MY UTMOST DEVOTIONAL BIBLE

———◆◆◆———

Presented to

_____

On this _____ *day of* _____

_____

_____

By _____

_____

———◆◆◆———

MY
UTMOST
DEVOTIONAL
BIBLE

NEW KING JAMES VERSION

Including selections from
MY UTMOST FOR HIS HIGHEST
and numerous other works
by Oswald Chambers

THOMAS NELSON PUBLISHERS
Nashville

Introduction to
My Utmost Devotional Bible

Seventy-five years ago a cable was sent from Egypt to Great Britain. "Oswald in His Presence" it read. This was the brief announcement of the death of Oswald Chambers who was taken at age forty-three while serving God at the vast military encampment of the Mediterranean Expeditionary Force on the open desert near Cairo. It was November 15, 1917.

Chambers once wrote concerning his ministry: "I feel I shall be buried for a time, hidden away in obscurity; then suddenly I shall flame out, do my work and be gone." His prophecy was accurate, but the profound effect of his words on believers in the twentieth century through the astounding proliferation of books he never knew would be printed, including the publication of this devotional Bible, prove that although he is gone, his work remains. Oswald Chambers' life was a light set on a hill that flamed into the dark storm of World War I and has illuminated the twentieth century ever since.

Clarence Chambers was a Baptist pastor in Aberdeen, Scotland, when his wife Hannah gave birth to their fourth son, Oswald, on July 24, 1874. His was a godly household. The pastor and his wife had both been baptized under the ministry of C. H. Spurgeon and in the first decade of Oswald's life served three churches in Scotland. While living in Perth, Oswald studied drawing at Sharps Institute. Eventually the family came to live in Southgate, London. There Oswald studied at the Kensington Art School. His talents and ambition in the arts earned him a scholarship for two years of study on the Continent. This he refused, fearing it would cause him a physical and moral decline.

In the meantime he experienced an evangelical conversion to Christ. While walking home with his father from a meeting directed by Spurgeon, the young man noted that he would have given his life to Christ that night had there been an opportunity. Clarence Chambers answered, "You can do it now, my boy." While they were there on the street, faith lit the flame of eternal life in Oswald Chambers.

Chambers was active among the young people of Rye Lane Baptist Church were he had been baptized. He taught their Sunday School, participated in evangelistic outreach, and joined in prayer meetings. Then, in 1895, he left his family in England and enrolled in the Arts Course of the University of Edinburgh. He studied Fine Art and Archaeology and supported himself painting portraits. But he also heard the Spirit of God calling: "Whom shall I send, and who will go for Us?" (Is. 6:8). He said this call to enter the ministry perplexed him tremendously. Writing to a friend, he admitted that he "often stifled it [the call of the Spirit] back and down." But at the same time he responded "through all my weaknesses, my sinfulness, and my frailties . . . 'Here am I, send me.'" The die was finally cast when Chambers became aware of a voice saying, "I need you for My service, but I can do without you."

Dunoon College was chosen as the place of preparation for Oswald Chambers' service to God, and he seems to have been a first-class collegian. Within a year he became a student tutor in Logic, Moral Philosophy, and Psychology. Among other activities in the community, he started a Browning Society to share his pleasure in the great Scottish poet. He relaxed by hiking in the Highlands. The wife of the principal of Dunoon described him as ". . . not one man but many men . . . artist, poet, philosopher, preacher and teacher, comedian . . . ."

Dr. F. B. Meyer visited Dunoon and spoke on the subject of the Holy Spirit. Because of this Chambers said he went to his room and "asked God simply and definitely for the baptism of the Holy Spirit, whatever that meant." In answer God used the next four years to bring Chambers "to the point of utter despair, . . . I got to the place where I did not care whether everyone knew how bad I was." But God had also taken hold of him with Luke 11:13: "If you then, being evil, know how to give good gifts to your children, how much more will *your* heavenly Father give the Holy Spirit to those who ask Him!" God's detailed exposure of the utter worthlessness of Chambers's own nature was not a stone or a serpent. God was giving him bread and fish; He was giving Chambers the Holy Spirit he had asked for (Luke 11:11). Chambers recalled that in a meeting at that time he stood up to prove God's word in his life. He declared, "Either Christianity is a downright fraud, or I have not got hold of the right end of the stick. And then and there I claimed the gift of the Holy Spirit in dogged committal on Luke 11:13." It was evident to Chambers that at that time his life and work began to bear the mark of the Holy Spirit. He had at last "got hold of the right end of the stick."

In 1905, after seven years of laying the groundwork for his ministry, Chambers left Dunoon Collge. That year he came into close fellowship with Bishop Juji Nakada, the evangelist from Japan. Together for two years they traveled among the Christians in America and Japan. Chambers returned to London in 1907 by way of Hong Kong, the Suez, Rome, and Paris. There he persevered in his evangelistic work, especially in association with the League of Prayer in England, Ireland, and Scotland.

Oswald Chambers once explained Genesis 5:1, 2, saying, "The relationship of man and woman has been totally misrepresented. The revelation in the Bible is not that it is a question of the one being unequal to the other but of the two being one." So it was in 1910 that he married Gertrude Hobbs whose notes of her husband's talks would enrich the church in over thirty published volumes.

The League of Prayer had an interest in starting a center of spiritual training. At the same time Oswald Chambers received a burden from God to start a college where he could pass on to others his insight in the truth of the Bible. A building was purchased on Clapham Common, London; and on January 12, 1911, the Bible Training College opened its doors with an enrollment of one student. Although common in the United States today, the college was unique in Great Britain at that time. In the college syllabus prospective students were told, "The College provides also atmosphere and time for spiritual life to take root before it is placed in the full blaze of the intellectual problems and actual difficulties of the times in which we live." Students were drawn by their spiritual hunger and desire to serve God. Soon the school filled to capacity—about twenty-five students.

One student later said, "Every memory of my days at the B.T.C. is a fresh cause for praise and thanksgiving to God." Another wrote that "throughout the years of the College life, . . . the Figure of the Son of God— Crowned and Glorified—with the

Thorns, and the Nailprints, and the hastening Feet, . . . that Figure, that Voice, that Face, is what emerges, and stands, and abides when all the rest . . . falls away." Here Gertrude Chambers began to take shorthand notes of her husband's sermons and lectures.

In July, 1915, the Bible Training College was closed "for the period of the war." On October 12 the same year, Oswald Chambers sailed for Egypt to serve with the staff of the Y.M.C.A. at Zeitoun near Cairo. He was soon joined by his wife and child.

Certainly a military camp is not a religious place, and no one could charge the men who gathered in the large reed huts of the Y.M.C.A. with being religious. They were not attracted there by religion. Rather, Oswald Chambers was a man whose being was described as "the redemption of Jesus Christ manifested in daily hourly living." This made the huts at Zeitoun like "the shadow of a great rock in a weary land" (Is. 32:2) to the New Zealanders, Australians, Englishmen, and Scotsmen who made up the Mediterranean Expeditionary Force. Many who gathered there in those days were able to testify like Isaiah that "the eyes of those who see will not be dim, and the ears of those who hear will listen" (32:3).

Chambers in the desert was "a lithe figure in khaki, with the eyes of a prophet and the profile of a Savonarola." Speaking in a "delightful, sparkling, humorous way . . . he can get a crowd of Australians night after night attracted by nothing but the message of Redemption." There in the wind, which he portrayed as "rampaging with the old antique heat of leagues of desert," and in the heat, which he said was not "like the sun's heat, but the heat of blinding devastation," Oswald Chambers spoke "to make all see what *is* the fellowship of the mystery, which from the beginning of the ages has been hidden in God who created all things through Jesus Christ" (Eph. 3:9).

And there he died, after two years of service, of complications from appendicitis.

There is a simple stone in Old Cairo Cemetery that is inscribed A BELIEVER IN JESUS CHRIST, with a Bible opened to Luke 11:13, the promise Oswald Chambers courageously appropriated and through which he faithfully served.

But this is not the only marker of this man's passing. Chambers ministered to those who faced the terrors of the First World War. He was truly "in the full blaze of the intellectual problems and actual difficulties of the times in which we live." This helps account for the vitality and fresh meaning of his words as this century draws to a close. He often spoke of the underlying tragedy of human life, yet also imparted the overshadowing hope of the message of Jesus Christ.

The readings in this devotional Bible have been drawn from the printed legacy of Oswald Chambers, the books which were lovingly and prayerfully assembled by his widow and her associates. May their message bring "Peace to the brethren, and love with faith, from God the Father and the Lord Jesus Christ" (Eph. 6:23).

Daniel Partner, Editor
Old Saybrook, Connecticut

Using *My Utmost Devotional Bible*

My Utmost Devotional Bible unfolds the Scriptures in an orderly, easy-to-follow fashion. The entire text of the New King James Version is divided into 365 readings, each with a passage from the Old Testament, Psalms, Proverbs, and the New Testament. All the books and chapters within these four divisions are presented in biblical order. The Old Testament progresses from Genesis to Malachi. Psalms and Proverbs each start with chapter one and move in order through the book. And the New Testament order of Matthew through Revelation is retained. Here are the first four readings from each group of material:

Book	Reading 1	Reading 2	Reading 3	Reading 4
Genesis	1, 2	3, 4	5, 6	7, 8
Psalms	1	2:1–6	2:7–12	3:1–4
Proverbs	1:1–7	1:8, 9	1:10–19	1:20–22
Matthew	1	2	3	4

Opening each day's reading is a meditation from the works of Oswald Chambers. These meditations are related to one of the passages within the Bible reading for the day. For example, Reading 1, titled "Dust, Drudgery, and Deity," speaks to Genesis 2:7, which is highlighted with a light gray screen in the text. Reading 2, "The Serpent and Eve," picks up a theme found in Genesis 3:1, and so on. Turn to page 13 for a complete listing of the meditation titles by reading number.

Another way to study the Chambers material and related scriptures within this Bible is by topic. You'll find a listing of the meditations by topic on page 17.

Punctuating the text are more than 600 short quotations also drawn from the works of Oswald Chambers.

Explanation of Key

At the end of each reading or brief quotation from Oswald Chambers, you will see a word or words enclosed in parentheses. These are key words from the titles of the works being quoted. All of these books are published by the Oswald Chambers Publications Association Limited and are distributed by Christian Literature Crusade in Fort Washington, Pennsylvania. Listed below are the complete titles of the works with their abbreviations as they appear in *My Utmost Devotional Bible*:

Approved	*Approved unto God*, 1946, 1948
Ask	*If Ye Shall Ask*, 1958, 1985 (Chosen Books); 1989, *If You Will Ask* (Discovery House)
Baffled	*Baffled to Fight Better*, 1931, 1990 (Discovery House)
Bib. Ethics	*Biblical Ethics*, 1947
Bib. Psych.	*Biblical Psychology*, 1962
Brill. Heritage	*Our Brilliant Heritage*, 1929, 1930, 1931, 1975

CHR. DISCPL.	*Christian Disciplines,* 1973, 1990 (Oswald Chambers Publications Association Limited and Nova Publications Limited)
CHRIS. DIS. 1	*Christian Discipline, Volume 1,* 1935, 1936, 1985 (Zondervan)
CHRIS. DIS. 2	*Christian Discipline, Volume 2,* 1935, 1936, 1985 (Zondervan)
CONFORMED	*Conformed to His Image,* 1950, 1985, 1996
DISCIPLES	*Disciples Indeed,* 1955
GENESIS	*Our Portrait in Genesis,* 1957, 1989 (Discovery House—combined with *Not Knowing Whither* under the title *Not Knowing Where*)
GLORIFY	*He Shall Glorify Me,* 1946
GLORY	*Bringing Sons unto Glory,* 1943, 1990 (Discovery House—combined with *Making All Things New*)
GOD'S WORKMANSHIP	*God's Workmanship,* 1953
GOOD	*The Highest Good,* 1937, 1938, 1940, 1992 (Discovery House—combined with *The Shadow of an Agony*)
GROW	*Grow Up into Him,* 1931
LONELINESS	*The Discipline of Loneliness (Chris. Dis. 2),* 1935, 1936, 1985
LOVE OF GOD	*The Love of God,* 1938, 1973, 1985 (Chosen Books), 1988 (Discovery House)
MAKING NEW	*Making All Things New,* 1930, 1990 (Discovery House—formerly *The Psychology of Redemption;* combined with *Bringing Sons into Glory*)
MORAL FOUND.	*The Moral Foundations of Life,* 1966
NOT KNOWING	*Not Knowing Whither,* 1934, 1989 (Discovery House—combined with *Our Portrait in Genesis* under the title *Not Knowing Where*)
PERFECT	*If Thou Wilt Be Perfect,* 1941
PHIL. SIN	*The Philosophy of Sin,* 1960
PLACE HELP	*The Place of Help,* 1935, 1989 (Discovery House)
POSSIBLE	*Now Is It Possible—(The Love of God,* 1985, Chosen)
PRAYER	*The Discipline of Prayer (Chris. Dis. 2),* 1935, 1936, 1985
PSY. REDEMP.	*The Psychology of Redemption,* 1930, 1990 (Discovery House—combined with *Bringing Sons into Glory* under the title *Making All Things New*)
RUN	*Run Today's Race,* 1968
SEND I YOU	*So Send I You,* 1930
SERMON MT.	*Studies in the Sermon on the Mount,* 1960
SERVANT AS LORD	*The Servant as His Lord,* 1957
SHAD. AGONY	*The Shadow of an Agony,* 1934, 1992 (Discovery House—combined with *The Highest Good*)
SHADE	*Shade of His Hand,* 1936, 1991 (Discovery House)
SUFFERING	*The Discipline of Suffering (Chris. Dis. 1),* 1935, 1936, 1985
UTMOST	*My Utmost for His Highest,* 1935 (Dodd, Mead, & Co.; copyright renewed 1963), 1989 (Discovery House)
WALKED	*As He Walked,* 1930
WORKMEN	*Workmen of God,* 1937

Beginning Page for Each Bible Book and Abbreviations

Old Testament

New Testament

Meditations by Topic

Preface
to
The New King James Version

Purpose

In the preface to the 1611 edition, the translators of the Authorized Version, known popularly as the King James Bible, state that it was not their purpose "to make a new translation . . . but to make a good one better." Indebted to the earlier work of William Tyndale and others, they saw their best contribution to consist in revising and enhancing the excellence of the English versions which had sprung from the Reformation of the sixteenth century. In harmony with the purpose of the King James scholars, the translators and editors of the present work have not pursued a goal of innovation. They have perceived the Holy Bible, New King James Version, as a continuation of the labors of the earlier translators, thus unlocking for today's readers the spiritual treasures found especially in the Authorized Version of the Holy Scriptures.

A Living Legacy

For nearly four hundred years, and throughout several revisions of its English form, the King James Bible has been deeply revered among the English-speaking peoples of the world. The precision of translation for which it is historically renowned, and its majesty of style, have enabled that monumental version of the Word of God to become the mainspring of the religion, language, and legal foundations of our civilization.

Although the Elizabethan period and our own era share in zeal for technical advance, the former period was more aggressively devoted to classical learning. Along with this awakened concern for the classics came a flourishing companion interest in the Scriptures, an interest that was enlivened by the conviction that the manuscripts were providentially handed down and were a trustworthy record of the inspired Word of God. The King James translators were committed to producing an English Bible that would be a precise translation, and by no means a paraphrase or a broadly approximate rendering. On the one hand, the scholars were almost as familiar with the original languages of the Bible as with their native English. On the other hand, their reverence for the divine Author and His Word assured a translation of the Scriptures in which only a principle of utmost accuracy could be accepted.

In 1786 Catholic scholar Alexander Geddes said of the King James Bible, "If accuracy and strictest attention to the letter of the text be supposed to constitute an excellent version, this is of all versions the most excellent." George Bernard Shaw became a literary legend in our century because of his severe and often humorous criticisms of our most cherished values. Surprisingly, however, Shaw pays the following tribute to the scholars commissioned by King James: "The translation was extraordinarily well done because to the translators what they were translating was not merely a curious collection of ancient books written by different authors in different stages of culture, but the Word of God divinely revealed through His chosen and expressly inspired scribes. In this conviction they carried out their work with boundless reverence and care and achieved a beautifully artistic result." History agrees with these estimates. Therefore, while seeking to unveil the excellent *form* of the traditional English Bible, special care has also been taken in the present edition to preserve the work of *precision* which is the legacy of the 1611 translators.

Complete Equivalence in Translation

Where new translation has been necessary in the New King James Version, the most complete representation of the original has been rendered by considering the history of usage and etymology of words in their contexts. This principle of complete equivalence seeks to preserve *all* of the information in the text, while presenting it in good literary form. Dynamic equivalence, a recent procedure in Bible translation, commonly results in paraphrasing where a more literal rendering is needed to reflect a specific and vital sense. For example, complete equivalence truly renders the original text in expressions such as "lifted her voice and wept" (Gen. 21:16); "I gave you cleanness of teeth" (Amos 4:6); "Jesus met them, saying, 'Rejoice!' " (Matt. 28:9); and " 'Woman, what does your concern have to do with Me?' " (John 2:4). Complete equivalence translates fully, in order to provide an English text that is both accurate and readable.

In keeping with the principle of complete equivalence, it is the policy to translate interjections which are commonly omitted in modern language renderings of the Bible. As an example, the interjection *behold*, in the older King James editions, continues to have a place in English usage, especially in dramatically calling attention to a spectacular scene, or an event of profound importance such as the Immanuel prophecy of Isaiah 7:14. Consequently, *behold* is retained for these occasions in the present edition. However, the Hebrew and Greek originals for this word can be translated vari-

ously, depending on the circumstances in the passage. Therefore, in addition to *behold*, words such as *indeed, look, see,* and *surely* are also rendered to convey the appropriate sense suggested by the context in each case.

In faithfulness to God and to our readers, it was deemed appropriate that all participating scholars sign a statement affirming their belief in the verbal and plenary inspiration of Scripture, and in the inerrancy of the original autographs.

Devotional Quality

The King James scholars readily appreciated the intrinsic beauty of divine revelation. They accordingly disciplined their talents to render well-chosen English words of their time, as well as a graceful, often musical arrangement of language, which has stirred the hearts of Bible readers through the years. The translators, the committees, and the editors of the present edition, while sensitive to the late-twentieth-century English idiom, and while adhering faithfully to the Hebrew, Aramaic, and Greek texts, have sought to maintain those lyrical and devotional qualities that are so highly regarded in the Authorized Version. This devotional quality is especially apparent in the poetic and prophetic books, although even the relatively plain style of the Gospels and Epistles cannot strictly be likened, as sometimes suggested, to modern newspaper style. The Koine Greek of the New Testament is influenced by the Hebrew background of the writers, for whom even the Gospel narratives were not merely flat utterance, but often song in various degrees of rhythm.

The Style

Students of the Bible applaud the timeless devotional character of our historic Bible. Yet it is also universally understood that our language, like all living languages, has undergone profound change since 1611. Subsequent revisions of the King James Bible have sought to keep abreast of changes in English speech. The present work is a further step toward this objective. Where obsolescence and other reading difficulties exist, present-day vocabulary, punctuation, and grammar have been carefully integrated. Words representing ancient objects, such as *chariot* and *phylactery,* have no modern substitutes and are therefore retained.

A special feature of the New King James Version is its conformity to the thought flow of the 1611 Bible. The reader discovers that the sequence and selection of words, phrases, and clauses of the new edition, while much clearer, are so close to the traditional that there is remarkable ease in listening to the reading of either edition while following with the other.

In the discipline of translating biblical and other ancient languages, a standard method of transliteration, that is, the English spelling of untranslated words, such as names of persons and places, has never been commonly adopted. In keeping with the design of the present work, the King James spelling of untranslated words is retained, although made uniform throughout. For example, instead of the spellings *Isaiah* and *Elijah* in the Old Testament, and *Esaias* and *Elias* in the New Testament, *Isaiah* and *Elijah* now appear in both Testaments.

King James doctrinal and theological terms, for example, *propitiation, justification,* and *sanctification,* are generally familiar to English-speaking peoples. Such terms have been retained except where the original language indicates need for a more precise translation.

Readers of the Authorized Version will immediately be struck by the absence of several pronouns: *thee, thou,* and *ye* are replaced by the simple *you,* while *your* and *yours* are substituted for *thy* and *thine* as applicable. *Thee, thou,*

thy, and *thine* were once forms of address to express a special relationship to human as well as divine persons. These pronouns are no longer part of our language. However, reverence for God in the present work is preserved by capitalizing pronouns, including *You, Your,* and *Yours,* which refer to Him. Additionally, capitalization of these pronouns benefits the reader by clearly distinguishing divine and human persons referred to in a passage. Without such capitalization the distinction is often obscure, because the antecedent of a pronoun is not always clear in the English translation.

In addition to the pronoun usages of the seventeenth century, the *-eth* and *-est* verb endings, so familiar in the earlier King James editions, are now obsolete. Unless a speaker is schooled in these verb endings, there is common difficulty in selecting the correct form to be used with a given subject of the verb in vocal prayer. That is, should we use *love, loveth,* or *lovest? do, doeth, doest,* or *dost? have, hath,* or *hast?* Because these forms are obsolete, contemporary English usage has been substituted for the previous verb endings.

In older editions of the King James Version, the frequency of the connective *and* far exceeded the limits of present English usage. Also, biblical linguists agree that the Hebrew and Greek original words for this conjunction may commonly be translated otherwise, depending on the immediate context. Therefore, instead of *and,* alternatives such as *also, but, however, now, so, then,* and *thus* are accordingly rendered in the present edition, when the original language permits.

The real character of the Authorized Version does not reside in its archaic pronouns or verbs or other grammatical forms of the seventeenth century, but rather in the care taken by its scholars to impart the letter and spirit of the original text in a majestic and reverent style.

The Format

The format of the New King James Version is designed to enhance the vividness and devotional quality of the Holy Scriptures:

—Words or phrases in *italics* indicate expressions in the original language which require clarification by additional English words, as also done throughout the history of the King James Bible.

—Poetry is structured as contemporary verse to reflect the poetic form and beauty of the passage in the original language.

—The covenant name of God was usually translated from the Hebrew as "LORD" or "GOD" (using capital letters as shown) in the King James Old Testament. This tradition is maintained. In the present edition the name is so capitalized whenever the covenant name is quoted in the New Testament from a passage in the Old Testament.

The Old Testament Text

The Hebrew Bible has come down to us through the scrupulous care of ancient scribes who copied the original text in successive generations. By the sixth century A.D. the scribes were succeeded by a group known as the Masoretes, who continued to preserve the sacred Scriptures for another five hundred years in a form known as the Masoretic Text. Babylonia, Palestine, and Tiberias were the main centers of Masoretic activity; but by the tenth century A.D. the Masoretes of Tiberias, led by the family of ben Asher, gained the ascendancy. Through subsequent editions, the ben Asher text became in the twelfth century the only recognized form of the Hebrew Scriptures.

Daniel Bomberg printed the first Rabbinic Bible in 1516–17; that work was followed in 1524–25 by a second edition prepared by Jacob ben Chayyim and also published by Bomberg. The text of ben Chayyim was adopted in most subsequent Hebrew Bibles, including those used by the King James translators. The ben Chayyim text was also used for the first two editions of Rudolph Kittel's *Biblia Hebraica* of 1906 and 1912. In 1937 Paul Kahle published a third edition of *Biblia Hebraica*. This edition was based on the oldest dated manuscript of the ben Asher text, the Leningrad Manuscript B19a (A.D. 1008), which Kahle regarded as superior to that used by ben Chayyim.

For the New King James Version the text used was the 1967/1977 Stuttgart edition of the *Biblia Hebraica*, with frequent comparisons being made with the Bomberg edition of 1524–25. The Septuagint (Greek) Version of the Old Testament and the Latin Vulgate also were consulted. In addition to referring to a variety of ancient versions of the Hebrew Scriptures, the New King James Version draws on the resources of relevant manuscripts from the Dead Sea caves. In the few places where the Hebrew was so obscure that the 1611 King James was compelled to follow one of the versions, but where information is now available to resolve the problems, the New King James Version follows the Hebrew text.

The New Testament Text

There is more manuscript support for the New Testament than for any other body of ancient literature. Over five thousand Greek, eight thousand Latin, and many more manuscripts in other languages attest the integrity of the New Testament. There is only one basic New Testament used by Protestants, Roman Catholics, and Orthodox, by conservatives and liberals. Minor variations in hand copying have appeared through the centuries, before mechanical printing began about A.D. 1450.

Some variations exist in the spelling of Greek words, in word order, and in similar details. These ordinarily do not show up in translation and do not affect the sense of the text in any way.

Other manuscript differences such as omission or inclusion of a word or a clause, and two paragraphs in the Gospels, should not overshadow the overwhelming degree of *agreement* which exists among the ancient records. Bible readers may be assured that the most important differences in English New Testaments of today are due, not to manuscript divergence, but to the way in which translators view the task of translation: How literally should the text be rendered? How does the translator view the matter of biblical inspiration? Does the translator adopt a paraphrase when a literal rendering would be quite clear and more to the point? The New King James Version follows the historic precedent of the Authorized Version in maintaining a literal approach to translation, except where the idiom of the original language cannot be translated directly into our tongue.

The King James New Testament was based on the traditional text of the Greek-speaking churches, first published in 1516, and later called the Textus Receptus or Received Text. Although based on the relatively few available manuscripts, these were representative of many more which existed at the time but only became known later. In the late nineteenth century, B. Westcott and F. Hort taught that this text had been officially edited by the fourth-century church, but a total lack of historical evidence for this event has forced a revision of the theory. It is now widely held that the Byzantine Text that largely supports the Textus Receptus has as much right as the Alexandrian or any other tradition to be weighed in determining the text of the New Testament.

Since the 1880s most contemporary translations of the New Testament have relied upon a relatively few manuscripts discovered chiefly in the late nineteenth and early twentieth centuries. Such translations depend primarily on two manuscripts, Codex Vaticanus and Codex Sinaiticus, because of their greater age. The Greek text obtained by using these sources and the related papyri (our most ancient manuscripts) is known as the Alexandrian Text. However, some scholars have grounds for doubting the faithfulness of Vaticanus and Sinaiticus, since they often disagree with one another, and Sinaiticus exhibits excessive omission.

A third viewpoint of New Testament scholarship holds that the best text is based on the consensus of the majority of existing Greek manuscripts. The text is called the Majority Text. Most of these manuscripts are in substantial agreement. Even though many are late, and none is earlier than the fifth century, usually their readings are verified by papyri, ancient versions, quotations from the early church fathers, or a combination of these. The Majority Text is similar to the Textus Receptus, but it corrects those readings which have little or no support in the Greek manuscript tradition.

Today, scholars agree that the science of New Testament textual criticism is in a state of flux. Very few scholars still favor the Textus Receptus as such, and then often for its historical prestige as the text of Luther, Calvin, Tyndale, and the King James Version. For about a century most have followed a Critical Text (so called because it is edited according to specific principles of textual criticism) which depends heavily upon the Alexandrian type of text. More recently many have abandoned this Critical Text (which is quite similar to the one edited by Westcott and Hort) for one that is more eclectic. Finally, a small but growing number of scholars prefer the Majority Text, which is close to the traditional text except in the Revelation.

In light of these facts, and also because the New King James Version is the fifth revision of a historic document translated from specific Greek texts, the editors decided to retain the traditional text in the body of the New Testament. It is most important to emphasize that fully eighty-five percent of the New Testament text is the same in the Textus Receptus, the Alexandrian Text, and the Majority Text.

MY
UTMOST
DEVOTIONAL
BIBLE

Reading 1—Dust, Drudgery, and Deity
Genesis 2:7

God made man a mixture of dust and Deity—"And the LORD God formed man *of* the dust of the ground, and breathed into his nostrils the breath of life; and man became a living being" (Gen. 2:7). The dust of a man's body is his glory, not his shame. Jesus Christ manifested Himself in that dust, and He claims that He can presence any man with His own divinity. The New Testament teaches us how to keep the body under and make it a servant. Robert Browning, of all the poets, is the one who insists that we make headway not in spite of the flesh, but because of the flesh, and in no other way.

Drudgery is the outcome of sin, but it has no right to be the rule of life. It becomes the rule of life because we ignore the fact that the dust of the earth belongs to God, and that our chief end is to glorify God. Unless we can maintain the presence of Divinity in our dust, life becomes a miserable drudgery. If we live in order to hoard up the means of living, we do not live at all, we have no time to, we are taken up with one form of drudgery or another to keep things going.   (*SHADE*)

GENESIS 1:1—2:25

IN the beginning God created the heavens and the earth. 2 The earth was without form, and void; and darkness *was* on the face of the deep. And the Spirit of God was hovering over the face of the waters.

3 Then God said, "Let there be light"; and there was light. 4 And God saw the light, that *it was* good; and God divided the light from the darkness. 5 God called the light Day, and the darkness He called Night. So the evening and the morning were the first day.

6 Then God said, "Let there be a firmament in the midst of the waters, and let it divide the waters from the waters." 7 Thus God made the firmament, and divided the waters which *were* under the firmament from the waters which *were* above the firmament; and it was so. 8 And God called the firmament Heaven. So the evening and the morning were the second day.

9 Then God said, "Let the waters under the heavens be gathered together into one place, and let the dry *land* appear"; and it was so. 10 And God called the dry *land* Earth, and the gathering together of the waters He called Seas. And God saw that *it was* good.

11 Then God said, "Let the earth bring forth grass, the herb *that* yields seed, *and* the fruit tree *that* yields fruit according to its kind, whose seed *is* in itself, on the earth"; and it was so. 12 And the earth brought forth grass, the herb *that* yields seed according to its kind, and the tree *that* yields fruit, whose seed *is* in itself according to its kind. And God saw that *it was* good. 13 So the evening and the morning were the third day.

14 Then God said, "Let there be lights in the firmament of the heavens to divide the day from the night; and let them be for signs and seasons, and for days and years; 15 and let them be for lights in the firmament of the heavens to give light on the earth"; and it was so. 16 Then God made two great lights: the greater light to rule the day, and the lesser light to rule the night. *He made* the stars also. 17 God set them in the firmament of the heavens to give light on the earth, 18 and to rule over the day and over the night, and to divide the light from the darkness. And God saw that *it was* good. 19 So the evening and the morning were the fourth day.

20 Then God said, "Let the waters abound with an abundance of living creatures, and let birds fly above the earth across the face of the firmament of the heavens." 21 So God created great sea creatures and every living thing that moves, with which the waters abounded, according to their kind, and every winged bird according to its kind. And God saw that *it was* good. 22 And God blessed them, saying, "Be fruitful and multiply, and fill the waters in the seas, and let birds multiply on the earth." 23 So the evening and the morning were the fifth day.

24 Then God said, "Let the earth bring forth the living creature according to its

kind: cattle and creeping thing and beast of the earth, *each* according to its kind"; and it was so. 25 And God made the beast of the earth according to its kind, cattle according to its kind, and everything that creeps on the earth according to its kind. And God saw that *it was* good.

26 Then God said, "Let Us make man in Our image, according to Our likeness; let them have dominion over the fish of the sea, over the birds of the air, and over the cattle, over all the earth and over every creeping thing that creeps on the earth." 27 So God created man in His *own* image; in the image of God He created him; male and female He created them. 28 Then God blessed them, and God said to them, "Be fruitful and multiply; fill the earth and subdue it; have dominion over the fish of the sea, over the birds of the air, and over every living thing that moves on the earth."

29 And God said, "See, I have given you every herb *that* yields seed which *is* on the face of all the earth, and every tree whose fruit yields seed; to you it shall be for food. 30 Also, to every beast of the earth, to every bird of the air, and to everything that creeps on the earth, in which *there is* life, *I have given* every green herb for food"; and it was so. 31 Then God saw everything that He had made, and indeed *it was* very good. So the evening and the morning were the sixth day.

2 THUS the heavens and the earth, and all the host of them, were finished. 2 And on the seventh day God ended His work which He had done, and He rested on the seventh day from all His work which He had done. 3 Then God blessed the seventh day and sanctified it, because in it He rested from all His work which God had created and made.

4 This *is* the history of the heavens and the earth when they were created, in the day that the LORD God made the earth and the heavens, 5 before any plant of the field was in the earth and before any herb of the field had grown. For the LORD God had not caused it to rain on the earth, and *there was* no man to till the ground; 6 but a mist went up from the earth and watered the whole face of the ground. 7 And the LORD God formed man *of* the dust of the ground, and breathed into his nostrils the breath of life; and man became a living being.

8 The LORD God planted a garden eastward in Eden, and there He put the man whom He had formed. 9 And out of the ground the LORD God made every tree

God made man a mixture of dust and Deity. (SHADE)

grow that is pleasant to the sight and good for food. The tree of life *was* also in the midst of the garden, and the tree of the knowledge of good and evil.

10 Now a river went out of Eden to water the garden, and from there it parted and became four riverheads. 11 The name of the first *is* Pishon; it *is* the one which skirts the whole land of Havilah, where *there is* gold. 12 And the gold of that land *is* good. Bdellium and the onyx stone *are* there. 13 The name of the second river *is* Gihon; it *is* the one which goes around the whole land of Cush. 14 The name of the third river *is* Hiddekel; it *is* the one which goes toward the east of Assyria. The fourth river *is* the Euphrates.

15 Then the LORD God took the man and put him in the garden of Eden to tend and keep it. 16 And the LORD God commanded the man, saying, "Of every tree of the garden you may freely eat; 17 but of the tree of the knowledge of good and evil you shall not eat, for in the day that you eat of it you shall surely die."

18 And the LORD God said, "*It is* not good that man should be alone; I will make him a helper comparable to him." 19 Out of the ground the LORD God formed every beast of the field and every bird of the air, and brought *them* to Adam to see what he would call them. And whatever Adam called each living creature, that *was* its name. 20 So Adam gave names to all cattle, to the birds of the air, and to every beast of the field. But for Adam there was not found a helper comparable to him.

21 And the LORD God caused a deep sleep to fall on Adam, and he slept; and He took one of his ribs, and closed up the flesh in its place. 22 Then the rib which the LORD God had taken from man He made into a woman, and He brought her to the man.

23 And Adam said:

"This *is* now bone of my bones
    And flesh of my flesh;
She shall be called Woman,
    Because she was taken out of Man."

24 Therefore a man shall leave his father and mother and be joined to his wife, and they shall become one flesh. 25 And they were both naked, the man and his wife, and were not ashamed.

PSALM 1:1–6

1   BLESSED *is* the man
    Who walks not in the counsel of the
      ungodly,
      Nor stands in the path of sinners,
      Nor sits in the seat of the scornful;
2   But his delight *is* in the law of the LORD,
    And in His law he meditates day and
      night.
3   He shall be like a tree
      Planted by the rivers of water,
      That brings forth its fruit in its
        season,
      Whose leaf also shall not wither;
    And whatever he does shall prosper.

4   The ungodly *are* not so,
    But *are* like the chaff which the wind
      drives away.
5   Therefore the ungodly shall not stand
      in the judgment,
    Nor sinners in the congregation of the
      righteous.

6   For the LORD knows the way of the
      righteous,
    But the way of the ungodly shall perish.

PROVERBS 1:1–7

THE proverbs of Solomon the son of David, king of Israel:

2   To know wisdom and instruction,
    To perceive the words of
      understanding,
3   To receive the instruction of wisdom,
    Justice, judgment, and equity;
4   To give prudence to the simple,
    To the young man knowledge and
      discretion—
5   A wise *man* will hear and increase
      learning,
    And a man of understanding will attain
      wise counsel,
6   To understand a proverb and an
      enigma,
    The words of the wise and their riddles.

7   The fear of the LORD *is* the beginning
      of knowledge,
    But fools despise wisdom and
      instruction.

---

*When you fear God you fear
nothing else.*   (RUN)

MATTHEW 1:1–25

THE book of the genealogy of Jesus Christ, the Son of David, the Son of Abraham:

2 Abraham begot Isaac, Isaac begot Jacob, and Jacob begot Judah and his brothers. 3 Judah begot Perez and Zerah by Tamar, Perez begot Hezron, and Hezron begot Ram. 4 Ram begot Amminadab, Amminadab begot Nahshon, and Nahshon begot Salmon. 5 Salmon begot Boaz by Rahab, Boaz begot Obed by Ruth, Obed begot Jesse, 6 and Jesse begot David the king.

David the king begot Solomon by her *who had been the wife* of Uriah. 7 Solomon begot Rehoboam, Rehoboam begot Abijah, and Abijah begot Asa. 8 Asa begot Jehoshaphat, Jehoshaphat begot Joram, and Joram begot Uzziah. 9 Uzziah begot Jotham, Jotham begot Ahaz, and Ahaz begot Hezekiah. 10 Hezekiah begot Manasseh, Manasseh begot Amon, and Amon begot Josiah. 11 Josiah begot Jeconiah and his brothers about the time they were carried away to Babylon.

12 And after they were brought to Babylon, Jeconiah begot Shealtiel, and Shealtiel begot Zerubbabel. 13 Zerubbabel begot Abiud, Abiud begot Eliakim, and Eliakim begot Azor. 14 Azor begot Zadok, Zadok begot Achim, and Achim begot Eliud. 15 Eliud begot Eleazar, Eleazar begot Matthan, and Matthan begot Jacob. 16 And Jacob begot Joseph the husband of Mary, of whom was born Jesus who is called Christ.

17 So all the generations from Abraham to David *are* fourteen generations, from David until the captivity in Babylon *are* fourteen generations, and from the captivity in Babylon until the Christ *are* fourteen generations.

18 Now the birth of Jesus Christ was as follows: After His mother Mary was betrothed to Joseph, before they came together, she was found with child of the Holy Spirit. 19 Then Joseph her husband, being a just *man,* and not wanting to make her a public example, was minded to put her away secretly. 20 But while he thought about these things, behold, an angel of the Lord appeared to him in a dream, saying, "Joseph, son of David, do not be afraid to take to you Mary your wife, for that which is conceived in her is of the Holy Spirit. 21 And she will bring forth a Son, and you shall call His name JESUS, for He will save His people from their sins."

22 So all this was done that it might be fulfilled which was spoken by the Lord

through the prophet, saying: 23 "Behold, the virgin shall be with child, and bear a Son, and they shall call His name Immanuel," which is translated, "God with us."

24 Then Joseph, being aroused from sleep, did as the angel of the Lord commanded him and took to him his wife, 25 and did not know her till she had brought forth her firstborn Son. And he called His name JESUS.

◆◆◆◆

Reading 2—The Serpent and Eve
Genesis 3:1

Why did Satan come *via* the serpent, and to Eve?—why did he not go direct to Adam? In thinking of man and woman as they were first created, it is extremely difficult, especially nowadays, to present the subject without introducing small, petty and disreputable ideas relative to the distinctions between man and woman. In Adam and Eve we are dealing with the primal creations of God. Adam was created immediately by the hand of God; Eve was created mediately. Eve stands for the soul side, the psychic side, of the human creation; all her sympathies and affinities were with the other creations of God around. Adam stands for the spirit side, the kingly, Godward side. Adam and Eve together are the likeness of God, "Then God said, Let Us make man in Our image, . . . male and female He created them." The revelation made here is not that woman stands as inferior to man, but that she stands in quite a different relation to all things, and that both man and woman are required for the complete creation of God referred to by the big general term 'Man.' (*BIB. PSYCH.*)

GENESIS 3:1—4:26

NOW the serpent was more cunning than any beast of the field which the LORD God had made. And he said to the woman, "Has God indeed said, 'You shall not eat of every tree of the garden'?"

2 And the woman said to the serpent, "We may eat the fruit of the trees of the garden; 3 but of the fruit of the tree which *is* in the midst of the garden, God has said, 'You shall not eat it, nor shall you touch it, lest you die.'"

4 Then the serpent said to the woman, "You will not surely die. 5 For God knows that in the day you eat of it your eyes will be opened, and you will be like God, knowing good and evil."

6 So when the woman saw that the tree *was* good for food, that it *was* pleasant to the eyes, and a tree desirable to make *one* wise, she took of its fruit and ate. She also gave to her husband with her, and he ate. 7 Then the eyes of both of them were opened, and they knew that they *were* naked; and they sewed fig leaves together and made themselves coverings.

Adam's sin was the perfect conscious realization of what he was doing. (PHIL. SIN)

8 And they heard the sound of the LORD God walking in the garden in the cool of the day, and Adam and his wife hid themselves from the presence of the LORD God among the trees of the garden.

9 Then the LORD God called to Adam and said to him, "Where *are* you?"

10 So he said, "I heard Your voice in the garden, and I was afraid because I was naked; and I hid myself."

11 And He said, "Who told you that you *were* naked? Have you eaten from the tree of which I commanded you that you should not eat?"

12 Then the man said, "The woman whom You gave *to be* with me, she gave me of the tree, and I ate."

13 And the LORD God said to the woman, "What *is* this you have done?"

The woman said, "The serpent deceived me, and I ate."

14 So the LORD God said to the serpent:

"Because you have done this,
You *are* cursed more than all cattle,
And more than every beast of the field;
On your belly you shall go,
And you shall eat dust
All the days of your life.
15 And I will put enmity
Between you and the woman,
And between your seed and her Seed;
He shall bruise your head,
And you shall bruise His heel."

16 To the woman He said:

"I will greatly multiply your sorrow
and your conception;
In pain you shall bring forth children;
Your desire *shall be* for your husband,
And he shall rule over you."

17 Then to Adam He said, "Because you have heeded the voice of your wife, and have eaten from the tree of which I commanded you, saying, 'You shall not eat of it':

"Cursed *is* the ground for your sake;
In toil you shall eat *of* it
All the days of your life.
18 Both thorns and thistles it shall bring forth for you,
And you shall eat the herb of the field.
19 In the sweat of your face you shall eat bread
Till you return to the ground,
For out of it you were taken;
For dust you *are*,
And to dust you *shall return.*"

20 And Adam called his wife's name Eve, because she was the mother of all *living.*
21 Also for Adam and his wife the LORD God made tunics of skin, and clothed them.
22 Then the LORD God said, "Behold, the man has become like one of Us, to know good and evil. And now, lest he put out his hand and take also of the tree of life, and eat, and live forever"— 23 therefore the LORD God sent him out of the garden of Eden to till the ground from which he was taken. 24 So He drove out the man; and He placed cherubim at the east of the garden of Eden, and a flaming sword which turned every way, to guard the way to the tree of life.

4 NOW Adam knew Eve *his* wife, and she conceived and bore *Cain*, and said, "I have acquired a man from the LORD." 2 Then she bore again, this time his brother Abel. Now Abel was a keeper of sheep, but Cain was a tiller of the ground. 3 And in the process of time it came to pass that Cain brought an offering of the fruit of the ground to the LORD. 4 Abel also brought of the firstborn of his flock and of their fat. And the LORD respected Abel and his offering, 5 but He did not respect Cain and his offering. And Cain was very angry, and his countenance fell.

The spirit of Cain is jealousy, spite and envy. (GLORIFY)

6 So the LORD said to Cain, "Why are you angry? And why has your countenance fallen? 7 If you do well, will you not be accepted? And if you do not do well, sin lies at the door. And its desire *is* for you, but you should rule over it."

8 Now Cain talked with Abel his brother; and it came to pass, when they were in the field, that Cain rose up against Abel his brother and killed him.

9 Then the LORD said to Cain, "Where is Abel your brother?"

He said, "I do not know. *Am* I my brother's keeper?"

10 And He said, "What have you done? The voice of your brother's blood cries out to Me from the ground. 11 So now you are cursed from the earth, which has opened its mouth to receive your brother's blood from your hand. 12 When you till the ground, it shall no longer yield its strength to you. A fugitive and a vagabond you shall be on the earth."

13 And Cain said to the LORD, "My punishment *is* greater than I can bear! 14 Surely You have driven me out this day from the face of the ground; I shall be hidden from Your face; I shall be a fugitive and a vagabond on the earth, and it will happen *that* anyone who finds me will kill me."

15 And the LORD said to him, "Therefore, whoever kills Cain, vengeance shall be taken on him sevenfold." And the LORD set a mark on Cain, lest anyone finding him should kill him.

16 Then Cain went out from the presence of the LORD and dwelt in the land of Nod on the east of Eden. 17 And Cain knew his wife, and she conceived and bore Enoch. And he built a city, and called the name of the city after the name of his son—Enoch.

18 To Enoch was born Irad; and Irad begot Mehujael, and Mehujael begot Methushael, and Methushael begot Lamech.

19 Then Lamech took for himself two wives: the name of one *was* Adah, and the name of the second *was* Zillah. 20 And Adah bore Jabal. He was the father of those who dwell in tents and have livestock. 21 His brother's name *was* Jubal. He was the father of all those who play the harp and flute. 22 And as for Zillah, she also bore Tubal-Cain, an instructor of every craftsman in bronze and iron. And the sister of Tubal-Cain *was* Naamah.

23 Then Lamech said to his wives:

"Adah and Zillah, hear my voice;
Wives of Lamech, listen to my speech!
For I have killed a man for wounding me,
Even a young man for hurting me.
24 If Cain shall be avenged seven,
Then Lamech seventy-sevenfo

25 And Adam knew his wife aga
she bore a son and named him Set
God has appointed another seed
instead of Abel, whom Cain
26 And as for Seth, to him also a s
born; and he named him Enosh. T
began to call on the name of the

PSALM 2:1-6

1 WHY do the nations rage,
And the people plot a vain t
2 The kings of the earth set th's,
And the rulers take counsel r,
Against the LORD and again
Anointed, *saying,*
3 "Let us break Their bonds i
And cast away Their cords is."

4 He who sits in the heavens ugh;
The LORD shall hold them ision.
5 Then He shall speak to then His wrath,
And distress them in His de displeasure:
6 "Yet I have set My King
On My holy hill of Zion."

PROVERBS 1:8, 9

8 MY son, hear the instruction of your father,
And do not forsake the law of your mother;

9 For they *will be* a graceful ornament on your head,
And chains about your neck.

MATTHEW 2:1-23

NOW after Jesus was born in Bethlehem of Judea in the days of Herod the king, behold, wise men from the East came to Jerusalem, 2 saying, "Where is He who has been born King of the Jews? For we have seen His star in the East and have come to worship Him."

3 When Herod the king heard *this,* he was troubled, and all Jerusalem with him. 4 And when he had gathered all the chief priests and scribes of the people together, he inquired of them where the Christ was to be born.

5 So they said to him, "In Bethlehem of Judea, for thus it is written by the prophet:

6 'But you, Bethlehem, *in* the land of Judah,
Are not the least among the rulers of Judah;
For out of you shall come a Ruler
Who will shepherd My people Israel.' "

7 Then Herod, when he had secretly called the wise men, determined from them what time the star appeared. 8 And he sent them to Bethlehem and said, "Go and search carefully for the young Child, and when you have found *Him,* bring back word to me, that I may come and worship Him also."

9 When they heard the king, they departed; and behold, the star which they had seen in the East went before them, till it came and stood over where the young Child was. 10 When they saw the star, they rejoiced with exceedingly great joy. 11 And when they had come into the house, they saw the young Child with Mary His mother, and fell down and worshiped Him. And when they had opened their treasures, they presented gifts to Him: gold, frankincense, and myrrh.

12 Then, being divinely warned in a dream that they should not return to Herod, they departed for their own country another way.

13 Now when they had departed, behold, an angel of the Lord appeared to Joseph in a dream, saying, "Arise, take the young Child and His mother, flee to Egypt, and stay there until I bring you word; for Herod will seek the young Child to destroy Him."

14 When he arose, he took the young Child and His mother by night and departed for Egypt, 15 and was there until the death of Herod, that it might be fulfilled which was spoken by the Lord through the prophet, saying, "Out of Egypt I called My Son."

16 Then Herod, when he saw that he was deceived by the wise men, was exceedingly angry; and he sent forth and put to death all the male children who were in Bethlehem and in all its districts, from two years old and under, according to the time which he had determined from the wise men. 17 Then was fulfilled what was spoken by Jeremiah the prophet, saying:

18 "A voice was heard in Ramah,
Lamentation, weeping, and great mourning,

Rachel weeping *for* her children,
Refusing to be comforted,
Because they are no more."

19 Now when Herod was dead, behold, an angel of the Lord appeared in a dream to Joseph in Egypt, 20 saying, "Arise, take the young Child and His mother, and go to the land of Israel, for those who sought the young Child's life are dead." 21 Then he arose, took the young Child and His mother, and came into the land of Israel.

22 But when he heard that Archelaus was reigning over Judea instead of his father Herod, he was afraid to go there. And being warned by God in a dream, he turned aside into the region of Galilee. 23 And he came and dwelt in a city called Nazareth, that it might be fulfilled which was spoken by the prophets, "He shall be called a Nazarene."

◆◆◆

Reading 3—Noah Builds the Impossible
Genesis 6:14, 17, 18

The ark stands as a reminder that nothing *is* until it is. Whenever we say a thing is impossible the reason is twofold: either our prejudices don't wish it to be, or we wish it so much that it seems too wonderful to be possible. Yet God only does the impossible.

In the realm of what is humanly possible, we don't need God; common sense is our god. We don't pray to God; we pray to some edifice of our common sense. It is God who is the architect of salvation; therefore salvation is not a commonsense design. What we have to do is to get inside that salvation.

If we put our faith in any construction of our own—our vows and decisions, our consecration—we are building something for ourselves. Picture Noah sitting down and saying, "God has given me a wonderful plan. I'm going to sit here and watch it happen." If he had done that, the water would have soon been over his head. Instead, it says, "Thus Noah did; according to all that God commanded him" (Gen. 6:22).

Still, the initiative springs from the mind of almighty God: "And behold, I Myself am bringing. . . ." It is not the natural consequence of cause and effect. And the result was a covenant with the new humanity after the Flood.

(*Not Knowing*)

GENESIS 5:1—6:22

THIS is the book of the genealogy of Adam. In the day that God created man, He made him in the likeness of God. 2 He created them male and female, and blessed them and called them Mankind in the day they were created. 3 And Adam lived one hundred and thirty years, and begot *a son* in his own likeness, after his image, and named him Seth. 4 After he begot Seth, the days

of Adam were eight hundred years; and he had sons and daughters. 5 So all the days that Adam lived were nine hundred and thirty years; and he died.

Both man and woman are required for the complete creation of God. (Bib. Psych.)

6 Seth lived one hundred and five years, and begot Enosh. 7 After he begot Enosh, Seth lived eight hundred and seven years, and had sons and daughters. 8 So all the days of Seth were nine hundred and twelve years; and he died.

9 Enosh lived ninety years, and begot Cainan. 10 After he begot Cainan, Enosh lived eight hundred and fifteen years, and had sons and daughters. 11 So all the days of Enosh were nine hundred and five years; and he died.

12 Cainan lived seventy years, and begot Mahalalel. 13 After he begot Mahalalel, Cainan lived eight hundred and forty years, and had sons and daughters. 14 So all the days of Cainan were nine hundred and ten years; and he died.

15 Mahalalel lived sixty-five years, and begot Jared. 16 After he begot Jared, Mahalalel lived eight hundred and thirty years, and had sons and daughters. 17 So all the days of Mahalalel were eight hundred and ninety-five years; and he died.

18 Jared lived one hundred and sixty-two years, and begot Enoch. 19 After he begot Enoch, Jared lived eight hundred years, and had sons and daughters. 20 So all the days of Jared were nine hundred and sixty-two years; and he died.

21 Enoch lived sixty-five years, and begot Methuselah. 22 After he begot Methuselah, Enoch walked with God three hundred years, and had sons and daughters. 23 So all the days of Enoch were three hundred and sixty-five years. 24 And Enoch walked with God; and he *was* not, for God took him.

25 Methuselah lived one hundred and eighty-seven years, and begot Lamech. 26 After he begot Lamech, Methuselah lived seven hundred and eighty-two years, and had sons and daughters. 27 So all the days of Methuselah were nine hundred and sixty-nine years; and he died.

28 Lamech lived one hundred and eighty-two years, and had a son. 29 And he called his name Noah, saying, "This *one* will comfort us concerning our work and the toil of our hands, because of the ground which the LORD has cursed." 30 After he begot Noah, Lamech lived five hundred and ninety-five years, and had sons and daughters. 31 So all the days of Lamech were seven hundred and seventy-seven years; and he died.

32 And Noah was five hundred years old, and Noah begot Shem, Ham, and Japheth.

6 NOW it came to pass, when men began to multiply on the face of the earth, and daughters were born to them, 2 that the sons of God saw the daughters of men, that they *were* beautiful; and they took wives for themselves of all whom they chose.

3 And the LORD said, "My Spirit shall not strive with man forever, for he *is* indeed flesh; yet his days shall be one hundred and twenty years." 4 There were giants on the earth in those days, and also afterward, when the sons of God came in to the daughters of men and they bore *children* to them. Those *were* the mighty men who *were* of old, men of renown.

5 Then the LORD saw that the wickedness of man *was* great in the earth, and *that* every intent of the thoughts of his heart *was* only evil continually. 6 And the LORD was sorry that He had made man on the earth, and He was grieved in His heart. 7 So the LORD said, "I will destroy man whom I have created from the face of the earth, both man and beast, creeping thing and birds of the air, for I am sorry that I have made them." 8 But Noah found grace in the eyes of the LORD.

9 This is the genealogy of Noah. Noah was a just man, perfect in his generations. Noah walked with God. 10 And Noah begot three sons: Shem, Ham, and Japheth.

11 The earth also was corrupt before God, and the earth was filled with violence. 12 So God looked upon the earth, and indeed it was corrupt; for all flesh had corrupted their way on the earth.

13 And God said to Noah, "The end of all flesh has come before Me, for the earth is filled with violence through them; and behold, I will destroy them with the earth. 14 Make yourself an ark of gopherwood; make rooms in the ark, and cover it inside and outside with pitch. 15 And this is how you shall make it: The length of the ark *shall be* three hundred cubits, its width fifty cubits, and its height thirty cubits. 16 You shall make a window for the ark, and you shall finish it to a cubit from above; and set the door of the ark in its side. You shall make it *with* lower, second, and third *decks*. 17 And behold, I Myself am bringing floodwaters on the earth, to destroy from under heaven all flesh in which *is* the breath of life; everything that *is* on the earth shall die. 18 But I will establish My covenant with you; and you shall go into the ark—you, your sons, your wife, and your sons' wives with you. 19 And of every living thing of all flesh you shall bring two of every *sort* into the ark, to keep *them* alive with you; they shall be male and female. 20 Of the birds after their kind, of animals after their kind, and of every creeping thing of the

earth after its kind, two of every *kind* will come to you to keep *them* alive. 21 And you shall take for yourself of all food that is eaten, and you shall gather *it* to yourself; and it shall be food for you and for them."

22 Thus Noah did; according to all that God commanded him, so he did.

PSALM 2:7–12

7 "I will declare the decree:
The LORD has said to Me,
'You *are* My Son,
Today I have begotten You.

8 Ask of Me, and I will give *You*
The nations *for* Your inheritance,
And the ends of the earth *for* Your possession.

9 You shall break them with a rod of iron;
You shall dash them to pieces like a potter's vessel.' "

10 Now therefore, be wise, O kings;
Be instructed, you judges of the earth.

11 Serve the LORD with fear,
And rejoice with trembling.

12 Kiss the Son, lest He be angry,
And you perish *in* the way,
When His wrath is kindled but a little.
Blessed *are* all those who put their trust in Him.

PROVERBS 1:10–19

10 MY son, if sinners entice you,
Do not consent.

11 If they say, "Come with us,
Let us lie in wait to *shed* blood;
Let us lurk secretly for the innocent without cause;

12 Let us swallow them alive like Sheol,
And whole, like those who go down to the Pit;

13 We shall find all *kinds* of precious possessions,
We shall fill our houses with spoil;

14 Cast in your lot among us,
Let us all have one purse"—

15 My son, do not walk in the way with them,
Keep your foot from their path;

16 For their feet run to evil,
And they make haste to shed blood.

17 Surely, in vain the net is spread
In the sight of any bird;

18 But they lie in wait for their *own* blood,
They lurk secretly for their *own* lives.

19 So *are* the ways of everyone who is greedy for gain;
It takes away the life of its owners.

MATTHEW 3:1–17

IN those days John the Baptist came preaching in the wilderness of Judea, 2 and saying, "Repent, for the kingdom of heaven is at hand!" 3 For this is he who was spoken of by the prophet Isaiah, saying:

"The voice of one crying in the wilderness:
'Prepare the way of the LORD;
Make His paths straight.' "

4 Now John himself was clothed in camel's hair, with a leather belt around his waist; and his food was locusts and wild honey. 5 Then Jerusalem, all Judea, and all the region around the Jordan went out to him 6 and were baptized by him in the Jordan, confessing their sins.

7 But when he saw many of the Pharisees and Sadducees coming to his baptism, he said to them, "Brood of vipers! Who warned you to flee from the wrath to come? 8 Therefore bear fruits worthy of repentance, 9 and do not think to say to yourselves, 'We have Abraham as *our* father.' For I say to you that God is able to raise up children to Abraham from these stones. 10 And even now the ax is laid to the root of the trees. Therefore every tree which does not bear good fruit is cut down and thrown into the fire. 11 I indeed baptize you with water unto repentance, but He who is coming after me is mightier than I, whose sandals I am not worthy to carry. He will baptize you with the Holy Spirit and fire. 12 His winnowing fan *is* in His hand, and He will thoroughly clean out His threshing floor, and gather His wheat into the barn; but He will burn up the chaff with unquenchable fire."

13 Then Jesus came from Galilee to John at the Jordan to be baptized by him. 14 And John *tried to* prevent Him, saying, "I need to be baptized by You, and are You coming to me?"

15 But Jesus answered and said to him, "Permit *it to be so* now, for thus it is fitting for us to fulfill all righteousness." Then he allowed Him.

16 When He had been baptized, Jesus came up immediately from the water; and

---

The baptism of our Lord was an extraordinary spiritual experience to Himself. (PSY. REDEMP.)

behold, the heavens were opened to Him, and He saw the Spirit of God descending like a dove and alighting upon Him.

17 And suddenly a voice *came* from heaven, saying, "This is My beloved Son, in whom I am well pleased."

◆◆◆◆

Reading 4—The Vision of the Long Way
Matthew 4:1–10

Each of the temptations presented to our Lord by Satan had this as its center: "You will get the kingship of men and the saviorhood of the world if You will take a 'shortcut'—put man's needs first, and he will crown You king; do something extraordinarily wonderful, indicative of Your power, and man will crown You king; compromise with evil, and You will get the kingship of men." Jesus could have brought the whole thing about suddenly (see John 6:15); but He did not. He withstood Satan and took the stupendously long way.

When we obey Jesus Christ it is never a question of what it costs us—it does not cost us anything, it is a delight—but of what it costs those whom we love, and there is always the danger of yielding to the temptation of the "shortcut." Am I prepared to let my obedience to God cost other people something? Jesus deliberately took the long trail, and He says, "*A* disciple is not above *his* teacher." "Because you have kept My command to persevere. . . ." We want to hurry things up by revivals. Over and over again we take the Devil's advice and say, "It must be done quickly—the need is the call; men must be saved." An understanding of the inwardness of our Lord's temptation will throw light on the progress of Christian history as well as on personal experience.   (*Place Help*)

GENESIS 7:1—8:22

THEN the Lord said to Noah, "Come into the ark, you and all your household, because I have seen *that* you *are* righteous before Me in this generation. 2 You shall take with you seven each of every clean animal, a male and his female; two each of animals that *are* unclean, a male and his female; 3 also seven each of birds of the air, male and female, to keep the species alive on the face of all the earth. 4 For after seven more days I will cause it to rain on the earth forty days and forty nights, and I will destroy from the face of the earth all living things that I have made." 5 And Noah did according to all that the Lord commanded him. 6 Noah *was* six hundred years old when the floodwaters were on the earth.

7 So Noah, with his sons, his wife, and his sons' wives, went into the ark because of the waters of the flood. 8 Of clean animals, of animals that *are* unclean, of birds, and of everything that creeps on the earth,

9 two by two they went into the ark to Noah, male and female, as God had commanded Noah. 10 And it came to pass after seven days that the waters of the flood were on the earth. 11 In the six hundredth year of Noah's life, in the second month, the seventeenth day of the month, on that day all the fountains of the great deep were broken up, and the windows of heaven were opened. 12 And the rain was on the earth forty days and forty nights.

13 On the very same day Noah and Noah's sons, Shem, Ham, and Japheth, and Noah's wife and the three wives of his sons with them, entered the ark— 14 they and every beast after its kind, all cattle after their kind, every creeping thing that creeps on the earth after its kind, and every bird after its kind, every bird of every sort. 15 And they went into the ark to Noah, two by two, of all flesh in which *is* the breath of life. 16 So those that entered, male and female of all flesh, went in as God had commanded him; and the Lord shut him in.

17 Now the flood was on the earth forty days. The waters increased and lifted up

the ark, and it rose high above the earth.
18 The waters prevailed and greatly increased on the earth, and the ark moved about on the surface of the waters.
19 And the waters prevailed exceedingly on the earth, and all the high hills under the whole heaven were covered. 20 The waters prevailed fifteen cubits upward, and the mountains were covered. 21 And all flesh died that moved on the earth: birds and cattle and beasts and every creeping thing that creeps on the earth, and every man.
22 All in whose nostrils *was* the breath of the spirit of life, all that *was* on the dry *land,* died. 23 So He destroyed all living things which were on the face of the ground: both man and cattle, creeping thing and bird of the air. They were destroyed from the earth. Only Noah and those who *were* with him in the ark remained *alive.*
24 And the waters prevailed on the earth one hundred and fifty days.

8 THEN God remembered Noah, and every living thing, and all the animals that *were* with him in the ark. And God made a wind to pass over the earth, and the waters subsided. 2 The fountains of the deep and the windows of heaven were also stopped, and the rain from heaven was restrained. 3 And the waters receded continually from the earth. At the end of the hundred and fifty days the waters decreased. 4 Then the ark rested in the seventh month, the seventeenth day of the month, on the mountains of Ararat. 5 And the waters decreased continually until the tenth month. In the tenth *month,* on the first *day* of the month, the tops of the mountains were seen.

6 So it came to pass, at the end of forty days, that Noah opened the window of the ark which he had made. 7 Then he sent out a raven, which kept going to and fro until the waters had dried up from the earth.
8 He also sent out from himself a dove, to see if the waters had receded from the face of the ground. 9 But the dove found no resting place for the sole of her foot, and she returned into the ark to him, for the waters *were* on the face of the whole earth. So he put out his hand and took her, and drew her into the ark to himself. 10 And he waited yet another seven days, and again he sent the dove out from the ark. 11 Then the dove came to him in the evening, and behold, a freshly plucked olive leaf *was* in her mouth; and Noah knew that the waters had receded from the earth. 12 So he waited yet another seven days and sent out the dove, which did not return again to him anymore.

13 And it came to pass in the six hundred and first year, in the first *month,* the first *day* of the month, that the waters were dried up from the earth; and Noah removed the covering of the ark and looked, and indeed the surface of the ground was dry. 14 And in the second month, on the twenty-seventh day of the month, the earth was dried.

15 Then God spoke to Noah, saying, 16 "Go out of the ark, you and your wife, and your sons and your sons' wives with you. 17 Bring out with you every living thing of all flesh that *is* with you: birds and cattle and every creeping thing that creeps on the earth, so that they may abound on the earth, and be fruitful and multiply on the earth." 18 So Noah went out, and his sons and his wife and his sons' wives with him. 19 Every animal, every creeping thing, every bird, *and* whatever creeps on the earth, according to their families, went out of the ark.

20 Then Noah built an altar to the LORD, and took of every clean animal and of every clean bird, and offered burnt offerings on the altar. 21 And the LORD smelled a soothing aroma. Then the LORD said in His heart, "I will never again curse the ground for man's sake, although the imagination of man's heart *is* evil from his youth; nor will I again destroy every living thing as I have done.

22 "While the earth remains,
      Seedtime and harvest,
      Cold and heat,
      Winter and summer,
      And day and night
      Shall not cease."

PSALM 3:1–4

1   LORD, how they have increased who
      trouble me!
    Many *are* they who rise up against me.
2   Many *are* they who say of me,
    "*There is* no help for him in God."
                                          Selah

3   But You, O LORD, *are* a shield for me,
    My glory and the One who lifts up
      my head.

---

*P*rayer is not logical, it is a
*mysterious moral working of the Holy
Spirit.*   (CHRIS. DIS. 2)

4 I cried to the LORD with my voice,
And He heard me from His holy hill.
                                    Selah

PROVERBS 1:20–22

20 WISDOM calls aloud outside;
She raises her voice in the open squares.
21 She cries out in the chief concourses,
At the openings of the gates in the city
She speaks her words:
22 "How long, you simple ones, will you
love simplicity?
For scorners delight in their scorning,
And fools hate knowledge.

MATTHEW 4:1–25

THEN Jesus was led up by the Spirit into
the wilderness to be tempted by the devil.

*His temptations went on from the
first moment of His conscious life
to the last.*   (LOVE OF GOD)

2 And when He had fasted forty days and
forty nights, afterward He was hungry.
3 Now when the tempter came to Him,
he said, "If You are the Son of God, command that these stones become bread."
4 But He answered and said, "It is written, 'Man shall not live by bread alone, but
by every word that proceeds from the
mouth of God.'"
5 Then the devil took Him up into the
holy city, set Him on the pinnacle of the
temple, 6 and said to Him, "If You are
the Son of God, throw Yourself down. For
it is written:

'He shall give His angels charge over
you,'

and,

'In *their* hands they shall bear you
up,
Lest you dash your foot against a
stone.'"

7 Jesus said to him, "It is written again,
'You shall not tempt the LORD your
God.'"
8 Again, the devil took Him up on an
exceedingly high mountain, and showed
Him all the kingdoms of the world and
their glory. 9 And he said to Him, "All these
things I will give You if You will fall down
and worship me."
10 Then Jesus said to him, "Away with
you, Satan! For it is written, 'You shall worship the LORD your God, and Him only
you shall serve.'"
11 Then the devil left Him, and behold,
angels came and ministered to Him.
12 Now when Jesus heard that John had
been put in prison, He departed to Galilee.
13 And leaving Nazareth, He came and
dwelt in Capernaum, which is by the sea,
in the regions of Zebulun and Naphtali,
14 that it might be fulfilled which was spoken by Isaiah the prophet, saying:

15 "The land of Zebulun and the land
of Naphtali,
By the way of the sea, beyond the
Jordan,
Galilee of the Gentiles:
16 The people who sat in darkness have
seen a great light,
And upon those who sat in the region
and shadow of death
Light has dawned."

17 From that time Jesus began to preach
and to say, "Repent, for the kingdom of
heaven is at hand."
18 And Jesus, walking by the Sea of Galilee, saw two brothers, Simon called Peter,
and Andrew his brother, casting a net into
the sea; for they were fishermen. 19 Then
He said to them, "Follow Me, and I will
make you fishers of men." 20 They immediately left *their* nets and followed Him.
21 Going on from there, He saw two
other brothers, James *the son* of Zebedee,
and John his brother, in the boat with Zebedee their father, mending their nets. He
called them, 22 and immediately they left
the boat and their father, and followed Him.
23 And Jesus went about all Galilee,
teaching in their synagogues, preaching the
gospel of the kingdom, and healing all kinds
of sickness and all kinds of disease among
the people. 24 Then His fame went throughout all Syria; and they brought to Him all
sick people who were afflicted with various
diseases and torments, and those who were
demon-possessed, epileptics, and paralytics;
and He healed them. 25 Great multitudes
followed Him—from Galilee, and *from* Decapolis, Jerusalem, Judea, and beyond the
Jordan.

*Reading 5—*The Abiding Relationship
Genesis 9:8, 9

God does not do certain things without the cooperation of man. We continually ask, "Why doesn't God do the thing instead of waiting for me?" The answer is that He chooses not to do so. It is like the difference between God's order and His permissive will. His permissive will allows the Devil to do his worst and allows me to sin as I choose, until I choose to resist the Devil, quit sinning, and come to God in the right relationship through Jesus Christ. It is God's will that human beings should get into moral relationship with Him, and His covenants are for that purpose. "Why doesn't God save me?" some ask. He has saved them, but they have not entered into relationship with Him.

All the great blessings of God are finished and complete, but they cannot be ours until we enter into relationship with Him on the basis of His covenant. Salvation is not an edict of God; salvation is something wrought out on the human plane through God becoming man. Waiting for God somehow to do something in us so we can trust in this is incarnate unbelief; it means we have no faith in Him. We have to go out of ourselves to enter into the covenant with God, just as God went out of Himself to enter into His covenant with man (Phil. 2:7, 8).   (*Not Knowing*)

GENESIS 9:1—10:32

SO God blessed Noah and his sons, and said to them: "Be fruitful and multiply, and fill the earth. 2 And the fear of you and the dread of you shall be on every beast of the earth, on every bird of the air, on all that move *on* the earth, and on all the fish of the sea. They are given into your hand. 3 Every moving thing that lives shall be food for you. I have given you all things, even as the green herbs. 4 But you shall not eat flesh with its life, *that is,* its blood. 5 Surely for your lifeblood I will demand *a reckoning;* from the hand of every beast I will require it, and from the hand of man. From the hand of every man's brother I will require the life of man.

6   "Whoever sheds man's blood,
      By man his blood shall be shed;
      For in the image of God
      He made man.
7   And as for you, be fruitful and
      multiply;
      Bring forth abundantly in the earth
      And multiply in it."

8 Then God spoke to Noah and to his sons with him, saying: 9 "And as for Me, behold, I establish My covenant with you and with your descendants after you, 10 and with every living creature that *is* with

you: the birds, the cattle, and every beast of the earth with you, of all that go out of the ark, every beast of the earth. 11 Thus I establish My covenant with you: Never again shall all flesh be cut off by the waters of the flood; never again shall there be a flood to destroy the earth."

12 And God said: "This *is* the sign of the covenant which I make between Me and you, and every living creature that *is* with you, for perpetual generations: 13 I set My rainbow in the cloud, and it shall be for the sign of the covenant between Me and the earth. 14 It shall be, when I bring a cloud over the earth, that the rainbow shall be seen in the cloud; 15 and I will remember My covenant which *is* between Me and you and every living creature of all flesh; the waters shall never again become a flood to destroy all flesh. 16 The rainbow shall be in the cloud, and I will look on it to remember the everlasting covenant between God and every living creature of all flesh that *is* on the earth." 17 And God said to Noah, "This *is* the sign of the covenant which I have established between Me and all flesh that *is* on the earth."

18 Now the sons of Noah who went out of the ark were Shem, Ham, and Japheth. And Ham *was* the father of Canaan. 19 These three *were* the sons of Noah, and from these the whole earth was populated.

20 And Noah began *to be* a farmer, and he planted a vineyard. 21 Then he drank of the wine and was drunk, and became uncovered in his tent. 22 And Ham, the father of Canaan, saw the nakedness of his father, and told his two brothers outside. 23 But Shem and Japheth took a garment, laid *it* on both their shoulders, and went backward and covered the nakedness of their father. Their faces *were* turned away, and they did not see their father's nakedness.

24 So Noah awoke from his wine, and knew what his younger son had done to him. 25 Then he said:

"Cursed *be* Canaan;
A servant of servants
He shall be to his brethren."

26 And he said:

"Blessed *be* the LORD,
The God of Shem,
And may Canaan be his servant.
27   May God enlarge Japheth,
And may he dwell in the tents of
    Shem;
And may Canaan be his servant."

28 And Noah lived after the flood three hundred and fifty years. 29 So all the days of Noah were nine hundred and fifty years; and he died.

10 NOW this *is* the genealogy of the sons of Noah: Shem, Ham, and Japheth. And sons were born to them after the flood.

2 The sons of Japheth *were* Gomer, Magog, Madai, Javan, Tubal, Meshech, and Tiras. 3 The sons of Gomer *were* Ashkenaz, Riphath, and Togarmah. 4 The sons of Javan *were* Elishah, Tarshish, Kittim, and Dodanim. 5 From these the coastland *peoples* of the Gentiles were separated into their lands, everyone according to his language, according to their families, into their nations.

6 The sons of Ham *were* Cush, Mizraim, Put, and Canaan. 7 The sons of Cush *were* Seba, Havilah, Sabtah, Raamah, and Sabtechah; and the sons of Raamah *were* Sheba and Dedan.

8 Cush begot Nimrod; he began to be a mighty one on the earth. 9 He was a mighty hunter before the LORD; therefore it is said, "Like Nimrod the mighty hunter before the LORD." 10 And the beginning of his kingdom was Babel, Erech, Accad, and Calneh, in the land of Shinar. 11 From that land he went to Assyria and built Nineveh, Rehoboth Ir, Calah, 12 and Resen between Nineveh and Calah (that *is* the principal city).

13 Mizraim begot Ludim, Anamim, Lehabim, Naphtuhim, 14 Pathrusim, and Casluhim (from whom came the Philistines and Caphtorim).

15 Canaan begot Sidon his firstborn, and Heth; 16 the Jebusite, the Amorite, and the Girgashite; 17 the Hivite, the Arkite, and the Sinite; 18 the Arvadite, the Zemarite, and the Hamathite. Afterward the families of the Canaanites were dispersed. 19 And the border of the Canaanites was from Sidon as you go toward Gerar, as far as Gaza; then as you go toward Sodom, Gomorrah, Admah, and Zeboiim, as far as Lasha. 20 These *were* the sons of Ham, according to their families, according to their languages, in their lands *and* in their nations.

21 And *children* were born also to Shem, the father of all the children of Eber, the brother of Japheth the elder. 22 The sons of Shem *were* Elam, Asshur, Arphaxad, Lud, and Aram. 23 The sons of Aram *were* Uz, Hul, Gether, and Mash. 24 Arphaxad begot Salah, and Salah begot Eber. 25 To Eber were born two sons: the name of one *was* Peleg, for in his days the earth was divided; and his brother's name *was* Joktan. 26 Joktan begot Almodad, Sheleph, Hazarmaveth, Jerah, 27 Hadoram, Uzal, Diklah, 28 Obal, Abimael, Sheba, 29 Ophir, Havilah, and Jobab. All these *were* the sons of Joktan. 30 And their dwelling place was from Mesha as you go toward Sephar, the mountain of the east. 31 These *were* the sons of Shem, according to their families, according to their languages, in their lands, according to their nations.

32 These *were* the families of the sons of Noah, according to their generations, in their nations; and from these the nations were divided on the earth after the flood.

PSALM 3:5–8

5   I lay down and slept;
    I awoke, for the LORD sustained me.
6   I will not be afraid of ten thousands
        of people
    Who have set *themselves* against me all
        around.

7   Arise, O LORD;
    Save me, O my God!
    For You have struck all my enemies
        on the cheekbone;
    You have broken the teeth of the
        ungodly.

8 Salvation *belongs* to the LORD.
   Your blessing *is* upon Your people.
                                        Selah

---

*O*ur *salvation comes to us so
easily because it cost God
so much*.   (PLACE HELP)

PROVERBS 1:23–27

23 TURN at my rebuke;
    Surely I will pour out my spirit on you;
    I will make my words known to you.
24 Because I have called and you refused,
    I have stretched out my hand and no
    one regarded,
25 Because you disdained all my counsel,
    And would have none of my rebuke,
26 I also will laugh at your calamity;
    I will mock when your terror comes;
27 When your terror comes like a storm,
    And your destruction comes like a
    whirlwind,
    When distress and anguish come upon
    you.

MATTHEW 5:1–26

AND seeing the multitudes, He went up
on a mountain, and when He was seated
His disciples came to Him. 2 Then He
opened His mouth and taught them, saying:

3   "Blessed *are* the poor in spirit,
       For theirs is the kingdom of
       heaven.
4   Blessed *are* those who mourn,
       For they shall be comforted.
5   Blessed *are* the meek,
       For they shall inherit the earth.
6   Blessed *are* those who hunger and
       thirst for righteousness,
       For they shall be filled.
7   Blessed *are* the merciful,
       For they shall obtain mercy.
8   Blessed *are* the pure in heart,
       For they shall see God.
9   Blessed *are* the peacemakers,
       For they shall be called sons of
       God.
10   Blessed are those who are persecuted
       for righteousness' sake,
       For theirs is the kingdom of
       heaven.

11 "Blessed are you when they revile and
persecute you, and say all kinds of evil
against you falsely for My sake. 12 Rejoice

and be exceedingly glad, for great *is* your
reward in heaven, for so they persecuted
the prophets who were before you.
13 "You are the salt of the earth; but if
the salt loses its flavor, how shall it be seasoned? It is then good for nothing but to
be thrown out and trampled underfoot by
men.
14 "You are the light of the world. A city
that is set on a hill cannot be hidden.
15 Nor do they light a lamp and put it under
a basket, but on a lampstand, and it gives
light to all *who are* in the house. 16 Let your
light so shine before men, that they may
see your good works and glorify your Father
in heaven.
17 "Do not think that I came to destroy
the Law or the Prophets. I did not come
to destroy but to fulfill. 18 For assuredly,
I say to you, till heaven and earth pass away,
one jot or one tittle will by no means pass
from the law till all is fulfilled. 19 Whoever
therefore breaks one of the least of these
commandments, and teaches men so, shall
be called least in the kingdom of heaven;
but whoever does and teaches *them,* he shall
be called great in the kingdom of heaven.
20 For I say to you, that unless your righteousness exceeds *the righteousness* of the
scribes and Pharisees, you will by no means
enter the kingdom of heaven.

---

*T*o *preach the Sermon on the Mount
apart from the Cross is to preach an
impossibility*.   (BIB. ETHICS)

---

21 "You have heard that it was said to
those of old, 'You shall not murder, and
whoever murders will be in danger of the
judgment.' 22 But I say to you that whoever
is angry with his brother without a cause
shall be in danger of the judgment. And
whoever says to his brother, 'Raca!' shall
be in danger of the council. But whoever
says, 'You fool!' shall be in danger of hell
fire. 23 Therefore if you bring your gift to
the altar, and there remember that your
brother has something against you,
24 leave your gift there before the altar, and
go your way. First be reconciled to your
brother, and then come and offer your gift.
25 Agree with your adversary quickly, while
you are on the way with him, lest your
adversary deliver you to the judge, the judge
hand you over to the officer, and you be
thrown into prison. 26 Assuredly, I say to
you, you will by no means get out of there
till you have paid the last penny.

Reading 6—The Calling of Abraham

Genesis 12:1

Personal acquaintance with God shows itself in separation, symbolized by Abraham's physical separation from his country and his kindred. Jesus Himself emphasized this need for separation (see Luke 14:26). Nowadays, such separation often involves a moral rather than a physical severance as we detach ourselves from the way those nearest and dearest to us think and look at things, if they do not have a personal relationship with God.

Those who would argue against obeying the call of God frequently take the shape of country and kindred, and if we listen to them, our ears will soon become dull to God's call. Their sympathy competes with God for the throne of our life, and we dissolve into the most commonplace Christians imaginable because we have no courage to strike out in faith. We have seen and heard but have not gone on. If we accept sympathy from those who have not heard the call of God, it will so blunt our own sense of His call that we become useless to Him.

Ultimately, every saint stands alone before God. And when He calls us to step out in faith, we begin the walk of faith alone, seeking no other comrade than the One who has called us for His purpose. (*NOT KNOWING*)

GENESIS 11:1—12:20

NOW the whole earth had one language and one speech. 2 And it came to pass, as they journeyed from the east, that they found a plain in the land of Shinar, and they dwelt there. 3 Then they said to one another, "Come, let us make bricks and bake *them* thoroughly." They had brick for stone, and they had asphalt for mortar. 4 And they said, "Come, let us build ourselves a city, and a tower whose top *is* in the heavens; let us make a name for ourselves, lest we be scattered abroad over the face of the whole earth."

5 But the LORD came down to see the city and the tower which the sons of men had built. 6 And the LORD said, "Indeed the people *are* one and they all have one language, and this is what they begin to do; now nothing that they propose to do will be withheld from them. 7 Come, let Us go down and there confuse their language, that they may not understand one another's speech." 8 So the LORD scattered them abroad from there over the face of all the earth, and they ceased building the city. 9 Therefore its name is called Babel, because there the LORD confused the language of all the earth; and from there the LORD scattered them abroad over the face of all the earth.

10 This *is* the genealogy of Shem: Shem *was* one hundred years old, and begot Arphaxad two years after the flood. 11 After he begot Arphaxad, Shem lived five hundred years, and begot sons and daughters.

12 Arphaxad lived thirty-five years, and begot Salah. 13 After he begot Salah, Arphaxad lived four hundred and three years, and begot sons and daughters.

14 Salah lived thirty years, and begot Eber. 15 After he begot Eber, Salah lived four hundred and three years, and begot sons and daughters.

16 Eber lived thirty-four years, and begot Peleg. 17 After he begot Peleg, Eber lived four hundred and thirty years, and begot sons and daughters.

18 Peleg lived thirty years, and begot Reu. 19 After he begot Reu, Peleg lived two hundred and nine years, and begot sons and daughters.

20 Reu lived thirty-two years, and begot Serug. 21 After he begot Serug, Reu lived two hundred and seven years, and begot sons and daughters.

22 Serug lived thirty years, and begot Nahor. 23 After he begot Nahor, Serug lived two hundred years, and begot sons and daughters.

24 Nahor lived twenty-nine years, and begot Terah. 25 After he begot Terah, Nahor lived one hundred and nineteen years, and begot sons and daughters.

26 Now Terah lived seventy years, and begot Abram, Nahor, and Haran.

27 This *is* the genealogy of Terah: Terah begot Abram, Nahor, and Haran. Haran begot Lot. 28 And Haran died before his father Terah in his native land, in Ur of the Chaldeans. 29 Then Abram and Nahor took wives: the name of Abram's wife *was* Sarai, and the name of Nahor's wife, Milcah, the daughter of Haran the father of Milcah and the father of Iscah. 30 But Sarai was barren; she had no child.

31 And Terah took his son Abram and his grandson Lot, the son of Haran, and his daughter-in-law Sarai, his son Abram's wife, and they went out with them from Ur of the Chaldeans to go to the land of Canaan; and they came to Haran and dwelt there. 32 So the days of Terah were two hundred and five years, and Terah died in Haran.

12 NOW the Lord had said to Abram:

"Get out of your country,
From your family
And from your father's house,
To a land that I will show you.
2   I will make you a great nation;
I will bless you
And make your name great;
And you shall be a blessing.
3   I will bless those who bless you,
And I will curse him who curses you;
And in you all the families of the earth shall be blessed."

To be brought into the zone of the call of God is to be profoundly altered.   (UTMOST)

4 So Abram departed as the Lord had spoken to him, and Lot went with him. And Abram *was* seventy-five years old when he departed from Haran. 5 Then Abram took Sarai his wife and Lot his brother's son, and all their possessions that they had gathered, and the people whom they had acquired in Haran, and they departed to go to the land of Canaan. So they came to the land of Canaan. 6 Abram passed through the land to the place of Shechem, as far as the terebinth tree of Moreh. And the Canaanites *were* then in the land.

7 Then the Lord appeared to Abram and said, "To your descendants I will give this land." And there he built an altar to the Lord, who had appeared to him. 8 And he moved from there to the mountain east of Bethel, and he pitched his tent *with* Bethel

on the west and Ai on the east; there he built an altar to the Lord and called on the name of the Lord. 9 So Abram journeyed, going on still toward the South.

10 Now there was a famine in the land, and Abram went down to Egypt to dwell there, for the famine *was* severe in the land. 11 And it came to pass, when he was close to entering Egypt, that he said to Sarai his wife, "Indeed I know that you *are* a woman of beautiful countenance. 12 Therefore it will happen, when the Egyptians see you, that they will say, 'This *is* his wife'; and they will kill me, but they will let you live. 13 Please say you *are* my sister, that it may be well with me for your sake, and that I may live because of you."

14 So it was, when Abram came into Egypt, that the Egyptians saw the woman, that she *was* very beautiful. 15 The princes of Pharaoh also saw her and commended her to Pharaoh. And the woman was taken to Pharaoh's house. 16 He treated Abram well for her sake. He had sheep, oxen, male donkeys, male and female servants, female donkeys, and camels.

17 But the Lord plagued Pharaoh and his house with great plagues because of Sarai, Abram's wife. 18 And Pharaoh called Abram and said, "What *is* this you have done to me? Why did you not tell me that she *was* your wife? 19 Why did you say, 'She *is* my sister'? I might have taken her as my wife. Now therefore, here is your wife; take *her* and go your way." 20 So Pharaoh commanded *his* men concerning him; and they sent him away, with his wife and all that he had.

PSALM 4:1–3

1   HEAR me when I call, O God of my righteousness!
You have relieved me in *my* distress;
Have mercy on me, and hear my prayer.

2   How long, O you sons of men,
Will you turn my glory to shame?
How long will you love worthlessness
And seek falsehood?   Selah
3   But know that the Lord has set apart for Himself him who is godly;
The Lord will hear when I call to Him.

PROVERBS 1:28–33

28 "THEN they will call on me, but I will not answer;
They will seek me diligently, but they will not find me.

29   Because they hated knowledge
     And did not choose the fear of the
        LORD,
30   They would have none of my counsel
     And despised my every rebuke.
31   Therefore they shall eat the fruit of their
        own way,
     And be filled to the full with their own
        fancies.
32   For the turning away of the simple will
        slay them,
     And the complacency of fools will
        destroy them;
33   But whoever listens to me will dwell
        safely,
     And will be secure, without fear of evil."

MATTHEW 5:27–48

"YOU have heard that it was said to those
of old, 'You shall not commit adultery.'
28 But I say to you that whoever looks at
a woman to lust for her has already committed adultery with her in his heart.
29 If your right eye causes you to sin, pluck
it out and cast *it* from you; for it is more
profitable for you that one of your members
perish, than for your whole body to be cast
into hell. 30 And if your right hand causes
you to sin, cut it off and cast *it* from you;
for it is more profitable for you that one
of your members perish, than for your
whole body to be cast into hell.

31 "Furthermore it has been said, 'Whoever divorces his wife, let him give her a
certificate of divorce.' 32 But I say to you
that whoever divorces his wife for any reason except sexual immorality causes her to
commit adultery; and whoever marries a
woman who is divorced commits adultery.

33 "Again you have heard that it was said
to those of old, 'You shall not swear falsely,
but shall perform your oaths to the Lord.'

34 But I say to you, do not swear at all:
neither by heaven, for it is God's throne;
35 nor by the earth, for it is His footstool;
nor by Jerusalem, for it is the city of the
great King. 36 Nor shall you swear by your
head, because you cannot make one hair
white or black. 37 But let your 'Yes' be 'Yes,'
and your 'No,' 'No.' For whatever is more
than these is from the evil one.

38 "You have heard that it was said, 'An
eye for an eye and a tooth for a tooth.'
39 But I tell you not to resist an evil person.
But whoever slaps you on your right cheek,
turn the other to him also. 40 If anyone
wants to sue you and take away your tunic,
let him have *your* cloak also. 41 And whoever
compels you to go one mile, go with him
two. 42 Give to him who asks you, and from
him who wants to borrow from you do
not turn away.

43 "You have heard that it was said, 'You
shall love your neighbor and hate your enemy.' 44 But I say to you, love your enemies,
bless those who curse you, do good to those
who hate you, and pray for those who spitefully use you and persecute you, 45 that you
may be sons of your Father in heaven; for
He makes His sun rise on the evil and on
the good, and sends rain on the just and
on the unjust. 46 For if you love those who
love you, what reward have you? Do not
even the tax collectors do the same?

---

*L*ove is not measured by what it gets
but by what it costs.   (PSY. REDEMP.)

---

47 And if you greet your brethren only, what
do you do more *than others?* Do not even
the tax collectors do so? 48 Therefore you
shall be perfect, just as your Father in heaven
is perfect.

◆◆◆◆

Reading 7—The Selected Place

Matthew 6:6

Did you ever say anything like this to yourself, "It is so difficult to select
a place"? What about the time when you were in love, was it impossible
to select a place to meet in? No, it was far from impossible; and beware of
self-indulgence. Think how long our Lord has waited for you; you have seen
Him in your visions, now pray to Him; get a place, not a mood, but a definite
material place and resort to it constantly, and pray to God as His Spirit in
you will help you. Bring to earth the promised life you have longed for, curb

your impulsive undisciplined wayward nature to His use, and rule in your body like a king where now, even in strength and honesty, you walk sentenced to be a prey to baser and less spiritual things. Do not say, "If I only had so and so"; you have not got so and so; but you can, if you will, select a place where you are actually. We can always do what we want to do if we want to do it sufficiently keenly. Do it now, "go into your room"; and remember, it is a place selected to pray in, not to make little addresses in, or for any other purpose than to pray in, never forget that.   (CHR. DISCPL.)

GENESIS 13:1—14:24

THEN Abram went up from Egypt, he and his wife and all that he had, and Lot with him, to the South. 2 Abram *was* very rich in livestock, in silver, and in gold. 3 And he went on his journey from the South as far as Bethel, to the place where his tent had been at the beginning, between Bethel and Ai, 4 to the place of the altar which he had made there at first. And there Abram called on the name of the LORD.

5 Lot also, who went with Abram, had flocks and herds and tents. 6 Now the land was not able to support them, that they might dwell together, for their possessions were so great that they could not dwell together. 7 And there was strife between the herdsmen of Abram's livestock and the herdsmen of Lot's livestock. The Canaanites and the Perizzites then dwelt in the land.

8 So Abram said to Lot, "Please let there be no strife between you and me, and between my herdsmen and your herdsmen; for we *are* brethren. 9 *Is* not the whole land before you? Please separate from me. If *you take* the left, then I will go to the right; or, if *you go* to the right, then I will go to the left."

10 And Lot lifted his eyes and saw all the plain of Jordan, that it *was* well watered everywhere (before the LORD destroyed Sodom and Gomorrah) like the garden of the LORD, like the land of Egypt as you go toward Zoar. 11 Then Lot chose for himself all the plain of Jordan, and Lot journeyed east. And they separated from each other. 12 Abram dwelt in the land of Canaan, and Lot dwelt in the cities of the plain and pitched *his* tent even as far as Sodom. 13 But the men of Sodom *were* exceedingly wicked and sinful against the LORD.

14 And the LORD said to Abram, after Lot had separated from him: "Lift your eyes now and look from the place where you are—northward, southward, eastward, and westward; 15 for all the land which you see I give to you and your descendants forever. 16 And I will make your descendants as the dust of the earth; so that if a man could number the dust of the earth, *then* your descendants also could be numbered. 17 Arise, walk in the land through its length and its width, for I give it to you."

18 Then Abram moved *his* tent, and went and dwelt by the terebinth trees of Mamre, which *are* in Hebron, and built an altar there to the LORD.

14 AND it came to pass in the days of Amraphel king of Shinar, Arioch king of Ellasar, Chedorlaomer king of Elam, and Tidal king of nations, 2 *that* they made war with Bera king of Sodom, Birsha king of Gomorrah, Shinab king of Admah, Shemeber king of Zeboiim, and the king of Bela (that is, Zoar). 3 All these joined together in the Valley of Siddim (that is, the Salt Sea). 4 Twelve years they served Chedorlaomer, and in the thirteenth year they rebelled.

5 In the fourteenth year Chedorlaomer and the kings that *were* with him came and attacked the Rephaim in Ashteroth Karnaim, the Zuzim in Ham, the Emim in Shaveh Kiriathaim, 6 and the Horites in their mountain of Seir, as far as El Paran, which *is* by the wilderness. 7 Then they turned back and came to En Mishpat (that *is*, Kadesh), and attacked all the country of the Amalekites, and also the Amorites who dwelt in Hazezon Tamar.

8 And the king of Sodom, the king of Gomorrah, the king of Admah, the king of Zeboiim, and the king of Bela (that *is*, Zoar) went out and joined together in battle in the Valley of Siddim 9 against Chedorlaomer king of Elam, Tidal king of nations, Amraphel king of Shinar, and Arioch king of Ellasar—four kings against five. 10 Now the Valley of Siddim *was full of* asphalt pits; and the kings of Sodom and Gomorrah fled; *some* fell there, and the remainder fled to the mountains. 11 Then they took all the goods of Sodom and Gomorrah, and all their provisions, and went their way. 12 They also took Lot, Abram's brother's

son who dwelt in Sodom, and his goods, and departed.

13 Then one who had escaped came and told Abram the Hebrew, for he dwelt by the terebinth trees of Mamre the Amorite, brother of Eshcol and brother of Aner; and they *were* allies with Abram. 14 Now when Abram heard that his brother was taken captive, he armed his three hundred and eighteen trained *servants* who were born in his own house, and went in pursuit as far as Dan. 15 He divided his forces against them by night, and he and his servants attacked them and pursued them as far as Hobah, which *is* north of Damascus. 16 So he brought back all the goods, and also brought back his brother Lot and his goods, as well as the women and the people.

17 And the king of Sodom went out to meet him at the Valley of Shaveh (that *is,* the King's Valley), after his return from the defeat of Chedorlaomer and the kings who *were* with him.

18 Then Melchizedek king of Salem brought out bread and wine; he *was* the priest of God Most High. 19 And he blessed him and said:

"Blessed be Abram of God Most High, Possessor of heaven and earth;
20   And blessed be God Most High, Who has delivered your enemies into your hand."

And he gave him a tithe of all.

21 Now the king of Sodom said to Abram, "Give me the persons, and take the goods for yourself."

22 But Abram said to the king of Sodom, "I have raised my hand to the LORD, God Most High, the Possessor of heaven and earth, 23 that I *will take* nothing, from a thread to a sandal strap, and that I will not take anything that *is* yours, lest you should say, 'I have made Abram rich'— 24 except only what the young men have eaten, and the portion of the men who went with me: Aner, Eshcol, and Mamre; let them take their portion."

PSALM 4:4–8

4   BE angry, and do not sin.
Meditate within your heart on your
bed, and be still.   Selah
5   Offer the sacrifices of righteousness,
And put your trust in the LORD.

6   *There are* many who say,
"Who will show us *any* good?"

LORD, lift up the light of Your countenance upon us.
7   You have put gladness in my heart, More than in the season that their grain and wine increased.
8   I will both lie down in peace, and sleep; For You alone, O LORD, make me dwell in safety.

PROVERBS 2:1–5

1   MY son, if you receive my words, And treasure my commands within you,
2   So that you incline your ear to wisdom, *And* apply your heart to understanding;

---

*T*he world of wisdom is arrant stupidity to the wisdom of the world.   (SHADE)

---

3   Yes, if you cry out for discernment, *And* lift up your voice for understanding,
4   If you seek her as silver, And search for her as *for* hidden treasures;
5   Then you will understand the fear of the LORD, And find the knowledge of God.

MATTHEW 6:1–18

"TAKE heed that you do not do your charitable deeds before men, to be seen by them. Otherwise you have no reward from your Father in heaven. 2 Therefore, when you do a charitable deed, do not sound a trumpet before you as the hypocrites do in the synagogues and in the streets, that they may have glory from men. Assuredly, I say to you, they have their reward. 3 But when you do a charitable deed, do not let your left hand know what your right hand is doing, 4 that your charitable deed may be in secret; and your Father who sees in secret will Himself reward you openly.

5 "And when you pray, you shall not be like the hypocrites. For they love to pray standing in the synagogues and on the corners of the streets, that they may be seen by men. Assuredly, I say to you, they have their reward. 6 But you, when you pray, go into your room, and when you have shut your door, pray to your Father who *is* in the secret *place;* and your Father who sees in secret will reward you openly.

7 And when you pray, do not use vain repetitions as the heathen *do*. For they think that they will be heard for their many words.

Jesus Christ does not pay any attention to the gift of "religious gab." (ASK)

---

8 "Therefore do not be like them. For your Father knows the things you have need of before you ask Him. 9 In this manner, therefore, pray:

Our Father in heaven,
Hallowed be Your name.
10 Your kingdom come.
Your will be done
On earth as *it is* in heaven.
11 Give us this day our daily bread.
12 And forgive us our debts,

As we forgive our debtors.
13 And do not lead us into temptation,
But deliver us from the evil one.
For Yours is the kingdom and the
power and the glory forever.
Amen.

14 "For if you forgive men their trespasses, your heavenly Father will also forgive you. 15 But if you do not forgive men their trespasses, neither will your Father forgive your trespasses.

16 "Moreover, when you fast, do not be like the hypocrites, with a sad countenance. For they disfigure their faces that they may appear to men to be fasting. Assuredly, I say to you, they have their reward. 17 But you, when you fast, anoint your head and wash your face, 18 so that you do not appear to men to be fasting, but to your Father who *is* in the secret *place;* and your Father who sees in secret will reward you openly.

◆◆◆◆

Reading 8—A Star-Hitched Wagon
Genesis 15:4, 5

In this chapter we fathom the depths of all that the New Testament unfolds. Abraham the childless is to become the father of nations. How mad the promise sounds! God points Abraham away from his wagon in the mud to that starry night and hitches the two together by His own word. God's appeal to the stars is not to furnish proof for a doubting mind, but to provide nourishment for a faltering faith. Nature to the saint is a sacrament of God, not merely a series of facts; not symbols and signs, but the real evidence of the coming of God as a sacrament to His faithful children.

The whole discipline of the life of faith is to mix together the light of heaven and the sordid actuality of earth. Contemplation and consideration must go together. We must take our plan for what we do on earth from the altitude of heaven; let contemplation of the stars be mixed with what we build on earth. (*NOT KNOWING*)

GENESIS 15:1—16:16

AFTER these things the word of the LORD came to Abram in a vision, saying, "Do not be afraid, Abram. I *am* your shield, your exceedingly great reward."

2 But Abram said, "Lord GOD, what will You give me, seeing I go childless, and the heir of my house *is* Eliezer of Damascus?" 3 Then Abram said, "Look, You have given me no offspring; indeed one born in my house is my heir!"

4 And behold, the word of the LORD *came* to him, saying, "This one shall not be your heir, but one who will come from your own body shall be your heir." 5 Then He brought him outside and said, "Look now toward heaven, and count the stars if you are able to number them." And He said to him, "So shall your descendants be."

6 And he believed in the LORD, and He accounted it to him for righteousness.

7 Then He said to him, "I *am* the LORD,

who brought you out of Ur of the Chaldeans, to give you this land to inherit it."

8 And he said, "Lord GOD, how shall I know that I will inherit it?"

9 So He said to him, "Bring Me a three-year-old heifer, a three-year-old female goat, a three-year-old ram, a turtledove, and a young pigeon." 10 Then he brought all these to Him and cut them in two, down the middle, and placed each piece opposite the other; but he did not cut the birds in two. 11 And when the vultures came down on the carcasses, Abram drove them away.

12 Now when the sun was going down, a deep sleep fell upon Abram; and behold, horror *and* great darkness fell upon him. 13 Then He said to Abram: "Know certainly that your descendants will be strangers in a land *that is* not theirs, and will serve them, and they will afflict them four hundred years. 14 And also the nation whom they serve I will judge; afterward they shall come out with great possessions. 15 Now as for you, you shall go to your fathers in peace; you shall be buried at a good old age. 16 But in the fourth generation they shall return here, for the iniquity of the Amorites *is* not yet complete."

17 And it came to pass, when the sun went down and it was dark, that behold, there appeared a smoking oven and a burning torch that passed between those pieces. 18 On the same day the LORD made a covenant with Abram, saying:

"To your descendants I have given this land, from the river of Egypt to the great river, the River Euphrates— 19 the Kenites, the Kenezzites, the Kadmonites, 20 the Hittites, the Perizzites, the Rephaim, 21 the Amorites, the Canaanites, the Girgashites, and the Jebusites."

16 NOW Sarai, Abram's wife, had borne him no *children*. And she had an Egyptian maidservant whose name was Hagar. 2 So Sarai said to Abram, "See now, the LORD has restrained me from bearing *children*. Please, go in to my maid; perhaps I shall obtain children by her." And Abram heeded the voice of Sarai. 3 Then Sarai, Abram's wife, took Hagar her maid, the Egyptian, and gave her to her husband Abram to be his wife, after Abram had dwelt ten years in the land of Canaan. 4 So he went in to Hagar, and she conceived. And when she saw that she had conceived, her mistress became despised in her eyes.

5 Then Sarai said to Abram, "My wrong *be* upon you! I gave my maid into your embrace; and when she saw that she had conceived, I became despised in her eyes.

The LORD judge between you and me."

6 So Abram said to Sarai, "Indeed your maid *is* in your hand; do to her as you please." And when Sarai dealt harshly with her, she fled from her presence.

7 Now the Angel of the LORD found her by a spring of water in the wilderness, by the spring on the way to Shur. 8 And He said, "Hagar, Sarai's maid, where have you come from, and where are you going?"

She said, "I am fleeing from the presence of my mistress Sarai."

9 The Angel of the LORD said to her, "Return to your mistress, and submit yourself under her hand." 10 Then the Angel of the LORD said to her, "I will multiply your descendants exceedingly, so that they shall not be counted for multitude." 11 And the Angel of the LORD said to her:

"Behold, you *are* with child,
And you shall bear a son.
You shall call his name Ishmael,
Because the LORD has heard your
affliction.
12 He shall be a wild man;
His hand *shall be* against every man,
And every man's hand against him.
And he shall dwell in the presence
of all his brethren."

13 Then she called the name of the LORD who spoke to her, You-Are-the-God-Who-Sees; for she said, "Have I also here seen Him who sees me?" 14 Therefore the well was called Beer Lahai Roi; observe, *it is* between Kadesh and Bered.

15 So Hagar bore Abram a son; and Abram named his son, whom Hagar bore, Ishmael. 16 Abram *was* eighty-six years old when Hagar bore Ishmael to Abram.

PSALM 5:1–7

1 GIVE ear to my words, O LORD,
   Consider my meditation.
2 Give heed to the voice of my cry,
   My King and my God,
   For to You I will pray.
3 My voice You shall hear in the morning,
   O LORD;
   In the morning I will direct *it* to You,
   And I will look up.

4 For You *are* not a God who takes
   pleasure in wickedness,
   Nor shall evil dwell with You.
5 The boastful shall not stand in Your
   sight;
   You hate all workers of iniquity.

6   You shall destroy those who speak
    falsehood;
    The LORD abhors the bloodthirsty and
    deceitful man.

7   But as for me, I will come into Your
    house in the multitude of Your
    mercy;
    In fear of You I will worship toward
    Your holy temple.

PROVERBS 2:6–9

6   FOR the LORD gives wisdom;
    From His mouth *come* knowledge and
    understanding;
7   He stores up sound wisdom for the
    upright;
    He is a shield to those who walk
    uprightly;
8   He guards the paths of justice,
    And preserves the way of His saints.

---

*Justice means rightness with God,
nothing is just until it is adjusted
to God.*   (MORAL FOUND.)

---

9   Then you will understand righteousness
    and justice,
    Equity *and* every good path.

MATTHEW 6:19–34

"DO not lay up for yourselves treasures
on earth, where moth and rust destroy and
where thieves break in and steal; 20 but lay
up for yourselves treasures in heaven, where
neither moth nor rust destroys and where
thieves do not break in and steal. 21 For
where your treasure is, there your heart will
be also.
22 "The lamp of the body is the eye. If
therefore your eye is good, your whole body

will be full of light. 23 But if your eye is
bad, your whole body will be full of darkness. If therefore the light that is in you is
darkness, how great *is* that darkness!
24 "No one can serve two masters; for
either he will hate the one and love the
other, or else he will be loyal to the one
and despise the other. You cannot serve
God and mammon.
25 "Therefore I say to you, do not worry
about your life, what you will eat or what
you will drink; nor about your body, what
you will put on. Is not life more than food
and the body more than clothing? 26 Look
at the birds of the air, for they neither sow
nor reap nor gather into barns; yet your
heavenly Father feeds them. Are you not
of more value than they? 27 Which of you
by worrying can add one cubit to his
stature?

---

*Imagine the sparrows and blackbirds
and thrushes worrying about their
feathers!*   (SERMON MT.)

---

28 "So why do you worry about clothing?
Consider the lilies of the field, how they
grow: they neither toil nor spin; 29 and yet
I say to you that even Solomon in all his
glory was not arrayed like one of these.
30 Now if God so clothes the grass of the
field, which today is, and tomorrow is
thrown into the oven, *will He* not much
more *clothe* you, O you of little faith?
31 "Therefore do not worry, saying,
'What shall we eat?' or 'What shall we
drink?' or 'What shall we wear?' 32 For after
all these things the Gentiles seek. For your
heavenly Father knows that you need all
these things. 33 But seek first the kingdom
of God and His righteousness, and all these
things shall be added to you. 34 Therefore
do not worry about tomorrow, for tomorrow will worry about its own things. Sufficient for the day *is* its own trouble.

◆◆◆◆

---

*Reading 9—*The Power of Publicity
Matthew 7:19, 20

The thing that enraged our Lord's enemies was the public manner in
which He did things; His miracles were the public manifestation of His
power. Today people are annoyed at public testimony. It is no use saying,
"Oh yes, I live a holy life, but I don't say anything about it." . . . If a thing

has its root in the heart of God, it will want to be public, to get out, it must do things in the external and the open, and Jesus not only encouraged this publicity. He insisted upon it. . . . "There is nothing covered that will not be revealed, and hidden that will not be known." It is God's law that men cannot hide what they really are. If they are His disciples it will be publicly portrayed. In Matthew 10 Jesus warned His disciples of what would happen when they publicly testified, but, He said, "Don't hide your light under a bushel for fear of wolfish men; be careful only that you don't go contrary to your duty and have your soul destroyed in hell as well as your body. Be wise as serpents and harmless as doves." . . . As surely as God is on His throne, the inevitable principle must work, the revealing of what men really are.   (*SERMON MT.*)

GENESIS 17:1—18:33

WHEN Abram was ninety-nine years old, the LORD appeared to Abram and said to him, "I *am* Almighty God; walk before Me and be blameless. 2 And I will make My covenant between Me and you, and will multiply you exceedingly." 3 Then Abram fell on his face, and God talked with him, saying: 4 "As for Me, behold, My covenant is with you, and you shall be a father of many nations. 5 No longer shall your name be called Abram, but your name shall be Abraham; for I have made you a father of many nations. 6 I will make you exceedingly fruitful; and I will make nations of you, and kings shall come from you. 7 And I will establish My covenant between Me and you and your descendants after you in their generations, for an everlasting covenant, to be God to you and your descendants after you. 8 Also I give to you and your descendants after you the land in which you are a stranger, all the land of Canaan, as an everlasting possession; and I will be their God."

9 And God said to Abraham: "As for you, you shall keep My covenant, you and your descendants after you throughout their generations. 10 This *is* My covenant which you shall keep, between Me and you and your descendants after you: Every male child among you shall be circumcised; 11 and you shall be circumcised in the flesh of your foreskins, and it shall be a sign of the covenant between Me and you. 12 He who is eight days old among you shall be circumcised, every male child in your generations, he who is born in your house or bought with money from any foreigner who is not your descendant. 13 He who is born in your house and he who is bought with your money must be circumcised, and My covenant shall be in your flesh for an everlasting

covenant. 14 And the uncircumcised male child, who is not circumcised in the flesh of his foreskin, that person shall be cut off from his people; he has broken My covenant."

15 Then God said to Abraham, "As for Sarai your wife, you shall not call her name Sarai, but Sarah *shall be* her name. 16 And I will bless her and also give you a son by her; then I will bless her, and she shall be *a mother of* nations; kings of peoples shall be from her."

17 Then Abraham fell on his face and laughed, and said in his heart, "Shall *a child* be born to a man who is one hundred years old? And shall Sarah, who is ninety years old, bear *a child?*" 18 And Abraham said to God, "Oh, that Ishmael might live before You!"

19 Then God said: "No, Sarah your wife shall bear you a son, and you shall call his name Isaac; I will establish My covenant with him for an everlasting covenant, *and* with his descendants after him. 20 And as for Ishmael, I have heard you. Behold, I have blessed him, and will make him fruitful, and will multiply him exceedingly. He shall beget twelve princes, and I will make him a great nation. 21 But My covenant I will establish with Isaac, whom Sarah shall bear to you at this set time next year." 22 Then He finished talking with him, and God went up from Abraham.

23 So Abraham took Ishmael his son, all who were born in his house and all who were bought with his money, every male among the men of Abraham's house, and circumcised the flesh of their foreskins that very same day, as God had said to him. 24 Abraham *was* ninety-nine years old when he was circumcised in the flesh of his foreskin. 25 And Ishmael his son *was* thirteen years old when he was circumcised in the flesh of his foreskin. 26 That very same day Abraham was circumcised, and his son

Ishmael; 27 and all the men of his house, born in the house or bought with money from a foreigner, were circumcised with him.

18 THEN the LORD appeared to him by the terebinth trees of Mamre, as he was sitting in the tent door in the heat of the day. 2 So he lifted his eyes and looked, and behold, three men were standing by him; and when he saw *them,* he ran from the tent door to meet them, and bowed himself to the ground, 3 and said, "My Lord, if I have now found favor in Your sight, do not pass on by Your servant. 4 Please let a little water be brought, and wash your feet, and rest yourselves under the tree. 5 And I will bring a morsel of bread, that you may refresh your hearts. After that you may pass by, inasmuch as you have come to your servant."

They said, "Do as you have said."

6 So Abraham hurried into the tent to Sarah and said, "Quickly, make ready three measures of fine meal; knead *it* and make cakes." 7 And Abraham ran to the herd, took a tender and good calf, gave *it* to a young man, and he hastened to prepare it. 8 So he took butter and milk and the calf which he had prepared, and set *it* before them; and he stood by them under the tree as they ate.

9 Then they said to him, "Where *is* Sarah your wife?"

So he said, "Here, in the tent."

10 And He said, "I will certainly return to you according to the time of life, and behold, Sarah your wife shall have a son." (Sarah was listening in the tent door which *was* behind him.) 11 Now Abraham and Sarah were old, well advanced in age; *and* Sarah had passed the age of childbearing. 12 Therefore Sarah laughed within herself, saying, "After I have grown old, shall I have pleasure, my lord being old also?"

13 And the LORD said to Abraham, "Why did Sarah laugh, saying, 'Shall I surely bear *a child,* since I am old?' 14 Is anything too hard for the LORD? At the appointed time I will return to you, according to the time of life, and Sarah shall have a son."

15 But Sarah denied *it,* saying, "I did not laugh," for she was afraid.

And He said, "No, but you did laugh!"

16 Then the men rose from there and looked toward Sodom, and Abraham went with them to send them on the way. 17 And the LORD said, "Shall I hide from Abraham what I am doing, 18 since Abraham shall surely become a great and mighty nation, and all the nations of the earth shall be blessed in him? 19 For I have known him, in order that he may command his children and his household after him, that they keep the way of the LORD, to do righteousness and justice, that the LORD may bring to Abraham what He has spoken to him." 20 And the LORD said, "Because the outcry against Sodom and Gomorrah is great, and because their sin is very grave, 21 I will go down now and see whether they have done altogether according to the outcry against it that has come to Me; and if not, I will know."

22 Then the men turned away from there and went toward Sodom, but Abraham still stood before the LORD. 23 And Abraham came near and said, "Would You also destroy the righteous with the wicked? 24 Suppose there were fifty righteous within the city; would You also destroy the place and not spare *it* for the fifty righteous that were in it? 25 Far be it from You to do such a thing as this, to slay the righteous with the wicked, so that the righteous should be as the wicked; far be it from You! Shall not the Judge of all the earth do right?"

26 So the LORD said, "If I find in Sodom fifty righteous within the city, then I will spare all the place for their sakes."

27 Then Abraham answered and said, "Indeed now, I who *am but* dust and ashes have taken it upon myself to speak to the Lord: 28 Suppose there were five less than the fifty righteous; would You destroy all of the city for *lack of* five?"

So He said, "If I find there forty-five, I will not destroy *it.*"

29 And he spoke to Him yet again and said, "Suppose there should be forty found there?"

So He said, "I will not do *it* for the sake of forty."

30 Then he said, "Let not the Lord be angry, and I will speak: Suppose thirty should be found there?"

So He said, "I will not do *it* if I find thirty there."

31 And he said, "Indeed now, I have taken it upon myself to speak to the Lord: Suppose twenty should be found there?"

So He said, "I will not destroy *it* for the sake of twenty."

32 Then he said, "Let not the Lord be angry, and I will speak but once more: Suppose ten should be found there?"

And He said, "I will not destroy *it* for the sake of ten." 33 So the LORD went His way as soon as He had finished speaking with Abraham; and Abraham returned to his place.

PSALM 5:8–12

8 LEAD me, O LORD, in Your
      righteousness because of my enemies;
      Make Your way straight before my face.

9 For *there is* no faithfulness in their
      mouth;
      Their inward part *is* destruction;
      Their throat *is* an open tomb;
      They flatter with their tongue.
10 Pronounce them guilty, O God!
      Let them fall by their own counsels;
      Cast them out in the multitude of their
      transgressions,
      For they have rebelled against You.

11 But let all those rejoice who put their
      trust in You;
      Let them ever shout for joy, because
      You defend them;
      Let those also who love Your name
      Be joyful in You.

---

*Beware of trusting in your trust
and see that you trust in the
Lord.*   (NOT KNOWING)

---

12 For You, O LORD, will bless the
      righteous;
      With favor You will surround him as
      with a shield.

PROVERBS 2:10–22

10 WHEN wisdom enters your heart,
      And knowledge is pleasant to your soul,
11 Discretion will preserve you;
      Understanding will keep you,
12 To deliver you from the way of evil,
      From the man who speaks perverse
      things,
13 From those who leave the paths of
      uprightness
      To walk in the ways of darkness;
14 Who rejoice in doing evil,
      And delight in the perversity of the
      wicked;
15 Whose ways *are* crooked,
      And *who are* devious in their paths;
16 To deliver you from the immoral
      woman,
      From the seductress *who* flatters with
      her words,
17 Who forsakes the companion of her
      youth,
      And forgets the covenant of her God.

18 For her house leads down to death,
      And her paths to the dead;
19 None who go to her return,
      Nor do they regain the paths of life—
20 So you may walk in the way of
      goodness,
      And keep *to* the paths of righteousness.
21 For the upright will dwell in the land,
      And the blameless will remain in it;
22 But the wicked will be cut off from
      the earth,
      And the unfaithful will be uprooted
      from it.

MATTHEW 7:1–29

"JUDGE not, that you be not judged.
2 For with what judgment you judge, you
will be judged; and with the measure you
use, it will be measured back to you.
3 And why do you look at the speck in
your brother's eye, but do not consider the
plank in your own eye? 4 Or how can you
say to your brother, 'Let me remove the
speck from your eye'; and look, a plank *is*
in your own eye? 5 Hypocrite! First remove
the plank from your own eye, and then
you will see clearly to remove the speck
from your brother's eye.

---

*There is always one fact more in
every life of which we know
nothing.*   (SERMON MT.)

---

6 "Do not give what is holy to the dogs;
nor cast your pearls before swine, lest they
trample them under their feet, and turn and
tear you in pieces.
7 "Ask, and it will be given to you; seek,
and you will find; knock, and it will be
opened to you. 8 For everyone who asks
receives, and he who seeks finds, and to
him who knocks it will be opened.
9 Or what man is there among you who,
if his son asks for bread, will give him a
stone? 10 Or if he asks for a fish, will he
give him a serpent? 11 If you then, being
evil, know how to give good gifts to your
children, how much more will your Father
who is in heaven give good things to those
who ask Him! 12 Therefore, whatever you
want men to do to you, do also to them,
for this is the Law and the Prophets.
13 "Enter by the narrow gate; for wide
is the gate and broad *is* the way that leads
to destruction, and there are many who

go in by it. 14 Because narrow *is* the gate and difficult *is* the way which leads to life, and there are few who find it.

15 "Beware of false prophets, who come to you in sheep's clothing, but inwardly they are ravenous wolves. 16 You will know them by their fruits. Do men gather grapes from thornbushes or figs from thistles? 17 Even so, every good tree bears good fruit, but a bad tree bears bad fruit. 18 A good tree cannot bear bad fruit, nor *can* a bad tree bear good fruit. 19 Every tree that does not bear good fruit is cut down and thrown into the fire. 20 Therefore by their fruits you will know them.

21 "Not everyone who says to Me, 'Lord, Lord,' shall enter the kingdom of heaven, but he who does the will of My Father in heaven. 22 Many will say to Me in that day, 'Lord, Lord, have we not prophesied in Your name, cast out demons in Your name, and done many wonders in Your name?'

23 And then I will declare to them, 'I never knew you; depart from Me, you who practice lawlessness!'

24 "Therefore whoever hears these sayings of Mine, and does them, I will liken him to a wise man who built his house on the rock: 25 and the rain descended, the floods came, and the winds blew and beat on that house; and it did not fall, for it was founded on the rock.

26 "But everyone who hears these sayings of Mine, and does not do them, will be like a foolish man who built his house on the sand: 27 and the rain descended, the floods came, and the winds blew and beat on that house; and it fell. And great was its fall."

28 And so it was, when Jesus had ended these sayings, that the people were astonished at His teaching, 29 for He taught them as one having authority, and not as the scribes.

◆◆◆◆

Reading 10—Humiliation and Honor
Genesis 20:11–18

The way in which Abraham offers his apologies reveals clearly that he was ashamed. The fear of man that had driven him earlier was awakened afresh by what he had so recently seen in Sodom, and he was suspicious of human nature everywhere. Abraham ashamedly explains his motive and his equivocation (Gen. 20:11). He admits that Sarah is not his sister, but he also indicates that his reason for lying has deservedly brought him humiliation. There was none of the sneaky element in Abraham that we see later in Jacob; Abraham was trying to guard Sarah for God because of the promised child. . . .

Our Lord never evidenced the slightest sign of fear or cunning or diplomacy. He was never suspicious of anyone; yet He trusted in no one except His Father. Consequently He was never vindictive, nor was He ever humiliated. It is only possible to be humiliated when we are serving our own pride.

Abraham's defects are clear and his sins obvious, but his nobility is extraordinary. Phases of his life may be used as a type of sanctification, but Abraham himself is a living example of the life of faith with both its failures and its successes. Sanctification is not something our Lord does in us; sanctification is *Himself* in us. "But of Him you are in Christ Jesus, who became for us wisdom from God—and righteousness and sanctification and redemption" (1 Cor. 1:30).   (*Not Knowing*)

GENESIS 19:1—20:18

NOW the two angels came to Sodom in the evening, and Lot was sitting in the gate of Sodom. When Lot saw *them,* he rose to meet them, and he bowed himself with his face toward the ground. 2 And he said, "Here now, my lords, please turn in to your servant's house and spend the night, and wash your feet; then you may rise early and go on your way."

And they said, "No, but we will spend the night in the open square."

3 But he insisted strongly; so they turned in to him and entered his house. Then he made them a feast, and baked unleavened bread, and they ate.

4 Now before they lay down, the men of the city, the men of Sodom, both old and young, all the people from every quarter, surrounded the house. 5 And they called to Lot and said to him, "Where are the men who came to you tonight? Bring them out to us that we may know them *carnally.*"

6 So Lot went out to them through the doorway, shut the door behind him, 7 and said, "Please, my brethren, do not do so wickedly! 8 See now, I have two daughters who have not known a man; please, let me bring them out to you, and you may do to them as you wish; only do nothing to these men, since this is the reason they have come under the shadow of my roof."

9 And they said, "Stand back!" Then they said, "This one came in to stay *here,* and he keeps acting as a judge; now we will deal worse with you than with them." So they pressed hard against the man Lot, and came near to break down the door. 10 But the men reached out their hands and pulled Lot into the house with them, and shut the door. 11 And they struck the men who *were* at the doorway of the house with blindness, both small and great, so that they became weary *trying* to find the door.

12 Then the men said to Lot, "Have you anyone else here? Son-in-law, your sons, your daughters, and whomever you have in the city—take *them* out of this place! 13 For we will destroy this place, because the outcry against them has grown great before the face of the LORD, and the LORD has sent us to destroy it."

14 So Lot went out and spoke to his sons-in-law, who had married his daughters, and said, "Get up, get out of this place; for the LORD will destroy this city!" But to his sons-in-law he seemed to be joking.

15 When the morning dawned, the angels urged Lot to hurry, saying, "Arise, take your wife and your two daughters who are here, lest you be consumed in the punishment of the city." 16 And while he lingered, the men took hold of his hand, his wife's hand, and the hands of his two daughters, the LORD being merciful to him, and they brought him out and set him outside the city. 17 So it came to pass, when they had brought them outside, that he said, "Escape for your life! Do not look behind you nor stay anywhere in the plain. Escape to the mountains, lest you be destroyed."

18 Then Lot said to them, "Please, no, my lords! 19 Indeed now, your servant has found favor in your sight, and you have increased your mercy which you have shown me by saving my life; but I cannot escape to the mountains, lest some evil overtake me and I die. 20 See now, this city *is* near *enough* to flee to, and it *is* a little one; please let me escape there (*is* it not a little one?) and my soul shall live."

21 And he said to him, "See, I have favored you concerning this thing also, in that I will not overthrow this city for which you have spoken. 22 Hurry, escape there. For I cannot do anything until you arrive there."

Therefore the name of the city was called Zoar.

23 The sun had risen upon the earth when Lot entered Zoar. 24 Then the LORD rained brimstone and fire on Sodom and Gomorrah, from the LORD out of the heavens. 25 So He overthrew those cities, all the plain, all the inhabitants of the cities, and what grew on the ground. 26 But his wife looked back behind him, and she became a pillar of salt.

27 And Abraham went early in the morning to the place where he had stood before the LORD. 28 Then he looked toward Sodom and Gomorrah, and toward all the land of the plain; and he saw, and behold, the smoke of the land which went up like the smoke of a furnace. 29 And it came to pass, when God destroyed the cities of the plain, that God remembered Abraham, and sent Lot out of the midst of the overthrow, when He overthrew the cities in which Lot had dwelt.

30 Then Lot went up out of Zoar and dwelt in the mountains, and his two daughters were with him; for he was afraid to dwell in Zoar. And he and his two daughters dwelt in a cave. 31 Now the firstborn said to the younger, "Our father *is* old, and *there is* no man on the earth to come in to us as is the custom of all the earth. 32 Come, let us make our father drink wine, and we

will lie with him, that we may preserve the lineage of our father." 33 So they made their father drink wine that night. And the firstborn went in and lay with her father, and he did not know when she lay down or when she arose.

34 It happened on the next day that the firstborn said to the younger, "Indeed I lay with my father last night; let us make him drink wine tonight also, and you go in *and* lie with him, that we may preserve the lineage of our father." 35 Then they made their father drink wine that night also. And the younger arose and lay with him, and he did not know when she lay down or when she arose.

36 Thus both the daughters of Lot were with child by their father. 37 The firstborn bore a son and called his name Moab; he *is* the father of the Moabites to this day. 38 And the younger, she also bore a son and called his name Ben-Ammi; he *is* the father of the people of Ammon to this day.

20 AND Abraham journeyed from there to the South, and dwelt between Kadesh and Shur, and stayed in Gerar. 2 Now Abraham said of Sarah his wife, "She *is* my sister." And Abimelech king of Gerar sent and took Sarah.

3 But God came to Abimelech in a dream by night, and said to him, "Indeed you *are* a dead man because of the woman whom you have taken, for she *is* a man's wife."

4 But Abimelech had not come near her; and he said, "Lord, will You slay a righteous nation also? 5 Did he not say to me, 'She *is* my sister'? And she, even she herself said, 'He *is* my brother.' In the integrity of my heart and innocence of my hands I have done this."

6 And God said to him in a dream, "Yes, I know that you did this in the integrity of your heart. For I also withheld you from sinning against Me; therefore I did not let you touch her. 7 Now therefore, restore the man's wife; for he *is* a prophet, and he will pray for you and you shall live. But if you do not restore *her,* know that you shall surely die, you and all who *are* yours."

---

*I*ndependence from God on the part
of Abraham . . . brought
trouble on the house of
Abimelech.   (NOT KNOWING)

---

8 So Abimelech rose early in the morning, called all his servants, and told all these things in their hearing; and the men were very much afraid. 9 And Abimelech called Abraham and said to him, "What have you done to us? How have I offended you, that you have brought on me and on my kingdom a great sin? You have done deeds to me that ought not to be done." 10 Then Abimelech said to Abraham, "What did you have in view, that you have done this thing?"

11 And Abraham said, "Because I thought, surely the fear of God *is* not in this place; and they will kill me on account of my wife. 12 But indeed *she is* truly my sister. She *is* the daughter of my father, but not the daughter of my mother; and she became my wife. 13 And it came to pass, when God caused me to wander from my father's house, that I said to her, 'This *is* your kindness that you should do for me: in every place, wherever we go, say of me, "He *is* my brother." ' "

14 Then Abimelech took sheep, oxen, and male and female servants, and gave *them* to Abraham; and he restored Sarah his wife to him. 15 And Abimelech said, "See, my land *is* before you; dwell where it pleases you." 16 Then to Sarah he said, "Behold, I have given your brother a thousand *pieces* of silver; indeed this vindicates you before all who *are* with you and before everybody." Thus she was rebuked.

17 So Abraham prayed to God; and God healed Abimelech, his wife, and his female servants. Then they bore *children;* 18 for the LORD had closed up all the wombs of the house of Abimelech because of Sarah, Abraham's wife.

PSALM 6:1–5

1   O LORD, do not rebuke me in Your
         anger,
    Nor chasten me in Your hot displeasure.
2   Have mercy on me, O LORD, for I *am*
         weak;
    O LORD, heal me, for my bones are
         troubled.
3   My soul also is greatly troubled;
    But You, O LORD—how long?
4   Return, O LORD, deliver me!
    Oh, save me for Your mercies' sake!
5   For in death *there is* no remembrance
         of You;
    In the grave who will give You thanks?

PROVERBS 3:1–4

1   MY son, do not forget my law,
    But let your heart keep my commands;

2   For length of days and long life
     And peace they will add to you.

3   Let not mercy and truth forsake you;
     Bind them around your neck,
     Write them on the tablet of your heart,
4   *And* so find favor and high esteem
     In the sight of God and man.

MATTHEW 8:1–17

WHEN He had come down from the mountain, great multitudes followed Him. 2 And behold, a leper came and worshiped Him, saying, "Lord, if You are willing, You can make me clean."

3 Then Jesus put out *His* hand and touched him, saying, "I am willing; be cleansed." Immediately his leprosy was cleansed.

4 And Jesus said to him, "See that you tell no one; but go your way, show yourself to the priest, and offer the gift that Moses commanded, as a testimony to them."

5 Now when Jesus had entered Capernaum, a centurion came to Him, pleading with Him, 6 saying, "Lord, my servant is lying at home paralyzed, dreadfully tormented."

7 And Jesus said to him, "I will come and heal him."

8 The centurion answered and said, "Lord, I am not worthy that You should come under my roof. But only speak a word, and my servant will be healed. 9 For I also am a man under authority, having soldiers under me. And I say to this *one,* 'Go,' and he goes; and to another, 'Come,' and he comes; and to my servant, 'Do this,' and he does *it.*"

10 When Jesus heard *it,* He marveled, and said to those who followed, "Assuredly, I say to you, I have not found such great faith, not even in Israel! 11 And I say to you that many will come from east and west, and sit down with Abraham, Isaac, and Jacob in the kingdom of heaven. 12 But the sons of the kingdom will be cast out into outer darkness. There will be weeping and gnashing of teeth." 13 Then Jesus said to the centurion, "Go your way; and as you have believed, *so* let it be done for you." And his servant was healed that same hour.

14 Now when Jesus had come into Peter's house, He saw his wife's mother lying sick with a fever. 15 So He touched her hand, and the fever left her. And she arose and served them.

When He touches, there is no convalescence.   (SEND I YOU)

---

16 When evening had come, they brought to Him many who were demon-possessed. And He cast out the spirits with a word, and healed all who were sick, 17 that it might be fulfilled which was spoken by Isaiah the prophet, saying:

"He Himself took our infirmities
And bore *our* sicknesses."

◆◆◆◆

Reading 11—The Duty of Diligence
Genesis 22:3

Here we see that Abraham "rose early in the morning." This phrase is characteristic not only of men and women in the Bible, but of God Himself. The revelation of God in the Old Testament is that of a working God. Unlike other religions that worship gods who rule in lofty disdain, the true God is one who is both diligent and suffering. The God who reveals Himself to Abraham is One ever intent on the fulfillment of His great designs; and He expects His people to do likewise. If God is diligent, surely we ought to be diligent in doing our duty to Him. Think how patient and how diligent God has been with us! Over and over again He gets us near the point, and then by some petty individual sulk we spoil it all, and He patiently begins all over again. Think of His vision for us: "whiter than snow shine." Has God had to begin all over again from where we left off last time, or have we said, "I will be true to God at all costs, no matter what the isolation"?

(NOT KNOWING)

GENESIS 21:1—22:24

AND the LORD visited Sarah as He had said, and the LORD did for Sarah as He had spoken. 2 For Sarah conceived and bore Abraham a son in his old age, at the set time of which God had spoken to him. 3 And Abraham called the name of his son who was born to him—whom Sarah bore to him—Isaac. 4 Then Abraham circumcised his son Isaac when he was eight days old, as God had commanded him. 5 Now Abraham was one hundred years old when his son Isaac was born to him. 6 And Sarah said, "God has made me laugh, *and* all who hear will laugh with me." 7 She also said, "Who would have said to Abraham that Sarah would nurse children? For I have borne *him* a son in his old age."

8 So the child grew and was weaned. And Abraham made a great feast on the same day that Isaac was weaned.

9 And Sarah saw the son of Hagar the Egyptian, whom she had borne to Abraham, scoffing. 10 Therefore she said to Abraham, "Cast out this bondwoman and her son; for the son of this bondwoman shall not be heir with my son, *namely* with Isaac." 11 And the matter was very displeasing in Abraham's sight because of his son.

12 But God said to Abraham, "Do not let it be displeasing in your sight because of the lad or because of your bondwoman. Whatever Sarah has said to you, listen to her voice; for in Isaac your seed shall be called. 13 Yet I will also make a nation of the son of the bondwoman, because he *is* your seed."

14 So Abraham rose early in the morning, and took bread and a skin of water; and putting *it* on her shoulder, he gave *it* and the boy to Hagar, and sent her away. Then she departed and wandered in the Wilderness of Beersheba. 15 And the water in the skin was used up, and she placed the boy under one of the shrubs. 16 Then she went and sat down across from *him* at a distance of about a bowshot; for she said to herself, "Let me not see the death of the boy." So she sat opposite *him,* and lifted her voice and wept.

17 And God heard the voice of the lad. Then the angel of God called to Hagar out of heaven, and said to her, "What ails you, Hagar? Fear not, for God has heard the voice of the lad where he *is.* 18 Arise, lift up the lad and hold him with your hand, for I will make him a great nation."

19 Then God opened her eyes, and she saw a well of water. And she went and filled the skin with water, and gave the lad a drink. 20 So God was with the lad; and he grew and dwelt in the wilderness, and became an archer. 21 He dwelt in the Wilderness of Paran; and his mother took a wife for him from the land of Egypt.

22 And it came to pass at that time that Abimelech and Phichol, the commander of his army, spoke to Abraham, saying, "God *is* with you in all that you do. 23 Now therefore, swear to me by God that you will not deal falsely with me, with my offspring, or with my posterity; but that according to the kindness that I have done to you, you will do to me and to the land in which you have dwelt."

24 And Abraham said, "I will swear."

25 Then Abraham rebuked Abimelech because of a well of water which Abimelech's servants had seized. 26 And Abimelech said, "I do not know who has done this thing; you did not tell me, nor had I heard *of it* until today." 27 So Abraham took sheep and oxen and gave them to Abimelech, and the two of them made a covenant. 28 And Abraham set seven ewe lambs of the flock by themselves.

29 Then Abimelech asked Abraham, "What *is the meaning of* these seven ewe lambs which you have set by themselves?"

30 And he said, "You will take *these* seven ewe lambs from my hand, that they may be my witness that I have dug this well." 31 Therefore he called that place Beersheba, because the two of them swore an oath there.

32 Thus they made a covenant at Beersheba. So Abimelech rose with Phichol, the commander of his army, and they returned to the land of the Philistines. 33 Then *Abraham* planted a tamarisk tree in Beersheba, and there called on the name of the LORD, the Everlasting God. 34 And Abraham stayed in the land of the Philistines many days.

22 NOW it came to pass after these things that God tested Abraham, and said to him, "Abraham!"

And he said, "Here I am."

2 Then He said, "Take now your son, your only *son* Isaac, whom you love, and go to the land of Moriah, and offer him there as a burnt offering on one of the mountains of which I shall tell you."

3 So Abraham rose early in the morning and saddled his donkey, and took two of his young men with him, and Isaac his son; and he split the wood for the burnt offering, and arose and went to the place of which God had told him. 4 Then on the third day Abraham lifted his eyes and saw the place

afar off. 5 And Abraham said to his young men, "Stay here with the donkey; the lad and I will go yonder and worship, and we will come back to you."

6 So Abraham took the wood of the burnt offering and laid *it* on Isaac his son; and he took the fire in his hand, and a knife, and the two of them went together. 7 But Isaac spoke to Abraham his father and said, "My father!"

And he said, "Here I am, my son."

Then he said, "Look, the fire and the wood, but where *is* the lamb for a burnt offering?"

8 And Abraham said, "My son, God will provide for Himself the lamb for a burnt offering." So the two of them went together.

9 Then they came to the place of which God had told him. And Abraham built an altar there and placed the wood in order; and he bound Isaac his son and laid him on the altar, upon the wood. 10 And Abraham stretched out his hand and took the knife to slay his son.

11 But the Angel of the Lord called to him from heaven and said, "Abraham, Abraham!"

So he said, "Here I am."

12 And He said, "Do not lay your hand on the lad, or do anything to him; for now I know that you fear God, since you have not withheld your son, your only *son*, from Me."

---

*S*acrifice . . . *is the exuberant passionate love-gift of the best I have to the one I love best.*   (MORAL FOUND.)

---

13 Then Abraham lifted his eyes and looked, and there behind *him was* a ram caught in a thicket by its horns. So Abraham went and took the ram, and offered it up for a burnt offering instead of his son. 14 And Abraham called the name of the place, The-Lord-Will-Provide; as it is said *to* this day, "In the Mount of the Lord it shall be provided."

15 Then the Angel of the Lord called to Abraham a second time out of heaven, 16 and said: "By Myself I have sworn, says the Lord, because you have done this thing, and have not withheld your son, your only *son*— 17 blessing I will bless you, and multiplying I will multiply your descendants as the stars of the heaven and as the sand which *is* on the seashore; and your descendants shall possess the gate of their enemies. 18 In your seed all the nations of the earth

shall be blessed, because you have obeyed My voice." 19 So Abraham returned to his young men, and they rose and went together to Beersheba; and Abraham dwelt at Beersheba.

20 Now it came to pass after these things that it was told Abraham, saying, "Indeed Milcah also has borne children to your brother Nahor: 21 Huz his firstborn, Buz his brother, Kemuel the father of Aram, 22 Chesed, Hazo, Pildash, Jidlaph, and Bethuel." 23 And Bethuel begot Rebekah. These eight Milcah bore to Nahor, Abraham's brother. 24 His concubine, whose name was Reumah, also bore Tebah, Gaham, Thahash, and Maachah.

PSALM 6:6–10

6   I am weary with my groaning;
    All night I make my bed swim;
    I drench my couch with my tears.
7   My eye wastes away because of grief;
    It grows old because of all my enemies.

8   Depart from me, all you workers of
        iniquity;
    For the Lord has heard the voice of
        my weeping.
9   The Lord has heard my supplication;
    The Lord will receive my prayer.
10 Let all my enemies be ashamed and
        greatly troubled;
    Let them turn back *and* be ashamed
        suddenly.

PROVERBS 3:5, 6

5   TRUST in the Lord with all your
        heart,
    And lean not on your own
        understanding;
6   In all your ways acknowledge Him,
    And He shall direct your paths.

MATTHEW 8:18–34

AND when Jesus saw great multitudes about Him, He gave a command to depart to the other side. 19 Then a certain scribe came and said to Him, "Teacher, I will follow You wherever You go."

20 And Jesus said to him, "Foxes have holes and birds of the air *have* nests, but the Son of Man has nowhere to lay *His* head."

21 Then another of His disciples said to Him, "Lord, let me first go and bury my father."

22 But Jesus said to him, "Follow Me, and let the dead bury their own dead."

23 Now when He got into a boat, His disciples followed Him. 24 And suddenly a great tempest arose on the sea, so that the boat was covered with the waves. But He was asleep. 25 Then His disciples came to *Him* and awoke Him, saying, "Lord, save us! We are perishing!"

26 But He said to them, "Why are you fearful, O you of little faith?" Then He arose and rebuked the winds and the sea, and there was a great calm. 27 So the men marveled, saying, "Who can this be, that even the winds and the sea obey Him?"

28 When He had come to the other side, to the country of the Gergesenes, there met Him two demon-possessed *men*, coming out of the tombs, exceedingly fierce, so that no one could pass that way. 29 And suddenly they cried out, saying, "What have we to do with You, Jesus, You Son of God? Have You come here to torment us before the time?"

30 Now a good way off from them there was a herd of many swine feeding. 31 So the demons begged Him, saying, "If You cast us out, permit us to go away into the herd of swine."

32 And He said to them, "Go." So when they had come out, they went into the herd of swine. And suddenly the whole herd of swine ran violently down the steep place into the sea, and perished in the water.

33 Then those who kept *them* fled; and they went away into the city and told everything, including what *had happened* to the demon-possessed *men*. 34 And behold, the whole city came out to meet Jesus. And when they saw Him, they begged *Him* to depart from their region.

> *F*aith is unutterable trust in God, trust which never dreams that He will not stand by us. (UTMOST)

❖❖❖❖

Reading 12—Solemn Sacredness of Serving
Genesis 24:2, 3

"The oldest servant of [Abraham's] house, who ruled over all that he had" was probably Eliezer of Damascus. Eliezer in many respects is representative of what a disciple of the Lord should be; the whole molding of his life was his devotion to his master, not to a sense of right or duty. We know very little about devotion to Jesus Christ. We know about devotion to right and to duty, but none of that is saintly; it is purely natural. Our sense of duty and right can never be God's. If we can state what our duty is, we have become gods in that particular. There is only One who knows what my duty is as a Christian, and that is God. The Sermon on the Mount nowhere tells us what our duty is; it tells us the things a saint will do. Be renewed in the spirit of your mind, says Paul, not that you may do your duty, but that you may make out what God's will is.

All Eliezer seeks is the happiness of his master; self-remembrance in him is dead. He is shrewd and practical, yet as guileless as a child—the exact embodiment of 1 Corinthians 4:2: "Moreover it is required in stewards that one be found faithful." (*NOT KNOWING*)

GENESIS 23:1—24:67

SARAH lived one hundred and twenty-seven years; *these were* the years of the life of Sarah. 2 So Sarah died in Kirjath Arba (that *is,* Hebron) in the land of Canaan, and Abraham came to mourn for Sarah and to weep for her.

> *F*aith does not deny death, . . . faith is not insensible to sorrow. (NOT KNOWING)

3 Then Abraham stood up from before his dead, and spoke to the sons of Heth,

saying, 4 "I *am* a foreigner and a visitor among you. Give me property for a burial place among you, that I may bury my dead out of my sight."

5 And the sons of Heth answered Abraham, saying to him, 6 "Hear us, my lord: You *are* a mighty prince among us; bury your dead in the choicest of our burial places. None of us will withhold from you his burial place, that you may bury your dead."

7 Then Abraham stood up and bowed himself to the people of the land, the sons of Heth. 8 And he spoke with them, saying, "If it is your wish that I bury my dead out of my sight, hear me, and meet with Ephron the son of Zohar for me, 9 that he may give me the cave of Machpelah which he has, which *is* at the end of his field. Let him give it to me at the full price, as property for a burial place among you."

10 Now Ephron dwelt among the sons of Heth; and Ephron the Hittite answered Abraham in the presence of the sons of Heth, all who entered at the gate of his city, saying, 11 "No, my lord, hear me: I give you the field and the cave that *is* in it; I give it to you in the presence of the sons of my people. I give it to you. Bury your dead!"

12 Then Abraham bowed himself down before the people of the land; 13 and he spoke to Ephron in the hearing of the people of the land, saying, "If you *will give it,* please hear me. I will give you money for the field; take *it* from me and I will bury my dead there."

14 And Ephron answered Abraham, saying to him, 15 "My lord, listen to me; the land *is worth* four hundred shekels of silver. What *is* that between you and me? So bury your dead." 16 And Abraham listened to Ephron; and Abraham weighed out the silver for Ephron which he had named in the hearing of the sons of Heth, four hundred shekels of silver, currency of the merchants.

17 So the field of Ephron which *was* in Machpelah, which *was* before Mamre, the field and the cave which *was* in it, and all the trees that *were* in the field, which *were* within all the surrounding borders, were deeded 18 to Abraham as a possession in the presence of the sons of Heth, before all who went in at the gate of his city.

19 And after this, Abraham buried Sarah his wife in the cave of the field of Machpelah, before Mamre (that *is,* Hebron) in the land of Canaan. 20 So the field and the cave that *is* in it were deeded to Abraham by the sons of Heth as property for a burial place.

24 NOW Abraham was old, well advanced in age; and the LORD had blessed Abraham in all things. 2 So Abraham said to the oldest servant of his house, who ruled over all that he had, "Please, put your hand under my thigh, 3 and I will make you swear by the LORD, the God of heaven and the God of the earth, that you will not take a wife for my son from the daughters of the Canaanites, among whom I dwell; 4 but you shall go to my country and to my family, and take a wife for my son Isaac."

5 And the servant said to him, "Perhaps the woman will not be willing to follow me to this land. Must I take your son back to the land from which you came?"

6 But Abraham said to him, "Beware that you do not take my son back there. 7 The LORD God of heaven, who took me from my father's house and from the land of my family, and who spoke to me and swore to me, saying, 'To your descendants I give this land,' He will send His angel before you, and you shall take a wife for my son from there. 8 And if the woman is not willing to follow you, then you will be released from this oath; only do not take my son back there." 9 So the servant put his hand under the thigh of Abraham his master, and swore to him concerning this matter.

10 Then the servant took ten of his master's camels and departed, for all his master's goods *were in* his hand. And he arose and went to Mesopotamia, to the city of Nahor. 11 And he made his camels kneel down outside the city by a well of water at evening time, the time when women go out to draw *water.* 12 Then he said, "O LORD God of my master Abraham, please give me success this day, and show kindness to my master Abraham. 13 Behold, *here* I stand by the well of water, and the daughters of the men of the city are coming out to draw water. 14 Now let it be that the young woman to whom I say, 'Please let down your pitcher that I may drink,' and she says, 'Drink, and I will also give your camels a drink'—*let her be the one* You have appointed for Your servant Isaac. And by this I will know that You have shown kindness to my master."

15 And it happened, before he had finished speaking, that behold, Rebekah, who was born to Bethuel, son of Milcah, the wife of Nahor, Abraham's brother, came out with her pitcher on her shoulder. 16 Now the young woman *was* very beautiful to behold, a virgin; no man had known her. And she went down to the well, filled her pitcher, and came up. 17 And the servant

ran to meet her and said, "Please let me drink a little water from your pitcher."

18 So she said, "Drink, my lord." Then she quickly let her pitcher down to her hand, and gave him a drink. 19 And when she had finished giving him a drink, she said, "I will draw *water* for your camels also, until they have finished drinking." 20 Then she quickly emptied her pitcher into the trough, ran back to the well to draw *water,* and drew for all his camels. 21 And the man, wondering at her, remained silent so as to know whether the LORD had made his journey prosperous or not.

22 So it was, when the camels had finished drinking, that the man took a golden nose ring weighing half a shekel, and two bracelets for her wrists weighing ten *shekels* of gold, 23 and said, "Whose daughter *are* you? Tell me, please, is there room *in* your father's house for us to lodge?"

24 So she said to him, "I *am* the daughter of Bethuel, Milcah's son, whom she bore to Nahor." 25 Moreover she said to him, "We have both straw and feed enough, and room to lodge."

26 Then the man bowed down his head and worshiped the LORD. 27 And he said, "Blessed *be* the LORD God of my master Abraham, who has not forsaken His mercy and His truth toward my master. As for me, being on the way, the LORD led me to the house of my master's brethren." 28 So the young woman ran and told her mother's household these things.

29 Now Rebekah had a brother whose name *was* Laban, and Laban ran out to the man by the well. 30 So it came to pass, when he saw the nose ring, and the bracelets on his sister's wrists, and when he heard the words of his sister Rebekah, saying, "Thus the man spoke to me," that he went to the man. And there he stood by the camels at the well. 31 And he said, "Come in, O blessed of the LORD! Why do you stand outside? For I have prepared the house, and a place for the camels."

32 Then the man came to the house. And he unloaded the camels, and provided straw and feed for the camels, and water to wash his feet and the feet of the men who *were* with him. 33 *Food* was set before him to eat, but he said, "I will not eat until I have told about my errand."

And he said, "Speak on."

34 So he said, "I *am* Abraham's servant. 35 The LORD has blessed my master greatly, and he has become great; and He has given him flocks and herds, silver and gold, male and female servants, and camels and donkeys. 36 And Sarah my master's wife bore

a son to my master when she was old; and to him he has given all that he has. 37 Now my master made me swear, saying, 'You shall not take a wife for my son from the daughters of the Canaanites, in whose land I dwell; 38 but you shall go to my father's house and to my family, and take a wife for my son.' 39 And I said to my master, 'Perhaps the woman will not follow me.' 40 But he said to me, 'The LORD, before whom I walk, will send His angel with you and prosper your way; and you shall take a wife for my son from my family and from my father's house. 41 You will be clear from this oath when you arrive among my family; for if they will not give *her* to you, then you will be released from my oath.'

42 "And this day I came to the well and said, 'O LORD God of my master Abraham, if You will now prosper the way in which I go, 43 behold, I stand by the well of water; and it shall come to pass that when the virgin comes out to draw *water,* and I say to her, "Please give me a little water from your pitcher to drink," 44 and she says to me, "Drink, and I will draw for your camels also,"—*let* her *be* the woman whom the LORD has appointed for my master's son.'

45 "But before I had finished speaking in my heart, there was Rebekah, coming out with her pitcher on her shoulder; and she went down to the well and drew *water.* And I said to her, 'Please let me drink.' 46 And she made haste and let her pitcher down from her *shoulder,* and said, 'Drink, and I will give your camels a drink also.' So I drank, and she gave the camels a drink also. 47 Then I asked her, and said, 'Whose daughter *are* you?' And she said, 'The daughter of Bethuel, Nahor's son, whom Milcah bore to him.' So I put the nose ring on her nose and the bracelets on her wrists. 48 And I bowed my head and worshiped the LORD, and blessed the LORD God of my master Abraham, who had led me in the way of truth to take the daughter of my master's brother for his son. 49 Now if you will deal kindly and truly with my master, tell me. And if not, tell me, that I may turn to the right hand or to the left."

50 Then Laban and Bethuel answered and said, "The thing comes from the LORD; we cannot speak to you either bad or good. 51 Here *is* Rebekah before you; take *her* and go, and let her be your master's son's wife, as the LORD has spoken."

52 And it came to pass, when Abraham's servant heard their words, that he worshiped the LORD, *bowing himself* to the earth. 53 Then the servant brought out jewelry of

silver, jewelry of gold, and clothing, and gave *them* to Rebekah. He also gave precious things to her brother and to her mother.

54 And he and the men who *were* with him ate and drank and stayed all night. Then they arose in the morning, and he said, "Send me away to my master."

55 But her brother and her mother said, "Let the young woman stay with us *a few* days, at least ten; after that she may go."

56 And he said to them, "Do not hinder me, since the LORD has prospered my way; send me away so that I may go to my master."

57 So they said, "We will call the young woman and ask her personally." 58 Then they called Rebekah and said to her, "Will you go with this man?"

And she said, "I will go."

59 So they sent away Rebekah their sister and her nurse, and Abraham's servant and his men. 60 And they blessed Rebekah and said to her:

> "Our sister, *may* you *become*
> The *mother of* thousands of ten
>   thousands;
> And may your descendants possess
> The gates of those who hate them."

61 Then Rebekah and her maids arose, and they rode on the camels and followed the man. So the servant took Rebekah and departed.

62 Now Isaac came from the way of Beer Lahai Roi, for he dwelt in the South. 63 And Isaac went out to meditate in the field in the evening; and he lifted his eyes and looked, and there, the camels *were* coming. 64 Then Rebekah lifted her eyes, and when she saw Isaac she dismounted from her camel; 65 for she had said to the servant, "Who *is* this man walking in the field to meet us?"

The servant said, "It *is* my master." So she took a veil and covered herself.

66 And the servant told Isaac all the things that he had done. 67 Then Isaac brought her into his mother Sarah's tent; and he took Rebekah and she became his wife, and he loved her. So Isaac was comforted after his mother's *death*.

PSALM 7:1–5

1   O LORD my God, in You I put my
        trust;
    Save me from all those who persecute
        me;

And deliver me,
2   Lest they tear me like a lion,
    Rending *me* in pieces, while *there is*
        none to deliver.

To live worthily of the name of Christian is to suffer persecution. (CHRIS. DIS. 1)

---

3   O LORD my God, if I have done this:
    If there is iniquity in my hands,
4   If I have repaid evil to him who was
        at peace with me,
    Or have plundered my enemy without
        cause,
5   Let the enemy pursue me and overtake
        me;
    Yes, let him trample my life to the earth,
    And lay my honor in the dust.
                                      Selah

PROVERBS 3:7, 8

7   DO not be wise in your own eyes;
    Fear the LORD and depart from evil.
8   It will be health to your flesh,
    And strength to your bones.

MATTHEW 9:1–17

SO He got into a boat, crossed over, and came to His own city. 2 Then behold, they brought to Him a paralytic lying on a bed. When Jesus saw their faith, He said to the paralytic, "Son, be of good cheer; your sins are forgiven you."

3 And at once some of the scribes said within themselves, "This Man blasphemes!"

4 But Jesus, knowing their thoughts, said, "Why do you think evil in your hearts? 5 For which is easier, to say, '*Your* sins are forgiven you,' or to say, 'Arise and walk'? 6 But that you may know that the Son of Man has power on earth to forgive sins"— then He said to the paralytic, "Arise, take up your bed, and go to your house." 7 And he arose and departed to his house.

8 Now when the multitudes saw *it*, they marveled and glorified God, who had given such power to men.

9 As Jesus passed on from there, He saw a man named Matthew sitting at the tax office. And He said to him, "Follow Me." So he arose and followed Him.

10 Now it happened, as Jesus sat at the

The Christianity of the New Testament is not individual, it is personal. (GLORIFY)

table in the house, *that* behold, many tax collectors and sinners came and sat down with Him and His disciples. 11 And when the Pharisees saw *it*, they said to His disciples, "Why does your Teacher eat with tax collectors and sinners?"

12 When Jesus heard *that*, He said to them, "Those who are well have no need of a physician, but those who are sick. 13 But go and learn what *this* means: 'I desire mercy and not sacrifice.' For I did not come to call the righteous, but sinners, to repentance."

14 Then the disciples of John came to Him, saying, "Why do we and the Pharisees fast often, but Your disciples do not fast?"

15 And Jesus said to them, "Can the friends of the bridegroom mourn as long as the bridegroom is with them? But the days will come when the bridegroom will be taken away from them, and then they will fast. 16 No one puts a piece of unshrunk cloth on an old garment; for the patch pulls away from the garment, and the tear is made worse. 17 Nor do they put new wine into old wineskins, or else the wineskins break, the wine is spilled, and the wineskins are ruined. But they put new wine into new wineskins, and both are preserved."

Reading 13—Therefore Pray
Matthew 9:38

The reason prayer is so important is, first of all, because our Lord told us that prayer on the ground of His redemption is the most mighty factor He has put into our hands. Second, it is important because of the personal presence of the Holy Spirit in the day in which we live. We receive our knowledge of the Holy Spirit not by experience first, but by the testimony of the Lord Jesus Christ. The testimony of Jesus Christ regarding the Holy Spirit is that He is here, and the real living experience the Holy Spirit works in us is that all His emphasis is laid on glorifying our Lord Jesus Christ. We know the Holy Spirit first by the testimony of Jesus, and then by the conscious enjoyment of His presence.

"Therefore pray." Prayer is labor, not agony, but labor on the ground of our Lord's redemption in simple confidence in Him. Prayer is simple to us because it cost Him so much to make it possible. God grant that we may work His victories for Him by taking His way about it. (ASK)

GENESIS 25:1—26:35

ABRAHAM again took a wife, and her name *was* Keturah. 2 And she bore him Zimran, Jokshan, Medan, Midian, Ishbak, and Shuah. 3 Jokshan begot Sheba and Dedan. And the sons of Dedan were Asshurim, Letushim, and Leummim. 4 And the sons of Midian *were* Ephah, Epher, Hanoch, Abidah, and Eldaah. All these *were* the children of Keturah.

5 And Abraham gave all that he had to Isaac. 6 But Abraham gave gifts to the sons of the concubines which Abraham had; and while he was still living he sent them east-ward, away from Isaac his son, to the country of the east.

7 This *is* the sum of the years of Abraham's life which he lived: one hundred and seventy-five years. 8 Then Abraham breathed his last and died in a good old age, an old man and full *of years,* and was gathered to his people. 9 And his sons Isaac and Ishmael buried him in the cave of Machpelah, which *is* before Mamre, in the field of Ephron the son of Zohar the Hittite, 10 the field which Abraham purchased from the sons of Heth. There Abraham was buried, and Sarah his wife. 11 And it came to pass, after the death of Abraham, that God

blessed his son Isaac. And Isaac dwelt at Beer Lahai Roi.

12 Now this *is* the genealogy of Ishmael, Abraham's son, whom Hagar the Egyptian, Sarah's maidservant, bore to Abraham. 13 And these *were* the names of the sons of Ishmael, by their names, according to their generations: The firstborn of Ishmael, Nebajoth; then Kedar, Adbeel, Mibsam, 14 Mishma, Dumah, Massa, 15 Hadar, Tema, Jetur, Naphish, and Kedemah. 16 These *were* the sons of Ishmael and these *were* their names, by their towns and their settlements, twelve princes according to their nations. 17 These *were* the years of the life of Ishmael: one hundred and thirty-seven years; and he breathed his last and died, and was gathered to his people. 18 (They dwelt from Havilah as far as Shur, which *is* east of Egypt as you go toward Assyria.) He died in the presence of all his brethren.

19 This *is* the genealogy of Isaac, Abraham's son. Abraham begot Isaac. 20 Isaac was forty years old when he took Rebekah as wife, the daughter of Bethuel the Syrian of Padan Aram, the sister of Laban the Syrian. 21 Now Isaac pleaded with the Lord for his wife, because she *was* barren; and the Lord granted his plea, and Rebekah his wife conceived. 22 But the children struggled together within her; and she said, "If *all is* well, why *am I* like this? " So she went to inquire of the Lord.

23 And the Lord said to her:

"Two nations *are* in your womb,
Two peoples shall be separated from your body;
One people shall be stronger than the other,
And the older shall serve the younger."

24 So when her days were fulfilled *for her* to give birth, indeed *there were* twins in her womb. 25 And the first came out red. *He was* like a hairy garment all over; so they called his name Esau. 26 Afterward his brother came out, and his hand took hold of Esau's heel; so his name was called Jacob. Isaac *was* sixty years old when she bore them.

27 So the boys grew. And Esau was a skillful hunter, a man of the field; but Jacob was a mild man, dwelling in tents. 28 And Isaac loved Esau because he ate *of his* game, but Rebekah loved Jacob.

29 Now Jacob cooked a stew; and Esau came in from the field, and he *was* weary. 30 And Esau said to Jacob, "Please feed me with that same red *stew,* for I *am* weary." Therefore his name was called Edom.

31 But Jacob said, "Sell me your birthright as of this day."

32 And Esau said, "Look, I *am* about to die; so what *is* this birthright to me?"

33 Then Jacob said, "Swear to me as of this day."

So he swore to him, and sold his birthright to Jacob. 34 And Jacob gave Esau bread and stew of lentils; then he ate and drank, arose, and went his way. Thus Esau despised *his* birthright.

26 THERE was a famine in the land, besides the first famine that was in the days of Abraham. And Isaac went to Abimelech king of the Philistines, in Gerar.

2 Then the Lord appeared to him and said: "Do not go down to Egypt; live in the land of which I shall tell you. 3 Dwell in this land, and I will be with you and bless you; for to you and your descendants I give all these lands, and I will perform the oath which I swore to Abraham your father. 4 And I will make your descendants multiply as the stars of heaven; I will give to your descendants all these lands; and in your seed all the nations of the earth shall be blessed; 5 because Abraham obeyed My voice and kept My charge, My commandments, My statutes, and My laws."

6 So Isaac dwelt in Gerar. 7 And the men of the place asked about his wife. And he said, "She *is* my sister"; for he was afraid to say, "She *is* my wife," *because he thought,* "lest the men of the place kill me for Rebekah, because she *is* beautiful to behold." 8 Now it came to pass, when he had been there a long time, that Abimelech king of the Philistines looked through a window, and saw, and there was Isaac, showing endearment to Rebekah his wife. 9 Then Abimelech called Isaac and said, "Quite obviously she *is* your wife; so how could you say, 'She *is* my sister'?"

Isaac said to him, "Because I said, 'Lest I die on account of her.' "

10 And Abimelech said, "What *is* this you have done to us? One of the people might soon have lain with your wife, and you would have brought guilt on us." 11 So Abimelech charged all *his* people, saying, "He who touches this man or his wife shall surely be put to death."

12 Then Isaac sowed in that land, and reaped in the same year a hundredfold; and the Lord blessed him. 13 The man began to prosper, and continued prospering until he became very prosperous; 14 for he had possessions of flocks and possessions of

herds and a great number of servants. So the Philistines envied him. 15 Now the Philistines had stopped up all the wells which his father's servants had dug in the days of Abraham his father, and they had filled them with earth. 16 And Abimelech said to Isaac, "Go away from us, for you are much mightier than we."

17 Then Isaac departed from there and pitched his tent in the Valley of Gerar, and dwelt there. 18 And Isaac dug again the wells of water which they had dug in the days of Abraham his father, for the Philistines had stopped them up after the death of Abraham. He called them by the names which his father had called them.

19 Also Isaac's servants dug in the valley, and found a well of running water there. 20 But the herdsmen of Gerar quarreled with Isaac's herdsmen, saying, "The water *is* ours." So he called the name of the well Esek, because they quarreled with him. 21 Then they dug another well, and they quarreled over that *one* also. So he called its name Sitnah. 22 And he moved from there and dug another well, and they did not quarrel over it. So he called its name Rehoboth, because he said, "For now the LORD has made room for us, and we shall be fruitful in the land."

23 Then he went up from there to Beersheba. 24 And the LORD appeared to him the same night and said, "I *am* the God of your father Abraham; do not fear, for I *am* with you. I will bless you and multiply your descendants for My servant Abraham's sake." 25 So he built an altar there and called on the name of the LORD, and he pitched his tent there; and there Isaac's servants dug a well.

26 Then Abimelech came to him from Gerar with Ahuzzath, one of his friends, and Phichol the commander of his army. 27 And Isaac said to them, "Why have you come to me, since you hate me and have sent me away from you?" 28 But they said, "We have certainly seen that the LORD is with you. So we said, 'Let there now be an oath between us, between you and us; and let us make a covenant with you, 29 that you will do us no harm, since we have not touched you, and since we have done nothing to you but good and have sent you away in peace. You *are* now the blessed of the LORD.'"

30 So he made them a feast, and they ate and drank. 31 Then they arose early in the morning and swore an oath with one another; and Isaac sent them away, and they departed from him in peace.

32 It came to pass the same day that Isaac's servants came and told him about the well which they had dug, and said to him, "We have found water." 33 So he called it Shebah. Therefore the name of the city *is* Beersheba to this day.

34 When Esau was forty years old, he took as wives Judith the daughter of Beeri the Hittite, and Basemath the daughter of Elon the Hittite. 35 And they were a grief of mind to Isaac and Rebekah.

PSALM 7:6–8

6   ARISE, O LORD, in Your anger;
      Lift Yourself up because of the rage
         of my enemies;
      Rise up for me *to* the judgment You
         have commanded!

7   So the congregation of the peoples shall
         surround You;
      For their sakes, therefore, return on
         high.

8   The LORD shall judge the peoples;
      Judge me, O LORD, according to my
         righteousness,
      And according to my integrity within
         me.

PROVERBS 3:9, 10

9   HONOR the LORD with your
         possessions,
      And with the firstfruits of all your
         increase;

---

*R*emember that the honor of Jesus
   is at stake in your bodily
   life. (MORAL FOUND.)

---

10   So your barns will be filled with plenty,
      And your vats will overflow with new
         wine.

MATTHEW 9:18–38

WHILE He spoke these things to them, behold, a ruler came and worshiped Him, saying, "My daughter has just died, but come and lay Your hand on her and she will live." 19 So Jesus arose and followed him, and so *did* His disciples.

20 And suddenly, a woman who had a flow of blood for twelve years came from behind and touched the hem of His garment. 21 For she said to herself, "If only I may touch His garment, I shall be made well." 22 But Jesus turned around, and when

He saw her He said, "Be of good cheer, daughter; your faith has made you well." And the woman was made well from that hour.

23 When Jesus came into the ruler's house, and saw the flute players and the noisy crowd wailing, 24 He said to them, "Make room, for the girl is not dead, but sleeping." And they ridiculed Him. 25 But when the crowd was put outside, He went in and took her by the hand, and the girl arose. 26 And the report of this went out into all that land.

27 When Jesus departed from there, two blind men followed Him, crying out and saying, "Son of David, have mercy on us!" 28 And when He had come into the house, the blind men came to Him. And Jesus said to them, "Do you believe that I am able to do this?"

They said to Him, "Yes, Lord." 29 Then He touched their eyes, saying, "According to your faith let it be to you." 30 And their eyes were opened. And Jesus sternly warned them, saying, "See *that* no one knows *it*." 31 But when they had departed, they spread the news about Him in all that country.

> *The salvation of Jesus Christ enables a man to see for the first time in his life.* (SHADE)

32 As they went out, behold, they brought to Him a man, mute and demon-possessed. 33 And when the demon was cast out, the mute spoke. And the multitudes marveled, saying, "It was never seen like this in Israel!"

34 But the Pharisees said, "He casts out demons by the ruler of the demons."

35 Then Jesus went about all the cities and villages, teaching in their synagogues, preaching the gospel of the kingdom, and healing every sickness and every disease among the people. 36 But when He saw the multitudes, He was moved with compassion for them, because they were weary and scattered, like sheep having no shepherd. 37 Then He said to His disciples, "The harvest truly *is* plentiful, but the laborers *are* few. 38 Therefore pray the Lord of the harvest to send out laborers into His harvest."

Reading 14—Yearning to Recover God
Genesis 28:12

If the vision had come to a man like Joseph or Daniel, fine unsullied men of God, we should not have been surprised, but the vision came to a mean man. The dream was a preincarnation vision of God, symbolizing that communication between God and man is open, there is no break now. (John 1:51, "And He said to him, 'Most assuredly, I say to you, hereafter you shall see heaven open, and the angels of God ascending and descending upon the Son of Man.'") The only being in whom that ever took place was Jesus Christ, and He claims that He can put us where we can have the vision fulfilled in our own lives. Never say that God intends man to have a domain of dreaming, having mighty visions of God, and living an actual life that is dead to God at the same time. Jesus Christ claims that He can put into us the thing that connects the two. . . . . When we feel our deadness the consolation is that this vision came to Jacob. God transformed Jacob into "Israel," indicating one who strives with God. When a man is born again of the Spirit of God he has the nature of Jesus Christ imparted to him. If we are yearning to recover God, what we need is to get to the point of deciding against the self-assertiveness of our own hearts, and letting God teach us how to pay the price of our dreams. (PLACE HELP)

GENESIS 27:1—28:22

NOW it came to pass, when Isaac was old and his eyes were so dim that he could not see, that he called Esau his older son and said to him, "My son."

And he answered him, "Here I am."

2 Then he said, "Behold now, I am old. I do not know the day of my death. 3 Now therefore, please take your weapons, your quiver and your bow, and go out to the field and hunt game for me. 4 And make me savory food, such as I love, and bring *it* to me that I may eat, that my soul may bless you before I die."

5 Now Rebekah was listening when Isaac spoke to Esau his son. And Esau went to the field to hunt game and to bring *it.* 6 So Rebekah spoke to Jacob her son, saying, "Indeed I heard your father speak to Esau your brother, saying, 7 'Bring me game and make savory food for me, that I may eat it and bless you in the presence of the LORD before my death.' 8 Now therefore, my son, obey my voice according to what I command you. 9 Go now to the flock and bring me from there two choice kids of the goats, and I will make savory food from them for your father, such as he loves. 10 Then you shall take *it* to your father, that he may eat *it,* and that he may bless you before his death."

11 And Jacob said to Rebekah his mother, "Look, Esau my brother *is* a hairy man, and I *am* a smooth-*skinned* man. 12 Perhaps my father will feel me, and I shall seem to be a deceiver to him; and I shall bring a curse on myself and not a blessing."

13 But his mother said to him, "*Let* your curse *be* on me, my son; only obey my voice, and go, get *them* for me." 14 And he went and got *them* and brought *them* to his mother, and his mother made savory food, such as his father loved. 15 Then Rebekah took the choice clothes of her elder son Esau, which *were* with her in the house, and put them on Jacob her younger son. 16 And she put the skins of the kids of the goats on his hands and on the smooth part of his neck. 17 Then she gave the savory food and the bread, which she had prepared, into the hand of her son Jacob.

18 So he went to his father and said, "My father."

And he said, "Here I am. Who *are* you, my son?"

19 Jacob said to his father, "I *am* Esau your firstborn; I have done just as you told me; please arise, sit and eat of my game, that your soul may bless me."

20 But Isaac said to his son, "How *is* it that you have found *it* so quickly, my son?"

And he said, "Because the LORD your God brought *it* to me."

21 Isaac said to Jacob, "Please come near, that I may feel you, my son, whether you *are* really my son Esau or not." 22 So Jacob went near to Isaac his father, and he felt him and said, "The voice *is* Jacob's voice, but the hands *are* the hands of Esau." 23 And he did not recognize him, because his hands were hairy like his brother Esau's hands; so he blessed him.

24 Then he said, "*Are* you really my son Esau?"

He said, "I *am.*"

25 He said, "Bring *it* near to me, and I will eat of my son's game, so that my soul may bless you." So he brought *it* near to him, and he ate; and he brought him wine, and he drank. 26 Then his father Isaac said to him, "Come near now and kiss me, my son." 27 And he came near and kissed him; and he smelled the smell of his clothing, and blessed him and said:

"Surely, the smell of my son
    Is like the smell of a field
    Which the LORD has blessed.
28 Therefore may God give you
    Of the dew of heaven,
    Of the fatness of the earth,
    And plenty of grain and wine.
29 Let peoples serve you,
    And nations bow down to you.
    Be master over your brethren,
    And let your mother's sons bow
      down to you.
    Cursed *be* everyone who curses you,
    And blessed *be* those who bless you!"

30 Now it happened, as soon as Isaac had finished blessing Jacob, and Jacob had scarcely gone out from the presence of Isaac his father, that Esau his brother came in from his hunting. 31 He also had made savory food, and brought it to his father, and said to his father, "Let my father arise and eat of his son's game, that your soul may bless me."

32 And his father Isaac said to him, "Who *are* you?"

So he said, "I *am* your son, your firstborn, Esau."

33 Then Isaac trembled exceedingly, and said, "Who? Where *is* the one who hunted game and brought *it* to me? I ate all *of it* before you came, and I have blessed him— *and* indeed he shall be blessed."

34 When Esau heard the words of his father, he cried with an exceedingly great and bitter cry, and said to his father, "Bless me— me also, O my father!"

35 But he said, "Your brother came with deceit and has taken away your blessing."

36 And *Esau* said, "Is he not rightly named Jacob? For he has supplanted me these two times. He took away my birthright, and now look, he has taken away my blessing!" And he said, "Have you not reserved a blessing for me?"

37 Then Isaac answered and said to Esau, "Indeed I have made him your master, and all his brethren I have given to him as servants; with grain and wine I have sustained him. What shall I do now for you, my son?"

38 And Esau said to his father, "Have you only one blessing, my father? Bless me—me also, O my father!" And Esau lifted up his voice and wept.

39 Then Isaac his father answered and said to him:

"Behold, your dwelling shall be of the
 fatness of the earth,
And of the dew of heaven from
 above.
40 By your sword you shall live,
 And you shall serve your brother;
 And it shall come to pass, when you
  become restless,
 That you shall break his yoke from
  your neck."

41 So Esau hated Jacob because of the blessing with which his father blessed him, and Esau said in his heart, "The days of mourning for my father are at hand; then I will kill my brother Jacob."

42 And the words of Esau her older son were told to Rebekah. So she sent and called Jacob her younger son, and said to him, "Surely your brother Esau comforts himself concerning you *by intending* to kill you. 43 Now therefore, my son, obey my voice: arise, flee to my brother Laban in Haran. 44 And stay with him a few days, until your brother's fury turns away, 45 until your brother's anger turns away from you, and he forgets what you have done to him; then I will send and bring you from there. Why should I be bereaved also of you both in one day?"

46 And Rebekah said to Isaac, "I am weary of my life because of the daughters of Heth; if Jacob takes a wife of the daughters of Heth, like these *who are* the daughters of the land, what good will my life be to me?"

28 THEN Isaac called Jacob and blessed him, and charged him, and said to him: "You shall not take a wife from the daughters of Canaan. 2 Arise, go to Padan Aram, to the house of Bethuel your mother's father; and take yourself a wife from there of the daughters of Laban your mother's brother.

3 "May God Almighty bless you,
 And make you fruitful and multiply
  you,
 That you may be an assembly of
  peoples;
4 And give you the blessing of
  Abraham,
 To you and your descendants with
  you,
 That you may inherit the land
 In which you are a stranger,
 Which God gave to Abraham."

5 So Isaac sent Jacob away, and he went to Padan Aram, to Laban the son of Bethuel the Syrian, the brother of Rebekah, the mother of Jacob and Esau.

6 Esau saw that Isaac had blessed Jacob and sent him away to Padan Aram to take himself a wife from there, *and that* as he blessed him he gave him a charge, saying, "You shall not take a wife from the daughters of Canaan," 7 and that Jacob had obeyed his father and his mother and had gone to Padan Aram. 8 Also Esau saw that the daughters of Canaan did not please his father Isaac. 9 So Esau went to Ishmael and took Mahalath the daughter of Ishmael, Abraham's son, the sister of Nebajoth, to be his wife in addition to the wives he had.

10 Now Jacob went out from Beersheba and went toward Haran. 11 So he came to a certain place and stayed there all night, because the sun had set. And he took one of the stones of that place and put it at his head, and he lay down in that place to sleep. 12 Then he dreamed, and behold, a ladder *was* set up on the earth, and its top reached to heaven; and there the angels of God were ascending and descending on it.

13 And behold, the LORD stood above it and said: "I *am* the LORD God of Abraham your father and the God of Isaac; the land on which you lie I will give to you and your descendants. 14 Also your descendants shall be as the dust of the earth; you shall spread abroad to the west and the east, to the north and the south; and in you and in your seed all the families of the earth shall be blessed. 15 Behold, I *am* with you and will keep you wherever you go, and will bring you back to this land; for I will not leave you until I have done what I have spoken to you."

16 Then Jacob awoke from his sleep and said, "Surely the LORD is in this place, and

I did not know *it*." 17 And he was afraid and said, "How awesome *is* this place! This *is* none other than the house of God, and this *is* the gate of heaven!"

18 Then Jacob rose early in the morning, and took the stone that he had put at his head, set it up as a pillar, and poured oil on top of it. 19 And he called the name of that place Bethel; but the name of that city had been Luz previously. 20 Then Jacob made a vow, saying, "If God will be with me, and keep me in this way that I am going, and give me bread to eat and clothing to put on, 21 so that I come back to my father's house in peace, then the LORD shall be my God. 22 And this stone which I have set as a pillar shall be God's house, and of all that You give me I will surely give a tenth to You."

PSALM 7:9–17

9 OH, let the wickedness of the wicked
   come to an end,
   But establish the just;
   For the righteous God tests the hearts
   and minds.
10 My defense *is* of God,
   Who saves the upright in heart.

11 God *is* a just judge,
   And God is angry *with the wicked* every
   day.
12 If he does not turn back,
   He will sharpen His sword;
   He bends His bow and makes it ready.
13 He also prepares for Himself
   instruments of death;
   He makes His arrows into fiery shafts.

14 Behold, *the wicked* brings forth iniquity;
   Yes, he conceives trouble and brings
   forth falsehood.
15 He made a pit and dug it out,
   And has fallen into the ditch *which* he
   made.
16 His trouble shall return upon his own
   head,
   And his violent dealing shall come
   down on his own crown.

17 I will praise the LORD according to His
   righteousness,

---

*P*raising God is the ultimate end
and aim of all we go
through.   (APPROVED)

And will sing praise to the name of
the LORD Most High.

PROVERBS 3:11, 12

11 MY son, do not despise the chastening
   of the LORD,
   Nor detest His correction;
12 For whom the LORD loves He corrects,
   Just as a father the son *in whom* he
   delights.

MATTHEW 10:1–20

AND when He had called His twelve disciples to *Him,* He gave them power *over* unclean spirits, to cast them out, and to heal all kinds of sickness and all kinds of disease. 2 Now the names of the twelve apostles are these: first, Simon, who is called Peter, and Andrew his brother; James the *son* of Zebedee, and John his brother; 3 Philip and Bartholomew; Thomas and Matthew the tax collector; James the *son* of Alphaeus, and Lebbaeus, whose surname was Thaddaeus; 4 Simon the Cananite, and Judas Iscariot, who also betrayed Him.

5 These twelve Jesus sent out and commanded them, saying: "Do not go into the way of the Gentiles, and do not enter a city of the Samaritans. 6 But go rather to the lost sheep of the house of Israel. 7 And as you go, preach, saying, 'The kingdom of heaven is at hand.' 8 Heal the sick, cleanse the lepers, raise the dead, cast out demons. Freely you have received, freely give. 9 Provide neither gold nor silver nor copper in your money belts, 10 nor bag for *your* journey, nor two tunics, nor sandals, nor staffs; for a worker is worthy of his food.

---

*T*he knowledge of my poverty brings
me to the frontier where Jesus Christ
works.   (CONFORMED)

---

11 "Now whatever city or town you enter, inquire who in it is worthy, and stay there till you go out. 12 And when you go into a household, greet it. 13 If the household is worthy, let your peace come upon it. But if it is not worthy, let your peace return to you. 14 And whoever will not receive you nor hear your words, when you depart from that house or city, shake off the dust from your feet. 15 Assuredly, I say to you, it will be more tolerable for the

land of Sodom and Gomorrah in the day of judgment than for that city!

16 "Behold, I send you out as sheep in the midst of wolves. Therefore be wise as serpents and harmless as doves. 17 But beware of men, for they will deliver you up to councils and scourge you in their synagogues. 18 You will be brought before gov-

ernors and kings for My sake, as a testimony to them and to the Gentiles. 19 But when they deliver you up, do not worry about how or what you should speak. For it will be given to you in that hour what you should speak; 20 for it is not you who speak, but the Spirit of your Father who speaks in you.

◆◆◆◆

Reading 15—Listening in Darkness
Matthew 10:27

Let it be understood that the darkness our Lord speaks of is not darkness caused by sin or disobedience, but rather darkness caused from excess of light. There are times in the life of every disciple when things are not clear or easy, when it is not possible to know what to do or say. Such times of darkness come as a discipline to the character and as the means of fuller knowledge of the Lord. Such darkness is a time for listening, not for speaking. This aspect of darkness as a necessary side to fellowship with God is not unusual in the Bible (see Is. 5:30; 50:10; 1 Pet. 1:6, 7). The Lord shares the darkness with His disciple: "Whatever I tell you in the dark. . . ." He is there. He knows all about it. The sense of mystery must always be, for mystery means being guided by obedience to someone who knows more than I do. On the Mount of Transfiguration this darkness from excess of light is brought out. "They were fearful as they entered the cloud," but in the cloud "they saw no one anymore, but only Jesus with themselves."   (*PLACE HELP*)

GENESIS 29:1—30:43

SO Jacob went on his journey and came to the land of the people of the East. 2 And he looked, and saw a well in the field; and behold, there *were* three flocks of sheep lying by it; for out of that well they watered the flocks. A large stone *was* on the well's mouth. 3 Now all the flocks would be gathered there; and they would roll the stone from the well's mouth, water the sheep, and put the stone back in its place on the well's mouth.

4 And Jacob said to them, "My brethren, where *are* you from?"

And they said, "We *are* from Haran."

5 Then he said to them, "Do you know Laban the son of Nahor?"

And they said, "We know him."

6 So he said to them, "Is he well?"

And they said, "*He is* well. And look, his daughter Rachel is coming with the sheep."

7 Then he said, "Look, *it is* still high day; *it is* not time for the cattle to be gathered

together. Water the sheep, and go and feed *them.*"

8 But they said, "We cannot until all the flocks are gathered together, and they have rolled the stone from the well's mouth; then we water the sheep."

9 Now while he was still speaking with them, Rachel came with her father's sheep, for she was a shepherdess. 10 And it came to pass, when Jacob saw Rachel the daughter of Laban his mother's brother, and the sheep of Laban his mother's brother, that Jacob went near and rolled the stone from the well's mouth, and watered the flock of Laban his mother's brother. 11 Then Jacob kissed Rachel, and lifted up his voice and wept. 12 And Jacob told Rachel that he *was* her father's relative and that he *was* Rebekah's son. So she ran and told her father.

13 Then it came to pass, when Laban heard the report about Jacob his sister's son, that he ran to meet him, and embraced him and kissed him, and brought him to his house. So he told Laban all these things. 14 And Laban said to him, "Surely you *are*

14 For her proceeds *are* better than the
profits of silver,
And her gain than fine gold.
15 She *is* more precious than rubies,
And all the things you may desire
cannot compare with her.
16 Length of days *is* in her right hand,
In her left hand riches and honor.
17 Her ways *are* ways of pleasantness,
And all her paths *are* peace.
18 She *is* a tree of life to those who take
hold of her,
And happy *are all* who retain her.

MATTHEW 10:21–42

"NOW brother will deliver up brother to
death, and a father *his* child; and children
will rise up against parents and cause them
to be put to death. 22 And you will be hated
by all for My name's sake. But he who endures to the end will be saved. 23 When
they persecute you in this city, flee to another. For assuredly, I say to you, you will
not have gone through the cities of Israel
before the Son of Man comes.

24 "A disciple is not above *his* teacher,
nor a servant above his master. 25 It is
enough for a disciple that he be like his
teacher, and a servant like his master. If
they have called the master of the house
Beelzebub, how much more *will they call*
those of his household! 26 Therefore do not
fear them. For there is nothing covered that
will not be revealed, and hidden that will
not be known.

27 "Whatever I tell you in the dark, speak
in the light; and what you hear in the ear,
preach on the housetops. 28 And do not
fear those who kill the body but cannot
kill the soul. But rather fear Him who is
able to destroy both soul and body in hell.
29 Are not two sparrows sold for a copper

coin? And not one of them falls to the
ground apart from your Father's will.
30 But the very hairs of your head are all
numbered. 31 Do not fear therefore; you
are of more value than many sparrows.

32 "Therefore whoever confesses Me before men, him I will also confess before
My Father who is in heaven. 33 But whoever
denies Me before men, him I will also deny
before My Father who is in heaven.

34 "Do not think that I came to bring
peace on earth. I did not come to bring
peace but a sword. 35 For I have come to
'set a man against his father, a daughter
against her mother, and a daughter-in-law
against her mother-in-law'; 36 and 'a man's
enemies will be those of his *own* household.'
37 He who loves father or mother more than
Me is not worthy of Me. And he who loves
son or daughter more than Me is not worthy
of Me. 38 And he who does not take his
cross and follow after Me is not worthy
of Me. 39 He who finds his life will lose
it, and he who loses his life for My sake
will find it.

---

*O*ur cross is the steady exhibition
of the fact that we are not our
own.   (PHIL. SIN)

---

40 "He who receives you receives Me, and
he who receives Me receives Him who sent
Me. 41 He who receives a prophet in the
name of a prophet shall receive a prophet's
reward. And he who receives a righteous
man in the name of a righteous man shall
receive a righteous man's reward. 42 And
whoever gives one of these little ones only
a cup of cold *water* in the name of a disciple,
assuredly, I say to you, he shall by no means
lose his reward."

◆◆◆◆

Reading 16—The Face of God
Genesis 32:30

*P*eniel means "Face of God," and it recalls the words that will come to
Moses generations later: "You cannot see My face; for no man shall see
Me, and live" (Ex. 33:20). These words give peculiar force to Jacob's words,
"I have seen God face to face, and my life is preserved," for Jacob did see
God face to face, and he did die—so profound a death that God gave him a
new name. "Your name shall no longer be called Jacob, but Israel."

That is always the test of the reality of sanctification: not so much that I have received something, but that I have ceased to be my old self. Through disillusionment and shattering Jacob comes out on God's side with a changed name; we drag the purpose of God through our own plans and change His name. We have to learn to distinguish between the impression made on us by a vision and identification with the One who gave us the vision. The love of God and His forgiveness are the first things we experience; we are not prepared as yet to recognize His other attributes of holiness and justice because that will mean death to everything that does not partake of God's nature.

(*Not Knowing*)

GENESIS 31:1—32:32

NOW *Jacob* heard the words of Laban's sons, saying, "Jacob has taken away all that was our father's, and from what was our father's he has acquired all this wealth." 2 And Jacob saw the countenance of Laban, and indeed it *was* not *favorable* toward him as before. 3 Then the LORD said to Jacob, "Return to the land of your fathers and to your family, and I will be with you."

4 So Jacob sent and called Rachel and Leah to the field, to his flock, 5 and said to them, "I see your father's countenance, that it *is* not *favorable* toward me as before; but the God of my father has been with me. 6 And you know that with all my might I have served your father. 7 Yet your father has deceived me and changed my wages ten times, but God did not allow him to hurt me. 8 If he said thus: 'The speckled shall be your wages,' then all the flocks bore speckled. And if he said thus: 'The streaked shall be your wages,' then all the flocks bore streaked. 9 So God has taken away the livestock of your father and given *them* to me. 10 "And it happened, at the time when the flocks conceived, that I lifted my eyes and saw in a dream, and behold, the rams which leaped upon the flocks *were* streaked, speckled, and gray-spotted. 11 Then the Angel of God spoke to me in a dream, saying, 'Jacob.' And I said, 'Here I am.' 12 And He said, 'Lift your eyes now and see, all the rams which leap on the flocks *are* streaked, speckled, and gray-spotted; for I have seen all that Laban is doing to you. 13 I *am* the God of Bethel, where you anointed the pillar *and* where you made a vow to Me. Now arise, get out of this land, and return to the land of your family.' "

14 Then Rachel and Leah answered and said to him, "Is there still any portion or inheritance for us in our father's house? 15 Are we not considered strangers by him? For he has sold us, and also completely consumed our money. 16 For all these riches which God has taken from our father are

really ours and our children's; now then, whatever God has said to you, do it."

17 Then Jacob rose and set his sons and his wives on camels. 18 And he carried away all his livestock and all his possessions which he had gained, his acquired livestock which he had gained in Padan Aram, to go to his father Isaac in the land of Canaan. 19 Now Laban had gone to shear his sheep, and Rachel had stolen the household idols that were her father's. 20 And Jacob stole away, unknown to Laban the Syrian, in that he did not tell him that he intended to flee. 21 So he fled with all that he had. He arose and crossed the river, and headed toward the mountains of Gilead.

22 And Laban was told on the third day that Jacob had fled. 23 Then he took his brethren with him and pursued him for seven days' journey, and he overtook him in the mountains of Gilead. 24 But God had come to Laban the Syrian in a dream by night, and said to him, "Be careful that you speak to Jacob neither good nor bad."

25 So Laban overtook Jacob. Now Jacob had pitched his tent in the mountains, and Laban with his brethren pitched in the mountains of Gilead.

26 And Laban said to Jacob: "What have you done, that you have stolen away unknown to me, and carried away my daughters like captives *taken* with the sword? 27 Why did you flee away secretly, and steal away from me, and not tell me; for I might have sent you away with joy and songs, with timbrel and harp? 28 And you did not allow me to kiss my sons and my daughters. Now you have done foolishly in *so* doing. 29 It is in my power to do you harm, but the God of your father spoke to me last night, saying, 'Be careful that you speak to Jacob neither good nor bad.' 30 And now you have surely gone because you greatly long for your father's house, *but* why did you steal my gods?"

31 Then Jacob answered and said to Laban, "Because I was afraid, for I said, 'Perhaps you would take your daughters from

me by force.' 32 With whomever you find your gods, do not let him live. In the presence of our brethren, identify what I have of yours and take *it* with you." For Jacob did not know that Rachel had stolen them.

33 And Laban went into Jacob's tent, into Leah's tent, and into the two maids' tents, but he did not find *them*. Then he went out of Leah's tent and entered Rachel's tent. 34 Now Rachel had taken the household idols, put them in the camel's saddle, and sat on them. And Laban searched all about the tent but did not find *them*. 35 And she said to her father, "Let it not displease my lord that I cannot rise before you, for the manner of women *is* with me." And he searched but did not find the household idols.

36 Then Jacob was angry and rebuked Laban, and Jacob answered and said to Laban: "What *is* my trespass? What *is* my sin, that you have so hotly pursued me? 37 Although you have searched all my things, what part of your household things have you found? Set *it* here before my brethren and your brethren, that they may judge between us both! 38 These twenty years I *have been* with you; your ewes and your female goats have not miscarried their young, and I have not eaten the rams of your flock. 39 That which was torn *by beasts* I did not bring to you; I bore the loss of it. You required it from my hand, *whether* stolen by day or stolen by night. 40 *There* I was! In the day the drought consumed me, and the frost by night, and my sleep departed from my eyes. 41 Thus I have been in your house twenty years; I served you fourteen years for your two daughters, and six years for your flock, and you have changed my wages ten times. 42 Unless the God of my father, the God of Abraham and the Fear of Isaac, had been with me, surely now you would have sent me away empty-handed. God has seen my affliction and the labor of my hands, and rebuked *you* last night."

43 And Laban answered and said to Jacob, *"These* daughters *are* my daughters, and *these* children *are* my children, and *this* flock *is* my flock; all that you see *is* mine. But what can I do this day to these my daughters or to their children whom they have borne? 44 Now therefore, come, let us make a covenant, you and I, and let it be a witness between you and me."

45 So Jacob took a stone and set it up *as* a pillar. 46 Then Jacob said to his brethren, "Gather stones." And they took stones and made a heap, and they ate there on the heap. 47 Laban called it Jegar Sahadu-

tha, but Jacob called it Galeed. 48 And Laban said, "This heap *is* a witness between you and me this day." Therefore its name was called Galeed, 49 also Mizpah, because he said, "May the LORD watch between you and me when we are absent one from another. 50 If you afflict my daughters, or if you take *other* wives besides my daughters, *although* no man *is* with us—see, God *is* witness between you and me!"

51 Then Laban said to Jacob, "Here is this heap and here is *this* pillar, which I have placed between you and me. 52 This heap *is* a witness, and *this* pillar *is* a witness, that I will not pass beyond this heap to you, and you will not pass beyond this heap and this pillar to me, for harm. 53 The God of Abraham, the God of Nahor, and the God of their father judge between us." And Jacob swore by the Fear of his father Isaac. 54 Then Jacob offered a sacrifice on the mountain, and called his brethren to eat bread. And they ate bread and stayed all night on the mountain. 55 And early in the morning Laban arose, and kissed his sons and daughters and blessed them. Then Laban departed and returned to his place.

32 SO Jacob went on his way, and the angels of God met him. 2 When Jacob saw them, he said, "This *is* God's camp." And he called the name of that place Mahanaim.

3 Then Jacob sent messengers before him to Esau his brother in the land of Seir, the country of Edom. 4 And he commanded them, saying, "Speak thus to my lord Esau, 'Thus your servant Jacob says: "I have dwelt with Laban and stayed there until now. 5 I have oxen, donkeys, flocks, and male and female servants; and I have sent to tell my lord, that I may find favor in your sight." ' "

6 Then the messengers returned to Jacob, saying, "We came to your brother Esau, and he also is coming to meet you, and four hundred men *are* with him." 7 So Jacob was greatly afraid and distressed; and he divided the people that *were* with him, and the flocks and herds and camels, into two companies. 8 And he said, "If Esau comes to the one company and attacks it, then the other company which is left will escape."

9 Then Jacob said, "O God of my father Abraham and God of my father Isaac, the LORD who said to me, 'Return to your country and to your family, and I will deal well with you': 10 I am not worthy of the least of all the mercies and of all the truth which You have shown Your servant; for I crossed over this Jordan with my staff,

and now I have become two companies.
11 Deliver me, I pray, from the hand of my brother, from the hand of Esau; for I fear him, lest he come and attack me *and* the mother with the children. 12 For You said, 'I will surely treat you well, and make your descendants as the sand of the sea, which cannot be numbered for multitude.' "

13 So he lodged there that same night, and took what came to his hand as a present for Esau his brother: 14 two hundred female goats and twenty male goats, two hundred ewes and twenty rams, 15 thirty milk camels with their colts, forty cows and ten bulls, twenty female donkeys and ten foals. 16 Then he delivered *them* to the hand of his servants, every drove by itself, and said to his servants, "Pass over before me, and put some distance between successive droves." 17 And he commanded the first one, saying, "When Esau my brother meets you and asks you, saying, 'To whom do you belong, and where are you going? Whose *are* these in front of you?' 18 then you shall say, 'They *are* your servant Jacob's. It *is* a present sent to my lord Esau; and behold, he also *is* behind us.' " 19 So he commanded the second, the third, and all who followed the droves, saying, "In this manner you shall speak to Esau when you find him; 20 and also say, 'Behold, your servant Jacob *is* behind us.' " For he said, "I will appease him with the present that goes before me, and afterward I will see his face; perhaps he will accept me." 21 So the present went on over before him, but he himself lodged that night in the camp.

22 And he arose that night and took his two wives, his two female servants, and his eleven sons, and crossed over the ford of Jabbok. 23 He took them, sent them over the brook, and sent over what he had. 24 Then Jacob was left alone; and a Man wrestled with him until the breaking of day. 25 Now when He saw that He did not prevail against him, He touched the socket of his hip; and the socket of Jacob's hip was out of joint as He wrestled with him.

---

*T*he natural is not sinful, but the natural is not spiritual.   (PSY. REDEMP.)

---

26 And He said, "Let Me go, for the day breaks."

But he said, "I will not let You go unless You bless me!"

27 So He said to him, "What *is* your name?"

He said, "Jacob."

28 And He said, "Your name shall no longer be called Jacob, but Israel; for you have struggled with God and with men, and have prevailed."

29 Then Jacob asked, saying, "Tell *me* Your name, I pray."

And He said, "Why *is* it *that* you ask about My name?" And He blessed him there.

30 So Jacob called the name of the place Peniel: "For I have seen God face to face, and my life is preserved." 31 Just as he crossed over Penuel the sun rose on him, and he limped on his hip. 32 Therefore to this day the children of Israel do not eat the muscle that shrank, which *is* on the hip socket, because He touched the socket of Jacob's hip in the muscle that shrank.

PSALM 8:6–9

6   YOU have made him to have dominion
        over the works of Your hands;
     You have put all *things* under his feet,
7   All sheep and oxen—
        Even the beasts of the field,
8   The birds of the air,
        And the fish of the sea
     That pass through the paths of the seas.

9   O LORD, our Lord,
        How excellent *is* Your name in all the
        earth!

PROVERBS 3:19, 20

19   THE LORD by wisdom founded the
        earth;
     By understanding He established the
        heavens;
20   By His knowledge the depths were
        broken up,
     And clouds drop down the dew.

MATTHEW 11:1–30

NOW it came to pass, when Jesus finished commanding His twelve disciples, that He departed from there to teach and to preach in their cities.

2 And when John had heard in prison about the works of Christ, he sent two of his disciples 3 and said to Him, "Are You the Coming One, or do we look for another?"

4 Jesus answered and said to them, "Go and tell John the things which you hear and see: 5 *The* blind see and *the* lame walk;

the lepers are cleansed and *the* deaf hear; *the* dead are raised up and *the* poor have the gospel preached to them. 6 And blessed is he who is not offended because of Me."

7 As they departed, Jesus began to say to the multitudes concerning John: "What did you go out into the wilderness to see? A reed shaken by the wind? 8 But what did you go out to see? A man clothed in soft garments? Indeed, those who wear soft *clothing* are in kings' houses. 9 But what did you go out to see? A prophet? Yes, I say to you, and more than a prophet. 10 For this is *he* of whom it is written:

'Behold, I send My messenger before Your face,
Who will prepare Your way before You.'

11 "Assuredly, I say to you, among those born of women there has not risen one greater than John the Baptist; but he who is least in the kingdom of heaven is greater than he. 12 And from the days of John the Baptist until now the kingdom of heaven suffers violence, and the violent take it by force. 13 For all the prophets and the law prophesied until John. 14 And if you are willing to receive *it,* he is Elijah who is to come. 15 He who has ears to hear, let him hear!

Before we can hear certain things, we must be trained.   (BRILL. HERITAGE)

---

16 "But to what shall I liken this generation? It is like children sitting in the marketplaces and calling to their companions, 17 and saying:

'We played the flute for you,
And you did not dance;

We mourned to you,
And you did not lament.'

18 For John came neither eating nor drinking, and they say, 'He has a demon.' 19 The Son of Man came eating and drinking, and they say, 'Look, a glutton and a winebibber, a friend of tax collectors and sinners!' But wisdom is justified by her children."

20 Then He began to rebuke the cities in which most of His mighty works had been done, because they did not repent: 21 "Woe to you, Chorazin! Woe to you, Bethsaida! For if the mighty works which were done in you had been done in Tyre and Sidon, they would have repented long ago in sackcloth and ashes. 22 But I say to you, it will be more tolerable for Tyre and Sidon in the day of judgment than for you. 23 And you, Capernaum, who are exalted to heaven, will be brought down to Hades; for if the mighty works which were done in you had been done in Sodom, it would have remained until this day. 24 But I say to you that it shall be more tolerable for the land of Sodom in the day of judgment than for you."

25 At that time Jesus answered and said, "I thank You, Father, Lord of heaven and earth, that You have hidden these things from *the* wise and prudent and have revealed them to babes. 26 Even so, Father, for so it seemed good in Your sight. 27 All things have been delivered to Me by My Father, and no one knows the Son except the Father. Nor does anyone know the Father except the Son, and *the one* to whom the Son wills to reveal *Him.* 28 Come to Me, all *you* who labor and are heavy laden, and I will give you rest. 29 Take My yoke upon you and learn from Me, for I am gentle and lowly in heart, and you will find rest for your souls. 30 For My yoke *is* easy and My burden is light."

◆◆◆◆

Reading 17—Expansion and Concentration
Genesis 33:18; 34:2, 25–29

In the meeting with Esau and the marvelous experience of reconciliation with him, Jacob had an expansion of heart, but he did not pay for it afterward in concentration. He lived loosely in the exalted peace of the expanded life, and suddenly a terrible tragedy breaks up the whole thing.

In our personal lives every expansion of heart . . . must be paid for by watchfulness; if it is not, looseness, ending in moral collapse, is sure to result.

Because people do not understand the way they are made, havoc is produced in the lives of those who really have had times with God and have experienced expansions of heart. But they have forgotten to concentrate, and the general feeling of looseness is a sure sign that God's presence has gone.

Jacob settled down in the peace of Shechem, Dinah went to hell, and her brothers to the Devil. Then God spoke to Jacob. If you forget to concentrate on God, the thing that happened in Jacob's domestic life on the big scale will happen in your bodily life on the narrow scale. The vision of what God wants must be paid for by concentration on your part; if it is not, in come the "little foxes," in come a hundred and one things that were never there before—and down you go. It is not that these things *may* happen; they *will* happen as sure as God is God, unless you watch and pray—that is, unless you concentrate until you are confirmed in the ways of God. (*NOT KNOWING*)

GENESIS 33:1—34:31

NOW Jacob lifted his eyes and looked, and there, Esau was coming, and with him were four hundred men. So he divided the children among Leah, Rachel, and the two maidservants. 2 And he put the maidservants and their children in front, Leah and her children behind, and Rachel and Joseph last. 3 Then he crossed over before them and bowed himself to the ground seven times, until he came near to his brother.

4 But Esau ran to meet him, and embraced him, and fell on his neck and kissed him, and they wept. 5 And he lifted his eyes and saw the women and children, and said, "Who *are* these with you?"

So he said, "The children whom God has graciously given your servant." 6 Then the maidservants came near, they and their children, and bowed down. 7 And Leah also came near with her children, and they bowed down. Afterward Joseph and Rachel came near, and they bowed down.

8 Then Esau said, "What *do* you *mean* by all this company which I met?"

And he said, "*These are* to find favor in the sight of my lord."

9 But Esau said, "I have enough, my brother; keep what you have for yourself."

10 And Jacob said, "No, please, if I have now found favor in your sight, then receive my present from my hand, inasmuch as I have seen your face as though I had seen the face of God, and you were pleased with me. 11 Please, take my blessing that is

brought to you, because God has dealt graciously with me, and because I have enough." So he urged him, and he took *it*.

12 Then Esau said, "Let us take our journey; let us go, and I will go before you."

13 But Jacob said to him, "My lord knows that the children *are* weak, and the flocks and herds which are nursing *are* with me. And if the men should drive them hard one day, all the flock will die. 14 Please let my lord go on ahead before his servant. I will lead on slowly at a pace which the livestock that go before me, and the children, are able to endure, until I come to my lord in Seir."

15 And Esau said, "Now let me leave with you *some* of the people who *are* with me."

But he said, "What need is there? Let me find favor in the sight of my lord." 16 So Esau returned that day on his way to Seir. 17 And Jacob journeyed to Succoth, built himself a house, and made booths for his livestock. Therefore the name of the place is called Succoth.

18 Then Jacob came safely to the city of Shechem, which *is* in the land of Canaan, when he came from Padan Aram; and he pitched his tent before the city. 19 And he bought the parcel of land, where he had pitched his tent, from the children of Hamor, Shechem's father, for one hundred pieces of money. 20 Then he erected an altar there and called it El Elohe Israel.

34 NOW Dinah the daughter of Leah, whom she had borne to Jacob, went out to see the daughters of the land. 2 And when Shechem the son of Hamor the Hivite, prince of the country, saw her, he took her and lay with her, and violated her. 3 His soul was strongly attracted to Dinah the daughter of Jacob, and he loved the young woman and spoke kindly to the

---

*G*od alters the inevitable when we get in touch with Him. (PERFECT)

young woman. 4 So Shechem spoke to his father Hamor, saying, "Get me this young woman as a wife."

5 And Jacob heard that he had defiled Dinah his daughter. Now his sons were with his livestock in the field; so Jacob held his peace until they came. 6 Then Hamor the father of Shechem went out to Jacob to speak with him. 7 And the sons of Jacob came in from the field when they heard *it;* and the men were grieved and very angry, because he had done a disgraceful thing in Israel by lying with Jacob's daughter, a thing which ought not to be done. 8 But Hamor spoke with them, saying, "The soul of my son Shechem longs for your daughter. Please give her to him as a wife. 9 And make marriages with us; give your daughters to us, and take our daughters to yourselves. 10 So you shall dwell with us, and the land shall be before you. Dwell and trade in it, and acquire possessions for yourselves in it."

11 Then Shechem said to her father and her brothers, "Let me find favor in your eyes, and whatever you say to me I will give. 12 Ask me ever so much dowry and gift, and I will give according to what you say to me; but give me the young woman as a wife."

13 But the sons of Jacob answered Shechem and Hamor his father, and spoke deceitfully, because he had defiled Dinah their sister. 14 And they said to them, "We cannot do this thing, to give our sister to one who is uncircumcised, for that *would be* a reproach to us. 15 But on this *condition* we will consent to you: If you will become as we *are,* if every male of you is circumcised, 16 then we will give our daughters to you, and we will take your daughters to us; and we will dwell with you, and we will become one people. 17 But if you will not heed us and be circumcised, then we will take our daughter and be gone."

18 And their words pleased Hamor and Shechem, Hamor's son. 19 So the young man did not delay to do the thing, because he delighted in Jacob's daughter. He *was* more honorable than all the household of his father.

20 And Hamor and Shechem his son came to the gate of their city, and spoke with the men of their city, saying: 21 "These men *are* at peace with us. Therefore let them dwell in the land and trade in it. For indeed the land *is* large enough for them. Let us take their daughters to us as wives, and let us give them our daughters. 22 Only on this *condition* will the men consent to dwell with us, to be one people: if every male among us is circumcised as they *are* circumcised. 23 *Will* not their livestock, their property, and every animal of theirs *be* ours? Only let us consent to them, and they will dwell with us." 24 And all who went out of the gate of his city heeded Hamor and Shechem his son; every male was circumcised, all who went out of the gate of his city.

25 Now it came to pass on the third day, when they were in pain, that two of the sons of Jacob, Simeon and Levi, Dinah's brothers, each took his sword and came boldly upon the city and killed all the males. 26 And they killed Hamor and Shechem his son with the edge of the sword, and took Dinah from Shechem's house, and went out. 27 The sons of Jacob came upon the slain, and plundered the city, because their sister had been defiled. 28 They took their sheep, their oxen, and their donkeys, what *was* in the city and what *was* in the field, 29 and all their wealth. All their little ones and their wives they took captive; and they plundered even all that *was* in the houses.

30 Then Jacob said to Simeon and Levi, "You have troubled me by making me obnoxious among the inhabitants of the land, among the Canaanites and the Perizzites; and since I *am* few in number, they will gather themselves together against me and kill me. I shall be destroyed, my household and I."

31 But they said, "Should he treat our sister like a harlot?"

PSALM 9:1–5

1 I will praise *You,* O LORD, with my whole heart;
   I will tell of all Your marvelous works.
2 I will be glad and rejoice in You;
   I will sing praise to Your name, O Most High.
3 When my enemies turn back,
   They shall fall and perish at Your presence.
4 For You have maintained my right and my cause;
   You sat on the throne judging in righteousness.
5 You have rebuked the nations,
   You have destroyed the wicked;
   You have blotted out their name forever and ever.

PROVERBS 3:21–26

21 MY son, let them not depart from your eyes—

Keep sound wisdom and discretion;
22 So they will be life to your soul
And grace to your neck.
23 Then you will walk safely in your way,
And your foot will not stumble.
24 When you lie down, you will not be afraid;
Yes, you will lie down and your sleep will be sweet.
25 Do not be afraid of sudden terror,
Nor of trouble from the wicked when it comes;
26 For the LORD will be your confidence,
And will keep your foot from being caught.

If you are walking with God it is impossible to be in the sulks. (NOT KNOWING)

MATTHEW 12:1–21

AT that time Jesus went through the grainfields on the Sabbath. And His disciples were hungry, and began to pluck heads of grain and to eat. 2 And when the Pharisees saw *it,* they said to Him, "Look, Your disciples are doing what is not lawful to do on the Sabbath!"

3 But He said to them, "Have you not read what David did when he was hungry, he and those who were with him: 4 how he entered the house of God and ate the showbread which was not lawful for him to eat, nor for those who were with him, but only for the priests? 5 Or have you not read in the law that on the Sabbath the priests in the temple profane the Sabbath, and are blameless? 6 Yet I say to you that in this place there is *One* greater than the temple. 7 But if you had known what *this* means, 'I desire mercy and not sacrifice,' you would not have condemned the guiltless. 8 For the Son of Man is Lord even of the Sabbath."

9 Now when He had departed from there, He went into their synagogue. 10 And behold, there was a man who had a withered hand. And they asked Him, saying, "Is it lawful to heal on the Sabbath?"—that they might accuse Him.

11 Then He said to them, "What man is there among you who has one sheep, and if it falls into a pit on the Sabbath, will not lay hold of it and lift *it* out? 12 Of how much more value then is a man than a sheep? Therefore it is lawful to do good on the Sabbath." 13 Then He said to the man, "Stretch out your hand." And he stretched *it* out, and it was restored as whole as the other. 14 Then the Pharisees went out and plotted against Him, how they might destroy Him.

15 But when Jesus knew *it,* He withdrew from there. And great multitudes followed Him, and He healed them all. 16 Yet He warned them not to make Him known, 17 that it might be fulfilled which was spoken by Isaiah the prophet, saying:

18 "Behold! My Servant whom I have chosen,
My Beloved in whom My soul is well pleased!
I will put My Spirit upon Him,
And He will declare justice to the Gentiles.
19 He will not quarrel nor cry out,
Nor will anyone hear His voice in the streets.
20 A bruised reed He will not break,
And smoking flax He will not quench,
Till He sends forth justice to victory;
21 And in His name Gentiles will trust."

Reading 18—Birthplace of Words
Matthew 12:34

The heart is the first thing to live in physical birth and in spiritual birth. It is a wonderful thing that God can cleanse and purify the thinking of our hearts. That is why our Lord says, "Out of the abundance of the heart his mouth speaks" (Luke 6:45). The Bible says that words are born in the heart, not in the head. "Will they not teach you and tell you, and utter words from their heart?" (Job 8:10). (See also Matt. 12:34.)

Jesus Christ said He always spoke as His Father wished Him to. Did His Father write out the words and tell Him to learn them by heart? No, the mainspring of the heart of Jesus Christ was the mainspring of the heart of God the Father, consequently the words Jesus Christ spoke were the exact expression of God's thought. In our Lord the tongue was in its right place; He never spoke from His head, but always from His heart. "If anyone among you thinks he is religious, and does not bridle his tongue . . . this one's religion *is* useless" (James 1:26), there is nothing in it. The tongue and the brain are under our control, not God's.   (*BIB. PSYCH.*)

GENESIS 35:1—36:43

THEN God said to Jacob, "Arise, go up to Bethel and dwell there; and make an altar there to God, who appeared to you when you fled from the face of Esau your brother."

2 And Jacob said to his household and to all who *were* with him, "Put away the foreign gods that *are* among us, purify yourselves, and change your garments. 3 Then let us arise and go up to Bethel; and I will make an altar there to God, who answered me in the day of my distress and has been with me in the way which I have gone." 4 So they gave Jacob all the foreign gods which *were* in their hands, and the earrings which *were* in their ears; and Jacob hid them under the terebinth tree which *was* by Shechem.

5 And they journeyed, and the terror of God was upon the cities that *were* all around them, and they did not pursue the sons of Jacob. 6 So Jacob came to Luz (that *is,* Bethel), which *is* in the land of Canaan, he and all the people who *were* with him. 7 And he built an altar there and called the place El Bethel, because there God appeared to him when he fled from the face of his brother.

8 Now Deborah, Rebekah's nurse, died, and she was buried below Bethel under the terebinth tree. So the name of it was called Allon Bachuth.

9 Then God appeared to Jacob again, when he came from Padan Aram, and blessed him. 10 And God said to him, "Your name *is* Jacob; your name shall not be called Jacob anymore, but Israel shall be your name." So He called his name Israel. 11 Also God said to him: "I *am* God Almighty. Be fruitful and multiply; a nation and a company of nations shall proceed from you, and kings shall come from your body. 12 The land which I gave Abraham and Isaac I give to you; and to your descendants after you I give this land." 13 Then God went up from him in the place where

He talked with him. 14 So Jacob set up a pillar in the place where He talked with him, a pillar of stone; and he poured a drink offering on it, and he poured oil on it. 15 And Jacob called the name of the place where God spoke with him, Bethel.

To be brought within the zone of God's voice is to be profoundly altered.   (SEND I YOU)

---

16 Then they journeyed from Bethel. And when there was but a little distance to go to Ephrath, Rachel labored *in childbirth,* and she had hard labor. 17 Now it came to pass, when she was in hard labor, that the midwife said to her, "Do not fear; you will have this son also." 18 And so it was, as her soul was departing (for she died), that she called his name Ben-Oni; but his father called him Benjamin. 19 So Rachel died and was buried on the way to Ephrath (that *is,* Bethlehem). 20 And Jacob set a pillar on her grave, which *is* the pillar of Rachel's grave to this day.

21 Then Israel journeyed and pitched his tent beyond the tower of Eder. 22 And it happened, when Israel dwelt in that land, that Reuben went and lay with Bilhah his father's concubine; and Israel heard *about it.*

Now the sons of Jacob were twelve: 23 the sons of Leah *were* Reuben, Jacob's firstborn, and Simeon, Levi, Judah, Issachar, and Zebulun; 24 the sons of Rachel *were* Joseph and Benjamin; 25 the sons of Bilhah, Rachel's maidservant, *were* Dan and Naphtali; 26 and the sons of Zilpah, Leah's maidservant, *were* Gad and Asher. These *were* the sons of Jacob who were born to him in Padan Aram.

27 Then Jacob came to his father Isaac at Mamre, or Kirjath Arba (that *is,* Hebron), where Abraham and Isaac had dwelt. 28 Now the days of Isaac were one hundred and eighty years. 29 So Isaac breathed his

last and died, and was gathered to his people, *being* old and full of days. And his sons Esau and Jacob buried him.

36 NOW this *is* the genealogy of Esau, who is Edom. 2 Esau took his wives from the daughters of Canaan: Adah the daughter of Elon the Hittite; Aholibamah the daughter of Anah, the daughter of Zibeon the Hivite; 3 and Basemath, Ishmael's daughter, sister of Nebajoth. 4 Now Adah bore Eliphaz to Esau, and Basemath bore Reuel. 5 And Aholibamah bore Jeush, Jaalam, and Korah. These *were* the sons of Esau who were born to him in the land of Canaan.

6 Then Esau took his wives, his sons, his daughters, and all the persons of his household, his cattle and all his animals, and all his goods which he had gained in the land of Canaan, and went to a country away from the presence of his brother Jacob. 7 For their possessions were too great for them to dwell together, and the land where they were strangers could not support them because of their livestock. 8 So Esau dwelt in Mount Seir. Esau *is* Edom.

9 And this *is* the genealogy of Esau the father of the Edomites in Mount Seir. 10 These *were* the names of Esau's sons: Eliphaz the son of Adah the wife of Esau, and Reuel the son of Basemath the wife of Esau. 11 And the sons of Eliphaz were Teman, Omar, Zepho, Gatam, and Kenaz.

12 Now Timna was the concubine of Eliphaz, Esau's son, and she bore Amalek to Eliphaz. These *were* the sons of Adah, Esau's wife.

13 These *were* the sons of Reuel: Nahath, Zerah, Shammah, and Mizzah. These were the sons of Basemath, Esau's wife.

14 These were the sons of Aholibamah, Esau's wife, the daughter of Anah, the daughter of Zibeon. And she bore to Esau: Jeush, Jaalam, and Korah.

15 These *were* the chiefs of the sons of Esau. The sons of Eliphaz, the firstborn *son* of Esau, were Chief Teman, Chief Omar, Chief Zepho, Chief Kenaz, 16 Chief Korah, Chief Gatam, *and* Chief Amalek. These *were* the chiefs of Eliphaz in the land of Edom. They *were* the sons of Adah.

17 These *were* the sons of Reuel, Esau's son: Chief Nahath, Chief Zerah, Chief Shammah, and Chief Mizzah. These *were* the chiefs of Reuel in the land of Edom. These *were* the sons of Basemath, Esau's wife.

18 And these *were* the sons of Aholibamah, Esau's wife: Chief Jeush, Chief Jaalam, and Chief Korah. These *were* the chiefs *who descended* from Aholibamah, Esau's wife, the daughter of Anah. 19 These *were* the sons of Esau, who is Edom, and these *were* their chiefs.

20 These *were* the sons of Seir the Horite who inhabited the land: Lotan, Shobal, Zibeon, Anah, 21 Dishon, Ezer, and Dishan. These *were* the chiefs of the Horites, the sons of Seir, in the land of Edom.

22 And the sons of Lotan were Hori and Hemam. Lotan's sister *was* Timna.

23 These *were* the sons of Shobal: Alvan, Manahath, Ebal, Shepho, and Onam.

24 These *were* the sons of Zibeon: both Ajah and Anah. This *was the* Anah who found the water in the wilderness as he pastured the donkeys of his father Zibeon. 25 These *were* the children of Anah: Dishon and Aholibamah the daughter of Anah.

26 These *were* the sons of Dishon: Hemdan, Eshban, Ithran, and Cheran. 27 These *were* the sons of Ezer: Bilhan, Zaavan, and Akan. 28 These *were* the sons of Dishan: Uz and Aran.

29 These *were* the chiefs of the Horites: Chief Lotan, Chief Shobal, Chief Zibeon, Chief Anah, 30 Chief Dishon, Chief Ezer, and Chief Dishan. These *were* the chiefs of the Horites, according to their chiefs in the land of Seir.

31 Now these *were* the kings who reigned in the land of Edom before any king reigned over the children of Israel: 32 Bela the son of Beor reigned in Edom, and the name of his city *was* Dinhabah. 33 And when Bela died, Jobab the son of Zerah of Bozrah reigned in his place. 34 When Jobab died, Husham of the land of the Temanites reigned in his place. 35 And when Husham died, Hadad the son of Bedad, who attacked Midian in the field of Moab, reigned in his place. And the name of his city *was* Avith. 36 When Hadad died, Samlah of Masrekah reigned in his place. 37 And when Samlah died, Saul of Rehoboth-*by*-the-River reigned in his place. 38 When Saul died, Baal-Hanan the son of Achbor reigned in his place. 39 And when Baal-Hanan the son of Achbor died, Hadar reigned in his place; and the name of his city *was* Pau. His wife's name *was* Mehetabel, the daughter of Matred, the daughter of Mezahab.

40 And these *were* the names of the chiefs of Esau, according to their families and their places, by their names: Chief Timnah, Chief Alvah, Chief Jetheth, 41 Chief Aholibamah, Chief Elah, Chief Pinon, 42 Chief Kenaz, Chief Teman, Chief Mibzar, 43 Chief Magdiel, and Chief Iram. These *were* the chiefs of Edom, according to their dwelling places

in the land of their possession. Esau *was* the father of the Edomites.

PSALM 9:6–10

6 O enemy, destructions are finished
     forever!
   And you have destroyed cities;
   Even their memory has perished.
7 But the LORD shall endure forever;
   He has prepared His throne for
     judgment.
8 He shall judge the world in
     righteousness,
   And He shall administer judgment for
     the peoples in uprightness.

9 The LORD also will be a refuge for the
     oppressed,
   A refuge in times of trouble.
10 And those who know Your name will
     put their trust in You;
   For You, LORD, have not forsaken those
     who seek You.

PROVERBS 3:27–30

27 DO not withhold good from those to
     whom it is due,
   When it is in the power of your hand
     to do *so.*
28 Do not say to your neighbor,
   "Go, and come back,
   And tomorrow I will give *it,*"
   When *you have* it with you.
29 Do not devise evil against your
     neighbor,
   For he dwells by you for safety's sake.
30 Do not strive with a man without cause,
   If he has done you no harm.

MATTHEW 12:22–50

THEN one was brought to Him who was demon-possessed, blind and mute; and He healed him, so that the blind and mute man both spoke and saw. 23 And all the multitudes were amazed and said, "Could this be the Son of David?"

24 Now when the Pharisees heard *it* they said, "This *fellow* does not cast out demons except by Beelzebub, the ruler of the demons."

25 But Jesus knew their thoughts, and said to them: "Every kingdom divided against itself is brought to desolation, and every city or house divided against itself will not stand. 26 If Satan casts out Satan,

he is divided against himself. How then will his kingdom stand? 27 And if I cast out demons by Beelzebub, by whom do your sons cast *them* out? Therefore they shall be your judges. 28 But if I cast out demons by the Spirit of God, surely the kingdom of God has come upon you.

No creed or school of thought or experience can monopolize the Spirit of God.   (BIB. ETHICS)

---

29 Or how can one enter a strong man's house and plunder his goods, unless he first binds the strong man? And then he will plunder his house. 30 He who is not with Me is against Me, and he who does not gather with Me scatters abroad.

31 "Therefore I say to you, every sin and blasphemy will be forgiven men, but the blasphemy *against* the Spirit will not be forgiven men. 32 Anyone who speaks a word against the Son of Man, it will be forgiven him; but whoever speaks against the Holy Spirit, it will not be forgiven him, either in this age or in the *age* to come.

33 "Either make the tree good and its fruit good, or else make the tree bad and its fruit bad; for a tree is known by *its* fruit. 34 Brood of vipers! How can you, being evil, speak good things? For out of the abundance of the heart the mouth speaks. 35 A good man out of the good treasure of his heart brings forth good things, and an evil man out of the evil treasure brings forth evil things. 36 But I say to you that for every idle word men may speak, they will give account of it in the day of judgment. 37 For by your words you will be justified, and by your words you will be condemned."

38 Then some of the scribes and Pharisees answered, saying, "Teacher, we want to see a sign from You."

39 But He answered and said to them, "An evil and adulterous generation seeks after a sign, and no sign will be given to it except the sign of the prophet Jonah. 40 For as Jonah was three days and three nights in the belly of the great fish, so will the Son of Man be three days and three nights in the heart of the earth. 41 The men of Nineveh will rise up in the judgment with this generation and condemn it, because they repented at the preaching of Jonah; and indeed a greater than Jonah *is* here. 42 The queen of the South will rise up in the judgment with this generation and condemn it, for she came from the ends

of the earth to hear the wisdom of Solomon; and indeed a greater than Solomon *is* here.

43 "When an unclean spirit goes out of a man, he goes through dry places, seeking rest, and finds none. 44 Then he says, 'I will return to my house from which I came.' And when he comes, he finds *it* empty, swept, and put in order. 45 Then he goes and takes with him seven other spirits more wicked than himself, and they enter and dwell there; and the last *state* of that man is worse than the first. So shall it also be with this wicked generation."

46 While He was still talking to the multitudes, behold, His mother and brothers stood outside, seeking to speak with Him. 47 Then one said to Him, "Look, Your mother and Your brothers are standing outside, seeking to speak with You." 48 But He answered and said to the one who told Him, "Who is My mother and who are My brothers?" 49 And He stretched out His hand toward His disciples and said, "Here are My mother and My brothers! 50 For whoever does the will of My Father in heaven is My brother and sister and mother."

◆◆◆◆

Reading 19—Reverence for Dreams
Genesis 37:2, 5, 18

The Bible always incarnates ideals in great personalities, and Joseph stands for the magnificent integrity of boyhood. No man thinks so clearly or has such high ideals as he does in his teens; but unless we live out our ideals, they become a mockery. Joseph was amazingly susceptible to God, and he "dreamed dreams." The dreams of the Old Testament are the touch of God on the spirit of a man; but Joseph's brothers did not reverence such dreams.

Beware what you brood on in secret, for the fateful opportunity will come when God and the Devil will meet in your soul, and you will do according to your brooding, swept beyond all control. This is a law as sure as God is God. Beware of saying, "Oh well, it doesn't matter much what I think about in secret." It does, for the time will come when what you think about in secret will find expression in an act. The fateful opportunity came to Joseph's brothers. The Bible always speaks of sin as it appears in its final analysis. Jesus did not say, "You must not covet because it will lead to stealing." He said, "You must not covet because it *is* stealing." He did not say, "You must not be angry with your brother because it will lead to murder." He said, "You must not be angry with your brother because it *is* murder." When the climax of these things is reached, we begin to see the meaning of Calvary.   (*Not Knowing*)

GENESIS 37:1—38:30

NOW Jacob dwelt in the land where his father was a stranger, in the land of Canaan. 2 This *is* the history of Jacob.

Joseph, *being* seventeen years old, was feeding the flock with his brothers. And the lad *was* with the sons of Bilhah and the sons of Zilpah, his father's wives; and Joseph brought a bad report of them to his father.

3 Now Israel loved Joseph more than all his children, because he *was* the son of his old age. Also he made him a tunic of *many* colors. 4 But when his brothers saw that their father loved him more than all his brothers, they hated him and could not speak peaceably to him.

5 Now Joseph had a dream, and he told *it* to his brothers; and they hated him even more. 6 So he said to them, "Please hear this dream which I have dreamed: 7 There we were, binding sheaves in the field. Then behold, my sheaf arose and also stood upright; and indeed your sheaves stood all around and bowed down to my sheaf."

8 And his brothers said to him, "Shall you indeed reign over us? Or shall you in-

deed have dominion over us?" So they hated him even more for his dreams and for his words.

9 Then he dreamed still another dream and told it to his brothers, and said, "Look, I have dreamed another dream. And this time, the sun, the moon, and the eleven stars bowed down to me."

10 So he told *it* to his father and his brothers; and his father rebuked him and said to him, "What *is* this dream that you have dreamed? Shall your mother and I and your brothers indeed come to bow down to the earth before you?" 11 And his brothers envied him, but his father kept the matter *in mind.*

12 Then his brothers went to feed their father's flock in Shechem. 13 And Israel said to Joseph, "Are not your brothers feeding *the flock* in Shechem? Come, I will send you to them."

So he said to him, "Here I am."

14 Then he said to him, "Please go and see if it is well with your brothers and well with the flocks, and bring back word to me." So he sent him out of the Valley of Hebron, and he went to Shechem.

15 Now a certain man found him, and there he was, wandering in the field. And the man asked him, saying, "What are you seeking?"

16 So he said, "I am seeking my brothers. Please tell me where they are feeding *their flocks.*"

17 And the man said, "They have departed from here, for I heard them say, 'Let us go to Dothan.'" So Joseph went after his brothers and found them in Dothan.

18 Now when they saw him afar off, even before he came near them, they conspired against him to kill him. 19 Then they said to one another, "Look, this dreamer is coming! 20 Come therefore, let us now kill him and cast him into some pit; and we shall say, 'Some wild beast has devoured him.' We shall see what will become of his dreams!"

21 But Reuben heard *it,* and he delivered him out of their hands, and said, "Let us not kill him." 22 And Reuben said to them, "Shed no blood, *but* cast him into this pit which *is* in the wilderness, and do not lay a hand on him"—that he might deliver him out of their hands, and bring him back to his father.

23 So it came to pass, when Joseph had come to his brothers, that they stripped Joseph *of* his tunic, the tunic of *many* colors that *was* on him. 24 Then they took him and cast him into a pit. And the pit *was* empty; *there was* no water in it.

25 And they sat down to eat a meal. Then they lifted their eyes and looked, and there was a company of Ishmaelites, coming from Gilead with their camels, bearing spices, balm, and myrrh, on their way to carry *them* down to Egypt. 26 So Judah said to his brothers, "What profit *is there* if we kill our brother and conceal his blood? 27 Come and let us sell him to the Ishmaelites, and let not our hand be upon him, for he *is* our brother *and* our flesh." And his brothers listened. 28 Then Midianite traders passed by; so *the brothers* pulled Joseph up and lifted him out of the pit, and sold him to the Ishmaelites for twenty *shekels* of silver. And they took Joseph to Egypt.

29 Then Reuben returned to the pit, and indeed Joseph *was* not in the pit; and he tore his clothes. 30 And he returned to his brothers and said, "The lad *is* no *more;* and I, where shall I go?"

31 So they took Joseph's tunic, killed a kid of the goats, and dipped the tunic in the blood. 32 Then they sent the tunic of *many* colors, and they brought *it* to their father and said, "We have found this. Do you know whether it *is* your son's tunic or not?"

33 And he recognized it and said, "*It is* my son's tunic. A wild beast has devoured him. Without doubt Joseph is torn to pieces." 34 Then Jacob tore his clothes, put sackcloth on his waist, and mourned for his son many days. 35 And all his sons and all his daughters arose to comfort him; but he refused to be comforted, and he said, "For I shall go down into the grave to my son in mourning." Thus his father wept for him.

36 Now the Midianites had sold him in Egypt to Potiphar, an officer of Pharaoh *and* captain of the guard.

38 IT came to pass at that time that Judah departed from his brothers, and visited a certain Adullamite whose name *was* Hirah. 2 And Judah saw there a daughter of a certain Canaanite whose name *was* Shua, and he married her and went in to her. 3 So she conceived and bore a son, and he called his name Er. 4 She conceived again and bore a son, and she called his name Onan. 5 And she conceived yet again and bore a son, and called his name Shelah. He was at Chezib when she bore him.

6 Then Judah took a wife for Er his firstborn, and her name *was* Tamar. 7 But Er, Judah's firstborn, was wicked in the sight of the LORD, and the LORD killed him. 8 And Judah said to Onan, "Go in to your brother's wife and marry her, and raise up

an heir to your brother." 9 But Onan knew that the heir would not be his; and it came to pass, when he went in to his brother's wife, that he emitted on the ground, lest he should give an heir to his brother. 10 And the thing which he did displeased the Lord; therefore He killed him also.

11 Then Judah said to Tamar his daughter-in-law, "Remain a widow in your father's house till my son Shelah is grown." For he said, "Lest he also die like his brothers." And Tamar went and dwelt in her father's house.

12 Now in the process of time the daughter of Shua, Judah's wife, died; and Judah was comforted, and went up to his sheepshearers at Timnah, he and his friend Hirah the Adullamite. 13 And it was told Tamar, saying, "Look, your father-in-law is going up to Timnah to shear his sheep." 14 So she took off her widow's garments, covered *herself* with a veil and wrapped herself, and sat in an open place which *was* on the way to Timnah; for she saw that Shelah was grown, and she was not given to him as a wife. 15 When Judah saw her, he thought she *was* a harlot, because she had covered her face. 16 Then he turned to her by the way, and said, "Please let me come in to you"; for he did not know that she *was* his daughter-in-law.

So she said, "What will you give me, that you may come in to me?"

17 And he said, "I will send a young goat from the flock."

So she said, "Will you give *me* a pledge till you send *it?* "

18 Then he said, "What pledge shall I give you?"

So she said, "Your signet and cord, and your staff that *is* in your hand." Then he gave *them* to her, and went in to her, and she conceived by him. 19 So she arose and went away, and laid aside her veil and put on the garments of her widowhood.

20 And Judah sent the young goat by the hand of his friend the Adullamite, to receive *his* pledge from the woman's hand, but he did not find her. 21 Then he asked the men of that place, saying, "Where is the harlot who *was* openly by the roadside?"

And they said, "There was no harlot in this *place.*"

22 So he returned to Judah and said, "I cannot find her. Also, the men of the place said there was no harlot in this *place.*"

23 Then Judah said, "Let her take *them* for herself, lest we be shamed; for I sent this young goat and you have not found her."

24 And it came to pass, about three months after, that Judah was told, saying, "Tamar your daughter-in-law has played the harlot; furthermore she *is* with child by harlotry."

So Judah said, "Bring her out and let her be burned!"

25 When she *was* brought out, she sent to her father-in-law, saying, "By the man to whom these belong, I *am* with child." And she said, "Please determine whose these *are*—the signet and cord, and staff."

26 So Judah acknowledged *them* and said, "She has been more righteous than I, because I did not give her to Shelah my son." And he never knew her again.

27 Now it came to pass, at the time for giving birth, that behold, twins *were* in her womb. 28 And so it was, when she was giving birth, that *the one* put out *his* hand; and the midwife took a scarlet *thread* and bound it on his hand, saying, "This one came out first." 29 Then it happened, as he drew back his hand, that his brother came out unexpectedly; and she said, "How did you break through? *This* breach *be* upon you!" Therefore his name was called Perez. 30 Afterward his brother came out who had the scarlet *thread* on his hand. And his name was called Zerah.

PSALM 9:11–20

11 SING praises to the Lord, who dwells in Zion!
  Declare His deeds among the people.
12 When He avenges blood, He remembers them;
  He does not forget the cry of the humble.

13 Have mercy on me, O Lord!
  Consider my trouble from those who hate me,
  You who lift me up from the gates of death,
14 That I may tell of all Your praise
  In the gates of the daughter of Zion.
  I will rejoice in Your salvation.

15 The nations have sunk down in the pit *which* they made;
  In the net which they hid, their own foot is caught.
16 The Lord is known *by* the judgment He executes;
  The wicked is snared in the work of his own hands.
                    Meditation.   Selah

17 The wicked shall be turned into hell,
  And all the nations that forget God.

18 For the needy shall not always be
      forgotten;
   The expectation of the poor shall *not*
      perish forever.

19 Arise, O LORD,
   Do not let man prevail;
   Let the nations be judged in Your sight.
20 Put them in fear, O LORD,
   That the nations may know themselves
      to be but men.   Selah

PROVERBS 3:31–35

31 DO not envy the oppressor,
   And choose none of his ways;
32 For the perverse *person is* an
      abomination to the LORD,
   But His secret counsel *is* with the
      upright.
33 The curse of the LORD *is* on the house
      of the wicked,
   But He blesses the home of the just.
34 Surely He scorns the scornful,
   But gives grace to the humble.
35 The wise shall inherit glory,
   But shame shall be the legacy of fools.

MATTHEW 13:1–30

ON the same day Jesus went out of the
house and sat by the sea. 2 And great multitudes were gathered together to Him, so
that He got into a boat and sat; and the
whole multitude stood on the shore.

3 Then He spoke many things to them
in parables, saying: "Behold, a sower went
out to sow. 4 And as he sowed, some *seed*
fell by the wayside; and the birds came and
devoured them. 5 Some fell on stony places,
where they did not have much earth; and
they immediately sprang up because they
had no depth of earth. 6 But when the sun
was up they were scorched, and because
they had no root they withered away.
7 And some fell among thorns, and the
thorns sprang up and choked them.
8 But others fell on good ground and
yielded a crop: some a hundredfold, some
sixty, some thirty. 9 He who has ears to
hear, let him hear!"

10 And the disciples came and said to
Him, "Why do You speak to them in
parables?"

11 He answered and said to them, "Because it has been given to you to know
the mysteries of the kingdom of heaven,
but to them it has not been given. 12 For
whoever has, to him more will be given,
and he will have abundance; but whoever
does not have, even what he has will be
taken away from him. 13 Therefore I speak
to them in parables, because seeing they
do not see, and hearing they do not hear,
nor do they understand. 14 And in them
the prophecy of Isaiah is fulfilled, which
says:

'Hearing you will hear and shall not
      understand,
And seeing you will see and not
      perceive;
15 For the hearts of this people have
      grown dull.
Their ears are hard of hearing,
And their eyes they have closed,
Lest they should see with *their* eyes
      and hear with *their* ears,
Lest they should understand with
      their hearts and turn,
So that I should heal them.'

16 But blessed *are* your eyes for they see,
and your ears for they hear; 17 for assuredly,
I say to you that many prophets and righteous *men* desired to see what you see, and
did not see *it,* and to hear what you hear,
and did not hear *it.*

18 "Therefore hear the parable of the
sower: 19 When anyone hears the word of
the kingdom, and does not understand *it,*
then the wicked *one* comes and snatches
away what was sown in his heart. This is
he who received seed by the wayside.
20 But he who received the seed on stony
places, this is he who hears the word and
immediately receives it with joy; 21 yet he
has no root in himself, but endures only
for a while. For when tribulation or persecution arises because of the word, immediately
he stumbles. 22 Now he who received seed
among the thorns is he who hears the word,
and the cares of this world and the deceitfulness of riches choke the word, and he becomes unfruitful. 23 But he who received
seed on the good ground is he who hears
the word and understands *it,* who indeed
bears fruit and produces: some a hundredfold, some sixty, some thirty."

---

*We can always gauge where we
are by the teachings of Jesus
Christ.*   (LOVE OF GOD)

---

24 Another parable He put forth to them,
saying: "The kingdom of heaven is like a
man who sowed good seed in his field;

25 but while men slept, his enemy came and sowed tares among the wheat and went his way. 26 But when the grain had sprouted and produced a crop, then the tares also appeared. 27 So the servants of the owner came and said to him, 'Sir, did you not sow good seed in your field? How then does it have tares?' 28 He said to them, 'An enemy has done this.' The servants said to him, 'Do you want us then to go and gather them up?' 29 But he said, 'No, lest while you gather up the tares you also uproot the wheat with them. 30 Let both grow together until the harvest, and at the time of harvest I will say to the reapers, "First gather together the tares and bind them in bundles to burn them, but gather the wheat into my barn." ' "

◆◆◆

Reading 20—The Supreme Barrier
Matthew 13:58

Redemption is the great outside fact of the Christian faith; it has to do not only with a man's experience of salvation, but with the basis of his thinking. The revelation of redemption means that Jesus Christ came here in order that by means of His death on the cross He might put the whole human race on a redemptive basis, so making it possible for every man to get back into perfect communion with God. "I have finished the work which You have given Me to do." What was finished? The redemption of the world. Men are not *going* to be redeemed; they *are* redeemed. "It is finished." It was not the salvation of individual men and women like you and me that was finished: the whole human race was put on the basis of redemption. Do I believe it? Let me think of the worst man I know, the man for whom I have no affinity, the man who is a continual thorn in my flesh, who is as mean as can be; can I imagine that man being presented "perfect in Christ Jesus"? If I can, I have got the beginning of Christian thinking. It ought to be an easy thing for the Christian who thinks to conceive of any and every kind of man being presented "perfect in Christ Jesus," but how seldom we do think! If I am an earnest evangelical preacher I may say to a man, "Oh yes, I believe God can save you," while in my heart of hearts I don't believe there is much hope for him. Our unbelief stands as the supreme barrier to Jesus Christ's work in men's souls. "Now He did not do many mighty works there because of their unbelief."   (CONFORMED)

GENESIS 39:1—40:23

NOW Joseph had been taken down to Egypt. And Potiphar, an officer of Pharaoh, captain of the guard, an Egyptian, bought him from the Ishmaelites who had taken him down there. 2 The LORD was with Joseph, and he was a successful man; and he was in the house of his master the Egyptian. 3 And his master saw that the LORD *was* with him and that the LORD made all he did to prosper in his hand. 4 So Joseph found favor in his sight, and served him. Then he made him overseer of his house, and all *that* he had he put under his authority. 5 So it was, from the time *that* he had made him overseer of his house and all that he had, that the LORD blessed the Egyptian's house for Joseph's sake; and the blessing of the LORD was on all that he had in the house and in the field. 6 Thus he left all that he had in Joseph's hand, and he did not know what he had except for the bread which he ate.

Now Joseph was handsome in form and appearance.

7 And it came to pass after these things that his master's wife cast longing eyes on Joseph, and she said, "Lie with me."

8 But he refused and said to his master's wife, "Look, my master does not know what *is* with me in the house, and he has commit-

ted all that he has to my hand. 9 *There is* no one greater in this house than I, nor has he kept back anything from me but you, because you *are* his wife. How then can I do this great wickedness, and sin against God?"

10 So it was, as she spoke to Joseph day by day, that he did not heed her, to lie with her *or* to be with her.

11 But it happened about this time, when Joseph went into the house to do his work, and none of the men of the house *was* inside, 12 that she caught him by his garment, saying, "Lie with me." But he left his garment in her hand, and fled and ran outside. 13 And so it was, when she saw that he had left his garment in her hand and fled outside, 14 that she called to the men of her house and spoke to them, saying, "See, he has brought in to us a Hebrew to mock us. He came in to me to lie with me, and I cried out with a loud voice. 15 And it happened, when he heard that I lifted my voice and cried out, that he left his garment with me, and fled and went outside."

16 So she kept his garment with her until his master came home. 17 Then she spoke to him with words like these, saying, "The Hebrew servant whom you brought to us came in to me to mock me; 18 so it happened, as I lifted my voice and cried out, that he left his garment with me and fled outside."

19 So it was, when his master heard the words which his wife spoke to him, saying, "Your servant did to me after this manner," that his anger was aroused. 20 Then Joseph's master took him and put him into the prison, a place where the king's prisoners *were* confined. And he was there in the prison. 21 But the LORD was with Joseph and showed him mercy, and He gave him favor in the sight of the keeper of the prison. 22 And the keeper of the prison committed to Joseph's hand all the prisoners who *were* in the prison; whatever they did there, it was his doing. 23 The keeper of the prison did not look into anything *that was* under *Joseph's* authority, because the LORD was with him; and whatever he did, the LORD made *it* prosper.

Whatever happens, happens by God's permission. (GOD'S WORKMANSHIP)

---

40 IT came to pass after these things *that* the butler and the baker of the king of Egypt offended their lord, the king

of Egypt. 2 And Pharaoh was angry with his two officers, the chief butler and the chief baker. 3 So he put them in custody in the house of the captain of the guard, in the prison, the place where Joseph *was* confined. 4 And the captain of the guard charged Joseph with them, and he served them; so they were in custody for a while.

5 Then the butler and the baker of the king of Egypt, who *were* confined in the prison, had a dream, both of them, each man's dream in one night *and* each man's dream with its *own* interpretation. 6 And Joseph came in to them in the morning and looked at them, and saw that they *were* sad. 7 So he asked Pharaoh's officers who *were* with him in the custody of his lord's house, saying, "Why do you look *so* sad today?"

8 And they said to him, "We each have had a dream, and *there is* no interpreter of it."

So Joseph said to them, "Do not interpretations belong to God? Tell *them* to me, please."

9 Then the chief butler told his dream to Joseph, and said to him, "Behold, in my dream a vine *was* before me, 10 and in the vine *were* three branches; it *was* as though it budded, its blossoms shot forth, and its clusters brought forth ripe grapes. 11 Then Pharaoh's cup *was* in my hand; and I took the grapes and pressed them into Pharaoh's cup, and placed the cup in Pharaoh's hand."

12 And Joseph said to him, "This *is* the interpretation of it: The three branches *are* three days. 13 Now within three days Pharaoh will lift up your head and restore you to your place, and you will put Pharaoh's cup in his hand according to the former manner, when you were his butler. 14 But remember me when it is well with you, and please show kindness to me; make mention of me to Pharaoh, and get me out of this house. 15 For indeed I was stolen away from the land of the Hebrews; and also I have done nothing here that they should put me into the dungeon."

16 When the chief baker saw that the interpretation was good, he said to Joseph, "I also *was* in my dream, and there *were* three white baskets on my head. 17 In the uppermost basket *were* all kinds of baked goods for Pharaoh, and the birds ate them out of the basket on my head."

18 So Joseph answered and said, "This *is* the interpretation of it: The three baskets *are* three days. 19 Within three days Pharaoh will lift off your head from you and hang

you on a tree; and the birds will eat your flesh from you."

20 Now it came to pass on the third day, *which was* Pharaoh's birthday, that he made a feast for all his servants; and he lifted up the head of the chief butler and of the chief baker among his servants. 21 Then he restored the chief butler to his butlership again, and he placed the cup in Pharaoh's hand. 22 But he hanged the chief baker, as Joseph had interpreted to them. 23 Yet the chief butler did not remember Joseph, but forgot him.

PSALM 10:1–11

1   WHY do You stand afar off, O LORD?
    Why do You hide in times of trouble?
2   The wicked in *his* pride persecutes the
        poor;
    Let them be caught in the plots which
        they have devised.

3   For the wicked boasts of his heart's
        desire;
    He blesses the greedy *and* renounces
        the LORD.
4   The wicked in his proud countenance
        does not seek *God;*
    God *is* in none of his thoughts.

5   His ways are always prospering;
    Your judgments *are* far above, out of
        his sight;
    As for all his enemies, he sneers at them.
6   He has said in his heart, "I shall not
        be moved;
    I shall never be in adversity."
7   His mouth is full of cursing and deceit
        and oppression;
    Under his tongue *is* trouble and
        iniquity.

8   He sits in the lurking places of the
        villages;
    In the secret places he murders the
        innocent;
    His eyes are secretly fixed on the
        helpless.
9   He lies in wait secretly, as a lion in
        his den;
    He lies in wait to catch the poor;
    He catches the poor when he draws
        him into his net.
10 So he crouches, he lies low,
    That the helpless may fall by his
        strength.
11 He has said in his heart,
    "God has forgotten;

He hides His face;
He will never see."

PROVERBS 4:1–6

1   HEAR, *my* children, the instruction
        of a father,
    And give attention to know
        understanding;
2   For I give you good doctrine:
    Do not forsake my law.
3   When I was my father's son,
    Tender and the only one in the sight
        of my mother,
4   He also taught me, and said to me:
    "Let your heart retain my words;
    Keep my commands, and live.
5   Get wisdom! Get understanding!
    Do not forget, nor turn away from the
        words of my mouth.
6   Do not forsake her, and she will
        preserve you;
    Love her, and she will keep you.

MATTHEW 13:31–58

ANOTHER parable He put forth to them, saying: "The kingdom of heaven is like a mustard seed, which a man took and sowed in his field, 32 which indeed is the least of all the seeds; but when it is grown it is greater than the herbs and becomes a tree, so that the birds of the air come and nest in its branches."

33 Another parable He spoke to them: "The kingdom of heaven is like leaven, which a woman took and hid in three measures of meal till it was all leavened."

34 All these things Jesus spoke to the multitude in parables; and without a parable He did not speak to them, 35 that it might be fulfilled which was spoken by the prophet, saying:

"I will open My mouth in parables;
I will utter things kept secret from
    the foundation of the world."

36 Then Jesus sent the multitude away and went into the house. And His disciples came to Him, saying, "Explain to us the parable of the tares of the field."

37 He answered and said to them: "He who sows the good seed is the Son of Man. 38 The field is the world, the good seeds are the sons of the kingdom, but the tares are the sons of the wicked *one.* 39 The enemy who sowed them is the devil, the harvest is the end of the age, and the reapers are

the angels. 40 Therefore as the tares are gathered and burned in the fire, so it will be at the end of this age. 41 The Son of Man will send out His angels, and they will gather out of His kingdom all things that offend, and those who practice lawlessness, 42 and will cast them into the furnace of fire. There will be wailing and gnashing of teeth. 43 Then the righteous will shine forth as the sun in the kingdom of their Father. He who has ears to hear, let him hear!

44 "Again, the kingdom of heaven is like treasure hidden in a field, which a man found and hid; and for joy over it he goes and sells all that he has and buys that field.

45 "Again, the kingdom of heaven is like a merchant seeking beautiful pearls, 46 who, when he had found one pearl of great price, went and sold all that he had and bought it.

47 "Again, the kingdom of heaven is like a dragnet that was cast into the sea and gathered some of every kind, 48 which, when it was full, they drew to shore; and they sat down and gathered the good into vessels, but threw the bad away. 49 So it will be at the end of the age. The angels will come forth, separate the wicked from among the just, 50 and cast them into the furnace of fire. There will be wailing and gnashing of teeth."

51 Jesus said to them, "Have you understood all these things?"

They said to Him, "Yes, Lord."

52 Then He said to them, "Therefore every scribe instructed concerning the kingdom of heaven is like a householder who brings out of his treasure *things* new and old."

53 Now it came to pass, when Jesus had finished these parables, that He departed from there. 54 When He had come to His own country, He taught them in their synagogue, so that they were astonished and said, "Where did this *Man* get this wisdom and *these* mighty works? 55 Is this not the carpenter's son? Is not His mother called Mary? And His brothers James, Joses, Simon, and Judas? 56 And His sisters, are they not all with us? Where then did this *Man* get all these things?" 57 So they were offended at Him.

Jesus Christ's teaching never beats about the bush.   (GENESIS)

But Jesus said to them, "A prophet is not without honor except in his own country and in his own house." 58 Now He did not do many mighty works there because of their unbelief.

◆◆◆◆

Reading 21—In Union with God
Genesis 41:1, 14, 42

It is the will of God that human beings should get into moral relationship with Him, and His covenants are for this purpose. Why does not God save me? He has saved me, but I have not entered into relationship with Him. Why does not God do this and that? He has done it, the point is—Will I step into covenant relationship? All the great blessings of God are finished and complete, but they are not mine until I enter into relationship with Him on the basis of His covenant.

Waiting for God is incarnate unbelief, it means that I have no faith in Him; I wait for Him to do something in me that I may trust in that. God will not do it, because that is not the basis of the God-and-man relationship. Man has to go out of himself in his covenant with God as God goes out of Himself in His covenant with man. It is a question of faith in God—the rarest thing; we have faith only in our feelings. I do not believe God unless He will give me something in my hand whereby I may know I have it, then I say—"Now I believe." There is no faith there. "Look to Me, and be saved."

When I have really transacted business with God on His covenant and have let go entirely, there is no sense of merit, no human ingredient in it at all, but a complete overwhelming sense of being brought into union with God, and the whole thing is transfigured with peace and joy.   (*UTMOST*)

GENESIS 41:1—42:38

THEN it came to pass, at the end of two full years, that Pharaoh had a dream; and behold, he stood by the river. 2 Suddenly there came up out of the river seven cows, fine looking and fat; and they fed in the meadow. 3 Then behold, seven other cows came up after them out of the river, ugly and gaunt, and stood by the *other* cows on the bank of the river. 4 And the ugly and gaunt cows ate up the seven fine looking and fat cows. So Pharaoh awoke. 5 He slept and dreamed a second time; and suddenly seven heads of grain came up on one stalk, plump and good. 6 Then behold, seven thin heads, blighted by the east wind, sprang up after them. 7 And the seven thin heads devoured the seven plump and full heads. So Pharaoh awoke, and indeed, *it was* a dream. 8 Now it came to pass in the morning that his spirit was troubled, and he sent and called for all the magicians of Egypt and all its wise men. And Pharaoh told them his dreams, but *there was* no one who could interpret them for Pharaoh.

9 Then the chief butler spoke to Pharaoh, saying: "I remember my faults this day. 10 When Pharaoh was angry with his servants, and put me in custody in the house of the captain of the guard, *both* me and the chief baker, 11 we each had a dream in one night, he and I. Each of us dreamed according to the interpretation of his *own* dream. 12 Now there *was* a young Hebrew man with us there, a servant of the captain of the guard. And we told him, and he interpreted our dreams for us; to each man he interpreted according to his *own* dream. 13 And it came to pass, just as he interpreted for us, so it happened. He restored me to my office, and he hanged him."

14 Then Pharaoh sent and called Joseph, and they brought him quickly out of the dungeon; and he shaved, changed his clothing, and came to Pharaoh. 15 And Pharaoh said to Joseph, "I have had a dream, and *there is* no one who can interpret it. But I have heard it said of you *that* you can understand a dream, to interpret it."

16 So Joseph answered Pharaoh, saying, "*It is* not in me; God will give Pharaoh an answer of peace."

17 Then Pharaoh said to Joseph: "Behold, in my dream I stood on the bank of the river. 18 Suddenly seven cows came up out of the river, fine looking and fat; and they fed in the meadow. 19 Then behold, seven other cows came up after them, poor and very ugly and gaunt, such ugliness as I have never seen in all the land of Egypt. 20 And the gaunt and ugly cows ate up the first seven, the fat cows. 21 When they had eaten them up, no one would have known that they had eaten them, for they *were* just as ugly as at the beginning. So I awoke. 22 Also I saw in my dream, and suddenly seven heads came up on one stalk, full and good. 23 Then behold, seven heads, withered, thin, *and* blighted by the east wind, sprang up after them. 24 And the thin heads devoured the seven good heads. So I told *this* to the magicians, but *there was* no one who could explain *it* to me."

25 Then Joseph said to Pharaoh, "The dreams of Pharaoh *are* one; God has shown Pharaoh what He *is* about to do: 26 The seven good cows *are* seven years, and the seven good heads *are* seven years; the dreams *are* one. 27 And the seven thin and ugly cows which came up after them *are* seven years, and the seven empty heads blighted by the east wind are seven years of famine. 28 This *is* the thing which I have spoken to Pharaoh. God has shown Pharaoh what He *is* about to do. 29 Indeed seven years of great plenty will come throughout all the land of Egypt; 30 but after them seven years of famine will arise, and all the plenty will be forgotten in the land of Egypt; and the famine will deplete the land. 31 So the plenty will not be known in the land because of the famine following, for it *will be* very severe. 32 And the dream was repeated to Pharaoh twice because the thing *is* established by God, and God will shortly bring it to pass.

33 "Now therefore, let Pharaoh select a discerning and wise man, and set him over the land of Egypt. 34 Let Pharaoh do *this,* and let him appoint officers over the land, to collect one-fifth *of the produce* of the land of Egypt in the seven plentiful years. 35 And let them gather all the food of those good years that are coming, and store up grain under the authority of Pharaoh, and let them keep food in the cities. 36 Then that food shall be as a reserve for the land for the seven years of famine which shall be in the land of Egypt, that the land may not perish during the famine."

37 So the advice was good in the eyes of Pharaoh and in the eyes of all his servants. 38 And Pharaoh said to his servants, "Can we find *such a one* as this, a man in whom *is* the Spirit of God?"

39 Then Pharaoh said to Joseph, "Inasmuch as God has shown you all this, *there is* no one as discerning and wise as you. 40 You shall be over my house, and all my people shall be ruled according to your word; only in regard to the throne will I be greater than you." 41 And Pharaoh said to Joseph, "See, I have set you over all the land of Egypt."

42 Then Pharaoh took his signet ring off his hand and put it on Joseph's hand; and he clothed him in garments of fine linen and put a gold chain around his neck. 43 And he had him ride in the second chariot which he had; and they cried out before him, "Bow the knee!" So he set him over all the land of Egypt. 44 Pharaoh also said to Joseph, "I *am* Pharaoh, and without your consent no man may lift his hand or foot in all the land of Egypt." 45 And Pharaoh called Joseph's name Zaphnath-Paaneah. And he gave him as a wife Asenath, the daughter of Poti-Pherah priest of On. So Joseph went out over *all* the land of Egypt.

46 Joseph was thirty years old when he stood before Pharaoh king of Egypt. And Joseph went out from the presence of Pharaoh, and went throughout all the land of Egypt. 47 Now in the seven plentiful years the ground brought forth abundantly. 48 So he gathered up all the food of the seven years which were in the land of Egypt, and laid up the food in the cities; he laid up in every city the food of the fields which surrounded them. 49 Joseph gathered very much grain, as the sand of the sea, until he stopped counting, for *it was* immeasurable.

50 And to Joseph were born two sons before the years of famine came, whom Asenath, the daughter of Poti-Pherah priest of On, bore to him. 51 Joseph called the name of the firstborn Manasseh: "For God has made me forget all my toil and all my father's house." 52 And the name of the second he called Ephraim: "For God has caused me to be fruitful in the land of my affliction."

53 Then the seven years of plenty which were in the land of Egypt ended, 54 and the seven years of famine began to come, as Joseph had said. The famine was in all lands, but in all the land of Egypt there was bread. 55 So when all the land of Egypt was famished, the people cried to Pharaoh for bread. Then Pharaoh said to all the Egyptians, "Go to Joseph; whatever he says to you, do." 56 The famine was over all the face of the earth, and Joseph opened all the storehouses and sold to the Egyptians. And the famine became severe in the land of Egypt. 57 So all countries came to Joseph in Egypt to buy *grain,* because the famine was severe in all lands.

42 WHEN Jacob saw that there was grain in Egypt, Jacob said to his sons, "Why do you look at one another?" 2 And he said, "Indeed I have heard that there is grain in Egypt; go down to that place and buy for us there, that we may live and not die."

3 So Joseph's ten brothers went down to buy grain in Egypt. 4 But Jacob did not send Joseph's brother Benjamin with his brothers, for he said, "Lest some calamity befall him." 5 And the sons of Israel went to buy *grain* among those who journeyed, for the famine was in the land of Canaan.

6 Now Joseph *was* governor over the land; and it was he who sold to all the people of the land. And Joseph's brothers came and bowed down before him with *their* faces to the earth. 7 Joseph saw his brothers and recognized them, but he acted as a stranger to them and spoke roughly to them. Then he said to them, "Where do you come from?"

And they said, "From the land of Canaan to buy food."

8 So Joseph recognized his brothers, but they did not recognize him. 9 Then Joseph remembered the dreams which he had dreamed about them, and said to them, "You *are* spies! You have come to see the nakedness of the land!"

According to the Bible, things do not go as we expect them to. (SEND I YOU)

---

10 And they said to him, "No, my lord, but your servants have come to buy food. 11 We *are* all one man's sons; we *are* honest *men;* your servants are not spies."

12 But he said to them, "No, but you have come to see the nakedness of the land."

13 And they said, "Your servants *are* twelve brothers, the sons of one man in the land of Canaan; and in fact, the youngest *is* with our father today, and one *is* no more."

14 But Joseph said to them, "It *is* as I spoke to you, saying, 'You *are* spies!' 15 In this *manner* you shall be tested: By the life of Pharaoh, you shall not leave this

place unless your youngest brother comes here. 16 Send one of you, and let him bring your brother; and you shall be kept in prison, that your words may be tested to see whether *there is* any truth in you; or else, by the life of Pharaoh, surely you *are* spies!" 17 So he put them all together in prison three days.

18 Then Joseph said to them the third day, "Do this and live, *for* I fear God: 19 If you *are* honest *men,* let one of your brothers be confined to your prison house; but you, go and carry grain for the famine of your houses. 20 And bring your youngest brother to me; so your words will be verified, and you shall not die."

And they did so. 21 Then they said to one another, "We *are* truly guilty concerning our brother, for we saw the anguish of his soul when he pleaded with us, and we would not hear; therefore this distress has come upon us."

22 And Reuben answered them, saying, "Did I not speak to you, saying, 'Do not sin against the boy'; and you would not listen? Therefore behold, his blood is now required of us." 23 But they did not know that Joseph understood *them,* for he spoke to them through an interpreter. 24 And he turned himself away from them and wept. Then he returned to them again, and talked with them. And he took Simeon from them and bound him before their eyes.

25 Then Joseph gave a command to fill their sacks with grain, to restore every man's money to his sack, and to give them provisions for the journey. Thus he did for them. 26 So they loaded their donkeys with the grain and departed from there. 27 But as one *of them* opened his sack to give his donkey feed at the encampment, he saw his money; and there it was, in the mouth of his sack. 28 So he said to his brothers, "My money has been restored, and there it is, in my sack!" Then their hearts failed *them* and they were afraid, saying to one another, "What *is* this *that* God has done to us?"

29 Then they went to Jacob their father in the land of Canaan and told him all that had happened to them, saying: 30 "The man *who is* lord of the land spoke roughly to us, and took us for spies of the country. 31 But we said to him, 'We *are* honest *men;* we are not spies. 32 We *are* twelve brothers, sons of our father; one *is* no *more,* and the youngest *is* with our father this day in the land of Canaan.' 33 Then the man, the lord of the country, said to us, 'By this I will know that you *are* honest *men:* Leave one of your brothers *here* with me, take *food*

for the famine of your households, and be gone. 34 And bring your youngest brother to me; so I shall know that you *are* not spies, but *that* you *are* honest *men.* I will grant your brother to you, and you may trade in the land.' "

35 Then it happened as they emptied their sacks, that surprisingly each man's bundle of money *was* in his sack; and when they and their father saw the bundles of money, they were afraid. 36 And Jacob their father said to them, "You have bereaved me: Joseph is no *more,* Simeon is no *more,* and you want to take Benjamin. All these things are against me."

37 Then Reuben spoke to his father, saying, "Kill my two sons if I do not bring him *back* to you; put him in my hands, and I will bring him back to you."

38 But he said, "My son shall not go down with you, for his brother is dead, and he is left alone. If any calamity should befall him along the way in which you go, then you would bring down my gray hair with sorrow to the grave."

PSALM 10:12–18

12 ARISE, O LORD!
    O God, lift up Your hand!
    Do not forget the humble.
13 Why do the wicked renounce God?
    He has said in his heart,
    "You will not require *an account.*"

14 But You have seen, for You observe
         trouble and grief,
    To repay *it* by Your hand.
    The helpless commits himself to You;
    You are the helper of the fatherless.
15 Break the arm of the wicked and the
         evil *man;*
    Seek out his wickedness *until* You find
         none.

16 The LORD *is* King forever and ever;
    The nations have perished out of His
         land.
17 LORD, You have heard the desire of
         the humble;
    You will prepare their heart;
    You will cause Your ear to hear,
18 To do justice to the fatherless and the
         oppressed,
    That the man of the earth may oppress
         no more.

PROVERBS 4:7–9

7   WISDOM *is* the principal thing;
    Therefore get wisdom.

And in all your getting, get
understanding.

8 Exalt her, and she will promote you;
She will bring you honor, when you
embrace her.

9 She will place on your head an
ornament of grace;
A crown of glory she will deliver to
you."

MATTHEW 14:1–21

AT that time Herod the tetrarch heard the report about Jesus 2 and said to his servants, "This is John the Baptist; he is risen from the dead, and therefore these powers are at work in him." 3 For Herod had laid hold of John and bound him, and put *him* in prison for the sake of Herodias, his brother Philip's wife. 4 Because John had said to him, "It is not lawful for you to have her." 5 And although he wanted to put him to death, he feared the multitude, because they counted him as a prophet.

6 But when Herod's birthday was celebrated, the daughter of Herodias danced before them and pleased Herod. 7 Therefore he promised with an oath to give her whatever she might ask.

8 So she, having been prompted by her mother, said, "Give me John the Baptist's head here on a platter."

9 And the king was sorry; nevertheless, because of the oaths and because of those who sat with him, he commanded *it* to be given to *her*. 10 So he sent and had John beheaded in prison. 11 And his head was brought on a platter and given to the girl, and she brought *it* to her mother. 12 Then his disciples came and took away the body and buried it, and went and told Jesus.

13 When Jesus heard *it*, He departed from there by boat to a deserted place by Himself. But when the multitudes heard it, they followed Him on foot from the cities. 14 And when Jesus went out He saw a great multitude; and He was moved with compassion for them, and healed their sick. 15 When it was evening, His disciples came to Him, saying, "This is a deserted place, and the hour is already late. Send the multitudes away, that they may go into the villages and buy themselves food."

16 But Jesus said to them, "They do not need to go away. You give them something to eat."

17 And they said to Him, "We have here only five loaves and two fish."

18 He said, "Bring them here to Me." 19 Then He commanded the multitudes to sit down on the grass. And He took the five loaves and the two fish, and looking up to heaven, He blessed and broke and gave the loaves to the disciples; and the disciples gave to the multitudes. 20 So they all ate and were filled, and they took up twelve baskets full of the fragments that remained. 21 Now those who had eaten were about five thousand men, besides women and children.

There is nothing logical about faith; it is of the nature of life. (Psy. Redemp.)

◆◆◆

Reading 22—Walking on Dry Land
Matthew 14:29

Passionate, genuine affection for Jesus will lead to all sorts of vows and promises which it is impossible to fulfill. It is an attitude of mind and heart that sees only the heroic. We are called to be unobtrusive disciples, not heroes. When we are right with God, the tiniest thing done out of love to Him is more precious to Him than any eloquent preaching of a sermon. . . . We all have a lurking desire to be exhibitions for God, to be put, as it were, in His showroom. Jesus does not want us to be specimens, He wants us to be so taken up with Him that we never think about ourselves, and the only impression left on others by our life is that Jesus Christ is having unhindered way.

Walking on water is easy to impulsive pluck, but walking on dry land as a disciple of Jesus Christ is different. Peter walked on the water to go to Jesus, but he followed Him afar off on the land. We do not need the grace of God to stand crises; human nature and our pride will do it. We can buck up and face the music of a crisis magnificently, but it does require the supernatural grace of God to live twenty-four hours of the day as a saint, to go through drudgery as a saint, to go through poverty as a saint, to go through an ordinary, unobtrusive, ignored existence as a saint, unnoted and unnoticeable. The "show business," which is so incorporated into our view of Christian work today, has caused us to drift far from our Lord's conception of discipleship. It is instilled in us to think that we have to do exceptional things for God; we have not. We have to be exceptional in ordinary things, to be holy in mean streets, among mean people, surrounded by sordid sinners. That is not learned in five minutes.   (*Send I You*)

GENESIS 43:1—44:34

NOW the famine *was* severe in the land. 2 And it came to pass, when they had eaten up the grain which they had brought from Egypt, that their father said to them, "Go back, buy us a little food."

3 But Judah spoke to him, saying, "The man solemnly warned us, saying, 'You shall not see my face unless your brother *is* with you.' 4 If you send our brother with us, we will go down and buy you food. 5 But if you will not send *him*, we will not go down; for the man said to us, 'You shall not see my face unless your brother *is* with you.' "

6 And Israel said, "Why did you deal *so* wrongfully with me *as* to tell the man whether you had still *another* brother?"

7 But they said, "The man asked us pointedly about ourselves and our family, saying, '*Is* your father still alive? Have you *another* brother?' And we told him according to these words. Could we possibly have known that he would say, 'Bring your brother down'?"

8 Then Judah said to Israel his father, "Send the lad with me, and we will arise and go, that we may live and not die, both we and you *and* also our little ones. 9 I myself will be surety for him; from my hand you shall require him. If I do not bring him *back* to you and set him before you, then let me bear the blame forever. 10 For if we had not lingered, surely by now we would have returned this second time."

11 And their father Israel said to them, "If *it must be* so, then do this: Take some of the best fruits of the land in your vessels and carry down a present for the man—a little balm and a little honey, spices and myrrh, pistachio nuts and almonds. 12 Take double money in your hand, and take back in your hand the money that was returned in the mouth of your sacks; perhaps it was an oversight. 13 Take your brother also, and arise, go back to the man. 14 And may God Almighty give you mercy before the man, that he may release your other brother and Benjamin. If I am bereaved, I am bereaved!"

15 So the men took that present and Benjamin, and they took double money in their hand, and arose and went down to Egypt; and they stood before Joseph. 16 When Joseph saw Benjamin with them, he said to the steward of his house, "Take *these* men to my home, and slaughter an animal and make ready; for *these* men will dine with me at noon." 17 Then the man did as Joseph ordered, and the man brought the men into Joseph's house.

18 Now the men were afraid because they were brought into Joseph's house; and they said, "*It is* because of the money, which was returned in our sacks the first time, that we are brought in, so that he may make a case against us and seize us, to take us as slaves with our donkeys."

19 When they drew near to the steward of Joseph's house, they talked with him at the door of the house, 20 and said, "O sir, we indeed came down the first time to buy food; 21 but it happened, when we came to the encampment, that we opened our sacks, and there, *each* man's money *was* in the mouth of his sack, our money in full weight; so we have brought it back in our hand. 22 And we have brought down other money in our hands to buy food. We do not know who put our money in our sacks."

23 But he said, "Peace *be* with you, do not be afraid. Your God and the God of your father has given you treasure in your

sacks; I had your money." Then he brought Simeon out to them.

24 So the man brought the men into Joseph's house and gave *them* water, and they washed their feet; and he gave their donkeys feed. 25 Then they made the present ready for Joseph's coming at noon, for they heard that they would eat bread there.

26 And when Joseph came home, they brought him the present which *was* in their hand into the house, and bowed down before him to the earth. 27 Then he asked them about *their* well-being, and said, "*Is* your father well, the old man of whom you spoke? *Is* he still alive?"

28 And they answered, "Your servant our father *is* in good health; he *is* still alive." And they bowed their heads down and prostrated themselves.

29 Then he lifted his eyes and saw his brother Benjamin, his mother's son, and said, "*Is* this your younger brother of whom you spoke to me?" And he said, "God be gracious to you, my son." 30 Now his heart yearned for his brother; so Joseph made haste and sought *somewhere* to weep. And he went into *his* chamber and wept there. 31 Then he washed his face and came out; and he restrained himself, and said, "Serve the bread."

32 So they set him a place by himself, and them by themselves, and the Egyptians who ate with him by themselves; because the Egyptians could not eat food with the Hebrews, for that *is* an abomination to the Egyptians. 33 And they sat before him, the firstborn according to his birthright and the youngest according to his youth; and the men looked in astonishment at one another. 34 Then he took servings to them from before him, but Benjamin's serving was five times as much as any of theirs. So they drank and were merry with him.

44 AND he commanded the steward of his house, saying, "Fill the men's sacks with food, as much as they can carry, and put each man's money in the mouth of his sack. 2 Also put my cup, the silver cup, in the mouth of the sack of the youngest, and his grain money." So he did according to the word that Joseph had spoken. 3 As soon as the morning dawned, the men were sent away, they and their donkeys. 4 When they had gone out of the city, *and* were not *yet* far off, Joseph said to his steward, "Get up, follow the men; and when you overtake them, say to them, 'Why have you repaid evil for good? 5 *Is* not this *the one* from which my lord drinks, and with

which he indeed practices divination? You have done evil in so doing.' "

6 So he overtook them, and he spoke to them these same words. 7 And they said to him, "Why does my lord say these words? Far be it from us that your servants should do such a thing. 8 Look, we brought back to you from the land of Canaan the money which we found in the mouth of our sacks. How then could we steal silver or gold from your lord's house? 9 With whomever of your servants it is found, let him die, and we also will be my lord's slaves."

10 And he said, "Now also *let* it *be* according to your words; he with whom it is found shall be my slave, and you shall be blameless." 11 Then each man speedily let down his sack to the ground, and each opened his sack. 12 So he searched. He began with the oldest and left off with the youngest; and the cup was found in Benjamin's sack. 13 Then they tore their clothes, and each man loaded his donkey and returned to the city.

14 So Judah and his brothers came to Joseph's house, and he *was* still there; and they fell before him on the ground. 15 And Joseph said to them, "What deed *is* this you have done? Did you not know that such a man as I can certainly practice divination?"

16 Then Judah said, "What shall we say to my lord? What shall we speak? Or how shall we clear ourselves? God has found out the iniquity of your servants; here we are, my lord's slaves, both we and *he* also with whom the cup was found."

17 But he said, "Far be it from me that I should do so; the man in whose hand the cup was found, he shall be my slave. And as for you, go up in peace to your father."

18 Then Judah came near to him and said: "O my lord, please let your servant speak a word in my lord's hearing, and do not let your anger burn against your servant; for you *are* even like Pharaoh. 19 My lord asked his servants, saying, 'Have you a father or a brother?' 20 And we said to my lord, 'We have a father, an old man, and a child of *his* old age, *who is* young; his brother is dead, and he alone is left of his mother's children, and his father loves him.' 21 Then you said to your servants, 'Bring him down to me, that I may set my eyes on him.' 22 And we said to my lord, 'The lad cannot leave his father, for *if* he should leave his father, *his father* would die.' 23 But you said to your servants, 'Unless your youngest brother comes down with you, you shall see my face no more.'

24 "So it was, when we went up to your servant my father, that we told him the words of my lord. 25 And our father said, 'Go back *and* buy us a little food.' 26 But we said, 'We cannot go down; if our youngest brother is with us, then we will go down; for we may not see the man's face unless our youngest brother *is* with us.' 27 Then your servant my father said to us, 'You know that my wife bore me two sons; 28 and the one went out from me, and I said, "Surely he is torn to pieces"; and I have not seen him since. 29 But if you take this one also from me, and calamity befalls him, you shall bring down my gray hair with sorrow to the grave.'

30 "Now therefore, when I come to your servant my father, and the lad *is* not with us, since his life is bound up in the lad's life, 31 it will happen, when he sees that the lad *is* not *with us,* that he will die. So your servants will bring down the gray hair of your servant our father with sorrow to the grave. 32 For your servant became surety for the lad to my father, saying, 'If I do not bring him *back* to you, then I shall bear the blame before my father forever.' 33 Now therefore, please let your servant remain instead of the lad as a slave to my lord, and let the lad go up with his brothers. 34 For how shall I go up to my father if the lad *is* not with me, lest perhaps I see the evil that would come upon my father?"

PSALM 11:1–7

1 IN the LORD I put my trust;
   How can you say to my soul,
   "Flee *as* a bird to your mountain"?

2 For look! The wicked bend *their* bow,
   They make ready their arrow on the
      string,
   That they may shoot secretly at the
      upright in heart.

3 If the foundations are destroyed,
   What can the righteous do?

4 The LORD *is* in His holy temple,
   The LORD's throne *is* in heaven;
   His eyes behold,
   His eyelids test the sons of men.

5 The LORD tests the righteous,
   But the wicked and the one who loves
      violence His soul hates.

6 Upon the wicked He will rain coals;
   Fire and brimstone and a burning wind
   Shall be the portion of their cup.

7 For the LORD *is* righteous,
   He loves righteousness;
   His countenance beholds the upright.

PROVERBS 4:10–13

10 HEAR, my son, and receive my sayings,
    And the years of your life will be many.

11 I have taught you in the way of wisdom;
    I have led you in right paths.

12 When you walk, your steps will not
       be hindered,
    And when you run, you will not
       stumble.

13 Take firm hold of instruction, do not
       let go;
    Keep her, for she *is* your life.

MATTHEW 14:22–36

IMMEDIATELY Jesus made His disciples get into the boat and go before Him to the other side, while He sent the multitudes away. 23 And when He had sent the multitudes away, He went up on the mountain by Himself to pray. Now when evening came, He was alone there. 24 But the boat was now in the middle of the sea, tossed by the waves, for the wind was contrary.

25 Now in the fourth watch of the night Jesus went to them, walking on the sea. 26 And when the disciples saw Him walking on the sea, they were troubled, saying, "It is a ghost!" And they cried out for fear.

27 But immediately Jesus spoke to them, saying, "Be of good cheer! It is I; do not be afraid."

28 And Peter answered Him and said, "Lord, if it is You, command me to come to You on the water."

29 So He said, "Come." And when Peter had come down out of the boat, he walked on the water to go to Jesus. 30 But when he saw that the wind *was* boisterous, he was afraid; and beginning to sink he cried out, saying, "Lord, save me!"

31 And immediately Jesus stretched out *His* hand and caught him, and said to him, "O you of little faith, why did you doubt?" 32 And when they got into the boat, the wind ceased.

33 Then those who were in the boat came and worshiped Him, saying, "Truly You are the Son of God."

34 When they had crossed over, they came to the land of Gennesaret. 35 And when the men of that place recognized Him, they sent out into all that surrounding region, brought to Him all who were sick, 36 and begged Him that they might only touch the hem of His garment. And as many as touched *it* were made perfectly well.

Reading 23—A Fool's Paradise
Matthew 15:19

Our Lord seemed to go so easily and calmly amongst all kinds of men—when He met a man who could sink to the level of Judas He never turned cynical, never lost heart or got discouraged; and when He met a loyal loving heart like John's He was not unduly elated, He never overpraised him. When we meet extra goodness we feel amazingly hopeful about everybody, and when we meet extra badness we feel exactly the opposite; but Jesus "knew what was in man." He knew exactly what human beings were like and what they needed; and He saw in them something no one else ever saw—hope for the most degraded. Jesus had a tremendous hopefulness about man.

(CONFORMED)

In Matthew 15, our Lord tells His disciples what the human heart is like—. "Out of the heart proceed . . ." and then follows the ugly catalogue. We say, "I never felt any of those things in my heart," and we prefer to trust our innocent ignorance rather than Jesus Christ's penetration. Either Jesus Christ must be the supreme Authority on the human heart, or He is not worth listening to. If I make conscious innocence the test, I am likely to come to a place where I will find with a shuddering awakening that what Jesus said is true, and I will be appalled at the possibility of evil in me. If I have never been a blackguard, the reason is a mixture of cowardice and the protection of civilized life; but when I am undressed before God I find that Jesus Christ is right in His diagnosis. As long as I remain under the refuge of innocence, I am living in a fool's paradise. (SERMON MT.)

GENESIS 45:1—46:34

THEN Joseph could not restrain himself before all those who stood by him, and he cried out, "Make everyone go out from me!" So no one stood with him while Joseph made himself known to his brothers. 2 And he wept aloud, and the Egyptians and the house of Pharaoh heard *it*.

3 Then Joseph said to his brothers, "I *am* Joseph; does my father still live?" But his brothers could not answer him, for they were dismayed in his presence. 4 And Joseph said to his brothers, "Please come near to me." So they came near. Then he said: "I *am* Joseph your brother, whom you sold into Egypt. 5 But now, do not therefore be grieved or angry with yourselves because you sold me here; for God sent me before you to preserve life. 6 For these two years the famine *has been* in the land, and *there are* still five years in which *there will be* neither plowing nor harvesting. 7 And God sent me before you to preserve a posterity for you in the earth, and to save your lives by a great deliverance. 8 So now *it was* not you *who* sent me here, but God; and He has made me a father to Pharaoh, and lord of all his house, and a ruler throughout all the land of Egypt.

> *God does not tell us what He is going to do, He reveals to you who He is.* (LOVE OF GOD)

9 "Hurry and go up to my father, and say to him, 'Thus says your son Joseph: "God has made me lord of all Egypt; come down to me, do not tarry. 10 You shall dwell in the land of Goshen, and you shall be near to me, you and your children, your children's children, your flocks and your herds, and all that you have. 11 There I will provide for you, lest you and your household, and all that you have, come to poverty; for *there are* still five years of famine." '

12 "And behold, your eyes and the eyes of my brother Benjamin see that *it is* my mouth that speaks to you. 13 So you shall tell my father of all my glory in Egypt, and of all that you have seen; and you shall hurry and bring my father down here."

14 Then he fell on his brother Benjamin's neck and wept, and Benjamin wept on his neck. 15 Moreover he kissed all his brothers and wept over them, and after that his brothers talked with him.

16 Now the report of it was heard in Pharaoh's house, saying, "Joseph's brothers have

come." So it pleased Pharaoh and his servants well. 17 And Pharaoh said to Joseph, "Say to your brothers, 'Do this: Load your animals and depart; go to the land of Canaan. 18 Bring your father and your households and come to me; I will give you the best of the land of Egypt, and you will eat the fat of the land. 19 Now you are commanded—do this: Take carts out of the land of Egypt for your little ones and your wives; bring your father and come. 20 Also do not be concerned about your goods, for the best of all the land of Egypt *is* yours.' "

21 Then the sons of Israel did so; and Joseph gave them carts, according to the command of Pharaoh, and he gave them provisions for the journey. 22 He gave to all of them, to each man, changes of garments; but to Benjamin he gave three hundred *pieces* of silver and five changes of garments. 23 And he sent to his father these *things:* ten donkeys loaded with the good things of Egypt, and ten female donkeys loaded with grain, bread, and food for his father for the journey. 24 So he sent his brothers away, and they departed; and he said to them, "See that you do not become troubled along the way."

25 Then they went up out of Egypt, and came to the land of Canaan to Jacob their father. 26 And they told him, saying, "Joseph *is* still alive, and he *is* governor over all the land of Egypt." And Jacob's heart stood still, because he did not believe them. 27 But when they told him all the words which Joseph had said to them, and when he saw the carts which Joseph had sent to carry him, the spirit of Jacob their father revived. 28 Then Israel said, "*It is* enough. Joseph my son *is* still alive. I will go and see him before I die."

46 SO Israel took his journey with all that he had, and came to Beersheba, and offered sacrifices to the God of his father Isaac. 2 Then God spoke to Israel in the visions of the night, and said, "Jacob, Jacob!"

And he said, "Here I am."

3 So He said, "I *am* God, the God of your father; do not fear to go down to Egypt, for I will make of you a great nation there. 4 I will go down with you to Egypt, and I will also surely bring you up *again;* and Joseph will put his hand on your eyes."

5 Then Jacob arose from Beersheba; and the sons of Israel carried their father Jacob, their little ones, and their wives, in the carts which Pharaoh had sent to carry him.

6 So they took their livestock and their goods, which they had acquired in the land of Canaan, and went to Egypt, Jacob and all his descendants with him. 7 His sons and his sons' sons, his daughters and his sons' daughters, and all his descendants he brought with him to Egypt.

8 Now these *were* the names of the children of Israel, Jacob and his sons, who went to Egypt: Reuben *was* Jacob's firstborn. 9 The sons of Reuben *were* Hanoch, Pallu, Hezron, and Carmi. 10 The sons of Simeon *were* Jemuel, Jamin, Ohad, Jachin, Zohar, and Shaul, the son of a Canaanite woman. 11 The sons of Levi *were* Gershon, Kohath, and Merari. 12 The sons of Judah *were* Er, Onan, Shelah, Perez, and Zerah (but Er and Onan died in the land of Canaan). The sons of Perez were Hezron and Hamul. 13 The sons of Issachar *were* Tola, Puvah, Job, and Shimron. 14 The sons of Zebulun *were* Sered, Elon, and Jahleel. 15 These *were* the sons of Leah, whom she bore to Jacob in Padan Aram, with his daughter Dinah. All the persons, his sons and his daughters, *were* thirty-three.

16 The sons of Gad *were* Ziphion, Haggi, Shuni, Ezbon, Eri, Arodi, and Areli. 17 The sons of Asher *were* Jimnah, Ishuah, Isui, Beriah, and Serah, their sister. And the sons of Beriah *were* Heber and Malchiel. 18 These *were* the sons of Zilpah, whom Laban gave to Leah his daughter; and these she bore to Jacob: sixteen persons.

19 The sons of Rachel, Jacob's wife, *were* Joseph and Benjamin. 20 And to Joseph in the land of Egypt were born Manasseh and Ephraim, whom Asenath, the daughter of Poti-Pherah priest of On, bore to him. 21 The sons of Benjamin *were* Belah, Becher, Ashbel, Gera, Naaman, Ehi, Rosh, Muppim, Huppim, and Ard. 22 These *were* the sons of Rachel, who were born to Jacob: fourteen persons in all.

23 The son of Dan *was* Hushim. 24 The sons of Naphtali *were* Jahzeel, Guni, Jezer, and Shillem. 25 These *were* the sons of Bilhah, whom Laban gave to Rachel his daughter, and she bore these to Jacob: seven persons in all.

26 All the persons who went with Jacob to Egypt, who came from his body, besides Jacob's sons' wives, *were* sixty-six persons in all. 27 And the sons of Joseph who were born to him in Egypt *were* two persons. All the persons of the house of Jacob who went to Egypt were seventy.

28 Then he sent Judah before him to Joseph, to point out before him *the way* to Goshen. And they came to the land of Goshen. 29 So Joseph made ready his char-

iot and went up to Goshen to meet his father Israel; and he presented himself to him, and fell on his neck and wept on his neck a good while.

30 And Israel said to Joseph, "Now let me die, since I have seen your face, because you *are* still alive."

31 Then Joseph said to his brothers and to his father's household, "I will go up and tell Pharaoh, and say to him, 'My brothers and those of my father's house, who *were* in the land of Canaan, have come to me. 32 And the men *are* shepherds, for their occupation has been to feed livestock; and they have brought their flocks, their herds, and all that they have.' 33 So it shall be, when Pharaoh calls you and says, 'What is your occupation?' 34 that you shall say, 'Your servants' occupation has been with livestock from our youth even till now, both we *and* also our fathers,' that you may dwell in the land of Goshen; for every shepherd *is* an abomination to the Egyptians.'"

PSALM 12:1–8

1 HELP, LORD, for the godly man ceases!
   For the faithful disappear from among
      the sons of men.
2 They speak idly everyone with his
      neighbor;
   With flattering lips *and* a double heart
      they speak.

3 May the LORD cut off all flattering lips,
   And the tongue that speaks proud
      things,
4 Who have said,
   "With our tongue we will prevail;
   Our lips *are* our own;
   Who *is* lord over us?"

5 "For the oppression of the poor, for the
      sighing of the needy,
   Now I will arise," says the LORD;
   "I will set *him* in the safety for which
      he yearns."

6 The words of the LORD *are* pure words,
   Like silver tried in a furnace of earth,
   Purified seven times.
7 You shall keep them, O LORD,
   You shall preserve them from this
      generation forever.

8 The wicked prowl on every side,
   When vileness is exalted among the sons
      of men.

PROVERBS 4:14–17

14 DO not enter the path of the wicked,
   And do not walk in the way of evil.
15 Avoid it, do not travel on it;
   Turn away from it and pass on.
16 For they do not sleep unless they have
      done evil;
   And their sleep is taken away unless
      they make *someone* fall.
17 For they eat the bread of wickedness,
   And drink the wine of violence.

MATTHEW 15:1–20

THEN the scribes and Pharisees who were from Jerusalem came to Jesus, saying, 2 "Why do Your disciples transgress the tradition of the elders? For they do not wash their hands when they eat bread."

3 He answered and said to them, "Why do you also transgress the commandment of God because of your tradition? 4 For God commanded, saying, 'Honor your father and your mother'; and, 'He who curses father or mother, let him be put to death.' 5 But you say, 'Whoever says to his father or mother, "Whatever profit you might have received from me *is* a gift *to God*"— 6 then he need not honor his father or mother.' Thus you have made the commandment of God of no effect by your tradition. 7 Hypocrites! Well did Isaiah prophesy about you, saying:

8 'These people draw near to Me with
      their mouth,
   And honor Me with *their* lips,
   But their heart is far from Me.
9 And in vain they worship Me,
   Teaching *as* doctrines the
      commandments of men.' "

10 When He had called the multitude to *Himself*, He said to them, "Hear and understand: 11 Not what goes into the mouth defiles a man; but what comes out of the mouth, this defiles a man."

12 Then His disciples came and said to Him, "Do You know that the Pharisees were offended when they heard this saying?"

13 But He answered and said, "Every plant which My heavenly Father has not planted will be uprooted. 14 Let them alone. They are blind leaders of the blind. And if the blind leads the blind, both will fall into a ditch."

15 Then Peter answered and said to Him, "Explain this parable to us."

16 So Jesus said, "Are you also still without understanding? 17 Do you not yet understand that whatever enters the mouth goes into the stomach and is eliminated? 18 But those things which proceed out of the mouth come from the heart, and they defile a man. 19 For out of the heart proceed evil thoughts, murders, adulteries, fornications, thefts, false witness, blasphemies. 20 These are *the things* which defile a man, but to eat with unwashed hands does not defile a man."

---

*T*he tiniest bit of sin is an indication of the vast corruption that is in the human heart.   (CONFORMED)

Reading 24—Great Is Your Faith
Matthew 15:22–28

Common sense is not faith, and faith is not common sense; they stand in the relation of the natural and the spiritual; of impulse and inspiration. Nothing Jesus Christ ever said is common sense, it is revelation sense, and it reaches the shores where common sense fails. . . .

For every detail of the common-sense life, there is a revelation fact of God whereby we can prove in practical experience what we believe God to be. Faith is a tremendously active principle which always puts Jesus Christ first— Lord, You have said so-and-so (for example, Matt. 6:33), it looks mad, but I am going to venture on Your word. To turn head faith into a personal possession is a fight *always,* not sometimes. God brings us into circumstances in order to educate our faith, because the nature of faith is to make its object real. Until we know Jesus, God is a mere abstraction, we cannot have faith in Him; but immediately we hear Jesus say—"He that has seen Me has seen the Father," we have something that is real, and faith is boundless. Faith is the whole man rightly related to God by the power of the Spirit of Jesus Christ.   (*UTMOST*)

GENESIS 47:1—48:22

THEN Joseph went and told Pharaoh, and said, "My father and my brothers, their flocks and their herds and all that they possess, have come from the land of Canaan; and indeed they *are* in the land of Goshen." 2 And he took five men from among his brothers and presented them to Pharaoh. 3 Then Pharaoh said to his brothers, "What *is* your occupation?"

And they said to Pharaoh, "Your servants *are* shepherds, both we *and* also our fathers." 4 And they said to Pharaoh, "We have come to dwell in the land, because your servants have no pasture for their flocks, for the famine *is* severe in the land of Canaan. Now therefore, please let your servants dwell in the land of Goshen."

5 Then Pharaoh spoke to Joseph, saying, "Your father and your brothers have come to you. 6 The land of Egypt *is* before you. Have your father and brothers dwell in the best of the land; let them dwell in the land of Goshen. And if you know *any* competent men among them, then make them chief herdsmen over my livestock."

7 Then Joseph brought in his father Jacob and set him before Pharaoh; and Jacob blessed Pharaoh. 8 Pharaoh said to Jacob, "How old *are* you?"

9 And Jacob said to Pharaoh, "The days of the years of my pilgrimage *are* one hundred and thirty years; few and evil have been the days of the years of my life, and they have not attained to the days of the years of the life of my fathers in the days of their pilgrimage." 10 So Jacob blessed Pharaoh, and went out from before Pharaoh.

11 And Joseph situated his father and his brothers, and gave them a possession in the land of Egypt, in the best of the land,

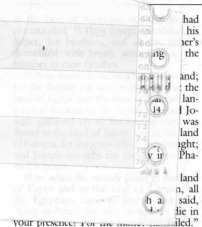

had
his
...er's
...ng   the
and;
: the
lan-
14   Jo-
was
land
ight;
v ir   Pha-

land
n, all
h a   said,
lie in
your presence? For the money ...iled."

16 Then Joseph said, "Give your livestock, and I will give you *bread* for your livestock, if the money is gone." 17 So they brought their livestock to Joseph, and Joseph gave them bread *in exchange* for the horses, the flocks, the cattle of the herds, and for the donkeys. Thus he fed them with bread *in exchange* for all their livestock that year.

18 When that year had ended, they came to him the next year and said to him, "We will not hide from my lord that our money is gone; my lord also has our herds of livestock. There is nothing left in the sight of my lord but our bodies and our lands. 19 Why should we die before your eyes, both we and our land? Buy us and our land for bread, and we and our land will be servants of Pharaoh; give *us* seed, that we may live and not die, that the land may not be desolate."

20 Then Joseph bought all the land of Egypt for Pharaoh; for every man of the Egyptians sold his field, because the famine was severe upon them. So the land became Pharaoh's. 21 And as for the people, he moved them into the cities, from *one* end of the borders of Egypt to the *other* end. 22 Only the land of the priests he did not buy; for the priests had rations *allotted to them* by Pharaoh, and they ate their rations which Pharaoh gave them; therefore they did not sell their lands.

23 Then Joseph said to the people, "Indeed I have bought you and your land this day for Pharaoh. Look, *here is* seed for you, and you shall sow the land. 24 And it shall come to pass in the harvest that you shall give one-fifth to Pharaoh. Four-fifths shall be your own, as seed for the field and for your food, for those of your households and as food for your little ones."

25 So they said, "You have saved our lives; let us find favor in the sight of my lord, and we will be Pharaoh's servants." 26 And Joseph made it a law over the land of Egypt to this day, *that* Pharaoh should have one-fifth, except for the land of the priests only, *which* did not become Pharaoh's.

27 So Israel dwelt in the land of Egypt, in the country of Goshen; and they had possessions there and grew and multiplied exceedingly. 28 And Jacob lived in the land of Egypt seventeen years. So the length of Jacob's life was one hundred and forty-seven years. 29 When the time drew near that Israel must die, he called his son Joseph and said to him, "Now if I have found favor in your sight, please put your hand under my thigh, and deal kindly and truly with me. Please do not bury me in Egypt, 30 but let me lie with my fathers; you shall carry me out of Egypt and bury me in their burial place."

And he said, "I will do as you have said." 31 Then he said, "Swear to me." And he swore to him. So Israel bowed himself on the head of the bed.

48 NOW it came to pass after these things that Joseph was told, "Indeed your father *is* sick"; and he took with him his two sons, Manasseh and Ephraim. 2 And Jacob was told, "Look, your son Joseph is coming to you"; and Israel strengthened himself and sat up on the bed. 3 Then Jacob said to Joseph: "God Almighty appeared to me at Luz in the land of Canaan and blessed me, 4 and said to me, 'Behold, I will make you fruitful and multiply you, and I will make of you a multitude of people, and give this land to your descendants after you *as* an everlasting possession.' 5 And now your two sons, Ephraim and Manasseh, who were born to you in the land of Egypt before I came to you in Egypt, *are* mine; as Reuben and Simeon, they shall be mine. 6 Your offspring whom you beget after them shall be yours; they will be called by the name of their brothers in their inheritance. 7 But as for me, when I came from Padan, Rachel died beside me in the land of Canaan on the way, when *there was* but a little distance to go to Ephrath; and I buried her there on the way to Ephrath (that is, Bethlehem)."

8 Then Israel saw Joseph's sons, and said, "Who *are* these?"

9 Joseph said to his father, "They *are* my sons, whom God has given me in this *place*."

And he said, "Please bring them to me, and I will bless them." 10 Now the eyes of

Israel were dim with age, *so that* he could not see. Then Joseph brought them near him, and he kissed them and embraced them. 11 And Israel said to Joseph, "I had not thought to see your face; but in fact, God has also shown me your offspring!"

12 So Joseph brought them from beside his knees, and he bowed down with his face to the earth. 13 And Joseph took them both, Ephraim with his right hand toward Israel's left hand, and Manasseh with his left hand toward Israel's right hand, and brought *them* near him. 14 Then Israel stretched out his right hand and laid *it* on Ephraim's head, who *was* the younger, and his left hand on Manasseh's head, guiding his hands knowingly, for Manasseh *was* the firstborn. 15 And he blessed Joseph, and said:

"God, before whom my fathers
   Abraham and Isaac walked,
The God who has fed me all my life
   long to this day,
16 The Angel who has redeemed me
   from all evil,
Bless the lads;
Let my name be named upon them,
And the name of my fathers Abraham
   and Isaac;
And let them grow into a multitude
   in the midst of the earth."

17 Now when Joseph saw that his father laid his right hand on the head of Ephraim, it displeased him; so he took hold of his father's hand to remove it from Ephraim's head to Manasseh's head. 18 And Joseph said to his father, "Not so, my father, for this *one is* the firstborn; put your right hand on his head."

19 But his father refused and said, "I know, my son, I know. He also shall become a people, and he also shall be great; but truly his younger brother shall be greater than he, and his descendants shall become a multitude of nations."

20 So he blessed them that day, saying, "By you Israel will bless, saying, 'May God make you as Ephraim and as Manasseh!'" And thus he set Ephraim before Manasseh.

21 Then Israel said to Joseph, "Behold, I am dying, but God will be with you and bring you back to the land of your fathers. 22 Moreover I have given to you one portion above your brothers, which I took from the hand of the Amorite with my sword and my bow."

PSALM 13:1–6

1 HOW long, O LORD? Will You forget
      me forever?
   How long will You hide Your face from
      me?

---

*If God is first, you can never
think of anything He will
   forget.*   (RUN)

---

2 How long shall I take counsel in my
      soul,
   Having sorrow in my heart daily?
   How long will my enemy be exalted
      over me?

3 Consider *and* hear me, O LORD my
      God;
   Enlighten my eyes,
   Lest I sleep the *sleep of* death;

4 Lest my enemy say,
   "I have prevailed against him";
   Lest those who trouble me rejoice when
      I am moved.

5 But I have trusted in Your mercy;
   My heart shall rejoice in Your salvation.

6 I will sing to the LORD,
   Because He has dealt bountifully with
      me.

PROVERBS 4:18, 19

18 BUT the path of the just *is* like the
       shining sun,
    That shines ever brighter unto the
       perfect day.

19 The way of the wicked *is* like darkness;
    They do not know what makes them
       stumble.

MATTHEW 15:21–39

THEN Jesus went out from there and departed to the region of Tyre and Sidon. 22 And behold, a woman of Canaan came from that region and cried out to Him, saying, "Have mercy on me, O Lord, Son of David! My daughter is severely demon-possessed."

---

*It is the nobodies that Jesus Christ
came to save.*   (CONFORMED)

23 But He answered her not a word.

And His disciples came and urged Him, saying, "Send her away, for she cries out after us."

24 But He answered and said, "I was not sent except to the lost sheep of the house of Israel."

25 Then she came and worshiped Him, saying, "Lord, help me!"

26 But He answered and said, "It is not good to take the children's bread and throw *it* to the little dogs."

27 And she said, "Yes, Lord, yet even the little dogs eat the crumbs which fall from their masters' table."

28 Then Jesus answered and said to her, "O woman, great *is* your faith! Let it be to you as you desire." And her daughter was healed from that very hour.

29 Jesus departed from there, skirted the Sea of Galilee, and went up on the mountain and sat down there. 30 Then great multitudes came to Him, having with them *the* lame, blind, mute, maimed, and many others; and they laid them down at Jesus' feet, and He healed them. 31 So the multitude marveled when they saw *the* mute speaking, *the* maimed made whole, *the* lame walking,

and *the* blind seeing; and they glorified the God of Israel.

32 Now Jesus called His disciples to *Himself* and said, "I have compassion on the multitude, because they have now continued with Me three days and have nothing to eat. And I do not want to send them away hungry, lest they faint on the way."

33 Then His disciples said to Him, "Where could we get enough bread in the wilderness to fill such a great multitude?"

34 Jesus said to them, "How many loaves do you have?"

And they said, "Seven, and a few little fish."

35 So He commanded the multitude to sit down on the ground. 36 And He took the seven loaves and the fish and gave thanks, broke *them* and gave *them* to His disciples; and the disciples *gave* to the multitude. 37 So they all ate and were filled, and they took up seven large baskets full of the fragments that were left. 38 Now those who ate were four thousand men, besides women and children. 39 And He sent away the multitude, got into the boat, and came to the region of Magdala.

◆◆◆

Reading 25—Spiritual Discipleship
Matthew 16:25

There is a difference between being saved and being a disciple. Some of us are saved, "yet so as through fire." We are grateful to God for saving us from sin, but we are of no use to Him in so far as our actual life is concerned. We are not spiritual disciples. Our Lord's last command was not, "Go and save men," but, "Go, . . . and make disciples." We cannot make disciples of others unless we are disciples ourselves. When a man comes to Jesus it is not sin that is in the way, but self-realization, pride, his claim to himself. "I must realize myself, I must be educated and trained, I must do those things that will help me to develop myself." Self-realization is anti-Christian. All this is vigorous paganism, it is not Christianity. Jesus Christ's attitude is always that of *anti*-self-realization. His purpose is not the development of man at all; His purpose is to make man exactly like Himself, and the characteristic of the Son of God is not self-realization but self-expenditure. Spiritual selfishness must go—am I prepared for it to go? "If anyone desires to come after Me, let him deny himself," that is, "let him give up his right to himself in Me."

(*Place Help*)

GENESIS 49:1—50:26

AND Jacob called his sons and said, "Gather together, that I may tell you what shall befall you in the last days:

2 "Gather together and hear, you sons of Jacob,
   And listen to Israel your father.

3 "Reuben, you are my firstborn,
   My might and the beginning of my strength,
   The excellency of dignity and the excellency of power.
4 Unstable as water, you shall not excel,
   Because you went up to your father's bed;
   Then you defiled *it*—
   He went up to my couch.

5 "Simeon and Levi *are* brothers;
   Instruments of cruelty *are in* their dwelling place.
6 Let not my soul enter their council;
   Let not my honor be united to their assembly;
   For in their anger they slew a man,
   And in their self-will they hamstrung an ox.
7 Cursed *be* their anger, for *it is* fierce;
   And their wrath, for it is cruel!
   I will divide them in Jacob
   And scatter them in Israel.

8 "Judah, you *are he* whom your brothers shall praise;
   Your hand *shall be* on the neck of your enemies;
   Your father's children shall bow down before you.
9 Judah *is* a lion's whelp;
   From the prey, my son, you have gone up.
   He bows down, he lies down as a lion;
   And as a lion, who shall rouse him?
10 The scepter shall not depart from Judah,
   Nor a lawgiver from between his feet,
   Until Shiloh comes;
   And to Him *shall be* the obedience of the people.
11 Binding his donkey to the vine,
   And his donkey's colt to the choice vine,
   He washed his garments in wine,
   And his clothes in the blood of grapes.
12 His eyes *are* darker than wine,
   And his teeth whiter than milk.

13 "Zebulun shall dwell by the haven of the sea;
   He *shall become* a haven for ships,
   And his border shall adjoin Sidon.

14 "Issachar is a strong donkey,
   Lying down between two burdens;
15 He saw that rest *was* good,
   And that the land *was* pleasant;
   He bowed his shoulder to bear *a burden,*
   And became a band of slaves.

16 "Dan shall judge his people
   As one of the tribes of Israel.
17 Dan shall be a serpent by the way,
   A viper by the path,
   That bites the horse's heels
   So that its rider shall fall backward.
18 I have waited for your salvation,
   O Lord!

19 "Gad, a troop shall tramp upon him,
   But he shall triumph at last.

20 "Bread from Asher *shall be* rich,
   And he shall yield royal dainties.

21 "Naphtali *is* a deer let loose;
   He uses beautiful words.

22 "Joseph *is* a fruitful bough,
   A fruitful bough by a well;
   His branches run over the wall.
23 The archers have bitterly grieved him,
   Shot *at him* and hated him.
24 But his bow remained in strength,
   And the arms of his hands were made strong
   By the hands of the Mighty *God* of Jacob
   (From there *is* the Shepherd, the Stone of Israel),
25 By the God of your father who will help you,
   And by the Almighty who will bless you
   With blessings of heaven above,
   Blessings of the deep that lies beneath,
   Blessings of the breasts and of the womb.
26 The blessings of your father
   Have excelled the blessings of my ancestors,
   Up to the utmost bound of the everlasting hills.
   They shall be on the head of Joseph,
   And on the crown of the head of him who was separate from his brothers.

27 "Benjamin is a ravenous wolf;
In the morning he shall devour the prey,
And at night he shall divide the spoil."

28 All these *are* the twelve tribes of Israel, and this *is* what their father spoke to them. And he blessed them; he blessed each one according to his own blessing.

29 Then he charged them and said to them: "I am to be gathered to my people; bury me with my fathers in the cave that *is* in the field of Ephron the Hittite, 30 in the cave that *is* in the field of Machpelah, which *is* before Mamre in the land of Canaan, which Abraham bought with the field of Ephron the Hittite as a possession for a burial place. 31 There they buried Abraham and Sarah his wife, there they buried Isaac and Rebekah his wife, and there I buried Leah. 32 The field and the cave that *is* there *were* purchased from the sons of Heth." 33 And when Jacob had finished commanding his sons, he drew his feet up into the bed and breathed his last, and was gathered to his people.

50 THEN Joseph fell on his father's face and wept over him, and kissed him. 2 And Joseph commanded his servants the physicians to embalm his father. So the physicians embalmed Israel. 3 Forty days were required for him, for such are the days required for those who are embalmed; and the Egyptians mourned for him seventy days.

4 Now when the days of his mourning were past, Joseph spoke to the household of Pharaoh, saying, "If now I have found favor in your eyes, please speak in the hearing of Pharaoh, saying, 5 'My father made me swear, saying, "Behold, I am dying; in my grave which I dug for myself in the land of Canaan, there you shall bury me." Now therefore, please let me go up and bury my father, and I will come back.' "

6 And Pharaoh said, "Go up and bury your father, as he made you swear."

7 So Joseph went up to bury his father; and with him went up all the servants of Pharaoh, the elders of his house, and all the elders of the land of Egypt, 8 as well as all the house of Joseph, his brothers, and his father's house. Only their little ones, their flocks, and their herds they left in the land of Goshen. 9 And there went up with him both chariots and horsemen, and it was a very great gathering.

10 Then they came to the threshing floor of Atad, which *is* beyond the Jordan, and they mourned there with a great and very solemn lamentation. He observed seven days of mourning for his father. 11 And when the inhabitants of the land, the Canaanites, saw the mourning at the threshing floor of Atad, they said, "This *is* a deep mourning of the Egyptians." Therefore its name was called Abel Mizraim, which *is* beyond the Jordan.

12 So his sons did for him just as he had commanded them. 13 For his sons carried him to the land of Canaan, and buried him in the cave of the field of Machpelah, before Mamre, which Abraham bought with the field from Ephron the Hittite as property for a burial place. 14 And after he had buried his father, Joseph returned to Egypt, he and his brothers and all who went up with him to bury his father.

15 When Joseph's brothers saw that their father was dead, they said, "Perhaps Joseph will hate us, and may actually repay us for all the evil which we did to him." 16 So they sent *messengers* to Joseph, saying, "Before your father died he commanded, saying, 17 'Thus you shall say to Joseph: "I beg you, please forgive the trespass of your brothers and their sin; for they did evil to you." ' Now, please, forgive the trespass of the servants of the God of your father." And Joseph wept when they spoke to him.

18 Then his brothers also went and fell down before his face, and they said, "Behold, we *are* your servants."

19 Joseph said to them, "Do not be afraid, for *am* I in the place of God? 20 But as for you, you meant evil against me; *but* God meant it for good, in order to bring it about as *it is* this day, to save many people alive. 21 Now therefore, do not be afraid; I will provide for you and your little ones." And he comforted them and spoke kindly to them.

22 So Joseph dwelt in Egypt, he and his father's household. And Joseph lived one hundred and ten years. 23 Joseph saw Ephraim's children to the third *generation*. The children of Machir, the son of Manasseh, were also brought up on Joseph's knees.

24 And Joseph said to his brethren, "I am dying; but God will surely visit you, and bring you out of this land to the land of which He swore to Abraham, to Isaac, and to Jacob." 25 Then Joseph took an oath from the children of Israel, saying, "God will surely visit you, and you shall carry up my bones from here." 26 So Joseph died, *being* one hundred and ten years old; and they embalmed him, and he was put in a coffin in Egypt.

PSALM 14:1–7

1 THE fool has said in his heart,
"*There is* no God."
They are corrupt,
They have done abominable works,
There is none who does good.

---

*A*theism is what the Bible calls it:
the belief of a fool.   (BIB. PSYCH.)

---

2 The LORD looks down from heaven
upon the children of men,
To see if there are any who understand,
who seek God.
3 They have all turned aside,
They have together become corrupt;
There is none who does good,
No, not one.

4 Have all the workers of iniquity no
knowledge,
Who eat up my people *as* they eat bread,
And do not call on the LORD?
5 There they are in great fear,
For God *is* with the generation of the
righteous.
6 You shame the counsel of the poor,
But the LORD *is* his refuge.

7 Oh, that the salvation of Israel *would
come* out of Zion!
When the LORD brings back the
captivity of His people,
Let Jacob rejoice *and* Israel be glad.

PROVERBS 4:20–24

20 MY son, give attention to my words;
Incline your ear to my sayings.
21 Do not let them depart from your eyes;
Keep them in the midst of your heart;
22 For they *are* life to those who find them,
And health to all their flesh.
23 Keep your heart with all diligence,
For out of it *spring* the issues of life.
24 Put away from you a deceitful mouth,
And put perverse lips far from you.

MATTHEW 16:1–28

THEN the Pharisees and Sadducees came,
and testing Him asked that He would show
them a sign from heaven. 2 He answered
and said to them, "When it is evening you
say, '*It will be* fair weather, for the sky is
red'; 3 and in the morning, '*It will be* foul
weather today, for the sky is red and threatening.' Hypocrites! You know how to discern the face of the sky, but you cannot
discern the signs of the times. 4 A wicked
and adulterous generation seeks after a sign,
and no sign shall be given to it except the
sign of the prophet Jonah." And He left
them and departed.

5 Now when His disciples had come to
the other side, they had forgotten to take
bread. 6 Then Jesus said to them, "Take
heed and beware of the leaven of the Pharisees and the Sadducees."

7 And they reasoned among themselves,
saying, "*It is* because we have taken no
bread."

8 But Jesus, being aware of *it*, said to
them, "O you of little faith, why do you
reason among yourselves because you have
brought no bread? 9 Do you not yet understand, or remember the five loaves of the
five thousand and how many baskets you
took up? 10 Nor the seven loaves of the
four thousand and how many large baskets
you took up? 11 How is it you do not understand that I did not speak to you concerning
bread?—*but* to beware of the leaven of the
Pharisees and Sadducees." 12 Then they understood that He did not tell *them* to beware
of the leaven of bread, but of the doctrine
of the Pharisees and Sadducees.

13 When Jesus came into the region of
Caesarea Philippi, He asked His disciples,
saying, "Who do men say that I, the Son
of Man, am?"

14 So they said, "Some *say* John the Baptist, some Elijah, and others Jeremiah or
one of the prophets."

15 He said to them, "But who do you
say that I am?"

16 Simon Peter answered and said, "You
are the Christ, the Son of the living God."

17 Jesus answered and said to him,
"Blessed are you, Simon Bar-Jonah, for flesh
and blood has not revealed *this* to you, but
My Father who is in heaven. 18 And I also
say to you that you are Peter, and on this
rock I will build My church, and the gates
of Hades shall not prevail against it.
19 And I will give you the keys of the kingdom of heaven, and whatever you bind on
earth will be bound in heaven, and whatever
you loose on earth will be loosed in heaven."

20 Then He commanded His disciples
that they should tell no one that He was
Jesus the Christ.

21 From that time Jesus began to show
to His disciples that He must go to Jerusalem, and suffer many things from the elders
and chief priests and scribes, and be killed,
and be raised the third day.

22 Then Peter took Him aside and began to rebuke Him, saying, "Far be it from You, Lord; this shall not happen to You!"

23 But He turned and said to Peter, "Get behind Me, Satan! You are an offense to Me, for you are not mindful of the things of God, but the things of men."

24 Then Jesus said to His disciples, "If anyone desires to come after Me, let him deny himself, and take up his cross, and follow Me. 25 For whoever desires to save his life will lose it, but whoever loses his life for My sake will find it. 26 For what profit is it to a man if he gains the whole world, and loses his own soul? Or what will a man give in exchange for his soul? 27 For the Son of Man will come in the glory of His Father with His angels, and then He will reward each according to his works. 28 Assuredly, I say to you, there are some standing here who shall not taste death till they see the Son of Man coming in His kingdom."

◆◆◆

Reading 26—Getting into God's Stride
Exodus 2:11–14

We may have the vision of God, a very clear understanding of what God wants—wrongs to be righted, the salvation of sinners, and the sanctification of believers; we are certain we see the way out, and we start to do the thing. Then comes something equivalent to the forty years in the wilderness, discouragement, disaster, upset, as if God had ignored the whole thing. When we are thoroughly flattened out, God comes back and revives the call, and we get the quaver in, and say, "Oh, who am I, that I should go?" We have to learn the first great stride of God—"I AM WHO I AM . . . has sent . . . you." We have to learn that our individual effort for God is an impertinence; our individuality must be rendered incandescent by a personal relationship to God, and that is not learned easily. The individual man is lost in his personal union with God, and what is manifested is the stride and the power of God. . . .

Moses had to learn this, and our Lord taught His disciples the same thing, "You did not choose Me, but I chose you and appointed you that you should go and bear fruit, and *that* your fruit should remain, that whatever you ask the Father in My name He may give you" (John 15:16), and He emphasizes it in John 17—"that they may be one just as We are one." (*PLACE HELP*)

EXODUS 1:1—2:25

NOW these *are* the names of the children of Israel who came to Egypt; each man and his household came with Jacob: 2 Reuben, Simeon, Levi, and Judah; 3 Issachar, Zebulun, and Benjamin; 4 Dan, Naphtali, Gad, and Asher. 5 All those who were descendants of Jacob were seventy persons (for Joseph was in Egypt *already*). 6 And Joseph died, all his brothers, and all that generation. 7 But the children of Israel were fruitful and increased abundantly, multiplied and grew exceedingly mighty; and the land was filled with them.

8 Now there arose a new king over Egypt, who did not know Joseph. 9 And he said to his people, "Look, the people of the children of Israel *are* more and mightier than we; 10 come, let us deal shrewdly with them, lest they multiply, and it happen, in the event of war, that they also join our enemies and fight against us, and *so* go up out of the land." 11 Therefore they set taskmasters over them to afflict them with their burdens. And they built for Pharaoh supply cities, Pithom and Raamses. 12 But the more they afflicted them, the more they multiplied and grew. And they were in dread of the children of Israel. 13 So the Egyptians made the children of Israel serve with rigor. 14 And they made their lives bitter with hard bondage—in mortar, in brick, and in all manner of service in the field. All their service in which they made them serve *was* with rigor.

15 Then the king of Egypt spoke to the Hebrew midwives, of whom the name of one *was* Shiphrah and the name of the other Puah; 16 and he said, "When you do the duties of a midwife for the Hebrew women, and see *them* on the birthstools, if it *is* a son, then you shall kill him; but if it *is* a daughter, then she shall live." 17 But the midwives feared God, and did not do as the king of Egypt commanded them, but saved the male children alive. 18 So the king of Egypt called for the midwives and said to them, "Why have you done this thing, and saved the male children alive?"

19 And the midwives said to Pharaoh, "Because the Hebrew women *are* not like the Egyptian women; for they *are* lively and give birth before the midwives come to them."

20 Therefore God dealt well with the midwives, and the people multiplied and grew very mighty. 21 And so it was, because the midwives feared God, that He provided households for them.

We impoverish God's ministry to us the moment we forget He is almighty. (RUN)

---

22 So Pharaoh commanded all his people, saying, "Every son who is born you shall cast into the river, and every daughter you shall save alive."

2 AND a man of the house of Levi went and took *as wife* a daughter of Levi. 2 So the woman conceived and bore a son. And when she saw that he *was* a beautiful *child,* she hid him three months. 3 But when she could no longer hide him, she took an ark of bulrushes for him, daubed it with asphalt and pitch, put the child in it, and laid *it* in the reeds by the river's bank. 4 And his sister stood afar off, to know what would be done to him.

5 Then the daughter of Pharaoh came down to bathe at the river. And her maidens walked along the riverside; and when she saw the ark among the reeds, she sent her maid to get it. 6 And when she opened *it,* she saw the child, and behold, the baby wept. So she had compassion on him, and said, "This is one of the Hebrews' children."

7 Then his sister said to Pharaoh's daughter, "Shall I go and call a nurse for you from the Hebrew women, that she may nurse the child for you?"

8 And Pharaoh's daughter said to her, "Go." So the maiden went and called the child's mother. 9 Then Pharaoh's daughter said to her, "Take this child away and nurse him for me, and I will give *you* your wages." So the woman took the child and nursed him. 10 And the child grew, and she brought him to Pharaoh's daughter, and he became her son. So she called his name Moses, saying, "Because I drew him out of the water."

11 Now it came to pass in those days, when Moses was grown, that he went out to his brethren and looked at their burdens. And he saw an Egyptian beating a Hebrew, one of his brethren. 12 So he looked this way and that way, and when he saw no one, he killed the Egyptian and hid him in the sand. 13 And when he went out the second day, behold, two Hebrew men were fighting, and he said to the one who did the wrong, "Why are you striking your companion?"

14 Then he said, "Who made you a prince and a judge over us? Do you intend to kill me as you killed the Egyptian?"

So Moses feared and said, "Surely this thing is known!" 15 When Pharaoh heard of this matter, he sought to kill Moses. But Moses fled from the face of Pharaoh and dwelt in the land of Midian; and he sat down by a well.

16 Now the priest of Midian had seven daughters. And they came and drew water, and they filled the troughs to water their father's flock. 17 Then the shepherds came and drove them away; but Moses stood up and helped them, and watered their flock.

18 When they came to Reuel their father, he said, "How *is it that* you have come so soon today?"

19 And they said, "An Egyptian delivered us from the hand of the shepherds, and he also drew enough water for us and watered the flock."

20 So he said to his daughters, "And where *is* he? Why *is it that* you have left the man? Call him, that he may eat bread."

21 Then Moses was content to live with the man, and he gave Zipporah his daughter to Moses. 22 And she bore *him* a son. He called his name Gershom, for he said, "I have been a stranger in a foreign land."

23 Now it happened in the process of time that the king of Egypt died. Then the children of Israel groaned because of the bondage, and they cried out; and their cry came up to God because of the bondage. 24 So God heard their groaning, and God remembered His covenant with Abraham, with Isaac, and with Jacob. 25 And God looked upon the children of Israel, and God acknowledged *them.*

PSALM 15:1–5

1 LORD, who may abide in Your
      tabernacle?
    Who may dwell in Your holy hill?

2 He who walks uprightly,
     And works righteousness,
     And speaks the truth in his heart;
3 He *who* does not backbite with his
      tongue,
     Nor does evil to his neighbor,
     Nor does he take up a reproach
      against his friend;
4 In whose eyes a vile person is despised,
     But he honors those who fear the
      LORD;
     He *who* swears to his own hurt and
      does not change;
5 He *who* does not put out his money
      at usury,
     Nor does he take a bribe against the
      innocent.

    He who does these *things* shall never
     be moved.

PROVERBS 4:25–27

25 LET your eyes look straight ahead,
      And your eyelids look right before you.
26 Ponder the path of your feet,
      And let all your ways be established.
27 Do not turn to the right or the left;
      Remove your foot from evil.

MATTHEW 17:1–27

NOW after six days Jesus took Peter, James, and John his brother, led them up on a high mountain by themselves; 2 and He was transfigured before them. His face shone like the sun, and His clothes became as white as the light. 3 And behold, Moses and Elijah appeared to them, talking with Him. 4 Then Peter answered and said to Jesus, "Lord, it is good for us to be here; if You wish, let us make here three tabernacles: one for You, one for Moses, and one for Elijah."

The first and foremost relationship in Christianity is the sovereign preference for Jesus Christ. (BIB. ETHICS)

---

5 While he was still speaking, behold, a bright cloud overshadowed them; and suddenly a voice came out of the cloud, saying, "This is My beloved Son, in whom I am well pleased. Hear Him!" 6 And when the disciples heard *it,* they fell on their faces and were greatly afraid. 7 But Jesus came and touched them and said, "Arise, and do not be afraid." 8 When they had lifted up their eyes, they saw no one but Jesus only.

9 Now as they came down from the mountain, Jesus commanded them, saying, "Tell the vision to no one until the Son of Man is risen from the dead."

10 And His disciples asked Him, saying, "Why then do the scribes say that Elijah must come first?"

11 Jesus answered and said to them, "Indeed, Elijah is coming first and will restore all things. 12 But I say to you that Elijah has come already, and they did not know him but did to him whatever they wished. Likewise the Son of Man is also about to suffer at their hands." 13 Then the disciples understood that He spoke to them of John the Baptist.

14 And when they had come to the multitude, a man came to Him, kneeling down to Him and saying, 15 "Lord, have mercy on my son, for he is an epileptic and suffers severely; for he often falls into the fire and often into the water. 16 So I brought him to Your disciples, but they could not cure him."

17 Then Jesus answered and said, "O faithless and perverse generation, how long shall I be with you? How long shall I bear with you? Bring him here to Me." 18 And Jesus rebuked the demon, and it came out of him; and the child was cured from that very hour.

19 Then the disciples came to Jesus privately and said, "Why could we not cast it out?"

20 So Jesus said to them, "Because of your unbelief; for assuredly, I say to you, if you have faith as a mustard seed, you will say to this mountain, 'Move from here to there,' and it will move; and nothing will be impossible for you. 21 However, this kind does not go out except by prayer and fasting."

22 Now while they were staying in Galilee, Jesus said to them, "The Son of Man is about to be betrayed into the hands of men, 23 and they will kill Him, and the third day He will be raised up." And they were exceedingly sorrowful.

24 When they had come to Capernaum, those who received the *temple* tax came to

Peter and said, "Does your Teacher not pay the *temple* tax?"

25 He said, "Yes."

And when he had come into the house, Jesus anticipated him, saying, "What do you think, Simon? From whom do the kings of the earth take customs or taxes, from their sons or from strangers?"

26 Peter said to Him, "From strangers." Jesus said to him, "Then the sons are free. 27 Nevertheless, lest we offend them, go to the sea, cast in a hook, and take the fish that comes up first. And when you have opened its mouth, you will find a piece of money; take that and give it to them for Me and you."

◄◄◄◄

Reading 27—Approaching Holy Ground
Exodus 3:5

"Strip off your commonplace moods," God says; "if you are going to see into this thing, you must put on the right mood for discerning it." The agony of a man's affliction is often necessary to put him into the right mood to face the fundamental things of life. The psalmist says, "Before I was afflicted I went astray, but now I keep Your word." The Bible is full of the fact that there has to be an approach to the holy ground. If I am not willing to be lifted up, it is no use talking about the higher heights. In putting John the Baptist to death, Herod committed moral suicide. He ordered the voice of God to be silent in his life, and when Jesus Christ stood before him, "he questioned Him with many words," for "he hoped to see some miracle done by Him"; but we read that Jesus "answered him nothing." It is quite possible for any man among us to get to a place where there is no such thing as truth or purity, and no man gets there without himself being to blame. . . . No man can do wrong in his heart and see right afterwards. If I am going to approach the holy ground, I must get into the right frame of mind—the excellency of a broken heart.   (*Shad. Agony*)

EXODUS 3:1—4:31

NOW Moses was tending the flock of Jethro his father-in-law, the priest of Midian. And he led the flock to the back of the desert, and came to Horeb, the mountain of God. 2 And the Angel of the Lord appeared to him in a flame of fire from the midst of a bush. So he looked, and behold, the bush was burning with fire, but the bush *was* not consumed. 3 Then Moses said, "I will now turn aside and see this great sight, why the bush does not burn."

4 So when the Lord saw that he turned aside to look, God called to him from the midst of the bush and said, "Moses, Moses!"

And he said, "Here I am."

5 Then He said, "Do not draw near this place. Take your sandals off your feet, for the place where you stand *is* holy ground."

6 Moreover He said, "I *am* the God of your

father—the God of Abraham, the God of Isaac, and the God of Jacob." And Moses hid his face, for he was afraid to look upon God.

7 And the Lord said: "I have surely seen the oppression of My people who *are* in Egypt, and have heard their cry because of their taskmasters, for I know their sorrows. 8 So I have come down to deliver them out of the hand of the Egyptians, and to bring them up from that land to a good and large land, to a land flowing with milk and honey, to the place of the Canaanites and the Hittites and the Amorites and the Perizzites and the Hivites and the Jebusites. 9 Now therefore, behold, the cry of the children of Israel has come to Me, and I have also seen the oppression with which the Egyptians oppress them. 10 Come now, therefore, and I will send you to Pharaoh that you may bring My people, the children of Israel, out of Egypt."

11 But Moses said to God, "Who *am* I

that I should go to Pharaoh, and that I should bring the children of Israel out of Egypt?"

12 So He said, "I will certainly be with you. And this *shall be* a sign to you that I have sent you: When you have brought the people out of Egypt, you shall serve God on this mountain."

13 Then Moses said to God, "Indeed, *when* I come to the children of Israel and say to them, 'The God of your fathers has sent me to you,' and they say to me, 'What *is* His name?' what shall I say to them?"

14 And God said to Moses, "I AM WHO I AM." And He said, "Thus you shall say to the children of Israel, 'I AM has sent me to you.' " 15 Moreover God said to Moses, "Thus you shall say to the children of Israel: 'The LORD God of your fathers, the God of Abraham, the God of Isaac, and the God of Jacob, has sent me to you. This

---

*T*he mystery of God is now, this minute, not in what is going to be. (GOD'S WORKMANSHIP)

---

is My name forever, and this *is* My memorial to all generations.' 16 Go and gather the elders of Israel together, and say to them, 'The LORD God of your fathers, the God of Abraham, of Isaac, and of Jacob, appeared to me, saying, "I have surely visited you and *seen* what is done to you in Egypt; 17 and I have said I will bring you up out of the affliction of Egypt to the land of the Canaanites and the Hittites and the Amorites and the Perizzites and the Hivites and the Jebusites, to a land flowing with milk and honey." ' 18 Then they will heed your voice; and you shall come, you and the elders of Israel, to the king of Egypt; and you shall say to him, 'The LORD God of the Hebrews has met with us; and now, please, let us go three days' journey into the wilderness, that we may sacrifice to the LORD our God.' 19 But I am sure that the king of Egypt will not let you go, no, not even by a mighty hand. 20 So I will stretch out My hand and strike Egypt with all My wonders which I will do in its midst; and after that he will let you go. 21 And I will give this people favor in the sight of the Egyptians; and it shall be, when you go, that you shall not go empty-handed. 22 But every woman shall ask of her neighbor, namely, of her who dwells near her house, articles of silver, articles of gold, and clothing; and you shall put *them* on your

sons and on your daughters. So you shall plunder the Egyptians."

4 THEN Moses answered and said, "But suppose they will not believe me or listen to my voice; suppose they say, 'The LORD has not appeared to you.' "

2 So the LORD said to him, "What *is* that in your hand?"

He said, "A rod."

3 And He said, "Cast it on the ground." So he cast it on the ground, and it became a serpent; and Moses fled from it. 4 Then the LORD said to Moses, "Reach out your hand and take *it* by the tail" (and he reached out his hand and caught it, and it became a rod in his hand), 5 "that they may believe that the LORD God of their fathers, the God of Abraham, the God of Isaac, and the God of Jacob, has appeared to you."

6 Furthermore the LORD said to him, "Now put your hand in your bosom." And he put his hand in his bosom, and when he took it out, behold, his hand *was* leprous, like snow. 7 And He said, "Put your hand in your bosom again." So he put his hand in his bosom again, and drew it out of his bosom, and behold, it was restored like his *other* flesh. 8 "Then it will be, if they do not believe you, nor heed the message of the first sign, that they may believe the message of the latter sign. 9 And it shall be, if they do not believe even these two signs, or listen to your voice, that you shall take water from the river and pour *it* on the dry *land*. The water which you take from the river will become blood on the dry *land*."

10 Then Moses said to the LORD, "O my Lord, I *am* not eloquent, neither before nor since You have spoken to Your servant; but I *am* slow of speech and slow of tongue."

11 So the LORD said to him, "Who has made man's mouth? Or who makes the mute, the deaf, the seeing, or the blind? *Have* not I, the LORD? 12 Now therefore, go, and I will be with your mouth and teach you what you shall say."

13 But he said, "O my Lord, please send by the hand of whomever *else* You may send."

14 So the anger of the LORD was kindled against Moses, and He said: "Is not Aaron the Levite your brother? I know that he can speak well. And look, he is also coming out to meet you. When he sees you, he will be glad in his heart. 15 Now you shall speak to him and put the words in his mouth. And I will be with your mouth and with his mouth, and I will teach you

what you shall do. 16 So he shall be your spokesman to the people. And he himself shall be as a mouth for you, and you shall be to him as God. 17 And you shall take this rod in your hand, with which you shall do the signs."

18 So Moses went and returned to Jethro his father-in-law, and said to him, "Please let me go and return to my brethren who *are* in Egypt, and see whether they are still alive."

And Jethro said to Moses, "Go in peace."

19 Now the LORD said to Moses in Midian, "Go, return to Egypt; for all the men who sought your life are dead." 20 Then Moses took his wife and his sons and set them on a donkey, and he returned to the land of Egypt. And Moses took the rod of God in his hand.

21 And the LORD said to Moses, "When you go back to Egypt, see that you do all those wonders before Pharaoh which I have put in your hand. But I will harden his heart, so that he will not let the people go. 22 Then you shall say to Pharaoh, 'Thus says the LORD: "Israel *is* My son, My first-born. 23 So I say to you, let My son go that he may serve Me. But if you refuse to let him go, indeed I will kill your son, your firstborn."' "

24 And it came to pass on the way, at the encampment, that the LORD met him and sought to kill him. 25 Then Zipporah took a sharp stone and cut off the foreskin of her son and cast *it* at *Moses'* feet, and said, "Surely you *are* a husband of blood to me!" 26 So He let him go. Then she said, "*You are* a husband of blood!"—because of the circumcision.

27 And the LORD said to Aaron, "Go into the wilderness to meet Moses." So he went and met him on the mountain of God, and kissed him. 28 So Moses told Aaron all the words of the LORD who had sent him, and all the signs which He had commanded him. 29 Then Moses and Aaron went and gathered together all the elders of the children of Israel. 30 And Aaron spoke all the words which the LORD had spoken to Moses. Then he did the signs in the sight of the people. 31 So the people believed; and when they heard that the LORD had visited the children of Israel and that He had looked on their affliction, then they bowed their heads and worshiped.

PSALM 16:1–6

1   PRESERVE me, O God, for in You
        I put my trust.

2   *O my soul,* you have said to the LORD,
        "You *are* my Lord,
        My goodness is nothing apart from
            You."

3   As for the saints who *are* on the earth,
        "They are the excellent ones, in whom
            is all my delight."

4   Their sorrows shall be multiplied who
            hasten *after* another *god;*
        Their drink offerings of blood I will
            not offer,
        Nor take up their names on my lips.

5   O LORD, *You are* the portion of my
            inheritance and my cup;
        You maintain my lot.

6   The lines have fallen to me in pleasant
            places;
        Yes, I have a good inheritance.

PROVERBS 5:1–6

1   MY son, pay attention to my wisdom;
        Lend your ear to my understanding,

2   That you may preserve discretion,
        And your lips may keep knowledge.

3   For the lips of an immoral woman drip
            honey,
        And her mouth *is* smoother than oil;

4   But in the end she is bitter as
            wormwood,
        Sharp as a two-edged sword.

5   Her feet go down to death,
        Her steps lay hold of hell.

6   Lest you ponder *her* path of life—
        Her ways are unstable;
        You do not know *them.*

MATTHEW 18:1–20

AT that time the disciples came to Jesus, saying, "Who then is greatest in the kingdom of heaven?"

2 Then Jesus called a little child to Him, set him in the midst of them, 3 and said, "Assuredly, I say to you, unless you are converted and become as little children, you will by no means enter the kingdom of heaven. 4 Therefore whoever humbles himself as this little child is the greatest in the kingdom of heaven. 5 Whoever receives one little child like this in My name receives Me.

6 "Whoever causes one of these little ones who believe in Me to sin, it would be better for him if a millstone were hung around his neck, and he were drowned in the depth of the sea. 7 Woe to the world because of

offenses! For offenses must come, but woe to that man by whom the offense comes!

8 "If your hand or foot causes you to sin, cut it off and cast *it* from you. It is better for you to enter into life lame or maimed, rather than having two hands or two feet, to be cast into the everlasting fire. 9 And if your eye causes you to sin, pluck it out and cast *it* from you. It is better for you to enter into life with one eye, rather than having two eyes, to be cast into hell fire.

I am not saved by believing; I realize I am saved by believing. (UTMOST)

10 "Take heed that you do not despise one of these little ones, for I say to you that in heaven their angels always see the face of My Father who is in heaven. 11 For the Son of Man has come to save that which was lost.

12 "What do you think? If a man has a hundred sheep, and one of them goes astray, does he not leave the ninety-nine and go to the mountains to seek the one that is straying? 13 And if he should find it, assuredly, I say to you, he rejoices more over that *sheep* than over the ninety-nine that did not go astray. 14 Even so it is not the will of your Father who is in heaven that one of these little ones should perish.

15 "Moreover if your brother sins against you, go and tell him his fault between you and him alone. If he hears you, you have gained your brother. 16 But if he will not hear, take with you one or two more, that 'by the mouth of two or three witnesses every word may be established.' 17 And if he refuses to hear them, tell *it* to the church. But if he refuses even to hear the church, let him be to you like a heathen and a tax collector.

18 "Assuredly, I say to you, whatever you bind on earth will be bound in heaven, and whatever you loose on earth will be loosed in heaven.

19 "Again I say to you that if two of you agree on earth concerning anything that they ask, it will be done for them by My Father in heaven. 20 For where two or three are gathered together in My name, I am there in the midst of them.'"

Reading 28—Straw Justice
Exodus 5:6–9

Wherever God sends us, He will guard our lives. Our personal property and possessions are a matter of indifference, we have to sit loosely to all those things; if we do not, there will be panic and heartbreak and distress. That is the inwardness of the overshadowing of personal deliverance.

The Sermon on the Mount indicates that when we are on Jesus Christ's errands, there is no time to stand up for ourselves. Jesus says, in effect, Do not be bothered with whether you are being justly dealt with or not. To look for justice is a sign of deflection from devotion to Him. Never look for justice in this world, but never cease to give it. If we look for justice, we will begin to grouse and to indulge in the discontent of self-pity—Why should I be treated like this? If we are devoted to Jesus Christ we have nothing to do with what we meet, whether it is just or unjust. Jesus says—Go steadily on with what I have told you to do and I will guard your life. If you try to guard it yourself, you remove yourself from My deliverance. The most devout among us become atheistic in this connection; we do not believe God, we enthrone common sense and tack the name of God on to it. We do lean to our own understanding, instead of trusting God with all our hearts. (*UTMOST*)

EXODUS 5:1—6:30

AFTERWARD Moses and Aaron went in and told Pharaoh, "Thus says the LORD God of Israel: 'Let My people go, that they may hold a feast to Me in the wilderness.'"

2 And Pharaoh said, "Who *is* the LORD, that I should obey His voice to let Israel go? I do not know the LORD, nor will I let Israel go."

3 So they said, "The God of the Hebrews has met with us. Please, let us go three days' journey into the desert and sacrifice to the LORD our God, lest He fall upon us with pestilence or with the sword."

4 Then the king of Egypt said to them, "Moses and Aaron, why do you take the people from their work? Get *back* to your labor." 5 And Pharaoh said, "Look, the people of the land *are* many now, and you make them rest from their labor!"

6 So the same day Pharaoh commanded the taskmasters of the people and their officers, saying, 7 "You shall no longer give the people straw to make brick as before. Let them go and gather straw for themselves. 8 And you shall lay on them the quota of bricks which they made before. You shall not reduce it. For they are idle; therefore they cry out, saying, 'Let us go *and* sacrifice to our God.' 9 Let more work be laid on the men, that they may labor in it, and let them not regard false words."

10 And the taskmasters of the people and their officers went out and spoke to the people, saying, "Thus says Pharaoh: 'I will not give you straw. 11 Go, get yourselves straw where you can find it; yet none of your work will be reduced.'" 12 So the people were scattered abroad throughout all the land of Egypt to gather stubble instead of straw. 13 And the taskmasters forced *them* to hurry, saying, "Fulfill your work, *your* daily quota, as when there was straw."

Much that we call the trial of our faith is the inevitable result of being alive. (NOT KNOWING)

---

14 Also the officers of the children of Israel, whom Pharaoh's taskmasters had set over them, were beaten *and* were asked, "Why have you not fulfilled your task in making brick both yesterday and today, as before?"

15 Then the officers of the children of Israel came and cried out to Pharaoh, saying, "Why are you dealing thus with your servants? 16 There is no straw given to your servants, and they say to us, 'Make brick!' And indeed your servants *are* beaten, but the fault *is* in your *own* people."

17 But he said, "You *are* idle! Idle! Therefore you say, 'Let us go *and* sacrifice to the LORD.' 18 Therefore go now *and* work; for no straw shall be given you, yet you shall deliver the quota of bricks." 19 And the officers of the children of Israel saw *that* they *were* in trouble after it was said, "You shall not reduce *any* bricks from your daily quota."

20 Then, as they came out from Pharaoh, they met Moses and Aaron who stood there to meet them. 21 And they said to them, "Let the LORD look on you and judge, because you have made us abhorrent in the sight of Pharaoh and in the sight of his servants, to put a sword in their hand to kill us."

22 So Moses returned to the LORD and said, "Lord, why have You brought trouble on this people? Why *is* it You have sent me? 23 For since I came to Pharaoh to speak in Your name, he has done evil to this people; neither have You delivered Your people at all."

6 THEN the LORD said to Moses, "Now you shall see what I will do to Pharaoh. For with a strong hand he will let them go, and with a strong hand he will drive them out of his land."

2 And God spoke to Moses and said to him: "I *am* the LORD. 3 I appeared to Abraham, to Isaac, and to Jacob, as God Almighty, but *by* My name LORD I was not known to them. 4 I have also established My covenant with them, to give them the land of Canaan, the land of their pilgrimage, in which they were strangers. 5 And I have also heard the groaning of the children of Israel whom the Egyptians keep in bondage, and I have remembered My covenant. 6 Therefore say to the children of Israel: 'I *am* the LORD; I will bring you out from under the burdens of the Egyptians, I will rescue you from their bondage, and I will redeem you with an outstretched arm and with great judgments. 7 I will take you as My people, and I will be your God. Then you shall know that I *am* the LORD your God who brings you out from under the burdens of the Egyptians. 8 And I will bring you into the land which I swore to give to Abraham, Isaac, and Jacob; and I will give it to you *as* a heritage: I *am* the LORD.'"

9 So Moses spoke thus to the children of Israel; but they did not heed Moses, because of anguish of spirit and cruel bondage.

10 And the LORD spoke to Moses, saying,

11 "Go in, tell Pharaoh king of Egypt to let the children of Israel go out of his land."

12 And Moses spoke before the LORD, saying, "The children of Israel have not heeded me. How then shall Pharaoh heed me, for I *am* of uncircumcised lips?"

13 Then the LORD spoke to Moses and Aaron, and gave them a command for the children of Israel and for Pharaoh king of Egypt, to bring the children of Israel out of the land of Egypt.

14 These *are* the heads of their fathers' houses: The sons of Reuben, the firstborn of Israel, *were* Hanoch, Pallu, Hezron, and Carmi. These are the families of Reuben. 15 And the sons of Simeon *were* Jemuel, Jamin, Ohad, Jachin, Zohar, and Shaul the son of a Canaanite woman. These *are* the families of Simeon. 16 These *are* the names of the sons of Levi according to their generations: Gershon, Kohath, and Merari. And the years of the life of Levi *were* one hundred and thirty-seven. 17 The sons of Gershon *were* Libni and Shimi according to their families. 18 And the sons of Kohath *were* Amram, Izhar, Hebron, and Uzziel. And the years of the life of Kohath *were* one hundred and thirty-three. 19 The sons of Merari *were* Mahli and Mushi. These *are* the families of Levi according to their generations.

20 Now Amram took for himself Jochebed, his father's sister, as wife; and she bore him Aaron and Moses. And the years of the life of Amram *were* one hundred and thirty-seven. 21 The sons of Izhar *were* Korah, Nepheg, and Zichri. 22 And the sons of Uzziel *were* Mishael, Elzaphan, and Zithri. 23 Aaron took to himself Elisheba, daughter of Amminadab, sister of Nahshon, as wife; and she bore him Nadab, Abihu, Eleazar, and Ithamar. 24 And the sons of Korah *were* Assir, Elkanah, and Abiasaph. These are the families of the Korahites. 25 Eleazar, Aaron's son, took for himself one of the daughters of Putiel as wife; and she bore him Phinehas. These *are* the heads of the fathers' houses of the Levites according to their families.

26 These *are the same* Aaron and Moses to whom the LORD said, "Bring out the children of Israel from the land of Egypt according to their armies." 27 These *are* the ones who spoke to Pharaoh king of Egypt, to bring out the children of Israel from Egypt. These *are the same* Moses and Aaron.

28 And it came to pass, on the day the LORD spoke to Moses in the land of Egypt, 29 that the LORD spoke to Moses, saying, "I *am* the LORD. Speak to Pharaoh king of Egypt all that I say to you."

30 But Moses said before the LORD, "Behold, I *am* of uncircumcised lips, and how shall Pharaoh heed me?"

PSALM 16:7–11

7　I will bless the LORD who has given
　　me counsel;
　　My heart also instructs me in the night
　　seasons.
8　I have set the LORD always before me;
　　Because *He is* at my right hand I shall
　　not be moved.

9　Therefore my heart is glad, and my
　　glory rejoices;
　　My flesh also will rest in hope.
10　For You will not leave my soul in Sheol,
　　Nor will You allow Your Holy One
　　to see corruption.
11　You will show me the path of life;
　　In Your presence *is* fullness of joy;
　　At Your right hand *are* pleasures
　　forevermore.

In the life of a saint there is no such thing as chance.　　(UTMOST)

PROVERBS 5:7–14

7　THEREFORE hear me now, *my*
　　children,
　　And do not depart from the words of
　　my mouth.
8　Remove your way far from her,
　　And do not go near the door of her
　　house,
9　Lest you give your honor to others,
　　And your years to the cruel *one;*
10　Lest aliens be filled with your wealth,
　　And your labors *go* to the house of a
　　foreigner;
11　And you mourn at last,
　　When your flesh and your body are
　　consumed,
12　And say:
　"How I have hated instruction,
　　And my heart despised correction!
13　I have not obeyed the voice of my
　　teachers,
　　Nor inclined my ear to those who
　　instructed me!
14　I was on the verge of total ruin,
　　In the midst of the assembly and
　　congregation."

MATTHEW 18:21–35

THEN Peter came to Him and said, "Lord, how often shall my brother sin against me, and I forgive him? Up to seven times?"

22 Jesus said to him, "I do not say to you, up to seven times, but up to seventy times seven. 23 Therefore the kingdom of heaven is like a certain king who wanted to settle accounts with his servants. 24 And when he had begun to settle accounts, one was brought to him who owed him ten thousand talents. 25 But as he was not able to pay, his master commanded that he be sold, with his wife and children and all that he had, and that payment be made. 26 The servant therefore fell down before him, saying, 'Master, have patience with me, and I will pay you all.' 27 Then the master of that servant was moved with compassion, released him, and forgave him the debt.

28 "But that servant went out and found one of his fellow servants who owed him a hundred denarii; and he laid hands on him and took *him* by the throat, saying, 'Pay me what you owe!' 29 So his fellow servant fell down at his feet and begged him, saying, 'Have patience with me, and I will pay you all.' 30 And he would not, but went and threw him into prison till he should pay the debt. 31 So when his fellow servants saw what had been done, they were very grieved, and came and told their master all that had been done. 32 Then his master, after he had called him, said to him, 'You wicked servant! I forgave you all that debt because you begged me. 33 Should you not also have had compassion on your fellow servant, just as I had pity on you?' 34 And his master was angry, and delivered him to the torturers until he should pay all that was due to him.

35 "So My heavenly Father also will do to you if each of you, from his heart, does not forgive his brother his trespasses."

◆◆◆◆

Reading 29—Of the Renewal of Youth
Matthew 19:14

Jesus Christ uses the child-spirit as a touchstone for the character of a disciple. He did not put up a child before His disciples as an ideal, but as an expression of the simple-hearted life they would live when they were born again. The life of a little child is expectant, full of wonder, and free from self-consciousness, and Jesus said, "Unless you are converted and become as little children, you will by no means enter the kingdom of heaven." . . . How many of us thought about how we should live before we were born? Why, none. But numbers of people try to think of how to live as Christians before they are born again. "Do not marvel that I said to you, 'You must be born again,' " that is, become as little children, with openhearted, unprejudiced minds in relation to God. . . . The most seriously minded Christian is the one who has just become a Christian; the mature saint is just like a young child, absolutely simple, and joyful and gay. Read the Sermon on the Mount—"Do not worry," (that is, have no care) "about your life." . . . The Christianity of Jesus Christ refuses to be careworn. Our Lord is indicating that we have to be carefully careless about everything saving our relationship to Him. Fuss is always a sign of fever. A great many people mistake perspiration in service for inspiration in devotion. The characteristic of a man who has come to God is that you cannot get him to take anyone seriously but God.　(*PLACE HELP*)

EXODUS 7:1—8:32

SO the LORD said to Moses: "See, I have made you *as* God to Pharaoh, and Aaron your brother shall be your prophet. 2 You shall speak all that I command you. And Aaron your brother shall tell Pharaoh to send the children of Israel out of his land. 3 And I will harden Pharaoh's heart, and multiply My signs and My wonders in the land of Egypt. 4 But Pharaoh will not heed you, so that I may lay My hand on Egypt and bring My armies *and* My people, the children of Israel, out of the land of Egypt by great judgments. 5 And the Egyptians shall know that I *am* the LORD, when I stretch out My hand on Egypt and bring out the children of Israel from among them."

6 Then Moses and Aaron did *so;* just as the LORD commanded them, so they did. 7 And Moses *was* eighty years old and Aaron eighty-three years old when they spoke to Pharaoh.

8 Then the LORD spoke to Moses and Aaron, saying, 9 "When Pharaoh speaks to you, saying, 'Show a miracle for yourselves,' then you shall say to Aaron, 'Take your rod and cast *it* before Pharaoh, *and* let it become a serpent.' " 10 So Moses and Aaron went in to Pharaoh, and they did so, just as the LORD commanded. And Aaron cast down his rod before Pharaoh and before his servants, and it became a serpent. 11 But Pharaoh also called the wise men and the sorcerers; so the magicians of Egypt, they also did in like manner with their enchantments. 12 For every man threw down his rod, and they became serpents. But Aaron's rod swallowed up their rods. 13 And Pharaoh's heart grew hard, and he did not heed them, as the LORD had said.

14 So the LORD said to Moses: "Pharaoh's heart *is* hard; he refuses to let the people go. 15 Go to Pharaoh in the morning, when he goes out to the water, and you shall stand by the river's bank to meet him; and the rod which was turned to a serpent you shall take in your hand. 16 And you shall say to him, 'The LORD God of the Hebrews has sent me to you, saying, "Let My people go, that they may serve Me in the wilderness"; but indeed, until now you would not hear! 17 Thus says the LORD: "By this you shall know that I *am* the LORD. Behold, I will strike the waters which *are* in the river with the rod that *is* in my hand, and they shall be turned to blood. 18 And the fish that *are* in the river shall die, the river

shall stink, and the Egyptians will loathe to drink the water of the river." ' "

19 Then the LORD spoke to Moses, "Say to Aaron, 'Take your rod and stretch out your hand over the waters of Egypt, over their streams, over their rivers, over their ponds, and over all their pools of water, that they may become blood. And there shall be blood throughout all the land of Egypt, both in *buckets of* wood and *pitchers of* stone.' " 20 And Moses and Aaron did so, just as the LORD commanded. So he lifted up the rod and struck the waters that *were* in the river, in the sight of Pharaoh and in the sight of his servants. And all the waters that *were* in the river were turned to blood. 21 The fish that *were* in the river died, the river stank, and the Egyptians could not drink the water of the river. So there was blood throughout all the land of Egypt.

22 Then the magicians of Egypt did so with their enchantments; and Pharaoh's heart grew hard, and he did not heed them, as the LORD had said. 23 And Pharaoh turned and went into his house. Neither was his heart moved by this. 24 So all the Egyptians dug all around the river for water to drink, because they could not drink the water of the river. 25 And seven days passed after the LORD had struck the river.

8 AND the LORD spoke to Moses, "Go to Pharaoh and say to him, 'Thus says the LORD: "Let My people go, that they may serve Me. 2 But if you refuse to let *them* go, behold, I will smite all your territory with frogs. 3 So the river shall bring forth frogs abundantly, which shall go up and come into your house, into your bedroom, on your bed, into the houses of your servants, on your people, into your ovens, and into your kneading bowls. 4 And the frogs shall come up on you, on your people, and on all your servants." ' "

5 Then the LORD spoke to Moses, "Say to Aaron, 'Stretch out your hand with your rod over the streams, over the rivers, and over the ponds, and cause frogs to come up on the land of Egypt.' " 6 So Aaron stretched out his hand over the waters of Egypt, and the frogs came up and covered the land of Egypt. 7 And the magicians did so with their enchantments, and brought up frogs on the land of Egypt.

8 Then Pharaoh called for Moses and Aaron, and said, "Entreat the LORD that He may take away the frogs from me and from my people; and I will let the people go, that they may sacrifice to the LORD."

9 And Moses said to Pharaoh, "Accept

the honor of saying when I shall intercede for you, for your servants, and for your people, to destroy the frogs from you and your houses, *that* they may remain in the river only."

10 So he said, "Tomorrow." And he said, "*Let it be* according to your word, that you may know that *there is* no one like the LORD our God. 11 And the frogs shall depart from you, from your houses, from your servants, and from your people. They shall remain in the river only."

12 Then Moses and Aaron went out from Pharaoh. And Moses cried out to the LORD concerning the frogs which He had brought against Pharaoh. 13 So the LORD did according to the word of Moses. And the frogs died out of the houses, out of the courtyards, and out of the fields. 14 They gathered them together in heaps, and the land stank. 15 But when Pharaoh saw that there was relief, he hardened his heart and did not heed them, as the LORD had said.

16 So the LORD said to Moses, "Say to Aaron, 'Stretch out your rod, and strike the dust of the land, so that it may become lice throughout all the land of Egypt.'" 17 And they did so. For Aaron stretched out his hand with his rod and struck the dust of the earth, and it became lice on man and beast. All the dust of the land became lice throughout all the land of Egypt.

18 Now the magicians so worked with their enchantments to bring forth lice, but they could not. So there were lice on man and beast. 19 Then the magicians said to Pharaoh, "This *is* the finger of God." But Pharaoh's heart grew hard, and he did not heed them, just as the LORD had said.

20 And the LORD said to Moses, "Rise early in the morning and stand before Pharaoh as he comes out to the water. Then say to him, 'Thus says the LORD: "Let My people go, that they may serve Me. 21 Or else, if you will not let My people go, behold, I will send swarms *of flies* on you and your servants, on your people and into your houses. The houses of the Egyptians shall be full of swarms *of flies,* and also the ground on which they *stand.* 22 And in that day I will set apart the land of Goshen, in which My people dwell, that no swarms *of flies* shall be there, in order that you may know that I *am* the LORD in the midst of the land. 23 I will make a difference between My people and your people. Tomorrow this sign shall be."'" 24 And the LORD did so. Thick swarms *of flies* came into the house of Pharaoh, *into* his servants' houses, and into all the land

of Egypt. The land was corrupted because of the swarms *of flies.*

25 Then Pharaoh called for Moses and Aaron, and said, "Go, sacrifice to your God in the land."

26 And Moses said, "It is not right to do so, for we would be sacrificing the abomination of the Egyptians to the LORD our God. If we sacrifice the abomination of the Egyptians before their eyes, then will they not stone us? 27 We will go three days' journey into the wilderness and sacrifice to the LORD our God as He will command us."

---

*W*hat an imperturbable certainty there is about the man who is in contact with the real God! (NOT KNOWING)

---

28 So Pharaoh said, "I will let you go, that you may sacrifice to the LORD your God in the wilderness; only you shall not go very far away. Intercede for me."

29 Then Moses said, "Indeed I am going out from you, and I will entreat the LORD, that the swarms *of flies* may depart tomorrow from Pharaoh, from his servants, and from his people. But let Pharaoh not deal deceitfully anymore in not letting the people go to sacrifice to the LORD."

30 So Moses went out from Pharaoh and entreated the LORD. 31 And the LORD did according to the word of Moses; He removed the swarms *of flies* from Pharaoh, from his servants, and from his people. Not one remained. 32 But Pharaoh hardened his heart at this time also; neither would he let the people go.

PSALM 17:1–7

1   HEAR a just cause, O LORD,
    Attend to my cry;
    Give ear to my prayer *which is* not from
        deceitful lips.

2   Let my vindication come from Your
        presence;
    Let Your eyes look on the things that
        are upright.

3   You have tested my heart;
    You have visited *me* in the night;
    You have tried me and have found
        nothing;
    I have purposed that my mouth shall
        not transgress.

4 Concerning the works of men,
By the word of Your lips,
I have kept away from the paths of the
destroyer.
5 Uphold my steps in Your paths,
That my footsteps may not slip.

6 I have called upon You, for You will
hear me, O God;
Incline Your ear to me, *and* hear my
speech.
7 Show Your marvelous lovingkindness
by Your right hand,
O You who save those who trust *in
You*
From those who rise up *against them.*

PROVERBS 5:15–20

15 DRINK water from your own cistern,
And running water from your own well.
16 Should your fountains be dispersed
abroad,
Streams of water in the streets?
17 Let them be only your own,
And not for strangers with you.
18 Let your fountain be blessed,
And rejoice with the wife of your youth.
19 *As a* loving deer and a graceful doe,
Let her breasts satisfy you at all times;
And always be enraptured with her love.
20 For why should you, my son, be
enraptured by an immoral woman,
And be embraced in the arms of a
seductress?

MATTHEW 19:1–30

NOW it came to pass, when Jesus had finished these sayings, *that* He departed from
Galilee and came to the region of Judea
beyond the Jordan. 2 And great multitudes
followed Him, and He healed them there.
3 The Pharisees also came to Him, testing
Him, and saying to Him, "Is it lawful for
a man to divorce his wife for *just* any
reason?"
4 And He answered and said to them,
"Have you not read that He who made
them at the beginning 'made them male and
female,' 5 and said, 'For this reason a man
shall leave his father and mother and be
joined to his wife, and the two shall become one flesh' ? 6 So then, they are no
longer two but one flesh. Therefore what
God has joined together, let not man
separate."
7 They said to Him, "Why then did Moses command to give a certificate of divorce,
and to put her away?"
8 He said to them, "Moses, because of
the hardness of your hearts, permitted you
to divorce your wives, but from the beginning it was not so. 9 And I say to you,
whoever divorces his wife, except for sexual
immorality, and marries another, commits
adultery; and whoever marries her who is
divorced commits adultery."
10 His disciples said to Him, "If such is
the case of the man with *his* wife, it is better
not to marry."
11 But He said to them, "All cannot accept this saying, but only *those* to whom
it has been given: 12 For there are eunuchs
who were born thus from *their* mother's
womb, and there are eunuchs who were
made eunuchs by men, and there are eunuchs who have made themselves eunuchs
for the kingdom of heaven's sake. He who
is able to accept *it,* let him accept *it."*
13 Then little children were brought to
Him that He might put *His* hands on them
and pray, but the disciples rebuked them.
14 But Jesus said, "Let the little children
come to Me, and do not forbid them; for
of such is the kingdom of heaven."
15 And He laid *His* hands on them and departed from there.
16 Now behold, one came and said to
Him, "Good Teacher, what good thing shall
I do that I may have eternal life?"
17 So He said to him, "Why do you call
Me good? No one *is* good but One, *that
is,* God. But if you want to enter into life,
keep the commandments."
18 He said to Him, "Which ones?"
Jesus said, " 'You shall not murder,' 'You
shall not commit adultery,' 'You shall not
steal,' 'You shall not bear false witness,'
19 'Honor your father and *your* mother,'
and, 'You shall love your neighbor as
yourself.' "
20 The young man said to Him, "All these
things I have kept from my youth. What
do I still lack?"
21 Jesus said to him, "If you want to be
perfect, go, sell what you have and give
to the poor, and you will have treasure in
heaven; and come, follow Me."
22 But when the young man heard that
saying, he went away sorrowful, for he had
great possessions.

---

*To be willingly poor for God is to strip
myself of all things for the sake of Jesus
Christ.* (PERFECT)

23 Then Jesus said to His disciples, "Assuredly, I say to you that it is hard for a rich man to enter the kingdom of heaven. 24 And again I say to you, it is easier for a camel to go through the eye of a needle than for a rich man to enter the kingdom of God."

25 When His disciples heard *it*, they were greatly astonished, saying, "Who then can be saved?"

26 But Jesus looked at *them* and said to them, "With men this is impossible, but with God all things are possible."

27 Then Peter answered and said to Him,

"See, we have left all and followed You. Therefore what shall we have?"

28 So Jesus said to them, "Assuredly I say to you, that in the regeneration, when the Son of Man sits on the throne of His glory, you who have followed Me will also sit on twelve thrones, judging the twelve tribes of Israel. 29 And everyone who has left houses or brothers or sisters or father or mother or wife or children or lands, for My name's sake, shall receive a hundredfold, and inherit eternal life. 30 But many *who are* first will be last, and the last first.

Reading 30—The Overflow of Service
Exodus 9:1

The call of God is not a call to any particular service; my interpretation of it may be because contact with the nature of God has made me realize what I would like to do for Him. The call of God is essentially expressive of His nature; service is the outcome of what is fitted to my nature. The vocation of the natural life is stated by the apostle Paul—"When it pleased God to reveal His Son in me that I might preach Him" (that is, sacramentally express) "among the Gentiles."

Service is the overflow of superabounding devotion; but, profoundly speaking, there is no *call* to that, it is my own little actual bit and is the echo of my identification with the nature of God. Service is the natural part of my life. God gets me into a relationship with Himself whereby I understand His call, then I do things out of sheer love for Him on my own account. To serve God is the deliberate love-gift of a nature that has heard the call of God. Service is expressive of that which is fitted to my nature: God's call is expressive of His nature; consequently when I receive His nature and hear His call, the voice of the Divine nature sounds in both and the two work together. The Son of God reveals Himself in me, and I serve Him in the ordinary ways of life out of devotion to Him.   (*Utmost*)

EXODUS 9:1—10:29

THEN the LORD said to Moses, "Go in to Pharaoh and tell him, 'Thus says the LORD God of the Hebrews: "Let My people go, that they may serve Me. 2 For if you refuse to let *them* go, and still hold them, 3 behold, the hand of the LORD will be on your cattle in the field, on the horses, on the donkeys, on the camels, on the oxen, and on the sheep—a very severe pestilence. 4 And the LORD will make a difference between the livestock of Israel and the livestock of Egypt. So nothing shall die of all *that* belongs to the children of Israel." ' "

5 Then the LORD appointed a set time, saying, "Tomorrow the LORD will do this thing in the land."

6 So the LORD did this thing on the next day, and all the livestock of Egypt died; but of the livestock of the children of Israel, not one died. 7 Then Pharaoh sent, and indeed, not even one of the livestock of the Israelites was dead. But the heart of Pharaoh became hard, and he did not let the people go.

8 So the LORD said to Moses and Aaron, "Take for yourselves handfuls of ashes from a furnace, and let Moses scatter it toward the heavens in the sight of Pharaoh. 9 And it will become fine dust in all the

land of Egypt, and it will cause boils that break out in sores on man and beast throughout all the land of Egypt." 10 Then they took ashes from the furnace and stood before Pharaoh, and Moses scattered *them* toward heaven. And *they* caused boils that break out in sores on man and beast. 11 And the magicians could not stand before Moses because of the boils, for the boils were on the magicians and on all the Egyptians. 12 But the LORD hardened the heart of Pharaoh; and he did not heed them, just as the LORD had spoken to Moses.

13 Then the LORD said to Moses, "Rise early in the morning and stand before Pharaoh, and say to him, 'Thus says the LORD God of the Hebrews: "Let My people go, that they may serve Me, 14 for at this time I will send all My plagues to your very heart, and on your servants and on your people, that you may know that *there is* none like Me in all the earth. 15 Now if I had stretched out My hand and struck you and your people with pestilence, then you would have been cut off from the earth. 16 But indeed for this *purpose* I have raised you up, that I may show My power *in* you, and that My name may be declared in all the earth. 17 As yet you exalt yourself against My people in that you will not let them go. 18 Behold, tomorrow about this time I will cause very heavy hail to rain down, such as has not been in Egypt since its founding until now. 19 Therefore send now *and* gather your livestock and all that you have in the field, for the hail shall come down on every man and every animal which is found in the field and is not brought home; and they shall die." ' "

20 He who feared the word of the LORD among the servants of Pharaoh made his servants and his livestock flee to the houses. 21 But he who did not regard the word of the LORD left his servants and his livestock in the field.

22 Then the LORD said to Moses, "Stretch out your hand toward heaven, that there may be hail in all the land of Egypt—on man, on beast, and on every herb of the field, throughout the land of Egypt." 23 And Moses stretched out his rod toward heaven; and the LORD sent thunder and hail, and fire darted to the ground. And the LORD rained hail on the land of Egypt. 24 So there was hail, and fire mingled with the hail, so very heavy that there was none like it in all the land of Egypt since it became a nation. 25 And the hail struck throughout the whole land of Egypt, all that *was* in the field, both man and beast; and the hail struck every herb of the field and broke

every tree of the field. 26 Only in the land of Goshen, where the children of Israel *were,* there was no hail.

27 And Pharaoh sent and called for Moses and Aaron, and said to them, "I have sinned this time. The LORD *is* righteous, and my people and I *are* wicked. 28 Entreat the LORD, that there may be no *more* mighty thundering and hail, for *it is* enough. I will let you go, and you shall stay no longer." 29 So Moses said to him, "As soon as I have gone out of the city, I will spread out my hands to the LORD; the thunder will cease, and there will be no more hail, that you may know that the earth *is* the LORD's. 30 But as for you and your servants, I know that you will not yet fear the LORD God."

31 Now the flax and the barley were struck, for the barley *was* in the head and the flax *was* in bud. 32 But the wheat and the spelt were not struck, for they *are* late crops.

33 So Moses went out of the city from Pharaoh and spread out his hands to the LORD; then the thunder and the hail ceased, and the rain was not poured on the earth. 34 And when Pharaoh saw that the rain, the hail, and the thunder had ceased, he sinned yet more; and he hardened his heart, he and his servants. 35 So the heart of Pharaoh was hard; neither would he let the children of Israel go, as the LORD had spoken by Moses.

10 NOW the LORD said to Moses, "Go in to Pharaoh; for I have hardened his heart and the hearts of his servants, that I may show these signs of Mine before him, 2 and that you may tell in the hearing of your son and your son's son the mighty things I have done in Egypt, and My signs which I have done among them, that you may know that I *am* the LORD."

3 So Moses and Aaron came in to Pharaoh and said to him, "Thus says the LORD God of the Hebrews: 'How long will you refuse to humble yourself before Me? Let My people go, that they may serve Me. 4 Or else, if you refuse to let My people go, behold, tomorrow I will bring locusts into your territory. 5 And they shall cover the face of the earth, so that no one will be able to see the earth; and they shall eat the residue of what is left, which remains to you from the hail, and they shall eat every tree which grows up for you out of the field. 6 They shall fill your houses, the houses of all your servants, and the houses of all the Egyptians—which neither your fathers nor your fathers' fathers have seen,

since the day that they were on the earth to this day.'" And he turned and went out from Pharaoh.

7 Then Pharaoh's servants said to him, "How long shall this man be a snare to us? Let the men go, that they may serve the LORD their God. Do you not yet know that Egypt is destroyed?"

8 So Moses and Aaron were brought again to Pharaoh, and he said to them, "Go, serve the LORD your God. Who *are* the ones that are going?"

9 And Moses said, "We will go with our young and our old; with our sons and our daughters, with our flocks and our herds we will go, for we must hold a feast to the LORD."

10 Then he said to them, "The LORD had better be with you when I let you and your little ones go! Beware, for evil is ahead of you. 11 Not so! Go now, you *who are* men, and serve the LORD, for that is what you desired." And they were driven out from Pharaoh's presence.

12 Then the LORD said to Moses, "Stretch out your hand over the land of Egypt for the locusts, that they may come upon the land of Egypt, and eat every herb of the land—all that the hail has left." 13 So Moses stretched out his rod over the land of Egypt, and the LORD brought an east wind on the land all that day and all *that* night. When it was morning, the east wind brought the locusts. 14 And the locusts went up over all the land of Egypt and rested on all the territory of Egypt. *They were* very severe; previously there had been no such locusts as they, nor shall there be such after them. 15 For they covered the face of the whole earth, so that the land was darkened; and they ate every herb of the land and all the fruit of the trees which the hail had left. So there remained nothing green on the trees or on the plants of the field throughout all the land of Egypt.

16 Then Pharaoh called for Moses and Aaron in haste, and said, "I have sinned against the LORD your God and against you. 17 Now therefore, please forgive my sin only this once, and entreat the LORD your God, that He may take away from me this death only." 18 So he went out from Pharaoh and entreated the LORD. 19 And the LORD turned a very strong west wind,

which took the locusts away and blew them into the Red Sea. There remained not one locust in all the territory of Egypt. 20 But the LORD hardened Pharaoh's heart, and he did not let the children of Israel go.

21 Then the LORD said to Moses, "Stretch out your hand toward heaven, that there may be darkness over the land of Egypt, darkness *which* may even be felt." 22 So Moses stretched out his hand toward heaven, and there was thick darkness in all the land of Egypt three days. 23 They did not see one another; nor did anyone rise from his place for three days. But all the children of Israel had light in their dwellings.

24 Then Pharaoh called to Moses and said, "Go, serve the LORD; only let your flocks and your herds be kept back. Let your little ones also go with you."

25 But Moses said, "You must also give us sacrifices and burnt offerings, that we may sacrifice to the LORD our God. 26 Our livestock also shall go with us; not a hoof shall be left behind. For we must take some of them to serve the LORD our God, and even we do not know with what we must serve the LORD until we arrive there."

27 But the LORD hardened Pharaoh's heart, and he would not let them go. 28 Then Pharaoh said to him, "Get away from me! Take heed to yourself and see my face no more! For in the day you see my face you shall die!"

29 So Moses said, "You have spoken well. I will never see your face again."

PSALM 17:8–15

8　KEEP me as the apple of Your eye;
　　Hide me under the shadow of Your
　　　　wings,
9　From the wicked who oppress me,
　　From my deadly enemies who surround
　　　　me.

10　They have closed up their fat *hearts;*
　　With their mouths they speak proudly.
11　They have now surrounded us in our
　　　　steps;
　　They have set their eyes, crouching
　　　　down to the earth,
12　As a lion is eager to tear his prey,
　　And like a young lion lurking in secret
　　　　places.

13　Arise, O LORD,
　　Confront him, cast him down;
　　Deliver my life from the wicked with
　　　　Your sword,

The thing that preserves a man from panic is his relationship to God. (RUN)

14 With Your hand from men, O LORD,
   From men of the world *who have* their
       portion in *this* life,
   And whose belly You fill with Your
       hidden treasure.
   They are satisfied with children,
   And leave the rest of their *possession* for
       their babes.

15 As for me, I will see Your face in
       righteousness;
   I shall be satisfied when I awake in Your
       likeness.

PROVERBS 5:21–23

21 FOR the ways of man *are* before the
       eyes of the LORD,
   And He ponders all his paths.
22 His own iniquities entrap the wicked
   man,
   And he is caught in the cords of his
       sin.
23 He shall die for lack of instruction,
   And in the greatness of his folly he shall
       go astray.

MATTHEW 20:1–16

"FOR the kingdom of heaven is like a landowner who went out early in the morning to hire laborers for his vineyard. 2 Now when he had agreed with the laborers for a denarius a day, he sent them into his vineyard. 3 And he went out about the third hour and saw others standing idle in the marketplace, 4 and said to them, 'You also go into the vineyard, and whatever is right I will give you.' So they went. 5 Again he went out about the sixth and the ninth hour, and did likewise. 6 And about the eleventh hour he went out and found others standing idle, and said to them, 'Why have you been standing here idle all day?' 7 They said to him, 'Because no one hired us.' He said to them, 'You also go into the vineyard, and whatever is right you will receive.'

8 "So when evening had come, the owner of the vineyard said to his steward, 'Call the laborers and give them *their* wages, beginning with the last to the first.' 9 And when those came who *were hired* about the eleventh hour, they each received a denarius. 10 But when the first came, they supposed that they would receive more; and they likewise received each a denarius. 11 And when they had received *it,* they complained against the landowner, 12 saying, 'These last *men* have worked *only* one hour, and you made them equal to us who have borne the burden and the heat of the day.' 13 But he answered one of them and said, 'Friend, I am doing you no wrong. Did you not agree with me for a denarius? 14 Take *what is* yours and go your way. I wish to give to this last man *the same* as to you. 15 Is it not lawful for me to do what I wish with my own things? Or is your eye evil because I am good?' 16 So the last will be first, and the first last. For many are called, but few chosen."

*F*ew *prove themselves the chosen ones.*   (UTMOST)

Reading 31—The Desire to Serve
Matthew 20:22

The disciples would have gone to any length to prove their devotion to Jesus. It was true devotion, but it wilted because it was based on an entire ignorance of themselves. In the end they "all forsook Him and fled," not because they wanted to, but because they did not know how to go on. Jesus put the disciples through crises to reveal them to themselves and bring them to the place of receiving the Holy Spirit. They could not see their need to receive the Holy Spirit until they found out that they were spiritual paupers. "Simon, Simon! Indeed, Satan has asked for you, that he may sift *you* as wheat" (Luke 22:31). Jesus allowed Peter to go over a moral precipice and deny that he ever knew Him before Peter realized what it was that kept him from being a disciple. It is not necessary for everyone to go the way of Peter's sifting, but the sifting must come in some form or other. The preaching of the gospel of temperament will not do for the making of disciples; nor will Jesus shield us in the slightest degree from any of the requirements of discipleship.

(*LOVE OF GOD*)

EXODUS 11:1—12:51

AND the LORD said to Moses, "I will bring one more plague on Pharaoh and on Egypt. Afterward he will let you go from here. When he lets *you* go, he will surely drive you out of here altogether. 2 Speak now in the hearing of the people, and let every man ask from his neighbor and every woman from her neighbor, articles of silver and articles of gold." 3 And the LORD gave the people favor in the sight of the Egyptians. Moreover the man Moses *was* very great in the land of Egypt, in the sight of Pharaoh's servants and in the sight of the people.

4 Then Moses said, "Thus says the LORD: 'About midnight I will go out into the midst of Egypt; 5 and all the firstborn in the land of Egypt shall die, from the firstborn of Pharaoh who sits on his throne, even to the firstborn of the female servant who *is* behind the handmill, and all the firstborn of the animals. 6 Then there shall be a great cry throughout all the land of Egypt, such as was not like it *before,* nor shall be like it again. 7 But against none of the children of Israel shall a dog move its tongue, against man or beast, that you may know that the LORD does make a difference between the Egyptians and Israel.' 8 And all these your servants shall come down to me and bow down to me, saying, 'Get out, and all the people who follow you!' After that I will go out." Then he went out from Pharaoh in great anger.

9 But the LORD said to Moses, "Pharaoh will not heed you, so that My wonders may be multiplied in the land of Egypt." 10 So Moses and Aaron did all these wonders before Pharaoh; and the LORD hardened Pharaoh's heart, and he did not let the children of Israel go out of his land.

12 NOW the LORD spoke to Moses and Aaron in the land of Egypt, saying, 2 "This month *shall be* your beginning of months; it *shall be* the first month of the year to you. 3 Speak to all the congregation of Israel, saying: 'On the tenth of this month every man shall take for himself a lamb, according to the house of *his* father, a lamb for a household. 4 And if the house-

hold is too small for the lamb, let him and his neighbor next to his house take *it* according to the number of the persons; according to each man's need you shall make your count for the lamb. 5 Your lamb shall be without blemish, a male of the first year. You may take *it* from the sheep or from the goats. 6 Now you shall keep it until the fourteenth day of the same month. Then the whole assembly of the congregation of Israel shall kill it at twilight. 7 And they shall take *some* of the blood and put *it* on the two doorposts and on the lintel of the houses where they eat it. 8 Then they shall eat the flesh on that night; roasted in fire, with unleavened bread *and* with bitter *herbs* they shall eat it. 9 Do not eat it raw, nor boiled at all with water, but roasted in fire— its head with its legs and its entrails. 10 You shall let none of it remain until morning, and what remains of it until morning you shall burn with fire. 11 And thus you shall eat it: *with* a belt on your waist, your sandals on your feet, and your staff in your hand. So you shall eat it in haste. It *is* the LORD's Passover.

12 'For I will pass through the land of Egypt on that night, and will strike all the firstborn in the land of Egypt, both man and beast; and against all the gods of Egypt I will execute judgment: I *am* the LORD. 13 Now the blood shall be a sign for you on the houses where you *are.* And when I see the blood, I will pass over you; and the plague shall not be on you to destroy *you* when I strike the land of Egypt.

14 'So this day shall be to you a memorial; and you shall keep it as a feast to the LORD throughout your generations. You shall keep it as a feast by an everlasting ordinance. 15 Seven days you shall eat unleavened bread. On the first day you shall remove leaven from your houses. For whoever eats leavened bread from the first day until the seventh day, that person shall be cut off from Israel. 16 On the first day *there shall be* a holy convocation, and on the seventh day there shall be a holy convocation for you. No manner of work shall be done on them; but *that* which everyone must eat— that only may be prepared by you. 17 So you shall observe *the Feast of* Unleavened Bread, for on this same day I will have brought your armies out of the land

of Egypt. Therefore you shall observe this day throughout your generations as an everlasting ordinance. 18 In the first *month,* on the fourteenth day of the month at evening, you shall eat unleavened bread, until the twenty-first day of the month at evening. 19 For seven days no leaven shall be found in your houses, since whoever eats what is leavened, that same person shall be cut off from the congregation of Israel, whether *he is* a stranger or a native of the land. 20 You shall eat nothing leavened; in all your dwellings you shall eat unleavened bread.' "

21 Then Moses called for all the elders of Israel and said to them, "Pick out and take lambs for yourselves according to your families, and kill the Passover *lamb.* 22 And you shall take a bunch of hyssop, dip *it* in the blood that *is* in the basin, and strike the lintel and the two doorposts with the blood that *is* in the basin. And none of you shall go out of the door of his house until morning. 23 For the LORD will pass through to strike the Egyptians; and when He sees the blood on the lintel and on the two doorposts, the LORD will pass over the door and not allow the destroyer to come into your houses to strike *you.* 24 And you shall observe this thing as an ordinance for you and your sons forever. 25 It will come to pass when you come to the land which the LORD will give you, just as He promised, that you shall keep this service. 26 And it shall be, when your children say to you, 'What do you mean by this service?' 27 that you shall say, 'It *is* the Passover sacrifice of the LORD, who passed over the houses of the children of Israel in Egypt when He struck the Egyptians and delivered our households.' " So the people bowed their heads and worshiped. 28 Then the children of Israel went away and did *so;* just as the LORD had commanded Moses and Aaron, so they did.

29 And it came to pass at midnight that the LORD struck all the firstborn in the land of Egypt, from the firstborn of Pharaoh who sat on his throne to the firstborn of the captive who *was* in the dungeon, and all the firstborn of livestock. 30 So Pharaoh rose in the night, he, all his servants, and all the Egyptians; and there was a great cry in Egypt, for *there was* not a house where *there was* not one dead. 31 Then he called for Moses and Aaron by night, and said, "Rise, go out from among my people, both you and the children of Israel. And go, serve the LORD as you have said. 32 Also take your flocks and your herds, as you have said, and be gone; and bless me also."

33 And the Egyptians urged the people, that they might send them out of the land in haste. For they said, "We *shall* all *be* dead." 34 So the people took their dough before it was leavened, having their kneading bowls bound up in their clothes on their shoulders. 35 Now the children of Israel had done according to the word of Moses, and they had asked from the Egyptians articles of silver, articles of gold, and clothing. 36 And the LORD had given the people favor in the sight of the Egyptians, so that they granted them *what they requested.* Thus they plundered the Egyptians.

37 Then the children of Israel journeyed from Rameses to Succoth, about six hundred thousand men on foot, besides children. 38 A mixed multitude went up with them also, and flocks and herds—a great deal of livestock. 39 And they baked unleavened cakes of the dough which they had brought out of Egypt; for it was not leavened, because they were driven out of Egypt and could not wait, nor had they prepared provisions for themselves.

40 Now the sojourn of the children of Israel who lived in Egypt *was* four hundred and thirty years. 41 And it came to pass at the end of the four hundred and thirty years—on that very same day—it came to pass that all the armies of the LORD went out from the land of Egypt. 42 It *is* a night of solemn observance to the LORD for bringing them out of the land of Egypt. This *is* that night of the LORD, a solemn observance for all the children of Israel throughout their generations.

43 And the LORD said to Moses and Aaron, "This *is* the ordinance of the Passover: No foreigner shall eat it. 44 But every man's servant who is bought for money, when you have circumcised him, then he may eat it. 45 A sojourner and a hired servant shall not eat it. 46 In one house it shall be eaten; you shall not carry any of the flesh outside the house, nor shall you break one of its bones. 47 All the congregation of Israel shall keep it. 48 And when a stranger dwells with you *and wants* to keep the Passover to the LORD, let all his males be circumcised, and then let him come near and keep it; and he shall be as a native of the land. For no uncircumcised person shall eat it. 49 One law shall be for the native-born and for the stranger who dwells among you."

50 Thus all the children of Israel did; as the LORD commanded Moses and Aaron, so they did. 51 And it came to pass, on that very same day, that the LORD brought

the children of Israel out of the land of Egypt according to their armies.

PSALM 18:1–12

1 I will love You, O LORD, my strength.
2 The LORD is my rock and my fortress
     and my deliverer;
   My God, my strength, in whom I will
     trust;
   My shield and the horn of my salvation,
     my stronghold.
3 I will call upon the LORD, *who is worthy*
     to be praised;
   So shall I be saved from my enemies.

4 The pangs of death surrounded me,
   And the floods of ungodliness made
     me afraid.
5 The sorrows of Sheol surrounded me;
   The snares of death confronted me.
6 In my distress I called upon the LORD,
   And cried out to my God;
   He heard my voice from His temple,
   And my cry came before Him, *even* to
     His ears.

7 Then the earth shook and trembled;
   The foundations of the hills also quaked
     and were shaken,
   Because He was angry.
8 Smoke went up from His nostrils,
   And devouring fire from His mouth;
   Coals were kindled by it.
9 He bowed the heavens also, and came
     down
   With darkness under His feet.
10 And He rode upon a cherub, and flew;
   He flew upon the wings of the wind.
11 He made darkness His secret place;
   His canopy around Him *was* dark
     waters
   And thick clouds of the skies.

---

*G*od *is in secret, and He sees us from
   the secret place.*   (UTMOST)

---

12 From the brightness before Him,
   His thick clouds passed with hailstones
     and coals of fire.

PROVERBS 6:1–5

1 MY son, if you become surety for your
     friend,
   If you have shaken hands in pledge for
     a stranger,

2 You are snared by the words of your
     mouth;
   You are taken by the words of your
     mouth.
3 So do this, my son, and deliver yourself;
   For you have come into the hand of
     your friend:
   Go and humble yourself;
   Plead with your friend.
4 Give no sleep to your eyes,
   Nor slumber to your eyelids.
5 Deliver yourself like a gazelle from the
     hand *of the hunter,*
   And like a bird from the hand of the
     fowler.

MATTHEW 20:17–34

NOW Jesus, going up to Jerusalem, took the twelve disciples aside on the road and said to them, 18 "Behold, we are going up to Jerusalem, and the Son of Man will be betrayed to the chief priests and to the scribes; and they will condemn Him to death, 19 and deliver Him to the Gentiles to mock and to scourge and to crucify. And the third day He will rise again."

20 Then the mother of Zebedee's sons came to Him with her sons, kneeling down and asking something from Him.

21 And He said to her, "What do you wish?"

She said to Him, "Grant that these two sons of mine may sit, one on Your right hand and the other on the left, in Your kingdom."

22 But Jesus answered and said, "You do not know what you ask. Are you able to drink the cup that I am about to drink, and be baptized with the baptism that I am baptized with?"

They said to Him, "We are able."

23 So He said to them, "You will indeed drink My cup, and be baptized with the baptism that I am baptized with; but to sit on My right hand and on My left is not Mine to give, but *it is for those* for whom it is prepared by My Father."

24 And when the ten heard *it,* they were greatly displeased with the two brothers. 25 But Jesus called them to *Himself* and said, "You know that the rulers of the Gentiles lord it over them, and those who are great exercise authority over them. 26 Yet it shall not be so among you; but whoever desires to become great among you, let him be your servant. 27 And whoever desires to be first among you, let him be your slave— 28 just as the Son of Man did not come to

be served, but to serve, and to give His life a ransom for many."

29 Now as they went out of Jericho, a great multitude followed Him. 30 And behold, two blind men sitting by the road, when they heard that Jesus was passing by, cried out, saying, "Have mercy on us, O Lord, Son of David!"

31 Then the multitude warned them that they should be quiet; but they cried out all the more, saying, "Have mercy on us, O Lord, Son of David!"

32 So Jesus stood still and called them,

God loves the man who needs Him.   (GENESIS)

and said, "What do you want Me to do for you?"

33 They said to Him, "Lord, that our eyes may be opened." 34 So Jesus had compassion and touched their eyes. And immediately their eyes received sight, and they followed Him.

◆◆◆

Reading 32—Cross the Red Sea
Exodus 14:11–14

I am impressed with the wonder of what God says, but He cannot expect me really to live it out in the details of my life!" When it comes to facing Jesus Christ on His own merits, our attitude is one of pious superiority—Your ideals are high and they impress us, but in touch with actual things, it cannot be done. Each of us thinks about Jesus in this way in some particular. . . . It is all very well to say "Trust in the Lord," but a man must live, and Jesus has nothing to draw with—nothing whereby to give us these things. Beware of the pious fraud in you which says—I have no misgivings about Jesus, only about myself. None of us ever had misgivings about ourselves; we know exactly what we cannot do, but we do have misgivings about Jesus. We are rather hurt at the idea that He can do what we cannot.

My misgivings arise from the fact that I ransack my own person to find out how He will be able to do it. My questions spring from the depths of my own inferiority. If I detect these misgivings in myself, let me bring them to the light and confess them—"Lord, I have had misgivings about You, I have not believed in Your wits apart from my own; I have not believed in Your almighty power apart from my finite understanding of it."   (*UTMOST*)

EXODUS 13:1—14:31

THEN the LORD spoke to Moses, saying, 2 "Consecrate to Me all the firstborn, whatever opens the womb among the children of Israel, *both* of man and beast; it is Mine."

3 And Moses said to the people: "Remember this day in which you went out of Egypt, out of the house of bondage; for by strength of hand the LORD brought you out of this *place*. No leavened bread shall be eaten. 4 On this day you are going out, in the month Abib. 5 And it shall be, when the LORD brings you into the land of the Canaanites and the Hittites and the Amorites and the Hivites and the Jebusites, which He swore to your fathers to give

you, a land flowing with milk and honey, that you shall keep this service in this month. 6 Seven days you shall eat unleavened bread, and on the seventh day *there shall be* a feast to the LORD. 7 Unleavened bread shall be eaten seven days. And no leavened bread shall be seen among you, nor shall leaven be seen among you in all your quarters. 8 And you shall tell your son in that day, saying, '*This is done* because of what the LORD did for me when I came up from Egypt.' 9 It shall be as a sign to you on your hand and as a memorial between your eyes, that the LORD's law may be in your mouth; for with a strong hand the LORD has brought you out of Egypt. 10 You shall therefore keep this ordinance in its season from year to year.

11 "And it shall be, when the Lord brings you into the land of the Canaanites, as He swore to you and your fathers, and gives it to you, 12 that you shall set apart to the Lord all that open the womb, that is, every firstborn that comes from an animal which you have; the males *shall be* the Lord's. 13 But every firstborn of a donkey you shall redeem with a lamb; and if you will not redeem *it,* then you shall break its neck. And all the firstborn of man among your sons you shall redeem. 14 So it shall be, when your son asks you in time to come, saying, 'What *is* this?' that you shall say to him, 'By strength of hand the Lord brought us out of Egypt, out of the house of bondage. 15 And it came to pass, when Pharaoh was stubborn about letting us go, that the Lord killed all the firstborn in the land of Egypt, both the firstborn of man and the firstborn of beast. Therefore I sacrifice to the Lord all males that open the womb, but all the firstborn of my sons I redeem.' 16 It shall be as a sign on your hand and as frontlets between your eyes, for by strength of hand the Lord brought us out of Egypt."

17 Then it came to pass, when Pharaoh had let the people go, that God did not lead them *by* way of the land of the Philistines, although that *was* near; for God said, "Lest perhaps the people change their minds when they see war, and return to Egypt."

When we are related to God, He guards from dangers seen and unseen.   (SHADE)

---

18 So God led the people around *by* way of the wilderness of the Red Sea. And the children of Israel went up in orderly ranks out of the land of Egypt.

19 And Moses took the bones of Joseph with him, for he had placed the children of Israel under solemn oath, saying, "God will surely visit you, and you shall carry up my bones from here with you."

20 So they took their journey from Succoth and camped in Etham at the edge of the wilderness. 21 And the Lord went before them by day in a pillar of cloud to lead the way, and by night in a pillar of fire to give them light, so as to go by day and night. 22 He did not take away the pillar of cloud by day or the pillar of fire by night *from* before the people.

14 NOW the Lord spoke to Moses, saying: 2 "Speak to the children of Israel, that they turn and camp before Pi Hahiroth, between Migdol and the sea, opposite Baal Zephon; you shall camp before it by the sea. 3 For Pharaoh will say of the children of Israel, 'They *are* bewildered by the land; the wilderness has closed them in.' 4 Then I will harden Pharaoh's heart, so that he will pursue them; and I will gain honor over Pharaoh and over all his army, that the Egyptians may know that I *am* the Lord." And they did so.

5 Now it was told the king of Egypt that the people had fled, and the heart of Pharaoh and his servants was turned against the people; and they said, "Why have we done this, that we have let Israel go from serving us?" 6 So he made ready his chariot and took his people with him. 7 Also, he took six hundred choice chariots, and all the chariots of Egypt with captains over every one of them. 8 And the Lord hardened the heart of Pharaoh king of Egypt, and he pursued the children of Israel; and the children of Israel went out with boldness. 9 So the Egyptians pursued them, all the horses *and* chariots of Pharaoh, his horsemen and his army, and overtook them camping by the sea beside Pi Hahiroth, before Baal Zephon.

10 And when Pharaoh drew near, the children of Israel lifted their eyes, and behold, the Egyptians marched after them. So they were very afraid, and the children of Israel cried out to the Lord. 11 Then they said to Moses, "Because *there were* no graves in Egypt, have you taken us away to die in the wilderness? Why have you so dealt with us, to bring us up out of Egypt? 12 *Is* this not the word that we told you in Egypt, saying, 'Let us alone that we may serve the Egyptians'? For *it would have been* better for us to serve the Egyptians than that we should die in the wilderness."

13 And Moses said to the people, "Do not be afraid. Stand still, and see the salvation of the Lord, which He will accomplish for you today. For the Egyptians whom you see today, you shall see again no more forever. 14 The Lord will fight for you, and you shall hold your peace."

15 And the Lord said to Moses, "Why do you cry to Me? Tell the children of Israel to go forward. 16 But lift up your rod, and stretch out your hand over the sea and divide it. And the children of Israel shall go on dry *ground* through the midst of the sea. 17 And I indeed will harden the hearts of the Egyptians, and they shall follow

them. So I will gain honor over Pharaoh and over all his army, his chariots, and his horsemen. 18 Then the Egyptians shall know that I *am* the LORD, when I have gained honor for Myself over Pharaoh, his chariots, and his horsemen."

19 And the Angel of God, who went before the camp of Israel, moved and went behind them; and the pillar of cloud went from before them and stood behind them. 20 So it came between the camp of the Egyptians and the camp of Israel. Thus it was a cloud and darkness *to the one,* and it gave light by night *to the other,* so that the one did not come near the other all that night.

21 Then Moses stretched out his hand over the sea; and the LORD caused the sea to go *back* by a strong east wind all that night, and made the sea into dry *land,* and the waters were divided. 22 So the children of Israel went into the midst of the sea on the dry *ground,* and the waters *were* a wall to them on their right hand and on their left. 23 And the Egyptians pursued and went after them into the midst of the sea, all Pharaoh's horses, his chariots, and his horsemen.

24 Now it came to pass, in the morning watch, that the LORD looked down upon the army of the Egyptians through the pillar of fire and cloud, and He troubled the army of the Egyptians. 25 And He took off their chariot wheels, so that they drove them with difficulty; and the Egyptians said, "Let us flee from the face of Israel, for the LORD fights for them against the Egyptians."

26 Then the LORD said to Moses, "Stretch out your hand over the sea, that the waters may come back upon the Egyptians, on their chariots, and on their horsemen." 27 And Moses stretched out his hand over the sea; and when the morning appeared, the sea returned to its full depth, while the Egyptians were fleeing into it. So the LORD overthrew the Egyptians in the midst of the sea. 28 Then the waters returned and covered the chariots, the horsemen, *and* all the army of Pharaoh that came into the sea after them. Not so much as one of them remained. 29 But the children of Israel had walked on dry *land* in the midst of the sea, and the waters *were* a wall to them on their right hand and on their left.

30 So the LORD saved Israel that day out of the hand of the Egyptians, and Israel saw the Egyptians dead on the seashore. 31 Thus Israel saw the great work which the LORD had done in Egypt; so the people feared the LORD, and believed the LORD and His servant Moses.

PSALM 18:13–19

13 THE LORD thundered from heaven,
And the Most High uttered His voice,
Hailstones and coals of fire.
14 He sent out His arrows and scattered the foe,
Lightnings in abundance, and He vanquished them.
15 Then the channels of the sea were seen,
The foundations of the world were uncovered
At Your rebuke, O LORD,
At the blast of the breath of Your nostrils.
16 He sent from above, He took me;
He drew me out of many waters.
17 He delivered me from my strong enemy,
From those who hated me,
For they were too strong for me.
18 They confronted me in the day of my calamity,
But the LORD was my support.
19 He also brought me out into a broad place;
He delivered me because He delighted in me.

PROVERBS 6:6–11

6 GO to the ant, you sluggard!
Consider her ways and be wise,
7 Which, having no captain,
Overseer or ruler,
8 Provides her supplies in the summer,
And gathers her food in the harvest.
9 How long will you slumber, O sluggard?
When will you rise from your sleep?
10 A little sleep, a little slumber,
A little folding of the hands to sleep—
11 So shall your poverty come on you like a prowler,
And your need like an armed man.

MATTHEW 21:1–22

NOW when they drew near Jerusalem, and came to Bethphage, at the Mount of Olives, then Jesus sent two disciples, 2 saying to them, "Go into the village opposite you, and immediately you will find a donkey tied, and a colt with her. Loose *them* and bring *them* to Me. 3 And if anyone says anything to you, you shall say, 'The Lord has need of them,' and immediately he will send them."

4 All this was done that it might be fulfilled which was spoken by the prophet, saying:

5 "Tell the daughter of Zion,
  'Behold, your King is coming to you,
  Lowly, and sitting on a donkey,
  A colt, the foal of a donkey.' "

6 So the disciples went and did as Jesus commanded them. 7 They brought the donkey and the colt, laid their clothes on them, and set *Him* on them. 8 And a very great multitude spread their clothes on the road; others cut down branches from the trees and spread *them* on the road. 9 Then the multitudes who went before and those who followed cried out, saying:

  "Hosanna to the Son of David!
  'Blessed *is* He who comes in the name of the LORD!'
  Hosanna in the highest!"

10 And when He had come into Jerusalem, all the city was moved, saying, "Who is this?"
11 So the multitudes said, "This is Jesus, the prophet from Nazareth of Galilee."
12 Then Jesus went into the temple of God and drove out all those who bought and sold in the temple, and overturned the tables of the money changers and the seats of those who sold doves. 13 And He said to them, "It is written, 'My house shall be called a house of prayer,' but you have made it a 'den of thieves.' "
14 Then *the* blind and *the* lame came to Him in the temple, and He healed them.

15 But when the chief priests and scribes saw the wonderful things that He did, and the children crying out in the temple and saying, "Hosanna to the Son of David!" they were indignant 16 and said to Him, "Do You hear what these are saying?"
    And Jesus said to them, "Yes. Have you never read,

  'Out of the mouth of babes and nursing infants
  You have perfected praise'? "

---

*O*nly a child gets prayer answered; a wise man does not.   (UTMOST)

---

17 Then He left them and went out of the city to Bethany, and He lodged there.
18 Now in the morning, as He returned to the city, He was hungry. 19 And seeing a fig tree by the road, He came to it and found nothing on it but leaves, and said to it, "Let no fruit grow on you ever again." Immediately the fig tree withered away.
20 And when the disciples saw *it,* they marveled, saying, "How did the fig tree wither away so soon?"
21 So Jesus answered and said to them, "Assuredly, I say to you, if you have faith and do not doubt, you will not only do what was done to the fig tree, but also if you say to this mountain, 'Be removed and be cast into the sea,' it will be done.
22 And whatever things you ask in prayer, believing, you will receive."

◆◆◆

Reading 33—The Very Essence of Sin
Matthew 21:31

Read the New Testament, and you will find that Jesus Christ did not get into a moral panic over the things that rouse us. We are staggered at immorality, but Jesus faced those things in the most amazingly calm way. When He was roused to a state of passionate indignation it was by people who were never guilty of such things. What our Lord continually faced was the disposition behind either the morality or the immorality. "If I had not come and spoken to them, they would have no sin . . ." (John 15:22). Any man would have known without His coming that it was wrong to take life, the law is written in him; any man would have known that immorality was wrong; but no man apart from Jesus Christ would believe that "my right to myself" is the very essence of sin. When we realize what Jesus means when He says, "If you would be My disciple, give up your right to yourself to Me," we begin to understand that "the carnal mind *is* enmity against God." "I will not give up my right to myself; I will serve God as I choose." Jesus Christ came to remove this disposition of self-realization.   (*GLORY*)

EXODUS 15:1—16:36

THEN Moses and the children of Israel sang this song to the LORD, and spoke, saying:

> "I will sing to the LORD,
> For He has triumphed gloriously!
> The horse and its rider
> He has thrown into the sea!
> 2 The LORD *is* my strength and song,
> And He has become my salvation;
> He *is* my God, and I will praise Him;
> My father's God, and I will exalt Him.

The true joy of a man's life is in his relationship to God.   (SHADE)

---

3 The LORD *is* a man of war;
  The LORD *is* His name.
4 Pharaoh's chariots and his army He
  has cast into the sea;
  His chosen captains also are drowned
  in the Red Sea.
5 The depths have covered them;
  They sank to the bottom like a stone.

6 "Your right hand, O LORD, has
  become glorious in power;
  Your right hand, O LORD, has dashed
  the enemy in pieces.
7 And in the greatness of Your
  excellence
  You have overthrown those who rose
  against You;
  You sent forth Your wrath;
  It consumed them like stubble.
8 And with the blast of Your nostrils
  The waters were gathered together;
  The floods stood upright like a heap;
  The depths congealed in the heart
  of the sea.
9 The enemy said, 'I will pursue,
  I will overtake,
  I will divide the spoil;
  My desire shall be satisfied on them.
  I will draw my sword,
  My hand shall destroy them.'
10 You blew with Your wind,
  The sea covered them;
  They sank like lead in the mighty
  waters.

11 "Who *is* like You, O LORD, among
  the gods?
  Who *is* like You, glorious in holiness,
  Fearful in praises, doing wonders?
12 You stretched out Your right hand;
  The earth swallowed them.
13 You in Your mercy have led forth
  The people whom You have
  redeemed;
  You have guided *them* in Your
  strength
  To Your holy habitation.

14 "The people will hear *and* be afraid;
  Sorrow will take hold of the
  inhabitants of Philistia.
15 Then the chiefs of Edom will be
  dismayed;
  The mighty men of Moab,
  Trembling will take hold of them;
  All the inhabitants of Canaan will
  melt away.
16 Fear and dread will fall on them;
  By the greatness of Your arm
  They will be *as* still as a stone,
  Till Your people pass over, O LORD,
  Till the people pass over
  Whom You have purchased.
17 You will bring them in and plant
  them
  In the mountain of Your inheritance,
  In the place, O LORD, *which* You have
  made
  For Your own dwelling,
  The sanctuary, O LORD, *which* Your
  hands have established.

18 "The LORD shall reign forever and
  ever."

19 For the horses of Pharaoh went with his chariots and his horsemen into the sea, and the LORD brought back the waters of the sea upon them. But the children of Israel went on dry *land* in the midst of the sea. 20 Then Miriam the prophetess, the sister of Aaron, took the timbrel in her hand; and all the women went out after her with timbrels and with dances. 21 And Miriam answered them:

> "Sing to the LORD,
> For He has triumphed gloriously!
> The horse and its rider
> He has thrown into the sea!"

22 So Moses brought Israel from the Red Sea; then they went out into the Wilderness of Shur. And they went three days in the wilderness and found no water. 23 Now when they came to Marah, they could not drink the waters of Marah, for they *were* bitter. Therefore the name of it was called Marah. 24 And the people complained against Moses, saying, "What shall we drink?" 25 So he cried out to the LORD, and the LORD showed him a tree. When he cast *it* into the waters, the waters were made sweet.

There He made a statute and an ordinance for them, and there He tested them, 26 and said, "If you diligently heed the voice of the LORD your God and do what is right in His sight, give ear to His commandments and keep all His statutes, I will put none of the diseases on you which I have brought on the Egyptians. For I *am* the LORD who heals you."

27 Then they came to Elim, where there *were* twelve wells of water and seventy palm trees; so they camped there by the waters.

16 AND they journeyed from Elim, and all the congregation of the children of Israel came to the Wilderness of Sin, which is between Elim and Sinai, on the fifteenth day of the second month after they departed from the land of Egypt. 2 Then the whole congregation of the children of Israel complained against Moses and Aaron in the wilderness. 3 And the children of Israel said to them, "Oh, that we had died by the hand of the LORD in the land of Egypt, when we sat by the pots of meat *and* when we ate bread to the full! For you have brought us out into this wilderness to kill this whole assembly with hunger."

4 Then the LORD said to Moses, "Behold, I will rain bread from heaven for you. And the people shall go out and gather a certain quota every day, that I may test them, whether they will walk in My law or not. 5 And it shall be on the sixth day that they shall prepare what they bring in, and it shall be twice as much as they gather daily."

6 Then Moses and Aaron said to all the children of Israel, "At evening you shall know that the LORD has brought you out of the land of Egypt; 7 And in the morning you shall see the glory of the LORD; for He hears your complaints against the LORD. But what *are* we, that you complain against us?" 8 Also Moses said, "*This shall be seen* when the LORD gives you meat to eat in the evening, and in the morning bread to the full; for the LORD hears your complaints

which you make against Him. And what *are* we? Your complaints *are* not against us but against the LORD."

9 Then Moses spoke to Aaron, "Say to all the congregation of the children of Israel, 'Come near before the LORD, for He has heard your complaints.' " 10 Now it came to pass, as Aaron spoke to the whole congregation of the children of Israel, that they looked toward the wilderness, and behold, the glory of the LORD appeared in the cloud.

11 And the LORD spoke to Moses, saying, 12 "I have heard the complaints of the children of Israel. Speak to them, saying, 'At twilight you shall eat meat, and in the morning you shall be filled with bread. And you shall know that I *am* the LORD your God.' "

13 So it was that quails came up at evening and covered the camp, and in the morning the dew lay all around the camp. 14 And when the layer of dew lifted, there, on the surface of the wilderness, was a small round substance, *as* fine as frost on the ground. 15 So when the children of Israel saw *it,* they said to one another, "What is it?" For they did not know what it *was.*

And Moses said to them, "This *is* the bread which the LORD has given you to eat. 16 This is the thing which the LORD has commanded: 'Let every man gather it according to each one's need, one omer for each person, *according to the* number of persons; let every man take for *those* who *are* in his tent.' "

17 Then the children of Israel did so and gathered, some more, some less. 18 So when they measured *it* by omers, he who gathered much had nothing left over, and he who gathered little had no lack. Every man had gathered according to each one's need. 19 And Moses said, "Let no one leave any of it till morning." 20 Notwithstanding they did not heed Moses. But some of them left part of it until morning, and it bred worms and stank. And Moses was angry with them. 21 So they gathered it every morning, every man according to his need. And when the sun became hot, it melted.

22 And so it was, on the sixth day, *that* they gathered twice as much bread, two omers for each one. And all the rulers of the congregation came and told Moses. 23 Then he said to them, "This *is what* the LORD has said: 'Tomorrow *is* a Sabbath rest, a holy Sabbath to the LORD. Bake what you will bake *today,* and boil what you will boil; and lay up for yourselves all that remains, to be kept until morning.' " 24 So they laid it up till morning, as Moses commanded; and it did not stink, nor were there any worms in it. 25 Then Moses said,

"Eat that today, for today *is* a Sabbath to the LORD; today you will not find it in the field. 26 Six days you shall gather it, but on the seventh day, the Sabbath, there will be none."

27 Now it happened *that some* of the people went out on the seventh day to gather, but they found none. 28 And the LORD said to Moses, "How long do you refuse to keep My commandments and My laws? 29 See! For the LORD has given you the Sabbath; therefore He gives you on the sixth day bread for two days. Let every man remain in his place; let no man go out of his place on the seventh day." 30 So the people rested on the seventh day.

31 And the house of Israel called its name Manna. And it *was* like white coriander seed, and the taste of it *was* like wafers *made* with honey.

32 Then Moses said, "This *is* the thing which the LORD has commanded: 'Fill an omer with it, to be kept for your generations, that they may see the bread with which I fed you in the wilderness, when I brought you out of the land of Egypt.'" 33 And Moses said to Aaron, "Take a pot and put an omer of manna in it, and lay it up before the LORD, to be kept for your generations." 34 As the LORD commanded Moses, so Aaron laid it up before the Testimony, to be kept. 35 And the children of Israel ate manna forty years, until they came to an inhabited land; they ate manna until they came to the border of the land of Canaan. 36 Now an omer *is* one-tenth of an ephah.

PSALM 18:20–27

20 THE LORD rewarded me according to my righteousness;
   According to the cleanness of my hands He has recompensed me.
21 For I have kept the ways of the LORD,
   And have not wickedly departed from my God.
22 For all His judgments *were* before me,
   And I did not put away His statutes from me.
23 I was also blameless before Him,
   And I kept myself from my iniquity.
24 Therefore the LORD has recompensed me according to my righteousness,
   According to the cleanness of my hands in His sight.

25 With the merciful You will show Yourself merciful;

With a blameless man You will show Yourself blameless;
26 With the pure You will show Yourself pure;
   And with the devious You will show Yourself shrewd.
27 For You will save the humble people,
   But will bring down haughty looks.

PROVERBS 6:12–15

12 A worthless person, a wicked man,
   Walks with a perverse mouth;
13 He winks with his eyes,
   He shuffles his feet,
   He points with his fingers;
14 Perversity *is* in his heart,
   He devises evil continually,
   He sows discord.
15 Therefore his calamity shall come suddenly;
   Suddenly he shall be broken without remedy.

MATTHEW 21:23–46

NOW when He came into the temple, the chief priests and the elders of the people confronted Him as He was teaching, and said, "By what authority are You doing these things? And who gave You this authority?"

24 But Jesus answered and said to them, "I also will ask you one thing, which if you tell Me, I likewise will tell you by what authority I do these things: 25 The baptism of John—where was it from? From heaven or from men?"

And they reasoned among themselves, saying, "If we say, 'From heaven,' He will say to us, 'Why then did you not believe him?' 26 But if we say, 'From men,' we fear the multitude, for all count John as a prophet." 27 So they answered Jesus and said, "We do not know."

And He said to them, "Neither will I tell you by what authority I do these things.

28 "But what do you think? A man had two sons, and he came to the first and said, 'Son, go, work today in my vineyard.' 29 He answered and said, 'I will not,' but afterward he regretted it and went. 30 Then he came to the second and said likewise. And he answered and said, 'I *go*, sir,' but he did not go. 31 Which of the two did the will of *his* father?"

They said to Him, "The first."

Jesus said to them, "Assuredly, I say to you that tax collectors and harlots enter the kingdom of God before you. 32 For John came to you in the way of righteousness, and you did not believe him; but tax collectors and harlots believed him; and when you saw *it,* you did not afterward relent and believe him.

33 "Hear another parable: There was a certain landowner who planted a vineyard and set a hedge around it, dug a winepress in it and built a tower. And he leased it to vinedressers and went into a far country. 34 Now when vintage-time drew near, he sent his servants to the vinedressers, that they might receive its fruit. 35 And the vinedressers took his servants, beat one, killed one, and stoned another. 36 Again he sent other servants, more than the first, and they did likewise to them. 37 Then last of all he sent his son to them, saying, 'They will respect my son.' 38 But when the vinedressers saw the son, they said among themselves, 'This is the heir. Come, let us kill him and seize his inheritance.' 39 So they took him and cast *him* out of the vineyard and killed *him.*

40 "Therefore, when the owner of the vineyard comes, what will he do to those vinedressers?"

41 They said to Him, "He will destroy those wicked men miserably, and lease *his*

vineyard to other vinedressers who will render to him the fruits in their seasons."

42 Jesus said to them, "Have you never read in the Scriptures:

'The stone which the builders rejected
Has become the chief cornerstone.
This was the Lord's doing,
And it is marvelous in our eyes' ?

43 "Therefore I say to you, the kingdom of God will be taken from you and given to a nation bearing the fruits of it. 44 And whoever falls on this stone will be broken; but on whomever it falls, it will grind him to powder."

The gospel of Jesus Christ awakens an intense craving and an equally intense resentment.   (APPROVED)

---

45 Now when the chief priests and Pharisees heard His parables, they perceived that He was speaking of them. 46 But when they sought to lay hands on Him, they feared the multitudes, because they took Him for a prophet.

◆◆◆◆

Reading 34—Obey God
Matthew 22:21

The golden rule for understanding spiritually is not intellect, but obedience. If a man wants scientific knowledge, intellectual curiosity is his guide; but if he wants insight into what Jesus Christ teaches, he can only get it by obedience. If things are dark to me, then I may be sure there is something I will not do. Intellectual darkness comes through ignorance; spiritual darkness comes because of something I do not intend to obey.

No man ever receives a word from God without instantly being put to the test over it. We disobey and then wonder why we don't go on spiritually. "If when you come to the altar," said Jesus, "there you remember that your brother has something against you . . . don't say another word to Me, but first go and put that thing right." The teaching of Jesus hits us where we live. We cannot stand as humbugs before Him for one second. He educates us down to the scruple. The Spirit of God unearths the spirit of self-vindication; He makes us sensitive to things we never thought of before.

When Jesus brings a thing home by His word, don't shirk it. If you do, you will become a religious humbug. Watch the things you shrug your shoulders over, and you will know why you do not go on spiritually. *First go*—at the risk of being thought fanatical you must obey what God tells you.   (*UTMOST*)

EXODUS 17:1—18:27

THEN all the congregation of the children of Israel set out on their journey from the Wilderness of Sin, according to the commandment of the LORD, and camped in Rephidim; but *there was* no water for the people to drink. 2 Therefore the people contended with Moses, and said, "Give us water, that we may drink."

So Moses said to them, "Why do you contend with me? Why do you tempt the LORD?"

3 And the people thirsted there for water, and the people complained against Moses, and said, "Why *is* it you have brought us up out of Egypt, to kill us and our children and our livestock with thirst?"

4 So Moses cried out to the LORD, saying, "What shall I do with this people? They are almost ready to stone me!"

5 And the LORD said to Moses, "Go on before the people, and take with you some of the elders of Israel. Also take in your hand your rod with which you struck the river, and go. 6 Behold, I will stand before you there on the rock in Horeb; and you shall strike the rock, and water will come out of it, that the people may drink."

And Moses did so in the sight of the elders of Israel. 7 So he called the name of the place Massah and Meribah, because of the contention of the children of Israel, and because they tempted the LORD, saying, "Is the LORD among us or not?"

8 Now Amalek came and fought with Israel in Rephidim. 9 And Moses said to Joshua, "Choose us some men and go out, fight with Amalek. Tomorrow I will stand on the top of the hill with the rod of God in my hand." 10 So Joshua did as Moses said to him, and fought with Amalek. And Moses, Aaron, and Hur went up to the top of the hill. 11 And so it was, when Moses held up his hand, that Israel prevailed; and when he let down his hand, Amalek prevailed. 12 But Moses' hands *became* heavy; so they took a stone and put *it* under him, and he sat on it. And Aaron and Hur supported his hands, one on one side, and the other on the other side; and his hands were steady until the going down of the sun. 13 So Joshua defeated Amalek and his people with the edge of the sword.

14 Then the LORD said to Moses, "Write this *for* a memorial in the book and recount *it* in the hearing of Joshua, that I will utterly blot out the remembrance of Amalek from under heaven." 15 And Moses built an altar and called its name, The-LORD-Is-My-Banner; 16 for he said, "Because the LORD

has sworn: the LORD *will have* war with Amalek from generation to generation."

18 AND Jethro, the priest of Midian, Moses' father-in-law, heard of all that God had done for Moses and for Israel His people—that the LORD had brought Israel out of Egypt. 2 Then Jethro, Moses' father-in-law, took Zipporah, Moses' wife, after he had sent her back, 3 with her two sons, of whom the name of one *was* Gershom (for he said, "I have been a stranger in a foreign land") 4 and the name of the other *was* Eliezer (for *he said*, "The God of my father *was* my help, and delivered me from the sword of Pharaoh"); 5 and Jethro, Moses' father-in-law, came with his sons and his wife to Moses in the wilderness, where he was encamped at the mountain of God. 6 Now he had said to Moses, "I, your father-in-law Jethro, am coming to you with your wife and her two sons with her."

7 So Moses went out to meet his father-in-law, bowed down, and kissed him. And they asked each other about *their* well-being; and they went into the tent. 8 And Moses told his father-in-law all that the LORD had done to Pharaoh and to the Egyptians for Israel's sake, all the hardship that had come upon them on the way, and *how* the LORD had delivered them. 9 Then Jethro rejoiced for all the good which the LORD had done for Israel, whom He had delivered out of the hand of the Egyptians. 10 And Jethro said, "Blessed *be* the LORD, who has delivered you out of the hand of the Egyptians and out of the hand of Pharaoh, *and* who has delivered the people from under the hand of the Egyptians. 11 Now I know that the LORD *is* greater than all the gods; for in the very thing in which they behaved proudly, *He was* above them." 12 Then Jethro, Moses' father-in-law, took a burnt offering and *other* sacrifices *to offer* to God. And Aaron came with all the elders of Israel to eat bread with Moses' father-in-law before God.

13 And so it was, on the next day, that Moses sat to judge the people; and the people stood before Moses from morning until evening. 14 So when Moses' father-in-law saw all that he did for the people, he said, "What *is* this thing that you are doing for the people? Why do you alone sit, and all the people stand before you from morning until evening?"

15 And Moses said to his father-in-law, "Because the people come to me to inquire of God. 16 When they have a difficulty, they come to me, and I judge between one and

another; and I make known the statutes of God and His laws."

17 So Moses' father-in-law said to him, "The thing that you do *is* not good. 18 Both you and these people who *are* with you will surely wear yourselves out. For this thing *is* too much for you; you are not able to perform it by yourself. 19 Listen now to my voice; I will give you counsel, and God will be with you: Stand before God for the people, so that you may bring the difficulties to God. 20 And you shall teach them the statutes and the laws, and show them the way in which they must walk and the work they must do. 21 Moreover you shall select from all the people able men, such as fear God, men of truth, hating covetousness; and place *such* over them *to be* rulers of thousands, rulers of hundreds, rulers of fifties, and rulers of tens. 22 And let them judge the people at all times. Then it will be *that* every great matter they shall bring to you, but every small matter they themselves shall judge. So it will be easier for you, for they will bear *the burden* with you. 23 If you do this thing, and God *so* commands you, then you will be able to endure, and all this people will also go to their place in peace."

24 So Moses heeded the voice of his father-in-law and did all that he had said. 25 And Moses chose able men out of all Israel, and made them heads over the people: rulers of thousands, rulers of hundreds, rulers of fifties, and rulers of tens. 26 So they judged the people at all times; the hard cases they brought to Moses, but they judged every small case themselves.

27 Then Moses let his father-in-law depart, and he went his way to his own land.

PSALM 18:28–36

28 FOR You will light my lamp;
The LORD my God will enlighten my darkness.

Spiritual darkness comes because of something I do not intend to obey. (SERMON MT.)

---

29 For by You I can run against a troop,
By my God I can leap over a wall.
30 *As for* God, His way *is* perfect;
The word of the LORD is proven;
He *is* a shield to all who trust in Him.

31 For who *is* God, except the LORD?
And who *is* a rock, except our God?
32 *It is* God who arms me with strength,
And makes my way perfect.
33 He makes my feet like the *feet of* deer,
And sets me on my high places.
34 He teaches my hands to make war,
So that my arms can bend a bow of bronze.

35 You have also given me the shield of Your salvation;
Your right hand has held me up,
Your gentleness has made me great.
36 You enlarged my path under me,
So my feet did not slip.

PROVERBS 6:16–19

16 THESE six *things* the LORD hates,
Yes, seven *are* an abomination to Him:
17 A proud look,
A lying tongue,
Hands that shed innocent blood,
18 A heart that devises wicked plans,
Feet that are swift in running to evil,
19 A false witness *who* speaks lies,
And one who sows discord among brethren.

A lie is a truth told with bad intent. (SHADE)

MATTHEW 22:1–22

AND Jesus answered and spoke to them again by parables and said: 2 "The kingdom of heaven is like a certain king who arranged a marriage for his son, 3 and sent out his servants to call those who were invited to the wedding; and they were not willing to come. 4 Again, he sent out other servants, saying, 'Tell those who are invited, "See, I have prepared my dinner; my oxen and fatted cattle *are* killed, and all things *are* ready. Come to the wedding." ' 5 But they made light of it and went their ways, one to his own farm, another to his business. 6 And the rest seized his servants, treated *them* spitefully, and killed *them*. 7 But when the king heard *about it,* he was furious. And he sent out his armies, destroyed those murderers, and burned up their city. 8 Then he said to his servants, 'The wedding is ready, but those who were invited were not worthy. 9 Therefore go into the highways, and as many as you find, invite to the wedding.' 10 So those servants went out into the highways and gathered together all whom they found, both bad and good. And the wedding *hall* was filled with guests.

11 "But when the king came in to see the guests, he saw a man there who did not have on a wedding garment. 12 So he said to him, 'Friend, how did you come in here without a wedding garment?' And he was speechless. 13 Then the king said to the servants, 'Bind him hand and foot, take him away, and cast *him* into outer darkness; there will be weeping and gnashing of teeth.'

14 "For many are called, but few *are* chosen."

15 Then the Pharisees went and plotted how they might entangle Him in *His* talk. 16 And they sent to Him their disciples with the Herodians, saying, "Teacher, we know that You are true, and teach the way of God in truth; nor do You care about anyone, for You do not regard the person of men. 17 Tell us, therefore, what do You think? Is it lawful to pay taxes to Caesar, or not?"

18 But Jesus perceived their wickedness, and said, "Why do you test Me, *you* hypocrites? 19 Show Me the tax money."

So they brought Him a denarius.

20 And He said to them, "Whose image and inscription *is* this?"

21 They said to Him, "Caesar's."

And He said to them, "Render therefore to Caesar the things that are Caesar's, and to God the things that are God's." 22 When they had heard *these words,* they marveled, and left Him and went their way.

◆◆◆

Reading 35—The Lover of God
Matthew 22:37, 38

Before we can love God we must have the Lover of God in us, namely, the Holy Spirit. When the Holy Spirit has shed abroad the love of God in our hearts, then that love requires cultivation. No love on earth will develop without being cultivated. We have to dedicate ourselves to love, which means identifying ourselves with God's interests in other people, and God is interested in some funny people, namely, in you and in me! We must beware of letting natural affinities hinder our walking in love. One of the most cruel ways of killing love is by disdain built on natural affinities. To be guided by our affinities is a natural tendency, but spiritually this tendency must be denied, and as we deny it we find that God gives us affinity with those for whom we have no natural affinity. Is there anyone in your life who would not be there if you were not a Christian? The love of God is not mere sentimentality; it is most practical thing for the saint to love as God loves. The springs of love are in God, not in us. The love of God is only in us when it has been shed abroad in our hearts by the Holy Spirit, and the evidence that it is there is the spontaneous way in which it is manifested.   (*WALKED*)

EXODUS 19:1—20:26

IN the third month after the children of Israel had gone out of the land of Egypt, on the same day, they came *to* the Wilderness of Sinai. 2 For they had departed from Rephidim, had come *to* the Wilderness of Sinai, and camped in the wilderness. So Israel camped there before the mountain.

3 And Moses went up to God, and the LORD called to him from the mountain, saying, "Thus you shall say to the house of Jacob, and tell the children of Israel: 4 'You have seen what I did to the Egyptians, and *how* I bore you on eagles' wings and brought you to Myself. 5 Now therefore, if you will indeed obey My voice and keep My covenant, then you shall be a special treasure to Me above all people; for all the earth *is* Mine. 6 And you shall be to Me a kingdom of priests and a holy nation.' These *are* the words which you shall speak to the children of Israel."

7 So Moses came and called for the elders of the people, and laid before them all these words which the LORD commanded him. 8 Then all the people answered together and said, "All that the LORD has spoken we will do." So Moses brought back the words of the people to the LORD. 9 And the LORD said to Moses, "Behold, I come to you in the thick cloud, that the people may hear when I speak with you, and believe you forever."

So Moses told the words of the people to the LORD.

10 Then the LORD said to Moses, "Go to the people and consecrate them today and tomorrow, and let them wash their clothes. 11 And let them be ready for the third day. For on the third day the LORD will come down upon Mount Sinai in the sight of all the people. 12 You shall set bounds for the people all around, saying, 'Take heed to yourselves that you do *not* go up to the mountain or touch its base. Whoever touches the mountain shall surely be put to death. 13 Not a hand shall touch him, but he shall surely be stoned or shot *with an arrow;* whether man or beast, he shall not live.' When the trumpet sounds long, they shall come near the mountain."

14 So Moses went down from the mountain to the people and sanctified the people, and they washed their clothes. 15 And he said to the people, "Be ready for the third day; do not come near *your* wives."

16 Then it came to pass on the third day, in the morning, that there were thunderings and lightnings, and a thick cloud on the mountain; and the sound of the trumpet was very loud, so that all the people who *were* in the camp trembled. 17 And Moses brought the people out of the camp to meet with God, and they stood at the foot of the mountain. 18 Now Mount Sinai *was* completely in smoke, because the LORD descended upon it in fire. Its smoke ascended like the smoke of a furnace, and the whole mountain quaked greatly. 19 And when the blast of the trumpet sounded long and became louder and louder, Moses spoke, and God answered him by voice. 20 Then the LORD came down upon Mount Sinai, on the top of the mountain. And the LORD called Moses to the top of the mountain, and Moses went up.

21 And the LORD said to Moses, "Go down and warn the people, lest they break through to gaze at the LORD, and many of them perish. 22 Also let the priests who come near the LORD consecrate themselves, lest the LORD break out against them."

23 But Moses said to the LORD, "The peo-ple cannot come up to Mount Sinai; for You warned us, saying, 'Set bounds around the mountain and consecrate it.' "

24 Then the LORD said to him, "Away! Get down and then come up, you and Aaron with you. But do not let the priests and the people break through to come up to the LORD, lest He break out against them." 25 So Moses went down to the people and spoke to them.

20 AND God spoke all these words, saying:

2 "I *am* the LORD your God, who brought you out of the land of Egypt, out of the house of bondage.

3 "You shall have no other gods before Me.

The true blessedness of the saint is in determinedly making and keeping God first.   (SERMON MT.)

---

4 "You shall not make for yourself a carved image—any likeness *of anything* that *is* in heaven above, or that *is* in the earth beneath, or that *is* in the water under the earth; 5 you shall not bow down to them nor serve them. For I, the LORD your God, *am* a jealous God, visiting the iniquity of the fathers upon the children to the third and fourth *generations* of those who hate Me, 6 but showing mercy to thousands, to those who love Me and keep My commandments.

7 "You shall not take the name of the LORD your God in vain, for the LORD will not hold *him* guiltless who takes His name in vain.

8 "Remember the Sabbath day, to keep it holy. 9 Six days you shall labor and do all your work, 10 but the seventh day *is* the Sabbath of the LORD your God. *In it* you shall do no work: you, nor your son, nor your daughter, nor your male servant, nor your female servant, nor your cattle, nor your stranger who *is* within your gates. 11 For *in* six days the LORD made the heavens and the earth, the sea, and all that *is* in them, and rested the seventh day. Therefore the LORD blessed the Sabbath day and hallowed it.

12 "Honor your father and your mother, that your days may be long upon the land which the LORD your God is giving you.

13 "You shall not murder.

14 "You shall not commit adultery.

15 "You shall not steal.

16 "You shall not bear false witness against your neighbor.

17 "You shall not covet your neighbor's house; you shall not covet your neighbor's wife, nor his male servant, nor his female servant, nor his ox, nor his donkey, nor anything that *is* your neighbor's."

18 Now all the people witnessed the thunderings, the lightning flashes, the sound of the trumpet, and the mountain smoking; and when the people saw *it*, they trembled and stood afar off. 19 Then they said to Moses, "You speak with us, and we will hear; but let not God speak with us, lest we die."

20 And Moses said to the people, "Do not fear; for God has come to test you, and that His fear may be before you, so that you may not sin." 21 So the people stood afar off, but Moses drew near the thick darkness where God *was.*

22 Then the LORD said to Moses, "Thus you shall say to the children of Israel: 'You have seen that I have talked with you from heaven. 23 You shall not make *anything to be* with Me—gods of silver or gods of gold you shall not make for yourselves. 24 An altar of earth you shall make for Me, and you shall sacrifice on it your burnt offerings and your peace offerings, your sheep and your oxen. In every place where I record My name I will come to you, and I will bless you. 25 And if you make Me an altar of stone, you shall not build it of hewn stone; for if you use your tool on it, you have profaned it. 26 Nor shall you go up by steps to My altar, that your nakedness may not be exposed on it.'

PSALM 18:37–45

37 I have pursued my enemies and overtaken them;
Neither did I turn back again till they were destroyed.

38 I have wounded them,
So that they could not rise;
They have fallen under my feet.

39 For You have armed me with strength for the battle;
You have subdued under me those who rose up against me.

40 You have also given me the necks of my enemies,
So that I destroyed those who hated me.

41 They cried out, but *there was* none to save;
Even to the LORD, but He did not answer them.

42 Then I beat them as fine as the dust before the wind;
I cast them out like dirt in the streets.

43 You have delivered me from the strivings of the people;
You have made me the head of the nations;
A people I have not known shall serve me.

44 As soon as they hear of me they obey me;
The foreigners submit to me.

45 The foreigners fade away,
And come frightened from their hideouts.

PROVERBS 6:20–25

20 MY son, keep your father's command,
And do not forsake the law of your mother.

21 Bind them continually upon your heart;
Tie them around your neck.

22 When you roam, they will lead you;
When you sleep, they will keep you;
And *when* you awake, they will speak with you.

23 For the commandment *is* a lamp,
And the law a light;
Reproofs of instruction *are* the way of life,

24 To keep you from the evil woman,
From the flattering tongue of a seductress.

25 Do not lust after her beauty in your heart,
Nor let her allure you with her eyelids.

MATTHEW 22:23–46

THE same day the Sadducees, who say there is no resurrection, came to Him and asked Him, 24 saying: "Teacher, Moses said that if a man dies, having no children, his brother shall marry his wife and raise up offspring for his brother. 25 Now there were with us seven brothers. The first died after he had married, and having no offspring, left his wife to his brother. 26 Likewise the second also, and the third, even to the seventh.

27 Last of all the woman died also.
28 Therefore, in the resurrection, whose
wife of the seven will she be? For they all
had her."

29 Jesus answered and said to them, "You
are mistaken, not knowing the Scriptures
nor the power of God. 30 For in the resurrection they neither marry nor are given
in marriage, but are like angels of God in
heaven. 31 But concerning the resurrection
of the dead, have you not read what was
spoken to you by God, saying, 32 'I am the
God of Abraham, the God of Isaac, and
the God of Jacob'? God is not the God
of the dead, but of the living." 33 And when
the multitudes heard *this,* they were astonished at His teaching.

34 But when the Pharisees heard that He
had silenced the Sadducees, they gathered
together. 35 Then one of them, a lawyer,
asked *Him a question,* testing Him, and saying, 36 "Teacher, which *is* the great commandment in the law?"

37 Jesus said to him, " 'You shall love the
LORD your God with all your heart, with
all your soul, and with all your mind.'
38 This is *the* first and great commandment.

---

*L*ove Him personally, passionately
and devotedly beyond any of the closest
ties on earth.   (UTMOST)

---

39 And *the* second *is* like it: 'You shall love
your neighbor as yourself.' 40 On these two
commandments hang all the Law and the
Prophets."

41 While the Pharisees were gathered together, Jesus asked them, 42 saying, "What
do you think about the Christ? Whose Son
is He?"

They said to Him, "*The Son* of David."

43 He said to them, "How then does David in the Spirit call Him 'Lord,' saying:

44 'The LORD said to my Lord,
  "Sit at My right hand,
    Till I make Your enemies Your
      footstool" '?

45 If David then calls Him 'Lord,' how is
He his Son?" 46 And no one was able to
answer Him a word, nor from that day
on did anyone dare question Him anymore.

◆◆◆◆

Reading 36—The Greatest Teacher
Matthew 23:10

The ecclesiastical idea of a servant of God is not Jesus Christ's idea. His
idea is that we serve Him by being the servants of other men. Jesus
Christ out-socialists the socialists. He says that in His Kingdom he that is
greatest shall be the servant of all. The real test of the saint is not preaching
the gospel, but washing disciples' feet, that is, doing the things that do not
count in the actual estimate of men but count everything in the estimate of
God. Paul delighted to spend himself out for God's interests in other people,
and he did not care what it cost. We come in with our economical notions—
"Suppose God wants me to go there—what about the salary? What about the
climate? How shall I be looked after? A man must consider these things." All
that is an indication that we are serving God with a reserve. Paul focuses
Jesus Christ's idea of a New Testament saint in his life, namely, not one who
proclaims the Gospel merely, but one who becomes broken bread and poured
out wine in the hands of Jesus Christ for other lives.   (*UTMOST*)

EXODUS 21:1—22:31

"NOW these *are* the judgments which you
shall set before them: 2 If you buy a Hebrew
servant, he shall serve six years; and in the
seventh he shall go out free and pay nothing.

3 If he comes in by himself, he shall go
out by himself; if he *comes in* married, then
his wife shall go out with him. 4 If his master
has given him a wife, and she has borne
him sons or daughters, the wife and her
children shall be her master's, and he shall
go out by himself. 5 But if the servant plainly

says, 'I love my master, my wife, and my children; I will not go out free,' 6 then his master shall bring him to the judges. He shall also bring him to the door, or to the doorpost, and his master shall pierce his ear with an awl; and he shall serve him forever.

7 "And if a man sells his daughter to be a female slave, she shall not go out as the male slaves do. 8 If she does not please her master, who has betrothed her to himself, then he shall let her be redeemed. He shall have no right to sell her to a foreign people, since he has dealt deceitfully with her. 9 And if he has betrothed her to his son, he shall deal with her according to the custom of daughters. 10 If he takes another *wife,* he shall not diminish her food, her clothing, and her marriage rights. 11 And if he does not do these three for her, then she shall go out free, without *paying* money.

12 "He who strikes a man so that he dies shall surely be put to death. 13 However, if he did not lie in wait, but God delivered *him* into his hand, then I will appoint for you a place where he may flee.

14 "But if a man acts with premeditation against his neighbor, to kill him by treachery, you shall take him from My altar, that he may die.

15 "And he who strikes his father or his mother shall surely be put to death.

16 "He who kidnaps a man and sells him, or if he is found in his hand, shall surely be put to death.

17 "And he who curses his father or his mother shall surely be put to death.

18 "If men contend with each other, and one strikes the other with a stone or with *his* fist, and he does not die but is confined to *his* bed, 19 if he rises again and walks about outside with his staff, then he who struck *him* shall be acquitted. He shall only pay *for* the loss of his time, and shall provide *for him* to be thoroughly healed.

20 "And if a man beats his male or female servant with a rod, so that he dies under his hand, he shall surely be punished. 21 Notwithstanding, if he remains alive a day or two, he shall not be punished; for he *is* his property.

22 "If men fight, and hurt a woman with child, so that she gives birth prematurely, yet no harm follows, he shall surely be punished accordingly as the woman's husband imposes on him; and he shall pay as the judges *determine.* 23 But if *any* harm follows, then you shall give life for life, 24 eye for eye, tooth for tooth, hand for hand, foot for foot, 25 burn for burn, wound for wound, stripe for stripe.

26 "If a man strikes the eye of his male or female servant, and destroys it, he shall let him go free for the sake of his eye. 27 And if he knocks out the tooth of his male or female servant, he shall let him go free for the sake of his tooth.

28 "If an ox gores a man or a woman to death, then the ox shall surely be stoned, and its flesh shall not be eaten; but the owner of the ox *shall be* acquitted. 29 But if the ox tended to thrust with its horn in times past, and it has been made known to his owner, and he has not kept it confined, so that it has killed a man or a woman, the ox shall be stoned and its owner also shall be put to death. 30 If there is imposed on him a sum of money, then he shall pay to redeem his life, whatever is imposed on him. 31 Whether it has gored a son or gored a daughter, according to this judgment it shall be done to him. 32 If the ox gores a male or female servant, he shall give to their master thirty shekels of silver, and the ox shall be stoned.

33 "And if a man opens a pit, or if a man digs a pit and does not cover it, and an ox or a donkey falls in it, 34 the owner of the pit shall make *it* good; he shall give money to their owner, but the dead *animal* shall be his.

35 "If one man's ox hurts another's, so that it dies, then they shall sell the live ox and divide the money from it; and the dead *ox* they shall also divide. 36 Or if it was known that the ox tended to thrust in time past, and its owner has not kept it confined, he shall surely pay ox for ox, and the dead animal shall be his own.

22 "IF a man steals an ox or a sheep, and slaughters it or sells it, he shall restore five oxen for an ox and four sheep for a sheep. 2 If the thief is found breaking in, and he is struck so that he dies, *there shall be* no guilt for his bloodshed. 3 If the sun has risen on him, *there shall be* guilt for his bloodshed. He should make full restitution; if he has nothing, then he shall be sold for his theft. 4 If the theft is certainly found alive in his hand, whether it is an ox or donkey or sheep, he shall restore double.

5 "If a man causes a field or vineyard to be grazed, and lets loose his animal, and it feeds in another man's field, he shall make restitution from the best of his own field and the best of his own vineyard.

6 "If fire breaks out and catches in thorns, so that stacked grain, standing grain, or the field is consumed, he who kindled the fire shall surely make restitution.

7 "If a man delivers to his neighbor money or articles to keep, and it is stolen out of the man's house, if the thief is found, he shall pay double. 8 If the thief is not found, then the master of the house shall be brought to the judges *to see* whether he has put his hand into his neighbor's goods.

9 "For any kind of trespass, *whether it concerns* an ox, a donkey, a sheep, or clothing, *or* for any kind of lost thing which *another* claims to be his, the cause of both parties shall come before the judges; *and* whomever the judges condemn shall pay double to his neighbor. 10 If a man delivers to his neighbor a donkey, an ox, a sheep, or any animal to keep, and it dies, is hurt, or driven away, no one seeing *it*, 11 *then* an oath of the Lord shall be between them both, that he has not put his hand into his neighbor's goods; and the owner of it shall accept *that*, and he shall not make *it* good. 12 But if, in fact, it is stolen from him, he shall make restitution to the owner of it. 13 If it is torn to pieces *by a beast, then* he shall bring it as evidence, *and* he shall not make good what was torn.

14 "And if a man borrows *anything* from his neighbor, and it becomes injured or dies, the owner of it not *being* with it, he shall surely make *it* good. 15 If its owner *was* with it, he shall not make *it* good; if it *was* hired, it came for its hire.

16 "If a man entices a virgin who is not betrothed, and lies with her, he shall surely pay the bride-price for her *to be* his wife. 17 If her father utterly refuses to give her to him, he shall pay money according to the bride-price of virgins.

18 "You shall not permit a sorceress to live.

19 "Whoever lies with an animal shall surely be put to death.

20 "He who sacrifices to *any* god, except to the Lord only, he shall be utterly destroyed.

21 "You shall neither mistreat a stranger nor oppress him, for you were strangers in the land of Egypt.

22 "You shall not afflict any widow or fatherless child. 23 If you afflict them in any way, *and* they cry at all to Me, I will surely hear their cry; 24 and My wrath will become hot, and I will kill you with the sword; your wives shall be widows, and your children fatherless.

25 "If you lend money to *any of* My people *who are* poor among you, you shall not be like a moneylender to him; you shall not charge him interest. 26 If you ever take your neighbor's garment as a pledge, you shall return it to him before the sun goes down. 27 For that *is* his only covering, it *is* his garment for his skin. What will he sleep in? And it will be that when he cries to Me, I will hear, for I *am* gracious.

28 "You shall not revile God, nor curse a ruler of your people.

29 "You shall not delay *to offer* the first of your ripe produce and your juices. The firstborn of your sons you shall give to Me. 30 Likewise you shall do with your oxen *and* your sheep. It shall be with its mother seven days; on the eighth day you shall give it to Me.

31 "And you shall be holy men to Me: you shall not eat meat torn *by beasts* in the field; you shall throw it to the dogs.

PSALM 18:46–50

46   THE Lord lives!
     Blessed *be* my Rock!
     Let the God of my salvation be exalted.

---

*T*he Rock of Ages is the great sheltering encirclement.   (RUN)

---

47   *It is* God who avenges me,
     And subdues the peoples under me;
48   He delivers me from my enemies.
     You also lift me up above those who
         rise against me;
     You have delivered me from the violent
         man.
49   Therefore I will give thanks to You,
         O Lord, among the Gentiles,
     And sing praises to Your name.

50   Great deliverance He gives to His king,
     And shows mercy to His anointed,
     To David and his descendants
         forevermore.

PROVERBS 6:26–29

26   FOR by means of a harlot
     A man is reduced to a crust of bread;
     And an adulteress will prey upon his
         precious life.
27   Can a man take fire to his bosom,
     And his clothes not be burned?
28   Can one walk on hot coals,
     And his feet not be seared?
29   So *is* he who goes in to his neighbor's
         wife;
     Whoever touches her shall not be
         innocent.

MATTHEW 23:1–22

THEN Jesus spoke to the multitudes and to His disciples, 2 saying: "The scribes and the Pharisees sit in Moses' seat. 3 Therefore whatever they tell you to observe, *that* observe and do, but do not do according to their works; for they say, and do not do. 4 For they bind heavy burdens, hard to bear, and lay *them* on men's shoulders; but they *themselves* will not move them with one of their fingers. 5 But all their works they do to be seen by men. They make their phylacteries broad and enlarge the borders of their garments. 6 They love the best places at feasts, the best seats in the synagogues, 7 greetings in the marketplaces, and to be called by men, 'Rabbi, Rabbi.' 8 But you, do not be called 'Rabbi'; for One is your Teacher, the Christ, and you are all brethren. 9 Do not call anyone on earth your father; for One is your Father, He who is in heaven. 10 And do not be called teachers; for One is your Teacher, the Christ. 11 But he who is greatest among you shall be your servant. 12 And whoever exalts himself will be humbled, and he who humbles himself will be exalted.

13 "But woe to you, scribes and Pharisees, hypocrites! For you shut up the kingdom of heaven against men; for you neither go in *yourselves*, nor do you allow those who are entering to go in. 14 Woe to you, scribes and Pharisees, hypocrites! For you devour widows' houses, and for a pretense make long prayers. Therefore you will receive greater condemnation.

15 "Woe to you, scribes and Pharisees, hypocrites! For you travel land and sea to win one proselyte, and when he is won, you make him twice as much a son of hell as yourselves.

16 "Woe to you, blind guides, who say, 'Whoever swears by the temple, it is nothing; but whoever swears by the gold of the temple, he is obliged *to perform it.*' 17 Fools and blind! For which is greater, the gold or the temple that sanctifies the gold? 18 And, 'Whoever swears by the altar, it is nothing; but whoever swears by the gift that is on it, he is obliged *to perform it.*' 19 Fools and blind! For which is greater, the gift or the altar that sanctifies the gift? 20 Therefore he who swears by the altar, swears by it and by all things on it. 21 He who swears by the temple, swears by it and by Him who dwells in it. 22 And he who swears by heaven, swears by the throne of God and by Him who sits on it.

The great characteristic of the saint is humility. (SERMON MT.)

Reading 37—No Second Best
Matthew 23:31

In the spiritual life we do not go from good to better, and from better to best; because there is only One to whom we go, and that One is The Best, namely, God Himself. There can be no such thing as God's second best. We can perversely put ourselves out of God's order into His permissive will, but that is a different matter. In seeking the Best we soon find that our enemy is our good things, not our bad. The things that keep us back from God's best are not sin and imperfection, but the things that are right and good and noble from the natural standpoint. To discern that the natural virtues antagonize surrender to God is to bring our soul at once into the center of our greatest battlefield. Very few of us debate with the sordid and the wrong, but we do debate with the good; and the higher up we go in the scale of the natural virtues, the more intense is the opposition to Jesus Christ, which is in inverse ratio to what one would naturally imagine. (*NOT KNOWING*)

EXODUS 23:1—24:18

"YOU shall not circulate a false report. Do not put your hand with the wicked to be an unrighteous witness. 2 You shall not follow a crowd to do evil; nor shall you testify in a dispute so as to turn aside after many to pervert *justice*. 3 You shall not show partiality to a poor man in his dispute.

4 "If you meet your enemy's ox or his donkey going astray, you shall surely bring it back to him again. 5 If you see the donkey of one who hates you lying under its burden, and you would refrain from helping it, you shall surely help him with it.

6 "You shall not pervert the judgment of your poor in his dispute. 7 Keep yourself far from a false matter; do not kill the innocent and righteous. For I will not justify the wicked. 8 And you shall take no bribe, for a bribe blinds the discerning and perverts the words of the righteous.

9 "Also you shall not oppress a stranger, for you know the heart of a stranger, because you were strangers in the land of Egypt.

10 "Six years you shall sow your land and gather in its produce, 11 but the seventh *year* you shall let it rest and lie fallow, that the poor of your people may eat; and what they leave, the beasts of the field may eat. In like manner you shall do with your vineyard *and* your olive grove. 12 Six days you shall do your work, and on the seventh day you shall rest, that your ox and your donkey may rest, and the son of your female servant and the stranger may be refreshed.

13 "And in all that I have said to you, be circumspect and make no mention of the name of other gods, nor let it be heard from your mouth.

14 "Three times you shall keep a feast to Me in the year: 15 You shall keep the Feast of Unleavened Bread (you shall eat unleavened bread seven days, as I commanded you, at the time appointed in the month of Abib, for in it you came out of Egypt; none shall appear before Me empty); 16 and the Feast of Harvest, the firstfruits of your labors which you have sown in the field; and the Feast of Ingathering at the end of the year, when you have gathered in *the fruit of* your labors from the field.

17 "Three times in the year all your males shall appear before the Lord GOD.

18 "You shall not offer the blood of My sacrifice with leavened bread; nor shall the fat of My sacrifice remain until morning. 19 The first of the firstfruits of your land you shall bring into the house of the LORD your God. You shall not boil a young goat in its mother's milk.

20 "Behold, I send an Angel before you to keep you in the way and to bring you into the place which I have prepared. 21 Beware of Him and obey His voice; do not provoke Him, for He will not pardon your transgressions; for My name *is* in Him. 22 But if you indeed obey His voice and do all that I speak, then I will be an enemy to your enemies and an adversary to your adversaries. 23 For My Angel will go before

---

We have the power to obey, and consequently the power to disobey. (SERMON MT.)

---

you and bring you in to the Amorites and the Hittites and the Perizzites and the Canaanites and the Hivites and the Jebusites; and I will cut them off. 24 You shall not bow down to their gods, nor serve them, nor do according to their works; but you shall utterly overthrow them and completely break down their *sacred* pillars.

25 "So you shall serve the LORD your God, and He will bless your bread and your water. And I will take sickness away from the midst of you. 26 No one shall suffer miscarriage or be barren in your land; I will fulfill the number of your days.

27 "I will send My fear before you, I will cause confusion among all the people to whom you come, and will make all your enemies turn *their* backs to you. 28 And I will send hornets before you, which shall drive out the Hivite, the Canaanite, and the Hittite from before you. 29 I will not drive them out from before you in one year, lest the land become desolate and the beasts of the field become too numerous for you. 30 Little by little I will drive them out from before you, until you have increased, and you inherit the land. 31 And I will set your bounds from the Red Sea to the sea, Philistia, and from the desert to the River. For I will deliver the inhabitants of the land into your hand, and you shall drive them out before you. 32 You shall make no covenant with them, nor with their gods. 33 They shall not dwell in your land, lest they make you sin against Me. For *if* you serve their gods, it will surely be a snare to you."

24 NOW He said to Moses, "Come up to the LORD, you and Aaron, Nadab and Abihu, and seventy of the elders of Israel, and worship from afar. 2 And Moses alone shall come near the LORD, but they shall not come near; nor shall the people go up with him."

3 So Moses came and told the people all the words of the LORD and all the judgments. And all the people answered with one voice and said, "All the words which the LORD has said we will do." 4 And Moses wrote all the words of the LORD. And he rose early in the morning, and built an altar at the foot of the mountain, and twelve pillars according to the twelve tribes of Israel. 5 Then he sent young men of the children of Israel, who offered burnt offerings and sacrificed peace offerings of oxen to the LORD. 6 And Moses took half the blood and put *it* in basins, and half the blood he sprinkled on the altar. 7 Then he took the Book of the Covenant and read in the hearing of the people. And they said, "All that the LORD has said we will do, and be obedient." 8 And Moses took the blood, sprinkled *it* on the people, and said, "This is the blood of the covenant which the LORD has made with you according to all these words."

9 Then Moses went up, also Aaron, Nadab, and Abihu, and seventy of the elders of Israel, 10 and they saw the God of Israel. And *there was* under His feet as it were a paved work of sapphire stone, and it was like the very heavens in *its* clarity. 11 But on the nobles of the children of Israel He did not lay His hand. So they saw God, and they ate and drank.

12 Then the LORD said to Moses, "Come up to Me on the mountain and be there; and I will give you tablets of stone, and the law and commandments which I have written, that you may teach them."

13 So Moses arose with his assistant Joshua, and Moses went up to the mountain of God. 14 And he said to the elders, "Wait here for us until we come back to you. Indeed, Aaron and Hur *are* with you. If any man has a difficulty, let him go to them." 15 Then Moses went up into the mountain, and a cloud covered the mountain.

16 Now the glory of the LORD rested on Mount Sinai, and the cloud covered it six days. And on the seventh day He called to Moses out of the midst of the cloud. 17 The sight of the glory of the LORD *was* like a consuming fire on the top of the mountain in the eyes of the children of Israel. 18 So Moses went into the midst of the cloud and went up into the mountain. And Moses was on the mountain forty days and forty nights.

PSALM 19:1–6

1　THE heavens declare the glory of God;
　　And the firmament shows His
　　　handiwork.
2　Day unto day utters speech,
　　And night unto night reveals
　　　knowledge.
3　*There is* no speech nor language
　　Where their voice is not heard.
4　Their line has gone out through all the
　　　earth,
　　And their words to the end of the world.

　　In them He has set a tabernacle for
　　　the sun,
5　Which *is* like a bridegroom coming out
　　　of his chamber,
　　And rejoices like a strong man to run
　　　its race.
6　Its rising *is* from one end of heaven,
　　And its circuit to the other end;
　　And there is nothing hidden from its
　　　heat.

PROVERBS 6:30, 31

30　*PEOPLE* do not despise a thief
　　If he steals to satisfy himself when he
　　　is starving.
31　Yet *when* he is found, he must restore
　　　sevenfold;
　　He may have to give up all the substance
　　　of his house.

MATTHEW 23:23–39

23 "WOE to you, scribes and Pharisees, hypocrites! For you pay tithe of mint and anise and cummin, and have neglected the weightier *matters* of the law: justice and mercy and faith. These you ought to have done, without leaving the others undone. 24 Blind guides, who strain out a gnat and swallow a camel!

25 "Woe to you, scribes and Pharisees, hypocrites! For you cleanse the outside of the cup and dish, but inside they are full of extortion and self-indulgence. 26 Blind Pharisee, first cleanse the inside of the cup and dish, that the outside of them may be clean also.

The nature of Pharisaism is that it must stand on tiptoe and be superior. (BAFFLED)

27 "Woe to you, scribes and Pharisees, hypocrites! For you are like whitewashed tombs which indeed appear beautiful outwardly, but inside are full of dead *men's* bones and all uncleanness. 28 Even so you also outwardly appear righteous to men, but inside you are full of hypocrisy and lawlessness.

29 "Woe to you, scribes and Pharisees, hypocrites! Because you build the tombs of the prophets and adorn the monuments of the righteous, 30 and say, 'If we had lived in the days of our fathers, we would not have been partakers with them in the blood of the prophets.'

31 "Therefore you are witnesses against yourselves that you are sons of those who murdered the prophets. 32 Fill up, then, the measure of your fathers' *guilt.* 33 Serpents, brood of vipers! How can you escape the condemnation of hell? 34 Therefore, indeed,

I send you prophets, wise men, and scribes: *some* of them you will kill and crucify, and *some* of them you will scourge in your synagogues and persecute from city to city, 35 that on you may come all the righteous blood shed on the earth, from the blood of righteous Abel to the blood of Zechariah, son of Berechiah, whom you murdered between the temple and the altar. 36 Assuredly, I say to you, all these things will come upon this generation.

37 "O Jerusalem, Jerusalem, the one who kills the prophets and stones those who are sent to her! How often I wanted to gather your children together, as a hen gathers her chicks under *her* wings, but you were not willing! 38 See! Your house is left to you desolate; 39 for I say to you, you shall see Me no more till you say, 'Blessed *is* He who comes in the name of the Lord!' "

◆◆◆◆

Reading 38—God's Grace at Work
Matthew 24:6

That [Matthew 24:6] is either the statement of a madman or of a Being who has power to put something into a man and keep him free from panic, even in the midst of the awful terror of war. The basis of panic is always cowardice. Our Lord teaches us to look things full in the face. He says—"When you hear of wars, don't be scared." It is the most natural thing in the world to be scared, and the clearest evidence that God's grace is at work in our hearts is when we do not get into panics. Our Lord insists on the inevitableness of peril. . . . Men may have lived undisturbed over a volcano for a long while, when suddenly an eruption occurs. Jesus Christ did not say— "You will understand why war has come," but—"Don't be scared when it does come, do not be in a panic." It is astonishing how we ignore Jesus Christ's words. He said that nations would end in war and bloodshed and havoc. We ignore His warnings; and when war comes we lose our wits and exhibit panic.   (*SHAD. AGONY*)

EXODUS 25:1—26:37

THEN the Lord spoke to Moses, saying: 2 "Speak to the children of Israel, that they bring Me an offering. From everyone who gives it willingly with his heart you shall take My offering. 3 And this *is* the offering which you shall take from them: gold, silver, and bronze; 4 blue, purple, and scarlet *thread,* fine linen, and goats' *hair;* 5 ram skins dyed red, badger skins, and acacia wood; 6 oil for the light, and spices for the

anointing oil and for the sweet incense; 7 onyx stones, and stones to be set in the ephod and in the breastplate. 8 And let them make Me a sanctuary, that I may dwell among them. 9 According to all that I show you, *that is,* the pattern of the tabernacle and the pattern of all its furnishings, just so you shall make *it.*

10 "And they shall make an ark of acacia wood; two and a half cubits *shall be* its length, a cubit and a half its width, and a cubit and a half its height. 11 And you shall overlay it with pure gold, inside and out

you shall overlay it, and shall make on it a molding of gold all around. 12 You shall cast four rings of gold for it, and put *them* in its four corners; two rings *shall be* on one side, and two rings on the other side. 13 And you shall make poles *of* acacia wood, and overlay them with gold. 14 You shall put the poles into the rings on the sides of the ark, that the ark may be carried by them. 15 The poles shall be in the rings of the ark; they shall not be taken from it. 16 And you shall put into the ark the Testimony which I will give you.

17 "You shall make a mercy seat of pure gold; two and a half cubits *shall be* its length and a cubit and a half its width. 18 And you shall make two cherubim of gold; of hammered work you shall make them at the two ends of the mercy seat. 19 Make one cherub at one end, and the other cherub at the other end; you shall make the cherubim at the two ends of it *of one piece* with the mercy seat. 20 And the cherubim shall stretch out *their* wings above, covering the mercy seat with their wings, and they shall face one another; the faces of the cherubim *shall be* toward the mercy seat. 21 You shall put the mercy seat on top of the ark, and in the ark you shall put the Testimony that I will give you. 22 And there I will meet with you, and I will speak with you from above the mercy seat, from between the two cherubim which *are* on the ark of the Testimony, about everything which I will give you in commandment to the children of Israel.

23 "You shall also make a table of acacia wood; two cubits *shall be* its length, a cubit its width, and a cubit and a half its height. 24 And you shall overlay it with pure gold, and make a molding of gold all around. 25 You shall make for it a frame of a handbreadth all around, and you shall make a gold molding for the frame all around. 26 And you shall make for it four rings of gold, and put the rings on the four corners that *are* at its four legs. 27 The rings shall be close to the frame, as holders for the poles to bear the table. 28 And you shall make the poles of acacia wood, and overlay them with gold, that the table may be carried with them. 29 You shall make its dishes, its pans, its pitchers, and its bowls for pouring. You shall make them of pure gold. 30 And you shall set the showbread on the table before Me always.

31 "You shall also make a lampstand of pure gold; the lampstand shall be of hammered work. Its shaft, its branches, its bowls, its *ornamental* knobs, and flowers shall be *of one piece*. 32 And six branches

shall come out of its sides: three branches of the lampstand out of one side, and three branches of the lampstand out of the other side. 33 Three bowls *shall be* made like almond *blossoms* on one branch, *with* an *ornamental* knob and a flower, and three bowls made like almond *blossoms* on the other branch, *with* an *ornamental* knob and a flower—and so for the six branches that come out of the lampstand. 34 On the lampstand itself four bowls *shall be* made like almond *blossoms, each with* its *ornamental* knob and flower. 35 And *there shall be* a knob under the *first* two branches of the same, a knob under the *second* two branches of the same, and a knob under the *third* two branches of the same, according to the six branches that extend from the lampstand. 36 Their knobs and their branches *shall be of one piece;* all of it *shall be* one hammered piece of pure gold. 37 You shall make seven lamps for it, and they shall arrange its lamps so that they give light in front of it. 38 And its wick-trimmers and their trays *shall be* of pure gold. 39 It shall be made of a talent of pure gold, with all these utensils. 40 And see to it that you make *them* according to the pattern which was shown you on the mountain.

26 "MOREOVER you shall make the tabernacle *with* ten curtains *of* fine woven linen and blue, purple, and scarlet *thread;* with artistic designs of cherubim you shall weave them. 2 The length of each curtain *shall be* twenty-eight cubits, and the width of each curtain four cubits. And every one of the curtains shall have the same measurements. 3 Five curtains shall be coupled to one another, and *the other* five curtains *shall be* coupled to one another. 4 And you shall make loops of blue *yarn* on the edge of the curtain on the selvedge of *one* set, and likewise you shall do on the outer edge of *the other* curtain of the second set. 5 Fifty loops you shall make in the one curtain, and fifty loops you shall make on the edge of the curtain that *is* on the end of the second set, that the loops may be clasped to one another. 6 And you shall make fifty clasps of gold, and couple the curtains together with the clasps, so that it may be one tabernacle.

7 "You shall also make curtains of goats' *hair,* to be a tent over the tabernacle. You shall make eleven curtains. 8 The length of each curtain *shall be* thirty cubits, and the width of each curtain four cubits; and the eleven curtains shall all have the same measurements. 9 And you shall couple five

curtains by themselves and six curtains by themselves, and you shall double over the sixth curtain at the forefront of the tent. 10 You shall make fifty loops on the edge of the curtain that is outermost in *one* set, and fifty loops on the edge of the curtain of the second set. 11 And you shall make fifty bronze clasps, put the clasps into the loops, and couple the tent together, that it may be one. 12 The remnant that remains of the curtains of the tent, the half curtain that remains, shall hang over the back of the tabernacle. 13 And a cubit on one side and a cubit on the other side, of what remains of the length of the curtains of the tent, shall hang over the sides of the tabernacle, on this side and on that side, to cover it.

14 "You shall also make a covering of ram skins dyed red for the tent, and a covering of badger skins above that.

15 "And for the tabernacle you shall make the boards of acacia wood, standing upright. 16 Ten cubits *shall be* the length of a board, and a cubit and a half *shall be* the width of each board. 17 Two tenons *shall be* in each board for binding one to another. Thus you shall make for all the boards of the tabernacle. 18 And you shall make the boards for the tabernacle, twenty boards for the south side. 19 You shall make forty sockets of silver under the twenty boards: two sockets under each of the boards for its two tenons. 20 And for the second side of the tabernacle, the north side, *there shall be* twenty boards 21 and their forty sockets of silver: two sockets under each of the boards. 22 For the far side of the tabernacle, westward, you shall make six boards. 23 And you shall also make two boards for the two back corners of the tabernacle. 24 They shall be coupled together at the bottom and they shall be coupled together at the top by one ring. Thus it shall be for both of them. They shall be for the two corners. 25 So there shall be eight boards with their sockets of silver—sixteen sockets—two sockets under each of the boards.

26 "And you shall make bars of acacia wood: five for the boards on one side of the tabernacle, 27 five bars for the boards on the other side of the tabernacle, and five bars for the boards of the side of the tabernacle, for the far side westward. 28 The middle bar shall pass through the midst of the boards from end to end. 29 You shall overlay the boards with gold, make their rings of gold *as* holders for the bars, and overlay the bars with gold. 30 And you shall raise up the tabernacle according to its pattern which you were shown on the mountain.

31 "You shall make a veil woven of blue, purple, and scarlet *thread,* and fine woven linen. It shall be woven with an artistic design of cherubim. 32 You shall hang it upon the four pillars of acacia *wood* overlaid with gold. Their hooks *shall be* gold, upon four sockets of silver. 33 And you shall hang the veil from the clasps. Then you shall bring the ark of the Testimony in there, behind the veil. The veil shall be a divider for you between the holy *place* and the Most Holy. 34 You shall put the mercy seat upon the ark of the Testimony in the Most Holy. 35 You shall set the table outside the veil, and the lampstand across from the table on the side of the tabernacle toward the south; and you shall put the table on the north side.

36 "You shall make a screen for the door of the tabernacle, *woven of* blue, purple, and scarlet *thread,* and fine woven linen, made by a weaver. 37 And you shall make for the screen five pillars of acacia *wood,* and overlay them with gold; their hooks *shall be* gold, and you shall cast five sockets of bronze for them.

PSALM 19:7–14

7 THE law of the LORD *is* perfect,
   converting the soul;
   The testimony of the LORD *is* sure,
   making wise the simple;
8 The statutes of the LORD *are* right,
   rejoicing the heart;
   The commandment of the LORD *is* pure,
   enlightening the eyes;
9 The fear of the LORD *is* clean, enduring
   forever;
   The judgments of the LORD *are* true
   and righteous altogether.
10 More to be desired *are they* than gold,
   Yea, than much fine gold;
   Sweeter also than honey and the
   honeycomb.
11 Moreover by them Your servant is
   warned,
   And in keeping them *there is* great
   reward.

12 Who can understand *his* errors?
   Cleanse me from secret *faults.*

There are possibilities below the threshold of our lives which no one but God knows. (BIB. PSYCH.)

13 Keep back Your servant also from
      presumptuous *sins;*
    Let them not have dominion over me.
    Then I shall be blameless,
    And I shall be innocent of great
      transgression.

14 Let the words of my mouth and the
      meditation of my heart
    Be acceptable in Your sight,
    O LORD, my strength and my
      Redeemer.

PROVERBS 6:32–35

32 WHOEVER commits adultery with a
      woman lacks understanding;
    He *who* does so destroys his own soul.
33 Wounds and dishonor he will get,
    And his reproach will not be wiped
      away.
34 For jealousy *is* a husband's fury;
    Therefore he will not spare in the day
      of vengeance.
35 He will accept no recompense,
    Nor will he be appeased though you
      give many gifts.

MATTHEW 24:1–28

THEN Jesus went out and departed from
the temple, and His disciples came up to
show Him the buildings of the temple.
2 And Jesus said to them, "Do you not see
all these things? Assuredly, I say to you,
not *one* stone shall be left here upon another, that shall not be thrown down."

3 Now as He sat on the Mount of Olives,
the disciples came to Him privately, saying,
"Tell us, when will these things be? And
what *will be* the sign of Your coming, and
of the end of the age?"

4 And Jesus answered and said to them:
"Take heed that no one deceives you.
5 For many will come in My name, saying,
'I am the Christ,' and will deceive many.
6 And you will hear of wars and rumors
of wars. See that you are not troubled; for
all *these things* must come to pass, but the
end is not yet. 7 For nation will rise against
nation, and kingdom against kingdom. And
there will be famines, pestilences, and earthquakes in various places. 8 All these *are* the
beginning of sorrows.

9 "Then they will deliver you up to tribulation and kill you, and you will be hated
by all nations for My name's sake. 10 And
then many will be offended, will betray one
another, and will hate one another.
11 Then many false prophets will rise up
and deceive many. 12 And because lawlessness will abound, the love of many will
grow cold. 13 But he who endures to the
end shall be saved. 14 And this gospel of
the kingdom will be preached in all the
world as a witness to all the nations, and
then the end will come.

15 "Therefore when you see the 'abomination of desolation,' spoken of by Daniel
the prophet, standing in the holy place"
(whoever reads, let him understand),
16 "then let those who are in Judea flee to
the mountains. 17 Let him who is on the
housetop not go down to take anything
out of his house. 18 And let him who is in
the field not go back to get his clothes.
19 But woe to those who are pregnant and
to those who are nursing babies in those
days! 20 And pray that your flight may not
be in winter or on the Sabbath. 21 For then
there will be great tribulation, such as has
not been since the beginning of the world
until this time, no, nor ever shall be.
22 And unless those days were shortened,
no flesh would be saved; but for the elect's
sake those days will be shortened.

23 "Then if anyone says to you, 'Look,
here *is* the Christ!' or 'There!' do not believe
it. 24 For false christs and false prophets
will rise and show great signs and wonders
to deceive, if possible, even the elect.
25 See, I have told you beforehand.
26 "Therefore if they say to you, 'Look,
He is in the desert!' do not go out; *or* 'Look,
He is in the inner rooms!' do not believe
it. 27 For as the lightning comes from the
east and flashes to the west, so also will
the coming of the Son of Man be. 28 For
wherever the carcass is, there the eagles will
be gathered together.

---

*The reason we do not pray is that
we do not own Jesus Christ as
Master.* (SEND I YOU)

◆◆◆◆

Reading 39—Holiness to the Lord
Exodus 28:36–38

Continually restate to yourself what the purpose of your life is. The destined end of man is not happiness, nor health, but holiness. . . . The one thing that matters is whether a man will accept the God who will make him holy. At all costs a man must be rightly related to God. . . .

God has one destined end for mankind, namely, holiness. His one aim is the production of saints. God is not an eternal blessing-machine for men; He did not come to save men out of pity: He came to save men because He had created them to be holy. The Atonement means that God can put me back into perfect union with Himself, without a shadow between, through the death of Jesus Christ.

Never tolerate through sympathy with yourself or with others any practice that is not in keeping with a holy God. Holiness means unsullied walking with the feet, unsullied talking with the tongue, unsullied thinking with the mind—every detail of the life under the scrutiny of God. Holiness is not only what God gives me, but what I manifest that God has given me.   (*Utmost*)

EXODUS 27:1—28:43

"YOU shall make an altar of acacia wood, five cubits long and five cubits wide—the altar shall be square—and its height *shall be* three cubits. 2 You shall make its horns on its four corners; its horns shall be of one piece with it. And you shall overlay it with bronze. 3 Also you shall make its pans to receive its ashes, and its shovels and its basins and its forks and its firepans; you shall make all its utensils of bronze. 4 You shall make a grate for it, a network of bronze; and on the network you shall make four bronze rings at its four corners. 5 You shall put it under the rim of the altar beneath, that the network may be midway up the altar. 6 And you shall make poles for the altar, poles of acacia wood, and overlay them with bronze. 7 The poles shall be put in the rings, and the poles shall be on the two sides of the altar to bear it. 8 You shall make it hollow with boards; as it was shown you on the mountain, so shall they make *it.*

9 "You shall also make the court of the tabernacle. For the south side *there shall be* hangings for the court *made of* fine woven linen, one hundred cubits long for one side. 10 And its twenty pillars and their twenty sockets *shall be* bronze. The hooks of the pillars and their bands *shall be* silver. 11 Likewise along the length of the north side *there shall be* hangings one hundred *cubits* long, with its twenty

pillars and their twenty sockets of bronze, and the hooks of the pillars and their bands of silver.

12 "And along the width of the court on the west side *shall be* hangings of fifty cubits, with their ten pillars and their ten sockets. 13 The width of the court on the east side *shall be* fifty cubits. 14 The hangings on *one* side *of the gate shall be* fifteen cubits, *with* their three pillars and their three sockets. 15 And on the other side *shall be* hangings of fifteen *cubits, with* their three pillars and their three sockets.

16 "For the gate of the court *there shall be* a screen twenty cubits long, *woven of* blue, purple, and scarlet *thread,* and fine woven linen, made by a weaver. It *shall have* four pillars and four sockets. 17 All the pillars around the court shall have bands of silver; their hooks *shall be* of silver and their sockets of bronze. 18 The length of the court *shall be* one hundred cubits, the width fifty throughout, and the height five cubits, *made of* fine woven linen, and its sockets of bronze. 19 All the utensils of the tabernacle for all its service, all its pegs, and all the pegs of the court, *shall be* of bronze.

20 "And you shall command the children of Israel that they bring you pure oil of pressed olives for the light, to cause the lamp to burn continually. 21 In the tabernacle of meeting, outside the veil which *is* before the Testimony, Aaron and his sons shall tend it from evening until morning before the LORD. *It shall be* a statute forever

to their generations on behalf of the children of Israel.

28 "NOW take Aaron your brother, and his sons with him, from among the children of Israel, that he may minister to Me as priest, Aaron *and* Aaron's sons: Nadab, Abihu, Eleazar, and Ithamar. 2 And you shall make holy garments for Aaron your brother, for glory and for beauty. 3 So you shall speak to all *who are* gifted artisans, whom I have filled with the spirit of wisdom, that they may make Aaron's garments, to consecrate him, that he may minister to Me as priest. 4 And these *are* the garments which they shall make: a breastplate, an ephod, a robe, a skillfully woven tunic, a turban, and a sash. So they shall make holy garments for Aaron your brother and his sons, that he may minister to Me as priest.

5 "They shall take the gold, blue, purple, and scarlet *thread,* and the fine linen, 6 and they shall make the ephod of gold, blue, purple, *and* scarlet *thread,* and fine woven linen, artistically worked. 7 It shall have two shoulder straps joined at its two edges, and *so* it shall be joined together. 8 And the intricately woven band of the ephod, which *is* on it, shall be of the same workmanship, *made of* gold, blue, purple, and scarlet *thread,* and fine woven linen.

9 "Then you shall take two onyx stones and engrave on them the names of the sons of Israel: 10 six of their names on one stone and six names on the other stone, in order of their birth. 11 With the work of an engraver in stone, *like* the engravings of a signet, you shall engrave the two stones with the names of the sons of Israel. You shall set them in settings of gold. 12 And you shall put the two stones on the shoulders of the ephod *as* memorial stones for the sons of Israel. So Aaron shall bear their names before the LORD on his two shoulders as a memorial. 13 You shall also make settings of gold, 14 and you shall make two chains of pure gold like braided cords, and fasten the braided chains to the settings.

15 "You shall make the breastplate of judgment. Artistically woven according to the workmanship of the ephod you shall make it: of gold, blue, purple, and scarlet *thread,* and fine woven linen, you shall make it. 16 It shall be doubled into a square: a span *shall be* its length, and a span *shall be* its width. 17 And you shall put settings of stones in it, four rows of stones: *The first* row *shall be* a sardius, a topaz, and an emerald; *this shall be* the first row; 18 the second row *shall be* a turquoise, a sapphire, and a

diamond; 19 the third row, a jacinth, an agate, and an amethyst; 20 and the fourth row, a beryl, an onyx, and a jasper. They shall be set in gold settings. 21 And the stones shall have the names of the sons of Israel, twelve according to their names, *like* the engravings of a signet, each one with its own name; they shall be according to the twelve tribes.

22 "You shall make chains for the breastplate at the end, like braided cords of pure gold. 23 And you shall make two rings of gold for the breastplate, and put the two rings on the two ends of the breastplate. 24 Then you shall put the two braided *chains* of gold in the two rings which are on the ends of the breastplate; 25 and the *other* two ends of the two braided *chains* you shall fasten to the two settings, and put them on the shoulder straps of the ephod in the front.

26 "You shall make two rings of gold, and put them on the two ends of the breastplate, on the edge of it, which is on the inner side of the ephod. 27 And two *other* rings of gold you shall make, and put them on the two shoulder straps, underneath the ephod toward its front, right at the seam above the intricately woven band of the ephod. 28 They shall bind the breastplate by means of its rings to the rings of the ephod, using a blue cord, so that it is above the intricately woven band of the ephod, and so that the breastplate does not come loose from the ephod.

29 "So Aaron shall bear the names of the sons of Israel on the breastplate of judgment over his heart, when he goes into the holy *place,* as a memorial before the LORD continually. 30 And you shall put in the breastplate of judgment the Urim and the Thummim, and they shall be over Aaron's heart when he goes in before the LORD. So Aaron shall bear the judgment of the children of Israel over his heart before the LORD continually.

31 "You shall make the robe of the ephod all of blue. 32 There shall be an opening for his head in the middle of it; it shall have a woven binding all around its opening, like the opening in a coat of mail, so that it does not tear. 33 And upon its hem you shall make pomegranates of blue, purple, and scarlet, all around its hem, and bells of gold between them all around: 34 a golden bell and a pomegranate, a golden bell and a pomegranate, upon the hem of the robe all around. 35 And it shall be upon Aaron when he ministers, and its sound will be heard when he goes into the holy *place* before the LORD and when he comes out, that he may not die.

36 "You shall also make a plate of pure gold and engrave on it, *like* the engraving of a signet:

HOLINESS TO THE LORD.

Jesus Christ stands for holiness.   (SHAD. AGONY)

37 And you shall put it on a blue cord, that it may be on the turban; it shall be on the front of the turban. 38 So it shall be on Aaron's forehead, that Aaron may bear the iniquity of the holy things which the children of Israel hallow in all their holy gifts; and it shall always be on his forehead, that they may be accepted before the LORD. 39 "You shall skillfully weave the tunic of fine linen *thread,* you shall make the turban of fine linen, and you shall make the sash of woven work.

40 "For Aaron's sons you shall make tunics, and you shall make sashes for them. And you shall make hats for them, for glory and beauty. 41 So you shall put them on Aaron your brother and on his sons with him. You shall anoint them, consecrate them, and sanctify them, that they may minister to Me as priests. 42 And you shall make for them linen trousers to cover their nakedness; they shall reach from the waist to the thighs. 43 They shall be on Aaron and on his sons when they come into the tabernacle of meeting, or when they come near the altar to minister in the holy *place,* that they do not incur iniquity and die. *It shall be* a statute forever to him and his descendants after him.

PSALM 20:1–5

1   MAY the LORD answer you in the day of trouble;
    May the name of the God of Jacob defend you;
2   May He send you help from the sanctuary,
    And strengthen you out of Zion;
3   May He remember all your offerings,
    And accept your burnt sacrifice.
                                    Selah

4   May He grant you according to your heart's *desire,*
    And fulfill all your purpose.
5   We will rejoice in your salvation,

A great deal depends on what is the real deep desire of our hearts.   (PERFECT)

And in the name of our God we will set up *our* banners!
May the LORD fulfill all your petitions.

PROVERBS 7:1–5

1   MY son, keep my words,
    And treasure my commands within you.
2   Keep my commands and live,
    And my law as the apple of your eye.
3   Bind them on your fingers;
    Write them on the tablet of your heart.
4   Say to wisdom, "You *are* my sister,"
    And call understanding *your* nearest kin,
5   That they may keep you from the immoral woman,
    From the seductress *who* flatters with her words.

MATTHEW 24:29–51

"IMMEDIATELY after the tribulation of those days the sun will be darkened, and the moon will not give its light; the stars will fall from heaven, and the powers of the heavens will be shaken. 30 Then the sign of the Son of Man will appear in heaven, and then all the tribes of the earth will mourn, and they will see the Son of Man coming on the clouds of heaven with power and great glory. 31 And He will send His angels with a great sound of a trumpet, and they will gather together His elect from the four winds, from one end of heaven to the other.

32 "Now learn this parable from the fig tree: When its branch has already become tender and puts forth leaves, you know that summer *is* near. 33 So you also, when you see all these things, know that it is near—at the doors! 34 Assuredly, I say to you, this generation will by no means pass away till all these things take place. 35 Heaven and earth will pass away, but My words will by no means pass away.

36 "But of that day and hour no one knows, not even the angels of heaven, but My Father only. 37 But as the days of Noah *were,* so also will the coming of the Son of Man be. 38 For as in the days before the flood, they were eating and drinking,

marrying and giving in marriage, until the day that Noah entered the ark, 39 and did not know until the flood came and took them all away, so also will the coming of the Son of Man be. 40 Then two *men* will be in the field: one will be taken and the other left. 41 Two *women will be* grinding at the mill: one will be taken and the other left. 42 Watch therefore, for you do not know what hour your Lord is coming. 43 But know this, that if the master of the house had known what hour the thief would come, he would have watched and not allowed his house to be broken into. 44 Therefore you also be ready, for the Son of Man is coming at an hour you do not expect.

45 "Who then is a faithful and wise servant, whom his master made ruler over his household, to give them food in due season? 46 Blessed *is* that servant whom his master, when he comes, will find so doing. 47 Assuredly, I say to you that he will make him ruler over all his goods. 48 But if that evil servant says in his heart, 'My master is delaying his coming,' 49 and begins to beat *his* fellow servants, and to eat and drink with the drunkards, 50 the master of that servant will come on a day when he is not looking for *him* and at an hour that he is not aware of, 51 and will cut him in two and appoint *him* his portion with the hypocrites. There shall be weeping and gnashing of teeth.

◆◆◆◆

Reading 40—The Divine Estimate of Life
Matthew 25:1–30

The modern Christian laughs at the idea of a final judgment. That shows how far we can stray away if we imbibe the idea that the modern mind is infallible and not our Lord. To His mind at least the finality of moral decision is reached in this life. There is no aspect of our Lord's mind that the modern mind detests so fundamentally as this one. . . .

The parables in the twenty-fifth chapter of St. Matthew are three aspects of the Divine estimate of life. The parable of the ten virgins reveals that it is fatal from our Lord's standpoint to live this life without preparation for the life to come. That is not the exegesis, it is the obvious underlying principle.

The parable of the talents is our Lord's statement with regard to the danger of leaving undone the work of a lifetime.

And the description of the last judgment is the picture of genuine astonishment on the part of both the losers and the gainers of what they had never once thought about.

To be accustomed to our Lord's teaching is not to ask, "What must I do to be good?" but, "What must I do to be saved?" How long does it take us to know what the true meaning of our life is? One-half second.   (GOOD)

EXODUS 29:1—30:38

"AND this is what you shall do to them to hallow them for ministering to Me as priests: Take one young bull and two rams without blemish, 2 and unleavened bread, unleavened cakes mixed with oil, and unleavened wafers anointed with oil (you shall make them of wheat flour). 3 You shall put them in one basket and bring them in the basket, with the bull and the two rams.
4 "And Aaron and his sons you shall bring

to the door of the tabernacle of meeting, and you shall wash them with water. 5 Then you shall take the garments, put the tunic on Aaron, and the robe of the ephod, the ephod, and the breastplate, and gird him with the intricately woven band of the ephod. 6 You shall put the turban on his head, and put the holy crown on the turban. 7 And you shall take the anointing oil, pour *it* on his head, and anoint him. 8 Then you shall bring his sons and put tunics on them. 9 And you shall gird them with sashes, Aaron and his sons, and put the hats on them. The priesthood shall be theirs for a perpetual statute. So you shall consecrate Aaron and his sons.

10 "You shall also have the bull brought before the tabernacle of meeting, and Aaron and his sons shall put their hands on the head of the bull. 11 Then you shall kill the bull before the LORD, *by* the door of the tabernacle of meeting. 12 You shall take *some* of the blood of the bull and put *it* on the horns of the altar with your finger, and pour all the blood beside the base of the altar. 13 And you shall take all the fat that covers the entrails, the fatty lobe *attached* to the liver, and the two kidneys and the fat that *is* on them, and burn *them* on the altar. 14 But the flesh of the bull, with its skin and its offal, you shall burn with fire outside the camp. It *is* a sin offering.

15 "You shall also take one ram, and Aaron and his sons shall put their hands on the head of the ram; 16 and you shall kill the ram, and you shall take its blood and sprinkle *it* all around on the altar. 17 Then you shall cut the ram in pieces, wash its entrails and its legs, and put *them* with its pieces and with its head. 18 And you shall burn the whole ram on the altar. It *is* a burnt offering to the LORD; it *is* a sweet aroma, an offering made by fire to the LORD.

19 "You shall also take the other ram, and Aaron and his sons shall put their hands on the head of the ram. 20 Then you shall kill the ram, and take some of its blood and put *it* on the tip of the right ear of Aaron and on the tip of the right ear of his sons, on the thumb of their right hand and on the big toe of their right foot, and sprinkle the blood all around on the altar. 21 And you shall take some of the blood that is on the altar, and some of the anointing oil, and sprinkle *it* on Aaron and on his garments, on his sons and on the garments of his sons with him; and he and his garments shall be hallowed, and his sons and his sons' garments with him.

22 "Also you shall take the fat of the ram, the fat tail, the fat that covers the entrails, the fatty lobe *attached to* the liver, the two kidneys and the fat on them, the right thigh (for it *is* a ram of consecration), 23 one loaf of bread, one cake *made with* oil, and one wafer from the basket of the unleavened bread that *is* before the LORD; 24 and you shall put all these in the hands of Aaron and in the hands of his sons, and you shall wave them *as* a wave offering before the LORD. 25 You shall receive them back from their hands and burn *them* on the altar as a burnt offering, as a sweet aroma before

the LORD. It *is* an offering made by fire to the LORD.

26 "Then you shall take the breast of the ram of Aaron's consecration and wave it *as* a wave offering before the LORD; and it shall be your portion. 27 And from the ram of the consecration you shall consecrate the breast of the wave offering which is waved, and the thigh of the heave offering which is raised, of *that* which *is* for Aaron and of *that* which is for his sons. 28 It shall be from the children of Israel *for* Aaron and his sons by a statute forever. For it is a heave offering; it shall be a heave offering from the children of Israel from the sacrifices of their peace offerings, *that is,* their heave offering to the LORD.

29 "And the holy garments of Aaron shall be his sons' after him, to be anointed in them and to be consecrated in them. 30 That son who becomes priest in his place shall put them on for seven days, when he enters the tabernacle of meeting to minister in the holy *place*.

31 "And you shall take the ram of the consecration and boil its flesh in the holy place. 32 Then Aaron and his sons shall eat the flesh of the ram, and the bread that *is* in the basket, *by* the door of the tabernacle of meeting. 33 They shall eat those things with which the atonement was made, to consecrate *and* to sanctify them; but an outsider shall not eat *them,* because they *are* holy. 34 And if any of the flesh of the consecration offerings, or of the bread, remains until the morning, then you shall burn the remainder with fire. It shall not be eaten, because it *is* holy.

35 "Thus you shall do to Aaron and his sons, according to all that I have commanded you. Seven days you shall consecrate them. 36 And you shall offer a bull every day *as* a sin offering for atonement. You shall cleanse the altar when you make atonement for it, and you shall anoint it to sanctify it. 37 Seven days you shall make atonement for the altar and sanctify it. And the altar shall be most holy. Whatever touches the altar must be holy.

38 "Now this *is* what you shall offer on the altar: two lambs of the first year, day by day continually. 39 One lamb you shall offer in the morning, and the other lamb you shall offer at twilight. 40 With the one lamb shall be one-tenth *of an ephah* of flour mixed with one-fourth of a hin of pressed oil, and one-fourth of a hin of wine *as* a drink offering. 41 And the other lamb you shall offer at twilight; and you shall offer with it the grain offering and the drink offering, as in the morning, for a sweet aroma,

an offering made by fire to the Lord. 42 *This shall be* a continual burnt offering throughout your generations *at* the door of the tabernacle of meeting before the Lord, where I will meet you to speak with you. 43 And there I will meet with the children of Israel, and *the tabernacle* shall be sanctified by My glory. 44 So I will consecrate the tabernacle of meeting and the altar. I will also consecrate both Aaron and his sons to minister to Me as priests. 45 I will dwell among the children of Israel and will be their God. 46 And they shall know that I *am* the Lord their God, who brought them up out of the land of Egypt, that I may dwell among them. I *am* the Lord their God.

30 "YOU shall make an altar to burn incense on; you shall make it of acacia wood. 2 A cubit *shall be* its length and a cubit its width—it shall be square—and two cubits *shall be* its height. Its horns *shall be* of one piece with it. 3 And you shall overlay its top, its sides all around, and its horns with pure gold; and you shall make for it a molding of gold all around. 4 Two gold rings you shall make for it, under the molding on both its sides. You shall place *them* on its two sides, and they will be holders for the poles with which to bear it. 5 You shall make the poles of acacia wood, and overlay them with gold. 6 And you shall put it before the veil that *is* before the ark of the Testimony, before the mercy seat that *is* over the Testimony, where I will meet with you.

7 "Aaron shall burn on it sweet incense every morning; when he tends the lamps, he shall burn incense on it. 8 And when Aaron lights the lamps at twilight, he shall burn incense on it, a perpetual incense before the Lord throughout your generations. 9 You shall not offer strange incense on it, or a burnt offering, or a grain offering; nor shall you pour a drink offering on it. 10 And Aaron shall make atonement upon its horns once a year with the blood of the sin offering of atonement; once a year he shall make atonement upon it throughout your generations. It *is* most holy to the Lord."

11 Then the Lord spoke to Moses, saying: 12 "When you take the census of the children of Israel for their number, then every man shall give a ransom for himself to the Lord, when you number them, that there may be no plague among them when *you* number them. 13 This is what everyone among those who are numbered shall give: half a shekel according to the shekel of the

sanctuary (a shekel *is* twenty gerahs). The half-shekel *shall be* an offering to the Lord. 14 Everyone included among those who are numbered, from twenty years old and above, shall give an offering to the Lord. 15 The rich shall not give more and the poor shall not give less than half a shekel, when *you* give an offering to the Lord, to make atonement for yourselves. 16 And you shall take the atonement money of the children of Israel, and shall appoint it for the service of the tabernacle of meeting, that it may be a memorial for the children of Israel before the Lord, to make atonement for yourselves."

17 Then the Lord spoke to Moses, saying: 18 "You shall also make a laver of bronze, with its base also of bronze, for washing. You shall put it between the tabernacle of meeting and the altar. And you shall put water in it, 19 for Aaron and his sons shall wash their hands and their feet in water from it. 20 When they go into the tabernacle of meeting, or when they come near the altar to minister, to burn an offering made by fire to the Lord, they shall wash with water, lest they die. 21 So they shall wash their hands and their feet, lest they die. And it shall be a statute forever to them—to him and his descendants throughout their generations."

22 Moreover the Lord spoke to Moses, saying: 23 "Also take for yourself quality spices—five hundred *shekels* of liquid myrrh, half as much sweet-smelling cinnamon (two hundred and fifty *shekels*), two hundred and fifty *shekels* of sweet-smelling cane, 24 five hundred *shekels* of cassia, according to the shekel of the sanctuary, and a hin of olive oil. 25 And you shall make from these a holy anointing oil, an ointment compounded according to the art of the perfumer. It shall be a holy anointing oil. 26 With it you shall anoint the tabernacle of meeting and the ark of the Testimony; 27 the table and all its utensils, the lampstand and its utensils, and the altar of incense; 28 the altar of burnt offering with all its utensils, and the laver and its base. 29 You shall consecrate them, that they may be most holy; whatever touches them must be holy. 30 And you shall anoint Aaron and his sons, and consecrate them, that *they* may minister to Me as priests.

31 "And you shall speak to the children of Israel, saying: 'This shall be a holy anointing oil to Me throughout your generations. 32 It shall not be poured on man's flesh; nor shall you make *any other* like it, according to its composition. It *is* holy, *and* it shall be holy to you. 33 Whoever com-

pounds *any* like it, or whoever puts *any* of it on an outsider, shall be cut off from his people.' "

34 And the LORD said to Moses: "Take sweet spices, stacte and onycha and galbanum, and pure frankincense with *these* sweet spices; there shall be equal amounts of each. 35 You shall make of these an incense, a compound according to the art of the perfumer, salted, pure, *and* holy. 36 And you shall beat *some* of it very fine, and put some of it before the Testimony in the tabernacle of meeting where I will meet with you. It shall be most holy to you. 37 But *as for* the incense which you shall make, you shall not make any for yourselves, according to its composition. It shall be to you holy for the LORD. 38 Whoever makes *any* like it, to smell it, he shall be cut off from his people."

PSALM 20:6–9

6 NOW I know that the LORD saves His anointed;
He will answer him from His holy heaven
With the saving strength of His right hand.

7 Some *trust* in chariots, and some in horses;
But we will remember the name of the LORD our God.

Trustfulness is based on confidence in God whose ways I do not understand. (GLORIFY)

8 They have bowed down and fallen;
But we have risen and stand upright.

9 Save, LORD!
May the King answer us when we call.

PROVERBS 7:6–23

6 FOR at the window of my house
I looked through my lattice,

7 And saw among the simple,
I perceived among the youths,
A young man devoid of understanding,

8 Passing along the street near her corner;
And he took the path to her house

9 In the twilight, in the evening,
In the black and dark night.

10 And there a woman met him,
With the attire of a harlot, and a crafty heart.

11 She *was* loud and rebellious,
Her feet would not stay at home.

12 At times *she was* outside, at times in the open square,
Lurking at every corner.

13 So she caught him and kissed him;
With an impudent face she said to him:

14 "*I have* peace offerings with me;
Today I have paid my vows.

15 So I came out to meet you,
Diligently to seek your face,
And I have found you.

16 I have spread my bed with tapestry,
Colored coverings of Egyptian linen.

17 I have perfumed my bed
With myrrh, aloes, and cinnamon.

18 Come, let us take our fill of love until morning;
Let us delight ourselves with love.

19 For my husband *is* not at home;
He has gone on a long journey;

20 He has taken a bag of money with him,
And will come home on the appointed day."

21 With her enticing speech she caused him to yield,
With her flattering lips she seduced him.

22 Immediately he went after her, as an ox goes to the slaughter,
Or as a fool to the correction of the stocks,

23 Till an arrow struck his liver.
As a bird hastens to the snare,
He did not know it *would cost* his life.

MATTHEW 25:1–30

"THEN the kingdom of heaven shall be likened to ten virgins who took their lamps and went out to meet the bridegroom. 2 Now five of them were wise, and five *were* foolish. 3 Those who *were* foolish took their lamps and took no oil with them, 4 but the wise took oil in their vessels with their lamps. 5 But while the bridegroom was delayed, they all slumbered and slept.

6 "And at midnight a cry was *heard:* 'Behold, the bridegroom is coming; go out to meet him!' 7 Then all those virgins arose and trimmed their lamps. 8 And the foolish said to the wise, 'Give us *some* of your oil, for our lamps are going out.' 9 But the wise answered, saying, '*No,* lest there should not be enough for us and you; but go rather to those who sell, and buy for yourselves.' 10 And while they went to buy, the bride-

groom came, and those who were ready went in with him to the wedding; and the door was shut.

11 "Afterward the other virgins came also, saying, 'Lord, Lord, open to us!' 12 But he answered and said, 'Assuredly, I say to you, I do not know you.'

13 "Watch therefore, for you know neither the day nor the hour in which the Son of Man is coming.

14 "For *the kingdom of heaven is* like a man traveling to a far country, *who* called his own servants and delivered his goods to them. 15 And to one he gave five talents, to another two, and to another one, to each according to his own ability; and immediately he went on a journey. 16 Then he who had received the five talents went and traded with them, and made another five talents. 17 And likewise he who *had received* two gained two more also. 18 But he who had received one went and dug in the ground, and hid his lord's money. 19 After a long time the lord of those servants came and settled accounts with them.

20 "So he who had received five talents came and brought five other talents, saying, 'Lord, you delivered to me five talents; look, I have gained five more talents besides them.' 21 His lord said to him, 'Well *done,* good and faithful servant; you were faithful over a few things, I will make you ruler over many things. Enter into the joy of your lord.' 22 He also who had received two talents came and said, 'Lord, you deliv-

ered to me two talents; look, I have gained two more talents besides them.' 23 His lord said to him, 'Well *done,* good and faithful servant; you have been faithful over a few things, I will make you ruler over many things. Enter into the joy of your lord.'

24 "Then he who had received the one talent came and said, 'Lord, I knew you to be a hard man, reaping where you have not sown, and gathering where you have not scattered seed. 25 And I was afraid, and went and hid your talent in the ground. Look, *there* you have *what is* yours.'

26 "But his lord answered and said to him, 'You wicked and lazy servant, you knew that I reap where I have not sown, and gather where I have not scattered seed.

---

*T*he only cure for laziness is to be filled with the life of God.   (WORKMEN)

---

27 So you ought to have deposited my money with the bankers, and at my coming I would have received back my own with interest. 28 So take the talent from him, and give *it* to him who has ten talents.

29 'For to everyone who has, more will be given, and he will have abundance; but from him who does not have, even what he has will be taken away. 30 And cast the unprofitable servant into the outer darkness. There will be weeping and gnashing of teeth.'

◆◆◆◆

Reading 41—God's Motives and Ours
Matthew 25:37–40

Do good until it is an unconscious habit of the life and you do not know you are doing it. . . . "Lord, when did we see You hungry and feed *You?* . . . inasmuch as You did *it* to one of the least of these My brethren, you did *it* to Me." That is our Lord's magnanimous interpretation of kind acts that people have never allowed themselves to think of. Get into the habit of having such a relationship to God . . . then you will no longer trust your own impulse, or your own judgment, you will trust only the inspiration of the Spirit of God. The mainspring of your motives will be the Father's heart, not your own; the Father's understanding, not your own. When once you are rightly related to God, He will use you as a channel through which His disposition will flow.

Much of our modern philanthropy is based on the motive of giving to the poor man because he deserves it, or because we are distressed at seeing him poor. Jesus never taught charity from those motives: He said, "Give to him who asks you, not because he deserves it, but because I tell you to." The great motive in all giving is Jesus Christ's command. We can always find a hundred and one reasons for not obeying our Lord's commands, because we will trust our reasoning rather than His reason, and our reason does not take God into calculation. How does civilization argue? "Does this man deserve what I am giving him?" Immediately you talk like that, the Spirit of God says, "Who are you? Do *you* deserve more than other men the blessings you have?"   (SERMON MT.)

EXODUS 31:1—32:35

THEN the LORD spoke to Moses, saying: 2 "See, I have called by name Bezalel the son of Uri, the son of Hur, of the tribe of Judah. 3 And I have filled him with the Spirit of God, in wisdom, in understanding, in knowledge, and in all *manner of* workmanship, 4 to design artistic works, to work in gold, in silver, in bronze, 5 in cutting jewels for setting, in carving wood, and to work in all *manner of* workmanship.

6 "And I, indeed I, have appointed with him Aholiab the son of Ahisamach, of the tribe of Dan; and I have put wisdom in the hearts of all the gifted artisans, that they may make all that I have commanded you: 7 the tabernacle of meeting, the ark of the Testimony and the mercy seat that *is* on it, and all the furniture of the tabernacle— 8 the table and its utensils, the pure *gold* lampstand with all its utensils, the altar of incense, 9 the altar of burnt offering with all its utensils, and the laver and its base— 10 the garments of ministry, the holy garments for Aaron the priest and the garments of his sons, to minister as priests, 11 and the anointing oil and sweet incense for the holy *place*. According to all that I have commanded you they shall do."

12 And the LORD spoke to Moses, saying, 13 "Speak also to the children of Israel, saying: 'Surely My Sabbaths you shall keep, for it *is* a sign between Me and you throughout your generations, that *you* may know that I *am* the LORD who sanctifies you. 14 You shall keep the Sabbath, therefore, for *it is* holy to you. Everyone who profanes it shall surely be put to death; for whoever does *any* work on it, that person shall be cut off from among his people. 15 Work shall be done for six days, but the seventh *is* the Sabbath of rest, holy to the LORD. Whoever does *any* work on the Sabbath day, he shall surely be put to death. 16 Therefore the children of Israel shall keep the Sabbath, to observe the Sabbath throughout their generations *as* a perpetual covenant. 17 It *is* a sign between Me and the children of Israel forever; for *in* six days

the LORD made the heavens and the earth, and on the seventh day He rested and was refreshed.' "

18 And when He had made an end of speaking with him on Mount Sinai, He gave Moses two tablets of the Testimony, tablets of stone, written with the finger of God.

32 NOW when the people saw that Moses delayed coming down from the mountain, the people gathered together to Aaron, and said to him, "Come, make us gods that shall go before us; for *as for* this Moses, the man who brought us up out of the land of Egypt, we do not know what has become of him."

2 And Aaron said to them, "Break off the golden earrings which *are* in the ears of your wives, your sons, and your daughters, and bring *them* to me." 3 So all the people broke off the golden earrings which *were* in their ears, and brought *them* to Aaron. 4 And he received *the gold* from their hand, and he fashioned it with an engraving tool, and made a molded calf.

Then they said, "This *is* your god, O Israel, that brought you out of the land of Egypt!"

5 So when Aaron saw *it,* he built an altar before it. And Aaron made a proclamation and said, "Tomorrow *is* a feast to the LORD." 6 Then they rose early on the next day, offered burnt offerings, and brought peace offerings; and the people sat down to eat and drink, and rose up to play.

7 And the LORD said to Moses, "Go, get down! For your people whom you brought out of the land of Egypt have corrupted *themselves.* 8 They have turned aside quickly out of the way which I commanded them. They have made themselves a molded calf, and worshiped it and sacrificed to it, and said, 'This *is* your god, O Israel, that brought you out of the land of Egypt!' " 9 And the LORD said to Moses, "I have seen this people, and indeed it *is* a stiff-necked people! 10 Now therefore, let Me alone, that My wrath may burn hot against them and I may consume them. And I will make of you a great nation."

11 Then Moses pleaded with the LORD

his God, and said: "LORD, why does Your wrath burn hot against Your people whom You have brought out of the land of Egypt with great power and with a mighty hand? 12 Why should the Egyptians speak, and say, 'He brought them out to harm them, to kill them in the mountains, and to consume them from the face of the earth'? Turn from Your fierce wrath, and relent from this harm to Your people. 13 Remember Abraham, Isaac, and Israel, Your servants, to whom You swore by Your own self, and said to them, 'I will multiply your descendants as the stars of heaven; and all this land that I have spoken of I give to your descendants, and they shall inherit *it* forever.'" 14 So the LORD relented from the harm which He said He would do to His people.

15 And Moses turned and went down from the mountain, and the two tablets of the Testimony *were* in his hand. The tablets *were* written on both sides; on the one *side* and on the other they were written. 16 Now the tablets *were* the work of God, and the writing *was* the writing of God engraved on the tablets.

17 And when Joshua heard the noise of the people as they shouted, he said to Moses, "*There is* a noise of war in the camp." 18 But he said:

> "*It is* not the noise of the shout of
>   victory,
>   Nor the noise of the cry of defeat,
> *But* the sound of singing I hear."

19 So it was, as soon as he came near the camp, that he saw the calf *and* the dancing. So Moses' anger became hot, and he cast the tablets out of his hands and broke them at the foot of the mountain. 20 Then he took the calf which they had made, burned *it* in the fire, and ground *it* to powder; and he scattered *it* on the water and made the children of Israel drink *it*. 21 And Moses said to Aaron, "What did this people do to you that you have brought *so* great a sin upon them?"

22 So Aaron said, "Do not let the anger of my lord become hot. You know the people, that they *are set* on evil. 23 For they said to me, 'Make us gods that shall go before us; *as for* this Moses, the man who brought us out of the land of Egypt, we do not know what has become of him.' 24 And I said to them, 'Whoever has any gold, let them break *it* off.' So they gave *it* to me, and I cast it into the fire, and this calf came out."

25 Now when Moses saw that the people *were* unrestrained (for Aaron had not restrained them, to *their* shame among their enemies), 26 then Moses stood in the entrance of the camp, and said, "Whoever *is* on the LORD's side—*come* to me!" And all the sons of Levi gathered themselves together to him. 27 And he said to them, "Thus says the LORD God of Israel: 'Let every man put his sword on his side, and go in and out from entrance to entrance throughout the camp, and let every man kill his brother, every man his companion, and every man his neighbor.'" 28 So the sons of Levi did according to the word of Moses. And about three thousand men of the people fell that day. 29 Then Moses said, "Consecrate yourselves today to the LORD, that He may bestow on you a blessing this day, for every man has opposed his son and his brother."

---

*C*onsecration is our part,
   sanctification is God's
      part. (UTMOST)

---

30 Now it came to pass on the next day that Moses said to the people, "You have committed a great sin. So now I will go up to the LORD; perhaps I can make atonement for your sin." 31 Then Moses returned to the LORD and said, "Oh, these people have committed a great sin, and have made for themselves a god of gold! 32 Yet now, if You will forgive their sin—but if not, I pray, blot me out of Your book which You have written."

33 And the LORD said to Moses, "Whoever has sinned against Me, I will blot him out of My book. 34 Now therefore, go, lead the people to *the place* of which I have spoken to you. Behold, My Angel shall go before you. Nevertheless, in the day when I visit for punishment, I will visit punishment upon them for their sin."

35 So the LORD plagued the people because of what they did with the calf which Aaron made.

PSALM 21:1–7

1   THE king shall have joy in Your
       strength, O LORD;
     And in Your salvation how greatly shall
       he rejoice!
2   You have given him his heart's desire,
     And have not withheld the request of
       his lips.   Selah

3   For You meet him with the blessings
    of goodness;
    You set a crown of pure gold upon
    his head.
4   He asked life from You, *and* You gave
    it to him—
    Length of days forever and ever.
5   His glory *is* great in Your salvation;
    Honor and majesty You have placed
    upon him.
6   For You have made him most blessed
    forever;
    You have made him exceedingly glad
    with Your presence.
7   For the king trusts in the LORD,
    And through the mercy of the Most
    High he shall not be moved.

PROVERBS 7:24–27

24 NOW therefore, listen to me, *my*
    children;
    Pay attention to the words of my
    mouth:
25 Do not let your heart turn aside to her
    ways,
    Do not stray into her paths;
26 For she has cast down many wounded,
    And all who were slain by her were
    strong *men.*
27 Her house *is* the way to hell,
    Descending to the chambers of death.

MATTHEW 25:31–46

"WHEN the Son of Man comes in His
glory, and all the holy angels with Him,
then He will sit on the throne of His glory.

---

*When the Lord does come it will be
as natural as breathing.*   (GENESIS)

32 All the nations will be gathered before
Him, and He will separate them one from
another, as a shepherd divides *his* sheep
from the goats. 33 And He will set the sheep
on His right hand, but the goats on the
left. 34 Then the King will say to those on
His right hand, 'Come, you blessed of My
Father, inherit the kingdom prepared for
you from the foundation of the world:
35 for I was hungry and you gave Me food;
I was thirsty and you gave Me drink; I
was a stranger and you took Me in;
36 I *was* naked and you clothed Me; I was
sick and you visited Me; I was in prison
and you came to Me.'

37 "Then the righteous will answer Him,
saying, 'Lord, when did we see You hungry
and feed *You*, or thirsty and give *You* drink?
38 When did we see You a stranger and
take *You* in, or naked and clothe *You*?
39 Or when did we see You sick, or in
prison, and come to You?' 40 And the King
will answer and say to them, 'Assuredly, I
say to you, inasmuch as you did *it* to one
of the least of these My brethren, you did
it to Me.'

41 "Then He will also say to those on
the left hand, 'Depart from Me, you cursed,
into the everlasting fire prepared for the
devil and his angels: 42 for I was hungry
and you gave Me no food; I was thirsty
and you gave Me no drink; 43 I was a
stranger and you did not take Me in, naked
and you did not clothe Me, sick and in
prison and you did not visit Me.'

44 "Then they also will answer Him, saying, 'Lord, when did we see You hungry
or thirsty or a stranger or naked or sick
or in prison, and did not minister to You?'
45 Then He will answer them, saying, 'Assuredly, I say to you, inasmuch as you did
not do *it* to one of the least of these, you
did not do *it* to Me.' 46 And these will go
away into everlasting punishment, but the
righteous into eternal life."

◆◆◆

Reading 42—The Cross of Christ
Matthew 26:1, 2

There are two views of Jesus Christ's death. One is that He was a martyr—
that is not the New Testament view; the other is that the Cross of Jesus
Christ was the Cross of God, not of a man at all—not a man doing his level
best for God, but "God doing the very best for man." The Cross of Jesus
Christ is the point where God and sinful man merge with a crash, and the
way to life is opened; but the crash is on the heart of God. The Cross is the

presentation of God having done His "bit," that which man could never do. . . . The foundation of the Christian faith is that the basis of human life is redemptive, and on that basis God performs His miracles. Jesus Christ told His disciples that He came here on purpose to die. The death of Jesus Christ is God's verdict on self-realization and every form of sin there is. If self-realization is to be the goal and end of the human race, then damned be God; if Jesus Christ is to be God, then damned be self-realization—the two cannot exist together. "If you would be My disciple, give up your right to yourself."

(*SHAD. AGONY*)

EXODUS 33:1—34:35

THEN the Lord said to Moses, "Depart *and* go up from here, you and the people whom you have brought out of the land of Egypt, to the land of which I swore to Abraham, Isaac, and Jacob, saying, 'To your descendants I will give it.' 2 And I will send *My* Angel before you, and I will drive out the Canaanite and the Amorite and the Hittite and the Perizzite and the Hivite and the Jebusite. 3 *Go up* to a land flowing with milk and honey; for I will not go up in your midst, lest I consume you on the way, for you *are* a stiff-necked people."

4 And when the people heard this bad news, they mourned, and no one put on his ornaments. 5 For the Lord had said to Moses, "Say to the children of Israel, 'You *are* a stiff-necked people. I could come up into your midst in one moment and consume you. Now therefore, take off your ornaments, that I may know what to do to you.' " 6 So the children of Israel stripped themselves of their ornaments by Mount Horeb.

7 Moses took his tent and pitched it outside the camp, far from the camp, and called it the tabernacle of meeting. And it came to pass *that* everyone who sought the Lord went out to the tabernacle of meeting which *was* outside the camp. 8 So it was, whenever Moses went out to the tabernacle, *that* all the people rose, and each man stood *at* his tent door and watched Moses until he had gone into the tabernacle. 9 And it came to pass, when Moses entered the tabernacle, that the pillar of cloud descended and stood *at* the door of the tabernacle, and *the* Lord talked with Moses. 10 All the people saw the pillar of cloud standing *at* the tabernacle door, and all the people rose and worshiped, each man *in* his tent door. 11 So the Lord spoke to Moses face to face, as a man speaks to his friend. And he would return to the camp, but his servant Joshua the son of Nun, a young man, did not depart from the tabernacle.

12 Then Moses said to the Lord, "See, You say to me, 'Bring up this people.' But You have not let me know whom You will send with me. Yet You have said, 'I know you by name, and you have also found grace in My sight.' 13 Now therefore, I pray, if I have found grace in Your sight, show me now Your way, that I may know You and that I may find grace in Your sight. And consider that this nation *is* Your people."

14 And He said, "My Presence will go *with you,* and I will give you rest."

15 Then he said to Him, "If Your Presence does not go *with us,* do not bring us up from here. 16 For how then will it be known that Your people and I have found grace in Your sight, except You go with us? So we shall be separate, Your people and I, from all the people who *are* upon the face of the earth."

17 So the Lord said to Moses, "I will also do this thing that you have spoken; for you have found grace in My sight, and I know you by name."

18 And he said, "Please, show me Your glory."

19 Then He said, "I will make all My goodness pass before you, and I will proclaim the name of the Lord before you. I will be gracious to whom I will be gracious, and I will have compassion on whom I will have compassion." 20 But He said, "You cannot see My face; for no man shall see Me, and live." 21 And the Lord said, "Here is a place by Me, and you shall stand on the rock. 22 So it shall be, while My glory passes by, that I will put you in the cleft of the rock, and will cover you with My hand while I pass by. 23 Then I will take away My hand, and you shall see My back; but My face shall not be seen."

34 AND the Lord said to Moses, "Cut two tablets of stone like the first *ones,* and I will write on *these* tablets the words that were on the first tablets which you broke. 2 So be ready in the morning, and come up in the morning to Mount Sinai, and present yourself to Me there on the top of the mountain. 3 And no man shall come up with you, and let no man be seen throughout all the mountain; let neither flocks nor herds feed before that mountain."

4 So he cut two tablets of stone like the first *ones.* Then Moses rose early in the morning and went up Mount Sinai, as the LORD had commanded him; and he took in his hand the two tablets of stone.

5 Now the LORD descended in the cloud and stood with him there, and proclaimed the name of the LORD. 6 And the LORD passed before him and proclaimed, "The LORD, the LORD God, merciful and gracious, longsuffering, and abounding in goodness and truth, 7 keeping mercy for thousands, forgiving iniquity and transgression and sin, by no means clearing *the guilty,* visiting the iniquity of the fathers upon the children and the children's children to the third and the fourth generation."

8 So Moses made haste and bowed his head toward the earth, and worshiped. 9 Then he said, "If now I have found grace in Your sight, O Lord, let my Lord, I pray, go among us, even though we *are* a stiff-necked people; and pardon our iniquity and our sin, and take us as Your inheritance."

10 And He said: "Behold, I make a covenant. Before all your people I will do marvels such as have not been done in all the earth, nor in any nation; and all the people among whom you *are* shall see the work of the LORD. For it *is* an awesome thing that I will do with you. 11 Observe what I command you this day. Behold, I am driving out from before you the Amorite and the Canaanite and the Hittite and the Perizzite and the Hivite and the Jebusite. 12 Take heed to yourself, lest you make a covenant with the inhabitants of the land where you are going, lest it be a snare in your midst. 13 But you shall destroy their altars, break their *sacred* pillars, and cut down their wooden images 14 (for you shall worship no other god, for the LORD, whose name *is* Jealous, *is* a jealous God), 15 lest you make a covenant with the inhabitants of the land, and they play the harlot with their gods and make sacrifice to their gods, and *one of them* invites you and you eat of his sacrifice, 16 and you take of his daughters for your sons, and his daughters play the harlot with their gods and make your sons play the harlot with their gods.

17 "You shall make no molded gods for yourselves.

18 "The Feast of Unleavened Bread you shall keep. Seven days you shall eat unleavened bread, as I commanded you, in the appointed time of the month of Abib; for in the month of Abib you came out from Egypt.

19 "All that open the womb *are* Mine, and every male firstborn among your livestock, *whether* ox or sheep. 20 But the firstborn of a donkey you shall redeem with a lamb. And if you will not redeem *him,* then you shall break his neck. All the firstborn of your sons you shall redeem.

"And none shall appear before Me empty-handed.

21 "Six days you shall work, but on the seventh day you shall rest; in plowing time and in harvest you shall rest.

22 "And you shall observe the Feast of Weeks, of the firstfruits of wheat harvest, and the Feast of Ingathering at the year's end.

23 "Three times in the year all your men shall appear before the Lord, the LORD God of Israel. 24 For I will cast out the nations before you and enlarge your borders; neither will any man covet your land when you go up to appear before the LORD your God three times in the year.

25 "You shall not offer the blood of My sacrifice with leaven, nor shall the sacrifice of the Feast of the Passover be left until morning.

26 "The first of the firstfruits of your land you shall bring to the house of the LORD your God. You shall not boil a young goat in its mother's milk."

27 Then the LORD said to Moses, "Write these words, for according to the tenor of these words I have made a covenant with you and with Israel." 28 So he was there with the LORD forty days and forty nights; he neither ate bread nor drank water. And He wrote on the tablets the words of the covenant, the Ten Commandments.

29 Now it was so, when Moses came down from Mount Sinai (and the two tablets of the Testimony *were* in Moses' hand when he came down from the mountain), that Moses did not know that the skin of his face shone while he talked with Him. 30 So when Aaron and all the children of Israel saw Moses, behold, the skin of his face shone, and they were afraid to come near him. 31 Then Moses called to them, and Aaron and all the rulers of the congregation returned to him; and Moses talked with them. 32 Afterward all the children of Israel came near, and he gave them as commandments all that the LORD had spoken with him on Mount Sinai. 33 And when Moses had finished speaking with them, he put a veil on his face. 34 But whenever Moses went in before the LORD to speak with Him, he would take the veil off until he came

out; and he would come out and speak to the children of Israel whatever he had been commanded. 35 And whenever the children of Israel saw the face of Moses, that the skin of Moses' face shone, then Moses would put the veil on his face again, until he went in to speak with Him.

PSALM 21:8–13

8   YOUR hand will find all Your enemies;
     Your right hand will find those who
       hate You.
9   You shall make them as a fiery oven
       in the time of Your anger;
     The LORD shall swallow them up in
       His wrath,
     And the fire shall devour them.
10 Their offspring You shall destroy from
       the earth,
     And their descendants from among the
       sons of men.
11 For they intended evil against You;
     They devised a plot *which* they are not
       able *to perform.*
12 Therefore You will make them turn
       their back;
     You will make ready *Your arrows* on
       Your string toward their faces.

13 Be exalted, O LORD, in Your own
       strength!
     We will sing and praise Your power.

PROVERBS 8:1–5

1   DOES not wisdom cry out,
     And understanding lift up her voice?
2   She takes her stand on the top of the
       high hill,
     Beside the way, where the paths meet.
3   She cries out by the gates, at the entry
       of the city,
     At the entrance of the doors:
4   "To you, O men, I call,
     And my voice *is* to the sons of men.
5   O you simple ones, understand
       prudence,
     And you fools, be of an understanding
       heart.

MATTHEW 26:1–25

NOW it came to pass, when Jesus had finished all these sayings, *that* He said to His disciples, 2 "You know that after two days is the Passover, and the Son of Man will be delivered up to be crucified."

3 Then the chief priests, the scribes, and the elders of the people assembled at the palace of the high priest, who was called Caiaphas, 4 and plotted to take Jesus by trickery and kill *Him.* 5 But they said, "Not during the feast, lest there be an uproar among the people."

6 And when Jesus was in Bethany at the house of Simon the leper, 7 a woman came to Him having an alabaster flask of very costly fragrant oil, and she poured *it* on His head as He sat *at the table.* 8 But when His disciples saw *it,* they were indignant, saying, "Why this waste? 9 For this fragrant oil might have been sold for much and given to *the* poor."

10 But when Jesus was aware of *it,* He said to them, "Why do you trouble the woman? For she has done a good work for Me. 11 For you have the poor with you always, but Me you do not have always. 12 For in pouring this fragrant oil on My body, she did *it* for My burial. 13 Assuredly, I say to you, wherever this gospel is preached in the whole world, what this woman has done will also be told as a memorial to her."

*R*emember, God calls us to proclaim the gospel. (APPROVED)

14 Then one of the twelve, called Judas Iscariot, went to the chief priests 15 and said, "What are you willing to give me if I deliver Him to you?" And they counted out to him thirty pieces of silver. 16 So from that time he sought opportunity to betray Him.

17 Now on the first *day of the Feast* of Unleavened Bread the disciples came to Jesus, saying to Him, "Where do You want us to prepare for You to eat the Passover?"

18 And He said, "Go into the city to a certain man, and say to him, 'The Teacher says, "My time is at hand; I will keep the Passover at your house with My disciples." ' "

19 So the disciples did as Jesus had directed them; and they prepared the Passover.

20 When evening had come, He sat down with the twelve. 21 Now as they were eating, He said, "Assuredly, I say to you, one of you will betray Me."

22 And they were exceedingly sorrowful, and each of them began to say to Him, "Lord, is it I?"

23 He answered and said, "He who dipped *his* hand with Me in the dish will betray Me. 24 The Son of Man indeed goes just as it is written of Him, but woe to that man by whom the Son of Man is be-trayed! It would have been good for that man if he had not been born."

25 Then Judas, who was betraying Him, answered and said, "Rabbi, is it I?"

He said to him, "You have said it."

◆◆◆◆

Reading 43—Sit Here
Matthew 26:36

Are we devotees to a cause or disciples of the Lord Jesus Christ? He said to the disciples, "Sit here." If they had been like some of us they would have said, "No, it is absurd. We must go and do something."

The more we get into the atmosphere of the New Testament the more we discover the unfathomable and unhasting leisure of our Lord's life, no matter what His agony. The difficulty is that when we do what God wants us to do, our friends say, "It is all very well, but suppose we all did that?" Our Lord did not tell all the disciples to sit there while He prayed; He told only three of them. The point is that we must take as from God the haphazard arrangements of our lives. If we accept the Lord Jesus Christ and the domination of His lordship, we also accept that nothing happens by chance, because we know that God orders and engineers circumstances; the fuss has gone, the amateur providence has gone, the amateur disposer has gone, and we know that "all things work together for good to those who love God." If Jesus says "Sit here, while I go and pray over there," the only appropriate thing we can do is to sit there. (*Ask*)

EXODUS 35:1—36:38

THEN Moses gathered all the congregation of the children of Israel together, and said to them, "These *are* the words which the LORD has commanded *you* to do: 2 Work shall be done for six days, but the seventh day shall be a holy day for you, a Sabbath of rest to the LORD. Whoever does any work on it shall be put to death. 3 You shall kindle no fire throughout your dwellings on the Sabbath day."

4 And Moses spoke to all the congregation of the children of Israel, saying, "This *is* the thing which the LORD commanded, saying: 5 'Take from among you an offering to the LORD. Whoever *is* of a willing heart, let him bring it as an offering to the LORD: gold, silver, and bronze; 6 blue, purple, and scarlet *thread,* fine linen, and goats' *hair;* 7 ram skins dyed red, badger skins, and acacia wood; 8 oil for the light, and spices for the anointing oil and for the sweet incense; 9 onyx stones, and stones to be set in the ephod and in the breastplate.

10 'All *who are* gifted artisans among you shall come and make all that the LORD has commanded: 11 the tabernacle, its tent, its covering, its clasps, its boards, its bars, its pillars, and its sockets; 12 the ark and its poles, *with* the mercy seat, and the veil of the covering; 13 the table and its poles, all its utensils, and the showbread; 14 also the lampstand for the light, its utensils, its lamps, and the oil for the light; 15 the incense altar, its poles, the anointing oil, the sweet incense, and the screen for the door at the entrance of the tabernacle; 16 the altar of burnt offering with its bronze grating, its poles, all its utensils, *and* the laver and its base; 17 the hangings of the court, its pillars, their sockets, and the screen for the gate of the court; 18 the pegs of the tabernacle, the pegs of the court, and their cords; 19 the garments of ministry, for ministering in the holy *place*—the holy garments for Aaron the priest and the garments of his sons, to minister as priests.' "

20 And all the congregation of the children of Israel departed from the presence of Moses. 21 Then everyone came whose

heart was stirred, and everyone whose spirit was willing, *and* they brought the LORD's offering for the work of the tabernacle of meeting, for all its service, and for the holy garments. 22 They came, both men and women, as many as had a willing heart, *and* brought earrings and nose rings, rings and necklaces, all jewelry of gold, that is, every man who *made* an offering of gold to the LORD. 23 And every man, with whom was found blue, purple, and scarlet *thread,* fine linen, goats' *hair,* red skins of rams, and badger skins, brought *them.* 24 Everyone who offered an offering of silver or bronze brought the LORD's offering. And everyone with whom was found acacia wood for any work of the service, brought *it.* 25 All the women *who were* gifted artisans spun yarn with their hands, and brought what they had spun, of blue, purple, *and* scarlet, and fine linen. 26 And all the women whose hearts stirred with wisdom spun yarn of goats' *hair.* 27 The rulers brought onyx stones, and the stones to be set in the ephod and in the breastplate, 28 and spices and oil for the light, for the anointing oil, and for the sweet incense. 29 The children of Israel brought a freewill offering to the LORD, all the men and women whose hearts were willing to bring *material* for all kinds of work which the LORD, by the hand of Moses, had commanded to be done.

30 And Moses said to the children of Israel, "See, the LORD has called by name Bezalel the son of Uri, the son of Hur, of the tribe of Judah; 31 and He has filled him with the Spirit of God, in wisdom and understanding, in knowledge and all manner of workmanship, 32 to design artistic works, to work in gold and silver and bronze, 33 in cutting jewels for setting, in carving wood, and to work in all manner of artistic workmanship.

34 "And He has put in his heart the ability to teach, *in* him and Aholiab the son of Ahisamach, of the tribe of Dan. 35 He has filled them with skill to do all manner of work of the engraver and the designer and the tapestry maker, in blue, purple, and scarlet *thread,* and fine linen, and of the weaver—those who do every work and those who design artistic works.

36 "AND Bezalel and Aholiab, and every gifted artisan in whom the LORD has put wisdom and understanding, to know how to do all manner of work for the service of the sanctuary, shall do according to all that the LORD has commanded."

2 Then Moses called Bezalel and Aholiab, and every gifted artisan in whose heart the LORD had put wisdom, everyone whose heart was stirred, to come and do the work. 3 And they received from Moses all the offering which the children of Israel had brought for the work of the service of making the sanctuary. So they continued bringing to him freewill offerings every morning. 4 Then all the craftsmen who were doing all the work of the sanctuary came, each from the work he was doing, 5 and they spoke to Moses, saying, "The people bring much more than enough for the service of the work which the LORD commanded *us* to do."

6 So Moses gave a commandment, and they caused it to be proclaimed throughout the camp, saying, "Let neither man nor woman do any more work for the offering of the sanctuary." And the people were restrained from bringing, 7 for the material they had was sufficient for all the work to be done—indeed too much.

8 Then all the gifted artisans among them who worked on the tabernacle made ten curtains woven of fine linen, and of blue, purple, and scarlet thread; *with* artistic designs of cherubim they made them. 9 The length of each curtain *was* twenty-eight cubits, and the width of each curtain four cubits; the curtains *were* all the same size. 10 And he coupled five curtains to one another, and *the other* five curtains he coupled to one another. 11 He made loops of blue *yarn* on the edge of the curtain on the selvedge of one set; likewise he did on the outer edge of *the other* curtain of the second set. 12 Fifty loops he made on one curtain, and fifty loops he made on the edge of the curtain on the end of the second set; the loops held one *curtain* to another. 13 And he made fifty clasps of gold, and coupled the curtains to one another with the clasps, that it might be one tabernacle.

14 He made curtains of goats' *hair* for the tent over the tabernacle; he made eleven curtains. 15 The length of each curtain *was* thirty cubits, and the width of each curtain four cubits; the eleven curtains *were* the same size. 16 He coupled five curtains by themselves and six curtains by themselves. 17 And he made fifty loops on the edge of the curtain that is outermost in one set, and fifty loops he made on the edge of the curtain of the second set. 18 He also made fifty bronze clasps to couple the tent together, that it might be one. 19 Then he made a covering for the tent of ram skins dyed red, and a covering of badger skins above *that.*

20 For the tabernacle he made boards of acacia wood, standing upright. 21 The

length of each board *was* ten cubits, and the width of each board a cubit and a half. 22 Each board had two tenons for binding one to another. Thus he made for all the boards of the tabernacle. 23 And he made boards for the tabernacle, twenty boards for the south side. 24 Forty sockets of silver he made to go under the twenty boards: two sockets under each of the boards for its two tenons. 25 And for the other side of the tabernacle, the north side, he made twenty boards 26 and their forty sockets of silver: two sockets under each of the boards. 27 For the west side of the tabernacle he made six boards. 28 He also made two boards for the two back corners of the tabernacle. 29 And they were coupled at the bottom and coupled together at the top by one ring. Thus he made both of them for the two corners. 30 So there were eight boards and their sockets—sixteen sockets of silver—two sockets under each of the boards.

31 And he made bars of acacia wood: five for the boards on one side of the tabernacle, 32 five bars for the boards on the other side of the tabernacle, and five bars for the boards of the tabernacle on the far side westward. 33 And he made the middle bar to pass through the boards from one end to the other. 34 He overlaid the boards with gold, made their rings of gold *to be* holders for the bars, and overlaid the bars with gold.

35 And he made a veil of blue, purple, and scarlet *thread,* and fine woven linen; it was worked *with* an artistic design of cherubim. 36 He made for it four pillars of acacia *wood,* and overlaid them with gold, with their hooks of gold; and he cast four sockets of silver for them.

37 He also made a screen for the tabernacle door, of blue, purple, and scarlet *thread,* and fine woven linen, made by a weaver, 38 and its five pillars with their hooks. And he overlaid their capitals and their rings with gold, but their five sockets *were* bronze.

PSALM 22:1–8

1   MY God, My God, why have You forsaken Me?
      Why are You so far from helping Me,
      And from the words of My groaning?

The basis of things must always be found in a personal relationship to a personal God.   (BAFFLED)

---

2   O My God, I cry in the daytime, but You do not hear;
      And in the night season, and am not silent.

3   But You *are* holy,
      Enthroned in the praises of Israel.

4   Our fathers trusted in You;
      They trusted, and You delivered them.

5   They cried to You, and were delivered;
      They trusted in You, and were not ashamed.

6   But I *am* a worm, and no man;
      A reproach of men, and despised by the people.

7   All those who see Me ridicule Me;
      They shoot out the lip, they shake the head, *saying,*

8   "He trusted in the LORD, let Him rescue Him;
      Let Him deliver Him, since He delights in Him!"

PROVERBS 8:6–11

6   LISTEN, for I will speak of excellent things,
      And from the opening of my lips *will come* right things;

7   For my mouth will speak truth;
      Wickedness *is* an abomination to my lips.

8   All the words of my mouth *are* with righteousness;
      Nothing crooked or perverse *is* in them.

9   They *are* all plain to him who understands,
      And right to those who find knowledge.

10   Receive my instruction, and not silver,
      And knowledge rather than choice gold;

11   For wisdom *is* better than rubies,
      And all the things one may desire cannot be compared with her.

MATTHEW 26:26–50

AND as they were eating, Jesus took bread, blessed and broke *it,* and gave *it* to the disciples and said, "Take, eat; this is My body."

27 Then He took the cup, and gave thanks, and gave *it* to them, saying, "Drink from it, all of you. 28 For this is My blood of the new covenant, which is shed for many for the remission of sins. 29 But I say to you, I will not drink of this fruit of the vine from now on until that day when I

drink it new with you in My Father's kingdom."

30 And when they had sung a hymn, they went out to the Mount of Olives.

31 Then Jesus said to them, "All of you will be made to stumble because of Me this night, for it is written:

'I will strike the Shepherd,
    And the sheep of the flock will be
      scattered.'

32 But after I have been raised, I will go before you to Galilee."

33 Peter answered and said to Him, "Even if all are made to stumble because of You, I will never be made to stumble."

34 Jesus said to him, "Assuredly, I say to you that this night, before the rooster crows, you will deny Me three times."

35 Peter said to Him, "Even if I have to die with You, I will not deny You!"

And so said all the disciples.

36 Then Jesus came with them to a place called Gethsemane, and said to the disciples, "Sit here while I go and pray over there."

37 And He took with Him Peter and the two sons of Zebedee, and He began to be sorrowful and deeply distressed. 38 Then He said to them, "My soul is exceedingly sorrowful, even to death. Stay here and watch with Me."

39 He went a little farther and fell on His face, and prayed, saying, "O My Father, if it is possible, let this cup pass from Me; nevertheless, not as I will, but as You *will*."

40 Then He came to the disciples and found them sleeping, and said to Peter, "What! Could you not watch with Me one

hour? 41 Watch and pray, lest you enter into temptation. The spirit indeed *is* willing, but the flesh *is* weak."

---

*E*very temptation of Satan will certainly seem right to us unless we have the Spirit of God.   (PSY. REDEMP.)

---

42 Again, a second time, He went away and prayed, saying, "O My Father, if this cup cannot pass away from Me unless I drink it, Your will be done." 43 And He came and found them asleep again, for their eyes were heavy.

44 So He left them, went away again, and prayed the third time, saying the same words. 45 Then He came to His disciples and said to them, "Are *you* still sleeping and resting? Behold, the hour is at hand, and the Son of Man is being betrayed into the hands of sinners. 46 Rise, let us be going. See, My betrayer is at hand."

47 And while He was still speaking, behold, Judas, one of the twelve, with a great multitude with swords and clubs, came from the chief priests and elders of the people.

48 Now His betrayer had given them a sign, saying, "Whomever I kiss, He is the One; seize Him." 49 Immediately he went up to Jesus and said, "Greetings, Rabbi!" and kissed Him.

50 But Jesus said to him, "Friend, why have you come?"

Then they came and laid hands on Jesus and took Him.

◆◆◆

Reading 44—Death by Divine Decree
Psalm 22:15

The death of Jesus Christ is the performance in history of the very Mind of God. There is no room for looking on Jesus Christ as a martyr; His death was not something that happened to Him which might have been prevented: His death was the very reason why He came. . . .

God could forgive men in no other way than by the death of His Son, and Jesus is exalted to be Savior because of His death. "We see Jesus . . . because of the suffering of death, crowned with glory and honor." The greatest note of triumph that ever sounded in the ears of a startled universe was that sounded on the Cross of Christ—*"It is finished."* That is the last word in the redemption of man.

Anything that belittles or obliterates the holiness of God by a false view of the love of God is untrue to the revelation of God given by Jesus Christ.

Never allow the thought that Jesus Christ stands with us against God out of pity and compassion; that He became a curse for us out of sympathy with us. Jesus Christ became a curse for us by the Divine decree. Our portion of realizing the terrific meaning of the curse is conviction of sin, the gift of shame and penitence is given us—this is the great mercy of God. Jesus Christ hates the wrong in man, and Calvary is the estimate of His hatred.   (*UTMOST*)

EXODUS 37:1—38:31

THEN Bezalel made the ark of acacia wood; two and a half cubits *was* its length, a cubit and a half its width, and a cubit and a half its height. 2 He overlaid it with pure gold inside and outside, and made a molding of gold all around it. 3 And he cast for it four rings of gold *to be set* in its four corners: two rings on one side, and two rings on the other side of it. 4 He made poles of acacia wood, and overlaid them with gold. 5 And he put the poles into the rings at the sides of the ark, to bear the ark. 6 He also made the mercy seat of pure gold; two and a half cubits *was* its length and a cubit and a half its width. 7 He made two cherubim of beaten gold; he made them of one piece at the two ends of the mercy seat: 8 one cherub at one end on this side, and the other cherub at the *other* end on that side. He made the cherubim at the two ends *of one piece* with the mercy seat. 9 The cherubim spread out *their* wings above, *and* covered the mercy seat with their wings. They faced one another; the faces of the cherubim were toward the mercy seat.

10 He made the table of acacia wood; two cubits *was* its length, a cubit its width, and a cubit and a half its height. 11 And he overlaid it with pure gold, and made a molding of gold all around it. 12 Also he made a frame of a handbreadth all around it, and made a molding of gold for the frame all around it. 13 And he cast for it four rings of gold, and put the rings on the four corners that *were* at its four legs. 14 The rings were close to the frame, as holders for the poles to bear the table. 15 And he made the poles of acacia wood to bear the table, and overlaid them with gold. 16 He made of pure gold the utensils which were on the table: its dishes, its cups, its bowls, and its pitchers for pouring.

17 He also made the lampstand of pure gold; of hammered work he made the lampstand. Its shaft, its branches, its bowls, its *ornamental* knobs, and its flowers were of the same piece. 18 And six branches came out of its sides: three branches of the lampstand out of one side, and three branches of the lampstand out of the other side. 19 There were three bowls made like almond *blossoms* on one branch, with an *ornamental* knob and a flower, and three bowls made like almond *blossoms* on the other branch, with an *ornamental* knob and a flower—and so for the six branches coming out of the lampstand. 20 And on the lampstand itself *were* four bowls made like almond *blossoms, each with* its *ornamental* knob and flower. 21 *There was* a knob under the *first* two branches of the same, a knob under the *second* two branches of the same, and a knob under the *third* two branches of the same, according to the six branches extending from it. 22 Their knobs and their branches were of one piece; all of it *was* one hammered piece of pure gold. 23 And he made its seven lamps, its wick-trimmers, and its trays of pure gold. 24 Of a talent of pure gold he made it, with all its utensils.

25 He made the incense altar of acacia wood. Its length *was* a cubit and its width a cubit—*it was* square—and two cubits *was* its height. Its horns were *of one piece* with it. 26 And he overlaid it with pure gold: its top, its sides all around, and its horns. He also made for it a molding of gold all around it. 27 He made two rings of gold for it under its molding, by its two corners on both sides, as holders for the poles with which to bear it. 28 And he made the poles of acacia wood, and overlaid them with gold.

29 He also made the holy anointing oil and the pure incense of sweet spices, according to the work of the perfumer.

38 HE made the altar of burnt offering of acacia wood; five cubits *was* its length and five cubits its width—*it was* square—and its height *was* three cubits. 2 He made its horns on its four corners; the horns were *of one piece* with it. And he overlaid it with bronze. 3 He made all the utensils for the altar: the pans, the shovels, the basins, the forks, and the firepans; all its utensils he made of bronze. 4 And he made a grate of bronze network for the altar, under its rim, midway from the bottom. 5 He cast four rings for the four corners of the bronze grating, *as* holders for the poles. 6 And he made the poles of acacia wood, and overlaid them with bronze. 7 Then he put the poles into the rings on the sides of the altar, with which to bear it. He made the altar hollow with boards.

8 He made the laver of bronze and its base of bronze, from the bronze mirrors of the serving women who assembled at the door of the tabernacle of meeting.

9 Then he made the court on the south side; the hangings of the court *were of* fine woven linen, one hundred cubits long. 10 There *were* twenty pillars for them, with twenty bronze sockets. The hooks of the pillars and their bands *were* silver. 11 On the north side *the hangings were* one hundred cubits *long,* with twenty pillars and their twenty bronze sockets. The hooks of the pillars and their bands *were* silver. 12 And on the west side *there were* hangings of fifty cubits, with ten pillars and their ten sockets. The hooks of the pillars and their bands *were* silver. 13 For the east side *the hangings were* fifty cubits. 14 The hangings of one side *of the gate were* fifteen cubits *long, with* their three pillars and their three sockets, 15 and the same for the other side of the court gate; on this side and that *were* hangings of fifteen cubits, *with* their three pillars and their three sockets. 16 All the hangings of the court all around *were of* fine woven linen. 17 The sockets for the pillars *were* bronze, the hooks of the pillars and their bands *were* silver, and the overlay of their capitals *was* silver; and all the pillars of the court had bands of silver. 18 The screen for the gate of the court *was* woven of blue, purple, and scarlet *thread,* and of fine woven linen. The length *was* twenty cubits, and the height along its width *was* five cubits, corresponding to the hangings of the court. 19 And *there were* four pillars *with* their four sockets of bronze; their hooks *were* silver, and the overlay of their capitals and their bands *was* silver. 20 All the pegs of the tabernacle, and of the court all around, *were* bronze.

21 This is the inventory of the tabernacle, the tabernacle of the Testimony, which was counted according to the commandment of Moses, for the service of the Levites, by the hand of Ithamar, son of Aaron the priest.

22 Bezalel the son of Uri, the son of Hur, of the tribe of Judah, made all that the LORD had commanded Moses. 23 And with him *was* Aholiab the son of Ahisamach, of the tribe of Dan, an engraver and designer, a weaver of blue, purple, and scarlet *thread,* and of fine linen.

24 All the gold that was used in all the work of the holy *place,* that is, the gold of the offering, was twenty-nine talents and seven hundred and thirty shekels, according to the shekel of the sanctuary. 25 And the silver from those who were numbered of the congregation *was* one hundred talents and one thousand seven hundred and seventy-five shekels, according to the shekel of the sanctuary: 26 a bekah for each man (*that is,* half a shekel, according to the shekel of the sanctuary), for everyone included in the numbering from twenty years old and above, for six hundred and three thousand, five hundred and fifty *men.* 27 And from the hundred talents of silver were cast the sockets of the sanctuary and the bases of the veil: one hundred sockets from the hundred talents, one talent for each socket. 28 Then from the one thousand seven hundred and seventy-five *shekels* he made hooks for the pillars, overlaid their capitals, and made bands for them.

29 The offering of bronze *was* seventy talents and two thousand four hundred shekels. 30 And with it he made the sockets for the door of the tabernacle of meeting, the bronze altar, the bronze grating for it, and all the utensils for the altar, 31 the sockets for the court all around, the bases for the court gate, all the pegs for the tabernacle, and all the pegs for the court all around.

PSALM 22:9–15

9   BUT You *are* He who took Me out of the womb;
You made Me trust *while* on My mother's breasts.

10 I was cast upon You from birth.
From My mother's womb You *have been* My God.

11 Be not far from Me,
For trouble *is* near;
For *there is* none to help.

12 Many bulls have surrounded Me;
Strong *bulls* of Bashan have encircled Me.

13 They gape at Me *with* their mouths,
Like a raging and roaring lion.

14 I am poured out like water,
And all My bones are out of joint;
My heart is like wax;
It has melted within Me.

15 My strength is dried up like a potsherd,
And My tongue clings to My jaws;

You have brought Me to the dust of
death.

PROVERBS 8:12–21

12 "I, wisdom, dwell with prudence,
And find out knowledge *and* discretion.
13 The fear of the LORD *is* to hate evil;
Pride and arrogance and the evil way
And the perverse mouth I hate.
14 Counsel *is* mine, and sound wisdom;
I *am* understanding, I have strength.
15 By me kings reign,
And rulers decree justice.
16 By me princes rule, and nobles,
All the judges of the earth.
17 I love those who love me,
And those who seek me diligently will
find me.
18 Riches and honor *are* with me,
Enduring riches and righteousness.
19 My fruit *is* better than gold, yes, than
fine gold,
And my revenue than choice silver.
20 I traverse the way of righteousness,
In the midst of the paths of justice,
21 That I may cause those who love me
to inherit wealth,
That I may fill their treasuries.

*H*e leads us in the paths of
righteousness wherever we are
placed.   (GOD'S WORKMANSHIP)

MATTHEW 26:51–75

AND suddenly, one of those *who were* with
Jesus stretched out *his* hand and drew his
sword, struck the servant of the high priest,
and cut off his ear.
52 But Jesus said to him, "Put your sword
in its place, for all who take the sword will
perish by the sword. 53 Or do you think
that I cannot now pray to My Father, and
He will provide Me with more than twelve
legions of angels? 54 How then could the
Scriptures be fulfilled, that it must happen
thus?"
55 In that hour Jesus said to the multitudes, "Have you come out, as against a
robber, with swords and clubs to take Me?
I sat daily with you, teaching in the temple,
and you did not seize Me. 56 But all this
was done that the Scriptures of the prophets
might be fulfilled."
Then all the disciples forsook Him and
fled.

57 And those who had laid hold of Jesus
led *Him* away to Caiaphas the high priest,
where the scribes and the elders were assembled. 58 But Peter followed Him at a distance to the high priest's courtyard. And
he went in and sat with the servants to
see the end.
59 Now the chief priests, the elders, and
all the council sought false testimony against
Jesus to put Him to death, 60 but found
none. Even though many false witnesses
came forward, they found none. But at last
two false witnesses came forward 61 and
said, "This *fellow* said, 'I am able to destroy
the temple of God and to build it in three
days.'"
62 And the high priest arose and said to
Him, "Do You answer nothing? What *is
it* these men testify against You?" 63 But
Jesus kept silent. And the high priest answered and said to Him, "I put You under
oath by the living God: Tell us if You are
the Christ, the Son of God!"
64 Jesus said to him, "*It is as* you said.
Nevertheless, I say to you, hereafter you
will see the Son of Man sitting at the right
hand of the Power, and coming on the
clouds of heaven."
65 Then the high priest tore his clothes,
saying, "He has spoken blasphemy! What
further need do we have of witnesses? Look,
now you have heard His blasphemy!
66 What do you think?"
They answered and said, "He is deserving
of death."
67 Then they spat in His face and beat
Him; and others struck *Him* with the palms
of their hands, 68 saying, "Prophesy to
us, Christ! Who is the one who struck
You?"
69 Now Peter sat outside in the courtyard.
And a servant girl came to him, saying,
"You also were with Jesus of Galilee."
70 But he denied it before *them* all, saying,
"I do not know what you are saying."
71 And when he had gone out to the gateway, another *girl* saw him and said to those
who were there, "This *fellow* also was with
Jesus of Nazareth."
72 But again he denied with an oath, "I
do not know the Man!"
73 And a little later those who stood by
came up and said to Peter, "Surely you also
are *one* of them, for your speech betrays
you."
74 Then he began to curse and swear,
saying, "I do not know the Man!"
Immediately a rooster crowed. 75 And
Peter remembered the word of Jesus who
had said to him, "Before the rooster crows,
you will deny Me three times." So he went
out and wept bitterly.

Reading 45—The Blessing of Obedience
Exodus 40:32

Our Lord never insists upon obedience; He tells us very emphatically what we ought to do, but He never takes means to make us do it. We have to obey Him out of a oneness of spirit. . . .

The Lord does not give me rules, He makes His standard very clear, and if my relationship to Him is that of love, I will do what He says without any hesitation. If I hesitate, it is because I love someone else in competition with Him, namely, myself. Jesus Christ will not help me to obey Him, I must obey Him; and when I do obey Him, I fulfill my spiritual destiny. My personal life may be crowded with small petty incidents, altogether unnoticeable and mean; but if I obey Jesus Christ in the haphazard circumstances, they become pinholes through which I see the face of God, and when I stand face to face with God I will discover that through my obedience thousands were blessed. When once God's redemption comes to the point of obedience in a human soul, it always creates. If I obey Jesus Christ, the redemption of God will rush through me to other lives, because behind the deed of obedience is the reality of Almighty God. (*Utmost*)

EXODUS 39:1—40:38

OF the blue, purple, and scarlet *thread* they made garments of ministry, for ministering in the holy *place,* and made the holy garments for Aaron, as the Lord had commanded Moses.

2 He made the ephod of gold, blue, purple, and scarlet *thread,* and of fine woven linen. 3 And they beat the gold into thin sheets and cut *it into* threads, to work *it* in *with* the blue, purple, and scarlet *thread,* and the fine linen, *into* artistic designs. 4 They made shoulder straps for it to couple *it* together; it was coupled together at its two edges. 5 And the intricately woven band of his ephod that *was* on it *was* of the same workmanship, *woven of* gold, blue, purple, and scarlet *thread,* and of fine woven linen, as the Lord had commanded Moses.

6 And they set onyx stones, enclosed in settings of gold; they were engraved, as signets are engraved, with the names of the sons of Israel. 7 He put them on the shoulders of the ephod *as* memorial stones for the sons of Israel, as the Lord had commanded Moses.

8 And he made the breastplate, artistically woven like the workmanship of the ephod, of gold, blue, purple, and scarlet *thread,* and of fine woven linen. 9 They made the breastplate square by doubling it; a span *was* its length and a span its width when doubled. 10 And they set in it four rows of stones: a row with a sardius, a topaz, and an emerald was the first row; 11 the second row, a turquoise, a sapphire, and a diamond; 12 the third row, a jacinth, an agate, and an amethyst; 13 the fourth row, a beryl, an onyx, and a jasper. *They were* enclosed in settings of gold in their mountings. 14 *There were* twelve stones according to the names of the sons of Israel: according to their names, *engraved like* a signet, each one with its own name according to the twelve tribes. 15 And they made chains for the breastplate at the ends, like braided cords of pure gold. 16 They also made two settings of gold and two gold rings, and put the two rings on the two ends of the breastplate. 17 And they put the two braided *chains* of gold in the two rings on the ends of the breastplate. 18 The two ends of the two braided *chains* they fastened in the two settings, and put them on the shoulder straps of the ephod in the front. 19 And they made two rings of gold and put *them* on the two ends of the breastplate, on the edge of it, which *was* on the inward side of the ephod. 20 They made two *other* gold rings and put them on the two shoulder straps, underneath the ephod toward its front, right at the seam above the intricately woven band of the ephod. 21 And they bound the breastplate by means of its rings to the rings of the ephod with a blue cord, so that it would be above the intricately woven band of the ephod, and that the breastplate would not come loose from the ephod, as the Lord had commanded Moses.

22 He made the robe of the ephod of woven work, all of blue. 23 And *there was* an opening in the middle of the robe, like the opening in a coat of mail, *with* a woven binding all around the opening, so that it would not tear. 24 They made on the hem of the robe pomegranates of blue, purple, and scarlet, and of fine woven *linen*. 25 And they made bells of pure gold, and put the bells between the pomegranates on the hem of the robe all around between the pomegranates: 26 a bell and a pomegranate, a bell and a pomegranate, all around the hem of the robe to minister in, as the Lord had commanded Moses.

27 They made tunics, artistically woven of fine linen, for Aaron and his sons, 28 a turban of fine linen, exquisite hats of fine linen, short trousers of fine woven linen, 29 and a sash of fine woven linen with blue, purple, and scarlet *thread*, made by a weaver, as the Lord had commanded Moses.

30 Then they made the plate of the holy crown of pure gold, and wrote on it an inscription *like* the engraving of a signet:

HOLINESS TO THE LORD.

31 And they tied to it a blue cord, to fasten *it* above on the turban, as the Lord had commanded Moses.

32 Thus all the work of the tabernacle of the tent of meeting was finished. And the children of Israel did according to all that the Lord had commanded Moses; so they did. 33 And they brought the tabernacle to Moses, the tent and all its furnishings: its clasps, its boards, its bars, its pillars, and its sockets; 34 the covering of ram skins dyed red, the covering of badger skins, and the veil of the covering; 35 the ark of the Testimony with its poles, and the mercy seat; 36 the table, all its utensils, and the showbread; 37 the pure *gold* lampstand with its lamps (the lamps set in order), all its utensils, and the oil for light; 38 the gold altar, the anointing oil, and the sweet incense; the screen for the tabernacle door; 39 the bronze altar, its grate of bronze, its poles, and all its utensils; the laver with its base; 40 the hangings of the court, its pillars and its sockets, the screen for the court gate, its cords, and its pegs; all the utensils for the service of the tabernacle, for the tent of meeting; 41 and the garments of ministry, to minister in the holy *place:* the holy garments for Aaron the priest, and his sons' garments, to minister as priests.

42 According to all that the Lord had commanded Moses, so the children of Israel did all the work. 43 Then Moses looked over all the work, and indeed they had done it; as the Lord had commanded, just so they had done it. And Moses blessed them.

40 THEN the Lord spoke to Moses, saying: 2 "On the first day of the first month you shall set up the tabernacle of the tent of meeting. 3 You shall put in it the ark of the Testimony, and partition off the ark with the veil. 4 You shall bring in the table and arrange the things that are to be set in order on it; and you shall bring in the lampstand and light its lamps. 5 You shall also set the altar of gold for the incense before the ark of the Testimony, and put up the screen for the door of the tabernacle. 6 Then you shall set the altar of the burnt offering before the door of the tabernacle of the tent of meeting. 7 And you shall set the laver between the tabernacle of meeting and the altar, and put water in it. 8 You shall set up the court all around, and hang up the screen at the court gate.

9 "And you shall take the anointing oil, and anoint the tabernacle and all that *is* in it; and you shall hallow it and all its utensils, and it shall be holy. 10 You shall anoint the altar of the burnt offering and all its utensils, and consecrate the altar. The altar shall be most holy. 11 And you shall anoint the laver and its base, and consecrate it.

12 "Then you shall bring Aaron and his sons to the door of the tabernacle of meeting and wash them with water. 13 You shall put the holy garments on Aaron, and anoint him and consecrate him, that he may minister to Me as priest. 14 And you shall bring his sons and clothe them with tunics. 15 You shall anoint them, as you anointed their father, that they may minister to Me as priests; for their anointing shall surely be an everlasting priesthood throughout their generations."

16 Thus Moses did; according to all that the Lord had commanded him, so he did.

17 And it came to pass in the first month of the second year, on the first *day* of the month, *that* the tabernacle was raised up. 18 So Moses raised up the tabernacle, fastened its sockets, set up its boards, put in its bars, and raised up its pillars. 19 And he spread out the tent over the tabernacle and put the covering of the tent on top of it, as the Lord had commanded Moses. 20 He took the Testimony and put *it* into the ark, inserted the poles through the rings of the ark, and put the mercy seat on top of the ark. 21 And he brought the ark into the tabernacle, hung up the veil of the cover-

ing, and partitioned off the ark of the Testimony, as the LORD had commanded Moses. 22 He put the table in the tabernacle of meeting, on the north side of the tabernacle, outside the veil; 23 and he set the bread in order upon it before the LORD, as the LORD had commanded Moses. 24 He put the lampstand in the tabernacle of meeting, across from the table, on the south side of the tabernacle; 25 and he lit the lamps before the LORD, as the LORD had commanded Moses. 26 He put the gold altar in the tabernacle of meeting in front of the veil; 27 and he burned sweet incense on it, as the LORD had commanded Moses. 28 He hung up the screen *at* the door of the tabernacle. 29 And he put the altar of burnt offering *before* the door of the tabernacle of the tent of meeting, and offered upon it the burnt offering and the grain offering, as the LORD had commanded Moses. 30 He set the laver between the tabernacle of meeting and the altar, and put water there for washing; 31 and Moses, Aaron, and his sons would wash their hands and their feet *with water* from it. 32 Whenever they went into the tabernacle of meeting, and when they came near the altar, they washed, as the LORD had commanded Moses. 33 And he raised up the court all around the tabernacle and the altar, and hung up the screen of the court gate. So Moses finished the work.

34 Then the cloud covered the tabernacle of meeting, and the glory of the LORD filled the tabernacle. 35 And Moses was not able to enter the tabernacle of meeting, because the cloud rested above it, and the glory of the LORD filled the tabernacle. 36 Whenever the cloud was taken up from above the tabernacle, the children of Israel would go onward in all their journeys. 37 But if the cloud was not taken up, then they did not journey till the day that it was taken up. 38 For the cloud of the LORD *was* above the tabernacle by day, and fire was over it by night, in the sight of all the house of Israel, throughout all their journeys.

PSALM 22:16–21

16 FOR dogs have surrounded Me;
      The congregation of the wicked has
         enclosed Me.
      They pierced My hands and My feet;
17 I can count all My bones.
      They look *and* stare at Me.
18 They divide My garments among them,
      And for My clothing they cast lots.

The death of Jesus was the death of God Incarnate.   (PHIL. SIN)

19 But You, O LORD, do not be far from
         Me;
      O My Strength, hasten to help Me!
20 Deliver Me from the sword,
      My precious *life* from the power of the
         dog.
21 Save Me from the lion's mouth
      And from the horns of the wild oxen!

      You have answered Me.

PROVERBS 8:22–31

22 "THE LORD possessed me at the
         beginning of His way,
      Before His works of old.
23 I have been established from
         everlasting,
      From the beginning, before there was
         ever an earth.
24 When *there were* no depths I was
         brought forth,
      When *there were* no fountains
         abounding with water.
25 Before the mountains were settled,
      Before the hills, I was brought forth;
26 While as yet He had not made the earth
         or the fields,
      Or the primal dust of the world.
27 When He prepared the heavens, I *was*
         there,
      When He drew a circle on the face of
         the deep,
28 When He established the clouds above,
      When He strengthened the fountains
         of the deep,
29 When He assigned to the sea its limit,
      So that the waters would not transgress
         His command,
      When He marked out the foundations
         of the earth,
30 Then I was beside Him *as* a master
         craftsman;
      And I was daily *His* delight,
      Rejoicing always before Him,
31 Rejoicing in His inhabited world,
      And my delight *was* with the sons of
         men.

MATTHEW 27:1–26

WHEN morning came, all the chief priests and elders of the people plotted against

Jesus to put Him to death. 2 And when they had bound Him, they led Him away and delivered Him to Pontius Pilate the governor.

3 Then Judas, His betrayer, seeing that He had been condemned, was remorseful and brought back the thirty pieces of silver to the chief priests and elders, 4 saying, "I have sinned by betraying innocent blood."

And they said, "What *is that* to us? You see *to it!*"

5 Then he threw down the pieces of silver in the temple and departed, and went and hanged himself.

6 But the chief priests took the silver pieces and said, "It is not lawful to put them into the treasury, because they are the price of blood." 7 And they consulted together and bought with them the potter's field, to bury strangers in. 8 Therefore that field has been called the Field of Blood to this day.

9 Then was fulfilled what was spoken by Jeremiah the prophet, saying, "And they took the thirty pieces of silver, the value of Him who was priced, whom they of the children of Israel priced, 10 and gave them for the potter's field, as the LORD directed me."

11 Now Jesus stood before the governor. And the governor asked Him, saying, "Are You the King of the Jews?"

Jesus said to him, "*It is as* you say." 12 And while He was being accused by the chief priests and elders, He answered nothing.

13 Then Pilate said to Him, "Do You not hear how many things they testify against You?" 14 But He answered him not one word, so that the governor marveled greatly.

15 Now at the feast the governor was accustomed to releasing to the multitude one prisoner whom they wished. 16 And at that time they had a notorious prisoner called Barabbas. 17 Therefore, when they had gathered together, Pilate said to them, "Whom do you want me to release to you? Barabbas, or Jesus who is called Christ?" 18 For he knew that they had handed Him over because of envy.

19 While he was sitting on the judgment seat, his wife sent to him, saying, "Have nothing to do with that just Man, for I have suffered many things today in a dream because of Him."

20 But the chief priests and elders persuaded the multitudes that they should ask for Barabbas and destroy Jesus. 21 The governor answered and said to them, "Which of the two do you want me to release to you?"

They said, "Barabbas!"

22 Pilate said to them, "What then shall I do with Jesus who is called Christ?"

They all said to him, "Let Him be crucified!"

23 Then the governor said, "Why, what evil has He done?"

But they cried out all the more, saying, "Let Him be crucified!"

The Bible makes more of the death of Jesus than of His life and His teaching.   (CONFORMED)

---

24 When Pilate saw that he could not prevail at all, but rather *that* a tumult was rising, he took water and washed *his* hands before the multitude, saying, "I am innocent of the blood of this just Person. You see *to it.*"

25 And all the people answered and said, "His blood *be* on us and on our children!"

26 Then he released Barabbas to them; and when he had scourged Jesus, he delivered *Him* to be crucified.

◆◆◆◆

Reading 46—Vanishing Vision of God
Matthew 27:46

Who is it that experiences God-forsakenness? Is it the lonely missionary with no comradeship? He is the one who knows the nearness of God. The ones who understand the experience of God-forsakenness are men like Cain: "My punishment *is* greater than I can bear!" (Gen. 4:13); men like Esau: ". . . an exceedingly great and bitter cry"; men like Saul: "God has departed from me and does not answer me anymore."

If our Lord had never known the "vanishing vision of God," He could not have been a complete Savior. Agony that has God behind it can be turned into triumph; but think of agony in which there is no God, neither in heaven above nor earth beneath, only the terror of an accusing conscience. No human sympathy can touch that desolation. In all probability the person is to blame for it, and just because he is, no human sympathy can reach him. Anyone can have a fellow feeling for a poor, unfortunate being and can sympathize with him, but who among us can understand agony that goes deeper down than can be put into words? Who but Jesus Christ?   (*GLORY*)

LEVITICUS 1:1—2:16

NOW the LORD called to Moses, and spoke to him from the tabernacle of meeting, saying, 2 "Speak to the children of Israel, and say to them: 'When any one of you brings an offering to the LORD, you shall bring your offering of the livestock—of the herd and of the flock.

3 'If his offering *is* a burnt sacrifice of the herd, let him offer a male without blemish; he shall offer it of his own free will at the door of the tabernacle of meeting before the LORD. 4 Then he shall put his hand on the head of the burnt offering, and it will be accepted on his behalf to make atonement for him. 5 He shall kill the bull before the LORD; and the priests, Aaron's sons, shall bring the blood and sprinkle the blood all around on the altar that *is by* the door of the tabernacle of meeting. 6 And he shall skin the burnt offering and cut it into its pieces. 7 The sons of Aaron the priest shall put fire on the altar, and lay the wood in order on the fire. 8 Then the priests, Aaron's sons, shall lay the parts, the head, and the fat in order on the wood that *is* on the fire upon the altar; 9 but he shall wash its entrails and its legs with water. And the priest shall burn all on the altar as a burnt sacrifice, an offering made by fire, a sweet aroma to the LORD.

10 'If his offering *is* of the flocks—of the sheep or of the goats—as a burnt sacrifice, he shall bring a male without blemish. 11 He shall kill it on the north side of the altar before the LORD; and the priests, Aaron's sons, shall sprinkle its blood all around on the altar. 12 And he shall cut it into its pieces, with its head and its fat; and the priest shall lay them in order on the wood that *is* on the fire upon the altar; 13 but he shall wash the entrails and the legs with water. Then the priest shall bring *it* all and burn *it* on the altar; it *is* a burnt sacrifice, an offering made by fire, a sweet aroma to the LORD.

14 'And if the burnt sacrifice of his offering to the LORD *is* of birds, then he shall bring his offering of turtledoves or young pigeons. 15 The priest shall bring it to the altar, wring off its head, and burn *it* on the altar; its blood shall be drained out at the side of the altar. 16 And he shall remove its crop with its feathers and cast it beside the altar on the east side, into the place for ashes. 17 Then he shall split it at its wings, *but* shall not divide *it* completely; and the priest shall burn it on the altar, on the wood that *is* on the fire. It *is* a burnt sacrifice, an offering made by fire, a sweet aroma to the LORD.

2 'WHEN anyone offers a grain offering to the LORD, his offering shall be *of* fine flour. And he shall pour oil on it, and put frankincense on it. 2 He shall bring it to Aaron's sons, the priests, one of whom shall take from it his handful of fine flour and oil with all the frankincense. And the priest shall burn *it as* a memorial on the altar, an offering made by fire, a sweet aroma to the LORD. 3 The rest of the grain offering *shall be* Aaron's and his sons'. *It is* most holy of the offerings to the LORD made by fire.

4 'And if you bring as an offering a grain offering baked in the oven, *it shall be* unleavened cakes of fine flour mixed with oil, or unleavened wafers anointed with oil. 5 But if your offering *is* a grain offering *baked* in a pan, *it shall be of* fine flour, unleavened, mixed with oil. 6 You shall break it in pieces and pour oil on it; it *is* a grain offering.

7 'If your offering *is* a grain offering *baked* in a covered pan, it shall be made *of* fine flour with oil. 8 You shall bring the grain offering that is made of these things to the LORD. And when it is presented to the priest, he shall bring it to the altar. 9 Then the priest shall take from the grain offering a memorial portion, and burn *it* on the altar. *It is* an offering made by fire, a sweet aroma to the LORD. 10 And what

is left of the grain offering *shall be* Aaron's and his sons'. *It is* most holy of the offerings to the LORD made by fire.

11 'No grain offering which you bring to the LORD shall be made with leaven, for you shall burn no leaven nor any honey in any offering to the LORD made by fire. 12 As for the offering of the firstfruits, you shall offer them to the LORD, but they shall not be burned on the altar for a sweet aroma. 13 And every offering of your grain offering you shall season with salt; you shall not allow the salt of the covenant of your God to be lacking from your grain offering. With all your offerings you shall offer salt.

14 'If you offer a grain offering of your firstfruits to the LORD, you shall offer for the grain offering of your firstfruits green heads of grain roasted on the fire, grain beaten from full heads. 15 And you shall put oil on it, and lay frankincense on it. It *is* a grain offering. 16 Then the priest shall burn the memorial portion: *part* of its beaten grain and *part* of its oil, with all the frankincense, as an offering made by fire to the LORD.

PSALM 22:22–31

22 I will declare Your name to My brethren;
   In the midst of the assembly I will praise You.
23 You who fear the LORD, praise Him!
   All you descendants of Jacob, glorify Him,
   And fear Him, all you offspring of Israel!
24 For He has not despised nor abhorred the affliction of the afflicted;
   Nor has He hidden His face from Him;
   But when He cried to Him, He heard.

25 My praise *shall be* of You in the great assembly;
   I will pay My vows before those who fear Him.
26 The poor shall eat and be satisfied;
   Those who seek Him will praise the LORD.
   Let your heart live forever!

27 All the ends of the world
   Shall remember and turn to the LORD,

The world must be born again just as individuals are. (GOOD)

And all the families of the nations
   Shall worship before You.
28 For the kingdom *is* the LORD's,
   And He rules over the nations.

29 All the prosperous of the earth
   Shall eat and worship;
   All those who go down to the dust
   Shall bow before Him,
   Even he who cannot keep himself alive.

30 A posterity shall serve Him.
   It will be recounted of the Lord to the *next* generation,
31 They will come and declare His righteousness to a people who will be born,
   That He has done *this*.

PROVERBS 8:32–36

32 "NOW therefore, listen to me, *my* children,
   For blessed *are those who* keep my ways.
33 Hear instruction and be wise,
   And do not disdain *it*.
34 Blessed is the man who listens to me,
   Watching daily at my gates,
   Waiting at the posts of my doors.
35 For whoever finds me finds life,
   And obtains favor from the LORD;
36 But he who sins against me wrongs his own soul;
   All those who hate me love death."

MATTHEW 27:27–54

THEN the soldiers of the governor took Jesus into the Praetorium and gathered the whole garrison around Him. 28 And they stripped Him and put a scarlet robe on Him. 29 When they had twisted a crown of thorns, they put *it* on His head, and a reed in His right hand. And they bowed the knee before Him and mocked Him, saying, "Hail, King of the Jews!" 30 Then they spat on Him, and took the reed and struck Him on the head. 31 And when they had mocked Him, they took the robe off Him, put His *own* clothes on Him, and led Him away to be crucified.

32 Now as they came out, they found a man of Cyrene, Simon by name. Him they compelled to bear His cross. 33 And when they had come to a place called Golgotha, that is to say, Place of a Skull, 34 they gave Him sour wine mingled with gall to drink.

But when He had tasted *it,* He would not drink.

35 Then they crucified Him, and divided His garments, casting lots, that it might be fulfilled which was spoken by the prophet:

> "They divided My garments among them,
> And for My clothing they cast lots."

36 Sitting down, they kept watch over Him there. 37 And they put up over His head the accusation written against Him:

THIS IS JESUS
THE KING OF THE JEWS.

38 Then two robbers were crucified with Him, one on the right and another on the left.

39 And those who passed by blasphemed Him, wagging their heads 40 and saying, "You who destroy the temple and build *it* in three days, save Yourself! If You are the Son of God, come down from the cross."

41 Likewise the chief priests also, mocking with the scribes and elders, said, 42 "He saved others; Himself He cannot save. If He is the King of Israel, let Him now come down from the cross, and we will believe Him. 43 He trusted in God; let Him deliver Him now if He will have Him; for He said, 'I am the Son of God.' "

44 Even the robbers who were crucified with Him reviled Him with the same thing.

45 Now from the sixth hour until the ninth hour there was darkness over all the land. 46 And about the ninth hour Jesus cried out with a loud voice, saying, "Eli, Eli, lama sabachthani?" that is, "My God, My God, why have You forsaken Me?"

47 Some of those who stood there, when they heard *that,* said, "This Man is calling for Elijah!" 48 Immediately one of them ran and took a sponge, filled *it* with sour wine and put *it* on a reed, and offered it to Him to drink.

49 The rest said, "Let Him alone; let us see if Elijah will come to save Him."

50 And Jesus cried out again with a loud voice, and yielded up His spirit.

The redemption of our Lord Jesus Christ is the great abiding reality. (PLACE HELP)

---

51 Then, behold, the veil of the temple was torn in two from top to bottom; and the earth quaked, and the rocks were split, 52 and the graves were opened; and many bodies of the saints who had fallen asleep were raised; 53 and coming out of the graves after His resurrection, they went into the holy city and appeared to many.

54 So when the centurion and those with him, who were guarding Jesus, saw the earthquake and the things that had happened, they feared greatly, saying, "Truly this was the Son of God!"

Reading 47—Identified with His Death
Leviticus 4:3, 4

The gospel of Jesus Christ always forces an issue of will. Do I accept God's verdict on sin in the Cross of Christ? Have I the slightest interest in the death of Jesus? Do I want to be identified with His death, to be killed right out to all interest in sin, in worldliness, in self—to be so identified with Jesus that I am spoilt for everything else but Him? The great privilege of discipleship is that I can sign on under His Cross, and that means death to sin. Get alone with Jesus and either tell Him that you do not want sin to die out in you; or else tell Him that at all costs you want to be identified with His death. Immediately you transact in confident faith in what Our Lord did on the Cross, a supernatural identification with His death takes place, and you will know with a knowledge that passes knowledge that your "old man" is crucified with Christ. The proof that your old man is crucified with Christ is the amazing ease with which the life of God in you enables you to obey the voice of Jesus Christ. (*UTMOST*)

LEVITICUS 3:1—4:35

'WHEN his offering *is* a sacrifice of a peace offering, if he offers *it* of the herd, whether male or female, he shall offer it without blemish before the LORD. 2 And he shall lay his hand on the head of his offering, and kill it *at* the door of the tabernacle of meeting; and Aaron's sons, the priests, shall sprinkle the blood all around on the altar. 3 Then he shall offer from the sacrifice of the peace offering an offering made by fire to the LORD. The fat that covers the entrails and all the fat that *is* on the entrails, 4 the two kidneys and the fat that *is* on them by the flanks, and the fatty lobe *attached* to the liver above the kidneys, he shall remove; 5 and Aaron's sons shall burn it on the altar upon the burnt sacrifice, which *is* on the wood that *is* on the fire, *as* an offering made by fire, a sweet aroma to the LORD.

6 'If his offering as a sacrifice of a peace offering to the LORD *is* of the flock, *whether* male or female, he shall offer it without blemish. 7 If he offers a lamb as his offering,

---

Sacrifice in the Bible means that we give to God the best we have. (LOVE OF GOD)

---

then he shall offer it before the LORD. 8 And he shall lay his hand on the head of his offering, and kill it before the tabernacle of meeting; and Aaron's sons shall sprinkle its blood all around on the altar.

9 'Then he shall offer from the sacrifice of the peace offering, as an offering made by fire to the LORD, its fat *and* the whole fat tail which he shall remove close to the backbone. And the fat that covers the entrails and all the fat that *is* on the entrails, 10 the two kidneys and the fat that *is* on them by the flanks, and the fatty lobe *attached* to the liver above the kidneys, he shall remove; 11 and the priest shall burn *them* on the altar *as* food, an offering made by fire to the LORD.

12 'And if his offering *is* a goat, then he shall offer it before the LORD. 13 He shall lay his hand on its head and kill it before the tabernacle of meeting; and the sons of Aaron shall sprinkle its blood all around on the altar. 14 Then he shall offer from it his offering, as an offering made by fire to the LORD. The fat that covers the entrails and all the fat that *is* on the entrails, 15 the two kidneys and the fat that *is* on

them by the flanks, and the fatty lobe *attached* to the liver above the kidneys, he shall remove; 16 and the priest shall burn them on the altar *as* food, an offering made by fire for a sweet aroma; all the fat *is* the LORD's.

17 'This shall be a perpetual statute throughout your generations in all your dwellings: you shall eat neither fat nor blood.' "

4 NOW the LORD spoke to Moses, saying, 2 "Speak to the children of Israel, saying: 'If a person sins unintentionally against any of the commandments of the LORD *in anything* which ought not to be done, and does any of them, 3 if the anointed priest sins, bringing guilt on the people, then let him offer to the LORD for his sin which he has sinned a young bull without blemish as a sin offering. 4 He shall bring the bull to the door of the tabernacle of meeting before the LORD, lay his hand on the bull's head, and kill the bull before the LORD. 5 Then the anointed priest shall take some of the bull's blood and bring it to the tabernacle of meeting. 6 The priest shall dip his finger in the blood and sprinkle some of the blood seven times before the LORD, in front of the veil of the sanctuary. 7 And the priest shall put some of the blood on the horns of the altar of sweet incense before the LORD, which is in the tabernacle of meeting; and he shall pour the remaining blood of the bull at the base of the altar of the burnt offering, which is at the door of the tabernacle of meeting. 8 He shall take from it all the fat of the bull as the sin offering. The fat that covers the entrails and all the fat which *is* on the entrails, 9 the two kidneys and the fat that *is* on them by the flanks, and the fatty lobe *attached* to the liver above the kidneys, he shall remove, 10 as it was taken from the bull of the sacrifice of the peace offering; and the priest shall burn them on the altar of the burnt offering. 11 But the bull's hide and all its flesh, with its head and legs, its entrails and offal— 12 the whole bull he shall carry outside the camp to a clean place, where the ashes are poured out, and burn it on wood with fire; where the ashes are poured out it shall be burned.

13 'Now if the whole congregation of Israel sins unintentionally, and the thing is hidden from the eyes of the assembly, and they have done *something against* any of the commandments of the LORD *in anything* which should not be done, and are guilty; 14 when the sin which they have committed becomes known, then the assembly shall

offer a young bull for the sin, and bring it before the tabernacle of meeting. 15 And the elders of the congregation shall lay their hands on the head of the bull before the LORD. Then the bull shall be killed before the LORD. 16 The anointed priest shall bring some of the bull's blood to the tabernacle of meeting. 17 Then the priest shall dip his finger in the blood and sprinkle *it* seven times before the LORD, in front of the veil. 18 And he shall put *some* of the blood on the horns of the altar which *is* before the LORD, which *is* in the tabernacle of meeting; and he shall pour the remaining blood at the base of the altar of burnt offering, which is at the door of the tabernacle of meeting. 19 He shall take all the fat from it and burn *it* on the altar. 20 And he shall do with the bull as he did with the bull as a sin offering; thus he shall do with it. So the priest shall make atonement for them, and it shall be forgiven them. 21 Then he shall carry the bull outside the camp, and burn it as he burned the first bull. It *is* a sin offering for the assembly.

22 'When a ruler has sinned, and done *something* unintentionally *against* any of the commandments of the LORD his God *in anything* which should not be done, and is guilty, 23 or if his sin which he has committed comes to his knowledge, he shall bring as his offering a kid of the goats, a male without blemish. 24 And he shall lay his hand on the head of the goat, and kill it at the place where they kill the burnt offering before the LORD. It *is* a sin offering. 25 The priest shall take some of the blood of the sin offering with his finger, put *it* on the horns of the altar of burnt offering, and pour its blood at the base of the altar of burnt offering. 26 And he shall burn all its fat on the altar, like the fat of the sacrifice of the peace offering. So the priest shall make atonement for him concerning his sin, and it shall be forgiven him.

27 'If anyone of the common people sins unintentionally by doing *something against* any of the commandments of the LORD *in anything* which ought not to be done, and is guilty, 28 or if his sin which he has committed comes to his knowledge, then he shall bring as his offering a kid of the goats, a female without blemish, for his sin which he has committed. 29 And he shall lay his hand on the head of the sin offering, and kill the sin offering at the place of the burnt offering. 30 Then the priest shall take *some* of its blood with his finger, put *it* on the horns of the altar of burnt offering, and pour all *the remaining* blood at the base of the altar. 31 He shall remove all its fat,

as fat is removed from the sacrifice of the peace offering; and the priest shall burn it on the altar for a sweet aroma to the LORD. So the priest shall make atonement for him, and it shall be forgiven him.

32 'If he brings a lamb as his sin offering, he shall bring a female without blemish. 33 Then he shall lay his hand on the head of the sin offering, and kill it as a sin offering at the place where they kill the burnt offering. 34 The priest shall take *some* of the blood of the sin offering with his finger, put *it* on the horns of the altar of burnt offering, and pour all *the remaining* blood at the base of the altar. 35 He shall remove all its fat, as the fat of the lamb is removed from the sacrifice of the peace offering. Then the priest shall burn it on the altar, according to the offerings made by fire to the LORD. So the priest shall make atonement for his sin that he has committed, and it shall be forgiven him.

PSALM 23:1–6

1   THE LORD *is* my shepherd;
    I shall not want.
2   He makes me to lie down in green
       pastures;
    He leads me beside the still waters.
3   He restores my soul;
    He leads me in the paths of
       righteousness
    For His name's sake.

4   Yea, though I walk through the valley
       of the shadow of death,
    I will fear no evil;
    For You *are* with me;
    Your rod and Your staff, they comfort
    me.

There is not only fear, but terrible danger, for the life unguarded by God. (PERFECT)

---

5   You prepare a table before me in the
       presence of my enemies;
    You anoint my head with oil;
    My cup runs over.
6   Surely goodness and mercy shall follow
    me
    All the days of my life;
    And I will dwell in the house of the
    LORD
    Forever.

PROVERBS 9:1–6

1 WISDOM has built her house,
   She has hewn out her seven pillars;
2 She has slaughtered her meat,
   She has mixed her wine,
   She has also furnished her table.
3 She has sent out her maidens,
   She cries out from the highest places
      of the city,
4 "Whoever *is* simple, let him turn in here!"
   As for him who lacks understanding,
      she says to him,
5 "Come, eat of my bread
   And drink of the wine I have mixed.
6 Forsake foolishness and live,
   And go in the way of understanding.

MATTHEW 27:55–66

AND many women who followed Jesus from Galilee, ministering to Him, were there looking on from afar, 56 among whom were Mary Magdalene, Mary the mother of James and Joses, and the mother of Zebedee's sons.

57 Now when evening had come, there came a rich man from Arimathea, named Joseph, who himself had also become a disciple of Jesus. 58 This man went to Pilate and asked for the body of Jesus. Then Pilate commanded the body to be given to him. 59 When Joseph had taken the body, he wrapped it in a clean linen cloth, 60 and laid it in his new tomb which he had hewn out of the rock; and he rolled a large stone against the door of the tomb, and departed. 61 And Mary Magdalene was there, and the other Mary, sitting opposite the tomb.

62 On the next day, which followed the Day of Preparation, the chief priests and Pharisees gathered together to Pilate, 63 saying, "Sir, we remember, while He was still alive, how that deceiver said, 'After three days I will rise.' 64 Therefore command that the tomb be made secure until the third day, lest His disciples come by night and steal Him *away*, and say to the people, 'He has risen from the dead.' So the last deception will be worse than the first."

65 Pilate said to them, "You have a guard; go your way, make *it* as secure as you know how." 66 So they went and made the tomb secure, sealing the stone and setting the guard.

◆◆◆

Reading 48—Room for the Impossible
Matthew 28:6

Jesus is not in the sitting by the tomb; He is not in the bitter tears; He is not in the sad communings. The place where we will find Jesus is just where common sense says it is impossible to find Him. It was no use for the disciples to imagine they were going to have a recurrence of those three years; it was impossible to recall the thrilling yesterdays; it was impossible for the two on the way to Emmaus to have a return of the fellowship they yearned for; but there was something infinitely better for them. "For He is risen, as He said." Impossibility had wedded itself to what Jesus had said. The proclamation of the impossible springs from the supernatural, not from common sense. The supernatural figures largely all through the life of our Lord. At His birth the angels proclaimed that He should be called Jesus "for He will save His people from their sins." We shall not think of our Lord as a savior if we look at Him in the light of our own minds, because no natural man imagines he needs to be saved. Do we make room in our faith for the impossible along the line of the supernatural? or have we reduced our religion to such common sense platitudes that there is no need for Jesus to have lived at all?

(PLACE HELP)

LEVITICUS 5:1—6:30

'IF a person sins in hearing the utterance of an oath, and *is* a witness, whether he has seen or known *of the matter*—if he does not tell *it*, he bears guilt.

2 'Or if a person touches any unclean thing, whether *it is* the carcass of an unclean beast, or the carcass of unclean livestock, or the carcass of unclean creeping things, and he is unaware of it, he also shall be unclean and guilty. 3 Or if he touches human uncleanness—whatever uncleanness with which a man may be defiled, and he is unaware of it—when he realizes *it,* then he shall be guilty.

4 'Or if a person swears, speaking thoughtlessly with *his* lips to do evil or to do good, whatever *it is* that a man may pronounce by an oath, and he is unaware of it—when he realizes *it,* then he shall be guilty in any of these *matters*.

5 'And it shall be, when he is guilty in any of these *matters,* that he shall confess that he has sinned in that *thing;* 6 and he shall bring his trespass offering to the LORD for his sin which he has committed, a female from the flock, a lamb or a kid of the goats as a sin offering. So the priest shall make atonement for him concerning his sin.

7 'If he is not able to bring a lamb, then he shall bring to the LORD, for his trespass which he has committed, two turtledoves or two young pigeons: one as a sin offering and the other as a burnt offering. 8 And he shall bring them to the priest, who shall offer *that* which *is* for the sin offering first, and wring off its head from its neck, but shall not divide *it* completely. 9 Then he shall sprinkle *some* of the blood of the sin offering on the side of the altar, and the rest of the blood shall be drained out at the base of the altar. It *is* a sin offering. 10 And he shall offer the second *as* a burnt offering according to the prescribed manner. So the priest shall make atonement on his behalf for his sin which he has committed, and it shall be forgiven him.

11 'But if he is not able to bring two turtledoves or two young pigeons, then he who sinned shall bring for his offering one-tenth of an ephah of fine flour as a sin offering. He shall put no oil on it, nor shall he put frankincense on it, for it *is* a sin offering.

Sacrifice is that I give as a love-gift the very best thing I have.   (RUN)

---

12 Then he shall bring it to the priest, and the priest shall take his handful of it as a memorial portion, and burn *it* on the altar according to the offerings made by fire to the LORD. It *is* a sin offering. 13 The priest shall make atonement for him, for his sin that he has committed in any of these matters; and it shall be forgiven him. *The rest* shall be the priest's as a grain offering.' "

14 Then the LORD spoke to Moses, saying: 15 "If a person commits a trespass, and sins unintentionally in regard to the holy things of the LORD, then he shall bring to the LORD as his trespass offering a ram without blemish from the flocks, with your valuation in shekels of silver according to the shekel of the sanctuary, as a trespass offering. 16 And he shall make restitution for the harm that he has done in regard to the holy thing, and shall add one-fifth to it and give it to the priest. So the priest shall make atonement for him with the ram of the trespass offering, and it shall be forgiven him.

17 "If a person sins, and commits any of these things which are forbidden to be done by the commandments of the LORD, though he does not know *it,* yet he is guilty and shall bear his iniquity. 18 And he shall bring to the priest a ram without blemish from the flock, with your valuation, as a trespass offering. So the priest shall make atonement for him regarding his ignorance in which he erred and did not know *it,* and it shall be forgiven him. 19 It is a trespass offering; he has certainly trespassed against the LORD."

6 AND the LORD spoke to Moses, saying: 2 "If a person sins and commits a trespass against the LORD by lying to his neighbor about what was delivered to him for safekeeping, or about a pledge, or about a robbery, or if he has extorted from his neighbor, 3 or if he has found what was lost and lies concerning it, and swears falsely—in any one of these things that a man may do in which he sins: 4 then it shall be, because he has sinned and is guilty, that he shall restore what he has stolen, or the thing which he has extorted, or what was delivered to him for safekeeping, or the lost thing which he found, 5 or all that about which he has sworn falsely. He shall restore its full value, add one-fifth more to it, *and* give it to whomever it belongs, on the day of his trespass offering. 6 And he shall bring his trespass offering to the LORD, a ram without blemish from the flock, with your valuation, as a trespass offering, to the priest. 7 So the priest shall

make atonement for him before the Lord, and he shall be forgiven for any one of these things that he may have done in which he trespasses."

8 Then the Lord spoke to Moses, saying, 9 "Command Aaron and his sons, saying, 'This *is* the law of the burnt offering: The burnt offering *shall be* on the hearth upon the altar all night until morning, and the fire of the altar shall be kept burning on it. 10 And the priest shall put on his linen garment, and his linen trousers he shall put on his body, and take up the ashes of the burnt offering which the fire has consumed on the altar, and he shall put them beside the altar. 11 Then he shall take off his garments, put on other garments, and carry the ashes outside the camp to a clean place. 12 And the fire on the altar shall be kept burning on it; it shall not be put out. And the priest shall burn wood on it every morning, and lay the burnt offering in order on it; and he shall burn on it the fat of the peace offerings. 13 A fire shall always be burning on the altar; it shall never go out.

14 'This *is* the law of the grain offering: The sons of Aaron shall offer it on the altar before the Lord. 15 He shall take from it his handful of the fine flour of the grain offering, with its oil, and all the frankincense which *is* on the grain offering, and shall burn *it* on the altar *for* a sweet aroma, as a memorial to the Lord. 16 And the remainder of it Aaron and his sons shall eat; with unleavened bread it shall be eaten in a holy place; in the court of the tabernacle of meeting they shall eat it. 17 It shall not be baked with leaven. I have given it *as* their portion of My offerings made by fire; it *is* most holy, like the sin offering and the trespass offering. 18 All the males among the children of Aaron may eat it. *It shall be* a statute forever in your generations concerning the offerings made by fire to the Lord. Everyone who touches them must be holy.' "

19 And the Lord spoke to Moses, saying, 20 "This *is* the offering of Aaron and his sons, which they shall offer to the Lord, *beginning* on the day when he is anointed: one-tenth of an ephah of fine flour as a daily grain offering, half of it in the morning and half of it at night. 21 It shall be made in a pan with oil. *When it is* mixed, you shall bring it in. The baked pieces of the grain offering you shall offer *for* a sweet aroma to the Lord. 22 The priest from among his sons, who is anointed in his place, shall offer it. *It is* a statute forever to the Lord. It shall be wholly burned. 23 For every grain offering for the priest shall be wholly burned. It shall not be eaten."

24 Also the Lord spoke to Moses, saying, 25 "Speak to Aaron and to his sons, saying, 'This *is* the law of the sin offering: In the place where the burnt offering is killed, the sin offering shall be killed before the Lord. It *is* most holy. 26 The priest who offers it for sin shall eat it. In a holy place it shall be eaten, in the court of the tabernacle of meeting. 27 Everyone who touches its flesh must be holy. And when its blood is sprinkled on any garment, you shall wash that on which it was sprinkled, in a holy place. 28 But the earthen vessel in which it is boiled shall be broken. And if it is boiled in a bronze pot, it shall be both scoured and rinsed in water. 29 All the males among the priests may eat it. It *is* most holy. 30 But no sin offering from which *any* of the blood is brought into the tabernacle of meeting, to make atonement in the holy *place,* shall be eaten. It shall be burned in the fire.

PSALM 24:1–6

1 THE earth *is* the Lord's, and all its
    fullness,
    The world and those who dwell therein.
2 For He has founded it upon the seas,
    And established it upon the waters.

3 Who may ascend into the hill of the
    Lord?
    Or who may stand in His holy place?
4 He who has clean hands and a pure
    heart,
    Who has not lifted up his soul to an
    idol,
    Nor sworn deceitfully.
5 He shall receive blessing from the
    Lord,
    And righteousness from the God of his
    salvation.
6 This *is* Jacob, the generation of those
    who seek Him,
    Who seek Your face.   Selah

PROVERBS 9:7–9

7 "HE who corrects a scoffer gets shame
    for himself,
    And he who rebukes a wicked *man only*
    harms himself.
8 Do not correct a scoffer, lest he hate
    you;
    Rebuke a wise *man,* and he will love
    you.

9   Give *instruction* to a wise *man,* and he
      will be still wiser;
      Teach a just *man,* and he will increase
      in learning.

MATTHEW 28:1–20

NOW after the Sabbath, as the first *day* of the week began to dawn, Mary Magdalene and the other Mary came to see the tomb. 2 And behold, there was a great earthquake; for an angel of the Lord descended from heaven, and came and rolled back the stone from the door, and sat on it. 3 His countenance was like lightning, and his clothing as white as snow. 4 And the guards shook for fear of him, and became like dead *men.*

5 But the angel answered and said to the women, "Do not be afraid, for I know that you seek Jesus who was crucified. 6 He is not here; for He is risen, as He said. Come, see the place where the Lord lay. 7 And go quickly and tell His disciples that He is risen from the dead, and indeed He is going before you into Galilee; there you will see Him. Behold, I have told you."

8 So they went out quickly from the tomb with fear and great joy, and ran to bring His disciples word.

9 And as they went to tell His disciples, behold, Jesus met them, saying, "Rejoice!" So they came and held Him by the feet and worshiped Him. 10 Then Jesus said to them, "Do not be afraid. Go *and* tell My brethren to go to Galilee, and there they will see Me."

11 Now while they were going, behold, some of the guard came into the city and reported to the chief priests all the things that had happened. 12 When they had assembled with the elders and consulted together, they gave a large sum of money to the soldiers, 13 saying, "Tell them, 'His disciples came at night and stole Him *away* while we slept.' 14 And if this comes to the governor's ears, we will appease him and make you secure." 15 So they took the money and did as they were instructed; and this saying is commonly reported among the Jews until this day.

16 Then the eleven disciples went away into Galilee, to the mountain which Jesus had appointed for them. 17 When they saw Him, they worshiped Him; but some doubted.

18 And Jesus came and spoke to them, saying, "All authority has been given to Me in heaven and on earth. 19 Go therefore and make disciples of all the nations, baptizing them in the name of the Father and of the Son and of the Holy Spirit, 20 teaching them to observe all things that I have commanded you; and lo, I am with you always, *even* to the end of the age." Amen.

> *We cannot make disciples of others unless we are disciples ourselves.* (PLACE HELP)

◆◆◆◆

Reading 49—The Dominating Sentiment
Mark 1:16–22

The average preaching of redemption deals mainly with the "scenic" cases; that is, those who have gone through exceptional experiences. But none of the early disciples had these scenic experiences, nor was their dominating sentiment a desire for deliverance from sin. They were elemental men in touch with the forces of nature, and there was something about Jesus Christ that fascinated them. When He said, "Follow Me," they followed Him at once; it was no cross to them. It would have been a cross not to follow, for the spell of Jesus was on them. We have come to the conclusion nowadays that a person must be a conscious sinner before Jesus Christ can do anything for him. The early disciples were not attracted to Jesus because they wanted to be saved from sin; they had no concept that they needed saving. They were attracted to Him by a dominating sincerity, by sentiments other than those which we say make men come to Jesus. . . . They did not follow Jesus because they wanted to be saved, but because they could not help following. Three years later when again Jesus said, "Follow Me," it was a different matter; many things had happened during those years. The first "Follow Me" meant an external following; now it was to be a following in internal martyrdom. (See John 21:18, 19.)   (*LOVE OF GOD*)

LEVITICUS 7:1—8:36

'LIKEWISE this *is* the law of the trespass offering (it *is* most holy): 2 In the place where they kill the burnt offering they shall kill the trespass offering. And its blood he shall sprinkle all around on the altar. 3 And he shall offer from it all its fat. The fat tail and the fat that covers the entrails, 4 the two kidneys and the fat that *is* on them by the flanks, and the fatty lobe *attached* to the liver above the kidneys, he shall remove; 5 and the priest shall burn them on the altar *as* an offering made by fire to the LORD. It *is* a trespass offering. 6 Every male among the priests may eat it. It shall be eaten in a holy place. It *is* most holy. 7 The trespass offering *is* like the sin offering; *there is* one law for them both: the priest who makes atonement with it shall have *it*. 8 And the priest who offers anyone's burnt offering, that priest shall have for himself the skin of the burnt offering which he has offered. 9 Also every grain offering that is baked in the oven and all that is prepared in the covered pan, or in a pan, shall be the priest's who offers it. 10 Every grain offering, *whether* mixed with oil or dry, shall belong to all the sons of Aaron, to one *as much* as the other.

11 'This *is* the law of the sacrifice of peace offerings which he shall offer to the LORD:

Sacrifice is the source of spiritual discipleship.   (PLACE HELP)

---

12 If he offers it for a thanksgiving, then he shall offer, with the sacrifice of thanksgiving, unleavened cakes mixed with oil, unleavened wafers anointed with oil, or cakes of blended flour mixed with oil. 13 Besides the cakes, *as* his offering he shall offer leavened bread with the sacrifice of thanksgiving of his peace offering. 14 And from it he shall offer one cake from each offering *as* a heave offering to the LORD. It shall belong to the priest who sprinkles the blood of the peace offering.

15 'The flesh of the sacrifice of his peace offering for thanksgiving shall be eaten the same day it is offered. He shall not leave any of it until morning. 16 But if the sacrifice of his offering *is* a vow or a voluntary offering, it shall be eaten the same day that he offers his sacrifice; but on the next day the remainder of it also may be eaten; 17 the remainder of the flesh of the sacrifice on the third day must be burned with fire. 18 And if *any* of the flesh of the sacrifice of his peace offering is eaten at all on the third day, it shall not be accepted, nor shall it be imputed *to* him who offers it; it shall be an abomination *to* him who offers it, and the person who eats of it shall bear guilt.

19 'The flesh that touches any unclean thing shall not be eaten. It shall be burned with fire. And as for the *clean* flesh, all who are clean may eat of it. 20 But the person who eats the flesh of the sacrifice of the peace offering that *belongs* to the LORD, while he is unclean, that person shall be cut off from his people. 21 Moreover the person who touches any unclean thing, *such as* human uncleanness, *an* unclean animal, or any abominable unclean thing, and who eats the flesh of the sacrifice of the peace offering that *belongs* to the LORD, that person shall be cut off from his people.' "

22 And the LORD spoke to Moses, saying, 23 "Speak to the children of Israel, saying: 'You shall not eat any fat, of ox or sheep or goat. 24 And the fat of an animal that dies *naturally*, and the fat of what is torn by wild beasts, may be used in any other way; but you shall by no means eat it. 25 For whoever eats the fat of the animal of which men offer an offering made by fire to the LORD, the person who eats *it* shall be cut off from his people. 26 Moreover you shall not eat any blood in any of your dwellings, *whether* of bird or beast. 27 Whoever eats any blood, that person shall be cut off from his people.' "

28 Then the LORD spoke to Moses, saying, 29 "Speak to the children of Israel, saying: 'He who offers the sacrifice of his peace offering to the LORD shall bring his offering to the LORD from the sacrifice of his peace offering. 30 His own hands shall bring the offerings made by fire to the LORD. The fat with the breast he shall bring, that the breast may be waved *as* a wave offering

before the LORD. 31 And the priest shall burn the fat on the altar, but the breast shall be Aaron's and his sons'. 32 Also the right thigh you shall give to the priest *as* a heave offering from the sacrifices of your peace offerings. 33 He among the sons of Aaron, who offers the blood of the peace offering and the fat, shall have the right thigh for *his* part. 34 For the breast of the wave offering and the thigh of the heave offering I have taken from the children of Israel, from the sacrifices of their peace offerings, and I have given them to Aaron the priest and to his sons from the children of Israel by a statute forever.' "

35 This *is* the consecrated portion for Aaron and his sons, from the offerings made by fire to the LORD, on the day when *Moses* presented them to minister to the LORD as priests. 36 The LORD commanded this to be given to them by the children of Israel, on the day that He anointed them, *by* a statute forever throughout their generations.

37 This *is* the law of the burnt offering, the grain offering, the sin offering, the trespass offering, the consecrations, and the sacrifice of the peace offering, 38 which the LORD commanded Moses on Mount Sinai, on the day when He commanded the children of Israel to offer their offerings to the LORD in the Wilderness of Sinai.

8 AND the LORD spoke to Moses, saying: 2 "Take Aaron and his sons with him, and the garments, the anointing oil, a bull as the sin offering, two rams, and a basket of unleavened bread; 3 and gather all the congregation together at the door of the tabernacle of meeting."

4 So Moses did as the LORD commanded him. And the congregation was gathered together at the door of the tabernacle of meeting. 5 And Moses said to the congregation, "This *is* what the LORD commanded to be done."

6 Then Moses brought Aaron and his sons and washed them with water. 7 And he put the tunic on him, girded him with the sash, clothed him with the robe, and put the ephod on him; and he girded him with the intricately woven band of the ephod, and with it tied *the ephod* on him. 8 Then he put the breastplate on him, and he put the Urim and the Thummim in the breastplate. 9 And he put the turban on his head. Also on the turban, on its front, he put the golden plate, the holy crown, as the LORD had commanded Moses.

10 Also Moses took the anointing oil, and anointed the tabernacle and all that *was* in

it, and consecrated them. 11 He sprinkled some of it on the altar seven times, anointed the altar and all its utensils, and the laver and its base, to consecrate them. 12 And he poured some of the anointing oil on Aaron's head and anointed him, to consecrate him.

13 Then Moses brought Aaron's sons and put tunics on them, girded them with sashes, and put hats on them, as the LORD had commanded Moses.

14 And he brought the bull for the sin offering. Then Aaron and his sons laid their hands on the head of the bull for the sin offering, 15 and Moses killed *it*. Then he took the blood, and put *some* on the horns of the altar all around with his finger, and purified the altar. And he poured the blood at the base of the altar, and consecrated it, to make atonement for it. 16 Then he took all the fat that *was* on the entrails, the fatty lobe *attached to* the liver, and the two kidneys with their fat, and Moses burned *them* on the altar. 17 But the bull, its hide, its flesh, and its offal, he burned with fire outside the camp, as the LORD had commanded Moses.

18 Then he brought the ram as the burnt offering. And Aaron and his sons laid their hands on the head of the ram, 19 and Moses killed *it*. Then he sprinkled the blood all around on the altar. 20 And he cut the ram into pieces; and Moses burned the head, the pieces, and the fat. 21 Then he washed the entrails and the legs in water. And Moses burned the whole ram on the altar. It *was* a burnt sacrifice for a sweet aroma, an offering made by fire to the LORD, as the LORD had commanded Moses.

22 And he brought the second ram, the ram of consecration. Then Aaron and his sons laid their hands on the head of the ram, 23 and Moses killed *it*. Also he took *some* of its blood and put it on the tip of Aaron's right ear, on the thumb of his right hand, and on the big toe of his right foot. 24 Then he brought Aaron's sons. And Moses put *some* of the blood on the tips of their right ears, on the thumbs of their right hands, and on the big toes of their right feet. And Moses sprinkled the blood all around on the altar. 25 Then he took the fat and the fat tail, all the fat that *was* on the entrails, the fatty lobe *attached to* the liver, the two kidneys and their fat, and the right thigh; 26 and from the basket of unleavened bread that was before the LORD he took one unleavened cake, a cake of bread *anointed with* oil, and one wafer, and put *them* on the fat and on the right thigh; 27 and he put all *these* in Aaron's hands and

in his sons' hands, and waved them *as* a wave offering before the LORD. 28 Then Moses took them from their hands and burned *them* on the altar, on the burnt offering. They *were* consecration offerings for a sweet aroma. That *was* an offering made by fire to the LORD. 29 And Moses took the breast and waved it *as* a wave offering before the LORD. It was Moses' part of the ram of consecration, as the LORD had commanded Moses.

30 Then Moses took some of the anointing oil and some of the blood which *was* on the altar, and sprinkled *it* on Aaron, on his garments, on his sons, and on the garments of his sons with him; and he consecrated Aaron, his garments, his sons, and the garments of his sons with him.

31 And Moses said to Aaron and his sons, "Boil the flesh *at* the door of the tabernacle of meeting, and eat it there with the bread that *is* in the basket of consecration offerings, as I commanded, saying, 'Aaron and his sons shall eat it.' 32 What remains of the flesh and of the bread you shall burn with fire. 33 And you shall not go outside the door of the tabernacle of meeting *for* seven days, until the days of your consecration are ended. For seven days he shall consecrate you. 34 As he has done this day, *so* the LORD has commanded to do, to make atonement for you. 35 Therefore you shall stay *at* the door of the tabernacle of meeting day and night for seven days, and keep the charge of the LORD, so that you may not die; for so I have been commanded." 36 So Aaron and his sons did all the things that the LORD had commanded by the hand of Moses.

PSALM 24:7–10

7 LIFT up your heads, O you gates!
And be lifted up, you everlasting doors!
And the King of glory shall come in.
8 Who *is* this King of glory?
The LORD strong and mighty,
The LORD mighty in battle.
9 Lift up your heads, O you gates!
Lift up, you everlasting doors!
And the King of glory shall come in.
10 Who is this King of glory?
The LORD of hosts,
He *is* the King of glory.   Selah

PROVERBS 9:10–12

10 "THE fear of the LORD *is* the beginning of wisdom,

And the knowledge of the Holy One *is* understanding.
11 For by me your days will be multiplied,
And years of life will be added to you.
12 If you are wise, you are wise for yourself,
And *if* you scoff, you will bear *it* alone."

MARK 1:1–22

THE beginning of the gospel of Jesus Christ, the Son of God. 2 As it is written in the Prophets:

"Behold, I send My messenger before Your face,
Who will prepare Your way before You."
3 "The voice of one crying in the wilderness:
'Prepare the way of the LORD;
Make His paths straight.' "

4 John came baptizing in the wilderness and preaching a baptism of repentance for the remission of sins. 5 Then all the land of Judea, and those from Jerusalem, went out to him and were all baptized by him in the Jordan River, confessing their sins. 6 Now John was clothed with camel's hair and with a leather belt around his waist, and he ate locusts and wild honey. 7 And he preached, saying, "There comes One after me who is mightier than I, whose sandal strap I am not worthy to stoop down and loose. 8 I indeed baptized you with water, but He will baptize you with the Holy Spirit."

9 It came to pass in those days *that* Jesus came from Nazareth of Galilee, and was baptized by John in the Jordan. 10 And immediately, coming up from the water, He saw the heavens parting and the Spirit descending upon Him like a dove. 11 Then a voice came from heaven, "You are My beloved Son, in whom I am well pleased."

12 Immediately the Spirit drove Him into the wilderness. 13 And He was there in the wilderness forty days, tempted by Satan, and was with the wild beasts; and the angels ministered to Him.

14 Now after John was put in prison, Jesus came to Galilee, preaching the gospel of the kingdom of God, 15 and saying, "The time is fulfilled, and the kingdom of God is at hand. Repent, and believe in the gospel."

16 And as He walked by the Sea of Galilee, He saw Simon and Andrew his brother cast-

ing a net into the sea; for they were fishermen. 17 Then Jesus said to them, "Follow Me, and I will make you become fishers of men." 18 They immediately left their nets and followed Him.

19 When He had gone a little farther from there, He saw James the *son* of Zebedee, and John his brother, who also *were* in the boat mending their nets. 20 And immedi-

ately He called them, and they left their father Zebedee in the boat with the hired servants, and went after Him.

21 Then they went into Capernaum, and immediately on the Sabbath He entered the synagogue and taught. 22 And they were astonished at His teaching, for He taught them as one having authority, and not as the scribes.

◆◆◆◆

Reading 50—Mercy's Healing
Mark 1:40, 41

When the soul is perplexed—and it certainly will be if we are going on with God, because we are a mark for Satan—and the sudden onslaught comes, as it did in the life of Job, we cry, "Heal me because of my pain," but there is no answer. Then we cry, "Heal me, not because I am in pain, but because my soul is perplexed; I cannot see any way out of it or why this thing should be"; still no answer; then at last we cry, "Heal me, O Lord, not because of my pain, nor because my soul is sick, but for Your mercies' sake." Then we have the answer, "The LORD has heard my supplication." The surroundings of the soul, the scenes which arise from our doings, do produce perplexity in the soul. The soul cannot be separated from the body, and bodily perplexities produce difficulties in the soul, and these difficulties go inward and at times intrude right to the very throne of God in the heart.

(BIB. PSYCH.)

LEVITICUS 9:1—10:20

IT came to pass on the eighth day that Moses called Aaron and his sons and the elders of Israel. 2 And he said to Aaron, "Take for yourself a young bull as a sin offering and a ram as a burnt offering, without blemish, and offer *them* before the LORD. 3 And to the children of Israel you shall speak, saying, 'Take a kid of the goats as a sin offering, and a calf and a lamb, *both* of the first year, without blemish, as a burnt offering, 4 also a bull and a ram as peace offerings, to sacrifice before the LORD, and a grain offering mixed with oil; for today the LORD will appear to you.'"

5 So they brought what Moses commanded before the tabernacle of meeting. And all the congregation drew near and stood before the LORD. 6 Then Moses said, "This *is* the thing which the LORD commanded you to do, and the glory of the LORD will appear to you." 7 And Moses said to Aaron, "Go to the altar, offer your sin offering and your burnt offering, and

make atonement for yourself and for the people. Offer the offering of the people, and make atonement for them, as the LORD commanded."

8 Aaron therefore went to the altar and killed the calf of the sin offering, which *was* for himself. 9 Then the sons of Aaron brought the blood to him. And he dipped his finger in the blood, put *it* on the horns of the altar, and poured the blood at the base of the altar. 10 But the fat, the kidneys, and the fatty lobe from the liver of the sin offering he burned on the altar, as the LORD had commanded Moses. 11 The flesh and the hide he burned with fire outside the camp.

12 And he killed the burnt offering; and Aaron's sons presented to him the blood, which he sprinkled all around on the altar. 13 Then they presented the burnt offering to him, with its pieces and head, and he burned *them* on the altar. 14 And he washed the entrails and the legs, and burned *them* with the burnt offering on the altar.

15 Then he brought the people's offering,

and took the goat, which *was* the sin offering for the people, and killed it and offered it for sin, like the first one. 16 And he brought the burnt offering and offered it according to the prescribed manner. 17 Then he brought the grain offering, took a handful of it, and burned *it* on the altar, besides the burnt sacrifice of the morning.

18 He also killed the bull and the ram *as* sacrifices of peace offerings, which *were* for the people. And Aaron's sons presented to him the blood, which he sprinkled all around on the altar, 19 and the fat from the bull and the ram—the fatty tail, what covers *the entrails* and the kidneys, and the fatty lobe *attached to* the liver; 20 and they put the fat on the breasts. Then he burned the fat on the altar; 21 but the breasts and the right thigh Aaron waved *as* a wave offering before the LORD, as Moses had commanded.

22 Then Aaron lifted his hand toward the people, blessed them, and came down from offering the sin offering, the burnt offering, and peace offerings. 23 And Moses and Aaron went into the tabernacle of meeting, and came out and blessed the people. Then the glory of the LORD appeared to all the people, 24 and fire came out from before the LORD and consumed the burnt offering and the fat on the altar. When all the people saw *it,* they shouted and fell on their faces.

10 THEN Nadab and Abihu, the sons of Aaron, each took his censer and put fire in it, put incense on it, and offered profane fire before the LORD, which He had not commanded them. 2 So fire went out from the LORD and devoured them, and they died before the LORD. 3 And Moses said to Aaron, "This is what the LORD spoke, saying:

'By those who come near Me
I must be regarded as holy;
And before all the people
I must be glorified.' "

So Aaron held his peace.
4 Then Moses called Mishael and Elzaphan, the sons of Uzziel the uncle of Aaron, and said to them, "Come near, carry your brethren from before the sanctuary out of the camp." 5 So they went near and carried them by their tunics out of the camp, as Moses had said.

6 And Moses said to Aaron, and to Eleazar and Ithamar, his sons, "Do not uncover your heads nor tear your clothes, lest you die, and wrath come upon all the people.

But let your brethren, the whole house of Israel, bewail the burning which the LORD has kindled. 7 You shall not go out from the door of the tabernacle of meeting, lest you die, for the anointing oil of the LORD *is* upon you." And they did according to the word of Moses.

8 Then the LORD spoke to Aaron, saying: 9 "Do not drink wine or intoxicating drink, you, nor your sons with you, when you go into the tabernacle of meeting, lest you die. *It shall be* a statute forever throughout your generations, 10 that you may distinguish between holy and unholy, and between unclean and clean, 11 and that you may teach the children of Israel all the statutes which the LORD has spoken to them by the hand of Moses."

12 And Moses spoke to Aaron, and to Eleazar and Ithamar, his sons who were left: "Take the grain offering that remains of the offerings made by fire to the LORD, and eat it without leaven beside the altar; for it *is* most holy. 13 You shall eat it in a holy place, because it *is* your due and your sons' due, of the sacrifices made by fire to the LORD; for so I have been commanded. 14 The breast of the wave offering and the thigh of the heave offering you shall eat in a clean place, you, your sons, and your daughters with you; for *they are* your due and your sons' due, *which* are given from the sacrifices of peace offerings of the children of Israel. 15 The thigh of the heave offering and the breast of the wave offering they shall bring with the offerings of fat made by fire, to offer *as* a wave offering before the LORD. And it shall be yours and your sons' with you, by a statute forever, as the LORD has commanded."

16 Then Moses made careful inquiry about the goat of the sin offering, and there it was—burned up. And he was angry with Eleazar and Ithamar, the sons of Aaron *who were* left, saying, 17 "Why have you not eaten the sin offering in a holy place, since it *is* most holy, and *God* has given it to you to bear the guilt of the congregation, to make atonement for them before the LORD? 18 See! Its blood was not brought inside the holy *place;* indeed you should have eaten it in a holy *place,* as I commanded."

19 And Aaron said to Moses, "Look, this day they have offered their sin offering and their burnt offering before the LORD, and such things have befallen me! *If* I had eaten the sin offering today, would it have been accepted in the sight of the LORD?" 20 So when Moses heard *that,* he was content.

PSALM 25:1–7

1 TO You, O LORD, I lift up my soul.
2 O my God, I trust in You;
Let me not be ashamed;
Let not my enemies triumph over me.

Soul is the rational expression of my personal spirit in my body. (MORAL FOUND.)

---

3 Indeed, let no one who waits on You
be ashamed;
Let those be ashamed who deal
treacherously without cause.

4 Show me Your ways, O LORD;
Teach me Your paths.
5 Lead me in Your truth and teach me,
For You *are* the God of my salvation;
On You I wait all the day.

6 Remember, O LORD, Your tender
mercies and Your lovingkindnesses,
For they *are* from of old.
7 Do not remember the sins of my youth,
nor my transgressions;
According to Your mercy remember
me,
For Your goodness' sake, O LORD.

PROVERBS 9:13–18

13 A foolish woman is clamorous;
She is simple, and knows nothing.
14 For she sits at the door of her house,
On a seat *by* the highest places of the
city,
15 To call to those who pass by,
Who go straight on their way:
16 "Whoever *is* simple, let him turn in here";
And *as for* him who lacks
understanding, she says to him,
17 "Stolen water is sweet,
And bread *eaten* in secret is pleasant."
18 But he does not know that the dead
are there,
That her guests *are* in the depths of
hell.

MARK 1:23–45

NOW there was a man in their synagogue
with an unclean spirit. And he cried out,
24 saying, "Let *us* alone! What have we to
do with You, Jesus of Nazareth? Did You
come to destroy us? I know who You are—
the Holy One of God!"

25 But Jesus rebuked him, saying, "Be
quiet, and come out of him!" 26 And when
the unclean spirit had convulsed him and
cried out with a loud voice, he came out
of him. 27 Then they were all amazed, so
that they questioned among themselves,
saying, "What is this? What new doctrine
is this? For with authority He commands
even the unclean spirits, and they obey
Him." 28 And immediately His fame spread
throughout all the region around Galilee.

29 Now as soon as they had come out
of the synagogue, they entered the house
of Simon and Andrew, with James and
John. 30 But Simon's wife's mother lay sick
with a fever, and they told Him about her
at once. 31 So He came and took her by
the hand and lifted her up, and immediately
the fever left her. And she served them.

32 At evening, when the sun had set, they
brought to Him all who were sick and those
who were demon-possessed. 33 And the
whole city was gathered together at the
door. 34 Then He healed many who were
sick with various diseases, and cast out many
demons; and He did not allow the demons
to speak, because they knew Him.

35 Now in the morning, having risen a
long while before daylight, He went out
and departed to a solitary place; and there
He prayed. 36 And Simon and those *who*

There is one prayer that God must answer, and that is the prayer of Jesus. (SEND I YOU)

---

were with Him searched for Him. 37 When
they found Him, they said to Him, "Everyone is looking for You."

38 But He said to them, "Let us go into
the next towns, that I may preach there
also, because for this purpose I have come
forth."

39 And He was preaching in their synagogues throughout all Galilee, and casting
out demons.

40 Now a leper came to Him, imploring
Him, kneeling down to Him and saying
to Him, "If You are willing, You can make
me clean."

41 Then Jesus, moved with compassion,
stretched out *His* hand and touched him,
and said to him, "I am willing; be cleansed."
42 As soon as He had spoken, immediately
the leprosy left him, and he was cleansed.
43 And He strictly warned him and sent

him away at once, 44 and said to him, "See that you say nothing to anyone; but go your way, show yourself to the priest, and offer for your cleansing those things which Moses commanded, as a testimony to them."

45 However, he went out and began to proclaim *it* freely, and to spread the matter, so that Jesus could no longer openly enter the city, but was outside in deserted places; and they came to Him from every direction.

◆◆◆◆

Reading 51—What Are You Haunted By?
Psalm 25:12

What are you haunted by? You will say—By nothing, but we are all haunted by something, generally by ourselves, or, if we are Christians, by our experience. The psalmist says we are to be haunted by God. The abiding consciousness of the life is to be God, not thinking about Him. The whole of our life inside and out is to be absolutely haunted by the presence of God. A child's consciousness is so mother-haunted that although the child is not consciously thinking of its mother, yet when calamity arises, the relationship that abides is that of the mother. So we are to live and move and have our being in God, to look at everything in relation to God, because the abiding consciousness of God pushes itself to the front all the time.

If we are haunted by God, nothing else can get in, no cares, no tribulation, no anxieties. We see now why our Lord so emphasized the sin of worry. How can we dare be so utterly unbelieving when God is round about us? To be haunted by God is to have an effective barricade against all the onslaughts of the enemy.   (*Utmost*)

LEVITICUS 11:1—12:8

NOW the Lord spoke to Moses and Aaron, saying to them, 2 "Speak to the children of Israel, saying, 'These *are* the animals which you may eat among all the animals that *are* on the earth: 3 Among the animals, whatever divides the hoof, having cloven hooves *and* chewing the cud—that you may eat. 4 Nevertheless these you shall not eat among those that chew the cud or those that have cloven hooves: the camel, because it chews the cud but does not have cloven hooves, is unclean to you; 5 the rock hyrax, because it chews the cud but does not have cloven hooves, *is* unclean to you; 6 the hare, because it chews the cud but does not have cloven hooves, *is* unclean to you; 7 and the swine, though it divides the hoof, having cloven hooves, yet does not chew the cud, *is* unclean to you. 8 Their flesh you shall not eat, and their carcasses you shall not touch. They *are* unclean to you.

9 'These you may eat of all that *are* in the water: whatever in the water has fins and scales, whether in the seas or in the rivers—that you may eat. 10 But all in the seas or in the rivers that do not have fins and scales, all that move in the water or any living thing which *is* in the water, they *are* an abomination to you. 11 They shall be an abomination to you; you shall not eat their flesh, but you shall regard their carcasses as an abomination. 12 Whatever in the water does not have fins or scales—that *shall be* an abomination to you.

13 'And these you shall regard as an abomination among the birds; they shall not be eaten, they *are* an abomination: the eagle, the vulture, the buzzard, 14 the kite, and the falcon after its kind; 15 every raven after its kind, 16 the ostrich, the short-eared owl, the sea gull, and the hawk after its kind; 17 the little owl, the fisher owl, and the screech owl; 18 the white owl, the jackdaw, and the carrion vulture; 19 the stork, the heron after its kind, the hoopoe, and the bat.

20 'All flying insects that creep on *all* fours *shall be* an abomination to you. 21 Yet these you may eat of every flying insect that creeps on *all* fours: those which have jointed legs above their feet with which to leap on the

earth. 22 These you may eat: the locust after its kind, the destroying locust after its kind, the cricket after its kind, and the grasshopper after its kind. 23 But all *other* flying insects which have four feet *shall be* an abomination to you.

24 'By these you shall become unclean; whoever touches the carcass of any of them shall be unclean until evening; 25 whoever carries part of the carcass of any of them shall wash his clothes and be unclean until evening. 26 *The carcass* of any animal which divides the foot, but is not cloven-hoofed or does not chew the cud, *is* unclean to you. Everyone who touches it shall be unclean. 27 And whatever goes on its paws, among all kinds of animals that go on *all* fours, those *are* unclean to you. Whoever touches any such carcass shall be unclean until evening. 28 Whoever carries *any such* carcass shall wash his clothes and be unclean until evening. It *is* unclean to you.

29 'These also *shall be* unclean to you among the creeping things that creep on the earth: the mole, the mouse, and the large lizard after its kind; 30 the gecko, the monitor lizard, the sand reptile, the sand lizard, and the chameleon. 31 These *are* unclean to you among all that creep. Whoever touches them when they are dead shall be unclean until evening. 32 Anything on which *any* of them falls, when they are dead shall be unclean, whether *it is* any item of wood or clothing or skin or sack, whatever item *it is*, in which *any* work is done, it must be put in water. And it shall be unclean until evening; then it shall be clean. 33 Any earthen vessel into which *any* of them falls you shall break; and whatever *is* in it shall be unclean: 34 in such a vessel, any edible food upon which water falls becomes unclean, and any drink that may be drunk from it becomes unclean. 35 And everything on which *a part* of *any such* carcass falls shall be unclean; *whether it is* an oven or cooking stove, it shall be broken down; *for* they *are* unclean, and shall be unclean to you. 36 Nevertheless a spring or a cistern, *in which there is* plenty of water, shall be clean, but whatever touches any such carcass becomes unclean. 37 And if a part of *any such* carcass falls on any planting seed which is to be sown, it *remains* clean. 38 But if water is put on the seed, and if *a part* of *any such* carcass falls on it, it *becomes* unclean to you.

39 'And if any animal which you may eat dies, he who touches its carcass shall be unclean until evening. 40 He who eats of its carcass shall wash his clothes and be unclean until evening. He also who carries its carcass shall wash his clothes and be unclean until evening.

41 'And every creeping thing that creeps on the earth *shall be* an abomination. It shall not be eaten. 42 Whatever crawls on its belly, whatever goes on *all* fours, or whatever has many feet among all creeping things that creep on the earth—these you shall not eat, for they *are* an abomination. 43 You shall not make yourselves abominable with any creeping thing that creeps; nor shall you make yourselves unclean with them, lest you be defiled by them. 44 For I *am* the LORD your God. You shall therefore consecrate yourselves, and you shall be holy; for I *am* holy. Neither shall you defile yourselves with any creeping thing that creeps on the earth. 45 For I *am* the LORD who brings you up out of the land of Egypt, to be your God. You shall therefore be holy, for I *am* holy.

We have to consecrate ourselves, and leave our gifts alone. (SEND I YOU)

---

46 'This *is* the law of the animals and the birds and every living creature that moves in the waters, and of every creature that creeps on the earth, 47 to distinguish between the unclean and the clean, and between the animal that may be eaten and the animal that may not be eaten.' "

12 THEN the LORD spoke to Moses, saying, 2 "Speak to the children of Israel, saying: 'If a woman has conceived, and borne a male child, then she shall be unclean seven days; as in the days of her customary impurity she shall be unclean. 3 And on the eighth day the flesh of his foreskin shall be circumcised. 4 She shall then continue in the blood of *her* purification thirty-three days. She shall not touch any hallowed thing, nor come into the sanctuary until the days of her purification are fulfilled.

5 'But if she bears a female child, then she shall be unclean two weeks, as in her customary impurity, and she shall continue in the blood of *her* purification sixty-six days.

6 'When the days of her purification are fulfilled, whether for a son or a daughter, she shall bring to the priest a lamb of the first year as a burnt offering, and a young pigeon or a turtledove as a sin offering, to the door of the tabernacle of meeting. 7 Then he shall offer it before the LORD, and make atonement for her. And she shall

be clean from the flow of her blood. This *is* the law for her who has borne a male or a female.

8 'And if she is not able to bring a lamb, then she may bring two turtledoves or two young pigeons—one as a burnt offering and the other as a sin offering. So the priest shall make atonement for her, and she will be clean.'"

PSALM 25:8–15

8 GOOD and upright *is* the LORD;
    Therefore He teaches sinners in the way.
9 The humble He guides in justice,
    And the humble He teaches His way.
10 All the paths of the LORD *are* mercy and truth,
    To such as keep His covenant and His testimonies.
11 For Your name's sake, O LORD,
    Pardon my iniquity, for it *is* great.
12 Who *is* the man that fears the LORD?
    Him shall He teach in the way He chooses.
13 He himself shall dwell in prosperity,
    And his descendants shall inherit the earth.
14 The secret of the LORD *is* with those who fear Him,
    And He will show them His covenant.
15 My eyes *are* ever toward the LORD,
    For He shall pluck my feet out of the net.

PROVERBS 10:1–3

THE proverbs of Solomon:

    A wise son makes a glad father,
    But a foolish son *is* the grief of his mother.

2 Treasures of wickedness profit nothing,
    But righteousness delivers from death.
3 The LORD will not allow the righteous soul to famish,
    But He casts away the desire of the wicked.

MARK 2:1–28

AND again He entered Capernaum after *some* days, and it was heard that He was in the house. 2 Immediately many gathered together, so that there was no longer room to receive *them*, not even near the door. And He preached the word to them. 3 Then they came to Him, bringing a paralytic who was carried by four *men*. 4 And when they could not come near Him because of the crowd, they uncovered the roof where He was. So when they had broken through, they let down the bed on which the paralytic was lying.

5 When Jesus saw their faith, He said to the paralytic, "Son, your sins are forgiven you."

6 And some of the scribes were sitting there and reasoning in their hearts, 7 "Why does this *Man* speak blasphemies like this? Who can forgive sins but God alone?"

8 But immediately, when Jesus perceived in His spirit that they reasoned thus within themselves, He said to them, "Why do you reason about these things in your hearts? 9 Which is easier, to say to the paralytic, '*Your* sins are forgiven you,' or to say, 'Arise, take up your bed and walk'? 10 But that you may know that the Son of Man has power on earth to forgive sins"—He said to the paralytic, 11 "I say to you, arise, take up your bed, and go to your house." 12 Immediately he arose, took up the bed, and went out in the presence of them all, so that all were amazed and glorified God, saying, "We never saw *anything* like this!"

13 Then He went out again by the sea; and all the multitude came to Him, and He taught them. 14 As He passed by, He saw Levi the *son* of Alphaeus sitting at the tax office. And He said to him, "Follow Me." So he arose and followed Him.

If you will give God your right to yourself, He will make a holy experiment out of you. (UTMOST)

15 Now it happened, as He was dining in *Levi's* house, that many tax collectors and sinners also sat together with Jesus and His disciples; for there were many, and they followed Him. 16 And when the scribes and Pharisees saw Him eating with the tax collectors and sinners, they said to His disciples, "How *is it* that He eats and drinks with tax collectors and sinners?"

17 When Jesus heard *it*, He said to them, "Those who are well have no need of a physician, but those who are sick. I did not come to call *the* righteous, but sinners, to repentance."

18 The disciples of John and of the Pharisees were fasting. Then they came and said

to Him, "Why do the disciples of John and of the Pharisees fast, but Your disciples do not fast?"

19 And Jesus said to them, "Can the friends of the bridegroom fast while the bridegroom is with them? As long as they have the bridegroom with them they cannot fast. 20 But the days will come when the bridegroom will be taken away from them, and then they will fast in those days. 21 No one sews a piece of unshrunk cloth on an old garment; or else the new piece pulls away from the old, and the tear is made worse. 22 And no one puts new wine into old wineskins; or else the new wine bursts the wineskins, the wine is spilled, and the wineskins are ruined. But new wine must be put into new wineskins."

23 Now it happened that He went through the grainfields on the Sabbath; and as they went His disciples began to pluck the heads of grain. 24 And the Pharisees said to Him, "Look, why do they do what is not lawful on the Sabbath?"

25 But He said to them, "Have you never read what David did when he was in need and hungry, he and those with him: 26 how he went into the house of God *in the days* of Abiathar the high priest, and ate the showbread, which is not lawful to eat except for the priests, and also gave some to those who were with him?"

27 And He said to them, "The Sabbath was made for man, and not man for the Sabbath. 28 Therefore the Son of Man is also Lord of the Sabbath."

◆◆◆

Reading 52—That He Might Send Them
Mark 3:14

How much Christian work there is today which has never been disciplined, but has simply sprung into being by impulse! In our Lord's life every project was disciplined to the will of His Father. There was not a movement of an impulse of His own will as distinct from His Father's—"The Son can do nothing of Himself." Then take ourselves—a vivid religious experience, and every project born of impulse put into action immediately, instead of being imprisoned and disciplined to obey Christ.

This is a day when practical work is overemphasized, and the saints who are bringing every project into captivity are criticized and told that they are not in earnest for God or for souls. True earnestness is found in obeying God, not in the inclination to serve Him that is born of undisciplined human nature. It is inconceivable, but true nevertheless, that saints are not bringing every project into captivity, but are doing work for God at the instigation of their own human nature which has not been spiritualized by determined discipline.   (*UTMOST*)

LEVITICUS 13:1–59

AND the LORD spoke to Moses and Aaron, saying: 2 "When a man has on the skin of his body a swelling, a scab, or a bright spot, and it becomes on the skin of his body *like* a leprous sore, then he shall be brought to Aaron the priest or to one of his sons the priests. 3 The priest shall examine the sore on the skin of the body; and if the hair on the sore has turned white, and the sore appears *to be* deeper than the skin of his body, it *is* a leprous sore. Then

the priest shall examine him, and pronounce him unclean. 4 But if the bright spot *is* white on the skin of his body, and does not appear *to be* deeper than the skin, and its hair has not turned white, then the priest shall isolate *the one who has* the sore seven days. 5 And the priest shall examine him on the seventh day; and indeed *if* the sore appears to be as it was, *and* the sore has not spread on the skin, then the priest shall isolate him another seven days. 6 Then the priest shall examine him again on the seventh day; and indeed *if* the sore has faded, *and* the sore has not spread on the skin, then the priest shall pronounce him clean; it *is only* a scab, and he shall wash his clothes and be clean. 7 But if the scab should at all spread over the skin, after he has been seen by the priest for his cleansing, he shall be seen by the priest again. 8 And *if* the priest sees that the scab has indeed spread on the skin, then the priest shall pronounce him unclean. It *is* leprosy.

9 "When the leprous sore is on a person, then he shall be brought to the priest. 10 And the priest shall examine *him;* and indeed *if* the swelling on the skin *is* white, and it has turned the hair white, and *there is* a spot of raw flesh in the swelling, 11 it *is* an old leprosy on the skin of his body. The priest shall pronounce him unclean, and shall not isolate him, for he *is* unclean.

12 "And if leprosy breaks out all over the skin, and the leprosy covers all the skin of *the one who has* the sore, from his head to his foot, wherever the priest looks, 13 then the priest shall consider; and indeed *if* the leprosy has covered all his body, he shall pronounce *him* clean *who has* the sore. It has all turned white. He *is* clean. 14 But when raw flesh appears on him, he shall be unclean. 15 And the priest shall examine the raw flesh and pronounce him to be unclean; *for* the raw flesh *is* unclean. It *is* leprosy. 16 Or if the raw flesh changes and turns white again, he shall come to the priest. 17 And the priest shall examine him; and indeed *if* the sore has turned white, then the priest shall pronounce *him* clean *who has* the sore. He *is* clean.

18 "If the body develops a boil in the skin, and it is healed, 19 and in the place of the boil there comes a white swelling or a bright spot, reddish-white, then it shall be shown to the priest; 20 and *if,* when the priest sees it, it indeed *appears* deeper than the skin, and its hair has turned white, the priest shall pronounce him unclean. It *is* a leprous sore which has broken out of the boil. 21 But if the priest examines it, and indeed *there are* no white hairs in it, and it *is* not deeper than the skin, but has faded, then the priest shall isolate him seven days; 22 and if it should at all spread over the skin, then the priest shall pronounce him unclean. It *is* a leprous sore. 23 But if the bright spot stays in one place, *and* has not spread, it *is* the scar of the boil; and the priest shall pronounce him clean.

24 "Or if the body receives a burn on its skin by fire, and the raw *flesh* of the burn becomes a bright spot, reddish-white or white, 25 then the priest shall examine it; and indeed *if* the hair of the bright spot has turned white, and it appears deeper than the skin, it *is* leprosy broken out in the burn. Therefore the priest shall pronounce him unclean. It *is* a leprous sore. 26 But if the priest examines it, and indeed *there are* no white hairs in the bright spot, and it *is* not deeper than the skin, but has faded, then the priest shall isolate him seven days. 27 And the priest shall examine him on the seventh day. If it has at all spread over the skin, then the priest shall pronounce him unclean. It *is* a leprous sore. 28 But if the bright spot stays in one place, *and* has not spread on the skin, but has faded, it *is* a swelling from the burn. The priest shall pronounce him clean, for it *is* the scar from the burn.

29 "If a man or woman has a sore on the head or the beard, 30 then the priest shall examine the sore; and indeed if it appears deeper than the skin, *and there is* in it thin yellow hair, then the priest shall pronounce him unclean. It *is* a scaly leprosy of the head or beard. 31 But if the priest examines the scaly sore, and indeed it does not appear deeper than the skin, and *there is* no black hair in it, then the priest shall isolate *the one who has* the scale seven days. 32 And on the seventh day the priest shall examine the sore; and indeed *if* the scale has not spread, and there is no yellow hair in it, and the scale does not appear deeper than the skin, 33 he shall shave himself, but the scale he shall not shave. And the priest shall isolate *the one who has* the scale another seven days. 34 On the seventh day the priest shall examine the scale; and indeed *if* the scale has not spread over the skin, and does not appear deeper than the skin, then the priest shall pronounce him clean. He shall wash his clothes and be clean. 35 But if the scale should at all spread over the skin after his cleansing, 36 then the priest shall examine him; and indeed *if* the scale has spread over the skin, the priest need not seek for yellow hair. He *is* unclean. 37 But if the scale appears to be at a standstill, and there is black hair grown up in it, the scale has healed. He *is* clean, and the priest shall pronounce him clean.

38 "If a man or a woman has bright spots on the skin of the body, *specifically* white bright spots, 39 then the priest shall look; and indeed *if* the bright spots on the skin of the body *are* dull white, it *is* a white spot *that* grows on the skin. He *is* clean.

40 "As for the man whose hair has fallen from his head, he *is* bald, *but* he *is* clean. 41 He whose hair has fallen from his forehead, he *is* bald on the forehead, *but* he *is* clean. 42 And if there is on the bald head

or bald forehead a reddish-white sore, it *is* leprosy breaking out on his bald head or his bald forehead. 43 Then the priest shall examine it; and indeed *if* the swelling of the sore *is* reddish-white on his bald head or on his bald forehead, as the appearance of leprosy on the skin of the body, 44 he is a leprous man. He *is* unclean. The priest shall surely pronounce him unclean; his sore *is* on his head.

45 "Now the leper on whom the sore *is,* his clothes shall be torn and his head bare; and he shall cover his mustache, and cry, 'Unclean! Unclean!' 46 He shall be unclean. All the days he has the sore he shall be unclean. He *is* unclean, and he shall dwell alone; his dwelling *shall be* outside the camp.

47 "Also, if a garment has a leprous plague in it, *whether it is* a woolen garment or a linen garment, 48 whether *it is* in the warp or woof of linen or wool, whether in leather or in anything made of leather, 49 and if the plague is greenish or reddish in the garment or in the leather, whether in the warp or in the woof, or in anything made of leather, it *is* a leprous plague and shall be shown to the priest. 50 The priest shall examine the plague and isolate *that which has* the plague seven days. 51 And he shall examine the plague on the seventh day. If the plague has spread in the garment, either in the warp or in the woof, in the leather *or* in anything made of leather, the plague *is* an active leprosy. It *is* unclean. 52 He shall therefore burn that garment in which is the plague, whether warp or woof, in wool or in linen, or anything of leather, for it *is* an active leprosy; *the garment* shall be burned in the fire.

53 "But if the priest examines *it,* and indeed the plague has not spread in the garment, either in the warp or in the woof, or in anything made of leather, 54 then the priest shall command that they wash *the thing* in which *is* the plague; and he shall isolate it another seven days. 55 Then the priest shall examine the plague after it has been washed; and indeed *if* the plague has not changed its color, though the plague has not spread, it *is* unclean, and you shall burn it in the fire; it continues eating away, *whether* the damage *is* outside or inside. 56 If the priest examines *it,* and indeed the plague has faded after washing it, then he shall tear it out of the garment, whether out of the warp or out of the woof, or out of the leather. 57 But if it appears again in the garment, either in the warp or in the woof, or in anything made of leather, it *is* a spreading *plague;* you shall burn with fire that in which is the plague. 58 And if

you wash the garment, either warp or woof, or whatever is made of leather, if the plague has disappeared from it, then it shall be washed a second time, and shall be clean.

59 "This *is* the law of the leprous plague in a garment of wool or linen, either in the warp or woof, or in anything made of leather, to pronounce it clean or to pronounce it unclean."

PSALM 25:16–22

16 TURN Yourself to me, and have mercy on me,
    For I *am* desolate and afflicted.
17 The troubles of my heart have enlarged;
    Bring me out of my distresses!
18 Look on my affliction and my pain,
    And forgive all my sins.

The value of a life can only be estimated by its spiritual relationship to God.   (GOD'S WORKMANSHIP)

---

19 Consider my enemies, for they are many;
    And they hate me with cruel hatred.
20 Keep my soul, and deliver me;
    Let me not be ashamed, for I put my trust in You.
21 Let integrity and uprightness preserve me,
    For I wait for You.

22 Redeem Israel, O God,
    Out of all their troubles!

PROVERBS 10:4, 5

4 HE who has a slack hand becomes poor,
   But the hand of the diligent makes rich.
5 He who gathers in summer *is* a wise son;
   He who sleeps in harvest *is* a son who causes shame.

MARK 3:1–19

AND He entered the synagogue again, and a man was there who had a withered hand. 2 So they watched Him closely, whether He would heal him on the Sabbath, so that they might accuse Him. 3 And He said to the man who had the withered hand, "Step forward." 4 Then He said to them, "Is it lawful on the Sabbath to do good or to do evil, to save life or to kill?" But they kept silent. 5 And when He had looked around at them with anger, being grieved by the hardness of their hearts, He said to the man, "Stretch out your hand." And he stretched *it* out, and his hand was restored as whole as the other. 6 Then the Pharisees went out and immediately plotted with the Herodians against Him, how they might destroy Him.

7 But Jesus withdrew with His disciples to the sea. And a great multitude from Galilee followed Him, and from Judea 8 and Jerusalem and Idumea and beyond the Jordan; and those from Tyre and Sidon, a great multitude, when they heard how many things He was doing, came to Him. 9 So He told His disciples that a small boat should be kept ready for Him because of the multitude, lest they should crush Him. 10 For He healed many, so that as many as had afflictions pressed about Him to touch Him. 11 And the unclean spirits, whenever they saw Him, fell down before Him and cried out, saying, "You are the Son of God." 12 But He sternly warned them that they should not make Him known.

13 And He went up on the mountain and called to *Him* those He Himself wanted. And they came to Him. 14 Then He appointed twelve, that they might be with Him and that He might send them out to preach, 15 and to have power to heal sicknesses and to cast out demons: 16 Simon, to whom He gave the name Peter; 17 James the *son* of Zebedee and John the brother of James, to whom He gave the name Boanerges, that is, "Sons of Thunder"; 18 Andrew, Philip, Bartholomew, Matthew, Thomas, James the *son* of Alphaeus, Thaddaeus, Simon the Cananite; 19 and Judas Iscariot, who also betrayed Him. And they went into a house.

◆◆◆◆

Reading 53—A Devil in the Company
Mark 3:21

These were the intimates our Lord grew up with in His own historic life. We say, "Oh, but the Lord must have had a sweet and delightful home life." But we are wrong: He had an exceedingly difficult home life. Jesus Christ's intimates were brothers and sisters who did not believe in Him, and He says that the disciple is not above his Master (Luke 6:40). The next time you feel inclined to grouse over uncongenial companions, remember that Jesus Christ had a devil in His company for three years.

Our Lord preached His first public sermon in the place where He was brought up, where He was most intimately known, and they smashed up His service and tried to kill Him. "Oh, but," we say, "I expected that when I was saved and sanctified, my father and mother and brothers and sisters would be made right, but instead they seem to be all wrong." If the mother of our Lord misunderstood Him, and His brethren did not believe in Him, the same things will happen to His life in us, and we must not think it strange concerning the misunderstandings of others. The life of the Son of God in us is brought into the same kind of circumstances that the historic life of Jesus Christ was brought into, and what was true of Him will be true also of His life in us.

(*PSY. REDEMP.*)

LEVITICUS 14:1–57

THEN the LORD spoke to Moses, saying, 2 "This shall be the law of the leper for the day of his cleansing: He shall be brought to the priest. 3 And the priest shall go out of the camp, and the priest shall examine *him*; and indeed, *if* the leprosy is healed in the leper, 4 then the priest shall command to take for him who is to be cleansed two living *and* clean birds, cedar wood, scarlet, and hyssop. 5 And the priest shall command that one of the birds be killed in an earthen vessel over running water. 6 As for the living bird, he shall take it, the cedar wood and the scarlet and the hyssop, and dip them and the living bird in the blood of the bird *that was* killed over the running water. 7 And he shall sprinkle it seven times on him who is to be cleansed from the leprosy, and shall pronounce him clean, and shall let the living bird loose in the open field. 8 He who is to be cleansed shall wash his clothes, shave off all his hair, and wash himself in water, that he may be clean. After that he shall come into the camp, and shall stay outside his tent seven days. 9 But on the seventh day he shall shave all the hair off his head and his beard and his eyebrows—all his hair he shall shave off. He shall wash his clothes and wash his body in water, and he shall be clean.

10 "And on the eighth day he shall take two male lambs without blemish, one ewe lamb of the first year without blemish, three-tenths *of an ephah* of fine flour mixed with oil as a grain offering, and one log of oil. 11 Then the priest who makes *him* clean shall present the man who is to be made clean, and those things, before the LORD, *at* the door of the tabernacle of meeting. 12 And the priest shall take one male lamb and offer it as a trespass offering, and the log of oil, and wave them *as* a wave offering before the LORD. 13 Then he shall kill the lamb in the place where he kills the sin offering and the burnt offering, in a holy place; for as the sin offering *is* the priest's, so *is* the trespass offering. It *is* most holy. 14 The priest shall take *some* of the blood of the trespass offering, and the priest shall put *it* on the tip of the right ear of him who is to be cleansed, on the thumb of his right hand, and on the big toe of his right foot. 15 And the priest shall take *some* of the log of oil, and pour *it* into the palm of his own left hand. 16 Then the priest shall dip his right finger in the oil that *is* in his left hand, and shall sprinkle some of the oil with his finger seven times before the LORD. 17 And of the rest of the oil in his hand, the priest shall put *some* on the tip of the right ear of him who is to be cleansed, on the thumb of his right hand, and on the big toe of his right foot, on the blood of the trespass offering. 18 The rest of the oil that *is* in the priest's hand he shall put on the head of him who is to be cleansed. So the priest shall make atonement for him before the LORD.

19 "Then the priest shall offer the sin offering, and make atonement for him who is to be cleansed from his uncleanness. Afterward he shall kill the burnt offering. 20 And the priest shall offer the burnt offering and the grain offering on the altar. So the priest shall make atonement for him, and he shall be clean.

21 "But if he *is* poor and cannot afford it, then he shall take one male lamb *as* a trespass offering to be waved, to make atonement for him, one-tenth *of an ephah* of fine flour mixed with oil as a grain offering, a log of oil, 22 and two turtledoves or two young pigeons, such as he is able to afford: one shall be a sin offering and the other a burnt offering. 23 He shall bring them to the priest on the eighth day for his cleansing, to the door of the tabernacle of meeting, before the LORD. 24 And the priest shall take the lamb of the trespass offering and the log of oil, and the priest shall wave them *as* a wave offering before the LORD. 25 Then he shall kill the lamb of the trespass offering, and the priest shall take *some* of the blood of the trespass offering and put *it* on the tip of the right ear of him who is to be cleansed, on the thumb of his right hand, and on the big toe of his right foot. 26 And the priest shall pour some of the oil into the palm of his own left hand. 27 Then the priest shall sprinkle with his right finger *some* of the oil that *is* in his left hand seven times before the LORD. 28 And the priest shall put *some* of the oil that *is* in his hand on the tip of the right ear of him who is to be cleansed, on the thumb of the right hand, and on the big toe of his right foot, on the place of the blood of the trespass offering. 29 The rest of the oil that *is* in the priest's hand he shall put on the head of him who is to be cleansed, to make atonement for him before the LORD. 30 And he shall offer one of the turtledoves or young pigeons, such as he can afford— 31 such as he is able to afford, the one *as* a sin offering and the other *as* a burnt offering, with the grain offering. So the priest shall make atonement for him who is to be cleansed before the LORD. 32 This *is* the law *for one* who had a leprous sore, who cannot afford the usual cleansing."

33 And the LORD spoke to Moses and Aaron, saying: 34 "When you have come into the land of Canaan, which I give you as a possession, and I put the leprous plague in a house in the land of your possession, 35 and he who owns the house comes and tells the priest, saying, 'It seems to me that *there is* some plague in the house,' 36 then the priest shall command that they empty the house, before the priest goes *into it* to examine the plague, that all that *is* in the house may not be made unclean; and afterward the priest shall go in to examine the house. 37 And he shall examine the plague;

and indeed *if* the plague *is* on the walls of the house with ingrained streaks, greenish or reddish, which appear to be deep in the wall, 38 then the priest shall go out of the house, to the door of the house, and shut up the house seven days. 39 And the priest shall come again on the seventh day and look; and indeed *if* the plague has spread on the walls of the house, 40 then the priest shall command that they take away the stones in which *is* the plague, and they shall cast them into an unclean place outside the city. 41 And he shall cause the house to be scraped inside, all around, and the dust that they scrape off they shall pour out in an unclean place outside the city. 42 Then they shall take other stones and put *them* in the place of *those* stones, and he shall take other mortar and plaster the house.

43 "Now if the plague comes back and breaks out in the house, after he has taken away the stones, after he has scraped the house, and after it is plastered, 44 then the priest shall come and look; and indeed *if* the plague has spread in the house, it *is* an active leprosy in the house. It *is* unclean. 45 And he shall break down the house, its stones, its timber, and all the plaster of the house, and he shall carry *them* outside the city to an unclean place. 46 Moreover he who goes into the house at all while it is shut up shall be unclean until evening. 47 And he who lies down in the house shall wash his clothes, and he who eats in the house shall wash his clothes.

48 "But if the priest comes in and examines *it*, and indeed the plague has not spread in the house after the house was plastered, then the priest shall pronounce the house clean, because the plague is healed. 49 And he shall take, to cleanse the house, two birds, cedar wood, scarlet, and hyssop. 50 Then he shall kill one of the birds in an earthen vessel over running water; 51 and he shall take the cedar wood, the hyssop, the scarlet, and the living bird, and dip them in the blood of the slain bird and in the running water, and sprinkle the house seven times. 52 And he shall cleanse the house with the blood of the bird and the running water and the living bird, with the cedar wood, the hyssop, and the scarlet. 53 Then he shall let the living bird loose outside the city in the open field, and make atonement for the house, and it shall be clean.

54 "This *is* the law for any leprous sore and scale, 55 for the leprosy of a garment and of a house, 56 for a swelling and a scab and a bright spot, 57 to teach when *it is* unclean and when *it is* clean. This *is* the law of leprosy."

PSALM 26:1–5

1   VINDICATE me, O Lord,
    For I have walked in my integrity.
    I have also trusted in the Lord;
    I shall not slip.
2   Examine me, O Lord, and prove me;
    Try my mind and my heart.

My relationship to God embraces every faculty.   (GOD'S WORKMANSHIP)

3   For Your lovingkindness *is* before my eyes,
    And I have walked in Your truth.
4   I have not sat with idolatrous mortals,
    Nor will I go in with hypocrites.
5   I have hated the assembly of evildoers,
    And will not sit with the wicked.

PROVERBS 10:6, 7

6   BLESSINGS *are* on the head of the righteous,
    But violence covers the mouth of the wicked.
7   The memory of the righteous *is* blessed,
    But the name of the wicked will rot.

MARK 3:20–35

THEN the multitude came together again, so that they could not so much as eat bread. 21 But when His own people heard *about this,* they went out to lay hold of Him, for they said, "He is out of His mind."

22 And the scribes who came down from Jerusalem said, "He has Beelzebub," and, "By the ruler of the demons He casts out demons."

23 So He called them to *Himself* and said to them in parables: "How can Satan cast out Satan? 24 If a kingdom is divided against itself, that kingdom cannot stand. 25 And if a house is divided against itself, that house cannot stand. 26 And if Satan has risen up against himself, and is divided, he cannot stand, but has an end. 27 No one can enter a strong man's house and plunder his goods, unless he first binds the strong man. And then he will plunder his house.

28 "Assuredly, I say to you, all sins will be forgiven the sons of men, and whatever blasphemies they may utter; 29 but he who blasphemes against the Holy Spirit never has forgiveness, but is subject to eternal

condemnation"— 30 because they said, "He has an unclean spirit."

31 Then His brothers and His mother came, and standing outside they sent to Him, calling Him. 32 And a multitude was sitting around Him; and they said to Him, "Look, Your mother and Your brothers are outside seeking You."

33 But He answered them, saying, "Who is My mother, or My brothers?" 34 And He looked around in a circle at those who sat about Him, and said, "Here are My mother and My brothers! 35 For whoever does the will of God is My brother and My sister and mother."

Doing God's will is never hard. The only thing that is hard is not doing His will.   (BRILL. HERITAGE)

Reading 54—Alone with God
Mark 4:10

When God gets us alone by affliction, heartbreak, or temptation, by disappointment, sickness, or by thwarted affection, by a broken friendship, or by a new friendship—when He gets us absolutely alone, and we are dumbfounded, and cannot ask one question, then He begins to expound. Watch Jesus Christ's training of the Twelve. It was the disciples, not the crowd outside, who were perplexed. They constantly asked Him questions, and He constantly expounded things to them; but they only understood after they had received the Holy Spirit (see John 14:26).

If you are going on with God, the only thing that is clear to you, and the only thing God intends to be clear, is the way He deals with your own soul. Your brother's sorrows and perplexities are an absolute confusion to you. We imagine we understand where the other person is, until God gives us a dose of the plague of our own hearts. There are whole tracts of stubbornness and ignorance to be revealed by the Holy Spirit in each one of us, and it can only be done when Jesus gets us alone. Are we alone with Him now, or are we taken up with little fussy notions, fussy comradeships in God's service, fussy ideas about our bodies? Jesus can expound nothing until we get through all the noisy questions of the head and are alone with Him.   (UTMOST)

LEVITICUS 15:1—16:34

AND the LORD spoke to Moses and Aaron, saying, 2 "Speak to the children of Israel, and say to them: 'When any man has a discharge from his body, his discharge *is* unclean. 3 And this shall be his uncleanness in regard to his discharge—whether his body runs with his discharge, or his body is stopped up by his discharge, it *is* his uncleanness. 4 Every bed is unclean on which he who has the discharge lies, and everything on which he sits shall be unclean. 5 And whoever touches his bed shall wash his clothes and bathe in water, and be unclean until evening. 6 He who sits on anything on which he who has the discharge sat shall wash his clothes and bathe in water, and be unclean until evening. 7 And he who touches the body of him who has the discharge shall wash his clothes and bathe in water, and be unclean until evening. 8 If he who has the discharge spits on him who is clean, then he shall wash his clothes and bathe in water, and be unclean until evening. 9 Any saddle on which he who has the discharge rides shall be unclean. 10 Whoever touches anything that was under him shall be unclean until evening. He who carries *any of* those things shall wash his clothes and bathe in water, and be unclean until evening. 11 And whomever the one who has the discharge touches, and has not rinsed his hands in water, he shall wash his clothes and bathe in water, and be unclean until evening. 12 The vessel of earth that he who has the discharge touches shall be broken, and every vessel of wood shall be rinsed in water.

13 'And when he who has a discharge is cleansed of his discharge, then he shall count for himself seven days for his cleansing, wash his clothes, and bathe his body in running water; then he shall be clean. 14 On the eighth day he shall take for himself two turtledoves or two young pigeons, and come before the LORD, to the door of the tabernacle of meeting, and give them to the priest. 15 Then the priest shall offer them, the one *as* a sin offering and the other *as* a burnt offering. So the priest shall make atonement for him before the LORD because of his discharge.

16 'If any man has an emission of semen, then he shall wash all his body in water, and be unclean until evening. 17 And any garment and any leather on which there is semen, it shall be washed with water, and be unclean until evening. 18 Also, when a woman lies with a man, and *there is* an emission of semen, they shall bathe in water, and be unclean until evening.

19 'If a woman has a discharge, *and* the discharge from her body is blood, she shall be set apart seven days; and whoever touches her shall be unclean until evening. 20 Everything that she lies on during her impurity shall be unclean; also everything that she sits on shall be unclean. 21 Whoever touches her bed shall wash his clothes and bathe in water, and be unclean until evening. 22 And whoever touches anything that she sat on shall wash his clothes and bathe in water, and be unclean until evening. 23 If *anything* is on *her* bed or on anything on which she sits, when he touches it, he shall be unclean until evening. 24 And if any man lies with her at all, so that her impurity is on him, he shall be unclean seven days; and every bed on which he lies shall be unclean.

25 'If a woman has a discharge of blood for many days, other than at the time of her *customary* impurity, or if it runs beyond her *usual time of* impurity, all the days of her unclean discharge shall be as the days of her *customary* impurity. She *shall be* unclean. 26 Every bed on which she lies all the days of her discharge shall be to her as the bed of her impurity; and whatever she sits on shall be unclean, as the uncleanness of her impurity. 27 Whoever touches those things shall be unclean; he shall wash his clothes and bathe in water, and be unclean until evening.

28 'But if she is cleansed of her discharge, then she shall count for herself seven days, and after that she shall be clean. 29 And on the eighth day she shall take for herself two turtledoves or two young pigeons, and bring them to the priest, to the door of the tabernacle of meeting. 30 Then the priest shall offer the one *as* a sin offering and the other *as* a burnt offering, and the priest shall make atonement for her before the LORD for the discharge of her uncleanness.

31 'Thus you shall separate the children of Israel from their uncleanness, lest they die in their uncleanness when they defile My tabernacle that *is* among them. 32 This *is* the law for one who has a discharge, and *for him* who emits semen and is unclean thereby, 33 and for her who is indisposed because of her *customary* impurity, and for one who has a discharge, either man or woman, and for him who lies with her who is unclean.' "

16 NOW the LORD spoke to Moses after the death of the two sons of Aaron, when they offered *profane fire* before the LORD, and died; 2 and the LORD said to Moses: "Tell Aaron your brother not to come at *just* any time into the Holy *Place* inside the veil, before the mercy seat which *is* on the ark, lest he die; for I will appear in the cloud above the mercy seat.

3 "Thus Aaron shall come into the Holy *Place:* with *the blood of* a young bull as a sin offering, and *of* a ram as a burnt offering. 4 He shall put the holy linen tunic and the linen trousers on his body; he shall be girded with a linen sash, and with the linen turban he shall be attired. These *are* holy garments. Therefore he shall wash his body in water, and put them on. 5 And he shall take from the congregation of the children of Israel two kids of the goats as a sin offering, and one ram as a burnt offering.

6 "Aaron shall offer the bull as a sin offering, which *is* for himself, and make atonement for himself and for his house. 7 He shall take the two goats and present them before the LORD *at* the door of the tabernacle of meeting. 8 Then Aaron shall cast lots for the two goats: one lot for the LORD and the other lot for the scapegoat. 9 And Aaron shall bring the goat on which the LORD's lot fell, and offer it *as* a sin offering. 10 But the goat on which the lot fell to be the scapegoat shall be presented alive before the LORD, to make atonement upon it, *and* to let it go as the scapegoat into the wilderness.

11 "And Aaron shall bring the bull of the sin offering, which is for himself, and make atonement for himself and for his house, and shall kill the bull as the sin offering

which *is* for himself. 12 Then he shall take a censer full of burning coals of fire from the altar before the LORD, with his hands full of sweet incense beaten fine, and bring *it* inside the veil. 13 And he shall put the incense on the fire before the LORD, that the cloud of incense may cover the mercy seat that *is* on the Testimony, lest he die. 14 He shall take some of the blood of the bull and sprinkle *it* with his finger on the mercy seat on the east *side;* and before the mercy seat he shall sprinkle some of the blood with his finger seven times.

15 "Then he shall kill the goat of the sin offering, which *is* for the people, bring its blood inside the veil, do with that blood as he did with the blood of the bull, and sprinkle it on the mercy seat and before the mercy seat. 16 So he shall make atonement for the Holy *Place,* because of the uncleanness of the children of Israel, and because of their transgressions, for all their sins; and so he shall do for the tabernacle of meeting which remains among them in the midst of their uncleanness. 17 There shall be no man in the tabernacle of meeting when he goes in to make atonement in the Holy *Place,* until he comes out, that he may make atonement for himself, for his household, and for all the assembly of Israel. 18 And he shall go out to the altar that *is* before the LORD, and make atonement for it, and shall take some of the blood of the bull and some of the blood of the goat, and put it on the horns of the altar all around. 19 Then he shall sprinkle some of the blood on it with his finger seven times, cleanse it, and consecrate it from the uncleanness of the children of Israel.

20 "And when he has made an end of atoning for the Holy *Place,* the tabernacle of meeting, and the altar, he shall bring the live goat. 21 Aaron shall lay both his hands on the head of the live goat, confess over it all the iniquities of the children of Israel, and all their transgressions, concerning all their sins, putting them on the head of the goat, and shall send *it* away into the wilderness by the hand of a suitable man. 22 The goat shall bear on itself all their iniquities to an uninhabited land; and he shall release the goat in the wilderness.

23 "Then Aaron shall come into the tabernacle of meeting, shall take off the linen garments which he put on when he went into the Holy *Place,* and shall leave them there. 24 And he shall wash his body with water in a holy place, put on his garments, come out and offer his burnt offering and the burnt offering of the people, and make atonement for himself and for the people. 25 The fat of the sin offering he shall burn on the altar. 26 And he who released the goat as the scapegoat shall wash his clothes and bathe his body in water, and afterward he may come into the camp. 27 The bull *for* the sin offering and the goat *for* the sin offering, whose blood was brought in to make atonement in the Holy *Place,* shall be carried outside the camp. And they shall burn in the fire their skins, their flesh, and their offal. 28 Then he who burns them shall wash his clothes and bathe his body in water, and afterward he may come into the camp.

29 "*This* shall be a statute forever for you: In the seventh month, on the tenth *day* of the month, you shall afflict your souls, and do no work at all, *whether* a native of your own country or a stranger who dwells among you. 30 For on that day *the priest* shall make atonement for you, to cleanse you, *that* you may be clean from all your sins before the LORD. 31 It *is* a sabbath of solemn rest for you, and you shall afflict your souls. *It is* a statute forever. 32 And the priest, who is anointed and consecrated to minister as priest in his father's place, shall make atonement, and put on the linen clothes, the holy garments; 33 then he shall make atonement for the Holy Sanctuary, and he shall make atonement for the tabernacle of meeting and for the altar, and he shall make atonement for the priests and for all the people of the assembly. 34 This shall be an everlasting statute for you, to make atonement for the children of Israel, for all their sins, once a year." And he did as the LORD commanded Moses.

PSALM 26:6–12

6 I will wash my hands in innocence;
   So I will go about Your altar, O LORD,
7 That I may proclaim with the voice of thanksgiving,
   And tell of all Your wondrous works.
8 LORD, I have loved the habitation of Your house,
   And the place where Your glory dwells.

9 Do not gather my soul with sinners,
   Nor my life with bloodthirsty men,
10 In whose hands *is* a sinister scheme,
   And whose right hand is full of bribes.

11 But as for me, I will walk in my integrity;
   Redeem me and be merciful to me.

A person cannot redeem himself.   (BAFFLED)

12   My foot stands in an even place;
     In the congregations I will bless the
     LORD.

PROVERBS 10:8

8   THE wise in heart will receive
     commands,
     But a prating fool will fall.

MARK 4:1–20

AND again He began to teach by the sea. And a great multitude was gathered to Him, so that He got into a boat and sat *in it* on the sea; and the whole multitude was on the land facing the sea. 2 Then He taught them many things by parables, and said to them in His teaching:

3 "Listen! Behold, a sower went out to sow. 4 And it happened, as he sowed, *that* some *seed* fell by the wayside; and the birds of the air came and devoured it. 5 Some fell on stony ground, where it did not have much earth; and immediately it sprang up because it had no depth of earth. 6 But when the sun was up it was scorched, and because it had no root it withered away. 7 And some *seed* fell among thorns; and the thorns grew up and choked it, and it yielded no crop. 8 But other *seed* fell on good ground and yielded a crop that sprang up, increased and produced: some thirtyfold, some sixty, and some a hundred."

9 And He said to them, "He who has ears to hear, let him hear!"

10 But when He was alone, those around Him with the twelve asked Him about the parable. 11 And He said to them, "To you it has been given to know the mystery of the kingdom of God; but to those who are outside, all things come in parables, 12 so that

'Seeing they may see and not perceive,
And hearing they may hear and not
     understand;
Lest they should turn,
And *their* sins be forgiven them.' "

13 And He said to them, "Do you not understand this parable? How then will you understand all the parables? 14 The sower sows the word. 15 And these are the ones by the wayside where the word is sown. When they hear, Satan comes immediately and takes away the word that was sown in their hearts. 16 These likewise are the ones sown on stony ground who, when they hear the word, immediately receive it with gladness; 17 and they have no root in themselves, and so endure only for a time. Afterward, when tribulation or persecution arises for the word's sake, immediately they stumble. 18 Now these are the ones sown among thorns; *they are* the ones who hear the word, 19 and the cares of this world, the deceitfulness of riches, and the desires for other things entering in choke the word, and it becomes unfruitful.

There is an enormous power in little things to distract our attention from God.   (GOOD)

20 But these are the ones sown on good ground, those who hear the word, accept *it,* and bear fruit: some thirtyfold, some sixty, and some a hundred."

◆◆◆◆

*Reading 55—*The Theology of Rest
Mark 4:35–41

The incident recorded in Mark 4:35–41 is not an incident in the life of a man, but in the life of God as man. This man asleep in the boat is God incarnate. Jesus had said to the disciples, "Let us cross over to the other side," but when the storm arose, instead of relying upon Him, they failed Him. The actual circumstances were so crushing that their common sense was up in alarm, their panic carried them off their feet, and in terror they awoke Him. When we are in fear, we can do nothing less than pray to God, but our Lord has the right to expect of those who name His Name and have His nature in them an understanding confidence in Him. Instead of that, when we are at our wits' end we go back to the elementary prayers of those who do not know Him, and prove that we have not the slightest atom of confidence in Him and in His government of the world: He is asleep—the tiller is not in His hand, and we sit down in nervous dread. God expects His children to be so confident in Him that in a crisis they are the ones upon whom He can rely. A great point is reached spiritually when we stop worrying God over personal matters or over any matter. God expects of us the one thing that glorifies Him—and that is to remain absolutely confident in Him, remembering what He has said beforehand, and sure that His purposes will be fulfilled.

(*PLACE HELP*)

LEVITICUS 17:1—18:30

AND the LORD spoke to Moses, saying, 2 "Speak to Aaron, to his sons, and to all the children of Israel, and say to them, 'This *is* the thing which the LORD has commanded, saying: 3 "Whatever man of the house of Israel who kills an ox or lamb or goat in the camp, or who kills *it* outside the camp, 4 and does not bring it to the door of the tabernacle of meeting to offer an offering to the LORD before the tabernacle of the LORD, the guilt of bloodshed shall be imputed to that man. He has shed blood; and that man shall be cut off from among his people, 5 to the end that the children of Israel may bring their sacrifices which they offer in the open field, that they may bring them to the LORD at the door of the tabernacle of meeting, to the priest, and offer them *as* peace offerings to the LORD. 6 And the priest shall sprinkle the blood on the altar of the LORD *at* the door of the tabernacle of meeting, and burn the fat for a sweet aroma to the LORD. 7 They shall no more offer their sacrifices to demons, after whom they have played the harlot. This shall be a statute forever for them throughout their generations." '

8 "Also you shall say to them: 'Whatever man of the house of Israel, or of the strangers who dwell among you, who offers a burnt offering or sacrifice, 9 and does not bring it to the door of the tabernacle of meeting, to offer it to the LORD, that man shall be cut off from among his people.

10 'And whatever man of the house of Israel, or of the strangers who dwell among you, who eats any blood, I will set My face against that person who eats blood, and will cut him off from among his people. 11 For the life of the flesh *is* in the blood, and I have given it to you upon the altar to make atonement for your souls; for it *is* the blood *that* makes atonement for the soul.' 12 Therefore I said to the children

of Israel, 'No one among you shall eat blood, nor shall any stranger who dwells among you eat blood.'

13 "Whatever man of the children of Israel, or of the strangers who dwell among you, who hunts and catches any animal or bird that may be eaten, he shall pour out its blood and cover it with dust; 14 for *it is* the life of all flesh. Its blood sustains its life. Therefore I said to the children of Israel, 'You shall not eat the blood of any flesh, for the life of all flesh is its blood. Whoever eats it shall be cut off.'

15 "And every person who eats what died *naturally* or what was torn *by beasts, whether he is* a native of your own country or a stranger, he shall both wash his clothes and bathe in water, and be unclean until evening. Then he shall be clean. 16 But if he does not wash *them* or bathe his body, then he shall bear his guilt."

18 THEN the LORD spoke to Moses, saying, 2 "Speak to the children of Israel, and say to them: 'I am the LORD your God. 3 According to the doings of the land of Egypt, where you dwelt, you shall not do; and according to the doings of the land of Canaan, where I am bringing you, you shall not do; nor shall you walk in their ordinances. 4 You shall observe My judgments and keep My ordinances, to walk in them: I *am* the LORD your God. 5 You shall therefore keep My statutes and My judgments, which if a man does, he shall live by them: I *am* the LORD.

6 'None of you shall approach anyone who is near of kin to him, to uncover his nakedness: I *am* the LORD. 7 The nakedness of your father or the nakedness of your mother you shall not uncover. She *is* your mother; you shall not uncover her nakedness. 8 The nakedness of your father's wife you shall not uncover; it *is* your father's nakedness. 9 The nakedness of your sister, the daughter of your father, or the daughter of your mother, *whether* born at home or

elsewhere, their nakedness you shall not uncover. 10 The nakedness of your son's daughter or your daughter's daughter, their nakedness you shall not uncover; for theirs *is* your own nakedness. 11 The nakedness of your father's wife's daughter, begotten by your father—she *is* your sister—you shall not uncover her nakedness. 12 You shall not uncover the nakedness of your father's sister; she *is* near of kin to your father. 13 You shall not uncover the nakedness of your mother's sister, for she *is* near of kin to your mother. 14 You shall not uncover the nakedness of your father's brother. You shall not approach his wife; she *is* your aunt. 15 You shall not uncover the nakedness of your daughter-in-law—she *is* your son's wife—you shall not uncover her nakedness. 16 You shall not uncover the nakedness of your brother's wife; it *is* your brother's nakedness. 17 You shall not uncover the nakedness of a woman and her daughter, nor shall you take her son's daughter or her daughter's daughter, to uncover her nakedness. They *are* near of kin to her. It *is* wickedness. 18 Nor shall you take a woman as a rival to her sister, to uncover her nakedness while the other is alive.

19 'Also you shall not approach a woman to uncover her nakedness as long as she is in her *customary* impurity. 20 Moreover you shall not lie carnally with your neighbor's wife, to defile yourself with her. 21 And you shall not let any of your descendants pass through *the fire* to Molech, nor shall you profane the name of your God: I *am* the LORD. 22 You shall not lie with a male as with a woman. It *is* an abomination. 23 Nor shall you mate with any animal, to defile yourself with it. Nor shall any woman stand before an animal to mate with it. It *is* perversion.

24 'Do not defile yourselves with any of these things; for by all these the nations are defiled, which I am casting out before you. 25 For the land is defiled; therefore I visit the punishment of its iniquity upon it, and the land vomits out its inhabitants. 26 You shall therefore keep My statutes and My judgments, and shall not commit *any* of these abominations, *either* any of your own nation or any stranger who dwells among you 27 (for all these abominations the men of the land have done, who *were* before you, and thus the land is defiled), 28 lest the land vomit you out also when you defile it, as it vomited out the nations that *were* before you. 29 For whoever commits any of these abominations, the persons who commit *them* shall be cut off from among their people.

30 'Therefore you shall keep My ordinance, so that *you* do not commit *any* of these abominable customs which were committed before you, and that you do not defile yourselves by them: I *am* the LORD your God.' "

PSALM 27:1–3

1   THE LORD *is* my light and my salvation;
Whom shall I fear?
The LORD *is* the strength of my life;
Of whom shall I be afraid?

God's grace is at work in our hearts . . . when we do not get into panics.   (SHAD. AGONY)

---

2   When the wicked came against me
To eat up my flesh,
My enemies and foes,
They stumbled and fell.
3   Though an army may encamp against me,
My heart shall not fear;
Though war may rise against me,
In this I *will be* confident.

PROVERBS 10:9

9   HE who walks with integrity walks securely,
But he who perverts his ways will become known.

MARK 4:21–41

ALSO He said to them, "Is a lamp brought to be put under a basket or under a bed? Is it not to be set on a lampstand? 22 For there is nothing hidden which will not be revealed, nor has anything been kept secret but that it should come to light. 23 If anyone has ears to hear, let him hear."

24 Then He said to them, "Take heed what you hear. With the same measure you use, it will be measured to you; and to you who hear, more will be given. 25 For whoever has, to him more will be given; but whoever does not have, even what he has will be taken away from him."

26 And He said, "The kingdom of God is as if a man should scatter seed on the ground, 27 and should sleep by night and

rise by day, and the seed should sprout and grow, he himself does not know how. 28 For the earth yields crops by itself: first the blade, then the head, after that the full grain in the head. 29 But when the grain ripens, immediately he puts in the sickle, because the harvest has come."

30 Then He said, "To what shall we liken the kingdom of God? Or with what parable shall we picture it? 31 *It is* like a mustard seed which, when it is sown on the ground, is smaller than all the seeds on earth; 32 but when it is sown, it grows up and becomes greater than all herbs, and shoots out large branches, so that the birds of the air may nest under its shade."

33 And with many such parables He spoke the word to them as they were able to hear *it*. 34 But without a parable He did not speak to them. And when they were alone, He explained all things to His disciples.

35 On the same day, when evening had come, He said to them, "Let us cross over to the other side." 36 Now when they had left the multitude, they took Him along in the boat as He was. And other little boats were also with Him. 37 And a great windstorm arose, and the waves beat into the boat, so that it was already filling. 38 But He was in the stern, asleep on a pillow. And they awoke Him and said to Him, "Teacher, do You not care that we are perishing?"

39 Then He arose and rebuked the wind, and said to the sea, "Peace, be still!" And the wind ceased and there was a great calm. 40 But He said to them, "Why are you so fearful? How *is it* that you have no faith?"

There is not only fear, but terrible danger, for the life unguarded by God.   (RUN)

---

41 And they feared exceedingly, and said to one another, "Who can this be, that even the wind and the sea obey Him!"

◆◆◆

Reading 56—What We Should Hate
Leviticus 19:17

A good way to use the "cursing" Psalms is in some such way as this— "Do not I hate them, O LORD, who hate You? . . . I hate them with perfect hatred." Ask yourself what is it that hates God? Nothing and no one hates God half as much as the wrong disposition in you does. "The carnal mind *is* enmity against God"; what we should hate is this principle that lusts against the Spirit of God and is determined to have our bodies and minds and rule them away from God. The Spirit of God awakens in us an unmeasured hatred of that power until we are not only sick of it, but sick to death of it, and we will gladly make the moral choice of going to its funeral. The meaning of Romans 6:6 is just this put into scriptural language: "Knowing this, that our old man was crucified with *Him*." The "old man" is the thing the Spirit of God will teach us to hate, and the love of God in our hearts concentrates our soul in horror against the wrong thing. Make no excuse for it. The next time you read those Psalms, which people think are so terrible, bring this interpretation to bear on them.   (BIB. PSYCH.)

LEVITICUS 19:1—20:27

AND the LORD spoke to Moses, saying, 2 "Speak to all the congregation of the children of Israel, and say to them: 'You shall be holy, for I the LORD your God *am* holy.

3 'Every one of you shall revere his mother and his father, and keep My Sabbaths: I *am* the LORD your God.

4 'Do not turn to idols, nor make for yourselves molded gods: I *am* the LORD your God.

5 'And if you offer a sacrifice of a peace offering to the LORD, you shall offer it of your own free will. 6 It shall be eaten the

same day you offer *it,* and on the next day. And if any remains until the third day, it shall be burned in the fire. 7 And if it is eaten at all on the third day, it *is* an abomination. It shall not be accepted. 8 Therefore *everyone* who eats it shall bear his iniquity, because he has profaned the hallowed *offering* of the LORD; and that person shall be cut off from his people.

9 'When you reap the harvest of your land, you shall not wholly reap the corners of your field, nor shall you gather the gleanings of your harvest. 10 And you shall not glean your vineyard, nor shall you gather *every* grape of your vineyard; you shall leave them for the poor and the stranger: I *am* the LORD your God.

11 'You shall not steal, nor deal falsely, nor lie to one another. 12 And you shall not swear by My name falsely, nor shall you profane the name of your God: I *am* the LORD.

13 'You shall not cheat your neighbor, nor rob *him.* The wages of him who is hired shall not remain with you all night until morning. 14 You shall not curse the deaf, nor put a stumbling block before the blind, but shall fear your God: I *am* the LORD.

15 'You shall do no injustice in judgment. You shall not be partial to the poor, nor honor the person of the mighty. In righteousness you shall judge your neighbor. 16 You shall not go about *as* a talebearer among your people; nor shall you take a stand against the life of your neighbor: I *am* the LORD.

17 'You shall not hate your brother in your heart. You shall surely rebuke your neighbor, and not bear sin because of him. 18 You shall not take vengeance, nor bear any grudge against the children of your people, but you shall love your neighbor as yourself: I *am* the LORD.

19 'You shall keep My statutes. You shall not let your livestock breed with another kind. You shall not sow your field with mixed seed. Nor shall a garment of mixed linen and wool come upon you.

20 'Whoever lies carnally with a woman who *is* betrothed to a man as a concubine, and who has not at all been redeemed nor given her freedom, for this there shall be scourging; *but* they shall not be put to death, because she was not free. 21 And he shall bring his trespass offering to the LORD, to the door of the tabernacle of meeting, a ram as a trespass offering. 22 The priest shall make atonement for him with the ram of the trespass offering before the LORD for his sin which he has committed. And

the sin which he has committed shall be forgiven him.

23 'When you come into the land, and have planted all kinds of trees for food, then you shall count their fruit as uncircumcised. Three years it shall be as uncircumcised to you. *It* shall not be eaten. 24 But in the fourth year all its fruit shall be holy, a praise to the LORD. 25 And in the fifth year you may eat its fruit, that it may yield to you its increase: I *am* the LORD your God.

26 'You shall not eat *anything* with the blood, nor shall you practice divination or soothsaying. 27 You shall not shave around the sides of your head, nor shall you disfigure the edges of your beard. 28 You shall not make any cuttings in your flesh for the dead, nor tattoo any marks on you: I *am* the LORD.

29 'Do not prostitute your daughter, to cause her to be a harlot, lest the land fall into harlotry, and the land become full of wickedness.

30 'You shall keep My Sabbaths and reverence My sanctuary: I *am* the LORD.

31 'Give no regard to mediums and familiar spirits; do not seek after them, to be defiled by them: I *am* the LORD your God.

32 'You shall rise before the gray headed and honor the presence of an old man, and fear your God: I *am* the LORD.

33 'And if a stranger dwells with you in your land, you shall not mistreat him. 34 The stranger who dwells among you shall be to you as one born among you, and you shall love him as yourself; for you were strangers in the land of Egypt: I *am* the LORD your God.

35 'You shall do no injustice in judgment, in measurement of length, weight, or volume. 36 You shall have honest scales, honest weights, an honest ephah, and an honest hin: I *am* the LORD your God, who brought you out of the land of Egypt.

37 'Therefore you shall observe all My statutes and all My judgments, and perform them: I *am* the LORD.' "

20 THEN the LORD spoke to Moses, saying, 2 "Again, you shall say to the children of Israel: 'Whoever of the children of Israel, or of the strangers who dwell in Israel, who gives *any* of his descendants to Molech, he shall surely be put to death. The people of the land shall stone him with stones. 3 I will set My face against that man, and will cut him off from his people, because he has given *some* of his descendants to Molech, to defile My sanctuary and profane My holy name. 4 And if the people of the

land should in any way hide their eyes from the man, when he gives *some* of his descendants to Molech, and they do not kill him, 5 then I will set My face against that man and against his family; and I will cut him off from his people, and all who prostitute themselves with him to commit harlotry with Molech.

6 'And the person who turns to mediums and familiar spirits, to prostitute himself with them, I will set My face against that person and cut him off from his people. 7 Consecrate yourselves therefore, and be holy, for I *am* the LORD your God. 8 And you shall keep My statutes, and perform them: I *am* the LORD who sanctifies you.

9 'For everyone who curses his father or his mother shall surely be put to death. He has cursed his father or his mother. His blood *shall be* upon him.

10 'The man who commits adultery with *another* man's wife, *he* who commits adultery with his neighbor's wife, the adulterer and the adulteress, shall surely be put to death. 11 The man who lies with his father's wife has uncovered his father's nakedness; both of them shall surely be put to death. Their blood *shall be* upon them. 12 If a man lies with his daughter-in-law, both of them shall surely be put to death. They have committed perversion. Their blood *shall be* upon them. 13 If a man lies with a male as he lies with a woman, both of them have committed an abomination. They shall surely be put to death. Their blood *shall be* upon them. 14 If a man marries a woman and her mother, it *is* wickedness. They shall be burned with fire, both he and they, that there may be no wickedness among you. 15 If a man mates with an animal, he shall surely be put to death, and you shall kill the animal. 16 If a woman approaches any animal and mates with it, you shall kill the woman and the animal. They shall surely be put to death. Their blood *is* upon them.

17 'If a man takes his sister, his father's daughter or his mother's daughter, and sees her nakedness and she sees his nakedness, it *is* a wicked thing. And they shall be cut off in the sight of their people. He has uncovered his sister's nakedness. He shall bear his guilt. 18 If a man lies with a woman during her sickness and uncovers her nakedness, he has exposed her flow, and she has uncovered the flow of her blood. Both of them shall be cut off from their people.

19 'You shall not uncover the nakedness of your mother's sister nor of your father's sister, for that would uncover his near of kin. They shall bear their guilt. 20 If a man lies with his uncle's wife, he has uncovered his uncle's nakedness. They shall bear their sin; they shall die childless. 21 If a man takes his brother's wife, it *is* an unclean thing. He has uncovered his brother's nakedness. They shall be childless.

22 'You shall therefore keep all My statutes and all My judgments, and perform them, that the land where I am bringing you to dwell may not vomit you out. 23 And you shall not walk in the statutes of the nation which I am casting out before you; for they commit all these things, and therefore I abhor them. 24 But I have said to you, "You shall inherit their land, and I will give it to you to possess, a land flowing with milk and honey." I *am* the LORD your God, who has separated you from the peoples. 25 You shall therefore distinguish between clean animals and unclean, between unclean birds and clean, and you shall not make yourselves abominable by beast or by bird, or by any kind of living thing that creeps on the ground, which I have separated from you as unclean. 26 And you shall be holy to Me, for I the LORD *am* holy, and have separated you from the peoples, that you should be Mine.

27 'A man or a woman who is a medium, or who has familiar spirits, shall surely be put to death; they shall stone them with stones. Their blood *shall be* upon them.' "

PSALM 27:4–10

4   ONE *thing* I have desired of the LORD,
      That will I seek:
      That I may dwell in the house of the
        LORD
      All the days of my life,
      To behold the beauty of the LORD,
      And to inquire in His temple.
5   For in the time of trouble
      He shall hide me in His pavilion;
      In the secret place of His tabernacle
      He shall hide me;
      He shall set me high upon a rock.

---

*T*he secret place convinces us
that He is our Father
and that He is righteousness
and love.   (CHRIS. DIS. 2)

---

6   And now my head shall be lifted up
        above my enemies all around me;
      Therefore I will offer sacrifices of joy
        in His tabernacle;
      I will sing, yes, I will sing praises to
        the LORD.

7   Hear, O LORD, *when* I cry with my
    voice!
    Have mercy also upon me, and answer
    me.
8   *When You said,* "Seek My face,"
    My heart said to You, "Your face,
    LORD, I will seek."
9   Do not hide Your face from me;
    Do not turn Your servant away in
    anger;
    You have been my help;
    Do not leave me nor forsake me,
    O God of my salvation.
10 When my father and my mother forsake
    me,
    Then the LORD will take care of me.

PROVERBS 10:10–12

10 HE who winks with the eye causes
    trouble,
    But a prating fool will fall.

11 The mouth of the righteous *is* a well
    of life,
    But violence covers the mouth of the
    wicked.

12 Hatred stirs up strife,
    But love covers all sins.

MARK 5:1–20

THEN they came to the other side of the
sea, to the country of the Gadarenes.
2 And when He had come out of the boat,
immediately there met Him out of the
tombs a man with an unclean spirit,
3 who had *his* dwelling among the tombs;
and no one could bind him, not even with
chains, 4 because he had often been bound
with shackles and chains. And the chains
had been pulled apart by him, and the shackles broken in pieces; neither could anyone
tame him. 5 And always, night and day,
he was in the mountains and in the tombs,
crying out and cutting himself with stones.

6 When he saw Jesus from afar, he ran
and worshiped Him. 7 And he cried out
with a loud voice and said, "What have I
to do with You, Jesus, Son of the Most
High God? I implore You by God that
You do not torment me."
8 For He said to him, "Come out of the
man, unclean spirit!" 9 Then He asked him,
"What *is* your name?"
And he answered, saying, "My name *is*
Legion; for we are many." 10 Also he
begged Him earnestly that He would not
send them out of the country.
11 Now a large herd of swine was feeding
there near the mountains. 12 So all the demons begged Him, saying, "Send us to the
swine, that we may enter them." 13 And
at once Jesus gave them permission. Then
the unclean spirits went out and entered
the swine (there were about two thousand);
and the herd ran violently down the steep
place into the sea, and drowned in the sea.
14 So those who fed the swine fled, and
they told *it* in the city and in the country.
And they went out to see what it was that
had happened. 15 Then they came to Jesus,
and saw the one *who had been* demon-
possessed and had the legion, sitting and
clothed and in his right mind. And they
were afraid. 16 And those who saw it told
them how it happened to him *who had been*
demon-possessed, and about the swine.
17 Then they began to plead with Him to
depart from their region.
18 And when He got into the boat, he
who had been demon-possessed begged
Him that he might be with Him.
19 However, Jesus did not permit him, but
said to him, "Go home to your friends,
and tell them what great things the Lord
has done for you, and how He has had
compassion on you." 20 And he departed
and began to proclaim in Decapolis all that
Jesus had done for him; and all marveled.

---

*J*udge *everything in the light of*
    Jesus Christ.   (GENESIS)

Reading 57—Know What You Should Do

Mark 5:28

When you know you should do a thing and you do it, immediately you will know more. If you revise where you are stodgy spiritually, you will find it goes back to the point where there was one thing you knew you should do, but you did not do it because there seemed no immediate call to, and now you have no perception, no discernment. Instead of being spiritually self-possessed at the time of crisis, you are spiritually distracted. It is a dangerous thing to refuse to go on knowing.

When the Spirit of God has opened your mind by His incoming and you are determining to know more, you will find that external circumstances and internal knowledge go together, and by obedience you begin to fulfill your spiritual destiny. The counterfeit of obedience is the state of mind in which you work up occasions to sacrifice yourself, ardor is mistaken for the discernment built on knowledge. "To obey is better than sacrifice." It is a great deal better to fulfill the purpose of God in your life by discerning His will than it is to perform great acts of self-sacrifice.   (BRILL. HERITAGE)

LEVITICUS 21:1—22:33

AND the LORD said to Moses, "Speak to the priests, the sons of Aaron, and say to them: 'None shall defile himself for the dead among his people, 2 except for his relatives who are nearest to him: his mother, his father, his son, his daughter, and his brother; 3 also his virgin sister who is near to him, who has had no husband, for her he may defile himself. 4 *Otherwise* he shall not defile himself, *being* a chief man among his people, to profane himself.

5 'They shall not make any bald *place* on their heads, nor shall they shave the edges of their beards nor make any cuttings in their flesh. 6 They shall be holy to their God and not profane the name of their God, for they offer the offerings of the LORD made by fire, *and* the bread of their God; therefore they shall be holy. 7 They shall not take a wife *who is* a harlot or a defiled woman, nor shall they take a woman divorced from her husband; for *the priest* is holy to his God. 8 Therefore you shall consecrate him, for he offers the bread of your God. He shall be holy to you, for I the LORD, who sanctify you, *am* holy. 9 The daughter of any priest, if she profanes herself by playing the harlot, she profanes her father. She shall be burned with fire.

10 '*He who is* the high priest among his brethren, on whose head the anointing oil was poured and who is consecrated to wear the garments, shall not uncover his head nor tear his clothes; 11 nor shall he go near

any dead body, nor defile himself for his father or his mother; 12 nor shall he go out of the sanctuary, nor profane the sanctuary of his God; for the consecration of the anointing oil of his God *is* upon him: I *am* the LORD. 13 And he shall take a wife in her virginity. 14 A widow or a divorced woman or a defiled woman *or* a harlot— these he shall not marry; but he shall take a virgin of his own people as wife. 15 Nor shall he profane his posterity among his people, for I the LORD sanctify him.' "

16 And the LORD spoke to Moses, saying, 17 "Speak to Aaron, saying: 'No man of your descendants in *succeeding* generations, who has *any* defect, may approach to offer the bread of his God. 18 For any man who has a defect shall not approach: a man blind or lame, who has a marred *face* or any *limb* too long, 19 a man who has a broken foot or broken hand, 20 or is a hunchback or a dwarf, or *a man* who has a defect in his eye, or eczema or scab, or is a eunuch. 21 No man of the descendants of Aaron the priest, who has a defect, shall come near to offer the offerings made by fire to the LORD. He has a defect; he shall not come near to offer the bread of his God. 22 He may eat the bread of his God, *both* the most holy and the holy; 23 only he shall not go near the veil or approach the altar, because he has a defect, lest he profane My sanctuaries; for I the LORD sanctify them.' "

24 And Moses told *it* to Aaron and his sons, and to all the children of Israel.

22 THEN the LORD spoke to Moses, saying, 2 "Speak to Aaron and his sons, that they separate themselves from the holy things of the children of Israel, and that they do not profane My holy name by what they dedicate to Me: I *am* the LORD. 3 Say to them: 'Whoever of all your descendants throughout your generations, who goes near the holy things which the children of Israel dedicate to the LORD, while he has uncleanness upon him, that person shall be cut off from My presence: I *am* the LORD.

4 'Whatever man of the descendants of Aaron, who *is* a leper or has a discharge, shall not eat the holy offerings until he is clean. And whoever touches anything made unclean *by* a corpse, or a man who has had an emission of semen, 5 or whoever touches any creeping thing by which he would be made unclean, or any person by whom he would become unclean, whatever his uncleanness may be— 6 the person who has touched any such thing shall be unclean until evening, and shall not eat the holy *offerings* unless he washes his body with water. 7 And when the sun goes down he shall be clean; and afterward he may eat the holy *offerings,* because it *is* his food. 8 Whatever dies *naturally* or is torn *by beasts* he shall not eat, to defile himself with it: I *am* the LORD.

9 'They shall therefore keep My ordinance, lest they bear sin for it and die thereby, if they profane it: I the LORD sanctify them.

10 'No outsider shall eat the holy *offering;* one who dwells with the priest, or a hired servant, shall not eat the holy thing. 11 But if the priest buys a person with his money, he may eat it; and one who is born in his house may eat his food. 12 If the priest's daughter is married to an outsider, she may not eat of the holy offerings. 13 But if the priest's daughter is a widow or divorced, and has no child, and has returned to her father's house as in her youth, she may eat her father's food; but no outsider shall eat it.

14 'And if a man eats the holy *offering* unintentionally, then he shall restore a holy *offering* to the priest, and add one-fifth to it. 15 They shall not profane the holy *offerings* of the children of Israel, which they offer to the LORD, 16 or allow them to bear the guilt of trespass when they eat their holy *offerings;* for I the LORD sanctify them.' "

17 And the LORD spoke to Moses, saying, 18 "Speak to Aaron and his sons, and to all the children of Israel, and say to them: 'Whatever man of the house of Israel, or of the strangers in Israel, who offers his sacrifice for any of his vows or for any of his freewill offerings, which they offer to the LORD as a burnt offering— 19 *you shall offer* of your own free will a male without blemish from the cattle, from the sheep, or from the goats. 20 Whatever has a defect, you shall not offer, for it shall not be acceptable on your behalf. 21 And whoever offers a sacrifice of a peace offering to the LORD, to fulfill *his* vow, or a freewill offering from the cattle or the sheep, it must be perfect to be accepted; there shall be no defect in it. 22 Those *that are* blind or broken or maimed, or have an ulcer or eczema or scabs, you shall not offer to the LORD, nor make an offering by fire of them on the altar to the LORD. 23 Either a bull or a lamb that has any limb too long or too short you may offer *as* a freewill offering, but for a vow it shall not be accepted.

24 'You shall not offer to the LORD what is bruised or crushed, or torn or cut; nor shall you make *any offering of them* in your land. 25 Nor from a foreigner's hand shall you offer any of these as the bread of your God, because their corruption *is* in them, *and* defects *are* in them. They shall not be accepted on your behalf.' "

26 And the LORD spoke to Moses, saying: 27 "When a bull or a sheep or a goat is born, it shall be seven days with its mother; and from the eighth day and thereafter it shall be accepted as an offering made by fire to the LORD. 28 *Whether it is* a cow or ewe, do not kill both her and her young on the same day. 29 And when you offer a sacrifice of thanksgiving to the LORD, offer *it* of your own free will. 30 On the same day it shall be eaten; you shall leave none of it until morning: I *am* the LORD.

31 "Therefore you shall keep My commandments, and perform them: I *am* the LORD. 32 You shall not profane My holy name, but I will be hallowed among the children of Israel. I *am* the LORD who sanctifies you, 33 who brought you out of the land of Egypt, to be your God: I *am* the LORD."

PSALM 27:11–14

11 TEACH me Your way, O LORD,
     And lead me in a smooth path, because of my enemies.
12 Do not deliver me to the will of my adversaries;
     For false witnesses have risen against me,
     And such as breathe out violence.

13 *I would have lost heart,* unless I had
   believed
   That I would see the goodness of the
   LORD
   In the land of the living.

14 Wait on the LORD;
   Be of good courage,
   And He shall strengthen your heart;
   Wait, I say, on the LORD!

God is never in a hurry.
(PLACE HELP)

PROVERBS 10:13–16

13 WISDOM is found on the lips of him
   who has understanding,
   But a rod *is* for the back of him who
   is devoid of understanding.

14 Wise *people* store up knowledge,
   But the mouth of the foolish *is* near
   destruction.

15 The rich man's wealth *is* his strong city;
   The destruction of the poor *is* their
   poverty.

16 The labor of the righteous *leads* to life,
   The wages of the wicked to sin.

MARK 5:21–43

NOW when Jesus had crossed over again
by boat to the other side, a great multitude
gathered to Him; and He was by the sea.
22 And behold, one of the rulers of the synagogue came, Jairus by name. And when
he saw Him, he fell at His feet 23 and begged
Him earnestly, saying, "My little daughter
lies at the point of death. Come and lay
Your hands on her, that she may be healed,
and she will live." 24 So *Jesus* went with
him, and a great multitude followed Him
and thronged Him.
25 Now a certain woman had a flow of
blood for twelve years, 26 and had suffered
many things from many physicians. She had

spent all that she had and was no better,
but rather grew worse. 27 When she heard
about Jesus, she came behind *Him* in the
crowd and touched His garment. 28 For
she said, "If only I may touch His clothes,
I shall be made well."
29 Immediately the fountain of her blood
was dried up, and she felt in *her* body that
she was healed of the affliction. 30 And
Jesus, immediately knowing in Himself that
power had gone out of Him, turned around
in the crowd and said, "Who touched My
clothes?"
31 But His disciples said to Him, "You
see the multitude thronging You, and You
say, 'Who touched Me?' "
32 And He looked around to see her who
had done this thing. 33 But the woman,
fearing and trembling, knowing what had
happened to her, came and fell down before
Him and told Him the whole truth.
34 And He said to her, "Daughter, your
faith has made you well. Go in peace, and
be healed of your affliction."
35 While He was still speaking, *some* came
from the ruler of the synagogue's *house* who
said, "Your daughter is dead. Why trouble
the Teacher any further?"
36 As soon as Jesus heard the word that
was spoken, He said to the ruler of the
synagogue, "Do not be afraid; only believe." 37 And He permitted no one to follow Him except Peter, James, and John
the brother of James. 38 Then He came to
the house of the ruler of the synagogue,
and saw a tumult and those who wept and
wailed loudly. 39 When He came in, He
said to them, "Why make this commotion
and weep? The child is not dead, but
sleeping."
40 And they ridiculed Him. But when
He had put them all outside, He took the
father and the mother of the child, and those
who were with Him, and entered where the
child was lying. 41 Then He took the child
by the hand, and said to her, "Talitha,
cumi," which is translated, "Little girl, I
say to you, arise." 42 Immediately the girl
arose and walked, for she was twelve years
of age. And they were overcome with great
amazement. 43 But He commanded them
strictly that no one should know it, and
said that *something* should be given her to
eat.

Reading 58—Pray About Everything
Psalm 28:1, 2

This solves the mystery of what we should pray for. If we are abiding in Jesus, we shall ask what He wants us to ask whether we are conscious of doing so or not. "Ask what you desire," that is, what your will is in. The meaning of prayer is that we recognize we are in the relationship of a child to his father. "Your Father knows the things you have need of before you ask Him." When once we realize that we can never think of anything our Father will forget, worry becomes impossible. Beware of getting into a panic. Panic is bad for the natural heart, and it is destructive to the spiritual life. "Let not your heart be troubled"—it is a command. Are we in the habit of constantly requesting, of continually talking to Jesus about everything? Where we go in the time of trial proves what the great underlying power in our lives is.

(BRILL. HERITAGE)

LEVITICUS 23:1—24:23

AND the LORD spoke to Moses, saying, 2 "Speak to the children of Israel, and say to them: 'The feasts of the LORD, which you shall proclaim to be holy convocations, these are My feasts.

3 'Six days shall work be done, but the seventh day is a Sabbath of solemn rest, a holy convocation. You shall do no work on it; it is the Sabbath of the LORD in all your dwellings.

4 'These are the feasts of the LORD, holy convocations which you shall proclaim at their appointed times. 5 On the fourteenth day of the first month at twilight is the LORD's Passover. 6 And on the fifteenth day of the same month is the Feast of Unleavened Bread to the LORD; seven days you must eat unleavened bread. 7 On the first day you shall have a holy convocation; you shall do no customary work on it. 8 But you shall offer an offering made by fire to the LORD for seven days. The seventh day shall be a holy convocation; you shall do no customary work on it.' "

9 And the LORD spoke to Moses, saying, 10 "Speak to the children of Israel, and say to them: 'When you come into the land which I give to you, and reap its harvest, then you shall bring a sheaf of the firstfruits of your harvest to the priest. 11 He shall wave the sheaf before the LORD, to be accepted on your behalf; on the day after the Sabbath the priest shall wave it. 12 And you shall offer on that day, when you wave the sheaf, a male lamb of the first year, without blemish, as a burnt offering to the LORD. 13 Its grain offering shall be two-tenths of an ephah of fine flour mixed with oil, an offering made by fire to the LORD, for a sweet aroma; and its drink offering shall be of wine, one-fourth of a hin. 14 You shall eat neither bread nor parched grain nor fresh grain until the same day that you have brought an offering to your God; it shall be a statute forever throughout your generations in all your dwellings.

15 'And you shall count for yourselves from the day after the Sabbath, from the day that you brought the sheaf of the wave offering: seven Sabbaths shall be completed. 16 Count fifty days to the day after the seventh Sabbath; then you shall offer a new grain offering to the LORD. 17 You shall bring from your dwellings two wave loaves of two-tenths of an ephah. They shall be of fine flour; they shall be baked with leaven. They are the firstfruits to the LORD. 18 And you shall offer with the bread seven lambs of the first year, without blemish, one young bull, and two rams. They shall be as a burnt offering to the LORD, with their grain offering and their drink offerings, an offering made by fire for a sweet aroma to the LORD. 19 Then you shall sacrifice one kid of the goats as a sin offering, and two male lambs of the first year as a sacrifice of a peace offering. 20 The priest shall wave them with the bread of the firstfruits as a wave offering before the LORD, with the two lambs. They shall be holy to the LORD for the priest. 21 And you shall proclaim on the same day that it is a holy convocation to you. You shall do no customary work on it. It shall be a statute forever in all your dwellings throughout your generations.

22 'When you reap the harvest of your land, you shall not wholly reap the corners of your field when you reap, nor shall you

gather any gleaning from your harvest. You shall leave them for the poor and for the stranger: I *am* the LORD your God.' "

23 Then the LORD spoke to Moses, saying, 24 "Speak to the children of Israel, saying: 'In the seventh month, on the first *day* of the month, you shall have a sabbath-*rest*, a memorial of blowing of trumpets, a holy convocation. 25 You shall do no customary work *on it;* and you shall offer an offering made by fire to the LORD.' "

26 And the LORD spoke to Moses, saying: 27 "Also the tenth *day* of this seventh month *shall be* the Day of Atonement. It shall be a holy convocation for you; you shall afflict your souls, and offer an offering made by fire to the LORD. 28 And you shall do no work on that same day, for *it is* the Day of Atonement, to make atonement for you before the LORD your God. 29 For any person who is not afflicted *in soul* on that same day shall be cut off from his people. 30 And any person who does any work on that same day, that person I will destroy from among his people. 31 You shall do no manner of work; *it shall be* a statute forever throughout your generations in all your dwellings. 32 It *shall be* to you a sabbath of *solemn* rest, and you shall afflict your souls; on the ninth *day* of the month at evening, from evening to evening, you shall celebrate your sabbath."

33 Then the LORD spoke to Moses, saying, 34 "Speak to the children of Israel, saying: 'The fifteenth day of this seventh month *shall be* the Feast of Tabernacles *for* seven days to the LORD. 35 On the first day *there shall be* a holy convocation. You shall do no customary work *on it.* 36 *For* seven days you shall offer an offering made by fire to the LORD. On the eighth day you shall have a holy convocation, and you shall offer an offering made by fire to the LORD. It *is* a sacred assembly, *and* you shall do no customary work *on it.*

37 'These *are* the feasts of the LORD which you shall proclaim *to be* holy convocations, to offer an offering made by fire to the LORD, a burnt offering and a grain offering, a sacrifice and drink offerings, everything on its day— 38 besides the Sabbaths of the LORD, besides your gifts, besides all your vows, and besides all your freewill offerings which you give to the LORD.

39 'Also on the fifteenth day of the seventh month, when you have gathered in the fruit of the land, you shall keep the feast of the LORD *for* seven days; on the first day *there shall be* a sabbath-*rest,* and on the eighth day a sabbath-*rest.* 40 And you shall take for yourselves on the first day the fruit of beautiful trees, branches of palm trees, the boughs of leafy trees, and willows of the brook; and you shall rejoice before the LORD your God for seven days. 41 You shall keep it as a feast to the LORD for seven days in the year. *It shall be* a statute forever in your generations. You shall celebrate it in the seventh month. 42 You shall dwell in booths for seven days. All who are native Israelites shall dwell in booths, 43 that your generations may know that I made the children of Israel dwell in booths when I brought them out of the land of Egypt: I *am* the LORD your God.' "

44 So Moses declared to the children of Israel the feasts of the LORD.

24 THEN the LORD spoke to Moses, saying: 2 "Command the children of Israel that they bring to you pure oil of pressed olives for the light, to make the lamps burn continually. 3 Outside the veil of the Testimony, in the tabernacle of meeting, Aaron shall be in charge of it from evening until morning before the LORD continually; *it shall be* a statute forever in your generations. 4 He shall be in charge of the lamps on the pure *gold* lampstand before the LORD continually.

5 "And you shall take fine flour and bake twelve cakes with it. Two-tenths *of an ephah* shall be in each cake. 6 You shall set them in two rows, six in a row, on the pure *gold* table before the LORD. 7 And you shall put pure frankincense on *each* row, that it may be on the bread for a memorial, an offering made by fire to the LORD. 8 Every Sabbath he shall set it in order before the LORD continually, *being taken* from the children of Israel by an everlasting covenant. 9 And it shall be for Aaron and his sons, and they shall eat it in a holy place; for it *is* most holy to him from the offerings of the LORD made by fire, by a perpetual statute."

10 Now the son of an Israelite woman, whose father *was* an Egyptian, went out among the children of Israel; and this Israelite *woman's* son and a man of Israel fought each other in the camp. 11 And the Israelite woman's son blasphemed the name *of the* LORD and cursed; and so they brought him to Moses. (His mother's name *was* Shelomith the daughter of Dibri, of the tribe of Dan.) 12 Then they put him in custody, that the mind of the LORD might be shown to them.

13 And the LORD spoke to Moses, saying, 14 "Take outside the camp him who has cursed; then let all who heard *him* lay their

hands on his head, and let all the congregation stone him.

15 "Then you shall speak to the children of Israel, saying: 'Whoever curses his God shall bear his sin. 16 And whoever blasphemes the name of the LORD shall surely be put to death. All the congregation shall certainly stone him, the stranger as well as him who is born in the land. When he blasphemes the name *of the LORD,* he shall be put to death.

17 'Whoever kills any man shall surely be put to death. 18 Whoever kills an animal shall make it good, animal for animal.

19 'If a man causes disfigurement of his neighbor, as he has done, so shall it be done to him— 20 fracture for fracture, eye for eye, tooth for tooth; as he has caused disfigurement of a man, so shall it be done to him. 21 And whoever kills an animal shall restore it; but whoever kills a man shall be put to death. 22 You shall have the same law for the stranger and for one from your own country; for I *am* the LORD your God.' "

23 Then Moses spoke to the children of Israel; and they took outside the camp him who had cursed, and stoned him with stones. So the children of Israel did as the LORD commanded Moses.

PSALM 28:1–5

1 TO You I will cry, O LORD my Rock:
Do not be silent to me,
Lest, if You *are* silent to me,
I become like those who go down to
the pit.

> *To silence the voice of God is
> damnation in time.* (PHIL. SIN)

2 Hear the voice of my supplications
When I cry to You,
When I lift up my hands toward Your
holy sanctuary.

3 Do not take me away with the wicked
And with the workers of iniquity,
Who speak peace to their neighbors,
But evil *is* in their hearts.
4 Give them according to their deeds,
And according to the wickedness of
their endeavors;
Give them according to the work of
their hands;
Render to them what they deserve.

5 Because they do not regard the works
of the LORD,
Nor the operation of His hands,
He shall destroy them
And not build them up.

PROVERBS 10:17, 18

17 HE who keeps instruction *is in* the way
of life,
But he who refuses correction goes
astray.

18 Whoever hides hatred *has* lying lips,
And whoever spreads slander *is* a fool.

MARK 6:1–29

THEN He went out from there and came to His own country, and His disciples followed Him. 2 And when the Sabbath had come, He began to teach in the synagogue. And many hearing *Him* were astonished, saying, "Where *did* this Man *get* these things? And what wisdom *is* this which is given to Him, that such mighty works are performed by His hands! 3 Is this not the carpenter, the Son of Mary, and brother of James, Joses, Judas, and Simon? And are not His sisters here with us?" So they were offended at Him.

> *Jesus Christ represents a
> character lived straight down in
> the ordinary amalgam of human
> life.* (SHAD. AGONY)

4 But Jesus said to them, "A prophet is not without honor except in his own country, among his own relatives, and in his own house." 5 Now He could do no mighty work there, except that He laid His hands on a few sick people and healed *them.* 6 And He marveled because of their unbelief. Then He went about the villages in a circuit, teaching.

7 And He called the twelve to *Himself,* and began to send them out two *by* two, and gave them power over unclean spirits. 8 He commanded them to take nothing for the journey except a staff—no bag, no bread, no copper in *their* money belts— 9 but to wear sandals, and not to put on two tunics.

10 Also He said to them, "In whatever place you enter a house, stay there till you

depart from that place. 11 And whoever will not receive you nor hear you, when you depart from there, shake off the dust under your feet as a testimony against them. Assuredly, I say to you, it will be more tolerable for Sodom and Gomorrah in the day of judgment than for that city!"

12 So they went out and preached that *people* should repent. 13 And they cast out many demons, and anointed with oil many who were sick, and healed *them*.

14 Now King Herod heard *of Him*, for His name had become well known. And he said, "John the Baptist is risen from the dead, and therefore these powers are at work in him."

15 Others said, "It is Elijah."

And others said, "It is the Prophet, or like one of the prophets."

16 But when Herod heard, he said, "This is John, whom I beheaded; he has been raised from the dead!" 17 For Herod himself had sent and laid hold of John, and bound him in prison for the sake of Herodias, his brother Philip's wife; for he had married her. 18 Because John had said to Herod, "It is not lawful for you to have your brother's wife."

19 Therefore Herodias held it against him and wanted to kill him, but she could not; 20 for Herod feared John, knowing that he *was* a just and holy man, and he protected him. And when he heard him, he did many things, and heard him gladly.

21 Then an opportune day came when Herod on his birthday gave a feast for his nobles, the high officers, and the chief *men* of Galilee. 22 And when Herodias' daughter herself came in and danced, and pleased Herod and those who sat with him, the king said to the girl, "Ask me whatever you want, and I will give *it* to you." 23 He also swore to her, "Whatever you ask me, I will give you, up to half my kingdom."

24 So she went out and said to her mother, "What shall I ask?"

And she said, "The head of John the Baptist!"

25 Immediately she came in with haste to the king and asked, saying, "I want you to give me at once the head of John the Baptist on a platter."

26 And the king was exceedingly sorry; *yet,* because of the oaths and because of those who sat with him, he did not want to refuse her. 27 Immediately the king sent an executioner and commanded his head to be brought. And he went and beheaded him in prison, 28 brought his head on a platter, and gave it to the girl; and the girl gave it to her mother. 29 When his disciples heard *of it,* they came and took away his corpse and laid it in a tomb.

◄◆◆►

Reading 59—The Rights of the Land
Leviticus 25:1–4

The twenty-fifth chapter of Leviticus is the great classic on the rights of the land. The establishment of men's rights on the earth is limited by the rights of the earth itself. If you keep taking from the land, never giving it any rest, in time it will stop giving to you. We talk about the rights of the land, and make it mean our right to grab as much from it as we can. In God's sight the land has rights just as human beings have, and many of the theories which are being advanced today go back to God's original prescription for the land. When God ordained "a sabbath of solemn rest for the land," it was a reiteration of the instructions given to Adam in the Garden of Eden— "Be fruitful and multiply; fill the earth and subdue it" (Gen. 1:28). Man was intended to replenish the earth by looking after it, being its lord not its tyrant; sin has made man its tyrant (see Rom. 8:19). The rights of the land will probably only be fully realized in the Millennium, because in this dispensation men ignore obedience to God's laws. (*Bib. Ethics*)

LEVITICUS 25:1–55

AND the LORD spoke to Moses on Mount Sinai, saying, 2 "Speak to the children of Israel, and say to them: 'When you come into the land which I give you, then the land shall keep a sabbath to the LORD. 3 Six years you shall sow your field, and six years you shall prune your vineyard, and gather its fruit; 4 but in the seventh year there shall be a sabbath of solemn rest for the land, a sabbath to the LORD. You shall neither sow your field nor prune your vineyard. 5 What grows of its own accord of your harvest you shall not reap, nor gather the grapes of your untended vine, *for* it is a year of rest for the land. 6 And the sabbath *produce* of the land shall be food for you: for you, your male and female servants, your hired man, and the stranger who dwells with you, 7 for your livestock and the beasts that *are* in your land—all its produce shall be for food.

8 'And you shall count seven sabbaths of years for yourself, seven times seven years; and the time of the seven sabbaths of years shall be to you forty-nine years. 9 Then you shall cause the trumpet of the Jubilee to sound on the tenth *day* of the seventh month; on the Day of Atonement you shall make the trumpet to sound throughout all your land. 10 And you shall consecrate the fiftieth year, and proclaim liberty throughout *all* the land to all its inhabitants. It shall be a Jubilee for you; and each of you shall return to his possession, and each of you shall return to his family. 11 That fiftieth year shall be a Jubilee to you; in it you shall neither sow nor reap what grows of its own accord, nor gather *the grapes* of your untended vine. 12 For it *is* the Jubilee; it shall be holy to you; you shall eat its produce from the field.

13 'In this Year of Jubilee, each of you shall return to his possession. 14 And if you sell anything to your neighbor or buy from your neighbor's hand, you shall not oppress one another. 15 According to the number of years after the Jubilee you shall buy from your neighbor, and according to the number of years of crops he shall sell to you. 16 According to the multitude of years you shall increase its price, and according to the fewer number of years you shall diminish its price; for he sells to you *according* to the number *of the years* of the crops. 17 Therefore you shall not oppress one another, but you shall fear your God; for I *am* the LORD your God.

18 'So you shall observe My statutes and keep My judgments, and perform them; and you will dwell in the land in safety. 19 Then the land will yield its fruit, and you will eat your fill, and dwell there in safety.

20 'And if you say, "What shall we eat in the seventh year, since we shall not sow nor gather in our produce?" 21 Then I will command My blessing on you in the sixth year, and it will bring forth produce enough for three years. 22 And you shall sow in the eighth year, and eat old produce until the ninth year; until its produce comes in, you shall eat *of* the old *harvest*.

23 'The land shall not be sold permanently, for the land *is* Mine; for you *are* strangers and sojourners with Me. 24 And in all the land of your possession you shall grant redemption of the land.

25 'If one of your brethren becomes poor, and has sold *some* of his possession, and if his redeeming relative comes to redeem it, then he may redeem what his brother sold. 26 Or if the man has no one to redeem it, but he himself becomes able to redeem it, 27 then let him count the years since its sale, and restore the remainder to the man to whom he sold it, that he may return to his possession. 28 But if he is not able to have *it* restored to himself, then what was sold shall remain in the hand of him who bought it until the Year of Jubilee; and in the Jubilee it shall be released, and he shall return to his possession.

29 'If a man sells a house in a walled city, then he may redeem it within a whole year after it is sold; *within* a full year he may redeem it. 30 But if it is not redeemed within the space of a full year, then the house in the walled city shall belong permanently to him who bought it, throughout his generations. It shall not be released in the Jubilee. 31 However the houses of villages which have no wall around them shall be counted as the fields of the country. They may be redeemed, and they shall be released in the Jubilee. 32 Nevertheless the cities of the Levites, *and* the houses in the cities of their possession, the Levites may redeem at any time. 33 And if a man purchases a house from the Levites, then the house that was sold in the city of his possession shall be released in the Jubilee; for the houses in the cities of the Levites *are* their possession among the children of Israel. 34 But the field of the common-land of their cities may not be sold, for it *is* their perpetual possession.

35 'If one of your brethren becomes poor, and falls into poverty among you, then you shall help him, like a stranger or a sojourner, that he may live with you. 36 Take no usury

or interest from him; but fear your God, that your brother may live with you. 37 You shall not lend him your money for usury, nor lend him your food at a profit. 38 I *am* the Lord your God, who brought you out of the land of Egypt, to give you the land of Canaan *and* to be your God.

39 'And if *one of* your brethren *who dwells* by you becomes poor, and sells himself to you, you shall not compel him to serve as a slave. 40 As a hired servant *and* a sojourner he shall be with you, *and* shall serve you until the Year of Jubilee. 41 And *then* he shall depart from you—he and his children with him—and shall return to his own family. He shall return to the possession of his fathers. 42 For they *are* My servants, whom I brought out of the land of Egypt; they shall not be sold as slaves. 43 You shall not rule over him with rigor, but you shall fear your God. 44 And as for your male and female slaves whom you may have—from the nations that are around you, from them you may buy male and female slaves. 45 Moreover you may buy the children of the strangers who dwell among you, and their families who are with you, which they beget in your land; and they shall become your property. 46 And you may take them as an inheritance for your children after you, to inherit *them as* a possession; they shall be your permanent slaves. But regarding your brethren, the children of Israel, you shall not rule over one another with rigor.

47 'Now if a sojourner or stranger close to you becomes rich, and *one of* your brethren *who dwells* by him becomes poor, and sells himself to the stranger *or* sojourner close to you, or to a member of the stranger's family, 48 after he is sold he may be redeemed again. One of his brothers may redeem him; 49 or his uncle or his uncle's son may redeem him; or *anyone* who is near of kin to him in his family may redeem him; or if he is able he may redeem himself. 50 Thus he shall reckon with him who bought him: The price of his release shall be according to the number of years, from the year that he was sold to him until the Year of Jubilee; *it shall be* according to the time of a hired servant for him. 51 If *there are* still many years *remaining*, according to them he shall repay the price of his redemption from the money with which he was bought. 52 And if there remain but a few years until the Year of Jubilee, then he shall reckon with him, *and* according to his years he shall repay him the price of his redemption. 53 He shall be with him as a yearly hired servant, and he shall not rule with rigor over him in your sight.

54 And if he is not redeemed in these *years*, then he shall be released in the Year of Jubilee—he and his children with him. 55 For the children of Israel *are* servants to Me; they *are* My servants whom I brought out of the land of Egypt: I *am* the Lord your God.

PSALM 28:6–9

6   BLESSED *be* the Lord,
     Because He has heard the voice of my
         supplications!
7   The Lord *is* my strength and my shield;
     My heart trusted in Him, and I am
         helped;
     Therefore my heart greatly rejoices,
     And with my song I will praise Him.

8   The Lord *is* their strength,
     And He *is* the saving refuge of His
         anointed.
9   Save Your people,
     And bless Your inheritance;
     Shepherd them also,
     And bear them up forever.

PROVERBS 10:19–21

19   IN the multitude of words sin is not
         lacking,
     But he who restrains his lips *is* wise.

*T*he *great test of a man's character is
his tongue.*   (SHADE)

20   The tongue of the righteous *is* choice
         silver;
     The heart of the wicked *is worth* little.
21   The lips of the righteous feed many,
     But fools die for lack of wisdom.

MARK 6:30–56

THEN the apostles gathered to Jesus and told Him all things, both what they had done and what they had taught. 31 And He said to them, "Come aside by yourselves to a deserted place and rest a while." For there were many coming and going, and they did not even have time to eat. 32 So they departed to a deserted place in the boat by themselves.

33 But the multitudes saw them departing, and many knew Him and ran there

on foot from all the cities. They arrived before them and came together to Him. 34 And Jesus, when He came out, saw a great multitude and was moved with compassion for them, because they were like sheep not having a shepherd. So He began to teach them many things. 35 When the day was now far spent, His disciples came to Him and said, "This is a deserted place, and already the hour *is* late. 36 Send them away, that they may go into the surrounding country and villages and buy themselves bread; for they have nothing to eat."

37 But He answered and said to them, "You give them something to eat."

And they said to Him, "Shall we go and buy two hundred denarii worth of bread and give them *something* to eat?"

38 But He said to them, "How many loaves do you have? Go and see."

And when they found out they said, "Five, and two fish."

39 Then He commanded them to make them all sit down in groups on the green grass. 40 So they sat down in ranks, in hundreds and in fifties. 41 And when He had taken the five loaves and the two fish, He looked up to heaven, blessed and broke the loaves, and gave *them* to His disciples to set before them; and the two fish He divided among *them* all. 42 So they all ate and were filled. 43 And they took up twelve baskets full of fragments and of the fish. 44 Now those who had eaten the loaves were about five thousand men.

45 Immediately He made His disciples get into the boat and go before Him to the other side, to Bethsaida, while He sent the multitude away. 46 And when He had sent them away, He departed to the mountain to pray. 47 Now when evening came, the boat was in the middle of the sea; and He *was* alone on the land. 48 Then He saw them straining at rowing, for the wind was against them. Now about the fourth watch of the night He came to them, walking on the sea, and would have passed them by. 49 And when they saw Him walking on the sea, they supposed it was a ghost, and cried out; 50 for they all saw Him and were troubled. But immediately He talked with them and said to them, "Be of good cheer! It is I; do not be afraid." 51 Then He went up into the boat to them, and the wind ceased. And they were greatly amazed in themselves beyond measure, and marveled. 52 For they had not understood about the loaves, because their heart was hardened.

53 When they had crossed over, they came to the land of Gennesaret and anchored there. 54 And when they came out of the boat, immediately the people recognized Him, 55 ran through that whole surrounding region, and began to carry about on beds those who were sick to wherever they heard He was. 56 Wherever He entered, into villages, cities, or the country, they laid the sick in the marketplaces, and begged Him that they might just touch the hem of His garment. And as many as touched Him were made well.

◆◆◆◆

*Reading 60—*Sow the Real Seed
Leviticus 26:16

There is nothing more impertinent than our crass infidelity in God. If He does not make us plowers and sowers and reapers all at once, we lose faith in Him. Modern evangelism makes the mistake of thinking that a worker must plow his field, sow the seed, and reap the harvest in half an hour. Our Lord was never in a hurry with the disciples. He kept on sowing the seed and paid no attention to whether they understood Him or not. He spoke the truth of God, and by His own life produced the right atmosphere for it to grow, and then left it alone, because He knew well that the seed had in it all the germinating power of God and would bring forth fruit after its kind once it was put in the right soil. We are never the same after listening to the truth; we may forget it, but we will hear it again. Sow the Word of God, and everyone who listens will get to God. If you sow vows, resolutions, aspirations, emotions, you will reap nothing but exhaustion: "And you shall sow your seed in vain, for your enemies shall eat it" (Lev. 26:16); but sow

the Word of God, and as sure as God is God, it will bring forth fruit. . . . A
man may not grasp all that is said, but something in him is intuitively held by
it. See that you sow the real seed of the Word of God, and then leave it
alone.   (*SERVANT AS LORD*)

LEVITICUS 26:1—27:34

1 'YOU shall not make idols for
     yourselves;
     neither a carved image nor a *sacred*
     pillar shall you rear up for
     yourselves;
     nor shall you set up an engraved stone
     in your land, to bow down to it;
     for I *am* the LORD your God.
2 You shall keep My Sabbaths and rev-
     erence My sanctuary:
     I *am* the LORD.

3 'If you walk in My statutes and keep
     My commandments, and perform
     them,
4 then I will give you rain in its season,
     the land shall yield its produce, and
     the trees of the field shall yield their
     fruit.
5 Your threshing shall last till the time
     of vintage, and the vintage shall
     last till the time of sowing;
     you shall eat your bread to the full,
     and dwell in your land safely.
6 I will give peace in the land, and you
     shall lie down, and none will make
     you afraid;
     I will rid the land of evil beasts,
     and the sword will not go through
     your land.
7 You will chase your enemies, and they
     shall fall by the sword before you.
8 Five of you shall chase a hundred,
     and a hundred of you shall put ten
     thousand to flight;
     your enemies shall fall by the sword
     before you.

9 'For I will look on you favorably and
     make you fruitful, multiply you
     and confirm My covenant with
     you.
10 You shall eat the old harvest, and
      clear out the old because of the
      new.
11 I will set My tabernacle among you,
      and My soul shall not abhor you.
12 I will walk among you and be your
      God, and you shall be My people.
13 I *am* the LORD your God, who
      brought you out of the land of
Egypt, that *you* should not be their
      slaves;
      I have broken the bands of your yoke
      and made you walk upright.

14 'But if you do not obey Me, and do
      not observe all these com-
      mandments,
15 and if you despise My statutes, or if
      your soul abhors My judgments,
      so that you do not perform all My
      commandments, *but* break My
      covenant,
16 I also will do this to you:
      I will even appoint terror over you,
      wasting disease and fever which
      shall consume the eyes and cause
      sorrow of heart.
      And you shall sow your seed in vain,
      for your enemies shall eat it.
17 I will set My face against you, and
      you shall be defeated by your
      enemies.
      Those who hate you shall reign over
      you, and you shall flee when no
      one pursues you.

18 'And after all this, if you do not obey
      Me, then I will punish you seven
      times more for your sins.
19 I will break the pride of your power;
      I will make your heavens like iron
      and your earth like bronze.
20 And your strength shall be spent in
      vain;
      for your land shall not yield its pro-
      duce, nor shall the trees of the land
      yield their fruit.

21 'Then, if you walk contrary to Me,
      and are not willing to obey Me,
      I will bring on you seven times
      more plagues, according to your
      sins.
22 I will also send wild beasts among
      you, which shall rob you of your
      children, destroy your livestock,
      and make you few in number;
      and your highways shall be desolate.

23 'And if by these things you are not
      reformed by Me, but walk contrary
      to Me,

24 then I also will walk contrary to you, and I will punish you yet seven times for your sins.

25 And I will bring a sword against you that will execute the vengeance of the covenant;
   when you are gathered together within your cities I will send pestilence among you;
   and you shall be delivered into the hand of the enemy.

26 When I have cut off your supply of bread, ten women shall bake your bread in one oven, and they shall bring back your bread by weight, and you shall eat and not be satisfied.

27 'And after all this, if you do not obey Me, but walk contrary to Me,

28 then I also will walk contrary to you in fury;
   and I, even I, will chastise you seven times for your sins.

29 You shall eat the flesh of your sons, and you shall eat the flesh of your daughters.

30 I will destroy your high places, cut down your incense altars, and cast your carcasses on the lifeless forms of your idols;
   and My soul shall abhor you.

*C*arelessness in spiritual matters is a crime. (Approved)

31 I will lay your cities waste and bring your sanctuaries to desolation, and I will not smell the fragrance of your sweet aromas.

32 I will bring the land to desolation, and your enemies who dwell in it shall be astonished at it.

33 I will scatter you among the nations and draw out a sword after you; your land shall be desolate and your cities waste.

34 Then the land shall enjoy its sabbaths as long as it lies desolate and you *are* in your enemies' land;
   then the land shall rest and enjoy its sabbaths.

35 As long as *it* lies desolate it shall rest—
   for the time it did not rest on your sabbaths when you dwelt in it.

36 'And as for those of you who are left, I will send faintness into their hearts in the lands of their enemies;
the sound of a shaken leaf shall cause them to flee;
they shall flee as though fleeing from a sword, and they shall fall when no one pursues.

37 They shall stumble over one another, as it were before a sword, when no one pursues;
   and you shall have no *power* to stand before your enemies.

38 You shall perish among the nations, and the land of your enemies shall eat you up.

39 And those of you who are left shall waste away in their iniquity in your enemies' lands;
   also in their fathers' iniquities, which are with them, they shall waste away.

40 '*But* if they confess their iniquity and the iniquity of their fathers, with their unfaithfulness in which they were unfaithful to Me, and that they also have walked contrary to Me,

41 and *that* I also have walked contrary to them and have brought them into the land of their enemies;
   if their uncircumcised hearts are humbled, and they accept their guilt—

42 then I will remember My covenant with Jacob, and My covenant with Isaac and My covenant with Abraham I will remember;
   I will remember the land.

43 The land also shall be left empty by them, and will enjoy its sabbaths while it lies desolate without them;
   they will accept their guilt, because they despised My judgments and because their soul abhorred My statutes.

44 Yet for all that, when they are in the land of their enemies, I will not cast them away, nor shall I abhor them, to utterly destroy them and break My covenant with them;
   for I *am* the LORD their God.

45 But for their sake I will remember the covenant of their ancestors, whom I brought out of the land of Egypt in the sight of the nations, that I might be their God:
   I *am* the LORD.' "

46 These *are* the statutes and judgments and laws which the LORD made between Himself and the children of Israel on Mount Sinai by the hand of Moses.

27 NOW the LORD spoke to Moses, saying, 2 "Speak to the children of Israel, and say to them: 'When a man consecrates by a vow certain persons to the LORD, according to your valuation, 3 if your valuation is of a male from twenty years old up to sixty years old, then your valuation shall be fifty shekels of silver, according to the shekel of the sanctuary. 4 If it *is* a female, then your valuation shall be thirty shekels; 5 and if from five years old up to twenty years old, then your valuation for a male shall be twenty shekels, and for a female ten shekels; 6 and if from a month old up to five years old, then your valuation for a male shall be five shekels of silver, and for a female your valuation shall be three shekels of silver; 7 and if from sixty years old and above, if *it is* a male, then your valuation shall be fifteen shekels, and for a female ten shekels.

8 'But if he is too poor to pay your valuation, then he shall present himself before the priest, and the priest shall set a value for him; according to the ability of him who vowed, the priest shall value him.

9 'If *it is* an animal that men may bring as an offering to the LORD, all that *anyone* gives to the LORD shall be holy. 10 He shall not substitute it or exchange it, good for bad or bad for good; and if he at all exchanges animal for animal, then both it and the one exchanged for it shall be holy. 11 If *it is* an unclean animal which they do not offer as a sacrifice to the LORD, then he shall present the animal before the priest; 12 and the priest shall set a value for it, whether it is good or bad; as you, the priest, value it, so it shall be. 13 But if he *wants* at all *to* redeem it, then he must add one-fifth to your valuation.

14 'And when a man dedicates his house *to be* holy to the LORD, then the priest shall set a value for it, whether it is good or bad; as the priest values it, so it shall stand. 15 If he who dedicated it *wants to* redeem his house, then he must add one-fifth of the money of your valuation to it, and it shall be his.

16 'If a man dedicates to the LORD *part* of a field of his possession, then your valuation shall be according to the seed for it. A homer of barley seed *shall be valued* at fifty shekels of silver. 17 If he dedicates his field from the Year of Jubilee, according to your valuation it shall stand. 18 But if he dedicates his field after the Jubilee, then the priest shall reckon to him the money due according to the years that remain till the Year of Jubilee, and it shall be deducted from your valuation. 19 And if he who dedicates the field ever wishes to redeem it, then he must add one-fifth of the money of your valuation to it, and it shall belong to him. 20 But if he does not want to redeem the field, or if he has sold the field to another man, it shall not be redeemed anymore; 21 but the field, when it is released in the Jubilee, shall be holy to the LORD, as a devoted field; it shall be the possession of the priest.

22 'And if a man dedicates to the LORD a field which he has bought, which is not the field of his possession, 23 then the priest shall reckon to him the worth of your valuation, up to the Year of Jubilee, and he shall give your valuation on that day *as* a holy *offering* to the LORD. 24 In the Year of Jubilee the field shall return to him from whom it was bought, to the one who *owned* the land as a possession. 25 And all your valuations shall be according to the shekel of the sanctuary: twenty gerahs to the shekel.

26 'But the firstborn of the animals, which should be the LORD's firstborn, no man shall dedicate; whether *it is* an ox or sheep, it *is* the LORD's. 27 And if *it is* an unclean animal, then he shall redeem *it* according to your valuation, and shall add one-fifth to it; or if it is not redeemed, then it shall be sold according to your valuation.

28 'Nevertheless no devoted *offering* that a man may devote to the LORD of all that he has, *both* man and beast, or the field of his possession, shall be sold or redeemed; every devoted *offering is* most holy to the LORD. 29 No person under the ban, who may become doomed to destruction among men, shall be redeemed, *but* shall surely be put to death. 30 And all the tithe of the land, *whether* of the seed of the land *or* of the fruit of the tree, *is* the LORD's. It *is* holy to the LORD. 31 If a man wants at all to redeem *any* of his tithes, he shall add one-fifth to it. 32 And concerning the tithe of the herd or the flock, of whatever passes under the rod, the tenth one shall be holy to the LORD. 33 He shall not inquire whether it is good or bad, nor shall he exchange it; and if he exchanges it at all, then both it and the one exchanged for it shall be holy; it shall not be redeemed.' "

34 These *are* the commandments which the LORD commanded Moses for the children of Israel on Mount Sinai.

PSALM 29:1–6

1   GIVE unto the LORD, O you mighty ones,
    Give unto the LORD glory and strength.

2   Give unto the LORD the glory due to
    His name;
    Worship the LORD in the beauty of
    holiness.

3   The voice of the LORD *is* over the
    waters;
    The God of glory thunders;
    The LORD *is* over many waters.
4   The voice of the LORD *is* powerful;
    The voice of the LORD *is* full of majesty.
5   The voice of the LORD breaks the
    cedars,
    Yes, the LORD splinters the cedars of
    Lebanon.
6   He makes them also skip like a calf,
    Lebanon and Sirion like a young wild
    ox.

PROVERBS 10:22–25

22 THE blessing of the LORD makes *one*
    rich,
    And He adds no sorrow with it.

23 To do evil *is* like sport to a fool,
    But a man of understanding has
    wisdom.
24 The fear of the wicked will come upon
    him,
    And the desire of the righteous will be
    granted.
25 When the whirlwind passes by, the
    wicked *is* no *more,*
    But the righteous *has* an everlasting
    foundation.

MARK 7:1–13

THEN the Pharisees and some of the scribes
came together to Him, having come from
Jerusalem. 2 Now when they saw some of
His disciples eat bread with defiled, that
is, with unwashed hands, they found fault.

3 For the Pharisees and all the Jews do not
eat unless they wash *their* hands in a special
way, holding the tradition of the elders.
4 *When they come* from the marketplace, they
do not eat unless they wash. And there are
many other things which they have received
and hold, *like* the washing of cups, pitchers,
copper vessels, and couches.
5 Then the Pharisees and scribes asked
Him, "Why do Your disciples not walk according to the tradition of the elders, but
eat bread with unwashed hands?"
6 He answered and said to them, "Well
did Isaiah prophesy of you hypocrites, as
it is written:

'This people honors Me with *their*
    lips,
    But their heart is far from Me.
7   And in vain they worship Me,
    Teaching *as* doctrines the
        commandments of men.'

8 For laying aside the commandment of
God, you hold the tradition of men—the
washing of pitchers and cups, and many
other such things you do."
9 He said to them, "*All too* well you reject
the commandment of God, that you may
keep your tradition. 10 For Moses said,
'Honor your father and your mother'; and,
'He who curses father or mother, let him
be put to death.' 11 But you say, 'If a man
says to his father or mother, "Whatever
profit you might have received from me *is*
Corban"—' (that is, a gift *to God*), 12 then
you no longer let him do anything for his
father or his mother, 13 making the word
of God of no effect through your tradition
which you have handed down. And many
such things you do."

---

*T*ake *heed to yourself, take heed how
you read, and above all don't
argue.*   (WORKMEN)

◆◆◆

Reading 61—Hand Over Your Heart
Mark 7:21, 22

This passage is detestable to an unspiritual person, it is in absolutely bad
taste, nine out of every ten people do not believe it because they are
grossly ignorant about the heart. In these verses Jesus Christ says, to put it in
modern language, "No crime has ever been committed that every human being

is not capable of committing." Do I believe that? Do you? If we do not, remember we pass a verdict straight off on the Lord Jesus Christ, we tell Him He does not know what He is talking about. We read that Jesus "knew what was in man," meaning that He knew men's hearts; and the apostle Paul emphasizes the same thing—"Don't glory in man; trust only the grace of God in yourself and in other people." No wonder Jesus Christ pleads with us to give over the keeping of our hearts to Him so that He can fill them with a new life! Every characteristic seen in the life of Jesus Christ becomes possible in our lives when once we hand over our hearts to Him to be filled with the Holy Spirit.

(*Bib. Psych.*)

NUMBERS 1:1—2:34

NOW the LORD spoke to Moses in the Wilderness of Sinai, in the tabernacle of meeting, on the first *day* of the second month, in the second year after they had come out of the land of Egypt, saying: 2 "Take a census of all the congregation of the children of Israel, by their families, by their fathers' houses, according to the number of names, every male individually, 3 from twenty years old and above—all who *are able to* go to war in Israel. You and Aaron shall number them by their armies.

The reason for [Israel's] survival is the purpose of God to be fulfilled through them. (GENESIS)

---

4 And with you there shall be a man from every tribe, each one the head of his father's house.

5 "These are the names of the men who shall stand with you: from Reuben, Elizur the son of Shedeur; 6 from Simeon, Shelumiel the son of Zurishaddai; 7 from Judah, Nahshon the son of Amminadab; 8 from Issachar, Nethanel the son of Zuar; 9 from Zebulun, Eliab the son of Helon; 10 from the sons of Joseph: from Ephraim, Elishama the son of Ammihud; from Manasseh, Gamaliel the son of Pedahzur; 11 from Benjamin, Abidan the son of Gideoni; 12 from Dan, Ahiezer the son of Ammishaddai; 13 from Asher, Pagiel the son of Ocran; 14 from Gad, Eliasaph the son of Deuel; 15 from Naphtali, Ahira the son of Enan." 16 These *were* chosen from the congregation, leaders of their fathers' tribes, heads of the divisions in Israel.

17 Then Moses and Aaron took these men who had been mentioned by name, 18 and they assembled all the congregation together on the first *day* of the second month; and they recited their ancestry by families, by their fathers' houses, according

to the number of names, from twenty years old and above, each one individually. 19 As the LORD commanded Moses, so he numbered them in the Wilderness of Sinai.

20 Now the children of Reuben, Israel's oldest son, their genealogies by their families, by their fathers' house, according to the number of names, every male individually, from twenty years old and above, all who *were able to* go to war: 21 those who were numbered of the tribe of Reuben *were* forty-six thousand five hundred.

22 From the children of Simeon, their genealogies by their families, by their fathers' house, of those who were numbered, according to the number of names, every male individually, from twenty years old and above, all who *were able to* go to war: 23 those who were numbered of the tribe of Simeon *were* fifty-nine thousand three hundred.

24 From the children of Gad, their genealogies by their families, by their fathers' house, according to the number of names, from twenty years old and above, all who *were able to* go to war: 25 those who were numbered of the tribe of Gad *were* forty-five thousand six hundred and fifty.

26 From the children of Judah, their genealogies by their families, by their fathers' house, according to the number of names, from twenty years old and above, all who *were able to* go to war: 27 those who were numbered of the tribe of Judah *were* seventy-four thousand six hundred.

28 From the children of Issachar, their genealogies by their families, by their fathers' house, according to the number of names, from twenty years old and above, all who *were able to* go to war: 29 those who were numbered of the tribe of Issachar *were* fifty-four thousand four hundred.

30 From the children of Zebulun, their genealogies by their families, by their fathers' house, according to the number of names, from twenty years old and above, all who *were able to* go to war: 31 those who were numbered of the tribe of Zebulun *were* fifty-seven thousand four hundred.

32 From the sons of Joseph, the children of Ephraim, their genealogies by their families, by their fathers' house, according to the number of names, from twenty years old and above, all who *were able to* go to war: 33 those who were numbered of the tribe of Ephraim *were* forty thousand five hundred.

34 From the children of Manasseh, their genealogies by their families, by their fathers' house, according to the number of names, from twenty years old and above, all who *were able to* go to war: 35 those who were numbered of the tribe of Manasseh *were* thirty-two thousand two hundred.

36 From the children of Benjamin, their genealogies by their families, by their fathers' house, according to the number of names, from twenty years old and above, all who *were able to* go to war: 37 those who were numbered of the tribe of Benjamin *were* thirty-five thousand four hundred.

38 From the children of Dan, their genealogies by their families, by their fathers' house, according to the number of names, from twenty years old and above, all who *were able to* go to war: 39 those who were numbered of the tribe of Dan *were* sixty-two thousand seven hundred.

40 From the children of Asher, their genealogies by their families, by their fathers' house, according to the number of names, from twenty years old and above, all who *were able to* go to war: 41 those who were numbered of the tribe of Asher *were* forty-one thousand five hundred.

42 From the children of Naphtali, their genealogies by their families, by their fathers' house, according to the number of names, from twenty years old and above, all who *were able to* go to war: 43 those who were numbered of the tribe of Naphtali *were* fifty-three thousand four hundred.

44 These are the ones who were numbered, whom Moses and Aaron numbered, with the leaders of Israel, twelve men, each one representing his father's house. 45 So all who were numbered of the children of Israel, by their fathers' houses, from twenty years old and above, all who *were able to* go to war in Israel— 46 all who were numbered were six hundred and three thousand five hundred and fifty.

47 But the Levites were not numbered among them by their fathers' tribe; 48 for the LORD had spoken to Moses, saying: 49 "Only the tribe of Levi you shall not number, nor take a census of them among the children of Israel; 50 but you shall appoint the Levites over the tabernacle of the Testimony, over all its furnishings, and over all things that belong to it; they shall carry the tabernacle and all its furnishings; they shall attend to it and camp around the tabernacle. 51 And when the tabernacle is to go forward, the Levites shall take it down; and when the tabernacle is to be set up, the Levites shall set it up. The outsider who comes near shall be put to death. 52 The children of Israel shall pitch their tents, everyone by his own camp, everyone by his own standard, according to their armies; 53 but the Levites shall camp around the tabernacle of the Testimony, that there may be no wrath on the congregation of the children of Israel; and the Levites shall keep charge of the tabernacle of the Testimony."

54 Thus the children of Israel did; according to all that the LORD commanded Moses, so they did.

2 AND the LORD spoke to Moses and Aaron, saying: 2 "Everyone of the children of Israel shall camp by his own standard, beside the emblems of his father's house; they shall camp some distance from the tabernacle of meeting. 3 On the east side, toward the rising of the sun, those of the standard of the forces with Judah shall camp according to their armies; and Nahshon the son of Amminadab *shall be* the leader of the children of Judah." 4 And his army was numbered at seventy-four thousand six hundred.

5 "Those who camp next to him *shall be* the tribe of Issachar, and Nethanel the son of Zuar *shall be* the leader of the children of Issachar." 6 And his army was numbered at fifty-four thousand four hundred.

7 "Then *comes* the tribe of Zebulun, and Eliab the son of Helon *shall be* the leader of the children of Zebulun." 8 And his army was numbered at fifty-seven thousand four hundred. 9 "All who were numbered according to their armies of the forces with Judah, one hundred and eighty-six thousand four hundred—these shall break camp first.

10 "On the south side *shall be* the standard of the forces with Reuben according to their armies, and the leader of the children of Reuben *shall be* Elizur the son of Shedeur." 11 And his army was numbered at forty-six thousand five hundred.

12 "Those who camp next to him *shall be* the tribe of Simeon, and the leader of the children of Simeon *shall be* Shelumiel the son of Zurishaddai." 13 And his army was numbered at fifty-nine thousand three hundred.

14 "Then *comes* the tribe of Gad, and the

leader of the children of Gad *shall be* Eliasaph the son of Reuel." 15 And his army was numbered at forty-five thousand six hundred and fifty. 16 "All who were numbered according to their armies of the forces with Reuben, one hundred and fifty-one thousand four hundred and fifty—they shall be the second to break camp.

17 "And the tabernacle of meeting shall move out with the camp of the Levites in the middle of the camps; as they camp, so they shall move out, everyone in his place, by their standards.

18 "On the west side *shall be* the standard of the forces with Ephraim according to their armies, and the leader of the children of Ephraim *shall be* Elishama the son of Ammihud." 19 And his army was numbered at forty thousand five hundred.

20 "Next to him *comes* the tribe of Manasseh, and the leader of the children of Manasseh *shall be* Gamaliel the son of Pedahzur." 21 And his army was numbered at thirty-two thousand two hundred.

22 "Then *comes* the tribe of Benjamin, and the leader of the children of Benjamin *shall be* Abidan the son of Gideoni." 23 And his army was numbered at thirty-five thousand four hundred. 24 "All who were numbered according to their armies of the forces with Ephraim, one hundred and eight thousand one hundred—they shall be the third to break camp.

25 "The standard of the forces with Dan *shall be* on the north side according to their armies, and the leader of the children of Dan *shall be* Ahiezer the son of Ammishaddai." 26 And his army was numbered at sixty-two thousand seven hundred.

27 "Those who camp next to him *shall be* the tribe of Asher, and the leader of the children of Asher *shall be* Pagiel the son of Ocran." 28 And his army was numbered at forty-one thousand five hundred.

29 "Then *comes* the tribe of Naphtali, and the leader of the children of Naphtali *shall be* Ahira the son of Enan." 30 And his army was numbered at fifty-three thousand four hundred. 31 "All who were numbered of the forces with Dan, one hundred and fifty-seven thousand six hundred—they shall break camp last, with their standards."

32 These *are* the ones who were numbered of the children of Israel by their fathers' houses. All who were numbered according to their armies of the forces *were* six hundred and three thousand five hundred and fifty. 33 But the Levites were not numbered among the children of Israel, just as the LORD commanded Moses.

34 Thus the children of Israel did according to all that the LORD commanded Moses; so they camped by their standards and so they broke camp, each one by his family, according to their fathers' houses.

PSALM 29:7–11

7 THE voice of the LORD divides the flames of fire.

8 The voice of the LORD shakes the wilderness;
The LORD shakes the Wilderness of Kadesh.
9 The voice of the LORD makes the deer give birth,
And strips the forests bare;
And in His temple everyone says, "Glory!"

10 The LORD sat *enthroned* at the Flood,
And the LORD sits as King forever.
11 The LORD will give strength to His people;
The LORD will bless His people with peace.

PROVERBS 10:26–29

26 AS vinegar to the teeth and smoke to the eyes,
So *is* the lazy *man* to those who send him.

27 The fear of the LORD prolongs days,
But the years of the wicked will be shortened.
28 The hope of the righteous *will be* gladness,
But the expectation of the wicked will perish.
29 The way of the LORD *is* strength for the upright,
But destruction *will come* to the workers of iniquity.

MARK 7:14–37

WHEN He had called all the multitude to *Himself,* He said to them, "Hear Me, everyone, and understand: 15 There is nothing that enters a man from outside which can defile him; but the things which come out of him, those are the things that defile a man. 16 If anyone has ears to hear, let him hear!"

Unless I have received the Holy Spirit my personality is dead to all God has to say.   (GLORY)

17 When He had entered a house away from the crowd, His disciples asked Him concerning the parable. 18 So He said to them, "Are you thus without understanding also? Do you not perceive that whatever enters a man from outside cannot defile him, 19 because it does not enter his heart but his stomach, and is eliminated, *thus* purifying all foods?" 20 And He said, "What comes out of a man, that defiles a man. 21 For from within, out of the heart of men, proceed evil thoughts, adulteries, fornications, murders, 22 thefts, covetousness, wickedness, deceit, lewdness, an evil eye, blasphemy, pride, foolishness. 23 All these evil things come from within and defile a man."

24 From there He arose and went to the region of Tyre and Sidon. And He entered a house and wanted no one to know *it*, but He could not be hidden. 25 For a woman whose young daughter had an unclean spirit heard about Him, and she came and fell at His feet. 26 The woman was a Greek, a Syro-Phoenician by birth, and she kept asking Him to cast the demon out of her daughter. 27 But Jesus said to her, "Let the children be filled first, for it is not good to take the children's bread and throw *it* to the little dogs."

28 And she answered and said to Him, "Yes, Lord, yet even the little dogs under the table eat from the children's crumbs."

29 Then He said to her, "For this saying go your way; the demon has gone out of your daughter."

30 And when she had come to her house, she found the demon gone out, and her daughter lying on the bed.

31 Again, departing from the region of Tyre and Sidon, He came through the midst of the region of Decapolis to the Sea of Galilee. 32 Then they brought to Him one who was deaf and had an impediment in his speech, and they begged Him to put His hand on him. 33 And He took him aside from the multitude, and put His fingers in his ears, and He spat and touched his tongue. 34 Then, looking up to heaven, He sighed, and said to him, "Ephphatha," that is, "Be opened."

35 Immediately his ears were opened, and the impediment of his tongue was loosed, and he spoke plainly. 36 Then He commanded them that they should tell no one; but the more He commanded them, the more widely they proclaimed *it*. 37 And they were astonished beyond measure, saying, "He has done all things well. He makes both the deaf to hear and the mute to speak."

Reading 62—The End of Prayer
Psalm 30:1, 2

Never *say* you will pray about a thing; *pray about it*. Our Lord's teaching about prayer is so amazingly simple but at the same time so amazingly profound that we are apt to miss His meaning. The danger is to water down what Jesus says about prayer and make it mean something more common sense; if it were only common sense, it was not worth His while to say it. The things Jesus says about prayer are supernatural revelations.

"For your Father knows the things you have need of before you ask Him" (Matt. 6:8). If God sees that my spiritual life will be furthered by giving the things for which I ask, then He will give them, but that is not the end of prayer. The end of prayer is that I come to know God Himself. If I allow my bodily needs to get out of relationship to God, then those needs will keep me morbidly interested in myself all the time, much to the Devil's enjoyment. We have to leave ourselves resolutely in God's hands and launch out into the work of intercession on the basis of faith in the perfect redemption of Jesus.

(BRILL. HERITAGE)

NUMBERS 3:1—4:49

NOW these *are* the records of Aaron and Moses when the Lord spoke with Moses on Mount Sinai. 2 And these *are* the names of the sons of Aaron: Nadab, the firstborn, and Abihu, Eleazar, and Ithamar. 3 These *are* the names of the sons of Aaron, the anointed priests, whom he consecrated to minister as priests. 4 Nadab and Abihu had died before the Lord when they offered profane fire before the Lord in the Wilderness of Sinai; and they had no children. So Eleazar and Ithamar ministered as priests in the presence of Aaron their father.

5 And the Lord spoke to Moses, saying: 6 "Bring the tribe of Levi near, and present them before Aaron the priest, that they may serve him. 7 And they shall attend to his needs and the needs of the whole congregation before the tabernacle of meeting, to do the work of the tabernacle. 8 Also they shall attend to all the furnishings of the tabernacle of meeting, and to the needs of the children of Israel, to do the work of the tabernacle. 9 And you shall give the Levites to Aaron and his sons; they *are* given entirely to him from among the children of Israel. 10 So you shall appoint Aaron and his sons, and they shall attend to their priesthood; but the outsider who comes near shall be put to death."

11 Then the Lord spoke to Moses, saying: 12 "Now behold, I Myself have taken the Levites from among the children of Israel instead of every firstborn who opens the womb among the children of Israel. Therefore the Levites shall be Mine, 13 because all the firstborn *are* Mine. On the day that I struck all the firstborn in the land of Egypt, I sanctified to Myself all the firstborn in Israel, both man and beast. They shall be Mine: I *am* the Lord."

14 Then the Lord spoke to Moses in the Wilderness of Sinai, saying: 15 "Number the children of Levi by their fathers' houses, by their families; you shall number every male from a month old and above."

16 So Moses numbered them according to the word of the Lord, as he was commanded. 17 These were the sons of Levi by their names: Gershon, Kohath, and Merari. 18 And these *are* the names of the sons of Gershon by their families: Libni and Shimei. 19 And the sons of Kohath by their families: Amram, Izehar, Hebron, and Uzziel. 20 And the sons of Merari by their families: Mahli and Mushi. These *are* the families of the Levites by their fathers' houses.

21 From Gershon *came* the family of the Libnites and the family of the Shimites; these *were* the families of the Gershonites. 22 Those who were numbered, according to the number of all the males from a month old and above—of those who were numbered *there were* seven thousand five hundred. 23 The families of the Gershonites were to camp behind the tabernacle westward. 24 And the leader of the father's house of the Gershonites *was* Eliasaph the son of Lael. 25 The duties of the children of Gershon in the tabernacle of meeting *included* the tabernacle, the tent with its covering, the screen for the door of the tabernacle of meeting, 26 the screen for the door of the court, the hangings of the court which *are* around the tabernacle and the altar, and their cords, according to all the work relating to them.

27 From Kohath *came* the family of the Amramites, the family of the Izharites, the family of the Hebronites, and the family of the Uzzielites; these *were* the families of the Kohathites. 28 According to the number of all the males, from a month old and above, *there were* eight thousand six hundred keeping charge of the sanctuary. 29 The families of the children of Kohath were to camp on the south side of the tabernacle. 30 And the leader of the fathers' house of the families of the Kohathites *was* Elizaphan the son of Uzziel. 31 Their duty *included* the ark, the table, the lampstand, the altars, the utensils of the sanctuary with which they ministered, the screen, and all the work relating to them.

32 And Eleazar the son of Aaron the priest *was to be* chief over the leaders of the Levites, *with* oversight of those who kept charge of the sanctuary.

33 From Merari *came* the family of the Mahlites and the family of the Mushites; these *were* the families of Merari. 34 And those who were numbered, according to the number of all the males from a month old and above, *were* six thousand two hundred. 35 The leader of the fathers' house of the families of Merari *was* Zuriel the son of Abihail. These *were* to camp on the north side of the tabernacle. 36 And the appointed duty of the children of Merari *included* the boards of the tabernacle, its bars, its pillars, its sockets, its utensils, all the work relating to them, 37 and the pillars of the court all around, with their sockets, their pegs, and their cords.

38 Moreover those who were to camp before the tabernacle on the east, before the tabernacle of meeting, *were* Moses, Aaron, and his sons, keeping charge of the sanctuary, to meet the needs of the children of

Israel; but the outsider who came near was to be put to death. 39 All who were numbered of the Levites, whom Moses and Aaron numbered at the commandment of the LORD, by their families, all the males from a month old and above, *were* twenty-two thousand.

40 Then the LORD said to Moses: "Number all the firstborn males of the children of Israel from a month old and above, and take the number of their names. 41 And you shall take the Levites for Me—I *am* the LORD—instead of all the firstborn among the children of Israel, and the livestock of the Levites instead of all the firstborn among the livestock of the children of Israel." 42 So Moses numbered all the firstborn among the children of Israel, as the LORD commanded him. 43 And all the firstborn males, according to the number of names from a month old and above, of those who were numbered of them, were twenty-two thousand two hundred and seventy-three.

44 Then the LORD spoke to Moses, saying: 45 "Take the Levites instead of all the firstborn among the children of Israel, and the livestock of the Levites instead of their livestock. The Levites shall be Mine: I *am* the LORD. 46 And for the redemption of the two hundred and seventy-three of the firstborn of the children of Israel, who are more than the number of the Levites, 47 you shall take five shekels for each one individually; you shall take *them* in the currency of the shekel of the sanctuary, the shekel of twenty gerahs. 48 And you shall give the money, with which the excess number of them is redeemed, to Aaron and his sons."

49 So Moses took the redemption money from those who were over and above those who were redeemed by the Levites. 50 From the firstborn of the children of Israel he took the money, one thousand three hundred and sixty-five *shekels,* according to the shekel of the sanctuary. 51 And Moses gave their redemption money to Aaron and his sons, according to the word of the LORD, as the LORD commanded Moses.

4 THEN the LORD spoke to Moses and Aaron, saying: 2 "Take a census of the sons of Kohath from among the children of Levi, by their families, by their fathers' house, 3 from thirty years old and above, even to fifty years old, all who enter the service to do the work in the tabernacle of meeting.

4 "This *is* the service of the sons of Kohath in the tabernacle of meeting, *relating to* the most holy things: 5 When the camp prepares to journey, Aaron and his sons shall come, and they shall take down the covering veil and cover the ark of the Testimony with it. 6 Then they shall put on it a covering of badger skins, and spread over *that* a cloth entirely of blue; and they shall insert its poles.

7 "On the table of showbread they shall spread a blue cloth, and put on it the dishes, the pans, the bowls, and the pitchers for pouring; and the showbread shall be on it. 8 They shall spread over them a scarlet cloth, and cover the same with a covering of badger skins; and they shall insert its poles. 9 And they shall take a blue cloth and cover the lampstand of the light, with its lamps, its wick-trimmers, its trays, and all its oil vessels, with which they service it. 10 Then they shall put it with all its utensils in a covering of badger skins, and put *it* on a carrying beam.

11 "Over the golden altar they shall spread a blue cloth, and cover it with a covering of badger skins; and they shall insert its poles. 12 Then they shall take all the utensils of service with which they minister in the sanctuary, put *them* in a blue cloth, cover them with a covering of badger skins, and put *them* on a carrying beam. 13 Also they shall take away the ashes from the altar, and spread a purple cloth over it. 14 They shall put on it all its implements with which they minister there—the firepans, the forks, the shovels, the basins, and all the utensils of the altar—and they shall spread on it a covering of badger skins, and insert its poles. 15 And when Aaron and his sons have finished covering the sanctuary and all the furnishings of the sanctuary, when the camp is set to go, then the sons of Kohath shall come to carry *them;* but they shall not touch any holy thing, lest they die.

"These *are* the things in the tabernacle of meeting which the sons of Kohath are to carry.

16 "The appointed duty of Eleazar the son of Aaron the priest *is* the oil for the light, the sweet incense, the daily grain offering, the anointing oil, the oversight of all the tabernacle, of all that *is* in it, with the sanctuary and its furnishings."

17 Then the LORD spoke to Moses and Aaron, saying: 18 "Do not cut off the tribe of the families of the Kohathites from among the Levites; 19 but do this in regard to them, that they may live and not die when they approach the most holy things: Aaron and his sons shall go in and appoint each of them to his service and his task. 20 But they shall not go in to watch while

the holy things are being covered, lest they die."

21 Then the LORD spoke to Moses, saying: 22 "Also take a census of the sons of Gershon, by their fathers' house, by their families. 23 From thirty years old and above, even to fifty years old, you shall number them, all who enter to perform the service, to do the work in the tabernacle of meeting. 24 This *is* the service of the families of the Gershonites, in serving and carrying: 25 They shall carry the curtains of the tabernacle and the tabernacle of meeting *with* its covering, the covering of badger skins that *is* on it, the screen for the door of the tabernacle of meeting, 26 the screen for the door of the gate of the court, the hangings of the court which *are* around the tabernacle and altar, and their cords, all the furnishings for their service and all that is made for these things: so shall they serve.

27 "Aaron and his sons shall assign all the service of the sons of the Gershonites, all their tasks and all their service. And you shall appoint to them all their tasks as their duty. 28 This *is* the service of the families of the sons of Gershon in the tabernacle of meeting. And their duties *shall be* under the authority of Ithamar the son of Aaron the priest.

29 "*As for* the sons of Merari, you shall number them by their families and by their fathers' house. 30 From thirty years old and above, even to fifty years old, you shall number them, everyone who enters the service to do the work of the tabernacle of meeting. 31 And this *is* what they must carry as all their service for the tabernacle of meeting: the boards of the tabernacle, its bars, its pillars, its sockets, 32 and the pillars around the court with their sockets, pegs, and cords, with all their furnishings and all their service; and you shall assign *to each man* by name the items he must carry. 33 This *is* the service of the families of the sons of Merari, as all their service for the tabernacle of meeting, under the authority of Ithamar the son of Aaron the priest."

34 And Moses, Aaron, and the leaders of the congregation numbered the sons of the Kohathites by their families and by their fathers' house, 35 from thirty years old and above, even to fifty years old, everyone who entered the service for work in the tabernacle of meeting; 36 and those who were numbered by their families were two thousand seven hundred and fifty. 37 These *were* the ones who were numbered of the families of the Kohathites, all who might serve in the tabernacle of meeting, whom Moses and Aaron numbered according to the commandment of the LORD by the hand of Moses.

38 And those who were numbered of the sons of Gershon, by their families and by their fathers' house, 39 from thirty years old and above, even to fifty years old, everyone who entered the service for work in the tabernacle of meeting— 40 those who were numbered by their families, by their fathers' house, were two thousand six hundred and thirty. 41 These *are* the ones who were numbered of the families of the sons of Gershon, of all who might serve in the tabernacle of meeting, whom Moses and Aaron numbered according to the commandment of the LORD.

42 Those of the families of the sons of Merari who were numbered, by their families, by their fathers' house, 43 from thirty years old and above, even to fifty years old, everyone who entered the service for work in the tabernacle of meeting— 44 those who were numbered by their families were three thousand two hundred. 45 These *are* the ones who were numbered of the families of the sons of Merari, whom Moses and Aaron numbered according to the word of the LORD by the hand of Moses.

46 All who were numbered of the Levites, whom Moses, Aaron, and the leaders of Israel numbered, by their families and by their fathers' houses, 47 from thirty years old and above, even to fifty years old, everyone who came to do the work of service and the work of bearing burdens in the tabernacle of meeting— 48 those who were numbered were eight thousand five hundred and eighty.

49 According to the commandment of the LORD they were numbered by the hand of Moses, each according to his service and according to his task; thus were they numbered by him, as the LORD commanded Moses.

PSALM 30:1–7

1 I will extol You, O LORD, for You have lifted me up,
And have not let my foes rejoice over me.

2 O LORD my God, I cried out to You,
And You healed me.

3 O LORD, You brought my soul up from the grave;
You have kept me alive, that I should not go down to the pit.

4 Sing praise to the LORD, you saints of His,

And give thanks at the remembrance
of His holy name.

5 For His anger *is but for* a moment,
His favor *is for* life;
Weeping may endure for a night,
But joy *comes* in the morning.

---

*H*appiness depends on what happens;
joy does not.   (RUN)

---

6 Now in my prosperity I said,
"I shall never be moved."
7 LORD, by Your favor You have made
my mountain stand strong;
You hid Your face, *and* I was troubled.

PROVERBS 10:30–32

30 THE righteous will never be removed,
But the wicked will not inhabit the
earth.
31 The mouth of the righteous brings forth
wisdom,
But the perverse tongue will be cut out.
32 The lips of the righteous know what
is acceptable,
But the mouth of the wicked *what is*
perverse.

MARK 8:1–21

IN those days, the multitude being very
great and having nothing to eat, Jesus called
His disciples *to Him* and said to them,
2 "I have compassion on the multitude, because they have now continued with Me
three days and have nothing to eat.
3 And if I send them away hungry to their
own houses, they will faint on the way;
for some of them have come from afar."
4 Then His disciples answered Him,
"How can one satisfy these people with
bread here in the wilderness?"
5 He asked them, "How many loaves do
you have?"
And they said, "Seven."
6 So He commanded the multitude to
sit down on the ground. And He took the

seven loaves and gave thanks, broke *them*
and gave *them* to His disciples to set before
them; and they set *them* before the multitude. 7 They also had a few small fish; and
having blessed them, He said to set them
also before *them.* 8 So they ate and were
filled, and they took up seven large baskets
of leftover fragments. 9 Now those who had
eaten were about four thousand. And He
sent them away, 10 immediately got into
the boat with His disciples, and came to
the region of Dalmanutha.

11 Then the Pharisees came out and began
to dispute with Him, seeking from Him a
sign from heaven, testing Him. 12 But He
sighed deeply in His spirit, and said, "Why
does this generation seek a sign? Assuredly,
I say to you, no sign shall be given to this
generation."

13 And He left them, and getting into
the boat again, departed to the other side.
14 Now the disciples had forgotten to take
bread, and they did not have more than
one loaf with them in the boat. 15 Then
He charged them, saying, "Take heed, beware of the leaven of the Pharisees and the
leaven of Herod."

16 And they reasoned among themselves,
saying, "*It is* because we have no bread."
17 But Jesus, being aware of *it,* said to
them, "Why do you reason because you
have no bread? Do you not yet perceive
nor understand? Is your heart still hardened? 18 Having eyes, do you not see? And

---

*U*ntil a man is born again what
Jesus says does not mean anything
to him.   (SERMON MT.)

---

having ears, do you not hear? And do you
not remember? 19 When I broke the five
loaves for the five thousand, how many baskets full of fragments did you take up?"
They said to Him, "Twelve."
20 "Also, when I broke the seven for the
four thousand, how many large baskets full
of fragments did you take up?"
And they said, "Seven."
21 So He said to them, "How *is it* you
do not understand?"

Reading 63—The Instant Spirit
Mark 8:34, 35

Jesus says if a man gains himself, he loses himself; and if he loses himself for His sake, he gains himself.

Beware of introducing the idea of time; the instant the Spirit of God touches your spirit, it is manifested in the body. Do not get the idea of a three-storied building with a vague, mysterious, ethereal upper story called spirit, a middle story called soul, and a lower story called body. We are personality, which shows itself in three phases—spirit, soul, and body. Never think that what energizes the spirit takes time before it gets into the soul and body, it shows itself instantly, from the crown of the head to the soles of the feet.

Jesus says that men are capable of missing the supreme good and His point of view is not acceptable to us because we do not believe we are capable of missing it. We are far removed from Jesus Christ's point of view today, we take the natural rationalistic line, and His teaching is no good whatever unless we believe the main gist of His gospel, namely, that we have to have something planted into us by supernatural grace. Jesus Christ's point of view is that a man may miss the chief good; we like to believe we will end all right somehow, but Jesus says we won't. If my feet are going in one direction, I cannot advance one step in the opposite direction unless I turn right round.   (*Good*)

NUMBERS 5:1—6:27

AND the LORD spoke to Moses, saying: 2 "Command the children of Israel that they put out of the camp every leper, everyone who has a discharge, and whoever becomes defiled by a corpse. 3 You shall put out both male and female; you shall put them outside the camp, that they may not defile their camps in the midst of which I dwell." 4 And the children of Israel did so, and put them outside the camp; as the LORD spoke to Moses, so the children of Israel did.

5 Then the LORD spoke to Moses, saying, 6 "Speak to the children of Israel: 'When a man or woman commits any sin that men commit in unfaithfulness against the LORD, and that person is guilty, 7 then he shall confess the sin which he has committed. He shall make restitution for his trespass in full, plus one-fifth of it, and give *it* to the one he has wronged. 8 But if the man has no relative to whom restitution may be made for the wrong, the restitution for the wrong *must go* to the LORD for the priest, in addition to the ram of the atonement with which atonement is made for him. 9 Every offering of all the holy things of the children of Israel, which they bring to the priest, shall be his. 10 And every man's holy things shall be his; whatever any man gives the priest shall be his.' "

11 And the LORD spoke to Moses, saying, 12 "Speak to the children of Israel, and say to them: 'If any man's wife goes astray and behaves unfaithfully toward him, 13 and a man lies with her carnally, and it is hidden from the eyes of her husband, and it is concealed that she has defiled herself, and *there was* no witness against her, nor was she caught— 14 if the spirit of jealousy comes upon him and he becomes jealous of his wife, who has defiled herself; or if the spirit of jealousy comes upon him and he becomes jealous of his wife, although she has not defiled herself— 15 then the man shall bring his wife to the priest. He shall bring the offering required for her, one-tenth of an ephah of barley meal; he shall pour no oil on it and put no frankincense on it, because it *is* a grain offering of jealousy, an offering for remembering, for bringing iniquity to remembrance.

16 'And the priest shall bring her near, and set her before the LORD. 17 The priest shall take holy water in an earthen vessel, and take some of the dust that is on the floor of the tabernacle and put *it* into the water. 18 Then the priest shall stand the woman before the LORD, uncover the woman's head, and put the offering for remembering in her hands, which *is* the grain offering of jealousy. And the priest shall have in his hand the bitter water that brings a curse. 19 And the priest shall put her under

oath, and say to the woman, "If no man has lain with you, and if you have not gone astray to uncleanness *while* under your husband's *authority,* be free from this bitter water that brings a curse. 20 But if you have gone astray *while* under your husband's *authority,* and if you have defiled yourself and some man other than your husband has lain with you"— 21 then the priest shall put the woman under the oath of the curse, and he shall say to the woman—"the Lord make you a curse and an oath among your people, when the Lord makes your thigh rot and your belly swell; 22 and may this water that causes the curse go into your stomach, and make *your* belly swell and *your* thigh rot."

'Then the woman shall say, "Amen, so be it."

23 'Then the priest shall write these curses in a book, and he shall scrape *them* off into the bitter water. 24 And he shall make the woman drink the bitter water that brings a curse, and the water that brings the curse shall enter her *to become* bitter. 25 Then the priest shall take the grain offering of jealousy from the woman's hand, shall wave the offering before the Lord, and bring it to the altar; 26 and the priest shall take a handful of the offering, as its memorial portion, burn *it* on the altar, and afterward make the woman drink the water. 27 When he has made her drink the water, then it shall be, if she has defiled herself and behaved unfaithfully toward her husband, that the water that brings a curse will enter her *and become* bitter, and her belly will swell, her thigh will rot, and the woman will become a curse among her people. 28 But if the woman has not defiled herself, and is clean, then she shall be free and may conceive children.

29 'This *is* the law of jealousy, when a wife, *while* under her husband's *authority,* goes astray and defiles herself, 30 or when the spirit of jealousy comes upon a man, and he becomes jealous of his wife; then he shall stand the woman before the Lord, and the priest shall execute all this law upon her. 31 Then the man shall be free from iniquity, but that woman shall bear her guilt.' "

6 THEN the Lord spoke to Moses, saying, 2 "Speak to the children of Israel, and say to them: 'When either a man or woman consecrates an offering to take the vow of a Nazirite, to separate himself to the Lord, 3 he shall separate himself from wine and *similar* drink; he shall drink neither vinegar made from wine nor vinegar made from *similar* drink; neither shall he drink any grape juice, nor eat fresh grapes or raisins. 4 All the days of his separation he shall eat nothing that is produced by the grapevine, from seed to skin.

5 'All the days of the vow of his separation no razor shall come upon his head; until the days are fulfilled for which he separated himself to the Lord, he shall be holy. *Then* he shall let the locks of the hair of his head grow. 6 All the days that he separates himself to the Lord he shall not go near a dead body. 7 He shall not make himself unclean even for his father or his mother, for his brother or his sister, when they die, because his separation to God *is* on his head. 8 All the days of his separation he shall be holy to the Lord.

9 'And if anyone dies very suddenly beside him, and he defiles his consecrated head, then he shall shave his head on the day of his cleansing; on the seventh day he shall shave it. 10 Then on the eighth day he shall bring two turtledoves or two young pigeons to the priest, to the door of the tabernacle of meeting; 11 and the priest shall offer one as a sin offering and *the* other as a burnt offering, and make atonement for him, because he sinned in regard to the corpse; and he shall sanctify his head that same day. 12 He shall consecrate to the Lord the days of his separation, and bring a male lamb in its first year as a trespass offering; but the former days shall be lost, because his separation was defiled.

13 'Now this *is* the law of the Nazirite: When the days of his separation are fulfilled, he shall be brought to the door of the tabernacle of meeting. 14 And he shall present his offering to the Lord: one male lamb in its first year without blemish as a burnt offering, one ewe lamb in its first year without blemish as a sin offering, one ram without blemish as a peace offering, 15 a basket of unleavened bread, cakes of fine flour mixed with oil, unleavened wafers anointed with oil, and their grain offering with their drink offerings.

16 'Then the priest shall bring *them* before the Lord and offer his sin offering and his burnt offering; 17 and he shall offer the ram as a sacrifice of a peace offering to the Lord, with the basket of unleavened bread; the priest shall also offer its grain offering and its drink offering. 18 Then the Nazirite shall shave his consecrated head *at* the door of the tabernacle of meeting, and shall take the hair from his consecrated head and put *it* on the fire which is under the sacrifice of the peace offering.

19 'And the priest shall take the boiled

shoulder of the ram, one unleavened cake from the basket, and one unleavened wafer, and put *them* upon the hands of the Nazirite after he has shaved his consecrated *hair,* 20 and the priest shall wave them as a wave offering before the LORD; they *are* holy for the priest, together with the breast of the wave offering and the thigh of the heave offering. After that the Nazirite may drink wine.'

21 "This is the law of the Nazirite who vows to the LORD the offering for his separation, and besides that, whatever else his hand is able to provide; according to the vow which he takes, so he must do according to the law of his separation."

22 And the LORD spoke to Moses, saying: 23 "Speak to Aaron and his sons, saying, 'This is the way you shall bless the children of Israel. Say to them:

24 "The LORD bless you and keep you;
25 The LORD make His face shine upon you,
   And be gracious to you;
26 The LORD lift up His countenance upon you,
   And give you peace." '

27 "So they shall put My name on the children of Israel, and I will bless them."

PSALM 30:8–12

8 I cried out to You, O LORD;
   And to the LORD I made supplication:
9 "What profit *is there* in my blood,
   When I go down to the pit?
   Will the dust praise You?
   Will it declare Your truth?
10 Hear, O LORD, and have mercy on me;
   LORD, be my helper!"

11 You have turned for me my mourning into dancing;
   You have put off my sackcloth and clothed me with gladness,
12 To the end that *my* glory may sing praise to You and not be silent.
   O LORD my God, I will give thanks to You forever.

PROVERBS 11:1–3

1 DISHONEST scales *are* an abomination to the LORD,
   But a just weight *is* His delight.

2 When pride comes, then comes shame;
   But with the humble *is* wisdom.

3 The integrity of the upright will guide them,
   But the perversity of the unfaithful will destroy them.

MARK 8:22–38

THEN He came to Bethsaida; and they brought a blind man to Him, and begged Him to touch him. 23 So He took the blind man by the hand and led him out of the town. And when He had spit on his eyes and put His hands on him, He asked him if he saw anything.

24 And he looked up and said, "I see men like trees, walking."

25 Then He put *His* hands on his eyes again and made him look up. And he was restored and saw everyone clearly. 26 Then He sent him away to his house, saying, "Neither go into the town, nor tell anyone in the town."

27 Now Jesus and His disciples went out to the towns of Caesarea Philippi; and on the road He asked His disciples, saying to them, "Who do men say that I am?"

28 So they answered, "John the Baptist; but some *say,* Elijah; and others, one of the prophets."

29 He said to them, "But who do you say that I am?"

Peter answered and said to Him, "You are the Christ."

30 Then He strictly warned them that they should tell no one about Him.

31 And He began to teach them that the Son of Man must suffer many things, and be rejected by the elders and chief priests and scribes, and be killed, and after three days rise again. 32 He spoke this word openly. Then Peter took Him aside and began to rebuke Him. 33 But when He had turned around and looked at His disciples, He rebuked Peter, saying, "Get behind Me, Satan! For you are not mindful of the things of God, but the things of men."

There is no royal road to sainthood and discipleship. (CHRIS. DIS. 2)

34 When He had called the people to *Himself,* with His disciples also, He said to them, "Whoever desires to come after Me, let him deny himself, and take up his cross, and follow Me. 35 For whoever desires to save his life will lose it, but whoever loses his life for My sake and the gospel's will save it. 36 For what will it profit a man

if he gains the whole world, and loses his own soul? 37 Or what will a man give in exchange for his soul? 38 For whoever is ashamed of Me and My words in this adul-terous and sinful generation, of him the Son of Man also will be ashamed when He comes in the glory of His Father with the holy angels."

◆◆◆

Reading 64—Is Christ Risen in Us?
Mark 9:9

"Tell no one . . . till the Son of Man had risen from the dead." Is Jesus Christ risen in us? Is He getting His way? When we look back on the choice of our life work, or of our friends, or of what we call our duty, is He really the dominating one? We can soon know whether He is. We say, "Now . . . we believe . . ." and Jesus says, "Do you now believe? Indeed, the hour is coming . . . that you . . . will leave Me alone.". . .

"Tell the vision to no one. . . ." So many do tell, they tell what they saw on the mount and testify to it, but the actual life does not tally with the vision; the Son of Man is not yet risen in them. The words sound all right, but He is not there. There is no communication of His life through the words, no illumination or understanding given to seeking souls, because the Son of Man is not yet risen in them. I wonder when He is going to be formed in us? "My little children, for whom I labor in birth again until Christ is formed in you" (Gal. 4:19). When are we going to believe that unbelievable thing, that we will leave Him alone, in spite of all we say?   (*PLACE HELP*)

NUMBERS 7:1—8:26

NOW it came to pass, when Moses had finished setting up the tabernacle, that he anointed it and consecrated it and all its furnishings, and the altar and all its utensils; so he anointed them and consecrated them. 2 Then the leaders of Israel, the heads of their fathers' houses, who *were* the leaders of the tribes and over those who were num-bered, made an offering. 3 And they brought their offering before the LORD, six covered carts and twelve oxen, a cart for *every* two of the leaders, and for each one an ox; and they presented them before the tabernacle.

4 Then the LORD spoke to Moses, saying, 5 "Accept *these* from them, that they may be used in doing the work of the tabernacle of meeting; and you shall give them to the Levites, *to* every man according to his ser-vice." 6 So Moses took the carts and the oxen, and gave them to the Levites. 7 Two carts and four oxen he gave to the sons of Gershon, according to their service; 8 and four carts and eight oxen he gave to the sons of Merari, according to their ser-vice, under the authority of Ithamar the son of Aaron the priest. 9 But to the sons of Kohath he gave none, because theirs *was* the service of the holy things, *which* they carried on their shoulders.

10 Now the leaders offered the dedication *offering* for the altar when it was anointed; so the leaders offered their offering before the altar. 11 For the LORD said to Moses, "They shall offer their offering, one leader each day, for the dedication of the altar."

12 And the one who offered his offering on the first day *was* Nahshon the son of Amminadab, from the tribe of Judah. 13 His offering *was* one silver platter, the weight of which *was* one hundred and thirty *shekels,* and one silver bowl of seventy shek-els, according to the shekel of the sanctuary, both of them full of fine flour mixed with oil as a grain offering; 14 one gold pan of ten *shekels,* full of incense; 15 one young bull, one ram, and one male lamb in its first year, as a burnt offering; 16 one kid of the goats as a sin offering; 17 and for the sacrifice of peace offerings: two oxen, five rams, five male goats, and five male lambs in their first year. This *was* the offering of Nahshon the son of Amminadab.

18 On the second day Nethanel the son of Zuar, leader of Issachar, presented *an offering.* 19 *For* his offering he offered one

silver platter, the weight of which *was* one hundred and thirty *shekels,* and one silver bowl of seventy shekels, according to the shekel of the sanctuary, both of them full of fine flour mixed with oil as a grain offering; 20 one gold pan of ten *shekels,* full of incense; 21 one young bull, one ram, and one male lamb in its first year, as a burnt offering; 22 one kid of the goats as a sin offering; 23 and as the sacrifice of peace offerings: two oxen, five rams, five male goats, and five male lambs in their first year. This *was* the offering of Nethanel the son of Zuar.

24 On the third day Eliab the son of Helon, leader of the children of Zebulun, *presented an offering.* 25 His offering *was* one silver platter, the weight of which *was* one hundred and thirty *shekels,* and one silver bowl of seventy shekels, according to the shekel of the sanctuary, both of them full of fine flour mixed with oil as a grain offering; 26 one gold pan of ten *shekels,* full of incense; 27 one young bull, one ram, and one male lamb in its first year, as a burnt offering; 28 one kid of the goats as a sin offering; 29 and for the sacrifice of peace offerings: two oxen, five rams, five male goats, and five male lambs in their first year. This *was* the offering of Eliab the son of Helon.

30 On the fourth day Elizur the son of Shedeur, leader of the children of Reuben, *presented an offering.* 31 His offering *was* one silver platter, the weight of which *was* one hundred and thirty *shekels,* and one silver bowl of seventy shekels, according to the shekel of the sanctuary, both of them full of fine flour mixed with oil as a grain offering; 32 one gold pan of ten *shekels,* full of incense; 33 one young bull, one ram, and one male lamb in its first year, as a burnt offering; 34 one kid of the goats as a sin offering; 35 and as the sacrifice of peace offerings: two oxen, five rams, five male goats, and five male lambs in their first year. This *was* the offering of Elizur the son of Shedeur.

36 On the fifth day Shelumiel the son of Zurishaddai, leader of the children of Simeon, *presented an offering.* 37 His offering *was* one silver platter, the weight of which *was* one hundred and thirty *shekels,* and one silver bowl of seventy shekels, according to the shekel of the sanctuary, both of them full of fine flour mixed with oil as a grain offering; 38 one gold pan of ten *shekels,* full of incense; 39 one young bull, one ram, and one male lamb in its first year, as a burnt offering; 40 one kid of the goats as a sin offering; 41 and as the sacrifice of peace of-

ferings: two oxen, five rams, five male goats, and five male lambs in their first year. This *was* the offering of Shelumiel the son of Zurishaddai.

42 On the sixth day Eliasaph the son of Deuel, leader of the children of Gad, *presented an offering.* 43 His offering *was* one silver platter, the weight of which *was* one hundred and thirty *shekels,* and one silver bowl of seventy shekels, according to the shekel of the sanctuary, both of them full of fine flour mixed with oil as a grain offering; 44 one gold pan of ten *shekels,* full of incense; 45 one young bull, one ram, and one male lamb in its first year, as a burnt offering; 46 one kid of the goats as a sin offering; 47 and as the sacrifice of peace offerings: two oxen, five rams, five male goats, and five male lambs in their first year. This *was* the offering of Eliasaph the son of Deuel.

48 On the seventh day Elishama the son of Ammihud, leader of the children of Ephraim, *presented an offering.* 49 His offering *was* one silver platter, the weight of which *was* one hundred and thirty *shekels,* and one silver bowl of seventy shekels, according to the shekel of the sanctuary, both of them full of fine flour mixed with oil as a grain offering; 50 one gold pan of ten *shekels,* full of incense; 51 one young bull, one ram, and one male lamb in its first year, as a burnt offering; 52 one kid of the goats as a sin offering; 53 and as the sacrifice of peace offerings: two oxen, five rams, five male goats, and five male lambs in their first year. This *was* the offering of Elishama the son of Ammihud.

54 On the eighth day Gamaliel the son of Pedahzur, leader of the children of Manasseh, *presented an offering.* 55 His offering *was* one silver platter, the weight of which *was* one hundred and thirty *shekels,* and one silver bowl of seventy shekels, according to the shekel of the sanctuary, both of them full of fine flour mixed with oil as a grain offering; 56 one gold pan of ten *shekels,* full of incense; 57 one young bull, one ram, and one male lamb in its first year, as a burnt offering; 58 one kid of the goats as a sin offering; 59 and as the sacrifice of peace offerings: two oxen, five rams, five male goats, and five male lambs in their first year. This *was* the offering of Gamaliel the son of Pedahzur.

60 On the ninth day Abidan the son of Gideoni, leader of the children of Benjamin, *presented an offering.* 61 His offering *was* one silver platter, the weight of which *was* one hundred and thirty *shekels,* and one silver bowl of seventy shekels, according to the

shekel of the sanctuary, both of them full of fine flour mixed with oil as a grain offering; 62 one gold pan of ten *shekels,* full of incense; 63 one young bull, one ram, and one male lamb in its first year, as a burnt offering; 64 one kid of the goats as a sin offering; 65 and as the sacrifice of peace offerings: two oxen, five rams, five male goats, and five male lambs in their first year. This *was* the offering of Abidan the son of Gideoni.

66 On the tenth day Ahiezer the son of Ammishaddai, leader of the children of Dan, *presented an offering.* 67 His offering *was* one silver platter, the weight of which *was* one hundred and thirty *shekels,* and one silver bowl of seventy shekels, according to the shekel of the sanctuary, both of them full of fine flour mixed with oil as a grain offering; 68 one gold pan of ten *shekels,* full of incense; 69 one young bull, one ram, and one male lamb in its first year, as a burnt offering; 70 one kid of the goats as a sin offering; 71 and as the sacrifice of peace offerings: two oxen, five rams, five male goats, and five male lambs in their first year. This *was* the offering of Ahiezer the son of Ammishaddai.

72 On the eleventh day Pagiel the son of Ocran, leader of the children of Asher, *presented an offering.* 73 His offering *was* one silver platter, the weight of which *was* one hundred and thirty *shekels,* and one silver bowl of seventy shekels, according to the shekel of the sanctuary, both of them full of fine flour mixed with oil as a grain offering; 74 one gold pan of ten *shekels,* full of incense; 75 one young bull, one ram, and one male lamb in its first year, as a burnt offering; 76 one kid of the goats as a sin offering; 77 and as the sacrifice of peace offerings: two oxen, five rams, five male goats, and five male lambs in their first year. This *was* the offering of Pagiel the son of Ocran.

78 On the twelfth day Ahira the son of Enan, leader of the children of Naphtali, *presented an offering.* 79 His offering *was* one silver platter, the weight of which *was* one hundred and thirty *shekels,* and one silver bowl of seventy shekels, according to the shekel of the sanctuary, both of them full of fine flour mixed with oil as a grain offering; 80 one gold pan of ten *shekels,* full of incense; 81 one young bull, one ram, and one male lamb in its first year, as a burnt offering; 82 one kid of the goats as a sin offering; 83 and as the sacrifice of peace offerings: two oxen, five rams, five male goats, and five male lambs in their first year. This *was* the offering of Ahira the son of Enan.

84 This *was* the dedication *offering* for the altar from the leaders of Israel, when it was anointed: twelve silver platters, twelve silver bowls, and twelve gold pans. 85 Each silver platter *weighed* one hundred and thirty *shekels* and each bowl seventy *shekels.* All the silver of the vessels *weighed* two thousand four hundred *shekels,* according to the shekel of the sanctuary. 86 The twelve gold pans full of incense *weighed* ten *shekels* apiece, according to the shekel of the sanctuary; all the gold of the pans *weighed* one hundred and twenty *shekels.* 87 All the oxen for the burnt offering *were* twelve young bulls, the rams twelve, the male lambs in their first year twelve, with their grain offering, and the kids of the goats as a sin offering twelve. 88 And all the oxen for the sacrifice of peace offerings were twenty-four bulls, the rams sixty, the male goats sixty, and the lambs in their first year sixty. This *was* the dedication *offering* for the altar after it was anointed.

89 Now when Moses went into the tabernacle of meeting to speak with Him, he heard the voice of One speaking to him from above the mercy seat that *was* on the ark of the Testimony, from between the two cherubim; thus He spoke to him.

8 AND the LORD spoke to Moses, saying: 2 "Speak to Aaron, and say to him, 'When you arrange the lamps, the seven lamps shall give light in front of the lampstand.'" 3 And Aaron did so; he arranged the lamps to face toward the front of the lampstand, as the LORD commanded Moses. 4 Now this workmanship of the lampstand *was* hammered gold; from its shaft to its flowers it *was* hammered work. According to the pattern which the LORD had shown Moses, so he made the lampstand.

5 Then the LORD spoke to Moses, saying: 6 "Take the Levites from among the children of Israel and cleanse them *ceremonially.* 7 Thus you shall do to them to cleanse them: Sprinkle water of purification on them, and let them shave all their body, and let them wash their clothes, and *so* make themselves clean. 8 Then let them take a young bull with its grain offering of fine flour mixed with oil, and you shall take another young bull as a sin offering. 9 And you shall bring the Levites before the tabernacle of meeting, and you shall gather together the whole congregation of the children of Israel. 10 So you shall bring the Levites before the LORD, and the children of Israel shall lay their hands on the Levites; 11 and Aaron shall offer the Levites before the LORD *like*

a wave offering from the children of Israel, that they may perform the work of the LORD. 12 Then the Levites shall lay their hands on the heads of the young bulls, and you shall offer one as a sin offering and the other as a burnt offering to the LORD, to make atonement for the Levites.

13 "And you shall stand the Levites before Aaron and his sons, and then offer them *like* a wave offering to the LORD. 14 Thus you shall separate the Levites from among the children of Israel, and the Levites shall be Mine. 15 After that the Levites shall go in to service the tabernacle of meeting. So you shall cleanse them and offer them *like* a wave offering. 16 For they *are* wholly given to Me from among the children of Israel; I have taken them for Myself instead of all who open the womb, the firstborn of all the children of Israel. 17 For all the firstborn among the children of Israel *are* Mine, *both* man and beast; on the day that I struck all the firstborn in the land of Egypt I sanctified them to Myself. 18 I have taken the Levites instead of all the firstborn of the children of Israel. 19 And I have given the Levites as a gift to Aaron and his sons from among the children of Israel, to do the work for the children of Israel in the tabernacle of meeting, and to make atonement for the children of Israel, that there be no plague among the children of Israel when the children of Israel come near the sanctuary."

20 Thus Moses and Aaron and all the congregation of the children of Israel did to the Levites; according to all that the LORD commanded Moses concerning the Levites, so the children of Israel did to them. 21 And the Levites purified themselves and washed their clothes; then Aaron presented them *like* a wave offering before the LORD, and Aaron made atonement for them to cleanse them. 22 After that the Levites went in to do their work in the tabernacle of meeting before Aaron and his sons; as the LORD commanded Moses concerning the Levites, so they did to them.

23 Then the LORD spoke to Moses, saying, 24 "This *is* what *pertains* to the Levites: From twenty-five years old and above one may enter to perform service in the work of the tabernacle of meeting; 25 and at the age of fifty years they must cease performing this work, and shall work no more. 26 They may minister with their brethren in the tabernacle of meeting, to attend to needs, but they *themselves* shall do no work. Thus you shall do to the Levites regarding their duties."

PSALM 31:1–5

1 IN You, O LORD, I put my trust;
   Let me never be ashamed;
   Deliver me in Your righteousness.
2 Bow down Your ear to me,
   Deliver me speedily;
   Be my rock of refuge,
   A fortress of defense to save me.

If our life is hid with Christ in God, He will keep us at ease. (RUN)

---

3 For You *are* my rock and my fortress;
   Therefore, for Your name's sake,
   Lead me and guide me.
4 Pull me out of the net which they have secretly laid for me,
   For You *are* my strength.
5 Into Your hand I commit my spirit;
   You have redeemed me, O LORD God of truth.

PROVERBS 11:4–6

4 RICHES do not profit in the day of wrath,
   But righteousness delivers from death.
5 The righteousness of the blameless will direct his way aright,
   But the wicked will fall by his own wickedness.
6 The righteousness of the upright will deliver them,
   But the unfaithful will be caught by *their* lust.

MARK 9:1–29

AND He said to them, "Assuredly, I say to you that there are some standing here who will not taste death till they see the kingdom of God present with power."

2 Now after six days Jesus took Peter, James, and John, and led them up on a high mountain apart by themselves; and He was transfigured before them. 3 His clothes became shining, exceedingly white, like snow, such as no launderer on earth

---

There was only one brilliant moment in the life of Jesus, . . . the Mount of Transfiguration. (GLORY)

---

can whiten them. 4 And Elijah appeared to them with Moses, and they were talking with Jesus. 5 Then Peter answered and said to Jesus, "Rabbi, it is good for us to be here; and let us make three tabernacles: one for You, one for Moses, and one for Elijah"— 6 because he did not know what to say, for they were greatly afraid.

7 And a cloud came and overshadowed them; and a voice came out of the cloud, saying, "This is My beloved Son. Hear Him!" 8 Suddenly, when they had looked around, they saw no one anymore, but only Jesus with themselves.

9 Now as they came down from the mountain, He commanded them that they should tell no one the things they had seen, till the Son of Man had risen from the dead. 10 So they kept this word to themselves, questioning what the rising from the dead meant.

11 And they asked Him, saying, "Why do the scribes say that Elijah must come first?"

12 Then He answered and told them, "Indeed, Elijah is coming first and restores all things. And how is it written concerning the Son of Man, that He must suffer many things and be treated with contempt? 13 But I say to you that Elijah has also come, and they did to him whatever they wished, as it is written of him."

14 And when He came to the disciples, He saw a great multitude around them, and scribes disputing with them. 15 Immediately, when they saw Him, all the people were greatly amazed, and running to *Him,* greeted Him. 16 And He asked the scribes, "What are you discussing with them?"

17 Then one of the crowd answered and said, "Teacher, I brought You my son, who has a mute spirit. 18 And wherever it seizes him, it throws him down; he foams at the mouth, gnashes his teeth, and becomes rigid. So I spoke to Your disciples, that they should cast it out, but they could not."

19 He answered him and said, "O faithless generation, how long shall I be with you? How long shall I bear with you? Bring him to Me." 20 Then they brought him to Him. And when he saw Him, immediately the spirit convulsed him, and he fell on the ground and wallowed, foaming at the mouth.

21 So He asked his father, "How long has this been happening to him?"

And he said, "From childhood. 22 And often he has thrown him both into the fire and into the water to destroy him. But if You can do anything, have compassion on us and help us."

23 Jesus said to him, "If you can believe, all things *are* possible to him who believes."

24 Immediately the father of the child cried out and said with tears, "Lord, I believe; help my unbelief!"

25 When Jesus saw that the people came running together, He rebuked the unclean spirit, saying to it, "Deaf and dumb spirit, I command you, come out of him and enter him no more!" 26 Then *the spirit* cried out, convulsed him greatly, and came out of him. And he became as one dead, so that many said, "He is dead." 27 But Jesus took him by the hand and lifted him up, and he arose.

28 And when He had come into the house, His disciples asked Him privately, "Why could we not cast it out?"

29 So He said to them, "This kind can come out by nothing but prayer and fasting."

◆◆◆◆

*Reading 65—*A Maimed Life
Mark 9:47

Sanctification means not only that we are delivered from sin, but that we start on a life of stern discipline. It is not a question of praying but of performing, of deliberately disciplining ourselves. There is no royal road there; we each have it entirely in our own hands. It is not wrong things that have to be sacrificed, but right things. "The good is the enemy of the best," not the bad, but the good that is not good enough. The danger is to argue on the line of giving up only what is wrong; Jesus Christ selected things essential to a full-orbed life—the right hand and the eye, these are not bad things, they are creations of God. Jesus Christ talked rugged, unmitigated truth. He was never ambiguous, and He says it is better to be maimed than damned. There was never a saint yet who did not have to start with a maimed life. Anyone will give up wrong things if he knows how to, but will I give up the best I have for Jesus Christ? If I am only willing to give up wrong things, never let me talk about being in love with Him! We say, "Why shouldn't I do it, there is no harm in it?" For pity's sake, go and do it, but remember that the construction of a spiritual character is doomed once you take that line. (*Bib. Ethics*)

NUMBERS 9:1—10:36

NOW the LORD spoke to Moses in the Wilderness of Sinai, in the first month of the second year after they had come out of the land of Egypt, saying: 2 "Let the children of Israel keep the Passover at its appointed time. 3 On the fourteenth day of this month, at twilight, you shall keep it at its appointed time. According to all its rites and ceremonies you shall keep it." 4 So Moses told the children of Israel that they should keep the Passover. 5 And they kept the Passover on the fourteenth day of the first month, at twilight, in the Wilderness of Sinai; according to all that the LORD commanded Moses, so the children of Israel did.

6 Now there were *certain* men who were defiled by a human corpse, so that they could not keep the Passover on that day; and they came before Moses and Aaron that day. 7 And those men said to him, "We *became* defiled by a human corpse. Why are we kept from presenting the offering of the LORD at its appointed time among the children of Israel?"

8 And Moses said to them, "Stand still, that I may hear what the LORD will command concerning you."

9 Then the LORD spoke to Moses, saying, 10 "Speak to the children of Israel, saying: 'If anyone of you or your posterity is unclean because of a corpse, or *is* far away on a journey, he may still keep the LORD's Passover. 11 On the fourteenth day of the second month, at twilight, they may keep it. They shall eat it with unleavened bread and bitter herbs. 12 They shall leave none of it until morning, nor break one of its bones. According to all the ordinances of the Passover they shall keep it. 13 But the man who *is* clean and is not on a journey, and ceases to keep the Passover, that same person shall be cut off from among his people, because he did not bring the offering of the LORD at its appointed time; that man shall bear his sin.

14 'And if a stranger dwells among you, and would keep the LORD's Passover, he must do so according to the rite of the Passover and according to its ceremony;

you shall have one ordinance, both for the stranger and the native of the land.' "

15 Now on the day that the tabernacle was raised up, the cloud covered the tabernacle, the tent of the Testimony; from evening until morning it was above the tabernacle like the appearance of fire. 16 So it was always: the cloud covered it *by day,* and the appearance of fire by night. 17 Whenever the cloud was taken up from above the tabernacle, after that the children of Israel would journey; and in the place where the cloud settled, there the children of Israel would pitch their tents. 18 At the command of the LORD the children of Israel would journey, and at the command of the LORD they would camp; as long as the cloud stayed above the tabernacle they remained encamped. 19 Even when the cloud continued long, many days above the tabernacle, the children of Israel kept the charge of the LORD and did not journey. 20 So it was, when the cloud was above the tabernacle a few days: according to the command of the LORD they would remain encamped, and according to the command of the LORD they would journey. 21 So it was, when the cloud remained only from evening until morning: when the cloud was taken up in the morning, then they would journey; whether by day or by night, whenever the cloud was taken up, they would journey. 22 *Whether it was* two days, a month, or a year that the cloud remained above the tabernacle, the children of Israel would remain encamped and not journey; but when it was taken up, they would journey. 23 At the command of the LORD they remained encamped, and at the command of the LORD they journeyed; they kept the charge of the LORD, at the command of the LORD by the hand of Moses.

10 AND the LORD spoke to Moses, saying: 2 "Make two silver trumpets for yourself; you shall make them of hammered work; you shall use them for calling the congregation and for directing the movement of the camps. 3 When they blow both of them, all the congregation shall gather before you at the door of the tabernacle of meeting. 4 But if they blow *only* one,

then the leaders, the heads of the divisions of Israel, shall gather to you. 5 When you sound the advance, the camps that lie on the east side shall then begin their journey. 6 When you sound the advance the second time, then the camps that lie on the south side shall begin their journey; they shall sound the call for them to begin their journeys. 7 And when the assembly is to be gathered together, you shall blow, but not sound the advance. 8 The sons of Aaron, the priests, shall blow the trumpets; and these shall be to you as an ordinance forever throughout your generations.

9 "When you go to war in your land against the enemy who oppresses you, then you shall sound an alarm with the trumpets, and you will be remembered before the LORD your God, and you will be saved from your enemies. 10 Also in the day of your gladness, in your appointed feasts, and at the beginning of your months, you shall blow the trumpets over your burnt offerings and over the sacrifices of your peace offerings; and they shall be a memorial for you before your God: I *am* the LORD your God."

11 Now it came to pass on the twentieth *day* of the second month, in the second year, that the cloud was taken up from above the tabernacle of the Testimony. 12 And the children of Israel set out from the Wilderness of Sinai on their journeys; then the cloud settled down in the Wilderness of Paran. 13 So they started out for the first time according to the command of the LORD by the hand of Moses.

14 The standard of the camp of the children of Judah set out first according to their armies; over their army was Nahshon the son of Amminadab. 15 Over the army of the tribe of the children of Issachar *was* Nethanel the son of Zuar. 16 And over the army of the tribe of the children of Zebulun *was* Eliab the son of Helon.

17 Then the tabernacle was taken down; and the sons of Gershon and the sons of Merari set out, carrying the tabernacle.

18 And the standard of the camp of Reuben set out according to their armies; over their army *was* Elizur the son of Shedeur. 19 Over the army of the tribe of the children of Simeon *was* Shelumiel the son of Zurishaddai. 20 And over the army of the tribe of the children of Gad *was* Eliasaph the son of Deuel.

21 Then the Kohathites set out, carrying the holy things. (The tabernacle would be prepared for their arrival.)

22 And the standard of the camp of the children of Ephraim set out according to their armies; over their army *was* Elishama

the son of Ammihud. 23 Over the army of the tribe of the children of Manasseh *was* Gamaliel the son of Pedahzur. 24 And over the army of the tribe of the children of Benjamin *was* Abidan the son of Gideoni.

25 Then the standard of the camp of the children of Dan (the rear guard of all the camps) set out according to their armies; over their army *was* Ahiezer the son of Ammishaddai. 26 Over the army of the tribe of the children of Asher *was* Pagiel the son of Ocran. 27 And over the army of the tribe of the children of Naphtali *was* Ahira the son of Enan.

28 Thus *was* the order of march of the children of Israel, according to their armies, when they began their journey.

29 Now Moses said to Hobab the son of Reuel the Midianite, Moses' father-in-law, "We are setting out for the place of which the LORD said, 'I will give it to you.' Come with us, and we will treat you well; for the LORD has promised good things to Israel."

30 And he said to him, "I will not go, but I will depart to my *own* land and to my relatives."

31 So *Moses* said, "Please do not leave, inasmuch as you know how we are to camp in the wilderness, and you can be our eyes. 32 And it shall be, if you go with us—indeed it shall be—that whatever good the LORD will do to us, the same we will do to you."

33 So they departed from the mountain of the LORD on a journey of three days; and the ark of the covenant of the LORD went before them for the three days' journey, to search out a resting place for them. 34 And the cloud of the LORD *was* above them by day when they went out from the camp.

35 So it was, whenever the ark set out, that Moses said:

> "Rise up, O LORD!
> Let Your enemies be scattered,
> And let those who hate You flee
>   before You."

36 And when it rested, he said:

> "Return, O LORD,
> *To* the many thousands of Israel."

PSALM 31:6–14

6   I have hated those who regard useless
      idols;
    But I trust in the LORD.
7   I will be glad and rejoice in Your mercy,
    For You have considered my trouble;
    You have known my soul in adversities,

8 And have not shut me up into the hand
   of the enemy;
   You have set my feet in a wide place.
9 Have mercy on me, O LORD, for I am
   in trouble;
   My eye wastes away with grief,
   Yes, my soul and my body!
10 For my life is spent with grief,
   And my years with sighing;
   My strength fails because of my
   iniquity,
   And my bones waste away.
11 I am a reproach among all my enemies,
   But especially among my neighbors,
   And *am* repulsive to my acquaintances;
   Those who see me outside flee from
   me.
12 I am forgotten like a dead man, out
   of mind;
   I am like a broken vessel.
13 For I hear the slander of many;
   Fear *is* on every side;
   While they take counsel together
   against me,
   They scheme to take away my life.
14 But as for me, I trust in You, O LORD;
   I say, "You *are* my God."

PROVERBS 11:7–11

7 WHEN a wicked man dies, *his*
   expectation will perish,
   And the hope of the unjust perishes.
8 The righteous is delivered from trouble,
   And it comes to the wicked instead.
9 The hypocrite with *his* mouth destroys
   his neighbor,
   But through knowledge the righteous
   will be delivered.
10 When it goes well with the righteous,
   the city rejoices;
   And when the wicked perish, *there is*
   jubilation.
11 By the blessing of the upright the city
   is exalted,
   But it is overthrown by the mouth of
   the wicked.

MARK 9:30–50

THEN they departed from there and passed
through Galilee, and He did not want anyone to know *it.* 31 For He taught His disciples and said to them, "The Son of Man
is being betrayed into the hands of men,
and they will kill Him. And after He is
killed, He will rise the third day." 32 But
they did not understand this saying, and
were afraid to ask Him.

33 Then He came to Capernaum. And
when He was in the house He asked them,
"What was it you disputed among yourselves on the road?" 34 But they kept silent,
for on the road they had disputed among
themselves who *would be* the greatest.
35 And He sat down, called the twelve, and
said to them, "If anyone desires to be first,
he shall be last of all and servant of all."
36 Then He took a little child and set him
in the midst of them. And when He had
taken him in His arms, He said to them,
37 "Whoever receives one of these little children in My name receives Me; and whoever
receives Me, receives not Me but Him who
sent Me."

---

*The only mind that understands
the things of God is the child
mind.* (MORAL FOUND.)

---

38 Now John answered Him, saying,
"Teacher, we saw someone who does not
follow us casting out demons in Your name,
and we forbade him because he does not
follow us."
39 But Jesus said, "Do not forbid him,
for no one who works a miracle in My
name can soon afterward speak evil of Me.
40 For he who is not against us is on our
side. 41 For whoever gives you a cup of
water to drink in My name, because you
belong to Christ, assuredly, I say to you,
he will by no means lose his reward.
42 "But whoever causes one of these little
ones who believe in Me to stumble, it would
be better for him if a millstone were hung
around his neck, and he were thrown into
the sea. 43 If your hand causes you to sin,
cut it off. It is better for you to enter into
life maimed, rather than having two hands,
to go to hell, into the fire that shall never
be quenched— 44 where

   'Their worm does not die
   And the fire is not quenched.'

45 And if your foot causes you to sin, cut
it off. It is better for you to enter life lame,
rather than having two feet, to be cast into
hell, into the fire that shall never be
quenched— 46 where

   'Their worm does not die
   And the fire is not quenched.'

47 And if your eye causes you to sin, pluck
it out. It is better for you to enter the

dom of God with one eye, rather than having two eyes, to be cast into hell fire—
48 where

> 'Their worm does not die
> And the fire is not quenched.'

49 "For everyone will be seasoned with fire, and every sacrifice will be seasoned with salt. 50 Salt *is* good, but if the salt loses its flavor, how will you season it? Have salt in yourselves, and have peace with one another."

Reading 66—Abandonment
Mark 10:28

Abandonment is not for anything at all. We have got so commercialized that we only go to God for something from Him, and not for Himself. It is like saying, "No, Lord, I don't want You, I want myself; but I want myself clean and filled with the Holy Ghost; I want to be put in Your showroom and be able to say—'This is what God has done for me.'" If we only give up something to God because we want more back, there is nothing of the Holy Spirit in our abandonment; it is miserable commercial self-interest. That we gain heaven, that we are delivered from sin, that we are made useful to God—these things never enter as considerations into real abandonment, which is a personal sovereign preference for Jesus Christ Himself.

When we come up against the barriers of natural relationship, where is Jesus Christ? Most of us desert Him—"Yes, Lord, I did hear Your call; but my mother is in the road, my wife, my self-interest, and I can go no further." "Then," Jesus says, "you cannot be My disciple."

The test of abandonment is always over the neck of natural devotion. Go over it, and God's own abandonment will embrace all those you had to hurt in abandoning. Beware of stopping short of abandonment to God. Most of us know abandonment in vision only.   (*Utmost*)

NUMBERS 11:1—12:16

NOW *when* the people complained, it displeased the Lord; for the Lord heard *it,* and His anger was aroused. So the fire of the Lord burned among them, and consumed *some* in the outskirts of the camp. 2 Then the people cried out to Moses, and when Moses prayed to the Lord, the fire was quenched. 3 So he called the name of the place Taberah, because the fire of the Lord had burned among them.

4 Now the mixed multitude who were among them yielded to intense craving; so the children of Israel also wept again and said: "Who will give us meat to eat? 5 We remember the fish which we ate freely in Egypt, the cucumbers, the melons, the leeks, the onions, and the garlic; 6 but now our whole being *is* dried up; *there is* nothing at all except this manna *before* our eyes!"

7 Now the manna *was* like coriander seed, and its color like the color of bdellium. 8 The people went about and gathered *it,* ground *it* on millstones or beat *it* in the mortar, cooked *it* in pans, and made cakes of it; and its taste was like the taste of pastry prepared with oil. 9 And when the dew fell on the camp in the night, the manna fell on it.

10 Then Moses heard the people weeping throughout their families, everyone at the door of his tent; and the anger of the Lord was greatly aroused; Moses also was displeased. 11 So Moses said to the Lord, "Why have You afflicted Your servant? And why have I not found favor in Your sight, that You have laid the burden of all these people on me? 12 Did I conceive all these people? Did I beget them, that You should say to me, 'Carry them in your bosom, as a guardian carries a nursing child,' to the land which You swore to their fathers? 13 Where am I to get meat to give to all

these people? For they weep all over me, saying, 'Give us meat, that we may eat.' 14 I am not able to bear all these people alone, because the burden *is* too heavy for me. 15 If You treat me like this, please kill me here and now—if I have found favor in Your sight—and do not let me see my wretchedness!"

16 So the LORD said to Moses: "Gather to Me seventy men of the elders of Israel, whom you know to be the elders of the people and officers over them; bring them to the tabernacle of meeting, that they may stand there with you. 17 Then I will come down and talk with you there. I will take of the Spirit that *is* upon you and will put *the same* upon them; and they shall bear the burden of the people with you, that you may not bear *it* yourself alone. 18 Then you shall say to the people, 'Consecrate yourselves for tomorrow, and you shall eat meat; for you have wept in the hearing of the LORD, saying, "Who will give us meat to eat? For *it was* well with us in Egypt." Therefore the LORD will give you meat, and you shall eat. 19 You shall eat, not one day, nor two days, nor five days, nor ten days, nor twenty days, 20 but *for* a whole month, until it comes out of your nostrils and becomes loathsome to you, because you have despised the LORD who is among you, and have wept before Him, saying, "Why did we ever come up out of Egypt?" ' "

21 And Moses said, "The people whom I *am* among *are* six hundred thousand men on foot; yet You have said, 'I will give them meat, that they may eat *for* a whole month.' 22 Shall flocks and herds be slaughtered for them, to provide enough for them? Or shall all the fish of the sea be gathered together for them, to provide enough for them?"

23 And the LORD said to Moses, "Has the LORD's arm been shortened? Now you shall see whether what I say will happen to you or not."

24 So Moses went out and told the people the words of the LORD, and he gathered the seventy men of the elders of the people and placed them around the tabernacle. 25 Then the LORD came down in the cloud, and spoke to him, and took of the Spirit that *was* upon him, and placed *the same* upon the seventy elders; and it happened, when the Spirit rested upon them, that they prophesied, although they never did *so* again.

26 But two men had remained in the camp: the name of one *was* Eldad, and the name of the other Medad. And the Spirit rested upon them. Now they *were* among those listed, but who had not gone out to the tabernacle; yet they prophesied in the camp. 27 And a young man ran and told Moses, and said, "Eldad and Medad are prophesying in the camp."

28 So Joshua the son of Nun, Moses' assistant, *one* of his choice men, answered and said, "Moses my lord, forbid them!"

29 Then Moses said to him, "Are you zealous for my sake? Oh, that all the LORD's people were prophets *and* that the LORD would put His Spirit upon them!" 30 And Moses returned to the camp, he and the elders of Israel.

31 Now a wind went out from the LORD, and it brought quail from the sea and left *them* fluttering near the camp, about a day's journey on this side and about a day's journey on the other side, all around the camp, and about two cubits above the surface of the ground. 32 And the people stayed up all that day, all night, and all the next day, and gathered the quail (he who gathered least gathered ten homers); and they spread *them* out for themselves all around the camp. 33 But while the meat *was* still between their teeth, before it was chewed, the wrath of the LORD was aroused against the people, and the LORD struck the people with a very great plague. 34 So he called the name of

---

*W*rath is the dark line in God's face, and is expressive of His hatred of sin. (CONFORMED)

---

that place Kibroth Hattaavah, because there they buried the people who had yielded to craving.

35 From Kibroth Hattaavah the people moved to Hazeroth, and camped at Hazeroth.

12 THEN Miriam and Aaron spoke against Moses because of the Ethiopian woman whom he had married; for he had married an Ethiopian woman. 2 So they said, "Has the LORD indeed spoken only through Moses? Has He not spoken through us also?" And the LORD heard *it*. 3 (Now the man Moses *was* very humble, more than all men who *were* on the face of the earth.)

4 Suddenly the LORD said to Moses, Aaron, and Miriam, "Come out, you three, to the tabernacle of meeting!" So the three came out. 5 Then the LORD came down in the pillar of cloud and stood *in* the door of the tabernacle, and called Aaron and

Miriam. And they both went forward.
6 Then He said,

"Hear now My words:
If there is a prophet among you,
I, the LORD, make Myself known to
him in a vision;
I speak to him in a dream.
7 Not so with My servant Moses;
He *is* faithful in all My house.
8 I speak with him face to face,
Even plainly, and not in dark sayings;
And he sees the form of the LORD.
Why then were you not afraid
To speak against My servant Moses?"

9 So the anger of the LORD was aroused
against them, and He departed. 10 And
when the cloud departed from above the
tabernacle, suddenly Miriam *became* leprous, as *white as* snow. Then Aaron turned
toward Miriam, and there she was, a leper.
11 So Aaron said to Moses, "Oh, my lord!
Please do not lay *this* sin on us, in which
we have done foolishly and in which
we have sinned. 12 Please do not let her
be as one dead, whose flesh is half consumed when he comes out of his mother's
womb!"
13 So Moses cried out to the LORD,
saying, "Please heal her, O God, I
pray!"
14 Then the LORD said to Moses, "If her
father had but spit in her face, would she
not be shamed seven days? Let her be shut
out of the camp seven days, and afterward
she may be received *again*." 15 So Miriam
was shut out of the camp seven days, and
the people did not journey till Miriam was
brought in *again*. 16 And afterward the people moved from Hazeroth and camped in
the Wilderness of Paran.

PSALM 31:15–18

15 MY times *are* in Your hand;
Deliver me from the hand of my
enemies,
And from those who persecute me.
16 Make Your face shine upon Your
servant;
Save me for Your mercies' sake.
17 Do not let me be ashamed, O LORD,
for I have called upon You;
Let the wicked be ashamed;
Let them be silent in the grave.
18 Let the lying lips be put to silence,
Which speak insolent things proudly
and contemptuously against the
righteous.

PROVERBS 11:12–14

12 HE who is devoid of wisdom despises
his neighbor,
But a man of understanding holds his
peace.

13 A talebearer reveals secrets,
But he who is of a faithful spirit conceals
a matter.

14 Where *there is* no counsel, the people
fall;
But in the multitude of counselors *there
is* safety.

MARK 10:1–31

THEN He arose from there and came to
the region of Judea by the other side of
the Jordan. And multitudes gathered to
Him again, and as He was accustomed, He
taught them again.
2 The Pharisees came and asked Him, "Is
it lawful for a man to divorce *his* wife?"
testing Him.
3 And He answered and said to them,
"What did Moses command you?"
4 They said, "Moses permitted *a man* to
write a certificate of divorce, and to dismiss
her."
5 And Jesus answered and said to them,
"Because of the hardness of your heart he
wrote you this precept. 6 But from the beginning of the creation, God 'made them
male and female.' 7 'For this reason a man
shall leave his father and mother and be
joined to his wife, 8 and the two shall become one flesh'; so then they are no longer
two, but one flesh. 9 Therefore what God
has joined together, let not man separate."
10 In the house His disciples also asked
Him again about the same *matter*. 11 So
He said to them, "Whoever divorces his
wife and marries another commits adultery
against her. 12 And if a woman divorces
her husband and marries another, she commits adultery."
13 Then they brought little children to
Him, that He might touch them; but the
disciples rebuked those who brought *them*.
14 But when Jesus saw *it*, He was greatly
displeased and said to them, "Let the little
children come to Me, and do not forbid
them; for of such is the kingdom of God.

A *child's life ought to be a child's
life, full of simplicity.*   (GLORY)

15 Assuredly, I say to you, whoever does not receive the kingdom of God as a little child will by no means enter it." 16 And He took them up in His arms, laid *His* hands on them, and blessed them.

17 Now as He was going out on the road, one came running, knelt before Him, and asked Him, "Good Teacher, what shall I do that I may inherit eternal life?"

18 So Jesus said to him, "Why do you call Me good? No one *is* good but One, *that is,* God. 19 You know the commandments: 'Do not commit adultery,' 'Do not murder,' 'Do not steal,' 'Do not bear false witness,' 'Do not defraud,' 'Honor your father and your mother.' "

20 And he answered and said to Him, "Teacher, all these things I have kept from my youth."

21 Then Jesus, looking at him, loved him, and said to him, "One thing you lack: Go your way, sell whatever you have and give to the poor, and you will have treasure in heaven; and come, take up the cross, and follow Me."

22 But he was sad at this word, and went away sorrowful, for he had great possessions.

23 Then Jesus looked around and said to His disciples, "How hard it is for those who have riches to enter the kingdom of God!" 24 And the disciples were astonished at His words. But Jesus answered again and said to them, "Children, how hard it is for those who trust in riches to enter the kingdom of God! 25 It is easier for a camel to go through the eye of a needle than for a rich man to enter the kingdom of God."

26 And they were greatly astonished, saying among themselves, "Who then can be saved?"

27 But Jesus looked at them and said, "With men *it is* impossible, but not with God; for with God all things are possible."

28 Then Peter began to say to Him, "See, we have left all and followed You."

29 So Jesus answered and said, "Assuredly, I say to you, there is no one who has left house or brothers or sisters or father or mother or wife or children or lands, for My sake and the gospel's, 30 who shall not receive a hundredfold now in this time—houses and brothers and sisters and mothers and children and lands, with persecutions—and in the age to come, eternal life. 31 But many *who are* first will be last, and the last first."

◆◆◆

Reading 67—The Sense of Awe
Mark 10:32

The disciples had been living in closest intimacy with Jesus, but now they begin to see that there is a dread side to His life. He has an attitude to things which is not easy to understand, and it fills them with fear. There are different kinds of fear. We know what fear is in the physical domain, and in the moral domain; but in the spiritual domain a man's fear is not for his own skin at all, but, as it were, fear that his hero won't get through. This was the disciples' fear; it seemed as if all they had expected Jesus to do would end in nothing. Not one of them knew what Jesus was after, but still they followed, and they were afraid. Many of us are supernaturally solemn about our religion because it is not real. As soon as our religion becomes real, it is possible to have humor in connection with it. There are occasions, nevertheless, when there is not only no humor, but when humor is unfit; there is a dread sense of detachment from our ordinary attitude to things which fills us with awe. We are all apt to interpret Jesus from our own standpoint; we get too familiar with Him, and a moral surgery of events is necessary before we can understand His standpoint.   (*PLACE HELP*)

NUMBERS 13:1—14:45

AND the LORD spoke to Moses, saying, 2 "Send men to spy out the land of Canaan, which I am giving to the children of Israel; from each tribe of their fathers you shall send a man, every one a leader among them."

3 So Moses sent them from the Wilderness of Paran according to the command of the LORD, all of them men who *were* heads of the children of Israel. 4 Now these *were* their names: from the tribe of Reuben, Shammua the son of Zaccur; 5 from the tribe of Simeon, Shaphat the son of Hori; 6 from the tribe of Judah, Caleb the son of Jephunneh; 7 from the tribe of Issachar, Igal the son of Joseph; 8 from the tribe of Ephraim, Hoshea the son of Nun; 9 from the tribe of Benjamin, Palti the son of Raphu; 10 from the tribe of Zebulun, Gaddiel the son of Sodi; 11 from the tribe of Joseph, *that is,* from the tribe of Manasseh, Gaddi the son of Susi; 12 from the tribe of Dan, Ammiel the son of Gemalli; 13 from the tribe of Asher, Sethur the son of Michael; 14 from the tribe of Naphtali, Nahbi the son of Vophsi; 15 from the tribe of Gad, Geuel the son of Machi.

16 These *are* the names of the men whom Moses sent to spy out the land. And Moses called Hoshea the son of Nun, Joshua.

17 Then Moses sent them to spy out the land of Canaan, and said to them, "Go up this *way* into the South, and go up to the mountains, 18 and see what the land is like: whether the people who dwell in it *are* strong or weak, few or many; 19 whether the land they dwell in *is* good or bad; whether the cities they inhabit *are* like camps or strongholds; 20 whether the land *is* rich or poor; and whether there are forests there or not. Be of good courage. And bring some of the fruit of the land." Now the time *was* the season of the first ripe grapes.

21 So they went up and spied out the land from the Wilderness of Zin as far as Rehob, near the entrance of Hamath. 22 And they went up through the South and came to Hebron; Ahiman, Sheshai, and Talmai, the descendants of Anak, *were* there. (Now Hebron was built seven years before Zoan in Egypt.) 23 Then they came to the Valley of Eshcol, and there cut down a branch with one cluster of grapes; they carried it between two of them on a pole. *They* also *brought* some of the pomegranates and figs. 24 The place was called the Valley of Eshcol, because of the cluster which the men of Israel cut down there. 25 And they

returned from spying out the land after forty days.

26 Now they departed and came back to Moses and Aaron and all the congregation of the children of Israel in the Wilderness of Paran, at Kadesh; they brought back word to them and to all the congregation, and showed them the fruit of the land. 27 Then they told him, and said: "We went to the land where you sent us. It truly flows with milk and honey, and this *is* its fruit. 28 Nevertheless the people who dwell in the land *are* strong; the cities *are* fortified *and* very large; moreover we saw the descendants of Anak there. 29 The Amalekites dwell in the land of the South; the Hittites, the Jebusites, and the Amorites dwell in the mountains; and the Canaanites dwell by the sea and along the banks of the Jordan."

30 Then Caleb quieted the people before Moses, and said, "Let us go up at once and take possession, for we are well able to overcome it."

You cannot overcome if there is nothing to overcome.   (MORAL FOUND.)

---

31 But the men who had gone up with him said, "We are not able to go up against the people, for they *are* stronger than we." 32 And they gave the children of Israel a bad report of the land which they had spied out, saying, "The land through which we have gone as spies *is* a land that devours its inhabitants, and all the people whom we saw in it *are* men of *great* stature. 33 There we saw the giants (the descendants of Anak came from the giants); and we were like grasshoppers in our own sight, and so we were in their sight."

14 SO all the congregation lifted up their voices and cried, and the people wept that night. 2 And all the children of Israel complained against Moses and Aaron, and the whole congregation said to them, "If only we had died in the land of Egypt! Or if only we had died in this wilderness! 3 Why has the LORD brought us to this land to fall by the sword, that our wives and children should become victims? Would it not be better for us to return to Egypt?" 4 So they said to one another, "Let us select a leader and return to Egypt."

5 Then Moses and Aaron fell on their faces before all the assembly of the congregation of the children of Israel.

6 But Joshua the son of Nun and Caleb

the son of Jephunneh, *who were* among those who had spied out the land, tore their clothes; 7 and they spoke to all the congregation of the children of Israel, saying: "The land we passed through to spy out *is* an exceedingly good land. 8 If the LORD delights in us, then He will bring us into this land and give it to us, 'a land which flows with milk and honey.' 9 Only do not rebel against the LORD, nor fear the people of the land, for they *are* our bread; their protection has departed from them, and the LORD *is* with us. Do not fear them."

10 And all the congregation said to stone them with stones. Now the glory of the LORD appeared in the tabernacle of meeting before all the children of Israel.

11 Then the LORD said to Moses: "How long will these people reject Me? And how long will they not believe Me, with all the signs which I have performed among them?

---

*W*ith our Lord to believe means to commit.   (APPROVED)

---

12 I will strike them with the pestilence and disinherit them, and I will make of you a nation greater and mightier than they."

13 And Moses said to the LORD: "Then the Egyptians will hear *it,* for by Your might You brought these people up from among them, 14 and they will tell *it* to the inhabitants of this land. They have heard that You, LORD, *are* among these people; that You, LORD, are seen face to face and Your cloud stands above them, and You go before them in a pillar of cloud by day and in a pillar of fire by night. 15 Now *if* You kill these people as one man, then the nations which have heard of Your fame will speak, saying, 16 'Because the LORD was not able to bring this people to the land which He swore to give them, therefore He killed them in the wilderness.' 17 And now, I pray, let the power of my Lord be great, just as You have spoken, saying, 18 'The LORD is longsuffering and abundant in mercy, forgiving iniquity and transgression; but He by no means clears *the guilty,* visiting the iniquity of the fathers on the children to the third and fourth *generation.'* 19 Pardon the iniquity of this people, I pray, according to the greatness of Your mercy, just as You have forgiven this people, from Egypt even until now."

20 Then the LORD said: "I have pardoned, according to your word; 21 but truly, as I live, all the earth shall be filled with the glory of the LORD— 22 because all these

men who have seen My glory and the signs which I did in Egypt and in the wilderness, and have put Me to the test now these ten times, and have not heeded My voice, 23 they certainly shall not see the land of which I swore to their fathers, nor shall any of those who rejected Me see it. 24 But My servant Caleb, because he has a different spirit in him and has followed Me fully, I will bring into the land where he went, and his descendants shall inherit it. 25 Now the Amalekites and the Canaanites dwell in the valley; tomorrow turn and move out into the wilderness by the Way of the Red Sea."

26 And the LORD spoke to Moses and Aaron, saying, 27 "How long *shall I bear with* this evil congregation who complain against Me? I have heard the complaints which the children of Israel make against Me. 28 Say to them, 'As I live,' says the LORD, 'just as you have spoken in My hearing, so I will do to you: 29 The carcasses of you who have complained against Me shall fall in this wilderness, all of you who were numbered, according to your entire number, from twenty years old and above. 30 Except for Caleb the son of Jephunneh and Joshua the son of Nun, you shall by no means enter the land which I swore I would make you dwell in. 31 But your little ones, whom you said would be victims, I will bring in, and they shall know the land which you have despised. 32 But *as for* you, your carcasses shall fall in this wilderness. 33 And your sons shall be shepherds in the wilderness forty years, and bear the brunt of your infidelity, until your carcasses are consumed in the wilderness. 34 According to the number of the days in which you spied out the land, forty days, for each day you shall bear your guilt one year, *namely* forty years, and you shall know My rejection. 35 I the LORD have spoken this. I will surely do so to all this evil congregation who are gathered together against Me. In this wilderness they shall be consumed, and there they shall die.'"

36 Now the men whom Moses sent to spy out the land, who returned and made all the congregation complain against him by bringing a bad report of the land, 37 those very men who brought the evil report about the land, died by the plague before the LORD. 38 But Joshua the son of Nun and Caleb the son of Jephunneh remained alive, of the men who went to spy out the land.

39 Then Moses told these words to all the children of Israel, and the people mourned greatly. 40 And they rose early in

the morning and went up to the top of the mountain, saying, "Here we are, and we will go up to the place which the LORD has promised, for we have sinned!"

41 And Moses said, "Now why do you transgress the command of the LORD? For this will not succeed. 42 Do not go up, lest you be defeated by your enemies, for the LORD *is* not among you. 43 For the Amalekites and the Canaanites *are* there before you, and you shall fall by the sword; because you have turned away from the LORD, the LORD will not be with you."

44 But they presumed to go up to the mountaintop. Nevertheless, neither the ark of the covenant of the LORD nor Moses departed from the camp. 45 Then the Amalekites and the Canaanites who dwelt in that mountain came down and attacked them, and drove them back as far as Hormah.

PSALM 31:19–24

19 OH, how great *is* Your goodness,
   Which You have laid up for those who fear You,
   Which You have prepared for those who trust in You
   In the presence of the sons of men!
20 You shall hide them in the secret place of Your presence
   From the plots of man;
   You shall keep them secretly in a pavilion
   From the strife of tongues.

21 Blessed *be* the LORD,
   For He has shown me His marvelous kindness in a strong city!
22 For I said in my haste,
   "I am cut off from before Your eyes";
   Nevertheless You heard the voice of my supplications
   When I cried out to You.

23 Oh, love the LORD, all you His saints!
   For the LORD preserves the faithful,
   And fully repays the proud person.

The evidence of our love for Him is the absolute spontaneity of our love. (UTMOST)

24 Be of good courage,
   And He shall strengthen your heart,
   All you who hope in the LORD.

PROVERBS 11:15

15 HE who is surety for a stranger will suffer,
   But one who hates being surety is secure.

MARK 10:32–52

NOW they were on the road, going up to Jerusalem, and Jesus was going before them; and they were amazed. And as they followed they were afraid. Then He took the twelve aside again and began to tell them the things that would happen to Him: 33 "Behold, we are going up to Jerusalem, and the Son of Man will be betrayed to the chief priests and to the scribes; and they will condemn Him to death and deliver Him to the Gentiles; 34 and they will mock Him, and scourge Him, and spit on Him, and kill Him. And the third day He will rise again."

35 Then James and John, the sons of Zebedee, came to Him, saying, "Teacher, we want You to do for us whatever we ask."

36 And He said to them, "What do you want Me to do for you?"

37 They said to Him, "Grant us that we may sit, one on Your right hand and the other on Your left, in Your glory."

38 But Jesus said to them, "You do not know what you ask. Are you able to drink the cup that I drink, and be baptized with the baptism that I am baptized with?"

39 They said to Him, "We are able."

So Jesus said to them, "You will indeed drink the cup that I drink, and with the baptism I am baptized with you will be baptized; 40 but to sit on My right hand and on My left is not Mine to give, but *it is for those* for whom it is prepared."

41 And when the ten heard *it,* they began to be greatly displeased with James and John. 42 But Jesus called them to *Himself* and said to them, "You know that those who are considered rulers over the Gentiles lord it over them, and their great ones exercise authority over them. 43 Yet it shall not be so among you; but whoever desires to become great among you shall be your servant. 44 And whoever of you desires to be first shall be slave of all. 45 For even the Son of Man did not come to be served, but to serve, and to give His life a ransom for many."

46 Now they came to Jericho. As He went out of Jericho with His disciples and a great multitude, blind Bartimaeus, the son of Timaeus, sat by the road begging. 47 And

when he heard that it was Jesus of Nazareth, he began to cry out and say, "Jesus, Son of David, have mercy on me!"

48 Then many warned him to be quiet; but he cried out all the more, "Son of David, have mercy on me!"

49 So Jesus stood still and commanded him to be called.

Then they called the blind man, saying to him, "Be of good cheer. Rise, He is calling you."

50 And throwing aside his garment, he rose and came to Jesus.

51 So Jesus answered and said to him, "What do you want Me to do for you?"

The blind man said to Him, "Rabboni, that I may receive my sight."

52 Then Jesus said to him, "Go your way; your faith has made you well." And immediately he received his sight and followed Jesus on the road.

◆◆◆◆

Reading 68—Passionate Zeal
Mark 11:15

We bring to the New Testament a sentimental conception of our Lord; we think of Him as the "meek and mild and gentle Jesus" and make it mean that He was of no practical account whatever. Our Lord *was* "gentle and lowly in heart," yet watch Him in the temple, meekness and gentleness were not the striking features there. We see instead a terrible Being with a whip of small cords in His hands, overturning the money changers' tables and driving out men and cattle. Is He the "meek and gentle Jesus" there? He is absolutely terrifying; no one dare interfere with Him. Why could He not have driven them out in a gentler way? Because passionate zeal had eaten Him up, with a detestation of everything that dared to call His Father's honor into disrepute. "Do not make my Father's house a house of merchandise!"—the deification of commercial enterprise. Everything of the nature of wrong must go when Jesus Christ begins to cleanse His Father's house. (*SERVANT AS LORD*)

NUMBERS 15:1—16:50

AND the LORD spoke to Moses, saying, 2 "Speak to the children of Israel, and say to them: 'When you have come into the land you are to inhabit, which I am giving to you, 3 and you make an offering by fire to the LORD, a burnt offering or a sacrifice, to fulfill a vow or as a freewill offering or in your appointed feasts, to make a sweet aroma to the LORD, from the herd or the flock, 4 then he who presents his offering to the LORD shall bring a grain offering of one-tenth *of an ephah* of fine flour mixed with one-fourth of a hin of oil; 5 and one-fourth of a hin of wine as a drink offering you shall prepare with the burnt offering or the sacrifice, for each lamb. 6 Or for a ram you shall prepare as a grain offering two-tenths *of an ephah* of fine flour mixed with one-third *of a hin* of oil; 7 and as a drink offering you shall offer one-third of a hin of wine as a sweet aroma to the LORD.

8 And when you prepare a young bull as a burnt offering, or as a sacrifice to fulfill a vow, or as a peace offering to the LORD, 9 then shall be offered with the young bull a grain offering of three-tenths *of an ephah* of fine flour mixed with half a hin of oil; 10 and you shall bring as the drink offering half a hin of wine *as* an offering made by fire, a sweet aroma to the LORD. 11 'Thus it shall be done for each young bull, for each ram, or for each lamb or young goat. 12 According to the number that you prepare, so you shall do with everyone according to their number. 13 All who are native-born shall do these things in this manner, in presenting an offering made by fire, a sweet aroma to the LORD. 14 And if a stranger dwells with you, or whoever *is* among you throughout your generations, and would present an offering made by fire, a sweet aroma to the LORD, just as you do, so shall he do. 15 One ordinance *shall be* for you of the assembly and for the

stranger who dwells *with you,* an ordinance forever throughout your generations; as you are, so shall the stranger be before the LORD. 16 One law and one custom shall be for you and for the stranger who dwells with you.' "

17 Again the LORD spoke to Moses, saying, 18 "Speak to the children of Israel, and say to them: 'When you come into the land to which I bring you, 19 then it will be, when you eat of the bread of the land, that you shall offer up a heave offering to the LORD. 20 You shall offer up a cake of the first of your ground meal *as* a heave offering; as a heave offering of the threshing floor, so shall you offer it up. 21 Of the first of your ground meal you shall give to the LORD a heave offering throughout your generations.

22 'If you sin unintentionally, and do not observe all these commandments which the LORD has spoken to Moses— 23 all that the LORD has commanded you by the hand of Moses, from the day the LORD gave commandment and onward throughout your generations— 24 then it will be, if it is unintentionally committed, without the knowledge of the congregation, that the whole congregation shall offer one young bull as a burnt offering, as a sweet aroma to the LORD, with its grain offering and its drink offering, according to the ordinance, and one kid of the goats as a sin offering. 25 So the priest shall make atonement for the whole congregation of the children of Israel, and it shall be forgiven them, for it was unintentional; they shall bring their offering, an offering made by fire to the LORD, and their sin offering before the LORD, for their unintended sin. 26 It shall be forgiven the whole congregation of the children of Israel and the stranger who dwells among them, because all the people *did it* unintentionally.

27 'And if a person sins unintentionally, then he shall bring a female goat in its first year as a sin offering. 28 So the priest shall make atonement for the person who sins unintentionally, when he sins unintentionally before the LORD, to make atonement for him; and it shall be forgiven him. 29 You shall have one law for him who sins unintentionally, *for* him who is native-born among the children of Israel and for the stranger who dwells among them.

30 'But the person who does *anything* presumptuously, *whether he is* native-born or a stranger, that one brings reproach on the LORD, and he shall be cut off from among his people. 31 Because he has despised the word of the LORD, and has broken His commandment, that person shall be completely cut off; his guilt *shall be* upon him.' "

32 Now while the children of Israel were in the wilderness, they found a man gathering sticks on the Sabbath day. 33 And those who found him gathering sticks brought him to Moses and Aaron, and to all the congregation. 34 They put him under guard, because it had not been explained what should be done to him.

35 Then the LORD said to Moses, "The man must surely be put to death; all the congregation shall stone him with stones outside the camp." 36 So, as the LORD commanded Moses, all the congregation brought him outside the camp and stoned him with stones, and he died.

37 Again the LORD spoke to Moses, saying, 38 "Speak to the children of Israel: Tell them to make tassels on the corners of their garments throughout their generations, and to put a blue thread in the tassels of the corners. 39 And you shall have the tassel, that you may look upon it and remember all the commandments of the LORD and do them, and that you *may* not follow the harlotry to which your own heart and your own eyes are inclined, 40 and that you may remember and do all My commandments, and be holy for your God. 41 I *am* the LORD your God, who brought you out of the land of Egypt, to be your God: I *am* the LORD your God."

16 NOW Korah the son of Izhar, the son of Kohath, the son of Levi, with Dathan and Abiram the sons of Eliab, and On the son of Peleth, sons of Reuben, took *men;* 2 and they rose up before Moses with some of the children of Israel, two hundred and fifty leaders of the congregation, representatives of the congregation, men of renown. 3 They gathered together against Moses and Aaron, and said to them, "*You take* too much upon yourselves, for all the congregation *is* holy, every one of them, and the LORD *is* among them. Why then do you exalt yourselves above the assembly of the LORD?"

4 So when Moses heard *it,* he fell on his face; 5 and he spoke to Korah and all his company, saying, "Tomorrow morning the LORD will show who *is* His and *who is* holy, and will cause *him* to come near to Him. That one whom He chooses He will cause to come near to Him. 6 Do this: Take censers, Korah and all your company; 7 put fire in them and put incense in them before the LORD tomorrow, and it shall be *that* the man whom the LORD chooses *is* the

holy one. *You take* too much upon yourselves, you sons of Levi!"

8 Then Moses said to Korah, "Hear now, you sons of Levi: 9 *Is it* a small thing to you that the God of Israel has separated you from the congregation of Israel, to bring you near to Himself, to do the work of the tabernacle of the Lord, and to stand before the congregation to serve them; 10 and that He has brought you near *to Himself,* you and all your brethren, the sons of Levi, with you? And are you seeking the priesthood also? 11 Therefore you and all your company *are* gathered together against the Lord. And what *is* Aaron that you complain against him?"

12 And Moses sent to call Dathan and Abiram the sons of Eliab, but they said, "We will not come up! 13 *Is it* a small thing that you have brought us up out of a land flowing with milk and honey, to kill us in the wilderness, that you should keep acting like a prince over us? 14 Moreover you have not brought us into a land flowing with milk and honey, nor given us inheritance of fields and vineyards. Will you put out the eyes of these men? We will not come up!"

15 Then Moses was very angry, and said to the Lord, "Do not respect their offering. I have not taken one donkey from them, nor have I hurt one of them."

16 And Moses said to Korah, "Tomorrow, you and all your company be present before the Lord—you and they, as well as Aaron. 17 Let each take his censer and put incense in it, and each of you bring his censer before the Lord, two hundred and fifty censers; both you and Aaron, each *with* his censer." 18 So every man took his censer, put fire in it, laid incense on it, and stood at the door of the tabernacle of meeting with Moses and Aaron. 19 And Korah gathered all the congregation against them at the door of the tabernacle of meeting. Then the glory of the Lord appeared to all the congregation.

20 And the Lord spoke to Moses and Aaron, saying, 21 "Separate yourselves from among this congregation, that I may consume them in a moment."

22 Then they fell on their faces, and said, "O God, the God of the spirits of all flesh, shall one man sin, and You be angry with all the congregation?"

23 So the Lord spoke to Moses, saying, 24 "Speak to the congregation, saying, 'Get away from the tents of Korah, Dathan, and Abiram.'"

25 Then Moses rose and went to Dathan and Abiram, and the elders of Israel followed him. 26 And he spoke to the congregation, saying, "Depart now from the tents of these wicked men! Touch nothing of theirs, lest you be consumed in all their sins." 27 So they got away from around the tents of Korah, Dathan, and Abiram; and Dathan and Abiram came out and stood at the door of their tents, with their wives, their sons, and their little children.

28 And Moses said: "By this you shall know that the Lord has sent me to do all these works, for *I have* not *done them* of my own will. 29 If these men die naturally like all men, or if they are visited by the common fate of all men, *then* the Lord has not sent me. 30 But if the Lord creates a new thing, and the earth opens its mouth and swallows them up with all that belongs to them, and they go down alive into the pit, then you will understand that these men have rejected the Lord."

31 Now it came to pass, as he finished speaking all these words, that the ground split apart under them, 32 and the earth opened its mouth and swallowed them up, with their households and all the men with Korah, with all *their* goods. 33 So they and all those with them went down alive into the pit; the earth closed over them, and they perished from among the assembly.

When a man becomes severed from God his life tumbles into turmoil and confusion. (Conformed)

34 Then all Israel who *were* around them fled at their cry, for they said, "Lest the earth swallow us up *also!*"

35 And a fire came out from the Lord and consumed the two hundred and fifty men who were offering incense.

36 Then the Lord spoke to Moses, saying: 37 "Tell Eleazar, the son of Aaron the priest, to pick up the censers out of the blaze, for they are holy, and scatter the fire some distance away. 38 The censers of these men who sinned against their own souls, let them be made into hammered plates as a covering for the altar. Because they presented them before the Lord, therefore they are holy; and they shall be a sign to the children of Israel." 39 So Eleazar the priest took the bronze censers, which those who were burned up had presented, and they were hammered out as a covering on the altar, 40 *to be* a memorial to the children of Israel that no outsider, who *is* not a descendant of Aaron, should come near to offer incense before the Lord, that he might

not become like Korah and his companions, just as the Lord had said to him through Moses.

41 On the next day all the congregation of the children of Israel complained against Moses and Aaron, saying, "You have killed the people of the Lord." 42 Now it happened, when the congregation had gathered against Moses and Aaron, that they turned toward the tabernacle of meeting; and suddenly the cloud covered it, and the glory of the Lord appeared. 43 Then Moses and Aaron came before the tabernacle of meeting.

44 And the Lord spoke to Moses, saying, 45 "Get away from among this congregation, that I may consume them in a moment."

And they fell on their faces.

46 So Moses said to Aaron, "Take a censer and put fire in it from the altar, put incense *on it,* and take it quickly to the congregation and make atonement for them; for wrath has gone out from the Lord. The plague has begun." 47 Then Aaron took *it* as Moses commanded, and ran into the midst of the assembly; and already the plague had begun among the people. So he put in the incense and made atonement for the people. 48 And he stood between the dead and the living; so the plague was stopped. 49 Now those who died in the plague were fourteen thousand seven hundred, besides those who died in the Korah incident. 50 So Aaron returned to Moses at the door of the tabernacle of meeting, for the plague had stopped.

PSALM 32:1–5

1   BLESSED *is he whose* transgression *is* forgiven,
    Whose sin *is* covered.
2   Blessed *is* the man to whom the Lord does not impute iniquity,
    And in whose spirit *there is* no deceit.

3   When I kept silent, my bones grew old Through my groaning all the day long.
4   For day and night Your hand was heavy upon me;
    My vitality was turned into the drought of summer.   Selah
5   I acknowledged my sin to You,
    And my iniquity I have not hidden.
    I said, "I will confess my transgressions to the Lord,"
    And You forgave the iniquity of my sin.   Selah

PROVERBS 11:16–18

16 A gracious woman retains honor,
    But ruthless *men* retain riches.
17 The merciful man does good for his own soul,
    But *he who is* cruel troubles his own flesh.
18 The wicked *man* does deceptive work,
    But he who sows righteousness *will have* a sure reward.

MARK 11:1–19

NOW when they drew near Jerusalem, to Bethphage and Bethany, at the Mount of Olives, He sent two of His disciples; 2 and He said to them, "Go into the village opposite you; and as soon as you have entered it you will find a colt tied, on which no one has sat. Loose it and bring *it.* 3 And if anyone says to you, 'Why are you doing this?' say, 'The Lord has need of it,' and immediately he will send it here."

4 So they went their way, and found the colt tied by the door outside on the street, and they loosed it. 5 But some of those who stood there said to them, "What are you doing, loosing the colt?" 6 And they spoke to them just as Jesus had commanded. So they let them go. 7 Then they brought the colt to Jesus and threw their clothes on it, and He sat on it. 8 And many spread their clothes on the road, and others cut down leafy branches from the trees and spread *them* on the road. 9 Then those who went before and those who followed cried out, saying:

    "Hosanna!
    'Blessed *is* He who comes in the name of the Lord!'
10 Blessed *is* the kingdom of our father David
    That comes in the name of the Lord! Hosanna in the highest!"

11 And Jesus went into Jerusalem and into the temple. So when He had looked around at all things, as the hour was already late, He went out to Bethany with the twelve.

12 Now the next day, when they had come out from Bethany, He was hungry. 13 And seeing from afar a fig tree having leaves, He went to see if perhaps He would find something on it. When He came to it, He found nothing but leaves, for it was not the season for figs. 14 In response Jesus said to it, "Let no one eat fruit from you ever again."

And His disciples heard *it*.

15 So they came to Jerusalem. Then Jesus went into the temple and began to drive out those who bought and sold in the temple, and overturned the tables of the money changers and the seats of those who sold doves. 16 And He would not allow anyone to carry wares through the temple. 17 Then He taught, saying to them, "Is it not written, 'My house shall be called a house of prayer for all nations'? But you have made it a 'den of thieves.'"

In the teaching of Jesus Christ prayer is the working of the miracle of redemption in me. (UTMOST)

18 And the scribes and chief priests heard it and sought how they might destroy Him; for they feared Him, because all the people were astonished at His teaching. 19 When evening had come, He went out of the city.

◆◆◆

*Reading 69—*The Hidden Life
Psalm 32:7

The most precarious thing is to try and live without God. If we are born again it is the easiest thing to live in right relationship to God and the most difficult thing to go wrong, if only we will heed God's warnings and keep in the light.

When we think of being delivered from sin, of being filled with the Spirit, and of walking in the light, we picture the peak of a great mountain, very high and wonderful, and we say—"Oh, but I could never live up there!" But when we do get there by God's grace, we find it is not a mountain peak, but a plateau where there is ample room to live and to grow. "You enlarged my path under me."

When you really see Jesus, I defy you to doubt Him. When He says—"Let not your heart be troubled," if you see Him I defy you to trouble your mind, it is a moral impossibility to doubt when He is there. Every time you get into personal contact with Jesus, His words are real. "My peace I give to you"; it is a peace all over from the crown of the head to the sole of the feet, an irrepressible confidence. "Your life is hid with Christ in God," and the imperturbable peace of Jesus Christ is imparted to you. (*UTMOST*)

NUMBERS 17:1—18:32

AND the LORD spoke to Moses, saying: 2 "Speak to the children of Israel, and get from them a rod from each father's house, all their leaders according to their fathers' houses—twelve rods. Write each man's name on his rod. 3 And you shall write Aaron's name on the rod of Levi. For there shall be one rod for the head of *each* father's house. 4 Then you shall place them in the tabernacle of meeting before the Testimony, where I meet with you. 5 And it shall be *that* the rod of the man whom I choose will blossom; thus I will rid Myself of the complaints of the children of Israel, which they make against you."

6 So Moses spoke to the children of Israel, and each of their leaders gave him a rod apiece, for each leader according to their fathers' houses, twelve rods; and the rod of Aaron *was* among their rods. 7 And Moses placed the rods before the LORD in the tabernacle of witness.

8 Now it came to pass on the next day that Moses went into the tabernacle of witness, and behold, the rod of Aaron, of the house of Levi, had sprouted and put forth buds, had produced blossoms and yielded ripe almonds. 9 Then Moses brought out all the rods from before the LORD to all the children of Israel; and they looked, and each man took his rod.

10 And the LORD said to Moses, "Bring

Aaron's rod back before the Testimony, to be kept as a sign against the rebels, that you may put their complaints away from Me, lest they die." 11 Thus did Moses; just as the LORD had commanded him, so he did.

12 So the children of Israel spoke to Moses, saying, "Surely we die, we perish, we all perish! 13 Whoever even comes near the tabernacle of the LORD must die. Shall we all utterly die?"

18 THEN the LORD said to Aaron: "You and your sons and your father's house with you shall bear the iniquity *related to* the sanctuary, and you and your sons with you shall bear the iniquity *associated with* your priesthood. 2 Also bring with you your brethren of the tribe of Levi, the tribe of your father, that they may be joined with you and serve you while you and your sons *are* with you before the tabernacle of witness. 3 They shall attend to your needs and all the needs of the tabernacle; but they shall not come near the articles of the sanctuary and the altar, lest they die—they and you also. 4 They shall be joined with you and attend to the needs of the tabernacle of meeting, for all the work of the tabernacle; but an outsider shall not come near you. 5 And you shall attend to the duties of the sanctuary and the duties of the altar, that there *may* be no more wrath on the children of Israel. 6 Behold, I Myself have taken your brethren the Levites from among the children of Israel; *they are* a gift to you, given by the LORD, to do the work of the tabernacle of meeting. 7 Therefore you and your sons with you shall attend to your priesthood for everything at the altar and behind the veil; and you shall serve. I give your priesthood *to you* as a gift for service, but the outsider who comes near shall be put to death."

8 And the LORD spoke to Aaron: "Here, I Myself have also given you charge of My heave offerings, all the holy gifts of the children of Israel; I have given them as a portion to you and your sons, as an ordinance forever. 9 This shall be yours of the most holy things *reserved* from the fire: every offering of theirs, every grain offering and every sin offering and every trespass offering which they render to Me, *shall be* most holy for you and your sons. 10 In a most holy *place* you shall eat it; every male shall eat it. It shall be holy to you.

11 "This also *is* yours: the heave offering of their gift, with all the wave offerings of the children of Israel; I have given them to you, and your sons and daughters with you, as an ordinance forever. Everyone who is clean in your house may eat it.

12 "All the best of the oil, all the best of the new wine and the grain, their firstfruits which they offer to the LORD, I have given them to you. 13 Whatever first ripe fruit is in their land, which they bring to the LORD, shall be yours. Everyone who is clean in your house may eat it.

14 "Every devoted thing in Israel shall be yours.

15 "Everything that first opens the womb of all flesh, which they bring to the LORD, whether man or beast, shall be yours; nevertheless the firstborn of man you shall surely redeem, and the firstborn of unclean animals you shall redeem. 16 And those redeemed of the devoted things you shall redeem when one month old, according to your valuation, for five shekels of silver, according to the shekel of the sanctuary, which *is* twenty gerahs. 17 But the firstborn of a cow, the firstborn of a sheep, or the firstborn of a goat you shall not redeem; they *are* holy. You shall sprinkle their blood on the altar, and burn their fat *as* an offering made by fire for a sweet aroma to the LORD. 18 And their flesh shall be yours, just as the wave breast and the right thigh are yours.

19 "All the heave offerings of the holy things, which the children of Israel offer to the LORD, I have given to you and your sons and daughters with you as an ordinance forever; it *is* a covenant of salt forever before the LORD with you and your descendants with you."

20 Then the LORD said to Aaron: "You shall have no inheritance in their land, nor shall you have any portion among them; I *am* your portion and your inheritance among the children of Israel.

21 "Behold, I have given the children of Levi all the tithes in Israel as an inheritance in return for the work which they perform, the work of the tabernacle of meeting. 22 Hereafter the children of Israel shall not come near the tabernacle of meeting, lest they bear sin and die. 23 But the Levites shall perform the work of the tabernacle of meeting, and they shall bear their iniquity; *it shall be* a statute forever, throughout your generations, that among the children of Israel they shall have no inheritance. 24 For the tithes of the children of Israel, which they offer up *as* a heave offering to the LORD, I have given to the Levites as an inheritance; therefore I have said to them, 'Among the children of Israel they shall have no inheritance.' "

25 Then the LORD spoke to Moses, say-

ing, 26 "Speak thus to the Levites, and say to them: 'When you take from the children of Israel the tithes which I have given you from them as your inheritance, then you shall offer up a heave offering of it to the LORD, a tenth of the tithe. 27 And your heave offering shall be reckoned to you as though *it were* the grain of the threshing floor and as the fullness of the winepress. 28 Thus you shall also offer a heave offering to the LORD from all your tithes which you receive from the children of Israel, and you shall give the LORD's heave offering from it to Aaron the priest. 29 Of all your gifts you shall offer up every heave offering due to the LORD, from all the best of them, the consecrated part of them.' 30 Therefore you shall say to them: 'When you have lifted up the best of it, then *the rest* shall be accounted to the Levites as the produce of the threshing floor and as the produce of the winepress. 31 You may eat it in any place, you and your households, for it *is* your reward for your work in the tabernacle of meeting. 32 And you shall bear no sin because of it, when you have lifted up the best of it. But you shall not profane the holy gifts of the children of Israel, lest you die.' "

PSALM 32:6–11

6 FOR this cause everyone who is godly shall pray to You
In a time when You may be found;
Surely in a flood of great waters
They shall not come near him.
7 You *are* my hiding place;
You shall preserve me from trouble;
You shall surround me with songs of deliverance.   Selah

Let your mind soak in the deliverance of God. (GOOD)

---

8 I will instruct you and teach you in the way you should go;
I will guide you with My eye.
9 Do not be like the horse *or* like the mule,
Which have no understanding,
Which must be harnessed with bit and bridle,
Else they will not come near you.
10 Many sorrows *shall be* to the wicked;
But he who trusts in the LORD, mercy shall surround him.

11 Be glad in the LORD and rejoice, you righteous;
And shout for joy, all *you* upright in heart!

PROVERBS 11:19–21

19 AS righteousness *leads* to life,
So he who pursues evil *pursues it* to his own death.
20 Those who are of a perverse heart *are* an abomination to the LORD,
But *the* blameless in their ways *are* His delight.
21 *Though they join* forces, the wicked will not go unpunished;
But the posterity of the righteous will be delivered.

MARK 11:20–33

NOW in the morning, as they passed by, they saw the fig tree dried up from the roots. 21 And Peter, remembering, said to Him, "Rabbi, look! The fig tree which You cursed has withered away."

22 So Jesus answered and said to them, "Have faith in God. 23 For assuredly, I say to you, whoever says to this mountain, 'Be removed and be cast into the sea,' and does not doubt in his heart, but believes that those things he says will be done, he will have whatever he says. 24 Therefore I say to you, whatever things you ask when you pray, believe that you receive *them,* and you will have *them.*

25 "And whenever you stand praying, if you have anything against anyone, forgive him, that your Father in heaven may also forgive you your trespasses. 26 But if you do not forgive, neither will your Father in heaven forgive your trespasses."

27 Then they came again to Jerusalem. And as He was walking in the temple, the chief priests, the scribes, and the elders came to Him. 28 And they said to Him, "By what authority are You doing these things? And who gave You this authority to do these things?"

29 But Jesus answered and said to them, "I also will ask you one question; then answer Me, and I will tell you by what authority I do these things: 30 The baptism of John—was it from heaven or from men? Answer Me."

31 And they reasoned among themselves, saying, "If we say, 'From heaven,' He will say, 'Why then did you not believe him?' 32 But if we say, 'From men' "—they feared

:ople, for all counted John to have a prophet indeed. 33 So they answered said to Jesus, "We do not know."

And Jesus answered and said to them, "Neither will I tell you by what authority I do these things."

◆◆◆

Reading 70—Question versus Revelation
Mark 12:18–27

Whenis "that day"? When the Ascended Lord makes you one with the Father. In that day you will be one with the Father as Jesus is. Until the resurrection life of Jesus is manifested in you, you want to ask this and that; then after a while you find all questions gone, you do not seem to have any left to ask. You have come to the place of entire reliance on the resurrection life of Jesus which brings you into perfect contact with the purpose of God. Are you living that life now? If not, why shouldn't you?

There may be any number of things dark to your understanding, but they do not come in between your heart and God. "And in that day you will ask Me nothing"—you do not need to, you are so certain that God will bring things out in accordance with His will. John 14:1 has become the real state of your heart, and there are no more questions to be asked. If anything is a mystery to you and it is coming in between you and God, never look for the explanation in your intellect, look for it in your disposition, it is that which is wrong. When once your disposition is willing to submit to the life of Jesus, the understanding will be perfectly clear, and you will get to the place where there is no distance between the Father and His child because the Lord has made you one, and "in that day you will ask Me nothing." (*UTMOST*)

NUMBERS 19:1—20:29

NOW the LORD spoke to Moses and Aaron, saying, 2 "This *is* the ordinance of the law which the LORD has commanded, saying: 'Speak to the children of Israel, that they bring you a red heifer without blemish, in which there *is* no defect *and* on which a yoke has never come. 3 You shall give it to Eleazar the priest, that he may take it outside the camp, and it shall be slaughtered before him; 4 and Eleazar the priest shall take some of its blood with his finger, and sprinkle some of its blood seven times directly in front of the tabernacle of meeting. 5 Then the heifer shall be burned in his sight: its hide, its flesh, its blood, and its offal shall be burned. 6 And the priest shall take cedar wood and hyssop and scarlet, and cast *them* into the midst of the fire burning the heifer. 7 Then the priest shall wash his clothes, he shall bathe in water, and afterward he shall come into the camp; the priest shall be unclean until evening. 8 And the one who burns it shall wash his clothes in water, bathe in water, and shall

be unclean until evening. 9 Then a man *who is* clean shall gather up the ashes of the heifer, and store *them* outside the camp in a clean place; and they shall be kept for the congregation of the children of Israel for the water of purification; it *is* for purifying from sin. 10 And the one who gathers the ashes of the heifer shall wash his clothes, and be unclean until evening. It shall be a statute forever to the children of Israel and to the stranger who dwells among them.

11 'He who touches the dead body of anyone shall be unclean seven days. 12 He shall purify himself with the water on the third day and on the seventh day; *then* he will be clean. But if he does not purify himself on the third day and on the seventh day, he will not be clean. 13 Whoever touches the body of anyone who has died, and does not purify himself, defiles the tabernacle of the LORD. That person hall be cut off from Israel. He shall be unclean, because the water of purification was not sprinkled on him; his uncleanness *is* still on him.

14 'This *is* the law when a man dies in a

tent: All who come into the tent and all who *are* in the tent shall be unclean seven days; 15 and every open vessel, which has no cover fastened on it, *is* unclean. 16 Whoever in the open field touches one who is slain by a sword or who has died, or a bone of a man, or a grave, shall be unclean seven days.

17 'And for an unclean *person* they shall take some of the ashes of the heifer burnt for purification from sin, and running water shall be put on them in a vessel. 18 A clean person shall take hyssop and dip *it* in the water, sprinkle *it* on the tent, on all the vessels, on the persons who were there, or on the one who touched a bone, the slain, the dead, or a grave. 19 The clean *person* shall sprinkle the unclean on the third day and on the seventh day; and on the seventh day he shall purify himself, wash his clothes, and bathe in water; and at evening he shall be clean.

20 'But the man who is unclean and does not purify himself, that person shall be cut off from among the assembly, because he has defiled the sanctuary of the LORD. The water of purification has not been sprinkled on him; he *is* unclean. 21 It shall be a perpetual statute for them. He who sprinkles the water of purification shall wash his clothes; and he who touches the water of purification shall be unclean until evening. 22 Whatever the unclean *person* touches shall be unclean; and the person who touches *it* shall be unclean until evening.' "

20 THEN the children of Israel, the whole congregation, came into the Wilderness of Zin in the first month, and the people stayed in Kadesh; and Miriam died there and was buried there.

2 Now there was no water for the congregation; so they gathered together against Moses and Aaron. 3 And the people contended with Moses and spoke, saying: "If only we had died when our brethren died before the LORD! 4 Why have you brought up the assembly of the LORD into this wilderness, that we and our animals should die here? 5 And why have you made us come up out of Egypt, to bring us to this evil place? It *is* not a place of grain or figs or vines or pomegranates; nor *is* there any water to drink." 6 So Moses and Aaron went from the presence of the assembly to the door of the tabernacle of meeting, and they fell on their faces. And the glory of the LORD appeared to them.

7 Then the LORD spoke to Moses, saying, 8 "Take the rod; you and your brother Aaron gather the congregation together.

Speak to the rock before their eyes, and it will yield its water; thus you shall bring water for them out of the rock, and give drink to the congregation and their animals." 9 So Moses took the rod from before the LORD as He commanded him.

10 And Moses and Aaron gathered the assembly together before the rock; and he said to them, "Hear now, you rebels! Must we bring water for you out of this rock?" 11 Then Moses lifted his hand and struck the rock twice with his rod; and water came out abundantly, and the congregation and their animals drank.

12 Then the LORD spoke to Moses and Aaron, "Because you did not believe Me, to hallow Me in the eyes of the children of Israel, therefore you shall not bring this assembly into the land which I have given them."

13 This *was* the water of Meribah, because the children of Israel contended with the LORD, and He was hallowed among them.

14 Now Moses sent messengers from Kadesh to the king of Edom. "Thus says your brother Israel: 'You know all the hardship that has befallen us, 15 how our fathers went down to Egypt, and we dwelt in Egypt a long time, and the Egyptians afflicted us and our fathers. 16 When we cried out to the LORD, He heard our voice and sent the Angel and brought us up out of Egypt; now here we are in Kadesh, a city on the edge of your border. 17 Please let us pass through your country. We will not pass through fields or vineyards, nor will we drink water from wells; we will go along the King's Highway; we will not turn aside to the right hand or to the left until we have passed through your territory.' "

18 Then Edom said to him, "You shall not pass through my *land,* lest I come out against you with the sword."

19 So the children of Israel said to him, "We will go by the Highway, and if I or my livestock drink any of your water, then I will pay for it; let me only pass through on foot, nothing *more.*"

20 Then he said, "You shall not pass through." So Edom came out against them with many men and with a strong hand. 21 Thus Edom refused to give Israel passage through his territory; so Israel turned away from him.

22 Now the children of Israel, the whole congregation, journeyed from Kadesh and came to Mount Hor. 23 And the LORD spoke to Moses and Aaron in Mount Hor by the border of the land of Edom, saying: 24 "Aaron shall be gathered to his people, for he shall not enter the land which I have

given to the children of Israel, because you rebelled against My word at the water of Meribah. 25 Take Aaron and Eleazar his son, and bring them up to Mount Hor; 26 and strip Aaron of his garments and put them on Eleazar his son; for Aaron shall be gathered *to his people* and die there." 27 So Moses did just as the LORD commanded, and they went up to Mount Hor in the sight of all the congregation. 28 Moses stripped Aaron of his garments and put them on Eleazar his son; and Aaron died there on the top of the mountain. Then Moses and Eleazar came down from the mountain. 29 Now when all the congregation saw that Aaron was dead, all the house of Israel mourned for Aaron thirty days.

PSALM 33:1–9

1   REJOICE in the LORD, O you
    righteous!
    For praise from the upright is beautiful.
2   Praise the LORD with the harp;
    Make melody to Him with an
        instrument of ten strings.
3   Sing to Him a new song;
    Play skillfully with a shout of joy.

4   For the word of the LORD *is* right,
    And all His work *is done* in truth.
5   He loves righteousness and justice;
    The earth is full of the goodness of the
        LORD.

6   By the word of the LORD the heavens
        were made,
    And all the host of them by the breath
        of His mouth.
7   He gathers the waters of the sea
        together as a heap;
    He lays up the deep in storehouses.

8   Let all the earth fear the LORD;
    Let all the inhabitants of the world
        stand in awe of Him.
9   For He spoke, and it was *done;*
    He commanded, and it stood fast.

PROVERBS 11:22–24

22 *AS* a ring of gold in a swine's snout,
    So is a lovely woman who lacks
        discretion.

23 The desire of the righteous *is* only good,
    But the expectation of the wicked *is*
        wrath.

24 There is *one* who scatters, yet increases
        more;
    And there is *one* who withholds more
        than is right,
    But it *leads* to poverty.

MARK 12:1–27

THEN He began to speak to them in parables: "A man planted a vineyard and set a hedge around *it,* dug *a place for* the wine vat and built a tower. And he leased it to vinedressers and went into a far country. 2 Now at vintage-time he sent a servant to the vinedressers, that he might receive some of the fruit of the vineyard from the vinedressers. 3 And they took *him* and beat him and sent *him* away empty-handed. 4 Again he sent them another servant, and at him they threw stones, wounded *him* in the head, and sent *him* away shamefully treated. 5 And again he sent another, and him they killed; and many others, beating some and killing some. 6 Therefore still having one son, his beloved, he also sent him to them last, saying, 'They will respect my son.' 7 But those vinedressers said among themselves, 'This is the heir. Come, let us kill him, and the inheritance will be ours.' 8 So they took him and killed *him* and cast *him* out of the vineyard.

9 "Therefore what will the owner of the vineyard do? He will come and destroy the vinedressers, and give the vineyard to others. 10 Have you not even read this Scripture:

'The stone which the builders rejected
    Has become the chief cornerstone.
11 This was the LORD's doing,
    And it is marvelous in our eyes'? "

12 And they sought to lay hands on Him, but feared the multitude, for they knew He had spoken the parable against them. So they left Him and went away.

13 Then they sent to Him some of the Pharisees and the Herodians, to catch Him in *His* words. 14 When they had come, they said to Him, "Teacher, we know that You are true, and care about no one; for You do not regard the person of men, but teach the way of God in truth. Is it lawful to pay taxes to Caesar, or not? 15 Shall we pay, or shall we not pay?"

But He, knowing their hypocrisy, said to them, "Why do you test Me? Bring Me a denarius that I may see *it.*" 16 So they brought *it.*

And He said to them, "Whose image and

inscription *is* this?" They said to Him, "Caesar's."

17 And Jesus answered and said to them, "Render to Caesar the things that are Caesar's, and to God the things that are God's."

And they marveled at Him.

18 Then *some* Sadducees, who say there is no resurrection, came to Him; and they asked Him, saying: 19 "Teacher, Moses wrote to us that if a man's brother dies, and leaves *his* wife behind, and leaves no children, his brother should take his wife and raise up offspring for his brother. 20 Now there were seven brothers. The first took a wife; and dying, he left no offspring. 21 And the second took her, and he died; nor did he leave any offspring. And the third likewise. 22 So the seven had her and left no offspring. Last of all the woman died also. 23 Therefore, in the resurrection, when they rise, whose wife will she be? For all seven had her as wife."

24 Jesus answered and said to them, "Are you not therefore mistaken, because you do not know the Scriptures nor the power of God? 25 For when they rise from the dead, they neither marry nor are given in marriage, but are like angels in heaven. 26 But concerning the dead, that they rise, have you not read in the book of Moses, in the *burning* bush *passage*, how God spoke to him, saying, 'I *am* the God of Abraham, the God of Isaac, and the God of Jacob'? 27 He is not the God of the dead, but the God of the living. You are therefore greatly mistaken."

*B*eware of the tendency to water down the supernatural in religion. (APPROVED)

Reading 71—The Embrace of Love
Mark 12:29, 30

My relationship to God embraces every faculty, I am to love Him with *all* my heart, *all* my soul, *all* my mind, *all* my strength, every detail is instinct with devotion to Him; if it is not I am disjointed somewhere. Think what you do for someone you love! The most amazingly minute details are perfectly transfigured because your whole nature is embraced, not one faculty only. You don't love a person with your heart and leave the rest of your nature out, you love with your whole being, from the crown of the head to the sole of the foot. That is the attitude of the New Testament all through. In 1 Corinthians 15 the apostle Paul has been speaking about the stupendous mystery of the resurrection, and suddenly, like a swinging lamp in a mine, he rushes it right straight down and says, "Now concerning the collection . . ." The New Testament is continually doing it—"Jesus knowing . . . that the Father had given all things into His hands . . . began to wash the disciples' feet." It takes God Incarnate to wash feet properly. It takes God Incarnate to do anything properly. (GOD'S WORKMANSHIP)

NUMBERS 21:1—22:41

THE king of Arad, the Canaanite, who dwelt in the South, heard that Israel was coming on the road to Atharim. Then he fought against Israel and took *some* of them prisoners. 2 So Israel made a vow to the LORD, and said, "If You will indeed deliver this people into my hand, then I will utterly destroy their cities." 3 And the LORD listened to the voice of Israel and delivered up the Canaanites, and they utterly destroyed them and their cities. So the name of that place was called Hormah.

4 Then they journeyed from Mount Hor by the Way of the Red Sea, to go around the land of Edom; and the soul of the people became very discouraged on the way.

5 And the people spoke against God and against Moses: "Why have you brought us up out of Egypt to die in the wilderness? For *there is* no food and no water, and our soul loathes this worthless bread." 6 So the LORD sent fiery serpents among the people, and they bit the people; and many of the people of Israel died.

7 Therefore the people came to Moses, and said, "We have sinned, for we have spoken against the LORD and against you; pray to the LORD that He take away the serpents from us." So Moses prayed for the people.

Get into the habit of dealing with God about everything.   (UTMOST)

---

8 Then the LORD said to Moses, "Make a fiery *serpent*, and set it on a pole; and it shall be that everyone who is bitten, when he looks at it, shall live." 9 So Moses made a bronze serpent, and put it on a pole; and so it was, if a serpent had bitten anyone, when he looked at the bronze serpent, he lived.

10 Now the children of Israel moved on and camped in Oboth. 11 And they journeyed from Oboth and camped at Ije Abarim, in the wilderness which *is* east of Moab, toward the sunrise. 12 From there they moved and camped in the Valley of Zered. 13 From there they moved and camped on the other side of the Arnon, which *is* in the wilderness that extends from the border of the Amorites; for the Arnon *is* the border of Moab, between Moab and the Amorites. 14 Therefore it is said in the Book of the Wars of the LORD:

> "Waheb in Suphah,
>   The brooks of the Arnon,
> 15 And the slope of the brooks
>   That reaches to the dwelling of Ar,
>   And lies on the border of Moab."

16 From there *they went* to Beer, which *is* the well where the LORD said to Moses, "Gather the people together, and I will give them water." 17 Then Israel sang this song:

> "Spring up, O well!
>   All of you sing to it—
> 18 The well the leaders sank,
>   Dug by the nation's nobles,
>   By the lawgiver, with their staves."

And from the wilderness *they went* to Mattanah, 19 from Mattanah to Nahaliel,

from Nahaliel to Bamoth, 20 and from Bamoth, *in* the valley that *is* in the country of Moab, to the top of Pisgah which looks down on the wasteland.

21 Then Israel sent messengers to Sihon king of the Amorites, saying, 22 "Let me pass through your land. We will not turn aside into fields or vineyards; we will not drink water from wells. We will go by the King's Highway until we have passed through your territory." 23 But Sihon would not allow Israel to pass through his territory. So Sihon gathered all his people together and went out against Israel in the wilderness, and he came to Jahaz and fought against Israel. 24 Then Israel defeated him with the edge of the sword, and took possession of his land from the Arnon to the Jabbok, as far as the people of Ammon; for the border of the people of Ammon *was* fortified. 25 So Israel took all these cities, and Israel dwelt in all the cities of the Amorites, in Heshbon and in all its villages. 26 For Heshbon *was* the city of Sihon king of the Amorites, who had fought against the former king of Moab, and had taken all his land from his hand as far as the Arnon. 27 Therefore those who speak in proverbs say:

> "Come to Heshbon, let it be built;
>   Let the city of Sihon be repaired.
>
> 28 "For fire went out from Heshbon,
>   A flame from the city of Sihon;
>   It consumed Ar of Moab,
>   The lords of the heights of the Arnon.
> 29 Woe to you, Moab!
>   You have perished, O people of
>   Chemosh!
>   He has given his sons as fugitives,
>   And his daughters into captivity,
>   To Sihon king of the Amorites.
>
> 30 "But we have shot at them;
>   Heshbon has perished as far as
>   Dibon.
>   Then we laid waste as far as Nophah,
>   Which *reaches* to Medeba."

31 Thus Israel dwelt in the land of the Amorites. 32 Then Moses sent to spy out Jazer; and they took its villages and drove out the Amorites who *were* there.

33 And they turned and went up by the way to Bashan. So Og king of Bashan went out against them, he and all his people, to battle at Edrei. 34 Then the LORD said to Moses, "Do not fear him, for I have delivered him into your hand, with all his people and his land; and you shall do to him as

you did to Sihon king of the Amorites, who dwelt at Heshbon." 35 So they defeated him, his sons, and all his people, until there was no survivor left him; and they took possession of his land.

22 THEN the children of Israel moved, and camped in the plains of Moab on the side of the Jordan *across from* Jericho.

2 Now Balak the son of Zippor saw all that Israel had done to the Amorites. 3 And Moab was exceedingly afraid of the people because they *were* many, and Moab was sick with dread because of the children of Israel. 4 So Moab said to the elders of Midian, "Now this company will lick up everything around us, as an ox licks up the grass of the field." And Balak the son of Zippor *was* king of the Moabites at that time. 5 Then he sent messengers to Balaam the son of Beor at Pethor, which *is* near the River in the land of the sons of his people, to call him, saying: "Look, a people has come from Egypt. See, they cover the face of the earth, and are settling next to me! 6 Therefore please come at once, curse this people for me, for they *are* too mighty for me. Perhaps I shall be able to defeat them and drive them out of the land, for I know that he whom you bless *is* blessed, and he whom you curse is cursed."

7 So the elders of Moab and the elders of Midian departed with the diviner's fee in their hand, and they came to Balaam and spoke to him the words of Balak. 8 And he said to them, "Lodge here tonight, and I will bring back word to you, as the LORD speaks to me." So the princes of Moab stayed with Balaam.

9 Then God came to Balaam and said, "Who *are* these men with you?"

10 So Balaam said to God, "Balak the son of Zippor, king of Moab, has sent to me, *saying,* 11 'Look, a people has come out of Egypt, and they cover the face of the earth. Come now, curse them for me; perhaps I shall be able to overpower them and drive them out.'"

12 And God said to Balaam, "You shall not go with them; you shall not curse the people, for they *are* blessed."

13 So Balaam rose in the morning and said to the princes of Balak, "Go back to your land, for the LORD has refused to give me permission to go with you."

14 And the princes of Moab rose and went to Balak, and said, "Balaam refuses to come with us."

15 Then Balak again sent princes, more numerous and more honorable than they. 16 And they came to Balaam and said to

him, "Thus says Balak the son of Zippor: 'Please let nothing hinder you from coming to me; 17 for I will certainly honor you greatly, and I will do whatever you say to me. Therefore please come, curse this people for me.'"

18 Then Balaam answered and said to the servants of Balak, "Though Balak were to give me his house full of silver and gold, I could not go beyond the word of the LORD my God, to do less or more. 19 Now therefore, please, you also stay here tonight, that I may know what more the LORD will say to me."

20 And God came to Balaam at night and said to him, "If the men come to call you, rise *and* go with them; but only the word which I speak to you—that you shall do."

21 So Balaam rose in the morning, saddled his donkey, and went with the princes of Moab.

22 Then God's anger was aroused because he went, and the Angel of the LORD took His stand in the way as an adversary against him. And he was riding on his donkey, and his two servants *were* with him. 23 Now the donkey saw the Angel of the LORD standing in the way with His drawn sword in His hand, and the donkey turned aside out of the way and went into the field. So Balaam struck the donkey to turn her back onto the road. 24 Then the Angel of the LORD stood in a narrow path between the vineyards, *with* a wall on this side and a wall on that side. 25 And when the donkey saw the Angel of the LORD, she pushed herself against the wall and crushed Balaam's foot against the wall; so he struck her again. 26 Then the Angel of the LORD went further, and stood in a narrow place where there *was* no way to turn either to the right hand or to the left. 27 And when the donkey saw the Angel of the LORD, she lay down under Balaam; so Balaam's anger was aroused, and he struck the donkey with his staff.

28 Then the LORD opened the mouth of the donkey, and she said to Balaam, "What have I done to you, that you have struck me these three times?"

29 And Balaam said to the donkey, "Because you have abused me. I wish there were a sword in my hand, for now I would kill you!"

30 So the donkey said to Balaam, "*Am* I not your donkey on which you have ridden, ever since *I became* yours, to this day? Was I ever disposed to do this to you?"

And he said, "No."

31 Then the LORD opened Balaam's eyes, and he saw the Angel of the LORD standing

in the way with His drawn sword in His hand; and he bowed his head and fell flat on his face. 32 And the Angel of the LORD said to him, "Why have you struck your donkey these three times? Behold, I have come out to stand against you, because *your* way is perverse before Me. 33 The donkey saw Me and turned aside from Me these three times. If she had not turned aside from Me, surely I would also have killed you by now, and let her live."

34 And Balaam said to the Angel of the LORD, "I have sinned, for I did not know You stood in the way against me. Now therefore, if it displeases You, I will turn back."

35 Then the Angel of the LORD said to Balaam, "Go with the men, but only the word that I speak to you, that you shall speak." So Balaam went with the princes of Balak.

36 Now when Balak heard that Balaam was coming, he went out to meet him at the city of Moab, which *is* on the border at the Arnon, the boundary of the territory. 37 Then Balak said to Balaam, "Did I not earnestly send to you, calling for you? Why did you not come to me? Am I not able to honor you?"

38 And Balaam said to Balak, "Look, I have come to you! Now, have I any power at all to say anything? The word that God puts in my mouth, that I must speak." 39 So Balaam went with Balak, and they came to Kirjath Huzoth. 40 Then Balak offered oxen and sheep, and he sent *some* to Balaam and to the princes who *were* with him.

41 So it was, the next day, that Balak took Balaam and brought him up to the high places of Baal, that from there he might observe the extent of the people.

PSALM 33:10–17

10 THE LORD brings the counsel of the nations to nothing;
He makes the plans of the peoples of no effect.
11 The counsel of the LORD stands forever,
The plans of His heart to all generations.
12 Blessed *is* the nation whose God *is* the LORD,
The people He has chosen as His own inheritance.
13 The LORD looks from heaven;
He sees all the sons of men.

14 From the place of His dwelling He looks
On all the inhabitants of the earth;
15 He fashions their hearts individually;
He considers all their works.
16 No king *is* saved by the multitude of an army;
A mighty man is not delivered by great strength.
17 A horse *is* a vain hope for safety;
Neither shall it deliver *any* by its great strength.

PROVERBS 11:25, 26

25 THE generous soul will be made rich,
And he who waters will also be watered himself.
26 The people will curse him who withholds grain,
But blessing *will be* on the head of him who sells *it*.

MARK 12:28–44

THEN one of the scribes came, and having heard them reasoning together, perceiving that He had answered them well, asked Him, "Which is the first commandment of all?"

29 Jesus answered him, "The first of all the commandments *is:* 'Hear, O Israel, the LORD our God, the LORD is one. 30 And you shall love the LORD your God with all your heart, with all your soul, with all your mind, and with all your strength.' This *is* the first commandment. 31 And the second, like *it, is* this: 'You shall love your neighbor as yourself.' There is no other commandment greater than these."

32 So the scribe said to Him, "Well *said*, Teacher. You have spoken the truth, for there is one God, and there is no other but He. 33 And to love Him with all the heart, with all the understanding, with all the soul, and with all the strength, and to love one's neighbor as oneself, is more than all the whole burnt offerings and sacrifices."

34 Now when Jesus saw that he answered wisely, He said to him, "You are not far from the kingdom of God."

But after that no one dared question Him.

35 Then Jesus answered and said, while He taught in the temple, "How *is it* that the scribes say that the Christ is the Son of David? 36 For David himself said by the Holy Spirit:

'The Lord said to my Lord,
"Sit at My right hand,
Till I make Your enemies Your
footstool." '

37 Therefore David himself calls Him 'Lord'; how is He *then* his Son?"

And the common people heard Him gladly.

38 Then He said to them in His teaching, "Beware of the scribes, who desire to go around in long robes, *love* greetings in the marketplaces, 39 the best seats in the synagogues, and the best places at feasts, 40 who devour widows' houses, and for a pretense make long prayers. These will receive greater condemnation."

41 Now Jesus sat opposite the treasury and saw how the people put money into the treasury. And many *who were* rich put in much. 42 Then one poor widow came and threw in two mites, which make a quadrans. 43 So He called His disciples to *Himself* and said to them, "Assuredly, I say to you that this poor widow has put in more than all those who have given to the treasury; 44 for they all put in out of their abundance, but she out of her poverty put in all that she had, her whole livelihood."

◆◆◆

Reading 72—The Basis of Panic
Mark 13:7

That is either the statement of a madman or of a Being who has power to put something into a man and keep him free from panic, even in the midst of the awful terror of war. The basis of panic is always cowardice. Our Lord teaches us to look things full in the face. He says—"When you hear of wars, don't be scared." It is the most natural thing in the world to be scared, and the clearest evidence that God's grace is at work in our hearts is when we do not get into panics. Our Lord insists on the inevitableness of peril. He says, "You must lay your account with war, with hatred, and with death." Men may have lived undisturbed over a volcano for a long while, when suddenly an eruption occurs. Jesus Christ did not say—"You will understand why war has come," but—"Don't be scared when it does come, do not be in a panic." It is astonishing how we ignore Jesus Christ's words. He said that nations would end in war and bloodshed and havoc. We ignore His warnings; and when war comes we lose our wits and exhibit panic.   (*Shad. Agony*)

NUMBERS 23:1—24:25

THEN Balaam said to Balak, "Build seven altars for me here, and prepare for me here seven bulls and seven rams."

2 And Balak did just as Balaam had spoken, and Balak and Balaam offered a bull and a ram on *each* altar. 3 Then Balaam said to Balak, "Stand by your burnt offering, and I will go; perhaps the Lord will come to meet me, and whatever He shows me I will tell you." So he went to a desolate height. 4 And God met Balaam, and he said to Him, "I have prepared the seven altars, and I have offered on *each* altar a bull and a ram."

5 Then the Lord put a word in Balaam's mouth, and said, "Return to Balak, and thus you shall speak." 6 So he returned to him, and there he was, standing by his burnt offering, he and all the princes of Moab.

7 And he took up his oracle and said:

"Balak the king of Moab has brought
   me from Aram,
From the mountains of the east.
'Come, curse Jacob for me,
   And come, denounce Israel!'

8 "How shall I curse whom God has
   not cursed?
And how shall I denounce *whom* the
   Lord has not denounced?
9 For from the top of the rocks I see
   him,
And from the hills I behold him;

> There! A people dwelling alone,
> Not reckoning itself among the
> nations.

10 "Who can count the dust of Jacob,
   Or number one-fourth of Israel?
   Let me die the death of the righteous,
   And let my end be like his!"

11 Then Balak said to Balaam, "What have you done to me? I took you to curse my enemies, and look, you have blessed *them* bountifully!"

12 So he answered and said, "Must I not take heed to speak what the LORD has put in my mouth?"

13 Then Balak said to him, "Please come with me to another place from which you may see them; you shall see only the outer part of them, and shall not see them all; curse them for me from there." 14 So he brought him to the field of Zophim, to the top of Pisgah, and built seven altars, and offered a bull and a ram on *each* altar.

15 And he said to Balak, "Stand here by your burnt offering while I meet *the* LORD over there."

16 Then the LORD met Balaam, and put a word in his mouth, and said, "Go back to Balak, and thus you shall speak." 17 So he came to him, and there he was, standing by his burnt offering, and the princes of Moab were with him. And Balak said to him, "What has the LORD spoken?"

18 Then he took up his oracle and said:

> "Rise up, Balak, and hear!
> Listen to me, son of Zippor!

19 "God *is* not a man, that He should
   lie,
   Nor a son of man, that He should
    repent.
   Has He said, and will He not do?
   Or has He spoken, and will He not
    make it good?

20 Behold, I have received *a command*
    to bless;
   He has blessed, and I cannot reverse
    it.

21 "He has not observed iniquity in
    Jacob,
   Nor has He seen wickedness in Israel.
   The LORD his God *is* with him,
   And the shout of a King *is* among
    them.

22 God brings them out of Egypt;
   He has strength like a wild ox.

23 "For *there is* no sorcery against Jacob,
   Nor any divination against Israel.

> It now must be said of Jacob
> And of Israel, 'Oh, what God has
> done!'

24 Look, a people rises like a lioness,
   And lifts itself up like a lion;
   It shall not lie down until it devours
    the prey,
   And drinks the blood of the slain."

25 Then Balak said to Balaam, "Neither curse them at all, nor bless them at all!"

26 So Balaam answered and said to Balak, "Did I not tell you, saying, 'All that the LORD speaks, that I must do'?"

27 Then Balak said to Balaam, "Please come, I will take you to another place; perhaps it will please God that you may curse them for me from there." 28 So Balak took Balaam to the top of Peor, that overlooks the wasteland. 29 Then Balaam said to Balak, "Build for me here seven altars, and prepare for me here seven bulls and seven rams." 30 And Balak did as Balaam had said, and offered a bull and a ram on *every* altar.

24 NOW when Balaam saw that it pleased the LORD to bless Israel, he did not go as at other times, to seek to use sorcery, but he set his face toward the wilderness. 2 And Balaam raised his eyes, and saw Israel encamped according to their tribes; and the Spirit of God came upon him.

3 Then he took up his oracle and said:

> "The utterance of Balaam the son of
> Beor,
> The utterance of the man whose eyes
> are opened,
4 The utterance of him who hears the
> words of God,
> Who sees the vision of the Almighty,
> Who falls down, with eyes wide
> open:

5 "How lovely are your tents, O Jacob!
   Your dwellings, O Israel!
6 Like valleys that stretch out,
   Like gardens by the riverside,
   Like aloes planted by the LORD,
   Like cedars beside the waters.
7 He shall pour water from his buckets,
   And his seed *shall be* in many waters.

> "His king shall be higher than Agag,
> And his kingdom shall be exalted.

8 "God brings him out of Egypt;
   He has strength like a wild ox;
   He shall consume the nations, his
    enemies;
   He shall break their bones

And pierce *them* with his arrows.
9 'He bows down, he lies down as a
    lion;
    And as a lion, who shall rouse him?'

"Blessed *is* he who blesses you,
And cursed *is* he who curses you."

10 Then Balak's anger was aroused against Balaam, and he struck his hands together; and Balak said to Balaam, "I called you to curse my enemies, and look, you have bountifully blessed *them* these three times! 11 Now therefore, flee to your place. I said I would greatly honor you, but in fact, the LORD has kept you back from honor."

12 So Balaam said to Balak, "Did I not also speak to your messengers whom you sent to me, saying, 13 'If Balak were to give me his house full of silver and gold, I could not go beyond the word of the LORD, to do good or bad of my own will. What the LORD says, that I must speak'? 14 And now, indeed, I am going to my people. Come, I will advise you what this people will do to your people in the latter days."

15 So he took up his oracle and said:

"The utterance of Balaam the son of
    Beor,
And the utterance of the man whose
    eyes are opened;
16   The utterance of him who hears the
    words of God,
And has the knowledge of the Most
    High,
Who sees the vision of the Almighty,
Who falls down, with eyes wide open:

17 "I see Him, but not now;
I behold Him, but not near;
A Star shall come out of Jacob;
A Scepter shall rise out of Israel,
And batter the brow of Moab,
And destroy all the sons of tumult.

18 "And Edom shall be a possession;
Seir also, his enemies, shall be a
    possession,
While Israel does valiantly.
19 Out of Jacob One shall have
    dominion,
And destroy the remains of the city."

20 Then he looked on Amalek, and he took up his oracle and said:

"Amalek *was* first among the nations,
But *shall be* last until he perishes."

21 Then he looked on the Kenites, and he took up his oracle and said:

"Firm is your dwelling place,
And your nest is set in the rock;
22 Nevertheless Kain shall be burned.
    How long until Asshur carries you
    away captive?"

23 Then he took up his oracle and said:

"Alas! Who shall live when God does
    this?
24 But ships *shall come* from the coasts
    of Cyprus,
And they shall afflict Asshur and
    afflict Eber,
And so shall *Amalek*, until he
    perishes."

25 So Balaam rose and departed and returned to his place; Balak also went his way.

PSALM 33:18–22

18 BEHOLD, the eye of the LORD *is* on
    those who fear Him,
    On those who hope in His mercy,
19 To deliver their soul from death,
    And to keep them alive in famine.

20 Our soul waits for the LORD;
    He *is* our help and our shield.
21 For our heart shall rejoice in Him,
    Because we have trusted in His holy
    name.
22 Let Your mercy, O LORD, be upon us,
    Just as we hope in You.

PROVERBS 11:27

27 HE who earnestly seeks good finds
    favor,
    But trouble will come to him who seeks
    evil.

MARK 13:1–20

THEN as He went out of the temple, one of His disciples said to Him, "Teacher, see what manner of stones and what buildings *are here!*"

2 And Jesus answered and said to him, "Do you see these great buildings? Not *one* stone shall be left upon another, that shall not be thrown down."

3 Now as He sat on the Mount of Olives opposite the temple, Peter, James, John, and Andrew asked Him privately, 4 "Tell

us, when will these things be? And what *will be* the sign when all these things will be fulfilled?"

5 And Jesus, answering them, began to say: "Take heed that no one deceives you. 6 For many will come in My name, saying, 'I am *He*,' and will deceive many. 7 But when you hear of wars and rumors of wars, do not be troubled; for *such things* must happen, but the end *is* not yet. 8 For nation will rise against nation, and kingdom against kingdom. And there will be earthquakes in various places, and there will be famines and troubles. These *are* the beginnings of sorrows.

9 "But watch out for yourselves, for they will deliver you up to councils, and you will be beaten in the synagogues. You will be brought before rulers and kings for My sake, for a testimony to them. 10 And the gospel must first be preached to all the nations. 11 But when they arrest *you* and de-

---

The Holy Spirit cannot bring back to our minds what we have never troubled to put there. (MORAL FOUND.)

---

liver you up, do not worry beforehand, or premeditate what you will speak. But whatever is given you in that hour, speak that; for it is not you who speak, but the Holy Spirit. 12 Now brother will betray brother to death, and a father *his* child; and children will rise up against parents and cause them to be put to death. 13 And you will be hated by all for My name's sake. But he who endures to the end shall be saved.

14 "So when you see the 'abomination of desolation,' spoken of by Daniel the prophet, standing where it ought not" (let the reader understand), "then let those who are in Judea flee to the mountains. 15 Let him who is on the housetop not go down into the house, nor enter to take anything out of his house. 16 And let him who is in the field not go back to get his clothes. 17 But woe to those who are pregnant and to those who are nursing babies in those days! 18 And pray that your flight may not be in winter. 19 For *in* those days there will be tribulation, such as has not been since the beginning of the creation which God created until this time, nor ever shall be. 20 And unless the Lord had shortened those days, no flesh would be saved; but for the elect's sake, whom He chose, He shortened the days.

Reading 73—United to Idols

Numbers 25:1–3

The psalmist prayed, "Unite my heart to fear Your name"—the whole spirit, soul and body so united with God that the soul does not think separately of body, soul or spirit, but only of God. There are false unities possible in a man's experience whereby man's spirit, soul and body are brought into harmony. Paul calls these things idolatry, because idolatry is the uniting of body, soul and spirit to the wrong god.

If we are despising the chastening of the Lord and fainting when rebuked of Him, it is because we do not understand what God is doing; He is weaning us from creatures to Himself, from the things we have been united to instead of being united to Him only. (*PERFECT*)

NUMBERS 25:1—26:65

NOW Israel remained in Acacia Grove, and the people began to commit harlotry with the women of Moab. 2 They invited the people to the sacrifices of their gods, and the people ate and bowed down to their gods. 3 So Israel was joined to Baal of Peor, and the anger of the LORD was aroused against Israel.

4 Then the LORD said to Moses, "Take all the leaders of the people and hang the offenders before the LORD, out in the sun, that the fierce anger of the LORD may turn away from Israel."

It is impossible for a man to know the views of Almighty God. (BAFFLED)

5 So Moses said to the judges of Israel, "Every one of you kill his men who were joined to Baal of Peor."

6 And indeed, one of the children of Israel came and presented to his brethren a Midianite woman in the sight of Moses and in the sight of all the congregation of the children of Israel, who *were* weeping at the door of the tabernacle of meeting. 7 Now when Phinehas the son of Eleazar, the son of Aaron the priest, saw *it*, he rose from among the congregation and took a javelin in his hand; 8 and he went after the man of Israel into the tent and thrust both of them through, the man of Israel, and the woman through her body. So the plague was stopped among the children of Israel. 9 And those who died in the plague were twenty-four thousand.

10 Then the LORD spoke to Moses, saying: 11 "Phinehas the son of Eleazar, the son of Aaron the priest, has turned back My wrath from the children of Israel, because he was zealous with My zeal among them, so that I did not consume the children of Israel in My zeal. 12 Therefore say, 'Behold, I give to him My covenant of peace; 13 and it shall be to him and his descendants after him a covenant of an everlasting priesthood, because he was zealous for his God, and made atonement for the children of Israel.' "

14 Now the name of the Israelite who was killed, who was killed with the Midianite woman, *was* Zimri the son of Salu, a leader of a father's house among the Simeonites. 15 And the name of the Midianite woman who was killed *was* Cozbi the daughter of Zur; he *was* head of the people of a father's house in Midian.

16 Then the LORD spoke to Moses, saying: 17 "Harass the Midianites, and attack them; 18 for they harassed you with their schemes by which they seduced you in the matter of Peor and in the matter of Cozbi, the daughter of a leader of Midian, their sister, who was killed in the day of the plague because of Peor."

26 AND it came to pass, after the plague, that the LORD spoke to Moses and Eleazar the son of Aaron the priest, saying: 2 "Take a census of all the congregation of the children of Israel from twenty years old and above, by their fathers' houses, all who are able to go to war in Israel."

3 So Moses and Eleazar the priest spoke with them in the plains of Moab by the Jordan, *across from* Jericho, saying: 4 *"Take a census of the people* from twenty years old and above, just as the LORD commanded Moses and the children of Israel who came out of the land of Egypt."

5 Reuben *was* the firstborn of Israel. The children of Reuben *were:* of Hanoch, the family of the Hanochites; of Pallu, the family of the Palluites; 6 of Hezron, the family of the Hezronites; of Carmi, the family of the Carmites. 7 These *are* the families of the Reubenites: those who were numbered of them were forty-three thousand seven hundred and thirty. 8 And the son of Pallu *was* Eliab. 9 The sons of Eliab *were* Nemuel, Dathan, and Abiram. These *are* the Dathan and Abiram, representatives of the congregation, who contended against Moses and Aaron in the company of Korah, when they contended against the LORD; 10 and the earth opened its mouth and swallowed them up together with Korah when that company died, when the fire devoured two hundred and fifty men; and they became a sign. 11 Nevertheless the children of Korah did not die.

12 The sons of Simeon according to their families *were:* of Nemuel, the family of the Nemuelites; of Jamin, the family of the Jaminites; of Jachin, the family of the Jachinites; 13 of Zerah, the family of the Zarhites; of Shaul, the family of the Shaulites. 14 These *are* the families of the Simeonites: twenty-two thousand two hundred.

15 The sons of Gad according to their families *were:* of Zephon, the family of the Zephonites; of Haggi, the family of the Haggites; of Shuni, the family of the Shunites; 16 of Ozni, the family of the Oznites; of Eri, the family of the Erites; 17 of Arod, the family of the Arodites; of Areli, the family of the Arelites. 18 These *are* the families of the sons of Gad according to those who were numbered of them: forty thousand five hundred.

19 The sons of Judah *were* Er and Onan; and Er and Onan died in the land of Canaan. 20 And the sons of Judah according to their families were: of Shelah, the family of the Shelanites; of Perez, the family of the Parzites; of Zerah, the family of the Zarhites. 21 And the sons of Perez were: of Hezron, the family of the Hezronites; of Hamul, the family of the Hamulites. 22 These *are* the families of Judah according to those who were numbered of them: seventy-six thousand five hundred.

23 The sons of Issachar according to their families *were:* of Tola, the family of the To-

laites; of Puah, the family of the Punites; 24 of Jashub, the family of the Jashubites; of Shimron, the family of the Shimronites. 25 These *are* the families of Issachar according to those who were numbered of them: sixty-four thousand three hundred.

26 The sons of Zebulun according to their families *were:* of Sered, the family of the Sardites; of Elon, the family of the Elonites; of Jahleel, the family of the Jahleelites. 27 These *are* the families of the Zebulunites according to those who were numbered of them: sixty thousand five hundred.

28 The sons of Joseph according to their families, by Manasseh and Ephraim, *were:* 29 The sons of Manasseh: of Machir, the family of the Machirites; and Machir begot Gilead; of Gilead, the family of the Gileadites. 30 These *are* the sons of Gilead: *of* Jeezer, the family of the Jeezerites; of Helek, the family of the Helekites; 31 *of* Asriel, the family of the Asrielites; *of* Shechem, the family of the Shechemites; 32 *of* Shemida, the family of the Shemidaites; *of* Hepher, the family of the Hepherites. 33 Now Zelophehad the son of Hepher had no sons, but daughters; and the names of the daughters of Zelophehad *were* Mahlah, Noah, Hoglah, Milcah, and Tirzah. 34 These *are* the families of Manasseh; and those who were numbered of them *were* fifty-two thousand five hundred.

35 These *are* the sons of Ephraim according to their families: of Shuthelah, the family of the Shuthalhites; of Becher, the family of the Bachrites; of Tahan, the family of the Tahanites. 36 And these *are* the sons of Shuthelah: of Eran, the family of the Eranites. 37 These *are* the families of the sons of Ephraim according to those who were numbered of them: thirty-two thousand five hundred.

These *are* the sons of Joseph according to their families.

38 The sons of Benjamin according to their families *were:* of Bela, the family of the Belaites; of Ashbel, the family of the Ashbelites; of Ahiram, the family of the Ahiramites; 39 of Shupham, the family of the Shuphamites; of Hupham, the family of the Huphamites. 40 And the sons of Bela were Ard and Naaman: *of Ard,* the family of the Ardites; of Naaman, the family of the Naamites. 41 These *are* the sons of Benjamin according to their families; and those who were numbered of them *were* forty-five thousand six hundred.

42 These *are* the sons of Dan according to their families: of Shuham, the family of the Shuhamites. These *are* the families of Dan according to their families. 43 All the families of the Shuhamites, according to those who were numbered of them, *were* sixty-four thousand four hundred.

44 The sons of Asher according to their families *were:* of Jimna, the family of the Jimnites; of Jesui, the family of the Jesuites; of Beriah, the family of the Beriites. 45 Of the sons of Beriah: of Heber, the family of the Heberites; of Malchiel, the family of the Malchielites. 46 And the name of the daughter of Asher *was* Serah. 47 These *are* the families of the sons of Asher according to those who were numbered of them: fifty-three thousand four hundred.

48 The sons of Naphtali according to their families *were:* of Jahzeel, the family of the Jahzeelites; of Guni, the family of the Gunites; 49 of Jezer, the family of the Jezerites; of Shillem, the family of the Shillemites. 50 These *are* the families of Naphtali according to their families; and those who were numbered of them *were* forty-five thousand four hundred.

51 These *are* those who were numbered of the children of Israel: six hundred and one thousand seven hundred and thirty.

52 Then the LORD spoke to Moses, saying: 53 "To these the land shall be divided as an inheritance, according to the number of names. 54 To a large *tribe* you shall give a larger inheritance, and to a small *tribe* you shall give a smaller inheritance. Each shall be given its inheritance according to those who were numbered of them. 55 But the land shall be divided by lot; they shall inherit according to the names of the tribes of their fathers. 56 According to the lot their inheritance shall be divided between the larger and the smaller."

57 And these *are* those who were numbered of the Levites according to their families: of Gershon, the family of the Gershonites; of Kohath, the family of the Kohathites; of Merari, the family of the Merarites. 58 These *are* the families of the Levites: the family of the Libnites, the family of the Hebronites, the family of the Mahlites, the family of the Mushites, and the family of the Korathites. And Kohath begot Amram. 59 The name of Amram's wife *was* Jochebed the daughter of Levi, who was born to Levi in Egypt; and to Amram she bore Aaron and Moses and their sister Miriam. 60 To Aaron were born Nadab and Abihu, Eleazar and Ithamar. 61 And Nadab and Abihu died when they offered profane fire before the LORD.

62 Now those who were numbered of them were twenty-three thousand, every male from a month old and above; for they were not numbered among the other chil-

dren of Israel, because there was no inheritance given to them among the children of Israel.

63 These *are* those who were numbered by Moses and Eleazar the priest, who numbered the children of Israel in the plains of Moab by the Jordan, *across from* Jericho. 64 But among these there was not a man of those who were numbered by Moses and Aaron the priest when they numbered the children of Israel in the Wilderness of Sinai. 65 For the LORD had said of them, "They shall surely die in the wilderness." So there was not left a man of them, except Caleb the son of Jephunneh and Joshua the son of Nun.

PSALM 34:1–7

1   I will bless the LORD at all times;
    His praise *shall* continually *be* in my
        mouth.
2   My soul shall make its boast in the
        LORD;
    The humble shall hear *of it* and be
        glad.
3   Oh, magnify the LORD with me,
    And let us exalt His name together.

4   I sought the LORD, and He heard
        me,
    And delivered me from all my fears.
5   They looked to Him and were radiant,
    And their faces were not ashamed.
6   This poor man cried out, and the LORD
        heard *him*,
    And saved him out of all his troubles.
7   The angel of the LORD encamps all
        around those who fear Him,
    And delivers them.

PROVERBS 11:28

28   HE who trusts in his riches will fall,
     But the righteous will flourish like
         foliage.

Ask yourself how does the advocacy of insurance agree with the Sermon on the Mount.   (GOOD)

MARK 13:21–37

"THEN if anyone says to you, 'Look, here *is* the Christ!' or, 'Look, *He is* there!' do not believe it. 22 For false christs and false prophets will rise and show signs and wonders to deceive, if possible, even the elect. 23 But take heed; see, I have told you all things beforehand.

24 "But in those days, after that tribulation, the sun will be darkened, and the moon will not give its light; 25 the stars of heaven will fall, and the powers in the heavens will be shaken. 26 Then they will see the Son of Man coming in the clouds with great power and glory. 27 And then He will send His angels, and gather together His elect from the four winds, from the farthest part of earth to the farthest part of heaven.

28 "Now learn this parable from the fig tree: When its branch has already become tender, and puts forth leaves, you know that summer is near. 29 So you also, when you see these things happening, know that it is near—at the doors! 30 Assuredly, I say to you, this generation will by no means pass away till all these things take place. 31 Heaven and earth will pass away, but My words will by no means pass away.

32 "But of that day and hour no one knows, not even the angels in heaven, nor the Son, but only the Father. 33 Take heed, watch and pray; for you do not know when the time is. 34 *It is* like a man going to a far country, who left his house and gave authority to his servants, and to each his work, and commanded the doorkeeper to watch. 35 Watch therefore, for you do not know when the master of the house is coming—in the evening, at midnight, at the crowing of the rooster, or in the morning— 36 lest, coming suddenly, he find you sleeping. 37 And what I say to you, I say to all: Watch!"

Reading 74—The Waste of Sentiment
Mark 14:3

It was an act no one else saw any occasion for; they said it was a waste. It was not an extraordinary occasion, and yet Mary broke the box of ointment and spilled the whole thing. It was not a useful thing, but an act of extravagant devotion, and Jesus commended her and said wherever His gospel was preached, this also should be spoken of for a memorial of her.

God spilled the life of His Son that the world might be saved. Am I prepared to spill my life out for Him? Our Lord is carried beyond Himself with delight when He sees any of us doing what Mary did, extravagantly wasting our substance for Him; not set for this or that economy, but being abandoned to Him.

In the Bible there is always a oneness between the spiritual and the material. It takes the incarnation of the Holy Spirit in a man's body to make him what Jesus Christ wants him to be. Unless the blessings of God can deal with our bodies and make them the temples of the Holy Spirit, then the religion of Jesus Christ is in the clouds. If I cannot exhibit the sentiment of the Holy Spirit in the sordid actualities of life and in doing menial things from the highest motive, I am not learning to pour out unto the Lord.   (*PLACE HELP*)

NUMBERS 27:1—28:31

THEN came the daughters of Zelophehad the son of Hepher, the son of Gilead, the son of Machir, the son of Manasseh, from the families of Manasseh the son of Joseph; and these *were* the names of his daughters: Mahlah, Noah, Hoglah, Milcah, and Tirzah. 2 And they stood before Moses, before Eleazar the priest, and before the leaders and all the congregation, *by* the doorway of the tabernacle of meeting, saying: 3 "Our father died in the wilderness; but he was not in the company of those who gathered together against the LORD, in company with Korah, but he died in his own sin; and he had no sons. 4 Why should the name of our father be removed from among his family because he had no son? Give us a possession among our father's brothers."

5 So Moses brought their case before the LORD.

6 And the LORD spoke to Moses, saying: 7 "The daughters of Zelophehad speak *what is* right; you shall surely give them a possession of inheritance among their father's brothers, and cause the inheritance of their father to pass to them. 8 And you shall speak to the children of Israel, saying: 'If a man dies and has no son, then you shall cause his inheritance to pass to his daughter. 9 If he has no daughter, then you shall give his inheritance to his brothers. 10 If he has no brothers, then you shall give his inheri-

tance to his father's brothers. 11 And if his father has no brothers, then you shall give his inheritance to the relative closest to him in his family, and he shall possess it.' " And it shall be to the children of Israel a statute of judgment, just as the LORD commanded Moses.

12 Now the LORD said to Moses: "Go up into this Mount Abarim, and see the land which I have given to the children of Israel. 13 And when you have seen it, you also shall be gathered to your people, as Aaron your brother was gathered. 14 For in the Wilderness of Zin, during the strife of the congregation, you rebelled against My command to hallow Me at the waters before their eyes." (These *are* the waters of Meribah, at Kadesh in the Wilderness of Zin.)

15 Then Moses spoke to the LORD, saying: 16 "Let the LORD, the God of the spirits of all flesh, set a man over the congregation, 17 who may go out before them and go in before them, who may lead them out and bring them in, that the congregation of the LORD may not be like sheep which have no shepherd."

18 And the LORD said to Moses: "Take Joshua the son of Nun with you, a man in whom *is* the Spirit, and lay your hand on him; 19 set him before Eleazar the priest and before all the congregation, and inaugurate him in their sight. 20 And you shall give *some* of your authority to him, that all the congregation of the children of Israel

may be obedient. 21 He shall stand before Eleazar the priest, who shall inquire before the LORD for him by the judgment of the Urim. At his word they shall go out, and at his word they shall come in, he and all the children of Israel with him—all the congregation."

22 So Moses did as the LORD commanded him. He took Joshua and set him before Eleazar the priest and before all the congregation. 23 And he laid his hands on him and inaugurated him, just as the LORD commanded by the hand of Moses.

28 NOW the LORD spoke to Moses, saying, 2 "Command the children of Israel, and say to them, 'My offering, My food' for My offerings made by fire as a sweet aroma to Me, you shall be careful to offer to Me at their appointed time.'

3 "And you shall say to them, 'This *is* the offering made by fire which you shall offer to the LORD: two male lambs in their first year without blemish, day by day, as a regular burnt offering. 4 The one lamb you shall offer in the morning, the other lamb you shall offer in the evening, 5 and one-tenth of an ephah of fine flour as a grain offering mixed with one-fourth of a hin of pressed oil. 6 *It is* a regular burnt offering which was ordained at Mount Sinai for a sweet aroma, an offering made by fire to the LORD. 7 And its drink offering *shall be* one-fourth of a hin for each lamb; in a holy *place* you shall pour out the drink to the LORD as an offering. 8 The other lamb you shall offer in the evening; as the morning grain offering and its drink offering, you shall offer *it* as an offering made by fire, a sweet aroma to the LORD.

9 'And on the Sabbath day two lambs in their first year, without blemish, and two-tenths *of an ephah* of fine flour as a grain offering, mixed with oil, with its drink offering— 10 *this is* the burnt offering for every Sabbath, besides the regular burnt offering with its drink offering.

11 'At the beginnings of your months you shall present a burnt offering to the LORD: two young bulls, one ram, and seven lambs in their first year, without blemish; 12 three-tenths *of an ephah* of fine flour as a grain offering, mixed with oil, for each bull; two-tenths *of an ephah* of fine flour as a grain offering, mixed with oil, for the one ram; 13 and one-tenth *of an ephah* of fine flour, mixed with oil, as a grain offering for each lamb, as a burnt offering of sweet aroma, an offering made by fire to the LORD. 14 Their drink offering shall be half a hin of wine for a bull, one-third of a hin for a

ram, and one-fourth of a hin for a lamb; this *is* the burnt offering for each month throughout the months of the year. 15 Also one kid of the goats as a sin offering to the LORD shall be offered, besides the regular burnt offering and its drink offering.

16 'On the fourteenth day of the first month *is* the Passover of the LORD. 17 And on the fifteenth day of this month *is* the feast; unleavened bread shall be eaten for seven days. 18 On the first day *you shall have* a holy convocation. You shall do no customary work. 19 And you shall present an offering made by fire as a burnt offering to the LORD: two young bulls, one ram, and seven lambs in their first year. Be sure they are without blemish. 20 Their grain offering shall be of fine flour mixed with oil: three-tenths *of an ephah* you shall offer for a bull, and two-tenths for a ram; 21 you shall offer one-tenth *of an ephah* for each of the seven lambs; 22 also one goat *as* a sin offering, to make atonement for you. 23 You shall offer these besides the burnt offering of the morning, which *is* for a regular burnt offering. 24 In this manner you shall offer the food of the offering made by fire daily for seven days, as a sweet aroma to the LORD; it shall be offered besides the regular burnt offering and its drink offering. 25 And on the seventh day you shall have a holy convocation. You shall do no customary work.

26 'Also on the day of the firstfruits, when you bring a new grain offering to the LORD at your *Feast of* Weeks, you shall have a holy convocation. You shall do no customary work. 27 You shall present a burnt offering as a sweet aroma to the LORD: two young bulls, one ram, and seven lambs in their first year, 28 with their grain offering of fine flour mixed with oil: three-tenths *of an ephah* for each bull, two-tenths for the one ram, 29 and one-tenth for each of the seven lambs; 30 *also* one kid of the goats, to make atonement for you. 31 Be sure they are without blemish. You shall present *them* with their drink offerings, besides the regular burnt offering with its grain offering.

PSALM 34:8–14

8 OH, taste and see that the LORD *is* good;
Blessed *is* the man *who* trusts in Him!
9 Oh, fear the LORD, you His saints!
There is no want to those who fear Him.
10 The young lions lack and suffer hunger;
But those who seek the LORD shall not lack any good *thing*.

11 Come, you children, listen to me;
    I will teach you the fear of the LORD.
12 Who *is* the man *who* desires life,
    And loves *many* days, that he may see
    good?
13 Keep your tongue from evil,
    And your lips from speaking deceit.
14 Depart from evil and do good;
    Seek peace and pursue it.

The peace that Jesus gives is never engineered by circumstances on the outside.   (PLACE HELP)

PROVERBS 11:29

29 HE who troubles his own house will
    inherit the wind,
    And the fool *will be* servant to the wise
    of heart.

MARK 14:1–26

AFTER two days it was the Passover and *the Feast* of Unleavened Bread. And the chief priests and the scribes sought how they might take Him by trickery and put *Him* to death. 2 But they said, "Not during the feast, lest there be an uproar of the people."

3 And being in Bethany at the house of Simon the leper, as He sat at the table, a woman came having an alabaster flask of very costly oil of spikenard. Then she broke the flask and poured *it* on His head. 4 But there were some who were indignant among themselves, and said, "Why was this fragrant oil wasted? 5 For it might have been sold for more than three hundred denarii and given to the poor." And they criticized her sharply.

6 But Jesus said, "Let her alone. Why do you trouble her? She has done a good work for Me. 7 For you have the poor with

---

Abandon to God is of more value than personal holiness.   (UTMOST)

---

you always, and whenever you wish you may do them good; but Me you do not

have always. 8 She has done what she could. She has come beforehand to anoint My body for burial. 9 Assuredly, I say to you, wherever this gospel is preached in the whole world, what this woman has done will also be told as a memorial to her."

10 Then Judas Iscariot, one of the twelve, went to the chief priests to betray Him to them. 11 And when they heard *it,* they were glad, and promised to give him money. So he sought how he might conveniently betray Him.

12 Now on the first day of Unleavened Bread, when they killed the Passover *lamb,* His disciples said to Him, "Where do You want us to go and prepare, that You may eat the Passover?"

13 And He sent out two of His disciples and said to them, "Go into the city, and a man will meet you carrying a pitcher of water; follow him. 14 Wherever he goes in, say to the master of the house, 'The Teacher says, "Where is the guest room in which I may eat the Passover with My disciples?" ' 15 Then he will show you a large upper room, furnished *and* prepared; there make ready for us."

16 So His disciples went out, and came into the city, and found it just as He had said to them; and they prepared the Passover.

17 In the evening He came with the twelve. 18 Now as they sat and ate, Jesus said, "Assuredly, I say to you, one of you who eats with Me will betray Me."

19 And they began to be sorrowful, and to say to Him one by one, "*Is* it I?" And another *said,* "*Is* it I?"

20 He answered and said to them, "*It is* one of the twelve, who dips with Me in the dish. 21 The Son of Man indeed goes just as it is written of Him, but woe to that man by whom the Son of Man is betrayed! It would have been good for that man if he had never been born."

22 And as they were eating, Jesus took bread, blessed and broke *it,* and gave *it* to them and said, "Take, eat; this is My body."

23 Then He took the cup, and when He had given thanks He gave *it* to them, and they all drank from it. 24 And He said to them, "This is My blood of the new covenant, which is shed for many. 25 Assuredly, I say to you, I will no longer drink of the fruit of the vine until that day when I drink it new in the kingdom of God."

26 And when they had sung a hymn, they went out to the Mount of Olives.

Reading 75—The Beauty of Self-Denial
Mark 14:36

Jesus Christ had no sin to deny, no wrong self to deny; He had only a holy Self. It was that Self He denied all the time, and it was that Self that Satan tried to make Him obey. What could be holier than the will of the holy Son of God? and yet all through He said, "not what I will, but as You *will*." It was the denying of His holy Self that made the marvelous beauty of our Lord's life.

If we have entered into the experience of sanctification, what are we doing with our holy selves? Do we every morning we waken thank God that we have a self to give to Him, a self that He has purified and adjusted and baptized with the Holy Ghost so that we might sacrifice it to Him? Sacrifice in its essence is the exuberant, passionate love-gift of the best I have to the one I love best. The best gift the Son of God had was His Holy Manhood, and He gave that as a love-gift to God that He might use it as an Atonement for the world. He poured out His soul unto death, and that is to be the characteristic of our lives. God is at perfect liberty to waste us if He chooses. We are sanctified for one purpose only, that we might sanctify our sanctification and give it to God. (*MORAL FOUND.*)

NUMBERS 29:1—30:16

'AND in the seventh month, on the first *day* of the month, you shall have a holy convocation. You shall do no customary work. For you it is a day of blowing the trumpets. 2 You shall offer a burnt offering as a sweet aroma to the LORD: one young bull, one ram, *and* seven lambs in their first year, without blemish. 3 Their grain offering *shall be* fine flour mixed with oil: three-tenths *of an ephah* for the bull, two-tenths for the ram, 4 and one-tenth for each of the seven lambs; 5 also one kid of the goats *as* a sin offering, to make atonement for you; 6 besides the burnt offering with its grain offering for the New Moon, the regular burnt offering with its grain offering, and their drink offerings, according to their ordinance, as a sweet aroma, an offering made by fire to the LORD.

7 'On the tenth *day* of this seventh month you shall have a holy convocation. You shall afflict your souls; you shall not do any work. 8 You shall present a burnt offering to the LORD *as* a sweet aroma: one young bull, one ram, *and* seven lambs in their first year. Be sure they are without blemish. 9 Their grain offering *shall be of* fine flour mixed with oil: three-tenths *of an ephah* for the bull, two-tenths for the one ram, 10 and one-tenth for each of the seven lambs; 11 also one kid of the goats *as* a sin offering, besides the sin offering for atonement, the regular burnt offering with its grain offering, and their drink offerings.

12 'On the fifteenth day of the seventh month you shall have a holy convocation. You shall do no customary work, and you shall keep a feast to the LORD seven days. 13 You shall present a burnt offering, an offering made by fire as a sweet aroma to the LORD: thirteen young bulls, two rams, *and* fourteen lambs in their first year. They shall be without blemish. 14 Their grain offering *shall be of* fine flour mixed with oil: three-tenths *of an ephah* for each of the thirteen bulls, two-tenths for each of the two rams, 15 and one-tenth for each of the fourteen lambs; 16 also one kid of the goats *as* a sin offering, besides the regular burnt offering, its grain offering, and its drink offering.

17 'On the second day *present* twelve young bulls, two rams, fourteen lambs in their first year without blemish, 18 and their grain offering and their drink offerings for the bulls, for the rams, and for the lambs, by their number, according to the ordinance; 19 also one kid of the goats *as* a sin offering, besides the regular burnt offering with its grain offering, and their drink offerings.

20 'On the third day *present* eleven bulls, two rams, fourteen lambs in their first year without blemish, 21 and their grain offering and their drink offerings for the bulls, for the rams, and for the lambs, by their num-

ber, according to the ordinance; 22 also one goat *as* a sin offering, besides the regular burnt offering, its grain offering, and its drink offering.

23 'On the fourth day *present* ten bulls, two rams, *and* fourteen lambs in their first year, without blemish, 24 and their grain offering and their drink offerings for the bulls, for the rams, and for the lambs, by their number, according to the ordinance; 25 also one kid of the goats *as* a sin offering, besides the regular burnt offering, its grain offering, and its drink offering.

26 'On the fifth day *present* nine bulls, two rams, *and* fourteen lambs in their first year without blemish, 27 and their grain offering and their drink offerings for the bulls, for the rams, and for the lambs, by their number, according to the ordinance; 28 also one goat *as* a sin offering, besides the regular burnt offering, its grain offering, and its drink offering.

29 'On the sixth day *present* eight bulls, two rams, *and* fourteen lambs in their first year without blemish, 30 and their grain offering and their drink offerings for the bulls, for the rams, and for the lambs, by their number, according to the ordinance; 31 also one goat *as* a sin offering, besides the regular burnt offering, its grain offering, and its drink offering.

32 'On the seventh day *present* seven bulls, two rams, *and* fourteen lambs in their first year without blemish, 33 and their grain offering and their drink offerings for the bulls, for the rams, and for the lambs, by their number, according to the ordinance; 34 also one goat *as* a sin offering, besides the regular burnt offering, its grain offering, and its drink offering.

35 'On the eighth day you shall have a sacred assembly. You shall do no customary work. 36 You shall present a burnt offering, an offering made by fire as a sweet aroma to the LORD: one bull, one ram, seven lambs in their first year without blemish, 37 and their grain offering and their drink offerings for the bull, for the ram, and for the lambs, by their number, according to the ordinance; 38 also one goat *as* a sin offering, besides the regular burnt offering, its grain offering, and its drink offering.

39 'These you shall present to the LORD at your appointed feasts (besides your vowed offerings and your freewill offerings) as your burnt offerings and your grain offerings, as your drink offerings and your peace offerings.' "

40 So Moses told the children of Israel everything, just as the LORD commanded Moses.

30 THEN Moses spoke to the heads of the tribes concerning the children of Israel, saying, "This *is* the thing which the LORD has commanded: 2 If a man makes a vow to the LORD, or swears an oath to bind himself by some agreement, he shall not break his word; he shall do according to all that proceeds out of his mouth.

3 "Or if a woman makes a vow to the LORD, and binds *herself* by some agreement while in her father's house in her youth, 4 and her father hears her vow and the agreement by which she has bound herself, and her father holds his peace, then all her vows shall stand, and every agreement with which she has bound herself shall stand. 5 But if her father overrules her on the day that he hears, then none of her vows nor her agreements by which she has bound herself shall stand; and the LORD will release her, because her father overruled her.

6 "If indeed she takes a husband, while bound by her vows or by a rash utterance from her lips by which she bound herself, 7 and her husband hears *it,* and makes no response to her on the day that he hears, then her vows shall stand, and her agreements by which she bound herself shall stand. 8 But if her husband overrules her on the day that he hears *it,* he shall make void her vow which she took and what she uttered with her lips, by which she bound herself, and the LORD will release her.

9 "Also any vow of a widow or a divorced woman, by which she has bound herself, shall stand against her.

10 "If she vowed in her husband's house, or bound herself by an agreement with an oath, 11 and her husband heard *it,* and made no response to her *and* did not overrule her, then all her vows shall stand, and every agreement by which she bound herself shall stand. 12 But if her husband truly made them void on the day he heard *them,* then whatever proceeded from her lips concerning her vows or concerning the agreement binding her, it shall not stand; her husband has made them void, and the LORD will release her. 13 Every vow and every binding oath to afflict her soul, her husband may confirm it, or her husband may make it void. 14 Now if her husband makes no response whatever to her from day to day, then he confirms all her vows or all the agreements that bind her; he confirms them, because he made no response to her on the day that he heard *them.* 15 But if he does make them void after he has heard *them,* then he shall bear her guilt."

16 These *are* the statutes which the LORD commanded Moses, between a man and his

wife, and between a father and his daughter in her youth in her father's house.

PSALM 34:15–22

15 THE eyes of the Lord *are* on the righteous,
   And His ears *are open* to their cry.
16 The face of the Lord *is* against those who do evil,
   To cut off the remembrance of them from the earth.

17 *The righteous* cry out, and the Lord hears,
   And delivers them out of all their troubles.
18 The Lord *is* near to those who have a broken heart,
   And saves such as have a contrite spirit.

Jesus does not alter our human nature, it does not need altering: He alters the mainspring.   (Sermon Mt.)

---

19 Many *are* the afflictions of the righteous,
   But the Lord delivers him out of them all.
20 He guards all his bones;
   Not one of them is broken.
21 Evil shall slay the wicked,
   And those who hate the righteous shall be condemned.
22 The Lord redeems the soul of His servants,
   And none of those who trust in Him shall be condemned.

PROVERBS 11:30, 31

30 THE fruit of the righteous *is a* tree of life,
   And he who wins souls *is* wise.

31 If the righteous will be recompensed on the earth,
   How much more the ungodly and the sinner.

MARK 14:27–54

THEN Jesus said to them, "All of you will be made to stumble because of Me this night, for it is written:

'I will strike the Shepherd,
   And the sheep will be scattered.'

28 "But after I have been raised, I will go before you to Galilee."
29 Peter said to Him, "Even if all are made to stumble, yet I *will* not *be*."
30 Jesus said to him, "Assuredly, I say to you that today, *even* this night, before the rooster crows twice, you will deny Me three times."
31 But he spoke more vehemently, "If I have to die with You, I will not deny You!" And they all said likewise.
32 Then they came to a place which was named Gethsemane; and He said to His disciples, "Sit here while I pray." 33 And He took Peter, James, and John with Him, and He began to be troubled and deeply distressed. 34 Then He said to them, "My soul is exceedingly sorrowful, *even* to death. Stay here and watch."
35 He went a little farther, and fell on the ground, and prayed that if it were possible, the hour might pass from Him. 36 And He said, "Abba, Father, all things *are* possible for You. Take this cup away from Me; nevertheless, not what I will, but what You *will*."

Our Lord in His agony was devoted to God's purpose.   (Psy. Redemp.)

---

37 Then He came and found them sleeping, and said to Peter, "Simon, are you sleeping? Could you not watch one hour? 38 Watch and pray, lest you enter into temptation. The spirit indeed *is* willing, but the flesh *is* weak."
39 Again He went away and prayed, and spoke the same words. 40 And when He returned, He found them asleep again, for their eyes were heavy; and they did not know what to answer Him.
41 Then He came the third time and said to them, "Are you still sleeping and resting? It is enough! The hour has come; behold, the Son of Man is being betrayed into the hands of sinners. 42 Rise, let us be going. See, My betrayer is at hand."
43 And immediately, while He was still speaking, Judas, one of the twelve, with a great multitude with swords and clubs, came from the chief priests and the scribes and the elders. 44 Now His betrayer had given them a signal, saying, "Whomever I kiss, He is the One; seize Him and lead *Him* away safely."
45 As soon as he had come, immediately

he went up to Him and said to Him, "Rabbi, Rabbi!" and kissed Him.

46 Then they laid their hands on Him and took Him. 47 And one of those who stood by drew his sword and struck the servant of the high priest, and cut off his ear.

48 Then Jesus answered and said to them, "Have you come out, as against a robber, with swords and clubs to take Me? 49 I was daily with you in the temple teaching, and you did not seize Me. But the Scriptures must be fulfilled."

50 Then they all forsook Him and fled. 51 Now a certain young man followed Him, having a linen cloth thrown around *his* naked *body*. And the young men laid hold of him, 52 and he left the linen cloth and fled from them naked.

53 And they led Jesus away to the high priest; and with him were assembled all the chief priests, the elders, and the scribes. 54 But Peter followed Him at a distance, right into the courtyard of the high priest. And he sat with the servants and warmed himself at the fire.

◆◆◆◆

Reading 76—Jesus Is Our Salvation
Psalm 35:3

Stand in implicit adoring faith in Him, *He* is made unto us "wisdom . . . and righteousness, and sanctification, and redemption." How can we talk of making a sacrifice for the Son of God! Our salvation is from hell and perdition, and then we talk about making sacrifices!

We have to get out into faith in Jesus Christ continually; not a prayer meeting Jesus Christ, nor a book Jesus Christ, but the New Testament Jesus Christ, who is God Incarnate, and who ought to strike us to His feet as dead. Our faith must be in the One from whom our experience springs. Jesus Christ wants our absolute abandon of devotion to Himself. We never can *experience* Jesus Christ, nor ever hold Him within the compass of our own hearts, but our faith must be built in strong emphatic confidence in Him.

It is along this line that we see the rugged impatience of the Holy Ghost against unbelief. All our fears are wicked, and we fear because we will not nourish ourselves in our faith. How can anyone who is identified with Jesus Christ suffer from doubt or fear! It ought to be an absolute paean of perfectly irrepressible, triumphant belief.   (*Utmost*)

NUMBERS 31:1—32:42

AND the Lord spoke to Moses, saying: 2 "Take vengeance on the Midianites for the children of Israel. Afterward you shall be gathered to your people."

3 So Moses spoke to the people, saying, "Arm some of yourselves for war, and let them go against the Midianites to take vengeance for the Lord on Midian. 4 A thousand from each tribe of all the tribes of Israel you shall send to the war."

5 So there were recruited from the divisions of Israel one thousand from *each* tribe, twelve thousand armed for war. 6 Then Moses sent them to the war, one thousand from *each* tribe; he sent them to the war with Phinehas the son of Eleazar the priest, with the holy articles and the signal trumpets in his hand. 7 And they warred against the Midianites, just as the Lord commanded Moses, and they killed all the males. 8 They killed the kings of Midian with *the rest of* those who were killed—Evi, Rekem, Zur, Hur, and Reba, the five kings of Midian. Balaam the son of Beor they also killed with the sword.

9 And the children of Israel took the women of Midian captive, with their little ones, and took as spoil all their cattle, all their flocks, and all their goods. 10 They also burned with fire all the cities where they dwelt, and all their forts. 11 And they took all the spoil and all the booty—of man and beast.

12 Then they brought the captives, the

booty, and the spoil to Moses, to Eleazar the priest, and to the congregation of the children of Israel, to the camp in the plains of Moab by the Jordan, *across from* Jericho. 13 And Moses, Eleazar the priest, and all the leaders of the congregation, went to meet them outside the camp. 14 But Moses was angry with the officers of the army, *with* the captains over thousands and captains over hundreds, who had come from the battle.

15 And Moses said to them: "Have you kept all the women alive? 16 Look, these *women* caused the children of Israel, through the counsel of Balaam, to trespass against the LORD in the incident of Peor, and there was a plague among the congregation of the LORD. 17 Now therefore, kill every male among the little ones, and kill every woman who has known a man intimately. 18 But keep alive for yourselves all the young girls who have not known a man intimately. 19 And as for you, remain outside the camp seven days; whoever has killed any person, and whoever has touched any slain, purify yourselves and your captives on the third day and on the seventh day. 20 Purify every garment, everything made of leather, everything woven of goats' *hair,* and everything made of wood."

21 Then Eleazar the priest said to the men of war who had gone to the battle, "This *is* the ordinance of the law which the LORD commanded Moses: 22 "Only the gold, the silver, the bronze, the iron, the tin, and the lead, 23 everything that can endure fire, you shall put through the fire, and it shall be clean; and it shall be purified with the water of purification. But all that cannot endure fire you shall put through water. 24 And you shall wash your clothes on the seventh day and be clean, and afterward you may come into the camp."

25 Now the LORD spoke to Moses, saying: 26 "Count up the plunder that was taken—of man and beast—you and Eleazar the priest and the chief fathers of the congregation; 27 and divide the plunder into two parts, between those who took part in the war, who went out to battle, and all the congregation. 28 And levy a tribute for the LORD on the men of war who went out to battle: one of every five hundred of the persons, the cattle, the donkeys, and the sheep; 29 take *it* from their half, and give *it* to Eleazar the priest as a heave offering to the LORD. 30 And from the children of Israel's half you shall take one of every fifty, drawn from the persons, the cattle, the donkeys, and the sheep, from all the livestock, and give them to the Levites who keep

charge of the tabernacle of the LORD." 31 So Moses and Eleazar the priest did as the LORD commanded Moses.

32 The booty remaining from the plunder, which the men of war had taken, was six hundred and seventy-five thousand sheep, 33 seventy-two thousand cattle, 34 sixty-one thousand donkeys, 35 and thirty-two thousand persons in all, of women who had not known a man intimately. 36 And the half, the portion for those who had gone out to war, was in number three hundred and thirty-seven thousand five hundred sheep; 37 and the LORD's tribute of the sheep was six hundred and seventy-five. 38 The cattle *were* thirty-six thousand, of which the LORD's tribute *was* seventy-two. 39 The donkeys *were* thirty thousand five hundred, of which the LORD's tribute *was* sixty-one. 40 The persons *were* sixteen thousand, of which the LORD's tribute *was* thirty-two persons. 41 So Moses gave the tribute *which was* the LORD's heave offering to Eleazar the priest, as the LORD commanded Moses.

42 And from the children of Israel's half, which Moses separated from the men who fought— 43 now the half belonging to the congregation was three hundred and thirty-seven thousand five hundred sheep, 44 thirty-six thousand cattle, 45 thirty thousand five hundred donkeys, 46 and sixteen thousand persons— 47 and from the children of Israel's half Moses took one of every fifty, drawn from man and beast, and gave them to the Levites, who kept charge of the tabernacle of the LORD, as the LORD commanded Moses.

48 Then the officers who *were* over thousands of the army, the captains of thousands and captains of hundreds, came near to Moses; 49 and they said to Moses, "Your servants have taken a count of the men of war who *are* under our command, and not a man of us is missing. 50 Therefore we have brought an offering for the LORD, what every man found of ornaments of gold: armlets and bracelets and signet rings and earrings and necklaces, to make atonement for ourselves before the LORD." 51 So Moses and Eleazar the priest received the gold from them, all the fashioned ornaments. 52 And all the gold of the offering that they offered to the LORD, from the captains of thousands and captains of hundreds, was sixteen thousand seven hundred and fifty shekels. 53 (The men of war had taken spoil, every man for himself.) 54 And Moses and Eleazar the priest received the gold from the captains of thousands and of hundreds, and brought it into

the tabernacle of meeting as a memorial for the children of Israel before the LORD.

32 NOW the children of Reuben and the children of Gad had a very great multitude of livestock; and when they saw the land of Jazer and the land of Gilead, that indeed the region *was* a place for livestock, 2 the children of Gad and the children of Reuben came and spoke to Moses, to Eleazar the priest, and to the leaders of the congregation, saying, 3 "Ataroth, Dibon, Jazer, Nimrah, Heshbon, Elealeh, Shebam, Nebo, and Beon, 4 the country which the LORD defeated before the congregation of Israel, *is* a land for livestock, and your servants have livestock." 5 Therefore they said, "If we have found favor in your sight, let this land be given to your servants as a possession. Do not take us over the Jordan."

6 And Moses said to the children of Gad and to the children of Reuben: "Shall your brethren go to war while you sit here? 7 Now why will you discourage the heart of the children of Israel from going over into the land which the LORD has given them? 8 Thus your fathers did when I sent them away from Kadesh Barnea to see the land. 9 For when they went up to the Valley of Eshcol and saw the land, they discouraged the heart of the children of Israel, so that they did not go into the land which the LORD had given them. 10 So the LORD's anger was aroused on that day, and He swore an oath, saying, 11 'Surely none of the men who came up from Egypt, from twenty years old and above, shall see the land of which I swore to Abraham, Isaac, and Jacob, because they have not wholly followed Me, 12 except Caleb the son of Jephunneh, the Kenizzite, and Joshua the son of Nun, for they have wholly followed the LORD.' 13 So the LORD's anger was aroused against Israel, and He made them wander in the wilderness forty years, until all the generation that had done evil in the sight of the LORD was gone. 14 And look! You have risen in your fathers' place, a brood of sinful men, to increase still more the fierce anger of the LORD against Israel. 15 For if you turn away from following Him, He will once again leave them in the wilderness, and you will destroy all these people."

16 Then they came near to him and said: "We will build sheepfolds here for our livestock, and cities for our little ones, 17 but we ourselves will be armed, ready *to go* before the children of Israel until we have brought them to their place; and our little ones will dwell in the fortified cities because of the inhabitants of the land. 18 We will not return to our homes until every one of the children of Israel has received his inheritance. 19 For we will not inherit with them on the other side of the Jordan and beyond, because our inheritance has fallen to us on this eastern side of the Jordan."

20 Then Moses said to them: "If you do this thing, if you arm yourselves before the LORD for the war, 21 and all your armed men cross over the Jordan before the LORD until He has driven out His enemies from before Him, 22 and the land is subdued before the LORD, then afterward you may return and be blameless before the LORD and before Israel; and this land shall be your possession before the LORD. 23 But if you do not do so, then take note, you have sinned against the LORD; and be sure your sin will find you out. 24 Build cities for your little ones and folds for your sheep, and do what has proceeded out of your mouth."

25 And the children of Gad and the children of Reuben spoke to Moses, saying: "Your servants will do as my lord commands. 26 Our little ones, our wives, our flocks, and all our livestock will be there in the cities of Gilead; 27 but your servants will cross over, every man armed for war, before the LORD to battle, just as my lord says."

28 So Moses gave command concerning them to Eleazar the priest, to Joshua the son of Nun, and to the chief fathers of the tribes of the children of Israel. 29 And Moses said to them: "If the children of Gad and the children of Reuben cross over the Jordan with you, every man armed for battle before the LORD, and the land is subdued before you, then you shall give them the land of Gilead as a possession. 30 But if they do not cross over armed with you, they shall have possessions among you in the land of Canaan."

31 Then the children of Gad and the children of Reuben answered, saying: "As the LORD has said to your servants, so we will do. 32 We will cross over armed before the LORD into the land of Canaan, but the possession of our inheritance *shall remain* with us on this side of the Jordan."

33 So Moses gave to the children of Gad, to the children of Reuben, and to half the tribe of Manasseh the son of Joseph, the kingdom of Sihon king of the Amorites and the kingdom of Og king of Bashan, the land with its cities within the borders, the cities of the surrounding country. 34 And the children of Gad built Dibon and Ataroth and Aroer, 35 Atroth and Sho-

phan and Jazer and Jogbehah, 36 Beth Nimrah and Beth Haran, fortified cities, and folds for sheep. 37 And the children of Reuben built Heshbon and Elealeh and Kirjathaim, 38 Nebo and Baal Meon (*their* names being changed) and Shibmah; and they gave *other* names to the cities which they built.

39 And the children of Machir the son of Manasseh went to Gilead and took it, and dispossessed the Amorites who *were* in it. 40 So Moses gave Gilead to Machir the son of Manasseh, and he dwelt in it. 41 Also Jair the son of Manasseh went and took its small towns, and called them Havoth Jair. 42 Then Nobah went and took Kenath and its villages, and he called it Nobah, after his own name.

PSALM 35:1–8

1 PLEAD *my cause,* O LORD, with those
      who strive with me;
   Fight against those who fight against
      me.
2 Take hold of shield and buckler,
   And stand up for my help.
3 Also draw out the spear,
   And stop those who pursue me.
   Say to my soul,
   "I *am* your salvation."

4 Let those be put to shame and brought
      to dishonor
   Who seek after my life;
   Let those be turned back and brought
      to confusion
   Who plot my hurt.
5 Let them be like chaff before the wind,
   And let the angel of the LORD chase
      them.
6 Let their way be dark and slippery,
   And let the angel of the LORD pursue
      them.
7 For without cause they have hidden
      their net for me *in* a pit,
   Which they have dug without cause for
      my life.
8 Let destruction come upon him
      unexpectedly,
   And let his net that he has hidden catch
      himself;
   Into that very destruction let him fall.

PROVERBS 12:1

1 WHOEVER loves instruction loves
      knowledge,
   But he who hates correction *is* stupid.

MARK 14:55–72

NOW the chief priests and all the council sought testimony against Jesus to put Him to death, but found none. 56 For many bore false witness against Him, but their testimonies did not agree.

57 Then some rose up and bore false witness against Him, saying, 58 "We heard Him say, 'I will destroy this temple made with hands, and within three days I will build another made without hands.'" 59 But not even then did their testimony agree.

60 And the high priest stood up in the midst and asked Jesus, saying, "Do You answer nothing? What *is it* these men testify against You?" 61 But He kept silent and answered nothing.

Again the high priest asked Him, saying to Him, "Are You the Christ, the Son of the Blessed?"

62 Jesus said, "I am. And you will see the Son of Man sitting at the right hand of the Power, and coming with the clouds of heaven."

63 Then the high priest tore his clothes and said, "What further need do we have of witnesses? 64 You have heard the blasphemy! What do you think?"

And they all condemned Him to be deserving of death.

65 Then some began to spit on Him, and to blindfold Him, and to beat Him, and to say to Him, "Prophesy!" And the officers struck Him with the palms of their hands.

God redeemed the whole human race when they were spitting in His face, as it were. (SHAD. AGONY)

66 Now as Peter was below in the courtyard, one of the servant girls of the high priest came. 67 And when she saw Peter warming himself, she looked at him and said, "You also were with Jesus of Nazareth."

68 But he denied it, saying, "I neither know nor understand what you are saying." And he went out on the porch, and a rooster crowed.

69 And the servant girl saw him again, and began to say to those who stood by, "This is one of them." 70 But he denied it again.

And a little later those who stood by said to Peter again, "Surely you are *one* of them; for you are a Galilean, and your speech shows *it.*"

71 Then he began to curse and swear, "I do not know this Man of whom you speak!"

72 A second time *the* rooster crowed.

Then Peter called to mind the word that Jesus had said to him, "Before the rooster crows twice, you will deny Me three times." And when he thought about it, he wept.

◆◆◆◆

Reading 77—Joy in the Lord
Psalm 35:9

J oy means the perfect fulfillment of that for which I was created and regenerated, not the successful doing of a thing. The joy our Lord had lay in doing what the Father sent Him to do, and He says—"As My Father has sent Me, even so am I sending you.". . . We have all to find our niche in life, and spiritually we find it when we receive our ministry from the Lord. In order to do this we must have companied with Jesus; we must know Him as more than a personal Savior. "I will show him how many things he must suffer for My name's sake."

"Do you love Me?" Then—"Feed My sheep." There is no choice of service, only absolute loyalty to our Lord's commission; loyalty to what you discern when you are in closest contact with God. If you have received a ministry from the Lord Jesus, you will know that the need is never the call: the need is the opportunity. The call is loyalty to the ministry you received when you were in real touch with Him. This does not imply that there is a campaign of service marked out for you, but it does mean that you will have to ignore the demands for service along other lines.   (*UTMOST*)

NUMBERS 33:1—34:29

THESE *are* the journeys of the children of Israel, who went out of the land of Egypt by their armies under the hand of Moses and Aaron. 2 Now Moses wrote down the starting points of their journeys at the command of the LORD. And these *are* their journeys according to their starting points:

3 They departed from Rameses in the first month, on the fifteenth day of the first month; on the day after the Passover the children of Israel went out with boldness in the sight of all the Egyptians. 4 For the Egyptians were burying all *their* firstborn, whom the LORD had killed among them. Also on their gods the LORD had executed judgments.

5 Then the children of Israel moved from Rameses and camped at Succoth. 6 They departed from Succoth and camped at Etham, which *is* on the edge of the wilderness. 7 They moved from Etham and turned back to Pi Hahiroth, which *is* east of Baal Zephon; and they camped near Migdol. 8 They departed from before Hahiroth and

passed through the midst of the sea into the wilderness, went three days' journey in the Wilderness of Etham, and camped at Marah. 9 They moved from Marah and came to Elim. At Elim *were* twelve springs of water and seventy palm trees; so they camped there.

10 They moved from Elim and camped by the Red Sea. 11 They moved from the Red Sea and camped in the Wilderness of Sin. 12 They journeyed from the Wilderness of Sin and camped at Dophkah. 13 They departed from Dophkah and camped at Alush. 14 They moved from Alush and camped at Rephidim, where there was no water for the people to drink.

15 They departed from Rephidim and camped in the Wilderness of Sinai. 16 They moved from the Wilderness of Sinai and camped at Kibroth Hattaavah. 17 They departed from Kibroth Hattaavah and camped at Hazeroth. 18 They departed from Hazeroth and camped at Rithmah. 19 They departed from Rithmah and camped at Rimmon Perez. 20 They departed from Rimmon Perez and camped at Libnah. 21 They moved from Libnah and camped

at Rissah. 22 They journeyed from Rissah and camped at Kehelathah. 23 They went from Kehelathah and camped at Mount Shepher. 24 They moved from Mount Shepher and camped at Haradah. 25 They moved from Haradah and camped at Makheloth. 26 They moved from Makheloth and camped at Tahath. 27 They departed from Tahath and camped at Terah. 28 They moved from Terah and camped at Mithkah. 29 They went from Mithkah and camped at Hashmonah. 30 They departed from Hashmonah and camped at Moseroth. 31 They departed from Moseroth and camped at Bene Jaakan. 32 They moved from Bene Jaakan and camped at Hor Hagidgad. 33 They went from Hor Hagidgad and camped at Jotbathah. 34 They moved from Jotbathah and camped at Abronah. 35 They departed from Abronah and camped at Ezion Geber. 36 They moved from Ezion Geber and camped in the Wilderness of Zin, which *is* Kadesh. 37 They moved from Kadesh and camped at Mount Hor, on the boundary of the land of Edom.

38 Then Aaron the priest went up to Mount Hor at the command of the LORD, and died there in the fortieth year after the children of Israel had come out of the land of Egypt, on the first *day* of the fifth month. 39 Aaron *was* one hundred and twenty-three years old when he died on Mount Hor.

40 Now the king of Arad, the Canaanite, who dwelt in the South in the land of Canaan, heard of the coming of the children of Israel.

41 So they departed from Mount Hor and camped at Zalmonah. 42 They departed from Zalmonah and camped at Punon. 43 They departed from Punon and camped at Oboth. 44 They departed from Oboth and camped at Ije Abarim, at the border of Moab. 45 They departed from Ijim and camped at Dibon Gad. 46 They moved from Dibon Gad and camped at Almon Diblathaim. 47 They moved from Almon Diblathaim and camped in the mountains of Abarim, before Nebo. 48 They departed from the mountains of Abarim and camped in the plains of Moab by the Jordan, *across from* Jericho. 49 They camped by the Jordan, from Beth Jesimoth as far as the Abel Acacia Grove in the plains of Moab.

50 Now the LORD spoke to Moses in the plains of Moab by the Jordan, *across from* Jericho, saying, 51 "Speak to the children of Israel, and say to them: 'When you have crossed the Jordan into the land of Canaan, 52 then you shall drive out all the inhabitants of the land from before you, destroy all their engraved stones, destroy all their

molded images, and demolish all their high places; 53 you shall dispossess *the inhabitants of* the land and dwell in it, for I have given you the land to possess. 54 And you shall divide the land by lot as an inheritance among your families; to the larger you shall give a larger inheritance, and to the smaller you shall give a smaller inheritance; there everyone's *inheritance* shall be whatever falls to him by lot. You shall inherit according to the tribes of your fathers. 55 But if you do not drive out the inhabitants of the land from before you, then it shall be that those whom you let remain *shall be* irritants in your eyes and thorns in your sides, and they shall harass you in the land where you dwell. 56 Moreover it shall be *that* I will do to you as I thought to do to them.' "

34 THEN the LORD spoke to Moses, saying, 2 "Command the children of Israel, and say to them: 'When you come into the land of Canaan, this *is* the land that shall fall to you as an inheritance—the land of Canaan to its boundaries. 3 Your southern border shall be from the Wilderness of Zin along the border of Edom; then your southern border shall extend eastward to the end of the Salt Sea; 4 your border shall turn from the southern side of the Ascent of Akrabbim, continue to Zin, and be on the south of Kadesh Barnea; then it shall go on to Hazar Addar, and continue to Azmon; 5 the border shall turn from Azmon to the Brook of Egypt, and it shall end at the Sea.

6 'As for the western border, you shall have the Great Sea for a border; this shall be your western border.

7 'And this shall be your northern border: From the Great Sea you shall mark out your *border* line to Mount Hor; 8 from Mount Hor you shall mark out *your border* to the entrance of Hamath; then the direction of the border shall be toward Zedad; 9 the border shall proceed to Ziphron, and it shall end at Hazar Enan. This shall be your northern border.

10 'You shall mark out your eastern border from Hazar Enan to Shepham; 11 the border shall go down from Shepham to Riblah on the east side of Ain; the border shall go down and reach to the eastern side of the Sea of Chinnereth; 12 the border shall go down along the Jordan, and it shall end at the Salt Sea. This shall be your land with its surrounding boundaries.' "

13 Then Moses commanded the children of Israel, saying: "This *is* the land which you shall inherit by lot, which the LORD has commanded to give to the nine tribes

and to the half-tribe. 14 For the tribe of the children of Reuben according to the house of their fathers, and the tribe of the children of Gad according to the house of their fathers, have received *their inheritance;* and the half-tribe of Manasseh has received its inheritance. 15 The two tribes and the half-tribe have received their inheritance on this side of the Jordan, *across from* Jericho eastward, toward the sunrise."

16 And the Lord spoke to Moses, saying, 17 "These *are* the names of the men who shall divide the land among you as an inheritance: Eleazar the priest and Joshua the son of Nun. 18 And you shall take one leader of every tribe to divide the land for the inheritance. 19 These *are* the names of the men: from the tribe of Judah, Caleb the son of Jephunneh; 20 from the tribe of the children of Simeon, Shemuel the son of Ammihud; 21 from the tribe of Benjamin, Elidad the son of Chislon; 22 a leader from the tribe of the children of Dan, Bukki the son of Jogli; 23 from the sons of Joseph: a leader from the tribe of the children of Manasseh, Hanniel the son of Ephod, 24 and a leader from the tribe of the children of Ephraim, Kemuel the son of Shiphtan; 25 a leader from the tribe of the children of Zebulun, Elizaphan the son of Parnach; 26 a leader from the tribe of the children of Issachar, Paltiel the son of Azzan; 27 a leader from the tribe of the children of Asher, Ahihud the son of Shelomi; 28 and a leader from the tribe of the children of Naphtali, Pedahel the son of Ammihud."

29 These *are* the ones the Lord commanded to divide the inheritance among the children of Israel in the land of Canaan.

PSALM 35:9–16

9 AND my soul shall be joyful in the Lord;
It shall rejoice in His salvation.

The Bible talks plentifully about joy, but it nowhere speaks about a "happy" Christian.   (Bib. Psych.)

---

10 All my bones shall say,
"Lord, who *is* like You,
Delivering the poor from him who is too strong for him,
Yes, the poor and the needy from him who plunders him?"

11 Fierce witnesses rise up;
They ask me *things* that I do not know.
12 They reward me evil for good,
To the sorrow of my soul.
13 But as for me, when they were sick,
My clothing *was* sackcloth;
I humbled myself with fasting;
And my prayer would return to my own heart.
14 I paced about as though *he were* my friend *or* brother;
I bowed down heavily, as one who mourns *for his* mother.

15 But in my adversity they rejoiced
And gathered together;
Attackers gathered against me,
And I did not know *it;*
They tore *at me* and did not cease;
16 With ungodly mockers at feasts
They gnashed at me with their teeth.

PROVERBS 12:2

2 A good *man* obtains favor from the Lord,
But a man of wicked intentions He will condemn.

MARK 15:1–24

IMMEDIATELY, in the morning, the chief priests held a consultation with the elders and scribes and the whole council; and they bound Jesus, led *Him* away, and delivered *Him* to Pilate. 2 Then Pilate asked Him, "Are You the King of the Jews?"

He answered and said to him, "*It is as* you say."

3 And the chief priests accused Him of many things, but He answered nothing. 4 Then Pilate asked Him again, saying, "Do You answer nothing? See how many things they testify against You!" 5 But Jesus still answered nothing, so that Pilate marveled.

6 Now at the feast he was accustomed to releasing one prisoner to them, whomever they requested. 7 And there was one named Barabbas, *who was* chained with his fellow rebels; they had committed murder in the rebellion. 8 Then the multitude, crying aloud, began to ask *him to do* just as he had always done for them. 9 But Pilate answered them, saying, "Do you want me to release to you the King of the Jews?" 10 For he knew that the chief priests had handed Him over because of envy.

11 But the chief priests stirred up the crowd, so that he should rather release Bar-

abbas to them. 12 Pilate answered and said to them again, "What then do you want me to do *with Him* whom you call the King of the Jews?"

13 So they cried out again, "Crucify Him!"

14 Then Pilate said to them, "Why, what evil has He done?"

But they cried out all the more, "Crucify Him!"

---

*T*he death of Jesus Christ holds
the secret of the mind
of God.   (GLORY)

---

15 So Pilate, wanting to gratify the crowd, released Barabbas to them; and he delivered Jesus, after he had scourged *Him,* to be crucified.

16 Then the soldiers led Him away into the hall called Praetorium, and they called together the whole garrison. 17 And they clothed Him with purple; and they twisted a crown of thorns, put it on His *head,* 18 and began to salute Him, "Hail, King of the Jews!" 19 Then they struck Him on the head with a reed and spat on Him; and bowing the knee, they worshiped Him. 20 And when they had mocked Him, they took the purple off Him, put His own clothes on Him, and led Him out to crucify Him.

21 Then they compelled a certain man, Simon a Cyrenian, the father of Alexander and Rufus, as he was coming out of the country and passing by, to bear His cross. 22 And they brought Him to the place Golgotha, which is translated, Place of a Skull. 23 Then they gave Him wine mingled with myrrh to drink, but He did not take *it.* 24 And when they crucified Him, they divided His garments, casting lots for them to determine what every man should take.

Reading 78—The Collision of God and Sin
Mark 15:25–37

There is nothing more certain in time or eternity than what Jesus Christ did on the Cross: He switched the whole of the human race back into a right relationship with God. He made redemption the basis of human life, that is, He made a way for every son of man to get into communion with God.

The Cross did not happen to Jesus: He came on purpose for it. He is "the Lamb slain from the foundation of the world." The whole meaning of the Incarnation is the Cross. . . . The Cross is the center of time and of eternity, the answer to the enigmas of both.

The Cross is not the cross of a man but the Cross of God, and the Cross of God can never be realized in human experience. The Cross is the exhibition of the nature of God, the gateway whereby any individual of the human race can enter into union with God. When we get to the Cross, we do not go through it; we abide in the life to which the Cross is the gateway.

The center of salvation is the Cross of Jesus, and the reason it is so easy to obtain salvation is because it cost God so much. The Cross is the point where God and sinful man merge with a crash and the way to life is opened—but the crash is on the heart of God.   (*UTMOST*)

NUMBERS 35:1—36:13

AND the LORD spoke to Moses in the plains of Moab by the Jordan *across from* Jericho, saying: 2 "Command the children of Israel that they give the Levites cities to dwell in from the inheritance of their possession, and you shall *also* give the Levites commonland around the cities. 3 They shall have the cities to dwell in; and their commonland shall be for their cattle, for their herds, and for all their animals. 4 The common-land of the cities which you will give the Levites *shall extend* from the wall of the city outward a thousand cubits all around. 5 And you shall measure outside the city on the east side two thousand cubits, on the south side two thousand cubits, on the west side two thousand cubits, and on the north side two thousand cubits. The city *shall be* in the middle. This shall belong to them as common-land for the cities.

6 "Now among the cities which you will give to the Levites *you shall appoint* six cities of refuge, to which a manslayer may flee. And to these you shall add forty-two cities. 7 So all the cities you will give to the Levites *shall be* forty-eight; these *you shall give* with their common-land. 8 And the cities which you will give *shall be* from the possession of the children of Israel; from the larger *tribe* you shall give many, from the smaller you shall give few. Each shall give some of its cities to the Levites, in proportion to the inheritance that each receives."

9 Then the LORD spoke to Moses, saying, 10 "Speak to the children of Israel, and say to them: 'When you cross the Jordan into the land of Canaan, 11 then you shall appoint cities to be cities of refuge for you, that the manslayer who kills any person accidentally may flee there. 12 They shall be cities of refuge for you from the avenger, that the manslayer may not die until he stands before the congregation in judgment. 13 And of the cities which you give, you shall have six cities of refuge. 14 You shall appoint three cities on this side of the Jordan, and three cities you shall appoint in the land of Canaan, *which* will be cities of refuge. 15 These six cities shall be for refuge for the children of Israel, for the stranger, and for the sojourner among them, that anyone who kills a person accidentally may flee there.

16 'But if he strikes him with an iron implement, so that he dies, he *is* a murderer; the murderer shall surely be put to death. 17 And if he strikes him with a stone in the hand, by which one could die, and he does die, he *is* a murderer; the murderer shall surely be put to death. 18 Or *if* he strikes him with a wooden hand weapon, by which one could die, and he does die, he *is* a murderer; the murderer shall surely be put to death. 19 The avenger of blood himself shall put the murderer to death; when he meets him, he shall put him to death. 20 If he pushes him out of hatred or, while lying in wait, hurls something at him so that he dies, 21 or in enmity he strikes him with his hand so that he dies, the one who struck *him* shall surely be put to death.

He *is* a murderer. The avenger of blood shall put the murderer to death when he meets him.

22 'However, if he pushes him suddenly without enmity, or throws anything at him without lying in wait, 23 or uses a stone, by which a man could die, throwing *it* at him without seeing *him,* so that he dies, while he was not his enemy or seeking his harm, 24 then the congregation shall judge between the manslayer and the avenger of blood according to these judgments. 25 So the congregation shall deliver the manslayer from the hand of the avenger of blood, and the congregation shall return him to the city of refuge where he had fled, and he shall remain there until the death of the high priest who was anointed with the holy oil. 26 But if the manslayer at any time goes outside the limits of the city of refuge where he fled, 27 and the avenger of blood finds him outside the limits of his city of refuge, and the avenger of blood kills the manslayer, he shall not be guilty of blood, 28 because he should have remained in his city of refuge until the death of the high priest. But after the death of the high priest the manslayer may return to the land of his possession.

29 'And these *things* shall be a statute of judgment to you throughout your generations in all your dwellings. 30 Whoever kills a person, the murderer shall be put to death on the testimony of witnesses; but one witness is not *sufficient* testimony against a person for the death *penalty.* 31 Moreover you shall take no ransom for the life of a murderer who *is* guilty of death, but he shall surely be put to death. 32 And you shall take no ransom for him who has fled to his city of refuge, that he may return to dwell in the land before the death of the priest. 33 So you shall not pollute the land where you *are;* for blood defiles the land, and no atonement can be made for the land, for the blood that is shed on it, except by the blood of him who shed it. 34 Therefore do not defile the land which you inhabit, in the midst of which I dwell; for I the LORD dwell among the children of Israel.' "

36 NOW the chief fathers of the families of the children of Gilead the son of Machir, the son of Manasseh, of the families of the sons of Joseph, came near and spoke before Moses and before the leaders, the chief fathers of the children of Israel. 2 And they said: "The LORD commanded my lord *Moses* to give the land as an inheritance by lot to the children of Israel, and my lord was commanded by the

LORD to give the inheritance of our brother Zelophehad to his daughters. 3 Now if they are married to any of the sons of the *other* tribes of the children of Israel, then their inheritance will be taken from the inheritance of our fathers, and it will be added to the inheritance of the tribe into which they marry; so it will be taken from the lot of our inheritance. 4 And when the Jubilee of the children of Israel comes, then their inheritance will be added to the inheritance of the tribe into which they marry; so their inheritance will be taken away from the inheritance of the tribe of our fathers."

5 Then Moses commanded the children of Israel according to the word of the LORD, saying: "What the tribe of the sons of Joseph speaks is right. 6 This *is* what the LORD commands concerning the daughters of Zelophehad, saying, 'Let them marry whom they think best, but they may marry only within the family of their father's tribe.' 7 So the inheritance of the children of Israel shall not change hands from tribe to tribe, for every one of the children of Israel shall keep the inheritance of the tribe of his fathers. 8 And every daughter who possesses an inheritance in any tribe of the children of Israel shall be the wife of one of the family of her father's tribe, so that the children of Israel each may possess the inheritance of his fathers. 9 Thus no inheritance shall change hands from *one* tribe to another, but every tribe of the children of Israel shall keep its own inheritance."

10 Just as the LORD commanded Moses, so did the daughters of Zelophehad; 11 for Mahlah, Tirzah, Hoglah, Milcah, and Noah, the daughters of Zelophehad, were married to the sons of their father's brothers. 12 They were married into the families of the children of Manasseh the son of Joseph, and their inheritance remained in the tribe of their father's family.

13 These *are* the commandments and the judgments which the LORD commanded the children of Israel by the hand of Moses in the plains of Moab by the Jordan, *across from* Jericho.

PSALM 35:17–28

17 LORD, how long will You look on? Rescue me from their destructions, My precious *life* from the lions.
18 I will give You thanks in the great assembly; I will praise You among many people.
19 Let them not rejoice over me who are wrongfully my enemies; Nor let them wink with the eye who hate me without a cause.
20 For they do not speak peace, But they devise deceitful matters Against *the* quiet ones in the land.
21 They also opened their mouth wide against me, *And* said, "Aha, aha! Our eyes have seen *it*."
22 *This* You have seen, O LORD; Do not keep silence. O Lord, do not be far from me.
23 Stir up Yourself, and awake to my vindication, To my cause, my God and my Lord.
24 Vindicate me, O LORD my God, according to Your righteousness; And let them not rejoice over me.
25 Let them not say in their hearts, "Ah, so we would have it!" Let them not say, "We have swallowed him up."
26 Let them be ashamed and brought to mutual confusion Who rejoice at my hurt; Let them be clothed with shame and dishonor Who exalt themselves against me.
27 Let them shout for joy and be glad, Who favor my righteous cause; And let them say continually, "Let the LORD be magnified, Who has pleasure in the prosperity of His servant."
28 And my tongue shall speak of Your righteousness *And* of Your praise all the day long.

PROVERBS 12:3

3 A man is not established by wickedness, But the root of the righteous cannot be moved.

MARK 15:25–47

NOW it was the third hour, and they crucified Him. 26 And the inscription of His accusation was written above:

THE KING OF THE JEWS.

27 With Him they also crucified two robbers, one on His right and the other on His left. 28 So the Scripture was fulfilled

which says, "And He was numbered with the transgressors."

29 And those who passed by blasphemed Him, wagging their heads and saying, "Aha! *You* who destroy the temple and build *it* in three days, 30 save Yourself, and come down from the cross!"

31 Likewise the chief priests also, mocking among themselves with the scribes, said, "He saved others; Himself He cannot save. 32 Let the Christ, the King of Israel, descend now from the cross, that we may see and believe."

Even those who were crucified with Him reviled Him.

33 Now when the sixth hour had come, there was darkness over the whole land until the ninth hour. 34 And at the ninth hour Jesus cried out with a loud voice, saying, "Eloi, Eloi, lama sabachthani?" which is translated, "My God, My God, why have You forsaken Me?"

35 Some of those who stood by, when they heard *that*, said, "Look, He is calling for Elijah!" 36 Then someone ran and filled a sponge full of sour wine, put *it* on a reed, and offered *it* to Him to drink, saying, "Let Him alone; let us see if Elijah will come to take Him down."

37 And Jesus cried out with a loud voice, and breathed His last.

38 Then the veil of the temple was torn in two from top to bottom. 39 So when the centurion, who stood opposite Him, saw that He cried out like this and breathed His last, he said, "Truly this Man was the Son of God!"

The whole purpose of the Redemption is to give back to man the original source of life.   (BIB. ETHICS)

---

40 There were also women looking on from afar, among whom were Mary Magdalene, Mary the mother of James the Less and of Joses, and Salome, 41 who also followed Him and ministered to Him when He was in Galilee, and many other women who came up with Him to Jerusalem.

42 Now when evening had come, because it was the Preparation Day, that is, the day before the Sabbath, 43 Joseph of Arimathea, a prominent council member, who was himself waiting for the kingdom of God, coming and taking courage, went in to Pilate and asked for the body of Jesus. 44 Pilate marveled that He was already dead; and summoning the centurion, he asked him if He had been dead for some time. 45 So when he found out from the centurion, he granted the body to Joseph. 46 Then he bought fine linen, took Him down, and wrapped Him in the linen. And he laid Him in a tomb which had been hewn out of the rock, and rolled a stone against the door of the tomb. 47 And Mary Magdalene and Mary *the mother* of Joses observed where He was laid.

Reading 79—Have I Seen Him?
Mark 16:12

Being saved and seeing Jesus are not the same thing. Many are partakers of God's grace who have never seen Jesus. When once you have seen Jesus, you can never be the same, other things do not appeal as they used to do.

Always distinguish between what you see Jesus to be, and what He has done for you. If you only know what He has done for you, you have not a big enough God; but if you have had a vision of Jesus as He is, experiences can come and go, you will endure "as seeing Him who is invisible." The man blind from his birth did not know who Jesus was until He appeared and revealed Himself to him. Jesus appears to those for whom He has done something; but we cannot dictate when He will come. Suddenly at any turn He may come. "Now I see Him!"

Jesus must appear to your friend as well as to you; no one can see Jesus with your eyes. Severance takes place where one and not the other has seen Jesus. You cannot bring your friend unless God brings him. Have you seen

Jesus? Then you will want others to see Him too. "And they went and told *it* to the rest, *but* they did not believe them either." You must tell, although they do not believe. (*UTMOST*)

DEUTERONOMY 1:1—2:37

THESE *are* the words which Moses spoke to all Israel on this side of the Jordan in the wilderness, in the plain opposite Suph, between Paran, Tophel, Laban, Hazeroth, and Dizahab. 2 *It is* eleven days' *journey* from Horeb by way of Mount Seir to Kadesh Barnea. 3 Now it came to pass in the fortieth year, in the eleventh month, on the first *day* of the month, *that* Moses spoke to the children of Israel according to all that the LORD had given him as commandments to them, 4 after he had killed Sihon king of the Amorites, who dwelt in Heshbon, and Og king of Bashan, who dwelt at Ashtaroth in Edrei.

5 On this side of the Jordan in the land of Moab, Moses began to explain this law, saying, 6 "The LORD our God spoke to us in Horeb, saying: 'You have dwelt long enough at this mountain. 7 Turn and take your journey, and go to the mountains of the Amorites, to all the neighboring *places* in the plain, in the mountains and in the lowland, in the South and on the seacoast, to the land of the Canaanites and to Lebanon, as far as the great river, the River Euphrates. 8 See, I have set the land before you; go in and possess the land which the LORD swore to your fathers—to Abraham, Isaac, and Jacob—to give to them and their descendants after them.'

9 "And I spoke to you at that time, saying: 'I alone am not able to bear you. 10 The LORD your God has multiplied you, and here you *are* today, as the stars of heaven in multitude. 11 May the LORD God of your fathers make you a thousand times more numerous than you are, and bless you as He has promised you! 12 How can I alone bear your problems and your burdens and your complaints? 13 Choose wise, understanding, and knowledgeable men from among your tribes, and I will make them heads over you.' 14 And you answered me and said, 'The thing which you have told *us* to do *is* good.' 15 So I took the heads of your tribes, wise and knowledgeable men, and made them heads over you, leaders of thousands, leaders of hundreds, leaders of fifties, leaders of tens, and officers for your tribes. 16 "Then I commanded your judges at

that time, saying, 'Hear *the cases* between your brethren, and judge righteously between a man and his brother or the stranger who is with him. 17 You shall not show partiality in judgment; you shall hear the small as well as the great; you shall not be afraid in any man's presence, for the judgment *is* God's. The case that is too hard for you, bring to me, and I will hear it.' 18 And I commanded you at that time all the things which you should do.

19 "So we departed from Horeb, and went through all that great and terrible wilderness which you saw on the way to the mountains of the Amorites, as the LORD our God had commanded us. Then we came to Kadesh Barnea. 20 And I said to you, 'You have come to the mountains of the Amorites, which the LORD our God is giving us. 21 Look, the LORD your God has set the land before you; go up *and* possess *it*, as the LORD God of your fathers has spoken to you; do not fear or be discouraged.'

22 "And every one of you came near to me and said, 'Let us send men before us, and let them search out the land for us, and bring back word to us of the way by which we should go up, and of the cities into which we shall come.'

23 "The plan pleased me well; so I took twelve of your men, one man from *each* tribe. 24 And they departed and went up into the mountains, and came to the Valley of Eshcol, and spied it out. 25 They also took *some* of the fruit of the land in their hands and brought *it* down to us; and they brought back word to us, saying, '*It is* a good land which the LORD our God is giving us.'

26 "Nevertheless you would not go up, but rebelled against the command of the LORD your God; 27 and you complained in your tents, and said, 'Because the LORD hates us, He has brought us out of the land of Egypt to deliver us into the hand of the Amorites, to destroy us. 28 Where can we go up? Our brethren have discouraged our hearts, saying, "The people *are* greater and taller than we; the cities *are* great and fortified up to heaven; moreover we have seen the sons of the Anakim there."'

29 "Then I said to you, 'Do not be terri-

fied, or afraid of them. 30 The Lord your God, who goes before you, He will fight for you, according to all He did for you in Egypt before your eyes, 31 and in the wilderness where you saw how the Lord your God carried you, as a man carries his son, in all the way that you went until you came to this place.' 32 Yet, for all that, you did not believe the Lord your God, 33 who went in the way before you to search out a place for you to pitch your tents, to show you the way you should go, in the fire by night and in the cloud by day.

34 "And the Lord heard the sound of your words, and was angry, and took an oath, saying, 35 'Surely not one of these men of this evil generation shall see that good land of which I swore to give to your fathers, 36 except Caleb the son of Jephunneh; he shall see it, and to him and his children I am giving the land on which he walked, because he wholly followed the Lord.' 37 The Lord was also angry with me for your sakes, saying, 'Even you shall not go in there. 38 Joshua the son of Nun, who stands before you, he shall go in there. Encourage him, for he shall cause Israel to inherit it.

39 'Moreover your little ones and your children, who you say will be victims, who today have no knowledge of good and evil, they shall go in there; to them I will give it, and they shall possess it. 40 But *as for* you, turn and take your journey into the wilderness by the Way of the Red Sea.'

41 "Then you answered and said to me, 'We have sinned against the Lord; we will go up and fight, just as the Lord our God commanded us.' And when everyone of you had girded on his weapons of war, you were ready to go up into the mountain.

42 "And the Lord said to me, 'Tell them, "Do not go up nor fight, for I *am* not among you; lest you be defeated before your enemies." ' 43 So I spoke to you; yet you would not listen, but rebelled against the command of the Lord, and presumptuously went up into the mountain. 44 And the Amorites who dwelt in that mountain came out against you and chased you as bees do, and drove you back from Seir to Hormah. 45 Then you returned and wept before the Lord, but the Lord would not listen to your voice nor give ear to you.

46 "So you remained in Kadesh many days, according to the days that you spent *there.*

2 "THEN we turned and journeyed into the wilderness of the Way of the Red

Sea, as the Lord spoke to me, and we skirted Mount Seir for many days.

2 "And the Lord spoke to me, saying: 3 'You have skirted this mountain long enough; turn northward. 4 And command the people, saying, "You *are about* to pass through the territory of your brethren, the descendants of Esau, who live in Seir; and they will be afraid of you. Therefore watch yourselves carefully. 5 Do not meddle with them, for I will not give you *any* of their land, no, not so much as one footstep, because I have given Mount Seir to Esau *as* a possession. 6 You shall buy food from them with money, that you may eat; and you shall also buy water from them with money, that you may drink.

7 "For the Lord your God has blessed you in all the work of your hand. He knows your trudging through this great wilderness. These forty years the Lord your God *has been* with you; you have lacked nothing." '

8 "And when we passed beyond our brethren, the descendants of Esau who dwell in Seir, away from the road of the plain, away from Elath and Ezion Geber, we turned and passed by way of the Wilderness of Moab. 9 Then the Lord said to me, 'Do not harass Moab, nor contend with them in battle, for I will not give you *any* of their land *as* a possession, because I have given Ar to the descendants of Lot *as* a possession.' "

10 (The Emim had dwelt there in times past, a people as great and numerous and tall as the Anakim. 11 They were also regarded as giants, like the Anakim, but the Moabites call them Emim. 12 The Horites formerly dwelt in Seir, but the descendants of Esau dispossessed them and destroyed them from before them, and dwelt in their place, just as Israel did to the land of their possession which the Lord gave them.)

13 " 'Now rise and cross over the Valley of the Zered.' So we crossed over the Valley of the Zered. 14 And the time we took to come from Kadesh Barnea until we crossed over the Valley of the Zered *was* thirty-eight years, until all the generation of the men of war was consumed from the midst of the camp, just as the Lord had sworn to them. 15 For indeed the hand of the Lord was against them, to destroy them from the midst of the camp until they were consumed.

16 "So it was, when all the men of war had finally perished from among the people, 17 that the Lord spoke to me, saying: 18 'This day you are to cross over at Ar, the boundary of Moab. 19 And *when* you

come near the people of Ammon, do not harass them or meddle with them, for I will not give you *any* of the land of the people of Ammon *as* a possession, because I have given it to the descendants of Lot *as* a possession.' "

20 (That was also regarded as a land of giants; giants formerly dwelt there. But the Ammonites call them Zamzummim, 21 a people as great and numerous and tall as the Anakim. But the LORD destroyed them before them, and they dispossessed them and dwelt in their place, 22 just as He had done for the descendants of Esau, who dwelt in Seir, when He destroyed the Horites from before them. They dispossessed them and dwelt in their place, even to this day. 23 And the Avim, who dwelt in villages as far as Gaza—the Caphtorim, who came from Caphtor, destroyed them and dwelt in their place.)

24 " 'Rise, take your journey, and cross over the River Arnon. Look, I have given into your hand Sihon the Amorite, king of Heshbon, and his land. Begin to possess *it,* and engage him in battle. 25 This day I will begin to put the dread and fear of you upon the nations under the whole heaven, who shall hear the report of you, and shall tremble and be in anguish because of you.'

26 "And I sent messengers from the Wilderness of Kedemoth to Sihon king of Heshbon, with words of peace, saying, 27 'Let me pass through your land; I will keep strictly to the road, and I will turn neither to the right nor to the left. 28 You shall sell me food for money, that I may eat, and give me water for money, that I may drink; only let me pass through on foot, 29 just as the descendants of Esau who dwell in Seir and the Moabites who dwell in Ar did for me, until I cross the Jordan to the land which the LORD our God is giving us.'

30 "But Sihon king of Heshbon would not let us pass through, for the LORD your God hardened his spirit and made his heart obstinate, that He might deliver him into your hand, as *it is* this day. 31 "And the LORD said to me, 'See, I have begun to give Sihon and his land over to you. Begin to possess *it,* that you may inherit his land.' 32 Then Sihon and all his people came out against us to fight at Jahaz. 33 And the LORD our God delivered him over to us; so we defeated him, his sons, and all his people. 34 We took all his cities at that time, and we utterly destroyed the men, women, and little ones of every city; we left none remaining. 35 We took only the livestock as plunder for ourselves, with

the spoil of the cities which we took. 36 From Aroer, which *is* on the bank of the River Arnon, and *from* the city that *is* in the ravine, as far as Gilead, there was not one city too strong for us; the LORD our God delivered all to us. 37 Only you did not go near the land of the people of Ammon—anywhere along the River Jabbok, or to the cities of the mountains, or wherever the LORD our God had forbidden us.

PSALM 36:1–6

1 AN oracle within my heart concerning
    the transgression of the wicked:
  There is no fear of God before his eyes.
2 For he flatters himself in his own eyes,
    When he finds out his iniquity *and*
    when he hates.
3 The words of his mouth *are* wickedness
    and deceit;
  He has ceased to be wise *and* to do
    good.
4 He devises wickedness on his bed;
  He sets himself in a way *that is* not
    good;
  He does not abhor evil.

5 Your mercy, O LORD, *is* in the heavens;
  Your faithfulness *reaches* to the clouds.
6 Your righteousness *is* like the great
    mountains;
  Your judgments *are* a great deep;
  O LORD, You preserve man and beast.

PROVERBS 12:4–6

4 AN excellent wife *is* the crown of her
    husband,
  But she who causes shame *is* like
    rottenness in his bones.

5 The thoughts of the righteous *are* right,
  But the counsels of the wicked *are*
    deceitful.
6 The words of the wicked *are,* "Lie in
    wait for blood,"
  But the mouth of the upright will
    deliver them.

MARK 16:1–20

NOW when the Sabbath was past, Mary Magdalene, Mary *the mother* of James, and Salome bought spices, that they might come and anoint Him. 2 Very early in the morning, on the first *day* of the week, they came to the tomb when the sun had risen. 3 And they said among themselves, "Who will roll away the stone from the door of the tomb for us?" 4 But when they looked up, they saw that the stone had been rolled away—for it was very large. 5 And entering the tomb, they saw a young man clothed in a long white robe sitting on the right side; and they were alarmed.

6 But he said to them, "Do not be alarmed. You seek Jesus of Nazareth, who was crucified. He is risen! He is not here. See the place where they laid Him. 7 But go, tell His disciples—and Peter—that He is going before you into Galilee; there you will see Him, as He said to you."

8 So they went out quickly and fled from the tomb, for they trembled and were amazed. And they said nothing to anyone, for they were afraid.

9 Now when *He* rose early on the first *day* of the week, He appeared first to Mary Magdalene, out of whom He had cast seven demons. 10 She went and told those who had been with Him, as they mourned and wept. 11 And when they heard that He was alive and had been seen by her, they did not believe.

12 After that, He appeared in another form to two of them as they walked and went into the country. 13 And they went

and told *it* to the rest, *but* they did not believe them either.

14 Later He appeared to the eleven as they sat at the table; and He rebuked their unbelief and hardness of heart, because they did not believe those who had seen Him after He had risen. 15 And He said to them, "Go into all the world and preach the gospel to every creature. 16 He who believes and is baptized will be saved; but he who does not believe will be condemned. 17 And these signs will follow those who believe: In My name they will cast out demons; they will speak with new tongues; 18 they will take up serpents; and if they drink anything deadly, it will by no means hurt them; they will lay hands on the sick, and they will recover."

19 So then, after the Lord had spoken to them, He was received up into heaven, and sat down at the right hand of God. 20 And they went out and preached everywhere, the Lord working with *them* and confirming the word through the accompanying signs. Amen.

---

*G*od *does not do anything* with *us, only* through *us.*   (SEND I YOU)

◆◆◆◆

Reading 80—The Circumstances of Prayer
Deuteronomy 3:23–25

Prayer is the battle; it is a matter of indifference where you are. Whichever way God engineers circumstances, the duty is to pray. Never allow the thought—"I am of no use where I am"; because you certainly can be of no use where you are not. Wherever God has dumped you down in circumstances pray, ejaculate to Him all the time. "Whatever you ask in My name, that I will do." We won't pray unless we get thrills, that is the intensest form of spiritual selfishness. We have to labor along the line of God's direction, and He says pray. "Pray the Lord of the harvest to send out laborers into His harvest."

There is nothing thrilling about a laboring man's work, but it is the laboring man who makes the conceptions of the genius possible; and it is the laboring saint who makes the conceptions of his Master possible. You labor at prayer and results happen all the time from His standpoint. What an astonishment it will be to find, when the veil is lifted, the souls that have been reaped by you, simply because you had been in the habit of taking your orders from Jesus Christ.   (UTMOST)

DEUTERONOMY 3:1—4:49

"THEN we turned and went up the road to Bashan; and Og king of Bashan came out against us, he and all his people, to battle at Edrei. 2 And the LORD said to me, 'Do not fear him, for I have delivered him and all his people and his land into your hand; you shall do to him as you did to Sihon king of the Amorites, who dwelt at Heshbon.'

3 "So the LORD our God also delivered into our hands Og king of Bashan, with all his people, and we attacked him until he had no survivors remaining. 4 And we took all his cities at that time; there was not a city which we did not take from them: sixty cities, all the region of Argob, the kingdom of Og in Bashan. 5 All these cities *were* fortified with high walls, gates, and bars, besides a great many rural towns. 6 And we utterly destroyed them, as we did to Sihon king of Heshbon, utterly destroying the men, women, and children of every city. 7 But all the livestock and the spoil of the cities we took as booty for ourselves.

8 "And at that time we took the land from the hand of the two kings of the Amorites who *were* on this side of the Jordan, from the River Arnon to Mount Hermon 9 (the Sidonians call Hermon Sirion, and the Amorites call it Senir), 10 all the cities of the plain, all Gilead, and all Bashan, as far as Salcah and Edrei, cities of the kingdom of Og in Bashan.

11 "For only Og king of Bashan remained of the remnant of the giants. Indeed his bedstead *was* an iron bedstead. (*Is it not* in Rabbah of the people of Ammon?) Nine cubits *is* its length and four cubits its width, according to the standard cubit.

12 "And this land, *which* we possessed at that time, from Aroer, which *is* by the River Arnon, and half the mountains of Gilead and its cities, I gave to the Reubenites and the Gadites. 13 The rest of Gilead, and all Bashan, the kingdom of Og, I gave to half the tribe of Manasseh. (All the region of Argob, with all Bashan, was called the land of the giants. 14 Jair the son of Manasseh took all the region of Argob, as far as the border of the Geshurites and the Maacha-thites, and called Bashan after his own name, Havoth Jair, to this day.)

15 "Also I gave Gilead to Machir. 16 And to the Reubenites and the Gadites I gave from Gilead as far as the River Arnon, the middle of the river as *the* border, as far as the River Jabbok, the border of the people of Ammon; 17 the plain also, with the Jordan as *the* border, from Chinnereth

as far as the east side of the Sea of the Arabah (the Salt Sea), below the slopes of Pisgah.

18 "Then I commanded you at that time, saying: 'The LORD your God has given you this land to possess. All you men of valor shall cross over armed before your brethren, the children of Israel. 19 But your wives, your little ones, and your livestock (I know that you have much livestock) shall stay in your cities which I have given you, 20 until the LORD has given rest to your brethren as to you, and they also possess the land which the LORD your God is giving them beyond the Jordan. Then each of you may return to his possession which I have given you.'

21 "And I commanded Joshua at that time, saying, 'Your eyes have seen all that the LORD your God has done to these two kings; so will the LORD do to all the kingdoms through which you pass. 22 You must not fear them, for the LORD your God Himself fights for you.'

23 "Then I pleaded with the LORD at that time, saying: 24 'O Lord GOD, You have begun to show Your servant Your greatness and Your mighty hand, for what god *is there* in heaven or on earth who can do *anything* like Your works and Your mighty *deeds*? 25 I pray, let me cross over and see the good land beyond the Jordan, those pleasant mountains, and Lebanon.'

26 "But the LORD was angry with me on your account, and would not listen to me. So the LORD said to me: 'Enough of that! Speak no more to Me of this matter. 27 Go up to the top of Pisgah, and lift your eyes toward the west, the north, the south, and the east; behold *it* with your eyes, for you shall not cross over this Jordan. 28 But command Joshua, and encourage him and strengthen him; for he shall go over before this people, and he shall cause them to inherit the land which you will see.'

29 "So we stayed in the valley opposite Beth Peor.

4 "NOW, O Israel, listen to the statutes and the judgments which I teach you to observe, that you may live, and go in and possess the land which the LORD God of your fathers is giving you. 2 You shall not add to the word which I command you, nor take from it, that you may keep the commandments of the LORD your God which I command you. 3 Your eyes have seen what the LORD did at Baal Peor; for the LORD your God has destroyed from among you all the men who followed Baal

of Peor. 4 But you who held fast to the Lord your God *are* alive today, every one of you.

5 "Surely I have taught you statutes and judgments, just as the Lord my God commanded me, that you should act according *to them* in the land which you go to possess. 6 Therefore be careful to observe *them;* for this *is* your wisdom and your understanding in the sight of the peoples who will hear all these statutes, and say, 'Surely this great nation *is* a wise and understanding people.'

7 "For what great nation *is there* that has God *so* near to it, as the Lord our God *is* to us, for whatever *reason* we may call upon Him? 8 And what great nation *is there* that has *such* statutes and righteous judgments as are in all this law which I set before you this day? 9 Only take heed to yourself, and diligently keep yourself, lest you forget the things your eyes have seen, and lest they depart from your heart all the days of your life. And teach them to your children and your grandchildren, 10 *especially concerning* the day you stood before the Lord your God in Horeb, when the Lord said to me, 'Gather the people to Me, and I will let them hear My words, that they may learn to fear Me all the days they live on the earth, and *that* they may teach their children.'

11 "Then you came near and stood at the foot of the mountain, and the mountain burned with fire to the midst of heaven, with darkness, cloud, and thick darkness. 12 And the Lord spoke to you out of the midst of the fire. You heard the sound of the words, but saw no form; *you* only *heard* a voice. 13 So He declared to you His covenant which He commanded you to perform, the Ten Commandments; and He wrote them on two tablets of stone. 14 And the Lord commanded me at that time to teach you statutes and judgments, that you might observe them in the land which you cross over to possess.

15 "Take careful heed to yourselves, for you saw no form when the Lord spoke to you at Horeb out of the midst of the fire, 16 lest you act corruptly and make for yourselves a carved image in the form of any figure: the likeness of male or female, 17 the likeness of any animal that *is* on the earth or the likeness of any winged bird that flies in the air, 18 the likeness of anything that creeps on the ground or the likeness of any fish that *is* in the water beneath the earth. 19 And *take heed,* lest you lift your eyes to heaven, and *when* you see the sun, the moon, and the stars, all the host of heaven, you feel driven to worship them

and serve them, which the Lord your God has given to all the peoples under the whole heaven as a heritage. 20 But the Lord has taken you and brought you out of the iron furnace, out of Egypt, to be His people, an inheritance, as you are this day. 21 Furthermore the Lord was angry with me for your sakes, and swore that I would not cross over the Jordan, and that I would not enter the good land which the Lord your God is giving you as an inheritance. 22 But I must die in this land, I must not cross over the Jordan; but you shall cross over and possess that good land. 23 Take heed to yourselves, lest you forget the covenant of the Lord your God which He made with you, and make for yourselves a carved image in the form of anything which the Lord your God has forbidden you. 24 For the Lord your God *is* a consuming fire, a jealous God.

25 "When you beget children and grandchildren and have grown old in the land, and act corruptly and make a carved image in the form of anything, and do evil in the sight of the Lord your God to provoke Him to anger, 26 I call heaven and earth to witness against you this day, that you will soon utterly perish from the land which you cross over the Jordan to possess; you will not prolong *your* days in it, but will be utterly destroyed. 27 And the Lord will scatter you among the peoples, and you will be left few in number among the nations where the Lord will drive you. 28 And there you will serve gods, the work of men's hands, wood and stone, which neither see nor hear nor eat nor smell. 29 But from there you will seek the Lord your God, and you will find *Him* if you seek Him with all your heart and with all your soul. 30 When you are in distress, and all these things come upon you in the latter days, when you turn to the Lord your God and obey His voice 31 (for the Lord your God *is* a merciful God), He will not forsake you nor destroy you, nor forget the covenant of your fathers which He swore to them.

32 "For ask now concerning the days that are past, which were before you, since the day that God created man on the earth, and *ask* from one end of heaven to the other, whether *any* great *thing* like this has happened, or *anything* like it has been heard. 33 Did *any* people *ever* hear the voice of God speaking out of the midst of the fire, as you have heard, and live? 34 Or did God *ever* try to go *and* take for Himself a nation from the midst of *another* nation, by trials, by signs, by wonders, by war, by a mighty

hand and an outstretched arm, and by great terrors, according to all that the Lord your God did for you in Egypt before your eyes? 35 To you it was shown, that you might know that the Lord Himself *is* God; *there is* none other besides Him. 36 Out of heaven He let you hear His voice, that He might instruct you; on earth He showed you His great fire, and you heard His words out of the midst of the fire. 37 And because He loved your fathers, therefore He chose their descendants after them; and He brought you out of Egypt with His Presence, with His mighty power, 38 driving out from be-

---

The whole almighty power of God is on our behalf. (Psy. Redemp.)

---

fore you nations greater and mightier than you, to bring you in, to give you their land *as* an inheritance, as *it is* this day. 39 Therefore know this day, and consider *it* in your heart, that the Lord Himself *is* God in heaven above and on the earth beneath; *there is* no other. 40 You shall therefore keep His statutes and His commandments which I command you today, that it may go well with you and with your children after you, and that you may prolong *your* days in the land which the Lord your God is giving you for all time."

41 Then Moses set apart three cities on this side of the Jordan, toward the rising of the sun, 42 that the manslayer might flee there, who kills his neighbor unintentionally, without having hated him in time past, and that by fleeing to one of these cities he might live: 43 Bezer in the wilderness on the plateau for the Reubenites, Ramoth in Gilead for the Gadites, and Golan in Bashan for the Manassites.

44 Now this *is* the law which Moses set before the children of Israel. 45 These *are* the testimonies, the statutes, and the judgments which Moses spoke to the children of Israel after they came out of Egypt, 46 on this side of the Jordan, in the valley opposite Beth Peor, in the land of Sihon king of the Amorites, who dwelt at Heshbon, whom Moses and the children of Israel defeated after they came out of Egypt. 47 And they took possession of his land and the land of Og king of Bashan, two kings of the Amorites, who *were* on this side of the Jordan, toward the rising of the sun, 48 from Aroer, which *is* on the bank of the River Arnon, even to Mount Sion (that is, Hermon), 49 and all the plain on the

east side of the Jordan as far as the Sea of the Arabah, below the slopes of Pisgah.

PSALM 36:7–12

7 HOW precious *is* Your lovingkindness, O God!
Therefore the children of men put their trust under the shadow of Your wings.
8 They are abundantly satisfied with the fullness of Your house,
And You give them drink from the river of Your pleasures.
9 For with You *is* the fountain of life;
In Your light we see light.

The only source of Life is the Lord Jesus Christ. (Utmost)

---

10 Oh, continue Your lovingkindness to those who know You,
And Your righteousness to the upright in heart.
11 Let not the foot of pride come against me,
And let not the hand of the wicked drive me away.
12 There the workers of iniquity have fallen;
They have been cast down and are not able to rise.

PROVERBS 12:7

7 THE wicked are overthrown and *are* no more,
But the house of the righteous will stand.

LUKE 1:1–20

INASMUCH as many have taken in hand to set in order a narrative of those things which have been fulfilled among us, 2 just as those who from the beginning were eyewitnesses and ministers of the word delivered them to us, 3 it seemed good to me also, having had perfect understanding of all things from the very first, to write to you an orderly account, most excellent Theophilus, 4 that you may know the certainty of those things in which you were instructed.

5 There was in the days of Herod, the king of Judea, a certain priest named Zacha-

rias, of the division of Abijah. His wife *was* of the daughters of Aaron, and her name *was* Elizabeth. 6 And they were both righteous before God, walking in all the commandments and ordinances of the Lord blameless. 7 But they had no child, because Elizabeth was barren, and they were both well advanced in years.

8 So it was, that while he was serving as priest before God in the order of his division, 9 according to the custom of the priesthood, his lot fell to burn incense when he went into the temple of the Lord. 10 And the whole multitude of the people was praying outside at the hour of incense. 11 Then an angel of the Lord appeared to him, standing on the right side of the altar of incense. 12 And when Zacharias saw *him,* he was troubled, and fear fell upon him.

13 But the angel said to him, "Do not be afraid, Zacharias, for your prayer is heard; and your wife Elizabeth will bear you a son, and you shall call his name John.

14 And you will have joy and gladness, and many will rejoice at his birth. 15 For he will be great in the sight of the Lord, and shall drink neither wine nor strong drink. He will also be filled with the Holy Spirit, even from his mother's womb. 16 And he will turn many of the children of Israel to the Lord their God. 17 He will also go before Him in the spirit and power of Elijah, 'to turn the hearts of the fathers to the children,' and the disobedient to the wisdom of the just, to make ready a people prepared for the Lord."

18 And Zacharias said to the angel, "How shall I know this? For I am an old man, and my wife is well advanced in years."

19 And the angel answered and said to him, "I am Gabriel, who stands in the presence of God, and was sent to speak to you and bring you these glad tidings. 20 But behold, you will be mute and not able to speak until the day these things take place, because you did not believe my words which will be fulfilled in their own time."

◆◆◆◆

Reading 81—Born from Above
Luke 1:35

Jesus Christ was born *into* this world, not *from* it. He came into history from the outside of history; He did not evolve out of history. Our Lord's birth was an advent; He did not come from the human race, He came into it from above. Jesus Christ is not the best human being, He is a Being who cannot be accounted for by the human race at all. He is God Incarnate, not man becoming God, but God coming into human flesh, coming into it from the outside. His Life is the Highest and the Holiest entering in at the lowliest door. Our Lord entered history by the Virgin Mary.

Just as our Lord came into human history from the outside, so He must come into us from the outside. Have we allowed our personal human lives to become a "Bethlehem" for the Son of God? . . . The conception of new birth in the New Testament is of something that enters into us, not of something that springs out of us.   (PSY. REDEMP.)

DEUTERONOMY 5:1—6:25

AND Moses called all Israel, and said to them: "Hear, O Israel, the statutes and judgments which I speak in your hearing today, that you may learn them and be careful to observe them. 2 The LORD our God made a covenant with us in Horeb. 3 The LORD did not make this covenant with our fathers, but with us, those who *are* here today, all of us who *are* alive. 4 The LORD talked with you face to face on the mountain from the midst of the fire. 5 I stood between the LORD and you at that time, to declare to you the word of the LORD; for you were afraid because of the fire, and you did not go up the mountain. *He* said:

6 'I *am* the LORD your God who

brought you out of the land of Egypt, out of the house of bondage.

7 'You shall have no other gods before Me.

8 'You shall not make for yourself a carved image—any likeness *of anything* that *is* in heaven above, or that *is* in the earth beneath, or that *is* in the water under the earth; 9 you shall not bow down to them nor serve them. For I, the LORD your God, *am* a jealous God, visiting the iniquity of the fathers upon the children to the third and fourth *generations* of those who hate Me, 10 but show-ing mercy to thousands, to those who love Me and keep My com-mandments.

11 'You shall not take the name of the LORD your God in vain, for the LORD will not hold *him* guiltless who takes His name in vain.

12 'Observe the Sabbath day, to keep it holy, as the LORD your God com-manded you. 13 Six days you shall labor and do all your work, 14 but the seventh day *is* the Sab-bath of the LORD your God. *In it* you shall do no work: you, nor your son, nor your daughter, nor your male servant, nor your fe-male servant, nor your ox, nor your donkey, nor any of your cat-tle, nor your stranger who *is* within your gates, that your male servant and your female servant may rest as well as you. 15 And remember that you were a slave in the land of Egypt, and the LORD your God brought you out from there by a mighty hand and by an outstretched arm; therefore the LORD your God commanded you to keep the Sabbath day.

16 'Honor your father and your mother, as the LORD your God has com-manded you, that your days may be long, and that it may be well with you in the land which the LORD your God is giving you.

17 'You shall not murder.

18 'You shall not commit adultery.

19 'You shall not steal.

20 'You shall not bear false witness against your neighbor.

21 'You shall not covet your neighbor's wife; and you shall not desire your neighbor's house, his field, his male servant, his female servant,

his ox, his donkey, or anything that *is* your neighbor's.'

22 "These words the LORD spoke to all your assembly, in the mountain from the midst of the fire, the cloud, and the thick darkness, with a loud voice; and He added no more. And He wrote them on two tablets of stone and gave them to me.

23 "So it was, when you heard the voice from the midst of the darkness, while the mountain was burning with fire, that you came near to me, all the heads of your tribes and your elders. 24 And you said: 'Surely the LORD our God has shown us His glory and His greatness, and we have heard His voice from the midst of the fire. We have seen this day that God speaks with man; yet he *still* lives. 25 Now therefore, why should we die? For this great fire will con-sume us; if we hear the voice of the LORD our God anymore, then we shall die. 26 For who *is there* of all flesh who has heard the voice of the living God speaking from the midst of the fire, as we *have,* and lived? 27 You go near and hear all that the LORD our God may say, and tell us all that the LORD our God says to you, and we will hear and do *it.*'

28 "Then the LORD heard the voice of your words when you spoke to me, and the LORD said to me: 'I have heard the voice of the words of this people which they have spoken to you. They are right *in* all that they have spoken. 29 Oh, that they had such a heart in them that they would fear Me and always keep all My com-mandments, that it might be well with them and with their children forever! 30 Go and say to them, "Return to your tents." 31 But as for you, stand here by Me, and I will speak to you all the commandments, the statutes, and the judgments which you shall teach them, that they may observe *them* in the land which I am giving them to possess.'

32 "Therefore you shall be careful to do as the LORD your God has commanded you; you shall not turn aside to the right hand or to the left. 33 You shall walk in all the ways which the LORD your God has com-manded you, that you may live and *that it may be* well with you, and *that* you may prolong *your* days in the land which you shall possess.

6 "NOW this *is* the commandment, *and these are* the statutes and judgments which the LORD your God has commanded to teach you, that you may observe *them* in the land which you are crossing over to possess, 2 that you may fear the LORD

your God, to keep all His statutes and His commandments which I command you, you and your son and your grandson, all the days of your life, and that your days may be prolonged. 3 Therefore hear, O Israel, and be careful to observe *it*, that it may be well with you, and that you may multiply greatly as the LORD God of your fathers has promised you—'a land flowing with milk and honey.'

4 "Hear, O Israel: The LORD our God, the LORD *is* one! 5 You shall love the LORD your God with all your heart, with all your soul, and with all your strength.

---

*S*oul is man's spirit becoming rational in the body, explaining itself. (ASK)

---

6 "And these words which I command you today shall be in your heart. 7 You shall teach them diligently to your children, and shall talk of them when you sit in your house, when you walk by the way, when you lie down, and when you rise up. 8 You shall bind them as a sign on your hand, and they shall be as frontlets between your eyes. 9 You shall write them on the doorposts of your house and on your gates.

10 "So it shall be, when the LORD your God brings you into the land of which He swore to your fathers, to Abraham, Isaac, and Jacob, to give you large and beautiful cities which you did not build, 11 houses full of all good things, which you did not fill, hewn-out wells which you did not dig, vineyards and olive trees which you did not plant—when you have eaten and are full— 12 *then* beware, lest you forget the LORD who brought you out of the land of Egypt, from the house of bondage. 13 You shall fear the LORD your God and serve Him, and shall take oaths in His name. 14 You shall not go after other gods, the gods of the peoples who *are* all around you 15 (for the LORD your God *is* a jealous God among you), lest the anger of the LORD your God be aroused against you and destroy you from the face of the earth.

16 "You shall not tempt the LORD your God as you tempted *Him* in Massah. 17 You shall diligently keep the commandments of the LORD your God, His testimonies, and His statutes which He has commanded you. 18 And you shall do *what is* right and good in the sight of the LORD, that it may be well with you, and that you may go in and possess the good land of

which the LORD swore to your fathers, 19 to cast out all your enemies from before you, as the LORD has spoken.

20 "When your son asks you in time to come, saying, 'What *is the meaning of* the testimonies, the statutes, and the judgments which the LORD our God has commanded you?' 21 then you shall say to your son: 'We were slaves of Pharaoh in Egypt, and the LORD brought us out of Egypt with a mighty hand; 22 and the LORD showed signs and wonders before our eyes, great and severe, against Egypt, Pharaoh, and all his household. 23 Then He brought us out from there, that He might bring us in, to give us the land of which He swore to our fathers. 24 And the LORD commanded us to observe all these statutes, to fear the LORD our God, for our good always, that He might preserve us alive, as *it is* this day. 25 Then it will be righteousness for us, if we are careful to observe all these commandments before the LORD our God, as He has commanded us.'

PSALM 37:1–4

1   DO not fret because of evildoers,
     Nor be envious of the workers of
         iniquity.
2   For they shall soon be cut down like
         the grass,
     And wither as the green herb.

3   Trust in the LORD, and do good;
     Dwell in the land, and feed on His
         faithfulness.
4   Delight yourself also in the LORD,
     And He shall give you the desires of
         your heart.

PROVERBS 12:8

8   A man will be commended according
         to his wisdom,
     But he who is of a perverse heart will
         be despised.

LUKE 1:21–38

AND the people waited for Zacharias, and marveled that he lingered so long in the temple. 22 But when he came out, he could not speak to them; and they perceived that he had seen a vision in the temple, for he beckoned to them and remained speechless.

23 So it was, as soon as the days of his service were completed, that he departed to his own house. 24 Now after those days

his wife Elizabeth conceived; and she hid herself five months, saying, 25 "Thus the Lord has dealt with me, in the days when He looked on *me,* to take away my reproach among people."

26 Now in the sixth month the angel Gabriel was sent by God to a city of Galilee named Nazareth, 27 to a virgin betrothed to a man whose name was Joseph, of the house of David. The virgin's name *was* Mary. 28 And having come in, the angel said to her, "Rejoice, highly favored *one,* the Lord *is* with you; blessed *are* you among women!"

29 But when she saw *him,* she was troubled at his saying, and considered what manner of greeting this was. 30 Then the angel said to her, "Do not be afraid, Mary, for you have found favor with God. 31 And behold, you will conceive in your womb and bring forth a Son, and shall call His name JESUS. 32 He will be great, and will be called the Son of the Highest; and the Lord God will give Him the throne of His father David. 33 And He will reign over the house of Jacob forever, and of His kingdom there will be no end."

34 Then Mary said to the angel, "How can this be, since I do not know a man?" 35 And the angel answered and said to her, *"The* Holy Spirit will come upon you, and the power of the Highest will overshadow you; therefore, also, that Holy One who is to be born will be called the Son of God. 36 Now indeed, Elizabeth your relative has also conceived a son in her old age; and this is now the sixth month for her who was called barren. 37 For with God nothing will be impossible."

The impossible is exactly what God does. (NOT KNOWING)

38 Then Mary said, "Behold the maidservant of the Lord! Let it be to me according to your word." And the angel departed from her.

Reading 82—One of God's Great Don'ts
Psalm 37:8

It is one thing to say "Fret not," but a very different thing to have such a disposition that you find yourself able not to fret. It sounds so easy to talk about "resting in the Lord" and "waiting patiently for Him" until the nest is upset—until we live, as so many are doing, in tumult and anguish; is it possible then to rest in the Lord? If this "don't" does not work there, it will work nowhere. This "don't" must work in days of perplexity as well as in days of peace, or it never will work. And if it will not work in your particular case, it will not work in anyone else's case. Resting in the Lord does not depend on external circumstances at all, but on your relationship to God Himself. . . .

Fretting springs from a determination to get our own way. Our Lord never worried and He was never anxious, because He was not "out" to realize His own ideas; He was "out" to realize God's ideas. Fretting is wicked if you are a child of God.

Have you been bolstering up that stupid soul of yours with the idea that your circumstances are too much for God? Put all "supposing" on one side and dwell in the shadow of the Almighty. Deliberately tell God that you will not fret about that thing. All our fret and worry is caused by calculating without God. (UTMOST)

DEUTERONOMY 7:1—8:20

"WHEN the LORD your God brings you into the land which you go to possess, and has cast out many nations before you, the Hittites and the Girgashites and the Amorites and the Canaanites and the Perizzites and the Hivites and the Jebusites, seven nations greater and mightier than you, 2 and when the LORD your God delivers them over to you, you shall conquer them *and* utterly destroy them. You shall make no covenant with them nor show mercy to them. 3 Nor shall you make marriages with them. You shall not give your daughter to their son, nor take their daughter for your son. 4 For they will turn your sons away from following Me, to serve other gods; so the anger of the LORD will be aroused against you and destroy you suddenly. 5 But thus you shall deal with them: you shall destroy their altars, and break down their *sacred* pillars, and cut down their wooden images, and burn their carved images with fire.

6 "For you *are* a holy people to the LORD your God; the LORD your God has chosen you to be a people for Himself, a special treasure above all the peoples on the face of the earth. 7 The LORD did not set His

---

It is not that you have got God but that He has got you.   (UTMOST)

---

love on you nor choose you because you were more in number than any other people, for you were the least of all peoples; 8 but because the LORD loves you, and because He would keep the oath which He swore to your fathers, the LORD has brought you out with a mighty hand, and redeemed you from the house of bondage, from the hand of Pharaoh king of Egypt. 9 "Therefore know that the LORD your God, He *is* God, the faithful God who keeps covenant and mercy for a thousand generations with those who love Him and keep His commandments; 10 and He repays those who hate Him to their face, to destroy them. He will not be slack with him who hates Him; He will repay him to his face. 11 Therefore you shall keep the commandment, the statutes, and the judgments which I command you today, to observe them.

12 "Then it shall come to pass, because you listen to these judgments, and keep and do them, that the LORD your God will keep with you the covenant and the mercy

which He swore to your fathers. 13 And He will love you and bless you and multiply you; He will also bless the fruit of your womb and the fruit of your land, your grain and your new wine and your oil, the increase of your cattle and the offspring of your flock, in the land of which He swore to your fathers to give you. 14 You shall be blessed above all peoples; there shall not be a male or female barren among you or among your livestock. 15 And the LORD will take away from you all sickness, and will afflict you with none of the terrible diseases of Egypt which you have known, but will lay *them* on all those who hate you. 16 Also you shall destroy all the peoples whom the LORD your God delivers over to you; your eye shall have no pity on them; nor shall you serve their gods, for that *will be* a snare to you.

17 "If you should say in your heart, 'These nations are greater than I; how can I dispossess them?'— 18 you shall not be afraid of them, *but* you shall remember well what the LORD your God did to Pharaoh and to all Egypt: 19 the great trials which your eyes saw, the signs and the wonders, the mighty hand and the outstretched arm, by which the LORD your God brought you out. So shall the LORD your God do to all the peoples of whom you are afraid. 20 Moreover the LORD your God will send the hornet among them until those who are left, who hide themselves from you, are destroyed. 21 You shall not be terrified of them; for the LORD your God, the great and awesome God, *is* among you. 22 And the LORD your God will drive out those nations before you little by little; you will be unable to destroy them at once, lest the beasts of the field become *too* numerous for you. 23 But the LORD your God will deliver them over to you, and will inflict defeat upon them until they are destroyed. 24 And He will deliver their kings into your hand, and you will destroy their name from under heaven; no one shall be able to stand against you until you have destroyed them. 25 You shall burn the carved images of their gods with fire; you shall not covet the silver or gold *that is* on them, nor take *it* for yourselves, lest you be snared by it; for it *is* an abomination to the LORD your God. 26 Nor shall you bring an abomination into your house, lest you be doomed to destruction like it. You shall utterly detest it and utterly abhor it, for it *is* an accursed thing.

8 "EVERY commandment which I command you today you must be careful to observe, that you may live and multiply, and go in and possess the land of which the LORD swore to your fathers. 2 And you shall remember that the LORD your God led you all the way these forty years in the wilderness, to humble you *and* test you, to know what *was* in your heart, whether you would keep His commandments or not. 3 So He humbled you, allowed you to hunger, and fed you with manna which you did not know nor did your fathers know, that He might make you know that man shall not live by bread alone; but man lives by every *word* that proceeds from the mouth of the LORD. 4 Your garments did not wear out on you, nor did your foot swell these forty years. 5 You should know in your heart that as a man chastens his son, *so* the LORD your God chastens you.

6 "Therefore you shall keep the commandments of the LORD your God, to walk in His ways and to fear Him. 7 For the LORD your God is bringing you into a good land, a land of brooks of water, of fountains and springs, that flow out of valleys and hills; 8 a land of wheat and barley, of vines and fig trees and pomegranates, a land of olive oil and honey; 9 a land in which you will eat bread without scarcity, in which you will lack nothing; a land whose stones *are* iron and out of whose hills you can dig copper. 10 When you have eaten and are full, then you shall bless the LORD your God for the good land which He has given you.

11 "Beware that you do not forget the LORD your God by not keeping His commandments, His judgments, and His statutes which I command you today, 12 lest— when you have eaten and are full, and have built beautiful houses and dwell *in them;* 13 and *when* your herds and your flocks multiply, and your silver and your gold are multiplied, and all that you have is multiplied; 14 when your heart is lifted up, and you forget the LORD your God who brought you out of the land of Egypt, from the house of bondage; 15 who led you through that great and terrible wilderness, *in which were* fiery serpents and scorpions and thirsty land where there was no water; who brought water for you out of the flinty rock; 16 who fed you in the wilderness with manna, which your fathers did not know, that He might humble you and that He might test you, to do you good in the end— 17 then you say in your heart, 'My power and the might of my hand have gained me this wealth.' 18 "And you shall remember the LORD your God, for *it is* He who gives you power to get wealth, that He may establish His covenant which He swore to your fathers, as *it is* this day. 19 Then it shall be, if you by any means forget the LORD your God, and follow other gods, and serve them and worship them, I testify against you this day that you shall surely perish. 20 As the nations which the LORD destroys before you, so you shall perish, because you would not be obedient to the voice of the LORD your God.

PSALM 37:5–11

5 COMMIT your way to the LORD,
Trust also in Him,
And He shall bring *it* to pass.
6 He shall bring forth your righteousness
as the light,
And your justice as the noonday.

7 Rest in the LORD, and wait patiently
for Him;
Do not fret because of him who
prospers in his way,
Because of the man who brings wicked
schemes to pass.
8 Cease from anger, and forsake wrath;
Do not fret—*it* only *causes* harm.

9 For evildoers shall be cut off;
But those who wait on the LORD,
They shall inherit the earth.
10 For yet a little while and the wicked
shall be no *more;*
Indeed, you will look carefully for his
place,
But it *shall be* no *more.*
11 But the meek shall inherit the earth,
And shall delight themselves in the
abundance of peace.

*H*e keeps us in perfect peace while He whispers His secrets and reveals His counsels.   (BRILL. HERITAGE)

PROVERBS 12:9, 10

9 BETTER *is the one* who is slighted but
has a servant,
Than he who honors himself but lacks
bread.

10 A righteous *man* regards the life of his
animal,
But the tender mercies of the wicked
are cruel.

LUKE 1:39–56

NOW Mary arose in those days and went into the hill country with haste, to a city of Judah, 40 and entered the house of Zacharias and greeted Elizabeth. 41 And it happened, when Elizabeth heard the greeting of Mary, that the babe leaped in her womb; and Elizabeth was filled with the Holy Spirit. 42 Then she spoke out with a loud voice and said, "Blessed *are* you among women, and blessed *is* the fruit of your womb! 43 But why *is* this *granted* to me, that the mother of my Lord should come to me? 44 For indeed, as soon as the voice of your greeting sounded in my ears, the babe leaped in my womb for joy. 45 Blessed *is* she who believed, for there will be a fulfillment of those things which were told her from the Lord."

46 And Mary said:

"My soul magnifies the Lord,

The whole meaning of the soul is to express the spirit.   (BIB. PSYCH.)

---

47   And my spirit has rejoiced in God my Savior.
48   For He has regarded the lowly state of His maidservant;
       For behold, henceforth all generations will call me blessed.
49   For He who is mighty has done great things for me,
       And holy *is* His name.
50   And His mercy *is* on those who fear Him
       From generation to generation.
51   He has shown strength with His arm;
       He has scattered *the* proud in the imagination of their hearts.
52   He has put down the mighty from *their* thrones,
       And exalted *the* lowly.
53   He has filled *the* hungry with good things,
       And *the* rich He has sent away empty.
54   He has helped His servant Israel,
       In remembrance of *His* mercy,
55   As He spoke to our fathers,
       To Abraham and to his seed forever."

56 And Mary remained with her about three months, and returned to her house.

◆◆◆◆

Reading 83—Knowledge of Salvation
Luke 1:77

The first sovereign work of grace is summed up in the words—"that they may receive forgiveness of sins." When a man fails in personal Christian experience, it is nearly always because he has never *received* anything. The only sign that a man is saved is that he has received something from Jesus Christ. Our part as workers for God is to open men's eyes that they may turn themselves from darkness to light; but that is not salvation, that is conversion—the effort of a roused human being. I do not think it is too sweeping to say that the majority of nominal Christians are of this order; their eyes are opened, but they have received nothing. Conversion is not regeneration. This is one of the neglected factors in our preaching today. When a man is born again, he knows that it is because he has received something as a gift from Almighty God and not because of his own decision. People register their vows, and sign their pledges, and determine to go through, but none of this is salvation. Salvation means that we are brought to the place where we are able to receive something from God on the authority of Jesus Christ, namely, remission of sins.

(*UTMOST*)

DEUTERONOMY 9:1—10:22

"HEAR, O Israel: You *are* to cross over the Jordan today, and go in to dispossess nations greater and mightier than yourself, cities great and fortified up to heaven, 2 a people great and tall, the descendants of the Anakim, whom you know, and *of whom* you heard *it said,* 'Who can stand before the descendants of Anak?' 3 Therefore understand today that the LORD your God *is* He who goes over before you *as* a consuming fire. He will destroy them and bring them down before you; so you shall drive them out and destroy them quickly, as the LORD has said to you.

4 "Do not think in your heart, after the LORD your God has cast them out before you, saying, 'Because of my righteousness the LORD has brought me in to possess this land'; but *it is* because of the wickedness of these nations *that* the LORD is driving them out from before you. 5 *It is* not because of your righteousness or the uprightness of your heart *that* you go in to possess their land, but because of the wickedness of these nations *that* the LORD your God drives them out from before you, and that He may fulfill the word which the LORD swore to your fathers, to Abraham, Isaac, and Jacob. 6 Therefore understand that the LORD your God is not giving you this good land to possess because of your righteousness, for you *are* a stiff-necked people.

7 "Remember! Do not forget how you provoked the LORD your God to wrath in the wilderness. From the day that you departed from the land of Egypt until you came to this place, you have been rebellious against the LORD. 8 Also in Horeb you provoked the LORD to wrath, so that the LORD was angry *enough* with you to have destroyed you. 9 When I went up into the mountain to receive the tablets of stone, the tablets of the covenant which the LORD made with you, then I stayed on the mountain forty days and forty nights. I neither ate bread nor drank water. 10 Then the LORD delivered to me two tablets of stone written with the finger of God, and on them *were* all the words which the LORD had spoken to you on the mountain from the midst of the fire in the day of the assembly. 11 And it came to pass, at the end of forty days and forty nights, *that* the LORD gave me the two tablets of stone, the tablets of the covenant. 12 "Then the LORD said to me, 'Arise, go down quickly from here, for your people whom you brought out of Egypt have acted corruptly; they have quickly turned aside

from the way which I commanded them; they have made themselves a molded image.'

13 "Furthermore the LORD spoke to me, saying, 'I have seen this people, and indeed they are a stiff-necked people. 14 Let Me alone, that I may destroy them and blot out their name from under heaven; and I will make of you a nation mightier and greater than they.'

15 "So I turned and came down from the mountain, and the mountain burned with fire; and the two tablets of the covenant *were* in my two hands. 16 And I looked, and behold, you had sinned against the LORD your God—had made for yourselves a molded calf! You had turned aside quickly from the way which the LORD had commanded you. 17 Then I took the two tablets and threw them out of my two hands and broke them before your eyes. 18 And I fell down before the LORD, as at the first, forty days and forty nights; I neither ate bread nor drank water, because of all your sin which you committed in doing wickedly in the sight of the LORD, to provoke Him to anger. 19 For I was afraid of the anger and hot displeasure with which the LORD was angry with you, to destroy you. But the LORD listened to me at that time also. 20 And the LORD was very angry with Aaron *and* would have destroyed him; so I prayed for Aaron also at the same time. 21 Then I took your sin, the calf which you had made, and burned it with fire and crushed it *and* ground *it* very small, until it was as fine as dust; and I threw its dust into the brook that descended from the mountain.

22 "Also at Taberah and Massah and Kibroth Hattaavah you provoked the LORD to wrath. 23 Likewise, when the LORD sent you from Kadesh Barnea, saying, 'Go up and possess the land which I have given you,' then you rebelled against the commandment of the LORD your God, and you did not believe Him nor obey His voice. 24 You have been rebellious against the LORD from the day that I knew you.

25 "Thus I prostrated myself before the LORD; forty days and forty nights I kept prostrating myself, because the LORD had said He would destroy you. 26 Therefore I prayed to the LORD, and said: 'O Lord GOD, do not destroy Your people and Your inheritance whom You have redeemed through Your greatness, whom You have brought out of Egypt with a mighty hand. 27 Remember Your servants, Abraham, Isaac, and Jacob; do not look on the stubbornness of this people, or on their wickedness or their sin, 28 lest the land from which

You brought us should say, "Because the LORD was not able to bring them to the land which He promised them, and because He hated them, He has brought them out to kill them in the wilderness." 29 Yet they *are* Your people and Your inheritance, whom You brought out by Your mighty power and by Your outstretched arm.'

10 "AT that time the LORD said to me, 'Hew for yourself two tablets of stone like the first, and come up to Me on the mountain and make yourself an ark of wood. 2 And I will write on the tablets the words that were on the first tablets, which you broke; and you shall put them in the ark.'

3 "So I made an ark of acacia wood, hewed two tablets of stone like the first, and went up the mountain, having the two tablets in my hand. 4 And He wrote on the tablets according to the first writing, the Ten Commandments, which the LORD had spoken to you in the mountain from the midst of the fire in the day of the assembly; and the LORD gave them to me. 5 Then I turned and came down from the mountain, and put the tablets in the ark which I had made; and there they are, just as the LORD commanded me."

6 (Now the children of Israel journeyed from the wells of Bene Jaakan to Moserah, where Aaron died, and where he was buried; and Eleazar his son ministered as priest in his stead. 7 From there they journeyed to Gudgodah, and from Gudgodah to Jotbathah, a land of rivers of water. 8 At that time the LORD separated the tribe of Levi to bear the ark of the covenant of the LORD, to stand before the LORD to minister to Him and to bless in His name, to this day. 9 Therefore Levi has no portion nor inheritance with his brethren; the LORD *is* his inheritance, just as the LORD your God promised him.)

10 "As at the first time, I stayed in the mountain forty days and forty nights; the LORD also heard me at that time, *and* the LORD chose not to destroy you. 11 Then the LORD said to me, 'Arise, begin *your* journey before the people, that they may go in and possess the land which I swore to their fathers to give them.'

12 "And now, Israel, what does the LORD your God require of you, but to fear the LORD your God, to walk in all His ways and to love Him, to serve the LORD your God with all your heart and with all your soul, 13 *and* to keep the commandments of the LORD and His statutes which I command you today for your good? 14 Indeed

heaven and the highest heavens belong to the LORD your God, *also* the earth with all that *is* in it. 15 The LORD delighted only in your fathers, to love them; and He chose their descendants after them, you above all peoples, as *it is* this day. 16 Therefore circumcise the foreskin of your heart, and be stiff-necked no longer. 17 For the LORD your God *is* God of gods and Lord of lords, the great God, mighty and awesome, who shows no partiality nor takes a bribe.

It is a great thing to have a God big enough to believe in.   (APPROVED)

18 He administers justice for the fatherless and the widow, and loves the stranger, giving him food and clothing. 19 Therefore love the stranger, for you were strangers in the land of Egypt. 20 You shall fear the LORD your God; you shall serve Him, and to Him you shall hold fast, and take oaths in His name. 21 He *is* your praise, and He *is* your God, who has done for you these great and awesome things which your eyes have seen. 22 Your fathers went down to Egypt with seventy persons, and now the LORD your God has made you as the stars of heaven in multitude.

PSALM 37:12–17

12   THE wicked plots against the just,
      And gnashes at him with his teeth.
13   The Lord laughs at him,
      For He sees that his day is coming.
14   The wicked have drawn the sword
      And have bent their bow,
      To cast down the poor and needy,
      To slay those who are of upright
          conduct.
15   Their sword shall enter their own heart,
      And their bows shall be broken.

16   A little that a righteous man has
      Is better than the riches of many wicked.
17   For the arms of the wicked shall be
          broken,
      But the LORD upholds the righteous.

PROVERBS 12:11

11   HE who tills his land will be satisfied
          with bread,
      But he who follows frivolity *is* devoid
          of understanding.

LUKE 1:57–80

NOW Elizabeth's full time came for her to be delivered, and she brought forth a son. 58 When her neighbors and relatives heard how the Lord had shown great mercy to her, they rejoiced with her.

59 So it was, on the eighth day, that they came to circumcise the child; and they would have called him by the name of his father, Zacharias. 60 His mother answered and said, "No; he shall be called John."

61 But they said to her, "There is no one among your relatives who is called by this name." 62 So they made signs to his father—what he would have him called.

63 And he asked for a writing tablet, and wrote, saying, "His name is John." So they all marveled. 64 Immediately his mouth was opened and his tongue *loosed*, and he spoke, praising God. 65 Then fear came on all who dwelt around them; and all these sayings were discussed throughout all the hill country of Judea. 66 And all those who heard *them* kept *them* in their hearts, saying, "What kind of child will this be?" And the hand of the Lord was with him.

67 Now his father Zacharias was filled with the Holy Spirit, and prophesied, saying:

68 "Blessed *is* the Lord God of Israel,
    For He has visited and redeemed His
    people,
69 And has raised up a horn of salvation
    for us
    In the house of His servant David,
70 As He spoke by the mouth of His
    holy prophets,
    Who *have been* since the world began,

71 That we should be saved from our
    enemies
    And from the hand of all who hate
    us,
72 To perform the mercy *promised* to our
    fathers
    And to remember His holy covenant,
73 The oath which He swore to our
    father Abraham:
74 To grant us that we,
    Being delivered from the hand of our
    enemies,
    Might serve Him without fear,
75 In holiness and righteousness before
    Him all the days of our life.

76 "And you, child, will be called the
    prophet of the Highest;
    For you will go before the face of
    the Lord to prepare His ways,
77 To give knowledge of salvation to
    His people
    By the remission of their sins,
78 Through the tender mercy of our
    God,
    With which the Dayspring from on
    high has visited us;
79 To give light to those who sit in
    darkness and the shadow of death,
    To guide our feet into the way of
    peace."

His peace is a direct gift through the personal presence of the Holy Ghost. (SEND I YOU)

---

80 So the child grew and became strong in spirit, and was in the deserts till the day of his manifestation to Israel.

◆◆◆

Reading 84—Supreme Sacrifice
Deuteronomy 12:13, 14

The altar of God's choosing is not approached by feelings of devotion or emotions of worship; that is why it is difficult to discover it. All natural religion reaches its climax in ritual, in the beauties of aesthetic and sensuous worship. God's altar is discerned only by the Holy Spirit when that Spirit is in a man.

The dissipation of devotion is seen over and over again in the practical issues of our lives. People give their lives to many things they have no business to. No one has any right to give up the right to himself or to herself to anyone but God Almighty, and devotion to a cause, no matter how noble or how beautiful, nowhere touches the profundity of this lesson. When we are told we must give up our right to ourselves to Jesus Christ, we are bound to ask— if we do not ask, we have not grasped the situation thoroughly "Who is it that asks this tremendous devotion? Is there any principle, any cause, any enterprise on the face of the earth of such importance that a man has to give the very highest he has, namely, his right to himself, for it?" The only being who dare ask of me this supreme sacrifice is the Lord Jesus Christ.

(*PLACE HELP*)

DEUTERONOMY 11:1—12:32

"THEREFORE you shall love the LORD your God, and keep His charge, His statutes, His judgments, and His commandments always. 2 Know today that *I do* not *speak* with your children, who have not known and who have not seen the chastening of the LORD your God, His greatness and His mighty hand and His outstretched arm— 3 His signs and His acts which He did in the midst of Egypt, to Pharaoh king of Egypt, and to all his land; 4 what He did to the army of Egypt, to their horses and their chariots: how He made the waters of the Red Sea overflow them as they pursued you, and *how* the LORD has destroyed them to this day; 5 what He did for you in the wilderness until you came to this place; 6 and what He did to Dathan and Abiram the sons of Eliab, the son of Reuben: how the earth opened its mouth and swallowed them up, their households, their tents, and all the substance that *was* in their possession, in the midst of all Israel— 7 but your eyes have seen every great act of the LORD which He did.

8 "Therefore you shall keep every commandment which I command you today, that you may be strong, and go in and possess the land which you cross over to possess, 9 and that you may prolong *your* days in the land which the LORD swore to give your fathers, to them and their descendants, 'a land flowing with milk and honey.' 10 For the land which you go to possess *is* not like the land of Egypt from which you have come, where you sowed your seed and watered *it* by foot, as a vegetable garden; 11 but the land which you cross over to possess *is* a land of hills and valleys, which drinks water from the rain of heaven, 12 a land for which the LORD your God cares; the eyes of the LORD your God *are* always on it, from the beginning of the year to the very end of the year.

13 'And it shall be that if you earnestly obey My commandments which I command you today, to love the LORD your God and serve Him with all your heart and with all

your soul, 14 then I will give *you* the rain for your land in its season, the early rain and the latter rain, that you may gather in your grain, your new wine, and your oil. 15 And I will send grass in your fields for your livestock, that you may eat and be filled.' 16 Take heed to yourselves, lest your heart be deceived, and you turn aside and serve other gods and worship them, 17 lest the LORD's anger be aroused against you, and He shut up the heavens so that there be no rain, and the land yield no produce, and you perish quickly from the good land which the LORD is giving you.

18 "Therefore you shall lay up these words of mine in your heart and in your soul, and bind them as a sign on your hand, and they shall be as frontlets between your eyes. 19 You shall teach them to your children, speaking of them when you sit in your house, when you walk by the way, when you lie down, and when you rise up. 20 And you shall write them on the doorposts of your house and on your gates, 21 that your days and the days of your children may be multiplied in the land of which the LORD swore to your fathers to give them, like the days of the heavens above the earth.

22 "For if you carefully keep all these commandments which I command you to do— to love the LORD your God, to walk in all His ways, and to hold fast to Him— 23 then the LORD will drive out all these nations from before you, and you will dispossess greater and mightier nations than yourselves. 24 Every place on which the sole of your foot treads shall be yours: from the wilderness and Lebanon, from the river, the River Euphrates, even to the Western Sea, shall be your territory. 25 No man shall be able to stand against you; the LORD your God will put the dread of you and the fear of you upon all the land where you tread, just as He has said to you.

26 "Behold, I set before you today a blessing and a curse: 27 the blessing, if you obey the commandments of the LORD your God which I command you today; 28 and the curse, if you do not obey the command-

ments of the LORD your God, but turn aside from the way which I command you today, to go after other gods which you have not known. 29 Now it shall be, when the LORD your God has brought you into the land which you go to possess, that you shall put the blessing on Mount Gerizim and the curse on Mount Ebal. 30 *Are* they not on the other side of the Jordan, toward the setting sun, in the land of the Canaanites who dwell in the plain opposite Gilgal, beside the terebinth trees of Moreh? 31 For you will cross over the Jordan and go in to possess the land which the LORD your God is giving you, and you will possess it and dwell in it. 32 And you shall be careful to observe all the statutes and judgments which I set before you today.

12 "THESE *are* the statutes and judgments which you shall be careful to observe in the land which the LORD God of your fathers is giving you to possess, all the days that you live on the earth. 2 You shall utterly destroy all the places where the nations which you shall dispossess served their gods, on the high mountains and on the hills and under every green tree. 3 And you shall destroy their altars, break their *sacred* pillars, and burn their wooden images with fire; you shall cut down the carved images of their gods and destroy their names from that place. 4 You shall not worship the LORD your God *with* such *things*.

5 "But you shall seek the place where the LORD your God chooses, out of all your tribes, to put His name for His dwelling place; and there you shall go. 6 There you shall take your burnt offerings, your sacrifices, your tithes, the heave offerings of your hand, your vowed offerings, your freewill offerings, and the firstborn of your herds and flocks. 7 And there you shall eat before the LORD your God, and you shall rejoice in all to which you have put your hand, you and your households, in which the LORD your God has blessed you.

8 "You shall not at all do as we are doing here today—every man doing whatever *is* right in his own eyes— 9 for as yet you have not come to the rest and the inheritance which the LORD your God is giving you. 10 But *when* you cross over the Jordan and dwell in the land which the LORD your God is giving you to inherit, and He gives you rest from all your enemies round about, so that you dwell in safety, 11 then there will be the place where the LORD your God chooses to make His name abide. There you shall bring all that I command you:

your burnt offerings, your sacrifices, your tithes, the heave offerings of your hand, and all your choice offerings which you vow to the LORD. 12 And you shall rejoice before the LORD your God, you and your sons and your daughters, your male and female servants, and the Levite who *is* within your gates, since he has no portion nor inheritance with you. 13 Take heed to yourself that you do not offer your burnt offerings in every place that you see; 14 but in the place which the LORD chooses, in one of your tribes, there you shall offer your burnt offerings, and there you shall do all that I command you.

15 "However, you may slaughter and eat meat within all your gates, whatever your heart desires, according to the blessing of the LORD your God which He has given you; the unclean and the clean may eat of it, of the gazelle and the deer alike. 16 Only you shall not eat the blood; you shall pour it on the earth like water. 17 You may not eat within your gates the tithe of your grain or your new wine or your oil, of the firstborn of your herd or your flock, of any of your offerings which you vow, of your freewill offerings, or of the heave offering of your hand. 18 But you must eat them before the LORD your God in the place which the LORD your God chooses, you and your son and your daughter, your male servant and your female servant, and the Levite who *is* within your gates; and you shall rejoice before the LORD your God in all to which you put your hands. 19 Take heed to yourself that you do not forsake the Levite as long as you live in your land.

20 "When the LORD your God enlarges your border as He has promised you, and you say, 'Let me eat meat,' because you long to eat meat, you may eat as much meat as your heart desires. 21 If the place where the LORD your God chooses to put His name is too far from you, then you may slaughter from your herd and from your flock which the LORD has given you, just as I have commanded you, and you may eat within your gates as much as your heart desires. 22 Just as the gazelle and the deer are eaten, so you may eat them; the unclean and the clean alike may eat them. 23 Only be sure that you do not eat the blood, for the blood *is* the life; you may not eat the life with the meat. 24 You shall not eat it; you shall pour it on the earth like water. 25 You shall not eat it, that it may go well with you and your children after you, when you do *what is* right in the sight of the LORD. 26 Only the holy

things which you have, and your vowed offerings, you shall take and go to the place which the LORD chooses. 27 And you shall offer your burnt offerings, the meat and the blood, on the altar of the LORD your God; and the blood of your sacrifices shall be poured out on the altar of the LORD your God, and you shall eat the meat. 28 Observe and obey all these words which I command you, that it may go well with you and your children after you forever, when you do *what is* good and right in the sight of the LORD your God.

29 "When the LORD your God cuts off from before you the nations which you go to dispossess, and you displace them and dwell in their land, 30 take heed to yourself that you are not ensnared to follow them, after they are destroyed from before you, and that you do not inquire after their gods, saying, 'How did these nations serve their gods? I also will do likewise.' 31 You shall not worship the LORD your God in that way; for every abomination to the LORD which He hates they have done to their gods; for they burn even their sons and daughters in the fire to their gods. 32 "Whatever I command you, be careful to observe it; you shall not add to it nor take away from it.

PSALM 37:18–22

18 THE LORD knows the days of the
    upright,
And their inheritance shall be forever.
19 They shall not be ashamed in the evil
    time,
And in the days of famine they shall
    be satisfied.
20 But the wicked shall perish;
And the enemies of the LORD,
Like the splendor of the meadows, shall
    vanish.
Into smoke they shall vanish away.
21 The wicked borrows and does not
    repay,
But the righteous shows mercy and
    gives.
22 For *those* blessed by Him shall inherit
    the earth,
But *those* cursed by Him shall be cut
    off.

PROVERBS 12:12–14

12 THE wicked covet the catch of evil *men*,
But the root of the righteous yields
    fruit.

13 The wicked is ensnared by the
    transgression of *his* lips,
But the righteous will come through
    trouble.
14 A man will be satisfied with good by
    the fruit of *his* mouth,
And the recompense of a man's hands
    will be rendered to him.

LUKE 2:1–24

AND it came to pass in those days *that* a decree went out from Caesar Augustus that all the world should be registered. 2 This census first took place while Quirinius was governing Syria. 3 So all went to be registered, everyone to his own city.

4 Joseph also went up from Galilee, out of the city of Nazareth, into Judea, to the city of David, which is called Bethlehem, because he was of the house and lineage of David, 5 to be registered with Mary, his betrothed wife, who was with child. 6 So it was, that while they were there, the days were completed for her to be delivered. 7 And she brought forth her firstborn Son, and wrapped Him in swaddling cloths, and laid Him in a manger, because there was no room for them in the inn.

The power of God is proved in His becoming a Baby.   (APPROVED)

---

8 Now there were in the same country shepherds living out in the fields, keeping watch over their flock by night. 9 And behold, an angel of the Lord stood before them, and the glory of the Lord shone around them, and they were greatly afraid. 10 Then the angel said to them, "Do not be afraid, for behold, I bring you good tidings of great joy which will be to all people. 11 For there is born to you this day in the city of David a Savior, who is Christ the Lord. 12 And this *will be* the sign to you: You will find a Babe wrapped in swaddling cloths, lying in a manger."

13 And suddenly there was with the angel a multitude of the heavenly host praising God and saying:

14 "Glory to God in the highest,
    And on earth peace, goodwill toward
    men!"

15 So it was, when the angels had gone away from them into heaven, that the shepherds said to one another, "Let us now

go to Bethlehem and see this thing that has come to pass, which the Lord has made known to us." 16 And they came with haste and found Mary and Joseph, and the Babe lying in a manger. 17 Now when they had seen *Him*, they made widely known the saying which was told them concerning this Child. 18 And all those who heard *it* marveled at those things which were told them by the shepherds. 19 But Mary kept all these things and pondered *them* in her heart. 20 Then the shepherds returned, glorifying and praising God for all the things that they had heard and seen, as it was told them.

21 And when eight days were completed for the circumcision of the Child, His name was called Jesus, the name given by the angel before He was conceived in the womb.

22 Now when the days of her purification according to the law of Moses were completed, they brought Him to Jerusalem to present *Him* to the Lord 23 (as it is written in the law of the Lord, "Every male who opens the womb shall be called holy to the Lord"), 24 and to offer a sacrifice according to what is said in the law of the Lord, "A pair of turtledoves or two young pigeons."

Reading 85—The Submission of Life
Luke 2:51

An amazing submission! For thirty years Jesus lived at home with brothers and sisters who did not believe in Him, and when He began His ministry they said He was mad. "As He is, so are we in this world." We say, "When I was born again I thought it would be a time of great illumination and service, and instead of that I have had to stay at home with people who have criticized me and limited me on the right hand and on the left; I have been misunderstood and misrepresented." "The disciple is not above *his* teacher" (Matt. 10:24). Do we think our lot ought to be better than Jesus Christ's? We can easily escape the submissions if we like, but if we do not submit, the Spirit of God will produce in us the most ghastly humiliation before long. . . .

God is not concerned about our aims. He does not say, "Do you want to go through this bereavement, this upset?" He allows these things for His own purpose. We may say what we like, but God does allow the devil, He does allow sin, He does allow bad men to triumph and tyrants to rule, and these things either make us fiends or they make us saints, it depends entirely on our relationship with God. If we say, "Your will be done," we get the tremendous consolation of knowing that our Father is working everything according to His own wisdom. If we understand what God is after, we shall be saved from being mean and cynical. (ASK)

DEUTERONOMY 13:1—14:29

"IF there arises among you a prophet or a dreamer of dreams, and he gives you a sign or a wonder, 2 and the sign or the wonder comes to pass, of which he spoke to you, saying, 'Let us go after other gods'—which you have not known—'and let us serve them,' 3 you shall not listen to the words of that prophet or that dreamer of dreams, for the Lord your God is testing you to know whether you love the Lord your God

with all your heart and with all your soul. 4 You shall walk after the Lord your God and fear Him, and keep His commandments and obey His voice; you shall serve Him and hold fast to Him. 5 But that prophet or that dreamer of dreams shall be put to death, because he has spoken in order to turn *you* away from the Lord your God, who brought you out of the land of Egypt and redeemed you from the house of bondage, to entice you from the way in which the Lord your God commanded you to walk. So you shall put away the evil from your midst.

6 "If your brother, the son of your mother, your son or your daughter, the wife of your bosom, or your friend who is as your own soul, secretly entices you, saying, 'Let us go and serve other gods,' which you have not known, neither you nor your fathers, 7 of the gods of the people which *are* all around you, near to you or far off from you, from *one* end of the earth to the *other* end of the earth, 8 you shall not consent to him or listen to him, nor shall your eye pity him, nor shall you spare him or conceal him; 9 but you shall surely kill him; your hand shall be first against him to put him to death, and afterward the hand of all the people. 10 And you shall stone him with stones until he dies, because he sought to entice you away from the LORD your God, who brought you out of the land of Egypt, from the house of bondage. 11 So all Israel shall hear and fear, and not again do such wickedness as this among you.

12 "If you hear someone in one of your cities, which the LORD your God gives you to dwell in, saying, 13 'Corrupt men have gone out from among you and enticed the inhabitants of their city, saying, "Let us go and serve other gods" '—which you have not known— 14 then you shall inquire, search out, and ask diligently. And *if it is* indeed true *and* certain *that* such an abomination was committed among you, 15 you shall surely strike the inhabitants of that city with the edge of the sword, utterly destroying it, all that is in it and its livestock—with the edge of the sword. 16 And you shall gather all its plunder into the middle of the street, and completely burn with fire the city and all its plunder, for the LORD your God. It shall be a heap forever; it shall not be built again. 17 So none of the accursed things shall remain in your hand, that the LORD may turn from the fierceness of His anger and show you mercy, have compassion on you and multiply you, just as He swore to your fathers, 18 because you have listened to the voice of the LORD your God, to keep all His commandments which I command you today, to do *what is* right in the eyes of the LORD your God.

14 "YOU *are* the children of the LORD your God; you shall not cut yourselves nor shave the front of your head for the dead. 2 For you *are* a holy people to the LORD your God, and the LORD has chosen you to be a people for Himself, a special treasure above all the peoples who *are* on the face of the earth.

3 "You shall not eat any detestable thing. 4 These *are* the animals which you may eat: the ox, the sheep, the goat, 5 the deer, the gazelle, the roe deer, the wild goat, the mountain goat, the antelope, and the mountain sheep. 6 And you may eat every animal with cloven hooves, having the hoof split into two parts, *and that* chews the cud, among the animals. 7 Nevertheless, of those that chew the cud or have cloven hooves, you shall not eat, *such as* these: the camel, the hare, and the rock hyrax; for they chew the cud but do not have cloven hooves; they *are* unclean for you. 8 Also the swine is unclean for you, because it has cloven hooves, yet *does* not *chew* the cud; you shall not eat their flesh or touch their dead carcasses.

9 "These you may eat of all that *are* in the waters: you may eat all that have fins and scales. 10 And whatever does not have fins and scales you shall not eat; it *is* unclean for you.

11 "All clean birds you may eat. 12 But these you shall not eat: the eagle, the vulture, the buzzard, 13 the red kite, the falcon, and the kite after their kinds; 14 every raven after its kind; 15 the ostrich, the short-eared owl, the sea gull, and the hawk after their kinds; 16 the little owl, the screech owl, the white owl, 17 the jackdaw, the carrion vulture, the fisher owl, 18 the stork, the heron after its kind, and the hoopoe and the bat.

19 "Also every creeping thing that flies is unclean for you; they shall not be eaten.

20 "You may eat all clean birds.

21 "You shall not eat anything that dies *of itself*; you may give it to the alien who *is* within your gates, that he may eat it, or you may sell it to a foreigner; for you *are* a holy people to the LORD your God.

"You shall not boil a young goat in its mother's milk.

22 "You shall truly tithe all the increase of your grain that the field produces year by year. 23 And you shall eat before the LORD your God, in the place where He chooses to make His name abide, the tithe of your grain and your new wine and your oil, of the firstborn of your herds and your flocks, that you may learn to fear the LORD your God always. 24 But if the journey is too long for you, so that you are not able to carry *the tithe, or* if the place where the LORD your God chooses to put His name is too far from you, when the LORD your God has blessed you, 25 then you shall exchange *it* for money, take the money in your hand, and go to the place which the

LORD your God chooses. 26 And you shall spend that money for whatever your heart desires: for oxen or sheep, for wine or similar drink, for whatever your heart desires; you shall eat there before the LORD your God, and you shall rejoice, you and your household. 27 You shall not forsake the Levite who *is* within your gates, for he has no part nor inheritance with you.

28 "At the end of *every* third year you shall bring out the tithe of your produce of that year and store *it* up within your gates. 29 And the Levite, because he has no portion nor inheritance with you, and the stranger and the fatherless and the widow who *are* within your gates, may come and eat and be satisfied, that the LORD your God may bless you in all the work of your hand which you do.

PSALM 37:23–29

23 THE steps of a *good* man are ordered by the LORD,
And He delights in his way.
24 Though he fall, he shall not be utterly cast down;
For the LORD upholds *him with* His hand.

25 I have been young, and *now* am old;
Yet I have not seen the righteous forsaken,
Nor his descendants begging bread.
26 *He is* ever merciful, and lends;
And his descendants *are* blessed.

27 Depart from evil, and do good;
And dwell forevermore.
28 For the LORD loves justice,
And does not forsake His saints;
They are preserved forever,
But the descendants of the wicked shall be cut off.

---

*T*he work of Jesus is the creation of saints.   (GLORY)

---

29 The righteous shall inherit the land,
And dwell in it forever.

PROVERBS 12:15, 16

15 THE way of a fool *is* right in his own eyes,
But he who heeds counsel *is* wise.
16 A fool's wrath is known at once,
But a prudent *man* covers shame.

LUKE 2:25–52

AND behold, there was a man in Jerusalem whose name was Simeon, and this man was just and devout, waiting for the Consolation of Israel, and the Holy Spirit was upon him. 26 And it had been revealed to him by the Holy Spirit that he would not see death before he had seen the Lord's Christ. 27 So he came by the Spirit into the temple. And when the parents brought in the Child Jesus, to do for Him according to the custom of the law, 28 he took Him up in his arms and blessed God and said:

29 "Lord, now You are letting Your servant depart in peace,
According to Your word;
30 For my eyes have seen Your salvation
31 Which You have prepared before the face of all peoples,
32 A light to *bring* revelation to the Gentiles,
And the glory of Your people Israel."

33 And Joseph and His mother marveled at those things which were spoken of Him. 34 Then Simeon blessed them, and said to Mary His mother, "Behold, this *Child* is destined for the fall and rising of many in Israel, and for a sign which will be spoken against 35 (yes, a sword will pierce through your own soul also), that the thoughts of many hearts may be revealed."

36 Now there was one, Anna, a prophetess, the daughter of Phanuel, of the tribe of Asher. She was of a great age, and had lived with a husband seven years from her virginity; 37 and this woman *was* a widow of about eighty-four years, who did not depart from the temple, but served *God* with fastings and prayers night and day. 38 And coming in that instant she gave thanks to the Lord, and spoke of Him to all those who looked for redemption in Jerusalem.

39 So when they had performed all things according to the law of the Lord, they returned to Galilee, to their *own* city, Nazareth. 40 And the Child grew and became strong in spirit, filled with wisdom; and the grace of God was upon Him.

41 His parents went to Jerusalem every year at the Feast of the Passover. 42 And when He was twelve years old, they went up to Jerusalem according to the custom of the feast. 43 When they had finished the days, as they returned, the Boy Jesus lingered behind in Jerusalem. And Joseph and His mother did not know *it;* 44 but supposing Him to have been in the company, they

went a day's journey, and sought Him among *their* relatives and acquaintances. 45 So when they did not find Him, they returned to Jerusalem, seeking Him. 46 Now so it was *that* after three days they found Him in the temple, sitting in the midst of the teachers, both listening to them and asking them questions. 47 And all who heard Him were astonished at His understanding and answers. 48 So when they saw Him, they were amazed; and His mother said to Him, "Son, why have You done this to us? Look, Your father and I have sought You anxiously."

49 And He said to them, "Why did you seek Me? Did you not know that I must be about My Father's business?" 50 But they did not understand the statement which He spoke to them.

51 Then He went down with them and came to Nazareth, and was subject to them, but His mother kept all these things in her heart. 52 And Jesus increased in wisdom and stature, and in favor with God and men.

We grow spiritually as our Lord grew physically, by a life of simple, unobtrusive obedience. (SERVANT AS LORD)

◆◆◆◆

Reading 86—The Enduement Regally
Luke 3:21, 22

We read that Jesus was in communion with His Father at the time of His baptism ("Jesus also was baptized; and . . . prayed . . ."—an inconceivable communion). And what happened? ". . . heaven was opened. And the Holy Spirit descended in bodily form like a dove upon Him, and a voice came from heaven which said, 'You are My beloved Son; in You I am well pleased.'" It was a purely personal experience. The Holy Spirit descended upon Jesus, and the voice of the Father said to Him, "You are My beloved Son." This Man, who was known to men as the humble Nazarene carpenter, was almighty God presented in the guise of a human life.

"Opened heaven" to our Lord means opened heaven to everyone. The Holy Spirit descending as a dove is symbolic of the Holy Spirit life that Jesus can communicate to every person. The New Testament records two personal descents of the Holy Spirit: one on our Lord as Son of Man at His baptism, the other on the Day of Pentecost—"Therefore being exalted to the right hand of God, and having received from the Father the promise of the Holy Spirit, He poured out this which you now see and hear" (Acts 2:33). By right of His death and resurrection and ascension our Lord can impart the Holy Spirit to any and every person (Luke 11:33; John 20:22). (*GLORY*)

DEUTERONOMY 15:1—16:22

"AT the end of *every* seven years you shall grant a release *of debts.* 2 And this *is* the form of the release: Every creditor who has lent *anything* to his neighbor shall release *it;* he shall not require *it* of his neighbor or his brother, because it is called the LORD's release. 3 Of a foreigner you may require *it;* but you shall give up your claim to what is owed by your brother, 4 except when there may be no poor among you; for the LORD will greatly bless you in the land which the LORD your God is giving you to possess *as* an inheritance— 5 only if you carefully obey the voice of the LORD your God, to observe with care all these commandments which I command you today. 6 For the LORD your God will bless you just as He promised you; you shall lend to many nations, but you shall not borrow; you shall reign over many nations, but they shall not reign over you.

7 "If there is among you a poor man of

your brethren, within any of the gates in your land which the LORD your God is giving you, you shall not harden your heart nor shut your hand from your poor brother, 8 but you shall open your hand wide to him and willingly lend him sufficient for his need, whatever he needs. 9 Beware lest there be a wicked thought in your heart, saying, 'The seventh year, the year of release, is at hand,' and your eye be evil against your poor brother and you give him nothing, and he cry out to the LORD against you, and it become sin among you. 10 You shall surely give to him, and your heart should not be grieved when you give to him, because for this thing the LORD your God will bless you in all your works and in all to which you put your hand. 11 For the poor will never cease from the land; therefore I command you, saying, 'You shall open your hand wide to your brother, to your poor and your needy, in your land.'

12 "If your brother, a Hebrew man, or a Hebrew woman, is sold to you and serves you six years, then in the seventh year you shall let him go free from you. 13 And when you send him away free from you, you shall not let him go away empty-handed; 14 you shall supply him liberally from your flock, from your threshing floor, and from your winepress. *From what* the LORD has blessed you with, you shall give to him. 15 You shall remember that you were a slave in the land of Egypt, and the LORD your God redeemed you; therefore I command you this thing today. 16 And if it happens that he says to you, 'I will not go away from you,' because he loves you and your house, since he prospers with you, 17 then you shall take an awl and thrust *it* through his ear to the door, and he shall be your servant forever. Also to your female servant you shall do likewise. 18 It shall not seem hard to you when you send him away free from you; for he has been worth a double hired servant in serving you six years. Then the LORD your God will bless you in all that you do.

19 "All the firstborn males that come from your herd and your flock you shall sanctify to the LORD your God; you shall do no work with the firstborn of your herd, nor shear the firstborn of your flock. 20 You and your household shall eat *it* before the LORD your God year by year in the place which the LORD chooses. 21 But if there is a defect in it, *if it is* lame or blind *or has* any serious defect, you shall not sacrifice it to the LORD your God. 22 You may eat it within your gates; the

unclean and the clean *person* alike *may eat it,* as *if it were* a gazelle or a deer. 23 Only you shall not eat its blood; you shall pour it on the ground like water.

16 "OBSERVE the month of Abib, and keep the Passover to the LORD your God, for in the month of Abib the LORD your God brought you out of Egypt by night. 2 Therefore you shall sacrifice the Passover to the LORD your God, from the flock and the herd, in the place where the LORD chooses to put His name. 3 You shall eat no leavened bread with it; seven days you shall eat unleavened bread with it, *that is,* the bread of affliction (for you came out of the land of Egypt in haste), that you may remember the day in which you came out of the land of Egypt all the days of your life. 4 And no leaven shall be seen among you in all your territory for seven days, nor shall *any* of the meat which you sacrifice the first day at twilight remain overnight until morning.

5 "You may not sacrifice the Passover within any of your gates which the LORD your God gives you; 6 but at the place where the LORD your God chooses to make His name abide, there you shall sacrifice the Passover at twilight, at the going down of the sun, at the time you came out of Egypt. 7 And you shall roast and eat *it* in the place which the LORD your God chooses, and in the morning you shall turn and go to your tents. 8 Six days you shall eat unleavened bread, and on the seventh day there *shall be* a sacred assembly to the LORD your God. You shall do no work *on it.*

9 "You shall count seven weeks for yourself; begin to count the seven weeks from *the time* you begin to *put* the sickle to the grain. 10 Then you shall keep the Feast of Weeks to the LORD your God with the tribute of a freewill offering from your hand, which you shall give as the LORD your God blesses you. 11 You shall rejoice before the LORD your God, you and your son and your daughter, your male servant and your female servant, the Levite who *is* within your gates, the stranger and the fatherless and the widow who *are* among you, at the place where the LORD your God chooses to make His name abide. 12 And you shall remember that you were a slave in Egypt, and you shall be careful to observe these statutes.

13 "You shall observe the Feast of Tabernacles seven days, when you have gathered from your threshing floor and from your winepress. 14 And you shall rejoice in your feast, you and your son and your daughter,

your male servant and your female servant and the Levite, the stranger and the fatherless and the widow, who *are* within your gates. 15 Seven days you shall keep a sacred feast to the LORD your God in the place which the LORD chooses, because the LORD your God will bless you in all your produce and in all the work of your hands, so that you surely rejoice.

16 "Three times a year all your males shall appear before the LORD your God in the place which He chooses: at the Feast of Unleavened Bread, at the Feast of Weeks, and at the Feast of Tabernacles; and they shall not appear before the LORD empty-handed. 17 Every man *shall give* as he is able, according to the blessing of the LORD your God which He has given you.

18 "You shall appoint judges and officers in all your gates, which the LORD your God gives you, according to your tribes, and they shall judge the people with just judgment. 19 You shall not pervert justice; you shall not show partiality, nor take a bribe, for a bribe blinds the eyes of the wise and twists the words of the righteous. 20 You shall follow what is altogether just, that you may live and inherit the land which the LORD your God is giving you.

21 "You shall not plant for yourself any tree, as a wooden image, near the altar which you build for yourself to the LORD your God. 22 You shall not set up a sacred pillar, which the LORD your God hates.

PSALM 37:30–36

30 THE mouth of the righteous speaks wisdom,
    And his tongue talks of justice.
31 The law of his God *is* in his heart;
    None of his steps shall slide.

32 The wicked watches the righteous,
    And seeks to slay him.
33 The LORD will not leave him in his hand,
    Nor condemn him when he is judged.

34 Wait on the LORD,
    And keep His way,
    And He shall exalt you to inherit the land;
    When the wicked are cut off, you shall see *it*.
35 I have seen the wicked in great power,
    And spreading himself like a native green tree.
36 Yet he passed away, and behold, he *was* no *more;*

Indeed I sought him, but he could not be found.

PROVERBS 12:17–19

17 HE *who* speaks truth declares righteousness,
    But a false witness, deceit.
18 There is one who speaks like the piercings of a sword,
    But the tongue of the wise *promotes* health.
19 The truthful lip shall be established forever,
    But a lying tongue *is* but for a moment.

LUKE 3:1–38

NOW in the fifteenth year of the reign of Tiberius Caesar, Pontius Pilate being governor of Judea, Herod being tetrarch of Galilee, his brother Philip tetrarch of Iturea and the region of Trachonitis, and Lysanias tetrarch of Abilene, 2 while Annas and Caiaphas were high priests, the word of God came to John the son of Zacharias in the wilderness. 3 And he went into all the region around the Jordan, preaching a baptism of repentance for the remission of sins, 4 as it is written in the book of the words of Isaiah the prophet, saying:

---

*T*he bedrock of Christianity is
    repentance.   (BAFFLED)

"The voice of one crying in the wilderness:
    'Prepare the way of the LORD;
    Make His paths straight.
5   Every valley shall be filled
    And every mountain and hill brought low;
    The crooked places shall be made straight
    And the rough ways smooth;
6   And all flesh shall see the salvation of God.' "

7 Then he said to the multitudes that came out to be baptized by him, "Brood of vipers! Who warned you to flee from the wrath to come? 8 Therefore bear fruits worthy of repentance, and do not begin to say to yourselves, 'We have Abraham as *our* father.' For I say to you that God is able to raise up children to Abraham from these stones. 9 And even now the ax is laid

to the root of the trees. Therefore every tree which does not bear good fruit is cut down and thrown into the fire."

10 So the people asked him, saying, "What shall we do then?"

11 He answered and said to them, "He who has two tunics, let him give to him who has none; and he who has food, let him do likewise."

12 Then tax collectors also came to be baptized, and said to him, "Teacher, what shall we do?"

13 And he said to them, "Collect no more than what is appointed for you."

14 Likewise the soldiers asked him, saying, "And what shall we do?"

So he said to them, "Do not intimidate anyone or accuse falsely, and be content with your wages."

15 Now as the people were in expectation, and all reasoned in their hearts about John, whether he was the Christ *or* not, 16 John answered, saying to all, "I indeed baptize you with water; but One mightier than I is coming, whose sandal strap I am not worthy to loose. He will baptize you with the Holy Spirit and fire. 17 His winnowing fan *is* in His hand, and He will thoroughly clean out His threshing floor, and gather the wheat into His barn; but the chaff He will burn with unquenchable fire."

18 And with many other exhortations he preached to the people. 19 But Herod the tetrarch, being rebuked by him concerning Herodias, his brother Philip's wife, and for all the evils which Herod had done, 20 also added this, above all, that he shut John up in prison.

21 When all the people were baptized, it came to pass that Jesus also was baptized; and while He prayed, the heaven was opened. 22 And the Holy Spirit descended in bodily form like a dove upon Him, and a voice came from heaven which said, "You are My beloved Son; in You I am well pleased."

23 Now Jesus Himself began *His ministry at* about thirty years of age, being (as was supposed) *the* son of Joseph, *the son* of Heli, 24 *the son* of Matthat, *the son* of Levi, *the son* of Melchi, *the son* of Janna, *the son* of Joseph, 25 *the son* of Mattathiah, *the son* of Amos, *the son* of Nahum, *the son* of Esli, *the son* of Naggai, 26 *the son* of Maath, *the son* of Mattathiah, *the son* of Semei, *the son* of Joseph, *the son* of Judah, 27 *the son* of Joannas, *the son* of Rhesa, *the son* of Zerubbabel, *the son* of Shealtiel, *the son* of Neri, 28 *the son* of Melchi, *the son* of Addi, *the son* of Cosam, *the son* of Elmodam, *the son* of Er, 29 *the son* of Jose, *the son* of Eliezer, *the son* of Jorim, *the son* of Matthat, *the son* of Levi, 30 *the son* of Simeon, *the son* of Judah, *the son* of Joseph, *the son* of Jonan, *the son* of Eliakim, 31 *the son* of Melea, *the son* of Menan, *the son* of Mattathah, *the son* of Nathan, *the son* of David, 32 *the son* of Jesse, *the son* of Obed, *the son* of Boaz, *the son* of Salmon, *the son* of Nahshon, 33 *the son* of Amminadab, *the son* of Ram, *the son* of Hezron, *the son* of Perez, *the son* of Judah, 34 *the son* of Jacob, *the son* of Isaac, *the son* of Abraham, *the son* of Terah, *the son* of Nahor, 35 *the son* of Serug, *the son* of Reu, *the son* of Peleg, *the son* of Eber, *the son* of Shelah, 36 *the son* of Cainan, *the son* of Arphaxad, *the son* of Shem, *the son* of Noah, *the son* of Lamech, 37 *the son* of Methuselah, *the son* of Enoch, *the son* of Jared, *the son* of Mahalalel, *the son* of Cainan, 38 *the son* of Enosh, *the son* of Seth, *the son* of Adam, *the son* of God.

◆◆◆◆

Reading 87—The Pinnacle of Temptation
Luke 4:9

The temptations of our Lord in the days of His flesh are the kind of temptations He is subjected to in the temple of our body. Watch when God shifts your circumstances and see whether you are going with Jesus or siding with the world, the flesh and the Devil. We wear His badge, but are we going with Him? "From that *time* many of His disciples went back and walked with Him no more."

The temptation may be to do some big startling thing in order to prove that we really are the children of God. Satan said to Jesus, "If You are the Son of God, throw Yourself down," and to us He says, "If you are saved and sanctified and true to God, everyone you know should be saved too." If that were true, Jesus Christ is wrong in His revelation of God. If by our salvation and right relationship to God, we can be the means of turning our world upside down, what has Jesus Christ been doing all these years? The temptation is to claim that God does something that will prove who we are and what He has done for us. It is a temptation of the Devil, and can only be detected as a temptation by the Spirit of God.   (POSSIBLE)

DEUTERONOMY 17:1—18:22

"YOU shall not sacrifice to the LORD your God a bull or sheep which has any blemish *or* defect, for that *is* an abomination to the LORD your God.

2 "If there is found among you, within any of your gates which the LORD your God gives you, a man or a woman who has been wicked in the sight of the LORD your God, in transgressing His covenant, 3 who has gone and served other gods and worshiped them, either the sun or moon or any of the host of heaven, which I have not commanded, 4 and it is told you, and you hear *of it,* then you shall inquire diligently. And if *it is* indeed true *and* certain that such an abomination has been committed in Israel, 5 then you shall bring out to your gates that man or woman who has committed that wicked thing, and shall stone to death that man or woman with stones. 6 Whoever is deserving of death shall be put to death on the testimony of two or three witnesses; he shall not be put to death on the testimony of one witness. 7 The hands of the witnesses shall be the first against him to put him to death, and afterward the hands of all the people. So you shall put away the evil from among you.

8 "If a matter arises which is too hard for you to judge, between degrees of guilt for bloodshed, between one judgment or another, or between one punishment or another, matters of controversy within your gates, then you shall arise and go up to the place which the LORD your God chooses. 9 And you shall come to the priests, the Levites, and to the judge *there* in those days, and inquire *of them;* they shall pronounce upon you the sentence of judgment. 10 You shall do according to the sentence which they pronounce upon you in that place which the LORD chooses. And you shall be careful to do according to all that they order you. 11 According to the sentence of the law in which they instruct you, according to the judgment which they tell

you, you shall do; you shall not turn aside *to* the right hand or *to* the left from the sentence which they pronounce upon you. 12 Now the man who acts presumptuously and will not heed the priest who stands to minister there before the LORD your God, or the judge, that man shall die. So you shall put away the evil from Israel. 13 And all the people shall hear and fear, and no longer act presumptuously.

14 "When you come to the land which the LORD your God is giving you, and possess it and dwell in it, and say, 'I will set a king over me like all the nations that *are* around me,' 15 you shall surely set a king over you whom the LORD your God chooses; *one* from among your brethren you shall set as king over you; you may not set a foreigner over you, who *is* not your brother. 16 But he shall not multiply horses for himself, nor cause the people to return to Egypt to multiply horses, for the LORD has said to you, 'You shall not return that way again.' 17 Neither shall he multiply wives for himself, lest his heart turn away; nor shall he greatly multiply silver and gold for himself.

18 "Also it shall be, when he sits on the throne of his kingdom, that he shall write for himself a copy of this law in a book, from *the one* before the priests, the Levites. 19 And it shall be with him, and he shall read it all the days of his life, that he may learn to fear the LORD his God and be careful to observe all the words of this law and these statutes, 20 that his heart may not be lifted above his brethren, that he may not turn aside from the commandment *to* the right hand or *to* the left, and that he may prolong *his* days in his kingdom, he and his children in the midst of Israel.

18 "THE priests, the Levites—all the tribe of Levi—shall have no part nor inheritance with Israel; they shall eat the offerings of the LORD made by fire, and His portion. 2 Therefore they shall have no inheritance among their brethren; the LORD is their inheritance, as He said to them.

3 "And this shall be the priest's due from the people, from those who offer a sacrifice, whether *it is* bull or sheep: they shall give to the priest the shoulder, the cheeks, and the stomach. 4 The firstfruits of your grain and your new wine and your oil, and the first of the fleece of your sheep, you shall give him. 5 For the LORD your God has chosen him out of all your tribes to stand to minister in the name of the LORD, him and his sons forever.

6 "So if a Levite comes from any of your gates, from where he dwells among all Israel, and comes with all the desire of his mind to the place which the LORD chooses, 7 then he may serve in the name of the LORD his God as all his brethren the Levites *do,* who stand there before the LORD. 8 They shall have equal portions to eat, besides what comes from the sale of his inheritance.

9 "When you come into the land which the LORD your God is giving you, you shall not learn to follow the abominations of those nations. 10 There shall not be found among you *anyone* who makes his son or his daughter pass through the fire, *or one* who practices witchcraft, *or* a soothsayer, or one who interprets omens, or a sorcerer, 11 or one who conjures spells, or a medium, or a spiritist, or one who calls up the dead. 12 For all who do these things *are* an abomination to the LORD, and because of these abominations the LORD your God drives them out from before you. 13 You shall be blameless before the LORD your God. 14 For these nations which you will dispossess listened to soothsayers and diviners; but as for you, the LORD your God has not appointed such for you.

15 "The LORD your God will raise up for you a Prophet like me from your midst, from your brethren. Him you shall hear, 16 according to all you desired of the LORD your God in Horeb in the day of the assembly, saying, 'Let me not hear again the voice of the LORD my God, nor let me see this great fire anymore, lest I die.'

17 "And the LORD said to me: 'What they have spoken is good. 18 I will raise up for them a Prophet like you from among their brethren, and will put My words in His mouth, and He shall speak to them all that I command Him. 19 And it shall be *that* whoever will not hear My words, which He speaks in My name, I will require *it* of him. 20 But the prophet who presumes to speak a word in My name, which I have not commanded him to speak, or who speaks in the name of other gods, that prophet shall die.' 21 And if you say in your heart, 'How shall we know the word which

the LORD has not spoken?'— 22 when a prophet speaks in the name of the LORD, if the thing does not happen or come to pass, that *is* the thing which the LORD has not spoken; the prophet has spoken it presumptuously; you shall not be afraid of him.

PSALM 37:37–40

37 MARK the blameless *man,* and observe the upright;
For the future of *that* man *is* peace.
38 But the transgressors shall be destroyed together;
The future of the wicked shall be cut off.

39 But the salvation of the righteous *is* from the LORD;
He is their strength in the time of trouble.
40 And the LORD shall help them and deliver them;
He shall deliver them from the wicked,
And save them,
Because they trust in Him.

PROVERBS 12:20–22

20 DECEIT is in the heart of those who devise evil,
But counselors of peace have joy.
21 No grave trouble will overtake the righteous,
But the wicked shall be filled with evil.
22 Lying lips *are* an abomination to the LORD,
But those who deal truthfully *are* His delight.

LUKE 4:1–30

THEN Jesus, being filled with the Holy Spirit, returned from the Jordan and was led by the Spirit into the wilderness, 2 being tempted for forty days by the devil. And in those days He ate nothing, and afterward, when they had ended, He was hungry.

3 And the devil said to Him, "If You are the Son of God, command this stone to become bread."

4 But Jesus answered him, saying, "It is written, 'Man shall not live by bread alone, but by every word of God.' "

5 Then the devil, taking Him up on a high mountain, showed Him all the kingdoms of the world in a moment of time.

6 And the devil said to Him, "All this authority I will give You, and their glory; for *this* has been delivered to me, and I give it to whomever I wish. 7 Therefore, if You will worship before me, all will be Yours."

8 And Jesus answered and said to him, "Get behind Me, Satan! For it is written, 'You shall worship the LORD your God, and Him only you shall serve.'"

9 Then he brought Him to Jerusalem, set Him on the pinnacle of the temple, and said to Him, "If You are the Son of God, throw Yourself down from here. 10 For it is written:

'He shall give His angels charge over you,
     To keep you,'

11 and,

'In *their* hands they shall bear you up,
     Lest you dash your foot against a stone.'"

12 And Jesus answered and said to him, "It has been said, 'You shall not tempt the LORD your God.'"

13 Now when the devil had ended every temptation, he departed from Him until an opportune time.

"*R*esist the devil," not attack him.   (GLORY)

---

14 Then Jesus returned in the power of the Spirit to Galilee, and news of Him went out through all the surrounding region. 15 And He taught in their synagogues, being glorified by all.

16 So He came to Nazareth, where He had been brought up. And as His custom was, He went into the synagogue on the Sabbath day, and stood up to read. 17 And He was handed the book of the prophet Isaiah. And when He had opened the book, He found the place where it was written:

18 "The Spirit of the LORD *is* upon Me,
     Because He has anointed Me
     To preach the gospel to *the* poor;
     He has sent Me to heal the brokenhearted,
     To proclaim liberty to *the* captives
     And recovery of sight to *the* blind,
     To set at liberty those who are oppressed,

19   To proclaim the acceptable year of the LORD."

20 Then He closed the book, and gave *it* back to the attendant and sat down. And the eyes of all who were in the synagogue were fixed on Him. 21 And He began to say to them, "Today this Scripture is fulfilled in your hearing." 22 So all bore witness to Him, and marveled at the gracious words which proceeded out of His mouth. And they said, "Is this not Joseph's son?"

23 He said to them, "You will surely say this proverb to Me, 'Physician, heal yourself! Whatever we have heard done in Capernaum, do also here in Your country.'" 24 Then He said, "Assuredly, I say to you, no prophet is accepted in his own country. 25 But I tell you truly, many widows were in Israel in the days of Elijah, when the heaven was shut up three years and six months, and there was a great famine throughout all the land; 26 but to none of them was Elijah sent except to Zarephath, *in the region of* Sidon, to a woman *who was* a widow. 27 And many lepers were in Israel in the time of Elisha the prophet, and none of them was cleansed except Naaman the Syrian."

28 So all those in the synagogue, when they heard these things, were filled with wrath, 29 and rose up and thrust Him out of the city; and they led Him to the brow of the hill on which their city was built, that they might throw Him down over the cliff. 30 Then passing through the midst of them, He went His way.

*Reading 88—*Incarnate Laziness

Proverbs 12:24

We all have moments when we feel better than our best, and we say— "I feel fit for anything; if only I could be like this always!" We are not meant to be. Those moments are moments of insight which we have to live up to when we do not feel like it. Many of us are no good for this workaday world when there is no high hour. . . .

Never allow a feeling which was stirred in you in the high hour to evaporate. Don't put your mental feet on the mantelpiece and say—"What a marvelous state of mind to be in!" Act immediately, do something, if only because you would rather not do it. If in a prayer meeting God has shown you something to do, don't say—"I'll do it": *do it!* Take yourself by the scruff of the neck and shake off your incarnate laziness. Laziness is always seen in cravings for the high hour; we talk about working up to a time on the mount. We have to learn to live in the gray day according to what we saw on the mount.

Don't cave in because you have been baffled once, get at it again. Burn your bridges behind you, and stand committed to God by your own act. Never revise your decisions, but see that you make your decisions in the light of the high hour. (*UTMOST*)

DEUTERONOMY 19:1—20:20

"WHEN the LORD your God has cut off the nations whose land the LORD your God is giving you, and you dispossess them and dwell in their cities and in their houses, 2 you shall separate three cities for yourself in the midst of your land which the LORD your God is giving you to possess. 3 You shall prepare roads for yourself, and divide into three parts the territory of your land which the LORD your God is giving you to inherit, that any manslayer may flee there.

4 "And this *is* the case of the manslayer who flees there, that he may live: Whoever kills his neighbor unintentionally, not having hated him in time past— 5 as when *a man* goes to the woods with his neighbor to cut timber, and his hand swings a stroke with the ax to cut down the tree, and the head slips from the handle and strikes his neighbor so that he dies—he shall flee to one of these cities and live; 6 lest the avenger of blood, while his anger is hot, pursue the manslayer and overtake him, because the way is long, and kill him, though he *was* not deserving of death, since he had not hated the victim in time past. 7 Therefore I command you, saying, 'You shall separate three cities for yourself.'

8 "Now if the LORD your God enlarges your territory, as He swore to your fathers, and gives you the land which He promised to give to your fathers, 9 and if you keep all these commandments and do them, which I command you today, to love the LORD your God and to walk always in His ways, then you shall add three more cities for yourself besides these three, 10 lest innocent blood be shed in the midst of your land which the LORD your God is giving you *as* an inheritance, and *thus* guilt of bloodshed be upon you.

11 "But if anyone hates his neighbor, lies in wait for him, rises against him and strikes him mortally, so that he dies, and he flees to one of these cities, 12 then the elders of his city shall send and bring him from there, and deliver him over to the hand of the avenger of blood, that he may die. 13 Your eye shall not pity him, but you shall put away *the guilt of* innocent blood from Israel, that it may go well with you.

14 "You shall not remove your neighbor's landmark, which the men of old have set, in your inheritance which you will inherit in the land that the LORD your God is giving you to possess.

15 "One witness shall not rise against a man concerning any iniquity or any sin that he commits; by the mouth of two or three witnesses the matter shall be established. 16 If a false witness rises against any man to testify against him of wrongdoing, 17 then both men in the controversy shall stand before the LORD, before the priests and the judges who serve in those days.

18 And the judges shall make careful inquiry, and indeed, *if* the witness *is* a false witness, who has testified falsely against his brother, 19 then you shall do to him as he thought to have done to his brother; so you shall put away the evil from among you. 20 And those who remain shall hear and fear, and hereafter they shall not again commit such evil among you. 21 Your eye shall not pity: life *shall be* for life, eye for eye, tooth for tooth, hand for hand, foot for foot.

20 "WHEN you go out to battle against your enemies, and see horses and chariots *and* people more numerous than you, do not be afraid of them; for the LORD your God *is* with you, who brought you up from the land of Egypt. 2 So it shall be, when you are on the verge of battle, that the priest shall approach and speak to the people. 3 And he shall say to them, 'Hear, O Israel: Today you are on the verge of battle with your enemies. Do not let your heart faint, do not be afraid, and do not tremble or be terrified because of them; 4 for the LORD your God *is* He who goes with you, to fight for you against your enemies, to save you.'

5 "Then the officers shall speak to the people, saying: 'What man *is there* who has built a new house and has not dedicated it? Let him go and return to his house, lest he die in the battle and another man dedicate it. 6 Also what man *is there* who has planted a vineyard and has not eaten of it? Let him go and return to his house, lest he die in the battle and another man eat of it. 7 And what man *is there* who is betrothed to a woman and has not married her? Let him go and return to his house, lest he die in the battle and another man marry her.'

8 "The officers shall speak further to the people, and say, 'What man *is there who is* fearful and fainthearted? Let him go and return to his house, lest the heart of his brethren faint like his heart.' 9 And so it shall be, when the officers have finished speaking to the people, that they shall make captains of the armies to lead the people.

10 "When you go near a city to fight against it, then proclaim an offer of peace to it. 11 And it shall be that if they accept your offer of peace, and open to you, then all the people *who are* found in it shall be placed under tribute to you, and serve you. 12 Now if *the city* will not make peace with you, but war against you, then you shall besiege it. 13 And when the LORD your God delivers it into your hands, you shall strike every male in it with the edge of the sword. 14 But the women, the little ones, the live-stock, and all that is in the city, all its spoil, you shall plunder for yourself; and you shall eat the enemies' plunder which the LORD your God gives you. 15 Thus you shall do to all the cities *which are* very far from you, which *are* not of the cities of these nations.

16 "But of the cities of these peoples which the LORD your God gives you *as* an inheritance, you shall let nothing that breathes remain alive, 17 but you shall utterly destroy them: the Hittite and the Amorite and the Canaanite and the Perizzite and the Hivite and the Jebusite, just as the LORD your God has commanded you, 18 lest they teach you to do according to all their abominations which they have done for their gods, and you sin against the LORD your God.

19 "When you besiege a city for a long time, while making war against it to take it, you shall not destroy its trees by wielding an ax against them; if you can eat of them, do not cut them down to use in the siege, for the tree of the field *is* man's *food.* 20 Only the trees which you know *are* not trees for food you may destroy and cut down, to build siegeworks against the city that makes war with you, until it is subdued.

PSALM 38:1–8

1 O LORD, do not rebuke me in Your wrath,
    Nor chasten me in Your hot displeasure!

2 For Your arrows pierce me deeply,
    And Your hand presses me down.

3 *There is* no soundness in my flesh
    Because of Your anger,
    Nor *any* health in my bones
    Because of my sin.

Measure your growth in grace by your sensitiveness to sin.   (DISCIPLES)

4 For my iniquities have gone over my head;
    Like a heavy burden they are too heavy for me.

5 My wounds are foul *and* festering
    Because of my foolishness.

6 I am troubled, I am bowed down greatly;
    I go mourning all the day long.

7 For my loins are full of inflammation,

And *there is* no soundness in my flesh.
8 I am feeble and severely broken;
I groan because of the turmoil of my
heart.

PROVERBS 12:23–25

23 A prudent man conceals knowledge,
But the heart of fools proclaims
foolishness.

24 The hand of the diligent will rule,
But the lazy *man* will be put to forced
labor.

25 Anxiety in the heart of man causes
depression,
But a good word makes it glad.

LUKE 4:31–44

THEN He went down to Capernaum, a
city of Galilee, and was teaching them on
the Sabbaths. 32 And they were astonished
at His teaching, for His word was with
authority. 33 Now in the synagogue there

> *It is not . . . the insight of a
> marvelous man, but a question of
> speaking with authority.*   (PERFECT)

was a man who had a spirit of an unclean
demon. And he cried out with a loud voice,
34 saying, "Let *us* alone! What have we to
do with You, Jesus of Nazareth? Did You
come to destroy us? I know who You are—
the Holy One of God!"

35 But Jesus rebuked him, saying, "Be
quiet, and come out of him!" And when
the demon had thrown him in *their* midst,
it came out of him and did not hurt him.
36 Then they were all amazed and spoke
among themselves, saying, "What a word
this *is!* For with authority and power He
commands the unclean spirits, and they
come out." 37 And the report about Him
went out into every place in the surrounding region.

38 Now He arose from the synagogue
and entered Simon's house. But Simon's
wife's mother was sick with a high fever,
and they made request of Him concerning
her. 39 So He stood over her and rebuked
the fever, and it left her. And immediately
she arose and served them.

40 When the sun was setting, all those
who had any that were sick with various
diseases brought them to Him; and He laid
His hands on every one of them and healed
them. 41 And demons also came out of
many, crying out and saying, "You are the
Christ, the Son of God!"

And He, rebuking *them,* did not allow
them to speak, for they knew that He was
the Christ.

42 Now when it was day, He departed
and went into a deserted place. And the
crowd sought Him and came to Him, and
tried to keep Him from leaving them;
43 but He said to them, "I must preach the
kingdom of God to the other cities also,
because for this purpose I have been sent."
44 And He was preaching in the synagogues
of Galilee.

◆◆◆

Reading 89—The Heart Is the Center
Psalm 38:10

There are people you come in contact with who "freeze" you, you cannot
think, things do not "go," everything feels tight and mean; you come
into the zone of other people and all those bands disappear, you are surprised
at how clearly you can think, everything seems to "go" better. You take a
deep breath and say, "Why, I feel quite different; what has happened?" The
one personality brought an atmosphere that froze the heart not only physically,
but psychically; kept it cold, kept it down, kept it back; the other personality
gave the heart a chance to expand and develop and surge throughout the whole
body. Taken in the physical domain, if people knew that the circulation of the
blood and quickening of the heart life would remove distempers from the

body, there would be a great deal less medicine taken and a great deal more walking done. The heart is the center of all physical life and of all the imaginations of the mind. Anything that keeps the physical blood in good condition and the heart working properly, benefits the soul life and spirit life as well. That is why Jesus Christ said, "Take heed to yourselves, lest your hearts be weighed down with carousing, drunkenness, and cares of life. . . ." (Bib. Psych.)

DEUTERONOMY 21:1—22:30

"IF *anyone* is found slain, lying in the field in the land which the LORD your God is giving you to possess, *and* it is not known who killed him, 2 then your elders and your judges shall go out and measure *the distance* from the slain man to the surrounding cities. 3 And it shall be *that* the elders of the city nearest to the slain man will take a heifer which has not been worked *and* which has not pulled with a yoke. 4 The elders of that city shall bring the heifer down to a valley with flowing water, which is neither plowed nor sown, and they shall break the heifer's neck there in the valley. 5 Then the priests, the sons of Levi, shall come near, for the LORD your God has chosen them to minister to Him and to bless in the name of the LORD; by their word every controversy and every assault shall be *settled*. 6 And all the elders of that city nearest to the slain *man* shall wash their hands over the heifer whose neck was broken in the valley. 7 Then they shall answer and say, 'Our hands have not shed this blood, nor have our eyes seen *it*. 8 Provide atonement, O LORD, for Your people Israel, whom You have redeemed, and do not lay innocent blood to the charge of Your people Israel.' And atonement shall be provided on their behalf for the blood. 9 So you shall put away the *guilt of* innocent blood from among you when you do *what is* right in the sight of the LORD.

10 "When you go out to war against your enemies, and the LORD your God delivers them into your hand, and you take them captive, 11 and you see among the captives a beautiful woman, and desire her and would take her for your wife, 12 then you shall bring her home to your house, and she shall shave her head and trim her nails. 13 She shall put off the clothes of her captivity, remain in your house, and mourn her father and her mother a full month; after that you may go in to her and be her husband, and she shall be your wife. 14 And it shall be, if you have no delight in her, then you shall set her free, but you certainly shall not sell her for money; you shall not treat her brutally, because you have humbled her.

15 "If a man has two wives, one loved and the other unloved, and they have borne him children, *both* the loved and the unloved, and *if* the firstborn son is of her who is unloved, 16 then it shall be, on the day he bequeaths his possessions to his sons, *that* he must not bestow firstborn status on the son of the loved wife in preference to the son of the unloved, the *true* firstborn. 17 But he shall acknowledge the son of the unloved wife *as* the firstborn by giving him a double portion of all that he has, for he *is* the beginning of his strength; the right of the firstborn *is* his.

18 "If a man has a stubborn and rebellious son who will not obey the voice of his father or the voice of his mother, and *who*, when they have chastened him, will not heed them, 19 then his father and his mother shall take hold of him and bring him out to the elders of his city, to the gate of his city. 20 And they shall say to the elders of his city, 'This son of ours is stubborn and rebellious; he will not obey our voice; he is a glutton and a drunkard.' 21 Then all the men of his city shall stone him to death with stones; so you shall put away the evil from among you, and all Israel shall hear and fear.

22 "If a man has committed a sin deserving of death, and he is put to death, and you hang him on a tree, 23 his body shall not remain overnight on the tree, but you shall surely bury him that day, so that you do not defile the land which the LORD your God is giving you *as* an inheritance; for he who is hanged *is* accursed of God.

22 "YOU shall not see your brother's ox or his sheep going astray, and hide yourself from them; you shall certainly bring them back to your brother. 2 And if your brother *is* not near you, or if you do not know him, then you shall bring it to your own house, and it shall remain with you until your brother seeks it; then you shall restore it to him. 3 You shall do the same with his donkey, and so shall you do with his garment; with any lost thing of

your brother's, which he has lost and you have found, you shall do likewise; you must not hide yourself.

4 "You shall not see your brother's donkey or his ox fall down along the road, and hide yourself from them; you shall surely help him lift *them* up again.

5 "A woman shall not wear anything that pertains to a man, nor shall a man put on a woman's garment, for all who do so *are* an abomination to the LORD your God.

6 "If a bird's nest happens to be before you along the way, in any tree or on the ground, with young ones or eggs, with the mother sitting on the young or on the eggs, you shall not take the mother with the young; 7 you shall surely let the mother go, and take the young for yourself, that it may be well with you and *that* you may prolong *your* days.

8 "When you build a new house, then you shall make a parapet for your roof, that you may not bring guilt of bloodshed on your household if anyone falls from it.

9 "You shall not sow your vineyard with different kinds of seed, lest the yield of the seed which you have sown and the fruit of your vineyard be defiled.

10 "You shall not plow with an ox and a donkey together.

11 "You shall not wear a garment of different sorts, *such as* wool and linen mixed together.

12 "You shall make tassels on the four corners of the clothing with which you cover *yourself.*

13 "If any man takes a wife, and goes in to her, and detests her, 14 and charges her with shameful conduct, and brings a bad name on her, and says, 'I took this woman, and when I came to her I found she *was* not a virgin,' 15 then the father and mother of the young woman shall take and bring out *the evidence of* the young woman's virginity to the elders of the city at the gate. 16 And the young woman's father shall say to the elders, 'I gave my daughter to this man as wife, and he detests her. 17 Now he has charged her with shameful conduct, saying, "I found your daughter *was* not a virgin," and yet these *are the evidences of* my daughter's virginity.' And they shall spread the cloth before the elders of the city. 18 Then the elders of that city shall take that man and punish him; 19 and they shall fine him one hundred *shekels* of silver and give *them* to the father of the young woman, because he has brought a bad name on a virgin of Israel. And she shall be his wife; he cannot divorce her all his days.

20 "But if the thing is true, *and evidences* of virginity are not found for the young woman, 21 then they shall bring out the young woman to the door of her father's house, and the men of her city shall stone her to death with stones, because she has done a disgraceful thing in Israel, to play the harlot in her father's house. So you shall put away the evil from among you.

22 "If a man is found lying with a woman married to a husband, then both of them shall die—the man that lay with the woman, and the woman; so you shall put away the evil from Israel.

23 "If a young woman *who is* a virgin is betrothed to a husband, and a man finds her in the city and lies with her, 24 then you shall bring them both out to the gate of that city, and you shall stone them to death with stones, the young woman because she did not cry out in the city, and the man because he humbled his neighbor's wife; so you shall put away the evil from among you.

25 "But if a man finds a betrothed young woman in the countryside, and the man forces her and lies with her, then only the man who lay with her shall die. 26 But you shall do nothing to the young woman; *there is* in the young woman no sin *deserving* of death, for just as when a man rises against his neighbor and kills him, even so *is* this matter. 27 For he found her in the countryside, *and* the betrothed young woman cried out, but *there was* no one to save her.

28 "If a man finds a young woman *who is* a virgin, who is not betrothed, and he seizes her and lies with her, and they are found out, 29 then the man who lay with her shall give to the young woman's father fifty *shekels* of silver, and she shall be his wife because he has humbled her; he shall not be permitted to divorce her all his days.

30 "A man shall not take his father's wife, nor uncover his father's bed.

PSALM 38:9–22

9 LORD, all my desire *is* before You;
And my sighing is not hidden from You.

10 My heart pants, my strength fails me;
As for the light of my eyes, it also has gone from me.

11 My loved ones and my friends stand aloof from my plague,
And my relatives stand afar off.

12 Those also who seek my life lay snares *for me*;

Those who seek my hurt speak of
destruction,
And plan deception all the day long.

13 But I, like a deaf *man*, do not hear;
And *I am* like a mute *who* does not
open his mouth.

14 Thus I am like a man who does not
hear,
And in whose mouth *is* no response.

15 For in You, O LORD, I hope;
You will hear, O Lord my God.

16 For I said, *"Hear me,* lest they rejoice
over me,
Lest, when my foot slips, they exalt
themselves against me."

17 For I *am* ready to fall,
And my sorrow *is* continually before
me.

18 For I will declare my iniquity;
I will be in anguish over my sin.

19 But my enemies *are* vigorous, *and* they
are strong;
And those who hate me wrongfully
have multiplied.

20 Those also who render evil for good,
They are my adversaries, because I
follow *what is* good.

21 Do not forsake me, O LORD;
O my God, be not far from me!

22 Make haste to help me,
O Lord, my salvation!

PROVERBS 12:26–28

26 THE righteous should choose his
friends carefully,
For the way of the wicked leads them
astray.

27 The lazy *man* does not roast what he
took in hunting,
But diligence *is* man's precious
possession.

28 In the way of righteousness *is* life,
And in *its* pathway *there is* no death.

LUKE 5:1–16

SO it was, as the multitude pressed about
Him to hear the word of God, that He
stood by the Lake of Gennesaret, 2 and saw
two boats standing by the lake; but the
fishermen had gone from them and were
washing *their* nets. 3 Then He got into one
of the boats, which was Simon's, and asked
him to put out a little from the land. And
He sat down and taught the multitudes
from the boat.

4 When He had stopped speaking, He
said to Simon, "Launch out into the deep
and let down your nets for a catch."

5 But Simon answered and said to Him,
"Master, we have toiled all night and caught
nothing; nevertheless at Your word I will
let down the net." 6 And when they had
done this, they caught a great number of
fish, and their net was breaking. 7 So they
signaled to *their* partners in the other boat
to come and help them. And they came
and filled both the boats, so that they began
to sink. 8 When Simon Peter saw *it,* he fell
down at Jesus' knees, saying, "Depart from
me, for I am a sinful man, O Lord!"

9 For he and all who were with him were
astonished at the catch of fish which they
had taken; 10 and so also *were* James and
John, the sons of Zebedee, who were partners with Simon. And Jesus said to Simon,
"Do not be afraid. From now on you will
catch men." 11 So when they had brought

---

*There is no division into sacred and
secular, it is all one great glorious
life.*   (BRILL. HERITAGE)

---

their boats to land, they forsook all and
followed Him.

12 And it happened when He was in a
certain city, that behold, a man who was
full of leprosy saw Jesus; and he fell on
his face and implored Him, saying, "Lord,
if You are willing, You can make me clean."

13 Then He put out *His* hand and touched
him, saying, "I am willing; be cleansed."
Immediately the leprosy left him. 14 And
He charged him to tell no one, "But go
and show yourself to the priest, and make
an offering for your cleansing, as a testimony to them, just as Moses commanded."

15 However, the report went around concerning Him all the more; and great multitudes came together to hear, and to be
healed by Him of their infirmities. 16 So
He Himself *often* withdrew into the wilderness and prayed.

Reading 90—Redemption Is the Way Out
Luke 5:31

There is a type of suffering caused because we do not see the way out. A man may say that the basis of things is rational—"Get to the bottom of things and you will find it all simple and easy of explanation"—well, that simply is not true. The basis of things is not rational, but tragic, and when you enter the domain of suffering and sorrow you find that reason and logic are your guide amongst things as they are, but nothing more. Is it rational that I should be born with a heredity over which I have no control? Is it rational that nations that are nominally Christian should be at war? The basis of things is tragic, and the only way out is through the Redemption. Many a man in mental stress of weather is driven to utter what sounds like blasphemy, and yet he may be nearer God than in his complacent acceptance of beliefs that have never been tried. Never be afraid of the man who seems to you to talk blasphemously, he is up against problems you may never have met with; instead of being wrathful, be patient with him. The man to be afraid of is the one who is indifferent, what morality he has got is well within his own grasp, and Jesus Christ is of no account at all. (*BIB. ETHICS*)

DEUTERONOMY 23:1—24:22

"HE who is emasculated by crushing or mutilation shall not enter the assembly of the LORD.

2 "One of illegitimate birth shall not enter the assembly of the LORD; even to the tenth generation none of his *descendants* shall enter the assembly of the LORD.

3 "An Ammonite or Moabite shall not enter the assembly of the LORD; even to the tenth generation none of his *descendants* shall enter the assembly of the LORD forever, 4 because they did not meet you with bread and water on the road when you came out of Egypt, and because they hired against you Balaam the son of Beor from Pethor of Mesopotamia, to curse you. 5 Nevertheless the LORD your God would not listen to Balaam, but the LORD your God turned the curse into a blessing for you, because the LORD your God loves you. 6 You shall not seek their peace nor their prosperity all your days forever.

7 "You shall not abhor an Edomite, for he *is* your brother. You shall not abhor an Egyptian, because you were an alien in his land. 8 The children of the third generation born to them may enter the assembly of the LORD.

9 "When the army goes out against your enemies, then keep yourself from every wicked thing. 10 If there is any man among you who becomes unclean by some occurrence in the night, then he shall go outside the camp; he shall not come inside the camp. 11 But it shall be, when evening comes, that he shall wash with water; and when the sun sets, he may come into the camp.

12 "Also you shall have a place outside the camp, where you may go out; 13 and you shall have an implement among your equipment, and when you sit down outside, you shall dig with it and turn and cover your refuse. 14 For the LORD your God walks in the midst of your camp, to deliver you and give your enemies over to you; therefore your camp shall be holy, that He may see no unclean thing among you, and turn away from you.

15 "You shall not give back to his master the slave who has escaped from his master to you. 16 He may dwell with you in your midst, in the place which he chooses within one of your gates, where it seems best to him; you shall not oppress him.

17 "There shall be no *ritual* harlot of the daughters of Israel, or a perverted one of the sons of Israel. 18 You shall not bring the wages of a harlot or the price of a dog to the house of the LORD your God for any vowed offering, for both of these *are* an abomination to the LORD your God.

19 "You shall not charge interest to your brother—interest on money *or* food *or* anything that is lent out at interest. 20 To a foreigner you may charge interest, but to your brother you shall not charge interest,

that the LORD your God may bless you in all to which you set your hand in the land which you are entering to possess.

21 "When you make a vow to the LORD your God, you shall not delay to pay it; for the LORD your God will surely require it of you, and it would be sin to you. 22 But if you abstain from vowing, it shall not be sin to you. 23 That which has gone from your lips you shall keep and perform, for you voluntarily vowed to the LORD your God what you have promised with your mouth.

24 "When you come into your neighbor's vineyard, you may eat your fill of grapes at your pleasure, but you shall not put *any* in your container. 25 When you come into your neighbor's standing grain, you may pluck the heads with your hand, but you shall not use a sickle on your neighbor's standing grain.

24 "WHEN a man takes a wife and marries her, and it happens that she finds no favor in his eyes because he has found some uncleanness in her, and he writes her a certificate of divorce, puts *it* in her hand, and sends her out of his house, 2 when she has departed from his house, and goes and becomes another man's *wife,* 3 *if* the latter husband detests her and writes her a certificate of divorce, puts *it* in her hand, and sends her out of his house, or if the latter husband dies who took her as his wife, 4 *then* her former husband who divorced her must not take her back to be his wife after she has been defiled; for that *is* an abomination before the LORD, and you shall not bring sin on the land which the LORD your God is giving you *as* an inheritance.

5 "When a man has taken a new wife, he shall not go out to war or be charged with any business; he shall be free at home one year, and bring happiness to his wife whom he has taken.

6 "No man shall take the lower or the upper millstone in pledge, for he takes *one's* living in pledge.

7 "If a man is found kidnapping any of his brethren of the children of Israel, and mistreats him or sells him, then that kidnapper shall die; and you shall put away the evil from among you.

8 "Take heed in an outbreak of leprosy, that you carefully observe and do according to all that the priests, the Levites, shall teach you; just as I commanded them, *so* you shall be careful to do. 9 Remember what the LORD your God did to Miriam on the way when you came out of Egypt!

10 "When you lend your brother anything, you shall not go into his house to get his pledge. 11 You shall stand outside, and the man to whom you lend shall bring the pledge out to you. 12 And if the man *is* poor, you shall not keep his pledge overnight. 13 You shall in any case return the pledge to him again when the sun goes down, that he may sleep in his own garment and bless you; and it shall be righteousness to you before the LORD your God.

14 "You shall not oppress a hired servant *who is* poor and needy, *whether* one of your brethren or one of the aliens who *is* in your land within your gates. 15 Each day you shall give *him* his wages, and not let the sun go down on it, for he *is* poor and has set his heart on it; lest he cry out against you to the LORD, and it be sin to you.

16 "Fathers shall not be put to death for *their* children, nor shall children be put to death for *their* fathers; a person shall be put to death for his own sin.

17 "You shall not pervert justice due the stranger or the fatherless, nor take a widow's garment as a pledge. 18 But you shall remember that you were a slave in Egypt, and the LORD your God redeemed you from there; therefore I command you to do this thing.

19 "When you reap your harvest in your field, and forget a sheaf in the field, you shall not go back to get it; it shall be for the stranger, the fatherless, and the widow, that the LORD your God may bless you in all the work of your hands. 20 When you beat your olive trees, you shall not go over the boughs again; it shall be for the stranger, the fatherless, and the widow. 21 When you gather the grapes of your vineyard, you shall not glean *it* afterward; it shall be for the stranger, the fatherless, and the widow. 22 And you shall remember that you were a slave in the land of Egypt; therefore I command you to do this thing.

PSALM 39:1–6

1   I said, "I will guard my ways,
    Lest I sin with my tongue;
    I will restrain my mouth with a muzzle,
    While the wicked are before me."
2   I was mute with silence,
    I held my peace *even* from good;
    And my sorrow was stirred up.
3   My heart was hot within me;
    While I was musing, the fire burned.
    Then I spoke with my tongue:

4   "LORD, make me to know my end,
And what *is* the measure of my days,
That I may know how frail I *am*.
5   Indeed, You have made my days *as*
handbreadths,
And my age *is* as nothing before You;
Certainly every man at his best state *is*
but vapor.   Selah
6   Surely every man walks about like a
shadow;
Surely they busy themselves in vain;
He heaps up *riches,*
And does not know who will gather
them.

PROVERBS 13:1–3

1   A wise son *heeds* his father's instruction,
But a scoffer does not listen to rebuke.

2   A man shall eat well by the fruit of *his*
mouth,
But the soul of the unfaithful feeds on
violence.
3   He who guards his mouth preserves
his life,
But he who opens wide his lips shall
have destruction.

LUKE 5:17–39

NOW it happened on a certain day, as
He was teaching, that there were Pharisees
and teachers of the law sitting by, who had
come out of every town of Galilee, Judea,
and Jerusalem. And the power of the Lord
was *present* to heal them. 18 Then behold,
men brought on a bed a man who was
paralyzed, whom they sought to bring in
and lay before Him. 19 And when they
could not find how they might bring him
in, because of the crowd, they went up on
the housetop and let him down with *his*
bed through the tiling into the midst before
Jesus.
20 When He saw their faith, He said to
him, "Man, your sins are forgiven you."
21 And the scribes and the Pharisees began to reason, saying, "Who is this who
speaks blasphemies? Who can forgive sins
but God alone?"
22 But when Jesus perceived their
thoughts, He answered and said to them,
"Why are you reasoning in your hearts?
23 Which is easier, to say, 'Your sins are
forgiven you,' or to say, 'Rise up and walk'?

24 But that you may know that the Son of
Man has power on earth to forgive sins"—
He said to the man who was paralyzed,
"I say to you, arise, take up your bed, and
go to your house."
25 Immediately he rose up before them,
took up what he had been lying on, and
departed to his own house, glorifying God.
26 And they were all amazed, and they glorified God and were filled with fear, saying,
"We have seen strange things today!"
27 After these things He went out and
saw a tax collector named Levi, sitting at
the tax office. And He said to him, "Follow
Me." 28 So he left all, rose up, and followed
Him.
29 Then Levi gave Him a great feast in
his own house. And there were a great number of tax collectors and others who sat
down with them. 30 And their scribes and
the Pharisees complained against His disciples, saying, "Why do You eat and drink
with tax collectors and sinners?"
31 Jesus answered and said to them,
"Those who are well have no need of a
physician, but those who are sick. 32 I have
not come to call *the* righteous, but sinners,
to repentance."

*That kind of statement hits the
Pharisees to the very core of their
being.*   (GOOD)

33 Then they said to Him, "Why do the
disciples of John fast often and make prayers, and likewise those of the Pharisees, but
Yours eat and drink?"
34 And He said to them, "Can you make
the friends of the bridegroom fast while
the bridegroom is with them? 35 But the
days will come when the bridegroom will
be taken away from them; then they will
fast in those days."
36 Then He spoke a parable to them: "No
one puts a piece from a new garment on
an old one; otherwise the new makes a tear,
and also the piece that was *taken* out of
the new does not match the old. 37 And
no one puts new wine into old wineskins;
or else the new wine will burst the wineskins and be spilled, and the wineskins will
be ruined. 38 But new wine must be put
into new wineskins, and both are preserved.
39 And no one, having drunk old *wine,* immediately desires new; for he says, 'The old
is better.' "

Reading 91—Devote the Dawns to God
Luke 6:12, 13

I t is not a haphazard thing, but in the constitution of God, that there are certain times of the day when it not only seems easier, but it *is* easier, to meet God. If you have ever prayed in the dawn you will ask yourself why you were so foolish as not to do it always: it is difficult to get into communion with God in the midst of the hurly-burly of the day. George MacDonald said that if he did not open wide the door of his mind to God in the early morning he worked on the finite all the rest of the day—"stand on the finite, act upon the wrong." It is not sentiment but an implicit reality that the conditions of dawn and communion with God go together. When the day of God appears there will be no night, always dawn and day. There is nothing of the nature of strain in God's Day, it is all free and beautiful and fine. "And there shall be night no more". . .

We all know when we are at our best intellectually, and if instead of giving that time to God we give it to our own development, we not only rob God, but rob ourselves of the possibility of His life thriving in us. We heard it said that we shall suffer if we do not pray; I question it. What will suffer if we do not pray is the life of God in us; but when we do pray and devote the dawns to God His nature in us develops, there is less self-realization and more Christ-realization.   (*GLORIFY*)

DEUTERONOMY 25:1—26:19

"IF there is a dispute between men, and they come to court, that *the judges* may judge them, and they justify the righteous and condemn the wicked, 2 then it shall be, if the wicked man deserves to be beaten, that the judge will cause him to lie down and be beaten in his presence, according to his guilt, with a certain number of blows. 3 Forty blows he may give him *and* no more, lest he should exceed this and beat him with many blows above these, and your brother be humiliated in your sight.

4 "You shall not muzzle an ox while it treads out *the grain*.

5 "If brothers dwell together, and one of them dies and has no son, the widow of the dead man shall not be *married* to a stranger outside *the family;* her husband's brother shall go in to her, take her as his wife, and perform the duty of a husband's brother to her. 6 And it shall be *that* the firstborn son which she bears will succeed to the name of his dead brother, that his name may not be blotted out of Israel. 7 But if the man does not want to take his brother's wife, then let his brother's wife go up to the gate to the elders, and say, 'My husband's brother refuses to raise up a name to his brother in Israel; he will not

perform the duty of my husband's brother.' 8 Then the elders of his city shall call him and speak to him. But *if* he stands firm and says, 'I do not want to take her,' 9 then his brother's wife shall come to him in the presence of the elders, remove his sandal from his foot, spit in his face, and answer and say, 'So shall it be done to the man who will not build up his brother's house.' 10 And his name shall be called in Israel, 'The house of him who had his sandal removed.'

11 "If *two* men fight together, and the wife of one draws near to rescue her husband from the hand of the one attacking him, and puts out her hand and seizes him by the genitals, 12 then you shall cut off her hand; your eye shall not pity *her.*

13 "You shall not have in your bag differing weights, a heavy and a light. 14 You shall not have in your house differing measures, a large and a small. 15 You shall have a perfect and just weight, a perfect and just measure, that your days may be lengthened in the land which the LORD your God is giving you. 16 For all who do such things, all who behave unrighteously, *are* an abomination to the LORD your God.

17 "Remember what Amalek did to you on the way as you were coming out of Egypt, 18 how he met you on the way and

attacked your rear ranks, all the stragglers at your rear, when you *were* tired and weary; and he did not fear God. 19 Therefore it shall be, when the LORD your God has given you rest from your enemies all around, in the land which the LORD your God is giving you to possess *as* an inheritance, *that* you will blot out the remembrance of Amalek from under heaven. You shall not forget.

26 "AND it shall be, when you come into the land which the LORD your God is giving you *as* an inheritance, and you possess it and dwell in it, 2 that you shall take some of the first of all the produce of the ground, which you shall bring from your land that the LORD your God is giving you, and put *it* in a basket and go to the place where the LORD your God chooses to make His name abide. 3 And you shall go to the one who is priest in those days, and say to him, 'I declare today to the LORD your God that I have come to the country which the LORD swore to our fathers to give us.'

4 "Then the priest shall take the basket out of your hand and set it down before the altar of the LORD your God. 5 And you shall answer and say before the LORD your God: 'My father *was* a Syrian, about to perish, and he went down to Egypt and dwelt there, few in number; and there he became a nation, great, mighty, and populous. 6 But the Egyptians mistreated us, afflicted us, and laid hard bondage on us. 7 Then we cried out to the LORD God of our fathers, and the LORD heard our voice and looked on our affliction and our labor and our oppression. 8 So the LORD brought us out of Egypt with a mighty hand and with an outstretched arm, with great terror and with signs and wonders. 9 He has brought us to this place and has given us this land, "a land flowing with milk and honey"; 10 and now, behold, I have brought the firstfruits of the land which you, O LORD, have given me.'

"Then you shall set it before the LORD your God, and worship before the LORD your God. 11 So you shall rejoice in every good *thing* which the LORD your God has given to you and your house, you and the Levite and the stranger who *is* among you.

12 "When you have finished laying aside all the tithe of your increase in the third year—the year of tithing—and have given *it* to the Levite, the stranger, the fatherless, and the widow, so that they may eat within your gates and be filled, 13 then you shall say before the LORD your God: 'I have removed the holy *tithe* from *my* house, and

also have given them to the Levite, the stranger, the fatherless, and the widow, according to all Your commandments which You have commanded me; I have not transgressed Your commandments, nor have I forgotten *them*. 14 I have not eaten any of it when in mourning, nor have I removed *any* of it for an unclean *use*, nor given *any* of it for the dead. I have obeyed the voice of the LORD my God, and have done according to all that You have commanded me. 15 Look down from Your holy habitation, from heaven, and bless Your people Israel and the land which You have given us, just as You swore to our fathers, "a land flowing with milk and honey." '

16 "This day the LORD your God commands you to observe these statutes and judgments; therefore you shall be careful to observe them with all your heart and with all your soul. 17 Today you have proclaimed the LORD to be your God, and that you will walk in His ways and keep His statutes, His commandments, and His judgments, and that you will obey His voice. 18 Also today the LORD has proclaimed you to be His special people, just as He promised you, that *you* should keep all His commandments, 19 and that He will set you high above all nations which He has made, in praise, in name, and in honor, and that you may be a holy people to the LORD your God, just as He has spoken."

PSALM 39:7–11

7 "AND now, Lord, what do I wait for? My hope *is* in You.

If your hopes are being disappointed just now it means that they are being purified. (GOD'S WORKMANSHIP)

---

8 Deliver me from all my transgressions; Do not make me the reproach of the foolish.

9 I was mute, I did not open my mouth, Because it was You who did *it*.

10 Remove Your plague from me; I am consumed by the blow of Your hand.

11 When with rebukes You correct man for iniquity, You make his beauty melt away like a moth; Surely every man *is* vapor. Selah

PROVERBS 13:4–6

4   THE soul of a lazy *man* desires, and
    has nothing;
    But the soul of the diligent shall be
    made rich.

5   A righteous *man* hates lying,
    But a wicked *man* is loathsome and
    comes to shame.

6   Righteousness guards *him whose* way
    is blameless,
    But wickedness overthrows the sinner.

LUKE 6:1–26

NOW it happened on the second Sabbath
after the first that He went through the
grainfields. And His disciples plucked the
heads of grain and ate *them,* rubbing *them*
in *their* hands. 2 And some of the Pharisees
said to them, "Why are you doing what is
not lawful to do on the Sabbath?"

3 But Jesus answering them said, "Have
you not even read this, what David did
when he was hungry, he and those who
were with him: 4 how he went into the
house of God, took and ate the showbread,
and also gave some to those with him, which
is not lawful for any but the priests to eat?"
5 And He said to them, "The Son of Man
is also Lord of the Sabbath."

6 Now it happened on another Sabbath,
also, that He entered the synagogue and
taught. And a man was there whose right
hand was withered. 7 So the scribes and
Pharisees watched Him closely, whether He
would heal on the Sabbath, that they might
find an accusation against Him. 8 But He
knew their thoughts, and said to the man
who had the withered hand, "Arise and
stand here." And he arose and stood.
9 Then Jesus said to them, "I will ask you
one thing: Is it lawful on the Sabbath to
do good or to do evil, to save life or to
destroy?" 10 And when He had looked

---

*T*he motive at the back . . . of the
Sermon on the Mount is love of
God.   (SERMON MT.)

---

around at them all, He said to the man,
"Stretch out your hand." And he did so,
and his hand was restored as whole as the
other. 11 But they were filled with rage, and
discussed with one another what they
might do to Jesus.

12 Now it came to pass in those days that
He went out to the mountain to pray, and
continued all night in prayer to God.
13 And when it was day, He called His
disciples to *Himself;* and from them He
chose twelve whom He also named apostles:
14 Simon, whom He also named Peter, and
Andrew his brother; James and John; Philip
and Bartholomew; 15 Matthew and
Thomas; James the *son* of Alphaeus, and
Simon called the Zealot; 16 Judas *the son*
of James, and Judas Iscariot who also became a traitor.

17 And He came down with them and
stood on a level place with a crowd of His
disciples and a great multitude of people
from all Judea and Jerusalem, and from the
seacoast of Tyre and Sidon, who came to
hear Him and be healed of their diseases,
18 as well as those who were tormented with
unclean spirits. And they were healed.
19 And the whole multitude sought to touch
Him, for power went out from Him and
healed *them* all.

20 Then He lifted up His eyes toward
His disciples, and said:

"Blessed *are you* poor,
    For yours is the kingdom of God.
21 Blessed *are you* who hunger now,
    For you shall be filled.
    Blessed *are you* who weep now,
    For you shall laugh.
22 Blessed are you when men hate you,
    And when they exclude you,
    And revile *you,* and cast out your
        name as evil,
    For the Son of Man's sake.
23 Rejoice in that day and leap for joy!
    For indeed your reward *is* great
        in heaven,
    For in like manner their fathers did
        to the prophets.

24 "But woe to you who are rich,
    For you have received your
        consolation.
25 Woe to you who are full,
    For you shall hunger.
    Woe to you who laugh now,
    For you shall mourn and weep.
26 Woe to you when all men speak well
        of you,
    For so did their fathers to the false
        prophets.

Reading 92—Instant Social Reform
Luke 6:31

Over and over again we blame God for His neglect of people by our sympathy with them, we may not put it into words but by our attitude we imply that we are filling up what God has forgotten to do. Never allow that idea, never allow it to come into your mind. In all probability the Spirit of God will begin to show us that people are where they are because we have neglected to do what we ought. Today the great craze is socialism, and men are saying that Jesus Christ came as a social reformer. Nonsense! We are the social reformers; Jesus Christ came to alter us, and we try to shirk our responsibility by putting our work on Him. Jesus alters us and puts us right; then these principles of His instantly make us social reformers. They begin to work straightway where we live, in our relationship to our fathers and mothers, to our brothers and sisters, our friends, our employers, or employees. "Consider how God has dealt with you," says Jesus, "and then consider that you do likewise to others." (*SERMON MT.*)

DEUTERONOMY 27:1—28:68

NOW Moses, with the elders of Israel, commanded the people, saying: "Keep all the commandments which I command you today. 2 And it shall be, on the day when you cross over the Jordan to the land which the LORD your God is giving you, that you shall set up for yourselves large stones, and whitewash them with lime. 3 You shall write on them all the words of this law, when you have crossed over, that you may enter the land which the LORD your God is giving you, 'a land flowing with milk and honey,' just as the LORD God of your fathers promised you. 4 Therefore it shall be, when you have crossed over the Jordan, *that* on Mount Ebal you shall set up these stones, which I command you today, and you shall whitewash them with lime. 5 And there you shall build an altar to the LORD your God, an altar of stones; you shall not use an iron *tool* on them. 6 You shall build with whole stones the altar of the LORD your God, and offer burnt offerings on it to the LORD your God. 7 You shall offer peace offerings, and shall eat there, and rejoice before the LORD your God. 8 And you shall write very plainly on the stones all the words of this law."

9 Then Moses and the priests, the Levites, spoke to all Israel, saying, "Take heed and listen, O Israel: This day you have become the people of the LORD your God. 10 Therefore you shall obey the voice of the LORD your God, and observe His commandments and His statutes which I command you today."

11 And Moses commanded the people on the same day, saying, 12 "These shall stand on Mount Gerizim to bless the people, when you have crossed over the Jordan: Simeon, Levi, Judah, Issachar, Joseph, and Benjamin; 13 and these shall stand on Mount Ebal to curse: Reuben, Gad, Asher, Zebulun, Dan, and Naphtali.

14 "And the Levites shall speak with a loud voice and say to all the men of Israel: 15 'Cursed *is* the one who makes a carved or molded image, an abomination to the LORD, the work of the hands of the craftsman, and sets *it* up in secret.'

"And all the people shall answer and say, 'Amen!'

16 'Cursed *is* the one who treats his father or his mother with contempt.'

"And all the people shall say, 'Amen!'

17 'Cursed *is* the one who moves his neighbor's landmark.'

"And all the people shall say, 'Amen!'

18 'Cursed *is* the one who makes the blind to wander off the road.'

"And all the people shall say, 'Amen!'

19 'Cursed *is* the one who perverts the justice due the stranger, the fatherless, and widow.'

"And all the people shall say, 'Amen!'

20 'Cursed *is* the one who lies with his father's wife, because he has uncovered his father's bed.'

"And all the people shall say, 'Amen!'

21 'Cursed *is* the one who lies with any kind of animal.'

"And all the people shall say, 'Amen!'

22 'Cursed *is* the one who lies with his sister, the daughter of his father or the daughter of his mother.'

"And all the people shall say, 'Amen!'

23 'Cursed *is* the one who lies with his mother-in-law.'

"And all the people shall say, 'Amen!'

24 'Cursed *is* the one who attacks his neighbor secretly.'

"And all the people shall say, 'Amen!'

25 'Cursed *is* the one who takes a bribe to slay an innocent person.'

"And all the people shall say, 'Amen!'

26 'Cursed *is* the one who does not confirm *all* the words of this law.'

"And all the people shall say, 'Amen!' "

28 "NOW it shall come to pass, if you diligently obey the voice of the LORD your God, to observe carefully all His commandments which I command you today, that the LORD your God will set you high above all nations of the earth. 2 And all these blessings shall come upon you and overtake you, because you obey the voice of the LORD your God:

3 "Blessed *shall* you *be* in the city, and blessed *shall* you *be* in the country.

4 "Blessed *shall be* the fruit of your body, the produce of your ground and the increase of your herds, the increase of your cattle and the offspring of your flocks.

5 "Blessed *shall be* your basket and your kneading bowl.

6 "Blessed *shall* you *be* when you come in, and blessed *shall* you *be* when you go out.

7 "The LORD will cause your enemies who rise against you to be defeated before your face; they shall come out against you one way and flee before you seven ways.

8 "The LORD will command the blessing on you in your storehouses and in all to which you set your hand, and He will bless you in the land which the LORD your God is giving you.

9 "The LORD will establish you as a holy people to Himself, just as He has sworn to you, if you keep the commandments of the LORD your God and walk in His ways. 10 Then all peoples of the earth shall see that you are called by the name of the LORD, and they shall be afraid of you. 11 And the LORD will grant you plenty of goods, in the fruit of your body, in the increase of your livestock, and in the produce of your ground, in the land of which the LORD swore to your fathers to give you. 12 The LORD will open to you His good treasure, the heavens, to give the rain to your land

in its season, and to bless all the work of your hand. You shall lend to many nations, but you shall not borrow. 13 And the LORD will make you the head and not the tail; you shall be above only, and not be beneath, if you heed the commandments of the LORD your God, which I command you today, and are careful to observe *them*. 14 So you shall not turn aside from any of the words which I command you this day, *to* the right or the left, to go after other gods to serve them.

15 "But it shall come to pass, if you do not obey the voice of the LORD your God, to observe carefully all His commandments and His statutes which I command you today, that all these curses will come upon you and overtake you:

16 "Cursed *shall* you *be* in the city, and cursed *shall* you *be* in the country.

17 "Cursed *shall be* your basket and your kneading bowl.

18 "Cursed *shall be* the fruit of your body and the produce of your land, the increase of your cattle and the offspring of your flocks.

19 "Cursed *shall* you *be* when you come in, and cursed *shall* you *be* when you go out.

20 "The LORD will send on you cursing, confusion, and rebuke in all that you set your hand to do, until you are destroyed and until you perish quickly, because of the wickedness of your doings in which you have forsaken Me. 21 The LORD will make the plague cling to you until He has consumed you from the land which you are going to possess. 22 The LORD will strike you with consumption, with fever, with inflammation, with severe burning fever, with the sword, with scorching, and with mildew; they shall pursue you until you perish. 23 And your heavens which *are* over your head shall be bronze, and the earth which is under you *shall be* iron. 24 The LORD will change the rain of your land to powder and dust; from the heaven it shall come down on you until you are destroyed.

25 "The LORD will cause you to be defeated before your enemies; you shall go out one way against them and flee seven ways before them; and you shall become troublesome to all the kingdoms of the earth. 26 Your carcasses shall be food for all the birds of the air and the beasts of the earth, and no one shall frighten *them* away. 27 The LORD will strike you with the boils of Egypt, with tumors, with the scab, and with the itch, from which you cannot be healed. 28 The LORD will strike you with

madness and blindness and confusion of heart. 29 And you shall grope at noonday, as a blind man gropes in darkness; you shall not prosper in your ways; you shall be only oppressed and plundered continually, and no one shall save *you.*

30 "You shall betroth a wife, but another man shall lie with her; you shall build a house, but you shall not dwell in it; you shall plant a vineyard, but shall not gather its grapes. 31 Your ox *shall be* slaughtered before your eyes, but you shall not eat of it; your donkey *shall be* violently taken away from before you, and shall not be restored to you; your sheep *shall be* given to your enemies, and you shall have no one to rescue *them.* 32 Your sons and your daughters *shall be* given to another people, and your eyes shall look and fail *with longing* for them all day long; and *there shall be* no strength in your hand. 33 A nation whom you have not known shall eat the fruit of your land and the produce of your labor, and you shall be only oppressed and crushed continually. 34 So you shall be driven mad because of the sight which your eyes see. 35 The LORD will strike you in the knees and on the legs with severe boils which cannot be healed, and from the sole of your foot to the top of your head.

36 "The LORD will bring you and the king whom you set over you to a nation which neither you nor your fathers have known, and there you shall serve other gods—wood and stone. 37 And you shall become an astonishment, a proverb, and a byword among all nations where the LORD will drive you.

38 "You shall carry much seed out to the field but gather little in, for the locust shall consume it. 39 You shall plant vineyards and tend *them,* but you shall neither drink *of* the wine nor gather the *grapes;* for the worms shall eat them. 40 You shall have olive trees throughout all your territory, but you shall not anoint *yourself* with the oil; for your olives shall drop off. 41 You shall beget sons and daughters, but they shall not be yours; for they shall go into captivity. 42 Locusts shall consume all your trees and the produce of your land.

43 "The alien who *is* among you shall rise higher and higher above you, and you shall come down lower and lower. 44 He shall lend to you, but you shall not lend to him; he shall be the head, and you shall be the tail.

45 "Moreover all these curses shall come upon you and pursue and overtake you, until you are destroyed, because you did not obey the voice of the LORD your God,

to keep His commandments and His statutes which He commanded you. 46 And they shall be upon you for a sign and a wonder, and on your descendants forever.

47 "Because you did not serve the LORD your God with joy and gladness of heart, for the abundance of everything, 48 therefore you shall serve your enemies, whom the LORD will send against you, in hunger, in thirst, in nakedness, and in need of everything; and He will put a yoke of iron on your neck until He has destroyed you. 49 The LORD will bring a nation against you from afar, from the end of the earth, *as swift* as the eagle flies, a nation whose language you will not understand, 50 a nation of fierce countenance, which does not respect the elderly nor show favor to the young. 51 And they shall eat the increase of your livestock and the produce of your land, until you are destroyed; they shall not leave you grain or new wine or oil, *or* the increase of your cattle or the offspring of your flocks, until they have destroyed you.

52 "They shall besiege you at all your gates until your high and fortified walls, in which you trust, come down throughout all your land; and they shall besiege you at all your gates throughout all your land which the LORD your God has given you. 53 You shall eat the fruit of your own body, the flesh of your sons and your daughters whom the LORD your God has given you, in the siege and desperate straits in which your enemy shall distress you. 54 The sensitive and very refined man among you will be hostile toward his brother, toward the wife of his bosom, and toward the rest of his children whom he leaves behind, 55 so that he will not give any of them the flesh of his children whom he will eat, because he has nothing left in the siege and desperate straits in which your enemy shall distress you at all your gates. 56 The tender and delicate woman among you, who would not venture to set the sole of her foot on the ground because of her delicateness and sensitivity, will refuse to the husband of her bosom, and to her son and her daughter, 57 her placenta which comes out from between her feet and her children whom she bears; for she will eat them secretly for lack of everything in the siege and desperate straits in which your enemy shall distress you at all your gates.

58 "If you do not carefully observe all the words of this law that are written in this book, that you may fear this glorious and awesome name, THE LORD YOUR GOD, 59 then the LORD will bring upon you and your descendants extraordinary

plagues—great and prolonged plagues—and serious and prolonged sicknesses. 60 Moreover He will bring back on you all the diseases of Egypt, of which you were afraid, and they shall cling to you. 61 Also every sickness and every plague, which *is* not written in this Book of the Law, will the LORD bring upon you until you are destroyed. 62 You shall be left few in number, whereas you were as the stars of heaven in multitude, because you would not obey the voice of the LORD your God. 63 And it shall be, *that* just as the LORD rejoiced over you to do you good and multiply you, so the LORD will rejoice over you to destroy you and bring you to nothing; and you shall be plucked from off the land which you go to possess.

64 "Then the LORD will scatter you among all peoples, from one end of the earth to the other, and there you shall serve other gods, which neither you nor your fathers have known—wood and stone. 65 And among those nations you shall find no rest, nor shall the sole of your foot have a resting place; but there the LORD will give you a trembling heart, failing eyes, and anguish of soul. 66 Your life shall hang in doubt before you; you shall fear day and night, and have no assurance of life. 67 In the morning you shall say, 'Oh, that it were evening!' And at evening you shall say, 'Oh, that it were morning!' because of the fear which terrifies your heart, and because of the sight which your eyes see.

68 "And the LORD will take you back to Egypt in ships, by the way of which I said to you, 'You shall never see it again.' And there you shall be offered for sale to your enemies as male and female slaves, but no one will buy *you*."

PSALM 39:12, 13

12 "HEAR my prayer, O LORD,
    And give ear to my cry;
    Do not be silent at my tears;
    For I *am* a stranger with You,
    A sojourner, as all my fathers *were*.

It is not part of the life of a natural man to pray.   (BRILL. HERITAGE)

---

13 Remove Your gaze from me, that I may
    regain strength,
    Before I go away and am no more."

PROVERBS 13:7, 8

7   THERE is one who makes himself rich,
        yet *has* nothing;
    And one who makes himself poor, yet
        has great riches.

8   The ransom of a man's life *is* his riches,
    But the poor does not hear rebuke.

LUKE 6:27–49

"BUT I say to you who hear: Love your enemies, do good to those who hate you, 28 bless those who curse you, and pray for those who spitefully use you. 29 To him who strikes you on the *one* cheek, offer the other also. And from him who takes away your cloak, do not withhold *your* tunic either. 30 Give to everyone who asks of you. And from him who takes away your goods do not ask *them* back. 31 And just as you want men to do to you, you also do to them likewise.

32 "But if you love those who love you, what credit is that to you? For even sinners love those who love them. 33 And if you do good to those who do good to you, what credit is that to you? For even sinners do the same. 34 And if you lend *to those* from whom you hope to receive back, what credit is that to you? For even sinners lend to sinners to receive as much back. 35 But love your enemies, do good, and lend, hoping for nothing in return; and your reward will be great, and you will be sons of the Most High. For He is kind to the unthankful and evil. 36 Therefore be merciful, just as your Father also is merciful.

37 "Judge not, and you shall not be judged. Condemn not, and you shall not be condemned. Forgive, and you will be forgiven. 38 Give, and it will be given to

---

The average Christian is the most penetratingly critical individual.   (SERMON MT.)

---

you: good measure, pressed down, shaken together, and running over will be put into your bosom. For with the same measure that you use, it will be measured back to you."

39 And He spoke a parable to them: "Can the blind lead the blind? Will they not both fall into the ditch? 40 A disciple is not above his teacher, but everyone who is perfectly

trained will be like his teacher. 41 And why do you look at the speck in your brother's eye, but do not perceive the plank in your own eye? 42 Or how can you say to your brother, 'Brother, let me remove the speck that *is* in your eye,' when you yourself do not see the plank that *is* in your own eye? Hypocrite! First remove the plank from your own eye, and then you will see clearly to remove the speck that is in your brother's eye.

43 "For a good tree does not bear bad fruit, nor does a bad tree bear good fruit. 44 For every tree is known by its own fruit. For *men* do not gather figs from thorns, nor do they gather grapes from a bramble bush. 45 A good man out of the good treasure of his heart brings forth good; and an evil man out of the evil treasure of his heart brings forth evil. For out of the abundance of the heart his mouth speaks.

46 "But why do you call Me 'Lord, Lord,' and not do the things which I say? 47 Whoever comes to Me, and hears My sayings and does them, I will show you whom he is like: 48 He is like a man building a house, who dug deep and laid the foundation on the rock. And when the flood arose, the stream beat vehemently against that house, and could not shake it, for it was founded on the rock. 49 But he who heard and did nothing is like a man who built a house on the earth without a foundation, against which the stream beat vehemently; and immediately it fell. And the ruin of that house was great."

◆◆◆

Reading 93— "Leave Me Alone"
Luke 7:23

Job gives utterance to a mood which is not foreign to us when he says, "*Am* I a sea, or a sea serpent, that You set a guard over me?" In certain moods of anguish the human heart says to God, "I wish You would let me alone, why should I be used for things which have no appeal to me?" In the Christian life we are not being used for our own designs at all, but for the fulfillment of the prayer of Jesus Christ. He has prayed that we might be "one with Him as He is one with the Father"; consequently, God is concerned only about that one thing, and He never says "By your leave." Whether we like it or not, God will burn us in His fire until we are as pure as He is, and it is during the process that we cry, as Job did, "I wish You would leave me alone."

We have the idea that prosperity, or happiness, or morality, is the end of a man's existence; according to the Bible it is something other, namely, "to glorify God and enjoy Him forever." When a man is right with God, God puts His honor in that man's keeping. Job was one of those in whom God staked His honor, and it was during the process of His inexplicable ways that Job makes his appeal for mercy, and yet all through there comes out his implicit confidence in God. "And blessed is he who is not offended because of Me," said our Lord.   (*Baffled*)

DEUTERONOMY 29:1—30:20

THESE *are* the words of the covenant which the LORD commanded Moses to make with the children of Israel in the land of Moab, besides the covenant which He made with them in Horeb.

2 Now Moses called all Israel and said to them: "You have seen all that the LORD did before your eyes in the land of Egypt, to Pharaoh and to all his servants and to all his land— 3 the great trials which your eyes have seen, the signs, and those great wonders. 4 Yet the LORD has not given you a heart to perceive and eyes to see and ears to hear, to this *very* day. 5 And I have led you forty years in the wilderness. Your clothes have not worn out on you, and your

sandals have not worn out on your feet. 6 You have not eaten bread, nor have you drunk wine or *similar* drink, that you may know that I *am* the LORD your God. 7 And when you came to this place, Sihon king of Heshbon and Og king of Bashan came out against us to battle, and we conquered them. 8 We took their land and gave it as an inheritance to the Reubenites, to the Gadites, and to half the tribe of Manasseh. 9 Therefore keep the words of this covenant, and do them, that you may prosper in all that you do.

10 "All of you stand today before the LORD your God: your leaders and your tribes and your elders and your officers, all the men of Israel, 11 your little ones and your wives—also the stranger who *is* in your camp, from the one who cuts your wood to the one who draws your water— 12 that you may enter into covenant with the LORD your God, and into His oath, which the LORD your God makes with you today, 13 that He may establish you today as a people for Himself, and *that* He may be God to you, just as He has spoken to you, and just as He has sworn to your fathers, to Abraham, Isaac, and Jacob.

14 "I make this covenant and this oath, not with you alone, 15 but with *him* who stands here with us today before the LORD our God, as well as with *him* who *is* not here with us today 16 (for you know that we dwelt in the land of Egypt and that we came through the nations which you passed by, 17 and you saw their abominations and their idols which *were* among them—wood and stone and silver and gold); 18 so that there may not be among you man or woman or family or tribe, whose heart turns away today from the LORD our God, to go *and* serve the gods of these nations, and that there may not be among you a root bearing bitterness or wormwood; 19 and so it may not happen, when he hears the words of this curse, that he blesses himself in his heart, saying, 'I shall have peace, even though I follow the dictates of my heart'—as though the drunkard could be included with the sober.

20 "The LORD would not spare him; for then the anger of the LORD and His jealousy would burn against that man, and every curse that is written in this book would settle on him, and the LORD would blot out his name from under heaven. 21 And the LORD would separate him from all the tribes of Israel for adversity, according to all the curses of the covenant that are written in this Book of the Law, 22 so that the coming generation of your

children who rise up after you, and the foreigner who comes from a far land, would say, when they see the plagues of that land and the sicknesses which the LORD has laid on it:

23 'The whole land *is* brimstone, salt, and burning; it is not sown, nor does it bear, nor does any grass grow there, like the overthrow of Sodom and Gomorrah, Admah, and Zeboiim, which the LORD overthrew in His anger and His wrath.' 24 All nations would say, 'Why has the LORD done so to this land? What does the heat of this great anger mean?' 25 Then *people* would say: 'Because they have forsaken the covenant of the LORD God of their fathers, which He made with them when He brought them out of the land of Egypt; 26 for they went and served other gods and worshiped them, gods that they did not know and that He had not given to them. 27 Then the anger of the LORD was aroused against this land, to bring on it every curse that is written in this book. 28 And the LORD uprooted them from their land in anger, in wrath, and in great indignation, and cast them into another land, as *it is* this day.'

29 "The secret *things belong* to the LORD our God, but those *things which are* revealed *belong* to us and to our children forever, that *we* may do all the words of this law.

30 "NOW it shall come to pass, when all these things come upon you, the blessing and the curse which I have set before you, and you call *them* to mind among all the nations where the LORD your God drives you, 2 and you return to the LORD your God and obey His voice, according to all that I command you today, you and your children, with all your heart and with all your soul, 3 that the LORD your God will bring you back from captivity, and have compassion on you, and gather you again from all the nations where the LORD your God has scattered you. 4 If *any* of you are driven out to the farthest *parts* under heaven, from there the LORD your God will gather you, and from there He will bring you. 5 Then the LORD your God will bring you to the land which your fathers possessed, and you shall possess it. He will prosper you and multiply you more than your fathers. 6 And the LORD your God will circumcise your heart and the heart of your descendants, to love the LORD your God with all your heart and with all your soul, that you may live.

7 "Also the LORD your God will put all these curses on your enemies and on those who hate you, who persecuted you.

8 And you will again obey the voice of the LORD and do all His commandments which I command you today. 9 The LORD your God will make you abound in all the work of your hand, in the fruit of your body, in the increase of your livestock, and in the produce of your land for good. For the LORD will again rejoice over you for good as He rejoiced over your fathers, 10 if you obey the voice of the LORD your God, to keep His commandments and His statutes which are written in this Book of the Law, *and* if you turn to the LORD your God with all your heart and with all your soul.

11 "For this commandment which I command you today *is* not *too* mysterious for you, nor *is* it far off. 12 It *is* not in heaven, that you should say, 'Who will ascend into heaven for us and bring it to us, that we may hear it and do it?' 13 Nor *is* it beyond the sea, that you should say, 'Who will go over the sea for us and bring it to us, that we may hear it and do it?' 14 But the word *is* very near you, in your mouth and in your heart, that you may do it.

15 "See, I have set before you today life and good, death and evil, 16 in that I command you today to love the LORD your God, to walk in His ways, and to keep His commandments, His statutes, and His judgments, that you may live and multiply; and the LORD your God will bless you in the land which you go to possess. 17 But if your heart turns away so that you do not hear, and are drawn away, and worship other gods and serve them, 18 I announce to you today that you shall surely perish; you shall not prolong *your* days in the land which you cross over the Jordan to go in and possess. 19 I call heaven and earth as witnesses today against you, *that* I have set before you life and death, blessing and cursing; therefore choose life, that both you and your descendants may live; 20 that you may love the LORD your God, that you may obey His voice, and that you may cling to Him, for He *is* your life and the length of your days; and that you may dwell in the land which the LORD swore to your fathers, to Abraham, Isaac, and Jacob, to give them."

PSALM 40:1–5

1 I waited patiently for the LORD;
And He inclined to me,
And heard my cry.
2 He also brought me up out of a horrible
pit,

There are times of crisis when we must wait on God, but they are rare. (NOT KNOWING)

Out of the miry clay,
And set my feet upon a rock,
And established my steps.
3 He has put a new song in my mouth—
Praise to our God;
Many will see *it* and fear,
And will trust in the LORD.

4 Blessed *is* that man who makes the
LORD his trust,
And does not respect the proud, nor
such as turn aside to lies.
5 Many, O LORD my God, *are* Your
wonderful works
Which You have done;
And Your thoughts toward us
Cannot be recounted to You in order;
If I would declare and speak *of them*,
They are more than can be numbered.

PROVERBS 13:9, 10

9 THE light of the righteous rejoices,
But the lamp of the wicked will be put
out.

10 By pride comes nothing but strife,
But with the well-advised *is* wisdom.

LUKE 7:1–30

NOW when He concluded all His sayings in the hearing of the people, He entered Capernaum. 2 And a certain centurion's servant, who was dear to him, was sick and ready to die. 3 So when he heard about Jesus, he sent elders of the Jews to Him, pleading with Him to come and heal his servant. 4 And when they came to Jesus, they begged Him earnestly, saying that the one for whom He should do this was deserving, 5 "for he loves our nation, and has built us a synagogue."

6 Then Jesus went with them. And when He was already not far from the house, the centurion sent friends to Him, saying to Him, "Lord, do not trouble Yourself, for I am not worthy that You should enter under my roof. 7 Therefore I did not even think myself worthy to come to You. But say the word, and my servant will be healed. 8 For I also am a man placed under author-

ity, having soldiers under me. And I say to one, 'Go,' and he goes; and to another, 'Come,' and he comes; and to my servant, 'Do this,' and he does *it*."

9 When Jesus heard these things, He marveled at him, and turned around and said to the crowd that followed Him, "I say to you, I have not found such great faith, not even in Israel!" 10 And those who were sent, returning to the house, found the servant well who had been sick.

11 Now it happened, the day after, *that* He went into a city called Nain; and many of His disciples went with Him, and a large crowd. 12 And when He came near the gate of the city, behold, a dead man was being carried out, the only son of his mother; and she was a widow. And a large crowd from the city was with her. 13 When the Lord saw her, He had compassion on her and said to her, "Do not weep." 14 Then He came and touched the open coffin, and those who carried *him* stood still. And He said, "Young man, I say to you, arise." 15 So he who was dead sat up and began to speak. And He presented him to his mother.

Jesus Christ is the One who can transmute everything we come across.   (SHADE)

---

16 Then fear came upon all, and they glorified God, saying, "A great prophet has risen up among us"; and, "God has visited His people." 17 And this report about Him went throughout all Judea and all the surrounding region.

18 Then the disciples of John reported to him concerning all these things. 19 And John, calling two of his disciples to *him*, sent *them* to Jesus, saying, "Are

You the Coming One, or do we look for another?"

20 When the men had come to Him, they said, "John the Baptist has sent us to You, saying, 'Are You the Coming One, or do we look for another?'" 21 And that very hour He cured many of infirmities, afflictions, and evil spirits; and to many blind He gave sight.

22 Jesus answered and said to them, "Go and tell John the things you have seen and heard: that *the* blind see, *the* lame walk, *the* lepers are cleansed, *the* deaf hear, *the* dead are raised, *the* poor have the gospel preached to them. 23 And blessed is *he* who is not offended because of Me."

24 When the messengers of John had departed, He began to speak to the multitudes concerning John: "What did you go out into the wilderness to see? A reed shaken by the wind? 25 But what did you go out to see? A man clothed in soft garments? Indeed those who are gorgeously appareled and live in luxury are in kings' courts. 26 But what did you go out to see? A prophet? Yes, I say to you, and more than a prophet. 27 This is *he* of whom it is written:

'Behold, I send My messenger before
    Your face,
  Who will prepare Your way before
    You.'

28 For I say to you, among those born of women there is not a greater prophet than John the Baptist; but he who is least in the kingdom of God is greater than he." 29 And when all the people heard *Him*, even the tax collectors justified God, having been baptized with the baptism of John. 30 But the Pharisees and lawyers rejected the will of God for themselves, not having been baptized by him.

◆◆◆◆

Reading 94—God-Given Shallowness
Luke 7:34

We are all so abominably serious, so interested in our own characters, that we refuse to behave like Christians in the shallow concerns of life. Our safeguard is the God-given shallowness. It is the attitude of a spiritual prig to go about with a countenance that is a rebuke to others because you have the idea that they are shallower than you. Live the surface common-sense life in a common-sense way, and remember that the shallow concerns of life are as much of God as the profound concerns. It is not our devotion to God or our holiness that makes us refuse to be shallow, but our wish to impress others that we are not shallow, which is a sure sign that we are prigs. We are to be of the stamp of our Lord and Master, and the prigs of His day called Him a glutton and a winebibber, they said He was not dealing with the profound things. Beware of the production of contempt for others by thinking that they are shallow. To be shallow is not a sign of being wicked: the ocean has a shore. The shallow amenities of life are appointed of God and are the things in which our Lord lived, and He lived in them as the Son of God. It is easier for personal pride not to live in them. Beware of posing as a profound person; God became a Baby. (*NOT KNOWING*)

DEUTERONOMY 31:1—32:52

THEN Moses went and spoke these words to all Israel. 2 And he said to them: "I *am* one hundred and twenty years old today. I can no longer go out and come in. Also the LORD has said to me, 'You shall not cross over this Jordan.' 3 The LORD your God Himself crosses over before you; He will destroy these nations from before you, and you shall dispossess them. Joshua himself crosses over before you, just as the LORD has said. 4 And the LORD will do to them as He did to Sihon and Og, the kings of the Amorites and their land, when He destroyed them. 5 The LORD will give them over to you, that you may do to them according to every commandment which I have commanded you. 6 Be strong and of good courage, do not fear nor be afraid of them; for the LORD your God, He *is* the One who goes with you. He will not leave you nor forsake you."

7 Then Moses called Joshua and said to him in the sight of all Israel, "Be strong and of good courage, for you must go with this people to the land which the LORD has sworn to their fathers to give them, and you shall cause them to inherit it. 8 And the LORD, He *is* the One who goes before you. He will be with you, He will not leave you nor forsake you; do not fear nor be dismayed."

9 So Moses wrote this law and delivered it to the priests, the sons of Levi, who bore the ark of the covenant of the LORD, and to all the elders of Israel. 10 And Moses commanded them, saying: "At the end of *every* seven years, at the appointed time in the year of release, at the Feast of Tabernacles, 11 when all Israel comes to appear before the LORD your God in the place which He chooses, you shall read this law before all Israel in their hearing. 12 Gather the people together, men and women and little

ones, and the stranger who *is* within your gates, that they may hear and that they may learn to fear the LORD your God and carefully observe all the words of this law, 13 and *that* their children, who have not known it, may hear and learn to fear the LORD your God as long as you live in the land which you cross the Jordan to possess."

14 Then the LORD said to Moses, "Behold, the days approach when you must die; call Joshua, and present yourselves in the tabernacle of meeting, that I may inaugurate him."

So Moses and Joshua went and presented themselves in the tabernacle of meeting. 15 Now the LORD appeared at the tabernacle in a pillar of cloud, and the pillar of cloud stood above the door of the tabernacle.

16 And the LORD said to Moses: "Behold, you will rest with your fathers; and this people will rise and play the harlot with the gods of the foreigners of the land, where they go *to be* among them, and they will forsake Me and break My covenant which I have made with them. 17 Then My anger shall be aroused against them in that day, and I will forsake them, and I will hide My face from them, and they shall be devoured. And many evils and troubles shall befall them, so that they will say in that day, 'Have not these evils come upon us because our God *is* not among us?' 18 And I will surely hide My face in that day because of all the evil which they have done, in that they have turned to other gods.

19 "Now therefore, write down this song for yourselves, and teach it to the children of Israel; put it in their mouths, that this song may be a witness for Me against the children of Israel. 20 When I have brought them to the land flowing with milk and honey, of which I swore to their fathers, and they have eaten and filled themselves and grown fat, then they will turn to other

gods and serve them; and they will provoke Me and break My covenant. 21 Then it shall be, when many evils and troubles have come upon them, that this song will testify against them as a witness; for it will not be forgotten in the mouths of their descendants, for I know the inclination of their behavior today, even before I have brought them to the land of which I swore *to give them.*"

22 Therefore Moses wrote this song the same day, and taught it to the children of Israel. 23 Then He inaugurated Joshua the son of Nun, and said, "Be strong and of good courage; for you shall bring the children of Israel into the land of which I swore to them, and I will be with you."

24 So it was, when Moses had completed writing the words of this law in a book, when they were finished, 25 that Moses commanded the Levites, who bore the ark of the covenant of the LORD, saying: 26 "Take this Book of the Law, and put it beside the ark of the covenant of the LORD your God, that it may be there as a witness against you; 27 for I know your rebellion and your stiff neck. *If* today, while I am yet alive with you, you have been rebellious against the LORD, then how much more after my death? 28 Gather to me all the elders of your tribes, and your officers, that I may speak these words in their hearing and call heaven and earth to witness against them. 29 For I know that after my death you will become utterly corrupt, and turn aside from the way which I have commanded you. And evil will befall you in the latter days, because you will do evil in the sight of the LORD, to provoke Him to anger through the work of your hands."

30 Then Moses spoke in the hearing of all the assembly of Israel the words of this song until they were ended:

32 "GIVE ear, O heavens, and I will speak;
And hear, O earth, the words of my mouth.
2 Let my teaching drop as the rain,
My speech distill as the dew,
As raindrops on the tender herb,
And as showers on the grass.
3 For I proclaim the name of the LORD:
Ascribe greatness to our God.
4 *He is* the Rock, His work *is* perfect;
For all His ways *are* justice,
A God of truth and without injustice;
Righteous and upright *is* He.

5 "They have corrupted themselves;
They are not His children,
Because of their blemish:

A perverse and crooked generation.
6 Do you thus deal with the LORD,
O foolish and unwise people?
Is He not your Father, *who* bought you?
Has He not made you and established you?

7 "Remember the days of old,
Consider the years of many generations.
Ask your father, and he will show you;
Your elders, and they will tell you:
8 When the Most High divided their inheritance to the nations,
When He separated the sons of Adam,
He set the boundaries of the peoples
According to the number of the children of Israel.
9 For the LORD's portion *is* His people;
Jacob *is* the place of His inheritance.

10 "He found him in a desert land
And in the wasteland, a howling wilderness;
He encircled him, He instructed him,
He kept him as the apple of His eye.
11 As an eagle stirs up its nest,
Hovers over its young,
Spreading out its wings, taking them up,
Carrying them on its wings,
12 *So* the LORD alone led him,
And *there was* no foreign god with him.

13 "He made him ride in the heights of the earth,
That he might eat the produce of the fields;
He made him draw honey from the rock,
And oil from the flinty rock;
14 Curds from the cattle, and milk of the flock,
With fat of lambs;
And rams of the breed of Bashan, and goats,
With the choicest wheat;
And you drank wine, the blood of the grapes.

15 "But Jeshurun grew fat and kicked;
You grew fat, you grew thick,
You are obese!
Then he forsook God *who* made him,
And scornfully esteemed the Rock of his salvation.

16   They provoked Him to jealousy with
        foreign *gods;*
        With abominations they provoked
        Him to anger.
17   They sacrificed to demons, not to
        God,
        To gods they did not know,
        To new *gods,* new arrivals
        That your fathers did not fear.
18   Of the Rock *who* begot you, you are
        unmindful,
        And have forgotten the God who
        fathered you.

19   "And when the LORD saw *it,* He
        spurned *them,*
        Because of the provocation of His
        sons and His daughters.
20   And He said: 'I will hide My face
        from them,
        I will see what their end *will be,*
        For they *are* a perverse generation,
        Children in whom *is* no faith.
21   They have provoked Me to jealousy
        by *what* is not God;
        They have moved Me to anger by
        their foolish idols.
        But I will provoke them to jealousy
        by *those who are* not a nation;
        I will move them to anger by a foolish
        nation.
22   For a fire is kindled in My anger,
        And shall burn to the lowest hell;
        It shall consume the earth with her
        increase,
        And set on fire the foundations of
        the mountains.

23   'I will heap disasters on them;
        I will spend My arrows on them.
24   *They shall be* wasted with hunger,
        Devoured by pestilence and bitter
        destruction;
        I will also send against them the teeth
        of beasts,
        With the poison of serpents of the
        dust.
25   The sword shall destroy outside;
        There shall be terror within
        For the young man and virgin,
        The nursing child with the man of
        gray hairs.
26   I would have said, "I will dash them
        in pieces,
        I will make the memory of them to
        cease from among men,"
27   Had I not feared the wrath of the
        enemy,
        Lest their adversaries should
        misunderstand,

Lest they should say, "Our hand *is*
        high;
        And it is not the LORD who has done
        all this." '

28   "For they *are* a nation void of counsel,
        Nor *is there any* understanding in
        them.
29   Oh, that they were wise, *that* they
        understood this,
        That they would consider their latter
        end!
30   How could one chase a thousand,
        And two put ten thousand to flight,
        Unless their Rock had sold them,
        And the LORD had surrendered
        them?
31   For their rock *is* not like our Rock,
        Even our enemies themselves *being*
        judges.
32   For their vine *is* of the vine of Sodom
        And of the fields of Gomorrah;
        Their grapes *are* grapes of gall,
        Their clusters *are* bitter.
33   Their wine *is* the poison of serpents,
        And the cruel venom of cobras.

34   '*Is* this not laid up in store with Me,
        Sealed up among My treasures?
35   Vengeance is Mine, and recompense;
        Their foot shall slip in *due* time;
        For the day of their calamity *is* at
        hand,
        And the things to come hasten upon
        them.'

36   "For the LORD will judge His people
        And have compassion on His
        servants,
        When He sees that *their* power is
        gone,
        And *there is* no one *remaining,* bond
        or free.
37   He will say: 'Where *are* their gods,
        The rock in which they sought
        refuge?
38   Who ate the fat of their sacrifices,
        And drank the wine of their drink
        offering?
        Let them rise and help you,
        And be your refuge.

39   'Now see that I, *even* I, *am* He,
        And *there is* no God besides Me;
        I kill and I make alive;
        I wound and I heal;
        Nor *is there any* who can deliver from
        My hand.
40   For I raise My hand to heaven,
        And say, "*As* I live forever,
41   If I whet My glittering sword,

And My hand takes hold on
    judgment,
I will render vengeance to My
    enemies,
And repay those who hate Me.
42 I will make My arrows drunk with
    blood,
And My sword shall devour flesh,
    With the blood of the slain and the
    captives,
From the heads of the leaders of the
    enemy." '

43 "Rejoice, O Gentiles, *with* His people;
    For He will avenge the blood of His
    servants,
And render vengeance to His
    adversaries;
He will provide atonement for His
    land *and* His people."

44 So Moses came with Joshua the son of Nun and spoke all the words of this song in the hearing of the people. 45 Moses finished speaking all these words to all Israel, 46 and he said to them: "Set your hearts on all the words which I testify among you today, which you shall command your children to be careful to observe—all the words of this law. 47 For it *is* not a futile thing for you, because it *is* your life, and by this word you shall prolong *your* days in the land which you cross over the Jordan to possess."
48 Then the LORD spoke to Moses that very same day, saying: 49 "Go up this mountain of the Abarim, Mount Nebo, which *is* in the land of Moab, across from Jericho; view the land of Canaan, which I give to the children of Israel as a possession; 50 and die on the mountain which you ascend, and be gathered to your people, just as Aaron your brother died on Mount Hor and was gathered to his people; 51 because you trespassed against Me among the children of Israel at the waters of Meribah Kadesh, in the Wilderness of Zin, because you did not hallow Me in the midst of the children of Israel. 52 Yet you shall see the land before *you,* though you shall not go there, into the land which I am giving to the children of Israel."

PSALM 40:6–12

6 SACRIFICE and offering You did not
    desire;
My ears You have opened.
Burnt offering and sin offering You did
    not require.

7 Then I said, "Behold, I come;
    In the scroll of the book *it is* written
    of me.
8 I delight to do Your will, O my God,
    And Your law *is* within my heart."

9 I have proclaimed the good news of
    righteousness
In the great assembly;
Indeed, I do not restrain my lips,
    O LORD, You Yourself know.
10 I have not hidden Your righteousness
    within my heart;
I have declared Your faithfulness and
    Your salvation;
I have not concealed Your
    lovingkindness and Your truth
From the great assembly.

11 Do not withhold Your tender mercies
    from me, O LORD;
Let Your lovingkindness and Your
    truth continually preserve me.
12 For innumerable evils have surrounded
    me;
My iniquities have overtaken me, so
    that I am not able to look up;
They are more than the hairs of my
    head;
Therefore my heart fails me.

PROVERBS 13:11, 12

11 WEALTH *gained by* dishonesty will be
    diminished,
But he who gathers by labor will
    increase.

12 Hope deferred makes the heart sick,
But *when* the desire comes, *it is* a tree
    of life.

LUKE 7:31–50

AND the Lord said, "To what then shall I liken the men of this generation, and what are they like? 32 They are like children sitting in the marketplace and calling to one another, saying:

    'We played the flute for you,
        And you did not dance;
    We mourned to you,
        And you did not weep.'

33 For John the Baptist came neither eating bread nor drinking wine, and you say, 'He has a demon.' 34 The Son of Man has come eating and drinking, and you say, 'Look, a glutton and a winebibber, a friend of tax

collectors and sinners!' 35 But wisdom is justified by all her children."

36 Then one of the Pharisees asked Him to eat with him. And He went to the Pharisee's house, and sat down to eat. 37 And behold, a woman in the city who was a sinner, when she knew that *Jesus* sat at the table in the Pharisee's house, brought an alabaster flask of fragrant oil, 38 and stood at His feet behind *Him* weeping; and she began to wash His feet with her tears, and wiped *them* with the hair of her head; and she kissed His feet and anointed *them* with the fragrant oil. 39 Now when the Pharisee who had invited Him saw *this*, he spoke to himself, saying, "This Man, if He were a prophet, would know who and what manner of woman *this is* who is touching Him, for she is a sinner."

The scrutiny we give other people should be for ourselves. (DISCIPLES)

---

40 And Jesus answered and said to him, "Simon, I have something to say to you." So he said, "Teacher, say it."

41 "There was a certain creditor who had two debtors. One owed five hundred denarii, and the other fifty. 42 And when they had nothing with which to repay, he freely forgave them both. Tell Me, therefore, which of them will love him more?"

43 Simon answered and said, "I suppose the *one* whom he forgave more."

And He said to him, "You have rightly judged." 44 Then He turned to the woman and said to Simon, "Do you see this woman? I entered your house; you gave Me no water for My feet, but she has washed My feet with her tears and wiped *them* with the hair of her head. 45 You gave Me no kiss, but this woman has not ceased to kiss My feet since the time I came in. 46 You did not anoint My head with oil, but this woman has anointed My feet with fragrant oil. 47 Therefore I say to you, her sins, *which are* many, are forgiven, for she loved much. But to whom little is forgiven, *the same* loves little."

48 Then He said to her, "Your sins are forgiven."

49 And those who sat at the table with Him began to say to themselves, "Who is this who even forgives sins?"

50 Then He said to the woman, "Your faith has saved you. Go in peace."

◆◆◆◆

*Reading 95—*The Darkness of Desolation
Luke 8:22

"If you obey Jesus you will have a life of joy and delight." Well, it is not true. Jesus said to the disciples—"Let us cross over to the other side of the lake," and they were plunged into the biggest storm they had ever known. You say, "If I had not obeyed Jesus I should not have got into this complication." Exactly. The problems in our walk with God are to be accounted for along this line, and the temptation is to say, "God could never have told me to go there, if He had done so this would not have happened." We discover then whether we are going to trust God's integrity or listen to our own expressed skepticism. . . .

Darkness is not synonymous with sin; if there is darkness spiritually it is much more likely to be the shade of God's hand than darkness on account of sin; it may be the threshold of a new revelation coming through a big break in personal experience. Before the dawn there is desolation; but wait, the dawn will merge into glorious day—". . . the light of dawn, that shineth more and more unto the perfect day." If you are experiencing the darkness of desolation on individual lines, go through with it, and you will find yourself face to face with Jesus Christ as never before. "I have come that they may have life"—life in which there is no death—"and that they may have *it* more abundantly."

(*GLORIFY*)

DEUTERONOMY 33:1—34:12

NOW this *is* the blessing with which Moses the man of God blessed the children of Israel before his death. 2 And he said:

"The LORD came from Sinai,
And dawned on them from Seir;
He shone forth from Mount Paran,
And He came with ten thousands of saints;
From His right hand
Came a fiery law for them.
3   Yes, He loves the people;
All His saints *are* in Your hand;
They sit down at Your feet;
Everyone receives Your words.

---

*A*round the saints is the great power of God which keeps watch and ward over them.   (PHIL. SIN)

---

4   Moses commanded a law for us,
A heritage of the congregation of Jacob.
5   And He was King in Jeshurun,
When the leaders of the people were gathered,
All the tribes of Israel together.

6   "Let Reuben live, and not die,
Nor let his men be few."

7 And this he said of Judah:

"Hear, LORD, the voice of Judah,
And bring him to his people;
Let his hands be sufficient for him,
And may You be a help against his enemies."

8 And of Levi he said:

"*Let* Your Thummim and Your Urim *be* with Your holy one,
Whom You tested at Massah,
And with whom You contended at the waters of Meribah,
9   Who says of his father and mother,
'I have not seen them';
Nor did he acknowledge his brothers,
Or know his own children;
For they have observed Your word
And kept Your covenant.
10   They shall teach Jacob Your judgments,
And Israel Your law.
They shall put incense before You,

And a whole burnt sacrifice on Your altar.
11   Bless his substance, LORD,
And accept the work of his hands;
Strike the loins of those who rise against him,
And of those who hate him, that they rise not again."

12 Of Benjamin he said:

"The beloved of the LORD shall dwell in safety by Him,
Who shelters him all the day long;
And he shall dwell between His shoulders."

13 And of Joseph he said:

"Blessed of the LORD *is* his land,
With the precious things of heaven, with the dew,
And the deep lying beneath,
14   With the precious fruits of the sun,
With the precious produce of the months,
15   With the best things of the ancient mountains,
With the precious things of the everlasting hills,
16   With the precious things of the earth and its fullness,
And the favor of Him who dwelt in the bush.
Let *the blessing* come 'on the head of Joseph,
And on the crown of the head of him *who was* separate from his brothers.'
17   His glory *is like* a firstborn bull,
And his horns *like* the horns of the wild ox;
Together with them
He shall push the peoples
To the ends of the earth;
They *are* the ten thousands of Ephraim,
And they *are* the thousands of Manasseh."

18 And of Zebulun he said:

"Rejoice, Zebulun, in your going out,
And Issachar in your tents!
19   They shall call the peoples *to* the mountain;
There they shall offer sacrifices of righteousness;
For they shall partake *of* the abundance of the seas
And *of* treasures hidden in the sand."

20 And of Gad he said:

"Blessed *is* he who enlarges Gad;
He dwells as a lion,
And tears the arm and the crown of
his head.
21 He provided the first *part* for himself,
Because a lawgiver's portion was
reserved there.
He came *with* the heads of the people;
He administered the justice of the
LORD,
And His judgments with Israel."

22 And of Dan he said:

"Dan *is* a lion's whelp;
He shall leap from Bashan."

23 And of Naphtali he said:

"O Naphtali, satisfied with favor,
And full of the blessing of the LORD,
Possess the west and the south."

24 And of Asher he said:

"Asher *is* most blessed of sons;
Let him be favored by his brothers,
And let him dip his foot in oil.
25 Your sandals *shall be* iron and bronze;
As your days, *so shall* your strength
be.

26 "*There is* no one like the God of
Jeshurun,
Who rides the heavens to help you,
And in His excellency on the clouds.
27 The eternal God *is your* refuge,
And underneath *are* the everlasting
arms;
He will thrust out the enemy from
before you,
And will say, 'Destroy!'
28 Then Israel shall dwell in safety,
The fountain of Jacob alone,
In a land of grain and new wine;
His heavens shall also drop dew.
29 Happy *are* you, O Israel!
Who *is* like you, a people saved by
the LORD,
The shield of your help
And the sword of your majesty!
Your enemies shall submit to you,
And you shall tread down their high
places."

34 THEN Moses went up from the
plains of Moab to Mount Nebo,
to the top of Pisgah, which is across from
Jericho. And the LORD showed him all the

land of Gilead as far as Dan, 2 all Naphtali
and the land of Ephraim and Manasseh,
all the land of Judah as far as the Western
Sea, 3 the South, and the plain of the Valley
of Jericho, the city of palm trees, as far as
Zoar. 4 Then the LORD said to him, "This
is the land of which I swore to give Abraham, Isaac, and Jacob, saying, 'I will give
it to your descendants.' I have caused you
to see *it* with your eyes, but you shall not
cross over there."

5 So Moses the servant of the LORD died
there in the land of Moab, according to
the word of the LORD. 6 And He buried
him in a valley in the land of Moab, opposite
Beth Peor; but no one knows his grave to
this day. 7 Moses *was* one hundred and
twenty years old when he died. His eyes
were not dim nor his natural vigor diminished. 8 And the children of Israel wept for
Moses in the plains of Moab thirty days.
So the days of weeping *and* mourning for
Moses ended.

9 Now Joshua the son of Nun was full
of the spirit of wisdom, for Moses had laid
his hands on him; so the children of Israel
heeded him, and did as the LORD had commanded Moses.

10 But since then there has not arisen in
Israel a prophet like Moses, whom the LORD
knew face to face, 11 in all the signs and
wonders which the LORD sent him to do
in the land of Egypt, before Pharaoh, before
all his servants, and in all his land, 12 and
by all that mighty power and all the great
terror which Moses performed in the sight
of all Israel.

PSALM 40:13–17

13 BE pleased, O LORD, to deliver me;
O LORD, make haste to help me!
14 Let them be ashamed and brought to
mutual confusion
Who seek to destroy my life;
Let them be driven backward and
brought to dishonor
Who wish me evil.
15 Let them be confounded because of
their shame,
Who say to me, "Aha, aha!"

16 Let all those who seek You rejoice and
be glad in You;
Let such as love Your salvation say
continually,
"The LORD be magnified!"
17 But I *am* poor and needy;
Yet the LORD thinks upon me.

You *are* my help and my deliverer;
Do not delay, O my God.

PROVERBS 13:13, 14

13 HE who despises the word will be
destroyed,
But he who fears the commandment
will be rewarded.
14 The law of the wise *is* a fountain of
life,
To turn *one* away from the snares of
death.

LUKE 8:1–25

NOW it came to pass, afterward, that He
went through every city and village, preaching and bringing the glad tidings of the
kingdom of God. And the twelve *were* with
Him, 2 and certain women who had been
healed of evil spirits and infirmities—Mary
called Magdalene, out of whom had come
seven demons, 3 and Joanna the wife of
Chuza, Herod's steward, and Susanna, and
many others who provided for Him from
their substance.

4 And when a great multitude had gathered, and they had come to Him from every
city, He spoke by a parable: 5 "A sower
went out to sow his seed. And as he sowed,
some fell by the wayside; and it was trampled down, and the birds of the air devoured
it. 6 Some fell on rock; and as soon as it
sprang up, it withered away because it
lacked moisture. 7 And some fell among
thorns, and the thorns sprang up with it
and choked it. 8 But others fell on good
ground, sprang up, and yielded a crop a
hundredfold." When He had said these
things He cried, "He who has ears to hear,
let him hear!"

9 Then His disciples asked Him, saying,
"What does this parable mean?"

10 And He said, "To you it has been given
to know the mysteries of the kingdom of
God, but to the rest *it is given* in parables,
that

'Seeing they may not see,
And hearing they may not
understand.'

11 "Now the parable is this: The seed is
the word of God. 12 Those by the wayside
are the ones who hear; then the devil comes

and takes away the word out of their hearts,
lest they should believe and be saved.
13 But the ones on the rock *are those* who,
when they hear, receive the word with joy;
and these have no root, who believe for a
while and in time of temptation fall away.
14 Now the ones *that* fell among thorns
are those who, when they have heard, go
out and are choked with cares, riches, and
pleasures of life, and bring no fruit to maturity. 15 But the ones *that* fell on the good

---

*Refuse to be swamped by the cares of
this world.*   (SERMON MT.)

---

ground are those who, having heard the
word with a noble and good heart, keep
it and bear fruit with patience.

16 "No one, when he has lit a lamp, covers
it with a vessel or puts *it* under a bed, but
sets *it* on a lampstand, that those who enter
may see the light. 17 For nothing is secret
that will not be revealed, nor *anything* hidden that will not be known and come to
light. 18 Therefore take heed how you hear.
For whoever has, to him *more* will be given;
and whoever does not have, even what he
seems to have will be taken from him."

19 Then His mother and brothers came
to Him, and could not approach Him because of the crowd. 20 And it was told Him
by some, who said, "Your mother and Your
brothers are standing outside, desiring to
see You."

21 But He answered and said to them,
"My mother and My brothers are these who
hear the word of God and do it."

22 Now it happened, on a certain day,
that He got into a boat with His disciples.
And He said to them, "Let us cross over
to the other side of the lake." And they
launched out. 23 But as they sailed He fell
asleep. And a windstorm came down on
the lake, and they were filling *with water,*
and were in jeopardy. 24 And they came
to Him and awoke Him, saying, "Master,
Master, we are perishing!"

Then He arose and rebuked the wind
and the raging of the water. And they
ceased, and there was a calm. 25 But He
said to them, "Where is your faith?"

And they were afraid, and marveled, saying to one another, "Who can this be? For
He commands even the winds and water,
and they obey Him!"

Reading 96—Willing Poverty for God
Luke 8:46

To be willingly poor for God is to strip myself of all things for the sake of Jesus Christ. One of the greatest snares is built on what is really a great truth, namely, that every man has Christ in himself. The pernicious use that is made of that statement is that therefore man draws power from himself. Never! Jesus Christ never drew power from Himself: He drew it always from without Himself, namely, from His Father. "The Son can do nothing of Himself" (John 5:19, 30). Beware of being rich spiritually on earth, only be rich spiritually in heaven. Jesus said to the rich young ruler, "If you will strip yourself and have no riches here, you will lay up for yourself treasure in heaven." Treasure in heaven is faith that has been tried (cf. Rev. 3:18). Immediately we begin to have fellowship with Jesus we have to live the life of faith at all costs; it may be bitter to begin with, but afterward it is ineffably and indescribably sweet—willing poverty for God, a determined going outside myself and every earthly thing.   (PERFECT)

JOSHUA 1:1—2:24

AFTER the death of Moses the servant of the LORD, it came to pass that the LORD spoke to Joshua the son of Nun, Moses' assistant, saying: 2 "Moses My servant is dead. Now therefore, arise, go over this Jordan, you and all this people, to the land which I am giving to them—the children of Israel. 3 Every place that the sole of your foot will tread upon I have given you, as I said to Moses. 4 From the wilderness and this Lebanon as far as the great river, the River Euphrates, all the land of the Hittites, and to the Great Sea toward the going down of the sun, shall be your territory. 5 No man shall *be able to* stand before you all the days of your life; as I was with Moses, *so* I will be with you. I will not leave you nor forsake you. 6 Be strong and of good courage, for to this people you shall divide as an inheritance the land which I swore to their fathers to give them. 7 Only be strong and very courageous, that you may observe to do according to all the law which Moses My servant commanded you; do not turn from it to the right hand or to the left, that you may prosper wherever you go. 8 This Book of the Law shall not depart from your mouth, but you shall meditate in it day and night, that you may observe to do according to all that is written in it. For then you will make your way prosperous, and then you will have good success. 9 Have I not commanded you? Be strong and of good courage; do not be afraid, nor be dismayed, for the LORD your God *is* with you wherever you go."

10 Then Joshua commanded the officers of the people, saying, 11 "Pass through the camp and command the people, saying, 'Prepare provisions for yourselves, for within three days you will cross over this Jordan, to go in to possess the land which the LORD your God is giving you to possess.' "

12 And to the Reubenites, the Gadites, and half the tribe of Manasseh Joshua spoke, saying, 13 "Remember the word which Moses the servant of the LORD commanded you, saying, 'The LORD your God is giving you rest and is giving you this land.' 14 Your wives, your little ones, and your livestock shall remain in the land which Moses gave you on this side of the Jordan. But you shall pass before your brethren armed, all your mighty men of valor, and help them, 15 until the LORD has given your brethren rest, as He *gave* you, and they also have taken possession of the land which the LORD your God is giving them. Then you shall return to the land of your possession and enjoy it, which Moses the LORD's servant gave you on this side of the Jordan toward the sunrise."

16 So they answered Joshua, saying, "All that you command us we will do, and wherever you send us we will go. 17 Just as we heeded Moses in all things, so we will heed you. Only the LORD your God be with you,

as He was with Moses. 18 Whoever rebels against your command and does not heed your words, in all that you command him, shall be put to death. Only be strong and of good courage."

2 NOW Joshua the son of Nun sent out two men from Acacia Grove to spy secretly, saying, "Go, view the land, especially Jericho."

So they went, and came to the house of a harlot named Rahab, and lodged there. 2 And it was told the king of Jericho, saying, "Behold, men have come here tonight from the children of Israel to search out the country."

3 So the king of Jericho sent to Rahab, saying, "Bring out the men who have come to you, who have entered your house, for they have come to search out all the country."

4 Then the woman took the two men and hid them. So she said, "Yes, the men came to me, but I did not know where they *were* from. 5 And it happened as the gate was being shut, when it was dark, that the men went out. Where the men went I do not know; pursue them quickly, for you may overtake them." 6 (But she had brought them up to the roof and hidden them with the stalks of flax, which she had laid in order on the roof.) 7 Then the men pursued them by the road to the Jordan, to the fords. And as soon as those who pursued them had gone out, they shut the gate.

8 Now before they lay down, she came up to them on the roof, 9 and said to the men: "I know that the LORD has given you the land, that the terror of you has fallen on us, and that all the inhabitants of the land are fainthearted because of you. 10 For we have heard how the LORD dried up the water of the Red Sea for you when you came out of Egypt, and what you did to the two kings of the Amorites who *were* on the other side of the Jordan, Sihon and Og, whom you utterly destroyed. 11 And as soon as we heard *these things,* our hearts melted; neither did there remain any more courage in anyone because of you, for the LORD your God, He *is* God in heaven above and on earth beneath. 12 Now therefore, I beg you, swear to me by the LORD, since I have shown you kindness, that you also will show kindness to my father's house, and give me a true token, 13 and spare my father, my mother, my brothers, my sisters, and all that they have, and deliver our lives from death."

14 So the men answered her, "Our lives for yours, if none of you tell this business of ours. And it shall be, when the LORD has given us the land, that we will deal kindly and truly with you."

15 Then she let them down by a rope through the window, for her house *was* on the city wall; she dwelt on the wall. 16 And she said to them, "Get to the mountain, lest the pursuers meet you. Hide there three days, until the pursuers have returned. Afterward you may go your way."

17 So the men said to her: "We *will be* blameless of this oath of yours which you have made us swear, 18 unless, *when* we come into the land, you bind this line of scarlet cord in the window through which you let us down, and unless you bring your father, your mother, your brothers, and all your father's household to your own home. 19 So it shall be *that* whoever goes outside the doors of your house into the street, his blood *shall be* on his own head, and we *will be* guiltless. And whoever is with you in the house, his blood *shall be* on our head if a hand is laid on him. 20 And if you tell this business of ours, then we will be free from your oath which you made us swear."

21 Then she said, "According to your words, so *be* it." And she sent them away, and they departed. And she bound the scarlet cord in the window.

22 They departed and went to the mountain, and stayed there three days until the pursuers returned. The pursuers sought *them* all along the way, but did not find *them.* 23 So the two men returned, descended from the mountain, and crossed over; and they came to Joshua the son of Nun, and told him all that had befallen them. 24 And they said to Joshua, "Truly the LORD has delivered all the land into our hands, for indeed all the inhabitants of the country are fainthearted because of us."

PSALM 41:1–13

1 BLESSED *is* he who considers the
      poor;
   The LORD will deliver him in time of
      trouble.
2 The LORD will preserve him and keep
      him alive,
   And he will be blessed on the earth;
   You will not deliver him to the will
      of his enemies.
3 The LORD will strengthen him on his
      bed of illness;
   You will sustain him on his sickbed.

4 I said, "LORD, be merciful to me;
   Heal my soul, for I have sinned against
       You."
5 My enemies speak evil of me:
   "When will he die, and his name perish?"
6 And if he comes to see *me,* he speaks
       lies;
   His heart gathers iniquity to itself;
   When he goes out, he tells *it.*
7 All who hate me whisper together
       against me;
   Against me they devise my hurt.
8 "An evil disease," *they say,* "clings to him.
   And *now* that he lies down, he will rise
       up no more."
9 Even my own familiar friend in whom
       I trusted,
   Who ate my bread,
   Has lifted up *his* heel against me.

10 But You, O LORD, be merciful to me,
       and raise me up,
    That I may repay them.
11 By this I know that You are well pleased
       with me,
    Because my enemy does not triumph
       over me.

---

*T*he Cross was a superb triumph in
which the foundations of hell were
   shaken.   (UTMOST)

---

12 As for me, You uphold me in my
       integrity,
    And set me before Your face forever.

13 Blessed *be* the LORD God of Israel
    From everlasting to everlasting!
    Amen and Amen.

PROVERBS 13:15, 16

15 GOOD understanding gains favor,
    But the way of the unfaithful *is* hard.
16 Every prudent *man* acts with
       knowledge,
    But a fool lays open *his* folly.

LUKE 8:26–56

THEN they sailed to the country of the
Gadarenes, which is opposite Galilee.
27 And when He stepped out on the land,
there met Him a certain man from the city
who had demons for a long time. And he
wore no clothes, nor did he live in a house
but in the tombs. 28 When he saw Jesus,
he cried out, fell down before Him, and
with a loud voice said, "What have I to
do with You, Jesus, Son of the Most High
God? I beg You, do not torment me!"
29 For He had commanded the unclean
spirit to come out of the man. For it had
often seized him, and he was kept under
guard, bound with chains and shackles; and
he broke the bonds and was driven by the
demon into the wilderness.
30 Jesus asked him, saying, "What is your
name?"
    And he said, "Legion," because many de-
mons had entered him. 31 And they begged
Him that He would not command them
to go out into the abyss.
32 Now a herd of many swine was feeding
there on the mountain. So they begged Him
that He would permit them to enter them.
And He permitted them. 33 Then the demons went out of the man and entered
the swine, and the herd ran violently down
the steep place into the lake and drowned.
34 When those who fed *them* saw what
had happened, they fled and told *it* in the
city and in the country. 35 Then they went
out to see what had happened, and came
to Jesus, and found the man from whom
the demons had departed, sitting at the feet
of Jesus, clothed and in his right mind. And
they were afraid. 36 They also who had seen
it told them by what means he who had
been demon-possessed was healed. 37 Then
the whole multitude of the surrounding
region of the Gadarenes asked Him to depart from them, for they were seized with
great fear. And He got into the boat and
returned.
38 Now the man from whom the demons
had departed begged Him that he might
be with Him. But Jesus sent him away,
saying, 39 "Return to your own house, and
tell what great things God has done for
you." And he went his way and proclaimed
throughout the whole city what great things
Jesus had done for him.
40 So it was, when Jesus returned, that
the multitude welcomed Him, for they were
all waiting for Him. 41 And behold, there
came a man named Jairus, and he was a
ruler of the synagogue. And he fell down
at Jesus' feet and begged Him to come to
his house, 42 for he had an only daughter
about twelve years of age, and she was
dying.
    But as He went, the multitudes thronged
Him. 43 Now a woman, having a flow of
blood for twelve years, who had spent all
her livelihood on physicians and could not

be healed by any, 44 came from behind and touched the border of His garment. And immediately her flow of blood stopped.

45 And Jesus said, "Who touched Me?"

When all denied it, Peter and those with him said, "Master, the multitudes throng and press You, and You say, 'Who touched Me?' "

46 But Jesus said, "Somebody touched Me, for I perceived power going out from Me." 47 Now when the woman saw that she was not hidden, she came trembling; and falling down before Him, she declared to Him in the presence of all the people the reason she had touched Him and how she was healed immediately.

48 And He said to her, "Daughter, be

The only simple thing in human life is our relationship to God in Christ.   (SHAD. AGONY)

---

of good cheer; your faith has made you well. Go in peace."

49 While He was still speaking, someone came from the ruler of the synagogue's *house,* saying to him, "Your daughter is dead. Do not trouble the Teacher."

50 But when Jesus heard *it,* He answered him, saying, "Do not be afraid; only believe, and she will be made well." 51 When He came into the house, He permitted no one to go in except Peter, James, and John, and the father and mother of the girl. 52 Now all wept and mourned for her; but He said, "Do not weep; she is not dead, but sleeping." 53 And they ridiculed Him, knowing that she was dead.

54 But He put them all outside, took her by the hand and called, saying, "Little girl, arise." 55 Then her spirit returned, and she arose immediately. And He commanded that she be given *something* to eat. 56 And her parents were astonished, but He charged them to tell no one what had happened.

---

*Reading 97—*Empty and Free
Luke 9:2–6

Our Lord emptied Himself and had nothing all the days of His earthly life, consequently He was free for God to lavish His gifts through Him to others. Think of the rushes with which we come in front of our Heavenly Father; whenever we see an occasion we rush in and say, "I can do this, you need not trouble God." I wonder if we are learning determinedly to possess nothing? It is possessing things that makes us so conceited—"Oh yes, I can give prayer for you; I can give this and that for you." We have to get to the place about which Jesus talked to the rich young ruler where we are so absolutely empty and poor that we have nothing, and God knows we have nothing, then He can do through us what He likes. Would that we would quickly get rid of all we have, give it away till there is nothing left, then there is a chance for God to pour through in rivers for other people.   (*PERFECT*)

JOSHUA 3:1—4:24

THEN Joshua rose early in the morning; and they set out from Acacia Grove and came to the Jordan, he and all the children of Israel, and lodged there before they crossed over. 2 So it was, after three days, that the officers went through the camp; 3 and they commanded the people, saying, "When you see the ark of the covenant of the LORD your God, and the priests, the Levites, bearing it, then you shall set out from your place and go after it. 4 Yet there shall be a space between you and it, about two thousand cubits by measure. Do not come near it, that you may know the way by which you must go, for you have not passed *this* way before."

5 And Joshua said to the people, "Sanctify yourselves, for tomorrow the LORD will do

wonders among you." 6 Then Joshua spoke to the priests, saying, "Take up the ark of the covenant and cross over before the people."

So they took up the ark of the covenant and went before the people.

7 And the Lord said to Joshua, "This day I will begin to exalt you in the sight of all Israel, that they may know that, as I was with Moses, *so* I will be with you. 8 You shall command the priests who bear the ark of the covenant, saying, 'When you have come to the edge of the water of the Jordan, you shall stand in the Jordan.'"

9 So Joshua said to the children of Israel, "Come here, and hear the words of the Lord your God." 10 And Joshua said, "By this you shall know that the living God *is* among you, and *that* He will without fail drive out from before you the Canaanites and the Hittites and the Hivites and the Perizzites and the Girgashites and the Amorites and the Jebusites: 11 Behold, the ark of the covenant of the Lord of all the earth is crossing over before you into the Jordan. 12 Now therefore, take for yourselves twelve men from the tribes of Israel, one man from every tribe. 13 And it shall come to pass, as soon as the soles of the feet of the priests who bear the ark of the Lord, the Lord of all the earth, shall rest in the waters of the Jordan, *that* the waters of the Jordan shall be cut off, the waters that come down from upstream, and they shall stand as a heap."

14 So it was, when the people set out from their camp to cross over the Jordan, with the priests bearing the ark of the covenant before the people, 15 and as those who bore the ark came to the Jordan, and the feet of the priests who bore the ark dipped in the edge of the water (for the Jordan overflows all its banks during the whole time of harvest), 16 that the waters which came down from upstream stood *still, and* rose in a heap very far away at Adam, the city that *is* beside Zaretan. So the waters that went down into the Sea of the Arabah, the Salt Sea, failed, *and* were cut off; and the people crossed over opposite Jericho. 17 Then the priests who bore the ark of the covenant of the Lord stood firm on dry ground in the midst of the Jordan; and all Israel crossed over on dry ground, until all the people had crossed completely over the Jordan.

4 AND it came to pass, when all the people had completely crossed over the Jordan, that the Lord spoke to Joshua, saying: 2 "Take for yourselves twelve men from the people, one man from every tribe, 3 and command them, saying, 'Take for yourselves twelve stones from here, out of the midst of the Jordan, from the place where the priests' feet stood firm. You shall carry them over with you and leave them in the lodging place where you lodge tonight.'"

4 Then Joshua called the twelve men whom he had appointed from the children of Israel, one man from every tribe; 5 and Joshua said to them: "Cross over before the ark of the Lord your God into the midst of the Jordan, and each one of you take up a stone on his shoulder, according to the number of the tribes of the children of Israel, 6 that this may be a sign among you when your children ask in time to come, saying, 'What do these stones *mean* to you?' 7 Then you shall answer them that the waters of the Jordan were cut off before the ark of the covenant of the Lord; when it crossed over the Jordan, the waters of the Jordan were cut off. And these stones shall be for a memorial to the children of Israel forever."

8 And the children of Israel did so, just as Joshua commanded, and took up twelve stones from the midst of the Jordan, as the Lord had spoken to Joshua, according to the number of the tribes of the children of Israel, and carried them over with them to the place where they lodged, and laid them down there. 9 Then Joshua set up twelve stones in the midst of the Jordan, in the place where the feet of the priests who bore the ark of the covenant stood; and they are there to this day.

10 So the priests who bore the ark stood in the midst of the Jordan until everything was finished that the Lord had commanded Joshua to speak to the people, according to all that Moses had commanded Joshua; and the people hurried and crossed over. 11 Then it came to pass, when all the people had completely crossed over, that the ark of the Lord and the priests crossed over in the presence of the people. 12 And the men of Reuben, the men of Gad, and half the tribe of Manasseh crossed over armed before the children of Israel, as Moses had spoken to them. 13 About forty thousand prepared for war crossed over before the Lord for battle, to the plains of Jericho. 14 On that day the Lord exalted Joshua in the sight of all Israel; and they feared him, as they had feared Moses, all the days of his life.

15 Then the Lord spoke to Joshua, saying, 16 "Command the priests who bear the ark of the Testimony to come up from the

Jordan." 17 Joshua therefore commanded the priests, saying, "Come up from the Jordan." 18 And it came to pass, when the priests who bore the ark of the covenant of the LORD had come from the midst of the Jordan, *and* the soles of the priests' feet touched the dry land, that the waters of the Jordan returned to their place and overflowed all its banks as before.

19 Now the people came up from the Jordan on the tenth *day* of the first month, and they camped in Gilgal on the east border of Jericho. 20 And those twelve stones which they took out of the Jordan, Joshua set up in Gilgal. 21 Then he spoke to the children of Israel, saying: "When your children ask their fathers in time to come, saying, 'What *are* these stones?' 22 then you shall let your children know, saying, 'Israel crossed over this Jordan on dry land'; 23 for the LORD your God dried up the waters of the Jordan before you until you had crossed over, as the LORD your God did to the Red Sea, which He dried up before us until we had crossed over, 24 that all the peoples of the earth may know the hand of the LORD, that it *is* mighty, that you may fear the LORD your God forever."

When you fear God you fear nothing else. (GOOD)

PSALM 42:1–5

1   AS the deer pants for the water brooks,
     So pants my soul for You, O God.

Redemption is the great Reality that is continually creating within us a longing for God. (SERVANT AS LORD)

---

2   My soul thirsts for God, for the living
     God.
     When shall I come and appear before
     God?
3   My tears have been my food day and
     night,
     While they continually say to me,
     "Where *is* your God?"

4   When I remember these *things,*
     I pour out my soul within me.
     For I used to go with the multitude;
     I went with them to the house of God,

With the voice of joy and praise,
With a multitude that kept a pilgrim
feast.

5   Why are you cast down, O my soul?
     And *why* are you disquieted within me?
     Hope in God, for I shall yet praise Him
     For the help of His countenance.

PROVERBS 13:17, 18

17   A wicked messenger falls into trouble,
     But a faithful ambassador *brings* health.

18   Poverty and shame *will come* to him who
     disdains correction,
     But he who regards a rebuke will be
     honored.

LUKE 9:1–17

THEN He called His twelve disciples together and gave them power and authority over all demons, and to cure diseases. 2 He sent them to preach the kingdom of God and to heal the sick. 3 And He said to them, "Take nothing for the journey, neither staffs nor bag nor bread nor money; and do not have two tunics apiece.

No man can stand in front of Jesus Christ and say, "I want to make money." (MORAL FOUND.)

---

4 "Whatever house you enter, stay there, and from there depart. 5 And whoever will not receive you, when you go out of that city, shake off the very dust from your feet as a testimony against them."

6 So they departed and went through the towns, preaching the gospel and healing everywhere.

7 Now Herod the tetrarch heard of all that was done by Him; and he was perplexed, because it was said by some that John had risen from the dead, 8 and by some that Elijah had appeared, and by others that one of the old prophets had risen again. 9 Herod said, "John I have beheaded, but who is this of whom I hear such things?" So he sought to see Him.

10 And the apostles, when they had returned, told Him all that they had done. Then He took them and went aside privately into a deserted place belonging to the city called Bethsaida. 11 But when the multitudes knew *it,* they followed Him; and He

received them and spoke to them about the kingdom of God, and healed those who had need of healing. 12 When the day began to wear away, the twelve came and said to Him, "Send the multitude away, that they may go into the surrounding towns and country, and lodge and get provisions; for we are in a deserted place here."

13 But He said to them, "You give them something to eat."

And they said, "We have no more than five loaves and two fish, unless we go and buy food for all these people." 14 For there were about five thousand men.

Then He said to His disciples, "Make them sit down in groups of fifty." 15 And they did so, and made them all sit down.

16 Then He took the five loaves and the two fish, and looking up to heaven, He blessed and broke *them,* and gave *them* to the disciples to set before the multitude. 17 So they all ate and were filled, and twelve baskets of the leftover fragments were taken up by them.

◆◆◆◆

Reading 98—His Exceeding Majesty
Luke 9:32

The disciples were with Jesus Christ on the mount, and in his epistle, Peter records what they saw there. He says "we . . . were eyewitnesses of His majesty" (2 Pet. 1:16). Jesus Christ is no comrade to Peter, He is absolute King of Kings. In the Apocalypse, the apostle John gives the same revelation of the appalling and sublime majesty of Jesus Christ. The disciples are fully awake now and face-to-face with reality.

The disciples came down from the mount into the demon-possessed valley, but it was not until after the Cross and the Resurrection that they began to understand what they had seen, the reason being that what they had seen in vision on the mount had to be worked out into actual experience in their lives. By the presence of the Holy Spirit in us, we know who the Lord Jesus is. We know Him "according to the Spirit." The Holy Spirit glorifies the Lord Jesus to us and in us until we know who He is and know the exceeding majesty of Him who said, "All authority has been given to Me in heaven and on earth." We do not know this by our intellect or by our sensible reasoning, but by the real witness of the Paraclete of God. The eyes of the disciples needed to be opened by the impartation of quickening life from our Lord after the resurrection before they knew Him (see Luke 24:16, 31). And the only way in which we can know our Lord is by His Spirit.   (*GLORY*)

JOSHUA 5:1—6:27

SO it was, when all the kings of the Amorites who *were* on the west side of the Jordan, and all the kings of the Canaanites who *were* by the sea, heard that the LORD had dried up the waters of the Jordan from before the children of Israel until we had crossed over, that their heart melted; and there was no spirit in them any longer because of the children of Israel.

2 At that time the LORD said to Joshua, "Make flint knives for yourself, and circumcise the sons of Israel again the second time." 3 So Joshua made flint knives for himself, and circumcised the sons of Israel at the hill of the foreskins. 4 And this *is* the reason why Joshua circumcised them: All the people who came out of Egypt *who were* males, all the men of war, had died in the wilderness on the way, after they had come out of Egypt. 5 For all the people who came out had been circumcised, but all the people born in the wilderness, on the way as they came out of Egypt, had not been circumcised. 6 For the children of Israel walked forty years in the wilderness, till all the people *who were* men of

war, who came out of Egypt, were consumed, because they did not obey the voice of the Lord—to whom the Lord swore that He would not show them the land which the Lord had sworn to their fathers that He would give us, "a land flowing with milk and honey." 7 Then Joshua circumcised their sons *whom* He raised up in their place; for they were uncircumcised, because they had not been circumcised on the way.

8 So it was, when they had finished circumcising all the people, that they stayed in their places in the camp till they were healed. 9 Then the Lord said to Joshua, "This day I have rolled away the reproach of Egypt from you." Therefore the name of the place is called Gilgal to this day.

10 Now the children of Israel camped in Gilgal, and kept the Passover on the fourteenth day of the month at twilight on the plains of Jericho. 11 And they ate of the produce of the land on the day after the Passover, unleavened bread and parched grain, on the very same day. 12 Then the manna ceased on the day after they had eaten the produce of the land; and the children of Israel no longer had manna, but they ate the food of the land of Canaan that year.

13 And it came to pass, when Joshua was by Jericho, that he lifted his eyes and looked, and behold, a Man stood opposite him with His sword drawn in His hand. And Joshua went to Him and said to Him, "*Are* You for us or for our adversaries?"

14 So He said, "No, but *as* Commander of the army of the Lord I have now come."

And Joshua fell on his face to the earth and worshiped, and said to Him, "What does my Lord say to His servant?"

15 Then the Commander of the Lord's army said to Joshua, "Take your sandal off your foot, for the place where you stand *is* holy." And Joshua did so.

6 NOW Jericho was securely shut up because of the children of Israel; none went out, and none came in. 2 And the Lord said to Joshua: "See! I have given Jericho into your hand, its king, *and* the mighty men of valor. 3 You shall march around the city, all *you* men of war; you shall go all around the city once. This you shall do six days. 4 And seven priests shall bear seven trumpets of rams' horns before the ark. But the seventh day you shall march around the city seven times, and the priests shall blow the trumpets. 5 It shall come to pass, when they make a long *blast* with the ram's horn, *and* when you hear the sound of the trumpet, that all the people shall

shout with a great shout; then the wall of the city will fall down flat. And the people shall go up every man straight before him."

6 Then Joshua the son of Nun called the priests and said to them, "Take up the ark of the covenant, and let seven priests bear seven trumpets of rams' horns before the ark of the Lord." 7 And he said to the people, "Proceed, and march around the city, and let him who is armed advance before the ark of the Lord."

8 So it was, when Joshua had spoken to the people, that the seven priests bearing the seven trumpets of rams' horns before the Lord advanced and blew the trumpets, and the ark of the covenant of the Lord followed them. 9 The armed men went before the priests who blew the trumpets, and the rear guard came after the ark, while *the priests* continued blowing the trumpets. 10 Now Joshua had commanded the people, saying, "You shall not shout or make any noise with your voice, nor shall a word proceed out of your mouth, until the day I say to you, 'Shout!' Then you shall shout." 11 So he had the ark of the Lord circle the city, going around *it* once. Then they came into the camp and lodged in the camp.

12 And Joshua rose early in the morning, and the priests took up the ark of the Lord. 13 Then seven priests bearing seven trumpets of rams' horns before the ark of the Lord went on continually and blew with the trumpets. And the armed men went before them. But the rear guard came after the ark of the Lord, while *the priests* continued blowing the trumpets. 14 And the second day they marched around the city once and returned to the camp. So they did six days.

15 But it came to pass on the seventh day that they rose early, about the dawning of the day, and marched around the city seven times in the same manner. On that day only they marched around the city seven times. 16 And the seventh time it happened, when the priests blew the trumpets, that Joshua said to the people: "Shout, for the Lord has given you the city! 17 Now the city shall be doomed by the Lord to destruction, it and all who *are* in it. Only Rahab the harlot shall live, she and all who *are* with her in the house, because she hid the messengers that we sent. 18 And you, by all means abstain from the accursed things, lest you become accursed when you take of the accursed things, and make the camp of Israel a curse, and trouble it. 19 But all the silver and gold, and vessels of bronze and iron, *are* consecrated to the

LORD; they shall come into the treasury of the LORD."

20 So the people shouted when *the priests* blew the trumpets. And it happened when the people heard the sound of the trumpet, and the people shouted with a great shout, that the wall fell down flat. Then the people went up into the city, every man straight before him, and they took the city. 21 And they utterly destroyed all that *was* in the city, both man and woman, young and old, ox and sheep and donkey, with the edge of the sword.

22 But Joshua had said to the two men who had spied out the country, "Go into the harlot's house, and from there bring out the woman and all that she has, as you swore to her." 23 And the young men who had been spies went in and brought out Rahab, her father, her mother, her brothers, and all that she had. So they brought out all her relatives and left them outside the camp of Israel. 24 But they burned the city and all that *was* in it with fire. Only the silver and gold, and the vessels of bronze and iron, they put into the treasury of the house of the LORD. 25 And Joshua spared Rahab the harlot, her father's household, and all that she had. So she dwells in Israel to this day, because she hid the messengers whom Joshua sent to spy out Jericho.

26 Then Joshua charged *them* at that time, saying, "Cursed *be* the man before the LORD who rises up and builds this city Jericho; he shall lay its foundation with his firstborn, and with his youngest he shall set up its gates."

27 So the LORD was with Joshua, and his fame spread throughout all the country.

PSALM 42:6–11

6 O my God, my soul is cast down within me;
Therefore I will remember You from the land of the Jordan,
And from the heights of Hermon,
From the Hill Mizar.
7 Deep calls unto deep at the noise of Your waterfalls;
All Your waves and billows have gone over me.
8 The LORD will command His lovingkindness in the daytime,

In the Christian faith the basis of human life is redemption. (SHAD. AGONY)

And in the night His song *shall be* with me—
A prayer to the God of my life.
9 I will say to God my Rock,
"Why have You forgotten me?
Why do I go mourning because of the oppression of the enemy?"
10 *As* with a breaking of my bones,
My enemies reproach me,
While they say to me all day long,
"Where *is* your God?"

11 Why are you cast down, O my soul?
And why are you disquieted within me?
Hope in God;
For I shall yet praise Him,
The help of my countenance and my God.

PROVERBS 13:19–21

19 A desire accomplished is sweet to the soul,
But *it is* an abomination to fools to depart from evil.

20 He who walks with wise *men* will be wise,
But the companion of fools will be destroyed.

21 Evil pursues sinners,
But to the righteous, good shall be repaid.

LUKE 9:18–36

AND it happened, as He was alone praying, *that* His disciples joined Him, and He asked them, saying, "Who do the crowds say that I am?"

19 So they answered and said, "John the Baptist, but some *say* Elijah; and others *say* that one of the old prophets has risen again."

20 He said to them, "But who do you say that I am?"

Peter answered and said, "The Christ of God."

21 And He strictly warned and commanded them to tell this to no one, 22 saying, "The Son of Man must suffer many things, and be rejected by the elders and chief priests and scribes, and be killed, and be raised the third day."

23 Then He said to *them* all, "If anyone desires to come after Me, let him deny himself, and take up his cross daily, and follow Me. 24 For whoever desires to save his life

If I have been identified with the Cross of Christ it must show through my fingertips.   (BIB. ETHICS)

will lose it, but whoever loses his life for My sake will save it. 25 For what profit is it to a man if he gains the whole world, and is himself destroyed or lost? 26 For whoever is ashamed of Me and My words, of him the Son of Man will be ashamed when He comes in His *own* glory, and *in* His Father's, and of the holy angels. 27 But I tell you truly, there are some standing here who shall not taste death till they see the kingdom of God."

28 Now it came to pass, about eight days after these sayings, that He took Peter, John, and James and went up on the mountain to pray. 29 As He prayed, the appearance of His face was altered, and His robe *became* white *and* glistening. 30 And behold, two men talked with Him, who were Moses and Elijah, 31 who appeared in glory and spoke of His decease which He was about to accomplish at Jerusalem. 32 But Peter and those with him were heavy with sleep; and when they were fully awake, they saw His glory and the two men who stood with Him. 33 Then it happened, as they were parting from Him, *that* Peter said to Jesus, "Master, it is good for us to be here; and let us make three tabernacles: one for You, one for Moses, and one for Elijah"—not knowing what he said.

34 While he was saying this, a cloud came and overshadowed them; and they were fearful as they entered the cloud. 35 And a voice came out of the cloud, saying, "This is My beloved Son. Hear Him!" 36 When the voice had ceased, Jesus was found alone. But they kept quiet, and told no one in those days any of the things they had seen.

◆◆◆

Reading 99—A Religion of Relationship
Luke 9:58

Our Lord Jesus Christ became poor for our sakes not as an example, but to give us the unerring secret of His religion. Professional Christianity is a religion of possessions that are devoted to God; the religion of Jesus Christ is a religion of personal relationship to God, and has nothing whatever to do with possessions. The disciple is rich not in possessions, but in personal identity. Voluntary poverty was the marked condition of Jesus (Luke 9:58), and the poverty of God's children in all ages is a significant thing. Today we are ashamed and afraid to be poor. The reason we hear so little about the inner spiritual side of external poverty is that few of us are in the place of Jesus, or of Paul. The scare of poverty will knock the spiritual backbone out of us unless we have the relationship that holds. The attitude of our Lord's life was that He was disconnected with everything to do with things that chain people down to this world; consequently, He could go wherever His Father wanted Him to.   (*APPROVED*)

JOSHUA 7:1—8:35

BUT the children of Israel committed a trespass regarding the accursed things, for Achan the son of Carmi, the son of Zabdi, the son of Zerah, of the tribe of Judah, took of the accursed things; so the anger of the LORD burned against the children of Israel.

2 Now Joshua sent men from Jericho to Ai, which *is* beside Beth Aven, on the east side of Bethel, and spoke to them, saying, "Go up and spy out the country." So the men went up and spied out Ai. 3 And they returned to Joshua and said to him, "Do not let all the people go up, but let about two or three thousand men go up and attack Ai. Do not weary all the people there, for *the people of Ai are* few." 4 So about three thousand men went up there from the peo-

ple, but they fled before the men of Ai. 5 And the men of Ai struck down about thirty-six men, for they chased them *from* before the gate as far as Shebarim, and struck them down on the descent; therefore the hearts of the people melted and became like water.

6 Then Joshua tore his clothes, and fell to the earth on his face before the ark of the LORD until evening, he and the elders of Israel; and they put dust on their heads. 7 And Joshua said, "Alas, Lord GOD, why have You brought this people over the Jordan at all—to deliver us into the hand of the Amorites, to destroy us? Oh, that we had been content, and dwelt on the other side of the Jordan! 8 O Lord, what shall I say when Israel turns its back before its enemies? 9 For the Canaanites and all the inhabitants of the land will hear *it,* and surround us, and cut off our name from the earth. Then what will You do for Your great name?"

10 So the LORD said to Joshua: "Get up! Why do you lie thus on your face? 11 Israel has sinned, and they have also transgressed My covenant which I commanded them. For they have even taken some of the accursed things, and have both stolen and deceived; and they have also put *it* among their own stuff. 12 Therefore the children of Israel could not stand before their enemies, *but* turned *their* backs before their enemies, because they have become doomed to destruction. Neither will I be with you anymore, unless you destroy the accursed from among you. 13 Get up, sanctify the people, and say, 'Sanctify yourselves for tomorrow, because thus says the LORD God of Israel: "*There is* an accursed thing in your midst, O Israel; you cannot stand before your enemies until you take away the accursed thing from among you." 14 In the morning therefore you shall be brought according to your tribes. And it shall be *that* the tribe which the LORD takes shall come according to families; and the family which the LORD takes shall come by households; and the household which the LORD takes shall come man by man. 15 Then it shall be *that* he who is taken with the accursed thing shall be burned with fire, he and all that he has, because he has transgressed the covenant of the LORD, and because he has done a disgraceful thing in Israel.' "

16 So Joshua rose early in the morning and brought Israel by their tribes, and the tribe of Judah was taken. 17 He brought the clan of Judah, and he took the family of the Zarhites; and he brought the family of the Zarhites man by man, and Zabdi was taken. 18 Then he brought his household man by man, and Achan the son of Carmi, the son of Zabdi, the son of Zerah, of the tribe of Judah, was taken.

19 Now Joshua said to Achan, "My son, I beg you, give glory to the LORD God of Israel, and make confession to Him, and tell me now what you have done; do not hide *it* from me."

20 And Achan answered Joshua and said, "Indeed I have sinned against the LORD God of Israel, and this is what I have done: 21 When I saw among the spoils a beautiful Babylonian garment, two hundred shekels of silver, and a wedge of gold weighing fifty shekels, I coveted them and took them. And there they are, hidden in the earth in the midst of my tent, with the silver under it."

22 So Joshua sent messengers, and they ran to the tent; and there it was, hidden in his tent, with the silver under it. 23 And they took them from the midst of the tent, brought them to Joshua and to all the children of Israel, and laid them out before the LORD. 24 Then Joshua, and all Israel with him, took Achan the son of Zerah, the silver, the garment, the wedge of gold, his sons, his daughters, his oxen, his donkeys, his sheep, his tent, and all that he had, and they brought them to the Valley of Achor. 25 And Joshua said, "Why have you troubled us? The LORD will trouble you this day." So all Israel stoned him with stones; and they burned them with fire after they had stoned them with stones.

26 Then they raised over him a great heap of stones, still there to this day. So the LORD turned from the fierceness of His anger. Therefore the name of that place has been called the Valley of Achor to this day.

8 NOW the LORD said to Joshua: "Do not be afraid, nor be dismayed; take all the people of war with you, and arise, go up to Ai. See, I have given into your hand the king of Ai, his people, his city, and his land. 2 And you shall do to Ai and its king as you did to Jericho and its king. Only its spoil and its cattle you shall take as booty for yourselves. Lay an ambush for the city behind it."

3 So Joshua arose, and all the people of war, to go up against Ai; and Joshua chose thirty thousand mighty men of valor and sent them away by night. 4 And he commanded them, saying: "Behold, you shall lie in ambush against the city, behind the city. Do not go very far from the city, but all of you be ready. 5 Then I and all the

people who *are* with me will approach the city; and it will come about, when they come out against us as at the first, that we shall flee before them. 6 For they will come out after us till we have drawn them from the city, for they will say, 'They are fleeing before us as at the first.' Therefore we will flee before them. 7 Then you shall rise from the ambush and seize the city, for the LORD your God will deliver it into your hand. 8 And it will be, when you have taken the city, *that* you shall set the city on fire. According to the commandment of the LORD you shall do. See, I have commanded you."

9 Joshua therefore sent them out; and they went to lie in ambush, and stayed between Bethel and Ai, on the west side of Ai; but Joshua lodged that night among the people. 10 Then Joshua rose up early in the morning and mustered the people, and went up, he and the elders of Israel, before the people to Ai. 11 And all the people of war who *were* with him went up and drew near; and they came before the city and camped on the north side of Ai. Now a valley *lay* between them and Ai. 12 So he took about five thousand men and set them in ambush between Bethel and Ai, on the west side of the city. 13 And when they had set the people, all the army that *was* on the north of the city, and its rear guard on the west of the city, Joshua went that night into the midst of the valley.

14 Now it happened, when the king of Ai saw *it*, that the men of the city hurried and rose early and went out against Israel to battle, he and all his people, at an appointed place before the plain. But he did not know that *there was* an ambush against him behind the city. 15 And Joshua and all Israel made as if they were beaten before them, and fled by the way of the wilderness. 16 So all the people who *were* in Ai were called together to pursue them. And they pursued Joshua and were drawn away from the city. 17 There was not a man left in Ai or Bethel who did not go out after Israel. So they left the city open and pursued Israel.

18 Then the LORD said to Joshua, "Stretch out the spear that *is* in your hand toward Ai, for I will give it into your hand." And Joshua stretched out the spear that *was* in his hand toward the city. 19 So *those in* ambush arose quickly out of their place; they ran as soon as he had stretched out his hand, and they entered the city and took it, and hurried to set the city on fire. 20 And when the men of Ai looked behind them, they saw, and behold, the smoke of the city ascended to heaven. So they had no power to flee this way or that way, and the people

who had fled to the wilderness turned back on the pursuers.

21 Now when Joshua and all Israel saw that the ambush had taken the city and that the smoke of the city ascended, they turned back and struck down the men of Ai. 22 Then the others came out of the city against them; so they were *caught* in the midst of Israel, some on this side and some on that side. And they struck them down, so that they let none of them remain or escape. 23 But the king of Ai they took alive, and brought him to Joshua.

24 And it came to pass when Israel had made an end of slaying all the inhabitants of Ai in the field, in the wilderness where they pursued them, and when they all had fallen by the edge of the sword until they were consumed, that all the Israelites returned to Ai and struck it with the edge of the sword. 25 So it was *that* all who fell that day, both men and women, *were* twelve thousand—all the people of Ai. 26 For Joshua did not draw back his hand, with which he stretched out the spear, until he had utterly destroyed all the inhabitants of Ai. 27 Only the livestock and the spoil of that city Israel took as booty for themselves, according to the word of the LORD which He had commanded Joshua. 28 So Joshua burned Ai and made it a heap forever, a desolation to this day. 29 And the king of Ai he hanged on a tree until evening. And as soon as the sun was down, Joshua commanded that they should take his corpse down from the tree, cast it at the entrance of the gate of the city, and raise over it a great heap of stones *that remains* to this day.

30 Now Joshua built an altar to the LORD God of Israel in Mount Ebal, 31 as Moses the servant of the LORD had commanded the children of Israel, as it is written in the Book of the Law of Moses: "an altar of whole stones over which no man has wielded an iron *tool*." And they offered on it burnt offerings to the LORD, and sacrificed peace offerings. 32 And there, in the presence of the children of Israel, he wrote on the stones a copy of the law of Moses, which he had written. 33 Then all Israel, with their elders and officers and judges, stood on either side of the ark before the priests, the Levites, who bore the ark of the covenant of the LORD, the stranger as well as he who was born among them. Half of them *were* in front of Mount Gerizim and half of them in front of Mount Ebal, as Moses the servant of the LORD had commanded before, that they should bless the people of Israel. 34 And afterward he read all the words of

the law, the blessings and the cursings, according to all that is written in the Book of the Law. 35 There was not a word of all that Moses had commanded which Joshua did not read before all the assembly of Israel, with the women, the little ones, and the strangers who were living among them.

PSALM 43:1–5

1 VINDICATE me, O God,
And plead my cause against an ungodly nation;
Oh, deliver me from the deceitful and unjust man!

2 For You *are* the God of my strength;
Why do You cast me off?
Why do I go mourning because of the oppression of the enemy?

3 Oh, send out Your light and Your truth!
Let them lead me;
Let them bring me to Your holy hill
And to Your tabernacle.

4 Then I will go to the altar of God,
To God my exceeding joy;
And on the harp I will praise You,
O God, my God.

5 Why are you cast down, O my soul?
And why are you disquieted within me?
Hope in God;
For I shall yet praise Him,
The help of my countenance and my God.

PROVERBS 13:22, 23

22 A good *man* leaves an inheritance to his children's children,
But the wealth of the sinner is stored up for the righteous.

23 Much food *is in* the fallow *ground* of the poor,
And for lack of justice there is waste.

LUKE 9:37–62

NOW it happened on the next day, when they had come down from the mountain, that a great multitude met Him. 38 Suddenly a man from the multitude cried out, saying, "Teacher, I implore You, look on my son, for he is my only child. 39 And behold, a spirit seizes him, and he suddenly cries out; it convulses him so that he foams *at the mouth;* and it departs from him with great difficulty, bruising him. 40 So I implored Your disciples to cast it out, but they could not."

41 Then Jesus answered and said, "O faithless and perverse generation, how long shall I be with you and bear with you? Bring your son here." 42 And as he was still coming, the demon threw him down and convulsed *him.* Then Jesus rebuked the unclean spirit, healed the child, and gave him back to his father.

43 And they were all amazed at the majesty of God.

But while everyone marveled at all the things which Jesus did, He said to His disciples, 44 "Let these words sink down into your ears, for the Son of Man is about to be betrayed into the hands of men." 45 But they did not understand this saying, and it was hidden from them so that they did not perceive it; and they were afraid to ask Him about this saying.

46 Then a dispute arose among them as to which of them would be greatest. 47 And Jesus, perceiving the thought of their heart, took a little child and set him by Him, 48 and said to them, "Whoever receives this little child in My name receives Me; and whoever receives Me receives Him who sent Me. For he who is least among you all will be great."

49 Now John answered and said, "Master, we saw someone casting out demons in Your name, and we forbade him because he does not follow with us."

50 But Jesus said to him, "Do not forbid *him,* for he who is not against us is on our side."

51 Now it came to pass, when the time had come for Him to be received up, that He steadfastly set His face to go to Jerusalem, 52 and sent messengers before His face. And as they went, they entered a village of the Samaritans, to prepare for Him. 53 But they did not receive Him, because His face was *set* for the journey to Jerusalem. 54 And when His disciples James and John saw *this,* they said, "Lord, do You want us to command fire to come down from heaven and consume them, just as Elijah did?"

55 But He turned and rebuked them, and said, "You do not know what manner of spirit you are of. 56 For the Son of Man did not come to destroy men's lives but to save *them.*" And they went to another village.

57 Now it happened as they journeyed on the road, *that* someone said to Him, "Lord, I will follow You wherever You go."

58 And Jesus said to him, "Foxes have holes and birds of the air *have* nests, but the Son of Man has nowhere to lay *His* head."

59 Then He said to another, "Follow Me."

If we are followers of God, we cannot take the initiative. (LOVE OF GOD)

But he said, "Lord, let me first go and bury my father."

60 Jesus said to him, "Let the dead bury their own dead, but you go and preach the kingdom of God."

61 And another also said, "Lord, I will follow You, but let me first go *and* bid them farewell who are at my house."

62 But Jesus said to him, "No one, having put his hand to the plow, and looking back, is fit for the kingdom of God."

---

*Reading 100—*The Determination to Serve
Luke 10:20

The bedrock in Jesus Christ's kingdom is not sincerity, not deciding for Christ, not a determination to serve Him, but a complete and entire recognition that we cannot begin to do it; then, says Jesus, "Blessed are you." Jesus Christ can do wonderful things for the person who enters into His kingdom through the moral frontier of need. Decisions for Christ fail not because they are not made in earnest, but because the bedrock of Christianity is ignored. The bedrock of Christianity does not lie in vowing or in strength of will; to begin with it is not ethical at all, but simply the recognition of the fact that I have not the power within me to do what my spirit longs to do. "Come to Me," said Jesus, not "Decide for Me." When I realize my inability to be what the New Testament tells me I should be, I have to come to Jesus "just as I am." I realize that I am an abject pauper morally and spiritually; if ever I am going to be what Jesus wants me to be, He must come in and do it. Jesus Christ claims on the basis of His redemption that He can put into anyone who is consciously poor enough to receive it, His own disposition; that is, the ability not only to will but to do. (See Phil. 2:12, 13.) The knowledge of our own poverty brings us to the moral frontier where Jesus Christ works.

(*LOVE OF GOD*)

JOSHUA 9:1—10:43

AND it came to pass when all the kings who *were* on this side of the Jordan, in the hills and in the lowland and in all the coasts of the Great Sea toward Lebanon—the Hittite, the Amorite, the Canaanite, the Perizzite, the Hivite, and the Jebusite—heard *about it,* 2 that they gathered together to fight with Joshua and Israel with one accord.

3 But when the inhabitants of Gibeon heard what Joshua had done to Jericho and Ai, 4 they worked craftily, and went and pretended to be ambassadors. And they took old sacks on their donkeys, old wineskins torn and mended, 5 old and patched sandals on their feet, and old garments on themselves; and all the bread of their provision was dry *and* moldy. 6 And they went to Joshua, to the camp at Gilgal, and said to him and to the men of Israel, "We have come from a far country; now therefore, make a covenant with us."

7 Then the men of Israel said to the Hivites, "Perhaps you dwell among us; so how can we make a covenant with you?"

8 But they said to Joshua, "We *are* your servants."

And Joshua said to them, "Who *are* you, and where do you come from?"

9 So they said to him: "From a very far country your servants have come, because of the name of the LORD your God; for we have heard of His fame, and all that He did in Egypt, 10 and all that He did

to the two kings of the Amorites who *were* beyond the Jordan—to Sihon king of Heshbon, and Og king of Bashan, who was at Ashtaroth. 11 Therefore our elders and all the inhabitants of our country spoke to us, saying, 'Take provisions with you for the journey, and go to meet them, and say to them, "We *are* your servants; now therefore, make a covenant with us." ' 12 This bread of ours we took hot *for* our provision from our houses on the day we departed to come to you. But now look, it is dry and moldy. 13 And these wineskins which we filled *were* new, and see, they are torn; and these our garments and our sandals have become old because of the very long journey."

14 Then the men of Israel took some of their provisions; but they did not ask counsel of the LORD. 15 So Joshua made peace with them, and made a covenant with them to let them live; and the rulers of the congregation swore to them.

16 And it happened at the end of three days, after they had made a covenant with them, that they heard that they *were* their neighbors who dwelt near them. 17 Then the children of Israel journeyed and came to their cities on the third day. Now their cities *were* Gibeon, Chephirah, Beeroth, and Kirjath Jearim. 18 But the children of Israel did not attack them, because the rulers of the congregation had sworn to them by the LORD God of Israel. And all the congregation complained against the rulers.

19 Then all the rulers said to all the congregation, "We have sworn to them by the LORD God of Israel; now therefore, we may not touch them. 20 This we will do to them: We will let them live, lest wrath be upon us because of the oath which we swore to them." 21 And the rulers said to them, "Let them live, but let them be woodcutters and water carriers for all the congregation, as the rulers had promised them."

22 Then Joshua called for them, and he spoke to them, saying, "Why have you deceived us, saying, 'We *are* very far from you,' when you dwell near us? 23 Now therefore, you *are* cursed, and none of you shall be freed from being slaves—woodcutters and water carriers for the house of my God."

24 So they answered Joshua and said, "Because your servants were clearly told that the LORD your God commanded His servant Moses to give you all the land, and to destroy all the inhabitants of the land from before you; therefore we were very much afraid for our lives because of you, and have done this thing. 25 And now, here we are, in your hands; do with us as it seems good and right to do to us."

26 So he did to them, and delivered them out of the hand of the children of Israel, so that they did not kill them. 27 And that day Joshua made them woodcutters and water carriers for the congregation and for the altar of the LORD, in the place which He would choose, even to this day.

10 NOW it came to pass when Adoni-Zedek king of Jerusalem heard how Joshua had taken Ai and had utterly destroyed it—as he had done to Jericho and its king, so he had done to Ai and its king—and how the inhabitants of Gibeon had made peace with Israel and were among them, 2 that they feared greatly, because Gibeon *was* a great city, like one of the royal cities, and because it *was* greater than Ai, and all its men *were* mighty. 3 Therefore Adoni-Zedek king of Jerusalem sent to Hoham king of Hebron, Piram king of Jarmuth, Japhia king of Lachish, and Debir king of Eglon, saying, 4 "Come up to me and help me, that we may attack Gibeon, for it has made peace with Joshua and with the children of Israel." 5 Therefore the five kings of the Amorites, the king of Jerusalem, the king of Hebron, the king of Jarmuth, the king of Lachish, *and* the king of Eglon, gathered together and went up, they and all their armies, and camped before Gibeon and made war against it.

6 And the men of Gibeon sent to Joshua at the camp at Gilgal, saying, "Do not forsake your servants; come up to us quickly, save us and help us, for all the kings of the Amorites who dwell in the mountains have gathered together against us."

7 So Joshua ascended from Gilgal, he and all the people of war with him, and all the mighty men of valor. 8 And the LORD said to Joshua, "Do not fear them, for I have delivered them into your hand; not a man of them shall stand before you." 9 Joshua therefore came upon them suddenly, having marched all night from Gilgal. 10 So the LORD routed them before Israel, killed them with a great slaughter at Gibeon, chased them along the road that goes to Beth Horon, and struck them down as far as Azekah and Makkedah. 11 And it happened, as they fled before Israel *and* were on the descent of Beth Horon, that the LORD cast down large hailstones from heaven on them as far as Azekah, and they died. *There were* more who died from the hailstones than the children of Israel killed with the sword.

12 Then Joshua spoke to the LORD in the day when the LORD delivered up the

Amorites before the children of Israel, and he said in the sight of Israel:

"Sun, stand still over Gibeon;
And Moon, in the Valley of Aijalon."
13 So the sun stood still,
And the moon stopped,
Till the people had revenge
Upon their enemies.

Is this not written in the Book of Jasher? So the sun stood still in the midst of heaven, and did not hasten to go *down* for about a whole day. 14 And there has been no day like that, before it or after it, that the LORD heeded the voice of a man; for the LORD fought for Israel.

15 Then Joshua returned, and all Israel with him, to the camp at Gilgal.

16 But these five kings had fled and hidden themselves in a cave at Makkedah. 17 And it was told Joshua, saying, "The five kings have been found hidden in the cave at Makkedah."

18 So Joshua said, "Roll large stones against the mouth of the cave, and set men by it to guard them. 19 And do not stay *there* yourselves, *but* pursue your enemies, and attack their rear *guard*. Do not allow them to enter their cities, for the LORD your God has delivered them into your hand." 20 Then it happened, while Joshua and the children of Israel made an end of slaying them with a very great slaughter, till they had finished, that those who escaped entered fortified cities. 21 And all the people returned to the camp, to Joshua at Makkedah, in peace.

No one moved his tongue against any of the children of Israel.

22 Then Joshua said, "Open the mouth of the cave, and bring out those five kings to me from the cave." 23 And they did so, and brought out those five kings to him from the cave: the king of Jerusalem, the king of Hebron, the king of Jarmuth, the king of Lachish, *and* the king of Eglon.

24 So it was, when they brought out those kings to Joshua, that Joshua called for all the men of Israel, and said to the captains of the men of war who went with him, "Come near, put your feet on the necks of these kings." And they drew near and put their feet on their necks. 25 Then Joshua said to them, "Do not be afraid, nor be dismayed; be strong and of good courage, for thus the LORD will do to all your enemies against whom you fight." 26 And afterward Joshua struck them and killed them, and hanged them on five trees; and they were hanging on the trees until evening.

27 So it was at the time of the going down of the sun *that* Joshua commanded, and they took them down from the trees, cast them into the cave where they had been hidden, and laid large stones against the cave's mouth, *which remain* until this very day.

28 On that day Joshua took Makkedah, and struck it and its king with the edge of the sword. He utterly destroyed them—all the people who *were* in it. He let none remain. He also did to the king of Makkedah as he had done to the king of Jericho.

29 Then Joshua passed from Makkedah, and all Israel with him, to Libnah; and they fought against Libnah. 30 And the LORD also delivered it and its king into the hand of Israel; he struck it and all the people who *were* in it with the edge of the sword. He let none remain in it, but did to its king as he had done to the king of Jericho.

31 Then Joshua passed from Libnah, and all Israel with him, to Lachish; and they encamped against it and fought against it. 32 And the LORD delivered Lachish into the hand of Israel, who took it on the second day, and struck it and all the people who *were* in it with the edge of the sword, according to all that he had done to Libnah. 33 Then Horam king of Gezer came up to help Lachish; and Joshua struck him and his people, until he left him none remaining.

34 From Lachish Joshua passed to Eglon, and all Israel with him; and they encamped against it and fought against it. 35 They took it on that day and struck it with the edge of the sword; all the people who *were* in it he utterly destroyed that day, according to all that he had done to Lachish.

36 So Joshua went up from Eglon, and all Israel with him, to Hebron; and they fought against it. 37 And they took it and struck it with the edge of the sword—its king, all its cities, and all the people who *were* in it; he left none remaining, according to all that he had done to Eglon, but utterly destroyed it and all the people who *were* in it.

38 Then Joshua returned, and all Israel with him, to Debir; and they fought against it. 39 And he took it and its king and all its cities; they struck them with the edge of the sword and utterly destroyed all the people who *were* in it. He left none remaining; as he had done to Hebron, so he did to Debir and its king, as he had done also to Libnah and its king.

40 So Joshua conquered all the land: the mountain country and the South and the

lowland and the wilderness slopes, and all their kings; he left none remaining, but utterly destroyed all that breathed, as the LORD God of Israel had commanded. 41 And Joshua conquered them from Kadesh Barnea as far as Gaza, and all the country of Goshen, even as far as Gibeon. 42 All these kings and their land Joshua took at one time, because the LORD God of Israel fought for Israel. 43 Then Joshua returned, and all Israel with him, to the camp at Gilgal.

PSALM 44:1–3

1 WE have heard with our ears, O God,
   Our fathers have told us,
   The deeds You did in their days,
   In days of old:
2 You drove out the nations with Your hand,
   But them You planted;
   You afflicted the peoples, and cast them out.
3 For they did not gain possession of the land by their own sword,
   Nor did their own arm save them;
   But it was Your right hand, Your arm, and the light of Your countenance,
   Because You favored them.

PROVERBS 13:24, 25

24 HE who spares his rod hates his son,
   But he who loves him disciplines him promptly.

25 The righteous eats to the satisfying of his soul,
   But the stomach of the wicked shall be in want.

LUKE 10:1–24

AFTER these things the Lord appointed seventy others also, and sent them two by two before His face into every city and place where He Himself was about to go. 2 Then He said to them, "The harvest truly *is* great, but the laborers *are* few, therefore pray the Lord of the harvest to send out laborers into His harvest. 3 Go your way; behold, I send you out as lambs among wolves. 4 Carry neither money bag, knapsack, nor sandals; and greet no one along the road. 5 But whatever house you enter, first say, 'Peace to this house.' 6 And if a son of peace is there, your peace will rest on it; if not, it will return to you. 7 And remain in the same house, eating and drinking such things as they give, for the laborer is worthy of his wages. Do not go from house to house. 8 Whatever city you enter, and they receive you, eat such things as are set before you. 9 And heal the sick there, and say to them, 'The kingdom of God has come near to you.' 10 But whatever city you enter, and they do not receive you, go out into its streets and say, 11 'The very dust of your city which clings to us we wipe off against you. Nevertheless know this, that the kingdom of God has come near you.' 12 But I say to you that it will be more tolerable in that Day for Sodom than for that city.

13 "Woe to you, Chorazin! Woe to you, Bethsaida! For if the mighty works which were done in you had been done in Tyre and Sidon, they would have repented long ago, sitting in sackcloth and ashes. 14 But

---

*R*epentance does not spring out of the human heart.   (CONFORMED)

---

it will be more tolerable for Tyre and Sidon at the judgment than for you. 15 And you, Capernaum, who are exalted to heaven, will be brought down to Hades. 16 He who hears you hears Me, he who rejects you rejects Me, and he who rejects Me rejects Him who sent Me."

17 Then the seventy returned with joy, saying, "Lord, even the demons are subject to us in Your name."

18 And He said to them, "I saw Satan fall like lightning from heaven. 19 Behold, I give you the authority to trample on serpents and scorpions, and over all the power of the enemy, and nothing shall by any means hurt you. 20 Nevertheless do not rejoice in this, that the spirits are subject to you, but rather rejoice because your names are written in heaven."

21 In that hour Jesus rejoiced in the Spirit and said, "I thank You, Father, Lord of heaven and earth, that You have hidden these things from *the* wise and prudent and revealed them to babes. Even so, Father, for so it seemed good in Your sight. 22 All things have been delivered to Me by My Father, and no one knows who the Son is except the Father, and who the Father is except the Son, and *the one* to whom the Son wills to reveal *Him*."

23 Then He turned to *His* disciples and

said privately, "Blessed *are* the eyes which see the things you see; 24 for I tell you that many prophets and kings have desired to see what you see, and have not seen *it*, and to hear what you hear, and have not heard *it*."

◆◆◆

Reading 101—The Never-Failing God
Joshua 11:6

What line does my thought take? Does it turn to what God says or to what I fear? Am I learning to say not what God says, but to say something after I have heard what He says? "For He Himself has said, 'I will never leave you nor forsake you.' So we may boldly say: 'The LORD *is* my helper; I will not fear. What can man do to me?' "

"I will in no way fail you"—not for all my sin and selfishness and stubbornness and waywardness. Have I really let God say to me that He will never fail me? If I have listened to this say-so of God's, then let me listen again.

"Neither will I in any way forsake you." Sometimes it is not difficulty that makes me think God will forsake me, but drudgery. There is no Hill Difficulty to climb, no vision given, nothing wonderful or beautiful, just the commonplace day in and day out—can I hear God's say-so in these things?

We have the idea that God is going to do some exceptional thing, that He is preparing and fitting us for some extraordinary thing by and by, but as we go on in grace we find that God is glorifying Himself here and now, in the present minute. If we have God's say-so behind us, the most amazing strength comes, and we learn to sing in the ordinary days and ways.   (*UTMOST*)

JOSHUA 11:1—12:24

AND it came to pass, when Jabin king of Hazor heard *these things,* that he sent to Jobab king of Madon, to the king of Shimron, to the king of Achshaph, 2 and to the kings who *were* from the north, in the mountains, in the plain south of Chinneroth, in the lowland, and in the heights of Dor on the west, 3 to the Canaanites in the east and in the west, the Amorite, the Hittite, the Perizzite, the Jebusite in the mountains, and the Hivite below Hermon in the land of Mizpah. 4 So they went out, they and all their armies with them, *as* many people *as* the sand that *is* on the seashore in multitude, with very many horses and chariots. 5 And when all these kings had met together, they came and camped together at the waters of Merom to fight against Israel.

6 But the LORD said to Joshua, "Do not be afraid because of them, for tomorrow about this time I will deliver all of them slain before Israel. You shall hamstring their horses and burn their chariots with fire."
7 So Joshua and all the people of war with him came against them suddenly by the waters of Merom, and they attacked them. 8 And the LORD delivered them into the hand of Israel, who defeated them and chased them to Greater Sidon, to the Brook Misrephoth, and to the Valley of Mizpah eastward; they attacked them until they left none of them remaining. 9 So Joshua did to them as the LORD had told him: he hamstrung their horses and burned their chariots with fire.

10 Joshua turned back at that time and took Hazor, and struck its king with the sword; for Hazor was formerly the head of all those kingdoms. 11 And they struck all the people who *were* in it with the edge of the sword, utterly destroying *them*. There was none left breathing. Then he burned Hazor with fire.

12 So all the cities of those kings, and all their kings, Joshua took and struck with the edge of the sword. He utterly destroyed them, as Moses the servant of the LORD had commanded. 13 But *as for* the cities that stood on their mounds, Israel burned none of them, except Hazor only, *which* Joshua burned. 14 And all the spoil of these cities and the livestock, the children of Israel took as booty for themselves; but they struck

every man with the edge of the sword until they had destroyed them, and they left none breathing. 15 As the Lord had commanded Moses his servant, so Moses commanded Joshua, and so Joshua did. He left nothing undone of all that the Lord had commanded Moses.

16 Thus Joshua took all this land: the mountain country, all the South, all the land of Goshen, the lowland, and the Jordan plain—the mountains of Israel and its lowlands, 17 from Mount Halak and the ascent to Seir, even as far as Baal Gad in the Valley of Lebanon below Mount Hermon. He captured all their kings, and struck them down and killed them. 18 Joshua made war a long time with all those kings. 19 There was not a city that made peace with the children of Israel, except the Hivites, the inhabitants of Gibeon. All *the others* they took in battle. 20 For it was of the Lord to harden their hearts, that they should come against Israel in battle, that He might utterly destroy them, *and* that they might receive no mercy, but that He might destroy them, as the Lord had commanded Moses.

21 And at that time Joshua came and cut off the Anakim from the mountains: from Hebron, from Debir, from Anab, from all the mountains of Judah, and from all the mountains of Israel; Joshua utterly destroyed them with their cities. 22 None of the Anakim were left in the land of the children of Israel; they remained only in Gaza, in Gath, and in Ashdod.

23 So Joshua took the whole land, according to all that the Lord had said to Moses; and Joshua gave it as an inheritance to Israel according to their divisions by their tribes. Then the land rested from war.

12 THESE *are* the kings of the land whom the children of Israel defeated, and whose land they possessed on the other side of the Jordan toward the rising of the sun, from the River Arnon to Mount Hermon, and all the eastern Jordan plain: 2 *One king was* Sihon king of the Amorites, who dwelt in Heshbon *and* ruled half of Gilead, from Aroer, which is on the bank of the River Arnon, from the middle of that river, even as far as the River Jabbok, *which is* the border of the Ammonites, 3 and the eastern Jordan plain from the Sea of Chinneroth as far as the Sea of the Arabah (the Salt Sea), the road to Beth Jeshimoth, and southward below the slopes of Pisgah. 4 *The other king was* Og king of Bashan and his territory, *who was* of the remnant of the giants, who dwelt at Ashtaroth and at Edrei, 5 and reigned over Mount Hermon, over Salcah, over all Bashan, as far as the border of the Geshurites and the Maachathites, and over half of Gilead *to* the border of Sihon king of Heshbon.

6 These Moses the servant of the Lord and the children of Israel had conquered; and Moses the servant of the Lord had given it *as* a possession to the Reubenites, the Gadites, and half the tribe of Manasseh.

7 And these *are* the kings of the country which Joshua and the children of Israel conquered on this side of the Jordan, on the west, from Baal Gad in the Valley of Lebanon as far as Mount Halak and the ascent to Seir, which Joshua gave to the tribes of Israel *as* a possession according to their divisions, 8 in the mountain country, in the lowlands, in the *Jordan* plain, in the slopes, in the wilderness, and in the South—the Hittites, the Amorites, the Canaanites, the Perizzites, the Hivites, and the Jebusites: 9 the king of Jericho, one; the king of Ai, which *is* beside Bethel, one; 10 the king of Jerusalem, one; the king of Hebron, one; 11 the king of Jarmuth, one; the king of Lachish, one; 12 the king of Eglon, one; the king of Gezer, one; 13 the king of Debir, one; the king of Geder, one; 14 the king of Hormah, one; the king of Arad, one; 15 the king of Libnah, one; the king of Adullam, one; 16 the king of Makkedah, one; the king of Bethel, one; 17 the king of Tappuah, one; the king of Hepher, one; 18 the king of Aphek, one; the king of Lasharon, one; 19 the king of Madon, one; the king of Hazor, one; 20 the king of Shimron Meron, one; the king of Achshaph, one; 21 the king of Taanach, one; the king of Megiddo, one; 22 the king of Kedesh, one; the king of Jokneam in Carmel, one; 23 the king of Dor in the heights of Dor, one; the king of the people of Gilgal, one; 24 the king of Tirzah, one—all the kings, thirty-one.

PSALM 44:4–19

4 YOU are my King, O God;
   Command victories for Jacob.
5 Through You we will push down our
      enemies;
   Through Your name we will trample
      those who rise up against us.
6 For I will not trust in my bow,
   Nor shall my sword save me.
7 But You have saved us from our
      enemies,
   And have put to shame those who hated
      us.

8   In God we boast all day long,
    And praise Your name forever.
                                        Selah

9   But You have cast *us* off and put us
        to shame,
    And You do not go out with our armies.
10 You make us turn back from the enemy,
    And those who hate us have taken spoil
        for themselves.
11 You have given us up like sheep *intended*
        for food,
    And have scattered us among the
        nations.
12 You sell Your people for *next to*
        nothing,
    And are not enriched by selling them.

13 You make us a reproach to our
        neighbors,
    A scorn and a derision to those all
        around us.
14 You make us a byword among the
        nations,
    A shaking of the head among the
        peoples.
15 My dishonor *is* continually before me,
    And the shame of my face has covered
        me,
16 Because of the voice of him who
        reproaches and reviles,
    Because of the enemy and the avenger.

17 All this has come upon us;
    But we have not forgotten You,
    Nor have we dealt falsely with Your
        covenant.
18 Our heart has not turned back,
    Nor have our steps departed from Your
        way;
19 But You have severely broken us in the
        place of jackals,
    And covered us with the shadow of
        death.

PROVERBS 14:1, 2

1   THE wise woman builds her house,
    But the foolish pulls it down with her
        hands.

2   He who walks in his uprightness fears
        the LORD,
    But *he who is* perverse in his ways
        despises Him.

LUKE 10:25–42

AND behold, a certain lawyer stood up
and tested Him, saying, "Teacher, what
shall I do to inherit eternal life?"

26 He said to him, "What is written in
the law? What is your reading *of it*?"
27 So he answered and said, " 'You shall
love the LORD your God with all your
heart, with all your soul, with all your
strength, and with all your mind,' and 'your
neighbor as yourself.' "

---

*The only way to love God with all our
soul is to give up our lives for His
sake.*   (PERFECT)

---

28 And He said to him, "You have answered rightly; do this and you will live."
29 But he, wanting to justify himself, said
to Jesus, "And who is my neighbor?"
30 Then Jesus answered and said: "A certain *man* went down from Jerusalem to Jericho, and fell among thieves, who stripped
him of his clothing, wounded *him*, and departed, leaving *him* half dead. 31 Now by
chance a certain priest came down that road.
And when he saw him, he passed by on
the other side. 32 Likewise a Levite, when
he arrived at the place, came and looked,
and passed by on the other side. 33 But a
certain Samaritan, as he journeyed, came
where he was. And when he saw him, he
had compassion. 34 So he went to *him* and
bandaged his wounds, pouring on oil and
wine; and he set him on his own animal,
brought him to an inn, and took care of
him. 35 On the next day, when he departed,
he took out two denarii, gave *them* to the
innkeeper, and said to him, 'Take care of
him; and whatever more you spend, when
I come again, I will repay you.' 36 So which
of these three do you think was neighbor
to him who fell among the thieves?"
37 And he said, "He who showed mercy
on him."
Then Jesus said to him, "Go and do
likewise."
38 Now it happened as they went that
He entered a certain village; and a certain
woman named Martha welcomed Him into
her house. 39 And she had a sister called
Mary, who also sat at Jesus' feet and heard
His word. 40 But Martha was distracted
with much serving, and she approached
Him and said, "Lord, do You not care that
my sister has left me to serve alone? Therefore tell her to help me."
41 And Jesus answered and said to her,
"Martha, Martha, you are worried and troubled about many things. 42 But one thing
is needed, and Mary has chosen that good
part, which will not be taken away from
her."

Reading 102—Spiritual Confusion
Luke 11:5–8

There is a time in spiritual life when God does not seem to be a friend. Everything was clear and easily marked and understood for a while, but now we find ourselves in a condition of darkness and desolation. The parable of the persistent friend is the illustration Jesus gives of how the heavenly Father will appear in times of spiritual confusion—as a man who does not care for his friends. We are in need, or our friends or our families are in need, and though we go to God who has been our friend all through, He does nothing at all. It is as if Jesus said to His disciples, "There are times when the heavenly Father will look like that, but don't give up, remember I have told you, 'Everyone who asks receives.'" In the meantime the friendship of God is completely shrouded. There are things that have no explanation, but maintain your relationship to God, "hang in" in confidence in Him, and the time will come when everything will be explained. It is only by going through the confusion that we shall get at what God wants us to get at. . . .

Jesus said, "Everyone who asks receives." We say, "I have asked but I have not received." It is because we ask in spiritual confusion. Jesus said to James and John: "You do not know what you ask"; they were brought into fellowship with Jesus Christ's cup and baptism, but not in the way they expected.

(PLACE HELP)

JOSHUA 13:1—14:15

NOW Joshua was old, advanced in years. And the LORD said to him: "You are old, advanced in years, and there remains very much land yet to be possessed. 2 This is the land that yet remains: all the territory of the Philistines and all *that of* the Geshurites, 3 from Sihor, which *is* east of Egypt, as far as the border of Ekron northward (*which* is counted as Canaanite); the five lords of the Philistines—the Gazites, the Ashdodites, the Ashkelonites, the Gittites, and the Ekronites; also the Avites; 4 from the south, all the land of the Canaanites, and Mearah that belongs to the Sidonians as far as Aphek, to the border of the Amorites; 5 the land of the Gebalites, and all Lebanon, toward the sunrise, from Baal Gad below Mount Hermon as far as the entrance to Hamath; 6 all the inhabitants of the mountains from Lebanon as far as the Brook Misrephoth, *and* all the Sidonians—them I will drive out from before the children of Israel; only divide it by lot to Israel as an inheritance, as I have commanded you. 7 Now therefore, divide this land as an inheritance to the nine tribes and half the tribe of Manasseh."

8 With the other half-tribe the Reubenites and the Gadites received their inheritance, which Moses had given them, beyond the Jordan eastward, as Moses the servant of the LORD had given them: 9 from Aroer which *is* on the bank of the River Arnon, and the town that *is* in the midst of the ravine, and all the plain of Medeba as far as Dibon; 10 all the cities of Sihon king of the Amorites, who reigned in Heshbon, as far as the border of the children of Ammon; 11 Gilead, and the border of the Geshurites and Maachathites, all Mount Hermon, and all Bashan as far as Salcah; 12 all the kingdom of Og in Bashan, who reigned in Ashtaroth and Edrei, who remained of the remnant of the giants; for Moses had defeated and cast out these.

13 Nevertheless the children of Israel did not drive out the Geshurites or the Maachathites, but the Geshurites and the Maachathites dwell among the Israelites until this day.

14 Only to the tribe of Levi he had given no inheritance; the sacrifices of the LORD God of Israel made by fire *are* their inheritance, as He said to them.

15 And Moses had given to the tribe of the children of Reuben *an inheritance* according to their families. 16 Their territory was from Aroer, which *is* on the bank of the River Arnon, and the city that *is* in the midst of the ravine, and all the plain by Medeba; 17 Heshbon and all its cities

that *are* in the plain: Dibon, Bamoth Baal, Beth Baal Meon, 18 Jahaza, Kedemoth, Mephaath, 19 Kirjathaim, Sibmah, Zereth Shahar on the mountain of the valley, 20 Beth Peor, the slopes of Pisgah, and Beth Jeshimoth— 21 all the cities of the plain and all the kingdom of Sihon king of the Amorites, who reigned in Heshbon, whom Moses had struck with the princes of Midian: Evi, Rekem, Zur, Hur, and Reba, who *were* princes of Sihon dwelling in the country. 22 The children of Israel also killed with the sword Balaam the son of Beor, the soothsayer, among those who were killed by them. 23 And the border of the children of Reuben was the bank of the Jordan. This *was* the inheritance of the children of Reuben according to their families, the cities and their villages.

24 Moses also had given *an inheritance* to the tribe of Gad, to the children of Gad according to their families. 25 Their territory was Jazer, and all the cities of Gilead, and half the land of the Ammonites as far as Aroer, which *is* before Rabbah, 26 and from Heshbon to Ramath Mizpah and Betonim, and from Mahanaim to the border of Debir, 27 and in the valley Beth Haram, Beth Nimrah, Succoth, and Zaphon, the rest of the kingdom of Sihon king of Heshbon, with the Jordan as *its* border, as far as the edge of the Sea of Chinnereth, on the other side of the Jordan eastward. 28 This *is* the inheritance of the children of Gad according to their families, the cities and their villages.

29 Moses also had given *an inheritance* to half the tribe of Manasseh; it was for half the tribe of the children of Manasseh according to their families: 30 Their territory was from Mahanaim, all Bashan, all the kingdom of Og king of Bashan, and all the towns of Jair which are in Bashan, sixty cities; 31 half of Gilead, and Ashtaroth and Edrei, cities of the kingdom of Og in Bashan, *were* for the children of Machir the son of Manasseh, for half of the children of Machir according to their families.

32 These *are the areas* which Moses had distributed as an inheritance in the plains of Moab on the other side of the Jordan, by Jericho eastward. 33 But to the tribe of Levi Moses had given no inheritance; the LORD God of Israel *was* their inheritance, as He had said to them.

14 THESE *are the areas* which the children of Israel inherited in the land of Canaan, which Eleazar the priest, Joshua the son of Nun, and the heads of the fathers

of the tribes of the children of Israel distributed as an inheritance to them. 2 Their inheritance *was* by lot, as the LORD had commanded by the hand of Moses, for the nine tribes and the half-tribe. 3 For Moses had given the inheritance of the two tribes and the half-tribe on the other side of the Jordan; but to the Levites he had given no inheritance among them. 4 For the children of Joseph were two tribes: Manasseh and Ephraim. And they gave no part to the Levites in the land, except cities to dwell *in,* with their common-lands for their livestock and their property. 5 As the LORD had commanded Moses, so the children of Israel did; and they divided the land.

6 Then the children of Judah came to Joshua in Gilgal. And Caleb the son of Jephunneh the Kenizzite said to him: "You know the word which the LORD said to Moses the man of God concerning you and me in Kadesh Barnea. 7 I *was* forty years old when Moses the servant of the LORD sent me from Kadesh Barnea to spy out the land, and I brought back word to him as *it was* in my heart. 8 Nevertheless my brethren who went up with me made the heart of the people melt, but I wholly followed the LORD my God. 9 So Moses swore on that day, saying, 'Surely the land where your foot has trodden shall be your inheritance and your children's forever, because you have wholly followed the LORD my God.' 10 And now, behold, the LORD has kept me alive, as He said, these forty-five years, ever since the LORD spoke this word to Moses while Israel wandered in the wilderness; and now, here I am this day, eighty-five years old. 11 As yet I *am as* strong this day as on the day that Moses sent me; just as my strength *was* then, so now *is* my strength for war, both for going out and for coming in. 12 Now therefore, give me this mountain of which the LORD spoke in that day; for you heard in that day how the Anakim *were* there, and *that* the cities *were* great *and* fortified. It may be that the LORD *will be* with me, and I shall be able to drive them out as the LORD said."

13 And Joshua blessed him, and gave Hebron to Caleb the son of Jephunneh as an inheritance. 14 Hebron therefore became the inheritance of Caleb the son of Jephunneh the Kenizzite to this day, because he wholly followed the LORD God of Israel. 15 And the name of Hebron formerly was Kirjath Arba (*Arba was* the greatest man among the Anakim).

Then the land had rest from war.

PSALM 44:20–26

20 IF we had forgotten the name of our
     God,
       Or stretched out our hands to a foreign
       god,
21 Would not God search this out?
       For He knows the secrets of the heart.
22 Yet for Your sake we are killed all day
     long;
       We are accounted as sheep for the
       slaughter.

23 Awake! Why do You sleep, O Lord?
       Arise! Do not cast *us* off forever.
24 Why do You hide Your face,
       And forget our affliction and our
       oppression?
25 For our soul is bowed down to the
     dust;
       Our body clings to the ground.
26 Arise for our help,
       And redeem us for Your mercies' sake.

PROVERBS 14:3

3 IN the mouth of a fool *is* a rod of pride,
     But the lips of the wise will preserve
     them.

LUKE 11:1–28

NOW it came to pass, as He was praying
in a certain place, when He ceased, *that*
one of His disciples said to Him, "Lord,
teach us to pray, as John also taught his
disciples."

*T*he key to all our work for God
is in that one word . . .
"Pray." (ASK)

2 So He said to them, "When you pray,
say:

       Our Father in heaven,
       Hallowed be Your name.
       Your kingdom come.
       Your will be done
       On earth as *it is* in heaven.
3   Give us day by day our daily bread.
4   And forgive us our sins,
       For we also forgive everyone who
       is indebted to us.
       And do not lead us into temptation,
       But deliver us from the evil one."

5 And He said to them, "Which of you
shall have a friend, and go to him at midnight and say to him, 'Friend, lend me three
loaves; 6 for a friend of mine has come to
me on his journey, and I have nothing to
set before him'; 7 and he will answer from
within and say, 'Do not trouble me; the
door is now shut, and my children are with
me in bed; I cannot rise and give to you'?
8 I say to you, though he will not rise and
give to him because he is his friend, yet
because of his persistence he will rise and
give him as many as he needs.

9 "So I say to you, ask, and it will be
given to you; seek, and you will find; knock,
and it will be opened to you. 10 For everyone who asks receives, and he who seeks
finds, and to him who knocks it will be
opened. 11 If a son asks for bread from any
father among you, will he give him a stone?
Or if *he asks* for a fish, will he give him a
serpent instead of a fish? 12 Or if he asks
for an egg, will he offer him a scorpion?
13 If you then, being evil, know how to
give good gifts to your children, how
much more will *your* heavenly Father
give the Holy Spirit to those who ask
Him!"

14 And He was casting out a demon, and
it was mute. So it was, when the demon
had gone out, that the mute spoke; and
the multitudes marveled. 15 But some of
them said, "He casts out demons by Beelzebub, the ruler of the demons."

16 Others, testing *Him,* sought from Him
a sign from heaven. 17 But He, knowing
their thoughts, said to them: "Every kingdom divided against itself is brought to desolation, and a house *divided* against a house
falls. 18 If Satan also is divided against himself, how will his kingdom stand? Because
you say I cast out demons by Beelzebub.
19 And if I cast out demons by Beelzebub,
by whom do your sons cast *them* out? Therefore they will be your judges. 20 But if I
cast out demons with the finger of God,
surely the kingdom of God has come upon
you. 21 When a strong man, fully armed,
guards his own palace, his goods are in
peace. 22 But when a stronger than he comes
upon him and overcomes him, he takes from
him all his armor in which he trusted, and
divides his spoils. 23 He who is not with
Me is against Me, and he who does not
gather with Me scatters.

24 "When an unclean spirit goes out of
a man, he goes through dry places, seeking
rest; and finding none, he says, 'I will return
to my house from which I came.' 25 And
when he comes, he finds *it* swept and put
in order. 26 Then he goes and takes with

him seven other spirits more wicked than himself, and they enter and dwell there; and the last *state* of that man is worse than the first."

27 And it happened, as He spoke these things, that a certain woman from the crowd raised her voice and said to Him, "Blessed *is* the womb that bore You, and *the* breasts which nursed You!"

28 But He said, "More than that, blessed *are* those who hear the word of God and keep it!"

◆◆◆

Reading 103—The Rugged Words of Jesus
Luke 11:46–52

Jesus Christ said He always spoke as His Father wished Him to. Did His Father write out the words and tell Him to learn them by heart? No, the mainspring of the heart of Jesus Christ was the mainspring of the heart of God the Father; consequently, the words Jesus Christ spoke were the exact expression of God's thought. In our Lord the tongue was in its right place; He never spoke from His head, but always from His heart. "If anyone among you thinks he is religious, and does not bridle his tongue . . . this one's religion *is* useless" (James 1:26), there is nothing in it. The tongue and the brain are under our control, not God's. . . .

Speaking from the heart does not mean refinement of speech merely; sometimes Jesus Christ's speech sounded anything but nice to natural ears, for example, Matthew 22. Some of the words He used, and some applications He made of His truth were terrible and rugged. . . . Jesus Christ did not speak as a man there. He spoke as the Master of men, with an absolute knowledge of what the human heart is like. That is why He so continually pleads with us to hand the keeping of our hearts over to Him.   (BIB. PSYCH.)

JOSHUA 15:1—16:10

SO *this* was the lot of the tribe of the children of Judah according to their families:

The border of Edom at the Wilderness of Zin southward *was* the extreme southern boundary. 2 And their southern border began at the shore of the Salt Sea, from the bay that faces southward. 3 Then it went out to the southern side of the Ascent of Akrabbim, passed along to Zin, ascended on the south side of Kadesh Barnea, passed along to Hezron, went up to Adar, and went around to Karkaa. 4 *From there* it passed toward Azmon and went out to the Brook of Egypt; and the border ended at the sea. This shall be your southern border.

5 The east border *was* the Salt Sea as far as the mouth of the Jordan.

And the border on the northern quarter *began* at the bay of the sea at the mouth of the Jordan. 6 The border went up to Beth Hoglah and passed north of Beth Arabah; and the border went up to the stone of Bohan the son of Reuben. 7 Then the border went up toward Debir from the Valley of Achor, and it turned northward toward Gilgal, which *is* before the Ascent of Adummim, which *is* on the south side of the valley. The border continued toward the waters of En Shemesh and ended at En Rogel. 8 And the border went up by the Valley of the Son of Hinnom to the southern slope of the Jebusite *city* (which *is* Jerusalem). The border went up to the top of the mountain that *lies* before the Valley of Hinnom westward, which *is* at the end of the Valley of Rephaim northward. 9 Then the border went around from the top of the hill to the fountain of the water of Nephtoah, and extended to the cities of Mount Ephron. And the border went around to Baalah (which *is* Kirjath Jearim). 10 Then the border turned westward from Baalah to Mount Seir, passed along to the side of Mount Jearim on the north (which *is* Chesalon), went down to Beth Shemesh, and passed on to Timnah.

11 And the border went out to the side of Ekron northward. Then the border went around to Shicron, passed along to Mount Baalah, and extended to Jabneel; and the border ended at the sea.

12 The west border *was* the coastline of the Great Sea. This *is* the boundary of the children of Judah all around according to their families.

13 Now to Caleb the son of Jephunneh he gave a share among the children of Judah, according to the commandment of the LORD to Joshua, *namely,* Kirjath Arba, which *is* Hebron (*Arba was* the father of Anak). 14 Caleb drove out the three sons of Anak from there: Sheshai, Ahiman, and Talmai, the children of Anak. 15 Then he went up from there to the inhabitants of Debir (formerly the name of Debir *was* Kirjath Sepher).

16 And Caleb said, "He who attacks Kirjath Sepher and takes it, to him I will give Achsah my daughter as wife." 17 So Othniel the son of Kenaz, the brother of Caleb, took it; and he gave him Achsah his daughter as wife. 18 Now it was so, when she came *to him,* that she persuaded him to ask her father for a field. So she dismounted from *her* donkey, and Caleb said to her, "What do you wish?" 19 She answered, "Give me a blessing; since you have given me land in the South, give me also springs of water." So he gave her the upper springs and the lower springs.

20 This *was* the inheritance of the tribe of the children of Judah according to their families:

21 The cities at the limits of the tribe of the children of Judah, toward the border of Edom in the South, were Kabzeel, Eder, Jagur, 22 Kinah, Dimonah, Adadah, 23 Kedesh, Hazor, Ithnan, 24 Ziph, Telem, Bealoth, 25 Hazor, Hadattah, Kerioth, Hezron (which *is* Hazor), 26 Amam, Shema, Moladah, 27 Hazar Gaddah, Heshmon, Beth Pelet, 28 Hazar Shual, Beersheba, Bizjothjah, 29 Baalah, Ijim, Ezem, 30 Eltolad, Chesil, Hormah, 31 Ziklag, Madmannah, Sansannah, 32 Lebaoth, Shilhim, Ain, and Rimmon: all the cities *are* twenty-nine, with their villages.

33 In the lowland: Eshtaol, Zorah, Ashnah, 34 Zanoah, En Gannim, Tappuah, Enam, 35 Jarmuth, Adullam, Socoh, Azekah, 36 Sharaim, Adithaim, Gederah, and Gederothaim: fourteen cities with their villages; 37 Zenan, Hadashah, Migdal Gad, 38 Dilean, Mizpah, Joktheel, 39 Lachish, Bozkath, Eglon, 40 Cabbon, Lahmas, Kithlish, 41 Gederoth, Beth Dagon, Naamah,

and Makkedah: sixteen cities with their villages; 42 Libnah, Ether, Ashan, 43 Jiphtah, Ashnah, Nezib, 44 Keilah, Achzib, and Mareshah: nine cities with their villages; 45 Ekron, with its towns and villages; 46 from Ekron to the sea, all that *lay* near Ashdod, with their villages; 47 Ashdod with its towns and villages, Gaza with its towns and villages—as far as the Brook of Egypt and the Great Sea with *its* coastline.

48 And in the mountain country: Shamir, Jattir, Sochoh, 49 Dannah, Kirjath Sannah (which *is* Debir), 50 Anab, Eshtemoh, Anim, 51 Goshen, Holon, and Giloh: eleven cities with their villages; 52 Arab, Dumah, Eshean, 53 Janum, Beth Tappuah, Aphekah, 54 Humtah, Kirjath Arba (which *is* Hebron), and Zior: nine cities with their villages; 55 Maon, Carmel, Ziph, Juttah, 56 Jezreel, Jokdeam, Zanoah, 57 Kain, Gibeah, and Timnah: ten cities with their villages; 58 Halhul, Beth Zur, Gedor, 59 Maarath, Beth Anoth, and Eltekon: six cities with their villages; 60 Kirjath Baal (which *is* Kirjath Jearim) and Rabbah: two cities with their villages.

61 In the wilderness: Beth Arabah, Middin, Secacah, 62 Nibshan, the City of Salt, and En Gedi: six cities with their villages.

63 As for the Jebusites, the inhabitants of Jerusalem, the children of Judah could not drive them out; but the Jebusites dwell with the children of Judah at Jerusalem to this day.

16 THE lot fell to the children of Joseph from the Jordan, by Jericho, to the waters of Jericho on the east, to the wilderness that goes up from Jericho through the mountains to Bethel, 2 then went out from Bethel to Luz, passed along to the border of the Archites at Ataroth, 3 and went down westward to the boundary of the Japhletites, as far as the boundary of Lower Beth Horon to Gezer; and it ended at the sea.

4 So the children of Joseph, Manasseh and Ephraim, took their inheritance.

5 The border of the children of Ephraim, according to their families, was *thus:* The border of their inheritance on the east side was Ataroth Addar as far as Upper Beth Horon.

6 And the border went out toward the sea on the north side of Michmethath; then the border went around eastward to Taanath Shiloh, and passed by it on the east of Janoah. 7 Then it went down from Janohah to Ataroth and Naarah, reached to Jericho, and came out at the Jordan.

8 The border went out from Tappuah

westward to the Brook Kanah, and it ended at the sea. This *was* the inheritance of the tribe of the children of Ephraim according to their families. 9 The separate cities for the children of Ephraim *were* among the inheritance of the children of Manasseh, all the cities with their villages.

10 And they did not drive out the Canaanites who dwelt in Gezer; but the Canaanites dwell among the Ephraimites to this day and have become forced laborers.

PSALM 45:1–5

1 MY heart is overflowing with a good theme;
    I recite my composition concerning the King;
    My tongue *is* the pen of a ready writer.

2 You are fairer than the sons of men;
    Grace is poured upon Your lips;
    Therefore God has blessed You forever.

3 Gird Your sword upon *Your* thigh,
      O Mighty One,
    With Your glory and Your majesty.

4 And in Your majesty ride prosperously
      because of truth, humility, *and* righteousness;
    And Your right hand shall teach You awesome things.

5 Your arrows *are* sharp in the heart of the King's enemies;
    The peoples fall under You.

PROVERBS 14:4, 5

4 WHERE no oxen *are*, the trough *is* clean;
    But much increase *comes* by the strength of an ox.

5 A faithful witness does not lie,
    But a false witness will utter lies.

LUKE 11:29–54

29 AND while the crowds were thickly gathered together, He began to say, "This is an evil generation. It seeks a sign, and no sign will be given to it except the sign of Jonah the prophet. 30 For as Jonah became a sign to the Ninevites, so also the Son of Man will be to this generation. 31 The queen of the South will rise up in the judgment with the men of this generation and condemn them, for she came from the ends of the earth to hear the wisdom

of Solomon; and indeed a greater than Solomon *is* here. 32 The men of Nineveh will rise up in the judgment with this generation and condemn it, for they repented at the preaching of Jonah; and indeed a greater than Jonah *is* here.

33 "No one, when he has lit a lamp, puts *it* in a secret place or under a basket, but on a lampstand, that those who come in may see the light. 34 The lamp of the body is the eye. Therefore, when your eye is good, your whole body also is full of light. But when *your eye* is bad, your body also *is* full of darkness. 35 Therefore take heed that the

---

If you do not obey the light, it will turn into darkness.   (UTMOST)

---

light which is in you is not darkness. 36 If then your whole body *is* full of light, having no part dark, *the* whole *body* will be full of light, as when the bright shining of a lamp gives you light."

37 And as He spoke, a certain Pharisee asked Him to dine with him. So He went in and sat down to eat. 38 When the Pharisee saw *it,* he marveled that He had not first washed before dinner.

39 Then the Lord said to him, "Now you Pharisees make the outside of the cup and dish clean, but your inward part is full of greed and wickedness. 40 Foolish ones! Did not He who made the outside make the inside also? 41 But rather give alms of such things as you have; then indeed all things are clean to you.

42 "But woe to you Pharisees! For you tithe mint and rue and all manner of herbs, and pass by justice and the love of God. These you ought to have done, without leaving the others undone. 43 Woe to you Pharisees! For you love the best seats in the synagogues and greetings in the marketplaces. 44 Woe to you, scribes and Pharisees, hypocrites! For you are like graves which are not seen, and the men who walk over *them* are not aware *of them.*"

45 Then one of the lawyers answered and said to Him, "Teacher, by saying these things You reproach us also."

46 And He said, "Woe to you also, lawyers! For you load men with burdens hard to bear, and you yourselves do not touch the burdens with one of your fingers. 47 Woe to you! For you build the tombs of the prophets, and your fathers killed them. 48 In fact, you bear witness that you approve the deeds of your fathers; for they indeed killed them, and you build their

tombs. 49 Therefore the wisdom of God also said, 'I will send them prophets and apostles, and *some* of them they will kill and persecute,' 50 that the blood of all the prophets which was shed from the foundation of the world may be required of this generation, 51 from the blood of Abel to the blood of Zechariah who perished between the altar and the temple. Yes, I say to you, it shall be required of this generation.

52 "Woe to you lawyers! For you have taken away the key of knowledge. You did not enter in yourselves, and those who were entering in you hindered."

53 And as He said these things to them, the scribes and the Pharisees began to assail *Him* vehemently, and to cross-examine Him about many things, 54 lying in wait for Him, and seeking to catch Him in something He might say, that they might accuse Him.

◆◆◆◆

Reading 104—Beware of Covetousness
Luke 12:15

The thing about our Lord and His teaching which puts Him immeasurably away from us nowadays is that He is opposed to all possessions, not only of money and property, but any kind of possession. That is the thing that makes Him such a deep-rooted enemy to the modern attitude to things. . . .

Jesus Christ nowhere stands with the anti-property league. It is an easy business for me to mentally satirize the man who owns land and money when I don't. . . . It may be hard for a rich man to enter into the kingdom of heaven, but it is just as hard for a poor man to seek first the kingdom of God. It is not eternal perdition, it is the perdition of losing the soul for this life. Jesus thought as much of the possibility of losing the highest good through poverty as through riches. His own followers were poor, yet He said to them, "Seek first"—bread and cheese? money? a new situation? clothing? food? No, "the kingdom of God and His righteousness, and all these things shall be added to you." Did He know what He was talking about, this poor Carpenter who had not a pillow of His own and never enough money to pay a night's lodging and yet spoke like that, and who also said that "the cares of this world, the deceitfulness of riches, and the desires for other things entering in choke the word, and it becomes unfruitful"?   (*Good*)

JOSHUA 17:1—18:28

THERE was also a lot for the tribe of Manasseh, for he *was* the firstborn of Joseph: *namely* for Machir the firstborn of Manasseh, the father of Gilead, because he was a man of war; therefore he was given Gilead and Bashan. 2 And there was *a lot* for the rest of the children of Manasseh according to their families: for the children of Abiezer, the children of Helek, the children of Asriel, the children of Shechem, the children of Hepher, and the children of Shemida; these *were* the male children of Manasseh the son of Joseph according to their families.

3 But Zelophehad the son of Hepher, the son of Gilead, the son of Machir, the son of Manasseh, had no sons, but only daughters. And these *are* the names of his daughters: Mahlah, Noah, Hoglah, Milcah, and Tirzah. 4 And they came near before Eleazar the priest, before Joshua the son of Nun, and before the rulers, saying, "The LORD commanded Moses to give us an inheritance among our brothers." Therefore, according to the commandment of the LORD, he gave them an inheritance among their father's brothers. 5 Ten shares fell to Manasseh, besides the land of Gilead and Bashan, which *were* on the other side of the Jordan, 6 because the daughters of Manasseh re-

ceived an inheritance among his sons; and the rest of Manasseh's sons had the land of Gilead.

7 And the territory of Manasseh was from Asher to Michmethath, that *lies* east of Shechem; and the border went along south to the inhabitants of En Tappuah. 8 Manasseh had the land of Tappuah, but Tappuah on the border of Manasseh *belonged* to the children of Ephraim. 9 And the border descended to the Brook Kanah, southward to the brook. These cities of Ephraim *are* among the cities of Manasseh. The border of Manasseh *was* on the north side of the brook; and it ended at the sea. 10 Southward *it was* Ephraim's, northward *it was* Manasseh's, and the sea was its border. Manasseh's territory was adjoining Asher on the north and Issachar on the east. 11 And in Issachar and in Asher, Manasseh had Beth Shean and its towns, Ibleam and its towns, the inhabitants of Dor and its towns, the inhabitants of En Dor and its towns, the inhabitants of Taanach and its towns, and the inhabitants of Megiddo and its towns—three hilly regions. 12 Yet the children of Manasseh could not drive out *the inhabitants of* those cities, but the Canaanites were determined to dwell in that land. 13 And it happened, when the children of Israel grew strong, that they put the Canaanites to forced labor, but did not utterly drive them out.

14 Then the children of Joseph spoke to Joshua, saying, "Why have you given us *only* one lot and one share to inherit, since we *are* a great people, inasmuch as the LORD has blessed us until now?"

15 So Joshua answered them, "If you *are* a great people, *then* go up to the forest *country* and clear a place for yourself there in the land of the Perizzites and the giants, since the mountains of Ephraim are too confined for you."

16 But the children of Joseph said, "The mountain country is not enough for us; and all the Canaanites who dwell in the land of the valley have chariots of iron, *both those* who *are* of Beth Shean and its towns and *those* who *are* of the Valley of Jezreel."

17 And Joshua spoke to the house of Joseph—to Ephraim and Manasseh—saying, "You *are* a great people and have great power; you shall not have *only* one lot, 18 but the mountain country shall be yours. Although it *is* wooded, you shall cut it down, and its farthest extent shall be yours; for you shall drive out the Canaanites, though they have iron chariots *and* are strong."

18 NOW the whole congregation of the children of Israel assembled together at Shiloh, and set up the tabernacle of meeting there. And the land was subdued before them. 2 But there remained among the children of Israel seven tribes which had not yet received their inheritance.

3 Then Joshua said to the children of Israel: "How long will you neglect to go and possess the land which the LORD God of your fathers has given you? 4 Pick out from among you three men for *each* tribe, and I will send them; they shall rise and go through the land, survey it according to their inheritance, and come *back* to me. 5 And they shall divide it into seven parts. Judah shall remain in their territory on the south, and the house of Joseph shall remain in their territory on the north. 6 You shall therefore survey the land in seven parts and bring *the survey* here to me, that I may cast lots for you here before the LORD our God. 7 But the Levites have no part among you, for the priesthood of the LORD *is* their inheritance. And Gad, Reuben, and half the tribe of Manasseh have received their inheritance beyond the Jordan on the east, which Moses the servant of the LORD gave them."

8 Then the men arose to go away; and Joshua charged those who went to survey the land, saying, "Go, walk through the land, survey it, and come back to me, that I may cast lots for you here before the LORD in Shiloh." 9 So the men went, passed through the land, and wrote the survey in a book in seven parts by cities; and they came to Joshua at the camp in Shiloh. 10 Then Joshua cast lots for them in Shiloh before the LORD, and there Joshua divided the land to the children of Israel according to their divisions.

11 Now the lot of the tribe of the children of Benjamin came up according to their families, and the territory of their lot came out between the children of Judah and the children of Joseph. 12 Their border on the north side began at the Jordan, and the border went up to the side of Jericho on the north, and went up through the mountains westward; it ended at the Wilderness of Beth Aven. 13 The border went over from there toward Luz, to the side of Luz (which *is* Bethel) southward; and the border descended to Ataroth Addar, near the hill that *lies* on the south side of Lower Beth Horon.

14 Then the border extended around the west side to the south, from the hill that *lies* before Beth Horon southward; and it ended at Kirjath Baal (which *is* Kirjath Jearim), a city of the children of Judah. This *was* the west side.

15 The south side *began* at the end of Kirjath Jearim, and the border extended on the west and went out to the spring of the waters of Nephtoah. 16 Then the border came down to the end of the mountain that *lies* before the Valley of the Son of Hinnom, which *is* in the Valley of the Rephaim on the north, descended to the Valley of Hinnom, to the side of the Jebusite *city* on the south, and descended to En Rogel. 17 And it went around from the north, went out to En Shemesh, and extended toward Geliloth, which is before the Ascent of Adummim, and descended to the stone of Bohan the son of Reuben. 18 Then it passed along toward the north side of Arabah, and went down to Arabah. 19 And the border passed along to the north side of Beth Hoglah; then the border ended at the north bay at the Salt Sea, at the south end of the Jordan. This *was* the southern boundary.

20 The Jordan was its border on the east side. This *was* the inheritance of the children of Benjamin, according to its boundaries all around, according to their families.

21 Now the cities of the tribe of the children of Benjamin, according to their families, were Jericho, Beth Hoglah, Emek Keziz, 22 Beth Arabah, Zemaraim, Bethel, 23 Avim, Parah, Ophrah, 24 Chephar Haammoni, Ophni, and Gaba: twelve cities with their villages; 25 Gibeon, Ramah, Beeroth, 26 Mizpah, Chephirah, Mozah, 27 Rekem, Irpeel, Taralah, 28 Zelah, Eleph, Jebus (which *is* Jerusalem), Gibeath, *and* Kirjath: fourteen cities with their villages. This was the inheritance of the children of Benjamin according to their families.

PSALM 45:6–17

6 YOUR throne, O God, *is* forever and ever;
A scepter of righteousness *is* the scepter of Your kingdom.
7 You love righteousness and hate wickedness;
Therefore God, Your God, has anointed You
With the oil of gladness more than Your companions.
8 All Your garments are scented with myrrh and aloes *and* cassia,
Out of the ivory palaces, by which they have made You glad.
9 Kings' daughters *are* among Your honorable women;
At Your right hand stands the queen in gold from Ophir.

10 Listen, O daughter,
Consider and incline your ear;
Forget your own people also, and your father's house;
11 So the King will greatly desire your beauty;
Because He *is* your Lord, worship Him.
12 And the daughter of Tyre *will come* with a gift;
The rich among the people will seek your favor.

13 The royal daughter *is* all glorious within *the palace*;
Her clothing *is* woven with gold.
14 She shall be brought to the King in robes of many colors;
The virgins, her companions who follow her, shall be brought to You.
15 With gladness and rejoicing they shall be brought;
They shall enter the King's palace.

16 Instead of Your fathers shall be Your sons,
Whom You shall make princes in all the earth.
17 I will make Your name to be remembered in all generations;
Therefore the people shall praise You forever and ever.

PROVERBS 14:6

6 A scoffer seeks wisdom and does not *find it*,
But knowledge *is* easy to him who understands.

LUKE 12:1–31

IN the meantime, when an innumerable multitude of people had gathered together, so that they trampled one another, He began to say to His disciples first *of all*, "Beware of the leaven of the Pharisees, which is hypocrisy. 2 For there is nothing covered that will not be revealed, nor hidden that will not be known. 3 Therefore whatever you have spoken in the dark will be heard in the light, and what you have spoken in the ear in inner rooms will be proclaimed on the housetops.

4 "And I say to you, My friends, do not be afraid of those who kill the body, and after that have no more that they can do. 5 But I will show you whom you should fear: Fear Him who, after He has killed,

has power to cast into hell; yes, I say to you, fear Him!

6 "Are not five sparrows sold for two copper coins? And not one of them is forgotten before God. 7 But the very hairs of your head are all numbered. Do not fear therefore; you are of more value than many sparrows.

8 "Also I say to you, whoever confesses Me before men, him the Son of Man also will confess before the angels of God. 9 But he who denies Me before men will be denied before the angels of God.

10 "And anyone who speaks a word against the Son of Man, it will be forgiven him; but to him who blasphemes against the Holy Spirit, it will not be forgiven. 11 "Now when they bring you to the synagogues and magistrates and authorities, do not worry about how or what you should answer, or what you should say. 12 For the Holy Spirit will teach you in that very hour what you ought to say."

13 Then one from the crowd said to Him, "Teacher, tell my brother to divide the inheritance with me."

14 But He said to him, "Man, who made Me a judge or an arbitrator over you?" 15 And He said to them, "Take heed and beware of covetousness, for one's life does not consist in the abundance of the things he possesses."

16 Then He spoke a parable to them, saying: "The ground of a certain rich man yielded plentifully. 17 And he thought within himself, saying, 'What shall I do, since I have no room to store my crops?' 18 So he said, 'I will do this: I will pull down my barns and build greater, and there I will store all my crops and my goods. 19 And I will say to my soul, "Soul, you have many goods laid up for many years;

take your ease; eat, drink, *and* be merry." ' 20 But God said to him, 'Fool! This night your soul will be required of you; then whose will those things be which you have provided?'

21 "So *is* he who lays up treasure for himself, and is not rich toward God."

22 Then He said to His disciples, "Therefore I say to you, do not worry about your life, what you will eat; nor about the body, what you will put on. 23 Life is more than food, and the body *is more* than clothing. 24 Consider the ravens, for they neither sow nor reap, which have neither storehouse nor barn; and God feeds them. Of how much more value are you than the birds? 25 And which of you by worrying can add one cubit to his stature? 26 If you then are not able to do *the* least, why are you anxious for the rest? 27 Consider the lilies, how they grow: they neither toil nor spin; and yet I say to you, even Solomon in all his glory was not arrayed like one of these. 28 If then

---

*H*ow often do we look at clouds, or grass, at sparrows, or flowers? (BRILL. HERITAGE)

God so clothes the grass, which today is in the field and tomorrow is thrown into the oven, how much more *will He clothe* you, O *you* of little faith?

29 "And do not seek what you should eat or what you should drink, nor have an anxious mind. 30 For all these things the nations of the world seek after, and your Father knows that you need these things. 31 But seek the kingdom of God, and all these things shall be added to you.

◆◆◆◆

Reading 105—Our Devotion as Disciples
Luke 12:49

"**O**ur God *is* a consuming fire," and when God comes on to this earth in the effective working of the redemption of Jesus Christ, He brings pain and havoc and disaster (see Matt. 10:34). The first result of the redemption of Jesus Christ in human life is havoc. If any human life can stand before God on its own basis, Calvary is much ado about nothing. If it can be proved that rationalism is the basis of human life, then the New Testament is nonsense; instead of its being a revelation, it is a cunningly devised fable. There is no need for redemption; Jesus Christ is nothing but a martyr, of whom it was true that He was stricken, smitten of God and afflicted. If we can stand before God apart from Jesus Christ, we have proved that Calvary is not needed. As soon as Jesus Christ comes in, He produces havoc because the whole world system is arrayed against His redemption. It was the world system of His day, and particularly the religious system, that killed the Son of God. (*GLORY*)

JOSHUA 19:1—20:9

THE second lot came out for Simeon, for the tribe of the children of Simeon according to their families. And their inheritance was within the inheritance of the children of Judah. 2 They had in their inheritance Beersheba (Sheba), Moladah, 3 Hazar Shual, Balah, Ezem, 4 Eltolad, Bethul, Hormah, 5 Ziklag, Beth Marcaboth, Hazar Susah, 6 Beth Lebaoth, and Sharuhen: thirteen cities and their villages; 7 Ain, Rimmon, Ether, and Ashan: four cities and their villages; 8 and all the villages that *were* all around these cities as far as Baalath Beer, Ramah of the South. This *was* the inheritance of the tribe of the children of Simeon according to their families.

9 The inheritance of the children of Simeon *was included* in the share of the children of Judah, for the share of the children of Judah was too much for them. Therefore the children of Simeon had *their* inheritance within the inheritance of that people.

10 The third lot came out for the children of Zebulun according to their families, and the border of their inheritance was as far as Sarid. 11 Their border went toward the west and to Maralah, went to Dabbasheth, and extended along the brook that is east of Jokneam. 12 Then from Sarid it went eastward toward the sunrise along the border of Chisloth Tabor, and went out toward Daberath, bypassing Japhia. 13 And from there it passed along on the east of Gath Hepher, toward Eth Kazin, and extended to Rimmon, which borders on Neah. 14 Then the border went around it on the north side of Hannathon, and it ended in the Valley of Jiphthah El. 15 Included were Kattath, Nahallal, Shimron, Idalah, and Bethlehem: twelve cities with their villages. 16 This *was* the inheritance of the children of Zebulun according to their families, these cities with their villages.

17 The fourth lot came out to Issachar, for the children of Issachar according to their families. 18 And their territory went to Jezreel, and *included* Chesulloth, Shunem, 19 Haphraim, Shion, Anaharath, 20 Rabbith, Kishion, Abez, 21 Remeth, En Gannim, En Haddah, and Beth Pazzez. 22 And the border reached to Tabor, Shahazimah, and Beth Shemesh; their border ended at the Jordan: sixteen cities with their villages. 23 This *was* the inheritance of the tribe of the children of Issachar according to their families, the cities and their villages.

24 The fifth lot came out for the tribe of the children of Asher according to their families. 25 And their territory included Helkath, Hali, Beten, Achshaph, 26 Alammelech, Amad, and Mishal; it reached to Mount Carmel westward, along *the Brook* Shihor Libnath. 27 It turned toward the sunrise to Beth Dagon; and it reached to Zebulun and to the Valley of Jiphthah El, then northward beyond Beth Emek and Neiel, bypassing Cabul *which was* on the left, 28 including Ebron, Rehob, Hammon, and Kanah, as far as Greater Sidon. 29 And the border turned to Ramah and to the fortified city of Tyre; then the border turned to Hosah, and ended at the sea by the region of Achzib. 30 Also Ummah, Aphek, and Rehob *were included:* twenty-two cities with their villages. 31 This *was* the inheritance of the tribe of the children of Asher according to their families, these cities with their villages.

32 The sixth lot came out to the children of Naphtali, for the children of Naphtali according to their families. 33 And their border began at Heleph, enclosing the territory from the terebinth tree in Zaanannim, Adami Nekeb, and Jabneel, as far as Lakkum; it ended at the Jordan. 34 From Heleph the border extended westward to Aznoth Tabor, and went out from there toward Hukkok; it adjoined Zebulun on the south side and Asher on the west side, and ended at Judah by the Jordan toward the sunrise. 35 And the fortified cities *are* Ziddim, Zer, Hammath, Rakkath, Chinnereth, 36 Adamah, Ramah, Hazor, 37 Kedesh, Edrei, En Hazor, 38 Iron, Migdal El, Horem, Beth Anath, and Beth Shemesh: nineteen cities with their villages. 39 This *was* the inheritance of the tribe of the children of Naphtali according to their families, the cities and their villages.

40 The seventh lot came out for the tribe

of the children of Dan according to their families. 41 And the territory of their inheritance was Zorah, Eshtaol, Ir Shemesh, 42 Shaalabbin, Aijalon, Jethlah, 43 Elon, Timnah, Ekron, 44 Eltekeh, Gibbethon, Baalath, 45 Jehud, Bene Berak, Gath Rimmon, 46 Me Jarkon, and Rakkon, with the region near Joppa. 47 And the border of the children of Dan went beyond these, because the children of Dan went up to fight against Leshem and took it; and they struck it with the edge of the sword, took possession of it, and dwelt in it. They called Leshem, Dan, after the name of Dan their father. 48 This *is* the inheritance of the tribe of the children of Dan according to their families, these cities with their villages.

49 When they had made an end of dividing the land as an inheritance according to their borders, the children of Israel gave an inheritance among them to Joshua the son of Nun. 50 According to the word of the LORD they gave him the city which he asked for, Timnath Serah in the mountains of Ephraim; and he built the city and dwelt in it.

51 These *were* the inheritances which Eleazar the priest, Joshua the son of Nun, and the heads of the fathers of the tribes of the children of Israel divided as an inheritance by lot in Shiloh before the LORD, at the door of the tabernacle of meeting. So they made an end of dividing the country.

20 THE LORD also spoke to Joshua, saying, 2 "Speak to the children of Israel, saying: 'Appoint for yourselves cities of refuge, of which I spoke to you through Moses, 3 that the slayer who kills a person accidentally *or* unintentionally may flee there; and they shall be your refuge from the avenger of blood. 4 And when he flees to one of those cities, and stands at the entrance of the gate of the city, and declares his case in the hearing of the elders of that city, they shall take him into the city as one of them, and give him a place, that he may dwell among them. 5 Then if the avenger of blood pursues him, they shall not deliver the slayer into his hand, because he struck his neighbor unintentionally, but did not hate him beforehand. 6 And he shall dwell in that city until he stands before the congregation for judgment, *and* until the death of the one who is high priest in those days. Then the slayer may return and come to his own city and his own house, to the city from which he fled.' "

7 So they appointed Kedesh in Galilee, in the mountains of Naphtali, Shechem in the mountains of Ephraim, and Kirjath Arba (which *is* Hebron) in the mountains of Judah. 8 And on the other side of the Jordan, by Jericho eastward, they assigned Bezer in the wilderness on the plain, from the tribe of Reuben, Ramoth in Gilead, from the tribe of Gad, and Golan in Bashan, from the tribe of Manasseh. 9 These were the cities appointed for all the children of Israel and for the stranger who dwelt among them, that whoever killed a person accidentally might flee there, and not die by the hand of the avenger of blood until he stood before the congregation.

PSALM 46:1–6

1 GOD *is* our refuge and strength,
   A very present help in trouble.
2 Therefore we will not fear,
   Even though the earth be removed,
   And though the mountains be carried
      into the midst of the sea;
3 *Though* its waters roar *and* be troubled,
   Though the mountains shake with its
      swelling.   Selah

4 *There is* a river whose streams shall make
      glad the city of God,
   The holy *place* of the tabernacle of the
      Most High.
5 God *is* in the midst of her, she shall
      not be moved;
   God shall help her, just at the break
      of dawn.
6 The nations raged, the kingdoms were
      moved;
   He uttered His voice, the earth melted.

PROVERBS 14:7–11

7 GO from the presence of a foolish man,
   When you do not perceive *in him* the
      lips of knowledge.
8 The wisdom of the prudent *is* to
      understand his way,
   But the folly of fools *is* deceit.

9 Fools mock at sin,
   But among the upright *there is* favor.

10 The heart knows its own bitterness,
   And a stranger does not share its joy.

11 The house of the wicked will be
      overthrown,
   But the tent of the upright will flourish.

LUKE 12:32–59

"DO not fear, little flock, for it is your Father's good pleasure to give you the kingdom. 33 Sell what you have and give alms; provide yourselves money bags which do not grow old, a treasure in the heavens that does not fail, where no thief approaches nor moth destroys. 34 For where your treasure is, there your heart will be also.

35 "Let your waist be girded and *your* lamps burning; 36 and you yourselves be like men who wait for their master, when he will return from the wedding, that when he comes and knocks they may open to him immediately. 37 Blessed *are* those servants whom the master, when he comes, will find watching. Assuredly, I say to you that he will gird himself and have them sit down *to eat,* and will come and serve them. 38 And if he should come in the second watch, or come in the third watch, and find *them* so, blessed are those servants. 39 But know this, that if the master of the house had known what hour the thief would come, he would have watched and not allowed his house to be broken into. 40 Therefore you also be ready, for the Son of Man is coming at an hour you do not expect."

41 Then Peter said to Him, "Lord, do You speak this parable *only* to us, or to all *people?"*

42 And the Lord said, "Who then is that faithful and wise steward, whom *his* master will make ruler over his household, to give *them their* portion of food in due season? 43 Blessed *is* that servant whom his master will find so doing when he comes. 44 Truly, I say to you that he will make him ruler over all that he has. 45 But if that servant says in his heart, 'My master is delaying his coming,' and begins to beat the male and female servants, and to eat and drink and be drunk, 46 the master of that servant will come on a day when he is not looking for *him,* and at an hour when he is not aware, and will cut him in two and appoint *him* his portion with the unbelievers.

47 And that servant who knew his master's will, and did not prepare *himself* or do according to his will, shall be beaten with many *stripes.* 48 But he who did not know, yet committed things deserving of stripes, shall be beaten with few. For everyone to whom much is given, from him much will be required; and to whom much has been committed, of him they will ask the more.

49 "I came to send fire on the earth, and how I wish it were already kindled! 50 But I have a baptism to be baptized with, and how distressed I am till it is accomplished! 51 Do *you* suppose that I came to give peace on earth? I tell you, not at all, but rather division. 52 For from now on

---

*T*he coming of Jesus Christ is not a peaceful thing, it is a disturbing thing.   (PLACE HELP)

---

five in one house will be divided: three against two, and two against three. 53 Father will be divided against son and son against father, mother against daughter and daughter against mother, mother-in-law against her daughter-in-law and daughter-in-law against her mother-in-law."

54 Then He also said to the multitudes, "Whenever *you see* a cloud rising out of the west, immediately you say, 'A shower is coming'; and so it is. 55 And when you see the south wind blow, you say, 'There will be hot weather'; and there is. 56 Hypocrites! You can discern the face of the sky and of the earth, but how *is it* you do not discern this time?

57 "Yes, and why, even of yourselves, do you not judge what is right? 58 When you go with your adversary to the magistrate, make every effort along the way to settle with him, lest he drag you to the judge, the judge deliver you to the officer, and the officer throw you into prison. 59 I tell you, you shall not depart from there till you have paid the very last mite."

Reading 106—Spiritual Tenacity

Psalm 46:10

Tenacity is more than endurance, it is endurance combined with the absolute certainty that what we are looking for is going to transpire. Tenacity is more than hanging on, which may be but the weakness of being too afraid to fall off. Tenacity is the supreme effort of a man refusing to believe that his hero is going to be conquered. The greatest fear a man has is not that he will be damned, but that Jesus Christ will be worsted, that the things He stood for—love and justice and forgiveness and kindness among men—will not win out in the end; the things He stands for look like will-o'-the-wisps. Then comes the call to spiritual tenacity, not to hang on and do nothing, but to work deliberately on the certainty that God is not going to be worsted.

If our hopes are being disappointed just now, it means that they are being purified. There is nothing noble the human mind has ever hoped for or dreamed of that will not be fulfilled. One of the greatest strains in life is the strain of waiting for God. "Because you have kept My command to persevere."

Remain spiritually tenacious.   (UTMOST)

JOSHUA 21:1—22:34

THEN the heads of the fathers' *houses* of the Levites came near to Eleazar the priest, to Joshua the son of Nun, and to the heads of the fathers' *houses* of the tribes of the children of Israel. 2 And they spoke to them at Shiloh in the land of Canaan, saying, "The LORD commanded through Moses to give us cities to dwell in, with their common-lands for our livestock." 3 So the children of Israel gave to the Levites from their inheritance, at the commandment of the LORD, these cities and their common-lands:

4 Now the lot came out for the families of the Kohathites. And the children of Aaron the priest, *who were* of the Levites, had thirteen cities by lot from the tribe of Judah, from the tribe of Simeon, and from the tribe of Benjamin. 5 The rest of the children of Kohath had ten cities by lot from the families of the tribe of Ephraim, from the tribe of Dan, and from the half-tribe of Manasseh.

6 And the children of Gershon had thirteen cities by lot from the families of the tribe of Issachar, from the tribe of Asher, from the tribe of Naphtali, and from the half-tribe of Manasseh in Bashan.

7 The children of Merari according to their families had twelve cities from the tribe of Reuben, from the tribe of Gad, and from the tribe of Zebulun.

8 And the children of Israel gave these cities with their common-lands by lot to the Levites, as the LORD had commanded by the hand of Moses.

9 So they gave from the tribe of the children of Judah and from the tribe of the children of Simeon these cities which are designated by name, 10 which were for the children of Aaron, one of the families of the Kohathites, *who were* of the children of Levi; for the lot was theirs first. 11 And they gave them Kirjath Arba (*Arba was* the father of Anak), which *is* Hebron, in the mountains of Judah, with the common-land surrounding it. 12 But the fields of the city and its villages they gave to Caleb the son of Jephunneh as his possession.

13 Thus to the children of Aaron the priest they gave Hebron with its common-land (a city of refuge for the slayer), Libnah with its common-land, 14 Jattir with its common-land, Eshtemoa with its common-land, 15 Holon with its common-land, Debir with its common-land, 16 Ain with its common-land, Juttah with its common-land, and Beth Shemesh with its common-land: nine cities from those two tribes; 17 and from the tribe of Benjamin, Gibeon with its common-land, Geba with its common-land, 18 Anathoth with its common-land, and Almon with its common-land: four cities. 19 All the cities of the children of Aaron, the priests, *were* thirteen cities with their common-lands.

20 And the families of the children of Ko-

hath, the Levites, the rest of the children of Kohath, even they had the cities of their lot from the tribe of Ephraim. 21 For they gave them Shechem with its common-land in the mountains of Ephraim (a city of refuge for the slayer), Gezer with its common-land, 22 Kibzaim with its common-land, and Beth Horon with its common-land: four cities; 23 and from the tribe of Dan, Eltekeh with its common-land, Gibbethon with its common-land, 24 Aijalon with its common-land, *and* Gath Rimmon with its common-land: four cities; 25 and from the half-tribe of Manasseh, Tanach with its common-land and Gath Rimmon with its common-land: two cities. 26 All the ten cities with their common-lands were for the rest of the families of the children of Kohath.

27 Also to the children of Gershon, of the families of the Levites, from the *other* half-tribe of Manasseh, *they gave* Golan in Bashan with its common-land (a city of refuge for the slayer), and Be Eshterah with its common-land: two cities; 28 and from the tribe of Issachar, Kishion with its common-land, Daberath with its common-land, 29 Jarmuth with its common-land, *and* En Gannim with its common-land: four cities; 30 and from the tribe of Asher, Mishal with its common-land, Abdon with its common-land, 31 Helkath with its common-land, and Rehob with its common-land: four cities; 32 and from the tribe of Naphtali, Kedesh in Galilee with its common-land (a city of refuge for the slayer), Hammoth Dor with its common-land, and Kartan with its common-land: three cities. 33 All the cities of the Gershonites according to their families *were* thirteen cities with their common-lands.

34 And to the families of the children of Merari, the rest of the Levites, from the tribe of Zebulun, Jokneam with its common-land, Kartah with its common-land, 35 Dimnah with its common-land, *and* Nahalal with its common-land: four cities; 36 and from the tribe of Reuben, Bezer with its common-land, Jahaz with its common-land, 37 Kedemoth with its common-land, and Mephaath with its common-land: four cities; 38 and from the tribe of Gad, Ramoth in Gilead with its common-land (a city of refuge for the slayer), Mahanaim with its common-land, 39 Heshbon with its common-land, *and* Jazer with its common-land: four cities in all. 40 So all the cities for the children of Merari according to their families, the rest of the families of the Levites, were *by* their lot twelve cities.

41 All the cities of the Levites within the possession of the children of Israel *were* forty-eight cities with their common-lands. 42 Every one of these cities had its common-land surrounding it; thus *were* all these cities.

43 So the LORD gave to Israel all the land of which He had sworn to give to their fathers, and they took possession of it and dwelt in it. 44 The LORD gave them rest all around, according to all that He had sworn to their fathers. And not a man of all their enemies stood against them; the LORD delivered all their enemies into their hand. 45 Not a word failed of any good thing which the LORD had spoken to the house of Israel. All came to pass.

22 THEN Joshua called the Reubenites, the Gadites, and half the tribe of Manasseh, 2 and said to them: "You have kept all that Moses the servant of the LORD commanded you, and have obeyed my voice in all that I commanded you. 3 You have not left your brethren these many days, up to this day, but have kept the charge of the commandment of the LORD your God. 4 And now the LORD your God has given rest to your brethren, as He promised them; now therefore, return and go to your tents, *and* to the land of your possession, which Moses the servant of the LORD gave you on the other side of the Jordan. 5 But take careful heed to do the commandment and the law which Moses the servant of the LORD commanded you, to love the LORD your God, to walk in all His ways, to keep His commandments, to hold fast to Him, and to serve Him with all your heart and with all your soul." 6 So Joshua blessed them and sent them away, and they went to their tents.

7 Now to half the tribe of Manasseh Moses had given a possession in Bashan, but to the *other* half of it Joshua gave *a possession* among their brethren on this side of the Jordan, westward. And indeed, when Joshua sent them away to their tents, he blessed them, 8 and spoke to them, saying, "Return with much riches to your tents, with very much livestock, with silver, with gold, with bronze, with iron, and with very much clothing. Divide the spoil of your enemies with your brethren."

9 So the children of Reuben, the children of Gad, and half the tribe of Manasseh returned, and departed from the children of Israel at Shiloh, which *is* in the land of Canaan, to go to the country of Gilead, to the land of their possession, which they

had obtained according to the word of the LORD by the hand of Moses.

10 And when they came to the region of the Jordan which *is* in the land of Canaan, the children of Reuben, the children of Gad, and half the tribe of Manasseh built an altar there by the Jordan—a great, impressive altar. 11 Now the children of Israel heard *someone* say, "Behold, the children of Reuben, the children of Gad, and half the tribe of Manasseh have built an altar on the frontier of the land of Canaan, in the region of the Jordan—on the children of Israel's side." 12 And when the children of Israel heard *of it,* the whole congregation of the children of Israel gathered together at Shiloh to go to war against them.

13 Then the children of Israel sent Phinehas the son of Eleazar the priest to the children of Reuben, to the children of Gad, and to half the tribe of Manasseh, into the land of Gilead, 14 and with him ten rulers, one ruler each from the chief house of every tribe of Israel; and each one *was* the head of the house of his father among the divisions of Israel. 15 Then they came to the children of Reuben, to the children of Gad, and to half the tribe of Manasseh, to the land of Gilead, and they spoke with them, saying, 16 "Thus says the whole congregation of the LORD: 'What treachery *is* this that you have committed against the God of Israel, to turn away this day from following the LORD, in that you have built for yourselves an altar, that you might rebel this day against the LORD? 17 *Is* the iniquity of Peor not enough for us, from which we are not cleansed till this day, although there was a plague in the congregation of the LORD, 18 but that you must turn away this day from following the LORD? And it shall be, if you rebel today against the LORD, that tomorrow He will be angry with the whole congregation of Israel. 19 Nevertheless, if the land of your possession *is* unclean, *then* cross over to the land of the possession of the LORD, where the LORD's tabernacle stands, and take possession among us; but do not rebel against the LORD, nor rebel against us, by building yourselves an altar besides the altar of the LORD our God. 20 Did not Achan the son of Zerah commit a trespass in the accursed thing, and wrath fell on all the congregation of Israel? And that man did not perish alone in his iniquity.' "

21 Then the children of Reuben, the children of Gad, and half the tribe of Manasseh answered and said to the heads of the divisions of Israel: 22 "The LORD God of gods, the LORD God of gods, He knows, and let Israel itself know—if *it is* in rebellion, or if in treachery against the LORD, do not save us this day. 23 If we have built ourselves an altar to turn from following the LORD, or if to offer on it burnt offerings or grain offerings, or if to offer peace offerings on it, let the LORD Himself require *an account.* 24 But in fact we have done it for fear, for a reason, saying, 'In time to come your descendants may speak to our descendants, saying, "What have you to do with the LORD God of Israel? 25 For the LORD has made the Jordan a border between you and us, *you* children of Reuben and children of Gad. You have no part in the LORD." So your descendants would make our descendants cease fearing the LORD.' 26 Therefore we said, 'Let us now prepare to build ourselves an altar, not for burnt offering nor for sacrifice, 27 but *that* it *may be* a witness between you and us and our generations after us, that we may perform the service of the LORD before Him with our burnt offerings, with our sacrifices, and with our peace offerings; that your descendants may not say to our descendants in time to come, "You have no part in the LORD." ' 28 Therefore we said that it will be, when they say *this* to us or to our generations in time to come, that we may say, 'Here is the replica of the altar of the LORD which our fathers made, though not for burnt offerings nor for sacrifices; but it *is* a witness between you and us.' 29 Far be it from us that we should rebel against the LORD, and turn from following the LORD this day, to build an altar for burnt offerings, for grain offerings, or for sacrifices, besides the altar of the LORD our God which *is* before His tabernacle."

30 Now when Phinehas the priest and the rulers of the congregation, the heads of the divisions of Israel who *were* with him, heard the words that the children of Reuben, the children of Gad, and the children of Manasseh spoke, it pleased them. 31 Then Phinehas the son of Eleazar the priest said to the children of Reuben, the children of Gad, and the children of Manasseh, "This day we perceive that the LORD *is* among us, because you have not committed this treachery against the LORD. Now you have delivered the children of Israel out of the hand of the LORD."

32 And Phinehas the son of Eleazar the priest, and the rulers, returned from the children of Reuben and the children of Gad, from the land of Gilead to the land of Canaan, to the children of Israel, and brought back word to them. 33 So the thing pleased the children of Israel, and the children of

Israel blessed God; they spoke no more of going against them in battle, to destroy the land where the children of Reuben and Gad dwelt.

34 The children of Reuben and the children of Gad called the altar, *Witness*, "For *it is* a witness between us that the LORD *is* God."

PSALM 46:7–11

7 THE LORD of hosts *is* with us;
The God of Jacob *is* our refuge.
Selah

8 Come, behold the works of the LORD,
Who has made desolations in the earth.

9 He makes wars cease to the end of the earth;
He breaks the bow and cuts the spear in two;
He burns the chariot in the fire.

10 Be still, and know that I *am* God;
I will be exalted among the nations,
I will be exalted in the earth!

11 The LORD of hosts *is* with us;
The God of Jacob *is* our refuge.
Selah

PROVERBS 14:12, 13

12 THERE is a way *that seems* right to a man,
But its end *is* the way of death.

13 Even in laughter the heart may sorrow,
And the end of mirth *may be* grief.

LUKE 13:1–22

THERE were present at that season some who told Him about the Galileans whose blood Pilate had mingled with their sacrifices. 2 And Jesus answered and said to them, "Do you suppose that these Galileans were worse sinners than all *other* Galileans, because they suffered such things? 3 I tell you, no; but unless you repent you will all likewise perish. 4 Or those eighteen on whom the tower in Siloam fell and killed them, do you think that they were worse sinners than all *other* men who dwelt in Jerusalem? 5 I tell you, no; but unless you repent you will all likewise perish."

6 He also spoke this parable: "A certain *man* had a fig tree planted in his vineyard,

and he came seeking fruit on it and found none. 7 Then he said to the keeper of his vineyard, 'Look, for three years I have come seeking fruit on this fig tree and find none. Cut it down; why does it use up the ground?' 8 But he answered and said to him, 'Sir, let it alone this year also, until I dig around it and fertilize *it*. 9 And if it bears fruit, *well*. But if not, after that you can cut it down.'"

10 Now He was teaching in one of the synagogues on the Sabbath. 11 And behold, there was a woman who had a spirit of infirmity eighteen years, and was bent over and could in no way raise *herself* up. 12 But when Jesus saw her, He called *her* to *Him* and said to her, "Woman, you are loosed from your infirmity." 13 And He laid *His* hands on her, and immediately she was made straight, and glorified God.

14 But the ruler of the synagogue answered with indignation, because Jesus had healed on the Sabbath; and he said to the crowd, "There are six days on which men ought to work; therefore come and be healed on them, and not on the Sabbath day."

15 The Lord then answered him and said, "Hypocrite! Does not each one of you on the Sabbath loose his ox or donkey from the stall, and lead *it* away to water it?

It is an easy business to appear to be what we are not. (SERMON MT.)

16 So ought not this woman, being a daughter of Abraham, whom Satan has bound—think of it—for eighteen years, be loosed from this bond on the Sabbath?" 17 And when He said these things, all His adversaries were put to shame; and all the multitude rejoiced for all the glorious things that were done by Him.

18 Then He said, "What is the kingdom of God like? And to what shall I compare it? 19 It is like a mustard seed, which a man took and put in his garden; and it grew and became a large tree, and the birds of the air nested in its branches."

20 And again He said, "To what shall I liken the kingdom of God? 21 It is like leaven, which a woman took and hid in three measures of meal till it was all leavened."

22 And He went through the cities and villages, teaching, and journeying toward Jerusalem. 23 Then one said to Him, "Lord, are there few who are saved?"

Reading 107—Struggle for Self
Luke 13:24

Everyone has to begin with this struggle for self, and striving to enter in at the narrow gate is a picture of the struggle. Anything that does not enter in at the narrow gate, for example, selfishness, self-interest, self-indulgence, ends in destruction. The struggle to enter in, no matter with what it may be in connection, braces us morally. Self-indulgence is a refusal to struggle, a refusal to make ourselves fit. We must be right ourselves before we can help others to be right.

If you make a moral struggle and gain a moral victory, you will be a benefit to all you come across, whereas if you do not struggle, you act as a moral pollution. Gain a moral victory in chastity or in your emotional life, it may be known to no one but yourself, and you are an untold benefit to everyone else; but if you refuse to struggle everyone else is weakened. This is a recognized psychological law, although little known. Struggle to gain the mastery over selfishness, and you will be a tremendous assistance; but if you don't overcome the tendency to spiritual sluggishness and self-indulgence, you are a hindrance to all around you. These things are intangible, but they are there, and Jesus says to us, "Strive to enter through the narrow gate." You never get through alone. If you struggle to get through, others are the stronger and better for knowing you.   (PLACE HELP)

JOSHUA 23:1—24:33

NOW it came to pass, a long time after the LORD had given rest to Israel from all their enemies round about, that Joshua was old, advanced in age. 2 And Joshua called for all Israel, for their elders, for their heads, for their judges, and for their officers, and said to them:

"I am old, advanced in age. 3 You have seen all that the LORD your God has done to all these nations because of you, for the LORD your God is He who has fought for you. 4 See, I have divided to you by lot these nations that remain, to be an inheritance for your tribes, from the Jordan, with all the nations that I have cut off, as far as the Great Sea westward. 5 And the LORD your God will expel them from before you and drive them out of your sight. So you shall possess their land, as the LORD your God promised you. 6 Therefore be very courageous to keep and to do all that is written in the Book of the Law of Moses, lest you turn aside from it to the right hand or to the left, 7 and lest you go among these nations, these who remain among you. You shall not make mention of the name of their gods, nor cause anyone to swear by them; you shall not serve them nor bow down to them, 8 but you shall hold fast to the LORD your God, as you have done to this day. 9 For the LORD has driven out from before you great and strong nations; but as for you, no one has been able to stand against you to this day. 10 One man of you shall chase a thousand, for the LORD your God is He who fights for you, as He promised you. 11 Therefore take careful heed to yourselves, that you love the LORD your God. 12 Or else, if indeed you do go back, and cling to the remnant of these nations—these that remain among you—and make marriages with them, and go in to them and they to you, 13 know for certain that the LORD your God will no longer drive out these nations from before you. But they shall be snares and traps to you, and scourges on your sides and thorns in your eyes, until you perish from this good land which the LORD your God has given you.

14 "Behold, this day I am going the way of all the earth. And you know in all your hearts and in all your souls that not one thing has failed of all the good things which the LORD your God spoke concerning you. All have come to pass for you; not one word of them has failed. 15 Therefore it shall come to pass, that as all the good things have come upon you which the LORD your God promised you, so the LORD will bring upon you all harmful things, until He has

destroyed you from this good land which the LORD your God has given you. 16 When you have transgressed the covenant of the LORD your God, which He commanded you, and have gone and served other gods, and bowed down to them, then the anger of the LORD will burn against you, and you shall perish quickly from the good land which He has given you."

24 THEN Joshua gathered all the tribes of Israel to Shechem and called for the elders of Israel, for their heads, for their judges, and for their officers; and they presented themselves before God. 2 And Joshua said to all the people, "Thus says the LORD God of Israel: 'Your fathers, *including* Terah, the father of Abraham and the father of Nahor, dwelt on the other side of the River in old times; and they served other gods. 3 Then I took your father Abraham from the other side of the River, led him throughout all the land of Canaan, and multiplied his descendants and gave him Isaac. 4 To Isaac I gave Jacob and Esau. To Esau I gave the mountains of Seir to possess, but Jacob and his children went down to Egypt. 5 Also I sent Moses and Aaron, and I plagued Egypt, according to what I did among them. Afterward I brought you out.

6 'Then I brought your fathers out of Egypt, and you came to the sea; and the Egyptians pursued your fathers with chariots and horsemen to the Red Sea. 7 So they cried out to the LORD; and He put darkness between you and the Egyptians, brought the sea upon them, and covered them. And your eyes saw what I did in Egypt. Then you dwelt in the wilderness a long time. 8 And I brought you into the land of the Amorites, who dwelt on the other side of the Jordan, and they fought with you. But I gave them into your hand, that you might possess their land, and I destroyed them from before you. 9 Then Balak the son of Zippor, king of Moab, arose to make war against Israel, and sent and called Balaam the son of Beor to curse you. 10 But I would not listen to Balaam; therefore he continued to bless you. So I delivered you out of his hand. 11 Then you went over the Jordan and came to Jericho. And the men of Jericho fought against you—*also* the Amorites, the Perizzites, the Canaanites, the Hittites, the Girgashites, the Hivites, and the Jebusites. But I delivered them into your hand. 12 I sent the hornet before you which drove them out from before you, *also* the two kings of the Amorites, *but* not with your sword or with your bow. 13 I have given

you a land for which you did not labor, and cities which you did not build, and you dwell in them; you eat of the vineyards and olive groves which you did not plant.'

14 "Now therefore, fear the LORD, serve Him in sincerity and in truth, and put away the gods which your fathers served on the other side of the River and in Egypt. Serve the LORD! 15 And if it seems evil to you to serve the LORD, choose for yourselves this day whom you will serve, whether the gods which your fathers served that *were* on the other side of the River, or the gods of the Amorites, in whose land you dwell. But as for me and my house, we will serve the LORD."

16 So the people answered and said: "Far be it from us that we should forsake the LORD to serve other gods; 17 for the LORD our God *is* He who brought us and our fathers up out of the land of Egypt, from the house of bondage, who did those great signs in our sight, and preserved us in all the way that we went and among all the people through whom we passed. 18 And the LORD drove out from before us all the people, including the Amorites who dwelt in the land. We also will serve the LORD, for He *is* our God."

19 But Joshua said to the people, "You cannot serve the LORD, for He *is* a holy God. He *is* a jealous God; He will not forgive your transgressions nor your sins. 20 If you forsake the LORD and serve foreign gods, then He will turn and do you harm and consume you, after He has done you good."

21 And the people said to Joshua, "No, but we will serve the LORD!"

22 So Joshua said to the people, "You *are* witnesses against yourselves that you have chosen the LORD for yourselves, to serve Him."

And they said, "*We are* witnesses!"

23 "Now therefore," *he said*, "put away the foreign gods which *are* among you, and incline your heart to the LORD God of Israel."

24 And the people said to Joshua, "The LORD our God we will serve, and His voice we will obey!"

25 So Joshua made a covenant with the people that day, and made for them a statute and an ordinance in Shechem.

26 Then Joshua wrote these words in the Book of the Law of God. And he took a large stone, and set it up there under the oak that *was* by the sanctuary of the LORD. 27 And Joshua said to all the people, "Behold, this stone shall be a witness to us, for it has heard all the words of the LORD

which He spoke to us. It shall therefore be a witness to you, lest you deny your God." 28 So Joshua let the people depart, each to his own inheritance.

29 Now it came to pass after these things that Joshua the son of Nun, the servant of the LORD, died, *being* one hundred and ten years old. 30 And they buried him within the border of his inheritance at Timnath Serah, which *is* in the mountains of Ephraim, on the north side of Mount Gaash.

31 Israel served the LORD all the days of Joshua, and all the days of the elders who outlived Joshua, who had known all the works of the LORD which He had done for Israel.

32 The bones of Joseph, which the children of Israel had brought up out of Egypt, they buried at Shechem, in the plot of ground which Jacob had bought from the sons of Hamor the father of Shechem for one hundred pieces of silver, and which had become an inheritance of the children of Joseph.

33 And Eleazar the son of Aaron died. They buried him in a hill *belonging to* Phinehas his son, which was given to him in the mountains of Ephraim.

PSALM 47:1–9

1 OH, clap your hands, all you peoples!
   Shout to God with the voice of
      triumph!
2 For the LORD Most High *is* awesome;
   He is a great King over all the earth.
3 He will subdue the peoples under us,
   And the nations under our feet.
4 He will choose our inheritance for us,
   The excellence of Jacob whom He
      loves.   Selah

5 God has gone up with a shout,
   The LORD with the sound of a trumpet.
6 Sing praises to God, sing praises!
   Sing praises to our King, sing praises!
7 For God *is* the King of all the earth;
   Sing praises with understanding.

8 God reigns over the nations;
   God sits on His holy throne.
9 The princes of the people have gathered
      together,
   The people of the God of Abraham.
   For the shields of the earth *belong* to
      God;
   He is greatly exalted.

PROVERBS 14:14

14 THE backslider in heart will be filled
      with his own ways,
   But a good man *will be satisfied* from
      above.

[A backslider*] has forsaken
God and taken up with something
else.*   (WORKMEN)

LUKE 13:23–35

AND He said to them, 24 "Strive to enter through the narrow gate, for many, I say to you, will seek to enter and will not be able. 25 When once the Master of the house has risen up and shut the door, and you begin to stand outside and knock at the door, saying, 'Lord, Lord, open for us,' and He will answer and say to you, 'I do not know you, where you are from,'

---

*H*ave you ever realized who the Lord
is in your life?   (SEND I YOU)

---

26 then you will begin to say, 'We ate and drank in Your presence, and You taught in our streets.' 27 But He will say, 'I tell you I do not know you, where you are from. Depart from Me, all you workers of iniquity.' 28 There will be weeping and gnashing of teeth, when you see Abraham and Isaac and Jacob and all the prophets in the kingdom of God, and yourselves thrust out. 29 They will come from the east and the west, from the north and the south, and sit down in the kingdom of God. 30 And indeed there are last who will be first, and there are first who will be last."

31 On that very day some Pharisees came, saying to Him, "Get out and depart from here, for Herod wants to kill You."

32 And He said to them, "Go, tell that fox, 'Behold, I cast out demons and perform cures today and tomorrow, and the third *day* I shall be perfected.' 33 Nevertheless I must journey today, tomorrow, and the *day* following; for it cannot be that a prophet should perish outside of Jerusalem.

34 "O Jerusalem, Jerusalem, the one who kills the prophets and stones those who are sent to her! How often I wanted to gather your children together, as a hen *gathers* her

brood under *her* wings, but you were not willing! 35 See! Your house is left to you desolate; and assuredly, I say to you, you shall not see Me until *the time* comes when you say, 'Blessed is He who comes in the name of the LORD!' "

------------------- ◆◆◆◆ -------------------

Reading 108—Defiant Humility
Luke 14:11

Get into the habit of examining in the sight of God the things that sound humble before men, and you will be amazed at how staggeringly impertinent they are. "Oh, I shouldn't like to say I am sanctified; I'm not a saint." Say that before God; and it means—"No, Lord, it is impossible for You to save and sanctify me; there are chances I have not had; so many imperfections in my brain and body; no, Lord, it isn't possible." That may sound wonderfully humble before men, but before God it is an attitude of defiance.

Again, the things that sound humble before God may sound the opposite before men. To say, "Thank God, I know I am saved and sanctified" is in the sight of God the acme of humility, it means you have so completely abandoned yourself to God that you know He is true. Never bother your head as to whether what you say sounds humble before men or not, but always be humble before God, and let Him be all in all.

There is only one relationship that matters, and that is your personal relationship to a personal Redeemer and Lord. Let everything else go, but maintain that at all costs, and God will fulfill His purpose through your life. One individual life may be of priceless value to God's purposes, and yours may be that life.   (*UTMOST*)

JUDGES 1:1—2:23

NOW after the death of Joshua it came to pass that the children of Israel asked the LORD, saying, "Who shall be first to go up for us against the Canaanites to fight against them?"

2 And the LORD said, "Judah shall go up. Indeed I have delivered the land into his hand."

3 So Judah said to Simeon his brother, "Come up with me to my allotted territory, that we may fight against the Canaanites; and I will likewise go with you to your allotted territory." And Simeon went with him. 4 Then Judah went up, and the LORD delivered the Canaanites and the Perizzites into their hand; and they killed ten thousand men at Bezek. 5 And they found Adoni-Bezek in Bezek, and fought against him; and they defeated the Canaanites and the Perizzites. 6 Then Adoni-Bezek fled, and they pursued him and caught him and cut off his thumbs and big toes. 7 And Adoni-Bezek said, "Seventy kings with their thumbs and big toes cut off used to gather *scraps* under my table; as I have done, so God has repaid me." Then they brought him to Jerusalem, and there he died.

8 Now the children of Judah fought against Jerusalem and took it; they struck it with the edge of the sword and set the city on fire. 9 And afterward the children of Judah went down to fight against the Canaanites who dwelt in the mountains, in the South, and in the lowland. 10 Then Judah went against the Canaanites who dwelt in Hebron. (Now the name of Hebron *was* formerly Kirjath Arba.) And they killed Sheshai, Ahiman, and Talmai.

11 From there they went against the inhabitants of Debir. (The name of Debir *was* formerly Kirjath Sepher.)

12 Then Caleb said, "Whoever attacks Kirjath Sepher and takes it, to him I will give my daughter Achsah as wife." 13 And

Othniel the son of Kenaz, Caleb's younger brother, took it; so he gave him his daughter Achsah as wife. 14 Now it happened, when she came *to him,* that she urged him to ask her father for a field. And she dismounted from *her* donkey, and Caleb said to her, "What do you wish?" 15 So she said to him, "Give me a blessing; since you have given me land in the South, give me also springs of water."

And Caleb gave her the upper springs and the lower springs.

16 Now the children of the Kenite, Moses' father-in-law, went up from the City of Palms with the children of Judah into the Wilderness of Judah, which *lies* in the South *near* Arad; and they went and dwelt among the people. 17 And Judah went with his brother Simeon, and they attacked the Canaanites who inhabited Zephath, and utterly destroyed it. So the name of the city was called Hormah. 18 Also Judah took Gaza with its territory, Ashkelon with its territory, and Ekron with its territory. 19 So the LORD was with Judah. And they drove out the mountaineers, but they could not drive out the inhabitants of the lowland, because they had chariots of iron. 20 And they gave Hebron to Caleb, as Moses had said. Then he expelled from there the three sons of Anak. 21 But the children of Benjamin did not drive out the Jebusites who inhabited Jerusalem; so the Jebusites dwell with the children of Benjamin in Jerusalem to this day.

22 And the house of Joseph also went up against Bethel, and the LORD *was* with them. 23 So the house of Joseph sent men to spy out Bethel. (The name of the city *was* formerly Luz.) 24 And when the spies saw a man coming out of the city, they said to him, "Please show us the entrance to the city, and we will show you mercy." 25 So he showed them the entrance to the city, and they struck the city with the edge of the sword; but they let the man and all his family go. 26 And the man went to the land of the Hittites, built a city, and called its name Luz, which *is* its name to this day.

27 However, Manasseh did not drive out *the inhabitants of* Beth Shean and its villages, or Taanach and its villages, or the inhabitants of Dor and its villages, or the inhabitants of Ibleam and its villages, or the inhabitants of Megiddo and its villages; for the Canaanites were determined to dwell in that land. 28 And it came to pass, when Israel was strong, that they put the Canaanites under tribute, but did not completely drive them out.

29 Nor did Ephraim drive out the Canaanites who dwelt in Gezer; so the Canaanites dwelt in Gezer among them.

30 Nor did Zebulun drive out the inhabitants of Kitron or the inhabitants of Nahalol; so the Canaanites dwelt among them, and were put under tribute.

31 Nor did Asher drive out the inhabitants of Acco or the inhabitants of Sidon, or of Ahlab, Achzib, Helbah, Aphik, or Rehob. 32 So the Asherites dwelt among the Canaanites, the inhabitants of the land; for they did not drive them out.

33 Nor did Naphtali drive out the inhabitants of Beth Shemesh or the inhabitants of Beth Anath; but they dwelt among the Canaanites, the inhabitants of the land. Nevertheless the inhabitants of Beth Shemesh and Beth Anath were put under tribute to them.

34 And the Amorites forced the children of Dan into the mountains, for they would not allow them to come down to the valley; 35 and the Amorites were determined to dwell in Mount Heres, in Aijalon, and in Shaalbim; yet when the strength of the house of Joseph became greater, they were put under tribute. 36 Now the boundary of the Amorites *was* from the Ascent of Akrabbim, from Sela, and upward.

2 THEN the Angel of the LORD came up from Gilgal to Bochim, and said: "I led you up from Egypt and brought you to the land of which I swore to your fathers; and I said, 'I will never break My covenant with you. 2 And you shall make no covenant with the inhabitants of this land; you shall tear down their altars.' But you have not obeyed My voice. Why have you done this? 3 Therefore I also said, 'I will not drive them out before you; but they shall be *thorns* in your side, and their gods shall be a snare to you.'" 4 So it was, when the Angel of the LORD spoke these words to all the children of Israel, that the people lifted up their voices and wept.

5 Then they called the name of that place Bochim; and they sacrificed there to the LORD. 6 And when Joshua had dismissed the people, the children of Israel went each to his own inheritance to possess the land.

7 So the people served the LORD all the days of Joshua, and all the days of the elders who outlived Joshua, who had seen all the great works of the LORD which He had done for Israel. 8 Now Joshua the son of Nun, the servant of the LORD, died *when he was* one hundred and ten years old. 9 And they buried him within the border

of his inheritance at Timnath Heres, in the mountains of Ephraim, on the north side of Mount Gaash. 10 When all that generation had been gathered to their fathers, another generation arose after them who did not know the LORD nor the work which He had done for Israel.

11 Then the children of Israel did evil in the sight of the LORD, and served the Baals; 12 and they forsook the LORD God of their fathers, who had brought them out of the land of Egypt; and they followed other gods from *among* the gods of the people who *were* all around them, and they bowed down to them; and they provoked the LORD to anger. 13 They forsook the LORD and served Baal and the Ashtoreths. 14 And the anger of the LORD was hot against Israel. So He delivered them into the hands of plunderers who despoiled them; and He sold them into the hands of their enemies all around, so that they could no longer stand before their enemies. 15 Wherever they went out, the hand of the LORD was against them for calamity, as the LORD had said, and as the LORD had sworn to them. And they were greatly distressed.

16 Nevertheless, the LORD raised up judges who delivered them out of the hand of those who plundered them. 17 Yet they would not listen to their judges, but they played the harlot with other gods, and bowed down to them. They turned quickly from the way in which their fathers walked, in obeying the commandments of the LORD; they did not do so. 18 And when the LORD raised up judges for them, the LORD was with the judge and delivered them out of the hand of their enemies all the days of the judge; for the LORD was moved to pity by their groaning because of those who oppressed them and harassed them. 19 And it came to pass, when the judge was dead, that they reverted and behaved more corruptly than their fathers, by following other gods, to serve them and bow down to them. They did not cease from their own doings nor from their stubborn way.

20 Then the anger of the LORD was hot against Israel; and He said, "Because this nation has transgressed My covenant which I commanded their fathers, and has not heeded My voice, 21 I also will no longer drive out before them any of the nations which Joshua left when he died, 22 so that through them I may test Israel, whether they will keep the ways of the LORD, to walk in them as their fathers kept *them*, or not." 23 Therefore the LORD left those nations, without driving them out immediately; nor did He deliver them into the hand of Joshua.

PSALM 48:1–8

1   GREAT *is* the LORD, and greatly to
       be praised
     In the city of our God,
     In His holy mountain.
2   Beautiful in elevation,
     The joy of the whole earth,
     Is Mount Zion *on* the sides of the north,
     The city of the great King.
3   God *is* in her palaces;
     He is known as her refuge.

4   For behold, the kings assembled,
     They passed by together.
5   They saw *it, and* so they marveled;
     They were troubled, they hastened
       away.
6   Fear took hold of them there,
     And pain, as of a woman in birth pangs,
7   *As when* You break the ships of Tarshish
     With an east wind.

8   As we have heard,
     So we have seen
     In the city of the LORD of hosts,
     In the city of our God:
     God will establish it forever.   Selah

PROVERBS 14:15–17

15   THE simple believes every word,
      But the prudent considers well his steps.
16   A wise *man* fears and departs from evil,
      But a fool rages and is self-confident.
17   A quick-tempered *man* acts foolishly,
      And a man of wicked intentions is
        hated.

LUKE 14:1–24

NOW it happened, as He went into the house of one of the rulers of the Pharisees to eat bread on the Sabbath, that they watched Him closely. 2 And behold, there was a certain man before Him who had dropsy. 3 And Jesus, answering, spoke to the lawyers and Pharisees, saying, "Is it lawful to heal on the Sabbath?"

4 But they kept silent. And He took *him* and healed him, and let him go. 5 Then He answered them, saying, "Which of you, having a donkey or an ox that has fallen into a pit, will not immediately pull him out on the Sabbath day?" 6 And they could

not answer Him regarding these things.

7 So He told a parable to those who were invited, when He noted how they chose the best places, saying to them: 8 "When you are invited by anyone to a wedding feast, do not sit down in the best place, lest one more honorable than you be invited by him; 9 and he who invited you and him come and say to you, 'Give place to this man,' and then you begin with shame to take the lowest place. 10 But when you are invited, go and sit down in the lowest place, so that when he who invited you comes he may say to you, 'Friend, go up higher.' Then you will have glory in the presence of those who sit at the table with you. 11 For whoever exalts himself will be humbled, and he who humbles himself will be exalted."

There is something amazingly humbling, . . . in being loyal to God. (NOT KNOWING)

---

12 Then He also said to him who invited Him, "When you give a dinner or a supper, do not ask your friends, your brothers, your relatives, nor rich neighbors, lest they also invite you back, and you be repaid. 13 But when you give a feast, invite *the* poor, *the* maimed, *the* lame, *the* blind. 14 And you will be blessed, because they cannot repay you; for you shall be repaid at the resurrection of the just."

15 Now when one of those who sat at the table with Him heard these things, he said to Him, "Blessed *is* he who shall eat bread in the kingdom of God!"

16 Then He said to him, "A certain man gave a great supper and invited many, 17 and sent his servant at supper time to say to those who were invited, 'Come, for all things are now ready.' 18 But they all with one *accord* began to make excuses. The first said to him, 'I have bought a piece of ground, and I must go and see it. I ask you to have me excused.' 19 And another said, 'I have bought five yoke of oxen, and I am going to test them. I ask you to have me excused.' 20 Still another said, 'I have married a wife, and therefore I cannot come.' 21 So that servant came and reported these things to his master. Then the master of the house, being angry, said to his servant, 'Go out quickly into the streets and lanes of the city, and bring in here *the* poor and *the* maimed and *the* lame and *the* blind.' 22 And the servant said, 'Master, it is done as you commanded, and still there is room.' 23 Then the master said to the servant, 'Go out into the highways and hedges, and compel *them* to come in, that my house may be filled. 24 For I say to you that none of those men who were invited shall taste my supper.' "

◆◆◆◆

Reading 109—The Kernel of Consecration
Luke 14:26

You cannot consecrate yourself *and* your friends. If at the altar your heart imagines that loving arms are still around you, and that together, lovers as lovers, and friends as friends, can enter through this mighty gate of supreme sanctification, it is a fond dream, doomed to disillusionment. Alone! Relinquish all! You cannot consecrate your children, your wife, your lover, your friend, your father, your mother or your own life as yours. You must abandon all and fling yourself on God as a mere conscious being, and unperplexed, seeking you'll find Him. The teaching that presents consecration as giving to God our gifts, our possessions, our comrades, is a profound error. These are all abandoned, and we give up forever *our right to ourselves*. A sanctified soul may be an artist, or a musician; but he is not a sanctified artist or musician: he is one who expresses the message of God through a particular medium. As long as the artist or musician imagines he can consecrate his artistic gifts to God, he is deluded. Abandonment of ourselves is the kernel of consecration, not presenting our gifts, but presenting ourselves without reserve. (*LONELINESS*)

JUDGES 3:1—4:24

NOW these *are* the nations which the LORD left, that He might test Israel by them, *that is,* all who had not known any of the wars in Canaan 2 (*this was* only so that the generations of the children of Israel might be taught to know war, at least those who had not formerly known it), 3 *namely,* five lords of the Philistines, all the Canaanites, the Sidonians, and the Hivites who dwelt in Mount Lebanon, from Mount Baal Hermon to the entrance of Hamath. 4 And they were *left, that He might* test Israel by them, to know whether they would obey the commandments of the LORD, which He had commanded their fathers by the hand of Moses.

5 Thus the children of Israel dwelt among the Canaanites, the Hittites, the Amorites, the Perizzites, the Hivites, and the Jebusites. 6 And they took their daughters to be their wives, and gave their daughters to their sons; and they served their gods.

7 So the children of Israel did evil in the sight of the LORD. They forgot the LORD their God, and served the Baals and Asherahs. 8 Therefore the anger of the LORD was hot against Israel, and He sold them into the hand of Cushan-Rishathaim king of Mesopotamia; and the children of Israel served Cushan-Rishathaim eight years. 9 When the children of Israel cried out to the LORD, the LORD raised up a deliverer for the children of Israel, who delivered them: Othniel the son of Kenaz, Caleb's younger brother. 10 The Spirit of the LORD came upon him, and he judged Israel. He went out to war, and the LORD delivered Cushan-Rishathaim king of Mesopotamia into his hand; and his hand prevailed over Cushan-Rishathaim. 11 So the land had rest for forty years. Then Othniel the son of Kenaz died.

12 And the children of Israel again did evil in the sight of the LORD. So the LORD strengthened Eglon king of Moab against Israel, because they had done evil in the sight of the LORD. 13 Then he gathered to himself the people of Ammon and Amalek, went and defeated Israel, and took possession of the City of Palms. 14 So the children of Israel served Eglon king of Moab eighteen years.

15 But when the children of Israel cried out to the LORD, the LORD raised up a deliverer for them: Ehud the son of Gera, the Benjamite, a left-handed man. By him the children of Israel sent tribute to Eglon king of Moab. 16 Now Ehud made himself

If our problems can be solved by other men, they are not problems but simply muddles. (BAFFLED)

a dagger (it was double-edged and a cubit in length) and fastened it under his clothes on his right thigh. 17 So he brought the tribute to Eglon king of Moab. (Now Eglon *was* a very fat man.) 18 And when he had finished presenting the tribute, he sent away the people who had carried the tribute. 19 But he himself turned back from the stone images that *were* at Gilgal, and said, "I have a secret message for you, O king."

He said, "Keep silence!" And all who attended him went out from him.

20 So Ehud came to him (now he was sitting upstairs in his cool private chamber). Then Ehud said, "I have a message from God for you." So he arose from *his* seat. 21 Then Ehud reached with his left hand, took the dagger from his right thigh, and thrust it into his belly. 22 Even the hilt went in after the blade, and the fat closed over the blade, for he did not draw the dagger out of his belly; and his entrails came out. 23 Then Ehud went out through the porch and shut the doors of the upper room behind him and locked them.

24 When he had gone out, *Eglon's* servants came to look, and *to their* surprise, the doors of the upper room were locked. So they said, "He is probably attending to his needs in the cool chamber." 25 So they waited till they were embarrassed, and still he had not opened the doors of the upper room. Therefore they took the key and opened *them.* And there was their master, fallen dead on the floor.

26 But Ehud had escaped while they delayed, and passed beyond the stone images and escaped to Seirah. 27 And it happened, when he arrived, that he blew the trumpet in the mountains of Ephraim, and the children of Israel went down with him from the mountains; and he led them. 28 Then he said to them, "Follow *me,* for the LORD has delivered your enemies the Moabites into your hand." So they went down after him, seized the fords of the Jordan leading to Moab, and did not allow anyone to cross over. 29 And at that time they killed about ten thousand men of Moab, all stout men of valor; not a man escaped. 30 So Moab was subdued that day under the hand of Israel. And the land had rest for eighty years.

31 After him was Shamgar the son of Anath, who killed six hundred men of the

Philistines with an ox goad; and he also delivered Israel.

4 WHEN Ehud was dead, the children of Israel again did evil in the sight of the LORD. 2 So the LORD sold them into the hand of Jabin king of Canaan, who reigned in Hazor. The commander of his army *was* Sisera, who dwelt in Harosheth Hagoyim. 3 And the children of Israel cried out to the LORD; for Jabin had nine hundred chariots of iron, and for twenty years he had harshly oppressed the children of Israel.

4 Now Deborah, a prophetess, the wife of Lapidoth, was judging Israel at that time. 5 And she would sit under the palm tree of Deborah between Ramah and Bethel in the mountains of Ephraim. And the children of Israel came up to her for judgment. 6 Then she sent and called for Barak the son of Abinoam from Kedesh in Naphtali, and said to him, "Has not the LORD God of Israel commanded, 'Go and deploy *troops* at Mount Tabor; take with you ten thousand men of the sons of Naphtali and of the sons of Zebulun; 7 and against you I will deploy Sisera, the commander of Jabin's army, with his chariots and his multitude at the River Kishon; and I will deliver him into your hand'?"

8 And Barak said to her, "If you will go with me, then I will go; but if you will not go with me, I will not go!"

9 So she said, "I will surely go with you; nevertheless there will be no glory for you in the journey you are taking, for the LORD will sell Sisera into the hand of a woman." Then Deborah arose and went with Barak to Kedesh. 10 And Barak called Zebulun and Naphtali to Kedesh; he went up with ten thousand men under his command, and Deborah went up with him.

11 Now Heber the Kenite, of the children of Hobab the father-in-law of Moses, had separated himself from the Kenites and pitched his tent near the terebinth tree at Zaanaim, which *is* beside Kedesh.

12 And they reported to Sisera that Barak the son of Abinoam had gone up to Mount Tabor. 13 So Sisera gathered together all his chariots, nine hundred chariots of iron, and all the people who *were* with him, from Harosheth Hagoyim to the River Kishon.

14 Then Deborah said to Barak, "Up! For this *is* the day in which the LORD has delivered Sisera into your hand. Has not the LORD gone out before you?" So Barak went down from Mount Tabor with ten thousand men following him. 15 And the LORD routed Sisera and all *his* chariots and all *his* army with the edge of the sword before

Barak; and Sisera alighted from *his* chariot and fled away on foot. 16 But Barak pursued the chariots and the army as far as Harosheth Hagoyim, and all the army of Sisera fell by the edge of the sword; not a man was left.

17 However, Sisera had fled away on foot to the tent of Jael, the wife of Heber the Kenite; for *there was* peace between Jabin king of Hazor and the house of Heber the Kenite. 18 And Jael went out to meet Sisera, and said to him, "Turn aside, my lord, turn aside to me; do not fear." And when he had turned aside with her into the tent, she covered him with a blanket.

19 Then he said to her, "Please give me a little water to drink, for I am thirsty." So she opened a jug of milk, gave him a drink, and covered him. 20 And he said to her, "Stand at the door of the tent, and if any man comes and inquires of you, and says, 'Is there any man here?' you shall say, 'No.'"

21 Then Jael, Heber's wife, took a tent peg and took a hammer in her hand, and went softly to him and drove the peg into his temple, and it went down into the ground; for he was fast asleep and weary. So he died. 22 And then, as Barak pursued Sisera, Jael came out to meet him, and said to him, "Come, I will show you the man whom you seek." And when he went into her *tent*, there lay Sisera, dead with the peg in his temple.

23 So on that day God subdued Jabin king of Canaan in the presence of the children of Israel. 24 And the hand of the children of Israel grew stronger and stronger against Jabin king of Canaan, until they had destroyed Jabin king of Canaan.

PSALM 48:9–14

9 WE have thought, O God, on Your
      lovingkindness,
   In the midst of Your temple.
10 According to Your name, O God,
   So *is* Your praise to the ends of the
      earth;
   Your right hand is full of righteousness.
11 Let Mount Zion rejoice,
   Let the daughters of Judah be glad,
   Because of Your judgments.

12 Walk about Zion,
   And go all around her.
   Count her towers;
13 Mark well her bulwarks;
   Consider her palaces;

That you may tell *it* to the generation
following.
14 For this *is* God,
Our God forever and ever;
He will be our guide
Even to death.

PROVERBS 14:18, 19

18 THE simple inherit folly,
But the prudent are crowned with
knowledge.
19 The evil will bow before the good,
And the wicked at the gates of the
righteous.

LUKE 14:25–35

NOW great multitudes went with Him.
And He turned and said to them, 26 "If
anyone comes to Me and does not hate
his father and mother, wife and children,
brothers and sisters, yes, and his own life
also, he cannot be My disciple. 27 And
whoever does not bear his cross and come
after Me cannot be My disciple. 28 For

*Discipleship means personal,
passionate devotion to a Person, our
Lord Jesus Christ.* (UTMOST)

which of you, intending to build a tower,
does not sit down first and count the cost,
whether he has *enough* to finish *it*—
29 lest, after he has laid the foundation, and
is not able to finish, all who see *it* begin
to mock him, 30 saying, 'This man began
to build and was not able to finish.'
31 Or what king, going to make war against
another king, does not sit down first and
consider whether he is able with ten thousand to meet him who comes against him
with twenty thousand? 32 Or else, while the
other is still a great way off, he sends a
delegation and asks conditions of peace.
33 So likewise, whoever of you does not
forsake all that he has cannot be My disciple.
34 "Salt *is* good; but if the salt has lost
its flavor, how shall it be seasoned?
35 It is neither fit for the land nor for the
dunghill, *but* men throw it out. He who
has ears to hear, let him hear!"

◆◆◆◆

Reading 110—Pharisaic Invincibility
Luke 15:2, 3

For thirty years Jesus did nothing, then for three years He stormed every
time He went down to Jerusalem. Josephus says He tore through the
temple courts like a madman. We hear nothing about that Jesus Christ today.
The meek and mild Being pictured today makes us lose altogether the meaning
of the Cross. We have to find out why Jesus was beside Himself with rage
and indignation at the Pharisees and not with those given over to carnal sins.
Which state of society is going to stand a ripping and tearing Being like Jesus
Christ who drags to the ground the highest respected pillars of its civilized
society, and shows that their respectability and religiosity is built on a much
more abominable pride than the harlot's or the publican's? The latter are
disgusting and coarse, but these men have the very pride of the Devil in their
hearts.

Ask yourself, then, what is it that awakens indignation in your heart? Is it
the same kind of thing that awakened indignation in Jesus Christ? The thing
that awakens indignation in us is the thing that upsets our present state of
comfort and society. The thing that made Jesus Christ blaze was pride that
defied God and prevented Him from having His right with human hearts.
"Calvary" means "the Place of a Skull," and that is where our Lord is always
crucified, in the culture and intellect of men who will not have self-knowledge
given by the light of Jesus Christ.   (GOOD)

JUDGES 5:1—6:40

THEN Deborah and Barak the son of Abinoam sang on that day, saying:

2 "When leaders lead in Israel,
   When the people willingly offer
      themselves,
   Bless the LORD!

3 "Hear, O kings! Give ear, O princes!
   I, *even* I, will sing to the LORD;
   I will sing praise to the LORD God
      of Israel.

4 "LORD, when You went out from Seir,
   When You marched from the field
      of Edom,
   The earth trembled and the heavens
      poured,
   The clouds also poured water;
5   The mountains gushed before the
      LORD,
   This Sinai, before the LORD God of
      Israel.

6 "In the days of Shamgar, son of Anath,
   In the days of Jael,
   The highways were deserted,
   And the travelers walked along the
      byways.
7 Village life ceased, it ceased in Israel,
   Until I, Deborah, arose,
   Arose a mother in Israel.
8 They chose new gods;
   Then *there was* war in the gates;
   Not a shield or spear was seen among
      forty thousand in Israel.
9 My heart *is* with the rulers of Israel
   Who offered themselves willingly
      with the people.
   Bless the LORD!

10 "Speak, you who ride on white
      donkeys,
   Who sit in judges' attire,
   And who walk along the road.
11 Far from the noise of the archers,
      among the watering places,
   There they shall recount the
      righteous acts of the LORD,
   The righteous acts *for* His villagers
      in Israel;
   Then the people of the LORD shall
      go down to the gates.

12 "Awake, awake, Deborah!
   Awake, awake, sing a song!
   Arise, Barak, and lead your captives
      away,
   O son of Abinoam!

13 "Then the survivors came down, the
      people against the nobles;
   The LORD came down for me against
      the mighty.
14 From Ephraim *were* those whose
      roots were in Amalek.
   After you, Benjamin, with your
      peoples,
   From Machir rulers came down,
   And from Zebulun those who bear
      the recruiter's staff.
15 And the princes of Issachar *were* with
      Deborah;
   As Issachar, so *was* Barak
   Sent into the valley under his
      command;
   Among the divisions of Reuben
   There were great resolves of heart.
16 Why did you sit among the
      sheepfolds,
   To hear the pipings for the flocks?
   The divisions of Reuben have great
      searchings of heart.
17 Gilead stayed beyond the Jordan,
   And why did Dan remain on ships?
   Asher continued at the seashore,
   And stayed by his inlets.
18 Zebulun *is* a people *who* jeopardized
      their lives to the point of death,
   Naphtali also, on the heights of the
      battlefield.

19 "The kings came *and* fought,
   Then the kings of Canaan fought
   In Taanach, by the waters of
      Megiddo;
   They took no spoils of silver.
20 They fought from the heavens;
   The stars from their courses fought
      against Sisera.
21 The torrent of Kishon swept them
      away,
   That ancient torrent, the torrent of
      Kishon.
   O my soul, march on in strength!
22 Then the horses' hooves pounded,
   The galloping, galloping of his
      steeds.
23 'Curse Meroz,' said the angel of the
      LORD,
   'Curse its inhabitants bitterly,
   Because they did not come to the
      help of the LORD,
   To the help of the LORD against the
      mighty.'

24 "Most blessed among women is Jael,
   The wife of Heber the Kenite;
   Blessed is she among women in tents.
25 He asked for water, she gave milk;

She brought out cream in a lordly
bowl.

26 She stretched her hand to the tent
peg,
Her right hand to the workmen's
hammer;
She pounded Sisera, she pierced his
head,
She split and struck through his
temple.

27 At her feet he sank, he fell, he lay
still;
At her feet he sank, he fell;
Where he sank, there he fell dead.

28 "The mother of Sisera looked through
the window,
And cried out through the lattice,
'Why is his chariot *so* long in coming?
Why tarries the clatter of his
chariots?'

29 Her wisest ladies answered her,
Yes, she answered herself,

30 'Are they not finding and dividing the
spoil:
To every man a girl *or* two;
For Sisera, plunder of dyed garments,
Plunder of garments embroidered
and dyed,
Two pieces of dyed embroidery for
the neck of the looter?'

31 "Thus let all Your enemies perish,
O LORD!
But *let* those who love Him *be* like
the sun
When it comes out in full strength."

So the land had rest for forty years.

6 THEN the children of Israel did evil
in the sight of the LORD. So the LORD
delivered them into the hand of Midian
for seven years, 2 and the hand of Midian
prevailed against Israel. Because of the Midianites, the children of Israel made for themselves the dens, the caves, and the strongholds which *are* in the mountains. 3 So it
was, whenever Israel had sown, Midianites
would come up; also Amalekites and the
people of the East would come up against
them. 4 Then they would encamp against
them and destroy the produce of the earth
as far as Gaza, and leave no sustenance for
Israel, neither sheep nor ox nor donkey.
5 For they would come up with their livestock and their tents, coming in as numerous as locusts; both they and their camels
were without number; and they would enter
the land to destroy it. 6 So Israel was greatly
impoverished because of the Midianites,
and the children of Israel cried out to the
LORD.

7 And it came to pass, when the children
of Israel cried out to the LORD because of
the Midianites, 8 that the LORD sent a
prophet to the children of Israel, who said
to them, "Thus says the LORD God of Israel:
'I brought you up from Egypt and brought
you out of the house of bondage; 9 and I
delivered you out of the hand of the Egyptians and out of the hand of all who oppressed you, and drove them out before
you and gave you their land. 10 Also I said
to you, "I *am* the LORD your God; do not
fear the gods of the Amorites, in whose
land you dwell." But you have not obeyed
My voice.'"

11 Now the Angel of the LORD came and
sat under the terebinth tree which *was* in
Ophrah, which *belonged* to Joash the Abi-
ezrite, while his son Gideon threshed wheat
in the winepress, in order to hide *it* from
the Midianites. 12 And the Angel of the
LORD appeared to him, and said to him,
"The LORD *is* with you, you mighty man
of valor!"

13 Gideon said to Him, "O my lord, if
the LORD is with us, why then has all this
happened to us? And where *are* all His miracles which our fathers told us about, saying,
'Did not the LORD bring us up from Egypt?'
But now the LORD has forsaken us and
delivered us into the hands of the
Midianites."

14 Then the LORD turned to him and
said, "Go in this might of yours, and you
shall save Israel from the hand of the Midianites. Have I not sent you?"

15 So he said to Him, "O my Lord, how
can I save Israel? Indeed my clan *is* the weakest in Manasseh, and I *am* the least in my
father's house."

16 And the LORD said to him, "Surely I
will be with you, and you shall defeat the
Midianites as one man."

17 Then he said to Him, "If now I have
found favor in Your sight, then show me
a sign that it is You who talk with me.
18 Do not depart from here, I pray, until
I come to You and bring out my offering
and set *it* before You."

And He said, "I will wait until you come
back."

19 So Gideon went in and prepared a
young goat, and unleavened bread from an
ephah of flour. The meat he put in a basket,
and he put the broth in a pot; and he
brought *them* out to Him under the terebinth tree and presented *them*. 20 The Angel
of God said to him, "Take the meat and
the unleavened bread and lay *them* on this

rock, and pour out the broth." And he did so.

21 Then the Angel of the LORD put out the end of the staff that *was* in His hand, and touched the meat and the unleavened bread; and fire rose out of the rock and consumed the meat and the unleavened bread. And the Angel of the LORD departed out of his sight.

22 Now Gideon perceived that He *was* the Angel of the LORD. So Gideon said, "Alas, O Lord GOD! For I have seen the Angel of the LORD face to face."

23 Then the LORD said to him, "Peace *be* with you; do not fear, you shall not die." 24 So Gideon built an altar there to the LORD, and called it The-LORD-*Is*-Peace. To this day it *is* still in Ophrah of the Abiezrites.

25 Now it came to pass the same night that the LORD said to him, "Take your father's young bull, the second bull of seven years old, and tear down the altar of Baal that your father has, and cut down the wooden image that *is* beside it; 26 and build an altar to the LORD your God on top of this rock in the proper arrangement, and take the second bull and offer a burnt sacrifice with the wood of the image which you shall cut down." 27 So Gideon took ten men from among his servants and did as the LORD had said to him. But because he feared his father's household and the men of the city too much to do *it* by day, he did *it* by night.

28 And when the men of the city arose early in the morning, there was the altar of Baal, torn down; and the wooden image that *was* beside it was cut down, and the second bull was being offered on the altar *which had been* built. 29 So they said to one another, "Who has done this thing?" And when they had inquired and asked, they said, "Gideon the son of Joash has done this thing." 30 Then the men of the city said to Joash, "Bring out your son, that he may die, because he has torn down the altar of Baal, and because he has cut down the wooden image that *was* beside it."

31 But Joash said to all who stood against him, "Would you plead for Baal? Would you save him? Let the one who would plead for him be put to death by morning! If he *is* a god, let him plead for himself, because his altar has been torn down!" 32 Therefore on that day he called him Jerubbaal, saying, "Let Baal plead against him, because he has torn down his altar."

33 Then all the Midianites and Amalekites, the people of the East, gathered together; and they crossed over and encamped in the Valley of Jezreel. 34 But the Spirit of the LORD came upon Gideon; then he blew the trumpet, and the Abiezrites gathered behind him. 35 And he sent messengers throughout all Manasseh, who also gathered behind him. He also sent messengers to Asher, Zebulun, and Naphtali; and they came up to meet them.

36 So Gideon said to God, "If You will save Israel by my hand as You have said— 37 look, I shall put a fleece of wool on the threshing floor; if there is dew on the fleece only, and *it is* dry on all the ground, then I shall know that You will save Israel by my hand, as You have said." 38 And it was so. When he rose early the next morning and squeezed the fleece together, he wrung the dew out of the fleece, a bowlful of water. 39 Then Gideon said to God, "Do not be angry with me, but let me speak just once more: Let me test, I pray, just once more with the fleece; let it now be dry only on the fleece, but on all the ground let there be dew." 40 And God did so that night. It

---

Prayer is getting into perfect communion with God.   (UTMOST)

---

was dry on the fleece only, but there was dew on all the ground.

PSALM 49:1–9

1   HEAR this, all peoples;
     Give ear, all inhabitants of the world,
2   Both low and high,
     Rich and poor together.
3   My mouth shall speak wisdom,
     And the meditation of my heart *shall give* understanding.
4   I will incline my ear to a proverb;
     I will disclose my dark saying on the harp.

5   Why should I fear in the days of evil,
     When the iniquity at my heels surrounds me?
6   Those who trust in their wealth
     And boast in the multitude of their riches,
7   None *of them* can by any means redeem *his* brother,
     Nor give to God a ransom for him—
8   For the redemption of their souls *is* costly,
     And it shall cease forever—
9   That he should continue to live eternally,
     And not see the Pit.

PROVERBS 14:20, 21

20 THE poor *man* is hated even by his
     own neighbor,
     But the rich *has* many friends.
21 He who despises his neighbor sins;
     But he who has mercy on the poor,
     happy *is* he.

LUKE 15:1–10

THEN all the tax collectors and the sinners
drew near to Him to hear Him. 2 And the
Pharisees and scribes complained, saying,
"This Man receives sinners and eats with
them." 3 So He spoke this parable to them,
saying:

4 "What man of you, having a hundred
sheep, if he loses one of them, does not
leave the ninety-nine in the wilderness, and
go after the one which is lost until he finds
it? 5 And when he has found *it*, he lays *it*
on his shoulders, rejoicing. 6 And when he
comes home, he calls together *his* friends
and neighbors, saying to them, 'Rejoice
with me, for I have found my sheep which
was lost!' 7 I say to you that likewise there
will be more joy in heaven over one sinner
who repents than over ninety-nine just persons who need no repentance.

8 "Or what woman, having ten silver
coins, if she loses one coin, does not light
a lamp, sweep the house, and search carefully until she finds *it*? 9 And when she has
found *it*, she calls *her* friends and neighbors
together, saying, 'Rejoice with me, for I
have found the piece which I lost!'
10 Likewise, I say to you, there is joy in
the presence of the angels of God over one
sinner who repents."

◆◆◆◆

Reading 111—The Older Brother's Interests
Luke 15:28–31

A s long as you have a personal interest in your own character, or any set
ambition, you cannot get through into identification with God's interests.
You can only get there by losing forever any idea of yourself and by letting
God take you right out into His purpose for the world, and because your
goings are of the Lord, you can never understand your ways.

I have to learn that the aim in life is God's, not mine. God is using me
from His great personal standpoint, and all He asks of me is that I trust Him,
and never say—Lord, this gives me such heartache. . . . When I stop telling
God what I want, He can catch me up for what He wants without let or
hindrance. He can crumple me up or exalt me, He can do anything He chooses.
He simply asks me to have implicit faith in Himself and in His goodness.
Self-pity is of the Devil; if I go off on that line I cannot be used by God for
His purpose in the world. I have "a world within the world" in which I live,
and God will never be able to get me outside it because I am afraid of being
frostbitten. (*UTMOST*)

JUDGES 7:1—8:35

THEN Jerubbaal (that *is,* Gideon) and all
the people who *were* with him rose early
and encamped beside the well of Harod,
so that the camp of the Midianites was on
the north side of them by the hill of Moreh
in the valley.

2 And the LORD said to Gideon, "The
people who *are* with you *are* too many for
Me to give the Midianites into their hands,
lest Israel claim glory for itself against Me,
saying, 'My own hand has saved me.'
3 Now therefore, proclaim in the hearing
of the people, saying, 'Whoever *is* fearful
and afraid, let him turn and depart at once
from Mount Gilead.' " And twenty-two
thousand of the people returned, and ten
thousand remained.

4 But the LORD said to Gideon, "The

people *are* still *too* many; bring them down to the water, and I will test them for you there. Then it will be, *that* of whom I say to you, 'This one shall go with you,' the same shall go with you; and of whomever I say to you, 'This one shall not go with you,' the same shall not go." 5 So he brought the people down to the water. And the LORD said to Gideon, "Everyone who laps from the water with his tongue, as a dog laps, you shall set apart by himself; likewise everyone who gets down on his knees to drink." 6 And the number of those who lapped, *putting* their hand to their mouth, was three hundred men; but all the rest of the people got down on their knees to drink water. 7 Then the LORD said to Gideon, "By the three hundred men who lapped I will save you, and deliver the Midianites into your hand. Let all the *other* people go, every man to his place." 8 So the people took provisions and their trumpets in their hands. And he sent away all *the rest of* Israel, every man to his tent, and retained those three hundred men. Now the camp of Midian was below him in the valley.

9 It happened on the same night that the LORD said to him, "Arise, go down against the camp, for I have delivered it into your hand. 10 But if you are afraid to go down, go down to the camp with Purah your servant, 11 and you shall hear what they say; and afterward your hands shall be strengthened to go down against the camp." Then he went down with Purah his servant to the outpost of the armed men who *were* in the camp. 12 Now the Midianites and Amalekites, all the people of the East, were lying in the valley as numerous as locusts; and their camels *were* without number, as the sand by the seashore in multitude.

13 And when Gideon had come, there was a man telling a dream to his companion. He said, "I have had a dream: *To my* surprise, a loaf of barley bread tumbled into the camp of Midian; it came to a tent and struck it so that it fell and overturned, and the tent collapsed."

14 Then his companion answered and said, "This *is* nothing else but the sword of Gideon the son of Joash, a man of Israel! Into his hand God has delivered Midian and the whole camp."

15 And so it was, when Gideon heard the telling of the dream and its interpretation, that he worshiped. He returned to the camp of Israel, and said, "Arise, for the LORD has delivered the camp of Midian into your hand." 16 Then he divided the three hundred men *into* three companies,

and he put a trumpet into every man's hand, with empty pitchers, and torches inside the pitchers. 17 And he said to them, "Look at me and do likewise; watch, and when I come to the edge of the camp you shall do as I do: 18 When I blow the trumpet, I and all who *are* with me, then you also blow the trumpets on every side of the whole camp, and say, '*The sword of* the LORD and of Gideon!' "

19 So Gideon and the hundred men who *were* with him came to the outpost of the camp at the beginning of the middle watch, just as they had posted the watch; and they blew the trumpets and broke the pitchers that *were* in their hands. 20 Then the three companies blew the trumpets and broke the pitchers—they held the torches in their left hands and the trumpets in their right hands for blowing—and they cried, "The sword of the LORD and of Gideon!" 21 And every man stood in his place all around the camp; and the whole army ran and cried out and fled. 22 When the three hundred blew the trumpets, the LORD set every man's sword against his companion throughout the whole camp; and the army fled to Beth Acacia, toward Zererah, as far as the border of Abel Meholah, by Tabbath.

23 And the men of Israel gathered together from Naphtali, Asher, and all Manasseh, and pursued the Midianites.

24 Then Gideon sent messengers throughout all the mountains of Ephraim, saying, "Come down against the Midianites, and seize from them the watering places as far as Beth Barah and the Jordan." Then all the men of Ephraim gathered together and seized the watering places as far as Beth Barah and the Jordan. 25 And they captured two princes of the Midianites, Oreb and Zeeb. They killed Oreb at the rock of Oreb, and Zeeb they killed at the winepress of Zeeb. They pursued Midian and brought the heads of Oreb and Zeeb to Gideon on the other side of the Jordan.

8 NOW the men of Ephraim said to him, "Why have you done this to us by not calling us when you went to fight with the Midianites?" And they reprimanded him sharply.

2 So he said to them, "What have I done now in comparison with you? *Is* not the gleaning *of the grapes* of Ephraim better than the vintage of Abiezer? 3 God has delivered into your hands the princes of Midian, Oreb and Zeeb. And what was I able to do in comparison with you?" Then their anger toward him subsided when he said that.

4 When Gideon came to the Jordan, he

and the three hundred men who *were* with him crossed over, exhausted but still in pursuit. 5 Then he said to the men of Succoth, "Please give loaves of bread to the people who follow me, for they are exhausted, and I am pursuing Zebah and Zalmunna, kings of Midian."

6 And the leaders of Succoth said, "*Are* the hands of Zebah and Zalmunna now in your hand, that we should give bread to your army?"

7 So Gideon said, "For this cause, when the Lord has delivered Zebah and Zalmunna into my hand, then I will tear your flesh with the thorns of the wilderness and with briers!" 8 Then he went up from there to Penuel and spoke to them in the same way. And the men of Penuel answered him as the men of Succoth had answered. 9 So he also spoke to the men of Penuel, saying, "When I come back in peace, I will tear down this tower!"

10 Now Zebah and Zalmunna *were* at Karkor, and their armies with them, about fifteen thousand, all who were left of all the army of the people of the East; for one hundred and twenty thousand men who drew the sword had fallen. 11 Then Gideon went up by the road of those who dwell in tents on the east of Nobah and Jogbehah; and he attacked the army while the camp felt secure. 12 When Zebah and Zalmunna fled, he pursued them; and he took the two kings of Midian, Zebah and Zalmunna, and routed the whole army.

13 Then Gideon the son of Joash returned from battle, from the Ascent of Heres. 14 And he caught a young man of the men of Succoth and interrogated him; and he wrote down for him the leaders of Succoth and its elders, seventy-seven men. 15 Then he came to the men of Succoth and said, "Here are Zebah and Zalmunna, about whom you ridiculed me, saying, '*Are* the hands of Zebah and Zalmunna now in your hand, that we should give bread to your weary men?'" 16 And he took the elders of the city, and thorns of the wilderness and briers, and with them he taught the men of Succoth. 17 Then he tore down the tower of Penuel and killed the men of the city.

18 And he said to Zebah and Zalmunna, "What kind of men *were they* whom you killed at Tabor?"

So they answered, "As you *are*, so *were* they; each one resembled the son of a king."

19 Then he said, "They *were* my brothers, the sons of my mother. *As* the Lord lives, if you had let them live, I would not kill you." 20 And he said to Jether his firstborn, "Rise, kill them!" But the youth would not draw his sword; for he was afraid, because he *was* still a youth.

21 So Zebah and Zalmunna said, "Rise yourself, and kill us; for as a man *is*, *so is* his strength." So Gideon arose and killed Zebah and Zalmunna, and took the crescent ornaments that *were* on their camels' necks.

22 Then the men of Israel said to Gideon, "Rule over us, both you and your son, and your grandson also; for you have delivered us from the hand of Midian."

23 But Gideon said to them, "I will not rule over you, nor shall my son rule over you; the Lord shall rule over you." 24 Then Gideon said to them, "I would like to make a request of you, that each of you would give me the earrings from his plunder." For they had golden earrings, because they *were* Ishmaelites.

25 So they answered, "We will gladly give *them*." And they spread out a garment, and each man threw into it the earrings from his plunder. 26 Now the weight of the gold earrings that he requested was one thousand seven hundred *shekels* of gold, besides the crescent ornaments, pendants, and purple robes which *were* on the kings of Midian, and besides the chains that *were* around their camels' necks. 27 Then Gideon made it into an ephod and set it up in his city, Ophrah. And all Israel played the harlot with it there. It became a snare to Gideon and to his house.

28 Thus Midian was subdued before the children of Israel, so that they lifted their heads no more. And the country was quiet for forty years in the days of Gideon.

29 Then Jerubbaal the son of Joash went and dwelt in his own house. 30 Gideon had seventy sons who were his own offspring, for he had many wives. 31 And his concubine who *was* in Shechem also bore him a son, whose name he called Abimelech. 32 Now Gideon the son of Joash died at a good old age, and was buried in the tomb of Joash his father, in Ophrah of the Abiezrites.

33 So it was, as soon as Gideon was dead, that the children of Israel again played the harlot with the Baals, and made Baal-Berith their god. 34 Thus the children of Israel did not remember the Lord their God, who had delivered them from the hands of all their enemies on every side; 35 nor did they show kindness to the house of Jerubbaal (Gideon) in accordance with the good he had done for Israel.

PSALM 49:10–20

10 FOR he sees wise men die;
Likewise the fool and the senseless
person perish,
And leave their wealth to others.

11 Their inner thought *is that* their houses
will last forever,
Their dwelling places to all generations;
They call *their* lands after their own
names.

12 Nevertheless man, *though* in honor,
does not remain;
He is like the beasts *that* perish.

13 This is the way of those who *are*
foolish,
And of their posterity who approve
their sayings.   Selah

14 Like sheep they are laid in the grave;
Death shall feed on them;
The upright shall have dominion over
them in the morning;
And their beauty shall be consumed in
the grave, far from their dwelling.

15 But God will redeem my soul from the
power of the grave,
For He shall receive me.   Selah

16 Do not be afraid when one becomes
rich,
When the glory of his house is
increased;

17 For when he dies he shall carry nothing
away;
His glory shall not descend after him.

18 Though while he lives he blesses himself
(For *men* will praise you when you do
well for yourself),

19 He shall go to the generation of his
fathers;
They shall never see light.

20 A man *who is* in honor, yet does not
understand,
Is like the beasts *that* perish.

PROVERBS 14:22–24

22 DO they not go astray who devise
evil?
But mercy and truth *belong* to those
who devise good.

23 In all labor there is profit,
But idle chatter *leads* only to poverty.

24 The crown of the wise is their
riches,
But the foolishness of fools *is* folly.

LUKE 15:11–32

THEN He said: "A certain man had two
sons. 12 And the younger of them said to
his father, 'Father, give me the portion of
goods that falls *to me.*' So he divided to
them *his* livelihood. 13 And not many days
after, the younger son gathered all together,
journeyed to a far country, and there wasted
his possessions with prodigal living.
14 But when he had spent all, there arose
a severe famine in that land, and he began
to be in want. 15 Then he went and joined
himself to a citizen of that country, and
he sent him into his fields to feed swine.
16 And he would gladly have filled his stomach with the pods that the swine ate, and
no one gave him *anything.*

17 "But when he came to himself, he said,
'How many of my father's hired servants
have bread enough and to spare, and I perish with hunger! 18 I will arise and go to
my father, and will say to him, "Father, I
have sinned against heaven and before you,
19 and I am no longer worthy to be called
your son. Make me like one of your hired
servants." '

20 "And he arose and came to his father.
But when he was still a great way off, his
father saw him and had compassion, and
ran and fell on his neck and kissed him.
21 And the son said to him, 'Father, I have
sinned against heaven and in your sight,
and am no longer worthy to be called your
son.'

22 "But the father said to his servants,
'Bring out the best robe and put *it* on him,
and put a ring on his hand and sandals
on *his* feet. 23 And bring the fatted calf here
and kill *it,* and let us eat and be merry;
24 for this my son was dead and is alive
again; he was lost and is found.' And they
began to be merry.

---

*The springs of love are in God, not
in us.*   (BRILL. HERITAGE)

---

25 "Now his older son was in the field.
And as he came and drew near to the house,
he heard music and dancing. 26 So he called
one of the servants and asked what these
things meant. 27 And he said to him, 'Your
brother has come, and because he has received him safe and sound, your father has
killed the fatted calf.'

28 "But he was angry and would not go
in. Therefore his father came out and
pleaded with him. 29 So he answered and

said to *his* father, 'Lo, these many years I have been serving you; I never transgressed your commandment at any time; and yet you never gave me a young goat, that I might make merry with my friends. 30 But as soon as this son of yours came, who has devoured your livelihood with harlots, you killed the fatted calf for him.' 31 "And he said to him, 'Son, you are always with me, and all that I have is yours. 32 It was right that we should make merry and be glad, for your brother was dead and is alive again, and was lost and is found.' "

◆◆◆

Reading 112—The Absolute Moral Law
Luke 16:17

The moral law never alters, either for the noblest or for the weakest, it is eternally and abidingly the same. The moral law ordained by God does not make itself weak to the weak, it does not palliate our shortcomings, it remains absolute for all time and eternity. If we do not realize this, it is because we are less than alive; immediately we are alive, life becomes a tragedy. "I was alive without the law once: but when the commandment came, sin revived, and I died." When we realize this, then the Spirit of God convicts us of sin. Until a man gets there and sees that there is no hope, the Cross of Jesus Christ is a farce to him. Conviction of sin always brings a fearful binding sense of the law, it makes a man hopeless—*"sold under sin."* I, a guilty sinner, can never get right with God, it is impossible. There is only one way in which I can get right with God, and that is by the Death of Jesus Christ. I must get rid of the lurking idea that I can ever be right with God because of my obedience— which of us could ever obey God to absolute perfection!   (*UTMOST*)

JUDGES 9:1—10:18

THEN Abimelech the son of Jerubbaal went to Shechem, to his mother's brothers, and spoke with them and with all the family of the house of his mother's father, saying, 2 "Please speak in the hearing of all the men of Shechem: 'Which is better for you, that all seventy of the sons of Jerubbaal reign over you, or that one reign over you?' Remember that I *am* your own flesh and bone."

3 And his mother's brothers spoke all these words concerning him in the hearing of all the men of Shechem; and their heart was inclined to follow Abimelech, for they said, "He is our brother." 4 So they gave him seventy *shekels* of silver from the temple of Baal-Berith, with which Abimelech hired worthless and reckless men; and they followed him. 5 Then he went to his father's house at Ophrah and killed his brothers, the seventy sons of Jerubbaal, on one stone. But Jotham the youngest son of Jerubbaal was left, because he hid himself. 6 And all the men of Shechem gathered together, all of Beth Millo, and they went and made Abimelech king beside the terebinth tree at the pillar that *was* in Shechem.

7 Now when they told Jotham, he went and stood on top of Mount Gerizim, and lifted his voice and cried out. And he said to them:

"Listen to me, you men of Shechem,
   That God may listen to you!

8 "The trees once went forth to anoint
      a king over them.
   And they said to the olive tree,
   'Reign over us!'
9   But the olive tree said to them,
   'Should I cease giving my oil,
      With which they honor God and
         men,
      And go to sway over trees?'

10 "Then the trees said to the fig tree,
   'You come *and* reign over us!'
11   But the fig tree said to them,

'Should I cease my sweetness and my
   good fruit,
And go to sway over trees?'

12 "Then the trees said to the vine,
   'You come *and* reign over us!'
13 But the vine said to them,
   'Should I cease my new wine,
   Which cheers *both* God and men,
   And go to sway over trees?'

14 "Then all the trees said to the bramble,
   'You come *and* reign over us!'
15 And the bramble said to the trees,
   'If in truth you anoint me as king
      over you,
   Then come *and* take shelter in my
      shade;
   But if not, let fire come out of the
      bramble
   And devour the cedars of Lebanon!'

16 "Now therefore, if you have acted in
truth and sincerity in making Abimelech
king, and if you have dealt well with Jerubbaal and his house, and have done to him
as he deserves— 17 for my father fought
for you, risked his life, and delivered you
out of the hand of Midian; 18 but you have
risen up against my father's house this day,
and killed his seventy sons on one stone,
and made Abimelech, the son of his female
servant, king over the men of Shechem,
because he is your brother— 19 if then you
have acted in truth and sincerity with Jerubbaal and with his house this day, *then* rejoice
in Abimelech, and let him also rejoice in
you. 20 But if not, let fire come from Abimelech and devour the men of Shechem and
Beth Millo; and let fire come from the men
of Shechem and from Beth Millo and devour Abimelech!" 21 And Jotham ran away
and fled; and he went to Beer and dwelt
there, for fear of Abimelech his brother.

22 After Abimelech had reigned over Israel three years, 23 God sent a spirit of ill
will between Abimelech and the men of
Shechem; and the men of Shechem dealt
treacherously with Abimelech, 24 that the
crime *done* to the seventy sons of Jerubbaal
might be settled and their blood be laid
on Abimelech their brother, who killed
them, and on the men of Shechem, who
aided him in the killing of his brothers.
25 And the men of Shechem set men in ambush against him on the tops of the mountains, and they robbed all who passed by
them along that way; and it was told
Abimelech.

26 Now Gaal the son of Ebed came with
his brothers and went over to Shechem;
and the men of Shechem put their confidence in him. 27 So they went out into the
fields, and gathered *grapes* from their vineyards and trod *them,* and made merry. And
they went into the house of their god, and
ate and drank, and cursed Abimelech.
28 Then Gaal the son of Ebed said, "Who
is Abimelech, and who *is* Shechem, that
we should serve him? *Is he* not the son of
Jerubbaal, and *is not* Zebul his officer? Serve
the men of Hamor the father of Shechem;
but why should we serve him? 29 If only
this people were under my authority! Then
I would remove Abimelech." So he said
to Abimelech, "Increase your army and
come out!"

30 When Zebul, the ruler of the city,
heard the words of Gaal the son of Ebed,
his anger was aroused. 31 And he sent messengers to Abimelech secretly, saying, "Take
note! Gaal the son of Ebed and his brothers
have come to Shechem; and here they are,
fortifying the city against you. 32 Now
therefore, get up by night, you and the
people who *are* with you, and lie in wait
in the field. 33 And it shall be, as soon as
the sun is up in the morning, *that* you shall
rise early and rush upon the city; and *when*
he and the people who are with him come
out against you, you may then do to them
as you find opportunity."

34 So Abimelech and all the people who
were with him rose by night, and lay in
wait against Shechem in four companies.
35 When Gaal the son of Ebed went out
and stood in the entrance to the city gate,
Abimelech and the people who *were* with
him rose from lying in wait. 36 And when
Gaal saw the people, he said to Zebul,
"Look, people are coming down from the
tops of the mountains!"

But Zebul said to him, "You see the shadows of the mountains as *if they were* men."
37 So Gaal spoke again and said, "See,
people are coming down from the center
of the land, and another company is coming
from the Diviners' Terebinth Tree."
38 Then Zebul said to him, "Where indeed *is* your mouth now, with which you
said, 'Who is Abimelech, that we should
serve him?' *Are* not these the people whom
you despised? Go out, if you will, and fight
with them now."
39 So Gaal went out, leading the men
of Shechem, and fought with Abimelech.
40 And Abimelech chased him, and he fled
from him; and many fell wounded, to the
very entrance of the gate. 41 Then Abimelech
dwelt at Arumah, and Zebul drove out Gaal
and his brothers, so that they would not
dwell in Shechem.

42 And it came about on the next day that the people went out into the field, and they told Abimelech. 43 So he took his people, divided them into three companies, and lay in wait in the field. And he looked, and there were the people, coming out of the city; and he rose against them and attacked them. 44 Then Abimelech and the company that *was* with him rushed forward and stood at the entrance of the gate of the city; and the *other* two companies rushed upon all who *were* in the fields and killed them. 45 So Abimelech fought against the city all that day; he took the city and killed the people who *were* in it; and he demolished the city and sowed it with salt.

46 Now when all the men of the tower of Shechem had heard *that,* they entered the stronghold of the temple of the god Berith. 47 And it was told Abimelech that all the men of the tower of Shechem were gathered together. 48 Then Abimelech went up to Mount Zalmon, he and all the people who *were* with him. And Abimelech took an ax in his hand and cut down a bough from the trees, and took it and laid *it* on his shoulder; then he said to the people who were with him, "What you have seen me do, make haste *and* do as I *have done.*" 49 So each of the people likewise cut down his own bough and followed Abimelech, put *them* against the stronghold, and set the stronghold on fire above them, so that all the people of the tower of Shechem died, about a thousand men and women.

50 Then Abimelech went to Thebez, and he encamped against Thebez and took it. 51 But there was a strong tower in the city, and all the men and women—all the people of the city—fled there and shut themselves in; then they went up to the top of the tower. 52 So Abimelech came as far as the tower and fought against it; and he drew near the door of the tower to burn it with fire. 53 But a certain woman dropped an upper millstone on Abimelech's head and crushed his skull. 54 Then he called quickly to the young man, his armorbearer, and said to him, "Draw your sword and kill me, lest men say of me, 'A woman killed him.'" So his young man thrust him through, and he died. 55 And when the men of Israel saw that Abimelech was dead, they departed, every man to his place.

56 Thus God repaid the wickedness of Abimelech, which he had done to his father by killing his seventy brothers. 57 And all the evil of the men of Shechem God returned on their own heads, and on them came the curse of Jotham the son of Jerubbaal.

10 AFTER Abimelech there arose to save Israel Tola the son of Puah, the son of Dodo, a man of Issachar; and he dwelt in Shamir in the mountains of Ephraim. 2 He judged Israel twenty-three years; and he died and was buried in Shamir.

3 After him arose Jair, a Gileadite; and he judged Israel twenty-two years. 4 Now he had thirty sons who rode on thirty donkeys; they also had thirty towns, which are called "Havoth Jair" to this day, which *are* in the land of Gilead. 5 And Jair died and was buried in Camon.

6 Then the children of Israel again did evil in the sight of the LORD, and served the Baals and the Ashtoreths, the gods of Syria, the gods of Sidon, the gods of Moab, the gods of the people of Ammon, and the gods of the Philistines; and they forsook the LORD and did not serve Him. 7 So the anger of the LORD was hot against Israel; and He sold them into the hands of the Philistines and into the hands of the people of Ammon. 8 From that year they harassed and oppressed the children of Israel for eighteen years—all the children of Israel who *were* on the other side of the Jordan in the land of the Amorites, in Gilead. 9 Moreover the people of Ammon crossed over the Jordan to fight against Judah also, against Benjamin, and against the house of Ephraim, so that Israel was severely distressed.

10 And the children of Israel cried out to the LORD, saying, "We have sinned against You, because we have both forsaken our God and served the Baals!"

11 So the LORD said to the children of Israel, "*Did I* not *deliver you* from the Egyptians and from the Amorites and from the people of Ammon and from the Philistines? 12 Also the Sidonians and Amalekites and Maonites oppressed you; and you cried out to Me, and I delivered you from their hand. 13 Yet you have forsaken Me and served other gods. Therefore I will deliver you no more. 14 Go and cry out to the gods which you have chosen; let them deliver you in your time of distress."

---

*A*ll the distress and all the sacrifice in the world will never atone for sin. (PSY. REDEMP.)

---

15 And the children of Israel said to the LORD, "We have sinned! Do to us whatever seems best to You; only deliver us this day, we pray." 16 So they put away the foreign

gods from among them and served the LORD. And His soul could no longer endure the misery of Israel.

17 Then the people of Ammon gathered together and encamped in Gilead. And the children of Israel assembled together and encamped in Mizpah. 18 And the people, the leaders of Gilead, said to one another, "Who *is* the man who will begin the fight against the people of Ammon? He shall be head over all the inhabitants of Gilead."

PSALM 50:1–6

1 THE Mighty One, God the LORD,
 Has spoken and called the earth
 From the rising of the sun to its going down.
2 Out of Zion, the perfection of beauty,
 God will shine forth.
3 Our God shall come, and shall not keep silent;
 A fire shall devour before Him,
 And it shall be very tempestuous all around Him.

4 He shall call to the heavens from above,
 And to the earth, that He may judge His people:
5 "Gather My saints together to Me,
 Those who have made a covenant with Me by sacrifice."
6 Let the heavens declare His righteousness,
 For God Himself *is* Judge.   Selah

PROVERBS 14:25–27

25 A true witness delivers souls,
 But a deceitful *witness* speaks lies.

26 In the fear of the LORD *there is* strong confidence,
 And His children will have a place of refuge.
27 The fear of the LORD *is* a fountain of life,
 To turn *one* away from the snares of death.

LUKE 16:1–31

HE also said to His disciples: "There was a certain rich man who had a steward, and an accusation was brought to him that this man was wasting his goods. 2 So he called him and said to him, 'What is this I hear about you? Give an account of your stew-

ardship, for you can no longer be steward.'
3 "Then the steward said within himself, 'What shall I do? For my master is taking the stewardship away from me. I cannot dig; I am ashamed to beg. 4 I have resolved what to do, that when I am put out of the stewardship, they may receive me into their houses.'

5 "So he called every one of his master's debtors to *him,* and said to the first, 'How much do you owe my master?' 6 And he said, 'A hundred measures of oil.' So he said to him, 'Take your bill, and sit down quickly and write fifty.' 7 Then he said to another, 'And how much do you owe?' So he said, 'A hundred measures of wheat.' And he said to him, 'Take your bill, and write eighty.' 8 So the master commended the unjust steward because he had dealt shrewdly. For the sons of this world are more shrewd in their generation than the sons of light.

9 "And I say to you, make friends for yourselves by unrighteous mammon, that when you fail, they may receive you into an everlasting home. 10 He who *is* faithful in *what is* least is faithful also in much; and he who is unjust in *what is* least is unjust also in much. 11 Therefore if you have not been faithful in the unrighteous mammon, who will commit to your trust the true *riches?* 12 And if you have not been faithful in what is another man's, who will give you what is your own?

13 "No servant can serve two masters; for either he will hate the one and love the other, or else he will be loyal to the one and despise the other. You cannot serve God and mammon."

---

*M*ammon is the system of civilized life which organizes itself without any consideration of God.   (MORAL FOUND.)

---

14 Now the Pharisees, who were lovers of money, also heard all these things, and they derided Him. 15 And He said to them, "You are those who justify yourselves before men, but God knows your hearts. For what is highly esteemed among men is an abomination in the sight of God.
16 "The law and the prophets *were* until John. Since that time the kingdom of God has been preached, and everyone is pressing into it. 17 And it is easier for heaven and earth to pass away than for one tittle of the law to fail.

18 "Whoever divorces his wife and marries another commits adultery; and whoever marries her who is divorced from *her* husband commits adultery.

19 "There was a certain rich man who was clothed in purple and fine linen and fared sumptuously every day. 20 But there was a certain beggar named Lazarus, full of sores, who was laid at his gate, 21 desiring to be fed with the crumbs which fell from the rich man's table. Moreover, the dogs came and licked his sores. 22 So it was that the beggar died, and was carried by the angels to Abraham's bosom. The rich man also died and was buried. 23 And being in torments in Hades, he lifted up his eyes and saw Abraham afar off, and Lazarus in his bosom.

24 "Then he cried and said, 'Father Abraham, have mercy on me, and send Lazarus that he may dip the tip of his finger in water and cool my tongue; for I am tormented in this flame.' 25 But Abraham said, 'Son, remember that in your lifetime you received your good things, and likewise Lazarus evil things; but now he is comforted and you are tormented. 26 And besides all this, between us and you there is a great gulf fixed, so that those who want to pass from here to you cannot, nor can those from there pass to us.'

27 "Then he said, 'I beg you therefore, father, that you would send him to my father's house, 28 for I have five brothers, that he may testify to them, lest they also come to this place of torment.' 29 Abraham said to him, 'They have Moses and the prophets; let them hear them.' 30 And he said, 'No, father Abraham; but if one goes to them from the dead, they will repent.' 31 But he said to him, 'If they do not hear Moses and the prophets, neither will they be persuaded though one rise from the dead.' "

◆◆◆◆

Reading 113—The Ideal Faith Made Real
Luke 17:5, 6

Common sense is not faith, and faith is not common sense; they stand in the relation of the natural and the spiritual; of impulse and inspiration. Nothing Jesus Christ ever said is common sense, it is revelation sense, and it reaches the shores where common sense fails. . . . Faith always works on the personal line, the whole purpose of God being to see that the ideal faith is made real in His children.

For every detail of the commonsense life, there is a revelation fact of God whereby we can prove in practical experience what we believe God to be. Faith is a tremendously active principle which always puts Jesus Christ first— Lord, You have said so-and-so (for example, Matt. 6:33), it looks mad, but I am going to venture on Your word. To turn head faith into a personal possession is a fight *always,* not sometimes. God brings us into circumstances in order to educate our faith, because the nature of faith is to make its object real. Until we know Jesus, God is a mere abstraction, we cannot have faith in Him; but immediately we hear Jesus say—"He who has seen Me has seen the Father," we have something that is real, and faith is boundless. Faith is the whole man rightly related to God by the power of the Spirit of Jesus Christ.   (*Utmost*)

JUDGES 11:1—12:15

NOW Jephthah the Gileadite was a mighty man of valor, but he *was* the son of a harlot; and Gilead begot Jephthah. 2 Gilead's wife bore sons; and when his wife's sons grew up, they drove Jephthah out, and said to him, "You shall have no inheritance in our father's house, for you *are* the son of another woman." 3 Then Jephthah fled from his brothers and dwelt in the land of Tob; and worthless men banded together with Jephthah and went out *raiding* with him.

4 It came to pass after a time that the

people of Ammon made war against Israel.
5 And so it was, when the people of Ammon made war against Israel, that the elders of Gilead went to get Jephthah from the land of Tob. 6 Then they said to Jephthah, "Come and be our commander, that we may fight against the people of Ammon."

7 So Jephthah said to the elders of Gilead, "Did you not hate me, and expel me from my father's house? Why have you come to me now when you are in distress?"

8 And the elders of Gilead said to Jephthah, "That is why we have turned again to you now, that you may go with us and fight against the people of Ammon, and be our head over all the inhabitants of Gilead."

9 So Jephthah said to the elders of Gilead, "If you take me back home to fight against the people of Ammon, and the LORD delivers them to me, shall I be your head?"

10 And the elders of Gilead said to Jephthah, "The LORD will be a witness between us, if we do not do according to your words." 11 Then Jephthah went with the elders of Gilead, and the people made him head and commander over them; and Jephthah spoke all his words before the LORD in Mizpah.

12 Now Jephthah sent messengers to the king of the people of Ammon, saying, "What do you have against me, that you have come to fight against me in my land?"

13 And the king of the people of Ammon answered the messengers of Jephthah, "Because Israel took away my land when they came up out of Egypt, from the Arnon as far as the Jabbok, and to the Jordan. Now therefore, restore those *lands* peaceably."

14 So Jephthah again sent messengers to the king of the people of Ammon, 15 and said to him, "Thus says Jephthah: 'Israel did not take away the land of Moab, nor the land of the people of Ammon; 16 for when Israel came up from Egypt, they walked through the wilderness as far as the Red Sea and came to Kadesh. 17 Then Israel sent messengers to the king of Edom, saying, "Please let me pass through your land." But the king of Edom would not heed. And in like manner they sent to the king of Moab, but he would not *consent*. So Israel remained in Kadesh. 18 And they went along through the wilderness and bypassed the land of Edom and the land of Moab, came to the east side of the land of Moab, and encamped on the other side of the Arnon. But they did not enter the border of Moab, for the Arnon *was* the border of Moab. 19 Then Israel sent messengers to Sihon king of the Amorites, king of Heshbon; and Israel said to him, "Please let us pass through your land into our place." 20 But Sihon did not trust Israel to pass through his territory. So Sihon gathered all his people together, encamped in Jahaz, and fought against Israel. 21 And the LORD God of Israel delivered Sihon and all his people into the hand of Israel, and they defeated them. Thus Israel gained possession of all the land of the Amorites, who inhabited that country. 22 They took posses-

---

God is the controller of history.   (SERVANT AS LORD)

---

sion of all the territory of the Amorites, from the Arnon to the Jabbok and from the wilderness to the Jordan.

23 'And now the LORD God of Israel has dispossessed the Amorites from before His people Israel; should you then possess it? 24 Will you not possess whatever Chemosh your god gives you to possess? So whatever the LORD our God takes possession of before us, we will possess. 25 And now, *are* you any better than Balak the son of Zippor, king of Moab? Did he ever strive against Israel? Did he ever fight against them? 26 While Israel dwelt in Heshbon and its villages, in Aroer and its villages, and in all the cities along the banks of the Arnon, for three hundred years, why did you not recover *them* within that time? 27 Therefore I have not sinned against you, but you wronged me by fighting against me. May the LORD, the Judge, render judgment this day between the children of Israel and the people of Ammon.' " 28 However, the king of the people of Ammon did not heed the words which Jephthah sent him.

29 Then the Spirit of the LORD came upon Jephthah, and he passed through Gilead and Manasseh, and passed through Mizpah of Gilead; and from Mizpah of Gilead he advanced *toward* the people of Ammon. 30 And Jephthah made a vow to the LORD, and said, "If You will indeed deliver the people of Ammon into my hands, 31 then it will be that whatever comes out of the doors of my house to meet me, when I return in peace from the people of Ammon, shall surely be the LORD's, and I will offer it up as a burnt offering."

32 So Jephthah advanced toward the people of Ammon to fight against them, and the LORD delivered them into his hands. 33 And he defeated them from Aroer as far as Minnith—twenty cities—and to Abel

Keramim, with a very great slaughter. Thus the people of Ammon were subdued before the children of Israel.

34 When Jephthah came to his house at Mizpah, there was his daughter, coming out to meet him with timbrels and dancing; and she *was his* only child. Besides her he had neither son nor daughter. 35 And it came to pass, when he saw her, that he tore his clothes, and said, "Alas, my daughter! You have brought me very low! You are among those who trouble me! For I have given my word to the LORD, and I cannot go back on it."

36 So she said to him, "My father, *if* you have given your word to the LORD, do to me according to what has gone out of your mouth, because the LORD has avenged you of your enemies, the people of Ammon." 37 Then she said to her father, "Let this thing be done for me: let me alone for two months, that I may go and wander on the mountains and bewail my virginity, my friends and I."

38 So he said, "Go." And he sent her away *for* two months; and she went with her friends, and bewailed her virginity on the mountains. 39 And it was so at the end of two months that she returned to her father, and he carried out his vow with her which he had vowed. She knew no man.

And it became a custom in Israel 40 *that* the daughters of Israel went four days each year to lament the daughter of Jephthah the Gileadite.

12 THEN the men of Ephraim gathered together, crossed over toward Zaphon, and said to Jephthah, "Why did you cross over to fight against the people of Ammon, and did not call us to go with you? We will burn your house down on you with fire!"

2 And Jephthah said to them, "My people and I were in a great struggle with the people of Ammon; and when I called you, you did not deliver me out of their hands. 3 So when I saw that you would not deliver *me,* I took my life in my hands and crossed over against the people of Ammon; and the LORD delivered them into my hand. Why then have you come up to me this day to fight against me?" 4 Now Jephthah gathered together all the men of Gilead and fought against Ephraim. And the men of Gilead defeated Ephraim, because they said, "You Gileadites *are* fugitives of Ephraim among the Ephraimites *and* among the Manassites." 5 The Gileadites seized the fords of the Jordan before the Ephraimites *arrived.* And when *any* Ephraimite who es-

caped said, "Let me cross over," the men of Gilead would say to him, "*Are* you an Ephraimite?" If he said, "No," 6 then they would say to him, "Then say, 'Shibboleth'!" And he would say, "Sibboleth," for he could not pronounce *it* right. Then they would take him and kill him at the fords of the Jordan. There fell at that time forty-two thousand Ephraimites.

7 And Jephthah judged Israel six years. Then Jephthah the Gileadite died and was buried among the cities of Gilead.

8 After him, Ibzan of Bethlehem judged Israel. 9 He had thirty sons. And he gave away thirty daughters in marriage, and brought in thirty daughters from elsewhere for his sons. He judged Israel seven years. 10 Then Ibzan died and was buried at Bethlehem.

11 After him, Elon the Zebulunite judged Israel. He judged Israel ten years. 12 And Elon the Zebulunite died and was buried at Aijalon in the country of Zebulun.

13 After him, Abdon the son of Hillel the Pirathonite judged Israel. 14 He had forty sons and thirty grandsons, who rode on seventy young donkeys. He judged Israel eight years. 15 Then Abdon the son of Hillel the Pirathonite died and was buried in Pirathon in the land of Ephraim, in the mountains of the Amalekites.

PSALM 50:7–15

7 "HEAR, O My people, and I will speak,
O Israel, and I will testify against you;
I *am* God, your God!
8 I will not rebuke you for your sacrifices
Or your burnt offerings,
Which are continually before Me.
9 I will not take a bull from your house,
Nor goats out of your folds.
10 For every beast of the forest *is* Mine,
And the cattle on a thousand hills.
11 I know all the birds of the mountains,
And the wild beasts of the field *are* Mine.

12 "If I were hungry, I would not tell you;
For the world *is* Mine, and all its fullness.
13 Will I eat the flesh of bulls,
Or drink the blood of goats?
14 Offer to God thanksgiving,
And pay your vows to the Most High.
15 Call upon Me in the day of trouble;
I will deliver you, and you shall glorify Me."

PROVERBS 14:28

28 IN a multitude of people *is* a king's
     honor,
   But in the lack of people *is* the downfall
     of a prince.

LUKE 17:1–19

THEN He said to the disciples, "It is impossible that no offenses should come, but woe *to him* through whom they do come! 2 It would be better for him if a millstone were hung around his neck, and he were thrown into the sea, than that he should offend one of these little ones. 3 Take heed to yourselves. If your brother sins against you, rebuke him; and if he repents, forgive him. 4 And if he sins against you seven times in a day, and seven times in a day returns to you, saying, 'I repent,' you shall forgive him."

5 And the apostles said to the Lord, "Increase our faith."

6 So the Lord said, "If you have faith as a mustard seed, you can say to this mulberry tree, 'Be pulled up by the roots and be planted in the sea,' and it would obey you. 7 And which of you, having a servant plowing or tending sheep, will say to him when he has come in from the field, 'Come at once and sit down to eat'? 8 But will he not rather say to him, 'Prepare something for my supper, and gird yourself and serve me till I have eaten and drunk, and afterward you will eat and drink'? 9 Does he thank that servant because he did the things that were commanded him? I think not. 10 So likewise you, when you have done all those things which you are commanded, say, 'We are unprofitable servants. We have done what was our duty to do.'"

11 Now it happened as He went to Jerusalem that He passed through the midst of Samaria and Galilee. 12 Then as He entered a certain village, there met Him ten men who were lepers, who stood afar off. 13 And they lifted up *their* voices and said, "Jesus, Master, have mercy on us!"

14 So when He saw *them,* He said to them, "Go, show yourselves to the priests." And so it was that as they went, they were cleansed.

15 And one of them, when he saw that he was healed, returned, and with a loud voice glorified God, 16 and fell down on *his* face at His feet, giving Him thanks. And he was a Samaritan.

17 So Jesus answered and said, "Were there not ten cleansed? But where *are* the nine? 18 Were there not any found who returned to give glory to God except this foreigner?" 19 And He said to him, "Arise, go your way. Your faith has made you well."

◆◆◆◆

Reading 114—Our Liberty of Wonders
Luke 17:21

"The kingdom of God is within you," uncompromisingly within you. We must never compromise with the kingdoms of this world; the temptation the Devil presents is that we should compromise. We recognize his temptation in the teaching that proclaims there is no such being as the Devil and no such place as hell; much that is called sin is a mere defect; men and women are like poor babes lost in the wood, just be kind and gentle with them, talk about the fatherhood of God, about universalism and brotherhood, the kindness of Providence and the nobility of man. Our Lord's temptations reveal where the onslaught will come. Today, through an overabundance of Christian activities, Jesus Christ is being dethroned in hearts, and Christian wits and wisdom are taking His place; consequently, when trials and difficulties come, most of us are at our wits' end because we have succumbed to one or another of these temptations.   (*GLORY*)

JUDGES 13:1—14:20

AGAIN the children of Israel did evil in the sight of the LORD, and the LORD delivered them into the hand of the Philistines for forty years.

2 Now there was a certain man from Zorah, of the family of the Danites, whose name *was* Manoah; and his wife *was* barren and had no children. 3 And the Angel of the LORD appeared to the woman and said to her, "Indeed now, you are barren and have borne no children, but you shall conceive and bear a son. 4 Now therefore, please be careful not to drink wine or *similar* drink, and not to eat anything unclean. 5 For behold, you shall conceive and bear a son. And no razor shall come upon his head, for the child shall be a Nazirite to God from the womb; and he shall begin to deliver Israel out of the hand of the Philistines."

6 So the woman came and told her husband, saying, "A Man of God came to me, and His countenance *was* like the countenance of the Angel of God, very awesome; but I did not ask Him where He *was* from, and He did not tell me His name. 7 And He said to me, 'Behold, you shall conceive and bear a son. Now drink no wine or *similar* drink, nor eat anything unclean, for the child shall be a Nazirite to God from the womb to the day of his death.'"

8 Then Manoah prayed to the LORD, and said, "O my Lord, please let the Man of God whom You sent come to us again and teach us what we shall do for the child who will be born."

9 And God listened to the voice of Manoah, and the Angel of God came to the woman again as she was sitting in the field; but Manoah her husband *was* not with her. 10 Then the woman ran in haste and told her husband, and said to him, "Look, the Man who came to me the *other* day has just now appeared to me!"

11 So Manoah arose and followed his wife. When he came to the Man, he said to Him, "Are You the Man who spoke to this woman?"

And He said, "I *am*."

12 Manoah said, "Now let Your words come *to pass!* What will be the boy's rule of life, and his work?"

13 So the Angel of the LORD said to Manoah, "Of all that I said to the woman let her be careful. 14 She may not eat anything that comes from the vine, nor may she drink wine or *similar* drink, nor eat anything unclean. All that I commanded her let her observe."

15 Then Manoah said to the Angel of the LORD, "Please let us detain You, and we will prepare a young goat for You."

16 And the Angel of the LORD said to Manoah, "Though you detain Me, I will not eat your food. But if you offer a burnt offering, you must offer it to the LORD." (For Manoah did not know He *was* the Angel of the LORD.)

17 Then Manoah said to the Angel of the LORD, "What *is* Your name, that when Your words come *to pass* we may honor You?"

18 And the Angel of the LORD said to him, "Why do you ask My name, seeing it *is* wonderful?"

19 So Manoah took the young goat with the grain offering, and offered it upon the rock to the LORD. And He did a wondrous thing while Manoah and his wife looked on— 20 it happened as the flame went up toward heaven from the altar—the Angel of the LORD ascended in the flame of the altar! When Manoah and his wife saw *this,* they fell on their faces to the ground. 21 When the Angel of the LORD appeared no more to Manoah and his wife, then Manoah knew that He *was* the Angel of the LORD.

22 And Manoah said to his wife, "We shall surely die, because we have seen God!"

23 But his wife said to him, "If the LORD had desired to kill us, He would not have accepted a burnt offering and a grain offering from our hands, nor would He have shown us all these *things,* nor would He have told us *such things* as these at this time."

24 So the woman bore a son and called his name Samson; and the child grew, and the LORD blessed him. 25 And the Spirit of the LORD began to move upon him at Mahaneh Dan between Zorah and Eshtaol.

14 Now Samson went down to Timnah, and saw a woman in Timnah of the daughters of the Philistines. 2 So he went up and told his father and mother, saying, "I have seen a woman in Timnah of the daughters of the Philistines; now therefore, get her for me as a wife."

3 Then his father and mother said to him, "*Is there* no woman among the daughters of your brethren, or among all my people, that you must go and get a wife from the uncircumcised Philistines?"

And Samson said to his father, "Get her for me, for she pleases me well."

4 But his father and mother did not know that it was of the LORD—that He was seeking an occasion to move against the Philistines. For at that time the Philistines had dominion over Israel.

5 So Samson went down to Timnah with his father and mother, and came to the vineyards of Timnah.

Now *to his* surprise, a young lion *came* roaring against him. 6 And the Spirit of the LORD came mightily upon him, and he tore the lion apart as one would have torn apart a young goat, though *he had* nothing in his hand. But he did not tell his father or his mother what he had done.

7 Then he went down and talked with the woman; and she pleased Samson well. 8 After some time, when he returned to get her, he turned aside to see the carcass of the lion. And behold, a swarm of bees and honey *were* in the carcass of the lion. 9 He took some of it in his hands and went along, eating. When he came to his father and mother, he gave *some* to them, and they also ate. But he did not tell them that he had taken the honey out of the carcass of the lion.

10 So his father went down to the woman. And Samson gave a feast there, for young men used to do so. 11 And it happened, when they saw him, that they brought thirty companions to be with him.

12 Then Samson said to them, "Let me pose a riddle to you. If you can correctly solve and explain it to me within the seven days of the feast, then I will give you thirty linen garments and thirty changes of clothing. 13 But if you cannot explain *it* to me, then you shall give me thirty linen garments and thirty changes of clothing."

And they said to him, "Pose your riddle, that we may hear it."

14 So he said to them:

> "Out of the eater came something to eat,
>   And out of the strong came something sweet."

Now for three days they could not explain the riddle.

15 But it came to pass on the seventh day that they said to Samson's wife, "Entice your husband, that he may explain the riddle to us, or else we will burn you and your father's house with fire. Have you invited us in order to take what is ours? *Is that* not *so?*"

16 Then Samson's wife wept on him, and said, "You only hate me! You do not love me! You have posed a riddle to the sons of my people, but you have not explained *it* to me."

And he said to her, "Look, I have not explained *it* to my father or my mother; so should I explain *it* to you?" 17 Now she

had wept on him the seven days while their feast lasted. And it happened on the seventh day that he told her, because she pressed him so much. Then she explained the riddle to the sons of her people. 18 So then the men of the city said to him on the seventh day before the sun went down:

> "What *is* sweeter than honey?
>   And what *is* stronger than a lion?"

And he said to them:

> "If you had not plowed with my heifer,
>   You would not have solved my riddle!"

19 Then the Spirit of the LORD came upon him mightily, and he went down to Ashkelon and killed thirty of their men, took their apparel, and gave the changes *of clothing* to those who had explained the riddle. So his anger was aroused, and he went back up to his father's house. 20 And Samson's wife was *given* to his companion, who had been his best man.

PSALM 50:16–23

16 BUT to the wicked God says:
    "What *right* have you to declare My statutes,
        Or take My covenant in your mouth,
17 Seeing you hate instruction
    And cast My words behind you?
18 When you saw a thief, you consented with him,
    And have been a partaker with adulterers.
19 You give your mouth to evil,
    And your tongue frames deceit.
20 You sit *and* speak against your brother;
    You slander your own mother's son.
21 These *things* you have done, and I kept silent;
    You thought that I was altogether like you;
    But I will rebuke you,
    And set *them* in order before your eyes.

22 "Now consider this, you who forget God,
    Lest I tear *you* in pieces,
    And *there be* none to deliver:
23 Whoever offers praise glorifies Me;
    And to him who orders *his* conduct aright
    I will show the salvation of God."

PROVERBS 14:29, 30

29 *HE who is* slow to wrath has great
     understanding,
     But *he who is* impulsive exalts folly.

30 A sound heart *is* life to the body,
     But envy *is* rottenness to the bones.

LUKE 17:20–37

NOW when He was asked by the Pharisees when the kingdom of God would come, He answered them and said, "The kingdom of God does not come with observation; 21 nor will they say, 'See here!' or 'See there!' For indeed, the kingdom of God is within you."

Evidence of new birth is that we see the rule of God.   (PSY. REDEMP.)

---

22 Then He said to the disciples, "The days will come when you will desire to see one of the days of the Son of Man, and you will not see *it.* 23 And they will say to you, 'Look here!' or 'Look there!' Do not go after *them* or follow *them.* 24 For as the lightning that flashes out of one *part* under heaven shines to the other *part* under heaven, so also the Son of Man will be in His day. 25 But first He must suffer many things and be rejected by this generation. 26 And as it was in the days of Noah, so it will be also in the days of the Son of Man: 27 They ate, they drank, they married wives, they were given in marriage, until the day that Noah entered the ark, and the flood came and destroyed them all. 28 Likewise as it was also in the days of Lot: They ate, they drank, they bought, they sold, they planted, they built; 29 but on the day that Lot went out of Sodom it rained fire and brimstone from heaven and destroyed *them* all. 30 Even so will it be in the day when the Son of Man is revealed.

31 "In that day, he who is on the housetop, and his goods *are* in the house, let him not come down to take them away. And likewise the one who is in the field, let him not turn back. 32 Remember Lot's wife. 33 Whoever seeks to save his life will lose it, and whoever loses his life will preserve it. 34 I tell you, in that night there will be two *men* in one bed: the one will be taken and the other will be left. 35 Two *women* will be grinding together: the one will be taken and the other left. 36 Two *men* will be in the field: the one will be taken and the other left."

37 And they answered and said to Him, "Where, Lord?"

So He said to them, "Wherever the body is, there the eagles will be gathered together."

Reading 115—Toward Fuller Communion
Luke 18:1–8

There are times when the heavenly Father will look as if He were an unjust judge. But remember that Jesus says that He is not. In the meantime there is a cloud on the friendship of the heart, and even love itself has to wait often in pain and tears for the blessing of fuller communion. The time is coming when we shall see perfectly clearly, but it is only through confusion that we can get to a clear outline. . . .

Until we have been disciplined properly by means of spiritual confusion we shall always want to bank on God's miracles and refuse to do the moral thing ourselves. It is much easier to ask God to do our work for us than to do it ourselves—"Oh well, I will pray and ask God to clean this thing up for me." God won't. We must do our own work. Prayer is always a temptation to bank on a miracle instead of a moral issue until we are disciplined. God will do more than we can do, but only in relationship to our spiritual growth. When we have received the gift of the Holy Spirit, we have to learn to obey

God in every detail, then the shroudings will be lifted, the shadows will disappear, the strangeness will go, and we shall begin to understand the friendship and the fatherhood and the faithfulness of God with regard to our lives.

(*Place Help*)

JUDGES 15:1—16:31

AFTER a while, in the time of wheat harvest, it happened that Samson visited his wife with a young goat. And he said, "Let me go in to my wife, into *her* room." But her father would not permit him to go in.

2 Her father said, "I really thought that you thoroughly hated her; therefore I gave her to your companion. *Is* not her younger sister better than she? Please, take her instead."

3 And Samson said to them, "This time I shall be blameless regarding the Philistines if I harm them!" 4 Then Samson went and caught three hundred foxes; and he took torches, turned *the foxes* tail to tail, and put a torch between each pair of tails. 5 When he had set the torches on fire, he let *the foxes* go into the standing grain of the Philistines, and burned up both the shocks and the standing grain, as well as the vineyards *and* olive groves.

6 Then the Philistines said, "Who has done this?"

And they answered, "Samson, the son-in-law of the Timnite, because he has taken his wife and given her to his companion." So the Philistines came up and burned her and her father with fire.

7 Samson said to them, "Since you would do a thing like this, I will surely take revenge on you, and after that I will cease." 8 So he attacked them hip and thigh with a great slaughter; then he went down and dwelt in the cleft of the rock of Etam.

9 Now the Philistines went up, encamped in Judah, and deployed themselves against Lehi. 10 And the men of Judah said, "Why have you come up against us?"

So they answered, "We have come up to arrest Samson, to do to him as he has done to us."

11 Then three thousand men of Judah went down to the cleft of the rock of Etam, and said to Samson, "Do you not know that the Philistines rule over us? What *is* this you have done to us?"

And he said to them, "As they did to me, so I have done to them."

12 But they said to him, "We have come down to arrest you, that we may deliver you into the hand of the Philistines."

Then Samson said to them, "Swear to me that you will not kill me yourselves."

13 So they spoke to him, saying, "No, but we will tie you securely and deliver you into their hand; but we will surely not kill you." And they bound him with two new ropes and brought him up from the rock.

14 When he came to Lehi, the Philistines came shouting against him. Then the Spirit of the Lord came mightily upon him; and the ropes that *were* on his arms became like flax that is burned with fire, and his bonds broke loose from his hands. 15 He found a fresh jawbone of a donkey, reached out his hand and took it, and killed a thousand men with it. 16 Then Samson said:

> "With the jawbone of a donkey,
>   Heaps upon heaps,
> With the jawbone of a donkey
>   I have slain a thousand men!"

17 And so it was, when he had finished speaking, that he threw the jawbone from his hand, and called that place Ramath Lehi.

18 Then he became very thirsty; so he cried out to the Lord and said, "You have given this great deliverance by the hand of Your servant; and now shall I die of thirst and fall into the hand of the uncircumcised?" 19 So God split the hollow place that *is* in Lehi, and water came out, and he drank; and his spirit returned, and he revived. Therefore he called its name En Hakkore, which is in Lehi to this day. 20 And he judged Israel twenty years in the days of the Philistines.

16 NOW Samson went to Gaza and saw a harlot there, and went in to her. 2 *When* the Gazites *were told*, "Samson has come here!" they surrounded *the place* and lay in wait for him all night at the gate of the city. They were quiet all night, saying, "In the morning, when it is daylight, we will kill him." 3 And Samson lay *low* till midnight; then he arose at midnight, took hold of the doors of the gate of the city and the two gateposts, pulled them up, bar and all, put *them* on his shoulders, and carried them to the top of the hill that faces Hebron.

4 Afterward it happened that he loved a

woman in the Valley of Sorek, whose name *was* Delilah. 5 And the lords of the Philistines came up to her and said to her, "Entice him, and find out where his great strength *lies,* and by what *means* we may overpower him, that we may bind him to afflict him; and every one of us will give you eleven hundred *pieces* of silver."

6 So Delilah said to Samson, "Please tell me where your great strength *lies,* and with what you may be bound to afflict you."

7 And Samson said to her, "If they bind me with seven fresh bowstrings, not yet dried, then I shall become weak, and be like any *other* man."

8 So the lords of the Philistines brought up to her seven fresh bowstrings, not yet dried, and she bound him with them. 9 Now *men were* lying in wait, staying with her in the room. And she said to him, "The Philistines *are* upon you, Samson!" But he broke the bowstrings as a strand of yarn breaks when it touches fire. So the secret of his strength was not known.

10 Then Delilah said to Samson, "Look, you have mocked me and told me lies. Now, please tell me what you may be bound with."

11 So he said to her, "If they bind me securely with new ropes that have never been used, then I shall become weak, and be like any *other* man."

12 Therefore Delilah took new ropes and bound him with them, and said to him, "The Philistines *are* upon you, Samson!" And *men were* lying in wait, staying in the room. But he broke them off his arms like a thread.

13 Delilah said to Samson, "Until now you have mocked me and told me lies. Tell me what you may be bound with."

And he said to her, "If you weave the seven locks of my head into the web of the loom"—

14 So she wove *it* tightly with the batten of the loom, and said to him, "The Philistines *are* upon you, Samson!" But he awoke from his sleep, and pulled out the batten and the web from the loom.

15 Then she said to him, "How can you say, 'I love you,' when your heart *is* not with me? You have mocked me these three times, and have not told me where your great strength *lies.*" 16 And it came to pass, when she pestered him daily with her words and pressed him, *so* that his soul was vexed to death, 17 that he told her all his heart, and said to her, "No razor has ever come upon my head, for I *have been* a Nazirite to God from my mother's womb. If I am shaven, then my strength will leave me, and

I shall become weak, and be like any *other* man."

18 When Delilah saw that he had told her all his heart, she sent and called for the lords of the Philistines, saying, "Come up once more, for he has told me all his heart." So the lords of the Philistines came up to her and brought the money in their hand. 19 Then she lulled him to sleep on her knees, and called for a man and had him shave off the seven locks of his head. Then she began to torment him, and his strength left him. 20 And she said, "The Philistines *are* upon you, Samson!" So he awoke from his sleep, and said, "I will go out as before, at other times, and shake myself free!" But he did not know that the LORD had departed from him.

21 Then the Philistines took him and put out his eyes, and brought him down to Gaza. They bound him with bronze fetters, and he became a grinder in the prison. 22 However, the hair of his head began to grow again after it had been shaven.

23 Now the lords of the Philistines gathered together to offer a great sacrifice to Dagon their god, and to rejoice. And they said:

> "Our god has delivered into our hands
> Samson our enemy!"

24 When the people saw him, they praised their god; for they said:

> "Our god has delivered into our hands
> our enemy,
> The destroyer of our land,
> And the one who multiplied our
> dead."

25 So it happened, when their hearts were merry, that they said, "Call for Samson, that he may perform for us." So they called for Samson from the prison, and he performed for them. And they stationed him between the pillars. 26 Then Samson said to the lad who held him by the hand, "Let me feel the pillars which support the temple, so that I can lean on them." 27 Now the temple was full of men and women. All the lords of the Philistines *were* there— about three thousand men and women on the roof watching while Samson performed.

28 Then Samson called to the LORD, say-

---

*T*he man who prays ceases to
be a fool.   (BAFFLED)

ing, "O Lord GOD, remember me, I pray! Strengthen me, I pray, just this once, O God, that I may with one *blow* take vengeance on the Philistines for my two eyes!" 29 And Samson took hold of the two middle pillars which supported the temple, and he braced himself against them, one on his right and the other on his left. 30 Then Samson said, "Let me die with the Philistines!" And he pushed with *all his* might, and the temple fell on the lords and all the people who *were* in it. So the dead that he killed at his death were more than he had killed in his life.

31 And his brothers and all his father's household came down and took him, and brought *him* up and buried him between Zorah and Eshtaol in the tomb of his father Manoah. He had judged Israel twenty years.

PSALM 51:1–6

1   HAVE mercy upon me, O God,
     According to Your lovingkindness;
     According to the multitude of Your
        tender mercies,
     Blot out my transgressions.
2   Wash me thoroughly from my iniquity,
     And cleanse me from my sin.

3   For I acknowledge my transgressions,
     And my sin *is* always before me.
4   Against You, You only, have I sinned,
     And done *this* evil in Your sight—
     That You may be found just when You
        speak,
     And blameless when You judge.

5   Behold, I was brought forth in iniquity,
     And in sin my mother conceived me.
6   Behold, You desire truth in the inward
        parts,
     And in the hidden *part* You will make
        me to know wisdom.

PROVERBS 14:31, 32

31 HE who oppresses the poor reproaches
     his Maker,
     But he who honors Him has mercy on
        the needy.

32 The wicked is banished in his
        wickedness,
     But the righteous has a refuge in his
        death.

LUKE 18:1–23

THEN He spoke a parable to them, that men always ought to pray and not lose heart, 2 saying: "There was in a certain city a judge who did not fear God nor regard man. 3 Now there was a widow in that city; and she came to him, saying, 'Get justice for me from my adversary.' 4 And he would not for a while; but afterward he said within himself, 'Though I do not fear God nor regard man, 5 yet because this widow troubles me I will avenge her, lest by her continual coming she weary me.' "

6 Then the Lord said, "Hear what the unjust judge said. 7 And shall God not avenge His own elect who cry out day and night to Him, though He bears long with them? 8 I tell you that He will avenge them speedily. Nevertheless, when the Son of Man comes, will He really find faith on the earth?"

9 Also He spoke this parable to some who trusted in themselves that they were righteous, and despised others: 10 "Two men went up to the temple to pray, one a Pharisee and the other a tax collector. 11 The Pharisee stood and prayed thus with himself, 'God, I thank You that I am not like other men—extortioners, unjust, adulterers, or even as this tax collector. 12 I fast

---

In the religious life of the Pharisee, prayer becomes a rite, a ceremony.   (BAFFLED)

---

twice a week; I give tithes of all that I possess.' 13 And the tax collector, standing afar off, would not so much as raise *his* eyes to heaven, but beat his breast, saying, 'God, be merciful to me a sinner!' 14 I tell you, this man went down to his house justified *rather* than the other; for everyone who exalts himself will be humbled, and he who humbles himself will be exalted."

15 Then they also brought infants to Him that He might touch them; but when the disciples saw *it,* they rebuked them. 16 But Jesus called them to *Him* and said, "Let the little children come to Me, and do not forbid them; for of such is the kingdom of God. 17 Assuredly, I say to you, whoever does not receive the kingdom of God as a little child will by no means enter it."

18 Now a certain ruler asked Him, saying,

"Good Teacher, what shall I do to inherit eternal life?"

19 So Jesus said to him, "Why do you call Me good? No one *is* good but One, *that is,* God. 20 You know the commandments: 'Do not commit adultery,' 'Do not murder,' 'Do not steal,' 'Do not bear false witness,' 'Honor your father and your mother.'"

21 And he said, "All these things I have kept from my youth."

22 So when Jesus heard these things, He said to him, "You still lack one thing. Sell all that you have and distribute to the poor, and you will have treasure in heaven; and come, follow Me."

23 But when he heard this, he became very sorrowful, for he was very rich.

◆◆◆◆

Reading 116— The Brave Comradeship of God
Luke 18:31

The bravery of God in trusting us! It is a tremendously risky thing to do, it looks as if all the odds were against Him. The majority of us don't bother much about Him, and yet He deliberately stakes all He has on us, He stands by and lets the world, the flesh, and the Devil do their worst, confident we will come out all right. All our Lord succeeded in doing during His life on earth was to gather together a group of fishermen—the whole church of God and the enterprise of our Lord on earth in a fishing boat!

We say, "It seems out of all proportion that God should choose me—I am of no value"; the reason He chooses us is that we are not of any value. It is folly to think that because a man has natural ability, he must make a good Christian. People with the best natural equipment may make the worst disciples because they will "boss" themselves. It is not a question of our equipment, but of our poverty; not what we bring with us, but what He puts in us; not our natural virtues, our strength of character, our knowledge, our experience; all that is of no avail in this matter; the only thing that is of avail is that we are taken up into the big compelling of God and made His comrade (1 Cor. 1:26–28).   (*PLACE HELP*)

JUDGES 17:1—19:30

NOW there was a man from the mountains of Ephraim, whose name *was* Micah. 2 And he said to his mother, "The eleven hundred *shekels* of silver that were taken from you, and on which you put a curse, even saying it in my ears—here *is* the silver with me; I took it."

And his mother said, "*May you be* blessed by the LORD, my son!" 3 So when he had returned the eleven hundred *shekels* of silver to his mother, his mother said, "I had wholly dedicated the silver from my hand to the LORD for my son, to make a carved image and a molded image; now therefore, I will return it to you." 4 Thus he returned the silver to his mother. Then his mother took two hundred *shekels* of silver and gave them to the silversmith, and he made it into a carved image and a molded image; and they were in the house of Micah.

5 The man Micah had a shrine, and made an ephod and household idols; and he consecrated one of his sons, who became his priest. 6 In those days *there was* no king in Israel; everyone did *what was* right in his own eyes.

7 Now there was a young man from Bethlehem in Judah, of the family of Judah; he *was* a Levite, and was staying there. 8 The man departed from the city of Bethlehem in Judah to stay wherever he could find *a place*. Then he came to the mountains of Ephraim, to the house of Micah, as he journeyed. 9 And Micah said to him, "Where do you come from?"

So he said to him, "I *am* a Levite from

Bethlehem in Judah, and I am on my way to find *a place* to stay."

10 Micah said to him, "Dwell with me, and be a father and a priest to me, and I will give you ten *shekels* of silver per year, a suit of clothes, and your sustenance." So the Levite went in. 11 Then the Levite was content to dwell with the man; and the young man became like one of his sons to him. 12 So Micah consecrated the Levite, and the young man became his priest, and lived in the house of Micah. 13 Then Micah said, "Now I know that the Lord will be good to me, since I have a Levite as priest!"

18 IN those days *there was* no king in Israel. And in those days the tribe of the Danites was seeking an inheritance for itself to dwell in; for until that day *their* inheritance among the tribes of Israel had not fallen to them. 2 So the children of Dan sent five men of their family from their territory, men of valor from Zorah and Eshtaol, to spy out the land and search it. They said to them, "Go, search the land." So they went to the mountains of Ephraim, to the house of Micah, and lodged there. 3 While they *were* at the house of Micah, they recognized the voice of the young Levite. They turned aside and said to him, "Who brought you here? What are you doing in this *place*? What do you have here?"

4 He said to them, "Thus and so Micah did for me. He has hired me, and I have become his priest."

5 So they said to him, "Please inquire of God, that we may know whether the journey on which we go will be prosperous."

6 And the priest said to them, "Go in peace. The presence of the Lord *be* with you on your way."

7 So the five men departed and went to Laish. They saw the people who *were* there, how they dwelt safely, in the manner of the Sidonians, quiet and secure. *There were* no rulers in the land who might put *them* to shame for anything. They *were* far from the Sidonians, and they had no ties with anyone.

8 Then *the spies* came back to their brethren at Zorah and Eshtaol, and their brethren said to them, "What *is* your *report*?"

9 So they said, "Arise, let us go up against them. For we have seen the land, and indeed it *is* very good. *Would* you *do* nothing? Do not hesitate to go, *and* enter to possess the land. 10 When you go, you will come to a secure people and a large land. For God has given it into your hands, a place where

there *is* no lack of anything that *is* on the earth."

11 And six hundred men of the family of the Danites went from there, from Zorah and Eshtaol, armed with weapons of war. 12 Then they went up and encamped in Kirjath Jearim in Judah. (Therefore they call that place Mahaneh Dan to this day. There *it is*, west of Kirjath Jearim.) 13 And they passed from there to the mountains of Ephraim, and came to the house of Micah.

14 Then the five men who had gone to spy out the country of Laish answered and said to their brethren, "Do you know that there are in these houses an ephod, household idols, a carved image, and a molded image? Now therefore, consider what you should do." 15 So they turned aside there, and came to the house of the young Levite man—to the house of Micah—and greeted him. 16 The six hundred men armed with their weapons of war, who *were* of the children of Dan, stood by the entrance of the gate. 17 Then the five men who had gone to spy out the land went up. Entering there, they took the carved image, the ephod, the household idols, and the molded image. The priest stood at the entrance of the gate with the six hundred men *who were* armed with weapons of war.

18 When these went into Micah's house and took the carved image, the ephod, the household idols, and the molded image, the priest said to them, "What are you doing?"

19 And they said to him, "Be quiet, put your hand over your mouth, and come with us; be a father and a priest to us. *Is it* better for you to be a priest to the household of one man, or that you be a priest to a tribe and a family in Israel?" 20 So the priest's heart was glad; and he took the ephod, the household idols, and the carved image, and took his place among the people.

21 Then they turned and departed, and put the little ones, the livestock, and the goods in front of them. 22 When they were a good way from the house of Micah, the men who *were* in the houses near Micah's house gathered together and overtook the children of Dan. 23 And they called out to the children of Dan. So they turned around and said to Micah, "What ails you, that you have gathered such a company?"

24 So he said, "You have taken away my gods which I made, and the priest, and you have gone away. Now what more do I have? How can you say to me, 'What ails you?'"

25 And the children of Dan said to him, "Do not let your voice be heard among

us, lest angry men fall upon you, and you lose your life, with the lives of your household!" 26 Then the children of Dan went their way. And when Micah saw that they *were* too strong for him, he turned and went back to his house.

27 So they took *the things* Micah had made, and the priest who had belonged to him, and went to Laish, to a people quiet and secure; and they struck them with the edge of the sword and burned the city with fire. 28 *There was* no deliverer, because it *was* far from Sidon, and they had no ties with anyone. It was in the valley that belongs to Beth Rehob. So they rebuilt the city and dwelt there. 29 And they called the name of the city Dan, after the name of Dan their father, who was born to Israel. However, the name of the city formerly *was* Laish.

30 Then the children of Dan set up for themselves the carved image; and Jonathan the son of Gershom, the son of Manasseh, and his sons were priests to the tribe of Dan until the day of the captivity of the land. 31 So they set up for themselves Micah's carved image which he made, all the time that the house of God was in Shiloh.

19 AND it came to pass in those days, when *there was* no king in Israel, that there was a certain Levite staying in the remote mountains of Ephraim. He took for himself a concubine from Bethlehem in Judah. 2 But his concubine played the harlot against him, and went away from him to her father's house at Bethlehem in Judah, and was there four whole months. 3 Then her husband arose and went after her, to speak kindly to her *and* bring her back, having his servant and a couple of donkeys with him. So she brought him into her father's house; and when the father of the young woman saw him, he was glad to meet him. 4 Now his father-in-law, the young woman's father, detained him; and he stayed with him three days. So they ate and drank and lodged there.

5 Then it came to pass on the fourth day that they arose early in the morning, and he stood to depart; but the young woman's father said to his son-in-law, "Refresh your heart with a morsel of bread, and afterward go your way."

6 So they sat down, and the two of them ate and drank together. Then the young woman's father said to the man, "Please be content to stay all night, and let your heart be merry." 7 And when the man stood to depart, his father-in-law urged him; so he lodged there again. 8 Then he arose early

in the morning on the fifth day to depart, but the young woman's father said, "Please refresh your heart." So they delayed until afternoon; and both of them ate.

9 And when the man stood to depart— he and his concubine and his servant—his father-in-law, the young woman's father, said to him, "Look, the day is now drawing toward evening; please spend the night. See, the day is coming to an end; lodge here, that your heart may be merry. Tomorrow go your way early, so that you may get home."

10 However, the man was not willing to spend that night; so he rose and departed, and came opposite Jebus (that is, Jerusalem). With him were the two saddled donkeys; his concubine *was* also with him. 11 They *were* near Jebus, and the day was far spent; and the servant said to his master, "Come, please, and let us turn aside into this city of the Jebusites and lodge in it."

12 But his master said to him, "We will not turn aside here into a city of foreigners, who *are* not of the children of Israel; we will go on to Gibeah." 13 So he said to his servant, "Come, let us draw near to one of these places, and spend the night in Gibeah or in Ramah." 14 And they passed by and went their way; and the sun went down on them near Gibeah, which belongs to Benjamin. 15 They turned aside there to go in to lodge in Gibeah. And when he went in, he sat down in the open square of the city, for no one would take them into *his* house to spend the night.

16 Just then an old man came in from his work in the field at evening, who also *was* from the mountains of Ephraim; he was staying in Gibeah, whereas the men of the place *were* Benjamites. 17 And when he raised his eyes, he saw the traveler in the open square of the city; and the old man said, "Where are you going, and where do you come from?"

18 So he said to him, "We *are* passing from Bethlehem in Judah toward the remote mountains of Ephraim; I *am* from there. I went to Bethlehem in Judah; *now* I am going to the house of the LORD. But there *is* no one who will take me into his house, 19 although we have both straw and fodder for our donkeys, and bread and wine for myself, for your female servant, and for the young man *who is* with your servant; *there is* no lack of anything."

20 And the old man said, "Peace *be* with you! However, *let* all your needs *be* my responsibility; only do not spend the night in the open square." 21 So he brought him into his house, and gave fodder to the

donkeys. And they washed their feet, and ate and drank.

22 As they were enjoying themselves, suddenly certain men of the city, perverted men, surrounded the house *and* beat on the door. They spoke to the master of the house, the old man, saying, "Bring out the man who came to your house, that we may know him *carnally!*"

23 But the man, the master of the house, went out to them and said to them, "No, my brethren! I beg you, do not act *so* wickedly! Seeing this man has come into my house, do not commit this outrage. 24 Look, *here is* my virgin daughter and *the man's* concubine; let me bring them out now. Humble them, and do with them as you please; but to this man do not do such a vile thing!" 25 But the men would not heed him. So the man took his concubine and brought *her* out to them. And they knew her and abused her all night until morning; and when the day began to break, they let her go.

26 Then the woman came as the day was dawning, and fell down at the door of the man's house where her master *was,* till it was light.

27 When her master arose in the morning, and opened the doors of the house and went out to go his way, there was his concubine, fallen *at* the door of the house with her hands on the threshold. 28 And he said to her, "Get up and let us be going." But there was no answer. So the man lifted her onto the donkey; and the man got up and went to his place.

29 When he entered his house he took a knife, laid hold of his concubine, and divided her into twelve pieces, limb by limb, and sent her throughout all the territory of Israel. 30 And so it was that all who saw it said, "No such deed has been done or seen from the day that the children of Israel came up from the land of Egypt until this day. Consider it, confer, and speak up!"

PSALM 51:7–11

7 PURGE me with hyssop, and I shall be clean;
   Wash me, and I shall be whiter than snow.
8 Make me hear joy and gladness,
   That the bones You have broken may rejoice.
9 Hide Your face from my sins,
   And blot out all my iniquities.
10 Create in me a clean heart, O God,
   And renew a steadfast spirit within me.

11 Do not cast me away from Your presence,
   And do not take Your Holy Spirit from me.

PROVERBS 14:33–35

33 WISDOM rests in the heart of him who has understanding,
   But *what is* in the heart of fools is made known.

34 Righteousness exalts a nation,
   But sin *is* a reproach to *any* people.

35 The king's favor *is* toward a wise servant,
   But his wrath *is against* him who causes shame.

LUKE 18:24–43

AND when Jesus saw that he became very sorrowful, He said, "How hard it is for those who have riches to enter the kingdom of God! 25 For it is easier for a camel to go through the eye of a needle than for a rich man to enter the kingdom of God."

26 And those who heard it said, "Who then can be saved?"

27 But He said, "The things which are impossible with men are possible with God."

28 Then Peter said, "See, we have left all and followed You."

29 So He said to them, "Assuredly, I say to you, there is no one who has left house or parents or brothers or wife or children, for the sake of the kingdom of God, 30 who shall not receive many times more in this present time, and in the age to come eternal life."

31 Then He took the twelve aside and said to them, "Behold, we are going up to Jerusalem, and all things that are written by the prophets concerning the Son of Man will be accomplished. 32 For He will be delivered to the Gentiles and will be mocked and insulted and spit upon. 33 They will scourge *Him* and kill Him. And the third day He will rise again."

34 But they understood none of these things; this saying was hidden from them, and they did not know the things which were spoken.

35 Then it happened, as He was coming near Jericho, that a certain blind man sat by the road begging. 36 And hearing a multitude passing by, he asked what it meant.

37 So they told him that Jesus of Nazareth was passing by. 38 And he cried out, saying, "Jesus, Son of David, have mercy on me!"

39 Then those who went before warned him that he should be quiet; but he cried out all the more, "Son of David, have mercy on me!"

40 So Jesus stood still and commanded him to be brought to Him. And when he had come near, He asked him, 41 saying, "What do you want Me to do for you?"

He said, "Lord, that I may receive my sight."

42 Then Jesus said to him, "Receive your sight; your faith has made you well."

No one is surprised over what God does when once he has faith in Him. (LOVE OF GOD)

---

43 And immediately he received his sight, and followed Him, glorifying God. And all the people, when they saw *it*, gave praise to God.

◆◆◆

Reading 117—He Can Save Anybody
Luke 19:5

The thing we have to learn by contact with Jesus Christ is this, that if the whole human race—everybody, good, bad and indifferent—is lost, we must have the boundless confidence of Jesus Christ Himself about us, that is, we must know that He can save anybody and everybody. There is a great deal of importance to be attached to this point. Just reflect in your mind and think of some lives you know that are frozen; there is no conviction of sin; they are dishonorable, and they know it; they are abnormal, off the main track altogether, but they are not a bit troubled about it; talk to them about their wrong doing and they are totally indifferent to you. You have to learn how to introduce the atmosphere of the Lord Jesus Christ around those souls. As soon as you do, something happens. Look what happened to Zacchaeus— "Then Zacchaeus stood and said to the Lord, 'Look, Lord, I give half of my goods to the poor; and if I have taken anything from anyone by false accusation, I restore fourfold.'" Who had been talking to him about his doings? Not a soul. Jesus had never said a word about his evil doings. What awakened him? What suddenly made him know where he was? The presence of Jesus!

(WORKMEN)

JUDGES 20:1—21:25

SO all the children of Israel came out, from Dan to Beersheba, as well as from the land of Gilead, and the congregation gathered together as one man before the LORD at Mizpah. 2 And the leaders of all the people, all the tribes of Israel, presented themselves in the assembly of the people of God, four hundred thousand foot soldiers who drew the sword. 3 (Now the children of Benjamin heard that the children of Israel had gone up to Mizpah.)

Then the children of Israel said, "Tell *us*, how did this wicked deed happen?"

4 So the Levite, the husband of the woman who was murdered, answered and said, "My concubine and I went into Gibeah, which belongs to Benjamin, to spend the night. 5 And the men of Gibeah rose against me, and surrounded the house at night because of me. They intended to kill me, but instead they ravished my concubine so that she died. 6 So I took hold of my concubine, cut her in pieces, and sent her throughout all the territory of the inheritance of Israel, because they committed lewdness and outrage in Israel. 7 Look! All of you *are* children of Israel; give your advice and counsel here and now!"

8 So all the people arose as one man, saying, "None *of us* will go to his tent, nor will any turn back to his house; 9 but now this *is* the thing which we will do to Gibeah:

We will go up against it by lot. 10 We will take ten men out of *every* hundred throughout all the tribes of Israel, a hundred out of *every* thousand, and a thousand out of *every* ten thousand, to make provisions for the people, that when they come to Gibeah in Benjamin, they may repay all the vileness that they have done in Israel." 11 So all the men of Israel were gathered against the city, united together as one man.

12 Then the tribes of Israel sent men through all the tribe of Benjamin, saying, "What *is* this wickedness that has occurred among you? 13 Now therefore, deliver up the men, the perverted men who *are* in Gibeah, that we may put them to death and remove the evil from Israel!" But the children of Benjamin would not listen to the voice of their brethren, the children of Israel. 14 Instead, the children of Benjamin gathered together from their cities to Gibeah, to go to battle against the children of Israel. 15 And from their cities at that time the children of Benjamin numbered twenty-six thousand men who drew the sword, besides the inhabitants of Gibeah, who numbered seven hundred select men. 16 Among all this people *were* seven hundred select men *who were* left-handed; every one could sling a stone at a hair's *breadth* and not miss. 17 Now besides Benjamin, the men of Israel numbered four hundred thousand men who drew the sword; all of these *were* men of war.

18 Then the children of Israel arose and went up to the house of God to inquire of God. They said, "Which of us shall go up first to battle against the children of Benjamin?"

The LORD said, "Judah first!"

19 So the children of Israel rose in the morning and encamped against Gibeah. 20 And the men of Israel went out to battle against Benjamin, and the men of Israel put themselves in battle array to fight against them at Gibeah. 21 Then the children of Benjamin came out of Gibeah, and on that day cut down to the ground twenty-two thousand men of the Israelites. 22 And the people, that is, the men of Israel, encouraged themselves and again formed the battle line at the place where they had put themselves in array on the first day. 23 Then the children of Israel went up and wept before the LORD until evening, and asked counsel of the LORD, saying, "Shall I again draw near for battle against the children of my brother Benjamin?"

And the LORD said, "Go up against him."

24 So the children of Israel approached the children of Benjamin on the second day.

25 And Benjamin went out against them from Gibeah on the second day, and cut down to the ground eighteen thousand more of the children of Israel; all these drew the sword.

26 Then all the children of Israel, that is, all the people, went up and came to the house of God and wept. They sat there before the LORD and fasted that day until evening; and they offered burnt offerings and peace offerings before the LORD. 27 So the children of Israel inquired of the LORD (the ark of the covenant of God *was* there in those days, 28 and Phinehas the son of Eleazar, the son of Aaron, stood before it in those days), saying, "Shall I yet again go out to battle against the children of my brother Benjamin, or shall I cease?"

And the LORD said, "Go up, for tomorrow I will deliver them into your hand."

29 Then Israel set men in ambush all around Gibeah. 30 And the children of Israel went up against the children of Benjamin on the third day, and put themselves in battle array against Gibeah as at the other times. 31 So the children of Benjamin went out against the people, *and* were drawn away from the city. They began to strike down *and* kill some of the people, as at the other times, in the highways (one of which goes up to Bethel and the other to Gibeah) and in the field, about thirty men of Israel. 32 And the children of Benjamin said, "They *are* defeated before us, as at first."

But the children of Israel said, "Let us flee and draw them away from the city to the highways." 33 So all the men of Israel rose from their place and put themselves in battle array at Baal Tamar. Then Israel's men in ambush burst forth from their position in the plain of Geba. 34 And ten thousand select men from all Israel came against Gibeah, and the battle was fierce. But *the Benjamites* did not know that disaster *was* upon them. 35 The LORD defeated Benjamin before Israel. And the children of Israel destroyed that day twenty-five thousand one hundred Benjamites; all these drew the sword.

36 So the children of Benjamin saw that they were defeated. The men of Israel had given ground to the Benjamites, because they relied on the men in ambush whom they had set against Gibeah. 37 And the men in ambush quickly rushed upon Gibeah; the men in ambush spread out and struck the whole city with the edge of the sword. 38 Now the appointed signal between the men of Israel and the men in ambush was

that they would make a great cloud of smoke rise up from the city, 39 whereupon the men of Israel would turn in battle. Now Benjamin had begun to strike *and* kill about thirty of the men of Israel. For they said, "Surely they are defeated before us, as *in* the first battle." 40 But when the cloud began to rise from the city in a column of smoke, the Benjamites looked behind them, and there was the whole city going up *in smoke* to heaven. 41 And when the men of Israel turned back, the men of Benjamin panicked, for they saw that disaster had come upon them. 42 Therefore they turned *their backs* before the men of Israel in the direction of the wilderness; but the battle overtook them, and whoever *came* out of the cities they destroyed in their midst. 43 They surrounded the Benjamites, chased them, *and* easily trampled them down as far as the front of Gibeah toward the east. 44 And eighteen thousand men of Benjamin fell; all these *were* men of valor. 45 Then they turned and fled toward the wilderness to the rock of Rimmon; and they cut down five thousand of them on the highways. Then they pursued them relentlessly up to Gidom, and killed two thousand of them. 46 So all who fell of Benjamin that day were twenty-five thousand men who drew the sword; all these *were* men of valor.

47 But six hundred men turned and fled toward the wilderness to the rock of Rimmon, and they stayed at the rock of Rimmon for four months. 48 And the men of Israel turned back against the children of Benjamin, and struck them down with the edge of the sword—from *every* city, men and beasts, all who were found. They also set fire to all the cities they came to.

21 NOW the men of Israel had sworn an oath at Mizpah, saying, "None of us shall give his daughter to Benjamin as a wife." 2 Then the people came to the house of God, and remained there before God till evening. They lifted up their voices and wept bitterly, 3 and said, "O LORD God of Israel, why has this come to pass in Israel, that today there should be one tribe *missing* in Israel?"

4 So it was, on the next morning, that the people rose early and built an altar there, and offered burnt offerings and peace offerings. 5 The children of Israel said, "Who *is there* among all the tribes of Israel who did not come up with the assembly to the LORD?" For they had made a great oath concerning anyone who had not come up to the LORD at Mizpah, saying, "He shall surely be put to death." 6 And the children

of Israel grieved for Benjamin their brother, and said, "One tribe is cut off from Israel today. 7 What shall we do for wives for those who remain, seeing we have sworn by the LORD that we will not give them our daughters as wives?"

8 And they said, "What one *is there* from the tribes of Israel who did not come up to Mizpah to the LORD?" And, in fact, no one had come to the camp from Jabesh Gilead to the assembly. 9 For when the people were counted, indeed, not one of the inhabitants of Jabesh Gilead *was* there. 10 So the congregation sent out there twelve thousand of their most valiant men, and commanded them, saying, "Go and strike the inhabitants of Jabesh Gilead with the edge of the sword, including the women and children. 11 And this *is* the thing that you shall do: You shall utterly destroy every male, and every woman who has known a man intimately." 12 So they found among the inhabitants of Jabesh Gilead four hundred young virgins who had not known a man intimately; and they brought them to the camp at Shiloh, which is in the land of Canaan.

13 Then the whole congregation sent *word* to the children of Benjamin who *were* at the rock of Rimmon, and announced peace to them. 14 So Benjamin came back at that time, and they gave them the women whom they had saved alive of the women of Jabesh Gilead; and yet they had not found enough for them.

15 And the people grieved for Benjamin, because the LORD had made a void in the tribes of Israel.

16 Then the elders of the congregation said, "What shall we do for wives for those who remain, since the women of Benjamin have been destroyed?" 17 And they said, "*There must be* an inheritance for the survivors of Benjamin, that a tribe may not be destroyed from Israel. 18 However, we cannot give them wives from our daughters, for the children of Israel have sworn an oath, saying, 'Cursed *be* the one who gives a wife to Benjamin.'" 19 Then they said, "In fact, *there is* a yearly feast of the LORD in Shiloh, which *is* north of Bethel, on the east side of the highway that goes up from Bethel to Shechem, and south of Lebonah."

20 Therefore they instructed the children of Benjamin, saying, "Go, lie in wait in the vineyards, 21 and watch; and just when the daughters of Shiloh come out to perform their dances, then come out from the vineyards, and every man catch a wife for himself from the daughters of Shiloh; then go to the land of Benjamin. 22 Then it shall

be, when their fathers or their brothers come to us to complain, that we will say to them, 'Be kind to them for our sakes, because we did not take a wife for any of them in the war; for *it is* not *as though* you have given the *women* to them at this time, making yourselves guilty of your oath.'"

23 And the children of Benjamin did so; they took enough wives for their number from those who danced, whom they caught. Then they went and returned to their inheritance, and they rebuilt the cities and dwelt in them. 24 So the children of Israel departed from there at that time, every man to his tribe and family; they went out from there, every man to his inheritance.

25 In those days *there was* no king in Israel; everyone did *what was* right in his own eyes.

PSALM 51:12–19

12 RESTORE to me the joy of Your salvation,
And uphold me *by Your* generous Spirit.
13 *Then* I will teach transgressors Your ways,
And sinners shall be converted to You.

14 Deliver me from the guilt of bloodshed, O God,
The God of my salvation,
And my tongue shall sing aloud of Your righteousness.
15 O Lord, open my lips,
And my mouth shall show forth Your praise.
16 For You do not desire sacrifice, or else I would give *it;*
You do not delight in burnt offering.
17 The sacrifices of God *are* a broken spirit,
A broken and a contrite heart—
These, O God, You will not despise.

18 Do good in Your good pleasure to Zion;
Build the walls of Jerusalem.
19 Then You shall be pleased with the sacrifices of righteousness,
With burnt offering and whole burnt offering;
Then they shall offer bulls on Your altar.

PROVERBS 15:1–3

1 A soft answer turns away wrath,
But a harsh word stirs up anger.
2 The tongue of the wise uses knowledge rightly,

But the mouth of fools pours forth foolishness.

3 The eyes of the LORD *are* in every place,
Keeping watch on the evil and the good.

LUKE 19:1–27

THEN *Jesus* entered and passed through Jericho. 2 Now behold, *there was* a man named Zacchaeus who was a chief tax collector, and he was rich. 3 And he sought to see who Jesus was, but could not because of the crowd, for he was of short stature. 4 So he ran ahead and climbed up into a sycamore tree to see Him, for He was going to pass that *way.* 5 And when Jesus came to the place, He looked up and saw him, and said to him, "Zacchaeus, make haste and come down, for today I must stay at your house." 6 So he made haste and came down, and received Him joyfully. 7 But when they saw *it,* they all complained, saying, "He has gone to be a guest with a man who is a sinner."

8 Then Zacchaeus stood and said to the Lord, "Look, Lord, I give half of my goods to the poor; and if I have taken anything from anyone by false accusation, I restore fourfold."

*N*othing has any power to alter a man save the incoming of the life of Jesus.   (RUN)

9 And Jesus said to him, "Today salvation has come to this house, because he also is a son of Abraham; 10 for the Son of Man has come to seek and to save that which was lost."

11 Now as they heard these things, He spoke another parable, because He was near Jerusalem and because they thought the kingdom of God would appear immediately. 12 Therefore He said: "A certain nobleman went into a far country to receive for himself a kingdom and to return. 13 So he called ten of his servants, delivered to them ten minas, and said to them, 'Do business till I come.' 14 But his citizens hated him, and sent a delegation after him, saying, 'We will not have this *man* to reign over us.'

15 "And so it was that when he returned, having received the kingdom, he then commanded these servants, to whom he had given the money, to be called to him, that

he might know how much every man had gained by trading. 16 Then came the first, saying, 'Master, your mina has earned ten minas.' 17 And he said to him, 'Well *done,* good servant; because you were faithful in a very little, have authority over ten cities.' 18 And the second came, saying, 'Master, your mina has earned five minas.' 19 Likewise he said to him, 'You also be over five cities.'

20 "Then another came, saying, 'Master, here is your mina, which I have kept put away in a handkerchief. 21 For I feared you, because you are an austere man. You collect what you did not deposit, and reap what you did not sow.' 22 And he said to him, 'Out of your own mouth I will judge you, *you* wicked servant. You knew that I was an austere man, collecting what I did not deposit and reaping what I did not sow. 23 Why then did you not put my money in the bank, that at my coming I might have collected it with interest?'

24 "And he said to those who stood by, 'Take the mina from him, and give *it* to him who has ten minas.' 25 (But they said to him, 'Master, he has ten minas.') 26 'For I say to you, that to everyone who has will be given; and from him who does not have, even what he has will be taken away from him. 27 But bring here those enemies of mine, who did not want me to reign over them, and slay *them* before me.' "

◆◆◆◆

Reading 118—If You Had Known!
Luke 19:42

What is it that blinds me in this "my day"? Have I a strange god—not a disgusting monster, but a disposition that rules me? More than once God has brought me face-to-face with the strange god and I thought I should have to yield, but I did not do it. I got through the crisis by the skin of my teeth and I find myself in the possession of the strange god still; I am blind to the things which belong to my peace. It is an appalling thing that we can be in the place where the Spirit of God should be getting at us unhinderedly, and yet increase our condemnation in God's sight.

"If you had known"—God goes direct to the heart, with the tears of Jesus behind. These words imply culpable responsibility; God holds us responsible for what we do not see. "Now they are hidden from your eyes"—because the disposition has never been yielded. The unfathomable sadness of the "might have been"! God never opens doors that have been closed. He opens other doors, but He reminds us that there are doors which we have shut, doors which need never have been shut, imaginations which need never have been sullied. Never be afraid when God brings back the past. Let memory have its way. It is a minister of God with its rebuke and chastisement and sorrow. God will turn the "might have been" into a wonderful culture for the future. (*Utmost*)

RUTH 1:1—2:23

NOW it came to pass, in the days when the judges ruled, that there was a famine in the land. And a certain man of Bethlehem, Judah, went to dwell in the country of Moab, he and his wife and his two sons. 2 The name of the man *was* Elimelech, the name of his wife *was* Naomi, and the names of his two sons *were* Mahlon and Chilion—Ephrathites of Bethlehem, Judah. And they went to the country of Moab and remained there. 3 Then Elimelech, Naomi's husband, died; and she was left, and her two sons. 4 Now they took wives of the women of Moab: the name of the one *was* Orpah, and the name of the other Ruth. And they dwelt there about ten years. 5 Then both

Mahlon and Chilion also died; so the woman survived her two sons and her husband.

6 Then she arose with her daughters-in-law that she might return from the country of Moab, for she had heard in the country of Moab that the Lord had visited His people by giving them bread. 7 Therefore she went out from the place where she was, and her two daughters-in-law with her; and they went on the way to return to the land of Judah. 8 And Naomi said to her two daughters-in-law, "Go, return each to her mother's house. The Lord deal kindly with you, as you have dealt with the dead and with me. 9 The Lord grant that you may find rest, each in the house of her husband."

So she kissed them, and they lifted up their voices and wept. 10 And they said to her, "Surely we will return with you to your people."

11 But Naomi said, "Turn back, my daughters; why will you go with me? *Are* there still sons in my womb, that they may be your husbands? 12 Turn back, my daughters, go—for I am too old to have a husband. If I should say I have hope, *if* I should have a husband tonight and should also bear sons, 13 would you wait for them till they were grown? Would you restrain yourselves from having husbands? No, my daughters; for it grieves me very much for your sakes that the hand of the Lord has gone out against me!"

14 Then they lifted up their voices and wept again; and Orpah kissed her mother-in-law, but Ruth clung to her.

15 And she said, "Look, your sister-in-law has gone back to her people and to her gods; return after your sister-in-law."

16 But Ruth said:

"Entreat me not to leave you,
   Or to turn back from following after
      you;
   For wherever you go, I will go;
   And wherever you lodge, I will lodge;
   Your people *shall be* my people,
   And your God, my God.
17 Where you die, I will die,
   And there will I be buried.
   The Lord do so to me, and more
      also,
   If *anything but* death parts you and
      me."

18 When she saw that she was determined to go with her, she stopped speaking to her.

19 Now the two of them went until they came to Bethlehem. And it happened, when they had come to Bethlehem, that all the city was excited because of them; and the women said, "*Is* this Naomi?"

20 But she said to them, "Do not call me Naomi; call me Mara, for the Almighty has dealt very bitterly with me. 21 I went out full, and the Lord has brought me home again empty. Why do you call me Naomi, since the Lord has testified against me, and the Almighty has afflicted me?"

22 So Naomi returned, and Ruth the Moabitess her daughter-in-law with her, who returned from the country of Moab. Now they came to Bethlehem at the beginning of barley harvest.

2 THERE was a relative of Naomi's husband, a man of great wealth, of the family of Elimelech. His name *was* Boaz. 2 So Ruth the Moabitess said to Naomi, "Please let me go to the field, and glean heads of grain after *him* in whose sight I may find favor."

And she said to her, "Go, my daughter."

3 Then she left, and went and gleaned in the field after the reapers. And she happened to come to the part of the field *belonging* to Boaz, who *was* of the family of Elimelech.

4 Now behold, Boaz came from Bethlehem, and said to the reapers, "The Lord *be* with you!"

And they answered him, "The Lord bless you!"

5 Then Boaz said to his servant who was in charge of the reapers, "Whose young woman *is* this?"

6 So the servant who was in charge of the reapers answered and said, "It *is* the young Moabite woman who came back with Naomi from the country of Moab. 7 And she said, 'Please let me glean and gather after the reapers among the sheaves.' So she came and has continued from morning until now, though she rested a little in the house."

8 Then Boaz said to Ruth, "You will listen, my daughter, will you not? Do not go to glean in another field, nor go from here, but stay close by my young women. 9 *Let* your eyes *be* on the field which they reap, and go after them. Have I not commanded the young men not to touch you? And when you are thirsty, go to the vessels and drink from what the young men have drawn."

10 So she fell on her face, bowed down to the ground, and said to him, "Why have I found favor in your eyes, that you should take notice of me, since I *am* a foreigner?"

11 And Boaz answered and said to her, "It has been fully reported to me, all that you have done for your mother-in-law since the death of your husband, and *how* you have left your father and your mother and the land of your birth, and have come to a people whom you did not know before. 12 The LORD repay your work, and a full reward be given you by the LORD God of Israel, under whose wings you have come for refuge."

13 Then she said, "Let me find favor in your sight, my lord; for you have comforted me, and have spoken kindly to your maidservant, though I am not like one of your maidservants."

14 Now Boaz said to her at mealtime, "Come here, and eat of the bread, and dip your piece of bread in the vinegar." So she sat beside the reapers, and he passed parched *grain* to her; and she ate and was satisfied, and kept some back. 15 And when she rose up to glean, Boaz commanded his young men, saying, "Let her glean even among the sheaves, and do not reproach her. 16 Also let *grain* from the bundles fall purposely for her; leave *it* that she may glean, and do not rebuke her."

17 So she gleaned in the field until evening, and beat out what she had gleaned, and it was about an ephah of barley. 18 Then she took *it* up and went into the city, and her mother-in-law saw what she had gleaned. So she brought out and gave to her what she had kept back after she had been satisfied.

19 And her mother-in-law said to her, "Where have you gleaned today? And where did you work? Blessed be the one who took notice of you."

So she told her mother-in-law with whom she had worked, and said, "The man's name with whom I worked today *is* Boaz."

20 Then Naomi said to her daughter-in-law, "Blessed *be* he of the LORD, who has not forsaken His kindness to the living and the dead!" And Naomi said to her, "This man *is* a relation of ours, one of our close relatives."

21 Ruth the Moabitess said, "He also said to me, 'You shall stay close by my young men until they have finished all my harvest.'"

22 And Naomi said to Ruth her daughter-in-law, "*It is* good, my daughter, that you go out with his young women, and that people do not meet you in any other field." 23 So she stayed close by the young women of Boaz, to glean until the end of barley harvest and wheat harvest; and she dwelt with her mother-in-law.

PSALM 52:1–5

1 WHY do you boast in evil, O mighty
    man?
    The goodness of God *endures*
      continually.
2 Your tongue devises destruction,
    Like a sharp razor, working deceitfully.
3 You love evil more than good,
    Lying rather than speaking
      righteousness.   Selah
4 You love all devouring words,
    You deceitful tongue.

5 God shall likewise destroy you forever;
    He shall take you away, and pluck you
      out of *your* dwelling place,
    And uproot you from the land of the
      living.   Selah

PROVERBS 15:4, 5

4 A wholesome tongue *is* a tree of life,
    But perverseness in it breaks the spirit.

5 A fool despises his father's instruction,
    But he who receives correction is
    prudent.

LUKE 19:28–48

WHEN He had said this, He went on ahead, going up to Jerusalem. 29 And it came to pass, when He drew near to Bethphage and Bethany, at the mountain called Olivet, *that* He sent two of His disciples, 30 saying, "Go into the village opposite *you,* where as you enter you will find a colt tied, on which no one has ever sat. Loose it and bring *it* here. 31 And if anyone asks you, 'Why are you loosing *it?*' thus you shall say to him, 'Because the Lord has need of it.'"

32 So those who were sent went their way and found *it* just as He had said to them. 33 But as they were loosing the colt, the owners of it said to them, "Why are you loosing the colt?"

34 And they said, "The Lord has need of him." 35 Then they brought him to Jesus. And they threw their own clothes on the colt, and they set Jesus on him. 36 And as He went, *many* spread their clothes on the road.

37 Then, as He was now drawing near the descent of the Mount of Olives, the whole multitude of the disciples began to rejoice and praise God with a loud voice

for all the mighty works they had seen, 38 saying:

> " 'Blessed *is* the King who comes in
> the name of the LORD!'
> Peace in heaven and glory in the
> highest!"

39 And some of the Pharisees called to Him from the crowd, "Teacher, rebuke Your disciples."

40 But He answered and said to them, "I tell you that if these should keep silent, the stones would immediately cry out."

41 Now as He drew near, He saw the city and wept over it, 42 saying, "If you had known, even you, especially in this your day, the things *that make* for your peace! But now they are hidden from your eyes.

43 For days will come upon you when your enemies will build an embankment around you, surround you and close you in on every side, 44 and level you, and your children within you, to the ground; and they will not leave in you one stone upon another, because you did not know the time of your visitation."

45 Then He went into the temple and began to drive out those who bought and sold in it, 46 saying to them, "It is written, 'My house is a house of prayer,' but you have made it a 'den of thieves.' "

47 And He was teaching daily in the temple. But the chief priests, the scribes, and the leaders of the people sought to destroy Him, 48 and were unable to do anything; for all the people were very attentive to hear Him.

◆◆◆

Reading 119—The Theology of Trust
Psalm 52:8

When we are in fear we can do nothing less than pray to God, but our Lord has a right to expect that those who name His name should have an understanding confidence in Him. God expects His children to be so confident in Him that in any crisis they are the reliable ones. Our trust is in God up to a certain point, then we go back to the elementary panic prayers of those who do not know God. We get to our wits' end, showing that we have not the slightest confidence in Him and His government of the world; He seems to be asleep, and we see nothing but breakers ahead.

"O you of little faith!" What a pang must have shot through the disciples—"Missed it again!" And what a pang will go through us when we suddenly realize that we might have produced downright joy in the heart of Jesus by remaining absolutely confident in Him, no matter what was ahead.

There are stages in life when there is no storm, no crisis, when we do our human best; it is when a crisis arises that we instantly reveal upon whom we rely. If we have been learning to worship God and to trust Him, the crisis will reveal that we will go to the breaking point and not break in our confidence in Him.   (*UTMOST*)

RUTH 3:1—4:22

THEN Naomi her mother-in-law said to her, "My daughter, shall I not seek security for you, that it may be well with you? 2 Now Boaz, whose young women you were with, *is he* not our relative? In fact, he is winnowing barley tonight at the threshing floor. 3 Therefore wash yourself and anoint yourself, put on your *best* gar-

ment and go down to the threshing floor; *but* do not make yourself known to the man until he has finished eating and drinking. 4 Then it shall be, when he lies down, that you shall notice the place where he lies; and you shall go in, uncover his feet, and lie down; and he will tell you what you should do."

5 And she said to her, "All that you say to me I will do."

6 So she went down to the threshing floor

and did according to all that her mother-in-law instructed her. 7 And after Boaz had eaten and drunk, and his heart was cheerful, he went to lie down at the end of the heap of grain; and she came softly, uncovered his feet, and lay down.

8 Now it happened at midnight that the man was startled, and turned himself; and there, a woman was lying at his feet. 9 And he said, "Who *are* you?"

So she answered, "I *am* Ruth, your maidservant. Take your maidservant under your wing, for you are a close relative."

10 Then he said, "Blessed *are* you of the LORD, my daughter! For you have shown more kindness at the end than at the beginning, in that you did not go after young men, whether poor or rich. 11 And now, my daughter, do not fear. I will do for you all that you request, for all the people of my town know that you *are* a virtuous woman. 12 Now it is true that I *am* a close relative; however, there is a relative closer than I. 13 Stay this night, and in the morning it shall be *that* if he will perform the duty of a close relative for you—good; let him do it. But if he does not want to perform the duty for you, then I will perform the duty for you, *as* the LORD lives! Lie down until morning."

14 So she lay at his feet until morning, and she arose before one could recognize another. Then he said, "Do not let it be known that the woman came to the threshing floor." 15 Also he said, "Bring the shawl that *is* on you and hold it." And when she held it, he measured six *ephahs* of barley, and laid *it* on her. Then she went into the city.

16 When she came to her mother-in-law, she said, "*Is* that you, my daughter?"

Then she told her all that the man had done for her. 17 And she said, "These six *ephahs* of barley he gave me; for he said to me, 'Do not go empty-handed to your mother-in-law.'"

18 Then she said, "Sit still, my daughter, until you know how the matter will turn out; for the man will not rest until he has concluded the matter this day."

4 NOW Boaz went up to the gate and sat down there; and behold, the close relative of whom Boaz had spoken came by. So Boaz said, "Come aside, friend, sit down here." So he came aside and sat down. 2 And he took ten men of the elders of the city, and said, "Sit down here." So they sat down. 3 Then he said to the close relative, "Naomi, who has come back from the country of Moab, sold the piece of land which *belonged* to our brother Elimelech. 4 And I thought to inform you, saying, 'Buy *it* back in the presence of the inhabitants and the elders of my people. If you will redeem *it,* redeem *it;* but if you will not redeem *it, then* tell me, that I may know; for *there is* no one but you to redeem *it,* and I *am* next after you.'"

And he said, "I will redeem *it.*"

5 Then Boaz said, "On the day you buy the field from the hand of Naomi, you must also buy *it* from Ruth the Moabitess, the wife of the dead, to perpetuate the name of the dead through his inheritance."

6 And the close relative said, "I cannot redeem *it* for myself, lest I ruin my own inheritance. You redeem my right of redemption for yourself, for I cannot redeem *it.*"

7 Now this *was the custom* in former times in Israel concerning redeeming and exchanging, to confirm anything: one man took off his sandal and gave *it* to the other, and this *was* a confirmation in Israel.

8 Therefore the close relative said to Boaz, "Buy *it* for yourself." So he took off his sandal. 9 And Boaz said to the elders and all the people, "You *are* witnesses this day that I have bought all that was Elimelech's, and all that *was* Chilion's and Mahlon's, from the hand of Naomi. 10 Moreover, Ruth the Moabitess, the widow of Mahlon, I have acquired as my wife, to perpetuate the name of the dead through his inheritance, that the name of the dead may not be cut off from among his brethren and from his position at the gate. You *are* witnesses this day."

11 And all the people who *were* at the gate, and the elders, said, "*We are* witnesses. The LORD make the woman who is coming to your house like Rachel and Leah, the two who built the house of Israel; and may you prosper in Ephrathah and be famous in Bethlehem. 12 May your house be like the house of Perez, whom Tamar bore to Judah, because of the offspring which the LORD will give you from this young woman."

13 So Boaz took Ruth and she became his wife; and when he went in to her, the LORD gave her conception, and she bore a son. 14 Then the women said to Naomi, "Blessed *be* the LORD, who has not left you this day without a close relative; and may his name be famous in Israel! 15 And may he be to you a restorer of life and a nourisher of your old age; for your daughter-in-law, who loves you, who is better to you than seven sons, has borne him." 16 Then Naomi took the child and laid him on her bosom,

and became a nurse to him. 17 Also the neighbor women gave him a name, saying, "There is a son born to Naomi." And they called his name Obed. He *is* the father of Jesse, the father of David.

18 Now this *is* the genealogy of Perez: Perez begot Hezron; 19 Hezron begot Ram, and Ram begot Amminadab; 20 Amminadab begot Nahshon, and Nahshon begot Salmon; 21 Salmon begot Boaz, and Boaz begot Obed; 22 Obed begot Jesse, and Jesse begot David.

PSALM 52:6–9

6   THE righteous also shall see and fear,
    And shall laugh at him, *saying,*
7   "Here is the man *who* did not make God his strength,
    But trusted in the abundance of his riches,
    And strengthened himself in his wickedness."
8   But I *am* like a green olive tree in the house of God;
    I trust in the mercy of God forever and ever.
9   I will praise You forever,
    Because You have done *it;*
    And in the presence of Your saints
    I will wait on Your name, for *it is* good.

*T*he characteristic of the life of a saint is essential elemental simplicity.   (PHIL. SIN)

PROVERBS 15:6, 7

6   IN the house of the righteous *there is* much treasure,
    But in the revenue of the wicked is trouble.

7   The lips of the wise disperse knowledge,
    But the heart of the fool *does* not *do* so.

LUKE 20:1–26

NOW it happened on one of those days, as He taught the people in the temple and preached the gospel, *that* the chief priests and the scribes, together with the elders, confronted *Him* 2 and spoke to Him, saying, "Tell us, by what authority are You doing these things? Or who is he who gave You this authority?"

3 But He answered and said to them, "I also will ask you one thing, and answer Me: 4 The baptism of John—was it from heaven or from men?"

5 And they reasoned among themselves, saying, "If we say, 'From heaven,' He will say, 'Why then did you not believe him?' 6 But if we say, 'From men,' all the people will stone us, for they are persuaded that John was a prophet." 7 So they answered that they did not know where *it was* from.

8 And Jesus said to them, "Neither will I tell you by what authority I do these things."

9 Then He began to tell the people this parable: "A certain man planted a vineyard, leased it to vinedressers, and went into a far country for a long time. 10 Now at vintage-time he sent a servant to the vinedressers, that they might give him some of the fruit of the vineyard. But the vinedressers beat him and sent *him* away empty-handed. 11 Again he sent another servant; and they beat him also, treated *him* shamefully, and sent *him* away empty-handed. 12 And again he sent a third; and they wounded him also and cast *him* out.

13 "Then the owner of the vineyard said, 'What shall I do? I will send my beloved son. Probably they will respect *him* when they see him.' 14 But when the vinedressers saw him, they reasoned among themselves, saying, 'This is the heir. Come, let us kill him, that the inheritance may be ours.' 15 So they cast him out of the vineyard and killed *him.* Therefore what will the owner of the vineyard do to them? 16 He will come and destroy those vinedressers and give the vineyard to others."

And when they heard *it* they said, "Certainly not!"

17 Then He looked at them and said, "What then is this that is written:

'The stone which the builders rejected Has become the chief cornerstone' ?

18 Whoever falls on that stone will be broken; but on whomever it falls, it will grind him to powder."

19 And the chief priests and the scribes that very hour sought to lay hands on Him, but they feared the people—for they knew He had spoken this parable against them.

20 So they watched *Him,* and sent spies who pretended to be righteous, that they might seize on His words, in order to deliver

Him to the power and the authority of the governor.

21 Then they asked Him, saying, "Teacher, we know that You say and teach rightly, and You do not show personal favoritism, but teach the way of God in truth: 22 Is it lawful for us to pay taxes to Caesar or not?"

23 But He perceived their craftiness, and said to them, "Why do you test Me?

24 Show Me a denarius. Whose image and inscription does it have?"

They answered and said, "Caesar's."

25 And He said to them, "Render therefore to Caesar the things that are Caesar's, and to God the things that are God's."

26 But they could not catch Him in His words in the presence of the people. And they marveled at His answer and kept silent.

◆◆◆◆

Reading 120—The Dilemma of Obedience
1 Samuel 3:15

God never speaks to us in startling ways, but in ways that are easy to misunderstand, and we say, "I wonder if that is God's voice?" Isaiah said that the Lord spoke to him "with a strong hand," that is, by the pressure of circumstances. Nothing touches our lives but it is God Himself speaking. Do we discern His hand or only mere occurrence?

Get into the habit of saying, "Speak, Lord," and life will become a romance. Every time circumstances press, say, "Speak, Lord"; make time to listen. Chastening is more than a means of discipline, it is meant to get me to the place of saying, "Speak, Lord." Recall the time when God did speak to you. Have you forgotten what He said? Was it Luke 11:13, or was it 1 Thessalonians 5:23? As we listen, our ear gets acute, and, like Jesus, we shall hear God all the time.

Shall I tell my "Eli" what God has shown to me? That is where the dilemma of obedience comes in. We disobey God by becoming amateur providences— I must shield "Eli," the best people we know. God did not tell Samuel to tell Eli; he had to decide that for himself. God's call to you may hurt your "Eli"; but if you try to prevent the suffering in another life, it will prove an obstruction between your soul and God. (*UTMOST*)

1 SAMUEL 1:1—3:21

NOW there was a certain man of Ramathaim Zophim, of the mountains of Ephraim, and his name *was* Elkanah the son of Jeroham, the son of Elihu, the son of Tohu, the son of Zuph, an Ephraimite. 2 And he had two wives: the name of one *was* Hannah, and the name of the other Peninnah. Peninnah had children, but Hannah had no children. 3 This man went up from his city yearly to worship and sacrifice to the LORD of hosts in Shiloh. Also the two sons of Eli, Hophni and Phinehas, the priests of the LORD, *were* there. 4 And whenever the time came for Elkanah to make an offering, he would give portions to Peninnah his wife and to all her sons and

daughters. 5 But to Hannah he would give a double portion, for he loved Hannah, although the LORD had closed her womb. 6 And her rival also provoked her severely, to make her miserable, because the LORD had closed her womb. 7 So it was, year by year, when she went up to the house of the LORD, that she provoked her; therefore she wept and did not eat.

8 Then Elkanah her husband said to her, "Hannah, why do you weep? Why do you not eat? And why is your heart grieved? *Am* I not better to you than ten sons?"

9 So Hannah arose after they had finished eating and drinking in Shiloh. Now Eli the priest was sitting on the seat by the doorpost of the tabernacle of the LORD. 10 And she *was* in bitterness of soul, and prayed to the

Lord and wept in anguish. 11 Then she made a vow and said, "O Lord of hosts, if You will indeed look on the affliction of Your maidservant and remember me, and not forget Your maidservant, but will give Your maidservant a male child, then I will give him to the Lord all the days of his life, and no razor shall come upon his head."

12 And it happened, as she continued praying before the Lord, that Eli watched her mouth. 13 Now Hannah spoke in her heart; only her lips moved, but her voice was not heard. Therefore Eli thought she was drunk. 14 So Eli said to her, "How long will you be drunk? Put your wine away from you!"

15 But Hannah answered and said, "No, my lord, I *am* a woman of sorrowful spirit. I have drunk neither wine nor intoxicating drink, but have poured out my soul before the Lord. 16 Do not consider your maidservant a wicked woman, for out of the abundance of my complaint and grief I have spoken until now."

17 Then Eli answered and said, "Go in peace, and the God of Israel grant your petition which you have asked of Him."

18 And she said, "Let your maidservant find favor in your sight." So the woman went her way and ate, and her face was no longer *sad.*

19 Then they rose early in the morning and worshiped before the Lord, and returned and came to their house at Ramah. And Elkanah knew Hannah his wife, and the Lord remembered her. 20 So it came to pass in the process of time that Hannah conceived and bore a son, and called his name Samuel, *saying,* "Because I have asked for him from the Lord."

21 Now the man Elkanah and all his house went up to offer to the Lord the yearly sacrifice and his vow. 22 But Hannah did not go up, for she said to her husband, "*Not* until the child is weaned; then I will take him, that he may appear before the Lord and remain there forever."

23 So Elkanah her husband said to her, "Do what seems best to you; wait until you have weaned him. Only let the Lord establish His word." Then the woman stayed and nursed her son until she had weaned him.

24 Now when she had weaned him, she took him up with her, with three bulls, one ephah of flour, and a skin of wine, and brought him to the house of the Lord in Shiloh. And the child *was* young. 25 Then they slaughtered a bull, and brought the child to Eli. 26 And she said, "O my lord! As your soul lives, my lord,

I *am* the woman who stood by you here, praying to the Lord. 27 For this child I prayed, and the Lord has granted me my petition which I asked of Him. 28 Therefore I also have lent him to the Lord; as long as he lives he shall be lent to the Lord." So they worshiped the Lord there.

2 AND Hannah prayed and said:

"My heart rejoices in the Lord;
My horn is exalted in the Lord.
I smile at my enemies,
Because I rejoice in Your salvation.

---

*P*rayer is the instrument of the life of worship, it is not worship itself.   (Chris. Dis. 2)

---

2 "No one is holy like the Lord,
For *there is* none besides You,
Nor *is there* any rock like our God.

3 "Talk no more so very proudly;
Let no arrogance come from your mouth,
For the Lord *is* the God of knowledge;
And by Him actions are weighed.

4 "The bows of the mighty men *are* broken,
And those who stumbled are girded with strength.
5 *Those who were* full have hired themselves out for bread,
And the hungry have ceased *to hunger.*
Even the barren has borne seven,
And she who has many children has become feeble.

6 "The Lord kills and makes alive;
He brings down to the grave and brings up.
7 The Lord makes poor and makes rich;
He brings low and lifts up.
8 He raises the poor from the dust
And lifts the beggar from the ash heap,
To set *them* among princes
And make them inherit the throne of glory.

"For the pillars of the earth *are* the Lord's,
And He has set the world upon them.
9 He will guard the feet of His saints,

But the wicked shall be silent in
darkness.

"For by strength no man shall
prevail.

10 The adversaries of the LORD shall be
broken in pieces;
From heaven He will thunder against
them.
The LORD will judge the ends of the
earth.

"He will give strength to His king,
And exalt the horn of His anointed."

11 Then Elkanah went to his house at Ramah. But the child ministered to the LORD
before Eli the priest.

12 Now the sons of Eli *were* corrupt; they
did not know the LORD. 13 And the priests'
custom with the people *was that* when any
man offered a sacrifice, the priest's servant
would come with a three-pronged fleshhook in his hand while the meat was boiling.
14 Then he would thrust *it* into the pan,
or kettle, or caldron, or pot; and the priest
would take for himself all that the fleshhook
brought up. So they did in Shiloh to all
the Israelites who came there. 15 Also, before they burned the fat, the priest's servant
would come and say to the man who sacrificed, "Give meat for roasting to the priest,
for he will not take boiled meat from you,
but raw."

16 And *if* the man said to him, "They
should really burn the fat first; *then* you
may take *as much* as your heart desires,"
he would then answer him, "*No,* but you
must give *it* now; and if not, I will take *it*
by force."

17 Therefore the sin of the young men
was very great before the LORD, for men
abhorred the offering of the LORD.

18 But Samuel ministered before the
LORD, *even as* a child, wearing a linen ephod.
19 Moreover his mother used to make him
a little robe, and bring *it* to him year by
year when she came up with her husband
to offer the yearly sacrifice. 20 And Eli would
bless Elkanah and his wife, and say, "The
LORD give you descendants from this
woman for the loan that was given to the
LORD." Then they would go to their own
home.

21 And the LORD visited Hannah, so that
she conceived and bore three sons and two
daughters. Meanwhile the child Samuel
grew before the LORD.

22 Now Eli was very old; and he heard
everything his sons did to all Israel, and
how they lay with the women who assembled at the door of the tabernacle of meet-

ing. 23 So he said to them, "Why do you
do such things? For I hear of your evil dealings from all the people. 24 No, my sons!
For *it is* not a good report that I hear. You
make the LORD's people transgress.
25 If one man sins against another, God
will judge him. But if a man sins against
the LORD, who will intercede for him?"
Nevertheless they did not heed the voice
of their father, because the LORD desired
to kill them.

26 And the child Samuel grew in stature,
and in favor both with the LORD and
men.

27 Then a man of God came to Eli and
said to him, "Thus says the LORD: 'Did I
not clearly reveal Myself to the house of
your father when they were in Egypt in
Pharaoh's house? 28 Did I not choose him
out of all the tribes of Israel *to be* My priest,
to offer upon My altar, to burn incense,
and to wear an ephod before Me? And did
I not give to the house of your father all
the offerings of the children of Israel made
by fire? 29 Why do you kick at My sacrifice
and My offering which I have commanded
in My dwelling place, and honor your sons
more than Me, to make yourselves fat with
the best of all the offerings of Israel My
people?' 30 Therefore the LORD God of Israel says: 'I said indeed *that* your house
and the house of your father would walk
before Me forever.' But now the LORD says:
'Far be it from Me; for those who honor
Me I will honor, and those who despise
Me shall be lightly esteemed. 31 Behold, the
days are coming that I will cut off your
arm and the arm of your father's house,
so that there will not be an old man in
your house. 32 And you will see an enemy
in My dwelling place, *despite* all the good
which God does for Israel. And there shall
not be an old man in your house forever.
33 But any of your men *whom* I do not cut
off from My altar shall consume your eyes
and grieve your heart. And all the descendants of your house shall die in the flower
of their age. 34 Now this *shall be* a sign to
you that will come upon your two sons,
on Hophni and Phinehas: in one day they
shall die, both of them. 35 Then I will raise
up for Myself a faithful priest *who* shall do
according to what *is* in My heart and in
My mind. I will build him a sure house,
and he shall walk before My anointed forever. 36 And it shall come to pass that everyone who is left in your house will come
and bow down to him for a piece of silver
and a morsel of bread, and say, "Please,
put me in one of the priestly positions, that
I may eat a piece of bread." ' "

3 NOW the boy Samuel ministered to the LORD before Eli. And the word of the LORD was rare in those days; *there was* no widespread revelation. 2 And it came to pass at that time, while Eli *was* lying down in his place, and when his eyes had begun to grow so dim that he could not see, 3 and before the lamp of God went out in the tabernacle of the LORD where the ark of God *was*, and while Samuel was lying down, 4 that the LORD called Samuel. And he answered, "Here I am!" 5 So he

---

When once the call of God comes, begin to go and never stop going. (UTMOST)

---

ran to Eli and said, "Here I am, for you called me."

And he said, "I did not call; lie down again." And he went and lay down.

6 Then the LORD called yet again, "Samuel!"

So Samuel arose and went to Eli, and said, "Here I am, for you called me." He answered, "I did not call, my son; lie down again." 7 (Now Samuel did not yet know the LORD, nor was the word of the LORD yet revealed to him.)

8 And the LORD called Samuel again the third time. So he arose and went to Eli, and said, "Here I am, for you did call me."

Then Eli perceived that the LORD had called the boy. 9 Therefore Eli said to Samuel, "Go, lie down; and it shall be, if He calls you, that you must say, 'Speak, LORD, for Your servant hears.'" So Samuel went and lay down in his place.

10 Now the LORD came and stood and called as at other times, "Samuel! Samuel!"

And Samuel answered, "Speak, for Your servant hears."

11 Then the LORD said to Samuel: "Behold, I will do something in Israel at which both ears of everyone who hears it will tingle. 12 In that day I will perform against Eli all that I have spoken concerning his house, from beginning to end. 13 For I have told him that I will judge his house forever for the iniquity which he knows, because his sons made themselves vile, and he did not restrain them. 14 And therefore I have sworn to the house of Eli that the iniquity of Eli's house shall not be atoned for by sacrifice or offering forever."

15 So Samuel lay down until morning, and opened the doors of the house of the LORD. And Samuel was afraid to tell Eli the vision. 16 Then Eli called Samuel and said, "Samuel, my son!"

He answered, "Here I am."

17 And he said, "What *is* the word that *the* LORD spoke to you? Please do not hide *it* from me. God do so to you, and more also, if you hide anything from me of all the things that He said to you." 18 Then Samuel told him everything, and hid nothing from him. And he said, "It *is* the LORD. Let Him do what seems good to Him."

19 So Samuel grew, and the LORD was with him and let none of his words fall to the ground. 20 And all Israel from Dan to Beersheba knew that Samuel *had been* established as a prophet of the LORD. 21 Then the LORD appeared again in Shiloh. For the LORD revealed Himself to Samuel in Shiloh by the word of the LORD.

PSALM 53:1–6

1   THE fool has said in his heart,
"*There is* no God."
They are corrupt, and have done
    abominable iniquity;
There is none who does good.

2   God looks down from heaven upon the
        children of men,
To see if there are *any* who understand,
    who seek God.

3   Every one of them has turned aside;
They have together become corrupt;
There is none who does good,
No, not one.

4   Have the workers of iniquity no
        knowledge,
Who eat up my people *as* they eat bread,
And do not call upon God?

5   There they are in great fear
Where no fear was,
For God has scattered the bones of him
    who encamps against you;
You have put *them* to shame,
Because God has despised them.

6   Oh, that the salvation of Israel would
        come out of Zion!
When God brings back the captivity
    of His people,
Let Jacob rejoice *and* Israel be glad.

PROVERBS 15:8–11

8   THE sacrifice of the wicked *is* an
        abomination to the LORD,

But the prayer of the upright *is* His
delight.

9 The way of the wicked *is* an
abomination to the LORD,
But He loves him who follows
righteousness.

10 Harsh discipline *is* for him who forsakes
the way,
And he who hates correction will
die.

11 Hell and Destruction *are* before the
LORD;
So how much more the hearts of the
sons of men.

LUKE 20:27–47

THEN some of the Sadducees, who deny
that there is a resurrection, came to *Him*
and asked Him, 28 saying: "Teacher, Moses
wrote to us *that* if a man's brother dies,
having a wife, and he dies without children,
his brother should take his wife and raise
up offspring for his brother. 29 Now there
were seven brothers. And the first took a
wife, and died without children. 30 And the
second took her as wife, and he died childless. 31 Then the third took her, and in like
manner the seven also; and they left no
children, and died. 32 Last of all the woman
died also. 33 Therefore, in the resurrection,
whose wife does she become? For all seven
had her as wife."

34 Jesus answered and said to them, "The
sons of this age marry and are given in
marriage. 35 But those who are counted
worthy to attain that age, and the resurrection from the dead, neither marry nor
are given in marriage; 36 nor can they die
anymore, for they are equal to the angels
and are sons of God, being sons of the
resurrection. 37 But even Moses showed in
the *burning* bush *passage* that the dead are
raised, when he called the Lord 'the God
of Abraham, the God of Isaac, and the God
of Jacob.' 38 For He is not the God of
the dead but of the living, for all live to
Him."

39 Then some of the scribes answered and
said, "Teacher, You have spoken well."
40 But after that they dared not question
Him anymore.

41 And He said to them, "How can they
say that the Christ is the Son of David?
42 Now David himself said in the Book of
Psalms:

'The LORD said to my Lord,
"Sit at My right hand,
43 Till I make Your enemies Your
footstool." '

44 Therefore David calls Him 'Lord'; how
is He then his Son?"

45 Then, in the hearing of all the people,
He said to His disciples, 46 "Beware of the
scribes, who desire to go around in long
robes, love greetings in the marketplaces,
the best seats in the synagogues, and the
best places at feasts, 47 who devour widows'
houses, and for a pretense make long prayers. These will receive greater condemnation."

◆◆◆◆

*Reading 121—*Quarrels of Nations
Luke 21:10, 11

"Is war of the Devil or of God?" It is of neither. It is of man, though
both God and the Devil are behind it. War is a conflict of wills, either
of individuals or of nations. National quarrels are everywhere today and it is
these quarrels which make men say—"Well, blot out nations altogether; the
only thing to do is to ignore the fact that there are nations; let us look forward
to a time when there will be none." This attitude is a revolt which is a mere
safety valve. The vision of a time when there will be no nations is right, but
ignoring the fact that there are nations just now is not the way to establish
the vision.

After the war the elemental will take its place again, and we shall recover
what we had lost in over-civilization. . . . In the final issue some things belonging
to civilization will be found to be fine, and some disastrous. The preaching of

the "gospel of temperament" and all such shallow optimism has been hit on
the head by the war; there are some clouds with no "silver lining," and the
injunction to "cheer up" is an insult.   (SHAD. AGONY)

1 SAMUEL 4:1—5:12

AND the word of Samuel came to all Israel.

Now Israel went out to battle against
the Philistines, and encamped beside Ebenezer; and the Philistines encamped in
Aphek. 2 Then the Philistines put themselves in battle array against Israel. And
when they joined battle, Israel was defeated
by the Philistines, who killed about four
thousand men of the army in the field.
3 And when the people had come into the
camp, the elders of Israel said, "Why has
the LORD defeated us today before the Philistines? Let us bring the ark of the covenant
of the LORD from Shiloh to us, that when
it comes among us it may save us from
the hand of our enemies." 4 So the people
sent to Shiloh, that they might bring from
there the ark of the covenant of the LORD
of hosts, who dwells *between* the cherubim.
And the two sons of Eli, Hophni and Phinehas, *were* there with the ark of the covenant
of God.

5 And when the ark of the covenant of
the LORD came into the camp, all Israel
shouted so loudly that the earth shook.
6 Now when the Philistines heard the noise
of the shout, they said, "What *does* the sound
of this great shout in the camp of the Hebrews *mean?*" Then they understood that
the ark of the LORD had come into the
camp. 7 So the Philistines were afraid, for
they said, "God has come into the camp!"
And they said, "Woe to us! For such a thing
has never happened before. 8 Woe to us!
Who will deliver us from the hand of these
mighty gods? These *are* the gods who struck
the Egyptians with all the plagues in the
wilderness. 9 Be strong and conduct yourselves like men, you Philistines, that you
do not become servants of the Hebrews,
as they have been to you. Conduct yourselves like men, and fight!"

10 So the Philistines fought, and Israel
was defeated, and every man fled to his
tent. There was a very great slaughter, and
there fell of Israel thirty thousand foot soldiers. 11 Also the ark of God was captured;
and the two sons of Eli, Hophni and Phinehas, died.

12 Then a man of Benjamin ran from the
battle line the same day, and came to Shiloh
with his clothes torn and dirt on his head.

13 Now when he came, there was Eli, sitting
on a seat by the wayside watching, for his
heart trembled for the ark of God. And
when the man came into the city and told
it, all the city cried out. 14 When Eli heard
the noise of the outcry, he said, "What *does*
the sound of this tumult *mean?*" And the
man came quickly and told Eli. 15 Eli was
ninety-eight years old, and his eyes were
so dim that he could not see.

16 Then the man said to Eli, "I *am* he
who came from the battle. And I fled today
from the battle line."

And he said, "What happened, my son?"

17 So the messenger answered and said,
"Israel has fled before the Philistines, and
there has been a great slaughter among the
people. Also your two sons, Hophni and
Phinehas, are dead; and the ark of God
has been captured."

18 Then it happened, when he made mention of the ark of God, that Eli fell off the
seat backward by the side of the gate; and
his neck was broken and he died, for the
man was old and heavy. And he had judged
Israel forty years.

19 Now his daughter-in-law, Phinehas'
wife, was with child, *due* to be delivered;
and when she heard the news that the ark
of God was captured, and that her father-
in-law and her husband were dead, she
bowed herself and gave birth, for her labor
pains came upon her. 20 And about the time
of her death the women who stood by her
said to her, "Do not fear, for you have borne
a son." But she did not answer, nor did
she regard *it.* 21 Then she named the child
Ichabod, saying, "The glory has departed
from Israel!" because the ark of God had
been captured and because of her father-
in-law and her husband. 22 And she said,
"The glory has departed from Israel, for
the ark of God has been captured."

5 THEN the Philistines took the ark of
God and brought it from Ebenezer to
Ashdod. 2 When the Philistines took the
ark of God, they brought it into the house
of Dagon and set it by Dagon. 3 And when
the people of Ashdod arose early in the
morning, there was Dagon, fallen on its
face to the earth before the ark of the LORD.
So they took Dagon and set it in its place
again. 4 And when they arose early the next
morning, there was Dagon, fallen on its

face to the ground before the ark of the LORD. The head of Dagon and both the palms of its hands *were* broken off on the threshold; only Dagon's torso was left of it. 5 Therefore neither the priests of Dagon nor any who come into Dagon's house tread on the threshold of Dagon in Ashdod to this day.

6 But the hand of the LORD was heavy on the people of Ashdod, and He ravaged them and struck them with tumors, *both* Ashdod and its territory. 7 And when the men of Ashdod saw how *it was,* they said, "The ark of the God of Israel must not remain with us, for His hand is harsh toward us and Dagon our god." 8 Therefore they sent and gathered to themselves all the lords of the Philistines, and said, "What shall we do with the ark of the God of Israel?"

And they answered, "Let the ark of the God of Israel be carried away to Gath." So they carried the ark of the God of Israel away. 9 So it was, after they had carried it away, that the hand of the LORD was against the city with a very great destruction; and He struck the men of the city, both small and great, and tumors broke out on them.

10 Therefore they sent the ark of God to Ekron. So it was, as the ark of God came to Ekron, that the Ekronites cried out, saying, "They have brought the ark of the God of Israel to us, to kill us and our people!" 11 So they sent and gathered together all the lords of the Philistines, and said, "Send away the ark of the God of Israel, and let it go back to its own place, so that it does not kill us and our people." For there was a deadly destruction throughout all the city; the hand of God was very heavy there. 12 And the men who did not die were stricken with the tumors, and the cry of the city went up to heaven.

PSALM 54:1–7

1 SAVE me, O God, by Your name,
And vindicate me by Your strength.
2 Hear my prayer, O God;
Give ear to the words of my mouth.

When we cling to God we learn to kneel for the first time. (GENESIS)

---

3 For strangers have risen up against me,
And oppressors have sought after my life;
They have not set God before them.
Selah

4 Behold, God *is* my helper;
The Lord *is* with those who uphold my life.
5 He will repay my enemies for their evil.
Cut them off in Your truth.

6 I will freely sacrifice to You;
I will praise Your name, O LORD, for *it is* good.
7 For He has delivered me out of all trouble;
And my eye has seen *its desire* upon my enemies.

PROVERBS 15:12, 13

12 A scoffer does not love one who corrects him,
Nor will he go to the wise.

13 A merry heart makes a cheerful countenance,
But by sorrow of the heart the spirit is broken.

LUKE 21:1–19

AND He looked up and saw the rich putting their gifts into the treasury, 2 and He saw also a certain poor widow putting in two mites. 3 So He said, "Truly I say to you that this poor widow has put in more than all; 4 for all these out of their abundance have put in offerings for God, but she out of her poverty put in all the livelihood that she had."

The bedrock in Jesus Christ's kingdom is poverty, not possession. (GLORIFY)

---

5 Then, as some spoke of the temple, how it was adorned with beautiful stones and donations, He said, 6 "These things which you see—the days will come in which not *one* stone shall be left upon another that shall not be thrown down."

7 So they asked Him, saying, "Teacher, but when will these things be? And what sign *will there be* when these things are about to take place?"

8 And He said: "Take heed that you not be deceived. For many will come in My name, saying, 'I am *He,*' and, 'The time has drawn near.' Therefore do not go after them. 9 But when you hear of wars and

commotions, do not be terrified; for these things must come to pass first, but the end *will not come* immediately."

10 Then He said to them, "Nation will rise against nation, and kingdom against kingdom. 11 And there will be great earthquakes in various places, and famines and pestilences; and there will be fearful sights and great signs from heaven. 12 But before all these things, they will lay their hands on you and persecute *you*, delivering *you* up to the synagogues and prisons. You will be brought before kings and rulers for My name's sake. 13 But it will turn out for you as an occasion for testimony. 14 Therefore settle *it* in your hearts not to meditate beforehand on what you will answer; 15 for I will give you a mouth and wisdom which all your adversaries will not be able to contradict or resist. 16 You will be betrayed even by parents and brothers, relatives and friends; and they will put *some* of you to death. 17 And you will be hated by all for My name's sake. 18 But not a hair of your head shall be lost. 19 By your patience possess your souls.

————————— ◆◆◆◆ —————————

Reading 122—The Childlike Habit of Prayer
Psalm 55:1, 2

We think rightly or wrongly about prayer according to the conception we have in our minds of prayer. If we think of prayer as the breath in our lungs and the blood from our hearts, we think rightly. The blood flows ceaselessly, and breathing continues ceaselessly; we are not conscious of it, but it is always going on. We are not always conscious of Jesus keeping us in perfect joint with God, but if we are obeying Him, He always is. Prayer is not an exercise, it is the life. Beware of anything that stops ejaculatory prayer. "Pray without ceasing," keep the childlike habit of ejaculatory prayer in your heart to God all the time.

Jesus never mentioned unanswered prayer; He had the boundless certainty that prayer is always answered. Have we by the Spirit the unspeakable certainty that Jesus had about prayer, or do we think of the times when God does not seem to have answered prayer? "Everyone who asks receives." We say— "But. . . , but . . ." God answers prayer in the best way, not sometimes, but every time, although the immediate manifestation of the answer in the domain in which we want it may not always follow. Do we expect God to answer prayer?   (*UTMOST*)

1 SAMUEL 6:1—7:17

NOW the ark of the LORD was in the country of the Philistines seven months. 2 And the Philistines called for the priests and the diviners, saying, "What shall we do with the ark of the LORD? Tell us how we should send it to its place."

3 So they said, "If you send away the ark of the God of Israel, do not send it empty; but by all means return *it* to Him *with* a trespass offering. Then you will be healed, and it will be known to you why His hand is not removed from you."

4 Then they said, "What *is* the trespass offering which we shall return to Him?"

They answered, "Five golden tumors and five golden rats, *according to* the number of the lords of the Philistines. For the same plague *was* on all of you and on your lords. 5 Therefore you shall make images of your tumors and images of your rats that ravage the land, and you shall give glory to the God of Israel; perhaps He will lighten His hand from you, from your gods, and from your land. 6 Why then do you harden your hearts as the Egyptians and Pharaoh hardened their hearts? When He did mighty things among them, did they not let the people go, that they might depart? 7 Now therefore, make a new cart, take two milk cows which have never been yoked, and hitch the cows to the cart; and take their calves home, away from them. 8 Then take the ark of the LORD and set it on the cart; and put the articles of gold which you are returning to Him *as* a trespass offering in a chest by its side. Then send it away, and let it go. 9 And watch: if it goes up the road to its own territory, to Beth Shemesh, *then* He has done us this great evil. But if not, then we shall know that *it is* not His hand *that* struck us—it happened to us by chance."

10 Then the men did so; they took two milk cows and hitched them to the cart, and shut up their calves at home. 11 And they set the ark of the LORD on the cart, and the chest with the gold rats and the images of their tumors. 12 Then the cows headed straight for the road to Beth Shemesh, *and* went along the highway, lowing as they went, and did not turn aside to the right hand or the left. And the lords of the Philistines went after them to the border of Beth Shemesh.

13 Now *the people of* Beth Shemesh *were* reaping their wheat harvest in the valley; and they lifted their eyes and saw the ark, and rejoiced to see *it.* 14 Then the cart came into the field of Joshua of Beth Shemesh, and stood there; a large stone *was* there. So they split the wood of the cart and offered the cows as a burnt offering to the LORD. 15 The Levites took down the ark of the LORD and the chest that *was* with it, in which *were* the articles of gold, and put *them* on the large stone. Then the men of Beth Shemesh offered burnt offerings and made sacrifices the same day to the LORD. 16 So when the five lords of the Philistines had seen *it,* they returned to Ekron the same day.

17 These *are* the golden tumors which the Philistines returned *as* a trespass offering to the LORD: one for Ashdod, one for Gaza, one for Ashkelon, one for Gath, one for Ekron; 18 and the golden rats, *according to* the number of all the cities of the Philistines *belonging* to the five lords, *both* fortified cities and country villages, even as far as the large *stone of* Abel on which they set the ark of the LORD, *which stone remains* to this day in the field of Joshua of Beth Shemesh. 19 Then He struck the men of Beth Shemesh, because they had looked into the ark of the LORD. He struck fifty thousand and seventy men of the people, and the people lamented because the LORD had struck the people with a great slaughter.

20 And the men of Beth Shemesh said, "Who is able to stand before this holy LORD God? And to whom shall it go up from us?" 21 So they sent messengers to the inhabitants of Kirjath Jearim, saying, "The Philistines have brought back the ark of the LORD; come down *and* take it up with you."

7 THEN the men of Kirjath Jearim came and took the ark of the LORD, and brought it into the house of Abinadab on the hill, and consecrated Eleazar his son to keep the ark of the LORD.

2 So it was that the ark remained in Kirjath Jearim a long time; it was there twenty years. And all the house of Israel lamented after the LORD.

3 Then Samuel spoke to all the house of Israel, saying, "If you return to the LORD with all your hearts, *then* put away the foreign gods and the Ashtoreths from among you, and prepare your hearts for the LORD, and serve Him only; and He will deliver you from the hand of the Philistines." 4 So the children of Israel put away the Baals and the Ashtoreths, and served the LORD only.

5 And Samuel said, "Gather all Israel to Mizpah, and I will pray to the LORD for

---

*O*ur spiritual certainty in prayer is God's divine certainty.   (CHRIS. DIS. 2)

---

you." 6 So they gathered together at Mizpah, drew water, and poured *it* out before the LORD. And they fasted that day, and said there, "We have sinned against the LORD." And Samuel judged the children of Israel at Mizpah.

7 Now when the Philistines heard that the children of Israel had gathered together at Mizpah, the lords of the Philistines went up against Israel. And when the children of Israel heard *of it,* they were afraid of the Philistines. 8 So the children of Israel said to Samuel, "Do not cease to cry out to the LORD our God for us, that He may save us from the hand of the Philistines."

9 And Samuel took a suckling lamb and offered *it as* a whole burnt offering to the LORD. Then Samuel cried out to the LORD for Israel, and the LORD answered him. 10 Now as Samuel was offering up the burnt offering, the Philistines drew near to battle against Israel. But the LORD thundered with a loud thunder upon the Philistines that day, and so confused them that they were overcome before Israel. 11 And the men of Israel went out of Mizpah and pursued the Philistines, and drove them back as far as

below Beth Car. 12 Then Samuel took a stone and set *it* up between Mizpah and Shen, and called its name Ebenezer, saying, "Thus far the LORD has helped us."

13 So the Philistines were subdued, and they did not come anymore into the territory of Israel. And the hand of the LORD was against the Philistines all the days of Samuel. 14 Then the cities which the Philistines had taken from Israel were restored to Israel, from Ekron to Gath; and Israel recovered its territory from the hands of the Philistines. Also there was peace between Israel and the Amorites.

15 And Samuel judged Israel all the days of his life. 16 He went from year to year on a circuit to Bethel, Gilgal, and Mizpah, and judged Israel in all those places. 17 But he always returned to Ramah, for his home *was* there. There he judged Israel, and there he built an altar to the LORD.

PSALM 55:1–8

1   GIVE ear to my prayer, O God,
     And do not hide Yourself from my
        supplication.

Prayer is an effort of will. (MORAL FOUND.)

---

2   Attend to me, and hear me;
     I am restless in my complaint, and moan
        noisily,
3   Because of the voice of the enemy,
     Because of the oppression of the
        wicked;
     For they bring down trouble upon me,
     And in wrath they hate me.

4   My heart is severely pained within me,
     And the terrors of death have fallen
        upon me.
5   Fearfulness and trembling have come
        upon me,
     And horror has overwhelmed me.
6   So I said, "Oh, that I had wings like
        a dove!
     I would fly away and be at rest.
7   Indeed, I would wander far off,
     And remain in the wilderness.   Selah
8   I would hasten my escape
     From the windy storm *and* tempest."

PROVERBS 15:14

14   THE heart of him who has
        understanding seeks knowledge,

But the mouth of fools feeds on foolishness.

LUKE 21:20–38

"BUT when you see Jerusalem surrounded by armies, then know that its desolation is near. 21 Then let those who are in Judea flee to the mountains, let those who are in the midst of her depart, and let not those who are in the country enter her. 22 For these are the days of vengeance, that all things which are written may be fulfilled. 23 But woe to those who are pregnant and to those who are nursing babies in those days! For there will be great distress in the land and wrath upon this people. 24 And they will fall by the edge of the sword, and be led away captive into all nations. And Jerusalem will be trampled by Gentiles until the times of the Gentiles are fulfilled.

25 "And there will be signs in the sun, in the moon, and in the stars; and on the earth distress of nations, with perplexity, the sea and the waves roaring; 26 men's hearts failing them from fear and the expectation of those things which are coming on the earth, for the powers of the heavens will be shaken. 27 Then they will see the Son of Man coming in a cloud with power and great glory. 28 Now when these things begin to happen, look up and lift up your heads, because your redemption draws near."

29 Then He spoke to them a parable: "Look at the fig tree, and all the trees. 30 When they are already budding, you see and know for yourselves that summer is now near. 31 So you also, when you see these things happening, know that the kingdom of God is near. 32 Assuredly, I say to you, this generation will by no means pass away till all things take place. 33 Heaven and earth will pass away, but My words will by no means pass away.

34 "But take heed to yourselves, lest your hearts be weighed down with carousing, drunkenness, and cares of this life, and that

---

Be careful of anything that is going to deflect your attention from God. (GOOD)

Day come on you unexpectedly. 35 For it will come as a snare on all those who dwell on the face of the whole earth. 36 Watch therefore, and pray always that you may be counted worthy to escape all these things that will come to pass, and to stand before the Son of Man."

37 And in the daytime He was teaching in the temple, but at night He went out and stayed on the mountain called Olivet. 38 Then early in the morning all the people came to Him in the temple to hear Him.

◆◆◆◆

Reading 123—The More Exceeding Worship
Luke 22:19, 20

Worship is giving the best we have unreservedly to God. Jesus Christ was entirely merciful because He kept nothing at all. We are merciful in spots, in a fragmentary way, because we will stick to our opinionettes. Whatever makes us spiritually satisfied will twist our mercy at once, because an opinionette is attached to every spot where we are satisfied, and when anyone comes in contact with that spot of satisfaction we are merciless to them. Jesus Christ was never merciless, and it is only as we draw on His life that we are like our Father in heaven. The only safety is to live the life hid with Christ in God. As long as we are consciously there, we are not there. It is only when we are there that it never occurs to us that we are, but the evidence is strong because others are getting the blessings of God through us and are helping themselves to us, even as Jesus Christ was made broken bread and poured-out wine for us. God cannot make some of us into broken bread because there are bits of unbaked dough in us that would produce indigestion. We have to go into the furnace again to be baked properly until we are no more like Ephraim, "a cake unturned."   (*Perfect*)

1 SAMUEL 8:1—9:27

NOW it came to pass when Samuel was old that he made his sons judges over Israel. 2 The name of his firstborn was Joel, and the name of his second, Abijah; *they were* judges in Beersheba. 3 But his sons did not walk in his ways; they turned aside after dishonest gain, took bribes, and perverted justice.

4 Then all the elders of Israel gathered together and came to Samuel at Ramah, 5 and said to him, "Look, you are old, and your sons do not walk in your ways. Now make us a king to judge us like all the nations."

6 But the thing displeased Samuel when they said, "Give us a king to judge us." So Samuel prayed to the LORD. 7 And the LORD said to Samuel, "Heed the voice of the people in all that they say to you; for they have not rejected you, but they have rejected Me, that I should not reign over them. 8 According to all the works which they have done since the day that I brought them up out of Egypt, even to this day—

with which they have forsaken Me and served other gods—so they are doing to you also. 9 Now therefore, heed their voice. However, you shall solemnly forewarn them, and show them the behavior of the king who will reign over them."

10 So Samuel told all the words of the LORD to the people who asked him for a king. 11 And he said, "This will be the behavior of the king who will reign over you: He will take your sons and appoint *them* for his own chariots and *to be* his horsemen, and *some* will run before his chariots. 12 He will appoint captains over his thousands and captains over his fifties, *will set some* to plow his ground and reap his harvest, and *some* to make his weapons of war and equipment for his chariots. 13 He will take your daughters *to be* perfumers, cooks, and bakers. 14 And he will take the best of your fields, your vineyards, and your olive groves, and give *them* to his servants. 15 He will take a tenth of your grain and your vintage, and give it to his officers and servants. 16 And he will take your male servants, your female servants, your finest

young men, and your donkeys, and put *them* to his work. 17 He will take a tenth of your sheep. And you will be his servants. 18 And you will cry out in that day because of your king whom you have chosen for yourselves, and the LORD will not hear you in that day."

19 Nevertheless the people refused to obey the voice of Samuel; and they said, "No, but we will have a king over us, 20 that we also may be like all the nations, and that our king may judge us and go out before us and fight our battles."

21 And Samuel heard all the words of the people, and he repeated them in the hearing of the LORD. 22 So the LORD said to Samuel, "Heed their voice, and make them a king."

And Samuel said to the men of Israel, "Every man go to his city."

9 THERE was a man of Benjamin whose name *was* Kish the son of Abiel, the son of Zeror, the son of Bechorath, the son of Aphiah, a Benjamite, a mighty man of power. 2 And he had a choice and handsome son whose name *was* Saul. *There was* not a more handsome person than he among the children of Israel. From his shoulders upward *he was* taller than any of the people.

The last thing we learn is not to glory in men. (GLORIFY)

---

3 Now the donkeys of Kish, Saul's father, were lost. And Kish said to his son Saul, "Please take one of the servants with you, and arise, go and look for the donkeys." 4 So he passed through the mountains of Ephraim and through the land of Shalisha, but they did not find *them*. Then they passed through the land of Shaalim, and *they were* not *there*. Then he passed through the land of the Benjamites, but they did not find *them*. 5 When they had come to the land of Zuph, Saul said to his servant who *was* with him, "Come, let us return, lest my father cease *caring* about the donkeys and become worried about us."

6 And he said to him, "Look now, *there is* in this city a man of God, and *he is* an honorable man; all that he says surely comes to pass. So let us go there; perhaps he can show us the way that we should go."

7 Then Saul said to his servant, "But look, *if* we go, what shall we bring the man? For the bread in our vessels is all gone,

and *there is* no present to bring to the man of God. What do we have?"

8 And the servant answered Saul again and said, "Look, I have here at hand one-fourth of a shekel of silver. I will give *that* to the man of God, to tell us our way." 9 (Formerly in Israel, when a man went to inquire of God, he spoke thus: "Come, let us go to the seer"; for *he who is* now *called* a prophet was formerly called a seer.)

10 Then Saul said to his servant, "Well said; come, let us go." So they went to the city where the man of God *was*. 11 As they went up the hill to the city, they met some young women going out to draw water, and said to them, "Is the seer here?"

12 And they answered them and said, "Yes, there he is, just ahead of you. Hurry now; for today he came to this city, because there is a sacrifice of the people today on the high place. 13 As soon as you come into the city, you will surely find him before he goes up to the high place to eat. For the people will not eat until he comes, because he must bless the sacrifice; afterward those who are invited will eat. Now therefore, go up, for about this time you will find him." 14 So they went up to the city. As they were coming into the city, there was Samuel, coming out toward them on his way up to the high place.

15 Now the LORD had told Samuel in his ear the day before Saul came, saying, 16 "Tomorrow about this time I will send you a man from the land of Benjamin, and you shall anoint him commander over My people Israel, that he may save My people from the hand of the Philistines; for I have looked upon My people, because their cry has come to Me."

17 So when Samuel saw Saul, the LORD said to him, "There he is, the man of whom I spoke to you. This one shall reign over My people." 18 Then Saul drew near to Samuel in the gate, and said, "Please tell me, where *is* the seer's house?"

19 Samuel answered Saul and said, "I *am* the seer. Go up before me to the high place, for you shall eat with me today; and tomorrow I will let you go and will tell you all that *is* in your heart. 20 But as for your donkeys that were lost three days ago, do not be anxious about them, for they have been found. And on whom *is* all the desire of Israel? *Is it* not on you and on all your father's house?"

21 And Saul answered and said, "*Am* I not a Benjamite, of the smallest of the tribes of Israel, and my family the least of all the

families of the tribe of Benjamin? Why then do you speak like this to me?"

22 Now Samuel took Saul and his servant and brought them into the hall, and had them sit in the place of honor among those who were invited; there *were* about thirty persons. 23 And Samuel said to the cook, "Bring the portion which I gave you, of which I said to you, 'Set it apart.'" 24 So the cook took up the thigh with its upper part and set *it* before Saul. And *Samuel* said, "Here it is, what was kept back. *It* was set apart for you. Eat; for until this time it has been kept for you, since I said I invited the people." So Saul ate with Samuel that day.

25 When they had come down from the high place into the city, *Samuel* spoke with Saul on the top of the house. 26 They arose early; and it was about the dawning of the day that Samuel called to Saul on the top of the house, saying, "Get up, that I may send you on your way." And Saul arose, and both of them went outside, he and Samuel.

27 As they were going down to the outskirts of the city, Samuel said to Saul, "Tell the servant to go on ahead of us." And he went on. "But you stand here awhile, that I may announce to you the word of God."

PSALM 55:9–15

9 DESTROY, O Lord, *and* divide their tongues,
For I have seen violence and strife in the city.
10 Day and night they go around it on its walls;
Iniquity and trouble *are* also in the midst of it.
11 Destruction *is* in its midst;
Oppression and deceit do not depart from its streets.

12 For *it is* not an enemy *who* reproaches me;
Then I could bear *it*.
Nor *is it* one *who* hates me who has exalted *himself* against me;
Then I could hide from him.
13 But *it was* you, a man my equal,
My companion and my acquaintance.
14 We took sweet counsel together,
And walked to the house of God in the throng.
15 Let death seize them;
Let them go down alive into hell,

For wickedness *is* in their dwellings *and* among them.

PROVERBS 15:15–17

15 ALL the days of the afflicted *are* evil,
But he who is of a merry heart *has* a continual feast.

16 Better *is* a little with the fear of the LORD,
Than great treasure with trouble.
17 Better *is* a dinner of herbs where love is,
Than a fatted calf with hatred.

LUKE 22:1–23

NOW the Feast of Unleavened Bread drew near, which is called Passover. 2 And the chief priests and the scribes sought how they might kill Him, for they feared the people.

3 Then Satan entered Judas, surnamed Iscariot, who was numbered among the twelve. 4 So he went his way and conferred with the chief priests and captains, how he might betray Him to them. 5 And they were glad, and agreed to give him money. 6 So he promised and sought opportunity to betray Him to them in the absence of the multitude.

7 Then came the Day of Unleavened Bread, when the Passover must be killed. 8 And He sent Peter and John, saying, "Go and prepare the Passover for us, that we may eat."

9 So they said to Him, "Where do You want us to prepare?"

10 And He said to them, "Behold, when you have entered the city, a man will meet you carrying a pitcher of water; follow him into the house which he enters. 11 Then you shall say to the master of the house, 'The Teacher says to you, "Where is the guest room where I may eat the Passover with My disciples?"' 12 Then he will show you a large, furnished upper room; there make ready."

13 So they went and found it just as He had said to them, and they prepared the Passover.

14 When the hour had come, He sat down, and the twelve apostles with Him. 15 Then He said to them, "With *fervent* desire I have desired to eat this Passover with you before I suffer; 16 for I say to you, I will no longer eat of it until it is fulfilled in the kingdom of God."

17 Then He took the cup, and gave thanks, and said, "Take this and divide *it* among yourselves; 18 for I say to you, I will not drink of the fruit of the vine until the kingdom of God comes."

19 And He took bread, gave thanks and broke *it*, and gave *it* to them, saying, "This is My body which is given for you; do this in remembrance of Me."

20 Likewise He also *took* the cup after supper, saying, "This cup *is* the new covenant in My blood, which is shed for you. 21 But behold, the hand of My betrayer *is* with Me on the table. 22 And truly the Son of Man goes as it has been determined, but woe to that man by whom He is betrayed!"

23 Then they began to question among themselves, which of them it was who would do this thing.

There are two Bodies of Christ: the Historic Body and the Mystical Body.   (GLORIFY)

◆◆◆◆

Reading 124—A Life of Temptation
Luke 22:28

Jesus Christ looked upon His life as one of temptation; and He goes through the same kind of temptation in us as He went through in the days of His flesh. The essence of Christianity is that we give the Son of God a chance to live and move and have His being in us, and the meaning of all spiritual growth is that He has an increasing opportunity to manifest Himself in our mortal flesh. The temptations of Jesus are not those of a man as man, but the temptations of God as man. "Therefore, in all things He had to be made like *His* brethren" (Heb. 2:17). Jesus Christ's temptations and ours move in different spheres until we become His brethren by being born from above. "For both He who sanctifies and those who are being sanctified *are* all of one, for which reason He is not ashamed to call them brethren" (Heb. 2:11). By regeneration the Son of God is formed in me and He has the same setting in my life as He had when on earth. The honor of Jesus Christ is at stake in my bodily life; am I remaining loyal to Him in the temptations which beset His life in me?   (PLACE HELP)

---

1 SAMUEL 10:1—11:15

THEN Samuel took a flask of oil and poured *it* on his head, and kissed him and said: "*Is it* not because the LORD has anointed you commander over His inheritance? 2 When you have departed from me today, you will find two men by Rachel's tomb in the territory of Benjamin at Zelzah; and they will say to you, 'The donkeys which you went to look for have been found. And now your father has ceased caring about the donkeys and is worrying about you, saying, "What shall I do about my son?"' 3 Then you shall go on forward from there and come to the terebinth tree of Tabor. There three men going up to God at Bethel will meet you, one carrying three young goats, another carrying three loaves of bread, and another carrying a skin of wine. 4 And they will greet you and give you two *loaves* of bread, which you shall receive from their hands. 5 After that you shall come to the hill of God where the Philistine garrison *is*. And it will happen, when you have come there to the city, that you will meet a group of prophets coming down from the high place with a stringed instrument, a tambourine, a flute, and a harp before them; and they will be prophesying. 6 Then the Spirit of the LORD will come upon you, and you will prophesy with them and be turned into another man. 7 And let it be, when these signs come to you, *that* you do as the occasion demands; for God *is* with you. 8 You shall go down before me to Gilgal;

and surely I will come down to you to offer burnt offerings *and* make sacrifices of peace offerings. Seven days you shall wait, till I come to you and show you what you should do."

9 So it was, when he had turned his back to go from Samuel, that God gave him another heart; and all those signs came to pass that day. 10 When they came there to the hill, there was a group of prophets to meet him; then the Spirit of God came upon him, and he prophesied among them. 11 And it happened, when all who knew him formerly saw that he indeed prophesied among the prophets, that the people said to one another, "What *is* this *that* has come upon the son of Kish? *Is* Saul also among the prophets?" 12 Then a man from there answered and said, "But who *is* their father?" Therefore it became a proverb: "*Is* Saul also among the prophets?" 13 And when he had finished prophesying, he went to the high place.

14 Then Saul's uncle said to him and his servant, "Where did you go?"

So he said, "To look for the donkeys. When we saw that *they were* nowhere *to be found,* we went to Samuel."

15 And Saul's uncle said, "Tell me, please, what Samuel said to you."

16 So Saul said to his uncle, "He told us plainly that the donkeys had been found." But about the matter of the kingdom, he did not tell him what Samuel had said.

17 Then Samuel called the people together to the LORD at Mizpah, 18 and said to the children of Israel, "Thus says the LORD God of Israel: 'I brought up Israel out of Egypt, and delivered you from the hand of the Egyptians *and* from the hand of all kingdoms and from those who oppressed you.' 19 But you have today rejected your God, who Himself saved you from all your adversities and your tribulations; and you have said to Him, 'No, set a king over us!' Now therefore, present yourselves before the LORD by your tribes and by your clans."

20 And when Samuel had caused all the tribes of Israel to come near, the tribe of Benjamin was chosen. 21 When he had caused the tribe of Benjamin to come near by their families, the family of Matri was chosen. And Saul the son of Kish was chosen. But when they sought him, he could not be found. 22 Therefore they inquired of the LORD further, "Has the man come here yet?"

And the LORD answered, "There he is, hidden among the equipment."

23 So they ran and brought him from there; and when he stood among the people, he was taller than any of the people from his shoulders upward. 24 And Samuel said to all the people, "Do you see him whom the LORD has chosen, that *there is* no one like him among all the people?"

So all the people shouted and said, "Long live the king!"

25 Then Samuel explained to the people the behavior of royalty, and wrote *it* in a book and laid *it* up before the LORD. And Samuel sent all the people away, every man to his house. 26 And Saul also went home to Gibeah; and valiant *men* went with him, whose hearts God had touched. 27 But some rebels said, "How can this man save us?" So they despised him, and brought him no presents. But he held his peace.

11 THEN Nahash the Ammonite came up and encamped against Jabesh Gilead; and all the men of Jabesh said to Nahash, "Make a covenant with us, and we will serve you."

2 And Nahash the Ammonite answered them, "On this *condition* I will make *a covenant* with you, that I may put out all your right eyes, and bring reproach on all Israel."

3 Then the elders of Jabesh said to him, "Hold off for seven days, that we may send messengers to all the territory of Israel. And then, if *there is* no one to save us, we will come out to you."

4 So the messengers came to Gibeah of Saul and told the news in the hearing of the people. And all the people lifted up their voices and wept. 5 Now there was Saul, coming behind the herd from the field; and Saul said, "What *troubles* the people, that they weep?" And they told him the words of the men of Jabesh. 6 Then the Spirit of God came upon Saul when he heard this news, and his anger was greatly aroused. 7 So he took a yoke of oxen and cut them in pieces, and sent *them* throughout all the territory of Israel by the hands of messengers, saying, "Whoever does not go out with Saul and Samuel to battle, so it shall be done to his oxen."

And the fear of the LORD fell on the people, and they came out with one consent. 8 When he numbered them in Bezek, the children of Israel were three hundred thousand, and the men of Judah thirty thousand. 9 And they said to the messengers who came, "Thus you shall say to the men of Jabesh Gilead: 'Tomorrow, by *the time* the sun is hot, you shall have help.' " Then the messengers came and reported *it* to the men of Jabesh, and they were glad. 10 Therefore the men of Jabesh said, "Tomorrow we will come out to you, and you may do with us whatever seems good to you."

11 So it was, on the next day, that Saul put the people in three companies; and they came into the midst of the camp in the morning watch, and killed Ammonites until the heat of the day. And it happened that those who survived were scattered, so that no two of them were left together.

12 Then the people said to Samuel, "Who *is* he who said, 'Shall Saul reign over us?' Bring the men, that we may put them to death."

13 But Saul said, "Not a man shall be put to death this day, for today the LORD has accomplished salvation in Israel."

14 Then Samuel said to the people, "Come, let us go to Gilgal and renew the kingdom there." 15 So all the people went to Gilgal, and there they made Saul king before the LORD in Gilgal. There they made sacrifices of peace offerings before the LORD, and there Saul and all the men of Israel rejoiced greatly.

PSALM 55:16–23

16   AS for me, I will call upon God,
       And the LORD shall save me.

17   Evening and morning and at noon
       I will pray, and cry aloud,
       And He shall hear my voice.

18   He has redeemed my soul in peace from
          the battle *that was* against me,
       For there were many against me.

19   God will hear, and afflict them,
       Even He who abides from of old.
                                      Selah

       Because they do not change,
       Therefore they do not fear God.

20   He has put forth his hands against those
          who were at peace with him;
       He has broken his covenant.

21   *The words* of his mouth were smoother
          than butter,
       But war *was* in his heart;
       His words were softer than oil,
       Yet they *were* drawn swords.

22   Cast your burden on the LORD,
       And He shall sustain you;
       He shall never permit the righteous to
          be moved.

23   But You, O God, shall bring them down
          to the pit of destruction;
       Bloodthirsty and deceitful men shall not
          live out half their days;
       But I will trust in You.

PROVERBS 15:18–20

18   A wrathful man stirs up strife,
       But *he who is* slow to anger allays
          contention.

19   The way of the lazy *man is* like a hedge
          of thorns,
       But the way of the upright *is* a highway.

20   A wise son makes a father glad,
       But a foolish man despises his mother.

LUKE 22:24–46

NOW there was also a dispute among them, as to which of them should be considered the greatest. 25 And He said to them, "The kings of the Gentiles exercise lordship over them, and those who exercise authority over them are called 'benefactors.' 26 But not so *among* you; on the contrary, he who is greatest among you, let him be as the younger, and he who governs as he who serves. 27 For who *is* greater, he who sits at the table, or he who serves? *Is* it not he who sits at the table? Yet I am among you as the One who serves.

28 "But you are those who have continued with Me in My trials. 29 And I bestow upon you a kingdom, just as My Father bestowed *one* upon Me, 30 that you may eat and drink at My table in My kingdom, and sit on thrones judging the twelve tribes of Israel."

31 And the Lord said, "Simon, Simon! Indeed, Satan has asked for you, that he may sift *you* as wheat. 32 But I have prayed for you, that your faith should not fail; and when you have returned to *Me,* strengthen your brethren."

33 But he said to Him, "Lord, I am ready to go with You, both to prison and to death."

34 Then He said, "I tell you, Peter, the rooster shall not crow this day before you will deny three times that you know Me."

35 And He said to them, "When I sent you without money bag, knapsack, and sandals, did you lack anything?"

So they said, "Nothing."

36 Then He said to them, "But now, he who has a money bag, let him take *it,* and likewise a knapsack; and he who has no sword, let him sell his garment and buy one. 37 For I say to you that this which is written must still be accomplished in Me: 'And He was numbered with the transgressors.' For the things concerning Me have an end."

38 So they said, "Lord, look, here *are* two swords."

And He said to them, "It is enough."

39 Coming out, He went to the Mount of Olives, as He was accustomed, and His disciples also followed Him. 40 When He came to the place, He said to them, "Pray that you may not enter into temptation."

41 And He was withdrawn from them about a stone's throw, and He knelt down and prayed, 42 saying, "Father, if it is Your will, take this cup away from Me; nevertheless not My will, but Yours, be done." 43 Then an angel appeared to Him from heaven, strengthening Him. 44 And being in agony, He prayed more earnestly. Then His sweat became like great drops of blood falling down to the ground.

---

*A*gony which has God behind it can be turned into triumph. (GLORY)

---

45 When He rose up from prayer, and had come to His disciples, He found them sleeping from sorrow. 46 Then He said to them, "Why do you sleep? Rise and pray, lest you enter into temptation."

◆◆◆◆

Reading 125—The Test of Loyalty
Luke 22:55–60

It is only the loyal soul who believes that God engineers circumstances. We take such liberty with our circumstances, we do not believe God engineers them, although we say we do; we treat the things that happen as if they were engineered by men. To be faithful in every circumstance means that we have only one loyalty, and that is to our Lord. Suddenly God breaks up a particular set of circumstances, and the realization comes that we have been disloyal to Him by not recognizing that He had ordered them; we never saw what He was after, and that particular thing will never be repeated all the days of our life. The test of loyalty always comes just there. If we learn to worship God in the trying circumstances, He will alter them in two seconds when He chooses.

Loyalty to Jesus Christ is the thing that we "stick at" today. We will be loyal to work, to service, to anything, but do not ask us to be loyal to Jesus Christ. Many Christians are intensely impatient of talking about loyalty to Jesus. Our Lord is dethroned more emphatically by Christian workers than by the world. God is made a machine for blessing men, and Jesus Christ is made a Worker among workers. (*UTMOST*)

1 SAMUEL 12:1—13:23

NOW Samuel said to all Israel: "Indeed I have heeded your voice in all that you said to me, and have made a king over you. 2 And now here is the king, walking before you; and I am old and grayheaded, and look, my sons *are* with you. I have walked before you from my childhood to this day. 3 Here I am. Witness against me before the LORD and before His anointed: Whose ox have I taken, or whose donkey have I taken, or whom have I cheated? Whom have I oppressed, or from whose hand have I received *any* bribe with which to blind my eyes? I will restore *it* to you."

4 And they said, "You have not cheated us or oppressed us, nor have you taken anything from any man's hand."

5 Then he said to them, "The LORD *is* witness against you, and His anointed *is* witness this day, that you have not found anything in my hand."

And they answered, "*He is* witness."

6 Then Samuel said to the people, "*It is* the LORD who raised up Moses and Aaron, and who brought your fathers up from the land of Egypt. 7 Now therefore, stand still,

that I may reason with you before the LORD concerning all the righteous acts of the LORD which He did to you and your fathers: 8 When Jacob had gone into Egypt, and your fathers cried out to the LORD, then the LORD sent Moses and Aaron, who brought your fathers out of Egypt and made them dwell in this place. 9 And when they forgot the LORD their God, He sold them into the hand of Sisera, commander of the army of Hazor, into the hand of the Philistines, and into the hand of the king of Moab; and they fought against them. 10 Then they cried out to the LORD, and said, 'We have sinned, because we have forsaken the LORD and served the Baals and Ashtoreths; but now deliver us from the hand of our enemies, and we will serve You.' 11 And the LORD sent Jerubbaal, Bedan, Jephthah, and Samuel, and delivered you out of the hand of your enemies on every side; and you dwelt in safety. 12 And when you saw that Nahash king of the Ammonites came against you, you said to me, 'No, but a king shall reign over us,' when the LORD your God *was* your king.

13 "Now therefore, here is the king whom you have chosen *and* whom you have desired. And take note, the LORD has set a king over you. 14 If you fear the LORD and serve Him and obey His voice, and do not rebel against the commandment of the LORD, then both you and the king who reigns over you will continue following the LORD your God. 15 However, if you do not obey the voice of the LORD, but rebel against the commandment of the LORD, then the hand of the LORD will be against you, as *it was* against your fathers.

The one word ringing out over our mental life is "Obey! Obey!" (BIB. PSYCH.)

---

16 "Now therefore, stand and see this great thing which the LORD will do before your eyes: 17 *Is* today not the wheat harvest? I will call to the LORD, and He will send thunder and rain, that you may perceive and see that your wickedness *is* great, which you have done in the sight of the LORD, in asking a king for yourselves."

18 So Samuel called to the LORD, and the LORD sent thunder and rain that day; and all the people greatly feared the LORD and Samuel.

19 And all the people said to Samuel, "Pray for your servants to the LORD your God, that we may not die; for we have added to all our sins the evil of asking a king for ourselves."

20 Then Samuel said to the people, "Do not fear. You have done all this wickedness; yet do not turn aside from following the LORD, but serve the LORD with all your heart. 21 And do not turn aside; for *then you would go* after empty things which cannot profit or deliver, for they *are* nothing. 22 For the LORD will not forsake His people, for His great name's sake, because it has pleased the LORD to make you His people. 23 Moreover, as for me, far be it from me that I should sin against the LORD in ceasing to pray for you; but I will teach you the good and the right way. 24 Only fear the LORD, and serve Him in truth with all your heart; for consider what great things He has done for you. 25 But if you still do wickedly, you shall be swept away, both you and your king."

13 SAUL reigned one year; and when he had reigned two years over Israel, 2 Saul chose for himself three thousand *men* of Israel. Two thousand were with Saul in Michmash and in the mountains of Bethel, and a thousand were with Jonathan in Gibeah of Benjamin. The rest of the people he sent away, every man to his tent.

3 And Jonathan attacked the garrison of the Philistines that *was* in Geba, and the Philistines heard *of it*. Then Saul blew the trumpet throughout all the land, saying, "Let the Hebrews hear!" 4 Now all Israel heard it said *that* Saul had attacked a garrison of the Philistines, and *that* Israel had also become an abomination to the Philistines. And the people were called together to Saul at Gilgal.

5 Then the Philistines gathered together to fight with Israel, thirty thousand chariots and six thousand horsemen, and people as the sand which *is* on the seashore in multitude. And they came up and encamped in Michmash, to the east of Beth Aven. 6 When the men of Israel saw that they were in danger (for the people were distressed), then the people hid in caves, in thickets, in rocks, in holes, and in pits. 7 And *some of* the Hebrews crossed over the Jordan to the land of Gad and Gilead.

As for Saul, he *was* still in Gilgal, and all the people followed him trembling. 8 Then he waited seven days, according to the time set by Samuel. But Samuel did not come to Gilgal; and the people were scattered from him. 9 So Saul said, "Bring a burnt offering and peace offerings here to me." And he offered the burnt offering. 10 Now it happened, as soon as he had finished presenting the burnt offering, that Samuel came; and Saul went out to meet him, that he might greet him.

11 And Samuel said, "What have you done?"

Saul said, "When I saw that the people were scattered from me, and *that* you did not come within the days appointed, and *that* the Philistines gathered together at Michmash, 12 then I said, 'The Philistines will now come down on me at Gilgal, and I have not made supplication to the LORD.' Therefore I felt compelled, and offered a burnt offering."

13 And Samuel said to Saul, "You have done foolishly. You have not kept the commandment of the LORD your God, which He commanded you. For now the LORD would have established your kingdom over Israel forever. 14 But now your kingdom shall not continue. The LORD has sought for Himself a man after His own heart, and the LORD has commanded him *to be* commander over His people, because you have not kept what the LORD commanded you."

15 Then Samuel arose and went up from Gilgal to Gibeah of Benjamin. And Saul numbered the people present with him, about six hundred men.

16 Saul, Jonathan his son, and the people present with them remained in Gibeah of Benjamin. But the Philistines encamped in Michmash. 17 Then raiders came out of the camp of the Philistines in three companies. One company turned onto the road to Ophrah, to the land of Shual, 18 another company turned to the road *to* Beth Horon, and another company turned *to* the road of the border that overlooks the Valley of Zeboim toward the wilderness.

19 Now there was no blacksmith to be found throughout all the land of Israel, for the Philistines said, "Lest the Hebrews make swords or spears." 20 But all the Israelites would go down to the Philistines to sharpen each man's plowshare, his mattock, his ax, and his sickle; 21 and the charge for a sharpening was a pim for the plowshares, the mattocks, the forks, and the axes, and to set the points of the goads. 22 So it came about, on the day of battle, that there was neither sword nor spear found in the hand of any of the people who *were* with Saul and Jonathan. But they were found with Saul and Jonathan his son.

23 And the garrison of the Philistines went out to the pass of Michmash.

PSALM 56:1–13

1 BE merciful to me, O God, for man
would swallow me up;
Fighting all day he oppresses me.

2 My enemies would hound *me* all day,
For *there are* many who fight against
me, O Most High.

3 Whenever I am afraid,
I will trust in You.

4 In God (I will praise His word),
In God I have put my trust;
I will not fear.
What can flesh do to me?

5 All day they twist my words;
All their thoughts *are* against me for
evil.

6 They gather together,
They hide, they mark my steps,
When they lie in wait for my life.

7 Shall they escape by iniquity?
In anger cast down the peoples, O God!

8 You number my wanderings;
Put my tears into Your bottle;
Are they not in Your book?

Remember, we go through nothing that God does not know about.   (BRILL. HERITAGE)

---

9 When I cry out *to You,*
Then my enemies will turn back;
This I know, because God *is* for me.

10 In God (I will praise *His* word),
In the LORD (I will praise *His* word),

11 In God I have put my trust;
I will not be afraid.
What can man do to me?

12 Vows *made* to You *are binding* upon
me, O God;
I will render praises to You,

13 For You have delivered my soul from
death.
Have You not *kept* my feet from falling,
That I may walk before God
In the light of the living?

PROVERBS 15:21–23

21 FOLLY *is* joy *to him who is* destitute
of discernment,
But a man of understanding walks
uprightly.

22 Without counsel, plans go awry,
   But in the multitude of counselors they
   are established.

23 A man has joy by the answer of his
   mouth,
   And a word *spoken* in due season, how
   good *it is!*

LUKE 22:47–71

AND while He was still speaking, behold, a multitude; and he who was called Judas, one of the twelve, went before them and drew near to Jesus to kiss Him. 48 But Jesus said to him, "Judas, are you betraying the Son of Man with a kiss?"

49 When those around Him saw what was going to happen, they said to Him, "Lord, shall we strike with the sword?" 50 And one of them struck the servant of the high priest and cut off his right ear.

51 But Jesus answered and said, "Permit even this." And He touched his ear and healed him.

52 Then Jesus said to the chief priests, captains of the temple, and the elders who had come to Him, "Have you come out, as against a robber, with swords and clubs? 53 When I was with you daily in the temple, you did not try to seize Me. But this is your hour, and the power of darkness."

54 Having arrested Him, they led *Him* and brought Him into the high priest's house. But Peter followed at a distance. 55 Now when they had kindled a fire in the midst of the courtyard and sat down together, Peter sat among them. 56 And a certain servant girl, seeing him as he sat by the fire, looked intently at him and said, "This man was also with Him."

57 But he denied Him, saying, "Woman, I do not know Him."

58 And after a little while another saw him and said, "You also are of them."

But Peter said, "Man, I am not!"

59 Then after about an hour had passed, another confidently affirmed, saying, "Surely this *fellow* also was with Him, for he is a Galilean."

60 But Peter said, "Man, I do not know what you are saying!"

Immediately, while he was still speaking, the rooster crowed. 61 And the Lord turned and looked at Peter. Then Peter remembered the word of the Lord, how He had said to him, "Before the rooster crows, you will deny Me three times." 62 So Peter went out and wept bitterly.

63 Now the men who held Jesus mocked Him and beat Him. 64 And having blindfolded Him, they struck Him on the face and asked Him, saying, "Prophesy! Who is the one who struck You?" 65 And many other things they blasphemously spoke against Him.

66 As soon as it was day, the elders of the people, both chief priests and scribes, came together and led Him into their council, saying, 67 "If You are the Christ, tell us."

But He said to them, "If I tell you, you will by no means believe. 68 And if I also ask *you,* you will by no means answer Me or let *Me* go. 69 Hereafter the Son of Man will sit on the right hand of the power of God."

70 Then they all said, "Are You then the Son of God?"

So He said to them, "You *rightly* say that I am."

71 And they said, "What further testimony do we need? For we have heard it ourselves from His own mouth."

◆◆◆◆

Reading 126—Exhibit Christ Crucified
Luke 23:21

Very few of us have any understanding of the reason why Jesus Christ died. If sympathy is all that human beings need, then the Cross of Christ is a farce, there was no need for it. What the world needs is not "a little bit of love," but a surgical operation.

When you are face-to-face with a soul in difficulty spiritually, remind yourself of Jesus Christ on the cross. If that soul can get to God on any other line, then the Cross of Jesus Christ is unnecessary. If you can help others by your sympathy or understanding, you are a traitor to Jesus Christ. You have to keep your soul rightly related to God and pour out for others on His line, not pour out on the human line and ignore God. The great note today is amiable religiosity.

The one thing we have to do is to exhibit Jesus Christ crucified, to lift Him up all the time. Every doctrine that is not imbedded in the Cross of Jesus will lead astray. If the worker himself believes in Jesus Christ and is banking on the reality of redemption, the people he talks to *must* be concerned. The thing that remains and deepens is the worker's simple relationship to Jesus Christ; his usefulness to God depends on that and that alone.   (*Utmost*)

1 SAMUEL 14:1—15:35

NOW it happened one day that Jonathan the son of Saul said to the young man who bore his armor, "Come, let us go over to the Philistines' garrison that *is* on the other side." But he did not tell his father. 2 And Saul was sitting in the outskirts of Gibeah under a pomegranate tree which *is* in Migron. The people who *were* with him *were* about six hundred men. 3 Ahijah the son of Ahitub, Ichabod's brother, the son of Phinehas, the son of Eli, the LORD's priest in Shiloh, was wearing an ephod. But the people did not know that Jonathan had gone.

4 Between the passes, by which Jonathan sought to go over to the Philistines' garrison, *there was* a sharp rock on one side and a sharp rock on the other side. And the name of one *was* Bozez, and the name of the other Seneh. 5 The front of one faced northward opposite Michmash, and the other southward opposite Gibeah.

6 Then Jonathan said to the young man who bore his armor, "Come, let us go over to the garrison of these uncircumcised; it may be that the LORD will work for us. For nothing restrains the LORD from saving by many or by few."

7 So his armorbearer said to him, "Do all that is in your heart. Go then; here I am with you, according to your heart."

8 Then Jonathan said, "Very well, let us cross over to *these* men, and we will show ourselves to them. 9 If they say thus to us, 'Wait until we come to you,' then we will stand still in our place and not go up to them. 10 But if they say thus, 'Come up to us,' then we will go up. For the LORD has delivered them into our hand, and this *will be* a sign to us."

11 So both of them showed themselves to the garrison of the Philistines. And the Philistines said, "Look, the Hebrews are coming out of the holes where they have hidden." 12 Then the men of the garrison called to Jonathan and his armorbearer, and said, "Come up to us, and we will show you something."

Jonathan said to his armorbearer, "Come up after me, for the LORD has delivered them into the hand of Israel." 13 And Jonathan climbed up on his hands and knees with his armorbearer after him; and they fell before Jonathan. And as he came after him, his armorbearer killed them. 14 That first slaughter which Jonathan and his armorbearer made was about twenty men within about half an acre of land.

15 And there was trembling in the camp, in the field, and among all the people. The garrison and the raiders also trembled; and the earth quaked, so that it was a very great trembling. 16 Now the watchmen of Saul in Gibeah of Benjamin looked, and *there* was the multitude, melting away; and they went here and there. 17 Then Saul said to the people who *were* with him, "Now call the roll and see who has gone from us." And when they had called the roll, surprisingly, Jonathan and his armorbearer *were* not *there*. 18 And Saul said to Ahijah, "Bring the ark of God here" (for at that time the ark of God was with the children of Israel). 19 Now it happened, while Saul talked to the priest, that the noise which *was* in the camp of the Philistines continued to increase; so Saul said to the priest, "Withdraw your hand." 20 Then Saul and all the people who *were* with him assembled, and they went to the battle; and indeed every man's sword was against his neighbor, *and there was* very great confusion. 21 Moreover the Hebrews *who* were with the Philistines before that time, who went up with them into the camp *from the* surrounding *country*, they also joined the Israelites who *were* with Saul and Jonathan. 22 Likewise all the men of Israel who had hidden in the mountains of Ephraim, *when* they heard that the Philistines fled, they also followed hard after them

in the battle. 23 So the LORD saved Israel that day, and the battle shifted to Beth Aven.

24 And the men of Israel were distressed that day, for Saul had placed the people under oath, saying, "Cursed *is* the man who eats *any* food until evening, before I have taken vengeance on my enemies." So none of the people tasted food. 25 Now all *the people* of the land came to a forest; and there was honey on the ground. 26 And when the people had come into the woods, there was the honey, dripping; but no one put his hand to his mouth, for the people feared the oath. 27 But Jonathan had not heard his father charge the people with the oath; therefore he stretched out the end of the rod *that was* in his hand and dipped it in a honeycomb, and put his hand to his mouth; and his countenance brightened. 28 Then one of the people said, "Your father strictly charged the people with an oath, saying, 'Cursed *is* the man who eats food this day.' " And the people were faint.

29 But Jonathan said, "My father has troubled the land. Look now, how my countenance has brightened because I tasted a little of this honey. 30 How much better if the people had eaten freely today of the spoil of their enemies which they found! For now would there not have been a much greater slaughter among the Philistines?"

31 Now they had driven back the Philistines that day from Michmash to Aijalon. So the people were very faint. 32 And the people rushed on the spoil, and took sheep, oxen, and calves, and slaughtered *them* on the ground; and the people ate *them* with the blood. 33 Then they told Saul, saying, "Look, the people are sinning against the LORD by eating with the blood!"

So he said, "You have dealt treacherously; roll a large stone to me this day." 34 Then Saul said, "Disperse yourselves among the people, and say to them, 'Bring me here every man's ox and every man's sheep, slaughter *them* here, and eat; and do not sin against the LORD by eating with the blood.' " So every one of the people brought his ox with him that night, and slaughtered *it* there. 35 Then Saul built an altar to the LORD. This was the first altar that he built to the LORD.

36 Now Saul said, "Let us go down after the Philistines by night, and plunder them until the morning light; and let us not leave a man of them."

And they said, "Do whatever seems good to you."

Then the priest said, "Let us draw near to God here."

37 So Saul asked counsel of God, "Shall I go down after the Philistines? Will You deliver them into the hand of Israel?" But He did not answer him that day. 38 And Saul said, "Come over here, all you chiefs of the people, and know and see what this sin was today. 39 For *as* the LORD lives, who saves Israel, though it be in Jonathan my son, he shall surely die." But not a man among all the people answered him. 40 Then he said to all Israel, "You be on one side, and my son Jonathan and I will be on the other side."

And the people said to Saul, "Do what seems good to you."

41 Therefore Saul said to the LORD God of Israel, "Give a perfect *lot*." So Saul and Jonathan were taken, but the people escaped. 42 And Saul said, "Cast *lots* between my son Jonathan and me." So Jonathan was taken. 43 Then Saul said to Jonathan, "Tell me what you have done."

And Jonathan told him, and said, "I only tasted a little honey with the end of the rod that *was* in my hand. So now I must die!"

44 Saul answered, "God do so and more also; for you shall surely die, Jonathan."

45 But the people said to Saul, "Shall Jonathan die, who has accomplished this great deliverance in Israel? Certainly not! *As* the LORD lives, not one hair of his head shall fall to the ground, for he has worked with God this day." So the people rescued Jonathan, and he did not die.

46 Then Saul returned from pursuing the Philistines, and the Philistines went to their own place.

47 So Saul established his sovereignty over Israel, and fought against all his enemies on every side, against Moab, against the people of Ammon, against Edom, against the kings of Zobah, and against the Philistines. Wherever he turned, he harassed *them*. 48 And he gathered an army and attacked the Amalekites, and delivered Israel from the hands of those who plundered them.

49 The sons of Saul were Jonathan, Jishui, and Malchishua. And the names of his two daughters *were these:* the name of the first-born Merab, and the name of the younger Michal. 50 The name of Saul's wife *was* Ahinoam the daughter of Ahimaaz. And the name of the commander of his army *was* Abner the son of Ner, Saul's uncle. 51 Kish *was* the father of Saul, and Ner the father of Abner *was* the son of Abiel.

52 Now there was fierce war with the Philistines all the days of Saul. And when Saul saw any strong man or any valiant man, he took him for himself.

15 SAMUEL also said to Saul, "The LORD sent me to anoint you king over His people, over Israel. Now therefore, heed the voice of the words of the LORD. 2 Thus says the LORD of hosts: 'I will punish Amalek *for* what he did to Israel, how he ambushed him on the way when he came up from Egypt. 3 Now go and attack Amalek, and utterly destroy all that they have, and do not spare them. But kill both man and woman, infant and nursing child, ox and sheep, camel and donkey.'"

4 So Saul gathered the people together and numbered them in Telaim, two hundred thousand foot soldiers and ten thousand men of Judah. 5 And Saul came to a city of Amalek, and lay in wait in the valley.

6 Then Saul said to the Kenites, "Go, depart, get down from among the Amalekites, lest I destroy you with them. For you showed kindness to all the children of Israel when they came up out of Egypt." So the Kenites departed from among the Amalekites. 7 And Saul attacked the Amalekites, from Havilah all the way to Shur, which is east of Egypt. 8 He also took Agag king of the Amalekites alive, and utterly destroyed all the people with the edge of the sword. 9 But Saul and the people spared Agag and the best of the sheep, the oxen, the fatlings, the lambs, and all *that was* good, and were unwilling to utterly destroy them. But everything despised and worthless, that they utterly destroyed.

10 Now the word of the LORD came to Samuel, saying, 11 "I greatly regret that I have set up Saul *as* king, for he has turned back from following Me, and has not performed My commandments." And it grieved Samuel, and he cried out to the LORD all night. 12 So when Samuel rose early in the morning to meet Saul, it was told Samuel, saying, "Saul went to Carmel, and indeed, he set up a monument for himself; and he has gone on around, passed by, and gone down to Gilgal." 13 Then Samuel went to Saul, and Saul said to him, "Blessed *are* you of the LORD! I have performed the commandment of the LORD."

14 But Samuel said, "What then *is* this bleating of the sheep in my ears, and the lowing of the oxen which I hear?"

15 And Saul said, "They have brought them from the Amalekites; for the people spared the best of the sheep and the oxen, to sacrifice to the LORD your God; and the rest we have utterly destroyed."

16 Then Samuel said to Saul, "Be quiet! And I will tell you what the LORD said to me last night."

And he said to him, "Speak on."

17 So Samuel said, "When you *were* little in your own eyes, *were* you not head of the tribes of Israel? And did not the LORD anoint you king over Israel? 18 Now the LORD sent you on a mission, and said, 'Go, and utterly destroy the sinners, the Amalekites, and fight against them until they are

---

Sin must be destroyed, not corrected; it is the destruction of something in order to lead to emancipation. (PHIL. SIN)

---

consumed.' 19 Why then did you not obey the voice of the LORD? Why did you swoop down on the spoil, and do evil in the sight of the LORD?"

20 And Saul said to Samuel, "But I have obeyed the voice of the LORD, and gone on the mission on which the LORD sent me, and brought back Agag king of Amalek; I have utterly destroyed the Amalekites. 21 But the people took of the plunder, sheep and oxen, the best of the things which should have been utterly destroyed, to sacrifice to the LORD your God in Gilgal."

22 So Samuel said:

"Has the LORD *as great* delight in
    burnt offerings and sacrifices,
    As in obeying the voice of the LORD?
    Behold, to obey is better than
       sacrifice,
    And to heed than the fat of rams.
23 For rebellion *is as* the sin of
       witchcraft,
    And stubbornness *is as* iniquity and
       idolatry.
    Because you have rejected the word
       of the LORD,
    He also has rejected you from *being*
       king."

24 Then Saul said to Samuel, "I have sinned, for I have transgressed the commandment of the LORD and your words, because I feared the people and obeyed their voice. 25 Now therefore, please pardon my sin, and return with me, that I may worship the LORD."

26 But Samuel said to Saul, "I will not return with you, for you have rejected the word of the LORD, and the LORD has rejected you from being king over Israel."

27 And as Samuel turned around to go away, *Saul* seized the edge of his robe, and it tore. 28 So Samuel said to him, "The LORD has torn the kingdom of Israel from

you today, and has given it to a neighbor of yours, *who is* better than you. 29 And also the Strength of Israel will not lie nor relent. For He *is* not a man, that He should relent."

30 Then he said, "I have sinned; *yet* honor me now, please, before the elders of my people and before Israel, and return with me, that I may worship the LORD your God." 31 So Samuel turned back after Saul, and Saul worshiped the LORD.

32 Then Samuel said, "Bring Agag king of the Amalekites here to me." So Agag came to him cautiously.

And Agag said, "Surely the bitterness of death is past."

33 But Samuel said, "As your sword has made women childless, so shall your mother be childless among women." And Samuel hacked Agag in pieces before the LORD in Gilgal.

34 Then Samuel went to Ramah, and Saul went up to his house at Gibeah of Saul. 35 And Samuel went no more to see Saul until the day of his death. Nevertheless Samuel mourned for Saul, and the LORD regretted that He had made Saul king over Israel.

PSALM 57:1–3

1   BE merciful to me, O God, be merciful
     to me!
     For my soul trusts in You;
     And in the shadow of Your wings I
       will make my refuge,
     Until *these* calamities have passed by.

2   I will cry out to God Most High,
     To God who performs *all things* for
       me.

3   He shall send from heaven and save
       me;
     He reproaches the one who would
       swallow me up.   Selah
     God shall send forth His mercy and
       His truth.

PROVERBS 15:24, 25

24   THE way of life *winds* upward for the
       wise,
     That he may turn away from hell below.

25   The LORD will destroy the house of
       the proud,
     But He will establish the boundary of
       the widow.

LUKE 23:1–25

THEN the whole multitude of them arose and led Him to Pilate. 2 And they began to accuse Him, saying, "We found this *fellow* perverting the nation, and forbidding to pay taxes to Caesar, saying that He Himself is Christ, a King."

3 Then Pilate asked Him, saying, "Are You the King of the Jews?"

He answered him and said, "*It is as* you say."

4 So Pilate said to the chief priests and the crowd, "I find no fault in this Man."

5 But they were the more fierce, saying, "He stirs up the people, teaching throughout all Judea, beginning from Galilee to this place."

6 When Pilate heard of Galilee, he asked if the Man were a Galilean. 7 And as soon as he knew that He belonged to Herod's jurisdiction, he sent Him to Herod, who was also in Jerusalem at that time. 8 Now when Herod saw Jesus, he was exceedingly glad; for he had desired for a long *time* to see Him, because he had heard many things about Him, and he hoped to see some miracle done by Him. 9 Then he questioned Him with many words, but He answered him nothing. 10 And the chief priests and scribes stood and vehemently accused Him. 11 Then Herod, with his men of war, treated Him with contempt and mocked *Him,* arrayed Him in a gorgeous robe, and sent Him back to Pilate. 12 That very day Pilate and Herod became friends with each other, for previously they had been at enmity with each other.

13 Then Pilate, when he had called together the chief priests, the rulers, and the people, 14 said to them, "You have brought this Man to me, as one who misleads the people. And indeed, having examined *Him* in your presence, I have found no fault in this Man concerning those things of which you accuse Him; 15 no, neither did Herod, for I sent you back to him; and indeed nothing deserving of death has been done by Him. 16 I will therefore chastise Him and release *Him*" 17 (for it was necessary for him to release one to them at the feast).

18 And they all cried out at once, saying, "Away with this *Man,* and release to us Barabbas"— 19 who had been thrown into prison for a certain rebellion made in the city, and for murder.

20 Pilate, therefore, wishing to release Jesus, again called out to them. 21 But they shouted, saying, "Crucify *Him,* crucify Him!"

22 Then he said to them the third time, "Why, what evil has He done? I have found no reason for death in Him. I will therefore chastise Him and let *Him* go."

23 But they were insistent, demanding with loud voices that He be crucified. And the voices of these men and of the chief priests prevailed. 24 So Pilate gave sentence that it should be as they requested. 25 And he released to them the one they requested, who for rebellion and murder had been thrown into prison; but he delivered Jesus to their will.

◆◆◆

Reading 127—The Victorious Voice for God
Luke 23:46

The Cross is a tragedy to man, but a tremendous triumph to God, an absolute triumph. Listen to the clear, ringing voice: "Father, into Your hands I commit My spirit!" The spirit of the Son of God only? No, the spirit of the whole human race incarnated in the Savior of the world. My spirit was there, your spirit was there, and by God's mighty grace and the gift of His Spirit given by our Lord after He ascended, we can know experientially His complete salvation for body, soul, and spirit.

Never consider this passage in a shallow way—that on the cross the physical sufferings of Jesus were so great that His mind was blinded and He imagined His Father had gone from Him. That understanding does not touch the depths of identification with sin to which our Lord went. Neither is it true to say that God was angry and hid His face from Him. If one may put it so, God was never more pleased with His Son than when He bridged the gulf between God and man by the sacrifice of Himself. (*GLORY*)

1 SAMUEL 16:1—17:58

NOW the LORD said to Samuel, "How long will you mourn for Saul, seeing I have rejected him from reigning over Israel? Fill your horn with oil, and go; I am sending you to Jesse the Bethlehemite. For I have provided Myself a king among his sons."

2 And Samuel said, "How can I go? If Saul hears *it,* he will kill me."

But the LORD said, "Take a heifer with you, and say, 'I have come to sacrifice to the LORD.' 3 Then invite Jesse to the sacrifice, and I will show you what you shall do; you shall anoint for Me the one I name to you."

4 So Samuel did what the LORD said, and went to Bethlehem. And the elders of the town trembled at his coming, and said, "Do you come peaceably?"

5 And he said, "Peaceably; I have come to sacrifice to the LORD. Sanctify yourselves, and come with me to the sacrifice." Then he consecrated Jesse and his sons, and invited them to the sacrifice.

6 So it was, when they came, that he looked at Eliab and said, "Surely the LORD's anointed *is* before Him!"

7 But the LORD said to Samuel, "Do not look at his appearance or at his physical stature, because I have refused him. For *the LORD does* not *see* as man sees; for man looks at the outward appearance, but the LORD looks at the heart."

A man can develop an amazing perfection of character without a spark of the grace of God. (DISCIPLES)

8 So Jesse called Abinadab, and made him pass before Samuel. And he said, "Neither has the LORD chosen this one." 9 Then Jesse made Shammah pass by. And he said, "Neither has the LORD chosen this one." 10 Thus Jesse made seven of his sons pass before Samuel. And Samuel said to Jesse, "The LORD has not chosen these." 11 And Samuel said to Jesse, "Are all the young

men here?" Then he said, "There remains yet the youngest, and there he is, keeping the sheep."

And Samuel said to Jesse, "Send and bring him. For we will not sit down till he comes here." 12 So he sent and brought him in. Now he *was* ruddy, with bright eyes, and good-looking. And the LORD said, "Arise, anoint him; for this *is* the one!" 13 Then Samuel took the horn of oil and anointed him in the midst of his brothers; and the Spirit of the LORD came upon David from that day forward. So Samuel arose and went to Ramah.

14 But the Spirit of the LORD departed from Saul, and a distressing spirit from the LORD troubled him. 15 And Saul's servants said to him, "Surely, a distressing spirit from God is troubling you. 16 Let our master now command your servants, *who are* before you, to seek out a man *who is* a skillful player on the harp. And it shall be that he will play it with his hand when the distressing spirit from God is upon you, and you shall be well."

17 So Saul said to his servants, "Provide me now a man who can play well, and bring *him* to me."

18 Then one of the servants answered and said, "Look, I have seen a son of Jesse the Bethlehemite, *who is* skillful in playing, a mighty man of valor, a man of war, prudent in speech, and a handsome person; and the LORD *is* with him."

19 Therefore Saul sent messengers to Jesse, and said, "Send me your son David, who *is* with the sheep." 20 And Jesse took a donkey *loaded with* bread, a skin of wine, and a young goat, and sent *them* by his son David to Saul. 21 So David came to Saul and stood before him. And he loved him greatly, and he became his armorbearer. 22 Then Saul sent to Jesse, saying, "Please let David stand before me, for he has found favor in my sight." 23 And so it was, whenever the spirit from God was upon Saul, that David would take a harp and play *it* with his hand. Then Saul would become refreshed and well, and the distressing spirit would depart from him.

17 NOW the Philistines gathered their armies together to battle, and were gathered at Sochoh, which *belongs* to Judah; they encamped between Sochoh and Azekah, in Ephes Dammim. 2 And Saul and the men of Israel were gathered together, and they encamped in the Valley of Elah, and drew up in battle array against the Philistines. 3 The Philistines stood on a mountain on one side, and Israel stood on a mountain on the other side, with a valley between them.

4 And a champion went out from the camp of the Philistines, named Goliath, from Gath, whose height *was* six cubits and a span. 5 *He had* a bronze helmet on his head, and he *was* armed with a coat of mail, and the weight of the coat *was* five thousand shekels of bronze. 6 And *he had* bronze armor on his legs and a bronze javelin between his shoulders. 7 Now the staff of his spear *was* like a weaver's beam, and his iron spearhead *weighed* six hundred shekels; and a shield-bearer went before him. 8 Then he stood and cried out to the armies of Israel, and said to them, "Why have you come out to line up for battle? *Am* I not a Philistine, and you the servants of Saul? Choose a man for yourselves, and let him come down to me. 9 If he is able to fight with me and kill me, then we will be your servants. But if I prevail against him and kill him, then you shall be our servants and serve us." 10 And the Philistine said, "I defy the armies of Israel this day; give me a man, that we may fight together." 11 When Saul and all Israel heard these words of the Philistine, they were dismayed and greatly afraid.

12 Now David *was* the son of that Ephrathite of Bethlehem Judah, whose name *was* Jesse, and who had eight sons. And the man was old, advanced *in years,* in the days of Saul. 13 The three oldest sons of Jesse had gone to follow Saul to the battle. The names of his three sons who went to the battle *were* Eliab the firstborn, next to him Abinadab, and the third Shammah. 14 David *was* the youngest. And the three oldest followed Saul. 15 But David occasionally went and returned from Saul to feed his father's sheep at Bethlehem.

16 And the Philistine drew near and presented himself forty days, morning and evening.

17 Then Jesse said to his son David, "Take now for your brothers an ephah of this dried *grain* and these ten loaves, and run to your brothers at the camp. 18 And carry these ten cheeses to the captain of *their* thousand, and see how your brothers fare, and bring back news of them." 19 Now Saul and they and all the men of Israel *were* in the Valley of Elah, fighting with the Philistines.

20 So David rose early in the morning, left the sheep with a keeper, and took *the things* and went as Jesse had commanded him. And he came to the camp as the army was going out to the fight and shouting for the battle. 21 For Israel and the Philistines had drawn up in battle array, army

against army. 22 And David left his supplies in the hand of the supply keeper, ran to the army, and came and greeted his brothers. 23 Then as he talked with them, there was the champion, the Philistine of Gath, Goliath by name, coming up from the armies of the Philistines; and he spoke according to the same words. So David heard *them.* 24 And all the men of Israel, when they saw the man, fled from him and were dreadfully afraid. 25 So the men of Israel said, "Have you seen this man who has come up? Surely he has come up to defy Israel; and it shall be *that* the man who kills him the king will enrich with great riches, will give him his daughter, and give his father's house exemption *from taxes* in Israel."

26 Then David spoke to the men who stood by him, saying, "What shall be done for the man who kills this Philistine and takes away the reproach from Israel? For who *is* this uncircumcised Philistine, that he should defy the armies of the living God?"

27 And the people answered him in this manner, saying, "So shall it be done for the man who kills him."

28 Now Eliab his oldest brother heard when he spoke to the men; and Eliab's anger was aroused against David, and he said, "Why did you come down here? And with whom have you left those few sheep in the wilderness? I know your pride and the insolence of your heart, for you have come down to see the battle."

29 And David said, "What have I done now? *Is there* not a cause?" 30 Then he turned from him toward another and said the same thing; and these people answered him as the first ones *did.*

31 Now when the words which David spoke were heard, they reported *them* to Saul; and he sent for him. 32 Then David said to Saul, "Let no man's heart fail because of him; your servant will go and fight with this Philistine."

33 And Saul said to David, "You are not able to go against this Philistine to fight with him; for you *are* a youth, and he a man of war from his youth."

34 But David said to Saul, "Your servant used to keep his father's sheep, and when a lion or a bear came and took a lamb out of the flock, 35 I went out after it and struck it, and delivered *the lamb* from its mouth; and when it arose against me, I caught *it* by its beard, and struck and killed it. 36 Your servant has killed both lion and bear; and this uncircumcised Philistine will be like one of them, seeing he has defied

the armies of the living God." 37 Moreover David said, "The LORD, who delivered me from the paw of the lion and from the paw of the bear, He will deliver me from the hand of this Philistine."

And Saul said to David, "Go, and the LORD be with you!"

38 So Saul clothed David with his armor, and he put a bronze helmet on his head; he also clothed him with a coat of mail. 39 David fastened his sword to his armor and tried to walk, for he had not tested *them.* And David said to Saul, "I cannot walk with these, for I have not tested *them.*" So David took them off.

40 Then he took his staff in his hand; and he chose for himself five smooth stones from the brook, and put them in a shepherd's bag, in a pouch which he had, and his sling was in his hand. And he drew near to the Philistine. 41 So the Philistine came, and began drawing near to David, and the man who bore the shield *went* before him. 42 And when the Philistine looked about and saw David, he disdained him; for he was *only* a youth, ruddy and good-looking. 43 So the Philistine said to David, "*Am* I a dog, that you come to me with sticks?" And the Philistine cursed David by his gods. 44 And the Philistine said to David, "Come to me, and I will give your flesh to the birds of the air and the beasts of the field!"

45 Then David said to the Philistine, "You come to me with a sword, with a spear, and with a javelin. But I come to you in the name of the LORD of hosts, the God of the armies of Israel, whom you have defied. 46 This day the LORD will deliver you into my hand, and I will strike you and take your head from you. And this day I will give the carcasses of the camp of the Philistines to the birds of the air and the wild beasts of the earth, that all the earth may know that there is a God in Israel. 47 Then all this assembly shall know that the LORD does not save with sword and spear; for the battle *is* the LORD's, and He will give you into our hands."

48 So it was, when the Philistine arose and came and drew near to meet David, that David hurried and ran toward the army to meet the Philistine. 49 Then David put his hand in his bag and took out a stone; and he slung *it* and struck the Philistine in his forehead, so that the stone sank into his forehead, and he fell on his face to the earth. 50 So David prevailed over the Philistine with a sling and a stone, and struck the Philistine and killed him. But *there was* no sword in the hand of David. 51 Therefore

David ran and stood over the Philistine, took his sword and drew it out of its sheath and killed him, and cut off his head with it.

And when the Philistines saw that their champion was dead, they fled. 52 Now the men of Israel and Judah arose and shouted, and pursued the Philistines as far as the entrance of the valley and to the gates of Ekron. And the wounded of the Philistines fell along the road to Shaaraim, even as far as Gath and Ekron. 53 Then the children of Israel returned from chasing the Philistines, and they plundered their tents. 54 And David took the head of the Philistine and brought it to Jerusalem, but he put his armor in his tent.

55 When Saul saw David going out against the Philistine, he said to Abner, the commander of the army, "Abner, whose son *is* this youth?"

And Abner said, "As your soul lives, O king, I do not know."

56 So the king said, "Inquire whose son this young man *is*."

57 Then, as David returned from the slaughter of the Philistine, Abner took him and brought him before Saul with the head of the Philistine in his hand. 58 And Saul said to him, "Whose son *are* you, young man?"

So David answered, "*I am* the son of your servant Jesse the Bethlehemite."

PSALM 57:4–11

4   MY soul *is* among lions;
      I lie *among* the sons of men
      Who are set on fire,
      Whose teeth *are* spears and arrows,
      And their tongue a sharp sword.

5   Be exalted, O God, above the heavens;
      Let Your glory *be* above all the earth.

6   They have prepared a net for my steps;
      My soul is bowed down;
      They have dug a pit before me;
      Into the midst of it they *themselves* have
        fallen.   Selah

7   My heart is steadfast, O God, my heart
      is steadfast;
      I will sing and give praise.

8   Awake, my glory!
      Awake, lute and harp!
      I will awaken the dawn.

9   I will praise You, O Lord, among the
      peoples;
      I will sing to You among the nations.

10   For Your mercy reaches unto the
      heavens,
      And Your truth unto the clouds.

11   Be exalted, O God, above the heavens;
      Let Your glory *be* above all the earth.

PROVERBS 15:26

26   THE thoughts of the wicked *are* an
      abomination to the Lord,
      But *the words* of the pure *are* pleasant.

LUKE 23:26–56

NOW as they led Him away, they laid hold of a certain man, Simon a Cyrenian, who was coming from the country, and on him they laid the cross that he might bear *it* after Jesus.

27 And a great multitude of the people followed Him, and women who also mourned and lamented Him. 28 But Jesus, turning to them, said, "Daughters of Jerusalem, do not weep for Me, but weep for yourselves and for your children. 29 For indeed the days are coming in which they will say, 'Blessed *are* the barren, wombs that never bore, and breasts which never nursed!' 30 Then they will begin 'to say to the mountains, "Fall on us!" and to the hills, "Cover us!" ' 31 For if they do these things in the green wood, what will be done in the dry?"

32 There were also two others, criminals, led with Him to be put to death. 33 And when they had come to the place called Calvary, there they crucified Him, and the criminals, one on the right hand and the

---

Jesus Christ hates the wrong in man, and Calvary is the estimate of His hatred.   (UTMOST)

---

other on the left. 34 Then Jesus said, "Father, forgive them, for they do not know what they do."

And they divided His garments and cast lots. 35 And the people stood looking on. But even the rulers with them sneered, saying, "He saved others; let Him save Himself if He is the Christ, the chosen of God."

36 The soldiers also mocked Him, coming and offering Him sour wine, 37 and saying, "If You are the King of the Jews, save Yourself."

38 And an inscription also was written over Him in letters of Greek, Latin, and Hebrew:

THIS IS THE KING OF THE JEWS.

39 Then one of the criminals who were hanged blasphemed Him, saying, "If You are the Christ, save Yourself and us."

40 But the other, answering, rebuked him, saying, "Do you not even fear God, seeing you are under the same condemnation? 41 And we indeed justly, for we receive the due reward of our deeds; but this Man has done nothing wrong." 42 Then he said to Jesus, "Lord, remember me when You come into Your kingdom."

43 And Jesus said to him, "Assuredly, I say to you, today you will be with Me in Paradise."

44 Now it was about the sixth hour, and there was darkness over all the earth until the ninth hour. 45 Then the sun was darkened, and the veil of the temple was torn in two. 46 And when Jesus had cried out with a loud voice, He said, "Father, 'into Your hands I commit My spirit.'" Having said this, He breathed His last.

47 So when the centurion saw what had happened, he glorified God, saying, "Certainly this was a righteous Man!"

48 And the whole crowd who came together to that sight, seeing what had been done, beat their breasts and returned. 49 But all His acquaintances, and the women who followed Him from Galilee, stood at a distance, watching these things.

50 Now behold, *there was* a man named Joseph, a council member, a good and just man. 51 He had not consented to their decision and deed. *He was* from Arimathea, a city of the Jews, who himself was also waiting for the kingdom of God. 52 This man went to Pilate and asked for the body of Jesus. 53 Then he took it down, wrapped it in linen, and laid it in a tomb *that was* hewn out of the rock, where no one had ever lain before. 54 That day was the Preparation, and the Sabbath drew near.

55 And the women who had come with Him from Galilee followed after, and they observed the tomb and how His body was laid. 56 Then they returned and prepared spices and fragrant oils. And they rested on the Sabbath according to the commandment.

*Reading 128—*The Commitment of Faith
Luke 24:25

To believe is literally to commit. Belief is a moral act, and Jesus makes an enormous demand of a man when He asks him to believe in Him. To be "a believer in Jesus" means to bank our confidence in Him, to stake our soul upon His honor—"I know whom I have believed. . . ." We pray, "Lord, increase our faith," and we try to pump up faith, but it does not come. What is wrong? The moral surrender to Jesus has not taken place. Will I surrender to Jesus from the real center of my life, and deliberately and willfully stake my confidence in what He says? Many of us use religious jargon; we talk about believing in God, but our actual life proves that we do not really believe onetenth of what we profess.

If you can solve your problems without Jesus, then solve them, but don't blink any of the facts. "Let not your heart be troubled," says Jesus. Does Jesus really mean that He wants us to be untroubled in heart? "Believe also in Me"— that is, make room for Me, especially in the matters where you cannot go. As we bring the child mind to what Jesus says about things, we will begin to manifest the miracle of an undisturbed heart. In the Cross our Lord deals with everything that keeps a man's heart disturbed. (*Place Help*)

1 SAMUEL 18:1—19:24

NOW when he had finished speaking to Saul, the soul of Jonathan was knit to the soul of David, and Jonathan loved him as his own soul. 2 Saul took him that day, and would not let him go home to his father's house anymore. 3 Then Jonathan and David made a covenant, because he loved him as his own soul. 4 And Jonathan took off the robe that *was* on him and gave it to David, with his armor, even to his sword and his bow and his belt.

5 So David went out wherever Saul sent him, *and* behaved wisely. And Saul set him over the men of war, and he was accepted in the sight of all the people and also in the sight of Saul's servants. 6 Now it had happened as they were coming *home*, when David was returning from the slaughter of the Philistine, that the women had come out of all the cities of Israel, singing and dancing, to meet King Saul, with tambourines, with joy, and with musical instruments. 7 So the women sang as they danced, and said:

"Saul has slain his thousands,
And David his ten thousands."

8 Then Saul was very angry, and the saying displeased him; and he said, "They have ascribed to David ten thousands, and to me they have ascribed *only* thousands. Now *what* more can he have but the kingdom?" 9 So Saul eyed David from that day forward.

10 And it happened on the next day that the distressing spirit from God came upon Saul, and he prophesied inside the house. So David played *music* with his hand, as at other times; but *there was* a spear in Saul's hand. 11 And Saul cast the spear, for he said, "I will pin David to the wall!" But David escaped his presence twice.

12 Now Saul was afraid of David, because the LORD was with him, but had departed from Saul. 13 Therefore Saul removed him from his presence, and made him his captain over a thousand; and he went out and came in before the people. 14 And David behaved wisely in all his ways, and the LORD *was* with him. 15 Therefore, when Saul saw that he behaved very wisely, he was afraid of him. 16 But all Israel and Judah loved David, because he went out and came in before them.

17 Then Saul said to David, "Here is my older daughter Merab; I will give her to you as a wife. Only be valiant for me, and fight the LORD's battles." For Saul thought, "Let my hand not be against him, but let the hand of the Philistines be against him."

18 So David said to Saul, "Who *am* I, and what *is* my life *or* my father's family in Israel, that I should be son-in-law to the king?" 19 But it happened at the time when Merab, Saul's daughter, should have been given to David, that she was given to Adriel the Meholathite as a wife.

20 Now Michal, Saul's daughter, loved David. And they told Saul, and the thing pleased him. 21 So Saul said, "I will give her to him, that she may be a snare to him, and that the hand of the Philistines may be against him." Therefore Saul said to David a second time, "You shall be my son-in-law today."

22 And Saul commanded his servants, "Communicate with David secretly, and say, 'Look, the king has delight in you, and all his servants love you. Now therefore, become the king's son-in-law.'"

23 So Saul's servants spoke those words in the hearing of David. And David said, "Does it seem to you *a* light *thing* to be a king's son-in-law, seeing I *am* a poor and lightly esteemed man?" 24 And the servants of Saul told him, saying, "In this manner David spoke."

25 Then Saul said, "Thus you shall say to David: 'The king does not desire any dowry but one hundred foreskins of the Philistines, to take vengeance on the king's enemies.'" But Saul thought to make David fall by the hand of the Philistines. 26 So when his servants told David these words, it pleased David well to become the king's son-in-law. Now the days had not expired; 27 therefore David arose and went, he and his men, and killed two hundred men of the Philistines. And David brought their foreskins, and they gave them in full count to the king, that he might become the king's son-in-law. Then Saul gave him Michal his daughter as a wife.

28 Thus Saul saw and knew that the LORD *was* with David, and *that* Michal, Saul's daughter, loved him; 29 and Saul was still more afraid of David. So Saul became David's enemy continually. 30 Then the princes of the Philistines went out *to war*. And so it was, whenever they went out, *that* David behaved more wisely than all the servants of Saul, so that his name became highly esteemed.

19 NOW Saul spoke to Jonathan his son and to all his servants, that they should kill David; but Jonathan, Saul's son, delighted greatly in David. 2 So Jonathan told David, saying, "My father Saul seeks to kill you. Therefore please be on your

guard until morning, and stay in a secret *place* and hide. 3 And I will go out and

---

*A*ny soul who has not that solitary place alone with God is in supreme peril spiritually.   (GLORIFY)

---

stand beside my father in the field where you *are*, and I will speak with my father about you. Then what I observe, I will tell you."

4 Thus Jonathan spoke well of David to Saul his father, and said to him, "Let not the king sin against his servant, against David, because he has not sinned against you, and because his works *have been* very good toward you. 5 For he took his life in his hands and killed the Philistine, and the LORD brought about a great deliverance for all Israel. You saw *it* and rejoiced. Why then will you sin against innocent blood, to kill David without a cause?"

6 So Saul heeded the voice of Jonathan, and Saul swore, "*As* the LORD lives, he shall not be killed." 7 Then Jonathan called David, and Jonathan told him all these things. So Jonathan brought David to Saul, and he was in his presence as in times past.

8 And there was war again; and David went out and fought with the Philistines, and struck them with a mighty blow, and they fled from him.

9 Now the distressing spirit from the LORD came upon Saul as he sat in his house with his spear in his hand. And David was playing *music* with *his* hand. 10 Then Saul sought to pin David to the wall with the spear, but he slipped away from Saul's presence; and he drove the spear into the wall. So David fled and escaped that night.

11 Saul also sent messengers to David's house to watch him and to kill him in the morning. And Michal, David's wife, told him, saying, "If you do not save your life tonight, tomorrow you will be killed." 12 So Michal let David down through a window. And he went and fled and escaped. 13 And Michal took an image and laid *it* in the bed, put a cover of goats' *hair* for his head, and covered *it* with clothes. 14 So when Saul sent messengers to take David, she said, "He *is* sick."

15 Then Saul sent the messengers *back* to see David, saying, "Bring him up to me in the bed, that I may kill him." 16 And when the messengers had come in, there was the image in the bed, with a cover of goats' *hair* for his head. 17 Then Saul said to Michal, "Why have you deceived me like this, and sent my enemy away, so that he has escaped?"

And Michal answered Saul, "He said to me, 'Let me go! Why should I kill you?' "

18 So David fled and escaped, and went to Samuel at Ramah, and told him all that Saul had done to him. And he and Samuel went and stayed in Naioth. 19 Now it was told Saul, saying, "Take note, David *is* at Naioth in Ramah!" 20 Then Saul sent messengers to take David. And when they saw the group of prophets prophesying, and Samuel standing *as* leader over them, the Spirit of God came upon the messengers of Saul, and they also prophesied. 21 And when Saul was told, he sent other messengers, and they prophesied likewise. Then Saul sent messengers again the third time, and they prophesied also. 22 Then he also went to Ramah, and came to the great well that *is* at Sechu. So he asked, and said, "Where *are* Samuel and David?"

And *someone* said, "Indeed *they are* at Naioth in Ramah." 23 So he went there to Naioth in Ramah. Then the Spirit of God was upon him also, and he went on and prophesied until he came to Naioth in Ramah. 24 And he also stripped off his clothes and prophesied before Samuel in like manner, and lay down naked all that day and all that night. Therefore they say, "*Is* Saul also among the prophets?"

PSALM 58:1–11

1   DO you indeed speak righteousness,
       you silent ones?
     Do you judge uprightly, you sons of
       men?
2   No, in heart you work wickedness;
     You weigh out the violence of your
       hands in the earth.

3   The wicked are estranged from the
       womb;
     They go astray as soon as they are born,
       speaking lies.
4   Their poison *is* like the poison of a
       serpent;
     They are like the deaf cobra *that* stops
       its ear,
5   Which will not heed the voice of
       charmers,
     Charming ever so skillfully.

6   Break their teeth in their mouth,
       O God!
     Break out the fangs of the young lions,
       O LORD!

7 Let them flow away as waters *which*
    run continually;
When he bends *his bow,*
Let his arrows be as if cut in pieces.

8 *Let them be* like a snail which melts away
    as it goes,
Like a stillborn child of a woman, that
    they may not see the sun.

9 Before your pots can feel *the burning*
    thorns,
He shall take them away as with a
    whirlwind,
As in His living and burning wrath.

10 The righteous shall rejoice when he sees
    the vengeance;
He shall wash his feet in the blood of
    the wicked.

11 So that men will say,
"Surely *there is* a reward for the
    righteous;
Surely He is God who judges in the
    earth."

PROVERBS 15:27–30

27 HE who is greedy for gain troubles
    his own house,
But he who hates bribes will live.

28 The heart of the righteous studies how
    to answer,
But the mouth of the wicked pours
    forth evil.

29 The LORD *is* far from the wicked,
But He hears the prayer of the
    righteous.

30 The light of the eyes rejoices the heart,
And a good report makes the bones
    healthy.

LUKE 24:1–35

NOW on the first *day* of the week, very
early in the morning, they, and certain *other
women* with them, came to the tomb bringing the spices which they had prepared.
2 But they found the stone rolled away from
the tomb. 3 Then they went in and did not
find the body of the Lord Jesus. 4 And it
happened, as they were greatly perplexed
about this, that behold, two men stood by
them in shining garments. 5 Then, as they
were afraid and bowed *their* faces to the
earth, they said to them, "Why do you seek
the living among the dead? 6 He is not here,
but is risen! Remember how He spoke to
you when He was still in Galilee, 7 saying,
'The Son of Man must be delivered into
the hands of sinful men, and be crucified,
and the third day rise again.' "

8 And they remembered His words.
9 Then they returned from the tomb and
told all these things to the eleven and to
all the rest. 10 It was Mary Magdalene,
Joanna, Mary *the mother* of James, and the
other *women* with them, who told these
things to the apostles. 11 And their words
seemed to them like idle tales, and they
did not believe them. 12 But Peter arose
and ran to the tomb; and stooping down,
he saw the linen cloths lying by themselves;
and he departed, marveling to himself at
what had happened.

13 Now behold, two of them were traveling that same day to a village called Emmaus, which was seven miles from Jerusalem. 14 And they talked together of all these
things which had happened. 15 So it was,
while they conversed and reasoned, that Jesus Himself drew near and went with them.
16 But their eyes were restrained, so that
they did not know Him.

17 And He said to them, "What kind of
conversation *is* this that you have with one
another as you walk and are sad?"

18 Then the one whose name was Cleopas
answered and said to Him, "Are You the
only stranger in Jerusalem, and have You
not known the things which happened
there in these days?"

19 And He said to them, "What things?"

So they said to Him, "The things concerning Jesus of Nazareth, who was a
Prophet mighty in deed and word before
God and all the people, 20 and how the
chief priests and our rulers delivered Him
to be condemned to death, and crucified
Him. 21 But we were hoping that it was
He who was going to redeem Israel. Indeed,
besides all this, today is the third day since
these things happened. 22 Yes, and certain
women of our company, who arrived at
the tomb early, astonished us. 23 When they
did not find His body, they came saying
that they had also seen a vision of angels
who said He was alive. 24 And certain of
those *who were* with us went to the tomb
and found *it* just as the women had said;
but Him they did not see."

25 Then He said to them, "O foolish ones,
and slow of heart to believe in all that the
prophets have spoken! 26 Ought not the
Christ to have suffered these things and
to enter into His glory?" 27 And beginning
at Moses and all the Prophets, He expounded to them in all the Scriptures the
things concerning Himself.

28 Then they drew near to the village where they were going, and He indicated that He would have gone farther. 29 But they constrained Him, saying, "Abide with us, for it is toward evening, and the day is far spent." And He went in to stay with them.

30 Now it came to pass, as He sat at the table with them, that He took bread, blessed and broke *it*, and gave it to them. 31 Then their eyes were opened and they knew Him; and He vanished from their sight.

32 And they said to one another, "Did not our heart burn within us while He talked with us on the road, and while He opened the Scriptures to us?" 33 So they

The key to my understanding of the Bible is . . . personal relationship to Jesus Christ. (APPROVED)

rose up that very hour and returned to Jerusalem, and found the eleven and those *who were* with them gathered together, 34 saying, "The Lord is risen indeed, and has appeared to Simon!" 35 And they told about the things *that had happened* on the road, and how He was known to them in the breaking of bread.

◆◆◆

Reading 129—The Promise of the Highest
Luke 24:49–53

The reason the disciples had to tarry until the day of Pentecost was not merely that they might be fitted to receive the promise: They had to wait until the Lord was glorified historically, for the Holy Spirit did not descend until the fullness of time was reached and the Son of God was glorified and ascended to the right hand of the Father (see John 15:26; Acts 2:33). The parenthesis in John 7:39 "(for the Holy Spirit was not yet *given*, because Jesus was not yet glorified)" does not apply to us. The Holy Spirit has been given; Jesus has been glorified; now the waiting depends upon our fitness, not upon God's providence. The reception of the Holy Spirit in His fullness depends entirely upon moral preparation. I must abide in the light which the Holy Spirit sheds and be obedient to the word of God; then when the power of God comes upon such obedience there will be the manifestation of a strong family likeness to Jesus. It is easier to be swayed by emotions than to live a life shot through with the Holy Spirit, a life in which Jesus is glorified. The Holy Spirit is absolutely honest; He indicates the things that are right and the things that are wrong. (*LOVE OF GOD*)

1 SAMUEL 20:1—21:15

THEN David fled from Naioth in Ramah, and went and said to Jonathan, "What have I done? What *is* my iniquity, and what *is* my sin before your father, that he seeks my life?"

2 So Jonathan said to him, "By no means! You shall not die! Indeed, my father will do nothing either great or small without first telling me. And why should my father hide this thing from me? It *is* not *so!*"

3 Then David took an oath again, and said, "Your father certainly knows that I have found favor in your eyes, and he has said, 'Do not let Jonathan know this, lest he be grieved.' But truly, *as* the LORD lives and *as* your soul lives, *there is* but a step between me and death."

4 So Jonathan said to David, "Whatever you yourself desire, I will do *it* for you."

5 And David said to Jonathan, "Indeed tomorrow *is* the New Moon, and I should not fail to sit with the king to eat. But let me go, that I may hide in the field until the third *day* at evening. 6 If your father misses me at all, then say, 'David earnestly asked *permission* of me that he might run

over to Bethlehem, his city, for *there is* a yearly sacrifice there for all the family.' 7 If he says thus: '*It is* well,' your servant will be safe. But if he is very angry, be sure that evil is determined by him. 8 Therefore you shall deal kindly with your servant, for you have brought your servant into a covenant of the Lord with you. Nevertheless, if there is iniquity in me, kill me yourself, for why should you bring me to your father?"

9 But Jonathan said, "Far be it from you! For if I knew certainly that evil was determined by my father to come upon you, then would I not tell you?"

10 Then David said to Jonathan, "Who will tell me, or what *if* your father answers you roughly?"

11 And Jonathan said to David, "Come, let us go out into the field." So both of them went out into the field. 12 Then Jonathan said to David: "The Lord God of Israel *is witness!* When I have sounded out my father sometime tomorrow, *or* the third *day,* and indeed *there is* good toward David, and I do not send to you and tell you, 13 may the Lord do so and much more to Jonathan. But if it pleases my father *to do* you evil, then I will report it to you and send you away, that you may go in safety. And the Lord be with you as He has been with my father. 14 And you shall not only show me the kindness of the Lord while I still live, that I may not die; 15 but you shall not cut off your kindness from my house forever, no, not when the Lord has cut off every one of the enemies of David from the face of the earth." 16 So Jonathan made *a covenant* with the house of David, *saying,* "Let the Lord require *it* at the hand of David's enemies."

17 Now Jonathan again caused David to vow, because he loved him; for he loved him as he loved his own soul. 18 Then Jonathan said to David, "Tomorrow *is* the New Moon; and you will be missed, because your seat will be empty. 19 And *when* you have stayed three days, go down quickly and come to the place where you hid on the day of the deed; and remain by the stone Ezel. 20 Then I will shoot three arrows to the side, as though I shot at a target; 21 and there I will send a lad, *saying,* 'Go, find the arrows.' If I expressly say to the lad, 'Look, the arrows *are* on this side of you; get them and come'—then, as the Lord lives, *there is* safety for you and no harm. 22 But if I say thus to the young man, 'Look, the arrows *are* beyond you'— go your way, for the Lord has sent you away. 23 And as for the matter which you

and I have spoken of, indeed the Lord *be* between you and me forever."

24 Then David hid in the field. And when the New Moon had come, the king sat down to eat the feast. 25 Now the king sat on his seat, as at other times, on a seat by the wall. And Jonathan arose, and Abner sat by Saul's side, but David's place was empty. 26 Nevertheless Saul did not say anything that day, for he thought, "Something has happened to him; he *is* unclean, surely he *is* unclean." 27 And it happened the next day, the second *day* of the month, that David's place was empty. And Saul said to Jonathan his son, "Why has the son of Jesse not come to eat, either yesterday or today?"

28 So Jonathan answered Saul, "David earnestly asked *permission* of me *to go* to Bethlehem. 29 And he said, 'Please let me go, for our family has a sacrifice in the city, and my brother has commanded me *to be there*. And now, if I have found favor in your eyes, please let me get away and see my brothers.' Therefore he has not come to the king's table."

30 Then Saul's anger was aroused against Jonathan, and he said to him, "You son of a perverse, rebellious *woman!* Do I not know that you have chosen the son of Jesse to your own shame and to the shame of your mother's nakedness? 31 For as long as the son of Jesse lives on the earth, you shall not be established, nor your kingdom. Now therefore, send and bring him to me, for he shall surely die."

32 And Jonathan answered Saul his father, and said to him, "Why should he be killed? What has he done?" 33 Then Saul cast a spear at him to kill him, by which Jonathan knew that it was determined by his father to kill David.

34 So Jonathan arose from the table in fierce anger, and ate no food the second day of the month, for he was grieved for David, because his father had treated him shamefully.

35 And so it was, in the morning, that Jonathan went out into the field at the time appointed with David, and a little lad *was* with him. 36 Then he said to his lad, "Now run, find the arrows which I shoot." As the lad ran, he shot an arrow beyond him. 37 When the lad had come to the place where the arrow was which Jonathan had shot, Jonathan cried out after the lad and said, "*Is* not the arrow beyond you?" 38 And Jonathan cried out after the lad, "Make haste, hurry, do not delay!" So Jonathan's lad gathered up the arrows and came back to his master. 39 But the lad did not know anything. Only Jonathan and David

knew of the matter. 40 Then Jonathan gave his weapons to his lad, and said to him, "Go, carry *them* to the city."

41 As soon as the lad had gone, David arose from *a place* toward the south, fell on his face to the ground, and bowed down three times. And they kissed one another; and they wept together, but David more so. 42 Then Jonathan said to David, "Go in peace, since we have both sworn in the name of the LORD, saying, 'May the LORD be between you and me, and between your descendants and my descendants, forever.' " So he arose and departed, and Jonathan went into the city.

21 NOW David came to Nob, to Ahimelech the priest. And Ahimelech was afraid when he met David, and said to him, "Why *are* you alone, and no one is with you?"

2 So David said to Ahimelech the priest, "The king has ordered me on some business, and said to me, 'Do not let anyone know anything about the business on which I send you, or what I have commanded you.' And I have directed *my* young men to such and such a place. 3 Now therefore, what have you on hand? Give *me* five *loaves of* bread in my hand, or whatever can be found."

4 And the priest answered David and said, "*There is* no common bread on hand; but there is holy bread, if the young men have at least kept themselves from women."

5 Then David answered the priest, and said to him, "Truly, women *have been* kept from us about three days since I came out. And the vessels of the young men are holy, and *the bread is* in effect common, even though it was consecrated in the vessel this day."

6 So the priest gave him holy *bread;* for there was no bread there but the showbread which had been taken from before the LORD, in order to put hot bread *in its place* on the day when it was taken away.

7 Now a certain man of the servants of Saul *was* there that day, detained before the LORD. And his name *was* Doeg, an Edomite, the chief of the herdsmen who *belonged* to Saul.

8 And David said to Ahimelech, "Is there not here on hand a spear or a sword? For I have brought neither my sword nor my weapons with me, because the king's business required haste."

9 So the priest said, "The sword of Goliath the Philistine, whom you killed in the Valley of Elah, there it is, wrapped in a cloth behind the ephod. If you will take that, take *it*. For *there is* no other except that one here."

And David said, "*There is* none like it; give it to me."

10 Then David arose and fled that day from before Saul, and went to Achish the king of Gath. 11 And the servants of Achish said to him, "*Is* this not David the king of the land? Did they not sing of him to one another in dances, saying:

'Saul has slain his thousands,
And David his ten thousands'?"

12 Now David took these words to heart, and was very much afraid of Achish the king of Gath. 13 So he changed his behavior before them, pretended madness in their hands, scratched on the doors of the gate, and let his saliva fall down on his beard. 14 Then Achish said to his servants, "Look, you see the man is insane. Why have you brought him to me? 15 Have I need of madmen, that you have brought this *fellow* to play the madman in my presence? Shall this *fellow* come into my house?"

PSALM 59:1–5

1   DELIVER me from my enemies,
     O my God;
   Defend me from those who rise up
     against me.
2   Deliver me from the workers of
     iniquity,
   And save me from bloodthirsty men.

3   For look, they lie in wait for my life;
   The mighty gather against me,
   Not *for* my transgression nor *for* my
     sin, O LORD.
4   They run and prepare themselves
     through no fault *of mine.*

   Awake to help me, and behold!
5   You therefore, O LORD God of hosts,
     the God of Israel,
   Awake to punish all the nations;
   Do not be merciful to any wicked
     transgressors.   Selah

PROVERBS 15:31–33

31   THE ear that hears the rebukes of life
     Will abide among the wise.
32   He who disdains instruction despises
     his own soul,
   But he who heeds rebuke gets
     understanding.

33 The fear of the LORD *is* the instruction of wisdom,
And before honor *is* humility.

LUKE 24:36–53

NOW as they said these things, Jesus Himself stood in the midst of them, and said to them, "Peace to you." 37 But they were

---

*P*eace is the deepest thing a human personality can know, it is almighty.   (SERVANT AS LORD)

---

terrified and frightened, and supposed they had seen a spirit. 38 And He said to them, "Why are you troubled? And why do doubts arise in your hearts? 39 Behold My hands and My feet, that it is I Myself. Handle Me and see, for a spirit does not have flesh and bones as you see I have."

40 When He had said this, He showed them His hands and His feet. 41 But while they still did not believe for joy, and marveled, He said to them, "Have you any food here?" 42 So they gave Him a piece of a broiled fish and some honeycomb. 43 And He took *it* and ate in their presence.

44 Then He said to them, "These *are* the words which I spoke to you while I was still with you, that all things must be fulfilled which were written in the Law of Moses and *the* Prophets and *the* Psalms concerning Me." 45 And He opened their understanding, that they might comprehend the Scriptures.

46 Then He said to them, "Thus it is written, and thus it was necessary for the Christ to suffer and to rise from the dead the third day, 47 and that repentance and remission of sins should be preached in His name to all nations, beginning at Jerusalem. 48 And you are witnesses of these things. 49 Behold, I send the Promise of My Father upon you; but tarry in the city of Jerusalem until you are endued with power from on high."

50 And He led them out as far as Bethany, and He lifted up His hands and blessed them. 51 Now it came to pass, while He blessed them, that He was parted from them and carried up into heaven. 52 And they worshiped Him, and returned to Jerusalem with great joy, 53 and were continually in the temple praising and blessing God. Amen.

◆◆◆

Reading 130—His Faithful Face of God
John 1:14

If we want to know what God is like, let us study the Lord Jesus. "He who has seen Me has seen the Father." How did people see Him in the days of His flesh? By their natural eyes? No, after His resurrection they received Holy Spirit, and their eyes were opened and they knew Him. We do not know Him by the reasoning of our minds, but by the new life. Jesus Christ is to us the faithful face of God. Could anyone be in doubt any more after they had seen Jesus Christ by the Holy Spirit? Think of the absurd, painful, distressing, never-to-be-answered questions we ask: "Shall I know those whom I love after death?" Wild, vagrant, wrong, stupid, painful questions. Look at Jesus Christ, get into contact with Him by the Holy Spirit, and those questions are impossible. He says, "Let not your heart be troubled; you believe in God, believe also in Me." The face of God is the Lord Jesus Christ. It always comes back to the simple point, "Come to Me."   (GLORY)

1 SAMUEL 22:1—23:29

DAVID therefore departed from there and escaped to the cave of Adullam. So when his brothers and all his father's house heard *it*, they went down there to him. 2 And everyone *who was* in distress, everyone *who was* in debt, and everyone *who was* discontented gathered to him. So he became captain over them. And there were about four hundred men with him.

3 Then David went from there to Mizpah of Moab; and he said to the king of Moab, "Please let my father and mother come here with you, till I know what God will do for me." 4 So he brought them before the king of Moab, and they dwelt with him all the time that David was in the stronghold.

5 Now the prophet Gad said to David, "Do not stay in the stronghold; depart, and go to the land of Judah." So David departed and went into the forest of Hereth.

6 When Saul heard that David and the men who *were* with him had been discovered—now Saul was staying in Gibeah under a tamarisk tree in Ramah, with his spear in his hand, and all his servants standing about him— 7 then Saul said to his servants who stood about him, "Hear now, you Benjamites! Will the son of Jesse give every one of you fields and vineyards, *and* make you all captains of thousands and captains of hundreds? 8 All of you have conspired against me, and *there is* no one who reveals to me that my son has made a covenant with the son of Jesse; and *there is* not one of you who is sorry for me or reveals to me that my son has stirred up my servant against me, to lie in wait, as *it is* this day."

9 Then answered Doeg the Edomite, who was set over the servants of Saul, and said, "I saw the son of Jesse going to Nob, to Ahimelech the son of Ahitub. 10 And he inquired of the LORD for him, gave him provisions, and gave him the sword of Goliath the Philistine."

11 So the king sent to call Ahimelech the priest, the son of Ahitub, and all his father's house, the priests who *were* in Nob. And they all came to the king. 12 And Saul said, "Hear now, son of Ahitub!"

He answered, "Here I am, my lord."

13 Then Saul said to him, "Why have you conspired against me, you and the son of Jesse, in that you have given him bread and a sword, and have inquired of God for him, that he should rise against me, to lie in wait, as it is this day?"

14 So Ahimelech answered the king and said, "And who among all your servants *is* as faithful as David, who is the king's son-in-law, who goes at your bidding, and is honorable in your house? 15 Did I then begin to inquire of God for him? Far be it from me! Let not the king impute anything to his servant, *or* to any in the house of my father. For your servant knew nothing of all this, little or much."

16 And the king said, "You shall surely die, Ahimelech, you and all your father's house!" 17 Then the king said to the guards who stood about him, "Turn and kill the priests of the LORD, because their hand also *is* with David, and because they knew when he fled and did not tell it to me." But the servants of the king would not lift their hands to strike the priests of the LORD. 18 And the king said to Doeg, "You turn and kill the priests!" So Doeg the Edomite turned and struck the priests, and killed on that day eighty-five men who wore a linen ephod. 19 Also Nob, the city of the priests, he struck with the edge of the sword, both men and women, children and nursing infants, oxen and donkeys and sheep—with the edge of the sword.

20 Now one of the sons of Ahimelech the son of Ahitub, named Abiathar, escaped and fled after David. 21 And Abiathar told David that Saul had killed the LORD's priests. 22 So David said to Abiathar, "I knew that day, when Doeg the Edomite *was* there, that he would surely tell Saul. I have caused *the death* of all the persons of your father's house. 23 Stay with me; do not fear. For he who seeks my life seeks your life, but with me you *shall be* safe."

23 THEN they told David, saying, "Look, the Philistines are fighting against Keilah, and they are robbing the threshing floors."

2 Therefore David inquired of the LORD, saying, "Shall I go and attack these Philistines?"

And the LORD said to David, "Go and attack the Philistines, and save Keilah."

3 But David's men said to him, "Look, we are afraid here in Judah. How much more then if we go to Keilah against the armies of the Philistines?" 4 Then David inquired of the LORD once again.

And the LORD answered him and said, "Arise, go down to Keilah. For I will deliver the Philistines into your hand." 5 And David and his men went to Keilah and fought with the Philistines, struck them with a mighty blow, and took away their livestock. So David saved the inhabitants of Keilah.

6 Now it happened, when Abiathar the son of Ahimelech fled to David at Keilah,

that he went down *with* an ephod in his hand.

7 And Saul was told that David had gone to Keilah. So Saul said, "God has delivered him into my hand, for he has shut himself in by entering a town that has gates and bars." 8 Then Saul called all the people together for war, to go down to Keilah to besiege David and his men.

9 When David knew that Saul plotted evil against him, he said to Abiathar the priest, "Bring the ephod here." 10 Then David said, "O Lord God of Israel, Your servant has certainly heard that Saul seeks to come to Keilah to destroy the city for my sake. 11 Will the men of Keilah deliver me into his hand? Will Saul come down, as Your servant has heard? O Lord God of Israel, I pray, tell Your servant."

And the Lord said, "He will come down."

12 Then David said, "Will the men of Keilah deliver me and my men into the hand of Saul?"

And the Lord said, "They will deliver *you.*"

13 So David and his men, about six hundred, arose and departed from Keilah and went wherever they could go. Then it was told Saul that David had escaped from Keilah; so he halted the expedition.

14 And David stayed in strongholds in the wilderness, and remained in the mountains in the Wilderness of Ziph. Saul sought him every day, but God did not deliver him into his hand. 15 So David saw that Saul had come out to seek his life. And David *was* in the Wilderness of Ziph in a forest. 16 Then Jonathan, Saul's son, arose and went to David in the woods and strengthened his hand in God. 17 And he said to him, "Do not fear, for the hand of Saul my father shall not find you. You shall be king over Israel, and I shall be next to you. Even my father Saul knows that." 18 So the two of them made a covenant before the Lord. And David stayed in the woods, and Jonathan went to his own house.

19 Then the Ziphites came up to Saul at Gibeah, saying, "Is David not hiding with us in strongholds in the woods, in the hill of Hachilah, which *is* on the south of Jeshimon? 20 Now therefore, O king, come down according to all the desire of your soul to come down; and our part *shall be* to deliver him into the king's hand."

21 And Saul said, "Blessed *are* you of the Lord, for you have compassion on me. 22 Please go and find out for sure, and see the place where his hideout is, *and* who

has seen him there. For I am told he is very crafty. 23 See therefore, and take knowledge of all the lurking places where he hides; and come back to me with certainty, and I will go with you. And it shall be, if he is in the land, that I will search for him throughout all the clans of Judah."

24 So they arose and went to Ziph before Saul. But David and his men *were* in the Wilderness of Maon, in the plain on the south of Jeshimon. 25 When Saul and his men went to seek *him,* they told David. Therefore he went down to the rock, and stayed in the Wilderness of Maon. And when Saul heard *that,* he pursued David in the Wilderness of Maon. 26 Then Saul went on one side of the mountain, and David and his men on the other side of the mountain. So David made haste to get away from Saul, for Saul and his men were encircling David and his men to take them. 27 But a messenger came to Saul, saying, "Hurry and come, for the Philistines have invaded the land!" 28 Therefore Saul returned from pursuing David, and went against the Philistines; so they called that place the Rock of Escape. 29 Then David went up from there and dwelt in strongholds at En Gedi.

PSALM 59:6–17

6   AT evening they return,
    They growl like a dog,
    And go all around the city.
7   Indeed, they belch with their mouth;
    Swords *are* in their lips;
    For *they say,* "Who hears?"

8   But You, O Lord, shall laugh at them;
    You shall have all the nations in
      derision.
9   I will wait for You, O You his Strength;
    For God *is* my defense.
10 My God of mercy shall come to meet
      me;
    God shall let me see *my desire* on my
      enemies.

11 Do not slay them, lest my people
      forget;
    Scatter them by Your power,
    And bring them down,
    O Lord our shield.
12 *For* the sin of their mouth *and* the
      words of their lips,
    Let them even be taken in their pride,
    And for the cursing and lying *which*
      they speak.

13 Consume *them* in wrath, consume *them*,
That they *may* not *be;*
And let them know that God rules in
Jacob
To the ends of the earth.   Selah

14 And at evening they return,
They growl like a dog,
And go all around the city.
15 They wander up and down for food,
And howl if they are not satisfied.

16 But I will sing of Your power;
Yes, I will sing aloud of Your mercy
in the morning;
For You have been my defense
And refuge in the day of my trouble.
17 To You, O my Strength, I will sing
praises;
For God *is* my defense,
My God of mercy.

PROVERBS 16:1, 2

1 THE preparations of the heart *belong*
to man,
But the answer of the tongue *is* from
the LORD.

2 All the ways of a man *are* pure in his
own eyes,
But the LORD weighs the spirits.

JOHN 1:1–28

IN the beginning was the Word, and the
Word was with God, and the Word was
God. 2 He was in the beginning with God.
3 All things were made through Him, and
without Him nothing was made that was
made. 4 In Him was life, and the life was
the light of men. 5 And the light shines in
the darkness, and the darkness did not comprehend it.

6 There was a man sent from God, whose
name *was* John. 7 This man came for a witness, to bear witness of the Light, that all
through him might believe. 8 He was not
that Light, but *was sent* to bear witness of
that Light. 9 That was the true Light which
gives light to every man coming into the
world.

10 He was in the world, and the world
was made through Him, and the world did
not know Him. 11 He came to His own,
and His own did not receive Him.
12 But as many as received Him, to them
He gave the right to become children of
God, to those who believe in His name:

---

*If I believe the character of Jesus,
am I living up to what I
believe?*   (DISCIPLES)

---

13 who were born, not of blood, nor of
the will of the flesh, nor of the will of man,
but of God.
14 And the Word became flesh and dwelt
among us, and we beheld His glory, the
glory as of the only begotten of the Father,
full of grace and truth.
15 John bore witness of Him and cried
out, saying, "This was He of whom I said,
'He who comes after me is preferred before
me, for He was before me.' "
16 And of His fullness we have all received, and grace for grace. 17 For the law
was given through Moses, *but* grace and
truth came through Jesus Christ. 18 No one
has seen God at any time. The only begotten
Son, who is in the bosom of the Father,
He has declared *Him.*
19 Now this is the testimony of John,
when the Jews sent priests and Levites from
Jerusalem to ask him, "Who are you?"
20 He confessed, and did not deny, but
confessed, "I am not the Christ."
21 And they asked him, "What then? Are
you Elijah?"
He said, "I am not."
"Are you the Prophet?"
And he answered, "No."
22 Then they said to him, "Who are you,
that we may give an answer to those who
sent us? What do you say about yourself?"
23 He said: "I *am*

'The voice of one crying in the
wilderness:
"Make straight the way of the LORD," '

as the prophet Isaiah said."
24 Now those who were sent were from
the Pharisees. 25 And they asked him, saying, "Why then do you baptize if you are
not the Christ, nor Elijah, nor the Prophet?"
26 John answered them, saying, "I baptize
with water, but there stands One among
you whom you do not know. 27 It is He
who, coming after me, is preferred before
me, whose sandal strap I am not worthy
to loose."
28 These things were done in Bethabara
beyond the Jordan, where John was baptizing.

◆◆◆◆

*Reading 131—*Christ's Vocation
John 1:29

At the outset of our Lord's public ministry He accepted His vocation, which was to "[take] away the sin of the world." We must never forget that. John's baptism was a baptism of repentance for the remission of sins, and that was the baptism with which Jesus was baptized. "Permit *it to be so* now, for thus it is fitting for us to fulfill all righteousness"; and right through to the end, our Lord was identified with that one thing—that is, sin.

The agony in Gethsemane reveals the last reach of the unfathomable depths to which our Lord went in that identification. "Christ has redeemed us from the curse of the law, having become a curse for us." "Behold! The Lamb of God who takes away the sin of the world!" These were almost the first words John the Baptist spoke about Jesus. And almost the last words Jesus spoke were to a criminal: "Today you will be with Me in Paradise." The last possible reach of faith is the cry of a sinner who begins to realize that God can save him. As soon as he cries out to God he will find the marvel of Jesus Christ's salvation wrought in his personal experience.   (*GLORY*)

1 SAMUEL 24:1—25:44

NOW it happened, when Saul had returned from following the Philistines, that it was told him, saying, "Take note! David *is* in the Wilderness of En Gedi." 2 Then Saul took three thousand chosen men from all Israel, and went to seek David and his men on the Rocks of the Wild Goats. 3 So he came to the sheepfolds by the road, where there *was* a cave; and Saul went in to attend to his needs. (David and his men were staying in the recesses of the cave.) 4 Then the men of David said to him, "This is the day of which the LORD said to you, 'Behold, I will deliver your enemy into your hand, that you may do to him as it seems good to you.'" And David arose and secretly cut off a corner of Saul's robe. 5 Now it happened afterward that David's heart troubled him because he had cut Saul's *robe.* 6 And he said to his men, "The LORD forbid that I should do this thing to my master, the LORD's anointed, to stretch out my hand against him, seeing he *is* the anointed of the LORD." 7 So David restrained his servants with *these* words, and did not allow them to rise against Saul. And Saul got up from the cave and went on *his* way.

8 David also arose afterward, went out of the cave, and called out to Saul, saying, "My lord the king!" And when Saul looked behind him, David stooped with his face to the earth, and bowed down. 9 And David said to Saul: "Why do you listen to the words of men who say, 'Indeed David seeks

your harm'? 10 Look, this day your eyes have seen that the LORD delivered you today into my hand in the cave, and *someone* urged *me* to kill you. But *my eye* spared you, and I said, 'I will not stretch out my hand against my lord, for he *is* the LORD's anointed.' 11 Moreover, my father, see! Yes, see the corner of your robe in my hand! For in that I cut off the corner of your robe, and did not kill you, know and see that *there is* neither evil nor rebellion in my hand, and I have not sinned against you. Yet you hunt my life to take it. 12 Let the LORD judge between you and me, and let the LORD avenge me on you. But my hand shall not be against you. 13 As the proverb of the ancients says, 'Wickedness proceeds from the wicked.' But my hand shall not be against you. 14 After whom has the king of Israel come out? Whom do you pursue? A dead dog? A flea? 15 Therefore let the LORD be judge, and judge between you and me, and see and plead my case, and deliver me out of your hand."

16 So it was, when David had finished speaking these words to Saul, that Saul said, "*Is* this your voice, my son David?" And Saul lifted up his voice and wept. 17 Then he said to David: "You *are* more righteous than I; for you have rewarded me with good, whereas I have rewarded you with evil. 18 And you have shown this day how you have dealt well with me; for when the LORD delivered me into your hand, you did not kill me. 19 For if a man finds his enemy, will he let him get away safely?

Therefore may the LORD reward you with good for what you have done to me this day. 20 And now I know indeed that you shall surely be king, and that the kingdom of Israel shall be established in your hand. 21 Therefore swear now to me by the LORD that you will not cut off my descendants after me, and that you will not destroy my name from my father's house."

22 So David swore to Saul. And Saul went home, but David and his men went up to the stronghold.

25 THEN Samuel died; and the Israelites gathered together and lamented for him, and buried him at his home in Ramah. And David arose and went down to the Wilderness of Paran.

2 Now *there was* a man in Maon whose business *was* in Carmel, and the man *was* very rich. He had three thousand sheep and a thousand goats. And he was shearing his sheep in Carmel. 3 The name of the man *was* Nabal, and the name of his wife Abigail. And *she was* a woman of good understanding and beautiful appearance; but the man *was* harsh and evil in *his* doings. He *was of the house of* Caleb.

4 When David heard in the wilderness that Nabal was shearing his sheep, 5 David sent ten young men; and David said to the young men, "Go up to Carmel, go to Nabal, and greet him in my name. 6 And thus you shall say to him who lives *in prosperity:* 'Peace *be* to you, peace to your house, and peace to all that you have! 7 Now I have heard that you have shearers. Your shepherds were with us, and we did not hurt them, nor was there anything missing from them all the while they were in Carmel. 8 Ask your young men, and they will tell you. Therefore let *my* young men find favor in your eyes, for we come on a feast day. Please give whatever comes to your hand to your servants and to your son David.' "

9 So when David's young men came, they spoke to Nabal according to all these words in the name of David, and waited.

10 Then Nabal answered David's servants, and said, "Who *is* David, and who *is* the son of Jesse? There are many servants nowadays who break away each one from his master. 11 Shall I then take my bread and my water and my meat that I have killed for my shearers, and give *it* to men when I do not know where they *are* from?"

12 So David's young men turned on their heels and went back; and they came and told him all these words. 13 Then David said to his men, "Every man gird on his sword." So every man girded on his sword, and David also girded on his sword. And about four hundred men went with David, and two hundred stayed with the supplies.

14 Now one of the young men told Abigail, Nabal's wife, saying, "Look, David sent messengers from the wilderness to greet our master; and he reviled them. 15 But the men *were* very good to us, and we were not hurt, nor did we miss anything as long as we accompanied them, when we were in the fields. 16 They were a wall to us both by night and day, all the time we were with them keeping the sheep. 17 Now therefore, know and consider what you will do, for harm is determined against our master and against all his household. For he *is such* a scoundrel that *one* cannot speak to him."

18 Then Abigail made haste and took two hundred *loaves* of bread, two skins of wine, five sheep already dressed, five seahs of roasted *grain,* one hundred clusters of raisins, and two hundred cakes of figs, and loaded *them* on donkeys. 19 And she said to her servants, "Go on before me; see, I am coming after you." But she did not tell her husband Nabal.

20 So it was, *as* she rode on the donkey, that she went down under cover of the hill; and there were David and his men, coming down toward her, and she met them. 21 Now David had said, "Surely in vain I have protected all that this *fellow* has in the wilderness, so that nothing was missed of all that *belongs* to him. And he has repaid me evil for good. 22 May God do so, and more also, to the enemies of David, if I leave one male of all who *belong* to him by morning light."

23 Now when Abigail saw David, she dismounted quickly from the donkey, fell on her face before David, and bowed down to the ground. 24 So she fell at his feet and said: "On me, my lord, *on me let* this iniquity *be!* And please let your maidservant speak in your ears, and hear the words of your maidservant. 25 Please, let not my lord regard this scoundrel Nabal. For as his name *is,* so *is* he: Nabal *is* his name, and folly *is* with him! But I, your maidservant, did not see the young men of my lord whom you sent. 26 Now therefore, my lord, *as* the LORD lives and *as* your soul lives, since the LORD has held you back from coming to bloodshed and from avenging yourself with your own hand, now then, let your enemies and those who seek harm for my lord be as Nabal. 27 And now this present which your maidservant has brought to my lord, let it be given to the young men who follow my lord. 28 Please forgive the trespass of your maidservant. For the LORD will

certainly make for my lord an enduring house, because my lord fights the battles of the LORD, and evil is not found in you throughout your days. 29 Yet a man has risen to pursue you and seek your life, but the life of my lord shall be bound in the bundle of the living with the LORD your God; and the lives of your enemies He shall sling out, *as from* the pocket of a sling.

Your life and mine is a bundle of chance. (SHADE)

---

30 And it shall come to pass, when the LORD has done for my lord according to all the good that He has spoken concerning you, and has appointed you ruler over Israel, 31 that this will be no grief to you, nor offense of heart to my lord, either that you have shed blood without cause, or that my lord has avenged himself. But when the LORD has dealt well with my lord, then remember your maidservant."

32 Then David said to Abigail: "Blessed *is* the LORD God of Israel, who sent you this day to meet me! 33 And blessed *is* your advice and blessed *are* you, because you have kept me this day from coming to bloodshed and from avenging myself with my own hand. 34 For indeed, *as* the LORD God of Israel lives, who has kept me back from hurting you, unless you had hurried and come to meet me, surely by morning light no males would have been left to Nabal!" 35 So David received from her hand what she had brought him, and said to her, "Go up in peace to your house. See, I have heeded your voice and respected your person."

36 Now Abigail went to Nabal, and there he was, holding a feast in his house, like the feast of a king. And Nabal's heart *was* merry within him, for he *was* very drunk; therefore she told him nothing, little or much, until morning light. 37 So it was, in the morning, when the wine had gone from Nabal, and his wife had told him these things, that his heart died within him, and he became *like* a stone. 38 Then it happened, *after* about ten days, that the LORD struck Nabal, and he died.

39 So when David heard that Nabal was dead, he said, "Blessed *be* the LORD, who has pleaded the cause of my reproach from the hand of Nabal, and has kept His servant from evil! For the LORD has returned the wickedness of Nabal on his own head."

And David sent and proposed to Abigail, to take her as his wife. 40 When the servants of David had come to Abigail at Carmel, they spoke to her saying, "David sent us to you, to ask you to become his wife."

41 Then she arose, bowed her face to the earth, and said, "Here is your maidservant, a servant to wash the feet of the servants of my lord." 42 So Abigail rose in haste and rode on a donkey, attended by five of her maidens; and she followed the messengers of David, and became his wife. 43 David also took Ahinoam of Jezreel, and so both of them were his wives.

44 But Saul had given Michal his daughter, David's wife, to Palti the son of Laish, who *was* from Gallim.

PSALM 60:1–5

1   O God, You have cast us off;
    You have broken us down;
    You have been displeased;
    Oh, restore us again!
2   You have made the earth tremble;
    You have broken it;
    Heal its breaches, for it is shaking.
3   You have shown Your people hard
        things;
    You have made us drink the wine of
        confusion.

4   You have given a banner to those who
        fear You,
    That it may be displayed because of
        the truth.   Selah
5   That Your beloved may be delivered,
    Save *with* Your right hand, and hear
        me.

PROVERBS 16:3

3   COMMIT your works to the LORD,
    And your thoughts will be established.

JOHN 1:29–51

THE next day John saw Jesus coming toward him, and said, "Behold! The Lamb of God who takes away the sin of the world!

Sin is not an act, but a hereditary disposition. (SHAD. AGONY)

---

30 This is He of whom I said, 'After me comes a Man who is preferred before me, for He was before me.' 31 I did not know Him; but that He should be revealed to

Israel, therefore I came baptizing with water."

32 And John bore witness, saying, "I saw the Spirit descending from heaven like a dove, and He remained upon Him. 33 I did not know Him, but He who sent me to baptize with water said to me, 'Upon whom you see the Spirit descending, and remaining on Him, this is He who baptizes with the Holy Spirit.' 34 And I have seen and testified that this is the Son of God."

35 Again, the next day, John stood with two of his disciples. 36 And looking at Jesus as He walked, he said, "Behold the Lamb of God!"

37 The two disciples heard him speak, and they followed Jesus. 38 Then Jesus turned, and seeing them following, said to them, "What do you seek?"

They said to Him, "Rabbi" (which is to say, when translated, Teacher), "where are You staying?"

39 He said to them, "Come and see." They came and saw where He was staying, and remained with Him that day (now it was about the tenth hour).

40 One of the two who heard John *speak,* and followed Him, was Andrew, Simon Peter's brother. 41 He first found his own brother Simon, and said to him, "We have found the Messiah" (which is translated, the Christ). 42 And he brought him to Jesus.

Now when Jesus looked at him, He said,

"You are Simon the son of Jonah. You shall be called Cephas" (which is translated, A Stone).

43 The following day Jesus wanted to go to Galilee, and He found Philip and said to him, "Follow Me." 44 Now Philip was from Bethsaida, the city of Andrew and Peter. 45 Philip found Nathanael and said to him, "We have found Him of whom Moses in the law, and also the prophets, wrote—Jesus of Nazareth, the son of Joseph."

46 And Nathanael said to him, "Can anything good come out of Nazareth?"

Philip said to him, "Come and see."

47 Jesus saw Nathanael coming toward Him, and said of him, "Behold, an Israelite indeed, in whom is no deceit!"

48 Nathanael said to Him, "How do You know me?"

Jesus answered and said to him, "Before Philip called you, when you were under the fig tree, I saw you."

49 Nathanael answered and said to Him, "Rabbi, You are the Son of God! You are the King of Israel!"

50 Jesus answered and said to him, "Because I said to you, 'I saw you under the fig tree,' do you believe? You will see greater things than these." 51 And He said to him, "Most assuredly, I say to you, hereafter you shall see heaven open, and the angels of God ascending and descending upon the Son of Man."

◆◆◆

Reading 132—He Knew What Was in Man
John 2:25

There is a sentimental notion that makes us make ourselves out worse than we think we are, because we have a lurking suspicion that if we make ourselves out amazingly bad, someone will say, "Oh no, you are not as bad as that"; but Jesus says we are worse. Our Lord never trusted any man, "for He knew what was in man"; but He was not a cynic for He had the profoundest confidence in what He could do for every man; consequently, He was never in a moral or intellectual panic, as we are, because we will put our confidence in man and in the things that Jesus put no confidence in. Paul says, "Don't glory in men; don't say, I am of Paul, or I am of Apollos, and don't think of yourself more highly than you ought to think, but think according to the measure of faith, that is, according to what the grace of God has done in you." Never trust (in the fundamental meaning of the word) any other saving Jesus Christ. That will mean you will never be unkind to anybody on the face of the earth, whether it be a degraded criminal or an upright moral man, because you have learned that the only thing to depend on in a man is what God has done in him. When you come to work for Jesus Christ, always ask yourself, "Do I believe Jesus Christ can do anything for that case?" Am I as confident in His power as He is in His own? If you deal with people without any faith in Jesus Christ it will crush the very life out of you. If we believe in Jesus Christ, we can face every problem the world holds.   (*GOOD*)

1 SAMUEL 26:1—27:12

NOW the Ziphites came to Saul at Gibeah, saying, "Is David not hiding in the hill of Hachilah, opposite Jeshimon?" 2 Then Saul arose and went down to the Wilderness of Ziph, having three thousand chosen men of Israel with him, to seek David in the Wilderness of Ziph. 3 And Saul encamped in the hill of Hachilah, which *is* opposite Jeshimon, by the road. But David stayed in the wilderness, and he saw that Saul came after him into the wilderness. 4 David therefore sent out spies, and understood that Saul had indeed come.

5 So David arose and came to the place where Saul had encamped. And David saw the place where Saul lay, and Abner the son of Ner, the commander of his army. Now Saul lay within the camp, with the people encamped all around him. 6 Then David answered, and said to Ahimelech the Hittite and to Abishai the son of Zeruiah, brother of Joab, saying, "Who will go down with me to Saul in the camp?"

And Abishai said, "I will go down with you."

7 So David and Abishai came to the people by night; and there Saul lay sleeping within the camp, with his spear stuck in the ground by his head. And Abner and the people lay all around him. 8 Then Abishai said to David, "God has delivered your enemy into your hand this day. Now therefore, please, let me strike him at once with the spear, right to the earth; and I will not *have to strike* him a second time!"

9 But David said to Abishai, "Do not destroy him; for who can stretch out his hand against the LORD's anointed, and be guiltless?" 10 David said furthermore, "*As* the LORD lives, the LORD shall strike him, or his day shall come to die, or he shall go out to battle and perish. 11 The LORD forbid that I should stretch out my hand against the LORD's anointed. But please, take now the spear and the jug of water that *are* by his head, and let us go." 12 So David took the spear and the jug of water *by* Saul's head, and they got away; and no man saw or knew *it* or awoke. For

they *were* all asleep, because a deep sleep from the LORD had fallen on them.

13 Now David went over to the other side, and stood on the top of a hill afar off, a great distance *being* between them. 14 And David called out to the people and to Abner the son of Ner, saying, "Do you not answer, Abner?"

Then Abner answered and said, "Who *are* you, calling out to the king?"

15 So David said to Abner, "*Are* you not a man? And who *is* like you in Israel? Why then have you not guarded your lord the king? For one of the people came in to destroy your lord the king. 16 This thing that you have done *is* not good. *As* the LORD lives, you deserve to die, because you have not guarded your master, the LORD's anointed. And now see where the king's spear *is*, and the jug of water that *was* by his head."

17 Then Saul knew David's voice, and said, "*Is* that your voice, my son David?"

David said, "*It is* my voice, my lord, O king." 18 And he said, "Why does my lord thus pursue his servant? For what have I done, or what evil *is* in my hand? 19 Now therefore, please, let my lord the king hear the words of his servant: If the LORD has stirred you up against me, let Him accept an offering. But if *it is* the children of men, *may* they *be* cursed before the LORD, for they have driven me out this day from sharing in the inheritance of the LORD, saying, 'Go, serve other gods.' 20 So now, do not let my blood fall to the earth before the face of the LORD. For the king of Israel has come out to seek a flea, as when one hunts a partridge in the mountains."

21 Then Saul said, "I have sinned. Return, my son David. For I will harm you no more, because my life was precious in your eyes this day. Indeed I have played the fool and erred exceedingly."

22 And David answered and said, "Here is the king's spear. Let one of the young men come over and get it. 23 May the LORD repay every man *for* his righteousness and his faithfulness; for the LORD delivered you into *my* hand today, but I would not stretch out my hand against the LORD's anointed.

*R*ighteousness—conformity to a right
standard, where no one but God
sees us.   (BIB. ETHICS)

24 And indeed, as your life was valued much
this day in my eyes, so let my life be valued
much in the eyes of the LORD, and let Him
deliver me out of all tribulation."

25 Then Saul said to David, *"May* you
be blessed, my son David! You shall both
do great things and also still prevail."

So David went on his way, and Saul returned to his place.

27 AND David said in his heart, "Now
I shall perish someday by the hand
of Saul. *There is* nothing better for me than
that I should speedily escape to the land
of the Philistines; and Saul will despair of
me, to seek me anymore in any part of Israel.
So I shall escape out of his hand." 2 Then
David arose and went over with the six
hundred men who *were* with him to Achish
the son of Maoch, king of Gath. 3 So David
dwelt with Achish at Gath, he and his men,
each man with his household, *and* David
with his two wives, Ahinoam the Jezreelitess, and Abigail the Carmelitess, Nabal's
widow. 4 And it was told Saul that David
had fled to Gath; so he sought him no more.

5 Then David said to Achish, "If I have
now found favor in your eyes, let them
give me a place in some town in the country,
that I may dwell there. For why should
your servant dwell in the royal city with
you?" 6 So Achish gave him Ziklag that
day. Therefore Ziklag has belonged to the
kings of Judah to this day. 7 Now the time
that David dwelt in the country of the Philistines was one full year and four months.

8 And David and his men went up and
raided the Geshurites, the Girzites, and the
Amalekites. For those nations were the inhabitants of the land from of old, as you
go to Shur, even as far as the land of Egypt.
9 Whenever David attacked the land, he left
neither man nor woman alive, but took
away the sheep, the oxen, the donkeys, the
camels, and the apparel, and returned and
came to Achish. 10 Then Achish would say,
"Where have you made a raid today?" And
David would say, "Against the southern
area of Judah, or against the southern *area*
of the Jerahmeelites, or against the southern
area of the Kenites." 11 David would save
neither man nor woman alive, to bring *news*
to Gath, saying, "Lest they should inform
on us, saying, 'Thus David did.' " And thus

was his behavior all the time he dwelt in
the country of the Philistines. 12 So Achish
believed David, saying, "He has made his
people Israel utterly abhor him; therefore
he will be my servant forever."

PSALM 60:6–12

6   GOD has spoken in His holiness:
    "I will rejoice;
    I will divide Shechem
    And measure out the Valley of Succoth.
7   Gilead *is* Mine, and Manasseh *is* Mine;
    Ephraim also *is* the helmet for My head;
    Judah *is* My lawgiver.
8   Moab *is* My washpot;
    Over Edom I will cast My shoe;
    Philistia, shout in triumph because of
    Me."

9   Who will bring me *to* the strong city?
    Who will lead me to Edom?
10 *Is it* not You, O God, *who* cast us off?
    And You, O God, *who* did not go out
    with our armies?
11 Give us help from trouble,
    For the help of man *is* useless.
12 Through God we will do valiantly,
    For *it is* He *who* shall tread down our
    enemies.

PROVERBS 16:4, 5

4   THE LORD has made all for Himself,
    Yes, even the wicked for the day of
    doom.

5   Everyone proud in heart *is* an
        abomination to the LORD;
    Though they join forces, none will go
    unpunished.

JOHN 2:1–25

ON the third day there was a wedding in
Cana of Galilee, and the mother of Jesus
was there. 2 Now both Jesus and His disciples were invited to the wedding. 3 And
when they ran out of wine, the mother of
Jesus said to Him, "They have no wine."

4 Jesus said to her, "Woman, what does
your concern have to do with Me? My hour
has not yet come."

5 His mother said to the servants, "Whatever He says to you, do *it.*"

6 Now there were set there six waterpots
of stone, according to the manner of purification of the Jews, containing twenty or

thirty gallons apiece. 7 Jesus said to them, "Fill the waterpots with water." And they filled them up to the brim. 8 And He said to them, "Draw *some* out now, and take *it* to the master of the feast." And they took *it*. 9 When the master of the feast had tasted the water that was made wine, and did not know where it came from (but the servants who had drawn the water knew), the master of the feast called the bridegroom. 10 And he said to him, "Every man at the beginning sets out the good wine, and when the *guests* have well drunk, then the inferior. You have kept the good wine until now!"

11 This beginning of signs Jesus did in Cana of Galilee, and manifested His glory; and His disciples believed in Him.

12 After this He went down to Capernaum, He, His mother, His brothers, and His disciples; and they did not stay there many days.

13 Now the Passover of the Jews was at hand, and Jesus went up to Jerusalem. 14 And He found in the temple those who sold oxen and sheep and doves, and the money changers doing business. 15 When He had made a whip of cords, He drove them all out of the temple, with the sheep and the oxen, and poured out the changers' money and overturned the tables. 16 And He said to those who sold doves, "Take these things away! Do not make My Father's house a house of merchandise!"

17 Then His disciples remembered that it was written, "Zeal for Your house has eaten Me up."

18 So the Jews answered and said to Him, "What sign do You show to us, since You do these things?"

19 Jesus answered and said to them, "Destroy this temple, and in three days I will raise it up."

20 Then the Jews said, "It has taken forty-six years to build this temple, and will You raise it up in three days?"

21 But He was speaking of the temple of His body. 22 Therefore, when He had risen from the dead, His disciples remembered that He had said this to them; and they believed the Scripture and the word which Jesus had said.

23 Now when He was in Jerusalem at the Passover, during the feast, many believed in His name when they saw the signs which He did. 24 But Jesus did not commit Himself to them, because He knew all *men,*

The only Being who understands me is the Being who made me. (MORAL FOUND.)

---

25 and had no need that anyone should testify of man, for He knew what was in man.

Reading 133—The Need for New Birth
John 3:3

Every man has need of new birth. "Most assuredly, I say to you, unless one is born again, he cannot see the kingdom of God" (John 3:3). Jesus did not speak these words to a man down and out in sin, but to a sterling, worthy, upright man. The concept of new birth in the New Testament is not a concept of something that springs out of us: but of something that enters into us. Just as our Lord came into human history from without, so He must come into us from without. Our new birth is the birth of the life of the Son of God into our old human nature, and our human nature has to be transfigured by the indwelling life of the Son of God. Have I allowed my personal human life to become a "Bethlehem" for the Son of God? It is not that God patches up my natural virtues, but that I learn by obedience to make room for Jesus Christ to exhibit His disposition in me. It is impossible to imitate the disposition of Jesus. Am I becoming the birthplace of the Son of God (Luke 1:35), or do I only know the miracle of God's changing grace? (*LOVE OF GOD*)

1 SAMUEL 28:1–25

NOW it happened in those days that the Philistines gathered their armies together for war, to fight with Israel. And Achish said to David, "You assuredly know that you will go out with me to battle, you and your men."

2 So David said to Achish, "Surely you know what your servant can do."

And Achish said to David, "Therefore I will make you one of my chief guardians forever."

3 Now Samuel had died, and all Israel had lamented for him and buried him in Ramah, in his own city. And Saul had put the mediums and the spiritists out of the land.

4 Then the Philistines gathered together, and came and encamped at Shunem. So Saul gathered all Israel together, and they encamped at Gilboa. 5 When Saul saw the army of the Philistines, he was afraid, and his heart trembled greatly. 6 And when Saul inquired of the LORD, the LORD did not answer him, either by dreams or by Urim or by the prophets.

7 Then Saul said to his servants, "Find me a woman who is a medium, that I may go to her and inquire of her."

And his servants said to him, "In fact, *there is* a woman who is a medium at En Dor."

8 So Saul disguised himself and put on other clothes, and he went, and two men with him; and they came to the woman by night. And he said, "Please conduct a séance for me, and bring up for me the one I shall name to you."

9 Then the woman said to him, "Look, you know what Saul has done, how he has cut off the mediums and the spiritists from the land. Why then do you lay a snare for my life, to cause me to die?"

10 And Saul swore to her by the LORD, saying, "*As* the LORD lives, no punishment shall come upon you for this thing."

11 Then the woman said, "Whom shall I bring up for you?"

And he said, "Bring up Samuel for me."

12 When the woman saw Samuel, she cried out with a loud voice. And the woman spoke to Saul, saying, "Why have you deceived me? For you *are* Saul!"

13 And the king said to her, "Do not be afraid. What did you see?"

And the woman said to Saul, "I saw a spirit ascending out of the earth."

14 So he said to her, "What *is* his form?" And she said, "An old man is coming up, and he *is* covered with a mantle." And Saul perceived that it *was* Samuel, and he stooped with *his* face to the ground and bowed down.

15 Now Samuel said to Saul, "Why have you disturbed me by bringing me up?"

And Saul answered, "I am deeply distressed; for the Philistines make war against me, and God has departed from me and does not answer me anymore, neither by prophets nor by dreams. Therefore I have called you, that you may reveal to me what I should do."

16 Then Samuel said: "So why do you ask me, seeing the LORD has departed from you and has become your enemy? 17 And the LORD has done for Himself as He spoke by me. For the LORD has torn the kingdom out of your hand and given it to your neighbor, David. 18 Because you did not obey the voice of the LORD nor execute His fierce wrath upon Amalek, therefore the LORD has done this thing to you this day. 19 Moreover the LORD will also deliver Israel with you into the hand of the Philistines. And tomorrow you and your sons *will be* with me. The LORD will also deliver the army of Israel into the hand of the Philistines."

20 Immediately Saul fell full length on the ground, and was dreadfully afraid because of the words of Samuel. And there was no strength in him, for he had eaten no food all day or all night.

21 And the woman came to Saul and saw that he was severely troubled, and said to him, "Look, your maidservant has obeyed your voice, and I have put my life in my hands and heeded the words which you spoke to me. 22 Now therefore, please, heed also the voice of your maidservant, and let me set a piece of bread before you; and eat, that you may have strength when you go on *your* way."

23 But he refused and said, "I will not eat."

So his servants, together with the woman, urged him; and he heeded their voice. Then he arose from the ground and sat on the bed. 24 Now the woman had a fatted calf in the house, and she hastened to kill it. And she took flour and kneaded *it,* and baked unleavened bread from it. 25 So she brought *it* before Saul and his servants, and they ate. Then they rose and went away that night.

PSALM 61:1–4

1 HEAR my cry, O God;
Attend to my prayer.

2   From the end of the earth I will cry
    to You,
    When my heart is overwhelmed;
    Lead me to the rock that is higher
    than I.

3   For You have been a shelter for me,
    A strong tower from the enemy.

---

*We are apt to forget that the enemy
is unseen and that he is supernatural.*   (GOD'S WORKMANSHIP)

---

4   I will abide in Your tabernacle forever;
    I will trust in the shelter of Your wings.
                                    Selah

PROVERBS 16:6

6   IN mercy and truth
    Atonement is provided for iniquity;
    And by the fear of the LORD *one* departs
    from evil.

JOHN 3:1–18

THERE was a man of the Pharisees named
Nicodemus, a ruler of the Jews. 2 This man
came to Jesus by night and said to Him,
"Rabbi, we know that You are a teacher
come from God; for no one can do these
signs that You do unless God is with him."

3 Jesus answered and said to him, "Most
assuredly, I say to you, unless one is born
again, he cannot see the kingdom of God."

4 Nicodemus said to Him, "How can a
man be born when he is old? Can he enter
a second time into his mother's womb and
be born?"

5 Jesus answered, "Most assuredly, I say

to you, unless one is born of water and
the Spirit, he cannot enter the kingdom
of God. 6 That which is born of the flesh
is flesh, and that which is born of the Spirit
is spirit. 7 Do not marvel that I said to you,
'You must be born again.' 8 The wind blows
where it wishes, and you hear the sound
of it, but cannot tell where it comes from
and where it goes. So is everyone who is
born of the Spirit."

9 Nicodemus answered and said to Him,
"How can these things be?"

10 Jesus answered and said to him, "Are
you the teacher of Israel, and do not know
these things? 11 Most assuredly, I say to
you, We speak what We know and testify
what We have seen, and you do not receive
Our witness. 12 If I have told you earthly
things and you do not believe, how will
you believe if I tell you heavenly things?
13 No one has ascended to heaven but He
who came down from heaven, *that is,* the
Son of Man who is in heaven. 14 And as
Moses lifted up the serpent in the wilderness, even so must the Son of Man be lifted
up, 15 that whoever believes in Him should
not perish but have eternal life. 16 For God
so loved the world that He gave His only
begotten Son, that whoever believes in Him
should not perish but have everlasting life.

---

*The love of God is not in
accordance with human standards in
any way.*   (LOVE OF GOD)

---

17 For God did not send His Son into the
world to condemn the world, but that the
world through Him might be saved.

18 "He who believes in Him is not condemned; but he who does not believe is
condemned already, because he has not believed in the name of the only begotten
Son of God.

◆◆◆◆

Reading 134—Rejoice in God's Provision
John 3:30

When once you see a soul in sight of the claims of Jesus, you know
your influence has been in the right direction, and instead of putting
out a hand to withhold the throes, pray that they grow ten times stronger
until no power on earth or in hell can ever hold that soul from Jesus Christ
(cf. Luke 14:26). Beware of rejoicing in the wrong thing with a soul, but see
that you rejoice at the right thing. "The friend of the bridegroom, who stands

and hears him, rejoices greatly because of the bridegroom's voice. Therefore this joy of mine is fulfilled."

It is not sin that hinders, but our not living as friends of the bridegroom. Suppose you talk about depending on God and how wonderful it is, and then others see that in your own immediate concerns you do not depend on Him a bit, but on your own wits. It makes them say, "Well, after all, it's a big pretense, there is no almighty Christ to depend on anywhere, it is all mere sentiment." The impression left is that Jesus Christ is not real to you. "John performed no sign, but all the things that John spoke about this Man were true" (John 10:41).   (*Place Help*)

1 SAMUEL 29:1—31:13

THEN the Philistines gathered together all their armies at Aphek, and the Israelites encamped by a fountain which *is* in Jezreel. 2 And the lords of the Philistines passed in review by hundreds and by thousands, but David and his men passed in review at the rear with Achish. 3 Then the princes of the Philistines said, "What *are* these Hebrews *doing here?*"

And Achish said to the princes of the Philistines, "*Is* this not David, the servant of Saul king of Israel, who has been with me these days, or these years? And to this day I have found no fault in him since he defected *to me*."

4 But the princes of the Philistines were angry with him; so the princes of the Philistines said to him, "Make this fellow return, that he may go back to the place which you have appointed for him, and do not let him go down with us to battle, lest in the battle he become our adversary. For with what could he reconcile himself to his master, if not with the heads of these men? 5 *Is* this not David, of whom they sang to one another in dances, saying:

'Saul has slain his thousands,
 And David his ten thousands'?"

6 Then Achish called David and said to him, "Surely, *as* the LORD lives, you have been upright, and your going out and your coming in with me in the army *is* good in my sight. For to this day I have not found evil in you since the day of your coming to me. Nevertheless the lords do not favor you. 7 Therefore return now, and go in peace, that you may not displease the lords of the Philistines."

8 So David said to Achish, "But what have I done? And to this day what have you found in your servant as long as I have been with you, that I may not go and fight against the enemies of my lord the king?"

9 Then Achish answered and said to David, "I know that you *are* as good in my sight as an angel of God; nevertheless the princes of the Philistines have said, 'He shall not go up with us to the battle.' 10 Now therefore, rise early in the morning with your master's servants who have come with you. And as soon as you are up early in the morning and have light, depart."

11 So David and his men rose early to depart in the morning, to return to the land of the Philistines. And the Philistines went up to Jezreel.

30 NOW it happened, when David and his men came to Ziklag, on the third day, that the Amalekites had invaded the South and Ziklag, attacked Ziklag and burned it with fire, 2 and had taken captive the women and those who *were* there, from small to great; they did not kill anyone, but carried *them* away and went their way. 3 So David and his men came to the city, and there it was, burned with fire; and their wives, their sons, and their daughters had been taken captive. 4 Then David and the people who *were* with him lifted up their voices and wept, until they had no more power to weep. 5 And David's two wives, Ahinoam the Jezreelitess, and Abigail the widow of Nabal the Carmelite, had been taken captive. 6 Now David was greatly distressed, for the people spoke of stoning him, because the soul of all the people was grieved, every man for his sons and his daughters. But David strengthened himself in the LORD his God.

7 Then David said to Abiathar the priest, Ahimelech's son, "Please bring the ephod here to me." And Abiathar brought the ephod to David. 8 So David inquired of the LORD, saying, "Shall I pursue this troop? Shall I overtake them?"

And He answered him, "Pursue, for you shall surely overtake *them* and without fail recover *all*."

9 So David went, he and the six hundred men who *were* with him, and came to the Brook Besor, where those stayed who were left behind. 10 But David pursued, he and four hundred men; for two hundred stayed *behind*, who were so weary that they could not cross the Brook Besor.

11 Then they found an Egyptian in the field, and brought him to David; and they gave him bread and he ate, and they let him drink water. 12 And they gave him a piece of a cake of figs and two clusters of raisins. So when he had eaten, his strength came back to him; for he had eaten no bread nor drunk water for three days and three nights. 13 Then David said to him, "To whom do you *belong,* and where *are* you from?"

And he said, "I *am* a young man from Egypt, servant of an Amalekite; and my master left me behind, because three days ago I fell sick. 14 We made an invasion of the southern *area* of the Cherethites, in the *territory* which *belongs* to Judah, and of the southern *area* of Caleb; and we burned Ziklag with fire."

15 And David said to him, "Can you take me down to this troop?"

So he said, "Swear to me by God that you will neither kill me nor deliver me into the hands of my master, and I will take you down to this troop."

16 And when he had brought him down, there they were, spread out over all the land, eating and drinking and dancing, because of all the great spoil which they had taken from the land of the Philistines and from the land of Judah. 17 Then David attacked them from twilight until the evening of the next day. Not a man of them escaped, except four hundred young men who rode on camels and fled. 18 So David recovered all that the Amalekites had carried away, and David rescued his two wives. 19 And nothing of theirs was lacking, either small or great, sons or daughters, spoil or anything which they had taken from them; David recovered all. 20 Then David took all the flocks and herds they had driven before those *other* livestock, and said, "This *is* David's spoil."

21 Now David came to the two hundred men who had been so weary that they could not follow David, whom they also had made to stay at the Brook Besor. So they went out to meet David and to meet the people who *were* with him. And when David came near the people, he greeted them. 22 Then all the wicked and worthless men of those who went with David answered and said, "Because they did not go with us, we will

not give them *any* of the spoil that we have recovered, except for every man's wife and children, that they may lead *them* away and depart."

23 But David said, "My brethren, you shall not do so with what the Lord has given us, who has preserved us and delivered into our hand the troop that came against us. 24 For who will heed you in this matter? But as his part *is* who goes down to the battle, so *shall* his part *be* who stays by the supplies; they shall share alike." 25 So it was, from that day forward; he made it a statute and an ordinance for Israel to this day.

26 Now when David came to Ziklag, he sent *some* of the spoil to the elders of Judah, to his friends, saying, "Here is a present for you from the spoil of the enemies of the Lord"— 27 to *those* who *were* in Bethel, *those* who *were* in Ramoth of the South, *those* who *were* in Jattir, 28 *those* who *were* in Aroer, *those* who *were* in Siphmoth, *those* who *were* in Eshtemoa, 29 *those* who *were* in Rachal, *those* who *were* in the cities of the Jerahmeelites, *those* who *were* in the cities of the Kenites, 30 *those* who *were* in Hormah, *those* who *were* in Chorashan, *those* who *were* in Athach, 31 *those* who *were* in Hebron, and to all the places where David himself and his men were accustomed to rove.

31 NOW the Philistines fought against Israel; and the men of Israel fled from before the Philistines, and fell slain on Mount Gilboa. 2 Then the Philistines followed hard after Saul and his sons. And the Philistines killed Jonathan, Abinadab, and Malchishua, Saul's sons. 3 The battle became fierce against Saul. The archers hit him, and he was severely wounded by the archers.

4 Then Saul said to his armorbearer, "Draw your sword, and thrust me through with it, lest these uncircumcised men come and thrust me through and abuse me."

But his armorbearer would not, for he was greatly afraid. Therefore Saul took a sword and fell on it. 5 And when his armorbearer saw that Saul was dead, he also fell on his sword, and died with him. 6 So Saul,

---

*T*he Bible reveals that the basis of things is not reasonable, but tragic. (Baffled)

---

his three sons, his armorbearer, and all his men died together that same day.

7 And when the men of Israel who *were* on the other side of the valley, and *those* who *were* on the other side of the Jordan, saw that the men of Israel had fled and that Saul and his sons were dead, they forsook the cities and fled; and the Philistines came and dwelt in them. 8 So it happened the next day, when the Philistines came to strip the slain, that they found Saul and his three sons fallen on Mount Gilboa. 9 And they cut off his head and stripped off his armor, and sent *word* throughout the land of the Philistines, to proclaim *it in* the temple of their idols and among the people. 10 Then they put his armor in the temple of the Ashtoreths, and they fastened his body to the wall of Beth Shan.

11 Now when the inhabitants of Jabesh Gilead heard what the Philistines had done to Saul, 12 all the valiant men arose and traveled all night, and took the body of Saul and the bodies of his sons from the wall of Beth Shan; and they came to Jabesh and burned them there. 13 Then they took their bones and buried *them* under the tamarisk tree at Jabesh, and fasted seven days.

PSALM 61:5–8

5 FOR You, O God, have heard my vows;
You have given *me* the heritage of those who fear Your name.

6 You will prolong the king's life,
His years as many generations.

7 He shall abide before God forever.
Oh, prepare mercy and truth, *which* may preserve him!

8 So I will sing praise to Your name forever,
That I may daily perform my vows.

PROVERBS 16:7–9

7 WHEN a man's ways please the LORD,
He makes even his enemies to be at peace with him.

8 Better *is* a little with righteousness,
Than vast revenues without justice.

9 A man's heart plans his way,
But the LORD directs his steps.

JOHN 3:19–36

AND this is the condemnation, that the light has come into the world, and men loved darkness rather than light, because their deeds were evil. 20 For everyone practicing evil hates the light and does not come to the light, lest his deeds should be exposed. 21 But he who does the truth comes to the light, that his deeds may be clearly seen, that they have been done in God."

22 After these things Jesus and His disciples came into the land of Judea, and there He remained with them and baptized. 23 Now John also was baptizing in Aenon near Salim, because there was much water there. And they came and were baptized. 24 For John had not yet been thrown into prison.

25 Then there arose a dispute between *some* of John's disciples and the Jews about purification. 26 And they came to John and said to him, "Rabbi, He who was with you beyond the Jordan, to whom you have testified—behold, He is baptizing, and all are coming to Him!"

27 John answered and said, "A man can receive nothing unless it has been given to him from heaven. 28 You yourselves bear me witness, that I said, 'I am not the Christ,' but, 'I have been sent before Him.' 29 He who has the bride is the bridegroom; but the friend of the bridegroom, who stands and hears him, rejoices greatly because of the bridegroom's voice. Therefore this joy of mine is fulfilled. 30 He must increase, but I *must* decrease. 31 He who comes from above is above all; he who is of the earth is earthly and speaks of the earth. He who comes from heaven is above all. 32 And what He has seen and heard, that He testifies; and no one receives His testimony. 33 He who has received His testimony has certified that God is true. 34 For He whom God has sent speaks the words of God, for God does not give the Spirit by measure. 35 The Father loves the Son, and has given all things into His hand. 36 He who believes in the Son has everlasting life; and he who does not believe the Son shall not see life, but the wrath of God abides on him."

Reading 135—God's Haphazard Order
John 4:4

One great thing to notice is that God's order comes to us in the haphazard. We try to plan our ways and work things out for ourselves, but they go wrong because there are more facts than we know; whereas if we just go on with the days as they come, we find that God's order comes to us in that apparently haphazard way. The man who does not know God depends entirely on his own wits and forecasting. If instead of arranging our own programs we will trust to the wisdom of God and concentrate all our efforts on the duty that lies nearest, we shall find that we meet God in that way and in no other. When we become "amateur providences" and arrange times and meetings, we may cause certain things to happen, but we very rarely meet God in that way; we meet Him most effectively as we go on in the ordinary ways. Where you look for God, He does not appear; where you do not look for Him, there He is—a trick of the weather, a letter, and suddenly you are face-to-face with the best thing you ever met. This comes out all through the life of Jesus Christ; it was the most natural thing for Him to go through Samaria.

(*GLORIFY*)

2 SAMUEL 1:1—2:32

NOW it came to pass after the death of Saul, when David had returned from the slaughter of the Amalekites, and David had stayed two days in Ziklag, 2 on the third day, behold, it happened that a man came from Saul's camp with his clothes torn and dust on his head. So it was, when he came to David, that he fell to the ground and prostrated himself.

3 And David said to him, "Where have you come from?"

So he said to him, "I have escaped from the camp of Israel."

4 Then David said to him, "How did the matter go? Please tell me."

And he answered, "The people have fled from the battle, many of the people are fallen and dead, and Saul and Jonathan his son are dead also."

5 So David said to the young man who told him, "How do you know that Saul and Jonathan his son are dead?"

6 Then the young man who told him said, "As I happened by chance *to be* on Mount Gilboa, there was Saul, leaning on his spear; and indeed the chariots and horsemen followed hard after him. 7 Now when he looked behind him, he saw me and called to me. And I answered, 'Here I am.'
8 And he said to me, 'Who *are* you?' So I answered him, 'I *am* an Amalekite.'
9 He said to me again, 'Please stand over me and kill me, for anguish has come upon me, but my life still *remains* in me.'

10 So I stood over him and killed him, because I was sure that he could not live after he had fallen. And I took the crown that *was* on his head and the bracelet that *was* on his arm, and have brought them here to my lord."

11 Therefore David took hold of his own clothes and tore them, and *so did* all the men who *were* with him. 12 And they mourned and wept and fasted until evening for Saul and for Jonathan his son, for the people of the LORD and for the house of Israel, because they had fallen by the sword.

13 Then David said to the young man who told him, "Where *are* you from?"

And he answered, "I *am* the son of an alien, an Amalekite."

14 So David said to him, "How was it you were not afraid to put forth your hand to destroy the LORD's anointed?" 15 Then David called one of the young men and said, "Go near, *and* execute him!" And he struck him so that he died. 16 So David said to him, "Your blood *is* on your own head, for your own mouth has testified against you, saying, 'I have killed the LORD's anointed.'"

17 Then David lamented with this lamentation over Saul and over Jonathan his son, 18 and he told *them* to teach the children of Judah *the Song of* the Bow; indeed *it is* written in the Book of Jasher:

19 "The beauty of Israel is slain on your high places!
How the mighty have fallen!

20 Tell *it* not in Gath,
Proclaim *it* not in the streets of
Ashkelon—
Lest the daughters of the Philistines
rejoice,
Lest the daughters of the
uncircumcised triumph.

21 "O mountains of Gilboa,
Let there be no dew nor rain upon
you,
Nor fields of offerings.
For the shield of the mighty is cast
away there!
The shield of Saul, not anointed with
oil.

22 From the blood of the slain,
From the fat of the mighty,
The bow of Jonathan did not turn
back,
And the sword of Saul did not return
empty.

23 "Saul and Jonathan *were* beloved and
pleasant in their lives,
And in their death they were not
divided;
They were swifter than eagles,
They were stronger than lions.

24 "O daughters of Israel, weep over
Saul,
Who clothed you in scarlet, with
luxury;
Who put ornaments of gold on your
apparel.

25 "How the mighty have fallen in the
midst of the battle!
Jonathan *was* slain in your high
places.

26 I am distressed for you, my brother
Jonathan;
You have been very pleasant to me;
Your love to me was wonderful,
Surpassing the love of women.

27 "How the mighty have fallen,
And the weapons of war perished!"

2 IT happened after this that David inquired of the Lord, saying, "Shall I
go up to any of the cities of Judah?"
And the Lord said to him, "Go up."
David said, "Where shall I go up?"
And He said, "To Hebron."
2 So David went up there, and his two
wives also, Ahinoam the Jezreelitess, and
Abigail the widow of Nabal the Carmelite.
3 And David brought up the men who *were*
with him, every man with his household.

So they dwelt in the cities of Hebron.
4 Then the men of Judah came, and there
they anointed David king over the house
of Judah. And they told David, saying, "The
men of Jabesh Gilead *were the ones* who
buried Saul." 5 So David sent messengers
to the men of Jabesh Gilead, and said to
them, "You *are* blessed of the Lord, for
you have shown this kindness to your lord,
to Saul, and have buried him. 6 And now
may the Lord show kindness and truth
to you. I also will repay you this kindness,
because you have done this thing. 7 Now
therefore, let your hands be strengthened,
and be valiant; for your master Saul is dead,
and also the house of Judah has anointed
me king over them."

8 But Abner the son of Ner, commander
of Saul's army, took Ishbosheth the son
of Saul and brought him over to Mahanaim;
9 and he made him king over Gilead, over
the Ashurites, over Jezreel, over Ephraim,
over Benjamin, and over all Israel.
10 Ishbosheth, Saul's son, *was* forty years
old when he began to reign over Israel,
and he reigned two years. Only the house
of Judah followed David. 11 And the time
that David was king in Hebron over the
house of Judah was seven years and six
months.
12 Now Abner the son of Ner, and the
servants of Ishbosheth the son of Saul, went
out from Mahanaim to Gibeon. 13 And Joab
the son of Zeruiah, and the servants of David, went out and met them by the pool
of Gibeon. So they sat down, one on one
side of the pool and the other on the other
side of the pool. 14 Then Abner said to Joab,
"Let the young men now arise and compete
before us."
And Joab said, "Let them arise."
15 So they arose and went over by number, twelve from Benjamin, *followers* of Ishbosheth the son of Saul, and twelve from
the servants of David. 16 And each one
grasped his opponent by the head and *thrust*
his sword in his opponent's side; so they
fell down together. Therefore that place was
called the Field of Sharp Swords, which *is*
in Gibeon. 17 So there was a very fierce
battle that day, and Abner and the men
of Israel were beaten before the servants
of David.
18 Now the three sons of Zeruiah were
there: Joab and Abishai and Asahel. And
Asahel *was as* fleet of foot as a wild gazelle.
19 So Asahel pursued Abner, and in going
he did not turn to the right hand or to
the left from following Abner.
20 Then Abner looked behind him and
said, "*Are* you Asahel?"

He answered, "I *am*."

21 And Abner said to him, "Turn aside to your right hand or to your left, and lay hold on one of the young men and take his armor for yourself." But Asahel would not turn aside from following him. 22 So Abner said again to Asahel, "Turn aside from following me. Why should I strike you to the ground? How then could I face your brother Joab?" 23 However, he refused to turn aside. Therefore Abner struck him in the stomach with the blunt end of the spear, so that the spear came out of his back; and he fell down there and died on the spot. So it was *that* as many as came to the place where Asahel fell down and died, stood still.

24 Joab and Abishai also pursued Abner. And the sun was going down when they came to the hill of Ammah, which *is* before Giah by the road to the Wilderness of Gibeon. 25 Now the children of Benjamin gathered together behind Abner and became a unit, and took their stand on top of a hill. 26 Then Abner called to Joab and said, "Shall the sword devour forever? Do you not know that it will be bitter in the latter end? How long will it be then until you tell the people to return from pursuing their brethren?"

27 And Joab said, "*As* God lives, unless you had spoken, surely then by morning all the people would have given up pursuing their brethren." 28 So Joab blew a trumpet; and all the people stood still and did not pursue Israel anymore, nor did they fight anymore. 29 Then Abner and his men went on all that night through the plain, crossed over the Jordan, and went through all Bithron; and they came to Mahanaim.

30 So Joab returned from pursuing Abner. And when he had gathered all the people together, there were missing of David's servants nineteen men and Asahel. 31 But the servants of David had struck down, of Benjamin and Abner's men, three hundred and sixty men who died. 32 Then they took up Asahel and buried him in his father's tomb, which *was in* Bethlehem. And Joab and his men went all night, and they came to Hebron at daybreak.

PSALM 62:1–4

1   TRULY my soul silently *waits* for God;
     From Him *comes* my salvation.
2   He only *is* my rock and my salvation;
     He is my defense;
     I shall not be greatly moved.

A rock conveys the idea of an encircling guard. (RUN)

3   How long will you attack a man?
     You shall be slain, all of you,
     Like a leaning wall and a tottering fence.
4   They only consult to cast *him* down
        from his high position;
     They delight in lies;
     They bless with their mouth,
     But they curse inwardly.   Selah

PROVERBS 16:10–12

10   DIVINATION *is* on the lips of the king;
      His mouth must not transgress in judgment.
11   Honest weights and scales *are* the LORD's;
      All the weights in the bag *are* His work.
12   *It is* an abomination for kings to commit wickedness,
      For a throne is established by righteousness.

JOHN 4:1–30

THEREFORE, when the Lord knew that the Pharisees had heard that Jesus made and baptized more disciples than John 2 (though Jesus Himself did not baptize, but His disciples), 3 He left Judea and departed again to Galilee. 4 But He needed to go through Samaria.

5 So He came to a city of Samaria which is called Sychar, near the plot of ground that Jacob gave to his son Joseph. 6 Now Jacob's well was there. Jesus therefore, being wearied from *His* journey, sat thus by the well. It was about the sixth hour.

7 A woman of Samaria came to draw water. Jesus said to her, "Give Me a drink." 8 For His disciples had gone away into the city to buy food.

9 Then the woman of Samaria said to Him, "How is it that You, being a Jew, ask a drink from me, a Samaritan woman?" For Jews have no dealings with Samaritans.

10 Jesus answered and said to her, "If you knew the gift of God, and who it is who says to you, 'Give Me a drink,' you would have asked Him, and He would have given you living water."

11 The woman said to Him, "Sir, You have nothing to draw with, and the well

*T*he one perfect Personality is our
Lord.   (PERFECT)

is deep. Where then do You get that living water? 12 Are You greater than our father Jacob, who gave us the well, and drank from it himself, as well as his sons and his livestock?"

13 Jesus answered and said to her, "Whoever drinks of this water will thirst again, 14 but whoever drinks of the water that I shall give him will never thirst. But the water that I shall give him will become in him a fountain of water springing up into everlasting life."

15 The woman said to Him, "Sir, give me this water, that I may not thirst, nor come here to draw."

16 Jesus said to her, "Go, call your husband, and come here."

17 The woman answered and said, "I have no husband."

Jesus said to her, "You have well said, 'I have no husband,' 18 for you have had five husbands, and the one whom you now have is not your husband; in that you spoke truly."

19 The woman said to Him, "Sir, I perceive that You are a prophet. 20 Our fathers worshiped on this mountain, and you *Jews* say that in Jerusalem is the place where one ought to worship."

21 Jesus said to her, "Woman, believe Me, the hour is coming when you will neither on this mountain, nor in Jerusalem, worship the Father. 22 You worship what you do not know; we know what we worship, for salvation is of the Jews. 23 But the hour is coming, and now is, when the true worshipers will worship the Father in spirit and truth; for the Father is seeking such to worship Him. 24 God *is* Spirit, and those who worship Him must worship in spirit and truth."

25 The woman said to Him, "I know that Messiah is coming" (who is called Christ). "When He comes, He will tell us all things."

26 Jesus said to her, "I who speak to you am *He*."

27 And at this *point* His disciples came, and they marveled that He talked with a woman; yet no one said, "What do You seek?" or, "Why are You talking with her?"

28 The woman then left her waterpot, went her way into the city, and said to the men, 29 "Come, see a Man who told me all things that I ever did. Could this be the Christ?" 30 Then they went out of the city and came to Him.

Reading 136—The Guarding Rock
Psalm 62:5, 6

"He only *is* my rock." A rock conveys the idea of an encircling guard, as that of a mother watching her child who is learning to walk; should the child fall, he falls into the encircling love and watchfulness of the mother's care. "The LORD is my rock," my encircling guard. Where did the psalmist learn this truth? In the school of silent waiting upon God. The Rock of Ages is the great sheltering encirclement; we are watched over by the mother-guardianship of God. "I am el-Shaddai," the father-mother God. "He is my strong tower [fortress] and my defense." The Lord Himself is our inviolable place of safety. There is a loftiness and an inaccessibility about the heavenly places in Christ Jesus. The higher you climb the purer the air until you come to the place where the least microbe is unable to live, and spiritually there is an inaccessible place of absolute security. "You have set Your house of defense [fortress] very high."   (*PLACE HELP*)

2 SAMUEL 3:1—4:12

NOW there was a long war between the house of Saul and the house of David. But David grew stronger and stronger, and the house of Saul grew weaker and weaker.

2 Sons were born to David in Hebron: His firstborn was Amnon by Ahinoam the Jezreelitess; 3 his second, Chileab, by Abigail the widow of Nabal the Carmelite; the third, Absalom the son of Maacah, the daughter of Talmai, king of Geshur; 4 the fourth, Adonijah the son of Haggith; the fifth, Shephatiah the son of Abital; 5 and the sixth, Ithream, by David's wife Eglah. These were born to David in Hebron.

6 Now it was so, while there was war between the house of Saul and the house of David, that Abner was strengthening *his* hold on the house of Saul.

7 And Saul had a concubine, whose name *was* Rizpah, the daughter of Aiah. So Ishbosheth said to Abner, "Why have you gone in to my father's concubine?"

8 Then Abner became very angry at the words of Ishbosheth, and said, "*Am* I a dog's head that belongs to Judah? Today I show loyalty to the house of Saul your father, to his brothers, and to his friends, and have not delivered you into the hand of David; and you charge me today with a fault concerning this woman? 9 May God do so to Abner, and more also, if I do not do for David as the LORD has sworn to him— 10 to transfer the kingdom from the house of Saul, and set up the throne of David over Israel and over Judah, from Dan to Beersheba." 11 And he could not answer Abner another word, because he feared him.

12 Then Abner sent messengers on his behalf to David, saying, "Whose *is* the land?" saying *also*, "Make your covenant with me, and indeed my hand *shall be* with you to bring all Israel to you."

13 And *David* said, "Good, I will make a covenant with you. But one thing I require of you: you shall not see my face unless you first bring Michal, Saul's daughter, when you come to see my face." 14 So David sent messengers to Ishbosheth, Saul's son, saying, "Give *me* my wife Michal, whom I betrothed to myself for a hundred foreskins of the Philistines." 15 And Ishbosheth sent and took her from *her* husband, from Paltiel the son of Laish. 16 Then her husband went along with her to Bahurim, weeping behind her. So Abner said to him, "Go, return!" And he returned.

17 Now Abner had communicated with the elders of Israel, saying, "In time past you were seeking for David *to be* king over you. 18 Now then, do *it!* For the LORD has spoken of David, saying, 'By the hand of My servant David, I will save My people Israel from the hand of the Philistines and the hand of all their enemies.'" 19 And Abner also spoke in the hearing of Benjamin. Then Abner also went to speak in the hearing of David in Hebron all that seemed good to Israel and the whole house of Benjamin.

20 So Abner and twenty men with him came to David at Hebron. And David made a feast for Abner and the men who *were* with him. 21 Then Abner said to David, "I will arise and go, and gather all Israel to my lord the king, that they may make a covenant with you, and that you may reign over all that your heart desires." So David sent Abner away, and he went in peace.

22 At that moment the servants of David and Joab came from a raid and brought much spoil with them. But Abner *was* not with David in Hebron, for he had sent him away, and he had gone in peace. 23 When Joab and all the troops that *were* with him had come, they told Joab, saying, "Abner the son of Ner came to the king, and he sent him away, and he has gone in peace." 24 Then Joab came to the king and said, "What have you done? Look, Abner came to you; why *is* it *that* you sent him away, and he has already gone? 25 Surely you realize that Abner the son of Ner came to deceive you, to know your going out and your coming in, and to know all that you are doing."

26 And when Joab had gone from David's presence, he sent messengers after Abner, who brought him back from the well of Sirah. But David did not know *it.* 27 Now when Abner had returned to Hebron, Joab took him aside in the gate to speak with him privately, and there stabbed him in the stomach, so that he died for the blood of Asahel his brother.

28 Afterward, when David heard *it,* he said, "My kingdom and I *are* guiltless before the LORD forever of the blood of Abner the son of Ner. 29 Let it rest on the head of Joab and on all his father's house; and let there never fail to be in the house of Joab one who has a discharge or is a leper, who leans on a staff or falls by the sword, or who lacks bread." 30 So Joab and Abishai his brother killed Abner, because he had killed their brother Asahel at Gibeon in the battle.

31 Then David said to Joab and to all

the people who were with him, "Tear your clothes, gird yourselves with sackcloth, and mourn for Abner." And King David followed the coffin. 32 So they buried Abner in Hebron; and the king lifted up his voice and wept at the grave of Abner, and all the people wept. 33 And the king sang *a lament* over Abner and said:

"Should Abner die as a fool dies?
34   Your hands were not bound
         Nor your feet put into fetters;
         As a man falls before wicked men,
         so you fell."

Then all the people wept over him again. 35 And when all the people came to persuade David to eat food while it was still day, David took an oath, saying, "God do so to me, and more also, if I taste bread or anything else till the sun goes down!" 36 Now all the people took note *of it,* and it pleased them, since whatever the king did pleased all the people. 37 For all the people and all Israel understood that day that it had not been the king's *intent* to kill Abner the son of Ner. 38 Then the king said to his servants, "Do you not know that a prince and a great man has fallen this day in Israel? 39 And I *am* weak today, though anointed king; and these men, the sons of Zeruiah, *are* too harsh for me. The LORD shall repay the evildoer according to his wickedness."

4 WHEN Saul's son heard that Abner had died in Hebron, he lost heart, and all Israel was troubled. 2 Now Saul's son *had* two men *who were* captains of troops. The name of one *was* Baanah and the name of the other Rechab, the sons of Rimmon the Beerothite, of the children of Benjamin. (For Beeroth also was *part* of Benjamin, 3 because the Beerothites fled to Gittaim and have been sojourners there until this day.)

4 Jonathan, Saul's son, had a son *who was* lame in *his* feet. He was five years old when the news about Saul and Jonathan came from Jezreel; and his nurse took him up and fled. And it happened, as she made haste to flee, that he fell and became lame. His name *was* Mephibosheth.

5 Then the sons of Rimmon the Beerothite, Rechab and Baanah, set out and came at about the heat of the day to the house of Ishbosheth, who was lying on his bed at noon. 6 And they came there, all the way into the house, *as though* to get wheat, and they stabbed him in the stomach. Then Rechab and Baanah his brother escaped.

7 For when they came into the house, he was lying on his bed in his bedroom; then they struck him and killed him, beheaded him and took his head, and were all night escaping through the plain. 8 And they brought the head of Ishbosheth to David at Hebron, and said to the king, "Here is the head of Ishbosheth, the son of Saul your enemy, who sought your life; and the LORD has avenged my lord the king this day of Saul and his descendants."

9 But David answered Rechab and Baanah his brother, the sons of Rimmon the Beerothite, and said to them, "*As* the LORD lives, who has redeemed my life from all adversity, 10 when someone told me, saying, 'Look, Saul is dead,' thinking to have brought good news, I arrested him and had him executed in Ziklag—the one who *thought* I would give him a reward for *his* news. 11 How much more, when wicked men have killed a righteous person in his own house on his bed? Therefore, shall I not now require his blood at your hand and remove you from the earth?" 12 So David commanded his young men, and they executed them, cut off their hands and feet, and hanged *them* by the pool in Hebron. But they took the head of Ishbosheth and buried *it* in the tomb of Abner in Hebron.

PSALM 62:5–12

5   MY soul, wait silently for God alone,
      For my expectation *is* from Him.

To wait upon God is the perfection of activity.   (PLACE HELP)

6   He only *is* my rock and my salvation;
      He is my defense;
      I shall not be moved.
7   In God *is* my salvation and my glory;
      The rock of my strength,
      And my refuge, *is* in God.

8   Trust in Him at all times, you people;
      Pour out your heart before Him;
      God *is* a refuge for us.   Selah

9   Surely men of low degree *are* a vapor,
      Men of high degree *are* a lie;
      If they are weighed on the scales,
      They *are* altogether *lighter* than vapor.
10   Do not trust in oppression,
      Nor vainly hope in robbery;
      If riches increase,
      Do not set *your* heart *on them.*

11 God has spoken once,
   Twice I have heard this:
   That power *belongs* to God.
12 Also to You, O Lord, *belongs* mercy;
   For You render to each one according
   to his work.

PROVERBS 16:13–15

13 RIGHTEOUS lips *are* the delight of
   kings,
   And they love him who speaks *what is*
   right.
14 As messengers of death *is* the king's
   wrath,
   But a wise man will appease it.
15 In the light of the king's face *is* life,
   And his favor *is* like a cloud of the latter
   rain.

JOHN 4:31–54

IN the meantime His disciples urged Him,
saying, "Rabbi, eat."
32 But He said to them, "I have food to
eat of which you do not know."
33 Therefore the disciples said to one another, "Has anyone brought Him *anything*
to eat?"
34 Jesus said to them, "My food is to
do the will of Him who sent Me, and to
finish His work. 35 Do you not say, 'There
are still four months and *then* comes the
harvest'? Behold, I say to you, lift up your
eyes and look at the fields, for they are already white for harvest! 36 And he who
reaps receives wages, and gathers fruit for
eternal life, that both he who sows and he
who reaps may rejoice together. 37 For in
this the saying is true: 'One sows and another reaps.' 38 I sent you to reap that for
which you have not labored; others have
labored, and you have entered into their
labors."
39 And many of the Samaritans of that
city believed in Him because of the word

of the woman who testified, "He told me
all that I *ever* did." 40 So when the Samaritans had come to Him, they urged Him
to stay with them; and He stayed there
two days. 41 And many more believed because of His own word.
42 Then they said to the woman, "Now
we believe, not because of what you said,
for we ourselves have heard *Him* and we
know that this is indeed the Christ, the
Savior of the world."
43 Now after the two days He departed
from there and went to Galilee. 44 For Jesus
Himself testified that a prophet has no
honor in his own country. 45 So when He
came to Galilee, the Galileans received Him,
having seen all the things He did in Jerusalem at the feast; for they also had gone to
the feast.
46 So Jesus came again to Cana of Galilee
where He had made the water wine. And
there was a certain nobleman whose son
was sick at Capernaum. 47 When he heard
that Jesus had come out of Judea into Galilee, he went to Him and implored Him
to come down and heal his son, for he
was at the point of death. 48 Then Jesus
said to him, "Unless you *people* see signs
and wonders, you will by no means believe."
49 The nobleman said to Him, "Sir, come
down before my child dies!"
50 Jesus said to him, "Go your way; your
son lives." So the man believed the word
that Jesus spoke to him, and he went his
way. 51 And as he was now going down,
his servants met him and told *him,* saying,
"Your son lives!"
52 Then he inquired of them the hour
when he got better. And they said to him,
"Yesterday at the seventh hour the fever
left him." 53 So the father knew that *it was*
at the same hour in which Jesus said to
him, "Your son lives." And he himself believed, and his whole household.
54 This again *is* the second sign Jesus did
when He had come out of Judea into
Galilee.

◆◆◆◆

Reading 137—Submitted to God
John 5:19

T he secret of our Lord's holy speech was that He habitually submitted
His intelligence to His Father. Whenever problems pressed on the human
side, as they did in the temptation, our Lord had within Himself the divine
remembrance that every problem had been solved in counsel with His Father

before He became incarnate (cf. Rev. 13:8), and that therefore the one thing for Him was to do the will of His Father, and to do it in His Father's way. Satan tried to hasten Him, tried to make Him face the problems as a Man, and do God's will in His own way: "The Son can do nothing of Himself, but what He sees the Father do" (John 5:19, RV). . . .

The danger with us is that we will only submit our minds to New Testament teaching where the light of our experience shines. "If we walk in the light"—as our experience is in the light? No, "if we walk in the light as He is in the light . . ." We have to keep in the light that God is in, not in the rays of the light of our experience. There are phases of God's truth that cannot be experienced, and as long as we stay in the narrow grooves of our experience we shall never become God-like, but specialists in certain doctrines—Christian oddities. We have to be specialists in devotion to Jesus Christ and in nothing else. If we want to know Jesus Christ's idea of a saint and to find out what holiness means, we must not only read pamphlets about sanctification, we must face ourselves with Jesus Christ, and as we do so He will make us face ourselves with God. (*MORAL FOUND.*)

2 SAMUEL 5:1—6:23

THEN all the tribes of Israel came to David at Hebron and spoke, saying, "Indeed we *are* your bone and your flesh. 2 Also, in time past, when Saul was king over us, you were the one who led Israel out and brought them in; and the LORD said to you, 'You shall shepherd My people Israel, and be ruler over Israel.' " 3 Therefore all the elders of Israel came to the king at Hebron, and King David made a covenant with them at Hebron before the LORD. And they anointed David king over Israel. 4 David *was* thirty years old when he began to reign, *and* he reigned forty years. 5 In Hebron he reigned over Judah seven years and six months, and in Jerusalem he reigned thirty-three years over all Israel and Judah.

6 And the king and his men went to Jerusalem against the Jebusites, the inhabitants of the land, who spoke to David, saying, "You shall not come in here; but the blind and the lame will repel you," thinking, "David cannot come in here." 7 Nevertheless David took the stronghold of Zion (that *is,* the City of David).

8 Now David said on that day, "Whoever climbs up by way of the water shaft and defeats the Jebusites (the lame and the blind, *who are* hated by David's soul), *he shall be chief and captain.*" Therefore they say, "The blind and the lame shall not come into the house."

9 Then David dwelt in the stronghold, and called it the City of David. And David built all around from the Millo and inward. 10 So David went on and became great, and the LORD God of hosts *was* with him.

11 Then Hiram king of Tyre sent messengers to David, and cedar trees, and carpenters and masons. And they built David a house. 12 So David knew that the LORD had established him as king over Israel, and that He had exalted His kingdom for the sake of His people Israel.

13 And David took more concubines and wives from Jerusalem, after he had come from Hebron. Also more sons and daughters were born to David. 14 Now these *are* the names of those who were born to him in Jerusalem: Shammua, Shobab, Nathan, Solomon, 15 Ibhar, Elishua, Nepheg, Japhia, 16 Elishama, Eliada, and Eliphelet.

17 Now when the Philistines heard that they had anointed David king over Israel, all the Philistines went up to search for David. And David heard *of it* and went down to the stronghold. 18 The Philistines also went and deployed themselves in the Valley of Rephaim. 19 So David inquired of the LORD, saying, "Shall I go up against the Philistines? Will You deliver them into my hand?"

And the LORD said to David, "Go up, for I will doubtless deliver the Philistines into your hand."

20 So David went to Baal Perazim, and David defeated them there; and he said, "The LORD has broken through my enemies before me, like a breakthrough of water." Therefore he called the name of that place Baal Perazim. 21 And they left their images there, and David and his men carried them away.

22 Then the Philistines went up once again and deployed themselves in the Valley of Rephaim. 23 Therefore David inquired

of the LORD, and He said, "You shall not go up; circle around behind them, and come upon them in front of the mulberry trees. 24 And it shall be, when you hear the sound of marching in the tops of the mulberry trees, then you shall advance quickly. For then the LORD will go out before you to strike the camp of the Philistines." 25 And David did so, as the LORD commanded him; and he drove back the Philistines from Geba as far as Gezer.

6 AGAIN David gathered all *the* choice men of Israel, thirty thousand. 2 And David arose and went with all the people who *were* with him from Baale Judah to bring up from there the ark of God, whose name is called by the Name, the LORD of Hosts, who dwells *between* the cherubim. 3 So they set the ark of God on a new cart, and brought it out of the house of Abinadab, which *was* on the hill; and Uzzah and Ahio, the sons of Abinadab, drove the new cart. 4 And they brought it out of the house of Abinadab, which *was* on the hill, accompanying the ark of God; and Ahio went before the ark. 5 Then David and all the house of Israel played *music* before the LORD on all kinds of *instruments of* fir wood, on harps, on stringed instruments, on tambourines, on sistrums, and on cymbals.

6 And when they came to Nachon's threshing floor, Uzzah put out *his hand* to the ark of God and took hold of it, for the oxen stumbled. 7 Then the anger of the LORD was aroused against Uzzah, and God struck him there for *his* error; and he died there by the ark of God. 8 And David became angry because of the LORD's outbreak against Uzzah; and he called the name of the place Perez Uzzah to this day.

9 David was afraid of the LORD that day; and he said, "How can the ark of the LORD come to me?" 10 So David would not move the ark of the LORD with him into the City of David; but David took it aside into the house of Obed-Edom the Gittite. 11 The ark of the LORD remained in the house of Obed-Edom the Gittite three months. And the LORD blessed Obed-Edom and all his household.

12 Now it was told King David, saying, "The LORD has blessed the house of Obed-Edom and all that *belongs* to him, because of the ark of God." So David went and brought up the ark of God from the house of Obed-Edom to the City of David with gladness. 13 And so it was, when those bearing the ark of the LORD had gone six paces, that he sacrificed oxen and fatted sheep. 14 Then David danced before the LORD

with all *his* might; and David *was* wearing a linen ephod. 15 So David and all the house of Israel brought up the ark of the LORD with shouting and with the sound of the trumpet.

16 Now as the ark of the LORD came into the City of David, Michal, Saul's daughter, looked through a window and saw King David leaping and whirling before the LORD; and she despised him in her heart. 17 So they brought the ark of the LORD, and set it in its place in the midst of the tabernacle that David had erected for it. Then David offered burnt offerings and peace offerings before the LORD. 18 And when David had finished offering burnt offerings and peace offerings, he blessed the people in the name of the LORD of hosts. 19 Then he distributed among all the people, among the whole multitude of Israel, both the women and the men, to everyone a loaf of bread, a piece *of meat,* and a cake of raisins. So all the people departed, everyone to his house.

20 Then David returned to bless his household. And Michal the daughter of Saul came out to meet David, and said, "How glorious was the king of Israel today, uncovering himself today in the eyes of the maids of his servants, as one of the base fellows shamelessly uncovers himself!"

21 So David said to Michal, "*It was* before the LORD, who chose me instead of your father and all his house, to appoint me ruler over the people of the LORD, over Israel. Therefore I will play *music* before the LORD. 22 And I will be even more undignified than this, and will be humble in my own sight. But as for the maidservants of whom you have spoken, by them I will be held in honor."

23 Therefore Michal the daughter of Saul had no children to the day of her death.

PSALM 63:1–11

1   O God, You *are* my God;
    Early will I seek You;
    My soul thirsts for You;
    My flesh longs for You
    In a dry and thirsty land
    Where there is no water.

2   So I have looked for You in the
        sanctuary,
    To see Your power and Your glory.

3   Because Your lovingkindness *is* better
        than life,
    My lips shall praise You.

*T*he springs of love are in God,
not in us.   (UTMOST)

4   Thus I will bless You while I live;
I will lift up my hands in Your name.
5   My soul shall be satisfied as with
marrow and fatness,
And my mouth shall praise You with
joyful lips.

6   When I remember You on my bed,
I meditate on You in the *night* watches.
7   Because You have been my help,
Therefore in the shadow of Your wings
I will rejoice.
8   My soul follows close behind You;
Your right hand upholds me.

9   But those *who* seek my life, to destroy
it,
Shall go into the lower parts of the
earth.
10   They shall fall by the sword;
They shall be a portion for jackals.

11   But the king shall rejoice in God;
Everyone who swears by Him shall
glory;
But the mouth of those who speak lies
shall be stopped.

PROVERBS 16:16, 17

16   HOW much better to get wisdom than
gold!
And to get understanding is to be
chosen rather than silver.

17   The highway of the upright *is* to depart
from evil;
He who keeps his way preserves his
soul.

JOHN 5:1–23

AFTER this there was a feast of the Jews,
and Jesus went up to Jerusalem. 2 Now
there is in Jerusalem by the Sheep *Gate* a
pool, which is called in Hebrew, Bethesda,
having five porches. 3 In these lay a great
multitude of sick people, blind, lame, paralyzed, waiting for the moving of the water.
4 For an angel went down at a certain time
into the pool and stirred up the water; then
whoever stepped in first, after the stirring
of the water, was made well of whatever
disease he had. 5 Now a certain man was
there who had an infirmity thirty-eight
years. 6 When Jesus saw him lying there,
and knew that he already had been *in that
condition* a long time, He said to him, "Do
you want to be made well?"

7 The sick man answered Him, "Sir, I
have no man to put me into the pool when
the water is stirred up; but while I am coming, another steps down before me."

8 Jesus said to him, "Rise, take up your
bed and walk." 9 And immediately the man
was made well, took up his bed, and walked.

And that day was the Sabbath. 10 The
Jews therefore said to him who was cured,
"It is the Sabbath; it is not lawful for you
to carry your bed."

11 He answered them, "He who made
me well said to me, 'Take up your bed and
walk.' "

12 Then they asked him, "Who is the Man
who said to you, 'Take up your bed and
walk'?" 13 But the one who was healed did
not know who it was, for Jesus had withdrawn, a multitude being in *that* place.
14 Afterward Jesus found him in the temple,
and said to him, "See, you have been made
well. Sin no more, lest a worse thing come
upon you."

15 The man departed and told the Jews
that it was Jesus who had made him well.

16 For this reason the Jews persecuted
Jesus, and sought to kill Him, because He
had done these things on the Sabbath.
17 But Jesus answered them, "My Father
has been working until now, and I have
been working."

18 Therefore the Jews sought all the more
to kill Him, because He not only broke
the Sabbath, but also said that God was
His Father, making Himself equal with
God. 19 Then Jesus answered and said to
them, "Most assuredly, I say to you, the
Son can do nothing of Himself, but what
He sees the Father do; for whatever He
does, the Son also does in like manner.

*O*ur Lord never drew power from
Himself, He drew it always . . . from
His Father.   (MORAL FOUND.)

20 For the Father loves the Son, and shows
Him all things that He Himself does; and
He will show Him greater works than these,
that you may marvel. 21 For as the Father
raises the dead and gives life to *them*, even
so the Son gives life to whom He will.
22 For the Father judges no one, but has
committed all judgment to the Son,

23 that all should honor the Son just as they honor the Father. He who does not honor the Son does not honor the Father who sent Him.

◆◆◆

Reading 138—Beyond Convictions
John 5:44

Up to the time of the Resurrection, the disciples saw only along the line of their old narrow Jewish prejudices. When they received the Holy Spirit from the risen Lord, the operation performed on the inside enabled them to see along the line of Christ's revelation (see Luke 24:31, 45). What takes place at the new birth is an explosion on the inside (a literal explosion, not a theoretical one) that opens all the doors that have been closed. Life becomes larger; there is the incoming of a totally new point of view.

The way a searchlight works is a very good illustration for prejudice. A searchlight illumines only so much and no more; but let daylight come, and you find a thousand and one things the searchlight did not reveal. . . .

Christianity is not walking in the light of our convictions, but walking in the light of the Lord, a very different thing. Convictions are necessary, but only as stepping-stones to all that God wants us to be. . . . We have to get into the white light of Jesus Christ where He is easily first—not our experience of Him first, but Jesus Christ Himself first, and our experience the evidence that we have seen Him.   (*GLORY*)

2 SAMUEL 7:1—8:18

NOW it came to pass when the king was dwelling in his house, and the LORD had given him rest from all his enemies all around, 2 that the king said to Nathan the prophet, "See now, I dwell in a house of cedar, but the ark of God dwells inside tent curtains."

3 Then Nathan said to the king, "Go, do all that *is* in your heart, for the LORD *is* with you."

4 But it happened that night that the word of the LORD came to Nathan, saying, 5 "Go and tell My servant David, 'Thus says the LORD: "Would you build a house for Me to dwell in? 6 For I have not dwelt in a house since the time that I brought the children of Israel up from Egypt, even to this day, but have moved about in a tent and in a tabernacle. 7 Wherever I have moved about with all the children of Israel, have I ever spoken a word to anyone from the tribes of Israel, whom I commanded to shepherd My people Israel, saying, 'Why have you not built Me a house of cedar?' " ' 8 Now therefore, thus shall you say to My servant David, 'Thus says the LORD of hosts: "I took you from the sheepfold, from following the sheep, to be ruler over My people, over Israel. 9 And I have been with you wherever you have gone, and have cut off all your enemies from before you, and have made you a great name, like the name of the great men who *are* on the earth. 10 Moreover I will appoint a place for My people Israel, and will plant them, that they may dwell in a place of their own and move no more; nor shall the sons of wickedness oppress them anymore, as previously, 11 since the time that I commanded judges *to be* over My people Israel, and have caused you to rest from all your enemies. Also the LORD tells you that He will make you a house.

12 "When your days are fulfilled and you rest with your fathers, I will set up your seed after you, who will come from your body, and I will establish his kingdom. 13 He shall build a house for My name, and I will establish the throne of his kingdom forever. 14 I will be his Father, and he shall be My son. If he commits iniquity, I will chasten him with the rod of men and with the blows of the sons of men. 15 But My mercy shall not depart from him,

as I took *it* from Saul, whom I removed from before you. 16 And your house and your kingdom shall be established forever before you. Your throne shall be established forever.' " "

17 According to all these words and according to all this vision, so Nathan spoke to David.

18 Then King David went in and sat before the LORD; and he said: "Who *am* I, O Lord GOD? And what is my house, that You have brought me this far? 19 And yet this was a small thing in Your sight, O Lord GOD; and You have also spoken of Your servant's house for a great while to come. *Is* this the manner of man, O Lord GOD? 20 Now what more can David say to You? For You, Lord GOD, know Your servant. 21 For Your word's sake, and according to Your own heart, You have done all these great things, to make Your servant know *them.* 22 Therefore You are great, O Lord GOD. For *there is* none like You, nor *is there any* God besides You, according to all that we have heard with our ears. 23 And who *is* like Your people, like Israel, the one nation on the earth whom God went to redeem for Himself as a people, to make for Himself a name—and to do for Yourself great and awesome deeds for Your land—before Your people whom You redeemed for Yourself from Egypt, the nations, and their gods? 24 For You have made Your people Israel Your very own people forever; and You, LORD, have become their God.

25 "Now, O LORD God, the word which You have spoken concerning Your servant and concerning his house, establish *it* forever and do as You have said. 26 So let Your name be magnified forever, saying, 'The LORD of hosts *is* the God over Israel.' And let the house of Your servant David be established before You. 27 For You, O LORD of hosts, God of Israel, have revealed *this* to Your servant, saying, 'I will build you a house.' Therefore Your servant has found it in his heart to pray this prayer to You.

---

*T*he majority of us waste our time in mere impulses in prayer. (BIB. PSYCH.)

---

28 "And now, O Lord GOD, You are God, and Your words are true, and You have promised this goodness to Your servant. 29 Now therefore, let it please You to bless the house of Your servant, that it may continue before You forever; for You, O Lord GOD, have spoken *it,* and with Your blessing let the house of Your servant be blessed forever."

8 AFTER this it came to pass that David attacked the Philistines and subdued them. And David took Metheg Ammah from the hand of the Philistines.

2 Then he defeated Moab. Forcing them down to the ground, he measured them off with a line. With two lines he measured off those to be put to death, and with one full line those to be kept alive. So the Moabites became David's servants, *and* brought tribute.

3 David also defeated Hadadezer the son of Rehob, king of Zobah, as he went to recover his territory at the River Euphrates. 4 David took from him one thousand *chariots,* seven hundred horsemen, and twenty thousand foot soldiers. Also David hamstrung all the chariot horses, except that he spared *enough* of them for one hundred chariots.

5 When the Syrians of Damascus came to help Hadadezer king of Zobah, David killed twenty-two thousand of the Syrians. 6 Then David put garrisons in Syria of Damascus; and the Syrians became David's servants, *and* brought tribute. So the LORD preserved David wherever he went. 7 And David took the shields of gold that had belonged to the servants of Hadadezer, and brought them to Jerusalem. 8 Also from Betah and from Berothai, cities of Hadadezer, King David took a large amount of bronze.

9 When Toi king of Hamath heard that David had defeated all the army of Hadadezer, 10 then Toi sent Joram his son to King David, to greet him and bless him, because he had fought against Hadadezer and defeated him (for Hadadezer had been at war with Toi); and *Joram* brought with him articles of silver, articles of gold, and articles of bronze. 11 King David also dedicated these to the LORD, along with the silver and gold that he had dedicated from all the nations which he had subdued—12 from Syria, from Moab, from the people of Ammon, from the Philistines, from Amalek, and from the spoil of Hadadezer the son of Rehob, king of Zobah.

13 And David made *himself* a name when he returned from killing eighteen thousand Syrians in the Valley of Salt. 14 He also put garrisons in Edom; throughout all Edom he put garrisons, and all the Edomites became David's servants. And the LORD preserved David wherever he went.

15 So David reigned over all Israel; and David administered judgment and justice

to all his people. 16 Joab the son of Zeruiah *was* over the army; Jehoshaphat the son of Ahilud *was* recorder; 17 Zadok the son of Ahitub and Ahimelech the son of Abiathar *were* the priests; Seraiah *was* the scribe; 18 Benaiah the son of Jehoiada *was over* both the Cherethites and the Pelethites; and David's sons were chief ministers.

PSALM 64:1–10

1 HEAR my voice, O God, in my meditation;
   Preserve my life from fear of the enemy.
2 Hide me from the secret plots of the wicked,
   From the rebellion of the workers of iniquity,
3 Who sharpen their tongue like a sword,
   And bend *their bows to shoot* their arrows—bitter words,
4 That they may shoot in secret at the blameless;
   Suddenly they shoot at him and do not fear.

5 They encourage themselves *in* an evil matter;
   They talk of laying snares secretly;
   They say, "Who will see them?"
6 They devise iniquities:
   "We have perfected a shrewd scheme."
   Both the inward thought and the heart of man are deep.

7 But God shall shoot at them *with* an arrow;
   Suddenly they shall be wounded.
8 So He will make them stumble over their own tongue;
   All who see them shall flee away.
9 All men shall fear,
   And shall declare the work of God;
   For they shall wisely consider His doing.

10 The righteous shall be glad in the LORD, and trust in Him.
   And all the upright in heart shall glory.

PROVERBS 16:18, 19

18 PRIDE *goes* before destruction,
   And a haughty spirit before a fall.
19 Better *to be* of a humble spirit with the lowly,
   Than to divide the spoil with the proud.

JOHN 5:24–47

"MOST assuredly, I say to you, he who hears My word and believes in Him who sent Me has everlasting life, and shall not come into judgment, but has passed from death into life. 25 Most assuredly, I say to you, the hour is coming, and now is, when the dead will hear the voice of the Son of God; and those who hear will live. 26 For as the Father has life in Himself, so He has granted the Son to have life in Himself; 27 and has given Him authority to execute judgment also, because He is the Son of Man. 28 Do not marvel at this; for the hour is coming in which all who are in the graves will hear His voice 29 and come forth—those who have done good, to the resurrection of life, and those who have done evil, to the resurrection of condemnation. 30 I can of Myself do nothing. As I hear, I judge; and My judgment is righteous, because I do not seek My own will but the will of the Father who sent Me.

31 "If I bear witness of Myself, My witness is not true. 32 There is another who bears witness of Me, and I know that the witness which He witnesses of Me is true. 33 You have sent to John, and he has borne witness to the truth. 34 Yet I do not receive testimony from man, but I say these things that you may be saved. 35 He was the burning and shining lamp, and you were willing for a time to rejoice in his light. 36 But I have a greater witness than John's; for the works which the Father has given Me to finish—the very works that I do—bear witness of Me, that the Father has sent Me. 37 And the Father Himself, who sent Me, has testified of Me. You have neither heard His voice at any time, nor seen His form. 38 But you do not have His word abiding in you, because whom He sent, Him you do not believe. 39 You search the Scriptures, for in them you think you have eternal life; and these are they which testify of Me.

---

*O*ur Lord's life is the exhibition of eternal life in time.   (GOOD)

---

40 But you are not willing to come to Me that you may have life.
41 "I do not receive honor from men. 42 But I know you, that you do not have the love of God in you. 43 I have come in My Father's name, and you do not receive Me; if another comes in his own name,

him you will receive. 44 How can you believe, who receive honor from one another, and do not seek the honor that *comes* from the only God? 45 Do not think that I shall accuse you to the Father; there is *one* who accuses you—Moses, in whom you trust. 46 For if you believed Moses, you would believe Me; for he wrote about Me. 47 But if you do not believe his writings, how will you believe My words?"

▰▰▰▰

Reading 139—Trust in Fact
Proverbs 16:20

It is not easy to say that God is love when everything that happens actually gives the lie to it. Everyone's soul represents some kind of battlefield. The point for each one is whether we will hang in, as Job did, and say "Though things look black, I will trust in God." *(BAFFLED)*

It is very easy to trust in God when there is no difficulty, but that is not trust at all, it is simply letting the mind rest in a complacent mood; but when there is sickness in the house, when there is trouble, when there is death, where is our trust in God? *(CHRIS. DIS. 1)*

God has to deal with us on the death side as well as on the life side. It is all very well to know in theory that there are things we must not trust in, but another thing to know it in fact. When God deals with us on the death side He puts the sentence of death on everything we should not trust in, and we have a miserable time until we learn never anymore to trust in it, never anymore to look anywhere else than to God. It sometimes happens that hardly a day passes without God saying, "Don't trust there, that is dead."

(GOD'S WORKMANSHIP)

2 SAMUEL 9:1—10:19

NOW David said, "Is there still anyone who is left of the house of Saul, that I may show him kindness for Jonathan's sake?"

2 And *there was* a servant of the house of Saul whose name *was* Ziba. So when they had called him to David, the king said to him, "*Are* you Ziba?"

He said, "At your service!"

3 Then the king said, "*Is* there not still someone of the house of Saul, to whom I may show the kindness of God?"

And Ziba said to the king, "There is still a son of Jonathan *who is* lame in *his* feet."

4 So the king said to him, "Where *is* he?"

And Ziba said to the king, "Indeed he *is* in the house of Machir the son of Ammiel, in Lo Debar."

5 Then King David sent and brought him out of the house of Machir the son of Ammiel, from Lo Debar.

6 Now when Mephibosheth the son of Jonathan, the son of Saul, had come to David, he fell on his face and prostrated himself. Then David said, "Mephibosheth?"

And he answered, "Here is your servant!"

7 So David said to him, "Do not fear, for I will surely show you kindness for Jonathan your father's sake, and will restore to you all the land of Saul your grandfather; and you shall eat bread at my table continually."

8 Then he bowed himself, and said, "What *is* your servant, that you should look upon such a dead dog as I?"

9 And the king called to Ziba, Saul's servant, and said to him, "I have given to your master's son all that belonged to Saul and to all his house. 10 You therefore, and your sons and your servants, shall work the land for him, and you shall bring in *the harvest,* that your master's son may have food to eat. But Mephibosheth your master's son shall eat bread at my table always." Now Ziba had fifteen sons and twenty servants.

11 Then Ziba said to the king, "According to all that my lord the king has commanded his servant, so will your servant do."

"As for Mephibosheth," *said the king,* "he shall eat at my table like one of the king's sons." 12 Mephibosheth had a young son whose name *was* Micha. And all who dwelt in the house of Ziba *were* servants of Mephibosheth. 13 So Mephibosheth dwelt in Jerusalem, for he ate continually at the king's table. And he was lame in both his feet.

10 IT happened after this that the king of the people of Ammon died, and Hanun his son reigned in his place. 2 Then David said, "I will show kindness to Hanun the son of Nahash, as his father showed kindness to me."

So David sent by the hand of his servants to comfort him concerning his father. And David's servants came into the land of the people of Ammon. 3 And the princes of the people of Ammon said to Hanun their lord, "Do you think that David really honors your father because he has sent comforters to you? Has David not *rather* sent his servants to you to search the city, to spy it out, and to overthrow it?"

4 Therefore Hanun took David's servants, shaved off half of their beards, cut off their garments in the middle, at their buttocks, and sent them away. 5 When they told David, he sent to meet them, because the men were greatly ashamed. And the king said, "Wait at Jericho until your beards have grown, and *then* return."

6 When the people of Ammon saw that they had made themselves repulsive to David, the people of Ammon sent and hired the Syrians of Beth Rehob and the Syrians of Zoba, twenty thousand foot soldiers; and from the king of Maacah one thousand men, and from Ish-Tob twelve thousand men. 7 Now when David heard *of it*, he sent Joab and all the army of the mighty men. 8 Then the people of Ammon came out and put themselves in battle array at the entrance of the gate. And the Syrians of Zoba, Beth Rehob, Ish-Tob, and Maacah *were* by themselves in the field.

9 When Joab saw that the battle line was against him before and behind, he chose some of Israel's best and put *them* in battle array against the Syrians. 10 And the rest of the people he put under the command of Abishai his brother, that he might set *them* in battle array against the people of Ammon. 11 Then he said, "If the Syrians are too strong for me, then you shall help me; but if the people of Ammon are too strong for you, then I will come and help you. 12 Be of good courage, and let us be strong for our people and for the cities of our God. And may the LORD do *what is* good in His sight."

13 So Joab and the people who *were* with him drew near for the battle against the Syrians, and they fled before him. 14 When the people of Ammon saw that the Syrians were fleeing, they also fled before Abishai, and entered the city. So Joab returned from the people of Ammon and went to Jerusalem.

15 When the Syrians saw that they had been defeated by Israel, they gathered together. 16 Then Hadadezer sent and brought out the Syrians who *were* beyond the River, and they came to Helam. And Shobach the commander of Hadadezer's army *went* before them. 17 When it was told David, he gathered all Israel, crossed over the Jordan, and came to Helam. And the Syrians set themselves in battle array against David and fought with him. 18 Then the Syrians fled before Israel; and David killed seven hundred charioteers and forty thousand horsemen of the Syrians, and struck Shobach the commander of their army, who died there. 19 And when all the kings *who were* servants to Hadadezer saw that they were defeated by Israel, they made peace with Israel and served them. So the Syrians were afraid to help the people of Ammon anymore.

PSALM 65:1–8

1 PRAISE is awaiting You, O God, in Zion;
And to You the vow shall be performed.

2 O You who hear prayer,
To You all flesh will come.

3 Iniquities prevail against me;
As for our transgressions,
You will provide atonement for them.

4 Blessed *is the man* You choose,
And cause to approach *You,*
That he may dwell in Your courts.
We shall be satisfied with the goodness of Your house,
Of Your holy temple.

5 *By* awesome deeds in righteousness You will answer us,
O God of our salvation,
You who are the confidence of all the ends of the earth,
And of the far-off seas;

It is always a wonder when God answers prayer. (ASK)

6 Who established the mountains by His strength,

Being clothed with power;

7 You who still the noise of the seas,
The noise of their waves,
And the tumult of the peoples.

8 They also who dwell in the farthest parts
are afraid of Your signs;
You make the outgoings of the morning
and evening rejoice.

PROVERBS 16:20, 21

20 HE who heeds the word wisely will
find good,
And whoever trusts in the LORD, happy
is he.

21 The wise in heart will be called prudent,
And sweetness of the lips increases
learning.

JOHN 6:1–21

AFTER these things Jesus went over the Sea of Galilee, which is *the Sea* of Tiberias. 2 Then a great multitude followed Him, because they saw His signs which He performed on those who were diseased. 3 And Jesus went up on the mountain, and there He sat with His disciples.

4 Now the Passover, a feast of the Jews, was near. 5 Then Jesus lifted up *His* eyes, and seeing a great multitude coming toward Him, He said to Philip, "Where shall we buy bread, that these may eat?" 6 But this He said to test him, for He Himself knew what He would do.

7 Philip answered Him, "Two hundred denarii worth of bread is not sufficient for them, that every one of them may have a little."

8 One of His disciples, Andrew, Simon Peter's brother, said to Him, 9 "There is a lad here who has five barley loaves and two small fish, but what are they among so many?"

10 Then Jesus said, "Make the people sit down." Now there was much grass in the place. So the men sat down, in number about five thousand. 11 And Jesus took the loaves, and when He had given thanks He distributed *them* to the disciples, and the disciples to those sitting down; and likewise of the fish, as much as they wanted. 12 So when they were filled, He said to His disciples, "Gather up the fragments that remain, so that nothing is lost." 13 Therefore they gathered *them* up, and filled twelve baskets with the fragments of the five barley loaves which were left over by those who had eaten. 14 Then those men, when they had seen the sign that Jesus did, said, "This is truly the Prophet who is to come into the world."

15 Therefore when Jesus perceived that they were about to come and take Him by force to make Him king, He departed again to the mountain by Himself alone.

16 Now when evening came, His disciples went down to the sea, 17 got into the boat, and went over the sea toward Capernaum. And it was already dark, and Jesus had not come to them. 18 Then the sea arose because a great wind was blowing. 19 So when they had rowed about three or four miles, they saw Jesus walking on the sea and drawing near the boat; and they were afraid. 20 But He said to them, "It is I; do not be afraid." 21 Then they willingly received Him into the boat, and immediately the boat was at the land where they were going.

◆◆◆

*Reading 140—*Our Eternal Life
John 6:47

Holy Spirit, salvation, and eternal life are interchangeable terms. "Holy Spirit" is the experiential name for eternal life working in human beings here and now. The only thing that makes eternal life actual is the entrance of the Holy Spirit by commitment to Jesus Christ. Our beliefs will mock us unless something comes into us from God, because nothing has any power to alter us except the incoming of the life of God. The Holy Spirit is the One who makes experientially real in us what Jesus Christ did for us. The Holy Spirit is the deity in proceeding power who applies the atonement to our experience.

Jesus Christ came to redeem us, to put us right with God, to deliver us from the power of death, to reveal God the Father. When we receive the Holy Spirit, He will make experientially real in us all that Jesus Christ came to do. The great need for men and women is to receive the Holy Spirit. Our creeds teach us to believe in the Holy Spirit; the New Testament says we must receive Him (see Luke 11:13). Are you powerless in your life? Then get at reality! Ask God for the Holy Spirit; that is, His eternal life, and you will begin to manifest in your mortal flesh the life of Jesus.   (GLORY)

2 SAMUEL 11:1—12:31

IT happened in the spring of the year, at the time when kings go out *to battle,* that David sent Joab and his servants with him, and all Israel; and they destroyed the people of Ammon and besieged Rabbah. But David remained at Jerusalem.

2 Then it happened one evening that David arose from his bed and walked on the roof of the king's house. And from the roof he saw a woman bathing, and the woman *was* very beautiful to behold. 3 So David sent and inquired about the woman. And *someone* said, *"Is* this not Bathsheba, the daughter of Eliam, the wife of Uriah the Hittite?" 4 Then David sent messengers, and took her; and she came to him, and he lay with her, for she was cleansed from her impurity; and she returned to her house. 5 And the woman conceived; so she sent and told David, and said, "I *am* with child."

6 Then David sent to Joab, *saying,* "Send me Uriah the Hittite." And Joab sent Uriah to David. 7 When Uriah had come to him, David asked how Joab was doing, and how the people were doing, and how the war prospered. 8 And David said to Uriah, "Go down to your house and wash your feet." So Uriah departed from the king's house, and a gift *of food* from the king followed him. 9 But Uriah slept at the door of the king's house with all the servants of his lord, and did not go down to his house. 10 So when they told David, saying, "Uriah did not go down to his house," David said to Uriah, "Did you not come from a journey? Why did you not go down to your house?"

11 And Uriah said to David, "The ark and Israel and Judah are dwelling in tents, and my lord Joab and the servants of my lord are encamped in the open fields. Shall I then go to my house to eat and drink, and to lie with my wife? *As* you live, and *as* your soul lives, I will not do this thing."

12 Then David said to Uriah, "Wait here today also, and tomorrow I will let you depart." So Uriah remained in Jerusalem that day and the next. 13 Now when David called him, he ate and drank before him; and he made him drunk. And at evening he went out to lie on his bed with the servants of his lord, but he did not go down to his house.

14 In the morning it happened that David wrote a letter to Joab and sent *it* by the hand of Uriah. 15 And he wrote in the letter, saying, "Set Uriah in the forefront of the hottest battle, and retreat from him, that he may be struck down and die." 16 So it was, while Joab besieged the city, that he assigned Uriah to a place where he knew there *were* valiant men. 17 Then the men of the city came out and fought with Joab. And *some* of the people of the servants of David fell; and Uriah the Hittite died also.

18 Then Joab sent and told David all the things concerning the war, 19 and charged the messenger, saying, "When you have finished telling the matters of the war to the king, 20 if it happens that the king's wrath rises, and he says to you: 'Why did you approach so near to the city when you fought? Did you not know that they would shoot from the wall? 21 Who struck Abimelech the son of Jerubbesheth? Was it not a woman who cast a piece of a millstone on him from the wall, so that he died in Thebez? Why did you go near the wall?'— then you shall say, 'Your servant Uriah the Hittite is dead also.' "

22 So the messenger went, and came and told David all that Joab had sent by him. 23 And the messenger said to David, "Surely the men prevailed against us and came out to us in the field; then we drove them back as far as the entrance of the gate. 24 The archers shot from the wall at your servants; and *some* of the king's servants are dead, and your servant Uriah the Hittite is dead also."

25 Then David said to the messenger, "Thus you shall say to Joab: 'Do not let this thing displease you, for the sword de-

vours one as well as another. Strengthen your attack against the city, and overthrow it.' So encourage him."

26 When the wife of Uriah heard that Uriah her husband was dead, she mourned for her husband. 27 And when her mourning was over, David sent and brought her to his house, and she became his wife and bore him a son. But the thing that David had done displeased the LORD.

12 THEN the LORD sent Nathan to David. And he came to him, and said to him: "There were two men in one city, one rich and the other poor. 2 The rich *man* had exceedingly many flocks and herds. 3 But the poor *man* had nothing, except one little ewe lamb which he had bought and nourished; and it grew up together with him and with his children. It ate of his own food and drank from his own cup and lay in his bosom; and it was like a daughter to him. 4 And a traveler came to the rich man, who refused to take from his own flock and from his own herd to prepare one for the wayfaring man who had come to him; but he took the poor man's lamb and prepared it for the man who had come to him."

5 So David's anger was greatly aroused against the man, and he said to Nathan, "*As* the LORD lives, the man who has done this shall surely die! 6 And he shall restore fourfold for the lamb, because he did this thing and because he had no pity."

7 Then Nathan said to David, "You *are* the man! Thus says the LORD God of Israel: 'I anointed you king over Israel, and I delivered you from the hand of Saul. 8 I gave you your master's house and your master's wives into your keeping, and gave you the house of Israel and Judah. And if *that had been* too little, I also would have given you much more! 9 Why have you despised the commandment of the LORD, to do evil in His sight? You have killed Uriah the Hittite with the sword; you have taken his wife *to be* your wife, and have killed him with the sword of the people of Ammon. 10 Now therefore, the sword shall never depart from your house, because you have despised Me, and have taken the wife of Uriah the Hittite to be your wife.' 11 Thus says the LORD: 'Behold, I will raise up adversity against you from your own house; and I will take your wives before your eyes and give *them* to your neighbor, and he shall lie with your wives in the sight of this sun. 12 For you did *it* secretly, but I will do this thing before all Israel, before the sun.' "

13 So David said to Nathan, "I have sinned against the LORD."

And Nathan said to David, "The LORD also has put away your sin; you shall not die. 14 However, because by this deed you have given great occasion to the enemies of the LORD to blaspheme, the child also *who is* born to you shall surely die." 15 Then Nathan departed to his house.

And the LORD struck the child that Uriah's wife bore to David, and it became ill. 16 David therefore pleaded with God for the child, and David fasted and went in and lay all night on the ground. 17 So the elders of his house arose *and went* to him, to raise him up from the ground. But he would not, nor did he eat food with them. 18 Then on the seventh day it came to pass that the child died. And the servants of David were afraid to tell him that the child was dead. For they said, "Indeed, while the child was alive, we spoke to him, and he would not heed our voice. How can we tell him that the child is dead? He may do some harm!"

19 When David saw that his servants were whispering, David perceived that the child was dead. Therefore David said to his servants, "Is the child dead?"

And they said, "He is dead."

20 So David arose from the ground, washed and anointed himself, and changed his clothes; and he went into the house of the LORD and worshiped. Then he went to his own house; and when he requested, they set food before him, and he ate. 21 Then his servants said to him, "What *is* this that you have done? You fasted and wept for the child *while he was* alive, but when the child died, you arose and ate food."

22 And he said, "While the child was alive, I fasted and wept; for I said, 'Who can tell *whether* the LORD will be gracious to me, that the child may live?' 23 But now he is dead; why should I fast? Can I bring him back again? I shall go to him, but he shall not return to me."

24 Then David comforted Bathsheba his wife, and went in to her and lay with her. So she bore a son, and he called his name Solomon. Now the LORD loved him, 25 and He sent *word* by the hand of Nathan the prophet: So he called his name Jedidiah, because of the LORD.

26 Now Joab fought against Rabbah of the people of Ammon, and took the royal city. 27 And Joab sent messengers to David, and said, "I have fought against Rabbah, and I have taken the city's water *supply*. 28 Now therefore, gather the rest of the

people together and encamp against the city and take it, lest I take the city and it be called after my name." 29 So David gathered all the people together and went to Rabbah, fought against it, and took it. 30 Then he took their king's crown from his head. Its weight *was* a talent of gold, with precious stones. And it was *set* on David's head. Also he brought out the spoil of the city in great abundance. 31 And he brought out the people who *were* in it, and put *them to work* with saws and iron picks and iron axes, and made them cross over to the brick works. So he did to all the cities of the people of Ammon. Then David and all the people returned to Jerusalem.

PSALM 65:9–13

9 YOU visit the earth and water it,
    You greatly enrich it;
    The river of God is full of water;
    You provide their grain,
    For so You have prepared it.
10 You water its ridges abundantly,
    You settle its furrows;
    You make it soft with showers,
    You bless its growth.

11 You crown the year with Your
        goodness,
    And Your paths drip *with* abundance.
12 They drop *on* the pastures of the
        wilderness,
    And the little hills rejoice on every side.
13 The pastures are clothed with flocks;
    The valleys also are covered with grain;
    They shout for joy, they also sing.

The joy of anything, from a blade of grass upwards, is to fulfill its created purpose.   (LOVE OF GOD)

PROVERBS 16:22–24

22 UNDERSTANDING *is* a wellspring
        of life to him who has it.
    But the correction of fools *is* folly.

23 The heart of the wise teaches his mouth,
    And adds learning to his lips.

24 Pleasant words *are like* a honeycomb,
    Sweetness to the soul and health to the
        bones.

JOHN 6:22–51

ON the following day, when the people who were standing on the other side of the sea saw that there was no other boat there, except that one which His disciples had entered, and that Jesus had not entered the boat with His disciples, but His disciples had gone away alone— 23 however, other boats came from Tiberias, near the place where they ate bread after the Lord had given thanks— 24 when the people therefore saw that Jesus was not there, nor His disciples, they also got into boats and came to Capernaum, seeking Jesus. 25 And when they found Him on the other side of the sea, they said to Him, "Rabbi, when did You come here?"

26 Jesus answered them and said, "Most assuredly, I say to you, you seek Me, not because you saw the signs, but because you ate of the loaves and were filled. 27 Do not labor for the food which perishes, but for the food which endures to everlasting life, which the Son of Man will give you, because God the Father has set His seal on Him."

28 Then they said to Him, "What shall we do, that we may work the works of God?"

29 Jesus answered and said to them, "This is the work of God, that you believe in Him whom He sent."

30 Therefore they said to Him, "What sign will You perform then, that we may see it and believe You? What work will You do? 31 Our fathers ate the manna in the desert; as it is written, 'He gave them bread from heaven to eat.' "

32 Then Jesus said to them, "Most assuredly, I say to you, Moses did not give you the bread from heaven, but My Father gives you the true bread from heaven. 33 For the bread of God is He who comes down from heaven and gives life to the world."

34 Then they said to Him, "Lord, give us this bread always."

35 And Jesus said to them, "I am the bread of life. He who comes to Me shall never hunger, and he who believes in Me shall never thirst. 36 But I said to you that you have seen Me and yet do not believe. 37 All that the Father gives Me will come to Me, and the one who comes to Me I will by no means cast out. 38 For I have come down from heaven, not to do My own will, but the will of Him who sent Me. 39 This is the will of the Father who sent Me, that of all He has given Me I should lose nothing, but should raise it up

at the last day. 40 And this is the will of Him who sent Me, that everyone who sees the Son and believes in Him may have everlasting life; and I will raise him up at the last day."

41 The Jews then complained about Him, because He said, "I am the bread which came down from heaven." 42 And they said, "Is not this Jesus, the son of Joseph, whose father and mother we know? How is it then that He says, 'I have come down from heaven'?"

43 Jesus therefore answered and said to them, "Do not murmur among yourselves. 44 No one can come to Me unless the Father who sent Me draws him; and I will raise him up at the last day. 45 It is written in the prophets, 'And they shall all be taught by God.' Therefore everyone who has heard and learned from the Father comes to Me. 46 Not that anyone has seen the Father, except He who is from God; He has seen the Father. 47 Most assuredly, I say to you, he who believes in Me has everlasting life. 48 I am the bread of life. 49 Your fathers ate the manna in the wilderness, and are dead. 50 This is the bread which comes down from heaven, that one may eat of it and not die. 51 I am the living bread which came down from heaven. If anyone eats of this bread, he will live forever; and the bread that I shall give is My flesh, which I shall give for the life of the world."

◆◆◆◆

Reading 141—The White Funeral
John 6:68

John 6 contains a description of the sifting out of the disciples from the crowd round about, until there were just the twelve left, and to them Jesus says—"Do you also want to go away?" Some who had been following Jesus had not gone too far to turn back, and "they went back and walked with Him no more." But Peter has gone too far to turn back and he says, "Lord, to whom shall we go?" There is a stage like that in our spiritual experience, we do not see the Guide ahead of us, we do not feel the joy of the Lord, there is no exhilaration, yet we have gone too far to go back, we are up against it now. It might be illustrated in the spiritual life by Tennyson's phrase, "a white funeral." When we go through the moral death to self-will we find we have committed ourselves, there are many things that must go to the "white funeral." At the first we have the idea that everything apart from Christ is bad; but there is much in our former life that is fascinating, any amount of paganism that is clear and vigorous, virtues that are good morally. But we have to discover they are not stamped with the right image and superscription, and if we are going to live the life of a saint we must go to the moral death of those things, make a termination of them, turn these good natural things into the spiritual.   (*Place Help*)

2 SAMUEL 13:1—14:33

AFTER this Absalom the son of David had a lovely sister, whose name *was* Tamar; and Amnon the son of David loved her. 2 Amnon was so distressed over his sister Tamar that he became sick; for she *was* a virgin. And it was improper for Amnon to do anything to her. 3 But Amnon had a friend whose name *was* Jonadab the son of Shimeah, David's brother. Now Jonadab *was* a very crafty man. 4 And he said to him, "Why *are* you, the king's son, becoming thinner day after day? Will you not tell me?"

Amnon said to him, "I love Tamar, my brother Absalom's sister."

5 So Jonadab said to him, "Lie down on your bed and pretend to be ill. And when your father comes to see you, say to him,

'Please let my sister Tamar come and give me food, and prepare the food in my sight, that I may see *it* and eat it from her hand.' " 6 Then Amnon lay down and pretended to be ill; and when the king came to see him, Amnon said to the king, "Please let Tamar my sister come and make a couple of cakes for me in my sight, that I may eat from her hand."

7 And David sent home to Tamar, saying, "Now go to your brother Amnon's house, and prepare food for him." 8 So Tamar went to her brother Amnon's house; and he was lying down. Then she took flour and kneaded *it,* made cakes in his sight, and baked the cakes. 9 And she took the pan and placed *them* out before him, but he refused to eat. Then Amnon said, "Have everyone go out from me." And they all went out from him. 10 Then Amnon said to Tamar, "Bring the food into the bedroom, that I may eat from your hand." And Tamar took the cakes which she had made, and brought *them* to Amnon her brother in the bedroom. 11 Now when she had brought *them* to him to eat, he took hold of her and said to her, "Come, lie with me, my sister."

12 But she answered him, "No, my brother, do not force me, for no such thing should be done in Israel. Do not do this disgraceful thing! 13 And I, where could I take my shame? And as for you, you would be like one of the fools in Israel. Now therefore, please speak to the king; for he will not withhold me from you." 14 However, he would not heed her voice; and being stronger than she, he forced her and lay with her.

15 Then Amnon hated her exceedingly, so that the hatred with which he hated her *was* greater than the love with which he had loved her. And Amnon said to her, "Arise, be gone!"

16 So she said to him, "No, indeed! This evil of sending me away *is* worse than the other that you did to me."

But he would not listen to her. 17 Then he called his servant who attended him, and said, "Here! Put this *woman* out, away from me, and bolt the door behind her." 18 Now she had on a robe of many colors, for the king's virgin daughters wore such apparel. And his servant put her out and bolted the door behind her.

19 Then Tamar put ashes on her head, and tore her robe of many colors that *was* on her, and laid her hand on her head and went away crying bitterly. 20 And Absalom her brother said to her, "Has Amnon your brother been with you? But now hold your peace, my sister. He *is* your brother; do not take this thing to heart." So Tamar remained desolate in her brother Absalom's house.

21 But when King David heard of all these things, he was very angry. 22 And Absalom spoke to his brother Amnon neither good nor bad. For Absalom hated Amnon, because he had forced his sister Tamar.

23 And it came to pass, after two full years, that Absalom had sheepshearers in Baal Hazor, which *is* near Ephraim; so Absalom invited all the king's sons. 24 Then Absalom came to the king and said, "Kindly note, your servant has sheepshearers; please, let the king and his servants go with your servant."

25 But the king said to Absalom, "No, my son, let us not all go now, lest we be a burden to you." Then he urged him, but he would not go; and he blessed him.

26 Then Absalom said, "If not, please let my brother Amnon go with us."

And the king said to him, "Why should he go with you?" 27 But Absalom urged him; so he let Amnon and all the king's sons go with him.

28 Now Absalom had commanded his servants, saying, "Watch now, when Amnon's heart is merry with wine, and when I say to you, 'Strike Amnon!' then kill him. Do not be afraid. Have I not commanded you? Be courageous and valiant." 29 So the servants of Absalom did to Amnon as Absalom had commanded. Then all the king's sons arose, and each one got on his mule and fled.

30 And it came to pass, while they were on the way, that news came to David, saying, "Absalom has killed all the king's sons, and not one of them is left!" 31 So the king arose and tore his garments and lay on the ground, and all his servants stood by with their clothes torn. 32 Then Jonadab the son of Shimeah, David's brother, answered and said, "Let not my lord suppose they have killed all the young men, the king's sons, for only Amnon is dead. For by the command of Absalom this has been determined from the day that he forced his sister Tamar. 33 Now therefore, let not my lord the king take the thing to his heart, to think that all the king's sons are dead. For only Amnon is dead."

34 Then Absalom fled. And the young man who was keeping watch lifted his eyes and looked, and there, many people were coming from the road on the hillside behind him. 35 And Jonadab said to the king, "Look, the king's sons are coming; as your servant said, so it is." 36 So it was, as soon

as he had finished speaking, that the king's sons indeed came, and they lifted up their voice and wept. Also the king and all his servants wept very bitterly.

37 But Absalom fled and went to Talmai the son of Ammihud, king of Geshur. And *David* mourned for his son every day. 38 So Absalom fled and went to Geshur, and was there three years. 39 And King David longed to go to Absalom. For he had been comforted concerning Amnon, because he was dead.

14 SO Joab the son of Zeruiah perceived that the king's heart *was* concerned about Absalom. 2 And Joab sent to Tekoa and brought from there a wise woman, and said to her, "Please pretend to be a mourner, and put on mourning apparel; do not anoint yourself with oil, but act like a woman who has been mourning a long time for the dead. 3 Go to the king and speak to him in this manner." So Joab put the words in her mouth.

4 And when the woman of Tekoa spoke to the king, she fell on her face to the ground and prostrated herself, and said, "Help, O king!"

5 Then the king said to her, "What troubles you?"

And she answered, "Indeed I *am* a widow, my husband is dead. 6 Now your maidservant had two sons; and the two fought with each other in the field, and *there was* no one to part them, but the one struck the other and killed him. 7 And now the whole family has risen up against your maidservant, and they said, 'Deliver him who struck his brother, that we may execute him for the life of his brother whom he killed; and we will destroy the heir also.' So they would extinguish my ember that is left, and leave to my husband *neither* name nor remnant on the earth."

8 Then the king said to the woman, "Go to your house, and I will give orders concerning you."

9 And the woman of Tekoa said to the king, "My lord, O king, *let* the iniquity *be* on me and on my father's house, and the king and his throne *be* guiltless."

10 So the king said, "Whoever says *anything* to you, bring him to me, and he shall not touch you anymore."

11 Then she said, "Please let the king remember the Lord your God, and do not permit the avenger of blood to destroy anymore, lest they destroy my son."

And he said, "*As* the Lord lives, not one hair of your son shall fall to the ground."

12 Therefore the woman said, "Please, let your maidservant speak *another* word to my lord the king."

And he said, "Say on."

13 So the woman said: "Why then have you schemed such a thing against the people of God? For the king speaks this thing as one who is guilty, *in that* the king does not bring his banished one home again. 14 For we will surely die and *become* like water spilled on the ground, which cannot be gathered up again. Yet God does not take away a life; but He devises means, so that His banished ones are not expelled from Him. 15 Now therefore, I have come to speak of this thing to my lord the king because the people have made me afraid. And your maidservant said, 'I will now speak to the king; it may be that the king will perform the request of his maidservant. 16 For the king will hear and deliver his maidservant from the hand of the man *who would* destroy me and my son together from the inheritance of God.' 17 Your maidservant said, 'The word of my lord the king will now be comforting; for as the angel of God, so *is* my lord the king in discerning good and evil. And may the Lord your God be with you.'"

18 Then the king answered and said to the woman, "Please do not hide from me anything that I ask you."

And the woman said, "Please, let my lord the king speak."

19 So the king said, "*Is* the hand of Joab with you in all this?" And the woman answered and said, "*As* you live, my lord the king, no one can turn to the right hand or to the left from anything that my lord the king has spoken. For your servant Joab commanded me, and he put all these words in the mouth of your maidservant. 20 To bring about this change of affairs your servant Joab has done this thing; but my lord *is* wise, according to the wisdom of the angel of God, to know everything that *is* in the earth."

21 And the king said to Joab, "All right, I have granted this thing. Go therefore, bring back the young man Absalom."

22 Then Joab fell to the ground on his face and bowed himself, and thanked the king. And Joab said, "Today your servant knows that I have found favor in your sight, my lord, O king, in that the king has fulfilled the request of his servant." 23 So Joab arose and went to Geshur, and brought Absalom to Jerusalem. 24 And the king said, "Let him return to his own house, but do not let him see my face." So Absalom returned to his own house, but did not see the king's face.

25 Now in all Israel there was no one who was praised as much as Absalom for his good looks. From the sole of his foot to the crown of his head there was no blemish in him. 26 And when he cut the hair of his head—at the end of every year he cut *it* because it was heavy on him—when he cut it, he weighed the hair of his head at two hundred shekels according to the king's standard. 27 To Absalom were born three sons, and one daughter whose name *was* Tamar. She was a woman of beautiful appearance.

28 And Absalom dwelt two full years in Jerusalem, but did not see the king's face. 29 Therefore Absalom sent for Joab, to send him to the king, but he would not come to him. And when he sent again the second time, he would not come. 30 So he said to his servants, "See, Joab's field is near mine, and he has barley there; go and set it on fire." And Absalom's servants set the field on fire.

31 Then Joab arose and came to Absalom's house, and said to him, "Why have your servants set my field on fire?"

32 And Absalom answered Joab, "Look, I sent to you, saying, 'Come here, so that I may send you to the king, to say, "Why have I come from Geshur? *It would be* better for me *to be* there still." ' Now therefore, let me see the king's face; but if there is iniquity in me, let him execute me."

33 So Joab went to the king and told him. And when he had called for Absalom, he came to the king and bowed himself on his face to the ground before the king. Then the king kissed Absalom.

PSALM 66:1–7

1 MAKE a joyful shout to God, all the earth!

2 Sing out the honor of His name; Make His praise glorious.

3 Say to God, "How awesome are Your works! Through the greatness of Your power Your enemies shall submit themselves to You.

4 All the earth shall worship You And sing praises to You; They shall sing praises *to* Your name."   Selah

5 Come and see the works of God; *He is* awesome *in His* doing toward the sons of men.

6 He turned the sea into dry *land;* They went through the river on foot.

There we will rejoice in Him.

7 He rules by His power forever; His eyes observe the nations; Do not let the rebellious exalt themselves.   Selah

PROVERBS 16:25, 26

25 THERE is a way *that seems* right to a man, But its end *is* the way of death.

26 The person who labors, labors for himself, For his *hungry* mouth drives him *on.*

JOHN 6:52–71

THE Jews therefore quarreled among themselves, saying, "How can this Man give us *His* flesh to eat?"

53 Then Jesus said to them, "Most assuredly, I say to you, unless you eat the flesh of the Son of Man and drink His blood, you have no life in you. 54 Whoever eats My flesh and drinks My blood has eternal life, and I will raise him up at the last day. 55 For My flesh is food indeed, and My blood is drink indeed. 56 He who eats My flesh and drinks My blood abides in Me, and I in him. 57 As the living Father sent Me, and I live because of the Father, so he who feeds on Me will live because of Me. 58 This is the bread which came down from heaven—not as your fathers ate the manna, and are dead. He who eats this bread will live forever."

59 These things He said in the synagogue as He taught in Capernaum.

60 Therefore many of His disciples, when they heard *this,* said, "This is a hard saying; who can understand it?"

61 When Jesus knew in Himself that His disciples complained about this, He said to them, "Does this offend you? 62 *What* then if you should see the Son of Man ascend where He was before? 63 It is the Spirit who gives life; the flesh profits nothing. The words that I speak to you are spirit, and *they* are life. 64 But there are some of

*N*othing Jesus Christ ever said is common sense, it is revelation sense.   (UTMOST)

you who do not believe." For Jesus knew from the beginning who they were who did not believe, and who would betray Him. 65 And He said, "Therefore I have said to you that no one can come to Me unless it has been granted to him by My Father."

66 From that *time* many of His disciples went back and walked with Him no more. 67 Then Jesus said to the twelve, "Do you also want to go away?"

68 But Simon Peter answered Him,

"Lord, to whom shall we go? You have the words of eternal life. 69 Also we have come to believe and know that You are the Christ, the Son of the living God."

70 Jesus answered them, "Did I not choose you, the twelve, and one of you is a devil?" 71 He spoke of Judas Iscariot, *the son* of Simon, for it was he who would betray Him, being one of the twelve.

◆◆◆◆

Reading 142—Go on Knowing
John 7:17

If you believe in Jesus, you will not spend all your time in the smooth waters just inside the harbor, full of exhilaration and delight, but always moored; you will have to go out through the harbor bar into the great deeps of God and begin to know for yourself, begin to get spiritual discernment. If you do not cut the moorings, God will have to break them with a storm and send you out. Why not unloosen and launch all on God and go out on the great swelling tide of His purpose?

"If anyone wills to do His will, he shall know . . ." When you know you should do a thing and you do it, immediately you will know more. If you revise where you are stodgy spiritually, you will find it goes back to the point where there was one thing you knew you should do, but you did not do it because there seemed no immediate call to, and now you have no perception, no discernment. Instead of being spiritually self-possessed at the time of crisis, you are spiritually distracted. It is a dangerous thing to refuse to go on knowing.   (*WALKED*)

2 SAMUEL 15:1—16:23

AFTER this it happened that Absalom provided himself with chariots and horses, and fifty men to run before him. 2 Now Absalom would rise early and stand beside the way to the gate. *So* it was, whenever anyone who had a lawsuit came to the king for a decision, that Absalom would call to him and say, "What city *are* you from?" And he would say, "Your servant *is* from such and such a tribe of Israel." 3 Then Absalom would say to him, "Look, your case *is* good and right; but *there is* no deputy of the king to hear you." 4 Moreover Absalom would say, "Oh, that I were made judge in the land, and everyone who has any suit or cause would come to me; then I would give him justice." 5 And *so* it was, whenever anyone came near to bow down to him, that he would put out his hand and take him and kiss him. 6 In this manner Absalom

acted toward all Israel who came to the king for judgment. So Absalom stole the hearts of the men of Israel.

7 Now it came to pass after forty years that Absalom said to the king, "Please, let me go to Hebron and pay the vow which I made to the LORD. 8 For your servant took a vow while I dwelt at Geshur in Syria, saying, 'If the LORD indeed brings me back to Jerusalem, then I will serve the LORD.' " 9 And the king said to him, "Go in peace." So he arose and went to Hebron.

10 Then Absalom sent spies throughout all the tribes of Israel, saying, "As soon as you hear the sound of the trumpet, then you shall say, 'Absalom reigns in Hebron!' " 11 And with Absalom went two hundred men invited from Jerusalem, and they went along innocently and did not know anything. 12 Then Absalom sent for Ahithophel the Gilonite, David's counselor, from his city—from Giloh—while he offered sacri-

fices. And the conspiracy grew strong, for the people with Absalom continually increased in number.

13 Now a messenger came to David, saying, "The hearts of the men of Israel are with Absalom."

14 So David said to all his servants who *were* with him at Jerusalem, "Arise, and let us flee, or we shall not escape from Absalom. Make haste to depart, lest he overtake us suddenly and bring disaster upon us, and strike the city with the edge of the sword."

15 And the king's servants said to the king, "We *are* your servants, *ready to do* whatever my lord the king commands."

16 Then the king went out with all his household after him. But the king left ten women, concubines, to keep the house.

17 And the king went out with all the people after him, and stopped at the outskirts.

18 Then all his servants passed before him; and all the Cherethites, all the Pelethites, and all the Gittites, six hundred men who had followed him from Gath, passed before the king.

19 Then the king said to Ittai the Gittite, "Why are you also going with us? Return and remain with the king. For you *are* a foreigner and also an exile from your own place. 20 In fact, you came *only* yesterday. Should I make you wander up and down with us today, since I go I know not where? Return, and take your brethren back. Mercy and truth *be* with you."

21 But Ittai answered the king and said, "*As* the LORD lives, and *as* my lord the king lives, surely in whatever place my lord the king shall be, whether in death or life, even there also your servant will be."

22 So David said to Ittai, "Go, and cross over." Then Ittai the Gittite and all his men and all the little ones who *were* with him crossed over. 23 And all the country wept with a loud voice, and all the people crossed over. The king himself also crossed over the Brook Kidron, and all the people crossed over toward the way of the wilderness.

24 There was Zadok also, and all the Levites with him, bearing the ark of the covenant of God. And they set down the ark of God, and Abiathar went up until all the people had finished crossing over from the city. 25 Then the king said to Zadok, "Carry the ark of God back into the city. If I find favor in the eyes of the LORD, He will bring me back and show me *both* it and His dwelling place. 26 But *if* He says thus: 'I have no delight in you,' here I am, let Him do to me as seems good to Him." 27 The king also said to Zadok the priest, "*Are* you *not*

a seer? Return to the city in peace, and your two sons with you, Ahimaaz your son, and Jonathan the son of Abiathar. 28 See, I will wait in the plains of the wilderness until word comes from you to inform me." 29 Therefore Zadok and Abiathar carried the ark of God back to Jerusalem. And they remained there.

30 So David went up by the Ascent of the *Mount of* Olives, and wept as he went up; and he had his head covered and went barefoot. And all the people who *were* with him covered their heads and went up, weeping as they went up. 31 Then *someone* told David, saying, "Ahithophel *is* among the conspirators with Absalom." And David said, "O LORD, I pray, turn the counsel of Ahithophel into foolishness!"

32 Now it happened when David had come to the top *of the mountain,* where he worshiped God—there was Hushai the Archite coming to meet him with his robe torn and dust on his head. 33 David said to him, "If you go on with me, then you will become a burden to me. 34 But if you return to the city, and say to Absalom, 'I will be your servant, O king; *as* I *was* your father's servant previously, so I *will* now also *be* your servant,' then you may defeat the counsel of Ahithophel for me. 35 And *do* you not *have* Zadok and Abiathar the priests with you there? Therefore it will be *that* whatever you hear from the king's house, you shall tell to Zadok and Abiathar the priests. 36 Indeed *they have* there with them their two sons, Ahimaaz, Zadok's *son,* and Jonathan, Abiathar's *son;* and by them you shall send me everything you hear."

37 So Hushai, David's friend, went into the city. And Absalom came into Jerusalem.

16 WHEN David was a little past the top *of the mountain,* there was Ziba the servant of Mephibosheth, who met him with a couple of saddled donkeys, and on them two hundred *loaves* of bread, one hundred clusters of raisins, one hundred summer fruits, and a skin of wine. 2 And the king said to Ziba, "What do you mean to do with these?"

So Ziba said, "The donkeys *are* for the king's household to ride on, the bread and summer fruit for the young men to eat, and the wine for those who are faint in the wilderness to drink."

3 Then the king said, "And where *is* your master's son?"

And Ziba said to the king, "Indeed he is staying in Jerusalem, for he said, 'Today the house of Israel will restore the kingdom of my father to me.'"

4 So the king said to Ziba, "Here, all that *belongs* to Mephibosheth *is* yours."

And Ziba said, "I humbly bow before you, *that* I may find favor in your sight, my lord, O king!"

5 Now when King David came to Bahurim, there was a man from the family of the house of Saul, whose name *was* Shimei the son of Gera, coming from there. He came out, cursing continuously as he came. 6 And he threw stones at David and at all the servants of King David. And all the people and all the mighty men *were* on his right hand and on his left. 7 Also Shimei said thus when he cursed: "Come out! Come out! You bloodthirsty man, you rogue! 8 The LORD has brought upon you all the blood of the house of Saul, in whose place you have reigned; and the LORD has delivered the kingdom into the hand of Absalom your son. So now you *are caught* in your own evil, because you are a bloodthirsty man!"

9 Then Abishai the son of Zeruiah said to the king, "Why should this dead dog curse my lord the king? Please, let me go over and take off his head!"

10 But the king said, "What have I to do with you, you sons of Zeruiah? So let him curse, because the LORD has said to him, 'Curse David.' Who then shall say, 'Why have you done so?' "

11 And David said to Abishai and all his servants, "See how my son who came from my own body seeks my life. How much more now *may this* Benjamite? Let him alone, and let him curse; for so the LORD has ordered him. 12 It may be that the LORD will look on my affliction, and that the LORD will repay me with good for his cursing this day." 13 And as David and his men went along the road, Shimei went along the hillside opposite him and cursed as he went, threw stones at him and kicked up dust. 14 Now the king and all the people who *were* with him became weary; so they refreshed themselves there.

15 Meanwhile Absalom and all the people, the men of Israel, came to Jerusalem; and Ahithophel *was* with him. 16 And so it was, when Hushai the Archite, David's friend, came to Absalom, that Hushai said to Absalom, "*Long* live the king! *Long* live the king!"

17 So Absalom said to Hushai, "*Is* this your loyalty to your friend? Why did you not go with your friend?"

18 And Hushai said to Absalom, "No, but whom the LORD and this people and all the men of Israel choose, his I will be, and with him I will remain. 19 "Furthermore, whom should I serve? *Should I* not *serve* in the presence of his son? As I have served in your father's presence, so will I be in your presence."

20 Then Absalom said to Ahithophel, "Give advice as to what we should do."

21 And Ahithophel said to Absalom, "Go in to your father's concubines, whom he has left to keep the house; and all Israel will hear that you are abhorred by your father. Then the hands of all who are with you will be strong." 22 So they pitched a tent for Absalom on the top of the house, and Absalom went in to his father's concubines in the sight of all Israel.

23 Now the advice of Ahithophel, which he gave in those days, *was* as if one had inquired at the oracle of God. So *was* all the advice of Ahithophel both with David and with Absalom.

PSALM 66:8–15

8   OH, bless our God, you peoples!
    And make the voice of His praise to
      be heard,
9   Who keeps our soul among the
      living,
    And does not allow our feet to be
      moved.
10 For You, O God, have tested us;
    You have refined us as silver is
      refined.

Faith must be tried, and it is the trial of faith that is precious. (NOT KNOWING)

---

11 You brought us into the net;
    You laid affliction on our backs.
12 You have caused men to ride over our
      heads;
    We went through fire and through
      water;
    But You brought us out to rich
      fulfillment.
13 I will go into Your house with burnt
      offerings;
    I will pay You my vows,
14 Which my lips have uttered
    And my mouth has spoken when I was
      in trouble.
15 I will offer You burnt sacrifices of fat
      animals,
    With the sweet aroma of rams;
    I will offer bulls with goats.   Selah

PROVERBS 16:27–30

27 AN ungodly man digs up evil,
And *it is* on his lips like a burning fire.
28 A perverse man sows strife,
And a whisperer separates the best of
friends.
29 A violent man entices his neighbor,
And leads him in a way *that is* not good.
30 He winks his eye to devise perverse
things;
He purses his lips *and* brings about evil.

JOHN 7:1–27

AFTER these things Jesus walked in Galilee; for He did not want to walk in Judea, because the Jews sought to kill Him. 2 Now the Jews' Feast of Tabernacles was at hand. 3 His brothers therefore said to Him, "Depart from here and go into Judea, that Your disciples also may see the works that You are doing. 4 For no one does anything in secret while he himself seeks to be known openly. If You do these things, show Yourself to the world." 5 For even His brothers did not believe in Him.

6 Then Jesus said to them, "My time has not yet come, but your time is always ready. 7 The world cannot hate you, but it hates Me because I testify of it that its works are evil. 8 You go up to this feast. I am not yet going up to this feast, for My time has not yet fully come." 9 When He had said these things to them, He remained in Galilee.

10 But when His brothers had gone up, then He also went up to the feast, not openly, but as it were in secret. 11 Then the Jews sought Him at the feast, and said, "Where is He?" 12 And there was much complaining among the people concerning

Him. Some said, "He is good"; others said, "No, on the contrary, He deceives the people." 13 However, no one spoke openly of Him for fear of the Jews.

14 Now about the middle of the feast Jesus went up into the temple and taught. 15 And the Jews marveled, saying, "How does this Man know letters, having never studied?"

16 Jesus answered them and said, "My doctrine is not Mine, but His who sent Me. 17 If anyone wills to do His will, he shall know concerning the doctrine, whether it is from God or *whether* I speak on My own *authority*. 18 He who speaks from himself seeks his own glory; but He who seeks the glory of the One who sent Him is true, and no unrighteousness is in Him. 19 Did not Moses give you the law, yet none of you keeps the law? Why do you seek to kill Me?"

20 The people answered and said, "You have a demon. Who is seeking to kill You?"

21 Jesus answered and said to them, "I did one work, and you all marvel. 22 Moses therefore gave you circumcision (not that it is from Moses, but from the fathers), and you circumcise a man on the Sabbath. 23 If a man receives circumcision on the Sabbath, so that the law of Moses should not be broken, are you angry with Me because I made a man completely well on the Sabbath? 24 Do not judge according to appearance, but judge with righteous judgment."

25 Now some of them from Jerusalem said, "Is this not He whom they seek to kill? 26 But look! He speaks boldly, and they say nothing to Him. Do the rulers know indeed that this is truly the Christ? 27 However, we know where this Man is from; but when the Christ comes, no one knows where He is from."

◆◆◆◆

Reading 143—The Sacrament of Sacrifice
John 7:38

Jesus Christ did not say, "He who believes in Me, in himself shall realize the blessing of the fullness of God," but, in effect, "out of him shall escape everything he has received." Our Lord always preaches anti-self-realization; He is not after developing a man at all, He is after making a man exactly like Himself, and the measure of the Son of God is self-expenditure. If we believe on Jesus Christ it is not what we gain but what He pours through us that counts. It is not that God makes us beautifully rounded grapes, but that He squeezes the sweetness out of us. We cannot measure our lives by spiritual success, but only by what God pours through us, and we cannot measure that at all. Who can measure the influence of a star or of a lily? Yet these are the things our Lord told us to consider. "He who believes in Me"—through him will He pour everything, leaving him nothing. A sacrament is the real presence in the actual elements; in this connection the actual elements are our lives.

(PLACE HELP)

2 SAMUEL 17:1—18:33

MOREOVER Ahithophel said to Absalom, "Now let me choose twelve thousand men, and I will arise and pursue David tonight. 2 I will come upon him while he *is* weary and weak, and make him afraid. And all the people who *are* with him will flee, and I will strike only the king. 3 Then I will bring back all the people to you. When all return except the man whom you seek, all the people will be at peace." 4 And the saying pleased Absalom and all the elders of Israel.

5 Then Absalom said, "Now call Hushai the Archite also, and let us hear what he says too." 6 And when Hushai came to Absalom, Absalom spoke to him, saying, "Ahithophel has spoken in this manner. Shall we do as he says? If not, speak up."

7 So Hushai said to Absalom: "The advice that Ahithophel has given *is* not good at this time. 8 For," said Hushai, "you know your father and his men, that they *are* mighty men, and they *are* enraged in their minds, like a bear robbed of her cubs in the field; and your father *is* a man of war, and will not camp with the people. 9 Surely by now he is hidden in some pit, or in some *other* place. And it will be, when some of them are overthrown at the first, that whoever hears *it* will say, 'There is a slaughter among the people who follow Absalom.' 10 And even he *who is* valiant, whose heart *is* like the heart of a lion, will melt completely. For all Israel knows that your father *is* a mighty man, and *those* who *are* with him *are* valiant men. 11 Therefore I advise that all Israel be fully gathered to you, from Dan to Beersheba, like the sand that *is* by the sea for multitude, and that you go to battle in person. 12 So we will come upon him in some place where he may be found, and we will fall on him as the dew falls on the ground. And of him and all the men who *are* with him there shall not be left so much as one. 13 Moreover, if he has withdrawn into a city, then all Israel shall bring ropes to that city; and we will pull it into the river, until there is not one small stone found there."

14 So Absalom and all the men of Israel said, "The advice of Hushai the Archite *is* better than the advice of Ahithophel." For the LORD had purposed to defeat the good advice of Ahithophel, to the intent that the LORD might bring disaster on Absalom.

15 Then Hushai said to Zadok and Abiathar the priests, "Thus and so Ahithophel advised Absalom and the elders of Israel, and thus and so I have advised. 16 Now therefore, send quickly and tell David, saying, 'Do not spend this night in the plains of the wilderness, but speedily cross over, lest the king and all the people who *are* with him be swallowed up.' " 17 Now Jonathan and Ahimaaz stayed at En Rogel, for they dared not be seen coming into the city; so a female servant would come and tell them, and they would go and tell King David. 18 Nevertheless a lad saw them, and told Absalom. But both of them went away quickly and came to a man's house in Bahurim, who had a well in his court; and they went down into it. 19 Then the woman took and spread a covering over the well's mouth, and spread ground grain on it; and the thing was not known. 20 And when Absalom's servants came to the woman at the house, they said, "Where *are* Ahimaaz and Jonathan?"

So the woman said to them, "They have gone over the water brook."

And when they had searched and could not find *them*, they returned to Jerusalem. 21 Now it came to pass, after they had departed, that they came up out of the well and went and told King David, and said to David, "Arise and cross over the water quickly. For thus has Ahithophel advised against you." 22 So David and all the people who *were* with him arose and crossed over the Jordan. By morning light not one of them was left who had not gone over the Jordan.

23 Now when Ahithophel saw that his advice was not followed, he saddled a donkey, and arose and went home to his house, to his city. Then he put his household in order, and hanged himself, and died; and he was buried in his father's tomb.

24 Then David went to Mahanaim. And

Absalom crossed over the Jordan, he and all the men of Israel with him. 25 And Absalom made Amasa captain of the army instead of Joab. This Amasa *was* the son of a man whose name *was* Jithra, an Israelite, who had gone in to Abigail the daughter of Nahash, sister of Zeruiah, Joab's mother. 26 So Israel and Absalom encamped in the land of Gilead.

27 Now it happened, when David had come to Mahanaim, that Shobi the son of Nahash from Rabbah of the people of Ammon, Machir the son of Ammiel from Lo Debar, and Barzillai the Gileadite from Rogelim, 28 brought beds and basins, earthen vessels and wheat, barley and flour, parched *grain* and beans, lentils and parched *seeds,* 29 honey and curds, sheep and cheese of the herd, for David and the people who *were* with him to eat. For they said, "The people are hungry and weary and thirsty in the wilderness."

18 AND David numbered the people who *were* with him, and set captains of thousands and captains of hundreds over them. 2 Then David sent out one third of the people under the hand of Joab, one third under the hand of Abishai the son of Zeruiah, Joab's brother, and one third under the hand of Ittai the Gittite. And the king said to the people, "I also will surely go out with you myself."

3 But the people answered, "You shall not go out! For if we flee away, they will not care about us; nor if half of us die, will they care about us. But *you are* worth ten thousand of us now. For you are now more help to us in the city."

4 Then the king said to them, "Whatever seems best to you I will do." So the king stood beside the gate, and all the people went out by hundreds and by thousands. 5 Now the king had commanded Joab, Abishai, and Ittai, saying, "*Deal* gently for my sake with the young man Absalom." And all the people heard when the king gave all the captains orders concerning Absalom.

6 So the people went out into the field of battle against Israel. And the battle was in the woods of Ephraim. 7 The people of Israel were overthrown there before the servants of David, and a great slaughter of twenty thousand took place there that day. 8 For the battle there was scattered over the face of the whole countryside, and the woods devoured more people that day than the sword devoured.

9 Then Absalom met the servants of David. Absalom rode on a mule. The mule went under the thick boughs of a great terebinth tree, and his head caught in the terebinth; so he was left hanging between heaven and earth. And the mule which *was* under him went on. 10 Now a certain man saw *it* and told Joab, and said, "I just saw Absalom hanging in a terebinth tree!"

11 So Joab said to the man who told him, "You just saw *him!* And why did you not strike him there to the ground? I would have given you ten *shekels* of silver and a belt."

12 But the man said to Joab, "Though I were to receive a thousand *shekels* of silver in my hand, I would not raise my hand against the king's son. For in our hearing the king commanded you and Abishai and Ittai, saying, 'Beware lest anyone *touch* the young man Absalom!' 13 Otherwise I would have dealt falsely against my own life. For there is nothing hidden from the king, and you yourself would have set yourself against *me.*"

14 Then Joab said, "I cannot linger with you." And he took three spears in his hand and thrust them through Absalom's heart, while he was *still* alive in the midst of the terebinth tree. 15 And ten young men who bore Joab's armor surrounded Absalom, and struck and killed him.

16 So Joab blew the trumpet, and the people returned from pursuing Israel. For Joab held back the people. 17 And they took Absalom and cast him into a large pit in the woods, and laid a very large heap of stones over him. Then all Israel fled, everyone to his tent.

18 Now Absalom in his lifetime had taken and set up a pillar for himself, which *is* in the King's Valley. For he said, "I have no son to keep my name in remembrance." He called the pillar after his own name. And to this day it is called Absalom's Monument.

19 Then Ahimaaz the son of Zadok said, "Let me run now and take the news to the king, how the LORD has avenged him of his enemies."

20 And Joab said to him, "You shall not take the news this day, for you shall take the news another day. But today you shall take no news, because the king's son is dead." 21 Then Joab said to the Cushite, "Go, tell the king what you have seen." So the Cushite bowed himself to Joab and ran.

22 And Ahimaaz the son of Zadok said again to Joab, "But whatever happens, please let me also run after the Cushite."

So Joab said, "Why will you run, my son, since you have no news ready?"

23 "But whatever happens," *he said,* "let me run."

So he said to him, "Run." Then Ahimaaz ran by way of the plain, and outran the Cushite.

24 Now David was sitting between the two gates. And the watchman went up to the roof over the gate, to the wall, lifted his eyes and looked, and there was a man, running alone. 25 Then the watchman cried out and told the king. And the king said, "If he *is* alone, *there is* news in his mouth." And he came rapidly and drew near.

26 Then the watchman saw *another* man running, and the watchman called to the gatekeeper and said, "There is *another* man, running alone!"

And the king said, "He also brings news."

27 So the watchman said, "I think the running of the first is like the running of Ahimaaz the son of Zadok."

And the king said, "He *is* a good man, and comes with good news."

28 So Ahimaaz called out and said to the king, "All is well!" Then he bowed down with his face to the earth before the king, and said, "Blessed *be* the LORD your God, who has delivered up the men who raised their hand against my lord the king!"

29 The king said, "Is the young man Absalom safe?"

Ahimaaz answered, "When Joab sent the king's servant and *me* your servant, I saw a great tumult, but I did not know what *it was about.*"

30 And the king said, "Turn aside *and* stand here." So he turned aside and stood still.

31 Just then the Cushite came, and the Cushite said, "There is good news, my lord the king! For the LORD has avenged you this day of all those who rose against you."

32 And the king said to the Cushite, "Is the young man Absalom safe?"

So the Cushite answered, "May the enemies of my lord the king, and all who rise against you to do harm, be like *that* young man!"

33 Then the king was deeply moved, and went up to the chamber over the gate, and wept. And as he went, he said thus: "O my son Absalom—my son, my son Absalom—if only I had died in your place! O Absalom my son, my son!"

PSALM 66:16–20

16 COME *and* hear, all you who fear God,
And I will declare what He has done
for my soul.

17 I cried to Him with my mouth,
And He was extolled with my tongue.

18 If I regard iniquity in my heart,
The Lord will not hear.

19 *But* certainly God has heard *me;*
He has attended to the voice of my
prayer.

20 Blessed *be* God,
Who has not turned away my prayer,
Nor His mercy from me!

---

*P*rayer is easy to us because of
what it cost God to enable us
to pray.   (ASK)

PROVERBS 16:31, 32

31 THE silver-haired head *is* a crown of
glory,
If it is found in the way of righteousness.

32 *He who is* slow to anger *is* better than
the mighty,
And he who rules his spirit than he
who takes a city.

JOHN 7:28–53

THEN Jesus cried out, as He taught in the temple, saying, "You both know Me, and you know where I am from; and I have not come of Myself, but He who sent Me is true, whom you do not know. 29 But I know Him, for I am from Him, and He sent Me."

30 Therefore they sought to take Him; but no one laid a hand on Him, because His hour had not yet come. 31 And many of the people believed in Him, and said, "When the Christ comes, will He do more signs than these which this *Man* has done?"

32 The Pharisees heard the crowd murmuring these things concerning Him, and the Pharisees and the chief priests sent officers to take Him. 33 Then Jesus said to them, "I shall be with you a little while longer, and *then* I go to Him who sent Me. 34 You will seek Me and not find *Me,* and where I am you cannot come."

35 Then the Jews said among themselves, "Where does He intend to go that we shall not find Him? Does He intend to go to the Dispersion among the Greeks and teach the Greeks? 36 What is this thing that He

said, 'You will seek Me and not find Me, and where I am you cannot come'?"

37 On the last day, that great *day* of the feast, Jesus stood and cried out, saying, "If anyone thirsts, let him come to Me and drink. 38 He who believes in Me, as the Scripture has said, out of his heart will flow rivers of living water." 39 But this He spoke

---

*T*he Spirit of God is a well of water in the disciple, perennially fresh.   (BRILL. HERITAGE)

---

concerning the Spirit, whom those believing in Him would receive; for the Holy Spirit was not yet *given*, because Jesus was not yet glorified.

40 Therefore many from the crowd, when they heard this saying, said, "Truly this is the Prophet." 41 Others said, "This is the Christ."

But some said, "Will the Christ come out of Galilee? 42 Has not the Scripture said

that the Christ comes from the seed of David and from the town of Bethlehem, where David was?" 43 So there was a division among the people because of Him. 44 Now some of them wanted to take Him, but no one laid hands on Him.

45 Then the officers came to the chief priests and Pharisees, who said to them, "Why have you not brought Him?"

46 The officers answered, "No man ever spoke like this Man!"

47 Then the Pharisees answered them, "Are you also deceived? 48 Have any of the rulers or the Pharisees believed in Him? 49 But this crowd that does not know the law is accursed."

50 Nicodemus (he who came to Jesus by night, being one of them) said to them, 51 "Does our law judge a man before it hears him and knows what he is doing?"

52 They answered and said to him, "Are you also from Galilee? Search and look, for no prophet has arisen out of Galilee."

53 And everyone went to his *own* house.

◆◆◆

Reading 144—Believe in the Light
John 8:12

Supposing you are walking . . . at night, you know there is a path but it is too dark and obscure for you to see; then the moon struggles through the clouds and you see the path, a clear strip of white, straight across the hill; in a little while all is obscure again, but you have seen the path and you know the way to go. There are times in our experience when life is just like that. We do not see the path though we know it is there, then the light shines and we see it, and when darkness comes again we can step boldly. Sometimes the light is as the moonlight or the dawn, or it comes as a terrifying flash of lightning, when all of a sudden we see the way we should go. "While you have the light, believe in the light, that you may become sons of light" (John 12:36). Have we believed in the light we have had? Can we recall the time when the light of God in the face of Jesus Christ was clearer to us than anything else has ever been, when we saw perfectly clearly and understood exactly what the Lord wanted? Did we believe in that light; and have we walked up to the light? Can we say, "I was not disobedient unto the heavenly vision"? So many of us see the light, we see the way . . . by a sudden lightning flash of God's revealing grace we see the way to go, but we do not take it. We say, "Oh, yes, I did receive the Spirit of God, and I thought that it would be like this and that, but it has not been." The reason is that we did not believe in the light when it was given. . . .   (BRILL. HERITAGE)

2 SAMUEL 19:1—20:26

AND Joab was told, "Behold, the king is weeping and mourning for Absalom." 2 So the victory that day was *turned* into mourning for all the people. For the people heard it said that day, "The king is grieved for his son." 3 And the people stole back

---

The summing up of all practical life is that the basis of things is tragic.   (SHADE)

---

into the city that day, as people who are ashamed steal away when they flee in battle. 4 But the king covered his face, and the king cried out with a loud voice, "O my son Absalom! O Absalom, my son, my son!"

5 Then Joab came into the house to the king, and said, "Today you have disgraced all your servants who today have saved your life, the lives of your sons and daughters, the lives of your wives and the lives of your concubines, 6 in that you love your enemies and hate your friends. For you have declared today that you regard neither princes nor servants; for today I perceive that if Absalom had lived and all of us had died today, then it would have pleased you well. 7 Now therefore, arise, go out and speak comfort to your servants. For I swear by the LORD, if you do not go out, not one will stay with you this night. And that will be worse for you than all the evil that has befallen you from your youth until now." 8 Then the king arose and sat in the gate. And they told all the people, saying, "There is the king, sitting in the gate." So all the people came before the king.

For everyone of Israel had fled to his tent.

9 Now all the people were in a dispute throughout all the tribes of Israel, saying, "The king saved us from the hand of our enemies, he delivered us from the hand of the Philistines, and now he has fled from the land because of Absalom. 10 But Absalom, whom we anointed over us, has died in battle. Now therefore, why do you say nothing about bringing back the king?"

11 So King David sent to Zadok and Abiathar the priests, saying, "Speak to the elders of Judah, saying, 'Why are you the last to bring the king back to his house, since the words of all Israel have come to the king, to his *very* house? 12 You *are* my brethren, you *are* my bone and my flesh. Why then are you the last to bring back the king?'

13 And say to Amasa, '*Are* you not my bone and my flesh? God do so to me, and more also, if you are not commander of the army before me continually in place of Joab.'" 14 So he swayed the hearts of all the men of Judah, just as *the heart of* one man, so that they sent *this word* to the king: "Return, you and all your servants!"

15 Then the king returned and came to the Jordan. And Judah came to Gilgal, to go to meet the king, to escort the king across the Jordan. 16 And Shimei the son of Gera, a Benjamite, who *was* from Bahurim, hurried and came down with the men of Judah to meet King David. 17 *There were* a thousand men of Benjamin with him, and Ziba the servant of the house of Saul, and his fifteen sons and his twenty servants with him; and they went over the Jordan before the king. 18 Then a ferryboat went across to carry over the king's household, and to do what he thought good.

Now Shimei the son of Gera fell down before the king when he had crossed the Jordan. 19 Then he said to the king, "Do not let my lord impute iniquity to me, or remember what wrong your servant did on the day that my lord the king left Jerusalem, that the king should take *it* to heart. 20 For I, your servant, know that I have sinned. Therefore here I am, the first to come today of all the house of Joseph to go down to meet my lord the king."

21 But Abishai the son of Zeruiah answered and said, "Shall not Shimei be put to death for this, because he cursed the LORD's anointed?"

22 And David said, "What have I to do with you, you sons of Zeruiah, that you should be adversaries to me today? Shall any man be put to death today in Israel? For do I not know that today I *am* king over Israel?" 23 Therefore the king said to Shimei, "You shall not die." And the king swore to him.

24 Now Mephibosheth the son of Saul came down to meet the king. And he had not cared for his feet, nor trimmed his mustache, nor washed his clothes, from the day the king departed until the day he returned in peace. 25 So it was, when he had come to Jerusalem to meet the king, that the king said to him, "Why did you not go with me, Mephibosheth?"

26 And he answered, "My lord, O king, my servant deceived me. For your servant said, 'I will saddle a donkey for myself, that I may ride on it and go to the king,' because your servant *is* lame. 27 And he has slandered your servant to my lord the king, but my lord the king *is* like the angel of God.

Therefore do *what is* good in your eyes. 28 For all my father's house were but dead men before my lord the king. Yet you set your servant among those who eat at your own table. Therefore what right have I still to cry out anymore to the king?"

29 So the king said to him, "Why do you speak anymore of your matters? I have said, 'You and Ziba divide the land.' "

30 Then Mephibosheth said to the king, "Rather, let him take it all, inasmuch as my lord the king has come back in peace to his own house."

31 And Barzillai the Gileadite came down from Rogelim and went across the Jordan with the king, to escort him across the Jordan. 32 Now Barzillai was a very aged man, eighty years old. And he had provided the king with supplies while he stayed at Mahanaim, for he *was* a very rich man. 33 And the king said to Barzillai, "Come across with me, and I will provide for you while you are with me in Jerusalem."

34 But Barzillai said to the king, "How long have I to live, that I should go up with the king to Jerusalem? 35 I *am* today eighty years old. Can I discern between the good and bad? Can your servant taste what I eat or what I drink? Can I hear any longer the voice of singing men and singing women? Why then should your servant be a further burden to my lord the king? 36 Your servant will go a little way across the Jordan with the king. And why should the king repay me *with* such a reward? 37 Please let your servant turn back again, that I may die in my own city, near the grave of my father and mother. But here is your servant Chimham; let him cross over with my lord the king, and do for him what seems good to you."

38 And the king answered, "Chimham shall cross over with me, and I will do for him what seems good to you. Now whatever you request of me, I will do for you."

39 Then all the people went over the Jordan. And when the king had crossed over, the king kissed Barzillai and blessed him, and he returned to his own place.

40 Now the king went on to Gilgal, and Chimham went on with him. And all the people of Judah escorted the king, and also half the people of Israel. 41 Just then all the men of Israel came to the king, and said to the king, "Why have our brethren, the men of Judah, stolen you away and brought the king, his household, and all David's men with him across the Jordan?"

42 So all the men of Judah answered the men of Israel, "Because the king *is* a close relative of ours. Why then are you angry over this matter? Have we ever eaten at the king's *expense?* Or has he given us any gift?"

43 And the men of Israel answered the men of Judah, and said, "We have ten shares in the king; therefore we also have more *right* to David than you. Why then do you despise us—were we not the first to advise bringing back our king?"

Yet the words of the men of Judah were fiercer than the words of the men of Israel.

20 AND there happened to be there a rebel, whose name *was* Sheba the son of Bichri, a Benjamite. And he blew a trumpet, and said:

"We have no share in David,
    Nor do we have inheritance in the
        son of Jesse;
    Every man to his tents, O Israel!"

2 So every man of Israel deserted David, *and* followed Sheba the son of Bichri. But the men of Judah, from the Jordan as far as Jerusalem, remained loyal to their king.

3 Now David came to his house at Jerusalem. And the king took the ten women, his concubines whom he had left to keep the house, and put them in seclusion and supported them, but did not go in to them. So they were shut up to the day of their death, living in widowhood.

4 And the king said to Amasa, "Assemble the men of Judah for me within three days, and be present here yourself." 5 So Amasa went to assemble *the men of* Judah. But he delayed longer than the set time which David had appointed him. 6 And David said to Abishai, "Now Sheba the son of Bichri will do us more harm than Absalom. Take your lord's servants and pursue him, lest he find for himself fortified cities, and escape us." 7 So Joab's men, with the Cherethites, the Pelethites, and all the mighty men, went out after him. And they went out of Jerusalem to pursue Sheba the son of Bichri. 8 When they *were* at the large stone which *is* in Gibeon, Amasa came before them. Now Joab was dressed in battle armor; on it was a belt *with* a sword fastened in its sheath at his hips; and as he was going forward, it fell out. 9 Then Joab said to Amasa, "*Are* you in health, my brother?" And Joab took Amasa by the beard with his right hand to kiss him. 10 But Amasa did not notice the sword that *was* in Joab's hand. And he struck him with it in the stomach, and his entrails poured out on the ground; and he did not *strike* him again. Thus he died.

Then Joab and Abishai his brother pursued Sheba the son of Bichri. 11 Meanwhile one of Joab's men stood near Amasa, and said, "Whoever favors Joab and whoever *is* for David—follow Joab!" 12 But Amasa wallowed in *his* blood in the middle of the highway. And when the man saw that all the people stood still, he moved Amasa from the highway to the field and threw a garment over him, when he saw that everyone who came upon him halted. 13 When he was removed from the highway, all the people went on after Joab to pursue Sheba the son of Bichri.

14 And he went through all the tribes of Israel to Abel and Beth Maachah and all the Berites. So they were gathered together and also went after *Sheba*. 15 Then they came and besieged him in Abel of Beth Maachah; and they cast up a siege mound against the city, and it stood by the rampart. And all the people who *were* with Joab battered the wall to throw it down.

16 Then a wise woman cried out from the city, "Hear, hear! Please say to Joab, 'Come nearby, that I may speak with you.'" 17 When he had come near to her, the woman said, "*Are* you Joab?"

He answered, "I *am*."

Then she said to him, "Hear the words of your maidservant."

And he answered, "I am listening."

18 So she spoke, saying, "They used to talk in former times, saying, 'They shall surely seek *guidance* at Abel,' and so they would end *disputes*. 19 I *am among the* peaceable *and* faithful in Israel. You seek to destroy a city and a mother in Israel. Why would you swallow up the inheritance of the LORD?"

20 And Joab answered and said, "Far be it, far be it from me, that I should swallow up or destroy! 21 That *is* not so. But a man from the mountains of Ephraim, Sheba the son of Bichri by name, has raised his hand against the king, against David. Deliver him only, and I will depart from the city."

So the woman said to Joab, "Watch, his head will be thrown to you over the wall." 22 Then the woman in her wisdom went to all the people. And they cut off the head of Sheba the son of Bichri, and threw *it* out to Joab. Then he blew a trumpet, and they withdrew from the city, every man to his tent. So Joab returned to the king at Jerusalem.

23 And Joab *was* over all the army of Israel; Benaiah the son of Jehoiada *was* over the Cherethites and the Pelethites; 24 Adoram *was* in charge of revenue; Jehoshaphat the son of Ahilud *was* recorder; 25 Sheva *was* scribe; Zadok and Abiathar *were* the priests; 26 and Ira the Jairite was a chief minister under David.

PSALM 67:1–7

1 GOD be merciful to us and bless us,
 And cause His face to shine upon us,
   Selah
2 That Your way may be known on earth,
 Your salvation among all nations.

3 Let the peoples praise You, O God;
 Let all the peoples praise You.
4 Oh, let the nations be glad and sing
 for joy!
 For You shall judge the people
 righteously,
 And govern the nations on earth.
   Selah

5 Let the peoples praise You, O God;
 Let all the peoples praise You.
6 *Then* the earth shall yield her increase;
 God, our own God, shall bless us.
7 God shall bless us,
 And all the ends of the earth shall fear
 Him.

PROVERBS 16:33—17:1

33 THE lot is cast into the lap,
 But its every decision *is* from the LORD.

17 BETTER *is* a dry morsel with
 quietness,
 Than a house full of feasting *with* strife.

JOHN 8:1–27

BUT Jesus went to the Mount of Olives. 2 Now early in the morning He came again into the temple, and all the people came to Him; and He sat down and taught them. 3 Then the scribes and Pharisees brought to Him a woman caught in adultery. And when they had set her in the midst, 4 they said to Him, "Teacher, this woman was caught in adultery, in the very act. 5 Now Moses, in the law, commanded us that such should be stoned. But what do You say?" 6 This they said, testing Him, that they might have *something* of which to accuse Him. But Jesus stooped down and wrote on the ground with *His* finger, as though He did not hear.

7 So when they continued asking Him, He raised Himself up and said to them, "He who is without sin among you, let

him throw a stone at her first." 8 And again He stooped down and wrote on the ground. 9 Then those who heard *it*, being convicted by *their* conscience, went out one by one, beginning with the oldest *even* to the last. And Jesus was left alone, and the woman standing in the midst. 10 When Jesus had raised Himself up and saw no one but the woman, He said to her, "Woman, where are those accusers of yours? Has no one condemned you?"

11 She said, "No one, Lord."

And Jesus said to her, "Neither do I condemn you; go and sin no more."

12 Then Jesus spoke to them again, saying, "I am the light of the world. He who follows Me shall not walk in darkness, but have the light of life."

13 The Pharisees therefore said to Him, "You bear witness of Yourself; Your witness is not true."

14 Jesus answered and said to them, "Even if I bear witness of Myself, My witness is true, for I know where I came from and where I am going; but you do not know where I come from and where I am going. 15 You judge according to the flesh; I judge no one. 16 And yet if I do judge, My judgment is true; for I am not alone, but I *am* with the Father who sent Me.

17 It is also written in your law that the testimony of two men is true. 18 I am One who bears witness of Myself, and the Father who sent Me bears witness of Me."

19 Then they said to Him, "Where is Your Father?"

Jesus answered, "You know neither Me nor My Father. If you had known Me, you would have known My Father also."

20 These words Jesus spoke in the treasury, as He taught in the temple; and no one laid hands on Him, for His hour had not yet come.

21 Then Jesus said to them again, "I am going away, and you will seek Me, and will die in your sin. Where I go you cannot come."

22 So the Jews said, "Will He kill Himself, because He says, 'Where I go you cannot come'?"

23 And He said to them, "You are from beneath; I am from above. You are of this world; I am not of this world. 24 Therefore I said to you that you will die in your sins; for if you do not believe that I am *He*, you will die in your sins."

25 Then they said to Him, "Who are You?"

And Jesus said to them, "Just what I have been saying to you from the beginning. 26 I have many things to say and to judge concerning you, but He who sent Me is true; and I speak to the world those things which I heard from Him."

27 They did not understand that He spoke to them of the Father.

---

*Reading 145—*His Unaging Youth
John 8:58

Spiritually we never grow old; through the passing of things we grow so many years young. The characteristic of the spiritual life is its unaging youth, exactly the opposite of the natural life. "I am . . . the First and the Last." The Ancient of Days represents the eternal childhood. God Almighty became the weakest thing in His own creation, a baby. When He comes into us in new birth, we can easily kill His life in us, or else we can see to it that His life is nourished according to the dictates of the Spirit of God, so that we grow "to the measure of the stature of the fullness of Christ." The mature saint is just like a little child, absolutely simple and joyful and lively. Go on living the life that God would have you live, and you will grow younger instead of older. There is a marvelous rejuvenescence when once you let God have His way. If you are feeling very old, then get born again and begin to grow in His new life.   (MAKING NEW)

2 SAMUEL 21:1—22:51

NOW there was a famine in the days of David for three years, year after year; and David inquired of the LORD. And the LORD answered, "It *is* because of Saul and *his* bloodthirsty house, because he killed the Gibeonites." 2 So the king called the Gibeonites and spoke to them. Now the Gibeonites *were* not of the children of Israel, but of the remnant of the Amorites; the children of Israel had sworn protection to them, but Saul had sought to kill them in his zeal for the children of Israel and Judah.

3 Therefore David said to the Gibeonites, "What shall I do for you? And with what shall I make atonement, that you may bless the inheritance of the LORD?"

4 And the Gibeonites said to him, "We will have no silver or gold from Saul or from his house, nor shall you kill any man in Israel for us."

So he said, "Whatever you say, I will do for you."

5 Then they answered the king, "As for the man who consumed us and plotted against us, *that* we should be destroyed from remaining in any of the territories of Israel, 6 let seven men of his descendants be delivered to us, and we will hang them before the LORD in Gibeah of Saul, *whom* the LORD chose."

And the king said, "I will give *them*."

7 But the king spared Mephibosheth the son of Jonathan, the son of Saul, because of the LORD's oath that *was* between them, between David and Jonathan the son of Saul. 8 So the king took Armoni and Mephibosheth, the two sons of Rizpah the daughter of Aiah, whom she bore to Saul, and the five sons of Michal the daughter of Saul, whom she brought up for Adriel the son of Barzillai the Meholathite; 9 and he delivered them into the hands of the Gibeonites, and they hanged them on the hill before the LORD. So they fell, *all* seven together, and were put to death in the days of harvest, in the first *days,* in the beginning of barley harvest.

10 Now Rizpah the daughter of Aiah took sackcloth and spread it for herself on the rock, from the beginning of harvest until the late rains poured on them from heaven. And she did not allow the birds of the air to rest on them by day nor the beasts of the field by night.

11 And David was told what Rizpah the daughter of Aiah, the concubine of Saul, had done. 12 Then David went and took the bones of Saul, and the bones of Jonathan his son, from the men of Jabesh Gilead who had stolen them from the street of Beth Shan, where the Philistines had hung them up, after the Philistines had struck down Saul in Gilboa. 13 So he brought up the bones of Saul and the bones of Jonathan his son from there; and they gathered the bones of those who had been hanged. 14 They buried the bones of Saul and Jonathan his son in the country of Benjamin in Zelah, in the tomb of Kish his father. So they performed all that the king commanded. And after that God heeded the prayer for the land.

15 When the Philistines were at war again with Israel, David and his servants with him went down and fought against the Philistines; and David grew faint. 16 Then Ishbi-Benob, who *was* one of the sons of the giant, the weight of whose bronze spear *was* three hundred *shekels,* who was bearing a new *sword,* thought he could kill David. 17 But Abishai the son of Zeruiah came to his aid, and struck the Philistine and killed him. Then the men of David swore to him, saying, "You shall go out no more with us to battle, lest you quench the lamp of Israel."

18 Now it happened afterward that there was again a battle with the Philistines at Gob. Then Sibbechai the Hushathite killed Saph, who *was* one of the sons of the giant. 19 Again there was war at Gob with the Philistines, where Elhanan the son of Jaare-Oregim the Bethlehemite killed *the brother of* Goliath the Gittite, the shaft of whose spear *was* like a weaver's beam.

20 Yet again there was war at Gath, where there was a man of *great* stature, who had six fingers on each hand and six toes on each foot, twenty-four in number; and he also was born to the giant. 21 So when he defied Israel, Jonathan the son of Shimea, David's brother, killed him.

22 These four were born to the giant in Gath, and fell by the hand of David and by the hand of his servants.

22 THEN David spoke to the LORD the words of this song, on the day when the LORD had delivered him from the hand of all his enemies, and from the hand of Saul. 2 And he said:

"The LORD *is* my rock and my fortress
    and my deliverer;
3 The God of my strength, in whom
    I will trust;
My shield and the horn of my
    salvation,
My stronghold and my refuge;

My Savior, You save me from
violence.
4 I will call upon the Lord, *who is
worthy* to be praised;
So shall I be saved from my enemies.

5 "When the waves of death surrounded
me,
The floods of ungodliness made me
afraid.
6 The sorrows of Sheol surrounded
me;
The snares of death confronted me.
7 In my distress I called upon the
Lord,
And cried out to my God;
He heard my voice from His temple,
And my cry *entered* His ears.

8 "Then the earth shook and trembled;
The foundations of heaven quaked
and were shaken,
Because He was angry.
9 Smoke went up from His nostrils,
And devouring fire from His mouth;
Coals were kindled by it.
10 He bowed the heavens also, and came
down
With darkness under His feet.
11 He rode upon a cherub, and flew;
And He was seen upon the wings
of the wind.
12 He made darkness canopies around
Him,
Dark waters *and* thick clouds of the
skies.
13 From the brightness before Him
Coals of fire were kindled.

14 "The Lord thundered from heaven,
And the Most High uttered His
voice.
15 He sent out arrows and scattered
them;
Lightning bolts, and He vanquished
them.
16 Then the channels of the sea were
seen,
The foundations of the world were
uncovered,
At the rebuke of the Lord,
At the blast of the breath of His
nostrils.

17 "He sent from above, He took me,
He drew me out of many waters.
18 He delivered me from my strong
enemy,
From those who hated me;
For they were too strong for me.
19 They confronted me in the day of
my calamity,

But the Lord was my support.
20 He also brought me out into a broad
place;
He delivered me because He
delighted in me.

21 "The Lord rewarded me according
to my righteousness;
According to the cleanness of my
hands
He has recompensed me.
22 For I have kept the ways of the Lord,
And have not wickedly departed from
my God.
23 For all His judgments *were* before
me;
And *as for* His statutes, I did not
depart from them.
24 I was also blameless before Him,
And I kept myself from my iniquity.
25 Therefore the Lord has recompensed
me according to my righteousness,
According to my cleanness in His
eyes.

26 "With the merciful You will show
Yourself merciful;
With a blameless man You will show
Yourself blameless;
27 With the pure You will show Yourself
pure;
And with the devious You will show
Yourself shrewd.
28 You will save the humble people;
But Your eyes *are* on the haughty,
that You may bring *them* down.

29 "For You *are* my lamp, O Lord;
The Lord shall enlighten my
darkness.
30 For by You I can run against a troop;
By my God I can leap over a wall.
31 *As for* God, His way *is* perfect;
The word of the Lord *is* proven;
He *is* a shield to all who trust in Him.

---

*P*erfect life means the perfect
adjustment of all our relationships to
God.   (Bib. Psych.)

---

32 "For who *is* God, except the Lord?
And who *is* a rock, except our God?
33 God *is* my strength *and* power,
And He makes my way perfect.
34 He makes my feet like the *feet* of deer,
And sets me on my high places.
35 He teaches my hands to make war,
So that my arms can bend a bow of
bronze.

36 "You have also given me the shield
    of Your salvation;
Your gentleness has made me great.
37 You enlarged my path under me;
    So my feet did not slip.

38 "I have pursued my enemies and
    destroyed them;
Neither did I turn back again till they
    were destroyed.
39 And I have destroyed them and
    wounded them,
So that they could not rise;
They have fallen under my feet.
40 For You have armed me with
    strength for the battle;
You have subdued under me those
    who rose against me.
41 You have also given me the necks
    of my enemies,
So that I destroyed those who hated
    me.
42 They looked, but *there was* none to
    save;
Even to the LORD, but He did not
    answer them.
43 Then I beat them as fine as the dust
    of the earth;
I trod them like dirt in the streets,
And I spread them out.

44 "You have also delivered me from the
    strivings of my people;
You have kept me as the head of the
    nations.
A people I have not known shall serve
    me.
45 The foreigners submit to me;
As soon as they hear, they obey me.
46 The foreigners fade away,
And come frightened from their
    hideouts.

47 "The LORD lives!
Blessed *be* my Rock!
Let God be exalted,
The Rock of my salvation!
48 *It is* God who avenges me,
And subdues the peoples under me;
49 He delivers me from my enemies.
You also lift me up above those who
    rise against me;
You have delivered me from the
    violent man.
50 Therefore I will give thanks to You,
    O LORD, among the Gentiles,
And sing praises to Your name.

51 "*He is* the tower of salvation to His
    king,
And shows mercy to His anointed,

To David and his descendants
    forevermore."

PSALM 68:1–6

1 LET God arise,
Let His enemies be scattered;
Let those also who hate Him flee before
    Him.
2 As smoke is driven away,
So drive *them* away;
As wax melts before the fire,
So let the wicked perish at the presence
    of God.
3 But let the righteous be glad;
Let them rejoice before God;
Yes, let them rejoice exceedingly.

4 Sing to God, sing praises to His name;
Extol Him who rides on the clouds,
By His name YAH,
And rejoice before Him.

5 A father of the fatherless, a defender
    of widows,
Is God in His holy habitation.
6 God sets the solitary in families;
He brings out those who are bound
    into prosperity;
But the rebellious dwell in a dry *land.*

PROVERBS 17:2–4

2 A wise servant will rule over a son who
    causes shame,
And will share an inheritance among
    the brothers.

3 The refining pot *is* for silver and the
    furnace for gold,
But the LORD tests the hearts.

4 An evildoer gives heed to false lips;
A liar listens eagerly to a spiteful tongue.

JOHN 8:28–59

THEN Jesus said to them, "When you lift
up the Son of Man, then you will know
that I am *He,* and *that* I do nothing of
Myself; but as My Father taught Me, I speak
these things. 29 And He who sent Me is
with Me. The Father has not left Me alone,
for I always do those things that please
Him." 30 As He spoke these words, many
believed in Him.

31 Then Jesus said to those Jews who believed Him, "If you abide in My word, you

Discipleship carries an option with it. (APPROVED)

are My disciples indeed. 32 And you shall know the truth, and the truth shall make you free."

33 They answered Him, "We are Abraham's descendants, and have never been in bondage to anyone. How *can* You say, 'You will be made free'?"

34 Jesus answered them, "Most assuredly, I say to you, whoever commits sin is a slave of sin. 35 And a slave does not abide in the house forever, *but* a son abides forever. 36 Therefore if the Son makes you free, you shall be free indeed.

37 "I know that you are Abraham's descendants, but you seek to kill Me, because My word has no place in you. 38 I speak what I have seen with My Father, and you do what you have seen with your father."

39 They answered and said to Him, "Abraham is our father."

Jesus said to them, "If you were Abraham's children, you would do the works of Abraham. 40 But now you seek to kill Me, a Man who has told you the truth which I heard from God. Abraham did not do this. 41 You do the deeds of your father."

Then they said to Him, "We were not born of fornication; we have one Father—God."

42 Jesus said to them, "If God were your Father, you would love Me, for I proceeded forth and came from God; nor have I come of Myself, but He sent Me. 43 Why do you not understand My speech? Because you are not able to listen to My word. 44 You are of *your* father the devil, and the desires of your father you want to do. He was a murderer from the beginning, and does not stand in the truth, because there is no truth

in him. When he speaks a lie, he speaks from his own *resources,* for he is a liar and the father of it. 45 But because I tell the truth, you do not believe Me. 46 Which of you convicts Me of sin? And if I tell the truth, why do you not believe Me? 47 He who is of God hears God's words; therefore you do not hear, because you are not of God."

48 Then the Jews answered and said to Him, "Do we not say rightly that You are a Samaritan and have a demon?"

49 Jesus answered, "I do not have a demon; but I honor My Father, and you dishonor Me. 50 And I do not seek My *own* glory; there is One who seeks and judges. 51 Most assuredly, I say to you, if anyone keeps My word he shall never see death."

52 Then the Jews said to Him, "Now we know that You have a demon! Abraham is dead, and the prophets; and You say, 'If anyone keeps My word he shall never taste death.' 53 Are You greater than our father Abraham, who is dead? And the prophets are dead. Who do You make Yourself out to be?"

54 Jesus answered, "If I honor Myself, My honor is nothing. It is My Father who honors Me, of whom you say that He is your God. 55 Yet you have not known Him, but I know Him. And if I say, 'I do not know Him,' I shall be a liar like you; but I do know Him and keep His word. 56 Your father Abraham rejoiced to see My day, and he saw *it* and was glad."

57 Then the Jews said to Him, "You are not yet fifty years old, and have You seen Abraham?"

58 Jesus said to them, "Most assuredly, I say to you, before Abraham was, I AM."

59 Then they took up stones to throw at Him; but Jesus hid Himself and went out of the temple, going through the midst of them, and so passed by.

Reading 146—Sanctified to the Lord
2 Samuel 23:16

I can never sanctify to God that with which I long to satisfy myself. If I am going to satisfy myself with the blessings of God, they will corrupt me; I have to sacrifice them, pour them out, do with them what any common-sense man would say is an absurd waste. Take it in the case of friendship, or of blessing, or of spiritual experiences; as soon as I long to hold any of these for myself I cannot sanctify them to the Lord. David had the right idea when he poured out the water before the Lord.

What has been like water from the well of Bethlehem to you recently? Love, friendship, spiritual blessing? Then at the peril of your soul, you take it to satisfy yourself. If you do, you cannot pour out before the Lord. How am I to pour out spiritual gifts, or natural friendship, or love? How can I give them to the Lord? In one way only—in the determination of my mind, and that takes about two seconds. If I hold spiritual blessings or friendship for myself they will corrupt me, no matter how beautiful they are. I have to pour them out before the Lord, give them to Him in my mind, though it looks as if I am wasting them; even as when David poured the water out on the sand, to be instantly sucked up.　(*PLACE HELP*)

2 SAMUEL 23:1—24:25

NOW these *are* the last words of David.

> *Thus* says David the son of Jesse;
> *Thus* says the man raised up on high,
> The anointed of the God of Jacob,
> And the sweet psalmist of Israel:

2　"The Spirit of the LORD spoke by me,
　　And His word *was* on my tongue.
3　The God of Israel said,
　　The Rock of Israel spoke to me:
　　'He who rules over men *must be* just,
　　Ruling in the fear of God.
4　And *he shall be* like the light of the
　　　morning *when* the sun rises,
　　A morning without clouds,
　　Like the tender grass *springing* out
　　　of the earth,
　　By clear shining after rain.'

5　"Although my house *is* not so with
　　　God,
　　Yet He has made with me an
　　　everlasting covenant,
　　Ordered in all *things* and secure.
　　For *this is* all my salvation and all
　　　my desire;
　　Will He not make *it* increase?
6　But *the sons* of rebellion *shall* all *be*
　　　as thorns thrust away,
　　Because they cannot be taken with
　　　hands.
7　But the man *who* touches them
　　Must be armed with iron and the
　　　shaft of a spear,
　　And they shall be utterly burned with
　　　fire in *their* place."

8 These *are* the names of the mighty men whom David had: Josheb-Basshebeth the Tachmonite, chief among the captains. He was called Adino the Eznite, because he had killed eight hundred men at one time. 9 And after him *was* Eleazar the son of Dodo, the Ahohite, *one* of the three mighty men with David when they defied the Philistines *who* were gathered there for battle, and the men of Israel had retreated. 10 He arose and attacked the Philistines until his hand was weary, and his hand stuck to the sword. The LORD brought about a great victory that day; and the people returned after him only to plunder. 11 And after him *was* Shammah the son of Agee the Hararite. The Philistines had gathered together into a troop where there was a piece of ground full of lentils. So the people fled from the Philistines. 12 But he stationed himself in the middle of the field, defended it, and killed the Philistines. So the LORD brought about a great victory.

13 Then three of the thirty chief men went down at harvest time and came to David at the cave of Adullam. And the troop of Philistines encamped in the Valley of Rephaim. 14 David *was* then in the stronghold, and the garrison of the Philistines *was* then *in* Bethlehem. 15 And David said with longing, "Oh, that someone would give me a drink of the water from the well of Bethlehem, which *is* by the gate!" 16 So the three mighty men broke through the camp of the Philistines, drew water from the well of Bethlehem that *was* by the gate, and took it and brought *it* to David. Nevertheless he would not drink it, but poured it out to the LORD. 17 And he said, "Far be it from me, O LORD, that I should do this! Is *this not* the blood of the men who went in *jeopardy of* their lives?" Therefore he would not drink it.

These things were done by the three mighty men.

18 Now Abishai the brother of Joab, the son of Zeruiah, was chief of *another* three. He lifted his spear against three hundred

men, killed *them*, and won a name among *these* three. 19 Was he not the most honored of three? Therefore he became their captain. However, he did not attain to the *first* three.

20 Benaiah *was* the son of Jehoiada, the son of a valiant man from Kabzeel, who had done many deeds. He had killed two lion-like heroes of Moab. He also had gone down and killed a lion in the midst of a pit on a snowy day. 21 And he killed an Egyptian, a spectacular man. The Egyptian *had* a spear in his hand; so he went down to him with a staff, wrested the spear out of the Egyptian's hand, and killed him with his own spear. 22 These *things* Benaiah the son of Jehoiada did, and won a name among three mighty men. 23 He was more honored than the thirty, but he did not attain to the *first* three. And David appointed him over his guard.

24 Asahel the brother of Joab *was* one of the thirty; Elhanan the son of Dodo of Bethlehem, 25 Shammah the Harodite, Elika the Harodite, 26 Helez the Paltite, Ira the son of Ikkesh the Tekoite, 27 Abiezer the Anathothite, Mebunnai the Hushathite, 28 Zalmon the Ahohite, Maharai the Netophathite, 29 Heleb the son of Baanah (the Netophathite), Ittai the son of Ribai from Gibeah of the children of Benjamin, 30 Benaiah a Pirathonite, Hiddai from the brooks of Gaash, 31 Abi-Albon the Arbathite, Azmaveth the Barhumite, 32 Eliahba the Shaalbonite (of the sons of Jashen), Jonathan, 33 Shammah the Hararite, Ahiam the son of Sharar the Hararite, 34 Eliphelet the son of Ahasbai, the son of the Maachathite, Eliam the son of Ahithophel the Gilonite, 35 Hezrai the Carmelite, Paarai the Arbite, 36 Igal the son of Nathan of Zobah, Bani the Gadite, 37 Zelek the Ammonite, Naharai the Beerothite (armorbearer of Joab the son of Zeruiah), 38 Ira the Ithrite, Gareb the Ithrite, 39 *and* Uriah the Hittite: thirty-seven in all.

24 AGAIN the anger of the Lord was aroused against Israel, and He moved David against them to say, "Go, number Israel and Judah."

2 So the king said to Joab the commander of the army who *was* with him, "Now go throughout all the tribes of Israel, from Dan to Beersheba, and count the people, that I may know the number of the people."

3 And Joab said to the king, "Now may the Lord your God add to the people a hundred times more than there are, and may the eyes of my lord the king see *it*. But why does my lord the king desire this thing?" 4 Nevertheless the king's word prevailed against Joab and against the captains of the army. Therefore Joab and the captains of the army went out from the presence of the king to count the people of Israel.

5 And they crossed over the Jordan and camped in Aroer, on the right side of the town which *is* in the midst of the ravine of Gad, and toward Jazer. 6 Then they came to Gilead and to the land of Tahtim Hodshi; they came to Dan Jaan and around to Sidon; 7 and they came to the stronghold of Tyre and to all the cities of the Hivites and the Canaanites. Then they went out to South Judah *as far as* Beersheba. 8 So when they had gone through all the land, they came to Jerusalem at the end of nine months and twenty days. 9 Then Joab gave the sum of the number of the people to the king. And there were in Israel eight hundred thousand valiant men who drew the sword, and the men of Judah were five hundred thousand men.

10 And David's heart condemned him after he had numbered the people. So David said to the Lord, "I have sinned greatly in what I have done; but now, I pray, O Lord, take away the iniquity of Your servant, for I have done very foolishly."

11 Now when David arose in the morning, the word of the Lord came to the prophet Gad, David's seer, saying, 12 "Go and tell David, 'Thus says the Lord: "I offer you three *things;* choose one of them for yourself, that I may do *it* to you." ' " 13 So Gad came to David and told him; and he said to him, "Shall seven years of famine come to you in your land? Or shall you flee three months before your enemies, while they pursue you? Or shall there be three days' plague in your land? Now consider and see what answer I should take back to Him who sent me."

14 And David said to Gad, "I am in great distress. Please let us fall into the hand of the Lord, for His mercies *are* great; but do not let me fall into the hand of man."

15 So the Lord sent a plague upon Israel from the morning till the appointed time. From Dan to Beersheba seventy thousand men of the people died. 16 And when the angel stretched out His hand over Jerusalem to destroy it, the Lord relented from the destruction, and said to the angel who was destroying the people, "It is enough; now restrain your hand." And the angel of the Lord was by the threshing floor of Araunah the Jebusite.

17 Then David spoke to the Lord when he saw the angel who was striking the people, and said, "Surely I have sinned, and I have done wickedly; but these sheep, what

have they done? Let Your hand, I pray, be against me and against my father's house."

18 And Gad came that day to David and said to him, "Go up, erect an altar to the LORD on the threshing floor of Araunah the Jebusite." 19 So David, according to the word of Gad, went up as the LORD commanded. 20 Now Araunah looked, and saw the king and his servants coming toward him. So Araunah went out and bowed before the king with his face to the ground.

21 Then Araunah said, "Why has my lord the king come to his servant?"

And David said, "To buy the threshing floor from you, to build an altar to the LORD, that the plague may be withdrawn from the people."

22 Now Araunah said to David, "Let my lord the king take and offer up whatever *seems* good to him. Look, *here are* oxen for burnt sacrifice, and threshing implements and the yokes of the oxen for wood. 23 All these, O king, Araunah has given to the king."

And Araunah said to the king, "May the LORD your God accept you."

24 Then the king said to Araunah, "No, but I will surely buy *it* from you for a price; nor will I offer burnt offerings to the LORD my God with that which costs me nothing." So David bought the threshing floor and the oxen for fifty shekels of silver. 25 And David built there an altar to the LORD, and offered burnt offerings and peace offerings. So the LORD heeded the prayers for the land, and the plague was withdrawn from Israel.

---

*P*rayer based on the Redemption creates what could not be until the prayer is offered. (SERVANT AS LORD)

PSALM 68:7–10

7 O God, when You went out before Your people,
When You marched through the wilderness, Selah
8 The earth shook;
The heavens also dropped *rain* at the presence of God;
Sinai itself *was moved* at the presence of God, the God of Israel.
9 You, O God, sent a plentiful rain, Whereby You confirmed Your inheritance,

When it was weary.
10 Your congregation dwelt in it;
You, O God, provided from Your goodness for the poor.

PROVERBS 17:5, 6

5 HE who mocks the poor reproaches his Maker;
He who is glad at calamity will not go unpunished.

6 Children's children *are* the crown of old men,
And the glory of children *is* their father.

JOHN 9:1–23

NOW as *Jesus* passed by, He saw a man who was blind from birth. 2 And His disciples asked Him, saying, "Rabbi, who sinned, this man or his parents, that he was born blind?"

3 Jesus answered, "Neither this man nor his parents sinned, but that the works of God should be revealed in him. 4 I must work the works of Him who sent Me while it is day; *the* night is coming when no one can work. 5 As long as I am in the world, I am the light of the world."

6 When He had said these things, He spat on the ground and made clay with the saliva; and He anointed the eyes of the blind man with the clay. 7 And He said to him, "Go, wash in the pool of Siloam" (which is translated, Sent). So he went and washed, and came back seeing.

8 Therefore the neighbors and those who previously had seen that he was blind said, "Is not this he who sat and begged?"

9 Some said, "This is he." Others *said,* "He is like him."

He said, "I am *he.*"

10 Therefore they said to him, "How were your eyes opened?"

11 He answered and said, "A Man called Jesus made clay and anointed my eyes and said to me, 'Go to the pool of Siloam and wash.' So I went and washed, and I received sight."

---

*N*ever allow bodily infirmities to hinder you obeying the commands of Jesus. (PERFECT)

---

12 Then they said to him, "Where is He?" He said, "I do not know."

13 They brought him who formerly was blind to the Pharisees. 14 Now it was a Sabbath when Jesus made the clay and opened his eyes. 15 Then the Pharisees also asked him again how he had received his sight. He said to them, "He put clay on my eyes, and I washed, and I see."

16 Therefore some of the Pharisees said, "This Man is not from God, because He does not keep the Sabbath."

Others said, "How can a man who is a sinner do such signs?" And there was a division among them.

17 They said to the blind man again, "What do you say about Him because He opened your eyes?"

He said, "He is a prophet."

18 But the Jews did not believe concerning him, that he had been blind and received his sight, until they called the parents of him who had received his sight. 19 And they asked them, saying, "Is this your son, who you say was born blind? How then does he now see?"

20 His parents answered them and said, "We know that this is our son, and that he was born blind; 21 but by what means he now sees we do not know, or who opened his eyes we do not know. He is of age; ask him. He will speak for himself." 22 His parents said these *things* because they feared the Jews, for the Jews had agreed already that if anyone confessed *that* He *was* Christ, he would be put out of the synagogue. 23 Therefore his parents said, "He is of age; ask him."

◆◆◆◆

Reading 147—He Is the Judgment

John 9:39

Jesus Christ did not come to pronounce judgment, He Himself is the judgment; whenever we come across Him we are judged instantly.

One of the most remarkable things about Jesus Christ is that although He was full of love and gentleness, yet in His presence everyone not only felt benefited, but ashamed. It is His presence that judges us; we long to meet Him, yet we dread to . . .

If you look at a sheep in the summertime you would say it was white, but see it against the background of startling virgin snow and it looks like a blot on the landscape. If we judge ourselves by one another we do not feel condemned (see 2 Cor. 10:12); but immediately Jesus Christ is in the background—His life, His language, His looks, His labors, we feel judged instantly. "It is for judgment that I have come into the world." The judgment that Jesus Christ's presence brings makes us pronounce judgment on ourselves, we feel a sense of shame, or of missing the mark, and we determine never to do that thing again.   (*GLORIFY*)

1 KINGS 1:1—2:46

NOW King David was old, advanced in years; and they put covers on him, but he could not get warm. 2 Therefore his servants said to him, "Let a young woman, a virgin, be sought for our lord the king, and let her stand before the king, and let her care for him; and let her lie in your bosom, that our lord the king may be warm." 3 So they sought for a lovely young woman throughout all the territory of Israel, and found Abishag the Shunammite, and brought her to the king. 4 The young woman *was* very lovely; and she cared for the king, and served him; but the king did not know her.

5 Then Adonijah the son of Haggith exalted himself, saying, "I will be king"; and he prepared for himself chariots and horsemen, and fifty men to run before him. 6 (And his father had not rebuked him at any time by saying, "Why have you done so?" He *was* also very good-looking. *His mother* had borne him after Absalom.) 7 Then he conferred with Joab the son of

Zeruiah and with Abiathar the priest, and they followed and helped Adonijah. 8 But Zadok the priest, Benaiah the son of Jehoiada, Nathan the prophet, Shimei, Rei, and the mighty men who *belonged* to David were not with Adonijah.

9 And Adonijah sacrificed sheep and oxen and fattened cattle by the stone of Zoheleth, which *is* by En Rogel; he also invited all his brothers, the king's sons, and all the men of Judah, the king's servants. 10 But he did not invite Nathan the prophet, Benaiah, the mighty men, or Solomon his brother.

11 So Nathan spoke to Bathsheba the mother of Solomon, saying, "Have you not heard that Adonijah the son of Haggith has become king, and David our lord does not know *it*? 12 Come, please, let me now give you advice, that you may save your own life and the life of your son Solomon. 13 Go immediately to King David and say to him, 'Did you not, my lord, O king, swear to your maidservant, saying, "Assuredly your son Solomon shall reign after me, and he shall sit on my throne"? Why then has Adonijah become king?' 14 Then, while you are still talking there with the king, I also will come in after you and confirm your words."

15 So Bathsheba went into the chamber to the king. (Now the king was very old, and Abishag the Shunammite was serving the king.) 16 And Bathsheba bowed and did homage to the king. Then the king said, "What is your wish?"

17 Then she said to him, "My lord, you swore by the LORD your God to your maidservant, *saying,* 'Assuredly Solomon your son shall reign after me, and he shall sit on my throne.' 18 So now, look! Adonijah has become king; and now, my lord the king, you do not know about *it.* 19 He has sacrificed oxen and fattened cattle and sheep in abundance, and has invited all the sons of the king, Abiathar the priest, and Joab the commander of the army; but Solomon your servant he has not invited. 20 And as for you, my lord, O king, the eyes of all Israel *are* on you, that you should tell them who will sit on the throne of my lord the king after him. 21 Otherwise it will happen, when my lord the king rests with his fathers, that I and my son Solomon will be counted as offenders."

22 And just then, while she was still talking with the king, Nathan the prophet also came in. 23 So they told the king, saying, "Here is Nathan the prophet." And when he came in before the king, he bowed down before the king with his face to the ground.

24 And Nathan said, "My lord, O king, have you said, 'Adonijah shall reign after me, and he shall sit on my throne'? 25 For he has gone down today, and has sacrificed oxen and fattened cattle and sheep in abundance, and has invited all the king's sons, and the commanders of the army, and Abiathar the priest; and look! They are eating and drinking before him; and they say, '*Long* live King Adonijah!' 26 But he has not invited me—me your servant—nor Zadok the priest, nor Benaiah the son of Jehoiada, nor your servant Solomon. 27 Has this thing been done by my lord the king, and you have not told your servant who should sit on the throne of my lord the king after him?"

28 Then King David answered and said, "Call Bathsheba to me." So she came into the king's presence and stood before the king. 29 And the king took an oath and said, "*As* the LORD lives, who has redeemed my life from every distress, 30 just as I swore to you by the LORD God of Israel, saying, 'Assuredly Solomon your son shall be king after me, and he shall sit on my throne in my place,' so I certainly will do this day."

31 Then Bathsheba bowed with *her* face to the earth, and paid homage to the king, and said, "Let my lord King David live forever!"

32 And King David said, "Call to me Zadok the priest, Nathan the prophet, and Benaiah the son of Jehoiada." So they came before the king. 33 The king also said to them, "Take with you the servants of your lord, and have Solomon my son ride on my own mule, and take him down to Gihon. 34 There let Zadok the priest and Nathan the prophet anoint him king over Israel; and blow the horn, and say, '*Long* live King Solomon!' 35 Then you shall come up after him, and he shall come and sit on my throne, and he shall be king in my place. For I have appointed him to be ruler over Israel and Judah."

36 Benaiah the son of Jehoiada answered the king and said, "Amen! May the LORD God of my lord the king say so *too.* 37 As the LORD has been with my lord the king, even so may He be with Solomon, and make his throne greater than the throne of my lord King David."

38 So Zadok the priest, Nathan the prophet, Benaiah the son of Jehoiada, the Cherethites, and the Pelethites went down and had Solomon ride on King David's mule, and took him to Gihon. 39 Then Zadok the priest took a horn of oil from the tabernacle and anointed Solomon. And they blew the horn, and all the people said, "*Long*

live King Solomon!" 40 And all the people went up after him; and the people played the flutes and rejoiced with great joy, so that the earth *seemed to* split with their sound.

All degrees of joy reside in the heart. (BIB. PSYCH.)

---

41 Now Adonijah and all the guests who *were* with him heard *it* as they finished eating. And when Joab heard the sound of the horn, he said, "Why *is* the city in such a noisy uproar?" 42 While he was still speaking, there came Jonathan, the son of Abiathar the priest. And Adonijah said to him, "Come in, for you *are* a prominent man, and bring good news."

43 Then Jonathan answered and said to Adonijah, "No! Our lord King David has made Solomon king. 44 The king has sent with him Zadok the priest, Nathan the prophet, Benaiah the son of Jehoiada, the Cherethites, and the Pelethites; and they have made him ride on the king's mule. 45 So Zadok the priest and Nathan the prophet have anointed him king at Gihon; and they have gone up from there rejoicing, so that the city is in an uproar. This *is* the noise that you have heard. 46 Also Solomon sits on the throne of the kingdom. 47 And moreover the king's servants have gone to bless our lord King David, saying, 'May God make the name of Solomon better than your name, and may He make his throne greater than your throne.' Then the king bowed himself on the bed. 48 Also the king said thus, 'Blessed *be* the LORD God of Israel, who has given *one* to sit on my throne this day, while my eyes see *it!*' "

49 So all the guests who were with Adonijah were afraid, and arose, and each one went his way.

50 Now Adonijah was afraid of Solomon; so he arose, and went and took hold of the horns of the altar. 51 And it was told Solomon, saying, "Indeed Adonijah is afraid of King Solomon; for look, he has taken hold of the horns of the altar, saying, 'Let King Solomon swear to me today that he will not put his servant to death with the sword.' "

52 Then Solomon said, "If he proves himself a worthy man, not one hair of him shall fall to the earth; but if wickedness is found in him, he shall die." 53 So King Solomon sent them to bring him down from the altar. And he came and fell down before King Solomon; and Solomon said to him, "Go to your house."

2 NOW the days of David drew near that he should die, and he charged Solomon his son, saying: 2 "I go the way of all the earth; be strong, therefore, and prove yourself a man. 3 And keep the charge of the LORD your God: to walk in His ways, to keep His statutes, His commandments, His judgments, and His testimonies, as it is written in the Law of Moses, that you may prosper in all that you do and wherever you turn; 4 that the LORD may fulfill His word which He spoke concerning me, saying, 'If your sons take heed to their way, to walk before Me in truth with all their heart and with all their soul,' He said, 'you shall not lack a man on the throne of Israel.'

5 "Moreover you know also what Joab the son of Zeruiah did to me, *and* what he did to the two commanders of the armies of Israel, to Abner the son of Ner and Amasa the son of Jether, whom he killed. And he shed the blood of war in peacetime, and put the blood of war on his belt that *was* around his waist, and on his sandals that *were* on his feet. 6 Therefore do according to your wisdom, and do not let his gray hair go down to the grave in peace.

7 "But show kindness to the sons of Barzillai the Gileadite, and let them be among those who eat at your table, for so they came to me when I fled from Absalom your brother.

8 "And see, *you have* with you Shimei the son of Gera, a Benjamite from Bahurim, who cursed me with a malicious curse in the day when I went to Mahanaim. But he came down to meet me at the Jordan, and I swore to him by the LORD, saying, 'I will not put you to death with the sword.' 9 Now therefore, do not hold him guiltless, for you *are* a wise man and know what you ought to do to him; but bring his gray hair down to the grave with blood."

10 So David rested with his fathers, and was buried in the City of David. 11 The period that David reigned over Israel *was* forty years; seven years he reigned in Hebron, and in Jerusalem he reigned thirty-three years. 12 Then Solomon sat on the throne of his father David; and his kingdom was firmly established.

13 Now Adonijah the son of Haggith came to Bathsheba the mother of Solomon. So she said, "Do you come peaceably?"

And he said, "Peaceably." 14 Moreover he said, "I have something *to say* to you."

And she said, "Say it."

15 Then he said, "You know that the king-

dom was mine, and all Israel had set their expectations on me, that I should reign. However, the kingdom has been turned over, and has become my brother's; for it was his from the LORD. 16 Now I ask one petition of you; do not deny me."

And she said to him, "Say it."

17 Then he said, "Please speak to King Solomon, for he will not refuse you, that he may give me Abishag the Shunammite as wife."

18 So Bathsheba said, "Very well, I will speak for you to the king."

19 Bathsheba therefore went to King Solomon, to speak to him for Adonijah. And the king rose up to meet her and bowed down to her, and sat down on his throne and had a throne set for the king's mother; so she sat at his right hand. 20 Then she said, "I desire one small petition of you; do not refuse me."

And the king said to her, "Ask it, my mother, for I will not refuse you."

21 So she said, "Let Abishag the Shunammite be given to Adonijah your brother as wife."

22 And King Solomon answered and said to his mother, "Now why do you ask Abishag the Shunammite for Adonijah? Ask for him the kingdom also—for he *is* my older brother—for him, and for Abiathar the priest, and for Joab the son of Zeruiah." 23 Then King Solomon swore by the LORD, saying, "May God do so to me, and more also, if Adonijah has not spoken this word against his own life! 24 Now therefore, *as* the LORD lives, who has confirmed me and set me on the throne of David my father, and who has established a house for me, as He promised, Adonijah shall be put to death today!"

25 So King Solomon sent by the hand of Benaiah the son of Jehoiada; and he struck him down, and he died.

26 And to Abiathar the priest the king said, "Go to Anathoth, to your own fields, for you *are* deserving of death; but I will not put you to death at this time, because you carried the ark of the Lord GOD before my father David, and because you were afflicted every time my father was afflicted." 27 So Solomon removed Abiathar from being priest to the LORD, that he might fulfill the word of the LORD which He spoke concerning the house of Eli at Shiloh.

28 Then news came to Joab, for Joab had defected to Adonijah, though he had not defected to Absalom. So Joab fled to the tabernacle of the LORD, and took hold of the horns of the altar. 29 And King Solomon was told, "Joab has fled to the tabernacle

of the LORD; there *he is*, by the altar." Then Solomon sent Benaiah the son of Jehoiada, saying, "Go, strike him down." 30 So Benaiah went to the tabernacle of the LORD, and said to him, "Thus says the king, 'Come out!'"

And he said, "No, but I will die here." And Benaiah brought back word to the king, saying, "Thus said Joab, and thus he answered me."

31 Then the king said to him, "Do as he has said, and strike him down and bury him, that you may take away from me and from the house of my father the innocent blood which Joab shed. 32 So the LORD will return his blood on his head, because he struck down two men more righteous and better than he, and killed them with the sword—Abner the son of Ner, the commander of the army of Israel, and Amasa the son of Jether, the commander of the army of Judah—though my father David did not know *it*. 33 Their blood shall therefore return upon the head of Joab and upon the head of his descendants forever. But upon David and his descendants, upon his house and his throne, there shall be peace forever from the LORD."

34 So Benaiah the son of Jehoiada went up and struck and killed him; and he was buried in his own house in the wilderness. 35 The king put Benaiah the son of Jehoiada in his place over the army, and the king put Zadok the priest in the place of Abiathar.

36 Then the king sent and called for Shimei, and said to him, "Build yourself a house in Jerusalem and dwell there, and do not go out from there anywhere. 37 For it shall be, on the day you go out and cross the Brook Kidron, know for certain you shall surely die; your blood shall be on your own head."

38 And Shimei said to the king, "The saying *is* good. As my lord the king has said, so your servant will do." So Shimei dwelt in Jerusalem many days.

39 Now it happened at the end of three years, that two slaves of Shimei ran away to Achish the son of Maachah, king of Gath. And they told Shimei, saying, "Look, your slaves *are* in Gath!" 40 So Shimei arose, saddled his donkey, and went to Achish at Gath to seek his slaves. And Shimei went and brought his slaves from Gath. 41 And Solomon was told that Shimei had gone from Jerusalem to Gath and had come back. 42 Then the king sent and called for Shimei, and said to him, "Did I not make you swear by the LORD, and warn you, saying, 'Know for certain that on the day you go out and

travel anywhere, you shall surely die'? And you said to me, 'The word I have heard *is* good.' 43 Why then have you not kept the oath of the LORD and the commandment that I gave you?" 44 The king said moreover to Shimei, "You know, as your heart acknowledges, all the wickedness that you did to my father David; therefore the LORD will return your wickedness on your own head. 45 But King Solomon *shall be* blessed, and the throne of David shall be established before the LORD forever."

46 So the king commanded Benaiah the son of Jehoiada; and he went out and struck him down, and he died. Thus the kingdom was established in the hand of Solomon.

PSALM 68:11–14

11 THE Lord gave the word;
    Great *was* the company of those who proclaimed *it:*
12 "Kings of armies flee, they flee,
    And she who remains at home divides the spoil.
13 Though you lie down among the sheepfolds,
    You will be like the wings of a dove covered with silver,
    And her feathers with yellow gold."
14 When the Almighty scattered kings in it,
    It was *white* as snow in Zalmon.

PROVERBS 17:7–9

7 EXCELLENT speech is not becoming to a fool,
   Much less lying lips to a prince.

8 A present *is* a precious stone in the eyes of its possessor;
   Wherever he turns, he prospers.

9 He who covers a transgression seeks love,
   But he who repeats a matter separates friends.

JOHN 9:24–41

SO they again called the man who was blind, and said to him, "Give God the glory! We know that this Man is a sinner."

25 He answered and said, "Whether He is a sinner *or not* I do not know. One thing I know: that though I was blind, now I see."

26 Then they said to him again, "What did He do to you? How did He open your eyes?"

27 He answered them, "I told you already, and you did not listen. Why do you want to hear *it* again? Do you also want to become His disciples?"

28 Then they reviled him and said, "You are His disciple, but we are Moses' disciples. 29 We know that God spoke to Moses; *as for* this *fellow,* we do not know where He is from."

30 The man answered and said to them, "Why, this is a marvelous thing, that you do not know where He is from; yet He has opened my eyes! 31 Now we know that God does not hear sinners; but if anyone is a worshiper of God and does His will, He hears him. 32 Since the world began it has been unheard of that anyone opened the eyes of one who was born blind. 33 If this Man were not from God, He could do nothing."

34 They answered and said to him, "You were completely born in sins, and are you teaching us?" And they cast him out.

God never insists on our obedience; human authority does. (GLORIFY)

35 Jesus heard that they had cast him out; and when He had found him, He said to him, "Do you believe in the Son of God?"

36 He answered and said, "Who is He, Lord, that I may believe in Him?"

37 And Jesus said to him, "You have both seen Him and it is He who is talking with you."

38 Then he said, "Lord, I believe!" And he worshiped Him.

39 And Jesus said, "For judgment I have come into this world, that those who do not see may see, and that those who see may be made blind."

40 Then *some* of the Pharisees who were with Him heard these words, and said to Him, "Are we blind also?"

41 Jesus said to them, "If you were blind, you would have no sin; but now you say, 'We see.' Therefore your sin remains.

Reading 148—Enter in by the Door
John 10:9

This is a picture of the life we are to live as God's children—entering in by our Lord, who is the Door, not once for all, but every day, for everything. Is there trouble in the physical domain? Enter in by the Door and be saved. Trouble in mental matters? Enter in and be saved. A thousand and one things make up life as it is and in them all we have to learn to enter in by the Door. Entering in, in the name of Jesus, is the condition of daily salvation, not salvation from sin only, but a salvation that keeps us manifestly the Lord's sheep.

Are you experiencing daily salvation, or are you shut out from Jesus Christ just now in your bodily life, in your mind, in your circumstances? Is there any fog, any darkness, any weariness, any trouble? Every day there are things that seem to shut the way up, but you can always enter in by the Door and experience salvation. In the East it is the body of the shepherd himself that is the door of the fold.

We are apt to have the idea that salvation is a kind of watertight compartment and if we enter in all our liberty will be destroyed. That is not our Lord's conception; He says "he shall go in and go out." Are we entering in by the Door for our daily work or only at a devotional meeting? The going in and out is our Lord's picture of the freedom of a son. A servant cannot go in and out as he likes, but Jesus says, "No longer do I call you servants, . . . but I have called you friends." Nothing is closed to you once you enter in by the Door.   (GOD'S WORKMANSHIP)

1 KINGS 3:1—4:34

NOW Solomon made a treaty with Pharaoh king of Egypt, and married Pharaoh's daughter; then he brought her to the City of David until he had finished building his own house, and the house of the LORD, and the wall all around Jerusalem. 2 Meanwhile the people sacrificed at the high places, because there was no house built for the name of the LORD until those days. 3 And Solomon loved the LORD, walking in the statutes of his father David, except that he sacrificed and burned incense at the high places.

4 Now the king went to Gibeon to sacrifice there, for that *was* the great high place: Solomon offered a thousand burnt offerings on that altar. 5 At Gibeon the LORD appeared to Solomon in a dream by night; and God said, "Ask! What shall I give you?"

6 And Solomon said: "You have shown great mercy to Your servant David my father, because he walked before You in truth, in righteousness, and in uprightness of heart with You; You have continued this great kindness for him, and You have given him a son to sit on his throne, as *it is* this day.

7 Now, O LORD my God, You have made Your servant king instead of my father David, but I *am* a little child; I do not know *how* to go out or come in. 8 And Your servant *is* in the midst of Your people whom You have chosen, a great people, too numerous to be numbered or counted. 9 Therefore give to Your servant an understanding heart to judge Your people, that I may discern between good and evil. For who is able to judge this great people of Yours?"

10 The speech pleased the LORD, that Solomon had asked this thing. 11 Then God said to him: "Because you have asked this thing, and have not asked long life for yourself, nor have asked riches for yourself, nor have asked the life of your enemies, but have asked for yourself understanding to discern justice, 12 behold, I have done according to your words; see, I have given

---

*D*iscernment is the power to interpret what we see and hear.   (PERFECT)

you a wise and understanding heart, so that there has not been anyone like you before you, nor shall any like you arise after you. 13 And I have also given you what you have not asked: both riches and honor, so that there shall not be anyone like you among the kings all your days. 14 So if you walk in My ways, to keep My statutes and My commandments, as your father David walked, then I will lengthen your days."

15 Then Solomon awoke; and indeed it had been a dream. And he came to Jerusalem and stood before the ark of the covenant of the LORD, offered up burnt offerings, offered peace offerings, and made a feast for all his servants.

16 Now two women *who were* harlots came to the king, and stood before him. 17 And one woman said, "O my lord, this woman and I dwell in the same house; and I gave birth while she *was* in the house. 18 Then it happened, the third day after I had given birth, that this woman also gave birth. And we *were* together; no one *was* with us in the house, except the two of us in the house. 19 And this woman's son died in the night, because she lay on him. 20 So she arose in the middle of the night and took my son from my side, while your maidservant slept, and laid him in her bosom, and laid her dead child in my bosom. 21 And when I rose in the morning to nurse my son, there he was, dead. But when I had examined him in the morning, indeed, he was not my son whom I had borne."

22 Then the other woman said, "No! But the living one *is* my son, and the dead one *is* your son."

And the first woman said, "No! But the dead one *is* your son, and the living one *is* my son."

Thus they spoke before the king.

23 And the king said, "The one says, 'This *is* my son, who lives, and your son *is* the dead one'; and the other says, 'No! But your son *is* the dead one, and my son *is* the living one.'" 24 Then the king said, "Bring me a sword." So they brought a sword before the king. 25 And the king said, "Divide the living child in two, and give half to one, and half to the other."

26 Then the woman whose son *was* living spoke to the king, for she yearned with compassion for her son; and she said, "O my lord, give her the living child, and by no means kill him!"

But the other said, "Let him be neither mine nor yours, *but* divide *him*."

27 So the king answered and said, "Give the first woman the living child, and by no means kill him; she *is* his mother."

28 And all Israel heard of the judgment which the king had rendered; and they feared the king, for they saw that the wisdom of God *was* in him to administer justice.

4 SO King Solomon was king over all Israel. 2 And these *were* his officials: Azariah the son of Zadok, the priest; 3 Elihoreph and Ahijah, the sons of Shisha, scribes; Jehoshaphat the son of Ahilud, the recorder; 4 Benaiah the son of Jehoiada, over the army; Zadok and Abiathar, the priests; 5 Azariah the son of Nathan, over the officers; Zabud the son of Nathan, a priest *and* the king's friend; 6 Ahishar, over the household; and Adoniram the son of Abda, over the labor force.

7 And Solomon had twelve governors over all Israel, who provided food for the king and his household; each one made provision for one month of the year. 8 These *are* their names: Ben-Hur, in the mountains of Ephraim; 9 Ben-Deker, in Makaz, Shaalbim, Beth Shemesh, and Elon Beth Hanan; 10 Ben-Hesed, in Arubboth; to him *belonged* Sochoh and all the land of Hepher; 11 Ben-Abinadab, *in* all the regions of Dor; he had Taphath the daughter of Solomon as wife; 12 Baana the son of Ahilud, *in* Taanach, Megiddo, and all Beth Shean, which *is* beside Zaretan below Jezreel, from Beth Shean to Abel Meholah, as far as the other side of Jokneam; 13 Ben-Geber, in Ramoth Gilead; to him *belonged* the towns of Jair the son of Manasseh, in Gilead; to him *also belonged* the region of Argob in Bashan—sixty large cities with walls and bronze gate-bars; 14 Ahinadab the son of Iddo, *in* Mahanaim; 15 Ahimaaz, in Naphtali; he also took Basemath the daughter of Solomon as wife; 16 Baanah the son of Hushai, in Asher and Aloth; 17 Jehoshaphat the son of Paruah, in Issachar; 18 Shimei the son of Elah, in Benjamin; 19 Geber the son of Uri, in the land of Gilead, *in* the country of Sihon king of the Amorites, and of Og king of Bashan. *He was* the only governor who *was* in the land.

20 Judah and Israel *were* as numerous as the sand by the sea in multitude, eating and drinking and rejoicing. 21 So Solomon reigned over all kingdoms from the River *to* the land of the Philistines, as far as the border of Egypt. *They* brought tribute and served Solomon all the days of his life.

22 Now Solomon's provision for one day was thirty kors of fine flour, sixty kors of meal, 23 ten fatted oxen, twenty oxen from the pastures, and one hundred sheep, be-

sides deer, gazelles, roebucks, and fatted fowl.

24 For he had dominion over all *the region* on this side of the River from Tiphsah even to Gaza, namely over all the kings on this side of the River; and he had peace on every side all around him. 25 And Judah and Israel dwelt safely, each man under his vine and his fig tree, from Dan as far as Beersheba, all the days of Solomon.

26 Solomon had forty thousand stalls of horses for his chariots, and twelve thousand horsemen. 27 And these governors, each man in his month, provided food for King Solomon and for all who came to King Solomon's table. There was no lack in their supply. 28 They also brought barley and straw to the proper place, for the horses and steeds, each man according to his charge.

29 And God gave Solomon wisdom and exceedingly great understanding, and largeness of heart like the sand on the seashore. 30 Thus Solomon's wisdom excelled the wisdom of all the men of the East and all the wisdom of Egypt. 31 For he was wiser than all men—than Ethan the Ezrahite, and Heman, Chalcol, and Darda, the sons of Mahol; and his fame was in all the surrounding nations. 32 He spoke three thousand proverbs, and his songs were one thousand and five. 33 Also he spoke of trees, from the cedar tree of Lebanon even to the hyssop that springs out of the wall; he spoke also of animals, of birds, of creeping things, and of fish. 34 And men of all nations, from all the kings of the earth who had heard of his wisdom, came to hear the wisdom of Solomon.

PSALM 68:15–20

15 A mountain of God *is* the mountain of Bashan;
A mountain *of many* peaks *is* the mountain of Bashan.

16 Why do you fume with envy, you mountains of *many* peaks?
This is the mountain *which* God desires to dwell in;
Yes, the LORD will dwell *in it* forever.

17 The chariots of God *are* twenty thousand,
Even thousands of thousands;
The Lord is among them *as in* Sinai, in the Holy *Place.*

18 You have ascended on high,
You have led captivity captive;
You have received gifts among men,

Even *from* the rebellious,
That the LORD God might dwell *there.*

19 Blessed *be* the Lord,
Who daily loads us *with benefits,*
The God of our salvation!   Selah

20 Our God *is* the God of salvation;
And to GOD the Lord *belong* escapes from death.

PROVERBS 17:10–12

10 REBUKE is more effective for a wise *man*
Than a hundred blows on a fool.

11 An evil *man* seeks only rebellion;
Therefore a cruel messenger will be sent against him.

12 Let a man meet a bear robbed of her cubs,
Rather than a fool in his folly.

JOHN 10:1–23

"MOST assuredly, I say to you, he who does not enter the sheepfold by the door, but climbs up some other way, the same is a thief and a robber. 2 But he who enters by the door is the shepherd of the sheep. 3 To him the doorkeeper opens, and the sheep hear his voice; and he calls his own sheep by name and leads them out. 4 And when he brings out his own sheep, he goes before them; and the sheep follow him, for they know his voice. 5 Yet they will by no means follow a stranger, but will flee from him, for they do not know the voice of strangers." 6 Jesus used this illustration, but they did not understand the things which He spoke to them.

7 Then Jesus said to them again, "Most assuredly, I say to you, I am the door of the sheep. 8 All who *ever* came before Me are thieves and robbers, but the sheep did not hear them. 9 I am the door. If anyone enters by Me, he will be saved, and will go in and out and find pasture. 10 The thief does not come except to steal, and to kill, and to destroy. I have come that they may have life, and that they may have *it* more abundantly.

Our Lord was not anti *anything.*   (DISCIPLES)

11 "I am the good shepherd. The good shepherd gives His life for the sheep. 12 But a hireling, *he who is* not the shepherd, one who does not own the sheep, sees the wolf coming and leaves the sheep and flees; and the wolf catches the sheep and scatters them. 13 The hireling flees because he is a hireling and does not care about the sheep. 14 I am the good shepherd; and I know My *sheep*, and am known by My own. 15 As the Father knows Me, even so I know the Father; and I lay down My life for the sheep. 16 And other sheep I have which are not of this fold; them also I must bring, and they will hear My voice; and there will be one flock *and* one shepherd.

17 "Therefore My Father loves Me, be-cause I lay down My life that I may take it again. 18 No one takes it from Me, but I lay it down of Myself. I have power to lay it down, and I have power to take it again. This command I have received from My Father."

19 Therefore there was a division again among the Jews because of these sayings. 20 And many of them said, "He has a de-mon and is mad. Why do you listen to Him?"

21 Others said, "These are not the words of one who has a demon. Can a demon open the eyes of the blind?"

22 Now it was the Feast of Dedication in Jerusalem, and it was winter. 23 And Jesus walked in the temple, in Solomon's porch.

◆◆◆◆

Reading 149—Moral Dominion
John 10:28

Eternal life was the life which Jesus Christ exhibited on the human plane, and it is the same life, not a copy of it, which is manifested in our mortal flesh when we are born of God. Eternal life is not a gift from God, eternal life is the gift *of God*. The energy and the power which was manifested in Jesus will be manifested in us by the sheer sovereign grace of God when once we have made the moral decision about sin. . . .

The life that was in Jesus is made ours by means of His cross when once we make the decision to be identified with Him. If it is difficult to get right with God, it is because we will not decide definitely about sin. Immediately we do decide, the full life of God comes in. Jesus came to give us endless supplies of life: "that you may be filled with all the fullness of God.". . .

The weakest saint can experience the power of the deity of the Son of God if once he is willing to "let go." Any strand of our own energy will blur the life of Jesus. We have to keep letting go, and slowly and surely the great full life of God will invade us in every part, and men will take knowledge of us that we have been with Jesus.   (*Utmost*)

1 KINGS 5:1—6:38

NOW Hiram king of Tyre sent his servants to Solomon, because he heard that they had anointed him king in place of his father, for Hiram had always loved David. 2 Then Solomon sent to Hiram, saying:

3 You know how my father David could not build a house for the name of the Lord his God because of the wars which were fought against him on every side, until the Lord put *his foes* under the soles of his feet.

4 But now the Lord my God has given me rest on every side; *there is* neither adversary nor evil occurrence.

5 And behold, I propose to build a house for the name of the Lord my God, as the Lord spoke to my father David, saying, "Your son, whom I will set on your throne in your place, he shall build the house for My name."

6 Now therefore, command that they cut down cedars for me from Lebanon; and my servants will be with your servants, and I will pay

you wages for your servants according to whatever you say. For you know *there is* none among us who has skill to cut timber like the Sidonians.

7 So it was, when Hiram heard the words of Solomon, that he rejoiced greatly and said,

> Blessed *be* the LORD this day, for He has given David a wise son over this great people!

8 Then Hiram sent to Solomon, saying:

> I have considered *the message* which you sent me, *and* I will do all you desire concerning the cedar and cypress logs.

> 9   My servants shall bring *them* down from Lebanon to the sea; I will float them in rafts by sea to the place you indicate to me, and will have them broken apart there; then you can take *them* away. And you shall fulfill my desire by giving food for my household.

10 Then Hiram gave Solomon cedar and cypress logs *according to* all his desire. 11 And Solomon gave Hiram twenty thousand kors of wheat *as* food for his household, and twenty kors of pressed oil. Thus Solomon gave to Hiram year by year.

12 So the LORD gave Solomon wisdom, as He had promised him; and there was peace between Hiram and Solomon, and the two of them made a treaty together.

13 Then King Solomon raised up a labor force out of all Israel; and the labor force was thirty thousand men. 14 And he sent them to Lebanon, ten thousand a month in shifts: they were one month in Lebanon *and* two months at home; Adoniram *was* in charge of the labor force. 15 Solomon had seventy thousand who carried burdens, and eighty thousand who quarried *stone* in the mountains, 16 besides three thousand three hundred from the chiefs of Solomon's deputies, who supervised the people who labored in the work. 17 And the king commanded them to quarry large stones, costly stones, *and* hewn stones, to lay the foundation of the temple. 18 So Solomon's builders, Hiram's builders, and the Gebalites quarried *them;* and they prepared timber and stones to build the temple.

6 AND it came to pass in the four hundred and eightieth year after the chil-

dren of Israel had come out of the land of Egypt, in the fourth year of Solomon's reign over Israel, in the month of Ziv, which *is* the second month, that he began to build the house of the LORD. 2 Now the house which King Solomon built for the LORD, its length *was* sixty cubits, its width twenty, and its height thirty cubits. 3 The vestibule in front of the sanctuary of the house *was* twenty cubits long across the width of the house, *and* the width of *the vestibule extended* ten cubits from the front of the house. 4 And he made for the house windows with beveled frames.

5 Against the wall of the temple he built chambers all around, *against* the walls of the temple, all around the sanctuary and the inner sanctuary. Thus he made side chambers all around it. 6 The lowest chamber *was* five cubits wide, the middle *was* six cubits wide, and the third *was* seven cubits wide; for he made narrow ledges around the outside of the temple, so that *the support beams* would not be fastened into the walls of the temple. 7 And the temple, when it was being built, was built with stone finished at the quarry, so that no hammer or chisel *or* any iron tool was heard in the temple while it was being built. 8 The doorway for the middle story *was* on the right side of the temple. They went up by stairs to the middle *story,* and from the middle to the third.

9 So he built the temple and finished it, and he paneled the temple with beams and boards of cedar. 10 And he built side chambers against the entire temple, each five cubits high; they were attached to the temple with cedar beams.

11 Then the word of the LORD came to Solomon, saying: 12 *"Concerning* this temple which you are building, if you walk in My statutes, execute My judgments, keep all My commandments, and walk in them, then I will perform My word with you, which I spoke to your father David. 13 And I will dwell among the children of Israel, and will not forsake My people Israel."

14 So Solomon built the temple and finished it. 15 And he built the inside walls of the temple with cedar boards; from the floor of the temple to the ceiling he paneled the inside with wood; and he covered the floor of the temple with planks of cypress. 16 Then he built the twenty-cubit room at the rear of the temple, from floor to ceiling, with cedar boards; he built *it* inside as the inner sanctuary, as the Most Holy *Place.* 17 And in front of it the temple sanctuary was forty cubits *long.* 18 The inside of the

temple was cedar, carved with ornamental buds and open flowers. All *was* cedar; there was no stone *to be* seen.

19 And he prepared the inner sanctuary inside the temple, to set the ark of the covenant of the LORD there. 20 The inner sanctuary *was* twenty cubits long, twenty cubits wide, and twenty cubits high. He overlaid it with pure gold, and overlaid the altar of cedar. 21 So Solomon overlaid the inside of the temple with pure gold. He stretched gold chains across the front of the inner sanctuary, and overlaid it with gold. 22 The whole temple he overlaid with gold, until he had finished all the temple; also he overlaid with gold the entire altar that *was* by the inner sanctuary.

23 Inside the inner sanctuary he made two cherubim *of* olive wood, *each* ten cubits high. 24 One wing of the cherub *was* five cubits, and the other wing of the cherub five cubits: ten cubits from the tip of one wing to the tip of the other. 25 And the other cherub *was* ten cubits; both cherubim *were* of the same size and shape. 26 The height of one cherub *was* ten cubits, and so *was* the other cherub. 27 Then he set the cherubim inside the inner room; and they stretched out the wings of the cherubim so that the wing of the one touched *one* wall, and the wing of the other cherub touched the other wall. And their wings touched each other in the middle of the room. 28 Also he overlaid the cherubim with gold.

29 Then he carved all the walls of the temple all around, both the inner and outer *sanctuaries,* with carved figures of cherubim, palm trees, and open flowers. 30 And the floor of the temple he overlaid with gold, both the inner and outer *sanctuaries.*

31 For the entrance of the inner sanctuary he made doors *of* olive wood; the lintel *and* doorposts *were* one-fifth *of the wall.* 32 The two doors *were of* olive wood; and he carved on them figures of cherubim, palm trees, and open flowers, and overlaid *them* with gold; and he spread gold on the cherubim and on the palm trees. 33 So for the door of the sanctuary he also made doorposts *of* olive wood, one-fourth *of the wall.* 34 And the two doors *were of* cypress wood; two panels *comprised* one folding door, and two panels *comprised* the other folding door. 35 Then he carved cherubim, palm trees, and open flowers *on them,* and overlaid *them* with gold applied evenly on the carved work.

36 And he built the inner court with three rows of hewn stone and a row of cedar beams.

37 In the fourth year the foundation of the house of the LORD was laid, in the month of Ziv. 38 And in the eleventh year, in the month of Bul, which is the eighth month, the house was finished in all its details and according to all its plans. So he was seven years in building it.

PSALM 68:21–27

21 BUT God will wound the head of His enemies,
   The hairy scalp of the one who still goes on in his trespasses.
22 The Lord said, "I will bring back from Bashan,
   I will bring *them* back from the depths of the sea,
23 That your foot may crush *them* in blood,
   And the tongues of your dogs *may have* their portion from *your* enemies."

24 They have seen Your procession, O God,
   The procession of my God, my King, into the sanctuary.
25 The singers went before, the players on instruments *followed* after;
   Among *them were* the maidens playing timbrels.
26 Bless God in the congregations,
   The Lord, from the fountain of Israel.
27 There *is* little Benjamin, their leader,
   The princes of Judah *and* their company,
   The princes of Zebulun *and* the princes of Naphtali.

PROVERBS 17:13–15

13 WHOEVER rewards evil for good,
   Evil will not depart from his house.

14 The beginning of strife *is like* releasing water;
   Therefore stop contention before a quarrel starts.

15 He who justifies the wicked, and he who condemns the just,
   Both of them alike *are* an abomination to the LORD.

JOHN 10:24–42

THEN the Jews surrounded Him and said to Him, "How long do You keep us in doubt? If You are the Christ, tell us plainly."

25 Jesus answered them, "I told you, and you do not believe. The works that I do in My Father's name, they bear witness of Me. 26 But you do not believe, because you are not of My sheep, as I said to you. 27 My sheep hear My voice, and I know them, and they follow Me. 28 And I give them eternal life, and they shall never perish; neither shall anyone snatch them out of My hand. 29 My Father, who has given *them* to Me, is greater than all; and no one is able to snatch *them* out of My Father's hand. 30 I and *My* Father are one."

31 Then the Jews took up stones again to stone Him. 32 Jesus answered them, "Many good works I have shown you from My Father. For which of those works do you stone Me?"

33 The Jews answered Him, saying, "For a good work we do not stone You, but for blasphemy, and because You, being a Man, make Yourself God."

34 Jesus answered them, "Is it not written in your law, 'I said, "You are gods" '? 35 If He called them gods, to whom the word of God came (and the Scripture cannot be broken), 36 do you say of Him whom the Father sanctified and sent into the world, 'You are blaspheming,' because I said, 'I am the Son of God'? 37 If I do not do the works of My Father, do not believe Me; 38 but if I do, though you do not believe Me, believe the works, that you may know and believe that the Father *is* in Me, and I in Him." 39 Therefore they sought

No man can believe God unless God is in him. (NOT KNOWING)

again to seize Him, but He escaped out of their hand.

40 And He went away again beyond the Jordan to the place where John was baptizing at first, and there He stayed. 41 Then many came to Him and said, "John performed no sign, but all the things that John spoke about this Man were true." 42 And many believed in Him there.

Reading 150—God's Silence
John 11:5, 6

How many of us have been blind in our prayers? Look back and think of the prayers you thought had not been answered but now find that God has answered with a bigger manifestation than you ever dreamed. God has trusted you in the most intimate way He could trust you, with an absolute silence, not of despair but of pleasure, because He saw you could stand a much bigger revelation than you had at the time.

Some prayers are followed by silence because they are wrong, others because they are bigger than we can understand. Jesus stayed where He was—a positive staying, because He loved Martha and Mary. Did they get Lazarus back? They got infinitely more; they got to know the greatest truth mortal beings ever knew—that Jesus Christ is the Resurrection and the Life. It will be a wonderful moment when we stand before God and find that the prayers we clamored for in early days and imagined were never answered, have been answered in the most amazing way, and that God's silence has been the sign of the answer. If we always want to be able to point to something and say, "This is the way God answered my Prayer," God cannot trust us yet with His silence.   (ASK)

1 KINGS 7:1—8:66

BUT Solomon took thirteen years to build his own house; so he finished all his house.

2 He also built the House of the Forest of Lebanon; its length *was* one hundred cubits, its width fifty cubits, and its height thirty cubits, with four rows of cedar pillars, and cedar beams on the pillars. 3 And *it was* paneled with cedar above the beams that *were* on forty-five pillars, fifteen *to* a row. 4 *There were* windows *with beveled frames in* three rows, and window *was* opposite window *in* three tiers. 5 And all the doorways and doorposts *had* rectangular frames; and window *was* opposite window *in* three tiers.

6 He also made the Hall of Pillars: its length *was* fifty cubits, and its width thirty cubits; and in front of them *was* a portico with pillars, and a canopy *was* in front of them.

7 Then he made a hall for the throne, the Hall of Judgment, where he might judge; and *it was* paneled with cedar from floor to ceiling.

8 And the house where he dwelt *had* another court inside the hall, of like workmanship. Solomon also made a house like this hall for Pharaoh's daughter, whom he had taken *as wife*.

9 All these *were of* costly stones cut to size, trimmed with saws, inside and out, from the foundation to the eaves, and also on the outside to the great court. 10 The foundation *was of* costly stones, large stones, some ten cubits and some eight cubits. 11 And above *were* costly stones, hewn to size, and cedar wood. 12 The great court *was* enclosed with three rows of hewn stones and a row of cedar beams. So were the inner court of the house of the LORD and the vestibule of the temple.

13 Now King Solomon sent and brought Huram from Tyre. 14 He *was* the son of a widow from the tribe of Naphtali, and his father *was* a man of Tyre, a bronze worker; he was filled with wisdom and understanding and skill in working with all kinds of bronze work. So he came to King Solomon and did all his work.

15 And he cast two pillars of bronze, each one eighteen cubits high, and a line of twelve cubits measured the circumference of each. 16 Then he made two capitals *of* cast bronze, to set on the tops of the pillars. The height of one capital *was* five cubits, and the height of the other capital *was* five cubits. 17 *He made* a lattice network, with wreaths of chainwork, for the capitals which *were* on top of the pillars: seven chains for one capital and seven for the other capital. 18 So he made the pillars, and two rows of pomegranates above the network all around to cover the capitals that *were* on top; and thus he did for the other capital.

19 The capitals which *were* on top of the pillars in the hall *were* in the shape of lilies, four cubits. 20 The capitals on the two pillars also *had pomegranates* above, by the convex surface which *was* next to the network; and there *were* two hundred such pomegranates in rows on each of the capitals all around.

21 Then he set up the pillars by the vestibule of the temple; he set up the pillar on the right and called its name Jachin, and he set up the pillar on the left and called its name Boaz. 22 The tops of the pillars were in the shape of lilies. So the work of the pillars was finished.

23 And he made the Sea of cast bronze, ten cubits from one brim to the other; *it was* completely round. Its height *was* five cubits, and a line of thirty cubits measured its circumference.

24 Below its brim *were* ornamental buds encircling it all around, ten to a cubit, all the way around the Sea. The ornamental buds *were* cast in two rows when it was cast. 25 It stood on twelve oxen: three looking toward the north, three looking toward the west, three looking toward the south, and three looking toward the east; the Sea *was set* upon them, and all their back parts *pointed* inward. 26 It *was* a handbreadth thick; and its brim was shaped like the brim of a cup, *like* a lily blossom. It contained two thousand baths.

27 He also made ten carts of bronze; four cubits *was* the length of each cart, four cubits its width, and three cubits its height. 28 And this *was* the design of the carts: They had panels, and the panels *were* between frames; 29 on the panels that *were* between the frames *were* lions, oxen, and cherubim. And on the frames *was* a pedestal on top. Below the lions and oxen *were* wreaths of plaited work. 30 Every cart had four bronze wheels and axles of bronze, and its four feet had supports. Under the laver *were* supports of cast *bronze* beside each wreath. 31 Its opening inside the crown at the top *was* one cubit in diameter; and the opening *was* round, shaped *like* a pedestal, one and a half cubits in outside diameter; and also on the opening *were* engravings, but the panels were square, not round. 32 Under the panels *were* the four wheels, and the axles of the wheels *were joined* to the cart. The height of a wheel *was* one and a half cubits. 33 The workmanship of the wheels *was* like the workmanship of a chariot

wheel; their axle pins, their rims, their spokes, and their hubs *were* all of cast *bronze.* 34 And *there were* four supports at the four corners of each cart; its supports *were* part of the cart itself. 35 On the top of the cart, at the height of half a cubit, *it was* perfectly round. And on the top of the cart, its flanges and its panels *were* of the same casting. 36 On the plates of its flanges and on its panels he engraved cherubim, lions, and palm trees, wherever there was a clear space on each, with wreaths all around. 37 Thus he made the ten carts. All of them were of the same mold, one measure, *and* one shape.

38 Then he made ten lavers of bronze; each laver contained forty baths, *and* each laver *was* four cubits. On each of the ten carts *was* a laver. 39 And he put five carts on the right side of the house, and five on the left side of the house. He set the Sea on the right side of the house, toward the southeast.

40 Huram made the lavers and the shovels and the bowls. So Huram finished doing all the work that he was to do for King Solomon *for* the house of the LORD: 41 the two pillars, the *two* bowl-shaped capitals that *were* on top of the two pillars; the two networks covering the two bowl-shaped capitals which *were* on top of the pillars; 42 four hundred pomegranates for the two networks (two rows of pomegranates for each network, to cover the two bowl-shaped capitals that *were* on top of the pillars); 43 the ten carts, and ten lavers on the carts; 44 one Sea, and twelve oxen under the Sea; 45 the pots, the shovels, and the bowls.

All these articles which Huram made for King Solomon *for* the house of the LORD *were of* burnished bronze. 46 In the plain of Jordan the king had them cast in clay molds, between Succoth and Zaretan. 47 And Solomon did not weigh all the articles, because *there were* so many; the weight of the bronze was not determined.

48 Thus Solomon had all the furnishings made for the house of the LORD: the altar of gold, and the table of gold on which *was* the showbread; 49 the lampstands of pure gold, five on the right *side* and five on the left in front of the inner sanctuary, with the flowers and the lamps and the wick-trimmers of gold; 50 the basins, the trimmers, the bowls, the ladles, and the censers of pure gold; and the hinges of gold, *both* for the doors of the inner room (the Most Holy *Place*) *and* for the doors of the main hall of the temple.

51 So all the work that King Solomon had done for the house of the LORD was finished; and Solomon brought in the things which his father David had dedicated: the silver and the gold and the furnishings. He put them in the treasuries of the house of the LORD.

8 NOW Solomon assembled the elders of Israel and all the heads of the tribes, the chief fathers of the children of Israel, to King Solomon in Jerusalem, that they might bring up the ark of the covenant of the LORD from the City of David, which *is* Zion. 2 Therefore all the men of Israel assembled with King Solomon at the feast in the month of Ethanim, which *is* the seventh month. 3 So all the elders of Israel came, and the priests took up the ark. 4 Then they brought up the ark of the LORD, the tabernacle of meeting, and all the holy furnishings that *were* in the tabernacle. The priests and the Levites brought them up. 5 Also King Solomon, and all the congregation of Israel who were assembled with him, *were* with him before the ark, sacrificing sheep and oxen that could not be counted or numbered for multitude. 6 Then the priests brought in the ark of the covenant of the LORD to its place, into the inner sanctuary of the temple, to the Most Holy *Place,* under the wings of the cherubim. 7 For the cherubim spread *their* two wings over the place of the ark, and the cherubim overshadowed the ark and its poles. 8 The poles extended so that the ends of the poles could be seen from the holy *place,* in front of the inner sanctuary; but they could not be seen from outside. And they are there to this day. 9 Nothing *was* in the ark except the two tablets of stone which Moses put there at Horeb, when the LORD made *a covenant* with the children of Israel, when they came out of the land of Egypt.

10 And it came to pass, when the priests came out of the holy *place,* that the cloud filled the house of the LORD, 11 so that the priests could not continue ministering because of the cloud; for the glory of the LORD filled the house of the LORD.

12 Then Solomon spoke:

"The LORD said He would dwell in
    the dark cloud.
13 I have surely built You an exalted
    house,
    And a place for You to dwell in
    forever."

14 Then the king turned around and blessed the whole assembly of Israel, while all the assembly of Israel was standing.

15 And he said: "Blessed *be* the LORD God of Israel, who spoke with His mouth to my father David, and with His hand has fulfilled *it,* saying, 16 'Since the day that I brought My people Israel out of Egypt, I have chosen no city from any tribe of Israel *in which* to build a house, that My name might be there; but I chose David to be over My people Israel.' 17 Now it was in the heart of my father David to build a temple for the name of the LORD God of Israel. 18 But the LORD said to my father David, 'Whereas it was in your heart to build a temple for My name, you did well that it was in your heart. 19 Nevertheless you shall not build the temple, but your son who will come from your body, he shall build the temple for My name.' 20 So the LORD has fulfilled His word which He spoke; and I have filled the position of my father David, and sit on the throne of Israel, as the LORD promised; and I have built a temple for the name of the LORD God of Israel. 21 And there I have made a place for the ark, in which *is* the covenant of the LORD which He made with our fathers, when He brought them out of the land of Egypt."

22 Then Solomon stood before the altar of the LORD in the presence of all the assembly of Israel, and spread out his hands toward heaven; 23 and he said: "LORD God of Israel, *there is* no God in heaven above or on earth below like You, who keep *Your* covenant and mercy with Your servants who walk before You with all their hearts. 24 You have kept what You promised Your servant David my father; You have both spoken with Your mouth and fulfilled *it* with Your hand, as *it is* this day. 25 Therefore, LORD God of Israel, now keep what You promised Your servant David my father, saying, 'You shall not fail to have a man sit before Me on the throne of Israel, only if your sons take heed to their way, that they walk before Me as you have walked before Me.' 26 And now I pray, O God of Israel, let Your word come true, which You have spoken to Your servant David my father.

27 "But will God indeed dwell on the earth? Behold, heaven and the heaven of heavens cannot contain You. How much less this temple which I have built! 28 Yet regard the prayer of Your servant and his supplication, O LORD my God, and listen to the cry and the prayer which Your servant is praying before You today: 29 that Your eyes may be open toward this temple night and day, toward the place of which You said, 'My name shall be there,'

that You may hear the prayer which Your servant makes toward this place. 30 And may You hear the supplication of Your servant and of Your people Israel, when they pray toward this place. Hear in heaven Your dwelling place; and when You hear, forgive.

In forgiving He is able to deal with our past, with our present and our future. (GLORIFY)

---

31 "When anyone sins against his neighbor, and is forced to take an oath, and comes *and* takes an oath before Your altar in this temple, 32 then hear in heaven, and act, and judge Your servants, condemning the wicked, bringing his way on his head, and justifying the righteous by giving him according to his righteousness.

33 "When Your people Israel are defeated before an enemy because they have sinned against You, and when they turn back to You and confess Your name, and pray and make supplication to You in this temple, 34 then hear in heaven, and forgive the sin of Your people Israel, and bring them back to the land which You gave to their fathers.

35 "When the heavens are shut up and there is no rain because they have sinned against You, when they pray toward this place and confess Your name, and turn from their sin because You afflict them, 36 then hear in heaven, and forgive the sin of Your servants, Your people Israel, that You may teach them the good way in which they should walk; and send rain on Your land which You have given to Your people as an inheritance.

37 "When there is famine in the land, pestilence *or* blight *or* mildew, locusts *or* grasshoppers; when their enemy besieges them in the land of their cities; whatever plague or whatever sickness *there is;* 38 whatever prayer, whatever supplication is made by anyone, *or* by all Your people Israel, when each one knows the plague of his own heart, and spreads out his hands toward this temple: 39 then hear in heaven Your dwelling place, and forgive, and act, and give to everyone according to all his ways, whose heart You know (for You alone know the hearts of all the sons of men), 40 that they may fear You all the days that they live in the land which You gave to our fathers.

41 "Moreover, concerning a foreigner, who *is* not of Your people Israel, but has come from a far country for Your name's sake 42 (for they will hear of Your great

name and Your strong hand and Your outstretched arm), when he comes and prays toward this temple, 43 hear in heaven Your dwelling place, and do according to all for which the foreigner calls to You, that all peoples of the earth may know Your name and fear You, as *do* Your people Israel, and that they may know that this temple which I have built is called by Your name.

44 "When Your people go out to battle against their enemy, wherever You send them, and when they pray to the LORD toward the city which You have chosen and the temple which I have built for Your name, 45 then hear in heaven their prayer and their supplication, and maintain their cause.

46 "When they sin against You (for *there is* no one who does not sin), and You become angry with them and deliver them to the enemy, and they take them captive to the land of the enemy, far or near; 47 *yet* when they come to themselves in the land where they were carried captive, and repent, and make supplication to You in the land of those who took them captive, saying, 'We have sinned and done wrong, we have committed wickedness'; 48 and *when* they return to You with all their heart and with all their soul in the land of their enemies who led them away captive, and pray to You toward their land which You gave to their fathers, the city which You have chosen and the temple which I have built for Your name: 49 then hear in heaven Your dwelling place their prayer and their supplication, and maintain their cause, 50 and forgive Your people who have sinned against You, and all their transgressions which they have transgressed against You; and grant them compassion before those who took them captive, that they may have compassion on them 51 (for they *are* Your people and Your inheritance, whom You brought out of Egypt, out of the iron furnace), 52 that Your eyes may be open to the supplication of Your servant and the supplication of Your people Israel, to listen to them whenever they call to You. 53 For You separated them from among all the peoples of the earth *to be* Your inheritance, as You spoke by Your servant Moses, when You brought our fathers out of Egypt, O Lord GOD."

54 And so it was, when Solomon had finished praying all this prayer and supplication to the LORD, that he arose from before the altar of the LORD, from kneeling on his knees with his hands spread up to heaven. 55 Then he stood and blessed all the assembly of Israel with a loud voice, saying: 56 "Blessed *be* the LORD, who has given rest to His people Israel, according to all that He promised. There has not failed one word of all His good promise, which He promised through His servant Moses. 57 May the LORD our God be with us, as He was with our fathers. May He not leave us nor forsake us, 58 that He may incline our hearts to Himself, to walk in all His ways, and to keep His commandments and His statutes and His judgments, which He commanded our fathers. 59 And may these words of mine, with which I have made supplication before the LORD, be near the LORD our God day and night, that He may maintain the cause of His servant and the cause of His people Israel, as each day may require, 60 that all the peoples of the earth may know that the LORD *is* God; *there is* no other. 61 Let your heart therefore be loyal to the LORD our God, to walk in His statutes and keep His commandments, as at this day."

62 Then the king and all Israel with him offered sacrifices before the LORD. 63 And Solomon offered a sacrifice of peace offerings, which he offered to the LORD, twenty-two thousand bulls and one hundred and twenty thousand sheep. So the king and all the children of Israel dedicated the house of the LORD. 64 On the same day the king consecrated the middle of the court that *was* in front of the house of the LORD; for there he offered burnt offerings, grain offerings, and the fat of the peace offerings, because the bronze altar that *was* before the LORD *was* too small to receive the burnt offerings, the grain offerings, and the fat of the peace offerings.

65 At that time Solomon held a feast, and all Israel with him, a great assembly from the entrance of Hamath to the Brook of Egypt, before the LORD our God, seven days and seven *more* days—fourteen days. 66 On the eighth day he sent the people away; and they blessed the king, and went to their tents joyful and glad of heart for all the good that the LORD had done for His servant David, and for Israel His people.

PSALM 68:28–35

28 YOUR God has commanded your strength;
Strengthen, O God, what You have done for us.
29 Because of Your temple at Jerusalem, Kings will bring presents to You.
30 Rebuke the beasts of the reeds,

The herd of bulls with the calves of
the peoples,
Till everyone submits himself with pieces
of silver.
Scatter the peoples *who* delight in
war.
31 Envoys will come out of Egypt;
Ethiopia will quickly stretch out her
hands to God.

32 Sing to God, you kingdoms of the
earth;
Oh, sing praises to the Lord,   Selah
33 To Him who rides on the heaven of
heavens, *which were* of old!
Indeed, He sends out His voice, a
mighty voice.
34 Ascribe strength to God;
His excellence *is* over Israel,
And His strength *is* in the clouds.
35 O God, *You are* more awesome than
Your holy places.
The God of Israel *is* He who gives
strength and power to *His* people.

Blessed *be* God!

PROVERBS 17:16, 17

16 WHY *is there* in the hand of a fool the
purchase price of wisdom,
Since *he has* no heart *for it?*

17 A friend loves at all times,
And a brother is born for adversity.

JOHN 11:1–29

NOW a certain *man* was sick, Lazarus of
Bethany, the town of Mary and her sister
Martha. 2 It was *that* Mary who anointed
the Lord with fragrant oil and wiped His
feet with her hair, whose brother Lazarus
was sick. 3 Therefore the sisters sent to Him,
saying, "Lord, behold, he whom You love
is sick."
4 When Jesus heard *that*, He said, "This
sickness is not unto death, but for the glory
of God, that the Son of God may be glorified through it."
5 Now Jesus loved Martha and her sister
and Lazarus. 6 So, when He heard that he
was sick, He stayed two more days in the
place where He was. 7 Then after this He
said to *the* disciples, "Let us go to Judea
again."
8 *The* disciples said to Him, "Rabbi, lately
the Jews sought to stone You, and are You
going there again?"

9 Jesus answered, "Are there not twelve
hours in the day? If anyone walks in the
day, he does not stumble, because he sees
the light of this world. 10 But if one walks
in the night, he stumbles, because the light
is not in him." 11 These things He said,
and after that He said to them, "Our friend
Lazarus sleeps, but I go that I may wake
him up."
12 Then His disciples said, "Lord, if he
sleeps he will get well." 13 However, Jesus
spoke of his death, but they thought that
He was speaking about taking rest in
sleep.
14 Then Jesus said to them plainly, "Lazarus is dead. 15 And I am glad for your sakes
that I was not there, that you may believe.
Nevertheless let us go to him."
16 Then Thomas, who is called the Twin,
said to his fellow disciples, "Let us also
go, that we may die with Him."
17 So when Jesus came, He found that
he had already been in the tomb four days.
18 Now Bethany was near Jerusalem, about
two miles away. 19 And many of the Jews
had joined the women around Martha and
Mary, to comfort them concerning their
brother.
20 Now Martha, as soon as she heard that
Jesus was coming, went and met Him, but
Mary was sitting in the house. 21 Now Martha said to Jesus, "Lord, if You had been
here, my brother would not have died.
22 But even now I know that whatever You
ask of God, God will give You."
23 Jesus said to her, "Your brother will
rise again."
24 Martha said to Him, "I know that he
will rise again in the resurrection at the
last day."

---

*Today we have substituted credal
belief for personal belief.*   (UTMOST)

---

25 Jesus said to her, "I am the resurrection
and the life. He who believes in Me, though
he may die, he shall live. 26 And whoever
lives and believes in Me shall never die.
Do you believe this?"
27 She said to Him, "Yes, Lord, I believe
that You are the Christ, the Son of God,
who is to come into the world."
28 And when she had said these things,
she went her way and secretly called Mary
her sister, saying, "The Teacher has come
and is calling for you." 29 As soon as she
heard *that,* she arose quickly and came to
Him.

Reading 151—Confidence in Jesus

John 11:40

Can you trust Jesus Christ where your common sense cannot trust Him? Can you venture heroically on Jesus Christ's statements when the facts of your common-sense life shout—"It's a lie"? On the mount it is easy to say—"Oh, yes, I believe God can do it"; but you have to come down into the demon-possessed valley and meet with facts that laugh ironically at the whole of your mount-of-transfiguration belief. Every time my program of belief is clear to my own mind, I come across something that contradicts it. Let me say I believe God will supply all my need, and then let me run dry, with no outlook, and see whether I will go through the trial of faith, or whether I will sink back to something lower.

Faith must be tested, because it can be turned into a personal possession only through conflict. What is your faith up against just now? The test will either prove that your faith is right, or it will kill it. "Blessed is he whosoever shall not be offended in Me." The final thing is confidence in Jesus. Believe steadfastly on Him and all you come up against will develop your faith. There is continual testing in the life of faith, and the last great test is death. May God keep us in fighting trim! Faith is unutterable trust in God, trust which never dreams that He will not stand by us. (*Utmost*)

1 KINGS 9:1—10:29

AND it came to pass, when Solomon had finished building the house of the LORD and the king's house, and all Solomon's desire which he wanted to do, 2 that the LORD appeared to Solomon the second time, as He had appeared to him at Gibeon. 3 And the LORD said to him: "I have heard your prayer and your supplication that you have made before Me; I have consecrated this house which you have built to put My name there forever, and My eyes and My heart will be there perpetually. 4 Now if

---

The real reason for prayer is intimacy of relation with our Father. (CHRIS. DIS. 2)

---

you walk before Me as your father David walked, in integrity of heart and in uprightness, to do according to all that I have commanded you, *and* if you keep My statutes and My judgments, 5 then I will establish the throne of your kingdom over Israel forever, as I promised David your father, saying, 'You shall not fail to have a man on the throne of Israel.' 6 *But* if you or your sons at all turn from following Me, and

do not keep My commandments *and* My statutes which I have set before you, but go and serve other gods and worship them, 7 then I will cut off Israel from the land which I have given them; and this house which I have consecrated for My name I will cast out of My sight. Israel will be a proverb and a byword among all peoples. 8 And *as for* this house, *which* is exalted, everyone who passes by it will be astonished and will hiss, and say, 'Why has the LORD done thus to this land and to this house?' 9 Then they will answer, 'Because they forsook the LORD their God, who brought their fathers out of the land of Egypt, and have embraced other gods, and worshiped them and served them; therefore the LORD has brought all this calamity on them.'"

10 Now it happened at the end of twenty years, when Solomon had built the two houses, the house of the LORD and the king's house 11 (Hiram the king of Tyre had supplied Solomon with cedar and cypress and gold, as much as he desired), *that* King Solomon then gave Hiram twenty cities in the land of Galilee. 12 Then Hiram went from Tyre to see the cities which Solomon had given him, but they did not please him. 13 So he said, "What *kind of* cities *are* these which you have given me, my brother?" And he called them the land of Cabul, as they are to this day. 14 Then

Hiram sent the king one hundred and twenty talents of gold.

15 And this *is* the reason for the labor force which King Solomon raised: to build the house of the LORD, his own house, the Millo, the wall of Jerusalem, Hazor, Megiddo, and Gezer. 16 (Pharaoh king of Egypt had gone up and taken Gezer and burned it with fire, had killed the Canaanites who dwelt in the city, and had given it *as* a dowry to his daughter, Solomon's wife.) 17 And Solomon built Gezer, Lower Beth Horon, 18 Baalath, and Tadmor in the wilderness, in the land *of Judah,* 19 all the storage cities that Solomon had, cities for his chariots and cities for his cavalry, and whatever Solomon desired to build in Jerusalem, in Lebanon, and in all the land of his dominion.

20 All the people *who were* left of the Amorites, Hittites, Perizzites, Hivites, and Jebusites, who *were* not of the children of Israel— 21 that is, their descendants who were left in the land after them, whom the children of Israel had not been able to destroy completely—from these Solomon raised forced labor, as it is to this day. 22 But of the children of Israel Solomon made no forced laborers, because they *were* men of war and his servants: his officers, his captains, commanders of his chariots, and his cavalry.

23 Others *were* chiefs of the officials who *were* over Solomon's work: five hundred and fifty, who ruled over the people who did the work.

24 But Pharaoh's daughter came up from the City of David to her house which *Solomon* had built for her. Then he built the Millo.

25 Now three times a year Solomon offered burnt offerings and peace offerings on the altar which he had built for the LORD, and he burned incense with them *on the altar* that *was* before the LORD. So he finished the temple.

26 King Solomon also built a fleet of ships at Ezion Geber, which *is* near Elath on the shore of the Red Sea, in the land of Edom. 27 Then Hiram sent his servants with the fleet, seamen who knew the sea, to work with the servants of Solomon. 28 And they went to Ophir, and acquired four hundred and twenty talents of gold from there, and brought *it* to King Solomon.

10 NOW when the queen of Sheba heard of the fame of Solomon concerning the name of the LORD, she came to test him with hard questions. 2 She came to Jerusalem with a very great retinue, with camels that bore spices, very much gold, and precious stones; and when she came to Solomon, she spoke with him about all that was in her heart. 3 So Solomon answered all her questions; there was nothing so difficult for the king that he could not explain *it* to her. 4 And when the queen of Sheba had seen all the wisdom of Solomon, the house that he had built, 5 the food on his table, the seating of his servants, the service of his waiters and their apparel, his cupbearers, and his entryway by which he went up to the house of the LORD, there was no more spirit in her. 6 Then she said to the king: "It was a true report which I heard in my own land about your words and your wisdom. 7 However I did not believe the words until I came and saw with my own eyes; and indeed the half was not told me. Your wisdom and prosperity exceed the fame of which I heard. 8 Happy *are* your men and happy *are* these your servants, who stand continually before you *and* hear your wisdom! 9 Blessed be the LORD your God, who delighted in you, setting you on the throne of Israel! Because the LORD has loved Israel forever, therefore He made you king, to do justice and righteousness."

10 Then she gave the king one hundred and twenty talents of gold, spices in great quantity, and precious stones. There never again came such abundance of spices as the queen of Sheba gave to King Solomon. 11 Also, the ships of Hiram, which brought gold from Ophir, brought great *quantities* of almug wood and precious stones from Ophir. 12 And the king made steps of the almug wood for the house of the LORD and for the king's house, also harps and stringed instruments for singers. There never again came such almug wood, nor has the like been seen to this day.

13 Now King Solomon gave the queen of Sheba all she desired, whatever she asked, besides what Solomon had given her according to the royal generosity. So she turned and went to her own country, she and her servants.

14 The weight of gold that came to Solomon yearly was six hundred and sixty-six talents of gold, 15 besides *that* from the traveling merchants, from the income of traders, from all the kings of Arabia, and from the governors of the country.

16 And King Solomon made two hundred large shields *of* hammered gold; six hundred *shekels* of gold went into each shield. 17 He also *made* three hundred shields *of* hammered gold; three minas of gold went into each shield. The king put

them in the House of the Forest of Lebanon.

18 Moreover the king made a great throne of ivory, and overlaid it with pure gold. 19 The throne had six steps, and the top of the throne *was* round at the back; *there were* armrests on either side of the place of the seat, and two lions stood beside the armrests. 20 Twelve lions stood there, one on each side of the six steps; nothing like *this* had been made for any *other* kingdom.

21 All King Solomon's drinking vessels *were* gold, and all the vessels of the House of the Forest of Lebanon *were* pure gold. Not *one was* silver, for this was accounted as nothing in the days of Solomon. 22 For the king had merchant ships at sea with the fleet of Hiram. Once every three years the merchant ships came bringing gold, silver, ivory, apes, and monkeys. 23 So King Solomon surpassed all the kings of the earth in riches and wisdom.

24 Now all the earth sought the presence of Solomon to hear his wisdom, which God had put in his heart. 25 Each man brought his present: articles of silver and gold, garments, armor, spices, horses, and mules, at a set rate year by year.

26 And Solomon gathered chariots and horsemen; he had one thousand four hundred chariots and twelve thousand horsemen, whom he stationed in the chariot cities and with the king at Jerusalem. 27 The king made silver *as common* in Jerusalem as stones, and he made cedar trees as abundant as the sycamores which *are* in the lowland. 28 Also Solomon had horses imported from Egypt and Keveh; the king's merchants bought them in Keveh at the *current* price. 29 Now a chariot that was imported from Egypt cost six hundred *shekels* of silver, and a horse one hundred and fifty; and thus, through their agents, they exported *them* to all the kings of the Hittites and the kings of Syria.

PSALM 69:1–4

1   SAVE me, O God!
    For the waters have come up to *my* neck.
2   I sink in deep mire,
    Where *there is* no standing;
    I have come into deep waters,
    Where the floods overflow me.
3   I am weary with my crying;
    My throat is dry;
    My eyes fail while I wait for my God.

4   Those who hate me without a cause
    Are more than the hairs of my head;

They are mighty who would destroy me,
Being my enemies wrongfully;
Though I have stolen nothing,
I *still* must restore *it*.

PROVERBS 17:18, 19

18 A man devoid of understanding shakes hands in a pledge,
    And becomes surety for his friend.

19 He who loves transgression loves strife,
    And he who exalts his gate seeks destruction.

JOHN 11:30–57

NOW Jesus had not yet come into the town, but was in the place where Martha met Him. 31 Then the Jews who were with her in the house, and comforting her, when they saw that Mary rose up quickly and went out, followed her, saying, "She is going to the tomb to weep there."

32 Then, when Mary came where Jesus was, and saw Him, she fell down at His feet, saying to Him, "Lord, if You had been here, my brother would not have died."

33 Therefore, when Jesus saw her weeping, and the Jews who came with her weeping, He groaned in the spirit and was troubled. 34 And He said, "Where have you laid him?"

They said to Him, "Lord, come and see."

35 Jesus wept. 36 Then the Jews said, "See how He loved him!"

37 And some of them said, "Could not this Man, who opened the eyes of the blind, also have kept this man from dying?"

38 Then Jesus, again groaning in Himself, came to the tomb. It was a cave, and a stone lay against it. 39 Jesus said, "Take away the stone."

Martha, the sister of him who was dead, said to Him, "Lord, by this time there is a stench, for he has been *dead* four days."

40 Jesus said to her, "Did I not say to you that if you would believe you would see the glory of God?" 41 Then they took away the stone *from the place* where the dead man was lying. And Jesus lifted up *His* eyes and said, "Father, I thank You that You have heard Me. 42 And I know that You always hear Me, but because of the people who are standing by I said *this,* that they may believe that You sent Me." 43 Now

when He had said these things, He cried with a loud voice, "Lazarus, come forth!" 44 And he who had died came out bound hand and foot with graveclothes, and his face was wrapped with a cloth. Jesus said to them, "Loose him, and let him go."

45 Then many of the Jews who had come to Mary, and had seen the things Jesus did, believed in Him. 46 But some of them went away to the Pharisees and told them the things Jesus did. 47 Then the chief priests and the Pharisees gathered a council and said, "What shall we do? For this Man works many signs. 48 If we let Him alone like this, everyone will believe in Him, and the Romans will come and take away both our place and nation."

49 And one of them, Caiaphas, being high priest that year, said to them, "You know nothing at all, 50 nor do you consider that it is expedient for us that one man should die for the people, and not that the whole nation should perish." 51 Now this he did not say on his own *authority;* but being high priest that year he prophesied that Jesus would die for the nation, 52 and not for that nation only, but also that He would gather together in one the children of God who were scattered abroad.

53 Then, from that day on, they plotted to put Him to death. 54 Therefore Jesus no longer walked openly among the Jews, but went from there into the country near the wilderness, to a city called Ephraim, and there remained with His disciples.

55 And the Passover of the Jews was near, and many went from the country up to Jerusalem before the Passover, to purify themselves. 56 Then they sought Jesus, and spoke among themselves as they stood in the temple, "What do you think—that He will not come to the feast?" 57 Now both the chief priests and the Pharisees had given a command, that if anyone knew where He was, he should report *it,* that they might seize Him.

◆◆◆

Reading 152—God's Way of Giving Life
John 12:24

D eath is God's delightful way of giving us life. The monks in the early ages shut themselves away from everything to prove they were dead to it all, and when they got away they found themselves more alive than ever. Jesus never shut Himself away from things, the first place He took His disciples to was a marriage feast. He did not cut Himself off from society, He was not aloof, so much was He not aloof that they called Him "a glutton and a winebibber"! But there was one characteristic of Jesus—He was fundamentally dead to the whole thing, it had no appeal to Him. The "hundredfold" which Jesus promised means that God can trust a man anywhere and with anything when he is fundamentally dead to things. . . .

We use the phrase "drawing on the resurrection life of Jesus," but try it, you cannot draw on it when you like. You will never get one breath of that life until you are dead, that is, dead to any desire that you want a blessing for body or soul or spirit. Immediately you die to that, the life of God is in you, and you don't know where you are with the exuberance of it.   (*Perfect*)

1 KINGS 11:1—12:33

BUT King Solomon loved many foreign women, as well as the daughter of Pharaoh: women of the Moabites, Ammonites, Edomites, Sidonians, *and* Hittites— 2 from the nations of whom the Lord had said to the children of Israel, "You shall not intermarry with them, nor they with you. Surely they will turn away your hearts after their gods." Solomon clung to these in love. 3 And he had seven hundred wives, princesses, and three hundred concubines; and his wives turned away his heart.

4 For it was so, when Solomon was old, that his wives turned his heart after other gods; and his heart was not loyal to the LORD his God, as *was* the heart of his father David. 5 For Solomon went after Ashtoreth the goddess of the Sidonians, and after Milcom the abomination of the Ammonites. 6 Solomon did evil in the sight of the LORD, and did not fully follow the LORD, as *did* his father David. 7 Then Solomon built a high place for Chemosh the abomination of Moab, on the hill that *is* east of Jerusalem, and for Molech the abomination of the people of Ammon. 8 And he did likewise for all his foreign wives, who burned incense and sacrificed to their gods.

9 So the LORD became angry with Solomon, because his heart had turned from the LORD God of Israel, who had appeared to him twice, 10 and had commanded him concerning this thing, that he should not go after other gods; but he did not keep what the LORD had commanded. 11 Therefore the LORD said to Solomon, "Because you have done this, and have not kept My covenant and My statutes, which I have commanded you, I will surely tear the kingdom away from you and give it to your servant. 12 Nevertheless I will not do it in your days, for the sake of your father David; I will tear it out of the hand of your son. 13 However I will not tear away the whole kingdom; I will give one tribe to your son for the sake of my servant David, and for the sake of Jerusalem which I have chosen."

14 Now the LORD raised up an adversary against Solomon, Hadad the Edomite; he *was* a descendant of the king in Edom. 15 For it happened, when David was in Edom, and Joab the commander of the army had gone up to bury the slain, after he had killed every male in Edom 16 (because for six months Joab remained there with all Israel, until he had cut down every male in Edom), 17 that Hadad fled to go to Egypt, and certain Edomites of his father's servants with him. Hadad *was* still a little child. 18 Then they arose from Midian and came to Paran; and they took men with them from Paran and came to Egypt, to Pharaoh king of Egypt, who gave him a house, apportioned food for him, and gave him land. 19 And Hadad found great favor in the sight of Pharaoh, so that he gave him as wife the sister of his own wife, that is, the sister of Queen Tahpenes. 20 Then the sister of Tahpenes bore him Genubath his son, whom Tahpenes weaned in Pharaoh's house. And Genubath was in Pha-

raoh's household among the sons of Pharaoh.

21 So when Hadad heard in Egypt that David rested with his fathers, and that Joab the commander of the army was dead, Hadad said to Pharaoh, "Let me depart, that I may go to my own country."

22 Then Pharaoh said to him, "But what have you lacked with me, that suddenly you seek to go to your own country?"

So he answered, "Nothing, but do let me go anyway."

23 And God raised up *another* adversary against him, Rezon the son of Eliadah, who had fled from his lord, Hadadezer king of Zobah. 24 So he gathered men to him and became captain over a band *of raiders*, when David killed those *of Zobah*. And they went to Damascus and dwelt there, and reigned in Damascus. 25 He was an adversary of Israel all the days of Solomon (besides the trouble that Hadad *caused*); and he abhorred Israel, and reigned over Syria.

26 Then Solomon's servant, Jeroboam the son of Nebat, an Ephraimite from Zereda, whose mother's name *was* Zeruah, a widow, also rebelled against the king.

27 And this *is* what caused him to rebel against the king: Solomon had built the Millo *and* repaired the damages to the City of David his father. 28 The man Jeroboam *was* a mighty man of valor; and Solomon, seeing that the young man was industrious, made him the officer over all the labor force of the house of Joseph.

29 Now it happened at that time, when Jeroboam went out of Jerusalem, that the prophet Ahijah the Shilonite met him on the way; and he had clothed himself with a new garment, and the two *were* alone in the field. 30 Then Ahijah took hold of the new garment that *was* on him, and tore it *into* twelve pieces. 31 And he said to Jeroboam, "Take for yourself ten pieces, for thus says the LORD, the God of Israel: 'Behold, I will tear the kingdom out of the hand of Solomon and will give ten tribes to you 32 (but he shall have one tribe for the sake of My servant David, and for the sake of Jerusalem, the city which I have chosen out of all the tribes of Israel), 33 because they have forsaken Me, and worshiped Ashtoreth the goddess of the Sidonians, Chemosh the god of the Moabites, and Milcom the god of the people of Ammon, and have not walked in My ways to do *what is* right in My eyes and *keep* My statutes and My judgments, as *did* his father David. 34 However I will not take the whole kingdom out of his hand, because I have made him ruler all the days of his life for

the sake of My servant David, whom I chose because he kept My commandments and My statutes. 35 But I will take the kingdom out of his son's hand and give it to you—ten tribes. 36 And to his son I will give one tribe, that My servant David may always have a lamp before Me in Jerusalem, the city which I have chosen for Myself, to put My name there. 37 So I will take you, and you shall reign over all your heart desires, and you shall be king over Israel. 38 Then it shall be, if you heed all that I command you, walk in My ways, and do *what is* right in My sight, to keep My statutes and My commandments, as My servant David did, then I will be with you and build for you an enduring house, as I built for David, and will give Israel to you. 39 And I will afflict the descendants of David because of this, but not forever.' "

40 Solomon therefore sought to kill Jeroboam. But Jeroboam arose and fled to Egypt, to Shishak king of Egypt, and was in Egypt until the death of Solomon.

41 Now the rest of the acts of Solomon, all that he did, and his wisdom, *are* they not written in the book of the acts of Solomon? 42 And the period that Solomon reigned in Jerusalem over all Israel *was* forty years. 43 Then Solomon rested with his fathers, and was buried in the City of David his father. And Rehoboam his son reigned in his place.

12 AND Rehoboam went to Shechem, for all Israel had gone to Shechem to make him king. 2 So it happened, when Jeroboam the son of Nebat heard *it* (he was still in Egypt, for he had fled from the presence of King Solomon and had been dwelling in Egypt), 3 that they sent and called him. Then Jeroboam and the whole assembly of Israel came and spoke to Rehoboam, saying, 4 "Your father made our yoke heavy; now therefore, lighten the burdensome service of your father, and his heavy yoke which he put on us, and we will serve you."

5 So he said to them, "Depart *for* three days, then come back to me." And the people departed.

6 Then King Rehoboam consulted the elders who stood before his father Solomon while he still lived, and he said, "How do you advise *me* to answer these people?"

7 And they spoke to him, saying, "If you will be a servant to these people today, and serve them, and answer them, and speak good words to them, then they will be your servants forever."

8 But he rejected the advice which the elders had given him, and consulted the young men who had grown up with him, who stood before him. 9 And he said to them, "What advice do you give? How should we answer this people who have spoken to me, saying, 'Lighten the yoke which your father put on us'?"

10 Then the young men who had grown up with him spoke to him, saying, "Thus you should speak to this people who have spoken to you, saying, 'Your father made our yoke heavy, but you make *it* lighter on us'—thus you shall say to them: 'My little *finger* shall be thicker than my father's waist! 11 And now, whereas my father put a heavy yoke on you, I will add to your yoke; my father chastised you with whips, but I will chastise you with scourges!' "

12 So Jeroboam and all the people came to Rehoboam the third day, as the king had directed, saying, "Come back to me the third day." 13 Then the king answered the people roughly, and rejected the advice which the elders had given him; 14 and he spoke to them according to the advice of the young men, saying, "My father made your yoke heavy, but I will add to your yoke; my father chastised you with whips, but I will chastise you with scourges!" 15 So the king did not listen to the people; for the turn *of events* was from the LORD, that He might fulfill His word, which the LORD had spoken by Ahijah the Shilonite to Jeroboam the son of Nebat.

16 Now when all Israel saw that the king did not listen to them, the people answered the king, saying:

> "What share have we in David?
> *We have* no inheritance in the son
>   of Jesse.
> To your tents, O Israel!
> Now, see to your own house,
>   O David!"

So Israel departed to their tents. 17 But Rehoboam reigned over the children of Israel who dwelt in the cities of Judah.

18 Then King Rehoboam sent Adoram, who *was* in charge of the revenue; but all Israel stoned him with stones, and he died. Therefore King Rehoboam mounted his chariot in haste to flee to Jerusalem. 19 So Israel has been in rebellion against the house of David to this day.

20 Now it came to pass when all Israel heard that Jeroboam had come back, they sent for him and called him to the congregation, and made him king over all Israel. There was none who followed the house of David, but the tribe of Judah only.

21 And when Rehoboam came to Jerusalem, he assembled all the house of Judah with the tribe of Benjamin, one hundred and eighty thousand chosen *men* who were warriors, to fight against the house of Israel, that he might restore the kingdom to Rehoboam the son of Solomon. 22 But the word of God came to Shemaiah the man of God, saying, 23 "Speak to Rehoboam the son of Solomon, king of Judah, to all the house of Judah and Benjamin, and to the rest of the people, saying, 24 'Thus says the LORD: "You shall not go up nor fight against your brethren the children of Israel. Let every man return to his house, for this thing is from Me." ' " Therefore they obeyed the word of the LORD, and turned back, according to the word of the LORD.

25 Then Jeroboam built Shechem in the mountains of Ephraim, and dwelt there. Also he went out from there and built Penuel. 26 And Jeroboam said in his heart, "Now the kingdom may return to the house of David: 27 If these people go up to offer sacrifices in the house of the LORD at Jerusalem, then the heart of this people will turn back to their lord, Rehoboam king of Judah, and they will kill me and go back to Rehoboam king of Judah."

28 Therefore the king asked advice, made two calves of gold, and said to the people, "It is too much for you to go up to Jerusalem. Here are your gods, O Israel, which brought you up from the land of Egypt!" 29 And he set up one in Bethel, and the other he put in Dan. 30 Now this thing became a sin, for the people went *to worship* before the one as far as Dan. 31 He made shrines on the high places, and made priests from every class of people, who were not of the sons of Levi.

32 Jeroboam ordained a feast on the fifteenth day of the eighth month, like the feast that *was* in Judah, and offered sacrifices on the altar. So he did at Bethel, sacrificing to the calves that he had made. And at Bethel he installed the priests of the high places which he had made. 33 So he made offerings on the altar which he had made at Bethel on the fifteenth day of the eighth month, in the month which he had devised in his own heart. And he ordained a feast for the children of Israel, and offered sacrifices on the altar and burned incense.

PSALM 69:5–15

5 O God, You know my foolishness;
   And my sins are not hidden from You.
6 Let not those who wait for You,

O Lord GOD of hosts, be ashamed
   because of me;
Let not those who seek You be
   confounded because of me, O God
   of Israel.
7 Because for Your sake I have borne
   reproach;
Shame has covered my face.
8 I have become a stranger to my
   brothers,
And an alien to my mother's children;
9 Because zeal for Your house has eaten
   me up,
And the reproaches of those who
   reproach You have fallen on me.
10 When I wept *and chastened* my soul with
   fasting,
That became my reproach.
11 I also made sackcloth my garment;
I became a byword to them.
12 Those who sit in the gate speak against
   me,
And I *am* the song of the drunkards.

13 But as for me, my prayer *is* to You,
O LORD, *in* the acceptable time;
O God, in the multitude of Your
   mercy,
Hear me in the truth of Your salvation.

When you pray, things *remain the same, but* you *begin to be different.*   (RUN)

14 Deliver me out of the mire,
And let me not sink;
Let me be delivered from those who
   hate me,
And out of the deep waters.
15 Let not the floodwater overflow me,
Nor let the deep swallow me up;
And let not the pit shut its mouth on
   me.

PROVERBS 17:20–22

20 HE who has a deceitful heart finds no
   good,
And he who has a perverse tongue falls
   into evil.

21 He who begets a scoffer *does so* to his
   sorrow,
And the father of a fool has no joy.

22 A merry heart does good, *like*
   medicine,
But a broken spirit dries the bones.

JOHN 12:1–26

THEN, six days before the Passover, Jesus came to Bethany, where Lazarus was who had been dead, whom He had raised from the dead. 2 There they made Him a supper; and Martha served, but Lazarus was one of those who sat at the table with Him. 3 Then Mary took a pound of very costly oil of spikenard, anointed the feet of Jesus, and wiped His feet with her hair. And the house was filled with the fragrance of the oil.

God does not want our possessions, He wants us. (Perfect)

4 But one of His disciples, Judas Iscariot, Simon's *son,* who would betray Him, said, 5 "Why was this fragrant oil not sold for three hundred denarii and given to the poor?" 6 This he said, not that he cared for the poor, but because he was a thief, and had the money box; and he used to take what was put in it. 7 But Jesus said, "Let her alone; she has kept this for the day of My burial. 8 For the poor you have with you always, but Me you do not have always."

9 Now a great many of the Jews knew that He was there; and they came, not for Jesus' sake only, but that they might also see Lazarus, whom He had raised from the dead. 10 But the chief priests plotted to put Lazarus to death also, 11 because on account of him many of the Jews went away and believed in Jesus.

12 The next day a great multitude that had come to the feast, when they heard that Jesus was coming to Jerusalem, 13 took branches of palm trees and went out to meet Him, and cried out:

"Hosanna!
'Blessed *is* He who comes in the name of the Lord!'
The King of Israel!"

14 Then Jesus, when He had found a young donkey, sat on it; as it is written:

15 "Fear not, daughter of Zion;
Behold, your King is coming,
Sitting on a donkey's colt."

16 His disciples did not understand these things at first; but when Jesus was glorified, then they remembered that these things were written about Him and *that* they had done these things to Him.

17 Therefore the people, who were with Him when He called Lazarus out of his tomb and raised him from the dead, bore witness. 18 For this reason the people also met Him, because they heard that He had done this sign. 19 The Pharisees therefore said among themselves, "You see that you are accomplishing nothing. Look, the world has gone after Him!"

20 Now there were certain Greeks among those who came up to worship at the feast. 21 Then they came to Philip, who was from Bethsaida of Galilee, and asked him, saying, "Sir, we wish to see Jesus."

22 Philip came and told Andrew, and in turn Andrew and Philip told Jesus.

23 But Jesus answered them, saying, "The hour has come that the Son of Man should be glorified. 24 Most assuredly, I say to you, unless a grain of wheat falls into the ground and dies, it remains alone; but if it dies, it produces much grain. 25 He who loves his life will lose it, and he who hates his life in this world will keep it for eternal life. 26 If anyone serves Me, let him follow Me; and where I am, there My servant will be also. If anyone serves Me, him *My* Father will honor.

◆◆◆◆

Reading 153—The Intuitive Light
John 12:36

Intuition in the natural world means that we see or discern at sight, there is no reasoning in connection with it, we see at once. When the Spirit of God is in us He gives us intuitive discernment, we know exactly what He wants; then the point is, are we going through identification with our Lord in order that that intuitive light may become the discipline of our lives? It is this practical aspect that has been ignored. We have not sufficiently emphasized the fact that we have to live as saints, and that in our lives the honor at stake is not our personal honor, but the honor of Jesus Christ.

When we are beginning to be spiritual by means of the reception of the Holy Spirit, we get moments of intuitive light. We are not always dull, there are moments when we are brilliant, and Jesus says, "While you have the light, believe in the light." We are apt to believe what we saw in the dark, and consequently we believe wrongly. We have to believe what we saw when we were in the light, "hang in" to it, discipline the whole of our lives up to it. If the Holy Spirit is working in our hearts, all this becomes implicitly clear to us. The Holy Spirit is honest, and we know intuitively whether we have or have not been identified with the death of Jesus, whether we have or have not given over our self-will to the holy will of God.   (*Place Help*)

1 KINGS 13:1—14:31

AND behold, a man of God went from Judah to Bethel by the word of the LORD, and Jeroboam stood by the altar to burn incense. 2 Then he cried out against the altar by the word of the LORD, and said, "O altar, altar! Thus says the LORD: 'Behold, a child, Josiah by name, shall be born to the house of David; and on you he shall sacrifice the priests of the high places who burn incense on you, and men's bones shall be burned on you.'" 3 And he gave a sign the same day, saying, "This *is* the sign which the LORD has spoken: Surely the altar shall split apart, and the ashes on it shall be poured out."

4 So it came to pass when King Jeroboam heard the saying of the man of God, who cried out against the altar in Bethel, that he stretched out his hand from the altar, saying, "Arrest him!" Then his hand, which he stretched out toward him, withered, so that he could not pull it back to himself. 5 The altar also was split apart, and the ashes poured out from the altar, according to the sign which the man of God had given by the word of the LORD. 6 Then the king answered and said to the man of God, "Please entreat the favor of the LORD your God, and pray for me, that my hand may be restored to me."

So the man of God entreated the LORD, and the king's hand was restored to him, and became as before. 7 Then the king said to the man of God, "Come home with me and refresh yourself, and I will give you a reward."

8 But the man of God said to the king, "If you were to give me half your house, I would not go in with you; nor would I eat bread nor drink water in this place.

9 For so it was commanded me by the word of the LORD, saying, 'You shall not eat bread, nor drink water, nor return by the same way you came.'" 10 So he went another way and did not return by the way he came to Bethel.

11 Now an old prophet dwelt in Bethel, and his sons came and told him all the works that the man of God had done that day in Bethel; they also told their father the words which he had spoken to the king. 12 And their father said to them, "Which way did he go?" For his sons had seen which way the man of God went who came from Judah. 13 Then he said to his sons, "Saddle the donkey for me." So they saddled the donkey for him; and he rode on it, 14 and went after the man of God, and found him sitting under an oak. Then he said to him, "*Are* you the man of God who came from Judah?"

And he said, "I *am*."

15 Then he said to him, "Come home with me and eat bread."

16 And he said, "I cannot return with you nor go in with you; neither can I eat bread nor drink water with you in this place. 17 For I have been told by the word of the LORD, 'You shall not eat bread nor drink water there, nor return by going the way you came.'"

18 He said to him, "I too *am* a prophet as you *are,* and an angel spoke to me by the word of the LORD, saying, 'Bring him back with you to your house, that he may eat bread and drink water.'" (He was lying to him.)

19 So he went back with him, and ate bread in his house, and drank water.

20 Now it happened, as they sat at the table, that the word of the LORD came to the prophet who had brought him back;

21 and he cried out to the man of God who came from Judah, saying, "Thus says the LORD: 'Because you have disobeyed the word of the LORD, and have not kept the commandment which the LORD your God commanded you, 22 but you came back, ate bread, and drank water in the place of which *the* LORD said to you, "Eat no bread and drink no water," your corpse shall not come to the tomb of your fathers.' "

23 So it was, after he had eaten bread and after he had drunk, that he saddled the donkey for him, the prophet whom he had brought back. 24 When he was gone, a lion met him on the road and killed him. And his corpse was thrown on the road, and the donkey stood by it. The lion also stood by the corpse. 25 And there, men passed by and saw the corpse thrown on the road, and the lion standing by the corpse. Then they went and told *it* in the city where the old prophet dwelt.

26 Now when the prophet who had brought him back from the way heard *it,* he said, "It *is* the man of God who was disobedient to the word of the LORD. Therefore the LORD has delivered him to the lion, which has torn him and killed him, according to the word of the LORD which He spoke to him." 27 And he spoke to his sons, saying, "Saddle the donkey for me." So they saddled *it.* 28 Then he went and found his corpse thrown on the road, and the donkey and the lion standing by the corpse. The lion had not eaten the corpse nor torn the donkey. 29 And the prophet took up the corpse of the man of God, laid it on the donkey, and brought it back. So the old prophet came to the city to mourn, and to bury him. 30 Then he laid the corpse in his own tomb; and they mourned over him, *saying,* "Alas, my brother!" 31 So it was, after he had buried him, that he spoke to his sons, saying, "When I am dead, then bury me in the tomb where the man of God *is* buried; lay my bones beside his bones. 32 For the saying which he cried out by the word of the LORD against the altar in Bethel, and against all the shrines on the high places which *are* in the cities of Samaria, will surely come to pass."

33 After this event Jeroboam did not turn from his evil way, but again he made priests from every class of people for the high places; whoever wished, he consecrated him, and he became *one* of the priests of the high places. 34 And this thing was the sin of the house of Jeroboam, so as to exterminate and destroy *it* from the face of the earth.

14 AT that time Abijah the son of Jeroboam became sick. 2 And Jeroboam said to his wife, "Please arise, and disguise yourself, that they may not recognize you as the wife of Jeroboam, and go to Shiloh. Indeed, Ahijah the prophet *is* there, who told me that *I would be* king over this people. 3 Also take with you ten loaves, *some* cakes, and a jar of honey, and go to him; he will tell you what will become of the child." 4 And Jeroboam's wife did so; she arose and went to Shiloh, and came to the house of Ahijah. But Ahijah could not see, for his eyes were glazed by reason of his age.

5 Now the LORD had said to Ahijah, "Here is the wife of Jeroboam, coming to ask you something about her son, for he *is* sick. Thus and thus you shall say to her; for it will be, when she comes in, that she will pretend *to be* another *woman*."

6 And so it was, when Ahijah heard the sound of her footsteps as she came through the door, he said, "Come in, wife of Jeroboam. Why do you pretend *to be* another *person*? For I *have been* sent to you *with* bad *news*. 7 Go, tell Jeroboam, 'Thus says the LORD God of Israel: "Because I exalted you from among the people, and made you ruler over My people Israel, 8 and tore the kingdom away from the house of David, and gave it to you; and *yet* you have not been as My servant David, who kept My commandments and who followed Me with all his heart, to do only *what was* right in My eyes; 9 but you have done more evil than all who were before you, for you have gone and made for yourself other gods and molded images to provoke Me to anger, and have cast Me behind your back— 10 therefore behold! I will bring disaster on the house of Jeroboam, and will cut off from Jeroboam every male in Israel, bond and free; I will take away the remnant of the house of Jeroboam, as one takes away refuse until it is all gone. 11 The dogs shall eat whoever belongs to Jeroboam and dies in the city, and the birds of the air shall eat whoever dies in the field; for the LORD has spoken!" ' 12 Arise therefore, go to your own house. When your feet enter the city, the child shall die. 13 And all Israel shall mourn for him and bury him, for he is the only one of Jeroboam who shall come to the grave, because in him there is found something good toward the LORD God of Israel in the house of Jeroboam.

14 "Moreover the LORD will raise up for Himself a king over Israel who shall cut off the house of Jeroboam; this is the day. What? Even now! 15 For the LORD will strike Israel, as a reed is shaken in the water.

He will uproot Israel from this good land which He gave to their fathers, and will scatter them beyond the River, because they have made their wooden images, provoking the LORD to anger. 16 And He will give Israel up because of the sins of Jeroboam, who sinned and who made Israel sin."

17 Then Jeroboam's wife arose and departed, and came to Tirzah. When she came to the threshold of the house, the child died. 18 And they buried him; and all Israel mourned for him, according to the word of the LORD which He spoke through His servant Ahijah the prophet.

19 Now the rest of the acts of Jeroboam, how he made war and how he reigned, indeed they *are* written in the book of the chronicles of the kings of Israel. 20 The period that Jeroboam reigned *was* twenty-two years. So he rested with his fathers. Then Nadab his son reigned in his place.

21 And Rehoboam the son of Solomon reigned in Judah. Rehoboam *was* forty-one years old when he became king. He reigned seventeen years in Jerusalem, the city which the LORD had chosen out of all the tribes of Israel, to put His name there. His mother's name *was* Naamah, an Ammonitess. 22 Now Judah did evil in the sight of the LORD, and they provoked Him to jealousy with their sins which they committed, more than all that their fathers had done. 23 For they also built for themselves high places, *sacred* pillars, and wooden images on every high hill and under every green tree. 24 And there were also perverted persons in the land. They did according to all the abominations of the nations which the LORD had cast out before the children of Israel.

25 It happened in the fifth year of King Rehoboam *that* Shishak king of Egypt came up against Jerusalem. 26 And he took away the treasures of the house of the LORD and the treasures of the king's house; he took away everything. He also took away all the gold shields which Solomon had made. 27 Then King Rehoboam made bronze shields in their place, and committed *them* to the hands of the captains of the guard, who guarded the doorway of the king's house. 28 And whenever the king entered the house of the LORD, the guards carried them, then brought them back into the guardroom.

29 Now the rest of the acts of Rehoboam, and all that he did, *are* they not written in the book of the chronicles of the kings of Judah? 30 And there was war between Rehoboam and Jeroboam all *their* days. 31 So Rehoboam rested with his fathers,

and was buried with his fathers in the City of David. His mother's name *was* Naamah, an Ammonitess. Then Abijam his son reigned in his place.

PSALM 69:16–21

16 HEAR me, O LORD, for Your
  lovingkindness *is* good;
  Turn to me according to the multitude
  of Your tender mercies.
17 And do not hide Your face from Your
  servant,
  For I am in trouble;
  Hear me speedily.
18 Draw near to my soul, *and* redeem it;
  Deliver me because of my enemies.

19 You know my reproach, my shame, and
  my dishonor;
  My adversaries *are* all before You.
20 Reproach has broken my heart,
  And I am full of heaviness;
  I looked *for someone* to take pity, but
  there was none;
  And for comforters, but I found none.
21 They also gave me gall for my food,
  And for my thirst they gave me vinegar
  to drink.

PROVERBS 17:23, 24

23 A wicked *man* accepts a bribe behind
  the back
  To pervert the ways of justice.

24 Wisdom *is* in the sight of him who has
  understanding,
  But the eyes of a fool *are* on the ends
  of the earth.

JOHN 12:27–50

"NOW My soul is troubled, and what shall I say? 'Father, save Me from this hour'? But for this purpose I came to this hour. 28 Father, glorify Your name."

Then a voice came from heaven, *saying,* "I have both glorified *it* and will glorify *it* again."

29 Therefore the people who stood by and heard *it* said that it had thundered. Others said, "An angel has spoken to Him."

30 Jesus answered and said, "This voice did not come because of Me, but for your sake. 31 Now is the judgment of this world; now the ruler of this world will be cast out. 32 And I, if I am lifted up from the

earth, will draw all *peoples* to Myself."
33 This He said, signifying by what death He would die.

34 The people answered Him, "We have heard from the law that the Christ remains forever; and how *can* You say, 'The Son of Man must be lifted up'? Who is this Son of Man?"

35 Then Jesus said to them, "A little while longer the light is with you. Walk while you have the light, lest darkness overtake you; he who walks in darkness does not know where he is going. 36 While you have the light, believe in the light, that you may become sons of light." These things Jesus spoke, and departed, and was hidden from them.

37 But although He had done so many signs before them, they did not believe in Him, 38 that the word of Isaiah the prophet might be fulfilled, which he spoke:

"Lord, who has believed our report?
  And to whom has the arm of the
  LORD been revealed?"

39 Therefore they could not believe, because Isaiah said again:

40 "He has blinded their eyes and
      hardened their hearts,
  Lest they should see with *their* eyes,
  Lest they should understand with
      their hearts and turn,
  So that I should heal them."

41 These things Isaiah said when he saw His glory and spoke of Him.

42 Nevertheless even among the rulers many believed in Him, but because of the Pharisees they did not confess *Him,* lest they should be put out of the synagogue; 43 for they loved the praise of men more than the praise of God.

44 Then Jesus cried out and said, "He who believes in Me, believes not in Me but in Him who sent Me. 45 And he who sees Me sees Him who sent Me. 46 I have come *as* a light into the world, that whoever believes in Me should not abide in darkness.

Light is the description of clear, beautiful, moral character from God's standpoint.   (SHAD. AGONY)

---

47 And if anyone hears My words and does not believe, I do not judge him; for I did not come to judge the world but to save the world. 48 He who rejects Me, and does not receive My words, has that which judges him—the word that I have spoken will judge him in the last day. 49 For I have not spoken on My own *authority;* but the Father who sent Me gave Me a command, what I should say and what I should speak. 50 And I know that His command is everlasting life. Therefore, whatever I speak, just as the Father has told Me, so I speak."

◆◆◆

Reading 154—# The Great Conception
John 13:13

We must have our Christian conception right, and this is the right conception, that Jesus Christ is our master. We do not give enough time to brooding on this conception of our Lord; we do not do enough at it. An artist or a musician must know how to brood on his conception. It is no use being the home of furtive ideas and having conceptions that come floating through like sunrise clouds. The artist has to go after the idea and stick to it until it is wrought into the character of his conception. It is not easy to maintain the conception of Jesus Christ as master. Spiritual concentration is needed to do it.

The conception of mastership which we get from our natural life is totally different from the mastership of Jesus Christ, because He never insists on our obedience. He simply says, "If you love Me, keep My commandments." That is the end of it. If I do not keep His commandments, He does not come and tell me I have done the wrong thing, I know it, there is no getting away from it. If once I have been indwelt by the Holy Spirit, He will always discern that I have done the fundamentally wrong thing when I disobey Jesus Christ. Let me disobey Him, and I am the most miserable wretch out of hell. He never punishes, yet I know that His consciousness of Himself is right, that He is master. (*PLACE HELP*)

1 KINGS 15:1—16:34

IN the eighteenth year of King Jeroboam the son of Nebat, Abijam became king over Judah. 2 He reigned three years in Jerusalem. His mother's name *was* Maachah the granddaughter of Abishalom. 3 And he walked in all the sins of his father, which he had done before him; his heart was not loyal to the LORD his God, as was the heart of his father David. 4 Nevertheless for David's sake the LORD his God gave him a lamp in Jerusalem, by setting up his son after him and by establishing Jerusalem; 5 because David did *what was* right in the eyes of the LORD, and had not turned aside from anything that He commanded him all the days of his life, except in the matter of Uriah the Hittite. 6 And there was war between Rehoboam and Jeroboam all the days of his life. 7 Now the rest of the acts of Abijam, and all that he did, *are* they not written in the book of the chronicles of the kings of Judah? And there was war between Abijam and Jeroboam.

8 So Abijam rested with his fathers, and they buried him in the City of David. Then Asa his son reigned in his place.

9 In the twentieth year of Jeroboam king of Israel, Asa became king over Judah. 10 And he reigned forty-one years in Jerusalem. His grandmother's name *was* Maachah the granddaughter of Abishalom. 11 Asa did *what was* right in the eyes of the LORD, as *did* his father David. 12 And he banished the perverted persons from the land, and removed all the idols that his fathers had made. 13 Also he removed Maachah his grandmother from *being* queen mother, because she had made an obscene image of Asherah. And Asa cut down her obscene image and burned *it* by the Brook Kidron. 14 But the high places were not removed. Nevertheless Asa's heart was loyal to the LORD all his days. 15 He also brought into the house of the LORD the things which his father had dedicated, and the things which he himself had dedicated: silver and gold and utensils.

16 Now there was war between Asa and Baasha king of Israel all their days. 17 And Baasha king of Israel came up against Judah, and built Ramah, that he might let none go out or come in to Asa king of Judah. 18 Then Asa took all the silver and gold *that was* left in the treasuries of the house of the LORD and the treasuries of the king's house, and delivered them into the hand of his servants. And King Asa sent them to Ben-Hadad the son of Tabrimmon, the son of Hezion, king of Syria, who dwelt in Damascus, saying, 19 "*Let there be* a treaty between you and me, as there was between my father and your father. See, I have sent you a present of silver and gold. Come and break your treaty with Baasha king of Israel, so that he will withdraw from me."

20 So Ben-Hadad heeded King Asa, and sent the captains of his armies against the cities of Israel. He attacked Ijon, Dan, Abel Beth Maachah, and all Chinneroth, with all the land of Naphtali. 21 Now it happened, when Baasha heard *it,* that he stopped building Ramah, and remained in Tirzah.

22 Then King Asa made a proclamation throughout all Judah; none *was* exempted. And they took away the stones and timber of Ramah, which Baasha had used for building; and with them King Asa built Geba of Benjamin, and Mizpah.

23 The rest of all the acts of Asa, all his might, all that he did, and the cities which he built, *are* they not written in the book of the chronicles of the kings of Judah? But in the time of his old age he was diseased in his feet. 24 So Asa rested with his fathers, and was buried with his fathers in the City of David his father. Then Jehoshaphat his son reigned in his place.

25 Now Nadab the son of Jeroboam became king over Israel in the second year of Asa king of Judah, and he reigned over Israel two years. 26 And he did evil in the sight of the LORD, and walked in the way of his father, and in his sin by which he had made Israel sin.

27 Then Baasha the son of Ahijah, of the house of Issachar, conspired against him. And Baasha killed him at Gibbethon, which *belonged* to the Philistines, while Nadab and all Israel laid siege to Gibbethon. 28 Baasha killed him in the third year of Asa king of

Judah, and reigned in his place. 29 And it was so, when he became king, *that* he killed all the house of Jeroboam. He did not leave to Jeroboam anyone that breathed, until he had destroyed him, according to the word of the LORD which He had spoken by His servant Ahijah the Shilonite, 30 because of the sins of Jeroboam, which he had sinned and by which he had made Israel sin, because of his provocation with which he had provoked the LORD God of Israel to anger.

31 Now the rest of the acts of Nadab, and all that he did, *are* they not written in the book of the chronicles of the kings of Israel? 32 And there was war between Asa and Baasha king of Israel all their days.

33 In the third year of Asa king of Judah, Baasha the son of Ahijah became king over all Israel in Tirzah, and *reigned* twenty-four years. 34 He did evil in the sight of the LORD, and walked in the way of Jeroboam, and in his sin by which he had made Israel sin.

16 THEN the word of the LORD came to Jehu the son of Hanani, against Baasha, saying: 2 "Inasmuch as I lifted you out of the dust and made you ruler over My people Israel, and you have walked in the way of Jeroboam, and have made My people Israel sin, to provoke Me to anger with their sins, 3 surely I will take away the posterity of Baasha and the posterity of his house, and I will make your house like the house of Jeroboam the son of Nebat. 4 The dogs shall eat whoever belongs to Baasha and dies in the city, and the birds of the air shall eat whoever dies in the fields."

5 Now the rest of the acts of Baasha, what he did, and his might, *are* they not written in the book of the chronicles of the kings of Israel? 6 So Baasha rested with his fathers and was buried in Tirzah. Then Elah his son reigned in his place.

7 And also the word of the LORD came by the prophet Jehu the son of Hanani against Baasha and his house, because of all the evil that he did in the sight of the LORD in provoking Him to anger with the work of his hands, in being like the house of Jeroboam, and because he killed them.

8 In the twenty-sixth year of Asa king of Judah, Elah the son of Baasha became king over Israel, *and reigned* two years in Tirzah. 9 Now his servant Zimri, commander of half *his* chariots, conspired against him as he was in Tirzah drinking himself drunk in the house of Arza, steward of *his* house in Tirzah. 10 And Zimri went in and struck him and killed him in the twenty-seventh year of Asa king of Judah, and reigned in his place.

11 Then it came to pass, when he began to reign, as soon as he was seated on his throne, *that* he killed all the household of Baasha; he did not leave him one male, neither of his relatives nor of his friends. 12 Thus Zimri destroyed all the household of Baasha, according to the word of the LORD, which He spoke against Baasha by Jehu the prophet, 13 for all the sins of Baasha and the sins of Elah his son, by which they had sinned and by which they had made Israel sin, in provoking the LORD God of Israel to anger with their idols.

14 Now the rest of the acts of Elah, and all that he did, *are* they not written in the book of the chronicles of the kings of Israel?

15 In the twenty-seventh year of Asa king of Judah, Zimri had reigned in Tirzah seven days. And the people *were* encamped against Gibbethon, which *belonged* to the Philistines. 16 Now the people *who were* encamped heard it said, "Zimri has conspired and also has killed the king." So all Israel made Omri, the commander of the army, king over Israel that day in the camp. 17 Then Omri and all Israel with him went up from Gibbethon, and they besieged Tirzah. 18 And it happened, when Zimri saw that the city was taken, that he went into the citadel of the king's house and burned the king's house down upon himself with fire, and died, 19 because of the sins which he had committed in doing evil in the sight of the LORD, in walking in the way of Jeroboam, and in his sin which he had committed to make Israel sin.

20 Now the rest of the acts of Zimri, and the treason he committed, *are* they not written in the book of the chronicles of the kings of Israel?

21 Then the people of Israel were divided into two parts: half of the people followed Tibni the son of Ginath, to make him king, and half followed Omri. 22 But the people who followed Omri prevailed over the people who followed Tibni the son of Ginath. So Tibni died and Omri reigned. 23 In the thirty-first year of Asa king of Judah, Omri became king over Israel, *and reigned* twelve years. Six years he reigned in Tirzah. 24 And he bought the hill of Samaria from Shemer for two talents of silver; then he built on the hill, and called the name of the city which he built, Samaria, after the name of Shemer, owner of the hill. 25 Omri did evil in the eyes of the LORD, and did worse than all who *were* before him. 26 For he walked in all the ways of Jeroboam the son of Nebat, and in his sin

by which he had made Israel sin, provoking the LORD God of Israel to anger with their idols.

27 Now the rest of the acts of Omri which he did, and the might that he showed, *are* they not written in the book of the chronicles of the kings of Israel?

28 So Omri rested with his fathers and was buried in Samaria. Then Ahab his son reigned in his place.

29 In the thirty-eighth year of Asa king of Judah, Ahab the son of Omri became king over Israel; and Ahab the son of Omri reigned over Israel in Samaria twenty-two years. 30 Now Ahab the son of Omri did evil in the sight of the LORD, more than all who *were* before him. 31 And it came to pass, as though it had been a trivial thing for him to walk in the sins of Jeroboam the son of Nebat, that he took as wife Jezebel the daughter of Ethbaal, king of the Sidonians; and he went and served Baal and worshiped him. 32 Then he set up an altar for Baal in the temple of Baal, which he had built in Samaria. 33 And Ahab made a wooden image. Ahab did more to provoke the LORD God of Israel to anger than all the kings of Israel who were before him. 34 In his days Hiel of Bethel built Jericho. He laid its foundation with Abiram his firstborn, and with his youngest *son* Segub he set up its gates, according to the word of the LORD, which He had spoken through Joshua the son of Nun.

PSALM 69:22–28

22 LET their table become a snare before them,
And their well-being a trap.
23 Let their eyes be darkened, so that they do not see;
And make their loins shake continually.
24 Pour out Your indignation upon them,
And let Your wrathful anger take hold of them.
25 Let their dwelling place be desolate;
Let no one live in their tents.
26 For they persecute the *ones* You have struck,
And talk of the grief of those You have wounded.
27 Add iniquity to their iniquity,
And let them not come into Your righteousness.
28 Let them be blotted out of the book of the living,
And not be written with the righteous.

PROVERBS 17:25, 26

25 A foolish son *is* a grief to his father,
And bitterness to her who bore him.

26 Also, to punish the righteous *is* not good,
Nor to strike princes for *their* uprightness.

JOHN 13:1–20

NOW before the Feast of the Passover, when Jesus knew that His hour had come that He should depart from this world to the Father, having loved His own who were in the world, He loved them to the end.

2 And supper being ended, the devil having already put it into the heart of Judas Iscariot, Simon's *son*, to betray Him, 3 Jesus, knowing that the Father had given all things into His hands, and that He had come from God and was going to God, 4 rose from supper and laid aside His garments, took a towel and girded Himself. 5 After that, He poured water into a basin and began to wash the disciples' feet, and to wipe *them* with the towel with which He was girded. 6 Then He came to Simon

---

*G*od wants to use us as He used
His own Son.   (RUN)

Peter. And *Peter* said to Him, "Lord, are You washing my feet?"

7 Jesus answered and said to him, "What I am doing you do not understand now, but you will know after this."

8 Peter said to Him, "You shall never wash my feet!"

Jesus answered him, "If I do not wash you, you have no part with Me."

9 Simon Peter said to Him, "Lord, not my feet only, but also *my* hands and *my* head!"

10 Jesus said to him, "He who is bathed needs only to wash *his* feet, but is completely clean; and you are clean, but not all of you." 11 For He knew who would betray Him; therefore He said, "You are not all clean."

12 So when He had washed their feet, taken His garments, and sat down again, He said to them, "Do you know what I have done to you? 13 You call Me Teacher

and Lord, and you say well, for *so* I am. 14 If I then, *your* Lord and Teacher, have washed your feet, you also ought to wash one another's feet. 15 For I have given you an example, that you should do as I have done to you. 16 Most assuredly, I say to you, a servant is not greater than his master; nor is he who is sent greater than he who sent him. 17 If you know these things, blessed are you if you do them.

18 "I do not speak concerning all of you. I know whom I have chosen; but that the Scripture may be fulfilled, 'He who eats bread with Me has lifted up his heel against Me.' 19 Now I tell you before it comes, that when it does come to pass, you may believe that I am *He*. 20 Most assuredly, I say to you, he who receives whomever I send receives Me; and he who receives Me receives Him who sent Me."

◄◄◄◄

Reading 155—Waiting for God's Guidance
John 13:37

There are times when you cannot understand why you cannot do what you want to do. When God brings the blank space, see that you do not fill it in, but wait. The blank space may come in order to teach you what sanctification means, or it may come after sanctification to teach you what service means. Never run before God's guidance. If there is the slightest doubt, then He is not guiding. Whenever there is doubt—*don't*. . . .

Peter did not wait on God; he forecast in his mind where the test would come, and the test came where he did not expect it. "I will lay down my life for Your sake." Peter's declaration was honest but ignorant. "Jesus answered him, . . . 'the rooster shall not crow till you have denied Me three times.'" This was said with a deeper knowledge of Peter than Peter had of himself. He could not follow Jesus because he did not know himself, of what he was capable. Natural devotion may be all very well to attract us to Jesus, to make us feel His fascination, but it will never make us disciples. Natural devotion will always deny Jesus somewhere or other.   (*Utmost*)

1 KINGS 17:1—18:46

AND Elijah the Tishbite, of the inhabitants of Gilead, said to Ahab, "*As* the Lord God of Israel lives, before whom I stand, there shall not be dew nor rain these years, except at my word."

2 Then the word of the Lord came to him, saying, 3 "Get away from here and turn eastward, and hide by the Brook Cherith, which flows into the Jordan. 4 And it will be *that* you shall drink from the brook, and I have commanded the ravens to feed you there."

5 So he went and did according to the word of the Lord, for he went and stayed by the Brook Cherith, which flows into the Jordan. 6 The ravens brought him bread and meat in the morning, and bread and meat in the evening; and he drank from the brook. 7 And it happened after a while

that the brook dried up, because there had been no rain in the land.

8 Then the word of the Lord came to him, saying, 9 "Arise, go to Zarephath, which *belongs* to Sidon, and dwell there. See, I have commanded a widow there to provide for you." 10 So he arose and went to Zarephath. And when he came to the gate of the city, indeed a widow *was* there gathering sticks. And he called to her and said, "Please bring me a little water in a cup, that I may drink." 11 And as she was going to get *it*, he called to her and said, "Please bring me a morsel of bread in your hand."

12 So she said, "As the Lord your God lives, I do not have bread, only a handful of flour in a bin, and a little oil in a jar; and see, I *am* gathering a couple of sticks that I may go in and prepare it for myself and my son, that we may eat it, and die."

The knowledge of our own poverty brings us to the moral frontier where Jesus Christ works. (LOVE OF GOD)

13 And Elijah said to her, "Do not fear; go *and* do as you have said, but make me a small cake from it first, and bring *it* to me; and afterward make *some* for yourself and your son. 14 For thus says the LORD God of Israel: 'The bin of flour shall not be used up, nor shall the jar of oil run dry, until the day the LORD sends rain on the earth.' "

15 So she went away and did according to the word of Elijah; and she and he and her household ate for *many* days. 16 The bin of flour was not used up, nor did the jar of oil run dry, according to the word of the LORD which He spoke by Elijah.

17 Now it happened after these things *that* the son of the woman who owned the house became sick. And his sickness was so serious that there was no breath left in him. 18 So she said to Elijah, "What have I to do with you, O man of God? Have you come to me to bring my sin to remembrance, and to kill my son?"

19 And he said to her, "Give me your son." So he took him out of her arms and carried him to the upper room where he was staying, and laid him on his own bed. 20 Then he cried out to the LORD and said, "O LORD my God, have You also brought tragedy on the widow with whom I lodge, by killing her son?" 21 And he stretched himself out on the child three times, and cried out to the LORD and said, "O LORD my God, I pray, let this child's soul come back to him." 22 Then the LORD heard the voice of Elijah; and the soul of the child came back to him, and he revived.

23 And Elijah took the child and brought him down from the upper room into the house, and gave him to his mother. And Elijah said, "See, your son lives!"

24 Then the woman said to Elijah, "Now by this I know that you *are* a man of God, *and* that the word of the LORD in your mouth *is* the truth."

18 AND it came to pass *after* many days that the word of the LORD came to Elijah, in the third year, saying, "Go, present yourself to Ahab, and I will send rain on the earth."

2 So Elijah went to present himself to Ahab; and *there was* a severe famine in Samaria. 3 And Ahab had called Obadiah, who *was* in charge of *his* house. (Now Obadiah feared the LORD greatly. 4 For so it was, while Jezebel massacred the prophets of the LORD, that Obadiah had taken one hundred prophets and hidden them, fifty to a cave, and had fed them with bread and water.) 5 And Ahab had said to Obadiah, "Go into the land to all the springs of water and to all the brooks; perhaps we may find grass to keep the horses and mules alive, so that we will not have to kill any livestock." 6 So they divided the land between them to explore it; Ahab went one way by himself, and Obadiah went another way by himself.

7 Now as Obadiah was on his way, suddenly Elijah met him; and he recognized him, and fell on his face, and said, "*Is* that you, my lord Elijah?"

8 And he answered him, "*It is* I. Go, tell your master, 'Elijah *is here*.' "

9 So he said, "How have I sinned, that you are delivering your servant into the hand of Ahab, to kill me? 10 *As* the LORD your God lives, there is no nation or kingdom where my master has not sent someone to hunt for you; and when they said, '*He is* not *here*,' he took an oath from the kingdom or nation that they could not find you. 11 And now you say, 'Go, tell your master, "Elijah *is here*" '! 12 And it shall come to pass, *as soon as* I am gone from you, that the Spirit of the LORD will carry you to a place I do not know; so when I go and tell Ahab, and he cannot find you, he will kill me. But I your servant have feared the LORD from my youth. 13 Was it not reported to my lord what I did when Jezebel killed the prophets of the LORD, how I hid one hundred men of the LORD's prophets, fifty to a cave, and fed them with bread and water? 14 And now you say, 'Go, tell your master, "Elijah *is here*." ' He will kill me!"

15 Then Elijah said, "*As* the LORD of hosts lives, before whom I stand, I will surely present myself to him today."

16 So Obadiah went to meet Ahab, and told him; and Ahab went to meet Elijah.

17 Then it happened, when Ahab saw Elijah, that Ahab said to him, "*Is that* you, O troubler of Israel?"

18 And he answered, "I have not troubled Israel, but you and your father's house *have*, in that you have forsaken the commandments of the LORD and have followed the Baals. 19 Now therefore, send *and* gather all Israel to me on Mount Carmel, the four hundred and fifty prophets of Baal, and the four hundred prophets of Asherah, who eat at Jezebel's table."

20 So Ahab sent for all the children of

Israel, and gathered the prophets together on Mount Carmel. 21 And Elijah came to all the people, and said, "How long will you falter between two opinions? If the LORD *is* God, follow Him; but if Baal, follow him." But the people answered him not a word. 22 Then Elijah said to the people, "I alone am left a prophet of the LORD; but Baal's prophets *are* four hundred and fifty men. 23 Therefore let them give us two bulls; and let them choose one bull for themselves, cut it in pieces, and lay it on the wood, but put no fire *under it;* and I will prepare the other bull, and lay *it* on the wood, but put no fire *under it.* 24 Then you call on the name of your gods, and I will call on the name of the LORD; and the God who answers by fire, He is God."

So all the people answered and said, "It is well spoken."

25 Now Elijah said to the prophets of Baal, "Choose one bull for yourselves and prepare *it* first, for you *are* many; and call on the name of your god, but put no fire *under it.*"

26 So they took the bull which was given them, and they prepared *it,* and called on the name of Baal from morning even till noon, saying, "O Baal, hear us!" But *there was* no voice; no one answered. Then they leaped about the altar which they had made.

27 And so it was, at noon, that Elijah mocked them and said, "Cry aloud, for he *is* a god; either he is meditating, or he is busy, or he is on a journey, *or* perhaps he is sleeping and must be awakened." 28 So they cried aloud, and cut themselves, as was their custom, with knives and lances, until the blood gushed out on them. 29 And when midday was past, they prophesied until the *time* of the offering of the *evening* sacrifice. But *there was* no voice; no one answered, no one paid attention.

30 Then Elijah said to all the people, "Come near to me." So all the people came near to him. And he repaired the altar of the LORD *that was* broken down. 31 And Elijah took twelve stones, according to the number of the tribes of the sons of Jacob, to whom the word of the LORD had come, saying, "Israel shall be your name." 32 Then with the stones he built an altar in the name of the LORD; and he made a trench around the altar large enough to hold two seahs of seed. 33 And he put the wood in order, cut the bull in pieces, and laid *it* on the wood, and said, "Fill four waterpots with water, and pour *it* on the burnt sacrifice and on the wood." 34 Then he said, "Do *it* a second time," and they did *it* a second

time; and he said, "Do *it* a third time," and they did *it* a third time. 35 So the water ran all around the altar; and he also filled the trench with water.

36 And it came to pass, at *the time of* the offering of the *evening* sacrifice, that Elijah the prophet came near and said, "LORD God of Abraham, Isaac, and Israel, let it be known this day that You *are* God in Israel and I *am* Your servant, and *that* I have done all these things at Your word. 37 Hear me, O LORD, hear me, that this people may know that You *are* the LORD God, and *that* You have turned their hearts back *to You* again."

38 Then the fire of the LORD fell and consumed the burnt sacrifice, and the wood and the stones and the dust, and it licked up the water that *was* in the trench. 39 Now when all the people saw *it,* they fell on their faces; and they said, "The LORD, He *is* God! The LORD, He *is* God!"

40 And Elijah said to them, "Seize the prophets of Baal! Do not let one of them escape!" So they seized them; and Elijah brought them down to the Brook Kishon and executed them there.

41 Then Elijah said to Ahab, "Go up, eat and drink; for *there is* the sound of abundance of rain." 42 So Ahab went up to eat and drink. And Elijah went up to the top of Carmel; then he bowed down on the ground, and put his face between his knees, 43 and said to his servant, "Go up now, look toward the sea."

So he went up and looked, and said, "*There is* nothing." And seven times he said, "Go again."

44 Then it came to pass the seventh *time,* that he said, "There is a cloud, as small as a man's hand, rising out of the sea!" So he said, "Go up, say to Ahab, 'Prepare *your chariot,* and go down before the rain stops you.'"

45 Now it happened in the meantime that the sky became black with clouds and wind, and there was a heavy rain. So Ahab rode away and went to Jezreel. 46 Then the hand of the LORD came upon Elijah; and he girded up his loins and ran ahead of Ahab to the entrance of Jezreel.

PSALM 69:29–36

29 BUT I *am* poor and sorrowful;
    Let Your salvation, O God, set me up
        on high.
30 I will praise the name of God with a
        song,

And will magnify Him with
thanksgiving.

31 *This* also shall please the LORD better
than an ox *or* bull,
Which has horns and hooves.

32 The humble shall see *this and* be glad;
And you who seek God, your hearts
shall live.

33 For the LORD hears the poor,
And does not despise His prisoners.

34 Let heaven and earth praise Him,
The seas and everything that moves in
them.

35 For God will save Zion
And build the cities of Judah,
That they may dwell there and possess
it.

36 Also, the descendants of His servants
shall inherit it,
And those who love His name shall
dwell in it.

PROVERBS 17:27, 28

27 HE who has knowledge spares his
words,
And a man of understanding is of a
calm spirit.

28 Even a fool is counted wise when he
holds his peace;
When he shuts his lips, *he is considered*
perceptive.

JOHN 13:21–38

WHEN Jesus had said these things, He
was troubled in spirit, and testified and said,
"Most assuredly, I say to you, one of you
will betray Me." 22 Then the disciples
looked at one another, perplexed about
whom He spoke.

23 Now there was leaning on Jesus' bosom one of His disciples, whom Jesus loved.
24 Simon Peter therefore motioned to him
to ask who it was of whom He spoke.

25 Then, leaning back on Jesus' breast,
he said to Him, "Lord, who is it?"

*Our Lord's first requirement is
a personal relationship to
Himself.* (BIB. ETHICS)

26 Jesus answered, "It is he to whom I
shall give a piece of bread when I have
dipped *it.*" And having dipped the bread,
He gave *it* to Judas Iscariot, *the son* of Simon. 27 Now after the piece of bread, Satan
entered him. Then Jesus said to him, "What
you do, do quickly." 28 But no one at the
table knew for what reason He said this
to him. 29 For some thought, because Judas
had the money box, that Jesus had said to
him, "Buy *those things* we need for the feast,"
or that he should give something to the
poor.

30 Having received the piece of bread,
he then went out immediately. And it was
night.

31 So, when he had gone out, Jesus said,
"Now the Son of Man is glorified, and God
is glorified in Him. 32 If God is glorified
in Him, God will also glorify Him in Himself, and glorify Him immediately. 33 Little
children, I shall be with you a little while
longer. You will seek Me; and as I said to
the Jews, 'Where I am going, you cannot
come,' so now I say to you. 34 A new commandment I give to you, that you love one
another; as I have loved you, that you also
love one another. 35 By this all will know
that you are My disciples, if you have love
for one another."

36 Simon Peter said to Him, "Lord,
where are You going?"

Jesus answered him, "Where I am going
you cannot follow Me now, but you shall
follow Me afterward."

37 Peter said to Him, "Lord, why can I
not follow You now? I will lay down my
life for Your sake."

38 Jesus answered him, "Will you lay
down your life for My sake? Most assuredly, I say to you, the rooster shall
not crow till you have denied Me three
times.

*Reading 156—*Living Worship
John 14:6

Jesus does not take men and say, "This is the truth and if you don't believe it you will be damned." He simply shows us the truth—"I am the . . . truth," and leaves us alone. We name His name, but is He the truth to us in our bodily life, in our common-sense life, in our intellectual and emotional life? It takes a long while for us to begin to see that Jesus Christ is the truth. Truths exist that have no meaning for us until we get into the domain of their power, "Most assuredly, I say to you, unless one is born again, he cannot see the kingdom of God" (John 3:3). We want to get at truth by "shortcuts"; the wonder is our Lord's amazing patience. He never insists that we take His way; He simply says, "I am the way." We might as well learn to take His way at the beginning, but we won't, we are determined on our own way. . . .

We say, "But I am so-and-so, and I have had these experiences, and I have ideas of my own." Or we may not say it, but we think it. It takes a long time to realize what Jesus is after, and the person you need most patience with is yourself. (*Place Help*)

1 KINGS 19:1—20:43

AND Ahab told Jezebel all that Elijah had done, also how he had executed all the prophets with the sword. 2 Then Jezebel sent a messenger to Elijah, saying, "So let the gods do *to me,* and more also, if I do not make your life as the life of one of them by tomorrow about this time." 3 And when he saw *that,* he arose and ran for his life, and went to Beersheba, which *belongs* to Judah, and left his servant there.

4 But he himself went a day's journey into the wilderness, and came and sat down under a broom tree. And he prayed that he might die, and said, "It is enough! Now, Lord, take my life, for I *am* no better than my fathers!"

When a man is at his wits' end, it is not a cowardly thing to pray. (Ask)

---

5 Then as he lay and slept under a broom tree, suddenly an angel touched him, and said to him, "Arise *and* eat." 6 Then he looked, and there by his head *was* a cake baked on coals, and a jar of water. So he ate and drank, and lay down again. 7 And the angel of the Lord came back the second time, and touched him, and said, "Arise *and* eat, because the journey *is* too great for you." 8 So he arose, and ate and drank; and he went in the strength of that food forty days and forty nights as far as Horeb, the mountain of God.

9 And there he went into a cave, and spent the night in that place; and behold, the word of the Lord *came* to him, and He said to him, "What are you doing here, Elijah?"

10 So he said, "I have been very zealous for the Lord God of hosts; for the children of Israel have forsaken Your covenant, torn down Your altars, and killed Your prophets with the sword. I alone am left; and they seek to take my life."

11 Then He said, "Go out, and stand on the mountain before the Lord." And behold, the Lord passed by, and a great and strong wind tore into the mountains and broke the rocks in pieces before the Lord, *but* the Lord *was* not in the wind; and after the wind an earthquake, *but* the Lord *was* not in the earthquake; 12 and after the earthquake a fire, *but* the Lord *was* not in the fire; and after the fire a still small voice.

13 So it was, when Elijah heard *it,* that he wrapped his face in his mantle and went out and stood in the entrance of the cave. Suddenly a voice *came* to him, and said, "What are you doing here, Elijah?"

14 And he said, "I have been very zealous for the Lord God of hosts; because the children of Israel have forsaken Your covenant, torn down Your altars, and killed Your prophets with the sword. I alone am left; and they seek to take my life."

15 Then the Lord said to him: "Go, re-

turn on your way to the Wilderness of Damascus; and when you arrive, anoint Hazael *as* king over Syria. 16 Also you shall anoint Jehu the son of Nimshi *as* king over Israel. And Elisha the son of Shaphat of Abel Meholah you shall anoint *as* prophet in your place. 17 It shall be *that* whoever escapes the sword of Hazael, Jehu will kill; and whoever escapes the sword of Jehu, Elisha will kill. 18 Yet I have reserved seven thousand in Israel, all whose knees have not bowed to Baal, and every mouth that has not kissed him."

19 So he departed from there, and found Elisha the son of Shaphat, who *was* plowing *with* twelve yoke *of oxen* before him, and he was with the twelfth. Then Elijah passed by him and threw his mantle on him. 20 And he left the oxen and ran after Elijah, and said, "Please let me kiss my father and my mother, and *then* I will follow you."

And he said to him, "Go back again, for what have I done to you?"

21 So *Elisha* turned back from him, and took a yoke of oxen and slaughtered them and boiled their flesh, using the oxen's equipment, and gave it to the people, and they ate. Then he arose and followed Elijah, and became his servant.

20 NOW Ben-Hadad the king of Syria gathered all his forces together; thirty-two kings *were* with him, with horses and chariots. And he went up and besieged Samaria, and made war against it. 2 Then he sent messengers into the city to Ahab king of Israel, and said to him, "Thus says Ben-Hadad: 3 'Your silver and your gold *are* mine; your loveliest wives and children are mine.' "

4 And the king of Israel answered and said, "My lord, O king, just as you say, I and all that I have *are* yours."

5 Then the messengers came back and said, "Thus speaks Ben-Hadad, saying, 'Indeed I have sent to you, saying, "You shall deliver to me your silver and your gold, your wives and your children"; 6 but I will send my servants to you tomorrow about this time, and they shall search your house and the houses of your servants. And it shall be, *that* whatever is pleasant in your eyes, they will put *it* in their hands and take *it*.' "

7 So the king of Israel called all the elders of the land, and said, "Notice, please, and see how this *man* seeks trouble, for he sent to me for my wives, my children, my silver, and my gold; and I did not deny him."

8 And all the elders and all the people said to him, "Do not listen or consent."

9 Therefore he said to the messengers of Ben-Hadad, "Tell my lord the king, 'All that you sent for to your servant the first time I will do, but this thing I cannot do.' "

And the messengers departed and brought back word to him.

10 Then Ben-Hadad sent to him and said, "The gods do so to me, and more also, if enough dust is left of Samaria for a handful for each of the people who follow me."

11 So the king of Israel answered and said, "Tell *him*, 'Let not the one who puts on *his armor* boast like the one who takes *it* off.' "

12 And it happened when *Ben-Hadad* heard this message, as he and the kings *were* drinking at the command post, that he said to his servants, "Get ready." And they got ready to attack the city.

13 Suddenly a prophet approached Ahab king of Israel, saying, "Thus says the LORD: 'Have you seen all this great multitude? Behold, I will deliver it into your hand today, and you shall know that I *am* the LORD.' "

14 So Ahab said, "By whom?"

And he said, "Thus says the LORD: 'By the young leaders of the provinces.' "

Then he said, "Who will set the battle in order?"

And he answered, "You."

15 Then he mustered the young leaders of the provinces, and there were two hundred and thirty-two; and after them he mustered all the people, all the children of Israel—seven thousand.

16 So they went out at noon. Meanwhile Ben-Hadad and the thirty-two kings helping him were getting drunk at the command post. 17 The young leaders of the provinces went out first. And Ben-Hadad sent out *a patrol,* and they told him, saying, "Men are coming out of Samaria!" 18 So he said, "If they have come out for peace, take them alive; and if they have come out for war, take them alive."

19 Then these young leaders of the provinces went out of the city with the army which followed them. 20 And each one killed his man; so the Syrians fled, and Israel pursued them; and Ben-Hadad the king of Syria escaped on a horse with the cavalry. 21 Then the king of Israel went out and attacked the horses and chariots, and killed the Syrians with a great slaughter.

22 And the prophet came to the king of Israel and said to him, "Go, strengthen yourself; take note, and see what you should do, for in the spring of the year the king of Syria will come up against you."

23 Then the servants of the king of Syria said to him, "Their gods *are* gods of the

hills. Therefore they were stronger than we; but if we fight against them in the plain, surely we will be stronger than they. 24 So do this thing: Dismiss the kings, each from his position, and put captains in their places; 25 and you shall muster an army like the army that you have lost, horse for horse and chariot for chariot. Then we will fight against them in the plain; surely we will be stronger than they."

And he listened to their voice and did so.

26 So it was, in the spring of the year, that Ben-Hadad mustered the Syrians and went up to Aphek to fight against Israel. 27 And the children of Israel were mustered and given provisions, and they went against them. Now the children of Israel encamped before them like two little flocks of goats, while the Syrians filled the countryside.

28 Then a man of God came and spoke to the king of Israel, and said, "Thus says the LORD: 'Because the Syrians have said, "The LORD *is* God of the hills, but He *is* not God of the valleys," therefore I will deliver all this great multitude into your hand, and you shall know that I *am* the LORD.' " 29 And they encamped opposite each other for seven days. So it was that on the seventh day the battle was joined; and the children of Israel killed one hundred thousand foot soldiers *of* the Syrians in one day. 30 But the rest fled to Aphek, into the city; then a wall fell on twenty-seven thousand of the men *who were* left.

And Ben-Hadad fled and went into the city, into an inner chamber.

31 Then his servants said to him, "Look now, we have heard that the kings of the house of Israel *are* merciful kings. Please, let us put sackcloth around our waists and ropes around our heads, and go out to the king of Israel; perhaps he will spare your life." 32 So they wore sackcloth around their waists and *put* ropes around their heads, and came to the king of Israel and said, "Your servant Ben-Hadad says, 'Please let me live.' "

And he said, "*Is* he still alive? He *is* my brother."

33 Now the men were watching closely to see whether *any sign of mercy would come* from him; and they quickly grasped *at this word* and said, "Your brother Ben-Hadad."

So he said, "Go, bring him." Then Ben-Hadad came out to him; and he had him come up into the chariot.

34 So *Ben-Hadad* said to him, "The cities which my father took from your father I will restore; and you may set up market-places for yourself in Damascus, as my father did in Samaria."

Then *Ahab said,* "I will send you away with this treaty." So he made a treaty with him and sent him away.

35 Now a certain man of the sons of the prophets said to his neighbor by the word of the LORD, "Strike me, please." And the man refused to strike him. 36 Then he said to him, "Because you have not obeyed the voice of the LORD, surely, as soon as you depart from me, a lion shall kill you." And as soon as he left him, a lion found him and killed him.

37 And he found another man, and said, "Strike me, please." So the man struck him, inflicting a wound. 38 Then the prophet departed and waited for the king by the road, and disguised himself with a bandage over his eyes. 39 Now as the king passed by, he cried out to the king and said, "Your servant went out into the midst of the battle; and there, a man came over and brought a man to me, and said, 'Guard this man; if by any means he is missing, your life shall be for his life, or else you shall pay a talent of silver.' 40 While your servant was busy here and there, he was gone."

Then the king of Israel said to him, "So *shall* your judgment *be;* you yourself have decided *it.*"

41 And he hastened to take the bandage away from his eyes; and the king of Israel recognized him as one of the prophets. 42 Then he said to him, "Thus says the LORD: 'Because you have let slip out of *your* hand a man whom I appointed to utter destruction, therefore your life shall go for his life, and your people for his people.' "

43 So the king of Israel went to his house sullen and displeased, and came to Samaria.

PSALM 70:1–5

1   *MAKE haste,* O God, to deliver me!
     Make haste to help me, O LORD!

2   Let them be ashamed and confounded
     Who seek my life;
     Let them be turned back and confused
     Who desire my hurt.

3   Let them be turned back because of
        their shame,
     Who say, "Aha, aha!"

4   Let all those who seek You rejoice and
        be glad in You;
     And let those who love Your salvation
        say continually,
     "Let God be magnified!"

5 But I *am* poor and needy;
   Make haste to me, O God!
   You *are* my help and my deliverer;
   O LORD, do not delay.

PROVERBS 18:1, 2

1 A man who isolates himself seeks his
      own desire;
   He rages against all wise judgment.

2 A fool has no delight in understanding,
   But in expressing his own heart.

JOHN 14:1–31

"LET not your heart be troubled; you believe in God, believe also in Me. 2 In My

---

*I*f we believe in Jesus Christ, we
can face every problem the world
holds.   (GOOD)

Father's house are many mansions; if *it were*
not *so*, I would have told you. I go to prepare
a place for you. 3 And if I go and prepare
a place for you, I will come again and receive
you to Myself; that where I am, *there* you
may be also. 4 And where I go you know,
and the way you know."

5 Thomas said to Him, "Lord, we do
not know where You are going, and how
can we know the way?"

6 Jesus said to him, "I am the way, the
truth, and the life. No one comes to the
Father except through Me.

7 "If you had known Me, you would have
known My Father also; and from now on
you know Him and have seen Him."

8 Philip said to Him, "Lord, show us the
Father, and it is sufficient for us."

9 Jesus said to him, "Have I been with
you so long, and yet you have not known
Me, Philip? He who has seen Me has seen
the Father; so how can you say, 'Show us
the Father'? 10 Do you not believe that I
am in the Father, and the Father in Me?
The words that I speak to you I do not
speak on My own *authority;* but the Father
who dwells in Me does the works. 11 Believe
Me that I *am* in the Father and the Father
in Me, or else believe Me for the sake of
the works themselves.

12 "Most assuredly, I say to you, he who
believes in Me, the works that I do he will
do also; and greater *works* than these he

will do, because I go to My Father.
13 And whatever you ask in My name, that
I will do, that the Father may be glorified
in the Son. 14 If you ask anything in My
name, I will do *it*.

15 "If you love Me, keep My commandments. 16 And I will pray the Father, and
He will give you another Helper, that He
may abide with you forever— 17 the Spirit
of truth, whom the world cannot receive,
because it neither sees Him nor knows Him;
but you know Him, for He dwells with
you and will be in you. 18 I will not leave
you orphans; I will come to you.

19 "A little while longer and the world
will see Me no more, but you will see Me.
Because I live, you will live also. 20 At that
day you will know that I *am* in My Father,
and you in Me, and I in you. 21 He who
has My commandments and keeps them,
it is he who loves Me. And he who loves
Me will be loved by My Father, and I will
love him and manifest Myself to him."

22 Judas (not Iscariot) said to Him,
"Lord, how is it that You will manifest
Yourself to us, and not to the world?"

23 Jesus answered and said to him, "If
anyone loves Me, he will keep My word;
and My Father will love him, and We will
come to him and make Our home with
him. 24 He who does not love Me does
not keep My words; and the word which
you hear is not Mine but the Father's who
sent Me.

25 "These things I have spoken to you
while being present with you. 26 But the

---

*T*he only way we can explain Jesus
Christ is the way He explains
Himself.   (BIB. PSYCH.)

Helper, the Holy Spirit, whom the Father
will send in My name, He will teach you
all things, and bring to your remembrance
all things that I said to you. 27 Peace I leave
with you, My peace I give to you; not as
the world gives do I give to you. Let not
your heart be troubled, neither let it be
afraid. 28 You have heard Me say to you,
'I am going away and coming *back* to you.'
If you loved Me, you would rejoice because
I said, 'I am going to the Father,' for My
Father is greater than I.

29 "And now I have told you before it
comes, that when it does come to pass,
you may believe. 30 I will no longer talk
much with you, for the ruler of this world
is coming, and he has nothing in Me.

31 But that the world may know that I love the Father, and as the Father gave Me commandment, so I do. Arise, let us go from here.

◆◆◆◆

Reading 157—Fruitfulness of Friendship
John 15:15

The fruitfulness of friendship is described in verse 13: "Greater love has no one than this, than to lay down one's life for his friends." If I am a friend of Jesus Christ, I lay down my life for Him. That does not mean that I go through the big crisis of death; it means that I lay down my life deliberately. . . . I have this to lay out and expend: I have a day before me, and I am going to lay it out for Jesus Christ; I have my duty to perform, but I am going to lay it out in devotion to Jesus Christ all through. It is difficult, and thank God it is difficult. Salvation is easy because it cost God so much, but the manifestation of it in my life is difficult. God does expect a man to be a man. God saves a man and endues him with His Holy Spirit, and says in effect, "Now it is up to you to pro͟ ͏ it, work it out; be loyal to Me while the nature of things round about you would make you disloyal. I have called you friends, now stand loyal to your Friend." His honor is at stake in our bodily life.   (*PLACE HELP*)

1 KINGS 21:1—22:53

AND it came to pass after these things *that* Naboth the Jezreelite had a vineyard which *was* in Jezreel, next to the palace of Ahab king of Samaria. 2 So Ahab spoke to Naboth, saying, "Give me your vineyard, that I may have it for a vegetable garden, because it *is* near, next to my house; and for it I will give you a vineyard better than it. *Or,* if it seems good to you, I will give you its worth in money."

3 But Naboth said to Ahab, "The LORD forbid that I should give the inheritance of my fathers to you!"

4 So Ahab went into his house sullen and displeased because of the word which Naboth the Jezreelite had spoken to him; for he had said, "I will not give you the inheritance of my fathers." And he lay down on his bed, and turned away his face, and would eat no food. 5 But Jezebel his wife came to him, and said to him, "Why is your spirit so sullen that you eat no food?"

6 He said to her, "Because I spoke to Naboth the Jezreelite, and said to him, 'Give me your vineyard for money; or else, if it pleases you, I will give you *another* vineyard for it.' And he answered, 'I will not give you my vineyard.' "

7 Then Jezebel his wife said to him, "You now exercise authority over Israel! Arise, eat food, and let your heart be cheerful; I will give you the vineyard of Naboth the Jezreelite."

8 And she wrote letters in Ahab's name, sealed *them* with his seal, and sent the letters to the elders and the nobles who *were* dwelling in the city with Naboth. 9 She wrote in the letters, saying,

Proclaim a fast, and seat Naboth with
high honor among the people;
10 and seat two men, scoundrels,
before him to bear witness against
him, saying, You have blasphemed
God and the king. *Then* take him
out, and stone him, that he may die.

11 So the men of his city, the elders and nobles who were inhabitants of his city, did as Jezebel had sent to them, as it *was* written in the letters which she had sent to them. 12 They proclaimed a fast, and seated Naboth with high honor among the people. 13 And two men, scoundrels, came in and sat before him; and the scoundrels witnessed against him, against Naboth, in the presence of the people, saying, "Naboth has blasphemed God and the king!" Then

they took him outside the city and stoned him with stones, so that he died. 14 Then they sent to Jezebel, saying, "Naboth has been stoned and is dead."

15 And it came to pass, when Jezebel heard that Naboth had been stoned and was dead, that Jezebel said to Ahab, "Arise, take possession of the vineyard of Naboth the Jezreelite, which he refused to give you for money; for Naboth is not alive, but dead." 16 So it was, when Ahab heard that Naboth was dead, that Ahab got up and went down to take possession of the vineyard of Naboth the Jezreelite.

17 Then the word of the LORD came to Elijah the Tishbite, saying, 18 "Arise, go down to meet Ahab king of Israel, who *lives* in Samaria. There *he is,* in the vineyard of Naboth, where he has gone down to take possession of it. 19 You shall speak to him, saying, 'Thus says the LORD: "Have you murdered and also taken possession?" ' And you shall speak to him, saying, 'Thus says the LORD: "In the place where dogs licked the blood of Naboth, dogs shall lick your blood, even yours." ' "

20 So Ahab said to Elijah, "Have you found me, O my enemy?"

And he answered, "I have found *you,* because you have sold yourself to do evil in the sight of the LORD: 21 'Behold, I will bring calamity on you. I will take away your posterity, and will cut off from Ahab every male in Israel, both bond and free. 22 I will make your house like the house of Jeroboam the son of Nebat, and like the house of Baasha the son of Ahijah, because of the provocation with which you have provoked *Me* to anger, and made Israel sin.' 23 And concerning Jezebel the LORD also spoke, saying, 'The dogs shall eat Jezebel by the wall of Jezreel.' 24 The dogs shall eat whoever belongs to Ahab and dies in the city, and the birds of the air shall eat whoever dies in the field."

25 But there was no one like Ahab who sold himself to do wickedness in the sight of the LORD, because Jezebel his wife stirred him up. 26 And he behaved very abominably in following idols, according to all *that* the Amorites had done, whom the LORD had cast out before the children of Israel.

27 So it was, when Ahab heard those words, that he tore his clothes and put sackcloth on his body, and fasted and lay in sackcloth, and went about mourning.

28 And the word of the LORD came to Elijah the Tishbite, saying, 29 "See how Ahab has humbled himself before Me? Because he has humbled himself before Me, I will not bring the calamity in his days.

In the days of his son I will bring the calamity on his house."

22 NOW three years passed without war between Syria and Israel. 2 Then it came to pass, in the third year, that Jehoshaphat the king of Judah went down to *visit* the king of Israel.

3 And the king of Israel said to his servants, "Do you know that Ramoth in Gilead *is* ours, but we hesitate to take it out of the hand of the king of Syria?" 4 So he said to Jehoshaphat, "Will you go with me to fight at Ramoth Gilead?"

Jehoshaphat said to the king of Israel, "I *am* as you *are,* my people as your people, my horses as your horses." 5 Also Jehoshaphat said to the king of Israel, "Please inquire for the word of the LORD today."

6 Then the king of Israel gathered the prophets together, about four hundred men, and said to them, "Shall I go against Ramoth Gilead to fight, or shall I refrain?"

So they said, "Go up, for the Lord will deliver *it* into the hand of the king."

7 And Jehoshaphat said, "*Is there* not still a prophet of the LORD here, that we may inquire of Him?"

8 So the king of Israel said to Jehoshaphat, "*There is* still one man, Micaiah the son of Imlah, by whom we may inquire of the LORD; but I hate him, because he does not prophesy good concerning me, but evil."

And Jehoshaphat said, "Let not the king say such things!"

9 Then the king of Israel called an officer and said, "Bring Micaiah the son of Imlah quickly!"

10 The king of Israel and Jehoshaphat the king of Judah, having put on *their* robes, sat each on his throne, at a threshing floor at the entrance of the gate of Samaria; and all the prophets prophesied before them. 11 Now Zedekiah the son of Chenaanah had made horns of iron for himself; and he said, "Thus says the LORD: 'With these you shall gore the Syrians until they are destroyed.' " 12 And all the prophets prophesied so, saying, "Go up to Ramoth Gilead and prosper, for the LORD will deliver *it* into the king's hand."

13 Then the messenger who had gone to call Micaiah spoke to him, saying, "Now listen, the words of the prophets with one accord encourage the king. Please, let your word be like the word of one of them, and speak encouragement."

14 And Micaiah said, "*As* the LORD lives, whatever the LORD says to me, that I will speak."

15 Then he came to the king; and the king said to him, "Micaiah, shall we go to war against Ramoth Gilead, or shall we refrain?"

And he answered him, "Go and prosper, for the LORD will deliver *it* into the hand of the king!"

16 So the king said to him, "How many times shall I make you swear that you tell me nothing but the truth in the name of the LORD?"

17 Then he said, "I saw all Israel scattered on the mountains, as sheep that have no shepherd. And the LORD said, 'These have no master. Let each return to his house in peace.' "

18 And the king of Israel said to Jehoshaphat, "Did I not tell you he would not prophesy good concerning me, but evil?"

19 Then *Micaiah* said, "Therefore hear the word of the LORD: I saw the LORD sitting on His throne, and all the host of heaven standing by, on His right hand and on His left. 20 And the LORD said, 'Who will persuade Ahab to go up, that he may fall at Ramoth Gilead?' So one spoke in this manner, and another spoke in that manner. 21 Then a spirit came forward and stood before the LORD, and said, 'I will persuade him.' 22 The LORD said to him, 'In what way?' So he said, 'I will go out and be a lying spirit in the mouth of all his prophets.' And the LORD said, 'You shall persuade *him*, and also prevail. Go out and do so.' 23 Therefore look! The LORD has put a lying spirit in the mouth of all these prophets of yours, and the LORD has declared disaster against you."

24 Now Zedekiah the son of Chenaanah went near and struck Micaiah on the cheek, and said, "Which way did the spirit from the LORD go from me to speak to you?"

25 And Micaiah said, "Indeed, you shall see on that day when you go into an inner chamber to hide!"

26 So the king of Israel said, "Take Micaiah, and return him to Amon the governor of the city and to Joash the king's son; 27 and say, 'Thus says the king: "Put this *fellow* in prison, and feed him with bread of affliction and water of affliction, until I come in peace." ' "

28 But Micaiah said, "If you ever return in peace, the LORD has not spoken by me." And he said, "Take heed, all you people!"

29 So the king of Israel and Jehoshaphat the king of Judah went up to Ramoth Gilead. 30 And the king of Israel said to Jehoshaphat, "I will disguise myself and go into battle; but you put on your robes."

So the king of Israel disguised himself and went into battle.

31 Now the king of Syria had commanded the thirty-two captains of his chariots, saying, "Fight with no one small or great, but only with the king of Israel." 32 So it was, when the captains of the chariots saw Jehoshaphat, that they said, "Surely it *is* the king of Israel!" Therefore they turned aside to fight against him, and Jehoshaphat cried out. 33 And it happened, when the captains of the chariots saw that it *was* not the king of Israel, that they turned back from pursuing him. 34 Now a *certain* man drew a bow at random, and struck the king of Israel between the joints of his armor. So he said to the driver of his chariot, "Turn around and take me out of the battle, for I am wounded."

35 The battle increased that day; and the king was propped up in his chariot, facing the Syrians, and died at evening. The blood ran out from the wound onto the floor of the chariot. 36 Then, as the sun was going down, a shout went throughout the army, saying, "Every man to his city, and every man to his own country!"

37 So the king died, and was brought to Samaria. And they buried the king in Samaria. 38 Then *someone* washed the chariot at a pool in Samaria, and the dogs licked up his blood while the harlots bathed, according to the word of the LORD which He had spoken.

39 Now the rest of the acts of Ahab, and all that he did, the ivory house which he built and all the cities that he built, *are* they not written in the book of the chronicles of the kings of Israel? 40 So Ahab rested with his fathers. Then Ahaziah his son reigned in his place.

41 Jehoshaphat the son of Asa had become king over Judah in the fourth year of Ahab king of Israel. 42 Jehoshaphat *was* thirty-five years old when he became king, and he reigned twenty-five years in Jerusalem. His mother's name *was* Azubah the daughter of Shilhi. 43 And he walked in all the ways of his father Asa. He did not turn aside from them, doing *what was* right in the eyes of the LORD. Nevertheless the high places were not taken away, *for* the people offered sacrifices and burned incense on the high places. 44 Also Jehoshaphat made peace with the king of Israel.

45 Now the rest of the acts of Jehoshaphat, the might that he showed, and how he made war, *are* they not written in the book of the chronicles of the kings of Judah? 46 And the rest of the perverted persons, who remained in the days of his father Asa,

he banished from the land. 47 *There was* then no king in Edom, only a deputy of the king.

48 Jehoshaphat made merchant ships to go to Ophir for gold; but they never sailed, for the ships were wrecked at Ezion Geber. 49 Then Ahaziah the son of Ahab said to Jehoshaphat, "Let my servants go with your servants in the ships." But Jehoshaphat would not.

50 And Jehoshaphat rested with his fathers, and was buried with his fathers in the City of David his father. Then Jehoram his son reigned in his place.

51 Ahaziah the son of Ahab became king over Israel in Samaria in the seventeenth year of Jehoshaphat king of Judah, and reigned two years over Israel. 52 He did evil in the sight of the LORD, and walked in the way of his father and in the way of his mother and in the way of Jeroboam the son of Nebat, who had made Israel sin; 53 for he served Baal and worshiped him, and provoked the LORD God of Israel to anger, according to all that his father had done.

PSALM 71:1–8

1 IN You, O LORD, I put my trust;
  Let me never be put to shame.
2 Deliver me in Your righteousness, and cause me to escape;
  Incline Your ear to me, and save me.
3 Be my strong refuge,
  To which I may resort continually;
  You have given the commandment to save me,
  For You *are* my rock and my fortress.
4 Deliver me, O my God, out of the hand of the wicked,
  Out of the hand of the unrighteous and cruel man.
5 For You are my hope, O Lord GOD;
  You are my trust from my youth.
6 By You I have been upheld from birth;
  You are He who took me out of my mother's womb.
  My praise *shall be* continually of You.

7 I have become as a wonder to many,
  But You *are* my strong refuge.
8 Let my mouth be filled *with* Your praise
  And with Your glory all the day.

PROVERBS 18:3–5

3 WHEN the wicked comes, contempt comes also;
  And with dishonor *comes* reproach.

4 The words of a man's mouth *are* deep waters;
  The wellspring of wisdom *is* a flowing brook.

5 *It is* not good to show partiality to the wicked,
  Or to overthrow the righteous in judgment.

JOHN 15:1–27

"I am the true vine, and My Father is the vinedresser. 2 Every branch in Me that does not bear fruit He takes away; and every *branch* that bears fruit He prunes, that it may bear more fruit. 3 You are already clean because of the word which I have spoken to you. 4 Abide in Me, and I in you. As the branch cannot bear fruit of itself, unless it abides in the vine, neither can you, unless you abide in Me.

---

*D*etermine to abide in Jesus wherever you are placed.   (UTMOST)

---

5 "I am the vine, you *are* the branches. He who abides in Me, and I in him, bears much fruit; for without Me you can do nothing. 6 If anyone does not abide in Me, he is cast out as a branch and is withered; and they gather them and throw *them* into the fire, and they are burned. 7 If you abide in Me, and My words abide in you, you will ask what you desire, and it shall be done for you. 8 By this My Father is glorified, that you bear much fruit; so you will be My disciples.

9 "As the Father loved Me, I also have loved you; abide in My love. 10 If you keep My commandments, you will abide in My love, just as I have kept My Father's commandments and abide in His love.

11 "These things I have spoken to you, that My joy may remain in you, and *that* your joy may be full. 12 This is My commandment, that you love one another as I have loved you. 13 Greater love has no one than this, than to lay down one's life for his friends. 14 You are My friends if you do whatever I command you. 15 No longer do I call you servants, for a servant does not know what his master is doing; but I have called you friends, for all things that I heard from My Father I have made known to you. 16 You did not choose Me, but I chose you and appointed you that you

should go and bear fruit, and *that* your fruit should remain, that whatever you ask the Father in My name He may give you. 17 These things I command you, that you love one another.

18 "If the world hates you, you know that it hated Me before *it hated* you. 19 If you were of the world, the world would love its own. Yet because you are not of the world, but I chose you out of the world, therefore the world hates you. 20 Remember the word that I said to you, 'A servant is not greater than his master.' If they persecuted Me, they will also persecute you. If they kept My word, they will keep yours also. 21 But all these things they will do to you for My name's sake, because they do not know Him who sent Me. 22 If I had not come and spoken to them, they would have no sin, but now they have no excuse for their sin. 23 He who hates Me hates My Father also. 24 If I had not done among them the works which no one else did, they would have no sin; but now they have seen and also hated both Me and My Father. 25 But *this happened* that the word might be fulfilled which is written in their law, 'They hated Me without a cause.'

26 "But when the Helper comes, whom I shall send to you from the Father, the Spirit of truth who proceeds from the Father, He will testify of Me. 27 And you also will bear witness, because you have been with Me from the beginning.

◆◆◆

Reading 158—The Unquestioned Things
John 16:23

When is "that day"? When the resurrection life of the Lord Jesus is the portion of our life. In that day we shall be one with the Father as Jesus said we should be, because the Holy Spirit has brought us there. No one can receive the Holy Spirit unless he is convinced of his own poverty. When we receive the Holy Spirit, He imparts the risen life of Jesus and there is no distance between the Father and His child. Have we come to this unquestioning place where there is no more perplexity of heart in regard to God? Any number of things may be dark and unexplained, but they do not come in between the heart and God. "In that day you will ask Me nothing"— you do not need to, you are so certain that God will bring it all out in perfect accordance with His will; John 14:1 ("let not your heart be troubled") has become the real state of your life. Until the resurrection life of Jesus Christ is manifested, we do want to ask questions; whenever we take a new step in God's providence we want to ask this and that. When the point of entire reliance on the resurrection of Jesus is reached, and we are brought into perfect contact with the purpose of God, we find all our questions have gone. Are we living that life now? If not, why shouldn't we?   (*PLACE HELP*)

2 KINGS 1:1—2:25

MOAB rebelled against Israel after the death of Ahab.

2 Now Ahaziah fell through the lattice of his upper room in Samaria, and was injured; so he sent messengers and said to them, "Go, inquire of Baal-Zebub, the god of Ekron, whether I shall recover from this injury." 3 But the angel of the LORD said to Elijah the Tishbite, "Arise, go up to meet the messengers of the king of Samaria, and say to them, '*Is it* because *there is* no God in Israel *that* you are going to inquire of Baal-Zebub, the god of Ekron?' 4 Now therefore, thus says the LORD: 'You shall not come down from the bed to which you have gone up, but you shall surely die.' " So Elijah departed.

5 And when the messengers returned to him, he said to them, "Why have you come back?"

6 So they said to him, "A man came up to meet us, and said to us, 'Go, return to the king who sent you, and say to him, "Thus says the LORD: 'Is it because there is no God in Israel that you are sending to inquire of Baal-Zebub, the god of Ekron? Therefore you shall not come down from the bed to which you have gone up, but you shall surely die.' " ' "

7 Then he said to them, "What kind of man was it who came up to meet you and told you these words?"

8 So they answered him, "A hairy man wearing a leather belt around his waist."

And he said, "It is Elijah the Tishbite."

9 Then the king sent to him a captain of fifty with his fifty men. So he went up to him; and there he was, sitting on the top of a hill. And he spoke to him: "Man of God, the king has said, 'Come down!' "

10 So Elijah answered and said to the captain of fifty, "If I am a man of God, then let fire come down from heaven and consume you and your fifty men." And fire came down from heaven and consumed him and his fifty. 11 Then he sent to him another captain of fifty with his fifty men.

And he answered and said to him: "Man of God, thus has the king said, 'Come down quickly!' "

12 So Elijah answered and said to them, "If I am a man of God, let fire come down from heaven and consume you and your fifty men." And the fire of God came down from heaven and consumed him and his fifty.

13 Again, he sent a third captain of fifty with his fifty men. And the third captain of fifty went up, and came and fell on his knees before Elijah, and pleaded with him, and said to him: "Man of God, please let my life and the life of these fifty servants of yours be precious in your sight. 14 Look, fire has come down from heaven and burned up the first two captains of fifties with their fifties. But let my life now be precious in your sight."

15 And the angel of the LORD said to Elijah, "Go down with him; do not be afraid of him." So he arose and went down with him to the king. 16 Then he said to him, "Thus says the LORD: 'Because you have sent messengers to inquire of Baal-Zebub, the god of Ekron, is it because there is no God in Israel to inquire of His word? Therefore you shall not come down from the bed to which you have gone up, but you shall surely die.' "

17 So *Ahaziah* died according to the word of the LORD which Elijah had spoken. Be-

cause he had no son, Jehoram became king in his place, in the second year of Jehoram the son of Jehoshaphat, king of Judah.

18 Now the rest of the acts of Ahaziah which he did, are they not written in the book of the chronicles of the kings of Israel?

2 AND it came to pass, when the LORD was about to take up Elijah into heaven by a whirlwind, that Elijah went with Elisha from Gilgal. 2 Then Elijah said to Elisha, "Stay here, please, for the LORD has sent me on to Bethel."

But Elisha said, "As the LORD lives, and as your soul lives, I will not leave you!" So they went down to Bethel.

3 Now the sons of the prophets who were at Bethel came out to Elisha, and said to him, "Do you know that the LORD will take away your master from over you today?"

And he said, "Yes, I know; keep silent!"

4 Then Elijah said to him, "Elisha, stay here, please, for the LORD has sent me on to Jericho."

But he said, "As the LORD lives, and as your soul lives, I will not leave you!" So they came to Jericho.

5 Now the sons of the prophets who were at Jericho came to Elisha and said to him, "Do you know that the LORD will take away your master from over you today?"

So he answered, "Yes, I know; keep silent!"

6 Then Elijah said to him, "Stay here, please, for the LORD has sent me on to the Jordan."

But he said, "As the LORD lives, and as your soul lives, I will not leave you!" So the two of them went on. 7 And fifty men of the sons of the prophets went and stood facing them at a distance, while the two of them stood by the Jordan. 8 Now Elijah took his mantle, rolled it up, and struck the water; and it was divided this way and that, so that the two of them crossed over on dry ground.

9 And so it was, when they had crossed over, that Elijah said to Elisha, "Ask! What may I do for you, before I am taken away from you?"

Elisha said, "Please let a double portion of your spirit be upon me."

10 So he said, "You have asked a hard thing. *Nevertheless,* if you see me when I am taken from you, it shall be so for you; but if not, it shall not be so." 11 Then it happened, as they continued on and talked, that suddenly a chariot of fire appeared with horses of fire, and separated the two of

them; and Elijah went up by a whirlwind into heaven.

12 And Elisha saw *it,* and he cried out, "My father, my father, the chariot of Israel and its horsemen!" So he saw him no more. And he took hold of his own clothes and tore them into two pieces. 13 He also took up the mantle of Elijah that had fallen from him, and went back and stood by the bank of the Jordan. 14 Then he took the mantle of Elijah that had fallen from him, and struck the water, and said, "Where *is* the LORD God of Elijah?" And when he also had struck the water, it was divided this way and that; and Elisha crossed over.

15 Now when the sons of the prophets who *were* from Jericho saw him, they said, "The spirit of Elijah rests on Elisha." And they came to meet him, and bowed to the ground before him. 16 Then they said to him, "Look now, there are fifty strong men with your servants. Please let them go and search for your master, lest perhaps the Spirit of the LORD has taken him up and cast him upon some mountain or into some valley."

And he said, "You shall not send anyone."

17 But when they urged him till he was ashamed, he said, "Send *them!*" Therefore they sent fifty men, and they searched for three days but did not find him. 18 And when they came back to him, for he had stayed in Jericho, he said to them, "Did I not say to you, 'Do not go'?"

19 Then the men of the city said to Elisha, "Please notice, the situation of this city *is* pleasant, as my lord sees; but the water *is* bad, and the ground barren."

20 And he said, "Bring me a new bowl, and put salt in it." So they brought *it* to him. 21 Then he went out to the source of the water, and cast in the salt there, and said, "Thus says the LORD: 'I have healed this water; from it there shall be no more death or barrenness.' " 22 So the water remains healed to this day, according to the word of Elisha which he spoke.

23 Then he went up from there to Bethel; and as he was going up the road, some youths came from the city and mocked him, and said to him, "Go up, you baldhead! Go up, you baldhead!"

24 So he turned around and looked at them, and pronounced a curse on them in the name of the LORD. And two female bears came out of the woods and mauled forty-two of the youths.

25 Then he went from there to Mount Carmel, and from there he returned to Samaria.

PSALM 71:9–16

9   DO not cast me off in the time of old age;
    Do not forsake me when my strength fails.
10 For my enemies speak against me;
    And those who lie in wait for my life take counsel together,
11 Saying, "God has forsaken him;
    Pursue and take him, for *there is* none to deliver *him.*"

12 O God, do not be far from me;
    O my God, make haste to help me!
13 Let them be confounded *and* consumed Who are adversaries of my life;
    Let them be covered *with* reproach and dishonor
    Who seek my hurt.

14 But I will hope continually,
    And will praise You yet more and more.
15 My mouth shall tell of Your righteousness
    And Your salvation all the day,
    For I do not know *their* limits.
16 I will go in the strength of the Lord GOD;
    I will make mention of Your righteousness, of Yours only.

PROVERBS 18:6–8

6   A fool's lips enter into contention,
    And his mouth calls for blows.
7   A fool's mouth *is* his destruction,
    And his lips *are* the snare of his soul.
8   The words of a talebearer *are* like tasty trifles,
    And they go down into the inmost body.

JOHN 16:1–33

"THESE things I have spoken to you, that you should not be made to stumble. 2 They will put you out of the synagogues; yes, the time is coming that whoever kills you will think that he offers God service. 3 And these things they will do to you because they have not known the Father nor Me. 4 But these things I have told you, that when the time comes, you may remember that I told you of them.

"And these things I did not say to you at the beginning, because I was with you.

5 "But now I go away to Him who sent Me, and none of you asks Me, 'Where are

You going?' 6 But because I have said these things to you, sorrow has filled your heart. 7 Nevertheless I tell you the truth. It is to your advantage that I go away; for if I do not go away, the Helper will not come to you; but if I depart, I will send Him to you. 8 And when He has come, He will convict the world of sin, and of righteousness, and of judgment: 9 of sin, because they do not believe in Me; 10 of righteousness, because I go to My Father and you see Me no more; 11 of judgment, because the ruler of this world is judged.

Jesus Christ stands as the type of man, and the only type of man, who can come near to God. (PHIL. SIN)

12 "I still have many things to say to you, but you cannot bear *them* now. 13 However, when He, the Spirit of truth, has come, He will guide you into all truth; for He will not speak on His own *authority,* but whatever He hears He will speak; and He will tell you things to come. 14 He will glorify Me, for He will take of what is Mine and declare *it* to you. 15 All things that the Father has are Mine. Therefore I said that He will take of Mine and declare *it* to you.

16 "A little while, and you will not see Me; and again a little while, and you will see Me, because I go to the Father."

17 Then *some* of His disciples said among themselves, "What is this that He says to us, 'A little while, and you will not see Me; and again a little while, and you will see Me'; and, 'because I go to the Father'?" 18 They said therefore, "What is this that He says, 'A little while'? We do not know what He is saying."

19 Now Jesus knew that they desired to ask Him, and He said to them, "Are you inquiring among yourselves about what I said, 'A little while, and you will not see Me; and again a little while, and you will

see Me'? 20 Most assuredly, I say to you that you will weep and lament, but the world will rejoice; and you will be sorrowful, but your sorrow will be turned into joy. 21 A woman, when she is in labor, has sorrow because her hour has come; but as soon as she has given birth to the child, she no longer remembers the anguish, for joy that a human being has been born into the world. 22 Therefore you now have sorrow; but I will see you again and your heart will rejoice, and your joy no one will take from you.

23 "And in that day you will ask Me nothing. Most assuredly, I say to you, whatever you ask the Father in My name He will give you. 24 Until now you have asked nothing in My name. Ask, and you will receive, that your joy may be full.

25 "These things I have spoken to you in figurative language; but the time is coming when I will no longer speak to you in figurative language, but I will tell you plainly about the Father. 26 In that day you will ask in My name, and I do not say to you that I shall pray the Father for you; 27 for the Father Himself loves you, because you have loved Me, and have believed that I came forth from God. 28 I came forth from the Father and have come into the world. Again, I leave the world and go to the Father."

29 His disciples said to Him, "See, now You are speaking plainly, and using no figure of speech! 30 Now we are sure that You know all things, and have no need that anyone should question You. By this we believe that You came forth from God."

31 Jesus answered them, "Do you now believe? 32 Indeed the hour is coming, yes, has now come, that you will be scattered, each to his own, and will leave Me alone. And yet I am not alone, because the Father is with Me. 33 These things I have spoken to you, that in Me you may have peace. In the world you will have tribulation; but be of good cheer, I have overcome the world."

Reading 159—Christ's Transfiguration

John 17:5

When our Lord as a man had fulfilled all God's demands of Him, and when by obedience He had transformed His natural life into a spiritual life, earth had no more hold on Him. On the Mount of Transfiguration, His real nature, that is, His essential deity, broke throughout the natural, and He was transfigured. He had fulfilled all the requirements of His Father for His earthly life, and God's presence, symbolized in the cloud, waited to usher Him back into the glory that He had with the Father before the world was. But He turned His back on the glory and came down from the mount to identify Himself with fallen humanity, because through Calvary there was to issue the newly constructed humanity. If Jesus Christ had gone to heaven from the Mount of Transfiguration, He would have gone alone. He would have been to us a glorious figure, One who manifested the life of God's normal man . . . but what good would that have been to us? We can never live in the power of an ideal put before us. . . . But Jesus Christ did not go to heaven from the mount. Moses and Elijah talked with Him, not of His glory and not of His deity, but of His death—the issue that He was about to accomplish at Jerusalem. By His death on the cross, Jesus Christ made the way for every son of man to get into communion with God.   (GLORY)

2 KINGS 3:1—4:44

NOW Jehoram the son of Ahab became king over Israel at Samaria in the eighteenth year of Jehoshaphat king of Judah, and reigned twelve years. 2 And he did evil in the sight of the LORD, but not like his father and mother; for he put away the *sacred* pillar of Baal that his father had made. 3 Nevertheless he persisted in the sins of Jeroboam the son of Nebat, who had made Israel sin; he did not depart from them.

4 Now Mesha king of Moab was a sheep-breeder, and he regularly paid the king of Israel one hundred thousand lambs and the wool of one hundred thousand rams. 5 But it happened, when Ahab died, that the king of Moab rebelled against the king of Israel.

6 So King Jehoram went out of Samaria at that time and mustered all Israel. 7 Then he went and sent to Jehoshaphat king of Judah, saying, "The king of Moab has rebelled against me. Will you go with me to fight against Moab?"

And he said, "I will go up; I *am* as you *are,* my people as your people, my horses as your horses." 8 Then he said, "Which way shall we go up?"

And he answered, "By way of the Wilderness of Edom."

9 So the king of Israel went with the king of Judah and the king of Edom, and they marched on that roundabout route seven days; and there was no water for the army, nor for the animals that followed them. 10 And the king of Israel said, "Alas! For the LORD has called these three kings together to deliver them into the hand of Moab."

11 But Jehoshaphat said, "*Is there* no prophet of the LORD here, that we may inquire of the LORD by him?"

So one of the servants of the king of Israel answered and said, "Elisha the son of Shaphat *is* here, who poured water on the hands of Elijah."

12 And Jehoshaphat said, "The word of the LORD is with him." So the king of Israel and Jehoshaphat and the king of Edom went down to him.

13 Then Elisha said to the king of Israel, "What have I to do with you? Go to the prophets of your father and the prophets of your mother."

But the king of Israel said to him, "No, for the LORD has called these three kings *together* to deliver them into the hand of Moab."

14 And Elisha said, "*As* the LORD of hosts lives, before whom I stand, surely were it not that I regard the presence of Jehoshaphat king of Judah, I would not look at

you, nor see you. 15 But now bring me a musician."

Then it happened, when the musician played, that the hand of the LORD came upon him. 16 And he said, "Thus says the LORD: 'Make this valley full of ditches.' 17 For thus says the LORD: 'You shall not see wind, nor shall you see rain; yet that valley shall be filled with water, so that you, your cattle, and your animals may drink.' 18 And this is a simple matter in the sight of the LORD; He will also deliver the Moabites into your hand. 19 Also you shall attack every fortified city and every choice city, and shall cut down every good tree, and stop up every spring of water, and ruin every good piece of land with stones."

20 Now it happened in the morning, when the grain offering was offered, that suddenly water came by way of Edom, and the land was filled with water.

21 And when all the Moabites heard that the kings had come up to fight against them, all who were able to bear arms and older were gathered; and they stood at the border. 22 Then they rose up early in the morning, and the sun was shining on the water; and the Moabites saw the water on the other side *as* red as blood. 23 And they said, "This is blood; the kings have surely struck swords and have killed one another; now therefore, Moab, to the spoil!"

24 So when they came to the camp of Israel, Israel rose up and attacked the Moabites, so that they fled before them; and they entered *their* land, killing the Moabites. 25 Then they destroyed the cities, and each man threw a stone on every good piece of land and filled it; and they stopped up all the springs of water and cut down all the good trees. But they left the stones of Kir Haraseth *intact*. However the slingers surrounded and attacked it.

26 And when the king of Moab saw that the battle was too fierce for him, he took with him seven hundred men who drew swords, to break through to the king of Edom, but they could not. 27 Then he took his eldest son who would have reigned in his place, and offered him *as* a burnt offering upon the wall; and there was great indignation against Israel. So they departed from him and returned to *their own* land.

4 A certain woman of the wives of the sons of the prophets cried out to Elisha, saying, "Your servant my husband is dead, and you know that your servant feared the LORD. And the creditor is coming to take my two sons to be his slaves."

2 So Elisha said to her, "What shall I do for you? Tell me, what do you have in the house?" And she said, "Your maidservant has nothing in the house but a jar of oil."

3 Then he said, "Go, borrow vessels from everywhere, from all your neighbors—empty vessels; do not gather just a few. 4 And when you have come in, you shall shut the door behind you and your sons; then pour it into all those vessels, and set aside the full ones."

5 So she went from him and shut the door behind her and her sons, who brought *the vessels* to her; and she poured *it* out. 6 Now it came to pass, when the vessels were full, that she said to her son, "Bring me another vessel."

And he said to her, "*There is* not another vessel." So the oil ceased. 7 Then she came and told the man of God. And he said, "Go, sell the oil and pay your debt; and you *and* your sons live on the rest."

8 Now it happened one day that Elisha went to Shunem, where there *was* a notable woman, and she persuaded him to eat some food. So it was, as often as he passed by, he would turn in there to eat some food. 9 And she said to her husband, "Look now, I know that this *is* a holy man of God, who passes by us regularly. 10 Please, let us make a small upper room on the wall; and let us put a bed for him there, and a table and a chair and a lampstand; so it will be, whenever he comes to us, he can turn in there."

11 And it happened one day that he came there, and he turned in to the upper room and lay down there. 12 Then he said to Gehazi his servant, "Call this Shunammite woman." When he had called her, she stood before him. 13 And he said to him, "Say now to her, 'Look, you have been concerned for us with all this care. What *can I* do for you? Do you want me to speak on your behalf to the king or to the commander of the army?' "

She answered, "I dwell among my own people."

14 So he said, "What then *is* to be done for her?"

And Gehazi answered, "Actually, she has no son, and her husband is old."

15 So he said, "Call her." When he had called her, she stood in the doorway. 16 Then he said, "About this time next year you shall embrace a son."

And she said, "No, my lord. Man of God, do not lie to your maidservant!"

17 But the woman conceived, and bore

a son when the appointed time had come, of which Elisha had told her.

18 And the child grew. Now it happened one day that he went out to his father, to the reapers. 19 And he said to his father, "My head, my head!"

So he said to a servant, "Carry him to his mother." 20 When he had taken him and brought him to his mother, he sat on her knees till noon, and *then* died. 21 And she went up and laid him on the bed of the man of God, shut *the door* upon him, and went out. 22 Then she called to her husband, and said, "Please send me one of the young men and one of the donkeys, that I may run to the man of God and come back."

23 So he said, "Why are you going to him today? It *is* neither the New Moon nor the Sabbath."

And she said, "It *is* well." 24 Then she saddled a donkey, and said to her servant, "Drive, and go forward; do not slacken the pace for me unless I tell you." 25 And so she departed, and went to the man of God at Mount Carmel.

So it was, when the man of God saw her afar off, that he said to his servant Gehazi, "Look, the Shunammite woman! 26 Please run now to meet her, and say to her, 'Is *it* well with you? Is *it* well with your husband? Is *it* well with the child?' "

And she answered, "It *is* well." 27 Now when she came to the man of God at the hill, she caught him by the feet, but Gehazi came near to push her away. But the man of God said, "Let her alone; for her soul *is* in deep distress, and the LORD has hidden *it* from me, and has not told me."

28 So she said, "Did I ask a son of my lord? Did I not say, 'Do not deceive me'?"

29 Then he said to Gehazi, "Get yourself ready, and take my staff in your hand, and be on your way. If you meet anyone, do not greet him; and if anyone greets you, do not answer him; but lay my staff on the face of the child."

30 And the mother of the child said, "*As* the LORD lives, and *as* your soul lives, I will not leave you." So he arose and followed her. 31 Now Gehazi went on ahead of them, and laid the staff on the face of the child; but *there was* neither voice nor hearing. Therefore he went back to meet him, and told him, saying, "The child has not awakened."

32 When Elisha came into the house, there was the child, lying dead on his bed. 33 He went in therefore, shut the door behind the two of them, and prayed to the LORD. 34 And he went up and lay on the

The very powers of darkness are paralyzed by prayer.   (DISCIPLES)

child, and put his mouth on his mouth, his eyes on his eyes, and his hands on his hands; and he stretched himself out on the child, and the flesh of the child became warm. 35 He returned and walked back and forth in the house, and again went up and stretched himself out on him; then the child sneezed seven times, and the child opened his eyes. 36 And he called Gehazi and said, "Call this Shunammite woman." So he called her. And when she came in to him, he said, "Pick up your son." 37 So she went in, fell at his feet, and bowed to the ground; then she picked up her son and went out.

38 And Elisha returned to Gilgal, and *there was* a famine in the land. Now the sons of the prophets *were* sitting before him; and he said to his servant, "Put on the large pot, and boil stew for the sons of the prophets." 39 So one went out into the field to gather herbs, and found a wild vine, and gathered from it a lapful of wild gourds, and came and sliced *them* into the pot of stew, though they did not know *what they were*. 40 Then they served it to the men to eat. Now it happened, as they were eating the stew, that they cried out and said, "Man of God, *there is* death in the pot!" And they could not eat it.

41 So he said, "Then bring some flour." And he put *it* into the pot, and said, "Serve *it* to the people, that they may eat." And there was nothing harmful in the pot.

42 Then a man came from Baal Shalisha, and brought the man of God bread of the firstfruits, twenty loaves of barley bread, and newly ripened grain in his knapsack. And he said, "Give *it* to the people, that they may eat."

43 But his servant said, "What? Shall I set this before one hundred men?"

He said again, "Give it to the people, that they may eat; for thus says the LORD: 'They shall eat and have *some* left over.'"
44 So he set *it* before them; and they ate and had *some* left over, according to the word of the LORD.

PSALM 71:17–24

17   O God, You have taught me from my
       youth;
    And to this *day* I declare Your
      wondrous works.

18 Now also when *I am* old and
   grayheaded,
   O God, do not forsake me,
   Until I declare Your strength to *this*
   generation,
   Your power to everyone *who* is to come.

19 Also Your righteousness, O God, *is* very
   high,
   You who have done great things;
   O God, who *is* like You?
20 *You,* who have shown me great and
   severe troubles,
   Shall revive me again,
   And bring me up again from the depths
   of the earth.
21 You shall increase my greatness,
   And comfort me on every side.

22 Also with the lute I will praise You—
   And Your faithfulness, O my God!
   To You I will sing with the harp,
   O Holy One of Israel.
23 My lips shall greatly rejoice when I sing
   to You,
   And my soul, which You have
   redeemed.
24 My tongue also shall talk of Your
   righteousness all the day long;
   For they are confounded,
   For they are brought to shame
   Who seek my hurt.

PROVERBS 18:9

9 HE who is slothful in his work
   Is a brother to him who is a great
   destroyer.

JOHN 17:1–26

JESUS spoke these words, lifted up His
eyes to heaven, and said: "Father, the hour
has come. Glorify Your Son, that Your Son
also may glorify You, 2 as You have given
Him authority over all flesh, that He should
give eternal life to as many as You have
given Him. 3 And this is eternal life, that
they may know You, the only true God,
and Jesus Christ whom You have sent.
4 I have glorified You on the earth. I have
finished the work which You have given
Me to do. 5 And now, O Father, glorify

---

*The Holy Spirit will glorify
Jesus only.* (PERFECT)

Me together with Yourself, with the glory
which I had with You before the world
was.

6 "I have manifested Your name to the
men whom You have given Me out of the
world. They were Yours, You gave them
to Me, and they have kept Your word.
7 Now they have known that all things
which You have given Me are from You.
8 For I have given to them the words which
You have given Me; and they have received
them, and have known surely that I came
forth from You; and they have believed that
You sent Me.
9 "I pray for them. I do not pray for the
world but for those whom You have given
Me, for they are Yours. 10 And all Mine
are Yours, and Yours are Mine, and I am
glorified in them. 11 Now I am no longer
in the world, but these are in the world,
and I come to You. Holy Father, keep
through Your name those whom You have
given Me, that they may be one as We *are.*
12 While I was with them in the world, I
kept them in Your name. Those whom You
gave Me I have kept; and none of them
is lost except the son of perdition, that
the Scripture might be fulfilled. 13 But
now I come to You, and these things I
speak in the world, that they may have
My joy fulfilled in themselves. 14 I have
given them Your word; and the world has
hated them because they are not of the
world, just as I am not of the world.
15 I do not pray that You should take them
out of the world, but that You should keep
them from the evil one. 16 They are not
of the world, just as I am not of the world.
17 Sanctify them by Your truth. Your word
is truth. 18 As You sent Me into the
world, I also have sent them into the
world. 19 And for their sakes I sanctify Myself, that they also may be sanctified by the
truth.
20 "I do not pray for these alone, but
also for those who will believe in Me
through their word; 21 that they all may
be one, as You, Father, *are* in Me, and I
in You; that they also may be one in Us,
that the world may believe that You sent
Me. 22 And the glory which You gave Me
I have given them, that they may be one
just as We are one: 23 I in them, and You
in Me; that they may be made perfect in
one, and that the world may know that
You have sent Me, and have loved them
as You have loved Me.
24 "Father, I desire that they also whom
You gave Me may be with Me where I
am, that they may behold My glory which
You have given Me; for You loved Me

before the foundation of the world. 25 O righteous Father! The world has not known You, but I have known You; and these have known that You sent Me.

26 And I have declared to them Your name, and will declare *it*, that the love with which You loved Me may be in them, and I in them."

◆◆◆◆

Reading 160—Christ's Agony and Triumph
John 18:1

We can never fathom the agony in Gethsemane, but at least we need not misunderstand it. It is the agony of God and Man in one, face-to-face with sin. We know nothing about Gethsemane in personal experience. Gethsemane and Calvary stand for something unique; they are the gateway into Life for us.

It was not the death on the cross that Jesus feared in Gethsemane; He stated most emphatically that He came on purpose to die. In Gethsemane He feared lest He might not get through as Son of Man. He would get through as Son of God—Satan could not touch Him there; but Satan's onslaught was that He would get through as an isolated Figure only; and that would mean that He could be no Savior. . . .

The agony in Gethsemane is the agony of the Son of God in fulfilling His destiny as the Savior of the world. The veil is drawn aside to reveal all it cost Him to make it possible for us to become sons of God. His agony is the basis of the simplicity of our salvation. The Cross of Christ is a triumph for the *Son of Man*. It was not only a sign that our Lord had triumphed, but that He had triumphed to save the human race. Every human being can get through into the presence of God now because of what the Son of Man went through.   (*UTMOST*)

2 KINGS 5:1—6:33

NOW Naaman, commander of the army of the king of Syria, was a great and honorable man in the eyes of his master, because by him the LORD had given victory to Syria. He was also a mighty man of valor, *but* a leper. 2 And the Syrians had gone out on raids, and had brought back captive a young girl from the land of Israel. She waited on Naaman's wife. 3 Then she said to her mistress, "If only my master *were* with the prophet who *is* in Samaria! For he would heal him of his leprosy." 4 And *Naaman* went in and told his master, saying, "Thus and thus said the girl who *is* from the land of Israel."

5 Then the king of Syria said, "Go now, and I will send a letter to the king of Israel."

So he departed and took with him ten talents of silver, six thousand *shekels* of gold, and ten changes of clothing. 6 Then he brought the letter to the king of Israel, which said,

Now be advised, when this letter comes to you, that I have sent Naaman my servant to you, that you may heal him of his leprosy.

7 And it happened, when the king of Israel read the letter, that he tore his clothes and said, "*Am* I God, to kill and make alive, that this man sends a man to me to heal him of his leprosy? Therefore please consider, and see how he seeks a quarrel with me."

8 So it was, when Elisha the man of God heard that the king of Israel had torn his clothes, that he sent to the king, saying, "Why have you torn your clothes? Please let him come to me, and he shall know that there is a prophet in Israel."

9 Then Naaman went with his horses and chariot, and he stood at the door of Elisha's house. 10 And Elisha sent a messenger to him, saying, "Go and wash in the Jordan seven times, and your flesh shall be restored to you, and *you shall* be clean." 11 But Naa-

man became furious, and went away and said, "Indeed, I said to myself, 'He will surely come out *to me,* and stand and call on the name of the Lord his God, and wave his hand over the place, and heal the leprosy.' 12 *Are* not the Abanah and the Pharpar, the rivers of Damascus, better than all the waters of Israel? Could I not wash in them and be clean?" So he turned and went away in a rage. 13 And his servants came near and spoke to him, and said, "My father, *if* the prophet had told you *to do* something great, would you not have done *it?* How much more then, when he says to you, 'Wash, and be clean'?" 14 So he went down and dipped seven times in the Jordan, according to the saying of the man of God; and his flesh was restored like the flesh of a little child, and he was clean.

15 And he returned to the man of God, he and all his aides, and came and stood before him; and he said, "Indeed, now I know that *there is* no God in all the earth, except in Israel; now therefore, please take a gift from your servant."

16 But he said, "*As* the Lord lives, before whom I stand, I will receive nothing." And he urged him to take *it,* but he refused.

17 So Naaman said, "Then, if not, please let your servant be given two mule-loads of earth; for your servant will no longer offer either burnt offering or sacrifice to other gods, but to the Lord. 18 Yet in this thing may the Lord pardon your servant: when my master goes into the temple of Rimmon to worship there, and he leans on my hand, and I bow down in the temple of Rimmon—when I bow down in the temple of Rimmon, may the Lord please pardon your servant in this thing."

19 Then he said to him, "Go in peace." So he departed from him a short distance.

20 But Gehazi, the servant of Elisha the man of God, said, "Look, my master has spared Naaman this Syrian, while not receiving from his hands what he brought; but *as* the Lord lives, I will run after him and take something from him." 21 So Gehazi pursued Naaman. When Naaman saw *him* running after him, he got down from the chariot to meet him, and said, "*Is* all well?"

22 And he said, "All *is* well. My master has sent me, saying, 'Indeed, just now two young men of the sons of the prophets have come to me from the mountains of Ephraim. Please give them a talent of silver and two changes of garments.' "

23 So Naaman said, "Please, take two talents." And he urged him, and bound two talents of silver in two bags, with two

changes of garments, and handed *them* to two of his servants; and they carried *them* on ahead of him. 24 When he came to the citadel, he took *them* from their hand, and stored *them* away in the house; then he let the men go, and they departed. 25 Now he went in and stood before his master. Elisha said to him, "Where *did you go,* Gehazi?"

And he said, "Your servant did not go anywhere."

26 Then he said to him, "Did not my heart go *with you* when the man turned back from his chariot to meet you? *Is it* time to receive money and to receive clothing, olive groves and vineyards, sheep and oxen, male and female servants? 27 Therefore the leprosy of Naaman shall cling to you and your descendants forever." And he went out from his presence leprous, *as white* as snow.

6 AND the sons of the prophets said to Elisha, "See now, the place where we dwell with you is too small for us. 2 Please, let us go to the Jordan, and let every man take a beam from there, and let us make there a place where we may dwell."

So he answered, "Go."

3 Then one said, "Please consent to go with your servants."

And he answered, "I will go." 4 So he went with them. And when they came to the Jordan, they cut down trees. 5 But as one was cutting down a tree, the iron *ax head* fell into the water; and he cried out and said, "Alas, master! For it was borrowed."

6 So the man of God said, "Where did it fall?" And he showed him the place. So he cut off a stick, and threw *it* in there; and he made the iron float. 7 Therefore he said, "Pick *it* up for yourself." So he reached out his hand and took it.

8 Now the king of Syria was making war against Israel; and he consulted with his servants, saying, "My camp *will be* in such and such a place." 9 And the man of God sent to the king of Israel, saying, "Beware that you do not pass this place, for the Syrians are coming down there." 10 Then the king of Israel sent *someone* to the place of which the man of God had told him. Thus he warned him, and he was watchful there, not just once or twice.

11 Therefore the heart of the king of Syria was greatly troubled by this thing; and he called his servants and said to them, "Will you not show me which of us *is* for the king of Israel?"

12 And one of his servants said, "None,

my lord, O king; but Elisha, the prophet who *is* in Israel, tells the king of Israel the words that you speak in your bedroom."

13 So he said, "Go and see where he *is*, that I may send and get him."

And it was told him, saying, "Surely *he is* in Dothan."

14 Therefore he sent horses and chariots and a great army there, and they came by night and surrounded the city. 15 And when the servant of the man of God arose early and went out, there was an army, surrounding the city with horses and chariots. And his servant said to him, "Alas, my master! What shall we do?"

16 So he answered, "Do not fear, for those who *are* with us *are* more than those who *are* with them." 17 And Elisha prayed, and said, "Lord, I pray, open his eyes that he may see." Then the Lord opened the eyes of the young man, and he saw. And behold, the mountain *was* full of horses and chariots of fire all around Elisha. 18 So when *the Syrians* came down to him, Elisha prayed to the Lord, and said, "Strike this people, I pray, with blindness." And He struck them with blindness according to the word of Elisha.

19 Now Elisha said to them, "This *is* not the way, nor *is* this the city. Follow me, and I will bring you to the man whom you seek." But he led them to Samaria.

20 So it was, when they had come to Samaria, that Elisha said, "Lord, open the eyes of these *men*, that they may see." And the Lord opened their eyes, and they saw; and there *they were*, inside Samaria!

21 Now when the king of Israel saw them, he said to Elisha, "My father, shall I kill *them*? Shall I kill *them*?"

22 But he answered, "You shall not kill *them*. Would you kill those whom you have taken captive with your sword and your bow? Set food and water before them, that they may eat and drink and go to their master." 23 Then he prepared a great feast for them; and after they ate and drank, he sent them away and they went to their master. So the bands of Syrian *raiders* came no more into the land of Israel.

24 And it happened after this that Ben-Hadad king of Syria gathered all his army, and went up and besieged Samaria. 25 And there was a great famine in Samaria; and indeed they besieged it until a donkey's head was *sold* for eighty *shekels* of silver, and one-fourth of a kab of dove droppings for five *shekels* of silver.

26 Then, as the king of Israel was passing by on the wall, a woman cried out to him, saying, "Help, my lord, O king!"

27 And he said, "If the Lord does not help you, where can I find help for you? From the threshing floor or from the winepress?" 28 Then the king said to her, "What is troubling you?"

And she answered, "This woman said to me, 'Give your son, that we may eat him today, and we will eat my son tomorrow.' 29 So we boiled my son, and ate him. And I said to her on the next day, 'Give your son, that we may eat him'; but she has hidden her son."

30 Now it happened, when the king heard the words of the woman, that he tore his clothes; and as he passed by on the wall, the people looked, and there underneath *he had* sackcloth on his body. 31 Then he said, "God do so to me and more also, if the head of Elisha the son of Shaphat remains on him today!"

32 But Elisha was sitting in his house, and the elders were sitting with him. And *the king* sent a man ahead of him, but before the messenger came to him, he said to the elders, "Do you see how this son of a murderer has sent someone to take away my head? Look, when the messenger comes, shut the door, and hold him fast at the door. *Is* not the sound of his master's feet behind him?" 33 And while he was still talking with them, there was the messenger, coming down to him; and then *the king* said, "Surely this calamity *is* from the Lord; why should I wait for the Lord any longer?"

PSALM 72:1–7

1 GIVE the king Your judgments,
   O God,
   And Your righteousness to the king's
   Son.
2 He will judge Your people with
   righteousness,
   And Your poor with justice.
3 The mountains will bring peace to the
   people,
   And the little hills, by righteousness.
4 He will bring justice to the poor of
   the people;
   He will save the children of the needy,
   And will break in pieces the oppressor.

5 They shall fear You
   As long as the sun and moon endure,
   Throughout all generations.
6 He shall come down like rain upon the
   grass before mowing,
   Like showers *that* water the earth.

7 In His days the righteous shall flourish,
   And abundance of peace,
   Until the moon is no more.

PROVERBS 18:10, 11

10 THE name of the LORD *is* a strong
    tower;
    The righteous run to it and are safe.
11 The rich man's wealth *is* his strong city,
    And like a high wall in his own esteem.

JOHN 18:1–18

WHEN Jesus had spoken these words, He
went out with His disciples over the Brook
Kidron, where there was a garden, which
He and His disciples entered. 2 And Judas,
who betrayed Him, also knew the place;
for Jesus often met there with His disciples.
3 Then Judas, having received a detachment
of troops, and officers from the chief priests
and Pharisees, came there with lanterns,
torches, and weapons. 4 Jesus therefore,
knowing all things that would come upon
Him, went forward and said to them,
"Whom are you seeking?"
5 They answered Him, "Jesus of
Nazareth."
Jesus said to them, "I am *He.*" And Judas,
who betrayed Him, also stood with them.
6 Now when He said to them, "I am *He,*"
they drew back and fell to the ground.
7 Then He asked them again, "Whom
are you seeking?"
And they said, "Jesus of Nazareth."
8 Jesus answered, "I have told you that
I am *He.* Therefore, if you seek Me, let
these go their way," 9 that the saying might

*The model of the Christian's
spirit is Christ
Himself.* (GOD'S WORKMANSHIP)

be fulfilled which He spoke, "Of those
whom You gave Me I have lost none."
10 Then Simon Peter, having a sword,
drew it and struck the high priest's servant,
and cut off his right ear. The servant's name
was Malchus.
11 So Jesus said to Peter, "Put your sword
into the sheath. Shall I not drink the cup
which My Father has given Me?"
12 Then the detachment *of troops* and the
captain and the officers of the Jews arrested
Jesus and bound Him. 13 And they led Him
away to Annas first, for he was the father-
in-law of Caiaphas who was high priest that
year. 14 Now it was Caiaphas who advised
the Jews that it was expedient that one man
should die for the people.
15 And Simon Peter followed Jesus, and
so *did* another disciple. Now that disciple
was known to the high priest, and went
with Jesus into the courtyard of the high
priest. 16 But Peter stood at the door outside. Then the other disciple, who was
known to the high priest, went out and
spoke to her who kept the door, and
brought Peter in. 17 Then the servant girl
who kept the door said to Peter, "You are
not also *one* of this Man's disciples, are
you?"
He said, "I am not."
18 Now the servants and officers who had
made a fire of coals stood there, for it was
cold, and they warmed themselves. And
Peter stood with them and warmed himself.

◆◆◆

*Reading 161—*Supernatural Loyalty
John 18:25–27

Our Lord has told us how love to Him is to manifest itself. "Do you
love Me?" "Feed My sheep"—identify yourself with My interests in
other people, not, identify *Me* with *your* interests in other people. First
Corinthians 13:4–8 gives the character of this love, it is the love *of God* expressing
itself. The test of my love for Jesus is the practical one, all the rest is sentimental
jargon.
   Loyalty to Jesus Christ is the supernatural work of redemption wrought in
me by the Holy Ghost who sheds abroad the love of God in my heart, and
that love works efficaciously through me in contact with everyone I meet. I

remain loyal to His name although every common-sense fact gives the lie to Him, and declares that He has no more power than a morning mist.

The key to missionary devotion means being attached to nothing and no one saving our Lord Himself, not being detached from things externally. Our Lord was amazingly in and out among ordinary things; His detachment was on the inside toward God. External detachment is often an indication of a secret vital attachment to the things we keep away from externally.

The loyalty of a missionary is to keep his soul concentratedly open to the nature of the Lord Jesus Christ. The men and women our Lord sends out on His enterprises are the ordinary human stuff, plus dominating devotion to Himself wrought by the Holy Ghost.   (*Utmost*)

2 KINGS 7:1—8:29

THEN Elisha said, "Hear the word of the LORD. Thus says the LORD: 'Tomorrow about this time a seah of fine flour *shall be sold* for a shekel, and two seahs of barley for a shekel, at the gate of Samaria.' "

2 So an officer on whose hand the king leaned answered the man of God and said, "Look, *if* the LORD would make windows in heaven, could this thing be?"

And he said, "In fact, you shall see *it* with your eyes, but you shall not eat of it."

3 Now there were four leprous men at the entrance of the gate; and they said to one another, "Why are we sitting here until we die? 4 If we say, 'We will enter the city,' the famine *is* in the city, and we shall die there. And if we sit here, we die also. Now therefore, come, let us surrender to the army of the Syrians. If they keep us alive, we shall live; and if they kill us, we shall only die." 5 And they rose at twilight to go to the camp of the Syrians; and when they had come to the outskirts of the Syrian camp, to their surprise no one *was* there. 6 For the LORD had caused the army of the Syrians to hear the noise of chariots and the noise of horses—the noise of a great army; so they said to one another, "Look, the king of Israel has hired against us the kings of the Hittites and the kings of the Egyptians to attack us!" 7 Therefore they arose and fled at twilight, and left the camp intact—their tents, their horses, and their donkeys—and they fled for their lives. 8 And when these lepers came to the outskirts of the camp, they went into one tent and ate and drank, and carried from it silver and gold and clothing, and went and hid *them;* then they came back and entered another tent, and carried *some* from there *also,* and went and hid *it.*

9 Then they said to one another, "We are not doing right. This day *is* a day of good news, and we remain silent. If we wait until morning light, some punishment will come upon us. Now therefore, come, let us go and tell the king's household." 10 So they went and called to the gatekeepers of the city, and told them, saying, "We went to the Syrian camp, and surprisingly no one *was* there, not a human sound—only horses and donkeys tied, and the tents intact." 11 And the gatekeepers called out, and they told *it* to the king's household inside.

12 So the king arose in the night and said to his servants, "Let me now tell you what the Syrians have done to us. They know that we *are* hungry; therefore they have gone out of the camp to hide themselves in the field, saying, 'When they come out of the city, we shall catch them alive, and get into the city.' "

13 And one of his servants answered and said, "Please, let several *men* take five of the remaining horses which are left in the city. Look, they *may either become* like all the multitude of Israel that are left in it; or indeed, *I say,* they *may become* like all the multitude of Israel left from those who are consumed; so let us send them and see." 14 Therefore they took two chariots with horses; and the king sent them in the direction of the Syrian army, saying, "Go and see." 15 And they went after them to the Jordan; and indeed all the road *was* full of garments and weapons which the Syrians had thrown away in their haste. So the messengers returned and told the king. 16 Then the people went out and plundered the tents of the Syrians. So a seah of fine flour was *sold* for a shekel, and two seahs of barley for a shekel, according to the word of the LORD.

17 Now the king had appointed the officer on whose hand he leaned to have charge of the gate. But the people trampled him

in the gate, and he died, just as the man of God had said, who spoke when the king came down to him. 18 So it happened just as the man of God had spoken to the king, saying, "Two seahs of barley for a shekel, and a seah of fine flour for a shekel, shall be *sold* tomorrow about this time in the gate of Samaria."

19 Then that officer had answered the man of God, and said, "Now look, *if* the LORD would make windows in heaven, could such a thing be?"

And he had said, "In fact, you shall see *it* with your eyes, but you shall not eat of it." 20 And so it happened to him, for the people trampled him in the gate, and he died.

8 THEN Elisha spoke to the woman whose son he had restored to life, saying, "Arise and go, you and your household, and stay wherever you can; for the LORD has called for a famine, and furthermore, it will come upon the land for seven years." 2 So the woman arose and did according to the saying of the man of God, and she went with her household and dwelt in the land of the Philistines seven years.

3 It came to pass, at the end of seven years, that the woman returned from the land of the Philistines; and she went to make an appeal to the king for her house and for her land. 4 Then the king talked with Gehazi, the servant of the man of God, saying, "Tell me, please, all the great things Elisha has done." 5 Now it happened, as he was telling the king how he had restored the dead to life, that there was the woman whose son he had restored to life, appealing to the king for her house and for her land. And Gehazi said, "My lord, O king, this *is* the woman, and this *is* her son whom Elisha restored to life." 6 And when the king asked the woman, she told him.

So the king appointed a certain officer for her, saying, "Restore all that *was* hers, and all the proceeds of the field from the day that she left the land until now."

7 Then Elisha went to Damascus, and Ben-Hadad king of Syria was sick; and it was told him, saying, "The man of God has come here." 8 And the king said to Hazael, "Take a present in your hand, and go to meet the man of God, and inquire of the LORD by him, saying, 'Shall I recover from this disease?' " 9 So Hazael went to meet him and took a present with him, of every good thing of Damascus, forty camel-loads; and he came and stood before him, and said, "Your son Ben-Hadad king of

Syria has sent me to you, saying, 'Shall I recover from this disease?' "

10 And Elisha said to him, "Go, say to him, 'You shall certainly recover.' However the LORD has shown me that he will really die." 11 Then he set his countenance in a stare until he was ashamed; and the man of God wept. 12 And Hazael said, "Why is my lord weeping?"

He answered, "Because I know the evil that you will do to the children of Israel: Their strongholds you will set on fire, and their young men you will kill with the sword; and you will dash their children, and rip open their women with child."

13 So Hazael said, "But what *is* your servant—a dog, that he should do this gross thing?"

And Elisha answered, "The LORD has shown me that you *will become* king over Syria."

14 Then he departed from Elisha, and came to his master, who said to him, "What did Elisha say to you?" And he answered, "He told me you would surely recover." 15 But it happened on the next day that he took a thick cloth and dipped *it* in water, and spread *it* over his face so that he died; and Hazael reigned in his place.

16 Now in the fifth year of Joram the son of Ahab, king of Israel, Jehoshaphat *having been* king of Judah, Jehoram the son of Jehoshaphat began to reign as king of Judah. 17 He was thirty-two years old when he became king, and he reigned eight years in Jerusalem. 18 And he walked in the way of the kings of Israel, just as the house of Ahab had done, for the daughter of Ahab was his wife; and he did evil in the sight of the LORD. 19 Yet the LORD would not destroy Judah, for the sake of his servant David, as He promised him to give a lamp to him *and* his sons forever.

20 In his days Edom revolted against Judah's authority, and made a king over themselves. 21 So Joram went to Zair, and all his chariots with him. Then he rose by night and attacked the Edomites who had surrounded him and the captains of the chariots; and the troops fled to their tents. 22 Thus Edom has been in revolt against Judah's authority to this day. And Libnah revolted at that time.

23 Now the rest of the acts of Joram, and all that he did, *are* they not written in the book of the chronicles of the kings of Judah? 24 So Joram rested with his fathers, and was buried with his fathers in the City of David. Then Ahaziah his son reigned in his place.

25 In the twelfth year of Joram the son

of Ahab, king of Israel, Ahaziah the son of Jehoram, king of Judah, began to reign. 26 Ahaziah *was* twenty-two years old when he became king, and he reigned one year in Jerusalem. His mother's name *was* Athaliah the granddaughter of Omri, king of Israel. 27 And he walked in the way of the house of Ahab, and did evil in the sight of the LORD, like the house of Ahab, for he *was* the son-in-law of the house of Ahab.

28 Now he went with Joram the son of Ahab to war against Hazael king of Syria at Ramoth Gilead; and the Syrians wounded Joram. 29 Then King Joram went back to Jezreel to recover from the wounds which the Syrians had inflicted on him at Ramah, when he fought against Hazael king of Syria. And Ahaziah the son of Jehoram, king of Judah, went down to see Joram the son of Ahab in Jezreel, because he was sick.

PSALM 72:8–16

8　HE shall have dominion also from sea to sea,
　　And from the River to the ends of the earth.
9　Those who dwell in the wilderness will bow before Him,
　　And His enemies will lick the dust.
10　The kings of Tarshish and of the isles Will bring presents;
　　The kings of Sheba and Seba Will offer gifts.
11　Yes, all kings shall fall down before Him;
　　All nations shall serve Him.

12　For He will deliver the needy when he cries,
　　The poor also, and *him* who has no helper.
13　He will spare the poor and needy,
　　And will save the souls of the needy.
14　He will redeem their life from oppression and violence;
　　And precious shall be their blood in His sight.

15　And He shall live;
　　And the gold of Sheba will be given to Him;
　　Prayer also will be made for Him continually,
　　And daily He shall be praised.

16　There will be an abundance of grain in the earth,
　　On the top of the mountains;

Its fruit shall wave like Lebanon;
And *those* of the city shall flourish like grass of the earth.

PROVERBS 18:12, 13

12　BEFORE destruction the heart of a man is haughty,
　　And before honor *is* humility.

13　He who answers a matter before he hears *it*,
　　It *is* folly and shame to him.

JOHN 18:19–40

THE high priest then asked Jesus about His disciples and His doctrine.

20 Jesus answered him, "I spoke openly to the world. I always taught in synagogues and in the temple, where the Jews always meet, and in secret I have said nothing. 21 Why do you ask Me? Ask those who have heard Me what I said to them. Indeed they know what I said."

22 And when He had said these things, one of the officers who stood by struck Jesus with the palm of his hand, saying, "Do You answer the high priest like that?"

23 Jesus answered him, "If I have spoken evil, bear witness of the evil; but if well, why do you strike Me?"

24 Then Annas sent Him bound to Caiaphas the high priest.

25 Now Simon Peter stood and warmed himself. Therefore they said to him, "You are not also *one* of His disciples, are you?" He denied *it* and said, "I am not!"

26 One of the servants of the high priest, a relative *of him* whose ear Peter cut off, said, "Did I not see you in the garden with Him?" 27 Peter then denied again; and immediately a rooster crowed.

28 Then they led Jesus from Caiaphas to the Praetorium, and it was early morning. But they themselves did not go into the Praetorium, lest they should be defiled, but that they might eat the Passover. 29 Pilate then went out to them and said, "What accusation do you bring against this Man?"

30 They answered and said to him, "If He were not an evildoer, we would not have delivered Him up to you."

31 Then Pilate said to them, "You take Him and judge Him according to your law."

Therefore the Jews said to him, "It is not lawful for us to put anyone to death," 32 that the saying of Jesus might be fulfilled which He spoke, signifying by what death He would die.

33 Then Pilate entered the Praetorium again, called Jesus, and said to Him, "Are You the King of the Jews?"

34 Jesus answered him, "Are you speaking for yourself about this, or did others tell you this concerning Me?"

35 Pilate answered, "Am I a Jew? Your own nation and the chief priests have delivered You to me. What have You done?"

36 Jesus answered, "My kingdom is not of this world. If My kingdom were of this world, My servants would fight, so that I

The world is the system of things which man has erected on God's earth. (BIB. ETHICS)

---

should not be delivered to the Jews; but now My kingdom is not from here."

37 Pilate therefore said to Him, "Are You a king then?"

Jesus answered, "You say *rightly* that I am a king. For this cause I was born, and for this cause I have come into the world, that I should bear witness to the truth. Everyone who is of the truth hears My voice."

38 Pilate said to Him, "What is truth?" And when he had said this, he went out again to the Jews, and said to them, "I find no fault in Him at all.

39 "But you have a custom that I should release someone to you at the Passover. Do you therefore want me to release to you the King of the Jews?"

40 Then they all cried again, saying, "Not this Man, but Barabbas!" Now Barabbas was a robber.

Reading 162—His Cross versus My Cross
John 19:17

The Cross of Jesus is often wrongly taken as a type of the cross we have to carry. Jesus did not say, "If any man will come after Me, let him take up *My* cross," but, "Let him deny himself, and take up his cross, and follow Me." Our cross becomes our divinely appointed privilege by means of His Cross. We are never called upon to carry His Cross. We have so hallowed the Cross by twenty centuries of emotion and sentiment that it sounds a very beautiful and pathetic thing to talk about carrying our cross. But a wooden cross with iron nails in it is a clumsy thing to carry. The real cross was like that, and do we imagine that the external cross was more ugly than our actual one? Or that the thing that tore our Lord's hands and feet was not really so terrible as our imagination of it? (*PSY. REDEMP.*)

The Cross of Jesus Christ stands unique and alone. His Cross is not our cross. Our cross is that we manifest before the world the fact that we are sanctified to do nothing but the will of God. By means of His Cross, our cross becomes our divinely appointed privilege. It is necessary to emphasize this because there is so much right feeling and wrong teaching abroad on the subject. We are never called upon to carry Christ's Cross: His Cross is the center of Time and Eternity; the answer to the enigmas of both. (*SUFFERING*)

---

2 KINGS 9:1—10:36

AND Elisha the prophet called one of the sons of the prophets, and said to him, "Get yourself ready, take this flask of oil in your hand, and go to Ramoth Gilead. 2 Now when you arrive at that place, look there for Jehu the son of Jehoshaphat, the son of Nimshi, and go in and make him rise up from among his associates, and take him to an inner room. 3 Then take the flask of oil, and pour *it* on his head, and say, 'Thus says the LORD: "I have anointed you king over Israel." ' Then open the door and flee, and do not delay."

4 So the young man, the servant of the prophet, went to Ramoth Gilead. 5 And when he arrived, there *were* the captains of the army sitting; and he said, "I have a message for you, Commander."

Jehu said, "For which *one* of us?"

And he said, "For you, Commander." 6 Then he arose and went into the house. And he poured the oil on his head, and said to him, "Thus says the LORD God of Israel: 'I have anointed you king over the people of the LORD, over Israel. 7 You shall strike down the house of Ahab your master, that I may avenge the blood of My servants the prophets, and the blood of all the servants of the LORD, at the hand of Jezebel. 8 For the whole house of Ahab shall perish; and I will cut off from Ahab all the males in Israel, both bond and free. 9 So I will make the house of Ahab like the house of Jeroboam the son of Nebat, and like the house of Baasha the son of Ahijah. 10 The dogs shall eat Jezebel on the plot *of ground* at Jezreel, and *there shall be* none to bury *her.*' " And he opened the door and fled.

11 Then Jehu came out to the servants of his master, and *one* said to him, "*Is* all well? Why did this madman come to you?"

And he said to them, "You know the man and his babble."

12 And they said, "A lie! Tell us now."

So he said, "Thus and thus he spoke to me, saying, 'Thus says the LORD: "I have anointed you king over Israel." ' "

13 Then each man hastened to take his garment and put *it* under him on the top of the steps; and they blew trumpets, saying, "Jehu is king!"

14 So Jehu the son of Jehoshaphat, the son of Nimshi, conspired against Joram. (Now Joram had been defending Ramoth Gilead, he and all Israel, against Hazael king of Syria. 15 But King Joram had returned to Jezreel to recover from the wounds which the Syrians had inflicted on him when he fought with Hazael king of Syria.) And Jehu said, "If you are so minded, let no one leave *or* escape from the city to go and tell *it* in Jezreel." 16 So Jehu rode in a chariot and went to Jezreel, for Joram was laid up there; and Ahaziah king of Judah had come down to see Joram.

17 Now a watchman stood on the tower in Jezreel, and he saw the company of Jehu as he came, and said, "I see a company of men."

And Joram said, "Get a horseman and send him to meet them, and let him say, '*Is it* peace?' "

18 So the horseman went to meet him, and said, "Thus says the king: '*Is it* peace?' "

And Jehu said, "What have you to do with peace? Turn around and follow me."

So the watchman reported, saying, "The messenger went to them, but is not coming back."

19 Then he sent out a second horseman who came to them, and said, "Thus says the king: '*Is it* peace?' "

And Jehu answered, "What have you to do with peace? Turn around and follow me."

20 So the watchman reported, saying, "He went up to them and is not coming back; and the driving *is* like the driving of Jehu the son of Nimshi, for he drives furiously!"

21 Then Joram said, "Make ready." And his chariot was made ready. Then Joram king of Israel and Ahaziah king of Judah went out, each in his chariot; and they went out to meet Jehu, and met him on the property of Naboth the Jezreelite. 22 Now it happened, when Joram saw Jehu, that he said, "*Is it* peace, Jehu?"

So he answered, "What peace, as long as the harlotries of your mother Jezebel and her witchcraft *are so* many?"

23 Then Joram turned around and fled, and said to Ahaziah, "Treachery, Ahaziah!" 24 Now Jehu drew his bow with full strength and shot Jehoram between his arms; and the arrow came out at his heart, and he sank down in his chariot. Then *Jehu* said to Bidkar his captain, "Pick *him* up, *and* throw him into the tract of the field of Naboth the Jezreelite; for remember, when you and I were riding together behind Ahab his father, that the LORD laid this burden upon him: 26 'Surely I saw yesterday the blood of Naboth and the blood of his sons,' says the LORD, 'and I will repay you in this plot,' says the LORD. Now therefore, take *and* throw him on the plot *of ground*, according to the word of the LORD."

27 But when Ahaziah king of Judah saw *this*, he fled by the road to Beth Haggan. So Jehu pursued him, and said, "Shoot him also in the chariot." *And they shot him* at the Ascent of Gur, which is by Ibleam. Then he fled to Megiddo, and died there. 28 And his servants carried him in the chariot to Jerusalem, and buried him in his tomb with his fathers in the City of David. 29 In the eleventh year of Joram the son of Ahab, Ahaziah had become king over Judah.

30 Now when Jehu had come to Jezreel, Jezebel heard *of it;* and she put paint on her eyes and adorned her head, and looked through a window. 31 Then, as Jehu entered at the gate, she said, "*Is it* peace, Zimri, murderer of your master?"

32 And he looked up at the window, and said, "Who *is* on my side? Who?" So two *or* three eunuchs looked out at him. 33 Then he said, "Throw her down." So they threw her down, and *some* of her blood spattered on the wall and on the horses; and he trampled her underfoot. 34 And when he had gone in, he ate and drank. Then he said, "Go now, see to this accursed *woman,* and bury her, for she was a king's daughter." 35 So they went to bury her, but they found no more of her than the skull and the feet and the palms of *her* hands. 36 Therefore they came back and told him. And he said, "This *is* the word of the LORD, which He spoke by His servant Elijah the Tishbite, saying, 'On the plot *of ground* at Jezreel dogs shall eat the flesh of Jezebel; 37 and the corpse of Jezebel shall be as refuse on the surface of the field, in the plot at Jezreel, so that they shall not say, "Here *lies* Jezebel." ' "

10 NOW Ahab had seventy sons in Samaria. And Jehu wrote and sent letters to Samaria, to the rulers of Jezreel, to the elders, and to those who reared Ahab's *sons,* saying:

2 Now as soon as this letter comes to you, since your master's sons *are* with you, and you have chariots and horses, a fortified city also, and weapons, 3 choose the best qualified of your master's sons, set *him* on his father's throne, and fight for your master's house.

4 But they were exceedingly afraid, and said, "Look, two kings could not stand up to him; how then can we stand?" 5 And he who *was* in charge of the house, and he who *was* in charge of the city, the elders also, and those who reared *the sons,* sent to Jehu, saying, "We *are* your servants, we will do all you tell us; but we will not make anyone king. Do *what is* good in your sight." 6 Then he wrote a second letter to them, saying:

If you *are* for me and will obey my voice, take the heads of the men, your master's sons, and come to me at Jezreel by this time tomorrow.

Now the king's sons, seventy persons, *were* with the great men of the city, *who* were rearing them. 7 So it was, when the letter came to them, that they took the king's sons and slaughtered seventy persons, put their heads in baskets and sent *them* to him at Jezreel.

8 Then a messenger came and told him, saying, "They have brought the heads of the king's sons."

And he said, "Lay them in two heaps at the entrance of the gate until morning."

9 So it was, in the morning, that he went out and stood, and said to all the people, "You *are* righteous. Indeed I conspired against my master and killed him; but who killed all these? 10 Know now that nothing shall fall to the earth of the word of the LORD which the LORD spoke concerning the house of Ahab; for the LORD has done what He spoke by His servant Elijah." 11 So Jehu killed all who remained of the house of Ahab in Jezreel, and all his great men and his close acquaintances and his priests, until he left him none remaining.

12 And he arose and departed and went to Samaria. On the way, at Beth Eked of the Shepherds, 13 Jehu met with the brothers of Ahaziah king of Judah, and said, "Who *are* you?"

So they answered, "We *are* the brothers of Ahaziah; we have come down to greet the sons of the king and the sons of the queen mother."

14 And he said, "Take them alive!" So they took them alive, and killed them at the well of Beth Eked, forty-two men; and he left none of them.

15 Now when he departed from there, he met Jehonadab the son of Rechab, *coming* to meet him; and he greeted him and said to him, "Is your heart right, as my heart *is* toward your heart?"

And Jehonadab answered, "It is."

Jehu said, "If it is, give *me* your hand." So he gave *him* his hand, and he took him up to him into the chariot. 16 Then he said, "Come with me, and see my zeal for the LORD." So they had him ride in his chariot. 17 And when he came to Samaria, he killed all who remained to Ahab in Samaria, till he had destroyed them, according to the word of the LORD which He spoke to Elijah.

18 Then Jehu gathered all the people together, and said to them, "Ahab served Baal a little, Jehu will serve him much. 19 Now therefore, call to me all the prophets of Baal, all his servants, and all his priests. Let no one be missing, for I have a great sacrifice for Baal. Whoever is missing shall not live." But Jehu acted deceptively, with the intent

of destroying the worshipers of Baal. 20 And Jehu said, "Proclaim a solemn assembly for Baal." So they proclaimed *it*. 21 Then Jehu sent throughout all Israel; and all the worshipers of Baal came, so that there was not a man left who did not come. So they came into the temple of Baal, and the temple of Baal was full from one end to the other. 22 And he said to the one in charge of the wardrobe, "Bring out vestments for all the worshipers of Baal." So he brought out vestments for them. 23 Then Jehu and Jehonadab the son of Rechab went into the temple of Baal, and said to the worshipers of Baal, "Search and see that no servants of the LORD are here with you, but only the worshipers of Baal." 24 So they went in to offer sacrifices and burnt offerings. Now Jehu had appointed for himself eighty men on the outside, and had said, "*If* any of the men whom I have brought into your hands escapes, *whoever lets him escape, it shall be* his life for the life of the other."

25 Now it happened, as soon as he had made an end of offering the burnt offering, that Jehu said to the guard and to the captains, "Go in *and* kill them; let no one come out!" And they killed them with the edge of the sword; then the guards and the officers threw *them* out, and went into the inner room of the temple of Baal. 26 And they brought the *sacred* pillars out of the temple of Baal and burned them. 27 Then they broke down the *sacred* pillar of Baal, and tore down the temple of Baal and made it a refuse dump to this day. 28 Thus Jehu destroyed Baal from Israel.

29 However Jehu did not turn away from the sins of Jeroboam the son of Nebat, who had made Israel sin, *that is,* from the golden calves that *were* at Bethel and Dan. 30 And the LORD said to Jehu, "Because you have done well in doing *what is* right in My sight, *and* have done to the house of Ahab all that *was* in My heart, your sons shall sit on the throne of Israel to the fourth *generation*." 31 But Jehu took no heed to walk in the law of the LORD God of Israel with all his heart; for he did not depart from the sins of Jeroboam, who had made Israel sin.

32 In those days the LORD began to cut off *parts* of Israel; and Hazael conquered them in all the territory of Israel 33 from the Jordan eastward: all the land of Gilead—Gad, Reuben, and Manasseh—from Aroer, which *is* by the River Arnon, including Gilead and Bashan.

34 Now the rest of the acts of Jehu, all that he did, and all his might, *are* they not

written in the book of the chronicles of the kings of Israel? 35 So Jehu rested with his fathers, and they buried him in Samaria. Then Jehoahaz his son reigned in his place. 36 And the period that Jehu reigned over Israel in Samaria *was* twenty-eight years.

PSALM 72:17–20

17   HIS name shall endure forever;
     His name shall continue as long as the sun.
     And *men* shall be blessed in Him;
     All nations shall call Him blessed.

18   Blessed *be* the LORD God, the God of Israel,
     Who only does wondrous things!
19   And blessed *be* His glorious name forever!
     And let the whole earth be filled *with* His glory.
     Amen and Amen.

20   The prayers of David the son of Jesse are ended.

We are apt to think of prayer as an aesthetic religious exercise.   (PLACE HELP)

PROVERBS 18:14, 15

14   THE spirit of a man will sustain him in sickness,
     But who can bear a broken spirit?

15   The heart of the prudent acquires knowledge,
     And the ear of the wise seeks knowledge.

JOHN 19:1–22

SO then Pilate took Jesus and scourged *Him*. 2 And the soldiers twisted a crown of thorns and put *it* on His head, and they put on Him a purple robe. 3 Then they said, "Hail, King of the Jews!" And they struck Him with their hands.

4 Pilate then went out again, and said to them, "Behold, I am bringing Him out to you, that you may know that I find no fault in Him."

5 Then Jesus came out, wearing the

crown of thorns and the purple robe. And *Pilate* said to them, "Behold the Man!"

6 Therefore, when the chief priests and officers saw Him, they cried out, saying, "Crucify *Him,* crucify *Him!*"

Pilate said to them, "You take Him and crucify *Him,* for I find no fault in Him."

7 The Jews answered him, "We have a law, and according to our law He ought to die, because He made Himself the Son of God."

8 Therefore, when Pilate heard that saying, he was the more afraid, 9 and went again into the Praetorium, and said to Jesus, "Where are You from?" But Jesus gave him no answer.

10 Then Pilate said to Him, "Are You not speaking to me? Do You not know that I have power to crucify You, and power to release You?"

11 Jesus answered, "You could have no power at all against Me unless it had been given you from above. Therefore the one who delivered Me to you has the greater sin."

12 From then on Pilate sought to release Him, but the Jews cried out, saying, "If you let this Man go, you are not Caesar's friend. Whoever makes himself a king speaks against Caesar."

13 When Pilate therefore heard that saying, he brought Jesus out and sat down in the judgment seat in a place that is called *The* Pavement, but in Hebrew, Gabbatha. 14 Now it was the Preparation Day of the Passover, and about the sixth hour. And he said to the Jews, "Behold your King!"

15 But they cried out, "Away with *Him,* away with *Him!* Crucify Him!"

Pilate said to them, "Shall I crucify your King?"

The chief priests answered, "We have no king but Caesar!"

16 Then he delivered Him to them to be crucified. Then they took Jesus and led *Him* away.

17 And He, bearing His cross, went out to a place called *the Place* of a Skull, which is called in Hebrew, Golgotha, 18 where they crucified Him, and two others with Him, one on either side, and Jesus in the

---

Calvary is God's responsibility undertaken and carried through as redemption. (PSY. REDEMP.)

---

center. 19 Now Pilate wrote a title and put *it* on the cross. And the writing was:

JESUS OF NAZARETH,
THE KING OF THE JEWS.

20 Then many of the Jews read this title, for the place where Jesus was crucified was near the city; and it was written in Hebrew, Greek, *and* Latin.

21 Therefore the chief priests of the Jews said to Pilate, "Do not write, 'The King of the Jews,' but, 'He said, "I am the King of the Jews."'"

22 Pilate answered, "What I have written, I have written."

◆◆◆◆

Reading 163—Faith in God's Reign
Psalm 73:1–9

It is easy to *say* God reigns, and then to see Satan, suffering, and sin reigning, and God apparently powerless. Belief in God must be tried before it is of value to God or to a child of His. It is the trial of our faith that makes us wealthy in God's sight. We begin by saying, "I know that God is love, that He is just and holy and true"; then we come up against common-sense facts that flatly contradict what we said we believed. Are we going to succumb, as the psalmist nearly did, to pessimistic moods of intellect and say, "After all I must abandon that view of God"? If we try to answer the problems of this world by intellectual or scientific methods we shall go mad, or else deny that the problems exist. . . . Jesus Christ makes us open our eyes and look at these things. God is the only being who can stand the slander that arises because the Devil and pain and sin are in the world. Stand true to the life hid with Christ in God and to the facts you have to face. You will have no answer intellectually, but your faith in God will be so unshakably firm that others will begin to see there is an answer they have never guessed.　(*PLACE HELP*)

2 KINGS 11:1—13:25

WHEN Athaliah the mother of Ahaziah saw that her son was dead, she arose and destroyed all the royal heirs. 2 But Jehosheba, the daughter of King Joram, sister of Ahaziah, took Joash the son of Ahaziah, and stole him away from among the king's sons *who were* being murdered; and they hid him and his nurse in the bedroom, from Athaliah, so that he was not killed. 3 So he was hidden with her in the house of the LORD for six years, while Athaliah reigned over the land.

4 In the seventh year Jehoiada sent and brought the captains of hundreds—of the bodyguards and the escorts—and brought them into the house of the LORD to him. And he made a covenant with them and took an oath from them in the house of the LORD, and showed them the king's son. 5 Then he commanded them, saying, "This *is* what you shall do: One-third of you who come on duty on the Sabbath shall be keeping watch over the king's house, 6 one-third *shall be* at the gate of Sur, and one-third at the gate behind the escorts. You shall keep the watch of the house, lest it be broken down. 7 The two contingents of you who go off duty on the Sabbath shall keep the watch of the house of the LORD for the king. 8 But you shall surround the king on all sides, every man with his weapons in his hand; and whoever comes within range, let him be put to death. You are to be with the king as he goes out and as he comes in."

9 So the captains of the hundreds did according to all that Jehoiada the priest commanded. Each of them took his men who were to be on duty on the Sabbath, with those who were going off duty on the Sabbath, and came to Jehoiada the priest. 10 And the priest gave the captains of hundreds the spears and shields which *had belonged* to King David, that were in the temple of the LORD. 11 Then the escorts stood, every man with his weapons in his hand, all around the king, from the right side of the temple to the left side of the temple, by the altar and the house. 12 And he brought out the king's son, put the crown on him, and *gave him* the Testimony; they

made him king and anointed him, and they clapped their hands and said, "Long live the king!"

13 Now when Athaliah heard the noise of the escorts *and* the people, she came to the people *in* the temple of the LORD. 14 When she looked, there was the king standing by a pillar according to custom; and the leaders and the trumpeters were by the king. All the people of the land were rejoicing and blowing trumpets. So Athaliah tore her clothes and cried out, "Treason! Treason!"

15 And Jehoiada the priest commanded the captains of the hundreds, the officers of the army, and said to them, "Take her outside under guard, and slay with the sword whoever follows her." For the priest had said, "Do not let her be killed in the house of the LORD." 16 So they seized her; and she went by way of the horses' entrance *into* the king's house, and there she was killed.

17 Then Jehoiada made a covenant between the LORD, the king, and the people, that they should be the LORD's people, and *also* between the king and the people. 18 And all the people of the land went to the temple of Baal, and tore it down. They thoroughly broke in pieces its altars and images, and killed Mattan the priest of Baal before the altars. And the priest appointed officers over the house of the LORD. 19 Then he took the captains of hundreds, the bodyguards, the escorts, and all the people of the land; and they brought the king down from the house of the LORD, and went by way of the gate of the escorts to the king's house. Then he sat on the throne of the kings. 20 So all the people of the land rejoiced; and the city was quiet, for they had slain Athaliah with the sword *in* the king's house. 21 Jehoash *was* seven years old when he became king.

12 IN the seventh year of Jehu, Jehoash became king, and he reigned forty years in Jerusalem. His mother's name *was* Zibiah of Beersheba. 2 Jehoash did *what was* right in the sight of the LORD all the days in which Jehoiada the priest instructed him. 3 But the high places were not taken away; the people still sacrificed and burned incense on the high places.

4 And Jehoash said to the priests, "All the money of the dedicated gifts that are brought into the house of the LORD—each man's census money, each man's assessment money—*and* all the money that a man purposes in his heart to bring into the house of the LORD, 5 let the priests take *it* themselves, each from his constituency; and let them repair the damages of the temple, wherever any dilapidation is found."

6 Now it was so, by the twenty-third year of King Jehoash, *that* the priests had not repaired the damages of the temple. 7 So King Jehoash called Jehoiada the priest and the *other* priests, and said to them, "Why have you not repaired the damages of the temple? Now therefore, do not take *more* money from your constituency, but deliver it for repairing the damages of the temple." 8 And the priests agreed that they would neither receive *more* money from the people, nor repair the damages of the temple.

9 Then Jehoiada the priest took a chest, bored a hole in its lid, and set it beside the altar, on the right side as one comes into the house of the LORD; and the priests who kept the door put there all the money brought into the house of the LORD. 10 So it was, whenever they saw that *there was* much money in the chest, that the king's scribe and the high priest came up and put it in bags, and counted the money that was found in the house of the LORD. 11 Then they gave the money, which had been apportioned, into the hands of those who did the work, who had the oversight of the house of the LORD; and they paid it out to the carpenters and builders who worked on the house of the LORD, 12 and to masons and stonecutters, and for buying timber and hewn stone, to repair the damage of the house of the LORD, and for all that was paid out to repair the temple. 13 However there were not made for the house of the LORD basins of silver, trimmers, sprinkling-bowls, trumpets, any articles of gold or articles of silver, from the money brought into the house of the LORD. 14 But they gave that to the workmen, and they repaired the house of the LORD with it. 15 Moreover they did not require an account from the men into whose hand they delivered the money to be paid to workmen, for they dealt faithfully. 16 The money from the trespass offerings and the money from the sin offerings was not brought into the house of the LORD. It belonged to the priests.

17 Hazael king of Syria went up and fought against Gath, and took it; then Hazael set his face to go up to Jerusalem. 18 And Jehoash king of Judah took all the sacred things that his fathers, Jehoshaphat and Jehoram and Ahaziah, kings of Judah, had dedicated, and his own sacred things, and all the gold found in the treasuries of the house of the LORD and in the king's house, and sent *them* to Hazael king of Syria. Then he went away from Jerusalem.

19 Now the rest of the acts of Joash, and all that he did, *are* they not written in the book of the chronicles of the kings of Judah? 20 And his servants arose and formed a conspiracy, and killed Joash in the house of the Millo, which goes down to Silla. 21 For Jozachar the son of Shimeath and Jehozabad the son of Shomer, his servants, struck him. So he died, and they buried him with his fathers in the City of David. Then Amaziah his son reigned in his place.

13 IN the twenty-third year of Joash the son of Ahaziah, king of Judah, Jehoahaz the son of Jehu became king over Israel in Samaria, *and reigned* seventeen years. 2 And he did evil in the sight of the LORD, and followed the sins of Jeroboam the son of Nebat, who had made Israel sin. He did not depart from them.

3 Then the anger of the LORD was aroused against Israel, and He delivered them into the hand of Hazael king of Syria, and into the hand of Ben-Hadad the son of Hazael, all *their* days. 4 So Jehoahaz pleaded with the LORD, and the LORD listened to him; for He saw the oppression of Israel, because the king of Syria oppressed them. 5 Then the LORD gave Israel a deliverer, so that they escaped from under the hand of the Syrians; and the children of Israel dwelt in their tents as before. 6 Nevertheless they did not depart from the sins of the house of Jeroboam, who had made Israel sin, *but* walked in them; and the wooden image also remained in Samaria. 7 For He left of the army of Jehoahaz only fifty horsemen, ten chariots, and ten thousand foot soldiers; for the king of Syria had destroyed them and made them like the dust at threshing.

8 Now the rest of the acts of Jehoahaz, all that he did, and his might, *are* they not written in the book of the chronicles of the kings of Israel? 9 So Jehoahaz rested with his fathers, and they buried him in Samaria. Then Joash his son reigned in his place.

10 In the thirty-seventh year of Joash king of Judah, Jehoash the son of Jehoahaz became king over Israel in Samaria, *and reigned* sixteen years. 11 And he did evil in the sight of the LORD. He did not depart from all the sins of Jeroboam the son of

Nebat, who made Israel sin, *but* walked in them.

12 Now the rest of the acts of Joash, all that he did, and his might with which he fought against Amaziah king of Judah, *are* they not written in the book of the chronicles of the kings of Israel? 13 So Joash rested with his fathers. Then Jeroboam sat on his throne. And Joash was buried in Samaria with the kings of Israel.

14 Elisha had become sick with the illness of which he would die. Then Joash the king of Israel came down to him, and wept over his face, and said, "O my father, my father, the chariots of Israel and their horsemen!"

15 And Elisha said to him, "Take a bow and some arrows." So he took himself a bow and some arrows. 16 Then he said to the king of Israel, "Put your hand on the bow." So he put his hand *on it,* and Elisha put his hands on the king's hands. 17 And he said, "Open the east window"; and he opened *it.* Then Elisha said, "Shoot"; and he shot. And he said, "The arrow of the LORD's deliverance and the arrow of deliverance from Syria; for you must strike the Syrians at Aphek till you have destroyed *them.*" 18 Then he said, "Take the arrows"; so he took *them.* And he said to the king of Israel, "Strike the ground"; so he struck three times, and stopped. 19 And the man of God was angry with him, and said, "You should have struck five or six times; then you would have struck Syria till you had destroyed *it!* But now you will strike Syria *only* three times."

20 Then Elisha died, and they buried him. And the *raiding* bands from Moab invaded the land in the spring of the year. 21 So it was, as they were burying a man, that suddenly they spied a band of *raiders;* and they put the man in the tomb of Elisha; and when the man was let down and touched the bones of Elisha, he revived and stood on his feet.

22 And Hazael king of Syria oppressed Israel all the days of Jehoahaz. 23 But the LORD was gracious to them, had compassion on them, and regarded them, because of His covenant with Abraham, Isaac, and Jacob, and would not yet destroy them or cast them from His presence.

24 Now Hazael king of Syria died. Then Ben-Hadad his son reigned in his place. 25 And Jehoash the son of Jehoahaz recaptured from the hand of Ben-Hadad, the son of Hazael, the cities which he had taken out of the hand of Jehoahaz his father by war. Three times Joash defeated him and recaptured the cities of Israel.

PSALM 73:1–9

1 TRULY God *is* good to Israel,
   To such as are pure in heart.
2 But as for me, my feet had almost stumbled;
   My steps had nearly slipped.
3 For I *was* envious of the boastful,
   When I saw the prosperity of the wicked.

4 For *there are* no pangs in their death,
   But their strength *is* firm.
5 They *are* not in trouble *as other* men,
   Nor are they plagued like *other* men.
6 Therefore pride serves as their necklace;
   Violence covers them *like* a garment.

---

*P*ride is the deification of self.   (UTMOST)

---

7 Their eyes bulge with abundance;
   They have more than heart could wish.
8 They scoff and speak wickedly
   concerning oppression;
   They speak loftily.
9 They set their mouth against the heavens,
   And their tongue walks through the earth.

PROVERBS 18:16, 17

16 A man's gift makes room for him,
    And brings him before great men.

17 The first *one* to plead his cause *seems* right,
    Until his neighbor comes and examines him.

JOHN 19:23–42

THEN the soldiers, when they had crucified Jesus, took His garments and made four parts, to each soldier a part, and also the tunic. Now the tunic was without seam, woven from the top in one piece. 24 They said therefore among themselves, "Let us not tear it, but cast lots for it, whose it shall be," that the Scripture might be fulfilled which says:

   "They divided My garments among them,
   And for My clothing they cast lots."

Therefore the soldiers did these things. 25 Now there stood by the cross of Jesus His mother, and His mother's sister, Mary the *wife* of Clopas, and Mary Magdalene. 26 When Jesus therefore saw His mother, and the disciple whom He loved standing by, He said to His mother, "Woman, behold your son!" 27 Then He said to the disciple, "Behold your mother!" And from that hour that disciple took her to his own *home*.

28 After this, Jesus, knowing that all things were now accomplished, that the Scripture might be fulfilled, said, "I thirst!" 29 Now a vessel full of sour wine was sitting there; and they filled a sponge with sour wine, put *it* on hyssop, and put *it* to His mouth. 30 So when Jesus had received the sour wine, He said, "It is finished!" And bowing His head, He gave up His spirit.

---

*R*edemption is the great outside fact of the Christian faith. (CONFORMED)

---

31 Therefore, because it was the Preparation *Day,* that the bodies should not remain on the cross on the Sabbath (for that Sabbath was a high day), the Jews asked Pilate that their legs might be broken, and *that* they might be taken away. 32 Then the soldiers came and broke the legs of the first and of the other who was crucified with Him. 33 But when they came to Jesus and saw that He was already dead, they did not break His legs. 34 But one of the soldiers pierced His side with a spear, and immediately blood and water came out. 35 And he who has seen has testified, and his testimony is true; and he knows that he is telling the truth, so that you may believe. 36 For these things were done that the Scripture should be fulfilled, "Not *one* of His bones shall be broken." 37 And again another Scripture says, "They shall look on Him whom they pierced."

38 After this, Joseph of Arimathea, being a disciple of Jesus, but secretly, for fear of the Jews, asked Pilate that he might take away the body of Jesus; and Pilate gave *him* permission. So he came and took the body of Jesus. 39 And Nicodemus, who at first came to Jesus by night, also came, bringing a mixture of myrrh and aloes, about a hundred pounds. 40 Then they took the body of Jesus, and bound it in strips of linen with the spices, as the custom of the Jews is to bury. 41 Now in the place where He was crucified there was a garden, and in the garden a new tomb in which no one had yet been laid. 42 So there they laid Jesus, because of the Jews' Preparation *Day,* for the tomb was nearby.

◆◆◆

Reading 164—The Realization of Christ
John 20:28

T he one great characteristic of being born from above is that I know who Jesus is. It is a discernment; something has happened on the inside, the surgery of events has opened my eyes. Is Jesus Christ a revelation to me, or is He simply a historical character? How are we to get the revelation of who Jesus is? Very simply. Jesus said that the Holy Spirit would glorify Him, and we can receive the Holy Spirit by asking (Luke 11:13); then we too shall be in the same category with Peter, and Jesus will say, "Blessed are you . . . for flesh and blood has not revealed this to you, but My Father who is in heaven" (Matt. 16:17). . . .

When we receive the Holy Spirit, we receive the quickening life that lifts us into the domain where Jesus lives and we have the revelation of who He is. The secret of the Christian is that he knows the absolute deity of Jesus Christ. Has Jesus made any difference to us in our actual lives? The essence of Christianity is not a creed or a doctrine, but an illumination that emancipates us: "I see who Jesus is." It is always a surprise, never an intellectual concept. "The wind blows where it wishes, . . . So is everyone who is born of the Spirit" (John 3:8). (*LOVE OF GOD*)

2 KINGS 14:1–29

IN the second year of Joash the son of Jehoahaz, king of Israel, Amaziah the son of Joash, king of Judah, became king. 2 He was twenty-five years old when he became king, and he reigned twenty-nine years in Jerusalem. His mother's name was Jehoaddan of Jerusalem. 3 And he did *what was* right in the sight of the LORD, yet not like his father David; he did everything as his father Joash had done. 4 However the high places were not taken away, and the people still sacrificed and burned incense on the high places.

5 Now it happened, as soon as the kingdom was established in his hand, that he executed his servants who had murdered his father the king. 6 But the children of the murderers he did not execute, according to what is written in the Book of the Law of Moses, in which the LORD commanded, saying, "Fathers shall not be put to death for their children, nor shall children be put to death for their fathers; but a person shall be put to death for his own sin."

7 He killed ten thousand Edomites in the Valley of Salt, and took Sela by war, and called its name Joktheel to this day.

8 Then Amaziah sent messengers to Jehoash the son of Jehoahaz, the son of Jehu, king of Israel, saying, "Come, let us face one another *in battle*." 9 And Jehoash king of Israel sent to Amaziah king of Judah, saying, "The thistle that *was* in Lebanon sent to the cedar that *was* in Lebanon, saying, 'Give your daughter to my son as wife'; and a wild beast that *was* in Lebanon passed by and trampled the thistle. 10 You have indeed defeated Edom, and your heart has lifted you up. Glory *in that*, and stay at home; for why should you meddle with trouble so that you fall—you and Judah with you?"

11 But Amaziah would not heed. Therefore Jehoash king of Israel went out; so he and Amaziah king of Judah faced one another at Beth Shemesh, which *belongs* to Judah. 12 And Judah was defeated by Israel, and every man fled to his tent. 13 Then Jehoash king of Israel captured Amaziah king of Judah, the son of Jehoash, the son of Ahaziah, at Beth Shemesh; and he went to Jerusalem, and broke down the wall of Jerusalem from the Gate of Ephraim to the Corner Gate—four hundred cubits. 14 And he took all the gold and silver, all the articles that were found in the house of the LORD and in the treasuries of the king's house, and hostages, and returned to Samaria.

15 Now the rest of the acts of Jehoash which he did—his might, and how he fought with Amaziah king of Judah—*are* they not written in the book of the chronicles of the kings of Israel? 16 So Jehoash rested with his fathers, and was buried in Samaria with the kings of Israel. Then Jeroboam his son reigned in his place.

17 Amaziah the son of Joash, king of Judah, lived fifteen years after the death of Jehoash the son of Jehoahaz, king of Israel. 18 Now the rest of the acts of Amaziah, *are* they not written in the book of the chronicles of the kings of Judah? 19 And they formed a conspiracy against him in Jerusalem, and he fled to Lachish; but they sent after him to Lachish and killed him there. 20 Then they brought him on horses, and he was buried at Jerusalem with his fathers in the City of David.

21 And all the people of Judah took Azariah, who *was* sixteen years old, and made him king instead of his father Amaziah. 22 He built Elath and restored it to Judah, after the king rested with his fathers.

23 In the fifteenth year of Amaziah the son of Joash, king of Judah, Jeroboam the son of Joash, king of Israel, became king in Samaria, *and reigned* forty-one years. 24 And he did evil in the sight of the LORD; he did not depart from all the sins of Jeroboam the son of Nebat, who had made Israel sin. 25 He restored the territory of Israel from the entrance of Hamath to the Sea of the Arabah, according to the word of the LORD God of Israel, which He had spoken through His servant Jonah the son of Amittai, the prophet who *was* from Gath Hepher. 26 For the LORD saw *that* the affliction of Israel *was* very bitter; and whether bond or free, there was no helper for Israel. 27 And the LORD did not say that He would blot out the name of Israel from under heaven; but He saved them by the hand of Jeroboam the son of Joash.

28 Now the rest of the acts of Jeroboam, and all that he did—his might, how he made war, and how he recaptured for Israel, from Damascus and Hamath, *what had belonged* to Judah—*are* they not written in the book of the chronicles of the kings of Israel? 29 So Jeroboam rested with his fathers, the kings of Israel. Then Zechariah his son reigned in his place.

PSALM 73:10–20

10　THEREFORE his people return here,
　　　And waters of a full *cup* are drained
　　　by them.

11 And they say, "How does God know?
And is there knowledge in the Most
High?"

12 Behold, these *are* the ungodly,
Who are always at ease;
They increase *in* riches.

13 Surely I have cleansed my heart *in* vain,
And washed my hands in innocence.

14 For all day long I have been plagued,
And chastened every morning.

15 If I had said, "I will speak thus,"
Behold, I would have been untrue to
the generation of Your children.

16 When I thought *how* to understand this,
It *was* too painful for me—

17 Until I went into the sanctuary of God;
Then I understood their end.

18 Surely You set them in slippery places;
You cast them down to destruction.

19 Oh, how they are *brought* to desolation,
as in a moment!
They are utterly consumed with terrors.

20 As a dream when *one* awakes,
So, Lord, when You awake,
You shall despise their image.

PROVERBS 18:18, 19

18 CASTING lots causes contentions to
cease,
And keeps the mighty apart.

19 A brother offended *is harder to win* than
a strong city,
And contentions *are* like the bars of a
castle.

JOHN 20:1–31

NOW the first *day* of the week Mary Magdalene went to the tomb early, while it was still dark, and saw *that* the stone had been taken away from the tomb. 2 Then she ran and came to Simon Peter, and to the other disciple, whom Jesus loved, and said to them, "They have taken away the Lord out of the tomb, and we do not know where they have laid Him."

3 Peter therefore went out, and the other disciple, and were going to the tomb. 4 So they both ran together, and the other disciple outran Peter and came to the tomb first. 5 And he, stooping down and looking in, saw the linen cloths lying *there;* yet he did not go in. 6 Then Simon Peter came, following him, and went into the tomb; and he saw the linen cloths lying *there,*

7 and the handkerchief that had been around His head, not lying with the linen cloths, but folded together in a place by itself. 8 Then the other disciple, who came to the tomb first, went in also; and he saw and believed. 9 For as yet they did not know the Scripture, that He must rise again from the dead. 10 Then the disciples went away again to their own homes.

11 But Mary stood outside by the tomb weeping, and as she wept she stooped down *and looked* into the tomb. 12 And she saw two angels in white sitting, one at the head and the other at the feet, where the body of Jesus had lain. 13 Then they said to her, "Woman, why are you weeping?"

She said to them, "Because they have taken away my Lord, and I do not know where they have laid Him."

14 Now when she had said this, she turned around and saw Jesus standing *there,* and did not know that it was Jesus. 15 Jesus said to her, "Woman, why are you weeping? Whom are you seeking?"

She, supposing Him to be the gardener, said to Him, "Sir, if You have carried Him away, tell me where You have laid Him, and I will take Him away."

16 Jesus said to her, "Mary!"

She turned and said to Him, "Rabboni!" (which is to say, Teacher).

17 Jesus said to her, "Do not cling to Me, for I have not yet ascended to My Father; but go to My brethren and say to them, 'I am ascending to My Father and your Father, and *to* My God and your God.' "

18 Mary Magdalene came and told the disciples that she had seen the Lord, and *that* He had spoken these things to her.

19 Then, the same day at evening, being the first *day* of the week, when the doors were shut where the disciples were assembled, for fear of the Jews, Jesus came and stood in the midst, and said to them, "Peace *be* with you." 20 When He had said this, He showed them *His* hands and His side. Then the disciples were glad when they saw the Lord.

21 So Jesus said to them again, "Peace to you! As the Father has sent Me, I also send you." 22 And when He had said this, He breathed on *them,* and said to them, "Receive the Holy Spirit. 23 If you forgive the sins of any, they are forgiven them; if you retain the *sins* of any, they are retained."

24 Now Thomas, called the Twin, one of the twelve, was not with them when Jesus came. 25 The other disciples therefore said to him, "We have seen the Lord."

So he said to them, "Unless I see in His

hands the print of the nails, and put my finger into the print of the nails, and put my hand into His side, I will not believe."

26 And after eight days His disciples were again inside, and Thomas with them. Jesus came, the doors being shut, and stood in the midst, and said, "Peace to you!" 27 Then He said to Thomas, "Reach your finger here, and look at My hands; and reach your hand *here,* and put *it* into My side. Do not be unbelieving, but believing."

28 And Thomas answered and said to Him, "My Lord and my God!"

29 Jesus said to him, "Thomas, because you have seen Me, you have believed.

There is only one God for the Christian, and He is Jesus Christ. (SHAD. AGONY)

Blessed *are* those who have not seen and *yet* have believed."

30 And truly Jesus did many other signs in the presence of His disciples, which are not written in this book; 31 but these are written that you may believe that Jesus is the Christ, the Son of God, and that believing you may have life in His name.

Reading 165—Discipline of Divine Loyalty
John 21:15–17

Is that what we have been doing, feeding Jesus Christ's sheep? Take a rapid survey. Have we been nourishing the lives of people in the understanding of Jesus, or has our aim been to maintain our particular deposit of doctrine? According to Jesus, divine loyalty means that we feed His sheep in the knowledge of Him, not feed them with our doctrine. Peter had boasted earlier of his love for Jesus—"Even if all are made to stumble because of You, I will never be made to stumble." But there is no brag left in him now—"Lord, You know all things; You know that I love You." "Feed My sheep." The discipline of divine loyalty is not that I am true to a doctrine, but so true to Jesus that other people are nourished in the knowledge of Him. Get rid of the idea that you must do good things, and remember what Jesus says, "He who believes in Me, . . . out of his heart will flow rivers of living water." In the Christian life it is never "Do, do," but "Be, be, and I will do through you." The type of man produced by the Spirit of Jesus is the one who bears a growing family likeness to Jesus.   (*PLACE HELP*)

---

2 KINGS 15:1—16:20

IN the twenty-seventh year of Jeroboam king of Israel, Azariah the son of Amaziah, king of Judah, became king. 2 He was sixteen years old when he became king, and he reigned fifty-two years in Jerusalem. His mother's name *was* Jecholiah of Jerusalem. 3 And he did *what was* right in the sight of the LORD, according to all that his father Amaziah had done, 4 except that the high places were not removed; the people still sacrificed and burned incense on the high places. 5 Then the LORD struck the king, so that he was a leper until the day of his death; so he dwelt in an isolated house. And Jotham the king's son *was* over the *royal* house, judging the people of the land.

6 Now the rest of the acts of Azariah, and all that he did, *are* they not written in the book of the chronicles of the kings of Judah? 7 So Azariah rested with his fathers, and they buried him with his fathers in the City of David. Then Jotham his son reigned in his place.

8 In the thirty-eighth year of Azariah king of Judah, Zechariah the son of Jeroboam reigned over Israel in Samaria six months. 9 And he did evil in the sight of the LORD, as his fathers had done; he did not depart from the sins of Jeroboam the son of Nebat, who had made Israel sin. 10 Then Shallum the son of Jabesh conspired against him, and struck and killed him in front of the people; and he reigned in his place.

11 Now the rest of the acts of Zechariah,

indeed they *are* written in the book of the chronicles of the kings of Israel.

12 This *was* the word of the LORD which He spoke to Jehu, saying, "Your sons shall sit on the throne of Israel to the fourth *generation.*" And so it was.

13 Shallum the son of Jabesh became king in the thirty-ninth year of Uzziah king of Judah; and he reigned a full month in Samaria. 14 For Menahem the son of Gadi went up from Tirzah, came to Samaria, and struck Shallum the son of Jabesh in Samaria and killed him; and he reigned in his place.

15 Now the rest of the acts of Shallum, and the conspiracy which he led, indeed they *are* written in the book of the chronicles of the kings of Israel. 16 Then from Tirzah, Menahem attacked Tiphsah, all who *were* there, and its territory. Because they did not surrender, therefore he attacked *it.* All the women there who were with child he ripped open.

17 In the thirty-ninth year of Azariah king of Judah, Menahem the son of Gadi became king over Israel, *and reigned* ten years in Samaria. 18 And he did evil in the sight of the LORD; he did not depart all his days from the sins of Jeroboam the son of Nebat, who had made Israel sin. 19 Pul king of Assyria came against the land; and Menahem gave Pul a thousand talents of silver, that his hand might be with him to strengthen the kingdom under his control. 20 And Menahem exacted the money from Israel, from all the very wealthy, from each man fifty shekels of silver, to give to the king of Assyria. So the king of Assyria turned back, and did not stay there in the land.

21 Now the rest of the acts of Menahem, and all that he did, *are* they not written in the book of the chronicles of the kings of Israel? 22 So Menahem rested with his fathers. Then Pekahiah his son reigned in his place.

23 In the fiftieth year of Azariah king of Judah, Pekahiah the son of Menahem became king over Israel in Samaria, *and reigned* two years. 24 And he did evil in the sight of the LORD; he did not depart from the sins of Jeroboam the son of Nebat, who had made Israel sin. 25 Then Pekah the son of Remaliah, an officer of his, conspired against him and killed him in Samaria, in the citadel of the king's house, along with Argob and Arieh; and with him were fifty men of Gilead. He killed him and reigned in his place.

26 Now the rest of the acts of Pekahiah, and all that he did, indeed they *are* written in the book of the chronicles of the kings of Israel.

27 In the fifty-second year of Azariah king of Judah, Pekah the son of Remaliah became king over Israel in Samaria, *and reigned* twenty years. 28 And he did evil in the sight of the LORD; he did not depart from the sins of Jeroboam the son of Nebat, who had made Israel sin. 29 In the days of Pekah king of Israel, Tiglath-Pileser king of Assyria came and took Ijon, Abel Beth Maachah, Janoah, Kedesh, Hazor, Gilead, and Galilee, all the land of Naphtali; and he carried them captive to Assyria. 30 Then Hoshea the son of Elah led a conspiracy against Pekah the son of Remaliah, and struck and killed him; so he reigned in his place in the twentieth year of Jotham the son of Uzziah.

31 Now the rest of the acts of Pekah, and all that he did, indeed they *are* written in the book of the chronicles of the kings of Israel.

32 In the second year of Pekah the son of Remaliah, king of Israel, Jotham the son of Uzziah, king of Judah, began to reign. 33 He was twenty-five years old when he became king, and he reigned sixteen years in Jerusalem. His mother's name *was* Jerusha the daughter of Zadok. 34 And he did *what was* right in the sight of the LORD; he did according to all that his father Uzziah had done. 35 However the high places were not removed; the people still sacrificed and burned incense on the high places. He built the Upper Gate of the house of the LORD.

36 Now the rest of the acts of Jotham, and all that he did, *are* they not written in the book of the chronicles of the kings of Judah? 37 In those days the LORD began to send Rezin king of Syria and Pekah the son of Remaliah against Judah. 38 So Jotham rested with his fathers, and was buried with his fathers in the City of David his father. Then Ahaz his son reigned in his place.

16 IN the seventeenth year of Pekah the son of Remaliah, Ahaz the son of Jotham, king of Judah, began to reign. 2 Ahaz *was* twenty years old when he became king, and he reigned sixteen years in Jerusalem; and he did not do *what was* right in the sight of the LORD his God, as his father David *had done.* 3 But he walked in the way of the kings of Israel; indeed he made his son pass through the fire, according to the abominations of the nations whom the LORD had cast out from before the children of Israel. 4 And he sacrificed

and burned incense on the high places, on the hills, and under every green tree.

5 Then Rezin king of Syria and Pekah the son of Remaliah, king of Israel, came up to Jerusalem to *make* war; and they besieged Ahaz but could not overcome *him.* 6 At that time Rezin king of Syria captured Elath for Syria, and drove the men of Judah from Elath. Then the Edomites went to Elath, and dwell there to this day.

7 So Ahaz sent messengers to Tiglath-Pileser king of Assyria, saying, "I *am* your servant and your son. Come up and save me from the hand of the king of Syria and from the hand of the king of Israel, who rise up against me." 8 And Ahaz took the silver and gold that was found in the house of the LORD, and in the treasuries of the king's house, and sent *it as* a present to the king of Assyria. 9 So the king of Assyria heeded him; for the king of Assyria went up against Damascus and took it, carried *its people* captive to Kir, and killed Rezin.

10 Now King Ahaz went to Damascus to meet Tiglath-Pileser king of Assyria, and saw an altar that *was* at Damascus; and King Ahaz sent to Urijah the priest the design of the altar and its pattern, according to all its workmanship. 11 Then Urijah the priest built an altar according to all that King Ahaz had sent from Damascus. So Urijah the priest made *it* before King Ahaz came back from Damascus. 12 And when the king came back from Damascus, the king saw the altar; and the king approached the altar and made offerings on it. 13 So he burned his burnt offering and his grain offering; and he poured his drink offering and sprinkled the blood of his peace offerings on the altar. 14 He also brought the bronze altar which *was* before the LORD, from the front of the temple—from between the *new* altar and the house of the LORD—and put it on the north side of the *new* altar. 15 Then King Ahaz commanded Urijah the priest, saying, "On the great *new* altar burn the morning burnt offering, the evening grain offering, the king's burnt sacrifice, and his grain offering, with the burnt offering of all the people of the land, their grain offering, and their drink offerings; and sprinkle on it all the blood of the burnt offering and all the blood of the sacrifice. And the bronze altar shall be for me to inquire *by.*" 16 Thus did Urijah the priest, according to all that King Ahaz commanded.

17 And King Ahaz cut off the panels of the carts, and removed the lavers from them; and he took down the Sea from the bronze oxen that *were* under it, and put it on a pavement of stones. 18 Also he removed the Sabbath pavilion which they had built in the temple, and he removed the king's outer entrance from the house of the LORD, on account of the king of Assyria.

19 Now the rest of the acts of Ahaz which he did, *are* they not written in the book of the chronicles of the kings of Judah? 20 So Ahaz rested with his fathers, and was buried with his fathers in the City of David. Then Hezekiah his son reigned in his place.

PSALM 73:21–28

21 THUS my heart was grieved,
    And I was vexed in my mind.
22 I *was* so foolish and ignorant;
    I was *like* a beast before You.
23 Nevertheless I *am* continually with
        You;
    You hold *me* by my right hand.
24 You will guide me with Your counsel,
    And afterward receive me *to* glory.

25 Whom have I in heaven *but You?*
    And *there is* none upon earth *that* I
        desire besides You.

When we are detached from things on the inside the fury of desire burns itself out.   (GLORIFY)

---

26 My flesh and my heart fail;
    But God *is* the strength of my heart
        and my portion forever.

27 For indeed, those who are far from You
        shall perish;
    You have destroyed all those who desert
        You for harlotry.

28 But *it is* good for me to draw near to
        God;
    I have put my trust in the Lord GOD,
    That I may declare all Your works.

PROVERBS 18:20, 21

20 A man's stomach shall be satisfied from
        the fruit of his mouth;
    From the produce of his lips he shall
        be filled.

21 Death and life *are* in the power of the
        tongue,
    And those who love it will eat its fruit.

JOHN 21:1–25

AFTER these things Jesus showed Himself again to the disciples at the Sea of Tiberias, and in this way He showed *Himself:* 2 Simon Peter, Thomas called the Twin, Nathanael of Cana in Galilee, the *sons* of Zebedee, and two others of His disciples were together. 3 Simon Peter said to them, "I am going fishing."

They said to him, "We are going with you also." They went out and immediately got into the boat, and that night they caught nothing. 4 But when the morning had now come, Jesus stood on the shore; yet the disciples did not know that it was Jesus. 5 Then Jesus said to them, "Children, have you any food?"

They answered Him, "No."

6 And He said to them, "Cast the net on the right side of the boat, and you will find *some.*" So they cast, and now they were not able to draw it in because of the multitude of fish.

---

*I*t is easier to rely on God in big things than in little things.   (GOOD)

---

7 Therefore that disciple whom Jesus loved said to Peter, "It is the Lord!" Now when Simon Peter heard that it was the Lord, he put on *his* outer garment (for he had removed it), and plunged into the sea. 8 But the other disciples came in the little boat (for they were not far from land, but about two hundred cubits), dragging the net with fish. 9 Then, as soon as they had come to land, they saw a fire of coals there, and fish laid on it, and bread. 10 Jesus said to them, "Bring some of the fish which you have just caught."

11 Simon Peter went up and dragged the net to land, full of large fish, one hundred and fifty-three; and although there were so many, the net was not broken. 12 Jesus said to them, "Come *and* eat breakfast." Yet none of the disciples dared ask Him, "Who are You?"—knowing that it was the Lord. 13 Jesus then came and took the bread and gave it to them, and likewise the fish.

14 This *is* now the third time Jesus showed Himself to His disciples after He was raised from the dead.

15 So when they had eaten breakfast, Jesus said to Simon Peter, "Simon, *son* of Jonah, do you love Me more than these?"

He said to Him, "Yes, Lord; You know that I love You."

He said to him, "Feed My lambs."

16 He said to him again a second time, "Simon, *son* of Jonah, do you love Me?"

He said to Him, "Yes, Lord; You know that I love You."

He said to him, "Tend My sheep."

17 He said to him the third time, "Simon, *son* of Jonah, do you love Me?" Peter was grieved because He said to him the third time, "Do you love Me?"

And he said to Him, "Lord, You know all things; You know that I love You."

Jesus said to him, "Feed My sheep. 18 Most assuredly, I say to you, when you were younger, you girded yourself and walked where you wished; but when you are old, you will stretch out your hands, and another will gird you and carry *you* where you do not wish." 19 This He spoke, signifying by what death he would glorify God. And when He had spoken this, He said to him, "Follow Me."

20 Then Peter, turning around, saw the disciple whom Jesus loved following, who also had leaned on His breast at the supper, and said, "Lord, who is the one who betrays You?" 21 Peter, seeing him, said to Jesus, "But Lord, what *about* this man?"

22 Jesus said to him, "If I will that he remain till I come, what *is that* to you? You follow Me."

23 Then this saying went out among the brethren that this disciple would not die. Yet Jesus did not say to him that he would not die, but, "If I will that he remain till I come, what *is that* to you?"

24 This is the disciple who testifies of these things, and wrote these things; and we know that his testimony is true.

25 And there are also many other things that Jesus did, which if they were written one by one, I suppose that even the world itself could not contain the books that would be written. Amen.

◄◄◄◄ ◆◆◆

Reading 166—The Passion for Christ
Acts 1:8

These words of our risen Lord were spoken just before His ascension. We have to be careful lest we make the passionate watchwords "a passion for souls" and "a passion for Christ" into rival cries. The great passion which the Holy Spirit works in us, whereby He expresses the redemption of our Lord in and through us in practical ways is the passion for Jesus Christ Himself. "You shall be witnesses to Me"—not witnesses only to what Jesus has done or can do, but witnesses who are an infinite satisfaction to His own heart wherever they are placed. The danger in the modern form of Christianity is its departure more and more from the great central figure of the Lord Jesus Christ.

Christian experience does not mean we have thought through the way God works in human lives by His grace, or that we are able to state theologically that God gives the Holy Spirit to those who ask Him—that may be Christian thinking, but it is not Christian experience. Christian experience is living through all this by the marvelous power of the Holy Spirit.

The Holy Spirit working in me does not produce wonderful experiences that make people say, "What a wonderful life that man lives"; the Holy Spirit working in me makes me a passionate, devoted, absorbed lover of the Lord Jesus Christ. (*PLACE HELP*)

2 KINGS 17:1—18:37

IN the twelfth year of Ahaz king of Judah, Hoshea the son of Elah became king of Israel in Samaria, *and he reigned* nine years. 2 And he did evil in the sight of the LORD, but not as the kings of Israel who were before him. 3 Shalmaneser king of Assyria came up against him; and Hoshea became his vassal, and paid him tribute money. 4 And the king of Assyria uncovered a conspiracy by Hoshea; for he had sent messengers to So, king of Egypt, and brought no tribute to the king of Assyria, as *he had done* year by year. Therefore the king of Assyria shut him up, and bound him in prison.

5 Now the king of Assyria went throughout all the land, and went up to Samaria and besieged it for three years. 6 In the ninth year of Hoshea, the king of Assyria took Samaria and carried Israel away to Assyria, and placed them in Halah and by the Habor, the River of Gozan, and in the cities of the Medes.

7 For so it was that the children of Israel had sinned against the LORD their God, who had brought them up out of the land of Egypt, from under the hand of Pharaoh king of Egypt; and they had feared other gods, 8 and had walked in the statutes of the nations whom the LORD had cast out from before the children of Israel, and of the kings of Israel, which they had made. 9 Also the children of Israel secretly did against the LORD their God things that *were* not right, and they built for themselves high places in all their cities, from watchtower to fortified city. 10 They set up for themselves *sacred* pillars and wooden images on every high hill and under every green tree. 11 There they burned incense on all the high places, like the nations whom the LORD had carried away before them; and they did wicked things to provoke the LORD to anger, 12 for they served idols, of which the LORD had said to them, "You shall not do this thing."

13 Yet the LORD testified against Israel and against Judah, by all of His prophets, every seer, saying, "Turn from your evil ways, and keep My commandments *and* My statutes, according to all the law which I commanded your fathers, and which I sent to you by My servants the prophets." 14 Nevertheless they would not hear, but stiffened their necks, like the necks of their fathers, who did not believe in the LORD their God. 15 And they rejected His statutes and His covenant that He had made with their fathers, and His testimonies which He had testified against them; they followed idols, became idolaters, and *went* after the nations who *were* all around them, *concern-*

ing whom the LORD had charged them that they should not do like them. 16 So they left all the commandments of the LORD their God, made for themselves a molded image *and* two calves, made a wooden image and worshiped all the host of heaven, and served Baal. 17 And they caused their sons and daughters to pass through the fire, practiced witchcraft and soothsaying, and sold themselves to do evil in the sight of the LORD, to provoke Him to anger. 18 Therefore the LORD was very angry with Israel, and removed them from His sight; there was none left but the tribe of Judah alone.

19 Also Judah did not keep the commandments of the LORD their God, but walked in the statutes of Israel which they made. 20 And the LORD rejected all the descendants of Israel, afflicted them, and delivered them into the hand of plunderers, until He had cast them from His sight. 21 For He tore Israel from the house of David, and they made Jeroboam the son of Nebat king. Then Jeroboam drove Israel from following the LORD, and made them commit a great sin. 22 For the children of Israel walked in all the sins of Jeroboam which he did; they did not depart from them, 23 until the LORD removed Israel out of His sight, as He had said by all His servants the prophets. So Israel was carried away from their own land to Assyria, *as it is* to this day.

24 Then the king of Assyria brought *people* from Babylon, Cuthah, Ava, Hamath, and from Sepharvaim, and placed *them* in the cities of Samaria instead of the children of Israel; and they took possession of Samaria and dwelt in its cities. 25 And it was so, at the beginning of their dwelling there, *that* they did not fear the LORD; therefore the LORD sent lions among them, which killed *some* of them. 26 So they spoke to the king of Assyria, saying, "The nations whom you have removed and placed in the cities of Samaria do not know the rituals of the God of the land; therefore He has sent lions among them, and indeed, they are killing them because they do not know the rituals of the God of the land." 27 Then the king of Assyria commanded, saying, "Send there one of the priests whom you brought from there; let him go and dwell there, and let him teach them the rituals of the God of the land." 28 Then one of the priests whom they had carried away from Samaria came and dwelt in Bethel, and taught them how they should fear the LORD.

29 However every nation continued to make gods of its own, and put *them* in the shrines on the high places which the Samaritans had made, *every* nation in the cities

where they dwelt. 30 The men of Babylon made Succoth Benoth, the men of Cuth made Nergal, the men of Hamath made Ashima, 31 and the Avites made Nibhaz and Tartak; and the Sepharvites burned their children in fire to Adrammelech and Anammelech, the gods of Sepharvaim. 32 So they feared the LORD, and from every class they appointed for themselves priests of the high places, who sacrificed for them in the shrines of the high places. 33 They feared the LORD, yet served their own gods—according to the rituals of the nations from among whom they were carried away.

34 To this day they continue practicing the former rituals; they do not fear the LORD, nor do they follow their statutes or their ordinances, or the law and commandment which the LORD had commanded the children of Jacob, whom He named Israel, 35 with whom the LORD had made a covenant and charged them, saying: "You shall not fear other gods, nor bow down to them nor serve them nor sacrifice to them; 36 but the LORD, who brought you up from the land of Egypt with great power and an outstretched arm, Him you shall fear, Him you shall worship, and to Him you shall offer sacrifice. 37 And the statutes, the ordinances, the law, and the commandment which He wrote for you, you shall be careful to observe forever; you shall not fear other gods. 38 And the covenant that I have made with you, you shall not forget, nor shall you fear other gods. 39 But the LORD your God you shall fear; and He will deliver you from the hand of all your enemies." 40 However they did not obey, but they followed their former rituals. 41 So these nations feared the LORD, yet served their carved images; also their children and their children's children have continued doing as their fathers did, even to this day.

18 NOW it came to pass in the third year of Hoshea the son of Elah, king of Israel, *that* Hezekiah the son of Ahaz, king of Judah, began to reign. 2 He was twenty-five years old when he became king, and he reigned twenty-nine years in Jerusalem. His mother's name *was* Abi the daughter of Zechariah. 3 And he did *what was* right in the sight of the LORD, according to all that his father David had done.

4 He removed the high places and broke the *sacred* pillars, cut down the wooden image and broke in pieces the bronze serpent that Moses had made; for until those days the children of Israel burned incense to it, and called it Nehushtan. 5 He trusted in the LORD God of Israel, so that after him

was none like him among all the kings of Judah, nor who were before him. 6 For he held fast to the Lord; he did not depart from following Him, but kept His commandments, which the Lord had commanded Moses. 7 The Lord was with him; he prospered wherever he went. And he rebelled against the king of Assyria and did not serve him. 8 He subdued the Philistines, as far as Gaza and its territory, from watchtower to fortified city.

9 Now it came to pass in the fourth year of King Hezekiah, which *was* the seventh year of Hoshea the son of Elah, king of Israel, *that* Shalmaneser king of Assyria came up against Samaria and besieged it. 10 And at the end of three years they took it. In the sixth year of Hezekiah, that *is,* the ninth year of Hoshea king of Israel, Samaria was taken. 11 Then the king of Assyria carried Israel away captive to Assyria, and put them in Halah and by the Habor, the River of Gozan, and in the cities of the Medes, 12 because they did not obey the voice of the Lord their God, but transgressed His covenant *and* all that Moses the servant of the Lord had commanded; and they would neither hear nor do *them.*

13 And in the fourteenth year of King Hezekiah, Sennacherib king of Assyria came up against all the fortified cities of Judah and took them. 14 Then Hezekiah king of Judah sent to the king of Assyria at Lachish, saying, "I have done wrong; turn away from me; whatever you impose on me I will pay." And the king of Assyria assessed Hezekiah king of Judah three hundred talents of silver and thirty talents of gold. 15 So Hezekiah gave *him* all the silver that was found in the house of the Lord and in the treasuries of the king's house. 16 At that time Hezekiah stripped *the gold from* the doors of the temple of the Lord, and *from* the pillars which Hezekiah king of Judah had overlaid, and gave it to the king of Assyria.

17 Then the king of Assyria sent *the* Tartan, *the* Rabsaris, *and the* Rabshakeh from Lachish, with a great army against Jerusalem, to King Hezekiah. And they went up and came to Jerusalem. When they had come up, they went and stood by the aqueduct from the upper pool, which *was* on the highway to the Fuller's Field. 18 And when they had called to the king, Eliakim the son of Hilkiah, who *was* over the household, Shebna the scribe, and Joah the son of Asaph, the recorder, came out to them. 19 Then *the* Rabshakeh said to them, "Say now to Hezekiah, 'Thus says the great king, the king of Assyria: "What confidence *is* this in which you trust? 20 You speak of

having plans and power for war; but *they are* mere words. And in whom do you trust, that you rebel against me? 21 Now look! You are trusting in the staff of this broken reed, Egypt, on which if a man leans, it will go into his hand and pierce it. So *is* Pharaoh king of Egypt to all who trust in him. 22 But if you say to me, 'We trust in the Lord our God,' *is* it not He whose high places and whose altars Hezekiah has taken away, and said to Judah and Jerusalem, 'You shall worship before this altar in Jerusalem'?" ' 23 Now therefore, I urge you, give a pledge to my master the king of Assyria, and I will give you two thousand horses—if you are able on your part to put riders on them! 24 How then will you repel one captain of the least of my master's servants, and put your trust in Egypt for chariots and horsemen? 25 Have I now come up without the Lord against this place to destroy it? The Lord said to me, 'Go up against this land, and destroy it.' "

26 Then Eliakim the son of Hilkiah, Shebna, and Joah said to *the* Rabshakeh, "Please speak to your servants in Aramaic, for we understand *it;* and do not speak to us in Hebrew in the hearing of the people who *are* on the wall."

27 But *the* Rabshakeh said to them, "Has my master sent me to your master and to you to speak these words, and not to the men who sit on the wall, who will eat and drink their own waste with you?"

28 Then *the* Rabshakeh stood and called out with a loud voice in Hebrew, and spoke, saying, "Hear the word of the great king, the king of Assyria! 29 Thus says the king: 'Do not let Hezekiah deceive you, for he shall not be able to deliver you from his hand; 30 nor let Hezekiah make you trust in the Lord, saying, "The Lord will surely deliver us; this city shall not be given into the hand of the king of Assyria." ' 31 Do not listen to Hezekiah; for thus says the king of Assyria: 'Make *peace* with me by a present and come out to me; and every one of you eat from his own vine and every one from his own fig tree, and every one of you drink the waters of his own cistern; 32 until I come and take you away to a land like your own land, a land of grain and new wine, a land of bread and vineyards, a land of olive groves and honey, that you may live and not die. But do not listen to Hezekiah, lest he persuade you, saying, "The Lord will deliver us." 33 Has any of the gods of the nations at all delivered its land from the hand of the king of Assyria? 34 Where *are* the gods of Hamath and Arpad? Where *are* the gods of Sepharvaim

and Hena and Ivah? Indeed, have they delivered Samaria from my hand? 35 Who among all the gods of the lands have delivered their countries from my hand, that the LORD should deliver Jerusalem from my hand?' "

36 But the people held their peace and answered him not a word; for the king's commandment was, "Do not answer him." 37 Then Eliakim the son of Hilkiah, who *was* over the household, Shebna the scribe, and Joah the son of Asaph, the recorder, came to Hezekiah with *their* clothes torn, and told him the words of *the* Rabshakeh.

PSALM 74:1–8

1 O God, why have You cast *us* off
      forever?
      Why does Your anger smoke against
      the sheep of Your pasture?
2 Remember Your congregation, *which*
      You have purchased of old,
      The tribe of Your inheritance, *which*
      You have redeemed—
      This Mount Zion where You have
      dwelt.
3 Lift up Your feet to the perpetual
      desolations.
      The enemy has damaged everything in
      the sanctuary.
4 Your enemies roar in the midst of Your
      meeting place;
      They set up their banners *for* signs.
5 They seem like men who lift up
      Axes among the thick trees.
6 And now they break down its carved
      work, all at once,
      With axes and hammers.
7 They have set fire to Your sanctuary;
      They have defiled the dwelling place
      of Your name to the ground.
8 They said in their hearts,
      "Let us destroy them altogether."
      They have burned up all the meeting
      places of God in the land.

PROVERBS 18:22–24

22 HE *who* finds a wife finds a good *thing,*
       And obtains favor from the LORD.

23 The poor *man* uses entreaties,
       But the rich answers roughly.

24 A man *who has* friends must himself
       be friendly,
       But there is a friend *who* sticks closer
       than a brother.

Jesus guides us by making us His friends.   (SEND I YOU)

ACTS 1:1–26

THE former account I made, O Theophilus, of all that Jesus began both to do and teach, 2 until the day in which He was taken up, after He through the Holy Spirit had given commandments to the apostles whom He had chosen, 3 to whom He also presented Himself alive after His suffering by many infallible proofs, being seen by them during forty days and speaking of the things pertaining to the kingdom of God.

4 And being assembled together with *them,* He commanded them not to depart from Jerusalem, but to wait for the Promise of the Father, "which," *He said,* "you have heard from Me; 5 for John truly baptized with water, but you shall be baptized with the Holy Spirit not many days from now." 6 Therefore, when they had come together, they asked Him, saying, "Lord, will You at this time restore the kingdom to Israel?" 7 And He said to them, "It is not for you to know times or seasons which the Father has put in His own authority. 8 But you shall receive power when the Holy Spirit has come upon you; and you shall be witnesses to Me in Jerusalem, and in all Judea and Samaria, and to the end of the earth."

9 Now when He had spoken these things, while they watched, He was taken up, and a cloud received Him out of their sight.

Jesus Christ is the only One who has not only been on this earth, but beyond it.   (GLORIFY)

10 And while they looked steadfastly toward heaven as He went up, behold, two men stood by them in white apparel, 11 who also said, "Men of Galilee, why do you stand gazing up into heaven? This *same* Jesus, who was taken up from you into heaven, will so come in like manner as you saw Him go into heaven."

12 Then they returned to Jerusalem from the mount called Olivet, which is near Jerusalem, a Sabbath day's journey. 13 And when they had entered, they went up into the upper room where they were staying: Peter, James, John, and Andrew; Philip and Thomas; Bartholomew and Matthew;

James *the son* of Alphaeus and Simon the Zealot; and Judas *the son* of James. 14 These all continued with one accord in prayer and supplication, with the women and Mary the mother of Jesus, and with His brothers.

15 And in those days Peter stood up in the midst of the disciples (altogether the number of names was about a hundred and twenty), and said, 16 "Men *and* brethren, this Scripture had to be fulfilled, which the Holy Spirit spoke before by the mouth of David concerning Judas, who became a guide to those who arrested Jesus; 17 for he was numbered with us and obtained a part in this ministry."

18 (Now this man purchased a field with the wages of iniquity; and falling headlong, he burst open in the middle and all his entrails gushed out. 19 And it became known to all those dwelling in Jerusalem; so that field is called in their own language, Akel Dama, that is, Field of Blood.)

20 "For it is written in the Book of Psalms:

'Let his dwelling place be desolate,
And let no one live in it';

and,

'Let another take his office.'

21 "Therefore, of these men who have accompanied us all the time that the Lord Jesus went in and out among us, 22 beginning from the baptism of John to that day when He was taken up from us, one of these must become a witness with us of His resurrection."

23 And they proposed two: Joseph called Barsabas, who was surnamed Justus, and Matthias. 24 And they prayed and said, "You, O Lord, who know the hearts of all, show which of these two You have chosen 25 to take part in this ministry and apostleship from which Judas by transgression fell, that he might go to his own place." 26 And they cast their lots, and the lot fell on Matthias. And he was numbered with the eleven apostles.

◆◆◆◆

Reading 167—Experimental Revelation
Acts 2:1

What an unspeakably wonderful day the Day of Pentecost was! There is only one Bethlehem, one Calvary, one Pentecost; these are the landmarks of Time and Eternity, everything and everyone is judged by them.

Beware of thinking of Pentecost in the light of personal experience only. The descent of the Holy Ghost can never be experimental, it is historical. The reception of the Holy Ghost into our hearts is experimental. Those who insist on the experimental line are in danger of forgetting the revelation and of putting all the emphasis on experience, while those who emphasize the revelation are in danger of forgetting the practical experience. In the New Testament the two are one; the experimental must be based on and regulated by the revelation. We imagine that we have the monopoly of the teaching about the Holy Spirit when we deal with His work in individual lives, namely, His power to transform men on the inside—the most important phase to us, but in God's Book the tiniest phase of the work of the mighty Spirit of God.   (*GLORIFY*)

2 KINGS 19:1—21:26

AND so it was, when King Hezekiah heard *it*, that he tore his clothes, covered himself with sackcloth, and went into the house of the LORD. 2 Then he sent Eliakim, who *was* over the household, Shebna the scribe, and the elders of the priests, covered with sackcloth, to Isaiah the prophet, the son of Amoz. 3 And they said to him, "Thus says Hezekiah: 'This day *is* a day of trouble, and rebuke, and blasphemy; for the children have come to birth, but *there is* no strength to bring them forth. 4 It may be that the

LORD your God will hear all the words of *the* Rabshakeh, whom his master the king of Assyria has sent to reproach the living God, and will rebuke the words which the LORD your God has heard. Therefore lift up *your* prayer for the remnant that is left.' "

5 So the servants of King Hezekiah came to Isaiah. 6 And Isaiah said to them, "Thus you shall say to your master, 'Thus says the LORD: "Do not be afraid of the words which you have heard, with which the servants of the king of Assyria have blasphemed Me. 7 Surely I will send a spirit upon him, and he shall hear a rumor and return to his own land; and I will cause him to fall by the sword in his own land." ' "

8 Then *the* Rabshakeh returned and found the king of Assyria warring against Libnah, for he heard that he had departed from Lachish. 9 And the king heard concerning Tirhakah king of Ethiopia, "Look, he has come out to make war with you." So he again sent messengers to Hezekiah, saying, 10 "Thus you shall speak to Hezekiah king of Judah, saying: 'Do not let your God in whom you trust deceive you, saying, "Jerusalem shall not be given into the hand of the king of Assyria." 11 Look! You have heard what the kings of Assyria have done to all lands by utterly destroying them; and shall you be delivered? 12 Have the gods of the nations delivered those whom my fathers have destroyed, Gozan and Haran and Rezeph, and the people of Eden who *were* in Telassar? 13 Where *is* the king of Hamath, the king of Arpad, and the king of the city of Sepharvaim, Hena, and Ivah?' "

14 And Hezekiah received the letter from the hand of the messengers, and read it; and Hezekiah went up to the house of the LORD, and spread it before the LORD. 15 Then Hezekiah prayed before the LORD, and said: "O LORD God of Israel, *the One* who dwells *between* the cherubim, You are God, You alone, of all the kingdoms of the earth. You have made heaven and earth. 16 Incline Your ear, O LORD, and hear; open Your eyes, O LORD, and see; and hear the words of Sennacherib, which he has sent to reproach the living God. 17 Truly, LORD, the kings of Assyria have laid waste the nations and their lands, 18 and have cast their gods into the fire; for they *were* not gods, but the work of men's hands—wood and stone. Therefore they destroyed them. 19 Now therefore, O LORD our God, I pray, save us from his hand, that all the kingdoms of the earth may know that You *are* the LORD God, You alone."

20 Then Isaiah the son of Amoz sent to Hezekiah, saying, "Thus says the LORD God of Israel: 'Because you have prayed to Me against Sennacherib king of Assyria, I have heard.' 21 This *is* the word which the LORD has spoken concerning him:

'The virgin, the daughter of Zion,
Has despised you, laughed you to
    scorn;
The daughter of Jerusalem
Has shaken *her* head behind your
    back!

22 'Whom have you reproached and
    blasphemed?
Against whom have you raised *your*
    voice,
And lifted up your eyes on high?
Against the Holy *One* of Israel.
23 By your messengers you have
    reproached the Lord,
And said: "By the multitude of my
    chariots
I have come up to the height of the
    mountains,
To the limits of Lebanon;
I will cut down its tall cedars
And its choice cypress trees;
I will enter the extremity of its
    borders,
To its fruitful forest.
24 I have dug and drunk strange water,
And with the soles of my feet I have
    dried up
All the brooks of defense."

25 'Did you not hear long ago
How I made it,
From ancient times that I formed it?
Now I have brought it to pass,
That you should be
For crushing fortified cities *into* heaps
    of ruins.
26 Therefore their inhabitants had little
    power;
They were dismayed and
    confounded;
They were *as* the grass of the field
And the green herb,
As the grass on the housetops
And *grain* blighted before it is grown.

27 'But I know your dwelling place,
Your going out and your coming in,
And your rage against Me.
28 Because your rage against Me and
    your tumult
Have come up to My ears,
Therefore I will put My hook in your
    nose
And My bridle in your lips,

And I will turn you back
By the way which you came.

29 'This *shall be* a sign to you:

You shall eat this year such as grows
of itself,
And in the second year what springs
from the same;
Also in the third year sow and reap,
Plant vineyards and eat the fruit of
them.

30   And the remnant who have escaped
of the house of Judah
Shall again take root downward,
And bear fruit upward.
31   For out of Jerusalem shall go a
remnant,
And those who escape from Mount
Zion.
The zeal of the LORD of hosts will
do this.'

32 "Therefore thus says the LORD concerning the king of Assyria:

'He shall not come into this city,
Nor shoot an arrow there,
Nor come before it with shield,
Nor build a siege mound against it.
33   By the way that he came,
By the same shall he return;
And he shall not come into this city,'
Says the LORD.
34   'For I will defend this city,
to save it
For My own sake and for My servant
David's sake.' "

35 And it came to pass on a certain night
that the angel of the LORD went out, and
killed in the camp of the Assyrians one hundred and eighty-five thousand; and when
people arose early in the morning, there were
the corpses—all dead. 36 So Sennacherib
king of Assyria departed and went away,
returned *home,* and remained at Nineveh.
37 Now it came to pass, as he was worshiping in the temple of Nisroch his god, that
his sons Adrammelech and Sharezer struck
him down with the sword; and they escaped
into the land of Ararat. Then Esarhaddon
his son reigned in his place.

20 IN those days Hezekiah was sick
and near death. And Isaiah the
prophet, the son of Amoz, went to him
and said to him, "Thus says the LORD: 'Set
your house in order, for you shall die, and
not live.' "
2 Then he turned his face toward the wall,

and prayed to the LORD, saying, 3 "Remember now, O LORD, I pray, how I have
walked before You in truth and with a loyal
heart, and have done *what was* good in Your
sight." And Hezekiah wept bitterly.

---

*Tell Him what you know He knows
. . . get to know it as
He does.*   (GLORIFY)

---

4 And it happened, before Isaiah had
gone out into the middle court, that the
word of the LORD came to him, saying,
5 "Return and tell Hezekiah the leader of
My people, 'Thus says the LORD, the God
of David your father: "I have heard your
prayer, I have seen your tears; surely I will
heal you. On the third day you shall go
up to the house of the LORD. 6 And I will
add to your days fifteen years. I will deliver
you and this city from the hand of the king
of Assyria; and I will defend this city for
My own sake, and for the sake of My servant
David." ' "
7 Then Isaiah said, "Take a lump of figs."
So they took and laid *it* on the boil, and
he recovered.
8 And Hezekiah said to Isaiah, "What *is*
the sign that the LORD will heal me, and
that I shall go up to the house of the LORD
the third day?"
9 Then Isaiah said, "This is the sign to
you from the LORD, that the LORD will
do the thing which He has spoken: *shall*
the shadow go forward ten degrees or go
backward ten degrees?"
10 And Hezekiah answered, "It is an easy
thing for the shadow to go down ten degrees; no, but let the shadow go backward
ten degrees."
11 So Isaiah the prophet cried out to the
LORD, and He brought the shadow ten degrees backward, by which it had gone down
on the sundial of Ahaz.
12 At that time Berodach-Baladan the son
of Baladan, king of Babylon, sent letters
and a present to Hezekiah, for he heard
that Hezekiah had been sick. 13 And Hezekiah was attentive to them, and showed
them all the house of his treasures—the silver and gold, the spices and precious ointment, and all his armory—all that was found
among his treasures. There was nothing in
his house or in all his dominion that Hezekiah did not show them.
14 Then Isaiah the prophet went to King
Hezekiah, and said to him, "What did these
men say, and from where did they come
to you?"

So Hezekiah said, "They came from a far country, from Babylon."

15 And he said, "What have they seen in your house?"

So Hezekiah answered, "They have seen all that *is* in my house; there is nothing among my treasures that I have not shown them."

16 Then Isaiah said to Hezekiah, "Hear the word of the LORD: 17 'Behold, the days are coming when all that *is* in your house, and what your fathers have accumulated until this day, shall be carried to Babylon; nothing shall be left,' says the LORD. 18 'And they shall take away some of your sons who will descend from you, whom you will beget; and they shall be eunuchs in the palace of the king of Babylon.' "

19 So Hezekiah said to Isaiah, "The word of the LORD which you have spoken *is* good!" For he said, "Will there not be peace and truth at least in my days?"

20 Now the rest of the acts of Hezekiah—all his might, and how he made a pool and a tunnel and brought water into the city—*are* they not written in the book of the chronicles of the kings of Judah? 21 So Hezekiah rested with his fathers. Then Manasseh his son reigned in his place.

21 MANASSEH *was* twelve years old when he became king, and he reigned fifty-five years in Jerusalem. His mother's name *was* Hephzibah. 2 And he did evil in the sight of the LORD, according to the abominations of the nations whom the LORD had cast out before the children of Israel. 3 For he rebuilt the high places which Hezekiah his father had destroyed; he raised up altars for Baal, and made a wooden image, as Ahab king of Israel had done; and he worshiped all the host of heaven and served them. 4 He also built altars in the house of the LORD, of which the LORD had said, "In Jerusalem I will put My name." 5 And he built altars for all the host of heaven in the two courts of the house of the LORD. 6 Also he made his son pass through the fire, practiced soothsaying, used witchcraft, and consulted spiritists and mediums. He did much evil in the sight of the LORD, to provoke *Him* to anger. 7 He even set a carved image of Asherah that he had made, in the house of which the LORD had said to David and to Solomon his son, "In this house and in Jerusalem, which I have chosen out of all the tribes of Israel, I will put My name forever; 8 and I will not make the feet of Israel wander anymore from the land which I gave their fathers—only if they are careful

to do according to all that I have commanded them, and according to all the law that My servant Moses commanded them." 9 But they paid no attention, and Manasseh seduced them to do more evil than the nations whom the LORD had destroyed before the children of Israel.

10 And the LORD spoke by His servants the prophets, saying, 11 "Because Manasseh king of Judah has done these abominations (he has acted more wickedly than all the Amorites who *were* before him, and has also made Judah sin with his idols), 12 therefore thus says the LORD God of Israel: 'Behold, *I* am bringing *such* calamity upon Jerusalem and Judah, that whoever hears of it, both his ears will tingle. 13 And I will stretch over Jerusalem the measuring line of Samaria and the plummet of the house of Ahab; I will wipe Jerusalem as *one* wipes a dish, wiping *it* and turning *it* upside down. 14 So I will forsake the remnant of My inheritance and deliver them into the hand of their enemies; and they shall become victims of plunder to all their enemies, 15 because they have done evil in My sight, and have provoked Me to anger since the day their fathers came out of Egypt, even to this day.' "

16 Moreover Manasseh shed very much innocent blood, till he had filled Jerusalem from one end to another, besides his sin by which he made Judah sin, in doing evil in the sight of the LORD.

17 Now the rest of the acts of Manasseh—all that he did, and the sin that he committed—*are* they not written in the book of the chronicles of the kings of Judah? 18 So Manasseh rested with his fathers, and was buried in the garden of his own house, in the garden of Uzza. Then his son Amon reigned in his place.

19 Amon *was* twenty-two years old when he became king, and he reigned two years in Jerusalem. His mother's name *was* Meshullemeth the daughter of Haruz of Jotbah. 20 And he did evil in the sight of the LORD, as his father Manasseh had done. 21 So he walked in all the ways that his father had walked; and he served the idols that his father had served, and worshiped them. 22 He forsook the LORD God of his fathers, and did not walk in the way of the LORD.

23 Then the servants of Amon conspired against him, and killed the king in his own house. 24 But the people of the land executed all those who had conspired against King Amon. Then the people of the land made his son Josiah king in his place.

25 Now the rest of the acts of Amon

which he did, *are* they not written in the book of the chronicles of the kings of Judah? 26 And he was buried in his tomb in the garden of Uzza. Then Josiah his son reigned in his place.

PSALM 74:9–17

9   WE do not see our signs;
    There is no longer any prophet;
    Nor *is there* any among us who knows how long.
10 O God, how long will the adversary reproach?
    Will the enemy blaspheme Your name forever?
11 Why do You withdraw Your hand, even Your right hand?
    Take it out of Your bosom and destroy *them.*
12 For God *is* my King from of old,
    Working salvation in the midst of the earth.
13 You divided the sea by Your strength;
    You broke the heads of the sea serpents in the waters.
14 You broke the heads of Leviathan in pieces,
    And gave him *as* food to the people inhabiting the wilderness.
15 You broke open the fountain and the flood;
    You dried up mighty rivers.
16 The day *is* Yours, the night also *is* Yours;
    You have prepared the light and the sun.
17 You have set all the borders of the earth;
    You have made summer and winter.

PROVERBS 19:1, 2

1   BETTER *is* the poor who walks in his integrity
    Than *one who is* perverse in his lips, and is a fool.

2   Also it is not good *for* a soul *to be* without knowledge,
    And he sins who hastens with *his* feet.

ACTS 2:1–21

WHEN the Day of Pentecost had fully come, they were all with one accord in one place. 2 And suddenly there came a sound from heaven, as of a rushing mighty wind, and it filled the whole house where they were sitting. 3 Then there appeared to them divided tongues, as of fire, and *one* sat upon each of them. 4 And they were all filled with the Holy Spirit and began to speak with other tongues, as the Spirit gave them utterance.

5 And there were dwelling in Jerusalem Jews, devout men, from every nation under heaven. 6 And when this sound occurred, the multitude came together, and were confused, because everyone heard them speak in his own language. 7 Then they were all amazed and marveled, saying to one another, "Look, are not all these who speak Galileans? 8 And how *is it that* we hear, each in our own language in which we were born? 9 Parthians and Medes and Elamites, those dwelling in Mesopotamia, Judea and Cappadocia, Pontus and Asia, 10 Phrygia and Pamphylia, Egypt and the parts of Libya adjoining Cyrene, visitors from Rome, both Jews and proselytes, 11 Cretans and Arabs—we hear them speaking in our own tongues the wonderful works of God." 12 So they were all amazed and perplexed, saying to one another, "Whatever could this mean?"

13 Others mocking said, "They are full of new wine."

14 But Peter, standing up with the eleven, raised his voice and said to them, "Men of Judea and all who dwell in Jerusalem, let this be known to you, and heed my words. 15 For these are not drunk, as you suppose, since it is *only* the third hour of the day. 16 But this is what was spoken by the prophet Joel:

17 'And it shall come to pass in the last days, says God,
    That I will pour out of My Spirit on all flesh;
    Your sons and your daughters shall prophesy,
    Your young men shall see visions,
    Your old men shall dream dreams.
18 And on My menservants and on My maidservants
    I will pour out My Spirit in those days;
    And they shall prophesy.
19 I will show wonders in heaven above And signs in the earth beneath:
    Blood and fire and vapor of smoke.
20 The sun shall be turned into darkness,
    And the moon into blood,
    Before the coming of the great and awesome day of the LORD.
21 And it shall come to pass
    That whoever calls on the name of the LORD
    Shall be saved.'

Reading 168—God and Sin
Acts 2:36

The cross of Jesus Christ is a revelation; our cross is an experience. If we neglect for one moment the basal revelation of the cross, we will make shipwreck of our faith, no matter what our experience is. The test of our spiritual life is our understanding of the cross. The cross of Jesus is often wrongly taken as a type of the cross we have to carry. Jesus did not say, "If anyone will come after Me, let him take up My cross," but "let him deny himself, and take up his cross, and follow Me." Our cross becomes our divinely appointed privilege by means of His cross. We are never called upon to carry His cross. We have so hallowed the cross by twenty centuries of emotion and sentiment that it sounds a very beautiful and pathetic thing to talk about carrying our cross. But a wooden cross with iron nails in it is a clumsy thing to carry. The real cross was like that, and do we imagine that the external cross was more ugly than our actual one? Or that the thing that tore our Lord's hands and feet was not really so terrible as our imagination of it?   (GLORY)

2 KINGS 22:1—24:20

JOSIAH *was* eight years old when he became king, and he reigned thirty-one years in Jerusalem. His mother's name *was* Jedidah the daughter of Adaiah of Bozkath. 2 And he did *what was* right in the sight of the LORD, and walked in all the ways of his father David; he did not turn aside to the right hand or to the left.

3 Now it came to pass, in the eighteenth year of King Josiah, *that* the king sent Shaphan the scribe, the son of Azaliah, the son of Meshullam, to the house of the LORD, saying: 4 "Go up to Hilkiah the high priest, that he may count the money which has been brought into the house of the LORD, which the doorkeepers have gathered from the people. 5 And let them deliver it into the hand of those doing the work, who are the overseers in the house of the LORD; let them give it to those who *are* in the house of the LORD doing the work, to repair the damages of the house— 6 to carpenters and builders and masons— and to buy timber and hewn stone to repair the house. 7 However there need be no accounting made with them of the money delivered into their hand, because they deal faithfully."

8 Then Hilkiah the high priest said to Shaphan the scribe, "I have found the Book of the Law in the house of the LORD." And Hilkiah gave the book to Shaphan, and he read it. 9 So Shaphan the scribe went to the king, bringing the king word, saying, "Your servants have gathered the money

that was found in the house, and have delivered it into the hand of those who do the work, who oversee the house of the LORD." 10 Then Shaphan the scribe showed the king, saying, "Hilkiah the priest has given me a book." And Shaphan read it before the king.

11 Now it happened, when the king heard the words of the Book of the Law, that he tore his clothes. 12 Then the king commanded Hilkiah the priest, Ahikam the son of Shaphan, Achbor the son of Michaiah, Shaphan the scribe, and Asaiah a servant of the king, saying, 13 "Go, inquire of the LORD for me, for the people and for all Judah, concerning the words of this book that has been found; for great *is* the wrath of the LORD that is aroused against us, because our fathers have not obeyed the words of this book, to do according to all that is written concerning us."

14 So Hilkiah the priest, Ahikam, Achbor, Shaphan, and Asaiah went to Huldah the prophetess, the wife of Shallum the son of Tikvah, the son of Harhas, keeper of the wardrobe. (She dwelt in Jerusalem in the Second Quarter.) And they spoke with her. 15 Then she said to them, "Thus says the LORD God of Israel, 'Tell the man who sent you to Me, 16 "Thus says the LORD: 'Behold, I will bring calamity on this place and on its inhabitants—all the words of the book which the king of Judah has read— 17 because they have forsaken Me and burned incense to other gods, that they might provoke Me to anger with all the works of their hands. Therefore My wrath

shall be aroused against this place and shall not be quenched.'"' 18 But as for the king of Judah, who sent you to inquire of the LORD, in this manner you shall speak to him, 'Thus says the LORD God of Israel: "*Concerning* the words which you have heard— 19 because your heart was tender, and you humbled yourself before the LORD when you heard what I spoke against this place and against its inhabitants, that they would become a desolation and a curse, and you tore your clothes and wept before Me, I also have heard *you*," says the LORD. 20 Surely, therefore, I will gather you to your fathers, and you shall be gathered to your grave in peace; and your eyes shall not see all the calamity which I will bring on this place."'" So they brought back word to the king.

23 NOW the king sent them to gather all the elders of Judah and Jerusalem to him. 2 The king went up to the house of the LORD with all the men of Judah, and with him all the inhabitants of Jerusalem—the priests and the prophets and all the people, both small and great. And he read in their hearing all the words of the Book of the Covenant which had been found in the house of the LORD.

3 Then the king stood by a pillar and made a covenant before the LORD, to follow the LORD and to keep His commandments and His testimonies and His statutes, with all *his* heart and all *his* soul, to perform the words of this covenant that were written in this book. And all the people took a stand for the covenant. 4 And the king commanded Hilkiah the high priest, the priests of the second order, and the doorkeepers, to bring out of the temple of the LORD all the articles that were made for Baal, for Asherah, and for all the host of heaven; and he burned them outside Jerusalem in the fields of Kidron, and carried their ashes to Bethel. 5 Then he removed the idolatrous priests whom the kings of Judah had ordained to burn incense on the high places in the cities of Judah and in the places all around Jerusalem, and those who burned incense to Baal, to the sun, to the moon, to the constellations, and to all the host of heaven. 6 And he brought out the wooden image from the house of the LORD, to the Brook Kidron outside Jerusalem, burned it at the Brook Kidron and ground *it* to ashes, and threw its ashes on the graves of the common people. 7 Then he tore down the *ritual* booths of the perverted persons that *were* in the house of the LORD, where the women wove hangings for the wooden

image. 8 And he brought all the priests from the cities of Judah, and defiled the high places where the priests had burned incense, from Geba to Beersheba; also he broke down the high places at the gates which *were* at the entrance of the Gate of Joshua the governor of the city, which *were* to the left of the city gate. 9 Nevertheless the priests of the high places did not come up to the altar of the LORD in Jerusalem, but they ate unleavened bread among their brethren.

10 And he defiled Topheth, which *is* in the Valley of the Son of Hinnom, that no man might make his son or his daughter pass through the fire to Molech. 11 Then he removed the horses that the kings of Judah had dedicated to the sun, at the entrance to the house of the LORD, by the chamber of Nathan-Melech, the officer who *was* in the court; and he burned the chariots of the sun with fire. 12 The altars that *were* on the roof, the upper chamber of Ahaz, which the kings of Judah had made, and the altars which Manasseh had made in the two courts of the house of the LORD, the king broke down and pulverized there, and threw their dust into the Brook Kidron. 13 Then the king defiled the high places that *were* east of Jerusalem, which *were* on the south of the Mount of Corruption, which Solomon king of Israel had built for Ashtoreth the abomination of the Sidonians, for Chemosh the abomination of the Moabites, and for Milcom the abomination of the people of Ammon. 14 And he broke in pieces the *sacred* pillars and cut down the wooden images, and filled their places with the bones of men.

15 Moreover the altar that *was* at Bethel, *and* the high place which Jeroboam the son of Nebat, who made Israel sin, had made, both that altar and the high place he broke down; and he burned the high place *and* crushed *it* to powder, and burned the wooden image. 16 As Josiah turned, he saw the tombs that *were* there on the mountain. And he sent and took the bones out of the tombs and burned *them* on the altar, and defiled it according to the word of the LORD which the man of God proclaimed, who proclaimed these words. 17 Then he said, "What gravestone *is* this that I see?"

So the men of the city told him, "*It is* the tomb of the man of God who came from Judah and proclaimed these things which you have done against the altar of Bethel."

18 And he said, "Let him alone; let no one move his bones." So they let his bones

alone, with the bones of the prophet who came from Samaria.

19 Now Josiah also took away all the shrines of the high places that *were* in the cities of Samaria, which the kings of Israel had made to provoke the Lord to anger; and he did to them according to all the deeds he had done in Bethel. 20 He executed all the priests of the high places who *were* there, on the altars, and burned men's bones on them; and he returned to Jerusalem.

21 Then the king commanded all the people, saying, "Keep the Passover to the Lord your God, as *it is* written in this Book of the Covenant." 22 Such a Passover surely had never been held since the days of the judges who judged Israel, nor in all the days of the kings of Israel and the kings of Judah. 23 But in the eighteenth year of King Josiah this Passover was held before the Lord in Jerusalem. 24 Moreover Josiah put away those who consulted mediums and spiritists, the household gods and idols, all the abominations that were seen in the land of Judah and in Jerusalem, that he might perform the words of the law which were written in the book that Hilkiah the priest found in the house of the Lord. 25 Now before him there was no king like him, who turned to the Lord with all his heart, with all his soul, and with all his might, according to all the Law of Moses; nor after him did *any* arise like him.

26 Nevertheless the Lord did not turn from the fierceness of His great wrath, with which His anger was aroused against Judah, because of all the provocations with which Manasseh had provoked Him. 27 And the Lord said, "I will also remove Judah from My sight, as I have removed Israel, and will cast off this city Jerusalem which I have chosen, and the house of which I said, 'My name shall be there.'"

28 Now the rest of the acts of Josiah, and all that he did, *are* they not written in the book of the chronicles of the kings of Judah? 29 In his days Pharaoh Necho king of Egypt went to the aid of the king of Assyria, to the River Euphrates; and King Josiah went against him. And *Pharaoh Necho* killed him at Megiddo when he confronted him. 30 Then his servants moved his body in a chariot from Megiddo, brought him to Jerusalem, and buried him in his own tomb. And the people of the land took Jehoahaz the son of Josiah, anointed him, and made him king in his father's place.

31 Jehoahaz *was* twenty-three years old when he became king, and he reigned three months in Jerusalem. His mother's name

was Hamutal the daughter of Jeremiah of Libnah. 32 And he did evil in the sight of the Lord, according to all that his fathers had done. 33 Now Pharaoh Necho put him in prison at Riblah in the land of Hamath, that he might not reign in Jerusalem; and he imposed on the land a tribute of one hundred talents of silver and a talent of gold. 34 Then Pharaoh Necho made Eliakim the son of Josiah king in place of his father Josiah, and changed his name to Jehoiakim. And *Pharaoh* took Jehoahaz and went to Egypt, and he died there.

35 So Jehoiakim gave the silver and gold to Pharaoh; but he taxed the land to give money according to the command of Pharaoh; he exacted the silver and gold from the people of the land, from every one according to his assessment, to give *it* to Pharaoh Necho. 36 Jehoiakim *was* twenty-five years old when he became king, and he reigned eleven years in Jerusalem. His mother's name *was* Zebudah the daughter of Pedaiah of Rumah. 37 And he did evil in the sight of the Lord, according to all that his fathers had done.

24 IN his days Nebuchadnezzar king of Babylon came up, and Jehoiakim became his vassal *for* three years. Then he turned and rebelled against him. 2 And the Lord sent against him *raiding* bands of Chaldeans, bands of Syrians, bands of Moabites, and bands of the people of Ammon; He sent them against Judah to destroy it, according to the word of the Lord which He had spoken by His servants the prophets. 3 Surely at the commandment of the Lord *this* came upon Judah, to remove *them* from His sight because of the sins of Manasseh, according to all that he had done, 4 and also because of the innocent blood that he had shed; for he had filled Jerusalem with innocent blood, which the Lord would not pardon.

5 Now the rest of the acts of Jehoiakim, and all that he did, *are* they not written in the book of the chronicles of the kings of Judah? 6 So Jehoiakim rested with his fathers. Then Jehoiachin his son reigned in his place.

7 And the king of Egypt did not come out of his land anymore, for the king of Babylon had taken all that belonged to the king of Egypt from the Brook of Egypt to the River Euphrates.

8 Jehoiachin *was* eighteen years old when he became king, and he reigned in Jerusalem three months. His mother's name *was* Nehushta the daughter of Elnathan of Jerusalem. 9 And he did evil in the sight of the

LORD, according to all that his father had done.

10 At that time the servants of Nebuchadnezzar king of Babylon came up against Jerusalem, and the city was besieged. 11 And Nebuchadnezzar king of Babylon came against the city, as his servants were besieging it. 12 Then Jehoiachin king of Judah, his mother, his servants, his princes, and his officers went out to the king of Babylon; and the king of Babylon, in the eighth year of his reign, took him prisoner.

13 And he carried out from there all the treasures of the house of the LORD and the treasures of the king's house, and he cut in pieces all the articles of gold which Solomon king of Israel had made in the temple of the LORD, as the LORD had said. 14 Also he carried into captivity all Jerusalem: all the captains and all the mighty men of valor, ten thousand captives, and all the craftsmen and smiths. None remained except the poorest people of the land. 15 And he carried Jehoiachin captive to Babylon. The king's mother, the king's wives, his officers, and the mighty of the land he carried into captivity from Jerusalem to Babylon. 16 All the valiant men, seven thousand, and craftsmen and smiths, one thousand, all *who were* strong *and* fit for war, these the king of Babylon brought captive to Babylon.

17 Then the king of Babylon made Mattaniah, *Jehoiachin's* uncle, king in his place, and changed his name to Zedekiah.

18 Zedekiah *was* twenty-one years old when he became king, and he reigned eleven years in Jerusalem. His mother's name *was* Hamutal the daughter of Jeremiah of Libnah. 19 He also did evil in the sight of the LORD, according to all that Jehoiakim had done. 20 For because of the anger of the LORD *this* happened in Jerusalem and Judah, that He finally cast them out from His presence. Then Zedekiah rebelled against the king of Babylon.

PSALM 74:18–23

18 REMEMBER this, *that* the enemy has reproached, O LORD,
And *that* a foolish people has blasphemed Your name.
19 Oh, do not deliver the life of Your turtledove to the wild beast!
Do not forget the life of Your poor forever.
20 Have respect to the covenant;
For the dark places of the earth are full of the haunts of cruelty.

21 Oh, do not let the oppressed return ashamed!
Let the poor and needy praise Your name.
22 Arise, O God, plead Your own cause;
Remember how the foolish man reproaches You daily.
23 Do not forget the voice of Your enemies;
The tumult of those who rise up against You increases continually.

PROVERBS 19:3

3 THE foolishness of a man twists his way,
And his heart frets against the LORD.

Fretting springs from a determination to get our own way. (UTMOST)

ACTS 2:22–47

"MEN of Israel, hear these words: Jesus of Nazareth, a Man attested by God to you by miracles, wonders, and signs which God did through Him in your midst, as you yourselves also know— 23 Him, being delivered by the determined purpose and foreknowledge of God, you have taken by lawless hands, have crucified, and put to death; 24 whom God raised up, having loosed the pains of death, because it was not possible that He should be held by it. 25 For David says concerning Him:

'I foresaw the LORD always before my face,
For He is at my right hand, that I may not be shaken.
26 Therefore my heart rejoiced, and my tongue was glad;
Moreover my flesh also will rest in hope.
27 For You will not leave my soul in Hades,
Nor will You allow Your Holy One to see corruption.
28 You have made known to me the ways of life;
You will make me full of joy in Your presence.'

29 "Men *and* brethren, let *me* speak freely to you of the patriarch David, that he is

both dead and buried, and his tomb is with us to this day. 30 Therefore, being a prophet, and knowing that God had sworn with an oath to him that of the fruit of his body, according to the flesh, He would raise up the Christ to sit on his throne, 31 he, foreseeing this, spoke concerning the resurrection of the Christ, that His soul was not left in Hades, nor did His flesh see corruption. 32 This Jesus God has raised up, of which we are all witnesses. 33 Therefore being exalted to the right hand of God, and having received from the Father the promise of the Holy Spirit, He poured out this which you now see and hear.

34 "For David did not ascend into the heavens, but he says himself:

'The LORD said to my Lord,
"Sit at My right hand,
35 Till I make Your enemies Your
footstool." '

36 "Therefore let all the house of Israel know assuredly that God has made this Jesus, whom you crucified, both Lord and Christ."

---

*T*he New Testament idea is that Jesus Christ is the absolute Lord over His disciples.   (SEND I YOU)

---

37 Now when they heard *this,* they were cut to the heart, and said to Peter and the rest of the apostles, "Men *and* brethren, what shall we do?"

38 Then Peter said to them, "Repent, and let every one of you be baptized in the name of Jesus Christ for the remission of sins; and you shall receive the gift of the Holy Spirit. 39 For the promise is to you and to your children, and to all who are afar off, as many as the Lord our God will call."

40 And with many other words he testified and exhorted them, saying, "Be saved from this perverse generation." 41 Then those who gladly received his word were baptized; and that day about three thousand souls were added *to them.* 42 And they continued steadfastly in the apostles' doctrine and fellowship, in the breaking of bread, and in prayers. 43 Then fear came upon every soul, and many wonders and signs were done through the apostles. 44 Now all who believed were together, and had all things in common, 45 and sold their possessions and goods, and divided them among all, as anyone had need.

46 So continuing daily with one accord in the temple, and breaking bread from house to house, they ate their food with gladness and simplicity of heart, 47 praising God and having favor with all the people. And the Lord added to the church daily those who were being saved.

◆◆◆◆

---

*Reading 169—*Give the Best You Have
Acts 3:6

A s we draw on the grace of God He increases voluntary poverty all along the line. Always give the best you have got every time; never think about who you are giving it to, let other people take it or leave it as they choose. Pour out the best you have, and always be poor. Never reserve anything; never be diplomatic and careful about the treasure God gives.   (*APPROVED*)

"Give to him who asks you." Why do we always make this mean money? Our Lord makes no mention of money. The blood of most of us seems to run in gold. The reason we make it mean money is because that is where our heart is. Peter said, "Silver and gold I do not have, but what I do have I give you." God grant we may understand that the spring of giving is not impulse nor inclination, but the inspiration of the Holy Spirit, I give because Jesus tells me to. . . .

The way Christians wriggle and twist and compromise over this verse springs from infidelity in the ruling providence of our heavenly Father. We enthrone common sense as God and say, "It is absurd; if I give to everyone that asks, every beggar in the place will be at my door." Try it. I have yet to find the man who obeyed Jesus Christ's command and did not realize that God restrains those who beg.   (*SERMON MT.*)

2 KINGS 25:1–30

NOW it came to pass in the ninth year of his reign, in the tenth month, on the tenth *day* of the month, *that* Nebuchadnezzar king of Babylon and all his army came against Jerusalem and encamped against it; and they built a siege wall against it all around. 2 So the city was besieged until the eleventh year of King Zedekiah. 3 By the ninth *day* of the *fourth* month the famine had become so severe in the city that there was no food for the people of the land.

4 Then the city wall was broken through, and all the men of war *fled* at night by way of the gate between two walls, which was by the king's garden, even though the Chaldeans *were* still encamped all around against the city. And *the king* went by way of the plain. 5 But the army of the Chaldeans pursued the king, and they overtook him in the plains of Jericho. All his army was scattered from him. 6 So they took the king and brought him up to the king of Babylon at Riblah, and they pronounced judgment on him. 7 Then they killed the sons of Zedekiah before his eyes, put out the eyes of Zedekiah, bound him with bronze fetters, and took him to Babylon.

8 And in the fifth month, on the seventh *day* of the month (which *was* the nineteenth year of King Nebuchadnezzar king of Babylon), Nebuzaradan the captain of the guard, a servant of the king of Babylon, came to Jerusalem. 9 He burned the house of the LORD and the king's house; all the houses of Jerusalem, that is, all the houses of the great, he burned with fire. 10 And all the army of the Chaldeans who *were with* the captain of the guard broke down the walls of Jerusalem all around.

11 Then Nebuzaradan the captain of the guard carried away captive the rest of the people *who* remained in the city and the defectors who had deserted to the king of Babylon, with the rest of the multitude. 12 But the captain of the guard left *some* of the poor of the land as vinedressers and farmers. 13 The bronze pillars that *were* in the house of the LORD, and the carts and the bronze Sea that *were* in the house of the LORD, the Chaldeans broke in pieces, and carried their bronze to Babylon. 14 They also took away the pots, the shovels,

the trimmers, the spoons, and all the bronze utensils with which the priests ministered. 15 The firepans and the basins, the things of solid gold and solid silver, the captain of the guard took away. 16 The two pillars, one Sea, and the carts, which Solomon had made for the house of the LORD, the bronze of all these articles was beyond measure. 17 The height of one pillar *was* eighteen cubits, and the capital on it *was* of bronze. The height of the capital was three cubits, and the network and pomegranates all around the capital were all of bronze. The second pillar was the same, with a network.

18 And the captain of the guard took Seraiah the chief priest, Zephaniah the second priest, and the three doorkeepers. 19 He also took out of the city an officer who had charge of the men of war, five men of the king's close associates who were found in the city, the chief recruiting officer of the army, who mustered the people of the land, and sixty men of the people of the land *who were* found in the city. 20 So Nebuzaradan, captain of the guard, took these and brought them to the king of Babylon at Riblah. 21 Then the king of Babylon struck them and put them to death at Riblah in the land of Hamath. Thus Judah was carried away captive from its own land.

22 Then he made Gedaliah the son of Ahikam, the son of Shaphan, governor over the people who remained in the land of Judah, whom Nebuchadnezzar king of Babylon had left. 23 Now when all the captains of the armies, they and *their* men, heard that the king of Babylon had made Gedaliah governor, they came to Gedaliah at Mizpah—Ishmael the son of Nethaniah, Johanan the son of Careah, Seraiah the son of Tanhumeth the Netophathite, and Jaazaniah the son of a Maachathite, they and their men. 24 And Gedaliah took an oath before them and their men, and said to them, "Do not be afraid of the servants of the Chaldeans. Dwell in the land and serve the king of Babylon, and it shall be well with you."

25 But it happened in the seventh month that Ishmael the son of Nethaniah, the son of Elishama, of the royal family, came with ten men and struck and killed Gedaliah, the Jews, as well as the Chaldeans who were

with him at Mizpah. 26 And all the people, small and great, and the captains of the armies, arose and went to Egypt; for they were afraid of the Chaldeans.

27 Now it came to pass in the thirty-seventh year of the captivity of Jehoiachin king of Judah, in the twelfth month, on the twenty-seventh *day* of the month, *that* Evil-Merodach king of Babylon, in the year that he began to reign, released Jehoiachin king of Judah from prison. 28 He spoke kindly to him, and gave him a more prominent seat than those of the kings who *were* with him in Babylon. 29 So Jehoiachin changed from his prison garments, and he ate bread regularly before the king all the days of his life. 30 And as for his provisions, *there was* a regular ration given him by the king, a portion for each day, all the days of his life.

PSALM 75:1–10

1 WE give thanks to You, O God, we give thanks!
For Your wondrous works declare *that* Your name is near.

2 "When I choose the proper time,
I will judge uprightly.

3 The earth and all its inhabitants are dissolved;
I set up its pillars firmly.   Selah

4 "I said to the boastful, 'Do not deal boastfully,'
And to the wicked, 'Do not lift up the horn.

5 Do not lift up your horn on high;
Do *not* speak with a stiff neck.'"

6 For exaltation *comes* neither from the east
Nor from the west nor from the south.

7 But God *is* the Judge:
He puts down one,
And exalts another.

8 For in the hand of the LORD *there is* a cup,
And the wine is red;
It is fully mixed, and He pours it out;
Surely its dregs shall all the wicked of the earth
Drain *and* drink down.

9 But I will declare forever,
I will sing praises to the God of Jacob.

10 "All the horns of the wicked I will also cut off,

But the horns of the righteous shall be exalted."

PROVERBS 19:4, 5

4 WEALTH makes many friends,
But the poor is separated from his friend.

5 A false witness will not go unpunished,
And *he who* speaks lies will not escape.

ACTS 3:1–26

NOW Peter and John went up together to the temple at the hour of prayer, the ninth *hour.* 2 And a certain man lame from his mother's womb was carried, whom they laid daily at the gate of the temple which is called Beautiful, to ask alms from those who entered the temple; 3 who, seeing Peter and John about to go into the temple, asked for alms. 4 And fixing his eyes on him, with John, Peter said, "Look at us." 5 So he gave them his attention, expecting to receive something from them. 6 Then Peter said, "Silver and gold I do not have, but what I do have I give you: In the name of Jesus Christ of Nazareth, rise up and walk." 7 And he took him by the right hand and lifted *him* up, and immediately his feet and ankle bones received strength. 8 So he, leaping up, stood and walked and entered the temple with them—walking, leaping, and praising God. 9 And all the people saw him walking and praising God. 10 Then they knew that it was he who sat begging alms at the Beautiful Gate of the temple; and they were filled with wonder and amazement at what had happened to him.

11 Now as the lame man who was healed held on to Peter and John, all the people ran together to them in the porch which is called Solomon's, greatly amazed. 12 So when Peter saw *it,* he responded to the people: "Men of Israel, why do you marvel at this? Or why look so intently at us, as though by our own power or godliness we had made this man walk? 13 The God of Abraham, Isaac, and Jacob, the God of our fathers, glorified His Servant Jesus, whom you delivered up and denied in the presence of Pilate, when he was determined to let *Him* go. 14 But you denied the Holy One and the Just, and asked for a murderer to be granted to you, 15 and killed the Prince of life, whom God raised from the dead, of which we are witnesses. 16 And His name, through faith in His name, has made

this man strong, whom you see and know. Yes, the faith which *comes* through Him has given him this perfect soundness in the presence of you all.

17 "Yet now, brethren, I know that you did *it* in ignorance, as *did* also your rulers. 18 But those things which God foretold by the mouth of all His prophets, that the Christ would suffer, He has thus fulfilled. 19 Repent therefore and be converted, that your sins may be blotted out, so that times of refreshing may come from the presence of the Lord, 20 and that He may send Jesus Christ, who was preached to you before, 21 whom heaven must receive until the times of restoration of all things, which God has spoken by the mouth of all His holy prophets since the world began. 22 For Moses truly said to the fathers, 'The LORD your God will raise up for you a Prophet like me from your brethren. Him you shall hear

A witness is one who has deliberately given up his life to the ownership of another. (SEND I YOU)

in all things, whatever He says to you. 23 And it shall be *that* every soul who will not hear that Prophet shall be utterly destroyed from among the people.' 24 Yes, and all the prophets, from Samuel and those who follow, as many as have spoken, have also foretold these days. 25 You are sons of the prophets, and of the covenant which God made with our fathers, saying to Abraham, 'And in your seed all the families of the earth shall be blessed.' 26 To you first, God, having raised up His Servant Jesus, sent Him to bless you, in turning away every one *of you* from your iniquities."

◆◆◆

Reading 170—Missing It
Acts 4:18

We have, as Christian disciples, to continually recognize that much of what is called Christianity today is not the Christianity of the New Testament; it is distinctly different in generation and manifestation. Jesus is not the fountainhead of modern Christianity; He is scarcely thought about. Christian preachers, Sunday School teachers, religious books, all without any apology patronize Jesus Christ and put Him on one side. We have to learn that to stand true to Jesus Christ's point of view means ostracism, the ostracism that was brought on Him; most of us know nothing whatever about it. The modern view looks upon human nature as pathetic: men and women are poor ignorant babes in the wood who have lost themselves. Jesus Christ's view is totally different, He does not look on men and women as babes in the wood, but as sinners who need saving, and the modern mind detests His view. Our Lord's teaching is based on something we violently hate, namely His doctrine of sin; we do not believe it unless we have had a radical dealing with God on the line of His teaching.

Remember that a disciple is committed to much more than belief in Jesus; he is committed to his Lord's view of the world, of men, of God and of sin. Take stock of your views and compare them with the New Testament, and never get tricked into thinking that the Bible does not mean what it says when it disagrees with you. Disagree with what our Lord says by all means if you like, but never say that the Bible does not mean what it says. (GOOD)

1 CHRONICLES 1:1—2:55

ADAM, Seth, Enosh, 2 Cainan, Mahalalel, Jared, 3 Enoch, Methuselah, Lamech, 4 Noah, Shem, Ham, and Japheth.

5 The sons of Japheth *were* Gomer, Magog, Madai, Javan, Tubal, Meshech, and Tiras. 6 The sons of Gomer *were* Ashkenaz, Diphath, and Togarmah. 7 The sons of Javan *were* Elishah, Tarshishah, Kittim, and Rodanim.

8 The sons of Ham *were* Cush, Mizraim, Put, and Canaan. 9 The sons of Cush *were* Seba, Havilah, Sabta, Raama, and Sabtecha. The sons of Raama *were* Sheba and Dedan. 10 Cush begot Nimrod; he began to be a mighty one on the earth. 11 Mizraim begot Ludim, Anamim, Lehabim, Naphtuhim, 12 Pathrusim, Casluhim (from whom came the Philistines and the Caphtorim). 13 Canaan begot Sidon, his firstborn, and Heth; 14 the Jebusite, the Amorite, and the Girgashite; 15 the Hivite, the Arkite, and the Sinite; 16 the Arvadite, the Zemarite, and the Hamathite.

17 The sons of Shem *were* Elam, Asshur, Arphaxad, Lud, Aram, Uz, Hul, Gether, and Meshech. 18 Arphaxad begot Shelah, and Shelah begot Eber. 19 To Eber were born two sons: the name of one *was* Peleg, for in his days the earth was divided; and his brother's name *was* Joktan. 20 Joktan begot Almodad, Sheleph, Hazarmaveth, Jerah, 21 Hadoram, Uzal, Diklah, 22 Ebal, Abimael, Sheba, 23 Ophir, Havilah, and Jobab. All these *were* the sons of Joktan.

24 Shem, Arphaxad, Shelah, 25 Eber, Peleg, Reu, 26 Serug, Nahor, Terah, 27 and Abram, who *is* Abraham. 28 The sons of Abraham *were* Isaac and Ishmael.

29 These *are* their genealogies: The firstborn of Ishmael *was* Nebajoth; then Kedar, Adbeel, Mibsam, 30 Mishma, Dumah, Massa, Hadad, Tema, 31 Jetur, Naphish, and Kedemah. These *were* the sons of Ishmael.

32 Now the sons born to Keturah, Abraham's concubine, *were* Zimran, Jokshan, Medan, Midian, Ishbak, and Shuah. The sons of Jokshan *were* Sheba and Dedan. 33 The sons of Midian *were* Ephah, Epher, Hanoch, Abida, and Eldaah. All these were the children of Keturah.

34 And Abraham begot Isaac. The sons of Isaac *were* Esau and Israel. 35 The sons of Esau *were* Eliphaz, Reuel, Jeush, Jaalam, and Korah. 36 And the sons of Eliphaz *were* Teman, Omar, Zephi, Gatam, *and* Kenaz; and *by* Timna, Amalek. 37 The sons of Reuel *were* Nahath, Zerah, Shammah, and Mizzah.

38 The sons of Seir *were* Lotan, Shobal, Zibeon, Anah, Dishon, Ezer, and Dishan. 39 And the sons of Lotan *were* Hori and Homam; Lotan's sister *was* Timna. 40 The sons of Shobal *were* Alian, Manahath, Ebal, Shephi, and Onam. The sons of Zibeon *were* Ajah and Anah. 41 The son of Anah *was* Dishon. The sons of Dishon *were* Hamran, Eshban, Ithran, and Cheran. 42 The sons of Ezer *were* Bilhan, Zaavan, *and* Jaakan. The sons of Dishan *were* Uz and Aran.

43 Now these *were* the kings who reigned in the land of Edom before a king reigned over the children of Israel: Bela the son of Beor, and the name of his city was Dinhabah. 44 And when Bela died, Jobab the son of Zerah of Bozrah reigned in his place. 45 When Jobab died, Husham of the land of the Temanites reigned in his place. 46 And when Husham died, Hadad the son of Bedad, who attacked Midian in the field of Moab, reigned in his place. The name of his city *was* Avith. 47 When Hadad died, Samlah of Masrekah reigned in his place. 48 And when Samlah died, Saul of Rehoboth-by-the-River reigned in his place. 49 When Saul died, Baal-Hanan the son of Achbor reigned in his place. 50 And when Baal-Hanan died, Hadad reigned in his place; and the name of his city *was* Pai. His wife's name was Mehetabel the daughter of Matred, the daughter of Mezahab. 51 Hadad died also. And the chiefs of Edom were Chief Timnah, Chief Aliah, Chief Jetheth, 52 Chief Aholibamah, Chief Elah, Chief Pinon, 53 Chief Kenaz, Chief Teman, Chief Mibzar, 54 Chief Magdiel, and Chief Iram. These *were* the chiefs of Edom.

2 THESE *were* the sons of Israel: Reuben, Simeon, Levi, Judah, Issachar, Zebulun, 2 Dan, Joseph, Benjamin, Naphtali, Gad, and Asher.

3 The sons of Judah *were* Er, Onan, and Shelah. *These* three were born to him by the daughter of Shua, the Canaanitess. Er, the firstborn of Judah, was wicked in the sight of the LORD; so He killed him. 4 And Tamar, his daughter-in-law, bore him Perez and Zerah. All the sons of Judah *were* five.

5 The sons of Perez *were* Hezron and Hamul. 6 The sons of Zerah *were* Zimri, Ethan, Heman, Calcol, and Dara—five of them in all.

7 The son of Carmi *was* Achar, the troubler of Israel, who transgressed in the accursed thing.

8 The son of Ethan *was* Azariah.

9 Also the sons of Hezron who were born

to him *were* Jerahmeel, Ram, and Chelubai. 10 Ram begot Amminadab, and Amminadab begot Nahshon, leader of the children of Judah; 11 Nahshon begot Salma, and Salma begot Boaz; 12 Boaz begot Obed, and Obed begot Jesse; 13 Jesse begot Eliab his firstborn, Abinadab the second, Shimea the third, 14 Nethanel the fourth, Raddai the fifth, 15 Ozem the sixth, *and* David the seventh.

16 Now their sisters *were* Zeruiah and Abigail. And the sons of Zeruiah *were* Abishai, Joab, and Asahel—three. 17 Abigail bore Amasa; and the father of Amasa *was* Jether the Ishmaelite.

18 Caleb the son of Hezron had children by Azubah, *his* wife, and by Jerioth. Now these were her sons: Jesher, Shobab, and Ardon. 19 When Azubah died, Caleb took Ephrath as his wife, who bore him Hur. 20 And Hur begot Uri, and Uri begot Bezalel.

21 Now afterward Hezron went in to the daughter of Machir the father of Gilead, whom he married when he *was* sixty years old; and she bore him Segub. 22 Segub begot Jair, who had twenty-three cities in the land of Gilead. 23 (Geshur and Syria took from them the towns of Jair, with Kenath and its towns—sixty towns.) All these *belonged to* the sons of Machir the father of Gilead. 24 After Hezron died in Caleb Ephrathah, Hezron's wife Abijah bore him Ashhur the father of Tekoa.

25 The sons of Jerahmeel, the firstborn of Hezron, *were* Ram, the firstborn, and Bunah, Oren, Ozem, *and* Ahijah. 26 Jerahmeel had another wife, whose name was Atarah; she was the mother of Onam. 27 The sons of Ram, the firstborn of Jerahmeel, were Maaz, Jamin, and Eker. 28 The sons of Onam were Shammai and Jada. The sons of Shammai *were* Nadab and Abishur.

29 And the name of the wife of Abishur *was* Abihail, and she bore him Ahban and Molid. 30 The sons of Nadab *were* Seled and Appaim; Seled died without children. 31 The son of Appaim *was* Ishi, the son of Ishi *was* Sheshan, and Sheshan's son *was* Ahlai. 32 The sons of Jada, the brother of Shammai, *were* Jether and Jonathan; Jether died without children. 33 The sons of Jonathan *were* Peleth and Zaza. These were the sons of Jerahmeel.

34 Now Sheshan had no sons, only daughters. And Sheshan had an Egyptian servant whose name *was* Jarha. 35 Sheshan gave his daughter to Jarha his servant as wife, and she bore him Attai. 36 Attai begot Nathan, and Nathan begot Zabad;

37 Zabad begot Ephlal, and Ephlal begot Obed; 38 Obed begot Jehu, and Jehu begot Azariah; 39 Azariah begot Helez, and Helez begot Eleasah; 40 Eleasah begot Sismai, and Sismai begot Shallum; 41 Shallum begot Jekamiah, and Jekamiah begot Elishama.

42 The descendants of Caleb the brother of Jerahmeel *were* Mesha, his firstborn, who was the father of Ziph, and the sons of Mareshah the father of Hebron. 43 The sons of Hebron *were* Korah, Tappuah, Rekem, and Shema. 44 Shema begot Raham the father of Jorkoam, and Rekem begot Shammai. 45 And the son of Shammai *was* Maon, and Maon *was* the father of Beth Zur.

46 Ephah, Caleb's concubine, bore Haran, Moza, and Gazez; and Haran begot Gazez. 47 And the sons of Jahdai *were* Regem, Jotham, Geshan, Pelet, Ephah, and Shaaph.

48 Maachah, Caleb's concubine, bore Sheber and Tirhanah. 49 She also bore Shaaph the father of Madmannah, Sheva the father of Machbenah and the father of Gibea. And the daughter of Caleb *was* Achsah.

50 These were the descendants of Caleb: The sons of Hur, the firstborn of Ephrathah, *were* Shobal the father of Kirjath Jearim, 51 Salma the father of Bethlehem, *and* Hareph the father of Beth Gader.

52 And Shobal the father of Kirjath Jearim had descendants: Haroeh, *and* half of the families of Manuhoth. 53 The families of Kirjath Jearim *were* the Ithrites, the Puthites, the Shumathites, and the Mishraites. From these came the Zorathites and the Eshtaolites.

54 The sons of Salma *were* Bethlehem, the Netophathites, Atroth Beth Joab, half of the Manahethites, and the Zorites. 55 And the families of the scribes who dwelt at Jabez *were* the Tirathites, the Shimeathites, *and* the Suchathites. These *were* the Kenites who came from Hammath, the father of the house of Rechab.

PSALM 76:1–6

1   IN Judah God *is* known;
    His name *is* great in Israel.
2   In Salem also is His tabernacle,
    And His dwelling place in Zion.
3   There He broke the arrows of the bow,
    The shield and sword of battle.   Selah

4   You *are* more glorious and excellent
    Than the mountains of prey.
5   The stouthearted were plundered;
    They have sunk into their sleep;

And none of the mighty men have
found the use of their hands.
6   At Your rebuke, O God of Jacob,
Both the chariot and horse were cast
into a dead sleep.

PROVERBS 19:6, 7

6   MANY entreat the favor of the nobility,
And every man *is* a friend to one who
gives gifts.
7   All the brothers of the poor hate him;
How much more do his friends go far
from him!
He may pursue *them with* words, *yet*
they abandon *him.*

ACTS 4:1–22

NOW as they spoke to the people, the
priests, the captain of the temple, and the
Sadducees came upon them, 2 being greatly
disturbed that they taught the people and
preached in Jesus the resurrection from the
dead. 3 And they laid hands on them, and
put *them* in custody until the next day, for
it was already evening. 4 However, many
of those who heard the word believed; and
the number of the men came to be about
five thousand.
5 And it came to pass, on the next day,
that their rulers, elders, and scribes,
6 as well as Annas the high priest, Caiaphas,
John, and Alexander, and as many as were
of the family of the high priest, were gathered together at Jerusalem. 7 And when they
had set them in the midst, they asked, "By
what power or by what name have you
done this?"
8 Then Peter, filled with the Holy Spirit,
said to them, "Rulers of the people and
elders of Israel: 9 If we this day are judged
for a good deed *done* to a helpless man,
by what means he has been made well,
10 let it be known to you all, and to all

---

*The Holy Spirit never swamps our
personal spirit.*   (PERFECT)

---

the people of Israel, that by the name of
Jesus Christ of Nazareth, whom you crucified, whom God raised from the dead, by
Him this man stands here before you whole.
11 This is the 'stone which was rejected by
you builders, which has become the chief
cornerstone.' 12 Nor is there salvation in
any other, for there is no other name under
heaven given among men by which we must
be saved."
13 Now when they saw the boldness of
Peter and John, and perceived that they
were uneducated and untrained men, they
marveled. And they realized that they had
been with Jesus. 14 And seeing the man who
had been healed standing with them, they
could say nothing against it. 15 But when
they had commanded them to go aside out
of the council, they conferred among themselves, 16 saying, "What shall we do to these
men? For, indeed, that a notable miracle
has been done through them *is* evident to
all who dwell in Jerusalem, and we cannot
deny *it.* 17 But so that it spreads no further
among the people, let us severely threaten
them, that from now on they speak to no
man in this name."
18 So they called them and commanded
them not to speak at all nor teach in the
name of Jesus. 19 But Peter and John answered and said to them, "Whether it is
right in the sight of God to listen to you
more than to God, you judge. 20 For we
cannot but speak the things which we have
seen and heard." 21 So when they had further threatened them, they let them go, finding no way of punishing them, because of
the people, since they all glorified God for
what had been done. 22 For the man was
over forty years old on whom this miracle
of healing had been performed.

◆◆◆◆

---

*Reading 171—*The Dependent Life
Acts 4:32

Try and develop a holy life in private, and you find it cannot be done.
Individuals can only live the true life when they are dependent on one
another. After the Resurrection our Lord would not allow Mary to hold a
spiritual experience for herself, she must get into contact with the disciples

and convey a message to them—"Do not cling to Me, . . . but go to My brethren and say to them, 'I am ascending to My Father and your Father, and *to* My God and your God.' " After Peter's denial the isolation of misery would inevitably have seized on him and made him want to retire in the mood of "I can never forgive myself," had not our Lord forestalled this by giving him something positive to do—"and when you have returned to *Me*, strengthen your brethren." Immediately you try to develop holiness alone and fix your eyes on your own whiteness, you lose the whole meaning of Christianity. The Holy Spirit makes a man fix his eyes on his Lord and on intense activity for others. In the early Middle Ages people had the idea that Christianity meant living a holy life apart from the world and its sociability, apart from its work and citizenship. That type of holiness is foreign to the New Testament; it cannot be reconciled with the records of the life of Jesus. The people of His day called Him "a friend of tax collectors and sinners" because He spent so much time with them.   (*Bib. Ethics*)

1 CHRONICLES 3:1—4:43

NOW these were the sons of David who were born to him in Hebron: The firstborn *was* Amnon, by Ahinoam the Jezreelitess; the second, Daniel, by Abigail the Carmelitess; 2 the third, Absalom the son of Maacah, the daughter of Talmai, king of Geshur; the fourth, Adonijah the son of Haggith; 3 the fifth, Shephatiah, by Abital; the sixth, Ithream, by his wife Eglah.

4 *These* six were born to him in Hebron. There he reigned seven years and six months, and in Jerusalem he reigned thirty-three years. 5 And these were born to him in Jerusalem: Shimea, Shobab, Nathan, and Solomon—four by Bathshua the daughter of Ammiel. 6 Also *there* were Ibhar, Elishama, Eliphelet, 7 Nogah, Nepheg, Japhia, 8 Elishama, Eliada, and Eliphelet—nine *in all.* 9 *These were* all the sons of David, besides the sons of the concubines, and Tamar their sister.

10 Solomon's son *was* Rehoboam; Abijah *was* his son, Asa his son, Jehoshaphat his son, 11 Joram his son, Ahaziah his son, Joash his son, 12 Amaziah his son, Azariah his son, Jotham his son, 13 Ahaz his son, Hezekiah his son, Manasseh his son, 14 Amon his son, *and* Josiah his son. 15 The sons of Josiah *were* Johanan the firstborn, the second Jehoiakim, the third Zedekiah, and the fourth Shallum. 16 The sons of Jehoiakim *were* Jeconiah his son *and* Zedekiah his son.

17 And the sons of Jeconiah *were* Assir, Shealtiel his son, 18 *and* Malchiram, Pedaiah, Shenazzar, Jecamiah, Hoshama, and Nedabiah. 19 The sons of Pedaiah *were* Zerubbabel and Shimei. The sons of Zerubbabel *were* Meshullam, Hananiah, Shelomith their sister, 20 and Hashubah, Ohel, Bere-

chiah, Hasadiah, and Jushab-Hesed—five *in all.*

21 The sons of Hananiah *were* Pelatiah and Jeshaiah, the sons of Rephaiah, the sons of Arnan, the sons of Obadiah, and the sons of Shechaniah. 22 The son of Shechaniah was Shemaiah. The sons of Shemaiah *were* Hattush, Igal, Bariah, Neariah, and Shaphat—six *in all.* 23 The sons of Neariah *were* Elioenai, Hezekiah, and Azrikam—three *in all.* 24 The sons of Elioenai *were* Hodaviah, Eliashib, Pelaiah, Akkub, Johanan, Delaiah, and Anani—seven *in all.*

4 THE sons of Judah *were* Perez, Hezron, Carmi, Hur, and Shobal. 2 And Reaiah the son of Shobal begot Jahath, and Jahath begot Ahumai and Lahad. These *were* the families of the Zorathites. 3 These *were* the sons *of the father* of Etam: Jezreel, Ishma, and Idbash; and the name of their sister *was* Hazelelponi; 4 and Penuel *was* the father of Gedor, and Ezer *was the* father of Hushah.

These *were* the sons of Hur, the firstborn of Ephrathah the father of Bethlehem.

5 And Ashhur the father of Tekoa had two wives, Helah and Naarah. 6 Naarah bore him Ahuzzam, Hepher, Temeni, and Haahashtari. These *were* the sons of Naarah. 7 The sons of Helah *were* Zereth, Zohar, and Ethnan; 8 and Koz begot Anub, Zobebah, and the families of Aharhel the son of Harum.

9 Now Jabez was more honorable than his brothers, and his mother called his name Jabez, saying, "Because I bore *him* in pain." 10 And Jabez called on the God of Israel saying, "Oh, that You would bless me indeed, and enlarge my territory, that Your hand would be with me, and that You would keep *me* from evil, that I may not

cause pain!" So God granted him what he requested.

11 Chelub the brother of Shuhah begot Mehir, who *was* the father of Eshton. 12 And Eshton begot Beth-Rapha, Paseah, and Tehinnah the father of Ir-Nahash. These *were* the men of Rechah.

13 The sons of Kenaz *were* Othniel and Seraiah. The sons of Othniel *were* Hathath, 14 and Meonothai *who* begot Ophrah. Seraiah begot Joab the father of Ge Harashim, for they were craftsmen. 15 The sons of Caleb the son of Jephunneh *were* Iru, Elah, and Naam. The son of Elah *was* Kenaz. 16 The sons of Jehallelel *were* Ziph, Ziphah, Tiria, and Asarel. 17 The sons of Ezrah *were* Jether, Mered, Epher, and Jalon. And *Mered's wife bore* Miriam, Shammai, and Ishbah the father of Eshtemoa. 18 (His wife Jehudijah bore Jered the father of Gedor, Heber the father of Sochoh, and Jekuthiel the father of Zanoah.) And these were the sons of Bithiah the daughter of Pharaoh, whom Mered took.

19 The sons of Hodiah's wife, the sister of Naham, *were* the fathers of Keilah the Garmite and of Eshtemoa the Maachathite. 20 And the sons of Shimon *were* Amnon, Rinnah, Ben-Hanan, and Tilon. And the sons of Ishi *were* Zoheth and Ben-Zoheth.

21 The sons of Shelah the son of Judah *were* Er the father of Lecah, Laadah the father of Mareshah, and the families of the house of the linen workers of the house of Ashbea; 22 also Jokim, the men of Chozeba, and Joash; Saraph, who ruled in Moab, and Jashubi-Lehem. Now the records are ancient. 23 These *were* the potters and those who dwell at Netaim and Gederah; there they dwelt with the king for his work.

24 The sons of Simeon *were* Nemuel, Jamin, Jarib, Zerah, *and* Shaul, 25 Shallum his son, Mibsam his son, and Mishma his son. 26 And the sons of Mishma *were* Hamuel his son, Zacchur his son, and Shimei his son. 27 Shimei had sixteen sons and six daughters; but his brothers did not have many children, nor did any of their families multiply as much as the children of Judah.

28 They dwelt at Beersheba, Moladah, Hazar Shual, 29 Bilhah, Ezem, Tolad, 30 Bethuel, Hormah, Ziklag, 31 Beth Marcaboth, Hazar Susim, Beth Biri, and at Shaaraim. These *were* their cities until the reign of David. 32 And their villages *were* Etam, Ain, Rimmon, Tochen, and Ashan— five cities— 33 and all the villages that *were* around these cities as far as Baal. These *were* their dwelling places, and they maintained their genealogy: 34 Meshobab, Jam-

lech, and Joshah the son of Amaziah; 35 Joel, and Jehu the son of Joshibiah, the son of Seraiah, the son of Asiel; 36 Elioenai, Jaakobah, Jeshohaiah, Asaiah, Adiel, Jesimiel, and Benaiah; 37 Ziza the son of Shiphi, the son of Allon, the son of Jedaiah, the son of Shimri, the son of Shemaiah— 38 these mentioned by name *were* leaders in their families, and their father's house increased greatly.

39 So they went to the entrance of Gedor, as far as the east side of the valley, to seek pasture for their flocks. 40 And they found rich, good pasture, and the land *was* broad, quiet, and peaceful; for some Hamites formerly lived there.

41 These recorded by name came in the days of Hezekiah king of Judah; and they attacked their tents and the Meunites who were found there, and utterly destroyed them, as it is to this day. So they dwelt in their place, because *there was* pasture for their flocks there. 42 Now *some* of them, five hundred men of the sons of Simeon, went to Mount Seir, having as their captains Pelatiah, Neariah, Rephaiah, and Uzziel, the sons of Ishi. 43 And they defeated the rest of the Amalekites who had escaped. They have dwelt there to this day.

PSALM 76:7–12

7   YOU, Yourself, *are* to be feared;
     And who may stand in Your presence
     When once You are angry?
8   You caused judgment to be heard from
         heaven;
     The earth feared and was still,
9   When God arose to judgment,
     To deliver all the oppressed of the earth.
                                        Selah

10 Surely the wrath of man shall praise
         You;
     With the remainder of wrath You shall
         gird Yourself.

11 Make vows to the LORD your God, and
         pay *them;*
     Let all who are around Him bring
         presents to Him who ought to be
         feared.
12 He shall cut off the spirit of princes;
     He is awesome to the kings of the earth.

PROVERBS 19:8, 9

8   HE who gets wisdom loves his own
         soul;

He who keeps understanding will find good.

9   A false witness will not go unpunished,
And *he who* speaks lies shall perish.

ACTS 4:23–37

AND being let go, they went to their own *companions* and reported all that the chief priests and elders had said to them. 24 So when they heard that, they raised their voice to God with one accord and said: "Lord, You *are* God, who made heaven and earth and the sea, and all that is in them, 25 who by the mouth of Your servant David have said:

'Why did the nations rage,
    And the people plot vain things?
26 The kings of the earth took their
        stand,
    And the rulers were gathered
        together
    Against the LORD and against His
        Christ.'

27 "For truly against Your holy Servant Jesus, whom You anointed, both Herod and Pontius Pilate, with the Gentiles and the people of Israel, were gathered together 28 to do whatever Your hand and Your purpose determined before to be done. 29 Now, Lord, look on their threats, and grant to Your servants that with all boldness they may speak Your word, 30 by stretching out Your hand to heal, and that signs and wonders may be done through the name of Your holy Servant Jesus."

31 And when they had prayed, the place where they were assembled together was shaken; and they were all filled with the Holy Spirit, and they spoke the word of God with boldness.

There is only one thing we cannot imitate: We cannot imitate being full of the Holy Ghost.   (DISCIPLES)

---

32 Now the multitude of those who believed were of one heart and one soul; neither did anyone say that any of the things he possessed was his own, but they had all things in common. 33 And with great power the apostles gave witness to the resurrection of the Lord Jesus. And great grace was upon them all. 34 Nor was there anyone among them who lacked; for all who were possessors of lands or houses sold them, and brought the proceeds of the things that were sold, 35 and laid *them* at the apostles' feet; and they distributed to each as anyone had need.

36 And Joses, who was also named Barnabas by the apostles (which is translated Son of Encouragement), a Levite of the country of Cyprus, 37 having land, sold *it,* and brought the money and laid *it* at the apostles' feet.

◆◆◆◆

Reading 172—Speaking Your Belief
Acts 5:20

The revelation that perceives is that which recklessly states what it believes. When you stand up before your fellowmen and confess something about Jesus Christ, you feel you have no one to support you in the matter, but as you testify you begin to find the reality of your spiritual possessions, and there rushes into you the realization of a totally new life. "Be still, and know that I *am* God." When a man is able to state that he believes in God, it reacts on all his relationships. The thing that preserves a man from panic is his relationship to God; if he is only related to himself and to his own courage, there may come a moment when his courage gives out.

Some of us are living on too low a level, and remember, the door is shut on our side, not on God's. As soon as we will "say so," the door opens and the salvation for which we believe is ours in actual possession. Things only become clear as we say them. Too often we are like the child who will not do anything but murmur. We grouse and refuse to say the emancipating word which is within our reach all the time. As soon as we say the emancipating word, we undo the door and there rushes into us a higher and better life, and the revelation becomes real. "I must get out of this cabined, confined place"— then say the right word. If you have not received, ask; if you have not found, seek; if the door is shut, knock. (*PLACE HELP*)

1 CHRONICLES 5:1—6:81

NOW the sons of Reuben the firstborn of Israel—he *was* indeed the firstborn, but because he defiled his father's bed, his birthright was given to the sons of Joseph, the son of Israel, so that the genealogy is not listed according to the birthright; 2 yet Judah prevailed over his brothers, and from him *came* a ruler, although the birthright was Joseph's— 3 the sons of Reuben the firstborn of Israel were Hanoch, Pallu, Hezron, and Carmi.

4 The sons of Joel *were* Shemaiah his son, Gog his son, Shimei his son, 5 Micah his son, Reaiah his son, 6 and Beerah his son, whom Tiglath-Pileser king of Assyria carried into captivity. He *was* leader of the Reubenites. 7 And his brethren by their families, when the genealogy of their generations was registered: the chief, Jeiel, and Zechariah, 8 and Bela the son of Azaz, the son of Shema, the son of Joel, who dwelt in Aroer, as far as Nebo and Baal Meon. 9 Eastward they settled as far as the entrance of the wilderness this side of the River Euphrates, because their cattle had multiplied in the land of Gilead.

10 Now in the days of Saul they made war with the Hagrites, who fell by their hand; and they dwelt in their tents throughout the entire *area* east of Gilead.

11 And the children of Gad dwelt next to them in the land of Bashan as far as Salcah: 12 Joel *was* the chief, Shapham the next, then Jaanai and Shaphat in Bashan, 13 and their brethren of their father's house: Michael, Meshullam, Sheba, Jorai, Jachan, Zia, and Eber—seven *in all*. 14 These *were* the children of Abihail the son of Huri, the son of Jaroah, the son of Gilead, the son of Michael, the son of Jeshishai, the son of Jahdo, the son of Buz; 15 Ahi the son of Abdiel, the son of Guni, *was* chief of their father's house. 16 And *the Gadites* dwelt in Gilead, in Bashan and in its villages, and in all the common-lands of Sharon within their borders. 17 All these were registered by genealogies in the days of Jotham king of Judah, and in the days of Jeroboam king of Israel.

18 The sons of Reuben, the Gadites, and half the tribe of Manasseh *had* forty-four thousand seven hundred and sixty valiant men, men able to bear shield and sword, to shoot with the bow, and skillful in war, who went to war. 19 They made war with the Hagrites, Jetur, Naphish, and Nodab. 20 And they were helped against them, and the Hagrites were delivered into their hand, and all who *were* with them, for they cried out to God in the battle. He heeded their prayer, because they put their trust in Him.

Prayer is the battle. (ASK)

21 Then they took away their livestock— fifty thousand of their camels, two hundred and fifty thousand of their sheep, and two thousand of their donkeys—also one hundred thousand of their men; 22 for many fell dead, because the war *was* God's. And they dwelt in their place until the captivity.

23 So the children of the half-tribe of Manasseh dwelt in the land. Their *numbers* increased from Bashan to Baal Hermon, that is, to Senir, or Mount Hermon. 24 These *were* the heads of their fathers' houses: Epher, Ishi, Eliel, Azriel, Jeremiah, Hodaviah, and Jahdiel. They were mighty men of valor, famous men, *and* heads of their fathers' houses.

25 And they were unfaithful to the God of their fathers, and played the harlot after the gods of the peoples of the land, whom God had destroyed before them. 26 So the God of Israel stirred up the spirit of Pul king of Assyria, that is, Tiglath-Pileser king of Assyria. He carried the Reubenites, the Gadites, and the half-tribe of Manasseh into captivity. He took them to Halah, Habor, Hara, and the river of Gozan to this day.

6 THE sons of Levi *were* Gershon, Kohath, and Merari. 2 The sons of Kohath *were* Amram, Izhar, Hebron, and Uzziel. 3 The children of Amram *were* Aaron, Moses, and Miriam. And the sons of Aaron *were* Nadab, Abihu, Eleazar, and Ithamar.

4 Eleazar begot Phinehas, *and* Phinehas begot Abishua; 5 Abishua begot Bukki, and Bukki begot Uzzi; 6 Uzzi begot Zerahiah, and Zerahiah begot Meraioth; 7 Meraioth begot Amariah, and Amariah begot Ahitub; 8 Ahitub begot Zadok, and Zadok begot Ahimaaz; 9 Ahimaaz begot Azariah, and Azariah begot Johanan; 10 Johanan begot Azariah (it was he who ministered as priest in the temple that Solomon built in Jerusalem); 11 Azariah begot Amariah, and Amariah begot Ahitub; 12 Ahitub begot Zadok, and Zadok begot Shallum; 13 Shallum begot Hilkiah, and Hilkiah begot Azariah; 14 Azariah begot Seraiah, and Seraiah begot Jehozadak. 15 Jehozadak went *into captivity* when the LORD carried Judah and Jerusalem into captivity by the hand of Nebuchadnezzar.

16 The sons of Levi *were* Gershon, Kohath, and Merari. 17 These are the names of the sons of Gershon: Libni and Shimei. 18 The sons of Kohath *were* Amram, Izhar, Hebron, and Uzziel. 19 The sons of Merari *were* Mahli and Mushi. Now these *are* the families of the Levites according to their fathers: 20 Of Gershon *were* Libni his son, Jahath his son, Zimmah his son, 21 Joah his son, Iddo his son, Zerah his son, *and* Jeatherai his son. 22 The sons of Kohath *were* Amminadab his son, Korah his son, Assir his son, 23 Elkanah his son, Ebiasaph his son, Assir his son, 24 Tahath his son, Uriel his son, Uzziah his son, and Shaul his son. 25 The sons of Elkanah *were* Amasai and Ahimoth. 26 *As for* Elkanah, the sons of Elkanah *were* Zophai his son, Nahath his son, 27 Eliab his son, Jeroham his son, *and* Elkanah his son. 28 The sons of Samuel *were Joel* the firstborn, and Abijah the second. 29 The sons of Merari *were* Mahli, Libni his son, Shimei his son, Uzzah his son, 30 Shimea his son, Haggiah his son, *and* Asaiah his son.

31 Now these are the men whom David appointed over the service of song in the house of the LORD, after the ark came to rest. 32 They were ministering with music before the dwelling place of the tabernacle of meeting, until Solomon had built the house of the LORD in Jerusalem, and they served in their office according to their order.

33 And these *are* the ones who ministered with their sons: Of the sons of the Kohathites *were* Heman the singer, the son of Joel, the son of Samuel, 34 the son of Elkanah, the son of Jeroham, the son of Eliel, the son of Toah, 35 the son of Zuph, the son of Elkanah, the son of Mahath, the son of Amasai, 36 the son of Elkanah, the son of Joel, the son of Azariah, the son of Zephaniah, 37 the son of Tahath, the son of Assir, the son of Ebiasaph, the son of Korah, 38 the son of Izhar, the son of Kohath, the son of Levi, the son of Israel. 39 And his brother Asaph, who stood at his right hand, *was* Asaph the son of Berachiah, the son of Shimea, 40 the son of Michael, the son of Baaseiah, the son of Malchijah, 41 the son of Ethni, the son of Zerah, the son of Adaiah, 42 the son of Ethan, the son of Zimmah, the son of Shimei, 43 the son of Jahath, the son of Gershon, the son of Levi.

44 Their brethren, the sons of Merari, on the left hand, *were* Ethan the son of Kishi, the son of Abdi, the son of Malluch, 45 the son of Hashabiah, the son of Amaziah, the son of Hilkiah, 46 the son of Amzi, the son of Bani, the son of Shamer, 47 the son of Mahli, the son of Mushi, the son of Merari, the son of Levi.

48 And their brethren, the Levites, *were* appointed to every kind of service of the tabernacle of the house of God.

49 But Aaron and his sons offered sacrifices on the altar of burnt offering and on the altar of incense, for all the work of the Most Holy *Place,* and to make atonement for Israel, according to all that Moses the servant of God had commanded. 50 Now these *are* the sons of Aaron: Eleazar his son, Phinehas his son, Abishua his son, 51 Bukki his son, Uzzi his son, Zerahiah his son, 52 Meraioth his son, Amariah his son, Ahitub his son, 53 Zadok his son, *and* Ahimaaz his son.

54 Now these *are* their dwelling places throughout their settlements in their territory, for they were *given* by lot to the sons of Aaron, of the family of the Kohathites: 55 They gave them Hebron in the land of Judah, with its surrounding common-lands. 56 But the fields of the city and its villages they gave to Caleb the son of Jephunneh. 57 And to the sons of Aaron they gave *one of* the cities of refuge, Hebron; also Libnah with its common-lands, Jattir, Eshtemoa with its common-lands, 58 Hilen with its common-lands, Debir with its common-lands, 59 Ashan with its common-lands, and Beth Shemesh with its common-lands. 60 And from the tribe of Benjamin: Geba with its common-lands, Alemeth with its common-lands, and Anathoth with its common-lands. All their cities among their families *were* thirteen.

61 To the rest of the family of the tribe of the Kohathites *they gave* by lot ten cities from half the tribe of Manasseh. 62 And to the sons of Gershon, throughout their

families, *they gave* thirteen cities from the tribe of Issachar, from the tribe of Asher, from the tribe of Naphtali, and from the tribe of Manasseh in Bashan. 63 To the sons of Merari, throughout their families, *they gave* twelve cities from the tribe of Reuben, from the tribe of Gad, and from the tribe of Zebulun. 64 So the children of Israel gave *these* cities with their common-lands to the Levites. 65 And they gave by lot from the tribe of the children of Judah, from the tribe of the children of Simeon, and from the tribe of the children of Benjamin these cities which are called by *their* names.

66 Now some of the families of the sons of Kohath *were given* cities as their territory from the tribe of Ephraim. 67 And they gave them *one of* the cities of refuge, Shechem with its common-lands, in the mountains of Ephraim, also Gezer with its common-lands, 68 Jokmeam with its common-lands, Beth Horon with its common-lands, 69 Aijalon with its common-lands, and Gath Rimmon with its common-lands. 70 And from the half-tribe of Manasseh: Aner with its common-lands and Bileam with its common-lands, for the rest of the family of the sons of Kohath.

71 From the family of the half-tribe of Manasseh the sons of Gershon *were given* Golan in Bashan with its common-lands and Ashtaroth with its common-lands. 72 And from the tribe of Issachar: Kedesh with its common-lands, Daberath with its common-lands, 73 Ramoth with its common-lands, and Anem with its common-lands. 74 And from the tribe of Asher: Mashal with its common-lands, Abdon with its common-lands, 75 Hukok with its common-lands, and Rehob with its common-lands. 76 And from the tribe of Naphtali: Kedesh in Galilee with its common-lands, Hammon with its common-lands, and Kirjathaim with its common-lands.

77 From the tribe of Zebulun the rest of the children of Merari *were given* Rimmon with its common-lands and Tabor with its common-lands. 78 And on the other side of the Jordan, across from Jericho, on the east side of the Jordan, *they were given* from the tribe of Reuben: Bezer in the wilderness with its common-lands, Jahzah with its common-lands, 79 Kedemoth with its common-lands, and Mephaath with its common-lands. 80 And from the tribe of Gad: Ramoth in Gilead with its common-lands, Mahanaim with its common-lands, 81 Heshbon with its common-lands, and Jazer with its common-lands.

PSALM 77:1–3

1 I cried out to God with my voice—
   To God with my voice;
   And He gave ear to me.
2 In the day of my trouble I sought the Lord;
   My hand was stretched out in the night without ceasing;
   My soul refused to be comforted.
3 I remembered God, and was troubled;
   I complained, and my spirit was overwhelmed.   Selah

PROVERBS 19:10–12

10 LUXURY is not fitting for a fool,
   Much less for a servant to rule over princes.

11 The discretion of a man makes him slow to anger,
   And his glory *is* to overlook a transgression.

12 The king's wrath *is* like the roaring of a lion,
   But his favor *is* like dew on the grass.

ACTS 5:1–21

BUT a certain man named Ananias, with Sapphira his wife, sold a possession. 2 And he kept back *part* of the proceeds, his wife also being aware *of it,* and brought a certain part and laid *it* at the apostles' feet. 3 But Peter said, "Ananias, why has Satan filled your heart to lie to the Holy Spirit and keep back *part* of the price of the land for yourself? 4 While it remained, was it not your own? And after it was sold, was it not in your own control? Why have you conceived this thing in your heart? You have not lied to men but to God."

Whatever we possess for ourselves is of the nature of sin.   (MORAL FOUND.)

---

5 Then Ananias, hearing these words, fell down and breathed his last. So great fear came upon all those who heard these things. 6 And the young men arose and wrapped him up, carried *him* out, and buried *him.*

7 Now it was about three hours later when his wife came in, not knowing what

had happened. 8 And Peter answered her, "Tell me whether you sold the land for so much?"

She said, "Yes, for so much."

9 Then Peter said to her, "How is it that you have agreed together to test the Spirit of the Lord? Look, the feet of those who have buried your husband *are* at the door, and they will carry you out." 10 Then immediately she fell down at his feet and breathed her last. And the young men came in and found her dead, and carrying *her* out, buried *her* by her husband. 11 So great fear came upon all the church and upon all who heard these things.

12 And through the hands of the apostles many signs and wonders were done among the people. And they were all with one accord in Solomon's Porch. 13 Yet none of the rest dared join them, but the people esteemed them highly. 14 And believers were increasingly added to the Lord, multitudes of both men and women, 15 so that they brought the sick out into the streets and laid *them* on beds and couches, that at least the shadow of Peter passing by might fall on some of them. 16 Also a multitude gathered from the surrounding cities to Jerusalem, bringing sick people and those who were tormented by unclean spirits, and they were all healed.

17 Then the high priest rose up, and all those who *were* with him (which is the sect of the Sadducees), and they were filled with indignation, 18 and laid their hands on the apostles and put them in the common prison. 19 But at night an angel of the Lord opened the prison doors and brought them out, and said, 20 "Go, stand in the temple and speak to the people all the words of this life."

21 And when they heard *that,* they entered the temple early in the morning and taught. But the high priest and those with him came and called the council together, with all the elders of the children of Israel, and sent to the prison to have them brought.

◆◆◆◆

Reading 173—Finding What Is Important
Acts 5:29–32

I s Jesus Christ's mind infallible, or is the modern Western mind infallible? The tendency abroad today is to think ourselves infallible, and the Bible a jumble up of the most extraordinary stuff, good stuff, but we cannot be expected to accept all its views. That means, we believe ourselves more likely to be infallible than Jesus Christ. We would repudiate this statement if made baldly, but we all act as if it were true, we all take for granted that Jesus Christ's teachings are nonsense; we treat them with respect and reverence, but we do not do anything else with them, we do not carry them out. . . .

Today we hold conferences and conventions and give reports and make our programs. None of these things were in the life of Jesus, and yet every minute of His life He realized that He was fulfilling the purpose of His Father (see John 9:4). How did He do it? By maintaining the one relationship, and it is that one relationship He insists on in His disciples, and it is the one we have lost in the rubbish of modern civilization. If we try and live the life Jesus Christ lived, modern civilization will fling us out like waste material; we are no good, we do not add anything to the hard cash of the times we live in, and the sooner we are flung out the better.   (GOOD)

---

1 CHRONICLES 7:1—8:40

THE sons of Issachar *were* Tola, Puah, Jashub, and Shimron—four *in all.* 2 The sons of Tola *were* Uzzi, Rephaiah, Jeriel, Jahmai, Jibsam, and Shemuel, heads of their father's house. *The sons* of Tola *were* mighty men of valor in their generations; their number in the days of David *was* twenty-two thousand six hundred. 3 The son of Uzzi *was* Izrahiah, and the sons of Izrahiah *were* Michael, Obadiah, Joel, and Ishiah. All five of them *were* chief men. 4 And with them, by their generations, according to their fathers' houses, *were* thirty-six thousand troops ready for war; for they had many wives and sons.

5 Now their brethren among all the families of Issachar *were* mighty men of valor, listed by their genealogies, eighty-seven thousand in all.

6 *The sons* of Benjamin *were* Bela, Becher, and Jediael—three *in all.* 7 The sons of Bela were Ezbon, Uzzi, Uzziel, Jerimoth, and Iri—five *in all.* They *were* heads of *their* fathers' houses, and they were listed by their genealogies, twenty-two thousand and thirty-four mighty men of valor.

8 The sons of Becher *were* Zemirah, Joash, Eliezer, Elioenai, Omri, Jerimoth, Abijah, Anathoth, and Alemeth. All these *are* the sons of Becher. 9 And they were recorded by genealogy according to their generations, heads of their fathers' houses, twenty thousand two hundred mighty men of valor. 10 The son of Jediael *was* Bilhan, and the sons of Bilhan *were* Jeush, Benjamin, Ehud, Chenaanah, Zethan, Tharshish, and Ahishahar.

11 All these sons of Jediael *were* heads of their fathers' houses; *there were* seventeen thousand two hundred mighty men of valor fit to go out for war *and* battle. 12 Shuppim and Huppim *were* the sons of Ir, *and* Hushim *was* the son of Aher.

13 The sons of Naphtali *were* Jahziel, Guni, Jezer, and Shallum, the sons of Bilhah.

14 The descendants of Manasseh: his Syrian concubine bore him Machir the father of Gilead, the father of Asriel. 15 Machir took as his wife *the sister* of Huppim and Shuppim, whose name *was* Maachah. The name of *Gilead's* grandson *was* Zelophehad, but Zelophehad begot only daughters. 16 (Maachah the wife of Machir bore a son, and she called his name Peresh. The name of his brother *was* Sheresh, and his sons *were* Ulam and Rakem. 17 The son of Ulam *was* Bedan.) These *were* the descendants of Gilead the son of Machir, the son of Manasseh.

18 His sister Hammoleketh bore Ishhod, Abiezer, and Mahlah.

19 And the sons of Shemida were Ahian, Shechem, Likhi, and Aniam.

20 The sons of Ephraim *were* Shuthelah, Bered his son, Tahath his son, Eladah his son, Tahath his son, 21 Zabad his son, Shuthelah his son, and Ezer and Elead. The men of Gath who were born in *that* land killed *them* because they came down to take away their cattle. 22 Then Ephraim their father mourned many days, and his brethren came to comfort him.

23 And when he went in to his wife, she conceived and bore a son; and he called his name Beriah, because tragedy had come upon his house. 24 Now his daughter *was* Sheerah, who built Lower and Upper Beth Horon and Uzzen Sheerah; 25 and Rephah *was* his son, *as well* as Resheph, and Telah his son, Tahan his son, 26 Laadan his son, Ammihud his son, Elishama his son, 27 Nun his son, and Joshua his son.

28 Now their possessions and dwelling places *were* Bethel and its towns: to the east Naaran, to the west Gezer and its towns, and Shechem and its towns, as far as Ayyah and its towns; 29 and by the borders of the children of Manasseh *were* Beth Shean and its towns, Taanach and its towns, Megiddo and its towns, Dor and its towns. In these dwelt the children of Joseph, the son of Israel.

30 The sons of Asher *were* Imnah, Ishvah, Ishvi, Beriah, and their sister Serah. 31 The sons of Beriah *were* Heber and Malchiel, who was the father of Birzaith. 32 And Heber begot Japhlet, Shomer, Hotham, and their sister Shua. 33 The sons of Japhlet *were* Pasach, Bimhal, and Ashvath. These *were* the children of Japhlet. 34 The sons of Shemer *were* Ahi, Rohgah, Jehubbah, and Aram. 35 And the sons of his brother Helem *were* Zophah, Imna, Shelesh, and Amal. 36 The sons of Zophah *were* Suah, Harnepher, Shual, Beri, Imrah, 37 Bezer, Hod, Shamma, Shilshah, Jithran, and Beera. 38 The sons of Jether *were* Jephunneh, Pispah, and Ara. 39 The sons of Ulla *were* Arah, Haniel, and Rizia.

40 All these *were* the children of Asher, heads of *their* fathers' houses, choice men, mighty men of valor, chief leaders. And they were recorded by genealogies among the army fit for battle; their number *was* twenty-six thousand.

8 NOW Benjamin begot Bela his firstborn, Ashbel the second, Aharah the third, 2 Nohah the fourth, and Rapha the fifth. 3 The sons of Bela *were* Addar, Gera, Abihud, 4 Abishua, Naaman, Ahoah, 5 Gera, Shephuphan, and Huram.

6 These *are* the sons of Ehud, who were the heads of the fathers' *houses* of the inhabitants of Geba, and who forced them to move to Manahath: 7 Naaman, Ahijah, and Gera who forced them to move. He begot Uzza and Ahihud.

8 Also Shaharaim had children in the country of Moab, after he had sent away Hushim and Baara his wives. 9 By Hodesh

his wife he begot Jobab, Zibia, Mesha, Malcam, 10 Jeuz, Sachiah, and Mirmah. These *were* his sons, heads of their fathers' *houses.*

11 And by Hushim he begot Abitub and Elpaal. 12 The sons of Elpaal *were* Eber, Misham, and Shemed, who built Ono and Lod with its towns; 13 and Beriah and Shema, who *were* heads of their fathers' *houses* of the inhabitants of Aijalon, who drove out the inhabitants of Gath. 14 Ahio, Shashak, Jeremoth, 15 Zebadiah, Arad, Eder, 16 Michael, Ispah, and Joha *were* the sons of Beriah. 17 Zebadiah, Meshullam, Hizki, Heber, 18 Ishmerai, Jizliah, and Jobab *were* the sons of Elpaal. 19 Jakim, Zichri, Zabdi, 20 Elienai, Zillethai, Eliel, 21 Adaiah, Beraiah, and Shimrath *were* the sons of Shimei. 22 Ishpan, Eber, Eliel, 23 Abdon, Zichri, Hanan, 24 Hananiah, Elam, Antothijah, 25 Iphdeiah, and Penuel *were* the sons of Shashak. 26 Shamsherai, Shehariah, Athaliah, 27 Jaareshiah, Elijah, and Zichri *were* the sons of Jeroham.

28 These *were* heads of the fathers' *houses* by their generations, chief men. These dwelt in Jerusalem.

29 Now the father of Gibeon, whose wife's name *was* Maacah, dwelt at Gibeon. 30 And his firstborn son *was* Abdon, then Zur, Kish, Baal, Nadab, 31 Gedor, Ahio, Zecher, 32 and Mikloth, *who* begot Shimeah. They also dwelt alongside their relatives in Jerusalem, with their brethren. 33 Ner begot Kish, Kish begot Saul, and Saul begot Jonathan, Malchishua, Abinadab, and Esh-Baal. 34 The son of Jonathan *was* Merib-Baal, and Merib-Baal begot Micah. 35 The sons of Micah *were* Pithon, Melech, Tarea, and Ahaz. 36 And Ahaz begot Jehoaddah; Jehoaddah begot Alemeth, Azmaveth, and Zimri; and Zimri begot Moza. 37 Moza begot Binea, Raphah his son, Eleasah his son, *and* Azel his son.

38 Azel had six sons whose names *were* these: Azrikam, Bocheru, Ishmael, Sheariah, Obadiah, and Hanan. All these *were* the sons of Azel. 39 And the sons of Eshek his brother *were* Ulam his firstborn, Jeush the second, and Eliphelet the third.

40 The sons of Ulam were mighty men of valor—archers. *They* had many sons and grandsons, one hundred and fifty *in all.* These *were* all sons of Benjamin.

PSALM 77:4–9

4   YOU hold my eyelids *open;*
     I am so troubled that I cannot speak.
5   I have considered the days of old,
     The years of ancient times.

6   I call to remembrance my song in the night;
     I meditate within my heart,
     And my spirit makes diligent search.

7   Will the Lord cast off forever?
     And will He be favorable no more?
8   Has His mercy ceased forever?
     Has *His* promise failed forevermore?
9   Has God forgotten to be gracious?
     Has He in anger shut up His tender mercies?   Selah

PROVERBS 19:13, 14

13   A foolish son *is* the ruin of his father,
     And the contentions of a wife *are* a
       continual dripping.

14   Houses and riches *are* an inheritance
       from fathers,
     But a prudent wife *is* from the LORD.

ACTS 5:22–42

BUT when the officers came and did not find them in the prison, they returned and reported, 23 saying, "Indeed we found the prison shut securely, and the guards standing outside before the doors; but when we opened them, we found no one inside!" 24 Now when the high priest, the captain of the temple, and the chief priests heard these things, they wondered what the outcome would be. 25 So one came and told them, saying, "Look, the men whom you put in prison are standing in the temple and teaching the people!"

26 Then the captain went with the officers and brought them without violence, for they feared the people, lest they should be stoned. 27 And when they had brought them, they set *them* before the council. And the high priest asked them, 28 saying, "Did we not strictly command you not to teach in this name? And look, you have filled Jerusalem with your doctrine, and intend to bring this Man's blood on us!"

29 But Peter and the *other* apostles answered and said: "We ought to obey God rather than men. 30 The God of our fathers

The one thing essential to the new life is obedience to the Spirit of God.   (PERFECT)

raised up Jesus whom you murdered by hanging on a tree. 31 Him God has exalted to His right hand *to be* Prince and Savior, to give repentance to Israel and forgiveness of sins. 32 And we are His witnesses to these things, and *so* also *is* the Holy Spirit whom God has given to those who obey Him."

33 When they heard *this,* they were furious and plotted to kill them. 34 Then one in the council stood up, a Pharisee named Gamaliel, a teacher of the law held in respect by all the people, and commanded them to put the apostles outside for a little while. 35 And he said to them: "Men of Israel, take heed to yourselves what you intend to do regarding these men. 36 For some time ago Theudas rose up, claiming to be somebody. A number of men, about four hundred, joined him. He was slain, and all who obeyed him were scattered and came

to nothing. 37 After this man, Judas of Galilee rose up in the days of the census, and drew away many people after him. He also perished, and all who obeyed him were dispersed. 38 And now I say to you, keep away from these men and let them alone; for if this plan or this work is of men, it will come to nothing; 39 but if it is of God, you cannot overthrow it—lest you even be found to fight against God."

40 And they agreed with him, and when they had called for the apostles and beaten *them,* they commanded that they should not speak in the name of Jesus, and let them go. 41 So they departed from the presence of the council, rejoicing that they were counted worthy to suffer shame for His name. 42 And daily in the temple, and in every house, they did not cease teaching and preaching Jesus *as* the Christ.

◆◆◆◆

*Reading 174—*Systematic Vexation
Acts 6:9–15

Persecution is systematic vexation, it does not leave you alone, it is something that throngs you; but to be boycotted means to be left alone, destitute of the comrades you used to have—"they think it strange that you do not run with *them* in the same flood of dissipation, speaking evil of *you.*" But they don't know that you carry a wonderful kingdom within, a kingdom full of light and peace and joy no matter how destitute and alone you may be on the outside. That is the wonderful work of the Lord in a man's soul. "Rejoice in that day and leap for joy!"   (*Servant as Lord*)

When you begin to deport yourself among men as a saint, they will leave you absolutely alone, you will be reviled and persecuted. No man can stand that unless he is in love with Jesus Christ; he cannot do it for a conviction or a creed, but he can do it for a Being whom he loves. Devotion to a Person is the only thing that tells; devotion to death to a Person, not devotion to a creed or a doctrine.   (*Sermon Mt.*)

1 CHRONICLES 9:1—10:14

SO all Israel was recorded by genealogies, and indeed, they *were* inscribed in the book of the kings of Israel. But Judah was carried away captive to Babylon because of their unfaithfulness. 2 And the first inhabitants who *dwelt* in their possessions in their cities *were* Israelites, priests, Levites, and the Nethinim.

3 Now in Jerusalem the children of Judah

dwelt, and some of the children of Benjamin, and of the children of Ephraim and Manasseh: 4 Uthai the son of Ammihud, the son of Omri, the son of Imri, the son of Bani, of the descendants of Perez, the son of Judah. 5 Of the Shilonites: Asaiah the firstborn and his sons. 6 Of the sons of Zerah: Jeuel, and their brethren—six hundred and ninety. 7 Of the sons of Benjamin: Sallu the son of Meshullam, the son of Hodaviah, the son of Hassenuah;

8 Ibneiah the son of Jeroham; Elah the son of Uzzi, the son of Michri; Meshullam the son of Shephatiah, the son of Reuel, the son of Ibnijah; 9 and their brethren, according to their generations—nine hundred and fifty-six. All these men *were* heads of a father's *house* in their fathers' houses.

10 Of the priests: Jedaiah, Jehoiarib, and Jachin; 11 Azariah the son of Hilkiah, the son of Meshullam, the son of Zadok, the son of Meraioth, the son of Ahitub, the officer over the house of God; 12 Adaiah the son of Jeroham, the son of Pashur, the son of Malchijah; Maasai the son of Adiel, the son of Jahzerah, the son of Meshullam, the son of Meshillemith, the son of Immer; 13 and their brethren, heads of their fathers' *houses*—one thousand seven hundred and sixty. *They were* very able men for the work of the service of the house of God.

14 Of the Levites: Shemaiah the son of Hasshub, the son of Azrikam, the son of Hashabiah, of the sons of Merari; 15 Bakbakkar, Heresh, Galal, and Mattaniah the son of Micah, the son of Zichri, the son of Asaph; 16 Obadiah the son of Shemaiah, the son of Galal, the son of Jeduthun; and Berechiah the son of Asa, the son of Elkanah, who lived in the villages of the Netophathites.

17 And the gatekeepers *were* Shallum, Akkub, Talmon, Ahiman, and their brethren. Shallum *was* the chief. 18 Until then *they had been* gatekeepers for the camps of the children of Levi at the King's Gate on the east.

19 Shallum the son of Kore, the son of Ebiasaph, the son of Korah, and his brethren, from his father's house, the Korahites, *were* in charge of the work of the service, gatekeepers of the tabernacle. Their fathers had been keepers of the entrance to the camp of the Lord. 20 And Phinehas the son of Eleazar had been the officer over them in time past; the Lord *was* with him. 21 Zechariah the son of Meshelemiah *was* keeper of the door of the tabernacle of meeting.

22 All those chosen as gatekeepers *were* two hundred and twelve. They were recorded by their genealogy, in their villages. David and Samuel the seer had appointed them to their trusted office. 23 So they and their children *were* in charge of the gates of the house of the Lord, the house of the tabernacle, by assignment. 24 The gatekeepers were assigned to the four directions: the east, west, north, and south. 25 And their brethren in their villages *had* to come with them from time to time for seven days. 26 For in this trusted office *were* four chief

gatekeepers; they were Levites. And they had charge over the chambers and treasuries of the house of God. 27 And they lodged *all* around the house of God because they *had* the responsibility, and they *were* in charge of opening *it* every morning.

28 Now *some* of them were in charge of the serving vessels, for they brought them in and took them out by count. 29 *Some* of them *were* appointed over the furnishings and over all the implements of the sanctuary, and over the fine flour and the wine and the oil and the incense and the spices. 30 And *some* of the sons of the priests made the ointment of the spices.

31 Mattithiah of the Levites, the firstborn of Shallum the Korahite, had the trusted office over the things that were baked in the pans. 32 And some of their brethren of the sons of the Kohathites *were* in charge of preparing the showbread for every Sabbath.

33 These are the singers, heads of the fathers' *houses* of the Levites, *who lodged* in the chambers, *and were* free *from other duties;* for they were employed in *that* work day and night. 34 These heads of the fathers' *houses* of the Levites *were* heads throughout their generations. They dwelt at Jerusalem.

35 Jeiel the father of Gibeon, whose wife's name *was* Maacah, dwelt at Gibeon. 36 His firstborn son *was* Abdon, then Zur, Kish, Baal, Ner, Nadab, 37 Gedor, Ahio, Zechariah, and Mikloth. 38 And Mikloth begot Shimeam. They also dwelt alongside their relatives in Jerusalem, with their brethren. 39 Ner begot Kish, Kish begot Saul, and Saul begot Jonathan, Malchishua, Abinadab, and Esh-Baal. 40 The son of Jonathan *was* Merib-Baal, and Merib-Baal begot Micah. 41 The sons of Micah *were* Pithon, Melech, Tahrea, *and Ahaz.* 42 And Ahaz begot Jarah; Jarah begot Alemeth, Azmaveth, and Zimri; and Zimri begot Moza; 43 Moza begot Binea, Rephaiah his son, Eleasah his son, and Azel his son.

44 And Azel had six sons whose names *were* these: Azrikam, Bocheru, Ishmael, Sheariah, Obadiah, and Hanan; these *were* the sons of Azel.

10 NOW the Philistines fought against Israel; and the men of Israel fled from before the Philistines, and fell slain on Mount Gilboa. 2 Then the Philistines followed hard after Saul and his sons. And the Philistines killed Jonathan, Abinadab, and Malchishua, Saul's sons. 3 The battle became fierce against Saul. The archers hit

him, and he was wounded by the archers. 4 Then Saul said to his armorbearer, "Draw your sword, and thrust me through with it, lest these uncircumcised men come and abuse me." But his armorbearer would not, for he was greatly afraid. Therefore Saul took a sword and fell on it. 5 And when his armorbearer saw that Saul was dead, he also fell on his sword and died. 6 So Saul and his three sons died, and all his house died together. 7 And when all the men of Israel who *were* in the valley saw that they had fled and that Saul and his sons were dead, they forsook their cities and fled; then the Philistines came and dwelt in them.

8 So it happened the next day, when the Philistines came to strip the slain, that they found Saul and his sons fallen on Mount Gilboa. 9 And they stripped him and took his head and his armor, and sent word *throughout* the land of the Philistines to proclaim the news *in the temple* of their idols and among the people. 10 Then they put his armor in the temple of their gods, and fastened his head in the temple of Dagon.

11 And when all Jabesh Gilead heard all that the Philistines had done to Saul, 12 all the valiant men arose and took the body of Saul and the bodies of his sons; and they brought them to Jabesh, and buried their bones under the tamarisk tree at Jabesh, and fasted seven days.

13 So Saul died for his unfaithfulness which he had committed against the LORD, because he did not keep the word of the LORD, and also because he consulted a medium for guidance. 14 But *he* did not inquire of the LORD; therefore He killed him, and turned the kingdom over to David the son of Jesse.

PSALM 77:10–15

10 AND I said, "This *is* my anguish;
But I *will remember* the years of the right hand of the Most High."
11 I will remember the works of the LORD;
Surely I will remember Your wonders of old.
12 I will also meditate on all Your work,
And talk of Your deeds.
13 Your way, O God, *is* in the sanctuary;
Who *is* so great a God as *our* God?
14 You *are* the God who does wonders;
You have declared Your strength among the peoples.
15 You have with *Your* arm redeemed Your people,
The sons of Jacob and Joseph.   Selah

PROVERBS 19:15, 16

15 LAZINESS casts *one* into a deep sleep,
And an idle person will suffer hunger.

16 He who keeps the commandment keeps his soul,
But he who is careless of his ways will die.

ACTS 6:1–15

NOW in those days, when *the number of* the disciples was multiplying, there arose a complaint against the Hebrews by the Hellenists, because their widows were neglected in the daily distribution. 2 Then the twelve summoned the multitude of the disciples and said, "It is not desirable that we should leave the word of God and serve tables. 3 Therefore, brethren, seek out from among you seven men of *good* reputation, full of the Holy Spirit and wisdom, whom we may appoint over this business; 4 but we will give ourselves continually to prayer and to the ministry of the word."

5 And the saying pleased the whole multitude. And they chose Stephen, a man full of faith and the Holy Spirit, and Philip, Prochorus, Nicanor, Timon, Parmenas, and Nicolas, a proselyte from Antioch, 6 whom they set before the apostles; and when they had prayed, they laid hands on them.

7 Then the word of God spread, and the number of the disciples multiplied greatly in Jerusalem, and a great many of the priests were obedient to the faith.

8 And Stephen, full of faith and power, did great wonders and signs among the people. 9 Then there arose some from what is

The sanctified saint has to alter the horizon of other people's lives. (LOVE OF GOD)

called the Synagogue of the Freedmen (Cyrenians, Alexandrians, and those from Cilicia and Asia), disputing with Stephen. 10 And they were not able to resist the wisdom and the Spirit by which he spoke. 11 Then they secretly induced men to say, "We have heard him speak blasphemous words against Moses and God." 12 And they stirred up the people, the elders, and the scribes; and they came upon *him,* seized him, and brought *him* to the council. 13 They also set up false witnesses who said,

> "This man does not cease to speak blasphemous words against this holy place and the law; 14 for we have heard him say that this Jesus of Nazareth will destroy this place and change the customs which Moses delivered to us." 15 And all who sat in the council, looking steadfastly at him, saw his face as the face of an angel.

◆◆◆◆

Reading 175—The Power of Voluntary Choice
Proverbs 19:17

We never get credit spiritually for impulsive giving. If suddenly we feel we should give . . . to a poor man, we get no credit from God for giving it, there is no virtue in it whatever. As a rule, that sort of giving is a relief to our feelings; it is not an indication of a generous character, but rather an indication of a lack of generosity. God never estimates what we give from impulse. We are given credit for what we determine in our hearts to give; for the giving that is governed by a fixed determination. The Spirit of God revolutionizes our philanthropic instincts. Much of our philanthropy is simply the impulse to save ourselves an uncomfortable feeling. The Spirit of God alters all that. As saints our attitude toward giving is that we give for Jesus Christ's sake, and from no other motive. God holds us responsible for the way we use this power of voluntary choice.   (*BIB. PSYCH.*)

1 CHRONICLES 11:1—12:40

THEN all Israel came together to David at Hebron, saying, "Indeed we *are* your bone and your flesh. 2 Also, in time past, even when Saul was king, you *were* the one who led Israel out and brought them in; and the LORD your God said to you, 'You shall shepherd My people Israel, and be ruler over My people Israel.' " 3 Therefore all the elders of Israel came to the king at Hebron, and David made a covenant with them at Hebron before the LORD. And they anointed David king over Israel, according to the word of the LORD by Samuel.

4 And David and all Israel went to Jerusalem, which is Jebus, where the Jebusites *were,* the inhabitants of the land. 5 But the inhabitants of Jebus said to David, "You shall not come in here!" Nevertheless David took the stronghold of Zion (that is, the City of David). 6 Now David said, "Whoever attacks the Jebusites first shall be chief and captain." And Joab the son of Zeruiah went up first, and became chief. 7 Then David dwelt in the stronghold; therefore they called it the City of David. 8 And he built the city around it, from the Millo to the surrounding area. Joab repaired the rest of the city. 9 So David went on and became great, and the LORD of hosts *was* with him.

10 Now these *were* the heads of the mighty men whom David had, who strengthened themselves with him in his kingdom, with all Israel, to make him king, according to the word of the LORD concerning Israel.

11 And this *is* the number of the mighty men whom David had: Jashobeam the son of a Hachmonite, chief of the captains; he had lifted up his spear against three hundred, killed *by him* at one time.

12 After him *was* Eleazar the son of Dodo, the Ahohite, who *was one* of the three mighty men. 13 He was with David at Pasdammim. Now there the Philistines were gathered for battle, and there was a piece of ground full of barley. So the people fled from the Philistines. 14 But they stationed themselves in the middle of *that* field, defended it, and killed the Philistines. So the LORD brought about a great victory.

15 Now three of the thirty chief men went down to the rock to David, into the cave of Adullam; and the army of the Philistines encamped in the Valley of Rephaim. 16 David *was* then in the stronghold, and the garrison of the Philistines *was* then in Bethlehem. 17 And David said with longing, "Oh, that someone would give me a drink of water from the well of Bethlehem,

which is by the gate!" 18 So the three broke through the camp of the Philistines, drew water from the well of Bethlehem that *was* by the gate, and took *it* and brought *it* to David. Nevertheless David would not drink it, but poured it out to the LORD. 19 And he said, "Far be it from me, O my God, that I should do this! Shall I drink the blood of these men *who have put* their lives *in jeopardy?* For at the risk of their lives they brought it." Therefore he would not drink it. These things were done by the three mighty men.

20 Abishai the brother of Joab was chief of *another* three. He had lifted up his spear against three hundred *men*, killed *them*, and won a name among *these* three. 21 Of the three he was more honored than the other two men. Therefore he became their captain. However he did not attain to the *first* three.

22 Benaiah was the son of Jehoiada, the son of a valiant man from Kabzeel, who had done many deeds. He had killed two lion-like heroes of Moab. He also had gone down and killed a lion in the midst of a pit on a snowy day. 23 And he killed an Egyptian, a man of *great* height, five cubits tall. In the Egyptian's hand *there was* a spear like a weaver's beam; and he went down to him with a staff, wrested the spear out of the Egyptian's hand, and killed him with his own spear. 24 These *things* Benaiah the son of Jehoiada did, and won a name among three mighty men. 25 Indeed he was more honored than the thirty, but he did not attain to the *first* three. And David appointed him over his guard.

26 Also the mighty warriors *were* Asahel the brother of Joab, Elhanan the son of Dodo of Bethlehem, 27 Shammoth the Harorite, Helez the Pelonite, 28 Ira the son of Ikkesh the Tekoite, Abiezer the Anathothite, 29 Sibbechai the Hushathite, Ilai the Ahohite, 30 Maharai the Netophathite, Heled the son of Baanah the Netophathite, 31 Ithai the son of Ribai of Gibeah, of the sons of Benjamin, Benaiah the Pirathonite, 32 Hurai of the brooks of Gaash, Abiel the Arbathite, 33 Azmaveth the Baharumite, Eliahba the Shaalbonite, 34 the sons of Hashem the Gizonite, Jonathan the son of Shageh the Hararite, 35 Ahiam the son of Sacar the Hararite, Eliphal the son of Ur, 36 Hepher the Mecherathite, Ahijah the Pelonite, 37 Hezro the Carmelite, Naarai the son of Ezbai, 38 Joel the brother of Nathan, Mibhar the son of Hagri, 39 Zelek the Ammonite, Naharai the Berothite (the armorbearer of Joab the son of Zeruiah), 40 Ira the Ithrite, Gareb the Ithrite, 41 Uriah the Hittite, Zabad the son of Ahlai, 42 Adina the son of Shiza the Reubenite (a chief of the Reubenites) and thirty with him, 43 Hanan the son of Maachah, Joshaphat the Mithnite, 44 Uzzia the Ashterathite, Shama and Jeiel the sons of Hotham the Aroerite, 45 Jediael the son of Shimri, and Joha his brother, the Tizite, 46 Eliel the Mahavite, Jeribai and Joshaviah the sons of Elnaam, Ithmah the Moabite, 47 Eliel, Obed, and Jaasiel the Mezobaite.

12 NOW these *were* the men who came to David at Ziklag while he was still a fugitive from Saul the son of Kish; and they *were* among the mighty men, helpers in the war, 2 armed with bows, using both the right hand and the left in *hurling* stones and *shooting* arrows with the bow. *They were* of Benjamin, Saul's brethren.

3 The chief *was* Ahiezer, then Joash, the sons of Shemaah the Gibeathite; Jeziel and Pelet the sons of Azmaveth; Berachah, and Jehu the Anathothite; 4 Ishmaiah the Gibeonite, a mighty man among the thirty, and over the thirty; Jeremiah, Jahaziel, Johanan, and Jozabad the Gederathite; 5 Eluzai, Jerimoth, Bealiah, Shemariah, and Shephatiah the Haruphite; 6 Elkanah, Jisshiah, Azarel, Joezer, and Jashobeam, the Korahites; 7 and Joelah and Zebadiah the sons of Jeroham of Gedor.

8 *Some* Gadites joined David at the stronghold in the wilderness, mighty men of valor, men trained for battle, who could handle shield and spear, whose faces *were* like the faces of lions, and *were* as swift as gazelles on the mountains: 9 Ezer the first, Obadiah the second, Eliab the third, 10 Mishmannah the fourth, Jeremiah the fifth, 11 Attai the sixth, Eliel the seventh, 12 Johanan the eighth, Elzabad the ninth, 13 Jeremiah the tenth, and Machbanai the eleventh. 14 These *were* from the sons of Gad, captains of the army; the least was over a hundred, and the greatest was over a thousand. 15 These *are* the ones who crossed the Jordan in the first month, when it had overflowed all its banks; and they put to flight all *those* in the valleys, to the east and to the west.

16 Then some of the sons of Benjamin and Judah came to David at the stronghold. 17 And David went out to meet them, and answered and said to them, "If you have come peaceably to me to help me, my heart will be united with you; but if to betray me to my enemies, since *there is* no wrong in my hands, may the God of our fathers look and bring judgment." 18 Then the

Spirit came upon Amasai, chief of the captains, *and he said:*

"*We are* yours, O David;
We *are* on your side, O son of Jesse!
Peace, peace to you,
And peace to your helpers!
For your God helps you."

So David received them, and made them captains of the troop.

19 And *some* from Manasseh defected to David when he was going with the Philistines to battle against Saul; but they did not help them, for the lords of the Philistines sent him away by agreement, saying, "He may defect to his master Saul *and endanger* our heads." 20 When he went to Ziklag, those of Manasseh who defected to him were Adnah, Jozabad, Jediael, Michael, Jozabad, Elihu, and Zillethai, captains of the thousands who *were* from Manasseh. 21 And they helped David against the bands *of raiders,* for they *were* all mighty men of valor, and they *were* captains in the army. 22 For at *that* time they came to David day by day to help him, until *it was* a great army, like the army of God.

23 Now these *were* the numbers of the divisions *that were* equipped for war, *and* came to David at Hebron to turn *over* the kingdom of Saul to him, according to the word of the LORD: 24 of the sons of Judah bearing shield and spear, six thousand eight hundred armed for war; 25 of the sons of Simeon, mighty men of valor fit for war, seven thousand one hundred; 26 of the sons of Levi four thousand six hundred; 27 Jehoiada, the leader of the Aaronites, and with him three thousand seven hundred; 28 Zadok, a young man, a valiant warrior, and from his father's house twenty-two captains; 29 of the sons of Benjamin, relatives of Saul, three thousand (until then the greatest part of them had remained loyal to the house of Saul); 30 of the sons of Ephraim twenty thousand eight hundred, mighty men of valor, famous men throughout their father's house; 31 of the half-tribe of Manasseh eighteen thousand, who were designated by name to come and make David king; 32 of the sons of Issachar who had understanding of the times, to know what Israel ought to do, their chiefs were two hundred; and all their brethren were at their command; 33 of Zebulun there were fifty thousand who went out to battle, expert in war with all weapons of war, stouthearted men who could keep ranks; 34 of Naphtali one thousand captains, and with them thirty-seven thousand with shield

and spear; 35 of the Danites who could keep battle formation, twenty-eight thousand six hundred; 36 of Asher, those who could go out to war, able to keep battle formation, forty thousand; 37 of the Reubenites and the Gadites and the half-tribe of Manasseh, from the other side of the Jordan, one hundred and twenty thousand armed for battle with every *kind* of weapon of war.

38 All these men of war, who could keep ranks, came to Hebron with a loyal heart, to make David king over all Israel; and all the rest of Israel *were* of one mind to make David king. 39 And they were there with David three days, eating and drinking, for their brethren had prepared for them. 40 Moreover those who were near to them, from as far away as Issachar and Zebulun and Naphtali, were bringing food on donkeys and camels, on mules and oxen—provisions of flour and cakes of figs and cakes of raisins, wine and oil and oxen and sheep abundantly, for *there was* joy in Israel.

PSALM 77:16–20

16 THE waters saw You, O God;
The waters saw You, they were afraid;
The depths also trembled.
17 The clouds poured out water;
The skies sent out a sound;
Your arrows also flashed about.
18 The voice of Your thunder *was* in the whirlwind;
The lightnings lit up the world;
The earth trembled and shook.
19 Your way *was* in the sea,
Your path in the great waters,
And Your footsteps were not known.
20 You led Your people like a flock
By the hand of Moses and Aaron.

PROVERBS 19:17–19

17 HE who has pity on the poor lends to the LORD,
And He will pay back what he has given.

18 Chasten your son while there is hope,
And do not set your heart on his destruction.

19 *A man of* great wrath will suffer punishment;
For if you rescue *him,* you will have to do it again.

ACTS 7:1–21

THEN the high priest said, "Are these things so?"

2 And he said, "Brethren and fathers, listen: The God of glory appeared to our father Abraham when he was in Mesopotamia, before he dwelt in Haran, 3 and said to him, 'Get out of your country and from your relatives, and come to a land that I will show you.' 4 Then he came out of the land of the Chaldeans and dwelt in Haran. And from there, when his father was dead, He moved him to this land in which you now dwell. 5 And *God* gave him no inheritance in it, not even *enough* to set his foot on. But even when *Abraham* had no child, He promised to give it to him for a possession, and to his descendants after him. 6 But God spoke in this way: that his descendants would dwell in a foreign land, and that they would bring them into bondage and oppress *them* four hundred years. 7 'And the nation to whom they will be in bondage I will judge,' said God, 'and after that they shall come out and serve Me in this place.' 8 Then He gave him the covenant of circumcision; and so *Abraham* begot Isaac and circumcised him on the eighth day; and Isaac *begot* Jacob, and Jacob *begot* the twelve patriarchs.

9 "And the patriarchs, becoming envious, sold Joseph into Egypt. But God was with him 10 and delivered him out of all his troubles, and gave him favor and wisdom in the presence of Pharaoh, king of Egypt; and he made him governor over Egypt and

You can't indulge in pious pretense when you come to the atmosphere of the Bible. (BIB. ETHICS)

all his house. 11 Now a famine and great trouble came over all the land of Egypt and Canaan, and our fathers found no sustenance. 12 But when Jacob heard that there was grain in Egypt, he sent out our fathers first. 13 And the second *time* Joseph was made known to his brothers, and Joseph's family became known to the Pharaoh. 14 Then Joseph sent and called his father Jacob and all his relatives to *him,* seventy-five people. 15 So Jacob went down to Egypt; and he died, he and our fathers. 16 And they were carried back to Shechem and laid in the tomb that Abraham bought for a sum of money from the sons of Hamor, *the father* of Shechem.

17 "But when the time of the promise drew near which God had sworn to Abraham, the people grew and multiplied in Egypt 18 till another king arose who did not know Joseph. 19 This man dealt treacherously with our people, and oppressed our forefathers, making them expose their babies, so that they might not live. 20 At this time Moses was born, and was well pleasing to God; and he was brought up in his father's house for three months. 21 But when he was set out, Pharaoh's daughter took him away and brought him up as her own son.

———— ◆◆◆◆ ————

Reading 176—The Enormous Leisure of God
Acts 7:22–30

"Moses was learned in all the wisdom of the Egyptians," a man in a royal setting by the providence of God, and he saw the burden of God's people, and his whole heart and mind was ablaze with the vision that he was the man to deliver them. He *was* the man to deliver his people, but not yet, there was something in the road, and God sent him into the wilderness to feed sheep for forty years. Imagine what those years must have meant to Moses, realizing on the threshold of his manhood the vision of what he was to do; seeing, as no one else could see, the burdens of his people, and feeling in himself the certainty that he was the one to deliver them; how he would ponder over God's ways during those forty years. . . .

Think of the enormous leisure of God! He never is in a hurry. We are in such a frantic hurry. We get down before God and pray, then we get up and say, "It is all done now," and in the light of the glory of the vision we go forth to do the thing. But it is not real, and God has to take us into the valley and puts us through fires and floods to batter us into shape, until we get into the condition in which He can trust us with the reality of His recognition of us.   (*SEND I YOU*)

1 CHRONICLES 13:1—14:17

THEN David consulted with the captains of thousands and hundreds, *and* with every leader. 2 And David said to all the assembly of Israel, "If *it seems* good to you, and if it is of the LORD our God, let us send out to our brethren everywhere *who are* left in all the land of Israel, and with them to the priests and Levites *who are* in their cities *and* their common-lands, that they may gather together to us; 3 and let us bring the ark of our God back to us, for we have not inquired at it since the days of Saul." 4 Then all the assembly said that they would do so, for the thing was right in the eyes of all the people.

5 So David gathered all Israel together, from Shihor in Egypt to as far as the entrance of Hamath, to bring the ark of God from Kirjath Jearim. 6 And David and all Israel went up to Baalah, to Kirjath Jearim, which belonged to Judah, to bring up from there the ark of God the LORD, who dwells *between* the cherubim, where *His* name is proclaimed. 7 So they carried the ark of God on a new cart from the house of Abinadab, and Uzza and Ahio drove the cart. 8 Then David and all Israel played *music* before God with all *their* might, with singing, on harps, on stringed instruments, on tambourines, on cymbals, and with trumpets.

9 And when they came to Chidon's threshing floor, Uzza put out his hand to hold the ark, for the oxen stumbled. 10 Then the anger of the LORD was aroused against Uzza, and He struck him because he put his hand to the ark; and he died there before God. 11 And David became angry because of the LORD's outbreak against Uzza; therefore that place is called Perez Uzza to this day. 12 David was afraid of God that day, saying, "How can I bring the ark of God to me?" 13 So David would not move the ark with him into the City of David, but took it aside into the house of Obed-Edom the Gittite. 14 The ark of God remained with the family of Obed-Edom in his house three months. And the LORD blessed the house of Obed-Edom and all that he had.

14 NOW Hiram king of Tyre sent messengers to David, and cedar trees, with masons and carpenters, to build him a house. 2 So David knew that the LORD had established him as king over Israel, for his kingdom was highly exalted for the sake of His people Israel.

3 Then David took more wives in Jerusalem, and David begot more sons and daughters. 4 And these are the names of his children whom he had in Jerusalem: Shammua, Shobab, Nathan, Solomon, 5 Ibhar, Elishua, Elpelet, 6 Nogah, Nepheg, Japhia, 7 Elishama, Beeliada, and Eliphelet.

8 Now when the Philistines heard that David had been anointed king over all Israel, all the Philistines went up to search for David. And David heard *of it* and went out against them. 9 Then the Philistines went and made a raid on the Valley of Rephaim. 10 And David inquired of God, saying, "Shall I go up against the Philistines? Will You deliver them into my hand?"

The LORD said to him, "Go up, for I will deliver them into your hand."

11 So they went up to Baal Perazim, and David defeated them there. Then David said, "God has broken through my enemies by my hand like a breakthrough of water." Therefore they called the name of that place Baal Perazim. 12 And when they left their gods there, David gave a commandment, and they were burned with fire.

13 Then the Philistines once again made a raid on the valley. 14 Therefore David inquired again of God, and God said to him, "You shall not go up after them; circle around them, and come upon them in front of the mulberry trees. 15 And it shall be, when you hear a sound of marching in the tops of the mulberry trees, then you shall go out to battle, for God has gone out before you to strike the camp of the Philistines." 16 So David did as God commanded him, and they drove back the army of the Philistines from Gibeon as far as Gezer. 17 Then the fame of David went out into all lands, and the LORD brought the fear of him upon all nations.

PSALM 78:1–11

1 GIVE ear, O my people, *to* my law;
  Incline your ears to the words of my
    mouth.
2 I will open my mouth in a parable;
  I will utter dark sayings of old,
3 Which we have heard and known,
  And our fathers have told us.
4 We will not hide *them* from their
    children,
  Telling to the generation to come the
    praises of the LORD,
  And His strength and His wonderful
    works that He has done.

5 For He established a testimony in
    Jacob,
  And appointed a law in Israel,
  Which He commanded our fathers,
  That they should make them known
    to their children;
6 That the generation to come might
    know *them*,
  The children *who* would be born,
  That they may arise and declare *them*
    to their children,
7 That they may set their hope in
    God,
  And not forget the works of God,
  But keep His commandments;
8 And may not be like their fathers,
  A stubborn and rebellious generation,
  A generation *that* did not set its heart
    aright,
  And whose spirit was not faithful to
    God.

9 The children of Ephraim, *being* armed
    and carrying bows,
  Turned back in the day of battle.
10 They did not keep the covenant of
    God;
  They refused to walk in His law,
11 And forgot His works
  And His wonders that He had shown
    them.

PROVERBS 19:20, 21

20 LISTEN to counsel and receive
    instruction,
  That you may be wise in your latter
    days.

21 There are many plans in a man's
    heart,
  Nevertheless the LORD's counsel—
    that will stand.

ACTS 7:22–43

AND Moses was learned in all the wisdom
of the Egyptians, and was mighty in words
and deeds.
23 "Now when he was forty years old,
it came into his heart to visit his brethren,
the children of Israel. 24 And seeing one
of *them* suffer wrong, he defended and
avenged him who was oppressed, and struck
down the Egyptian. 25 For he supposed that
his brethren would have understood that
God would deliver them by his hand, but
they did not understand. 26 And the next
day he appeared to two of them as they
were fighting, and *tried to* reconcile them,
saying, 'Men, you are brethren; why do
you wrong one another?' 27 But he who
did his neighbor wrong pushed him away,
saying, 'Who made you a ruler and a judge
over us? 28 Do you want to kill me as you
did the Egyptian yesterday?' 29 Then, at this
saying, Moses fled and became a dweller
in the land of Midian, where he had two
sons.
30 "And when forty years had passed, an
Angel of the Lord appeared to him in a
flame of fire in a bush, in the wilderness
of Mount Sinai. 31 When Moses saw *it*, he
marveled at the sight; and as he drew near
to observe, the voice of the Lord came to
him, 32 *saying*, 'I *am* the God of your fathers—the God of Abraham, the God of
Isaac, and the God of Jacob.' And Moses
trembled and dared not look. 33 'Then the
LORD said to him, "Take your sandals off
your feet, for the place where you stand is
holy ground. 34 I have surely seen the oppression of My people who are in Egypt;
I have heard their groaning and have come
down to deliver them. And now come, I
will send you to Egypt." '
35 "This Moses whom they rejected, saying, 'Who made you a ruler and a judge?'
is the one God sent *to be* a ruler and a
deliverer by the hand of the Angel who
appeared to him in the bush. 36 He brought
them out, after he had shown wonders and
signs in the land of Egypt, and in the Red
Sea, and in the wilderness forty years.
37 "This is that Moses who said to the
children of Israel, 'The LORD your God will
raise up for you a Prophet like me from
your brethren. Him you shall hear.'

---

*H*ow few of us do speak! When
we talk to a soul, we talk like a
tract! (GOD'S WORKMANSHIP)

---

38 "This is he who was in the congregation in the wilderness with the Angel who spoke to him on Mount Sinai, and *with* our fathers, the one who received the living oracles to give to us, 39 whom our fathers would not obey, but rejected. And in their hearts they turned back to Egypt, 40 saying to Aaron, 'Make us gods to go before us; *as for* this Moses who brought us out of the land of Egypt, we do not know what has become of him.' 41 And they made a calf in those days, offered sacrifices to the idol, and rejoiced in the works of their own hands. 42 Then God turned and gave them up to worship the host of heaven, as it is written in the book of the Prophets:

'Did you offer Me slaughtered animals
  and sacrifices *during* forty years in
  the wilderness,
O house of Israel?
43 You also took up the tabernacle of
  Moloch,
And the star of your god
  Remphan,
Images which you made to
  worship;
And I will carry you away beyond
  Babylon.'

◆◆◆◆

Reading 177—"Receive My Spirit"
Acts 7:59

The Bible reveals that death is inevitable—"and thus death spread to all men." "It is appointed for men to die once." Repeat that over to yourself. It is appointed to everyone of us that we are going to cease to be as we are now, and the place that knows us now shall know us no more. We may shirk it, we may ignore it, we may be so full of robust health and spirits that the thought of death never enters, but it is inevitable.   (*SERVANT AS LORD*)

We all die. It is humiliating for our predications to remember that although the spirit of man is indestructible, the phase of life which we bank on naturally passes. We may have labor in it, and delight and satisfaction in it, but it will all pass. When a beast dies, his body disappears and his soul goes downward into entire nature; the spirit of a man goes straight back to God who made it; it is never absorbed into God.   (*SHADE*)

1 CHRONICLES 15:1—16:43

DAVID built houses for himself in the City of David; and he prepared a place for the ark of God, and pitched a tent for it. 2 Then David said, "No one may carry the ark of God but the Levites, for the LORD has chosen them to carry the ark of God and to minister before Him forever." 3 And David gathered all Israel together at Jerusalem, to bring up the ark of the LORD to its place, which he had prepared for it. 4 Then David assembled the children of Aaron and the Levites: 5 of the sons of Kohath, Uriel the chief, and one hundred and twenty of his brethren; 6 of the sons of Merari, Asaiah the chief, and two hundred and twenty of his brethren; 7 of the sons of Gershom, Joel the chief, and one hundred and thirty of his brethren; 8 of the sons of Elizaphan, Shemaiah the chief, and two hundred of his brethren; 9 of the sons of Hebron, Eliel the chief, and eighty of his brethren; 10 of the sons of Uzziel, Amminadab the chief, and one hundred and twelve of his brethren.

11 And David called for Zadok and Abiathar the priests, and for the Levites: for Uriel, Asaiah, Joel, Shemaiah, Eliel, and Amminadab. 12 He said to them, "You *are* the heads of the fathers' *houses* of the Levites; sanctify yourselves, you and your brethren, that you may bring up the ark of the LORD God of Israel to *the place* I have prepared for it. 13 For because you *did* not *do it* the first *time*, the LORD our God broke out against us, because we did not consult Him about the proper order."

14 So the priests and the Levites sanctified themselves to bring up the ark of the LORD God of Israel. 15 And the children of the Levites bore the ark of God on their shoulders, by its poles, as Moses had commanded according to the word of the LORD.

16 Then David spoke to the leaders of the Levites to appoint their brethren *to be* the singers accompanied by instruments of music, stringed instruments, harps, and cymbals, by raising the voice with resounding joy. 17 So the Levites appointed Heman the son of Joel; and of his brethren, Asaph the son of Berechiah; and of their brethren, the sons of Merari, Ethan the son of Kushaiah; 18 and with them their brethren of the second *rank:* Zechariah, Ben, Jaaziel, Shemiramoth, Jehiel, Unni, Eliab, Benaiah, Maaseiah, Mattithiah, Elipheleh, Mikneiah, Obed-Edom, and Jeiel, the gatekeepers; 19 the singers, Heman, Asaph, and Ethan, *were* to sound the cymbals of bronze; 20 Zechariah, Aziel, Shemiramoth, Jehiel, Unni, Eliab, Maaseiah, and Benaiah, with strings according to Alamoth; 21 Mattithiah, Elipheleh, Mikneiah, Obed-Edom, Jeiel, and Azaziah, to direct with harps on the Sheminith; 22 Chenaniah, leader of the Levites, was instructor *in charge of* the music, because he *was* skillful; 23 Berechiah and Elkanah *were* doorkeepers for the ark; 24 Shebaniah, Joshaphat, Nethanel, Amasai, Zechariah, Benaiah, and Eliezer, the priests, were to blow the trumpets before the ark of God; and Obed-Edom and Jehiah, doorkeepers for the ark.

25 So David, the elders of Israel, and the captains over thousands went to bring up the ark of the covenant of the LORD from the house of Obed-Edom with joy. 26 And so it was, when God helped the Levites who bore the ark of the covenant of the LORD, that they offered seven bulls and seven rams. 27 David was clothed with a robe of fine linen, as were all the Levites who bore the ark, the singers, and Chenaniah the music master *with* the singers. David also wore a linen ephod. 28 Thus all Israel brought up the ark of the covenant of the LORD with shouting and with the sound of the horn, with trumpets and with cymbals, making music with stringed instruments and harps.

29 And it happened, *as* the ark of the covenant of the LORD came to the City of David, that Michal, Saul's daughter, looked through a window and saw King David whirling and playing music; and she despised him in her heart.

> *Thinking takes place in the heart, not in the brain.*   (BIB. PSYCH.)

16 SO they brought the ark of God, and set it in the midst of the tabernacle that David had erected for it. Then they offered burnt offerings and peace offerings before God. 2 And when David had finished offering the burnt offerings and the peace offerings, he blessed the people in the name of the LORD. 3 Then he distributed to everyone of Israel, both man and woman, to everyone a loaf of bread, a piece *of meat,* and a cake of raisins.

4 And he appointed some of the Levites to minister before the ark of the LORD, to commemorate, to thank, and to praise the LORD God of Israel: 5 Asaph the chief, and next to him Zechariah, *then* Jeiel, Shemiramoth, Jehiel, Mattithiah, Eliab, Benaiah, and Obed-Edom: Jeiel with stringed instruments and harps, but Asaph made music with cymbals; 6 Benaiah and Jahaziel the priests regularly *blew* the trumpets before the ark of the covenant of God.

7 On that day David first delivered *this psalm* into the hand of Asaph and his brethren, to thank the LORD:

8   Oh, give thanks to the LORD!
     Call upon His name;
     Make known His deeds among the
        peoples!
9   Sing to Him, sing psalms to Him;
     Talk of all His wondrous works!
10   Glory in His holy name;
     Let the hearts of those rejoice who
        seek the LORD!
11   Seek the LORD and His strength;
     Seek His face evermore!
12   Remember His marvelous works
        which He has done,
     His wonders, and the judgments of
        His mouth,
13   O seed of Israel His servant,
     You children of Jacob, His chosen
        ones!

14   He *is* the LORD our God;
     His judgments *are* in all the earth.
15   Remember His covenant forever,
     The word which He commanded, for
        a thousand generations,
16   *The covenant which* He made with
        Abraham,
     And His oath to Isaac,
17   And confirmed it to Jacob for a
        statute,
     To Israel *for* an everlasting covenant,

18 Saying, "To you I will give the land
   of Canaan
   As the allotment of your inheritance,"
19 When you were few in number,
   Indeed very few, and strangers in it.

20 When they went from one nation to
   another,
   And from *one* kingdom to another
   people,
21 He permitted no man to do them
   wrong;
   Yes, He rebuked kings for their sakes,
22 *Saying*, "Do not touch My anointed
   ones,
   And do My prophets no harm."

23 Sing to the LORD, all the earth;
   Proclaim the good news of His
   salvation from day to day.
24 Declare His glory among the nations,
   His wonders among all peoples.

25 For the LORD *is* great and greatly
   to be praised;
   He *is* also to be feared above all gods.
26 For all the gods of the peoples *are*
   idols,
   But the LORD made the heavens.
27 Honor and majesty *are* before Him;
   Strength and gladness are in His
   place.

28 Give to the LORD, O families of the
   peoples,
   Give to the LORD glory and strength.
29 Give to the LORD the glory *due* His
   name;
   Bring an offering, and come before
   Him.
   Oh, worship the LORD in the beauty
   of holiness!
30 Tremble before Him, all the earth.
   The world also is firmly established,
   It shall not be moved.

31 Let the heavens rejoice, and let the
   earth be glad;
   And let them say among the nations,
   "The LORD reigns."
32 Let the sea roar, and all its fullness;
   Let the field rejoice, and all that *is*
   in it.
33 Then the trees of the woods shall
   rejoice before the LORD,
   For He is coming to judge the earth.

34 Oh, give thanks to the LORD, for *He
   is* good!
   For His mercy *endures* forever.

35 And say, "Save us, O God of our
   salvation;
   Gather us together, and deliver us
   from the Gentiles,
   To give thanks to Your holy
   name,
   To triumph in Your praise."

36 Blessed *be* the LORD God of Israel
   From everlasting to everlasting!

And all the people said, "Amen!" and
praised the LORD.

37 So he left Asaph and his brothers there
before the ark of the covenant of the LORD
to minister before the ark regularly, as every
day's work required; 38 and Obed-Edom
with his sixty-eight brethren, including
Obed-Edom the son of Jeduthun, and
Hosah, *to be* gatekeepers; 39 and Zadok the
priest and his brethren the priests, before
the tabernacle of the LORD at the high place
that *was* at Gibeon, 40 to offer burnt offerings to the LORD on the altar of burnt offering regularly morning and evening, and *to
do* according to all that is written in the
Law of the LORD which He commanded
Israel; 41 and with them Heman and Jeduthun and the rest who were chosen, who
were designated by name, to give thanks
to the LORD, because His mercy *endures*
forever; 42 and with them Heman and Jeduthun, to sound aloud with trumpets and
cymbals and the musical instruments of
God. Now the sons of Jeduthun *were*
gatekeepers.

43 Then all the people departed, every
man to his house; and David returned to
bless his house.

PSALM 78:12–16

12 MARVELOUS things He did in the
   sight of their fathers,
   In the land of Egypt, *in* the field of
   Zoan.
13 He divided the sea and caused them
   to pass through;
   And He made the waters stand up like
   a heap.
14 In the daytime also He led them with
   the cloud,
   And all the night with a light of fire.
15 He split the rocks in the wilderness,
   And gave *them* drink in abundance like
   the depths.
16 He also brought streams out of the
   rock,
   And caused waters to run down like
   rivers.

PROVERBS 19:22–24

22 WHAT is desired in a man is kindness,
And a poor man is better than a liar.

23 The fear of the LORD *leads* to life,
And *he who has it* will abide in
satisfaction;
He will not be visited with evil.

24 A lazy *man* buries his hand in the bowl,
And will not so much as bring it to
his mouth again.

ACTS 7:44–60

"OUR fathers had the tabernacle of witness in the wilderness, as He appointed, instructing Moses to make it according to the pattern that he had seen, 45 which our fathers, having received it in turn, also brought with Joshua into the land possessed by the Gentiles, whom God drove out before the face of our fathers until the days of David, 46 who found favor before God and asked to find a dwelling for the God of Jacob. 47 But Solomon built Him a house.

48 "However, the Most High does not dwell in temples made with hands, as the prophet says:

49 'Heaven *is* My throne,
And earth *is* My footstool.
What house will you build for Me?
says the LORD,
Or what *is* the place of My rest?
50 Has My hand not made all these
things?'

51 "*You* stiff-necked and uncircumcised in heart and ears! You always resist the Holy Spirit; as your fathers *did,* so *do* you.

> *T*he natural heart, we cannot repeat it too often, does not want the Gospel.   (BIB. PSYCH.)

52 Which of the prophets did your fathers not persecute? And they killed those who foretold the coming of the Just One, of whom you now have become the betrayers and murderers, 53 who have received the law by the direction of angels and have not kept *it.*"

54 When they heard these things they were cut to the heart, and they gnashed at him with *their* teeth. 55 But he, being full of the Holy Spirit, gazed into heaven and saw the glory of God, and Jesus standing at the right hand of God, 56 and said, "Look! I see the heavens opened and the Son of Man standing at the right hand of God!"

57 Then they cried out with a loud voice, stopped their ears, and ran at him with one accord; 58 and they cast *him* out of the city and stoned *him.* And the witnesses laid down their clothes at the feet of a young man named Saul. 59 And they stoned Stephen as he was calling on *God* and saying, "Lord Jesus, receive my spirit." 60 Then he knelt down and cried out with a loud voice, "Lord, do not charge them with this sin." And when he had said this, he fell asleep.

❧❧❧❧

Reading 178—Power for Change
Acts 8:17

The Holy Spirit's influence and power were at work before Pentecost, but *He* was not there. Immediately our Lord was glorified in Ascension, the Holy Spirit came into this world, and He has been here ever since. We have to receive the revelation that He is here. The reception of the Holy Spirit is the maintained attitude of a believer. When we receive the Holy Spirit, we receive quickening life from the ascended Lord.

It is not the baptism of the Holy Ghost which changes men, but the power of the ascended Christ coming into men's lives by the Holy Ghost that changes them. We too often divorce what the New Testament never divorces. The baptism of the Holy Ghost is not an experience apart from Jesus Christ: it is the evidence of the ascended Christ.

The baptism of the Holy Ghost does not make you think of Time or Eternity, it is one amazing glorious NOW. "This is eternal life, that they may know You." Begin to know Him now, and finish never.   (*Utmost*)

1 CHRONICLES 17:1—18:17

NOW it came to pass, when David was dwelling in his house, that David said to Nathan the prophet, "See now, I dwell in a house of cedar, but the ark of the covenant of the Lord *is* under tent curtains."

2 Then Nathan said to David, "Do all that *is* in your heart, for God *is* with you."

3 But it happened that night that the word of God came to Nathan, saying, 4 "Go and tell My servant David, 'Thus says the Lord: "You shall not build Me a house to dwell in. 5 For I have not dwelt in a house since the time that I brought up Israel, even to this day, but have gone from tent to tent, and from *one* tabernacle *to another*. 6 Wherever I have moved about with all Israel, have I ever spoken a word to any of the judges of Israel, whom I commanded to shepherd My people, saying, 'Why have you not built Me a house of cedar?' " ' 7 Now therefore, thus shall you say to My servant David, 'Thus says the Lord of hosts: "I took you from the sheepfold, from following the sheep, to be ruler over My people Israel. 8 And I have been with you wherever you have gone, and have cut off all your enemies from before you, and have made you a name like the name of the great men who *are* on the earth. 9 Moreover I will appoint a place for My people Israel, and will plant them, that they may dwell in a place of their own and move no more; nor shall the sons of wickedness oppress them anymore, as previously, 10 since the time that I commanded judges *to be* over My people Israel. Also I will subdue all your enemies. Furthermore I tell you that the Lord will build you a house. 11 And it shall be, when your days are fulfilled, when you must go *to be* with your fathers, that I will set up your seed after you, who will be of your sons; and I will establish his kingdom. 12 He shall build Me a house, and I will establish his throne forever. 13 I will be his Father, and he shall be My son; and I will not take My mercy away from him, as I took *it* from *him* who was before you. 14 And I will establish him in My house and in My kingdom forever; and his throne shall be established forever." ' "

15 According to all these words and according to all this vision, so Nathan spoke to David.

16 Then King David went in and sat before the Lord; and he said: "Who *am* I, O Lord God? And what is my house, that You have brought me this far? 17 And *yet* this was a small thing in Your sight, O God; and You have *also* spoken of Your servant's house for a great while to come, and have regarded me according to the rank of a man of high degree, O Lord God. 18 What more can David *say* to You for the honor of Your servant? For You know Your servant. 19 O Lord, for Your servant's sake, and according to Your own heart, You have done all this greatness, in making known all these great things. 20 O Lord, *there is* none like You, nor *is there any* God besides You, according to all that we have heard with our ears. 21 And who *is* like Your people Israel, the one nation on the earth whom God went to redeem for Himself *as* a people—to make for Yourself a name by great and awesome deeds, by driving out nations from before Your people whom You redeemed from Egypt? 22 For You have made Your people Israel Your very own people forever; and You, Lord, have become their God.

23 "And now, O Lord, the word which You have spoken concerning Your servant and concerning his house, *let it* be established forever, and do as You have said. 24 So let it be established, that Your name may be magnified forever, saying, 'The Lord of hosts, the God of Israel, *is* Israel's God.' And let the house of Your servant David be established before You. 25 For You, O my God, have revealed to Your servant that You will build him a house. Therefore Your servant has found it *in his heart* to pray before You. 26 And now,

---

*P*rayer is labor, not agony.   (ASK)

Lord, You are God, and have promised this goodness to Your servant. 27 Now You have been pleased to bless the house of Your servant, that it may continue before You forever; for You have blessed it, O Lord, and *it shall be* blessed forever."

18 AFTER this it came to pass that David attacked the Philistines, subdued them, and took Gath and its towns from the hand of the Philistines. 2 Then he defeated Moab, and the Moabites became David's servants, *and* brought tribute.

3 And David defeated Hadadezer king of Zobah *as far as* Hamath, as he went to establish his power by the River Euphrates. 4 David took from him one thousand chariots, seven thousand horsemen, and twenty thousand foot soldiers. Also David hamstrung all the chariot *horses,* except that he spared enough of them for one hundred chariots.

5 When the Syrians of Damascus came to help Hadadezer king of Zobah, David killed twenty-two thousand of the Syrians. 6 Then David put *garrisons* in Syria of Damascus; and the Syrians became David's servants, *and* brought tribute. So the LORD preserved David wherever he went. 7 And David took the shields of gold that were on the servants of Hadadezer, and brought them to Jerusalem. 8 Also from Tibhath and from Chun, cities of Hadadezer, David brought a large amount of bronze, with which Solomon made the bronze Sea, the pillars, and the articles of bronze.

9 Now when Tou king of Hamath heard that David had defeated all the army of Hadadezer king of Zobah, 10 he sent Hadoram his son to King David, to greet him and bless him, because he had fought against Hadadezer and defeated him (for Hadadezer had been at war with Tou); and *Hadoram brought with him* all kinds of articles of gold, silver, and bronze. 11 King David also dedicated these to the LORD, along with the silver and gold that he had brought from all *these* nations—from Edom, from Moab, from the people of Ammon, from the Philistines, and from Amalek.

12 Moreover Abishai the son of Zeruiah killed eighteen thousand Edomites in the Valley of Salt. 13 He also put garrisons in Edom, and all the Edomites became David's servants. And the LORD preserved David wherever he went.

14 So David reigned over all Israel, and administered judgment and justice to all his people. 15 Joab the son of Zeruiah *was* over the army; Jehoshaphat the son of Ahilud *was* recorder; 16 Zadok the son of Ahitub and Abimelech the son of Abiathar *were* the priests; Shavsha *was* the scribe; 17 Benaiah the son of Jehoiada *was* over the Cherethites and the Pelethites; and David's sons *were* chief ministers at the king's side.

PSALM 78:17–25

17 BUT they sinned even more against Him
By rebelling against the Most High in the wilderness.
18 And they tested God in their heart
By asking for the food of their fancy.
19 Yes, they spoke against God:
They said, "Can God prepare a table in the wilderness?
20 Behold, He struck the rock,
So that the waters gushed out,
And the streams overflowed.
Can He give bread also?
Can He provide meat for His people?"

21 Therefore the LORD heard *this* and was furious;
So a fire was kindled against Jacob,
And anger also came up against Israel,
22 Because they did not believe in God,
And did not trust in His salvation.
23 Yet He had commanded the clouds above,
And opened the doors of heaven,
24 Had rained down manna on them to eat,
And given them of the bread of heaven.
25 Men ate angels' food;
He sent them food to the full.

PROVERBS 19:25, 26

25 STRIKE a scoffer, and the simple will become wary;
Rebuke one who has understanding, *and* he will discern knowledge.

26 He who mistreats *his* father *and* chases away *his* mother
Is a son who causes shame and brings reproach.

ACTS 8:1–25

NOW Saul was consenting to his death.

At that time a great persecution arose against the church which was at Jerusalem; and they were all scattered throughout the regions of Judea and Samaria, except the apostles. 2 And devout men carried Stephen

---

***P**ersecution is the thing that tests our Christianity.* (SERVANT AS LORD)

---

to his burial, and made great lamentation over him.

3 As for Saul, he made havoc of the church, entering every house, and dragging off men and women, committing *them* to prison.

4 Therefore those who were scattered went everywhere preaching the word. 5 Then Philip went down to the city of Samaria and preached Christ to them. 6 And the multitudes with one accord heeded the things spoken by Philip, hearing and seeing the miracles which he did. 7 For unclean spirits, crying with a loud voice, came out of many who were possessed; and many who were paralyzed and lame were healed. 8 And there was great joy in that city.

9 But there was a certain man called Simon, who previously practiced sorcery in the city and astonished the people of Samaria, claiming that he was someone great, 10 to whom they all gave heed, from the least to the greatest, saying, "This man is the great power of God." 11 And they heeded him because he had astonished them with his sorceries for a long time. 12 But when they believed Philip as he preached the things concerning the kingdom of God and the name of Jesus Christ, both men and women were baptized. 13 Then Simon himself also believed; and when he was baptized he continued with Philip, and was amazed, seeing the miracles and signs which were done.

14 Now when the apostles who were at Jerusalem heard that Samaria had received the word of God, they sent Peter and John to them, 15 who, when they had come down, prayed for them that they might receive the Holy Spirit. 16 For as yet He had fallen upon none of them. They had only been baptized in the name of the Lord Jesus. 17 Then they laid hands on them, and they received the Holy Spirit.

18 And when Simon saw that through the laying on of the apostles' hands the Holy Spirit was given, he offered them money, 19 saying, "Give me this power also, that anyone on whom I lay hands may receive the Holy Spirit."

20 But Peter said to him, "Your money perish with you, because you thought that the gift of God could be purchased with money! 21 You have neither part nor portion in this matter, for your heart is not right in the sight of God. 22 Repent therefore of this your wickedness, and pray God if perhaps the thought of your heart may be forgiven you. 23 For I see that you are poisoned by bitterness and bound by iniquity."

24 Then Simon answered and said, "Pray to the Lord for me, that none of the things which you have spoken may come upon me."

25 So when they had testified and preached the word of the Lord, they returned to Jerusalem, preaching the gospel in many villages of the Samaritans.

◆◆◆◆

Reading 179—Peril for the Preacher
Acts 8:35

The more facile the expression in words, the less likely is the truth to be carried out in life. There is a peril for the preacher that the listener has not, the peril of expressing a thing and letting the expression react in the exhaustion of never doing it. That is where fasting has to be exercised—fasting from eloquence, from fine literary finish, from all that natural culture makes us esteem, if it is going to lead us into a hirpling walk with God. "This kind can come out by nothing but prayer and fasting."   (*SERMON MT.*)

When the message you have to deliver, brother preacher, strikes straight home, don't water it down just a little. Go straight for God if you come from Him. Neither for fear nor favor alter the message. What happened to John the Baptist? He went straight back to God, minus his head. That was the result of his message.   (*WORKMEN*)

Be a walking, talking, living example of what you preach, in every silent moment of your life, known and unknown; bear the scrutiny of God, until you prove that you are indeed an example of what He can do, and then "make disciples of all the nations." (*WORKMEN*)

1 CHRONICLES 19:1—20:8

IT happened after this that Nahash the king of the people of Ammon died, and his son reigned in his place. 2 Then David said, "I will show kindness to Hanun the son of Nahash, because his father showed kindness to me." So David sent messengers to comfort him concerning his father. And David's servants came to Hanun in the land of the people of Ammon to comfort him.

3 And the princes of the people of Ammon said to Hanun, "Do you think that David really honors your father because he has sent comforters to you? Did his servants not come to you to search and to overthrow and to spy out the land?"

4 Therefore Hanun took David's servants, shaved them, and cut off their garments in the middle, at their buttocks, and sent them away. 5 Then *some* went and told David about the men; and he sent to meet them, because the men were greatly ashamed. And the king said, "Wait at Jericho until your beards have grown, and *then* return."

6 When the people of Ammon saw that they had made themselves repulsive to David, Hanun and the people of Ammon sent a thousand talents of silver to hire for themselves chariots and horsemen from Mesopotamia, from Syrian Maacah, and from Zobah. 7 So they hired for themselves thirty-two thousand chariots, with the king of Maacah and his people, who came and encamped before Medeba. Also the people of Ammon gathered together from their cities, and came to battle.

8 Now when David heard *of it,* he sent Joab and all the army of the mighty men. 9 Then the people of Ammon came out and put themselves in battle array before the gate of the city, and the kings who had come *were* by themselves in the field.

10 When Joab saw that the battle line was against him before and behind, he chose some of Israel's best, and put *them* in battle array against the Syrians. 11 And the rest of the people he put under the command of Abishai his brother, and they set *themselves* in battle array against the people of Ammon. 12 Then he said, "If the Syrians are too strong for me, then you shall help me; but if the people of Ammon are too strong for you, then I will help you. 13 Be of good courage, and let us be strong for our people and for the cities of our God. And may the LORD do *what is* good in His sight."

14 So Joab and the people who *were* with him drew near for the battle against the Syrians, and they fled before him. 15 When the people of Ammon saw that the Syrians were fleeing, they also fled before Abishai his brother, and entered the city. So Joab went to Jerusalem.

16 Now when the Syrians saw that they had been defeated by Israel, they sent messengers and brought the Syrians who were beyond the River, and Shophach the commander of Hadadezer's army *went* before them. 17 When it was told David, he gathered all Israel, crossed over the Jordan and came upon them, and set up in battle array against them. So when David had set up in *battle* array against the Syrians, they fought with him. 18 Then the Syrians fled before Israel; and David killed seven thousand charioteers and forty thousand foot soldiers of the Syrians, and killed Shophach the commander of the army. 19 And when the servants of Hadadezer saw that they were defeated by Israel, they made peace with David and became his servants. So the Syrians were not willing to help the people of Ammon anymore.

20 IT happened in the spring of the year, at the time kings go out *to battle,* that Joab led out the armed forces and ravaged the country of the people of Ammon, and came and besieged Rabbah. But David stayed at Jerusalem. And Joab defeated Rabbah and overthrew it. 2 Then David took their king's crown from his head, and found it to weigh a talent of gold, and *there were* precious stones in it. And it was set on David's head. Also he brought out the spoil of the city in great abundance. 3 And he brought out the people who *were* in it, and put *them* to work with saws, with iron picks, and with axes. So David did to all the cities of the people of Ammon. Then David and all the people returned *to* Jerusalem.

4 Now it happened afterward that war

broke out at Gezer with the Philistines, at which time Sibbechai the Hushathite killed Sippai, *who was one* of the sons of the giant. And they were subdued.

5 Again there was war with the Philistines, and Elhanan the son of Jair killed Lahmi the brother of Goliath the Gittite, the shaft of whose spear *was* like a weaver's beam.

6 Yet again there was war at Gath, where there was a man of *great* stature, with twenty-four fingers and toes, six *on each hand* and six *on each foot;* and he also was born to the giant. 7 So when he defied Israel, Jonathan the son of Shimea, David's brother, killed him.

8 These were born to the giant in Gath, and they fell by the hand of David and by the hand of his servants.

PSALM 78:26–33

26 HE caused an east wind to blow in the heavens;
And by His power He brought in the south wind.
27 He also rained meat on them like the dust,
Feathered fowl like the sand of the seas;
28 And He let *them* fall in the midst of their camp,
All around their dwellings.
29 So they ate and were well filled,
For He gave them their own desire.
30 They were not deprived of their craving;
But while their food *was* still in their mouths,
31 The wrath of God came against them,
And slew the stoutest of them,
And struck down the choice *men* of Israel.

32 In spite of this they still sinned,
And did not believe in His wondrous works.
33 Therefore their days He consumed in futility,
And their years in fear.

PROVERBS 19:27–29

27 CEASE listening to instruction, my son,
And you will stray from the words of knowledge.

28 A disreputable witness scorns justice,
And the mouth of the wicked devours iniquity.

29 Judgments are prepared for scoffers,
And beatings for the backs of fools.

ACTS 8:26–40

NOW an angel of the Lord spoke to Philip, saying, "Arise and go toward the south along the road which goes down from Jerusalem to Gaza." This is desert. 27 So he arose and went. And behold, a man of Ethiopia, a eunuch of great authority under Candace the queen of the Ethiopians, who had charge of all her treasury, and had come to Jerusalem to worship, 28 was returning. And sitting in his chariot, he was reading Isaiah the prophet. 29 Then the Spirit said to Philip, "Go near and overtake this chariot."

30 So Philip ran to him, and heard him reading the prophet Isaiah, and said, "Do you understand what you are reading?"

31 And he said, "How can I, unless someone guides me?" And he asked Philip to come up and sit with him. 32 The place in the Scripture which he read was this:

"He was led as a sheep to the slaughter;
And as a lamb before its shearer *is* silent,
So He opened not His mouth.
33 In His humiliation His justice was taken away,
And who will declare His generation?
For His life is taken from the earth."

34 So the eunuch answered Philip and said, "I ask you, of whom does the prophet say this, of himself or of some other man?" 35 Then Philip opened his mouth, and beginning at this Scripture, preached Jesus to him. 36 Now as they went down the road,

---

*O*ur Lord never tells us to confess anything but Himself, "Whoever confesses Me before men. . . ." (SERMON MT.)

---

they came to some water. And the eunuch said, "See, *here is* water. What hinders me from being baptized?"

37 Then Philip said, "If you believe with all your heart, you may."

And he answered and said, "I believe that Jesus Christ is the Son of God."

38 So he commanded the chariot to stand still. And both Philip and the eunuch went

down into the water, and he baptized him. 39 Now when they came up out of the water, the Spirit of the Lord caught Philip away, so that the eunuch saw him no more; and he went on his way rejoicing. 40 But Philip was found at Azotus. And passing through, he preached in all the cities till he came to Caesarea.

◆◆◆◆ ──────────────

Reading 180—Inscrutable Disaster
Acts 9:9

W ho was Saul of Tarsus? A Pharisee of the Pharisees, a man of superb integrity and conscientiousness. . . . He was conscientious when he hounded the followers of Jesus Christ to death. Then came disaster, all his world was flung to pieces. God arrested him, "He was three days without sight, and neither ate nor drank"; but out of the inscrutable disaster and upset God brought him into a personal experience of Himself. "But when it pleased God, who separated me from my mother's womb and called *me* through His grace, to reveal His Son in me, . . ." (Gal. 1:15, 16). For three years Saul went round about Sinai while the Holy Spirit blazed into him the things that became his epistles. . . .

When I start walking with God, I have not taken three strides before I find He has outstripped me; He has different ways of doing things and I have to be trained and disciplined into His ways. . . . Discouragement is "disenchanted egotism." We learn spiritual truth by atmosphere not by intellectual reasoning; God's Spirit alters the atmosphere of our ways of looking at things, and things begin to be possible which never were possible before.

If you are going through a period of discouragement there is a big personal enlargement ahead. We have the stride of divine healing, of sanctification, of the Second Coming; all these are right, but the stride of God is never anything less than union with Himself. (PLACE HELP)

1 CHRONICLES 21:1—22:19

NOW Satan stood up against Israel, and moved David to number Israel. 2 So David

─────────────
Satan represents the self-interest of humanity. (GLORIFY)
─────────────

said to Joab and to the leaders of the people, "Go, number Israel from Beersheba to Dan, and bring the number of them to me that I may know *it*."

3 And Joab answered, "May the LORD make His people a hundred times more than they are. But, my lord the king, *are* they not all my lord's servants? Why then does my lord require this thing? Why should he be a cause of guilt in Israel?"

4 Nevertheless the king's word prevailed against Joab. Therefore Joab departed and went throughout all Israel and came to Jerusalem. 5 Then Joab gave the sum of the number of the people to David. All Israel *had* one million one hundred thousand men who drew the sword, and Judah *had* four hundred and seventy thousand men who drew the sword. 6 But he did not count Levi and Benjamin among them, for the king's word was abominable to Joab.

7 And God was displeased with this thing; therefore He struck Israel. 8 So David said to God, "I have sinned greatly, because I have done this thing; but now, I pray, take away the iniquity of Your servant, for I have done very foolishly."

9 Then the LORD spoke to Gad, David's seer, saying, 10 "Go and tell David, saying, 'Thus says the LORD: "I offer you three *things;* choose one of them for yourself, that I may do *it* to you." ' "

11 So Gad came to David and said to him, "Thus says the LORD: 'Choose for yourself, 12 either three years of famine, or three months to be defeated by your foes with the sword of your enemies overtaking *you*, or else for three days the sword of the LORD—the plague in the land, with the angel of the LORD destroying throughout all the territory of Israel.' Now consider what answer I should take back to Him who sent me."

13 And David said to Gad, "I am in great distress. Please let me fall into the hand of the LORD, for His mercies *are* very great; but do not let me fall into the hand of man."

14 So the LORD sent a plague upon Israel, and seventy thousand men of Israel fell. 15 And God sent an angel to Jerusalem to destroy it. As he was destroying, the LORD looked and relented of the disaster, and said to the angel who was destroying, "It is enough; now restrain your hand." And the angel of the LORD stood by the threshing floor of Ornan the Jebusite.

16 Then David lifted his eyes and saw the angel of the LORD standing between earth and heaven, having in his hand a drawn sword stretched out over Jerusalem. So David and the elders, clothed in sackcloth, fell on their faces. 17 And David said to God, "Was it not I who commanded the people to be numbered? I am the one who has sinned and done evil indeed; but these sheep, what have they done? Let Your hand, I pray, O LORD my God, be against me and my father's house, but not against Your people that they should be plagued."

18 Therefore, the angel of the LORD commanded Gad to say to David that David should go and erect an altar to the LORD on the threshing floor of Ornan the Jebusite. 19 So David went up at the word of Gad, which he had spoken in the name of the LORD. 20 Now Ornan turned and saw the angel; and his four sons *who were* with him hid themselves, but Ornan continued threshing wheat. 21 So David came to Ornan, and Ornan looked and saw David. And he went out from the threshing floor, and bowed before David with *his* face to the ground. 22 Then David said to Ornan, "Grant me the place of *this* threshing floor, that I may build an altar on it to the LORD. You shall grant it to me at the full price, that the plague may be withdrawn from the people."

23 But Ornan said to David, "Take *it* to yourself, and let my lord the king do *what is* good in his eyes. Look, I *also* give *you* the oxen for burnt offerings, the threshing implements for wood, and the wheat for the grain offering; I give *it* all."

24 Then King David said to Ornan, "No, but I will surely buy *it* for the full price, for I will not take what is yours for the LORD, nor offer burnt offerings with *that which* costs *me* nothing." 25 So David gave Ornan six hundred shekels of gold by weight for the place. 26 And David built there an altar to the LORD, and offered burnt offerings and peace offerings, and called on the LORD; and He answered him from heaven by fire on the altar of burnt offering.

27 So the LORD commanded the angel, and he returned his sword to its sheath.

28 At that time, when David saw that the LORD had answered him on the threshing floor of Ornan the Jebusite, he sacrificed there. 29 For the tabernacle of the LORD and the altar of the burnt offering, which Moses had made in the wilderness, *were* at that time at the high place in Gibeon. 30 But David could not go before it to inquire of God, for he was afraid of the sword of the angel of the LORD.

22 THEN David said, "This *is* the house of the LORD God, and this *is* the altar of burnt offering for Israel." 2 So David commanded to gather the aliens who *were* in the land of Israel; and he appointed masons to cut hewn stones to build the house of God. 3 And David prepared iron in abundance for the nails of the doors of the gates and for the joints, and bronze in abundance beyond measure, 4 and cedar trees in abundance; for the Sidonians and those from Tyre brought much cedar wood to David.

5 Now David said, "Solomon my son *is* young and inexperienced, and the house to be built for the LORD *must be* exceedingly magnificent, famous and glorious throughout all countries. I will now make preparation for it." So David made abundant preparations before his death.

6 Then he called for his son Solomon, and charged him to build a house for the LORD God of Israel. 7 And David said to Solomon: "My son, as for me, it was in my mind to build a house to the name of the LORD my God; 8 but the word of the LORD came to me, saying, 'You have shed much blood and have made great wars; you shall not build a house for My name, because you have shed much blood on the earth in My sight. 9 Behold, a son shall be born to you, who shall be a man of rest; and I will give him rest from all his enemies all around. His name shall be Solomon, for I will give peace and quietness to Israel

in his days. 10 He shall build a house for My name, and he shall be My son, and I *will be* his Father; and I will establish the throne of his kingdom over Israel forever.' 11 Now, my son, may the LORD be with you; and may you prosper, and build the house of the LORD your God, as He has said to you. 12 Only may the LORD give you wisdom and understanding, and give you charge concerning Israel, that you may keep the law of the LORD your God. 13 Then you will prosper, if you take care to fulfill the statutes and judgments with which the LORD charged Moses concerning Israel. Be strong and of good courage; do not fear nor be dismayed. 14 Indeed I have taken much trouble to prepare for the house of the LORD one hundred thousand talents of gold and one million talents of silver, and bronze and iron beyond measure, for it is so abundant. I have prepared timber and stone also, and you may add to them. 15 Moreover *there are* workmen with you in abundance: woodsmen and stone-cutters, and all types of skillful men for every kind of work. 16 Of gold and silver and bronze and iron *there is* no limit. Arise and begin working, and the LORD be with you."

17 David also commanded all the leaders of Israel to help Solomon his son, *saying,* 18 "*Is* not the LORD your God with you? And has He *not* given you rest on every side? For He has given the inhabitants of the land into my hand, and the land is subdued before the LORD and before His people. 19 Now set your heart and your soul to seek the LORD your God. Therefore arise and build the sanctuary of the LORD God, to bring the ark of the covenant of the LORD and the holy articles of God into the house that is to be built for the name of the LORD."

PSALM 78:34–39

34 WHEN He slew them, then they sought Him;
  And they returned and sought earnestly for God.
35 Then they remembered that God *was* their rock,
  And the Most High God their Redeemer.
36 Nevertheless they flattered Him with their mouth,
  And they lied to Him with their tongue;
37 For their heart was not steadfast with Him,
  Nor were they faithful in His covenant.

38 But He, *being* full of compassion, forgave *their* iniquity,
  And did not destroy *them.*
  Yes, many a time He turned His anger away,
  And did not stir up all His wrath;
39 For He remembered that they *were but* flesh,
  A breath that passes away and does not come again.

PROVERBS 20:1, 2

1 WINE *is* a mocker,
  Strong drink *is* a brawler,
  And whoever is led astray by it is not wise.

2 The wrath of a king *is* like the roaring of a lion;
  Whoever provokes him to anger sins *against* his own life.

ACTS 9:1–21

THEN Saul, still breathing threats and murder against the disciples of the Lord, went to the high priest 2 and asked letters from him to the synagogues of Damascus, so that if he found any who were of the Way, whether men or women, he might bring them bound to Jerusalem.

3 As he journeyed he came near Damascus, and suddenly a light shone around him from heaven. 4 Then he fell to the ground, and heard a voice saying to him, "Saul, Saul, why are you persecuting Me?"

5 And he said, "Who are You, Lord?"

Then the Lord said, "I am Jesus, whom you are persecuting. It *is* hard for you to kick against the goads."

6 So he, trembling and astonished, said, "Lord, what do You want me to do?"

Then the Lord *said* to him, "Arise and go into the city, and you will be told what you must do."

7 And the men who journeyed with him stood speechless, hearing a voice but seeing no one. 8 Then Saul arose from the ground, and when his eyes were opened he saw no one. But they led him by the hand and brought *him* into Damascus. 9 And he was three days without sight, and neither ate nor drank.

10 Now there was a certain disciple at Damascus named Ananias; and to him the Lord said in a vision, "Ananias."

And he said, "Here I am, Lord."

11 So the Lord *said* to him, "Arise and go to the street called Straight, and inquire at the house of Judas for *one* called Saul of Tarsus, for behold, he is praying. 12 And in a vision he has seen a man named Ananias coming in and putting *his* hand on him, so that he might receive his sight."

13 Then Ananias answered, "Lord, I have heard from many about this man, how much harm he has done to Your saints in Jerusalem. 14 And here he has authority

---

Jesus Christ can make the weakest man into a divine dreadnought, fearing nothing.   (SERVANT AS LORD)

---

from the chief priests to bind all who call on Your name."

15 But the Lord said to him, "Go, for he is a chosen vessel of Mine to bear My name before Gentiles, kings, and the children of Israel. 16 For I will show him how

many things he must suffer for My name's sake."

17 And Ananias went his way and entered the house; and laying his hands on him he said, "Brother Saul, the Lord Jesus, who appeared to you on the road as you came, has sent me that you may receive your sight and be filled with the Holy Spirit." 18 Immediately there fell from his eyes *something* like scales, and he received his sight at once; and he arose and was baptized.

19 So when he had received food, he was strengthened. Then Saul spent some days with the disciples at Damascus.

20 Immediately he preached the Christ in the synagogues, that He is the Son of God.

21 Then all who heard were amazed, and said, "Is this not he who destroyed those who called on this name in Jerusalem, and has come here for that purpose, so that he might bring them bound to the chief priests?"

◆◆◆◆

Reading 181—Devoted to a Person
Acts 9:26

The vision Paul had on the road to Damascus was no passing emotion, but a vision that had very clear and emphatic directions for him, and he says, "I was not disobedient to the heavenly vision." Our Lord said, in effect, to Paul—Your whole life is to be overmastered by Me; you are to have no end, no aim, and no purpose but Mine. *"I have chosen him."*

When we are born again we all have visions, if we are spiritual at all, of what Jesus wants us to be, and the great thing is to learn not to be disobedient to the vision, not to say that it cannot be attained. It is not sufficient to know that God has redeemed the world, and to know that the Holy Spirit can make all that Jesus did effectual in me; I must have the basis of a personal relationship to Him. Paul was not given a message or a doctrine to proclaim, he was brought into a vivid, personal, overmastering relationship to Jesus Christ. Acts 26:16 is immensely commanding—"to make you a minister and a witness." There is nothing there apart from the personal relationship. Paul was devoted to a Person not to a cause. He was absolutely Jesus Christ's, he saw nothing else, he lived for nothing else. "For I determined not to know anything among you except Jesus Christ and Him crucified."   (*UTMOST*)

---

1 CHRONICLES 23:1—25:31

SO when David was old and full of days, he made his son Solomon king over Israel.

2 And he gathered together all the leaders of Israel, with the priests and the Levites.

3 Now the Levites were numbered from the age of thirty years and above; and the number of individual males was thirty-eight thousand. 4 Of these, twenty-four thousand *were* to look after the work of the house of the LORD, six thousand *were* officers and

judges, 5 four thousand *were* gatekeepers, and four thousand praised the LORD with *musical* instruments, "which I made," *said David*, "for giving praise."

6 Also David separated them into divisions among the sons of Levi: Gershon, Kohath, and Merari.

7 Of the Gershonites: Laadan and Shimei. 8 The sons of Laadan: the first Jehiel, then Zetham and Joel—three *in all*. 9 The sons of Shimei: Shelomith, Haziel, and Haran—three *in all*. These were the heads of the fathers' *houses* of Laadan. 10 And the sons of Shimei: Jahath, Zina, Jeush, and Beriah. These *were* the four sons of Shimei. 11 Jahath was the first and Zizah the second. But Jeush and Beriah did not have many sons; therefore they were assigned as one father's house.

12 The sons of Kohath: Amram, Izhar, Hebron, and Uzziel—four *in all*. 13 The sons of Amram: Aaron and Moses; and Aaron was set apart, he and his sons forever, that he should sanctify the most holy things, to burn incense before the LORD, to minister to Him, and to give the blessing in His name forever. 14 Now the sons of Moses the man of God were reckoned to the tribe of Levi. 15 The sons of Moses *were* Gershon and Eliezer. 16 Of the sons of Gershon, Shebuel *was* the first. 17 Of the descendants of Eliezer, Rehabiah was the first. And Eliezer had no other sons, but the sons of Rehabiah were very many. 18 Of the sons of Izhar, Shelomith *was* the first. 19 Of the sons of Hebron, Jeriah *was* the first, Amariah the second, Jahaziel the third, and Jekameam the fourth. 20 Of the sons of Uzziel, Michah *was* the first and Jesshiah the second.

21 The sons of Merari *were* Mahli and Mushi. The sons of Mahli *were* Eleazar and Kish. 22 And Eleazar died, and had no sons, but only daughters; and their brethren, the sons of Kish, took them *as wives*. 23 The sons of Mushi *were* Mahli, Eder, and Jeremoth—three *in all*.

24 These *were* the sons of Levi by their fathers' houses—the heads of the fathers' *houses* as they were counted individually by the number of their names, who did the work for the service of the house of the LORD, from the age of twenty years and above.

25 For David said, "The LORD God of Israel has given rest to His people, that they may dwell in Jerusalem forever"; 26 and also to the Levites, "They shall no longer carry the tabernacle, or any of the articles for its service." 27 For by the last words of David the Levites *were* numbered from twenty years old and above; 28 because

their duty *was* to help the sons of Aaron in the service of the house of the LORD, in the courts and in the chambers, in the purifying of all holy things and the work of the service of the house of God, 29 both with the showbread and the fine flour for the grain offering, with the unleavened cakes and *what is baked in* the pan, with what is mixed and with all kinds of measures and sizes; 30 to stand every morning to thank and praise the LORD, and likewise at evening; 31 and at every presentation of a burnt offering to the LORD on the Sabbaths and on the New Moons and on the set feasts, by number according to the ordinance governing them, regularly before the LORD; 32 and that they should attend to the needs of the tabernacle of meeting, the needs of the holy *place*, and the needs of the sons of Aaron their brethren in the work of the house of the LORD.

24 NOW *these are* the divisions of the sons of Aaron. The sons of Aaron *were* Nadab, Abihu, Eleazar, and Ithamar. 2 And Nadab and Abihu died before their father, and had no children; therefore Eleazar and Ithamar ministered as priests. 3 Then David with Zadok of the sons of Eleazar, and Ahimelech of the sons of Ithamar, divided them according to the schedule of their service.

4 There were more leaders found of the sons of Eleazar than of the sons of Ithamar, and *thus* they were divided. Among the sons of Eleazar *were* sixteen heads of *their* fathers' houses, and eight heads of their fathers' houses among the sons of Ithamar. 5 Thus they were divided by lot, one group as another, for there were officials of the sanctuary and officials *of the house* of God, from the sons of Eleazar and from the sons of Ithamar. 6 And the scribe, Shemaiah the son of Nethanel, *one of* the Levites, wrote them down before the king, the leaders, Zadok the priest, Ahimelech the son of Abiathar, and the heads of the fathers' *houses* of the priests and Levites, one father's house taken for Eleazar and *one* for Ithamar.

7 Now the first lot fell to Jehoiarib, the second to Jedaiah, 8 the third to Harim, the fourth to Seorim, 9 the fifth to Malchijah, the sixth to Mijamin, 10 the seventh to Hakkoz, the eighth to Abijah, 11 the ninth to Jeshua, the tenth to Shecaniah, 12 the eleventh to Eliashib, the twelfth to Jakim, 13 the thirteenth to Huppah, the fourteenth to Jeshebeab, 14 the fifteenth to Bilgah, the sixteenth to Immer, 15 the seventeenth to Hezir, the eighteenth to Happizzez, 16 the nineteenth to Pethahiah, the

twentieth to Jehezekel, 17 the twenty-first to Jachin, the twenty-second to Gamul, 18 the twenty-third to Delaiah, the twenty-fourth to Maaziah.

19 This *was* the schedule of their service for coming into the house of the LORD according to their ordinance by the hand of Aaron their father, as the LORD God of Israel had commanded him.

20 And the rest of the sons of Levi: of the sons of Amram, Shubael; of the sons of Shubael, Jehdeiah. 21 Concerning Rehabiah, of the sons of Rehabiah, the first *was* Isshiah. 22 Of the Izharites, Shelomoth; of the sons of Shelomoth, Jahath. 23 Of the sons *of Hebron,* Jeriah *was the first,* Amariah the second, Jahaziel the third, *and* Jekameam the fourth. 24 *Of* the sons of Uzziel, Michah; of the sons of Michah, Shamir. 25 The brother of Michah, Isshiah; of the sons of Isshiah, Zechariah. 26 The sons of Merari *were* Mahli and Mushi; the son of Jaaziah, Beno. 27 The sons of Merari by Jaaziah *were* Beno, Shoham, Zaccur, and Ibri. 28 Of Mahli: Eleazar, who had no sons. 29 Of Kish: the son of Kish, Jerahmeel.

30 Also the sons of Mushi *were* Mahli, Eder, and Jerimoth. These *were* the sons of the Levites according to their fathers' houses.

31 These also cast lots just as their brothers the sons of Aaron did, in the presence of King David, Zadok, Ahimelech, and the heads of the fathers' *houses* of the priests and Levites. The chief fathers *did* just as their younger brethren.

25 MOREOVER David and the captains of the army separated for the service *some* of the sons of Asaph, of Heman, and of Jeduthun, who *should* prophesy with harps, stringed instruments, and cymbals. And the number of the skilled men performing their service was: 2 Of the sons of Asaph: Zaccur, Joseph, Nethaniah, and Asharelah; the sons of Asaph *were* under the direction of Asaph, who prophesied according to the order of the king. 3 Of Jeduthun, the sons of Jeduthun: Gedaliah, Zeri, Jeshaiah, Shimei, Hashabiah, and Mattithiah, six, under the direction of their father Jeduthun, who prophesied with a harp to give thanks and to praise the LORD. 4 Of Heman, the sons of Heman: Bukkiah, Mattaniah, Uzziel, Shebuel, Jerimoth, Hananiah, Hanani, Eliathah, Giddalti, Romamti-Ezer, Joshbekashah, Mallothi, Hothir, *and* Mahazioth. 5 All these *were* the sons of Heman the king's seer in the words of God, to exalt his horn. For God gave Heman fourteen sons and three daughters.

6 All these *were* under the direction of their father for the music *in* the house of the LORD, with cymbals, stringed instruments, and harps, for the service of the house of God. Asaph, Jeduthun, and Heman *were* under the authority of the king. 7 So the number of them, with their brethren who were instructed in the songs of the LORD, all who were skillful, *was* two hundred and eighty-eight.

8 And they cast lots for their duty, the small as well as the great, the teacher with the student.

9 Now the first lot for Asaph came out for Joseph; the second for Gedaliah, him with his brethren and sons, twelve; 10 the third for Zaccur, his sons and his brethren, twelve; 11 the fourth for Jizri, his sons and his brethren, twelve; 12 the fifth for Nethaniah, his sons and his brethren, twelve; 13 the sixth for Bukkiah, his sons and his brethren, twelve; 14 the seventh for Jesharelah, his sons and his brethren, twelve; 15 the eighth for Jeshaiah, his sons and his brethren, twelve; 16 the ninth for Mattaniah, his sons and his brethren, twelve; 17 the tenth for Shimei, his sons and his brethren, twelve; 18 the eleventh for Azarel, his sons and his brethren, twelve; 19 the twelfth for Hashabiah, his sons and his brethren, twelve; 20 the thirteenth for Shubael, his sons and his brethren, twelve; 21 the fourteenth for Mattithiah, his sons and his brethren, twelve; 22 the fifteenth for Jeremoth, his sons and his brethren, twelve; 23 the sixteenth for Hananiah, his sons and his brethren, twelve; 24 the seventeenth for Joshbekashah, his sons and his brethren, twelve; 25 the eighteenth for Hanani, his sons and his brethren, twelve; 26 the nineteenth for Mallothi, his sons and his brethren, twelve; 27 the twentieth for Eliathah, his sons and his brethren, twelve; 28 the twenty-first for Hothir, his sons and his brethren, twelve; 29 the twenty-second for Giddalti, his sons and his brethren, twelve; 30 the twenty-third for Mahazioth, his sons and his brethren, twelve; 31 the twenty-fourth for Romamti-Ezer, his sons and his brethren, twelve.

PSALM 78:40–55

40   HOW often they provoked Him in the wilderness,
And grieved Him in the desert!
41   Yes, again and again they tempted God,
And limited the Holy One of Israel.
42   They did not remember His power:

The day when He redeemed them from
the enemy,

*I*srael was despised, and a
despisable nation, intentionally
turning away from God into
idolatry. (SEND I YOU)

43 When He worked His signs in Egypt,
And His wonders in the field of Zoan;
44 Turned their rivers into blood,
And their streams, that they could not
drink.
45 He sent swarms of flies among them,
which devoured them,
And frogs, which destroyed them.
46 He also gave their crops to the
caterpillar,
And their labor to the locust.
47 He destroyed their vines with hail,
And their sycamore trees with frost.
48 He also gave up their cattle to the hail,
And their flocks to fiery lightning.
49 He cast on them the fierceness of His
anger,
Wrath, indignation, and trouble,
By sending angels of destruction *among
them.*
50 He made a path for His anger;
He did not spare their soul from death,
But gave their life over to the plague,
51 And destroyed all the firstborn in
Egypt,
The first of *their* strength in the tents
of Ham.
52 But He made His own people go forth
like sheep,
And guided them in the wilderness like
a flock;
53 And He led them on safely, so that they
did not fear;
But the sea overwhelmed their enemies.
54 And He brought them to His holy
border,
This mountain *which* His right hand
had acquired.
55 He also drove out the nations before
them,
Allotted them an inheritance by survey,
And made the tribes of Israel dwell in
their tents.

PROVERBS 20:3

3 IT *is* honorable for a man to stop
striving,
Since any fool can start a quarrel.

ACTS 9:22–43

BUT Saul increased all the more in strength,
and confounded the Jews who dwelt in Damascus, proving that this *Jesus* is the Christ.
23 Now after many days were past, the
Jews plotted to kill him. 24 But their plot
became known to Saul. And they watched
the gates day and night, to kill him.
25 Then the disciples took him by night and
let *him* down through the wall in a large
basket.
26 And when Saul had come to Jerusalem,
he tried to join the disciples; but they were
all afraid of him, and did not believe that
he was a disciple. 27 But Barnabas took him
and brought *him* to the apostles. And he
declared to them how he had seen the Lord
on the road, and that He had spoken to
him, and how he had preached boldly at
Damascus in the name of Jesus. 28 So he
was with them at Jerusalem, coming in and
going out. 29 And he spoke boldly in the
name of the Lord Jesus and disputed against
the Hellenists, but they attempted to kill
him. 30 When the brethren found out, they
brought him down to Caesarea and sent
him out to Tarsus.
31 Then the churches throughout all Judea, Galilee, and Samaria had peace and
were edified. And walking in the fear of
the Lord and in the comfort of the Holy
Spirit, they were multiplied.
32 Now it came to pass, as Peter went
through all *parts of the country,* that he also
came down to the saints who dwelt in
Lydda. 33 There he found a certain man
named Aeneas, who had been bedridden
eight years and was paralyzed. 34 And Peter
said to him, "Aeneas, Jesus the Christ heals
you. Arise and make your bed." Then he
arose immediately. 35 So all who dwelt at
Lydda and Sharon saw him and turned to
the Lord.
36 At Joppa there was a certain disciple
named Tabitha, which is translated Dorcas.
This woman was full of good works and
charitable deeds which she did. 37 But it
happened in those days that she became
sick and died. When they had washed her,
they laid *her* in an upper room. 38 And since
Lydda was near Joppa, and the disciples
had heard that Peter was there, they sent
two men to him, imploring *him* not to delay
in coming to them. 39 Then Peter arose and
went with them. When he had come, they
brought *him* to the upper room. And all
the widows stood by him weeping, showing
the tunics and garments which Dorcas had
made while she was with them. 40 But Peter
put them all out, and knelt down and

prayed. And turning to the body he said, "Tabitha, arise." And she opened her eyes, and when she saw Peter she sat up. 41 Then he gave her *his* hand and lifted her up; and when he had called the saints and widows, he presented her alive. 42 And it became known throughout all Joppa, and many believed on the Lord. 43 So it was that he stayed many days in Joppa with Simon, a tanner.

◆◆◆◆

Reading 182—Obey the Vision
Acts 10:17–19

When we are born again we all have visions, if we are spiritual at all, of what Jesus wants us to be, and the great thing is to learn not to be disobedient to the vision, not to say that it cannot be attained.   (MUH)

If the Holy Spirit has given you a vision in your private Bible study or during a meeting which made your heart glow, and your mind expand, and your will stir itself to grasp, you will have to pay to the last farthing in concentration along that line until all you saw in vision is made actual.   (*CONFORMED*)

The healthiest exercise for the mind of a Christian is to learn to apprehend the truth granted to it in vision. Every Christian with any experience at all has had a vision of some fundamental truth, either about the Atonement or the Holy Spirit or sin, and it is at the peril of their souls that they lose the vision. By prayer and determination we have to form the habit of keeping ourselves soaked in the vision God has given. The difficulty with the majority of us is that we will not seek to apprehend the vision, we get glimpses of it and then leave it alone.   (*PHIL. SIN*)

1 CHRONICLES 26:1—27:34

CONCERNING the divisions of the gatekeepers: of the Korahites, Meshelemiah the son of Kore, of the sons of Asaph. 2 And the sons of Meshelemiah *were* Zechariah the firstborn, Jediael the second, Zebadiah the third, Jathniel the fourth, 3 Elam the fifth, Jehohanan the sixth, Eliehoenai the seventh.

4 Moreover the sons of Obed-Edom *were* Shemaiah the firstborn, Jehozabad the second, Joah the third, Sacar the fourth, Nethanel the fifth, 5 Ammiel the sixth, Issachar the seventh, Peulthai the eighth; for God blessed him.

6 Also to Shemaiah his son were sons born who governed their fathers' houses, because they *were* men of great ability. 7 The sons of Shemaiah *were* Othni, Rephael, Obed, and Elzabad, whose brothers Elihu and Semachiah *were* able men.

8 All these *were* of the sons of Obed-Edom, they and their sons and their breth-ren, able men with strength for the work: sixty-two of Obed-Edom.

9 And Meshelemiah had sons and breth-ren, eighteen able men.

10 Also Hosah, of the children of Merari, had sons: Shimri the first (for *though* he was not the firstborn, his father made him the first), 11 Hilkiah the second, Tebaliah the third, Zechariah the fourth; all the sons and brethren of Hosah *were* thirteen.

12 Among these *were* the divisions of the gatekeepers, among the chief men, *having* duties just like their brethren, to serve in the house of the LORD. 13 And they cast lots for each gate, the small as well as the great, according to their father's house. 14 The lot for the East *Gate* fell to Shelemiah. Then they cast lots *for* his son Zechariah, a wise counselor, and his lot came out for the North Gate; 15 to Obed-Edom the South Gate, and to his sons the storehouse. 16 To Shuppim and Hosah *the lot came out* for the West Gate, with the Shallecheth Gate on the ascending highway—watchman opposite watchman. 17 On the

east were *six* Levites, on the north four each day, on the south four each day, and for the storehouse two by two. 18 As for the Parbar on the west, *there were* four on the highway *and* two at the Parbar. 19 These were the divisions of the gatekeepers among the sons of Korah and among the sons of Merari.

20 Of the Levites, Ahijah *was* over the treasuries of the house of God and over the treasuries of the dedicated things. 21 The sons of Laadan, the descendants of the Gershonites of Laadan, heads of their fathers' *houses,* of Laadan the Gershonite: Jehieli. 22 The sons of Jehieli, Zetham and Joel his brother, *were* over the treasuries of the house of the LORD. 23 Of the Amramites, the Izharites, the Hebronites, and the Uzzielites: 24 Shebuel the son of Gershom, the son of Moses, *was* overseer of the treasuries. 25 And his brethren by Eliezer *were* Rehabiah his son, Jeshaiah his son, Joram his son, Zichri his son, and Shelomith his son.

26 This Shelomith and his brethren *were* over all the treasuries of the dedicated things which King David and the heads of fathers' *houses,* the captains over thousands and hundreds, and the captains of the army, had dedicated. 27 Some of the spoils won in battles they dedicated to maintain the house of the LORD. 28 And all that Samuel the seer, Saul the son of Kish, Abner the son of Ner, and Joab the son of Zeruiah had dedicated, every dedicated *thing,* was under the hand of Shelomith and his brethren.

29 Of the Izharites, Chenaniah and his sons *performed* duties as officials and judges over Israel outside Jerusalem.

30 Of the Hebronites, Hashabiah and his brethren, one thousand seven hundred able men, had the oversight of Israel on the west side of the Jordan for all the business of the LORD, and in the service of the king. 31 Among the Hebronites, Jerijah *was* head of the Hebronites according to his genealogy of the fathers. In the fortieth year of the reign of David they were sought, and there were found among them capable men at Jazer of Gilead. 32 And his brethren *were* two thousand seven hundred able men, heads of fathers' *houses,* whom King David made officials over the Reubenites, the Gadites, and the half-tribe of Manasseh, for every matter pertaining to God and the affairs of the king.

27 AND the children of Israel, according to their number, the heads of fathers' *houses,* the captains of thousands and hundreds and their officers, served the king in every matter of the *military* divisions. *These divisions* came in and went out month by month throughout all the months of the year, each division *having* twenty-four thousand.

2 Over the first division for the first month *was* Jashobeam the son of Zabdiel, and in his division *were* twenty-four thousand; 3 *he was* of the children of Perez, and the chief of all the captains of the army for the first month. 4 Over the division of the second month *was* Dodai an Ahohite, and of his division Mikloth also *was* the leader; in his division *were* twenty-four thousand. 5 The third captain of the army for the third month *was* Benaiah, the son of Jehoiada the priest, who was chief; in his division *were* twenty-four thousand. 6 This was the Benaiah *who was* mighty *among* the thirty, and was over the thirty; in his division *was* Ammizabad his son. 7 The fourth *captain* for the fourth month *was* Asahel the brother of Joab, and Zebadiah his son after him; in his division *were* twenty-four thousand. 8 The fifth *captain* for the fifth month *was* Shamhuth the Izrahite; in his division were twenty-four thousand. 9 The sixth *captain* for the sixth month *was* Ira the son of Ikkesh the Tekoite; in his division *were* twenty-four thousand. 10 The seventh *captain* for the seventh month *was* Helez the Pelonite, of the children of Ephraim; in his division *were* twenty-four thousand. 11 The eighth *captain* for the eighth month *was* Sibbechai the Hushathite, of the Zarhites; in his division *were* twenty-four thousand. 12 The ninth *captain* for the ninth month *was* Abiezer the Anathothite, of the Benjamites; in his division *were* twenty-four thousand. 13 The tenth *captain* for the tenth month *was* Maharai the Netophathite, of the Zarhites; in his division *were* twenty-four thousand. 14 The eleventh *captain* for the eleventh month *was* Benaiah the Pirathonite, of the children of Ephraim; in his division *were* twenty-four thousand. 15 The twelfth *captain* for the twelfth month *was* Heldai the Netophathite, of Othniel; in his division *were* twenty-four thousand.

16 Furthermore, over the tribes of Israel: the officer over the Reubenites *was* Eliezer the son of Zichri; over the Simeonites, Shephatiah the son of Maachah; 17 *over* the Levites, Hashabiah the son of Kemuel; over the Aaronites, Zadok; 18 *over* Judah, Elihu, *one* of David's brothers; *over* Issachar, Omri the son of Michael; 19 *over* Zebulun, Ishmaiah the son of Obadiah; *over* Naphtali, Jerimoth the son of Azriel; 20 *over* the

children of Ephraim, Hoshea the son of Azaziah; *over* the half-tribe of Manasseh, Joel the son of Pedaiah; 21 *over* the half-*tribe* of Manasseh in Gilead, Iddo the son of Zechariah; *over* Benjamin, Jaasiel the son of Abner; 22 *over* Dan, Azarel the son of Jeroham. These *were* the leaders of the tribes of Israel.

23 But David did not take the number of those twenty years old and under, because the Lord had said He would multiply Israel like the stars of the heavens. 24 Joab the son of Zeruiah began a census, but he did not finish, for wrath came upon Israel because of this census; nor was the number recorded in the account of the chronicles of King David.

25 And Azmaveth the son of Adiel *was* over the king's treasuries; and Jehonathan the son of Uzziah was over the storehouses in the field, in the cities, in the villages, and in the fortresses. 26 Ezri the son of Chelub was over those who did the work of the field for tilling the ground. 27 And Shimei the Ramathite *was* over the vineyards, and Zabdi the Shiphmite was over the produce of the vineyards for the supply of wine. 28 Baal-Hanan the Gederite was over the olive trees and the sycamore trees that *were* in the lowlands, and Joash *was* over the store of oil. 29 And Shitrai the Sharonite *was* over the herds that fed in Sharon, and Shaphat the son of Adlai was over the herds *that were* in the valleys. 30 Obil the Ishmaelite *was* over the camels, Jehdeiah the Meronothite *was* over the donkeys, 31 and Jaziz the Hagrite *was* over the flocks. All these *were* the officials over King David's property.

32 Also Jehonathan, David's uncle, *was* a counselor, a wise man, and a scribe; and Jehiel the son of Hachmoni *was* with the king's sons. 33 Ahithophel *was* the king's counselor, and Hushai the Archite *was* the king's companion. 34 After Ahithophel *was* Jehoiada the son of Benaiah, then Abiathar. And the general of the king's army *was* Joab.

PSALM 78:56–66

56 YET they tested and provoked the Most
       High God,
       And did not keep His testimonies,
57 But turned back and acted unfaithfully
       like their fathers;
       They were turned aside like a deceitful
       bow.
58 For they provoked Him to anger with
       their high places,
       And moved Him to jealousy with their
       carved images.

59 When God heard *this,* He was furious,
       And greatly abhorred Israel,
60 So that He forsook the tabernacle of
       Shiloh,
       The tent He had placed among men,
61 And delivered His strength into
       captivity,
       And His glory into the enemy's hand.
62 He also gave His people over to the
       sword,
       And was furious with His inheritance.

---

*Their distress is due entirely to their
deliberate determination to use
themselves for a purpose other than
God's.* (SEND I YOU)

---

63 The fire consumed their young men,
       And their maidens were not given in
       marriage.
64 Their priests fell by the sword,
       And their widows made no
       lamentation.

65 Then the Lord awoke as *from* sleep,
       Like a mighty man who shouts because
       of wine.
66 And He beat back His enemies;
       He put them to a perpetual reproach.

PROVERBS 20:4, 5

4 THE lazy *man* will not plow because
      of winter;
      He will beg during harvest and *have*
      nothing.

5 Counsel in the heart of man *is like* deep
      water,
      But a man of understanding will draw
      it out.

ACTS 10:1–23

THERE was a certain man in Caesarea called Cornelius, a centurion of what was called the Italian Regiment, 2 a devout *man* and one who feared God with all his household, who gave alms generously to the people, and prayed to God always. 3 About the ninth hour of the day he saw clearly in a vision an angel of God coming in and saying to him, "Cornelius!"

4 And when he observed him, he was afraid, and said, "What is it, lord?"

So he said to him, "Your prayers and

your alms have come up for a memorial before God. 5 Now send men to Joppa, and send for Simon whose surname is Peter. 6 He is lodging with Simon, a tanner, whose house is by the sea. He will tell you what you must do." 7 And when the angel who spoke to him had departed, Cornelius called two of his household servants and a devout soldier from among those who waited on him continually. 8 So when he had explained all *these* things to them, he sent them to Joppa.

9 The next day, as they went on their journey and drew near the city, Peter went up on the housetop to pray, about the sixth hour. 10 Then he became very hungry and wanted to eat; but while they made ready, he fell into a trance 11 and saw heaven opened and an object like a great sheet bound at the four corners, descending to him and let down to the earth. 12 In it were all kinds of four-footed animals of the earth, wild beasts, creeping things, and birds of the air. 13 And a voice came to him, "Rise, Peter; kill and eat."

14 But Peter said, "Not so, Lord! For I have never eaten anything common or unclean."

15 And a voice *spoke* to him again the second time, "What God has cleansed you must not call common." 16 This was done three times. And the object was taken up into heaven again.

17 Now while Peter wondered within himself what this vision which he had seen meant, behold, the men who had been sent from Cornelius had made inquiry for Simon's house, and stood before the gate. 18 And they called and asked whether Simon, whose surname was Peter, was lodging there.

19 While Peter thought about the vision, the Spirit said to him, "Behold, three men are seeking you. 20 Arise therefore, go down and go with them, doubting nothing; for I have sent them."

21 Then Peter went down to the men who had been sent to him from Cornelius, and said, "Yes, I am he whom you seek. For what reason have you come?"

22 And they said, "Cornelius *the* centurion, a just man, one who fears God and has a good reputation among all the nation of the Jews, was divinely instructed by a holy angel to summon you to his house, and to hear words from you." 23 Then he invited them in and lodged *them*.

On the next day Peter went away with them, and some brethren from Joppa accompanied him.

◆◆◆

Reading 183—We Are Witnesses
Acts 10:36–41

One of the dangers of present-day teaching is that it makes us turn our eyes off Jesus Christ on to ourselves, off the Source of our salvation on to salvation itself. The effect of that is a morbid, hypersensitive life, totally unlike our Lord's life, it has not the passion of abandon that characterized Him. The New Testament never allows for a moment the idea that continually crops up in modern spiritual teaching—"I have to remember that I am a specimen of what God can do." That is inspired by the Devil, never by the Spirit of God. We are not here to be specimens of what God can do, but to have our life so hid with Christ in God that our Lord's words will be true of us, that men beholding our good works will glorify our Father in heaven. There was no "show business" in the life of the Son of God, and there is to be no "show business" in the life of the saint. Concentrate on God, let Him engineer circumstances as He will, and wherever He places you He is binding up the brokenhearted through you, setting at liberty the captives through you, doing His mighty soul-saving work through you, as you keep rightly related to Him. Self-conscious service is killed, self-conscious devotion is gone, only one thing remains—"witnesses to Me," Jesus Christ first, second and third.

(MORAL FOUND.)

1 CHRONICLES 28:1—29:30

NOW David assembled at Jerusalem all the leaders of Israel: the officers of the tribes and the captains of the divisions who served the king, the captains over thousands and captains over hundreds, and the stewards over all the substance and possessions of the king and of his sons, with the officials, the valiant men, and all the mighty men of valor. 2 Then King David rose to his feet and said, "Hear me, my brethren and my people: I *had* it in my heart to build a house of rest for the ark of the covenant of the LORD, and for the footstool of our God, and had made preparations to build it. 3 But God said to me, 'You shall not build a house for My name, because you *have been* a man of war and have shed blood.' 4 However the LORD God of Israel chose me above all the house of my father to be king over Israel forever, for He has chosen Judah *to be* the ruler. And of the house of Judah, the house of my father, and among the sons of my father, He was pleased with me to make *me* king over all Israel. 5 And of all my sons (for the LORD has given me many sons) He has chosen my son Solomon to sit on the throne of the kingdom of the LORD over Israel. 6 Now He said to me, 'It is your son Solomon *who* shall build My house and My courts; for I have chosen him *to be* My son, and I will be his Father. 7 Moreover I will establish his kingdom forever, if he is steadfast to observe My commandments and My judgments, as it is this day.' 8 Now therefore, in the sight of all Israel, the assembly of the LORD, and in the hearing of our God, be careful to seek out all the commandments of the LORD your God, that you may possess this good land, and leave *it* as an inheritance for your children after you forever.

9 "As for you, my son Solomon, know the God of your father, and serve Him with a loyal heart and with a willing mind; for the LORD searches all hearts and understands all the intent of the thoughts. If you seek Him, He will be found by you; but if you forsake Him, He will cast you off forever. 10 Consider now, for the LORD has chosen you to build a house for the sanctuary; be strong, and do it."

11 Then David gave his son Solomon the plans for the vestibule, its houses, its treasuries, its upper chambers, its inner chambers, and the place of the mercy seat; 12 and the plans for all that he had by the Spirit, of the courts of the house of the LORD, of all the chambers all around, of the treasuries of the house of God, and of the treasuries for the dedicated things; 13 also for the division of the priests and the Levites, for all the work of the service of the house of the LORD, and for all the articles of service in the house of the LORD. 14 *He gave* gold by weight for *things* of gold, for all articles used in every kind of service; also *silver* for all articles of silver by weight, for all articles used in every kind of service; 15 the weight for the lampstands of gold, and their lamps of gold, by weight for each lampstand and its lamps; for the lampstands of silver by weight, for the lampstand and its lamps, according to the use of each lampstand. 16 And by weight *he gave* gold for the tables of the showbread, for each table, and silver for the tables of silver; 17 also pure gold for the forks, the basins, the pitchers of pure gold, and the golden bowls—*he gave gold* by weight for every bowl; and for the silver bowls, *silver* by weight for every bowl; 18 and refined gold by weight for the altar of incense, and for the construction of the chariot, that is, the gold cherubim that spread *their wings* and overshadowed the ark of the covenant of the LORD. 19 "All *this," said David,* "the LORD made me understand in writing, by *His* hand upon me, all the works of these plans."

20 And David said to his son Solomon, "Be strong and of good courage, and do *it;* do not fear nor be dismayed, for the LORD God—my God—*will be* with you. He will not leave you nor forsake you, until you have finished all the work for the service of the house of the LORD. 21 *Here are* the divisions of the priests and the Levites for all the service of the house of God; and every willing craftsman *will be* with you for all manner of workmanship, for every kind of service; also the leaders and all the people *will be* completely at your command."

29 FURTHERMORE King David said to all the assembly: "My son Solomon, whom alone God has chosen, *is* young and inexperienced; and the work *is* great, because the temple *is* not for man but for the LORD God. 2 Now for the house of my God I have prepared with all my might: gold for *things to be made of* gold, silver for *things of* silver, bronze for *things of* bronze, iron for *things of* iron, wood for *things of* wood, onyx stones, *stones* to be set, glistening stones of various colors, all kinds of precious stones, and marble slabs in abundance. 3 Moreover, because I have set my affection on the house of my God, I have given to the house of my God, over and above all that I have prepared for the holy house, my own special treasure of gold and silver: 4 three thousand talents of gold, of the gold of Ophir, and seven thousand talents of refined silver, to overlay the walls of the houses; 5 the gold for *things of* gold and the silver for *things of* silver, and for all kinds of work *to be done* by the hands of craftsmen. Who *then* is willing to consecrate himself this day to the LORD?"

You must abandon all and fling yourself on God as a mere conscious being. (CHRIS. DIS. 2)

---

6 Then the leaders of the fathers' *houses,* leaders of the tribes of Israel, the captains of thousands and of hundreds, with the officers over the king's work, offered willingly. 7 They gave for the work of the house of God five thousand talents and ten thousand darics of gold, ten thousand talents of silver, eighteen thousand talents of bronze, and one hundred thousand talents of iron. 8 And whoever had *precious* stones gave *them* to the treasury of the house of the LORD, into the hand of Jehiel the Gershonite. 9 Then the people rejoiced, for they had offered willingly, because with a loyal heart they had offered willingly to the LORD; and King David also rejoiced greatly. 10 Therefore David blessed the LORD before all the assembly; and David said:

"Blessed are You, LORD God of Israel, our Father, forever and ever.
11 Yours, O LORD, *is* the greatness,
The power and the glory,
The victory and the majesty;
For all *that is* in heaven and in earth
is Yours;
Yours *is* the kingdom, O LORD,
And You are exalted as head over all.
12 Both riches and honor *come* from You,
And You reign over all.
In Your hand *is* power and might;
In Your hand *it is* to make great
And to give strength to all.

13 "Now therefore, our God,
We thank You
And praise Your glorious name.
14 But who *am* I, and who *are* my people,
That we should be able to offer so willingly as this?
For all things *come* from You,
And of Your own we have given You.

15 For we *are* aliens and pilgrims before You,
As *were* all our fathers;
Our days on earth *are* as a shadow,
And without hope.

16 "O LORD our God, all this abundance that we have prepared to build You a house for Your holy name is from Your hand, and *is* all Your own. 17 I know also, my God, that You test the heart and have pleasure in uprightness. As for me, in the uprightness of my heart I have willingly offered all these *things;* and now with joy I have seen Your people, who are present here to offer willingly to You. 18 O LORD God of Abraham, Isaac, and Israel, our fathers, keep this forever in the intent of the thoughts of the heart of Your people, and fix their heart toward You. 19 And give my son Solomon a loyal heart to keep Your commandments and Your testimonies and Your statutes, to do all *these things,* and to build the temple for which I have made provision."

20 Then David said to all the assembly, "Now bless the LORD your God." So all the assembly blessed the LORD God of their fathers, and bowed their heads and prostrated themselves before the LORD and the king.

21 And they made sacrifices to the LORD and offered burnt offerings to the LORD on the next day: a thousand bulls, a thousand rams, a thousand lambs, with their drink offerings, and sacrifices in abundance for all Israel. 22 So they ate and drank before the LORD with great gladness on that day. And they made Solomon the son of David king the second time, and anointed *him* before the LORD *to be* the leader, and Zadok *to be* priest. 23 Then Solomon sat on the throne of the LORD as king instead of David his father, and prospered; and all Israel obeyed him. 24 All the leaders and the mighty men, and also all the sons of King David, submitted themselves to King Solomon. 25 So the LORD exalted Solomon exceedingly in the sight of all Israel, and bestowed on him *such* royal majesty as had not been on any king before him in Israel.

26 Thus David the son of Jesse reigned over all Israel. 27 And the period that he reigned over Israel *was* forty years; seven years he reigned in Hebron, and thirty-three *years* he reigned in Jerusalem. 28 So he died in a good old age, full of days and riches and honor; and Solomon his son reigned in his place. 29 Now the acts of King David, first and last, indeed they *are* written in the book of Samuel the seer, in the book

of Nathan the prophet, and in the book of Gad the seer, 30 with all his reign and his might, and the events that happened to him, to Israel, and to all the kingdoms of the lands.

PSALM 78:67–72

67 MOREOVER He rejected the tent of Joseph,
And did not choose the tribe of Ephraim,
68 But chose the tribe of Judah,
Mount Zion which He loved.
69 And He built His sanctuary like the heights,
Like the earth which He has established forever.
70 He also chose David His servant,
And took him from the sheepfolds;
71 From following the ewes that had young He brought him,
To shepherd Jacob His people,
And Israel His inheritance.
72 So he shepherded them according to the integrity of his heart,
And guided them by the skillfulness of his hands.

PROVERBS 20:6, 7

6 MOST men will proclaim each his own goodness,
But who can find a faithful man?

7 The righteous *man* walks in his integrity;
His children *are* blessed after him.

ACTS 10:24–48

AND the following day they entered Caesarea. Now Cornelius was waiting for them, and had called together his relatives and close friends. 25 As Peter was coming in, Cornelius met him and fell down at his feet and worshiped *him.* 26 But Peter lifted him up, saying, "Stand up; I myself am also a man." 27 And as he talked with him, he went in and found many who had come together. 28 Then he said to them, "You know how unlawful it is for a Jewish man to keep company with or go to one of another nation. But God has shown me that I should not call any man common or unclean. 29 Therefore I came without objection as soon as I was sent for. I ask, then, for what reason have you sent for me?"

30 So Cornelius said, "Four days ago I was fasting until this hour; and at the ninth hour I prayed in my house, and behold, a man stood before me in bright clothing, 31 and said, 'Cornelius, your prayer has been heard, and your alms are remembered in the sight of God. 32 Send therefore to Joppa and call Simon here, whose surname is Peter. He is lodging in the house of Simon, a tanner, by the sea. When he comes, he will speak to you.' 33 So I sent to you immediately, and you have done well to come. Now therefore, we are all present before God, to hear all the things commanded you by God."

34 Then Peter opened *his* mouth and said: "In truth I perceive that God shows no partiality. 35 But in every nation whoever fears Him and works righteousness is accepted by Him. 36 The word which *God* sent to the children of Israel, preaching peace through Jesus Christ—He is Lord of all— 37 that word you know, which was proclaimed throughout all Judea, and began from Galilee after the baptism which John preached: 38 how God anointed Jesus of Nazareth with the Holy Spirit and with power, who went about doing good and healing all who were oppressed by the devil, for God was with Him. 39 And we are witnesses of all things which He did both in the land of the Jews and in Jerusalem, whom they killed by hanging on a tree. 40 Him God raised up on the third day, and showed Him openly, 41 not to all the people, but to witnesses chosen before by God, *even* to us who ate and drank with Him after He arose from the dead. 42 And He commanded us to preach to the people, and to testify that it is He who was ordained by God *to be* Judge of the living and the dead. 43 To Him all the prophets witness that, through His name, whoever believes in Him will receive remission of sins."

44 While Peter was still speaking these words, the Holy Spirit fell upon all those who heard the word. 45 And those of the

---

If I obey Jesus Christ, the redemption of God will rush through me to other lives.   (UTMOST)

---

circumcision who believed were astonished, as many as came with Peter, because the gift of the Holy Spirit had been poured out on the Gentiles also. 46 For they heard them speak with tongues and magnify God. Then Peter answered, 47 "Can anyone forbid water, that these should not be baptized who have received the Holy Spirit just as we *have?*" 48 And he commanded them to be baptized in the name of the Lord. Then they asked him to stay a few days.

◄◄◄◄◄

*Reading 184—*Have a Message and Be One
Acts 11:20

W e are not saved to be "channels only," but to be sons and daughters of God. We are not turned into spiritual mediums, but into spiritual messengers; the message must be part of ourselves. The Son of God was His own message, His words were spirit and life; and as His disciples our lives must be the sacrament of our message. The natural heart will do any amount of serving, but it takes the heart broken by conviction of sin, and baptized by the Holy Ghost, and crumpled into the purpose of God before the life becomes the sacrament of its message.

There is a difference between giving a testimony and preaching. A preacher is one who has realized the call of God and is determined to use his every power to proclaim God's truth. God takes us out of our own ideas for our lives and we are "batter'd to shape and use," as the disciples were after Pentecost. Pentecost did not teach the disciples anything; it made them the incarnation of what they preached—"You shall be witnesses to Me."

Let God have perfect liberty when you speak. Before God's message can liberate other souls, the liberation must be real in you. Gather your material, and set it alight when you speak.   (*UTMOST*)

2 CHRONICLES 1:1—2:18

NOW Solomon the son of David was strengthened in his kingdom, and the LORD his God *was* with him and exalted him exceedingly.

2 And Solomon spoke to all Israel, to the captains of thousands and of hundreds, to the judges, and to every leader in all Israel, the heads of the fathers' *houses.* 3 Then Solomon, and all the assembly with him, went to the high place that *was* at Gibeon; for the tabernacle of meeting with God was there, which Moses the servant of the LORD had made in the wilderness. 4 But David had brought up the ark of God from Kirjath Jearim to *the place* David had prepared for it, for he had pitched a tent for it at Jerusalem. 5 Now the bronze altar that Bezalel the son of Uri, the son of Hur, had made, he put before the tabernacle of the LORD; Solomon and the assembly sought Him *there.* 6 And Solomon went up there to the bronze altar before the LORD, which *was* at the tabernacle of meet-

ing, and offered a thousand burnt offerings on it.

7 On that night God appeared to Solomon, and said to him, "Ask! What shall I give you?"

8 And Solomon said to God: "You have shown great mercy to David my father, and have made me king in his place. 9 Now, O LORD God, let Your promise to David my father be established, for You have made me king over a people like the dust of the earth in multitude. 10 Now give me wisdom and knowledge, that I may go out and come in before this people; for who can judge this great people of Yours?"

11 Then God said to Solomon: "Because this was in your heart, and you have not asked riches or wealth or honor or the life of your enemies, nor have you asked long life—but have asked wisdom and knowledge for yourself, that you may judge My people over whom I have made you king— 12 wisdom and knowledge *are* granted to you; and I will give you riches and wealth and honor, such as none of the kings have

had who *were* before you, nor shall any after you have the like."

13 So Solomon came to Jerusalem from the high place that *was* at Gibeon, from before the tabernacle of meeting, and reigned over Israel. 14 And Solomon gathered chariots and horsemen; he had one thousand four hundred chariots and twelve thousand horsemen, whom he stationed in the chariot cities and with the king in Jerusalem. 15 Also the king made silver and gold as common in Jerusalem as stones, and he made cedars as abundant as the sycamores which *are* in the lowland. 16 And Solomon had horses imported from Egypt and Keveh; the king's merchants bought them in Keveh at the *current* price. 17 They also acquired and imported from Egypt a chariot for six hundred *shekels* of silver, and a horse for one hundred and fifty; thus, through their agents, they exported them to all the kings of the Hittites and the kings of Syria.

2 THEN Solomon determined to build a temple for the name of the LORD, and a royal house for himself. 2 Solomon selected seventy thousand men to bear burdens, eighty thousand to quarry *stone* in the mountains, and three thousand six hundred to oversee them.

3 Then Solomon sent to Hiram king of Tyre, saying:

As you have dealt with David my father, and sent him cedars to build himself a house to dwell in, *so deal with me.* 4 Behold, I am building a temple for the name of the LORD my God, to dedicate *it* to Him, to burn before Him sweet incense, for the continual showbread, for the burnt offerings morning and evening, on the Sabbaths, on the New Moons, and on the set feasts of the LORD our God. This *is an ordinance* forever to Israel.

5 And the temple which I build *will be* great, for our God is greater than all gods. 6 But who is able to build Him a temple, since heaven and the heaven of heavens cannot contain Him? Who *am* I then, that I should build Him a temple, except to burn sacrifice before Him?

7 Therefore send me at once a man skillful to work in gold and silver, in bronze and iron, in purple and crimson and blue, who has skill to engrave with the skillful men who are with me in Judah and Jerusalem, whom David my father provided. 8 Also send me cedar and cypress and algum logs from Lebanon, for I know that your servants have skill to cut timber in Lebanon; and indeed my servants *will be* with your servants, 9 to prepare timber for me in abundance, for the temple which I am about to build *shall be* great and wonderful.

10 And indeed I will give to your servants, the woodsmen who cut timber, twenty thousand kors of ground wheat, twenty thousand kors of barley, twenty thousand baths of wine, and twenty thousand baths of oil.

11 Then Hiram king of Tyre answered in writing, which he sent to Solomon:

Because the LORD loves His people, He has made you king over them.

12 Hiram also said:

Blessed *be* the LORD God of Israel, who made heaven and earth, for He has given King David a wise son, endowed with prudence and understanding, who will build a temple for the LORD and a royal house for himself!

13 And now I have sent a skillful man, endowed with understanding, Huram my master *craftsman* 14 (the son of a woman of the daughters of Dan, and his father was a man of Tyre), skilled to work in gold and silver, bronze and iron, stone and wood, purple and blue, fine linen and crimson, and to make any engraving and to accomplish any plan which may be given to him, with your skillful men and with the skillful men of my lord David your father.

15 Now therefore, the wheat, the barley, the oil, and the wine which my lord has spoken of, let him send to his servants. 16 And we will cut wood from Lebanon, as much as you need; we will bring it to you in rafts by sea to Joppa, and you will carry it up to Jerusalem.

17 Then Solomon numbered all the aliens who *were* in the land of Israel, after the

census in which David his father had numbered them; and there were found to be one hundred and fifty-three thousand six hundred. 18 And he made seventy thousand of them bearers of burdens, eighty thousand stonecutters in the mountain, and three thousand six hundred overseers to make the people work.

PSALM 79:1–4

1 O God, the nations have come into
   Your inheritance;
   Your holy temple they have defiled;
   They have laid Jerusalem in heaps.
2 The dead bodies of Your servants
   They have given *as* food for the birds
   of the heavens,
   The flesh of Your saints to the beasts
   of the earth.

*T*he life of God within the saint produces agony every now and again. (PHIL. SIN)

3 Their blood they have shed like water
   all around Jerusalem,
   And *there was* no one to bury *them.*
4 We have become a reproach to our
   neighbors,
   A scorn and derision to those who are
   around us.

PROVERBS 20:8, 9

8 A king who sits on the throne of
   judgment
   Scatters all evil with his eyes.

9 Who can say, "I have made my heart
   clean,
   I am pure from my sin"?

ACTS 11:1–30

NOW the apostles and brethren who were in Judea heard that the Gentiles had also received the word of God. 2 And when Peter came up to Jerusalem, those of the circumcision contended with him, 3 saying, "You went in to uncircumcised men and ate with them!"

4 But Peter explained *it* to them in order from the beginning, saying: 5 "I was in the city of Joppa praying; and in a trance I saw a vision, an object descending like a great sheet, let down from heaven by four corners; and it came to me. 6 When I observed it intently and considered, I saw four-footed animals of the earth, wild beasts, creeping things, and birds of the air. 7 And I heard a voice saying to me, 'Rise, Peter; kill and eat.' 8 But I said, 'Not so, Lord! For nothing common or unclean has at any time entered my mouth.' 9 But the voice answered me again from heaven, 'What God has cleansed you must not call common.' 10 Now this was done three

*T*he only basis of the spiritual is the sacrifice of the natural. (SERMON MT.)

times, and all were drawn up again into heaven. 11 At that very moment, three men stood before the house where I was, having been sent to me from Caesarea. 12 Then the Spirit told me to go with them, doubting nothing. Moreover these six brethren accompanied me, and we entered the man's house. 13 And he told us how he had seen an angel standing in his house, who said to him, 'Send men to Joppa, and call for Simon whose surname is Peter, 14 who will tell you words by which you and all your household will be saved.' 15 And as I began to speak, the Holy Spirit fell upon them, as upon us at the beginning. 16 Then I remembered the word of the Lord, how He said, 'John indeed baptized with water, but you shall be baptized with the Holy Spirit.' 17 If therefore God gave them the same gift as *He gave* us when we believed on the Lord Jesus Christ, who was I that I could withstand God?"

18 When they heard these things they became silent; and they glorified God, saying, "Then God has also granted to the Gentiles repentance to life."

19 Now those who were scattered after the persecution that arose over Stephen traveled as far as Phoenicia, Cyprus, and Antioch, preaching the word to no one but the Jews only. 20 But some of them were men from Cyprus and Cyrene, who, when they had come to Antioch, spoke to the Hellenists, preaching the Lord Jesus. 21 And the hand of the Lord was with them, and a great number believed and turned to the Lord.

22 Then news of these things came to the ears of the church in Jerusalem, and they sent out Barnabas to go as far as Antioch. 23 When he came and had seen the grace of God, he was glad, and encouraged

them all that with purpose of heart they should continue with the Lord. 24 For he was a good man, full of the Holy Spirit and of faith. And a great many people were added to the Lord.

25 Then Barnabas departed for Tarsus to seek Saul. 26 And when he had found him, he brought him to Antioch. So it was that for a whole year they assembled with the church and taught a great many people. And the disciples were first called Christians in Antioch.

27 And in these days prophets came from Jerusalem to Antioch. 28 Then one of them, named Agabus, stood up and showed by the Spirit that there was going to be a great famine throughout all the world, which also happened in the days of Claudius Caesar. 29 Then the disciples, each according to his ability, determined to send relief to the brethren dwelling in Judea. 30 This they also did, and sent it to the elders by the hands of Barnabas and Saul.

<hr>

Reading 185—But the Word of God Grew
Acts 12:24

Sow the word of God, and everyone who listens will get to God. If you sow vows, resolutions, aspirations, emotions, you will reap nothing but exhaustion, "and you shall sow your seed in vain, for your enemies shall eat it"; but sow the word of God, and as sure as God is God, it will bring forth fruit.   (SERVANT AS LORD)

No one is ever the same after listening to the word of God, you cannot be; you may imagine you have paid no attention to it, and yet months after maybe a crisis arises and suddenly the word of God comes and grips you by the throat, so to speak, and awakens all the terrors of hell in your life, and you say, "Wherever did that word come from?" Years ago, months ago, weeks ago, it sank straight into our unconscious mind, God knew it was there though you did not, and it did its damaging work, and now it has suddenly come to light.   (PHIL. SIN)

2 CHRONICLES 3:1—4:22

NOW Solomon began to build the house of the LORD at Jerusalem on Mount Moriah, where the LORD had appeared to his father David, at the place that David had prepared on the threshing floor of Ornan the Jebusite. 2 And he began to build on the second *day* of the second month in the fourth year of his reign.

3 This is the foundation which Solomon laid for building the house of God: The length *was* sixty cubits (by cubits according to the former measure) and the width twenty cubits. 4 And the vestibule that *was* in front of *the sanctuary* was twenty cubits long across the width of the house, and the height *was* one hundred and twenty. He overlaid the inside with pure gold. 5 The larger room he paneled with cypress which he overlaid with fine gold, and he carved palm trees and chainwork on it.

6 And he decorated the house with precious stones for beauty, and the gold *was* gold from Parvaim. 7 He also overlaid the house—the beams and doorposts, its walls and doors—with gold; and he carved cherubim on the walls.

8 And he made the Most Holy Place. Its length was according to the width of the house, twenty cubits, and its width twenty cubits. He overlaid it with six hundred talents of fine gold. 9 The weight of the nails *was* fifty shekels of gold; and he overlaid the upper area with gold. 10 In the Most Holy Place he made two cherubim, fashioned by carving, and overlaid them with gold. 11 The wings of the cherubim *were* twenty cubits in *overall* length: one wing *of the one cherub was* five cubits, touching the wall of the room, and the other wing *was* five cubits, touching the wing of the other cherub; 12 *one* wing of the other cherub *was* five cubits, touching the wall of

the room, and the other wing *also was* five cubits, touching the wing of the other cherub. 13 The wings of these cherubim spanned twenty cubits overall. They stood on their feet, and they faced inward. 14 And he made the veil of blue, purple, crimson, and fine linen, and wove cherubim into it.

15 Also he made in front of the temple two pillars thirty-five cubits high, and the capital that *was* on the top of each of *them* was five cubits. 16 He made wreaths of chainwork, as in the inner sanctuary, and put *them* on top of the pillars; and he made one hundred pomegranates, and put *them* on the wreaths of chainwork. 17 Then he set up the pillars before the temple, one on the right hand and the other on the left; he called the name of the one on the right hand Jachin, and the name of the one on the left Boaz.

4 MOREOVER he made a bronze altar: twenty cubits was its length, twenty cubits its width, and ten cubits its height.

2 Then he made the Sea of cast *bronze*, ten cubits from one brim to the other; *it was* completely round. Its height *was* five cubits, and a line of thirty cubits measured its circumference. 3 And under it *was* the likeness of oxen encircling it all around, ten to a cubit, all the way around the Sea. The oxen *were* cast in two rows, when it was cast. 4 It stood on twelve oxen: three looking toward the north, three looking toward the west, three looking toward the south, and three looking toward the east; the Sea *was set* upon them, and all their back parts *pointed* inward. 5 It *was* a handbreadth thick; and its brim was shaped like the brim of a cup, *like* a lily blossom. It contained three thousand baths.

6 He also made ten lavers, and put five on the right side and five on the left, to wash in them; such things as they offered for the burnt offering they would wash in them, but the Sea *was* for the priests to wash in. 7 And he made ten lampstands of gold according to their design, and set *them* in the temple, five on the right side and five on the left. 8 He also made ten tables, and placed *them* in the temple, five on the right side and five on the left. And he made one hundred bowls of gold.

9 Furthermore he made the court of the priests, and the great court and doors for the court; and he overlaid these doors with bronze. 10 He set the Sea on the right side, toward the southeast.

11 Then Huram made the pots and the shovels and the bowls. So Huram finished doing the work that he was to do for King Solomon for the house of God: 12 the two pillars and the bowl-shaped capitals *that were* on top of the two pillars; the two networks covering the two bowl-shaped capitals which *were* on top of the pillars; 13 four hundred pomegranates for the two networks (two rows of pomegranates for each network, to cover the two bowl-shaped capitals that *were* on the pillars); 14 he also made carts and the lavers on the carts; 15 one Sea and twelve oxen under it; 16 also the pots, the shovels, the forks—and all their articles Huram his master *craftsman* made of burnished bronze for King Solomon for the house of the LORD.

17 In the plain of Jordan the king had them cast in clay molds, between Succoth and Zeredah. 18 And Solomon had all these articles made in such great abundance that the weight of the bronze was not determined.

19 Thus Solomon had all the furnishings made for the house of God: the altar of gold and the tables on which *was* the showbread; 20 the lampstands with their lamps of pure gold, to burn in the prescribed manner in front of the inner sanctuary, 21 with the flowers and the lamps and the wick-trimmers of gold, of purest gold; 22 the trimmers, the bowls, the ladles, and the censers of pure gold. As for the entry of the sanctuary, its inner doors to the Most Holy *Place*, and the doors of the main hall of the temple, *were* gold.

PSALM 79:5–10

5 HOW long, LORD?
Will You be angry forever?
Will Your jealousy burn like fire?
6 Pour out Your wrath on the nations
that do not know You,
And on the kingdoms that do not call
on Your name.
7 For they have devoured Jacob,
And laid waste his dwelling place.

8 Oh, do not remember former iniquities
against us!
Let Your tender mercies come speedily
to meet us,
For we have been brought very low.
9 Help us, O God of our salvation,
For the glory of Your name;
And deliver us, and provide atonement
for our sins,
For Your name's sake!

10 Why should the nations say,
    "Where *is* their God?"
    Let there be known among the nations
       in our sight
    The avenging of the blood of Your
       servants *which has been* shed.

PROVERBS 20:10–12

10 DIVERSE weights *and* diverse
    measures,
    They *are* both alike, an abomination
    to the LORD.

11 Even a child is known by his deeds,
    Whether what he does *is* pure and right.

12 The hearing ear and the seeing eye,
    The LORD has made them both.

ACTS 12:1–25

NOW about that time Herod the king
stretched out *his* hand to harass some from
the church. 2 Then he killed James the
brother of John with the sword. 3 And because he saw that it pleased the Jews, he
proceeded further to seize Peter also. Now
it was *during* the Days of Unleavened
Bread. 4 So when he had arrested him, he
put *him* in prison, and delivered *him* to
four squads of soldiers to keep him, intending to bring him before the people after
Passover.

5 Peter was therefore kept in prison, but
constant prayer was offered to God for him
by the church. 6 And when Herod was

Prayer is an effort of will.   (UTMOST)

---

about to bring him out, that night Peter
was sleeping, bound with two chains between two soldiers; and the guards before
the door were keeping the prison. 7 Now
behold, an angel of the Lord stood by *him,*
and a light shone in the prison; and he
struck Peter on the side and raised him up,
saying, "Arise quickly!" And his chains fell
off *his* hands. 8 Then the angel said to him,
"Gird yourself and tie on your sandals";
and so he did. And he said to him, "Put
on your garment and follow me." 9 So he
went out and followed him, and did not
know that what was done by the angel was
real, but thought he was seeing a vision.
10 When they were past the first and the

second guard posts, they came to the iron
gate that leads to the city, which opened
to them of its own accord; and they went
out and went down one street, and immediately the angel departed from him.
11 And when Peter had come to himself,
he said, "Now I know for certain that the
Lord has sent His angel, and has delivered
me from the hand of Herod and *from* all
the expectation of the Jewish people."
12 So, when he had considered *this,* he
came to the house of Mary, the mother of
John whose surname was Mark, where
many were gathered together praying.
13 And as Peter knocked at the door of the
gate, a girl named Rhoda came to answer.
14 When she recognized Peter's voice, because of *her* gladness she did not open the
gate, but ran in and announced that Peter
stood before the gate. 15 But they said to
her, "You are beside yourself!" Yet she kept
insisting that it was so. So they said, "It
is his angel."
16 Now Peter continued knocking; and
when they opened *the door* and saw him,
they were astonished. 17 But motioning to
them with his hand to keep silent, he declared to them how the Lord had brought
him out of the prison. And he said, "Go,
tell these things to James and to the brethren." And he departed and went to another
place.
18 Then, as soon as it was day, there was
no small stir among the soldiers about what
had become of Peter. 19 But when Herod
had searched for him and not found him,
he examined the guards and commanded
that *they* should be put to death.
And he went down from Judea to
Caesarea, and stayed *there.*
20 Now Herod had been very angry with
the people of Tyre and Sidon; but they
came to him with one accord, and having
made Blastus the king's personal aide their
friend, they asked for peace, because their
country was supplied with food by the
king's *country.*
21 So on a set day Herod, arrayed in royal
apparel, sat on his throne and gave an ora-
tion to them. 22 And the people kept shouting, "The voice of a god and not of a man!"
23 Then immediately an angel of the Lord
struck him, because he did not give glory
to God. And he was eaten by worms and
died.
24 But the word of God grew and
multiplied.
25 And Barnabas and Saul returned from
Jerusalem when they had fulfilled *their* ministry, and they also took with them John
whose surname was Mark.

◆◆◆◆

Reading 186—The Cost of Prayer
2 Chronicles 5:6; 6:13

We ought to give much more time than we do—a great deal more time than we do—to brooding on the fundamental truths on which the Spirit of God works the simplicity of our Christian experience. The fundamental truths are redemption and the personal presence of the Holy Spirit, and these two are focused in one mighty personality, the Lord Jesus Christ. Thank God for the emphasis laid on the efficacy of the Holy Spirit to make experientially real the redemption of Jesus Christ in individual lives.

Remember, what makes prayer easy is not our wits or our understanding, but the tremendous agony of God in redemption. A thing is worth just what it costs. Prayer is not what it costs us, but what it cost God to enable us to pray. It cost God so much that a little child can pray. It cost God almighty so much that anyone can pray. But it is time those of us who name His name knew the secret of the cost, and the secret is here, "My soul is exceeding sorrowful, *even* to death." These words open the door to the autobiography of our Lord's agony. We find the real key to Gethsemane in Matthew 4, which records the temptations of our Lord. Here they come again in a deeper and more appealing manner than ever before. We are not looking here (as we do when we deal with the temptations) at the type of temptation we have to go through; we are dealing here with the grappling of God as Man in the last reaches of historical redemption.   (*Ask*)

2 CHRONICLES 5:1—6:42

SO all the work that Solomon had done for the house of the LORD was finished; and Solomon brought in the things which his father David had dedicated: the silver and the gold and all the furnishings. And he put *them* in the treasuries of the house of God.

2 Now Solomon assembled the elders of Israel and all the heads of the tribes, the chief fathers of the children of Israel, in Jerusalem, that they might bring the ark of the covenant of the LORD up from the City of David, which *is* Zion. 3 Therefore all the men of Israel assembled with the king at the feast, which *was* in the seventh month. 4 So all the elders of Israel came, and the Levites took up the ark. 5 Then they brought up the ark, the tabernacle of meeting, and all the holy furnishings that *were* in the tabernacle. The priests and the Levites brought them up. 6 Also King Solomon, and all the congregation of Israel who were assembled with him before the ark, were sacrificing sheep and oxen that could not be counted or numbered for multitude. 7 Then the priests brought in the ark of the covenant of the LORD to its place, into the inner sanctuary of the temple, to

the Most Holy *Place,* under the wings of the cherubim. 8 For the cherubim spread *their* wings over the place of the ark, and the cherubim overshadowed the ark and its poles. 9 The poles extended so that the ends of the poles of the ark could be seen from *the holy place,* in front of the inner sanctuary; but they could not be seen from outside. And they are there to this day. 10 Nothing was in the ark except the two tablets which Moses put *there* at Horeb, when the LORD made *a covenant* with the children of Israel, when they had come out of Egypt.

11 And it came to pass when the priests came out of the *Most Holy Place* (for all the priests who *were* present had sanctified themselves, without keeping to their divisions), 12 and the Levites *who were* the singers, all those of Asaph and Heman and Jeduthun, with their sons and their brethren, stood at the east end of the altar, clothed in white linen, having cymbals, stringed instruments and harps, and with them one hundred and twenty priests sounding with trumpets— 13 indeed it came to pass, when the trumpeters and singers *were* as one, to make one sound to be heard in praising and thanking the LORD, and when they lifted up their voice with the trumpets and

cymbals and instruments of music, and praised the LORD, *saying:*

"*For He is* good,
For His mercy *endures* forever,"

that the house, the house of the LORD, was filled with a cloud, 14 so that the priests could not continue ministering because of the cloud; for the glory of the LORD filled the house of God.

6 THEN Solomon spoke:

"The LORD said
He would dwell in the dark cloud.
2   I have surely built You an exalted house,
And a place for You to dwell in forever."

3 Then the king turned around and blessed the whole assembly of Israel, while all the assembly of Israel was standing. 4 And he said: "Blessed *be* the LORD God of Israel, who has fulfilled with His hands *what* He spoke with His mouth to my father David, saying, 5 'Since the day that I brought My people out of the land of Egypt, I have chosen no city from any tribe of Israel *in which* to build a house, that My name might be there, nor did I choose any man to be a ruler over My people Israel. 6 Yet I have chosen Jerusalem, that My name may be there, and I have chosen David to be over My people Israel.' 7 Now it was in the heart of my father David to build a temple for the name of the LORD God of Israel. 8 But the LORD said to my father David, 'Whereas it was in your heart to build a temple for My name, you did well in that it was in your heart. 9 Nevertheless you shall not build the temple, but your son who will come from your body, he shall build the temple for My name.' 10 So the LORD has fulfilled His word which He spoke, and I have filled the position of my father David, and sit on the throne of Israel, as the LORD promised; and I have built the temple for the name of the LORD God of Israel. 11 And there I have put the ark, in which *is* the covenant of the LORD which He made with the children of Israel."

12 Then *Solomon* stood before the altar of the LORD in the presence of all the assembly of Israel, and spread out his hands 13 (for Solomon had made a bronze platform five cubits long, five cubits wide, and three cubits high, and had set it in the midst of the court; and he stood on it, knelt down on his knees before all the assembly of Israel,

and spread out his hands toward heaven); 14 and he said: "LORD God of Israel, *there is* no God in heaven or on earth like You, who keep *Your* covenant and mercy with Your servants who walk before You with all their hearts. 15 You have kept what You promised Your servant David my father; You have both spoken with Your mouth and fulfilled *it* with Your hand, as *it is* this day. 16 Therefore, LORD God of Israel, now keep what You promised Your servant David my father, saying, 'You shall not fail to have a man sit before Me on the throne of Israel, only if your sons take heed to their way, that they walk in My law as you have walked before Me.' 17 And now, O LORD God of Israel, let Your word come true, which You have spoken to Your servant David.

18 "But will God indeed dwell with men on the earth? Behold, heaven and the heaven of heavens cannot contain You. How much less this temple which I have built! 19 Yet regard the prayer of Your servant and his supplication, O LORD my God, and listen to the cry and the prayer which Your servant is praying before You: 20 that Your

---

Prayer is an interruption to personal ambition. (ASK)

---

eyes may be open toward this temple day and night, toward the place where *You* said *You* would put Your name, that You may hear the prayer which Your servant makes toward this place. 21 And may You hear the supplications of Your servant and of Your people Israel, when they pray toward this place. Hear from heaven Your dwelling place, and when You hear, forgive.

22 "If anyone sins against his neighbor, and is forced to take an oath, and comes *and* takes an oath before Your altar in this temple, 23 then hear from heaven, and act, and judge Your servants, bringing retribution on the wicked by bringing his way on his own head, and justifying the righteous by giving him according to his righteousness.

24 "Or if Your people Israel are defeated before an enemy because they have sinned against You, and return and confess Your name, and pray and make supplication before You in this temple, 25 then hear from heaven and forgive the sin of Your people Israel, and bring them back to the land which You gave to them and their fathers.

26 "When the heavens are shut up and there is no rain because they have sinned

against You, when they pray toward this place and confess Your name, and turn from their sin because You afflict them, 27 then hear *in* heaven, and forgive the sin of Your servants, Your people Israel, that You may teach them the good way in which they should walk; and send rain on Your land which You have given to Your people as an inheritance.

28 "When there is famine in the land, pestilence or blight or mildew, locusts or grasshoppers; when their enemies besiege them in the land of their cities; whatever plague or whatever sickness *there is;* 29 whatever prayer, whatever supplication is *made* by anyone, or by all Your people Israel, when each one knows his own burden and his own grief, and spreads out his hands to this temple: 30 then hear from heaven Your dwelling place, and forgive, and give to everyone according to all his ways, whose heart You know (for You alone know the hearts of the sons of men), 31 that they may fear You, to walk in Your ways as long as they live in the land which You gave to our fathers.

32 "Moreover, concerning a foreigner, who is not of Your people Israel, but has come from a far country for the sake of Your great name and Your mighty hand and Your outstretched arm, when they come and pray in this temple; 33 then hear from heaven Your dwelling place, and do according to all for which the foreigner calls to You, that all peoples of the earth may know Your name and fear You, as *do* Your people Israel, and that they may know that this temple which I have built is called by Your name.

34 "When Your people go out to battle against their enemies, wherever You send them, and when they pray to You toward this city which You have chosen and the temple which I have built for Your name, 35 then hear from heaven their prayer and their supplication, and maintain their cause.

36 "When they sin against You (for *there is* no one who does not sin), and You become angry with them and deliver them to the enemy, and they take them captive to a land far or near; 37 *yet* when they come to themselves in the land where they were carried captive, and repent, and make supplication to You in the land of their captivity, saying, 'We have sinned, we have done wrong, and have committed wickedness'; 38 and *when* they return to You with all their heart and with all their soul in the land of their captivity, where they have been carried captive, and pray toward their land which You gave to their fathers, the city

which You have chosen, and toward the temple which I have built for Your name: 39 then hear from heaven Your dwelling place their prayer and their supplications, and maintain their cause, and forgive Your people who have sinned against You. 40 Now, my God, I pray, let Your eyes be open and *let* Your ears *be* attentive to the prayer *made* in this place.

41 "Now therefore,
Arise, O LORD God, to Your resting place,
You and the ark of Your strength.
Let Your priests, O LORD God, be clothed with salvation,
And let Your saints rejoice in goodness.

42 "O LORD God, do not turn away the face of Your Anointed;
Remember the mercies of Your servant David."

PSALM 79:11–13

11 LET the groaning of the prisoner come before You;
According to the greatness of Your power
Preserve those who are appointed to die;
12 And return to our neighbors sevenfold into their bosom
Their reproach with which they have reproached You, O Lord.

13 So we, Your people and sheep of Your pasture,
Will give You thanks forever;
We will show forth Your praise to all generations.

PROVERBS 20:13, 14

13 DO not love sleep, lest you come to poverty;
Open your eyes, *and* you will be satisfied with bread.

14 "*It is* good for nothing," cries the buyer;
But when he has gone his way, then he boasts.

ACTS 13:1–25

NOW in the church that was at Antioch there were certain prophets and teachers:

Barnabas, Simeon who was called Niger, Lucius of Cyrene, Manaen who had been brought up with Herod the tetrarch, and Saul. 2 As they ministered to the Lord and fasted, the Holy Spirit said, "Now separate to Me Barnabas and Saul for the work to which I have called them." 3 Then, having fasted and prayed, and laid hands on them, they sent *them* away.

4 So, being sent out by the Holy Spirit, they went down to Seleucia, and from there they sailed to Cyprus. 5 And when they arrived in Salamis, they preached the word of God in the synagogues of the Jews. They also had John as *their* assistant.

6 Now when they had gone through the island to Paphos, they found a certain sorcerer, a false prophet, a Jew whose name *was* Bar-Jesus, 7 who was with the proconsul, Sergius Paulus, an intelligent man. This man called for Barnabas and Saul and sought to hear the word of God. 8 But Elymas the sorcerer (for so his name is translated) withstood them, seeking to turn the proconsul away from the faith. 9 Then Saul, who also *is called* Paul, filled with the Holy Spirit, looked intently at him 10 and said, "O full of all deceit and all fraud, *you* son of the devil, *you* enemy of all righteousness, will you not cease perverting the straight ways of the Lord? 11 And now, indeed, the hand of the Lord *is* upon you, and you shall be blind, not seeing the sun for a time."

And immediately a dark mist fell on him, and he went around seeking someone to lead him by the hand. 12 Then the proconsul believed, when he saw what had been done,

---

We have to accept God's purpose in the providential jumble of things. (GOD'S WORKMANSHIP)

---

being astonished at the teaching of the Lord.

13 Now when Paul and his party set sail from Paphos, they came to Perga in Pamphylia; and John, departing from them, returned to Jerusalem. 14 But when they departed from Perga, they came to Antioch in Pisidia, and went into the synagogue on the Sabbath day and sat down. 15 And after the reading of the Law and the Prophets, the rulers of the synagogue sent to them, saying, "Men *and* brethren, if you have any word of exhortation for the people, say on."

16 Then Paul stood up, and motioning with *his* hand said, "Men of Israel, and you who fear God, listen: 17 The God of this people Israel chose our fathers, and exalted the people when they dwelt as strangers in the land of Egypt, and with an uplifted arm He brought them out of it. 18 Now for a time of about forty years He put up with their ways in the wilderness. 19 And when He had destroyed seven nations in the land of Canaan, He distributed their land to them by allotment.

20 "After that He gave *them* judges for about four hundred and fifty years, until Samuel the prophet. 21 And afterward they asked for a king; so God gave them Saul the son of Kish, a man of the tribe of Benjamin, for forty years. 22 And when He had removed him, He raised up for them David as king, to whom also He gave testimony and said, 'I have found David the *son* of Jesse, a man after My *own* heart, who will do all My will.' 23 From this man's seed, according to *the* promise, God raised up for Israel a Savior—Jesus— 24 after John had first preached, before His coming, the baptism of repentance to all the people of Israel. 25 And as John was finishing his course, he said, 'Who do you think I am? I am not *He*. But behold, there comes One after me, the sandals of whose feet I am not worthy to loose.'

◆◆◆◆

Reading 187—The Fire of Answered Prayer
2 Chronicles 7:1

Our Lord in His teaching regarding prayer never once referred to unanswered prayer; He said God always answers prayer. If our prayers are in the name of Jesus, that is, in accordance with His nature, the answers will not be in accordance with our nature, but with His. We are apt to forget this, and to say without thinking that God does not always answer prayer. He does every time, and when we are in close communion with Him, we realize that we have not been misled.   (*Ask*)

Prayer to us is not practical, it is stupid, and until we do see that prayer is stupid, that is, stupid from the ordinary natural common-sense point of view, we will never pray. "It is absurd to think that God is going to alter things in answer to prayer!" But that is what Jesus says He will do. It sounds stupid, but it is a stupidity based on His Redemption. The reason that our prayers are not answered is that we are not stupid enough to believe what Jesus says. It is a child, and only a child who has prayer answered; a wise and prudent man does not.   (*Send I You*)

2 CHRONICLES 7:1—8:18

WHEN Solomon had finished praying, fire came down from heaven and consumed the burnt offering and the sacrifices; and the glory of the LORD filled the temple. 2 And the priests could not enter the house of the LORD, because the glory of the LORD had filled the LORD's house. 3 When all the children of Israel saw how the fire came down, and the glory of the LORD on the temple, they bowed their faces to the ground on the pavement, and worshiped and praised the LORD, *saying:*

"For *He is* good,
For His mercy *endures* forever."

4 Then the king and all the people offered sacrifices before the LORD. 5 King Solomon offered a sacrifice of twenty-two thousand bulls and one hundred and twenty thousand sheep. So the king and all the people dedicated the house of God. 6 And the priests attended to their services; the Levites also with instruments of the music of the LORD, which King David had made to praise the LORD, saying, "For His mercy *endures* forever," whenever David offered praise by their ministry. The priests sounded trumpets opposite them, while all Israel stood.

7 Furthermore Solomon consecrated the middle of the court that *was* in front of the house of the LORD; for there he offered burnt offerings and the fat of the peace offerings, because the bronze altar which Solomon had made was not able to receive the burnt offerings, the grain offerings, and the fat.

8 At that time Solomon kept the feast seven days, and all Israel with him, a very great assembly from the entrance of Hamath to the Brook of Egypt. 9 And on the eighth day they held a sacred assembly, for they observed the dedication of the altar seven days, and the feast seven days. 10 On the twenty-third day of the seventh month he sent the people away to their tents, joyful and glad of heart for the good that the LORD had done for David, for Solomon, and for His people Israel. 11 Thus Solomon finished the house of the LORD and the king's house; and Solomon successfully accomplished all that came into his heart to make in the house of the LORD and in his own house.

12 Then the LORD appeared to Solomon by night, and said to him: "I have heard your prayer, and have chosen this place for Myself as a house of sacrifice. 13 When I shut up heaven and there is no rain, or command the locusts to devour the land, or send pestilence among My people, 14 if My people who are called by My name will humble themselves, and pray and seek My face, and turn from their wicked ways, then I will hear from heaven, and will forgive their sin and heal their land. 15 Now

---

The forgiveness of God does not work unless we turn.   (GLORIFY)

My eyes will be open and My ears attentive to prayer *made* in this place. 16 For now I have chosen and sanctified this house, that My name may be there forever; and My eyes and My heart will be there perpetually. 17 As for you, if you walk before Me as your father David walked, and do according to all that I have commanded you, and if you keep My statutes and My judgments, 18 then I will establish the throne of your kingdom, as I covenanted with David your father, saying, 'You shall not fail *to have* a man as ruler in Israel.'

19 "But if you turn away and forsake My statutes and My commandments which I have set before you, and go and serve other

gods, and worship them, 20 then I will uproot them from My land which I have given them; and this house which I have sanctified for My name I will cast out of My sight, and will make it a proverb and a byword among all peoples.

21 "And *as for* this house, which is exalted, everyone who passes by it will be astonished and say, 'Why has the LORD done thus to this land and this house?' 22 Then they will answer, 'Because they forsook the LORD God of their fathers, who brought them out of the land of Egypt, and embraced other gods, and worshiped them and served them; therefore He has brought all this calamity on them.' "

8 IT came to pass at the end of twenty years, when Solomon had built the house of the LORD and his own house, 2 that the cities which Hiram had given to Solomon, Solomon built them; and he settled the children of Israel there. 3 And Solomon went to Hamath Zobah and seized it. 4 He also built Tadmor in the wilderness, and all the storage cities which he built in Hamath. 5 He built Upper Beth Horon and Lower Beth Horon, fortified cities *with* walls, gates, and bars, 6 also Baalath and all the storage cities that Solomon had, and all the chariot cities and the cities of the cavalry, and all that Solomon desired to build in Jerusalem, in Lebanon, and in all the land of his dominion.

7 All the people *who were* left of the Hittites, Amorites, Perizzites, Hivites, and Jebusites, who *were* not of Israel— 8 that is, their descendants who were left in the land after them, whom the children of Israel did not destroy—from these Solomon raised forced labor, as it is to this day. 9 But Solomon did not make the children of Israel servants for his work. Some *were* men of war, captains of his officers, captains of his chariots, and his cavalry. 10 And others *were* chiefs of the officials of King Solomon: two hundred and fifty, who ruled over the people.

11 Now Solomon brought the daughter of Pharaoh up from the City of David to the house he had built for her, for he said, "My wife shall not dwell in the house of David king of Israel, because *the places* to which the ark of the LORD has come are holy."

12 Then Solomon offered burnt offerings to the LORD on the altar of the LORD which he had built before the vestibule, 13 according to the daily rate, offering according to the commandment of Moses, for the Sabbaths, the New Moons, and the three appointed yearly feasts—the Feast of Unleavened Bread, the Feast of Weeks, and the Feast of Tabernacles. 14 And, according to the order of David his father, he appointed the divisions of the priests for their service, the Levites for their duties (to praise and serve before the priests) as the duty of each day required, and the gatekeepers by their divisions at each gate; for so David the man of God had commanded. 15 They did not depart from the command of the king to the priests and Levites concerning any matter or concerning the treasuries.

16 Now all the work of Solomon was well-ordered from the day of the foundation of the house of the LORD until it was finished. So the house of the LORD was completed.

17 Then Solomon went to Ezion Geber and Elath on the seacoast, in the land of Edom. 18 And Hiram sent him ships by the hand of his servants, and servants who knew the sea. They went with the servants of Solomon to Ophir, and acquired four hundred and fifty talents of gold from there, and brought it to King Solomon.

PSALM 80:1–6

1 GIVE ear, O Shepherd of Israel,
You who lead Joseph like a flock;
You who dwell *between* the cherubim,
shine forth!

2 Before Ephraim, Benjamin, and
Manasseh,
Stir up Your strength,
And come *and* save us!

3 Restore us, O God;
Cause Your face to shine,
And we shall be saved!

4 O LORD God of hosts,
How long will You be angry
Against the prayer of Your people?

5 You have fed them with the bread of
tears,
And given them tears to drink in great
measure.

6 You have made us a strife to our
neighbors,
And our enemies laugh among
themselves.

PROVERBS 20:15

15 THERE is gold and a multitude of
rubies,
But the lips of knowledge *are* a precious
jewel.

ACTS 13:26–52

"MEN *and* brethren, sons of the family of Abraham, and those among you who fear God, to you the word of this salvation has been sent. 27 For those who dwell in Jerusalem, and their rulers, because they did not know Him, nor even the voices of the Prophets which are read every Sabbath, have fulfilled *them* in condemning *Him*. 28 And though they found no cause for death *in Him*, they asked Pilate that He should be put to death. 29 Now when they had fulfilled all that was written concerning Him, they took *Him* down from the tree and laid *Him* in a tomb. 30 But God raised Him from the dead. 31 He was seen for many days by those who came up with Him from Galilee to Jerusalem, who are His witnesses to the people. 32 And we declare to you glad tidings—that promise which was made to the fathers, 33 God has fulfilled this for us their children, in that He has raised up Jesus. As it is also written in the second Psalm:

'You are My Son,
Today I have begotten You.'

---

*T*he grace of God never fails us,
but we often fail the grace
of God. (MORAL FOUND.)

---

34 And that He raised Him from the dead, no more to return to corruption, He has spoken thus:

'I will give you the sure mercies of David.'

35 Therefore He also says in another *Psalm:*

'You will not allow Your Holy One to see corruption.'

36 "For David, after he had served his own generation by the will of God, fell asleep, was buried with his fathers, and saw corruption; 37 but He whom God raised up saw no corruption. 38 Therefore let it be known to you, brethren, that through this Man is preached to you the forgiveness of sins; 39 and by Him everyone who believes is justified from all things from which you could not be justified by the law of Moses. 40 Beware therefore, lest what has been spoken in the prophets come upon you:

41 'Behold, you despisers,
Marvel and perish!
For I work a work in your days,
A work which you will by no means believe,
Though one were to declare it to you.' "

42 So when the Jews went out of the synagogue, the Gentiles begged that these words might be preached to them the next Sabbath. 43 Now when the congregation had broken up, many of the Jews and devout proselytes followed Paul and Barnabas, who, speaking to them, persuaded them to continue in the grace of God.

44 On the next Sabbath almost the whole city came together to hear the word of God. 45 But when the Jews saw the multitudes, they were filled with envy; and contradicting and blaspheming, they opposed the things spoken by Paul. 46 Then Paul and Barnabas grew bold and said, "It was necessary that the word of God should be spoken to you first; but since you reject it, and judge yourselves unworthy of everlasting life, behold, we turn to the Gentiles. 47 For so the Lord has commanded us:

'I have set you as a light to the Gentiles,
That you should be for salvation to the ends of the earth.' "

48 Now when the Gentiles heard this, they were glad and glorified the word of the Lord. And as many as had been appointed to eternal life believed.

49 And the word of the Lord was being spread throughout all the region. 50 But the Jews stirred up the devout and prominent women and the chief men of the city, raised up persecution against Paul and Barnabas, and expelled them from their region. 51 But they shook off the dust from their feet against them, and came to Iconium. 52 And the disciples were filled with joy and with the Holy Spirit.

Reading 188—The Power to Suffer
Acts 14:22

Have we begun to walk the practical path in grace? Do we know anything about the practice of pain? Watch what the Bible has to say about suffering, and you will find the great characteristic of the life of a child of God is the power to suffer, and through that suffering the natural is transformed into the spiritual. The thing we kick against most is the question of pain and suffering. We have naturally the idea that if we are happy and peaceful we are all right. "I did not come to bring peace but a sword," said our Lord—a striking utterance from the Prince of Peace. Happiness is not a sign that we are right with God; happiness is a sign of satisfaction, that is all, and the majority of us can be satisfied on too low a level. Jesus Christ disturbs every kind of satisfaction that is less than delight in God. Every strand of sentimental satisfaction is an indication of how much farther we have to go before we understand the life of God, it is the satisfaction of a smug self-interest which God by circumstances and pain shocks out of us as we go in the discipline of life. (PERFECT)

2 CHRONICLES 9:1—10:19

NOW when the queen of Sheba heard of the fame of Solomon, she came to Jerusalem to test Solomon with hard questions, *having* a very great retinue, camels that bore spices, gold in abundance, and precious stones; and when she came to Solomon, she spoke with him about all that was in her heart. 2 So Solomon answered all her questions; there was nothing so difficult for Solomon that he could not explain it to her. 3 And when the queen of Sheba had seen the wisdom of Solomon, the house that he had built, 4 the food on his table, the seating of his servants, the service of his waiters and their apparel, his cupbearers and their apparel, and his entryway by which he went up to the house of the LORD, there was no more spirit in her.

5 Then she said to the king: "*It was* a true report which I heard in my own land about your words and your wisdom. 6 However I did not believe their words until I came and saw with my own eyes; and indeed the half of the greatness of your wisdom was not told me. You exceed the fame of which I heard. 7 Happy *are* your men and happy *are* these your servants, who stand continually before you and hear your wisdom! 8 Blessed be the LORD your God, who delighted in you, setting you on His throne *to be* king for the LORD your God! Because your God has loved Israel, to establish them forever, therefore He made you king over them, to do justice and righteousness."

9 And she gave the king one hundred and twenty talents of gold, spices in great abundance, and precious stones; there never were any spices such as those the queen of Sheba gave to King Solomon.

10 Also, the servants of Hiram and the servants of Solomon, who brought gold from Ophir, brought algum wood and precious stones. 11 And the king made walkways *of* the algum wood for the house of the LORD and for the king's house, also harps and stringed instruments for singers; and there were none such *as these* seen before in the land of Judah.

12 Now King Solomon gave to the queen of Sheba all she desired, whatever she asked, *much more* than she had brought to the king. So she turned and went to her own country, she and her servants.

13 The weight of gold that came to Solomon yearly was six hundred and sixty-six talents of gold, 14 besides *what* the traveling merchants and traders brought. And all the kings of Arabia and governors of the country brought gold and silver to Solomon. 15 And King Solomon made two hundred large shields of hammered gold; six hundred *shekels* of hammered gold went into each shield. 16 *He* also *made* three hundred shields of hammered gold; three hundred *shekels* of gold went into each shield. The king put them in the House of the Forest of Lebanon.

17 Moreover the king made a great throne of ivory, and overlaid it with pure gold. 18 The throne *had* six steps, with a footstool of gold, *which were* fastened to the throne;

there were armrests on either side of the place of the seat, and two lions stood beside the armrests. 19 Twelve lions stood there, one on each side of the six steps; nothing like *this* had been made for any *other* kingdom.

20 All King Solomon's drinking vessels *were* gold, and all the vessels of the House of the Forest of Lebanon *were* pure gold. Not *one was* silver, for this was accounted as nothing in the days of Solomon. 21 For the king's ships went to Tarshish with the servants of Hiram. Once every three years the merchant ships came, bringing gold, silver, ivory, apes, and monkeys.

22 So King Solomon surpassed all the kings of the earth in riches and wisdom. 23 And all the kings of the earth sought the presence of Solomon to hear his wisdom, which God had put in his heart. 24 Each man brought his present: articles of silver and gold, garments, armor, spices, horses, and mules, at a set rate year by year.

25 Solomon had four thousand stalls for horses and chariots, and twelve thousand horsemen whom he stationed in the chariot cities and with the king at Jerusalem.

26 So he reigned over all the kings from the River to the land of the Philistines, as far as the border of Egypt. 27 The king made silver *as common* in Jerusalem as stones, and he made cedar trees as abundant as the sycamores which *are* in the lowland. 28 And they brought horses to Solomon from Egypt and from all lands.

29 Now the rest of the acts of Solomon, first and last, *are* they not written in the book of Nathan the prophet, in the prophecy of Ahijah the Shilonite, and in the visions of Iddo the seer concerning Jeroboam the son of Nebat? 30 Solomon reigned in Jerusalem over all Israel forty years. 31 Then Solomon rested with his fathers, and was buried in the City of David his father. And Rehoboam his son reigned in his place.

10 AND Rehoboam went to Shechem, for all Israel had gone to Shechem to make him king. 2 So it happened, when Jeroboam the son of Nebat heard *it* (he was in Egypt, where he had fled from the presence of King Solomon), that Jeroboam returned from Egypt. 3 Then they sent for him and called him. And Jeroboam and all Israel came and spoke to Rehoboam, saying, 4 "Your father made our yoke heavy; now therefore, lighten the burdensome service of your father and his heavy yoke

which he put on us, and we will serve you."

5 So he said to them, "Come back to me after three days." And the people departed.

6 Then King Rehoboam consulted the elders who stood before his father Solomon while he still lived, saying, "How do you advise *me* to answer these people?"

7 And they spoke to him, saying, "If you are kind to these people, and please them, and speak good words to them, they will be your servants forever."

8 But he rejected the advice which the elders had given him, and consulted the young men who had grown up with him, who stood before him. 9 And he said to them, "What advice do you give? How should we answer this people who have spoken to me, saying, 'Lighten the yoke which your father put on us'?"

10 Then the young men who had grown up with him spoke to him, saying, "Thus you should speak to the people who have spoken to you, saying, 'Your father made our yoke heavy, but you make *it* lighter on us'—thus you shall say to them: 'My little *finger* shall be thicker than my father's waist! 11 And now, whereas my father put a heavy yoke on you, I will add to your yoke; my father chastised you with whips, but I *will chastise you* with scourges!' "

12 So Jeroboam and all the people came to Rehoboam on the third day, as the king had directed, saying, "Come back to me the third day." 13 Then the king answered them roughly. King Rehoboam rejected the advice of the elders, 14 and he spoke to them according to the advice of the young men, saying, "My father made your yoke heavy, but I will add to it; my father chastised you with whips, but I *will chastise you* with scourges!" 15 So the king did not listen to the people; for the turn *of events* was from God, that the LORD might fulfill His word, which He had spoken by the hand of Ahijah the Shilonite to Jeroboam the son of Nebat.

16 Now when all Israel *saw* that the king did not listen to them, the people answered the king, saying:

> "What share have we in David?
> *We have* no inheritance in the son
>   of Jesse.
> Every man to your tents, O Israel!
> Now see to your own house,
>   O David!"

So all Israel departed to their tents. 17 But Rehoboam reigned over the children of Israel who dwelt in the cities of Judah.

18 Then King Rehoboam sent Hadoram, who *was* in charge of revenue; but the children of Israel stoned him with stones, and he died. Therefore King Rehoboam mounted *his* chariot in haste to flee to Jerusalem. 19 So Israel has been in rebellion against the house of David to this day.

PSALM 80:7–13

7   RESTORE us, O God of hosts;
    Cause Your face to shine,
    And we shall be saved!

8   You have brought a vine out of Egypt;
    You have cast out the nations, and
        planted it.
9   You prepared *room* for it,
    And caused it to take deep root,
    And it filled the land.
10 The hills were covered with its shadow,
    And the mighty cedars with its boughs.
11 She sent out her boughs to the Sea,
    And her branches to the River.

12 Why have You broken down her
        hedges,
    So that all who pass by the way pluck
        her *fruit?*
13 The boar out of the woods uproots it,
    And the wild beast of the field devours
        it.

PROVERBS 20:16–18

16 TAKE the garment of one who is surety
        for a stranger,
    And hold it as a pledge *when it* is for
        a seductress.

17 Bread gained by deceit *is* sweet to a
        man,
    But afterward his mouth will be filled
        with gravel.

18 Plans are established by counsel;
    By wise counsel wage war.

ACTS 14:1–28

NOW it happened in Iconium that they went together to the synagogue of the Jews, and so spoke that a great multitude both of the Jews and of the Greeks believed.

2 But the unbelieving Jews stirred up the Gentiles and poisoned their minds against the brethren. 3 Therefore they stayed there a long time, speaking boldly in the Lord, who was bearing witness to the word of His grace, granting signs and wonders to be done by their hands.

4 But the multitude of the city was divided: part sided with the Jews, and part with the apostles. 5 And when a violent attempt was made by both the Gentiles and Jews, with their rulers, to abuse and stone them, 6 they became aware of it and fled to Lystra and Derbe, cities of Lycaonia, and to the surrounding region. 7 And they were preaching the gospel there.

8 And in Lystra a certain man without strength in his feet was sitting, a cripple from his mother's womb, who had never walked. 9 *This* man heard Paul speaking. Paul, observing him intently and seeing that he had faith to be healed, 10 said with a loud voice, "Stand up straight on your feet!" And he leaped and walked. 11 Now when the people saw what Paul had done, they raised their voices, saying in the Lycaonian *language,* "The gods have come down to us in the likeness of men!" 12 And Barnabas they called Zeus, and Paul, Hermes, because he was the chief speaker. 13 Then the priest of Zeus, whose temple was in front of their city, brought oxen and garlands to the gates, intending to sacrifice with the multitudes.

14 But when the apostles Barnabas and Paul heard this, they tore their clothes and ran in among the multitude, crying out 15 and saying, "Men, why are you doing these things? We also are men with the same nature as you, and preach to you that you should turn from these useless things to the living God, who made the heaven, the earth, the sea, and all things that are in them, 16 who in bygone generations allowed all nations to walk in their own ways. 17 Nevertheless He did not leave Himself without witness, in that He did good, gave us rain from heaven and fruitful seasons, filling our hearts with food and gladness." 18 And with these sayings they could scarcely restrain the multitudes from sacrificing to them.

19 Then Jews from Antioch and Iconium came there; and having persuaded the multitudes, they stoned Paul *and* dragged *him* out of the city, supposing him to be dead. 20 However, when the disciples gathered around him, he rose up and went into the city. And the next day he departed with Barnabas to Derbe.

21 And when they had preached the gos-

pel to that city and made many disciples, they returned to Lystra, Iconium, and Antioch, 22 strengthening the souls of the disciples, exhorting *them* to continue in the faith, and *saying*, "We must through many tribulations enter the kingdom of God." 23 So

---

Despair is always the gateway of faith. (GOOD)

---

when they had appointed elders in every church, and prayed with fasting, they commended them to the Lord in whom they had believed. 24 And after they had passed through Pisidia, they came to Pamphylia. 25 Now when they had preached the word in Perga, they went down to Attalia. 26 From there they sailed to Antioch, where they had been commended to the grace of God for the work which they had completed.

27 Now when they had come and gathered the church together, they reported all that God had done with them, and that He had opened the door of faith to the Gentiles. 28 So they stayed there a long time with the disciples.

Reading 189—Saved Through Grace
Acts 15:11

The surest sign that God has done a work of grace in my heart is that I love Jesus Christ best, not weakly and faintly, not intellectually, but passionately, personally and devotedly, overwhelming every other love of my life. (*BIB. PSYCH.*)

"Grace" is a theological word and is unfortunately used, because we usually mean by theology something remote that has to do with controversy, something whereby our mind is tied up in knots and our practical life left alone. In the Bible theology is immensely practical. "Grace" means the overflowing nature of God; we see it in Nature, we have no words to describe the lavishness of God. "The grace of our Lord Jesus Christ" is the overflowing of God's nature in entire and absolute forgiveness through His own sacrifice. (*GLORY*)

---

2 CHRONICLES 11:1—12:16

NOW when Rehoboam came to Jerusalem, he assembled from the house of Judah and Benjamin one hundred and eighty thousand chosen *men* who were warriors, to fight against Israel, that he might restore the kingdom to Rehoboam.

2 But the word of the LORD came to Shemaiah the man of God, saying, 3 "Speak to Rehoboam the son of Solomon, king of Judah, and to all Israel in Judah and Benjamin, saying, 4 'Thus says the LORD: "You shall not go up or fight against your brethren! Let every man return to his house, for this thing is from Me." ' " Therefore they obeyed the words of the LORD, and turned back from attacking Jeroboam.

5 So Rehoboam dwelt in Jerusalem, and built cities for defense in Judah. 6 And he built Bethlehem, Etam, Tekoa, 7 Beth Zur, Sochoh, Adullam, 8 Gath, Mareshah, Ziph, 9 Adoraim, Lachish, Azekah, 10 Zorah, Aijalon, and Hebron, which are in Judah and Benjamin, fortified cities. 11 And he fortified the strongholds, and put captains in them, and stores of food, oil, and wine. 12 Also in every city *he put* shields and spears, and made them very strong, having Judah and Benjamin on his side.

13 And from all their territories the priests and the Levites who *were* in all Israel took their stand with him. 14 For the Levites left their common-lands and their possessions and came to Judah and Jerusalem, for Jeroboam and his sons had rejected them from serving as priests to the LORD. 15 Then he appointed for himself priests for the high places, for the demons, and the calf idols which he had made. 16 And after *the Levites left,* those from all the tribes of Israel, such as set their heart to seek the LORD God

of Israel, came to Jerusalem to sacrifice to the LORD God of their fathers. 17 So they strengthened the kingdom of Judah, and made Rehoboam the son of Solomon strong for three years, because they walked in the way of David and Solomon for three years.

18 Then Rehoboam took for himself as wife Mahalath the daughter of Jerimoth the son of David, *and of* Abihail the daughter of Eliah the son of Jesse. 19 And she bore him children: Jeush, Shamariah, and Zaham. 20 After her he took Maachah the granddaughter of Absalom; and she bore him Abijah, Attai, Ziza, and Shelomith. 21 Now Rehoboam loved Maachah the granddaughter of Absalom more than all his wives and his concubines; for he took eighteen wives and sixty concubines, and begot twenty-eight sons and sixty daughters. 22 And Rehoboam appointed Abijah the son of Maachah as chief, *to be* leader among his brothers; for he *intended* to make him king. 23 He dealt wisely, and dispersed some of his sons throughout all the territories of Judah and Benjamin, to every fortified city; and he gave them provisions in abundance. He also sought many wives *for them.*

12 NOW it came to pass, when Rehoboam had established the kingdom and had strengthened himself, that he forsook the law of the LORD, and all Israel along with him. 2 And it happened in the fifth year of King Rehoboam *that* Shishak king of Egypt came up against Jerusalem, because they had transgressed against the LORD, 3 with twelve hundred chariots, sixty thousand horsemen, and people without number who came with him out of Egypt—the Lubim and the Sukkiim and the Ethiopians. 4 And he took the fortified cities of Judah and came to Jerusalem.

5 Then Shemaiah the prophet came to Rehoboam and the leaders of Judah, who were gathered together in Jerusalem because of Shishak, and said to them, "Thus says the LORD: 'You have forsaken Me, and therefore I also have left you in the hand of Shishak.' "

6 So the leaders of Israel and the king humbled themselves; and they said, "The LORD *is* righteous."

7 Now when the LORD saw that they humbled themselves, the word of the LORD came to Shemaiah, saying, "They have humbled themselves; *therefore* I will not destroy them, but I will grant them some deliverance. My wrath shall not be poured out on Jerusalem by the hand of Shishak.

8 Nevertheless they will be his servants, that they may distinguish My service from the service of the kingdoms of the nations."

9 So Shishak king of Egypt came up against Jerusalem, and took away the treasures of the house of the LORD and the treasures of the king's house; he took everything. He also carried away the gold shields which Solomon had made. 10 Then King Rehoboam made bronze shields in their place, and committed *them* to the hands of the captains of the guard, who guarded the doorway of the king's house. 11 And whenever the king entered the house of the LORD, the guard would go and bring them out; then they would take them back into the guardroom. 12 When he humbled himself, the wrath of the LORD turned from him, so as not to destroy *him* completely; and things also went well in Judah.

13 Thus King Rehoboam strengthened himself in Jerusalem and reigned. Now Rehoboam *was* forty-one years old when he became king; and he reigned seventeen years in Jerusalem, the city which the LORD had chosen out of all the tribes of Israel, to put His name there. His mother's name *was* Naamah, an Ammonitess. 14 And he did evil, because he did not prepare his heart to seek the LORD.

15 The acts of Rehoboam, first and last, *are* they not written in the book of Shemaiah the prophet, and of Iddo the seer concerning genealogies? And *there were* wars between Rehoboam and Jeroboam all their days. 16 So Rehoboam rested with his fathers, and was buried in the City of David. Then Abijah his son reigned in his place.

PSALM 80:14–19

14 RETURN, we beseech You, O God of hosts;
Look down from heaven and see,
And visit this vine
15 And the vineyard which Your right hand has planted,
And the branch *that* You made strong for Yourself.
16 *It is* burned with fire, *it is* cut down;
They perish at the rebuke of Your countenance.
17 Let Your hand be upon the man of Your right hand,
Upon the son of man *whom* You made strong for Yourself.
18 Then we will not turn back from You;
Revive us, and we will call upon Your name.

19 Restore us, O Lᴏʀᴅ God of hosts;
    Cause Your face to shine,
    And we shall be saved!

PROVERBS 20:19–21

19 HE who goes about *as* a talebearer
    reveals secrets;
    Therefore do not associate with one
    who flatters with his lips.

20 Whoever curses his father or his mother,
    His lamp will be put out in deep
    darkness.

21 An inheritance gained hastily at the
    beginning
    Will not be blessed at the end.

ACTS 15:1–21

AND certain *men* came down from Judea
and taught the brethren, "Unless you are
circumcised according to the custom of
Moses, you cannot be saved." 2 Therefore,
when Paul and Barnabas had no small dissension and dispute with them, they determined that Paul and Barnabas and certain
others of them should go up to Jerusalem,
to the apostles and elders, about this
question.

3 So, being sent on their way by the
church, they passed through Phoenicia and
Samaria, describing the conversion of the
Gentiles; and they caused great joy to all
the brethren. 4 And when they had come
to Jerusalem, they were received by the
church and the apostles and the elders; and
they reported all things that God had done
with them. 5 But some of the sect of the
Pharisees who believed rose up, saying, "It
is necessary to circumcise them, and to command *them* to keep the law of Moses."

6 Now the apostles and elders came together to consider this matter. 7 And when
there had been much dispute, Peter rose
up and said to them: "Men and brethren,
you know that a good while ago God chose
among us, that by my mouth the Gentiles
should hear the word of the gospel and
believe. 8 So God, who knows the heart,

acknowledged them by giving them the
Holy Spirit, just as *He did* to us, 9 and made
no distinction between us and them, purifying their hearts by faith. 10 Now therefore,
why do you test God by putting a yoke
on the neck of the disciples which neither
our fathers nor we were able to bear?

*We have no business to bow our
necks to any yoke saving the yoke
of . . . Jesus Christ.*   (Bɪʙ. Psʏᴄʜ.)

11 But we believe that through the grace
of the Lord Jesus Christ we shall be saved
in the same manner as they."

12 Then all the multitude kept silent and
listened to Barnabas and Paul declaring how
many miracles and wonders God had
worked through them among the Gentiles.
13 And after they had become silent, James
answered, saying, "Men *and* brethren, listen
to me: 14 Simon has declared how God at
the first visited the Gentiles to take out of
them a people for His name. 15 And with
this the words of the prophets agree, just
as it is written:

16 'After this I will return
    And will rebuild the tabernacle of
        David, which has fallen down;
    I will rebuild its ruins,
    And I will set it up;
17 So that the rest of mankind may seek
        the Lᴏʀᴅ,
    Even all the Gentiles who are called
        by My name,
    Says the Lᴏʀᴅ who does all these
        things.'

18 "Known to God from eternity are all
His works. 19 Therefore I judge that we
should not trouble those from among the
Gentiles who are turning to God, 20 but
that we write to them to abstain from things
polluted by idols, *from* sexual immorality,
from things strangled, and *from* blood.
21 For Moses has had throughout many
generations those who preach him in every
city, being read in the synagogues every
Sabbath."

Reading 190—Life with Uncommon Spirit
Psalm 81:5

A life with presence—that is, an uncommon spirit—redeems any situation from the commonplace. It may be cleaning boots or doing housework, any ordinary thing at all, but as soon as it is touched by a man or woman with presence it ceases to be commonplace. The rarest asset to a godly life is to be practically conscientious in every situation: "But the LORD was with Joseph . . . and He gave him favor in the sight of the keeper of the prison."

Joseph's adaptability was superb. Adaptability is not tact. Tact is frequently nothing but the moral counterpart of hypocrisy. Adaptability is the power to make a suitable environment for oneself out of any set of circumstances. Most of us are all right if we can live in our own particular setting, with our own crowd, but when we get pitchforked somewhere else, either we cannot adapt ourselves, or we adapt ourselves too easily and lose God. Joseph did not lose God. God was with Joseph in Egypt as He had been in Canaan; He was with him in the prison as He was in the house of his master.   (*NOT KNOWING*)

2 CHRONICLES 13:1—14:15

IN the eighteenth year of King Jeroboam, Abijah became king over Judah. 2 He reigned three years in Jerusalem. His mother's name *was* Michaiah the daughter of Uriel of Gibeah.

And there was war between Abijah and Jeroboam. 3 Abijah set the battle in order with an army of valiant warriors, four hundred thousand choice men. Jeroboam also drew up in battle formation against him with eight hundred thousand choice men, mighty men of valor.

4 Then Abijah stood on Mount Zemaraim, which *is* in the mountains of Ephraim, and said, "Hear me, Jeroboam and all Israel: 5 Should you not know that the LORD God of Israel gave the dominion over Israel to David forever, to him and his sons, by a covenant of salt? 6 Yet Jeroboam the son of Nebat, the servant of Solomon the son of David, rose up and rebelled against his lord. 7 Then worthless rogues gathered to him, and strengthened themselves against Rehoboam the son of Solomon, when Rehoboam was young and inexperienced and could not withstand them. 8 And now you think to withstand the kingdom of the LORD, which is in the hand of the sons of David; and you *are* a great multitude, and with you are the gold calves which Jeroboam made for you as gods. 9 Have you not cast out the priests of the LORD, the sons of Aaron, and the Levites, and made for yourselves priests, like the peoples of *other* lands, so that whoever comes to con-

secrate himself with a young bull and seven rams may be a priest of *things that are* not gods? 10 But as for us, the LORD *is* our God, and we have not forsaken Him; and the priests who minister to the LORD *are* the sons of Aaron, and the Levites *attend* to *their* duties. 11 And they burn to the LORD every morning and every evening burnt sacrifices and sweet incense; *they* also *set* the showbread *in order on* the pure *gold* table, and the lampstand of gold with its lamps to burn every evening; for we keep the command of the LORD our God, but you have forsaken Him. 12 Now look, God Himself is with us as *our* head, and His priests with sounding trumpets to sound the alarm against you. O children of Israel, do not fight against the LORD God of your fathers, for you shall not prosper!"

13 But Jeroboam caused an ambush to go around behind them; so they were in front of Judah, and the ambush *was* behind them. 14 And when Judah looked around, to their surprise the battle line *was* at both front and rear; and they cried out to the LORD, and the priests sounded the trumpets. 15 Then the men of Judah gave a shout; and as the men of Judah shouted, it happened that God struck Jeroboam and all Israel before Abijah and Judah. 16 And the children of Israel fled before Judah, and God delivered them into their hand. 17 Then Abijah and his people struck them with a great slaughter; so five hundred thousand choice men of Israel fell slain. 18 Thus the children of Israel were subdued at that time; and the children of Judah pre-

vailed, because they relied on the LORD God of their fathers.

19 And Abijah pursued Jeroboam and took cities from him: Bethel with its villages, Jeshanah with its villages, and Ephrain with its villages. 20 So Jeroboam did not recover strength again in the days of Abijah; and the LORD struck him, and he died.

21 But Abijah grew mighty, married fourteen wives, and begot twenty-two sons and sixteen daughters. 22 Now the rest of the acts of Abijah, his ways, and his sayings *are* written in the annals of the prophet Iddo.

14 SO Abijah rested with his fathers, and they buried him in the City of David. Then Asa his son reigned in his place. In his days the land was quiet for ten years.

2 Asa did *what was* good and right in the eyes of the LORD his God, 3 for he removed the altars of the foreign *gods* and the high places, and broke down the *sacred* pillars and cut down the wooden images. 4 He commanded Judah to seek the LORD God of their fathers, and to observe the law and the commandment. 5 He also removed the high places and the incense altars from all the cities of Judah, and the kingdom was quiet under him. 6 And he built fortified cities in Judah, for the land had rest; he had no war in those years, because the LORD had given him rest. 7 Therefore he said to Judah, "Let us build these cities and make walls around *them,* and towers, gates, and bars, *while* the land *is* yet before us, because we have sought the LORD our God; we have sought *Him,* and He has given us rest on every side." So they built and prospered. 8 And Asa had an army of three hundred thousand from Judah who carried shields and spears, and from Benjamin two hundred and eighty thousand men who carried shields and drew bows; all these *were* mighty men of valor.

9 Then Zerah the Ethiopian came out against them with an army of a million men and three hundred chariots, and he came to Mareshah. 10 So Asa went out against him, and they set the troops in battle array in the Valley of Zephathah at Mareshah. 11 And Asa cried out to the LORD his God, and said, "LORD, *it is* nothing for You to help, whether with many or with those who have no power; help us, O LORD our God, for we rest on You, and in Your name we go against this multitude. O LORD, You *are* our God; do not let man prevail against You!"

12 So the LORD struck the Ethiopians before Asa and Judah, and the Ethiopians fled. 13 And Asa and the people who *were* with him pursued them to Gerar. So the Ethiopians were overthrown, and they could not recover, for they were broken before the LORD and His army. And they carried away very much spoil. 14 Then they defeated all the cities around Gerar, for the fear of the LORD came upon them; and they plundered all the cities, for there was exceedingly much spoil in them. 15 They also attacked the livestock enclosures, and carried off sheep and camels in abundance, and returned to Jerusalem.

PSALM 81:1–5

1 SING aloud to God our strength;
Make a joyful shout to the God of Jacob.

2 Raise a song and strike the timbrel,
The pleasant harp with the lute.

3 Blow the trumpet at the time of the New Moon,
At the full moon, on our solemn feast day.

4 For this *is* a statute for Israel,
A law of the God of Jacob.

5 This He established in Joseph *as* a testimony,
When He went throughout the land of Egypt,
Where I heard a language I did not understand.

PROVERBS 20:22, 23

22 DO not say, "I will recompense evil";
Wait for the LORD, and He will save you.

23 Diverse weights *are* an abomination to the LORD,
And dishonest scales *are* not good.

ACTS 15:22–41

22 THEN it pleased the apostles and elders, with the whole church, to send chosen men of their own company to Antioch with Paul and Barnabas, *namely,* Judas who was also named Barsabas, and Silas, leading men among the brethren.

23 They wrote this *letter* by them:

The apostles, the elders, and the brethren,

To the brethren who are of the Gentiles in Antioch, Syria, and Cilicia:

Greetings.

24 Since we have heard that some who went out from us have troubled you with words, unsettling your souls, saying, *"You must* be circumcised and keep the law"—to whom we gave no *such* commandment— 25 it seemed good to us, being assembled with one accord, to send chosen men to you with our beloved Barnabas and Paul, 26 men who have risked their lives for the name of our Lord Jesus Christ.

A saint must measure his life by self-expenditure.   (PLACE HELP)

---

27 We have therefore sent Judas and Silas, who will also report the same things by word of mouth. 28 For it seemed good to the Holy Spirit, and to us, to lay upon you no greater burden than these necessary things: 29 that you abstain from things offered to idols, from blood, from things strangled, and from sexual immorality. If you keep yourselves from these, you will do well.

Farewell.

30 So when they were sent off, they came to Antioch; and when they had gathered the multitude together, they delivered the letter. 31 When they had read it, they rejoiced over its encouragement. 32 Now Judas and Silas, themselves being prophets also, exhorted and strengthened the brethren with many words. 33 And after they had stayed *there* for a time, they were sent back with greetings from the brethren to the apostles.

34 However, it seemed good to Silas to remain there. 35 Paul and Barnabas also remained in Antioch, teaching and preaching the word of the Lord, with many others also.

36 Then after some days Paul said to Barnabas, "Let us now go back and visit our brethren in every city where we have preached the word of the Lord, *and see* how they are doing." 37 Now Barnabas was determined to take with them John called Mark. 38 But Paul insisted that they should not take with them the one who had departed from them in Pamphylia, and had not gone with them to the work. 39 Then the contention became so sharp that they parted from one another. And so Barnabas took Mark and sailed to Cyprus; 40 but Paul chose Silas and departed, being commended by the brethren to the grace of God. 41 And he went through Syria and Cilicia, strengthening the churches.

◆◆◆◆

*Reading 191—*A Fearful Curiosity
Acts 16:16–19

The Bible reveals that the unseen world has rulers and majesties and tremendous beings with whom man can get into communication and be possessed by, but God pronounces His curse on the man or woman who dares to communicate with them.   (*SERVANT AS LORD*)

The good angels are a host and the bad angels are a host. Today spiritualism is having tremendous vogue; men and women are getting into communication with departed spirits and putting themselves in league with the unseen powers. If you have got as far as reading fortunes in tea cups, *stop*. If you have gone as far as telling fortunes by cards, *stop*. I will tell you why—the Devil uses these apparently harmless things to create a fearful curiosity in the minds of men and women, especially young men and women, and it may bring them into league with the angelic forces that hate God, into league with the principalities and the rulers of this world's darkness. Never say, "What is the harm in it?" Push it to its logical conclusion and ask—"Where will this end?"   (*SERVANT AS LORD*)

2 CHRONICLES 15:1—16:14

NOW the Spirit of God came upon Azariah the son of Oded. 2 And he went out to meet Asa, and said to him: "Hear me, Asa, and all Judah and Benjamin. The LORD *is* with you while you are with Him. If you seek Him, He will be found by you; but if you forsake Him, He will forsake you. 3 For a long time Israel *has been* without the true God, without a teaching priest, and without law; 4 but when in their trouble they turned to the LORD God of Israel, and sought Him, He was found by them. 5 And in those times *there was* no peace to the one who went out, nor to the one who came in, but great turmoil *was* on all the inhabitants of the lands. 6 So nation was destroyed by nation, and city by city, for God troubled them with every adversity. 7 But you, be strong and do not let your hands be weak, for your work shall be rewarded!"

8 And when Asa heard these words and the prophecy of Oded the prophet, he took courage, and removed the abominable idols from all the land of Judah and Benjamin and from the cities which he had taken in the mountains of Ephraim; and he restored the altar of the LORD that *was* before the vestibule of the LORD. 9 Then he gathered all Judah and Benjamin, and those who dwelt with them from Ephraim, Manasseh, and Simeon, for they came over to him in great numbers from Israel when they saw that the LORD his God was with him.

10 So they gathered together at Jerusalem in the third month, in the fifteenth year of the reign of Asa. 11 And they offered to the LORD at that time seven hundred bulls and seven thousand sheep from the spoil they had brought. 12 Then they entered into a covenant to seek the LORD God of their fathers with all their heart and with all their soul; 13 and whoever would not seek the LORD God of Israel was to be put to death, whether small or great, whether man or woman. 14 Then they took an oath before the LORD with a loud voice, with shouting and trumpets and rams' horns. 15 And all Judah rejoiced at the oath, for they had sworn with all their heart and sought Him with all their soul; and He was found by them, and the LORD gave them rest all around.

16 Also he removed Maachah, the mother of Asa the king, from *being* queen mother, because she had made an obscene image of Asherah; and Asa cut down her obscene image, then crushed and burned *it* by the Brook Kidron. 17 But the high places were not removed from Israel. Nevertheless the heart of Asa was loyal all his days.

18 He also brought into the house of God the things that his father had dedicated and that he himself had dedicated: silver and gold and utensils. 19 And there was no war until the thirty-fifth year of the reign of Asa.

16 IN the thirty-sixth year of the reign of Asa, Baasha king of Israel came up against Judah and built Ramah, that he might let none go out or come in to Asa king of Judah. 2 Then Asa brought silver and gold from the treasuries of the house of the LORD and of the king's house, and sent to Ben-Hadad king of Syria, who dwelt in Damascus, saying, 3 "*Let there be* a treaty between you and me, as there was between my father and your father. See, I have sent you silver and gold; come, break your treaty with Baasha king of Israel, so that he will withdraw from me."

4 So Ben-Hadad heeded King Asa, and sent the captains of his armies against the cities of Israel. They attacked Ijon, Dan, Abel Maim, and all the storage cities of Naphtali. 5 Now it happened, when Baasha heard *it*, that he stopped building Ramah and ceased his work. 6 Then King Asa took all Judah, and they carried away the stones and timber of Ramah, which Baasha had used for building; and with them he built Geba and Mizpah.

7 And at that time Hanani the seer came to Asa king of Judah, and said to him: "Because you have relied on the king of Syria, and have not relied on the LORD your God, therefore the army of the king of Syria has escaped from your hand. 8 Were the Ethiopians and the Lubim not a huge army with very many chariots and horsemen? Yet, because you relied on the LORD, He delivered them into your hand. 9 For the eyes of the LORD run to and fro throughout the whole earth, to show Himself strong on behalf of *those* whose heart *is* loyal to Him. In this you have done foolishly; therefore from now on you shall have wars." 10 Then Asa was angry with the seer, and put him in prison, for *he was* enraged at him because of this. And Asa oppressed *some* of the people at that time.

11 Note that the acts of Asa, first and last, are indeed written in the book of the kings of Judah and Israel. 12 And in the thirty-ninth year of his reign, Asa became diseased in his feet, and his malady was severe; yet in his disease he did not seek the LORD, but the physicians.

13 So Asa rested with his fathers; he died in the forty-first year of his reign. 14 They buried him in his own tomb, which he had made for himself in the City of David; and they laid him in the bed which was filled with spices and various ingredients prepared in a mixture of ointments. They made a very great burning for him.

PSALM 81:6–10

6   "I removed his shoulder from the burden;
    His hands were freed from the baskets.
7   You called in trouble, and I delivered you;
    I answered you in the secret place of thunder;
    I tested you at the waters of Meribah.
                     Selah

8   "Hear, O My people, and I will admonish you!
    O Israel, if you will listen to Me!
9   There shall be no foreign god among you;
    Nor shall you worship any foreign god.
10 I *am* the LORD your God,
    Who brought you out of the land of Egypt;
    Open your mouth wide, and I will fill it.

PROVERBS 20:24, 25

24 A man's steps *are* of the LORD;
    How then can a man understand his own way?

25 *It is* a snare for a man to devote rashly *something as* holy,
    And afterward to reconsider *his* vows.

ACTS 16:1–21

THEN he came to Derbe and Lystra. And behold, a certain disciple was there, named Timothy, *the* son of a certain Jewish woman who believed, but his father *was* Greek. 2 He was well spoken of by the brethren who were at Lystra and Iconium. 3 Paul wanted to have him go on with him. And he took *him* and circumcised him because of the Jews who were in that region, for they all knew that his father was Greek. 4 And as they went through the cities, they delivered to them the decrees to keep, which were determined by the apostles and elders at Jerusalem. 5 So the churches were strengthened in the faith, and increased in number daily.

6 Now when they had gone through Phrygia and the region of Galatia, they were forbidden by the Holy Spirit to preach the word in Asia. 7 After they had come to Mysia, they tried to go into Bithynia, but the Spirit did not permit them. 8 So passing by Mysia, they came down to Troas. 9 And a vision appeared to Paul in the night. A man of Macedonia stood and pleaded with him, saying, "Come over to Macedonia and help us." 10 Now after he had seen the vision, immediately we sought to go to Macedonia, concluding that the Lord had called us to preach the gospel to them.

11 Therefore, sailing from Troas, we ran a straight course to Samothrace, and the next *day* came to Neapolis, 12 and from there to Philippi, which is the foremost city of that part of Macedonia, a colony. And we were staying in that city for some days. 13 And on the Sabbath day we went out of the city to the riverside, where prayer was customarily made; and we sat down and spoke to the women who met *there*. 14 Now a certain woman named Lydia heard *us*. She was a seller of purple from the city of Thyatira, who worshiped God. The Lord opened her heart to heed the things spoken by Paul. 15 And when she and her household were baptized, she begged *us*, saying, "If you have judged me to be faithful to the Lord, come to my house and stay." So she persuaded us.

---

*F*aith gets us into the middle, which is God and God's purpose.   (MORAL FOUND.)

---

16 Now it happened, as we went to prayer, that a certain slave girl possessed with a spirit of divination met us, who brought her masters much profit by fortune-telling. 17 This girl followed Paul and us, and cried out, saying, "These men are the servants of the Most High God, who proclaim to us the way of salvation." 18 And this she did for many days.

But Paul, greatly annoyed, turned and said to the spirit, "I command you in the name of Jesus Christ to come out of her." And he came out that very hour. 19 But when her masters saw that their hope of profit was gone, they seized Paul and Silas and dragged *them* into the marketplace to the authorities.

20 And they brought them to the magis-trates, and said, "These men, being Jews, exceedingly trouble our city; 21 and they teach customs which are not lawful for us, being Romans, to receive or observe."

◆◆◆◆

Reading 192—The Immortal Part of a Man
Proverbs 20:27

Beware of dividing man up into body, soul and spirit. Man *is* body, soul and spirit. Soul is the expression of man's personal spirit in his body. Spirit means I, myself, the incalculable being that is "me," the essence that expresses itself in the soul. The immortal part of a man is not his soul, but his spirit. Man's spirit is as indestructible as Almighty God, the expression of his spirit in the soul depends on the body. In the Bible the soul is always referred to in connection with the body. The soul is the holder of the body and spirit together, and when the body disappears, the soul disappears, but the essential personality of the man remains. (*PSY. REDEMP.*)

Soul is the expression of spirit in the body; soul has no existence apart from spirit and body. Immediately body goes, the spirit returns to God who gave it, and soul is not. The resurrection is of body, not of spirit or soul. Spirit is the immortal, indestructible part of a man, and it goes back to God who gave it, with all the characteristics that marked it while it was on this earth. (*GLORY*)

2 CHRONICLES 17:1—18:34

THEN Jehoshaphat his son reigned in his place, and strengthened himself against Israel. 2 And he placed troops in all the fortified cities of Judah, and set garrisons in the land of Judah and in the cities of Ephraim which Asa his father had taken. 3 Now the LORD was with Jehoshaphat, because he walked in the former ways of his father David; he did not seek the Baals, 4 but sought the God of his father, and walked in His commandments and not according to the acts of Israel. 5 Therefore the LORD established the kingdom in his hand; and all Judah gave presents to Jehoshaphat, and he had riches and honor in abundance. 6 And his heart took delight in the ways of the LORD; moreover he removed the high places and wooden images from Judah.

7 Also in the third year of his reign he sent his leaders, Ben-Hail, Obadiah, Zechariah, Nethanel, and Michaiah, to teach in the cities of Judah. 8 And with them *he sent* Levites: Shemaiah, Nethaniah, Zebadiah, Asahel, Shemiramoth, Jehonathan, Adonijah, Tobijah, and Tobadonijah—the Levites; and with them Elishama and Jehoram, the priests. 9 So they taught in Judah, and *had* the Book of the Law of the LORD with them; they went throughout all the cities of Judah and taught the people.

10 And the fear of the LORD fell on all the kingdoms of the lands that *were* around Judah, so that they did not make war against Jehoshaphat. 11 Also *some* of the Philistines brought Jehoshaphat presents and silver as tribute; and the Arabians brought him flocks, seven thousand seven hundred rams and seven thousand seven hundred male goats.

12 So Jehoshaphat became increasingly powerful, and he built fortresses and storage cities in Judah. 13 He had much property in the cities of Judah; and the men of war, mighty men of valor, *were* in Jerusalem.

14 These *are* their numbers, according to their fathers' houses. Of Judah, the captains of thousands: Adnah the captain, and with him three hundred thousand mighty men of valor; 15 and next to him *was* Jehohanan the captain, and with him two hundred and eighty thousand; 16 and next to him *was* Amasiah the son of Zichri, who willingly offered himself to the LORD, and with him

two hundred thousand mighty men of valor. 17 Of Benjamin: Eliada a mighty man of valor, and with him two hundred thousand men armed with bow and shield; 18 and next to him *was* Jehozabad, and with him one hundred and eighty thousand prepared for war. 19 These served the king, besides those the king put in the fortified cities throughout all Judah.

18 JEHOSHAPHAT had riches and honor in abundance; and by marriage he allied himself with Ahab. 2 After some years he went down to *visit* Ahab in Samaria; and Ahab killed sheep and oxen in abundance for him and the people who were with him, and persuaded him to go up *with him* to Ramoth Gilead. 3 So Ahab king of Israel said to Jehoshaphat king of Judah, "Will you go with me *against* Ramoth Gilead?"

And he answered him, "I *am* as you *are*, and my people as your people; *we will be* with you in the war."

4 Also Jehoshaphat said to the king of Israel, "Please inquire for the word of the LORD today."

5 Then the king of Israel gathered the prophets together, four hundred men, and said to them, "Shall we go to war against Ramoth Gilead, or shall I refrain?"

So they said, "Go up, for God will deliver it into the king's hand."

6 But Jehoshaphat said, "*Is there* not still a prophet of the LORD here, that we may inquire of Him?"

7 So the king of Israel said to Jehoshaphat, "*There is* still one man by whom we may inquire of the LORD; but I hate him, because he never prophesies good concerning me, but always evil. He *is* Micaiah the son of Imla."

And Jehoshaphat said, "Let not the king say such things!"

8 Then the king of Israel called one *of his* officers and said, "Bring Micaiah the son of Imla quickly!"

9 The king of Israel and Jehoshaphat king of Judah, clothed in *their* robes, sat each on his throne; and they sat at a threshing floor at the entrance of the gate of Samaria; and all the prophets prophesied before them. 10 Now Zedekiah the son of Chenaanah had made horns of iron for himself; and he said, "Thus says the LORD: 'With these you shall gore the Syrians until they are destroyed.'"

11 And all the prophets prophesied so, saying, "Go up to Ramoth Gilead and prosper, for the LORD will deliver *it* into the king's hand."

12 Then the messenger who had gone to call Micaiah spoke to him, saying, "Now listen, the words of the prophets with one accord encourage the king. Therefore please let your word be like *the word of* one of them, and speak encouragement."

13 And Micaiah said, "*As* the LORD lives, whatever my God says, that I will speak."

14 Then he came to the king; and the king said to him, "Micaiah, shall we go to war against Ramoth Gilead, or shall I refrain?"

And he said, "Go and prosper, and they shall be delivered into your hand!"

15 So the king said to him, "How many times shall I make you swear that you tell me nothing but the truth in the name of the LORD?"

16 Then he said, "I saw all Israel scattered on the mountains, as sheep that have no shepherd. And the LORD said, 'These have no master. Let each return to his house in peace.'"

17 And the king of Israel said to Jehoshaphat, "Did I not tell you he would not prophesy good concerning me, but evil?"

18 Then *Micaiah* said, "Therefore hear the word of the LORD: I saw the LORD sitting on His throne, and all the host of heaven standing on His right hand and His left. 19 And the LORD said, 'Who will persuade Ahab king of Israel to go up, that he may fall at Ramoth Gilead?' So one spoke in this manner, and another spoke in that manner. 20 Then a spirit came forward and stood before the LORD, and said, 'I will persuade him.' The LORD said to him, 'In what way?' 21 So he said, 'I will go out and be a lying spirit in the mouth of all his prophets.' And *the* LORD said, 'You shall persuade *him* and also prevail; go out and do so.' 22 Therefore look! The LORD has put a lying spirit in the mouth of these prophets of yours, and the LORD has declared disaster against you."

23 Then Zedekiah the son of Chenaanah went near and struck Micaiah on the cheek, and said, "Which way did the spirit from the LORD go from me to speak to you?"

24 And Micaiah said, "Indeed you shall see on that day when you go into an inner chamber to hide!"

25 Then the king of Israel said, "Take Micaiah, and return him to Amon the governor of the city and to Joash the king's son; 26 and say, 'Thus says the king: "Put this *fellow* in prison, and feed him with bread of affliction and water of affliction, until I return in peace."'"

27 But Micaiah said, "If you ever return in peace, the LORD has not spoken by me." And he said, "Take heed, all you people!"

28 So the king of Israel and Jehoshaphat the king of Judah went up to Ramoth Gilead. 29 And the king of Israel said to Jehoshaphat, "I will disguise myself and go into battle; but you put on your robes." So the king of Israel disguised himself, and they went into battle.

30 Now the king of Syria had commanded the captains of the chariots who *were* with him, saying, "Fight with no one small or great, but only with the king of Israel."

31 So it was, when the captains of the chariots saw Jehoshaphat, that they said, "It *is* the king of Israel!" Therefore they surrounded him to attack; but Jehoshaphat cried out, and the LORD helped him, and God diverted them from him. 32 For so it was, when the captains of the chariots saw that it was not the king of Israel, that they turned back from pursuing him. 33 Now a certain man drew a bow at random, and struck the king of Israel between the joints of his armor. So he said to the driver of his chariot, "Turn around and take me out of the battle, for I am wounded." 34 The battle increased that day, and the king of Israel propped *himself* up in *his* chariot facing the Syrians until evening; and about the time of sunset he died.

PSALM 81:11–16

11 "BUT My people would not heed My voice,
   And Israel would *have* none of Me.
12 So I gave them over to their own stubborn heart,
   To walk in their own counsels.

A stubborn man is always a "small potato." (SHADE)

---

13 "Oh, that My people would listen to Me,
   That Israel would walk in My ways!
14 I would soon subdue their enemies,
   And turn My hand against their adversaries.
15 The haters of the LORD would pretend submission to Him,
   But their fate would endure forever.
16 He would have fed them also with the finest of wheat;
   And with honey from the rock I would have satisfied you."

PROVERBS 20:26–28

26 A wise king sifts out the wicked,
   And brings the threshing wheel over them.

27 The spirit of a man *is* the lamp of the LORD,
   Searching all the inner depths of his heart.

28 Mercy and truth preserve the king,
   And by lovingkindness he upholds his throne.

ACTS 16:22–40

THEN the multitude rose up together against them; and the magistrates tore off their clothes and commanded *them* to be beaten with rods. 23 And when they had laid many stripes on them, they threw *them* into prison, commanding the jailer to keep them securely. 24 Having received such a charge, he put them into the inner prison and fastened their feet in the stocks.

25 But at midnight Paul and Silas were praying and singing hymns to God, and the prisoners were listening to them.

In the New Testament, prayer is based on a relationship with God through Jesus Christ. (ASK)

---

26 Suddenly there was a great earthquake, so that the foundations of the prison were shaken; and immediately all the doors were opened and everyone's chains were loosed. 27 And the keeper of the prison, awaking from sleep and seeing the prison doors open, supposing the prisoners had fled, drew his sword and was about to kill himself. 28 But Paul called with a loud voice, saying, "Do yourself no harm, for we are all here."

29 Then he called for a light, ran in, and fell down trembling before Paul and Silas. 30 And he brought them out and said, "Sirs, what must I do to be saved?" 31 So they said, "Believe on the Lord Jesus Christ, and you will be saved, you and your household." 32 Then they spoke the word of the Lord to him and to all who were in his house. 33 And he took them the same hour of the night and washed

their stripes. And immediately he and all his family were baptized. 34 Now when he had brought them into his house, he set food before them; and he rejoiced, having believed in God with all his household.

35 And when it was day, the magistrates sent the officers, saying, "Let those men go."

36 So the keeper of the prison reported these words to Paul, saying, "The magistrates have sent to let you go. Now therefore depart, and go in peace."

37 But Paul said to them, "They have beaten us openly, uncondemned Romans, *and* have thrown *us* into prison. And now do they put us out secretly? No indeed! Let them come themselves and get us out."

38 And the officers told these words to the magistrates, and they were afraid when they heard that they were Romans. 39 Then they came and pleaded with them and brought *them* out, and asked *them* to depart from the city. 40 So they went out of the prison and entered *the house of* Lydia; and when they had seen the brethren, they encouraged them and departed.

◆◆◆◆

Reading 193—The Unbribed Soul
Psalm 82:3, 4

We have grown literally afraid of being poor. We despise anyone who elects to be poor in order to simplify and save his inner life. If he does not join the general scramble, and pant with the money-making street, we deem him spiritless and lacking in ambition. We have lost the power of imagining what the ancient idealization of poverty could have meant—the liberation from material attachments, the unbribed soul, the manlier indifference, the paying our way by what we are or do, and not by what we have; the right to fling away our life at any moment irresponsibly, the more athletic trim, in short, the moral fighting shape. (*Chris. Dis. 2*)

The thing in which I am blessed is my poverty. If I know I have no strength of will, no nobility of disposition, then, says Jesus, "Blessed are you," because it is through that poverty that I enter into the kingdom of heaven. I cannot enter the kingdom of heaven as a good man or woman; I can only enter the kingdom of heaven as a complete pauper. (*Love of God*)

2 CHRONICLES 19:1—20:37

THEN Jehoshaphat the king of Judah returned safely to his house in Jerusalem. 2 And Jehu the son of Hanani the seer went out to meet him, and said to King Jehoshaphat, "Should you help the wicked and love those who hate the LORD? Therefore the wrath of the LORD *is* upon you. 3 Nevertheless good things are found in you, in that you have removed the wooden images from the land, and have prepared your heart to seek God."

4 So Jehoshaphat dwelt at Jerusalem; and he went out again among the people from Beersheba to the mountains of Ephraim, and brought them back to the LORD God of their fathers. 5 Then he set judges in the land throughout all the fortified cities of Judah, city by city, 6 and said to the judges, "Take heed to what you are doing, for you do not judge for man but for the LORD, who *is* with you in the judgment. 7 Now therefore, let the fear of the LORD be upon you; take care and do *it*, for *there is* no iniquity with the LORD our God, no partiality, nor taking of bribes."

8 Moreover in Jerusalem, for the judgment of the LORD and for controversies, Jehoshaphat appointed some of the Levites and priests, and some of the chief fathers of Israel, when they returned to Jerusalem. 9 And he commanded them, saying, "Thus you shall act in the fear of the LORD, faithfully and with a loyal heart: 10 Whatever case comes to you from your brethren who

dwell in their cities, whether of bloodshed or offenses against law or commandment, against statutes or ordinances, you shall warn them, lest they trespass against the Lord and wrath come upon you and your brethren. Do this, and you will not be guilty. 11 And take notice: Amariah the chief priest *is* over you in all matters of the Lord; and Zebadiah the son of Ishmael, the ruler of the house of Judah, for all the king's matters; also the Levites *will be* officials before you. Behave courageously, and the Lord will be with the good."

20 IT happened after this *that* the people of Moab with the people of Ammon, and *others* with them besides the Ammonites, came to battle against Jehoshaphat. 2 Then some came and told Jehoshaphat, saying, "A great multitude is coming against you from beyond the sea, from Syria; and they are in Hazazon Tamar" (which *is* En Gedi). 3 And Jehoshaphat feared, and set himself to seek the Lord, and proclaimed a fast throughout all Judah. 4 So Judah gathered together to ask *help* from the Lord; and from all the cities of Judah they came to seek the Lord.

5 Then Jehoshaphat stood in the assembly of Judah and Jerusalem, in the house of the Lord, before the new court, 6 and said: "O Lord God of our fathers, *are* You not God in heaven, and do You *not* rule over all the kingdoms of the nations, and in Your hand *is there not* power and might, so that no one is able to withstand You? 7 *Are* You not our God, *who* drove out the inhabitants of this land before Your people Israel, and gave it to the descendants of Abraham Your friend forever? 8 And they dwell in it, and have built You a sanctuary in it for Your name, saying, 9 'If disaster comes upon us— sword, judgment, pestilence, or famine— we will stand before this temple and in Your presence (for Your name *is* in this temple), and cry out to You in our affliction, and You will hear and save.' 10 And now, here are the people of Ammon, Moab, and Mount Seir—whom You would not let Israel invade when they came out of the land of Egypt, but they turned from them and did not destroy them— 11 here they are, rewarding us by coming to throw us out of Your possession which You have given us to inherit. 12 O our God, will You not judge them? For we have no power against this great multitude that is coming against us; nor do we know what to do, but our eyes *are* upon You."

13 Now all Judah, with their little ones, their wives, and their children, stood before the Lord.

14 Then the Spirit of the Lord came upon Jahaziel the son of Zechariah, the son of Benaiah, the son of Jeiel, the son of Mattaniah, a Levite of the sons of Asaph, in the midst of the assembly. 15 And he said, "Listen, all you of Judah and you inhabitants of Jerusalem, and you, King Jehoshaphat! Thus says the Lord to you: 'Do not be afraid nor dismayed because of this great multitude, for the battle *is* not yours, but God's. 16 Tomorrow go down against them. They will surely come up by the Ascent of Ziz, and you will find them at the end of the brook before the Wilderness of Jeruel. 17 You will not *need* to fight in this *battle*. Position yourselves, stand still and see the salvation of the Lord, who is with you, O Judah and Jerusalem!' Do not fear or be dismayed; tomorrow go out against them, for the Lord *is* with you."

18 And Jehoshaphat bowed his head with *his* face to the ground, and all Judah and the inhabitants of Jerusalem bowed before the Lord, worshiping the Lord. 19 Then the Levites of the children of the Kohathites and of the children of the Korahites stood up to praise the Lord God of Israel with voices loud and high.

20 So they rose early in the morning and went out into the Wilderness of Tekoa; and as they went out, Jehoshaphat stood and said, "Hear me, O Judah and you inhabitants of Jerusalem: Believe in the Lord your God, and you shall be established; believe His prophets, and you shall prosper." 21 And when he had consulted with the people, he appointed those who should sing to the Lord, and who should praise the beauty of holiness, as they went out before the army and were saying:

"Praise the Lord,
For His mercy *endures* forever."

22 Now when they began to sing and to praise, the Lord set ambushes against the people of Ammon, Moab, and Mount Seir, who had come against Judah; and they were defeated. 23 For the people of Ammon and Moab stood up against the inhabitants of Mount Seir to utterly kill and destroy *them*. And when they had made an end of the inhabitants of Seir, they helped to destroy one another.

24 So when Judah came to a place overlooking the wilderness, they looked toward the multitude; and there *were* their dead bodies, fallen on the earth. No one had escaped.

25 When Jehoshaphat and his people came to take away their spoil, they found among them an abundance of valuables on the dead bodies, and precious jewelry, which they stripped off for themselves, more than they could carry away; and they were three days gathering the spoil because there was so much. 26 And on the fourth day they assembled in the Valley of Berachah, for there they blessed the LORD; therefore the name of that place was called The Valley of Berachah until this day. 27 Then they returned, every man of Judah and Jerusalem, with Jehoshaphat in front of them, to go back to Jerusalem with joy, for the LORD had made them rejoice over their enemies. 28 So they came to Jerusalem, with stringed instruments and harps and trumpets, to the house of the LORD. 29 And the fear of God was on all the kingdoms of *those* countries when they heard that the LORD had fought against the enemies of Israel. 30 Then the realm of Jehoshaphat was quiet, for his God gave him rest all around.

31 So Jehoshaphat was king over Judah. *He was* thirty-five years old when he became king, and he reigned twenty-five years in Jerusalem. His mother's name *was* Azubah the daughter of Shilhi. 32 And he walked in the way of his father Asa, and did not turn aside from it, doing *what was* right in the sight of the LORD. 33 Nevertheless the high places were not taken away, for as yet the people had not directed their hearts to the God of their fathers.

34 Now the rest of the acts of Jehoshaphat, first and last, indeed they *are* written in the book of Jehu the son of Hanani, which *is* mentioned in the book of the kings of Israel.

35 After this Jehoshaphat king of Judah allied himself with Ahaziah king of Israel, who acted very wickedly. 36 And he allied himself with him to make ships to go to Tarshish, and they made the ships in Ezion Geber. 37 But Eliezer the son of Dodavah of Mareshah prophesied against Jehoshaphat, saying, "Because you have allied yourself with Ahaziah, the LORD has destroyed your works." Then the ships were wrecked, so that they were not able to go to Tarshish.

PSALM 82:1–8

1   GOD stands in the congregation of the mighty;
     He judges among the gods.
2   How long will you judge unjustly,

And show partiality to the wicked?
                                        Selah
3   Defend the poor and fatherless;
     Do justice to the afflicted and needy.
4   Deliver the poor and needy;
     Free *them* from the hand of the wicked.

5   They do not know, nor do they understand;
     They walk about in darkness;
     All the foundations of the earth are unstable.

6   I said, "You *are* gods,
     And all of you *are* children of the Most High.
7   But you shall die like men,
     And fall like one of the princes."

8   Arise, O God, judge the earth;
     For You shall inherit all nations.

PROVERBS 20:29, 30

29 THE glory of young men *is* their strength,
     And the splendor of old men *is* their gray head.

30 Blows that hurt cleanse away evil,
     As *do* stripes the inner depths of the heart.

ACTS 17:1–15

NOW when they had passed through Amphipolis and Apollonia, they came to Thessalonica, where there was a synagogue of the Jews. 2 Then Paul, as his custom was, went in to them, and for three Sabbaths reasoned with them from the Scriptures, 3 explaining and demonstrating that the Christ had to suffer and rise again from the dead, and *saying,* "This Jesus whom I preach to you is the Christ." 4 And some of them were persuaded; and a great multitude of the devout Greeks, and not a few of the leading women, joined Paul and Silas.

5 But the Jews who were not persuaded, becoming envious, took some of the evil men from the marketplace, and gathering a mob, set all the city in an uproar and attacked the house of Jason, and sought to bring them out to the people. 6 But when

---

It is a dangerous thing to refuse to go on knowing.   (UTMOST)

they did not find them, they dragged Jason and some brethren to the rulers of the city, crying out, "These who have turned the world upside down have come here too. 7 Jason has harbored them, and these are all acting contrary to the decrees of Caesar, saying there is another king—Jesus." 8 And they troubled the crowd and the rulers of the city when they heard these things. 9 So when they had taken security from Jason and the rest, they let them go.

10 Then the brethren immediately sent Paul and Silas away by night to Berea. When they arrived, they went into the synagogue of the Jews. 11 These were more fair-minded than those in Thessalonica, in that they received the word with all readiness, and searched the Scriptures daily *to find out* whether these things were so. 12 Therefore many of them believed, and also not a few of the Greeks, prominent women as well as men. 13 But when the Jews from Thessalonica learned that the word of God was preached by Paul at Berea, they came there also and stirred up the crowds. 14 Then immediately the brethren sent Paul away, to go to the sea; but both Silas and Timothy remained there. 15 So those who conducted Paul brought him to Athens; and receiving a command for Silas and Timothy to come to him with all speed, they departed.

◆◆◆

Reading 194—Created in Regeneration
Acts 17:28

B y creation we are the children of God; we are not the sons and daughters of God by creation; Jesus Christ makes us sons and daughters of God by regeneration (John 1:12). The idea of the Fatherhood of Jesus is revealed in the Bible, though rarely mentioned. "Everlasting Father" refers to the Being we know as the Son of God. Paul in talking to the Athenians said, "We are the offspring of God." But the creator-power in Jesus Christ is vested in a more marvelous way even than when God created the world through Him for He has that in Himself whereby He can create His own image. God created the world and everything that was made through the Son, and that which has been made was life in Him"; therefore just as God created the world through Him, the Son is able to create His own image in anyone and everyone.   (BRILL. HERITAGE)

2 CHRONICLES 21:1—22:12

AND Jehoshaphat rested with his fathers, and was buried with his fathers in the City of David. Then Jehoram his son reigned in his place. 2 He had brothers, the sons of Jehoshaphat: Azariah, Jehiel, Zechariah, Azaryahu, Michael, and Shephatiah; all these *were* the sons of Jehoshaphat king of Israel. 3 Their father gave them great gifts of silver and gold and precious things, with fortified cities in Judah; but he gave the kingdom to Jehoram, because he *was* the firstborn.

4 Now when Jehoram was established over the kingdom of his father, he strengthened himself and killed all his brothers with the sword, and also *others* of the princes of Israel.

5 Jehoram *was* thirty-two years old when he became king, and he reigned eight years in Jerusalem. 6 And he walked in the way of the kings of Israel, just as the house of Ahab had done, for he had the daughter of Ahab as a wife; and he did evil in the sight of the LORD. 7 Yet the LORD would not destroy the house of David, because of the covenant that He had made with David, and since He had promised to give a lamp to him and to his sons forever.

8 In his days Edom revolted against Judah's authority, and made a king over themselves. 9 So Jehoram went out with his officers, and all his chariots with him. And he rose by night and attacked the Edomites who had surrounded him and the captains of the chariots. 10 Thus Edom has been in revolt against Judah's authority to this day.

At that time Libnah revolted against his rule, because he had forsaken the LORD God of his fathers. 11 Moreover he made high places in the mountains of Judah, and caused the inhabitants of Jerusalem to commit harlotry, and led Judah astray.

12 And a letter came to him from Elijah the prophet, saying,

Thus says the LORD God of your father David:
Because you have not walked in the ways of Jehoshaphat your father, or in the ways of Asa king of Judah, 13 but have walked in the way of the kings of Israel, and have made Judah and the inhabitants of Jerusalem to play the harlot like the harlotry of the house of Ahab, and also have killed your brothers, those of your father's household, *who were* better than yourself, 14 behold, the LORD will strike your people with a serious affliction—your children, your wives, and all your possessions; 15 and you *will become* very sick with a disease of your intestines, until your intestines come out by reason of the sickness, day by day.

16 Moreover the LORD stirred up against Jehoram the spirit of the Philistines and the Arabians who *were* near the Ethiopians. 17 And they came up into Judah and invaded it, and carried away all the possessions that were found in the king's house, and also his sons and his wives, so that there was not a son left to him except Jehoahaz, the youngest of his sons.

18 After all this the LORD struck him in his intestines with an incurable disease. 19 Then it happened in the course of time, after the end of two years, that his intestines came out because of his sickness; so he died in severe pain. And his people made no burning for him, like the burning for his fathers.

20 He was thirty-two years old when he became king. He reigned in Jerusalem eight years and, to no one's sorrow, departed. However they buried him in the City of David, but not in the tombs of the kings.

22 THEN the inhabitants of Jerusalem made Ahaziah his youngest son king in his place, for the raiders who came with the Arabians into the camp had killed all the older *sons*. So Ahaziah the son of Jehoram, king of Judah, reigned. 2 Ahaziah *was* forty-two years old when he became king,

and he reigned one year in Jerusalem. His mother's name *was* Athaliah the granddaughter of Omri. 3 He also walked in the ways of the house of Ahab, for his mother advised him to do wickedly. 4 Therefore he did evil in the sight of the LORD, like the house of Ahab; for they were his counselors after the death of his father, to his destruction. 5 He also followed their advice, and went with Jehoram the son of Ahab king of Israel to war against Hazael king of Syria at Ramoth Gilead; and the Syrians wounded Joram. 6 Then he returned to Jezreel to recover from the wounds which he had received at Ramah, when he fought against Hazael king of Syria. And Azariah the son of Jehoram, king of Judah, went down to see Jehoram the son of Ahab in Jezreel, because he was sick.

7 His going to Joram was God's occasion for Ahaziah's downfall; for when he arrived, he went out with Jehoram against Jehu the son of Nimshi, whom the LORD had anointed to cut off the house of Ahab. 8 And it happened, when Jehu was executing judgment on the house of Ahab, and found the princes of Judah and the sons of Ahaziah's brothers who served Ahaziah, that he killed them. 9 Then he searched for Ahaziah; and they caught him (he was hiding in Samaria), and brought him to Jehu. When they had killed him, they buried him, "because," they said, "he is the son of Jehoshaphat, who sought the LORD with all his heart."

So the house of Ahaziah had no one to assume power over the kingdom.

10 Now when Athaliah the mother of Ahaziah saw that her son was dead, she arose and destroyed all the royal heirs of the house of Judah. 11 But Jehoshabeath, the daughter of the king, took Joash the son of Ahaziah, and stole him away from among the king's sons who were being murdered, and put him and his nurse in a bedroom. So Jehoshabeath, the daughter of King Jehoram, the wife of Jehoiada the priest (for she was the sister of Ahaziah), hid him from Athaliah so that she did not kill him. 12 And he was hidden with them in the house of God for six years, while Athaliah reigned over the land.

PSALM 83:1–8

1   DO not keep silent, O God!
    Do not hold Your peace,
    And do not be still, O God!
2   For behold, Your enemies make a
        tumult;

And those who hate You have lifted
up their head.
3 They have taken crafty counsel against
Your people,
And consulted together against Your
sheltered ones.
4 They have said, "Come, and let us cut
them off from *being* a nation,
That the name of Israel may be
remembered no more."

5 For they have consulted together with
one consent;
They form a confederacy against You:
6 The tents of Edom and the Ishmaelites;
Moab and the Hagrites;
7 Gebal, Ammon, and Amalek;
Philistia with the inhabitants of Tyre;
8 Assyria also has joined with them;
They have helped the children of Lot.
Selah

PROVERBS 21:1

1 THE king's heart *is* in the hand of the
Lord,
Like the rivers of water; He turns it
wherever He wishes.

ACTS 17:16–34

NOW while Paul waited for them at Athens, his spirit was provoked within him when he saw that the city was given over to idols. 17 Therefore he reasoned in the synagogue with the Jews and with the *Gentile* worshipers, and in the marketplace daily with those who happened to be there. 18 Then certain Epicurean and Stoic philosophers encountered him. And some said, "What does this babbler want to say?"

Others said, "He seems to be a proclaimer of foreign gods," because he preached to them Jesus and the resurrection.

19 And they took him and brought him to the Areopagus, saying, "May we know what this new doctrine *is* of which you speak? 20 For you are bringing some strange things to our ears. Therefore we want to know what these things mean." 21 For all the Athenians and the foreigners who were there spent their time in nothing else but either to tell or to hear some new thing.

22 Then Paul stood in the midst of the Areopagus and said, "Men of Athens, I perceive that in all things you are very religious; 23 for as I was passing through and considering the objects of your worship, I even found an altar with this inscription:

TO THE UNKNOWN GOD.

Therefore, the One whom you worship without knowing, Him I proclaim to you:

A preacher has to bring the gospel of God to men's needs.   (APPROVED)

24 God, who made the world and everything in it, since He is Lord of heaven and earth, does not dwell in temples made with hands. 25 Nor is He worshiped with men's hands, as though He needed anything, since He gives to all life, breath, and all things. 26 And He has made from one blood every nation of men to dwell on all the face of the earth, and has determined their preappointed times and the boundaries of their dwellings, 27 so that they should seek the Lord, in the hope that they might grope for Him and find Him, though He is not far from each one of us; 28 for in Him we live and move and have our being, as also some of your own poets have said, 'For we are also His offspring.' 29 Therefore, since we are the offspring of God, we ought not to think that the Divine Nature is like gold or silver or stone, something shaped by art and man's devising. 30 Truly, these times of ignorance God overlooked, but now commands all men everywhere to repent, 31 because He has appointed a day on which He will judge the world in righteousness by the Man whom He has ordained. He has given assurance of this to all by raising Him from the dead."

32 And when they heard of the resurrection of the dead, some mocked, while others said, "We will hear you again on this *matter*." 33 So Paul departed from among them. 34 However, some men joined him and believed, among them Dionysius the Areopagite, a woman named Damaris, and others with them.

Reading 195—The Weight of the Center

Proverbs 21:2

The Bible always means more than we are apt to mean. The term "heart" in the Bible means the center of everything. The human soul has the spirit in and above it and the body by and about it; but the vital center of all is the heart. When we speak of the heart, figuratively or actually, we mean the mid-most part of a person. The Bible teaching differs from that of science in that it makes the heart the soul center and the spirit center as well. (*BIB. PSYCH.*)

If we try, as has been tried by psychologists, to take out of the Bible something that agrees with modern science, we shall have to omit many things the Bible says about the heart. According to the Bible the heart is the center of physical life, the center of memory, the center of damnation and of salvation, the center of God's working and the center from which everything works which molds the human mechanism. (*BIB. PSYCH.*)

2 CHRONICLES 23:1—24:27

IN the seventh year Jehoiada strengthened himself, *and made a* covenant with the captains of hundreds: Azariah the son of Jeroham, Ishmael the son of Jehohanan, Azariah the son of Obed, Maaseiah the son of Adaiah, and Elishaphat the son of Zichri. 2 And they went throughout Judah and gathered the Levites from all the cities of Judah, and the chief fathers of Israel, and they came to Jerusalem.

3 Then all the assembly made a covenant with the king in the house of God. And he said to them, "Behold, the king's son shall reign, as the LORD has said of the sons of David. 4 This *is* what you shall do: One-third of you entering on the Sabbath, of the priests and the Levites, *shall be* keeping watch over the doors; 5 one-third *shall be* at the king's house; and one-third at the Gate of the Foundation. All the people *shall be* in the courts of the house of the LORD. 6 But let no one come into the house of the LORD except the priests and those of the Levites who serve. They may go in, for they *are* holy; but all the people shall keep the watch of the LORD. 7 And the Levites shall surround the king on all sides, every man with his weapons in his hand; and whoever comes into the house, let him be put to death. You are to be with the king when he comes in and when he goes out."

8 So the Levites and all Judah did according to all that Jehoiada the priest commanded. And each man took his men who were to be on duty on the Sabbath, with those who were going *off duty* on the Sabbath; for Jehoiada the priest had not dismissed the divisions. 9 And Jehoiada the priest gave to the captains of hundreds the spears and the large and small shields which *had belonged* to King David, that *were* in the temple of God. 10 Then he set all the people, every man with his weapon in his hand, from the right side of the temple to the left side of the temple, along by the altar and by the temple, all around the king. 11 And they brought out the king's son, put the crown on him, *gave him* the Testimony, and made him king. Then Jehoiada and his sons anointed him, and said, "*Long* live the king!"

12 Now when Athaliah heard the noise of the people running and praising the king, she came to the people *in* the temple of the LORD. 13 *When* she looked, there was the king standing by his pillar at the entrance; and the leaders and the trumpeters *were* by the king. All the people of the land were rejoicing and blowing trumpets, also the singers with musical instruments, and those who led in praise. So Athaliah tore her clothes and said, "Treason! Treason!"

14 And Jehoiada the priest brought out the captains of hundreds who were set over the army, and said to them, "Take her outside under guard, and slay with the sword whoever follows her." For the priest had said, "Do not kill her in the house of the LORD."

15 So they seized her; and she went by way of the entrance of the Horse Gate *into* the king's house, and they killed her there.

16 Then Jehoiada made a covenant between himself, the people, and the king, that they should be the LORD's people. 17 And all the people went to the temple of Baal, and tore it down. They broke in pieces its altars and images, and killed Mattan the priest of Baal before the altars. 18 Also Jehoiada appointed the oversight of the house of the LORD to the hand of the priests, the Levites, whom David had assigned in the house of the LORD, to offer the burnt offerings of the LORD, as *it is* written in the Law of Moses, with rejoicing and with singing, *as it was established* by David. 19 And he set the gatekeepers at the gates of the house of the LORD, so that no one *who was* in any way unclean should enter.

20 Then he took the captains of hundreds, the nobles, the governors of the people, and all the people of the land, and brought the king down from the house of the LORD; and they went through the Upper Gate to the king's house, and set the king on the throne of the kingdom. 21 So all the people of the land rejoiced; and the city was quiet, for they had slain Athaliah with the sword.

24 JOASH *was* seven years old when he became king, and he reigned forty years in Jerusalem. His mother's name *was* Zibiah of Beersheba. 2 Joash did *what was* right in the sight of the LORD all the days of Jehoiada the priest. 3 And Jehoiada took two wives for him, and he had sons and daughters.

4 Now it happened after this *that* Joash set his heart on repairing the house of the LORD. 5 Then he gathered the priests and the Levites, and said to them, "Go out to the cities of Judah, and gather from all Israel money to repair the house of your God from year to year, and see that you do it quickly."

However the Levites did not do it quickly. 6 So the king called Jehoiada the chief *priest,* and said to him, "Why have you not required the Levites to bring in from Judah and from Jerusalem the collection, *according to the commandment* of Moses the servant of the LORD and of the assembly of Israel, for the tabernacle of witness?" 7 For the sons of Athaliah, that wicked woman, had broken into the house of God, and had also presented all the dedicated things of the house of the LORD to the Baals.

8 Then at the king's command they made a chest, and set it outside at the gate of the house of the LORD. 9 And they made a proclamation throughout Judah and Jerusalem to bring to the LORD the collection *that* Moses the servant of God *had imposed* on Israel in the wilderness. 10 Then all the leaders and all the people rejoiced, brought their contributions, and put *them* into the chest until all had given. 11 So it was, at that time, when the chest was brought to the king's official by the hand of the Levites, and when they saw that *there was* much money, that the king's scribe and the high priest's officer came and emptied the chest, and took it and returned it to its place. Thus they did day by day, and gathered money in abundance.

12 The king and Jehoiada gave it to those who did the work of the service of the house of the LORD; and they hired masons and carpenters to repair the house of the LORD, and also those who worked in iron and bronze to restore the house of the LORD. 13 So the workmen labored, and the work was completed by them; they restored the house of God to its original condition and reinforced it. 14 When they had finished, they brought the rest of the money before the king and Jehoiada; they made from it articles for the house of the LORD, articles for serving and offering, spoons and vessels of gold and silver. And they offered burnt offerings in the house of the LORD continually all the days of Jehoiada.

15 But Jehoiada grew old and was full of days, and he died; *he was* one hundred and thirty years old when he died. 16 And they buried him in the City of David among the kings, because he had done good in Israel, both toward God and His house.

17 Now after the death of Jehoiada the leaders of Judah came and bowed down to the king. And the king listened to them. 18 Therefore they left the house of the LORD God of their fathers, and served wooden images and idols; and wrath came upon Judah and Jerusalem because of their trespass. 19 Yet He sent prophets to them, to bring them back to the LORD; and they testified against them, but they would not listen.

20 Then the Spirit of God came upon Zechariah the son of Jehoiada the priest, who stood above the people, and said to them, "Thus says God: 'Why do you transgress the commandments of the LORD, so that you cannot prosper? Because you have forsaken the LORD, He also has forsaken you.'" 21 So they conspired against him, and at the command of the king they stoned him with stones in the court of the house of the LORD. 22 Thus Joash the king did

not remember the kindness which Jehoiada his father had done to him, but killed his son; and as he died, he said, "The LORD look on *it,* and repay!"

23 So it happened in the spring of the year *that* the army of Syria came up against him; and they came to Judah and Jerusalem, and destroyed all the leaders of the people from among the people, and sent all their spoil to the king of Damascus. 24 For the army of the Syrians came with a small company of men; but the LORD delivered a very great army into their hand, because they had forsaken the LORD God of their fathers. So they executed judgment against Joash. 25 And when they had withdrawn from him (for they left him severely wounded), his own servants conspired against him because of the blood of the sons of Jehoiada the priest, and killed him on his bed. So he died. And they buried him in the City of David, but they did not bury him in the tombs of the kings.

26 These are the ones who conspired against him: Zabad the son of Shimeath the Ammonitess, and Jehozabad the son of Shimrith the Moabitess. 27 Now *concerning* his sons, and the many oracles about him, and the repairing of the house of God, indeed they *are* written in the annals of the book of the kings. Then Amaziah his son reigned in his place.

PSALM 83:9–18

9   DEAL with them as *with* Midian,
     As *with* Sisera,
     As *with* Jabin at the Brook Kishon,
10 Who perished at En Dor,
     Who became *as* refuse on the earth.
11 Make their nobles like Oreb and like Zeeb,
     Yes, all their princes like Zebah and Zalmunna,
12 Who said, "Let us take for ourselves The pastures of God for a possession."

13 O my God, make them like the whirling dust,
     Like the chaff before the wind!
14 As the fire burns the woods,
     And as the flame sets the mountains on fire,
15 So pursue them with Your tempest,
     And frighten them with Your storm.
16 Fill their faces with shame,
     That they may seek Your name, O LORD.

17 Let them be confounded and dismayed forever;
     Yes, let them be put to shame and perish,
18 That they may know that You, whose name alone *is* the LORD,
     Are the Most High over all the earth.

PROVERBS 21:2, 3

2   EVERY way of a man *is* right in his own eyes,
     But the LORD weighs the hearts.

3   To do righteousness and justice
     Is more acceptable to the LORD than sacrifice.

ACTS 18:1–28

AFTER these things Paul departed from Athens and went to Corinth. 2 And he found a certain Jew named Aquila, born in Pontus, who had recently come from Italy with his wife Priscilla (because Claudius had commanded all the Jews to depart from Rome); and he came to them. 3 So, because he was of the same trade, he stayed with them and worked; for by occupation they were tentmakers. 4 And he

---

It takes all God's power in me to do the most commonplace things in His way. (UTMOST)

---

reasoned in the synagogue every Sabbath, and persuaded both Jews and Greeks.

5 When Silas and Timothy had come from Macedonia, Paul was compelled by the Spirit, and testified to the Jews *that* Jesus *is* the Christ. 6 But when they opposed him and blasphemed, he shook *his* garments and said to them, "Your blood *be* upon your *own* heads; I *am* clean. From now on I will go to the Gentiles." 7 And he departed from there and entered the house of a certain *man* named Justus, *one* who worshiped God, whose house was next door to the synagogue. 8 Then Crispus, the ruler of the synagogue, believed on the Lord with all his household. And many of the Corinthians, hearing, believed and were baptized.

9 Now the Lord spoke to Paul in the

night by a vision, "Do not be afraid, but speak, and do not keep silent; 10 for I am with you, and no one will attack you to hurt you; for I have many people in this city." 11 And he continued *there* a year and six months, teaching the word of God among them.

12 When Gallio was proconsul of Achaia, the Jews with one accord rose up against Paul and brought him to the judgment seat, 13 saying, "This *fellow* persuades men to worship God contrary to the law."

14 And when Paul was about to open *his* mouth, Gallio said to the Jews, "If it were a matter of wrongdoing or wicked crimes, O Jews, there would be reason why I should bear with you. 15 But if it is a question of words and names and your own law, look *to it* yourselves; for I do not want to be a judge of such *matters*." 16 And he drove them from the judgment seat. 17 Then all the Greeks took Sosthenes, the ruler of the synagogue, and beat *him* before the judgment seat. But Gallio took no notice of these things.

18 So Paul still remained a good while. Then he took leave of the brethren and sailed for Syria, and Priscilla and Aquila *were* with him. He had *his* hair cut off at Cenchrea, for he had taken a vow. 19 And he came to Ephesus, and left them there; but he himself entered the synagogue and reasoned with the Jews. 20 When they asked *him* to stay a longer time with them, he did not consent, 21 but took leave of them, saying, "I must by all means keep this coming feast in Jerusalem; but I will return again to you, God willing." And he sailed from Ephesus.

22 And when he had landed at Caesarea, and gone up and greeted the church, he went down to Antioch. 23 After he had spent some time *there,* he departed and went over the region of Galatia and Phrygia in order, strengthening all the disciples.

24 Now a certain Jew named Apollos, born at Alexandria, an eloquent man *and* mighty in the Scriptures, came to Ephesus. 25 This man had been instructed in the way of the Lord; and being fervent in spirit, he spoke and taught accurately the things of the Lord, though he knew only the baptism of John. 26 So he began to speak boldly in the synagogue. When Aquila and Priscilla heard him, they took him aside and explained to him the way of God more accurately. 27 And when he desired to cross to Achaia, the brethren wrote, exhorting the disciples to receive him; and when he arrived, he greatly helped those who had believed through grace; 28 for he vigorously refuted the Jews publicly, showing from the Scriptures that Jesus is the Christ.

◆◆◆◆

*Reading 196—*Bible Teachings on Souls
Psalm 84:2

One of the greatest difficulties in most of our colleges for training ministers, who are supposed to work for the cure of souls, is that they are never taught how to deal with souls. There is hardly a college anywhere for training ministers where the question of dealing with souls is ever mentioned. Ministers will bear me out in this, that everything they have learned they have had to learn out of their own experience. They are trained in everything but how to deal with the facts they have to deal with.   (*WORKMEN*)

In the Old Testament the word "soul," that is, animal soul, the soul that is present only in this order of beings, is mentioned about 460 times. In the New Testament the word "soul" is mentioned about fifty-seven times, with the same meaning. When the Bible mentions a thing over five hundred times, it is time that Christians examined the teaching about it with care. (*BIB. PSYCH.*)

2 CHRONICLES 25:1—27:9

AMAZIAH *was* twenty-five years old *when* he became king, and he reigned twenty-nine years in Jerusalem. His mother's name *was* Jehoaddan of Jerusalem. 2 And he did *what was* right in the sight of the LORD, but not with a loyal heart.

3 Now it happened, as soon as the kingdom was established for him, that he executed his servants who had murdered his father the king. 4 However he did not execute their children, but *did* as *it is* written in the Law in the Book of Moses, where the LORD commanded, saying, "The fathers shall not be put to death for their children, nor shall the children be put to death for their fathers; but a person shall die for his own sin."

5 Moreover Amaziah gathered Judah together and set over them captains of thousands and captains of hundreds, according to *their* fathers' houses, throughout all Judah and Benjamin; and he numbered them from twenty years old and above, and found them to be three hundred thousand choice *men, able* to go to war, who could handle spear and shield. 6 He also hired one hundred thousand mighty men of valor from Israel for one hundred talents of silver. 7 But a man of God came to him, saying, "O king, do not let the army of Israel go with you, for the LORD *is* not with Israel— *not with* any of the children of Ephraim. 8 But if you go, be gone! Be strong in battle! *Even so,* God shall make you fall before the enemy; for God has power to help and to overthrow."

9 Then Amaziah said to the man of God, "But what *shall we* do about the hundred talents which I have given to the troops of Israel?"

And the man of God answered, "The LORD is able to give you much more than this." 10 So Amaziah discharged the troops that had come to him from Ephraim, to go back home. Therefore their anger was greatly aroused against Judah, and they returned home in great anger.

11 Then Amaziah strengthened himself, and leading his people, he went to the Valley of Salt and killed ten thousand of the people of Seir. 12 Also the children of Judah took captive ten thousand alive, brought them to the top of the rock, and cast them down from the top of the rock, so that they all were dashed in pieces.

13 But as for the soldiers of the army which Amaziah had discharged, so that they would not go with him to battle, they raided the cities of Judah from Samaria to Beth

Horon, killed three thousand in them, and took much spoil.

14 Now it was so, after Amaziah came from the slaughter of the Edomites, that he brought the gods of the people of Seir, set them up *to be* his gods, and bowed down before them and burned incense to them. 15 Therefore the anger of the LORD was aroused against Amaziah, and He sent him a prophet who said to him, "Why have you sought the gods of the people, which could not rescue their own people from your hand?"

16 So it was, as he talked with him, that *the king* said to him, "Have we made you the king's counselor? Cease! Why should you be killed?"

Then the prophet ceased, and said, "I know that God has determined to destroy you, because you have done this and have not heeded my advice."

17 Now Amaziah king of Judah asked advice and sent to Joash the son of Jehoahaz, the son of Jehu, king of Israel, saying, "Come, let us face one another *in battle.*"

18 And Joash king of Israel sent to Amaziah king of Judah, saying, "The thistle that *was* in Lebanon sent to the cedar that was in Lebanon, saying, 'Give your daughter to my son as wife'; and a wild beast that *was* in Lebanon passed by and trampled the thistle. 19 Indeed you say that you have defeated the Edomites, and your heart is lifted up to boast. Stay at home now; why should you meddle with trouble, that you should fall—you and Judah with you?"

20 But Amaziah would not heed, for it *came* from God, that He might give them into the hand *of their enemies,* because they sought the gods of Edom. 21 So Joash king of Israel went out; and he and Amaziah king of Judah faced one another at Beth Shemesh, which *belongs* to Judah. 22 And Judah was defeated by Israel, and every man fled to his tent. 23 Then Joash the king of Israel captured Amaziah king of Judah, the son of Joash, the son of Jehoahaz, at Beth Shemesh; and he brought him to Jerusalem, and broke down the wall of Jerusalem from the Gate of Ephraim to the Corner Gate— four hundred cubits. 24 And *he took* all the gold and silver, all the articles that were found in the house of God with Obed-Edom, the treasures of the king's house, and hostages, and returned to Samaria.

25 Amaziah the son of Joash, king of Judah, lived fifteen years after the death of Joash the son of Jehoahaz, king of Israel. 26 Now the rest of the acts of Amaziah, from first to last, indeed *are* they not written in the book of the kings of Judah and Israel?

27 After the time that Amaziah turned away from following the LORD, they made a conspiracy against him in Jerusalem, and he fled to Lachish; but they sent after him to Lachish and killed him there. 28 Then they brought him on horses and buried him with his fathers in the City of Judah.

26 NOW all the people of Judah took Uzziah, who *was* sixteen years old, and made him king instead of his father Amaziah. 2 He built Elath and restored it to Judah, after the king rested with his fathers.

3 Uzziah *was* sixteen years old when he became king, and he reigned fifty-two years in Jerusalem. His mother's name was Jecholiah of Jerusalem. 4 And he did *what was* right in the sight of the LORD, according to all that his father Amaziah had done. 5 He sought God in the days of Zechariah, who had understanding in the visions of God; and as long as he sought the LORD, God made him prosper.

6 Now he went out and made war against the Philistines, and broke down the wall of Gath, the wall of Jabneh, and the wall of Ashdod; and he built cities *around* Ashdod and among the Philistines. 7 God helped him against the Philistines, against the Arabians who lived in Gur Baal, and against the Meunites. 8 Also the Ammonites brought tribute to Uzziah. His fame spread as far as the entrance of Egypt, for he became exceedingly strong.

9 And Uzziah built towers in Jerusalem at the Corner Gate, at the Valley Gate, and at the corner buttress of the wall; then he fortified them. 10 Also he built towers in the desert. He dug many wells, for he had much livestock, both in the lowlands and in the plains; *he also had* farmers and vinedressers in the mountains and in Carmel, for he loved the soil.

11 Moreover Uzziah had an army of fighting men who went out to war by companies, according to the number on their roll as prepared by Jeiel the scribe and Maaseiah the officer, under the hand of Hananiah, *one* of the king's captains. 12 The total number of chief officers of the mighty men of valor *was* two thousand six hundred. 13 And under their authority *was* an army of three hundred and seven thousand five hundred, that made war with mighty power, to help the king against the enemy. 14 Then Uzziah prepared for them, for the entire army, shields, spears, helmets, body armor, bows, and slings *to cast* stones. 15 And he made devices in Jerusalem, invented by skillful men, to be on the towers

and the corners, to shoot arrows and large stones. So his fame spread far and wide, for he was marvelously helped till he became strong.

16 But when he was strong his heart was lifted up, to *his* destruction, for he transgressed against the LORD his God by entering the temple of the LORD to burn incense on the altar of incense. 17 So Azariah the priest went in after him, and with him were eighty priests of the LORD—valiant men. 18 And they withstood King Uzziah, and said to him, "*It is* not for you, Uzziah, to burn incense to the LORD, but for the priests, the sons of Aaron, who are consecrated to burn incense. Get out of the sanctuary, for you have trespassed! You *shall have* no honor from the LORD God."

19 Then Uzziah became furious; and he *had* a censer in his hand to burn incense. And while he was angry with the priests, leprosy broke out on his forehead, before the priests in the house of the LORD, beside the incense altar. 20 And Azariah the chief priest and all the priests looked at him, and there, on his forehead, he *was* leprous; so they thrust him out of that place. Indeed he also hurried to get out, because the LORD had struck him.

21 King Uzziah was a leper until the day of his death. He dwelt in an isolated house, because he was a leper; for he was cut off from the house of the LORD. Then Jotham his son *was* over the king's house, judging the people of the land.

22 Now the rest of the acts of Uzziah, from first to last, the prophet Isaiah the son of Amoz wrote. 23 So Uzziah rested with his fathers, and they buried him with his fathers in the field of burial which *belonged* to the kings, for they said, "He is a leper." Then Jotham his son reigned in his place.

27 JOTHAM *was* twenty-five years old when he became king, and he reigned sixteen years in Jerusalem. His mother's name *was* Jerushah the daughter of Zadok. 2 And he did *what was* right in the sight of the LORD, according to all that his father Uzziah had done (although he did not enter the temple of the LORD). But still the people acted corruptly.

3 He built the Upper Gate of the house of the LORD, and he built extensively on the wall of Ophel. 4 Moreover he built cities in the mountains of Judah, and in the forests he built fortresses and towers. 5 He also fought with the king of the Ammonites and defeated them. And the people of Ammon gave him in that year one hundred

talents of silver, ten thousand kors of wheat, and ten thousand of barley. The people of Ammon paid this to him in the second and third years also. 6 So Jotham became mighty, because he prepared his ways before the LORD his God.

7 Now the rest of the acts of Jotham, and all his wars and his ways, indeed they *are* written in the book of the kings of Israel and Judah. 8 He was twenty-five years old when he became king, and he reigned sixteen years in Jerusalem. 9 So Jotham rested with his fathers, and they buried him in the City of David. Then Ahaz his son reigned in his place.

PSALM 84:1–7

1 HOW lovely *is* Your tabernacle,
   O LORD of hosts!
2 My soul longs, yes, even faints
   For the courts of the LORD;
   My heart and my flesh cry out for the
      living God.

3 Even the sparrow has found a home,
   And the swallow a nest for herself,
   Where she may lay her young—
   Even Your altars, O LORD of hosts,
   My King and my God.
4 Blessed *are* those who dwell in Your
      house;
   They will still be praising You.   Selah

5 Blessed *is* the man whose strength *is*
      in You,
   Whose heart *is* set on pilgrimage.
6 *As they* pass through the Valley of Baca,
   They make it a spring;
   The rain also covers it with pools.
7 They go from strength to strength;
   Each one appears before God in Zion.

PROVERBS 21:4, 5

4 A haughty look, a proud heart,
   And the plowing of the wicked *are* sin.

5 The plans of the diligent *lead* surely
      to plenty,
   But *those of* everyone *who is* hasty, surely
      to poverty.

ACTS 19:1–20

AND it happened, while Apollos was at Corinth, that Paul, having passed through the upper regions, came to Ephesus. And finding some disciples 2 he said to them, "Did you receive the Holy Spirit when you believed?"

So they said to him, "We have not so much as heard whether there is a Holy Spirit."

3 And he said to them, "Into what then were you baptized?"

So they said, "Into John's baptism."

4 Then Paul said, "John indeed baptized with a baptism of repentance, saying to the people that they should believe on Him who would come after him, that is, on Christ Jesus."

5 When they heard *this,* they were baptized in the name of the Lord Jesus. 6 And when Paul had laid hands on them, the Holy Spirit came upon them, and they spoke with tongues and prophesied. 7 Now the men were about twelve in all.

8 And he went into the synagogue and spoke boldly for three months, reasoning and persuading concerning the things of the kingdom of God. 9 But when some were hardened and did not believe, but spoke evil of the Way before the multitude, he departed from them and withdrew the disciples, reasoning daily in the school of Tyrannus. 10 And this continued for two years, so that all who dwelt in Asia heard the word of the Lord Jesus, both Jews and Greeks.

11 Now God worked unusual miracles by the hands of Paul, 12 so that even handkerchiefs or aprons were brought from his body to the sick, and the diseases left them and the evil spirits went out of them. 13 Then some of the itinerant Jewish exorcists took it upon themselves to call the name of the Lord Jesus over those who had evil spirits, saying, "We exorcise you by the Jesus whom Paul preaches." 14 Also there were seven sons of Sceva, a Jewish chief priest, who did so.

15 And the evil spirit answered and said, "Jesus I know, and Paul I know; but who are you?"

The strength of a real man or real woman cannot be estimated.   (GLORIFY)

---

16 Then the man in whom the evil spirit was leaped on them, overpowered them, and prevailed against them, so that they fled out of that house naked and wounded. 17 This became known both to all Jews and Greeks dwelling in Ephesus; and fear fell

on them all, and the name of the Lord Jesus was magnified. 18 And many who had believed came confessing and telling their deeds. 19 Also, many of those who had practiced magic brought their books together and burned *them* in the sight of all. And they counted up the value of them, and *it* totaled fifty thousand *pieces* of silver. 20 So the word of the Lord grew mightily and prevailed.

◆◆◆◆

Reading 197—The Pure Life
Proverbs 21:8

Jesus Christ demands that the heart of a disciple be fathomlessly pure, and unless He can give me His disposition, His teaching is tantalizing. If all He came to do was to mock me by telling me to be what I know I never can be, I can afford to ignore Him, but if He can give me His own disposition of holiness, then I begin to see how I can lay my account with purity. (*SERMON MT.*)

What do we mean by "pure in heart"? We mean nothing less and nothing else than what the Son of God was and is. When God raises us up into the heavenly places He imparts to us the very purity that is Jesus Christ's. That is what the sanctified life means—the undisturbable range of His peace, the unshakable, indefatigable power of His strength, and the unfathomable, crystalline purity of His holiness. There is plenty of room in the heavenly places to grow into the realization of the unfathomable depths of the purity of Christ's heart. (*BRILL. HERITAGE*)

2 CHRONICLES 28:1—29:36

AHAZ *was* twenty years old when he became king, and he reigned sixteen years in Jerusalem; and he did not do *what was* right in the sight of the LORD, as his father David *had done*. 2 For he walked in the ways of the kings of Israel, and made molded images for the Baals. 3 He burned incense in the Valley of the Son of Hinnom, and burned his children in the fire, according to the abominations of the nations whom the LORD had cast out before the children of Israel. 4 And he sacrificed and burned incense on the high places, on the hills, and under every green tree.

5 Therefore the LORD his God delivered him into the hand of the king of Syria. They defeated him, and carried away a great multitude of them as captives, and brought *them* to Damascus. Then he was also delivered into the hand of the king of Israel, who defeated him with a great slaughter. 6 For Pekah the son of Remaliah killed one hundred and twenty thousand in Judah in one day, all valiant men, because they had forsaken the LORD God of their fathers.

7 Zichri, a mighty man of Ephraim, killed Maaseiah the king's son, Azrikam the officer over the house, and Elkanah *who was* second to the king. 8 And the children of Israel carried away captive of their brethren two hundred thousand women, sons, and daughters; and they also took away much spoil from them, and brought the spoil to Samaria.

9 But a prophet of the LORD was there, whose name *was* Oded; and he went out before the army that came to Samaria, and said to them: "Look, because the LORD God of your fathers was angry with Judah, He has delivered them into your hand; but you have killed them in a rage *that* reaches up to heaven. 10 And now you propose to force the children of Judah and Jerusalem to be your male and female slaves; *but are* you not also guilty before the LORD your God? 11 Now hear me, therefore, and return the captives, whom you have taken captive from your brethren, for the fierce wrath of the LORD *is* upon you."

12 Then some of the heads of the children of Ephraim, Azariah the son of Johanan, Berechiah the son of Meshillemoth, Jehizkiah the son of Shallum, and Amasa the

son of Hadlai, stood up against those who came from the war, 13 and said to them, "You shall not bring the captives here, for we *already* have offended the LORD. You intend to add to our sins and to our guilt; for our guilt is great, and *there is* fierce wrath against Israel." 14 So the armed men left the captives and the spoil before the leaders and all the assembly. 15 Then the men who were designated by name rose up and took the captives, and from the spoil they clothed all who were naked among them, dressed them and gave them sandals, gave them food and drink, and anointed them; and they let all the feeble ones ride on donkeys. So they brought them to their brethren at Jericho, the city of palm trees. Then they returned to Samaria.

16 At the same time King Ahaz sent to the kings of Assyria to help him. 17 For again the Edomites had come, attacked Judah, and carried away captives. 18 The Philistines also had invaded the cities of the lowland and of the South of Judah, and had taken Beth Shemesh, Aijalon, Gederoth, Sochoh with its villages, Timnah with its villages, and Gimzo with its villages; and they dwelt there. 19 For the LORD brought Judah low because of Ahaz king of Israel, for he had encouraged moral decline in Judah and had been continually unfaithful to the LORD. 20 Also Tiglath-Pileser king of Assyria came to him and distressed him, and did not assist him. 21 For Ahaz took part *of the treasures* from the house of the LORD, from the house of the king, and from the leaders, and he gave *it* to the king of Assyria; but he did not help him.

22 Now in the time of his distress King Ahaz became increasingly unfaithful to the LORD. This *is that* King Ahaz. 23 For he sacrificed to the gods of Damascus which had defeated him, saying, "Because the gods of the kings of Syria help them, I will sacrifice to them that they may help me." But they were the ruin of him and of all Israel. 24 So Ahaz gathered the articles of the house of God, cut in pieces the articles of the house of God, shut up the doors of the house of the LORD, and made for himself altars in every corner of Jerusalem. 25 And in every single city of Judah he made high places to burn incense to other gods, and provoked to anger the LORD God of his fathers.

26 Now the rest of his acts and all his ways, from first to last, indeed they *are* written in the book of the kings of Judah and Israel. 27 So Ahaz rested with his fathers, and they buried him in the city, in Jerusalem; but they did not bring him into the tombs of the kings of Israel. Then Hezekiah his son reigned in his place.

29 HEZEKIAH became king *when he was* twenty-five years old, and he reigned twenty-nine years in Jerusalem. His mother's name *was* Abijah the daughter of Zechariah. 2 And he did *what was* right in the sight of the LORD, according to all that his father David had done.

3 In the first year of his reign, in the first month, he opened the doors of the house of the LORD and repaired them. 4 Then he brought in the priests and the Levites, and gathered them in the East Square, 5 and said to them: "Hear me, Levites! Now sanctify yourselves, sanctify the house of the LORD God of your fathers, and carry out the rubbish from the holy *place*. 6 For our fathers have trespassed and done evil in the eyes of the LORD our God; they have forsaken Him, have turned their faces away from the dwelling place of the LORD, and turned *their* backs *on Him.* 7 They have also shut up the doors of the vestibule, put out the lamps, and have not burned incense or offered burnt offerings in the holy *place* to the God of Israel. 8 Therefore the wrath of the LORD fell upon Judah and Jerusalem, and He has given them up to trouble, to desolation, and to jeering, as you see with your eyes. 9 For indeed, because of this our fathers have fallen by the sword; and our sons, our daughters, and our wives *are* in captivity.

10 "Now *it is* in my heart to make a covenant with the LORD God of Israel, that His fierce wrath may turn away from us. 11 My sons, do not be negligent now, for the LORD has chosen you to stand before Him, to serve Him, and that you should minister to Him and burn incense."

12 Then these Levites arose: Mahath the son of Amasai and Joel the son of Azariah, of the sons of the Kohathites; of the sons of Merari, Kish the son of Abdi and Azariah the son of Jehallelel; of the Gershonites, Joah the son of Zimmah and Eden the son of Joah; 13 of the sons of Elizaphan, Shimri and Jeiel; of the sons of Asaph, Zechariah and Mattaniah; 14 of the sons of Heman, Jehiel and Shimei; and of the sons of Jeduthun, Shemaiah and Uzziel.

15 And they gathered their brethren, sanctified themselves, and went according to the commandment of the king, at the words of the LORD, to cleanse the house of the LORD. 16 Then the priests went into

the inner part of the house of the LORD to cleanse *it,* and brought out all the debris that they found in the temple of the LORD to the court of the house of the LORD. And the Levites took *it* out and carried *it* to the Brook Kidron.

17 Now they began to sanctify on the first *day* of the first month, and on the eighth day of the month they came to the vestibule of the LORD. So they sanctified the house of the LORD in eight days, and on the sixteenth day of the first month they finished.

18 Then they went in to King Hezekiah and said, "We have cleansed all the house of the LORD, the altar of burnt offerings with all its articles, and the table of the showbread with all its articles. 19 Moreover all the articles which King Ahaz in his reign had cast aside in his transgression we have prepared and sanctified; and there they *are,* before the altar of the LORD."

20 Then King Hezekiah rose early, gathered the rulers of the city, and went up to the house of the LORD. 21 And they brought seven bulls, seven rams, seven lambs, and seven male goats for a sin offering for the kingdom, for the sanctuary, and for Judah. Then he commanded the priests, the sons of Aaron, to offer *them* on the altar of the LORD. 22 So they killed the bulls, and the priests received the blood and sprinkled *it* on the altar. Likewise they killed the rams and sprinkled the blood on the altar. They also killed the lambs and sprinkled the blood on the altar. 23 Then they brought out the male goats *for* the sin offering before the king and the assembly, and they laid their hands on them. 24 And the priests killed them; and they presented their blood on the altar as a sin offering to make an atonement for all Israel, for the king commanded *that* the burnt offering and the sin offering *be made* for all Israel.

25 And he stationed the Levites in the house of the LORD with cymbals, with stringed instruments, and with harps, according to the commandment of David, of Gad the king's seer, and of Nathan the prophet; for thus *was* the commandment of the LORD by his prophets. 26 The Levites stood with the instruments of David, and the priests with the trumpets. 27 Then Hezekiah commanded *them* to offer the burnt offering on the altar. And when the burnt offering began, the song of the LORD *also* began, with the trumpets and with the instruments of David king of Israel. 28 So all the assembly worshiped, the singers sang, and the trumpeters sounded; all *this continued* until the burnt offering was finished.

29 And when they had finished offering, the king and all who were present with him bowed and worshiped. 30 Moreover King Hezekiah and the leaders commanded the Levites to sing praise to the LORD with the words of David and of Asaph the seer. So they sang praises with gladness, and they bowed their heads and worshiped.

31 Then Hezekiah answered and said, "Now *that* you have consecrated yourselves to the LORD, come near, and bring sacrifices and thank offerings into the house of the LORD." So the assembly brought in sacrifices and thank offerings, and as many as were of a willing heart *brought* burnt offerings. 32 And the number of the burnt offerings which the assembly brought was seventy bulls, one hundred rams, *and* two hundred lambs; all these *were* for a burnt offering to the LORD. 33 The consecrated things *were* six hundred bulls and three thousand sheep. 34 But the priests were too few, so that they could not skin all the burnt offerings; therefore their brethren the Levites helped them until the work was ended and until the *other* priests had sanctified themselves, for the Levites were more diligent in sanctifying themselves than the priests. 35 Also the burnt offerings *were* in abundance, with the fat of the peace offerings and *with* the drink offerings for *every* burnt offering.

So the service of the house of the LORD was set in order. 36 Then Hezekiah and all the people rejoiced that God had prepared the people, since the events took place so suddenly.

PSALM 84:8–12

8   O LORD God of hosts, hear my prayer;
     Give ear, O God of Jacob!   Selah

---

*I*mpulsive prayer, the prayer that looks so futile, is the thing God needs more than anything else. (SEND I YOU)

---

9   O God, behold our shield,
     And look upon the face of Your
        anointed.

10   For a day in Your courts *is* better than
        a thousand.
     I would rather be a doorkeeper in the
        house of my God

Than dwell in the tents of wickedness.

11 For the LORD God *is* a sun and
        shield;
    The LORD will give grace and glory;
    No good *thing* will He withhold
    From those who walk uprightly.

12 O LORD of hosts,
    Blessed *is* the man who trusts in You!

PROVERBS 21:6–8

6   GETTING treasures by a lying tongue
    Is the fleeting fantasy of those who seek
        death.

7   The violence of the wicked will destroy
        them,
    Because they refuse to do justice.

8   The way of a guilty man *is* perverse;
    But *as for* the pure, his work *is*
        right.

ACTS 19:21–41

WHEN these things were accomplished,
Paul purposed in the Spirit, when he had
passed through Macedonia and Achaia, to
go to Jerusalem, saying, "After I have been
there, I must also see Rome." 22 So he sent
into Macedonia two of those who ministered to him, Timothy and Erastus, but he
himself stayed in Asia for a time.

23 And about that time there arose a great
commotion about the Way. 24 For a certain
man named Demetrius, a silversmith, who
made silver shrines of Diana, brought no
small profit to the craftsmen. 25 He called
them together with the workers of similar
occupation, and said: "Men, you know that
we have our prosperity by this trade.
26 Moreover you see and hear that not only
at Ephesus, but throughout almost all Asia,
this Paul has persuaded and turned away
many people, saying that they are not gods
which are made with hands. 27 So not only

is this trade of ours in danger of falling
into disrepute, but also the temple of the
great goddess Diana may be despised and
her magnificence destroyed, whom all Asia
and the world worship."

28 Now when they heard *this,* they were
full of wrath and cried out, saying, "Great
is Diana of the Ephesians!" 29 So the whole
city was filled with confusion, and rushed
into the theater with one accord, having
seized Gaius and Aristarchus, Macedonians,
Paul's travel companions. 30 And when Paul
wanted to go in to the people, the disciples
would not allow him. 31 Then some of the
officials of Asia, who were his friends, sent
to him pleading that he would not venture
into the theater. 32 Some therefore cried
one thing and some another, for the assembly was confused, and most of them did
not know why they had come together.
33 And they drew Alexander out of the multitude, the Jews putting him forward. And
Alexander motioned with his hand, and
wanted to make his defense to the people.
34 But when they found out that he was a
Jew, all with one voice cried out for about
two hours, "Great *is* Diana of the
Ephesians!"

35 And when the city clerk had quieted
the crowd, he said: "Men of Ephesus, what
man is there who does not know that the
city of the Ephesians is temple guardian
of the great goddess Diana, and of the *image*
which fell down from Zeus? 36 Therefore,
since these things cannot be denied, you
ought to be quiet and do nothing rashly.
37 For you have brought these men here
who are neither robbers of temples nor blasphemers of your goddess. 38 Therefore, if
Demetrius and his fellow craftsmen have
a case against anyone, the courts are open
and there are proconsuls. Let them bring
charges against one another. 39 But if you
have any other inquiry to make, it shall
be determined in the lawful assembly.
40 For we are in danger of being called in
question for today's uproar, there being no
reason which we may give to account for
this disorderly gathering." 41 And when he
had said these things, he dismissed the
assembly.

◄◄◄◄

Reading 198—Despicable Yet Chosen
Psalm 85:1, 2

There were no nations until after the flood. After the flood the human race was split up into nations, and God called off one stream of the human race in Abraham, and created a nation out of that one man. The Old Testament is not a history of the nations of the world, but the history of that one nation. In secular history Israel is disregarded as being merely a miserable horde of slaves, and justly so from the standpoint of the historian. The nations to which the Bible pays little attention are much finer to read about, but they have no importance in the redemptive purpose of God. His purpose was the creation of a nation to be His bondslave, that through that nation all the other nations should come to know Him. The idea that Israel was a magnificently developed type of nation is a mistaken one. Israel was a despised, and a despisable nation, continually turning away from God into idolatry but nothing ever altered the purpose of God for the nation. The despised element is always a noticeable element in the purpose of God. When the Savior of the world came, He came of that despised nation; He Himself was "despised and rejected by men," and in all Christian enterprise there is this same despised element, "things which are despised God has chosen." (*SEND I YOU*)

2 CHRONICLES 30:1—31:21

AND Hezekiah sent to all Israel and Judah, and also wrote letters to Ephraim and Manasseh, that they should come to the house of the LORD at Jerusalem, to keep the Passover to the LORD God of Israel. 2 For the king and his leaders and all the assembly in Jerusalem had agreed to keep the Passover in the second month. 3 For they could not keep it at the regular time, because a sufficient number of priests had not consecrated themselves, nor had the people gathered together at Jerusalem. 4 And the matter pleased the king and all the assembly. 5 So they resolved to make a proclamation throughout all Israel, from Beersheba to Dan, that they should come to keep the Passover to the LORD God of Israel at Jerusalem, since they had not done *it* for a long *time* in the *prescribed* manner.

6 Then the runners went throughout all Israel and Judah with the letters from the king and his leaders, and spoke according to the command of the king: "Children of Israel, return to the LORD God of Abraham, Isaac, and Israel; then He will return to the remnant of you who have escaped from the hand of the kings of Assyria. 7 And do not be like your fathers and your brethren, who trespassed against the LORD God of their fathers, so that He gave them up to desolation, as you see. 8 Now do not be stiff-necked, as your fathers *were, but* yield yourselves to the LORD; and enter His sanctuary, which He has sanctified forever, and serve the LORD your God, that the fierceness of His wrath may turn away from you. 9 For if you return to the LORD, your brethren and your children *will be treated* with compassion by those who lead them captive, so that they may come back to this land; for the LORD your God *is* gracious and merciful, and will not turn *His* face from you if you return to Him."

10 So the runners passed from city to city through the country of Ephraim and Manasseh, as far as Zebulun; but they laughed at them and mocked them. 11 Nevertheless some from Asher, Manasseh, and Zebulun humbled themselves and came to Jerusalem. 12 Also the hand of God was on Judah to give them singleness of heart to obey the command of the king and the leaders, at the word of the LORD.

13 Now many people, a very great assembly, gathered at Jerusalem to keep the Feast of Unleavened Bread in the second month. 14 They arose and took away the altars that *were* in Jerusalem, and they took away all the incense altars and cast *them* into the Brook Kidron. 15 Then they slaughtered the Passover *lambs* on the fourteenth *day* of the second month. The priests and the Levites were ashamed, and sanctified themselves, and brought the burnt offerings to the house of the LORD. 16 They stood in their place according to their custom, according to the Law of Moses the man of God; the priests sprinkled the blood *received*

from the hand of the Levites. 17 For *there were* many in the assembly who had not sanctified themselves; therefore the Levites had charge of the slaughter of the Passover *lambs* for everyone *who was* not clean, to sanctify *them* to the LORD. 18 For a multitude of the people, many from Ephraim, Manasseh, Issachar, and Zebulun, had not cleansed themselves, yet they ate the Passover contrary to what was written. But Hezekiah prayed for them, saying, "May the good LORD provide atonement for everyone 19 *who* prepares his heart to seek

---

The life of God in [*a man*] . . . *is nourished not by food but by prayer.* (ASK)

God, the LORD God of his fathers, though *he is* not *cleansed* according to the purification of the sanctuary." 20 And the LORD listened to Hezekiah and healed the people.

21 So the children of Israel who were present at Jerusalem kept the Feast of Unleavened Bread seven days with great gladness; and the Levites and the priests praised the LORD day by day, *singing* to the LORD, accompanied by loud instruments. 22 And Hezekiah gave encouragement to all the Levites who taught the good knowledge of the LORD; and they ate throughout the feast seven days, offering peace offerings and making confession to the LORD God of their fathers.

23 Then the whole assembly agreed to keep *the feast* another seven days, and they kept it *another* seven days with gladness. 24 For Hezekiah king of Judah gave to the assembly a thousand bulls and seven thousand sheep, and the leaders gave to the assembly a thousand bulls and ten thousand sheep; and a great number of priests sanctified themselves. 25 The whole assembly of Judah rejoiced, also the priests and Levites, all the assembly that came from Israel, the sojourners who came from the land of Israel, and those who dwelt in Judah. 26 So there was great joy in Jerusalem, for since the time of Solomon the son of David, king of Israel, *there had* been nothing like this in Jerusalem. 27 Then the priests, the Levites, arose and blessed the people, and their voice was heard; and their prayer came *up* to His holy dwelling place, to heaven.

31 NOW when all this was finished, all Israel who were present went out to the cities of Judah and broke the sacred pillars in pieces, cut down the wooden images, and threw down the high places and the altars—from all Judah, Benjamin, Ephraim, and Manasseh—until they had utterly destroyed them all. Then all the children of Israel returned to their own cities, every man to his possession.

2 And Hezekiah appointed the divisions of the priests and the Levites according to their divisions, each man according to his service, the priests and Levites for burnt offerings and peace offerings, to serve, to give thanks, and to praise in the gates of the camp of the LORD. 3 The king also *appointed* a portion of his possessions for the burnt offerings: for the morning and evening burnt offerings, the burnt offerings for the Sabbaths and the New Moons and the set feasts, as *it is* written in the Law of the LORD.

4 Moreover he commanded the people who dwelt in Jerusalem to contribute support for the priests and the Levites, that they might devote themselves to the Law of the LORD.

5 As soon as the commandment was circulated, the children of Israel brought in abundance the firstfruits of grain and wine, oil and honey, and of all the produce of the field; and they brought in abundantly the tithe of everything. 6 And the children of Israel and Judah, who dwelt in the cities of Judah, brought the tithe of oxen and sheep; also the tithe of holy things which were consecrated to the LORD their God they laid in heaps.

7 In the third month they began laying them in heaps, and they finished in the seventh month. 8 And when Hezekiah and the leaders came and saw the heaps, they blessed the LORD and His people Israel. 9 Then Hezekiah questioned the priests and the Levites concerning the heaps. 10 And Azariah the chief priest, from the house of Zadok, answered him and said, "Since *the people* began to bring the offerings into the house of the LORD, we have had enough to eat and have plenty left, for the LORD has blessed His people; and what is left *is* this great abundance."

11 Now Hezekiah commanded *them* to prepare rooms in the house of the LORD, and they prepared them. 12 Then they faithfully brought in the offerings, the tithes, and the dedicated things; Cononiah the Levite had charge of them, and Shimei his brother *was* the next. 13 Jehiel, Azaziah, Nahath, Asahel, Jerimoth, Jozabad, Eliel, Ismachiah, Mahath, and Benaiah *were* overseers under the hand of Cononiah and

Shimei his brother, at the commandment of Hezekiah the king and Azariah the ruler of the house of God. 14 Kore the son of Imnah the Levite, the keeper of the East Gate, *was* over the freewill offerings to God, to distribute the offerings of the LORD and the most holy things. 15 And under him *were* Eden, Miniamin, Jeshua, Shemaiah, Amariah, and Shecaniah, *his* faithful assistants in the cities of the priests, to distribute allotments to their brethren by divisions, to the great as well as the small.

16 Besides those males from three years old and up who were written in the genealogy, they distributed to everyone who entered the house of the LORD his daily portion for the work of his service, by his division, 17 and to the priests who were written in the genealogy according to their father's house, and to the Levites from twenty years old and up according to their work, by their divisions, 18 and to all who were written in the genealogy—their little ones and their wives, their sons and daughters—for in their faithfulness they sanctified themselves in holiness.

19 Also for the sons of Aaron the priests, *who were* in the fields of the common-lands of their cities, in every single city, *there were* men who were designated by name to distribute portions to all the males among the priests and to all who were listed by genealogies among the Levites.

20 Thus Hezekiah did throughout all Judah, and he did what *was* good and right and true before the LORD his God. 21 And in every work that he began in the service of the house of God, in the law and in the commandment, to seek his God, he did *it* with all his heart. So he prospered.

PSALM 85:1–7

1 LORD, You have been favorable to
    Your land;
   You have brought back the captivity
    of Jacob.
2 You have forgiven the iniquity of Your
    people;
   You have covered all their sin.   Selah
3 You have taken away all Your wrath;
   You have turned from the fierceness of
    Your anger.

4 Restore us, O God of our salvation,
   And cause Your anger toward us to
    cease.
5 Will You be angry with us forever?

Will You prolong Your anger to all
    generations?
6 Will You not revive us again,
   That Your people may rejoice in You?
7 Show us Your mercy, LORD,
   And grant us Your salvation.

PROVERBS 21:9–11

9 BETTER to dwell in a corner of a
    housetop,
   Than in a house shared with a
    contentious woman.

10 The soul of the wicked desires evil;
   His neighbor finds no favor in his
    eyes.

11 When the scoffer is punished, the simple
    is made wise;
   But when the wise is instructed, he
    receives knowledge.

ACTS 20:1–16

AFTER the uproar had ceased, Paul called the disciples to *himself*, embraced *them*, and departed to go to Macedonia. 2 Now when he had gone over that region and encouraged them with many words, he came to Greece 3 and stayed three months. And when the Jews plotted against him as he was about to sail to Syria, he decided to return through Macedonia. 4 And Sopater of Berea accompanied him to Asia—also Aristarchus and Secundus of the Thessalonians, and Gaius of Derbe, and Timothy, and Tychicus and Trophimus of Asia. 5 These men, going ahead, waited for us at Troas. 6 But we sailed away from Philippi after the Days of Unleavened Bread, and in five days joined them at Troas, where we stayed seven days.

7 Now on the first *day* of the week, when the disciples came together to break bread, Paul, ready to depart the next day, spoke to them and continued his message until midnight. 8 There were many lamps in the upper room where they were gathered together. 9 And in a window sat a certain young man named Eutychus, who was sinking into a deep sleep. He was overcome by sleep; and as Paul continued speaking, he fell down from the third story and was taken up dead. 10 But Paul went down, fell on him, and embracing *him* said, "Do not trouble yourselves, for his life is in him." 11 Now when he had come up, had broken

bread and eaten, and talked a long while, even till daybreak, he departed. 12 And they brought the young man in alive, and they were not a little comforted.

13 Then we went ahead to the ship and sailed to Assos, there intending to take Paul on board; for so he had given orders, intending himself to go on foot. 14 And when he met us at Assos, we took him on board

and came to Mitylene. 15 We sailed from there, and the next *day* came opposite Chios. The following *day* we arrived at Samos and stayed at Trogyllium. The next *day* we came to Miletus. 16 For Paul had decided to sail past Ephesus, so that he would not have to spend time in Asia; for he was hurrying to be at Jerusalem, if possible, on the Day of Pentecost.

◆◆◆

Reading 199—The Sacrament of God in Myself
Acts 20:24

"Nor do I count my life dear to myself." Paul was absolutely indifferent to any other consideration than that of fulfilling the ministry he had received. He could never be appealed to by those who urged him to remain in a certain place because he was being of so much use there. Watch our Lord also. He went through villages and cities where He was marvelously used, but the great characteristic of His earthly life was that He steadfastly set His face to go to Jerusalem; He never stayed in a place because He had been of use there (Mark 1:37, 38). Beware of the sweet sisters and beloved brothers who say to you, "Now do consider whether you will not be of more use here than anywhere else." Probably you will, and in the passing of the months, you will become moldy bread instead of eating bread. We have nothing to do with God's purpose but only with the sacrament of God in us, that is, the real presence of God coming through the common elements of our lives (see John 7:37–39). The measure of our service for God is not our usefulness to others. We have nothing to do with the estimate of others, nor with success in service; we have to see that we fulfill our ministry.   (*GLORY*)

2 CHRONICLES 32:1—33:25

AFTER these deeds of faithfulness, Sennacherib king of Assyria came and entered Judah; he encamped against the fortified cities, thinking to win them over to himself. 2 And when Hezekiah saw that Sennacherib had come, and that his purpose was to make war against Jerusalem, 3 he consulted with his leaders and commanders to stop the water from the springs which *were* outside the city; and they helped him. 4 Thus many people gathered together who stopped all the springs and the brook that ran through the land, saying, "Why should the kings of Assyria come and find much water?" 5 And he strengthened himself, built up all the wall that was broken, raised *it* up to the towers, and *built* another wall outside; also he repaired the Millo *in* the City of David, and made weapons and shields in abundance. 6 Then he set military captains

over the people, gathered them together to him in the open square of the city gate, and gave them encouragement, saying, 7 "Be strong and courageous; do not be afraid nor dismayed before the king of Assyria, nor before all the multitude that *is* with him; for *there are* more with us than with him. 8 With him *is* an arm of flesh; but with us *is* the LORD our God, to help us and to fight our battles." And the people were strengthened by the words of Hezekiah king of Judah.

9 After this Sennacherib king of Assyria sent his servants to Jerusalem (but he and all the forces with him *laid siege* against Lachish), to Hezekiah king of Judah, and to all Judah who *were* in Jerusalem, saying, 10 "Thus says Sennacherib king of Assyria: 'In what do you trust, that you remain under siege in Jerusalem? 11 Does not Hezekiah persuade you to give yourselves over to die by famine and by thirst, saying, "The LORD

our God will deliver us from the hand of the king of Assyria"? 12 Has not the same Hezekiah taken away His high places and His altars, and commanded Judah and Jerusalem, saying, "You shall worship before one altar and burn incense on it"? 13 Do you not know what I and my fathers have done to all the peoples of *other* lands? Were the gods of the nations of those lands in any way able to deliver their lands out of my hand? 14 Who *was there* among all the gods of those nations that my fathers utterly destroyed that could deliver his people from my hand, that your God should be able to deliver you from my hand? 15 Now therefore, do not let Hezekiah deceive you or persuade you like this, and do not believe him; for no god of any nation or kingdom was able to deliver his people from my hand or the hand of my fathers. How much less will your God deliver you from my hand?' "

16 Furthermore, his servants spoke against the LORD God and against His servant Hezekiah.

17 He also wrote letters to revile the LORD God of Israel, and to speak against Him, saying, "As the gods of the nations of *other* lands have not delivered their people from my hand, so the God of Hezekiah will not deliver His people from my hand." 18 Then they called out with a loud voice in Hebrew to the people of Jerusalem who *were* on the wall, to frighten them and trouble them, that they might take the city. 19 And they spoke against the God of Jerusalem, as against the gods of the people of the earth—the work of men's hands.

20 Now because of this King Hezekiah and the prophet Isaiah, the son of Amoz, prayed and cried out to heaven. 21 Then

---

It cost God everything to make it possible for us to pray. (ASK)

---

the LORD sent an angel who cut down every mighty man of valor, leader, and captain in the camp of the king of Assyria. So he returned shamefaced to his own land. And when he had gone into the temple of his god, some of his own offspring struck him down with the sword there.

22 Thus the LORD saved Hezekiah and the inhabitants of Jerusalem from the hand of Sennacherib the king of Assyria, and from the hand of all *others,* and guided them on every side. 23 And many brought gifts to the LORD at Jerusalem, and presents to Hezekiah king of Judah, so that he was exalted in the sight of all nations thereafter.

24 In those days Hezekiah was sick and near death, and he prayed to the LORD; and He spoke to him and gave him a sign. 25 But Hezekiah did not repay according to the favor *shown* him, for his heart was lifted up; therefore wrath was looming over him and over Judah and Jerusalem. 26 Then Hezekiah humbled himself for the pride of his heart, he and the inhabitants of Jerusalem, so that the wrath of the LORD did not come upon them in the days of Hezekiah.

27 Hezekiah had very great riches and honor. And he made himself treasuries for silver, for gold, for precious stones, for spices, for shields, and for all kinds of desirable items; 28 storehouses for the harvest of grain, wine, and oil; and stalls for all kinds of livestock, and folds for flocks. 29 Moreover he provided cities for himself, and possessions of flocks and herds in abundance; for God had given him very much property. 30 This same Hezekiah also stopped the water outlet of Upper Gihon, and brought the water by tunnel to the west side of the City of David. Hezekiah prospered in all his works.

31 However, *regarding* the ambassadors of the princes of Babylon, whom they sent to him to inquire about the wonder that was *done* in the land, God withdrew from him, in order to test him, that He might know all *that was* in his heart.

32 Now the rest of the acts of Hezekiah, and his goodness, indeed they *are* written in the vision of Isaiah the prophet, the son of Amoz, *and* in the book of the kings of Judah and Israel. 33 So Hezekiah rested with his fathers, and they buried him in the upper tombs of the sons of David; and all Judah and the inhabitants of Jerusalem honored him at his death. Then Manasseh his son reigned in his place.

33 MANASSEH *was* twelve years old when he became king, and he reigned fifty-five years in Jerusalem. 2 But he did evil in the sight of the LORD, according to the abominations of the nations whom the LORD had cast out before the children of Israel. 3 For he rebuilt the high places which Hezekiah his father had broken down; he raised up altars for the Baals, and made wooden images; and he worshiped all the host of heaven and served them. 4 He also built altars in the house of the LORD, of which the LORD had said, "In Jerusalem shall My name be forever." 5 And he built altars for all the host of heaven in the two courts of the house of the LORD. 6 Also he caused his sons to pass

through the fire in the Valley of the Son of Hinnom; he practiced soothsaying, used witchcraft and sorcery, and consulted mediums and spiritists. He did much evil in the sight of the LORD, to provoke Him to anger. 7 He even set a carved image, the idol which he had made, in the house of God, of which God had said to David and to Solomon his son, "In this house and in Jerusalem, which I have chosen out of all the tribes of Israel, I will put My name forever; 8 and I will not again remove the foot of Israel from the land which I have appointed for your fathers—only if they are careful to do all that I have commanded them, according to the whole law and the statutes and the ordinances by the hand of Moses." 9 So Manasseh seduced Judah and the inhabitants of Jerusalem to do more evil than the nations whom the LORD had destroyed before the children of Israel.

10 And the LORD spoke to Manasseh and his people, but they would not listen. 11 Therefore the LORD brought upon them the captains of the army of the king of Assyria, who took Manasseh with hooks, bound him with bronze *fetters,* and carried him off to Babylon. 12 Now when he was in affliction, he implored the LORD his God, and humbled himself greatly before the God of his fathers, 13 and prayed to Him; and He received his entreaty, heard his supplication, and brought him back to Jerusalem into his kingdom. Then Manasseh knew that the LORD *was* God.

14 After this he built a wall outside the City of David on the west side of Gihon, in the valley, as far as the entrance of the Fish Gate; and *it* enclosed Ophel, and he raised it to a very great height. Then he put military captains in all the fortified cities of Judah. 15 He took away the foreign gods and the idol from the house of the LORD, and all the altars that he had built in the mount of the house of the LORD and in Jerusalem; and he cast *them* out of the city. 16 He also repaired the altar of the LORD, sacrificed peace offerings and thank offerings on it, and commanded Judah to serve the LORD God of Israel. 17 Nevertheless the people still sacrificed on the high places, *but* only to the LORD their God.

18 Now the rest of the acts of Manasseh, his prayer to his God, and the words of the seers who spoke to him in the name of the LORD God of Israel, indeed they *are written* in the book of the kings of Israel. 19 Also his prayer and *how God* received his entreaty, and all his sin and trespass, and the sites where he built high places and set up wooden images and carved images,

before he was humbled, indeed they *are* written among the sayings of Hozai. 20 So Manasseh rested with his fathers, and they buried him in his own house. Then his son Amon reigned in his place.

21 Amon *was* twenty-two years old when he became king, and he reigned two years in Jerusalem. 22 But he did evil in the sight of the LORD, as his father Manasseh had done; for Amon sacrificed to all the carved images which his father Manasseh had made, and served them. 23 And he did not humble himself before the LORD, as his father Manasseh had humbled himself; but Amon trespassed more and more.

24 Then his servants conspired against him, and killed him in his own house. 25 But the people of the land executed all those who had conspired against King Amon. Then the people of the land made his son Josiah king in his place.

PSALM 85:8–13

8 I will hear what God the LORD will
     speak,
   For He will speak peace
   To His people and to His saints;
   But let them not turn back to folly.
9 Surely His salvation *is* near to those
     who fear Him,
   That glory may dwell in our land.

10 Mercy and truth have met together;
    Righteousness and peace have kissed.
11 Truth shall spring out of the earth,
    And righteousness shall look down
      from heaven.
12 Yes, the LORD will give *what is* good;
    And our land will yield its increase.
13 Righteousness will go before Him,
    And shall make His footsteps *our*
      pathway.

PROVERBS 21:12

12 THE righteous *God* wisely considers the
      house of the wicked,
    Overthrowing the wicked for *their*
      wickedness.

ACTS 20:17–38

FROM Miletus he sent to Ephesus and called for the elders of the church. 18 And when they had come to him, he said to them: "You know, from the first day that I came to Asia, in what manner I always lived among you, 19 serving the Lord with all humility, with many tears and trials which happened to me by the plotting of the Jews; 20 how I kept back nothing that was helpful, but proclaimed it to you, and taught you publicly and from house to house, 21 testifying to Jews, and also to Greeks, repentance toward God and faith toward our Lord Jesus Christ. 22 And see, now I go bound in the spirit to Jerusalem, not knowing the things that will happen to me there, 23 except that the Holy Spirit

---

*A*lways act according to the wish that is born in you by the Spirit of God. (MORAL FOUND.)

---

testifies in every city, saying that chains and tribulations await me. 24 But none of these things move me; nor do I count my life dear to myself, so that I may finish my race with joy, and the ministry which I received from the Lord Jesus, to testify to the gospel of the grace of God.

25 "And indeed, now I know that you all, among whom I have gone preaching the kingdom of God, will see my face no more. 26 Therefore I testify to you this day that I *am* innocent of the blood of all *men*. 27 For I have not shunned to declare to you the whole counsel of God. 28 Therefore take heed to yourselves and to all the flock, among which the Holy Spirit has made you overseers, to shepherd the church of God which He purchased with His own blood. 29 For I know this, that after my departure savage wolves will come in among you, not sparing the flock. 30 Also from among yourselves men will rise up, speaking perverse things, to draw away the disciples after themselves. 31 Therefore watch, and remember that for three years I did not cease to warn everyone night and day with tears.

32 "So now, brethren, I commend you to God and to the word of His grace, which is able to build you up and give you an inheritance among all those who are sanctified. 33 I have coveted no one's silver or gold or apparel. 34 Yes, you yourselves know that these hands have provided for my necessities, and for those who were with me. 35 I have shown you in every way, by laboring like this, that you must support the weak. And remember the words of the Lord Jesus, that He said, 'It is more blessed to give than to receive.' "

36 And when he had said these things, he knelt down and prayed with them all. 37 Then they all wept freely, and fell on Paul's neck and kissed him, 38 sorrowing most of all for the words which he spoke, that they would see his face no more. And they accompanied him to the ship.

◆◆◆◆

Reading 200—The Holiness of Abandonment
Psalm 86:2

Abandon in the profound sense is of infinitely more value than personal holiness. Personal holiness brings the attention to bear on my own whiteness, I dare not be indiscreet, or unreserved, I dare not do anything in case I incur a speck. God can't bless that sort of thing, it is as unlike His own character as could be. The holiness produced through the indwelling of His Son in me is a holiness which is never conscious of itself. There are some people in whom you cannot find a speck and yet they are not abundantly blessed of God, while others make grave indiscretions and get marvelously blessed; the reason being that the former have become devotees of personal holiness, conscientious to a degree; the latter are marked by abandonment to God. Whatever centers attention on anything other than our Lord Himself will always lead astray. The only way to be kept cleansed is by walking in the light, as God is in the light. Only as we walk in that light is the holiness of Jesus Christ not only imputed, but imparted, to us. (*GENESIS*)

2 CHRONICLES 34:1—36:23

JOSIAH *was* eight years old when he became king, and he reigned thirty-one years in Jerusalem. 2 And he did *what was* right in the sight of the LORD, and walked in the ways of his father David; *he* did *not* turn aside to the right hand or to the left.

3 For in the eighth year of his reign, while he was still young, he began to seek the God of his father David; and in the twelfth year he began to purge Judah and Jerusalem of the high places, the wooden images, the carved images, and the molded images. 4 They broke down the altars of the Baals in his presence, and the incense altars which *were* above them he cut down; and the wooden images, the carved images, and the molded images he broke in pieces, and made dust of them and scattered *it* on the graves of those who had sacrificed to them. 5 He also burned the bones of the priests on their altars, and cleansed Judah and Jerusalem. 6 And *so he did* in the cities of Manasseh, Ephraim, and Simeon, as far as Naphtali and all around, with axes. 7 When he had broken down the altars and the wooden images, had beaten the carved images into powder, and cut down all the incense altars throughout all the land of Israel, he returned to Jerusalem.

8 In the eighteenth year of his reign, when he had purged the land and the temple, he sent Shaphan the son of Azaliah, Maaseiah the governor of the city, and Joah the son of Joahaz the recorder, to repair the house of the LORD his God. 9 When they came to Hilkiah the high priest, they delivered the money that was brought into the house of God, which the Levites who kept the doors had gathered from the hand of Manasseh and Ephraim, from all the remnant of Israel, from all Judah and Benjamin, and *which* they had brought back to Jerusalem. 10 Then they put *it* in the hand of the foremen who had the oversight of the house of the LORD; and they gave it to the workmen who worked in the house of the LORD, to repair and restore the house. 11 They gave *it* to the craftsmen and builders to buy hewn stone and timber for beams, and to floor the houses which the kings of Judah had destroyed. 12 And the men did the work faithfully. Their overseers *were* Jahath and Obadiah the Levites, of the sons of Merari, and Zechariah and Meshullam, of the sons of the Kohathites, to supervise. *Others of* the Levites, all of whom were skillful with instruments of music, 13 *were* over the burden bearers and *were* overseers of all who did work in any kind of service.

And *some* of the Levites *were* scribes, officers, and gatekeepers.

14 Now when they brought out the money that was brought into the house of the LORD, Hilkiah the priest found the Book of the Law of the LORD *given* by Moses. 15 Then Hilkiah answered and said to Shaphan the scribe, "I have found the Book of the Law in the house of the LORD." And Hilkiah gave the book to Shaphan. 16 So Shaphan carried the book to the king, bringing the king word, saying, "All that was committed to your servants they are doing. 17 And they have gathered the money that was found in the house of the LORD, and have delivered it into the hand of the overseers and the workmen." 18 Then Shaphan the scribe told the king, saying, "Hilkiah the priest has given me a book." And Shaphan read it before the king.

19 Thus it happened, when the king heard the words of the Law, that he tore his clothes. 20 Then the king commanded Hilkiah, Ahikam the son of Shaphan, Abdon the son of Micah, Shaphan the scribe, and Asaiah a servant of the king, saying, 21 "Go, inquire of the LORD for me, and for those who are left in Israel and Judah, concerning the words of the book that is found; for great *is* the wrath of the LORD that is poured out on us, because our fathers have not kept the word of the LORD, to do according to all that is written in this book."

22 So Hilkiah and those the king *had appointed* went to Huldah the prophetess, the wife of Shallum the son of Tokhath, the son of Hasrah, keeper of the wardrobe. (She dwelt in Jerusalem in the Second Quarter.) And they spoke to her to that *effect*.

23 Then she answered them, "Thus says the LORD God of Israel, 'Tell the man who sent you to Me, 24 "Thus says the LORD: 'Behold, I will bring calamity on this place and on its inhabitants, all the curses that are written in the book which they have read before the king of Judah, 25 because they have forsaken Me and burned incense to other gods, that they might provoke Me to anger with all the works of their hands. Therefore My wrath will be poured out on this place, and not be quenched.'"' 26 But as for the king of Judah, who sent you to inquire of the LORD, in this manner you shall speak to him, 'Thus says the LORD God of Israel: "*Concerning* the words which you have heard— 27 because your heart was tender, and you humbled yourself before God when you heard His words against this place and against its inhabitants, and you humbled yourself before Me, and you

tore your clothes and wept before Me, I also have heard *you,*" says the LORD. 28 "Surely I will gather you to your fathers, and you shall be gathered to your grave in peace; and your eyes shall not see all the calamity which I will bring on this place and its inhabitants."'" So they brought back word to the king.

29 Then the king sent and gathered all the elders of Judah and Jerusalem. 30 The king went up to the house of the LORD, with all the men of Judah and the inhabitants of Jerusalem—the priests and the Levites, and all the people, great and small. And he read in their hearing all the words of the Book of the Covenant which had been found in the house of the LORD. 31 Then the king stood in his place and made a covenant before the LORD, to follow the LORD, and to keep His commandments and His testimonies and His statutes with all his heart and all his soul, to perform the words of the covenant that were written in this book. 32 And he made all who were present in Jerusalem and Benjamin take a stand. So the inhabitants of Jerusalem did according to the covenant of God, the God of their fathers. 33 Thus Josiah removed all the abominations from all the country that *belonged* to the children of Israel, and made all who were present in Israel diligently serve the LORD their God. All his days they did not depart from following the LORD God of their fathers.

35 NOW Josiah kept a Passover to the LORD in Jerusalem, and they slaughtered the Passover *lambs* on the fourteenth *day* of the first month. 2 And he set the priests in their duties and encouraged them for the service of the house of the LORD. 3 Then he said to the Levites who taught all Israel, who were holy to the LORD: "Put the holy ark in the house which Solomon the son of David, king of Israel, built. *It shall* no longer *be* a burden on *your* shoulders. Now serve the LORD your God and His people Israel. 4 Prepare *yourselves* according to your fathers' houses, according to your divisions, following the written instruction of David king of Israel and the written instruction of Solomon his son. 5 And stand in the holy *place* according to the divisions of the fathers' houses of your brethren the *lay* people, and *according to* the division of the father's house of the Levites. 6 So slaughter the Passover *offerings,* consecrate yourselves, and prepare *them* for your brethren, that *they* may do according to the word of the LORD by the hand of Moses."

7 Then Josiah gave the *lay* people lambs and young goats from the flock, all for Passover *offerings* for all who were present, to the number of thirty thousand, as well as three thousand cattle; these *were* from the king's possessions. 8 And his leaders gave willingly to the people, to the priests, and to the Levites. Hilkiah, Zechariah, and Jehiel, rulers of the house of God, gave to the priests for the Passover *offerings* two thousand six hundred *from the flock,* and three hundred cattle. 9 Also Conaniah, his brothers Shemaiah and Nethanel, and Hashabiah and Jeiel and Jozabad, chief of the Levites, gave to the Levites for Passover *offerings* five thousand *from the flock* and five hundred cattle.

10 So the service was prepared, and the priests stood in their places, and the Levites in their divisions, according to the king's command. 11 And they slaughtered the Passover *offerings;* and the priests sprinkled *the blood* with their hands, while the Levites skinned *the animals.* 12 Then they removed the burnt offerings that *they* might give them to the divisions of the fathers' houses of the *lay* people, to offer to the LORD, as *it is* written in the Book of Moses. And so *they did* with the cattle. 13 Also they roasted the Passover *offerings* with fire according to the ordinance; but the *other* holy *offerings* they boiled in pots, in caldrons, and in pans, and divided *them* quickly among all the *lay* people. 14 Then afterward they prepared portions for themselves and for the priests, because the priests, the sons of Aaron, *were busy* in offering burnt offerings and fat until night; therefore the Levites prepared portions for themselves and for the priests, the sons of Aaron. 15 And the singers, the sons of Asaph, *were* in their places, according to the command of David, Asaph, Heman, and Jeduthun the king's seer. Also the gatekeepers were at each gate; they did not have to leave their position, because their brethren the Levites prepared portions for them.

16 So all the service of the LORD was prepared the same day, to keep the Passover and to offer burnt offerings on the altar of the LORD, according to the command of King Josiah. 17 And the children of Israel who were present kept the Passover at that time, and the Feast of Unleavened Bread for seven days. 18 There had been no Passover kept in Israel like that since the days of Samuel the prophet; and none of the kings of Israel had kept such a Passover as Josiah kept, with the priests and the Levites, all Judah and Israel who were present, and the inhabitants of Jerusalem. 19 In the

eighteenth year of the reign of Josiah this Passover was kept.

20 After all this, when Josiah had prepared the temple, Necho king of Egypt came up to fight against Carchemish by the Euphrates; and Josiah went out against him. 21 But he sent messengers to him, saying, "What have I to do with you, king of Judah? *I have* not *come* against you this day, but against the house with which I have war; for God commanded me to make haste. Refrain *from meddling with* God, who *is* with me, lest He destroy you." 22 Nevertheless Josiah would not turn his face from him, but disguised himself so that he might fight with him, and did not heed the words of Necho from the mouth of God. So he came to fight in the Valley of Megiddo.

23 And the archers shot King Josiah; and the king said to his servants, "Take me away, for I am severely wounded." 24 His servants therefore took him out of that chariot and put him in the second chariot that he had, and they brought him to Jerusalem. So he died, and was buried in *one of* the tombs of his fathers. And all Judah and Jerusalem mourned for Josiah.

25 Jeremiah also lamented for Josiah. And to this day all the singing men and the singing women speak of Josiah in their lamentations. They made it a custom in Israel; and indeed they *are* written in the Laments.

26 Now the rest of the acts of Josiah and his goodness, according to *what was* written in the Law of the LORD, 27 and his deeds from first to last, indeed they *are* written in the book of the kings of Israel and Judah.

36 THEN the people of the land took Jehoahaz the son of Josiah, and made him king in his father's place in Jerusalem. 2 Jehoahaz *was* twenty-three years old when he became king, and he reigned three months in Jerusalem. 3 Now the king of Egypt deposed him at Jerusalem; and he imposed on the land a tribute of one hundred talents of silver and a talent of gold. 4 Then the king of Egypt made *Jehoahaz's* brother Eliakim king over Judah and Jerusalem, and changed his name to Jehoiakim. And Necho took Jehoahaz his brother and carried him off to Egypt.

5 Jehoiakim *was* twenty-five years old when he became king, and he reigned eleven years in Jerusalem. And he did evil in the sight of the LORD his God. 6 Nebuchadnezzar king of Babylon came up against him, and bound him in bronze *fetters* to carry him off to Babylon. 7 Nebuchadnezzar also carried off *some* of the articles from the house of the LORD to Babylon, and

put them in his temple at Babylon. 8 Now the rest of the acts of Jehoiakim, the abominations which he did, and what was found against him, indeed they *are* written in the book of the kings of Israel and Judah. Then Jehoiachin his son reigned in his place.

9 Jehoiachin *was* eight years old when he became king, and he reigned in Jerusalem three months and ten days. And he did evil in the sight of the LORD. 10 At the turn of the year King Nebuchadnezzar summoned *him* and took him to Babylon, with the costly articles from the house of the LORD, and made Zedekiah, *Jehoiakim's* brother, king over Judah and Jerusalem.

11 Zedekiah *was* twenty-one years old when he became king, and he reigned eleven years in Jerusalem. 12 He did evil in the sight of the LORD his God, *and* did not humble himself before Jeremiah the prophet, *who spoke* from the mouth of the LORD. 13 And he also rebelled against King Nebuchadnezzar, who had made him swear *an oath* by God; but he stiffened his neck and hardened his heart against turning to the LORD God of Israel. 14 Moreover all the leaders of the priests and the people transgressed more and more, *according* to all the abominations of the nations, and defiled the house of the LORD which He had consecrated in Jerusalem.

15 And the LORD God of their fathers sent *warnings* to them by His messengers, rising up early and sending *them,* because He had compassion on His people and on His dwelling place. 16 But they mocked the messengers of God, despised His words, and scoffed at His prophets, until the wrath of the LORD arose against His people, till *there was* no remedy.

17 Therefore He brought against them the king of the Chaldeans, who killed their young men with the sword in the house of their sanctuary, and had no compassion on young man or virgin, on the aged or the weak; He gave *them* all into his hand. 18 And all the articles from the house of God, great and small, the treasures of the house of the LORD, and the treasures of the king and of his leaders, all *these* he took to Babylon. 19 Then they burned the house of God, broke down the wall of Jerusalem, burned all its palaces with fire, and destroyed all its precious possessions. 20 And those who escaped from the sword he carried away to Babylon, where they became servants to him and his sons until the rule of the kingdom of Persia, 21 to fulfill the word of the LORD by the mouth of Jeremiah, until the land had enjoyed her

Sabbaths. As long as she lay desolate she kept Sabbath, to fulfill seventy years.

22 Now in the first year of Cyrus king of Persia, that the word of the LORD by the mouth of Jeremiah might be fulfilled, the LORD stirred up the spirit of Cyrus king of Persia, so that he made a proclamation throughout all his kingdom, and also *put it* in writing, saying,

23 Thus says Cyrus king of Persia:
All the kingdoms of the earth the LORD God of heaven has given me. And He has commanded me to build Him a house at Jerusalem which is in Judah. Who *is* among you of all His people? May the LORD his God *be* with him, and let him go up!

PSALM 86:1–5

1 BOW down Your ear, O LORD, hear me;
For I *am* poor and needy.
2 Preserve my life, for I *am* holy;
You are my God;
Save Your servant who trusts in You!

---

*T*he highest authority conceivable for a man is that of a holy character. (PERFECT)

---

3 Be merciful to me, O Lord,
For I cry to You all day long.
4 Rejoice the soul of Your servant,
For to You, O Lord, I lift up my soul.
5 For You, Lord, *are* good, and ready to forgive,
And abundant in mercy to all those who call upon You.

PROVERBS 21:13, 14

13 WHOEVER shuts his ears to the cry of the poor
Will also cry himself and not be heard.

14 A gift in secret pacifies anger,
And a bribe behind the back, strong wrath.

ACTS 21:1–17

NOW it came to pass, that when we had departed from them and set sail, running a straight course we came to Cos, the following *day* to Rhodes, and from there to Patara. 2 And finding a ship sailing over to Phoenicia, we went aboard and set sail. 3 When we had sighted Cyprus, we passed it on the left, sailed to Syria, and landed at Tyre; for there the ship was to unload her cargo. 4 And finding disciples, we stayed there seven days. They told Paul through the Spirit not to go up to Jerusalem. 5 When we had come to the end of those days, we departed and went on our way; and they all accompanied us, with wives and children, till *we were* out of the city. And we knelt down on the shore and prayed. 6 When we had taken our leave of one another, we boarded the ship, and they returned home.

7 And when we had finished *our* voyage from Tyre, we came to Ptolemais, greeted the brethren, and stayed with them one day. 8 On the next *day* we who were Paul's companions departed and came to Caesarea, and entered the house of Philip the evangelist, who was *one* of the seven, and stayed with him. 9 Now this man had four virgin daughters who prophesied. 10 And as we stayed many days, a certain prophet named Agabus came down from Judea. 11 When he had come to us, he took Paul's belt, bound his *own* hands and feet, and said, "Thus says the Holy Spirit, 'So shall the Jews at Jerusalem bind the man who owns this belt, and deliver *him* into the hands of the Gentiles.' "

12 Now when we heard these things, both we and those from that place pleaded with him not to go up to Jerusalem. 13 Then Paul answered, "What do you mean by weeping and breaking my heart? For I am ready not only to be bound, but also to die at Jerusalem for the name of the Lord Jesus."

14 So when he would not be persuaded, we ceased, saying, "The will of the Lord be done."

15 And after those days we packed and went up to Jerusalem. 16 Also some of the disciples from Caesarea went with us and brought with them a certain Mnason of Cyprus, an early disciple, with whom we were to lodge.

17 And when we had come to Jerusalem, the brethren received us gladly.

Reading 201—The Supplicating Voice
Psalm 86:6, 7

"Ask whatsoever you will," that is, not what you like, but ask that which your personal life is in. There is very little that our personal life is in when we pray, we spell out platitudes before God and call it prayer, but it is not prayer at all. (*PLACE HELP*)

Nothing is more difficult than to ask. We long, and desire, and crave, and suffer, but not until we are at the extreme limit will we *ask*. A sense of unreality makes us ask. We cannot bring ourselves up against spiritual reality when we like—all at once the staggering realization dawns that we are destitute of the Holy Spirit, ignorant of all that the Lord Jesus stands for. The first result of being brought up against reality is this realization of poverty, of the lack of wisdom, lack of the Holy Spirit, lack of power, lack of a grip of God. "If any of you lacks wisdom, let him ask of God," but be sure you do lack wisdom. (*BRILL. HERITAGE*)

EZRA 1:1—2:70

NOW in the first year of Cyrus king of Persia, that the word of the LORD by the mouth of Jeremiah might be fulfilled, the LORD stirred up the spirit of Cyrus king of Persia, so that he made a proclamation throughout all his kingdom, and also *put it* in writing, saying,

2 Thus says Cyrus king of Persia:
All the kingdoms of the earth the LORD God of heaven has given me. And He has commanded me to build Him a house at Jerusalem which *is* in Judah. 3 Who *is* among you of all His people? May his God be with him, and let him go up to Jerusalem which *is* in Judah, and build the house of the LORD God of Israel (He *is* God), which *is* in Jerusalem.
4 And whoever is left in any place where he dwells, let the men of his place help him with silver and gold, with goods and livestock, besides the freewill offerings for the house of God which *is* in Jerusalem.

5 Then the heads of the fathers' *houses* of Judah and Benjamin, and the priests and the Levites, with all whose spirits God had moved, arose to go up and build the house of the LORD which *is* in Jerusalem. 6 And all those who *were* around them encouraged them with articles of silver and gold, with goods and livestock, and with precious things, besides all *that* was willingly offered.
7 King Cyrus also brought out the articles of the house of the LORD, which Nebuchadnezzar had taken from Jerusalem and put in the temple of his gods; 8 and Cyrus king of Persia brought them out by the hand of Mithredath the treasurer, and counted them out to Sheshbazzar the prince of Judah. 9 This *is* the number of them: thirty gold platters, one thousand silver platters, twenty-nine knives, 10 thirty gold basins, four hundred and ten silver basins of a similar *kind, and* one thousand other articles. 11 All the articles of gold and silver *were* five thousand four hundred. All *these* Sheshbazzar took with the captives who were brought from Babylon to Jerusalem.

2 NOW these *are* the people of the province who came back from the captivity, of those who had been carried away, whom Nebuchadnezzar the king of Babylon had carried away to Babylon, and who returned to Jerusalem and Judah, everyone to his *own* city.
2 *Those* who came with Zerubbabel *were* Jeshua, Nehemiah, Seraiah, Reelaiah, Mordecai, Bilshan, Mispar, Bigvai, Rehum, *and* Baanah. The number of the men of the people of Israel: 3 the people of Parosh, two thousand one hundred and seventy-two; 4 the people of Shephatiah, three hundred and seventy-two; 5 the people of Arah, seven hundred and seventy-five; 6 the people of Pahath-Moab, of the people of Jeshua *and* Joab, two thousand eight hundred and twelve; 7 the people of Elam, one thousand two hundred and fifty-four; 8 the people of Zattu, nine hundred and forty-five; 9 the people of Zaccai, seven hundred and sixty; 10 the people of Bani, six hundred

and forty-two; 11 the people of Bebai, six hundred and twenty-three; 12 the people of Azgad, one thousand two hundred and twenty-two; 13 the people of Adonikam, six hundred and sixty-six; 14 the people of Bigvai, two thousand and fifty-six; 15 the people of Adin, four hundred and fifty-four; 16 the people of Ater of Hezekiah, ninety-eight; 17 the people of Bezai, three hundred and twenty-three; 18 the people of Jorah, one hundred and twelve; 19 the people of Hashum, two hundred and twenty-three; 20 the people of Gibbar, ninety-five; 21 the people of Bethlehem, one hundred and twenty-three; 22 the men of Netophah, fifty-six; 23 the men of Anathoth, one hundred and twenty-eight; 24 the people of Azmaveth, forty-two; 25 the people of Kirjath Arim, Chephirah, and Beeroth, seven hundred and forty-three; 26 the people of Ramah and Geba, six hundred and twenty-one; 27 the men of Michmas, one hundred and twenty-two; 28 the men of Bethel and Ai, two hundred and twenty-three; 29 the people of Nebo, fifty-two; 30 the people of Magbish, one hundred and fifty-six; 31 the people of the other Elam, one thousand two hundred and fifty-four; 32 the people of Harim, three hundred and twenty; 33 the people of Lod, Hadid, and Ono, seven hundred and twenty-five; 34 the people of Jericho, three hundred and forty-five; 35 the people of Senaah, three thousand six hundred and thirty.

36 The priests: the sons of Jedaiah, of the house of Jeshua, nine hundred and seventy-three; 37 the sons of Immer, one thousand and fifty-two; 38 the sons of Pashhur, one thousand two hundred and forty-seven; 39 the sons of Harim, one thousand and seventeen.

40 The Levites: the sons of Jeshua and Kadmiel, of the sons of Hodaviah, seventy-four.

41 The singers: the sons of Asaph, one hundred and twenty-eight.

42 The sons of the gatekeepers: the sons of Shallum, the sons of Ater, the sons of Talmon, the sons of Akkub, the sons of Hatita, and the sons of Shobai, one hundred and thirty-nine *in* all.

43 The Nethinim: the sons of Ziha, the sons of Hasupha, the sons of Tabbaoth, 44 the sons of Keros, the sons of Siaha, the sons of Padon, 45 the sons of Lebanah, the sons of Hagabah, the sons of Akkub, 46 the sons of Hagab, the sons of Shalmai, the sons of Hanan, 47 the sons of Giddel, the sons of Gahar, the sons of Reaiah, 48 the sons of Rezin, the sons of Nekoda, the sons of Gazzam, 49 the sons of Uzza,

the sons of Paseah, the sons of Besai, 50 the sons of Asnah, the sons of Meunim, the sons of Nephusim, 51 the sons of Bakbuk, the sons of Hakupha, the sons of Harhur, 52 the sons of Bazluth, the sons of Mehida, the sons of Harsha, 53 the sons of Barkos, the sons of Sisera, the sons of Tamah, 54 the sons of Neziah, and the sons of Hatipha.

55 The sons of Solomon's servants: the sons of Sotai, the sons of Sophereth, the sons of Peruda, 56 the sons of Jaala, the sons of Darkon, the sons of Giddel, 57 the sons of Shephatiah, the sons of Hattil, the sons of Pochereth of Zebaim, and the sons of Ami. 58 All the Nethinim and the children of Solomon's servants were three hundred and ninety-two.

59 And these *were* the ones who came up from Tel Melah, Tel Harsha, Cherub, Addan, and Immer; but they could not identify their father's house or their genealogy, whether they *were* of Israel: 60 the sons of Delaiah, the sons of Tobiah, and the sons of Nekoda, six hundred and fifty-two; 61 and of the sons of the priests: the sons of Habaiah, the sons of Koz, and the sons of Barzillai, who took a wife of the daughters of Barzillai the Gileadite, and was called by their name. 62 These sought their listing *among* those who were registered by genealogy, but they were not found; therefore they *were excluded* from the priesthood as defiled. 63 And the governor said to them that they should not eat of the most holy things till a priest could consult with the Urim and Thummim.

64 The whole assembly together *was* forty-two thousand three hundred *and* sixty, 65 besides their male and female servants, of whom *there were* seven thousand three hundred and thirty-seven; and they had two hundred men and women singers. 66 Their horses *were* seven hundred and thirty-six, their mules two hundred and forty-five, 67 their camels four hundred and thirty-five, and *their* donkeys six thousand seven hundred and twenty.

68 *Some* of the heads of the fathers' *houses,* when they came to the house of the LORD which *is* in Jerusalem, offered freely for the house of God, to erect it in its place: 69 According to their ability, they gave to the treasury for the work sixty-one thousand gold drachmas, five thousand minas of silver, and one hundred priestly garments.

70 So the priests and the Levites, *some* of the people, the singers, the gatekeepers, and the Nethinim, dwelt in their cities, and all Israel in their cities.

PSALM 86:6–10

6   GIVE ear, O Lord, to my prayer;
    And attend to the voice of my
    supplications.
7   In the day of my trouble I will call upon
    You,
    For You will answer me.

8   Among the gods *there is* none like You,
    O Lord;
    Nor *are there any works* like Your
    works.
9   All nations whom You have made
    Shall come and worship before You,
    O Lord,
    And shall glorify Your name.
10 For You *are* great, and do wondrous
    things;
    You alone *are* God.

PROVERBS 21:15, 16

15 *IT is* a joy for the just to do justice,
    But destruction *will come* to the workers
    of iniquity.

16 A man who wanders from the way of
    understanding
    Will rest in the assembly of the dead.

ACTS 21:18–40

ON the following *day* Paul went in with
us to James, and all the elders were present.
19 When he had greeted them, he told in
detail those things which God had done
among the Gentiles through his ministry.
20 And when they heard *it,* they glorified
the Lord. And they said to him, "You see,
brother, how many myriads of Jews there
are who have believed, and they are all zealous for the law; 21 but they have been informed about you that you teach all the
Jews who are among the Gentiles to forsake
Moses, saying that they ought not to circumcise *their* children nor to walk according
to the customs. 22 What then? The assembly
must certainly meet, for they will hear that
you have come. 23 Therefore do what we
tell you: We have four men who have taken
a vow. 24 Take them and be purified with
them, and pay their expenses so that they
may shave *their* heads, and that all may know
that those things of which they were informed concerning you are nothing, but
that you yourself also walk orderly and keep

the law. 25 But concerning the Gentiles who
believe, we have written *and* decided that
they should observe no such thing, except
that they should keep themselves from
things offered to idols, from blood, from
things strangled, and from sexual immorality."

26 Then Paul took the men, and the next
day, having been purified with them, entered the temple to announce the expiration
of the days of purification, at which time
an offering should be made for each one
of them.

27 Now when the seven days were almost
ended, the Jews from Asia, seeing him in
the temple, stirred up the whole crowd
and laid hands on him, 28 crying out,
"Men of Israel, help! This is the man who
teaches all *men* everywhere against the people, the law, and this place; and furthermore
he also brought Greeks into the temple
and has defiled this holy place." 29 (For

---

*If prosperity is the blessing of the Old
Testament, adversity is the blessing of
the New.*   (Baffled)

---

they had previously seen Trophimus the
Ephesian with him in the city, whom they
supposed that Paul had brought into the
temple.)

30 And all the city was disturbed; and
the people ran together, seized Paul, and
dragged him out of the temple; and immediately the doors were shut. 31 Now as they
were seeking to kill him, news came to the
commander of the garrison that all Jerusalem was in an uproar. 32 He immediately
took soldiers and centurions, and ran down
to them. And when they saw the commander and the soldiers, they stopped beating Paul. 33 Then the commander came near
and took him, and commanded *him* to be
bound with two chains; and he asked who
he was and what he had done. 34 And some
among the multitude cried one thing and
some another.

So when he could not ascertain the truth
because of the tumult, he commanded him
to be taken into the barracks. 35 When he
reached the stairs, he had to be carried by
the soldiers because of the violence of the
mob. 36 For the multitude of the people
followed after, crying out, "Away with
him!"

37 Then as Paul was about to be led into
the barracks, he said to the commander,
"May I speak to you?"

He replied, "Can you speak Greek? 38 Are you not the Egyptian who some time ago stirred up a rebellion and led the four thousand assassins out into the wilderness?"

39 But Paul said, "I am a Jew from Tarsus, in Cilicia, a citizen of no mean city; and I implore you, permit me to speak to the people."

40 So when he had given him permission, Paul stood on the stairs and motioned with his hand to the people. And when there was a great silence, he spoke to *them* in the Hebrew language, saying,

◆◆◆◆

Reading 202—Abundant in Truth
Psalm 86:15

The one great Truth to keep steadfastly before us is the Lord Jesus Christ; He is the Truth. Only the whole truth is the Truth, any part of the truth may become an error. If you have a ray of light on the Truth never call it the whole truth; follow it up and it will lead you to the central Truth, the Lord Jesus Christ.   (GLORY)

Our tendency is to make truth a logical statement, to make it a principle instead of a Person. Profoundly speaking there are no Christian principles, but the saint by abiding in Christ in the Way of the Fatherhood of God discerns the Truth of God in the passing moments. Confusion arises when we disassociate ourselves from our Lord and try to live up to a standard merely constructed on His word.   (CHRIS. DIS. 1)

Would that men who name the name of Christ realized that He *is* the Truth, not the proclaimer of it; that He *is* the Gospel, not the preacher of the Gospel; that He *is* the Way of the Fatherhood of God.   (CHRIS. DIS. 1)

EZRA 3:1—4:24

AND when the seventh month had come, and the children of Israel *were* in the cities, the people gathered together as one man to Jerusalem. 2 Then Jeshua the son of Jozadak and his brethren the priests, and Zerubbabel the son of Shealtiel and his brethren, arose and built the altar of the God of Israel, to offer burnt offerings on it, as *it is* written in the Law of Moses the man of God. 3 Though fear *had come* upon them because of the people of those countries, they set the altar on its bases; and they offered burnt offerings on it to the LORD, *both* the morning and evening burnt offerings. 4 They also kept the Feast of Tabernacles, as *it is* written, and *offered* the daily burnt offerings in the number required by ordinance for each day. 5 Afterwards *they offered* the regular burnt offering, and *those* for New Moons and for all the appointed feasts of the LORD that were consecrated, and *those* of everyone who willingly offered a freewill offering to the LORD. 6 From the first day of the seventh month they began to offer burnt offerings to the LORD, although the foundation of the temple of the LORD had not been laid. 7 They also gave money to the masons and the carpenters, and food, drink, and oil to the people of Sidon and Tyre to bring cedar logs from Lebanon to the sea, to Joppa, according to the permission which they had from Cyrus king of Persia.

8 Now in the second month of the second year of their coming to the house of God at Jerusalem, Zerubbabel the son of Shealtiel, Jeshua the son of Jozadak, and the rest of their brethren the priests and the Levites, and all those who had come out of the captivity to Jerusalem, began *work* and appointed the Levites from twenty years old and above to oversee the work of the house of the LORD. 9 Then Jeshua *with* his sons and brothers, Kadmiel *with* his sons, and the sons of Judah, arose as one to oversee those working on the house of God: the sons of Henadad *with* their sons and their brethren the Levites.

10 When the builders laid the foundation of the temple of the LORD, the priests stood in their apparel with trumpets, and the

Levites, the sons of Asaph, with cymbals, to praise the LORD, according to the ordinance of David king of Israel. 11 And they sang responsively, praising and giving thanks to the LORD:

"For *He is* good,
        For His mercy *endures* forever
        toward Israel."

Then all the people shouted with a great shout, when they praised the LORD, because the foundation of the house of the LORD was laid.

12 But many of the priests and Levites and heads of the fathers' *houses,* old men who had seen the first temple, wept with a loud voice when the foundation of this temple was laid before their eyes. Yet many shouted aloud for joy, 13 so that the people could not discern the noise of the shout of joy from the noise of the weeping of the people, for the people shouted with a loud shout, and the sound was heard afar off.

4 NOW when the adversaries of Judah and Benjamin heard that the descendants of the captivity were building the temple of the LORD God of Israel, 2 they came to Zerubbabel and the heads of the fathers' *houses,* and said to them, "Let us build with you, for we seek your God as you *do;* and we have sacrificed to Him since the days of Esarhaddon king of Assyria, who brought us here." 3 But Zerubbabel and Jeshua and the rest of the heads of the fathers' *houses* of Israel said to them, "You may do nothing with us to build a house for our God; but we alone will build to the LORD God of Israel, as King Cyrus the king of Persia has commanded us." 4 Then the people of the land tried to discourage the people of Judah. They troubled them in building, 5 and hired counselors against them to frustrate their purpose all the days of Cyrus king of Persia, even until the reign of Darius king of Persia.

6 In the reign of Ahasuerus, in the beginning of his reign, they wrote an accusation against the inhabitants of Judah and Jerusalem.

7 In the days of Artaxerxes also, Bishlam, Mithredath, Tabel, and the rest of their companions wrote to Artaxerxes king of Persia; and the letter *was* written in Aramaic script, and translated into the Aramaic language. 8 Rehum the commander and Shimshai the scribe wrote a letter against Jerusalem to King Artaxerxes in this fashion:

9   From Rehum the commander, Shimshai the scribe, and the rest of their companions—*representatives* of the Dinaites, the Apharsathchites, the Tarpelites, the people of Persia and Erech and Babylon and Shushan, the Dehavites, the Elamites, 10 and the rest of the nations whom the great and noble Osnapper took captive and settled in the cities of Samaria and the remainder beyond the River— and so forth.

11 (This *is* a copy of the letter that they sent him)

To King Artaxerxes from your servants, the men *of the region* beyond the River, and so forth:

12   Let it be known to the king that the Jews who came up from you have come to us at Jerusalem, and are building the rebellious and evil city, and are finishing *its* walls and repairing the foundations. 13 Let it now be known to the king that, if this city is built and the walls completed, they will not pay tax, tribute, or custom, and the king's treasury will be diminished. 14 Now because we receive support from the palace, it was not proper for us to see the king's dishonor; therefore we have sent and informed the king, 15 that search may be made in the book of the records of your fathers. And you will find in the book of the records and know that this city *is* a rebellious city, harmful to kings and provinces, and that they have incited sedition within the city in former times, for which cause this city was destroyed.

16   We inform the king that if this city is rebuilt and its walls are completed, the result will be that you will have no dominion beyond the River.

17 The king sent an answer:

To Rehum the commander, *to* Shimshai the scribe, *to* the rest of their companions who dwell in Samaria, and *to* the remainder beyond the River:

Peace, and so forth.

18   The letter which you sent to us has been clearly read before me. 19 And

I gave the command, and a search has been made, and it was found that this city in former times has revolted against kings, and rebellion and sedition have been fostered in it. 20 There have also been mighty kings over Jerusalem, who have ruled over all *the region* beyond the River; and tax, tribute, and custom were paid to them. 21 Now give the command to make these men cease, that this city may not be built until the command is given by me.

22 Take heed now that you do not fail to do this. Why should damage increase to the hurt of the kings?

23 Now when the copy of King Artaxerxes' letter *was* read before Rehum, Shimshai the scribe, and their companions, they went up in haste to Jerusalem against the Jews, and by force of arms made them cease. 24 Thus the work of the house of God which *is* at Jerusalem ceased, and it was discontinued until the second year of the reign of Darius king of Persia.

PSALM 86:11–17

11 TEACH me Your way, O LORD;
I will walk in Your truth;
Unite my heart to fear Your name.

We learn His truth by obeying it. (GLORIFY)

---

12 I will praise You, O Lord my God,
with all my heart,
And I will glorify Your name
forevermore.

13 For great *is* Your mercy toward me,
And You have delivered my soul from
the depths of Sheol.

14 O God, the proud have risen against
me,
And a mob of violent *men* have sought
my life,
And have not set You before them.

15 But You, O Lord, *are* a God full of
compassion, and gracious,
Longsuffering and abundant in mercy
and truth.

16 Oh, turn to me, and have mercy on
me!
Give Your strength to Your servant,

And save the son of Your maidservant.
17 Show me a sign for good,
That those who hate me may see *it* and
be ashamed,
Because You, LORD, have helped me
and comforted me.

PROVERBS 21:17, 18

17 HE who loves pleasure *will be* a poor
man;
He who loves wine and oil will not
be rich.

18 The wicked *shall be* a ransom for the
righteous,
And the unfaithful for the upright.

ACTS 22:1–30

"BRETHREN and fathers, hear my defense before you now." 2 And when they heard that he spoke to them in the Hebrew language, they kept all the more silent.

Then he said: 3 "I am indeed a Jew, born in Tarsus of Cilicia, but brought up in this city at the feet of Gamaliel, taught according to the strictness of our fathers' law, and was zealous toward God as you all are today. 4 I persecuted this Way to the death, binding and delivering into prisons both men and women, 5 as also the high priest bears me witness, and all the council of the elders, from whom I also received letters to the brethren, and went to Damascus to bring in chains even those who were there to Jerusalem to be punished.

6 "Now it happened, as I journeyed and came near Damascus at about noon, suddenly a great light from heaven shone around me. 7 And I fell to the ground and heard a voice saying to me, 'Saul, Saul, why are you persecuting Me?' 8 So I answered, 'Who are You, Lord?' And He said to me, 'I am Jesus of Nazareth, whom you are persecuting.'

9 "And those who were with me indeed saw the light and were afraid, but they did not hear the voice of Him who spoke to me. 10 So I said, 'What shall I do, Lord?' And the Lord said to me, 'Arise and go into Damascus, and there you will be told all things which are appointed for you to do.' 11 And since I could not see for the glory of that light, being led by the hand of those who were with me, I came into Damascus.

12 "Then a certain Ananias, a devout man according to the law, having a good

testimony with all the Jews who dwelt *there,* 13 came to me; and he stood and said to me, 'Brother Saul, receive your sight.' And at that same hour I looked up at him. 14 Then he said, 'The God of our fathers has chosen you that you should know His will, and see the Just One, and hear the voice of His mouth. 15 For you will be His witness to all men of what you have seen and heard. 16 And now why are you waiting? Arise and be baptized, and wash away your sins, calling on the name of the Lord.'

17 "Now it happened, when I returned to Jerusalem and was praying in the temple, that I was in a trance 18 and saw Him saying to me, 'Make haste and get out of Jerusalem quickly, for they will not receive your testimony concerning Me.' 19 So I said, 'Lord, they know that in every synagogue I imprisoned and beat those who believe on You. 20 And when the blood of Your martyr Stephen was shed, I also was standing by consenting to his death, and guarding the clothes of those who were killing him.' 21 Then He said to me, 'Depart, for I will send you far from here to the Gentiles.'"

> *To have brickbats and rotten eggs flung at you is not persecution.*   (SERVANT AS LORD)

22 And they listened to him until this word, and *then* they raised their voices and said, "Away with such a *fellow* from the earth, for he is not fit to live!" 23 Then, as they cried out and tore off *their* clothes and threw dust into the air, 24 the commander ordered him to be brought into the barracks, and said that he should be examined under scourging, so that he might know why they shouted so against him. 25 And as they bound him with thongs, Paul said to the centurion who stood by, "Is it lawful for you to scourge a man who is a Roman, and uncondemned?"

26 When the centurion heard *that,* he went and told the commander, saying, "Take care what you do, for this man is a Roman."

27 Then the commander came and said to him, "Tell me, are you a Roman?"

He said, "Yes."

28 The commander answered, "With a large sum I obtained this citizenship."

And Paul said, "But I was born *a citizen.*"

29 Then immediately those who were about to examine him withdrew from him; and the commander was also afraid after he found out that he was a Roman, and because he had bound him.

30 The next day, because he wanted to know for certain why he was accused by the Jews, he released him from *his* bonds, and commanded the chief priests and all their council to appear, and brought Paul down and set him before them.

Reading 203—Drawing on the Resurrection
Psalm 87:7

The life God plants in us develops its own virtues, not the virtues of Adam but of Jesus Christ. Watch how God will wither up your confidence in natural virtues after sanctification, and in any power you have, until you learn to draw your life from the reservoir of the resurrection life of Jesus. Thank God if you are going through a drying-up experience!

The sign that God is at work in us is that He corrupts confidence in the natural virtues, because they are not promises of what we are going to be, but remnants of what God created man to be. We will cling to the natural virtues, while all the time God is trying to get us into contact with the life of Jesus Christ which can never be described in terms of the natural virtues. It is the saddest thing to see people in the service of God depending on that which the grace of God never gave them, depending on what they have by the accident of heredity. God does not build up our natural virtues and transfigure them, because our natural virtues can never come anywhere near what Jesus Christ wants. No natural love, no natural patience, no natural purity can ever come up to His demands. But as we bring every bit of our bodily life into harmony with the new life which God has put in us, He will exhibit in us the virtues that were characteristic of the Lord Jesus. (*UTMOST*)

EZRA 5:1—6:22

THEN the prophet Haggai and Zechariah the son of Iddo, prophets, prophesied to the Jews who *were* in Judah and Jerusalem, in the name of the God of Israel, *who was* over them. 2 So Zerubbabel the son of Shealtiel and Jeshua the son of Jozadak rose up and began to build the house of God which *is* in Jerusalem; and the prophets of God *were* with them, helping them.

3 At the same time Tattenai the governor of *the region* beyond the River and Shethar-Boznai and their companions came to them and spoke thus to them: "Who has commanded you to build this temple and finish this wall?" 4 Then, accordingly, we told them the names of the men who were constructing this building. 5 But the eye of their God was upon the elders of the Jews, so that they could not make them cease till a report could go to Darius. Then a written answer was returned concerning this *matter*. 6 This is a copy of the letter that Tattenai sent:

The governor of *the region* beyond the River, and Shethar-Boznai, and his companions, the Persians who *were in the region* beyond the River, to Darius the king.

7 (They sent a letter to him, in which was written thus)

To Darius the king:

All peace.

8 Let it be known to the king that we went into the province of Judea, to the temple of the great God, which is being built with heavy stones, and timber is being laid in the walls; and this work goes on diligently and prospers in their hands.

9 Then we asked those elders, *and* spoke thus to them: "Who commanded you to build this temple and to finish these walls?" 10 We also asked their names to inform you, that we might write the names of the men who *were* chief among them.

11 And thus they returned us an answer, saying: "We are the servants of the God of heaven and earth, and we are rebuilding the temple that was built many years ago, which a great king of Israel built and completed. 12 But because our fathers provoked the God of heaven to wrath, He gave them into the hand of Nebuchadnezzar king of Babylon, the Chaldean, *who* destroyed this temple and carried the people away to Babylon. 13 However, in the first year of Cyrus king of Babylon, King Cyrus issued a decree to build this house of God. 14 Also, the gold and silver articles of the house of God, which Nebuchadnezzar had taken from the temple that *was* in Jerusalem and carried into the temple of Babylon—those King Cyrus took from the temple of Babylon, and they were given to one named Sheshbazzar, whom he had made governor. 15 And he said to him, 'Take these articles; go, carry them to the temple *site* that *is* in Jerusalem, and let the house of God be rebuilt on its former site.' 16 Then the same Sheshbazzar came *and* laid the foundation of the house of God which *is* in Jerusalem; but from that time even until now it has been under construction, and it is not finished."

17 Now therefore, if *it seems* good to the king, let a search be made in the king's treasure house, which *is* there in Babylon, whether it is *so* that a decree was issued by King Cyrus to build this house of God at Jerusalem, and let the king send us his pleasure concerning this *matter*.

6 THEN King Darius issued a decree, and a search was made in the archives, where the treasures were stored in Babylon. 2 And at Achmetha, in the palace that *is* in the province of Media, a scroll was found, and in it a record *was* written thus:

3 In the first year of King Cyrus, King Cyrus issued a decree *concerning* the house of God at Jerusalem: "Let the house be rebuilt, the place where they

offered sacrifices; and let the foundations of it be firmly laid, its height sixty cubits *and* its width sixty cubits, 4 *with* three rows of heavy stones and one row of new timber. Let the expenses be paid from the king's treasury. 5 Also let the gold and silver articles of the house of God, which Nebuchadnezzar took from the temple which *is* in Jerusalem and brought to Babylon, be restored and taken back to the temple which *is* in Jerusalem, *each* to its place; and deposit *them* in the house of God"—

6   Now *therefore,* Tattenai, governor of *the region* beyond the River, and Shethar-Boznai, and your companions the Persians who *are* beyond the River, keep yourselves far from there. 7 Let the work of this house of God alone; let the governor of the Jews and the elders of the Jews build this house of God on its site.

8   Moreover I issue a decree *as to* what you shall do for the elders of these Jews, for the building of this house of God: Let the cost be paid at the king's expense from taxes *on the region* beyond the River; this is to be given immediately to these men, so that they are not hindered. 9 And whatever they need—young bulls, rams, and lambs for the burnt offerings of the God of heaven, wheat, salt, wine, and oil, according to the request of the priests who *are* in Jerusalem—let it be given them day by day without fail, 10 that they may offer sacrifices of sweet aroma to the God of heaven, and pray for the life of the king and his sons.

11   Also I issue a decree that whoever alters this edict, let a timber be pulled from his house and erected, and let him be hanged on it; and let his house be made a refuse heap because of this. 12 And may the God who causes His name to dwell there destroy any king or people who put their hand to alter it, or to destroy this house of God which is in Jerusalem. I Darius issue a decree; let it be done diligently.

13 Then Tattenai, governor of *the region* beyond the River, Shethar-Boznai, and their companions diligently did according to what King Darius had sent. 14 So the elders of the Jews built, and they prospered through the prophesying of Haggai the prophet and Zechariah the son of Iddo. And they built and finished *it,* according to the commandment of the God of Israel, and according to the command of Cyrus, Darius, and Artaxerxes king of Persia. 15 Now the temple was finished on the third day of the month of Adar, which was in the sixth year of the reign of King Darius. 16 Then the children of Israel, the priests and the Levites and the rest of the descendants of the captivity, celebrated the dedication of this house of God with joy. 17 And they offered sacrifices at the dedication of this house of God, one hundred bulls, two hundred rams, four hundred lambs, and as a sin offering for all Israel twelve male goats, according to the number of the tribes of Israel. 18 They assigned the priests to their divisions and the Levites to their divisions, over the service of God in Jerusalem, as it is written in the Book of Moses.

19 And the descendants of the captivity kept the Passover on the fourteenth *day* of the first month. 20 For the priests and the Levites had purified themselves; all of them *were ritually* clean. And they slaughtered the Passover *lambs* for all the descendants of the captivity, for their brethren the priests, and for themselves. 21 Then the children of Israel who had returned from the captivity ate together with all who had separated themselves from the filth of the nations of the land in order to seek the LORD God of Israel. 22 And they kept the Feast of Unleavened Bread seven days with joy; for the LORD made them joyful, and turned the heart of the king of Assyria toward them, to strengthen their hands in the work of the house of God, the God of Israel.

PSALM 87:1–7

1   HIS foundation *is* in the holy mountains.
2   The LORD loves the gates of Zion More than all the dwellings of Jacob.
3   Glorious things are spoken of you, O city of God!   Selah

4   "I will make mention of Rahab and Babylon to those who know Me; Behold, O Philistia and Tyre, with Ethiopia: 'This *one* was born there.' "

5   And of Zion it will be said, "This *one* and that *one* were born in her;

And the Most High Himself shall
establish her."
6 The LORD will record,
When He registers the peoples:
"This *one* was born there."   Selah

7 Both the singers and the players on
instruments *say,*
"All my springs *are* in you."

PROVERBS 21:19, 20

19 BETTER to dwell in the wilderness,
Than with a contentious and angry
woman.

20 *There is* desirable treasure,
And oil in the dwelling of the wise,
But a foolish man squanders it.

ACTS 23:1–15

THEN Paul, looking earnestly at the council, said, "Men *and* brethren, I have lived
in all good conscience before God until this
day." 2 And the high priest Ananias commanded those who stood by him to strike
him on the mouth. 3 Then Paul said to him,
"God will strike you, *you* whitewashed wall!
For you sit to judge me according to the
law, and do you command me to be struck
contrary to the law?"
4 And those who stood by said, "Do you
revile God's high priest?"
5 Then Paul said, "I did not know, brethren, that he was the high priest; for it is
written, 'You shall not speak evil of a ruler
of your people.' "
6 But when Paul perceived that one part
were Sadducees and the other Pharisees,
he cried out in the council, "Men *and* brethren, I am a Pharisee, the son of a Pharisee;

concerning the hope and resurrection of
the dead I am being judged!"
7 And when he had said this, a dissension
arose between the Pharisees and the Sadducees; and the assembly was divided.
8 For Sadducees say that there is no resurrection—and no angel or spirit; but the
Pharisees confess both. 9 Then there arose
a loud outcry. And the scribes of the Pharisees' party arose and protested, saying, "We
find no evil in this man; but if a spirit or
an angel has spoken to him, let us not fight
against God."
10 Now when there arose a great dissension, the commander, fearing lest Paul
might be pulled to pieces by them, commanded the soldiers to go down and take
him by force from among them, and bring
him into the barracks.
11 But the following night the Lord stood
by him and said, "Be of good cheer, Paul;
for as you have testified for Me in Jerusalem,
so you must also bear witness at Rome."

---

*The Christian life is one of incarnate
spiritual pluck.*   (UTMOST)

---

12 And when it was day, some of the Jews
banded together and bound themselves under an oath, saying that they would neither
eat nor drink till they had killed Paul.
13 Now there were more than forty who
had formed this conspiracy. 14 They came
to the chief priests and elders, and said,
"We have bound ourselves under a great
oath that we will eat nothing until we have
killed Paul. 15 Now you, therefore, together
with the council, suggest to the commander
that he be brought down to you tomorrow,
as though you were going to make further
inquiries concerning him; but we are ready
to kill him before he comes near."

◆◆◆

*Reading 204—*Follow Righteousness
Proverbs 21:21

If I try to be right, it is a sure sign I am wrong; the only way to be right
is by stopping the humbug of trying to be and remaining steadfast in faith
in Jesus Christ. "He who practices righteousness is righteous, just as He is
righteous." (GOD'S WORKMANSHIP)
The majority of us know nothing whatever about the righteousness that is
gifted to us in Jesus Christ, we are still trying to bring human nature up to a

pitch it cannot reach, because there is something wrong with human nature. The old Puritanism which we are apt to ridicule did the same service for men that Pharisaism did for Saul, and that Roman Catholicism did for Luther; but nowadays we have no "iron" in us anywhere; we have no idea of righteousness, we do not care whether we are righteous or not. We have not only lost Jesus Christ's idea of righteousness, but we laugh at the Bible idea of righteousness; our god is the conventional righteousness of the society to which we belong.

(GOOD)

EZRA 7:1—8:36

NOW after these things, in the reign of Artaxerxes king of Persia, Ezra the son of Seraiah, the son of Azariah, the son of Hilkiah, 2 the son of Shallum, the son of Zadok, the son of Ahitub, 3 the son of Amariah, the son of Azariah, the son of Meraioth, 4 the son of Zerahiah, the son of Uzzi, the son of Bukki, 5 the son of Abishua, the son of Phinehas, the son of Eleazar, the son of Aaron the chief priest— 6 this Ezra came up from Babylon; and he *was* a skilled scribe in the Law of Moses, which the LORD God of Israel had given. The king granted him all his request, according to the hand of the LORD his God upon him. 7 *Some* of the children of Israel, the priests, the Levites, the singers, the gatekeepers, and the Nethinim came up to Jerusalem in the seventh year of King Artaxerxes. 8 And Ezra came to Jerusalem in the fifth month, which *was* in the seventh year of the king. 9 On the first *day* of the first month he began *his* journey from Babylon, and on the first *day* of the fifth month he came to Jerusalem, according to the good hand of his God upon him. 10 For Ezra had prepared his heart to seek the Law of the LORD, and to do *it,* and to teach statutes and ordinances in Israel.

11 This *is* a copy of the letter that King Artaxerxes gave Ezra the priest, the scribe, expert in the words of the commandments of the LORD, and of His statutes to Israel:

12 Artaxerxes, king of kings,

To Ezra the priest, a scribe of the Law of the God of heaven:

Perfect *peace,* and so forth.

13 I issue a decree that all those of the people of Israel and the priests and Levites in my realm, who volunteer to go up to Jerusalem, may go with you. 14 And whereas you are being sent by the king and his seven counselors to inquire concerning Judah and Jerusalem, with regard to the Law of your God which *is* in your hand; 15 and *whereas you are* to carry the silver and gold which the king and his counselors have freely offered to the God of Israel, whose dwelling *is* in Jerusalem; 16 and *whereas* all the silver and gold that you may find in all the province of Babylon, along with the freewill offering of the people and the priests, *are to be* freely offered for the house of their God in Jerusalem— 17 now therefore, be careful to buy with this money bulls, rams, and lambs, with their grain offerings and their drink offerings, and offer them on the altar of the house of your God in Jerusalem.

18 And whatever seems good to you and your brethren to do with the rest of the silver and the gold, do it according to the will of your God. 19 Also the articles that are given to you for the service of the house of your God, deliver in full before the God of Jerusalem. 20 And whatever more may be needed for the house of your God, which you may have occasion to provide, pay *for it* from the king's treasury.

21 And I, *even* I, Artaxerxes the king, issue a decree to all the treasurers who *are in the region* beyond the River, that whatever Ezra the priest, the scribe of the Law of the God of heaven, may require of you, let it be done diligently, 22 up to one hundred talents of silver, one hundred kors of wheat, one hundred baths of wine, one hundred baths of oil, and salt without prescribed limit. 23 Whatever is commanded by the God of heaven, let it diligently be done for the house of the God of heaven. For why should there be wrath against the realm of the king and his sons?

24 Also we inform you that it shall not be lawful to impose tax, tribute, or custom *on* any of the priests, Levites, singers, gatekeepers, Nethinim, or servants of this house of God. 25 And you, Ezra, according to your God-given wisdom, set magistrates and judges who may judge all the people who *are in the region* beyond the River, all such as know the laws of your God; and teach those who do not know *them*. 26 Whoever will not observe the law of your God and the law of the king, let judgment be executed speedily on him, whether *it be* death, or banishment, or confiscation of goods, or imprisonment.

27 Blessed *be* the LORD God of our fathers, who has put *such a thing* as this in the king's heart, to beautify the house of the LORD which *is* in Jerusalem, 28 and has extended mercy to me before the king and his counselors, and before all the king's mighty princes.

So I was encouraged, as the hand of the LORD my God *was* upon me; and I gathered leading men of Israel to go up with me.

8 THESE *are* the heads of their fathers' houses, and *this is* the genealogy of those who went up with me from Babylon, in the reign of King Artaxerxes: 2 of the sons of Phinehas, Gershom; of the sons of Ithamar, Daniel; of the sons of David, Hattush; 3 of the sons of Shecaniah, of the sons of Parosh, Zechariah; and registered with him *were* one hundred and fifty males; 4 of the sons of Pahath-Moab, Eliehoenai the son of Zerahiah, and with him two hundred males; 5 of the sons of Shechaniah, Ben-Jahaziel, and with him three hundred males; 6 of the sons of Adin, Ebed the son of Jonathan, and with him fifty males; 7 of the sons of Elam, Jeshaiah the son of Athaliah, and with him seventy males; 8 of the sons of Shephatiah, Zebadiah the son of Michael, and with him eighty males; 9 of the sons of Joab, Obadiah the son of Jehiel, and with him two hundred and eighteen males; 10 of the sons of Shelomith, Ben-Josiphiah, and with him one hundred and sixty males; 11 of the sons of Bebai, Zechariah the son of Bebai, and with him twenty-eight males; 12 of the sons of Azgad, Johanan the son of Hakkatan, and with him one hundred and ten males; 13 of the last sons of Adonikam, whose names *are* these—Eliphelet, Jeiel, and Shemaiah—and with them sixty males; 14 also of the sons of Bigvai, Uthai and Zabbud, and with them seventy males.

15 Now I gathered them by the river that flows to Ahava, and we camped there three days. And I looked among the people and the priests, and found none of the sons of Levi there. 16 Then I sent for Eliezer, Ariel, Shemaiah, Elnathan, Jarib, Elnathan, Nathan, Zechariah, and Meshullam, leaders; also for Joiarib and Elnathan, men of understanding. 17 And I gave them a command for Iddo the chief man at the place Casiphia, and I told them what they should say to Iddo *and* his brethren the Nethinim at the place Casiphia—that they should bring us servants for the house of our God. 18 Then, by the good hand of our God upon us, they brought us a man of understanding, of the sons of Mahli the son of Levi, the son of Israel, namely Sherebiah, with his sons and brothers, eighteen men; 19 and Hashabiah, and with him Jeshaiah of the sons of Merari, his brothers and their sons, twenty men; 20 also of the Nethinim, whom David and the leaders had appointed for the service of the Levites, two hundred and twenty Nethinim. All of them were designated by name.

21 Then I proclaimed a fast there at the river of Ahava, that we might humble ourselves before our God, to seek from Him the right way for us and our little ones and all our possessions. 22 For I was ashamed to request of the king an escort of soldiers and horsemen to help us against the enemy on the road, because we had spoken to the king, saying, "The hand of our God *is* upon all those for good who seek Him, but His power and His wrath *are* against all those who forsake Him." 23 So we fasted and entreated our God for this, and He answered our prayer.

---

*O*ur Lord in His teaching always made prayer, not preparation for work, but the work.   (ASK)

---

24 And I separated twelve of the leaders of the priests—Sherebiah, Hashabiah, and ten of their brethren with them— 25 and weighed out to them the silver, the gold, and the articles, the offering for the house of our God which the king and his counselors and his princes, and all Israel *who were* present, had offered. 26 I weighed into their hand six hundred and fifty talents of silver, silver articles *weighing* one hundred talents, one hundred talents of gold, 27 twenty gold basins *worth* a thousand drachmas, and two vessels of fine polished bronze, precious as

gold. 28 And I said to them, "You *are* holy to the LORD; the articles *are* holy also; and the silver and the gold *are* a freewill offering to the LORD God of your fathers. 29 Watch and keep *them* until you weigh *them* before the leaders of the priests and the Levites and heads of the fathers' *houses* of Israel in Jerusalem, *in* the chambers of the house of the LORD." 30 So the priests and the Levites received the silver and the gold and the articles by weight, to bring *them* to Jerusalem to the house of our God.

31 Then we departed from the river of Ahava on the twelfth *day* of the first month, to go to Jerusalem. And the hand of our God was upon us, and He delivered us from the hand of the enemy and from ambush along the road. 32 So we came to Jerusalem, and stayed there three days.

33 Now on the fourth day the silver and the gold and the articles were weighed in the house of our God by the hand of Meremoth the son of Uriah the priest, and with him *was* Eleazar the son of Phinehas; with them *were* the Levites, Jozabad the son of Jeshua and Noadiah the son of Binnui, 34 with the number *and* weight of everything. All the weight was written down at that time.

35 The children of those who had been carried away captive, who had come from the captivity, offered burnt offerings to the God of Israel: twelve bulls for all Israel, ninety-six rams, seventy-seven lambs, and twelve male goats *as* a sin offering. All *this was* a burnt offering to the LORD.

36 And they delivered the king's orders to the king's satraps and the governors *in the region* beyond the River. So they gave support to the people and the house of God.

PSALM 88:1–5

1   O LORD, God of my salvation,
    I have cried out day and night before
        You.
2   Let my prayer come before You;
    Incline Your ear to my cry.

Get your prayers inspired by God the Holy Ghost.   (SERMON MT.)

---

3   For my soul is full of troubles,
    And my life draws near to the grave.
4   I am counted with those who go down
        to the pit;
    I am like a man *who has* no strength,
5   Adrift among the dead,

Like the slain who lie in the grave,
Whom You remember no more,
And who are cut off from Your hand.

PROVERBS 21:21, 22

21 HE who follows righteousness and
        mercy
    Finds life, righteousness and honor.

22 A wise *man* scales the city of the mighty,
    And brings down the trusted
        stronghold.

ACTS 23:16–35

SO when Paul's sister's son heard of their ambush, he went and entered the barracks and told Paul. 17 Then Paul called one of the centurions to *him* and said, "Take this young man to the commander, for he has something to tell him." 18 So he took him and brought *him* to the commander and said, "Paul the prisoner called me to *him* and asked *me* to bring this young man to you. He has something to say to you."

19 Then the commander took him by the hand, went aside, and asked privately, "What is it that you have to tell me?"

20 And he said, "The Jews have agreed to ask that you bring Paul down to the council tomorrow, as though they were going to inquire more fully about him. 21 But do not yield to them, for more than forty of them lie in wait for him, men who have bound themselves by an oath that they will neither eat nor drink till they have killed him; and now they are ready, waiting for the promise from you."

22 So the commander let the young man depart, and commanded *him*, "Tell no one that you have revealed these things to me."

23 And he called for two centurions, saying, "Prepare two hundred soldiers, seventy horsemen, and two hundred spearmen to go to Caesarea at the third hour of the night; 24 and provide mounts to set Paul on, and bring *him* safely to Felix the governor." 25 He wrote a letter in the following manner:

26 Claudius Lysias,

    To the most excellent governor Felix:

    Greetings.

27 This man was seized by the Jews and
    was about to be killed by them.
    Coming with the troops I rescued
    him, having learned that he was a

Roman. 28 And when I wanted to know the reason they accused him, I brought him before their council. 29 I found out that he was accused concerning questions of their law, but had nothing charged against him deserving of death or chains. 30 And when it was told me that the Jews lay in wait for the man, I sent him immediately to you, and also commanded his accusers to state before you the charges against him.

Farewell.

31 Then the soldiers, as they were commanded, took Paul and brought *him* by night to Antipatris. 32 The next day they left the horsemen to go on with him, and returned to the barracks. 33 When they came to Caesarea and had delivered the letter to the governor, they also presented Paul to him. 34 And when the governor had read *it,* he asked what province he was from. And when he understood that *he was* from Cilicia, 35 he said, "I will hear you when your accusers also have come." And he commanded him to be kept in Herod's Praetorium.

$$\blacktriangleright\blacktriangleright\blacktriangleright\blacktriangleright$$

Reading 205—Keep Inner Vision Clear
Acts 24:16

Conscience is that faculty in me which attaches itself to the highest that I know, and tells me what the highest I know demands that I do. It is the eye of the soul which looks out either towards God or towards what it regards as the highest, and therefore conscience records differently in different people. If I am in the habit of steadily facing myself with God, my conscience will always introduce God's perfect law and indicate what I should do. The point is, will I obey? I have to make an effort to keep my conscience so sensitive that I walk without offense. I should be living in such perfect sympathy with God's Son, that in every circumstance the spirit of my mind is renewed, and I "make out" at once "what *is* that good and acceptable and perfect will of God."

God always educates us down to the scruple. Is my ear so keen to hear the tiniest whisper of the Spirit that I know what I should do? "Do not grieve the Holy Spirit." He does not come with a voice like thunder; His voice is so gentle that it is easy to ignore it. The one thing that keeps the conscience sensitive to Him is the continual habit of being open to God on the inside. When there is any debate, quit. "Why shouldn't I do this?" You are on the wrong track. There is no debate possible when conscience speaks. At your peril, you allow one thing to obscure your inner communion with God. Drop it, whatever it is, and see that you keep your inner vision clear.   (*UTMOST*)

EZRA 9:1—10:44

WHEN these things were done, the leaders came to me, saying, "The people of Israel and the priests and the Levites have not separated themselves from the peoples of the lands, with respect to the abominations of the Canaanites, the Hittites, the Perizzites, the Jebusites, the Ammonites, the Moabites, the Egyptians, and the Amorites. 2 For they have taken some of their daughters *as wives* for themselves and their sons, so that the holy seed is mixed with the peoples of *those* lands. Indeed, the hand of the leaders and rulers has been foremost in this trespass." 3 So when I heard this thing, I tore my garment and my robe, and plucked out some of the hair of my head and beard, and sat down astonished. 4 Then everyone who trembled at the words of the God of Israel assembled to me, because of the transgression of those who had been carried away captive, and I sat astonished until the evening sacrifice.

5 At the evening sacrifice I arose from my fasting; and having torn my garment and my robe, I fell on my knees and spread out my hands to the LORD my God. 6 And I said: "O my God, I am too ashamed and humiliated to lift up my face to You, my God; for our iniquities have risen higher than *our* heads, and our guilt has grown up to the heavens. 7 Since the days of our fathers to this day we *have been* very guilty, and for our iniquities we, our kings, *and* our priests have been delivered into the hand of the kings of the lands, to the sword, to captivity, to plunder, and to humiliation, as *it is* this day. 8 And now for a little while grace has been *shown* from the LORD our God, to leave us a remnant to escape, and to give us a peg in His holy place, that our God may enlighten our eyes and give us a measure of revival in our bondage.

God grant we may not hinder those who are battling their way slowly into the light. (WORKMEN)

---

9 For we *were* slaves. Yet our God did not forsake us in our bondage; but He extended mercy to us in the sight of the kings of Persia, to revive us, to repair the house of our God, to rebuild its ruins, and to give us a wall in Judah and Jerusalem. 10 And now, O our God, what shall we say after this? For we have forsaken Your commandments, 11 which You commanded by Your servants the prophets, saying, 'The land which you are entering to possess is an unclean land, with the uncleanness of the peoples of the lands, with their abominations which have filled it from one end to another with their impurity. 12 Now therefore, do not give your daughters as wives for their sons, nor take their daughters to your sons; and never seek their peace or prosperity, that you may be strong and eat the good of the land, and leave *it* as an inheritance to your children forever.' 13 And after all that has come upon us for our evil deeds and for our great guilt, since You our God have punished us less than our iniquities *deserve,* and have given us *such* deliverance as this, 14 should we again break Your commandments, and join in marriage with the people *committing* these abominations? Would You not be angry with us until You had consumed *us,* so that *there would be* no remnant or survivor? 15 O LORD God of Israel, You *are* righteous, for we are left as a remnant, as *it is* this day. Here we

are before You, in our guilt, though no one can stand before You because of this!"

10 NOW while Ezra was praying, and while he was confessing, weeping, and bowing down before the house of God, a very large assembly of men, women, and children gathered to him from Israel; for the people wept very bitterly. 2 And Shechaniah the son of Jehiel, *one* of the sons of Elam, spoke up and said to Ezra, "We have trespassed against our God, and have taken pagan wives from the peoples of the land; yet now there is hope in Israel in spite of this. 3 Now therefore, let us make a covenant with our God to put away all these wives and those who have been born to them, according to the advice of my master and of those who tremble at the commandment of our God; and let it be done according to the law. 4 Arise, for *this* matter *is* your *responsibility.* We also *are* with you. Be of good courage, and do *it.*"

5 Then Ezra arose, and made the leaders of the priests, the Levites, and all Israel swear an oath that they would do according to this word. So they swore an oath. 6 Then Ezra rose up from before the house of God, and went into the chamber of Jehohanan the son of Eliashib; and *when* he came there, he ate no bread and drank no water, for he mourned because of the guilt of those from the captivity.

7 And they issued a proclamation throughout Judah and Jerusalem to all the descendants of the captivity, that they must gather at Jerusalem, 8 and that whoever would not come within three days, according to the instructions of the leaders and elders, all his property would be confiscated, and he himself would be separated from the assembly of those from the captivity.

9 So all the men of Judah and Benjamin gathered at Jerusalem within three days. It *was* the ninth month, on the twentieth of the month; and all the people sat in the open square of the house of God, trembling because of *this* matter and because of heavy rain. 10 Then Ezra the priest stood up and said to them, "You have transgressed and have taken pagan wives, adding to the guilt of Israel. 11 Now therefore, make confession to the LORD God of your fathers, and do His will; separate yourselves from the peoples of the land, and from the pagan wives."

12 Then all the assembly answered and said with a loud voice, "Yes! As you have said, so we must do. 13 But *there are* many people; *it is* the season for heavy rain, and we are not able to stand outside. Nor *is*

this the work of one or two days, for *there are* many of us who have transgressed in this matter. 14 Please, let the leaders of our entire assembly stand; and let all those in our cities who have taken pagan wives come at appointed times, together with the elders and judges of their cities, until the fierce wrath of our God is turned away from us in this matter." 15 Only Jonathan the son of Asahel and Jahaziah the son of Tikvah opposed this, and Meshullam and Shabbethai the Levite gave them support.

16 Then the descendants of the captivity did so. And Ezra the priest, *with* certain heads of the fathers' *households,* were set apart by the fathers' *households,* each of them by name; and they sat down on the first day of the tenth month to examine the matter. 17 By the first day of the first month they finished *questioning* all the men who had taken pagan wives.

18 And among the sons of the priests who had taken pagan wives *the following* were found of the sons of Jeshua the son of Jozadak, and his brothers: Maaseiah, Eliezer, Jarib, and Gedaliah. 19 And they gave their promise that they would put away their wives; and *being* guilty, *they presented* a ram of the flock as their trespass offering.

20 Also of the sons of Immer: Hanani and Zebadiah; 21 of the sons of Harim: Maaseiah, Elijah, Shemaiah, Jehiel, and Uzziah; 22 of the sons of Pashhur: Elioenai, Maaseiah, Ishmael, Nethanel, Jozabad, and Elasah.

23 Also of the Levites: Jozabad, Shimei, Kelaiah (the same *is* Kelita), Pethahiah, Judah, and Eliezer.

24 Also of the singers: Eliashib; and of the gatekeepers: Shallum, Telem, and Uri.

25 And others of Israel: of the sons of Parosh: Ramiah, Jeziah, Malchiah, Mijamin, Eleazar, Malchijah, and Benaiah; 26 of the sons of Elam: Mattaniah, Zechariah, Jehiel, Abdi, Jeremoth, and Eliah; 27 of the sons of Zattu: Elioenai, Eliashib, Mattaniah, Jeremoth, Zabad, and Aziza; 28 of the sons of Bebai: Jehohanan, Hananiah, Zabbai, *and* Athlai; 29 of the sons of Bani: Meshullam, Malluch, Adaiah, Jashub, Sheal, *and* Ramoth; 30 of the sons of Pahath-Moab: Adna, Chelal, Benaiah, Maaseiah, Mattaniah, Bezalel, Binnui, and Manasseh; 31 *of* the sons of Harim: Eliezer, Ishijah, Malchijah, Shemaiah, Shimeon, 32 Benjamin, Malluch, *and* Shemariah; 33 of the sons of Hashum: Mattenai, Mattattah, Zabad, Eliphelet, Jeremai, Manasseh, *and* Shimei; 34 of the sons of Bani: Maadai, Amram, Uel, 35 Benaiah, Bedeiah, Cheluh, 36 Vaniah, Meremoth, Eliashib, 37 Mattaniah, Mattenai, Jaasai, 38 Bani, Binnui, Shimei, 39 Shelemiah, Nathan, Adaiah, 40 Machnadebai, Shashai, Sharai, 41 Azarel, Shelemiah, Shemariah, 42 Shallum, Amariah, *and* Joseph; 43 of the sons of Nebo: Jeiel, Mattithiah, Zabad, Zebina, Jaddai, Joel, *and* Benaiah.

44 All these had taken pagan wives, and *some* of them had wives *by whom* they had children.

PSALM 88:6–10

6   YOU have laid me in the lowest pit,
    In darkness, in the depths.
7   Your wrath lies heavy upon me,
    And You have afflicted *me* with all Your
      waves.   Selah
8   You have put away my acquaintances
      far from me;
    You have made me an abomination to
      them;
    I am shut up, and I cannot get out;
9   My eye wastes away because of
      affliction.

    LORD, I have called daily upon You;
    I have stretched out my hands to You.
10   Will You work wonders for the dead?
    Shall the dead arise *and* praise You?
                      Selah

PROVERBS 21:23, 24

23   WHOEVER guards his mouth and
      tongue
    Keeps his soul from troubles.

24   A proud *and* haughty *man*—
    "Scoffer" *is* his name;
    He acts with arrogant pride.

ACTS 24:1–27

NOW after five days Ananias the high priest came down with the elders and a certain orator *named* Tertullus. These gave evidence to the governor against Paul.

2 And when he was called upon, Tertullus began his accusation, saying: "Seeing that through you we enjoy great peace, and prosperity is being brought to this nation by your foresight, 3 we accept *it* always and in all places, most noble Felix, with all thankfulness. 4 Nevertheless, not to be tedious to you any further, I beg you to hear, by your courtesy, a few words from us. 5 For we have found this man a plague, a

creator of dissension among all the Jews throughout the world, and a ringleader of the sect of the Nazarenes. 6 He even tried to profane the temple, and we seized him, and wanted to judge him according to our law. 7 But the commander Lysias came by and with great violence took *him* out of our hands, 8 commanding his accusers to come to you. By examining him yourself you may ascertain all these things of which we accuse him." 9 And the Jews also assented, maintaining that these things were so.

10 Then Paul, after the governor had nodded to him to speak, answered: "Inasmuch as I know that you have been for many years a judge of this nation, I do the more cheerfully answer for myself, 11 because you may ascertain that it is no more than twelve days since I went up to Jerusalem to worship. 12 And they neither found me in the temple disputing with anyone nor inciting the crowd, either in the synagogues or in the city. 13 Nor can they prove the things of which they now accuse me. 14 But this I confess to you, that according to the Way which they call a sect, so I worship the God of my fathers, believing all things which are written in the Law and in the Prophets. 15 I have hope in God, which they themselves also accept, that there will be a resurrection of *the* dead, both of *the* just and *the* unjust. 16 This *being* so, I myself always strive to have a conscience without offense toward God and men.

17 "Now after many years I came to bring alms and offerings to my nation, 18 in the midst of which some Jews from Asia found me purified in the temple, neither with a mob nor with tumult. 19 They ought to

> *When a man gets rightly adjusted to God his conscience staggers him.* (SHAD. AGONY)

have been here before you to object if they had anything against me. 20 Or else let those who are *here* themselves say if they found any wrongdoing in me while I stood before the council, 21 unless *it is* for this one statement which I cried out, standing among them, 'Concerning the resurrection of the dead I am being judged by you this day.'"

22 But when Felix heard these things, having more accurate knowledge of *the* Way, he adjourned the proceedings and said, "When Lysias the commander comes down, I will make a decision on your case." 23 So he commanded the centurion to keep Paul and to let *him* have liberty, and told him not to forbid any of his friends to provide for or visit him.

24 And after some days, when Felix came with his wife Drusilla, who was Jewish, he sent for Paul and heard him concerning the faith in Christ. 25 Now as he reasoned about righteousness, self-control, and the judgment to come, Felix was afraid and answered, "Go away for now; when I have a convenient time I will call for you." 26 Meanwhile he also hoped that money would be given him by Paul, that he might release him. Therefore he sent for him more often and conversed with him.

27 But after two years Porcius Festus succeeded Felix; and Felix, wanting to do the Jews a favor, left Paul bound.

◆◆◆◆

Reading 206—Personal Responsibility
Acts 25:11

The apostle Paul, who said he had "the mind of Christ," wrote to the Corinthians: "Why do you not rather accept wrong? Why do you not rather *let yourselves* be cheated?" (1 Cor. 6:7); and yet when being tried himself, he said, "I appeal to Caesar" (Acts 25:11).

God Himself, our Lord Jesus Christ, and the saints, are examples of contradiction judged by every standard saving one, namely, the standard of personal responsibility to God on the basis of personal character.

In testing circumstances saints decide differently—may all the different decisions be correct? Unquestionably they may, for the decisions are made on the basis of pesonal character in its responsibility to God. The blunder of the saint lies in saying, "Because I decide thus in this crisis, therefore is the rule for all." Nonsense! God is Sovereign and His ways are discernible according to the attainment of the particular character. . . . No saint knows what he will do in circumstances he has never been in. "I would have you without carefulness," says the apostle Paul. A saint is a creature of vast possibilities, knit into shape by the ruling personality of God. (CHR. DISCPL.)

NEHEMIAH 1:1—2:20

THE words of Nehemiah the son of Hachaliah.

It came to pass in the month of Chislev, *in* the twentieth year, as I was in Shushan the citadel, 2 that Hanani one of my brethren came with men from Judah; and I asked them concerning the Jews who had escaped, who had survived the captivity, and concerning Jerusalem. 3 And they said to me, "The survivors who are left from the captivity in the province *are* there in great distress and reproach. The wall of Jerusalem *is* also broken down, and its gates *are* burned with fire."

4 So it was, when I heard these words, that I sat down and wept, and mourned *for many* days; I was fasting and praying before the God of heaven.

5 And I said: "I pray, LORD God of heaven, O great and awesome God, *You* who keep *Your* covenant and mercy with those who love You and observe Your commandments, 6 please let Your ear be attentive and Your eyes open, that You may hear the prayer of Your servant which I pray before You now, day and night, for the children of Israel Your servants, and confess the sins of the children of Israel which we have sinned against You. Both my father's house and I have sinned. 7 We have acted very corruptly against You, and have not kept the commandments, the statutes, nor the ordinances which You commanded Your servant Moses. 8 Remember, I pray, the word that You commanded Your servant Moses, saying, '*If* you are unfaithful, I will scatter you among the nations; 9 but *if* you return to Me, and keep My commandments and do them, though some of you were cast out to the farthest part of the heavens, *yet* I will gather them from there, and bring them to the place which I have chosen as a dwelling for My name.' 10 Now these *are* Your servants and Your people, whom You have redeemed by Your great power, and by Your strong hand. 11 O Lord, I pray, please let Your ear be attentive to the prayer of Your servant, and to the prayer of Your servants who desire to fear Your name; and let Your servant prosper this day, I pray, and grant him mercy in the sight of this man."

For I was the king's cupbearer.

2 AND it came to pass in the month of Nisan, in the twentieth year of King Artaxerxes, *when* wine *was* before him, that I took the wine and gave it to the king. Now I had never been sad in his presence before. 2 Therefore the king said to me, "Why *is* your face sad, since you *are* not sick? This *is* nothing but sorrow of heart."

So I became dreadfully afraid, 3 and said to the king, "May the king live forever! Why should my face not be sad, when the city, the place of my fathers' tombs, *lies* waste, and its gates are burned with fire?"

4 Then the king said to me, "What do you request?"

So I prayed to the God of heaven. 5 And I said to the king, "If it pleases the

---

We are uncertain of the next step, but we are certain of God. (UTMOST)

---

king, and if your servant has found favor in your sight, I ask that you send me to Judah, to the city of my fathers' tombs, that I may rebuild it."

6 Then the king said to me (the queen also sitting beside him), "How long will your journey be? And when will you return?" So it pleased the king to send me; and I set him a time.

7 Furthermore I said to the king, "If it pleases the king, let letters be given to me for the governors *of the region* beyond the River, that they must permit me to pass through till I come to Judah, 8 and a letter to Asaph the keeper of the king's forest, that he must give me timber to make beams for the gates of the citadel which *pertains* to the temple, for the city wall, and for the house that I will occupy." And the king granted *them* to me according to the good hand of my God upon me.

9 Then I went to the governors *in the*

region beyond the River, and gave them the king's letters. Now the king had sent captains of the army and horsemen with me. 10 When Sanballat the Horonite and Tobiah the Ammonite official heard *of it,* they were deeply disturbed that a man had come to seek the well-being of the children of Israel.

11 So I came to Jerusalem and was there three days. 12 Then I arose in the night, I and a few men with me; I told no one what my God had put in my heart to do at Jerusalem; nor was there any animal with me, except the one on which I rode. 13 And I went out by night through the Valley Gate to the Serpent Well and the Refuse Gate, and viewed the walls of Jerusalem which were broken down and its gates which were burned with fire. 14 Then I went on to the Fountain Gate and to the King's Pool, but *there was* no room for the animal under me to pass. 15 So I went up in the night by the valley, and viewed the wall; then I turned back and entered by the Valley Gate, and so returned. 16 And the officials did not know where I had gone or what I had done; I had not yet told the Jews, the priests, the nobles, the officials, or the others who did the work.

17 Then I said to them, "You see the distress that we *are* in, how Jerusalem *lies* waste, and its gates are burned with fire. Come and let us build the wall of Jerusalem, that we may no longer be a reproach." 18 And I told them of the hand of my God which had been good upon me, and also of the king's words that he had spoken to me.

So they said, "Let us rise up and build." Then they set their hands to *this* good *work.*

19 But when Sanballat the Horonite, Tobiah the Ammonite official, and Geshem the Arab heard *of it,* they laughed at us and despised us, and said, "What *is* this thing that you are doing? Will you rebel against the king?"

20 So I answered them, and said to them, "The God of heaven Himself will prosper us; therefore we His servants will arise and build, but you have no heritage or right or memorial in Jerusalem."

PSALM 88:11–18

11 SHALL Your lovingkindness be
    declared in the grave?
    Or Your faithfulness in the place of
    destruction?
12 Shall Your wonders be known in the
    dark?

And Your righteousness in the land of
    forgetfulness?
13 But to You I have cried out, O LORD,
    And in the morning my prayer comes
    before You.
14 LORD, why do You cast off my soul?
    Why do You hide Your face from
    me?
15 I *have been* afflicted and ready to die
    from *my* youth;
    I suffer Your terrors;
    I am distraught.
16 Your fierce wrath has gone over me;
    Your terrors have cut me off.
17 They came around me all day long like
    water;
    They engulfed me altogether.
18 Loved one and friend You have put
    far from me,
    And my acquaintances into darkness.

PROVERBS 21:25, 26

25 THE desire of the lazy *man* kills him,
    For his hands refuse to labor.

Running all through [*the Bible is*]
*the awful curse on laziness and
spiritual sloth.*   (WORKMEN)

---

26 He covets greedily all day long,
    But the righteous gives and does not
    spare.

ACTS 25:1–27

NOW when Festus had come to the province, after three days he went up from Caesarea to Jerusalem. 2 Then the high priest and the chief men of the Jews informed him against Paul; and they petitioned him, 3 asking a favor against him, that he would summon him to Jerusalem— while *they* lay in ambush along the road to kill him. 4 But Festus answered that Paul should be kept at Caesarea, and that he himself was going *there* shortly. 5 "Therefore," he said, "let those who have authority among you go down with *me* and accuse this man, to see if there is any fault in him."

6 And when he had remained among them more than ten days, he went down to Caesarea. And the next day, sitting on the judgment seat, he commanded Paul to

be brought. 7 When he had come, the Jews who had come down from Jerusalem stood about and laid many serious complaints against Paul, which they could not prove, 8 while he answered for himself, "Neither against the law of the Jews, nor against the temple, nor against Caesar have I offended in anything at all."

9 But Festus, wanting to do the Jews a favor, answered Paul and said, "Are you willing to go up to Jerusalem and there be judged before me concerning these things?"

10 So Paul said, "I stand at Caesar's judgment seat, where I ought to be judged. To the Jews I have done no wrong, as you very well know. 11 For if I am an offender, or have committed anything deserving of death, I do not object to dying; but if there is nothing in these things of which these men accuse me, no one can deliver me to them. I appeal to Caesar."

12 Then Festus, when he had conferred with the council, answered, "You have appealed to Caesar? To Caesar you shall go!"

13 And after some days King Agrippa and Bernice came to Caesarea to greet Festus. 14 When they had been there many days, Festus laid Paul's case before the king, saying: "There is a certain man left a prisoner by Felix, 15 about whom the chief priests and the elders of the Jews informed *me*, when I was in Jerusalem, asking for a judgment against him. 16 To them I answered, 'It is not the custom of the Romans to deliver any man to destruction before the accused meets the accusers face to face, and has opportunity to answer for himself concerning the charge against him.' 17 Therefore when they had come together, without any delay, the next day I sat on the judgment seat and commanded the man to be brought in. 18 When the accusers stood up, they brought no accusation against him of such things as I supposed, 19 but had some questions against him about their own religion and about a certain Jesus, who had died, whom Paul affirmed to be alive. 20 And because I was uncertain of such questions, I asked whether he was willing to go to Jerusalem and there be judged concerning these matters. 21 But when Paul appealed to be reserved for the decision of Augustus, I commanded him to be kept till I could send him to Caesar."

22 Then Agrippa said to Festus, "I also would like to hear the man myself."

"Tomorrow," he said, "you shall hear him."

23 So the next day, when Agrippa and Bernice had come with great pomp, and had entered the auditorium with the commanders and the prominent men of the city, at Festus' command Paul was brought in. 24 And Festus said: "King Agrippa and all the men who are here present with us, you see this man about whom the whole assembly of the Jews petitioned me, both at Jerusalem and here, crying out that he was not fit to live any longer. 25 But when I found that he had committed nothing deserving of death, and that he himself had appealed to Augustus, I decided to send him. 26 I have nothing certain to write to my lord concerning him. Therefore I have brought him out before you, and especially before you, King Agrippa, so that after the examination has taken place I may have something to write. 27 For it seems to me unreasonable to send a prisoner and not to specify the charges against him."

◆◆◆

Reading 207—The Shape of the Vision
Acts 26:19

Thank God for the sight of all you have never yet been. The vision is not an ecstasy or a dream, but a perfect understanding of what God wants, it is the divine light making manifest the calling of God. You may call the vision an emotion or a desire, but it is something that absorbs you. Learn to thank God for making known His demands. You have had the vision, but you are not there yet by any means. You have seen what God wants you to be but what you are not yet. Are you prepared to have this "iron dug from central gloom" battered into "shape and use"? "Battering" conveys the idea of a blacksmith putting good metal into right useful shape. The batterings of God come in commonplace days and commonplace ways. God is using the anvil to bring us into the shape of the vision. The length of time it takes God to do it depends upon us. If we prefer to loll on the mount of transfiguration, to live on the memory of the vision, we are of no use to live with the ordinary stuff of which human life is made up. We have not to live always in ecstasy and conscious contemplation of God, but to live in reliance on what we saw in the vision when we are in the midst of actualities. It is when we are going through the valley to prove whether we will be the "choice" ones, that most of us turn tail; we are not prepared for the blows which must come if we are going to be turned into the shape of the vision.   (*Send I You*)

NEHEMIAH 3:1—5:19

THEN Eliashib the high priest rose up with his brethren the priests and built the Sheep Gate; they consecrated it and hung its doors. They built as far as the Tower of the Hundred, *and* consecrated it, then as far as the Tower of Hananel. 2 Next to *Eliashib* the men of Jericho built. And next to them Zaccur the son of Imri built.

3 Also the sons of Hassenaah built the Fish Gate; they laid its beams and hung its doors with its bolts and bars. 4 And next to them Meremoth the son of Urijah, the son of Koz, made repairs. Next to them Meshullam the son of Berechiah, the son of Meshezabel, made repairs. Next to them Zadok the son of Baana made repairs. 5 Next to them the Tekoites made repairs; but their nobles did not put their shoulders to the work of their Lord.

6 Moreover Jehoiada the son of Paseah and Meshullam the son of Besodeiah repaired the Old Gate; they laid its beams and hung its doors, with its bolts and bars. 7 And next to them Melatiah the Gibeonite, Jadon the Meronothite, the men of Gibeon and Mizpah, repaired the residence of the governor *of the region* beyond the River. 8 Next to him Uzziel the son of Harhaiah, one of the goldsmiths, made repairs. Also next to him Hananiah, one of the perfumers, made repairs; and they fortified Jerusalem as far as the Broad Wall. 9 And next to them Rephaiah the son of Hur, leader of half the district of Jerusalem, made repairs. 10 Next to them Jedaiah the son of Harumaph made repairs in front of his house. And next to him Hattush the son of Hashabniah made repairs.

11 Malchijah the son of Harim and Hashub the son of Pahath-Moab repaired another section, as well as the Tower of the Ovens. 12 And next to him was Shallum the son of Hallohesh, leader of half the

district of Jerusalem; he and his daughters made repairs.

13 Hanun and the inhabitants of Zanoah repaired the Valley Gate. They built it, hung its doors with its bolts and bars, and *repaired* a thousand cubits of the wall as far as the Refuse Gate.

14 Malchijah the son of Rechab, leader of the district of Beth Haccerem, repaired the Refuse Gate; he built it and hung its doors with its bolts and bars.

15 Shallun the son of Col-Hozeh, leader of the district of Mizpah, repaired the Fountain Gate; he built it, covered it, hung its doors with its bolts and bars, and repaired the wall of the Pool of Shelah by the King's Garden, as far as the stairs that go down from the City of David. 16 After him Nehemiah the son of Azbuk, leader of half the district of Beth Zur, made repairs as far as *the place* in front of the tombs of David, to the man-made pool, and as far as the House of the Mighty.

17 After him the Levites, *under* Rehum the son of Bani, made repairs. Next to him Hashabiah, leader of half the district of Keilah, made repairs for his district. 18 After him their brethren, *under* Bavai the son of Henadad, leader of the *other* half of the district of Keilah, made repairs. 19 And next to him Ezer the son of Jeshua, the leader of Mizpah, repaired another section in front of the Ascent to the Armory at the buttress. 20 After him Baruch the son of Zabbai carefully repaired the other section, from the buttress to the door of the house of Eliashib the high priest. 21 After him Meremoth the son of Urijah, the son of Koz, repaired another section, from the door of the house of Eliashib to the end of the house of Eliashib.

22 And after him the priests, the men of the plain, made repairs. 23 After him Benjamin and Hasshub made repairs opposite their house. After them Azariah the son of Maaseiah, the son of Ananiah, made re-

pairs by his house. 24 After him Binnui the son of Henadad repaired another section, from the house of Azariah to the buttress, even as far as the corner. 25 Palal the son of Uzai *made repairs* opposite the buttress, and on the tower which projects from the king's upper house that *was* by the court of the prison. After him Pedaiah the son of Parosh *made repairs.*

26 Moreover the Nethinim who dwelt in Ophel *made repairs* as far as *the place* in front of the Water Gate toward the east, and on the projecting tower. 27 After them the Tekoites repaired another section, next to the great projecting tower, and as far as the wall of Ophel.

28 Beyond the Horse Gate the priests made repairs, each in front of his *own* house. 29 After them Zadok the son of Immer made repairs in front of his *own* house. After him Shemaiah the son of Shechaniah, the keeper of the East Gate, made repairs. 30 After him Hananiah the son of Shelemiah, and Hanun, the sixth son of Zalaph, repaired another section. After him Meshullam the son of Berechiah made repairs in front of his dwelling. 31 After him Malchijah, one of the goldsmiths, made repairs as far as the house of the Nethinim and of the merchants, in front of the Miphkad Gate, and as far as the upper room at the corner. 32 And between the upper room at the corner, as far as the Sheep Gate, the goldsmiths and the merchants made repairs.

4 BUT it so happened, when Sanballat heard that we were rebuilding the wall, that he was furious and very indignant, and mocked the Jews. 2 And he spoke before his brethren and the army of Samaria, and said, "What are these feeble Jews doing? Will they fortify themselves? Will they offer sacrifices? Will they complete it in a day? Will they revive the stones from the heaps of rubbish—*stones* that are burned?"

3 Now Tobiah the Ammonite *was* beside him, and he said, "Whatever they build, if even a fox goes up *on it,* he will break down their stone wall."

4 Hear, O our God, for we are despised; turn their reproach on their own heads, and give them as plunder to a land of captivity! 5 Do not cover their iniquity, and do not let their sin be blotted out from before You; for they have provoked *You* to anger before the builders.

6 So we built the wall, and the entire wall was joined together up to half its *height,* for the people had a mind to work.

Prayer imparts the power to walk and not faint. (ASK)

---

7 Now it happened, when Sanballat, Tobiah, the Arabs, the Ammonites, and the Ashdodites heard that the walls of Jerusalem were being restored and the gaps were beginning to be closed, that they became very angry, 8 and all of them conspired together to come *and* attack Jerusalem and create confusion. 9 Nevertheless we made our prayer to our God, and because of them we set a watch against them day and night.

10 Then Judah said, "The strength of the laborers is failing, and *there is* so much rubbish that we are not able to build the wall."

11 And our adversaries said, "They will neither know nor see anything, till we come into their midst and kill them and cause the work to cease."

12 So it was, when the Jews who dwelt near them came, that they told us ten times, "From whatever place you turn, *they will be* upon us."

13 Therefore I positioned *men* behind the lower parts of the wall, at the openings; and I set the people according to their families, with their swords, their spears, and their bows. 14 And I looked, and arose and said to the nobles, to the leaders, and to the rest of the people, "Do not be afraid of them. Remember the Lord, great and awesome, and fight for your brethren, your sons, your daughters, your wives, and your houses."

15 And it happened, when our enemies heard that it was known to us, and *that* God had brought their plot to nothing, that all of us returned to the wall, everyone to his work. 16 So it was, from that time on, *that* half of my servants worked at construction, while the other half held the spears, the shields, the bows, and *wore* armor; and the leaders *were* behind all the house of Judah. 17 Those who built on the wall, and those who carried burdens, loaded themselves so that with one hand they worked at construction, and with the other held a weapon. 18 Every one of the builders had his sword girded at his side as he built. And the one who sounded the trumpet *was* beside me.

19 Then I said to the nobles, the rulers, and the rest of the people, "The work *is* great and extensive, and we are separated far from one another on the wall. 20 Wherever you hear the sound of the trumpet, rally to us there. Our God will fight for us."

21 So we labored in the work, and half of *the men* held the spears from daybreak until the stars appeared. 22 At the same time I also said to the people, "Let each man and his servant stay at night in Jerusalem, that they may be our guard by night and a working party by day." 23 So neither I, my brethren, my servants, nor the men of the guard who followed me took off our clothes, *except* that everyone took them off for washing.

5 AND there was a great outcry of the people and their wives against their Jewish brethren. 2 For there were those who said, "We, our sons, and our daughters *are* many; therefore let us get grain, that we may eat and live."

3 There were also *some* who said, "We have mortgaged our lands and vineyards and houses, that we might buy grain because of the famine."

4 There were also those who said, "We have borrowed money for the king's tax *on* our lands and vineyards. 5 Yet now our flesh *is* as the flesh of our brethren, our children as their children; and indeed we are forcing our sons and our daughters to be slaves, and *some* of our daughters have been brought into slavery. *It is* not in our power *to redeem them,* for other men have our lands and vineyards."

6 And I became very angry when I heard their outcry and these words. 7 After serious thought, I rebuked the nobles and rulers, and said to them, "Each of you is exacting usury from his brother." So I called a great assembly against them. 8 And I said to them, "According to our ability we have redeemed our Jewish brethren who were sold to the nations. Now indeed, will you even sell your brethren? Or should they be sold to us?"

Then they were silenced and found nothing *to say.* 9 Then I said, "What you are doing *is* not good. Should you not walk in the fear of our God because of the reproach of the nations, our enemies? 10 I also, *with* my brethren and my servants, am lending them money and grain. Please, let us stop this usury! 11 Restore now to them, even this day, their lands, their vineyards, their olive groves, and their houses, also a hundredth of the money and the grain, the new wine and the oil, that you have charged them."

12 So they said, "We will restore *it,* and will require nothing from them; we will do as you say."

Then I called the priests, and required an oath from them that they would do according to this promise. 13 Then I shook out the fold of my garment and said, "So may God shake out each man from his house, and from his property, who does not perform this promise. Even thus may he be shaken out and emptied."

And all the assembly said, "Amen!" and praised the LORD. Then the people did according to this promise.

14 Moreover, from the time that I was appointed to be their governor in the land of Judah, from the twentieth year until the thirty-second year of King Artaxerxes, twelve years, neither I nor my brothers ate the governor's provisions. 15 But the former governors who *were* before me laid burdens on the people, and took from them bread and wine, besides forty shekels of silver. Yes, even their servants bore rule over the people, but I did not do so, because of the fear of God. 16 Indeed, I also continued the work on this wall, and we did not buy any land. All my servants *were* gathered there for the work.

17 And at my table *were* one hundred and fifty Jews and rulers, besides those who came to us from the nations around us. 18 Now *that* which was prepared daily *was* one ox *and* six choice sheep. Also fowl were prepared for me, and once every ten days an abundance of all kinds of wine. Yet in spite of this I did not demand the governor's provisions, because the bondage was heavy on this people.

19 Remember me, my God, for good, *according to* all that I have done for this people.

PSALM 89:1–4

1   I will sing of the mercies of the LORD forever;
     With my mouth will I make known
     Your faithfulness to all generations.
2   For I have said, "Mercy shall be built
     up forever;
     Your faithfulness You shall establish in
     the very heavens."

3   "I have made a covenant with My chosen,
     I have sworn to My servant David:
4   'Your seed I will establish forever,
     And build up your throne to all
     generations.' "   Selah

PROVERBS 21:27

27   THE sacrifice of the wicked *is* an
      abomination;
      How much more *when* he brings it with
      wicked intent!

ACTS 26:1–32

THEN Agrippa said to Paul, "You are permitted to speak for yourself."

So Paul stretched out his hand and answered for himself: 2 "I think myself happy, King Agrippa, because today I shall answer for myself before you concerning all the things of which I am accused by the Jews, 3 especially because you are expert in all customs and questions which have to do with the Jews. Therefore I beg you to hear me patiently.

4 "My manner of life from my youth, which was spent from the beginning among my own nation at Jerusalem, all the Jews know. 5 They knew me from the first, if they were willing to testify, that according to the strictest sect of our religion I lived a Pharisee. 6 And now I stand and am judged for the hope of the promise made by God to our fathers. 7 To this *promise* our twelve tribes, earnestly serving *God* night and day, hope to attain. For this hope's sake, King Agrippa, I am accused by the Jews. 8 Why should it be thought incredible by you that God raises the dead?

9 "Indeed, I myself thought I must do many things contrary to the name of Jesus of Nazareth. 10 This I also did in Jerusalem, and many of the saints I shut up in prison, having received authority from the chief priests; and when they were put to death, I cast my vote against *them*. 11 And I punished them often in every synagogue and compelled *them* to blaspheme; and being exceedingly enraged against them, I persecuted *them* even to foreign cities.

12 "While thus occupied, as I journeyed to Damascus with authority and commission from the chief priests, 13 at midday, O king, along the road I saw a light from heaven, brighter than the sun, shining around me and those who journeyed with me. 14 And when we all had fallen to the ground, I heard a voice speaking to me and saying in the Hebrew language, 'Saul, Saul, why are you persecuting Me? *It is* hard for you to kick against the goads.' 15 So I said, 'Who are You, Lord?' And He said, 'I am Jesus, whom you are persecuting. 16 But rise and stand on your feet; for I have appeared to you for this purpose, to make you a minister and a witness both of the things which you have seen and of the things which I will yet reveal to you. 17 I will deliver you from the *Jewish* people, as well as *from* the Gentiles, to whom I

now send you, 18 to open their eyes, *in order* to turn *them* from darkness to light, and *from* the power of Satan to God, that they may receive forgiveness of sins and an inheritance among those who are sanctified by faith in Me.'

Forgiveness means that I am forgiven into a recreated relationship to God.   (PLACE HELP)

---

19 "Therefore, King Agrippa, I was not disobedient to the heavenly vision, 20 but declared first to those in Damascus and in Jerusalem, and throughout all the region of Judea, and *then* to the Gentiles, that they should repent, turn to God, and do works befitting repentance. 21 For these reasons the Jews seized me in the temple and tried to kill *me*. 22 Therefore, having obtained help from God, to this day I stand, witnessing both to small and great, saying no other things than those which the prophets and Moses said would come— 23 that the Christ would suffer, that He would be the first to rise from the dead, and would proclaim light to the *Jewish* people and to the Gentiles."

24 Now as he thus made his defense, Festus said with a loud voice, "Paul, you are beside yourself! Much learning is driving you mad!"

25 But he said, "I am not mad, most noble Festus, but speak the words of truth and reason. 26 For the king, before whom I also speak freely, knows these things; for I am convinced that none of these things escapes his attention, since this thing was not done in a corner. 27 King Agrippa, do you believe the prophets? I know that you do believe."

28 Then Agrippa said to Paul, "You almost persuade me to become a Christian."

29 And Paul said, "I would to God that not only you, but also all who hear me today, might become both almost and altogether such as I am, except for these chains."

30 When he had said these things, the king stood up, as well as the governor and Bernice and those who sat with them; 31 and when they had gone aside, they talked among themselves, saying, "This man is doing nothing deserving of death or chains."

32 Then Agrippa said to Festus, "This man might have been set free if he had not appealed to Caesar."

Reading 208—The Strength of Weakness
Nehemiah 6:9

"He was crucified in weakness." Jesus Christ represents God limiting His own power for one purpose: He died for the weak, for the ungodly, for sinners, and for no one else. "I did not come to call the righteous, but sinners to repentance." No chain is stronger than its weakest link. (*MORAL FOUND.*)

The "strong man" idea is the one that appeals to men, the strong man physically, morally, strong in every way; the kingdoms of men are to be founded on strong men and the weakest are to go to the wall. History proves, however, that it is the strongest that go to the wall, not the weakest. (*GOD'S WORKMANSHIP*)

In all trade and commerce there is oppression, and we try to justify it by saying that the weakest must go to the wall. But is that so? Where are the mighty civilizations of other days? Where are the prehistoric animals, those colossal powerful creatures? It is they that have gone to the wall. The great blunder in all kingdoms among men is that we will demand strong men, consequently, each kingdom in its turn goes to the wall because no chain is stronger than its weakest link. (*SHADE*)

NEHEMIAH 6:1—7:73

NOW it happened when Sanballat, Tobiah, Geshem the Arab, and the rest of our enemies heard that I had rebuilt the wall, and *that* there were no breaks left in it (though at that time I had not hung the doors in the gates), 2 that Sanballat and Geshem sent to me, saying, "Come, let us meet together among the villages in the plain of Ono." But they thought to do me harm.

3 So I sent messengers to them, saying, "I *am* doing a great work, so that I cannot come down. Why should the work cease while I leave it and go down to you?"

4 But they sent me this message four times, and I answered them in the same manner.

5 Then Sanballat sent his servant to me as before, the fifth time, with an open letter in his hand. 6 In it *was* written:

It is reported among the nations, and Geshem says, *that* you and the Jews plan to rebel; therefore, according to these rumors, you are rebuilding the wall, that you may be their king. 7 And you have also appointed prophets to proclaim concerning you at Jerusalem, saying, "*There is* a king in Judah!" Now these matters will be reported to the king. So come, therefore, and let us consult together.

8 Then I sent to him, saying, "No such things as you say are being done, but you invent them in your own heart."

9 For they all *were trying to* make us afraid, saying, "Their hands will be weakened in the work, and it will not be done." Now therefore, *O God,* strengthen my hands.

10 Afterward I came to the house of Shemaiah the son of Delaiah, the son of Mehetabel, who *was* a secret informer; and he said, "Let us meet together in the house of God, within the temple, and let us close the doors of the temple, for they are coming to kill you; indeed, at night they will come to kill you."

11 And I said, "Should such a man as I flee? And who *is there* such as I who would go into the temple to save his life? I will not go in!" 12 Then I perceived that God had not sent him at all, but that he pronounced *this* prophecy against me because Tobiah and Sanballat had hired him. 13 For this reason he *was* hired, that I should be afraid and act that way and sin, so *that* they might have *cause* for an evil report, that they might reproach me.

14 My God, remember Tobiah and Sanballat, according to these their works, and the prophetess Noadiah and the rest of the prophets who would have made me afraid.

15 So the wall was finished on the twenty-fifth *day* of Elul, in fifty-two days. 16 And

it happened, when all our enemies heard *of it*, and all the nations around us saw *these things*, that they were very disheartened in their own eyes; for they perceived that this work was done by our God.

17 Also in those days the nobles of Judah sent many letters to Tobiah, and *the letters of* Tobiah came to them. 18 For many in Judah were pledged to him, because he was the son-in-law of Shechaniah the son of Arah, and his son Jehohanan had married the daughter of Meshullam the son of Berechiah. 19 Also they reported his good deeds before me, and reported my words to him. Tobiah sent letters to frighten me.

7 THEN it was, when the wall was built and I had hung the doors, when the gatekeepers, the singers, and the Levites had been appointed, 2 that I gave the charge of Jerusalem to my brother Hanani, and Hananiah the leader of the citadel, for he *was* a faithful man and feared God more than many.

3 And I said to them, "Do not let the gates of Jerusalem be opened until the sun is hot; and while they stand *guard*, let them shut and bar the doors; and appoint guards from among the inhabitants of Jerusalem, one at his watch station and another in front of his own house."

4 Now the city *was* large and spacious, but the people in it *were* few, and the houses *were* not rebuilt. 5 Then my God put it into my heart to gather the nobles, the rulers, and the people, that they might be registered by genealogy. And I found a register of the genealogy of those who had come up in the first *return*, and found written in it:

6   These *are* the people of the province who came back from the captivity, of those who had been carried away, whom Nebuchadnezzar the king of Babylon had carried away, and who returned to Jerusalem and Judah, everyone to his city.

7   Those who came with Zerubbabel *were* Jeshua, Nehemiah, Azariah, Raamiah, Nahamani, Mordecai, Bilshan, Mispereth, Bigvai, Nehum, and Baanah.

The number of the men of the people of Israel: 8 the sons of Parosh, two thousand one hundred and seventy-two;

9 the sons of Shephatiah, three hundred and seventy-two;

10 the sons of Arah, six hundred and fifty-two;

11 the sons of Pahath-Moab, of the sons of Jeshua and Joab, two thousand eight hundred and eighteen;

12 the sons of Elam, one thousand two hundred and fifty-four;

13 the sons of Zattu, eight hundred and forty-five;

14 the sons of Zaccai, seven hundred and sixty;

15 the sons of Binnui, six hundred and forty-eight;

16 the sons of Bebai, six hundred and twenty-eight;

17 the sons of Azgad, two thousand three hundred and twenty-two;

18 the sons of Adonikam, six hundred and sixty-seven;

19 the sons of Bigvai, two thousand and sixty-seven;

20 the sons of Adin, six hundred and fifty-five;

21 the sons of Ater of Hezekiah, ninety-eight;

22 the sons of Hashum, three hundred and twenty-eight;

23 the sons of Bezai, three hundred and twenty-four;

24 the sons of Hariph, one hundred and twelve;

25 the sons of Gibeon, ninety-five;

26 the men of Bethlehem and Netophah, one hundred and eighty-eight;

27 the men of Anathoth, one hundred and twenty-eight;

28 the men of Beth Azmaveth, forty-two;

29 the men of Kirjath Jearim, Chephirah, and Beeroth, seven hundred and forty-three;

30 the men of Ramah and Geba, six hundred and twenty-one;

31 the men of Michmas, one hundred and twenty-two;

32 the men of Bethel and Ai, one hundred and twenty-three;

33 the men of the other Nebo, fifty-two;

34 the sons of the other Elam, one thousand two hundred and fifty-four;

35 the sons of Harim, three hundred and twenty;

36 the sons of Jericho, three hundred and forty-five;

37 the sons of Lod, Hadid, and Ono, seven hundred and twenty-one;

38 the sons of Senaah, three thousand nine hundred and thirty.

39 The priests: the sons of Jedaiah, of the house of Jeshua, nine hundred and seventy-three; 40 the sons of Immer, one thousand and fifty-two; 41 the sons of Pashhur, one thousand two hundred and forty-seven; 42 the sons of Harim, one thousand and seventeen.

43 The Levites: the sons of Jeshua, of Kadmiel,
and of the sons of Hodevah, seventy-four.

44 The singers: the sons of Asaph, one hundred and forty-eight.

45 The gatekeepers: the sons of Shallum, the sons of Ater, the sons of Talmon, the sons of Akkub, the sons of Hatita, the sons of Shobai, one hundred and thirty-eight.

46 The Nethinim: the sons of Ziha, the sons of Hasupha, the sons of Tabbaoth, 47 the sons of Keros, the sons of Sia, the sons of Padon, 48 the sons of Lebana, the sons of Hagaba, the sons of Salmai, 49 the sons of Hanan, the sons of Giddel, the sons of Gahar, 50 the sons of Reaiah, the sons of Rezin, the sons of Nekoda, 51 the sons of Gazzam, the sons of Uzza, the sons of Paseah, 52 the sons of Besai, the sons of Meunim, the sons of Nephishesim, 53 the sons of Bakbuk, the sons of Hakupha, the sons of Harhur, 54 the sons of Bazlith, the sons of Mehida, the sons of Harsha, 55 the sons of Barkos, the sons of Sisera, the sons of Tamah, 56 the sons of Neziah, and the sons of Hatipha.

57 The sons of Solomon's servants: the sons of Sotai,

the sons of Sophereth, the sons of Perida, 58 the sons of Jaala, the sons of Darkon, the sons of Giddel, 59 the sons of Shephatiah, the sons of Hattil, the sons of Pochereth of Zebaim, and the children of Amon.
60 All the Nethinim, and the sons of Solomon's servants, *were* three hundred and ninety-two.

61 And these *were* the ones who came up from Tel Melah, Tel Harsha, Cherub, Addon, and Immer, but they could not identify their father's house nor their lineage, whether they *were* of Israel: 62 the sons of Delaiah, the sons of Tobiah, the sons of Nekoda, six hundred and forty-two;
63 and of the priests: the sons of Habaiah, the sons of Koz, the sons of Barzillai, who took a wife of the daughters of Barzillai the Gileadite, and was called by their name.
64 These sought their listing *among* those who were registered by genealogy, but it was not found; therefore they were excluded from the priesthood as defiled. 65 And the governor said to them that they should not eat of the most holy things till a priest could consult with the Urim and Thummim.

66 Altogether the whole assembly *was* forty-two thousand three hundred and sixty, 67 besides their male and female servants, of whom *there were* seven thousand three hundred and thirty-seven; and they had two hundred and forty-five men and women singers. 68 Their horses were seven hundred and thirty-six, their mules two hundred and forty-five, 69 *their* camels four hundred and thirty-five, *and* donkeys six thousand seven hundred and twenty.

70 And some of the heads of the fathers' houses gave to the work. The governor gave to the treasury one thousand gold drachmas, fifty basins, and five hundred and thirty priestly garments. 71 Some of the heads of the fathers' *houses* gave to the treasury of the work twenty thousand gold

drachmas, and two thousand two hundred silver minas. 72 And that which the rest of the people gave *was* twenty thousand gold drachmas, two thousand silver minas, and sixty-seven priestly garments.

73 So the priests, the Levites, the gate-keepers, the singers, *some* of the people, the Nethinim, and all Israel dwelt in their cities.

When the seventh month came, the children of Israel *were* in their cities.

PSALM 89:5–10

5 AND the heavens will praise Your wonders, O LORD;
Your faithfulness also in the assembly of the saints.

6 For who in the heavens can be compared to the LORD?
Who among the sons of the mighty can be likened to the LORD?

7 God is greatly to be feared in the assembly of the saints,
And to be held in reverence by all *those* around Him.

8 O LORD God of hosts,
Who *is* mighty like You, O LORD?
Your faithfulness also surrounds You.

9 You rule the raging of the sea;
When its waves rise, You still them.

10 You have broken Rahab in pieces, as one who is slain;
You have scattered Your enemies with Your mighty arm.

PROVERBS 21:28

28 A false witness shall perish,
But the man who hears *him* will speak endlessly.

ACTS 27:1–26

AND when it was decided that we should sail to Italy, they delivered Paul and some other prisoners to *one* named Julius, a centurion of the Augustan Regiment. 2 So, entering a ship of Adramyttium, we put to sea, meaning to sail along the coasts of Asia. Aristarchus, a Macedonian of Thessalonica, was with us. 3 And the next *day* we landed at Sidon. And Julius treated Paul kindly and gave *him* liberty to go to his friends and receive care. 4 When we had put to sea from there, we sailed under *the shelter of* Cyprus, because the winds were contrary.

5 And when we had sailed over the sea which is off Cilicia and Pamphylia, we came to Myra, *a city* of Lycia. 6 There the centurion found an Alexandrian ship sailing to Italy, and he put us on board.

7 When we had sailed slowly many days, and arrived with difficulty off Cnidus, the wind not permitting us to proceed, we sailed under *the shelter of* Crete off Salmone. 8 Passing it with difficulty, we came to a place called Fair Havens, near the city *of* Lasea.

9 Now when much time had been spent, and sailing was now dangerous because the Fast was already over, Paul advised them, 10 saying, "Men, I perceive that this voyage will end with disaster and much loss, not only of the cargo and ship, but also our lives." 11 Nevertheless the centurion was more persuaded by the helmsman and the owner of the ship than by the things spoken by Paul. 12 And because the harbor was not suitable to winter in, the majority advised to set sail from there also, if by any means they could reach Phoenix, a harbor of Crete opening toward the southwest and northwest, *and* winter *there*.

13 When the south wind blew softly, supposing that they had obtained *their* desire, putting out to sea, they sailed close by Crete. 14 But not long after, a tempestuous head wind arose, called Euroclydon. 15 So when the ship was caught, and could not head into the wind, we let *her* drive. 16 And running under *the shelter of* an island called Clauda, we secured the skiff with difficulty. 17 When they had taken it on board, they used cables to undergird the ship; and fearing lest they should run aground on the Syrtis *Sands*, they struck sail and so were driven. 18 And because we were exceedingly tempest-tossed, the next *day* they lightened the ship. 19 On the third *day* we threw the ship's tackle overboard with our own hands. 20 Now when neither sun nor stars appeared for many days, and no small tempest beat on *us*, all hope that we would be saved was finally given up.

21 But after long abstinence from food, then Paul stood in the midst of them and said, "Men, you should have listened to me, and not have sailed from Crete and incurred this disaster and loss. 22 And now

The one thing God is after is character. (GOOD)

I urge you to take heart, for there will be no loss of life among you, but only of the ship. 23 For there stood by me this night an angel of the God to whom I belong and whom I serve, 24 saying, 'Do not be afraid, Paul; you must be brought before Caesar; and indeed God has granted you all those who sail with you.' 25 Therefore take heart, men, for I believe God that it will be just as it was told me. 26 However, we must run aground on a certain island."

◆◆◆◆

Reading 209—The Earth Also Is Yours
Psalm 89:11, 12

Those who deal with the great secrets of the universe imply that our planet is such a tiny spot in the tremendous universe that it is a piece of stupid conceit on our part to think that God watches over us. And to make our planet the center where God performed the marvelous drama of His own history of the Incarnation and Atonement is absurd, they say. But watch a simple-minded person, one who is right with God and is not terrified by the reasonings of men, as he looks at the stars and exclaims, "when I consider Your heavens, the work of Your fingers, the moon and the stars, which You have ordained; what is man, that You are mindful of him?" It is said not in despair, but in adoring wonder.   (*SERVANT AS LORD*)

Look at the world either through a telescope or a microscope and you will be dwarfed into terror by the infinitely great or the infinitely little. Naturalists tell us that there are no two blades of grass alike, and close inspection of a bee's wing under a microscope reveals how marvelously it is made. What do I read in the Bible? I read that the God of heaven counts the hairs of our heads. Jesus says so. I read that the mighty God watches the sparrows so intimately that not one of them falls on the ground without His notice. I read that the God who holds the seas in the hollow of His hand and guides the stars in their courses, clothes the grass of the field. Through the love of God in Christ Jesus we are brought into a wonderful intimacy with the infinitely great and the infinitely little.   (*SERVANT AS LORD*)

NEHEMIAH 8:1—9:38

NOW all the people gathered together as one man in the open square that *was* in front of the Water Gate; and they told Ezra the scribe to bring the Book of the Law of Moses, which the LORD had commanded Israel. 2 So Ezra the priest brought the Law before the assembly of men and women and all who *could* hear with understanding on the first day of the seventh month. 3 Then he read from it in the open square that *was* in front of the Water Gate from morning until midday, before the men and women and those who could understand; and the ears of all the people *were attentive* to the Book of the Law.

4 So Ezra the scribe stood on a platform of wood which they had made for the pur-

pose; and beside him, at his right hand, stood Mattithiah, Shema, Anaiah, Urijah, Hilkiah, and Maaseiah; and at his left hand Pedaiah, Mishael, Malchijah, Hashum, Hashbadana, Zechariah, *and* Meshullam. 5 And Ezra opened the book in the sight of all the people, for he was *standing* above all the people; and when he opened it, all the people stood up. 6 And Ezra blessed the LORD, the great God.

Then all the people answered, "Amen, Amen!" while lifting up their hands. And they bowed their heads and worshiped the LORD with *their* faces to the ground.

7 Also Jeshua, Bani, Sherebiah, Jamin, Akkub, Shabbethai, Hodijah, Maaseiah, Kelita, Azariah, Jozabad, Hanan, Pelaiah, and the Levites, helped the people to understand the Law; and the people *stood* in their

place. 8 So they read distinctly from the book, in the Law of God; and they gave the sense, and helped *them* to understand the reading.

9 And Nehemiah, who *was* the governor, Ezra the priest *and* scribe, and the Levites who taught the people said to all the people, "This day *is* holy to the Lord your God; do not mourn nor weep." For all the people wept, when they heard the words of the Law.

10 Then he said to them, "Go your way, eat the fat, drink the sweet, and send portions to those for whom nothing is prepared; for *this* day *is* holy to our Lord. Do not sorrow, for the joy of the Lord is your strength."

11 So the Levites quieted all the people, saying, "Be still, for the day *is* holy; do not be grieved." 12 And all the people went their way to eat and drink, to send portions and rejoice greatly, because they understood the words that were declared to them.

13 Now on the second day the heads of the fathers' *houses* of all the people, with the priests and Levites, were gathered to Ezra the scribe, in order to understand the words of the Law. 14 And they found written in the Law, which the Lord had commanded by Moses, that the children of Israel should dwell in booths during the feast of the seventh month, 15 and that they should announce and proclaim in all their cities and in Jerusalem, saying, "Go out to the mountain, and bring olive branches, branches of oil trees, myrtle branches, palm branches, and branches of leafy trees, to make booths, as *it is* written."

16 Then the people went out and brought *them* and made themselves booths, each one on the roof of his house, or in their courtyards or the courts of the house of God, and in the open square of the Water Gate and in the open square of the Gate of Ephraim. 17 So the whole assembly of those who had returned from the captivity made booths and sat under the booths; for since the days of Joshua the son of Nun until that day the children of Israel had not done so. And there was very great gladness. 18 Also day by day, from the first day until the last day, he read from the Book of the Law of God. And they kept the feast seven days; and on the eighth day *there was* a sacred assembly, according to the *prescribed* manner.

9 NOW on the twenty-fourth day of this month the children of Israel were as-

sembled with fasting, in sackcloth, and with dust on their heads. 2 Then those of Israelite lineage separated themselves from all foreigners; and they stood and confessed their sins and the iniquities of their fathers. 3 And they stood up in their place and read from the Book of the Law of the Lord their God *for one*-fourth of the day; and *for another* fourth they confessed and worshiped the Lord their God.

4 Then Jeshua, Bani, Kadmiel, Shebaniah, Bunni, Sherebiah, Bani, *and* Chenani stood on the stairs of the Levites and cried out with a loud voice to the Lord their God. 5 And the Levites, Jeshua, Kadmiel, Bani, Hashabniah, Sherebiah, Hodijah, Shebaniah, *and* Pethahiah, said:

"Stand up *and* bless the Lord your
    God
Forever and ever!

"Blessed be Your glorious name,
    Which is exalted above all blessing
    and praise!
6 You alone *are* the Lord;
    You have made heaven,
    The heaven of heavens, with all their
    host,
    The earth and everything on it,
    The seas and all that is in them,
    And You preserve them all.
    The host of heaven worships You.

7 "You *are* the Lord God,
    Who chose Abram,
    And brought him out of Ur of the
    Chaldeans,
    And gave him the name Abraham;
8 You found his heart faithful before
    You,
    And made a covenant with him
    To give the land of the Canaanites,
    The Hittites, the Amorites,
    The Perizzites, the Jebusites,
    And the Girgashites—
    To give *it* to his descendants.
    You have performed Your words,
    For You *are* righteous.

9 "You saw the affliction of our fathers
    in Egypt,
    And heard their cry by the Red Sea.
10 You showed signs and wonders
    against Pharaoh,
    Against all his servants,
    And against all the people of his land.
    For You knew that they acted
    proudly against them.
    So You made a name for Yourself,
    as *it is* this day.

11 And You divided the sea before them,
    So that they went through the midst
        of the sea on the dry land;
    And their persecutors You threw into
        the deep,
    As a stone into the mighty waters.
12 Moreover You led them by day with
        a cloudy pillar,
    And by night with a pillar of fire,
    To give them light on the road
    Which they should travel.

13 "You came down also on Mount Sinai,
    And spoke with them from heaven,
    And gave them just ordinances and
        true laws,
    Good statutes and commandments.
14 You made known to them Your holy
        Sabbath,
    And commanded them precepts,
        statutes and laws,
    By the hand of Moses Your servant.
15 You gave them bread from heaven
        for their hunger,
    And brought them water out of the
        rock for their thirst,
    And told them to go in to possess
        the land
    Which You had sworn to give them.

16 "But they and our fathers acted
        proudly,
    Hardened their necks,
    And did not heed Your
        commandments.
17 They refused to obey,
    And they were not mindful of Your
        wonders
    That You did among them.
    But they hardened their necks,
    And in their rebellion
    They appointed a leader
    To return to their bondage.
    But You *are* God,
    Ready to pardon,
    Gracious and merciful,
    Slow to anger,
    Abundant in kindness,
    And did not forsake them.

18 "Even when they made a molded calf
        for themselves,
    And said, 'This *is* your god
    That brought you up out of Egypt,'
    And worked great provocations,
19 Yet in Your manifold mercies
    You did not forsake them in the
        wilderness.
    The pillar of the cloud did not depart
        from them by day,
    To lead them on the road;

    Nor the pillar of fire by night,
    To show them light,
    And the way they should go.
20 You also gave Your good Spirit to
        instruct them,
    And did not withhold Your manna
        from their mouth,
    And gave them water for their thirst.
21 Forty years You sustained them in
        the wilderness;
    They lacked nothing;
    Their clothes did not wear out
    And their feet did not swell.

22 "Moreover You gave them kingdoms
        and nations,
    And divided them into districts.
    So they took possession of the land
        of Sihon,
    The land of the king of Heshbon,
    And the land of Og king of Bashan.
23 You also multiplied their children as
        the stars of heaven,
    And brought them into the land
    Which You had told their fathers
    To go in and possess.
24 So the people went in
    And possessed the land;
    You subdued before them the
        inhabitants of the land,
    The Canaanites,
    And gave them into their hands,
    With their kings
    And the people of the land,
    That they might do with them as they
        wished.
25 And they took strong cities and a
        rich land,
    And possessed houses full of all
        goods,
    Cisterns *already* dug, vineyards, olive
        groves,
    And fruit trees in abundance.
    So they ate and were filled and grew
        fat,
    And delighted themselves in Your
        great goodness.

26 "Nevertheless they were disobedient
    And rebelled against You,
    Cast Your law behind their backs
    And killed Your prophets, who
        testified against them
    To turn them to Yourself;
    And they worked great provocations.
27 Therefore You delivered them into
        the hand of their enemies,
    Who oppressed them;
    And in the time of their trouble,
    When they cried to You,
    You heard from heaven;

And according to Your abundant
mercies
You gave them deliverers who saved
them
From the hand of their enemies.

28 "But after they had rest,
They again did evil before You.
Therefore You left them in the hand
of their enemies,
So that they had dominion over
them;
Yet when they returned and cried out
to You,
You heard from heaven;
And many times You delivered them
according to Your mercies,
29 And testified against them,
That You might bring them back to
Your law.
Yet they acted proudly,
And did not heed Your
commandments,
But sinned against Your judgments,
'Which if a man does, he shall live
by them.'
And they shrugged their shoulders,
Stiffened their necks,
And would not hear.
30 Yet for many years You had patience
with them,
And testified against them by Your
Spirit in Your prophets.
Yet they would not listen;
Therefore You gave them into the
hand of the peoples of the lands.
31 Nevertheless in Your great mercy
You did not utterly consume them
nor forsake them;
For You *are* God, gracious and
merciful.

32 "Now therefore, our God,
The great, the mighty, and awesome
God,
Who keeps covenant and mercy:
Do not let all the trouble seem small
before You
That has come upon us,
Our kings and our princes,
Our priests and our prophets,
Our fathers and on all Your people,
From the days of the kings of Assyria
until this day.
33 However You *are* just in all that has
befallen us;
For You have dealt faithfully,
But we have done wickedly.
34 Neither our kings nor our princes,
Our priests nor our fathers,
Have kept Your law,

Nor heeded Your commandments
and Your testimonies,
With which You testified against
them.
35 For they have not served You in their
kingdom,
Or in the many good *things* that You
gave them,
Or in the large and rich land which
You set before them;
Nor did they turn from their wicked
works.

36 "Here we *are*, servants today!
And the land that You gave to our
fathers,
To eat its fruit and its bounty,
Here we *are*, servants in it!
37 And it yields much increase to the
kings
You have set over us,
Because of our sins;
Also they have dominion over our
bodies and our cattle
At their pleasure;
And we *are* in great distress.

38 "And because of all this,
We make a sure *covenant* and write
it;
Our leaders, our Levites, *and* our
priests seal *it.*"

PSALM 89:11–18

11 THE heavens *are* Yours, the earth also
is Yours;
The world and all its fullness, You have
founded them.
12 The north and the south, You have
created them;
Tabor and Hermon rejoice in Your
name.
13 You have a mighty arm;
Strong is Your hand, *and* high is Your
right hand.
14 Righteousness and justice *are* the
foundation of Your throne;
Mercy and truth go before Your face.
15 Blessed *are* the people who know the
joyful sound!
They walk, O LORD, in the light of
Your countenance.
16 In Your name they rejoice all day long,
And in Your righteousness they are
exalted.
17 For You *are* the glory of their strength,
And in Your favor our horn is exalted.
18 For our shield *belongs* to the LORD,
And our king to the Holy One of
Israel.

PROVERBS 21:29–31

29 A wicked man hardens his face,
    But *as for* the upright, he establishes
    his way.

30 *There is* no wisdom or understanding
    Or counsel against the LORD.

31 The horse *is* prepared for the day of
    battle,
    But deliverance *is* of the LORD.

---

*H*e destroys the wrong and the evil
*for one purpose only, the deliverance
of the good.*   (PHIL. SIN)

ACTS 27:27–44

NOW when the fourteenth night had come,
as we were driven up and down in the Adri-
atic *Sea,* about midnight the sailors sensed
that they were drawing near some land.
28 And they took soundings and found *it*
to be twenty fathoms; and when they had
gone a little farther, they took soundings
again and found *it* to be fifteen fathoms.
29 Then, fearing lest we should run aground
on the rocks, they dropped four anchors
from the stern, and prayed for day to come.
30 And as the sailors were seeking to escape
from the ship, when they had let down
the skiff into the sea, under pretense of
putting out anchors from the prow, 31 Paul
said to the centurion and the soldiers, "Unless these men stay in the ship, you cannot
be saved." 32 Then the soldiers cut away
the ropes of the skiff and let it fall off.
33 And as day was about to dawn, Paul

implored *them* all to take food, saying, "Today is the fourteenth day you have waited
and continued without food, and eaten
nothing. 34 Therefore I urge you to take
nourishment, for this is for your survival,
since not a hair will fall from the head of
any of you." 35 And when he had said these
things, he took bread and gave thanks to
God in the presence of them all; and when
he had broken *it* he began to eat. 36 Then

---

*C*haracter is always revealed in
crises.   (GOD'S WORKMANSHIP)

---

they were all encouraged, and also took
food themselves. 37 And in all we were two
hundred and seventy-six persons on the
ship. 38 So when they had eaten enough,
they lightened the ship and threw out the
wheat into the sea.
39 When it was day, they did not recognize the land; but they observed a bay with
a beach, onto which they planned to run
the ship if possible. 40 And they let go the
anchors and left *them* in the sea, meanwhile
loosing the rudder ropes; and they hoisted
the mainsail to the wind and made for shore.
41 But striking a place where two seas met,
they ran the ship aground; and the prow
stuck fast and remained immovable, but the
stern was being broken up by the violence
of the waves.
42 And the soldiers' plan was to kill the
prisoners, lest any of them should swim
away and escape. 43 But the centurion,
wanting to save Paul, kept them from *their*
purpose, and commanded that those who
could swim should jump *overboard* first
and get to land, 44 and the rest, some on
boards and some on *parts* of the ship. And
so it was that they all escaped safely to
land.

◆◆◆◆

---

*Reading 210—*An Ordinary Life
Acts 28:31

*W*ho is God? I have never seen God, or spoken to Him. An omnipresent,
omniscient, omnipotent Being does not amount to anything to me;
He is an abstract finding of a man's intellect. Can God take on hands and feet
and man's ways of doing things, and manifest Himself on the plane on which
we live? The Bible says that that is what God did do. Jesus Christ lived a
human life on this earth, and He exhibited a disposition not yours and not
mine.   (SHADE)

The majority of us make the character of God out of our own heads; therefore He does not amount to anything at all. That God is called an omnipresent, omniscient, omnipotent Being who rules the universe does not matter one iota to me. But the New Testament reveals the essential nature of God to be not omnipotence, omnipresence, and omniscience, but holiness. God became the weakest thing in His own creation, namely, a Baby; He entered human history on that line. He was so ordinary that the folks of His day paid no attention to Him, and the religious people said He was making a farce of religion.   (*Shad. Agony*)

NEHEMIAH 10:1—11:36

NOW those who placed *their* seal on *the document were:*

Nehemiah the governor, the son of Hacaliah, and Zedekiah, 2 Seraiah, Azariah, Jeremiah, 3 Pashhur, Amariah, Malchijah, 4 Hattush, Shebaniah, Malluch, 5 Harim, Meremoth, Obadiah, 6 Daniel, Ginnethon, Baruch, 7 Meshullam, Abijah, Mijamin, 8 Maaziah, Bilgai, *and* Shemaiah. These *were* the priests.

9   The Levites: Jeshua the son of Azaniah, Binnui of the sons of Henadad, *and* Kadmiel.

10   Their brethren: Shebaniah, Hodijah, Kelita, Pelaiah, Hanan, 11 Micha, Rehob, Hashabiah, 12 Zaccur, Sherebiah, Shebaniah, 13 Hodijah, Bani, *and* Beninu.

14   The leaders of the people: Parosh, Pahath-Moab, Elam, Zattu, Bani, 15 Bunni, Azgad, Bebai, 16 Adonijah, Bigvai, Adin, 17 Ater, Hezekiah, Azzur, 18 Hodijah, Hashum, Bezai, 19 Hariph, Anathoth, Nebai, 20 Magpiash, Meshullam, Hezir, 21 Meshezabel, Zadok, Jaddua, 22 Pelatiah, Hanan, Anaiah, 23 Hoshea, Hananiah, Hasshub, 24 Hallohesh, Pilha, Shobek, 25 Rehum, Hashabnah, Maaseiah, 26 Ahijah, Hanan, Anan, 27 Malluch, Harim, *and* Baanah.

28 Now the rest of the people—the priests, the Levites, the gatekeepers, the singers, the Nethinim, and all those who had separated themselves from the peoples of the lands to the Law of God, their wives, their sons, and their daughters, everyone who had knowledge and understanding— 29 these joined with their brethren, their nobles, and entered into a curse and an oath to walk in God's Law, which was given by Moses the servant of God, and to observe and do all the commandments of the Lord our Lord, and His ordinances and His statutes: 30 We would not give our daughters as wives to the peoples of the land, nor take their daughters for our sons; 31 *if* the peoples of the land brought wares or any grain to sell on the Sabbath day, we would not buy it from them on the Sabbath, or on a holy day; and we would forego the seventh year's *produce* and the exacting of every debt.

32 Also we made ordinances for ourselves, to exact from ourselves yearly one-third of a shekel for the service of the house of our God: 33 for the showbread, for the regular grain offering, for the regular burnt offering of the Sabbaths, the New Moons, and the set feasts; for the holy things, for the sin offerings to make atonement for Israel, and all the work of the house of our God. 34 We cast lots among the priests, the Levites, and the people, for *bringing* the wood offering into the house of our God, according to our fathers' houses, at the appointed times year by year, to burn on the altar of the Lord our God as *it is* written in the Law.

35 And *we made ordinances* to bring the firstfruits of our ground and the firstfruits of all fruit of all trees, year by year, to the house of the Lord; 36 to bring the firstborn of our sons and our cattle, as *it is* written in the Law, and the firstborn of our herds and our flocks, to the house of our God, to the priests who minister in the house of our God; 37 to bring the firstfruits of our dough, our offerings, the fruit from all kinds of trees, *the* new wine and oil, to the priests, to the storerooms of the house of our God; and to bring the tithes of our land to the Levites, for the Levites should receive the tithes in all our farming communities. 38 And the priest, the descendant of Aaron, shall be with the Levites when the Levites receive tithes; and the Levites shall

bring up a tenth of the tithes to the house of our God, to the rooms of the storehouse. 39 For the children of Israel and the children of Levi shall bring the offering of the grain, of the new wine and the oil, to the storerooms where the articles of the sanctuary *are, where* the priests who minister and the gatekeepers and the singers *are;* and we will not neglect the house of our God.

11 NOW the leaders of the people dwelt at Jerusalem; the rest of the people cast lots to bring one out of ten to dwell in Jerusalem, the holy city, and nine-tenths *were to dwell* in *other* cities. 2 And the people blessed all the men who willingly offered themselves to dwell at Jerusalem. 3 These *are* the heads of the province who dwelt in Jerusalem. (But in the cities of Judah everyone dwelt in his own possession in their cities—Israelites, priests, Levites, Nethinim, and descendants of Solomon's servants.) 4 Also in Jerusalem dwelt *some* of the children of Judah and of the children of Benjamin.

The children of Judah: Athaiah the son of Uzziah, the son of Zechariah, the son of Amariah, the son of Shephatiah, the son of Mahalalel, of the children of Perez; 5 and Maaseiah the son of Baruch, the son of Col-Hozeh, the son of Hazaiah, the son of Adaiah, the son of Joiarib, the son of Zechariah, the son of Shiloni. 6 All the sons of Perez who dwelt at Jerusalem *were* four hundred and sixty-eight valiant men.

7 And these are the sons of Benjamin: Sallu the son of Meshullam, the son of Joed, the son of Pedaiah, the son of Kolaiah, the son of Maaseiah, the son of Ithiel, the son of Jeshaiah; 8 and after him Gabbai *and* Sallai, nine hundred and twenty-eight. 9 Joel the son of Zichri *was* their overseer, and Judah the son of Senuah *was* second over the city.

10 Of the priests: Jedaiah the son of Joiarib, and Jachin; 11 Seraiah the son of Hilkiah, the son of Meshullam, the son of Zadok, the son of Meraioth, the son of Ahitub, *was* the leader of the house of God. 12 Their brethren who did the work of the house *were* eight hundred and twenty-two; and Adaiah the son of Jeroham, the son of Pelaliah, the son of Amzi, the son of Zechariah, the son of Pashhur, the son of Malchijah, 13 and his brethren, heads of the fathers' *houses, were* two hundred and forty-two; and Amashai the son of Azarel, the son of Ahzai, the son of Meshillemoth, the son of Immer, 14 and their brethren, mighty men of valor, *were* one hundred and

twenty-eight. Their overseer *was* Zabdiel the son of *one of* the great men.

15 Also of the Levites: Shemaiah the son of Hasshub, the son of Azrikam, the son of Hashabiah, the son of Bunni; 16 Shab-bethai and Jozabad, of the heads of the Levites, *had* the oversight of the business outside of the house of God; 17 Mattaniah the son of Micha, the son of Zabdi, the son of Asaph, the leader *who* began the thanksgiving with prayer; Bakbu-kiah, the second among his brethren; and Abda the son of Shammua, the son of Galal, the son of Jeduthun. 18 All the Levites in the holy city *were* two hundred and eighty-four.

19 Moreover the gatekeepers, Akkub, Talmon, and their brethren who kept the gates, *were* one hundred and seventy-two.

20 And the rest of Israel, of the priests *and* Levites, *were* in all the cities of Judah, everyone in his inheritance. 21 But the Nethinim dwelt in Ophel. And Ziha and Gishpa *were* over the Nethinim.

22 Also the overseer of the Levites at Jerusalem *was* Uzzi the son of Bani, the son of Hashabiah, the son of Mattaniah, the son of Micha, of the sons of Asaph, the singers in charge of the service of the house of God. 23 For *it was* the king's command concerning them that a certain portion should be for the singers, a quota day by day. 24 Pethahiah the son of Meshezabel, of the children of Zerah the son of Judah, *was* the king's deputy in all matters concerning the people.

25 And as for the villages with their fields, *some* of the children of Judah dwelt in Kirjath Arba and its villages, Dibon and its villages, Jekabzeel and its villages; 26 in Jeshua, Moladah, Beth Pelet, 27 Hazar Shual, and Beersheba and its villages; 28 in Ziklag and Meconah and its villages; 29 in En Rimmon, Zorah, Jarmuth, 30 Zanoah, Adullam, and their villages; in Lachish and its fields; in Azekah and its villages. They dwelt from Beersheba to the Valley of Hinnom.

31 Also the children of Benjamin from Geba *dwelt* in Michmash, Aija, and Bethel, and their villages; 32 in Anathoth, Nob, Ananiah; 33 in Hazor, Ramah, Gittaim; 34 in Hadid, Zeboim, Neballat; 35 in Lod, Ono, *and* the Valley of Craftsmen. 36 Some of the Judean divisions of Levites *were* in Benjamin.

PSALM 89:19–29

19 THEN You spoke in a vision to Your holy one,

And said: "I have given help to *one who is* mighty;
I have exalted one chosen from the people.
20 I have found My servant David;
With My holy oil I have anointed him,
21 With whom My hand shall be established;
Also My arm shall strengthen him.
22 The enemy shall not outwit him,
Nor the son of wickedness afflict him.
23 I will beat down his foes before his face,
And plague those who hate him.

24 "But My faithfulness and My mercy *shall be* with him,
And in My name his horn shall be exalted.
25 Also I will set his hand over the sea,
And his right hand over the rivers.
26 He shall cry to Me, 'You *are* my Father,
My God, and the rock of my salvation.'
27 Also I will make him *My* firstborn,
The highest of the kings of the earth.
28 My mercy I will keep for him forever,
And My covenant shall stand firm with him.
29 His seed also I will make *to endure* forever,
And his throne as the days of heaven.

PROVERBS 22:1, 2

1 A *good* name is to be chosen rather than great riches,
Loving favor rather than silver and gold.

2 The rich and the poor have this in common,
The LORD *is* the maker of them all.

ACTS 28:1–31

NOW when they had escaped, they then found out that the island was called Malta. 2 And the natives showed us unusual kindness; for they kindled a fire and made us all welcome, because of the rain that was falling and because of the cold. 3 But when Paul had gathered a bundle of sticks and laid *them* on the fire, a viper came out because of the heat, and fastened on his hand. 4 So when the natives saw the creature hanging from his hand, they said to one another, "No doubt this man is a murderer, whom, though he has escaped the sea, yet justice does not allow to live." 5 But he shook off the creature into the fire and suffered no harm. 6 However, they were expecting that he would swell up or suddenly fall down dead. But after they had looked for a long time and saw no harm come to him, they changed their minds and said that he was a god.

7 In that region there was an estate of the leading citizen of the island, whose name was Publius, who received us and entertained us courteously for three days. 8 And it happened that the father of Publius lay sick of a fever and dysentery. Paul went in to him and prayed, and he laid his hands on him and healed him. 9 So when this was done, the rest of those on the island who had diseases also came and were healed. 10 They also honored us in many ways; and when we departed, they provided such things as were necessary.

11 After three months we sailed in an Alexandrian ship whose figurehead was the Twin Brothers, which had wintered at the island. 12 And landing at Syracuse, we stayed three days. 13 From there we circled round and reached Rhegium. And after one day the south wind blew; and the next day we came to Puteoli, 14 where we found brethren, and were invited to stay with them seven days. And so we went toward Rome. 15 And from there, when the brethren heard about us, they came to meet us as far as Appii Forum and Three Inns. When Paul saw them, he thanked God and took courage.

16 Now when we came to Rome, the centurion delivered the prisoners to the captain of the guard; but Paul was permitted to dwell by himself with the soldier who guarded him.

17 And it came to pass after three days that Paul called the leaders of the Jews together. So when they had come together, he said to them: "Men *and* brethren, though I have done nothing against our people or the customs of our fathers, yet I was delivered as a prisoner from Jerusalem into the hands of the Romans, 18 who, when they had examined me, wanted to let *me* go, because there was no cause for putting me to death. 19 But when the Jews spoke against *it*, I was compelled to appeal to Caesar, not that I had anything of which to accuse my nation. 20 For this reason

---

*G*od sows His saints in the places
that are most useless according
to the judgment of the
world. (SEND I YOU)

therefore I have called for you, to see *you* and speak with *you,* because for the hope of Israel I am bound with this chain."

21 Then they said to him, "We neither received letters from Judea concerning you, nor have any of the brethren who came reported or spoken any evil of you. 22 But we desire to hear from you what you think; for concerning this sect, we know that it is spoken against everywhere."

23 So when they had appointed him a day, many came to him at *his* lodging, to whom he explained and solemnly testified of the kingdom of God, persuading them concerning Jesus from both the Law of Moses and the Prophets, from morning till evening. 24 And some were persuaded by the things which were spoken, and some disbelieved. 25 So when they did not agree among themselves, they departed after Paul had said one word: "The Holy Spirit spoke rightly through Isaiah the prophet to our fathers, 26 saying,

'Go to this people and say:
"Hearing you will hear, and shall not understand;
And seeing you will see, and not perceive;

27 For the hearts of this people have grown dull.
Their ears are hard of hearing,
And their eyes they have closed,
Lest they should see with *their* eyes and hear with *their* ears,
Lest they should understand with *their* hearts and turn,
So that I should heal them."'

We must never take our Lord's words and interpret them by our own human reason.   (PSY. REDEMP.)

---

28 "Therefore let it be known to you that the salvation of God has been sent to the Gentiles, and they will hear it!" 29 And when he had said these words, the Jews departed and had a great dispute among themselves.

30 Then Paul dwelt two whole years in his own rented house, and received all who came to him, 31 preaching the kingdom of God and teaching the things which concern the Lord Jesus Christ with all confidence, no one forbidding him.

Reading 211—Loss of Communion with God
Romans 1:21–25

Up to the time of the Fall man drew all his sustenance from God; when he fell, he lost that harmony completely; and the danger now is that although man's spirit is as immortal as God, it receives no sustenance from God. The first thing that happened was that man became his own god, exactly what the Devil said would happen.   (GLORY)

The fundamental basis of the life of man was the life of God and communion with God, and until he fell Adam's spirit and soul and body were in absolute harmony with God. What do we mean by the Fall? God intended man to progress from innocence to holiness by a series of deliberate moral choices in which he was to sacrifice the life of nature to the will of God. Adam refused to do this, and that constitutes the Fall. When Adam fell the Spirit of God was withdrawn instantly, not after a time. The real seat of death is in man's spirit, the dissolution of the body is a mere incident; the point God's Book emphasizes is the instant withdrawal of life, the withdrawal of the Spirit which held man's spirit, soul and body in living communion with God.   (GLORY)

NEHEMIAH 12:1—13:31

NOW these *are* the priests and the Levites who came up with Zerubbabel the son of Shealtiel, and Jeshua: Seraiah, Jeremiah, Ezra, 2 Amariah, Malluch, Hattush, 3 Shechaniah, Rehum, Meremoth, 4 Iddo, Ginnethoi, Abijah, 5 Mijamin, Maadiah, Bilgah, 6 Shemaiah, Joiarib, Jedaiah, 7 Sallu, Amok, Hilkiah, *and* Jedaiah.

These *were* the heads of the priests and their brethren in the days of Jeshua.

8 Moreover the Levites *were* Jeshua, Binnui, Kadmiel, Sherebiah, Judah, *and* Mattaniah *who led* the thanksgiving *psalms*, he and his brethren. 9 Also Bakbukiah and Unni, their brethren, *stood* across from them in *their* duties.

10 Jeshua begot Joiakim, Joiakim begot Eliashib, Eliashib begot Joiada, 11 Joiada begot Jonathan, and Jonathan begot Jaddua.

12 Now in the days of Joiakim, the priests, the heads of the fathers' *houses were:* of Seraiah, Meraiah; of Jeremiah, Hananiah; 13 of Ezra, Meshullam; of Amariah, Jehohanan; 14 of Melichu, Jonathan; of Shebaniah, Joseph; 15 of Harim, Adna; of Meraioth, Helkai; 16 of Iddo, Zechariah; of Ginnethon, Meshullam; 17 of Abijah, Zichri; *the son* of Minjamin; of Moadiah, Piltai; 18 of Bilgah, Shammua; of Shemaiah, Jehonathan; 19 of Joiarib, Mattenai; of Jedaiah, Uzzi; 20 of Sallai, Kallai; of Amok, Eber; 21 of Hilkiah, Hashabiah; *and* of Jedaiah, Nethanel.

22 During the reign of Darius the Persian, a record *was also kept* of the Levites and priests *who had been* heads of their fathers' *houses* in the days of Eliashib, Joiada, Johanan, and Jaddua. 23 The sons of Levi, the heads of the fathers' *houses* until the days of Johanan the son of Eliashib, *were* written in the book of the chronicles.

24 And the heads of the Levites *were* Hashabiah, Sherebiah, and Jeshua the son of Kadmiel, with their brothers across from them, to praise *and* give thanks, group alternating with group, according to the command of David the man of God. 25 Mattaniah, Bakbukiah, Obadiah, Meshullam, Talmon, and Akkub *were* gatekeepers keeping the watch at the storerooms of the gates. 26 These *lived* in the days of Joiakim the son of Jeshua, the son of Jozadak, and in the days of Nehemiah the governor, and of Ezra the priest, the scribe.

27 Now at the dedication of the wall of Jerusalem they sought out the Levites in all their places, to bring them to Jerusalem to celebrate the dedication with gladness, both with thanksgivings and singing, *with* cymbals and stringed instruments and harps. 28 And the sons of the singers gathered together from the countryside around Jerusalem, from the villages of the Netophathites, 29 from the house of Gilgal, and from the fields of Geba and Azmaveth; for the singers had built themselves villages all around Jerusalem. 30 Then the priests and Levites purified themselves, and purified the people, the gates, and the wall.

31 So I brought the leaders of Judah up on the wall, and appointed two large thanksgiving choirs. *One* went to the right hand on the wall toward the Refuse Gate. 32 After them went Hoshaiah and half of the leaders of Judah, 33 and Azariah, Ezra, Meshullam, 34 Judah, Benjamin, Shemaiah, Jeremiah, 35 and some of the priests' sons with trumpets—Zechariah the son of Jonathan, the son of Shemaiah, the son of Mattaniah, the son of Michaiah, the son of Zaccur, the son of Asaph, 36 and his brethren, Shemaiah, Azarel, Milalai, Gilalai, Maai, Nethanel, Judah, *and* Hanani, with the musical instruments of David the man of God. And Ezra the scribe *went* before them. 37 By the Fountain Gate, in front of them, they went up the stairs of the City of David, on the stairway of the wall, beyond the house of David, as far as the Water Gate eastward.

38 The other thanksgiving choir went the opposite *way,* and I *was* behind them with half of the people on the wall, going past the Tower of the Ovens as far as the Broad Wall, 39 and above the Gate of Ephraim, above the Old Gate, above the Fish Gate, the Tower of Hananel, the Tower of the Hundred, as far as the Sheep Gate; and they stopped by the Gate of the Prison.

40 So the two thanksgiving choirs stood in the house of God, likewise I and the half of the rulers with me; 41 and the priests, Eliakim, Maaseiah, Minjamin, Michaiah, Elioenai, Zechariah, *and* Hananiah, with trumpets; 42 also Maaseiah, Shemaiah, Eleazar, Uzzi, Jehohanan, Malchijah, Elam, and Ezer. The singers sang loudly with Jezrahiah the director.

43 Also that day they offered great sacrifices, and rejoiced, for God had made them rejoice with great joy; the women and the children also rejoiced, so that the joy of Jerusalem was heard afar off.

44 And at the same time some were appointed over the rooms of the storehouse for the offerings, the firstfruits, and the tithes, to gather into them from the fields of the cities the portions specified by the Law for the priests and Levites; for Judah

rejoiced over the priests and Levites who ministered. 45 Both the singers and the gatekeepers kept the charge of their God and the charge of the purification, according to the command of David *and* Solomon his son. 46 For in the days of David and Asaph of old *there were* chiefs of the singers, and songs of praise and thanksgiving to God. 47 In the days of Zerubbabel and in the days of Nehemiah all Israel gave the portions for the singers and the gatekeepers, a portion for each day. They also consecrated *holy things* for the Levites, and the Levites consecrated *them* for the children of Aaron.

13 ON that day they read from the Book of Moses in the hearing of the people, and in it was found written that no Ammonite or Moabite should ever come into the assembly of God, 2 because they had not met the children of Israel with bread and water, but hired Balaam against them to curse them. However, our God turned the curse into a blessing. 3 So it was, when they had heard the Law, that they separated all the mixed multitude from Israel.

4 Now before this, Eliashib the priest, having authority over the storerooms of the house of our God, *was* allied with Tobiah. 5 And he had prepared for him a large room, where previously they had stored the grain offerings, the frankincense, the articles, the tithes of grain, the new wine and oil, which were commanded *to be given* to the Levites and singers and gatekeepers, and the offerings for the priests. 6 But during all this I was not in Jerusalem, for in the thirty-second year of Artaxerxes king of Babylon I had returned to the king. Then after certain days I obtained leave from the king, 7 and I came to Jerusalem and discovered the evil that Eliashib had done for Tobiah, in preparing a room for him in the courts of the house of God. 8 And it grieved me bitterly; therefore I threw all the household goods of Tobiah out of the room. 9 Then I commanded them to cleanse the rooms; and I brought back into them the articles of the house of God, with the grain offering and the frankincense.

10 I also realized that the portions for the Levites had not been given *them;* for each of the Levites and the singers who did the work had gone back to his field. 11 So I contended with the rulers, and said, "Why is the house of God forsaken?" And I gathered them together and set them in their place. 12 Then all Judah brought the tithe of the grain and the new wine and

the oil to the storehouse. 13 And I appointed as treasurers over the storehouse Shelemiah the priest and Zadok the scribe, and of the Levites, Pedaiah; and next to them *was* Hanan the son of Zaccur, the son of Mattaniah; for they were considered faithful, and their task *was* to distribute to their brethren.

14 Remember me, O my God, concerning this, and do not wipe out my good deeds that I have done for the house of my God, and for its services!

15 In those days I saw *people* in Judah treading wine presses on the Sabbath, and bringing in sheaves, and loading donkeys with wine, grapes, figs, and all *kinds of* burdens, which they brought into Jerusalem on the Sabbath day. And I warned *them* about the day on which they were selling provisions. 16 Men of Tyre dwelt there also, who brought in fish and all kinds of goods, and sold *them* on the Sabbath to the children of Judah, and in Jerusalem.

17 Then I contended with the nobles of Judah, and said to them, "What evil thing *is* this that you do, by which you profane the Sabbath day? 18 Did not your fathers do thus, and did not our God bring all this disaster on us and on this city? Yet you bring added wrath on Israel by profaning the Sabbath."

19 So it was, at the gates of Jerusalem, as it began to be dark before the Sabbath, that I commanded the gates to be shut, and charged that they must not be opened till after the Sabbath. Then I posted *some* of my servants at the gates, *so that* no burdens would be brought in on the Sabbath day. 20 Now the merchants and sellers of all kinds of wares lodged outside Jerusalem once or twice. 21 Then I warned them, and said to them, "Why do you spend the night around the wall? If you do *so* again, I will lay hands on you!" From that time on they came no *more* on the Sabbath. 22 And I commanded the Levites that they should cleanse themselves, and that they should go and guard the gates, to sanctify the Sabbath day.

Remember me, O my God, *concerning* this also, and spare me according to the greatness of Your mercy!

23 In those days I also saw Jews *who* had married women of Ashdod, Ammon, *and* Moab. 24 And half of their children spoke the language of Ashdod, and could not speak the language of Judah, but spoke according to the language of one or the other people. 25 So I contended with them and cursed them, struck some of them and pulled out their hair, and made them swear by God,

saying, "You shall not give your daughters as wives to their sons, nor take their daughters for your sons or yourselves. 26 Did not Solomon king of Israel sin by these things? Yet among many nations there was no king like him, who was beloved of his God; and God made him king over all Israel. Nevertheless pagan women caused even him to sin. 27 Should we then hear of your doing all this great evil, transgressing against our God by marrying pagan women?"

28 And *one* of the sons of Joiada, the son of Eliashib the high priest, *was* a son-in-law of Sanballat the Horonite; therefore I drove him from me.

29 Remember them, O my God, because they have defiled the priesthood and the covenant of the priesthood and the Levites.

30 Thus I cleansed them of everything pagan. I also assigned duties to the priests and the Levites, each to his service, 31 and *to bringing* the wood offering and the firstfruits at appointed times.

Remember me, O my God, for good!

PSALM 89:30–37

30 "IF his sons forsake My law
   And do not walk in My judgments,
31 If they break My statutes
   And do not keep My commandments,
32 Then I will punish their transgression
     with the rod,
   And their iniquity with stripes.
33 Nevertheless My lovingkindness I will
     not utterly take from him,
   Nor allow My faithfulness to fail.
34 My covenant I will not break,
   Nor alter the word that has gone out
     of My lips.
35 Once I have sworn by My holiness;
   I will not lie to David:
36 His seed shall endure forever,
   And his throne as the sun before Me;
37 It shall be established forever like the
     moon,
   Even *like* the faithful witness in the sky."
                  Selah

PROVERBS 22:3, 4

3 A prudent *man* foresees evil and hides
   himself,
   But the simple pass on and are
   punished.

4 By humility *and* the fear of the Lord
   Are riches and honor and life.

ROMANS 1:1–32

PAUL, a bondservant of Jesus Christ, called *to be* an apostle, separated to the gospel of God 2 which He promised before through His prophets in the Holy Scriptures, 3 concerning His Son Jesus Christ our Lord, who was born of the seed of David according to the flesh, 4 *and* declared *to be* the Son of God with power according to the Spirit of holiness, by the resurrection from the dead. 5 Through Him we have received

---

In Him we deal with God as Man, the God-Man.   (GLORY)

---

grace and apostleship for obedience to the faith among all nations for His name, 6 among whom you also are the called of Jesus Christ;

7 To all who are in Rome, beloved of God, called *to be* saints:

Grace to you and peace from God our Father and the Lord Jesus Christ.

8 First, I thank my God through Jesus Christ for you all, that your faith is spoken of throughout the whole world. 9 For God is my witness, whom I serve with my spirit in the gospel of His Son, that without ceasing I make mention of you always in my prayers, 10 making request if, by some means, now at last I may find a way in the will of God to come to you. 11 For I long to see you, that I may impart to you some spiritual gift, so that you may be established— 12 that is, that I may be encouraged together with you by the mutual faith both of you and me.

13 Now I do not want you to be unaware, brethren, that I often planned to come to you (but was hindered until now), that I might have some fruit among you also, just as among the other Gentiles. 14 I am a debtor both to Greeks and to barbarians, both to wise and to unwise. 15 So, as much as is in me, *I am* ready to preach the gospel to you who are in Rome also.

16 For I am not ashamed of the gospel of Christ, for it is the power of God to salvation for everyone who believes, for the Jew first and also for the Greek. 17 For in it the righteousness of God is revealed from faith to faith; as it is written, "The just shall live by faith."

18 For the wrath of God is revealed from heaven against all ungodliness and

unrighteousness of men, who suppress the truth in unrighteousness, 19 because what may be known of God is manifest in them, for God has shown *it* to them. 20 For since the creation of the world His invisible *attributes* are clearly seen, being understood by the things that are made, *even* His eternal power and Godhead, so that they are without excuse, 21 because, although they knew God, they did not glorify *Him* as God, nor were thankful, but became futile in their thoughts, and their foolish hearts were darkened. 22 Professing to be wise, they became fools, 23 and changed the glory of the incorruptible God into an image made like corruptible man—and birds and four-footed animals and creeping things.

24 Therefore God also gave them up to uncleanness, in the lusts of their hearts, to dishonor their bodies among themselves, 25 who exchanged the truth of God for the lie, and worshiped and served the creature rather than the Creator, who is blessed forever. Amen.

26 For this reason God gave them up to vile passions. For even their women exchanged the natural use for what is against nature. 27 Likewise also the men, leaving the natural use of the woman, burned in their lust for one another, men with men committing what is shameful, and receiving in themselves the penalty of their error which was due.

28 And even as they did not like to retain God in *their* knowledge, God gave them over to a debased mind, to do those things which are not fitting; 29 being filled with all unrighteousness, sexual immorality, wickedness, covetousness, maliciousness; full of envy, murder, strife, deceit, evilmindedness; *they are* whisperers, 30 backbiters, haters of God, violent, proud, boasters, inventors of evil things, disobedient to parents, 31 undiscerning, untrustworthy, unloving, unforgiving, unmerciful; 32 who, knowing the righteous judgment of God, that those who practice such things are deserving of death, not only do the same but also approve of those who practice them.

◆◆◆

Reading 212—In the Vision of the Gospel
Romans 2:16

Thank God for the sight of all you have never yet been. You have had the vision, but you are not there yet by any means. It is when we are in the valley, where we prove whether we will be the choice ones, that most of us turn back. We are not quite prepared for the blows which must come if we are going to be turned into the shape of the vision. We have seen what we are not, and what God wants us to be, but are we willing to have the vision "batter'd to shape and use" by God? The batterings always come in commonplace ways and through commonplace people.

There are times when we do know what God's purpose is; whether we will let the vision be turned into actual character depends upon us, not upon God. If we prefer to loll on the mount and live in the memory of the vision, we will be of no use actually in the ordinary stuff of which human life is made up. We have to learn to live in reliance on what we saw in the vision, not in ecstasies and conscious contemplation of God, but to live in actualities in the light of the vision until we get to the veritable reality. Every bit of our training is in that direction. Learn to thank God for making known His demands.

(*Utmost*)

ESTHER 1:1—2:23

NOW it came to pass in the days of Ahasuerus (this *was* the Ahasuerus who reigned over one hundred and twenty-seven provinces, from India to Ethiopia), 2 in those days when King Ahasuerus sat on the throne of his kingdom, which *was* in Shushan the citadel, 3 *that* in the third year of his reign he made a feast for all his officials and servants—the powers of Persia and Media, the nobles, and the princes of the provinces *being* before him— 4 when he showed the riches of his glorious kingdom and the splendor of his excellent majesty for many days, one hundred and eighty days *in all*.

5 And when these days were completed, the king made a feast lasting seven days for all the people who were present in Shushan the citadel, from great to small, in the court of the garden of the king's palace. 6 *There were* white and blue linen *curtains* fastened with cords of fine linen and purple on silver rods and marble pillars; *and the* couches *were* of gold and silver on a *mosaic* pavement of alabaster, turquoise, and white and black marble. 7 And they served drinks in golden vessels, each vessel being different from the other, with royal wine in abundance, according to the generosity of the king. 8 In accordance with the law, the drinking was not compulsory; for so the king had ordered all the officers of his household, that they should do according to each man's pleasure.

9 Queen Vashti also made a feast for the women *in* the royal palace which *belonged* to King Ahasuerus.

10 On the seventh day, when the heart of the king was merry with wine, he commanded Mehuman, Biztha, Harbona, Bigtha, Abagtha, Zethar, and Carcas, seven eunuchs who served in the presence of King Ahasuerus, 11 to bring Queen Vashti before the king, *wearing* her royal crown, in order to show her beauty to the people and the officials, for she *was* beautiful to behold. 12 But Queen Vashti refused to come at the king's command *brought* by *his* eunuchs; therefore the king was furious, and his anger burned within him.

13 Then the king said to the wise men who understood the times (for this *was* the king's manner toward all who knew law and justice, 14 those closest to him *being* Carshena, Shethar, Admatha, Tarshish, Meres, Marsena, and Memucan, the seven princes of Persia and Media, who had access to the king's presence, *and* who ranked highest in the kingdom): 15 "What *shall we* do to Queen Vashti, according to law, because she did not obey the command of King Ahasuerus *brought to her* by the eunuchs?"

16 And Memucan answered before the king and the princes: "Queen Vashti has not only wronged the king, but also all the princes, and all the people who *are* in all the provinces of King Ahasuerus. 17 For the queen's behavior will become known to all women, so that they will despise their husbands in their eyes, when they report, 'King Ahasuerus commanded Queen Vashti to be brought in before him, but she did not come.' 18 This very day the *noble* ladies of Persia and Media will say to all the king's officials that they have heard of the behavior of the queen. Thus *there will be* excessive contempt and wrath. 19 If it pleases the king, let a royal decree go out from him, and let it be recorded in the laws of the Persians and the Medes, so that it will not be altered, that Vashti shall come no more before King Ahasuerus; and let the king give her royal position to another who is better than she. 20 When the king's decree which he will make is proclaimed throughout all his empire (for it is great), all wives will honor their husbands, both great and small."

21 And the reply pleased the king and the princes, and the king did according to the word of Memucan. 22 Then he sent letters to all the king's provinces, to each province in its own script, and to every people in their own language, that each man should be master in his own house, and speak in the language of his own people.

2 AFTER these things, when the wrath of King Ahasuerus subsided, he remembered Vashti, what she had done, and what had been decreed against her. 2 Then the king's servants who attended him said: "Let beautiful young virgins be sought for the king; 3 and let the king appoint officers in all the provinces of his kingdom, that they may gather all the beautiful young virgins to Shushan the citadel, into the women's quarters, under the custody of Hegai the king's eunuch, custodian of the women. And let beauty preparations be given *them*. 4 Then let the young woman who pleases the king be queen instead of Vashti."

This thing pleased the king, and he did so.

5 In Shushan the citadel there was a certain Jew whose name *was* Mordecai the son of Jair, the son of Shimei, the son of Kish, a Benjamite. 6 *Kish* had been carried away from Jerusalem with the captives who had been captured with Jeconiah king of Judah, whom Nebuchadnezzar the king of Babylon had carried away. 7 And *Mordecai* had brought up Hadassah, that *is*, Esther, his uncle's daughter, for she had neither father nor mother. The young woman *was* lovely and beautiful. When her father and mother died, Mordecai took her as his own daughter.

8 So it was, when the king's command and decree were heard, and when many

young women were gathered at Shushan the citadel, *under* the custody of Hegai, that Esther also was taken to the king's palace, into the care of Hegai the custodian of the women. 9 Now the young woman pleased him, and she obtained his favor; so he readily gave beauty preparations to her, besides her allowance. Then seven choice maidservants were provided for her from the king's palace, and he moved her and her maidservants to the best *place* in the house of the women.

10 Esther had not revealed her people or family, for Mordecai had charged her not to reveal *it.* 11 And every day Mordecai paced in front of the court of the women's quarters, to learn of Esther's welfare and what was happening to her.

12 Each young woman's turn came to go in to King Ahasuerus after she had completed twelve months' preparation, according to the regulations for the women, for thus were the days of their preparation apportioned: six months with oil of myrrh, and six months with perfumes and preparations for beautifying women. 13 Thus *prepared, each* young woman went to the king, and she was given whatever she desired to take with her from the women's quarters to the king's palace. 14 In the evening she went, and in the morning she returned to the second house of the women, to the custody of Shaashgaz, the king's eunuch who kept the concubines. She would not go in to the king again unless the king delighted in her and called for her by name.

15 Now when the turn came for Esther the daughter of Abihail the uncle of Mordecai, who had taken her as his daughter, to go in to the king, she requested nothing but what Hegai the king's eunuch, the custodian of the women, advised. And Esther obtained favor in the sight of all who saw her. 16 So Esther was taken to King Ahasuerus, into his royal palace, in the tenth month, which *is* the month of Tebeth, in the seventh year of his reign. 17 The king loved Esther more than all the *other* women, and she obtained grace and favor in his sight more than all the virgins; so he set the royal crown upon her head and made her queen instead of Vashti. 18 Then the king made a great feast, the Feast of Esther, for all his officials and servants; and he proclaimed a holiday in the provinces and gave gifts according to the generosity of a king.

19 When virgins were gathered together a second time, Mordecai sat within the king's gate. 20 *Now* Esther had not revealed her family and her people, just as Mordecai had charged her, for Esther obeyed the command of Mordecai as when she was brought up by him.

21 In those days, while Mordecai sat within the king's gate, two of the king's eunuchs, Bigthan and Teresh, doorkeepers, became furious and sought to lay hands on King Ahasuerus. 22 So the matter became known to Mordecai, who told Queen Esther, and Esther informed the king in Mordecai's name. 23 And when an inquiry was made into the matter, it was confirmed, and both were hanged on a gallows; and it was written in the book of the chronicles in the presence of the king.

PSALM 89:38–45

38 BUT You have cast off and abhorred,
   You have been furious with Your
      anointed.
39 You have renounced the covenant of
      Your servant;
   You have profaned his crown *by casting
      it* to the ground.
40 You have broken down all his hedges;
   You have brought his strongholds to
      ruin.
41 All who pass by the way plunder
      him;
   He is a reproach to his neighbors.
42 You have exalted the right hand of his
      adversaries;
   You have made all his enemies rejoice.
43 You have also turned back the edge of
      his sword,
   And have not sustained him in the
      battle.
44 You have made his glory cease,
   And cast his throne down to the
      ground.
45 The days of his youth You have
      shortened;
   You have covered him with shame.
                                    Selah

PROVERBS 22:5, 6

5 THORNS *and* snares *are* in the way
      of the perverse;
   He who guards his soul will be far from
      them.

6 Train up a child in the way he should
      go,
   And when he is old he will not depart
      from it.

ROMANS 2:1–29

THEREFORE you are inexcusable, O man, whoever you are who judge, for in whatever you judge another you condemn yourself; for you who judge practice the same things. 2 But we know that the judgment of God is according to truth against those who practice such things. 3 And do you think this, O man, you who judge those practicing such things, and doing the same, that you will escape the judgment of God? 4 Or do you despise the riches of His goodness, forbearance, and longsuffering, not knowing that the goodness of God leads you to repentance? 5 But in accordance with your hardness and your impenitent heart you are treasuring up for yourself wrath in the day of wrath and revelation of the righteous judgment of God, 6 who "will render to each one according to his deeds": 7 eternal life to those who by patient continuance in doing good seek for glory, honor, and immortality; 8 but to those who are self-seeking and do not obey the truth, but obey unrighteousness—indignation and wrath, 9 tribulation and anguish, on every soul of man who does evil, of the Jew first and also of the Greek; 10 but glory, honor, and peace to everyone who works what is good, to the Jew first and also to the Greek. 11 For there is no partiality with God.

12 For as many as have sinned without law will also perish without law, and as many as have sinned in the law will be judged by the law 13 (for not the hearers of the law *are* just in the sight of God, but the doers of the law will be justified; 14 for when Gentiles, who do not have the law, by nature do the things in the law, these, although not having the law, are a law to themselves, 15 who show the work of the law written in their hearts, their conscience also bearing witness, and between themselves *their* thoughts accusing or else excusing *them*) 16 in the day when God will judge the secrets of men by Jesus Christ, according to my gospel.

17 Indeed you are called a Jew, and rest on the law, and make your boast in God, 18 and know *His* will, and approve the things that are excellent, being instructed out of the law, 19 and are confident that you yourself are a guide to the blind, a light to those who are in darkness, 20 an instructor of the foolish, a teacher of babes, having the form of knowledge and truth in the law. 21 You, therefore, who teach another, do you not teach yourself? You who preach that a man should not steal, do you steal? 22 You who say, "Do not commit adultery," do you commit adultery? You who abhor idols, do you rob temples? 23 You who make your boast in the law, do you dishonor God through breaking the law? 24 For "the name of God is blasphemed among the Gentiles because of you," as it is written.

25 For circumcision is indeed profitable if you keep the law; but if you are a breaker of the law, your circumcision has become uncircumcision. 26 Therefore, if an uncircumcised man keeps the righteous requirements of the law, will not his uncircumcision be counted as circumcision? 27 And will not the physically uncircumcised, if he fulfills the law, judge you who, *even* with *your* written *code* and circumcision, *are* a transgressor of the law? 28 For he is not a Jew who *is one* outwardly, nor *is* circumcision that which *is* outward in the flesh; 29 but *he is* a Jew who *is one* inwardly; and circumcision *is that* of the heart, in the Spirit, not in the letter; whose praise *is* not from men but from God.

> *Every man has a conscience, although every man does not know God.* (BIB. ETHICS)

Reading 213—Have Faith in Jesus
Romans 3:24–26

Is it not humiliating to be told that we must come to Jesus! Think of the things we will not come to Jesus Christ about. If you want to know how real you are, test yourself by these words—"Come to Me." In every degree in which you are not real, you will dispute rather than come, you will quibble rather than come, you will go through sorrow rather than come, you will do anything rather than come the last lap of unutterable foolishness—"Just as I am.". . .

"Come to Me." When you hear those words you will know that something must happen in you before you can come. The Holy Spirit will show you what you have to do, anything at all that will put the ax at the root of the thing which is preventing you from getting through. You will never get further until you are willing to do that one thing. The Holy Spirit will locate the one impregnable thing in you, but He cannot budge it unless you are willing to let Him.

How often have you come to God with your requests and gone away with the feeling—Oh, well, I have done it this time! And yet you go away with nothing, while all the time God has stood with outstretched hands not only to take you, but for you to take Him. Think of the invincible, unconquerable, unwearying patience of Jesus—"Come to Me."   (*UTMOST*)

ESTHER 3:1—4:17

AFTER these things King Ahasuerus promoted Haman, the son of Hammedatha the Agagite, and advanced him and set his seat above all the princes who *were* with him. 2 And all the king's servants who *were* within the king's gate bowed and paid homage to Haman, for so the king had commanded concerning him. But Mordecai would not bow or pay homage. 3 Then the king's servants who *were* within the king's gate said to Mordecai, "Why do you transgress the king's command?" 4 Now it happened, when they spoke to him daily and he would not listen to them, that they told *it* to Haman, to see whether Mordecai's words would stand; for *Mordecai* had told them that he *was* a Jew. 5 When Haman saw that Mordecai did not bow or pay him homage, Haman was filled with wrath. 6 But he disdained to lay hands on Mordecai alone, for they had told him of the people of Mordecai. Instead, Haman sought to destroy all the Jews who *were* throughout the whole kingdom of Ahasuerus—the people of Mordecai.

7 In the first month, which is the month of Nisan, in the twelfth year of King Ahasuerus, they cast Pur (that *is*, the lot), before Haman to determine the day and the month, until *it fell on the* twelfth *month*, which *is* the month of Adar.

8 Then Haman said to King Ahasuerus, "There is a certain people scattered and dispersed among the people in all the provinces of your kingdom; their laws *are* different from all *other* people's, and they do not keep the king's laws. Therefore it *is* not fitting for the king to let them remain. 9 If it pleases the king, let *a decree* be written

that they be destroyed, and I will pay ten thousand talents of silver into the hands of those who do the work, to bring *it* into the king's treasuries."

10 So the king took his signet ring from his hand and gave it to Haman, the son of Hammedatha the Agagite, the enemy of the Jews. 11 And the king said to Haman, "The money and the people *are* given to you, to do with them as seems good to you."

12 Then the king's scribes were called on the thirteenth day of the first month, and *a decree* was written according to all that Haman commanded—to the king's satraps, to the governors who *were* over each province, to the officials of all people, to every province according to its script, and to every people in their language. In the name of King Ahasuerus it was written, and sealed with the king's signet ring. 13 And the letters were sent by couriers into all the king's provinces, to destroy, to kill, and to annihilate all the Jews, both young and old, little children and women, in one day, on the thirteenth *day* of the twelfth *month*, which *is* the month of Adar, and to plunder their possessions. 14 A copy of the document was to be issued as law in every province, being published for all people, that they should be ready for that day. 15 The couriers went out, hastened by the king's command; and the decree was proclaimed in Shushan the citadel. So the king and Haman sat down to drink, but the city of Shushan was perplexed.

4 WHEN Mordecai learned all that had happened, he tore his clothes and put on sackcloth and ashes, and went out into the midst of the city. He cried out with a

loud and bitter cry. 2 He went as far as the front of the king's gate, for no one *might* enter the king's gate clothed with sackcloth. 3 And in every province where the king's command and decree arrived, *there was* great mourning among the Jews, with fasting, weeping, and wailing; and many lay in sackcloth and ashes.

4 So Esther's maids and eunuchs came and told her, and the queen was deeply distressed. Then she sent garments to clothe Mordecai and take his sackcloth away from him, but he would not accept *them*. 5 Then Esther called Hathach, *one* of the king's eunuchs whom he had appointed to attend her, and she gave him a command concerning Mordecai, to learn what and why this *was*. 6 So Hathach went out to Mordecai in the city square that *was* in front of the king's gate. 7 And Mordecai told him all that had happened to him, and the sum of money that Haman had promised to pay into the king's treasuries to destroy the Jews. 8 He also gave him a copy of the written decree for their destruction, which was given at Shushan, that he might show it to Esther and explain it to her, and that he might command her to go in to the king to make supplication to him and plead before him for her people. 9 So Hathach returned and told Esther the words of Mordecai.

10 Then Esther spoke to Hathach, and gave him a command for Mordecai: 11 "All the king's servants and the people of the king's provinces know that any man or woman who goes into the inner court to the king, who has not been called, *he has* but one law: put *all* to death, except the one to whom the king holds out the golden scepter, that he may live. Yet I myself have not been called to go in to the king these thirty days." 12 So they told Mordecai Esther's words.

13 And Mordecai told *them* to answer Esther: "Do not think in your heart that you will escape in the king's palace any more than all the other Jews. 14 For if you remain completely silent at this time, relief and deliverance will arise for the Jews from another place, but you and your father's house will perish. Yet who knows whether you have come to the kingdom for *such* a time as this?"

15 Then Esther told *them* to reply to Mordecai: 16 "Go, gather all the Jews who are present in Shushan, and fast for me; neither eat nor drink for three days, night or day. My maids and I will fast likewise. And so I will go to the king, which *is* against the law; and if I perish, I perish!"

17 So Mordecai went his way and did according to all that Esther commanded him.

PSALM 89:46–52

46 HOW long, LORD?
   Will You hide Yourself forever?
   Will Your wrath burn like fire?
47 Remember how short my time is;
   For what futility have You created all
      the children of men?
48 What man can live and not see death?
   Can he deliver his life from the power
      of the grave?   Selah

49 Lord, where *are* Your former
      lovingkindnesses,
   Which You swore to David in Your
      truth?
50 Remember, Lord, the reproach of
      Your servants—
   How I bear in my bosom *the reproach
      of* all the many peoples,
51 With which Your enemies have
      reproached, O LORD,
   With which they have reproached the
      footsteps of Your anointed.

52 Blessed *be* the LORD forevermore!
   Amen and Amen.

PROVERBS 22:7, 8

7 THE rich rules over the poor,
   And the borrower *is* servant to the
      lender.

8 He who sows iniquity will reap sorrow,
   And the rod of his anger will fail.

ROMANS 3:1–31

WHAT advantage then has the Jew, or what *is* the profit of circumcision? 2 Much in every way! Chiefly because to them were committed the oracles of God. 3 For what if some did not believe? Will their unbelief make the faithfulness of God without effect? 4 Certainly not! Indeed, let God be true but every man a liar. As it is written:

   "That You may be justified in Your
      words,
      And may overcome when You are
         judged."

5 But if our unrighteousness demonstrates the righteousness of God, what shall

we say? *Is* God unjust who inflicts wrath? (I speak as a man.) 6 Certainly not! For then how will God judge the world?

7 For if the truth of God has increased through my lie to His glory, why am I also still judged as a sinner? 8 And *why* not *say,* "Let us do evil that good may come"?— as we are slanderously reported and as some affirm that we say. Their condemnation is just.

9 What then? Are we better *than they?* Not at all. For we have previously charged both Jews and Greeks that they are all under sin.

10 As it is written:

"There is none righteous, no, not one;
11   There is none who understands;
        There is none who seeks after God.
12   They have all turned aside;
        They have together become
           unprofitable;
        There is none who does good, no,
           not one."
13 "Their throat *is* an open tomb;
        With their tongues they have
           practiced deceit";
    "The poison of asps *is* under their
        lips";
14 "Whose mouth *is* full of cursing and
        bitterness."
15 "Their feet *are* swift to shed blood;
16   Destruction and misery *are* in their
        ways;
17   And the way of peace they have not
        known."
18 "There is no fear of God before their
        eyes."

19 Now we know that whatever the law says, it says to those who are under the law, that every mouth may be stopped, and all the world may become guilty before God. 20 Therefore by the deeds of the law no flesh will be justified in His sight, for by the law *is* the knowledge of sin.

21 But now the righteousness of God apart from the law is revealed, being witnessed by the Law and the Prophets, 22 even the righteousness of God, through faith in Jesus Christ, to all and on all who believe. For there is no difference; 23 for all have sinned and fall short of the glory of God, 24 being justified freely by His grace through the redemption that is in Christ Jesus, 25 whom God set forth *as* a propitia-

---

God never justifies men outside Christ.   (GOOD)

---

tion by His blood, through faith, to demonstrate His righteousness, because in His forbearance God had passed over the sins that were previously committed, 26 to demonstrate at the present time His righteousness, that He might be just and the justifier of the one who has faith in Jesus.

27 Where *is* boasting then? It is excluded. By what law? Of works? No, but by the law of faith. 28 Therefore we conclude that a man is justified by faith apart from the deeds of the law. 29 Or *is He* the God of the Jews only? *Is He* not also the God of the Gentiles? Yes, of the Gentiles also, 30 since *there is* one God who will justify the circumcised by faith and the uncircumcised through faith. 31 Do we then make void the law through faith? Certainly not! On the contrary, we establish the law.

Reading 214—The Great Solution
Romans 4:3

God hitched Abraham's wagon to the stars He had created, by His word. In our personal lives the great solution is always found in the words of our Lord when we have His Spirit. Jesus Christ is God incarnate, and He makes His words spirit and life to us. Our little human wagons are hitched to the star of God's sacramental purpose by the words of Jesus and in no other way. Whenever we indulge in hurry or in the dumps and refuse to pay attention to His words, we smash the connecting line and go off on our own.

"And he believed in the LORD, and He accounted it to him for righteousness." This is the act by which Abraham goes out of himself and relies upon God for righteousness and grace. Abraham had manifested many noble qualities of heart and many virtues in his walk of faith, but these did not make him righteous before God. That was accomplished through his living confidence in God.

This verse is the first germ of the great doctrine of "the Lord our Righteousness." Righteousness must never be made to mean less than a guiltless position in the presence of justice and right. The justification of every sinner is by faith, and by faith alone. But it is our just walk that proves Him just in saving us. If we do not walk in the life of faith, we are a slander to God.

(*Not Knowing*)

ESTHER 5:1—6:14

NOW it happened on the third day that Esther put on *her* royal *robes* and stood in the inner court of the king's palace, across from the king's house, while the king sat on his royal throne in the royal house, facing the entrance of the house. 2 So it was, when the king saw Queen Esther standing in the court, *that* she found favor in his sight, and the king held out to Esther the golden scepter that *was* in his hand. Then Esther went near and touched the top of the scepter.

3 And the king said to her, "What do you wish, Queen Esther? What *is* your request? It shall be given to you—up to half the kingdom!"

4 So Esther answered, "If it pleases the king, let the king and Haman come today to the banquet that I have prepared for him."

5 Then the king said, "Bring Haman quickly, that he may do as Esther has said." So the king and Haman went to the banquet that Esther had prepared.

6 At the banquet of wine the king said to Esther, "What *is* your petition? It shall be granted you. What *is* your request, up to half the kingdom? It shall be done!"

7 Then Esther answered and said, "My petition and request *is this:* 8 If I have found favor in the sight of the king, and if it pleases the king to grant my petition and fulfill my request, then let the king and Haman come to the banquet which I will prepare for them, and tomorrow I will do as the king has said."

9 So Haman went out that day joyful and with a glad heart; but when Haman saw Mordecai in the king's gate, and that he did not stand or tremble before him, he was filled with indignation against Mordecai. 10 Nevertheless Haman restrained himself and went home, and he sent and called for his friends and his wife Zeresh. 11 Then Haman told them of his great riches, the multitude of his children, everything in which the king had promoted him,

and how he had advanced him above the officials and servants of the king.

12 Moreover Haman said, "Besides, Queen Esther invited no one but me to come in with the king to the banquet that she prepared; and tomorrow I am again invited by her, along with the king. 13 Yet all this avails me nothing, so long as I see Mordecai the Jew sitting at the king's gate."

14 Then his wife Zeresh and all his friends said to him, "Let a gallows be made, fifty cubits high, and in the morning suggest to the king that Mordecai be hanged on it; then go merrily with the king to the banquet."

And the thing pleased Haman; so he had the gallows made.

6 THAT night the king could not sleep. So one was commanded to bring the book of the records of the chronicles; and they were read before the king. 2 And it was found written that Mordecai had told of Bigthana and Teresh, two of the king's eunuchs, the doorkeepers who had sought to lay hands on King Ahasuerus. 3 Then the king said, "What honor or dignity has been bestowed on Mordecai for this?"

And the king's servants who attended him said, "Nothing has been done for him."

4 So the king said, "Who *is* in the court?" Now Haman had *just* entered the outer court of the king's palace to suggest that the king hang Mordecai on the gallows that he had prepared for him.

5 The king's servants said to him, "Haman is there, standing in the court."

And the king said, "Let him come in."

6 So Haman came in, and the king asked him, "What shall be done for the man whom the king delights to honor?"

Now Haman thought in his heart, "Whom would the king delight to honor more than me?" 7 And Haman answered the king, "*For* the man whom the king delights to honor, 8 let a royal robe be brought which the king has worn, and a horse on which the king has ridden, which has a royal

crest placed on its head. 9 Then let this robe
and horse be delivered to the hand of one
of the king's most noble princes, that he
may array the man whom the king delights
to honor. Then parade him on horseback
through the city square, and proclaim before him: 'Thus shall it be done to the man
whom the king delights to honor!' "

10 Then the king said to Haman, "Hurry,
take the robe and the horse, as you have
suggested, and do so for Mordecai the
Jew who sits within the king's gate! Leave
nothing undone of all that you have
spoken."

11 So Haman took the robe and the horse,
arrayed Mordecai and led him on horse
back through the city square, and proclaimed before him, "Thus shall it be done
to the man whom the king delights to
honor!"

12 Afterward Mordecai went back to the
king's gate. But Haman hurried to his
house, mourning and with his head covered.
13 When Haman told his wife Zeresh and
all his friends everything that had happened
to him, his wise men and his wife Zeresh
said to him, "If Mordecai, before whom
you have begun to fall, is of Jewish descent,
you will not prevail against him but will
surely fall before him."

14 While they *were* still talking with him,
the king's eunuchs came, and hastened to
bring Haman to the banquet which Esther
had prepared.

PSALM 90:1–6

1   LORD, You have been our dwelling
     place in all generations.
2   Before the mountains were brought
     forth,
     Or ever You had formed the earth and
     the world,
     Even from everlasting to everlasting,
     You *are* God.

3   You turn man to destruction,
     And say, "Return, O children of
     men."
4   For a thousand years in Your sight
     Are like yesterday when it is past,
     And *like* a watch in the night.
5   You carry them away *like* a flood;
     They are like a sleep.
     In the morning they are like grass *which*
     grows up:
6   In the morning it flourishes and grows
     up;
     In the evening it is cut down and
     withers.

PROVERBS 22:9

9   HE who has a generous eye will be
     blessed,
     For he gives of his bread to the
     poor.

ROMANS 4:1–25

WHAT then shall we say that Abraham
our father has found according to the flesh?
2 For if Abraham was justified by works,
he has *something* to boast about, but not
before God. 3 For what does the Scripture
say? "Abraham believed God, and it was
accounted to him for righteousness."
4 Now to him who works, the wages are
not counted as grace but as debt.

5 But to him who does not work but
believes on Him who justifies the ungodly,
his faith is accounted for righteousness,

*T*he justification of every sinner
is by faith and by faith
alone.   (NOT KNOWING)

6 just as David also describes the blessedness
of the man to whom God imputes righteousness apart from works:

7   "Blessed *are those* whose lawless deeds
     are forgiven,
     And whose sins are covered;
8   Blessed *is the* man to whom the LORD
     shall not impute sin."

9 *Does* this blessedness then *come* upon
the circumcised *only,* or upon the uncircumcised also? For we say that faith was accounted to Abraham for righteousness.
10 How then was it accounted? While he
was circumcised, or uncircumcised? Not
while circumcised, but while uncircumcised. 11 And he received the sign of circumcision, a seal of the righteousness of the
faith which *he had while still* uncircumcised,
that he might be the father of all those
who believe, though they are uncircumcised, that righteousness might be imputed
to them also, 12 and the father of circumcision to those who not only *are* of the circumcision, but who also walk in the steps
of the faith which our father Abraham *had
while still* uncircumcised.

13 For the promise that he would be the
heir of the world *was* not to Abraham or

to his seed through the law, but through the righteousness of faith. 14 For if those who are of the law *are* heirs, faith is made void and the promise made of no effect, 15 because the law brings about wrath; for where there is no law *there is* no transgression.

16 Therefore *it is* of faith that *it might be* according to grace, so that the promise might be sure to all the seed, not only to those who are of the law, but also to those who are of the faith of Abraham, who is the father of us all 17 (as it is written, "I have made you a father of many nations") in the presence of Him whom he believed—God, who gives life to the dead and calls those things which do not exist as though they did; 18 who, contrary to hope, in hope believed, so that he became the father of many nations, according to what was spoken, "So shall your descendants be." 19 And not being weak in faith, he did not consider his own body, already dead (since he was about a hundred years old), and the deadness of Sarah's womb. 20 He did not waver at the promise of God through unbelief, but was strengthened in faith, giving glory to God, 21 and being fully convinced that what He had promised He was also able to perform. 22 And therefore "it was accounted to him for righteousness."

23 Now it was not written for his sake alone that it was imputed to him, 24 but also for us. It shall be imputed to us who believe in Him who raised up Jesus our Lord from the dead, 25 who was delivered up because of our offenses, and was raised because of our justification.

*Reading 215—*At the Wall of the World
Romans 5:7–9

The great fundamental revelation regarding the human race is that God has redeemed us; and redemption enters into our lives when we are upset enough to see we need it. There is too much common sense used, "pills to cure an earthquake" given; and "the gospel of temperament" preached. It is an insult today to tell some men and women to cheer up. One of the most shallow petty things that can be said is that "every cloud has a silver lining." There are some clouds that are black all through. At the wall of the world stands God with His arms outstretched; and when a man or woman is driven there, the consolations of Jesus Christ are given. Through the agonies in human life we do not make redemption, but we see why it was necessary for God to make it. It is not necessary for every man to go through these agonies, but it takes a time of agony to get the shallow scepticism knocked out of us. It is a good thing to be reverent with what we do not understand. A moral agony gives a man "a second wind," and he runs better after it, and is a good deal more likely to win.   (*SHAD. AGONY*)

ESTHER 7:1—8:17

SO the king and Haman went to dine with Queen Esther. 2 And on the second day, at the banquet of wine, the king again said to Esther, "What *is* your petition, Queen Esther? It shall be granted you. And what *is* your request, up to half the kingdom? It shall be done!"

3 Then Queen Esther answered and said, "If I have found favor in your sight, O king, and if it pleases the king, let my life be given me at my petition, and my people at my request. 4 For we have been sold, my people and I, to be destroyed, to be killed, and to be annihilated. Had we been sold as male and female slaves, I would have held my tongue, although the enemy could never compensate for the king's loss."

5 So King Ahasuerus answered and said to Queen Esther, "Who is he, and where is he, who would dare presume in his heart to do such a thing?"

6 And Esther said, "The adversary and enemy *is* this wicked Haman!"

So Haman was terrified before the king and queen.

7 Then the king arose in his wrath from the banquet of wine *and went* into the palace garden; but Haman stood before Queen Esther, pleading for his life, for he saw that evil was determined against him by the king. 8 When the king returned from the palace garden to the place of the banquet of wine, Haman had fallen across the couch where Esther *was*. Then the king said, "Will he also assault the queen while I *am* in the house?"

As the word left the king's mouth, they covered Haman's face. 9 Now Harbonah, one of the eunuchs, said to the king, "Look! The gallows, fifty cubits high, which Haman made for Mordecai, who spoke good on the king's behalf, is standing at the house of Haman."

Then the king said, "Hang him on it!"

10 So they hanged Haman on the gallows that he had prepared for Mordecai. Then the king's wrath subsided.

8 ON that day King Ahasuerus gave Queen Esther the house of Haman, the enemy of the Jews. And Mordecai came before the king, for Esther had told how he *was related* to her. 2 So the king took off his signet ring, which he had taken from Haman, and gave it to Mordecai; and Esther appointed Mordecai over the house of Haman.

3 Now Esther spoke again to the king, fell down at his feet, and implored him with tears to counteract the evil of Haman the Agagite, and the scheme which he had devised against the Jews. 4 And the king held out the golden scepter toward Esther. So Esther arose and stood before the king, 5 and said, "If it pleases the king, and if I have found favor in his sight and the thing *seems* right to the king and I am pleasing in his eyes, let it be written to revoke the letters devised by Haman, the son of Hammedatha the Agagite, which he wrote to annihilate the Jews who *are* in all the king's provinces. 6 For how can I endure to see the evil that will come to my people? Or how can I endure to see the destruction of my countrymen?"

7 Then King Ahasuerus said to Queen Esther and Mordecai the Jew, "Indeed, I have given Esther the house of Haman, and they have hanged him on the gallows because he *tried to* lay his hand on the Jews. 8 You yourselves write *a decree* concerning the Jews, as you please, in the king's name, and seal *it* with the king's signet ring; for whatever is written in the king's name and sealed with the king's signet ring no one can revoke."

9 So the king's scribes were called at that time, in the third month, which *is* the month of Sivan, on the twenty-third *day;* and it was written, according to all that Mordecai commanded, to the Jews, the satraps, the governors, and the princes of the provinces from India to Ethiopia, one hundred and twenty-seven provinces *in all,* to every province in its own script, to every people in their own language, and to the Jews in their own script and language. 10 And he wrote in the name of King Ahasuerus, sealed *it* with the king's signet ring, and sent letters by couriers on horseback, riding on royal horses bred from swift steeds.

11 By these letters the king permitted the Jews who *were* in every city to gather together and protect their lives—to destroy, kill, and annihilate all the forces of any people or province that would assault them, *both* little children and women, and to plunder their possessions, 12 on one day in all the provinces of King Ahasuerus, on the thirteenth *day* of the twelfth month, which *is* the month of Adar. 13 A copy of the document was to be issued as a decree in every province and published for all people, so that the Jews would be ready on that day to avenge themselves on their enemies. 14 The couriers who rode on royal horses went out, hastened and pressed on by the king's command. And the decree was issued in Shushan the citadel.

15 So Mordecai went out from the presence of the king in royal apparel of blue and white, with a great crown of gold and a garment of fine linen and purple; and the city of Shushan rejoiced and was glad. 16 The Jews had light and gladness, joy and honor. 17 And in every province and city, wherever the king's command and decree came, the Jews had joy and gladness, a feast and a holiday. Then many of the people of the land became Jews, because fear of the Jews fell upon them.

PSALM 90:7–17

7   FOR we have been consumed by Your anger,
     And by Your wrath we are terrified.
8   You have set our iniquities before You,
     Our secret *sins* in the light of Your countenance.
9   For all our days have passed away in Your wrath;
     We finish our years like a sigh.
10   The days of our lives *are* seventy years;

And if by reason of strength *they are*
    eighty years,
Yet their boast *is* only labor and sorrow;
For it is soon cut off, and we fly away.
11 Who knows the power of Your anger?
    For as the fear of You, *so is* Your wrath.
12 So teach *us* to number our days,
    That we may gain a heart of wisdom.

13 Return, O LORD!
    How long?
    And have compassion on Your servants.
14 Oh, satisfy us early with Your mercy,
    That we may rejoice and be glad all
    our days!
15 Make us glad according to the days *in*
    which You have afflicted us,
    The years *in which* we have seen evil.
16 Let Your work appear to Your servants,
    And Your glory to their children.
17 And let the beauty of the LORD our
    God be upon us,
    And establish the work of our hands
    for us;
    Yes, establish the work of our hands.

---

*True Christian experience brings
us face-to-face with spiritual
beauty.*   (SERVANT AS LORD)

PROVERBS 22:10, 11

10 CAST out the scoffer, and contention
    will leave;
    Yes, strife and reproach will cease.

11 He who loves purity of heart
    And has grace on his lips,
    The king *will be* his friend.

ROMANS 5:1–21

THEREFORE, having been justified by
faith, we have peace with God through our
Lord Jesus Christ, 2 through whom also
we have access by faith into this grace in
which we stand, and rejoice in hope of the
glory of God. 3 And not only *that,* but we
also glory in tribulations, knowing that
tribulation produces perseverance; 4 and
perseverance, character; and character,
hope. 5 Now hope does not disappoint, because the love of God has been poured out
in our hearts by the Holy Spirit who was
given to us.
6 For when we were still without
strength, in due time Christ died for the
ungodly. 7 For scarcely for a righteous man

will one die; yet perhaps for a good man
someone would even dare to die. 8 But God
demonstrates His own love toward us, in
that while we were still sinners, Christ died
for us. 9 Much more then, having now been
justified by His blood, we shall be saved
from wrath through Him. 10 For if when
we were enemies we were reconciled to God
through the death of His Son, much more,
having been reconciled, we shall be saved
by His life. 11 And not only *that,* but we
also rejoice in God through our Lord Jesus
Christ, through whom we have now received the reconciliation.
12 Therefore, just as through one man
sin entered the world, and death through
sin, and thus death spread to all men, because all sinned— 13 (For until the law sin
was in the world, but sin is not imputed
when there is no law. 14 Nevertheless death
reigned from Adam to Moses, even over
those who had not sinned according to the
likeness of the transgression of Adam, who
is a type of Him who was to come.
15 But the free gift *is* not like the offense.
For if by the one man's offense many died,
much more the grace of God and the gift
by the grace of the one Man, Jesus Christ,
abounded to many. 16 And the gift *is* not
like *that which came* through the one who
sinned. For the judgment *which came* from
one *offense resulted* in condemnation, but
the free gift *which came* from many offenses
resulted in justification. 17 For if by the one
man's offense death reigned through the
one, much more those who receive abundance of grace and of the gift of righteousness will reign in life through the One, Jesus
Christ.)
18 Therefore, as through one man's offense *judgment* came to all men, resulting
in condemnation, even so through one
Man's righteous act *the free gift came* to all
men, resulting in justification of life.
19 For as by one man's disobedience many
were made sinners, so also by one Man's
obedience many will be made righteous.
20 Moreover the law entered that the offense might abound. But where sin
abounded, grace abounded much more,
21 so that as sin reigned in death, even so
grace might reign through righteousness
to eternal life through Jesus Christ our
Lord.

---

*Keep your mind on the "much
more" of your Heavenly
Father.*   (RUN)

Reading 216—Yield Yourselves to God

Romans 6:12, 13

When I am born again my human nature is not different, it is the same as before, I am related to life in the same way, I have the same bodily organs, but the mainspring is different, and I have to see now that all my members are dominated by the new disposition (see Romans 5:13, 19). There is only one kind of human nature, and that is the human nature we have all got; and there is only one kind of holiness, the holiness of Jesus Christ. Give Him "elbowroom," and He will manifest Himself in you, and other people will recognize Him. Human beings know human beings too well to mistake where goodness comes from; when they see certain characteristics they will know they come only from the indwelling of Jesus. It is not the manifestation of noble human traits, but of a real family likeness of Jesus. It is *His* gentleness, *His* patience, *His* purity, never mine. The whole art of spirituality is that my human nature should retire and let the new disposition have its way.   (*CONFORMED*)

As we go on, we find every place God brings us into is the means of enabling us to realize with growing joy that the life of Christ within is more than a match, not only for the enemy on the outside, but for the impaired body that comes between. Paul urges with passionate pleading, that we present our bodies a living sacrifice, and then realize, not presumptuously, but with slow, sure, overwhelming certainty that every command of Christ can be obeyed in our bodily life through the Atonement.   (*PERFECT*)

ESTHER 9:1—10:3

NOW in the twelfth month, that *is*, the month of Adar, on the thirteenth day, *the time* came for the king's command and his decree to be executed. On the day that the enemies of the Jews had hoped to overpower them, the opposite occurred, in that the Jews themselves overpowered those who hated them. 2 The Jews gathered together in their cities throughout all the provinces of King Ahasuerus to lay hands on those who sought their harm. And no one could withstand them, because fear of them fell upon all people. 3 And all the officials of the provinces, the satraps, the governors, and all those doing the king's work, helped the Jews, because the fear of Mordecai fell upon them. 4 For Mordecai *was* great in the king's palace, and his fame spread throughout all the provinces; for this man Mordecai became increasingly prominent. 5 Thus the Jews defeated all their enemies with the stroke of the sword, with slaughter and destruction, and did what they pleased with those who hated them.

6 And in Shushan the citadel the Jews killed and destroyed five hundred men. 7 Also Parshandatha, Dalphon, Aspatha, 8 Poratha, Adalia, Aridatha, 9 Parmashta, Arisai, Aridai, and Vajezatha— 10 the ten sons of Haman the son of Hammedatha, the enemy of the Jews—they killed; but they did not lay a hand on the plunder.

11 On that day the number of those who were killed in Shushan the citadel was brought to the king. 12 And the king said to Queen Esther, "The Jews have killed and destroyed five hundred men in Shushan the citadel, and the ten sons of Haman. What have they done in the rest of the king's provinces? Now what *is* your petition? It shall be granted to you. Or what *is* your further request? It shall be done."

13 Then Esther said, "If it pleases the king, let it be granted to the Jews who *are* in Shushan to do again tomorrow according to today's decree, and let Haman's ten sons be hanged on the gallows."

14 So the king commanded this to be done; the decree was issued in Shushan, and they hanged Haman's ten sons.

15 And the Jews who *were* in Shushan gathered together again on the fourteenth day of the month of Adar and killed three hundred men at Shushan; but they did not lay a hand on the plunder.

16 The remainder of the Jews in the king's

provinces gathered together and protected their lives, had rest from their enemies, and killed seventy-five thousand of their enemies; but they did not lay a hand on the plunder. 17 *This was* on the thirteenth day of the month of Adar. And on the fourteenth of *the month* they rested and made it a day of feasting and gladness.

18 But the Jews who *were* at Shushan assembled together on the thirteenth *day,* as well as on the fourteenth; and on the fifteenth of *the month* they rested, and made it a day of feasting and gladness. 19 Therefore the Jews of the villages who dwelt in the unwalled towns celebrated the fourteenth day of the month of Adar *with* gladness and feasting, as a holiday, and for sending presents to one another.

20 And Mordecai wrote these things and sent letters to all the Jews, near and far, who *were* in all the provinces of King Ahasuerus, 21 to establish among them that they should celebrate yearly the fourteenth and fifteenth days of the month of Adar, 22 as the days on which the Jews had rest from their enemies, as the month which was turned from sorrow to joy for them, and from mourning to a holiday; that they should make them days of feasting and joy, of sending presents to one another and gifts to the poor. 23 So the Jews accepted the custom which they had begun, as Mordecai had written to them, 24 because Haman, the son of Hammedatha the Agagite, the enemy of all the Jews, had plotted against the Jews to annihilate them, and had cast Pur (that *is,* the lot), to consume them and destroy them; 25 but when *Esther* came before the king, he commanded by letter that this wicked plot which *Haman* had devised against the Jews should return on his own head, and that he and his sons should be hanged on the gallows.

26 So they called these days Purim, after the name Pur. Therefore, because of all the words of this letter, what they had seen concerning this matter, and what had happened to them, 27 the Jews established and imposed it upon themselves and their descendants and all who would join them, that without fail they should celebrate these two days every year, according to the written *instructions* and according to the *prescribed* time, 28 *that* these days *should be* remembered and kept throughout every

generation, every family, every province, and every city, that these days of Purim should not fail *to be observed* among the Jews, and *that* the memory of them should not perish among their descendants.

29 Then Queen Esther, the daughter of Abihail, with Mordecai the Jew, wrote with full authority to confirm this second letter about Purim. 30 And *Mordecai* sent letters to all the Jews, to the one hundred and twenty-seven provinces of the kingdom of Ahasuerus, *with* words of peace and truth, 31 to confirm these days of Purim at their *appointed* time, as Mordecai the Jew and Queen Esther had prescribed for them, and as they had decreed for themselves and their descendants concerning matters of their fasting and lamenting. 32 So the decree of Esther confirmed these matters of Purim, and it was written in the book.

10 AND King Ahasuerus imposed tribute on the land and *on* the islands of the sea. 2 Now all the acts of his power and his might, and the account of the greatness of Mordecai, to which the king advanced him, *are* they not written in the book of the chronicles of the kings of Media and Persia? 3 For Mordecai the Jew *was* second to King Ahasuerus, and was great among the Jews and well received by the multitude of his brethren, seeking the good of his people and speaking peace to all his countrymen.

PSALM 91:1–6

1 HE who dwells in the secret place of the Most High
Shall abide under the shadow of the Almighty.
2 I will say of the LORD, "*He is* my refuge and my fortress;
My God, in Him I will trust."

3 Surely He shall deliver you from the snare of the fowler
And from the perilous pestilence.
4 He shall cover you with His feathers, And under His wings you shall take refuge;
His truth *shall be your* shield and buckler.
5 You shall not be afraid of the terror by night,
Nor of the arrow *that* flies by day,
6 *Nor* of the pestilence *that* walks in darkness,
Nor of the destruction *that* lays waste at noonday.

Memory is a spiritual thing and exists in the heart. (BIB. PSYCH.)

PROVERBS 22:12

12 THE eyes of the LORD preserve
     knowledge,
     But He overthrows the words of the
     faithless.

ROMANS 6:1–23

WHAT shall we say then? Shall we continue
in sin that grace may abound? 2 Certainly
not! How shall we who died to sin live
any longer in it? 3 Or do you not know
that as many of us as were baptized into
Christ Jesus were baptized into His death?
4 Therefore we were buried with Him
through baptism into death, that just as
Christ was raised from the dead by the glory
of the Father, even so we also should walk
in newness of life.

5 For if we have been united together
in the likeness of His death, certainly we
also shall be *in the likeness of His* resurrection, 6 knowing this, that our old man
was crucified with *Him,* that the body of
sin might be done away with, that we
should no longer be slaves of sin. 7 For
he who has died has been freed from sin.
8 Now if we died with Christ, we believe
that we shall also live with Him, 9 knowing
that Christ, having been raised from the
dead, dies no more. Death no longer has
dominion over Him. 10 For *the death* that
He died, He died to sin once for all; but
the life that He lives, He lives to God.
11 Likewise you also, reckon yourselves to
be dead indeed to sin, but alive to God in
Christ Jesus our Lord.

12 Therefore do not let sin reign in your
mortal body, that you should obey it in
its lusts. 13 And do not present your members *as* instruments of unrighteousness to
sin, but present yourselves to God as being
alive from the dead, and your members *as*
instruments of righteousness to God.
14 For sin shall not have dominion over
you, for you are not under law but under
grace.

15 What then? Shall we sin because we
are not under law but under grace? Certainly
not! 16 Do you not know that to whom
you present yourselves slaves to obey, you
are that one's slaves whom you obey,
whether of sin *leading* to death, or of obedience *leading* to righteousness? 17 But God
be thanked that *though* you were slaves of
sin, yet you obeyed from the heart that
form of doctrine to which you were delivered. 18 And having been set free from sin,
you became slaves of righteousness.
19 I speak in human *terms* because of the
weakness of your flesh. For just as you
presented your members *as* slaves of uncleanness, and of lawlessness *leading* to
more lawlessness, so now present your
members *as* slaves *of* righteousness for
holiness.

20 For when you were slaves of sin, you
were free in regard to righteousness.
21 What fruit did you have then in the things
of which you are now ashamed? For the
end of those things *is* death. 22 But now
having been set free from sin, and having
become slaves of God, you have your fruit
to holiness, and the end, everlasting life.
23 For the wages of sin *is* death, but the
gift of God *is* eternal life in Christ Jesus
our Lord.

*E*ternal life is not a present
given to me by God, it is
Himself.   (PSY. REDEMP.)

Reading 217—When Disaster Comes
Job 1:13–19

All that a man possesses is at times not in the hand of God, but in the
hand of the Adversary, because God has never withdrawn that authority
from Satan. The disasters that attend a man's possessions are satanic in their
origin and not of the haphazard order they seem to be. When Jesus Christ
talked about discipleship, He indicated that a disciple must be detached from
property and possessions, for if a man's life is in what he possesses, when
disaster comes to his possessions, his life goes too (see Luke 12:15).

Satan had been allowed to attack Job's possessions; now his power is increased, and he is free to attack Job's personal inheritance directly. When a man is hit by undeserved destruction, the immediate result is a slander against God—"Why should God allow this thing to happen?"

There are people today who are going through an onslaught of destruction that paralyzes all our platitudes and preaching; the only thing that will bring relief is the consolations of Christ. . . .   (BAFFLED)

JOB 1:1—2:13

THERE was a man in the land of Uz, whose name *was* Job; and that man was blameless and upright, and one who feared God and shunned evil. 2 And seven sons and three daughters were born to him. 3 Also, his possessions were seven thousand sheep, three thousand camels, five hundred yoke of oxen, five hundred female donkeys, and a very large household, so that this man was the greatest of all the people of the East.

4 And his sons would go and feast *in their* houses, each on his *appointed* day, and would send and invite their three sisters to eat and drink with them. 5 So it was, when the days of feasting had run their course, that Job would send and sanctify them, and he would rise early in the morning and offer burnt offerings *according to* the number of them all. For Job said, "It may be that my sons have sinned and cursed God in their hearts." Thus Job did regularly.

6 Now there was a day when the sons of God came to present themselves before the LORD, and Satan also came among them. 7 And the LORD said to Satan, "From where do you come?"

So Satan answered the LORD and said, "From going to and fro on the earth, and from walking back and forth on it."

8 Then the LORD said to Satan, "Have you considered My servant Job, that *there is* none like him on the earth, a blameless and upright man, one who fears God and shuns evil?"

9 So Satan answered the LORD and said, "Does Job fear God for nothing? 10 Have You not made a hedge around him, around his household, and around all that he has on every side? You have blessed the work of his hands, and his possessions have increased in the land. 11 But now, stretch out Your hand and touch all that he has, and he will surely curse You to Your face!"

12 And the LORD said to Satan, "Behold, all that he has *is* in your power; only do not lay a hand on his *person*."

So Satan went out from the presence of the LORD.

13 Now there was a day when his sons and daughters *were* eating and drinking wine in their oldest brother's house; 14 and a messenger came to Job and said, "The oxen were plowing and the donkeys feeding beside them, 15 when the Sabeans raided *them* and took them away—indeed they have killed the servants with the edge of the sword; and I alone have escaped to tell you!"

16 While he *was* still speaking, another also came and said, "The fire of God fell from heaven and burned up the sheep and the servants, and consumed them; and I alone have escaped to tell you!"

17 While he *was* still speaking, another also came and said, "The Chaldeans formed three bands, raided the camels and took them away, yes, and killed the servants with the edge of the sword; and I alone have escaped to tell you!"

18 While he *was* still speaking, another also came and said, "Your sons and daughters *were* eating and drinking wine in their oldest brother's house, 19 and suddenly a great wind came from across the wilderness and struck the four corners of the house, and it fell on the young people, and they are dead; and I alone have escaped to tell you!"

20 Then Job arose, tore his robe, and shaved his head; and he fell to the ground and worshiped. 21 And he said:

"Naked I came from my mother's womb,
   And naked shall I return there.
The LORD gave, and the LORD has taken away;
   Blessed be the name of the LORD."

22 In all this Job did not sin nor charge God with wrong.

2 AGAIN there was a day when the sons of God came to present themselves before the LORD, and Satan came also among them to present himself before the LORD. 2 And the LORD said to Satan, "From where do you come?"

Satan answered the LORD and said,

"From going to and fro on the earth, and from walking back and forth on it."

3 Then the LORD said to Satan, "Have you considered My servant Job, that *there is* none like him on the earth, a blameless and upright man, one who fears God and shuns evil? And still he holds fast to his integrity, although you incited Me against him, to destroy him without cause."

4 So Satan answered the LORD and said, "Skin for skin! Yes, all that a man has he will give for his life. 5 But stretch out Your hand now, and touch his bone and his flesh, and he will surely curse You to Your face!"

6 And the LORD said to Satan, "Behold, he *is* in your hand, but spare his life."

7 So Satan went out from the presence of the LORD, and struck Job with painful boils from the sole of his foot to the crown of his head. 8 And he took for himself a potsherd with which to scrape himself while he sat in the midst of the ashes.

9 Then his wife said to him, "Do you still hold fast to your integrity? Curse God and die!"

10 But he said to her, "You speak as one of the foolish women speaks. Shall we indeed accept good from God, and shall we not accept adversity?" In all this Job did not sin with his lips.

11 Now when Job's three friends heard of all this adversity that had come upon him, each one came from his own place— Eliphaz the Temanite, Bildad the Shuhite, and Zophar the Naamathite. For they had made an appointment together to come and mourn with him, and to comfort him. 12 And when they raised their eyes from afar, and did not recognize him, they lifted their voices and wept; and each one tore his robe and sprinkled dust on his head toward heaven. 13 So they sat down with him on the ground seven days and seven nights, and no one spoke a word to him, for they saw that *his* grief was very great.

PSALM 91:7–13

7   A thousand may fall at your side,
     And ten thousand at your right hand;
     But it shall not come near you.
8   Only with your eyes shall you look,
     And see the reward of the wicked.

9   Because you have made the LORD, *who is* my refuge,
     Even the Most High, your dwelling place,
10   No evil shall befall you,

Nor shall any plague come near your dwelling;
11   For He shall give His angels charge over you,
     To keep you in all your ways.
12   In *their* hands they shall bear you up,
     Lest you dash your foot against a stone.
13   You shall tread upon the lion and the cobra,
     The young lion and the serpent you shall trample underfoot.

PROVERBS 22:13, 14

13   THE lazy *man* says, "*There is* a lion outside!
     I shall be slain in the streets!"

14   The mouth of an immoral woman *is* a deep pit;
     He who is abhorred by the LORD will fall there.

ROMANS 7:1–25

OR do you not know, brethren (for I speak to those who know the law), that the law has dominion over a man as long as he lives? 2 For the woman who has a husband is bound by the law to *her* husband as long as he lives. But if the husband dies, she is released from the law of *her* husband. 3 So then if, while *her* husband lives, she marries another man, she will be called an adulteress; but if her husband dies, she is free from that law, so that she is no adulteress, though she has married another man. 4 Therefore, my brethren, you also have become dead to the law through the body of Christ, that you may be married to another—to Him who was raised from the dead, that we should bear fruit to God. 5 For when we were in the flesh, the sinful passions which were aroused by the law were at work in our members to bear fruit to death. 6 But now we have been delivered from the law, having died to what we were held by, so that we should serve in the newness of the Spirit and not *in* the oldness of the letter.

7 What shall we say then? *Is* the law sin? Certainly not! On the contrary, I would not have known sin except through the law. For I would not have known covetousness unless the law had said, "You shall not covet." 8 But sin, taking opportunity by the commandment, produced in me all *manner of evil* desire. For apart from the law sin *was* dead. 9 I was alive once without the

law, but when the commandment came, sin revived and I died. 10 And the commandment, which *was* to *bring* life, I found to *bring* death. 11 For sin, taking occasion by the commandment, deceived me, and by it killed *me*. 12 Therefore the law *is* holy, and the commandment holy and just and good.

13 Has then what is good become death to me? Certainly not! But sin, that it might appear sin, was producing death in me through what is good, so that sin through the commandment might become exceedingly sinful. 14 For we know that the law is spiritual, but I am carnal, sold under sin. 15 For what I am doing, I do not understand. For what I will to do, that I do not practice; but what I hate, that I do. 16 If, then, I do what I will not to do, I agree with the law that *it is* good. 17 But now, *it is* no longer I who do it, but sin that dwells in me. 18 For I know that in me (that is, in my flesh) nothing good dwells; for to will is present with me, but *how* to perform what is good I do not find. 19 For the good that I will *to do,* I do not

do; but the evil I will not *to do,* that I practice. 20 Now if I do what I will not *to do,* it is no longer I who do it, but sin that dwells in me.

21 I find then a law, that evil is present with me, the one who wills to do good. 22 For I delight in the law of God according to the inward man. 23 But I see another law in my members, warring against the law of my mind, and bringing me into captivity to the law of sin which is in my members. 24 O wretched man that I am! Who will deliver me from this body of death?

Be yourself first, then go to your own funeral, and let God forever after be All in all. (PERFECT)

---

25 I thank God—through Jesus Christ our Lord!

So then, with the mind I myself serve the law of God, but with the flesh the law of sin.

◄◄◄◄

Reading 218—The Inherited Baffling
Job 3:23–26

We may not experience the sense of being baffled by reason of any terrific sorrow, but if we really face the teachings of Jesus Christ in the Sermon on the Mount honestly and drastically, we shall know something of what Job was going through. The teachings of Jesus Christ must produce despair, because if He means what He says, where are we in regard to it? "Blessed *are* the pure in heart"—blessed is the man who has nothing in him for God to censure. Can I come up to that standard? Yet Jesus says only the pure in heart can stand before God. The New Testament never says that Jesus Christ came primarily to teach men; it says that He came to reveal that He has put the basis of human life on redemption, that is, He has made it possible for any and every man to be born into the kingdom where He lives (see John 3:3). Then when we are born again His teaching becomes a description of what God has undertaken to make a man if he will let His power work through him. So long as a man has his morality well within his own grasp he does not need Jesus Christ—"For I did not come to call the righteous, but sinners," said Jesus. When a man has been hard hit and realizes his own helplessness he finds that it is not a cowardly thing to turn to Jesus Christ, but the way out which God has made for him. (*BAFFLED*)

JOB 3:1—4:21

AFTER this Job opened his mouth and cursed the day of his *birth*. 2 And Job spoke, and said:

3   "May the day perish on which I was born,
    And the night *in which* it was said,
    'A male child is conceived.'

4   May that day be darkness;
    May God above not seek it,
    Nor the light shine upon it.

5   May darkness and the shadow of death claim it;
    May a cloud settle on it;
    May the blackness of the day terrify it.

6   *As for* that night, may darkness seize it;
    May it not rejoice among the days of the year,
    May it not come into the number of the months.

7   Oh, may that night be barren!
    May no joyful shout come into it!

8   May those curse it who curse the day,
    Those who are ready to arouse Leviathan.

9   May the stars of its morning be dark;
    May it look for light, but *have* none,
    And not see the dawning of the day;

10   Because it did not shut up the doors of my *mother's* womb,
    Nor hide sorrow from my eyes.

11   "Why did I not die at birth?
    Why did I *not* perish when I came from the womb?

12   Why did the knees receive me?
    Or why the breasts, that I should nurse?

13   For now I would have lain still and been quiet,
    I would have been asleep;
    Then I would have been at rest

14   With kings and counselors of the earth,
    Who built ruins for themselves,

15   Or with princes who had gold,
    Who filled their houses *with* silver;

16   Or *why* was I not hidden like a stillborn child,
    Like infants who never saw light?

17   There the wicked cease *from* troubling,
    And there the weary are at rest.

18   *There* the prisoners rest together;
    They do not hear the voice of the oppressor.

19   The small and great are there,
    And the servant *is* free from his master.

20   "Why is light given to him who is in misery,
    And life to the bitter of soul,

21   Who long for death, but it does not *come*,
    And search for it more than hidden treasures;

22   Who rejoice exceedingly,
    And are glad when they can find the grave?

23   *Why is light given* to a man whose way is hidden,
    And whom God has hedged in?

24   For my sighing comes before I eat,
    And my groanings pour out like water.

25   For the thing I greatly feared has come upon me,
    And what I dreaded has happened to me.

26   I am not at ease, nor am I quiet;
    I have no rest, for trouble comes."

4 THEN Eliphaz the Temanite answered and said:

Don't take the part of Job's friends and say you can explain the whole thing. (DISCIPLES)

---

2   "*If* one attempts a word with you, will you become weary?
    But who can withhold himself from speaking?

3   Surely you have instructed many,
    And you have strengthened weak hands.

4   Your words have upheld him who was stumbling,
    And you have strengthened the feeble knees;

5   But now it comes upon you, and you are weary;
    It touches you, and you are troubled.

6   *Is* not your reverence your confidence?
    And the integrity of your ways your hope?

7   "Remember now, who *ever* perished being innocent?
    Or where were the upright *ever* cut off?

8   Even as I have seen,
    Those who plow iniquity

And sow trouble reap the same.
9 By the blast of God they perish,
And by the breath of His anger they are consumed.
10 The roaring of the lion,
The voice of the fierce lion,
And the teeth of the young lions are broken.
11 The old lion perishes for lack of prey,
And the cubs of the lioness are scattered.

12 "Now a word was secretly brought to me,
And my ear received a whisper of it.
13 In disquieting thoughts from the visions of the night,
When deep sleep falls on men,
14 Fear came upon me, and trembling,
Which made all my bones shake.
15 Then a spirit passed before my face;
The hair on my body stood up.
16 It stood still,
But I could not discern its appearance.
A form *was* before my eyes;
There was silence;
Then I heard a voice *saying*:
17 'Can a mortal be more righteous than God?
Can a man be more pure than his Maker?
18 If He puts no trust in His servants,
If He charges His angels with error,
19 How much more those who dwell in houses of clay,
Whose foundation is in the dust,
Who are crushed before a moth?
20 They are broken in pieces from morning till evening;
They perish forever, with no one regarding.
21 Does not their own excellence go away?
They die, even without wisdom.'

PSALM 91:14–16

14 "BECAUSE he has set his love upon Me, therefore I will deliver him;
I will set him on high, because he has known My name.

A child of God never prays to be conscious that God answers prayer. (UTMOST)

---

15 He shall call upon Me, and I will answer him;
I *will be* with him in trouble;
I will deliver him and honor him.
16 With long life I will satisfy him,
And show him My salvation."

PROVERBS 22:15

15 FOOLISHNESS *is* bound up in the heart of a child;
The rod of correction will drive it far from him.

ROMANS 8:1–21

THERE *is* therefore now no condemnation to those who are in Christ Jesus, who do not walk according to the flesh, but according to the Spirit. 2 For the law of the Spirit of life in Christ Jesus has made me free from the law of sin and death. 3 For what the law could not do in that it was weak through the flesh, God *did* by sending His own Son in the likeness of sinful flesh, on account of sin: He condemned sin in the flesh, 4 that the righteous requirement of the law might be fulfilled in us who do not walk according to the flesh but according to the Spirit. 5 For those who live according to the flesh set their minds on the things of the flesh, but those *who live* according to the Spirit, the things of the Spirit. 6 For to be carnally minded *is* death, but to be spiritually minded *is* life and peace. 7 Because the carnal mind *is* enmity against God; for it is not subject to the law of God, nor indeed can be. 8 So then, those who are in the flesh cannot please God.

9 But you are not in the flesh but in the Spirit, if indeed the Spirit of God dwells in you. Now if anyone does not have the Spirit of Christ, he is not His. 10 And if Christ *is* in you, the body *is* dead because of sin, but the Spirit *is* life because of righteousness. 11 But if the Spirit of Him who raised Jesus from the dead dwells in you, He who raised Christ from the dead will also give life to your mortal bodies through His Spirit who dwells in you.

12 Therefore, brethren, we are debtors—not to the flesh, to live according to the flesh. 13 For if you live according to the flesh you will die; but if by the Spirit you put to death the deeds of the body, you will live. 14 For as many as are led by the Spirit of God, these are sons of God. 15 For you did not receive the spirit of

bondage again to fear, but you received the Spirit of adoption by whom we cry out, "Abba, Father." 16 The Spirit Himself bears witness with our spirit that we are children of God, 17 and if children, then heirs—heirs of God and joint heirs with Christ, if indeed we suffer with *Him,* that we may also be glorified together.

18 For I consider that the sufferings of this present time are not worthy *to be com-* *pared* with the glory which shall be revealed in us. 19 For the earnest expectation of the creation eagerly waits for the revealing of the sons of God. 20 For the creation was subjected to futility, not willingly, but because of Him who subjected *it* in hope; 21 because the creation itself also will be delivered from the bondage of corruption into the glorious liberty of the children of God.

◆◆◆◆

Reading 219—The Spirit's Intercession
Romans 8:27

The Spirit imparts a solemnity to our circumstances and makes us understand something of the travail of Jesus Christ. It is not that we enter into the agony of intercession, it is that we intercede for the people He has placed around us; we present their cases before Him and give the Holy Spirit a chance to intercede for them. We bring the particular people and circumstances before God's throne, and the Holy Spirit in us has a chance to intercede for them. That is how God is going to sweep the whole world by His saints.

Are we making the Holy Spirit's work difficult by being indefinite, or by trying to do His work for Him? We must be the human side of the intercession, and the human side is the circumstances we are in, the people with whom we are in contact. We have to use our common sense in keeping our conscious life and our circumstances as a shrine of the Holy Spirit, and as we bring the different ones before God, the Holy Spirit presents them before the throne all the time. The Holy Spirit does the interceding, but we must do our part; we must do the human side while He does the divine. So never think it strange concerning the circumstances you are in.   (Ask)

JOB 5:1—6:30

1 "CALL out now;
  Is there anyone who will answer you?
  And to which of the holy ones will
    you turn?
2 For wrath kills a foolish man,
  And envy slays a simple one.
3 I have seen the foolish taking root,
  But suddenly I cursed his dwelling
    place.
4 His sons are far from safety,
  They are crushed in the gate,
  And *there is* no deliverer.
5 Because the hungry eat up his harvest,
  Taking it even from the thorns,
  And a snare snatches their substance.
6 For affliction does not come from
    the dust,

Nor does trouble spring from the
    ground;
7 Yet man is born to trouble,
  As the sparks fly upward.

8 "But as for me, I would seek God,
  And to God I would commit my
    cause—
9 Who does great things, and
    unsearchable,
  Marvelous things without number.
10 He gives rain on the earth,
  And sends waters on the fields.
11 He sets on high those who are lowly,
  And those who mourn are lifted to
    safety.
12 He frustrates the devices of the crafty,
  So that their hands cannot carry out
    their plans.

13 He catches the wise in their own
craftiness,
And the counsel of the cunning
comes quickly upon them.
14 They meet with darkness in the
daytime,
And grope at noontime as in the
night.
15 But He saves the needy from the
sword,
From the mouth of the mighty,
And from their hand.
16 So the poor have hope,
And injustice shuts her mouth.

17 "Behold, happy *is* the man whom God
corrects;
Therefore do not despise the
chastening of the Almighty.
18 For He bruises, but He binds up;
He wounds, but His hands make
whole.
19 He shall deliver you in six troubles,
Yes, in seven no evil shall touch you.
20 In famine He shall redeem you from
death,
And in war from the power of the
sword.
21 You shall be hidden from the scourge
of the tongue,
And you shall not be afraid of
destruction when it comes.
22 You shall laugh at destruction and
famine,
And you shall not be afraid of the
beasts of the earth.
23 For you shall have a covenant with
the stones of the field,
And the beasts of the field shall be
at peace with you.
24 You shall know that your tent *is* in
peace;
You shall visit your dwelling and find
nothing amiss.

---

*T*he path of peace for us is to hand
ourselves over to God. (BIB. PSYCH.)

---

25 You shall also know that your
descendants *shall be* many,
And your offspring like the grass of
the earth.
26 You shall come to the grave at a full
age,
As a sheaf of grain ripens in its season.
27 Behold, this we have searched out;
It *is* true.
Hear it, and know for yourself."

6 THEN Job answered and said:

2 "Oh, that my grief were fully weighed,
And my calamity laid with it on the
scales!
3 For then it would be heavier than
the sand of the sea—
Therefore my words have been rash.
4 For the arrows of the Almighty *are*
within me;
My spirit drinks in their poison;
The terrors of God are arrayed
against me.
5 Does the wild donkey bray when it
has grass,
Or does the ox low over its fodder?
6 Can flavorless food be eaten without
salt?
Or is there *any* taste in the white of
an egg?
7 My soul refuses to touch *them*;
They *are* as loathsome food to me.

8 "Oh, that I might have my request,
That God would grant *me* the thing
that I long for!
9 That it would please God to crush
me,
That He would loose His hand and
cut me off!
10 Then I would still have comfort;
Though in anguish I would exult,
He will not spare;
For I have not concealed the words
of the Holy One.

11 "What strength do I have, that I
should hope?
And what *is* my end, that I should
prolong my life?
12 *Is* my strength the strength of stones?
Or is my flesh bronze?
13 *Is* my help not within me?
And is success driven from me?

14 "To him who is afflicted, kindness
should be shown by his friend,
Even though he forsakes the fear of
the Almighty.
15 My brothers have dealt deceitfully
like a brook,
Like the streams of the brooks that
pass away,
16 Which are dark because of the ice,
And into which the snow vanishes.
17 When it is warm, they cease to flow;
When it is hot, they vanish from their
place.
18 The paths of their way turn aside,
They go nowhere and perish.
19 The caravans of Tema look,

The travelers of Sheba hope for them.
20 They are disappointed because they
    were confident;
    They come there and are confused.
21 For now you are nothing,
    You see terror and are afraid.
22 Did I ever say, 'Bring *something* to
    me'?
    Or, 'Offer a bribe for me from your
    wealth'?
23 Or, 'Deliver me from the enemy's
    hand'?
    Or, 'Redeem me from the hand of
    oppressors'?

24 "Teach me, and I will hold my tongue;
    Cause me to understand wherein I
    have erred.
25 How forceful are right words!
    But what does your arguing prove?
26 Do you intend to rebuke *my* words,
    And the speeches of a desperate one,
    which are as wind?
27 Yes, you overwhelm the fatherless,
    And you undermine your friend.
28 Now therefore, be pleased to look
    at me;
    For I would never lie to your face.
29 Yield now, let there be no injustice!
    Yes, concede, my righteousness still
    stands!
30 Is there injustice on my tongue?
    Cannot my taste discern the
    unsavory?

PSALM 92:1–7

1 *IT is* good to give thanks to the Lord,
    And to sing praises to Your name,
      O Most High;
2 To declare Your lovingkindness in the
      morning,
    And Your faithfulness every night,
3 On an instrument of ten strings,
    On the lute,
    And on the harp,
    With harmonious sound.
4 For You, Lord, have made me glad
      through Your work;
    I will triumph in the works of Your
    hands.

5 O Lord, how great are Your works!
    Your thoughts are very deep.
6 A senseless man does not know,
    Nor does a fool understand this.
7 When the wicked spring up like grass,
    And when all the workers of iniquity
      flourish,
    It is that they may be destroyed forever.

PROVERBS 22:16

16 HE who oppresses the poor to increase
    his *riches,*
    And he who gives to the rich, *will* surely
    come to poverty.

ROMANS 8:22–39

FOR we know that the whole creation
groans and labors with birth pangs together
until now. 23 Not only *that,* but we also
who have the firstfruits of the Spirit, even
we ourselves groan within ourselves, eagerly
waiting for the adoption, the redemption
of our body. 24 For we were saved in this
hope, but hope that is seen is not hope;
for why does one still hope for what he
sees? 25 But if we hope for what we do
not see, we eagerly wait for *it* with perseverance.

26 Likewise the Spirit also helps in our
weaknesses. For we do not know what we
should pray for as we ought, but the Spirit
Himself makes intercession for us with
groanings which cannot be uttered.
27 Now He who searches the hearts knows
what the mind of the Spirit *is,* because He
makes intercession for the saints according
to *the will of* God.

28 And we know that all things work together for good to those who love God,
to those who are the called according to
His purpose. 29 For whom He foreknew,
He also predestined *to be* conformed to the
image of His Son, that He might be the
firstborn among many brethren. 30 Moreover whom He predestined, these He also
called; whom He called, these He also justified; and whom He justified, these He also
glorified.

31 What then shall we say to these things?
If God *is* for us, who *can be* against us?
32 He who did not spare His own Son,
but delivered Him up for us all, how shall
He not with Him also freely give us all
things? 33 Who shall bring a charge against
God's elect? *It is* God who justifies.
34 Who *is* he who condemns? *It is* Christ
who died, and furthermore is also risen,
who is even at the right hand of God, who
also makes intercession for us. 35 Who shall
separate us from the love of Christ? *Shall*
tribulation, or distress, or persecution, or
famine, or nakedness, or peril, or sword?
36 As it is written:

    "For Your sake we are killed all day
      long;

We are accounted as sheep for the slaughter."

37 Yet in all these things we are more than conquerors through Him who loved us. 38 For I am persuaded that neither death nor life, nor angels nor principalities nor powers, nor things present nor things to come, 39 nor height nor depth, nor any other created thing, shall be able to separate us from the love of God which is in Christ Jesus our Lord.

No power on earth or in hell can conquer the Spirit of God in a human spirit. (UTMOST)

◆◆◆◆

Reading 220—The Pose of Platitude
Job 8:7–10

The biggest thing you can do for those who are suffering is not to talk platitudes, not to ask questions, but to get into contact with God, and the "greater *works*" will be done by prayer (John 14:12, 13). Job's friends never once prayed for him; all they did was try to prove a point to enrich their own creed out of his sufferings. We are not intended to understand life. I cannot understand or define life; I cannot understand or define God; consequently, I am master of neither. Logic and reason are always on the hunt for definition, and anything that cannot be defined is apt to be defied. Rationalism usually defies God and defies life; it will not have anything that cannot be defined on a rational basis, forgetting that the things that make up elemental human life cannot be defined.

There are teachers today who play the fool on these elemental lines; they declare that they can give guidance, but they only succeed in doing a fathomless amount of harm. A man is a criminal for knowing some things when he has no right to know them. The primal curse of God was on Adam when he ate the fruit from the tree of the knowledge of good and evil. Adam was intended to know good and evil, but not by eating of the fruit of the tree; God wanted him to know good and evil in the way Jesus Christ knew it, by simple obedience to His Father. (*BAFFLED*)

JOB 7:1—8:22

1 "IS *there* not a time of hard service
  for man on earth?
  Are not his days also like the days
  of a hired man?
2 Like a servant who earnestly desires
  the shade,
  And like a hired man who eagerly
  looks for his wages,
3 So I have been allotted months of
  futility,
  And wearisome nights have been
  appointed to me.
4 When I lie down, I say, 'When shall
  I arise,
  And the night be ended?'

For I have had my fill of tossing till
  dawn.
5 My flesh is caked with worms and
  dust,
  My skin is cracked and breaks out
  afresh.

6 "My days are swifter than a weaver's
  shuttle,
  And are spent without hope.
7 Oh, remember that my life *is* a breath!
  My eye will never again see good.
8 The eye of him who sees me will
  see me no *more;*
  While your *eyes* are upon me, I shall
  no longer *be.*
9 *As* the cloud disappears and vanishes
  away,

So he who goes down to the grave
does not come up.
10 He shall never return to his house,
Nor shall his place know him
anymore.

11 "Therefore I will not restrain my
mouth;
I will speak in the anguish of my
spirit;
I will complain in the bitterness of
my soul.
12 *Am* I a sea, or a sea serpent,
That You set a guard over me?
13 When I say, 'My bed will comfort
me,
My couch will ease my complaint,'
14 Then You scare me with dreams
And terrify me with visions,
15 So that my soul chooses strangling
And death rather than my body.
16 I loathe *my life;*
I would not live forever.
Let me alone,
For my days *are but* a breath.

17 "What *is* man, that You should exalt
him,
That You should set Your heart on
him,
18 That You should visit him every
morning,
And test him every moment?
19 How long?
Will You not look away from me,
And let me alone till I swallow my
saliva?
20 Have I sinned?
What have I done to You, O watcher
of men?
Why have You set me as Your target,
So that I am a burden to myself?
21 Why then do You not pardon my
transgression,
And take away my iniquity?
For now I will lie down in the dust,
And You will seek me diligently,
But I *will* no longer *be.*"

8 THEN Bildad the Shuhite answered
and said:

2 "How long will you speak these *things,*
And the words of your mouth *be like*
a strong wind?
3 Does God subvert judgment?
Or does the Almighty pervert justice?
4 If your sons have sinned against Him,
He has cast them away for their
transgression.

5 If you would earnestly seek God
And make your supplication to the
Almighty,
6 If you *were* pure and upright,
Surely now He would awake for
you,
And prosper your rightful dwelling
place.
7 Though your beginning was small,
Yet your latter end would increase
abundantly.

8 "For inquire, please, of the former age,
And consider the things discovered
by their fathers;
9 For we *were born* yesterday, and know
nothing,
Because our days on earth *are* a
shadow.
10 Will they not teach you and tell
you,
And utter words from their heart?

11 "Can the papyrus grow up without a
marsh?
Can the reeds flourish without
water?
12 While it *is* yet green *and* not cut
down,
It withers before any *other* plant.
13 So *are* the paths of all who forget
God;
And the hope of the hypocrite shall
perish,
14 Whose confidence shall be cut off,
And whose trust *is* a spider's web.
15 He leans on his house, but it does
not stand.
He holds it fast, but it does not
endure.
16 He grows green in the sun,
And his branches spread out in his
garden.
17 His roots wrap around the rock heap,
And look for a place in the stones.
18 If he is destroyed from his place,
Then *it* will deny him, *saying,* 'I have
not seen you.'

19 "Behold, this is the joy of His way,
And out of the earth others will grow.
20 Behold, God will not cast away the
blameless,
Nor will He uphold the evildoers.
21 He will yet fill your mouth with
laughing,
And your lips with rejoicing.
22 Those who hate you will be clothed
with shame,
And the dwelling place of the wicked
will come to nothing."

PSALM 92:8–15

8 BUT You, Lord, *are* on high forevermore.
9 For behold, Your enemies, O Lord,
For behold, Your enemies shall perish;
All the workers of iniquity shall be scattered.

10 But my horn You have exalted like a wild ox;
I have been anointed with fresh oil.

---

*H*ow are you to grow in knowledge of God? By remaining where you are. (SERMON MT.)

---

11 My eye also has seen *my desire* on my enemies;
My ears hear *my desire* on the wicked Who rise up against me.

12 The righteous shall flourish like a palm tree,
He shall grow like a cedar in Lebanon.
13 Those who are planted in the house of the Lord
Shall flourish in the courts of our God.
14 They shall still bear fruit in old age;
They shall be fresh and flourishing,
15 To declare that the Lord is upright;
He is my rock, and *there is* no unrighteousness in Him.

PROVERBS 22:17–21

17 INCLINE your ear and hear the words of the wise,
And apply your heart to my knowledge;
18 For *it is* a pleasant thing if you keep them within you;
Let them all be fixed upon your lips,
19 So that your trust may be in the Lord;
I have instructed you today, even you.
20 Have I not written to you excellent things
Of counsels and knowledge,
21 That I may make you know the certainty of the words of truth,

That you may answer words of truth
To those who send to you?

ROMANS 9:1–15

I tell the truth in Christ, I am not lying, my conscience also bearing me witness in the Holy Spirit, 2 that I have great sorrow and continual grief in my heart. 3 For I could wish that I myself were accursed from Christ for my brethren, my countrymen according to the flesh, 4 who are Israelites, to whom *pertain* the adoption, the glory, the covenants, the giving of the law, the service *of God,* and the promises; 5 of whom *are* the fathers and from whom, according to the flesh, Christ *came,* who is over all, *the* eternally blessed God. Amen.

---

*I*srael is still in the shadow of God's hand. (SEND I YOU)

---

6 But it is not that the word of God has taken no effect. For they *are* not all Israel who *are* of Israel, 7 nor *are they* all children because they are the seed of Abraham; but, "In Isaac your seed shall be called." 8 That is, those who *are* the children of the flesh, these *are* not the children of God; but the children of the promise are counted as the seed. 9 For this *is* the word of promise: "At this time I will come and Sarah shall have a son."

10 And not only *this,* but when Rebecca also had conceived by one man, *even* by our father Isaac 11 (for *the children* not yet being born, nor having done any good or evil, that the purpose of God according to election might stand, not of works but of Him who calls), 12 it was said to her, "The older shall serve the younger." 13 As it is written, "Jacob I have loved, but Esau I have hated."

14 What shall we say then? *Is there* unrighteousness with God? Certainly not! 15 For He says to Moses, "I will have mercy on whomever I will have mercy, and I will have compassion on whomever I will have compassion."

Reading 221—Conceptions for Rejection
Job 10:7, 8

Job's utterances are the last word in the expression of certain forms of grief. These particular views are stately and terrific; Job is trying to state to his own mind why God seems to have rejected him, and also why he should reject the way God is being presented to him . . .

All along Job bases his conceptions on the facts which he knows, and this is the only thing to do, although many of us would rather tell a lie for the honor of God than face the facts. A fanatic is one who entrenches himself in invincible ignorance. Job will not accept anything that contradicts the facts he knows; he is not melancholy, he does not say God is cruel, he simply states the facts—"It looks as though God is rejecting me without any reason, all the facts go to prove this and I am not going to avoid them." Job will not lay a flattering unction to his soul on the line of expediency. No man ever puts a stumbling block in the way of others by telling the truth; to tell the truth is more honoring to God than to tell a lie. If God has done something for you, you will know it unmistakably, but if He has not, never say He has for the sake of other people. Job sticks to facts, that is what confuses his friends; but in the end Job is brought face-to-face with God.   (*BAFFLED*)

JOB 9:1—10:22

THEN Job answered and said:

2 "Truly I know *it is* so,
But how can a man be righteous before God?

3 If one wished to contend with Him,
He could not answer Him one time out of a thousand.

4 *God is* wise in heart and mighty in strength.
Who has hardened *himself* against Him and prospered?

5 He removes the mountains, and they do not know
When He overturns them in His anger;

6 He shakes the earth out of its place,
And its pillars tremble;

7 He commands the sun, and it does not rise;
He seals off the stars;

8 He alone spreads out the heavens,
And treads on the waves of the sea;

9 He made the Bear, Orion, and the Pleiades,
And the chambers of the south;

10 He does great things past finding out,
Yes, wonders without number.

11 If He goes by me, I do not see *Him*;
If He moves past, I do not perceive Him;

12 If He takes away, who can hinder Him?
Who can say to Him, 'What are You doing?'

13 God will not withdraw His anger,
The allies of the proud lie prostrate beneath Him.

14 "How then can I answer Him,
And choose my words *to reason* with Him?

15 For though I were righteous, I could not answer Him;
I would beg mercy of my Judge.

16 If I called and He answered me,
I would not believe that He was listening to my voice.

17 For He crushes me with a tempest,
And multiplies my wounds without cause.

18 He will not allow me to catch my breath,
But fills me with bitterness.

19 If *it is a matter* of strength, indeed *He is* strong;
And if of justice, who will appoint my day *in court?*

20 Though I were righteous, my own mouth would condemn me;
Though I *were* blameless, it would prove me perverse.

21 "I am blameless, yet I do not know myself;

I despise my life.

22 It *is* all one *thing;*
Therefore I say, 'He destroys the
blameless and the wicked.'

23 If the scourge slays suddenly,
He laughs at the plight of the
innocent.

24 The earth is given into the hand of
the wicked.
He covers the faces of its judges.
If it is not *He,* who else could it be?

25 "Now my days are swifter than a
runner;
They flee away, they see no good.

26 They pass by like swift ships,
Like an eagle swooping on its prey.

27 If I say, 'I will forget my complaint,
I will put off my sad face and wear
a smile,'

28 I am afraid of all my sufferings;
I know that You will not hold me
innocent.

29 *If* I am condemned,
Why then do I labor in vain?

30 If I wash myself with snow water,
And cleanse my hands with soap,

31 Yet You will plunge me into the pit,
And my own clothes will abhor me.

32 "For *He is* not a man, as I *am,*
That I may answer Him,
And that we should go to court
together.

33 Nor is there any mediator
between us,
Who may lay his hand on us both.

34 Let Him take His rod away from me,
And do not let dread of Him
terrify me.

35 *Then* I would speak and not fear Him,
But it is not so with me.

10 "MY soul loathes my life;
I will give free course to my
complaint,
I will speak in the bitterness of my
soul.

---

*D*ig out the "root of bitterness,"
then there can be no fruit to sour
the life.   (WORKMEN)

---

2 I will say to God, 'Do not
condemn me;
Show me why You contend with me.

3 *Does it* seem good to You that You
should oppress,
That You should despise the work
of Your hands,
And smile on the counsel of the
wicked?

4 Do You have eyes of flesh?
Or do You see as man sees?

5 *Are* Your days like the days of a
mortal man?
Are Your years like the days of a
mighty man,

6 That You should seek for my iniquity
And search out my sin,

7 Although You know that I am not
wicked,
And *there is* no one who can deliver
from Your hand?

8 'Your hands have made me and
fashioned me,
An intricate unity;
Yet You would destroy me.

9 Remember, I pray, that You have
made me like clay.
And will You turn me into dust
again?

10 Did You not pour me out like milk,
And curdle me like cheese,

11 Clothe me with skin and flesh,
And knit me together with bones and
sinews?

12 You have granted me life and favor,
And Your care has preserved my
spirit.

13 'And these *things* You have hidden
in Your heart;
I know that this *was* with You:

14 If I sin, then You mark me,
And will not acquit me of my
iniquity.

15 If I am wicked, woe to me;
Even *if* I am righteous, I cannot lift
up my head.
I am full of disgrace;
See my misery!

16 If *my head* is exalted,
You hunt me like a fierce lion,
And again You show Yourself
awesome against me.

17 You renew Your witnesses against
me,
And increase Your indignation
toward me;
Changes and war are *ever* with me.

18 'Why then have You brought me out
of the womb?
Oh, that I had perished and no eye
had seen me!

19 I would have been as though I had
not been.

I would have been carried from the
womb to the grave.
20 Are not my days few?
Cease! Leave me alone, that I may
take a little comfort,
21 Before I go *to the place from which* I
shall not return,
To the land of darkness and the
shadow of death,
22 A land as dark as darkness *itself,*
As the shadow of death, without any
order,
Where even the light *is* like
darkness.' "

PSALM 93:1–5

1 THE Lord reigns, He is clothed with
majesty;
The Lord is clothed,
He has girded Himself with strength.
Surely the world is established, so that
it cannot be moved.
2 Your throne *is* established from of old;
You *are* from everlasting.

3 The floods have lifted up, O Lord,
The floods have lifted up their voice;
The floods lift up their waves.
4 The Lord on high *is* mightier
Than the noise of many waters,
Than the mighty waves of the sea.

5 Your testimonies are very sure;
Holiness adorns Your house,
O Lord, forever.

PROVERBS 22:22, 23

22 DO not rob the poor because he *is* poor,
Nor oppress the afflicted at the gate;
23 For the Lord will plead their cause,
And plunder the soul of those who
plunder them.

ROMANS 9:16–33

SO then *it is* not of him who wills, nor of
him who runs, but of God who shows
mercy. 17 For the Scripture says to the Pharaoh, "For this very purpose I have raised
you up, that I may show My power in you,
and that My name may be declared in all
the earth." 18 Therefore He has mercy on
whom He wills, and whom He wills He
hardens.
19 You will say to me then, "Why does

He still find fault? For who has resisted
His will?" 20 But indeed, O man, who are
you to reply against God? Will the thing
formed say to him who formed *it,* "Why
have you made me like this?" 21 Does not
the potter have power over the clay, from
the same lump to make one vessel for honor
and another for dishonor?
22 *What* if God, wanting to show *His*
wrath and to make His power known, endured with much longsuffering the vessels
of wrath prepared for destruction, 23 and
that He might make known the riches of
His glory on the vessels of mercy, which
He had prepared beforehand for glory,
24 *even* us whom He called, not of the Jews
only, but also of the Gentiles?
25 As He says also in Hosea:

"I will call them My people, who were
not My people,
And her beloved, who was not
beloved."
26 "And it shall come to pass in the place
where it was said to them,
'*You are* not My people,'
There they shall be called sons of the
living God."

27 Isaiah also cries out concerning Israel:

"Though the number of the children
of Israel be as the sand of the sea,
The remnant will be saved.
28 For He will finish the work and cut
it short in righteousness,
Because the Lord will make a short
work upon the earth."

29 And as Isaiah said before:

"Unless the Lord of Sabaoth had left
us a seed,
We would have become like Sodom,
And we would have been made like
Gomorrah."

30 What shall we say then? That Gentiles,
who did not pursue righteousness, have attained to righteousness, even the righteousness of faith; 31 but Israel, pursuing the law

---

*Faith in the Bible is faith in God
against everything that contradicts
Him.*   (Utmost)

---

of righteousness, has not attained to the
law of righteousness. 32 Why? Because *they*

did not *seek it* by faith, but as it were, by the works of the law. For they stumbled at that stumbling stone. 33 As it is written:

"Behold, I lay in Zion a stumbling stone and rock of offense,
And whoever believes on Him will not be put to shame."

◆◆◆◆

Reading 222—Confession of Belief
Romans 10:10

In the Bible confession and testimony are put in a prominent place, and the test of a man's moral caliber is the "say so." I may try and make myself believe a hundred and one things, but they will never be mine until I "say so." "With the heart one believes. . . ." "Heart" means all that is meant by "me." If I say with myself what I believe and confess it with my mouth, I am lifted into the domain of that thing. This is always the price of spiritual emancipation. If a child is to be taken out of his sulky mood he has to go across the disinclination of his reserve and *say* something; and this is true of all moral and spiritual life. If I will not confess with my mouth what I believe in my heart, that particular phase of believing will never be mine actually. Assurance of faith is never gained by reserve but only by abandonment. In the matter of human love it is a great emancipation to have it expressed; there may be intuitions of the love, but the realization of it is not ours until it is expressed. Morally and spiritually we live, as it were, in sections, and the door from one section to another is by means of words, and until we say the right word the door will not open. The right word is always based on the killing of the disinclination which belongs to a lower section.   (*PLACE HELP*)

JOB 11:1—12:25

THEN Zophar the Naamathite answered and said:

2 "Should not the multitude of words
   be answered?
   And should a man full of talk be
   vindicated?
3 Should your empty talk make men
   hold their peace?
   And when you mock, should no one
   rebuke you?
4 For you have said,
   'My doctrine *is* pure,
   And I am clean in your eyes.'
5 But oh, that God would speak,
   And open His lips against you,
6 That He would show you the secrets
   of wisdom!
   For *they would* double *your*
   prudence.
   Know therefore that God exacts from
   you
   Less than your iniquity *deserves*.

7 "Can you search out the deep things
   of God?
   Can you find out the limits of the
   Almighty?

◆◆

God Himself is the key to the riddle of the universe.   (*BAFFLED*)

8 *They are* higher than heaven—what
   can you do?
   Deeper than Sheol—what can you
   know?
9 Their measure *is* longer than the earth
   And broader than the sea.
10 "If He passes by, imprisons, and
   gathers *to judgment*,
   Then who can hinder Him?
11 For He knows deceitful men;
   He sees wickedness also.
   Will He not then consider *it*?
12 For an empty-headed man will be
   wise,

When a wild donkey's colt is born
   a man.

13 "If you would prepare your heart,
   And stretch out your hands toward
     Him;
14 If iniquity *were* in your hand, *and*
   you put it far away,
   And would not let wickedness dwell
     in your tents;
15 Then surely you could lift up your
     face without spot;
   Yes, you could be steadfast, and not
     fear;
16 Because you would forget *your*
     misery,
   And remember *it* as waters *that have*
     passed away,
17 And *your* life would be brighter than
     noonday.
   Though you were dark, you would
     be like the morning.
18 And you would be secure, because
     there is hope;
   Yes, you would dig *around you, and*
     take your rest in safety.
19 You would also lie down, and no
     one would make *you* afraid;
   Yes, many would court your favor.
20 But the eyes of the wicked will fail,
   And they shall not escape,
   And their hope—loss of life!"

12 THEN Job answered and said:

2 "No doubt you *are* the people,
   And wisdom will die with you!
3 But I have understanding as well as
     you;
   I *am* not inferior to you.
   Indeed, who does not *know* such
     things as these?

4 "I am one mocked by his friends,
   Who called on God, and He
     answered him,
   The just and blameless *who is*
     ridiculed.
5 A lamp is despised in the thought
     of one who is at ease;
   It is made ready for those whose feet
     slip.
6 The tents of robbers prosper,
   And those who provoke God are
     secure—
   In what God provides by His hand.

7 "But now ask the beasts, and they will
     teach you;
   And the birds of the air, and they
     will tell you;

8 Or speak to the earth, and it will teach
     you;
   And the fish of the sea will explain
     to you.
9 Who among all these does not know
   That the hand of the LORD has done
     this,
10 In whose hand *is* the life of every
     living thing,
   And the breath of all mankind?
11 Does not the ear test words
   And the mouth taste its food?
12 Wisdom *is* with aged men,
   And with length of days,
     understanding.

13 "With Him *are* wisdom and strength,
   He has counsel and understanding.
14 If He breaks *a thing* down, it cannot
     be rebuilt;
   If He imprisons a man, there can be
     no release.
15 If He withholds the waters, they dry
     up;
   If He sends them out, they
     overwhelm the earth.
16 With Him *are* strength and prudence.
   The deceived and the deceiver *are*
     His.
17 He leads counselors away plundered,
   And makes fools of the judges.
18 He loosens the bonds of kings,
   And binds their waist with a belt.
19 He leads princes away plundered,
   And overthrows the mighty.
20 He deprives the trusted ones of
     speech,
   And takes away the discernment of
     the elders.
21 He pours contempt on princes,
   And disarms the mighty.
22 He uncovers deep things out of
     darkness,
   And brings the shadow of death to
     light.
23 He makes nations great, and destroys
     them;
   He enlarges nations, and guides
     them.
24 He takes away the understanding of
     the chiefs of the people of the earth,
   And makes them wander in a pathless
     wilderness.
25 They grope in the dark without light,
   And He makes them stagger like a
     drunken *man.*

PSALM 94:1–11

1 O LORD God, to whom vengeance
     belongs—

O God, to whom vengeance belongs,
  shine forth!
2 Rise up, O Judge of the earth;
  Render punishment to the proud.
3 LORD, how long will the wicked,
  How long will the wicked triumph?

4 They utter speech, *and* speak insolent
    things;
  All the workers of iniquity boast in
    themselves.
5 They break in pieces Your people,
    O LORD,
  And afflict Your heritage.
6 They slay the widow and the stranger,
  And murder the fatherless.
7 Yet they say, "The LORD does not see,
  Nor does the God of Jacob
    understand."

8 Understand, you senseless among the
    people;
  And *you* fools, when will you be wise?
9 He who planted the ear, shall He not
    hear?
  He who formed the eye, shall He not
    see?
10 He who instructs the nations, shall He
    not correct,
  He who teaches man knowledge?
11 The LORD knows the thoughts of man,
  That they *are* futile.

PROVERBS 22:24, 25

24 MAKE no friendship with an angry
    man,
  And with a furious man do not go,
25 Lest you learn his ways
  And set a snare for your soul.

ROMANS 10:1–21

BRETHREN, my heart's desire and prayer
to God for Israel is that they may be saved.
2 For I bear them witness that they have a
zeal for God, but not according to knowledge. 3 For they being ignorant of God's
righteousness, and seeking to establish their
own righteousness, have not submitted to
the righteousness of God. 4 For Christ *is*
the end of the law for righteousness to
everyone who believes.
  5 For Moses writes about the righteousness which is of the law, "The man who
does those things shall live by them."
6 But the righteousness of faith speaks in
this way, "Do not say in your heart, 'Who
will ascend into heaven?' " (that is, to bring
Christ down *from above*) 7 or, " 'Who will

descend into the abyss?' " (that is, to bring
Christ up from the dead). 8 But what does
it say? "The word is near you, in your mouth
and in your heart" (that is, the word of
faith which we preach): 9 that if you confess
with your mouth the Lord Jesus and believe
in your heart that God has raised Him from
the dead, you will be saved. 10 For with

---

*The believer is one who bases all on
Jesus Christ's sacrifice.* (GOOD)

---

the heart one believes unto righteousness,
and with the mouth confession is made unto
salvation. 11 For the Scripture says, "Whoever believes on Him will not be put to
shame." 12 For there is no distinction between Jew and Greek, for the same Lord
over all is rich to all who call upon Him.
13 For "whoever calls on the name of the
LORD shall be saved."
  14 How then shall they call on Him in
whom they have not believed? And how
shall they believe in Him of whom they
have not heard? And how shall they hear
without a preacher? 15 And how shall they
preach unless they are sent? As it is written:

  "How beautiful are the feet of those
      who preach the gospel of peace,
    Who bring glad tidings of good
      things!"

16 But they have not all obeyed the gospel.
For Isaiah says, "LORD, who has believed
our report?" 17 So then faith *comes* by hearing, and hearing by the word of God.
  18 But I say, have they not heard? Yes
indeed:

  "Their sound has gone out to all the
      earth,
    And their words to the ends of the
      world."

19 But I say, did Israel not know? First
Moses says:

  "I will provoke you to jealousy by *those
      who are* not a nation,
    I will move you to anger by a foolish
      nation."

20 But Isaiah is very bold and says:

  "I was found by those who did not
      seek Me;
    I was made manifest to those who
      did not ask for Me."

21 But to Israel he says:

"All day long I have stretched out My hands

To a disobedient and contrary people."

Reading 223—Instinctive Integrity
Job 13:13–28

Job feels that in spite of all that is happening, God's integrity remains, and his own integrity. He cannot explain his sufferings by saying, "I am being punished because I have done wrong," or, "I am suffering because I needed to be perfected." The friends have accused Job of being a hypocrite and imply that he is also an atheist, but just at this very time Job gives expression to the most sublime utterance of faith in the whole of the Old Testament—"Though He slay me, yet will I trust Him." "Though He, whom you are misrepresenting and whom I cannot state in words—though He slay me, I will trust in the fact that He is full of the integrity I believe Him to be, and I will wait for Him. I will face my own common-sense integrity, and dedicate my instinctive sense of God's integrity, and in the end I know that both will work out into one."

Always remain true to facts and to the intuitive certainty that God must be just, and do not try to justify Him too quickly. The juggling trick tries to justify God for allowing sin and war. Sin and war are absolutely unjustifiable, and yet the instinct of every Christian is—"I know that in the end God will justify Himself." Meantime you can justify Him only by a venture of faith which cannot be logically demonstrated. (BAFFLED)

JOB 13:1—14:22

1 "BEHOLD, my eye has seen all *this*,
   My ear has heard and understood it.
2 What you know, I also know;
   I *am* not inferior to you.
3 But I would speak to the Almighty,
   And I desire to reason with God.
4 But you forgers of lies,
   You *are* all worthless physicians.
5 Oh, that you would be silent,
   And it would be your wisdom!
6 Now hear my reasoning,
   And heed the pleadings of my lips.
7 Will you speak wickedly for God,
   And talk deceitfully for Him?
8 Will you show partiality for Him?
   Will you contend for God?
9 Will it be well when He searches you out?
   Or can you mock Him as one mocks a man?
10 He will surely rebuke you
   If you secretly show partiality.
11 Will not His excellence make you afraid,

And the dread of Him fall upon you?
12 Your platitudes *are* proverbs of ashes,
   Your defenses are defenses of clay.

13 "Hold your peace with me, and let me speak,
   Then let come on me what *may!*
14 Why do I take my flesh in my teeth,
   And put my life in my hands?
15 Though He slay me, yet will I trust Him.
   Even so, I will defend my own ways before Him.
16 He also *shall* be my salvation,
   For a hypocrite could not come before Him.
17 Listen carefully to my speech,
   And to my declaration with your ears.
18 See now, I have prepared *my* case,
   I know that I shall be vindicated.
19 Who *is* he *who* will contend with me?
   If now I hold my tongue, I perish.

20 "Only two *things* do not do to me,
   Then I will not hide myself from You:
21 Withdraw Your hand far from me,

And let not the dread of You make
me afraid.
22 Then call, and I will answer;
Or let me speak, then You respond
to me.
23 How many *are* my iniquities and sins?
Make me know my transgression and
my sin.
24 Why do You hide Your face,
And regard me as Your enemy?
25 Will You frighten a leaf driven to
and fro?
And will You pursue dry stubble?
26 For You write bitter things
against me,
And make me inherit the iniquities
of my youth.
27 You put my feet in the stocks,
And watch closely all my paths.
You set a limit for the soles of my
feet.

28 "*Man* decays like a rotten thing,
Like a garment that is moth-eaten.

14 "MAN *who is* born of woman
Is of few days and full of trouble.
2 He comes forth like a flower and fades
away;
He flees like a shadow and does not
continue.
3 And do You open Your eyes on such
a one,
And bring me to judgment with
Yourself?
4 Who can bring a clean *thing* out of
an unclean?
No one!
5 Since his days *are* determined,
The number of his months *is* with
You;
You have appointed his limits, so that
he cannot pass.
6 Look away from him that he may
rest,
Till like a hired man he finishes his
day.

7 "For there is hope for a tree,
If it is cut down, that it will sprout
again,
And that its tender shoots will not
cease.
8 Though its root may grow old in
the earth,
And its stump may die in the ground,
9 *Yet* at the scent of water it will bud
And bring forth branches like a plant.
10 But man dies and is laid away;
Indeed he breathes his last
And where *is* he?

11 *As* water disappears from the sea,
And a river becomes parched and
dries up,
12 So man lies down and does not rise.
Till the heavens *are* no more,
They will not awake
Nor be roused from their sleep.

13 "Oh, that You would hide me in the
grave,
That You would conceal me until
Your wrath is past,
That You would appoint me a set
time, and remember me!
14 If a man dies, shall he live *again?*
All the days of my hard service I will
wait,
Till my change comes.
15 You shall call, and I will answer You;
You shall desire the work of Your
hands.
16 For now You number my steps,
But do not watch over my sin.
17 My transgression *is* sealed up in a
bag,
And You cover my iniquity.

18 "But *as* a mountain falls *and* crumbles
away,
And *as* a rock is moved from its place;
19 *As* water wears away stones,
And as torrents wash away the soil
of the earth;
So You destroy the hope of man.
20 You prevail forever against him, and
he passes on;
You change his countenance and send
him away.
21 His sons come to honor, and he does
not know *it;*
They are brought low, and he does
not perceive *it.*
22 But his flesh will be in pain over it,
And his soul will mourn over it."

PSALM 94:12–19

12 BLESSED *is* the man whom You
instruct, O Lord,
And teach out of Your law,
13 That You may give him rest from the
days of adversity,
Until the pit is dug for the wicked.
14 For the Lord will not cast off His
people,
Nor will He forsake His inheritance.
15 But judgment will return to
righteousness,
And all the upright in heart will
follow it.

16 Who will rise up for me against the
    evildoers?
    Who will stand up for me against the
    workers of iniquity?
17 Unless the LORD *had been* my help,
    My soul would soon have settled in
    silence.

---

*The characteristics of God Almighty
are mirrored for us in Jesus
Christ.* (BIB. PSYCH.)

---

18 If I say, "My foot slips,"
    Your mercy, O LORD, will hold me up.
19 In the multitude of my anxieties within
    me,
    Your comforts delight my soul.

PROVERBS 22:26, 27

26 DO not be one of those who shakes
    hands in a pledge,
    One of those who is surety for debts;
27 If you have nothing *with which* to pay,
    Why should he take away your bed from
    under you?

ROMANS 11:1–18

I say then, has God cast away His people?
Certainly not! For I also am an Israelite,
of the seed of Abraham, *of* the tribe of Benjamin. 2 God has not cast away His people
whom He foreknew. Or do you not know
what the Scripture says of Elijah, how he
pleads with God against Israel, saying,
3 "LORD, they have killed Your prophets
and torn down Your altars, and I alone
am left, and they seek my life"? 4 But what
does the divine response say to him? "I

---

*God's predestinations are the
voluntary choosing of the sanctified
soul.* (SEND I YOU)

---

have reserved for Myself seven thousand
men who have not bowed the knee to Baal."
5 Even so then, at this present time there
is a remnant according to the election of
grace. 6 And if by grace, then *it is* no longer
of works; otherwise grace is no longer grace.
But if *it is* of works, it is no longer grace;
otherwise work is no longer work.

7 What then? Israel has not obtained what
it seeks; but the elect have obtained it, and
the rest were blinded. 8 Just as it is written:

> "God has given them a spirit of stupor,
>   Eyes that they should not see
>   And ears that they should not hear,
> To this very day."

9 And David says:

> "Let their table become a snare and
>   a trap,
> A stumbling block and a recompense
>   to them.
10 Let their eyes be darkened, so that
>   they do not see,
> And bow down their back always."

11 I say then, have they stumbled that
they should fall? Certainly not! But through
their fall, to provoke them to jealousy, salvation *has come* to the Gentiles. 12 Now if
their fall *is* riches for the world, and their
failure riches for the Gentiles, how much
more their fullness!

13 For I speak to you Gentiles; inasmuch
as I am an apostle to the Gentiles, I magnify
my ministry, 14 if by any means I may provoke to jealousy *those who are* my flesh and
save some of them. 15 For if their being
cast away *is* the reconciling of the world,
what *will* their acceptance *be* but life from
the dead?

16 For if the firstfruit *is* holy, the lump
is also *holy;* and if the root *is* holy, so *are*
the branches. 17 And if some of the branches
were broken off, and you, being a wild olive
tree, were grafted in among them, and with
them became a partaker of the root and
fatness of the olive tree, 18 do not boast
against the branches. But if you do boast,
remember that you do not support the root,
but the root supports you.

Reading 224—What Is Man?
Job 15:14–16

Theology is the science of religion, an intellectual attempt to systematize the consciousness of God. If we take the doctrine of the Trinity (which is a noble attempt of the mind of man to put into a theological formula the Godhead as revealed in the Bible) and say—"That is God," every other attempt at a statement of the Godhead is met by a sledgehammer blow of finality. My theology has taken the place of God and I have to say, "That it is blasphemy." Theology is second, not first; in its place it is a handmaid of religion, but it becomes a tyrant if put in the first place. The great doctrines of predestination and election are secondary matters; they are attempts at definition, but if we take sides with the theological method we will damn those who differ from us without a minute's hesitation. Is there any form of belief which has taken the place of God with me? We only believe what we conceive of God, and when things happen contrary to that line, we deny the experience and remain true to our theological method. Job is on the right trail.   (BAFFLED)

JOB 15:1—16:22

THEN Eliphaz the Temanite answered and said:

2 "Should a wise man answer with
      empty knowledge,
   And fill himself with the east wind?
3 Should he reason with unprofitable
      talk,
   Or by speeches with which he can
      do no good?
4 Yes, you cast off fear,
   And restrain prayer before God.
5 For your iniquity teaches your
      mouth,
   And you choose the tongue of the
      crafty.
6 Your own mouth condemns you, and
      not I;
   Yes, your own lips testify against you.

7 "Are you the first man who was born?
   Or were you made before the hills?
8 Have you heard the counsel of God?
   Do you limit wisdom to yourself?
9 What do you know that we do not
      know?
   What do you understand that is not
      in us?
10 Both the gray-haired and the aged
      are among us,
   Much older than your father.
11 Are the consolations of God too small
      for you,
   And the word spoken gently with you?
12 Why does your heart carry you away,

And what do your eyes wink at,
13 That you turn your spirit against
      God,
   And let such words go out of your
      mouth?

14 "What is man, that he could be pure?
   And he who is born of a woman, that
      he could be righteous?
15 If God puts no trust in His saints,
   And the heavens are not pure in His
      sight,
16 How much less man, who is
      abominable and filthy,
   Who drinks iniquity like water!

17 "I will tell you, hear me;
   What I have seen I will declare,
18 What wise men have told,
   Not hiding anything received from
      their fathers,
19 To whom alone the land was given,
   And no alien passed among them:
20 The wicked man writhes with pain
      all his days,
   And the number of years is hidden
      from the oppressor.
21 Dreadful sounds are in his ears;
   In prosperity the destroyer comes
      upon him.
22 He does not believe that he will
      return from darkness,
   For a sword is waiting for him.
23 He wanders about for bread, saying,
      'Where is it?'
   He knows that a day of darkness is
      ready at his hand.

24 Trouble and anguish make him
   afraid;
   They overpower him, like a king
   ready for battle.
25 For he stretches out his hand against
   God,
   And acts defiantly against the
   Almighty,

Never accept an explanation that travesties God's character. (DISCIPLES)

---

26 Running stubbornly against Him
   With his strong, embossed shield.

27 "Though he has covered his face with
   his fatness,
   And made *his* waist heavy with fat,
28 He dwells in desolate cities,
   In houses which no one inhabits,
   Which are destined to become ruins.
29 He will not be rich,
   Nor will his wealth continue,
   Nor will his possessions overspread
   the earth.
30 He will not depart from darkness;
   The flame will dry out his branches,
   And by the breath of His mouth he
   will go away.
31 Let him not trust in futile *things,*
   deceiving himself,
   For futility will be his reward.
32 It will be accomplished before his
   time,
   And his branch will not be green.
33 He will shake off his unripe grape
   like a vine,
   And cast off his blossom like an olive
   tree.
34 For the company of hypocrites *will
   be* barren,
   And fire will consume the tents of
   bribery.
35 They conceive trouble and bring
   forth futility;
   Their womb prepares deceit."

16 THEN Job answered and said:

2 "I have heard many such things;
   Miserable comforters *are* you all!
3 Shall words of wind have an end?
   Or what provokes you that you
   answer?
4 I also could speak as you *do,*
   If your soul were in my soul's place.
   I could heap up words against you,
   And shake my head at you;

5 *But* I would strengthen you with my
   mouth,
   And the comfort of my lips would
   relieve *your grief.*

6 "Though I speak, my grief is not
   relieved;
   And *if* I remain silent, how am I
   eased?
7 But now He has worn me out;
   You have made desolate all my
   company.
8 You have shriveled me up,
   And it is a witness *against me;*
   My leanness rises up against me
   And bears witness to my face.
9 He tears *me* in His wrath, and hates
   me;
   He gnashes at me with His teeth;
   My adversary sharpens His gaze on
   me.
10 They gape at me with their mouth,
   They strike me reproachfully on the
   cheek,
   They gather together against me.
11 God has delivered me to the ungodly,
   And turned me over to the hands
   of the wicked.
12 I was at ease, but He has shattered
   me;
   He also has taken *me* by my neck,
   and shaken me to pieces;
   He has set me up for His target,
13 His archers surround me.
   He pierces my heart and does not
   pity;
   He pours out my gall on the ground.
14 He breaks me with wound upon
   wound;
   He runs at me like a warrior.

15 "I have sewn sackcloth over my skin,
   And laid my head in the dust.
16 My face is flushed from weeping,
   And on my eyelids *is* the shadow of
   death;
17 Although no violence *is* in my hands,
   And my prayer *is* pure.

18 "O earth, do not cover my blood,
   And let my cry have no *resting* place!
19 Surely even now my witness *is* in
   heaven,
   And my evidence *is* on high.
20 My friends scorn me;
   My eyes pour out *tears* to God.
21 Oh, that one might plead for a man
   with God,
   As a man *pleads* for his neighbor!
22 For when a few years are finished,
   I shall go the way of no return.

PSALM 94:20–23

20 SHALL the throne of iniquity, which
devises evil by law,
Have fellowship with You?
21 They gather together against the life
of the righteous,
And condemn innocent blood.
22 But the Lord has been my defense,
And my God the rock of my refuge.
23 He has brought on them their own
iniquity,
And shall cut them off in their own
wickedness;
The Lord our God shall cut them off.

PROVERBS 22:28, 29

28 DO not remove the ancient landmark
Which your fathers have set.

29 Do you see a man *who* excels in his
work?
He will stand before kings;
He will not stand before unknown *men.*

ROMANS 11:19–36

YOU will say then, "Branches were broken
off that I might be grafted in." 20 Well *said.*
Because of unbelief they were broken off,
and you stand by faith. Do not be haughty,
but fear. 21 For if God did not spare the
natural branches, He may not spare you
either. 22 Therefore consider the goodness
and severity of God: on those who fell,
severity; but toward you, goodness, if you
continue in *His* goodness. Otherwise you
also will be cut off. 23 And they also, if
they do not continue in unbelief, will be
grafted in, for God is able to graft them
in again. 24 For if you were cut out of the
olive tree which is wild by nature, and were
grafted contrary to nature into a cultivated
olive tree, how much more will these, who

are natural *branches,* be grafted into their
own olive tree?
25 For I do not desire, brethren, that you
should be ignorant of this mystery, lest you
should be wise in your own opinion, that
blindness in part has happened to Israel
until the fullness of the Gentiles has come
in. 26 And so all Israel will be saved, as it
is written:

"The Deliverer will come out of Zion,
And He will turn away ungodliness
from Jacob;
27 For this *is* My covenant with them,
When I take away their sins."

28 Concerning the gospel *they are* enemies
for your sake, but concerning the election
they are beloved for the sake of the fathers.

---

*The love of God is revealed in that
He laid down His life for His
enemies.* (Sermon Mt.)

---

29 For the gifts and the calling of God *are*
irrevocable. 30 For as you were once disobedient to God, yet have now obtained mercy
through their disobedience, 31 even so these
also have now been disobedient, that
through the mercy shown you they also
may obtain mercy. 32 For God has committed them all to disobedience, that He might
have mercy on all.
33 Oh, the depth of the riches both of
the wisdom and knowledge of God! How
unsearchable *are* His judgments and His
ways past finding out!

34 "For who has known the mind of the
Lord?
Or who has become His counselor?"
35 "Or who has first given to Him
And it shall be repaid to him?"

36 For of Him and through Him and to
Him *are* all things, to whom *be* glory forever. Amen.

Reading 225—In the Despair Before Men
Job 17:11–16

Acertain type of religious hypocrisy makes men hide what they feel, but Job has come to the place where he cannot hide it—"I cannot pretend that I am comforted of God," he says. If only Job could have taken on the pose that he had the comfort of God, his friends would not have challenged him, but he says, "I have no comfort; I do not see God, neither can I talk to Him; all I know is that my creed and former belief must be wrong. I do not know what to accept, but I am certain God will prove that He is just and true and right, and I refuse to tell a lie in order to help Him out."

This attitude of religious faith is finely expressed by the psalmist—"Then I will go to the altar of God, to God my exceeding joy" (Ps. 43:4). This is sublime faith, the faith that Jesus demanded of John the Baptist. "Blessed is he who is not offended because of Me." Will I stick to it, without any presence or humbug, that God is righteous, although everything in my actual experience seems to prove that He is cruel? Most of us are hypocrites—too afraid to state the thing as Job did. We say right out, "God is cruel to allow me to go through this, and I refuse to believe in Him anymore." Job stuck to his point that when everything was known it would not be to God's dishonor, but to His honor. (*BAFFLED*)

JOB 17:1—18:21

1 "MY spirit is broken,
My days are extinguished,
The grave *is ready* for me.
2 *Are* not mockers with me?
And does not my eye dwell
on their provocation?

3 "Now put down a pledge for me with
Yourself.
Who *is* he *who* will shake hands
with me?
4 For You have hidden their heart from
understanding;
Therefore You will not exalt *them*.
5 He who speaks flattery to *his* friends,
Even the eyes of his children will fail.

6 "But He has made me a byword of
the people,
And I have become one in whose
face men spit.
7 My eye has also grown dim because
of sorrow,
And all my members *are* like
shadows.
8 Upright *men* are astonished at this,
And the innocent stirs himself up
against the hypocrite.
9 Yet the righteous will hold to his way,
And he who has clean hands will be
stronger and stronger.

10 "But please, come back again, all of
you,
For I shall not find *one* wise *man*
among you.
11 My days are past,
My purposes are broken off,
Even the thoughts of my heart.
12 They change the night into day;
'The light *is* near,' *they say*, in the face
of darkness.
13 If I wait *for* the grave *as* my house,
If I make my bed in the darkness,
14 If I say to corruption, 'You *are* my
father,'
And to the worm, 'You *are* my
mother and my sister,'
15 Where then *is* my hope?
As for my hope, who can see it?
16 *Will* they go down to the gates of
Sheol?
Shall *we have* rest together in the
dust?"

18 THEN Bildad the Shuhite answered and said:

2 "How long *till* you put an end to
words?
Gain understanding, and afterward
we will speak.
3 Why are we counted as beasts,
And regarded as stupid in your sight?
4 You who tear yourself in anger,

Shall the earth be forsaken for you?
Or shall the rock be removed from
its place?

5 "The light of the wicked indeed goes
out,
And the flame of his fire does not
shine.
6 The light is dark in his tent,
And his lamp beside him is put out.
7 The steps of his strength are
shortened,
And his own counsel casts him down.
8 For he is cast into a net by his own
feet,
And he walks into a snare.
9 The net takes *him* by the heel,
And a snare lays hold of him.
10 A noose *is* hidden for him on the
ground,
And a trap for him in the road.
11 Terrors frighten him on every side,
And drive him to his feet.
12 His strength is starved,
And destruction *is* ready at his side.
13 It devours patches of his skin;
The firstborn of death devours his
limbs.
14 He is uprooted from the shelter of
his tent,
And they parade him before the king
of terrors.
15 They dwell in his tent *who are* none
of his;
Brimstone is scattered on his
dwelling.
16 His roots are dried out below,
And his branch withers above.
17 The memory of him perishes from
the earth,
And he has no name among the
renowned.
18 He is driven from light into darkness,
And chased out of the world.
19 He has neither son nor posterity
among his people,
Nor any remaining in his dwellings.
20 Those in the west are astonished at
his day,
As those in the east are frightened.
21 Surely such *are* the dwellings of the
wicked,
And this *is* the place *of him who* does
not know God."

PSALM 95:1–5

1 OH come, let us sing to the LORD!
Let us shout joyfully to the Rock of
our salvation.

2 Let us come before His presence with
thanksgiving;
Let us shout joyfully to Him with
psalms.
3 For the LORD *is* the great God,
And the great King above all gods.

---

*T*he Bible statements *[defining God]
stand like eternal monuments,
shrouded in ineffable
glory.* (CHRIS. DIS. 1)

---

4 In His hand *are* the deep places of the
earth;
The heights of the hills *are* His also.
5 The sea *is* His, for He made it;
And His hands formed the dry *land.*

PROVERBS 23:1–3

1 WHEN you sit down to eat with a ruler,
Consider carefully what *is* before you;
2 And put a knife to your throat
If you *are* a man given to appetite.
3 Do not desire his delicacies,
For they *are* deceptive food.

ROMANS 12:1–21

I beseech you therefore, brethren, by the
mercies of God, that you present your bodies a living sacrifice, holy, acceptable to God,
which is your reasonable service. 2 And do
not be conformed to this world, but be
transformed by the renewing of your mind,
that you may prove what *is* that good and
acceptable and perfect will of God.

---

*D*o not ask God to take your body, but
give your body to God.* (PLACE HELP)

---

3 For I say, through the grace given to
me, to everyone who is among you, not
to think *of himself* more highly than he
ought to think, but to think soberly, as
God has dealt to each one a measure of
faith. 4 For as we have many members in
one body, but all the members do not have
the same function, 5 so we, *being* many,
are one body in Christ, and individually
members of one another. 6 Having then
gifts differing according to the grace that
is given to us, *let us use them:* if prophecy,
let us prophesy in proportion to our faith;

7 or ministry, *let us use it* in *our* ministering; he who teaches, in teaching; 8 he who exhorts, in exhortation; he who gives, with liberality; he who leads, with diligence; he who shows mercy, with cheerfulness.

9 *Let* love *be* without hypocrisy. Abhor what is evil. Cling to what is good. 10 *Be* kindly affectionate to one another with brotherly love, in honor giving preference to one another; 11 not lagging in diligence, fervent in spirit, serving the Lord; 12 rejoicing in hope, patient in tribulation, continuing steadfastly in prayer; 13 distributing to the needs of the saints, given to hospitality.

14 Bless those who persecute you; bless and do not curse. 15 Rejoice with those who rejoice, and weep with those who weep. 16 Be of the same mind toward one another.

Do not set your mind on high things, but associate with the humble. Do not be wise in your own opinion.

17 Repay no one evil for evil. Have regard for good things in the sight of all men. 18 If it is possible, as much as depends on you, live peaceably with all men. 19 Beloved, do not avenge yourselves, but *rather* give place to wrath; for it is written, "Vengeance *is* Mine, I will repay," says the Lord. 20 Therefore

"If your enemy is hungry, feed him;
    If he is thirsty, give him a drink;
    For in so doing you will heap coals
        of fire on his head."

21 Do not be overcome by evil, but overcome evil with good.

◆◆◆◆

Reading 226—The Account of Desolateness
Job 19:6, 7

Job's statements are not colored; he simply states what has happened to him—everything has gone and no explanation has been given him. There is no bright side to some troubles. There is no reasonable hope for countless lives on account of this war, and it is shallow nonsense to tell them to "cheer up"; life to them is a hell of darkness of the most appalling order. The one who preaches at such a time is an impertinence, but the one who says "I don't know why you are going through this, it is black and desperate, but I will wait with you," is an unspeakable benediction and sustaining. Job has no one to do this for him, his onetime friends simply add to his bitterness; they too have been hit along the line of their creed, and they are indignant and talk only on the religious line.   (*BAFFLED*)

JOB 19:1—20:29

THEN Job answered and said:

2 "How long will you torment my soul,
    And break me in pieces with words?
3 These ten times you have reproached
        me;
    You are not ashamed *that* you have
        wronged me.
4 And if indeed I have erred,
    My error remains with me.
5 If indeed you exalt *yourselves* against
        me,
    And plead my disgrace against me,

6 Know then that God has wronged
        me,
    And has surrounded me with His net.
7 "If I cry out concerning wrong, I am
        not heard.
    If I cry aloud, *there is* no justice.
8 He has fenced up my way, so that I
        cannot pass;
    And He has set darkness in my paths.
9 He has stripped me of my glory,
    And taken the crown *from* my head.
10 He breaks me down on every side,
    And I am gone;
    My hope He has uprooted like a tree.

11 He has also kindled His wrath against
me,
And He counts me as *one of* His
enemies.

12 His troops come together
And build up their road against me;
They encamp all around my tent.

13 "He has removed my brothers far from
me,
And my acquaintances are completely
estranged from me.

14 My relatives have failed,
And my close friends have forgotten
me.

15 Those who dwell in my house, and
my maidservants,
Count me as a stranger;
I am an alien in their sight.

16 I call my servant, but he gives no
answer;
I beg him with my mouth.

17 My breath is offensive to my wife,
And I am repulsive to the children
of my own body.

18 Even young children despise me;
I arise, and they speak against me.

19 All my close friends abhor me,
And those whom I love have turned
against me.

20 My bone clings to my skin and to
my flesh,
And I have escaped by the skin of
my teeth.

21 "Have pity on me, have pity on me,
O you my friends,
For the hand of God has struck me!

22 Why do you persecute me as God
does,
And are not satisfied with my flesh?

23 "Oh, that my words were written!
Oh, that they were inscribed in a
book!

24 That they were engraved on a rock
With an iron pen and lead, forever!

25 For I know *that* my Redeemer lives,
And He shall stand at last on the
earth;

26 And after my skin is destroyed, this
I know,
That in my flesh I shall see God,

27 Whom I shall see for myself,
And my eyes shall behold, and not
another.
How my heart yearns within me!

28 If you should say, 'How shall we
persecute him?'—
Since the root of the matter is found
in me,

29 Be afraid of the sword for yourselves;
For wrath *brings* the punishment of
the sword,
That you may know *there is* a
judgment."

20 THEN Zophar the Naamathite answered and said:

2 "Therefore my anxious thoughts make
me answer,
Because of the turmoil within me.

---

*If thinking gives you a headache,
it is a sign that you have
brains.* (MORAL FOUND.)

---

3 I have heard the rebuke that
reproaches me,
And the spirit of my understanding
causes me to answer.

4 "Do you *not* know this of old,
Since man was placed on earth,

5 That the triumphing of the wicked
is short,
And the joy of the hypocrite is *but*
for a moment?

6 Though his haughtiness mounts up
to the heavens,
And his head reaches to the clouds,

7 *Yet* he will perish forever like his own
refuse;
Those who have seen him will say,
'Where is he?'

8 He will fly away like a dream, and
not be found;
Yes, he will be chased away like a
vision of the night.

9 The eye *that* saw him will *see him*
no more,
Nor will his place behold him
anymore.

10 His children will seek the favor of
the poor,
And his hands will restore his wealth.

11 His bones are full of his youthful
vigor,
But it will lie down with him in the
dust.

12 "Though evil is sweet in his mouth,
And he hides it under his tongue,

13 *Though* he spares it and does not
forsake it,
But still keeps it in his mouth,

14 *Yet* his food in his stomach turns
sour;
It becomes cobra venom within him.

15 He swallows down riches
And vomits them up again;
God casts them out of his belly.

16 He will suck the poison of cobras;
The viper's tongue will slay him.

17 He will not see the streams,
The rivers flowing with honey and
cream.

18 He will restore that for which he
labored,
And will not swallow *it* down;
From the proceeds of business
He will get no enjoyment.

19 For he has oppressed *and* forsaken
the poor,
He has violently seized a house which
he did not build.

20 "Because he knows no quietness in
his heart,
He will not save anything he desires.

21 Nothing is left for him to eat;
Therefore his well-being will not last.

22 In his self-sufficiency he will be in
distress;
Every hand of misery will come
against him.

23 *When* he is about to fill his stomach,
God will cast on him the fury of His
wrath,
And will rain *it* on him while he is
eating.

24 He will flee from the iron weapon;
A bronze bow will pierce him
through.

25 It is drawn, and comes out of the
body;
Yes, the glittering *point comes* out of
his gall.
Terrors *come* upon him;

26 Total darkness *is* reserved for his
treasures.
An unfanned fire will consume him;
It shall go ill with him who is left
in his tent.

27 The heavens will reveal his iniquity,
And the earth will rise up against
him.

28 The increase of his house will depart,
And his goods will flow away in the
day of His wrath.

29 This *is* the portion from God for a
wicked man,
The heritage appointed to him by
God."

PSALM 95:6–11

6 OH come, let us worship and bow
down;

Let us kneel before the LORD our
Maker.

7 For He *is* our God,
And we *are* the people of His pasture,
And the sheep of His hand.

Today, if you will hear His voice:

8 "Do not harden your hearts, as in the
rebellion,
As *in* the day of trial in the wilderness,

9 When your fathers tested Me;
They tried Me, though they saw My
work.

10 For forty years I was grieved with *that*
generation,
And said, 'It *is* a people who go astray
in their hearts,
And they do not know My ways.'

11 So I swore in My wrath,
'They shall not enter My rest.'"

PROVERBS 23:4, 5

4 DO not overwork to be rich;
Because of your own understanding,
cease!

5 Will you set your eyes on that which
is not?
For *riches* certainly make themselves
wings;
They fly away like an eagle *toward*
heaven.

ROMANS 13:1–14

LET every soul be subject to the governing
authorities. For there is no authority except
from God, and the authorities that exist
are appointed by God. 2 Therefore whoever
resists the authority resists the ordinance
of God, and those who resist will bring
judgment on themselves. 3 For rulers are

*It is only the unworthy in a man
that does not bow down to worthy
authority.*   (BAFFLED)

not a terror to good works, but to evil.
Do you want to be unafraid of the authority? Do what is good, and you will have
praise from the same. 4 For he is God's minister to you for good. But if you do evil,
be afraid; for he does not bear the sword
in vain; for he is God's minister, an avenger
to *execute* wrath on him who practices evil.
5 Therefore *you* must be subject, not only
because of wrath but also for conscience'

sake. 6 For because of this you also pay taxes, for they are God's ministers attending continually to this very thing. 7 Render therefore to all their due: taxes to whom taxes *are due,* customs to whom customs, fear to whom fear, honor to whom honor.

8 Owe no one anything except to love one another, for he who loves another has fulfilled the law. 9 For the commandments, "You shall not commit adultery," "You shall not murder," "You shall not steal," "You shall not bear false witness," "You shall not covet," and if *there is* any other commandment, are *all* summed up in this saying, namely, "You shall love your neighbor as

yourself." 10 Love does no harm to a neighbor; therefore love *is* the fulfillment of the law.

11 And *do* this, knowing the time, that now *it is* high time to awake out of sleep; for now our salvation *is* nearer than when we *first* believed. 12 The night is far spent, the day is at hand. Therefore let us cast off the works of darkness, and let us put on the armor of light. 13 Let us walk properly, as in the day, not in revelry and drunkenness, not in lewdness and lust, not in strife and envy. 14 But put on the Lord Jesus Christ, and make no provision for the flesh, to *fulfill its* lusts.

◆◆◆◆

Reading 227—The Sense of Perverseness
Job 21:15, 19, 27, 34

Job persists in stating that the basis of things is not clear, nor easy to understand. "It is absurd to say, as you are doing," he says, "that God punishes the evil man and looks after the good; there is so much perversity at the basis of things that that explanation won't do." The friends give this explanation because they are true to their creed, and Job says, "I held the same creed as you do until I came to my great trouble." Their creed was based on sound principles, but what is needed is a sound relationship at the basis of things. When things are suddenly altered by bereavement or by some tension in personal experience, we find ourselves wonderfully at home with what Job says. There is a wildness about things, and we revolt against the people who explain everything on the basis of sound principles. They have everything ready at hand, and can tell you just where everyone goes wrong; but Job's contention is that when a man is face-to-face with things as they are, easy explanations won't do, for things are not easy; there is a perverseness all through. If Job is not right in his contention, then the Redemption is "much ado about nothing." (*BAFFLED*)

JOB 21:1—22:30

THEN Job answered and said:

2 "Listen carefully to my speech,
  And let this be your consolation.
3 Bear with me that I may speak,
  And after I have spoken, keep mocking.

4 "As for me, *is* my complaint against man?
  And if *it were,* why should I not be impatient?
5 Look at me and be astonished;

Put *your* hand over *your* mouth.
6 Even when I remember I am terrified,
  And trembling takes hold of my flesh.
7 Why do the wicked live *and* become old,
  Yes, become mighty in power?
8 Their descendants are established with them in their sight,
  And their offspring before their eyes.
9 Their houses *are* safe from fear,
  Neither *is* the rod of God upon them.
10 Their bull breeds without failure;
  Their cow calves without miscarriage.

11 They send forth their little ones like
a flock,
And their children dance.
12 They sing to the tambourine and
harp,
And rejoice to the sound of the flute.
13 They spend their days in wealth,
And in a moment go down to the
grave.
14 Yet they say to God, 'Depart
from us,
For we do not desire the knowledge
of Your ways.
15 Who *is* the Almighty, that we should
serve Him?
And what profit do we have if we
pray to Him?'
16 Indeed their prosperity *is* not in their
hand;
The counsel of the wicked is far
from me.

17 "How often is the lamp of the wicked
put out?
How often does their destruction
come upon them,
The sorrows *God* distributes in His
anger?
18 They are like straw before the wind,
And like chaff that a storm carries
away.
19 *They say,* 'God lays up one's iniquity
for his children';
Let Him recompense him, that he
may know *it*.
20 Let his eyes see his destruction,
And let him drink of the wrath of
the Almighty.
21 For what does he care about his
household after him,
When the number of his months is
cut in half?

22 "Can *anyone* teach God knowledge,
Since He judges those on high?
23 One dies in his full strength,
Being wholly at ease and secure;
24 His pails are full of milk,
And the marrow of his bones is moist.
25 Another man dies in the bitterness
of his soul,
Never having eaten with pleasure.
26 They lie down alike in the dust,
And worms cover them.

27 "Look, I know your thoughts,
And the schemes *with which* you
would wrong me.
28 For you say,
'Where *is* the house of the prince?
And where *is* the tent,

The dwelling place of the wicked?'
29 Have you not asked those who travel
the road?
And do you not know their signs?
30 For the wicked are reserved for the
day of doom;
They shall be brought out on the day
of wrath.
31 Who condemns his way to his face?
And who repays him *for what* he has
done?
32 Yet he shall be brought to the grave,
And a vigil kept over the tomb.
33 The clods of the valley shall be sweet
to him;
Everyone shall follow him,
As countless *have gone* before him.

34 How then can you comfort me with
empty words,
Since falsehood remains in your
answers?"

22 THEN Eliphaz the Temanite answered and said:

2 "Can a man be profitable to God,
Though he who is wise may be
profitable to himself?
3 *Is it* any pleasure to the Almighty
that you are righteous?
Or *is it* gain *to Him* that you make
your ways blameless?

4 "Is it because of your fear of Him that
He corrects you,
And enters into judgment with you?
5 *Is* not your wickedness great,
And your iniquity without end?
6 For you have taken pledges from your
brother for no reason,
And stripped the naked of their
clothing.
7 You have not given the weary water
to drink,
And you have withheld bread from
the hungry.
8 But the mighty man possessed the
land,
And the honorable man dwelt in it.
9 You have sent widows away empty,
And the strength of the fatherless was
crushed.
10 Therefore snares *are* all around you,
And sudden fear troubles you,
11 Or darkness *so that* you cannot see;
And an abundance of water covers
you.

12 "*Is* not God in the height of heaven?
And see the highest stars, how lofty
they are!

13 And you say, 'What does God know?
Can He judge through the deep
darkness?

14 Thick clouds cover Him, so that He
cannot see,
And He walks above the circle of
heaven.'

15 Will you keep to the old way
Which wicked men have trod,

16 Who were cut down before their
time,
Whose foundations were swept away
by a flood?

17 They said to God, 'Depart from us!
What can the Almighty do to them?'

18 Yet He filled their houses with good
things;
But the counsel of the wicked is far
from me.

19 "The righteous see *it* and are glad,
And the innocent laugh at them:

20 'Surely our adversaries are cut down,
And the fire consumes their remnant.'

21 "Now acquaint yourself with Him,
and be at peace;
Thereby good will come to you.

22 Receive, please, instruction from His
mouth,
And lay up His words in your heart.

23 If you return to the Almighty, you
will be built up;
You will remove iniquity far from
your tents.

---

*G*od is so almightily simple that
it is impossible to complicate
Him. (CONFORMED)

---

24 Then you will lay your gold in the
dust,
And the *gold* of Ophir among the
stones of the brooks.

25 Yes, the Almighty will be your gold
And your precious silver;

26 For then you will have your delight
in the Almighty,
And lift up your face to God.

27 You will make your prayer to Him,
He will hear you,
And you will pay your vows.

28 You will also declare a thing,
And it will be established for you;
So light will shine on your ways.

29 When they cast *you* down, and you
say, 'Exaltation *will come!*'
Then He will save the humble *person.*

30 He will *even* deliver one who is not
innocent;
Yes, he will be delivered by the purity
of your hands."

PSALM 96:1–6

1 OH, sing to the LORD a new song!
Sing to the LORD, all the earth.

2 Sing to the LORD, bless His name;
Proclaim the good news of His
salvation from day to day.

3 Declare His glory among the nations,
His wonders among all peoples.

4 For the LORD *is* great and greatly to
be praised;
He *is* to be feared above all gods.

5 For all the gods of the peoples *are* idols,
But the LORD made the heavens.

6 Honor and majesty *are* before Him;
Strength and beauty *are* in His
sanctuary.

PROVERBS 23:6–8

6 DO not eat the bread of a miser,
Nor desire his delicacies;

7 For as he thinks in his heart, so *is* he.
"Eat and drink!" he says to you,
But his heart is not with you.

8 The morsel you have eaten, you will
vomit up,
And waste your pleasant words.

ROMANS 14:1–23

RECEIVE one who is weak in the faith,
but not to disputes over doubtful things.
2 For one believes he may eat all things,
but he who is weak eats *only* vegetables.
3 Let not him who eats despise him who
does not eat, and let not him who does
not eat judge him who eats; for God has
received him. 4 Who are you to judge another's servant? To his own master he stands
or falls. Indeed, he will be made to stand,
for God is able to make him stand.

5 One person esteems *one* day above another; another esteems every day *alike.* Let
each be fully convinced in his own mind.
6 He who observes the day, observes *it* to
the Lord; and he who does not observe
the day, to the Lord he does not observe
it. He who eats, eats to the Lord, for he
gives God thanks; and he who does not
eat, to the Lord he does not eat, and gives
God thanks. 7 For none of us lives to himself, and no one dies to himself. 8 For if

we live, we live to the Lord; and if we die, we die to the Lord. Therefore, whether we live or die, we are the Lord's. 9 For to this end Christ died and rose and lived again, that He might be Lord of both the dead and the living. 10 But why do you judge your brother? Or why do you show contempt for your brother? For we shall all stand before the judgment seat of Christ. 11 For it is written:

> "*As* I live, says the Lord,
> Every knee shall bow to Me,
> And every tongue shall confess to God."

12 So then each of us shall give account of himself to God. 13 Therefore let us not judge one another anymore, but rather resolve this, not to put a stumbling block or a cause to fall in *our* brother's way.

14 I know and am convinced by the Lord Jesus that *there is* nothing unclean of itself; but to him who considers anything to be unclean, to him *it is* unclean. 15 Yet if your brother is grieved because of *your* food, you are no longer walking in love. Do not destroy with your food the one for whom Christ died. 16 Therefore do not let your good be spoken of as evil; 17 for the kingdom of God is not eating and drinking, but righteousness and peace and joy in the Holy Spirit. 18 For he who serves Christ

---

The central meaning of the kingdom is my personal relationship to my Lord. (GOD'S WORKMANSHIP)

---

in these things *is* acceptable to God and approved by men.

19 Therefore let us pursue the things *which make* for peace and the things by which one may edify another. 20 Do not destroy the work of God for the sake of food. All things indeed *are* pure, but *it is* evil for the man who eats with offense. 21 *It is* good neither to eat meat nor drink wine nor *do anything* by which your brother stumbles or is offended or is made weak. 22 Do you have faith? Have *it* to yourself before God. Happy *is* he who does not condemn himself in what he approves. 23 But he who doubts is condemned if he eats, because *he does* not *eat* from faith; for whatever *is* not from faith is sin.

◆◆◆◆

Reading 228—Seeking Faith's Foundation
Job 23:3, 4

The reason the experience of redemption is so easy is because it cost God so much. . . . It is men like Job and the apostle Paul who bring us to the basis of things, not the average Christian among us, who knows no more why the basis of his salvation is redemption than the average common-sense man knows the basis of ordinary human life. We must get hold of the great souls, the men who have been hard hit and have gone to the basis of things, and whose experiences have been preserved for us by God, that we may know where we stand. One of the reasons for the futility of pseudo-evangelism is that it bases its doctrine on the shallow weak things it has saved. Thank God, Christianity does save the shallow weak things, but they are not the ones who diagnose Christianity, they are the expression of the last reach of Christianity. Paul said: "Not many mighty, not many noble, *are called*"; he did not say "not any mighty, not any noble." It is our Lord Himself, and men like Job in the Old Testament and Paul in the New, who give us the indication of where we are to look for the foundation of our faith when it is being shaken.

(*BAFFLED*)

JOB 23:1—25:6

THEN Job answered and said:

2 "Even today my complaint is bitter;
My hand is listless because of my
groaning.
3 Oh, that I knew where I might find
Him,
That I might come to His seat!
4 I would present *my* case before Him,
And fill my mouth with arguments.
5 I would know the words *which* He
would answer me,
And understand what He would say
to me.
6 Would He contend with me in His
great power?
No! But He would take *note* of me.
7 There the upright could reason with
Him,
And I would be delivered forever
from my Judge.

8 "Look, I go forward, but He is not
there,
And backward, but I cannot perceive
Him;
9 When He works on the left hand, I
cannot behold *Him;*
When He turns to the right hand, I
cannot see *Him.*
10 But He knows the way that I take;
When He has tested me, I shall come
forth as gold.
11 My foot has held fast to His steps;
I have kept His way and not turned
aside.
12 I have not departed from the
commandment of His lips;
I have treasured the words of His
mouth
More than my necessary *food.*

13 "But He *is* unique, and who can make
Him change?
And *whatever* His soul desires, *that*
He does.
14 For He performs *what is* appointed
for me,
And many such *things are* with Him.
15 Therefore I am terrified at His
presence;
When I consider *this,* I am afraid of
Him.
16 For God made my heart weak,
And the Almighty terrifies me;
17 Because I was not cut off from the
presence of darkness,
And He did *not* hide deep darkness
from my face.

24 "*SINCE* times are not hidden from
the Almighty,
Why do those who know Him see
not His days?

2 "*Some* remove landmarks;
They seize flocks violently and feed
on them;
3 They drive away the donkey of the
fatherless;
They take the widow's ox as a pledge.
4 They push the needy off the road;
All the poor of the land are forced
to hide.
5 Indeed, *like* wild donkeys in the
desert,
They go out to their work, searching
for food.
The wilderness *yields* food for them
and for *their* children.
6 They gather their fodder in the field
And glean in the vineyard of the
wicked.
7 They spend the night naked, without
clothing,
And have no covering in the cold.
8 They are wet with the showers of
the mountains,
And huddle around the rock for want
of shelter.

9 "*Some* snatch the fatherless from the
breast,
And take a pledge from the poor.
10 They cause *the poor* to go naked,
without clothing;
And they take away the sheaves from
the hungry.
11 They press out oil within their walls,
And tread winepresses, yet suffer
thirst.
12 The dying groan in the city,
And the souls of the wounded cry
out;
Yet God does not charge *them* with
wrong.

13 "There are those who rebel against
the light;
They do not know its ways
Nor abide in its paths.
14 The murderer rises with the light;
He kills the poor and needy;
And in the night he is like a thief.
15 The eye of the adulterer waits for
the twilight,
Saying, 'No eye will see me';
And he disguises *his* face.
16 In the dark they break into houses
Which they marked for themselves
in the daytime;

They do not know the light.
17 For the morning is the same to them
       as the shadow of death;
    If *someone* recognizes *them,*
    They are in the terrors of the shadow
       of death.

18 "They *should be* swift on the face of
       the waters,
    Their portion *should be* cursed in the
       earth,
    So that no *one would* turn into the
       way of their vineyards.
19 As drought and heat consume the
       snow waters,
    So the grave *consumes those who* have
       sinned.
20 The womb *should* forget him,
    The worm *should* feed sweetly on
       him;
    He *should* be remembered no more,
    And wickedness *should* be broken like
       a tree.
21 For he preys on the barren *who* do
       not bear,
    And does no good for the widow.

22 "But *God* draws the mighty away with
       His power;
    He rises up, but no *man* is sure of
       life.
23 He gives them security, and they rely
       on it;
    Yet His eyes *are* on their ways.
24 They are exalted for a little while,
    Then they are gone.
    They are brought low;
    They are taken out of the way like
       all *others;*
    They dry out like the heads of grain.

25 "Now if *it is* not *so,* who will prove
       me a liar,
    And make my speech worth
       nothing?"

25 THEN Bildad the Shuhite an-
       swered and said:

2   "Dominion and fear *belong* to Him;
    He makes peace in His high places.
3   Is there any number to His armies?
    Upon whom does His light not rise?
4   How then can man be righteous
       before God?
    Or how can he be pure *who is* born
       of a woman?
5   If even the moon does not shine,
    And the stars are not pure in His
       sight,
6   How much less man, *who is* a maggot,
    And a son of man, *who is* a worm?"

PSALM 96:7–10

7   GIVE to the LORD, O families of the
       peoples,
    Give to the LORD glory and strength.
8   Give to the LORD the glory *due* His
       name;
    Bring an offering, and come into His
       courts.
9   Oh, worship the LORD in the beauty
       of holiness!
    Tremble before Him, all the earth.

10 Say among the nations, "The LORD
       reigns;
    The world also is firmly established,
    It shall not be moved;
    He shall judge the peoples righteously."

PROVERBS 23:9

9   DO not speak in the hearing of a fool,
    For he will despise the wisdom of your
       words.

ROMANS 15:1–24

WE then who are strong ought to bear
with the scruples of the weak, and not to
please ourselves. 2 Let each of us please *his*
neighbor for *his* good, leading to edification. 3 For even Christ did not please Himself; but as it is written, "The reproaches
of those who reproached You fell on Me."
4 For whatever things were written before
were written for our learning, that we
through the patience and comfort of the
Scriptures might have hope. 5 Now may
the God of patience and comfort grant you
to be like-minded toward one another, according to Christ Jesus, 6 that you may with
one mind *and* one mouth glorify the God
and Father of our Lord Jesus Christ.

7 Therefore receive one another, just as
Christ also received us, to the glory of God.
8 Now I say that Jesus Christ has become
a servant to the circumcision for the truth
of God, to confirm the promises *made* to
the fathers, 9 and that the Gentiles might
glorify God for *His* mercy, as it is written:

> "For this reason I will confess to You
>   among the Gentiles,
> And sing to Your name."

10 And again he says:

> "Rejoice, O Gentiles, with His
>   people!"

11 And again:

"Praise the LORD, all you Gentiles!
Laud Him, all you peoples!"

12 And again, Isaiah says:

"There shall be a root of Jesse;
And He who shall rise to reign over
the Gentiles,
In Him the Gentiles shall hope."

13 Now may the God of hope fill you with all joy and peace in believing, that you may abound in hope by the power of the Holy Spirit.
14 Now I myself am confident concerning you, my brethren, that you also are full of goodness, filled with all knowledge, able also to admonish one another. 15 Nevertheless, brethren, I have written more boldly to you on *some* points, as reminding you, because of the grace given to me by God, 16 that I might be a minister of Jesus Christ to the Gentiles, ministering the gospel of God, that the offering of the Gentiles might be acceptable, sanctified by the Holy Spirit. 17 Therefore I have reason to glory in Christ Jesus in the things *which pertain* to God. 18 For I will not dare to speak of any of those things which Christ has not accomplished through me, in word and deed, to make the Gentiles obedient— 19 in mighty signs and wonders, by the power of the Spirit of God, so that from Jerusalem and round about to Illyricum I have fully preached the gospel of Christ. 20 And so I

Never water down the word of God, preach it in its undiluted sternness.   (UTMOST)

---

have made it my aim to preach the gospel, not where Christ was named, lest I should build on another man's foundation, 21 but as it is written:

"To whom He was not announced,
they shall see;
And those who have not heard shall
understand."

22 For this reason I also have been much hindered from coming to you. 23 But now no longer having a place in these parts, and having a great desire these many years to come to you, 24 whenever I journey to Spain, I shall come to you. For I hope to see you on my journey, and to be helped on my way there by you, if first I may enjoy your *company* for a while.

◆◆◆◆

---

*Reading 229—*God Must Step In
Job 26:1–14

In the Book of Job, nature is always referred to as being wild; this is a point of view we have forgotten nowadays. We talk about laws and findings, we give scientific explanations of thunder and of a sunset, and come to the conclusion that there is no unexplained sublimity in nature at all. The wildness of nature has to be recognized, there are forces in the earth and air and sea which baffle attempts at explanation or of control; all we can do is to give a direction for thought along certain lines.

Neither logic nor science can explain the sublimities of nature. Supposing a scientist with a diseased olfactory nerve says that there is no perfume in a rose, and to prove his statement he dissects the rose and tabulates every part, and then says, "Where is the perfume? It is a fiction; I have demonstrated that there is none." There is always one fact more that science cannot explain, and the best thing to do is not to deny it in order to preserve your sanity, but to say, as Job did, "No, the one fact more which you cannot explain means that God must step in just there, or there is no explanation to be had."   (BAFFLED)

JOB 26:1–14

BUT Job answered and said:

2   "How have you helped *him who is* without power?
    How have you saved the arm *that has* no strength?

3   How have you counseled *one who has* no wisdom?
    And *how* have you declared sound advice to many?

4   To whom have you uttered words?
    And whose spirit came from you?

5   "The dead tremble,
    Those under the waters and those inhabiting them.

6   Sheol *is* naked before Him,
    And Destruction has no covering.

7   He stretches out the north over empty space;
    He hangs the earth on nothing.

8   He binds up the water in His thick clouds,
    Yet the clouds are not broken under it.

9   He covers the face of *His* throne,
    And spreads His cloud over it.

10 He drew a circular horizon on the face of the waters,
    At the boundary of light and darkness.

11 The pillars of heaven tremble,
    And are astonished at His rebuke.

12 He stirs up the sea with His power,
    And by His understanding He breaks up the storm.

13 By His Spirit He adorned the heavens;
    His hand pierced the fleeing serpent.

14 Indeed these *are* the mere edges of His ways,
    And how small a whisper we hear of Him!
    But the thunder of His power who can understand?"

PSALM 96:11–13

11 LET the heavens rejoice, and let the earth be glad;
    Let the sea roar, and all its fullness;

12 Let the field be joyful, and all that *is* in it.

Then all the trees of the woods will rejoice before the LORD.

13 For He is coming, for He is coming to judge the earth.
    He shall judge the world with righteousness,
    And the peoples with His truth.

PROVERBS 23:10–12

10 DO not remove the ancient landmark,
    Nor enter the fields of the fatherless;

11 For their Redeemer *is* mighty;
    He will plead their cause against you.

12 Apply your heart to instruction,
    And your ears to words of knowledge.

ROMANS 15:25–33

BUT now I am going to Jerusalem to minister to the saints. 26 For it pleased those from Macedonia and Achaia to make a certain contribution for the poor among the saints who are in Jerusalem. 27 It pleased them

---

It takes the supernatural power of God to keep us as saints in the drab commonplace days.   (SEND I YOU)

---

indeed, and they are their debtors. For if the Gentiles have been partakers of their spiritual things, their duty is also to minister to them in material things. 28 Therefore, when I have performed this and have sealed to them this fruit, I shall go by way of you to Spain. 29 But I know that when I come to you, I shall come in the fullness of the blessing of the gospel of Christ. 30 Now I beg you, brethren, through the Lord Jesus Christ, and through the love of the Spirit, that you strive together with me in prayers to God for me, 31 that I may be delivered from those in Judea who do not believe, and that my service for Jerusalem may be acceptable to the saints, 32 that I may come to you with joy by the will of God, and may be refreshed together with you. 33 Now the God of peace *be* with you all. Amen.

◆◆◆◆

Reading 230—The Way Out
Job 28:20, 28

Every common-sense fact requires something for its explanation which common sense cannot give. The facts of every day and night reveal things our own minds cannot explain. When a scientific man comes across a gap in his explanations, instead of saying, "There is no gap here," let him recognize that there is a gap he cannot bridge, and that he must be reverent with what he cannot understand. The tendency is to deny that a fact has any existence because it cannot be fitted into any explanation as yet. That "the exception proves the rule" is not true: the exception proves that the rule won't do; the rule is useful only in the greatest number of cases. When scientists treat a thesis as a fact, they mean that it is based on the highest degree of probability. There are no "infallible" findings, and the man who bows down to scientific findings may be as big a fool as the man who refuses to do so. The man who prays ceases to be a fool, while the man who refuses to pray nourishes a blind life within his own brain and he will find no way out on that road. Job cries out that prayer is the only way out in all these matters. (*BAFFLED*)

JOB 27:1—28:28

MOREOVER Job continued his discourse, and said:

2 "*As* God lives, *who* has taken away my justice,
And the Almighty, *who* has made my soul bitter,
3 As long as my breath *is* in me,
And the breath of God in my nostrils,
4 My lips will not speak wickedness,
Nor my tongue utter deceit.
5 Far be it from me
That I should say you are right;
Till I die I will not put away my integrity from me.
6 My righteousness I hold fast, and will not let it go;
My heart shall not reproach *me* as long as I live.

7 "May my enemy be like the wicked,
And he who rises up against me like the unrighteous.
8 For what is the hope of the hypocrite,
Though he may gain *much*,
If God takes away his life?
9 Will God hear his cry
When trouble comes upon him?
10 Will he delight himself in the Almighty?
Will he always call on God?

11 "I will teach you about the hand of God;
What *is* with the Almighty I will not conceal.
12 Surely all of you have seen *it*;
Why then do you behave with complete nonsense?

13 "This is the portion of a wicked man with God,
And the heritage of oppressors, received from the Almighty:
14 If his children are multiplied, *it is* for the sword;
And his offspring shall not be satisfied with bread.
15 Those who survive him shall be buried in death,
And their widows shall not weep,
16 Though he heaps up silver like dust,
And piles up clothing like clay—
17 He may pile *it* up, but the just will wear *it*,
And the innocent will divide the silver.
18 He builds his house like a moth,
Like a booth *which* a watchman makes.
19 The rich man will lie down,
But not be gathered *up*;
He opens his eyes,
And he *is* no more.
20 Terrors overtake him like a flood;
A tempest steals him away in the night.
21 The east wind carries him away, and he is gone;
It sweeps him out of his place.

22 It hurls against him and does not
spare;
He flees desperately from its power.
23 *Men* shall clap their hands at him,
And shall hiss him out of his place.

28 "SURELY there is a mine for silver,
And a place *where* gold is refined.
2 Iron is taken from the earth,
And copper *is* smelted *from* ore.
3 *Man* puts an end to darkness,
And searches every recess
For ore in the darkness and the
shadow of death.
4 He breaks open a shaft away from
people;
In places forgotten by feet
They hang far away from men;
They swing to and fro.
5 *As for* the earth, from it comes bread,
But underneath it is turned up as by
fire;
6 Its stones *are* the source of sapphires,
And it contains gold dust.
7 *That* path no bird knows,
Nor has the falcon's eye seen it.
8 The proud lions have not
trodden it,
Nor has the fierce lion passed
over it.
9 He puts his hand on the flint;
He overturns the mountains at the
roots.
10 He cuts out channels in the rocks,
And his eye sees every precious thing.
11 He dams up the streams from
trickling;
What is hidden he brings forth to
light.

12 "But where can wisdom be found?
And where *is* the place of
understanding?
13 Man does not know its value,
Nor is it found in the land of the
living.
14 The deep says, *'It is* not in me';
And the sea says, *'It is* not with
me.'
15 It cannot be purchased for gold,
Nor can silver be weighed *for* its price.
16 It cannot be valued in the gold of
Ophir,
In precious onyx or sapphire.
17 Neither gold nor crystal can
equal it,
Nor can it be exchanged for jewelry
of fine gold.
18 No mention shall be made of coral
or quartz,
For the price of wisdom *is* above
rubies.

19 The topaz of Ethiopia cannot
equal it,
Nor can it be valued in pure gold.

20 "From where then does wisdom
come?
And where *is* the place of
understanding?
21 It is hidden from the eyes of all living,
And concealed from the birds of the
air.
22 Destruction and Death say,
'We have heard a report about it with
our ears.'
23 God understands its way,
And He knows its place.
24 For He looks to the ends of the earth,
And sees under the whole heavens,
25 To establish a weight for the wind,
And apportion the waters by
measure.
26 When He made a law for the rain,
And a path for the thunderbolt,
27 Then He saw *wisdom* and
declared it;
He prepared it, indeed, He searched
it out.
28 And to man He said,
'Behold, the fear of the Lord, that *is*
wisdom,
And to depart from evil *is*
understanding.' "

PSALM 97:1–6

1 THE Lord reigns;
Let the earth rejoice;
Let the multitude of isles be glad!

2 Clouds and darkness surround Him;
Righteousness and justice *are* the
foundation of His throne.

---

*When clouds are around
the saint knows that they are but the
dust of the Father's feet.*   (ASK)

---

3 A fire goes before Him,
And burns up His enemies round
about.
4 His lightnings light the world;
The earth sees and trembles.
5 The mountains melt like wax at the
presence of the Lord,
At the presence of the Lord of the
whole earth.
6 The heavens declare His righteousness,
And all the peoples see His glory.

PROVERBS 23:13, 14

13 DO not withhold correction from a child,
For *if* you beat him with a rod, he will not die.
14 You shall beat him with a rod,
And deliver his soul from hell.

ROMANS 16:1–27

I commend to you Phoebe our sister, who is a servant of the church in Cenchrea, 2 that you may receive her in the Lord in a manner worthy of the saints, and assist her in whatever business she has need of you; for indeed she has been a helper of many and of myself also.

3 Greet Priscilla and Aquila, my fellow workers in Christ Jesus, 4 who risked their own necks for my life, to whom not only I give thanks, but also all the churches of the Gentiles. 5 Likewise *greet* the church that is in their house.

Greet my beloved Epaenetus, who is the firstfruits of Achaia to Christ. 6 Greet Mary, who labored much for us. 7 Greet Andronicus and Junia, my countrymen and my fellow prisoners, who are of note among the apostles, who also were in Christ before me.

8 Greet Amplias, my beloved in the Lord. 9 Greet Urbanus, our fellow worker in Christ, and Stachys, my beloved. 10 Greet Apelles, approved in Christ. Greet those who are of the *household* of Aristobulus. 11 Greet Herodion, my countryman. Greet those who are of the *household* of Narcissus who are in the Lord.

12 Greet Tryphena and Tryphosa, who have labored in the Lord. Greet the beloved Persis, who labored much in the Lord. 13 Greet Rufus, chosen in the Lord, and his mother and mine. 14 Greet Asyncritus, Phlegon, Hermas, Patrobas, Hermes, and the brethren who are with them. 15 Greet Philologus and Julia, Nereus and his sister, and Olympas, and all the saints who are with them.

16 Greet one another with a holy kiss. The churches of Christ greet you.

17 Now I urge you, brethren, note those who cause divisions and offenses, contrary to the doctrine which you learned, and avoid them. 18 For those who are such do not serve our Lord Jesus Christ, but their own belly, and by smooth words and flattering speech deceive the hearts of the simple. 19 For your obedience has become known to all. Therefore I am glad on your behalf; but I want you to be wise in what is good, and simple concerning evil. 20 And the God

---

The characteristic of a saint's life is this bent of obedience. (PERFECT)

---

of peace will crush Satan under your feet shortly.

The grace of our Lord Jesus Christ *be* with you. Amen.

21 Timothy, my fellow worker, and Lucius, Jason, and Sosipater, my countrymen, greet you.

22 I, Tertius, who wrote *this* epistle, greet you in the Lord.

23 Gaius, my host and *the host* of the whole church, greets you. Erastus, the treasurer of the city, greets you, and Quartus, a brother. 24 The grace of our Lord Jesus Christ *be* with you all. Amen.

25 Now to Him who is able to establish you according to my gospel and the preaching of Jesus Christ, according to the revelation of the mystery kept secret since the world began 26 but now made manifest, and

---

Slowly and surely we learn the great secret of eternal life, which is to know God. (BRILL. HERITAGE)

---

by the prophetic Scriptures made known to all nations, according to the commandment of the everlasting God, for obedience to the faith— 27 to God, alone wise, *be* glory through Jesus Christ forever. Amen.

────────────── ◆◆◆◆ ──────────────

Reading 231—Proclaiming Christ's Cross
1 Corinthians 1:17, 18

It seems so remote from actual things to say that the preaching of the cross conveys the presence of God, but God has chosen to save in this way. "It pleased God through the foolishness of the message preached to save those who believe," because behind the preaching of the gospel is the creative redemption of God at work in the souls of men. That is the miracle of God. If you can tell how a grain of wheat when put into the ground will bring forth what it never was before, you can also tell how the Word of God put into a man's soul will bring forth what was not there before—a new life. The same God is the author of both. How are men born of the Spirit? By the proclaiming of the historic cross of Christ. "The wind blows where it wishes, . . . So is everyone who is born of the Spirit." The simple proclaiming of the gospel of God creates the need for the gospel. Nothing can satisfy the need but that which creates the need. The inner reality of redemption is that it creates all the time. "And I, if I am lifted up from the earth, will draw all *peoples* to Myself." Once let Jesus be lifted up and the Spirit of God creates the need for Him.   (*Place Help*)

JOB 29:1—30:31

JOB further continued his discourse, and said:

2 "Oh, that I were as *in* months past,
As *in* the days *when* God watched over me;
3 When His lamp shone upon my head,
And when by His light I walked *through* darkness;
4 Just as I was in the days of my prime,
When the friendly counsel of God *was* over my tent;
5 When the Almighty *was* yet with me,
When my children *were* around me;
6 When my steps were bathed with cream,
And the rock poured out rivers of oil for me!

7 "When I went out to the gate by the city,
When I took my seat in the open square,
8 The young men saw me and hid,
And the aged arose *and* stood;
9 The princes refrained from talking,
And put *their* hand on their mouth;
10 The voice of nobles was hushed,
And their tongue stuck to the roof of their mouth.
11 When the ear heard, then it blessed me,

And when the eye saw, then it approved me;
12 Because I delivered the poor who cried out,
The fatherless and *the one who* had no helper.
13 The blessing of a perishing *man* came upon me,
And I caused the widow's heart to sing for joy.
14 I put on righteousness, and it clothed me;
My justice *was* like a robe and a turban.
15 I *was* eyes to the blind,
And I *was* feet to the lame.
16 I *was* a father to the poor,
And I searched out the case *that* I did not know.
17 I broke the fangs of the wicked,
And plucked the victim from his teeth.

18 "Then I said, 'I shall die in my nest,
And multiply *my* days as the sand.
19 My root *is* spread out to the waters,
And the dew lies all night on my branch.
20 My glory *is* fresh within me,
And my bow is renewed in my hand.'

21 "*Men* listened to me and waited,
And kept silence for my counsel.
22 After my words they did not speak again,

And my speech settled on them *as dew*.

23 They waited for me *as* for the rain,
And they opened their mouth wide *as* for the spring rain.

24 *If* I mocked at them, they did not believe *it*,
And the light of my countenance they did not cast down.

25 I chose the way for them, and sat as chief;
So I dwelt as a king in the army,
As one *who* comforts mourners.

30 "BUT now they mock at me, *men* younger than I,
Whose fathers I disdained to put with the dogs of my flock.

2 Indeed, what *profit* is the strength of their hands to me?
Their vigor has perished.

3 *They are* gaunt from want and famine,
Fleeing late to the wilderness, desolate and waste,

4 Who pluck mallow by the bushes,
And broom tree roots *for* their food.

5 They were driven out from among *men*,
They shouted at them as *at* a thief.

6 *They had* to live in the clefts of the valleys,
In caves of the earth and the rocks.

7 Among the bushes they brayed,
Under the nettles they nestled.

8 *They were* sons of fools,
Yes, sons of vile men;
They were scourged from the land.

9 "And now I am their taunting song;
Yes, I am their byword.

10 They abhor me, they keep far from me;
They do not hesitate to spit in my face.

11 Because He has loosed my bowstring and afflicted me,
They have cast off restraint before me.

12 At *my* right *hand* the rabble arises;
They push away my feet,
And they raise against me their ways of destruction.

13 They break up my path,
They promote my calamity;
They have no helper.

14 They come as broad breakers;
Under the ruinous storm they roll along.

15 Terrors are turned upon me;
They pursue my honor as the wind,

And my prosperity has passed like a cloud.

16 "And now my soul is poured out because of my *plight*;
The days of affliction take hold of me.

17 My bones are pierced in me at night,
And my gnawing pains take no rest.

18 By great force my garment is disfigured;
It binds me about as the collar of my coat.

19 He has cast me into the mire,
And I have become like dust and ashes.

20 "I cry out to You, but You do not answer me;
I stand up, and You regard me.

There is a time in spiritual life when God does not seem to be a friend. (PLACE HELP)

---

21 *But* You have become cruel to me;
With the strength of Your hand You oppose me.

22 You lift me up to the wind and cause me to ride *on it*;
You spoil my success.

23 For I know *that* You will bring me *to* death,
And *to* the house appointed for all living.

24 "Surely He would not stretch out *His* hand against a heap of ruins,
If they cry out when He destroys *it*.

25 Have I not wept for him who was in trouble?
Has *not* my soul grieved for the poor?

26 But when I looked for good, evil came *to me*;
And when I waited for light, then came darkness.

27 My heart is in turmoil and cannot rest;
Days of affliction confront me.

28 I go about mourning, but not in the sun;
I stand up in the assembly *and* cry out for help.

29 I am a brother of jackals,
And a companion of ostriches.

30 My skin grows black and falls from me;
My bones burn with fever.

31 My harp is *turned* to mourning,
And my flute to the voice of those
who weep.

PSALM 97:7–12

7 LET all be put to shame who serve
carved images,
Who boast of idols.
Worship Him, all *you* gods.
8 Zion hears and is glad,
And the daughters of Judah rejoice
Because of Your judgments, O LORD.
9 For You, LORD, *are* most high above
all the earth;
You are exalted far above all gods.

10 You who love the LORD, hate evil!
He preserves the souls of His saints;
He delivers them out of the hand of
the wicked.
11 Light is sown for the righteous,
And gladness for the upright in heart.
12 Rejoice in the LORD, you righteous,
And give thanks at the remembrance
of His holy name.

PROVERBS 23:15, 16

15 MY son, if your heart is wise,
My heart will rejoice—indeed, I myself;
16 Yes, my inmost being will rejoice
When your lips speak right things.

1 CORINTHIANS 1:1–31

PAUL, called *to be* an apostle of Jesus Christ
through the will of God, and Sosthenes
our brother,

2 To the church of God which is at Corinth, to those who are sanctified in Christ
Jesus, called *to be* saints, with all who in
every place call on the name of Jesus Christ
our Lord, both theirs and ours:

3 Grace to you and peace from God our
Father and the Lord Jesus Christ.

4 I thank my God always concerning you
for the grace of God which was given to
you by Christ Jesus, 5 that you were enriched in everything by Him in all utterance
and all knowledge, 6 even as the testimony
of Christ was confirmed in you, 7 so that
you come short in no gift, eagerly waiting
for the revelation of our Lord Jesus Christ,
8 who will also confirm you to the end,
that you may be blameless in the day of our
Lord Jesus Christ. 9 God *is* faithful, by
whom you were called into the fellowship
of His Son, Jesus Christ our Lord.

10 Now I plead with you, brethren, by
the name of our Lord Jesus Christ, that
you all speak the same thing, and *that* there
be no divisions among you, but *that* you
be perfectly joined together in the same
mind and in the same judgment. 11 For it
has been declared to me concerning you,
my brethren, by those of Chloe's *household,*
that there are contentions among you.
12 Now I say this, that each of you says,
"I am of Paul," or "I am of Apollos," or
"I am of Cephas," or "I am of Christ."
13 Is Christ divided? Was Paul crucified for
you? Or were you baptized in the name
of Paul?

14 I thank God that I baptized none of
you except Crispus and Gaius, 15 lest anyone should say that I had baptized in my
own name. 16 Yes, I also baptized the household of Stephanas. Besides, I do not know
whether I baptized any other. 17 For Christ
did not send me to baptize, but to preach
the gospel, not with wisdom of words, lest
the cross of Christ should be made of no
effect.
18 For the message of the cross is foolishness to those who are perishing, but to us
who are being saved it is the power of God.
19 For it is written:

"I will destroy the wisdom of the wise,
And bring to nothing the
understanding of the prudent."

20 Where *is* the wise? Where *is* the scribe?
Where *is* the disputer of this age? Has not
God made foolish the wisdom of this world?
21 For since, in the wisdom of God, the
world through wisdom did not know God,
it pleased God through the foolishness of
the message preached to save those who
believe. 22 For Jews request a sign, and
Greeks seek after wisdom; 23 but we preach
Christ crucified, to the Jews a stumbling
block and to the Greeks foolishness,

---

*Jesus Christ is a source of deep
offense to the educated mind
of today.* (UTMOST)

---

24 but to those who are called, both Jews
and Greeks, Christ the power of God and
the wisdom of God. 25 Because the foolishness of God is wiser than men, and the
weakness of God is stronger than men.

26 For you see your calling, brethren, that not many wise according to the flesh, not many mighty, not many noble, *are called*. 27 But God has chosen the foolish things of the world to put to shame the wise, and God has chosen the weak things of the world to put to shame the things which are mighty; 28 and the base things of the world and the things which are despised God has chosen, and the things which are not, to bring to nothing the things that are, 29 that no flesh should glory in His presence. 30 But of Him you are in Christ Jesus, who became for us wisdom from God—and righteousness and sanctification and redemption— 31 that, as it is written, "He who glories, let him glory in the LORD."

◆◆◆◆

Reading 232—The Passion for Authority
Job 32:1–6

In Elihu the passion for authority is represented. The average man in Job's condition is apt to break away from all authority. A lesser man than Job would have become a philosopher and said that every man is a law unto himself, that is, his own inner consciousness is sufficient law. Job was not of this order; neither was Elihu. The passion for authority is a noble one, but Elihu missed out on the fact that authority to be worthy arises out of the nature of a superior moral integrity, and not simply from one who happens to be higher up in the scale than ourselves. Elihu comes with the idea that because God has said a thing, therefore it is authoritative. Job wants to know what kind of God it was who said it; is He a being whose character does not contradict the moral basis of life? Authority must be of a moral, not a superstitious character. Elihu's contention is, "Because God has said so," that is sufficient; or, "Because the creed says so," therefore it must be blindly accepted. To be without any authority is to be lawless, but to have only an internal authority is as bad as having a blind external authority; the two must meet together somehow.   (*BAFFLED*)

JOB 31:1—32:22

1 "I have made a covenant with my eyes; Why then should I look upon a young woman?
2 For what *is* the allotment of God from above, And the inheritance of the Almighty from on high?
3 *Is* it not destruction for the wicked, And disaster for the workers of iniquity?
4 Does He not see my ways, And count all my steps?

5 "If I have walked with falsehood, Or if my foot has hastened to deceit,
6 Let me be weighed on honest scales, That God may know my integrity.
7 If my step has turned from the way, Or my heart walked after my eyes, Or if any spot adheres to my hands,

God knows all the deepest possibilities there are in me.   (BIB. ETHICS)

8 *Then* let me sow, and another eat; Yes, let my harvest be rooted out.

9 "If my heart has been enticed by a woman, Or *if* I have lurked at my neighbor's door,
10 *Then* let my wife grind for another, And let others bow down over her.
11 For that *would be* wickedness; Yes, it *would be* iniquity *deserving of* judgment.
12 For that *would be* a fire *that* consumes to destruction, And would root out all my increase.

13 "If I have despised the cause of my male or female servant
When they complained against me,
14 What then shall I do when God rises up?
When He punishes, how shall I answer Him?
15 Did not He who made me in the womb make them?
Did not the same One fashion us in the womb?

16 "If I have kept the poor from *their* desire,
Or caused the eyes of the widow to fail,
17 Or eaten my morsel by myself,
So that the fatherless could not eat of it
18 (But from my youth I reared him as a father,
And from my mother's womb I guided *the widow*);
19 If I have seen anyone perish for lack of clothing,
Or any poor *man* without covering;
20 If his heart has not blessed me,
And *if* he was *not* warmed with the fleece of my sheep;
21 If I have raised my hand against the fatherless,
When I saw I had help in the gate;
22 *Then* let my arm fall from my shoulder,
Let my arm be torn from the socket.
23 For destruction *from* God *is* a terror to me,
And because of His magnificence I cannot endure.

24 "If I have made gold my hope,
Or said to fine gold, 'You are my confidence';
25 If I have rejoiced because my wealth *was* great,
And because my hand had gained much;
26 If I have observed the sun when it shines,
Or the moon moving *in* brightness,
27 So that my heart has been secretly enticed,
And my mouth has kissed my hand;
28 This also *would be* an iniquity *deserving of* judgment,
For I would have denied God *who is* above.

29 "If I have rejoiced at the destruction of him who hated me,
Or lifted myself up when evil found him

30 (Indeed I have not allowed my mouth to sin
By asking for a curse on his soul);
31 If the men of my tent have not said,
'Who is there that has not been satisfied with his meat?'
32 (*But* no sojourner had to lodge in the street,
For I have opened my doors to the traveler);
33 If I have covered my transgressions as Adam,
By hiding my iniquity in my bosom,
34 Because I feared the great multitude,
And dreaded the contempt of families,
So that I kept silence
And did not go out of the door—
35 Oh, that I had one to hear me!
Here is my mark.
Oh, that the Almighty would answer me,
That my Prosecutor had written a book!
36 Surely I would carry it on my shoulder,
And bind it on me *like* a crown;
37 I would declare to Him the number of my steps;
Like a prince I would approach Him.

38 "If my land cries out against me,
And its furrows weep together;
39 If I have eaten its fruit without money,
Or caused its owners to lose their lives;
40 *Then* let thistles grow instead of wheat,
And weeds instead of barley."

The words of Job are ended.

32 SO these three men ceased answering Job, because he *was* righteous in his own eyes. 2 Then the wrath of Elihu, the son of Barachel the Buzite, of the family of Ram, was aroused against Job; his wrath was aroused because he justified himself rather than God. 3 Also against his three friends his wrath was aroused, because they had found no answer, and *yet* had condemned Job.

4 Now because they *were* years older than he, Elihu had waited to speak to Job. 5 When Elihu saw that *there was* no answer in the mouth of these three men, his wrath was aroused.

6 So Elihu, the son of Barachel the Buzite, answered and said:

"I *am* young in years, and you *are* very old;
Therefore I was afraid,
And dared not declare my opinion to you.

7 I said, 'Age should speak,
And multitude of years should teach wisdom.'

8 But *there is* a spirit in man,
And the breath of the Almighty gives him understanding.

9 Great men are not *always* wise,
Nor do the aged *always* understand justice.

10 "Therefore I say, 'Listen to me,
I also will declare my opinion.'

11 Indeed I waited for your words,
I listened to your reasonings, while you searched out what to say.

12 I paid close attention to you;
And surely not one of you convinced Job,
Or answered his words—

13 Lest you say,
'We have found wisdom';
God will vanquish him, not man.

14 Now he has not directed *his* words against me;
So I will not answer him with your words.

15 "They are dismayed and answer no more;
Words escape them.

16 And I have waited, because they did not speak,
Because they stood still *and* answered no more.

17 I also will answer my part,
I too will declare my opinion.

18 For I am full of words;
The spirit within me compels me.

19 Indeed my belly *is* like wine *that* has no vent;
It is ready to burst like new wineskins.

20 I will speak, that I may find relief;
I must open my lips and answer.

21 Let me not, I pray, show partiality to anyone;
Nor let me flatter any man.

22 For I do not know how to flatter,
Else my Maker would soon take me away.

PSALM 98:1–3

1 OH, sing to the Lord a new song!
For He has done marvelous things;

His right hand and His holy arm have gained Him the victory.

2 The Lord has made known His salvation;
His righteousness He has revealed in the sight of the nations.

3 He has remembered His mercy and His faithfulness to the house of Israel;
All the ends of the earth have seen the salvation of our God.

PROVERBS 23:17, 18

17 DO not let your heart envy sinners,
But *be zealous* for the fear of the Lord all the day;

18 For surely there is a hereafter,
And your hope will not be cut off.

1 CORINTHIANS 2:1–16

AND I, brethren, when I came to you, did not come with excellence of speech or of wisdom declaring to you the testimony of God. 2 For I determined not to know anything among you except Jesus Christ and Him crucified. 3 I was with you in weakness, in fear, and in much trembling. 4 And my speech and my preaching *were* not with persuasive words of human wisdom, but in demonstration of the Spirit and of power, 5 that your faith should not be in the wisdom of men but in the power of God.

6 However, we speak wisdom among those who are mature, yet not the wisdom of this age, nor of the rulers of this age, who are coming to nothing. 7 But we speak the wisdom of God in a mystery, the hidden *wisdom* which God ordained before the ages for our glory, 8 which none of the rulers

---

*M*ystery *means being guided by obedience to Someone who knows more than I do.*   (Place Help)

---

of this age knew; for had they known, they would not have crucified the Lord of glory. 9 But as it is written:

"Eye has not seen, nor ear heard,
Nor have entered into the heart of man
The things which God has prepared for those who love Him."

10 But God has revealed *them* to us through His Spirit. For the Spirit searches all things,

yes, the deep things of God. 11 For what man knows the things of a man except the spirit of the man which is in him? Even so no one knows the things of God except the Spirit of God. 12 Now we have received, not the spirit of the world, but the Spirit who is from God, that we might know the things that have been freely given to us by God.

13 These things we also speak, not in words which man's wisdom teaches but which the Holy Spirit teaches, comparing spiritual things with spiritual. 14 But the natural man does not receive the things of the Spirit of God, for they are foolishness to him; nor can he know *them*, because they are spiritually discerned. 15 But he who is spiritual judges all things, yet he himself is *rightly* judged by no one. 16 For "who has known the mind of the LORD that he may instruct Him?" But we have the mind of Christ.

◆◆◆◆

Reading 233—The Worthiness of God
Job 33:12, 13

It is dangerous to be conscious of submission to a spiritual power. The difference between fatalism and faith lies just here. Fatalism means, "My number's up; I have to bow to the power whether I like it or not; I do not know the character of the power, but it is greater than I am, and I must submit." The submission of faith is that I do know the character of the Power, and this was the line Job took: "Though He slay me, yet I will trust the fact that His character is worthy." This is the attitude of faith all through—I submit to One whose character I know but whose ways are obscured in mystery just now.

We do know the character of God, if we are Christians, because we have it revealed to us in Jesus Christ: "He who has seen Me has seen the Father." Anything that contradicts the manifestations given in and through the Lord Jesus Christ cannot be true of God. Therefore we know that the character of God is noble and true and right, and any authority from God is based, not on autocracy or mere blind power, but on worthiness which everything in me recognizes as worthy, therefore I submit.   (*BAFFLED*)

JOB 33:1—34:37

1 "BUT please, Job, hear my speech,
   And listen to all my words.
2 Now, I open my mouth;
   My tongue speaks in my mouth.
3 My words *come* from my upright heart;
   My lips utter pure knowledge.
4 The Spirit of God has made me,
   And the breath of the Almighty gives me life.
5 If you can answer me,
   Set *your words* in order before me;
   Take your stand.
6 Truly I *am* as your spokesman before God;
   I also have been formed out of clay.

God made man a mixture of dust and deity.   (SHADE)

7 Surely no fear of me will terrify you,
   Nor will my hand be heavy on you.
8 "Surely you have spoken in my hearing,
   And I have heard the sound of *your* words, *saying,*
9 'I *am* pure, without transgression;
   I *am* innocent, and *there is* no iniquity in me.
10 Yet He finds occasions against me,
   He counts me as His enemy;

11 He puts my feet in the stocks,
He watches all my paths.'

12 "Look, *in* this you are not righteous.
I will answer you,
For God is greater than man.

13 Why do you contend with Him?
For He does not give an accounting
of any of His words.

14 For God may speak in one way, or
in another,
Yet man does not perceive it.

15 In a dream, in a vision of the night,
When deep sleep falls upon men,
While slumbering on their beds,

16 Then He opens the ears of men,
And seals their instruction.

17 In order to turn man *from his* deed,
And conceal pride from man,

18 He keeps back his soul from the Pit,
And his life from perishing by the
sword.

19 "*Man* is also chastened with pain on
his bed,
And with strong *pain* in many of his
bones,

20 So that his life abhors bread,
And his soul succulent food.

21 His flesh wastes away from sight,
And his bones stick out *which once*
were not seen.

22 Yes, his soul draws near the Pit,
And his life to the executioners.

23 "If there is a messenger for him,
A mediator, one among a thousand,
To show man His uprightness,

24 Then He is gracious to him, and
says,
'Deliver him from going down to the
Pit;
I have found a ransom';

25 His flesh shall be young like a child's,
He shall return to the days of his
youth.

26 He shall pray to God, and He will
delight in him,
He shall see His face with joy,
For He restores to man His
righteousness.

27 Then he looks at men and says,
'I have sinned, and perverted *what was*
right,
And it did not profit me.'

28 He will redeem his soul from going
down to the Pit,
And his life shall see the light.

29 "Behold, God works all these *things,*
Twice, *in fact,* three *times* with a man,

30 To bring back his soul from the Pit,
That he may be enlightened with the
light of life.

31 "Give ear, Job, listen to me;
Hold your peace, and I will speak.

32 If you have anything to say,
answer me;
Speak, for I desire to justify you.

33 If not, listen to me;
Hold your peace, and I will teach
you wisdom."

34 ELIHU further answered and said:

2 "Hear my words, you wise *men;*
Give ear to me, you who have
knowledge.

3 For the ear tests words
As the palate tastes food.

4 Let us choose justice for ourselves;
Let us know among ourselves what
is good.

5 "For Job has said, 'I am righteous,
But God has taken away my justice;

6 Should I lie concerning my right?
My wound *is* incurable, *though I am*
without transgression.'

7 What man *is* like Job,
Who drinks scorn like water,

8 Who goes in company with the
workers of iniquity,
And walks with wicked men?

9 For he has said, 'It profits a man
nothing
That he should delight in God.'

10 "Therefore listen to me, you men of
understanding:
Far be it from God *to do* wickedness,
And *from* the Almighty to *commit*
iniquity.

11 For He repays man *according to* his
work,
And makes man to find a reward
according to *his* way.

12 Surely God will never do wickedly,
Nor will the Almighty pervert justice.

13 Who gave Him charge over the earth?
Or who appointed *Him over* the
whole world?

14 If He should set His heart on it,
If He should gather to Himself His
Spirit and His breath,

15 All flesh would perish together,
And man would return to dust.

16 "If *you have* understanding, hear this;
Listen to the sound of my words:

17 Should one who hates justice
govern?

Will you condemn *Him who is* most just?

18 *Is it fitting* to say to a king, '*You are* worthless,'
And to nobles, '*You are* wicked'?

19 Yet He is not partial to princes,
Nor does He regard the rich more than the poor;
For they *are* all the work of His hands.

20 In a moment they die, in the middle of the night;
The people are shaken and pass away;
The mighty are taken away without a hand.

21 "For His eyes *are* on the ways of man,
And He sees all his steps.

22 There is no darkness nor shadow of death
Where the workers of iniquity may hide themselves.

23 For He need not further consider a man,
That he should go before God in judgment.

24 He breaks in pieces mighty men without inquiry,
And sets others in their place.

25 Therefore He knows their works;
He overthrows *them* in the night,
And they are crushed.

26 He strikes them as wicked *men*
In the open sight of others,

27 Because they turned back from Him,
And would not consider any of His ways,

28 So that they caused the cry of the poor to come to Him;
For He hears the cry of the afflicted.

29 When He gives quietness, who then can make trouble?
And when He hides *His* face, who then can see Him,
Whether *it is* against a nation or a man alone?—

30 That the hypocrite should not reign,
Lest the people be ensnared.

31 "For has *anyone* said to God,
'I have borne *chastening;*
I will offend no more;

32 Teach me *what* I do not see;
If I have done iniquity, I will do no more'?

33 Should He repay *it* according to your *terms,*
Just because you disavow it?
You must choose, and not I;
Therefore speak what you know.

34 "Men of understanding say to me,
Wise men who listen to me:

35 'Job speaks without knowledge,
His words *are* without wisdom.'

36 Oh, that Job were tried to the utmost,
Because *his* answers *are like* those of wicked men!

37 For he adds rebellion to his sin;
He claps *his hands* among us,
And multiplies his words against God."

PSALM 98:4–9

4 SHOUT joyfully to the LORD, all the earth;
Break forth in song, rejoice, and sing praises.

5 Sing to the LORD with the harp,
With the harp and the sound of a psalm,

6 With trumpets and the sound of a horn;
Shout joyfully before the LORD, the King.

7 Let the sea roar, and all its fullness,
The world and those who dwell in it;

8 Let the rivers clap *their* hands;
Let the hills be joyful together before the LORD,

9 For He is coming to judge the earth.
With righteousness He shall judge the world,
And the peoples with equity.

PROVERBS 23:19–21

19 HEAR, my son, and be wise;
And guide your heart in the way.

20 Do not mix with winebibbers,
Or with gluttonous eaters of meat;

21 For the drunkard and the glutton will come to poverty,
And drowsiness will clothe *a man* with rags.

We get much more concerned about not offending other people than about offending our Lord. (LOVE OF GOD)

---

1 CORINTHIANS 3:1–23

AND I, brethren, could not speak to you as to spiritual *people* but as to carnal, as to babes in Christ. 2 I fed you with milk and not with solid food; for until now you were not able *to receive it,* and even now you are still not able; 3 for you are still carnal. For where *there are* envy, strife, and divisions among you, are you not carnal and behaving like *mere* men? 4 For when one says, "I am of Paul," and another, "I *am* of Apollos," are you not carnal?

5 Who then is Paul, and who *is* Apollos, but ministers through whom you believed, as the Lord gave to each one? 6 I planted, Apollos watered, but God gave the increase. 7 So then neither he who plants is anything, nor he who waters, but God who gives the increase. 8 Now he who plants and he who waters are one, and each one will receive his own reward according to his own labor.

9 For we are God's fellow workers; you are God's field, *you are* God's building. 10 According to the grace of God which was given to me, as a wise master builder I have laid the foundation, and another builds on it. But let each one take heed how he builds on it. 11 For no other foundation can anyone lay than that which is laid, which is Jesus Christ. 12 Now if anyone builds on this foundation *with* gold, silver, precious stones, wood, hay, straw, 13 each one's work will become clear; for the Day will declare it, because it will be revealed by fire; and the fire will test each one's work, of what sort it is. 14 If anyone's work which he has built on *it* endures, he will receive a reward. 15 If anyone's work is burned, he will suffer loss; but he himself will be saved, yet so as through fire.

16 Do you not know that you are the temple of God and *that* the Spirit of God dwells in you? 17 If anyone defiles the tem-

---

From God's standpoint man's chief glory is his body. (BIB. PSYCH.)

---

ple of God, God will destroy him. For the temple of God is holy, which *temple* you are.

18 Let no one deceive himself. If anyone among you seems to be wise in this age, let him become a fool that he may become wise. 19 For the wisdom of this world is foolishness with God. For it is written, "He catches the wise in their *own* craftiness"; 20 and again, "The LORD knows the thoughts of the wise, that they are futile." 21 Therefore let no one boast in men. For all things are yours: 22 whether Paul or Apollos or Cephas, or the world or life or death, or things present or things to come— all are yours. 23 And you *are* Christ's, and Christ *is* God's.

◆◆◆◆

*Reading 234—*The Essence of Christianity
Job 36:22

There is always a tendency to produce an absolute authority; we accept the authority of the church, or of the Bible, or of a creed, and often refuse to do anymore thinking on the matter; and in so doing we ignore the essential nature of Christianity which is based on a personal relationship to Jesus Christ, and works on the basis of our responsibility. On the ground of the Redemption I am saved and God puts His Holy Spirit into me; then He expects me to react on the basis of that relationship. I can evade it by dumping my responsibility onto a church, or a book or a creed, forgetting what Jesus said: "You search the Scriptures, for in them you think you have eternal life; and these are they which testify of Me. But you are not willing to come to Me that you may have life." The only way to understand the Scriptures is not to accept them blindly, but to read them in the light of a personal relationship to Jesus Christ. . . . A scientist can explain the universe in which common-sense people live, but the scientific explanation is not first; life is first. The same with theology; theology is the systematizing of the intellectual expression of life from God; it is a mighty thing, but it is second, not first. (*BAFFLED*)

JOB 35:1—36:33

MOREOVER Elihu answered and said:

2 "Do you think this is right?
Do you say,
'My righteousness is more than
God's'?

3 For you say,
'What advantage will it be to You?
What profit shall I have, more than
if I had sinned?'

4 "I will answer you,
And your companions with you.

5 Look to the heavens and see;
And behold the clouds—
They are higher than you.

6 If you sin, what do you accomplish
against Him?
Or, *if* your transgressions are
multiplied, what do you do to
Him?

7 If you are righteous, what do you
give Him?
Or what does He receive from your
hand?

8 Your wickedness affects a man such
as you,
And your righteousness a son of man.

9 "Because of the multitude of
oppressions they cry out;
They cry out for help because of the
arm of the mighty.

10 But no one says, 'Where *is* God my
Maker,
Who gives songs in the night,

11 Who teaches us more than the beasts
of the earth,
And makes us wiser than the birds
of heaven?'

12 There they cry out, but He does not
answer,
Because of the pride of evil men.

13 Surely God will not listen to empty
talk,
Nor will the Almighty regard it.

14 Although you say you do not see
Him,
Yet justice *is* before Him, and you
must wait for Him.

15 And now, because He has not
punished in His anger,
Nor taken much notice of folly,

16 Therefore Job opens his mouth in
vain;
He multiplies words without
knowledge."

36 ELIHU also proceeded and said:

2 "Bear with me a little, and I will show
you
That *there are* yet words to speak on
God's behalf.

3 I will fetch my knowledge from afar;
I will ascribe righteousness to my
Maker.

4 For truly my words *are* not false;
One who is perfect in knowledge *is*
with you.

5 "Behold, God *is* mighty, but despises
no one;
He *is* mighty in strength of
understanding.

6 He does not preserve the life of the
wicked,
But gives justice to the oppressed.

7 He does not withdraw His eyes from
the righteous;
But *they are* on the throne with kings,
For He has seated them forever,
And they are exalted.

8 And if *they are* bound in fetters,
Held in the cords of affliction,

9 Then He tells them their work and
their transgressions—
That they have acted defiantly.

10 He also opens their ear to instruction,
And commands that they turn from
iniquity.

11 If they obey and serve *Him,*
They shall spend their days in
prosperity,
And their years in pleasures.

12 But if they do not obey,
They shall perish by the sword,
And they shall die without
knowledge.

13 "But the hypocrites in heart store up
wrath;
They do not cry for help when He
binds them.

14 They die in youth,
And their life *ends* among the
perverted persons.

15 He delivers the poor in their
affliction,
And opens their ears in oppression.

16 "Indeed He would have brought you
out of dire distress,
Into a broad place where *there is* no
restraint;
And what is set on your table *would
be* full of richness.

17 But you are filled with the judgment
due the wicked;

Judgment and justice take hold *of you.*

18 Because *there is* wrath, *beware* lest He take you away with *one* blow;
For a large ransom would not help you avoid *it.*

19 Will your riches,
Or all the mighty forces,
Keep you from distress?

20 Do not desire the night,
When people are cut off in their place.

21 Take heed, do not turn to iniquity,
For you have chosen this rather than affliction.

22 "Behold, God is exalted by His power;
Who teaches like Him?

23 Who has assigned Him His way,
Or who has said, 'You have done wrong'?

24 "Remember to magnify His work,
Of which men have sung.

25 Everyone has seen it;
Man looks on *it* from afar.

26 "Behold, God *is* great, and we do not know *Him;*
Nor can the number of His years *be* discovered.

27 For He draws up drops of water,
Which distill as rain from the mist,

28 Which the clouds drop down
And pour abundantly on man.

29 Indeed, can *anyone* understand the spreading of clouds,
The thunder from His canopy?

30 Look, He scatters His light upon it,
And covers the depths of the sea.

31 For by these He judges the peoples;
He gives food in abundance.

32 He covers *His* hands with lightning,
And commands it to strike.

33 His thunder declares it,
The cattle also, concerning the rising *storm.*

PSALM 99:1–9

1 THE LORD reigns;
Let the peoples tremble!
He dwells *between* the cherubim;
Let the earth be moved!

2 The LORD *is* great in Zion,
And He *is* high above all the peoples.

3 Let them praise Your great and awesome name—
He *is* holy.

4 The King's strength also loves justice;
You have established equity;

You have executed justice and righteousness in Jacob.

5 Exalt the LORD our God,
And worship at His footstool—
He *is* holy.

6 Moses and Aaron were among His priests,
And Samuel was among those who called upon His name;
They called upon the LORD, and He answered them.

7 He spoke to them in the cloudy pillar;
They kept His testimonies and the ordinance He gave them.

8 You answered them, O LORD our God;
You were to them God-Who-Forgives,
Though You took vengeance on their deeds.

9 Exalt the LORD our God,
And worship at His holy hill;
For the LORD our God *is* holy.

PROVERBS 23:22–25

22 LISTEN to your father who begot you,
And do not despise your mother when she is old.

23 Buy the truth, and do not sell *it,*
Also wisdom and instruction and understanding.

24 The father of the righteous will greatly rejoice,
And he who begets a wise *child* will delight in him.

25 Let your father and your mother be glad,
And let her who bore you rejoice.

1 CORINTHIANS 4:1–21

LET a man so consider us, as servants of Christ and stewards of the mysteries of God. 2 Moreover it is required in stewards that one be found faithful. 3 But with me it is a very small thing that I should be judged by you or by a human court. In fact, I do not even judge myself. 4 For I know of nothing against myself, yet I am not justified by this; but He who judges me is the Lord. 5 Therefore judge nothing before the time, until the Lord comes, who will both bring to light the hidden things of darkness and reveal the counsels of the hearts. Then each one's praise will come from God.

6 Now these things, brethren, I have

figuratively transferred to myself and Apollos for your sakes, that you may learn in us not to think beyond what is written, that none of you may be puffed up on behalf of one against the other. 7 For who makes you differ *from another?* And what do you have that you did not receive? Now if you did indeed receive *it,* why do you boast as if you had not received *it?*

8 You are already full! You are already rich! You have reigned as kings without us—and indeed I could wish you did reign, that we also might reign with you! 9 For I think that God has displayed us, the apostles, last, as men condemned to death; for we have been made a spectacle to the world, both to angels and to men. 10 We *are* fools for Christ's sake, but you *are* wise in Christ! We *are* weak, but you *are* strong! You *are* distinguished, but we *are* dishonored! 11 To the present hour we both hunger and thirst, and we are poorly clothed, and beaten, and homeless. 12 And we labor, working with our own hands. Being reviled, we bless; being persecuted, we endure; 13 being defamed, we entreat. We have been made as the filth of the world, the offscouring of all things until now.

If it was God's will to bruise His own Son, why should it not be His will to bruise you? (NOT KNOWING)

14 I do not write these things to shame you, but as my beloved children I warn *you.* 15 For though you might have ten thousand instructors in Christ, yet *you do* not *have* many fathers; for in Christ Jesus I have begotten you through the gospel. 16 Therefore I urge you, imitate me. 17 For this reason I have sent Timothy to you, who is my beloved and faithful son in the Lord, who will remind you of my ways in Christ, as I teach everywhere in every church.

18 Now some are puffed up, as though I were not coming to you. 19 But I will come to you shortly, if the Lord wills, and I will know, not the word of those who are puffed up, but the power. 20 For the kingdom of God *is* not in word but in power. 21 What do you want? Shall I come to you with a rod, or in love and a spirit of gentleness?

Reading 235—The Condemnation of Sanity
Job 37:23, 24

Elihu condemns Job sorrowfully, but absolutely; he declares that not only has Job made shipwreck of his faith, but he has become defiant in silencing the friends.

Job will not accept anything blindly; he says, "I must see that it does not contradict what I know." The apostle Paul speaks of "the foolishness of God" as pitted against "the wisdom of men," when men said of Jesus Christ, "That cannot be God." When the Judaic ritualists saw Jesus Christ, they said, "You are a blasphemer; You do not express God at all." Anna and Simeon were the only two of the descendants of Abraham who recognized who Jesus was, hence the condemnation of the crowd. If two who had lived a life of communion with God could detect Jehovah [Yahweh] as the Babe of Bethlehem within the symbolism, the others who did not recognize Him are to be condemned. They did not see Him because they had become blinded on the line of absolute authority, the line of symbolism or creed, and when that which was symbolized appeared, they could not see Him. (*BAFFLED*)

JOB 37:1—38:41

1 "AT this also my heart trembles,
And leaps from its place.

2 Hear attentively the thunder of His voice,
And the rumbling *that* comes from His mouth.

3 He sends it forth under the whole heaven,
His lightning to the ends of the earth.

4 After it a voice roars;
He thunders with His majestic voice,
And He does not restrain them when His voice is heard.

5 God thunders marvelously with His voice;
He does great things which we cannot comprehend.

6 For He says to the snow, 'Fall *on* the earth';
Likewise to the gentle rain and the heavy rain of His strength.

7 He seals the hand of every man,
That all men may know His work.

8 The beasts go into dens,
And remain in their lairs.

9 From the chamber *of the south* comes the whirlwind,
And cold from the scattering winds *of the north*.

10 By the breath of God ice is given,
And the broad waters are frozen.

11 Also with moisture He saturates the thick clouds;
He scatters His bright clouds.

12 And they swirl about, being turned by His guidance,
That they may do whatever He commands them
On the face of the whole earth.

13 He causes it to come,
Whether for correction,
Or for His land,
Or for mercy.

14 "Listen to this, O Job;
Stand still and consider the wondrous works of God.

15 Do you know when God dispatches them,
And causes the light of His cloud to shine?

16 Do you know how the clouds are balanced,
Those wondrous works of Him who is perfect in knowledge?

17 Why *are* your garments hot,
When He quiets the earth by the south *wind*?

18 With Him, have you spread out the skies,
Strong as a cast metal mirror?

19 "Teach us what we should say to Him,
For we can prepare nothing because of the darkness.

20 Should He be told that I *wish to* speak?
If a man were to speak, surely he would be swallowed up.

21 Even now *men* cannot look at the light *when it is* bright in the skies,
When the wind has passed and cleared them.

22 He comes from the north *as* golden *splendor;*
With God *is* awesome majesty.

23 *As for* the Almighty, we cannot find Him;
He is excellent in power,
In judgment and abundant justice;
He does not oppress.

24 Therefore men fear Him;
He shows no partiality to any *who are* wise of heart."

38 THEN the LORD answered Job out of the whirlwind, and said:

2 "Who *is* this who darkens counsel
By words without knowledge?

3 Now prepare yourself like a man;
I will question you, and you shall answer Me.

4 "Where were you when I laid the foundations of the earth?
Tell *Me*, if you have understanding.

5 Who determined its measurements?
Surely you know!
Or who stretched the line upon it?

6 To what were its foundations fastened?
Or who laid its cornerstone,

7 When the morning stars sang together,
And all the sons of God shouted for joy?

Who were these "sons of God"? . . . They were unquestionably angels and archangels. (BIB. PSYCH.)

8 "Or *who* shut in the sea with doors,
When it burst forth *and* issued from the womb;

9 When I made the clouds its garment,

And thick darkness its swaddling
band;

10 When I fixed My limit for it,
And set bars and doors;

11 When I said,
'This far you may come, but no
farther,
And here your proud waves must
stop!'

12 "Have you commanded the morning
since your days *began,*
And caused the dawn to know its
place,

13 That it might take hold of the ends
of the earth,
And the wicked be shaken out of it?

14 It takes on form like clay *under* a
seal,
And stands out like a garment.

15 From the wicked their light is
withheld,
And the upraised arm is broken.

16 "Have you entered the springs of the
sea?
Or have you walked in search of the
depths?

17 Have the gates of death been revealed
to you?
Or have you seen the doors of the
shadow of death?

18 Have you comprehended the breadth
of the earth?
Tell *Me,* if you know all this.

19 "Where *is* the way *to* the dwelling of
light?
And darkness, where *is* its place,

20 That you may take it to its territory,
That you may know the paths *to* its
home?

21 Do you know *it,* because you were
born then,
Or *because* the number of your days
is great?

22 "Have you entered the treasury of
snow,
Or have you seen the treasury of hail,

23 Which I have reserved for the time
of trouble,
For the day of battle and war?

24 By what way is light diffused,
Or the east wind scattered over the
earth?

25 "Who has divided a channel for the
overflowing *water,*
Or a path for the thunderbolt,

26 To cause it to rain on a land *where
there is* no one,
A wilderness in which *there is* no man;

27 To satisfy the desolate waste,
And cause to spring forth the growth
of tender grass?

28 Has the rain a father?
Or who has begotten the drops of
dew?

29 From whose womb comes the ice?
And the frost of heaven, who gives
it birth?

30 The waters harden like stone,
And the surface of the deep is frozen.

31 "Can you bind the cluster of the
Pleiades,
Or loose the belt of Orion?

32 Can you bring out Mazzaroth in its
season?
Or can you guide the Great Bear with
its cubs?

33 Do you know the ordinances of the
heavens?
Can you set their dominion over the
earth?

34 "Can you lift up your voice to the
clouds,
That an abundance of water may
cover you?

35 Can you send out lightnings, that
they may go,
And say to you, 'Here we *are!*'?

36 Who has put wisdom in the mind?
Or who has given understanding to
the heart?

---

*B*eware of blaspheming the
Creator by calling the natural
sinful. (NOT KNOWING)

---

37 Who can number the clouds by
wisdom?
Or who can pour out the bottles of
heaven,

38 When the dust hardens in clumps,
And the clods cling together?

39 "Can you hunt the prey for the lion,
Or satisfy the appetite of the young
lions,

40 When they crouch in *their* dens,
Or lurk in their lairs to lie in wait?

41 Who provides food for the raven,
When its young ones cry to God,
And wander about for lack of food?

PSALM 100:1–5

1   MAKE a joyful shout to the Lord, all
     you lands!
2   Serve the Lord with gladness;
     Come before His presence with singing.
3   Know that the Lord, He *is* God;
     It is He *who* has made us, and not we
     ourselves;
     We are His people and the sheep of
     His pasture.

4   Enter into His gates with thanksgiving,
     And into His courts with praise.
     Be thankful to Him, *and* bless His
     name.
5   For the Lord *is* good;
     His mercy *is* everlasting,
     And His truth *endures* to all generations.

PROVERBS 23:26–28

26   MY son, give me your heart,
     And let your eyes observe my ways.
27   For a harlot *is* a deep pit,
     And a seductress *is* a narrow well.
28   She also lies in wait as *for* a victim,
     And increases the unfaithful among
     men.

1 CORINTHIANS 5:1–13

IT is actually reported *that there is* sexual
immorality among you, and such sexual immorality as is not even named among the
Gentiles—that a man has his father's wife!
2 And you are puffed up, and have not rather
mourned, that he who has done this deed
might be taken away from among you.
3 For I indeed, as absent in body but present
in spirit, have already judged (as though I
were present) him who has so done this
deed. 4 In the name of our Lord Jesus
Christ, when you are gathered together,
along with my spirit, with the power of
our Lord Jesus Christ, 5 deliver such a one
to Satan for the destruction of the flesh,
that his spirit may be saved in the day of
the Lord Jesus.

6 Your glorying *is* not good. Do you not
know that a little leaven leavens the whole
lump? 7 Therefore purge out the old leaven,
that you may be a new lump, since you
truly are unleavened. For indeed Christ, our
Passover, was sacrificed for us. 8 Therefore
let us keep the feast, not with old leaven,
nor with the leaven of malice and wickedness, but with the unleavened *bread* of sincerity and truth.

9 I wrote to you in my epistle not to
keep company with sexually immoral people. 10 Yet *I* certainly *did* not *mean* with
the sexually immoral people of this world,
or with the covetous, or extortioners, or
idolaters, since then you would need to go
out of the world. 11 But now I have written
to you not to keep company with anyone
named a brother, who is sexually immoral,
or covetous, or an idolater, or a reviler,
or a drunkard, or an extortioner—not even
to eat with such a person.

12 For what *have* I *to do* with judging
those also who are outside? Do you not
judge those who are inside? 13 But those
who are outside God judges. Therefore "put
away from yourselves the evil person."

◆◆◆◆

Reading 236—The Wild Universe
Job 39:1–30

In these chapters the whole of the universe is symbolized, and whatever
the universe is, it is not tame. A certain type of modern science would
have us believe it is, that we can harness the sea and air and earth. Quite true,
you can, if you only read scientific manuals and deal with successful experiments;
but before long you discover elements which knock all your calculations on
the head and prove that the universe is wild and unmanageable. And yet in
the beginning God intended man to control it; the reason he cannot is because
he twisted God's order; instead of recognizing God's dominion over himself,
man became his own god, and by so doing lost control of everything else (see
Gen. 3).

When Jesus Christ came He was easily Master of the life in the air and earth and sea, and in Him we see the order God originally intended for man. If you want to know what the human race is to be like on the basis of the redemption, you will find it mirrored in Jesus Christ—a perfect oneness between God and man, no gap; in the meantime there is a gap, and the universe is wild, not tame. Every type of superstition pretends it can rule the universe; the scientific quack proclaims he can control the weather, that he has occult powers and can take the untamable universe and tame it. God says it cannot be done.   (BAFFLED)

JOB 39:1—40:24

1 "DO you know the time when the wild mountain goats bear young? *Or* can you mark when the deer gives birth?

2 Can you number the months *that* they fulfill? Or do you know the time when they bear young?

3 They bow down, They bring forth their young, They deliver their offspring.

4 Their young ones are healthy, They grow strong with grain; They depart and do not return to them.

5 "Who set the wild donkey free? Who loosed the bonds of the onager,

6 Whose home I have made the wilderness, And the barren land his dwelling?

7 He scorns the tumult of the city; He does not heed the shouts of the driver.

8 The range of the mountains *is* his pasture, And he searches after every green thing.

9 "Will the wild ox be willing to serve you? Will he bed by your manger?

10 Can you bind the wild ox in the furrow with ropes? Or will he plow the valleys behind you?

11 Will you trust him because his strength *is* great? Or will you leave your labor to him?

12 Will you trust him to bring home your grain, And gather it to your threshing floor?

13 "The wings of the ostrich wave proudly,

But are her wings and pinions *like the* kindly stork's?

14 For she leaves her eggs on the ground, And warms them in the dust;

15 She forgets that a foot may crush them, Or that a wild beast may break them.

16 She treats her young harshly, as though *they were* not hers; Her labor is in vain, without concern,

17 Because God deprived her of wisdom, And did not endow her with understanding.

18 When she lifts herself on high, She scorns the horse and its rider.

19 "Have you given the horse strength? Have you clothed his neck with thunder?

20 Can you frighten him like a locust? His majestic snorting strikes terror.

21 He paws in the valley, and rejoices in *his* strength; He gallops into the clash of arms.

22 He mocks at fear, and is not frightened; Nor does he turn back from the sword.

23 The quiver rattles against him, The glittering spear and javelin.

24 He devours the distance with fierceness and rage; Nor does he come to a halt because the trumpet *has* sounded.

25 At *the blast of* the trumpet he says, 'Aha!' He smells the battle from afar, The thunder of captains and shouting.

26 "Does the hawk fly by your wisdom, *And* spread its wings toward the south?

27 Does the eagle mount up at your command,

And make its nest on high?

28 On the rock it dwells and resides,
    On the crag of the rock and the
       stronghold.
29 From there it spies out the prey;
    Its eyes observe from afar.
30 Its young ones suck up blood;
    And where the slain *are*, there it *is*."

40 MOREOVER the LORD answered Job, and said:

2 "Shall the one who contends with the
       Almighty correct *Him*?
   He who rebukes God, let him
       answer it."

3 Then Job answered the LORD and said:

4 "Behold, I am vile;
   What shall I answer You?
   I lay my hand over my mouth.
5 Once I have spoken, but I will not
       answer;
   Yes, twice, but I will proceed no
       further."

6 Then the LORD answered Job out of the whirlwind, and said:

7 "Now prepare yourself like a man;
   I will question you, and you shall
       answer Me:

8 "Would you indeed annul My
       judgment?
   Would you condemn Me that you
       may be justified?
9 Have you an arm like God?
   Or can you thunder with a voice like
       His?
10 Then adorn yourself *with* majesty and
       splendor,
   And array yourself with glory and
       beauty.
11 Disperse the rage of your wrath;
   Look on everyone *who is* proud, and
       humble him.
12 Look on everyone *who is* proud, *and*
       bring him low;
   Tread down the wicked in their place.
13 Hide them in the dust together,
   Bind their faces in hidden *darkness*.
14 Then I will also confess to you
   That your own right hand can save
       you.

15 "Look now at the behemoth, which
       I made *along* with you;
   He eats grass like an ox.
16 See now, his strength *is* in his hips,

And his power *is* in his stomach
       muscles.
17 He moves his tail like a cedar;
   The sinews of his thighs are tightly
       knit.
18 His bones *are like* beams of bronze,
   His ribs like bars of iron.
19 He *is* the first of the ways of God;
   Only He who made him can bring
       near His sword.
20 Surely the mountains yield food for
       him,
   And all the beasts of the field play
       there.
21 He lies under the lotus trees,
   In a covert of reeds and marsh.
22 The lotus trees cover him *with* their
       shade;
   The willows by the brook surround
       him.
23 Indeed the river may rage,
   Yet he is not disturbed;
   He is confident, though the Jordan
       gushes into his mouth,
24 *Though* he takes it in his eyes,
   Or one pierces *his* nose with a snare.

PSALM 101:1–4

1 I will sing of mercy and justice;
   To You, O LORD, I will sing praises.

2 I will behave wisely in a perfect way.
   Oh, when will You come to me?
   I will walk within my house with a
       perfect heart.

Christian perfection is the perfection of a relationship to God.   (NOT KNOWING)

---

3 I will set nothing wicked before my
       eyes;
   I hate the work of those who fall away;
   It shall not cling to me.
4 A perverse heart shall depart from me;
   I will not know wickedness.

PROVERBS 23:29, 30

29 WHO has woe?
   Who has sorrow?
   Who has contentions?
   Who has complaints?
   Who has wounds without cause?
   Who has redness of eyes?

30 Those who linger long at the wine,
   Those who go in search of mixed wine.

1 CORINTHIANS 6:1–20

DARE any of you, having a matter against another, go to law before the unrighteous, and not before the saints? 2 Do you not know that the saints will judge the world? And if the world will be judged by you, are you unworthy to judge the smallest matters? 3 Do you not know that we shall judge angels? How much more, things that pertain to this life? 4 If then you have judgments concerning things pertaining to this life, do you appoint those who are least esteemed by the church to judge? 5 I say this to your shame. Is it so, that there is not a wise man among you, not even one, who will be able to judge between his brethren? 6 But brother goes to law against brother, and that before unbelievers!

7 Now therefore, it is already an utter failure for you that you go to law against one another. Why do you not rather accept wrong? Why do you not rather *let yourselves* be cheated? 8 No, you yourselves do wrong and cheat, and *you do* these things *to your* brethren! 9 Do you not know that the unrighteous will not inherit the kingdom of God? Do not be deceived. Neither fornicators, nor idolaters, nor adulterers, nor homosexuals, nor sodomites, 10 nor thieves, nor covetous, nor drunkards, nor revilers, nor extortioners will inherit the kingdom of God. 11 And such were some of you. But you were washed, but you were sancti-

fied, but you were justified in the name of the Lord Jesus and by the Spirit of our God.

12 All things are lawful for me, but all things are not helpful. All things are lawful for me, but I will not be brought under the power of any. 13 Foods for the stomach and the stomach for foods, but God will destroy both it and them. Now the body *is* not for sexual immorality but for the Lord, and the Lord for the body. 14 And God both raised up the Lord and will also raise us up by His power.

15 Do you not know that your bodies are members of Christ? Shall I then take the members of Christ and make *them* members of a harlot? Certainly not! 16 Or do you not know that he who is joined to a harlot is one body *with her*? For "the two," He says, "shall become one flesh." 17 But he who is joined to the Lord is one spirit *with Him*.

18 Flee sexual immorality. Every sin that a man does is outside the body, but he who commits sexual immorality sins against his own body. 19 Or do you not know that your body is the temple of the Holy Spirit *who is* in you, whom you have from God, and you are not your own? 20 For you were

---

*T*he Bible gives the body a very high place indeed. (BIB. PSYCH.)

---

bought at a price; therefore glorify God in your body and in your spirit, which are God's.

◆◆◆◆

Reading 237—Keeping Clean
Job 42:1–6

Sin is not man's problem, but God's. God has taken the problem of sin into His own hands and solved it, and the proof that He has is the cross of Calvary. The cross is the cross of God. On the ground of the Redemption I can "wash my robes, and make them white in the blood of the Lamb." Pseudo-evangelism has twisted the revelation and made it mean—"Now that God has saved me, I do not need to do anything." The New Testament revelation is that now I am saved by God's grace, I must work on that basis and keep myself clean. It does not matter what a man's heredity is, or what tendencies there are in him; on the basis of the Redemption he can become all that God's Book indicates he should be. The essential truth of Christianity in thinking is that I can "wash my robes, and make them clean in the blood of the Lamb." That is the exposition of the Redemption in actual experience. Are we thinking along this line, or on the pagan line which makes out that the basis of things is rational, and leaves out God, and Jesus Christ, and the Redemption altogether? (*BAFFLED*)

JOB 41:1—42:17

1 "CAN you draw out Leviathan with a hook,
Or *snare* his tongue with a line *which* you lower?

2 Can you put a reed through his nose,
Or pierce his jaw with a hook?

3 Will he make many supplications to you?
Will he speak softly to you?

4 Will he make a covenant with you?
Will you take him as a servant forever?

5 Will you play with him as *with* a bird,
Or will you leash him for your maidens?

6 Will *your* companions make a banquet of him?
Will they apportion him among the merchants?

7 Can you fill his skin with harpoons,
Or his head with fishing spears?

8 Lay your hand on him;
Remember the battle—
Never do it again!

9 Indeed, *any* hope of *overcoming* him is false;
Shall *one not* be overwhelmed at the sight of him?

10 No one is *so* fierce that he would dare stir him up.
Who then is able to stand against Me?

11 Who has preceded Me, that I should pay *him*?
Everything under heaven is Mine.

12 "I will not conceal his limbs,
His mighty power, or his graceful proportions.

13 Who can remove his outer coat?
Who can approach *him* with a double bridle?

14 Who can open the doors of his face,
With his terrible teeth all around?

15 *His* rows of scales are *his* pride,
Shut up tightly *as with* a seal;

16 One is so near another
That no air can come between them;

17 They are joined one to another,
They stick together and cannot be parted.

18 His sneezings flash forth light,

And his eyes *are* like the eyelids of the morning.

19 Out of his mouth go burning lights;
Sparks of fire shoot out.

20 Smoke goes out of his nostrils,
As *from* a boiling pot and burning rushes.

21 His breath kindles coals,
And a flame goes out of his mouth.

22 Strength dwells in his neck,
And sorrow dances before him.

23 The folds of his flesh are joined together;
They are firm on him and cannot be moved.

24 His heart is as hard as stone,
Even as hard as the lower *millstone*.

25 When he raises himself up, the mighty are afraid;
Because of his crashings they are beside themselves.

26 *Though* the sword reaches him, it cannot avail;
Nor does spear, dart, or javelin.

27 He regards iron as straw,
And bronze as rotten wood.

28 The arrow cannot make him flee;
Slingstones become like stubble to him.

29 Darts are regarded as straw;
He laughs at the threat of javelins.

30 His undersides *are* like sharp potsherds;
He spreads pointed *marks* in the mire.

31 He makes the deep boil like a pot;
He makes the sea like a pot of ointment.

32 He leaves a shining wake behind him;
One would think the deep had white hair.

33 On earth there is nothing like him,
Which is made without fear.

34 He beholds every high *thing*;
He *is* king over all the children of pride."

42 THEN Job answered the LORD and said:

2 "I know that You can do everything,
And that no purpose *of Yours* can be withheld from You.

3 *You asked,* 'Who *is* this who hides counsel without knowledge?'

> Therefore I have uttered what I did
>   not understand,
> Things too wonderful for me, which
>   I did not know.
> 4 Listen, please, and let me speak;
>   *You said,* 'I will question you, and
>   you shall answer Me.'
>
> 5 "I have heard of You by the hearing
>   of the ear,
>   But now my eye sees You.
> 6 Therefore I abhor *myself,*
>   And repent in dust and ashes."

7 And so it was, after the LORD had spoken these words to Job, that the LORD said to Eliphaz the Temanite, "My wrath is aroused against you and your two friends, for you have not spoken of Me *what is* right, as My servant Job *has.* 8 Now therefore, take for yourselves seven bulls and seven rams, go to My servant Job, and offer up for yourselves a burnt offering; and My servant Job shall pray for you. For I will accept him, lest I deal with you *according to your* folly; because you have not spoken of Me *what is* right, as My servant Job *has.*"

9 So Eliphaz the Temanite and Bildad the Shuhite *and* Zophar the Naamathite went and did as the LORD commanded them; for the LORD had accepted Job. 10 And the LORD restored Job's losses when he prayed for his friends. Indeed the LORD gave Job twice as much as he had before.

When you get into the inner place I defy you to go on praying for yourself. (NOT KNOWING)

---

11 Then all his brothers, all his sisters, and all those who had been his acquaintances before, came to him and ate food with him in his house; and they consoled him and comforted him for all the adversity that the LORD had brought upon him. Each one gave him a piece of silver and each a ring of gold. 12 Now the LORD blessed the latter *days* of Job more than his beginning; for he had fourteen thousand sheep, six thousand camels, one thousand yoke of oxen, and one thousand female donkeys. 13 He also had seven sons and three daughters. 14 And he called the name of the first Jemimah, the name of the second Keziah, and the name of the third Keren-Happuch. 15 In all the land were found no women *so* beautiful as the daughters of Job; and their father gave them an inheritance among their brothers.

16 After this Job lived one hundred and forty years, and saw his children and grandchildren *for* four generations. 17 So Job died, old and full of days.

PSALM 101:5–8

> 5 WHOEVER secretly slanders his
>   neighbor,
>   Him I will destroy;
>   The one who has a haughty look and
>   a proud heart,
>   Him I will not endure.
> 6 My eyes *shall be* on the faithful of the
>   land,
>   That they may dwell with me;
>   He who walks in a perfect way,
>   He shall serve me.
> 7 He who works deceit shall not dwell
>   within my house;
>   He who tells lies shall not continue in
>   my presence.
> 8 Early I will destroy all the wicked of
>   the land,
>   That I may cut off all the evildoers from
>   the city of the LORD.

PROVERBS 23:31–35

> 31 DO not look on the wine when it is
>   red,
>   When it sparkles in the cup,
>   *When* it swirls around smoothly;
> 32 At the last it bites like a serpent,
>   And stings like a viper.
> 33 Your eyes will see strange things,
>   And your heart will utter perverse
>   things.
> 34 Yes, you will be like one who lies down
>   in the midst of the sea,
>   Or like one who lies at the top of the
>   mast, *saying:*
> 35 "They have struck me, *but* I was not
>   hurt;
>   They have beaten me, but I did not
>   feel *it.*
>   When shall I awake, that I may seek
>   another *drink?*"

1 CORINTHIANS 7:1–19

NOW concerning the things of which you wrote to me:

It is good for a man not to touch a woman. 2 Nevertheless, because of sexual immorality, let each man have his own wife, and let each woman have her own husband.

3 Let the husband render to his wife the affection due her, and likewise also the wife to her husband. 4 The wife does not have authority over her own body, but the husband *does*. And likewise the husband does not have authority over his own body, but the wife *does*. 5 Do not deprive one another except with consent for a time, that you may give yourselves to fasting and prayer; and come together again so that Satan does not tempt you because of your lack of self-control. 6 But I say this as a concession, not as a commandment. 7 For I wish that all men were even as I myself. But each one has his own gift from God, one in this manner and another in that.

8 But I say to the unmarried and to the widows: It is good for them if they remain even as I am; 9 but if they cannot exercise self-control, let them marry. For it is better to marry than to burn *with passion*.

10 Now to the married I command, *yet* not I but the Lord: A wife is not to depart from *her* husband. 11 But even if she does depart, let her remain unmarried or be reconciled to *her* husband. And a husband is not to divorce *his* wife.

12 But to the rest I, not the Lord, say: If any brother has a wife who does not believe, and she is willing to live with him, let him not divorce her. 13 And a woman who has a husband who does not believe, if he is willing to live with her, let her not divorce him. 14 For the unbelieving hus-

---

A spiritual saint never believes circumstances to be haphazard.   (UTMOST)

---

band is sanctified by the wife, and the unbelieving wife is sanctified by the husband; otherwise your children would be unclean, but now they are holy. 15 But if the unbeliever departs, let him depart; a brother or a sister is not under bondage in such *cases*. But God has called us to peace. 16 For how do you know, O wife, whether you will save *your* husband? Or how do you know, O husband, whether you will save *your* wife?

17 But as God has distributed to each one, as the Lord has called each one, so let him walk. And so I ordain in all the churches. 18 Was anyone called while circumcised? Let him not become uncircumcised. Was anyone called while uncircumcised? Let him not be circumcised. 19 Circumcision is nothing and uncircumcision is nothing, but keeping the commandments of God *is what matters*.

◆◆◆

Reading 238—The Way Out of Tragedy
Ecclesiastes 1:1–11

No man who thinks and faces life as it actually is, can be other than pessimistic. There is no way out unless he finds it by religious faith or is blinded by his temperament. The summing up of all practical life is that the basis of things is tragic. Sum up your life as it actually is, and, unless you look at actual things from a religious or a temperamental or an intellectual standpoint, everything is to be said for this philosophy: Eat, drink, and be merry, for tomorrow we die. If rationalism is the basis of things, that is undoubtedly the most reasonable thing to do. But if the basis of things is tragic, then the Bible standpoint comes nearer the solution, and Nietzsche is nearer the truth than any rationalist. Nietzsche declares that the basis of things is tragic, and that the way out is by the merciless superman: the Bible reveals that the basis of things is tragic, and that the way out is by redemption. We say that man is in process of evolution—a magnificent promise of what he is going to be! The wisdom of Hebrews looks at man's history and attainments and says—What a magnificent ruin of what he was created to be!   (*SHADE*)

ECCLESIASTES 1:1—2:26

THE words of the Preacher, the son of David, king in Jerusalem.

2 "Vanity of vanities," says the Preacher;
   "Vanity of vanities, all *is* vanity."

3 What profit has a man from all his labor
   In which he toils under the sun?
4 *One* generation passes away, and *another* generation comes;
   But the earth abides forever.
5 The sun also rises, and the sun goes down,
   And hastens to the place where it arose.
6 The wind goes toward the south,
   And turns around to the north;
   The wind whirls about continually,
   And comes again on its circuit.
7 All the rivers run into the sea,
   Yet the sea *is* not full;
   To the place from which the rivers come,
   There they return again.
8 All things *are* full of labor;
   Man cannot express *it.*
   The eye is not satisfied with seeing,
   Nor the ear filled with hearing.

9 That which has been *is* what will be,
   That which *is* done is what will be done,
   And *there is* nothing new under the sun.
10 Is there anything of which it may be said,
   "See, this *is* new"?
   It has already been in ancient times before us.
11 *There is* no remembrance of former *things,*
   Nor will there be any remembrance of *things* that are to come
   By *those* who will come after.

12 I, the Preacher, was king over Israel in Jerusalem. 13 And I set my heart to seek and search out by wisdom concerning all that is done under heaven; this burdensome task God has given to the sons of man, by which they may be exercised. 14 I have seen all the works that are done under the sun; and indeed, all *is* vanity and grasping for the wind.

15 *What is* crooked cannot be made straight,
   And what is lacking cannot be numbered.

16 I communed with my heart, saying, "Look, I have attained greatness, and have gained more wisdom than all who were before me in Jerusalem. My heart has understood great wisdom and knowledge." 17 And I set my heart to know wisdom and to know madness and folly. I perceived that this also is grasping for the wind.

18 For in much wisdom *is* much grief,
   And he who increases knowledge increases sorrow.

2 I said in my heart, "Come now, I will test you with mirth; therefore enjoy pleasure"; but surely, this also *was* vanity. 2 I said of laughter—"Madness!"; and of mirth, "What does it accomplish?" 3 I searched in my heart *how* to gratify my flesh with wine, while guiding my heart with wisdom, and how to lay hold on folly, till I might see what *was* good for the sons of men to do under heaven all the days of their lives.

4 I made my works great, I built myself houses, and planted myself vineyards. 5 I made myself gardens and orchards, and I planted all *kinds* of fruit trees in them. 6 I made myself water pools from which to water the growing trees of the grove. 7 I acquired male and female servants, and had servants born in my house. Yes, I had greater possessions of herds and flocks than all who were in Jerusalem before me. 8 I also gathered for myself silver and gold and the special treasures of kings and of the provinces. I acquired male and female singers, the delights of the sons of men, *and* musical instruments of all kinds.

9 So I became great and excelled more than all who were before me in Jerusalem. Also my wisdom remained with me.

10 Whatever my eyes desired I did not keep from them.
   I did not withhold my heart from any pleasure,
   For my heart rejoiced in all my labor;
   And this was my reward from all my labor.
11 Then I looked on all the works that my hands had done
   And on the labor in which I had toiled;
   And indeed all *was* vanity and grasping for the wind.
   There was no profit under the sun.

> *What we possess often possesses us—we are possessed by possessions.* (GLORY)

12 Then I turned myself to consider
     wisdom and madness and folly;
   For what *can* the man *do* who
     succeeds the king?—
   Only what he has already done.
13 Then I saw that wisdom excels folly
   As light excels darkness.
14 The wise man's eyes *are* in his head,
   But the fool walks in darkness.
   Yet I myself perceived
   That the same event happens to them
     all.

15 So I said in my heart,
   "As it happens to the fool,
   It also happens to me,
   And why was I then more wise?"
   Then I said in my heart,
   "This also *is* vanity."
16 For *there is* no more remembrance
     of the wise than of the fool forever,
   Since all that now *is* will be forgotten
     in the days to come.
   And how does a wise *man* die?
   As the fool!

17 Therefore I hated life because the work that was done under the sun *was* distressing to me, for all *is* vanity and grasping for the wind. 18 Then I hated all my labor in which I had toiled under the sun, because I must leave it to the man who will come after me. 19 And who knows whether he will be wise or a fool? Yet he will rule over all my labor in which I toiled and in which I have shown myself wise under the sun. This also *is* vanity. 20 Therefore I turned my heart and despaired of all the labor in which I had toiled under the sun. 21 For there is a man whose labor *is* with wisdom, knowledge, and skill; yet he must leave his heritage to a man who has not labored for it. This also *is* vanity and a great evil. 22 For what has man for all his labor, and for the striving of his heart with which he has toiled under the sun? 23 For all his days *are* sorrowful, and his work burdensome; even in the night his heart takes no rest. This also is vanity.

24 Nothing *is* better for a man *than* that he should eat and drink, and *that* his soul should enjoy good in his labor. This also, I saw, was from the hand of God. 25 For who can eat, or who can have enjoyment, more than I? 26 For *God* gives wisdom and knowledge and joy to a man who *is* good in His sight; but to the sinner He gives the work of gathering and collecting, that he may give to *him who is* good before God. This also *is* vanity and grasping for the wind.

PSALM 102:1–11

1 HEAR my prayer, O LORD,
   And let my cry come to You.
2 Do not hide Your face from me in the
     day of my trouble;
   Incline Your ear to me;
   In the day that I call, answer me
     speedily.

3 For my days are consumed like smoke,
   And my bones are burned like a hearth.
4 My heart is stricken and withered like
     grass,
   So that I forget to eat my bread.
5 Because of the sound of my groaning
   My bones cling to my skin.
6 I am like a pelican of the wilderness;
   I am like an owl of the desert.
7 I lie awake,
   And am like a sparrow alone on the
     housetop.

8 My enemies reproach me all day long;
   Those who deride me swear an oath
     against me.
9 For I have eaten ashes like bread,
   And mingled my drink with weeping,
10 Because of Your indignation and Your
     wrath;
   For You have lifted me up and cast
     me away.
11 My days *are* like a shadow that
     lengthens,
   And I wither away like grass.

PROVERBS 24:1, 2

1 DO not be envious of evil men,
   Nor desire to be with them;
2 For their heart devises violence,
   And their lips talk of troublemaking.

1 CORINTHIANS 7:20–40

LET each one remain in the same calling in which he was called. 21 Were you called *while* a slave? Do not be concerned about it; but if you can be made free, rather use *it*. 22 For he who is called in the Lord *while* a slave is the Lord's freedman. Likewise he who is called *while* free is Christ's slave.

23 You were bought at a price; do not become slaves of men. 24 Brethren, let each one remain with God in that *state* in which he was called.

25 Now concerning virgins: I have no commandment from the Lord; yet I give judgment as one whom the Lord in His mercy *has made* trustworthy. 26 I suppose therefore that this is good because of the present distress—that *it is* good for a man to remain as he is: 27 Are you bound to a wife? Do not seek to be loosed. Are you loosed from a wife? Do not seek a wife. 28 But even if you do marry, you have not sinned; and if a virgin marries, she has not sinned. Nevertheless such will have trouble in the flesh, but I would spare you.

29 But this I say, brethren, the time *is* short, so that from now on even those who have wives should be as though they had none, 30 those who weep as though they did not weep, those who rejoice as though they did not rejoice, those who buy as though they did not possess, 31 and those who use this world as not misusing *it*. For the form of this world is passing away.

32 But I want you to be without care.

A clean cut from everything that savors of the world . . . is essential for the Christian.   (BIB. ETHICS)

He who is unmarried cares for the things of the Lord—how he may please the Lord. 33 But he who is married cares about the things of the world—how he may please *his* wife. 34 There is a difference between a wife and a virgin. The unmarried woman cares about the things of the Lord, that she may be holy both in body and in spirit. But she who is married cares about the things of the world—how she may please *her* husband. 35 And this I say for your own profit, not that I may put a leash on you, but for what is proper, and that you may serve the Lord without distraction.

36 But if any man thinks he is behaving improperly toward his virgin, if she is past the flower of youth, and thus it must be, let him do what he wishes. He does not sin; let them marry. 37 Nevertheless he who stands steadfast in his heart, having no necessity, but has power over his own will, and has so determined in his heart that he will keep his virgin, does well. 38 So then he who gives *her* in marriage does well, but he who does not give *her* in marriage does better.

39 A wife is bound by law as long as her husband lives; but if her husband dies, she is at liberty to be married to whom she wishes, only in the Lord. 40 But she is happier if she remains as she is, according to my judgment—and I think I also have the Spirit of God.

◆◆◆◆

Reading 239—To Kill or to Heal?
Ecclesiastes 3:3

Every art, every healing, and every good, can be used for an opposite purpose. Every possibility I have of producing a fine character in time, I can use to produce the opposite; I have that liberty from the Creator. God will not prevent my disobeying Him; if He did, my obedience would not be worth anything. Some of us complain that God should have made the universe and human life like a foolproof machine, so simple that there would be no possibility of going wrong. If He had, we would have been like jellyfish. If there is no possibility of being damned, there is no need for salvation.

In the time between birth and death, most of us are in our "shell." There is something in us which makes us peck, and when the crack comes, instead if its being the gentle light and dawn of a new day, it is like a lightning flash. The universe we awaken to is not one of order, but a great big howling confusion, and it takes time to get adjusted. The distresses we reap in between God's decrees for us, we, together with other human beings, are personally responsible for. If we make our life a muddle, it is to a large extent because we have not discerned the great underlying relationship to God.   (*SHADE*)

ECCLESIASTES 3:1–22

1 TO everything *there is* a season,
A time for every purpose under
heaven:

2 A time to be born,
And a time to die;
A time to plant,
And a time to pluck *what is*
planted;

3 A time to kill,
And a time to heal;
A time to break down,
And a time to build up;

4 A time to weep,
And a time to laugh;
A time to mourn,
And a time to dance;

5 A time to cast away stones,
And a time to gather stones;
A time to embrace,
And a time to refrain from
embracing;

6 A time to gain,
And a time to lose;
A time to keep,
And a time to throw away;

7 A time to tear,
And a time to sew;
A time to keep silence,
And a time to speak;

8 A time to love,
And a time to hate;
A time of war,
And a time of peace.

9 What profit has the worker from that in which he labors? 10 I have seen the God-given task with which the sons of men are to be occupied. 11 He has made everything beautiful in its time. Also He has put eternity in their hearts, except that no one can find out the work that God does from beginning to end.

12 I know that nothing *is* better for them than to rejoice, and to do good in their lives, 13 and also that every man should eat and drink and enjoy the good of all his labor—it *is* the gift of God.

14 I know that whatever God does,
It shall be forever.
Nothing can be added to it,
And nothing taken from it.
God does *it*, that men should fear
before Him.

15 That which is has already been,
And what is to be has already been;
And God requires an account of what
is past.

16 Moreover I saw under the sun:

In the place of judgment,
Wickedness *was* there;
And *in* the place of righteousness,
Iniquity *was* there.

17 I said in my heart,

"God shall judge the righteous and
the wicked,
For *there is* a time there for every
purpose and for every work."

18 I said in my heart, "Concerning the condition of the sons of men, God tests them, that they may see that they themselves are *like* animals." 19 For what happens to the sons of men also happens to animals; one thing befalls them: as one dies, so dies the other. Surely, they all have one breath; man has no advantage over animals, for all *is* vanity. 20 All go to one place: all are from the dust, and all return to dust. 21 Who knows the spirit of the sons of men, which goes upward, and the spirit of the animal, which goes down to the earth? 22 So I perceived that nothing *is* better than that a man should rejoice in his own works, for that *is* his heritage. For who can bring him to see what will happen after him?

PSALM 102:12–17

12 BUT You, O LORD, shall endure
forever,
And the remembrance of Your name
to all generations.

*G*od is true to the laws of His own
nature. (DISCIPLES)

13 You will arise *and* have mercy on Zion;
For the time to favor her,
Yes, the set time, has come.

14 For Your servants take pleasure in her
stones,
And show favor to her dust.

15 So the nations shall fear the name of
the LORD,
And all the kings of the earth Your
glory.

16 For the LORD shall build up Zion;
He shall appear in His glory.

17 He shall regard the prayer of the
destitute,
And shall not despise their prayer.

PROVERBS 24:3, 4

3　THROUGH wisdom a house is built,
　And by understanding it is established;
4　By knowledge the rooms are filled
　With all precious and pleasant riches.

1 CORINTHIANS 8:1–13

NOW concerning things offered to idols:
We know that we all have knowledge.
Knowledge puffs up, but love edifies.

The majority of spiritual Christians . . . are too cocksure and certain there is nothing more to know.　(PERFECT)

---

2 And if anyone thinks that he knows anything, he knows nothing yet as he ought to know. 3 But if anyone loves God, this one is known by Him.

4 Therefore concerning the eating of things offered to idols, we know that an idol *is* nothing in the world, and that *there*

is no other God but one. 5 For even if there are so-called gods, whether in heaven or on earth (as there are many gods and many lords), 6 yet for us *there is* one God, the Father, of whom *are* all things, and we for Him; and one Lord Jesus Christ, through whom *are* all things, and through whom we *live*.

7 However, *there is* not in everyone that knowledge; for some, with consciousness of the idol, until now eat *it* as a thing offered to an idol; and their conscience, being weak, is defiled. 8 But food does not commend us to God; for neither if we eat are we the better, nor if we do not eat are we the worse.

9 But beware lest somehow this liberty of yours become a stumbling block to those who are weak. 10 For if anyone sees you who have knowledge eating in an idol's temple, will not the conscience of him who is weak be emboldened to eat those things offered to idols? 11 And because of your knowledge shall the weak brother perish, for whom Christ died? 12 But when you thus sin against the brethren, and wound their weak conscience, you sin against Christ. 13 Therefore, if food makes my brother stumble, I will never again eat meat, lest I make my brother stumble.

◆◆◆◆

Reading 240—The Oppression of Trade
Ecclesiastes 4:4

If you go back to the origin of civilization, you find it was founded by a murderer. Among the good things, the shielding and protecting things, that are the outcome of civilization, what Solomon mentions is always to be found—the crushing of someone in order to get gain. It may be done kindly or brutally, but the basis of success must be the crushing of something or someone. There is a rivalry between men, and we have made it a good thing; we have made ambition and competition the very essence of civilized life. No wonder there is no room for Jesus Christ, and no room for the Bible. We are all so scientifically orthodox nowadays, so materialistic and certain that rationalism is the basis of things, that we make the Bible out to be the most revolutionary, unorthodox and heretical of books. Jesus Christ echoes Solomon's attitude: "For one's life does not consist in the abundance of the things which he possesses."

At the basis of trade and civilized life lie oppression and tyranny. Whether you are king or subject, says Solomon, you cannot find joy in any system of civilized life, or in trade or commerce; for underneath there is a rivalry that stings and bites, and the kindest man will put his heel on his greatest friend. These are not the blind statements of a disappointed man, but statements of facts discerned by the wisest man that ever lived.　(SHADE)

ECCLESIASTES 4:1—6:12

THEN I returned and considered all the oppression that is done under the sun:

> And look! The tears of the oppressed,
> But they have no comforter—
> On the side of their oppressors *there is* power,
> But they have no comforter.

2 Therefore I praised the dead who were already dead,
> More than the living who are still alive.

3 Yet, better than both *is he* who has never existed,
> Who has not seen the evil work that is done under the sun.

4 Again, I saw that for all toil and every skillful work a man is envied by his neighbor. This also *is* vanity and grasping for the wind.

5 The fool folds his hands
> And consumes his own flesh.

6 Better a handful *with* quietness
> Than both hands full, *together with* toil and grasping for the wind.

7 Then I returned, and I saw vanity under the sun:

8 There is one alone, without companion:
> He has neither son nor brother.
> Yet *there is* no end to all his labors,
> Nor is his eye satisfied with riches.
> *But he never asks,*
> "For whom do I toil and deprive myself of good?"
> This also *is* vanity and a grave misfortune.

9 Two *are* better than one,
> Because they have a good reward for their labor.

10 For if they fall, one will lift up his companion.
> But woe to him *who is* alone when he falls,
> For *he has* no one to help him up.

11 Again, if two lie down together, they will keep warm;
> But how can one be warm *alone?*

12 Though one may be overpowered by another, two can withstand him.
> And a threefold cord is not quickly broken.

13 Better a poor and wise youth
> Than an old and foolish king who will be admonished no more.

14 For he comes out of prison to be king,
> Although he was born poor in his kingdom.

15 I saw all the living who walk under the sun;
> They were with the second youth who stands in his place.

16 *There was* no end of all the people over whom he was made king;
> Yet those who come afterward will not rejoice in him.
> Surely this also *is* vanity and grasping for the wind.

5 WALK prudently when you go to the house of God; and draw near to hear rather than to give the sacrifice of fools, for they do not know that they do evil.

2 Do not be rash with your mouth,
> And let not your heart utter anything hastily before God.
> For God *is* in heaven, and you on earth;
> Therefore let your words be few.

3 For a dream comes through much activity,
> And a fool's voice *is known* by *his* many words.

4 When you make a vow to God, do not delay to pay it;
> For *He has* no pleasure in fools.
> Pay what you have vowed—

5 Better not to vow than to vow and not pay.

6 Do not let your mouth cause your flesh to sin, nor say before the messenger *of God* that it *was* an error. Why should God be angry at your excuse and destroy the work of your hands? 7 For in the multitude of dreams and many words *there is* also vanity. But fear God.

8 If you see the oppression of the poor, and the violent perversion of justice and righteousness in a province, do not marvel at the matter; for high official watches over high official, and higher officials are over them.

9 Moreover the profit of the land is for all; *even* the king is served from the field.

10 He who loves silver will not be satisfied with silver;
> Nor he who loves abundance, with increase.
> This also *is* vanity.

11 When goods increase,
They increase who eat them;
So what profit have the owners
Except to see *them* with their eyes?

12 The sleep of a laboring man *is* sweet,
Whether he eats little or much;
But the abundance of the rich will
not permit him to sleep.

13 There is a severe evil *which* I have
seen under the sun:
Riches kept for their owner to his
hurt.

14 But those riches perish through
misfortune;
When he begets a son, *there is* nothing
in his hand.

15 As he came from his mother's womb,
naked shall he return,
To go as he came;
And he shall take nothing from his
labor
Which he may carry away in his hand.

16 And this also *is* a severe evil—
Just exactly as he came, so shall
he go.
And what profit has he who has
labored for the wind?

17 All his days he also eats in darkness,
And *he has* much sorrow and sickness
and anger.

18 Here is what I have seen: *It is* good
and fitting *for one* to eat and drink, and to
enjoy the good of all his labor in which
he toils under the sun all the days of his
life which God gives him; for it *is* his heritage. 19 As for every man to whom God
has given riches and wealth, and given him
power to eat of it, to receive his heritage
and rejoice in his labor—this *is* the gift of
God. 20 For he will not dwell unduly on
the days of his life, because God keeps *him*
busy with the joy of his heart.

---

*G*od can take any man and put
the miracle of His joy into
him. (GLORIFY)

---

6 THERE is an evil which I have seen
under the sun, and it *is* common among
men: 2 A man to whom God has given
riches and wealth and honor, so that he
lacks nothing for himself of all he desires;
yet God does not give him power to eat
of it, but a foreigner consumes it. This *is*
vanity, and it *is* an evil affliction.

3 If a man begets a hundred *children* and
lives many years, so that the days of his
years are many, but his soul is not satisfied
with goodness, or indeed he has no burial,
I say *that* a stillborn child *is* better than
he— 4 for it comes in vanity and departs
in darkness, and its name is covered with
darkness. 5 Though it has not seen the sun
or known *anything,* this has more rest than
that man, 6 even if he lives a thousand years
twice—but has not seen goodness. Do not
all go to one place?

7 All the labor of man *is* for his mouth,
And yet the soul is not satisfied.
8 For what more has the wise *man* than
the fool?
What does the poor man have,
Who knows *how* to walk before the
living?
9 Better *is* the sight of the eyes than
the wandering of desire.
This also *is* vanity and grasping for
the wind.

10 Whatever one is, he has been named
already,
For it is known that he *is* man;
And he cannot contend with Him
who is mightier than he.
11 Since there are many things that
increase vanity,
How *is* man the better?

12 For who knows what *is* good for man
in life, all the days of his vain life which
he passes like a shadow? Who can tell a
man what will happen after him under the
sun?

PSALM 102:18–28

18 THIS will be written for the generation
to come,
That a people yet to be created may
praise the LORD.
19 For He looked down from the height
of His sanctuary;
From heaven the LORD viewed the
earth,
20 To hear the groaning of the prisoner,
To release those appointed to death,
21 To declare the name of the LORD in
Zion,
And His praise in Jerusalem,
22 When the peoples are gathered
together,
And the kingdoms, to serve the LORD.

23 He weakened my strength in the way;
He shortened my days.

24 I said, "O my God,
Do not take me away in the midst of
my days;
Your years *are* throughout all
generations.
25 Of old You laid the foundation of the
earth,
And the heavens *are* the work of Your
hands.
26 They will perish, but You will endure;
Yes, they will all grow old like a
garment;
Like a cloak You will change them,
And they will be changed.
27 But You *are* the same,
And Your years will have no end.
28 The children of Your servants will
continue,
And their descendants will be
established before You."

PROVERBS 24:5, 6

5 A wise man *is* strong,
Yes, a man of knowledge increases
strength;
6 For by wise counsel you will wage your
own war,
And in a multitude of counselors *there*
is safety.

1 CORINTHIANS 9:1–27

AM I not an apostle? Am I not free? Have
I not seen Jesus Christ our Lord? Are you
not my work in the Lord? 2 If I am not
an apostle to others, yet doubtless I am to
you. For you are the seal of my apostleship
in the Lord.

3 My defense to those who examine me
is this: 4 Do we have no right to eat and
drink? 5 Do we have no right to take along
a believing wife, as *do* also the other apostles,
the brothers of the Lord, and Cephas?
6 Or *is it* only Barnabas and I *who* have
no right to refrain from working? 7 Who
ever goes to war at his own expense? Who
plants a vineyard and does not eat of its
fruit? Or who tends a flock and does not
drink of the milk of the flock?

8 Do I say these things as a *mere* man?
Or does not the law say the same also?
9 For it is written in the law of Moses, "You
shall not muzzle an ox while it treads out
the grain." Is it oxen God is concerned
about? 10 Or does He say *it* altogether for
our sakes? For our sakes, no doubt, *this* is
written, that he who plows shou!d plow
in hope, and he who threshes in hope should
be partaker of his hope. 11 If we have sown
spiritual things for you, *is it* a great thing

if we reap your material things? 12 If others
are partakers of *this* right over you, *are* we
not even more?

Nevertheless we have not used this right,
but endure all things lest we hinder the
gospel of Christ. 13 Do you not know that
those who minister the holy things eat *of
the things* of the temple, and those who
serve at the altar partake of *the offerings of*
the altar? 14 Even so the Lord has commanded that those who preach the gospel
should live from the gospel.

15 But I have used none of these things,
nor have I written these things that it should
be done so to me; for it *would be* better
for me to die than that anyone should make
my boasting void. 16 For if I preach the
gospel, I have nothing to boast of, for necessity is laid upon me; yes, woe is me if I
do not preach the gospel! 17 For if I do
this willingly, I have a reward; but if against
my will, I have been entrusted with a stewardship. 18 What is my reward then? That
when I preach the gospel, I may present
the gospel of Christ without charge, that
I may not abuse my authority in the gospel.

19 For though I am free from all *men*, I
have made myself a servant to all, that I
might win the more; 20 and to the Jews
I became as a Jew, that I might win Jews;
to those *who are* under the law, as under
the law, that I might win those *who are*
under the law; 21 to those *who are* without
law, as without law (not being without law
toward God, but under law toward Christ),
that I might win those *who are* without
law; 22 to the weak I became as weak, that
I might win the weak. I have become all
things to all *men*, that I might by all means
save some. 23 Now this I do for the gospel's
sake, that I may be partaker of it with *you*.

24 Do you not know that those who run
in a race all run, but one receives the prize?
Run in such a way that you may obtain
it. 25 And everyone who competes *for the
prize* is temperate in all things. Now they
do it to obtain a perishable crown, but we
for an imperishable *crown*. 26 Therefore I
run thus: not with uncertainty. Thus I fight:
not as *one who* beats the air. 27 But I discipline my body and bring *it* into subjection,
lest, when I have preached to others, I myself should become disqualified.

*In forming a new habit it is
vitally important to insist on
bringing the body under control
first.* (MORAL FOUND.)

Reading 241—Shame of the Gospel
Ecclesiastes 7:7

A wise person who has built his life in confidence in God will appear a fool when he is among people who are sleek and cunning. . . . The wisdom of God is arrant stupidity to the wisdom of the world, until all of a sudden God makes the wisdom of the world foolish (see 1 Cor. 1:23–25).

If you stand true to your faith in God, there will be situations in which you will come across extortioners, cunning, crafty people, who use their wits instead of worshiping God, and you will appear a fool. Are you prepared to appear a fool for Christ's sake? Very few of us know anything about suffering for Christ's sake for conscience or conviction's sake. To suffer for Christ's sake is to suffer because of being personally related to Him.

If you are going to be true to God, you will appear a fool among those who do not believe in God, and you must lay your account with this. Jesus said, "Therefore whoever confesses ME before men . . ." and it tests a man for all he is worth to confess Jesus Christ, because the confession has to be made in the set he belongs to and esteems. The "shame" of the gospel. "I am not ashamed of the gospel of Christ," says Paul.   (*SHADE*)

ECCLESIASTES 7:1–29

1 A good name *is* better than precious
  ointment,
  And the day of death than the day
  of one's birth;

2 Better to go to the house of mourning
  Than to go to the house of feasting,
  For that *is* the end of all men;
  And the living will take *it* to heart.

3 Sorrow *is* better than laughter,
  For by a sad countenance the heart
  is made better.

4 The heart of the wise *is* in the house
  of mourning,
  But the heart of fools *is* in the house
  of mirth.

5 *It is* better to hear the rebuke of the
  wise
  Than for a man to hear the song of
  fools.

6 For like the crackling of thorns under
  a pot,
  So *is* the laughter of the fool.
  This also is vanity.

7 Surely oppression destroys a wise
  man's reason,
  And a bribe debases the heart.

8 The end of a thing *is* better than its
  beginning;
  The patient in spirit *is* better than
  the proud in spirit.

9 Do not hasten in your spirit to be
  angry,
  For anger rests in the bosom of fools.

10 Do not say,
  "Why were the former days better than
  these?"
  For you do not inquire wisely
  concerning this.

11 Wisdom *is* good with an inheritance,
  And profitable to those who see the
  sun.

12 For wisdom *is* a defense *as* money *is*
  a defense,
  But the excellence of knowledge *is*
  that wisdom gives life to those who
  have it.

13 Consider the work of God;
  For who can make straight what He
  has made crooked?

The revelation of God in the Old Testament is that of a working God.   (NOT KNOWING)

---

14 In the day of prosperity be joyful,
  But in the day of adversity consider:
  Surely God has appointed the one
  as well as the other,
  So that man can find out nothing
  that will come after him.

15 I have seen everything in my days of vanity:

> There is a just *man* who perishes in his righteousness,
> And there is a wicked *man* who prolongs *life* in his wickedness.

16 Do not be overly righteous,
Nor be overly wise:
Why should you destroy yourself?
17 Do not be overly wicked,
Nor be foolish:
Why should you die before your time?
18 *It is* good that you grasp this,
And also not remove your hand from the other;
For he who fears God will escape them all.

19 Wisdom strengthens the wise
More than ten rulers of the city.

20 For *there is* not a just man on earth who does good
And does not sin.

21 Also do not take to heart everything people say,
Lest you hear your servant cursing you.
22 For many times, also, your own heart has known
That even you have cursed others.

23 All this I have proved by wisdom.
I said, "I will be wise";
But it *was* far from me.
24 As for that which is far off and exceedingly deep,
Who can find it out?
25 I applied my heart to know,
To search and seek out wisdom and the reason *of things,*
To know the wickedness of folly,
Even of foolishness *and* madness.
26 And I find more bitter than death
The woman whose heart *is* snares and nets,
Whose hands *are* fetters.
He who pleases God shall escape from her,
But the sinner shall be trapped by her.

27 "Here is what I have found," says the Preacher,
"*Adding* one thing to the other to find out the reason,

28 Which my soul still seeks but I cannot find:
One man among a thousand I have found,
But a woman among all these I have not found.
29 Truly, this only I have found:
That God made man upright,
But they have sought out many schemes."

PSALM 103:1–5

1 BLESS the LORD, O my soul;
And all that is within me, *bless* His holy name!
2 Bless the LORD, O my soul,
And forget not all His benefits:
3 Who forgives all your iniquities,
Who heals all your diseases,
4 Who redeems your life from destruction,
Who crowns you with lovingkindness and tender mercies,
5 Who satisfies your mouth with good *things,*
So that your youth is renewed like the eagle's.

PROVERBS 24:7–9

7 WISDOM *is* too lofty for a fool;
He does not open his mouth in the gate.

8 He who plots to do evil
Will be called a schemer.
9 The devising of foolishness *is* sin,
And the scoffer *is* an abomination to men.

1 CORINTHIANS 10:1–18

MOREOVER, brethren, I do not want you to be unaware that all our fathers were under the cloud, all passed through the sea, 2 all were baptized into Moses in the cloud and in the sea, 3 all ate the same spiritual food, 4 and all drank the same spiritual drink. For they drank of that spiritual Rock that followed them, and that Rock was Christ. 5 But with most of them God was not well pleased, for *their bodies* were scattered in the wilderness.

6 Now these things became our examples, to the intent that we should not lust after evil things as they also lusted. 7 And do not become idolaters as *were* some of them.

As it is written, "The people sat down to eat and drink, and rose up to play." 8 Nor let us commit sexual immorality, as some of them did, and in one day twenty-three thousand fell; 9 nor let us tempt Christ, as some of them also tempted, and were destroyed by serpents; 10 nor complain, as some of them also complained, and were destroyed by the destroyer. 11 Now all these things happened to them as examples, and they were written for our admonition, upon whom the ends of the ages have come.

12 Therefore let him who thinks he stands take heed lest he fall. 13 No temptation has overtaken you except such as is common to man; but God *is* faithful, who will not allow you to be tempted beyond what you are able, but with the temptation will also make the way of escape, that you may be able to bear *it*.

---

*G*od does not keep us from temptation, He succors us in the midst of it.   (Psy. Redemp.)

---

14 Therefore, my beloved, flee from idolatry. 15 I speak as to wise men; judge for yourselves what I say. 16 The cup of blessing which we bless, is it not the communion of the blood of Christ? The bread which we break, is it not the communion of the body of Christ? 17 For we, *though* many, are one bread *and* one body; for we all partake of that one bread.

18 Observe Israel after the flesh: Are not those who eat of the sacrifices partakers of the altar?

◆◆◆

Reading 242—The Interim of Life
Ecclesiastes 9:3, 4

The interim between birth and death is a school training, a program of which we have not the laying out. We may calculate and say we are going to do this and that, but "you do not know what shall be on the morrow." It is a haphazard life, and we have to bank on God's wisdom, not on our own. It looks as if Solomon were counseling the Bohemian life, and as if Jesus Christ did the same when He said, "Therefore I say to you, do not worry about your life." A Bohemian is careless about everything, and neither Jesus Christ nor Solomon teaches that. Jesus Christ taught that a man is to be carefully careless about everything except his relationship to God. The great care of the life, Jesus says, is to make the relationship to God the one care. Most of us are careful about everything except that.

The life we are living has a program which we fulfill but about which we know nothing. We have been put into a program that we have no say in, and we bungle our part by trying to be our own organizers.

"There's a divinity that shapes our ends,
   Rough-hew them how we will."   (*Shade*)

ECCLESIASTES 8:1—10:20

1   WHO *is* like a wise *man*?
      And who knows the interpretation
         of a thing?
      A man's wisdom makes his face shine,
      And the sternness of his face is
         changed.

2 I *say,* "Keep the king's commandment for the sake of your oath to God. 3 Do not be hasty to go from his presence. Do not take your stand for an evil thing, for he does whatever pleases him."

4   Where the word of a king *is, there*
         is power;

And who may say to him, "What are
you doing?"

5 He who keeps his command will
experience nothing harmful;
And a wise man's heart discerns both
time and judgment,

6 Because for every matter there is a
time and judgment,
Though the misery of man increases
greatly.

7 For he does not know what will
happen;
So who can tell him when it will
occur?

8 No one has power over the spirit to
retain the spirit,
And no one has power in the day
of death.
There is no release from that war,
And wickedness will not deliver those
who are given to it.

9 All this I have seen, and applied my
heart to every work that is done under the
sun: *There is* a time in which one man rules
over another to his own hurt.

10 Then I saw the wicked buried, who
had come and gone from the place of holiness, and they were forgotten in the city
where they had so done. This also *is* vanity.

11 Because the sentence against an evil work
is not executed speedily, therefore the heart
of the sons of men is fully set in them to
do evil. 12 Though a sinner does evil a hundred *times,* and his *days* are prolonged, yet
I surely know that it will be well with those
who fear God, who fear before Him.

13 But it will not be well with the wicked;
nor will he prolong *his* days, *which are* as
a shadow, because he does not fear before
God.

14 There is a vanity which occurs on earth,
that there are just *men* to whom it happens
according to the work of the wicked; again,
there are wicked *men* to whom it happens
according to the work of the righteous. I
said that this also *is* vanity.

15 So I commended enjoyment, because
a man has nothing better under the sun
than to eat, drink, and be merry; for this
will remain with him in his labor *all* the
days of his life which God gives him under
the sun.

16 When I applied my heart to know wisdom and to see the business that is done
on earth, even though one sees no sleep
day or night, 17 then I saw all the work of
God, that a man cannot find out the work
that is done under the sun. For though a
man labors to discover *it,* yet he will not
find *it;* moreover, though a wise *man* at-

tempts to know *it,* he will not be able to
find *it.*

9 FOR I considered all this in my heart,
so that I could declare it all: that the
righteous and the wise and their works *are*
in the hand of God. People know neither
love nor hatred *by* anything *they see* before
them. 2 All things *come* alike to all:

One event *happens* to the righteous
and the wicked;
To the good, the clean, and the
unclean;
To him who sacrifices and him who
does not sacrifice.
As is the good, so *is* the sinner;
He who takes an oath as *he* who fears
an oath.

3 This *is* an evil in all that is done under
the sun: that one thing *happens* to all. Truly
the hearts of the sons of men are full of
evil; madness *is* in their hearts while they
live, and after that *they go* to the dead.
4 But for him who is joined to all the living
there is hope, for a living dog is better than
a dead lion.

5 For the living know that they will
die;
But the dead know nothing,
And they have no more reward,
For the memory of them is forgotten.

6 Also their love, their hatred, and their
envy have now perished;
Nevermore will they have a share
In anything done under the sun.

7 Go, eat your bread with joy,
And drink your wine with a merry
heart;
For God has already accepted your
works.

8 Let your garments always be white,
And let your head lack no oil.

9 Live joyfully with the wife whom you
love all the days of your vain life which
He has given you under the sun, all your
days of vanity; for that *is* your portion in
life, and in the labor which you perform
under the sun.

10 Whatever your hand finds to do, do
it with your might; for *there is* no work
or device or knowledge or wisdom in the
grave where you are going.

11 I returned and saw under the sun
that—

The race *is* not to the swift,
Nor the battle to the strong,

Nor bread to the wise,
Nor riches to men of understanding,
Nor favor to men of skill;
But time and chance happen to them
all.

12 For man also does not know his time:
Like fish taken in a cruel net,
Like birds caught in a snare,
So the sons of men *are* snared in an
evil time,
When it falls suddenly upon them.

13 This wisdom I have also seen under
the sun, and it *seemed* great to me: 14 *There
was* a little city with few men in it; and a
great king came against it, besieged it, and
built great snares around it. 15 Now there
was found in it a poor wise man, and he
by his wisdom delivered the city. Yet no
one remembered that same poor man.
16 Then I said:

"Wisdom *is* better than strength.
Nevertheless the poor man's wisdom
is despised,
And his words are not heard.
17 Words of the wise, *spoken* quietly,
should be heard
Rather than the shout of a ruler of
fools.
18 Wisdom *is* better than weapons of
war;
But one sinner destroys much good."

10 DEAD flies putrefy the perfumer's
ointment,
And cause it to give off a foul odor;
So does a little folly to one respected
for wisdom *and* honor.
2 A wise man's heart *is* at his right hand,
But a fool's heart at his left.
3 Even when a fool walks along the
way,
He lacks wisdom,
And he shows everyone *that* he *is* a
fool.
4 If the spirit of the ruler rises against
you,
Do not leave your post;
For conciliation pacifies great
offenses.

5 There is an evil I have seen under
the sun,
As an error proceeding from the
ruler:
6 Folly is set in great dignity,
While the rich sit in a lowly place.
7 I have seen servants on horses,
While princes walk on the ground
like servants.

8 He who digs a pit will fall into it,
And whoever breaks through a wall
will be bitten by a serpent.
9 He who quarries stones may be hurt
by them,
And he who splits wood may be
endangered by it.
10 If the ax is dull,
And one does not sharpen the edge,
Then he must use more strength;
But wisdom brings success.

11 A serpent may bite when *it is* not
charmed;
The babbler is no different.
12 The words of a wise man's mouth
are gracious,
But the lips of a fool shall swallow
him up;
13 The words of his mouth begin with
foolishness,
And the end of his talk *is* raving
madness.
14 A fool also multiplies words.
No man knows what is to be;
Who can tell him what will be after
him?
15 The labor of fools wearies them,
For they do not even know how to
go to the city!

16 Woe to you, O land, when your king
is a child,
And your princes feast in the
morning!
17 Blessed *are* you, O land, when your
king *is* the son of nobles,
And your princes feast at the proper
time—
For strength and not for
drunkenness!
18 Because of laziness the building
decays,
And through idleness of hands the
house leaks.

---

*T*ake heed to yourself, and never allow
anything to produce laziness and
sloth.   (WORKMEN)

---

19 A feast is made for laughter,
And wine makes merry;
But money answers everything.

20 Do not curse the king, even in your
thought;
Do not curse the rich, even in your
bedroom;

For a bird of the air may carry your
voice,
And a bird in flight may tell the
matter.

PSALM 103:6–14

6 THE LORD executes righteousness
And justice for all who are oppressed.
7 He made known His ways to Moses,
His acts to the children of Israel.
8 The LORD *is* merciful and gracious,
Slow to anger, and abounding in mercy.
9 He will not always strive *with us,*
Nor will He keep *His anger* forever.
10 He has not dealt with us according to
our sins,
Nor punished us according to our
iniquities.
11 For as the heavens are high above the
earth,
So great is His mercy toward those who
fear Him;
12 As far as the east is from the west,
So far has He removed our
transgressions from us.
13 As a father pities *his* children,
So the LORD pities those who fear Him.
14 For He knows our frame;
He remembers that we *are* dust.

PROVERBS 24:10–12

10 IF you faint in the day of adversity,
Your strength *is* small.
11 Deliver *those who* are drawn toward
death,
And hold back *those* stumbling to the
slaughter.
12 If you say, "Surely we did not know
this,"
Does not He who weighs the hearts
consider *it*?
He who keeps your soul, does He *not*
know *it*?
And will He *not* render to *each* man
according to his deeds?

1 CORINTHIANS 10:19–33

WHAT am I saying then? That an idol is
anything, or what is offered to idols is anything? 20 Rather, that the things which the
Gentiles sacrifice they sacrifice to demons
and not to God, and I do not want you
to have fellowship with demons. 21 You
cannot drink the cup of the Lord and the
cup of demons; you cannot partake of the
Lord's table and of the table of demons.
22 Or do we provoke the Lord to jealousy?
Are we stronger than He?

23 All things are lawful for me, but not
all things are helpful; all things are lawful
for me, but not all things edify. 24 Let no
one seek his own, but each one the other's
well-being.

25 Eat whatever is sold in the meat market, asking no questions for conscience'
sake; 26 for "the earth *is* the LORD's, and
all its fullness."

---

*"If only God would not be so holy
as my conscience tells me
He is."* (GENESIS)

---

27 If any of those who do not believe
invites you *to dinner,* and you desire to go,
eat whatever is set before you, asking no
question for conscience' sake. 28 But if anyone says to you, "This was offered to idols,"
do not eat it for the sake of the one who
told you, and for conscience' sake; for "the
earth *is* the LORD's, and all its fullness."
29 "Conscience," I say, not your own, but
that of the other. For why is my liberty
judged by another *man's* conscience?
30 But if I partake with thanks, why am I
evil spoken of for *the food* over which I
give thanks?

31 Therefore, whether you eat or drink,
or whatever you do, do all to the glory of
God. 32 Give no offense, either to the Jews
or to the Greeks or to the church of God,
33 just as I also please all *men* in all *things,*
not seeking my own profit, but the *profit*
of many, that they may be saved.

Reading 243—Power to Slay Weariness
Ecclesiastes 12:5

Solomon is describing the last lap of a man's life when his nerves give way, and little things become an intolerable burden. There are things like this that come across us naturally and we have difficulty in tracing where they come from; they make us irritable or melancholy. Times when a fly or a mosquito is more annoying than the Devil himself. And the same thing is true spiritually; there are times when little things pester and annoy and there is nothing in us big enough to cope with them. This verse is a picture of the shadows which come across a man's soul not because he has done wrong or has backslidden; there is nothing definite about it, but he finds himself belittling everything; there is no vision or power or grandeur in anything. . . . "What is the good of anything at all? What is the good of having done my duty? of praying, or believing in God?" . . .

What is the cure? The cure is that of a right vision. Every man has the power to slay his own weariness, not by "bucking up" as you do physically, but by suddenly looking at things from a different standpoint. "Why are you cast down, O my soul? And why are you disquieted within me? Hope in God; for I shall yet praise Him, the help of my countenance and my God" (Ps. 43:5). It is a tremendous thing to know that God reigns and rules and rejoices, and that His joy is our strength. The confidence of a Christian is that God is . . . "the Father of lights, with whom there is no variation or shadow of turning." (*PLACE HELP*)

ECCLESIASTES 11:1—12:14

1 CAST your bread upon the waters,
For you will find it after many days.
2 Give a serving to seven, and also to eight,
For you do not know what evil will be on the earth.

3 If the clouds are full of rain,
They empty *themselves* upon the earth;
And if a tree falls to the south or the north,
In the place where the tree falls, there it shall lie.
4 He who observes the wind will not sow,
And he who regards the clouds will not reap.

5 As you do not know what *is* the way of the wind,
Or how the bones *grow* in the womb of her who is with child,
So you do not know the works of God who makes everything.
6 In the morning sow your seed,
And in the evening do not withhold your hand;

For you do not know which will prosper,
Either this or that,
Or whether both alike *will be* good.

7 Truly the light is sweet,
And *it is* pleasant for the eyes to behold the sun;
8 But if a man lives many years
And rejoices in them all,
Yet let him remember the days of darkness,
For they will be many.
All that is coming *is* vanity.

9 Rejoice, O young man, in your youth,
And let your heart cheer you in the days of your youth;
Walk in the ways of your heart,
And in the sight of your eyes;
But know that for all these
God will bring you into judgment.
10 Therefore remove sorrow from your heart,
And put away evil from your flesh,
For childhood and youth *are* vanity.

12 REMEMBER now your Creator in the days of your youth,

Before the difficult days come,
And the years draw near when you
  say,
"I have no pleasure in them":

---

*The one word in the spiritual
vocabulary is* now.   (LOVE OF GOD)

---

2 While the sun and the light,
   The moon and the stars,
   Are not darkened,
   And the clouds do not return after
     the rain;
3 In the day when the keepers of the
     house tremble,
   And the strong men bow down;
   When the grinders cease because they
     are few,
   And those that look through the
     windows grow dim;
4 When the doors are shut in the
     streets,
   And the sound of grinding is low;
   When one rises up at the sound of
     a bird,
   And all the daughters of music are
     brought low.
5 Also they are afraid of height,
   And of terrors in the way;
   When the almond tree blossoms,
   The grasshopper is a burden,
   And desire fails.
   For man goes to his eternal
     home,
   And the mourners go about the
     streets.

6 *Remember your Creator* before the
     silver cord is loosed,
   Or the golden bowl is broken,
   Or the pitcher shattered at the
     fountain,
   Or the wheel broken at the well.
7 Then the dust will return to the earth
     as it was,
   And the spirit will return to God who
     gave it.

8 "Vanity of vanities," says the Preacher,
   "All *is* vanity."

9 And moreover, because the Preacher
was wise, he still taught the people knowledge; yes, he pondered and sought out *and*
set in order many proverbs. 10 The Preacher
sought to find acceptable words; and *what
was* written *was* upright—words of truth.
11 The words of the wise are like goads,

and the words of scholars are like well-
driven nails, given by one Shepherd.
12 And further, my son, be admonished by
these. Of making many books *there is* no
end, and much study *is* wearisome to the
flesh.

13 Let us hear the conclusion of the whole
matter:

   Fear God and keep His
     commandments,
   For this is man's all.
14 For God will bring every work into
     judgment,
   Including every secret thing,
   Whether good or evil.

PSALM 103:15–22

15 *AS for* man, his days *are* like grass;
   As a flower of the field, so he flourishes.
16 For the wind passes over it, and it is
     gone,
   And its place remembers it no
     more.
17 But the mercy of the LORD *is* from
     everlasting to everlasting
   On those who fear Him,
   And His righteousness to children's
     children,
18 To such as keep His covenant,
   And to those who remember His
     commandments to do them.

19 The LORD has established His throne
     in heaven,
   And His kingdom rules over all.

20 Bless the LORD, you His angels,
   Who excel in strength, who do His
     word,
   Heeding the voice of His word.
21 Bless the LORD, all *you* His hosts,
   You ministers of His, who do His
     pleasure.
22 Bless the LORD, all His works,
   In all places of His dominion.

   Bless the LORD, O my soul!

PROVERBS 24:13, 14

13 MY son, eat honey because *it is* good,
   And the honeycomb *which is* sweet to
     your taste;
14 So *shall* the knowledge of wisdom *be*
     to your soul;
   If you have found *it*, there is a prospect,
   And your hope will not be cut off.

1 CORINTHIANS 11:1–16

IMITATE me, just as I also *imitate* Christ.

The great meaning of following is that we imitate as children, not as monkeys. (LOVE OF GOD)

---

2 Now I praise you, brethren, that you remember me in all things and keep the traditions just as I delivered *them* to you. 3 But I want you to know that the head of every man is Christ, the head of woman *is* man, and the head of Christ *is* God. 4 Every man praying or prophesying, having *his* head covered, dishonors his head. 5 But every woman who prays or prophesies with *her* head uncovered dishonors her head, for that is one and the same as if her head were shaved. 6 For if a woman is not covered, let her also be shorn. But if it is shameful for a woman to be shorn or shaved, let her be covered. 7 For a man indeed ought not to cover *his* head, since he is the image and glory of God; but woman is the glory of man. 8 For man is not from woman, but woman from man. 9 Nor was man created for the woman, but woman for the man. 10 For this reason the woman ought to have *a symbol of* authority on *her* head, because of the angels. 11 Nevertheless, neither *is* man independent of woman, nor woman independent of man, in the Lord. 12 For as woman *came* from man, even so man also *comes* through woman; but all things are from God.

13 Judge among yourselves. Is it proper for a woman to pray to God with her head uncovered? 14 Does not even nature itself teach you that if a man has long hair, it is a dishonor to him? 15 But if a woman has long hair, it is a glory to her; for *her* hair is given to her for a covering. 16 But if anyone seems to be contentious, we have no such custom, nor *do* the churches of God.

◆◆◆

Reading 244—The Lily in the Bush
Song of Solomon 2:2

The lily Solomon refers to is as common as our daisy, but a perfume pervades it. The illustration is as if a traveler were passing a field and suddenly a fragrant aroma was wafted to him from a bush. Marveling at the sweetness, he looked into the bush and found a lily growing in its bosom. People come to a good but worldly home, and say, "What a beautiful influence comes from that home." But begin to draw aside the ordinary commonplace things of the home and you discover that tucked away somewhere is a mother or a daughter who is really a "lily" of the Lord. Or take it in connection with individual lives, we may see a man who is generally disadvantaged in appearance or in education, a thoroughly commonplace man, yet a marvelous influence radiates from him. Our Lord is spoken of as "a root out of dry ground"—thoroughly disadvantaged. That is what Isaiah says the hero of God will be like.

The true character of the loveliness that tells for God is always unconscious. Conscious influence is priggish and unChristian. . . . Who are the people who have influenced us most? Certainly not the priggish men and women, but our mothers, our fathers, our sisters—the ones who had not the remotest idea that they were influencing us. (*LOVE OF GOD*)

SONG OF SOLOMON 1:1—2:17

THE song of songs, which *is* Solomon's.

2 Let him kiss me with the kisses of
   his mouth—
  For your love *is* better than wine.
3 Because of the fragrance of your good
   ointments,
  Your name *is* ointment poured forth;
  Therefore the virgins love you.
4 Draw me away!

We will run after you.

The king has brought me into his
  chambers.

We will be glad and rejoice in you.

We will remember your love more
  than wine.

Rightly do they love you.

5 I *am* dark, but lovely,
  O daughters of Jerusalem,
  Like the tents of Kedar,
  Like the curtains of Solomon.
6 Do not look upon me, because I *am*
   dark,
  Because the sun has tanned me.
  My mother's sons were angry with
   me;
  They made me the keeper of the
   vineyards,
  But my own vineyard I have not kept.
7 Tell me, O you whom I love,
  Where you feed *your flock,*
  Where you make *it* rest at noon.
  For why should I be as one who veils
   herself
  By the flocks of your companions?
8 If you do not know, O fairest among
   women,
  Follow in the footsteps of the flock,
  And feed your little goats
  Beside the shepherds' tents.
9 I have compared you, my love,
  To my filly among Pharaoh's
   chariots.
10 Your cheeks are lovely with
   ornaments,
  Your neck with chains *of gold.*

11 We will make you ornaments of gold
  With studs of silver.

12 While the king *is* at his table,
  My spikenard sends forth its
   fragrance.
13 A bundle of myrrh *is* my beloved to
   me,
  That lies all night between my
   breasts.
14 My beloved *is* to me a cluster of
   henna *blooms*
  In the vineyards of En Gedi.

15 Behold, you *are* fair, my love!
  Behold, you *are* fair!
  You *have* dove's eyes.

16 Behold, you *are* handsome, my
   beloved!
  Yes, pleasant!
  Also our bed *is* green.
17 The beams of our houses *are* cedar,
  And our rafters of fir.

2 I *am* the rose of Sharon,
  And the lily of the valleys.

2 Like a lily among thorns,
  So is my love among the daughters.

3 Like an apple tree among the trees
   of the woods,
  So *is* my beloved among the sons.
  I sat down in his shade with great
   delight,
  And his fruit *was* sweet to my taste.

---

*Fall in love, and you will see beauty
in everything.* (SHAD. AGONY)

---

4 He brought me to the banqueting
   house,
  And his banner over me *was* love.
5 Sustain me with cakes of raisins,
  Refresh me with apples,
  For I *am* lovesick.

6 His left hand *is* under my head,
  And his right hand embraces me.
7 I charge you, O daughters of
   Jerusalem,
  By the gazelles or by the does of the
   field,
  Do not stir up nor awaken love
  Until it pleases.

8 The voice of my beloved!
  Behold, he comes
  Leaping upon the mountains,
  Skipping upon the hills.

9   My beloved is like a gazelle or a young
        stag.
    Behold, he stands behind our wall;
    He is looking through the windows,
    Gazing through the lattice.

10   My beloved spoke, and said to me:
    "Rise up, my love, my fair one,
    And come away.
11   For lo, the winter is past,
    The rain is over *and* gone.
12   The flowers appear on the earth;
    The time of singing has come,
    And the voice of the turtledove
    Is heard in our land.
13   The fig tree puts forth her green figs,
    And the vines *with* the tender grapes
    Give a good smell.
    Rise up, my love, my fair one,
    And come away!

14   "O my dove, in the clefts of the rock,
    In the secret *places* of the cliff,
    Let me see your face,
    Let me hear your voice;
    For your voice *is* sweet,
    And your face *is* lovely."

15   Catch us the foxes,
    The little foxes that spoil the vines,
    For our vines *have* tender grapes.

16   My beloved *is* mine, and I *am* his.
    He feeds *his flock* among the lilies.

17   Until the day breaks
    And the shadows flee away,
    Turn, my beloved,
    And be like a gazelle
    Or a young stag
    Upon the mountains of Bether.

PSALM 104:1–9

1   BLESS the Lord, O my soul!

    O Lord my God, You are very great:
    You are clothed with honor and
        majesty,
2   Who cover *Yourself* with light as *with*
        a garment,
    Who stretch out the heavens like a
        curtain.

3   He lays the beams of His upper
        chambers in the waters,
    Who makes the clouds His chariot,
    Who walks on the wings of the wind,
4   Who makes His angels spirits,
    His ministers a flame of fire.

5   *You who* laid the foundations of the
        earth,
    So *that* it should not be moved forever,
6   You covered it with the deep as *with*
        a garment;
    The waters stood above the mountains.
7   At Your rebuke they fled;
    At the voice of Your thunder they
        hastened away.
8   They went up over the mountains;
    They went down into the valleys,
    To the place which You founded for
        them.
9   You have set a boundary that they may
        not pass over,
    That they may not return to cover the
        earth.

PROVERBS 24:15, 16

15   DO not lie in wait, O wicked *man,*
        against the dwelling of the righteous;
    Do not plunder his resting place;
16   For a righteous *man* may fall seven
        times
    And rise again,
    But the wicked shall fall by calamity.

1 CORINTHIANS 11:17–34

NOW in giving these instructions I do not
praise *you*, since you come together not for
the better but for the worse. 18 For first
of all, when you come together as a church,
I hear that there are divisions among you,
and in part I believe it. 19 For there must
also be factions among you, that those who
are approved may be recognized among
you. 20 Therefore when you come together
in one place, it is not to eat the Lord's
Supper. 21 For in eating, each one takes
his own supper ahead of *others;* and one
is hungry and another is drunk. 22 What!
Do you not have houses to eat and drink
in? Or do you despise the church of God
and shame those who have nothing? What
shall I say to you? Shall I praise you in
this? I do not praise *you*.

23 For I received from the Lord that
which I also delivered to you: that the Lord
Jesus on the *same* night in which He was
betrayed took bread; 24 and when He had
given thanks, He broke *it* and said, "Take,
eat; this is My body which is broken for
you; do this in remembrance of Me."
25 In the same manner *He* also *took* the cup
after supper, saying, "This cup is the new
covenant in My blood. This do, as often
as you drink *it,* in remembrance of Me."

26 For as often as you eat this bread and drink this cup, you proclaim the Lord's death till He comes.

---

*T*he ordinance of the Lord's Supper is a symbol of what we should be doing all the time.   (NOT KNOWING)

---

27 Therefore whoever eats this bread or drinks *this* cup of the Lord in an unworthy manner will be guilty of the body and blood of the Lord. 28 But let a man examine himself, and so let him eat of the bread and drink of the cup. 29 For he who eats and drinks in an unworthy manner eats and drinks judgment to himself, not discerning the Lord's body. 30 For this reason many *are* weak and sick among you, and many sleep. 31 For if we would judge ourselves, we would not be judged. 32 But when we are judged, we are chastened by the Lord, that we may not be condemned with the world.

33 Therefore, my brethren, when you come together to eat, wait for one another. 34 But if anyone is hungry, let him eat at home, lest you come together for judgment. And the rest I will set in order when I come.

◆◆◆◆

Reading 245—Regeneration
1 Corinthians 12:12–27

*T*he doctrine of substitution is twofold. Not only is Jesus Christ identified with my sin, but I am identified with Him so that His ruling disposition is in me, and the moral transaction on my part is agreement with God's verdict on sin in the Cross of Jesus Christ. Redemption means that God through Jesus Christ can take the most miserable wreck and turn him into a son of God. As long as a man has his morality well within his own grasp, Jesus Christ does not amount to anything to him, but when a man gets to his wits' end by agony and says involuntarily, "My God, what am I up against? there is something underneath I never knew was there," he begins to pay attention to what Jesus Christ says. A moral preparation is necessary before we can believe; truth is a moral vision, and does not exist for a man until he sees it. There is a frontier outside which Jesus Christ does not tell; but when once we get over that frontier, He becomes all in all. God takes us through circumstances until we enter the moral frontiers where Jesus Christ tells.

When you come to your wits' end, remember there is a way out, namely, personal relationship to God through the Redemption of Jesus Christ.

(SHAD. AGONY)

SONG OF SOLOMON 3:1—4:16

1   BY night on my bed I sought the one I love;
    I sought him, but I did not find him.
2   "I will rise now," *I said,*
    "And go about the city;
    In the streets and in the squares
    I will seek the one I love."
    I sought him, but I did not find him.
3   The watchmen who go about the city found me;

I said,
    "Have you seen the one I love?"

4   Scarcely had I passed by them,
    When I found the one I love.
    I held him and would not let him go,
    Until I had brought him to the house of my mother,
    And into the chamber of her who conceived me.

5   I charge you, O daughters of Jerusalem,

By the gazelles or by the does of the
  field,
Do not stir up nor awaken love
Until it pleases.

6 Who *is* this coming out of the
     wilderness
   Like pillars of smoke,
   Perfumed with myrrh and
     frankincense,
   With all the merchant's fragrant
     powders?
7 Behold, it *is* Solomon's couch,
   With sixty valiant men around it,
   Of the valiant of Israel.
8 They all hold swords,
   Being expert in war.
   Every man *has* his sword on his thigh
   Because of fear in the night.

9 Of the wood of Lebanon
   Solomon the King
   Made himself a palanquin:
10 He made its pillars *of* silver,
   Its support *of* gold,
   Its seat *of* purple,
   Its interior paved *with* love
   By the daughters of Jerusalem.
11 Go forth, O daughters of Zion,
   And see King Solomon with the
     crown
   With which his mother crowned him
   On the day of his wedding,
   The day of the gladness of his heart.

4 BEHOLD, you *are* fair, my love!
   Behold, you *are* fair!
   You *have* dove's eyes behind your
     veil.
   Your hair *is* like a flock of goats,
   Going down from Mount Gilead.
2 Your teeth *are* like a flock of shorn
     sheep
   Which have come up from the
     washing,
   Every one of which bears twins,
   And none *is* barren among them.
3 Your lips *are* like a strand of scarlet,
   And your mouth is lovely.
   Your temples behind your veil
   Are like a piece of pomegranate.
4 Your neck *is* like the tower of David,
   Built for an armory,
   On which hang a thousand bucklers,
   All shields of mighty men.
5 Your two breasts *are* like two fawns,
   Twins of a gazelle,
   Which feed among the lilies.

6 Until the day breaks
   And the shadows flee away,

I will go my way to the mountain
  of myrrh
And to the hill of frankincense.

7 You *are* all fair, my love,
   And *there is* no spot in you.
8 Come with me from Lebanon, *my*
     spouse,
   With me from Lebanon.
   Look from the top of Amana,
   From the top of Senir and Hermon,
   From the lions' dens,
   From the mountains of the leopards.

9 You have ravished my heart,
   My sister, *my* spouse;
   You have ravished my heart
   With one *look* of your eyes,
   With one link of your necklace.
10 How fair is your love,
   My sister, *my* spouse!
   How much better than wine is your
     love,
   And the scent of your perfumes
   Than all spices!
11 Your lips, O *my* spouse,
   Drip as the honeycomb;
   Honey and milk *are* under your
     tongue;
   And the fragrance of your garments
   Is like the fragrance of Lebanon.

12 A garden enclosed
   Is my sister, *my* spouse,
   A spring shut up,
   A fountain sealed.
13 Your plants *are* an orchard of
     pomegranates
   With pleasant fruits,
   Fragrant henna with spikenard,
14 Spikenard and saffron,
   Calamus and cinnamon,
   With all trees of frankincense,
   Myrrh and aloes,
   With all the chief spices—
15 A fountain of gardens,
   A well of living waters,
   And streams from Lebanon.

16 Awake, O north *wind*,
   And come, O south!
   Blow upon my garden,
   That its spices may flow out.
   Let my beloved come to his garden
   And eat its pleasant fruits.

PSALM 104:10–23

10 HE sends the springs into the valleys;
   They flow among the hills.

11 They give drink to every beast of the field;
The wild donkeys quench their thirst.
12 By them the birds of the heavens have their home;
They sing among the branches.
13 He waters the hills from His upper chambers;
The earth is satisfied with the fruit of Your works.

14 He causes the grass to grow for the cattle,
And vegetation for the service of man,
That he may bring forth food from the earth,
15 And wine *that* makes glad the heart of man,
Oil to make *his* face shine,
And bread *which* strengthens man's heart.
16 The trees of the LORD are full *of sap,*
The cedars of Lebanon which He planted,
17 Where the birds make their nests;
The stork has her home in the fir trees.
18 The high hills *are* for the wild goats;
The cliffs are a refuge for the rock badgers.

19 He appointed the moon for seasons;
The sun knows its going down.
20 You make darkness, and it is night,
In which all the beasts of the forest creep about.
21 The young lions roar after their prey,
And seek their food from God.
22 *When* the sun rises, they gather together
And lie down in their dens.
23 Man goes out to his work
And to his labor until the evening.

PROVERBS 24:17, 18

17 DO not rejoice when your enemy falls,
And do not let your heart be glad when he stumbles;
18 Lest the LORD see *it,* and it displease Him,
And He turn away His wrath from him.

1 CORINTHIANS 12:1–31

NOW concerning spiritual *gifts,* brethren, I do not want you to be ignorant: 2 You know that you were Gentiles, carried away to these dumb idols, however you were led. 3 Therefore I make known to you that no one speaking by the Spirit of God calls Jesus accursed, and no one can say that Jesus is Lord except by the Holy Spirit.

4 There are diversities of gifts, but the same Spirit. 5 There are differences of ministries, but the same Lord. 6 And there are diversities of activities, but it is the same God who works all in all. 7 But the manifestation of the Spirit is given to each one for the profit *of all:* 8 for to one is given the word of wisdom through the Spirit, to another the word of knowledge through the same Spirit, 9 to another faith by the same Spirit, to another gifts of healings by the same Spirit, 10 to another the working of miracles, to another prophecy, to another discerning of spirits, to another *different* kinds of tongues, to another the interpretation of tongues. 11 But one and the same Spirit works all these things, distributing to each one individually as He wills.

12 For as the body is one and has many members, but all the members of that one body, being many, are one body, so also *is* Christ. 13 For by one Spirit we were all

The body of Christ is an organism, not an organization. (GLORIFY)

baptized into one body—whether Jews or Greeks, whether slaves or free—and have all been made to drink into one Spirit. 14 For in fact the body is not one member but many.

15 If the foot should say, "Because I am not a hand, I am not of the body," is it therefore not of the body? 16 And if the ear should say, "Because I am not an eye, I am not of the body," is it therefore not of the body? 17 If the whole body *were* an eye, where *would be* the hearing? If the whole *were* hearing, where *would be* the smelling? 18 But now God has set the members, each one of them, in the body just as He pleased. 19 And if they *were* all one member, where *would* the body *be?*

20 But now indeed *there are* many members, yet one body. 21 And the eye cannot say to the hand, "I have no need of you"; nor again the head to the feet, "I have no need of you." 22 No, much rather, those members of the body which seem to be weaker are necessary. 23 And those *members* of the body which we think to be less honorable, on these we bestow greater honor; and our unpresentable *parts* have greater modesty, 24 but our presentable *parts* have no need. But God composed the body, having given greater honor to that *part* which

lacks it, 25 that there should be no schism in the body, but *that* the members should have the same care for one another. 26 And if one member suffers, all the members suffer with *it*; or if one member is honored, all the members rejoice with *it*.

27 Now you are the body of Christ, and members individually. 28 And God has appointed these in the church: first apostles, second prophets, third teachers, after that miracles, then gifts of healings, helps, administrations, varieties of tongues. 29 *Are* all apostles? *Are* all prophets? *Are* all teachers? *Are* all workers of miracles? 30 Do all have gifts of healings? Do all speak with tongues? Do all interpret? 31 But earnestly desire the best gifts. And yet I show you a more excellent way.

◆◆◆

Reading 246—Direction of Divine Living
1 Corinthians 13:4–8

"Love suffers long *and* is kind; love does not envy; love . . . does not seek its own, is not provoked, thinks no evil; . . . bears all things, believes all things, hopes all things, endures all things. Love never fails." That is Christian living in actual life. If I have the disposition of a faultfinder, I am a most uncomfortable person to live with, but if the love of God has been shed abroad in my heart, I begin to see extraordinary self-sacrifice under the roughest of exteriors. I begin to see nobility where before I only saw meanness, because I see only what I bring with me the power of seeing—a most humiliating thing to realize!

The direction of divine living is that I identify myself with God's interests in other people, and He is interested in some funny people, namely, you and me! We see the humor of our heavenly Father in the way He brings around us the type of people who are to us what we have been to Him; now He will watch how we behave to them. How did Jesus treat us? With infinite patience, with amplitude of forgiveness and generosity. Then He says that we are to treat them in the same way. "But if you do not forgive men their trespasses, neither will your Father forgive your trespasses."   (*PLACE HELP*)

SONG OF SOLOMON 5:1—6:13

1 I have come to my garden, my sister,
  my spouse;
  I have gathered my myrrh with my
  spice;
  I have eaten my honeycomb with my
  honey;
  I have drunk my wine with my milk.

  Eat, O friends!
  Drink, yes, drink deeply,
  O beloved ones!

2 I sleep, but my heart is awake;
  It is the voice of my beloved!
  He knocks, *saying,*
  "Open for me, my sister, my love,
  My dove, my perfect one;
  For my head is covered with dew,
  My locks with the drops of the
    night."

3 I have taken off my robe;
  How can I put it on *again?*
  I have washed my feet;
  How can I defile them?

4 My beloved put his hand
  By the latch of *the door,*
  And my heart yearned for him.

5 I arose to open for my beloved,
  And my hands dripped *with* myrrh,
  My fingers with liquid myrrh,
  On the handles of the lock.

6 I opened for my beloved,
  But my beloved had turned away *and*
  was gone.
  My heart leaped up when he spoke.
  I sought him, but I could not find
  him;

I called him, but he gave me no
answer.

7 The watchmen who went about the
city found me.
They struck me, they wounded me;
The keepers of the walls
Took my veil away from me.

8 I charge you, O daughters of
Jerusalem,
If you find my beloved,
That you tell him I *am* lovesick!

9 What *is* your beloved
More than *another* beloved,
O fairest among women?
What *is* your beloved
More than *another* beloved,
That you so charge us?

10 My beloved *is* white and ruddy,
Chief among ten thousand.

11 His head *is like* the finest gold;
His locks *are* wavy,
And black as a raven.

12 His eyes *are* like doves
By the rivers of waters,
Washed with milk,
And fitly set.

13 His cheeks *are* like a bed of spices,
Banks of scented herbs.
His lips *are* lilies,
Dripping liquid myrrh.

14 His hands *are* rods of gold
Set with beryl.
His body *is* carved ivory
Inlaid *with* sapphires.

15 His legs *are* pillars of marble
Set on bases of fine gold.
His countenance *is* like Lebanon,
Excellent as the cedars.

16 His mouth *is* most sweet,
Yes, he *is* altogether lovely.
This *is* my beloved,
And this *is* my friend,
O daughters of Jerusalem!

6 WHERE has your beloved gone,
O fairest among women?
Where has your beloved turned aside,
That we may seek him with you?

2 My beloved has gone to his garden,
To the beds of spices,
To feed *his flock* in the gardens,
And to gather lilies.

3 I *am* my beloved's,
And my beloved *is* mine.
He feeds *his flock* among the lilies.

4 O my love, you *are as* beautiful as
Tirzah,

Lovely as Jerusalem,
Awesome as *an army* with banners!

5 Turn your eyes away from me,
For they have overcome me.
Your hair *is* like a flock of goats
Going down from Gilead.

6 Your teeth *are* like a flock of sheep
Which have come up from the
washing;
Every one bears twins,
And none *is* barren among them.

7 Like a piece of pomegranate
Are your temples behind your veil.

8 There are sixty queens
And eighty concubines,
And virgins without number.

9 My dove, my perfect one,
Is the only one,
The only one of her mother,
The favorite of the one who bore
her.
The daughters saw her
And called her blessed,
The queens and the concubines,
And they praised her.

10 Who is she who looks forth as the
morning,
Fair as the moon,
Clear as the sun,
Awesome as *an army* with banners?

11 I went down to the garden of nuts
To see the verdure of the valley,
To see whether the vine had budded
And the pomegranates had bloomed.

12 Before I was even aware,
My soul had made me
As the chariots of my noble people.

13 Return, return, O Shulamite;
Return, return, that we may look
upon you!
What would you see in the
Shulamite—
As it were, the dance of the two
camps?

PSALM 104:24–30

24 O LORD, how manifold are Your
works!
In wisdom You have made them all.
The earth is full of Your possessions—

25 This great and wide sea,
In which *are* innumerable teeming
things,
Living things both small and great.

26 There the ships sail about;

There is that Leviathan
Which You have made to play there.

27 These all wait for You,
That You may give *them* their food in
due season.

28 *What* You give them they gather in;
You open Your hand, they are filled
with good.

29 You hide Your face, they are troubled;
You take away their breath, they die
and return to their dust.

30 You send forth Your Spirit, they are
created;
And You renew the face of the earth.

PROVERBS 24:19, 20

19 DO not fret because of evildoers,
Nor be envious of the wicked;

20 For there will be no prospect for the
evil *man;*
The lamp of the wicked will be put
out.

1 CORINTHIANS 13:1–13

THOUGH I speak with the tongues of men
and of angels, but have not love, I have
become sounding brass or a clanging cym-
bal. 2 And though I have *the gift of* prophecy,
and understand all mysteries and all knowledge, and though I have all faith, so that
I could remove mountains, but have not
love, I am nothing. 3 And though I bestow
all my goods to feed *the poor,* and though
I give my body to be burned, but have
not love, it profits me nothing.

4 Love suffers long *and* is kind; love does
not envy; love does not parade itself, is
not puffed up; 5 does not behave rudely,
does not seek its own, is not provoked,
thinks no evil; 6 does not rejoice in iniquity,
but rejoices in the truth; 7 bears all things,
believes all things, hopes all things, endures
all things.

8 Love never fails. But whether *there are*
prophecies, they will fail; whether *there are*
tongues, they will cease; whether *there is*
knowledge, it will vanish away. 9 For we
know in part and we prophesy in part.
10 But when that which is perfect has come,
then that which is in part will be done away.

11 When I was a child, I spoke as a child,
I understood as a child, I thought as a child;
but when I became a man, I put away
childish things. 12 For now we see in a mirror, dimly, but then face to face. Now I
know in part, but then I shall know just
as I also am known.

---

*God wants to make eternally our
own what we only possessed
intermittently.*   (NOT KNOWING)

13 And now abide faith, hope, love, these
three; but the greatest of these *is* love.

◆◆◆

Reading 247—Into the Middle of Things
Psalm 104:34

Meditation means getting to the middle of a thing, pinning yourself
down to a certain thing and concentratedly brooding upon it. The
majority of us attend only to the "muddle" of things; consequently, we get
spiritual indigestion, the counterpart of physical indigestion, a desperately
gloomy state of affairs. We cannot see anything rightly, and all we do see is
stars. "Faith is . . . the evidence of things not seen." Suppose Jesus suddenly
lifted the veil from our eyes and let us see angels ministering to us, His own
Presence with us, the Holy Ghost in us, and the Father around us, how amazed
we should be! We have lived in the "muddle" of things instead of in the middle
of things. Faith gets us into the middle, which is God and God's purpose.

(MORAL FOUND.)

SONG OF SOLOMON 7:1—8:14

1 HOW beautiful are your feet in sandals,
O prince's daughter!
The curves of your thighs *are* like jewels,
The work of the hands of a skillful workman.

2 Your navel *is* a rounded goblet;
It lacks no blended beverage.
Your waist *is* a heap of wheat
Set about with lilies.

3 Your two breasts *are* like two fawns,
Twins of a gazelle.

4 Your neck *is* like an ivory tower,
Your eyes *like* the pools in Heshbon
By the gate of Bath Rabbim.
Your nose *is* like the tower of Lebanon
Which looks toward Damascus.

5 Your head *crowns* you like *Mount Carmel,*
And the hair of your head *is* like purple;
A king *is* held captive by *your* tresses.

6 How fair and how pleasant you are,
O love, with your delights!

7 This stature of yours is like a palm tree,
And your breasts *like* its clusters.

8 I said, "I will go up to the palm tree,
I will take hold of its branches."
Let now your breasts be like clusters of the vine,
The fragrance of your breath like apples,

9 And the roof of your mouth like the best wine.

The wine goes *down* smoothly for my beloved,
Moving gently the lips of sleepers.

10 I *am* my beloved's,
And his desire *is* toward me.

---

*N*either natural love nor divine love will remain unless it is cultivated.   (BRILL. HERITAGE)

---

11 Come, my beloved,
Let us go forth to the field;
Let us lodge in the villages.

12 Let us get up early to the vineyards;
Let us see if the vine has budded,
Whether the grape blossoms are open,
And the pomegranates are in bloom.
There I will give you my love.

13 The mandrakes give off a fragrance,
And at our gates *are* pleasant *fruits,*
All manner, new and old,
Which I have laid up for you, my beloved.

8 OH, that you were like my brother,
Who nursed at my mother's breasts!
If I should find you outside,
I would kiss you;
I would not be despised.

2 I would lead you *and* bring you
Into the house of my mother,
She *who* used to instruct me.
I would cause you to drink of spiced wine,
Of the juice of my pomegranate.

3 His left hand *is* under my head,
And his right hand embraces me.

4 I charge you, O daughters of Jerusalem,
Do not stir up nor awaken love
Until it pleases.

5 Who *is* this coming up from the wilderness,
Leaning upon her beloved?

I awakened you under the apple tree.
There your mother brought you forth;
There she *who* bore you brought *you* forth.

6 Set me as a seal upon your heart,
As a seal upon your arm;
For love *is as* strong as death,
Jealousy *as* cruel as the grave;
Its flames *are* flames of fire,
A most vehement flame.

7 Many waters cannot quench love,
Nor can the floods drown it.
If a man would give for love
All the wealth of his house,
It would be utterly despised.

8 We have a little sister,
And she has no breasts.
What shall we do for our sister
In the day when she is spoken for?

9 If she *is* a wall,
We will build upon her
A battlement of silver;
And if she *is* a door,
We will enclose her
With boards of cedar.

10 I *am* a wall,
And my breasts like towers;
Then I became in his eyes
As one who found peace.

11 Solomon had a vineyard at Baal
Hamon;
He leased the vineyard to keepers;
Everyone was to bring for its fruit
A thousand silver coins.

12 My own vineyard *is* before me.
You, O Solomon, *may have* a
thousand,
And those who tend its fruit two
hundred.

13 You who dwell in the gardens,
The companions listen for your
voice—
Let me hear it!

14 Make haste, my beloved,
And be like a gazelle
Or a young stag
On the mountains of spices.

PSALM 104:31–35

31 MAY the glory of the LORD endure
forever;
May the LORD rejoice in His works.

32 He looks on the earth, and it trembles;
He touches the hills, and they smoke.

33 I will sing to the LORD as long as I
live;
I will sing praise to my God while I
have my being.

34 May my meditation be sweet to Him;
I will be glad in the LORD.

A life of intimacy with God is
characterized by joy.   (GLORIFY)

---

35 May sinners be consumed from the
earth,
And the wicked be no more.

Bless the LORD, O my soul!
Praise the LORD!

PROVERBS 24:21, 22

21 MY son, fear the LORD and the king;
Do not associate with those given to
change;

22 For their calamity will rise suddenly,
And who knows the ruin those two
can bring?

1 CORINTHIANS 14:1–20

PURSUE love, and desire spiritual *gifts,*
but especially that you may prophesy.
2 For he who speaks in a tongue does not
speak to men but to God, for no one understands *him;* however, in the spirit he speaks
mysteries. 3 But he who prophesies speaks
edification and exhortation and comfort to
men. 4 He who speaks in a tongue edifies
himself, but he who prophesies edifies the
church. 5 I wish you all spoke with tongues,
but even more that you prophesied; for
he who prophesies *is* greater than he who
speaks with tongues, unless indeed he interprets, that the church may receive edification.

6 But now, brethren, if I come to you
speaking with tongues, what shall I profit
you unless I speak to you either by revelation, by knowledge, by prophesying, or by
teaching? 7 Even things without life,
whether flute or harp, when they make a
sound, unless they make a distinction in
the sounds, how will it be known what is
piped or played? 8 For if the trumpet makes
an uncertain sound, who will prepare for
battle? 9 So likewise you, unless you utter
by the tongue words easy to understand,
how will it be known what is spoken? For
you will be speaking into the air. 10 There
are, it may be, so many kinds of languages
in the world, and none of them *is* without
significance. 11 Therefore, if I do not know
the meaning of the language, I shall be a
foreigner to him who speaks, and he who
speaks *will be* a foreigner to me. 12 Even
so you, since you are zealous for spiritual
gifts, let it be for the edification of the church
that you seek to excel.

13 Therefore let him who speaks in a
tongue pray that he may interpret. 14 For
if I pray in a tongue, my spirit prays, but
my understanding is unfruitful. 15 What is
the conclusion then? I will pray with the
spirit, and I will also pray with the understanding. I will sing with the spirit, and I
will also sing with the understanding.
16 Otherwise, if you bless with the spirit,
how will he who occupies the place of the
uninformed say "Amen" at your giving of
thanks, since he does not understand what
you say? 17 For you indeed give thanks well,
but the other is not edified.

18 I thank my God I speak with tongues
more than you all; 19 yet in the church I

would rather speak five words with my understanding, that I may teach others also, than ten thousand words in a tongue.

20 Brethren, do not be children in understanding; however, in malice be babes, but in understanding be mature.

◆◆◆

*Reading 248—*Pay Attention to the Fog
1 Corinthians 14:33

At times in spiritual life there is confusion, and the usual way out is to say there ought to be no confusion. Some of us are inclined to be fanatical, we won't pay any attention to things that are not black or white, right or wrong. There are very few things that are black or white, right or wrong, and until we recognize this we are apt to be insolent or indifferent toward anything in between. A fog is as real as clear sunshine; if we don't pay any attention to the fog, we shall come to disaster. There are things in the spiritual life which are confused, not because we have disobeyed, but owing to the very nature of things. The confusion arises from being unschooled spiritually.   (*PLACE HELP*)

It is not a question of right and wrong, but a question of God taking you by a way which in the meantime you do not understand, and it is only by going through the confusion that you will get at what God wants.   (*UTMOST*)

ISAIAH 1:1—2:22

THE vision of Isaiah the son of Amoz, which he saw concerning Judah and Jerusalem in the days of Uzziah, Jotham, Ahaz, *and* Hezekiah, kings of Judah.

2   Hear, O heavens, and give ear,
      O earth!
    For the LORD has spoken:
    "I have nourished and brought up
      children,
    And they have rebelled against Me;
3   The ox knows its owner
    And the donkey its master's crib;
    But Israel does not know,
    My people do not consider."

4   Alas, sinful nation,
    A people laden with iniquity,
    A brood of evildoers,
    Children who are corrupters!
    They have forsaken the LORD,
    They have provoked to anger
    The Holy One of Israel,
    They have turned away backward.

5   Why should you be stricken again?
    You will revolt more and more.
    The whole head is sick,
    And the whole heart faints.
6   From the sole of the foot even to
      the head,
    There is no soundness in it,
    But wounds and bruises and
      putrefying sores;
    They have not been closed or bound
      up,
    Or soothed with ointment.

7   Your country *is* desolate,
    Your cities *are* burned with fire;
    Strangers devour your land in your
      presence;
    And *it is* desolate, as overthrown by
      strangers.
8   So the daughter of Zion is left as a
      booth in a vineyard,
    As a hut in a garden of cucumbers,
    As a besieged city.
9   Unless the LORD of hosts
    Had left to us a very small remnant,
    We would have become like Sodom,
    We would have been made like
      Gomorrah.

10   Hear the word of the LORD,
    You rulers of Sodom;
    Give ear to the law of our God,
    You people of Gomorrah:

11 "To what purpose *is* the multitude of
     your sacrifices to Me?"
   Says the LORD.
   "I have had enough of burnt offerings
      of rams
   And the fat of fed cattle.
   I do not delight in the blood of bulls,
   Or of lambs or goats.

12 "When you come to appear before Me,
     Who has required this from your
       hand,
   To trample My courts?
13 Bring no more futile sacrifices;
   Incense is an abomination to Me.
   The New Moons, the Sabbaths, and
     the calling of assemblies—
   I cannot endure iniquity and the
     sacred meeting.
14 Your New Moons and your
     appointed feasts
   My soul hates;
   They are a trouble to Me,
   I am weary of bearing *them*.
15 When you spread out your hands,
   I will hide My eyes from you;
   Even though you make many prayers,
   I will not hear.
   Your hands are full of blood.

16 "Wash yourselves, make yourselves
     clean;
   Put away the evil of your doings from
     before My eyes.
   Cease to do evil,
17 Learn to do good;
   Seek justice,
   Rebuke the oppressor;
   Defend the fatherless,
   Plead for the widow.

18 "Come now, and let us reason
     together,"
   Says the LORD,
   "Though your sins are like scarlet,
   They shall be as white as snow;
   Though they are red like crimson,
   They shall be as wool.
19 If you are willing and obedient,
   You shall eat the good of the land;
20 But if you refuse and rebel,
   You shall be devoured by the sword";
   For the mouth of the LORD has
     spoken.

21 How the faithful city has become a
     harlot!
   It was full of justice;
   Righteousness lodged in it,
   But now murderers.
22 Your silver has become dross,

   Your wine mixed with water.
23 Your princes *are* rebellious,
   And companions of thieves;
   Everyone loves bribes,
   And follows after rewards.
   They do not defend the fatherless,
   Nor does the cause of the widow
     come before them.

24 Therefore the Lord says,
   The LORD of hosts, the Mighty One
     of Israel,
   "Ah, I will rid Myself of My
     adversaries,
   And take vengeance on My enemies.
25 I will turn My hand against you,
   And thoroughly purge away your
     dross,
   And take away all your alloy.
26 I will restore your judges as at the
     first,
   And your counselors as at the
     beginning.
   Afterward you shall be called the city
     of righteousness, the faithful city."

27 Zion shall be redeemed with justice,
   And her penitents with
     righteousness.
28 The destruction of transgressors and
     of sinners *shall be* together,
   And those who forsake the LORD
     shall be consumed.
29 For they shall be ashamed of the
     terebinth trees
   Which you have desired;
   And you shall be embarrassed
     because of the gardens
   Which you have chosen.
30 For you shall be as a terebinth whose
     leaf fades,
   And as a garden that has no water.
31 The strong shall be as tinder,
   And the work of it as a spark;
   Both will burn together,
   And no one shall quench *them*.

2 THE word that Isaiah the son of Amoz
  saw concerning Judah and Jerusalem.

2 Now it shall come to pass in the latter
     days
   That the mountain of the LORD's
     house
   Shall be established on the top of
     the mountains,
   And shall be exalted above the hills;
   And all nations shall flow to it.
3 Many people shall come and say,
   "Come, and let us go up to the
     mountain of the LORD,

To the house of the God of Jacob;
He will teach us His ways,
And we shall walk in His paths."
For out of Zion shall go forth the
   law,
And the word of the LORD from
   Jerusalem.
4 He shall judge between the nations,
And rebuke many people;
They shall beat their swords into
   plowshares,
And their spears into pruning hooks;
Nation shall not lift up sword against
   nation,
Neither shall they learn war anymore.
5 O house of Jacob, come and let us
   walk
In the light of the LORD.

---

*K*eep *continually coming to the
light, don't keep anything covered
up.* (PLACE HELP)

---

6 For You have forsaken Your people,
   the house of Jacob,
Because they are filled with eastern
   ways;
They *are* soothsayers like the
   Philistines,
And they are pleased with the
   children of foreigners.
7 Their land is also full of silver and
   gold,
And there is no end to their treasures;
Their land is also full of horses,
And there is no end to their chariots.
8 Their land is also full of idols;
They worship the work of their own
   hands,
That which their own fingers have
   made.
9 People bow down,
And each man humbles himself;
Therefore do not forgive them.
10 Enter into the rock, and hide in the
   dust,
From the terror of the LORD
And the glory of His majesty.
11 The lofty looks of man shall be
   humbled,
The haughtiness of men shall be
   bowed down,
And the LORD alone shall be exalted
   in that day.
12 For the day of the LORD of hosts
Shall come upon everything proud
   and lofty,

Upon everything lifted up—
And it shall be brought low—
13 Upon all the cedars of Lebanon *that
are* high and lifted up,
And upon all the oaks of Bashan;
14 Upon all the high mountains,
And upon all the hills *that are*
   lifted up;
15 Upon every high tower,
And upon every fortified wall;
16 Upon all the ships of Tarshish,
And upon all the beautiful sloops.
17 The loftiness of man shall be bowed
   down,
And the haughtiness of men shall be
   brought low;
The LORD alone will be exalted in
   that day,
18 But the idols He shall utterly abolish.

19 They shall go into the holes of the
   rocks,
And into the caves of the earth,
From the terror of the LORD
And the glory of His majesty,
When He arises to shake the earth
   mightily.

20 In that day a man will cast away his
   idols of silver
And his idols of gold,
Which they made, *each* for himself
   to worship,
To the moles and bats,
21 To go into the clefts of the rocks,
And into the crags of the rugged
   rocks,
From the terror of the LORD
And the glory of His majesty,
When He arises to shake the earth
   mightily.

22 Sever yourselves from such a man,
Whose breath *is* in his nostrils;
For of what account is he?

PSALM 105:1–6

1 OH, give thanks to the LORD!
Call upon His name;
Make known His deeds among the
   peoples!
2 Sing to Him, sing psalms to Him;
Talk of all His wondrous works!
3 Glory in His holy name;
Let the hearts of those rejoice who seek
   the LORD!
4 Seek the LORD and His strength;
Seek His face evermore!

5 Remember His marvelous works which
He has done,
His wonders, and the judgments of His
mouth,
6 O seed of Abraham His servant,
You children of Jacob, His chosen ones!

PROVERBS 24:23–25

23 THESE *things* also *belong* to the wise:

It is not good to show partiality in
judgment.
24 He who says to the wicked, "You *are*
righteous,"
Him the people will curse;
Nations will abhor him.
25 But those who rebuke *the wicked* will
have delight,
And a good blessing will come upon
them.

1 CORINTHIANS 14:21–40

IN the law it is written:

"With *men of* other tongues and other
lips
I will speak to this people;
And yet, for all that, they will not
hear Me,"

says the Lord. 22 Therefore tongues are for a sign, not
to those who believe but to unbelievers;
but prophesying is not for unbelievers but
for those who believe. 23 Therefore if the
whole church comes together in one place,
and all speak with tongues, and there come
in *those who are* uninformed or unbelievers,
will they not say that you are out of your
mind? 24 But if all prophesy, and an unbeliever or an uninformed person comes
in, he is convinced by all, he is convicted
by all. 25 And thus the secrets of his heart
are revealed; and so, falling down on *his*
face, he will worship God and report that
God is truly among you.

26 How is it then, brethren? Whenever
you come together, each of you has a psalm,
has a teaching, has a tongue, has a revelation, has an interpretation. Let all things
be done for edification. 27 If anyone speaks
in a tongue, *let there be* two or at the most
three, *each* in turn, and let one interpret.
28 But if there is no interpreter, let him
keep silent in church, and let him speak
to himself and to God. 29 Let two or three
prophets speak, and let the others judge.
30 But if *anything* is revealed to another who
sits by, let the first keep silent. 31 For you
can all prophesy one by one, that all may
learn and all may be encouraged. 32 And
the spirits of the prophets are subject to
the prophets. 33 For God is not *the author*
of confusion but of peace, as in all the
churches of the saints.

34 Let your women keep silent in the
churches, for they are not permitted to
speak; but *they are* to be submissive, as the
law also says. 35 And if they want to learn
something, let them ask their own husbands
at home; for it is shameful for women to
speak in church.

36 Or did the word of God come *originally*
from you? Or *was it* you only that it reached?
37 If anyone thinks himself to be a prophet
or spiritual, let him acknowledge that the
things which I write to you are the commandments of the Lord. 38 But if anyone
is ignorant, let him be ignorant.

39 Therefore, brethren, desire earnestly
to prophesy, and do not forbid to speak
with tongues. 40 Let all things be done de-
cently and in order.

◆◆◆◆

Reading 249—His Fulfilled Fitness in God
1 Corinthians 15:28

Redemption does not only mean personal salvation and the redemption
of our body; it means the absolute and complete redemption of the
whole material earth in every iota, and not only the earth, but the whole material
universe: "a new heaven and a new earth." It means that all relegated authority
shall pass, and God will be the absolute authority: "That God may be all in
all." There is a time coming, thank God, when everything shall be under the

direct rule of God in every detail. We look for a new heaven and a new earth, and then will the human race stand before God as Jesus Christ stood before Him when He was here. Jesus Christ, Son of God and Son of Man, is not a mere individual; He is the One who represents the whole human race. To see the human race as God intends it to be, look at the life of Jesus, and by the redemption the human race is to be brought there. When the human race is actually there, Jesus Christ as Son of Man ceases to be and becomes absolute deity again. The Son becomes subject to the Father, and God remains all in all. Our Lord's prayer is answered. "And now, O Father, glorify Me together with Yourself, with the glory which I had with You before the world was." That glory is to be in God.   (*GLORY*)

ISAIAH 3:1—4:6

1 FOR behold, the Lord, the LORD of hosts,
   Takes away from Jerusalem and from Judah
   The stock and the store,
   The whole supply of bread and the whole supply of water;
2 The mighty man and the man of war,
   The judge and the prophet,
   And the diviner and the elder;
3 The captain of fifty and the honorable man,
   The counselor and the skillful artisan,
   And the expert enchanter.

4 "I will give children *to be* their princes,
   And babes shall rule over them.
5 The people will be oppressed,
   Every one by another and every one by his neighbor;
   The child will be insolent toward the elder,
   And the base toward the honorable."

6 When a man takes hold of his brother
   In the house of his father, *saying*,
   "You have clothing;
   You be our ruler,
   And *let* these ruins *be* under your power,"
7 In that day he will protest, saying,
   "I cannot cure *your* ills,
   For in my house *is* neither food nor clothing;
   Do not make me a ruler of the people."

8 For Jerusalem stumbled,
   And Judah is fallen,
   Because their tongue and their doings
   Are against the LORD,
   To provoke the eyes of His glory.
9 The look on their countenance witnesses against them,

And they declare their sin as Sodom;
   They do not hide *it*.
   Woe to their soul!
   For they have brought evil upon themselves.

10 "Say to the righteous that *it shall be* well *with them*,
   For they shall eat the fruit of their doings.
11 Woe to the wicked! *It shall be* ill *with him*,
   For the reward of his hands shall be given him.
12 *As for* My people, children *are* their oppressors,
   And women rule over them.
   O My people! Those who lead you cause *you* to err,
   And destroy the way of your paths."

13 The LORD stands up to plead,
   And stands to judge the people.
14 The LORD will enter into judgment
   With the elders of His people
   And His princes:
   "For you have eaten up the vineyard;
   The plunder of the poor *is* in your houses.
15 What do you mean by crushing My people
   And grinding the faces of the poor?"
   Says the Lord GOD of hosts.

16 Moreover the LORD says:

   "Because the daughters of Zion are haughty,
   And walk with outstretched necks
   And wanton eyes,
   Walking and mincing *as* they go,
   Making a jingling with their feet,
17 Therefore the Lord will strike with a scab
   The crown of the head of the daughters of Zion,

And the LORD will uncover their secret parts."

18 In that day the Lord will take away the finery:
The jingling anklets, the scarves, and the crescents;
19 The pendants, the bracelets, and the veils;
20 The headdresses, the leg ornaments, and the headbands;
The perfume boxes, the charms,
21 and the rings;
The nose jewels,
22 the festal apparel, and the mantles;
The outer garments, the purses,
23 and the mirrors;
The fine linen, the turbans, and the robes.

24 And so it shall be:

Instead of a sweet smell there will be a stench;
Instead of a sash, a rope;
Instead of well-set hair, baldness;
Instead of a rich robe, a girding of sackcloth;
And branding instead of beauty.
25 Your men shall fall by the sword,
And your mighty in the war.

26 Her gates shall lament and mourn,
And she *being* desolate shall sit on the ground.

4 AND in that day seven women shall take hold of one man, saying,
"We will eat our own food and wear our own apparel;
Only let us be called by your name,
To take away our reproach."
2 In that day the Branch of the LORD shall be beautiful and glorious;
And the fruit of the earth *shall be* excellent and appealing
For those of Israel who have escaped.

3 And it shall come to pass that *he who is* left in Zion and remains in Jerusalem will be called holy—everyone who is recorded among the living in Jerusalem. 4 When the Lord has washed away the filth of the daughters of Zion, and purged the blood of Jerusalem from her midst, by the spirit of judgment and by the spirit of burning, 5 then the LORD will create above every dwelling place of Mount Zion, and above her assemblies, a cloud and smoke by day and the shining of a flaming fire by night. For over all the glory there *will*

be a covering. 6 And there will be a tabernacle for shade in the daytime from the heat, for a place of refuge, and for a shelter from storm and rain.

PSALM 105:7–22

7 HE *is* the LORD our God;
His judgments *are* in all the earth.
8 He remembers His covenant forever,
The word *which* He commanded, for a thousand generations,
9 *The covenant* which He made with Abraham,
And His oath to Isaac,
10 And confirmed it to Jacob for a statute,
To Israel *as* an everlasting covenant,
11 Saying, "To you I will give the land of Canaan
As the allotment of your inheritance,"
12 When they were few in number,
Indeed very few, and strangers in it.

13 When they went from one nation to another,
From *one* kingdom to another people,
14 He permitted no one to do them wrong;
Yes, He rebuked kings for their sakes,
15 *Saying*, "Do not touch My anointed ones,
And do My prophets no harm."

16 Moreover He called for a famine in the land;
He destroyed all the provision of bread.
17 He sent a man before them—
Joseph—*who* was sold as a slave.
18 They hurt his feet with fetters,
He was laid in irons.
19 Until the time that his word came to pass,
The word of the LORD tested him.
20 The king sent and released him,
The ruler of the people let him go free.
21 He made him lord of his house,
And ruler of all his possessions,
22 To bind his princes at his pleasure,
And teach his elders wisdom.

PROVERBS 24:26, 27

26 HE who gives a right answer kisses the lips.

27 Prepare your outside work,
Make it fit for yourself in the field;
And afterward build your house.

1 CORINTHIANS 15:1–28

MOREOVER, brethren, I declare to you the gospel which I preached to you, which also you received and in which you stand, 2 by which also you are saved, if you hold fast that word which I preached to you—unless you believed in vain.

3 For I delivered to you first of all that which I also received: that Christ died for our sins according to the Scriptures, 4 and that He was buried, and that He rose again the third day according to the Scriptures, 5 and that He was seen by Cephas, then by the twelve. 6 After that He was seen by over five hundred brethren at once, of whom the greater part remain to the present, but some have fallen asleep. 7 After that He was seen by James, then by all the apostles. 8 Then last of all He was seen by me also, as by one born out of due time.

9 For I am the least of the apostles, who am not worthy to be called an apostle, because I persecuted the church of God. 10 But by the grace of God I am what I am, and His grace toward me was not in vain; but I labored more abundantly than they all, yet not I, but the grace of God *which was* with me. 11 Therefore, whether *it was* I or they, so we preach and so you believed.

12 Now if Christ is preached that He has been raised from the dead, how do some among you say that there is no resurrection of the dead? 13 But if there is no resurrection of the dead, then Christ is not risen. 14 And if Christ is not risen, then our preaching *is* empty and your faith *is* also empty. 15 Yes, and we are found false wit-

There are only two Men in the Bible: Adam and Jesus Christ. (GLORY)

nesses of God, because we have testified of God that He raised up Christ, whom He did not raise up—if in fact the dead do not rise. 16 For if *the* dead do not rise, then Christ is not risen. 17 And if Christ is not risen, your faith *is* futile; you are still in your sins! 18 Then also those who have fallen asleep in Christ have perished. 19 If in this life only we have hope in Christ, we are of all men the most pitiable.

20 But now Christ is risen from the dead, *and* has become the firstfruits of those who have fallen asleep. 21 For since by man *came* death, by Man also *came* the resurrection of the dead. 22 For as in Adam all die, even so in Christ all shall be made alive. 23 But each one in his own order: Christ the firstfruits, afterward those *who are* Christ's at His coming. 24 Then *comes* the end, when He delivers the kingdom to God the Father, when He puts an end to all rule and all authority and power. 25 For He must reign till He has put all enemies under His feet. 26 The last enemy *that* will be destroyed *is* death. 27 For "He has put all things under His feet." But when He says "all things are put under *Him*," *it is* evident that He who put all things under Him is excepted. 28 Now when all things are made subject to Him, then the Son Himself will also be subject to Him who put all things under Him, that God may be all in all.

♦♦♦♦

Reading 250—The Last Adam's Gift
1 Corinthians 15:45

Jesus Christ came into the human race from the outside, and when we are born again, His life comes into us from the outside. Jesus Christ is the normal man, and in His relationship to God, to the Devil, to sin and to man we see the expression in human nature of what He calls "eternal life." We try to enter the life of Jesus in the wrong way. We do not enter into His life by imitation: we enter into it by its entering into us by means of His death. Jesus Christ gives us His life, namely, Holy Spirit. When we ask God for the Holy Spirit, we receive the very nature of God, *Holy* Spirit. We become regenerate, born from above, by the gift of life from the last Adam, then we have to live in obedience to that Spirit which has come into our spirit.

The records in the Gospels are given, not so much that we might understand the Person of our Lord from the natural standpoint, but that we might understand how to exhibit His life in us when we are born from above. We have to take our instructions for this from Jesus Christ. The danger is lest we praise God's salvation and sovereign grace while we refuse to manifest His salvation in our human nature.   (PSY. REDEMP.)

ISAIAH 5:1—6:13

1 NOW let me sing to my
      Well-beloved
   A song of my Beloved regarding
      His vineyard:

   My Well-beloved has a vineyard
   On a very fruitful hill.
2 He dug it up and cleared out its
      stones,
   And planted it with the choicest vine.
   He built a tower in its midst,
   And also made a winepress in it;
   So He expected *it* to bring forth
      good grapes,
   But it brought forth wild grapes.

3 "And now, O inhabitants of
      Jerusalem and men of Judah,
   Judge, please, between Me and My
      vineyard.
4 What more could have been done
      to My vineyard
   That I have not done in it?
   Why then, when I expected *it* to bring
      forth *good* grapes,
   Did it bring forth wild grapes?
5 And now, please let Me tell you what
      I will do to My vineyard:
   I will take away its hedge, and it shall
      be burned;
   And break down its wall, and it shall
      be trampled down.
6 I will lay it waste;
   It shall not be pruned or dug,
   But there shall come up briers and
      thorns.
   I will also command the clouds
   That they rain no rain on it."

7 For the vineyard of the LORD of hosts
      is the house of Israel,
   And the men of Judah are His
      pleasant plant.
   He looked for justice, but behold,
      oppression;
   For righteousness, but behold, a cry
      for help.

8 Woe to those who join house to
      house;

   They add field to field,
   Till *there is* no place
   Where they may dwell alone in the
      midst of the land!
9 In my hearing the LORD of hosts *said,*
   "Truly, many houses shall be desolate,
   Great and beautiful ones, without
      inhabitant.
10 For ten acres of vineyard shall yield
      one bath,
   And a homer of seed shall yield one
      ephah."

11 Woe to those who rise early in the
      morning,
   That they may follow intoxicating
      drink;
   Who continue until night, *till* wine
      inflames them!
12 The harp and the strings,
   The tambourine and flute,
   And wine are in their feasts;
   But they do not regard the work of
      the LORD,
   Nor consider the operation of His
      hands.

13 Therefore my people have gone into
      captivity,
   Because *they have* no knowledge;
   Their honorable men *are* famished,
   And their multitude dried up with
      thirst.
14 Therefore Sheol has enlarged itself
   And opened its mouth beyond
      measure;
   Their glory and their multitude and
      their pomp,
   And he who is jubilant, shall descend
      into it.
15 People shall be brought down,
   Each man shall be humbled,
   And the eyes of the lofty shall be
      humbled.
16 But the LORD of hosts shall be
      exalted in judgment,
   And God who is holy shall be
      hallowed in righteousness.
17 Then the lambs shall feed in their
      pasture,
   And in the waste places of the fat
      ones strangers shall eat.

18 Woe to those who draw iniquity with
cords of vanity,
And sin as if with a cart rope;
19 That say, "Let Him make speed *and*
hasten His work,
That we may see *it;*
And let the counsel of the Holy One
of Israel draw near and come,
That we may know *it.*"

20 Woe to those who call evil good, and
good evil;
Who put darkness for light, and light
for darkness;
Who put bitter for sweet, and sweet
for bitter!

I am not judged by the light I have,
but by the light I have refused to
accept.   (SHAD. AGONY)

---

21 Woe to *those who are* wise in their
own eyes,
And prudent in their own sight!

22 Woe to men mighty at drinking wine,
Woe to men valiant for mixing
intoxicating drink,
23 Who justify the wicked for a bribe,
And take away justice from the
righteous man!

24 Therefore, as the fire devours the
stubble,
And the flame consumes the chaff,
So their root will be as rottenness,
And their blossom will ascend like
dust;
Because they have rejected the law
of the LORD of hosts,
And despised the word of the Holy
One of Israel.
25 Therefore the anger of the LORD is
aroused against His people;
He has stretched out His hand
against them
And stricken them,
And the hills trembled.
Their carcasses *were* as refuse in the
midst of the streets.

For all this His anger is not turned
away,
But His hand *is* stretched out still.

26 He will lift up a banner to the nations
from afar,
And will whistle to them from the
end of the earth;

Surely they shall come with speed,
swiftly.
27 No one will be weary or stumble
among them,
No one will slumber or sleep;
Nor will the belt on their loins be
loosed,
Nor the strap of their sandals be
broken;
28 Whose arrows *are* sharp,
And all their bows bent;
Their horses' hooves will seem like
flint,
And their wheels like a whirlwind.
29 Their roaring *will be* like a lion,
They will roar like young lions;
Yes, they will roar
And lay hold of the prey;
They will carry *it* away safely,
And no one will deliver.
30 In that day they will roar against them
Like the roaring of the sea.
And if *one* looks to the land,
Behold, darkness *and* sorrow;
And the light is darkened by the
clouds.

6 IN the year that King Uzziah died, I
saw the Lord sitting on a throne, high
and lifted up, and the train of His *robe* filled
the temple. 2 Above it stood seraphim; each
one had six wings: with two he covered
his face, with two he covered his feet, and
with two he flew. 3 And one cried to another
and said:

"Holy, holy, holy *is* the LORD of
hosts;
The whole earth *is* full of His
glory!"

4 And the posts of the door were shaken
by the voice of him who cried out, and
the house was filled with smoke.
5 So I said:

"Woe *is* me, for I am undone!
Because I *am* a man of unclean lips,
And I dwell in the midst of a people
of unclean lips;
For my eyes have seen the King,
The LORD of hosts."

6 Then one of the seraphim flew to me,
having in his hand a live coal *which* he had
taken with the tongs from the altar.
7 And he touched my mouth *with it,* and
said:

"Behold, this has touched your lips;
Your iniquity is taken away,
And your sin purged."

8 Also I heard the voice of the Lord, saying:

"Whom shall I send,
And who will go for Us?"

Then I said, "Here *am* I! Send me."

Very few of us hear the call of God because we are not in the place to answer.   (SEND I YOU)

---

9 And He said, "Go, and tell this people:

'Keep on hearing, but do not understand;
Keep on seeing, but do not perceive.'

10 "Make the heart of this people dull,
And their ears heavy,
And shut their eyes;
Lest they see with their eyes,
And hear with their ears,
And understand with their heart,
And return and be healed."

11 Then I said, "Lord, how long?"
And He answered:

"Until the cities are laid waste and without inhabitant,
The houses are without a man,
The land is utterly desolate,
12 The LORD has removed men far away,
And the forsaken places *are* many in the midst of the land.
13 But yet a tenth *will be* in it,
And will return and be for consuming,
As a terebinth tree or as an oak,
Whose stump *remains* when it is cut down.
So the holy seed *shall be* its stump."

PSALM 105:23–36

23 ISRAEL also came into Egypt,
And Jacob dwelt in the land of Ham.
24 He increased His people greatly,
And made them stronger than their enemies.
25 He turned their heart to hate His people,
To deal craftily with His servants.

26 He sent Moses His servant,
And Aaron whom He had chosen.

27 They performed His signs among them,
And wonders in the land of Ham.
28 He sent darkness, and made *it* dark;
And they did not rebel against His word.
29 He turned their waters into blood,
And killed their fish.
30 Their land abounded with frogs,
Even in the chambers of their kings.
31 He spoke, and there came swarms of flies,
And lice in all their territory.
32 He gave them hail for rain,
And flaming fire in their land.
33 He struck their vines also, and their fig trees,
And splintered the trees of their territory.
34 He spoke, and locusts came,
Young locusts without number,
35 And ate up all the vegetation in their land,
And devoured the fruit of their ground.
36 He also destroyed all the firstborn in their land,
The first of all their strength.

PROVERBS 24:28, 29

28 DO not be a witness against your neighbor without cause,
For would you deceive with your lips?
29 Do not say, "I will do to him just as he has done to me;
I will render to the man according to his work."

1 CORINTHIANS 15:29–58

OTHERWISE, what will they do who are baptized for the dead, if the dead do not rise at all? Why then are they baptized for the dead? 30 And why do we stand in jeopardy every hour? 31 I affirm, by the boasting in you which I have in Christ Jesus our Lord, I die daily. 32 If, in the manner of men, I have fought with beasts at Ephesus, what advantage *is it* to me? If *the* dead do not rise, "Let us eat and drink, for tomorrow we die!"

33 Do not be deceived: "Evil company corrupts good habits." 34 Awake to righteousness, and do not sin; for some do not have the knowledge of God. I speak *this* to your shame.

35 But someone will say, "How are the dead raised up? And with what body do they come?" 36 Foolish one, what you sow

is not made alive unless it dies. 37 And what you sow, you do not sow that body that shall be, but mere grain—perhaps wheat or some other *grain*. 38 But God gives it a body as He pleases, and to each seed its own body.

39 All flesh *is* not the same flesh, but *there is* one *kind of* flesh of men, another flesh of animals, another of fish, *and* another of birds.

40 *There are* also celestial bodies and terrestrial bodies; but the glory of the celestial *is* one, and the *glory* of the terrestrial *is* another. 41 *There is* one glory of the sun, another glory of the moon, and another glory of the stars; for *one* star differs from *another* star in glory.

42 So also *is* the resurrection of the dead. *The body* is sown in corruption, it is raised in incorruption. 43 It is sown in dishonor, it is raised in glory. It is sown in weakness, it is raised in power. 44 It is sown a natural body, it is raised a spiritual body. There is a natural body, and there is a spiritual body. 45 And so it is written, "The first man Adam became a living being." The last Adam *became* a life-giving spirit.

46 However, the spiritual is not first, but the natural, and afterward the spiritual. 47 The first man *was* of the earth, *made* of dust; the second Man *is* the Lord from heaven. 48 As *was* the *man* of dust, so also

are those *who are made* of dust; and as *is* the heavenly *Man,* so also *are* those *who are* heavenly. 49 And as we have borne the image of the *man* of dust, we shall also bear the image of the heavenly *Man.*

50 Now this I say, brethren, that flesh and blood cannot inherit the kingdom of God; nor does corruption inherit incorruption. 51 Behold, I tell you a mystery: We shall not all sleep, but we shall all be changed— 52 in a moment, in the twinkling of an eye, at the last trumpet. For the trumpet will sound, and the dead will be raised incorruptible, and we shall be changed. 53 For this corruptible must put on incorruption, and this mortal *must* put on immortality. 54 So when this corruptible has put on incorruption, and this mortal has put on immortality, then shall be brought to pass the saying that is written: "Death is swallowed up in victory."

55 "O Death, where *is* your sting?
    O Hades, where *is* your victory?"

56 The sting of death *is* sin, and the strength of sin *is* the law. 57 But thanks *be* to God, who gives us the victory through our Lord Jesus Christ.

58 Therefore, my beloved brethren, be steadfast, immovable, always abounding in the work of the Lord, knowing that your labor is not in vain in the Lord.

◆◆◆◆

Reading 251—His Birth and Our New Birth
Isaiah 7:14

His Birth in History. "Therefore, also, that Holy One who is to be born will be called the Son of God." (Luke 1:35). Jesus Christ was born *into* this world, not *from* it. He did not evolve out of history; He came into history from the outside. Jesus Christ is not the best human being. He is a Being who cannot be accounted for by the human race at all. He is not man becoming God, but God Incarnate, God coming into human flesh, coming into it from outside. His life is the Highest and the Holiest entering in at the Lowliest door. Our Lord's birth was an advent.

His Birth in Me. "For whom I labor in birth again until Christ is formed in you" (Gal. 4:19). Just as our Lord came into human history from outside, so He must come into me from outside. Have I allowed my personal human life to become a "Bethlehem" for the Son of God? I cannot enter into the realm of the kingdom of God unless I am born from above by a birth totally unlike natural birth. "You must be born again." This is not a command, it is a foundation fact. The characteristic of the new birth is that I yield myself so completely to God that Christ is formed in me. Immediately Christ is formed in me, His nature begins to work through me.

God manifest in the flesh—that is what is made profoundly possible for you and me by the Redemption.   (UTMOST)

ISAIAH 7:1—8:22

NOW it came to pass in the days of Ahaz the son of Jotham, the son of Uzziah, king of Judah, *that* Rezin king of Syria and Pekah the son of Remaliah, king of Israel, went up to Jerusalem to *make* war against it, but could not prevail against it. 2 And it was told to the house of David, saying, "Syria's forces are deployed in Ephraim." So his heart and the heart of his people were moved as the trees of the woods are moved with the wind.

3 Then the LORD said to Isaiah, "Go out now to meet Ahaz, you and Shear-Jashub your son, at the end of the aqueduct from the upper pool, on the highway to the Fuller's Field, 4 and say to him: 'Take heed, and be quiet; do not fear or be fainthearted for these two stubs of smoking firebrands, for the fierce anger of Rezin and Syria, and the son of Remaliah. 5 Because Syria, Ephraim, and the son of Remaliah have plotted evil against you, saying, 6 "Let us go up against Judah and trouble it, and let us make a gap in its wall for ourselves, and set a king over them, the son of Tabel"— 7 thus says the Lord GOD:

"It shall not stand,
     Nor shall it come to pass.
8   For the head of Syria *is* Damascus,
     And the head of Damascus *is* Rezin.
     Within sixty-five years Ephraim will
          be broken,
     So that it will not *be* a people.
9   The head of Ephraim *is* Samaria,
     And the head of Samaria *is*
          Remaliah's son.
     If you will not believe,
     Surely you shall not be
          established." ' "

10 Moreover the LORD spoke again to Ahaz, saying, 11 "Ask a sign for yourself from the LORD your God; ask it either in the depth or in the height above."

12 But Ahaz said, "I will not ask, nor will I test the LORD!"

13 Then he said, "Hear now, O house of David! *Is it* a small thing for you to weary men, but will you weary my God also? 14 Therefore the Lord Himself will give you a sign: Behold, the virgin shall conceive and bear a Son, and shall call His name Immanuel. 15 Curds and honey He

---

*G*od Almighty became the
weakest thing in His own creation,
a Baby.   (PSY. REDEMP.)

---

shall eat, that He may know to refuse the evil and choose the good. 16 For before the Child shall know to refuse the evil and choose the good, the land that you dread will be forsaken by both her kings. 17 The LORD will bring the king of Assyria upon you and your people and your father's house—days that have not come since the day that Ephraim departed from Judah."

18   And it shall come to pass in that day
          That the LORD will whistle for the
               fly
          That *is* in the farthest part of the rivers
               of Egypt,
          And for the bee that *is* in the land
               of Assyria.
19   They will come, and all of them will
               rest
          In the desolate valleys and in the
               clefts of the rocks,
          And on all thorns and in all pastures.

20   In the same day the Lord will shave
               with a hired razor,
          With those from beyond the River,
               with the king of Assyria,
          The head and the hair of the legs,
          And will also remove the beard.

21   It shall be in that day
          That a man will keep alive a young
               cow and two sheep;
22   So it shall be, from the abundance
               of milk they give,
          That he will eat curds;
          For curds and honey everyone will
               eat who is left in the land.

23   It shall happen in that day,
          That wherever there could be a
               thousand vines

Worth a thousand *shekels* of silver,
It will be for briers and thorns.
24 With arrows and bows men will come
there,
Because all the land will become
briers and thorns.

25 And to any hill which could be dug
with the hoe,
You will not go there for fear of briers
and thorns;
But it will become a range for oxen
And a place for sheep to roam.

8 MOREOVER the Lord said to me,
"Take a large scroll, and write on it
with a man's pen concerning Maher-Shalal-
Hash-Baz. 2 And I will take for Myself
faithful witnesses to record, Uriah the priest
and Zechariah the son of Jeberechiah."

---

*The faithful few . . . are the
disguised citizens of the kingdom of
God.* (GOD'S WORKMANSHIP)

---

3 Then I went to the prophetess, and she
conceived and bore a son. Then the LORD
said to me, "Call his name Maher-Shalal-
Hash-Baz; 4 for before the child shall have
knowledge to cry 'My father' and 'My
mother,' the riches of Damascus and the
spoil of Samaria will be taken away before
the king of Assyria."

5 The LORD also spoke to me again,
saying:

6 "Inasmuch as these people refused
The waters of Shiloah that flow
softly,
And rejoice in Rezin and in
Remaliah's son;
7 Now therefore, behold, the Lord
brings up over them
The waters of the River, strong and
mighty—
The king of Assyria and all his glory;
He will go up over all his channels
And go over all his banks.
8 He will pass through Judah,
He will overflow and pass over,
He will reach up to the neck;
And the stretching out of his wings
Will fill the breadth of Your land,
O Immanuel.

9 "Be shattered, O you peoples, and be
broken in pieces!
Give ear, all you from far countries.

Gird yourselves, but be broken in
pieces;
Gird yourselves, but be broken in
pieces.
10 Take counsel together, but it will
come to nothing;
Speak the word, but it will not stand,
For God *is* with us."

11 For the LORD spoke thus to me with
a strong hand, and instructed me that I
should not walk in the way of this people,
saying:

12 "Do not say, 'A conspiracy,'
Concerning all that this people call
a conspiracy,
Nor be afraid of their threats, nor
be troubled.
13 The LORD of hosts, Him you shall
hallow;
Let Him *be* your fear,
And *let* Him *be* your dread.
14 He will be as a sanctuary,
But a stone of stumbling and a rock
of offense
To both the houses of Israel,
As a trap and a snare to the
inhabitants of Jerusalem.
15 And many among them shall
stumble;
They shall fall and be broken,
Be snared and taken."

16 Bind up the testimony,
Seal the law among my disciples.
17 And I will wait on the LORD,
Who hides His face from the house
of Jacob;
And I will hope in Him.
18 Here am I and the children whom
the LORD has given me!
We are for signs and wonders in Israel
From the LORD of hosts,
Who dwells in Mount Zion.

19 And when they say to you, "Seek those
who are mediums and wizards, who whisper and mutter," should not a people seek
their God? *Should they seek* the dead on behalf of the living? 20 To the law and to
the testimony! If they do not speak according to this word, *it is* because *there is* no
light in them.
21 They will pass through it hard-pressed
and hungry; and it shall happen, when they
are hungry, that they will be enraged and
curse their king and their God, and look
upward. 22 Then they will look to the earth,
and see trouble and darkness, gloom of anguish; and *they will be* driven into darkness.

PSALM 105:37–45

37 HE also brought them out with silver
and gold,
And *there was* none feeble among His
tribes.

38 Egypt was glad when they departed,
For the fear of them had fallen upon
them.

39 He spread a cloud for a covering,
And fire to give light in the night.

40 *The people* asked, and He brought quail,
And satisfied them with the bread of
heaven.

41 He opened the rock, and water gushed
out;
It ran in the dry places *like* a river.

42 For He remembered His holy promise,
And Abraham His servant.

43 He brought out His people with joy,
His chosen ones with gladness.

44 He gave them the lands of the Gentiles,
And they inherited the labor of the
nations,

45 That they might observe His statutes
And keep His laws.

Praise the LORD!

PROVERBS 24:30–34

30 I went by the field of the lazy *man*,
And by the vineyard of the man devoid
of understanding;

31 And there it was, all overgrown with
thorns;
Its surface was covered with nettles;
Its stone wall was broken down.

32 When I saw *it*, I considered *it* well;
I looked on *it and* received instruction:

33 A little sleep, a little slumber,
A little folding of the hands to rest;

34 So shall your poverty come *like* a
prowler,
And your need like an armed man.

1 CORINTHIANS 16:1–24

NOW concerning the collection for the
saints, as I have given orders to the churches
of Galatia, so you must do also: 2 On the
first *day* of the week let each one of you
lay something aside, storing up as he may
prosper, that there be no collections when
I come. 3 And when I come, whomever
you approve by *your* letters I will send to
bear your gift to Jerusalem. 4 But if it
is fitting that I go also, they will go with
me.

5 Now I will come to you when I pass
through Macedonia (for I am passing
through Macedonia). 6 And it may be that
I will remain, or even spend the winter with
you, that you may send me on my journey,
wherever I go. 7 For I do not wish to see
you now on the way; but I hope to stay a
while with you, if the Lord permits.

8 But I will tarry in Ephesus until Pentecost. 9 For a great and effective door has
opened to me, and *there are* many adversaries.

10 And if Timothy comes, see that he may
be with you without fear; for he does the
work of the Lord, as I also *do*. 11 Therefore
let no one despise him. But send him on
his journey in peace, that he may come to
me; for I am waiting for him with the
brethren.

12 Now concerning *our* brother Apollos,
I strongly urged him to come to you with
the brethren, but he was quite unwilling
to come at this time; however, he will come
when he has a convenient time.

13 Watch, stand fast in the faith, be brave,
be strong. 14 Let all *that* you *do* be done
with love.

15 I urge you, brethren—you know the
household of Stephanas, that it is the firstfruits of Achaia, and *that* they have devoted
themselves to the ministry of the saints—
16 that you also submit to such, and to
everyone who works and labors with *us*.

17 I am glad about the coming of Stephanas, Fortunatus, and Achaicus, for what
was lacking on your part they supplied.
18 For they refreshed my spirit and yours.
Therefore acknowledge such men.

19 The churches of Asia greet you. Aquila
and Priscilla greet you heartily in the Lord,
with the church that is in their house.
20 All the brethren greet you.

Greet one another with a holy kiss.

21 The salutation with my own hand—
Paul's.

22 If anyone does not love the Lord Jesus
Christ, let him be accursed. O Lord, come!

23 The grace of our Lord Jesus Christ
be with you. 24 My love *be* with you all in
Christ Jesus. Amen.

Reading 252—Disasters of Fellowship
2 Corinthians 1:8

There are disasters to be faced by the one who is in real fellowship with the Lord Jesus Christ. God has never promised to keep us immune from trouble; He says, "I *will be* with him in trouble," which is a very different thing. Paul was "an apostle of Jesus Christ by the will of God," and it is this fact that accounts for the crushing criticism and the spiteful treatment to which he was subjected by those who could not discern on what authority he based his apostleship. Paul was a Pharisee of the Pharisees, he stood in the fore rank of learning until Jesus appeared to him, staggered him, blinded him, extinguished all his personal aims, and sent him out to be an apostle to the Gentiles—"I have chosen him." That was the ground Paul stood on, and that only—he was an apostle "by the will of God" (see Gal. 1:15, 16).

If you are experiencing the disasters of fellowship, don't get into despair, remain unswervingly and unhesitatingly faithful to the Lord Jesus Christ and refuse to compromise for one second. Don't say "it can't be done" because you see a thing is going to crush your physical life. Calculate on the disaster of fellowship, because through it God is going to bring you into fellowship with His Son.   (*PLACE HELP*)

ISAIAH 9:1—10:34

1 NEVERTHELESS the gloom *will*
  not *be* upon her who *is* distressed,
As when at first He lightly esteemed
The land of Zebulun and the land
  of Naphtali,
And afterward more heavily
  oppressed *her,*
By the way of the sea, beyond the
  Jordan,
In Galilee of the Gentiles.
2 The people who walked in darkness
Have seen a great light;
Those who dwelt in the land of the
  shadow of death,
Upon them a light has shined.

3 You have multiplied the nation
And increased its joy;
They rejoice before You
According to the joy of harvest,
As *men* rejoice when they divide the
  spoil.
4 For You have broken the yoke of
  his burden
And the staff of his shoulder,
The rod of his oppressor,
As in the day of Midian.
5 For every warrior's sandal from the
  noisy battle,
And garments rolled in blood,
Will be used for burning *and* fuel
  of fire.

6 For unto us a Child is born,
Unto us a Son is given;
And the government will be upon
  His shoulder.
And His name will be called
Wonderful, Counselor, Mighty
  God,
Everlasting Father, Prince of Peace.

The secret of the Christian is that he knows the absolute deity of the Lord Jesus Christ.   (GOOD)

---

7 Of the increase of *His* government
  and peace
There will be no end,
Upon the throne of David and over
  His kingdom,
To order it and establish it with
  judgment and justice
From that time forward, even
  forever.
The zeal of the LORD of hosts will
  perform this.

8 The Lord sent a word against Jacob,
And it has fallen on Israel.
9 All the people will know—
Ephraim and the inhabitant of
  Samaria—

Who say in pride and arrogance of
   heart:
10 "The bricks have fallen down,
   But we will rebuild with hewn stones;
   The sycamores are cut down,
   But we will replace *them* with cedars."
11 Therefore the Lord shall set up
   The adversaries of Rezin against him,
   And spur his enemies on,
12 The Syrians before and the Philistines
   behind;
   And they shall devour Israel with an
   open mouth.

For all this His anger is not turned
   away,
But His hand *is* stretched out still.

13 For the people do not turn to Him
   who strikes them,
   Nor do they seek the Lord of hosts.
14 Therefore the Lord will cut off head
   and tail from Israel,
   Palm branch and bulrush in one day.
15 The elder and honorable, he *is* the
   head;
   The prophet who teaches lies, he *is*
   the tail.
16 For the leaders of this people cause
   them to err,
   And *those who are* led by them are
   destroyed.
17 Therefore the Lord will have no joy
   in their young men,
   Nor have mercy on their fatherless
   and widows;
   For everyone *is* a hypocrite and an
   evildoer,
   And every mouth speaks folly.

For all this His anger is not turned
   away,
But His hand *is* stretched out still.

18 For wickedness burns as the fire;
   It shall devour the briers and thorns,
   And kindle in the thickets of the
   forest;
   They shall mount up *like* rising
   smoke.
19 Through the wrath of the Lord of
   hosts
   The land is burned up,
   And the people shall be as fuel for
   the fire;
   No man shall spare his brother.
20 And he shall snatch on the right hand
   And be hungry;
   He shall devour on the left hand
   And not be satisfied;

Every man shall eat the flesh of his
   own arm.
21 Manasseh *shall devour* Ephraim, and
   Ephraim Manasseh;
   Together they *shall be* against Judah.

For all this His anger is not turned
   away,
But His hand *is* stretched out still.

10 "WOE to those who decree
       unrighteous decrees,
   Who write misfortune,
   Which they have prescribed
2 To rob the needy of justice,
   And to take what is right from the
   poor of My people,
   That widows may be their prey,
   And *that* they may rob the fatherless.
3 What will you do in the day of
   punishment,
   And in the desolation *which* will
   come from afar?
   To whom will you flee for help?
   And where will you leave your glory?
4 Without Me they shall bow down
   among the prisoners,
   And they shall fall among the slain."

For all this His anger is not turned
   away,
But His hand *is* stretched out still.

5 "Woe to Assyria, the rod of My anger
   And the staff in whose hand is My
   indignation.
6 I will send him against an ungodly
   nation,
   And against the people of My wrath
   I will give him charge,
   To seize the spoil, to take the prey,
   And to tread them down like the mire
   of the streets.
7 Yet he does not mean so,
   Nor does his heart think so;
   But *it is* in his heart to destroy,
   And cut off not a few nations.
8 For he says,
   'Are not my princes altogether kings?
9 Is not Calno like Carchemish?
   Is not Hamath like Arpad?
   Is not Samaria like Damascus?
10 As my hand has found the kingdoms
   of the idols,
   Whose carved images excelled those
   of Jerusalem and Samaria,
11 As I have done to Samaria and her
   idols,
   Shall I not do also to Jerusalem and
   her idols?' "

12 Therefore it shall come to pass, when the Lord has performed all His work on Mount Zion and on Jerusalem, *that He will say,* "I will punish the fruit of the arrogant heart of the king of Assyria, and the glory of his haughty looks."

13 For he says:

> "By the strength of my hand I have done *it,*
> And by my wisdom, for I am prudent;
> Also I have removed the boundaries of the people,
> And have robbed their treasuries;
> So I have put down the inhabitants like a valiant *man.*
>
> 14 My hand has found like a nest the riches of the people,
> And as one gathers eggs *that are* left,
> I have gathered all the earth;
> And there was no one who moved *his* wing,
> Nor opened *his* mouth with even a peep."

15 Shall the ax boast itself against him who chops with it?
Or shall the saw exalt itself against him who saws with it?
As if a rod could wield *itself* against those who lift it up,
Or as if a staff could lift up, *as if it were* not wood!

16 Therefore the Lord, the Lord of hosts,
Will send leanness among his fat ones;
And under his glory
He will kindle a burning
Like the burning of a fire.

17 So the Light of Israel will be for a fire,
And his Holy One for a flame;
It will burn and devour
His thorns and his briers in one day.

18 And it will consume the glory of his forest and of his fruitful field,
Both soul and body;
And they will be as when a sick man wastes away.

19 Then the rest of the trees of his forest
Will be so few in number
That a child may write them.

20 And it shall come to pass in that day
That the remnant of Israel,
And such as have escaped of the house of Jacob,
Will never again depend on him who defeated them,

But will depend on the LORD, the Holy One of Israel, in truth.

21 The remnant will return, the remnant of Jacob,
To the Mighty God.

22 For though your people, O Israel, be as the sand of the sea,
A remnant of them will return;
The destruction decreed shall overflow with righteousness.

23 For the Lord GOD of hosts
Will make a determined end
In the midst of all the land.

24 Therefore thus says the Lord GOD of hosts: "O My people, who dwell in Zion, do not be afraid of the Assyrian. He shall strike you with a rod and lift up his staff against you, in the manner of Egypt. 25 For yet a very little while and the indignation will cease, as will My anger in their destruction." 26 And the LORD of hosts will stir up a scourge for him like the slaughter of Midian at the rock of Oreb; *as* His rod was on the sea, so will He lift it up in the manner of Egypt.

27 It shall come to pass in that day
That his burden will be taken away from your shoulder,
And his yoke from your neck,
And the yoke will be destroyed because of the anointing oil.

28 He has come to Aiath,
He has passed Migron;
At Michmash he has attended to his equipment.

29 They have gone along the ridge,
They have taken up lodging at Geba.
Ramah is afraid,
Gibeah of Saul has fled.

30 Lift up your voice,
O daughter of Gallim!
Cause it to be heard as far as Laish—
O poor Anathoth!

31 Madmenah has fled,
The inhabitants of Gebim seek refuge.

32 As yet he will remain at Nob that day;
He will shake his fist at the mount of the daughter of Zion,
The hill of Jerusalem.

33 Behold, the Lord,
The LORD of hosts,
Will lop off the bough with terror;
Those of high stature *will be* hewn down,
And the haughty will be humbled.

34 He will cut down the thickets of the
forest with iron,
And Lebanon will fall by the Mighty
One.

PSALM 106:1–5

1 PRAISE the Lord!

Oh, give thanks to the Lord, for *He
is* good!
For His mercy *endures* forever.

2 Who can utter the mighty acts of the
Lord?
Who can declare all His praise?
3 Blessed *are* those who keep justice,
And he who does righteousness at all
times!

4 Remember me, O Lord, with the favor
You have toward Your people.
Oh, visit me with Your salvation,
5 That I may see the benefit of Your
chosen ones,
That I may rejoice in the gladness of
Your nation,
That I may glory with Your inheritance.

PROVERBS 25:1, 2

THESE also *are* proverbs of Solomon which the men of Hezekiah king of
Judah copied:

2 *It is* the glory of God to conceal a
matter,
But the glory of kings *is* to search out
a matter.

2 CORINTHIANS 1:1–24

PAUL, an apostle of Jesus Christ by the
will of God, and Timothy *our* brother,

To the church of God which is at Corinth,
with all the saints who are in all Achaia:

2 Grace to you and peace from God our
Father and the Lord Jesus Christ.

---

*I have to see that I allow the peace
of God to regulate all that
I do.*   (Good)

---

3 Blessed *be* the God and Father of our
Lord Jesus Christ, the Father of mercies

and God of all comfort, 4 who comforts
us in all our tribulation, that we may be
able to comfort those who are in any trouble, with the comfort with which we ourselves are comforted by God. 5 For as the
sufferings of Christ abound in us, so our
consolation also abounds through Christ.
6 Now if we are afflicted, *it is* for your consolation and salvation, which is effective
for enduring the same sufferings which we
also suffer. Or if we are comforted, *it is* for
your consolation and salvation. 7 And our
hope for you *is* steadfast, because we know
that as you are partakers of the sufferings, so also *you will partake* of the consolation.

8 For we do not want you to be ignorant,
brethren, of our trouble which came to us
in Asia: that we were burdened beyond
measure, above strength, so that we despaired even of life. 9 Yes, we had the sentence of death in ourselves, that we should
not trust in ourselves but in God who raises
the dead, 10 who delivered us from so great
a death, and does deliver us; in whom we
trust that He will still deliver *us,* 11 you
also helping together in prayer for us, that
thanks may be given by many persons on
our behalf for the gift *granted* to us through
many.

12 For our boasting is this: the testimony
of our conscience that we conducted ourselves in the world in simplicity and godly
sincerity, not with fleshly wisdom but by
the grace of God, and more abundantly
toward you. 13 For we are not writing any
other things to you than what you read
or understand. Now I trust you will understand, even to the end 14 (as also you have
understood us in part), that we are your
boast as you also *are* ours, in the day of
the Lord Jesus.

15 And in this confidence I intended to
come to you before, that you might have
a second benefit— 16 to pass by way of you
to Macedonia, to come again from Macedonia to you, and be helped by you on my
way to Judea. 17 Therefore, when I was
planning this, did I do it lightly? Or the
things I plan, do I plan according to the
flesh, that with me there should be Yes,
Yes, and No, No? 18 But *as* God *is* faithful,
our word to you was not Yes and No.
19 For the Son of God, Jesus Christ, who
was preached among you by us—by me,
Silvanus, and Timothy—was not Yes and
No, but in Him was Yes. 20 For all the
promises of God in Him *are* Yes, and in
Him Amen, to the glory of God through
us. 21 Now He who establishes us with you
in Christ and has anointed us *is* God,

22 who also has sealed us and given us the Spirit in our hearts as a guarantee.

23 Moreover I call God as witness against my soul, that to spare you I came no more to Corinth. 24 Not that we have dominion over your faith, but are fellow workers for your joy; for by faith you stand.

◆◆◆◆

*Reading 253—*The Viewpoint
2 Corinthians 2:14

The viewpoint of a worker for God must not be as near the highest as he can get, it must be *the* highest. Be careful to maintain strenuously God's point of view, it has to be done every day, bit by bit; don't think on the finite. No outside power can touch the viewpoint.

The viewpoint to maintain is that we are here for one purpose only, namely, to be captives in the train of Christ's triumphs. We are not in God's showroom, we are here to exhibit one thing—the absolute captivity of our lives to Jesus Christ. How small the other points of view are—I am standing alone battling for Jesus; I have to maintain the cause of Christ and hold this fort for Him. Paul says—I am in the train of a conqueror, and it does not matter what the difficulties are, I am always led in triumph. Is this idea being worked out practically in us? Paul's secret joy was that God took him, a red-handed rebel against Jesus Christ, and made him a captive, and now that is all he is here for. Paul's joy was to be a captive of the Lord, he had no other interest in heaven or in earth. It is a shameful thing for a Christian to talk about getting the victory. The Victor ought to have got us so completely that it is His victory all the time, and we are more than conquerors through Him.   (*Utmost*)

ISAIAH 11:1—12:6

1 THERE shall come forth a Rod from the stem of Jesse,
And a Branch shall grow out of his roots.

2 The Spirit of the Lord shall rest upon Him,
The Spirit of wisdom and understanding,
The Spirit of counsel and might,
The Spirit of knowledge and of the fear of the Lord.

3 His delight *is* in the fear of the Lord,
And He shall not judge by the sight of His eyes,
Nor decide by the hearing of His ears;

4 But with righteousness He shall judge the poor,
And decide with equity for the meek of the earth;
He shall strike the earth with the rod of His mouth,
And with the breath of His lips He shall slay the wicked.

5 Righteousness shall be the belt of His loins,
And faithfulness the belt of His waist.

6 "The wolf also shall dwell with the lamb,
The leopard shall lie down with the young goat,
The calf and the young lion and the fatling together;
And a little child shall lead them.

7 The cow and the bear shall graze;
Their young ones shall lie down together;
And the lion shall eat straw like the ox.

8 The nursing child shall play by the cobra's hole,

And the weaned child shall put his
    hand in the viper's den.
9 They shall not hurt nor destroy in
    all My holy mountain,
    For the earth shall be full of the
    knowledge of the LORD
    As the waters cover the sea.

10 "And in that day there shall be a
    Root of Jesse,
    Who shall stand as a banner to the
    people;
    For the Gentiles shall seek Him,
    And His resting place shall be
    glorious."

11 It shall come to pass in that day
    That the Lord shall set His hand
    again the second time
    To recover the remnant of His
    people who are left,
    From Assyria and Egypt,
    From Pathros and Cush,
    From Elam and Shinar,
    From Hamath and the islands of the
    sea.

12 He will set up a banner for the
    nations,
    And will assemble the outcasts of
    Israel,
    And gather together the dispersed of
    Judah
    From the four corners of the earth.
13 Also the envy of Ephraim shall
    depart,
    And the adversaries of Judah shall
    be cut off;
    Ephraim shall not envy Judah,
    And Judah shall not harass Ephraim.
14 But they shall fly down upon the
    shoulder of the Philistines toward
    the west;
    Together they shall plunder the
    people of the East;
    They shall lay their hand on Edom
    and Moab;
    And the people of Ammon shall obey
    them.
15 The LORD will utterly destroy the
    tongue of the Sea of Egypt;
    With His mighty wind He will shake
    His fist over the River,
    And strike it in the seven streams,
    And make *men* cross over dryshod.
16 There will be a highway for the
    remnant of His people
    Who will be left from Assyria,
    As it was for Israel
    In the day that he came up from the
    land of Egypt.

12 AND in that day you will say:

    "O LORD, I will praise You;
    Though You were angry with me,
    Your anger is turned away, and You
    comfort me.
2 Behold, God *is* my salvation,
    I will trust and not be afraid;
    'For YAH, the LORD, *is* my strength
    and song;
    He also has become my salvation.'"

3 Therefore with joy you will draw
    water
    From the wells of salvation.

---

*The joy of the Lord takes us into the
consciousness of God.*   (PSY. REDEMP.)

---

4 And in that day you will say:

    "Praise the LORD, call upon His name;
    Declare His deeds among the
    peoples,
    Make mention that His name is
    exalted.
5 Sing to the LORD,
    For He has done excellent things;
    This *is* known in all the earth.
6 Cry out and shout, O inhabitant of
    Zion,
    For great *is* the Holy One of Israel
    in your midst!"

PSALM 106:6–18

6 WE have sinned with our fathers,
    We have committed iniquity,
    We have done wickedly.
7 Our fathers in Egypt did not
    understand Your wonders;
    They did not remember the multitude
    of Your mercies,
    But rebelled by the sea—the Red Sea.

8 Nevertheless He saved them for His
    name's sake,
    That He might make His mighty power
    known.
9 He rebuked the Red Sea also, and it
    dried up;
    So He led them through the depths,
    As through the wilderness.
10 He saved them from the hand of him
    who hated *them,*
    And redeemed them from the hand of
    the enemy.
11 The waters covered their enemies;

There was not one of them left.

12 Then they believed His words;
They sang His praise.

13 They soon forgot His works;
They did not wait for His counsel,

14 But lusted exceedingly in the
wilderness,
And tested God in the desert.

15 And He gave them their request,
But sent leanness into their soul.

16 When they envied Moses in the camp,
And Aaron the saint of the LORD,

17 The earth opened up and swallowed
Dathan,
And covered the faction of Abiram.

18 A fire was kindled in their company;
The flame burned up the wicked.

PROVERBS 25:3–5

3 *AS* the heavens for height and the earth
for depth,
So the heart of kings *is* unsearchable.

4 Take away the dross from silver,
And it will go to the silversmith *for*
jewelry.

5 Take away the wicked from before the
king,
And his throne will be established in
righteousness.

2 CORINTHIANS 2:1–17

BUT I determined this within myself, that
I would not come again to you in sorrow.
2 For if I make you sorrowful, then who
is he who makes me glad but the one who
is made sorrowful by me?

3 And I wrote this very thing to you,
lest, when I came, I should have sorrow
over those from whom I ought to have
joy, having confidence in you all that my
joy is *the joy* of you all. 4 For out of much

affliction and anguish of heart I wrote to
you, with many tears, not that you should
be grieved, but that you might know the
love which I have so abundantly for you.

5 But if anyone has caused grief, he has
not grieved me, but all of you to some extent—not to be too severe. 6 This punishment which *was inflicted* by the majority *is*
sufficient for such a man, 7 so that, on the
contrary, you *ought* rather to forgive and
comfort *him,* lest perhaps such a one be
swallowed up with too much sorrow.
8 Therefore I urge you to reaffirm *your* love
to him. 9 For to this end I also wrote, that
I might put you to the test, whether you
are obedient in all things. 10 Now whom
you forgive anything, I also *forgive.* For if
indeed I have forgiven anything, I have forgiven that one for your sakes in the presence of Christ, 11 lest Satan should take advantage of us; for we are not ignorant of
his devices.

12 Furthermore, when I came to Troas
to *preach* Christ's gospel, and a door was
opened to me by the Lord, 13 I had no
rest in my spirit, because I did not find
Titus my brother; but taking my leave of
them, I departed for Macedonia.

14 Now thanks *be* to God who always
leads us in triumph in Christ, and through
us diffuses the fragrance of His knowledge
in every place. 15 For we are to God the
fragrance of Christ among those who are
being saved and among those who are perishing. 16 To the one *we are* the aroma of
death *leading* to death, and to the other
the aroma of life *leading* to life. And who
is sufficient for these things? 17 For we are

---

*The natural man does not want to be
born again.* (PSY. REDEMP.)

---

not, as so many, peddling the word of God;
but as of sincerity, but as from God, we
speak in the sight of God in Christ.

◆◆◆◆

*Reading 254—*Epistles and Experts

2 Corinthians 3:2

An "epistle of Christ" means a reincarnation of Jesus. Thank God for
experiences, for the power to be enchanted, but this is the thing that
tells—"Christ in you." I may be able to expound the Word of God, I may be
an expert in a great many things, but unless my experience shows in expression

a strong family likeness to Jesus, it is making me spiritually inefficient; I may be enchanted with the truth, but unless my enchantment is transformed into the energy which bears the mark of the disposition of Jesus, it is making for spiritual inefficiency. I may be expert in the knowledge of Scripture and expert in Christian work, but if all this is not turning me into an epistle in which men can read "Jesus," it is making for spiritual inefficiency. Is the expression in my life more and more the expression of the indwelling Holy Spirit? Is my energy the energy that comes direct from my risen Lord? Is my life an epistle that spells only one thing—God? Is the dominating interest in my life God? Have I any other dominating interest? If I have, then none of my energy or expert knowledge is telling in the tiniest degree for Jesus.   (*Place Help*)

ISAIAH 13:1—14:32

THE burden against Babylon which Isaiah the son of Amoz saw.

2 "Lift up a banner on the high mountain,
   Raise your voice to them;
   Wave your hand, that they may enter the gates of the nobles.
3 I have commanded My sanctified ones;
   I have also called My mighty ones for My anger—
   Those who rejoice in My exaltation."

4 The noise of a multitude in the mountains,
   Like that of many people!
   A tumultuous noise of the kingdoms of nations gathered together!
   The LORD of hosts musters The army for battle.
5 They come from a far country,
   From the end of heaven—
   The LORD and His weapons of indignation,
   To destroy the whole land.

6 Wail, for the day of the LORD *is* at hand!
   It will come as destruction from the Almighty.
7 Therefore all hands will be limp,
   Every man's heart will melt,
8 And they will be afraid.
   Pangs and sorrows will take hold of *them;*
   They will be in pain as a woman in childbirth;
   They will be amazed at one another;
   Their faces *will be like* flames.

9 Behold, the day of the LORD comes,
   Cruel, with both wrath and fierce anger,
   To lay the land desolate;
   And He will destroy its sinners from it.
10 For the stars of heaven and their constellations
    Will not give their light;
    The sun will be darkened in its going forth,
    And the moon will not cause its light to shine.

11 "I will punish the world for *its* evil,
    And the wicked for their iniquity;
    I will halt the arrogance of the proud,
    And will lay low the haughtiness of the terrible.
12 I will make a mortal more rare than fine gold,
    A man more than the golden wedge of Ophir.
13 Therefore I will shake the heavens,
    And the earth will move out of her place,
    In the wrath of the LORD of hosts
    And in the day of His fierce anger.
14 It shall be as the hunted gazelle,
    And as a sheep that no man takes up;
    Every man will turn to his own people,
    And everyone will flee to his own land.
15 Everyone who is found will be thrust through,
    And everyone who is captured will fall by the sword.
16 Their children also will be dashed to pieces before their eyes;
    Their houses will be plundered And their wives ravished.

17 "Behold, I will stir up the Medes against them,
    Who will not regard silver;

And *as for* gold, they will not delight in it.

18 Also *their* bows will dash the young men to pieces,
And they will have no pity on the fruit of the womb;
Their eye will not spare children.

19 And Babylon, the glory of kingdoms,
The beauty of the Chaldeans' pride,
Will be as when God overthrew Sodom and Gomorrah.

20 It will never be inhabited,
Nor will it be settled from generation to generation;
Nor will the Arabian pitch tents there,
Nor will the shepherds make their sheepfolds there.

21 But wild beasts of the desert will lie there,
And their houses will be full of owls;
Ostriches will dwell there,
And wild goats will caper there.

22 The hyenas will howl in their citadels,
And jackals in their pleasant palaces.
Her time *is* near to come,
And her days will not be prolonged."

14 FOR the Lord will have mercy on Jacob, and will still choose Israel, and settle them in their own land. The strangers will be joined with them, and they will cling to the house of Jacob. 2 Then people will take them and bring them to their place, and the house of Israel will possess them for servants and maids in the land of the LORD; they will take them captive whose captives they were, and rule over their oppressors.

3 It shall come to pass in the day the LORD gives you rest from your sorrow, and from your fear and the hard bondage in which you were made to serve, 4 that you will take up this proverb against the king of Babylon, and say:

"How the oppressor has ceased,
The golden city ceased!

5 The LORD has broken the staff of the wicked,
The scepter of the rulers;

6 He who struck the people in wrath with a continual stroke,
He who ruled the nations in anger,
Is persecuted *and* no one hinders.

7 The whole earth is at rest *and* quiet;
They break forth into singing.

8 Indeed the cypress trees rejoice over you,
And the cedars of Lebanon,
Saying, 'Since you were cut down,

No woodsman has come up against us.'

9 "Hell from beneath is excited about you,
To meet *you* at your coming;
It stirs up the dead for you,
All the chief ones of the earth;
It has raised up from their thrones
All the kings of the nations.

10 They all shall speak and say to you:
'Have you also become as weak as we?
Have you become like us?

11 Your pomp is brought down to Sheol,
And the sound of your stringed instruments;
The maggot is spread under you,
And worms cover you.'

12 "How you are fallen from heaven,
O Lucifer, son of the morning!
How you are cut down to the ground,
You who weakened the nations!

An angel next in power to God is revealed to be the originator of sin. (PHIL. SIN)

---

13 For you have said in your heart:
'I will ascend into heaven,
I will exalt my throne above the stars of God;
I will also sit on the mount of the congregation
On the farthest sides of the north;

14 I will ascend above the heights of the clouds,
I will be like the Most High.'

15 Yet you shall be brought down to Sheol,
To the lowest depths of the Pit.

16 "Those who see you will gaze at you,
And consider you, *saying:*
'*Is* this the man who made the earth tremble,
Who shook kingdoms,

17 Who made the world as a wilderness
And destroyed its cities,
Who did not open the house of his prisoners?'

18 "All the kings of the nations,
All of them, sleep in glory,
Everyone in his own house;

19 But you are cast out of your grave

Like an abominable branch,
Like the garment of those who are
    slain,
Thrust through with a sword,
Who go down to the stones of the
    pit,
Like a corpse trodden underfoot.
20 You will not be joined with them
    in burial,
Because you have destroyed your
    land
And slain your people.
The brood of evildoers shall never
    be named.
21 Prepare slaughter for his children
Because of the iniquity of their
    fathers,
Lest they rise up and possess the
    land,
And fill the face of the world with
    cities."

22 "For I will rise up against them," says
    the LORD of hosts,
"And cut off from Babylon the name
    and remnant,
And offspring and posterity," says the
    LORD.
23 "I will also make it a possession for
    the porcupine,
And marshes of muddy water;
I will sweep it with the broom of
    destruction," says the LORD of
    hosts.

24 The LORD of hosts has sworn,
    saying,
"Surely, as I have thought, so it shall
    come to pass,
And as I have purposed, *so* it shall
    stand:
25 That I will break the Assyrian in My
    land,
And on My mountains tread him
    underfoot.
Then his yoke shall be removed from
    them,
And his burden removed from their
    shoulders.
26 This *is* the purpose that is purposed
    against the whole earth,
And this *is* the hand that is stretched
    out over all the nations.
27 For the LORD of hosts has purposed,
    And who will annul *it*?
His hand *is* stretched out,
And who will turn it back?"

28 This is the burden which came in the
year that King Ahaz died.

29 "Do not rejoice, all you of Philistia,
Because the rod that struck you is
    broken;
For out of the serpent's roots will
    come forth a viper,
And its offspring *will be* a fiery flying
    serpent.
30 The firstborn of the poor will feed,
And the needy will lie down in safety;
I will kill your roots with famine,
And it will slay your remnant.
31 Wail, O gate! Cry, O city!
All you of Philistia *are* dissolved;
For smoke will come from the north,
And no one *will be* alone in his
    appointed times."

32 What will they answer the messengers
    of the nation?
That the LORD has founded Zion,
And the poor of His people shall take
    refuge in it.

PSALM 106:19–23

19 THEY made a calf in Horeb,
And worshiped the molded image.
20 Thus they changed their glory
Into the image of an ox that eats grass.
21 They forgot God their Savior,
Who had done great things in Egypt,
22 Wondrous works in the land of Ham,
Awesome things by the Red Sea.
23 Therefore He said that He would
    destroy them,
Had not Moses His chosen one stood
    before Him in the breach,
To turn away His wrath, lest He destroy
    them.

PROVERBS 25:6, 7

6 DO not exalt yourself in the presence
    of the king,
And do not stand in the place of the
    great;
7 For *it is* better that he say to you,
"Come up here,"
Than that you should be put lower in
    the presence of the prince,
Whom your eyes have seen.

2 CORINTHIANS 3:1–18

DO we begin again to commend ourselves?
Or do we need, as some *others*, epistles of
commendation to you or *letters* of commendation from you? 2 You are our epistle writ-

ten in our hearts, known and read by all men; 3 clearly *you are* an epistle of Christ, ministered by us, written not with ink but by the Spirit of the living God, not on tablets of stone but on tablets of flesh, *that is,* of the heart.

4 And we have such trust through Christ toward God. 5 Not that we are sufficient of ourselves to think of anything as *being* from ourselves, but our sufficiency *is* from God, 6 who also made us sufficient as ministers of the new covenant, not of the letter but of the Spirit; for the letter kills, but the Spirit gives life.

7 But if the ministry of death, written *and* engraved on stones, was glorious, so that the children of Israel could not look steadily at the face of Moses because of the glory of his countenance, which *glory* was passing away, 8 how will the ministry of the Spirit not be more glorious? 9 For if the ministry of condemnation *had* glory, the ministry of righteousness exceeds much more in glory. 10 For even what was made glorious had no glory in this respect, because of the glory that excels. 11 For if what is passing away *was* glorious, what remains *is* much more glorious.

12 Therefore, since we have such hope, we use great boldness of speech— 13 unlike Moses, *who* put a veil over his face so that the children of Israel could not look steadily at the end of what was passing away. 14 But their minds were blinded. For until this day the same veil remains unlifted in the reading of the Old Testament, because the *veil* is taken away in Christ. 15 But even to this day, when Moses is read, a veil lies on their heart. 16 Nevertheless when one turns to the Lord, the veil is taken away.

---

*T*he only way we can understand the Bible is by personal contact with the Living Word.   (GLORY)

---

17 Now the Lord is the Spirit; and where the Spirit of the Lord *is,* there *is* liberty. 18 But we all, with unveiled face, beholding as in a mirror the glory of the Lord, are being transformed into the same image from glory to glory, just as by the Spirit of the Lord.

---

*Reading 255—*Basic Tragedy
2 Corinthians 4:17

T he basis of human life is tragedy. It is difficult to realize this until one gets through the experiences that are on the surface of life, and we discover we are built with a bigger capacity for pain than for joy, that the undertone of all our life is sorrow, and the great expression and revelation of God in the world is the revelation of the Cross, not of joy. It is one of the things which makes the Bible seem so utterly unreal so long as we are healthy and full of life and spirits. Tragedy is something in which all the forces make for disaster. Paul in writing about human life always wrote from the Bible standpoint, which is, that the basis of things is not reasonable but tragic. Sin has made a gap between God and the human race; and, consequently, when we try to explain our lives on the line of logic or reason, we find things don't work out that way. . . . Jesus Christ stands outside the majority of our lives in the usual run because He deals with the fundamentals; we do not, we deal with the external actuals, and it is only when the external actuals are plowed into by sorrow or bereavement that we begin to find there is only one reality—our Lord Jesus Christ, and only one book that brings light.   (*PLACE HELP*)

ISAIAH 15:1—16:14

THE burden against Moab.

Because in the night Ar of Moab is
laid waste
And destroyed,
Because in the night Kir of Moab
is laid waste
And destroyed,
2   He has gone up to the temple and
Dibon,
To the high places to weep.
Moab will wail over Nebo and over
Medeba;
On all their heads *will be* baldness,
And every beard cut off.
3   In their streets they will clothe
themselves with sackcloth;
On the tops of their houses
And in their streets
Everyone will wail, weeping
bitterly.
4   Heshbon and Elealeh will cry out,
Their voice shall be heard as far as
Jahaz;
Therefore the armed soldiers of
Moab will cry out;
His life will be burdensome to
him.

5   "My heart will cry out for Moab;
His fugitives *shall flee* to Zoar,
Like a three-year-old heifer.
For by the Ascent of Luhith
They will go up with weeping;
For in the way of Horonaim
They will raise up a cry of
destruction,
6   For the waters of Nimrim will be
desolate,
For the green grass has withered
away;
The grass fails, there is nothing
green.
7   Therefore the abundance they have
gained,
And what they have laid up,
They will carry away to the Brook
of the Willows.
8   For the cry has gone all around the
borders of Moab,
Its wailing to Eglaim
And its wailing to Beer Elim.
9   For the waters of Dimon will be full
of blood;
Because I will bring more upon
Dimon,
Lions upon him who escapes from
Moab,
And on the remnant of the land."

16 SEND the lamb to the ruler of the
land,
From Sela to the wilderness,
To the mount of the daughter of
Zion.
2   For it shall be as a wandering bird
thrown out of the nest;
So shall be the daughters of Moab
at the fords of the Arnon.

3   "Take counsel, execute judgment;
Make your shadow like the night in
the middle of the day;
Hide the outcasts,
Do not betray him who escapes.
4   Let My outcasts dwell with you,
O Moab;
Be a shelter to them from the face
of the spoiler.
For the extortioner is at an end,
Devastation ceases,
The oppressors are consumed out of
the land.
5   In mercy the throne will be
established;
And One will sit on it in truth, in
the tabernacle of David,
Judging and seeking justice and
hastening righteousness."

6   We have heard of the pride of
Moab—
He is very proud—
Of his haughtiness and his pride and
his wrath;
But his lies *shall* not *be* so.
7   Therefore Moab shall wail for Moab;
Everyone shall wail.
For the foundations of Kir Hareseth
you shall mourn;
Surely *they are* stricken.

8   For the fields of Heshbon languish,
And the vine of Sibmah;
The lords of the nations have broken
down its choice plants,
Which have reached to Jazer
And wandered through the
wilderness.
Her branches are stretched out,
They are gone over the sea.
9   Therefore I will bewail the vine of
Sibmah,
With the weeping of Jazer;
I will drench you with my tears,
O Heshbon and Elealeh;
For battle cries have fallen
Over your summer fruits and your
harvest.

10 Gladness is taken away,
And joy from the plentiful field;

In the vineyards there will be no
singing,
Nor will there be shouting;
No treaders will tread out wine in
the presses;
I have made their shouting cease.
11 Therefore my heart shall resound like
a harp for Moab,
And my inner being for Kir Heres.

12 And it shall come to pass,
When it is seen that Moab is weary
on the high place,
That he will come to his sanctuary
to pray;
But he will not prevail.

13 This *is* the word which the LORD has
spoken concerning Moab since that time.
14 But now the LORD has spoken, saying,
"Within three years, as the years of a hired
man, the glory of Moab will be despised
with all that great multitude, and the remnant *will be* very small *and* feeble."

PSALM 106:24–31

24 THEN they despised the pleasant land;
They did not believe His word,
25 But complained in their tents,
And did not heed the voice of the
LORD.
26 Therefore He raised His hand *in an
oath* against them,
To overthrow them in the wilderness,
27 To overthrow their descendants among
the nations,
And to scatter them in the lands.

28 They joined themselves also to Baal of
Peor,
And ate sacrifices made to the dead.
29 Thus they provoked *Him* to anger with
their deeds,
And the plague broke out among them.
30 Then Phinehas stood up and
intervened,
And the plague was stopped.
31 And that was accounted to him for
righteousness
To all generations forevermore.

PROVERBS 25:8–10

8 DO not go hastily to court;
For what will you do in the end,
When your neighbor has put you to
shame?
9 Debate your case with your neighbor,

And do not disclose the secret to
another;
10 Lest he who hears *it* expose your shame,
And your reputation be ruined.

2 CORINTHIANS 4:1–18

THEREFORE, since we have this ministry,
as we have received mercy, we do not lose
heart. 2 But we have renounced the hidden
things of shame, not walking in craftiness
nor handling the word of God deceitfully,
but by manifestation of the truth com-
mending ourselves to every man's conscience in the sight of God. 3 But even if
our gospel is veiled, it is veiled to those
who are perishing, 4 whose minds the god
of this age has blinded, who do not believe,
lest the light of the gospel of the glory of
Christ, who is the image of God, should
shine on them. 5 For we do not preach ourselves, but Christ Jesus the Lord, and ourselves your bondservants for Jesus' sake.
6 For it is the God who commanded light
to shine out of darkness, who has shone
in our hearts to *give* the light of the knowledge of the glory of God in the face of
Jesus Christ.

7 But we have this treasure in earthen
vessels, that the excellence of the power
may be of God and not of us. 8 *We are*
hard-pressed on every side, yet not crushed;
we are perplexed, but not in despair;
9 persecuted, but not forsaken; struck
down, but not destroyed— 10 always carrying about in the body the dying of the Lord
Jesus, that the life of Jesus also may be
manifested in our body. 11 For we who live
are always delivered to death for Jesus' sake,
that the life of Jesus also may be manifested
in our mortal flesh. 12 So then death is working in us, but life in you.

---

*O*ur bodies are not our shame, but
our glory. (SERVANT AS LORD)

---

13 And since we have the same spirit of
faith, according to what is written, "I believed and therefore I spoke," we also believe and therefore speak, 14 knowing that
He who raised up the Lord Jesus will also
raise us up with Jesus, and will present *us*
with you. 15 For all things *are* for your
sakes, that grace, having spread through
the many, may cause thanksgiving to
abound to the glory of God.
16 Therefore we do not lose heart. Even

though our outward man is perishing, yet the inward *man* is being renewed day by day. 17 For our light affliction, which is but for a moment, is working for us a far more exceeding *and* eternal weight of glory, 18 while we do not look at the things which are seen, but at the things which are not seen. For the things which are seen *are* temporary, but the things which are not seen *are* eternal.

◆◆◆◆

Reading 256—The Christian Meaning
2 Corinthians 5:17

If we are saved by the grace of God it means not only that we are delivered from destruction, but that we are a new creation. The condemnation is to know a thing and not work it out. We know we have experienced the grace of God, but are we living the life of regeneration in our actual experience? We take the Christian view up to a certain point and exploit it according to our belief. The average Christian says, "Oh, yes, I am saved." Well, produce your goods! Where are the characteristics in you that Jesus Christ taught us to expect in a Christian? In what way are you different from other men? Are you just as hard in driving a bargain as they are? If Christianity does not affect my money and my marriage relationships, it is not worth anything. Today men are asking not so much if Christianity is true, but if it is real? Does it amount to anything in actual life? If I have a personal relationship to Jesus on the basis of His redemption, it will show in the way I live, in the way I act toward men; "old things have passed away; behold, all things have become new." (PLACE HELP)

ISAIAH 17:1—18:7

THE burden against Damascus.

"Behold, Damascus will cease from
    being a city,
And it will be a ruinous heap.
2 The cities of Aroer *are* forsaken;
    They will be for flocks
Which lie down, and no one will
    make *them* afraid.
3 The fortress also will cease from
    Ephraim,
The kingdom from Damascus,
    And the remnant of Syria;
They will be as the glory of the
    children of Israel,"
Says the LORD of hosts.

4 "In that day it shall come to pass
    That the glory of Jacob will wane,
And the fatness of his flesh grow lean.
5 It shall be as when the harvester
    gathers the grain,
And reaps the heads with his
    arm;

It shall be as he who gathers heads
    of grain
In the Valley of Rephaim.
6 Yet gleaning grapes will be left
    in it,
Like the shaking of an olive tree,
Two *or* three olives at the top of the
    uppermost bough,
Four *or* five in its most fruitful
    branches,"
Says the LORD God of Israel.

7 In that day a man will look to his
    Maker,
And his eyes will have respect for
    the Holy One of Israel.
8 He will not look to the altars,
    The work of his hands;
He will not respect what his fingers
    have made,
Nor the wooden images nor the
    incense altars.

9 In that day his strong cities will be
    as a forsaken bough
And an uppermost branch,

Which they left because of the
children of Israel;
And there will be desolation.

10 Because you have forgotten the God
of your salvation,
And have not been mindful of the
Rock of your stronghold,
Therefore you will plant pleasant
plants
And set out foreign seedlings;

11 In the day you will make your plant
to grow,
And in the morning you will make
your seed to flourish;
But the harvest *will be* a heap of ruins
In the day of grief and desperate
sorrow.

12 Woe to the multitude of many
people
Who make a noise like the roar of
the seas,
And to the rushing of nations
That make a rushing like the rushing
of mighty waters!

13 The nations will rush like the rushing
of many waters;
But *God* will rebuke them and they
will flee far away,
And be chased like the chaff of the
mountains before the wind,
Like a rolling thing before the
whirlwind.

14 Then behold, at eventide, trouble!
And before the morning, he *is* no
more.
This *is* the portion of those who
plunder us,
And the lot of those who rob us.

18 WOE to the land shadowed with
buzzing wings,
Which *is* beyond the rivers of
Ethiopia,

2 Which sends ambassadors by sea,
Even in vessels of reed on the waters,
saying,
"Go, swift messengers, to a nation tall
and smooth *of skin,*
To a people terrible from their
beginning onward,
A nation powerful and treading
down,
Whose land the rivers divide."

3 All inhabitants of the world and
dwellers on the earth:
When he lifts up a banner on the
mountains, you see *it;*

And when he blows a trumpet, you
hear *it.*

4 For so the Lord said to me,
"I will take My rest,
And I will look from My dwelling
place
Like clear heat in sunshine,
Like a cloud of dew in the heat of
harvest."

5 For before the harvest, when the bud
is perfect
And the sour grape is ripening in
the flower,
He will both cut off the sprigs with
pruning hooks
And take away *and* cut down the
branches.

6 They will be left together for the
mountain birds of prey
And for the beasts of the earth;
The birds of prey will summer on
them,
And all the beasts of the earth will
winter on them.

7 In that time a present will be brought
to the Lord of hosts
From a people tall and smooth *of skin,*
And from a people terrible from their
beginning onward,
A nation powerful and treading
down,
Whose land the rivers divide—
To the place of the name of the Lord
of hosts,
To Mount Zion.

PSALM 106:32–39

32 THEY angered *Him* also at the waters
of strife,
So that it went ill with Moses on
account of them;

33 Because they rebelled against His
Spirit,
So that he spoke rashly with his lips.

34 They did not destroy the peoples,
Concerning whom the Lord had
commanded them,

35 But they mingled with the Gentiles
And learned their works;

36 They served their idols,
Which became a snare to them.

37 They even sacrificed their sons
And their daughters to demons,

38 And shed innocent blood,
The blood of their sons and daughters,
Whom they sacrificed to the idols of
Canaan;

And the land was polluted with blood.
39 Thus they were defiled by their own
   works,
   And played the harlot by their own
   deeds.

PROVERBS 25:11, 12

11 A word fitly spoken *is like* apples of
   gold
   In settings of silver.
12 *Like* an earring of gold and an ornament
   of fine gold
   Is a wise rebuker to an obedient ear.

2 CORINTHIANS 5:1–21

FOR we know that if our earthly house,
this tent, is destroyed, we have a building
from God, a house not made with hands,
eternal in the heavens. 2 For in this we
groan, earnestly desiring to be clothed with
our habitation which is from heaven,
3 if indeed, having been clothed, we shall
not be found naked. 4 For we who are in
this tent groan, being burdened, not because
we want to be unclothed, but further
clothed, that mortality may be swallowed
up by life. 5 Now He who has prepared
us for this very thing *is* God, who also has
given us the Spirit as a guarantee.

6 So *we are* always confident, knowing
that while we are at home in the body we
are absent from the Lord. 7 For we walk
by faith, not by sight. 8 We are confident,
yes, well pleased rather to be absent from
the body and to be present with the Lord.

9 Therefore we make it our aim, whether
present or absent, to be well pleasing to
Him. 10 For we must all appear before the
judgment seat of Christ, that each one may
receive the things *done* in the body, according to what he has done, whether good

or bad. 11 Knowing, therefore, the terror
of the Lord, we persuade men; but we are
well known to God, and I also trust are
well known in your consciences.

12 For we do not commend ourselves
again to you, but give you opportunity to
boast on our behalf, that you may have
an answer for those who boast in appearance and not in heart. 13 For if we are beside
ourselves, *it is* for God; or if we are of
sound mind, *it is* for you. 14 For the love
of Christ compels us, because we judge
thus: that if One died for all, then all died;
15 and He died for all, that those who live
should live no longer for themselves, but
for Him who died for them and rose again.

16 Therefore, from now on, we regard
no one according to the flesh. Even though
we have known Christ according to the
flesh, yet now we know *Him thus* no
longer. 17 Therefore, if anyone *is* in Christ,
he is a new creation; old things have passed
away; behold, all things have become new.
18 Now all things *are* of God, who has reconciled us to Himself through Jesus Christ,
and has given us the ministry of reconciliation, 19 that is, that God was in Christ reconciling the world to Himself, not imputing
their trespasses to them, and has committed
to us the word of reconciliation.

---

*When we read of the sacrifice of
Jesus Christ, it is the sacrifice of
God also.*   (GLORY)

---

20 Now then, we are ambassadors for
Christ, as though God were pleading
through us: we implore *you* on Christ's behalf, be reconciled to God. 21 For He made
Him who knew no sin *to be* sin for us,
that we might become the righteousness
of God in Him.

◆◆◆◆

Reading 257—Mastery in Circumstances
2 Corinthians 6:4–18

Verses 4–18 are Paul's spiritual diary. They describe the outward hardships
which proved the hotbed for the graces of the Spirit—the working
together of outward hardships and inward grace. You have been asking the
Lord to give you the graces of the Spirit and then some set of circumstances
has come and given you a sharp twinge, and you say, "Well, I have asked

God to bring out in me the graces of the Spirit, but every time the Devil seems to get the better of me." What you are calling "the Devil" is the very thing God is using to manifest the graces of the Spirit in you. . . .

The worker learns the secret of the "campfires" where he can recount with other Christians the great hours when the Son of God walked with him in the fiery furnace. . . .

The fiery furnaces are there by God's direct permission. It is misleading to imagine that we are developed in spite of our circumstances—we are developed because of them. It is mastery in circumstances that is needed, not mastery over them. We have to manifest the graces of the Spirit among things as they are, not to wait for the Millennium.   (*LOVE OF GOD*)

ISAIAH 19:1—20:6

THE burden against Egypt.

> Behold, the LORD rides on a swift cloud,
> And will come into Egypt;
> The idols of Egypt will totter at His presence,
> And the heart of Egypt will melt in its midst.

2 "I will set Egyptians against Egyptians;
Everyone will fight against his brother,
And everyone against his neighbor,
City against city, kingdom against kingdom.
3 The spirit of Egypt will fail in its midst;
I will destroy their counsel,
And they will consult the idols and the charmers,
The mediums and the sorcerers.
4 And the Egyptians I will give
Into the hand of a cruel master,
And a fierce king will rule over them,"
Says the Lord, the LORD of hosts.

5 The waters will fail from the sea,
And the river will be wasted and dried up.
6 The rivers will turn foul;
The brooks of defense will be emptied and dried up;
The reeds and rushes will wither.
7 The papyrus reeds by the River, by the mouth of the River,
And everything sown by the River,
Will wither, be driven away, and be no more.
8 The fishermen also will mourn;
All those will lament who cast hooks into the River,

And they will languish who spread nets on the waters.
9 Moreover those who work in fine flax
And those who weave fine fabric will be ashamed;
10 And its foundations will be broken.
All who make wages *will be* troubled of soul.

11 Surely the princes of Zoan *are* fools;
Pharaoh's wise counselors give foolish counsel.
How do you say to Pharaoh, "I *am* the son of the wise,
The son of ancient kings?"
12 Where *are* they?
Where are your wise men?
Let them tell you now,
And let them know what the LORD of hosts has purposed against Egypt.
13 The princes of Zoan have become fools;
The princes of Noph are deceived;
They have also deluded Egypt,
Those who are the mainstay of its tribes.
14 The LORD has mingled a perverse spirit in her midst;
And they have caused Egypt to err in all her work,
As a drunken man staggers in his vomit.
15 Neither will there be *any* work for Egypt,
Which the head or tail,
Palm branch or bulrush, may do.

16 In that day Egypt will be like women, and will be afraid and fear because of the waving of the hand of the LORD of hosts, which He waves over it. 17 And the land of Judah will be a terror to Egypt; everyone

who makes mention of it will be afraid in himself, because of the counsel of the Lord of hosts which He has determined against it.

18 In that day five cities in the land of Egypt will speak the language of Canaan and swear by the Lord of hosts; one will be called the City of Destruction.

19 In that day there will be an altar to the Lord in the midst of the land of Egypt, and a pillar to the Lord at its border. 20 And it will be for a sign and for a witness to the Lord of hosts in the land of Egypt; for they will cry to the Lord because of the oppressors, and He will send them a Savior and a Mighty One, and He will deliver them. 21 Then the Lord will be known to Egypt, and the Egyptians will know the Lord in that day, and will make sacrifice and offering; yes, they will make a vow to the Lord and perform *it.* 22 And the Lord will strike Egypt, He will strike and heal *it;* they will return to the Lord, and He will be entreated by them and heal them.

23 In that day there will be a highway from Egypt to Assyria, and the Assyrian will come into Egypt and the Egyptian into Assyria, and the Egyptians will serve with the Assyrians.

24 In that day Israel will be one of three with Egypt and Assyria—a blessing in the midst of the land, 25 whom the Lord of hosts shall bless, saying, "Blessed *is* Egypt My people, and Assyria the work of My hands, and Israel My inheritance."

20 IN the year that Tartan came to Ashdod, when Sargon the king of Assyria sent him, and he fought against Ashdod and took it, 2 at the same time the Lord spoke by Isaiah the son of Amoz, saying, "Go, and remove the sackcloth from your body, and take your sandals off your feet." And he did so, walking naked and barefoot.

3 Then the Lord said, "Just as My servant Isaiah has walked naked and barefoot three years *for* a sign and a wonder against Egypt and Ethiopia, 4 so shall the king of Assyria lead away the Egyptians as prisoners and the Ethiopians as captives, young and old, naked and barefoot, with their buttocks uncovered, to the shame of Egypt. 5 Then they shall be afraid and ashamed of Ethiopia their expectation and Egypt their glory. 6 And the inhabitant of this territory will say in that day, 'Surely such *is* our expectation, wherever we flee for help to be delivered from the king of Assyria; and how shall we escape?'"

PSALM 106:40–48

40 THEREFORE the wrath of the Lord was kindled against His people,
So that He abhorred His own inheritance.

41 And He gave them into the hand of the Gentiles,
And those who hated them ruled over them.

42 Their enemies also oppressed them,
And they were brought into subjection under their hand.

43 Many times He delivered them;
But they rebelled in their counsel,
And were brought low for their iniquity.

44 Nevertheless He regarded their affliction,
When He heard their cry;

45 And for their sake He remembered His covenant,
And relented according to the multitude of His mercies.

46 He also made them to be pitied
By all those who carried them away captive.

47 Save us, O Lord our God,
And gather us from among the Gentiles,
To give thanks to Your holy name,
To triumph in Your praise.

48 Blessed *be* the Lord God of Israel
From everlasting to everlasting!
And let all the people say, "Amen!"

Praise the Lord!

PROVERBS 25:13

13 LIKE the cold of snow in time of harvest
Is a faithful messenger to those who send him,
For he refreshes the soul of his masters.

2 CORINTHIANS 6:1–18

WE then, *as* workers together *with Him* also plead with *you* not to receive the grace of God in vain. 2 For He says:

"In an acceptable time I have heard you,
And in the day of salvation I have helped you."

Behold, now *is* the accepted time; behold, now *is* the day of salvation.

3 We give no offense in anything, that our ministry may not be blamed. 4 But in all *things* we commend ourselves as ministers of God: in much patience, in tribulations, in needs, in distresses, 5 in stripes,

---

*B*eware *of egging God on; possess your soul in patience.* (GENESIS)

---

in imprisonments, in tumults, in labors, in sleeplessness, in fastings; 6 by purity, by knowledge, by longsuffering, by kindness, by the Holy Spirit, by sincere love, 7 by the word of truth, by the power of God, by the armor of righteousness on the right hand and on the left, 8 by honor and dishonor, by evil report and good report; as deceivers, and *yet* true; 9 as unknown, and *yet* well known; as dying, and behold we live; as chastened, and *yet* not killed; 10 as sorrowful, yet always rejoicing; as poor, yet making many rich; as having nothing, and *yet* possessing all things. 11 O Corinthians! We have spoken openly to you, our heart is wide open.

12 You are not restricted by us, but you are restricted by your *own* affections. 13 Now in return for the same (I speak as to children), you also be open.

14 Do not be unequally yoked together with unbelievers. For what fellowship has righteousness with lawlessness? And what communion has light with darkness? 15 And what accord has Christ with Belial? Or what part has a believer with an unbeliever? 16 And what agreement has the temple of God with idols? For you are the temple of the living God. As God has said:

> "I will dwell in them
> And walk among *them*.
> I will be their God,
> And they shall be My people."

17 Therefore

> "Come out from among them
> And be separate, says the Lord.
> Do not touch what is unclean,
> And I will receive you."

18 "I will be a Father to you,
> And you shall be My sons and
> daughters,
> Says the LORD Almighty."

◆◆◆

Reading 258—Voice and Vision
Psalm 107:2

We are apt to use words without having any idea of their meaning. In a crisis a word is really an "open sesame," and in certain spiritual, moral, and emotional crises if we do not say the word, emancipation will never be ours. Think of it in a simple way. When a child knows it has done something wrong and you want him to say he is sorry, the natural inclination of the child is stubbornly to refuse to say he is sorry; but until he does say so, there is no emancipation for him on to a higher level in his own life. This is the key to the way we are built all through; it is true not only in a child's life but in the moral domain, and emphatically true in the spiritual domain. Many of us are on the verge of a spiritual vision the realization of which never becomes ours because we will not open our mouths to "say so." We have to "say so" before we "feel so." The writer to the Hebrews speaks of the "sacrifice of praise." If we only praise when we feel like praising, it is simply an undisciplined expression, but if we deliberately go over the neck of our disinclination and offer the sacrifice of praise, we are emancipated by our very statements. We can slay a grousing mood by stating what we believe, and we are emancipated into a higher level of life immediately; but the "say so" must come before the emancipation is ours. (*PLACE HELP*)

ISAIAH 21:1—22:25

THE burden against the Wilderness of the Sea.

As whirlwinds in the South pass through,
So it comes from the desert, from a terrible land.

2 A distressing vision is declared to me;
The treacherous dealer deals treacherously,
And the plunderer plunders.
Go up, O Elam!
Besiege, O Media!
All its sighing I have made to cease.

3 Therefore my loins are filled with pain;
Pangs have taken hold of me, like the pangs of a woman in labor.
I was distressed when *I* heard *it;*
I was dismayed when *I* saw *it.*

4 My heart wavered, fearfulness frightened me;
The night for which I longed He turned into fear for me.

5 Prepare the table,
Set a watchman in the tower,
Eat and drink.
Arise, you princes,
Anoint the shield!

6 For thus has the Lord said to me:
"Go, set a watchman,
Let him declare what he sees."

7 And he saw a chariot *with* a pair of horsemen,
A chariot of donkeys, *and* a chariot of camels,
And he listened earnestly with great care.

8 Then he cried, "A lion, my Lord!
I stand continually on the watchtower in the daytime;
I have sat at my post every night.

9 And look, here comes a chariot of men *with* a pair of horsemen!"
Then he answered and said,
"Babylon is fallen, is fallen!
And all the carved images of her gods
He has broken to the ground."

10 Oh, my threshing and the grain of my floor!
That which I have heard from the Lord of hosts,
The God of Israel,
I have declared to you.

11 The burden against Dumah.

He calls to me out of Seir,
"Watchman, what of the night?
Watchman, what of the night?"

12 The watchman said,
"The morning comes, and also the night.
If you will inquire, inquire;
Return! Come back!"

13 The burden against Arabia.

In the forest in Arabia you will lodge,
O you traveling companies of Dedanites.

14 O inhabitants of the land of Tema,
Bring water to him who is thirsty;
With their bread they met him who fled.

15 For they fled from the swords, from the drawn sword,
From the bent bow, and from the distress of war.

16 For thus the Lord has said to me: "Within a year, according to the year of a hired man, all the glory of Kedar will fail; 17 and the remainder of the number of archers, the mighty men of the people of Kedar, will be diminished; for the Lord God of Israel has spoken *it.*"

22 THE burden against the Valley of Vision.

What ails you now, that you have all gone up to the housetops,

2 You who are full of noise,
A tumultuous city, a joyous city?
Your slain *men are* not slain with the sword,
Nor dead in battle.

3 All your rulers have fled together;
They are captured by the archers.
All who are found in you are bound together;
They have fled from afar.

4 Therefore I said, "Look away from me,
I will weep bitterly;
Do not labor to comfort me
Because of the plundering of the daughter of my people."

5 For *it is* a day of trouble and treading down and perplexity
By the Lord God of hosts
In the Valley of Vision—
Breaking down the walls
And of crying to the mountain.

6 Elam bore the quiver

With chariots of men *and* horsemen,
And Kir uncovered the shield.
7   It shall come to pass *that* your choicest valleys
Shall be full of chariots,
And the horsemen shall set themselves in array at the gate.

8   He removed the protection of Judah.
You looked in that day to the armor of the House of the Forest;
9   You also saw the damage to the city of David,
That it was great;
And you gathered together the waters of the lower pool.
10   You numbered the houses of Jerusalem,
And the houses you broke down To fortify the wall.
11   You also made a reservoir between the two walls
For the water of the old pool.
But you did not look to its Maker,
Nor did you have respect for Him who fashioned it long ago.

12   And in that day the Lord GOD of hosts
Called for weeping and for mourning,
For baldness and for girding with sackcloth.
13   But instead, joy and gladness,
Slaying oxen and killing sheep,
Eating meat and drinking wine:
"Let us eat and drink, for tomorrow we die!"

14   Then it was revealed in my hearing by the LORD of hosts,
"Surely for this iniquity there will be no atonement for you,
Even to your death," says the Lord GOD of hosts.

15   Thus says the Lord GOD of hosts:

"Go, proceed to this steward,
To Shebna, who *is* over the house, *and say:*
16   'What have you here, and whom have you here,
That you have hewn a sepulcher here,
As he who hews himself a sepulcher on high,
Who carves a tomb for himself in a rock?
17   Indeed, the LORD will throw you away violently,
O mighty man,

And will surely seize you.
18   He will surely turn violently and toss you like a ball
Into a large country;
There you shall die, and there your glorious chariots
Shall be the shame of your master's house.
19   So I will drive you out of your office,
And from your position he will pull you down.

20   'Then it shall be in that day,
That I will call My servant Eliakim the son of Hilkiah;
21   I will clothe him with your robe
And strengthen him with your belt;
I will commit your responsibility into his hand.
He shall be a father to the inhabitants of Jerusalem
And to the house of Judah.
22   The key of the house of David I will lay on his shoulder;
So he shall open, and no one shall shut;
And he shall shut, and no one shall open.
23   I will fasten him *as* a peg in a secure place,
And he will become a glorious throne to his father's house.

24   'They will hang on him all the glory of his father's house, the offspring and the posterity, all vessels of small quantity, from the cups to all the pitchers. 25 In that day,' says the LORD of hosts, 'the peg that is fastened in the secure place will be removed and be cut down and fall, and the burden that *was* on it will be cut off; for the LORD has spoken.' "

PSALM 107:1–9

1   OH, give thanks to the LORD, for *He is* good!
For His mercy *endures* forever.
2   Let the redeemed of the LORD say *so,*
Whom He has redeemed from the hand of the enemy,
3   And gathered out of the lands,
From the east and from the west,
From the north and from the south.

4   They wandered in the wilderness in a desolate way;
They found no city to dwell in.
5   Hungry and thirsty,
Their soul fainted in them.

6   Then they cried out to the LORD in
     their trouble,
     And He delivered them out of their
     distresses.
7   And He led them forth by the right
     way,
     That they might go to a city for a
     dwelling place.
8   Oh, that *men* would give thanks to the
     LORD *for* His goodness,
     And *for* His wonderful works to the
     children of men!
9   For He satisfies the longing soul,
     And fills the hungry soul with goodness.

---

*It is only when we get hungry
spiritually that we receive the
Holy Spirit.*   (UTMOST)

PROVERBS 25:14–16

14   WHOEVER falsely boasts of giving
     Is like clouds and wind without rain.

15   By long forbearance a ruler is
     persuaded,
     And a gentle tongue breaks a bone.

16   Have you found honey?
     Eat only as much as you need,
     Lest you be filled with it and vomit.

2 CORINTHIANS 7:1–16

THEREFORE, having these promises, beloved, let us cleanse ourselves from all filthiness of the flesh and spirit, perfecting holiness in the fear of God.

---

*He is working out His ultimate
perfection all the time.*   (UTMOST)

---

2 Open *your hearts* to us. We have
wronged no one, we have corrupted no
one, we have cheated no one. 3 I do not
say *this* to condemn; for I have said before

that you are in our hearts, to die together
and to live together. 4 Great *is* my boldness
of speech toward you, great *is* my boasting
on your behalf. I am filled with comfort.
I am exceedingly joyful in all our tribulation.

5 For indeed, when we came to Macedonia, our bodies had no rest, but we were
troubled on every side. Outside *were* con-
flicts, inside *were* fears. 6 Nevertheless God,
who comforts the downcast, comforted us
by the coming of Titus, 7 and not only by
his coming, but also by the consolation with
which he was comforted in you, when he
told us of your earnest desire, your mourning, your zeal for me, so that I rejoiced
even more.

8 For even if I made you sorry with my
letter, I do not regret it; though I did regret
it. For I perceive that the same epistle made
you sorry, though only for a while.
9 Now I rejoice, not that you were made
sorry, but that your sorrow led to repentance. For you were made sorry in a godly
manner, that you might suffer loss from
us in nothing. 10 For godly sorrow produces repentance *leading* to salvation, not
to be regretted; but the sorrow of the world
produces death. 11 For observe this very
thing, that you sorrowed in a godly manner:
What diligence it produced in you, *what*
clearing *of yourselves, what* indignation, *what*
fear, *what* vehement desire, *what* zeal,
what vindication! In all *things* you proved
yourselves to be clear in this matter.
12 Therefore, although I wrote to you, *I
did* not *do it* for the sake of him who had
done the wrong, nor for the sake of him
who suffered wrong, but that our care for
you in the sight of God might appear to
you.

13 Therefore we have been comforted in
your comfort. And we rejoiced exceedingly
more for the joy of Titus, because his spirit
has been refreshed by you all. 14 For if in
anything I have boasted to him about you,
I am not ashamed. But as we spoke all things
to you in truth, even so our boasting to
Titus was found true. 15 And his affections
are greater for you as he remembers the
obedience of you all, how with fear and
trembling you received him. 16 Therefore
I rejoice that I have confidence in you in
everything.

Reading 259—Self-Expenditure
2 Corinthians 8:9

Grace means the overflowing nature of God. We see it in nature; we have no words to describe the lavishness of God. "The grace of our Lord Jesus Christ" is the overflowing of God's nature in entire and absolute forgiveness through His own sacrifice. Do we discern that grace? We talk about the sacrifice of the Son of God and forget that it was the sacrifice of God Himself. "God was in Christ, reconciling the world to Himself."

". . . that you through His poverty might become rich." Rich in what? Not in possessions, but in personal identity. Our Lord Jesus Christ became poor, not as an example, but to give us the secret of His religion. The religion of Jesus Christ is a religion of personal relationship to God and has nothing to do with possessions. Professional Christianity is a religion of possessions that are devoted to God. The disciple realizes that his life does not consist in the abundance of things he possesses, because what we possess often possesses us; we are possessed by possessions. "This is mine; you must not touch it!" When we become rich toward God, it will show in the details of our actual life.   (GLORY)

ISAIAH 23:1—24:23

THE burden against Tyre.

Wail, you ships of Tarshish!
For it is laid waste,
So that there is no house, no harbor;
From the land of Cyprus it is revealed to them.

2 Be still, you inhabitants of the coastland,
You merchants of Sidon,
Whom those who cross the sea have filled.

3 And on great waters the grain of Shihor,
The harvest of the River, *is* her revenue;
And she is a marketplace for the nations.

4 Be ashamed, O Sidon;
For the sea has spoken,
The strength of the sea, saying,
"I do not labor, nor bring forth children;
Neither do I rear young men,
Nor bring up virgins."

5 When the report *reaches* Egypt,
They also will be in agony at the report of Tyre.

6 Cross over to Tarshish;
Wail, you inhabitants of the coastland!

7 *Is* this your joyous *city,*
Whose antiquity *is* from ancient days,
Whose feet carried her far off to dwell?

8 Who has taken this counsel against Tyre, the crowning *city,*
Whose merchants *are* princes,
Whose traders *are* the honorable of the earth?

9 The LORD of hosts has purposed it,
To bring to dishonor the pride of all glory,
To bring into contempt all the honorable of the earth.

10 Overflow through your land like the River,
O daughter of Tarshish;
There is no more strength.

11 He stretched out His hand over the sea,
He shook the kingdoms;
The LORD has given a commandment against Canaan
To destroy its strongholds.

12 And He said, "You will rejoice no more,
O you oppressed virgin daughter of Sidon.

Arise, cross over to Cyprus;
There also you will have no rest."

13 Behold, the land of the Chaldeans,
This people *which* was not;
Assyria founded it for wild beasts of
the desert.
They set up its towers,
They raised up its palaces,
And brought it to ruin.

14 Wail, you ships of Tarshish!
For your strength is laid waste.

15 Now it shall come to pass in that day
that Tyre will be forgotten seventy years,
according to the days of one king. At the
end of seventy years it will happen to Tyre
as *in* the song of the harlot:

16 "Take a harp, go about the city,
You forgotten harlot;
Make sweet melody, sing many
songs,
That you may be remembered."

17 And it shall be, at the end of seventy
years, that the LORD will deal with Tyre.
She will return to her hire, and commit
fornication with all the kingdoms of the
world on the face of the earth. 18 Her gain
and her pay will be set apart for the LORD;
it will not be treasured nor laid up, for
her gain will be for those who dwell before
the LORD, to eat sufficiently, and for fine
clothing.

24 BEHOLD, the LORD makes the
earth empty and makes it waste,
Distorts its surface
And scatters abroad its inhabitants.
2 And it shall be:
As with the people, so with the priest;
As with the servant, so with his
master;
As with the maid, so with her
mistress;
As with the buyer, so with the seller;
As with the lender, so with the
borrower;
As with the creditor, so with the
debtor.
3 The land shall be entirely emptied
and utterly plundered,
For the LORD has spoken this word.

4 The earth mourns *and* fades away,
The world languishes *and* fades away;
The haughty people of the earth
languish.
5 The earth is also defiled under its
inhabitants,

Because they have transgressed the
laws,
Changed the ordinance,
Broken the everlasting covenant.
6 Therefore the curse has devoured the
earth,
And those who dwell in it are
desolate.
Therefore the inhabitants of the earth
are burned,
And few men *are* left.

7 The new wine fails, the vine
languishes,
All the merry-hearted sigh.
8 The mirth of the tambourine ceases,
The noise of the jubilant ends,
The joy of the harp ceases.
9 They shall not drink wine with a
song;
Strong drink is bitter to those who
drink it.
10 The city of confusion is broken
down;
Every house is shut up, so that none
may go in.
11 *There is* a cry for wine in the streets,
All joy is darkened,
The mirth of the land is gone.
12 In the city desolation is left,
And the gate is stricken with
destruction.
13 When it shall be thus in the midst
of the land among the people,
It shall be like the shaking of an olive
tree,
Like the gleaning of grapes when the
vintage is done.

14 They shall lift up their voice, they
shall sing;
For the majesty of the LORD
They shall cry aloud from the sea.
15 Therefore glorify the LORD in the
dawning light,
The name of the LORD God of Israel
in the coastlands of the sea.
16 From the ends of the earth we have
heard songs:
"Glory to the righteous!"
But I said, "I am ruined, ruined!
Woe to me!
The treacherous dealers have dealt
treacherously,
Indeed, the treacherous dealers have
dealt very treacherously."

17 Fear and the pit and the snare
Are upon you, O inhabitant of the
earth.
18 And it shall be

That he who flees from the noise of
the fear
Shall fall into the pit,
And he who comes up from the
midst of the pit
Shall be caught in the snare;
For the windows from on high are
open,
And the foundations of the earth are
shaken.

19 The earth is violently broken,
The earth is split open,
The earth is shaken exceedingly.
20 The earth shall reel to and fro like a
drunkard,
And shall totter like a hut;
Its transgression shall be heavy upon
it,
And it will fall, and not rise again.

21 It shall come to pass in that day
That the LORD will punish on high
the host of exalted ones,
And on the earth the kings of the
earth.
22 They will be gathered together,
As prisoners are gathered in the pit,
And will be shut up in the prison;
After many days they will be
punished.
23 Then the moon will be disgraced
And the sun ashamed;
For the LORD of hosts will reign
On Mount Zion and in Jerusalem
And before His elders, gloriously.

PSALM 107:10–22

10 THOSE who sat in darkness and in
the shadow of death,
Bound in affliction and irons—

---

*"Darkness" is my own
point of view, my prejudices
and preconceived
determinations.*   (BIB. PSYCH.)

---

11 Because they rebelled against the words
of God,
And despised the counsel of the Most
High,
12 Therefore He brought down their
heart with labor;
They fell down, and *there was* none to
help.

13 Then they cried out to the LORD in
their trouble,
And He saved them out of their
distresses.
14 He brought them out of darkness and
the shadow of death,
And broke their chains in pieces.
15 Oh, that *men* would give thanks to the
LORD *for* His goodness,
And *for* His wonderful works to the
children of men!
16 For He has broken the gates of bronze,
And cut the bars of iron in two.

17 Fools, because of their transgression,
And because of their iniquities, were
afflicted.
18 Their soul abhorred all manner of food,
And they drew near to the gates of
death.
19 Then they cried out to the LORD in
their trouble,
And He saved them out of their
distresses.
20 He sent His word and healed them,
And delivered *them* from their
destructions.
21 Oh, that *men* would give thanks to the
LORD *for* His goodness,
And *for* His wonderful works to the
children of men!
22 Let them sacrifice the sacrifices of
thanksgiving,
And declare His works with rejoicing.

PROVERBS 25:17

17 SELDOM set foot in your neighbor's
house,
Lest he become weary of you and hate
you.

2 CORINTHIANS 8:1–24

MOREOVER, brethren, we make known
to you the grace of God bestowed on the
churches of Macedonia: 2 that in a great
trial of affliction the abundance of their joy
and their deep poverty abounded in the
riches of their liberality. 3 For I bear witness
that according to *their* ability, yes, and beyond *their* ability, *they were* freely willing,
4 imploring us with much urgency that we
would receive the gift and the fellowship
of the ministering to the saints. 5 And not
only as we had hoped, but they first gave
themselves to the Lord, and *then* to us by
the will of God. 6 So we urged Titus, that
as he had begun, so he would also complete

this grace in you as well. 7 But as you abound in everything—in faith, in speech, in knowledge, in all diligence, and in your love for us—*see* that you abound in this grace also.

We are here to be living monuments of God's grace. (UTMOST)

---

8 I speak not by commandment, but I am testing the sincerity of your love by the diligence of others. 9 For you know the grace of our Lord Jesus Christ, that though He was rich, yet for your sakes He became poor, that you through His poverty might become rich.

10 And in this I give advice: It is to your advantage not only to be doing what you began and were desiring to do a year ago; 11 but now you also must complete the doing *of it;* that as *there was* a readiness to desire *it,* so *there* also *may be* a completion out of what *you* have. 12 For if there is first a willing mind, *it is* accepted according to what one has, *and* not according to what he does not have.

13 For *I do* not *mean* that others should be eased and you burdened; 14 but by an equality, *that* now at this time your abun-dance *may supply* their lack, that their abundance also may supply your lack—that there may be equality. 15 As it is written, "He who *gathered* much had nothing left over, and he who *gathered* little had no lack."

16 But thanks *be* to God who puts the same earnest care for you into the heart of Titus. 17 For he not only accepted the exhortation, but being more diligent, he went to you of his own accord. 18 And we have sent with him the brother whose praise *is* in the gospel throughout all the churches, 19 and not only *that,* but who was also chosen by the churches to travel with us with this gift, which is administered by us to the glory of the Lord Himself and *to show* your ready mind, 20 avoiding this: that anyone should blame us in this lavish gift which is administered by us— 21 providing honorable things, not only in the sight of the Lord, but also in the sight of men.

22 And we have sent with them our brother whom we have often proved diligent in many things, but now much more diligent, because of the great confidence which *we have* in you. 23 If *anyone inquires* about Titus, *he is* my partner and fellow worker concerning you. Or if our brethren *are inquired about, they are* messengers of the churches, the glory of Christ. 24 Therefore show to them, and before the churches the proof of your love and of our boasting on your behalf.

◆◆◆◆

Reading 260—Give Money; Give Sympathy
2 Corinthians 9:6–15

The greatest motive in all giving is Jesus Christ's command.
(SERMON MT.)

As long as we have something to give, we must give. How does civilization argue? "Does this man deserve that I should give to him?" "If I give that man money, I know what he will do with it." Jesus Christ says, "Give to him who asks you," not because he deserves it, but "because I tell you to." (SHADE)

As Christians our giving is to be proportionate to all we have received of the infinite giving of God. "Freely you have received, freely give." Not how much we give, but what we do not give, is the test of our Christianity. When we speak of giving we nearly always think only of money. Money is the lifeblood of most of us. We have a remarkable trick—when we give money we don't give sympathy; and when we give sympathy we don't give money.
(CONFORMED)

ISAIAH 25:1—26:21

1 O LORD, You *are* my God.
I will exalt You,
I will praise Your name,
For You have done wonderful *things;*
Your counsels of old *are* faithfulness
and truth.

2 For You have made a city a ruin,
A fortified city a ruin,
A palace of foreigners to be a city
no more;
It will never be rebuilt.

3 Therefore the strong people will
glorify You;
The city of the terrible nations will
fear You.

4 For You have been a strength to the
poor,
A strength to the needy in his distress,
A refuge from the storm,
A shade from the heat;
For the blast of the terrible ones *is*
as a storm *against* the wall.

5 You will reduce the noise of aliens,
As heat in a dry place;
As heat in the shadow of a cloud,
The song of the terrible ones will
be diminished.

6 And in this mountain
The LORD of hosts will make for all
people
A feast of choice pieces,
A feast of wines on the lees,
Of fat things full of marrow,
Of well-refined wines on the lees.

7 And He will destroy on this
mountain
The surface of the covering cast over
all people,
And the veil that is spread over all
nations.

8 He will swallow up death forever,
And the Lord GOD will wipe away
tears from all faces;
The rebuke of His people
He will take away from all the earth;
For the LORD has spoken.

9 And it will be said in that day:
"Behold, this *is* our God;
We have waited for Him, and He
will save us.
This *is* the LORD;
We have waited for Him;
We will be glad and rejoice in His
salvation."

10 For on this mountain the hand of
the LORD will rest,

And Moab shall be trampled down
under Him,
As straw is trampled down for the
refuse heap.

11 And He will spread out His hands
in their midst
As a swimmer reaches out to swim,
And He will bring down their pride
Together with the trickery of their
hands.

12 The fortress of the high fort of your
walls
He will bring down, lay low,
And bring to the ground, down to
the dust.

26 IN that day this song will be sung
in the land of Judah:

"We have a strong city;
God will appoint salvation *for* walls
and bulwarks.

2 Open the gates,
That the righteous nation which
keeps the truth may enter in.

3 You will keep *him* in perfect peace,
Whose mind *is* stayed *on You,*
Because he trusts in You.

4 Trust in the LORD forever,
For in YAH, the LORD, *is* everlasting
strength.

5 For He brings down those who dwell
on high,
The lofty city;
He lays it low,
He lays it low to the ground,
He brings it down to the dust.

6 The foot shall tread it down—
The feet of the poor
And the steps of the needy."

7 The way of the just *is* uprightness;
O Most Upright,
You weigh the path of the just.

8 Yes, in the way of Your judgments,
O LORD, we have waited for You;
The desire of *our* soul *is* for Your
name
And for the remembrance of You.

9 With my soul I have desired You in
the night,
Yes, by my spirit within me I will
seek You early;
For when Your judgments *are* in the
earth,
The inhabitants of the world will
learn righteousness.

---

*The struggle of spirit is to get itself
expressed in the soul.* (BIB. PSYCH.)

10 Let grace be shown to the wicked,
   Yet he will not learn righteousness;
   In the land of uprightness he will
   deal unjustly,
   And will not behold the majesty of
   the LORD.
11 LORD, *when* Your hand is lifted up,
   they will not see.
   But they will see and be ashamed
   For *their* envy of people;
   Yes, the fire of Your enemies shall
   devour them.

12 LORD, You will establish peace for
   us,
   For You have also done all our works
   in us.
13 O LORD our God, masters besides
   You
   Have had dominion over us;
   But by You only we make mention
   of Your name.
14 *They are* dead, they will not live;
   They are deceased, they will not rise.
   Therefore You have punished and
   destroyed them,
   And made all their memory to perish.
15 You have increased the nation,
   O LORD,
   You have increased the nation;
   You are glorified;
   You have expanded all the borders
   of the land.

16 LORD, in trouble they have visited
   You,
   They poured out a prayer *when* Your
   chastening *was* upon them.
17 As a woman with child
   Is in pain and cries out in her pangs,
   When she draws near the time of her
   delivery,
   So have we been in Your sight,
   O LORD.
18 We have been with child, we have
   been in pain;
   We have, as it were, brought forth
   wind;
   We have not accomplished any
   deliverance in the earth,
   Nor have the inhabitants of the world
   fallen.

19 Your dead shall live;
   Together with my dead body they shall
   arise.
   Awake and sing, you who dwell in
   dust;
   For your dew *is like* the dew of herbs,
   And the earth shall cast out the dead.

20 Come, my people, enter your
   chambers,
   And shut your doors behind you;
   Hide yourself, as it were, for a little
   moment,
   Until the indignation is past.
21 For behold, the LORD comes out of
   His place
   To punish the inhabitants of the earth
   for their iniquity;
   The earth will also disclose her blood,
   And will no more cover her slain.

PSALM 107:23–32

23 THOSE who go down to the sea in
   ships,
   Who do business on great waters,
24 They see the works of the LORD,
   And His wonders in the deep.
25 For He commands and raises the stormy
   wind,
   Which lifts up the waves of the sea.
26 They mount up to the heavens,
   They go down again to the depths;
   Their soul melts because of trouble.
27 They reel to and fro, and stagger like
   a drunken man,
   And are at their wits' end.
28 Then they cry out to the LORD in their
   trouble,
   And He brings them out of their
   distresses.
29 He calms the storm,
   So that its waves are still.
30 Then they are glad because they are
   quiet;
   So He guides them to their desired
   haven.
31 Oh, that *men* would give thanks to the
   LORD *for* His goodness,
   And *for* His wonderful works to the
   children of men!
32 Let them exalt Him also in the assembly
   of the people,
   And praise Him in the company of the
   elders.

PROVERBS 25:18, 19

18 A man who bears false witness against
   his neighbor
   Is like a club, a sword, and a sharp
   arrow.

19 Confidence in an unfaithful *man* in
   time of trouble
   Is like a bad tooth and a foot out of
   joint.

2 CORINTHIANS 9:1–15

NOW concerning the ministering to the saints, it is superfluous for me to write to you; 2 for I know your willingness, about which I boast of you to the Macedonians, that Achaia was ready a year ago; and your zeal has stirred up the majority. 3 Yet I have sent the brethren, lest our boasting of you should be in vain in this respect, that, as I said, you may be ready; 4 lest if *some* Macedonians come with me and find you unprepared, we (not to mention you!) should be ashamed of this confident boasting. 5 Therefore I thought it necessary to exhort the brethren to go to you ahead of time, and prepare your generous gift beforehand, which *you had* previously promised, that it may be ready as *a matter of* generosity and not as a grudging obligation.

6 But this *I say:* He who sows sparingly will also reap sparingly, and he who sows bountifully will also reap bountifully. 7 *So let* each one *give* as he purposes in his heart, not grudgingly or of necessity; for God loves a cheerful giver. 8 And God *is* able to make all grace abound toward you, that you, always having all sufficiency in all *things,* may have an abundance for every good work. 9 As it is written:

> "He has dispersed abroad,
> He has given to the poor;
> His righteousness endures forever."

10 Now may He who supplies seed to the sower, and bread for food, supply and multiply the seed you have *sown* and increase the fruits of your righteousness, 11 while *you are* enriched in everything for all liberality, which causes thanksgiving through us to God. 12 For the administration of this service not only supplies the needs of the saints, but also is abounding through many thanksgivings to God, 13 while, through the proof of this ministry, they glorify God for the obedience of your confession to the gospel of Christ, and for *your* liberal sharing with them and all *men,* 14 and by their prayer for you, who long for you because of the exceeding grace of God in you. 15 Thanks *be* to God for His indescribable gift!

What do we do to earn a gift? Nothing; we take it. (BRILL. HERITAGE)

Reading 261—Where the Battle Is Won
2 Corinthians 10:3–5

The battle is lost or won in the secret places of the will before God, never first in the external world. The Spirit of God apprehends me and I am obliged to get alone with God and fight the battle out before Him. Until this is done, I lose every time. . . .

If I say, "I will wait till I get into the circumstances and then put God to the test," I shall find I cannot. I must get the thing settled between myself and God in the secret places of my soul where no stranger intermeddles, and then I can go forth with the certainty that the battle is won. Lose it there, and calamity and disaster and upset are as sure as God's decree. The reason the battle is not won is because I try to win it in the external world first. Get alone with God, fight it out before Him, settle the matter there once and for all.

In dealing with other people, the line to take is to push them to an issue of will. That is the way abandonment begins. Every now and again, not often, but sometimes, God brings us to a point of climax. That is the Great Divide in the life; from that point we either go toward a more and more dilatory and useless type of Christian life, or we become more and more ablaze for the glory of God—My Utmost for *His* Highest. (*UTMOST*)

ISAIAH 27:1—28:29

1 IN that day the LORD with His
  severe sword, great and strong,
  Will punish Leviathan the fleeing
  serpent,
  Leviathan that twisted serpent;
  And He will slay the reptile that *is*
  in the sea.

2 In that day sing to her,
  "A vineyard of red wine!
3 I, the LORD, keep it,
  I water it every moment;
  Lest any hurt it,
  I keep it night and day.
4 Fury *is* not in Me.
  Who would set briers *and* thorns
  Against Me in battle?
  I would go through them,
  I would burn them together.
5 Or let him take hold of My strength,
  That he may make peace with Me;
  And he shall make peace with Me."

6 Those who come He shall cause to
  take root in Jacob;
  Israel shall blossom and bud,
  And fill the face of the world with
  fruit.

7 Has He struck Israel as He struck
  those who struck him?
  Or has He been slain according to
  the slaughter of those who were
  slain by Him?
8 In measure, by sending it away,
  You contended with it.
  He removes *it* by His rough wind
  In the day of the east wind.
9 Therefore by this the iniquity of
  Jacob will be covered;
  And this *is* all the fruit of taking away
  his sin:
  When he makes all the stones of the
  altar
  Like chalkstones that are beaten to
  dust,
  Wooden images and incense altars
  shall not stand.

10 Yet the fortified city *will be* desolate,
  The habitation forsaken and left like
  a wilderness;
  There the calf will feed, and there it
  will lie down
  And consume its branches.
11 When its boughs are withered, they
  will be broken off;
  The women come *and* set them on
  fire.

For it *is* a people of no understanding;
  Therefore He who made them will
  not have mercy on them,
  And He who formed them will show
  them no favor.

12 And it shall come to pass in that day
  That the LORD will thresh,
  From the channel of the River to the
  Brook of Egypt;
  And you will be gathered one by one,
  O you children of Israel.

13 So it shall be in that day:
  The great trumpet will be blown;
  They will come, who are about to
  perish in the land of Assyria,
  And they who are outcasts in the land
  of Egypt,
  And shall worship the LORD in the
  holy mount at Jerusalem.

28 WOE to the crown of pride, to the
  drunkards of Ephraim,
  Whose glorious beauty *is* a fading
  flower
  Which *is* at the head of the verdant
  valleys,
  To those who are overcome with
  wine!
2 Behold, the Lord has a mighty and
  strong one,
  Like a tempest of hail and a
  destroying storm,
  Like a flood of mighty waters
  overflowing,
  Who will bring *them* down to the
  earth with *His* hand.
3 The crown of pride, the drunkards
  of Ephraim,
  Will be trampled underfoot;
4 And the glorious beauty is a fading
  flower
  Which *is* at the head of the verdant
  valley,
  Like the first fruit before the summer,
  Which an observer sees;
  He eats it up while it is still in his
  hand.

5 In that day the LORD of hosts
  will be
  For a crown of glory and a diadem
  of beauty
  To the remnant of His people,
6 For a spirit of justice to him who
  sits in judgment,
  And for strength to those who turn
  back the battle at the gate.

7 But they also have erred through
  wine,

And through intoxicating drink are
  out of the way;
The priest and the prophet have
  erred through intoxicating drink,
They are swallowed up by wine,
They are out of the way through
  intoxicating drink;
They err in vision, they stumble *in*
  judgment.
8 For all tables are full of vomit *and*
  filth;
  No place *is clean.*

9 "Whom will he teach knowledge?
  And whom will he make to
    understand the message?
  Those *just* weaned from milk?
  Those *just* drawn from the breasts?
10 For precept *must be* upon precept,
    precept upon precept,
  Line upon line, line upon line,
  Here a little, there a little."

11 For with stammering lips and
    another tongue
  He will speak to this people,
12 To whom He said, "This *is* the rest
    with which
  You may cause the weary to rest,"
  And, "This *is* the refreshing";
  Yet they would not hear.
13 But the word of the Lord was to
    them,
  "Precept upon precept, precept upon
    precept,
  Line upon line, line upon line,
  Here a little, there a little,"
  That they might go and fall
    backward, and be broken
  And snared and caught.

14 Therefore hear the word of the Lord,
    you scornful men,
  Who rule this people who *are* in
    Jerusalem,
15 Because you have said, "We have
    made a covenant with death,
  And with Sheol we are in agreement.
  When the overflowing scourge passes
    through,
  It will not come to us,
  For we have made lies our refuge,
  And under falsehood we have hidden
    ourselves."

16 Therefore thus says the Lord God:

  "Behold, I lay in Zion a stone for a
    foundation,
  A tried stone, a precious cornerstone,
    a sure foundation;

Whoever believes will not act hastily.
17 Also I will make justice the
    measuring line,
  And righteousness the plummet;
  The hail will sweep away the refuge
    of lies,
  And the waters will overflow the
    hiding place.
18 Your covenant with death will be
    annulled,
  And your agreement with Sheol will
    not stand;
  When the overflowing scourge
    passes through,
  Then you will be trampled down
    by it.
19 As often as it goes out it will take
    you;
  For morning by morning it will pass
    over,
  And by day and by night;
  It will be a terror just to understand
    the report."

20 For the bed is too short to stretch
    out *on,*
  And the covering so narrow that one
    cannot wrap himself *in it.*
21 For the Lord will rise up as *at* Mount
    Perazim,
  He will be angry as in the Valley of
    Gibeon—
  That He may do His work, His
    awesome work,
  And bring to pass His act, His
    unusual act.
22 Now therefore, do not be mockers,
  Lest your bonds be made strong;
  For I have heard from the Lord God
    of hosts,
  A destruction determined even upon
    the whole earth.

23 Give ear and hear my voice,
  Listen and hear my speech.
24 Does the plowman keep plowing all
    day to sow?
  Does he keep turning his soil and
    breaking the clods?
25 When he has leveled its surface,
  Does he not sow the black cummin
  And scatter the cummin,
  Plant the wheat in rows,
  The barley in the appointed place,
  And the spelt in its place?
26 For He instructs him in right
    judgment,
  His God teaches him.

27 For the black cummin is not threshed
    with a threshing sledge,

Nor is a cartwheel rolled over the
  cummin;
But the black cummin is beaten out
  with a stick,
And the cummin with a rod.
28 Bread *flour* must be ground;
  Therefore he does not thresh it
  forever,
  Break *it with* his cartwheel,
  Or crush it *with* his horsemen.
29 This also comes from the LORD of
  hosts,
  Who is wonderful in counsel *and*
  excellent in guidance.

PSALM 107:33–43

33 HE turns rivers into a wilderness,
  And the watersprings into dry ground;
34 A fruitful land into barrenness,
  For the wickedness of those who dwell
  in it.
35 He turns a wilderness into pools of
  water,
  And dry land into watersprings.
36 There He makes the hungry dwell,
  That they may establish a city for a
  dwelling place,
37 And sow fields and plant vineyards,
  That they may yield a fruitful harvest.
38 He also blesses them, and they multiply
  greatly;
  And He does not let their cattle
  decrease.

39 When they are diminished and brought
  low
  Through oppression, affliction and
  sorrow,
40 He pours contempt on princes,
  And causes them to wander in the
  wilderness *where there is* no way;
41 Yet He sets the poor on high, far from
  affliction,
  And makes *their* families like a flock.
42 The righteous see *it* and rejoice,
  And all iniquity stops its mouth.

43 Whoever *is* wise will observe these
  things,
  And they will understand the
  lovingkindness of the LORD.

PROVERBS 25:20

20 *LIKE* one who takes away a garment
  in cold weather,
  And like vinegar on soda,
  Is one who sings songs to a heavy heart.

2 CORINTHIANS 10:1–18

NOW I, Paul, myself am pleading with you
by the meekness and gentleness of Christ—
who in presence *am* lowly among you, but
being absent am bold toward you. 2 But I
beg *you* that when I am present I may not
be bold with that confidence by which I
intend to be bold against some, who think
of us as if we walked according to the flesh.
3 For though we walk in the flesh, we do
not war according to the flesh. 4 For the
weapons of our warfare *are* not carnal but
mighty in God for pulling down strongholds, 5 casting down arguments and every
high thing that exalts itself against the
knowledge of God, bringing every thought
into captivity to the obedience of Christ,

*Until a man is born again,
he cannot think as a
Christian.*   (PSY. REDEMP.)

6 and being ready to punish all disobedience
when your obedience is fulfilled.

7 Do you look at things according to the
outward appearance? If anyone is convinced
in himself that he is Christ's, let him again
consider this in himself, that just as he *is*
Christ's, even so we *are* Christ's. 8 For even
if I should boast somewhat more about our
authority, which the Lord gave us for edification and not for your destruction, I shall
not be ashamed— 9 lest I seem to terrify
you by letters. 10 "For *his* letters," they say,
"*are* weighty and powerful, but *his* bodily
presence *is* weak, and *his* speech contempt-
ible." 11 Let such a person consider this,
that what we are in word by letters when
we are absent, such *we will* also *be* in deed
when we are present.

12 For we dare not class ourselves or compare ourselves with those who commend
themselves. But they, measuring themselves
by themselves, and comparing themselves
among themselves, are not wise. 13 We,
however, will not boast beyond measure,
but within the limits of the sphere which
God appointed us—a sphere which especially includes you. 14 For we are not over-
extending ourselves (as though *our authority*
did not extend to you), for it was to you
that we came with the gospel of Christ;
15 not boasting of things beyond measure,
that is, in other men's labors, but having
hope, *that* as your faith is increased, we
shall be greatly enlarged by you in our
sphere, 16 to preach the gospel in the *regions*

beyond you, *and* not to boast in another man's sphere of accomplishment.

17 But "he who glories, let him glory in the LORD." 18 For not he who commends himself is approved, but whom the Lord commends.

◆◆◆

Reading 262—The Importance of the Cross
2 Corinthians 11:3

Today any number of religious books set out to expound Jesus Christ from a philosophical point of view. They are entrancing and apparently helpful, but in reality they do a great deal of harm, because instead of helping us to form the mind of Christ and understand His point of view, they serve to confuse our mind. When people ask for the "simple gospel" to be preached, they generally mean, "Preach us the thing we have always listened to, the thing that keeps us sound asleep. Don't present us with anything new." That means the mind is not open to accept facts, not open to entering into a relationship with God.

The Cross is the symbol of Christian living and it is also the symbol of Christian thinking. Until a man is born again, his thinking goes round and round in a circle and he becomes intoxicated with his own importance. When he is born again, there is a violent readjustment in his actual life, and when he begins to think along Jesus Christ's line, there is just as tremendous a revolution in his thinking processes. To ignore the Cross in either living or thinking is to become a traitor to Jesus Christ.   (*GLORY*)

ISAIAH 29:1–24

1 "WOE to Ariel, to Ariel, the city
        where David dwelt!
    Add year to year;
    Let feasts come around.
2 Yet I will distress Ariel;
    There shall be heaviness and sorrow,
    And it shall be to Me as Ariel.
3 I will encamp against you all
        around,
    I will lay siege against you with a
        mound,
    And I will raise siegeworks against
        you.
4 You shall be brought down,
    You shall speak out of the ground;
    Your speech shall be low, out of the
        dust;
    Your voice shall be like a medium's,
        out of the ground;
    And your speech shall whisper out
        of the dust.

5 "Moreover the multitude of your
        foes
    Shall be like fine dust,

    And the multitude of the terrible
        ones
    Like chaff that passes away;
    Yes, it shall be in an instant,
        suddenly.
6 You will be punished by the LORD
        of hosts
    With thunder and earthquake and
        great noise,
    With storm and tempest
    And the flame of devouring fire.
7 The multitude of all the nations who
        fight against Ariel,
    Even all who fight against her and
        her fortress,
    And distress her,
    Shall be as a dream of a night vision.
8 It shall even be as when a hungry
        man dreams,
    And look—he eats;
    But he awakes, and his soul is still
        empty;
    Or as when a thirsty man dreams,
    And look—he drinks;
    But he awakes, and indeed *he is*
        faint,
    And his soul still craves:

So the multitude of all the nations
   shall be,
Who fight against Mount Zion."
9 Pause and wonder!
   Blind yourselves and be blind!
   They are drunk, but not with wine;
   They stagger, but not with
      intoxicating drink.
10 For the LORD has poured out on you
   The spirit of deep sleep,
   And has closed your eyes, namely,
      the prophets;
   And He has covered your heads,
      namely, the seers.

11 The whole vision has become to you
like the words of a book that is sealed, which
men deliver to one who is literate, saying,
"Read this, please."
And he says, "I cannot, for it *is* sealed."
12 Then the book is delivered to one who
is illiterate, saying, "Read this, please."
And he says, "I am not literate."
13 Therefore the Lord said:

"Inasmuch as these people draw near
   with their mouths
And honor Me with their lips,
But have removed their hearts far
   from Me,
And their fear toward Me is taught
   by the commandment of men,
14 Therefore, behold, I will again do a
      marvelous work
   Among this people,
   A marvelous work and a wonder;
   For the wisdom of their wise *men*
      shall perish,
   And the understanding of their
      prudent *men* shall be hidden."

15 Woe to those who seek deep to hide
      their counsel far from the LORD,
   And their works are in the dark;
   They say, "Who sees us?" and, "Who
      knows us?"

A man is what he is in the
   dark.   (PLACE HELP)

---

16 Surely you have things turned
      around!
   Shall the potter be esteemed as the
      clay;
   For shall the thing made say of him
      who made it,
   "He did not make me"?
   Or shall the thing formed say of him
      who formed it,

"He has no understanding"?

17 *Is* it not yet a very little while
   Till Lebanon shall be turned into a
      fruitful field,
   And the fruitful field be esteemed as
      a forest?
18 In that day the deaf shall hear the
      words of the book,
   And the eyes of the blind shall see
      out of obscurity and out of
      darkness.
19 The humble also shall increase *their*
      joy in the LORD,
   And the poor among men shall
      rejoice
   In the Holy One of Israel.
20 For the terrible one is brought to
      nothing,
   The scornful one is consumed,
   And all who watch for iniquity are
      cut off—
21 Who make a man an offender by a
      word,
   And lay a snare for him who reproves
      in the gate,
   And turn aside the just by empty
      words.

22 Therefore thus says the LORD, who
redeemed Abraham, concerning the house
of Jacob:

"Jacob shall not now be ashamed,
   Nor shall his face now grow pale;
23 But when he sees his children,
   The work of My hands, in his midst,
   They will hallow My name,
   And hallow the Holy One of Jacob,
   And fear the God of Israel.
24 These also who erred in spirit will
      come to understanding,
   And those who complained will learn
      doctrine."

PSALM 108:1–6

1 O God, my heart is steadfast;
   I will sing and give praise, even with
      my glory.
2 Awake, lute and harp!
   I will awaken the dawn.
3 I will praise You, O LORD, among the
      peoples,
   And I will sing praises to You among
      the nations.
4 For Your mercy *is* great above the
      heavens,
   And Your truth *reaches* to the clouds.

5 Be exalted, O God, above the heavens,
And Your glory above all the earth;

6 That Your beloved may be delivered,
Save *with* Your right hand, and hear
me.

PROVERBS 25:21, 22

21 IF your enemy is hungry, give him
bread to eat;
And if he is thirsty, give him water to
drink;

22 For *so* you will heap coals of fire on
his head,
And the LORD will reward you.

2 CORINTHIANS 11:1–15

OH, that you would bear with me in a
little folly—and indeed you do bear with
me. 2 For I am jealous for you with godly
jealousy. For I have betrothed you to one
husband, that I may present *you as* a chaste
virgin to Christ. 3 But I fear, lest somehow,
as the serpent deceived Eve by his craftiness,
so your minds may be corrupted from the
simplicity that is in Christ. 4 For if he who
comes preaches another Jesus whom we
have not preached, or *if* you receive a different spirit which you have not received, or
a different gospel which you have not accepted—you may well put up with it!

5 For I consider that I am not at all inferior to the most eminent apostles. 6 Even
though *I am* untrained in speech, yet *I
am* not in knowledge. But we have been
thoroughly manifested among you in all
things.

7 Did I commit sin in humbling myself
that you might be exalted, because I
preached the gospel of God to you free of
charge? 8 I robbed other churches, taking
wages *from them* to minister to you.
9 And when I was present with you, and
in need, I was a burden to no one, for
what I lacked the brethren who came from
Macedonia supplied. And in everything I
kept myself from being burdensome to
you, and so I will keep *myself.* 10 As the
truth of Christ is in me, no one shall stop
me from this boasting in the regions of
Achaia. 11 Why? Because I do not love you?
God knows!

12 But what I do, I will also continue
to do, that I may cut off the opportunity
from those who desire an opportunity to
be regarded just as we are in the things of
which they boast. 13 For such *are* false
apostles, deceitful workers, transforming
themselves into apostles of Christ. 14 And
no wonder! For Satan himself transforms
himself into an angel of light. 15 Therefore
it is no great thing if his ministers also transform themselves into ministers of righteousness, whose end will be according to their
works.

◆◆◆◆

Reading 263—Testing Spiritual Maturity
Isaiah 30:21

The surest test of maturity is the power to look back without blinking
anything. When we look back we get either hopelessly despairing or
hopelessly conceited. The difference between the natural backward look and
the spiritual backward look is in what we forget. Forgetting in the natural
domain is the outcome of vanity—the only things I intend to remember are
those in which I figure as being a very fine person! Forgetting in the spiritual
domain is the gift of God. The Spirit of God never allows us to forget what
we have been, but He does make us forget what we have attained to, which
is quite unnatural. The surest sign that you are growing in mature appreciation
of your salvation is that as you look back you never think now of the things
you used to bank on before. Think of the difference between your first realization
of God's forgiveness, and your realization of what it cost God to forgive you;
the hilarity in the one case has been merged into holiness, you have become
intensely devoted to God who forgave you. (*CONFORMED*)

ISAIAH 30:1—32:20

1 "WOE to the rebellious children,"
    says the Lord,
"Who take counsel, but not of Me,
    And who devise plans, but not of
      My Spirit,
    That they may add sin to sin;
2 Who walk to go down to Egypt,
    And have not asked My advice,
    To strengthen themselves in the
      strength of Pharaoh,
    And to trust in the shadow of Egypt!
3 Therefore the strength of Pharaoh
    Shall be your shame,
    And trust in the shadow of Egypt
    Shall be *your* humiliation.
4 For his princes were at Zoan,
    And his ambassadors came to Hanes.
5 They were all ashamed of a people
    who could not benefit them,
    Or be help or benefit,
    But a shame and also a reproach."

6 The burden against the beasts of the
South.

    Through a land of trouble and
      anguish,
    From which *came* the lioness and
      lion,
    The viper and fiery flying serpent,
    They will carry their riches on the
      backs of young donkeys,
    And their treasures on the humps of
      camels,
    To a people *who* shall not profit;
7 For the Egyptians shall help in vain
    and to no purpose.
    Therefore I have called her
    Rahab-Hem-Shebeth.

8 Now go, write it before them on a
    tablet,
    And note it on a scroll,
    That it may be for time to come,
    Forever and ever:
9 That this *is* a rebellious people,
    Lying children,
    Children *who* will not hear the law
      of the Lord;
10 Who say to the seers, "Do not see,"
    And to the prophets, "Do not
      prophesy to us right things;
    Speak to us smooth things, prophesy
      deceits.
11 Get out of the way,
    Turn aside from the path,
    Cause the Holy One of Israel
    To cease from before us."

12 Therefore thus says the Holy One of
Israel:

"Because you despise this word,
    And trust in oppression and
      perversity,
    And rely on them,
13 Therefore this iniquity shall be to you
    Like a breach ready to fall,
    A bulge in a high wall,
    Whose breaking comes suddenly, in
      an instant.
14 And He shall break it like the
      breaking of the potter's vessel,
    Which is broken in pieces;
    He shall not spare.
    So there shall not be found among
      its fragments
    A shard to take fire from the hearth,
    Or to take water from the cistern."

15 For thus says the Lord God, the Holy
One of Israel:

"In returning and rest you shall be
      saved;
    In quietness and confidence shall be
      your strength."
    But you would not,
16 And you said, "No, for we will flee
      on horses"—
    Therefore you shall flee!
    And, "We will ride on swift *horses*"—
    Therefore those who pursue you shall
      be swift!

17 One thousand *shall flee* at the threat
      of one,
    At the threat of five you shall flee,
    Till you are left as a pole on top of
      a mountain
    And as a banner on a hill.

18 Therefore the Lord will wait, that
      He may be gracious to you;
    And therefore He will be exalted, that
      He may have mercy on you.
    For the Lord *is* a God of justice;
    Blessed *are* all those who wait for
      Him.

19 For the people shall dwell in Zion
      at Jerusalem;
    You shall weep no more.
    He will be very gracious to you at
      the sound of your cry;
    When He hears it, He will answer
      you.
20 And *though* the Lord gives you
    The bread of adversity and the water
      of affliction,

Yet your teachers will not be moved
into a corner anymore,
But your eyes shall see your teachers.
21 Your ears shall hear a word behind
you, saying,
"This *is* the way, walk in it,"
Whenever you turn to the right
hand
Or whenever you turn to the left.
22 You will also defile the covering of
your images of silver,
And the ornament of your molded
images of gold.
You will throw them away as an
unclean thing;
You will say to them, "Get away!"

23 Then He will give the rain for your
seed
With which you sow the ground,
And bread of the increase of the
earth;
It will be fat and plentiful.
In that day your cattle will feed
In large pastures.
24 Likewise the oxen and the young
donkeys that work the ground
Will eat cured fodder,
Which has been winnowed with the
shovel and fan.
25 There will be on every high
mountain
And on every high hill
Rivers *and* streams of waters,
In the day of the great slaughter,
When the towers fall.
26 Moreover the light of the moon will
be as the light of the sun,
And the light of the sun will be
sevenfold,
As the light of seven days,
In the day that the LORD binds up
the bruise of His people
And heals the stroke of their
wound.

27 Behold, the name of the LORD comes
from afar,
Burning *with* His anger,
And *His* burden *is* heavy;
His lips are full of indignation,
And His tongue like a devouring
fire.
28 His breath is like an overflowing
stream,
Which reaches up to the neck,
To sift the nations with the sieve of
futility;
And *there shall be* a bridle in the jaws
of the people,
Causing *them* to err.

29 You shall have a song
As in the night *when* a holy festival
is kept,
And gladness of heart as when one
goes with a flute,
To come into the mountain of the
LORD,
To the Mighty One of Israel.
30 The LORD will cause His glorious
voice to be heard,
And show the descent of His arm,
With the indignation of *His* anger
And the flame of a devouring fire,
With scattering, tempest, and
hailstones.
31 For through the voice of the LORD
Assyria will be beaten down,
As He strikes with the rod.
32 And *in* every place where the staff
of punishment passes,
Which the LORD lays on him,
It will be with tambourines and
harps;
And in battles of brandishing He will
fight with it.
33 For Tophet *was* established of old,
Yes, for the king it is prepared.
He has made *it* deep and large;
Its pyre *is* fire with much wood;
The breath of the LORD, like a stream
of brimstone,
Kindles it.

31 WOE to those who go down to
Egypt for help,
And rely on horses,
Who trust in chariots because *they
are* many,
And in horsemen because they are
very strong,
But who do not look to the Holy
One of Israel,
Nor seek the LORD!
2 Yet He also *is* wise and will bring
disaster,
And will not call back His words,
But will arise against the house of
evildoers,
And against the help of those who
work iniquity.
3 Now the Egyptians *are* men, and not
God;
And their horses are flesh, and not
spirit.
When the LORD stretches out His
hand,
Both he who helps will fall,
And he who is helped will fall down;
They all will perish together.

4 For thus the LORD has spoken to me:

"As a lion roars,
And a young lion over his prey
(When a multitude of shepherds is
summoned against him,
He will not be afraid of their voice
Nor be disturbed by their noise),
So the LORD of hosts will come down
To fight for Mount Zion and for its
hill.

5 Like birds flying about,
So will the LORD of hosts defend
Jerusalem.
Defending, He will also deliver *it;*
Passing over, He will preserve *it.*"

6 Return *to Him* against whom the children of Israel have deeply revolted. 7 For in that day every man shall throw away his idols of silver and his idols of gold—sin, which your own hands have made for yourselves.

8 "Then Assyria shall fall by a sword
not of man,
And a sword not of mankind shall
devour him.
But he shall flee from the sword,
And his young men shall become
forced labor.

9 He shall cross over to his stronghold
for fear,
And his princes shall be afraid of the
banner,"
Says the LORD,
Whose fire *is* in Zion
And whose furnace *is* in Jerusalem.

32 BEHOLD, a king will reign in
righteousness,
And princes will rule with justice.

2 A man will be as a hiding place from
the wind,
And a cover from the tempest,
As rivers of water in a dry place,
As the shadow of a great rock in a
weary land.

3 The eyes of those who see will not
be dim,
And the ears of those who hear will
listen.

4 Also the heart of the rash will
understand knowledge,
And the tongue of the stammerers
will be ready to speak plainly.

5 The foolish person will no longer be
called generous,
Nor the miser said *to be* bountiful;

6 For the foolish person will speak
foolishness,
And his heart will work iniquity:

To practice ungodliness,
To utter error against the LORD,
To keep the hungry unsatisfied,
And he will cause the drink of the
thirsty to fail.

7 Also the schemes of the schemer *are*
evil;
He devises wicked plans
To destroy the poor with lying
words,
Even when the needy speaks justice.

8 But a generous man devises generous
things,
And by generosity he shall stand.

9 Rise up, you women who are at ease,
Hear my voice;
You complacent daughters,
Give ear to my speech.

10 In a year and *some* days
You will be troubled, you complacent
women;
For the vintage will fail,
The gathering will not come.

11 Tremble, you *women* who are at ease;
Be troubled, you complacent ones;
Strip yourselves, make yourselves
bare,
And gird *sackcloth* on *your* waists.

12 People shall mourn upon their breasts
For the pleasant fields, for the fruitful
vine.

13 On the land of my people will come
up thorns *and* briers,
Yes, on all the happy homes *in* the
joyous city;

14 Because the palaces will be forsaken,
The bustling city will be deserted.
The forts and towers will become lairs
forever,
A joy of wild donkeys, a pasture of
flocks—

15 Until the Spirit is poured upon us
from on high,
And the wilderness becomes a fruitful
field,
And the fruitful field is counted as
a forest.

16 Then justice will dwell in the
wilderness,
And righteousness remain in the
fruitful field.

17 The work of righteousness will be
peace,
And the effect of righteousness,
quietness and assurance forever.

18 My people will dwell in a peaceful
habitation,
In secure dwellings, and in quiet
resting places,

19 Though hail comes down on the forest,
And the city is brought low in humiliation.

20 Blessed *are* you who sow beside all waters,
Who send out freely the feet of the ox and the donkey.

PSALM 108:7–13

7   GOD has spoken in His holiness:
"I will rejoice;
I will divide Shechem
And measure out the Valley of Succoth.
8   Gilead *is* Mine; Manasseh *is* Mine;
Ephraim also *is* the helmet for My head;
Judah *is* My lawgiver.
9   Moab *is* My washpot;
Over Edom I will cast My shoe;
Over Philistia I will triumph."

10 Who will bring me *into* the strong city?
Who will lead me to Edom?
11 *Is it* not *You*, O God, *who* cast us off?
And *You*, O God, *who* did not go out with our armies?
12 Give us help from trouble,
For the help of man is useless.
13 Through God we will do valiantly,
For *it is* He *who* shall tread down our enemies.

PROVERBS 25:23, 24

23 THE north wind brings forth rain,
And a backbiting tongue an angry countenance.

24 *It is* better to dwell in a corner of a housetop,
Than in a house shared with a contentious woman.

2 CORINTHIANS 11:16–33

I say again, let no one think me a fool. If otherwise, at least receive me as a fool, that I also may boast a little. 17 What I speak, I speak not according to the Lord, but as it were, foolishly, in this confidence of boasting. 18 Seeing that many boast according to the flesh, I also will boast. 19 For you put up with fools gladly, since you *yourselves* are wise! 20 For you put up with it if one brings you into bondage, if one devours *you*, if one takes *from you*, if one exalts himself, if one strikes you on the face. 21 To *our* shame I say that we were too weak for that! But in whatever anyone is bold—I speak foolishly—I am bold also.

22 Are they Hebrews? So *am* I. Are they Israelites? So *am* I. Are they the seed of Abraham? So *am* I. 23 Are they ministers of Christ?—I speak as a fool—I *am* more: in labors more abundant, in stripes above measure, in prisons more frequently, in deaths often. 24 From the Jews five times I received forty *stripes* minus one. 25 Three

---

*N*ever yield to a power unless you know its character.   (LOVE OF GOD)

---

times I was beaten with rods; once I was stoned; three times I was shipwrecked; a night and a day I have been in the deep; 26 *in* journeys often, *in* perils of waters, *in* perils of robbers, *in* perils of *my own* countrymen, *in* perils of the Gentiles, *in* perils in the city, *in* perils in the wilderness, *in* perils in the sea, *in* perils among false brethren; 27 in weariness and toil, in sleeplessness often, in hunger and thirst, in fastings often, in cold and nakedness— 28 besides the other things, what comes upon me daily: my deep concern for all the churches. 29 Who is weak, and I am not weak? Who is made to stumble, and I do not burn *with indignation*?

30 If I must boast, I will boast in the things which concern my infirmity. 31 The God and Father of our Lord Jesus Christ, who is blessed forever, knows that I am not lying. 32 In Damascus the governor, under Aretas the king, was guarding the city of the Damascenes with a garrison, desiring to arrest me; 33 but I was let down in a basket through a window in the wall, and escaped from his hands.

Reading 264—The Delight of Sacrifice
2 Corinthians 12:15

When the Spirit of God has shed abroad the love of God in our hearts, we begin deliberately to identify ourselves with Jesus Christ's interests in other people, and Jesus Christ is interested in every kind of man there is. We have no right in Christian work to be guided by our affinities; this is one of the biggest tests of our relationship to Jesus Christ. The delight of sacrifice is that I lay down my life for my Friend, not fling it away, but deliberately lay my life out for Him and His interests in other people, not for a cause. Paul spent himself for one purpose only—that he might win men to Jesus Christ. Paul attracted to Jesus all the time, never to himself. "I have become all things to all *men*, that I might by all means save some." When a man says he must develop a holy life alone with God, he is of no more use to his fellowmen: he puts himself on a pedestal, away from the common run of men. Paul became a sacramental personality; wherever he went, Jesus Christ helped Himself to his life. Many of us are after our own ends, and Jesus Christ cannot help Himself to our lives. If we are abandoned to Jesus, we have no ends of our own to serve.   (*Utmost*)

ISAIAH 33:1—34:17

1 WOE to you who plunder, though
   you *have* not *been* plundered;
   And you who deal treacherously,
   though they have not dealt
   treacherously with you!
   When you cease plundering,
   You will be plundered;
   When you make an end of dealing
   treacherously,
   They will deal treacherously with
   you.

2 O Lord, be gracious to us;
   We have waited for You.
   Be their arm every morning,
   Our salvation also in the time of
   trouble.

3 At the noise of the tumult the people
   shall flee;
   When You lift Yourself up, the
   nations shall be scattered;

4 And Your plunder shall be gathered
   Like the gathering of the caterpillar;
   As the running to and fro of locusts,
   He shall run upon them.

5 The Lord is exalted, for He dwells
   on high;
   He has filled Zion with justice and
   righteousness.

6 Wisdom and knowledge will be the
   stability of your times,
   And the strength of salvation;
   The fear of the Lord *is* His
   treasure.

7 Surely their valiant ones shall cry
   outside,
   The ambassadors of peace shall weep
   bitterly.

8 The highways lie waste,
   The traveling man ceases.
   He has broken the covenant,
   He has despised the cities,
   He regards no man.

9 The earth mourns *and* languishes,
   Lebanon is shamed *and* shriveled;
   Sharon is like a wilderness,
   And Bashan and Carmel shake off
   their fruits.

10 "Now I will rise," says the Lord;
   "Now I will be exalted,
   Now I will lift Myself up.

11 You shall conceive chaff,
   You shall bring forth stubble;
   Your breath, *as* fire, shall devour
   you.

12 And the people shall be *like* the
   burnings of lime;
   Like thorns cut up they shall be
   burned in the fire.

13 Hear, you *who are* afar off, what I
   have done;
   And you *who are* near, acknowledge
   My might."

14 The sinners in Zion are afraid;
Fearfulness has seized the
hypocrites:
"Who among us shall dwell with the
devouring fire?
Who among us shall dwell with
everlasting burnings?"

15 He who walks righteously and speaks
uprightly,
He who despises the gain of
oppressions,
Who gestures with his hands,
refusing bribes,
Who stops his ears from hearing of
bloodshed,
And shuts his eyes from seeing evil:

16 He will dwell on high;
His place of defense *will be* the
fortress of rocks;
Bread will be given him,
His water *will be* sure.

17 Your eyes will see the King in His
beauty;
They will see the land that is very
far off.

18 Your heart will meditate on terror:
"Where *is* the scribe?
Where *is* he who weighs?
Where *is* he who counts the towers?"

19 You will not see a fierce people,
A people of obscure speech, beyond
perception,
Of a stammering tongue *that you*
cannot understand.

20 Look upon Zion, the city of our
appointed feasts;
Your eyes will see Jerusalem, a quiet
home,
A tabernacle *that* will not be taken
down;
Not one of its stakes will ever be
removed,
Nor will any of its cords be broken.

21 But there the majestic LORD *will be*
for us
A place of broad rivers *and* streams,
In which no galley with oars will sail,
Nor majestic ships pass by

22 (For the LORD *is* our Judge,
The LORD *is* our Lawgiver,
The LORD *is* our King;
He will save us);

23 Your tackle is loosed,
They could not strengthen their mast,
They could not spread the sail.

Then the prey of great plunder is
divided;
The lame take the prey.

24 And the inhabitant will not say, "I
am sick";
The people who dwell in it *will be*
forgiven *their* iniquity.

34 COME near, you nations, to hear;
And heed, you people!
Let the earth hear, and all that is
in it,
The world and all things that come
forth from it.

2 For the indignation of the LORD *is*
against all nations,
And *His* fury against all their armies;
He has utterly destroyed them,
He has given them over to the
slaughter.

3 Also their slain shall be thrown out;
Their stench shall rise from their
corpses,
And the mountains shall be melted
with their blood.

4 All the host of heaven shall be
dissolved,
And the heavens shall be rolled up
like a scroll;
All their host shall fall down
As the leaf falls from the vine,
And as *fruit* falling from a fig tree.

5 "For My sword shall be bathed in
heaven;
Indeed it shall come down on Edom,
And on the people of My curse, for
judgment.

6 The sword of the LORD is filled with
blood,
It is made overflowing with fatness,
With the blood of lambs and goats,
With the fat of the kidneys of rams.
For the LORD has a sacrifice in
Bozrah,
And a great slaughter in the land of
Edom.

7 The wild oxen shall come down with
them,
And the young bulls with the mighty
bulls;
Their land shall be soaked with
blood,
And their dust saturated with
fatness."

8 For *it is* the day of the LORD's
vengeance,
The year of recompense for the cause
of Zion.

9 Its streams shall be turned into pitch,
And its dust into brimstone;
Its land shall become burning pitch.

10 It shall not be quenched night or day;

Its smoke shall ascend forever.
From generation to generation it
shall lie waste;
No one shall pass through it forever
and ever.
11 But the pelican and the porcupine
shall possess it,
Also the owl and the raven shall dwell
in it.
And He shall stretch out over it
The line of confusion and the stones
of emptiness.
12 They shall call its nobles to the
kingdom,
But none *shall be* there, and all its
princes shall be nothing.

13 And thorns shall come up in its
palaces,
Nettles and brambles in its fortresses;
It shall be a habitation of jackals,
A courtyard for ostriches.
14 The wild beasts of the desert shall
also meet with the jackals,
And the wild goat shall bleat to its
companion;
Also the night creature shall rest
there,
And find for herself a place of rest.
15 There the arrow snake shall make her
nest and lay *eggs*
And hatch, and gather *them* under
her shadow;
There also shall the hawks be
gathered,
Every one with her mate.

16 "Search from the book of the LORD,
and read:
Not one of these shall fail;
Not one shall lack her mate.
For My mouth has commanded it,
and His Spirit has gathered them.
17 He has cast the lot for them,
And His hand has divided it among
them with a measuring line.
They shall possess it forever;
From generation to generation they
shall dwell in it."

PSALM 109:1–5

1   DO not keep silent,
O God of my praise!
2   For the mouth of the wicked and the
mouth of the deceitful
Have opened against me;
They have spoken against me with a
lying tongue.

3   They have also surrounded me with
words of hatred,
And fought against me without a cause.
4   In return for my love they are my
accusers,
But I *give myself to* prayer.

---

*Prayer is not its own cause, but
the effect of the life of God
in me.*   (CHRIS. DIS. 2)

---

5   Thus they have rewarded me evil for
good,
And hatred for my love.

PROVERBS 25:25, 26

25 *AS* cold water to a weary soul,
So *is* good news from a far country.

26 A righteous *man* who falters before the
wicked
Is like a murky spring and a polluted
well.

2 CORINTHIANS 12:1–21

IT is doubtless not profitable for me to
boast. I will come to visions and revelations
of the Lord: 2 I know a man in Christ who
fourteen years ago—whether in the body
I do not know, or whether out of the body
I do not know, God knows—such a one
was caught up to the third heaven.
3 And I know such a man—whether in the
body or out of the body I do not know,
God knows— 4 how he was caught up into
Paradise and heard inexpressible words,
which it is not lawful for a man to utter.
5 Of such a one I will boast; yet of myself
I will not boast, except in my infirmities.
6 For though I might desire to boast, I will
not be a fool; for I will speak the truth.
But I refrain, lest anyone should think of
me above what he sees me *to be* or hears
from me.

7 And lest I should be exalted above measure by the abundance of the revelations,
a thorn in the flesh was given to me, a
messenger of Satan to buffet me, lest I be
exalted above measure. 8 Concerning this
thing I pleaded with the Lord three times
that it might depart from me. 9 And He
said to me, "My grace is sufficient for you,
for My strength is made perfect in weakness." Therefore most gladly I will rather
boast in my infirmities, that the power of

Christ may rest upon me. 10 Therefore I take pleasure in infirmities, in reproaches, in needs, in persecutions, in distresses, for Christ's sake. For when I am weak, then I am strong.

11 I have become a fool in boasting; you have compelled me. For I ought to have been commended by you; for in nothing was I behind the most eminent apostles, though I am nothing. 12 Truly the signs of an apostle were accomplished among you with all perseverance, in signs and wonders and mighty deeds. 13 For what is it in which you were inferior to other churches, except that I myself was not burdensome to you? Forgive me this wrong!

14 Now *for* the third time I am ready to come to you. And I will not be burdensome to you; for I do not seek yours, but you. For the children ought not to lay up for the parents, but the parents for the children. 15 And I will very gladly spend and be spent for your souls; though the more abundantly I love you, the less I am loved.

16 But be that *as it may*, I did not burden you. Nevertheless, being crafty, I caught you by cunning! 17 Did I take advantage of you by any of those whom I sent to you? 18 I urged Titus, and sent our brother with *him*. Did Titus take advantage of you? Did we not walk in the same spirit? Did *we* not *walk* in the same steps?

19 Again, do you think that we excuse ourselves to you? We speak before God in Christ. But *we do* all things, beloved, for your edification. 20 For I fear lest, when I come, I shall not find you such as I wish, and *that* I shall be found by you such as you do not wish; lest *there be* contentions, jealousies, outbursts of wrath, selfish ambitions, backbitings, whisperings, conceits, tumults; 21 lest, when I come again, my God will humble me among you, and I shall mourn for many who have sinned before and have not repented of the uncleanness, fornication, and lewdness which they have practiced.

---

*R*epentance is the sign that I realize what God has done in Christ Jesus.   (UTMOST)

◆◆◆

Reading 265—Vision and Reality
Isaiah 35:7

God gives us the vision, then He takes us down to the valley to batter us into the shape of the vision, and it is in the valley that so many of us faint and give way. Every vision will be made real if we will have patience. Think of the enormous leisure of God! He is never in a hurry. We are always in such a frantic hurry. In the light of the glory of the vision we go forth to do things, but the vision is not real in us yet; and God has to take us into the valley, and put us through fires and floods to batter us into shape, until we get to the place where He can trust us with the veritable reality. Ever since we had the vision God has been at work, getting us into the shape of the ideal, and over and over again we escape from His hand and try to batter ourselves into our own shape.

The vision is not a castle in the air, but a vision of what God wants you to be. Let Him put you on His wheel and whirl you as He likes, and as sure as God is God and you are you, you will turn out exactly in accordance with the vision. Don't lose heart in the process. If you have ever had the vision of God, you may try as you like to be satisfied on a lower level, but God will never let you.   (*UTMOST*)

ISAIAH 35:1—36:22

1   THE wilderness and the wasteland
      shall be glad for them,
      And the desert shall rejoice and
      blossom as the rose;
2   It shall blossom abundantly and
      rejoice,
      Even with joy and singing.
      The glory of Lebanon shall be given
      to it,
      The excellence of Carmel and Sharon.
      They shall see the glory of the LORD,
      The excellency of our God.

3   Strengthen the weak hands,
      And make firm the feeble knees.
4   Say to those *who are* fearful-hearted,
      "Be strong, do not fear!
      Behold, your God will come *with*
      vengeance,
      With the recompense of God;
      He will come and save you."

5   Then the eyes of the blind shall be
      opened,
      And the ears of the deaf shall be
      unstopped.
6   Then the lame shall leap like a deer,
      And the tongue of the dumb sing.
      For waters shall burst forth in the
      wilderness,
      And streams in the desert.
7   The parched ground shall become a
      pool,
      And the thirsty land springs of water;
      In the habitation of jackals, where
      each lay,
      There shall be grass with reeds and
      rushes.

8   A highway shall be there, and a road,
      And it shall be called the Highway
      of Holiness.
      The unclean shall not pass over it,
      But it *shall be* for others.
      Whoever walks the road, although
      a fool,
      Shall not go astray.
9   No lion shall be there,
      Nor shall *any* ravenous beast go up
      on it;
      It shall not be found there.
      But the redeemed shall walk *there,*
10 And the ransomed of the LORD shall
      return,
      And come to Zion with singing,
      With everlasting joy on their heads.
      They shall obtain joy and gladness,
      And sorrow and sighing shall flee
      away.

The way God's life manifests itself in joy is in a peace which has no desire for praise. (LOVE OF GOD)

36 NOW it came to pass in the fourteenth year of King Hezekiah *that*
Sennacherib king of Assyria came up against
all the fortified cities of Judah and took
them. 2 Then the king of Assyria sent *the*
Rabshakeh with a great army from Lachish
to King Hezekiah at Jerusalem. And he
stood by the aqueduct from the upper pool,
on the highway to the Fuller's Field.
3 And Eliakim the son of Hilkiah, who was
over the household, Shebna the scribe, and
Joah the son of Asaph, the recorder, came
out to him.

4 Then *the* Rabshakeh said to them, "Say
now to Hezekiah, 'Thus says the great king,
the king of Assyria: "What confidence is
this in which you trust? 5 I say you speak
of having plans and power for war; but
they are mere words. Now in whom do
you trust, that you rebel against me?
6 Look! You are trusting in the staff of this
broken reed, Egypt, on which if a man leans,
it will go into his hand and pierce it. So
is Pharaoh king of Egypt to all who trust
in him.
7 "But if you say to me, 'We trust in the
LORD our God,' *is it* not He whose high
places and whose altars Hezekiah has taken
away, and said to Judah and Jerusalem,
'You shall worship before this altar'?" '
8 Now therefore, I urge you, give a pledge
to my master the king of Assyria, and I
will give you two thousand horses—if you
are able on your part to put riders on them!
9 How then will you repel one captain of
the least of my master's servants, and put
your trust in Egypt for chariots and horsemen? 10 Have I now come up without the
LORD against this land to destroy it? The
LORD said to me, 'Go up against this land,
and destroy it.' "

11 Then Eliakim, Shebna, and Joah said
to *the* Rabshakeh, "Please speak to your
servants in Aramaic, for we understand *it;*
and do not speak to us in Hebrew in the
hearing of the people who *are* on the wall."
12 But *the* Rabshakeh said, "Has my master sent me to your master and to you to
speak these words, and not to the men who
sit on the wall, who will eat and drink their
own waste with you?"
13 Then *the* Rabshakeh stood and called
out with a loud voice in Hebrew, and said,
"Hear the words of the great king, the king

of Assyria! 14 Thus says the king: 'Do not let Hezekiah deceive you, for he will not be able to deliver you; 15 nor let Hezekiah make you trust in the LORD, saying, "The LORD will surely deliver us; this city will not be given into the hand of the king of Assyria." ' 16 Do not listen to Hezekiah; for thus says the king of Assyria: 'Make *peace* with me *by a* present and come out to me; and every one of you eat from his own vine and every one from his own fig tree, and every one of you drink the waters of his own cistern; 17 until I come and take you away to a land like your own land, a land of grain and new wine, a land of bread and vineyards. 18 *Beware* lest Hezekiah persuade you, saying, "The LORD will deliver us." Has any one of the gods of the nations delivered its land from the hand of the king of Assyria? 19 Where *are* the gods of Hamath and Arpad? Where *are* the gods of Sepharvaim? Indeed, have they delivered Samaria from my hand? 20 Who among all the gods of these lands have delivered their countries from my hand, that the LORD should deliver Jerusalem from my hand?' "

21 But they held their peace and answered him not a word; for the king's commandment was, "Do not answer him." 22 Then Eliakim the son of Hilkiah, who *was* over the household, Shebna the scribe, and Joah the son of Asaph, the recorder, came to Hezekiah with *their* clothes torn, and told him the words of *the* Rabshakeh.

PSALM 109:6–13

6   SET a wicked man over him,
     And let an accuser stand at his right
        hand.
7   When he is judged, let him be found
        guilty,
     And let his prayer become sin.
8   Let his days be few,
     And let another take his office.
9   Let his children be fatherless,
     And his wife a widow.
10   Let his children continually be
        vagabonds, and beg;
     Let them seek *their bread* also from their
        desolate places.
11   Let the creditor seize all that he has,
     And let strangers plunder his labor.
12   Let there be none to extend mercy to
        him,
     Nor let there be any to favor his
        fatherless children.
13   Let his posterity be cut off,
     And in the generation following let their
        name be blotted out.

PROVERBS 25:27, 28

27   IT *is* not good to eat much honey;
     So to seek one's own glory *is not* glory.

28   Whoever *has* no rule over his own spirit
     Is like a city broken down, without
        walls.

2 CORINTHIANS 13:1–14

THIS *will be* the third *time* I am coming to you. "By the mouth of two or three witnesses every word shall be established." 2 I have told you before, and foretell as if I were present the second time, and now being absent I write to those who have sinned before, and to all the rest, that if I come again I will not spare— 3 since you seek a proof of Christ speaking in me, who is not weak toward you, but mighty in you. 4 For though He was crucified in weakness, yet He lives by the power of God. For we also are weak in Him, but we shall live with Him by the power of God toward you.

5 Examine yourselves *as to* whether you are in the faith. Test yourselves. Do you not know yourselves, that Jesus Christ is in you?—unless indeed you are disqualified. 6 But I trust that you will know that we are not disqualified.

7 Now I pray to God that you do no evil, not that we should appear approved, but that you should do what is honorable, though we may seem disqualified. 8 For we can do nothing against the truth, but for the truth. 9 For we are glad when we are weak and you are strong. And this also we pray, that you may be made complete. 10 Therefore I write these things being absent, lest being present I should use sharpness, according to the authority which the Lord has given me for edification and not for destruction.

11 Finally, brethren, farewell. Become complete. Be of good comfort, be of one mind, live in peace; and the God of love and peace will be with you.

12 Greet one another with a holy kiss. 13 All the saints greet you.

14 The grace of the Lord Jesus Christ, and the love of God, and the communion of the Holy Spirit *be* with you all. Amen.

Very few of us know what love of God *is, we know what* love of moral good *is.*   (DISCIPLES)

The Need for Disillusionment
Isaiah 38:15–20

Most of the suffering in human life comes because we refuse to be disillusioned. For instance, if I love a human being, and do not love God, I demand of that man or woman an infinite satisfaction which they cannot give. I demand of them every perfection and every rectitude, and when I do not get it, I become cruel and vindictive and jealous. Think of the average married life after, say, five or ten years; too often it sinks down into the most commonplace drudgery. The reason is that the husband and wife have not known God rightly, they have not gone through the transfiguration of love, nor entered through the discipline of disillusionment into satisfaction in God, and consequently they have begun to endure one another instead of having one another for enjoyment in God. The human heart must have satisfaction, but there is only one being who can satisfy the last aching abyss of the human heart, and that is our Lord Jesus Christ. That is why He is apparently so severe in regard to every human relationship. He says if we are going to be His disciples, occasion may arise when we must hate both father and mother, and every closest tie there is. Our Lord has no illusions about men, and He knows that every relationship in life that is not based on loyalty to Him will end in disaster. (*PLACE HELP*)

ISAIAH 37:1—38:22

AND so it was, when King Hezekiah heard *it,* that he tore his clothes, covered himself with sackcloth, and went into the house of the LORD. 2 Then he sent Eliakim, who *was* over the household, Shebna the scribe, and the elders of the priests, covered with sackcloth, to Isaiah the prophet, the son of Amoz. 3 And they said to him, "Thus says Hezekiah: 'This day *is* a day of trouble and rebuke and blasphemy; for the children have come to birth, but *there is* no strength to bring them forth. 4 It may be that the LORD your God will hear the words of *the* Rabshakeh, whom his master the king of Assyria has sent to reproach the living God, and will rebuke the words which the LORD your God has heard. Therefore lift up *your* prayer for the remnant that is left.' "

Whenever our Lord spoke of importunity in intercession it was never for ourselves but for others. (NOT KNOWING)

5 So the servants of King Hezekiah came to Isaiah. 6 And Isaiah said to them, "Thus you shall say to your master, 'Thus says the LORD: "Do not be afraid of the words which you have heard, with which the servants of the king of Assyria have blasphemed Me. 7 Surely I will send a spirit upon him, and he shall hear a rumor and return to his own land; and I will cause him to fall by the sword in his own land." ' "

8 Then *the* Rabshakeh returned, and found the king of Assyria warring against Libnah, for he heard that he had departed from Lachish. 9 And the king heard concerning Tirhakah king of Ethiopia, "He has come out to make war with you." So when he heard *it,* he sent messengers to Hezekiah, saying, 10 "Thus you shall speak to Hezekiah king of Judah, saying: 'Do not let your God in whom you trust deceive you, saying, "Jerusalem shall not be given into the hand of the king of Assyria." 11 Look! You have heard what the kings of Assyria have done to all lands by utterly destroying them; and shall you be delivered? 12 Have the gods of the nations delivered those whom my fathers have destroyed, Gozan and Haran and Rezeph, and the people of Eden who *were* in Telassar? 13 Where *is* the king of Hamath, the king of Arpad, and the king of the city of Sepharvaim, Hena, and Ivah?' "

14 And Hezekiah received the letter from the hand of the messengers, and read it; and Hezekiah went up to the house of the

LORD, and spread it before the LORD. 15 Then Hezekiah prayed to the LORD, saying: 16 "O LORD of hosts, God of Israel, *the One* who dwells *between* the cherubim, You *are* God, You alone, of all the kingdoms of the earth. You have made heaven and earth. 17 Incline Your ear, O LORD, and hear; open Your eyes, O LORD, and see; and hear all the words of Sennacherib, which he has sent to reproach the living God. 18 Truly, LORD, the kings of Assyria have laid waste all the nations and their lands, 19 and have cast their gods into the fire; for they *were* not gods, but the work of men's hands—wood and stone. Therefore they destroyed them. 20 Now therefore, O LORD our God, save us from his hand, that all the kingdoms of the earth may know that You *are* the LORD, You alone."

21 Then Isaiah the son of Amoz sent to Hezekiah, saying, "Thus says the LORD God of Israel, 'Because you have prayed to Me against Sennacherib king of Assyria, 22 this *is* the word which the LORD has spoken concerning him:

"The virgin, the daughter of Zion,
Has despised you, laughed you to
scorn;
The daughter of Jerusalem
Has shaken *her* head behind your
back!

23 "Whom have you reproached and
blasphemed?
Against whom have you raised *your*
voice,
And lifted up your eyes on high?
Against the Holy One of Israel.
24 By your servants you have reproached
the Lord,
And said, 'By the multitude of my
chariots
I have come up to the height of the
mountains,
To the limits of Lebanon;
I will cut down its tall cedars
And its choice cypress trees;
I will enter its farthest height,
To its fruitful forest.
25 I have dug and drunk water,
And with the soles of my feet I have
dried up
All the brooks of defense.'

26 "Did you not hear long ago
How I made it,
From ancient times that I formed it?
Now I have brought it to pass,
That you should be

For crushing fortified cities *into* heaps
of ruins.
27 Therefore their inhabitants *had* little
power;
They were dismayed and
confounded;
They were *as* the grass of the field
And the green herb,
As the grass on the housetops
And grain blighted before it is grown.

28 "But I know your dwelling place,
Your going out and your coming in,
And your rage against Me.
29 Because your rage against Me and
your tumult
Have come up to My ears,
Therefore I will put My hook in your
nose
And My bridle in your lips,
And I will turn you back
By the way which you came." '

30 "This *shall be* a sign to you:

You shall eat this year such as grows
of itself,
And the second year what springs
from the same;
Also in the third year sow and reap,
Plant vineyards and eat the fruit of
them.
31 And the remnant who have escaped
of the house of Judah
Shall again take root downward,
And bear fruit upward.
32 For out of Jerusalem shall go a
remnant,
And those who escape from Mount
Zion.
The zeal of the LORD of hosts will
do this.

33 "Therefore thus says the LORD concerning the king of Assyria:

'He shall not come into this city,
Nor shoot an arrow there,
Nor come before it with shield,
Nor build a siege mound against it.
34 By the way that he came,
By the same shall he return;
And he shall not come into this city,'
Says the LORD.
35 'For I will defend this city, to
save it
For My own sake and for My servant
David's sake.' "

36 Then the angel of the LORD went out, and killed in the camp of the Assyrians

one hundred and eighty-five thousand; and when *people* arose early in the morning, there were the corpses—all dead. 37 So Sennacherib king of Assyria departed and went away, returned *home,* and remained at Nineveh. 38 Now it came to pass, as he was worshiping in the house of Nisroch his god, that his sons Adrammelech and Sharezer struck him down with the sword; and they escaped into the land of Ararat. Then Esarhaddon his son reigned in his place.

38 IN those days Hezekiah was sick and near death. And Isaiah the prophet, the son of Amoz, went to him and said to him, "Thus says the LORD: 'Set your house in order, for you shall die and not live.' "

2 Then Hezekiah turned his face toward the wall, and prayed to the LORD, 3 and said, "Remember now, O LORD, I pray, how I have walked before You in truth and with a loyal heart, and have done *what is* good in Your sight." And Hezekiah wept bitterly.

4 And the word of the LORD came to Isaiah, saying, 5 "Go and tell Hezekiah, 'Thus says the LORD, the God of David your father: "I have heard your prayer, I have seen your tears; surely I will add to your days fifteen years. 6 I will deliver you and this city from the hand of the king of Assyria, and I will defend this city." ' 7 And this *is* the sign to you from the LORD, that the LORD will do this thing which He has spoken: 8 Behold, I will bring the shadow on the sundial, which has gone down with the sun on the sundial of Ahaz, ten degrees backward." So the sun returned ten degrees on the dial by which it had gone down.

9 This is the writing of Hezekiah king of Judah, when he had been sick and had recovered from his sickness:

10 I said,
    "In the prime of my life
    I shall go to the gates of Sheol;
    I am deprived of the remainder of
       my years."
11 I said,
    "I shall not see YAH,
    The LORD in the land of the living;
    I shall observe man no more among
       the inhabitants of the world.
12 My life span is gone,
    Taken from me like a shepherd's tent;
    I have cut off my life like a weaver.
    He cuts me off from the loom;
    From day until night You make an
       end of me.

13 I have considered until morning—
    Like a lion,
    So He breaks all my bones;
    From day until night You make an
       end of me.
14 Like a crane *or* a swallow, so I
       chattered;
    I mourned like a dove;
    My eyes fail *from looking* upward.
    O LORD, I am oppressed;
    Undertake for me!

15 "What shall I say?
    He has both spoken to me,
    And He Himself has done *it.*
    I shall walk carefully all my years
    In the bitterness of my soul.
16 O Lord, by these *things men* live;
    And in all these *things is* the life of
       my spirit;
    So You will restore me and make me
       live.
17 Indeed *it was* for *my own* peace
    That I had great bitterness;
    But You have lovingly *delivered* my
       soul from the pit of corruption,
    For You have cast all my sins behind
       Your back.
18 For Sheol cannot thank You,
    Death cannot praise You;
    Those who go down to the pit cannot
       hope for Your truth.
19 The living, the living man, he shall
       praise You,
    As I *do* this day;
    The father shall make known Your
       truth to the children.

20 "The LORD *was ready* to save me;
    Therefore we will sing my songs with
       stringed instruments
    All the days of our life, in the house
       of the LORD."

21 Now Isaiah had said, "Let them take a lump of figs, and apply *it* as a poultice on the boil, and he shall recover."

22 And Hezekiah had said, "What *is* the sign that I shall go up to the house of the LORD?"

PSALM 109:14–20

14 LET the iniquity of his fathers be
       remembered before the LORD,
    And let not the sin of his mother be
       blotted out.
15 Let them be continually before the
       LORD,

That He may cut off the memory of
them from the earth;

16 Because he did not remember to show
mercy,
But persecuted the poor and needy
man,
That he might even slay the broken in
heart.

17 As he loved cursing, so let it come to
him;
As he did not delight in blessing, so
let it be far from him.

18 As he clothed himself with cursing as
with his garment,
So let it enter his body like water,
And like oil into his bones.

19 Let it be to him like the garment which
covers him,
And for a belt with which he girds
himself continually.

20 *Let* this *be* the LORD's reward to my
accusers,
And to those who speak evil against
my person.

PROVERBS 26:1

1 AS snow in summer and rain in
harvest,
So honor is not fitting for a fool.

GALATIANS 1:1–24

PAUL, an apostle (not from men nor
through man, but through Jesus Christ and
God the Father who raised Him from the
dead), 2 and all the brethren who are with
me,

To the churches of Galatia:

3 Grace to you and peace from God the
Father and our Lord Jesus Christ, 4 who
gave Himself for our sins, that He might
deliver us from this present evil age, according to the will of our God and Father,
5 to whom *be* glory forever and ever. Amen.

6 I marvel that you are turning away so
soon from Him who called you in the grace
of Christ, to a different gospel, 7 which is
not another; but there are some who trouble
you and want to pervert the gospel of
Christ. 8 But even if we, or an angel from
heaven, preach any other gospel to you
than what we have preached to you, let
him be accursed. 9 As we have said before,
so now I say again, if anyone preaches any
other gospel to you than what you have
received, let him be accursed.

10 For do I now persuade men, or God?
Or do I seek to please men? For if I still
pleased men, I would not be a bondservant
of Christ.

11 But I make known to you, brethren,
that the gospel which was preached by me
is not according to man. 12 For I neither
received it from man, nor was I taught *it,*
but *it came* through the revelation of Jesus
Christ.

13 For you have heard of my former conduct in Judaism, how I persecuted the
church of God beyond measure and *tried
to* destroy it. 14 And I advanced in Judaism

---

*Persecution is systematic
vexation.* (SERVANT AS LORD)

---

beyond many of my contemporaries in my
own nation, being more exceedingly zealous for the traditions of my fathers.

15 But when it pleased God, who separated me from my mother's womb and
called *me* through His grace, 16 to reveal
His Son in me, that I might preach Him
among the Gentiles, I did not immediately
confer with flesh and blood, 17 nor did I
go up to Jerusalem to those *who were* apostles before me; but I went to Arabia, and
returned again to Damascus.

18 Then after three years I went up to
Jerusalem to see Peter, and remained with
him fifteen days. 19 But I saw none of the
other apostles except James, the Lord's
brother. 20 (Now *concerning* the things
which I write to you, indeed, before God,
I do not lie.)

21 Afterward I went into the regions of
Syria and Cilicia. 22 And I was unknown
by face to the churches of Judea which *were*
in Christ. 23 But they were hearing only,
"He who formerly persecuted us now
preaches the faith which he once *tried to*
destroy." 24 And they glorified God in me.

Reading 267—Bent of Regeneration
Galatians 2:20

The New Testament's teaching about Christianity is that the Son of God is formed in me on the basis of His marvelous regeneration until, as Paul says, "the *life* which I now live in the flesh"—not the life I am going to live when I get to heaven, but the life I now live in this flesh, the life that all see and know—"I live by the faith of the Son of God, who loved me, and gave Himself for me." What has happened to Paul? He has gone through his battle of the margins, he has gone through a moral decision with Jesus Christ, not an intellectual one; he has said—I agree with God in the things that He condemns in the Cross, self-interest, self-realization, though these have been dearer to me than my life; "I count all things loss for the excellence of the knowledge of Christ Jesus my Lord." It may take four minutes or forty years to be identified with Jesus Christ; it depends on whether I am willing to face the music, that is, forgo my hereditary right to my claim to myself and let Him take His claim to me.   (*SHAD. AGONY*)

ISAIAH 39:1—40:31

AT that time Merodach-Baladan the son of Baladan, king of Babylon, sent letters and a present to Hezekiah, for he heard that he had been sick and had recovered. 2 And Hezekiah was pleased with them, and showed them the house of his treasures—the silver and gold, the spices and precious ointment, and all his armory—all that was found among his treasures. There was nothing in his house or in all his dominion that Hezekiah did not show them.

3 Then Isaiah the prophet went to King Hezekiah, and said to him, "What did these men say, and from where did they come to you?"

So Hezekiah said, "They came to me from a far country, from Babylon."

4 And he said, "What have they seen in your house?"

So Hezekiah answered, "They have seen all that *is* in my house; there is nothing among my treasures that I have not shown them."

5 Then Isaiah said to Hezekiah, "Hear the word of the LORD of hosts: 6 'Behold, the days are coming when all that *is* in your house, and what your fathers have accumulated until this day, shall be carried to Babylon; nothing shall be left,' says the LORD. 7 'And they shall take away *some* of your sons who will descend from you, whom you will beget; and they shall be eunuchs in the palace of the king of Babylon.' "

8 So Hezekiah said to Isaiah, "The word of the LORD which you have spoken *is* good!" For he said, "At least there will be peace and truth in my days."

40 "COMFORT, yes, comfort My people!"
Says your God.
2 "Speak comfort to Jerusalem, and cry out to her,
That her warfare is ended,
That her iniquity is pardoned;
For she has received from the LORD's hand
Double for all her sins."

3 The voice of one crying in the wilderness:
"Prepare the way of the LORD;
Make straight in the desert
A highway for our God.
4 Every valley shall be exalted
And every mountain and hill brought low;
The crooked places shall be made straight
And the rough places smooth;
5 The glory of the LORD shall be revealed,
And all flesh shall see *it* together;
For the mouth of the LORD has spoken."

6 The voice said, "Cry out!"
And he said, "What shall I cry?"

"All flesh *is* grass,
And all its loveliness *is* like the flower of the field.

7   The grass withers, the flower fades,
     Because the breath of the LORD blows
          upon it;
     Surely the people *are* grass.
8   The grass withers, the flower
          fades,
     But the word of our God stands
          forever."

9   O Zion,
     You who bring good tidings,
     Get up into the high mountain;
     O Jerusalem,
     You who bring good tidings,
     Lift up your voice with strength,
     Lift *it* up, be not afraid;
     Say to the cities of Judah, "Behold
          your God!"

10   Behold, the Lord GOD shall come
          with a strong *hand,*
     And His arm shall rule for Him;
     Behold, His reward *is* with Him,
     And His work before Him.
11   He will feed His flock like a shepherd;
     He will gather the lambs with His
          arm,
     And carry *them* in His bosom,
     And gently lead those who are with
          young.

12   Who has measured the waters in the
          hollow of His hand,
     Measured heaven with a span
     And calculated the dust of the earth
          in a measure?
     Weighed the mountains in scales
     And the hills in a balance?
13   Who has directed the Spirit of the
          LORD,
     Or *as* His counselor has taught Him?
14   With whom did He take counsel, and
          who instructed Him,
     And taught Him in the path of
          justice?
     Who taught Him knowledge,
     And showed Him the way of
          understanding?

15   Behold, the nations *are* as a drop in
          a bucket,
     And are counted as the small dust
          on the scales;
     Look, He lifts up the isles as a very
          little thing.
16   And Lebanon *is* not sufficient to
          burn,
     Nor its beasts sufficient for a burnt
          offering.
17   All nations before Him *are* as
          nothing,

And they are counted by Him less
     than nothing and worthless.

18   To whom then will you liken God?
     Or what likeness will you compare
          to Him?
19   The workman molds an image,
     The goldsmith overspreads it with
          gold,
     And the silversmith casts silver
          chains.
20   Whoever *is* too impoverished for *such*
          a contribution
     Chooses a tree *that* will not rot;
     He seeks for himself a skillful
          workman
     To prepare a carved image *that* will
          not totter.

21   Have you not known?
     Have you not heard?
     Has it not been told you from the
          beginning?
     Have you not understood from the
          foundations of the earth?
22   *It is* He who sits above the circle of
          the earth,
     And its inhabitants *are* like
          grasshoppers,
     Who stretches out the heavens like
          a curtain,
     And spreads them out like a tent to
          dwell in.
23   He brings the princes to nothing;
     He makes the judges of the earth
          useless.

24   Scarcely shall they be planted,
     Scarcely shall they be sown,
     Scarcely shall their stock take root
          in the earth,
     When He will also blow on them,
     And they will wither,
     And the whirlwind will take them
          away like stubble.

25   "To whom then will you liken Me,
     Or *to whom* shall I be equal?" says
          the Holy One.
26   Lift up your eyes on high,
     And see who has created these
          things,
     Who brings out their host by
          number;

Six days God labored, thinking
Creation, until, as He thought,
so it was.   (GENESIS)

He calls them all by name,
By the greatness of His might
And the strength of *His* power;
Not one is missing.

27 Why do you say, O Jacob,
And speak, O Israel:
"My way is hidden from the LORD,
And my just claim is passed over by
my God"?
28 Have you not known?
Have you not heard?
The everlasting God, the LORD,
The Creator of the ends of the earth,
Neither faints nor is weary.
His understanding is unsearchable.
29 He gives power to the weak,
And to *those who have* no might He
increases strength.
30 Even the youths shall faint and be
weary,
And the young men shall utterly fall,
31 But those who wait on the LORD
Shall renew *their* strength;
They shall mount up with wings like
eagles,
They shall run and not be weary,
They shall walk and not faint.

PSALM 109:21–25

21 BUT You, O GOD the Lord,
Deal with me for Your name's sake;
Because Your mercy *is* good,
deliver me.
22 For I *am* poor and needy,
And my heart is wounded within me.
23 I am gone like a shadow when it
lengthens;
I am shaken off like a locust.
24 My knees are weak through fasting,
And my flesh is feeble from lack of
fatness.
25 I also have become a reproach to them;
When they look at me, they shake their
heads.

PROVERBS 26:2

2 LIKE a flitting sparrow, like a flying
swallow,
So a curse without cause shall not
alight.

GALATIANS 2:1–21

THEN after fourteen years I went up again
to Jerusalem with Barnabas, and also took
Titus with *me*. 2 And I went up by revelation, and communicated to them that gospel
which I preach among the Gentiles, but
privately to those who were of reputation,
lest by any means I might run, or had run,
in vain. 3 Yet not even Titus who *was* with
me, being a Greek, was compelled to be
circumcised. 4 And *this occurred* because of
false brethren secretly brought in (who
came in by stealth to spy out our liberty
which we have in Christ Jesus, that they
might bring us into bondage), 5 to whom
we did not yield submission even for an
hour, that the truth of the gospel might
continue with you.

6 But from those who seemed to be something—whatever they were, it makes no difference to me; God shows personal favoritism to no man—for those who seemed *to
be something* added nothing to me. 7 But
on the contrary, when they saw that the
gospel for the uncircumcised had been committed to me, as *the gospel* for the circumcised *was* to Peter 8 (for He who worked
effectively in Peter for the apostleship to
the circumcised also worked effectively in
me toward the Gentiles), 9 and when James,
Cephas, and John, who seemed to be pillars,
perceived the grace that had been given to
me, they gave me and Barnabas the right
hand of fellowship, that we *should go* to
the Gentiles and they to the circumcised.
10 *They desired* only that we should remember the poor, the very thing which I also
was eager to do.

11 Now when Peter had come to Antioch,
I withstood him to his face, because he
was to be blamed; 12 for before certain men
came from James, he would eat with the
Gentiles; but when they came, he withdrew
and separated himself, fearing those who
were of the circumcision. 13 And the rest
of the Jews also played the hypocrite with
him, so that even Barnabas was carried away
with their hypocrisy.

14 But when I saw that they were not
straightforward about the truth of the gospel, I said to Peter before *them* all, "If you,
being a Jew, live in the manner of Gentiles
and not as the Jews, why do you compel
Gentiles to live as Jews? 15 We *who are* Jews
by nature, and not sinners of the Gentiles,
16 knowing that a man is not justified by
the works of the law but by faith in Jesus
Christ, even we have believed in Christ
Jesus, that we might be justified by faith
in Christ and not by the works of the law;
for by the works of the law no flesh shall
be justified.
17 "But if, while we seek to be justified
by Christ, we ourselves also are found sin-

ners, *is* Christ therefore a minister of sin? Certainly not! 18 For if I build again those things which I destroyed, I make myself a transgressor. 19 For I through the law died to the law that I might live to God. 20 I have been crucified with Christ; it is no longer I who live, but Christ lives in me; and the *life* which I now live in the flesh I live by faith in the Son of God, who loved me and gave Himself for me.

21 I do not set aside the grace of God; for if righteousness *comes* through the law, then Christ died in vain."

*I*f excellence of character is made the test, the grace of God is "made void." (DISCIPLES)

*Reading 268—*Readjusted to God
Galatians 3:11

I f all Jesus came to do was to tell me I must have an unsullied career, when my past has been blasted by sin and wickedness on my own part, then He but tantalizes me. If He is simply a teacher, He only increases our capacity for misery, for He sets up standards that stagger us.

But the teaching of Jesus Christ is not an ideal, it is the statement of the life we will live when we are readjusted to God by the Atonement. The type of life Jesus lived, the type of character He expressed, is possible for us by His death, and only by His death, because by means of His death we receive the life to which His teaching applies. (*BIB. ETHICS*)

Our Lord is not the great Teacher of the world, He is the Savior of the world and the Teacher of those who believe in Him, which is a radically different matter. His teaching is of no use saving to agonize mankind with its unattainable ideals until men are made anew through the Cross. Unless I am born from above the only result of the teachings of Jesus is to produce despair. People say that Jesus Christ came to teach us to be good; He never did! All the teaching in the world about a man having a pure heart won't make it pure. Our Lord's teaching has no power in it unless I possess His nature.

(*CONFORMED*)

ISAIAH 41:1—42:25

1 "KEEP silence before Me,
   O coastlands,
   And let the people renew *their* strength!
   Let them come near, then let them speak;
   Let us come near together for judgment.

2 "Who raised up one from the east?
   Who in righteousness called him to His feet?
   Who gave the nations before him,
   And made *him* rule over kings?
   Who gave *them* as the dust *to* his sword,

As driven stubble to his bow?
3 Who pursued them, *and* passed safely
   By the way *that* he had not gone with his feet?
4 Who has performed and done *it,*
   Calling the generations from the beginning?
   'I, the LORD, am the first;
   And with the last I *am* He.' "

5 The coastlands saw *it* and feared,
   The ends of the earth were afraid;
   They drew near and came.
6 Everyone helped his neighbor,
   And said to his brother,
   "Be of good courage!"
7 So the craftsman encouraged the goldsmith;

He who smooths *with* the hammer
    inspired him who strikes the anvil,
Saying, "It *is* ready for the soldering";
Then he fastened it with pegs,
    That it might not totter.

8 "But you, Israel, *are* My servant,
    Jacob whom I have chosen,
    The descendants of Abraham My
        friend.
9 *You* whom I have taken from the ends
        of the earth,
    And called from its farthest regions,
    And said to you,
    'You *are* My servant,
    I have chosen you and have not cast
        you away:
10 Fear not, for I *am* with you;
    Be not dismayed, for I *am* your God.
    I will strengthen you,
    Yes, I will help you,
    I will uphold you with My righteous
        right hand.'

11 "Behold, all those who were incensed
        against you
    Shall be ashamed and disgraced;
    They shall be as nothing,
    And those who strive with you shall
        perish.
12 You shall seek them and not find
        them—
    Those who contended with you.
    Those who war against you
    Shall be as nothing,
    As a nonexistent thing.
13 For I, the LORD your God, will hold
        your right hand,
    Saying to you, 'Fear not, I will help
        you.'

14 "Fear not, you worm Jacob,
    You men of Israel!
    I will help you," says the LORD
    And your Redeemer, the Holy One
        of Israel.
15 "Behold, I will make you into a new
        threshing sledge with sharp teeth;
    You shall thresh the mountains and
        beat *them* small,
    And make the hills like chaff.
16 You shall winnow them, the wind
        shall carry them away,
    And the whirlwind shall scatter them;
    You shall rejoice in the LORD,
    And glory in the Holy One of Israel.

17 "The poor and needy seek water, but
        there is none,
    Their tongues fail for thirst.
    I, the LORD, will hear them;

I, the God of Israel, will not forsake
    them.
18 I will open rivers in desolate heights,
    And fountains in the midst of the
        valleys;
    I will make the wilderness a pool of
        water,
    And the dry land springs of water.
19 I will plant in the wilderness the cedar
        and the acacia tree,
    The myrtle and the oil tree;
    I will set in the desert the cypress
        tree *and* the pine
    And the box tree together,
20 That they may see and know,
    And consider and understand
        together,
    That the hand of the LORD has done
        this,
    And the Holy One of Israel has
        created it.

21 "Present your case," says the LORD.
    "Bring forth your strong *reasons*," says
        the King of Jacob.
22 "Let them bring forth and show us
        what will happen;
    Let them show the former things,
        what they *were*,
    That we may consider them,
    And know the latter end of them;
    Or declare to us things to come.
23 Show the things that are to come
        hereafter,
    That we may know that you *are*
        gods;
    Yes, do good or do evil,
    That we may be dismayed and see
        it together.
24 Indeed you *are* nothing,
    And your work *is* nothing;
    He who chooses you *is* an
        abomination.

25 "I have raised up one from the north,
    And he shall come;
    From the rising of the sun he shall
        call on My name;
    And he shall come against princes
        as *though* mortar,
    As the potter treads clay.
26 Who has declared from the
        beginning, that we may know?
    And former times, that we may say,
        '*He is* righteous'?
    Surely *there is* no one who shows,
    Surely *there is* no one who declares,
    Surely *there is* no one who hears your
        words.
27 The first time *I said* to Zion,
    'Look, there they are!'

And I will give to Jerusalem one who brings good tidings.

28 For I looked, and *there was* no man;
I looked among them, but *there was* no counselor,
Who, when I asked of them, could answer a word.

29 Indeed they *are* all worthless;
Their works *are* nothing;
Their molded images *are* wind and confusion.

42
"BEHOLD! My Servant whom I uphold,
My Elect One *in whom* My soul delights!
I have put My Spirit upon Him;
He will bring forth justice to the Gentiles.

2 He will not cry out, nor raise *His voice,*
Nor cause His voice to be heard in the street.

3 A bruised reed He will not break,
And smoking flax He will not quench;
He will bring forth justice for truth.

4 He will not fail nor be discouraged,
Till He has established justice in the earth;
And the coastlands shall wait for His law."

5 Thus says God the LORD,
Who created the heavens and stretched them out,
Who spread forth the earth and that which comes from it,
Who gives breath to the people on it,
And spirit to those who walk on it:

6 "I, the LORD, have called You in righteousness,
And will hold Your hand;
I will keep You and give You as a covenant to the people,
As a light to the Gentiles,

7 To open blind eyes,
To bring out prisoners from the prison,
Those who sit in darkness from the prison house.

8 I *am* the LORD, that *is* My name;
And My glory I will not give to another,
Nor My praise to carved images.

9 Behold, the former things have come to pass,
And new things I declare;
Before they spring forth I tell you of them."

10 Sing to the LORD a new song,
And His praise from the ends of the earth,
You who go down to the sea, and all that is in it,
You coastlands and you inhabitants of them!

11 Let the wilderness and its cities lift up *their voice,*
The villages *that* Kedar inhabits.
Let the inhabitants of Sela sing,
Let them shout from the top of the mountains.

12 Let them give glory to the LORD,
And declare His praise in the coastlands.

13 The LORD shall go forth like a mighty man;
He shall stir up *His* zeal like a man of war.
He shall cry out, yes, shout aloud;
He shall prevail against His enemies.

14 "I have held My peace a long time,
I have been still and restrained Myself.
Now I will cry like a woman in labor,
I will pant and gasp at once.

15 I will lay waste the mountains and hills,
And dry up all their vegetation;
I will make the rivers coastlands,
And I will dry up the pools.

16 I will bring the blind by a way they did not know;
I will lead them in paths they have not known.
I will make darkness light before them,
And crooked places straight.
These things I will do for them,
And not forsake them.

17 They shall be turned back,
They shall be greatly ashamed,
Who trust in carved images,
Who say to the molded images,
'You *are* our gods.'

18 "Hear, you deaf;
And look, you blind, that you may see.

19 Who *is* blind but My servant,
Or deaf as My messenger *whom* I send?
Who *is* blind as *he who is* perfect,
And blind as the LORD's servant?

20 Seeing many things, but you do not observe;
Opening the ears, but he does not hear."

21 The LORD is well pleased for His
    righteousness' sake;
    He will exalt the law and make *it*
    honorable.
22 But this *is* a people robbed and
    plundered;
    All of them are snared in holes,
    And they are hidden in prison houses;
    They are for prey, and no one
    delivers;
    For plunder, and no one says,
    "Restore!"

23 Who among you will give ear to this?
    Who will listen and hear for the time
    to come?
24 Who gave Jacob for plunder, and
    Israel to the robbers?
    Was it not the LORD,
    He against whom we have sinned?
    For they would not walk in His ways,
    Nor were they obedient to His law.
25 Therefore He has poured on him the
    fury of His anger
    And the strength of battle;
    It has set him on fire all around,
    Yet he did not know;
    And it burned him,
    Yet he did not take *it* to heart.

PSALM 109:26–31

26 HELP me, O LORD my God!
    Oh, save me according to Your mercy,
27 That they may know that this *is* Your
    hand—
    That You, LORD, have done it!
28 Let them curse, but You bless;
    When they arise, let them be ashamed,
    But let Your servant rejoice.
29 Let my accusers be clothed with shame,
    And let them cover themselves with
    their own disgrace as with a mantle.

30 I will greatly praise the LORD with my
    mouth;
    Yes, I will praise Him among the
    multitude.
31 For He shall stand at the right hand
    of the poor,
    To save *him* from those who condemn
    him.

PROVERBS 26:3, 4

3 A whip for the horse,
    A bridle for the donkey,
    And a rod for the fool's back.

4 Do not answer a fool according to his
    folly,
    Lest you also be like him.

GALATIANS 3:1–29

O foolish Galatians! Who has bewitched
you that you should not obey the truth,
before whose eyes Jesus Christ was clearly
portrayed among you as crucified? 2 This
only I want to learn from you: Did you
receive the Spirit by the works of the law,
or by the hearing of faith? 3 Are you so
foolish? Having begun in the Spirit, are
you now being made perfect by the flesh?
4 Have you suffered so many things in
vain—if indeed *it was* in vain?

5 Therefore He who supplies the Spirit
to you and works miracles among you, *does
He do it* by the works of the law, or by
the hearing of faith?— 6 just as Abraham
"believed God, and it was accounted to
him for righteousness." 7 Therefore know
that *only* those who are of faith are sons
of Abraham. 8 And the Scripture, foreseeing
that God would justify the Gentiles by faith,
preached the gospel to Abraham beforehand, *saying*, "In you all the nations shall
be blessed." 9 So then those who *are* of
faith are blessed with believing Abraham.

10 For as many as are of the works of
the law are under the curse; for it is written,
"Cursed *is* everyone who does not continue
in all things which are written in the book
of the law, to do them." 11 But that no
one is justified by the law in the sight of
God *is* evident, for "the just shall live by
faith." 12 Yet the law is not of faith, but
"the man who does them shall live by
them."

13 Christ has redeemed us from the curse
of the law, having become a curse for us
(for it is written, "Cursed *is* everyone who
hangs on a tree"), 14 that the blessing of

---

*Jesus Christ became a curse for us by
the divine decree.*   (UTMOST)

Abraham might come upon the Gentiles
in Christ Jesus, that we might receive the
promise of the Spirit through faith.

15 Brethren, I speak in the manner of
men: Though *it is* only a man's covenant,
yet *if it is* confirmed, no one annuls or adds
to it. 16 Now to Abraham and his Seed were
the promises made. He does not say, "And
to seeds," as of many, but as of one, "And
to your Seed," who is Christ. 17 And this

I say, *that* the law, which was four hundred and thirty years later, cannot annul the covenant that was confirmed before by God in Christ, that it should make the promise of no effect. 18 For if the inheritance *is* of the law, *it is* no longer of promise; but God gave *it* to Abraham by promise.

19 What purpose then *does* the law *serve?* It was added because of transgressions, till the Seed should come to whom the promise was made; *and it was* appointed through angels by the hand of a mediator. 20 Now a mediator does not *mediate* for one *only,* but God is one.

21 *Is* the law then against the promises of God? Certainly not! For if there had been a law given which could have given life, truly righteousness would have been by the law. 22 But the Scripture has confined all under sin, that the promise by faith in Jesus Christ might be given to those who believe. 23 But before faith came, we were kept under guard by the law, kept for the faith which would afterward be revealed. 24 Therefore the law was our tutor *to bring us* to Christ, that we might be justified by faith. 25 But after faith has come, we are no longer under a tutor.

26 For you are all sons of God through faith in Christ Jesus. 27 For as many of you as were baptized into Christ have put on Christ. 28 There is neither Jew nor Greek, there is neither slave nor free, there is neither male nor female; for you are all one in Christ Jesus. 29 And if you *are* Christ's, then you are Abraham's seed, and heirs according to the promise.

◆◆◆◆

Reading 269—In the Days of His Resurrection
Galatians 4:19

Jesus put the early disciples through crises until they discovered that they could not be disciples by means of ordinary human sincerity and devotion. Human earnestness and vowing cannot make a person a disciple of Jesus Christ any more than it can turn him into an angel; something must be received by each person and that is the meaning of being born again. When one is struck by his need of the Holy Spirit, God will put the Holy Spirit into his spirit. In regeneration, the personal spirit is energized by the Holy Spirit, and the Son of God is formed in him (Gal. 1:15, 16; 4:19). This is the New Testament evangel, and it needs to be restated. New birth refers not only to a person's eternal salvation, but to his being of value to God in this order of things; it means infinitely more than being delivered from sin and from hell. The gift of the essential nature of God is made efficacious in us by the entering in of the Holy Spirit; He imparts to us the quickening life of the Son of God, and we are lifted into the domain where Jesus lives. (See John 3:5.)   (*LOVE OF GOD*)

ISAIAH 43:1—44:28

1   BUT now, thus says the LORD, who
       created you, O Jacob,
     And He who formed you, O Israel:
     "Fear not, for I have redeemed you;
     I have called *you* by your name;
     You *are* Mine.
2   When you pass through the waters,
       I *will be* with you;
     And through the rivers, they shall
       not overflow you.

He created us susceptible of all the blessedness which He had ordained for us.   (LOVE OF GOD)

When you walk through the fire, you
  shall not be burned,
Nor shall the flame scorch you.
3   For I *am* the LORD your God,
     The Holy One of Israel, your Savior;
     I gave Egypt for your ransom,

Ethiopia and Seba in your place.
4   Since you were precious in My sight,
     You have been honored,
     And I have loved you;
     Therefore I will give men for you,
     And people for your life.
5   Fear not, for I *am* with you;
     I will bring your descendants from
       the east,
     And gather you from the west;
6   I will say to the north, 'Give them
       up!'
     And to the south, 'Do not keep them
       back!'
     Bring My sons from afar,
     And My daughters from the ends of
       the earth—
7   Everyone who is called by My name,
     Whom I have created for My glory;
     I have formed him, yes, I have made
       him."

8   Bring out the blind people who have
       eyes,
     And the deaf who have ears.
9   Let all the nations be gathered
       together,
     And let the people be assembled.
     Who among them can declare this,
     And show us former things?
     Let them bring out their witnesses,
       that they may be justified;
     Or let them hear and say, "*It is*
       truth."
10   "You *are* My witnesses," says the
       LORD,
     "And My servant whom I have
       chosen,
     That you may know and believe Me,
     And understand that I *am* He.
     Before Me there was no God formed,
     Nor shall there be after Me.
11   I, *even* I, *am* the LORD,
     And besides Me *there is* no savior.
12   I have declared and saved,
     I have proclaimed,
     And *there was* no foreign *god* among
       you;
     Therefore you *are* My witnesses,"
     Says the LORD, "that I *am* God.
13   Indeed before the day *was*, I *am* He;
     And *there is* no one who can deliver
       out of My hand;
     I work, and who will reverse it?"

14   Thus says the LORD, your
       Redeemer,
     The Holy One of Israel:
     "For your sake I will send to Babylon,
     And bring them all down as
       fugitives—

The Chaldeans, who rejoice in their
  ships.
15   I *am* the LORD, your Holy One,
     The Creator of Israel, your King."

16   Thus says the LORD, who makes a
       way in the sea
     And a path through the mighty
       waters,
17   Who brings forth the chariot and
       horse,
     The army and the power
     (They shall lie down together, they
       shall not rise;
     They are extinguished, they are
       quenched like a wick):
18   "Do not remember the former things,
     Nor consider the things of old.
19   Behold, I will do a new thing,
     Now it shall spring forth;
     Shall you not know it?
     I will even make a road in the
       wilderness
     And rivers in the desert.
20   The beast of the field will honor Me,
     The jackals and the ostriches,
     Because I give waters in the
       wilderness
     And rivers in the desert,
     To give drink to My people, My
       chosen.
21   This people I have formed for
       Myself;
     They shall declare My praise.

22   "But you have not called upon Me,
       O Jacob;
     And you have been weary of Me,
       O Israel.
23   You have not brought Me the sheep
       for your burnt offerings,
     Nor have you honored Me with your
       sacrifices.
     I have not caused you to serve with
       grain offerings,
     Nor wearied you with incense.
24   You have bought Me no sweet cane
       with money,
     Nor have you satisfied Me with the
       fat of your sacrifices;
     But you have burdened Me with your
       sins,
     You have wearied Me with your
       iniquities.

25   "I, *even* I, *am* He who blots out your
       transgressions for My own sake;
     And I will not remember your
       sins.
26   Put Me in remembrance;
     Let us contend together;

State your *case,* that you may be
acquitted.

27   Your first father sinned,
And your mediators have
transgressed against Me.

28   Therefore I will profane the princes
of the sanctuary;
I will give Jacob to the curse,
And Israel to reproaches.

44   "YET hear me now, O Jacob My
servant,
And Israel whom I have chosen.

2   Thus says the LORD who made you
And formed you from the womb,
who will help you:
'Fear not, O Jacob My servant;
And you, Jeshurun, whom I have
chosen.

3   For I will pour water on him who
is thirsty,
And floods on the dry ground;
I will pour My Spirit on your
descendants,
And My blessing on your offspring;

4   They will spring up among the grass
Like willows by the watercourses.'

5   One will say, 'I *am* the LORD's';
Another will call *himself* by the name
of Jacob;
Another will write *with* his hand,
'The LORD's,'
And name *himself* by the name of
Israel.

6   "Thus says the LORD, the King of
Israel,
And his Redeemer, the LORD of
hosts:
'I *am* the First and I *am* the Last;
Besides Me *there is* no God.

7   And who can proclaim as I do?
Then let him declare it and set it in
order for Me,
Since I appointed the ancient people.
And the things that are coming and
shall come,
Let them show these to them.

8   Do not fear, nor be afraid;
Have I not told you from that time,
and declared *it?*
You *are* My witnesses.
Is there a God besides Me?
Indeed *there is* no other Rock;
I know not *one.'* "

9   Those who make an image, all of
them *are* useless,
And their precious things shall not
profit;
They *are* their own witnesses;

They neither see nor know, that they
may be ashamed.

10   Who would form a god or mold an
image
That profits him nothing?

11   Surely all his companions would be
ashamed;
And the workmen, they *are* mere
men.
Let them all be gathered together,
Let them stand up;
Yet they shall fear,
They shall be ashamed together.

12   The blacksmith with the tongs works
one in the coals,
Fashions it with hammers,
And works it with the strength of
his arms.
Even so, he is hungry, and his
strength fails;
He drinks no water and is faint.

13   The craftsman stretches out *his* rule,
He marks one out with chalk;
He fashions it with a plane,
He marks it out with the compass,
And makes it like the figure of a man,
According to the beauty of a man,
that it may remain in the house.

14   He cuts down cedars for himself,
And takes the cypress and the oak;
He secures *it* for himself among the
trees of the forest.
He plants a pine, and the rain
nourishes *it.*

15   Then it shall be for a man to burn,
For he will take some of it and warm
himself;
Yes, he kindles *it* and bakes bread;
Indeed he makes a god and
worships *it;*
He makes it a carved image, and falls
down to it.

16   He burns half of it in the fire;
With this half he eats meat;
He roasts a roast, and is satisfied.
He even warms *himself* and says,
"Ah! I am warm,
I have seen the fire."

17   And the rest of it he makes into a
god,
His carved image.
He falls down before it and
worships *it,*
Prays to it and says,
"Deliver me, for you *are* my god!"

18   They do not know nor understand;
For He has shut their eyes, so that
they cannot see,

And their hearts, so that they cannot
understand.

19 And no one considers in his heart,
Nor *is there* knowledge nor
understanding to say,
"I have burned half of it in the fire,
Yes, I have also baked bread on its
coals;
I have roasted meat and eaten *it;*
And shall I make the rest of it an
abomination?
Shall I fall down before a block of
wood?"

20 He feeds on ashes;
A deceived heart has turned him
aside;
And he cannot deliver his soul,
Nor say, "*Is there* not a lie in my
right hand?"

21 "Remember these, O Jacob,
And Israel, for you *are* My servant;
I have formed you, you *are* My
servant;
O Israel, you will not be forgotten
by Me!

22 I have blotted out, like a thick cloud,
your transgressions,
And like a cloud, your sins.
Return to Me, for I have redeemed
you."

23 Sing, O heavens, for the LORD has
done *it!*
Shout, you lower parts of the earth;
Break forth into singing, you
mountains,
O forest, and every tree in it!
For the LORD has redeemed Jacob,
And glorified Himself in Israel.

24 Thus says the LORD, your Redeemer,
And He who formed you from the
womb:
"I *am* the LORD, who makes all
things,
Who stretches out the heavens all
alone,
Who spreads abroad the earth by
Myself;

25 Who frustrates the signs of the
babblers,
And drives diviners mad;
Who turns wise men backward,
And makes their knowledge
foolishness;

26 Who confirms the word of His
servant,
And performs the counsel of His
messengers;

Who says to Jerusalem, 'You shall
be inhabited,'
To the cities of Judah, 'You shall be
built,'
And I will raise up her waste places;

27 Who says to the deep, 'Be dry!
And I will dry up your rivers';

28 Who says of Cyrus, '*He is* My
shepherd,
And he shall perform all My pleasure,
Saying to Jerusalem, "You shall be
built,"
And to the temple, "Your foundation
shall be laid." ' "

PSALM 110:1–7

1 THE LORD said to my Lord,
"Sit at My right hand,
Till I make Your enemies Your
footstool."

2 The LORD shall send the rod of Your
strength out of Zion.
Rule in the midst of Your enemies!

3 Your people *shall be* volunteers
In the day of Your power;
In the beauties of holiness, from the
womb of the morning,
You have the dew of Your youth.

4 The LORD has sworn
And will not relent,
"You *are* a priest forever
According to the order of
Melchizedek."

5 The Lord *is* at Your right hand;
He shall execute kings in the day of
His wrath.

6 He shall judge among the nations,
He shall fill *the places* with dead
bodies,
He shall execute the heads of many
countries.

7 He shall drink of the brook by the
wayside;
Therefore He shall lift up the head.

PROVERBS 26:5–9

5 ANSWER a fool according to his folly,
Lest he be wise in his own eyes.

6 He who sends a message by the hand
of a fool
Cuts off *his own* feet *and* drinks violence.

7 *Like* the legs of the lame that hang limp
Is a proverb in the mouth of fools.

8 Like one who binds a stone in a sling
Is he who gives honor to a fool.

9 *Like* a thorn *that* goes into the hand
of a drunkard
Is a proverb in the mouth of fools.

GALATIANS 4:1–31

NOW I say *that* the heir, as long as he is
a child, does not differ at all from a slave,
though he is master of all, 2 but is under
guardians and stewards until the time appointed by the father. 3 Even so we, when
we were children, were in bondage under
the elements of the world. 4 But when the
fullness of the time had come, God sent
forth His Son, born of a woman, born
under the law, 5 to redeem those who were

Jesus Christ was born into *this
world, not* from *it.*   (Utmost)

---

under the law, that we might receive the
adoption as sons.

6 And because you are sons, God has sent
forth the Spirit of His Son into your hearts,
crying out, "Abba, Father!" 7 Therefore
you are no longer a slave but a son, and
if a son, then an heir of God through
Christ.

8 But then, indeed, when you did not
know God, you served those which by nature are not gods. 9 But now after you have
known God, or rather are known by God,
how *is it that* you turn again to the weak
and beggarly elements, to which you desire
again to be in bondage? 10 You observe
days and months and seasons and years.
11 I am afraid for you, lest I have labored
for you in vain.

12 Brethren, I urge you to become like
me, for I *became* like you. You have not
injured me at all. 13 You know that because
of physical infirmity I preached the gospel
to you at the first. 14 And my trial which
was in my flesh you did not despise or reject,
but you received me as an angel of God,
even as Christ Jesus. 15 What then was the
blessing you *enjoyed?* For I bear you witness

that, if possible, you would have plucked
out your own eyes and given them to me.
16 Have I therefore become your enemy because I tell you the truth?

17 They zealously court you, *but* for no
good; yes, they want to exclude you, that
you may be zealous for them. 18 But it is
good to be zealous in a good thing always,
and not only when I am present with you.
19 My little children, for whom I labor in
birth again until Christ is formed in you,
20 I would like to be present with you now
and to change my tone; for I have doubts
about you.

21 Tell me, you who desire to be under
the law, do you not hear the law? 22 For
it is written that Abraham had two sons:
the one by a bondwoman, the other by a
freewoman. 23 But he *who was* of the bondwoman was born according to the flesh,
and he of the freewoman through promise,
24 which things are symbolic. For these are
the two covenants: the one from Mount
Sinai which gives birth to bondage, which
is Hagar— 25 for this Hagar is Mount Sinai
in Arabia, and corresponds to Jerusalem
which now is, and is in bondage with her
children— 26 but the Jerusalem above is
free, which is the mother of us all. 27 For
it is written:

"Rejoice, O barren,
You who do not bear!
Break forth and shout,
You who are not in labor!
For the desolate has many more
children
Than she who has a husband."

28 Now we, brethren, as Isaac *was,* are
children of promise. 29 But, as he who was
born according to the flesh then persecuted
him *who was born* according to the Spirit,
even so *it is* now. 30 Nevertheless what does
the Scripture say? "Cast out the bondwoman and her son, for the son of the
bondwoman shall not be heir with the son
of the freewoman." 31 So then, brethren,
we are not children of the bondwoman but
of the free.

Reading 270—Spiritual Undertow
Galatians 5:7

An undertow is an undercurrent flowing in a different direction from the water at the surface. It is the undercurrent that drowns; a swimmer will never plunge into an undercurrent, a fool will. The spiritual undertow that switched away the Galatians was Judaism, formalism. It was not dominant, but hidden; it ran in exactly the opposite direction to the current of liberty into which they were being brought by Christ. Instead of going out to sea, out into the glorious liberty of the children of God, they were being switched away. "You ran well. . . ." They had been heading straight for the ocean, but the undercurrent of ritualism bewitched them, hindered them from obeying the truth. After a big transaction with God the current of your life heads you straight out to sea, right over the harbor bar, every sail set; now be alert for the spiritual undertow that would suck you back. The undercurrent is always most dangerous just where the river merges with the sea. The undercurrent is of the same nature as the river and will take you back into its swirling current; not out into the main stream, but back to the shipwrecks on the bank. The most pitiable of all wrecks are those inside the harbor.   (PLACE HELP)

ISAIAH 45:1—46:13

1 "THUS says the Lord to His
  anointed,
To Cyrus, whose right hand I have
  held—
To subdue nations before him
And loose the armor of kings,
To open before him the double
  doors,
So that the gates will not be shut:
2 'I will go before you
And make the crooked places
  straight;
I will break in pieces the gates of
  bronze
And cut the bars of iron.
3 I will give you the treasures of
  darkness
And hidden riches of secret places,
That you may know that I, the LORD,
Who call *you* by your name,
Am the God of Israel.
4 For Jacob My servant's sake,
And Israel My elect,
I have even called you by your name;
I have named you, though you have
  not known Me.
5 I *am* the LORD, and *there is* no other;
There is no God besides Me.
I will gird you, though you have not
  known Me,
6 That they may know from the rising
  of the sun to its setting

That *there is* none besides Me.
I *am* the LORD, and *there is* no other;
7 I form the light and create darkness,
I make peace and create calamity;
I, the LORD, do all these *things*.'

8 "Rain down, you heavens, from
  above,
And let the skies pour down
  righteousness;
Let the earth open, let them bring
  forth salvation,
And let righteousness spring up
  together.
I, the LORD, have created it.

9 "Woe to him who strives with his
  Maker!
Let the potsherd *strive* with the
  potsherds of the earth!
Shall the clay say to him who forms
  it, 'What are you making?'
Or shall your handiwork *say*, 'He has
  no hands'?
10 Woe to him who says to *his* father,
  'What are you begetting?'
Or to the woman, 'What have you
  brought forth?' "

11 Thus says the LORD,
The Holy One of Israel, and his
  Maker:
"Ask Me of things to come
  concerning My sons;

And concerning the work of My
hands, you command Me.
12 I have made the earth,
And created man on it.
I—My hands—stretched out the
heavens,
And all their host I have commanded.

Matter did not exist before God created it. (BIB. PSYCH.)

---

13 I have raised him up in righteousness,
And I will direct all his ways;
He shall build My city
And let My exiles go free,
Not for price nor reward,"
Says the LORD of hosts.

14 Thus says the LORD:

"The labor of Egypt and merchandise
of Cush
And of the Sabeans, men of stature,
Shall come over to you, and they shall
be yours;
They shall walk behind you,
They shall come over in chains;
And they shall bow down to you.
They will make supplication to you,
saying, 'Surely God *is* in you,
And *there is* no other;
There is no other God.' "

15 Truly You *are* God, who hide
Yourself,
O God of Israel, the Savior!
16 They shall be ashamed
And also disgraced, all of them;
They shall go in confusion together,
Who are makers of idols.
17 *But* Israel shall be saved by the LORD
With an everlasting salvation;
You shall not be ashamed or
disgraced
Forever and ever.

18 For thus says the LORD,
Who created the heavens,
Who is God,
Who formed the earth and made it,
Who has established it,
Who did not create it in vain,
Who formed it to be inhabited:
"I *am* the LORD, and *there is* no other.
19 I have not spoken in secret,
In a dark place of the earth;
I did not say to the seed of Jacob,
'Seek Me in vain';

I, the LORD, speak righteousness,
I declare things that are right.

20 "Assemble yourselves and come;
Draw near together,
You *who have* escaped from the
nations.
They have no knowledge,
Who carry the wood of their carved
image,
And pray to a god *that* cannot save.
21 Tell and bring forth *your case;*
Yes, let them take counsel together.
Who has declared this from ancient
time?
Who has told it from that time?
Have not I, the LORD?
And *there is* no other God
besides Me,
A just God and a Savior;
There is none besides Me.

22 "Look to Me, and be saved,
All you ends of the earth!
For I *am* God, and *there is* no other.
23 I have sworn by Myself;
The word has gone out of My mouth
in righteousness,
And shall not return,
That to Me every knee shall bow,
Every tongue shall take an oath.
24 He shall say,
'Surely in the LORD I have
righteousness and strength.
To Him *men* shall come,
And all shall be ashamed
Who are incensed against Him.
25 In the LORD all the descendants
of Israel
Shall be justified, and shall glory.' "

46 BEL bows down, Nebo stoops;
Their idols were on the beasts
and on the cattle.
Your carriages *were* heavily loaded,
A burden to the weary *beast.*
2 They stoop, they bow down
together;
They could not deliver the burden,
But have themselves gone into
captivity.

3 "Listen to Me, O house of Jacob,
And all the remnant of the house of
Israel,
Who have been upheld *by Me* from
birth,
Who have been carried from the
womb:
4 Even to *your* old age, I *am* He,

And *even* to gray hairs I will carry
  you!
I have made, and I will bear;
Even I will carry, and will deliver
  you.

5   "To whom will you liken Me, and
      make *Me* equal
    And compare Me, that we should be
      alike?
6   They lavish gold out of the bag,
    And weigh silver on the scales;
    They hire a goldsmith, and he makes
      it a god;
    They prostrate themselves, yes, they
      worship.
7   They bear it on the shoulder, they
      carry it
    And set it in its place, and it stands;
    From its place it shall not move.
    Though *one* cries out to it, yet it
      cannot answer
    Nor save him out of his trouble.

8   "Remember this, and show yourselves
      men;
    Recall to mind, O you transgressors.
9   Remember the former things of old,
    For I *am* God, and *there is* no other;
    I am God, and *there is* none like Me,
10 Declaring the end from the
      beginning,
    And from ancient times *things* that
      are not *yet* done,
    Saying, 'My counsel shall stand,
    And I will do all My pleasure,'
11 Calling a bird of prey from the east,
    The man who executes My counsel,
      from a far country.
    Indeed I have spoken *it;*
    I will also bring it to pass.
    I have purposed *it;*
    I will also do it.

12 "Listen to Me, you stubborn-hearted,
    Who *are* far from righteousness:
13 I bring My righteousness near,
      it shall not be far off;
    My salvation shall not linger.
    And I will place salvation in Zion,
    For Israel My glory.

PSALM 111:1–6

1   PRAISE the LORD!

    I will praise the LORD with *my* whole
      heart,
    In the assembly of the upright and *in*
      the congregation.

2   The works of the LORD *are* great,
    Studied by all who have pleasure in
      them.
3   His work *is* honorable and glorious,
    And His righteousness endures
      forever.
4   He has made His wonderful works to
      be remembered;
    The LORD *is* gracious and full of
      compassion.
5   He has given food to those who fear
      Him;
    He will ever be mindful of His
      covenant.
6   He has declared to His people the
      power of His works,
    In giving them the heritage of the
      nations.

PROVERBS 26:10

10 THE great *God* who formed
      everything
    Gives the fool *his* hire and the
      transgressor *his* wages.

GALATIANS 5:1–26

STAND fast therefore in the liberty by
which Christ has made us free, and do not
be entangled again with a yoke of bondage.
2 Indeed I, Paul, say to you that if you become circumcised, Christ will profit you
nothing. 3 And I testify again to every man
who becomes circumcised that he is a
debtor to keep the whole law. 4 You have
become estranged from Christ, you who
attempt to be justified by law; you have fallen
from grace. 5 For we through the Spirit
eagerly wait for the hope of righteousness
by faith. 6 For in Christ Jesus neither circumcision nor uncircumcision avails anything, but faith working through love.
7 You ran well. Who hindered you from
obeying the truth? 8 This persuasion does
not *come* from Him who calls you. 9 A little
leaven leavens the whole lump. 10 I have
confidence in you, in the Lord, that you
will have no other mind; but he who troubles you shall bear his judgment, whoever
he is.
11 And I, brethren, if I still preach circumcision, why do I still suffer persecution?
Then the offense of the cross has ceased.
12 I could wish that those who trouble you
would even cut themselves off!
13 For you, brethren, have been called
to liberty; only do not *use* liberty as an
opportunity for the flesh, but through love

serve one another. 14 For all the law is fulfilled in one word, *even* in this: "You shall
love your neighbor as yourself." 15 But if
you bite and devour one another, beware
lest you be consumed by one another!

16 I say then: Walk in the Spirit, and you
shall not fulfill the lust of the flesh.
17 For the flesh lusts against the Spirit, and
the Spirit against the flesh; and these are
contrary to one another, so that you do
not do the things that you wish. 18 But if
you are led by the Spirit, you are not under
the law.

19 Now the works of the flesh are evident,
which are: adultery, fornication, uncleanness, lewdness, 20 idolatry, sorcery, hatred,
contentions, jealousies, outbursts of wrath,
selfish ambitions, dissensions, heresies,
21 envy, murders, drunkenness, revelries,
and the like; of which I tell you beforehand,
just as I also told *you* in time past, that
those who practice such things will not inherit the kingdom of God.

22 But the fruit of the Spirit is love, joy,
peace, longsuffering, kindness, goodness,
faithfulness, 23 gentleness, self-control.

---

*We cannot imitate the disposition of
Jesus Christ; it is either there or it
isn't.* (SHAD. AGONY)

Against such there is no law. 24 And those
who are Christ's have crucified the flesh with
its passions and desires. 25 If we live in the
Spirit, let us also walk in the Spirit.
26 Let us not become conceited, provoking
one another, envying one another.

◆◆◆◆

Reading 271—Jargon of Sanctimoniousness
Galatians 6:14

The Galatians were relapsing not into sin, but into fixity; they had the
jargon of sanctimoniousness, but no real vigorous life. It is easy to think
that we are to be specimens of what God can do. According to the New
Testament, a saint is a piece of rugged human stuff remade by the Atonement
into oneness with God by the power of the Holy Spirit. The tendency to
stereotype Christian experience is an abiding danger; it leads to the amateur
providence attitude—"I am not likely to go wrong, but you are." I become,
as it were, god almighty over a particular doctrine and imagine that everyone
else is off on a side track. For example, when I think I can define what sanctification
is, I have done something God refuses to do. Books about sanctification are
much clearer than the Bible. The Bible is uncommonly confusing, so is human
life. There is only one thing that is simple, and that is our relationship to
Jesus Christ. What is needed today is not so much a revival as a resurgent
form of awakening, the incoming of the tremendous life of God in a new
form. (*PLACE HELP*)

ISAIAH 47:1—48:22

1 "COME down and sit in the dust,
    O virgin daughter of Babylon;
    Sit on the ground without a
        throne,
    O daughter of the Chaldeans!
    For you shall no more be called
    Tender and delicate.
2 Take the millstones and grind meal.
    Remove your veil,

Take off the skirt,
Uncover the thigh,
Pass through the rivers.
3 Your nakedness shall be uncovered,
    Yes, your shame will be seen;
    I will take vengeance,
    And I will not arbitrate with a man."

4 *As for* our Redeemer, the LORD of
        hosts *is* His name,
    The Holy One of Israel.

5 "Sit in silence, and go into darkness,
    O daughter of the Chaldeans;
    For you shall no longer be called
    The Lady of Kingdoms.
6 I was angry with My people;
    I have profaned My inheritance,
    And given them into your hand.
    You showed them no mercy;
    On the elderly you laid your yoke
        very heavily.
7 And you said, 'I shall be a lady
        forever,'
    So that you did not take these *things*
        to heart,
    Nor remember the latter end of
        them.

8 "Therefore hear this now, *you who are*
        given to pleasures,
    Who dwell securely,
    Who say in your heart, 'I *am,* and
        there is no one else besides me;
    I shall not sit *as* a widow,
    Nor shall I know the loss of children';
9 But these two *things* shall come to
        you
    In a moment, in one day:
    The loss of children, and
        widowhood.
    They shall come upon you in their
        fullness
    Because of the multitude of your
        sorceries,
    For the great abundance of your
        enchantments.

10 "For you have trusted in your
        wickedness;
    You have said, 'No one sees me';
    Your wisdom and your knowledge
        have warped you;
    And you have said in your heart,
    'I *am,* and *there is* no one else
        besides me.'
11 Therefore evil shall come upon you;
    You shall not know from where it
        arises.
    And trouble shall fall upon you;
    You will not be able to put it off.
    And desolation shall come upon you
        suddenly,
    Which you shall not know.

12 "Stand now with your enchantments
    And the multitude of your sorceries,
    In which you have labored from your
        youth—
    Perhaps you will be able to profit,
    Perhaps you will prevail.
13 You are wearied in the multitude of
        your counsels;

Let now the astrologers, the
        stargazers,
    And the monthly prognosticators
    Stand up and save you
    From what shall come upon you.
14 Behold, they shall be as stubble,
    The fire shall burn them;
    They shall not deliver themselves
    From the power of the flame;
    It shall not *be* a coal to be
        warmed by,
    Nor a fire to sit before!
15 Thus shall they be to you
    With whom you have labored,
    Your merchants from your youth;
    They shall wander each one to his
        quarter.
    No one shall save you.

48 "HEAR this, O house of Jacob,
        Who are called by the name of
            Israel,
    And have come forth from the
        wellsprings of Judah;
    Who swear by the name of the LORD,
    And make mention of the God of
        Israel,
    But not in truth or in righteousness;
2 For they call themselves after the
        holy city,
    And lean on the God of Israel;
    The LORD of hosts *is* His name:

3 "I have declared the former things
        from the beginning;
    They went forth from My mouth,
        and I caused them to hear it.
    Suddenly I did *them,* and they came
        to pass.
4 Because I knew that you *were*
        obstinate,
    And your neck *was* an iron sinew,
    And your brow bronze,
5 Even from the beginning I have
        declared *it* to you;
    Before it came to pass I proclaimed
        it to you,
    Lest you should say, 'My idol has
        done them,
    And my carved image and my molded
        image
    Have commanded them.'
6 "You have heard;
    See all this.
    And will you not declare *it?*
    I have made you hear new things
        from this time,
    Even hidden things, and you did not
        know them.
7 They are created now and not from
        the beginning;

And before this day you have not
heard them,
Lest you should say, 'Of course I
knew them.'
8 Surely you did not hear,
Surely you did not know;
Surely from long ago your ear was
not opened.
For I knew that you would deal very
treacherously,
And were called a transgressor from
the womb.

9 "For My name's sake I will defer My
anger,
And *for* My praise I will restrain it
from you,
So that I do not cut you off.
10 Behold, I have refined you, but not
as silver;
I have tested you in the furnace of
affliction.
11 For My own sake, for My own sake,
I will do *it;*
For how should *My name* be
profaned?
And I will not give My glory to
another.

12 "Listen to Me, O Jacob,
And Israel, My called:
I *am* He, I *am* the First,
I *am* also the Last.
13 Indeed My hand has laid the
foundation of the earth,
And My right hand has stretched out
the heavens;
When I call to them,
They stand up together.

14 "All of you, assemble yourselves, and
hear!
Who among them has declared these
things?
The LORD loves him;
He shall do His pleasure on Babylon,
And His arm *shall be against* the
Chaldeans.
15 I, *even* I, have spoken;
Yes, I have called him,
I have brought him, and his way will
prosper.

16 "Come near to Me, hear this:
I have not spoken in secret from the
beginning;
From the time that it was, I *was* there.
And now the Lord GOD and His
Spirit
Have sent Me."

17 Thus says the LORD, your
Redeemer,
The Holy One of Israel:
"I *am* the LORD your God,
Who teaches you to profit,
Who leads you by the way you
should go.
18 Oh, that you had heeded My
commandments!
Then your peace would have been
like a river,
And your righteousness like the
waves of the sea.
19 Your descendants also would have
been like the sand,
And the offspring of your body like
the grains of sand;
His name would not have been
cut off
Nor destroyed from before Me."

20 Go forth from Babylon!
Flee from the Chaldeans!
With a voice of singing,
Declare, proclaim this,
Utter it to the end of the earth;
Say, "The LORD has redeemed
His servant Jacob!"
21 And they did not thirst
When He led them through the
deserts;
He caused the waters to flow from
the rock for them;
He also split the rock, and the waters
gushed out.

22 *"There is* no peace," says the LORD,
"for the wicked."

PSALM 111:7–10

7 THE works of His hands *are* verity
and justice;
All His precepts *are* sure.
8 They stand fast forever and ever,
And are done in truth and uprightness.
9 He has sent redemption to His people;
He has commanded His covenant
forever:
Holy and awesome *is* His name.

---

*T*he Bible reveals that the only
way out is through the
Redemption.   (BAFFLED)

---

10 The fear of the LORD *is* the beginning
of wisdom;

A good understanding have all those
who do *His commandments*.
His praise endures forever.

PROVERBS 26:11, 12

11 AS a dog returns to his own vomit,
    So a fool repeats his folly.
12 Do you see a man wise in his own
    eyes?
    There is more hope for a fool than for
    him.

GALATIANS 6:1–18

BRETHREN, if a man is overtaken in any
trespass, you who *are* spiritual restore such
a one in a spirit of gentleness, considering
yourself lest you also be tempted. 2 Bear
one another's burdens, and so fulfill the
law of Christ. 3 For if anyone thinks himself
to be something, when he is nothing, he
deceives himself. 4 But let each one examine
his own work, and then he will have rejoicing in himself alone, and not in another.
5 For each one shall bear his own load.

6 Let him who is taught the word share
in all good things with him who teaches.

7 Do not be deceived, God is not
mocked; for whatever a man sows, that he
will also reap. 8 For he who sows to his
flesh will of the flesh reap corruption, but
he who sows to the Spirit will of the Spirit
reap everlasting life. 9 And let us not grow
weary while doing good, for in due season
we shall reap if we do not lose heart.
10 Therefore, as we have opportunity, let
us do good to all, especially to those who
are of the household of faith.

11 See with what large letters I have written to you with my own hand! 12 As many
as desire to make a good showing in the
flesh, these *would* compel you to be circumcised, only that they may not suffer persecution for the cross of Christ. 13 For not
even those who are circumcised keep the
law, but they desire to have you circumcised
that they may boast in your flesh. 14 But
God forbid that I should boast except in
the cross of our Lord Jesus Christ, by whom
the world has been crucified to me, and I
to the world. 15 For in Christ Jesus neither
circumcision nor uncircumcision avails
anything, but a new creation.

16 And as many as walk according to this
rule, peace and mercy *be* upon them, and
upon the Israel of God.

17 From now on let no one trouble me,
for I bear in my body the marks of the
Lord Jesus.

18 Brethren, the grace of our Lord Jesus
Christ *be* with your spirit. Amen.

◆◆◆◆

Reading 272—The New Testament Passion
Ephesians 1:12

The joy of anything, from a blade of grass upward, is to fulfill its created
purpose "that we who first trusted in Christ should be to the praise of
His glory" (Eph. 1:12). We are not here to win souls, to do good to others.
That is the natural outcome but it is not our aim, and this is where so many
of us cease to be followers. We will follow God as long as He makes us a
blessing to others, but when He does not, we will not follow. Suppose our
Lord had measured His life by whether or not He was a blessing to others.
Why, He was a "stone of stumbling" to thousands, actually to His own neighbors,
to His own nation, because through Him they blasphemed the Holy Spirit,
and in His own country "He did not many mighty works there because of
their unbelief" (Matt. 13:58). If our Lord had measured His life by its actual
results, He would have been full of misery. We get switched off when instead
of following God we follow Christian work and workers. We are much more
concerned over the passion for souls than the passion for Christ. . . . The
passion for souls is not a New Testament idea at all, but religious commercialism.
When we are taken up with this passion, the joy of the Lord is never ours
but only an excitable joy which always leaves a snare behind.   (*LOVE OF GOD*)

ISAIAH 49:1—50:11

1 "LISTEN, O coastlands, to Me,
   And take heed, you peoples from
      afar!
   The LORD has called Me from the
      womb;
   From the matrix of My mother He
      has made mention of My name.
2 And He has made My mouth like a
      sharp sword;
   In the shadow of His hand He has
      hidden Me,
   And made Me a polished shaft;
   In His quiver He has hidden Me."

3 "And He said to me,
   'You *are* My servant, O Israel,
   In whom I will be glorified.'
4 Then I said, 'I have labored in vain,
   I have spent my strength for nothing
      and in vain;
   Yet surely my just reward *is* with the
      LORD,
   And my work with my God.' "

5 "And now the LORD says,
   Who formed Me from the womb *to
      be* His Servant,
   To bring Jacob back to Him,
   So that Israel is gathered to Him
   (For I shall be glorious in the eyes
      of the LORD,
   And My God shall be My strength),
6 Indeed He says,
   'It is too small a thing that You should
      be My Servant
   To raise up the tribes of Jacob,
   And to restore the preserved ones
      of Israel;
   I will also give You as a light to the
      Gentiles,
   That You should be My salvation to
      the ends of the earth.' "

7 Thus says the LORD,
   The Redeemer of Israel, their Holy
      One,
   To Him whom man despises,
   To Him whom the nation abhors,
   To the Servant of rulers:
   "Kings shall see and arise,
   Princes also shall worship,
   Because of the LORD who is faithful,
   The Holy One of Israel;
   And He has chosen You."

8 Thus says the LORD:

   "In an acceptable time I have heard
      You,

And in the day of salvation I have
   helped You;
I will preserve You and give You
As a covenant to the people,
To restore the earth,
To cause them to inherit the desolate
   heritages;
9 That You may say to the prisoners,
   'Go forth,'
To those who *are* in darkness, 'Show
   yourselves.'

"They shall feed along the roads,
   And their pastures *shall be* on all
      desolate heights.
10 They shall neither hunger nor thirst,
   Neither heat nor sun shall strike
      them;
   For He who has mercy on them will
      lead them,
   Even by the springs of water He will
      guide them.
11 I will make each of My mountains
      a road,
   And My highways shall be elevated.
12 Surely these shall come from afar;
   Look! Those from the north and the
      west,
   And these from the land of Sinim."

13 Sing, O heavens!
   Be joyful, O earth!
   And break out in singing,
      O mountains!
   For the LORD has comforted His
      people,
   And will have mercy on His afflicted.

14 But Zion said, "The LORD has
      forsaken me,
   And my Lord has forgotten me."

15 "Can a woman forget her nursing
      child,
   And not have compassion on the son
      of her womb?
   Surely they may forget,
   Yet I will not forget you.

---

*There was never a human breast that
beat with more tenderness than Jesus
Christ's.*   (PERFECT)

---

16 See, I have inscribed you on the
      palms *of My hands;*
   Your walls *are* continually before Me.
17 Your sons shall make haste;
   Your destroyers and those who laid
      you waste

Shall go away from you.

18 Lift up your eyes, look around and
see;
All these gather together *and* come
to you.
As I live," says the Lord,
"You shall surely clothe yourselves
with them all as an ornament,
And bind them *on you* as a bride
does.

19 "For your waste and desolate places,
And the land of your destruction,
Will even now be too small for the
inhabitants;
And those who swallowed you up
will be far away.

20 The children you will have,
After you have lost the others,
Will say again in your ears,
'The place *is* too small for me;
Give me a place where I may dwell.'

21 Then you will say in your heart,
'Who has begotten these for me,
Since I have lost my children and
am desolate,
A captive, and wandering to and fro?
And who has brought these up?
There I was, left alone;
But these, where *were* they?' "

22 Thus says the Lord God:

"Behold, I will lift My hand in an oath
to the nations,
And set up My standard for the
peoples;
They shall bring your sons in *their*
arms,
And your daughters shall be carried
on *their* shoulders;

23 Kings shall be your foster fathers,
And their queens your nursing
mothers;
They shall bow down to you with
their faces to the earth,
And lick up the dust of your feet.
Then you will know that I *am* the
Lord,
For they shall not be ashamed who
wait for Me."

24 Shall the prey be taken from the
mighty,
Or the captives of the righteous be
delivered?

25 But thus says the Lord:

"Even the captives of the mighty shall
be taken away,

And the prey of the terrible be
delivered;
For I will contend with him who
contends with you,
And I will save your children.

26 I will feed those who oppress you
with their own flesh,
And they shall be drunk with their
own blood as with sweet wine.
All flesh shall know
That I, the Lord, *am* your Savior,
And your Redeemer, the Mighty
One of Jacob."

50 THUS says the Lord:

"Where *is* the certificate of your
mother's divorce,
Whom I have put away?
Or which of My creditors *is it* to
whom I have sold you?
For your iniquities you have sold
yourselves,
And for your transgressions your
mother has been put away.

2 Why, when I came, *was there* no man?
Why, when I called, *was there* none
to answer?
Is My hand shortened at all that it
cannot redeem?
Or have I no power to deliver?
Indeed with My rebuke I dry up the
sea,
I make the rivers a wilderness;
Their fish stink because *there is* no
water,
And die of thirst.

3 I clothe the heavens with blackness,
And I make sackcloth their
covering."

4 "The Lord God has given Me
The tongue of the learned,
That I should know how to speak
A word in season to *him who is*
weary.
He awakens Me morning by
morning,
He awakens My ear
To hear as the learned.

5 The Lord God has opened My ear;
And I was not rebellious,
Nor did I turn away.

6 I gave My back to those who struck
Me,
And My cheeks to those who plucked
out the beard;
I did not hide My face from shame
and spitting.

7 "For the Lord God will help Me;
Therefore I will not be disgraced;

Therefore I have set My face like a flint,
And I know that I will not be ashamed.
8 *He is* near who justifies Me;
Who will contend with Me?
Let us stand together.
Who *is* My adversary?
Let him come near Me.
9 Surely the Lord GOD will help Me;
Who *is* he *who* will condemn Me?
Indeed they will all grow old like a garment;
The moth will eat them up.

10 "Who among you fears the LORD?
Who obeys the voice of His Servant?
Who walks in darkness
And has no light?
Let him trust in the name of the LORD
And rely upon his God.
11 Look, all you who kindle a fire,
Who encircle *yourselves* with sparks:
Walk in the light of your fire and
in the sparks you have kindled—
This you shall have from My hand:
You shall lie down in torment.

PSALM 112:1–4

1 PRAISE the LORD!

Blessed *is* the man *who* fears the LORD,
Who delights greatly in His commandments.

2 His descendants will be mighty on earth;
The generation of the upright will be blessed.
3 Wealth and riches *will be* in his house,
And his righteousness endures forever.
4 Unto the upright there arises light in the darkness;
He is gracious, and full of compassion, and righteous.

PROVERBS 26:13–15

13 THE lazy *man* says, "*There is* a lion in the road!
A fierce lion *is* in the streets!"
14 *As* a door turns on its hinges,
So *does* the lazy *man* on his bed.
15 The lazy *man* buries his hand in the bowl;
It wearies him to bring it back to his mouth.

EPHESIANS 1:1–23

PAUL, an apostle of Jesus Christ by the will of God,

To the saints who are in Ephesus, and faithful in Christ Jesus:

2 Grace to you and peace from God our Father and the Lord Jesus Christ.
3 Blessed *be* the God and Father of our Lord Jesus Christ, who has blessed us with every spiritual blessing in the heavenly *places* in Christ, 4 just as He chose us in Him before the foundation of the world, that we should be holy and without blame before Him in love, 5 having predestined us to adoption as sons by Jesus Christ to Himself, according to the good pleasure of His will, 6 to the praise of the glory of His grace, by which He made us accepted in the Beloved.

7 In Him we have redemption through His blood, the forgiveness of sins, according to the riches of His grace 8 which He made to abound toward us in all wisdom and prudence, 9 having made known to us the mystery of His will, according to His good pleasure which He purposed in Himself, 10 that in the dispensation of the fullness of the times He might gather together in one all things in Christ, both which are in heaven and which are on earth—in Him. 11 In Him also we have obtained an inheritance, being predestined according to the purpose of Him who works all things according to the counsel of His will, 12 that

---

*C*ontinually *restate to yourself what the purpose of your life is.* (UTMOST)

---

we who first trusted in Christ should be to the praise of His glory.
13 In Him you also *trusted,* after you heard the word of truth, the gospel of your salvation; in whom also, having believed, you were sealed with the Holy Spirit of promise, 14 who is the guarantee of our inheritance until the redemption of the purchased possession, to the praise of His glory.
15 Therefore I also, after I heard of your faith in the Lord Jesus and your love for all the saints, 16 do not cease to give thanks for you, making mention of you in my prayers: 17 that the God of our Lord Jesus Christ, the Father of glory, may give to you the spirit of wisdom and revelation in

the knowledge of Him, 18 the eyes of your understanding being enlightened; that you may know what is the hope of His calling, what are the riches of the glory of His inheritance in the saints, 19 and what *is* the exceeding greatness of His power toward us who believe, according to the working of His mighty power 20 which He worked in Christ when He raised Him from the dead and seated *Him* at His right hand in the heavenly *places,* 21 far above all principality and power and might and dominion, and every name that is named, not only in this age but also in that which is to come.

22 And He put all *things* under His feet, and gave Him *to be* head over all *things* to the church, 23 which is His body, the fullness of Him who fills all in all.

◆◆◆

Reading 273—Donation of Deity
Ephesians 2:5, 6

The moral miracle of Christianity is that when I know my limitations, when I reach the frontiers by weakness, not by will, Jesus Christ says, "Blessed are you, I will do the rest." But I have to get there; it is not that God will not do anything for me until I do, but that He cannot. God cannot put into me, a moral being, the disposition that is in Jesus Christ unless I am conscious I need it. I cannot receive that which I do not believe I need; but when I am struck by an agony, or the sense of helplessness with regard to Jesus Christ's teaching, I am ready then to receive the donation of deity. . . .

If I receive the Spirit of God and become a son of God by right of regeneration, God does not give me my Christian character, I have to make that. He gives me the disposition of His Son; He puts Holy Spirit into me, then He says, "Now, breast and back as they should be, and work it out." My disposition tells through my body on to outward circumstances, and as I obey the Spirit of God and the word of God, I slowly form the Christian character.

(SHAD. AGONY)

ISAIAH 51:1—52:15

1 "LISTEN to Me, you who follow
      after righteousness,
   You who seek the LORD:
   Look to the rock *from which* you were
      hewn,
   And to the hole of the pit *from which*
      you were dug.
2 Look to Abraham your father,
   And to Sarah *who* bore you;
   For I called him alone,
   And blessed him and increased
      him."

3 For the LORD will comfort Zion,
   He will comfort all her waste places;
   He will make her wilderness like
      Eden,
   And her desert like the garden of the
      LORD;

Joy and gladness will be found in
      it,
   Thanksgiving and the voice of
      melody.

4 "Listen to Me, My people;
   And give ear to Me, O My nation:
   For law will proceed from Me,
   And I will make My justice rest
   As a light of the peoples.
5 My righteousness *is* near,
   My salvation has gone forth,
   And My arms will judge the peoples;
   The coastlands will wait upon Me,
   And on My arm they will trust.
6 Lift up your eyes to the heavens,
   And look on the earth beneath.
   For the heavens will vanish away like
      smoke,
   The earth will grow old like a
      garment,

And those who dwell in it will die
   in like manner;
But My salvation will be forever,
And My righteousness will not be
   abolished.

7 "Listen to Me, you who know
      righteousness,
   You people in whose heart *is* My law:
   Do not fear the reproach of men,
   Nor be afraid of their insults.
8 For the moth will eat them up like
      a garment,
   And the worm will eat them like
      wool;
   But My righteousness will be forever,
   And My salvation from generation
      to generation."

9 Awake, awake, put on strength,
   O arm of the LORD!
   Awake as in the ancient days,
   In the generations of old.
   Are You not *the arm* that cut Rahab
      apart,
   And wounded the serpent?

10 *Are* You not *the One* who dried up
      the sea,
   The waters of the great deep;
   That made the depths of the sea a
      road
   For the redeemed to cross over?
11 So the ransomed of the LORD shall
      return,
   And come to Zion with singing,
   With everlasting joy on their heads.
   They shall obtain joy and gladness;
   Sorrow and sighing shall flee away.

12 "I, *even* I, *am* He who comforts you.
   Who *are* you that you should be
      afraid
   Of a man *who* will die,
   And of the son of a man *who* will
      be made like grass?
13 And you forget the LORD your
      Maker,
   Who stretched out the heavens
   And laid the foundations of the earth;
   You have feared continually
      every day
   Because of the fury of the oppressor,
   When *he has* prepared to destroy.
   And where *is* the fury of the
      oppressor?
14 The captive exile hastens, that he may
      be loosed,
   That he should not die in the pit,
   And that his bread should not fail.
15 But I *am* the LORD your God,

Who divided the sea whose waves
   roared—
The LORD of hosts *is* His name.
16 And I have put My words in your
      mouth;
   I have covered you with the shadow
      of My hand,
   That I may plant the heavens,
   Lay the foundations of the earth,
   And say to Zion, 'You *are* My
      people.'"

---

*N*o power outside, from the Devil
downward, can take us out of
         God's hand.   (GOOD)

---

17 Awake, awake!
   Stand up, O Jerusalem,
   You who have drunk at the hand of
      the LORD
   The cup of His fury;
   You have drunk the dregs of the cup
      of trembling,
   And drained *it* out.
18 *There is* no one to guide her
   Among all the sons she has
      brought forth;
   Nor *is there any* who takes her by
      the hand
   Among all the sons she has
      brought up.
19 These two *things* have come to you;
   Who will be sorry for you?—
   Desolation and destruction, famine
      and sword—
   By whom will I comfort you?
20 Your sons have fainted,
   They lie at the head of all the streets,
   Like an antelope in a net;
   They are full of the fury of the LORD,
   The rebuke of your God.

21 Therefore please hear this, you
      afflicted,
   And drunk but not with wine.
22 Thus says your Lord,
   The LORD and your God,
   Who pleads the cause of His people:
   "See, I have taken out of your hand
   The cup of trembling,
   The dregs of the cup of My fury;
   You shall no longer drink it.
23 But I will put it into the hand of
      those who afflict you,
   Who have said to you,
   'Lie down, that we may walk over
      you.'

And you have laid your body like
   the ground,
And as the street, for those who walk
   over."

52 AWAKE, awake!
   Put on your strength, O Zion;
Put on your beautiful garments,
O Jerusalem, the holy city!
For the uncircumcised and the
   unclean
Shall no longer come to you.
2   Shake yourself from the dust, arise;
Sit down, O Jerusalem!
Loose yourself from the bonds of
   your neck,
O captive daughter of Zion!

3 For thus says the LORD:

"You have sold yourselves for nothing,
And you shall be redeemed without
   money."

4 For thus says the Lord GOD:

"My people went down at first
Into Egypt to dwell there;
Then the Assyrian oppressed them
   without cause.
5   Now therefore, what have I here,"
   says the LORD,
"That My people are taken away for
   nothing?
Those who rule over them
Make them wail," says the LORD,
"And My name *is* blasphemed
   continually every day.
6   Therefore My people shall know My
   name;
Therefore *they shall know* in that day
That I *am* He who speaks:
'Behold, *it is* I.' "

7   How beautiful upon the mountains
Are the feet of him who brings good
   news,
Who proclaims peace,
Who brings glad tidings of good
   things,
Who proclaims salvation,
Who says to Zion,
"Your God reigns!"
8   Your watchmen shall lift up *their*
   voices,
With their voices they shall sing
   together;
For they shall see eye to eye
When the LORD brings back Zion.
9   Break forth into joy, sing together,
You waste places of Jerusalem!

For the LORD has comforted His
   people,
He has redeemed Jerusalem.
10   The LORD has made bare His holy
   arm
In the eyes of all the nations;
And all the ends of the earth shall
   see
The salvation of our God.

11   Depart! Depart! Go out from there,
Touch no unclean *thing;*
Go out from the midst of her,
Be clean,
You who bear the vessels of the
   LORD.
12   For you shall not go out with haste,
Nor go by flight;
For the LORD will go before you,
And the God of Israel *will be* your
   rear guard.

13   Behold, My Servant shall deal
   prudently;
He shall be exalted and extolled and
   be very high.
14   Just as many were astonished at you,
So His visage was marred more than
   any man,
And His form more than the sons
   of men;
15   So shall He sprinkle many nations.
Kings shall shut their mouths
   at Him;
For what had not been told them
   they shall see,
And what they had not heard they
   shall consider.

PSALM 112:5–10

5   A good man deals graciously and
   lends;
He will guide his affairs with
   discretion.

*The best of men are but the best
  of men.* (SHADE)

6   Surely he will never be shaken;
The righteous will be in everlasting
   remembrance.
7   He will not be afraid of evil tidings;
His heart is steadfast, trusting in the
   LORD.
8   His heart *is* established;
He will not be afraid,

Until he sees *his desire* upon his
enemies.

9 He has dispersed abroad,
He has given to the poor;
His righteousness endures forever;
His horn will be exalted with honor.
10 The wicked will see *it* and be grieved;
He will gnash his teeth and melt away;
The desire of the wicked shall perish.

PROVERBS 26:16

16 THE lazy *man is* wiser in his own
eyes
Than seven men who can answer
sensibly.

EPHESIANS 2:1–22

AND you He *made alive,* who were dead
in trespasses and sins, 2 in which you once
walked according to the course of this
world, according to the prince of the power
of the air, the spirit who now works in
the sons of disobedience, 3 among whom
also we all once conducted ourselves in the
lusts of our flesh, fulfilling the desires of
the flesh and of the mind, and were by
nature children of wrath, just as the others.
4 But God, who is rich in mercy, because
of His great love with which He loved us,
5 even when we were dead in trespasses,
made us alive together with Christ (by grace
you have been saved), 6 and raised *us* up
together, and made *us* sit together in the
heavenly *places* in Christ Jesus, 7 that in the
ages to come He might show the exceeding
riches of His grace in *His* kindness toward
us in Christ Jesus. 8 For by grace you have
been saved through faith, and that not of
yourselves; *it is* the gift of God, 9 not of
works, lest anyone should boast. 10 For we
are His workmanship, created in Christ

Jesus for good works, which God prepared
beforehand that we should walk in them.

---

*It is impossible for Christ to be where
you are, that is why He has put you
there.* (NOT KNOWING)

---

11 Therefore remember that you, once
Gentiles in the flesh—who are called Uncircumcision by what is called the Circumcision made in the flesh by hands— 12 that
at that time you were without Christ, being
aliens from the commonwealth of Israel and
strangers from the covenants of promise,
having no hope and without God in the
world. 13 But now in Christ Jesus you who
once were far off have been brought near
by the blood of Christ.
14 For He Himself is our peace, who has
made both one, and has broken down the
middle wall of separation, 15 having abolished in His flesh the enmity, *that is,* the
law of commandments *contained* in ordinances, so as to create in Himself one new
man *from* the two, *thus* making peace,
16 and that He might reconcile them both
to God in one body through the cross,
thereby putting to death the enmity.
17 And He came and preached peace to you
who were afar off and to those who were
near. 18 For through Him we both have
access by one Spirit to the Father.
19 Now, therefore, you are no longer
strangers and foreigners, but fellow citizens
with the saints and members of the household of God, 20 having been built on the
foundation of the apostles and prophets,
Jesus Christ Himself being the chief corner-
stone, 21 in whom the whole building, being
fitted together, grows into a holy temple
in the Lord, 22 in whom you also are being
built together for a dwelling place of God
in the Spirit.

Reading 274—Dimensions of Divine Love
Ephesians 3:18, 19

The first thing we need to be educated in spiritually is a knowledge of
the dimensions of divine love, its length and depth and width and height.
That God is love is a revelation. Unless I am born from above, what is the
use of telling me God is love? To me He is not love. Where is the love of

God in war? in suffering? in all the inevitable inequalities of life? No one who faces facts as they are could ever prove that God is love unless he accepts the revelation of His love made by Jesus Christ. John 3:16 does not begin to have any meaning to the natural man who knows nothing whatever of the domain Jesus Christ represents; but let him come up against things and be brought to his wits' end, and then let him read John 3:16. Not until we realize that there is something tragic at the basis of human life shall we recognize the love of God.

In the Cross we may see the dimensions of divine love. The Cross is not the cross of a man, but the exhibition of the heart of God. At the back of the wall of the world stands God with His arms outstretched, and every man driven there is driven into the arms of God. The Cross of Jesus is the supreme evidence of the love of God (Rom. 8:35–39). "Who shall separate us from the love of Christ?" (v. 35).   (*Place Help*)

ISAIAH 53:1—54:17

1   WHO has believed our report?
    And to whom has the arm of the
        Lord been revealed?
2   For He shall grow up before Him
        as a tender plant,
    And as a root out of dry ground.
    He has no form or comeliness;
    And when we see Him,
    There is no beauty that we should
        desire Him.
3   He is despised and rejected by men,
    A Man of sorrows and acquainted
        with grief.
    And we hid, as it were, *our* faces from
        Him;
    He was despised, and we did not
        esteem Him.

4   Surely He has borne our griefs
    And carried our sorrows;
    Yet we esteemed Him stricken,
    Smitten by God, and afflicted.
5   But He *was* wounded for our
        transgressions,
    He was bruised for our iniquities;
    The chastisement for our peace *was*
        upon Him,
    And by His stripes we are healed.
6   All we like sheep have gone astray;
    We have turned, every one, to his
        own way;
    And the Lord has laid on Him the
        iniquity of us all.

7   He was oppressed and He was
        afflicted,
    Yet He opened not His mouth;
    He was led as a lamb to the slaughter,
    And as a sheep before its shearers is
        silent,

    So He opened not His mouth.
8   He was taken from prison and from
        judgment,
    And who will declare His generation?
    For He was cut off from the land
        of the living;
    For the transgressions of My people
    He was stricken.
9   And they made His grave with the
        wicked—
    But with the rich at His death,
    Because He had done no violence,
    Nor *was any* deceit in His mouth.

10 Yet it pleased the Lord to bruise
        Him;
    He has put *Him* to grief.
    When You make His soul an offering
        for sin,
    He shall see *His* seed, He shall
        prolong *His* days,
    And the pleasure of the Lord shall
        prosper in His hand.

---

*T*he profundity of His agony has
to do with the fulfilling of His
destiny.   (Psy. Redemp.)

---

11 He shall see the labor of His soul,
    and be satisfied.
    By His knowledge My righteous
        Servant shall justify many,
    For He shall bear their iniquities.
12 Therefore I will divide Him a portion
        with the great,
    And He shall divide the spoil with
        the strong,
    Because He poured out His soul
        unto death,

And He was numbered with the
transgressors,
And He bore the sin of many,
And made intercession for the
transgressors.

54 "SING, O barren,
You *who* have not borne!
Break forth into singing, and cry
aloud,
You *who* have not labored with child!
For more *are* the children of the
desolate
Than the children of the married
woman," says the LORD.

2 "Enlarge the place of your tent,
And let them stretch out the curtains
of your dwellings;
Do not spare;
Lengthen your cords,
And strengthen your stakes.

3 For you shall expand to the right and
to the left,
And your descendants will inherit the
nations,
And make the desolate cities
inhabited.

4 "Do not fear, for you will not be
ashamed;
Neither be disgraced, for you will
not be put to shame;
For you will forget the shame of your
youth,
And will not remember the reproach
of your widowhood anymore.

5 For your Maker *is* your husband,
The LORD of hosts *is* His name;
And your Redeemer *is* the Holy One
of Israel;
He is called the God of the whole
earth.

6 For the LORD has called you
Like a woman forsaken and grieved
in spirit,
Like a youthful wife when you were
refused,"
Says your God.

7 "For a mere moment I have forsaken
you,
But with great mercies I will gather
you.

8 With a little wrath I hid My face from
you for a moment;
But with everlasting kindness I will
have mercy on you,"
Says the LORD, your Redeemer.

9 "For this *is* like the waters of Noah
to Me;
For as I have sworn

That the waters of Noah would no
longer cover the earth,
So have I sworn
That I would not be angry with you,
nor rebuke you.

10 For the mountains shall depart
And the hills be removed,
But My kindness shall not depart
from you,
Nor shall My covenant of peace be
removed,"
Says the LORD, who has mercy on
you.

11 "O you afflicted one,
Tossed with tempest, *and* not
comforted,
Behold, I will lay your stones with
colorful gems,
And lay your foundations with
sapphires.

12 I will make your pinnacles of rubies,
Your gates of crystal,
And all your walls of precious stones.

13 All your children *shall be* taught by
the LORD,
And great *shall be* the peace of your
children.

14 In righteousness you shall be
established;
You shall be far from oppression, for
you shall not fear;
And from terror, for it shall not come
near you.

15 Indeed they shall surely assemble, *but*
not because of Me.
Whoever assembles against you shall
fall for your sake.

16 "Behold, I have created the blacksmith
Who blows the coals in the fire,
Who brings forth an instrument for
his work;
And I have created the spoiler to
destroy.

17 No weapon formed against you shall
prosper,
And every tongue *which* rises against
you in judgment
You shall condemn.
This *is* the heritage of the servants
of the LORD,
And their righteousness *is* from Me,"
Says the LORD.

PSALM 113:1–4

1 PRAISE the LORD!

Praise, O servants of the LORD,
Praise the name of the LORD!

2 Blessed be the name of the LORD
   From this time forth and forevermore!
3 From the rising of the sun to its going
   down
   The LORD's name *is* to be praised.

4 The LORD *is* high above all nations,
   His glory above the heavens.

PROVERBS 26:17–19

17 HE who passes by *and* meddles in a
   quarrel not his own
   Is like one who takes a dog by the ears.

18 Like a madman who throws
   firebrands, arrows, and death,
19 *Is* the man *who* deceives his neighbor,
   And says, "I was only joking!"

EPHESIANS 3:1–21

FOR this reason I, Paul, the prisoner of
Christ Jesus for you Gentiles— 2 if indeed
you have heard of the dispensation of the
grace of God which was given to me for
you, 3 how that by revelation He made
known to me the mystery (as I have briefly
written already, 4 by which, when you read,
you may understand my knowledge in the
mystery of Christ), 5 which in other ages
was not made known to the sons of men,
as it has now been revealed by the Spirit
to His holy apostles and prophets: 6 that
the Gentiles should be fellow heirs, of the
same body, and partakers of His promise
in Christ through the gospel, 7 of which I
became a minister according to the gift of
the grace of God given to me by the effective working of His power.
8 To me, who am less than the least of
all the saints, this grace was given, that I
should preach among the Gentiles the unsearchable riches of Christ, 9 and to make
all see what *is* the fellowship of the mystery,
which from the beginning of the ages has
been hidden in God who created all things
through Jesus Christ; 10 to the intent that
now the manifold wisdom of God might
be made known by the church to the principalities and powers in the heavenly *places,*
11 according to the eternal purpose which
He accomplished in Christ Jesus our Lord,
12 in whom we have boldness and access
with confidence through faith in Him.
13 Therefore I ask that you do not lose heart
at my tribulations for you, which is your
glory.
14 For this reason I bow my knees to
the Father of our Lord Jesus Christ,

---

*God must not be treated as a hospital
for our broken "toys," but as our
Father.* (NOT KNOWING)

---

15 from whom the whole family in heaven
and earth is named, 16 that He would grant
you, according to the riches of His glory,
to be strengthened with might through His
Spirit in the inner man, 17 that Christ may
dwell in your hearts through faith; that you,
being rooted and grounded in love,
18 may be able to comprehend with all the
saints what *is* the width and length and
depth and height— 19 to know the love
of Christ which passes knowledge; that
you may be filled with all the fullness of
God.
20 Now to Him who is able to do exceedingly abundantly above all that we ask or
think, according to the power that works
in us, 21 to Him *be* glory in the church by
Christ Jesus to all generations, forever and
ever. Amen.

Reading 275—Spiritual Evolution
Ephesians 4:13

The world today is obsessed with the idea of evolution. We hear speculations
about the superman, we are told we are getting better and better; but
what we are tending toward we don't know. The remarkable thing about the
spiritual evolution represented by Jesus Christ is that the goal is given to us
at the start, namely, Jesus Christ Himself. The natural view and the Bible's
view of man are different; the natural point of view is that man is a great

being in the making, his achievements are a wonderful promise of what he is going to be; the Bible's point of view is that man is a magnificent ruin of what God designed him to be. The Bible does not look forward to an evolution of mankind; the Bible talks of a revolution—"You must be born again." That is not a command but the statement of a foundation fact. . . . God and man as God created him were at one, but severance came with the introduction of sin; then Jesus Christ came, and in Him God and man are again made at one. Jesus Christ did not evolve out of history, He came into history from outside history; He is not the best human being the world has ever seen, He is a being who cannot be accounted for by the human race at all. . . . Paul uses the figure of Jesus as the goal to which the whole human race is to attain—"till we all come . . . to the measure of the stature of the fullness of Christ." (*PLACE HELP*)

ISAIAH 55:1—56:12

1 "HO! Everyone who thirsts,
    Come to the waters;
    And you who have no money,
    Come, buy and eat.
    Yes, come, buy wine and milk
    Without money and without price.
2 Why do you spend money for *what is* not bread,
    And your wages for *what* does not satisfy?
    Listen carefully to Me, and eat *what is* good,
    And let your soul delight itself in abundance.
3 Incline your ear, and come to Me.
    Hear, and your soul shall live;
    And I will make an everlasting covenant with you—
    The sure mercies of David.
4 Indeed I have given him *as* a witness to the people,
    A leader and commander for the people.
5 Surely you shall call a nation you do not know,
    And nations *who* do not know you shall run to you,
    Because of the LORD your God,
    And the Holy One of Israel;
    For He has glorified you."

6 Seek the LORD while He may be found,
    Call upon Him while He is near.
7 Let the wicked forsake his way,
    And the unrighteous man his thoughts;
    Let him return to the LORD,
    And He will have mercy on him;
    And to our God,
    For He will abundantly pardon.

8 "For My thoughts *are* not your thoughts,
    Nor *are* your ways My ways," says the LORD.
9 "For *as* the heavens are higher than the earth,
    So are My ways higher than your ways,
    And My thoughts than your thoughts.

10 "For as the rain comes down, and the snow from heaven,
    And do not return there,
    But water the earth,
    And make it bring forth and bud,
    That it may give seed to the sower
    And bread to the eater,
11 So shall My word be that goes forth from My mouth;
    It shall not return to Me void,
    But it shall accomplish what I please,
    And it shall prosper *in the thing* for which I sent it.

12 "For you shall go out with joy,
    And be led out with peace;
    The mountains and the hills
    Shall break forth into singing before you,
    And all the trees of the field shall clap *their* hands.

The Redemption covers more than men and women, it covers the whole earth.   (BIB. ETHICS)

---

13 Instead of the thorn shall come up the cypress tree,
    And instead of the brier shall come up the myrtle tree;

And it shall be to the LORD for a
name,
For an everlasting sign *that* shall not
be cut off."

56 THUS says the LORD:

"Keep justice, and do righteousness,
For My salvation *is* about to
come,
And My righteousness to be
revealed.

2 Blessed *is* the man *who* does this,
And the son of man *who* lays hold
on it;
Who keeps from defiling the
Sabbath,
And keeps his hand from doing any
evil."

3 Do not let the son of the foreigner
Who has joined himself to the LORD
Speak, saying,
"The LORD has utterly separated me
from His people";
Nor let the eunuch say,
"Here I am, a dry tree."
4 For thus says the LORD:
"To the eunuchs who keep My
Sabbaths,
And choose what pleases Me,
And hold fast My covenant,
5 Even to them I will give in My house
And within My walls a place and a
name
Better than that of sons and
daughters;
I will give them an everlasting name
That shall not be cut off.

6 "Also the sons of the foreigner
Who join themselves to the LORD,
to serve Him,
And to love the name of the LORD,
to be His servants—
Everyone who keeps from defiling
the Sabbath,
And holds fast My covenant—
7 Even them I will bring to My holy
mountain,
And make them joyful in My house
of prayer.
Their burnt offerings and their
sacrifices
Will be accepted on My altar;
For My house shall be called a house
of prayer for all nations."
8 The Lord GOD, who gathers the
outcasts of Israel, says,
"Yet I will gather to him
Others besides those who are
gathered to him."

9 All you beasts of the field, come to
devour,
All you beasts in the forest.
10 His watchmen *are* blind,
They are all ignorant;
They *are* all dumb dogs,
They cannot bark;
Sleeping, lying down, loving to
slumber.
11 Yes, *they are* greedy dogs
Which never have enough.
And they *are* shepherds
Who cannot understand;
They all look to their own way,
Every one for his own gain,
From his *own* territory.
12 "Come," *one says,* "I will bring wine,
And we will fill ourselves with
intoxicating drink;
Tomorrow will be as today,
And much more abundant."

PSALM 113:5–9

5 WHO *is* like the LORD our God,
Who dwells on high,
6 Who humbles Himself to behold
The things that are in the heavens and
in the earth?

7 He raises the poor out of the dust,
And lifts the needy out of the ash heap,
8 That He may seat *him* with princes—
With the princes of His people.
9 He grants the barren woman a home,
Like a joyful mother of children.

Praise the LORD!

PROVERBS 26:20, 21

20 WHERE *there is* no wood, the fire
goes out;
And where *there is* no talebearer, strife
ceases.
21 *As* charcoal *is* to burning coals, and
wood to fire,
So *is* a contentious man to kindle
strife.

EPHESIANS 4:1–32

I, therefore, the prisoner of the Lord, beseech you to walk worthy of the calling
with which you were called, 2 with all lowliness and gentleness, with longsuffering,
bearing with one another in love, 3 en-
deavoring to keep the unity of the Spirit

in the bond of peace. 4 *There is* one body and one Spirit, just as you were called in one hope of your calling; 5 one Lord, one faith, one baptism; 6 one God and Father of all, who *is* above all, and through all, and in you all.

7 But to each one of us grace was given according to the measure of Christ's gift. 8 Therefore He says:

"When He ascended on high,
He led captivity captive,
And gave gifts to men."

9 (Now this, "He ascended"—what does it mean but that He also first descended into the lower parts of the earth? 10 He who descended is also the One who ascended far above all the heavens, that He might fill all things.)

11 And He Himself gave some *to be* apostles, some prophets, some evangelists, and some pastors and teachers, 12 for the equipping of the saints for the work of ministry, for the edifying of the body of Christ, 13 till we all come to the unity of the faith and of the knowledge of the Son of God, to a perfect man, to the measure of the stature of the fullness of Christ; 14 that we should no longer be children, tossed to and fro and carried about with every wind of doctrine, by the trickery of men, in the cunning craftiness of deceitful plotting, 15 but, speaking the truth in love, may grow up in all things into Him who is the head—Christ— 16 from whom the whole body, joined and knit together by what every joint supplies, according to the effective working by which every part does its share, causes growth of the body for the edifying of itself in love.

17 This I say, therefore, and testify in the Lord, that you should no longer walk as the rest of the Gentiles walk, in the futility of their mind, 18 having their understand-ing darkened, being alienated from the life of God, because of the ignorance that is in them, because of the blindness of their heart; 19 who, being past feeling, have given themselves over to lewdness, to work all uncleanness with greediness.

20 But you have not so learned Christ, 21 if indeed you have heard Him and have been taught by Him, as the truth is in Jesus: 22 that you put off, concerning your former conduct, the old man which grows corrupt according to the deceitful lusts, 23 and be renewed in the spirit of your mind, 24 and that you put on the new man which was created according to God, in true righteousness and holiness.

Jesus Christ is the normal Man, the Man according to God's standard. (CONFORMED)

---

25 Therefore, putting away lying, "*Let* each one *of you* speak truth with his neighbor," for we are members of one another. 26 "Be angry, and do not sin": do not let the sun go down on your wrath, 27 nor give place to the devil. 28 Let him who stole steal no longer, but rather let him labor, working with *his* hands what is good, that he may have something to give him who has need. 29 Let no corrupt word proceed out of your mouth, but what is good for necessary edification, that it may impart grace to the hearers. 30 And do not grieve the Holy Spirit of God, by whom you were sealed for the day of redemption. 31 Let all bitterness, wrath, anger, clamor, and evil speaking be put away from you, with all malice. 32 And be kind to one another, tenderhearted, forgiving one another, even as God in Christ forgave you.

◆◆◆◆

Reading 276—Struggle for Correlation
Ephesians 5:1, 2

I f I struggle for myself on the right line, I struggle for others also, and the struggle establishes a correlation between God and myself, and the characteristic of the life is a strong family likeness to Jesus. A self indwelt by Jesus becomes like Him. "Walk in love, as Christ also has loved us." Jesus has loved me to the end of all my meanness and selfishness and sin; now, He says, show that same love to others. "For if you forgive men their trespasses, your heavenly Father will also forgive you"—that is, I am to ask to be forgiven, not on the ground of the Atonement, but because I forgive. "But if you do not forgive men their trespasses, neither will your Father forgive your trespasses." That is hard hitting. Am I prepared to show the man who does evil to me the love God has shown to me? I have to learn to identify myself with God's interests in other people, and God's interests are never my selfish interests, but always His interests. . . . The benefit of my life to others is in proportion to whether I am making this struggle for the self God designed me to be, and my worth to God is in proportion to my getting into correlation with Him, getting His point of view about everything.   (*PLACE HELP*)

ISAIAH 57:1—58:14

1   THE righteous perishes,
    And no man takes *it* to heart;
    Merciful men *are* taken away,
    While no one considers
    That the righteous is taken away
       from evil.
2   He shall enter into peace;
    They shall rest in their beds,
    Each one walking *in* his uprightness.

3   "But come here,
    You sons of the sorceress,
    You offspring of the adulterer and
       the harlot!
4   Whom do you ridicule?
    Against whom do you make a wide
       mouth
    And stick out the tongue?
    Are you not children of transgression,
    Offspring of falsehood,
5   Inflaming yourselves with gods
       under every green tree,
    Slaying the children in the valleys,
    Under the clefts of the rocks?
6   Among the smooth *stones* of the
       stream
    Is your portion;
    They, they, *are* your lot!
    Even to them you have poured a
       drink offering,
    You have offered a grain offering.
    Should I receive comfort in these?

7   "On a lofty and high mountain
    You have set your bed;
    Even there you went up
    To offer sacrifice.
8   Also behind the doors and their
       posts
    You have set up your remembrance;
    For you have uncovered yourself *to
       those other* than Me,
    And have gone up to them;

    You have enlarged your bed
    And made *a covenant* with them;
    You have loved their bed,
    Where you saw *their* nudity.
9   You went to the king with ointment,
    And increased your perfumes;
    You sent your messengers far off,
    And *even* descended to Sheol.
10 You are wearied in the length of your
       way;
    Yet you did not say, 'There is no
       hope.'
    You have found the life of your
       hand;
    Therefore you were not grieved.

11 "And of whom have you been afraid,
       or feared,
    That you have lied
    And not remembered Me,
    Nor taken *it* to your heart?
    Is it not because I have held My
       peace from of old
    That you do not fear Me?
12 I will declare your righteousness
    And your works,
    For they will not profit you.
13 When you cry out,
    Let your collection *of idols* deliver
       you.
    But the wind will carry them all away,
    A breath will take *them*.
    But he who puts his trust in Me shall
       possess the land,
    And shall inherit My holy mountain."

14 And one shall say,
    "Heap it up! Heap it up!
    Prepare the way,
    Take the stumbling block out of the
       way of My people."

15 For thus says the High and Lofty
       One

Who inhabits eternity, whose name
  is Holy:
"I dwell in the high and holy *place,*
  With him *who* has a contrite and
    humble spirit,
To revive the spirit of the humble,
And to revive the heart of the contrite
  ones.

16 For I will not contend forever,
  Nor will I always be angry;
For the spirit would fail before Me,
And the souls *which* I have made.

17 For the iniquity of his covetousness
  I was angry and struck him;
I hid and was angry,
And he went on backsliding in the
  way of his heart.

18 I have seen his ways, and will heal
  him;
I will also lead him,
And restore comforts to him
And to his mourners.

19 "I create the fruit of the lips:
Peace, peace to *him who is* far off and
  to *him who is* near,"
Says the LORD,
"And I will heal him."

20 But the wicked *are* like the troubled
  sea,
When it cannot rest,
Whose waters cast up mire and dirt.

21 "*There is* no peace,"
Says my God, "for the wicked."

58 "CRY aloud, spare not;
  Lift up your voice like a trumpet;
Tell My people their transgression,
And the house of Jacob their sins.

2 Yet they seek Me daily,
And delight to know My ways,
As a nation that did righteousness,
And did not forsake the ordinance
  of their God.
They ask of Me the ordinances of
  justice;
They take delight in approaching
  God.

3 'Why have we fasted,' *they say,* 'and
  You have not seen?
Why have we afflicted our souls, and
  You take no notice?'

"In fact, in the day of your fast you
  find pleasure,
And exploit all your laborers.

4 Indeed you fast for strife and debate,
And to strike with the fist of
  wickedness.
You will not fast as *you do* this day,

To make your voice heard on high.

5 Is it a fast that I have chosen,
A day for a man to afflict his soul?
Is it to bow down his head like a
  bulrush,
And to spread out sackcloth and
  ashes?
Would you call this a fast,
And an acceptable day to the LORD?

6 "*Is* this not the fast that I have chosen:
To loose the bonds of wickedness,
To undo the heavy burdens,
To let the oppressed go free,
And that you break every yoke?

7 *Is it* not to share your bread with
  the hungry,
And that you bring to your house
  the poor who are cast out;
When you see the naked, that you
  cover him,
And not hide yourself from your
  own flesh?

8 Then your light shall break forth like
  the morning,
Your healing shall spring forth
  speedily,
And your righteousness shall go
  before you;
The glory of the LORD shall be your
  rear guard.

9 Then you shall call, and the LORD
  will answer;
You shall cry, and He will say, 'Here
  I *am.*'

"If you take away the yoke from your
  midst,
The pointing of the finger, and
  speaking wickedness,

10 *If* you extend your soul to the
  hungry
And satisfy the afflicted soul,
Then your light shall dawn in the
  darkness,
And your darkness shall *be* as the
  noonday.

11 The LORD will guide you continually,
And satisfy your soul in drought,
And strengthen your bones;
You shall be like a watered garden,
And like a spring of water, whose
  waters do not fail.

12 Those from among you
Shall build the old waste places;
You shall raise up the foundations
  of many generations;
And you shall be called the Repairer
  of the Breach,
The Restorer of Streets to Dwell In.

13 "If you turn away your foot from
   the Sabbath,
   From doing your pleasure on My
   holy day,
   And call the Sabbath a delight,
   The holy *day* of the LORD honorable,
   And shall honor Him, not doing your
   own ways,
   Nor finding your own pleasure,
   Nor speaking *your own* words,
14 Then you shall delight yourself in the
   LORD;
   And I will cause you to ride on the
   high hills of the earth,
   And feed you with the heritage of
   Jacob your father.
   The mouth of the LORD has
   spoken."

PSALM 114:1–8

1 WHEN Israel went out of Egypt,
   The house of Jacob from a people of
   strange language,
2 Judah became His sanctuary,
   And Israel His dominion.

3 The sea saw *it* and fled;
   Jordan turned back.
4 The mountains skipped like rams,
   The little hills like lambs.
5 What ails you, O sea, that you fled?
   O Jordan, *that* you turned back?
6 O mountains, *that* you skipped like
   rams?
   O little hills, like lambs?

7 Tremble, O earth, at the presence of
   the Lord,
   At the presence of the God of Jacob,
8 Who turned the rock *into* a pool of
   water,
   The flint into a fountain of waters.

PROVERBS 26:22

22 THE words of a talebearer *are* like
   tasty trifles,
   And they go down into the inmost
   body.

EPHESIANS 5:1–16

THEREFORE be imitators of God as dear
children. 2 And walk in love, as Christ also
has loved us and given Himself for us, an
offering and a sacrifice to God for a sweet-
smelling aroma.

3 But fornication and all uncleanness or
covetousness, let it not even be named
among you, as is fitting for saints; 4 neither
filthiness, nor foolish talking, nor coarse
jesting, which are not fitting, but rather
giving of thanks. 5 For this you know, that
no fornicator, unclean person, nor covetous
man, who is an idolater, has any inheritance
in the kingdom of Christ and God.
6 Let no one deceive you with empty words,
for because of these things the wrath of
God comes upon the sons of disobedience.
7 Therefore do not be partakers with
them.

8 For you were once darkness, but now
you are light in the Lord. Walk as children
of light 9 (for the fruit of the Spirit *is* in
all goodness, righteousness, and truth),

---

*The fruit of the Spirit is the exact
expression of the disposition of
Jesus.* (PLACE HELP)

---

10 finding out what is acceptable to the
Lord. 11 And have no fellowship with the
unfruitful works of darkness, but rather expose *them.* 12 For it is shameful even to
speak of those things which are done by
them in secret. 13 But all things that are
exposed are made manifest by the light,
for whatever makes manifest is light.
14 Therefore He says:

   "Awake, you who sleep,
   Arise from the dead,
   And Christ will give you light."

15 See then that you walk circumspectly,
not as fools but as wise, 16 redeeming the
time, because the days are evil.

Reading 277—Enthusiastic and Capable
Ephesians 5:18

We think that sobriety and capability go together, but it is not always so. A man may be sober and incapable as well as drunk and incapable. Paul warns against the enthusiasm according to wine, but he says we have no business to be nondescript, negative people, drunk neither one way nor the other; we must be enthusiastic. In other words, "Be being filled." The teaching of the New Testament presents the passion of life. Stoicism has come so much into the idea of the Christian life that we imagine the stoic is the best type of Christian; but just where stoicism seems most like Christianity it is most adverse. A stoic overcomes the world by passionlessness, by eviscerating all personal interest out of life until he is a mere submissive recording machine. Christianity overcomes the world by passion, not by passionlessness. Passion is usually taken to mean something from which human nature suffers; in reality it stands for endurance and high enthusiasm, a radiant intensity of life, life at the highest pitch all the time without any reaction. That is what Paul means by being filled. (*PLACE HELP*)

ISAIAH 59:1—60:22

1 BEHOLD, the Lord's hand is not shortened,
That it cannot save;
Nor His ear heavy,
That it cannot hear.

2 But your iniquities have separated you from your God;
And your sins have hidden *His* face from you,
So that He will not hear.

3 For your hands are defiled with blood,
And your fingers with iniquity;
Your lips have spoken lies,
Your tongue has muttered perversity.

4 No one calls for justice,
Nor does *any* plead for truth.
They trust in empty words and speak lies;
They conceive evil and bring forth iniquity.

5 They hatch vipers' eggs and weave the spider's web;
He who eats of their eggs dies,
And *from* that which is crushed a viper breaks out.

6 Their webs will not become garments,
Nor will they cover themselves with their works;
Their works *are* works of iniquity,
And the act of violence *is* in their hands.

7 Their feet run to evil,
And they make haste to shed innocent blood;
Their thoughts *are* thoughts of iniquity;
Wasting and destruction *are* in their paths.

8 The way of peace they have not known,
And *there is* no justice in their ways;
They have made themselves crooked paths;
Whoever takes that way shall not know peace.

9 Therefore justice is far from us,
Nor does righteousness overtake us;
We look for light, but there is darkness!
For brightness, *but* we walk in blackness!

10 We grope for the wall like the blind,
And we grope as if *we had* no eyes;
We stumble at noonday as at twilight;
We are as dead *men* in desolate places.

11 We all growl like bears,
And moan sadly like doves;
We look for justice, but *there is* none;
For salvation, *but* it is far from us.

12 For our transgressions are multiplied before You,
And our sins testify against us;
For our transgressions *are* with us,

And *as for* our iniquities, we know
them:

13 In transgressing and lying against the
LORD,
And departing from our God,
Speaking oppression and revolt,
Conceiving and uttering from the
heart words of falsehood.

14 Justice is turned back,
And righteousness stands afar off;
For truth is fallen in the street,
And equity cannot enter.

15 So truth fails,
And he *who* departs from evil makes
himself a prey.

Then the LORD saw *it,* and it
displeased Him
That *there was* no justice.

16 He saw that *there was* no man,
And wondered that *there was* no
intercessor;
Therefore His own arm brought
salvation for Him;
And His own righteousness, it
sustained Him.

17 For He put on righteousness as a
breastplate,
And a helmet of salvation on His
head;
He put on the garments of
vengeance for clothing,
And was clad with zeal as a cloak.

18 According to *their* deeds, accordingly
He will repay,
Fury to His adversaries,
Recompense to His enemies;
The coastlands He will fully repay.

19 So shall they fear
The name of the LORD from the
west,
And His glory from the rising of the
sun;
When the enemy comes in like a
flood,
The Spirit of the LORD will lift up
a standard against him.

20 "The Redeemer will come to Zion,
And to those who turn from
transgression in Jacob,"
Says the LORD.

21 "As for Me," says the LORD, "this *is*
My covenant with them: My Spirit who *is*
upon you, and My words which I have
put in your mouth, shall not depart from
your mouth, nor from the mouth of your
descendants, nor from the mouth of your
descendants' descendants," says the LORD,
"from this time and forevermore."

60 Arise, shine;
For your light has come!
And the glory of the LORD is risen
upon you.

*Each of us has a particular
possession of light that no one else
can have.* (BRILL. HERITAGE)

2 For behold, the darkness shall cover
the earth,
And deep darkness the people;
But the LORD will arise over you,
And His glory will be seen upon you.

3 The Gentiles shall come to your light,
And kings to the brightness of your
rising.

4 "Lift up your eyes all around, and see:
They all gather together, they come
to you;
Your sons shall come from afar,
And your daughters shall be nursed
at *your* side.

5 Then you shall see and become
radiant,
And your heart shall swell with joy;
Because the abundance of the sea
shall be turned to you,
The wealth of the Gentiles shall come
to you.

6 The multitude of camels shall cover
your *land,*
The dromedaries of Midian and
Ephah;
All those from Sheba shall come;
They shall bring gold and incense,
And they shall proclaim the praises
of the LORD.

7 All the flocks of Kedar shall be
gathered together to you,
The rams of Nebaioth shall minister
to you;
They shall ascend with acceptance on
My altar,
And I will glorify the house of My
glory.

8 "Who *are* these *who* fly like a cloud,
And like doves to their roosts?

9 Surely the coastlands shall wait for
Me;
And the ships of Tarshish *will come*
first,
To bring your sons from afar,
Their silver and their gold with them,
To the name of the LORD your God,
And to the Holy One of Israel,
Because He has glorified you.

10 "The sons of foreigners shall build up
   your walls,
   And their kings shall minister to you;
   For in My wrath I struck you,
   But in My favor I have had mercy
   on you.

11 Therefore your gates shall be open
   continually;
   They shall not be shut day or night,
   That *men* may bring to you the wealth
   of the Gentiles,
   And their kings in procession.

12 For the nation and kingdom which
   will not serve you shall perish,
   And *those* nations shall be utterly
   ruined.

13 "The glory of Lebanon shall come to
   you,
   The cypress, the pine, and the box
   tree together,
   To beautify the place of My
   sanctuary;
   And I will make the place of My feet
   glorious.

14 Also the sons of those who afflicted
   you
   Shall come bowing to you,
   And all those who despised you shall
   fall prostrate at the soles of your
   feet;
   And they shall call you The City of
   the LORD,
   Zion of the Holy One of Israel.

15 "Whereas you have been forsaken and
   hated,
   So that no one went through *you*,
   I will make you an eternal excellence,
   A joy of many generations.

16 You shall drink the milk of the
   Gentiles,
   And milk the breast of kings;
   You shall know that I, the LORD,
   am your Savior
   And your Redeemer, the Mighty One
   of Jacob.

17 "Instead of bronze I will bring gold,
   Instead of iron I will bring silver,
   Instead of wood, bronze,
   And instead of stones, iron.
   I will also make your officers peace,
   And your magistrates righteousness.

18 Violence shall no longer be heard in
   your land,
   Neither wasting nor destruction
   within your borders;
   But you shall call your walls
   Salvation,
   And your gates Praise.

19 "The sun shall no longer be your light
   by day,
   Nor for brightness shall the moon
   give light to you;
   But the LORD will be to you an
   everlasting light,
   And your God your glory.

20 Your sun shall no longer go down,
   Nor shall your moon withdraw itself;
   For the LORD will be your everlasting
   light,
   And the days of your mourning shall
   be ended.

21 Also your people *shall* all *be*
   righteous;
   They shall inherit the land forever,
   The branch of My planting,
   The work of My hands,
   That I may be glorified.

22 A little one shall become a thousand,
   And a small one a strong nation.
   I, the LORD, will hasten it in its
   time."

PSALM 115:1–8

1 NOT unto us, O LORD, not unto us,
   But to Your name give glory,
   Because of Your mercy,
   Because of Your truth.

2 Why should the Gentiles say,
   "So where *is* their God?"

3 But our God *is* in heaven;
   He does whatever He pleases.

4 Their idols *are* silver and gold,
   The work of men's hands.

5 They have mouths, but they do not
   speak;
   Eyes they have, but they do not see;

6 They have ears, but they do not hear;
   Noses they have, but they do not smell;

7 They have hands, but they do not
   handle;
   Feet they have, but they do not walk;
   Nor do they mutter through their
   throat.

8 Those who make them are like them;
   So is everyone who trusts in them.

PROVERBS 26:23

23 FERVENT lips with a wicked heart
   Are like earthenware covered with silver
   dross.

EPHESIANS 5:17–33

THEREFORE do not be unwise, but
understand what the will of the Lord *is*.

18 And do not be drunk with wine, in which is dissipation; but be filled with the Spirit, 19 speaking to one another in psalms and hymns and spiritual songs, singing and making melody in your heart to the Lord, 20 giving thanks always for all things to God the Father in the name of our Lord Jesus Christ, 21 submitting to one another in the fear of God.

22 Wives, submit to your own husbands, as to the Lord. 23 For the husband is head of the wife, as also Christ is head of the church; and He is the Savior of the body. 24 Therefore, just as the church is subject to Christ, so *let* the wives *be* to their own husbands in everything.

25 Husbands, love your wives, just as Christ also loved the church and gave Himself for her, 26 that He might sanctify and cleanse her with the washing of water by the word, 27 that He might present her to Himself a glorious church, not having spot or wrinkle or any such thing, but that she should be holy and without blemish. 28 So husbands ought to love their own wives as their own bodies; he who loves his wife loves himself. 29 For no one ever hated his own flesh, but nourishes and cherishes it, just as the Lord *does* the church. 30 For we are members of His body, of His flesh and of His bones. 31 "For this reason a man shall leave his father and mother and be joined to his wife, and the two shall become one flesh." 32 This is a great mystery, but I speak concerning Christ and the church. 33 Nevertheless let each one of you in particular so love his own wife as himself, and let the wife *see* that she respects *her* husband.

❖❖❖❖

Reading 278—How Not to Fight
Ephesians 6:11–13

These verses are not a picture of how to fight, but of how not to fight. If you have not put on the armor, you will have to fight; but "having put on the whole armor of God, then *stand*," says Paul. There are times when God's servants are sent out to attack, to storm the citadel, but the counsel given here is as to how we are to hold the position which has been gained. We need to learn this conservation of energy, "having done all, to stand," manifesting the full power of God.

"For we do not wrestle against flesh and blood"—if we do, we are "out of it"; our warfare is against "the spiritual *hosts* of wickedness" which the world does not see. We are apt to forget that the enemy is unseen and that he is supernatural (see Dan. 10:12, 13). "Don't make any mistake," says Paul, "you are not wrestling against flesh and blood, you are wrestling against tremendous powers you will never be able to withstand unless you put on the whole armor of God. When you see men doing terrible things, remember you are not wrestling against them, they are the cat's-paw of the rulers of the darkness of this world." We are to be taken up with a much more difficult wrestling, namely, the wrestling against the spiritual hosts of wickedness in the heavenly places which prevent us from seeing God. . . .   (*GOD'S WORKMANSHIP*)

ISAIAH 61:1—62:12

1 "THE Spirit of the Lord God *is*
      upon Me,
    Because the LORD has anointed
      Me
    To preach good tidings to the poor;

He has sent Me to heal the
      brokenhearted,
    To proclaim liberty to the captives,
    And the opening of the prison to
      those who are bound;
2 To proclaim the acceptable year of
      the LORD,

And the day of vengeance of our
God;
To comfort all who mourn,

3 To console those who mourn in
Zion,
To give them beauty for ashes,
The oil of joy for mourning,
The garment of praise for the spirit
of heaviness;
That they may be called trees of
righteousness,
The planting of the LORD, that He
may be glorified."

4 And they shall rebuild the old ruins,
They shall raise up the former
desolations,
And they shall repair the ruined cities,
The desolations of many generations.

5 Strangers shall stand and feed your
flocks,
And the sons of the foreigner
Shall be your plowmen and your
vinedressers.

6 But you shall be named the priests
of the LORD,
They shall call you the servants of
our God.
You shall eat the riches of the
Gentiles,
And in their glory you shall boast.

7 Instead of your shame *you shall have*
double *honor,*
And *instead of* confusion they shall
rejoice in their portion.
Therefore in their land they shall
possess double;
Everlasting joy shall be theirs.

8 "For I, the LORD, love justice;
I hate robbery for burnt offering;
I will direct their work in truth,
And will make with them an
everlasting covenant.

9 Their descendants shall be known
among the Gentiles,
And their offspring among the
people.
All who see them shall acknowledge
them,
That they *are* the posterity *whom* the
LORD has blessed."

10 I will greatly rejoice in the LORD,
My soul shall be joyful in my God;
For He has clothed me with the
garments of salvation,
He has covered me with the robe
of righteousness,
As a bridegroom decks *himself* with
ornaments,

And as a bride adorns *herself* with
her jewels.

11 For as the earth brings forth its bud,
As the garden causes the things that
are sown in it to spring forth,
So the Lord GOD will cause
righteousness and praise to spring
forth before all the nations.

62

FOR Zion's sake I will not hold
My peace,
And for Jerusalem's sake I will not
rest,
Until her righteousness goes forth
as brightness,
And her salvation as a lamp *that*
burns.

2 The Gentiles shall see your
righteousness,
And all kings your glory.
You shall be called by a new name,
Which the mouth of the LORD will
name.

3 You shall also be a crown of glory
In the hand of the LORD,
And a royal diadem
In the hand of your God.

4 You shall no longer be termed
Forsaken,
Nor shall your land any more be
termed Desolate;
But you shall be called Hephzibah,
and your land Beulah;
For the LORD delights in you,
And your land shall be married.

5 For *as* a young man marries a virgin,
So shall your sons marry you;
And *as* the bridegroom rejoices over
the bride,
So shall your God rejoice over you.

6 I have set watchmen on your walls,
O Jerusalem;
They shall never hold their peace day
or night.
You who make mention of the
LORD, do not keep silent,

7 And give Him no rest till He
establishes
And till He makes Jerusalem a praise
in the earth.

8 The LORD has sworn by His right
hand
And by the arm of His strength:
"Surely I will no longer give your
grain
As food for your enemies;
And the sons of the foreigner shall
not drink your new wine,
For which you have labored.

9 But those who have gathered it shall
   eat it,
   And praise the LORD;
   Those who have brought it together
   shall drink it in My holy courts."

10 Go through,
   Go through the gates!
   Prepare the way for the people;
   Build up,
   Build up the highway!
   Take out the stones,
   Lift up a banner for the peoples!

11 Indeed the LORD has proclaimed
   To the end of the world:
   "Say to the daughter of Zion,
   'Surely your salvation is coming;
   Behold, His reward *is* with Him,
   And His work before Him.' "

12 And they shall call them The Holy
   People,
   The Redeemed of the LORD;
   And you shall be called Sought Out,
   A City Not Forsaken.

PSALM 115:9–13

9 O Israel, trust in the LORD;
   He *is* their help and their shield.
10 O house of Aaron, trust in the LORD;
   He *is* their help and their shield.
11 You who fear the LORD, trust in the
   LORD;
   He *is* their help and their shield.

12 The LORD has been mindful of *us;*
   He will bless us;
   He will bless the house of Israel;
   He will bless the house of Aaron.
13 He will bless those who fear the LORD,
   Both small and great.

PROVERBS 26:24–26

24 HE who hates, disguises *it* with his lips,
   And lays up deceit within himself;
25 When he speaks kindly, do not believe
   him,
   For *there are* seven abominations in his
   heart;
26 *Though his* hatred is covered by deceit,
   His wickedness will be revealed before
   the assembly.

EPHESIANS 6:1–24

CHILDREN, obey your parents in the
Lord, for this is right. 2 "Honor your father

and mother," which is the first commandment with promise: 3 "that it may be well
with you and you may live long on the
earth."

4 And you, fathers, do not provoke your
children to wrath, but bring them up in
the training and admonition of the Lord.

5 Bondservants, be obedient to those who
are your masters according to the flesh,
with fear and trembling, in sincerity of
heart, as to Christ; 6 not with eyeservice,
as men-pleasers, but as bondservants of
Christ, doing the will of God from the
heart, 7 with goodwill doing service, as to
the Lord, and not to men, 8 knowing that
whatever good anyone does, he will receive
the same from the Lord, whether *he is* a
slave or free.

9 And you, masters, do the same things
to them, giving up threatening, knowing
that your own Master also is in heaven,
and there is no partiality with Him.

10 Finally, my brethren, be strong in the
Lord and in the power of His might.
11 Put on the whole armor of God, that
you may be able to stand against the wiles
of the devil. 12 For we do not wrestle against

---

*I*t is God's own nature that is the
armor.   (BRILL. HERITAGE)

---

flesh and blood, but against principalities,
against powers, against the rulers of the
darkness of this age, against spiritual *hosts*
of wickedness in the heavenly *places.*
13 Therefore take up the whole armor of
God, that you may be able to withstand
in the evil day, and having done all, to stand.
14 Stand therefore, having girded your
waist with truth, having put on the breastplate of righteousness, 15 and having shod
your feet with the preparation of the gospel
of peace; 16 above all, taking the shield of
faith with which you will be able to quench
all the fiery darts of the wicked one.
17 And take the helmet of salvation, and
the sword of the Spirit, which is the word
of God; 18 praying always with all prayer
and supplication in the Spirit, being watchful to this end with all perseverance and
supplication for all the saints— 19 and for
me, that utterance may be given to me,
that I may open my mouth boldly to make
known the mystery of the gospel, 20 for
which I am an ambassador in chains; that
in it I may speak boldly, as I ought to speak.
21 But that you also may know my affairs
and how I am doing, Tychicus, a beloved

brother and faithful minister in the Lord, will make all things known to you; 22 whom I have sent to you for this very purpose, that you may know our affairs, and *that* he may comfort your hearts.

23 Peace to the brethren, and love with faith, from God the Father and the Lord Jesus Christ. 24 Grace *be* with all those who love our Lord Jesus Christ in sincerity. Amen.

◆◆◆◆

Reading 279—Sovereign Preference
Philippians 1:21

Love is literally the sovereign preference of my person for another person, and Jesus says that spiritually that preference must be for Himself. When Paul said, "For to me, to live *is* Christ," he did not mean that he did not live for anything else but that the dominant note, the great consuming passion underneath everything, was his love for Jesus Christ—it explained everything he did. We are not always conscious of the sovereign preference, but a crisis will reveal it. So many make the blunder of mistaking the ecstasy of the first introduction into the kingdom of God for the purpose of God in getting them there; the purpose of God for us is that we realize what the death of Christ meant for *us*. When we tell God that we want at all costs to be identified with the death of Jesus Christ, at that instant a supernatural identification with His death takes place, and we know with a knowledge that passes knowledge that our "old man" is crucified with Christ, and we prove it forever after by the amazing ease with which the supernatural life of God in us enables us to do His will. That is why the bedrock of Christianity is personal, passionate devotion to the Lord Jesus. (*Place Help*)

ISAIAH 63:1—64:12

1 WHO *is* this who comes from Edom,
  With dyed garments from Bozrah,
  This *One who is* glorious in His
    apparel,
  Traveling in the greatness of His
    strength?—

  "I who speak in righteousness, mighty
    to save."

2 Why *is* Your apparel red,
  And Your garments like one who
    treads in the winepress?

3 "I have trodden the winepress alone,
  And from the peoples no one *was*
    with Me.
  For I have trodden them in My anger,
  And trampled them in My fury;
  Their blood is sprinkled upon My
    garments,
  And I have stained all My robes.

4 For the day of vengeance *is* in My
    heart,
  And the year of My redeemed has
    come.

5 I looked, but *there was* no one to
    help,
  And I wondered
  That *there was* no one to uphold;
  Therefore My own arm brought
    salvation for Me;
  And My own fury, it sustained Me.

6 I have trodden down the peoples in
    My anger,
  Made them drunk in My fury,
  And brought down their strength to
    the earth."

7 I will mention the lovingkindnesses
    of the Lord
  And the praises of the Lord,
  According to all that the Lord has
    bestowed on us,
  And the great goodness toward the
    house of Israel,

Which He has bestowed on them
   according to His mercies,
According to the multitude of His
   lovingkindnesses.

8 For He said, "Surely they *are* My
   people,
Children *who* will not lie."
So He became their Savior.

9 In all their affliction He was afflicted,
And the Angel of His Presence saved
   them;
In His love and in His pity He
   redeemed them;
And He bore them and carried them
All the days of old.

10 But they rebelled and grieved His
   Holy Spirit;
So He turned Himself against them
   as an enemy,
And He fought against them.

11 Then he remembered the days of old,
Moses *and* his people, *saying:*
"Where *is* He who brought them up
   out of the sea
With the shepherd of His flock?
Where *is* He who put His Holy
   Spirit within them,

12 Who led *them* by the right hand of
   Moses,
With His glorious arm,
Dividing the water before them
To make for Himself an everlasting
   name,

13 Who led them through the deep,
As a horse in the wilderness,
That they might not stumble?"

14 As a beast goes down into the valley,
And the Spirit of the LORD causes
   him to rest,
So You lead Your people,
To make Yourself a glorious name.

15 Look down from heaven,
And see from Your habitation, holy
   and glorious.
Where *are* Your zeal and Your
   strength,
The yearning of Your heart and
   Your mercies toward me?
Are they restrained?

16 Doubtless You *are* our Father,
Though Abraham was ignorant
   of us,
And Israel does not acknowledge us.
You, O LORD, *are* our Father;
Our Redeemer from Everlasting *is*
   Your name.

17 O LORD, why have You made us stray
   from Your ways,

And hardened our heart from Your
   fear?
Return for Your servants' sake,
The tribes of Your inheritance.

18 Your holy people have possessed *it*
   but a little while;
Our adversaries have trodden down
   Your sanctuary.

19 We have become *like* those of old,
   over whom You never ruled,
Those who were never called by
   Your name.

64 OH, that You would rend the
   heavens!
That You would come down!
That the mountains might shake at
   Your presence—

2 As fire burns brushwood,
As fire causes water to boil—
To make Your name known to Your
   adversaries,
That the nations may tremble at
   Your presence!

3 When You did awesome things *for*
   which we did not look,
You came down,
The mountains shook at Your
   presence.

4 For since the beginning of the world
Men have not heard nor perceived
   by the ear,
Nor has the eye seen any God
   besides You,
Who acts for the one who waits for
   Him.

5 You meet him who rejoices and does
   righteousness,
Who remembers You in Your ways.
You are indeed angry, for we have
   sinned—
In these ways we continue;
And we need to be saved.

6 But we are all like an unclean *thing*,
And all our righteousnesses *are* like
   filthy rags;
We all fade as a leaf,
And our iniquities, like the wind,
Have taken us away.

7 And *there is* no one who calls on Your
   name,
Who stirs himself up to take hold
   of You;
For You have hidden Your face
   from us,
And have consumed us because of
   our iniquities.

8 But now, O LORD,
You *are* our Father;

We *are* the clay, and You our potter;
And all we *are* the work of Your hand.

9 Do not be furious, O LORD,
Nor remember iniquity forever;
Indeed, please look—we all *are* Your people!

10 Your holy cities are a wilderness,
Zion is a wilderness,
Jerusalem a desolation.

11 Our holy and beautiful temple,
Where our fathers praised You,
Is burned up with fire;
And all our pleasant things are laid waste.

12 Will You restrain Yourself because of these *things*, O LORD?
Will You hold Your peace, and afflict us very severely?

PSALM 115:14–18

14 MAY the LORD give you increase more and more,
You and your children.

15 *May* you *be* blessed by the LORD,
Who made heaven and earth.

16 The heaven, *even* the heavens, *are* the LORD's;
But the earth He has given to the children of men.

17 The dead do not praise the LORD,
Nor any who go down into silence.

18 But we will bless the LORD
From this time forth and forevermore.

Praise the LORD!

PROVERBS 26:27

27 WHOEVER digs a pit will fall into it,
And he who rolls a stone will have it roll back on him.

PHILIPPIANS 1:1–30

PAUL and Timothy, bondservants of Jesus Christ,

To all the saints in Christ Jesus who are in Philippi, with the bishops and deacons:

2 Grace to you and peace from God our Father and the Lord Jesus Christ.
3 I thank my God upon every remembrance of you, 4 always in every prayer of mine making request for you all with joy, 5 for your fellowship in the gospel from the first day until now, 6 being confident of this very thing, that He who has begun a good work in you will complete *it* until the day of Jesus Christ; 7 just as it is right for me to think this of you all, because I have you in my heart, inasmuch as both in my chains and in the defense and confirmation of the gospel, you all are partakers with me of grace. 8 For God is my witness, how greatly I long for you all with the affection of Jesus Christ.

9 And this I pray, that your love may abound still more and more in knowledge and all discernment, 10 that you may approve the things that are excellent, that you may be sincere and without offense till the day of Christ, 11 being filled with the fruits of righteousness which *are* by Jesus Christ, to the glory and praise of God.

12 But I want you to know, brethren, that the things *which happened* to me have actually turned out for the furtherance of the gospel, 13 so that it has become evident to the whole palace guard, and to all the rest, that my chains are in Christ; 14 and most of the brethren in the Lord, having become confident by my chains, are much more bold to speak the word without fear.

15 Some indeed preach Christ even from envy and strife, and some also from goodwill: 16 The former preach Christ from selfish ambition, not sincerely, supposing to add affliction to my chains; 17 but the latter out of love, knowing that I am appointed for the defense of the gospel. 18 What then? Only *that* in every way, whether in pretense or in truth, Christ is preached; and in this I rejoice, yes, and will rejoice.

19 For I know that this will turn out for my deliverance through your prayer and the supply of the Spirit of Jesus Christ,

Self-pity will prevent us appreciating God's deliverance. (GOOD)

20 according to my earnest expectation and hope that in nothing I shall be ashamed, but with all boldness, as always, so now also Christ will be magnified in my body, whether by life or by death. 21 For to me, to live *is* Christ, and to die *is* gain. 22 But if *I* live on in the flesh, this *will mean* fruit from *my* labor; yet what I shall choose I cannot tell. 23 For I am hard-pressed between the two, having a desire to depart

and be with Christ, *which is* far better. 24 Nevertheless to remain in the flesh *is* more needful for you. 25 And being confident of this, I know that I shall remain and continue with you all for your progress and joy of faith, 26 that your rejoicing for me may be more abundant in Jesus Christ by my coming to you again.

27 Only let your conduct be worthy of the gospel of Christ, so that whether I come and see you or am absent, I may hear of your affairs, that you stand fast in one spirit, with one mind striving together for the faith of the gospel, 28 and not in any way terrified by your adversaries, which is to them a proof of perdition, but to you of salvation, and that from God. 29 For to you it has been granted on behalf of Christ, not only to believe in Him, but also to suffer for His sake, 30 having the same conflict which you saw in me and now hear *is* in me.

◆◆◆

Reading 280—The Exercised Experience
Philippians 2:12, 13

If we have experienced regeneration, we must not only talk about the experience, we must exercise it and work out what God has worked in. We have to show it in our fingertips, in our tongue, and in our bodily contact with other people, and as we obey God, we find we have a wealth of power on the inside. The question of forming habits on the basis of the grace of God is a very vital one. To ignore it is to fall into the snare of the Pharisee: the grace of God is praised; Jesus Christ is praised; the Redemption is praised, but the practical everyday life evades working it out. If we refuse to practice, it is not God's grace that fails when a crisis comes, but our own nature. When the crisis comes, we ask God to help us, but He cannot if we have not made our nature an ally. The practicing is ours, not God's. God regenerates us and puts us in contact with all His divine resources, but He cannot make us walk according to His will. If we will obey the Spirit of God and practice through our physical life all that God has put in our hearts by His Spirit, then when the crisis comes, we shall find that we have not only God's grace to stand by us but our own nature also. The crisis is passed without any disaster, and the soul is built up into a stronger attitude toward God.   (*MAKING NEW*)

ISAIAH 65:1—66:24

1 "I was sought by *those who* did not
   ask *for Me;*
I was found by *those who* did not
   seek Me.
I said, 'Here I am, here I am,'
To a nation *that* was not called by
   My name.
2 I have stretched out My hands all
   day long to a rebellious people,
Who walk in a way *that is* not good,
According to their own thoughts;
3 A people who provoke Me to anger
   continually to My face;
Who sacrifice in gardens,
And burn incense on altars of brick;

4 Who sit among the graves,
And spend the night in the tombs;
Who eat swine's flesh,
And the broth of abominable things
   is *in* their vessels;
5 Who say, 'Keep to yourself,
Do not come near me,
For I am holier than you!'
These *are* smoke in My nostrils,
A fire that burns all the day.

6 "Behold, *it is* written before Me:
I will not keep silence, but will
   repay—
Even repay into their bosom—
7 Your iniquities and the iniquities of
   your fathers together,"

Says the L ORD,
"Who have burned incense on the
mountains
And blasphemed Me on the hills;
Therefore I will measure their former
work into their bosom."

8 Thus says the L ORD:

"As the new wine is found in the
cluster,
And *one* says, 'Do not destroy it,
For a blessing *is* in it,'
So will I do for My servants' sake,
That I may not destroy them all.
9 I will bring forth descendants from
Jacob,
And from Judah an heir of My
mountains;
My elect shall inherit it,
And My servants shall dwell there.
10 Sharon shall be a fold of flocks,
And the Valley of Achor a place for
herds to lie down,
For My people who have sought Me.

11 "But you *are* those who forsake the
L ORD,
Who forget My holy mountain,
Who prepare a table for Gad,
And who furnish a drink offering for
Meni.
12 Therefore I will number you for the
sword,
And you shall all bow down to the
slaughter;
Because, when I called, you did not
answer;
When I spoke, you did not hear,
But did evil before My eyes,
And chose *that* in which I do not
delight."

13 Therefore thus says the Lord G OD:

"Behold, My servants shall eat,
But you shall be hungry;
Behold, My servants shall drink,
But you shall be thirsty;
Behold, My servants shall rejoice,
But you shall be ashamed;
14 Behold, My servants shall sing for
joy of heart,
But you shall cry for sorrow of heart,
And wail for grief of spirit.
15 You shall leave your name as a curse
to My chosen;
For the Lord G OD will slay you,
And call His servants by another
name;

16 So that he who blesses himself in the
earth
Shall bless himself in the God of
truth;
And he who swears in the earth
Shall swear by the God of truth;
Because the former troubles are
forgotten,
And because they are hidden from
My eyes.

17 "For behold, I create new heavens and
a new earth;
And the former shall not be
remembered or come to mind.
18 But be glad and rejoice forever in
what I create;
For behold, I create Jerusalem *as* a
rejoicing,
And her people a joy.

---

*H*ave we ever let God tell us any of
His joys? (U TMOST)

---

19 I will rejoice in Jerusalem,
And joy in My people;
The voice of weeping shall no longer
be heard in her,
Nor the voice of crying.

20 "No more shall an infant from there
live but a few days,
Nor an old man who has not fulfilled
his days;
For the child shall die one hundred
years old,
But the sinner *being* one hundred
years old shall be accursed.
21 They shall build houses and inhabit
them;
They shall plant vineyards and eat
their fruit.
22 They shall not build and another
inhabit;
They shall not plant and another eat;
For as the days of a tree, *so shall be*
the days of My people,
And My elect shall long enjoy the
work of their hands.
23 They shall not labor in vain,
Nor bring forth children for trouble;
For they *shall be* the descendants of
the blessed of the L ORD,
And their offspring with them.

24 "It shall come to pass
That before they call, I will answer;
And while they are still speaking, I
will hear.

25 The wolf and the lamb shall feed
together,
The lion shall eat straw like the ox,
And dust *shall be* the serpent's food.
They shall not hurt nor destroy in
all My holy mountain,"
Says the LORD.

66

THUS says the LORD:

"Heaven *is* My throne,
And earth *is* My footstool.
Where *is* the house that you will build
Me?
And where *is* the place of My rest?
2 For all those *things* My hand has
made,
And all those *things* exist,"
Says the LORD.
"But on this *one* will I look:
On *him who is* poor and of a contrite
spirit,
And who trembles at My word.

3 "He who kills a bull *is as if* he slays a
man;
He who sacrifices a lamb, *as if* he
breaks a dog's neck;
He who offers a grain offering, *as if*
he offers swine's blood;
He who burns incense, *as if* he
blesses an idol.
Just as they have chosen their own
ways,
And their soul delights in their
abominations,
4 So will I choose their delusions,
And bring their fears on them;
Because, when I called, no one
answered,
When I spoke they did not hear;
But they did evil before My eyes,
And chose *that* in which I do not
delight."

5 Hear the word of the LORD,
You who tremble at His word:
"Your brethren who hated you,
Who cast you out for My name's
sake, said,
'Let the LORD be glorified,
That we may see your joy.'
But they shall be ashamed."

6 The sound of noise from the city!
A voice from the temple!
The voice of the LORD,
Who fully repays His enemies!

7 "Before she was in labor, she gave
birth;

Before her pain came,
She delivered a male child.
8 Who has heard such a thing?
Who has seen such things?
Shall the earth be made to give birth
in one day?
Or shall a nation be born at once?
For as soon as Zion was in labor,
She gave birth to her children.
9 Shall I bring to the time of birth,
and not cause delivery?" says the
LORD.
"Shall I who cause delivery shut up
the womb?" says your God.
10 "Rejoice with Jerusalem,
And be glad with her, all you who
love her;
Rejoice for joy with her, all you who
mourn for her;
11 That you may feed and be satisfied
With the consolation of her bosom,
That you may drink deeply and be
delighted
With the abundance of her glory."

12 For thus says the LORD:

"Behold, I will extend peace to her
like a river,
And the glory of the Gentiles like a
flowing stream.
Then you shall feed;
On *her* sides shall you be carried,
And be dandled on *her* knees.
13 As one whom his mother comforts,
So I will comfort you;
And you shall be comforted in
Jerusalem."

14 When you see *this,* your heart shall
rejoice,
And your bones shall flourish like
grass;
The hand of the LORD shall be
known to His servants,
And *His* indignation to His enemies.
15 For behold, the LORD will come
with fire
And with His chariots, like a
whirlwind,
To render His anger with fury,
And His rebuke with flames of fire.
16 For by fire and by His sword
The LORD will judge all flesh;
And the slain of the LORD shall be
many.

17 "Those who sanctify themselves and
purify themselves,
To go to the gardens
After an *idol* in the midst,

Eating swine's flesh and the
abomination and the mouse,
Shall be consumed together," says
the LORD.

18 "For I *know* their works and their
thoughts. It shall be that I will gather all
nations and tongues; and they shall come
and see My glory. 19 I will set a sign among
them; and those among them who escape
I will send to the nations: *to* Tarshish and
Pul and Lud, who draw the bow, and Tubal
and Javan, *to* the coastlands afar off who
have not heard My fame nor seen My glory.
And they shall declare My glory among the
Gentiles. 20 Then they shall bring all your
brethren for an offering to the LORD out
of all nations, on horses and in chariots
and in litters, on mules and on camels, to
My holy mountain Jerusalem," says the
LORD, "as the children of Israel bring an
offering in a clean vessel into the house of
the LORD. 21 And I will also take some of
them for priests *and* Levites," says the
LORD.

22 "For as the new heavens and the new
earth
Which I will make shall remain before
Me," says the LORD,
"So shall your descendants and your
name remain.
23 And it shall come to pass
That from one New Moon to
another,
And from one Sabbath to another,
All flesh shall come to worship before
Me," says the LORD.

24 "And they shall go forth and look
Upon the corpses of the men
Who have transgressed against Me.
For their worm does not die,
And their fire is not quenched.
They shall be an abhorrence to all
flesh."

PSALM 116:1–4

1 I love the LORD, because He has heard
My voice *and* my supplications.
2 Because He has inclined His ear to me,
Therefore I will call *upon Him* as long
as I live.

3 The pains of death surrounded me,
And the pangs of Sheol laid hold of
me;
I found trouble and sorrow.

4 Then I called upon the name of the
LORD:
"O LORD, I implore You, deliver my
soul!"

PROVERBS 26:28

28 A lying tongue hates *those who are*
crushed by it,
And a flattering mouth works ruin.

PHILIPPIANS 2:1–30

THEREFORE if *there is* any consolation
in Christ, if any comfort of love, if any
fellowship of the Spirit, if any affection and
mercy, 2 fulfill my joy by being like-minded,
having the same love, *being* of one accord,
of one mind. 3 *Let* nothing *be done* through
selfish ambition or conceit, but in lowliness
of mind let each esteem others better than
himself. 4 Let each of you look out not only
for his own interests, but also for the interests of others.

5 Let this mind be in you which was also
in Christ Jesus, 6 who, being in the form
of God, did not consider it robbery to be
equal with God, 7 but made Himself of no
reputation, taking the form of a bondservant, *and* coming in the likeness of men.
8 And being found in appearance as a man,
He humbled Himself and became obedient
to *the point of* death, even the death of the
cross. 9 Therefore God also has highly exalted Him and given Him the name which
is above every name, 10 that at the name
of Jesus every knee should bow, of those
in heaven, and of those on earth, and of
those under the earth, 11 and *that* every
tongue should confess that Jesus Christ *is*
Lord, to the glory of God the Father.
12 Therefore, my beloved, as you have
always obeyed, not as in my presence only,
but now much more in my absence, work
out your own salvation with fear and trembling; 13 for it is God who works in you
both to will and to do for *His* good pleasure.
14 Do all things without complaining and
disputing, 15 that you may become blameless and harmless, children of God without
fault in the midst of a crooked and perverse
generation, among whom you shine as

*We have to be blameless in all
our social relationships before
God.* (LOVE OF GOD)

lights in the world, 16 holding fast the word of life, so that I may rejoice in the day of Christ that I have not run in vain or labored in vain.

17 Yes, and if I am being poured out *as a drink offering* on the sacrifice and service of your faith, I am glad and rejoice with you all. 18 For the same reason you also be glad and rejoice with me.

19 But I trust in the Lord Jesus to send Timothy to you shortly, that I also may be encouraged when I know your state. 20 For I have no one like-minded, who will sincerely care for your state. 21 For all seek their own, not the things which are of Christ Jesus. 22 But you know his proven character, that as a son with *his* father he served with me in the gospel. 23 Therefore I hope to send him at once, as soon as I see how it goes with me. 24 But I trust in the

Lord that I myself shall also come shortly.

25 Yet I considered it necessary to send to you Epaphroditus, my brother, fellow worker, and fellow soldier, but your messenger and the one who ministered to my need; 26 since he was longing for you all, and was distressed because you had heard that he was sick. 27 For indeed he was sick almost unto death; but God had mercy on him, and not only on him but on me also, lest I should have sorrow upon sorrow. 28 Therefore I sent him the more eagerly, that when you see him again you may rejoice, and I may be less sorrowful. 29 Receive him therefore in the Lord with all gladness, and hold such men in esteem; 30 because for the work of Christ he came close to death, not regarding his life, to supply what was lacking in your service toward me.

◆◆◆

Reading 281—The Service of Memory
Philippians 3:13, 14

When Paul says "forgetting those things which are behind," he is not referring to his past life; Paul never forgot that he had been "a blasphemer, a persecutor, and an insolent man;" but he determinedly forgot all he had attained to in the Christian life, because he was always pressing on to "those things which are ahead." The gospel of the grace of God takes the stain of memory from a worker, not by making him ignore the past, but by enabling him to see that God can make it of service in his work for God. A worker should never tell people to forget the past; preachers of the gospel of temperament do that. If we forget the past we will be hard and obtuse. If we are hard, we are of no use to God; and unless we know the Cross of Christ as the power which takes the stinging stain out of memory and transforms it, we are of no use to others. Unless a worker has had the experience of the grace of God transforming the stain of memory into a personal experience of salvation, there will be a weak-kneed-ness and a feeble-handed-ness about him that will hinder God's message. . . . The gospel can never be preached by sinless lips, but only by the lips of those who have been saved from sin by the Atonement. Angels cannot preach the gospel, only beings such as Paul and you and I can preach the gospel. We say that Jesus preached the gospel, but He did more: He came that there might be a gospel to preach. (*PLACE HELP*)

JEREMIAH 1:1—2:37

THE words of Jeremiah the son of Hilkiah, of the priests who *were* in Anathoth in the land of Benjamin, 2 to whom the word of the LORD came in the days of Josiah the

son of Amon, king of Judah, in the thirteenth year of his reign. 3 It came also in the days of Jehoiakim the son of Josiah, king of Judah, until the end of the eleventh year of Zedekiah the son of Josiah, king of Judah, until the carrying away of Jerusalem captive in the fifth month.

4 Then the word of the LORD came to me, saying:

5 "Before I formed you in the womb I knew you;
Before you were born I sanctified you;
I ordained you a prophet to the nations."

Individual lives are the expression of a preexisting idea in the mind of God. (BIB. PSYCH.)

---

6 Then said I:

"Ah, Lord GOD!
Behold, I cannot speak, for I *am* a youth."

7 But the LORD said to me:

"Do not say, 'I *am* a youth,'
For you shall go to all to whom I send you,
And whatever I command you, you shall speak.
8 Do not be afraid of their faces,
For I *am* with you to deliver you,"
says the LORD.

9 Then the LORD put forth His hand and touched my mouth, and the LORD said to me:

"Behold, I have put My words in your mouth.
10 See, I have this day set you over the nations and over the kingdoms,
To root out and to pull down,
To destroy and to throw down,
To build and to plant."

11 Moreover the word of the LORD came to me, saying, "Jeremiah, what do you see?"
And I said, "I see a branch of an almond tree."
12 Then the LORD said to me, "You have seen well, for I am ready to perform My word."
13 And the word of the LORD came to me the second time, saying, "What do you see?"
And I said, "I see a boiling pot, and it is facing away from the north."
14 Then the LORD said to me:

"Out of the north calamity shall break forth

On all the inhabitants of the land.
15 For behold, I am calling
All the families of the kingdoms of the north," says the LORD;
"They shall come and each one set his throne
At the entrance of the gates of Jerusalem,
Against all its walls all around,
And against all the cities of Judah.
16 I will utter My judgments
Against them concerning all their wickedness,
Because they have forsaken Me,
Burned incense to other gods,
And worshiped the works of their own hands.

17 "Therefore prepare yourself and arise,
And speak to them all that I command you.
Do not be dismayed before their faces,
Lest I dismay you before them.
18 For behold, I have made you this day
A fortified city and an iron pillar,
And bronze walls against the whole land—
Against the kings of Judah,
Against its princes,
Against its priests,
And against the people of the land.
19 They will fight against you,
But they shall not prevail against you.
For I *am* with you," says the LORD,
"to deliver you."

2 MOREOVER the word of the LORD came to me, saying, 2 "Go and cry in the hearing of Jerusalem, saying, 'Thus says the LORD:

"I remember you,
The kindness of your youth,
The love of your betrothal,
When you went after Me in the wilderness,
In a land not sown.
3 Israel *was* holiness to the LORD,
The firstfruits of His increase.
All that devour him will offend;
Disaster will come upon them," says the LORD.' "

4 Hear the word of the LORD, O house of Jacob and all the families of the house of Israel. 5 Thus says the LORD:

"What injustice have your fathers found in Me,

That they have gone far from Me,
Have followed idols,
And have become idolaters?

6 Neither did they say, 'Where *is* the
   LORD,
   Who brought us up out of the land
   of Egypt,
   Who led us through the wilderness,
   Through a land of deserts and pits,
   Through a land of drought and the
   shadow of death,
   Through a land that no one crossed
   And where no one dwelt?'

7 I brought you into a bountiful
   country,
   To eat its fruit and its goodness.
   But when you entered, you defiled
   My land
   And made My heritage an
   abomination.

8 The priests did not say, 'Where *is* the
   LORD?'
   And those who handle the law did
   not know Me;
   The rulers also transgressed
   against Me;
   The prophets prophesied by Baal,
   And walked after *things that* do not
   profit.

9 "Therefore I will yet bring charges
   against you," says the LORD,
   "And against your children's children
   I will bring charges.

10 For pass beyond the coasts of Cyprus
   and see,
   Send to Kedar and consider
   diligently,
   And see if there has been such *a
   thing.*

11 Has a nation changed *its* gods,
   Which *are* not gods?
   But My people have changed their
   Glory
   For *what* does not profit.

12 Be astonished, O heavens, at this,
   And be horribly afraid;
   Be very desolate," says the LORD.

13 "For My people have committed two
   evils:
   They have forsaken Me, the fountain
   of living waters,
   And hewn themselves cisterns—
   broken cisterns that can hold no
   water.

14 "*Is* Israel a servant?
   Is he a homeborn *slave?*
   Why is he plundered?

15 The young lions roared at him, *and*
   growled;
   They made his land waste;

His cities are burned, without
inhabitant.

16 Also the people of Noph and
   Tahpanhes
   Have broken the crown of your head.

17 Have you not brought this on
   yourself,
   In that you have forsaken the LORD
   your God
   When He led you in the way?

18 And now why take the road to Egypt,
   To drink the waters of Sihor?
   Or why take the road to Assyria,
   To drink the waters of the River?

19 Your own wickedness will correct
   you,
   And your backslidings will rebuke
   you.
   Know therefore and see that *it is* an
   evil and bitter *thing*
   That you have forsaken the LORD
   your God,
   And the fear of Me *is* not in you,"
   Says the Lord GOD of hosts.

20 "For of old I have broken your yoke
   and burst your bonds;
   And you said, 'I will not transgress,'
   When on every high hill and under
   every green tree
   You lay down, playing the harlot.

21 Yet I had planted you a noble vine,
   a seed of highest quality.
   How then have you turned
   before Me
   Into the degenerate plant of an alien
   vine?

22 For though you wash yourself with
   lye, and use much soap,
   Yet your iniquity is marked before
   Me," says the Lord GOD.

23 "How can you say, 'I am not polluted,
   I have not gone after the Baals'?
   See your way in the valley;
   Know what you have done:
   You are a swift dromedary breaking
   loose in her ways,

24 A wild donkey used to the wilderness,
   That sniffs at the wind in her desire;
   In her time of mating, who can turn
   her away?
   All those who seek her will not weary
   themselves;
   In her month they will find her.

25 Withhold your foot from being
   unshod, and your throat from
   thirst.
   But you said, 'There is no hope.
   No! For I have loved aliens, and after
   them I will go.'

26 "As the thief is ashamed when he is
   found out,
   So is the house of Israel ashamed;
   They and their kings and their
   princes, and their priests and their
   prophets,
27 Saying to a tree, 'You *are* my father,'
   And to a stone, 'You gave birth
   to me.'
   For they have turned *their* back to
   Me, and not *their* face.
   But in the time of their trouble
   They will say, 'Arise and save us.'
28 But where *are* your gods that you
   have made for yourselves?
   Let them arise,
   If they can save you in the time of
   your trouble;
   For *according to* the number of your
   cities
   Are your gods, O Judah.

29 "Why will you plead with Me?
   You all have transgressed against
   Me," says the LORD.
30 "In vain I have chastened your
   children;
   They received no correction.
   Your sword has devoured your
   prophets
   Like a destroying lion.

31 "O generation, see the word of the
   LORD!
   Have I been a wilderness to Israel,
   Or a land of darkness?
   Why do My people say, 'We are lords;
   We will come no more to You'?
32 Can a virgin forget her ornaments,
   Or a bride her attire?
   Yet My people have forgotten Me
   days without number.

33 "Why do you beautify your way to
   seek love?
   Therefore you have also taught
   The wicked women your ways.
34 Also on your skirts is found
   The blood of the lives of the poor
   innocents.
   I have not found it by secret search,
   But plainly on all these things.
35 Yet you say, 'Because I am innocent,
   Surely His anger shall turn from me.'
   Behold, I will plead My case against
   you,
   Because you say, 'I have not sinned.'
36 Why do you gad about so much to
   change your way?
   Also you shall be ashamed of Egypt
   as you were ashamed of Assyria.

37 Indeed you will go forth from him
   With your hands on your head;
   For the LORD has rejected your
   trusted allies,
   And you will not prosper by them.

PSALM 116:5–14

5 GRACIOUS *is* the LORD, and
   righteous;
   Yes, our God *is* merciful.
6 The LORD preserves the simple;
   I was brought low, and He saved me.
7 Return to your rest, O my soul,
   For the LORD has dealt bountifully
   with you.

8 For You have delivered my soul from
   death,
   My eyes from tears,
   And my feet from falling.
9 I will walk before the LORD
   In the land of the living.

---

*We cannot talk to God unless we
walk with Him when we are not
talking.* (GLORIFY)

---

10 I believed, therefore I spoke,
   "I am greatly afflicted."
11 I said in my haste,
   "All men *are* liars."

12 What shall I render to the LORD
   For all His benefits toward me?
13 I will take up the cup of salvation,
   And call upon the name of the LORD.
14 I will pay my vows to the LORD
   Now in the presence of all His people.

PROVERBS 27:1

1 DO not boast about tomorrow,
   For you do not know what a day may
   bring forth.

PHILIPPIANS 3:1–21

FINALLY, my brethren, rejoice in the
Lord. For me to write the same things to
you *is* not tedious, but for you *it is* safe.

2 Beware of dogs, beware of evil workers,
beware of the mutilation! 3 For we are the
circumcision, who worship God in the
Spirit, rejoice in Christ Jesus, and have no
confidence in the flesh, 4 though I also

might have confidence in the flesh. If anyone else thinks he may have confidence in the flesh, I more so: 5 circumcised the eighth day, of the stock of Israel, *of* the tribe of Benjamin, a Hebrew of the Hebrews; concerning the law, a Pharisee; 6 concerning zeal, persecuting the church; concerning the righteousness which is in the law, blameless.

7 But what things were gain to me, these I have counted loss for Christ. 8 Yet indeed I also count all things loss for the excellence of the knowledge of Christ Jesus my Lord, for whom I have suffered the loss of all things, and count them as rubbish, that I may gain Christ 9 and be found in Him,

---

To commit myself to Jesus means there is nothing that is not committed.   (GOOD)

---

not having my own righteousness, which *is* from the law, but that which *is* through faith in Christ, the righteousness which is from God by faith; 10 that I may know Him and the power of His resurrection, and the fellowship of His sufferings, being conformed to His death, 11 if, by any means, I may attain to the resurrection from the dead.

12 Not that I have already attained, or am already perfected; but I press on, that I may lay hold of that for which Christ Jesus has also laid hold of me. 13 Brethren, I do not count myself to have apprehended; but one thing *I do,* forgetting those things which are behind and reaching forward to those things which are ahead, 14 I press toward the goal for the prize of the upward call of God in Christ Jesus.

15 Therefore let us, as many as are mature, have this mind; and if in anything you think otherwise, God will reveal even this to you. 16 Nevertheless, to *the degree* that we have already attained, let us walk by the same rule, let us be of the same mind.

17 Brethren, join in following my example, and note those who so walk, as you have us for a pattern. 18 For many walk, of whom I have told you often, and now tell you even weeping, *that they are* the enemies of the cross of Christ: 19 whose end *is* destruction, whose god *is their* belly, and *whose* glory *is* in their shame—who set their mind on earthly things. 20 For our citizenship is in heaven, from which we also eagerly wait for the Savior, the Lord Jesus Christ, 21 who will transform our lowly body that it may be conformed to His glorious body, according to the working by which He is able even to subdue all things to Himself.

◆◆◆◆

Reading 282—Method of Christian Thinking
Philippians 4:8, 9

In Philippians 4:8, 9 Paul gives the rule for the thinking life of the Christian. Have we ever given our brains the task of concentrated thinking along this line? "Finally, brethren, whatever things are true, whatever things *are* noble, whatever things *are* just, whatever things *are* pure, whatever things *are* lovely, whatever things *are* of good report; if *there is* any virtue and if *there is* anything praiseworthy—meditate on these things." It is because we will not bring every thought into captivity to the obedience of Christ that all the perplexities are produced regarding methods of thinking that look like Christianity. Strands are taken out of Jesus Christ's teaching, the Bible is exploited to agree with certain principles, but the Truth, our Lord Jesus Christ is ignored.

If we base our thinking on principles instead of on a Person we shall go wrong, no matter how devout or honest we are. The one great truth to keep steadfastly before us is the Lord Jesus Christ; He is the Truth. Only the whole truth is the truth; any part of the truth may become an error. If you have a ray of light on the truth, never call it the whole truth; follow it up and it will lead you to the central Truth, the Lord Jesus Christ.   (*GLORY*)

JEREMIAH 3:1—4:31

1   "THEY say, 'If a man divorces his
          wife,
      And she goes from him
      And becomes another man's,
      May he return to her again?'
      Would not that land be greatly
          polluted?
      But you have played the harlot with
          many lovers;
      Yet return to Me," says the LORD.

2   "Lift up your eyes to the desolate
          heights and see:
      Where have you not lain *with men?*
      By the road you have sat for them
      Like an Arabian in the wilderness;
      And you have polluted the land
      With your harlotries and your
          wickedness.
3   Therefore the showers have been
          withheld,
      And there has been no latter rain.
      You have had a harlot's forehead;
      You refuse to be ashamed.
4   Will you not from this time cry to
          Me,
      'My Father, You *are* the guide of my
          youth?
5   Will He remain angry forever?
      Will He keep it to the end?'
      Behold, you have spoken and done
          evil things,
      As you were able."

6 The LORD said also to me in the days
of Josiah the king: "Have you seen what
backsliding Israel has done? She has gone
up on every high mountain and under every
green tree, and there played the harlot.
7 And I said, after she had done all these
things, 'Return to Me.' But she did not return. And her treacherous sister Judah saw
it. 8 Then I saw that for all the causes for
which backsliding Israel had committed
adultery, I had put her away and given her
a certificate of divorce; yet her treacherous
sister Judah did not fear, but went and
played the harlot also. 9 So it came to pass,
through her casual harlotry, that she defiled
the land and committed adultery with
stones and trees. 10 And yet for all this her
treacherous sister Judah has not turned to
Me with her whole heart, but in pretense,"
says the LORD.
11 Then the LORD said to me, "Backsliding Israel has shown herself more righteous
than treacherous Judah. 12 Go and proclaim
these words toward the north, and say:

'Return, backsliding Israel,' says the
      LORD;
'I will not cause My anger to fall on
      you.
For I *am* merciful,' says the LORD;
'I will not remain angry forever.
13   Only acknowledge your iniquity,
      That you have transgressed against
          the LORD your God,
      And have scattered your charms
      To alien deities under every green
          tree,
      And you have not obeyed My voice,'
      says the LORD.

14 "Return, O backsliding children," says
the LORD; "for I am married to you. I will
take you, one from a city and two from a
family, and I will bring you to Zion.
15 And I will give you shepherds according
to My heart, who will feed you with knowledge and understanding.
16 "Then it shall come to pass, when you
are multiplied and increased in the land in
those days," says the LORD, "that they will
say no more, 'The ark of the covenant of
the LORD.' It shall not come to mind, nor
shall they remember it, nor shall they visit
it, nor shall it be made anymore.
17 "At that time Jerusalem shall be called
The Throne of the LORD, and all the
nations shall be gathered to it, to the name
of the LORD, to Jerusalem. No more shall
they follow the dictates of their evil hearts.
18 "In those days the house of Judah shall
walk with the house of Israel, and they shall
come together out of the land of the north
to the land that I have given as an inheritance to your fathers.
19 "But I said:

      'How can I put you among the
          children
      And give you a pleasant land,
      A beautiful heritage of the hosts of
          nations?'

"And I said:

      'You shall call Me, "My Father,"
      And not turn away from Me.'
20   Surely, *as* a wife treacherously departs
          from her husband,
      So have you dealt treacherously with
          Me,
      O house of Israel," says the LORD.

21   A voice was heard on the desolate
          heights,
      Weeping *and* supplications of the
          children of Israel.
      For they have perverted their way;

They have forgotten the Lord their God.

22 "Return, you backsliding children,
   And I will heal your backslidings."

"Indeed we do come to You,
For You are the Lord our God.
23 Truly, in vain *is salvation hoped for*
   from the hills,
   And from the multitude of
   mountains;
   Truly, in the Lord our God
   Is the salvation of Israel.
24 For shame has devoured
   The labor of our fathers from our
   youth—
   Their flocks and their herds,
   Their sons and their daughters.
25 We lie down in our shame,
   And our reproach covers us.
   For we have sinned against the Lord
   our God,
   We and our fathers,
   From our youth even to this day,
   And have not obeyed the voice of
   the Lord our God."

4 "IF you will return, O Israel," says the
   Lord,
   "Return to Me;
   And if you will put away your
   abominations out of My sight,
   Then you shall not be moved.
2 And you shall swear, 'The Lord
   lives,'
   In truth, in judgment, and in
   righteousness;
   The nations shall bless themselves in
   Him,
   And in Him they shall glory."

3 For thus says the Lord to the men of
Judah and Jerusalem:

"Break up your fallow ground,
And do not sow among thorns.
4 Circumcise yourselves to the Lord,
   And take away the foreskins of your
   hearts,
   You men of Judah and inhabitants
   of Jerusalem,
   Lest My fury come forth like fire,
   And burn so that no one can
   quench *it*,
   Because of the evil of your doings."

5 Declare in Judah and proclaim in
Jerusalem, and say:

"Blow the trumpet in the land;
Cry, 'Gather together,'

And say, 'Assemble yourselves,
And let us go into the fortified cities.'
6 Set up the standard toward Zion.
   Take refuge! Do not delay!
   For I will bring disaster from the
   north,
   And great destruction."

7 The lion has come up from his
   thicket,
   And the destroyer of nations is on
   his way.
   He has gone forth from his place
   To make your land desolate.
   Your cities will be laid waste,
   Without inhabitant.
8 For this, clothe yourself with
   sackcloth,
   Lament and wail.
   For the fierce anger of the Lord
   Has not turned back from us.

9 "And it shall come to pass in that day,"
   says the Lord,
   "*That* the heart of the king shall perish,
   And the heart of the princes;
   The priests shall be astonished,
   And the prophets shall wonder."

10 Then I said, "Ah, Lord God!
   Surely You have greatly deceived this
   people and Jerusalem,
   Saying, 'You shall have peace,'
   Whereas the sword reaches to the
   heart."

11 At that time it will be said
   To this people and to Jerusalem,
   "A dry wind of the desolate heights
   blows in the wilderness
   Toward the daughter of My people—
   Not to fan or to cleanse—
12 A wind too strong for these will come
   for Me;
   Now I will also speak judgment
   against them."

13 "Behold, he shall come up like clouds,
   And his chariots like a whirlwind.
   His horses are swifter than eagles.
   Woe to us, for we are plundered!"

14 O Jerusalem, wash your heart from
   wickedness,
   That you may be saved.
   How long shall your evil thoughts
   lodge within you?
15 For a voice declares from Dan
   And proclaims affliction from Mount
   Ephraim:
16 "Make mention to the nations,

Yes, proclaim against Jerusalem,
That watchers come from a far
country
And raise their voice against the cities
of Judah.
17 Like keepers of a field they are against
her all around,
Because she has been rebellious
against Me," says the LORD.
18 "Your ways and your doings
Have procured these *things* for you.
This *is* your wickedness,
Because it is bitter,
Because it reaches to your heart."

19 O my soul, my soul!
I am pained in my very heart!
My heart makes a noise in me;
I cannot hold my peace,
Because you have heard, O my soul,
The sound of the trumpet,
The alarm of war.
20 Destruction upon destruction is
cried,
For the whole land is plundered.
Suddenly my tents are plundered,
And my curtains in a moment.
21 How long will I see the standard,
And hear the sound of the trumpet?

22 "For My people *are* foolish,
They have not known Me.
They *are* silly children,
And they have no understanding.
They *are* wise to do evil,
But to do good they have no
knowledge."

23 I beheld the earth, and indeed *it was*
without form, and void;
And the heavens, they *had* no light.
24 I beheld the mountains, and indeed
they trembled,
And all the hills moved back and
forth.
25 I beheld, and indeed *there was* no
man,
And all the birds of the heavens had
fled.
26 I beheld, and indeed the fruitful land
was a wilderness,
And all its cities were broken down
At the presence of the LORD,
By His fierce anger.

27 For thus says the LORD:

"The whole land shall be desolate;
Yet I will not make a full end.
28 For this shall the earth mourn,
And the heavens above be black,

Because I have spoken.
I have purposed and will not relent,
Nor will I turn back from it.
29 The whole city shall flee from the
noise of the horsemen and
bowmen.
They shall go into thickets and climb
up on the rocks.
Every city *shall be* forsaken,
And not a man shall dwell in it.

30 "And *when* you *are* plundered,
What will you do?
Though you clothe yourself with
crimson,
Though you adorn *yourself* with
ornaments of gold,
Though you enlarge your eyes with
paint,
In vain you will make yourself fair;
Your lovers will despise you;
They will seek your life.

31 "For I have heard a voice as of a
woman in labor,
The anguish as of her who brings
forth her first child,
The voice of the daughter of Zion
bewailing herself;
She spreads her hands, *saying,*
'Woe *is* me now, for my soul is weary
Because of murderers!'

PSALM 116:15–19

15 PRECIOUS in the sight of the LORD
Is the death of His saints.

16 O LORD, truly I *am* Your servant;
I *am* Your servant, the son of Your
maidservant;
You have loosed my bonds.
17 I will offer to You the sacrifice of
thanksgiving,
And will call upon the name of the
LORD.

18 I will pay my vows to the LORD
Now in the presence of all His people,
19 In the courts of the LORD's house,
In the midst of you, O Jerusalem.

Praise the LORD!

PROVERBS 27:2

2 LET another man praise you, and not
your own mouth;
A stranger, and not your own lips.

PHILIPPIANS 4:1–23

THEREFORE, my beloved and longed-for brethren, my joy and crown, so stand fast in the Lord, beloved.

2 I implore Euodia and I implore Syntyche to be of the same mind in the Lord. 3 And I urge you also, true companion, help these women who labored with me in the gospel, with Clement also, and the rest of my fellow workers, whose names *are* in the Book of Life.

4 Rejoice in the Lord always. Again I will say, rejoice!

5 Let your gentleness be known to all men. The Lord *is* at hand.

6 Be anxious for nothing, but in everything by prayer and supplication, with thanksgiving, let your requests be made known to God; 7 and the peace of God, which surpasses all understanding, will guard your hearts and minds through Christ Jesus.

8 Finally, brethren, whatever things are true, whatever things *are* noble, whatever things *are* just, whatever things *are* pure, whatever things *are* lovely, whatever things *are* of good report, if *there is* any virtue and if *there is* anything praiseworthy—meditate on these things. 9 The things which you learned and received and heard

---

God gives us the Holy Spirit not only for holy living but for holy thinking. (MORAL FOUND.)

---

and saw in me, these do, and the God of peace will be with you.

10 But I rejoiced in the Lord greatly that now at last your care for me has flourished again; though you surely did care, but you lacked opportunity. 11 Not that I speak in regard to need, for I have learned in whatever state I am, to be content: 12 I know how to be abased, and I know how to abound. Everywhere and in all things I have learned both to be full and to be hungry, both to abound and to suffer need. 13 I can do all things through Christ who strengthens me.

14 Nevertheless you have done well that you shared in my distress. 15 Now you Philippians know also that in the beginning of the gospel, when I departed from Macedonia, no church shared with me concerning giving and receiving but you only. 16 For even in Thessalonica you sent *aid* once and again for my necessities. 17 Not that I seek the gift, but I seek the fruit that abounds to your account. 18 Indeed I have all and abound. I am full, having received from Epaphroditus the things *sent* from you, a sweet-smelling aroma, an acceptable sacrifice, well pleasing to God. 19 And my God shall supply all your need according to His riches in glory by Christ Jesus. 20 Now to our God and Father *be* glory forever and ever. Amen.

21 Greet every saint in Christ Jesus. The brethren who are with me greet you. 22 All the saints greet you, but especially those who are of Caesar's household.

23 The grace of our Lord Jesus Christ be with you all. Amen.

◆◆◆

Reading 283—The Sufferings That Remain
Colossians 1:24

The devotion of the saint is to "fill up in my flesh what is lacking in the afflictions of Christ, for the sake of His body," nothing remains behind to be filled up for redemption's sake. How did Jesus Christ suffer? Because people misunderstood Him? Because He was persecuted? Because He could not get on with me? No, He suffered for one thing only—that men might be saved; He let Almighty God do His whole will in and through Him without asking His permission. He suffered "according to the will of God."

How can we fill up the sufferings that remain behind? First John 5:16 is an indication of one way, that of intercession. Remember, no one has time to pray, he has to take time from other things that are valuable to understand how necessary time for prayer is. The things that act like thorns and stings in our personal lives will go away when we pray; we won't feel the smart anymore, because we have got God's point of view about them. Prayer means that we get into union with God's view of other people. Our devotion as saints is to identify ourselves with God's interests in other lives. God pays no attention to our personal affinities; He expects us to identify ourselves with His interests in others.   (GLORY)

JEREMIAH 5:1—6:30

1   "RUN to and fro through the streets
          of Jerusalem;
       See now and know;
       And seek in her open places
       If you can find a man,
       If there is *anyone* who executes
          judgment,
       Who seeks the truth,
       And I will pardon her.
2   Though they say, '*As* the LORD lives,'
       Surely they swear falsely."

3   O LORD, *are* not Your eyes on the
          truth?
       You have stricken them,
       But they have not grieved;
       You have consumed them,
       But they have refused to receive
          correction.
       They have made their faces harder
          than rock;
       They have refused to return.

4   Therefore I said, "Surely these *are*
          poor.
       They are foolish;
       For they do not know the way of
          the LORD,
       The judgment of their God.
5   I will go to the great men and speak
          to them,
       For they have known the way of the
          LORD,
       The judgment of their God."

       But these have altogether broken the
          yoke
       And burst the bonds.
6   Therefore a lion from the forest shall
          slay them,
       A wolf of the deserts shall destroy
          them;
       A leopard will watch over their cities.
       Everyone who goes out from there
          shall be torn in pieces,
       Because their transgressions are
          many;
       Their backslidings have increased.

7   "How shall I pardon you for this?
       Your children have forsaken Me
       And sworn by *those that are* not gods.
       When I had fed them to the full,
       Then they committed adultery
       And assembled themselves by troops
          in the harlots' houses.
8   They were *like* well-fed lusty
          stallions;
       Every one neighed after his
          neighbor's wife.
9   Shall I not punish *them* for these
          things?" says the LORD.
       "And shall I not avenge Myself on
          such a nation as this?

10   "Go up on her walls and destroy,
       But do not make a complete end.
       Take away her branches,
       For they *are* not the LORD's.
11   For the house of Israel and the
          house of Judah
       Have dealt very treacherously with
          Me," says the LORD.

12   They have lied about the LORD,
       And said, "*It is* not He.
       Neither will evil come upon us,
       Nor shall we see sword or famine.
13   And the prophets become wind,
       For the word *is* not in them.
       Thus shall it be done to them."

14 Therefore thus says the LORD God of
hosts:

       "Because you speak this word,
       Behold, I will make My words in your
          mouth fire,
       And this people wood,
       And it shall devour them.
15   Behold, I will bring a nation against
          you from afar,
       O house of Israel," says the LORD.
       "It *is* a mighty nation,
       It *is* an ancient nation,
       A nation whose language you do not
          know,
       Nor can you understand what they
          say.

16 Their quiver *is* like an open tomb;
    They *are* all mighty men.
17 And they shall eat up your harvest
        and your bread,
        Which your sons and daughters
            should eat.
    They shall eat up your flocks and your
        herds;
    They shall eat up your vines and your
        fig trees;
    They shall destroy your fortified
        cities,
    In which you trust, with the sword.

18 "Nevertheless in those days," says the
LORD, "I will not make a complete end of
you. 19 And it will be when you say, 'Why
does the LORD our God do all these *things*
to us?' then you shall answer them, 'Just
as you have forsaken Me and served foreign
gods in your land, so you shall serve aliens
in a land *that is* not yours.'

20 "Declare this in the house of Jacob
        And proclaim it in Judah, saying,
21 'Hear this now, O foolish people,
        Without understanding,
    Who have eyes and see not,
    And who have ears and hear not:
22 Do you not fear Me?' says the LORD.
    'Will you not tremble at My presence,
    Who have placed the sand as the
        bound of the sea,
    By a perpetual decree, that it cannot
        pass beyond it?
    And though its waves toss to and
        fro,
    Yet they cannot prevail;
    Though they roar, yet they cannot
        pass over it.
23 But this people has a defiant and
        rebellious heart;
    They have revolted and departed.
24 They do not say in their heart,
    "Let us now fear the LORD our God,
    Who gives rain, both the former and
        the latter, in its season.
    He reserves for us the appointed
        weeks of the harvest."
25 Your iniquities have turned these
        things away,
    And your sins have withheld good
        from you.

26 'For among My people are found
        wicked *men;*
    They lie in wait as one who sets
        snares;
    They set a trap;
    They catch men.
27 As a cage is full of birds,
        So their houses *are* full of deceit.

Therefore they have become great
    and grown rich.
28 They have grown fat, they are sleek;
    Yes, they surpass the deeds of the
        wicked;
    They do not plead the cause,
    The cause of the fatherless;
    Yet they prosper,
    And the right of the needy they do
        not defend.
29 Shall I not punish *them* for these
        things?' says the LORD.
    'Shall I not avenge Myself on such a
        nation as this?'

30 "An astonishing and horrible thing
        Has been committed in the land:
31 The prophets prophesy falsely,
    And the priests rule by their *own*
        power;
    And My people love *to have it* so.
    But what will you do in the end?

6   "O you children of Benjamin,
        Gather yourselves to flee from the
            midst of Jerusalem!
    Blow the trumpet in Tekoa,
    And set up a signal-fire in Beth
        Haccerem;
    For disaster appears out of the north,
    And great destruction.
2   I have likened the daughter of Zion
        To a lovely and delicate woman.
3   The shepherds with their flocks shall
        come to her.
    They shall pitch *their* tents against
        her all around.
    Each one shall pasture in his own
        place."

4   "Prepare war against her;
    Arise, and let us go up at noon.
    Woe to us, for the day goes away,
    For the shadows of the evening are
        lengthening.
5   Arise, and let us go by night,
    And let us destroy her palaces."

6 For thus has the LORD of hosts said:

    "Cut down trees,
        And build a mound against
            Jerusalem.
    This *is* the city to be punished.
    She *is* full of oppression in her midst.
7   As a fountain wells up with water,
        So she wells up with her wickedness.
    Violence and plundering are heard
        in her.
    Before Me continually *are* grief and
        wounds.

8 Be instructed, O Jerusalem,
  Lest My soul depart from you;
  Lest I make you desolate,
  A land not inhabited."

9 Thus says the LORD of hosts:

  "They shall thoroughly glean as a vine
    the remnant of Israel;
  As a grape gatherer, put your hand
    back into the branches."

10 To whom shall I speak and give
    warning,
   That they may hear?
   Indeed their ear *is* uncircumcised,
   And they cannot give heed.
   Behold, the word of the LORD is a
     reproach to them;
   They have no delight in it.
11 Therefore I am full of the fury of
    the LORD.
   I am weary of holding *it* in.
   "I will pour it out on the children
     outside,
   And on the assembly of young men
     together;
   For even the husband shall be taken
     with the wife,
   The aged with *him who is* full of days.
12 And their houses shall be turned
    over to others,
   Fields and wives together;
   For I will stretch out My hand
   Against the inhabitants of the land,"
   says the LORD.
13 "Because from the least of them even
    to the greatest of them,
   Everyone *is* given to covetousness;
   And from the prophet even to the
     priest,
   Everyone deals falsely.
14 They have also healed the hurt of
    My people slightly,
   Saying, 'Peace, peace!'
   When *there is* no peace.
15 Were they ashamed when they had
    committed abomination?
   No! They were not at all ashamed;
   Nor did they know how to blush.
   Therefore they shall fall among
     those who fall;
   At the time I punish them,
   They shall be cast down," says the
     LORD.

16 Thus says the LORD:

  "Stand in the ways and see,
  And ask for the old paths, where the
    good way *is,*

And walk in it;
  Then you will find rest for your souls.
  But they said, 'We will not walk
    in it.'
17 Also, I set watchmen over you,
    saying,
   'Listen to the sound of the trumpet!'
   But they said, 'We will not listen.'
18 Therefore hear, you nations,
   And know, O congregation, what *is*
     among them.
19 Hear, O earth!
   Behold, I will certainly bring calamity
     on this people—
   The fruit of their thoughts,
   Because they have not heeded My
     words
   Nor My law, but rejected it.
20 For what purpose to Me
   Comes frankincense from Sheba,
   And sweet cane from a far country?
   Your burnt offerings *are* not
     acceptable,
   Nor your sacrifices sweet to Me."

21 Therefore thus says the LORD:

  "Behold, I will lay stumbling blocks
    before this people,
  And the fathers and the sons together
    shall fall on them.
  The neighbor and his friend shall
    perish."

22 Thus says the LORD:

  "Behold, a people comes from the
    north country,
  And a great nation will be raised from
    the farthest parts of the earth.
23 They will lay hold on bow and spear;
   They *are* cruel and have no mercy;
   Their voice roars like the sea;
   And they ride on horses,
   As men of war set in array against
     you, O daughter of Zion."

24 We have heard the report of it;
   Our hands grow feeble.
   Anguish has taken hold of us,
   Pain as of a woman in labor.
25 Do not go out into the field,
   Nor walk by the way.
   Because of the sword of the enemy,
   Fear *is* on every side.
26 O daughter of my people,
   Dress in sackcloth
   And roll about in ashes!
   Make mourning *as for* an only son,
     most bitter lamentation;
   For the plunderer will suddenly come
     upon us.

27 "I have set you *as* an assayer *and* a
fortress among My people,
That you may know and test their
way.
28 They *are* all stubborn rebels, walking
as slanderers.
They are bronze and iron,
They *are* all corrupters;
29 The bellows blow fiercely,
The lead is consumed by the fire;
The smelter refines in vain,
For the wicked are not drawn off.
30 *People* will call them rejected silver,
Because the LORD has rejected them."

PSALM 117:1, 2

1 PRAISE the LORD, all you Gentiles!
Laud Him, all you peoples!
2 For His merciful kindness is great
toward us,
And the truth of the LORD *endures*
forever.

Praise the LORD!

PROVERBS 27:3, 4

3 A stone *is* heavy and sand *is* weighty,
But a fool's wrath *is* heavier than both
of them.

4 Wrath *is* cruel and anger a torrent,
But who *is* able to stand before jealousy?

COLOSSIANS 1:1–29

PAUL, an apostle of Jesus Christ by the
will of God, and Timothy our brother,

2 To the saints and faithful brethren in
Christ *who are* in Colosse:

Grace to you and peace from God our
Father and the Lord Jesus Christ.
3 We give thanks to the God and Father
of our Lord Jesus Christ, praying always
for you, 4 since we heard of your faith in
Christ Jesus and of your love for all the
saints; 5 because of the hope which is laid
up for you in heaven, of which you heard
before in the word of the truth of the gospel,
6 which has come to you, as *it has* also in
all the world, and is bringing forth fruit,
as *it is* also among you since the day you
heard and knew the grace of God in truth;
7 as you also learned from Epaphras, our
dear fellow servant, who is a faithful minis-

ter of Christ on your behalf, 8 who also
declared to us your love in the Spirit.
9 For this reason we also, since the day
we heard it, do not cease to pray for you,
and to ask that you may be filled with the
knowledge of His will in all wisdom and
spiritual understanding; 10 that you may
walk worthy of the Lord, fully pleasing
Him, being fruitful in every good work and
increasing in the knowledge of God;
11 strengthened with all might, according
to His glorious power, for all patience and
longsuffering with joy; 12 giving thanks to
the Father who has qualified us to be partakers of the inheritance of the saints in the
light. 13 He has delivered us from the power
of darkness and conveyed *us* into the kingdom of the Son of His love, 14 in whom
we have redemption through His blood,
the forgiveness of sins.
•15 He is the image of the invisible God,
the firstborn over all creation. 16 For by
Him all things were created that are in
heaven and that are on earth, visible and
invisible, whether thrones or dominions or
principalities or powers. All things were created through Him and for Him. 17 And
He is before all things, and in Him all things
consist. 18 And He is the head of the body,
the church, who is the beginning, the firstborn from the dead, that in all things He
may have the preeminence.
19 For it pleased *the Father that* in Him
all the fullness should dwell, 20 and by Him

---

*T*he secret of the Christian is that he
knows the absolute deity of Jesus
Christ.   (LOVE OF GOD)

---

to reconcile all things to Himself, by
Him, whether things on earth or things
in heaven, having made peace through the
blood of His cross.
21 And you, who once were alienated and
enemies in your mind by wicked works,
yet now He has reconciled 22 in the body
of His flesh through death, to present you
holy, and blameless, and above reproach
in His sight— 23 if indeed you continue
in the faith, grounded and steadfast, and
are not moved away from the hope of the
gospel which you heard, which was
preached to every creature under heaven,
of which I, Paul, became a minister.
24 I now rejoice in my sufferings for you,
and fill up in my flesh what is lacking in
the afflictions of Christ, for the sake of His
body, which is the church, 25 of which I
became a minister according to the steward-

ship from God which was given to me for you, to fulfill the word of God, 26 the mystery which has been hidden from ages and from generations, but now has been revealed to His saints. 27 To them God willed to make known what are the riches of the glory of this mystery among the Gen- tiles: which is Christ in you, the hope of glory. 28 Him we preach, warning every man and teaching every man in all wisdom, that we may present every man perfect in Christ Jesus. 29 To this *end* I also labor, striving according to His working which works in me mightily.

◆◆◆◆

Reading 284—The Reorganizing of Humanity
Colossians 2:8

Am I prepared to accept Jesus Christ's view of Himself, or have I a point of view? Will I come to Jesus Christ just as I am and face the fact that He says certain astounding things about Himself? Jesus Christ did not preach a gospel of hope; He came to reorganize humanity from the inside through a tremendous tragedy in His own life called the Cross, and through that Cross every member of the human race can be reinstated in God's favor and enter into a conscious inheritance of the atonement.

Jesus Christ is the only medium God Almighty has for revealing Himself: "Nor does anyone know the Father except the Son. . . ." Our Lord knows nothing about God being revealed in nature, in the love of our friends, and so on. The poet talks about God being revealed in nature, but the poet does not remember that there is sin in the world. He sees clearly what God's idea is for man, but he forgets that we belong to a fallen race. Consequently, his poetry is only a vision; it cannot be worked out on Mother Earth.   (*GLORY*)

JEREMIAH 7:1—8:22

THE word that came to Jeremiah from the LORD, saying, 2 "Stand in the gate of the LORD's house, and proclaim there this word, and say, 'Hear the word of the LORD, all *you of* Judah who enter in at these gates to worship the LORD!' " 3 Thus says the LORD of hosts, the God of Israel: "Amend your ways and your doings, and I will cause you to dwell in this place. 4 Do not trust in these lying words, saying, 'The temple of the LORD, the temple of the LORD, the temple of the LORD *are* these.'

5 "For if you thoroughly amend your ways and your doings, if you thoroughly execute judgment between a man and his neighbor, 6 *if* you do not oppress the stranger, the fatherless, and the widow, and do not shed innocent blood in this place, or walk after other gods to your hurt, 7 then I will cause you to dwell in this place, in the land that I gave to your fathers forever and ever.

8 "Behold, you trust in lying words that cannot profit. 9 Will you steal, murder, com- mit adultery, swear falsely, burn incense to Baal, and walk after other gods whom you do not know, 10 and *then* come and stand before Me in this house which is called by My name, and say, 'We are delivered to do all these abominations'? 11 Has this house, which is called by My name, become a den of thieves in your eyes? Behold, I, even I, have seen *it*," says the LORD.

12 "But go now to My place which *was* in Shiloh, where I set My name at the first, and see what I did to it because of the wickedness of My people Israel. 13 And now, because you have done all these works," says the LORD, "and I spoke to you, rising up early and speaking, but you did not hear, and I called you, but you did not answer, 14 therefore I will do to the house which is called by My name, in which you trust, and to this place which I gave to you and your fathers, as I have done to Shiloh. 15 And I will cast you out of My sight, as I have cast out all your brethren—the whole posterity of Ephraim.

16 "Therefore do not pray for this people, nor lift up a cry or prayer for them, nor make intercession to Me; for I will not hear you. 17 Do you not see what they do in the cities of Judah and in the streets of Jerusalem? 18 The children gather wood, the fathers kindle the fire, and the women knead dough, to make cakes for the queen of heaven; and *they* pour out drink offerings to other gods, that they may provoke Me to anger. 19 Do they provoke Me to anger?" says the LORD. "*Do they* not *provoke* themselves, to the shame of their own faces?"

20 Therefore thus says the Lord GOD: "Behold, My anger and My fury will be poured out on this place—on man and on beast, on the trees of the field and on the fruit of the ground. And it will burn and not be quenched."

21 Thus says the LORD of hosts, the God of Israel: "Add your burnt offerings to your sacrifices and eat meat. 22 For I did not speak to your fathers, or command them in the day that I brought them out of the land of Egypt, concerning burnt offerings or sacrifices. 23 But this is what I commanded them, saying, 'Obey My voice, and I will be your God, and you shall be My people. And walk in all the ways that I have commanded you, that it may be well with you.' 24 Yet they did not obey or incline their ear, but followed the counsels *and* the dictates of their evil hearts, and went backward and not forward. 25 Since the day that your fathers came out of the land of Egypt until this day, I have even sent to you all My servants the prophets, daily rising up early and sending *them*. 26 Yet they did not obey Me or incline their ear, but stiffened their neck. They did worse than their fathers.

27 "Therefore you shall speak all these words to them, but they will not obey you. You shall also call to them, but they will not answer you.

28 "So you shall say to them, 'This *is* a nation that does not obey the voice of the LORD their God nor receive correction. Truth has perished and has been cut off from their mouth. 29 Cut off your hair and cast *it* away, and take up a lamentation on the desolate heights; for the LORD has rejected and forsaken the generation of His wrath.' 30 For the children of Judah have done evil in My sight," says the LORD. "They have set their abominations in the house which is called by My name, to pollute it. 31 And they have built the high places of Tophet, which *is* in the Valley of the Son of Hinnom, to burn their sons and their daughters in the fire, which I did not command, nor did it come into My heart.

32 "Therefore behold, the days are coming," says the LORD, "when it will no more be called Tophet, or the Valley of the Son of Hinnom, but the Valley of Slaughter; for they will bury in Tophet until there is no room. 33 The corpses of this people will be food for the birds of the heaven and for the beasts of the earth. And no one will frighten *them away*. 34 Then I will cause to cease from the cities of Judah and from the streets of Jerusalem the voice of mirth and the voice of gladness, the voice of the bridegroom and the voice of the bride. For the land shall be desolate.

8 "AT that time," says the LORD, "they shall bring out the bones of the kings of Judah, and the bones of its princes, and the bones of the priests, and the bones of the prophets, and the bones of the inhabitants of Jerusalem, out of their graves. 2 They shall spread them before the sun and the moon and all the host of heaven, which they have loved and which they have served and after which they have walked, which they have sought and which they have worshiped. They shall not be gathered nor buried; they shall be like refuse on the face of the earth. 3 Then death shall be chosen rather than life by all the residue of those who remain of this evil family, who remain in all the places where I have driven them," says the LORD of hosts.

4 "Moreover you shall say to them, 'Thus says the LORD:

"Will they fall and not rise?
Will one turn away and not return?
5   Why has this people slidden back,
Jerusalem, in a perpetual backsliding?
They hold fast to deceit,
They refuse to return.
6   I listened and heard,
But they do not speak aright.
No man repented of his wickedness,
Saying, 'What have I done?'
Everyone turned to his own course,
As the horse rushes into the battle.

7   "Even the stork in the heavens
Knows her appointed times;
And the turtledove, the swift, and
the swallow
Observe the time of their coming.
But My people do not know the
judgment of the LORD.

8   "How can you say, 'We *are* wise,
And the law of the LORD *is* with us'?
Look, the false pen of the scribe
certainly works falsehood.

9 The wise men are ashamed,
  They are dismayed and taken.
  Behold, they have rejected the word
      of the LORD;
  So what wisdom do they have?
10 Therefore I will give their wives to
      others,
  And their fields to those who will
      inherit *them;*
  Because from the least even to the
      greatest
  Everyone is given to covetousness;
  From the prophet even to the priest
  Everyone deals falsely.
11 For they have healed the hurt of the
      daughter of My people slightly,
  Saying, 'Peace, peace!'
  When *there is* no peace.
12 Were they ashamed when they had
      committed abomination?
  No! They were not at all ashamed,
  Nor did they know how to blush.
  Therefore they shall fall among those
      who fall;
  In the time of their punishment
  They shall be cast down," says the
      LORD.

13 "I will surely consume them," says the
      LORD.
  "No grapes *shall be* on the vine,
  Nor figs on the fig tree,
  And the leaf shall fade;
  And *the things* I have given them shall
      pass away from them." ' "

14 "Why do we sit still?
  Assemble yourselves,
  And let us enter the fortified cities,
  And let us be silent there.
  For the LORD our God has put us
      to silence
  And given us water of gall to drink,
  Because we have sinned against the
      LORD.

15 "*We* looked for peace, but no good
      came;
  And for a time of health, and there
      was trouble!
16 The snorting of His horses was heard
      from Dan.
  The whole land trembled at the sound
      of the neighing of His strong ones;
  For they have come and devoured
      the land and all that is in it,
  The city and those who dwell in it."

17 "For behold, I will send serpents
      among you,
  Vipers which cannot be charmed,

And they shall bite you," says the
      LORD.

18 I would comfort myself in sorrow;
  My heart *is* faint in me.
19 Listen! The voice,
  The cry of the daughter of my people
  From a far country:
  "*Is* not the LORD in Zion?
  Is not her King in her?"

  "Why have they provoked Me to anger
  With their carved images—
  With foreign idols?"

20 "The harvest is past,
  The summer is ended,
  And we are not saved!"

21 For the hurt of the daughter of my
      people I am hurt.
  I am mourning;
  Astonishment has taken hold of me.
22 *Is there* no balm in Gilead,
  Is there no physician there?
  Why then is there no recovery
  For the health of the daughter of my
      people?

PSALM 118:1–4

1 OH, give thanks to the LORD, for
      He is good!
  For His mercy *endures* forever.

2 Let Israel now say,
  "His mercy *endures* forever."
3 Let the house of Aaron now say,
  "His mercy *endures* forever."
4 Let those who fear the LORD now say,
  "His mercy *endures* forever."

PROVERBS 27:5, 6

5 OPEN rebuke *is* better
  Than love carefully concealed.

6 Faithful *are* the wounds of a friend,
  But the kisses of an enemy *are* deceitful.

COLOSSIANS 2:1–23

FOR I want you to know what a great
conflict I have for you and those in Laodicea, and *for* as many as have not seen my
face in the flesh, 2 that their hearts may
be encouraged, being knit together in love,
and *attaining* to all riches of the full assurance of understanding, to the knowledge

of the mystery of God, both of the Father and of Christ, 3 in whom are hidden all the treasures of wisdom and knowledge.

4 Now this I say lest anyone should deceive you with persuasive words. 5 For though I am absent in the flesh, yet I am with you in spirit, rejoicing to see your *good* order and the steadfastness of your faith in Christ.

6 As you therefore have received Christ Jesus the Lord, so walk in Him, 7 rooted and built up in Him and established in the faith, as you have been taught, abounding in it with thanksgiving.

8 Beware lest anyone cheat you through philosophy and empty deceit, according to the tradition of men, according to the basic principles of the world, and not according to Christ. 9 For in Him dwells all the fullness of the Godhead bodily; 10 and you are complete in Him, who is the head of all principality and power.

11 In Him you were also circumcised with the circumcision made without hands, by putting off the body of the sins of the flesh, by the circumcision of Christ, 12 buried with Him in baptism, in which you also were raised with *Him* through faith in the working of God, who raised Him from the dead. 13 And you, being dead in your trespasses and the uncircumcision of your flesh, He has made alive together with Him, having forgiven you all trespasses, 14 having wiped out the handwriting of requirements that was against us, which was contrary to us. And He has taken it out of the way,

having nailed it to the cross. 15 Having disarmed principalities and powers, He made a public spectacle of them, triumphing over them in it.

In the Cross our Lord deals with everything that keeps a man's heart disturbed. (PLACE HELP)

---

16 So let no one judge you in food or in drink, or regarding a festival or a new moon or sabbaths, 17 which are a shadow of things to come, but the substance is of Christ. 18 Let no one cheat you of your reward, taking delight in *false* humility and worship of angels, intruding into those things which he has not seen, vainly puffed up by his fleshly mind, 19 and not holding fast to the Head, from whom all the body, nourished and knit together by joints and ligaments, grows with the increase *that is* from God.

20 Therefore, if you died with Christ from the basic principles of the world, why, as *though* living in the world, do you subject yourselves to regulations— 21 "Do not touch, do not taste, do not handle," 22 which all concern things which perish with the using—according to the commandments and doctrines of men? 23 These things indeed have an appearance of wisdom in self-imposed religion, *false* humility, and neglect of the body, *but are* of no value against the indulgence of the flesh.

◆◆◆◆

Reading 285—Our Entire Life
Colossians 3:1–4

"Your life is hidden with Christ in God." Christ is our entire life. When once we realize this, certain forms of doubt and perplexity vanish forever. If we set our affection on things above, those perplexities will never trouble us anymore because we know the Lord Jesus, and He is not distracted by these present perplexities. The things that are obscure to the natural man become clear to the penetration of the mind that sets itself on the things above. Such a one does not pretend not to have doubts; we know he has not got them. His is not a stoical calm. The reason is that he has been living for a long time in Colossians 3, the entire life is hid with Christ in God, the whole set of the mind is on the things above, and the things on earth are transfigured.

Thank God that the almighty power of Jesus Christ is for us. All power is vested in Him in heaven and on earth, and He says, "Lo, I am with you always." All the power of the deity of Christ is ours through His resurrection. (*GLORY*)

JEREMIAH 9:1—10:25

1 OH, that my head were waters,
   And my eyes a fountain of tears,
   That I might weep day and night
   For the slain of the daughter of my
      people!
2 Oh, that I had in the wilderness
   A lodging place for travelers;
   That I might leave my people,
   And go from them!
   For they *are* all adulterers,
   An assembly of treacherous men.

3 "And *like* their bow they have bent
      their tongues *for* lies.
   They are not valiant for the truth on
      the earth.
   For they proceed from evil to evil,
   And they do not know Me," says the
      LORD.
4 "Everyone take heed to his neighbor,
   And do not trust any brother;
   For every brother will utterly
      supplant,
   And every neighbor will walk with
      slanderers.
5 Everyone will deceive his neighbor,
   And will not speak the truth;
   They have taught their tongue to
      speak lies;
   They weary themselves to commit
      iniquity.
6 Your dwelling place *is* in the midst
      of deceit;
   Through deceit they refuse to know
      Me," says the LORD.

7 Therefore thus says the LORD of hosts:

   "Behold, I will refine them and try
      them;
   For how shall I deal with the
      daughter of My people?
8 Their tongue *is* an arrow shot out;
   It speaks deceit;
   One speaks peaceably to his neighbor
      with his mouth,
   But in his heart he lies in wait.
9 Shall I not punish them for these
      things?" says the LORD.
   "Shall I not avenge Myself on such a
      nation as this?"

10 I will take up a weeping and wailing
      for the mountains,
   And for the dwelling places of the
      wilderness a lamentation,
   Because they are burned up,
   So that no one can pass through;

Nor can *men* hear the voice of the
      cattle.
   Both the birds of the heavens and
      the beasts have fled;
   They are gone.

11 "I will make Jerusalem a heap of ruins,
      a den of jackals.
   I will make the cities of Judah
      desolate, without an inhabitant."

12 Who *is* the wise man who may understand this? And *who is he* to whom the mouth
of the LORD has spoken, that he may declare
it? Why does the land perish *and* burn up
like a wilderness, so that no one can pass
through?
13 And the LORD said, "Because they have
forsaken My law which I set before them,
and have not obeyed My voice, nor walked
according to it, 14 but they have walked
according to the dictates of their own hearts
and after the Baals, which their fathers
taught them," 15 therefore thus says the
LORD of hosts, the God of Israel: "Behold,
I will feed them, this people, with wormwood, and give them water of gall to drink.
16 I will scatter them also among the Gentiles, whom neither they nor their fathers
have known. And I will send a sword after
them until I have consumed them."
17 Thus says the LORD of hosts:

   "Consider and call for the mourning
      women,
   That they may come;
   And send for skillful wailing women,
   That they may come.
18 Let them make haste
   And take up a wailing for us,
   That our eyes may run with tears,
   And our eyelids gush with water.
19 For a voice of wailing is heard from
      Zion:
   'How we are plundered!
   We are greatly ashamed,
   Because we have forsaken the land,
   Because we have been cast out of our
      dwellings.'"

20 Yet hear the word of the LORD,
      O women,
   And let your ear receive the word
      of His mouth;
   Teach your daughters wailing,
   And everyone her neighbor a
      lamentation.
21 For death has come through our
      windows,
   Has entered our palaces,

To kill off the children—*no longer to
be* outside!
And the young men—*no longer* on
the streets!

22 Speak, "Thus says the LORD:

'Even the carcasses of men shall fall
as refuse on the open field,
Like cuttings after the harvester,
And no one shall gather *them*.' "

23 Thus says the LORD:

"Let not the wise *man* glory in his
wisdom,
Let not the mighty *man* glory in his
might,
Nor let the rich *man* glory in his
riches;
24 But let him who glories glory in this,
That he understands and knows Me,
That I *am* the LORD, exercising
lovingkindness, judgment, and
righteousness in the earth.
For in these I delight," says the LORD.

25 "Behold, the days are coming," says
the LORD, "that I will punish all *who are*
circumcised with the uncircumcised—
26 Egypt, Judah, Edom, the people of Ammon, Moab, and all *who are* in the farthest
corners, who dwell in the wilderness. For
all *these* nations *are* uncircumcised, and all
the house of Israel *are* uncircumcised in
the heart."

10 HEAR the word which the LORD
speaks to you, O house of Israel.
2 Thus says the LORD:

"Do not learn the way of the Gentiles;
Do not be dismayed at the signs of
heaven,
For the Gentiles are dismayed at
them.
3 For the customs of the peoples *are*
futile;
For *one* cuts a tree from the forest,
The work of the hands of the
workman, with the ax.
4 They decorate it with silver and gold;
They fasten it with nails and hammers
So that it will not topple.
5 They *are* upright, like a palm tree,
And they cannot speak;
They must be carried,
Because they cannot go *by themselves*.
Do not be afraid of them,
For they cannot do evil,
Nor can they do any good."

6 Inasmuch as *there is* none like You,
O LORD
(You *are* great, and Your name *is*
great in might),
7 Who would not fear You, O King
of the nations?
For this is Your rightful due.
For among all the wise *men* of the
nations,
And in all their kingdoms,
There is none like You.
8 But they are altogether dull-hearted
and foolish;
A wooden idol *is* a worthless
doctrine.
9 Silver is beaten into plates;
It is brought from Tarshish,
And gold from Uphaz,
The work of the craftsman
And of the hands of the metalsmith;
Blue and purple *are* their clothing;
They *are* all the work of skillful *men*.
10 But the LORD *is* the true God;
He *is* the living God and the
everlasting King.
At His wrath the earth will tremble,
And the nations will not be able to
endure His indignation.

11 Thus you shall say to them: "The gods
that have not made the heavens and the
earth shall perish from the earth and from
under these heavens."

12 He has made the earth by His power,
He has established the world by His
wisdom,
And has stretched out the heavens
at His discretion.
13 When He utters His voice,
There is a multitude of waters in the
heavens:
"And He causes the vapors to ascend
from the ends of the earth.
He makes lightning for the rain,
He brings the wind out of His
treasuries."

14 Everyone is dull-hearted, without
knowledge;
Every metalsmith is put to shame by
an image;
For his molded image *is* falsehood,
And *there is* no breath in them.
15 They *are* futile, a work of errors;
In the time of their punishment they
shall perish.
16 The Portion of Jacob *is* not like them,
For He *is* the Maker of all *things*,
And Israel *is* the tribe of His
inheritance;

The LORD of hosts *is* His name.

17 Gather up your wares from the land,
O inhabitant of the fortress!

18 For thus says the LORD:

"Behold, I will throw out at this time
The inhabitants of the land,
And will distress them,
That they may find *it so*."

19 Woe is me for my hurt!
My wound is severe.
But I say, "Truly this *is* an infirmity,
And I must bear it."

20 My tent is plundered,
And all my cords are broken;
My children have gone from me,
And they *are* no more.
There is no one to pitch my tent
anymore,
Or set up my curtains.

21 For the shepherds have become dull-
hearted,
And have not sought the LORD;
Therefore they shall not prosper,
And all their flocks shall be scattered.

22 Behold, the noise of the report has
come,
And a great commotion out of the
north country,
To make the cities of Judah desolate,
a den of jackals.

23 O LORD, I know the way of man *is*
not in himself;
It is not in man who walks to direct
his own steps.

24 O LORD, correct me, but with justice;
Not in Your anger, lest You bring
me to nothing.

25 Pour out Your fury on the Gentiles,
who do not know You,
And on the families who do not call
on Your name;
For they have eaten up Jacob,
Devoured him and consumed him,
And made his dwelling place
desolate.

PSALM 118:5–9

5 I called on the LORD in distress;
The LORD answered me *and set me* in
a broad place.

6 The LORD *is* on my side;
I will not fear.
What can man do to me?

7 The LORD is for me among those who
help me;
Therefore I shall see *my desire* on those
who hate me.

8 *It is* better to trust in the LORD
Than to put confidence in man.

9 *It is* better to trust in the LORD
Than to put confidence in princes.

PROVERBS 27:7

7 A satisfied soul loathes the
honeycomb,
But to a hungry soul every bitter thing
is sweet.

COLOSSIANS 3:1–25

IF then you were raised with Christ, seek
those things which are above, where Christ
is, sitting at the right hand of God.
2 Set your mind on things above, not on
things on the earth. 3 For you died, and
your life is hidden with Christ in God.
4 When Christ *who is* our life appears, then
you also will appear with Him in glory.
5 Therefore put to death your members
which are on the earth: fornication, uncleanness, passion, evil desire, and covetousness, which is idolatry. 6 Because of these
things the wrath of God is coming upon
the sons of disobedience, 7 in which you
yourselves once walked when you lived in
them.

8 But now you yourselves are to put off
all these: anger, wrath, malice, blasphemy,
filthy language out of your mouth. 9 Do
not lie to one another, since you have put
off the old man with his deeds, 10 and have
put on the new *man* who is renewed in
knowledge according to the image of Him
who created him, 11 where there is neither
Greek nor Jew, circumcised nor uncircumcised, barbarian, Scythian, slave *nor* free,
but Christ *is* all and in all.

12 Therefore, as *the* elect of God, holy
and beloved, put on tender mercies, kindness, humility, meekness, longsuffering;
13 bearing with one another, and forgiving
one another, if anyone has a complaint
against another; even as Christ forgave you,
so you also *must do.* 14 But above all these
things put on love, which is the bond of
perfection. 15 And let the peace of God rule

*The love which has God
as its center makes no
demands.* (GOD'S WORKMANSHIP)

in your hearts, to which also you were called in one body; and be thankful. 16 Let the word of Christ dwell in you richly in all wisdom, teaching and admonishing one another in psalms and hymns and spiritual songs, singing with grace in your hearts to the Lord. 17 And *whatever* you do in word or deed, *do* all in the name of the Lord Jesus, giving thanks to God the Father through Him.

18 Wives, submit to your own husbands, as is fitting in the Lord.

19 Husbands, love your wives and do not be bitter toward them.

20 Children, obey your parents in all things, for this is well pleasing to the Lord.

21 Fathers, do not provoke your children, lest they become discouraged.

22 Bondservants, obey in all things your masters according to the flesh, not with eyeservice, as men-pleasers, but in sincerity of heart, fearing God. 23 And whatever you do, do it heartily, as to the Lord and not to men, 24 knowing that from the Lord you will receive the reward of the inheritance; for you serve the Lord Christ. 25 But he who does wrong will be repaid for what he has done, and there is no partiality.

◆◆◆◆

Reading 286—The Sacrifice of Prayer
Colossians 4:2

It is comparatively easy to think or say apt things about private prayer, but it is not so easy to say things about public prayer, the reason probably being that few of us are willing to carry the cross of public prayer, or at least if we do, we repeat aloud to a large extent our own private concerns, which are much better told in secret and alone. It is easier too to evade self-consciousness in private prayer; emancipation from self-consciousness is like a deliverance from a terrible sickness, and one gets rather alarmed at the slightest symptom of it again. Probably this is the reason why many Christians, who ought to be the strength and safeguard of a public prayer meeting in a community of Christians, are not so; they keep silent and just one or two have merely the gift of devotional language are allowed to dominate the prayer meeting; and the mid-week prayer meeting is given up and becomes the mid-week service. We must remember that there is a sacrifice of prayer as well as a sacrifice of praise.   (*Chris. Dis. 2*)

JEREMIAH 11:1—12:17

THE word that came to Jeremiah from the LORD, saying, 2 "Hear the words of this covenant, and speak to the men of Judah and to the inhabitants of Jerusalem; 3 and say to them, 'Thus says the LORD God of Israel: "Cursed *is* the man who does not obey the words of this covenant 4 which I commanded your fathers in the day I brought them out of the land of Egypt, from the iron furnace, saying, 'Obey My voice, and do according to all that I command you; so shall you be My people, and I will be your God,' 5 that I may establish the oath which I have sworn to your fathers, to give them 'a land flowing with milk and honey,' as *it is* this day." ' "

And I answered and said, "So be it, LORD."

6 Then the LORD said to me, "Proclaim all these words in the cities of Judah and in the streets of Jerusalem, saying: 'Hear the words of this covenant and do them. 7 For I earnestly exhorted your fathers in the day I brought them up out of the land of Egypt, until this day, rising early and exhorting, saying, "Obey My voice." 8 Yet they did not obey or incline their ear, but everyone followed the dictates of his evil heart; therefore I will bring upon them all the words of this covenant, which I commanded *them* to do, but *which* they have not done.' "

9 And the LORD said to me, "A conspiracy has been found among the men of Judah

and among the inhabitants of Jerusalem. 10 They have turned back to the iniquities of their forefathers who refused to hear My words, and they have gone after other gods to serve them; the house of Israel and the house of Judah have broken My covenant which I made with their fathers."

11 Therefore thus says the LORD: "Behold, I will surely bring calamity on them which they will not be able to escape; and though they cry out to Me, I will not listen to them. 12 Then the cities of Judah and the inhabitants of Jerusalem will go and cry out to the gods to whom they offer incense, but they will not save them at all in the time of their trouble. 13 For *according to* the number of your cities were your gods, O Judah; and *according to* the number of the streets of Jerusalem you have set up altars to *that* shameful thing, altars to burn incense to Baal.

14 "So do not pray for this people, or lift up a cry or prayer for them; for I will not hear *them* in the time that they cry out to Me because of their trouble.

15 "What has My beloved to do in My house,
    Having done lewd deeds with many?
    And the holy flesh has passed from you.
    When you do evil, then you rejoice.
16 The LORD called your name,
    Green Olive Tree, Lovely *and* of Good Fruit.
    With the noise of a great tumult
    He has kindled fire on it,
    And its branches are broken.

17 "For the LORD of hosts, who planted you, has pronounced doom against you for the evil of the house of Israel and of the house of Judah, which they have done against themselves to provoke Me to anger in offering incense to Baal."

18 Now the LORD gave me knowledge *of it,* and I know *it;* for You showed me their doings. 19 But I *was* like a docile lamb brought to the slaughter; and I did not know that they had devised schemes against me, *saying,* "Let us destroy the tree with its fruit, and let us cut him off from the land of the living, that his name may be remembered no more."

20 But, O LORD of hosts,
    You who judge righteously,
    Testing the mind and the heart,
    Let me see Your vengeance on them,
    For to You I have revealed my cause.

21 "Therefore thus says the LORD concerning the men of Anathoth who seek your life, saying, 'Do not prophesy in the name of the LORD, lest you die by our hand'— 22 therefore thus says the LORD of hosts: 'Behold, I will punish them. The young men shall die by the sword, their sons and their daughters shall die by famine; 23 and there shall be no remnant of them, for I will bring catastrophe on the men of Anathoth, *even* the year of their punishment.' "

12 RIGHTEOUS *are* You, O LORD,
    when I plead with You;
    Yet let me talk with You about *Your* judgments.
    Why does the way of the wicked prosper?
    Why are those happy who deal so treacherously?
2   You have planted them, yes, they have taken root;
    They grow, yes, they bear fruit.
    You *are* near in their mouth
    But far from their mind.

3   But You, O LORD, know me;
    You have seen me,
    And You have tested my heart toward You.
    Pull them out like sheep for the slaughter,
    And prepare them for the day of slaughter.
4   How long will the land mourn,
    And the herbs of every field wither?
    The beasts and birds are consumed,
    For the wickedness of those who dwell there,
    Because they said, "He will not see our final end."

5   "If you have run with the footmen, and they have wearied you,
    Then how can you contend with horses?
    And *if* in the land of peace,
    In which you trusted, *they wearied you,*
    Then how will you do in the floodplain of the Jordan?
6   For even your brothers, the house of your father,
    Even they have dealt treacherously with you;
    Yes, they have called a multitude after you.
    Do not believe them,
    Even though they speak smooth words to you.

7 "I have forsaken My house, I have left
    My heritage;
  I have given the dearly beloved of
    My soul into the hand of her
    enemies.
8 My heritage is to Me like a lion in
    the forest;
  It cries out against Me;
  Therefore I have hated it.
9 My heritage *is* to Me *like* a speckled
    vulture;
  The vultures all around *are* against
    her.
  Come, assemble all the beasts of the
    field,
  Bring them to devour!

10 "Many rulers have destroyed My
    vineyard,
  They have trodden My portion
    underfoot;
  They have made My pleasant portion
    a desolate wilderness.
11 They have made it desolate;
  Desolate, it mourns to Me;
  The whole land is made desolate,
  Because no one takes *it* to heart.
12 The plunderers have come
  On all the desolate heights in the
    wilderness,
  For the sword of the LORD shall
    devour
  From *one* end of the land to the *other*
    end of the land;
  No flesh shall have peace.
13 They have sown wheat but reaped
    thorns;
  They have put themselves to pain *but*
    do not profit.
  But be ashamed of your harvest
  Because of the fierce anger of the
    LORD."

14 Thus says the LORD: "Against all My
evil neighbors who touch the inheritance
which I have caused My people Israel to
inherit—behold, I will pluck them out of
their land and pluck out the house of Judah
from among them. 15 Then it shall be, after
I have plucked them out, that I will return
and have compassion on them and bring
them back, everyone to his heritage and
everyone to his land. 16 And it shall be, if
they will learn carefully the ways of My
people, to swear by My name, 'As the LORD
lives,' as they taught My people to swear
by Baal, then they shall be established in
the midst of My people. 17 But if they do
not obey, I will utterly pluck up and destroy
that nation," says the LORD.

PSALM 118:10–14

10 ALL nations surrounded me,
  But in the name of the LORD I will
    destroy them.
11 They surrounded me,
  Yes, they surrounded me;
  But in the name of the LORD I will
    destroy them.
12 They surrounded me like bees;
  They were quenched like a fire of
    thorns;
  For in the name of the LORD I will
    destroy them.
13 You pushed me violently, that I might
    fall,
  But the LORD helped me.
14 The LORD *is* my strength and song,
  And He has become my salvation.

PROVERBS 27:8

8 LIKE a bird that wanders from its
    nest
  Is a man who wanders from his place.

COLOSSIANS 4:1–18

MASTERS, give your bondservants what
is just and fair, knowing that you also have
a Master in heaven.

2 Continue earnestly in prayer, being vigilant in it with thanksgiving; 3 meanwhile
praying also for us, that God would open
to us a door for the word, to speak the
mystery of Christ, for which I am also in
chains, 4 that I may make it manifest, as I
ought to speak.

5 Walk in wisdom toward those *who are*
outside, redeeming the time. 6 *Let* your
speech always *be* with grace, seasoned with
salt, that you may know how you ought
to answer each one.

---

*A man's spirit only expresses
itself as soul by means of
words.* (MORAL FOUND.)

---

7 Tychicus, a beloved brother, faithful
minister, and fellow servant in the Lord,
will tell you all the news about me.
8 I am sending him to you for this very
purpose, that he may know your circumstances and comfort your hearts, 9 with
Onesimus, a faithful and beloved brother,
who is *one* of you. They will make known

to you all things which *are happening* here.

10 Aristarchus my fellow prisoner greets you, with Mark the cousin of Barnabas (about whom you received instructions: if he comes to you, welcome him), 11 and Jesus who is called Justus. These *are my* only fellow workers for the kingdom of God who are of the circumcision; they have proved to be a comfort to me.

12 Epaphras, who is *one* of you, a bondservant of Christ, greets you, always laboring fervently for you in prayers, that you may stand perfect and complete in all the will of God. 13 For I bear him witness that he has a great zeal for you, and those who are in Laodicea, and those in Hierapolis. 14 Luke the beloved physician and Demas greet you. 15 Greet the brethren who are in Laodicea, and Nymphas and the church that *is* in his house.

16 Now when this epistle is read among you, see that it is read also in the church of the Laodiceans, and that you likewise read the epistle from Laodicea. 17 And say to Archippus, "Take heed to the ministry which you have received in the Lord, that you may fulfill it."

18 This salutation by my own hand—Paul. Remember my chains. Grace *be* with you. Amen.

Reading 287—The Church in God
1 Thessalonians 1:1

Our word "church" is connected with civilized organizations of religious people; our Lord's attitude to the church is different. He says it is composed of those who have had a personal revelation from God as to who Jesus Christ is, and have made a public declaration of the same.

(SHAD. AGONY)

The church is a separated band of people who are united to God by the regenerating power of the Spirit, and the bedrock of membership in the church is that we know who Jesus is by a personal revelation of Him. The indwelling Spirit is the supreme Guide, and He keeps us absorbed with our Lord. The emphasis today is placed on the furtherance of an organization; the note is, "We must keep this thing going." If we are in God's order the thing will go; if we are not in His order, it won't.   (CONFORMED)

JEREMIAH 13:1—14:22

THUS the LORD said to me: "Go and get yourself a linen sash, and put it around your waist, but do not put it in water." 2 So I got a sash according to the word of the LORD, and put *it* around my waist.

3 And the word of the LORD came to me the second time, saying, 4 "Take the sash that you acquired, which *is* around your waist, and arise, go to the Euphrates, and hide it there in a hole in the rock." 5 So I went and hid it by the Euphrates, as the LORD commanded me.

6 Now it came to pass after many days that the LORD said to me, "Arise, go to the Euphrates, and take from there the sash which I commanded you to hide there." 7 Then I went to the Euphrates and dug, and I took the sash from the place where I had hidden it; and there was the sash, ruined. It was profitable for nothing.

8 Then the word of the LORD came to me, saying, 9 "Thus says the LORD: 'In this manner I will ruin the pride of Judah and the great pride of Jerusalem. 10 This evil people, who refuse to hear My words, who follow the dictates of their hearts, and walk after other gods to serve them and worship them, shall be just like this sash which is profitable for nothing. 11 For as the sash clings to the waist of a man, so I have caused the whole house of Israel and the whole house of Judah to cling to Me,' says the LORD, 'that they may become My people, for renown, for praise, and for glory; but they would not hear.'

12 "Therefore you shall speak to them this word: 'Thus says the LORD God of Israel: "Every bottle shall be filled with wine." '

"And they will say to you, 'Do we not certainly know that every bottle will be filled with wine?'

13 "Then you shall say to them, 'Thus says the Lord: "Behold, I will fill all the inhabitants of this land—even the kings who sit on David's throne, the priests, the prophets, and all the inhabitants of Jerusalem—with drunkenness! 14 And I will dash them one against another, even the fathers and the sons together," says the Lord. "I will not pity nor spare nor have mercy, but will destroy them."'"

15 Hear and give ear:
  Do not be proud,
  For the Lord has spoken.
16 Give glory to the Lord your God
  Before He causes darkness,
  And before your feet stumble
  On the dark mountains,
  And while you are looking for light,
  He turns it into the shadow of death
  And makes *it* dense darkness.
17 But if you will not hear it,
  My soul will weep in secret for *your* pride;
  My eyes will weep bitterly
  And run down with tears,
  Because the Lord's flock has been taken captive.

18 Say to the king and to the queen mother,
  "Humble yourselves;
  Sit down,
  For your rule shall collapse, the crown of your glory."
19 The cities of the South shall be shut up,
  And no one shall open *them;*
  Judah shall be carried away captive, all of it;
  It shall be wholly carried away captive.

20 Lift up your eyes and see
  Those who come from the north.
  Where *is* the flock *that* was given to you,
  Your beautiful sheep?
21 What will you say when He punishes you?
  For you have taught them
  To be chieftains, to be head over you.
  Will not pangs seize you,
  Like a woman in labor?
22 And if you say in your heart,
  "Why have these things come upon me?"
  For the greatness of your iniquity

Your skirts have been uncovered,
  Your heels made bare.
23 Can the Ethiopian change his skin
  or the leopard its spots?
  Then may you also do good who are accustomed to do evil.

24 "Therefore I will scatter them like stubble
  That passes away by the wind of the wilderness.
25 This is your lot,
  The portion of your measures from Me," says the Lord,
  "Because you have forgotten Me
  And trusted in falsehood.
26 Therefore I will uncover your skirts over your face,
  That your shame may appear.
27 I have seen your adulteries
  And your *lustful* neighings,
  The lewdness of your harlotry,
  Your abominations on the hills in the fields.
  Woe to you, O Jerusalem!
  Will you still not be made clean?"

14 THE word of the Lord that came to Jeremiah concerning the droughts.

2 "Judah mourns,
  And her gates languish;
  They mourn for the land,
  And the cry of Jerusalem has gone up.
3 Their nobles have sent their lads for water;
  They went to the cisterns *and* found no water.
  They returned with their vessels empty;
  They were ashamed and confounded
  And covered their heads.
4 Because the ground is parched,
  For there was no rain in the land,
  The plowmen were ashamed;
  They covered their heads.
5 Yes, the deer also gave birth in the field,
  But left because there was no grass.
6 And the wild donkeys stood in the desolate heights;
  They sniffed at the wind like jackals;
  Their eyes failed because *there was* no grass."

7 O Lord, though our iniquities testify against us,
  Do it for Your name's sake;

For our backslidings are many,
We have sinned against You.
8 O the Hope of Israel, his Savior in
time of trouble,
Why should You be like a stranger
in the land,
And like a traveler *who* turns aside
to tarry for a night?
9 Why should You be like a man
astonished,
Like a mighty one *who* cannot save?
Yet You, O Lord, *are* in our midst,
And we are called by Your name;
Do not leave us!

10 Thus says the Lord to this people:

"Thus they have loved to wander;
They have not restrained their feet.
Therefore the Lord does not accept
them;
He will remember their iniquity
now,
And punish their sins."

11 Then the Lord said to me, "Do not
pray for this people, for *their* good.
12 When they fast, I will not hear their cry;
and when they offer burnt offering and
grain offering, I will not accept them. But
I will consume them by the sword, by the
famine, and by the pestilence."
13 Then I said, "Ah, Lord God! Behold,
the prophets say to them, 'You shall not
see the sword, nor shall you have famine,
but I will give you assured peace in this
place.' "
14 And the Lord said to me, "The prophets prophesy lies in My name. I have not
sent them, commanded them, nor spoken
to them; they prophesy to you a false vision,
divination, a worthless thing, and the deceit of their heart. 15 Therefore thus says
the Lord concerning the prophets who
prophesy in My name, whom I did not
send, and who say, 'Sword and famine shall
not be in this land'—'By sword and famine
those prophets shall be consumed! 16 And
the people to whom they prophesy shall
be cast out in the streets of Jerusalem because of the famine and the sword; they
will have no one to bury them—them nor
their wives, their sons nor their daughters—
for I will pour their wickedness on them.'
17 "Therefore you shall say this word to
them:

'Let my eyes flow with tears night
and day,
And let them not cease;
For the virgin daughter of my people

Has been broken with a mighty
stroke, with a very severe blow.
18 If I go out to the field,
Then behold, those slain with the
sword!
And if I enter the city,
Then behold, those sick from famine!
Yes, both prophet and priest go
about in a land they do not
know.' "

19 Have You utterly rejected Judah?
Has Your soul loathed Zion?
Why have You stricken us so that
there is no healing for us?
We looked for peace, but *there was*
no good;
And for the time of healing, and there
was trouble.
20 We acknowledge, O Lord, our
wickedness
And the iniquity of our fathers,
For we have sinned against You.
21 Do not abhor *us,* for Your name's
sake;
Do not disgrace the throne of Your
glory.
Remember, do not break Your
covenant with us.
22 Are there any among the idols of the
nations that can cause rain?
Or can the heavens give showers?
Are You not He, O Lord our God?
Therefore we will wait for You,
Since You have made all these.

PSALM 118:15–20

15 THE voice of rejoicing and salvation
Is in the tents of the righteous;
The right hand of the Lord does
valiantly.
16 The right hand of the Lord is exalted;
The right hand of the Lord does
valiantly.
17 I shall not die, but live,
And declare the works of the Lord.
18 The Lord has chastened me severely,
But He has not given me over to death.

19 Open to me the gates of righteousness;
I will go through them,
And I will praise the Lord.
20 This is the gate of the Lord,
Through which the righteous shall
enter.

PROVERBS 27:9

9 OINTMENT and perfume delight the
heart,

And the sweetness of a man's friend
gives delight by hearty counsel.

1 THESSALONIANS 1:1–10

PAUL, Silvanus, and Timothy,

To the church of the Thessalonians in
God the Father and the Lord Jesus Christ:

Grace to you and peace from God our
Father and the Lord Jesus Christ.
2 We give thanks to God always for you
all, making mention of you in our prayers,
3 remembering without ceasing your work
of faith, labor of love, and patience of hope
in our Lord Jesus Christ in the sight of
our God and Father, 4 knowing, beloved
brethren, your election by God. 5 For our
gospel did not come to you in word only,
but also in power, and in the Holy Spirit
and in much assurance, as you know what
kind of men we were among you for your
sake.

6 And you became followers of us and
of the Lord, having received the word in
much affliction, with joy of the Holy Spirit,

---

*One of the consolations of the new
way is the fathomless joy of the Holy
Ghost.*   (SEND I YOU)

---

7 so that you became examples to all in
Macedonia and Achaia who believe.
8 For from you the word of the Lord has
sounded forth, not only in Macedonia and
Achaia, but also in every place. Your faith
toward God has gone out, so that we do
not need to say anything. 9 For they themselves declare concerning us what manner
of entry we had to you, and how you turned
to God from idols to serve the living and
true God, 10 and to wait for His Son from
heaven, whom He raised from the dead,
even Jesus who delivers us from the wrath
to come.

◆◆◆

---

*Reading 288—*The Duty of Loyalty
Proverbs 27:10

"Greater love has no one than this, than to lay down one's life for his
friends." If I am a friend of Jesus Christ, I lay down my life for
Him. That does not mean that I go through the big crisis of death; it means
that I lay down my life deliberately as I would lay out a pound note. I have
this to lay out and expend; I have a day before me, and I am going to lay it
out for Jesus Christ; I have my duty to perform, but I am going to lay it out
in devotion to Jesus Christ all through. It is difficult, and thank God it is
difficult. Salvation is easy because it cost God so much, but the manifestation
of it in my life is difficult. God does expect a man to be a man. God saves a
man and endues him with His Holy Spirit, and says in effect, "Now it is up
to you to prove it, work it out; be loyal to Me while the nature of things
round about you would make you disloyal. I have called you friends, now
stand loyal to your Friend." His honor is at stake in our bodily life.

(*PLACE HELP*)

JEREMIAH 15:1—16:21

THEN the LORD said to me, "*Even* if
Moses and Samuel stood before Me, My
mind *would* not *be* favorable toward this
people. Cast *them* out of My sight, and
let them go forth. 2 And it shall be, if they

say to you, 'Where should we go?' then
you shall tell them, 'Thus says the LORD:

"Such as *are* for death, to death;
And such as *are* for the sword, to
the sword;
And such as *are* for the famine, to
the famine;

And such as *are* for the captivity, to the captivity." '

3 "And I will appoint over them four forms *of destruction*," says the LORD: "the sword to slay, the dogs to drag, the birds of the heavens and the beasts of the earth to devour and destroy. 4 I will hand them over to trouble, to all kingdoms of the earth, because of Manasseh the son of Hezekiah, king of Judah, for what he did in Jerusalem.

5 "For who will have pity on you,
  O Jerusalem?
  Or who will bemoan you?
  Or who will turn aside to ask how
    you are doing?
6 You have forsaken Me," says the
  LORD,
  "You have gone backward.
  Therefore I will stretch out My hand
    against you and destroy you;
  I am weary of relenting!
7 And I will winnow them with a
    winnowing fan in the gates of the
    land;
  I will bereave *them* of children;
  I will destroy My people,
  Since they do not return from their
    ways.
8 Their widows will be increased to
    Me more than the sand of the seas;
  I will bring against them,
  Against the mother of the young
    men,
  A plunderer at noonday;
  I will cause anguish and terror to fall
    on them suddenly.

9 "She languishes who has borne seven;
  She has breathed her last;
  Her sun has gone down
  While *it was* yet day;
  She has been ashamed and
    confounded.
  And the remnant of them I will
    deliver to the sword
  Before their enemies," says the LORD.

10 Woe is me, my mother,
  That you have borne me,
  A man of strife and a man of
    contention to the whole earth!
  I have neither lent for interest,
  Nor have men lent to me for interest.
  Every one of them curses me.

11 The LORD said:

"Surely it will be well with your
  remnant;

Surely I will cause the enemy to
  intercede with you
In the time of adversity and in the
  time of affliction.
12 Can anyone break iron,
  The northern iron and the bronze?
13 Your wealth and your treasures
  I will give as plunder without price,
  Because of all your sins,
  Throughout your territories.
14 And I will make *you* cross over with
    your enemies
  Into a land *which* you do not know;
  For a fire is kindled in My anger,
  Which shall burn upon you."

15 O LORD, You know;
  Remember me and visit me,
  And take vengeance for me on my
    persecutors.
  In Your enduring patience, do not
    take me away.
  Know that for Your sake I have
    suffered rebuke.
16 Your words were found, and I ate
    them,
  And Your word was to me the joy
    and rejoicing of my heart;
  For I am called by Your name,
  O LORD God of hosts.

---

*E*very bit of knowledge that we
have of God fills us with ineffable
joy. (BRILL, HERITAGE)

---

17 I did not sit in the assembly of the
    mockers,
  Nor did I rejoice;
  I sat alone because of Your hand,
  For You have filled me with
    indignation.
18 Why is my pain perpetual
  And my wound incurable,
  Which refuses to be healed?
  Will You surely be to me like an
    unreliable stream,
  As waters *that* fail?

19 Therefore thus says the LORD:

"If you return,
  Then I will bring you back;
  You shall stand before Me;
  If you take out the precious from
    the vile,
  You shall be as My mouth.
  Let them return to you,
  But you must not return to them.

20 And I will make you to this people
     a fortified bronze wall;
     And they will fight against you,
     But they shall not prevail against you;
     For I *am* with you to save you
     And deliver you," says the Lord.
21 "I will deliver you from the hand of
     the wicked,
     And I will redeem you from the grip
     of the terrible."

16 THE word of the Lord also came to me, saying, 2 "You shall not take a wife, nor shall you have sons or daughters in this place." 3 For thus says the Lord concerning the sons and daughters who are born in this place, and concerning their mothers who bore them and their fathers who begot them in this land: 4 "They shall die gruesome deaths; they shall not be lamented nor shall they be buried, *but* they shall be like refuse on the face of the earth. They shall be consumed by the sword and by famine, and their corpses shall be meat for the birds of heaven and for the beasts of the earth."

5 For thus says the Lord: "Do not enter the house of mourning, nor go to lament or bemoan them; for I have taken away My peace from this people," says the Lord, "lovingkindness and mercies. 6 Both the great and the small shall die in this land. They shall not be buried; neither shall men lament for them, cut themselves, nor make themselves bald for them. 7 Nor shall *men* break *bread* in mourning for them, to comfort them for the dead; nor shall *men* give them the cup of consolation to drink for their father or their mother. 8 Also you shall not go into the house of feasting to sit with them, to eat and drink."

9 For thus says the Lord of hosts, the God of Israel: "Behold, I will cause to cease from this place, before your eyes and in your days, the voice of mirth and the voice of gladness, the voice of the bridegroom and the voice of the bride.

10 "And it shall be, when you show this people all these words, and they say to you, 'Why has the Lord pronounced all this great disaster against us? Or what *is* our iniquity? Or what *is* our sin that we have committed against the Lord our God?' 11 then you shall say to them, 'Because your fathers have forsaken Me,' says the Lord; 'they have walked after other gods and have served them and worshiped them, and have forsaken Me and not kept My law. 12 And you have done worse than your fathers, for behold, each one follows the dictates of his own evil heart, so that no one

listens to Me. 13 Therefore I will cast you out of this land into a land that you do not know, neither you nor your fathers; and there you shall serve other gods day and night, where I will not show you favor.'

14 "Therefore behold, the days are coming," says the Lord, "that it shall no more be said, 'The Lord lives who brought up the children of Israel from the land of Egypt,' 15 but, 'The Lord lives who brought up the children of Israel from the land of the north and from all the lands where He had driven them.' For I will bring them back into their land which I gave to their fathers.

16 "Behold, I will send for many fishermen," says the Lord, "and they shall fish them; and afterward I will send for many hunters, and they shall hunt them from every mountain and every hill, and out of the holes of the rocks. 17 For My eyes *are* on all their ways; they are not hidden from My face, nor is their iniquity hidden from My eyes. 18 And first I will repay double for their iniquity and their sin, because they have defiled My land; they have filled My inheritance with the carcasses of their detestable and abominable idols."

19 O Lord, my strength and my
     fortress,
     My refuge in the day of affliction,
     The Gentiles shall come to You
     From the ends of the earth and say,
     "Surely our fathers have inherited lies,
     Worthlessness and unprofitable
     things."
20 Will a man make gods for himself,
     Which *are* not gods?

21 "Therefore behold, I will this once
     cause them to know,
     I will cause them to know
     My hand and My might;
     And they shall know that My name
     is the Lord.

PSALM 118:21–24

21 I will praise You,
     For You have answered me,
     And have become my salvation.

22 The stone *which* the builders rejected
     Has become the chief cornerstone.
23 This was the Lord's doing;
     It *is* marvelous in our eyes.
24 This *is* the day the Lord has made;
     We will rejoice and be glad in it.

PROVERBS 27:10

10 DO not forsake your own friend
       or your father's friend,
    Nor go to your brother's house in the
       day of your calamity;
    Better *is* a neighbor nearby than a
       brother far away.

1 THESSALONIANS 2:1–20

FOR you yourselves know, brethren, that our coming to you was not in vain. 2 But even after we had suffered before and were spitefully treated at Philippi, as you know, we were bold in our God to speak to you the gospel of God in much conflict.

Virtue can only be the outcome of conflict.   (BRILL. HERITAGE)

---

3 For our exhortation *did* not *come* from error or uncleanness, nor *was it* in deceit.

4 But as we have been approved by God to be entrusted with the gospel, even so we speak, not as pleasing men, but God who tests our hearts. 5 For neither at any time did we use flattering words, as you know, nor a cloak for covetousness—God *is* witness. 6 Nor did we seek glory from men, either from you or from others, when we might have made demands as apostles of Christ. 7 But we were gentle among you, just as a nursing *mother* cherishes her own children. 8 So, affectionately longing for you, we were well pleased to impart to you not only the gospel of God, but also our own lives, because you had become dear

to us. 9 For you remember, brethren, our labor and toil; for laboring night and day, that we might not be a burden to any of you, we preached to you the gospel of God.

10 You *are* witnesses, and God *also,* how devoutly and justly and blamelessly we behaved ourselves among you who believe; 11 as you know how we exhorted, and comforted, and charged every one of you, as a father *does* his own children, 12 that you would walk worthy of God who calls you into His own kingdom and glory.

13 For this reason we also thank God without ceasing, because when you received the word of God which you heard from us, you welcomed *it* not *as* the word of men, but as it is in truth, the word of God, which also effectively works in you who believe. 14 For you, brethren, became imitators of the churches of God which are in Judea in Christ Jesus. For you also suffered the same things from your own countrymen, just as they *did* from the Judeans, 15 who killed both the Lord Jesus and their own prophets, and have persecuted us; and they do not please God and are contrary to all men, 16 forbidding us to speak to the Gentiles that they may be saved, so as always to fill up *the measure of* their sins; but wrath has come upon them to the uttermost.

17 But we, brethren, having been taken away from you for a short time in presence, not in heart, endeavored more eagerly to see your face with great desire. 18 Therefore we wanted to come to you—even I, Paul, time and again—but Satan hindered us. 19 For what *is* our hope, or joy, or crown of rejoicing? *Is it* not even you in the presence of our Lord Jesus Christ at His coming? 20 For you are our glory and joy.

◆◆◆◆

Reading 289—Suffering as a Christian
1 Thessalonians 3:4

To "suffer as a Christian" is not to be marked peculiar because of your views, or because you will not bend to conventionality; these things are not Christian, but ordinary human traits from which all men suffer irrespective of creed or religion or no religion. To "suffer as a Christian" is to suffer because there is an essential difference between you and the world which rouses the contempt of the world, and the disgust and hatred of the spirit that is in the world. To "suffer as a Christian" is to have no answer when the world's satire is turned on you, as it was turned on Jesus Christ when He hung upon the cross, when they turned His words into jest and jeer; they will do the same to you. He gave no answer, neither can you. (CHRIS. DIS. 1)

Let it be said with reverence, even with bated breath, and in the atmosphere of the deepest humility, that suffering "according to the will of God" raises us to a freedom and felicity in the Highest that baffles all language to express. As ever, the only sufficient language is the language of Scripture.

(CHRIS. DIS. 1)

JEREMIAH 17:1—18:23

1 "THE sin of Judah *is* written with a
     pen of iron;
   With the point of a diamond *it is*
     engraved
   On the tablet of their heart,
   And on the horns of your altars,
2 While their children remember
   Their altars and their wooden images
   By the green trees on the high hills.
3 O My mountain in the field,
   I will give as plunder your wealth,
     all your treasures,
   And your high places of sin within
     all your borders.
4 And you, even yourself,
   Shall let go of your heritage which
     I gave you;
   And I will cause you to serve your
     enemies
   In the land which you do not know;
   For you have kindled a fire in My
     anger *which* shall burn forever."

5 Thus says the LORD:

   "Cursed *is* the man who trusts in man
   And makes flesh his strength,
   Whose heart departs from the LORD.
6 For he shall be like a shrub in the
     desert,
   And shall not see when good comes,
   But shall inhabit the parched places
     in the wilderness,
   In a salt land *which is* not inhabited.

7 "Blessed *is* the man who trusts in the
     LORD,
   And whose hope is the LORD.
8 For he shall be like a tree planted
     by the waters,
   Which spreads out its roots by the
     river,
   And will not fear when heat comes;
   But its leaf will be green,
   And will not be anxious in the year
     of drought,
   Nor will cease from yielding fruit.

9 "The heart *is* deceitful above all *things*,
   And desperately wicked;

Who can know it?
10 I, the LORD, search the heart,
    I test the mind,
    Even to give every man according
      to his ways,
    According to the fruit of his doings.

11 "*As* a partridge that broods but does
      not hatch,
    So is he who gets riches, but not by
      right;
    It will leave him in the midst of his
      days,
    And at his end he will be a fool."

12 A glorious high throne from the
      beginning
    Is the place of our sanctuary.
13 O LORD, the hope of Israel,
    All who forsake You shall be
      ashamed.

    "Those who depart from Me
    Shall be written in the earth,
    Because they have forsaken the LORD,
    The fountain of living waters."

14 Heal me, O LORD, and I shall be
      healed;
    Save me, and I shall be saved,
    For You *are* my praise.
15 Indeed they say to me,
    "Where *is* the word of the LORD?
    Let it come now!"
16 As for me, I have not hurried away
      from *being* a shepherd *who* follows
      You,
    Nor have I desired the woeful day;
    You know what came out of my lips;
    It was right there before You.
17 Do not be a terror to me;
    You *are* my hope in the day of doom.
18 Let them be ashamed who persecute
      me,
    But do not let me be put to shame;
    Let them be dismayed,
    But do not let me be dismayed.
    Bring on them the day of doom,
    And destroy them with double
      destruction!

19 Thus the LORD said to me: "Go and stand in the gate of the children of the peo-

ple, by which the kings of Judah come in and by which they go out, and in all the gates of Jerusalem; 20 and say to them, 'Hear the word of the LORD, you kings of Judah, and all Judah, and all the inhabitants of Jerusalem, who enter by these gates. 21 Thus says the LORD: "Take heed to yourselves, and bear no burden on the Sabbath day, nor bring *it* in by the gates of Jerusalem; 22 nor carry a burden out of your houses on the Sabbath day, nor do any work, but hallow the Sabbath day, as I commanded your fathers. 23 But they did not obey nor incline their ear, but made their neck stiff, that they might not hear nor receive instruction.

24 "And it shall be, if you heed Me carefully," says the LORD, "to bring no burden through the gates of this city on the Sabbath day, but hallow the Sabbath day, to do no work in it, 25 then shall enter the gates of this city kings and princes sitting on the throne of David, riding in chariots and on horses, they and their princes, accompanied by the men of Judah and the inhabitants of Jerusalem; and this city shall remain forever. 26 And they shall come from the cities of Judah and from the places around Jerusalem, from the land of Benjamin and from the lowland, from the mountains and from the South, bringing burnt offerings and sacrifices, grain offerings and incense, bringing sacrifices of praise to the house of the LORD.

27 "But if you will not heed Me to hallow the Sabbath day, such as not carrying a burden when entering the gates of Jerusalem on the Sabbath day, then I will kindle a fire in its gates, and it shall devour the palaces of Jerusalem, and it shall not be quenched." ' "

18 THE word which came to Jeremiah from the LORD, saying: 2 "Arise and go down to the potter's house, and there I will cause you to hear My words." 3 Then I went down to the potter's house, and there he was, making something at the wheel. 4 And the vessel that he made of clay was marred in the hand of the potter; so he made it again into another vessel, as it seemed good to the potter to make.

5 Then the word of the LORD came to me, saying: 6 "O house of Israel, can I not do with you as this potter?" says the LORD. "Look, as the clay *is* in the potter's hand, so *are* you in My hand, O house of Israel! 7 The instant I speak concerning a nation and concerning a kingdom, to pluck up, to pull down, and to destroy *it,* 8 if that nation against whom I have spoken turns from its evil, I will relent of the disaster

that I thought to bring upon it. 9 And the instant I speak concerning a nation and concerning a kingdom, to build and to plant *it,* 10 if it does evil in My sight so that it does not obey My voice, then I will relent concerning the good with which I said I would benefit it.

11 "Now therefore, speak to the men of Judah and to the inhabitants of Jerusalem, saying, 'Thus says the LORD: "Behold, I am fashioning a disaster and devising a plan against you. Return now every one from his evil way, and make your ways and your doings good." ' "

12 And they said, "That is hopeless! So we will walk according to our own plans, and we will every one obey the dictates of his evil heart."

13 Therefore thus says the LORD:

> "Ask now among the Gentiles,
> Who has heard such things?
> The virgin of Israel has done a very horrible thing.
> 14 Will *a man* leave the snow water of Lebanon,
> *Which comes* from the rock of the field?
> Will the cold flowing waters be forsaken for strange waters?

> 15 "Because My people have forgotten Me,
> They have burned incense to worthless idols.
> And they have caused themselves to stumble in their ways,
> *From* the ancient paths,
> To walk in pathways and not on a highway,
> 16 To make their land desolate *and* a perpetual hissing;
> Everyone who passes by it will be astonished
> And shake his head.
> 17 I will scatter them as with an east wind before the enemy;
> I will show them the back and not the face
> In the day of their calamity."

18 Then they said, "Come and let us devise plans against Jeremiah; for the law shall not perish from the priest, nor counsel from the wise, nor the word from the prophet. Come and let us attack him with the tongue, and let us not give heed to any of his words."

> 19 Give heed to me, O LORD,
> And listen to the voice of those who contend with me!

20 Shall evil be repaid for good?
    For they have dug a pit for my
      life.
    Remember that I stood before You
    To speak good for them,
    To turn away Your wrath from
      them.
21 Therefore deliver up their children
      to the famine,
    And pour out their *blood*
    By the force of the sword;
    Let their wives *become* widows
    And bereaved of their children.
    Let their men be put to death,
    Their young men *be* slain
    By the sword in battle.
22 Let a cry be heard from their houses,
    When You bring a troop suddenly
      upon them;
    For they have dug a pit to take
      me,
    And hidden snares for my feet.
23 Yet, LORD, You know all their
      counsel
    Which is against me, to slay *me*.
    Provide no atonement for their
      iniquity,
    Nor blot out their sin from Your
      sight;
    But let them be overthrown before
      You.
    Deal *thus* with them
    In the time of Your anger.

PSALM 118:25–29

25 SAVE now, I pray, O LORD;
    O LORD, I pray, send now prosperity.

---

*O*ne of the great words of God
in our spiritual calendar is
NOW.   (GLORIFY)

---

26 Blessed *is* he who comes in the name
      of the LORD!
    We have blessed you from the house
      of the LORD.
27 God *is* the LORD,
    And He has given us light;
    Bind the sacrifice with cords to the
      horns of the altar.
28 You *are* my God, and I will praise You;
    You are my God, I will exalt You.

29 Oh, give thanks to the LORD, for *He
    is* good!
    For His mercy *endures* forever.

PROVERBS 27:11, 12

11 MY son, be wise, and make my heart
      glad,
    That I may answer him who
      reproaches me.

12 A prudent *man* foresees evil *and* hides
      himself;
    The simple pass on *and* are punished.

1 THESSALONIANS 3:1–13

THEREFORE, when we could no longer
endure it, we thought it good to be left
in Athens alone, 2 and sent Timothy, our
brother and minister of God, and our fellow
laborer in the gospel of Christ, to establish
you and encourage you concerning your
faith, 3 that no one should be shaken by
these afflictions; for you yourselves know
that we are appointed to this. 4 For, in fact,
we told you before when we were with
you that we would suffer tribulation, just
as it happened, and you know. 5 For this
reason, when I could no longer endure it,
I sent to know your faith, lest by some
means the tempter had tempted you, and
our labor might be in vain.

6 But now that Timothy has come to us
from you, and brought us good news of
your faith and love, and that you always
have good remembrance of us, greatly desiring to see us, as we also *to see* you— 7 therefore, brethren, in all our affliction and
distress we were comforted concerning
you by your faith. 8 For now we live, if
you stand fast in the Lord.

9 For what thanks can we render to God
for you, for all the joy with which we rejoice
for your sake before our God, 10 night and
day praying exceedingly that we may see
your face and perfect what is lacking in
your faith?

11 Now may our God and Father Himself, and our Lord Jesus Christ, direct our
way to you. 12 And may the Lord make
you increase and abound in love to one
another and to all, just as we *do* to you,

---

*T*he more I love the more blessing
does He pour out on other
lives.   (GOD'S WORKMANSHIP)

---

13 so that He may establish your hearts
blameless in holiness before our God and
Father at the coming of our Lord Jesus
Christ with all His saints.

Reading 290—Is God's Will My Will?
1 Thessalonians 4:3

It is not a question of whether God is willing to sanctify me; is it *my* will? Am I willing to let God do in me all that has been made possible by the Atonement? Am I willing to let Jesus be made sanctification to me, and to let the life of Jesus be manifested in my mortal flesh? Beware of saying—Oh, I am longing to be sanctified. You are not, stop longing and make it a matter of transaction—"Nothing in my hands I bring." Receive Jesus Christ to be made sanctification to you in implicit faith, and the great marvel of the Atonement of Jesus will be made real in you. All that Jesus made possible is made mine by the free loving gift of God on the ground of what He performed, my attitude as a saved and sanctified soul is that of profound humble holiness (there is no such thing as proud holiness), a holiness based on agonizing repentance and a sense of unspeakable shame and degradation; and also on the amazing realization that the love of God commended itself to me in that while I cared nothing about Him, He completed everything for my salvation and sanctification (see Rom. 5:8, RV). No wonder Paul says nothing is "able to separate us from the love of God, which is in Christ Jesus our Lord."

(*UTMOST*)

JEREMIAH 19:1—20:18

THUS says the LORD: "Go and get a potter's earthen flask, and *take* some of the elders of the people and some of the elders of the priests. 2 And go out to the Valley of the Son of Hinnom, which *is* by the entry of the Potsherd Gate; and proclaim there the words that I will tell you, 3 and say, 'Hear the word of the LORD, O kings of Judah and inhabitants of Jerusalem. Thus says the LORD of hosts, the God of Israel: "Behold, I will bring such a catastrophe on this place, that whoever hears of it, his ears will tingle.

4 "Because they have forsaken Me and made this an alien place, because they have burned incense in it to other gods whom neither they, their fathers, nor the kings of Judah have known, and have filled this place with the blood of the innocents 5 (they have also built the high places of Baal, to burn their sons with fire *for* burnt offerings to Baal, which I did not command or speak, nor did it come into My mind), 6 therefore behold, the days are coming," says the LORD, "that this place shall no more be called Tophet or the Valley of the Son of Hinnom, but the Valley of Slaughter. 7 And I will make void the counsel of Judah and Jerusalem in this place, and I will cause them to fall by the sword before their enemies and by the hands of those who seek their lives; their corpses I will give as meat for the birds of the heaven and for the beasts of the earth. 8 I will make this city desolate and a hissing; everyone who passes by it will be astonished and hiss because of all its plagues. 9 And I will cause them to eat the flesh of their sons and the flesh of their daughters, and everyone shall eat the flesh of his friend in the siege and in the desperation with which their enemies and those who seek their lives shall drive them to despair." '

10 "Then you shall break the flask in the sight of the men who go with you, 11 and say to them, 'Thus says the LORD of hosts: "Even so I will break this people and this city, as *one* breaks a potter's vessel, which cannot be made whole again; and they shall bury *them* in Tophet till *there is* no place to bury. 12 Thus I will do to this place," says the LORD, "and to its inhabitants, and make this city like Tophet. 13 And the houses of Jerusalem and the houses of the kings of Judah shall be defiled like the place of Tophet, because of all the houses on whose roofs they have burned incense to all the host of heaven, and poured out drink offerings to other gods." ' "

14 Then Jeremiah came from Tophet, where the LORD had sent him to prophesy; and he stood in the court of the Lord's house and said to all the people, 15 "Thus says the LORD of hosts, the God of Israel: 'Behold, I will bring on this city and on all her towns all the doom that I have pronounced against it, because they have stiffened their necks that they might not hear My words.' "

20 NOW Pashhur the son of Immer, the priest who *was* also chief governor in the house of the LORD, heard that Jeremiah prophesied these things. 2 Then Pashhur struck Jeremiah the prophet, and put him in the stocks that *were* in the high gate of Benjamin, which *was* by the house of the LORD.

3 And it happened on the next day that Pashhur brought Jeremiah out of the stocks. Then Jeremiah said to him, "The LORD has not called your name Pashhur, but Magor-Missabib. 4 For thus says the LORD: 'Behold, I will make you a terror to yourself and to all your friends; and they shall fall by the sword of their enemies, and your eyes shall see *it*. I will give all Judah into the hand of the king of Babylon, and he shall carry them captive to Babylon and slay them with the sword. 5 Moreover I will deliver all the wealth of this city, all its produce, and all its precious things; all the treasures of the kings of Judah I will give into the hand of their enemies, who will plunder them, seize them, and carry them to Babylon. 6 And you, Pashhur, and all who dwell in your house, shall go into captivity. You shall go to Babylon, and there you shall die, and be buried there, you and all your friends, to whom you have prophesied lies.' "

7 O LORD, You induced me, and I was persuaded;
You are stronger than I, and have prevailed.
I am in derision daily;
Everyone mocks me.
8 For when I spoke, I cried out;
I shouted, "Violence and plunder!"
Because the word of the LORD was made to me
A reproach and a derision daily.
9 Then I said, "I will not make mention of Him,
Nor speak anymore in His name."
But *His word* was in my heart like a burning fire
Shut up in my bones;
I was weary of holding *it* back,
And I could not.
10 For I heard many mocking:
"Fear on every side!"
"Report," *they say,* "and we will report it!"
All my acquaintances watched for my stumbling, *saying,*
"Perhaps he can be induced;
Then we will prevail against him,
And we will take our revenge on him."

11 But the LORD *is* with me as a mighty, awesome One.
Therefore my persecutors will stumble, and will not prevail.
They will be greatly ashamed, for they will not prosper.
Their everlasting confusion will never be forgotten.
12 But, O LORD of hosts,
You who test the righteous,
And see the mind and heart,
Let me see Your vengeance on them;
For I have pleaded my cause before You.

13 Sing to the LORD! Praise the LORD!
For He has delivered the life of the poor
From the hand of evildoers.

14 Cursed *be* the day in which I was born!
Let the day not be blessed in which my mother bore me!
15 Let the man *be* cursed
Who brought news to my father, saying,
"A male child has been born to you!"
Making him very glad.
16 And let that man be like the cities
Which the LORD overthrew, and did not relent;
Let him hear the cry in the morning
And the shouting at noon,
17 Because he did not kill me from the womb,
That my mother might have been my grave,
And her womb always enlarged *with me.*
18 Why did I come forth from the womb to see labor and sorrow,
That my days should be consumed with shame?

PSALM 119:1–8

1 BLESSED *are* the undefiled in the way,
Who walk in the law of the LORD!
2 Blessed *are* those who keep His testimonies,
Who seek Him with the whole heart!
3 They also do no iniquity;
They walk in His ways.
4 You have commanded *us*
To keep Your precepts diligently.
5 Oh, that my ways were directed
To keep Your statutes!
6 Then I would not be ashamed,

When I look into all Your
commandments.
7 I will praise You with uprightness of
heart,
When I learn Your righteous
judgments.
8 I will keep Your statutes;
Oh, do not forsake me utterly!

PROVERBS 27:13

13 TAKE the garment of him who is surety
for a stranger,
And hold it in pledge *when* he is surety
for a seductress.

1 THESSALONIANS 4:1–18

FINALLY then, brethren, we urge and exhort in the Lord Jesus that you should
abound more and more, just as you received
from us how you ought to walk and to
please God; 2 for you know what commandments we gave you through the Lord Jesus.
3 For this is the will of God, your sanctification: that you should abstain from sexual
immorality; 4 that each of you should know
how to possess his own vessel in sanctification and honor, 5 not in passion of lust,
like the Gentiles who do not know God;
6 that no one should take advantage of and
defraud his brother in this matter, because
the Lord *is* the avenger of all such, as we
also forewarned you and testified. 7 For
God did not call us to uncleanness, but in
holiness. 8 Therefore he who rejects *this*
does not reject man, but God, who has
also given us His Holy Spirit.

9 But concerning brotherly love you have
no need that I should write to you, for
you yourselves are taught by God to love
one another; 10 and indeed you do so toward all the brethren who are in all Macedonia. But we urge you, brethren, that
you increase more and more; 11 that you
also aspire to lead a quiet life, to mind
your own business, and to work with
your own hands, as we commanded you,

---

*"Study to shut up and mind your
own business."*   (RUN)

---

12 that you may walk properly toward those
who are outside, and *that* you may lack
nothing.
13 But I do not want you to be ignorant,
brethren, concerning those who have fallen
asleep, lest you sorrow as others who have
no hope. 14 For if we believe that Jesus
died and rose again, even so God will bring
with Him those who sleep in Jesus.
15 For this we say to you by the word
of the Lord, that we who are alive *and*
remain until the coming of the Lord will
by no means precede those who are asleep.
16 For the Lord Himself will descend from
heaven with a shout, with the voice of an
archangel, and with the trumpet of God.
And the dead in Christ will rise first.
17 Then we who are alive *and* remain shall
be caught up together with them in the
clouds to meet the Lord in the air. And
thus we shall always be with the Lord.
18 Therefore comfort one another with
these words.

Reading 291—The Value of Calm
1 Thessalonians 5:23

One of the things we need to be cured of by the God of peace is the
petulant struggle of doing things for ourselves—"I can sanctify myself;
if I cut off this and that and the other I shall be all right." No, Paul says, "the
God of peace Himself sanctify you completely" (1 Thess. 5:23). Has the God
of peace brought you into a calm, or is there a clamor and a struggle still?
Are you still hanging onto some obstinate conviction of your own? Still struggling
with some particular line of things you want? "The God of peace Himself
sanctify you completely." If we are to be sanctified, it must be by the God of
peace Himself. The power that makes the life of the saint does not come from
our efforts at all; it comes from the heart of the God of peace.

Some use a phrase, "to pray through." What we have to "pray through" is all our petulant struggling after sanctification, all the inveterate suspicion in our hearts that God cannot sanctify us. When we are rid of all that and are right before God, then God lets us see how He alone does the work.   (*ASK*)

JEREMIAH 21:1—22:30

THE word which came to Jeremiah from the LORD when King Zedekiah sent to him Pashhur the son of Melchiah, and Zephaniah the son of Maaseiah, the priest, saying, 2 "Please inquire of the LORD for us, for Nebuchadnezzar king of Babylon makes war against us. Perhaps the LORD will deal with us according to all His wonderful works, that *the king* may go away from us."

3 Then Jeremiah said to them, "Thus you shall say to Zedekiah, 4 'Thus says the LORD God of Israel: "Behold, I will turn back the weapons of war that *are* in your hands, with which you fight against the king of Babylon and the Chaldeans who besiege you outside the walls; and I will assemble them in the midst of this city. 5 I Myself will fight against you with an outstretched hand and with a strong arm, even in anger and fury and great wrath. 6 I will strike the inhabitants of this city, both man and beast; they shall die of a great pestilence. 7 And afterward," says the LORD, "I will deliver Zedekiah king of Judah, his servants and the people, and such as are left in this city from the pestilence and the sword and the famine, into the hand of Nebuchadnezzar king of Babylon, into the hand of their enemies, and into the hand of those who seek their life; and he shall strike them with the edge of the sword. He shall not spare them, or have pity or mercy." '

8 "Now you shall say to this people, 'Thus says the LORD: "Behold, I set before you the way of life and the way of death. 9 He who remains in this city shall die by the sword, by famine, and by pestilence; but he who goes out and defects to the Chaldeans who besiege you, he shall live, and his life shall be as a prize to him. 10 For I have set My face against this city for adversity and not for good," says the LORD. "It shall be given into the hand of the king of Babylon, and he shall burn it with fire." '

11 "And concerning the house of the king of Judah, *say*, 'Hear the word of the LORD, 12 O house of David! Thus says the LORD:

"Execute judgment in the morning;
    And deliver *him who is* plundered

Out of the hand of the oppressor,
Lest My fury go forth like fire
And burn so that no one can
    quench *it*,
Because of the evil of your doings.

13 "Behold, I *am* against you,
    O inhabitant of the valley,
    And rock of the plain," says the LORD,
"Who say, 'Who shall come down
    against us?
Or who shall enter our dwellings?'
14   But I will punish you according to
    the fruit of your doings," says the
    LORD;
"I will kindle a fire in its forest,
    And it shall devour all things around
    it." ' "

22 THUS says the LORD: "Go down to the house of the king of Judah, and there speak this word, 2 and say, 'Hear the word of the LORD, O king of Judah, you who sit on the throne of David, you and your servants and your people who enter these gates! 3 Thus says the LORD: "Execute judgment and righteousness, and deliver the plundered out of the hand of the oppressor. Do no wrong and do no violence to the stranger, the fatherless, or the widow, nor shed innocent blood in this place. 4 For if you indeed do this thing, then shall enter the gates of this house, riding on horses and in chariots, accompanied by servants and people, kings who sit on the throne of David. 5 But if you will not hear these words, I swear by Myself," says the LORD, "that this house shall become a desolation." ' "

6 For thus says the LORD to the house of the king of Judah:

"You *are* Gilead to Me,
    The head of Lebanon;
    Yet I surely will make you a
        wilderness,
    Cities *which* are not inhabited.
7   I will prepare destroyers against you,
    Everyone with his weapons;
    They shall cut down your choice
        cedars
    And cast *them* into the fire.

8 And many nations will pass by this city; and everyone will say to his neighbor, 'Why

has the LORD done so to this great city?'
9 Then they will answer, 'Because they have
forsaken the covenant of the LORD their
God, and worshiped other gods and served
them.' "

10 Weep not for the dead, nor bemoan
       him;
     Weep bitterly for him who goes
       away,
     For he shall return no more,
     Nor see his native country.

11 For thus says the LORD concerning
Shallum the son of Josiah, king of Judah,
who reigned instead of Josiah his father,
who went from this place: "He shall not
return here anymore, 12 but he shall die
in the place where they have led him captive,
and shall see this land no more.

13 "Woe to him who builds his house
       by unrighteousness
     And his chambers by injustice,
     Who uses his neighbor's service
       without wages
     And gives him nothing for his work,
14   Who says, 'I will build myself a wide
       house with spacious chambers,
     And cut out windows for it,
     Paneling *it* with cedar
     And painting *it* with vermilion.'

15 "Shall you reign because you enclose
       yourself in cedar?
     Did not your father eat and drink,
     And do justice and righteousness?
     Then *it was* well with him.
16   He judged the cause of the poor and
       needy;
     Then *it was* well.
     Was not this knowing Me?" says the
       LORD.
17 "Yet your eyes and your heart *are* for
       nothing but your covetousness,
     For shedding innocent blood,
     And practicing oppression and
       violence."

18 Therefore thus says the LORD concerning Jehoiakim the son of Josiah, king
of Judah:

     "They shall not lament for him,
     Saying, 'Alas, my brother!' or 'Alas,
       my sister!'
     They shall not lament for him,
     Saying, 'Alas, master!' or 'Alas, his
       glory!'
19   He shall be buried with the burial
       of a donkey,

     Dragged and cast out beyond the
       gates of Jerusalem.

20 "Go up to Lebanon, and cry out,
     And lift up your voice in Bashan;
     Cry from Abarim,
     For all your lovers are destroyed.
21   I spoke to you in your prosperity,
     But you said, 'I will not hear.'
     This *has been* your manner from your
       youth,
     That you did not obey My voice.
22   The wind shall eat up all your rulers,
     And your lovers shall go into
       captivity;
     Surely then you will be ashamed and
       humiliated
     For all your wickedness.
23   O inhabitant of Lebanon,
     Making your nest in the cedars,
     How gracious will you be when
       pangs come upon you,
     Like the pain of a woman in labor?

24 "*As* I live," says the LORD, "though
Coniah the son of Jehoiakim, king of Judah,
were the signet on My right hand, yet I
would pluck you off; 25 and I will give you
into the hand of those who seek your life,
and into the hand *of those* whose face you
fear—the hand of Nebuchadnezzar king of
Babylon and the hand of the Chaldeans.
26 So I will cast you out, and your mother
who bore you, into another country where
you were not born; and there you shall
die. 27 But to the land to which they desire
to return, there they shall not return.

28 "Is this man Coniah a despised,
       broken idol—
     A vessel in which *is* no pleasure?
     Why are they cast out, he and his
       descendants,
     And cast into a land which they do
       not know?
29   O earth, earth, earth,
     Hear the word of the LORD!
30   Thus says the LORD:
     'Write this man down as childless,
     A man *who* shall not prosper in his
       days;
     For none of his descendants shall
       prosper,
     Sitting on the throne of David,
     And ruling anymore in Judah.' "

PSALM 119:9–16

9   HOW can a young man cleanse his
       way?

By taking heed according to Your word.

We must let God lift up our experience to the standard of His word. (PSY. REDEMP.)

---

10 With my whole heart I have sought You;
    Oh, let me not wander from Your commandments!
11 Your word I have hidden in my heart,
    That I might not sin against You.
12 Blessed *are* You, O LORD!
    Teach me Your statutes.
13 With my lips I have declared
    All the judgments of Your mouth.
14 I have rejoiced in the way of Your testimonies,
    As *much as* in all riches.
15 I will meditate on Your precepts,
    And contemplate Your ways.
16 I will delight myself in Your statutes;
    I will not forget Your word.

PROVERBS 27:14

14 HE who blesses his friend with a loud voice, rising early in the morning,
   It will be counted a curse to him.

1 THESSALONIANS 5:1–28

BUT concerning the times and the seasons, brethren, you have no need that I should write to you. 2 For you yourselves know perfectly that the day of the Lord so comes as a thief in the night. 3 For when they say, "Peace and safety!" then sudden destruction comes upon them, as labor pains upon a pregnant woman. And they shall not escape. 4 But you, brethren, are not in darkness, so that this Day should overtake you as a thief. 5 You are all sons of light and sons of the day. We are not of the night nor of darkness. 6 Therefore let us not sleep, as others *do*, but let us watch and be sober. 7 For those who sleep, sleep at night, and those who get drunk are drunk at night. 8 But let us who are of the day be sober, putting on the breastplate of faith and love, and *as* a helmet the hope of salvation. 9 For God did not appoint us to wrath, but to obtain salvation through our Lord Jesus Christ, 10 who died for us, that whether we wake or sleep, we should live together with Him.

11 Therefore comfort each other and edify one another, just as you also are doing.

12 And we urge you, brethren, to recognize those who labor among you, and are over you in the Lord and admonish you, 13 and to esteem them very highly in love for their work's sake. Be at peace among yourselves.

14 Now we exhort you, brethren, warn those who are unruly, comfort the fainthearted, uphold the weak, be patient with all. 15 See that no one renders evil for evil to anyone, but always pursue what is good both for yourselves and for all.

16 Rejoice always, 17 pray without ceasing, 18 in everything give thanks; for this is the will of God in Christ Jesus for you.

19 Do not quench the Spirit. 20 Do not despise prophecies. 21 Test all things; hold fast what is good. 22 Abstain from every form of evil.

23 Now may the God of peace Himself sanctify you completely; and may your whole spirit, soul, and body be preserved blameless at the coming of our Lord Jesus Christ. 24 He who calls you *is* faithful, who also will do *it*.

If God can keep you blameless this second, He can do it the next. (LOVE OF GOD)

---

25 Brethren, pray for us.

26 Greet all the brethren with a holy kiss.

27 I charge you by the Lord that this epistle be read to all the holy brethren.

28 The grace of our Lord Jesus Christ *be* with you. Amen.

Reading 292—Christ's Body, the Church
2 Thessalonians 1:1

T he church of Jesus Christ is an organism; we are built up into Him, baptized by one Spirit into one body. Churchianity is an organization; Christianity is an organism. Organization is an enormous benefit until it is mistaken for the life. God has no concern about our organizations. When their purpose is finished He allows them to be swept aside, and if we are attached to the organization, we shall go with it. Organization is a great necessity, but not an end in itself, and to live for any organization is a spiritual disaster. . . .

Our word "church" is connected with civilized organizations of religious people; our Lord's attitude to the church is different. He says it is composed of those who have had a personal revelation from God as to who Jesus Christ is, and have made a public declaration of the same (Matt. 16:13–20).

(Shad. Agony)

JEREMIAH 23:1—24:10

"WOE to the shepherds who destroy and scatter the sheep of My pasture!" says the LORD. 2 Therefore thus says the LORD God of Israel against the shepherds who feed My people: "You have scattered My flock, driven them away, and not attended to them. Behold, I will attend to you for the evil of your doings," says the LORD. 3 "But I will gather the remnant of My flock out of all countries where I have driven them, and bring them back to their folds; and they shall be fruitful and increase. 4 I will set up shepherds over them who will feed them; and they shall fear no more, nor be dismayed, nor shall they be lacking," says the LORD.

5 "Behold, *the* days are coming," says the LORD,
"That I will raise to David a Branch of righteousness;
A King shall reign and prosper,
And execute judgment and righteousness in the earth.
6 In His days Judah will be saved,
And Israel will dwell safely;
Now this *is* His name by which He will be called:

THE LORD OUR RIGHTEOUSNESS.

7 "Therefore, behold, *the* days are coming," says the LORD, "that they shall no longer say, 'As the LORD lives who brought up the children of Israel from the land of Egypt,' 8 but, 'As the LORD lives who brought up and led the descendants of the house of Israel from the north country

and from all the countries where I had driven them.' And they shall dwell in their own land."

9 My heart within me is broken
Because of the prophets;
All my bones shake.
I am like a drunken man,
And like a man whom wine has overcome,
Because of the LORD,
And because of His holy words.
10 For the land is full of adulterers;
For because of a curse the land mourns.
The pleasant places of the wilderness are dried up.
Their course of life is evil,
And their might *is* not right.

11 "For both prophet and priest are profane;
Yes, in My house I have found their wickedness," says the LORD.
12 "Therefore their way shall be to them
Like slippery *ways;*
In the darkness they shall be driven on
And fall in them;
For I will bring disaster on them,
The year of their punishment," says the LORD.
13 "And I have seen folly in the prophets of Samaria:
They prophesied by Baal
And caused My people Israel to err.
14 Also I have seen a horrible thing in the prophets of Jerusalem:
They commit adultery and walk in lies;

They also strengthen the hands of
evildoers,
So that no one turns back from his
wickedness.
All of them are like Sodom to Me,
And her inhabitants like Gomorrah.

15 "Therefore thus says the LORD of
hosts concerning the prophets:

'Behold, I will feed them with
wormwood,
And make them drink the water of
gall;
For from the prophets of Jerusalem
Profaneness has gone out into all the
land.' "

16 Thus says the LORD of hosts:

"Do not listen to the words of the
prophets who prophesy to you.
They make you worthless;
They speak a vision of their own
heart,
Not from the mouth of the LORD.
17 They continually say to those who
despise Me,
'The LORD has said, "You shall have
peace" ';
And *to* everyone who walks according
to the dictates of his own heart,
they say,
'No evil shall come upon you.' "

18 For who has stood in the counsel
of the LORD,
And has perceived and heard His
word?
Who has marked His word and
heard *it*?
19 Behold, a whirlwind of the LORD has
gone forth in fury—
A violent whirlwind!
It will fall violently on the head of
the wicked.
20 The anger of the LORD will not turn
back
Until He has executed and performed
the thoughts of His heart.
In the latter days you will understand
it perfectly.

21 "I have not sent these prophets, yet
they ran.
I have not spoken to them, yet they
prophesied.
22 But if they had stood in My counsel,
And had caused My people to hear
My words,

Then they would have turned them
from their evil way
And from the evil of their doings.

23 "*Am* I a God near at hand," says the
LORD,
"And not a God afar off?
24 Can anyone hide himself in secret
places,
So I shall not see him?" says the
LORD;
"Do I not fill heaven and earth?" says
the LORD.

25 "I have heard what the prophets have
said who prophesy lies in My name, saying,
'I have dreamed, I have dreamed!' 26 How
long will *this* be in the heart of the prophets
who prophesy lies? Indeed *they are* prophets
of the deceit of their own heart, 27 who
try to make My people forget My name
by their dreams which everyone tells his
neighbor, as their fathers forgot My name
for Baal.

28 "The prophet who has a dream, let
him tell a dream;
And he who has My word, let him
speak My word faithfully.
What *is* the chaff to the wheat?" says
the LORD.
29 "*Is* not My word like a fire?" says the
LORD,
"And like a hammer *that* breaks the
rock in pieces?

30 "Therefore behold, I *am* against the
prophets," says the LORD, "who steal My
words every one from his neighbor. 31 Behold, I *am* against the prophets," says the
LORD, "who use their tongues and say, 'He
says.' 32 Behold, I *am* against those who
prophesy false dreams," says the LORD,
"and tell them, and cause My people to
err by their lies and by their recklessness.
Yet I did not send them or command them;
therefore they shall not profit this people
at all," says the LORD.

33 "So when these people or the prophet
or the priest ask you, saying, 'What is the
oracle of the LORD?' you shall then say to
them, 'What oracle?' I will even forsake
you," says the LORD. 34 "And *as for* the
prophet and the priest and the people who
say, 'The oracle of the LORD!' I will even
punish that man and his house. 35 Thus
every one of you shall say to his neighbor,
and every one to his brother, 'What has
the LORD answered?' and, 'What has the
LORD spoken?' 36 And the oracle of the
LORD you shall mention no more. For

every man's word will be his oracle, for you have perverted the words of the living God, the LORD of hosts, our God. 37 Thus you shall say to the prophet, 'What has the LORD answered you?' and, 'What has the LORD spoken?' 38 But since you say, 'The oracle of the LORD!' therefore thus says the LORD: 'Because you say this word, "The oracle of the LORD!" and I have sent to you, saying, "Do not say, 'The oracle of the LORD!'" 39 therefore behold, I, even I, will utterly forget you and forsake you, and the city that I gave you and your fathers, and *will cast you* out of My presence. 40 And I will bring an everlasting reproach upon you, and a perpetual shame, which shall not be forgotten.' "

24 THE LORD showed me, and there were two baskets of figs set before the temple of the LORD, after Nebuchadnezzar king of Babylon had carried away captive Jeconiah the son of Jehoiakim, king of Judah, and the princes of Judah with the craftsmen and smiths, from Jerusalem, and had brought them to Babylon. 2 One basket *had* very good figs, like the figs *that are* first ripe; and the other basket *had* very bad figs which could not be eaten, they were so bad. 3 Then the LORD said to me, "What do you see, Jeremiah?"

And I said, "Figs, the good figs, very good; and the bad, very bad, which cannot be eaten, they are so bad."

4 Again the word of the LORD came to me, saying, 5 "Thus says the LORD, the God of Israel: 'Like these good figs, so will I acknowledge those who are carried away captive from Judah, whom I have sent out of this place for *their own* good, into the land of the Chaldeans. 6 For I will set My eyes on them for good, and I will bring them back to this land; I will build them and not pull *them* down, and I will plant them and not pluck *them* up. 7 Then I will give them a heart to know Me, that I *am* the LORD; and they shall be My people, and I will be their God, for they shall return to Me with their whole heart.

8 'And as the bad figs which cannot be eaten, they are so bad'—surely thus says the LORD—'so will I give up Zedekiah the king of Judah, his princes, the residue of Jerusalem who remain in this land, and those who dwell in the land of Egypt. 9 I will deliver them to trouble into all the kingdoms of the earth, for *their* harm, *to be* a reproach and a byword, a taunt and a curse, in all places where I shall drive them. 10 And I will send the sword, the famine, and the pestilence among them, till they

are consumed from the land that I gave to them and their fathers.' "

PSALM 119:17–24

17 DEAL bountifully with Your servant, *That* I may live and keep Your word.
18 Open my eyes, that I may see Wondrous things from Your law.
19 I *am* a stranger in the earth; Do not hide Your commandments from me.
20 My soul breaks with longing For Your judgments at all times.
21 You rebuke the proud—the cursed, Who stray from Your commandments.
22 Remove from me reproach and contempt, For I have kept Your testimonies.
23 Princes also sit *and* speak against me, *But* Your servant meditates on Your statutes.
24 Your testimonies also *are* my delight *And* my counselors.

PROVERBS 27:15, 16

15 A continual dripping on a very rainy day And a contentious woman are alike;
16 Whoever restrains her restrains the wind, And grasps oil with his right hand.

2 THESSALONIANS 1:1–12

PAUL, Silvanus, and Timothy,

To the church of the Thessalonians in God our Father and the Lord Jesus Christ:

2 Grace to you and peace from God our Father and the Lord Jesus Christ.

3 We are bound to thank God always for you, brethren, as it is fitting, because your faith grows exceedingly, and the love of every one of you all abounds toward each other, 4 so that we ourselves boast of you among the churches of God for your patience and faith in all your persecutions and tribulations that you endure, 5 *which is* manifest evidence of the righteous judgment of God, that you may be counted worthy of the kingdom of God, for which you also suffer; 6 since *it is* a righteous thing with God to repay with tribulation those who trouble you, 7 and to *give* you who are

*They don't know that you carry a
wonderful kingdom within, a
kingdom full of light and peace and
joy.* (SERVANT AS LORD)

troubled rest with us when the Lord Jesus
is revealed from heaven with His mighty
angels, 8 in flaming fire taking vengeance on
those who do not know God, and on those
who do not obey the gospel of our Lord
Jesus Christ. 9 These shall be punished with

everlasting destruction from the presence
of the Lord and from the glory of His
power, 10 when He comes, in that Day,
to be glorified in His saints and to be ad-
mired among all those who believe, because
our testimony among you was believed.

11 Therefore we also pray always for you
that our God would count you worthy of
this calling, and fulfill all the good pleasure
of *His* goodness and the work of faith with
power, 12 that the name of our Lord Jesus
Christ may be glorified in you, and you
in Him, according to the grace of our God
and the Lord Jesus Christ.

◆◆◆

Reading 293—The Solidarity of Sin
2 Thessalonians 2:3, 4

Anything that puts self-realization on top is part of the solidarity of sin,
which the Bible says will head up until it gets to the terrific and marvelous
figurehead Paul refers to in 2 Thessalonians, revered and respected of every
race and religion and nationality. The spirit in man, however religious, however
sweet and delightful it may appear to men, if it is not the Spirit of God must
be "scattering" away from Jesus. "He who does not gather with Me scatters."

Christianity is based on another universe of facts than the universe we get
at by our common sense; it is based on the universe of revelation facts which
we only get at by faith born of the Spirit of God. The revelation which Christianity
makes is that the essential nature of deity is holiness, and the might of God is
shown in that He became the weakest thing in His own creation. Jesus Christ
claims that, on the basis of redemption, He has put the whole of the human
race back to where God designed it to be, and individuals begin to see this
when they are awakened by their own agony.   (*SHAD. AGONY*)

JEREMIAH 25:1—26:24

THE word that came to Jeremiah concerning all the people of Judah, in the fourth
year of Jehoiakim the son of Josiah, king
of Judah (which *was* the first year of Nebuchadnezzar king of Babylon), 2 which Jeremiah the prophet spoke to all the people
of Judah and to all the inhabitants of Jerusalem, saying: 3 "From the thirteenth year of
Josiah the son of Amon, king of Judah,
even to this day, this *is* the twenty-third
year in which the word of the LORD has
come to me; and I have spoken to you,
rising early and speaking, but you have not
listened. 4 And the LORD has sent to you
all His servants the prophets, rising early
and sending *them,* but you have not listened
nor inclined your ear to hear. 5 They said,

'Repent now everyone of his evil way and
his evil doings, and dwell in the land that
the LORD has given to you and your fathers
forever and ever. 6 Do not go after other

*If any man has got out of touch
with God . . . he can get back
now.* (GLORIFY)

gods to serve them and worship them, and
do not provoke Me to anger with the works
of your hands; and I will not harm you.'
7 Yet you have not listened to Me," says
the LORD, "that you might provoke Me
to anger with the works of your hands to
your own hurt.

8 "Therefore thus says the LORD of

hosts: 'Because you have not heard My words, 9 behold, I will send and take all the families of the north,' says the LORD, 'and Nebuchadnezzar the king of Babylon, My servant, and will bring them against this land, against its inhabitants, and against these nations all around, and will utterly destroy them, and make them an astonishment, a hissing, and perpetual desolations. 10 Moreover I will take from them the voice of mirth and the voice of gladness, the voice of the bridegroom and the voice of the bride, the sound of the millstones and the light of the lamp. 11 And this whole land shall be a desolation *and* an astonishment, and these nations shall serve the king of Babylon seventy years.

12 'Then it will come to pass, when seventy years are completed, *that* I will punish the king of Babylon and that nation, the land of the Chaldeans, for their iniquity,' says the LORD; 'and I will make it a perpetual desolation. 13 So I will bring on that land all My words which I have pronounced against it, all that is written in this book, which Jeremiah has prophesied concerning all the nations. 14 (For many nations and great kings shall be served by them also; and I will repay them according to their deeds and according to the works of their own hands.)' "

15 For thus says the LORD God of Israel to me: "Take this wine cup of fury from My hand, and cause all the nations, to whom I send you, to drink it. 16 And they will drink and stagger and go mad because of the sword that I will send among them."

17 Then I took the cup from the LORD's hand, and made all the nations drink, to whom the LORD had sent me: 18 Jerusalem and the cities of Judah, its kings and its princes, to make them a desolation, an astonishment, a hissing, and a curse, as *it is* this day; 19 Pharaoh king of Egypt, his servants, his princes, and all his people; 20 all the mixed multitude, all the kings of the land of Uz, all the kings of the land of the Philistines (namely, Ashkelon, Gaza, Ekron, and the remnant of Ashdod); 21 Edom, Moab, and the people of Ammon; 22 all the kings of Tyre, all the kings of Sidon, and the kings of the coastlands which *are* across the sea; 23 Dedan, Tema, Buz, and all *who are* in the farthest corners; 24 all the kings of Arabia and all the kings of the mixed multitude who dwell in the desert; 25 all the kings of Zimri, all the kings of Elam, and all the kings of the Medes; 26 all the kings of the north, far and near, one with another; and all the kingdoms

of the world which *are* on the face of the earth. Also the king of Sheshach shall drink after them.

27 "Therefore you shall say to them, 'Thus says the LORD of hosts, the God of Israel: "Drink, be drunk, and vomit! Fall and rise no more, because of the sword which I will send among you." ' 28 And it shall be, if they refuse to take the cup from your hand to drink, then you shall say to them, 'Thus says the LORD of hosts: "You shall certainly drink! 29 For behold, I begin to bring calamity on the city which is called by My name, and should you be utterly unpunished? You shall not be unpunished, for I will call for a sword on all the inhabitants of the earth," says the LORD of hosts.'

30 "Therefore prophesy against them all these words, and say to them:

'The LORD will roar from on high,
    And utter His voice from His holy
        habitation;
    He will roar mightily against His
        fold.
    He will give a shout, as those who
        tread *the grapes,*
    Against all the inhabitants of the
        earth.
31   A noise will come to the ends of the
        earth—
    For the LORD has a controversy
        with the nations;
    He will plead His case with all
        flesh.
    He will give those *who are* wicked
        to the sword,' says the LORD."

32 Thus says the LORD of hosts:

"Behold, disaster shall go forth
From nation to nation,
And a great whirlwind shall be
    raised up
From the farthest parts of the earth.

33 "And at that day the slain of the LORD shall be from *one* end of the earth even to the *other* end of the earth. They shall not be lamented, or gathered, or buried; they shall become refuse on the ground.

34 "Wail, shepherds, and cry!
    Roll about in *the ashes,*
    You leaders of the flock!
    For the days of your slaughter and
        your dispersions are fulfilled;
    You shall fall like a precious vessel.
35   And the shepherds will have no way
        to flee,

Nor the leaders of the flock to escape.

36 A voice of the cry of the shepherds,
And a wailing of the leaders to the
flock *will be heard.*
For the LORD has plundered their
pasture,

37 And the peaceful dwellings are cut
down
Because of the fierce anger of the
LORD.

38 He has left His lair like the lion;
For their land is desolate
Because of the fierceness of the
Oppressor,
And because of His fierce anger."

26 IN the beginning of the reign of
Jehoiakim the son of Josiah, king
of Judah, this word came from the LORD,
saying, 2 "Thus says the LORD: 'Stand in
the court of the LORD's house, and speak
to all the cities of Judah, which come to
worship *in* the LORD's house, all the words
that I command you to speak to them. Do
not diminish a word. 3 Perhaps everyone
will listen and turn from his evil way, that
I may relent concerning the calamity which
I purpose to bring on them because of the
evil of their doings.' 4 And you shall say
to them, 'Thus says the LORD: "If you will
not listen to Me, to walk in My law which
I have set before you, 5 to heed the words
of My servants the prophets whom I sent
to you, both rising up early and sending
them (but you have not heeded), 6 then I
will make this house like Shiloh, and will
make this city a curse to all the nations of
the earth." ' "

7 So the priests and the prophets and all
the people heard Jeremiah speaking these
words in the house of the LORD. 8 Now
it happened, when Jeremiah had made an
end of speaking all that the LORD had commanded *him* to speak to all the people, that
the priests and the prophets and all the
people seized him, saying, "You will surely
die! 9 Why have you prophesied in the name
of the LORD, saying, 'This house shall be
like Shiloh, and this city shall be desolate,
without an inhabitant'?" And all the people
were gathered against Jeremiah in the
house of the LORD.

10 When the princes of Judah heard these
things, they came up from the king's house
to the house of the LORD and sat down
in the entry of the New Gate of the LORD's
house. 11 And the priests and the prophets
spoke to the princes and all the people,
saying, "This man deserves to die! For he
has prophesied against this city, as you
have heard with your ears."

12 Then Jeremiah spoke to all the princes
and all the people, saying: "The LORD sent
me to prophesy against this house and
against this city with all the words that you
have heard. 13 Now therefore, amend your
ways and your doings, and obey the voice
of the LORD your God; then the LORD will
relent concerning the doom that He has
pronounced against you. 14 As for me, here
I am, in your hand; do with me as seems
good and proper to you. 15 But know for
certain that if you put me to death, you
will surely bring innocent blood on yourselves, on this city, and on its inhabitants;
for truly the LORD has sent me to you to
speak all these words in your hearing."

16 So the princes and all the people said
to the priests and the prophets, "This man
does not deserve to die. For he has spoken
to us in the name of the LORD our God."

17 Then certain of the elders of the land
rose up and spoke to all the assembly of
the people, saying: 18 "Micah of Moresheth
prophesied in the days of Hezekiah king
of Judah, and spoke to all the people of
Judah, saying, 'Thus says the LORD of hosts:

"Zion shall be plowed *like* a field,
Jerusalem shall become heaps of
ruins,
And the mountain of the temple
Like the bare hills of the forest." '

19 Did Hezekiah king of Judah and all Judah
ever put him to death? Did he not fear
the LORD and seek the LORD's favor? And
the LORD relented concerning the doom
which He had pronounced against them.
But we are doing great evil against ourselves."

20 Now there was also a man who prophesied in the name of the LORD, Urijah the
son of Shemaiah of Kirjath Jearim, who
prophesied against this city and against this
land according to all the words of Jeremiah.
21 And when Jehoiakim the king, with all
his mighty men and all the princes, heard
his words, the king sought to put him to
death; but when Urijah heard *it,* he was
afraid and fled, and went to Egypt.
22 Then Jehoiakim the king sent men to
Egypt: Elnathan the son of Achbor, and
other men *who went* with him to Egypt.
23 And they brought Urijah from Egypt and
brought him to Jehoiakim the king, who
killed him with the sword and cast his dead
body into the graves of the common people.
24 Nevertheless the hand of Ahikam the
son of Shaphan was with Jeremiah, so that
they should not give him into the hand of
the people to put him to death.

PSALM 119:25–32

25 MY soul clings to the dust;
    Revive me according to Your word.
26 I have declared my ways, and You
       answered me;
    Teach me Your statutes.
27 Make me understand the way of Your
       precepts;
    So shall I meditate on Your wonderful
       works.
28 My soul melts from heaviness;
    Strengthen me according to Your
       word.
29 Remove from me the way of lying,
    And grant me Your law graciously.
30 I have chosen the way of truth;
    Your judgments I have laid *before me*.
31 I cling to Your testimonies;
    O LORD, do not put me to shame!
32 I will run the course of Your
       commandments,
    For You shall enlarge my heart.

PROVERBS 27:17

17 *AS* iron sharpens iron,
    So a man sharpens the countenance of
       his friend.

2 THESSALONIANS 2:1–17

NOW, brethren, concerning the coming of our Lord Jesus Christ and our gathering together to Him, we ask you, 2 not to be soon shaken in mind or troubled, either by spirit or by word or by letter, as if from us, as though the day of Christ had come. 3 Let no one deceive you by any means; for *that Day will not come* unless the falling away comes first, and the man of sin is revealed, the son of perdition, 4 who opposes and exalts himself above all that is called God or that is worshiped, so that he sits as God in the temple of God, showing himself that he is God.

5 Do you not remember that when I was still with you I told you these things? 6 And now you know what is restraining, that he may be revealed in his own time. 7 For the mystery of lawlessness is already at work; only He who now restrains *will do so* until He is taken out of the way. 8 And then the lawless one will be revealed, whom the Lord will consume with the breath of His mouth and destroy with the brightness of His coming. 9 The coming of the *lawless one* is according to the working of Satan, with all power, signs, and lying wonders, 10 and with all unrighteous deception among those who perish, because they did not receive the love of the truth, that they might be saved. 11 And for this reason God will send them strong delusion, that they should believe the lie, 12 that they all may be condemned who did not believe the truth but had pleasure in unrighteousness.

13 But we are bound to give thanks to God always for you, brethren beloved by the Lord, because God from the beginning chose you for salvation through sanctification by the Spirit and belief in the truth,

---

Sanctification means that his spirit becomes the birthplace of the Son of God.   (CONFORMED)

---

14 to which He called you by our gospel, for the obtaining of the glory of our Lord Jesus Christ. 15 Therefore, brethren, stand fast and hold the traditions which you were taught, whether by word or our epistle.

16 Now may our Lord Jesus Christ Himself, and our God and Father, who has loved us and given *us* everlasting consolation and good hope by grace, 17 comfort your hearts and establish you in every good word and work.

Reading 294—## Discernment of God
2 Thessalonians 3:10

Paul's counsel is that "if anyone will not work, neither shall he eat." There are plenty of folks who eat but don't work, and they suffer for it. If we are physically healthy, the benefit of the food we eat corresponds to the work we do, and the same is true in mental, moral and spiritual health. The prayer our Lord taught us is full of wisdom along this line, "Give us this day our daily bread." That does not mean that if we do not pray we shall not get it. The word "give" has the sense of "receiving." When we become children of God we receive our daily bread from Him, the basis of blessing lies there, otherwise we take it as an animal with no discernment of God. (*SHADE*)

Our Lord took care to say that "God makes His sun to rise on the evil and on the good, and sends His rain on the just and on the unjust." God's blessings are not to be taken as an indication of the integrity of the character blessed, yet on the other hand the discernment of God's character is determined entirely by the individual character of the person estimating God. (*GENESIS*)

JEREMIAH 27:1—28:17

IN the beginning of the reign of Jehoiakim the son of Josiah, king of Judah, this word came to Jeremiah from the LORD, saying, 2 "Thus says the LORD to me: 'Make for yourselves bonds and yokes, and put them on your neck, 3 and send them to the king of Edom, the king of Moab, the king of the Ammonites, the king of Tyre, and the king of Sidon, by the hand of the messengers who come to Jerusalem to Zedekiah king of Judah. 4 And command them to say to their masters, "Thus says the LORD of hosts, the God of Israel—thus you shall say to your masters: 5 'I have made the earth, the man and the beast that *are* on the ground, by My great power and by My outstretched arm, and have given it to whom it seemed proper to Me. 6 And now I have given all these lands into the hand of Nebuchadnezzar the king of Babylon, My servant; and the beasts of the field I have also given him to serve him. 7 So all nations shall serve him and his son and his son's son, until the time of his land comes; and then many nations and great kings shall make him serve them. 8 And it shall be, *that* the nation and kingdom which will not serve Nebuchadnezzar the king of Babylon, and which will not put its neck under the yoke of the king of Babylon, that nation I will punish,' says the LORD, 'with the sword, the famine, and the pestilence, until I have consumed them by his hand.

9 Therefore do not listen to your prophets, your diviners, your dreamers, your soothsayers, or your sorcerers, who speak to you, saying, "You shall not serve the king of Babylon." 10 For they prophesy a lie to you, to remove you far from your land; and I will drive you out, and you will perish. 11 But the nations that bring their necks under the yoke of the king of Babylon and serve him, I will let them remain in their own land,' says the LORD, 'and they shall till it and dwell in it.' "' "

12 I also spoke to Zedekiah king of Judah according to all these words, saying, "Bring your necks under the yoke of the king of Babylon, and serve him and his people, and live! 13 Why will you die, you and your people, by the sword, by the famine, and by the pestilence, as the LORD has spoken against the nation that will not serve the king of Babylon? 14 Therefore do not listen to the words of the prophets who speak to you, saying, 'You shall not serve the king of Babylon,' for they prophesy a lie to you; 15 for I have not sent them," says the LORD, "yet they prophesy a lie in My name, that I may drive you out, and that you may perish, you and the prophets who prophesy to you."

16 Also I spoke to the priests and to all this people, saying, "Thus says the LORD: 'Do not listen to the words of your prophets who prophesy to you, saying, "Behold, the vessels of the LORD's house will now shortly be brought back from Babylon"; for they

prophesy a lie to you. 17 Do not listen to them; serve the king of Babylon, and live! Why should this city be laid waste? 18 But if they *are* prophets, and if the word of the LORD is with them, let them now make intercession to the LORD of hosts, that the vessels which are left in the house of the LORD, *in* the house of the king of Judah, and at Jerusalem, do not go to Babylon.'

19 "For thus says the LORD of hosts concerning the pillars, concerning the Sea, concerning the carts, and concerning the remainder of the vessels that remain in this city, 20 which Nebuchadnezzar king of Babylon did not take, when he carried away captive Jeconiah the son of Jehoiakim, king of Judah, from Jerusalem to Babylon, and all the nobles of Judah and Jerusalem— 21 yes, thus says the LORD of hosts, the God of Israel, concerning the vessels that remain in the house of the LORD, and in the house of the king of Judah and of Jerusalem: 22 'They shall be carried to Babylon, and there they shall be until the day that I visit them,' says the LORD. 'Then I will bring them up and restore them to this place.' "

28 AND it happened in the same year, at the beginning of the reign of Zedekiah king of Judah, in the fourth year *and* in the fifth month, *that* Hananiah the son of Azur the prophet, who *was* from Gibeon, spoke to me in the house of the LORD in the presence of the priests and of all the people, saying, 2 "Thus speaks the LORD of hosts, the God of Israel, saying: 'I have broken the yoke of the king of Babylon. 3 Within two full years I will bring back to this place all the vessels of the LORD's house, that Nebuchadnezzar king of Babylon took away from this place and carried to Babylon. 4 And I will bring back to this place Jeconiah the son of Jehoiakim, king of Judah, with all the captives of Judah who went to Babylon,' says the LORD, 'for I will break the yoke of the king of Babylon.' "

5 Then the prophet Jeremiah spoke to the prophet Hananiah in the presence of the priests and in the presence of all the people who stood in the house of the LORD, 6 and the prophet Jeremiah said, "Amen! The LORD do so; the LORD perform your words which you have prophesied, to bring back the vessels of the LORD's house and all who were carried away captive, from Babylon to this place. 7 Nevertheless hear now this word that I speak in your hearing and in the hearing of all the people:

8 The prophets who have been before me and before you of old prophesied against many countries and great kingdoms—of war and disaster and pestilence. 9 As for the prophet who prophesies of peace, when the word of the prophet comes to pass, the prophet will be known *as* one whom the LORD has truly sent."

10 Then Hananiah the prophet took the yoke off the prophet Jeremiah's neck and broke it. 11 And Hananiah spoke in the presence of all the people, saying, "Thus says the LORD: 'Even so I will break the yoke of Nebuchadnezzar king of Babylon from the neck of all nations within the space of two full years.' " And the prophet Jeremiah went his way.

12 Now the word of the LORD came to Jeremiah, after Hananiah the prophet had broken the yoke from the neck of the prophet Jeremiah, saying, 13 "Go and tell Hananiah, saying, 'Thus says the LORD: "You have broken the yokes of wood, but you have made in their place yokes of iron." 14 For thus says the LORD of hosts, the God of Israel: "I have put a yoke of iron on the neck of all these nations, that they may serve Nebuchadnezzar king of Babylon; and they shall serve him. I have given him the beasts of the field also." ' "

15 Then the prophet Jeremiah said to Hananiah the prophet, "Hear now, Hananiah, the LORD has not sent you, but you make this people trust in a lie. 16 Therefore thus says the LORD: 'Behold, I will cast you from the face of the earth. This year you shall die, because you have taught rebellion against the LORD.' "

17 So Hananiah the prophet died the same year in the seventh month.

PSALM 119:33–40

33 TEACH me, O LORD, the way of Your statutes,
And I shall keep it *to* the end.
34 Give me understanding, and I shall keep Your law;
Indeed, I shall observe it with *my* whole heart.
35 Make me walk in the path of Your commandments,
For I delight in it.
36 Incline my heart to Your testimonies,
And not to covetousness.
37 Turn away my eyes from looking at worthless things,
And revive me in Your way.
38 Establish Your word to Your servant,
Who *is devoted* to fearing You.

39 Turn away my reproach which I
      dread,
   For Your judgments *are* good.
40 Behold, I long for Your precepts;
   Revive me in Your righteousness.

PROVERBS 27:18

18 WHOEVER keeps the fig tree will eat
     its fruit;
   So he who waits on his master will be
     honored.

2 THESSALONIANS 3:1–18

FINALLY, brethren, pray for us, that the
word of the Lord may run *swiftly* and be
glorified, just as *it is* with you, 2 and that
we may be delivered from unreasonable and
wicked men; for not all have faith.

3 But the Lord is faithful, who will establish you and guard *you* from the evil one.
4 And we have confidence in the Lord concerning you, both that you do and will do
the things we command you.

5 Now may the Lord direct your hearts
into the love of God and into the patience
of Christ.

---

*T*he whole meaning of the
Christian life from our Lord's
standpoint is to be ready for
Him.   (SEND I YOU)

---

6 But we command you, brethren, in the
name of our Lord Jesus Christ, that you
withdraw from every brother who walks
disorderly and not according to the tradition which he received from us. 7 For you
yourselves know how you ought to follow us, for we were not disorderly among
you; 8 nor did we eat anyone's bread
free of charge, but worked with labor and
toil night and day, that we might not be
a burden to any of you, 9 not because
we do not have authority, but to make
ourselves an example of how you should
follow us.

10 For even when we were with you, we
commanded you this: If anyone will not
work, neither shall he eat. 11 For we hear
that there are some who walk among you
in a disorderly manner, not working at all,
but are busybodies. 12 Now those who are
such we command and exhort through our
Lord Jesus Christ that they work in quietness and eat their own bread.

13 But *as for* you, brethren, do not grow
weary *in* doing good. 14 And if anyone does
not obey our word in this epistle, note that
person and do not keep company with him,
that he may be ashamed. 15 Yet do not count
him as an enemy, but admonish *him* as a
brother.

16 Now may the Lord of peace Himself
give you peace always in every way. The
Lord *be* with you all.

17 The salutation of Paul with my own
hand, which is a sign in every epistle; so I
write.

18 The grace of our Lord Jesus Christ
be with you all. Amen.

◆◆◆◆

Reading 295—The Bedrock of Christianity
1 Timothy 1:13–15

Because a man has altered his life it does not necessarily mean that he has
repented. A man may have lived a bad life and suddenly stopped being
bad, not because he has repented, but because he is like an exhausted volcano.
The fact that he has become good is no sign of his having become a Christian.
The bedrock of Christianity is repentance. The apostle Paul never forgot what
he had been; when he speaks of "forgetting those things which are behind,"
he is referring to what he has attained to; the Holy Spirit never allowed him
to forget what he had been (see 1 Cor. 15:9, Eph. 3:8, 1 Tim. 1:13–15).
Repentance means that I estimate exactly what I am in God's sight and I
am sorry for it, and on the basis of the Redemption I become the opposite.
The only repentant man is the holy man, that is, the one who becomes the

opposite of what he was because something has entered into him. Any man who knows himself knows that he cannot be holy; therefore, if he does become holy it is because God has "shipped" something into him; he is now "presenced with Divinity," and can begin to bring forth "fruits worthy of repentance". . .

Jesus Christ's claim is that He can put a new disposition, His own disposition, Holy Spirit, into any man, and it will be manifested in all that he does. But the disposition of the Son of God can only enter my life by the way of repentance. (BAFFLED)

JEREMIAH 29:1—30:24

NOW these *are* the words of the letter that Jeremiah the prophet sent from Jerusalem to the remainder of the elders who were carried away captive—to the priests, the prophets, and all the people whom Nebuchadnezzar had carried away captive from Jerusalem to Babylon. 2 (This happened after Jeconiah the king, the queen mother, the eunuchs, the princes of Judah and Jerusalem, the craftsmen, and the smiths had departed from Jerusalem.) 3 *The letter was sent* by the hand of Elasah the son of Shaphan, and Gemariah the son of Hilkiah, whom Zedekiah king of Judah sent to Babylon, to Nebuchadnezzar king of Babylon, saying,

4   Thus says the LORD of hosts, the God of Israel, to all who were carried away captive, whom I have caused to be carried away from Jerusalem to Babylon:

5   Build houses and dwell *in them;* plant gardens and eat their fruit. 6 Take wives and beget sons and daughters; and take wives for your sons and give your daughters to husbands, so that they may bear sons and daughters—that you may be increased there, and not diminished. 7 And seek the peace of the city where I have caused you to be carried away captive, and pray to the LORD for it; for in its peace you will have peace. 8 For thus says the LORD of hosts, the God of Israel: Do not let your prophets and your diviners who are in your midst deceive you, nor listen to your dreams which you cause to be dreamed. 9 For they prophesy falsely to you in My name; I have not sent them, says the LORD.

10   For thus says the LORD: After seventy years are completed at Babylon, I will visit you and perform My good word toward you, and cause you to return to this place. 11 For I know the thoughts that I think toward you, says the LORD, thoughts of peace and not of evil, to give you a future and a hope. 12 Then you will call upon Me and go and pray to Me, and I will listen to you. 13 And you will seek Me and find *Me,* when you search for Me with all your heart.

There is only one Being who can satisfy the last aching abyss of the human heart. (UTMOST)

---

14 I will be found by you, says the LORD, and I will bring you back from your captivity; I will gather you from all the nations and from all the places where I have driven you, says the LORD, and I will bring you to the place from which I cause you to be carried away captive.

15   Because you have said, "The LORD has raised up prophets for us in Babylon"— 16 therefore thus says the LORD concerning the king who sits on the throne of David, concerning all the people who dwell in this city, and concerning your brethren who have not gone out with you into captivity— 17 thus says the LORD of hosts: Behold, I will send on them the sword, the famine, and the pestilence, and will make them like rotten figs that cannot be eaten, they are so bad. 18 And I will pursue them with the sword, with famine, and with pestilence; and I will deliver them to trouble among all the kingdoms of the earth—to be a curse, an astonishment, a hissing, and a reproach among all the nations where I have driven them, 19 because they

have not heeded My words, says the LORD, which I sent to them by My servants the prophets, rising up early and sending *them;* neither would you heed, says the LORD. 20 Therefore hear the word of the LORD, all you of the captivity, whom I have sent from Jerusalem to Babylon.

21 Thus says the LORD of hosts, the God of Israel, concerning Ahab the son of Kolaiah, and Zedekiah the son of Maaseiah, who prophesy a lie to you in My name: Behold, I will deliver them into the hand of Nebuchadnezzar king of Babylon, and he shall slay them before your eyes. 22 And because of them a curse shall be taken up by all the captivity of Judah who *are* in Babylon, saying, "The LORD make you like Zedekiah and Ahab, whom the king of Babylon roasted in the fire"; 23 because they have done disgraceful things in Israel, have committed adultery with their neighbors' wives, and have spoken lying words in My name, which I have not commanded them. Indeed I know, and *am* a witness, says the LORD.

24 You shall also speak to Shemaiah the Nehelamite, saying, 25 Thus speaks the LORD of hosts, the God of Israel, saying: You have sent letters in your name to all the people who *are* at Jerusalem, to Zephaniah the son of Maaseiah the priest, and to all the priests, saying, 26 "The LORD has made you priest instead of Jehoiada the priest, so that there should be officers *in* the house of the LORD over every man *who* is demented and considers himself a prophet, that you should put him in prison and in the stocks. 27 Now therefore, why have you not rebuked Jeremiah of Anathoth who makes himself a prophet to you? 28 For he has sent to us *in* Babylon, saying, 'This *captivity is* long; build houses and dwell *in them,* and plant gardens and eat their fruit.' "

29 Now Zephaniah the priest read this letter in the hearing of Jeremiah the prophet. 30 Then the word of the LORD came to Jeremiah, saying: 31 Send to all those in captivity, saying, Thus says the LORD concerning Shemaiah the Nehelamite: Because Shemaiah has prophesied to you, and I have not sent him, and he has caused you to trust in a lie— 32 therefore thus says the LORD: Behold, I will punish Shemaiah the Nehelamite and his family: he shall not have anyone to dwell among this people, nor shall he see the good that I will do for My people, says the LORD, because he has taught rebellion against the LORD.

30 THE word that came to Jeremiah from the LORD, saying, 2 "Thus speaks the LORD God of Israel, saying: 'Write in a book for yourself all the words that I have spoken to you. 3 For behold, the days are coming,' says the LORD, 'that I will bring back from captivity My people Israel and Judah,' says the LORD. 'And I will cause them to return to the land that I gave to their fathers, and they shall possess it.' "

4 Now these *are* the words that the LORD spoke concerning Israel and Judah.

5 "For thus says the LORD:

'We have heard a voice of trembling,
Of fear, and not of peace.
6 Ask now, and see,
Whether a man is ever in labor with child?
So why do I see every man *with* his hands on his loins
Like a woman in labor,
And all faces turned pale?
7 Alas! For that day *is* great,
So that none *is* like it;
And it *is* the time of Jacob's trouble,
But he shall be saved out of it.

8 'For it shall come to pass in that day,'
Says the LORD of hosts,
'*That* I will break his yoke from your neck,
And will burst your bonds;
Foreigners shall no more enslave them.
9 But they shall serve the LORD their God,
And David their king,
Whom I will raise up for them.

10 'Therefore do not fear, O My servant Jacob,' says the LORD,
'Nor be dismayed, O Israel;
For behold, I will save you from afar,

And your seed from the land of their
captivity.
Jacob shall return, have rest and be
quiet,
And no one shall make *him* afraid.
11 For I *am* with you,' says the LORD,
'to save you;
Though I make a full end of all
nations where I have scattered you,
Yet I will not make a complete end
of you.
But I will correct you in justice,
And will not let you go altogether
unpunished.'

12 "For thus says the LORD:

'Your affliction *is* incurable,
Your wound *is* severe.
13 *There is* no one to plead your cause,
That you may be bound up;
You have no healing medicines.
14 All your lovers have forgotten you;
They do not seek you;
For I have wounded you with the
wound of an enemy,
With the chastisement of a cruel one,
For the multitude of your iniquities,
Because your sins have increased.
15 Why do you cry about your affliction?
Your sorrow *is* incurable.
Because of the multitude of your
iniquities,
Because your sins have increased,
I have done these things to you.

16 'Therefore all those who devour you
shall be devoured;
And all your adversaries, every one
of them, shall go into captivity;
Those who plunder you shall become
plunder,
And all who prey upon you I will
make a prey.
17 For I will restore health to you
And heal you of your wounds,' says
the LORD,
'Because they called you an outcast
saying:
"This *is* Zion;
No one seeks her." '

18 "Thus says the LORD:

'Behold, I will bring back the captivity
of Jacob's tents,
And have mercy on his dwelling
places;
The city shall be built upon its own
mound,

And the palace shall remain according
to its own plan.
19 Then out of them shall proceed
thanksgiving
And the voice of those who make
merry;
I will multiply them, and they shall
not diminish;
I will also glorify them, and they shall
not be small.
20 Their children also shall be as before,
And their congregation shall be
established before Me;
And I will punish all who oppress
them.
21 Their nobles shall be from among
them,
And their governor shall come from
their midst;
Then I will cause him to draw near,
And he shall approach Me;
For who *is* this who pledged his heart
to approach Me?' says the LORD.
22 'You shall be My people,
And I will be your God.' "

23 Behold, the whirlwind of the LORD
Goes forth with fury,
A continuing whirlwind;
It will fall violently on the head of
the wicked.
24 The fierce anger of the LORD will
not return until He has done it,
And until He has performed the
intents of His heart.

In the latter days you will
consider it.

PSALM 119:41–48

41 LET Your mercies come also to me,
O LORD—
Your salvation according to Your word.
42 So shall I have an answer for him who
reproaches me,
For I trust in Your word.
43 And take not the word of truth utterly
out of my mouth,
For I have hoped in Your ordinances.
44 So shall I keep Your law continually,
Forever and ever.
45 And I will walk at liberty,
For I seek Your precepts.
46 I will speak of Your testimonies also
before kings,
And will not be ashamed.
47 And I will delight myself in Your
commandments,
Which I love.

48 My hands also I will lift up to Your
    commandments,
Which I love,
And I will meditate on Your statutes.

PROVERBS 27:19

19 AS in water face *reflects* face,
So a man's heart *reveals* the man.

1 TIMOTHY 1:1–20

PAUL, an apostle of Jesus Christ, by the
commandment of God our Savior and the
Lord Jesus Christ, our hope,

2 To Timothy, a true son in the faith:

Grace, mercy, *and* peace from God our
Father and Jesus Christ our Lord.
3 As I urged you when I went into Macedonia—remain in Ephesus that you may
charge some that they teach no other doctrine, 4 nor give heed to fables and endless
genealogies, which cause disputes rather
than godly edification which is in faith.
5 Now the purpose of the commandment
is love from a pure heart, *from* a good conscience, and *from* sincere faith, 6 from which
some, having strayed, have turned aside to
idle talk, 7 desiring to be teachers of the
law, understanding neither what they say
nor the things which they affirm.
8 But we know that the law *is* good if
one uses it lawfully, 9 knowing this: that
the law is not made for a righteous person,
but for *the* lawless and insubordinate, for
the ungodly and for sinners, for *the* unholy
and profane, for murderers of fathers and
murderers of mothers, for manslayers,

10 for fornicators, for sodomites, for kid-
nappers, for liars, for perjurers, and if there
is any other thing that is contrary to sound
doctrine, 11 according to the glorious gospel of the blessed God which was committed to my trust.
12 And I thank Christ Jesus our Lord
who has enabled me, because He counted
me faithful, putting *me* into the ministry,
13 although I was formerly a blasphemer,
a persecutor, and an insolent man; but I
obtained mercy because I did *it* ignorantly
in unbelief. 14 And the grace of our Lord
was exceedingly abundant, with faith and
love which are in Christ Jesus. 15 This *is* a
faithful saying and worthy of all acceptance,
that Christ Jesus came into the world to
save sinners, of whom I am chief.

---

*C*onscience will always record
God whenever it has been faced
by God.   (SHAD. AGONY)

---

16 However, for this reason I obtained
mercy, that in me first Jesus Christ might
show all longsuffering, as a pattern to those
who are going to believe on Him for everlasting life. 17 Now to the King eternal, immortal, invisible, to God who alone is wise,
be honor and glory forever and ever. Amen.
18 This charge I commit to you, son
Timothy, according to the prophecies previously made concerning you, that by them
you may wage the good warfare, 19 having
faith and a good conscience, which some
having rejected, concerning the faith have
suffered shipwreck, 20 of whom are Hymenaeus and Alexander, whom I delivered to
Satan that they may learn not to blaspheme.

◆◆◆◆

Reading 296—The Serpent, Eve and Adam
1 Timothy 2:14

E ve, having affinity and sympathy with the other creations around, would
naturally listen with more unsuspecting interest to the suggestions which
came through the subtle creature which spoke to her. The Bible says that Eve
was deceived, it does not say that Adam was deceived; consequently, Adam is
far more responsible than Eve because he sinned deliberately. There was no
conscious intention to disobey in Eve's heart, she was deceived by the subtle
wisdom of Satan *via* the serpent. Adam, however, was not deceived, he sinned
with a deliberate understanding of what he was doing; so the Bible associates
"sin" with Adam ("Therefore, just as through one man sin entered the

world. . . ," Rom. 5:12) and "transgression" with Eve ("And Adam was not deceived, but the woman being deceived was in the transgression").

In this connection it is of importance to note that the Bible reveals that our Redeemer entered into the world through the woman. Man, as man, had no part whatever in the Redemption of the world; it was "the seed of the woman."   (BIB. PSYCH.)

JEREMIAH 31:1—32:44

"AT the same time," says the LORD, "I will be the God of all the families of Israel, and they shall be My people."
   2 Thus says the LORD:

> "The people who survived the sword
> Found grace in the wilderness—
> Israel, when I went to give him rest."

3   The LORD has appeared of old to
      me, *saying:*
   "Yes, I have loved you with an
      everlasting love;
   Therefore with lovingkindness I have
      drawn you.
4   Again I will build you, and you shall
      be rebuilt,
      O virgin of Israel!
   You shall again be adorned with your
      tambourines,
   And shall go forth in the dances of
      those who rejoice.
5   You shall yet plant vines on the
      mountains of Samaria;
   The planters shall plant and eat *them*
      as ordinary food.
6   For there shall be a day
      When the watchmen will cry on
      Mount Ephraim,
   'Arise, and let us go up *to* Zion,
   To the LORD our God.' "

7 For thus says the LORD:

> "Sing with gladness for Jacob,
> And shout among the chief of the
>   nations;
> Proclaim, give praise, and say,
> 'O LORD, save Your people,
> The remnant of Israel!'

8   Behold, I will bring them from the
      north country,
   And gather them from the ends of
      the earth,
   Among them the blind and the lame,
   The woman with child
   And the one who labors with child,
      together;
   A great throng shall return there.

9   They shall come with weeping,
   And with supplications I will lead
      them.
   I will cause them to walk by the rivers
      of waters,
   In a straight way in which they shall
      not stumble;
   For I am a Father to Israel,
   And Ephraim *is* My firstborn.

10 "Hear the word of the LORD,
      O nations,
   And declare *it* in the isles afar off,
      and say,
   'He who scattered Israel will gather
      him,
   And keep him as a shepherd *does* his
      flock.'
11   For the LORD has redeemed Jacob,
   And ransomed him from the hand
      of one stronger than he.
12   Therefore they shall come and sing
      in the height of Zion,
   Streaming to the goodness of the
      LORD—
   For wheat and new wine and oil,
   For the young of the flock and the
      herd;
   Their souls shall be like a
      well-watered garden,
   And they shall sorrow no more
      at all.

13 "Then shall the virgin rejoice in the
      dance,
   And the young men and the old,
      together;
   For I will turn their mourning to
      joy,
   Will comfort them,
   And make them rejoice rather than
      sorrow.
14   I will satiate the soul of the priests
      with abundance,
   And My people shall be satisfied with
      My goodness, says the LORD."

15 Thus says the LORD:

> "A voice was heard in Ramah,
> Lamentation *and* bitter weeping,

Rachel weeping for her children,
Refusing to be comforted for her
  children,
Because they *are* no more."

16 Thus says the Lord:

"Refrain your voice from weeping,
And your eyes from tears;
For your work shall be rewarded, says
  the Lord,
And they shall come back from the
  land of the enemy.
17 There is hope in your future, says
  the Lord,
That *your* children shall come back
  to their own border.

18 "I have surely heard Ephraim
  bemoaning himself:
'You have chastised me, and I was
  chastised,
Like an untrained bull;
Restore me, and I will return,
For You *are* the Lord my God.
19 Surely, after my turning, I repented;
And after I was instructed, I struck
  myself on the thigh;
I was ashamed, yes, even humiliated,
Because I bore the reproach of my
  youth.'
20 *Is* Ephraim My dear son?
Is he a pleasant child?
For though I spoke against him,
I earnestly remember him still;
Therefore My heart yearns for him;
I will surely have mercy on him, says
  the Lord.

21 "Set up signposts,
Make landmarks;
Set your heart toward the highway,
The way in *which* you went.
Turn back, O virgin of Israel,
Turn back to these your cities.
22 How long will you gad about,
O you backsliding daughter?
For the Lord has created a new thing
  in the earth—
A woman shall encompass a man."

23 Thus says the Lord of hosts, the God
of Israel: "They shall again use this speech
in the land of Judah and in its cities, when
I bring back their captivity: 'The Lord bless
you, O home of justice, *and* mountain of
holiness!' 24 And there shall dwell in Judah
itself, and in all its cities together, farmers
and those going out with flocks. 25 For I
have satiated the weary soul, and I have
replenished every sorrowful soul."

26 After this I awoke and looked around,
and my sleep was sweet to me.
27 "Behold, the days are coming, says the
Lord, that I will sow the house of Israel
and the house of Judah with the seed of
man and the seed of beast. 28 And it shall
come to pass, *that* as I have watched over
them to pluck up, to break down, to throw
down, to destroy, and to afflict, so I will
watch over them to build and to plant, says
the Lord. 29 In those days they shall say
no more:

'The fathers have eaten sour grapes,
And the children's teeth are set on
  edge.'

30 But every one shall die for his own iniquity; every man who eats the sour grapes,
his teeth shall be set on edge.
31 "Behold, the days are coming, says the
Lord, when I will make a new covenant
with the house of Israel and with the house
of Judah— 32 not according to the covenant
that I made with their fathers in the day
that I took them by the hand to lead them
out of the land of Egypt, My covenant
which they broke, though I was a husband
to them, says the Lord. 33 But this *is* the
covenant that I will make with the house
of Israel after those days, says the Lord:
I will put My law in their minds, and write
it on their hearts; and I will be their God,
and they shall be My people. 34 No more
shall every man teach his neighbor, and every man his brother, saying, 'Know the
Lord,' for they all shall know Me, from
the least of them to the greatest of them,
says the Lord. For I will forgive their iniquity, and their sin I will remember no
more."

35 Thus says the Lord,
Who gives the sun for a light by day,
The ordinances of the moon and the
  stars for a light by night,
Who disturbs the sea,
And its waves roar
(The Lord of hosts *is* His name):

36 "If those ordinances depart
From before Me, says the Lord,
Then the seed of Israel shall also
  cease
From being a nation before Me
  forever."

37 Thus says the Lord:

"If heaven above can be measured,
And the foundations of the earth
  searched out beneath,

I will also cast off all the seed of Israel For all that they have done, says the LORD.

38 "Behold, the days are coming, says the LORD, that the city shall be built for the LORD from the Tower of Hananel to the Corner Gate. 39 The surveyor's line shall again extend straight forward over the hill Gareb; then it shall turn toward Goath. 40 And the whole valley of the dead bodies and of the ashes, and all the fields as far as the Brook Kidron, to the corner of the Horse Gate toward the east, *shall be* holy to the LORD. It shall not be plucked up or thrown down anymore forever."

32 THE word that came to Jeremiah from the LORD in the tenth year of Zedekiah king of Judah, which was the eighteenth year of Nebuchadnezzar. 2 For then the king of Babylon's army besieged Jerusalem, and Jeremiah the prophet was shut up in the court of the prison, which *was in* the king of Judah's house. 3 For Zedekiah king of Judah had shut him up, saying, "Why do you prophesy and say, 'Thus says the LORD: "Behold, I will give this city into the hand of the king of Babylon, and he shall take it; 4 and Zedekiah king of Judah shall not escape from the hand of the Chaldeans, but shall surely be delivered into the hand of the king of Babylon, and shall speak with him face to face, and see him eye to eye; 5 then he shall lead Zedekiah to Babylon, and there he shall be until I visit him," says the LORD; "though you fight with the Chaldeans, you shall not succeed" '?"

6 And Jeremiah said, "The word of the LORD came to me, saying, 7 'Behold, Hanamel the son of Shallum your uncle will come to you, saying, "Buy my field which *is* in Anathoth, for the right of redemption *is* yours to buy *it*." ' 8 Then Hanamel my uncle's son came to me in the court of the prison according to the word of the LORD, and said to me, 'Please buy my field that *is* in Anathoth, which *is* in the country of Benjamin; for the right of inheritance *is* yours, and the redemption yours; buy *it* for yourself.' Then I knew that this was the word of the LORD. 9 So I bought the field from Hanamel, the son of my uncle who *was* in Anathoth, and weighed *out to* him the money—seventeen shekels of silver. 10 And I signed the deed and sealed *it,* took witnesses, and weighed the money on the scales. 11 So I took the purchase deed, *both* that which was sealed *according* to the law

and custom, and that which was open; 12 and I gave the purchase deed to Baruch the son of Neriah, son of Mahseiah, in the presence of Hanamel my uncle's *son,* and in the presence of the witnesses who signed the purchase deed, before all the Jews who sat in the court of the prison.

13 "Then I charged Baruch before them, saying, 14 'Thus says the LORD of hosts, the God of Israel: "Take these deeds, both this purchase deed which is sealed and this deed which is open, and put them in an earthen vessel, that they may last many days." 15 For thus says the LORD of hosts, the God of Israel: "Houses and fields and vineyards shall be possessed again in this land." '

16 "Now when I had delivered the purchase deed to Baruch the son of Neriah, I prayed to the LORD, saying: 17 'Ah, Lord GOD! Behold, You have made the heavens and the earth by Your great power and outstretched arm. There is nothing too hard for You. 18 *You* show lovingkindness to thousands, and repay the iniquity of the fathers into the bosom of their children after them—the Great, the Mighty God, whose name *is* the LORD of hosts. 19 *You are* great in counsel and mighty in work, for your eyes *are* open to all the ways of the sons of men, to give everyone according to his ways and according to the fruit of his doings. 20 You have set signs and wonders in the land of Egypt, to this day, and in Israel and among *other* men; and You have made Yourself a name, as it is this day. 21 You have brought Your people Israel out of the land of Egypt with signs and wonders, with a strong hand and an outstretched arm, and with great terror; 22 You have given them this land, of which You swore to their fathers to give them— "a land flowing with milk and honey." 23 And they came in and took possession of it, but they have not obeyed Your voice or walked in Your law. They have done nothing of all that You commanded them to do; therefore You have caused all this calamity to come upon them.

24 'Look, the siege mounds! They have come to the city to take it; and the city has been given into the hand of the Chaldeans who fight against it, because of the sword and famine and pestilence. What You have spoken has happened; there You see it! 25 And You have said to me, O Lord GOD, "Buy the field for money, and take witnesses"!—yet the city has been given into the hand of the Chaldeans.' "

26 Then the word of the LORD came to Jeremiah, saying, 27 "Behold, I *am* the

LORD, the God of all flesh. Is there anything too hard for Me? 28 Therefore thus says the LORD: 'Behold, I will give this city into the hand of the Chaldeans, into the hand of Nebuchadnezzar king of Babylon, and he shall take it. 29 And the Chaldeans who fight against this city shall come and set fire to this city and burn it, with the houses on whose roofs they have offered incense to Baal and poured out drink offerings to other gods, to provoke Me to anger; 30 because the children of Israel and the children of Judah have done only evil before Me from their youth. For the children of Israel have provoked Me only to anger with the work of their hands,' says the LORD. 31 'For this city has been to Me *a provocation of* My anger and My fury from the day that they built it, even to this day; so I will remove it from before My face 32 because of all the evil of the children of Israel and the children of Judah, which they have done to provoke Me to anger—they, their kings, their princes, their priests, their prophets, the men of Judah, and the inhabitants of Jerusalem. 33 And they have turned to Me the back, and not the face; though I taught them, rising up early and teaching *them,* yet they have not listened to receive instruction. 34 But they set their abominations in the house which is called by My name, to defile it. 35 And they built the high places of Baal which *are* in the Valley of the Son of Hinnom, to cause their sons and their daughters to pass through *the fire* to Molech, which I did not command them, nor did it come into My mind that they should do this abomination, to cause Judah to sin.'

36 "Now therefore, thus says the LORD, the God of Israel, concerning this city of which you say, 'It shall be delivered into the hand of the king of Babylon by the sword, by the famine, and by the pestilence: 37 Behold, I will gather them out of all countries where I have driven them in My anger, in My fury, and in great wrath; I will bring them back to this place, and I will cause them to dwell safely. 38 They shall be My people, and I will be their God; 39 then I will give them one heart and one way, that they may fear Me forever, for the good of them and their children after them. 40 And I will make an everlasting covenant with them, that I will not turn away from doing them good; but I will put My fear in their hearts so that they will not depart from Me. 41 Yes, I will rejoice over them to do them good, and I will assuredly plant them in this land, with all My heart and with all My soul.'

42 "For thus says the LORD: 'Just as I have brought all this great calamity on this people, so I will bring on them all the good that I have promised them. 43 And fields will be bought in this land of which you say, "*It is* desolate, without man or beast; it has been given into the hand of the Chaldeans." 44 Men will buy fields for money, sign deeds and seal *them,* and take witnesses, in the land of Benjamin, in the places around Jerusalem, in the cities of Judah, in the cities of the mountains, in the cities of the lowland, and in the cities of the South; for I will cause their captives to return,' says the LORD."

PSALM 119:49–56

49 REMEMBER the word to Your servant,
Upon which You have caused me to hope.
50 This *is* my comfort in my affliction,
For Your word has given me life.
51 The proud have me in great derision,
Yet I do not turn aside from Your law.
52 I remembered Your judgments of old, O LORD,
And have comforted myself.
53 Indignation has taken hold of me
Because of the wicked, who forsake Your law.
54 Your statutes have been my songs
In the house of my pilgrimage.
55 I remember Your name in the night, O LORD,
And I keep Your law.
56 This has become mine,
Because I kept Your precepts.

PROVERBS 27:20

20 HELL and Destruction are never full;
So the eyes of man are never satisfied.

1 TIMOTHY 2:1–15

THEREFORE I exhort first of all that supplications, prayers, intercessions, *and* giving of thanks be made for all men, 2 for kings and all who are in authority, that we may lead a quiet and peaceable life in all godliness and reverence. 3 For this *is* good and acceptable in the sight of God our Savior, 4 who desires all men to be saved and to come to the knowledge of the truth.

5 For *there is* one God and one Mediator between God and men, *the* Man Christ Jesus, 6 who gave Himself a ransom for all, to be testified in due time, 7 for which I was appointed a preacher and an apostle—I am speaking the truth in Christ *and* not lying—a teacher of the Gentiles in faith and truth.

8 I desire therefore that the men pray everywhere, lifting up holy hands, without wrath and doubting; 9 in like manner also, that the women adorn themselves in modest apparel, with propriety and moderation, not with braided hair or gold or pearls or costly clothing, 10 but, which is proper for women professing godliness, with good works. 11 Let a woman learn in silence with all submission. 12 And I do not permit a woman to teach or to have authority over a man, but to be in silence. 13 For Adam was formed first, then Eve. 14 And Adam was not deceived, but the woman being deceived, fell into transgression. 15 Never-

---

*T*he full force of God's judgment comes on the man, not on the woman.   (NOT KNOWING)

---

theless she will be saved in childbearing if they continue in faith, love, and holiness, with self-control.

◆◆◆◆

Reading 297—Truth in the House of God
1 Timothy 3:15

*T*he central truth is not Salvation, nor Sanctification, nor the Second Coming; the central truth is nothing less than Jesus Christ Himself. "I, if I am lifted up from the earth, will draw all *peoples* to Myself." Error always comes in when we take something Jesus Christ does and preach it as the truth. It is part of the truth, but if we take it to be the whole truth we become advocates of an idea instead of a Person, the Lord Himself.   (*SERMON MT.*)

The Truth is our Lord Himself; consequently, any part of the truth may be a lie unless it leads to a relation to *the* Truth. Salvation, sanctification, the Second Coming are all parts of the Truth, but none is the Truth; and they are only parts of the Truth as they are absorbed by the Truth, our Lord Himself.   (*PERFECT*)

The Personality of Truth is the great revelation of Christianity—"I am the Truth." Our Lord did not say He was "all truth" so that we could go to His statements as to a textbook and verify things; there are domains, such as science and art and history, which are distinctly man's domains and the boundaries of our knowledge must continually alter and be enlarged; God never encourages laziness.   (*GOD'S WORKMANSHIP*)

JEREMIAH 33:1—34:22

MOREOVER the word of the LORD came to Jeremiah a second time, while he was still shut up in the court of the prison, saying, 2 "Thus says the LORD who made it, the LORD who formed it to establish it (the LORD *is* His name): 3 'Call to Me, and I will answer you, and show you great and mighty things, which you do not know.'

4 "For thus says the LORD, the God of Israel, concerning the houses of this city and the houses of the kings of Judah, which have been pulled down *to fortify* against the siege mounds and the sword: 5 'They come to fight with the Chaldeans, but *only* to fill their places with the dead bodies of men whom I will slay in My anger and My fury, all for whose wickedness I have hidden My face from this city. 6 Behold, I will bring it health and healing; I will heal them and

reveal to them the abundance of peace and truth. 7 And I will cause the captives of Judah and the captives of Israel to return, and will rebuild those places as at the first. 8 I will cleanse them from all their iniquity by which they have sinned against Me, and I will pardon all their iniquities by which they have sinned and by which they have transgressed against Me. 9 Then it shall be to Me a name of joy, a praise, and an honor before all nations of the earth, who shall hear all the good that I do to them; they shall fear and tremble for all the goodness and all the prosperity that I provide for it.'

10 "Thus says the LORD: 'Again there shall be heard in this place—of which you say, "It *is* desolate, without man and without beast"—in the cities of Judah, in the streets of Jerusalem that are desolate, without man and without inhabitant and without beast, 11 the voice of joy and the voice of gladness, the voice of the bridegroom and the voice of the bride, the voice of those who will say:

"Praise the LORD of hosts,
    For the LORD *is* good,
    For His mercy *endures* forever"—

and of those *who will* bring the sacrifice of praise into the house of the LORD. For I will cause the captives of the land to return as at the first,' says the LORD.

12 "Thus says the LORD of hosts: 'In this place which is desolate, without man and without beast, and in all its cities, there shall again be a dwelling place of shepherds causing *their* flocks to lie down. 13 In the cities of the mountains, in the cities of the lowland, in the cities of the South, in the land of Benjamin, in the places around Jerusalem, and in the cities of Judah, the flocks shall again pass under the hands of him who counts *them*,' says the LORD.

14 'Behold, the days are coming,' says the LORD, 'that I will perform that good thing which I have promised to the house of Israel and to the house of Judah:

15 'In those days and at that time
    I will cause to grow up to David
    A Branch of righteousness;
    He shall execute judgment and
        righteousness in the earth.
16 In those days Judah will be saved,
    And Jerusalem will dwell safely.
    And this *is the name* by which she
        will be called:

THE LORD OUR RIGHTEOUSNESS.'

17 "For thus says the LORD: 'David shall never lack a man to sit on the throne of the house of Israel; 18 nor shall the priests, the Levites, lack a man to offer burnt offerings before Me, to kindle grain offerings, and to sacrifice continually.'"

19 And the word of the LORD came to Jeremiah, saying, 20 "Thus says the LORD: 'If you can break My covenant with the day and My covenant with the night, so that there will not be day and night in their season, 21 then My covenant may also be broken with David My servant, so that he shall not have a son to reign on his throne, and with the Levites, the priests, My ministers. 22 As the host of heaven cannot be numbered, nor the sand of the sea measured, so will I multiply the descendants of David My servant and the Levites who minister to Me.'"

23 Moreover the word of the LORD came to Jeremiah, saying, 24 "Have you not considered what these people have spoken, saying, 'The two families which the LORD has chosen, He has also cast them off'? Thus they have despised My people, as if they should no more be a nation before them.

25 "Thus says the LORD: 'If My covenant *is* not with day and night, *and if* I have not appointed the ordinances of heaven and earth, 26 then I will cast away the descendants of Jacob and David My servant, *so* that I will not take *any* of his descendants *to be* rulers over the descendants of Abraham, Isaac, and Jacob. For I will cause their captives to return, and will have mercy on them.'"

34 THE word which came to Jeremiah from the LORD, when Nebuchadnezzar king of Babylon and all his army, all the kingdoms of the earth under his dominion, and all the people, fought against Jerusalem and all its cities, saying, 2 "Thus says the LORD, the God of Israel: 'Go and speak to Zedekiah king of Judah and tell him, "Thus says the LORD: 'Behold, I will give this city into the hand of the king of Babylon, and he shall burn it with fire. 3 And you shall not escape from his hand, but shall surely be taken and delivered into his hand; your eyes shall see the eyes of the king of Babylon, he shall speak with you face to face, and you shall go to Babylon.'"' 4 Yet hear the word of the LORD, O Zedekiah king of Judah! Thus says the LORD concerning you: 'You shall not die by the sword. 5 You shall die in peace; as

in the ceremonies of your fathers, the former kings who were before you, so they shall burn incense for you and lament for you, *saying*, "Alas, lord!" For I have pronounced the word, says the LORD.' "

6 Then Jeremiah the prophet spoke all these words to Zedekiah king of Judah in Jerusalem, 7 when the king of Babylon's army fought against Jerusalem and all the cities of Judah that were left, against Lachish and Azekah; for *only* these fortified cities remained of the cities of Judah.

8 *This is* the word that came to Jeremiah from the LORD, after King Zedekiah had made a covenant with all the people who *were* at Jerusalem to proclaim liberty to them: 9 that every man should set free his male and female slave—a Hebrew man or woman—that no one should keep a Jewish brother in bondage. 10 Now when all the princes and all the people, who had entered into the covenant, heard that everyone should set free his male and female slaves, that no one should keep them in bondage anymore, they obeyed and let *them* go. 11 But afterward they changed their minds and made the male and female slaves return, whom they had set free, and brought them into subjection as male and female slaves.

12 Therefore the word of the LORD came to Jeremiah from the LORD, saying, 13 "Thus says the LORD, the God of Israel: 'I made a covenant with your fathers in the day that I brought them out of the land of Egypt, out of the house of bondage, saying, 14 "At the end of seven years let every man set free his Hebrew brother, who has been sold to him; and when he has served you six years, you shall let him go free from you." But your fathers did not obey Me nor incline their ear. 15 Then you recently turned and did what was right in My sight—every man proclaiming liberty to his neighbor; and you made a covenant before Me in the house which is called by My name. 16 Then you turned around and profaned My name, and every one of you brought back his male and female slaves, whom he had set at liberty, at their pleasure, and brought them back into subjection, to be your male and female slaves.'

17 "Therefore thus says the LORD: 'You have not obeyed Me in proclaiming liberty, every one to his brother and every one to his neighbor. Behold, I proclaim liberty to you,' says the LORD—'to the sword, to pestilence, and to famine! And I will deliver you to trouble among all the kingdoms of the earth. 18 And I will give the men who have transgressed My covenant, who have not performed the words of the covenant which they made before Me, when they cut the calf in two and passed between the parts of it— 19 the princes of Judah, the princes of Jerusalem, the eunuchs, the priests, and all the people of the land who passed between the parts of the calf— 20 I will give them into the hand of their enemies and into the hand of those who seek their life. Their dead bodies shall be for meat for the birds of the heaven and the beasts of the earth. 21 And I will give Zedekiah king of Judah and his princes into the hand of their enemies, into the hand of those who seek their life, and into the hand of the king of Babylon's army which has gone back from you. 22 Behold, I will command,' says the LORD, 'and cause them to return to this city. They will fight against it and take it and burn it with fire; and I will make the cities of Judah a desolation without inhabitant.' "

PSALM 119:57–64

57 YOU *are* my portion, O LORD;
I have said that I would keep Your words.
58 I entreated Your favor with *my* whole heart;
Be merciful to me according to Your word.
59 I thought about my ways,
And turned my feet to Your testimonies.
60 I made haste, and did not delay
To keep Your commandments.
61 The cords of the wicked have bound me,
But I have not forgotten Your law.
62 At midnight I will rise to give thanks to You,
Because of Your righteous judgments.
63 I *am* a companion of all who fear You,
And of those who keep Your precepts.
64 The earth, O LORD, is full of Your mercy;
Teach me Your statutes.

PROVERBS 27:21

21 THE refining pot *is* for silver and the furnace for gold,
And a man *is valued* by what others say of him.

1 TIMOTHY 3:1–16

THIS *is* a faithful saying: If a man desires the position of a bishop, he desires a good work. 2 A bishop then must be blameless, the husband of one wife, temperate, soberminded, of good behavior, hospitable, able to teach; 3 not given to wine, not violent, not greedy for money, but gentle, not quarrelsome, not covetous; 4 one who rules his own house well, having *his* children in submission with all reverence 5 (for if a man does not know how to rule his own house, how will he take care of the church of God?); 6 not a novice, lest being puffed up with pride he fall into the *same* condemnation as the devil. 7 Moreover he must have a good testimony among those who are outside, lest he fall into reproach and the snare of the devil.

8 Likewise deacons *must be* reverent, not double-tongued, not given to much wine, not greedy for money, 9 holding the mystery of the faith with a pure conscience. 10 But let these also first be tested; then let them serve as deacons, being *found* blameless. 11 Likewise, *their* wives *must be* reverent, not slanderers, temperate, faithful in all things. 12 Let deacons be the husbands of one wife, ruling *their* children and their own houses well. 13 For those who have

served well as deacons obtain for themselves a good standing and great boldness in the faith which is in Christ Jesus.

14 These things I write to you, though I hope to come to you shortly; 15 but if I am delayed, *I write* so that you may know how you ought to conduct yourself in the house of God, which is the church of the living God, the pillar and ground of the truth. 16 And without controversy great is the mystery of godliness:

> God was manifested in the flesh,
> Justified in the Spirit,
> Seen by angels,
> Preached among the Gentiles,
> Believed on in the world,
> Received up in glory.

A lmighty God is nothing but a mental abstraction unless He becomes concrete and actual.   (BAFFLED)

Reading 298—The Harness of Meditation
1 Timothy 4:15

Meditation is not being like a pebble in a brook, allowing the waters of thought to flow over us; that is reverie. Meditation is the most intense spiritual act, it brings every part of body and mind into harness. To be spiritual by effort is a sure sign of a false relationship to God; to be obedient by effort in the initial stages is a sure sign that we are determined to obey God at all costs. Take time. Remember we have all the time there is. The majority of us waste time and want to encroach on eternity. "Oh well, I will think about these things when I have time." The only time you will have is the day after you are dead, and that will be eternity. An hour, or half an hour, of daily attention to, and meditation on, our own spiritual life is the secret of progress.   (*MORAL FOUND.*)

There is a quietism of devotional self-indulgence which takes the place spiritually that loafing does socially. It is easy to call it meditative prayer, but meditation is only attained in actual life by the strenuous discipline of brooding in the center of a subject. . . . . A saint is never consciously a praying one. A saint endeavors consciously and strenuously to master the technical means of expressing God's life in himself. The place of prayer in the New Testament is just this one of severe technical training in which spiritual sympathies are sustained in unsecular strength, and manifested in the vulgar details of actual life.   (*PRAYER*)

JEREMIAH 35:1—36:32

THE word which came to Jeremiah from the LORD in the days of Jehoiakim the son of Josiah, king of Judah, saying, 2 "Go to the house of the Rechabites, speak to them, and bring them into the house of the LORD, into one of the chambers, and give them wine to drink."

3 Then I took Jaazaniah the son of Jeremiah, the son of Habazziniah, his brothers and all his sons, and the whole house of the Rechabites, 4 and I brought them into the house of the LORD, into the chamber of the sons of Hanan the son of Igdaliah, a man of God, which *was* by the chamber of the princes, above the chamber of Maaseiah the son of Shallum, the keeper of the door. 5 Then I set before the sons of the house of the Rechabites bowls full of wine, and cups; and I said to them, "Drink wine."

6 But they said, "We will drink no wine, for Jonadab the son of Rechab, our father, commanded us, saying, 'You shall drink no wine, you nor your sons, forever. 7 You shall not build a house, sow seed, plant a vineyard, nor have *any of these;* but all your days you shall dwell in tents, that you may live many days in the land where you are sojourners.' 8 Thus we have obeyed the voice of Jonadab the son of Rechab, our father, in all that he charged us, to drink no wine all our days, we, our wives, our sons, or our daughters, 9 nor to build ourselves houses to dwell in; nor do we have vineyard, field, or seed. 10 But we have dwelt in tents, and have obeyed and done according to all that Jonadab our father commanded us. 11 But it came to pass, when Nebuchadnezzar king of Babylon came up into the land, that we said, 'Come, let us go to Jerusalem for fear of the army of the Chaldeans and for fear of the army of the Syrians.' So we dwell at Jerusalem."

12 Then came the word of the LORD to Jeremiah, saying, 13 "Thus says the LORD of hosts, the God of Israel: 'Go and tell the men of Judah and the inhabitants of Jerusalem, "Will you not receive instruction to obey My words?" says the LORD. 14 "The words of Jonadab the son of Rechab, which he commanded his sons, not to drink wine, are performed; for to this day they drink none, and obey their father's commandment. But although I have spoken to you, rising early and speaking, you did not obey Me. 15 I have also sent to you all My servants the prophets, rising up early and sending *them,* saying, 'Turn now everyone from his evil way, amend your doings, and do not go after other gods to serve them; then you will dwell in the land which I have given you and your fathers.' But you have not inclined your ear, nor obeyed Me. 16 Surely the sons of Jonadab the son of Rechab have performed the commandment of their father, which he commanded them, but this people has not obeyed Me." '

17 "Therefore thus says the LORD God of hosts, the God of Israel: 'Behold, I will bring on Judah and on all the inhabitants of Jerusalem all the doom that I have pronounced against them; because I have spoken to them but they have not heard, and I have called to them but they have not answered.' "

18 And Jeremiah said to the house of the Rechabites, "Thus says the LORD of hosts, the God of Israel: 'Because you have obeyed the commandment of Jonadab your father, and kept all his precepts and done according to all that he commanded you, 19 therefore thus says the LORD of hosts, the God of Israel: "Jonadab the son of Rechab shall not lack a man to stand before Me forever." ' "

36 NOW it came to pass in the fourth year of Jehoiakim the son of Josiah, king of Judah, *that* this word came to Jeremiah from the LORD, saying: 2 "Take a scroll of a book and write on it all the words that I have spoken to you against Israel, against Judah, and against all the nations, from the day I spoke to you, from the days of Josiah even to this day. 3 It may be that the house of Judah will hear all the adversities which I purpose to bring upon them, that everyone may turn from his evil way, that I may forgive their iniquity and their sin."

4 Then Jeremiah called Baruch the son of Neriah; and Baruch wrote on a scroll of a book, at the instruction of Jeremiah, all the words of the LORD which He had spoken to him. 5 And Jeremiah commanded Baruch, saying, "I *am* confined, I cannot go into the house of the LORD. 6 You go, therefore, and read from the scroll which you have written at my instruction, the words of the LORD, in the hearing of the people in the LORD's house on the day of fasting. And you shall also read them in the hearing of all Judah who come from their cities. 7 It may be that they will present their supplication before the LORD, and everyone will turn from his evil way. For great *is* the anger and the fury that the LORD has pronounced against this people." 8 And Baruch the son of Neriah did according to all that Jeremiah the prophet com-

manded him, reading from the book the words of the LORD in the LORD's house.

9 Now it came to pass in the fifth year of Jehoiakim the son of Josiah, king of Judah, in the ninth month, *that* they proclaimed a fast before the LORD to all the people in Jerusalem, and to all the people who came from the cities of Judah to Jerusalem. 10 Then Baruch read from the book the words of Jeremiah in the house of the LORD, in the chamber of Gemariah the son of Shaphan the scribe, in the upper court at the entry of the New Gate of the LORD's house, in the hearing of all the people.

11 When Michaiah the son of Gemariah, the son of Shaphan, heard all the words of the LORD from the book, 12 he then went down to the king's house, into the scribe's chamber; and there all the princes were sitting—Elishama the scribe, Delaiah the son of Shemaiah, Elnathan the son of Achbor, Gemariah the son of Shaphan, Zedekiah the son of Hananiah, and all the princes. 13 Then Michaiah declared to them all the words that he had heard when Baruch read the book in the hearing of the people. 14 Therefore all the princes sent Jehudi the son of Nethaniah, the son of Shelemiah, the son of Cushi, to Baruch, saying, "Take in your hand the scroll from which you have read in the hearing of the people, and come." So Baruch the son of Neriah took the scroll in his hand and came to them. 15 And they said to him, "Sit down now, and read it in our hearing." So Baruch read *it* in their hearing.

16 Now it happened, when they had heard all the words, that they looked in fear from one to another, and said to Baruch, "We will surely tell the king of all these words." 17 And they asked Baruch, saying, "Tell us now, how did you write all these words—at his instruction?"

18 So Baruch answered them, "He proclaimed with his mouth all these words to me, and I wrote *them* with ink in the book."

19 Then the princes said to Baruch, "Go and hide, you and Jeremiah; and let no one know where you are."

20 And they went to the king, into the court; but they stored the scroll in the chamber of Elishama the scribe, and told all the words in the hearing of the king. 21 So the king sent Jehudi to bring the scroll, and he took it from Elishama the scribe's chamber. And Jehudi read it in the hearing of the king and in the hearing of all the princes who stood beside the king. 22 Now the king was sitting in the winter house in the ninth month, with *a fire* burning on the hearth before him. 23 And it happened, when Jehudi had read three or four columns, *that the king* cut it with the scribe's knife and cast *it* into the fire that *was* on the hearth, until all the scroll was consumed in the fire that *was* on the hearth. 24 Yet they were not afraid, nor did they tear their garments, the king nor any of his servants who heard all these words. 25 Nevertheless Elnathan, Delaiah, and Gemariah implored the king not to burn the scroll; but he would not listen to them. 26 And the king commanded Jerahmeel the king's son, Seraiah the son of Azriel, and Shelemiah the son of Abdeel, to seize Baruch the scribe and Jeremiah the prophet, but the LORD hid them.

27 Now after the king had burned the scroll with the words which Baruch had written at the instruction of Jeremiah, the word of the LORD came to Jeremiah, saying: 28 "Take yet another scroll, and write on it all the former words that were in the first scroll which Jehoiakim the king of Judah has burned. 29 And you shall say to Jehoiakim king of Judah, 'Thus says the LORD: "You have burned this scroll, saying, 'Why have you written in it that the king of Babylon will certainly come and destroy this land, and cause man and beast to cease from here?'" 30 Therefore thus says the LORD concerning Jehoiakim king of Judah: "He shall have no one to sit on the throne of David, and his dead body shall be cast out to the heat of the day and the frost of the night. 31 I will punish him, his family, and his servants for their iniquity; and I will bring on them, on the inhabitants of Jerusalem, and on the men of Judah all the doom that I have pronounced against them; but they did not heed."'"

32 Then Jeremiah took another scroll and gave it to Baruch the scribe, the son of Neriah, who wrote on it at the instruction of Jeremiah all the words of the book which Jehoiakim king of Judah had burned in the fire. And besides, there were added to them many similar words.

PSALM 119:65–72

65 YOU have dealt well with Your servant,
    O LORD, according to Your word.
66 Teach me good judgment and
       knowledge,
    For I believe Your commandments.
67 Before I was afflicted I went astray,
    But now I keep Your word.
68 You *are* good, and do good;
    Teach me Your statutes.

69 The proud have forged a lie against me,
   But I will keep Your precepts with *my*
   whole heart.
70 Their heart is as fat as grease,
   But I delight in Your law.
71 *It is* good for me that I have been
   afflicted,
   That I may learn Your statutes.
72 The law of Your mouth *is* better
   to me
   Than thousands of *coins of* gold and
   silver.

PROVERBS 27:22

22 THOUGH you grind a fool in a mortar
   with a pestle along with crushed
   grain,
   Yet his foolishness will not depart from
   him.

1 TIMOTHY 4:1–16

NOW the Spirit expressly says that in latter times some will depart from the faith, giving heed to deceiving spirits and doctrines of demons, 2 speaking lies in hypocrisy, having their own conscience seared with a hot iron, 3 forbidding to marry, *and commanding* to abstain from foods which God created to be received with thanksgiving by those who believe and know the truth. 4 For every creature of God *is* good, and nothing is to be refused if it is received with thanksgiving; 5 for it is sanctified by the word of God and prayer.

6 If you instruct the brethren in these things, you will be a good minister of Jesus Christ, nourished in the words of faith and of the good doctrine which you have carefully followed. 7 But reject profane and old wives' fables, and exercise yourself toward godliness. 8 For bodily exercise profits a little, but godliness is profitable for all things, having promise of the life that now is and of that which is to come. 9 This *is* a faithful saying and worthy of all acceptance. 10 For to this *end* we both labor and suffer reproach, because we trust in the living God, who is *the* Savior of all men, especially of those who believe. 11 These things command and teach.

12 Let no one despise your youth, but be an example to the believers in word, in conduct, in love, in spirit, in faith, in purity. 13 Till I come, give attention to reading, to exhortation, to doctrine. 14 Do not neglect the gift that is in you, which was given to you by prophecy with the laying on of the hands of the eldership. 15 Meditate on

---

I have to learn to identify myself with God's interests in other people.   (PLACE HELP)

---

these things; give yourself entirely to them, that your progress may be evident to all. 16 Take heed to yourself and to the doctrine. Continue in them, for in doing this you will save both yourself and those who hear you.

◆◆◆

Reading 299—The Fact of Sickness
1 Timothy 5:23

The Bible attitude [toward sickness] is not that God sends sickness or that sickness is of the Devil, but that sickness is a fact usable by both God and the Devil. Never base a principle on your own experience. My personal experience is this: I have never once in my life been sick without being to blame for it. As soon as I turned my mind to asking why the sickness was allowed, I learned a lesson that I have never forgotten, namely, that my physical health depends absolutely on my relationship to God.   (*PHIL. SIN*)

The fact of health and the fact of sickness are there; we have nothing to do with choosing them, they come and go. We have to get on to another platform, the moral platform, and then the spiritual platform, before we can begin to get an explanation of these facts.   (*PHIL. SIN*)

JEREMIAH 37:1—38:28

NOW King Zedekiah the son of Josiah reigned instead of Coniah the son of Jehoiakim, whom Nebuchadnezzar king of Babylon made king in the land of Judah. 2 But neither he nor his servants nor the people of the land gave heed to the words of the LORD which He spoke by the prophet Jeremiah.

3 And Zedekiah the king sent Jehucal the son of Shelemiah, and Zephaniah the son of Maaseiah, the priest, to the prophet Jeremiah, saying, "Pray now to the LORD our God for us." 4 Now Jeremiah was coming and going among the people, for they had not *yet* put him in prison. 5 Then Pharaoh's army came up from Egypt; and when the Chaldeans who were besieging Jerusalem heard news of them, they departed from Jerusalem.

We have to realize that prayer is stupid from the ordinary common-sense point of view. (UTMOST)

---

6 Then the word of the LORD came to the prophet Jeremiah, saying, 7 "Thus says the LORD, the God of Israel, 'Thus you shall say to the king of Judah, who sent you to Me to inquire of Me: "Behold, Pharaoh's army which has come up to help you will return to Egypt, to their own land. 8 And the Chaldeans shall come back and fight against this city, and take it and burn it with fire." ' 9 Thus says the LORD: 'Do not deceive yourselves, saying, "The Chaldeans will surely depart from us," for they will not depart. 10 For though you had defeated the whole army of the Chaldeans who fight against you, and there remained *only* wounded men among them, they would rise up, every man in his tent, and burn the city with fire.' "

11 And it happened, when the army of the Chaldeans left *the siege* of Jerusalem for fear of Pharaoh's army, 12 that Jeremiah went out of Jerusalem to go into the land of Benjamin to claim his property there among the people. 13 And when he was in the Gate of Benjamin, a captain of the guard *was* there whose name *was* Irijah the son of Shelemiah, the son of Hananiah; and he seized Jeremiah the prophet, saying, "You are defecting to the Chaldeans!"

14 Then Jeremiah said, "False! I am not defecting to the Chaldeans." But he did not listen to him.

So Irijah seized Jeremiah and brought him to the princes. 15 Therefore the princes were angry with Jeremiah, and they struck him and put him in prison in the house of Jonathan the scribe. For they had made that the prison.

16 When Jeremiah entered the dungeon and the cells, and Jeremiah had remained there many days, 17 then Zedekiah the king sent and took him *out*. The king asked him secretly in his house, and said, "Is there *any* word from the LORD?"

And Jeremiah said, "There is." Then he said, "You shall be delivered into the hand of the king of Babylon!"

18 Moreover Jeremiah said to King Zedekiah, "What offense have I committed against you, against your servants, or against this people, that you have put me in prison? 19 Where now *are* your prophets who prophesied to you, saying, 'The king of Babylon will not come against you or against this land?' 20 Therefore please hear now, O my lord the king. Please, let my petition be accepted before you, and do not make me return to the house of Jonathan the scribe, lest I die there."

21 Then Zedekiah the king commanded that they should commit Jeremiah to the court of the prison, and that they should give him daily a piece of bread from the bakers' street, until all the bread in the city was gone. Thus Jeremiah remained in the court of the prison.

38 NOW Shephatiah the son of Mattan, Gedaliah the son of Pashhur, Jucal the son of Shelemiah, and Pashhur the son of Malchiah heard the words that Jeremiah had spoken to all the people, saying, 2 "Thus says the LORD: 'He who remains in this city shall die by the sword, by famine, and by pestilence; but he who goes over to the Chaldeans shall live; his life shall be as a prize to him, and he shall live.' 3 Thus says the LORD: 'This city shall surely be given into the hand of the king of Babylon's army, which shall take it.' "

4 Therefore the princes said to the king, "Please, let this man be put to death, for thus he weakens the hands of the men of war who remain in this city, and the hands of all the people, by speaking such words to them. For this man does not seek the welfare of this people, but their harm."

5 Then Zedekiah the king said, "Look, he *is* in your hand. For the king can *do* nothing against you." 6 So they took Jeremiah and cast him into the dungeon of

Malchiah the king's son, which *was* in the court of the prison, and they let Jeremiah down with ropes. And in the dungeon *there was* no water, but mire. So Jeremiah sank in the mire.

7 Now Ebed-Melech the Ethiopian, one of the eunuchs, who was in the king's house, heard that they had put Jeremiah in the dungeon. When the king was sitting at the Gate of Benjamin, 8 Ebed-Melech went out of the king's house and spoke to the king, saying: 9 "My lord the king, these men have done evil in all that they have done to Jeremiah the prophet, whom they have cast into the dungeon, and he is likely to die from hunger in the place where he is. For *there is* no more bread in the city." 10 Then the king commanded Ebed-Melech the Ethiopian, saying, "Take from here thirty men with you, and lift Jeremiah the prophet out of the dungeon before he dies." 11 So Ebed-Melech took the men with him and went into the house of the king under the treasury, and took from there old clothes and old rags, and let them down by ropes into the dungeon to Jeremiah. 12 Then Ebed-Melech the Ethiopian said to Jeremiah, "Please put these old clothes and rags under your armpits, under the ropes." And Jeremiah did so. 13 So they pulled Jeremiah up with ropes and lifted him out of the dungeon. And Jeremiah remained in the court of the prison.

14 Then Zedekiah the king sent and had Jeremiah the prophet brought to him at the third entrance of the house of the LORD. And the king said to Jeremiah, "I will ask you something. Hide nothing from me."

15 Jeremiah said to Zedekiah, "If I declare *it* to you, will you not surely put me to death? And if I give you advice, you will not listen to me."

16 So Zedekiah the king swore secretly to Jeremiah, saying, "*As* the LORD lives, who made our very souls, I will not put you to death, nor will I give you into the hand of these men who seek your life."

17 Then Jeremiah said to Zedekiah, "Thus says the LORD, the God of hosts, the God of Israel: 'If you surely surrender to the king of Babylon's princes, then your soul shall live; this city shall not be burned with fire, and you and your house shall live. 18 But if you do not surrender to the king of Babylon's princes, then this city shall be given into the hand of the Chaldeans; they shall burn it with fire, and you shall not escape from their hand.' "

19 And Zedekiah the king said to Jeremiah, "I am afraid of the Jews who have defected to the Chaldeans, lest they deliver me into their hand, and they abuse me."

20 But Jeremiah said, "They shall not deliver *you*. Please, obey the voice of the LORD which I speak to you. So it shall be well with you, and your soul shall live. 21 But if you refuse to surrender, this *is* the word that the LORD has shown me: 22 'Now behold, all the women who are left in the king of Judah's house *shall be* surrendered to the king of Babylon's princes, and those *women* shall say:

"Your close friends have set upon you
And prevailed against you;
Your feet have sunk in the mire,
And they have turned away again.'

23 'So they shall surrender all your wives and children to the Chaldeans. You shall not escape from their hand, but shall be taken by the hand of the king of Babylon. And you shall cause this city to be burned with fire.' "

24 Then Zedekiah said to Jeremiah, "Let no one know of these words, and you shall not die. 25 But if the princes hear that I have talked with you, and they come to you and say to you, 'Declare to us now what you have said to the king, and also what the king said to you; do not hide *it* from us, and we will not put you to death,' 26 then you shall say to them, 'I presented my request before the king, that he would not make me return to Jonathan's house to die there.' "

27 Then all the princes came to Jeremiah and asked him. And he told them according to all these words that the king had commanded. So they stopped speaking with him, for the conversation had not been heard. 28 Now Jeremiah remained in the court of the prison until the day that Jerusalem was taken. And he was *there* when Jerusalem was taken.

PSALM 119:73–80

73 YOUR hands have made me and fashioned me;
Give me understanding, that I may learn Your commandments.
74 Those who fear You will be glad when they see me,
Because I have hoped in Your word.
75 I know, O LORD, that Your judgments *are* right,
And *that* in faithfulness You have afflicted me.
76 Let, I pray, Your merciful kindness be for my comfort,

According to Your word to Your servant.

Prayer is not meant to develop us, but to develop the life of God in us.   (PSY. REDEMP.)

---

77 Let Your tender mercies come to me,
      that I may live;
      For Your law *is* my delight.
78 Let the proud be ashamed,
      For they treated me wrongfully with
      falsehood;
      But I will meditate on Your precepts.
79 Let those who fear You turn to me,
      Those who know Your testimonies.
80 Let my heart be blameless regarding
      Your statutes,
      That I may not be ashamed.

PROVERBS 27:23–27

23 BE diligent to know the state of your
      flocks,
      And attend to your herds;
24 For riches *are* not forever,
      Nor does a crown *endure* to all
      generations.
25 *When* the hay is removed, and the
      tender grass shows itself,
      And the herbs of the mountains are
      gathered in,
26 The lambs *will provide* your clothing,
      And the goats the price of a field;
27 *You shall have* enough goats' milk for
      your food,
      For the food of your household,
      And the nourishment of your
      maidservants.

1 TIMOTHY 5:1–25

DO not rebuke an older man, but exhort *him* as a father, younger men as brothers, 2 older women as mothers, younger women as sisters, with all purity.
3 Honor widows who are really widows. 4 But if any widow has children or grandchildren, let them first learn to show piety at home and to repay their parents; for this is good and acceptable before God. 5 Now she who is really a widow, and left

alone, trusts in God and continues in supplications and prayers night and day. 6 But she who lives in pleasure is dead while she lives. 7 And these things command, that they may be blameless. 8 But if anyone does not provide for his own, and especially for those of his household, he has denied the faith and is worse than an unbeliever.

9 Do not let a widow under sixty years old be taken into the number, *and not unless* she has been the wife of one man, 10 well reported for good works: if she has brought up children, if she has lodged strangers, if she has washed the saints' feet, if she has relieved the afflicted, if she has diligently followed every good work.

11 But refuse *the* younger widows; for when they have begun to grow wanton against Christ, they desire to marry, 12 having condemnation because they have cast off their first faith. 13 And besides they learn *to be* idle, wandering about from house to house, and not only idle but also gossips and busybodies, saying things which they ought not. 14 Therefore I desire that *the* younger *widows* marry, bear children, manage the house, give no opportunity to the adversary to speak reproachfully. 15 For some have already turned aside after Satan. 16 If any believing man or woman has widows, let them relieve them, and do not let the church be burdened, that it may relieve those who are really widows.

17 Let the elders who rule well be counted worthy of double honor, especially those who labor in the word and doctrine. 18 For the Scripture says, "You shall not muzzle an ox while it treads out the grain," and, "The laborer *is* worthy of his wages." 19 Do not receive an accusation against an elder except from two or three witnesses. 20 Those who are sinning rebuke in the presence of all, that the rest also may fear. 21 I charge *you* before God and the Lord Jesus Christ and the elect angels that you observe these things without prejudice, doing nothing with partiality. 22 Do not lay hands on anyone hastily, nor share in other people's sins; keep yourself pure.

23 No longer drink only water, but use a little wine for your stomach's sake and your frequent infirmities.

24 Some men's sins are clearly evident, preceding *them* to judgment, but those of some *men* follow later. 25 Likewise, the good works *of some* are clearly evident, and those that are otherwise cannot be hidden.

Reading 300—God's Useless Superabundance
1 Timothy 6:17–19

To use the word "economy" in connection with God is to belittle and misunderstand Him. Where is the economy of God in His sunsets and sunrises, in the grass and flowers and trees? God has made a superabounding number of things that are of no *use* to anyone. How many of us bother our heads about the sunrises and sunsets? Yet they go on just the same. Lavish extravagance to an extraordinary degree is the characteristic of God, never economy. Grace is the overflowing favor of God. Imagine a man who is in love being economical! The characteristic of a man when he is awake is never that he is calculating and sensible.

Today we are so afraid of poverty that we never dream of doing anything that might involve us in being poor. We are out of the running of the medieval monks who took on the vow of poverty. Many of us are poor, but none of us chooses to be. These men chose to be poor, they believed it was the only way they could perfect their own inner life. Our attitude is that if we are extravagant a rainy day will come for which we have not laid up. You cannot lay up for a rainy day and justify it in the light of Jesus Christ's teaching. We are not Christians at heart, we don't believe in the wisdom of God, but only in our own. We go in for insurance and economy and speculation, everything that makes us secure in our own wisdom. (SHADE)

JEREMIAH 39:1—40:16

IN the ninth year of Zedekiah king of Judah, in the tenth month, Nebuchadnezzar king of Babylon and all his army came against Jerusalem, and besieged it. 2 In the eleventh year of Zedekiah, in the fourth month, on the ninth *day* of the month, the city was penetrated.

3 Then all the princes of the king of Babylon came in and sat in the Middle Gate: Nergal-Sharezer, Samgar-Nebo, Sarsechim, Rabsaris, Nergal-Sarezer, Rabmag, with the rest of the princes of the king of Babylon.

4 So it was, when Zedekiah the king of Judah and all the men of war saw them, that they fled and went out of the city by night, by way of the king's garden, by the gate between the two walls. And he went out by way of the plain. 5 But the Chaldean army pursued them and overtook Zedekiah in the plains of Jericho. And when they had captured him, they brought him up to Nebuchadnezzar king of Babylon, to Riblah in the land of Hamath, where he pronounced judgment on him. 6 Then the king of Babylon killed the sons of Zedekiah before his eyes in Riblah; the king of Babylon also killed all the nobles of Judah. 7 Moreover he put out Zedekiah's eyes, and bound him with bronze fetters to carry him off to Babylon. 8 And the Chaldeans burned the king's house and the houses of the people with fire, and broke down the walls of Jerusalem. 9 Then Nebuzaradan the captain of the guard carried away captive to Babylon the remnant of the people who remained in the city and those who defected to him, with the rest of the people who remained. 10 But Nebuzaradan the captain of the guard left in the land of Judah the poor people, who had nothing, and gave them vineyards and fields at the same time.

11 Now Nebuchadnezzar king of Babylon gave charge concerning Jeremiah to Nebuzaradan the captain of the guard, saying, 12 "Take him and look after him, and do him no harm; but do to him just as he says to you." 13 So Nebuzaradan the captain of the guard sent Nebushasban, Rabsaris, Nergal-Sharezer, Rabmag, and all the king of Babylon's chief officers; 14 then they sent *someone* to take Jeremiah from the court of the prison, and committed him to Gedaliah the son of Ahikam, the son of Shaphan, that he should take him home. So he dwelt among the people.

15 Meanwhile the word of the LORD had come to Jeremiah while he was shut up in the court of the prison, saying, 16 "Go and speak to Ebed-Melech the Ethiopian, saying, 'Thus says the LORD of hosts, the God

of Israel: "Behold, I will bring My words upon this city for adversity and not for good, and they shall be *performed* in that day before you. 17 But I will deliver you in that day," says the LORD, "and you shall not be given into the hand of the men of whom you *are* afraid. 18 For I will surely deliver you, and you shall not fall by the sword; but your life shall be as a prize to you, because you have put your trust in Me," says the LORD.' "

40 THE word that came to Jeremiah from the LORD after Nebuzaradan the captain of the guard had let him go from Ramah, when he had taken him bound in chains among all who were carried away captive from Jerusalem and Judah, who were carried away captive to Babylon.

2 And the captain of the guard took Jeremiah and said to him: "The LORD your God has pronounced this doom on this place. 3 Now the LORD has brought *it,* and has done just as He said. Because you *people* have sinned against the LORD, and not obeyed His voice, therefore this thing has come upon you. 4 And now look, I free you this day from the chains that *were* on your hand. If it seems good to you to come with me to Babylon, come, and I will look after you. But if it seems wrong for you to come with me to Babylon, remain here. See, all the land *is* before you; wherever it seems good and convenient for you to go, go there."

5 Now while Jeremiah had not yet gone back, *Nebuzaradan said,* "Go back to Gedaliah the son of Ahikam, the son of Shaphan, whom the king of Babylon has made governor over the cities of Judah, and dwell with him among the people. Or go wherever it seems convenient for you to go." So the captain of the guard gave him rations and a gift and let him go. 6 Then Jeremiah went to Gedaliah the son of Ahikam, to Mizpah, and dwelt with him among the people who were left in the land.

7 And when all the captains of the armies who *were* in the fields, they and their men, heard that the king of Babylon had made Gedaliah the son of Ahikam governor in the land, and had committed to him men, women, children, and the poorest of the land who had not been carried away captive to Babylon, 8 then they came to Gedaliah at Mizpah—Ishmael the son of Nethaniah, Johanan and Jonathan the sons of Kareah, Seraiah the son of Tanhumeth, the sons of Ephai the Netophathite, and Jezaniah the son of a Maachathite, they and their men. 9 And Gedaliah the son of Ahikam,

the son of Shaphan, took an oath before them and their men, saying, "Do not be afraid to serve the Chaldeans. Dwell in the land and serve the king of Babylon, and it shall be well with you. 10 As for me, I will indeed dwell at Mizpah and serve the Chaldeans who come to us. But you, gather wine and summer fruit and oil, put *them* in your vessels, and dwell in your cities that you have taken." 11 Likewise, when all the Jews who *were* in Moab, among the Ammonites, in Edom, and who *were* in all the countries, heard that the king of Babylon had left a remnant of Judah, and that he had set over them Gedaliah the son of Ahikam, the son of Shaphan, 12 then all the Jews returned out of all places where they had been driven, and came to the land of Judah, to Gedaliah at Mizpah, and gathered wine and summer fruit in abundance.

13 Moreover Johanan the son of Kareah and all the captains of the forces that *were* in the fields came to Gedaliah at Mizpah, 14 and said to him, "Do you certainly know that Baalis the king of the Ammonites has sent Ishmael the son of Nethaniah to murder you?" But Gedaliah the son of Ahikam did not believe them.

15 Then Johanan the son of Kareah spoke secretly to Gedaliah in Mizpah, saying, "Let me go, please, and I will kill Ishmael the son of Nethaniah, and no one will know *it.* Why should he murder you, so that all the Jews who are gathered to you would be scattered, and the remnant in Judah perish?"

16 But Gedaliah the son of Ahikam said to Johanan the son of Kareah, "You shall not do this thing, for you speak falsely concerning Ishmael."

PSALM 119:81–88

81 MY soul faints for Your salvation,
But I hope in Your word.
82 My eyes fail *from searching* Your word,
Saying, "When will You comfort me?"
83 For I have become like a wineskin in smoke,
Yet I do not forget Your statutes.
84 How many *are* the days of Your servant?
When will You execute judgment on those who persecute me?
85 The proud have dug pits for me,
Which *is* not according to Your law.
86 All Your commandments *are* faithful;
They persecute me wrongfully;
Help me!

87 They almost made an end of me on
   earth,
   But I did not forsake Your precepts.
88 Revive me according to Your
   lovingkindness,
   So that I may keep the testimony of
   Your mouth.

PROVERBS 28:1

1 THE wicked flee when no one
  pursues,
  But the righteous are bold as a lion.

1 TIMOTHY 6:1–21

LET as many bondservants as are under
the yoke count their own masters worthy
of all honor, so that the name of God and
His doctrine may not be blasphemed.
2 And those who have believing masters,
let them not despise *them* because they are
brethren, but rather serve *them* because
those who are benefited are believers and
beloved. Teach and exhort these things.

3 If anyone teaches otherwise and does
not consent to wholesome words, *even* the
words of our Lord Jesus Christ, and to
the doctrine which accords with godliness,
4 he is proud, knowing nothing, but is obsessed with disputes and arguments over
words, from which come envy, strife, reviling, evil suspicions, 5 useless wranglings of
men of corrupt minds and destitute of the
truth, who suppose that godliness is a *means
of* gain. From such withdraw yourself.

6 Now godliness with contentment is
great gain. 7 For we brought nothing into
this world, *and it is* certain we can carry
nothing out. 8 And having food and clothing, with these we shall be content.
9 But those who desire to be rich fall into
temptation and a snare, and *into* many foolish and harmful lusts which drown men
in destruction and perdition. 10 For the love

of money is a root of all *kinds of* evil, for
which some have strayed from the faith in
their greediness, and pierced themselves
through with many sorrows.

---

*One of the most besmirching
impurities lies in money
matters.*   (LOVE OF GOD)

---

11 But you, O man of God, flee these
things and pursue righteousness, godliness,
faith, love, patience, gentleness. 12 Fight the
good fight of faith, lay hold on eternal life,
to which you were also called and have confessed the good confession in the presence
of many witnesses. 13 I urge you in the sight
of God who gives life to all things, and
before Christ Jesus who witnessed the good
confession before Pontius Pilate, 14 that you
keep *this* commandment without spot,
blameless until our Lord Jesus Christ's appearing, 15 which He will manifest in His
own time, *He who is* the blessed and only
Potentate, the King of kings and Lord of
lords, 16 who alone has immortality, dwelling in unapproachable light, whom no man
has seen or can see, to whom *be* honor
and everlasting power. Amen.

17 Command those who are rich in this
present age not to be haughty, nor to trust
in uncertain riches but in the living God,
who gives us richly all things to enjoy.
18 *Let them* do good, that they be rich in
good works, ready to give, willing to share,
19 storing up for themselves a good foundation for the time to come, that they may
lay hold on eternal life.

20 O Timothy! Guard what was committed to your trust, avoiding the profane *and*
idle babblings and contradictions of what
is falsely called knowledge— 21 by professing it some have strayed concerning the
faith.

Grace *be* with you. Amen.

◆◆◆◆

Reading 301—A Pure Conscience
2 Timothy 1:3

Conscience is that innate faculty in a man's spirit that attaches itself to
the highest the man knows, whether he be an atheist or a Christian.
The highest the Christian knows is God: the highest the atheist knows is his
principles.   (PHIL. SIN)

When conscience has been enlightened by the Son of God being formed in me, I have to make an effort to keep my conscience so sensitive that I obey that which I perceive to be God's will. I have to be so keen in the scent of the Lord, so sensitive to the tiniest touch of His Spirit, that I know what I should do. If I keep my soul inwardly open to God, then when I come in contact with the affairs of life outside, I know immediately what I should do; if I do not, I am to blame.   (*Brill. Heritage*)

When conscience speaks there must be no debate whatever. In a crisis human nature is put on the strain, and we usually know what to do; but the sensitive conscience of the Christian is realized in the ordinary things of life, the humdrum things. We are apt to think of conscience only in connection with something outrageous.   (*Brill. Heritage*)

JEREMIAH 41:1—42:22

NOW it came to pass in the seventh month *that* Ishmael the son of Nethaniah, the son of Elishama, of the royal family and of the officers of the king, came with ten men to Gedaliah the son of Ahikam, at Mizpah. And there they ate bread together in Mizpah. 2 Then Ishmael the son of Nethaniah, and the ten men who were with him, arose and struck Gedaliah the son of Ahikam, the son of Shaphan, with the sword, and killed him whom the king of Babylon had made governor over the land. 3 Ishmael also struck down all the Jews who were with him, *that is,* with Gedaliah at Mizpah, and the Chaldeans who were found there, the men of war.

4 And it happened, on the second day after he had killed Gedaliah, when as yet no one knew *it,* 5 that certain men came from Shechem, from Shiloh, and from Samaria, eighty men with their beards shaved and their clothes torn, having cut themselves, with offerings and incense in their hand, to bring *them* to the house of the LORD. 6 Now Ishmael the son of Nethaniah went out from Mizpah to meet them, weeping as he went along; and it happened as he met them that he said to them, "Come to Gedaliah the son of Ahikam!" 7 So it was, when they came into the midst of the city, that Ishmael the son of Nethaniah killed them *and cast them* into the midst of a pit, he and the men who were with him. 8 But ten men were found among them who said to Ishmael, "Do not kill us, for we have treasures of wheat, barley, oil, and honey in the field." So he desisted and did not kill them among their brethren. 9 Now the pit into which Ishmael had cast all the dead bodies of the men whom he had slain, because of Gedaliah, *was* the same one Asa the king had made for fear of Baasha king of Israel. Ishmael the son of Nethaniah filled it with *the* slain. 10 Then Ishmael carried away captive all the rest of the people who *were* in Mizpah, the king's daughters and all the people who remained in Mizpah, whom Nebuzaradan the captain of the guard had committed to Gedaliah the son of Ahikam. And Ishmael the son of Nethaniah carried them away captive and departed to go over to the Ammonites.

11 But when Johanan the son of Kareah and all the captains of the forces that *were* with him heard of all the evil that Ishmael the son of Nethaniah had done, 12 they took all the men and went to fight with Ishmael the son of Nethaniah; and they found him by the great pool that *is* in Gibeon. 13 So it was, when all the people who *were* with Ishmael saw Johanan the son of Kareah, and all the captains of the forces who *were* with him, that they were glad. 14 Then all the people whom Ishmael had carried away captive from Mizpah turned around and came back, and went to Johanan the son of Kareah. 15 But Ishmael the son of Nethaniah escaped from Johanan with eight men and went to the Ammonites.

16 Then Johanan the son of Kareah, and all the captains of the forces that were with him, took from Mizpah all the rest of the people whom he had recovered from Ishmael the son of Nethaniah after he had murdered Gedaliah the son of Ahikam— the mighty men of war and the women and the children and the eunuchs, whom he had brought back from Gibeon. 17 And they departed and dwelt in the habitation of Chimham, which is near Bethlehem, as they went on their way to Egypt, 18 because of the Chaldeans; for they were afraid of them, because Ishmael the son of Nethaniah had murdered Gedaliah the son of Ahikam, whom the king of Babylon had made governor in the land.

42 NOW all the captains of the forces, Johanan the son of Kareah, Jezaniah the son of Hoshaiah, and all the people, from the least to the greatest, came near 2 and said to Jeremiah the prophet, "Please, let our petition be acceptable to you, and pray for us to the LORD your God, for all this remnant (since we are left *but* a few of many, as you can see), 3 that the LORD your God may show us the way in which we should walk and the thing we should do."

4 Then Jeremiah the prophet said to them, "I have heard. Indeed, I will pray to the LORD your God according to your words, and it shall be, *that* whatever the LORD answers you, I will declare *it* to you. I will keep nothing back from you."

5 So they said to Jeremiah, "Let the LORD be a true and faithful witness between us, if we do not do according to everything which the LORD your God sends us by you. 6 Whether *it is* pleasing or displeasing, we will obey the voice of the LORD our God to whom we send you, that it may be well with us when we obey the voice of the LORD our God."

7 And it happened after ten days that the word of the LORD came to Jeremiah. 8 Then he called Johanan the son of Kareah, all the captains of the forces which *were* with him, and all the people from the least even to the greatest, 9 and said to them, "Thus says the LORD, the God of Israel, to whom you sent me to present your petition before Him: 10 'If you will still remain in this land, then I will build you and not pull *you* down, and I will plant you and not pluck *you* up. For I relent concerning the disaster that I have brought upon you. 11 Do not be afraid of the king of Babylon, of whom you are afraid; do not be afraid of him,' says the LORD, 'for I *am* with you, to save you and deliver you from his hand. 12 And I will show you mercy, that he may have mercy on you and cause you to return to your own land.'

13 "But if you say, 'We will not dwell in this land,' disobeying the voice of the LORD your God, 14 saying, 'No, but we will go to the land of Egypt where we shall see no war, nor hear the sound of the trumpet, nor be hungry for bread, and there we will dwell'— 15 Then hear now the word of the LORD, O remnant of Judah! Thus says the LORD of hosts, the God of Israel: 'If you wholly set your faces to enter Egypt, and go to dwell there, 16 then it shall be *that* the sword which you feared shall overtake you there in the land of Egypt; the famine of which you were afraid shall follow

close after you there *in* Egypt; and there you shall die. 17 So shall it be with all the men who set their faces to go to Egypt to dwell there. They shall die by the sword, by famine, and by pestilence. And none of them shall remain or escape from the disaster that I will bring upon them.'

18 "For thus says the LORD of hosts, the God of Israel: 'As My anger and My fury have been poured out on the inhabitants of Jerusalem, so will My fury be poured out on you when you enter Egypt. And you shall be an oath, an astonishment, a curse, and a reproach; and you shall see this place no more.'

19 "The LORD has said concerning you, O remnant of Judah, 'Do not go to Egypt!' Know certainly that I have admonished you this day. 20 For you were hypocrites in your hearts when you sent me to the LORD your God, saying, 'Pray for us to the LORD our God, and according to all that the LORD your God says, so declare to us and we will do *it*.' 21 And I have this day declared *it* to you, but you have not obeyed the voice of the LORD your God, or anything which He has sent you by me. 22 Now therefore, know certainly that you shall die by the sword, by famine, and by pestilence in the place where you desire to go to dwell."

PSALM 119:89–96

89 FOREVER, O LORD,
    Your word is settled in heaven.
90 Your faithfulness *endures* to all
       generations;
    You established the earth, and it abides.
91 They continue this day according to
       Your ordinances,
    For all *are* Your servants.
92 Unless Your law *had been* my delight,
    I would then have perished in my
       affliction.
93 I will never forget Your precepts,
    For by them You have given me life.
94 I *am* Yours, save me;
    For I have sought Your precepts.
95 The wicked wait for me to destroy me,
    But I will consider Your testimonies.
96 I have seen the consummation of all
       perfection,

*C*hristian perfection is not and
never can be, human
perfection.   (NOT KNOWING)

But Your commandment *is* exceedingly broad.

PROVERBS 28:2

2   BECAUSE of the transgression of a
    land, many *are* its princes;
    But by a man of understanding *and*
    knowledge
    Right will be prolonged.

2 TIMOTHY 1:1–18

PAUL, an apostle of Jesus Christ by the will of God, according to the promise of life which is in Christ Jesus,

2 To Timothy, a beloved son:

Grace, mercy, *and* peace from God the Father and Christ Jesus our Lord. 3 I thank God, whom I serve with a pure conscience, as *my* forefathers *did*, as without ceasing I remember you in my prayers night and day, 4 greatly desiring to see you, being

---

*C*onscience is the internal perception of God's moral law.   (PHIL. SIN)

---

mindful of your tears, that I may be filled with joy, 5 when I call to remembrance the genuine faith that is in you, which dwelt first in your grandmother Lois and your mother Eunice, and I am persuaded is in you also. 6 Therefore I remind you to stir up the gift of God which is in you through

the laying on of my hands. 7 For God has not given us a spirit of fear, but of power and of love and of a sound mind.

8 Therefore do not be ashamed of the testimony of our Lord, nor of me His prisoner, but share with me in the sufferings for the gospel according to the power of God, 9 who has saved us and called *us* with a holy calling, not according to our works, but according to His own purpose and grace which was given to us in Christ Jesus before time began, 10 but has now been revealed by the appearing of our Savior Jesus Christ, *who* has abolished death and brought life and immortality to light through the gospel, 11 to which I was appointed a preacher, an apostle, and a teacher of the Gentiles. 12 For this reason I also suffer these things; nevertheless I am not ashamed, for I know whom I have believed and am persuaded that He is able to keep what I have committed to Him until that Day.

13 Hold fast the pattern of sound words which you have heard from me, in faith and love which are in Christ Jesus. 14 That good thing which was committed to you, keep by the Holy Spirit who dwells in us.

15 This you know, that all those in Asia have turned away from me, among whom are Phygellus and Hermogenes. 16 The Lord grant mercy to the household of Onesiphorus, for he often refreshed me, and was not ashamed of my chain; 17 but when he arrived in Rome, he sought me out very zealously and found *me*. 18 The Lord grant to him that he may find mercy from the Lord in that Day—and you know very well how many ways he ministered *to me* at Ephesus.

◆◆◆

Reading 302—A Loyal Soldier
2 Timothy 2:3

The first requirement of the worker is discipline voluntarily entered into. It is easy to be passionate, easy to be thrilled by spiritual influences, but it takes a heart in love with Jesus Christ to put the feet in His footprints, and to square the life to a steady "going up to Jerusalem" with Him. Discipline is the one thing the modern Christian knows nothing of; we won't stand discipline nowadays. God has given me an experience of His life and grace; therefore, I am a law unto myself.

The discipline of a worker is not in order to develop his own life, but for the purposes of his Commander. The reason there is so much failure is because we forget that we are here for that one thing, loyalty to Jesus Christ; otherwise we have no business to have taken the vows of God upon us. If a soldier is not prepared to be killed, he has no business to have enlisted as a soldier. The only way to keep true to God is by a steady persistent refusal to be interested in Christian work and to be interested alone in Jesus Christ. . . .

Our Lord Himself is the example of a disciplined life. He lived a holy life by sacrificing Himself to His Father; His words and His thinking were holy because He submitted His intelligence to His Father's word, and He worked the works of God because He steadily submitted His will to His Father's will; and as is the Master, so is the disciple. (*APPROVED*)

JEREMIAH 43:1—44:30

NOW it happened, when Jeremiah had stopped speaking to all the people all the words of the LORD their God, for which the LORD their God had sent him to them, all these words, 2 that Azariah the son of Hoshaiah, Johanan the son of Kareah, and all the proud men spoke, saying to Jeremiah, "You speak falsely! The LORD our God has not sent you to say, 'Do not go to Egypt to dwell there.' 3 But Baruch the son of Neriah has set you against us, to deliver us into the hand of the Chaldeans, that they may put us to death or carry us away captive to Babylon." 4 So Johanan the son of Kareah, all the captains of the forces, and all the people would not obey the voice of the LORD, to remain in the land of Judah. 5 But Johanan the son of Kareah and all the captains of the forces took all the remnant of Judah who had returned to dwell in the land of Judah, from all nations where they had been driven— 6 men, women, children, the king's daughters, and every person whom Nebuzaradan the captain of the guard had left with Gedaliah the son of Ahikam, the son of Shaphan, and Jeremiah the prophet and Baruch the son of Neriah. 7 So they went to the land of Egypt, for they did not obey the voice of the LORD. And they went as far as Tahpanhes.

8 Then the word of the LORD came to Jeremiah in Tahpanhes, saying, 9 "Take large stones in your hand, and hide them in the sight of the men of Judah, in the clay in the brick courtyard which *is* at the entrance to Pharaoh's house in Tahpanhes; 10 and say to them, 'Thus says the LORD of hosts, the God of Israel: "Behold, I will send and bring Nebuchadnezzar the king of Babylon, My servant, and will set his throne above these stones that I have hidden. And he will spread his royal pavilion over them. 11 When he comes, he shall strike the land of Egypt *and deliver* to death *those appointed* for death, and to captivity *those appointed* for captivity, and to the sword *those appointed* for the sword. 12 I will kindle a fire in the houses of the gods of Egypt, and he shall burn them and carry them away captive. And he shall array himself with the land of Egypt, as a shepherd puts on his garment, and he shall go out from there in peace. 13 He shall also break the sacred pillars of Beth Shemesh that *are* in the land of Egypt; and the houses of the gods of the Egyptians he shall burn with fire." ' "

44 THE word that came to Jeremiah concerning all the Jews who dwell in the land of Egypt, who dwell at Migdol, at Tahpanhes, at Noph, and in the country of Pathros, saying, 2 "Thus says the LORD of hosts, the God of Israel: 'You have seen all the calamity that I have brought on Jerusalem and on all the cities of Judah; and behold, this day they *are* a desolation, and no one dwells in them, 3 because of their wickedness which they have committed to provoke Me to anger, in that they went to burn incense *and* to serve other gods whom they did not know, they nor you nor your fathers. 4 However I have sent to you all My servants the prophets, rising early and sending *them*, saying, "Oh, do not do this abominable thing that I hate!" 5 But they did not listen or incline their ear to turn from their wickedness, to burn no incense to other gods. 6 So My fury and My anger were poured out and kindled in the cities of Judah and in the streets of Jerusalem; and they are wasted *and* desolate, as it is this day.'

7 "Now therefore, thus says the LORD, the God of hosts, the God of Israel: 'Why do you commit *this* great evil against yourselves, to cut off from you man and woman, child and infant, out of Judah, leaving none

to remain, 8 in that you provoke Me to wrath with the works of your hands, burning incense to other gods in the land of Egypt where you have gone to dwell, that you may cut yourselves off and be a curse and a reproach among all the nations of the earth? 9 Have you forgotten the wickedness of your fathers, the wickedness of the kings of Judah, the wickedness of their wives, your own wickedness, and the wickedness of your wives, which they committed in the land of Judah and in the streets of Jerusalem? 10 They have not been humbled, to this day, nor have they feared; they have not walked in My law or in My statutes that I set before you and your fathers.'

11 "Therefore thus says the LORD of hosts, the God of Israel: 'Behold, I will set My face against you for catastrophe and for cutting off all Judah. 12 And I will take the remnant of Judah who have set their faces to go into the land of Egypt to dwell there, and they shall all be consumed *and* fall in the land of Egypt. They shall be consumed by the sword *and* by famine. They shall die, from the least to the greatest, by the sword and by famine; and they shall be an oath, an astonishment, a curse and a reproach! 13 For I will punish those who dwell in the land of Egypt, as I have punished Jerusalem, by the sword, by famine, and by pestilence, 14 so that none of the remnant of Judah who have gone into the land of Egypt to dwell there shall escape or survive, lest they return to the land of Judah, to which they desire to return and dwell. For none shall return except those who escape.' "

15 Then all the men who knew that their wives had burned incense to other gods, with all the women who stood by, a great multitude, and all the people who dwelt in the land of Egypt, in Pathros, answered Jeremiah, saying: 16 "*As for* the word that you have spoken to us in the name of the LORD, we will not listen to you! 17 But we will certainly do whatever has gone out of our own mouth, to burn incense to the queen of heaven and pour out drink offerings to her, as we have done, we and our fathers, our kings and our princes, in the cities of Judah and in the streets of Jerusalem. For *then* we had plenty of food, were well-off, and saw no trouble. 18 But since we stopped burning incense to the queen of heaven and pouring out drink offerings to her, we have lacked everything and have been consumed by the sword and by famine."

19 *The women also said,* "And when we burned incense to the queen of heaven and poured out drink offerings to her, did we make cakes for her, to worship her, and pour out drink offerings to her without our husbands' *permission?*"

20 Then Jeremiah spoke to all the people—the men, the women, and all the people who had given him *that* answer—saying: 21 "The incense that you burned in the cities of Judah and in the streets of Jerusalem, you and your fathers, your kings and your princes, and the people of the land, did not the LORD remember them, and did it *not* come into His mind? 22 So the LORD could no longer bear *it,* because of the evil of your doings *and* because of the abominations which you committed. Therefore your land is a desolation, an astonishment, a curse, and without an inhabitant, as *it is* this day. 23 Because you have burned incense and because you have sinned against the LORD, and have not obeyed the voice of the LORD or walked in His law, in His statutes or in His testimonies, therefore this calamity has happened to you, as *at* this day."

24 Moreover Jeremiah said to all the people and to all the women, "Hear the word of the LORD, all Judah who *are* in the land of Egypt! 25 Thus says the LORD of hosts, the God of Israel, saying: 'You and your wives have spoken with your mouths and fulfilled with your hands, saying, "We will surely keep our vows that we have made, to burn incense to the queen of heaven and pour out drink offerings to her." You will surely keep your vows and perform your vows!' 26 Therefore hear the word of the LORD, all Judah who dwell in the land of Egypt: 'Behold, I have sworn by My great name,' says the LORD, 'that My name shall no more be named in the mouth of any man of Judah in all the land of Egypt, saying, "The Lord GOD lives." 27 Behold, I will watch over them for adversity and not for good. And all the men of Judah who *are* in the land of Egypt shall be consumed by the sword and by famine, until there is an end to them. 28 Yet a small number who escape the sword shall return from the land of Egypt to the land of Judah; and all the remnant of Judah, who have gone to the land of Egypt to dwell there, shall know whose words will stand, Mine or theirs. 29 And this *shall be* a sign to you,' says the LORD, 'that I will punish you in this place, that you may know that My words will surely stand against you for adversity.'

30 "Thus says the LORD: 'Behold, I will give Pharaoh Hophra king of Egypt into the hand of his enemies and into the hand of those who seek his life, as I gave Zedekiah

king of Judah into the hand of Nebuchadnezzar king of Babylon, his enemy who
sought his life.'"

PSALM 119:97–104

97 OH, how I love Your law!
     It *is* my meditation all the day.
98 You, through Your commandments,
        make me wiser than my enemies;
     For they *are* ever with me.
99 I have more understanding than all
        my teachers,
     For Your testimonies *are* my
        meditation.
100 I understand more than the ancients,
     Because I keep Your precepts.
101 I have restrained my feet from every
        evil way,
     That I may keep Your word.
102 I have not departed from Your
        judgments,
     For You Yourself have taught me.
103 How sweet are Your words to my
        taste,
     Sweeter than honey to my mouth!
104 Through Your precepts I get
        understanding;
     Therefore I hate every false way.

PROVERBS 28:3

3 A poor man who oppresses the poor
   Is like a driving rain which leaves no
   food.

2 TIMOTHY 2:1–26

YOU therefore, my son, be strong in the
grace that is in Christ Jesus. 2 And the things
that you have heard from me among many
witnesses, commit these to faithful men
who will be able to teach others also.
3 You therefore must endure hardship as a
good soldier of Jesus Christ. 4 No one en-
gaged in warfare entangles himself with the
affairs of *this* life, that he may please him
who enlisted him as a soldier. 5 And also
if anyone competes in athletics, he is not
crowned unless he competes according to
the rules. 6 The hardworking farmer must
be first to partake of the crops. 7 Consider
what I say, and may the Lord give you
understanding in all things.

8 Remember that Jesus Christ, of the seed
of David, was raised from the dead according to my gospel, 9 for which I suffer trouble
as an evildoer, *even* to the point of chains;
but the word of God is not chained.

10 Therefore I endure all things for the sake
of the elect, that they also may obtain the
salvation which is in Christ Jesus with eternal glory.

---

*We have to learn to live in the
reality of the eternal
things.*   (PLACE HELP)

---

11 *This is* a faithful saying:

For if we died with *Him*,
   We shall also live with *Him*.
12 If we endure,
       We shall also reign with *Him*.
     If we deny *Him*,
        He also will deny us.
13 If we are faithless,
       He remains faithful;
     He cannot deny Himself.

14 Remind *them* of these things, charging
them before the Lord not to strive about
words to no profit, to the ruin of the hearers.
15 Be diligent to present yourself approved
to God, a worker who does not need to
be ashamed, rightly dividing the word of
truth. 16 But shun profane *and* idle babblings, for they will increase to more ungodliness. 17 And their message will spread like
cancer. Hymenaeus and Philetus are of this
sort, 18 who have strayed concerning the
truth, saying that the resurrection is already
past; and they overthrow the faith of some.
19 Nevertheless the solid foundation of
God stands, having this seal: "The Lord
knows those who are His," and, "Let everyone who names the name of Christ depart
from iniquity."

20 But in a great house there are not only
vessels of gold and silver, but also of wood
and clay, some for honor and some for dishonor. 21 Therefore if anyone cleanses himself from the latter, he will be a vessel for
honor, sanctified and useful for the Master,
prepared for every good work. 22 Flee also
youthful lusts; but pursue righteousness,
faith, love, peace with those who call on
the Lord out of a pure heart. 23 But avoid
foolish and ignorant disputes, knowing that
they generate strife. 24 And a servant of the
Lord must not quarrel but be gentle to
all, able to teach, patient, 25 in humility cor-
recting those who are in opposition, if God
perhaps will grant them repentance, so that
they may know the truth, 26 and *that* they
may come to their senses *and escape* the
snare of the devil, having been taken captive
by him to *do* his will.

Reading 303—What Do You Want?
Jeremiah 45:5

Are you seeking great things for yourself? Not seeking to be a great one, but seeking great things from God for yourself. God wants you in a closer relationship to Himself than receiving His gifts, He wants you to get to know Him. A great thing is accidental, it comes and goes. God never gives us anything accidental. There is nothing easier than getting into a right relationship with God except when it is not God whom you want but only what He gives.

If you have only come the length of asking God for things, you have never come to the first strand of abandonment, you have become a Christian from a standpoint of your own. "I did ask God for the Holy Spirit, but He did not give me the rest and the peace I expected." Instantly God puts His finger on the reason—you are not seeking the Lord at all, you are seeking something for yourself. Jesus says—"Ask, and it will be given to you." Ask God for what you want, and you cannot ask if you are not asking for a right thing. When you draw near to God, you cease from asking for things. "Your Father knows the things you have need of before you ask Him." Then why ask? That you may get to know Him.   (UTMOST)

JEREMIAH 45:1—46:28

THE word that Jeremiah the prophet spoke to Baruch the son of Neriah, when he had written these words in a book at the instruction of Jeremiah, in the fourth year of Jehoiakim the son of Josiah, king of Judah, saying, 2 "Thus says the LORD, the God of Israel, to you, O Baruch: 3 'You said, "Woe is me now! For the LORD has added grief to my sorrow. I fainted in my sighing, and I find no rest." '

4 "Thus you shall say to him, 'Thus says the LORD: "Behold, what I have built I will break down, and what I have planted I will pluck up, that is, this whole land. 5 And do you seek great things for yourself? Do not seek them; for behold, I will bring adversity on all flesh," says the LORD. "But I will give your life to you as a prize in all places, wherever you go." ' "

46 THE word of the LORD which came to Jeremiah the prophet against the nations. 2 Against Egypt.

Concerning the army of Pharaoh Necho, king of Egypt, which was by the River Euphrates in Carchemish, and which Nebuchadnezzar king of Babylon defeated in the fourth year of Jehoiakim the son of Josiah, king of Judah:

3 "Order the buckler and shield,
    And draw near to battle!
4 Harness the horses,
    And mount up, you horsemen!
    Stand forth with your helmets,
    Polish the spears,
    Put on the armor!
5 Why have I seen them dismayed and
        turned back?
    Their mighty ones are beaten down;
    They have speedily fled,
    And did not look back,
    For fear was all around," says the
        LORD.
6 "Do not let the swift flee away,
    Nor the mighty man escape;
    They will stumble and fall
    Toward the north, by the River
        Euphrates.

7 "Who is this coming up like a flood,
    Whose waters move like the rivers?
8 Egypt rises up like a flood,
    And its waters move like the rivers;
    And he says, 'I will go up and cover
        the earth,
    I will destroy the city and its
        inhabitants.'
9 Come up, O horses, and rage,
        O chariots!
    And let the mighty men come forth:

The Ethiopians and the Libyans who
handle the shield,
And the Lydians who handle *and*
bend the bow.
10 For this *is* the day of the Lord GOD
of hosts,
A day of vengeance,
That He may avenge Himself on His
adversaries.
The sword shall devour;
It shall be satiated and made drunk
with their blood;
For the Lord GOD of hosts has a
sacrifice
In the north country by the River
Euphrates.

11 "Go up to Gilead and take balm,
O virgin, the daughter of Egypt;
In vain you will use many medicines;
You shall not be cured.
12 The nations have heard of your
shame,
And your cry has filled the land;
For the mighty man has stumbled
against the mighty;
They both have fallen together."

13 The word that the LORD spoke to
Jeremiah the prophet, how Nebuchadnezzar king of Babylon would come *and* strike
the land of Egypt.

14 "Declare in Egypt, and proclaim in
Migdol;
Proclaim in Noph and in Tahpanhes;
Say, 'Stand fast and prepare
yourselves,
For the sword devours all around
you.'
15 Why are your valiant *men* swept
away?
They did not stand
Because the LORD drove them away.
16 He made many fall;
Yes, one fell upon another.
And they said, 'Arise!
Let us go back to our own people
And to the land of our nativity
From the oppressing sword.'
17 They cried there,
'Pharaoh, king of Egypt, *is but* a noise.
He has passed by the appointed
time!'

18 "*As* I live," says the King,
Whose name *is* the LORD of hosts,
"Surely as Tabor *is* among the
mountains
And as Carmel by the sea, *so* he shall
come.
19 O you daughter dwelling in Egypt,

Prepare yourself to go into captivity!
For Noph shall be waste and
desolate, without inhabitant.

20 "Egypt *is* a very pretty heifer,
But destruction comes, it comes
from the north.
21 Also her mercenaries are in her midst
like fat bulls,
For they also are turned back,
They have fled away together.
They did not stand,
For the day of their calamity had
come upon them,
The time of their punishment.
22 Her noise shall go like a serpent,
For they shall march with an army
And come against her with axes,
Like those who chop wood.

23 "They shall cut down her forest," says
the LORD,
"Though it cannot be searched,
Because they *are* innumerable,
And more numerous than
grasshoppers.
24 The daughter of Egypt shall be
ashamed;
She shall be delivered into the hand
Of the people of the north."

25 The LORD of hosts, the God of Israel,
says: "Behold, I will bring punishment on
Amon of No, and Pharaoh and Egypt, with
their gods and their kings—Pharaoh and
those who trust in him. 26 And I will deliver
them into the hand of those who seek their
lives, into the hand of Nebuchadnezzar
king of Babylon and the hand of his servants. Afterward it shall be inhabited as
in the days of old," says the LORD.

27 "But do not fear, O My servant Jacob,
And do not be dismayed, O Israel!
For behold, I will save you from afar,
And your offspring from the land of
their captivity;
Jacob shall return, have rest and be
at ease;
No one shall make *him* afraid.
28 Do not fear, O Jacob My servant,"
says the LORD,
"For I *am* with you;
For I will make a complete end of
all the nations
To which I have driven you,
But I will not make a complete end
of you.
I will rightly correct you,
For I will not leave you wholly
unpunished."

PSALM 119:105–112

105 YOUR word *is* a lamp to my feet
     And a light to my path.
106 I have sworn and confirmed
     That I will keep Your righteous
        judgments.
107 I am afflicted very much;
     Revive me, O Lord, according to
        Your word.
108 Accept, I pray, the freewill offerings
        of my mouth, O Lord,
     And teach me Your judgments.
109 My life *is* continually in my hand,
     Yet I do not forget Your law.
110 The wicked have laid a snare for me,
     Yet I have not strayed from Your
        precepts.
111 Your testimonies I have taken as a
        heritage forever,
     For they *are* the rejoicing of my heart.
112 I have inclined my heart to perform
        Your statutes
     Forever, to the very end.

PROVERBS 28:4

4 THOSE who forsake the law praise the
      wicked,
   But such as keep the law contend with
      them.

2 TIMOTHY 3:1–17

BUT know this, that in the last days perilous
times will come: 2 For men will be lovers
of themselves, lovers of money, boasters,
proud, blasphemers, disobedient to parents,
unthankful, unholy, 3 unloving, unforgiving, slanderers, without self-control, brutal,
despisers of good, 4 traitors, headstrong,
haughty, lovers of pleasure rather than lovers of God, 5 having a form of godliness
but denying its power. And from such people turn away! 6 For of this sort are those
who creep into households and make captives of gullible women loaded down with
sins, led away by various lusts, 7 always
learning and never able to come to the
knowledge of the truth. 8 Now as Jannes
and Jambres resisted Moses, so do these
also resist the truth: men of corrupt minds,
disapproved concerning the faith; 9 but they
will progress no further, for their folly will
be manifest to all, as theirs also was.

10 But you have carefully followed my
doctrine, manner of life, purpose, faith,
longsuffering, love, perseverance, 11 persecutions, afflictions, which happened to
me at Antioch, at Iconium, at Lystra—
what persecutions I endured. And out of
them all the Lord delivered me. 12 Yes, and
all who desire to live godly in Christ Jesus
will suffer persecution. 13 But evil men and
impostors will grow worse and worse, deceiving and being deceived. 14 But you must
continue in the things which you have
learned and been assured of, knowing from
whom you have learned *them,* 15 and that
from childhood you have known the Holy
Scriptures, which are able to make you wise
for salvation through faith which is in Christ
Jesus.

16 All Scripture *is* given by inspiration
of God, and *is* profitable for doctrine, for
reproof, for correction, for instruction in
righteousness, 17 that the man of God may

---

*The mystery of the Bible is that
its inspiration was direct from
God.*   (MORAL FOUND.)

---

be complete, thoroughly equipped for every
good work.

Reading 304—Instant in Season
2 Timothy 4:2

Many of us suffer from the morbid tendency to be instant "out of season."
The season does not refer to time, but to us—"Be instant in season,
out of season," whether we feel like it or not. If we do only what we feel
inclined to do, some of us would do nothing forever and ever. There are
unemployables in the spiritual domain, spiritually decrepit people, who refuse
to do anything unless they are supernaturally inspired. The proof that we are

rightly related to God is that we do our best whether we feel inspired or not.

One of the great snares of the Christian worker is to make a fetish of his rare moments. When the Spirit of God gives you a time of inspiration and insight, you say, "Now I will always be like this for God." No, you will not, God will take care you are not. Those times are the gift of God entirely. You cannot give them to yourself when you choose. If you say you will only be at your best, you become an intolerable drag on God; you will never do anything unless God keeps you consciously inspired. If you make a god of your best moments, you will find that God will fade out of your life and never come back until you do the duty that lies nearest, and have learned not to make a fetish of your rare moments.   (*UTMOST*)

JEREMIAH 47:1—48:47

THE word of the LORD that came to Jeremiah the prophet against the Philistines, before Pharaoh attacked Gaza.

2 Thus says the LORD:

"Behold, waters rise out of the north,
    And shall be an overflowing flood;
They shall overflow the land and all
    that is in it,
The city and those who dwell within;
Then the men shall cry,
And all the inhabitants of the land
    shall wail.
3 At the noise of the stamping hooves
        of his strong horses,
    At the rushing of his chariots,
    At the rumbling of his wheels,
    The fathers will not look back for
        their children,
    Lacking courage,
4 Because of the day that comes to
        plunder all the Philistines,
    To cut off from Tyre and Sidon every
        helper who remains;
    For the LORD shall plunder the
        Philistines,
    The remnant of the country of
        Caphtor.
5 Baldness has come upon Gaza,
    Ashkelon is cut off
    With the remnant of their valley.
    How long will you cut yourself?

6 "O you sword of the LORD,
    How long until you are quiet?
    Put yourself up into your scabbard,
    Rest and be still!
7 How can it be quiet,
    Seeing the LORD has given it a charge
    Against Ashkelon and against the
        seashore?
    There He has appointed it."

48 AGAINST Moab.
    Thus says the LORD of hosts, the God of Israel:

"Woe to Nebo!
    For it is plundered,
    Kirjathaim is shamed *and* taken;
    The high stronghold is shamed and
        dismayed—
2 No more praise of Moab.
    In Heshbon they have devised evil
        against her:
    'Come, and let us cut her off as a
        nation.'
    You also shall be cut down,
        O Madmen!
    The sword shall pursue you;
3 A voice of crying *shall be* from
        Horonaim:
    'Plundering and great destruction!'

4 "Moab is destroyed;
    Her little ones have caused a cry to
        be heard;
5 For in the Ascent of Luhith they
        ascend with continual weeping;
    For in the descent of Horonaim the
        enemies have heard a cry of
        destruction.

6 "Flee, save your lives!
    And be like the juniper in the
        wilderness.
7 For because you have trusted in your
        works and your treasures,
    You also shall be taken.
    And Chemosh shall go forth into
        captivity,
    His priests and his princes together.
8 And the plunderer shall come against
        every city;
    No one shall escape.
    The valley also shall perish,
    And the plain shall be destroyed,
    As the LORD has spoken.

9 "Give wings to Moab,
   That she may flee and get away;
   For her cities shall be desolate,
   Without any to dwell in them.
10 Cursed *is* he who does the work of
      the Lord deceitfully,
   And cursed *is* he who keeps back his
      sword from blood.

11 "Moab has been at ease from his
      youth;
   He has settled on his dregs,
   And has not been emptied from
      vessel to vessel,
   Nor has he gone into captivity.
   Therefore his taste remained in him,
   And his scent has not changed.

---

*T*he natural life has to be turned into
the spiritual.   (MORAL FOUND.)

---

12 "Therefore behold, the days are
      coming," says the Lord,
   "That I shall send him wine workers
   Who will tip him over
   And empty his vessels
   And break the bottles.
13 Moab shall be ashamed of Chemosh,
   As the house of Israel was ashamed
      of Bethel, their confidence.

14 "How can you say, 'We *are* mighty
   And strong men for the war'?
15 Moab is plundered and gone up *from*
      her cities;
   Her chosen young men have gone
      down to the slaughter," says the
      King,
   Whose name *is* the Lord of hosts.

16 "The calamity of Moab *is* near at hand,
   And his affliction comes quickly.
17 Bemoan him, all you who are around
      him;
   And all you who know his name,
   Say, 'How the strong staff is broken,
   The beautiful rod!'

18 "O daughter inhabiting Dibon,
   Come down from *your* glory,
   And sit in thirst;
   For the plunderer of Moab has come
      against you,
   He has destroyed your strongholds.
19 O inhabitant of Aroer,
   Stand by the way and watch;
   Ask him who flees
   And her who escapes;

Say, 'What has happened?'
20 Moab is shamed, for he is broken
      down.
   Wail and cry!
   Tell it in Arnon, that Moab is
      plundered.

21 "And judgment has come on the plain
      country:
   On Holon and Jahzah and Mephaath,
22 On Dibon and Nebo and Beth
      Diblathaim,
23 On Kirjathaim and Beth Gamul and
      Beth Meon,
24 On Kerioth and Bozrah,
   On all the cities of the land of Moab,
   Far or near.
25 The horn of Moab is cut off,
   And his arm is broken," says the
      Lord.

26 "Make him drunk,
   Because he exalted *himself* against the
      Lord.
   Moab shall wallow in his vomit,
   And he shall also be in derision.
27 For was not Israel a derision to you?
   Was he found among thieves?
   For whenever you speak of him,
   You shake *your head in scorn*.
28 You who dwell in Moab,
   Leave the cities and dwell in the rock,
   And be like the dove *which* makes
      her nest
   In the sides of the cave's mouth.

29 "We have heard the pride of Moab
   (He *is* exceedingly proud),
   Of his loftiness and arrogance and
      pride,
   And of the haughtiness of his heart."

30 "I know his wrath," says the Lord,
   "But it *is* not right;
   His lies have made nothing right.
31 Therefore I will wail for Moab,
   And I will cry out for all Moab;
   I will mourn for the men of Kir
      Heres.
32 O vine of Sibmah! I will weep for
      you with the weeping of Jazer.
   Your plants have gone over the sea,
   They reach to the sea of Jazer.
   The plunderer has fallen on your
      summer fruit and your vintage.
33 Joy and gladness are taken
   From the plentiful field
   And from the land of Moab;
   I have caused wine to fail from the
      winepresses;

No one will tread with joyous
shouting—
Not joyous shouting!

34 "From the cry of Heshbon to Elealeh
and to Jahaz
They have uttered their voice,
From Zoar to Horonaim,
Like a three-year-old heifer;
For the waters of Nimrim also shall
be desolate.

35 "Moreover," says the LORD,
"I will cause to cease in Moab
The one who offers *sacrifices* in the
high places
And burns incense to his gods.

36 Therefore My heart shall wail like
flutes for Moab,
And like flutes My heart shall wail
For the men of Kir Heres.
Therefore the riches they have
acquired have perished.

37 "For every head *shall be* bald, and every
beard clipped;
On all the hands *shall be* cuts, and
on the loins sackcloth—

38 A general lamentation
On all the housetops of Moab,
And in its streets;
For I have broken Moab like a vessel
in which *is* no pleasure," says the
LORD.

39 "They shall wail:
'How she is broken down!
How Moab has turned her back with
shame!'
So Moab shall be a derision
And a dismay to all those about her."

40 For thus says the LORD:

"Behold, one shall fly like an eagle,
And spread his wings over Moab.

41 Kerioth is taken,
And the strongholds are surprised;
The mighty men's hearts in Moab
on that day shall be
Like the heart of a woman in birth
pangs.

42 And Moab shall be destroyed as a
people,
Because he exalted *himself* against the
LORD.

43 Fear and the pit and the snare *shall
be* upon you,
O inhabitant of Moab," says the
LORD.

44 "He who flees from the fear shall fall
into the pit,

And he who gets out of the pit shall
be caught in the snare.
For upon Moab, upon it I will bring
The year of their punishment," says
the LORD.

45 "Those who fled stood under the
shadow of Heshbon
Because of exhaustion.
But a fire shall come out of Heshbon,
A flame from the midst of Sihon,
And shall devour the brow of Moab,
The crown of the head of the sons
of tumult.

46 Woe to you, O Moab!
The people of Chemosh perish;
For your sons have been taken
captive,
And your daughters captive.

47 "Yet I will bring back the captives of
Moab
In the latter days," says the LORD.

Thus far *is* the judgment of Moab.

PSALM 119:113–120

113 I hate the double-minded,
But I love Your law.

*The man who does not put God first
in his calculations is always
double-minded.* (BRILL. HERITAGE)

114 You *are* my hiding place and my
shield;
I hope in Your word.

115 Depart from me, you evildoers,
For I will keep the commandments
of my God!

116 Uphold me according to Your word,
that I may live;
And do not let me be ashamed of my
hope.

117 Hold me up, and I shall be safe,
And I shall observe Your statutes
continually.

118 You reject all those who stray from
Your statutes,
For their deceit *is* falsehood.

119 You put away all the wicked of the
earth *like* dross;
Therefore I love Your testimonies.

120 My flesh trembles for fear of You,
And I am afraid of Your judgments.

PROVERBS 28:5

5 EVIL men do not understand justice,
  But those who seek the LORD
    understand all.

*The only thing to depend on in
a man is what God has done in
him.*   (GOOD)

2 TIMOTHY 4:1–22

I charge *you* therefore before God and the Lord Jesus Christ, who will judge the living and the dead at His appearing and His kingdom: 2 Preach the word! Be ready in season *and* out of season. Convince, rebuke, exhort, with all longsuffering and teaching. 3 For the time will come when they will not endure sound doctrine, but according to their own desires, *because* they have itching ears, they will heap up for themselves teachers; 4 and they will turn *their* ears away from the truth, and be turned aside to fables. 5 But you be watchful in all things, endure afflictions, do the work of an evangelist, fulfill your ministry.

6 For I am already being poured out as a drink offering, and the time of my departure is at hand. 7 I have fought the good fight, I have finished the race, I have kept the faith. 8 Finally, there is laid up for me the crown of righteousness, which the Lord, the righteous Judge, will give to me on that Day, and not to me only but also to all who have loved His appearing.

9 Be diligent to come to me quickly; 10 for Demas has forsaken me, having loved this present world, and has departed for Thessalonica—Crescens for Galatia, Titus for Dalmatia. 11 Only Luke is with me. Get Mark and bring him with you, for he is useful to me for ministry. 12 And Tychicus I have sent to Ephesus. 13 Bring the cloak that I left with Carpus at Troas when you come—and the books, especially the parchments.

14 Alexander the coppersmith did me much harm. May the Lord repay him according to his works. 15 You also must beware of him, for he has greatly resisted our words.

16 At my first defense no one stood with me, but all forsook me. May it not be charged against them.

17 But the Lord stood with me and strengthened me, so that the message might be preached fully through me, and *that* all the Gentiles might hear. Also I was delivered out of the mouth of the lion. 18 And the Lord will deliver me from every evil work and preserve *me* for His heavenly kingdom. To Him *be* glory forever and ever. Amen!

19 Greet Prisca and Aquila, and the household of Onesiphorus. 20 Erastus stayed in Corinth, but Trophimus I have left in Miletus sick.

21 Do your utmost to come before winter.

Eubulus greets you, as well as Pudens, Linus, Claudia, and all the brethren.

22 The Lord Jesus Christ be with your spirit. Grace be with you. Amen.

◆◆◆◆

Reading 305—Do Not Be a Spiritual Beggar
Titus 1:9

I t is not the thing on which we spend most time that molds us, but the thing that exerts the greatest power. Five minutes with God and His word is worth more than all the rest of the day. Do we come to the Bible to be spoken to by God, to be made "wise for salvation," or simply to hunt for texts on which to build addresses? There are people who vagabond through the Bible, taking sufficient only out of it for the making of sermons, they never let the word of God walk out of the Bible and talk to them. Beware of living from hand to mouth in spiritual matters; do not be a spiritual mendicant.   (*WALKED*)

Are we in the habit of listening to the words of Jesus? Do we realize that

Jesus knows more about our business than we do ourselves? Do we take His word for our clothes, our money, our domestic work; or do we think we can manage these things for ourselves? The Spirit of God has the habit of taking the words of Jesus out of their scriptural setting and putting them into the setting of our personal lives.   (*WALKED*)

JEREMIAH 49:1—50:46

AGAINST the Ammonites.
    Thus says the LORD:

    "Has Israel no sons?
    Has he no heir?
    Why *then* does Milcom inherit Gad,
    And his people dwell in its cities?
2   Therefore behold, the days are
        coming," says the LORD,
    "That I will cause to be heard an alarm
        of war
    In Rabbah of the Ammonites;
    It shall be a desolate mound,
    And her villages shall be burned with
        fire.
    Then Israel shall take possession of
        his inheritance," says the LORD.

3   "Wail, O Heshbon, for Ai is
        plundered!
    Cry, you daughters of Rabbah,
    Gird yourselves with sackcloth!
    Lament and run to and fro by the
        walls;
    For Milcom shall go into captivity
    With his priests and his princes
        together.
4   Why do you boast in the valleys,
    Your flowing valley, O backsliding
        daughter?
    Who trusted in her treasures, *saying*,
    'Who will come against me?'
5   Behold, I will bring fear upon you,"
    Says the Lord GOD of hosts,
    "From all those who are around you;
    You shall be driven out, everyone
        headlong,
    And no one will gather those who
        wander off.
6   But afterward I will bring back
    The captives of the people of
        Ammon," says the LORD.

7 Against Edom.
Thus says the LORD of hosts:

    "*Is* wisdom no more in Teman?
    Has counsel perished from the
        prudent?
    Has their wisdom vanished?

8   Flee, turn back, dwell in the depths,
        O inhabitants of Dedan!
    For I will bring the calamity of Esau
        upon him,
    The time *that* I will punish him.
9   If grape gatherers came to you,
    Would they not leave *some* gleaning
        grapes?
    If thieves by night,
    Would they not destroy until they
        have enough?
10 But I have made Esau bare;
    I have uncovered his secret places,
    And he shall not be able to hide
        himself.
    His descendants are plundered,
    His brethren and his neighbors,
    And he *is* no more.
11 Leave your fatherless children,
    I will preserve *them* alive;
    And let your widows trust in Me."

12 For thus says the LORD: "Behold, those whose judgment *was* not to drink of the cup have assuredly drunk. And *are* you the one who will altogether go unpunished? You shall not go unpunished, but you shall surely drink *of it*. 13 For I have sworn by Myself," says the LORD, "that Bozrah shall become a desolation, a reproach, a waste, and a curse. And all its cities shall be perpetual wastes."

14 I have heard a message from the
        LORD,
    And an ambassador has been sent to
        the nations:
    "Gather together, come against her,
    And rise up to battle!

15 "For indeed, I will make you small
        among nations,
    Despised among men.
16 Your fierceness has deceived you,
    The pride of your heart,
    O you who dwell in the clefts of the
        rock,
    Who hold the height of the hill!
    Though you make your nest as high
        as the eagle,
    I will bring you down from there,"
        says the LORD.

17 "Edom also shall be an astonishment;
　　Everyone who goes by it will be
　　　astonished
　　And will hiss at all its plagues.
18 As in the overthrow of Sodom and
　　　Gomorrah
　　And their neighbors," says the LORD,
　　"No one shall remain there,
　　Nor shall a son of man dwell in it.

19 "Behold, he shall come up like a lion
　　　from the floodplain of the Jordan
　　Against the dwelling place of the
　　　strong;
　　But I will suddenly make him run
　　　away from her.
　　And who *is* a chosen *man that* I may
　　　appoint over her?
　　For who *is* like Me?
　　Who will arraign Me?
　　And who *is* that shepherd
　　Who will withstand Me?"

20 Therefore hear the counsel of the
　　　LORD that He has taken against
　　　Edom,
　　And His purposes that He has
　　　proposed against the inhabitants
　　　of Teman:
　　Surely the least of the flock shall draw
　　　them out;
　　Surely He shall make their dwelling
　　　places desolate with them.
21 The earth shakes at the noise of their
　　　fall;
　　At the cry its noise is heard at the
　　　Red Sea.
22 Behold, He shall come up and fly
　　　like the eagle,
　　And spread His wings over Bozrah;
　　The heart of the mighty men of Edom
　　　in that day shall be
　　Like the heart of a woman in birth
　　　pangs.

23 Against Damascus.

　　"Hamath and Arpad are shamed,
　　For they have heard bad news.
　　They are fainthearted;
　　There is trouble on the sea;
　　It cannot be quiet.
24 Damascus has grown feeble;
　　She turns to flee,
　　And fear has seized *her*.
　　Anguish and sorrows have taken her
　　　like a woman in labor.
25 Why is the city of praise not deserted,
　　　the city of My joy?
26 Therefore her young men shall fall
　　　in her streets,

And all the men of war shall be cut
　　off in that day," says the LORD of
　　hosts.
27 "I will kindle a fire in the wall of
　　　Damascus,
　　And it shall consume the palaces of
　　　Ben-Hadad."

28 Against Kedar and against the kingdoms of Hazor, which Nebuchadnezzar
king of Babylon shall strike.
Thus says the LORD:

　　"Arise, go up to Kedar,
　　And devastate the men of the East!
29　Their tents and their flocks they shall
　　　take away.
　　They shall take for themselves their
　　　curtains,
　　All their vessels and their camels;
　　And they shall cry out to them,
　　'Fear *is* on every side!'

30 "Flee, get far away! Dwell in the
　　　depths,
　　O inhabitants of Hazor!" says the
　　　LORD.
　　"For Nebuchadnezzar king of Babylon
　　　has taken counsel against you,
　　And has conceived a plan against you.

31 "Arise, go up to the wealthy nation
　　　that dwells securely," says the
　　　LORD,
　　"Which has neither gates nor bars,
　　Dwelling alone.
32　Their camels shall be for booty,
　　And the multitude of their cattle for
　　　plunder.
　　I will scatter to all winds those in
　　　the farthest corners,
　　And I will bring their calamity from
　　　all its sides," says the LORD.
33 "Hazor shall be a dwelling for jackals,
　　　a desolation forever;
　　No one shall reside there,
　　Nor son of man dwell in it."

34 The word of the LORD that came to
Jeremiah the prophet against Elam, in the
beginning of the reign of Zedekiah king
of Judah, saying, 35 "Thus says the LORD
of hosts:

　　'Behold, I will break the bow of
　　　Elam,
　　The foremost of their might.
36　Against Elam I will bring the four
　　　winds
　　From the four quarters of heaven,
　　And scatter them toward all those
　　　winds;

There shall be no nations where the outcasts of Elam will not go.

37 For I will cause Elam to be dismayed before their enemies
And before those who seek their life.
I will bring disaster upon them,
My fierce anger,' says the LORD;
'And I will send the sword after them
Until I have consumed them.

38 I will set My throne in Elam,
And will destroy from there the king and the princes,' says the LORD.

39 'But it shall come to pass in the latter days:
I will bring back the captives of Elam,' says the LORD."

50

THE word that the LORD spoke against Babylon *and* against the land of the Chaldeans by Jeremiah the prophet.

2 "Declare among the nations,
Proclaim, and set up a standard;
Proclaim—do not conceal *it*—
Say, 'Babylon is taken, Bel is shamed.
Merodach is broken in pieces;
Her idols are humiliated,
Her images are broken in pieces.'

3 For out of the north a nation comes up against her,
Which shall make her land desolate,
And no one shall dwell therein.
They shall move, they shall depart,
Both man and beast.

4 "In those days and in that time," says the LORD,
"The children of Israel shall come,
They and the children of Judah together;
With continual weeping they shall come,
And seek the LORD their God.

5 They shall ask the way to Zion,
With their faces toward it, *saying,*
'Come and let us join ourselves to the LORD
In a perpetual covenant
That will not be forgotten.'

6 "My people have been lost sheep.
Their shepherds have led them astray;
They have turned them away *on* the mountains.
They have gone from mountain to hill;
They have forgotten their resting place.

7 All who found them have devoured them;
And their adversaries said, 'We have not offended,
Because they have sinned against the LORD, the habitation of justice,
The LORD, the hope of their fathers.'

8 "Move from the midst of Babylon,
Go out of the land of the Chaldeans;
And be like the rams before the flocks.

9 For behold, I will raise and cause to come up against Babylon
An assembly of great nations from the north country,
And they shall array themselves against her;
From there she shall be captured.
Their arrows *shall be* like *those* of an expert warrior;
None shall return in vain.

10 And Chaldea shall become plunder;
All who plunder her shall be satisfied," says the LORD.

11 "Because you were glad, because you rejoiced,
You destroyers of My heritage,
Because you have grown fat like a heifer threshing grain,
And you bellow like bulls,

12 Your mother shall be deeply ashamed;
She who bore you shall be ashamed.
Behold, the least of the nations *shall be* a wilderness,
A dry land and a desert.

13 Because of the wrath of the LORD
She shall not be inhabited,
But she shall be wholly desolate.
Everyone who goes by Babylon shall be horrified
And hiss at all her plagues.

14 "Put yourselves in array against Babylon all around,
All you who bend the bow;
Shoot at her, spare no arrows,
For she has sinned against the LORD.

15 Shout against her all around;
She has given her hand,
Her foundations have fallen,
Her walls are thrown down;
For it *is* the vengeance of the LORD.
Take vengeance on her.
As she has done, so do to her.

16 Cut off the sower from Babylon,

And him who handles the sickle at
　　harvest time.
For fear of the oppressing sword
Everyone shall turn to his own
　　people,
And everyone shall flee to his own
　　land.

17 "Israel *is* like scattered sheep;
　　The lions have driven *him* away.
　　First the king of Assyria devoured
　　　　him;
　　Now at last this Nebuchadnezzar
　　　　king of Babylon has broken his
　　　　bones."

18 Therefore thus says the LORD of
hosts, the God of Israel:

　"Behold, I will punish the king of
　　　Babylon and his land,
　　As I have punished the king of
　　　　Assyria.
19　But I will bring back Israel to his
　　　home,
　　And he shall feed on Carmel and
　　　　Bashan;
　　His soul shall be satisfied on Mount
　　　　Ephraim and Gilead.
20　In those days and in that time," says
　　　the LORD,
　　"The iniquity of Israel shall be sought,
　　　but *there shall be* none;
　　And the sins of Judah, but they shall
　　　　not be found;
　　For I will pardon those whom I
　　　　preserve.

21 "Go up against the land of Merathaim,
　　　against it,
　　And against the inhabitants of
　　　　Pekod.
　　Waste and utterly destroy them," says
　　　the LORD,
　　"And do according to all that I have
　　　　commanded you.
22　A sound of battle *is* in the land,
　　And of great destruction.
23　How the hammer of the whole earth
　　　has been cut apart and broken!
　　How Babylon has become a
　　　　desolation among the nations!
　　I have laid a snare for you;
24　You have indeed been trapped,
　　　O Babylon,
　　And you were not aware;
　　You have been found and also caught,
　　Because you have contended against
　　　　the LORD.
25　The LORD has opened His armory,

And has brought out the weapons
　　of His indignation;
For this *is* the work of the Lord GOD
　　of hosts
In the land of the Chaldeans.
26　Come against her from the farthest
　　　border;
　　Open her storehouses;
　　Cast her up as heaps of ruins,
　　And destroy her utterly;
　　Let nothing of her be left.
27　Slay all her bulls,
　　Let them go down to the slaughter.
　　Woe to them!
　　For their day has come, the time of
　　　　their punishment.
28　The voice of those who flee and
　　　escape from the land of Babylon
　　Declares in Zion the vengeance of
　　　the LORD our God,
　　The vengeance of His temple.

29 "Call together the archers against
　　　Babylon.
　　All you who bend the bow, encamp
　　　　against it all around;
　　Let none of them escape.
　　Repay her according to her work;
　　According to all she has done, do
　　　　to her;
　　For she has been proud against the
　　　　LORD,
　　Against the Holy One of Israel.
30　Therefore her young men shall fall
　　　in the streets,
　　And all her men of war shall be cut
　　　　off in that day," says the LORD.
31 "Behold, I *am* against you,
　　O most haughty one!" says the Lord
　　　GOD of hosts;
　　"For your day has come,
　　The time *that* I will punish you.
32　The most proud shall stumble and
　　　fall,
　　And no one will raise him up;
　　I will kindle a fire in his cities,
　　And it will devour all around
　　　　him."

33 Thus says the LORD of hosts:

　"The children of Israel *were*
　　　oppressed,
　　Along with the children of Judah;
　　All who took them captive have held
　　　　them fast;
　　They have refused to let them go.
34　Their Redeemer *is* strong;
　　The LORD of hosts *is* His name.
　　He will thoroughly plead their case,
　　That He may give rest to the land,

And disquiet the inhabitants of
Babylon.

35 "A sword *is* against the Chaldeans,"
says the LORD,
"Against the inhabitants of Babylon,
And against her princes and her wise
men.
36 A sword *is* against the soothsayers,
and they will be fools.
A sword *is* against her mighty men,
and they will be dismayed.
37 A sword *is* against their horses,
Against their chariots,
And against all the mixed peoples
who *are* in her midst;
And they will become like women.
A sword *is* against her treasures, and
they will be robbed.
38 A drought *is* against her waters, and
they will be dried up.
For it *is* the land of carved images,
And they are insane with *their* idols.

39 "Therefore the wild desert beasts shall
dwell *there* with the jackals,
And the ostriches shall dwell in it.
It shall be inhabited no more forever,
Nor shall it be dwelt in from
generation to generation.

*There is a gap and a wildness
in things.*   (BAFFLED)

40 As God overthrew Sodom and
Gomorrah
And their neighbors," says the LORD,
"*So* no one shall reside there,
Nor son of man dwell in it.

41 "Behold, a people shall come from the
north,
And a great nation and many kings
Shall be raised up from the ends of
the earth.
42 They shall hold the bow and the
lance;
They *are* cruel and shall not show
mercy.
Their voice shall roar like the sea;
They shall ride on horses,
Set in array, like a man for the battle,
Against you, O daughter of Babylon.

43 "The king of Babylon has heard the
report about them,
And his hands grow feeble;
Anguish has taken hold of him,
Pangs as of a woman in childbirth.

44 "Behold, he shall come up like a lion
from the floodplain of the Jordan
Against the dwelling place of the
strong;
But I will make them suddenly run
away from her.
And who *is* a chosen *man that* I may
appoint over her?
For who *is* like Me?
Who will arraign Me?
And who *is* that shepherd
Who will withstand Me?"

45 Therefore hear the counsel of the
LORD that He has taken against
Babylon,
And His purposes that He has
proposed against the land of the
Chaldeans:
Surely the least of the flock shall draw
them out;
Surely He will make their dwelling
place desolate with them.
46 At the noise of the taking of Babylon
The earth trembles,
And the cry is heard among the
nations.

PSALM 119:121–128

121 I have done justice and righteousness;
Do not leave me to my oppressors.
122 Be surety for Your servant for good;
Do not let the proud oppress me.
123 My eyes fail *from seeking* Your
salvation
And Your righteous word.
124 Deal with Your servant according to
Your mercy,
And teach me Your statutes.
125 I *am* Your servant;
Give me understanding,
That I may know Your testimonies.
126 *It is* time for *You* to act, O LORD,
For they have regarded Your law as
void.
127 Therefore I love Your commandments
More than gold, yes, than fine gold!
128 Therefore all *Your* precepts *concerning*
all *things*
I consider *to be* right;
I hate every false way.

PROVERBS 28:6

6 BETTER *is* the poor who walks in his
integrity
Than one perverse *in his* ways, though
he *be* rich.

TITUS 1:1–16

PAUL, a bondservant of God and an apostle of Jesus Christ, according to the faith of God's elect and the acknowledgment of the truth which accords with godliness, 2 in hope of eternal life which God, who cannot lie, promised before time began, 3 but has in due time manifested His word through preaching, which was committed to me according to the commandment of God our Savior;

4 To Titus, a true son in *our* common faith:

Grace, mercy, *and* peace from God the Father and the Lord Jesus Christ our Savior.

5 For this reason I left you in Crete, that you should set in order the things that are lacking, and appoint elders in every city as I commanded you— 6 if a man is blameless, the husband of one wife, having faithful children not accused of dissipation or insubordination. 7 For a bishop must be blameless, as a steward of God, not self-willed, not quick-tempered, not given to wine, not violent, not greedy for money, 8 but hospitable, a lover of what is good, sober-minded, just, holy, self-controlled,

9 holding fast the faithful word as he has been taught, that he may be able, by sound doctrine, both to exhort and convict those who contradict.

10 For there are many insubordinate, both idle talkers and deceivers, especially those of the circumcision, 11 whose mouths must be stopped, who subvert whole households, teaching things which they ought not, for the sake of dishonest gain. 12 One of them, a prophet of their own, said, "Cretans *are* always liars, evil beasts, lazy gluttons." 13 This testimony is true. Therefore rebuke them sharply, that they may be sound in the faith, 14 not giving heed to Jewish fables and commandments of men who turn from the truth. 15 To the pure all things are pure, but to those who are defiled and unbelieving nothing is pure; but even their mind and conscience are defiled. 16 They profess to know God,

---

*I*t is Satan, not God, who makes a man say everyone must be just as he is.   (BRILL. HERITAGE)

---

but in works they deny Him, being abominable, disobedient, and disqualified for every good work.

◆◆◆

Reading 306—The Garden of the Mind
Jeremiah 51:50

"And let Jerusalem," the God-lit city, "come to your mind." Ask yourself, *What do I let come into my mind?* If a man lets his garden alone, it pretty soon ceases to be a garden; and if a saint lets his mind alone, it will soon become a garbage patch for Satan's scarecrows. Read the terrible things that Paul says will grow in the mind of a saint unless he looks after it (see Col. 3:5). The command to let Jerusalem come into our mind means we have to watch our intellect and devote it for one purpose; let only those things come in that are worthy of the God-lit city. *"Let"* . . . it is a command. See to it by the careful watching of your mind that only those thoughts come in that are worthy of God. We do not sufficiently realize the need to pray when we lie down at night, "Deliver us from the evil one." It puts us in the attitude of asking the Lord to watch our minds and our dreams, and He will do it.

(*PHIL. SIN*)

JEREMIAH 51:1—52:34

THUS says the LORD:

"Behold, I will raise up against
  Babylon,
Against those who dwell in Leb
  Kamai,
A destroying wind.
2 And I will send winnowers to
     Babylon,
   Who shall winnow her and empty
     her land.
   For in the day of doom
   They shall be against her all around.
3 Against *her* let the archer bend his
     bow,
   And lift himself up against *her* in his
     armor.
   Do not spare her young men;
   Utterly destroy all her army.
4 Thus the slain shall fall in the land
     of the Chaldeans,
   And *those* thrust through in her
     streets.
5 For Israel is not forsaken, nor Judah,
   By his God, the LORD of hosts,
   Though their land was filled with sin
     against the Holy One of Israel."

6 Flee from the midst of Babylon,
   And every one save his life!
   Do not be cut off in her iniquity,
   For this *is* the time of the LORD's
     vengeance;
   He shall recompense her.
7 Babylon *was* a golden cup in the
     LORD's hand,
   That made all the earth drunk.
   The nations drank her wine;
   Therefore the nations are deranged.
8 Babylon has suddenly fallen and
     been destroyed.
   Wail for her!
   Take balm for her pain;
   Perhaps she may be healed.

9 We would have healed Babylon,
   But she is not healed.
   Forsake her, and let us go everyone
     to his own country;
   For her judgment reaches to heaven
     and is lifted up to the skies.
10 The LORD has revealed our
     righteousness.
   Come and let us declare in Zion the
     work of the LORD our God.

11 Make the arrows bright!
   Gather the shields!

The LORD has raised up the spirit
  of the kings of the Medes.
For His plan *is* against Babylon to
  destroy it,
Because it *is* the vengeance of the
  LORD,
The vengeance for His temple.
12 Set up the standard on the walls of
     Babylon;
   Make the guard strong,
   Set up the watchmen,
   Prepare the ambushes.
   For the LORD has both devised and
     done
   What He spoke against the
     inhabitants of Babylon.
13 O you who dwell by many waters,
   Abundant in treasures,
   Your end has come,
   The measure of your covetousness.
14 The LORD of hosts has sworn by
     Himself:
   "Surely I will fill you with men, as
     with locusts,
   And they shall lift up a shout against
     you."

15 He has made the earth by His power;
   He has established the world by His
     wisdom,
   And stretched out the heaven by His
     understanding.
16 When He utters *His* voice—
   There is a multitude of waters in the
     heavens:
   "He causes the vapors to ascend from
     the ends of the earth;
   He makes lightnings for the rain;
   He brings the wind out of His
     treasuries."

17 Everyone is dull-hearted, without
     knowledge;
   Every metalsmith is put to shame by
     the carved image;
   For his molded image *is* falsehood,
   And *there is* no breath in them.
18 They *are* futile, a work of errors;
   In the time of their punishment they
     shall perish.
19 The Portion of Jacob *is* not like them,
   For He *is* the Maker of all things;
   And *Israel is* the tribe of His
     inheritance.
   The LORD of hosts *is* His name.

20 "You *are* My battle-ax *and* weapons
     of war:
   For with you I will break the nation
     in pieces;
   With you I will destroy kingdoms;

21 With you I will break in pieces the
   horse and its rider;
   With you I will break in pieces the
   chariot and its rider;
22 With you also I will break in pieces
   man and woman;
   With you I will break in pieces old
   and young;
   With you I will break in pieces the
   young man and the maiden;
23 With you also I will break in pieces
   the shepherd and his flock;
   With you I will break in pieces the
   farmer and his yoke of oxen;
   And with you I will break in pieces
   governors and rulers.

24 "And I will repay Babylon
   And all the inhabitants of Chaldea
   For all the evil they have done
   In Zion in your sight," says the LORD.

25 "Behold, I *am* against you,
   O destroying mountain,
   Who destroys all the earth," says the
   LORD.
   "And I will stretch out My hand
   against you,
   Roll you down from the rocks,
   And make you a burnt mountain.
26 They shall not take from you a stone
   for a corner
   Nor a stone for a foundation,
   But you shall be desolate forever,"
   says the LORD.

27 Set up a banner in the land,
   Blow the trumpet among the nations!
   Prepare the nations against her,
   Call the kingdoms together against
   her:
   Ararat, Minni, and Ashkenaz.
   Appoint a general against her;
   Cause the horses to come up like the
   bristling locusts.
28 Prepare against her the nations,
   With the kings of the Medes,
   Its governors and all its rulers,
   All the land of his dominion.
29 And the land will tremble and
   sorrow;
   For every purpose of the LORD shall
   be performed against Babylon,
   To make the land of Babylon a
   desolation without inhabitant.
30 The mighty men of Babylon have
   ceased fighting,
   They have remained in their
   strongholds;
   Their might has failed,
   They became *like* women;

They have burned her dwelling
   places,
The bars of her *gate* are broken.
31 One runner will run to meet another,
   And one messenger to meet another,
   To show the king of Babylon that
   his city is taken on *all* sides;
32 The passages are blocked,
   The reeds they have burned with fire,
   And the men of war are terrified.

33 For thus says the LORD of hosts, the
God of Israel:

"The daughter of Babylon *is* like a
   threshing floor
   When it is time to thresh her;
   Yet a little while
   And the time of her harvest will
   come."

34 "Nebuchadnezzar the king of Babylon
   Has devoured me, he has crushed me;
   He has made me an empty vessel,
   He has swallowed me up like a
   monster,
   He has filled his stomach with my
   delicacies,
   He has spit me out.
35 Let the violence *done* to me and my
   flesh *be* upon Babylon,"
   The inhabitant of Zion will say;
   "And my blood be upon the
   inhabitants of Chaldea!"
   Jerusalem will say.

36 Therefore thus says the LORD:

"Behold, I will plead your case and
   take vengeance for you.
   I will dry up her sea and make her
   springs dry.
37 Babylon shall become a heap,
   A dwelling place for jackals,
   An astonishment and a hissing,
   Without an inhabitant.
38 They shall roar together like lions,
   They shall growl like lions' whelps.
39 In their excitement I will prepare
   their feasts;
   I will make them drunk,
   That they may rejoice,
   And sleep a perpetual sleep
   And not awake," says the LORD.
40 "I will bring them down
   Like lambs to the slaughter,
   Like rams with male goats.

41 "Oh, how Sheshach is taken!
   Oh, how the praise of the whole earth
   is seized!

How Babylon has become desolate
  among the nations!
42 The sea has come up over Babylon;
  She is covered with the multitude of
    its waves.
43 Her cities are a desolation,
  A dry land and a wilderness,
  A land where no one dwells,
  Through which no son of man passes.
44 I will punish Bel in Babylon,
  And I will bring out of his mouth
    what he has swallowed;
  And the nations shall not stream to
    him anymore.
  Yes, the wall of Babylon shall fall.

45 "My people, go out of the midst of
    her!
  And let everyone deliver himself
    from the fierce anger of the Lord.
46 And lest your heart faint,
  And you fear for the rumor that *will
    be* heard in the land
  (A rumor will come *one* year,
  And after that, in *another* year
  A rumor *will come,*
  And violence in the land,
  Ruler against ruler),
47 Therefore behold, the days are
    coming
  That I will bring judgment on the
    carved images of Babylon;
  Her whole land shall be ashamed,
  And all her slain shall fall in her midst.
48 Then the heavens and the earth and
    all that *is* in them
  Shall sing joyously over Babylon;
  For the plunderers shall come to her
    from the north," says the Lord.

49 As Babylon *has caused* the slain of
    Israel to fall,
  So at Babylon the slain of all the earth
    shall fall.
50 You who have escaped the sword,
  Get away! Do not stand still!
  Remember the Lord afar off,
  And let Jerusalem come to your
    mind.

51 We are ashamed because we have
    heard reproach.
  Shame has covered our faces,
  For strangers have come into the
    sanctuaries of the Lord's house.

52 "Therefore behold, the days are
    coming," says the Lord,
  "That I will bring judgment on her
    carved images,

And throughout all her land the
  wounded shall groan.
53 Though Babylon were to mount up
    to heaven,
  And though she were to fortify the
    height of her strength,
  Yet from Me plunderers would
    come to her," says the Lord.

54 The sound of a cry *comes* from
    Babylon,
  And great destruction from the land
    of the Chaldeans,
55 Because the Lord is plundering
    Babylon
  And silencing her loud voice,
  Though her waves roar like great
    waters,
  And the noise of their voice is
    uttered,
56 Because the plunderer comes against
    her, against Babylon,
  And her mighty men are taken.
  Every one of their bows is broken;
  For the Lord *is* the God of
    recompense,
  He will surely repay.

57 "And I will make drunk
  Her princes and wise men,
  Her governors, her deputies, and her
    mighty men.
  And they shall sleep a perpetual sleep
  And not awake," says the King,
  Whose name *is* the Lord of hosts.

58 Thus says the Lord of hosts:

"The broad walls of Babylon shall be
  utterly broken,
  And her high gates shall be burned
    with fire;
  The people will labor in vain,
  And the nations, because of the fire;
  And they shall be weary."

59 The word which Jeremiah the prophet
commanded Seraiah the son of Neriah, the
son of Mahseiah, when he went with Zedekiah the king of Judah to Babylon in the
fourth year of his reign. And Seraiah *was*
the quartermaster. 60 So Jeremiah wrote in
a book all the evil that would come upon
Babylon, all these words that are written
against Babylon. 61 And Jeremiah said to
Seraiah, "When you arrive in Babylon and
see it, and read all these words, 62 then you
shall say, 'O Lord, You have spoken against
this place to cut it off, so that none shall
remain in it, neither man nor beast, but it
shall be desolate forever.' 63 Now it shall

be, when you have finished reading this book, *that* you shall tie a stone to it and throw it out into the Euphrates. 64 Then you shall say, 'Thus Babylon shall sink and not rise from the catastrophe that I will bring upon her. And they shall be weary.' "

Thus far *are* the words of Jeremiah.

52 ZEDEKIAH *was* twenty-one years old when he became king, and he reigned eleven years in Jerusalem. His mother's name *was* Hamutal the daughter of Jeremiah of Libnah. 2 He also did evil in the sight of the LORD, according to all that Jehoiakim had done. 3 For because of the anger of the LORD *this* happened in Jerusalem and Judah, till He finally cast them out from His presence. Then Zedekiah rebelled against the king of Babylon.

4 Now it came to pass in the ninth year of his reign, in the tenth month, on the tenth *day* of the month, *that* Nebuchadnezzar king of Babylon and all his army came against Jerusalem and encamped against it; and *they* built a siege wall against it all around. 5 So the city was besieged until the eleventh year of King Zedekiah. 6 By the fourth month, on the ninth day of the month, the famine had become so severe in the city that there was no food for the people of the land. 7 Then the city wall was broken through, and all the men of war fled and went out of the city at night by way of the gate between the two walls, which *was* by the king's garden, even though the Chaldeans *were* near the city all around. And they went by way of the plain.

8 But the army of the Chaldeans pursued the king, and they overtook Zedekiah in the plains of Jericho. All his army was scattered from him. 9 So they took the king and brought him up to the king of Babylon at Riblah in the land of Hamath, and he pronounced judgment on him. 10 Then the king of Babylon killed the sons of Zedekiah before his eyes. And he killed all the princes of Judah in Riblah. 11 He also put out the eyes of Zedekiah; and the king of Babylon bound him in bronze fetters, took him to Babylon, and put him in prison till the day of his death.

12 Now in the fifth month, on the tenth *day* of the month (which *was* the nineteenth year of King Nebuchadnezzar king of Babylon), Nebuzaradan, the captain of the guard, *who* served the king of Babylon, came to Jerusalem. 13 He burned the house of the LORD and the king's house; all the houses of Jerusalem, that is, all the houses

of the great, he burned with fire. 14 And all the army of the Chaldeans who *were* with the captain of the guard broke down all the walls of Jerusalem all around. 15 Then Nebuzaradan the captain of the guard carried away captive *some* of the poor people, the rest of the people who remained in the city, the defectors who had deserted to the king of Babylon, and the rest of the craftsmen. 16 But Nebuzaradan the captain of the guard left *some* of the poor of the land as vinedressers and farmers.

17 The bronze pillars that *were* in the house of the LORD, and the carts and the bronze Sea that *were* in the house of the LORD, the Chaldeans broke in pieces, and carried all their bronze to Babylon. 18 They also took away the pots, the shovels, the trimmers, the bowls, the spoons, and all the bronze utensils with which the priests ministered. 19 The basins, the firepans, the bowls, the pots, the lampstands, the spoons, and the cups, whatever *was* solid gold and whatever *was* solid silver, the captain of the guard took away. 20 The two pillars, one Sea, the twelve bronze bulls which *were* under *it, and* the carts, which King Solomon had made for the house of the LORD—the bronze of all these articles was beyond measure. 21 Now *concerning* the pillars: the height of one pillar *was* eighteen cubits, a measuring line of twelve cubits could measure its circumference, and its thickness *was* four fingers; *it was* hollow. 22 A capital of bronze *was* on it; and the height of one capital *was* five cubits, with a network and pomegranates all around the capital, all of bronze. The second pillar, with pomegranates was the same. 23 There were ninety-six pomegranates on the sides; all the pomegranates, all around on the network, *were* one hundred.

24 The captain of the guard took Seraiah the chief priest, Zephaniah the second priest, and the three doorkeepers. 25 He also took out of the city an officer who had charge of the men of war, seven men of the king's close associates who were found in the city, the principal scribe of the army who mustered the people of the land, and sixty men of the people of the land who were found in the midst of the city. 26 And Nebuzaradan the captain of the guard took these and brought them to the king of Babylon at Riblah. 27 Then the king of Babylon struck them and put them to death at Riblah in the land of Hamath. Thus Judah was carried away captive from its own land.

28 These *are* the people whom Nebuchadnezzar carried away captive: in the seventh

year, three thousand and twenty-three Jews; 29 in the eighteenth year of Nebuchadnezzar he carried away captive from Jerusalem eight hundred and thirty-two persons; 30 in the twenty-third year of Nebuchadnezzar, Nebuzaradan the captain of the guard carried away captive of the Jews seven hundred and forty-five persons. All the persons *were* four thousand six hundred.

31 Now it came to pass in the thirty-seventh year of the captivity of Jehoiachin king of Judah, in the twelfth month, on the twenty-fifth *day* of the month, *that* Evil-Merodach king of Babylon, in the first *year* of his reign, lifted up the head of Jehoiachin king of Judah and brought him out of prison. 32 And he spoke kindly to him and gave him a more prominent seat than those of the kings who *were* with him in Babylon. 33 So Jehoiachin changed from his prison garments, and he ate bread regularly before the king all the days of his life. 34 And as for his provisions, there was a regular ration given him by the king of Babylon, a portion for each day until the day of his death, all the days of his life.

PSALM 119:129–136

129 YOUR testimonies are wonderful;
    Therefore my soul keeps them.
130 The entrance of Your words gives light;
    It gives understanding to the simple.
131 I opened my mouth and panted,
    For I longed for Your commandments.
132 Look upon me and be merciful to me,
    As Your custom *is* toward those who love Your name.
133 Direct my steps by Your word,
    And let no iniquity have dominion over me.
134 Redeem me from the oppression of man,
    That I may keep Your precepts.
135 Make Your face shine upon Your servant,
    And teach me Your statutes.
136 Rivers of water run down from my eyes,
    Because *men* do not keep Your law.

PROVERBS 28:7, 8

7 WHOEVER keeps the law *is* a discerning son,

But a companion of gluttons shames his father.

8 One who increases his possessions by usury and extortion
    Gathers it for him who will pity the poor.

TITUS 2:1–15

BUT as for you, speak the things which are proper for sound doctrine: 2 that the older men be sober, reverent, temperate, sound in faith, in love, in patience; 3 the older women likewise, that they be reverent in behavior, not slanderers, not given to much wine, teachers of good things— 4 that they admonish the young women to love their husbands, to love their children, 5 to be discreet, chaste, homemakers, good, obedient to their own husbands, that the word of God may not be blasphemed.

6 Likewise, exhort the young men to be sober-minded, 7 in all things showing yourself *to be* a pattern of good works; in doctrine *showing* integrity, reverence, incorruptibility, 8 sound speech that cannot be condemned, that one who is an opponent may be ashamed, having nothing evil to say of you.

9 *Exhort* bondservants to be obedient to their own masters, to be well pleasing in all *things,* not answering back, 10 not pilfering, but showing all good fidelity, that they may adorn the doctrine of God our Savior in all things.

11 For the grace of God that brings salvation has appeared to all men, 12 teaching

Everything we are that is not through the grace of God will be a dead clog on us. (PHIL. SIN)

us that, denying ungodliness and worldly lusts, we should live soberly, righteously, and godly in the present age, 13 looking for the blessed hope and glorious appearing of our great God and Savior Jesus Christ, 14 who gave Himself for us, that He might redeem us from every lawless deed and purify for Himself *His* own special people, zealous for good works.

15 Speak these things, exhort, and rebuke with all authority. Let no one despise you.

Reading 307—The Red-Handed Rebellion
Lamentations 1:20

The Bible looks on sin, not as a disease, but as red-handed rebellion against the domination of the Creator. The essence of sin is "I won't allow anybody to 'boss' me saving myself," and it may manifest itself in a morally good man as well as in a morally bad man. Sin has not to do with morality or immorality, it has to do with my claim to my right to myself, a deliberate and emphatic independence of God, though I veneer it over with Christian phraseology. (GENESIS)

The Bible looks upon the human race as it is as the result of a mutiny against God; consequently, you find in the Bible something you find in no other book or conception. The modern view of man is, What a marvelous promise of what he is going to be! The Bible looks at man and sees the ruin of what he once was. In the Bible everything is based on the fact that there is something wrong at the basis of things. (BIB. ETHICS)

LAMENTATIONS 1:1—2:22

1   HOW lonely sits the city
     That was full of people!
     How like a widow is she,
     Who *was* great among the nations!
     The princess among the provinces
     Has become a slave!

2   She weeps bitterly in the night,
     Her tears *are* on her cheeks;
     Among all her lovers
     She has none to comfort *her*.
     All her friends have dealt
          treacherously with her;
     They have become her enemies.

3   Judah has gone into captivity,
     Under affliction and hard servitude;
     She dwells among the nations,
     She finds no rest;
     All her persecutors overtake her in
          dire straits.

4   The roads to Zion mourn
     Because no one comes to the set
          feasts.
     All her gates are desolate;
     Her priests sigh,
     Her virgins are afflicted,
     And she *is* in bitterness.

5   Her adversaries have become the
          master,
     Her enemies prosper;
     For the LORD has afflicted her
     Because of the multitude of her
          transgressions.
     Her children have gone into captivity
     before the enemy.

6   And from the daughter of Zion
     All her splendor has departed.
     Her princes have become like deer
     That find no pasture,
     That flee without strength
     Before the pursuer.

7   In the days of her affliction and
          roaming,
     Jerusalem remembers all her pleasant
          things
     That she had in the days of old.
     When her people fell into the hand
          of the enemy,
     With no one to help her,
     The adversaries saw her
     And mocked at her downfall.

8   Jerusalem has sinned gravely,
     Therefore she has become vile.
     All who honored her despise her
     Because they have seen her
          nakedness;
     Yes, she sighs and turns away.

9   Her uncleanness *is* in her skirts;
     She did not consider her destiny;
     Therefore her collapse was awesome;
     She had no comforter.
     "O LORD, behold my affliction,
     For *the* enemy is exalted!"

10 The adversary has spread his hand
   Over all her pleasant things;
   For she has seen the nations enter
      her sanctuary,
   Those whom You commanded
   Not to enter Your assembly.

11 All her people sigh,
   They seek bread;
   They have given their valuables for
      food to restore life.
   "See, O LORD, and consider,
   For I am scorned."

12 "*Is it* nothing to you, all you who
      pass by?
   Behold and see
   If there is any sorrow like my sorrow,
   Which has been brought on me,
   Which the LORD has inflicted
   In the day of His fierce anger.

13 "From above He has sent fire into my
      bones,
   And it overpowered them;
   He has spread a net for my feet
   And turned me back;
   He has made me desolate
   And faint all the day.

14 "The yoke of my transgressions was
      bound;
   They were woven together by His
      hands,
   And thrust upon my neck.
   He made my strength fail;
   The Lord delivered me into the
      hands of *those whom* I am not able
      to withstand.

15 "The Lord has trampled underfoot
      all my mighty *men* in my midst;
   He has called an assembly against
      me
   To crush my young men;
   The Lord trampled *as* in a winepress
   The virgin daughter of Judah.

16 "For these *things* I weep;
   My eye, my eye overflows with
      water;
   Because the comforter, who should
      restore my life,
   Is far from me.
   My children are desolate
   Because the enemy prevailed."

17 Zion spreads out her hands,
   But no one comforts her;
   The LORD has commanded
      concerning Jacob

That those around him *become* his
   adversaries;
Jerusalem has become an unclean
   thing among them.

18 "The LORD is righteous,
   For I rebelled against His
      commandment.
   Hear now, all peoples,
   And behold my sorrow;
   My virgins and my young men
   Have gone into captivity.

19 "I called for my lovers,
   But they deceived me;
   My priests and my elders
   Breathed their last in the city,
   While they sought food
   To restore their life.

20 "See, O LORD, that I *am* in distress;
   My soul is troubled;
   My heart is overturned within me,
   For I have been very rebellious.
   Outside the sword bereaves,
   At home *it is* like death.

21 "They have heard that I sigh,
   But no one comforts me.
   All my enemies have heard of my
      trouble;
   They are glad that You have
      done *it*.
   Bring on the day You have
      announced,
   That they may become like me.

22 "Let all their wickedness come before
      You,
   And do to them as You have done
      to me
   For all my transgressions;
   For my sighs *are* many,
   And my heart *is* faint."

2 HOW the Lord has covered the
      daughter of Zion
   With a cloud in His anger!
   He cast down from heaven to the
      earth
   The beauty of Israel,
   And did not remember His footstool
   In the day of His anger.

2 The Lord has swallowed up and has
      not pitied
   All the dwelling places of Jacob.
   He has thrown down in His wrath
   The strongholds of the daughter of
      Judah;

He has brought *them* down to the
    ground;
He has profaned the kingdom and
    its princes.

3   He has cut off in fierce anger
     Every horn of Israel;
     He has drawn back His right hand
       From before the enemy.
     He has blazed against Jacob like a
       flaming fire
     Devouring all around.

4   Standing like an enemy, He has bent
     His bow;
     With His right hand, like an
       adversary,
     He has slain all *who were* pleasing to
       His eye;
     On the tent of the daughter of Zion,
     He has poured out His fury like fire.

5   The Lord was like an enemy.
     He has swallowed up Israel,
     He has swallowed up all her palaces;
     He has destroyed her strongholds,
     And has increased mourning and
       lamentation
     In the daughter of Judah.

6   He has done violence to His
       tabernacle,
     As if it were a garden;
     He has destroyed His place of
       assembly;
     The LORD has caused
     The appointed feasts and Sabbaths
       to be forgotten in Zion.
     In His burning indignation He has
       spurned the king and the priest.

7   The Lord has spurned His altar,
     He has abandoned His sanctuary;
     He has given up the walls of her
       palaces
     Into the hand of the enemy.
     They have made a noise in the house
       of the LORD
     As on the day of a set feast.

8   The LORD has purposed to destroy
     The wall of the daughter of Zion.
     He has stretched out a line;
     He has not withdrawn His hand from
       destroying;
     Therefore He has caused the rampart
       and wall to lament;
     They languished together.

9   Her gates have sunk into the ground;
     He has destroyed and broken her
       bars.

Her king and her princes *are* among
    the nations;
The Law *is* no *more*,
And her prophets find no vision from
    the LORD.

If I have disobeyed, the Word of God
is dried up, there is ''no open
vision.''   (DISCIPLES)

---

10   The elders of the daughter of Zion
     Sit on the ground *and* keep silence;
     They throw dust on their heads
     And gird themselves with sackcloth.
     The virgins of Jerusalem
     Bow their heads to the ground.

11   My eyes fail with tears,
     My heart is troubled;
     My bile is poured on the ground
     Because of the destruction of the
       daughter of my people,
     Because the children and the infants
     Faint in the streets of the city.

12   They say to their mothers,
     "Where *is* grain and wine?"
     As they swoon like the wounded
     In the streets of the city,
     As their life is poured out
     In their mothers' bosom.

13   How shall I console you?
     To what shall I liken you,
     O daughter of Jerusalem?
     What shall I compare with you, that
       I may comfort you,
     O virgin daughter of Zion?
     For your ruin *is* spread wide as the
       sea;
     Who can heal you?

14   Your prophets have seen for you
     False and deceptive visions;
     They have not uncovered your
       iniquity,
     To bring back your captives,
     But have envisioned for you false
       prophecies and delusions.

15   All who pass by clap *their* hands at
     you;
     They hiss and shake their heads
     At the daughter of Jerusalem:
     "*Is* this the city that is called
     'The perfection of beauty,
     The joy of the whole earth'?"

16 All your enemies have opened their
      mouth against you;
   They hiss and gnash *their* teeth.
   They say, "We have swallowed
      her up!
   Surely this *is* the day we have waited
      for;
   We have found *it,* we have seen *it!*"

17 The LORD has done what He
      purposed;
   He has fulfilled His word
   Which He commanded in days of
      old.
   He has thrown down and has not
      pitied,
   And He has caused an enemy to
      rejoice over you;
   He has exalted the horn of your
      adversaries.

18 Their heart cried out to the Lord,
   "O wall of the daughter of Zion,
   Let tears run down like a river day
      and night;
   Give yourself no relief;
   Give your eyes no rest.

19 "Arise, cry out in the night,
   At the beginning of the watches;
   Pour out your heart like water before
      the face of the Lord.
   Lift your hands toward Him
   For the life of your young children,
   Who faint from hunger at the head
      of every street."

20 "See, O LORD, and consider!
   To whom have You done this?
   Should the women eat their
      offspring,
   The children they have cuddled?
   Should the priest and prophet be slain
   In the sanctuary of the Lord?

21 "Young and old lie
   On the ground in the streets;
   My virgins and my young men
   Have fallen by the sword;
   You have slain *them* in the day of
      Your anger,
   You have slaughtered *and* not pitied.

22 "You have invited as to a feast day
   The terrors that surround me.
   In the day of the LORD's anger
   There was no refugee or survivor.
   Those whom I have borne and
      brought up
   My enemies have destroyed."

PSALM 119:137–144

137 RIGHTEOUS *are* You, O LORD,
    And upright *are* Your judgments.
138 Your testimonies, *which* You have
       commanded,
    Are righteous and very faithful.
139 My zeal has consumed me,
    Because my enemies have forgotten
       Your words.
140 Your word *is* very pure;
    Therefore Your servant loves it.
141 I *am* small and despised,
    Yet I do not forget Your precepts.
142 Your righteousness *is* an everlasting
       righteousness,
    And Your law *is* truth.
143 Trouble and anguish have
       overtaken me,
    Yet Your commandments *are* my
       delights.
144 The righteousness of Your testimonies
    is everlasting;
    Give me understanding, and I shall
       live.

PROVERBS 28:9, 10

9 ONE who turns away his ear from
      hearing the law,
   Even his prayer *is* an abomination.

10 Whoever causes the upright to go astray
      in an evil way,
   He himself will fall into his own pit;
   But the blameless will inherit good.

TITUS 3:1–15

REMIND them to be subject to rulers and
authorities, to obey, to be ready for every
good work, 2 to speak evil of no one, to
be peaceable, gentle, showing all humility
to all men. 3 For we ourselves were also
once foolish, disobedient, deceived, serving
various lusts and pleasures, living in malice
and envy, hateful and hating one another.

*God is interested in some strange
people.*   (GLORIFY)

4 But when the kindness and the love of
God our Savior toward man appeared,
5 not by works of righteousness which we
have done, but according to His mercy He

saved us, through the washing of regeneration and renewing of the Holy Spirit, 6 whom He poured out on us abundantly through Jesus Christ our Savior, 7 that having been justified by His grace we should become heirs according to the hope of eternal life.

8 This is a faithful saying, and these things I want you to affirm constantly, that those who have believed in God should be careful to maintain good works. These things are good and profitable to men.

9 But avoid foolish disputes, genealogies, contentions, and strivings about the law; for they are unprofitable and useless.

10 Reject a divisive man after the first and second admonition, 11 knowing that such a person is warped and sinning, being self-condemned.

12 When I send Artemas to you, or Tychicus, be diligent to come to me at Nicopolis, for I have decided to spend the winter there. 13 Send Zenas the lawyer and Apollos on their journey with haste, that they may lack nothing. 14 And let our *people* also learn to maintain good works, to *meet* urgent needs, that they may not be unfruitful.

15 All who *are* with me greet you. Greet those who love us in the faith.

Grace *be* with you all. Amen.

◆◆◆◆

Reading 308—Our Immortal Spirit
Philemon 25

Beware of dividing man up into body, soul and spirit: man *is* body, soul and spirit. Soul has no entity, it depends entirely upon the body, and yet there is a subtle spiritual element in it. Soul is the rational expression of my personal spirit in my body, the way I reason and think and work.   (*Moral Found.*)

Soul and body depend upon each other, spirit does not, spirit is immortal. Soul is simply the spirit expressing itself in the body. Immediately the body goes, the soul is gone, but the moment the body is brought back, soul is brought back, and spirit, soul and body will again be together. Spirit has never died, can never die, in the sense in which the body dies; the spirit is immortal, either in immortal life or in immortal death. There is no such thing as annihilation taught in the Bible. The separation of spirit from body and soul is temporary. The resurrection is the resurrection of the body.   (*Bib. Psych.*)

LAMENTATIONS 3:1—5:22

1 I *am* the man *who* has seen affliction
    by the rod of His wrath.
2 He has led me and made *me* walk
    In darkness and not *in* light.
3 Surely He has turned His hand
        against me
    Time and time again throughout the
        day.

4 He has aged my flesh and my skin,
    And broken my bones.
5 He has besieged me
    And surrounded *me* with bitterness
        and woe.
6 He has set me in dark places
    Like the dead of long ago.

7 He has hedged me in so that I cannot
        get out;
    He has made my chain heavy.
8 Even when I cry and shout,
    He shuts out my prayer.
9 He has blocked my ways with hewn
        stone;
    He has made my paths crooked.

10 He *has been* to me a bear lying in
        wait,
    Like a lion in ambush.
11 He has turned aside my ways and
        torn me in pieces;
    He has made me desolate.
12 He has bent His bow
    And set me up as a target for the
        arrow.

13 He has caused the arrows of His quiver
To pierce my loins.
14 I have become the ridicule of all my people—
Their taunting song all the day.
15 He has filled me with bitterness,
He has made me drink wormwood.

16 He has also broken my teeth with gravel,
And covered me with ashes.
17 You have moved my soul far from peace;
I have forgotten prosperity.
18 And I said, "My strength and my hope
Have perished from the LORD."

19 Remember my affliction and roaming,
The wormwood and the gall.
20 My soul still remembers
And sinks within me.
21 This I recall to my mind,
Therefore I have hope.

22 *Through* the LORD's mercies we are not consumed,
Because His compassions fail not.
23 *They are* new every morning;
Great *is* Your faithfulness.
24 "The LORD *is* my portion," says my soul,
"Therefore I hope in Him!"

25 The LORD *is* good to those who wait for Him,
To the soul *who* seeks Him.
26 *It is* good that *one* should hope and wait quietly
For the salvation of the LORD.
27 *It is* good for a man to bear
The yoke in his youth.

28 Let him sit alone and keep silent,
Because *God* has laid *it* on him;
29 Let him put his mouth in the dust—
There may yet be hope.
30 Let him give *his* cheek to the one who strikes him,
And be full of reproach.

31 For the Lord will not cast off forever.
32 Though He causes grief,
Yet He will show compassion
According to the multitude of His mercies.
33 For He does not afflict willingly,
Nor grieve the children of men.

34 To crush under one's feet
All the prisoners of the earth,
35 To turn aside the justice *due* a man
Before the face of the Most High,
36 Or subvert a man in his cause—
The Lord does not approve.

37 Who *is* he *who* speaks and it comes to pass,
When the Lord has not commanded *it*?
38 *Is it* not from the mouth of the Most High
That woe and well-being proceed?
39 Why should a living man complain,
A man for the punishment of his sins?

40 Let us search out and examine our ways,
And turn back to the LORD;
41 Let us lift our hearts and hands
To God in heaven.
42 We have transgressed and rebelled;
You have not pardoned.

43 You have covered *Yourself* with anger
And pursued us;
You have slain *and* not pitied.
44 You have covered Yourself with a cloud,
That prayer should not pass through.
45 You have made us an offscouring and refuse
In the midst of the peoples.

46 All our enemies
Have opened their mouths against us.
47 Fear and a snare have come upon us,
Desolation and destruction.
48 My eyes overflow with rivers of water
For the destruction of the daughter of my people.

49 My eyes flow and do not cease,
Without interruption,
50 Till the LORD from heaven
Looks down and sees.
51 My eyes bring suffering to my soul
Because of all the daughters of my city.

52 My enemies without cause
Hunted me down like a bird.

---

*I*t is the lives of the prophets that prefigure the Lord Jesus Christ.   (SEND I YOU)

53 They silenced my life in the pit
   And threw stones at me.
54 The waters flowed over my head;
   I said, "I am cut off!"
55 I called on Your name, O Lord,
   From the lowest pit.
56 You have heard my voice:
   "Do not hide Your ear
   From my sighing, from my cry for
      help."
57 You drew near on the day I called
      on You,
   And said, "Do not fear!"

58 O Lord, You have pleaded the case
      for my soul;
   You have redeemed my life.
59 O Lord, You have seen *how* I am
      wronged;
   Judge my case.
60 You have seen all their vengeance,
   All their schemes against me.

61 You have heard their reproach,
      O Lord,
   All their schemes against me,
62 The lips of my enemies
   And their whispering against me all
      the day.
63 Look at their sitting down and their
      rising up;
   I *am* their taunting song.

64 Repay them, O Lord,
   According to the work of their hands.
65 Give them a veiled heart;
   Your curse *be* upon them!
66 In Your anger,
   Pursue and destroy them
   From under the heavens of
      the Lord.

4 HOW the gold has become dim!
   How changed the fine gold!
   The stones of the sanctuary are
      scattered
   At the head of every street.

2 The precious sons of Zion,
   Valuable as fine gold,
   How they are regarded as clay pots,
   The work of the hands of the potter!

3 Even the jackals present their breasts
   To nurse their young;
   But the daughter of my people *is*
      cruel,
   Like ostriches in the wilderness.

4 The tongue of the infant clings
   To the roof of its mouth for thirst;

The young children ask for bread,
But no one breaks *it* for them.

5 Those who ate delicacies
   Are desolate in the streets;
   Those who were brought up in scarlet
   Embrace ash heaps.

6 The punishment of the iniquity of
      the daughter of my people
   Is greater than the punishment of the
      sin of Sodom,
   Which was overthrown in a moment,
   With no hand to help her!

7 Her Nazirites were brighter than
      snow
   And whiter than milk;
   They were more ruddy in body than
      rubies,
   Like sapphire in their appearance.

8 *Now* their appearance is blacker than
      soot;
   They go unrecognized in the streets;
   Their skin clings to their bones,
   It has become as dry as wood.

9 *Those* slain by the sword are better
      off
   Than *those* who die of hunger;
   For these pine away,
   Stricken *for lack* of the fruits of the
      field.

10 The hands of the compassionate
      women
   Have cooked their own children;
   They became food for them
   In the destruction of the daughter
      of my people.

11 The Lord has fulfilled His fury,
   He has poured out His fierce anger.
   He kindled a fire in Zion,
   And it has devoured its foundations.

12 The kings of the earth,
   And all inhabitants of the world,
   Would not have believed
   That the adversary and the enemy
   Could enter the gates of Jerusalem—

13 Because of the sins of her prophets
   And the iniquities of her priests,
   Who shed in her midst
   The blood of the just.

14 They wandered blind in the streets;
   They have defiled themselves with
      blood,

So that no one would touch their garments.

15 They cried out to them,
"Go away, unclean!
Go away, go away,
Do not touch us!"
When they fled and wandered,
Those among the nations said,
"They shall no longer dwell *here*."

16 The face of the LORD scattered them;
He no longer regards them.
The people do not respect the priests
Nor show favor to the elders.

17 Still our eyes failed us,
Watching vainly for our help;
In our watching we watched
For a nation *that* could not save *us*.

18 They tracked our steps
So that we could not walk in our streets.
Our end was near;
Our days were over,
For our end had come.

19 Our pursuers were swifter
Than the eagles of the heavens.
They pursued us on the mountains
And lay in wait for us in the wilderness.

20 The breath of our nostrils, the anointed of the LORD,
Was caught in their pits,
Of whom we said, "Under his shadow
We shall live among the nations."

21 Rejoice and be glad, O daughter of Edom,
You who dwell in the land of Uz!
The cup shall also pass over to you
And you shall become drunk and make yourself naked.

22 *The punishment of* your iniquity is accomplished,
O daughter of Zion;
He will no longer send you into captivity.
He will punish your iniquity,
O daughter of Edom;
He will uncover your sins!

5 REMEMBER, O LORD, what has come upon us;
Look, and behold our reproach!

2 Our inheritance has been turned over to aliens,
And our houses to foreigners.

3 We have become orphans and waifs,
Our mothers *are* like widows.

4 We pay for the water we drink,
And our wood comes at a price.

5 *They* pursue at our heels;
We labor *and* have no rest.

6 We have given our hand *to the* Egyptians
And the Assyrians, to be satisfied with bread.

7 Our fathers sinned *and are* no more,
But we bear their iniquities.

8 Servants rule over us;
There is none to deliver *us* from their hand.

9 We get our bread *at the risk* of our lives,
Because of the sword in the wilderness.

10 Our skin is hot as an oven,
Because of the fever of famine.

11 They ravished the women in Zion,
The maidens in the cities of Judah.

12 Princes were hung up by their hands,
And elders were not respected.

13 Young men ground at the millstones;
Boys staggered under *loads of* wood.

14 The elders have ceased *gathering at* the gate,
And the young men from their music.

15 The joy of our heart has ceased;
Our dance has turned into mourning.

16 The crown has fallen *from* our head.
Woe to us, for we have sinned!

17 Because of this our heart is faint;
Because of these *things* our eyes grow dim;

18 Because of Mount Zion which is desolate,
With foxes walking about on it.

19 You, O LORD, remain forever;
Your throne from generation to generation.

20 Why do You forget us forever,
And forsake us for so long a time?

21 Turn us back to You, O LORD, and we will be restored;
Renew our days as of old,

22 Unless You have utterly rejected us,
And are very angry with us!

PSALM 119:145–152

145   I cry out with *my* whole heart;
Hear me, O LORD!
I will keep Your statutes.

146   I cry out to You;
Save me, and I will keep Your
testimonies.

147   I rise before the dawning of the
morning,
And cry for help;
I hope in Your word.

148   My eyes are awake through the *night*
watches,
That I may meditate on Your word.

149   Hear my voice according to Your
lovingkindness;
O LORD, revive me according to Your
justice.

150   They draw near who follow after
wickedness;
They are far from Your law.

151   You *are* near, O LORD,
And all Your commandments *are*
truth.

152   Concerning Your testimonies,
I have known of old that You have
founded them forever.

PROVERBS 28:11

11   THE rich man *is* wise in his own eyes,
But the poor who has understanding
searches him out.

PHILEMON 1–25

PAUL, a prisoner of Christ Jesus, and
Timothy *our* brother,

To Philemon our beloved *friend* and fellow laborer, 2 to the beloved Apphia, Archippus our fellow soldier, and to the
church in your house:

3 Grace to you and peace from God our
Father and the Lord Jesus Christ.

4 I thank my God, making mention of
you always in my prayers, 5 hearing of your
love and faith which you have toward the
Lord Jesus and toward all the saints,
6 that the sharing of your faith may become
effective by the acknowledgment of every
good thing which is in you in Christ Jesus.
7 For we have great joy and consolation
in your love, because the hearts of the saints
have been refreshed by you, brother.

8 Therefore, though I might be very bold
in Christ to command you what is fitting,
9 yet for love's sake I rather appeal *to you*—
being such a one as Paul, the aged, and
now also a prisoner of Jesus Christ—
10 I appeal to you for my son Onesimus,
whom I have begotten *while* in my chains,
11 who once was unprofitable to you, but
now is profitable to you and to me.

---

*There was never a saint yet who
did not have to start with a
maimed life.*   (BIB. ETHICS)

---

12 I am sending him back. You therefore
receive him, that is, my own heart,
13 whom I wished to keep with me, that
on your behalf he might minister to me
in my chains for the gospel. 14 But without
your consent I wanted to do nothing, that
your good deed might not be by compulsion, as it were, but voluntary.

15 For perhaps he departed for a while
for this *purpose,* that you might receive him
forever, 16 no longer as a slave but more
than a slave—a beloved brother, especially
to me but how much more to you, both
in the flesh and in the Lord.

17 If then you count me as a partner, receive him as *you would* me. 18 But if he has
wronged you or owes anything, put that
on my account. 19 I, Paul, am writing with
my own hand. I will repay—not to mention
to you that you owe me even your own
self besides. 20 Yes, brother, let me have
joy from you in the Lord; refresh my heart
in the Lord.

21 Having confidence in your obedience,
I write to you, knowing that you will do
even more than I say. 22 But, meanwhile,
also prepare a guest room for me, for I
trust that through your prayers I shall be
granted to you.

23 Epaphras, my fellow prisoner in
Christ Jesus, greets you, 24 *as do* Mark,
Aristarchus, Demas, Luke, my fellow la-
borers.

25 The grace of our Lord Jesus Christ
be with your spirit. Amen.

Reading 309—The Voice of God's Nature

Ezekiel 1:28; 2:1

When we speak of the call of God, we are apt to forget the most important feature, namely, the nature of the One who calls. There is the call of the sea, the call of the mountains, the call of the great ice barriers, but these calls are only heard by the few. The call is the expression of the nature from which it comes, and we can only record the call if the same nature is in us. The call of God is the expression of God's nature, not of our nature. There are strands of the call of God providentially at work for us which we recognize and no one else does. It is the threading of God's voice to us in some particular matter, and it is no use consulting anyone else about it. We have to keep that profound relationship between our souls and God.

The call of God is not the echo of my nature; my affinities and personal temperament are not considered. As long as I consider my personal temperament and think about what I am fitted for, I shall never hear the call of God. But when I am brought into relationship with God, I am in the condition Isaiah was in. Isaiah's soul was so attuned to God by the tremendous crisis he had gone through that he recorded the call of God to his amazed soul. The majority of us have no ear for anything but ourselves, we cannot hear a thing God says. To be brought into the zone of the call of God is to be profoundly altered. (*Utmost*)

EZEKIEL 1:1—2:10

NOW it came to pass in the thirtieth year, in the fourth *month,* on the fifth *day* of the month, as I *was* among the captives by the River Chebar, *that* the heavens were opened and I saw visions of God. 2 On the fifth *day* of the month, which *was* in the fifth year of King Jehoiachin's captivity, 3 the word of the Lord came expressly to Ezekiel the priest, the son of Buzi, in the land of the Chaldeans by the River Chebar; and the hand of the Lord was upon him there.

4 Then I looked, and behold, a whirlwind was coming out of the north, a great cloud with raging fire engulfing itself; and brightness *was* all around it and radiating out of its midst like the color of amber, out of the midst of the fire. 5 Also from within it *came* the likeness of four living creatures. And this *was* their appearance: they had the likeness of a man. 6 Each one had four faces, and each one had four wings. 7 Their legs *were* straight, and the soles of their feet *were* like the soles of calves' feet. They sparkled like the color of burnished bronze. 8 The hands of a man *were* under their wings on their four sides; and each of the four had faces and wings. 9 Their wings touched one another. *The creatures* did not turn when they went, but each one went straight forward.

10 As for the likeness of their faces, *each* had the face of a man; each of the four had the face of a lion on the right side, each of the four had the face of an ox on the left side, and each of the four had the face of an eagle. 11 Thus *were* their faces. Their wings stretched upward; two *wings* of each one touched one another, and two covered their bodies. 12 And each one went straight forward; they went wherever the spirit wanted to go, and they did not turn when they went.

13 As for the likeness of the living creatures, their appearance *was* like burning coals of fire, like the appearance of torches going back and forth among the living creatures. The fire was bright, and out of the fire went lightning. 14 And the living creatures ran back and forth, in appearance like a flash of lightning.

15 Now as I looked at the living creatures, behold, a wheel *was* on the earth beside each living creature with its four faces. 16 The appearance of the wheels and their workings *was* like the color of beryl, and all four had the same likeness. The appearance of their workings *was,* as it were, a wheel in the middle of a wheel. 17 When they moved, they went toward any one of four directions; they did not turn aside

when they went. 18 As for their rims, they were so high they were awesome; and their rims *were* full of eyes, all around the four of them. 19 When the living creatures went, the wheels went beside them; and when the living creatures were lifted up from the earth, the wheels were lifted up. 20 Wherever the spirit wanted to go, they went, *because* there the spirit went; and the wheels were lifted together with them, for the spirit of the living creatures *was* in the wheels. 21 When those went, *these* went; when those stood, *these* stood; and when those were lifted up from the earth, the wheels were lifted up together with them, for the spirit of the living creatures *was* in the wheels.

22 The likeness of the firmament above the heads of the living creatures *was* like the color of an awesome crystal, stretched out over their heads. 23 And under the firmament their wings *spread out* straight, one toward another. Each one had two which covered one side, and each one had two which covered the other side of the body. 24 When they went, I heard the noise of their wings, like the noise of many waters, like the voice of the Almighty, a tumult like the noise of an army; and when they stood still, they let down their wings. 25 A voice came from above the firmament that *was* over their heads; whenever they stood, they let down their wings.

26 And above the firmament over their heads *was* the likeness of a throne, in appearance like a sapphire stone; on the likeness of the throne *was* a likeness with the appearance of a man high above it. 27 Also from the appearance of His waist and upward I saw, as it were, the color of amber with the appearance of fire all around within it; and from the appearance of His waist and downward I saw, as it were, the appearance of fire with brightness all around. 28 Like the appearance of a rainbow in a cloud on a rainy day, so *was* the appearance of the brightness all around it. This *was* the appearance of the likeness of the glory of the LORD.

So when I saw *it,* I fell on my face, and I heard a voice of One speaking.

2 AND He said to me, "Son of man, stand on your feet, and I will speak to you." 2 Then the Spirit entered me when He spoke to me, and set me on my feet; and I heard Him who spoke to me. 3 And He said to me: "Son of man, I am sending you to the children of Israel, to a rebellious nation that has rebelled against Me; they and their fathers have transgressed against Me to this very day. 4 For *they are* impudent and stubborn children. I am sending you to them, and you shall say to them, 'Thus says the Lord GOD.' 5 As for them, whether they hear or whether they refuse—for they *are* a rebellious house—yet they will know that a prophet has been among them.

6 "And you, son of man, do not be afraid of them nor be afraid of their words, though briers and thorns *are* with you and you dwell among scorpions; do not be afraid of their words or dismayed by their looks, though they *are* a rebellious house. 7 You shall speak My words to them, whether they hear or whether they refuse, for they *are* rebellious. 8 But you, son of man, hear what I say to you. Do not be rebellious like that rebellious house; open your mouth and eat what I give you."

9 Now when I looked, there was a hand stretched out to me; and behold, a scroll of a book *was* in it. 10 Then He spread it before me; and *there was* writing on the inside and on the outside, and written on it *were* lamentations and mourning and woe.

PSALM 119:153–160

153 CONSIDER my affliction and
        deliver me,
    For I do not forget Your law.
154 Plead my cause and redeem me;
    Revive me according to Your word.
155 Salvation *is* far from the wicked,
    For they do not seek Your statutes.
156 Great *are* Your tender mercies,
        O LORD;
    Revive me according to Your
        judgments.
157 Many *are* my persecutors and my
        enemies,
    Yet I do not turn from Your
        testimonies.
158 I see the treacherous, and am
        disgusted,
    Because they do not keep Your word.
159 Consider how I love Your precepts;
    Revive me, O LORD, according to
        Your lovingkindness.
160 The entirety of Your word *is* truth,
    And every one of Your righteous
        judgments *endures* forever.

PROVERBS 28:12

12 WHEN the righteous rejoice, *there is*
    great glory;

But when the wicked arise, men hide themselves.

HEBREWS 1:1–14

GOD, who at various times and in various ways spoke in time past to the fathers by the prophets, 2 has in these last days spoken to us by *His* Son, whom He has appointed heir of all things, through whom also He made the worlds; 3 who being the brightness of *His* glory and the express image of His person, and upholding all things by the word of His power, when He had by Himself purged our sins, sat down at the right hand of the Majesty on high,

---

*H*is glory was the glory of actual holiness. (PSY. REDEMP.)

---

4 having become so much better than the angels, as He has by inheritance obtained a more excellent name than they.

5 For to which of the angels did He ever say:

"You are My Son,
Today I have begotten You"?

And again:

"I will be to Him a Father,
And He shall be to Me a Son"?

6 But when He again brings the firstborn into the world, He says:

"Let all the angels of God worship Him."

7 And of the angels He says:

"Who makes His angels spirits
And His ministers a flame of fire."

8 But to the Son *He says:*

"Your throne, O God, *is* forever and ever;
A scepter of righteousness *is* the scepter of Your kingdom.
9   You have loved righteousness and hated lawlessness;
Therefore God, Your God, has anointed You
With the oil of gladness more than Your companions."

10 And:

"You, LORD, in the beginning laid the foundation of the earth,
And the heavens are the work of Your hands.
11   They will perish, but You remain;
And they will all grow old like a garment;
12   Like a cloak You will fold them up,
And they will be changed.
But You are the same,
And Your years will not fail."

13 But to which of the angels has He ever said:

"Sit at My right hand,
Till I make Your enemies Your footstool"?

14 Are they not all ministering spirits sent forth to minister for those who will inherit salvation?

◆◆◆◆

---

*Reading 310—*Temptations of God as Man
Hebrews 2:11, 17, 18

Jesus Christ looked upon His life as one of temptation; and He goes through the same kind of temptation in us as He went through in the days of His flesh. The essence of Christianity is that we give the Son of God a chance to live and move and have His being in us, and the meaning of all spiritual growth is that He has an increasing opportunity to manifest Himself in our mortal flesh. The temptations of Jesus are not those of a Man as man, but the temptations of God as Man. "Therefore, in all things He had to be made like *His* brethren" (Heb. 2:17). Jesus Christ's temptations and ours move in different spheres until we become His brethren by being born from above. "For both He who sanctifies and those who are being sanctified *are* all of one, for which reason He is not ashamed to call them brethren" (Heb. 2:11). By regeneration the Son of God is formed in me and He has the same setting in my life as He had when on earth. The honor of Jesus Christ is at stake in my bodily life; am I remaining loyal to Him in the temptations which beset His life in me?   (*PLACE HELP*)

We are apt to imagine that our Lord was only tempted once and that then His temptations were over. His temptations went on from the first moment of His conscious life to the last, because His holiness was not the holiness of Almighty God, but the holiness of man, which can only progress by means of the things that go against it (see Heb. 2:18; 4:15). Are we going with Jesus in His temptations? It is true that He is with us in our temptations, but are we with Him in His?   (*POSSIBLE*)

EZEKIEL 3:1—4:17

MOREOVER He said to me, "Son of man, eat what you find; eat this scroll, and go, speak to the house of Israel." 2 So I opened my mouth, and He caused me to eat that scroll.

3 And He said to me, "Son of man, feed your belly, and fill your stomach with this scroll that I give you." So I ate, and it was in my mouth like honey in sweetness.

You cannot prove facts; you have to swallow them.   (PHIL. SIN)

---

4 Then He said to me: "Son of man, go to the house of Israel and speak with My words to them. 5 For you *are* not sent to a people of unfamiliar speech and of hard language, *but* to the house of Israel, 6 not to many people of unfamiliar speech and of hard language, whose words you cannot understand. Surely, had I sent you to them, they would have listened to you. 7 But the house of Israel will not listen to you, because they will not listen to Me; for all the house of Israel *are* impudent and hard-hearted. 8 Behold, I have made your face strong against their faces, and your forehead strong against their foreheads. 9 Like adamant stone, harder than flint, I have made your forehead; do not be afraid of them, nor be dismayed at their looks, though they *are* a rebellious house."

10 Moreover He said to me: "Son of man, receive into your heart all My words that I speak to you, and hear with your ears. 11 And go, get to the captives, to the children of your people, and speak to them and tell them, 'Thus says the Lord GOD,' whether they hear, or whether they refuse."

12 Then the Spirit lifted me up, and I heard behind me a great thunderous voice: "Blessed *is* the glory of the LORD from His place!" 13 *I* also *heard* the noise of the wings of the living creatures that touched one another, and the noise of the wheels beside them, and a great thunderous noise. 14 So the Spirit lifted me up and took me away, and I went in bitterness, in the heat of my spirit; but the hand of the LORD was strong upon me. 15 Then I came to the captives at Tel Abib, who dwelt by the River Chebar; and I sat where they sat, and remained there astonished among them seven days.

16 Now it came to pass at the end of seven days that the word of the LORD came to me, saying, 17 "Son of man, I have made you a watchman for the house of Israel; therefore hear a word from My mouth, and give them warning from Me: 18 When I say to the wicked, 'You shall surely die,' and you give him no warning, nor speak to warn the wicked from his wicked way, to save his life, that same wicked *man* shall die in his iniquity; but his blood I will require at your hand. 19 Yet, if you warn the wicked, and he does not turn from his wickedness, nor from his wicked way, he shall die in his iniquity; but you have delivered your soul.

20 "Again, when a righteous *man* turns from his righteousness and commits iniquity, and I lay a stumbling block before him, he shall die; because you did not give him warning, he shall die in his sin, and his righteousness which he has done shall not be remembered; but his blood I will require at your hand. 21 Nevertheless if you warn the righteous *man* that the righteous should not sin, and he does not sin, he shall surely live because he took warning; also you will have delivered your soul."

22 Then the hand of the Lord was upon me there, and He said to me, "Arise, go out into the plain, and there I shall talk with you."

23 So I arose and went out into the plain, and behold, the glory of the Lord stood there, like the glory which I saw by the River Chebar; and I fell on my face. 24 Then the Spirit entered me and set me on my feet, and spoke with me and said to me: "Go, shut yourself inside your house. 25 And you, O son of man, surely they will put ropes on you and bind you with them, so that you cannot go out among them. 26 I will make your tongue cling to the roof of your mouth, so that you shall be mute and not be one to rebuke them, for they *are* a rebellious house. 27 But when I speak with you, I will open your mouth, and you shall say to them, 'Thus says the Lord God.' He who hears, let him hear; and he who refuses, let him refuse; for they *are* a rebellious house.

4 "YOU also, son of man, take a clay tablet and lay it before you, and portray on it a city, Jerusalem. 2 Lay siege against it, build a siege wall against it, and heap up a mound against it; set camps against it also, and place battering rams against it all around. 3 Moreover take for yourself an iron plate, and set it *as* an iron wall between you and the city. Set your face against it, and it shall be besieged, and you shall lay siege against it. This *will be* a sign to the house of Israel.

4 "Lie also on your left side, and lay the iniquity of the house of Israel upon it. *According* to the number of the days that you lie on it, you shall bear their iniquity. 5 For I have laid on you the years of their iniquity, according to the number of the days, three hundred and ninety days; so you shall bear the iniquity of the house of Israel. 6 And when you have completed them, lie again on your right side; then you shall bear the iniquity of the house of Judah forty days. I have laid on you a day for each year.

7 "Therefore you shall set your face toward the siege of Jerusalem; your arm *shall be* uncovered, and you shall prophesy against it. 8 And surely I will restrain you so that you cannot turn from one side to another till you have ended the days of your siege.

9 "Also take for yourself wheat, barley, beans, lentils, millet, and spelt; put them into one vessel, and make bread of them for yourself. *During* the number of days that you lie on your side, three hundred

and ninety days, you shall eat it. 10 And your food which you eat *shall be* by weight, twenty shekels a day; from time to time you shall eat it. 11 You shall also drink water by measure, one-sixth of a hin; from time to time you shall drink. 12 And you shall eat it *as* barley cakes; and bake it using fuel of human waste in their sight."

13 Then the Lord said, "So shall the children of Israel eat their defiled bread among the Gentiles, where I will drive them."

14 So I said, "Ah, Lord God! Indeed I have never defiled myself from my youth till now; I have never eaten what died of itself or was torn by beasts, nor has abominable flesh ever come into my mouth."

15 Then He said to me, "See, I am giving you cow dung instead of human waste, and you shall prepare your bread over it."

16 Moreover He said to me, "Son of man, surely I will cut off the supply of bread in Jerusalem; they shall eat bread by weight and with anxiety, and shall drink water by measure and with dread, 17 that they may lack bread and water, and be dismayed with one another, and waste away because of their iniquity.

PSALM 119:161–168

161 PRINCES persecute me without a cause,
But my heart stands in awe of Your word.
162 I rejoice at Your word
As one who finds great treasure.
163 I hate and abhor lying,
But I love Your law.
164 Seven times a day I praise You,
Because of Your righteous judgments.
165 Great peace have those who love Your law,
And nothing causes them to stumble.
166 Lord, I hope for Your salvation,
And I do Your commandments.
167 My soul keeps Your testimonies,
And I love them exceedingly.
168 I keep Your precepts and Your testimonies,
For all my ways *are* before You.

PROVERBS 28:13

13 HE who covers his sins will not prosper,
But whoever confesses and forsakes *them* will have mercy.

HEBREWS 2:1–18

THEREFORE we must give the more earnest heed to the things we have heard, lest we drift away. 2 For if the word spoken through angels proved steadfast, and every transgression and disobedience received a just reward, 3 how shall we escape if we neglect so great a salvation, which at the first began to be spoken by the Lord, and was confirmed to us by those who heard *Him*, 4 God also bearing witness both with signs and wonders, with various miracles, and gifts of the Holy Spirit, according to His own will?

5 For He has not put the world to come, of which we speak, in subjection to angels. 6 But one testified in a certain place, saying:

> "What is man that You are mindful of him,
>   Or the son of man that You take care of him?
> 7   You have made him a little lower than the angels;
>   You have crowned him with glory and honor,
>   And set him over the works of Your hands.
> 8   You have put all things in subjection under his feet."

For in that He put all in subjection under him, He left nothing *that is* not put under him. But now we do not yet see all things put under him. 9 But we see Jesus, who was made a little lower than the angels, for the suffering of death crowned with glory and honor, that He, by the grace of God, might taste death for everyone. 10 For it was fitting for Him, for whom *are* all things and by whom *are* all things, in bringing many sons to glory, to make the captain of their salvation perfect through sufferings. 11 For both He who sanctifies and those who are being sanctified *are* all of one, for which reason He is not ashamed to call them brethren, 12 saying:

---

*T*he sanctified life is a life that bears a strong family likeness to Jesus Christ.   (BRILL. HERITAGE)

> "I will declare Your name to My brethren;
>   In the midst of the assembly I will sing praise to You."

13 And again:

> "I will put My trust in Him."

And again:

> "Here am I and the children whom God has given Me."

14 Inasmuch then as the children have partaken of flesh and blood, He Himself likewise shared in the same, that through death He might destroy him who had the power of death, that is, the devil, 15 and release those who through fear of death were all their lifetime subject to bondage. 16 For indeed He does not give aid to angels, but He does give aid to the seed of Abraham. 17 Therefore, in all things He had to be made like *His* brethren, that He might be a merciful and faithful High Priest in things *pertaining* to God, to make propitiation for the sins of the people. 18 For in that He Himself has suffered, being tempted, He is able to aid those who are tempted.

◆◆◆◆

Reading 311—The "Why" of Judgment
Ezekiel 5:7, 8

It is not being reconciled to the fact of sin that produces all the disasters in life. You may talk about the nobility of human nature, but there is something in human nature which will laugh in the face of every ideal you have. If you refuse to agree with the fact that there is vice and self-seeking, something downright spiteful and wrong in human beings, instead of reconciling yourself to it, when it strikes your life, you will compromise with it and say it is of no use to battle against it. Have you made allowance for this hour and the power of darkness, or do you take a recognition of yourself that misses out sin? In your bodily relationships and friendships do you reconcile yourself to the fact of sin? If not, you will be caught round the next corner and you will compromise with it. If you reconcile yourself to the fact of sin, you will realize the danger at once—Yes, I see what that would mean. The recognition of sin does not destroy the basis of friendship; it establishes a mutual regard for the fact that the basis of life is tragic. Always beware of an estimate of life which does not recognize the fact that there is sin.   (*UTMOST*)

EZEKIEL 5:1—6:14

"AND you, son of man, take a sharp sword, take it as a barber's razor, and pass *it* over your head and your beard; then take scales to weigh and divide the hair. 2 You shall burn with fire one-third in the midst of the city, when the days of the siege are finished; then you shall take one-third and strike around *it* with the sword, and one-third you shall scatter in the wind: I will draw out a sword after them. 3 You shall also take a small number of them and bind them in the edge of your *garment*. 4 Then take some of them again and throw them into the midst of the fire, and burn them in the fire. From there a fire will go out into all the house of Israel.

5 "Thus says the Lord GOD: 'This *is* Jerusalem; I have set her in the midst of the nations and the countries all around her. 6 She has rebelled against My judgments by doing wickedness more than the nations, and against My statutes more than the countries that *are* all around her; for they have refused My judgments, and they have not walked in My statutes.' 7 Therefore thus says the Lord GOD: 'Because you have multiplied *disobedience* more than the nations that *are* all around you, have not walked in My statutes nor kept My judgments, nor even done according to the judgments of the nations that *are* all around you'— 8 therefore thus says the Lord GOD: 'Indeed I, even I, *am* against you and will execute judgments in your midst in the sight of the nations. 9 And I will do among you what I have never done, and the like of which I will never do again, because of all your abominations. 10 Therefore fathers shall eat *their* sons in your midst, and sons shall eat their fathers; and I will execute judgments among you, and all of you who remain I will scatter to all the winds.

11 'Therefore, *as* I live,' says the Lord GOD, 'surely, because you have defiled My sanctuary with all your detestable things and with all your abominations, therefore I will also diminish *you;* My eye will not spare, nor will I have any pity. 12 One-third of you shall die of the pestilence, and be consumed with famine in your midst; and one-third shall fall by the sword all around you; and I will scatter another third to all the winds, and I will draw out a sword after them.

13 'Thus shall My anger be spent, and I will cause My fury to rest upon them, and I will be avenged; and they shall know that I, the LORD, have spoken *it* in My zeal, when I have spent My fury upon them. 14 Moreover I will make you a waste and a reproach among the nations that *are* all around you, in the sight of all who pass by.

15 'So it shall be a reproach, a taunt, a lesson, and an astonishment to the nations that *are* all around you, when I execute judgments among you in anger and in fury and in furious rebukes. I, the LORD, have spoken. 16 When I send against them the terrible arrows of famine which shall be for destruction, which I will send to destroy you, I will increase the famine upon you and cut off your supply of bread. 17 So I will send against you famine and wild beasts, and they will bereave you. Pestilence and blood shall pass through you, and I will bring the sword against you. I, the LORD, have spoken.' "

6 NOW the word of the LORD came to me, saying: 2 "Son of man, set your face toward the mountains of Israel, and prophesy against them, 3 and say, 'O mountains of Israel, hear the word of the Lord GOD! Thus says the Lord GOD to the mountains, to the hills, to the ravines, and to the valleys: "Indeed I, *even* I, will bring a sword against you, and I will destroy your high places. 4 Then your altars shall be desolate, your incense altars shall be broken, and I will cast down your slain *men* before your idols. 5 And I will lay the corpses of

the children of Israel before their idols, and I will scatter your bones all around your altars. 6 In all your dwelling places the cities shall be laid waste, and the high places shall be desolate, so that your altars may be laid waste and made desolate, your idols may be broken and made to cease, your incense altars may be cut down, and your works may be abolished. 7 The slain shall fall in your midst, and you shall know that I *am* the LORD.

8 "Yet I will leave a remnant, so that you may have *some* who escape the sword among the nations, when you are scattered through the countries. 9 Then those of you who escape will remember Me among the nations where they are carried captive, because I was crushed by their adulterous heart which has departed from Me, and by their eyes which play the harlot after their idols; they will loathe themselves for the evils which they committed in all their abominations. 10 And they shall know that I *am* the LORD; I have not said in vain that I would bring this calamity upon them."

11 'Thus says the Lord GOD: "Pound your fists and stamp your feet, and say, 'Alas, for all the evil abominations of the house of Israel! For they shall fall by the sword, by famine, and by pestilence. 12 He who is far off shall die by the pestilence, he who is near shall fall by the sword, and he who remains and is besieged shall die by the famine. Thus will I spend My fury upon them. 13 Then you shall know that I *am* the LORD, when their slain are among their idols all around their altars, on every high hill, on all the mountaintops, under every green tree, and under every thick oak, wherever they offered sweet incense to all their idols. 14 So I will stretch out My hand against them and make the land desolate, yes, more desolate than the wilderness toward Diblah, in all their dwelling places. Then they shall know that I *am* the LORD.' " ' "

PSALM 119:169–176

169 LET my cry come before You,
O LORD;
Give me understanding according to
Your word.
170 Let my supplication come before You;
Deliver me according to Your word.
171 My lips shall utter praise,
For You teach me Your statutes.
172 My tongue shall speak of Your word,
For all Your commandments *are*
righteousness.

173 Let Your hand become my help,
For I have chosen Your precepts.
174 I long for Your salvation, O LORD,
And Your law *is* my delight.
175 Let my soul live, and it shall praise
You;
And let Your judgments help me.
176 I have gone astray like a lost sheep;
Seek Your servant,
For I do not forget Your
commandments.

PROVERBS 28:14

14 HAPPY *is* the man who is always
reverent,
But he who hardens his heart will fall
into calamity.

HEBREWS 3:1–19

THEREFORE, holy brethren, partakers of the heavenly calling, consider the Apostle and High Priest of our confession, Christ Jesus, 2 who was faithful to Him who appointed Him, as Moses also *was faithful* in all His house. 3 For this One has been counted worthy of more glory than Moses, inasmuch as He who built the house has more honor than the house. 4 For every house is built by someone, but He who built all things *is* God. 5 And Moses indeed *was* faithful in all His house as a servant, for a testimony of those things which would be spoken *afterward,* 6 but Christ as a Son over His own house, whose house we are if we hold fast the confidence and the rejoicing of the hope firm to the end.

7 Therefore, as the Holy Spirit says:

"Today, if you will hear His voice,
8 Do not harden your hearts as in the
rebellion,
In the day of trial in the wilderness,
9 Where your fathers tested Me,
tried Me,
And saw My works forty years.
10 Therefore I was angry with that
generation,
And said, 'They always go astray in
their heart,
And they have not known My ways.'
11 So I swore in My wrath,
'They shall not enter My rest.' "

12 Beware, brethren, lest there be in any of you an evil heart of unbelief in departing

Disbelief as often arises from temperament as from sin. (DISCIPLES)

"Today, if you will hear His voice,
Do not harden your hearts as in the rebellion."

16 For who, having heard, rebelled? Indeed, *was it* not all who came out of Egypt, *led* by Moses? 17 Now with whom was He angry forty years? *Was it* not with those who sinned, whose corpses fell in the wilderness? 18 And to whom did He swear that they would not enter His rest, but to those who did not obey? 19 So we see that they could not enter in because of unbelief.

from the living God; 13 but exhort one another daily, while it is called "Today," lest any of you be hardened through the deceitfulness of sin. 14 For we have become partakers of Christ if we hold the beginning of our confidence steadfast to the end, 15 while it is said:

Reading 312—Direction in Distress
Psalm 120:1

If I am a child of God, distress will lead me to Him for direction. The distress comes not because I have done wrong, it is part of the inevitable result of not being at home in the world, of being in contact with those who reason and live from a different standpoint. We blunder when we try to make out that the prosperity referred to in the Old Testament is intended for us in this dispensation. Plainly that prosperity has never yet been fulfilled in the history of the world; it is going to be fulfilled, but it does not refer to this dispensation, which is the dispensation of the humiliation of the saints, not of their glorification. One of Satan's greatest delusions is to decoy folks off on to blessings that are merely secondary. We become sidetracked if we make physical health our aim and imagine that because we are children of God we shall always be perfectly well; that there will be great manifestations of God's power, thousands saved, and so on. (GOOD)

EZEKIEL 7:1—8:18

MOREOVER the word of the LORD came to me, saying, 2 "And you, son of man, thus says the Lord GOD to the land of Israel:

'An end! The end has come upon the four corners of the land.
3 Now the end *has come* upon you,
And I will send My anger against you;
I will judge you according to your ways,
And I will repay you for all your abominations.
4 My eye will not spare you,
Nor will I have pity;
But I will repay your ways,
And your abominations will be in your midst;

Then you shall know that I *am* the LORD!'

5 "Thus says the Lord GOD:

'A disaster, a singular disaster;
Behold, it has come!
6 An end has come,
The end has come;
It has dawned for you;
Behold, it has come!
7 Doom has come to you, you who dwell in the land;
The time has come,
A day of trouble *is* near,
And not of rejoicing in the mountains.
8 Now upon you I will soon pour out My fury,
And spend My anger upon you;

I will judge you according to your
    ways,
And I will repay you for all your
    abominations.

9   'My eye will not spare,
    Nor will I have pity;
    I will repay you according to your
        ways,
    And your abominations will be in
        your midst.
    Then you shall know that I *am* the
        Lord who strikes.

10 'Behold, the day!
    Behold, it has come!
    Doom has gone out;
    The rod has blossomed,
    Pride has budded.

---

*W*herever there is natural pride the
Lord must inevitably be put to
shame.   (Not Knowing)

---

11 Violence has risen up into a rod of
        wickedness;
    None of them *shall remain,*
    None of their multitude,
    None of them;
    Nor *shall there be* wailing for them.
12 The time has come,
    The day draws near.

    'Let not the buyer rejoice,
    Nor the seller mourn,
    For wrath *is* on their whole
        multitude.
13 For the seller shall not return to what
        has been sold,
    Though he may still be alive;
    For the vision concerns the whole
        multitude,
    And it shall not turn back;
    No one will strengthen himself
    Who lives in iniquity.

14 'They have blown the trumpet and
        made everyone ready,
    But no one goes to battle;
    For My wrath *is* on all their
        multitude.
15 The sword *is* outside,
    And the pestilence and famine
        within.
    Whoever *is* in the field
    Will die by the sword;
    And whoever *is* in the city,
    Famine and pestilence will devour
        him.

16 'Those who survive will escape and
        be on the mountains
    Like doves of the valleys,
    All of them mourning,
    Each for his iniquity.
17 Every hand will be feeble,
    And every knee will be *as* weak *as*
        water.
18 They will also be girded with
        sackcloth;
    Horror will cover them;
    Shame *will be* on every face,
    Baldness on all their heads.

19 'They will throw their silver into the
        streets,
    And their gold will be like refuse;
    Their silver and their gold will not
        be able to deliver them
    In the day of the wrath of the
        Lord;
    They will not satisfy their souls,
    Nor fill their stomachs,
    Because it became their stumbling
        block of iniquity.

20 'As for the beauty of his ornaments,
    He set it in majesty;
    But they made from it
    The images of their abominations—
    Their detestable things;
    Therefore I have made it
    Like refuse to them.
21 I will give it as plunder
    Into the hands of strangers,
    And to the wicked of the earth as
        spoil;
    And they shall defile it.
22 I will turn My face from them,
    And they will defile My secret
        place;
    For robbers shall enter it and
        defile it.

23 'Make a chain,
    For the land is filled with crimes of
        blood,
    And the city is full of violence.
24 Therefore I will bring the worst of
        the Gentiles,
    And they will possess their houses;
    I will cause the pomp of the strong
        to cease,
    And their holy places shall be defiled.
25 Destruction comes;
    They will seek peace, but *there shall
    be* none.
26 Disaster will come upon disaster,
    And rumor will be upon rumor.
    Then they will seek a vision from a
        prophet;

But the law will perish from the
    priest,
And counsel from the elders.

27 'The king will mourn,
    The prince will be clothed with
      desolation,
    And the hands of the common people
      will tremble.
    I will do to them according to their
      way,
    And according to what they deserve
      I will judge them;
    Then they shall know that I *am* the
      Lord!'"

8 AND it came to pass in the sixth year,
in the sixth *month,* on the fifth *day* of
the month, as I sat in my house with the
elders of Judah sitting before me, that the
hand of the Lord God fell upon me there.
2 Then I looked, and there was a likeness,
like the appearance of fire—from the appearance of His waist and downward, fire;
and from His waist and upward, like the
appearance of brightness, like the color of
amber. 3 He stretched out the form of a
hand, and took me by a lock of my hair;
and the Spirit lifted me up between earth
and heaven, and brought me in visions of
God to Jerusalem, to the door of the north
gate of the inner *court,* where the seat of
the image of jealousy *was,* which provokes
to jealousy. 4 And behold, the glory of the
God of Israel *was* there, like the vision that
I saw in the plain.
5 Then He said to me, "Son of man, lift
your eyes now toward the north." So I lifted
my eyes toward the north, and there, north
of the altar gate, was this image of jealousy
in the entrance.
6 Furthermore He said to me, "Son of
man, do you see what they are doing, the
great abominations that the house of Israel
commits here, to make Me go far away
from My sanctuary? Now turn again, you
will see greater abominations." 7 So He
brought me to the door of the court; and
when I looked, there was a hole in the
wall. 8 Then He said to me, "Son of man,
dig into the wall"; and when I dug into
the wall, there was a door.
9 And He said to me, "Go in, and see
the wicked abominations which they are
doing there." 10 So I went in and saw, and
there—every sort of creeping thing, abominable beasts, and all the idols of the house
of Israel, portrayed all around on the walls.
11 And there stood before them seventy men
of the elders of the house of Israel, and in
their midst stood Jaazaniah the son of Sha-

phan. Each man had a censer in his hand,
and a thick cloud of incense went up.
12 Then He said to me, "Son of man, have
you seen what the elders of the house of
Israel do in the dark, every man in the room
of his idols? For they say, 'The Lord does
not see us, the Lord has forsaken the
land.'"
13 And He said to me, "Turn again, *and*
you will see greater abominations that they
are doing." 14 So He brought me to the
door of the north gate of the Lord's
house; and to my dismay, women were sitting there weeping for Tammuz.
15 Then He said to me, "Have you seen
this, O son of man? Turn again, you will
see greater abominations than these."
16 So He brought me into the inner court
of the Lord's house; and there, at the door
of the temple of the Lord, between the
porch and the altar, *were* about twenty-five
men with their backs toward the temple
of the Lord and their faces toward the
east, and they were worshiping the sun toward the east.
17 And He said to me, "Have you seen
this, O son of man? Is it a trivial thing to
the house of Judah to commit the abominations which they commit here? For they
have filled the land with violence; then they
have returned to provoke Me to anger. Indeed they put the branch to their nose.
18 Therefore I also will act in fury. My eye
will not spare nor will I have pity; and
though they cry in My ears with a loud
voice, I will not hear them."

PSALM 120:1–7

1   IN my distress I cried to the Lord,
     And He heard me.
2   Deliver my soul, O Lord, from lying
     lips
     And from a deceitful tongue.

3   What shall be given to you,
     Or what shall be done to you,
     You false tongue?
4   Sharp arrows of the warrior,
     With coals of the broom tree!

5   Woe is me, that I dwell in
     Meshech,
     That I dwell among the tents of
     Kedar!
6   My soul has dwelt too long
     With one who hates peace.
7   I *am for* peace;
     But when I speak, they *are* for war.

PROVERBS 28:15

15 *LIKE* a roaring lion and a charging
      bear
   Is a wicked ruler over poor people.

HEBREWS 4:1–16

THEREFORE, since a promise remains of
entering His rest, let us fear lest any of
you seem to have come short of it.
2 For indeed the gospel was preached to
us as well as to them; but the word which
they heard did not profit them, not being
mixed with faith in those who heard *it*.
3 For we who have believed do enter that
rest, as He has said:

> "So I swore in My wrath,
>   'They shall not enter My rest,' "

although the works were finished from the
foundation of the world. 4 For He has spoken in a certain place of the seventh *day*
in this way: "And God rested on the seventh
day from all His works"; 5 and again in
this *place:* "They shall not enter My rest."
6 Since therefore it remains that some
must enter it, and those to whom it was
first preached did not enter because of disobedience, 7 again He designates a certain
day, saying in David, "Today," after such
a long time, as it has been said:

> "Today, if you will hear His voice,
>   Do not harden your hearts."

8 For if Joshua had given them rest, then
He would not afterward have spoken of
another day. 9 There remains therefore a
rest for the people of God. 10 For he
who has entered His rest has himself also
ceased from his works as God *did* from
His.
11 Let us therefore be diligent to enter
that rest, lest anyone fall according to the
same example of disobedience. 12 For the
word of God *is* living and powerful, and
sharper than any two-edged sword, piercing
even to the division of soul and spirit, and
of joints and marrow, and is a discerner
of the thoughts and intents of the heart.
13 And there is no creature hidden from
His sight, but all things *are* naked and open
to the eyes of Him to whom we *must give*
account.

---

*There is no room for personal vanity
when the standard is seen to be
God Himself.*   (DISCIPLES)

---

14 Seeing then that we have a great High
Priest who has passed through the heavens,
Jesus the Son of God, let us hold fast *our*
confession. 15 For we do not have a High
Priest who cannot sympathize with our
weaknesses, but was in all *points* tempted
as *we are, yet* without sin. 16 Let us therefore come boldly to the throne of grace,
that we may obtain mercy and find grace
to help in time of need.

Reading 313—Help from the Lord
Psalm 121:1, 2

When we come to the New Testament interpretation of our Lord
we find He is not a teacher, we find He is a Savior. We find that
His teaching is but a statement of the kind of life we will live when we
have let Him remake us by means of His cross and by the incoming of His
Spirit. . . .
   I would like to commend this thought for the instruction and courage of
those whose hearts are fainting in the way, from whom the ideals of youth
have fled, to whom life holds out no more promises. For thirty years or more
it may be that life has been a boundless romance of possibilities; beckoning
signs from lofty mountain peaks have lured the spirit on; but now the burden
and the heat of the day have come and the mountaintops are obscured in a
dazing, dazzling heat, and the road is dusty and the mileage long, and the

feet are weak and the endeavor is exhausted. Let me bring the message contained in this psalm, even as a cup of water from the clear sparkling spring of life. "My help *comes* from the LORD, who made heaven and earth." (*PLACE HELP*)

EZEKIEL 9:1—10:22

THEN He called out in my hearing with a loud voice, saying, "Let those who have charge over the city draw near, each *with* a deadly weapon in his hand." 2 And suddenly six men came from the direction of the upper gate, which faces north, each with his battle-ax in his hand. One man among them *was* clothed with linen and had a writer's inkhorn at his side. They went in and stood beside the bronze altar.

3 Now the glory of the God of Israel had gone up from the cherub, where it had been, to the threshold of the temple. And He called to the man clothed with linen, who *had* the writer's inkhorn at his side; 4 and the LORD said to him, "Go through the midst of the city, through the midst of Jerusalem, and put a mark on the foreheads of the men who sigh and cry over all the abominations that are done within it."

5 To the others He said in my hearing, "Go after him through the city and kill; do not let your eye spare, nor have any pity. 6 Utterly slay old *and* young men, maidens and little children and women; but do not come near anyone on whom *is* the mark; and begin at My sanctuary." So they began with the elders who *were* before the temple. 7 Then He said to them, "Defile the temple, and fill the courts with the slain. Go out!" And they went out and killed in the city.

8 So it was, that while they were killing them, I was left *alone;* and I fell on my face and cried out, and said, "Ah, Lord GOD! Will You destroy all the remnant of Israel in pouring out Your fury on Jerusalem?"

9 Then He said to me, "The iniquity of the house of Israel and Judah *is* exceedingly great, and the land is full of bloodshed, and the city full of perversity; for they say, 'The LORD has forsaken the land, and the LORD does not see!' 10 And as for Me also, My eye will neither spare, nor will I have pity, *but* I will recompense their deeds on their own head."

11 Just then, the man clothed with linen, who *had* the inkhorn at his side, reported back and said, "I have done as You commanded me."

10 AND I looked, and there in the firmament that was above the head of the cherubim, there appeared something like a sapphire stone, having the appearance of the likeness of a throne. 2 Then He spoke to the man clothed with linen, and said, "Go in among the wheels, under the cherub, fill your hands with coals of fire from among the cherubim, and scatter *them* over the city." And he went in as I watched.

3 Now the cherubim were standing on the south side of the temple when the man went in, and the cloud filled the inner court. 4 Then the glory of the LORD went up from the cherub, *and paused* over the threshold of the temple; and the house was filled with the cloud, and the court was full of the brightness of the LORD's glory. 5 And the sound of the wings of the cherubim was heard *even* in the outer court, like the voice of Almighty God when He speaks.

6 Then it happened, when He commanded the man clothed in linen, saying, "Take fire from among the wheels, from among the cherubim," that he went in and stood beside the wheels. 7 And the cherub stretched out his hand from among the cherubim to the fire that *was* among the cherubim, and took *some of it* and put *it* into the hands of the *man* clothed with linen, who took *it* and went out. 8 The cherubim appeared to have the form of a man's hand under their wings.

9 And when I looked, there were four wheels by the cherubim, one wheel by one cherub and another wheel by each other cherub; the wheels appeared *to have* the color of a beryl stone. 10 *As for* their appearance, all four looked alike—as it were, a wheel in the middle of a wheel. 11 When they went, they went toward *any of* their four directions; they did not turn aside when they went, but followed in the direction the head was facing. They did not turn aside when they went. 12 And their whole body, with their back, their hands, their wings, and the wheels that the four had, *were* full of eyes all around. 13 As for the wheels, they were called in my hearing, "Wheel."

14 Each one had four faces: the first face *was* the face of a cherub, the second face the face of a man, the third the face of a

lion, and the fourth the face of an eagle. 15 And the cherubim were lifted up. This *was* the living creature I saw by the River Chebar. 16 When the cherubim went, the wheels went beside them; and when the cherubim lifted their wings to mount up from the earth, the same wheels also did not turn from beside them. 17 When *the cherubim* stood still, *the wheels* stood still, and when *one* was lifted up, *the other* lifted itself up, for the spirit of the living creature *was* in them.

18 Then the glory of the LORD departed from the threshold of the temple and stood over the cherubim. 19 And the cherubim lifted their wings and mounted up from the earth in my sight. When they went out, the wheels *were* beside them; and they stood at the door of the east gate of the LORD's house, and the glory of the God of Israel *was* above them.

20 This *is* the living creature I saw under the God of Israel by the River Chebar, and I knew they *were* cherubim. 21 Each one had four faces and each one four wings, and the likeness of the hands of a man *was* under their wings. 22 And the likeness of their faces *was* the same *as* the faces which I had seen by the River Chebar, their appearance and their persons. They each went straight forward.

PSALM 121:1–8

1   I will lift up my eyes to the hills—
    From whence comes my help?
2   My help *comes* from the LORD,
    Who made heaven and earth.

3   He will not allow your foot to be
    moved;
    He who keeps you will not slumber.
4   Behold, He who keeps Israel
    Shall neither slumber nor sleep.

5   The LORD *is* your keeper;
    The LORD *is* your shade at your right
    hand.
6   The sun shall not strike you by
    day,
    Nor the moon by night.

7   The LORD shall preserve you from all
    evil;
    He shall preserve your soul.
8   The LORD shall preserve your going
    out and your coming in
    From this time forth, and even
    forevermore.

PROVERBS 28:16

16   A ruler who lacks understanding *is* a
     great oppressor,
     But he who hates covetousness will
     prolong *his* days.

HEBREWS 5:1–14

FOR every high priest taken from among men is appointed for men in things *pertaining* to God, that he may offer both gifts and sacrifices for sins. 2 He can have compassion on those who are ignorant and going astray, since he himself is also subject to weakness. 3 Because of this he is required as for the people, so also for himself, to offer *sacrifices* for sins. 4 And no man takes this honor to himself, but he who is called by God, just as Aaron *was*.

5 So also Christ did not glorify Himself to become High Priest, *but it* was He who said to Him:

"You are My Son,
    Today I have begotten You."

6 As *He* also *says* in another *place*:

"You *are* a priest forever
    According to the order of
        Melchizedek";

7 who, in the days of His flesh, when He had offered up prayers and supplications, with vehement cries and tears to Him who was able to save Him from death, and was heard because of His godly fear, 8 though He was a Son, *yet* He learned obedience by the things which He suffered. 9 And having been perfected, He became the author of eternal salvation to all who obey

---

If Jesus Christ was a martyr, our salvation is a myth. (PHIL. SIN)

Him, 10 called by God as High Priest "according to the order of Melchizedek," 11 of whom we have much to say, and hard to explain, since you have become dull of hearing.

12 For though by this time you ought to be teachers, you need *someone* to teach you again the first principles of the oracles of God; and you have come to need milk and not solid food. 13 For everyone who

partakes *only* of milk *is* unskilled in the word of righteousness, for he is a babe. 14 But solid food belongs to those who are of full age, *that is,* those who by reason of use have their senses exercised to discern both good and evil.

◄◄◄◄

Reading 314—The Ministry of the Interior
Psalm 122:2

The gifts of our ascended Lord—"apostles, prophets, evangelists"—are "for the equipping of the saints." If you should be in advance of the rest of the community, God will take you into "the ministry of the interior." Spiritual insight is not for the purpose of making us realize we are better than other people, but in order that our responsibility might be added to. If we neglect to go to God about our communities, our ministers, we become criticizing centers instead of ministers of the interior. . . . Locusts in their flight over a stream may drown by the million, but others keep coming until there is a way for the live ones to go over their bodies. God uses His saints in the same way. . . . There are prominent names in works of faith, such as Müller and Quarrier, but there are thousands of others whose names are not known. It is the same truth our Lord uttered regarding Himself, "Unless a grain of wheat falls into the ground and dies, it remains alone; but if it dies, it produces much grain." The work in a community to begin with may be a wondrous delight, then it seems to die out, and if you do not know the teaching of our Lord you will say it is dead; it is not, it has fallen into the ground and died in its old form, but by and by it will bring forth fruit which will alter the whole landscape.   (*GOOD*)

EZEKIEL 11:1—12:28

THEN the Spirit lifted me up and brought me to the East Gate of the LORD's house, which faces eastward; and there at the door of the gate were twenty-five men, among whom I saw Jaazaniah the son of Azzur, and Pelatiah the son of Benaiah, princes of the people. 2 And He said to me: "Son of man, these *are* the men who devise iniquity and give wicked counsel in this city, 3 who say, 'The time *is* not near to build houses; this *city is* the caldron, and we *are* the meat.' 4 Therefore prophesy against them, prophesy, O son of man!"

5 Then the Spirit of the LORD fell upon me, and said to me, "Speak! 'Thus says the LORD: "Thus you have said, O house of Israel; for I know the things that come into your mind. 6 You have multiplied your slain in this city, and you have filled its streets with the slain." 7 Therefore thus says the Lord GOD: "Your slain whom you have laid in its midst, they *are* the meat, and this *city is* the caldron; but I shall bring

you out of the midst of it. 8 You have feared the sword; and I will bring a sword upon you," says the Lord GOD. 9 "And I will bring you out of its midst, and deliver you into the hands of strangers, and execute judgments on you. 10 You shall fall by the sword. I will judge you at the border of Israel. Then you shall know that I *am* the LORD. 11 This *city* shall not be your caldron, nor shall you be the meat in its midst. I will judge you at the border of Israel. 12 And you shall know that I *am* the LORD; for you have not walked in My statutes nor executed My judgments, but have done according to the customs of the Gentiles which *are* all around you." ' "

13 Now it happened, while I was prophesying, that Pelatiah the son of Benaiah died. Then I fell on my face and cried with a loud voice, and said, "Ah, Lord GOD! Will You make a complete end of the remnant of Israel?"

14 Again the word of the LORD came to me, saying, 15 "Son of man, your brethren, your relatives, your countrymen, and all the

house of Israel in its entirety, *are* those about whom the inhabitants of Jerusalem have said, 'Get far away from the LORD; this land has been given to us as a possession.' 16 Therefore say, 'Thus says the Lord GOD: "Although I have cast them far off among the Gentiles, and although I have scattered them among the countries, yet I shall be a little sanctuary for them in the countries where they have gone." '

17 Therefore say, 'Thus says the Lord GOD: "I will gather you from the peoples, assemble you from the countries where you have been scattered, and I will give you the land of Israel." ' 18 And they will go there, and they will take away all its detestable things and all its abominations from there. 19 Then I will give them one heart, and I will put a new spirit within them, and take the stony heart out of their flesh, and give them a heart of flesh, 20 that they may walk in My statutes and keep My judgments and do them; and they shall be My people, and I will be their God. 21 But *as for those* whose hearts follow the desire for their detestable things and their abominations, I will recompense their deeds on their own heads," says the Lord GOD.

22 So the cherubim lifted up their wings, with the wheels beside them, and the glory of the God of Israel *was* high above them. 23 And the glory of the LORD went up from the midst of the city and stood on the mountain, which *is* on the east side of the city.

24 Then the Spirit took me up and brought me in a vision by the Spirit of God into Chaldea, to those in captivity. And the vision that I had seen went up from me. 25 So I spoke to those in captivity of all the things the LORD had shown me.

12 NOW the word of the LORD came to me, saying: 2 "Son of man, you dwell in the midst of a rebellious house, which has eyes to see but does not see, and ears to hear but does not hear; for they *are* a rebellious house.

3 "Therefore, son of man, prepare your belongings for captivity, and go into captivity by day in their sight. You shall go from your place into captivity to another place in their sight. It may be that they will consider, though they *are* a rebellious house. 4 By day you shall bring out your belongings in their sight, as though going into captivity; and at evening you shall go in their sight, like those who go into captivity. 5 Dig through the wall in their sight, and carry your belongings out through it. 6 In their sight you shall bear *them* on *your*

shoulders *and* carry *them* out at twilight; you shall cover your face, so that you cannot see the ground, for I have made you a sign to the house of Israel."

7 So I did as I was commanded. I brought out my belongings by day, as though going into captivity, and at evening I dug through the wall with my hand. I brought *them* out at twilight, *and* I bore *them* on *my* shoulder in their sight.

8 And in the morning the word of the LORD came to me, saying, 9 "Son of man, has not the house of Israel, the rebellious house, said to you, 'What are you doing?' 10 Say to them, 'Thus says the Lord GOD: "This burden *concerns* the prince in Jerusalem and all the house of Israel who are among them." ' 11 Say, 'I *am* a sign to you. As I have done, so shall it be done to them; they shall be carried away into captivity.' 12 And the prince who *is* among them shall bear *his belongings* on *his* shoulder at twilight and go out. They shall dig through the wall to carry *them* out through it. He shall cover his face, so that he cannot see the ground with *his* eyes. 13 I will also spread My net over him, and he shall be caught in My snare. I will bring him to Babylon, *to* the land of the Chaldeans; yet he shall not see it, though he shall die there. 14 I will scatter to every wind all who *are* around him to help him, and all his troops; and I will draw out the sword after them.

15 "Then they shall know that I *am* the LORD, when I scatter them among the nations and disperse them throughout the countries. 16 But I will spare a few of their men from the sword, from famine, and from pestilence, that they may declare all their abominations among the Gentiles wherever they go. Then they shall know that I *am* the LORD."

17 Moreover the word of the LORD came to me, saying, 18 "Son of man, eat your bread with quaking, and drink your water with trembling and anxiety. 19 And say to the people of the land, 'Thus says the Lord GOD to the inhabitants of Jerusalem *and* to the land of Israel: "They shall eat their bread with anxiety, and drink their water with dread, so that her land may be emptied of all who are in it, because of the violence of all those who dwell in it. 20 Then the cities that are inhabited shall be laid waste, and the land shall become desolate; and you shall know that I *am* the LORD." ' "

21 And the word of the LORD came to me, saying, 22 "Son of man, what *is* this proverb *that* you *people* have about the land of Israel, which says, 'The days are prolonged, and every vision fails'? 23 Tell them

therefore, 'Thus says the Lord GOD: "I will lay this proverb to rest, and they shall no more use it as a proverb in Israel." But say to them, "The days are at hand, and the fulfillment of every vision. 24 For no more shall there be any false vision or flattering divination within the house of Israel. 25 For I *am* the LORD. I speak, and the word which I speak will come to pass; it will no more be postponed; for in your days, O rebellious house, I will say the word and perform it," says the Lord GOD.'"

26 Again the word of the LORD came to me, saying, 27 "Son of man, look, the house of Israel is saying, 'The vision that he sees *is* for many days *from now,* and he prophesies of times far off.' 28 Therefore say to them, 'Thus says the Lord GOD: "None of My words will be postponed any more, but the word which I speak will be done," says the Lord GOD.'"

PSALM 122:1–5

1 I was glad when they said to me,
   "Let us go into the house of the LORD."
2 Our feet have been standing
   Within your gates, O Jerusalem!

3 Jerusalem is built
   As a city that is compact together,
4 Where the tribes go up,
   The tribes of the LORD,
   To the Testimony of Israel,
   To give thanks to the name of the LORD.
5 For thrones are set there for judgment,
   The thrones of the house of David.

PROVERBS 28:17, 18

17 A man burdened with bloodshed will
    flee into a pit;
    Let no one help him.

18 Whoever walks blamelessly will be
    saved,
    But *he who is* perverse *in his* ways will
    suddenly fall.

HEBREWS 6:1–20

THEREFORE, leaving the discussion of the elementary *principles* of Christ, let us go on to perfection, not laying again the foundation of repentance from dead works and of faith toward God, 2 of the doctrine of baptisms, of laying on of hands, of resurrection of the dead, and of eternal judg-

ment. 3 And this we will do if God permits.

4 For *it is* impossible for those who were once enlightened, and have tasted the heavenly gift, and have become partakers of the Holy Spirit, 5 and have tasted the good word of God and the powers of the age to come, 6 if they fall away, to renew them again to repentance, since they crucify again for themselves the Son of God, and put *Him* to an open shame.

7 For the earth which drinks in the rain that often comes upon it, and bears herbs useful for those by whom it is cultivated, receives blessing from God; 8 but if it bears thorns and briers, *it is* rejected and near to being cursed, whose end *is* to be burned.

9 But, beloved, we are confident of better things concerning you, yes, things that accompany salvation, though we speak in this manner. 10 For God *is* not unjust to forget your work and labor of love which you have shown toward His name, *in that* you have ministered to the saints, and do minister. 11 And we desire that each one of you show the same diligence to the full assurance of hope until the end, 12 that you do not become sluggish, but imitate those who through faith and patience inherit the promises.

Our capacity in spiritual matters is measured by the promises of God. (RUN)

13 For when God made a promise to Abraham, because He could swear by no one greater, He swore by Himself, 14 saying, "Surely blessing I will bless you, and multiplying I will multiply you." 15 And so, after he had patiently endured, he obtained the promise. 16 For men indeed swear by the greater, and an oath for confirmation *is* for them an end of all dispute. 17 Thus God, determining to show more abundantly to the heirs of promise the immutability of His counsel, confirmed *it* by an oath, 18 that by two immutable things, in which it *is* impossible for God to lie, we might have strong consolation, who have fled for refuge to lay hold of the hope set before *us.*

19 This *hope* we have as an anchor of the soul, both sure and steadfast, and which enters the Presence *behind* the veil, 20 where the forerunner has entered for us, *even* Jesus, having become High Priest forever according to the order of Melchizedek.

◄◄◆◆

Reading 315—What to Pray For
Psalm 122:6

Y ou cannot intercede if you do not believe in the reality of the Redemption; you will turn intercession into futile sympathy with human beings which will only increase their submissive content to being out of touch with God. In intercession you bring the person or the circumstance that impinges on you before God until you are moved by His attitude toward that person or circumstance. Intercession means filling up "what is lacking in the afflictions of Christ," and that is why there are so few intercessors. Intercession is put on the line of—"Put yourself in his place." Never! Try to put yourself in God's place. . . .

Our work lies in coming into definite contact with God about everything, and we shirk it by becoming active workers. We do the things that can be tabulated but we will not intercede. Intercession is the one thing that has no snares, because it keeps our relationship with God completely open.

The thing to watch in intercession is that no soul is patched up; a soul must get through into contact with the life of God. Think of the number of souls God has brought about our path and we have dropped them! When we pray on the ground of redemption, God creates something He can create in no other way than through intercessory prayer.   (*Utmost*)

EZEKIEL 13:1—14:23

AND the word of the LORD came to me, saying, 2 "Son of man, prophesy against the prophets of Israel who prophesy, and say to those who prophesy out of their own heart, 'Hear the word of the LORD!' "

3 Thus says the Lord GOD: "Woe to the foolish prophets, who follow their own spirit and have seen nothing! 4 O Israel, your prophets are like foxes in the deserts. 5 You have not gone up into the gaps to build a wall for the house of Israel to stand in battle on the day of the LORD. 6 They have envisioned futility and false divination, saying, 'Thus says the LORD!' But the LORD has not sent them; yet they hope that the word may be confirmed. 7 Have you not seen a futile vision, and have you not spoken false divination? You say, 'The LORD says,' but I have not spoken."

8 Therefore thus says the Lord GOD: "Because you have spoken nonsense and envisioned lies, therefore I *am* indeed against you," says the Lord GOD. 9 "My hand will be against the prophets who envision futility and who divine lies; they shall not be in the assembly of My people, nor be written in the record of the house of Israel, nor shall they enter into the land of Israel. Then you shall know that I *am* the Lord GOD.

10 "Because, indeed, because they have seduced My people, saying, 'Peace!' when *there is* no peace—and one builds a wall, and they plaster it with untempered *mortar*— 11 say to those who plaster *it* with untempered *mortar,* that it will fall. There will be flooding rain, and you, O great hailstones, shall fall; and a stormy wind shall tear *it* down. 12 Surely, when the wall has fallen, will it not be said to you, 'Where *is* the mortar with which you plastered *it?* "

13 Therefore thus says the Lord GOD: "I will cause a stormy wind to break forth in My fury; and there shall be a flooding rain in My anger, and great hailstones in fury to consume *it*. 14 So I will break down the wall you have plastered with untempered *mortar,* and bring it down to the ground, so that its foundation will be uncovered; it will fall, and you shall be consumed in the midst of it. Then you shall know that I *am* the LORD.

15 "Thus will I accomplish My wrath on the wall and on those who have plastered it with untempered *mortar;* and I will say to you, 'The wall *is no more,* nor those who plastered it, 16 *that is,* the prophets of Israel who prophesy concerning Jerusalem, and who see visions of peace for her when *there is* no peace,' " says the Lord GOD.

17 "Likewise, son of man, set your face against the daughters of your people, who

prophesy out of their own heart; prophesy against them, 18 and say, 'Thus says the Lord GOD: "Woe to the *women* who sew *magic* charms on their sleeves and make veils for the heads of people of every height to hunt souls! Will you hunt the souls of My people, and keep yourselves alive? 19 And will you profane Me among My people for handfuls of barley and for pieces of bread, killing people who should not die, and keeping people alive who should not live, by your lying to My people who listen to lies?"

20 'Therefore thus says the Lord GOD: "Behold, I *am* against your *magic* charms by which you hunt souls there like birds. I will tear them from your arms, and let the souls go, the souls you hunt like birds. 21 I will also tear off your veils and deliver My people out of your hand, and they shall no longer be as prey in your hand. Then you shall know that I *am* the LORD.

22 "Because with lies you have made the heart of the righteous sad, whom I have not made sad; and you have strengthened the hands of the wicked, so that he does not turn from his wicked way to save his life. 23 Therefore you shall no longer envision futility nor practice divination; for I will deliver My people out of your hand, and you shall know that I *am* the LORD."'"

14 NOW some of the elders of Israel came to me and sat before me. 2 And the word of the LORD came to me, saying, 3 "Son of man, these men have set up their idols in their hearts, and put before them that which causes them to stumble into iniquity. Should I let Myself be inquired of at all by them?

4 "Therefore speak to them, and say to them, 'Thus says the Lord GOD: "Everyone of the house of Israel who sets up his idols in his heart, and puts before him what causes him to stumble into iniquity, and then comes to the prophet, I the LORD will answer him who comes, according to the multitude of his idols, 5 that I may seize the house of Israel by their heart, because they are all estranged from Me by their idols."'

6 "Therefore say to the house of Israel, 'Thus says the Lord GOD: "Repent, turn away from your idols, and turn your faces away from all your abominations. 7 For anyone of the house of Israel, or of the strangers who dwell in Israel, who separates himself from Me and sets up his idols in his heart and puts before him what causes him to stumble into iniquity, then comes to a prophet to inquire of him concerning Me, I the LORD will answer him by Myself.

8 I will set My face against that man and make him a sign and a proverb, and I will cut him off from the midst of My people. Then you shall know that I *am* the LORD.

9 "And if the prophet is induced to speak anything, I the LORD have induced that prophet, and I will stretch out My hand against him and destroy him from among My people Israel. 10 And they shall bear their iniquity; the punishment of the prophet shall be the same as the punishment of the one who inquired, 11 that the house of Israel may no longer stray from Me, nor be profaned anymore with all their transgressions, but that they may be My people and I may be their God," says the Lord GOD.' "

12 The word of the LORD came again to me, saying: 13 "Son of man, when a land sins against Me by persistent unfaithfulness, I will stretch out My hand against it; I will cut off its supply of bread, send famine on it, and cut off man and beast from it. 14 Even *if* these three men, Noah, Daniel, and Job, were in it, they would deliver *only* themselves by their righteousness," says the Lord GOD.

15 "If I cause wild beasts to pass through the land, and they empty it, and make it so desolate that no man may pass through because of the beasts, 16 *even though* these three men *were* in it, *as* I live," says the Lord GOD, "they would deliver neither sons nor daughters; only they would be delivered, and the land would be desolate.

17 "Or *if* I bring a sword on that land, and say, 'Sword, go through the land,' and I cut off man and beast from it, 18 even *though* these three men *were* in it, *as* I live," says the Lord GOD, "they would deliver neither sons nor daughters, but only they themselves would be delivered.

19 "Or *if* I send a pestilence into that land and pour out My fury on it in blood, and cut off from it man and beast, 20 even *though* Noah, Daniel, and Job *were* in it, *as* I live," says the Lord GOD, "they would deliver neither son nor daughter; they would deliver *only* themselves by their righteousness."

21 For thus says the Lord GOD: "How much more it shall be when I send My four severe judgments on Jerusalem—the sword and famine and wild beasts and pestilence—to cut off man and beast from it? 22 Yet behold, there shall be left in it a remnant who will be brought out, *both* sons and daughters; surely they will come out to you, and you will see their ways and their doings. Then you will be comforted concerning the disaster that I have brought

upon Jerusalem, all that I have brought upon it. 23 And they will comfort you, when you see their ways and their doings; and you shall know that I have done nothing without cause that I have done in it," says the Lord GOD.

PSALM 122:6–9

6   PRAY for the peace of Jerusalem:
     "May they prosper who love you.

Every time you pray your horizon is altered.   (RUN)

7   Peace be within your walls,
     Prosperity within your palaces."
8   For the sake of my brethren and
         companions,
     I will now say, "Peace *be* within you."
9   Because of the house of the LORD our
         God
     I will seek your good.

PROVERBS 28:19

19   HE who tills his land will have plenty
         of bread,
     But he who follows frivolity will have
         poverty enough!

HEBREWS 7:1–28

FOR this Melchizedek, king of Salem, priest of the Most High God, who met Abraham returning from the slaughter of the kings and blessed him, 2 to whom also Abraham gave a tenth part of all, first being translated "king of righteousness," and then also king of Salem, meaning "king of peace," 3 without father, without mother, without genealogy, having neither beginning of days nor end of life, but made like the Son of God, remains a priest continually.

4 Now consider how great this man *was,* to whom even the patriarch Abraham gave a tenth of the spoils. 5 And indeed those who are of the sons of Levi, who receive the priesthood, have a commandment to receive tithes from the people according to the law, that is, from their brethren, though they have come from the loins of Abraham; 6 but he whose genealogy is not derived from them received tithes from Abraham and blessed him who had the promises. 7 Now beyond all contradiction the lesser

is blessed by the better. 8 Here mortal men receive tithes, but there he *receives them,* of whom it is witnessed that he lives. 9 Even Levi, who receives tithes, paid tithes through Abraham, so to speak, 10 for he was still in the loins of his father when Melchizedek met him.

11 Therefore, if perfection were through the Levitical priesthood (for under it the people received the law), what further need *was there* that another priest should rise according to the order of Melchizedek, and not be called according to the order of Aaron? 12 For the priesthood being 'changed, of necessity there is also a change of the law. 13 For He of whom these things are spoken belongs to another tribe, from which no man has officiated at the altar.

14 For *it is* evident that our Lord arose from Judah, of which tribe Moses spoke nothing concerning priesthood. 15 And it is yet far more evident if, in the likeness of Melchizedek, there arises another priest 16 who has come, not according to the law of a fleshly commandment, but according to the power of an endless life. 17 For He testifies:

    "You *are* a priest forever
    According to the order of
        Melchizedek."

18 For on the one hand there is an annulling of the former commandment because of its weakness and unprofitableness, 19 for the law made nothing perfect; on the other hand, *there is the* bringing in of a better hope, through which we draw near to God.

Draw on the grace of God now.   (APPROVED)

20 And inasmuch as *He was* not *made priest* without an oath 21 (for they have become priests without an oath, but He with an oath by Him who said to Him:

    "The LORD has sworn
    And will not relent,
    'You *are* a priest forever
    According to the order of
        Melchizedek'"),

22 by so much more Jesus has become a surety of a better covenant.

23 Also there were many priests, because they were prevented by death from continu-

ing. 24 But He, because He continues forever, has an unchangeable priesthood. 25 Therefore He is also able to save to the uttermost those who come to God through Him, since He always lives to make intercession for them.

26 For such a High Priest was fitting for us, *who is* holy, harmless, undefiled, separate from sinners, and has become higher than the heavens; 27 who does not need daily, as those high priests, to offer up sacrifices, first for His own sins and then for the people's, for this He did once for all when He offered up Himself. 28 For the law appoints as high priests men who have weakness, but the word of the oath, which came after the law, *appoints* the Son who has been perfected forever.

◆◆◆◆

Reading 316—Attention to God
Psalm 123:2

God intends our attention to be arrested, He does not arrest it for us. The things Jesus tells us to consider are not things that compel our attention—"Consider the lilies of the field," "Look at the birds of the air." The Spirit of God instructs us to be attentive. Are our eyes so fixed upon God that we have spiritual discernment and can see His countenance in the dreadful cloud of war? Most of us are at our wits' end, we have no inkling of what God is doing because our eyes have not been waiting upon Him. We are apt to pay more attention to our newspaper than to God's Book, and spiritual leakage begins because we do not make the effort to lift up our eyes to God. This is a description of entire reliance on God. Be careful of anything that is going to deflect your attention from God. (GOOD)

EZEKIEL 15:1—16:63

THEN the word of the LORD came to me, saying: 2 "Son of man, how is the wood of the vine *better* than any other wood, the vine branch which is among the trees of the forest? 3 Is wood taken from it to make any object? Or can *men* make a peg from it to hang any vessel on? 4 Instead, it is thrown into the fire for fuel; the fire devours both ends of it, and its middle is burned. Is it useful for *any* work? 5 Indeed, when it was whole, no object could be made from it. How much less will it be useful for *any* work when the fire has devoured it, and it is burned?

6 "Therefore thus says the Lord GOD: 'Like the wood of the vine among the trees of the forest, which I have given to the fire for fuel, so I will give up the inhabitants of Jerusalem; 7 and I will set My face against them. They will go out from *one* fire, but *another* fire shall devour them. Then you shall know that I *am* the LORD, when I set My face against them. 8 Thus I will make the land desolate, because they have persisted in unfaithfulness,' says the Lord GOD."

16 AGAIN the word of the LORD came to me, saying, 2 "Son of man, cause Jerusalem to know her abominations, 3 and say, 'Thus says the Lord GOD to Jerusalem: "Your birth and your nativity *are* from the land of Canaan; your father *was* an Amorite and your mother a Hittite. 4 *As for* your nativity, on the day you were born your navel cord was not cut, nor were you washed in water to cleanse *you;* you were not rubbed with salt nor wrapped in swaddling cloths. 5 No eye pitied you, to do any of these things for you, to have compassion on you; but you were thrown out into the open field, when you yourself were loathed on the day you were born.

6 "And when I passed by you and saw you struggling in your own blood, I said to you in your blood, 'Live!' Yes, I said to you in your blood, 'Live!' 7 I made you thrive like a plant in the field; and you grew, matured, and became very beautiful. *Your* breasts were formed, your hair grew, but you *were* naked and bare.

8 "When I passed by you again and looked upon you, indeed your time *was* the time of love; so I spread My wing over you and covered your nakedness. Yes, I swore an oath to you and entered into a covenant with you, and you became Mine," says the Lord GOD.

9 "Then I washed you in water; yes, I thoroughly washed off your blood, and I anointed you with oil. 10 I clothed you in embroidered cloth and gave you sandals of badger skin; I clothed you with fine linen and covered you with silk. 11 I adorned you with ornaments, put bracelets on your wrists, and a chain on your neck. 12 And I put a jewel in your nose, earrings in your ears, and a beautiful crown on your head. 13 Thus you were adorned with gold and silver, and your clothing *was of* fine linen, silk, and embroidered cloth. You ate *pastry of* fine flour, honey, and oil. You were exceedingly beautiful, and succeeded to royalty. 14 Your fame went out among the nations because of your beauty, for it *was* perfect through My splendor which I had bestowed on you," says the Lord GOD.

15 "But you trusted in your own beauty, played the harlot because of your fame, and poured out your harlotry on everyone passing by who *would have* it. 16 You took some of your garments and adorned multicolored high places for yourself, and played the harlot on them. *Such* things should not happen, nor be. 17 You have also taken your beautiful jewelry from My gold and My silver, which I had given you, and made for yourself male images and played the harlot with them. 18 You took your embroidered garments and covered them, and you set My oil and My incense before them. 19 Also My food which I gave you—the pastry of fine flour, oil, and honey *which* I fed you— you set it before them as sweet incense; and *so* it was," says the Lord GOD.

20 "Moreover you took your sons and your daughters, whom you bore to Me, and these you sacrificed to them to be devoured. *Were* your *acts* of harlotry a small matter, 21 that you have slain My children and offered them up to them by causing them to pass through *the fire?* 22 And in all your abominations and acts of harlotry you did not remember the days of your youth, when you were naked and bare, struggling in your blood.

23 "Then it was so, after all your wickedness—'Woe, woe to you!' says the Lord GOD— 24 *that* you also built for yourself a shrine, and made a high place for yourself in every street. 25 You built your high places at the head of every road, and made your beauty to be abhorred. You offered yourself to everyone who passed by, and multiplied your acts of harlotry. 26 You also committed harlotry with the Egyptians, your very fleshly neighbors, and increased your acts of harlotry to provoke Me to anger.

27 "Behold, therefore, I stretched out My hand against you, diminished your allotment, and gave you up to the will of those who hate you, the daughters of the Philistines, who were ashamed of your lewd behavior. 28 You also played the harlot with the Assyrians, because you were insatiable; indeed you played the harlot with them and still were not satisfied. 29 Moreover you multiplied your acts of harlotry as far as the land of the trader, Chaldea; and even then you were not satisfied.

30 "How degenerate is your heart!" says the Lord GOD, "seeing you do all these *things*, the deeds of a brazen harlot.

God has paid the price of redeeming a race that had become degenerate.   (BIB. ETHICS)

---

31 "You erected your shrine at the head of every road, and built your high place in every street. Yet you were not like a harlot, because you scorned payment. 32 *You are* an adulterous wife, *who* takes strangers instead of her husband. 33 Men make payment to all harlots, but you made your payments to all your lovers, and hired them to come to you from all around for your harlotry. 34 You are the opposite of *other* women in your harlotry, because no one solicited you to be a harlot. In that you gave payment but no payment was given you, therefore you are the opposite."

35 'Now then, O harlot, hear the word of the LORD! 36 Thus says the Lord GOD: "Because your filthiness was poured out and your nakedness uncovered in your harlotry with your lovers, and with all your abominable idols, and because of the blood of your children which you gave to them, 37 surely, therefore, I will gather all your lovers with whom you took pleasure, all those you loved, *and* all those you hated; I will gather them from all around against you and will uncover your nakedness to them, that they may see all your nakedness. 38 And I will judge you as women who break wedlock or shed blood are judged; I will bring blood upon you in fury and jealousy. 39 I will also give you into their hand, and they shall throw down your shrines and break down your high places. They shall also strip you

of your clothes, take your beautiful jewelry, and leave you naked and bare.

40 "They shall also bring up an assembly against you, and they shall stone you with stones and thrust you through with their swords. 41 They shall burn your houses with fire, and execute judgments on you in the sight of many women; and I will make you cease playing the harlot, and you shall no longer hire lovers. 42 So I will lay to rest My fury toward you, and My jealousy shall depart from you. I will be quiet, and be angry no more. 43 Because you did not remember the days of your youth, but agitated Me with all these *things,* surely I will also recompense your deeds on *your own* head," says the Lord GOD. "And you shall not commit lewdness in addition to all your abominations.

44 "Indeed everyone who quotes proverbs will use *this* proverb against you: 'Like mother, like daughter!' 45 You *are* your mother's daughter, loathing husband and children; and you *are* the sister of your sisters, who loathed their husbands and children; your mother *was* a Hittite and your father an Amorite.

46 "Your elder sister *is* Samaria, who dwells with her daughters to the north of you; and your younger sister, who dwells to the south of you, *is* Sodom and her daughters. 47 You did not walk in their ways nor act according to their abominations; but, as *if that were* too little, you became more corrupt than they in all your ways.

48 "*As* I live," says the Lord GOD, "neither your sister Sodom nor her daughters have done as you and your daughters have done. 49 Look, this was the iniquity of your sister Sodom: She and her daughter had pride, fullness of food, and abundance of idleness; neither did she strengthen the hand of the poor and needy. 50 And they were haughty and committed abomination before Me; therefore I took them away as I saw *fit.*

51 "Samaria did not commit half of your sins; but you have multiplied your abominations more than they, and have justified your sisters by all the abominations which you have done. 52 You who judged your sisters, bear your own shame also, because the sins which you committed were more abominable than theirs; they are more righteous than you. Yes, be disgraced also, and bear your own shame, because you justified your sisters.

53 "When I bring back their captives, the captives of Sodom and her daughters, and the captives of Samaria and her daughters, then *I will also bring back* the captives of your captivity among them, 54 that you may bear your own shame and be disgraced by all that you did when you comforted them. 55 When your sisters, Sodom and her daughters, return to their former state, and Samaria and her daughters return to their former state, then you and your daughters will return to your former state. 56 For your sister Sodom was not a byword in your mouth in the days of your pride, 57 before your wickedness was uncovered. It was like the time of the reproach of the daughters of Syria and all *those* around her, and of the daughters of the Philistines, who despise you everywhere. 58 You have paid for your lewdness and your abominations," says the LORD. 59 For thus says the Lord GOD: "I will deal with you as you have done, who despised the oath by breaking the covenant.

60 "Nevertheless I will remember My covenant with you in the days of your youth, and I will establish an everlasting covenant with you. 61 Then you will remember your ways and be ashamed, when you receive your older and your younger sisters; for I will give them to you for daughters, but not because of My covenant with you. 62 And I will establish My covenant with you. Then you shall know that I *am* the LORD, 63 that you may remember and be ashamed, and never open your mouth anymore because of your shame, when I provide you an atonement for all you have done," says the Lord GOD.' "

PSALM 123:1–4

1   UNTO You I lift up my eyes,
       O You who dwell in the heavens.
2   Behold, as the eyes of servants *look* to
       the hand of their masters,
       As the eyes of a maid to the hand of
       her mistress,
       So our eyes *look* to the LORD our God,
       Until He has mercy on us.

You can only be profoundly moved by devotion. (NOT KNOWING)

---

3   Have mercy on us, O LORD, have mercy
       on us!
       For we are exceedingly filled with
       contempt.
4   Our soul is exceedingly filled
       With the scorn of those who are at ease,
       With the contempt of the proud.

PROVERBS 28:20

20 A faithful man will abound with
     blessings,
     But he who hastens to be rich will not
     go unpunished.

HEBREWS 8:1–13

NOW *this is* the main point of the things
we are saying: We have such a High Priest,
who is seated at the right hand of the throne
of the Majesty in the heavens, 2 a Minister
of the sanctuary and of the true tabernacle
which the Lord erected, and not man.

3 For every high priest is appointed to
offer both gifts and sacrifices. Therefore *it
is* necessary that this One also have something to offer. 4 For if He were on earth,
He would not be a priest, since there are
priests who offer the gifts according to the
law; 5 who serve the copy and shadow of
the heavenly things, as Moses was divinely
instructed when he was about to make the
tabernacle. For He said, "See *that* you make
all things according to the pattern shown
you on the mountain." 6 But now He has
obtained a more excellent ministry, inasmuch as He is also Mediator of a better

covenant, which was established on better
promises.

7 For if that first *covenant* had been faultless, then no place would have been sought
for a second. 8 Because finding fault with
them, He says: "Behold, the days are coming, says the LORD, when I will make a
new covenant with the house of Israel and
with the house of Judah— 9 not according
to the covenant that I made with their fathers in the day when I took them by the
hand to lead them out of the land of Egypt;
because they did not continue in My covenant, and I disregarded them, says the
LORD. 10 For this *is* the covenant that I
will make with the house of Israel after
those days, says the LORD: I will put My
laws in their mind and write them on their
hearts; and I will be their God, and they
shall be My people. 11 None of them shall
teach his neighbor, and none his brother,
saying, 'Know the LORD,' for all shall know
Me, from the least of them to the greatest
of them. 12 For I will be merciful to their
unrighteousness, and their sins and their
lawless deeds I will remember no
more."

13 In that He says, "A new *covenant*," He
has made the first obsolete. Now what is
becoming obsolete and growing old is
ready to vanish away.

◄◆►

Reading 317—Absurd Antipathy
Psalm 124:2, 3

A t heart men are antagonistic to the lordship of Jesus Christ. It is not
antagonism to creeds or points of view, but antagonism encountered
for My sake. Many of us awaken antagonism by our way of stating things; we
have to distinguish between being persecuted for some notion of our own
and being persecuted "for My sake." We are apt to think only of the bad
things as being against Jesus, but it is the refined things, the cultured things,
the religious things which are dead against Jesus Christ unless they are loyal
to Him. It was the religious people of our Lord's time who withstood Him,
not the worldly. "If the world hates you, you know that it hated Me before *it
hated* you" (John 15:18). These are the deliberate words of our Lord to His
disciples. In the measure in which we are loyal to Jesus Christ the same thing
happens to us; we are at a loss to understand why people should have the
most apparently absurd antipathy to us. Their anger is strangely unaccountable;
it is not irritation, but an inspired working against.   (*GOOD*)

EZEKIEL 17:1—18:32

AND the word of the LORD came to me, saying, 2 "Son of man, pose a riddle, and speak a parable to the house of Israel, 3 and say, 'Thus says the Lord GOD:

"A great eagle with large wings and
    long pinions,
Full of feathers of various colors,
Came to Lebanon
And took from the cedar the highest
    branch.
4   He cropped off its topmost young
    twig
And carried it to a land of trade;
He set it in a city of merchants.
5   Then he took some of the seed of
    the land
And planted it in a fertile field;
He placed *it* by abundant waters
And set it like a willow tree.
6   And it grew and became a spreading
    vine of low stature;
Its branches turned toward him,
But its roots were under it.
So it became a vine,
Brought forth branches,
And put forth shoots.

7   "But there was another great eagle
    with large wings and many
    feathers;
And behold, this vine bent its roots
    toward him,
And stretched its branches toward
    him,
From the garden terrace where it had
    been planted,
That he might water it.
8   It was planted in good soil by many
    waters,
To bring forth branches, bear fruit,
And become a majestic vine." '

9 "Say, 'Thus says the Lord GOD:

"Will it thrive?
Will he not pull up its roots,
Cut off its fruit,
And leave it to wither?
All of its spring leaves will wither,
And no great power or many people
Will be needed to pluck it up by its
    roots.
10   Behold, *it is* planted,
Will it thrive?
Will it not utterly wither when the
    east wind touches it?
It will wither in the garden terrace
    where it grew." ' "

11 Moreover the word of the LORD came to me, saying, 12 "Say now to the rebellious house: 'Do you not know what these *things* mean?' Tell *them,* 'Indeed the king of Babylon went to Jerusalem and took its king and princes, and led them with him to Babylon. 13 And he took the king's offspring, made a covenant with him, and put him under oath. He also took away the mighty of the land, 14 that the kingdom might be brought low and not lift itself up, *but* that by keeping his covenant it might stand. 15 But he rebelled against him by sending his ambassadors to Egypt, that they might give him horses and many people. Will he prosper? Will he who does such *things* escape? Can he break a covenant and still be delivered?

16 '*As* I live,' says the Lord GOD, 'surely in the place *where* the king *dwells* who made him king, whose oath he despised and whose covenant he broke—with him in the midst of Babylon he shall die. 17 Nor will Pharaoh with *his* mighty army and great company do anything in the war, when they heap up a siege mound and build a wall to cut off many persons. 18 Since he despised the oath by breaking the covenant, and in fact gave his hand and still did all these *things,* he shall not escape.' "

19 Therefore thus says the Lord GOD: "*As* I live, surely My oath which he despised, and My covenant which he broke, I will recompense on his own head. 20 I will spread My net over him, and he shall be taken in My snare. I will bring him to Babylon and try him there for the treason which he committed against Me. 21 All his fugitives with all his troops shall fall by the sword, and those who remain shall be scattered to every wind; and you shall know that I, the LORD, have spoken."

22 Thus says the Lord GOD: "I will take also *one* of the highest branches of the high cedar and set *it* out. I will crop off from the topmost of its young twigs a tender one, and will plant *it* on a high and prominent mountain. 23 On the mountain height of Israel I will plant it; and it will bring forth boughs, and bear fruit, and be a majestic cedar. Under it will dwell birds of every sort; in the shadow of its branches they will dwell. 24 And all the trees of the field shall know that I, the LORD, have brought down the high tree and exalted the low tree, dried up the green tree and made the dry tree flourish; I, the LORD, have spoken and have done *it.*"

18 THE word of the LORD came to me again, saying,

2 "What do you mean when you use this proverb concerning the land of Israel, saying:

'The fathers have eaten sour grapes,
And the children's teeth are set on edge'?

3 "*As* I live," says the Lord GOD, "you shall no longer use this proverb in Israel.

4   "Behold, all souls are Mine;
    The soul of the father
    As well as the soul of the son is Mine;
    The soul who sins shall die.
5   But if a man is just
    And does what is lawful and right;
6   If he has not eaten on the mountains,
    Nor lifted up his eyes to the idols
      of the house of Israel,
    Nor defiled his neighbor's wife,
    Nor approached a woman during her
      impurity;
7   If he has not oppressed anyone,
    But has restored to the debtor his
      pledge;
    Has robbed no one by violence,
    But has given his bread to the hungry
    And covered the naked with clothing;
8   If he has not exacted usury
    Nor taken any increase,
    But has withdrawn his hand from
      iniquity
    And executed true judgment between
      man and man;
9   *If* he has walked in My statutes
    And kept My judgments faithfully—
    He *is* just;
    He shall surely live!"
    Says the Lord GOD.

10 "If he begets a son *who is* a robber
    Or a shedder of blood,
    Who does any of these *things*
11 And does none of those *duties,*
    But has eaten on the mountains
    Or defiled his neighbor's wife;
12 If he has oppressed the poor and
      needy,
    Robbed by violence,
    Not restored the pledge,
    Lifted his eyes to the idols,
    Or committed abomination;
13 If he has exacted usury
    Or taken increase—
    Shall he then live?
    He shall not live!
    If he has done any of these
      abominations,
    He shall surely die;
    His blood shall be upon him.

14 "*If,* however, he begets a son
    Who sees all the sins which his father
      has done,
    And considers but does not do
      likewise;
15 *Who* has not eaten on the mountains,
    Nor lifted his eyes to the idols of
      the house of Israel,
    Nor defiled his neighbor's wife;
16 Has not oppressed anyone,
    Nor withheld a pledge,
    Nor robbed by violence,
    But has given his bread to the hungry
    And covered the naked with
      clothing;
17 *Who* has withdrawn his hand from
      the poor
    And not received usury or increase,
    But has executed My judgments
    And walked in My statutes—
    He shall not die for the iniquity of
      his father;
    He shall surely live!

18 "*As for* his father,
    Because he cruelly oppressed,
    Robbed his brother by violence,
    And did what *is* not good among
      his people,
    Behold, he shall die for his iniquity.

19 "Yet you say, 'Why should the son not bear the guilt of the father?' Because the son has done what is lawful and right, and has kept all My statutes and observed them, he shall surely live. 20 The soul who sins shall die. The son shall not bear the guilt of the father, nor the father bear the guilt of the son. The righteousness of the righteous shall be upon himself, and the wickedness of the wicked shall be upon himself.

21 "But if a wicked man turns from all his sins which he has committed, keeps all My statutes, and does what is lawful and right, he shall surely live; he shall not die. 22 None of the transgressions which he has committed shall be remembered against him; because of the righteousness which he has done, he shall live. 23 Do I have any pleasure at all that the wicked should die?" says the Lord GOD, "*and* not that he should turn from his ways and live?

24 "But when a righteous man turns away from his righteousness and commits iniquity, and does according to all the abominations that the wicked *man* does, shall he live? All the righteousness which he has done shall not be remembered; because of the unfaithfulness of which he is guilty and the sin which he has committed, because of them he shall die.

25 "Yet you say, 'The way of the Lord is not fair.' Hear now, O house of Israel, is it not My way which is fair, and your ways which are not fair? 26 When a righteous *man* turns away from his righteousness, commits iniquity, and dies in it, it is because of the iniquity which he has done that he dies. 27 Again, when a wicked *man* turns away from the wickedness which he committed, and does what is lawful and right, he preserves himself alive. 28 Because he considers and turns away from all the transgressions which he committed, he shall surely live; he shall not die. 29 Yet the house of Israel says, 'The way of the Lord is not fair.' O house of Israel, is it not My ways which are fair, and your ways which are not fair?

30 "Therefore I will judge you, O house of Israel, every one according to his ways," says the Lord God. "Repent, and turn from all your transgressions, so that iniquity will not be your ruin. 31 Cast away from you all the transgressions which you have committed, and get yourselves a new heart and a new spirit. For why should you die, O house of Israel? 32 For I have no pleasure in the death of one who dies," says the Lord God. "Therefore turn and live!"

PSALM 124:1–8

1 "IF it had not been the Lord who was on our side,"
Let Israel now say—
2 "If it had not been the Lord who was on our side,
When men rose up against us,
3 Then they would have swallowed us alive,
When their wrath was kindled against us;
4 Then the waters would have overwhelmed us,
The stream would have gone over our soul;
5 Then the swollen waters
Would have gone over our soul."

6 Blessed *be* the Lord,
Who has not given us *as* prey to their teeth.
7 Our soul has escaped as a bird from the snare of the fowlers;
The snare is broken, and we have escaped.
8 Our help *is* in the name of the Lord,
Who made heaven and earth.

PROVERBS 28:21

21 TO show partiality *is* not good,
Because for a piece of bread a man will transgress.

HEBREWS 9:1–28

THEN indeed, even the first *covenant* had ordinances of divine service and the earthly sanctuary. 2 For a tabernacle was prepared: the first *part,* in which *was* the lampstand, the table, and the showbread, which is called the sanctuary; 3 and behind the second veil, the part of the tabernacle which is called the Holiest of All, 4 which had the golden censer and the ark of the covenant overlaid on all sides with gold, in which *were* the golden pot that had the mānna, Aaron's rod that budded, and the tablets of the covenant; 5 and above it were the cherubim of glory overshadowing the mercy seat. Of these things we cannot now speak in detail.

6 Now when these things had been thus prepared, the priests always went into the first part of the tabernacle, performing *the services.* 7 But into the second part the high priest *went* alone once a year, not without blood, which he offered for himself and *for* the people's sins *committed* in ignorance; 8 the Holy Spirit indicating this, that the way into the Holiest of All was not yet made manifest while the first tabernacle was still standing. 9 It *was* symbolic for the present time in which both gifts and sacrifices are offered which cannot make him who performed the service perfect in regard to the conscience— 10 *concerned* only with foods and drinks, various washings, and fleshly ordinances imposed until the time of reformation.

11 But Christ came *as* High Priest of the good things to come, with the greater and more perfect tabernacle not made with hands, that is, not of this creation. 12 Not with the blood of goats and calves, but with His own blood He entered the Most Holy Place once for all, having obtained eternal redemption. 13 For if the blood of bulls and goats and the ashes of a heifer, sprinkling the unclean, sanctifies for the purifying of the flesh, 14 how much more shall the blood of Christ, who through the eternal Spirit offered Himself without spot to God, cleanse your conscience from dead works to serve the living God? 15 And for this reason He is the Mediator of the new covenant, by means of death, for the

Can God readjust a seared conscience and make it sensitive again? He can.   (BRILL. HERITAGE)

redemption of the transgressions under the first covenant, that those who are called may receive the promise of the eternal inheritance.

16 For where there *is* a testament, there must also of necessity be the death of the testator. 17 For a testament *is* in force after men are dead, since it has no power at all while the testator lives. 18 Therefore not even the first *covenant* was dedicated without blood. 19 For when Moses had spoken every precept to all the people according to the law, he took the blood of calves and goats, with water, scarlet wool, and hyssop, and sprinkled both the book itself and all the people, 20 saying, "This *is* the blood of the covenant which God has commanded you." 21 Then likewise he sprinkled with blood both the tabernacle and all the vessels of the ministry. 22 And according to the law almost all things are purified with blood, and without shedding of blood there is no remission.

23 Therefore *it was* necessary that the copies of the things in the heavens should be purified with these, but the heavenly things themselves with better sacrifices than these. 24 For Christ has not entered the holy places made with hands, *which are* copies of the true, but into heaven itself, now to appear in the presence of God for us; 25 not that He should offer Himself often, as the high priest enters the Most Holy Place every year with blood of another— 26 He then would have had to suffer often since the foundation of the world; but now, once at the end of the ages, He has appeared to put away sin by the sacrifice of Himself. 27 And as it is appointed for men to die once, but after this the judgment, 28 so Christ was offered once to bear the sins of many. To those who eagerly wait for Him He will appear a second time, apart from sin, for salvation.

◆◆◆◆

Reading 318—The Rod of the Wicked
Psalm 125:3

The rod [NKJV, *scepter*] means two things—it is used in counting in the sheep, and it is used to destroy the wild beast that suddenly springs out on the sheep (Ps. 25:4). The man of sin will have his rod, he will do clever tricks, he will put the mark of the beast on every business system that he sanctions, and those who do not have that mark on them can never do business under the regime of the man of sin. Suppose you find that the people who are "counted in" under the mark of the beast succeed, and you do not succeed, you may be tempted to negotiate the thing and say, "Well, I don't know, if I did this thing it would save me; I had better just compromise a bit." We must never do that. "The [rod] of the wicked shall not rest on the righteous," God says. There is no need to fear, if we keep within the moral frontiers of God we can say boldly, "The Lord *is* my helper." We do not need to mind how the wicked bluster and say, "If you don't do this and that, you will starve." Be faithful, make holiness your aim, holiness in every relationship—money, food, clothes, friendship—then you will see the Lord in all these domains.

(*GOOD*)

EZEKIEL 19:1—20:49

"MOREOVER take up a lamentation for the princes of Israel, 2 and say:

'What *is* your mother? A lioness:
She lay down among the lions;
Among the young lions she
    nourished her cubs.
3   She brought up one of her cubs,
And he became a young lion;
He learned to catch prey,
And he devoured men.
4   The nations also heard of him;
He was trapped in their pit,
And they brought him with chains
    to the land of Egypt.

5   'When she saw that she waited, *that*
    her hope was lost,
She took another of her cubs *and*
    made him a young lion.
6   He roved among the lions,
And became a young lion;
He learned to catch prey;
He devoured men.
7   He knew their desolate places,
And laid waste their cities;
The land with its fullness was
    desolated
By the noise of his roaring.
8   Then the nations set against him from
    the provinces on every side,
And spread their net over him;
He was trapped in their pit.
9   They put him in a cage with chains,
And brought him to the king of
    Babylon;
They brought him in nets,
That his voice should no longer be
    heard on the mountains of Israel.

10   'Your mother *was* like a vine in your
    bloodline,
Planted by the waters,
Fruitful and full of branches
Because of many waters.
11   She had strong branches for scepters
    of rulers.
She towered in stature above the
    thick branches,
And was seen in her height amid the
    dense foliage.
12   But she was plucked up in fury,
She was cast down to the ground,
And the east wind dried her fruit.
Her strong branches were broken and
    withered;
The fire consumed them.
13   And now she *is* planted in the
    wilderness,

In a dry and thirsty land.
14   Fire has come out from a rod of her
    branches
And devoured her fruit,
So that she has no strong branch—
    a scepter for ruling.'"

This *is* a lamentation, and has become a lamentation.

20   IT came to pass in the seventh year, in the fifth *month*, on the tenth *day* of the month, *that* certain of the elders of Israel came to inquire of the LORD, and sat before me. 2 Then the word of the LORD came to me, saying, 3 "Son of man, speak to the elders of Israel, and say to them, 'Thus says the Lord GOD: "Have you come to inquire of Me? *As* I live," says the Lord GOD, "I will not be inquired of by you." ' 4 Will you judge them, son of man, will you judge *them?* Then make known to them the abominations of their fathers.

5 "Say to them, 'Thus says the Lord GOD: "On the day when I chose Israel and raised My hand in an oath to the descendants of the house of Jacob, and made Myself known to them in the land of Egypt, I raised My hand in an oath to them, saying, 'I *am* the LORD your God.' 6 On that day I raised My hand in an oath to them, to bring them out of the land of Egypt into a land that I had searched out for them, 'flowing with milk and honey,' the glory of all lands. 7 Then I said to them, 'Each of you, throw away the abominations which are before his eyes, and do not defile yourselves with the idols of Egypt. I *am* the LORD your God.' 8 But they rebelled against Me and would not obey Me. They did not all cast away the abominations which were before their eyes, nor did they forsake the idols of Egypt. Then I said, 'I will pour out My fury on them and fulfill My anger against them in the midst of the land of Egypt.' 9 But I acted for My name's sake, that it should not be profaned before the Gentiles among whom they *were,* in whose sight I had made Myself known to them, to bring them out of the land of Egypt.

10 "Therefore I made them go out of the land of Egypt and brought them into the wilderness. 11 And I gave them My statutes and showed them My judgments, 'which, *if* a man does, he shall live by them.' 12 Moreover I also gave them My Sabbaths, to be a sign between them and Me, that they might know that I *am* the LORD who sanctifies them. 13 Yet the house of Israel rebelled against Me in the wilderness; they did not walk in My statutes; they despised

My judgments, 'which, *if* a man does, he shall live by them'; and they greatly defiled My Sabbaths. Then I said I would pour out My fury on them in the wilderness, to consume them. 14 But I acted for My name's sake, that it should not be profaned before the Gentiles, in whose sight I had brought them out. 15 So I also raised My hand in an oath to them in the wilderness, that I would not bring them into the land which I had given *them*, 'flowing with milk and honey,' the glory of all lands, 16 because they despised My judgments and did not walk in My statutes, but profaned My Sabbaths; for their heart went after their idols. 17 Nevertheless My eye spared them from destruction. I did not make an end of them in the wilderness.

18 "But I said to their children in the wilderness, 'Do not walk in the statutes of your fathers, nor observe their judgments, nor defile yourselves with their idols. 19 I *am* the LORD your God: Walk in My statutes, keep My judgments, and do them; 20 hallow My Sabbaths, and they will be a sign between Me and you, that you may know that I *am* the LORD your God.'

21 "Notwithstanding, the children rebelled against Me; they did not walk in My statutes, and were not careful to observe My judgments, 'which, *if* a man does, he shall live by them'; but they profaned My Sabbaths. Then I said I would pour out My fury on them and fulfill My anger against them in the wilderness. 22 Nevertheless I withdrew My hand and acted for My name's sake, that it should not be profaned in the sight of the Gentiles, in whose sight I had brought them out. 23 Also I raised My hand in an oath to those in the wilderness, that I would scatter them among the Gentiles and disperse them throughout the countries, 24 because they had not executed My judgments, but had despised My statutes, profaned My Sabbaths, and their eyes were fixed on their fathers' idols.

25 "Therefore I also gave them up to statutes *that were* not good, and judgments by which they could not live; 26 and I pronounced them unclean because of their ritual gifts, in that they caused all their firstborn to pass through *the fire*, that I might make them desolate and that they might know that I am the LORD." '

27 "Therefore, son of man, speak to the house of Israel, and say to them, 'Thus says the Lord GOD: "In this too your fathers have blasphemed Me, by being unfaithful to Me. 28 When I brought them into the land *concerning* which I had raised My hand

in an oath to give them, and they saw all the high hills and all the thick trees, there they offered their sacrifices and provoked Me with their offerings. There they also sent up their sweet aroma and poured out their drink offerings. 29 Then I said to them, 'What *is* this high place to which you go?' So its name is called Bamah to this day." '

30 Therefore say to the house of Israel, 'Thus says the Lord GOD: "Are you defiling yourselves in the manner of your fathers, and committing harlotry according to their abominations? 31 For when you offer your gifts and make your sons pass through the fire, you defile yourselves with all your idols, even to this day. So shall I be inquired of by you, O house of Israel? *As* I live," says the Lord GOD, "I will not be inquired of by you. 32 What you have in your mind shall never be, when you say, 'We will be like the Gentiles, like the families in other countries, serving wood and stone.'

33 "*As* I live," says the Lord GOD, "surely with a mighty hand, with an outstretched arm, and with fury poured out, I will rule over you. 34 I will bring you out from the peoples and gather you out of the countries where you are scattered, with a mighty hand, with an outstretched arm, and with fury poured out. 35 And I will bring you into the wilderness of the peoples, and there I will plead My case with you face to face. 36 Just as I pleaded My case with your fathers in the wilderness of the land of Egypt, so I will plead My case with you," says the Lord GOD.

37 "I will make you pass under the rod, and I will bring you into the bond of the covenant; 38 I will purge the rebels from among you, and those who transgress against Me; I will bring them out of the country where they dwell, but they shall not enter the land of Israel. Then you will know that I *am* the LORD.

39 "As for you, O house of Israel," thus says the Lord GOD: "Go, serve every one of you his idols—and hereafter—if you will not obey Me; but profane My holy name no more with your gifts and your idols. 40 For on My holy mountain, on the mountain height of Israel," says the Lord GOD, "there all the house of Israel, all of them in the land, shall serve Me; there I will accept them, and there I will require your offerings and the firstfruits of your sacrifices, together with all your holy things. 41 I will accept you as a sweet aroma when I bring you out from the peoples and gather you out of the countries where you have been scattered; and I will be hallowed in you

before the Gentiles. 42 Then you shall know that I *am* the LORD, when I bring you into the land of Israel, into the country *for* which I raised My hand in an oath to give to your fathers. 43 And there you shall remember your ways and all your doings with which you were defiled; and you shall loathe yourselves in your own sight because of all the evils that you have committed. 44 Then you shall know that I *am* the LORD, when I have dealt with you for My name's sake, not according to your wicked ways nor according to your corrupt doings, O house of Israel," says the Lord GOD.' "

45 Furthermore the word of the LORD came to me, saying, 46 "Son of man, set your face toward the south; preach against the south and prophesy against the forest land, the South, 47 and say to the forest of the South, 'Hear the word of the LORD! Thus says the Lord GOD: "Behold, I will kindle a fire in you, and it shall devour every green tree and every dry tree in you; the blazing flame shall not be quenched, and all faces from the south to the north shall be scorched by it. 48 All flesh shall see that I, the LORD, have kindled it; it shall not be quenched." ' "

49 Then I said, "Ah, Lord GOD! They say of me, 'Does he not speak parables?' "

PSALM 125:1–5

1 THOSE who trust in the LORD
  Are like Mount Zion,
  Which cannot be moved, *but* abides
    forever.
2 As the mountains surround
    Jerusalem,
  So the LORD surrounds His people
  From this time forth and forever.

3 For the scepter of wickedness shall not
    rest
  On the land allotted to the righteous,
  Lest the righteous reach out their hands
    to iniquity.

4 Do good, O LORD, to *those who are*
    good,
  And to *those who are* upright in their
    hearts.

5 As for such as turn aside to their
    crooked ways,
  The LORD shall lead them away
  With the workers of iniquity.

  Peace *be* upon Israel!

PROVERBS 28:22

22 A man with an evil eye hastens after
    riches,
  And does not consider that poverty will
    come upon him.

HEBREWS 10:1–18

FOR the law, having a shadow of the good things to come, *and* not the very image of the things, can never with these same sacrifices, which they offer continually year by year, make those who approach perfect. 2 For then would they not have ceased to be offered? For the worshipers, once purified, would have had no more consciousness of sins. 3 But in those *sacrifices there is* a reminder of sins every year. 4 For *it is* not possible that the blood of bulls and goats could take away sins.

5 Therefore, when He came into the world, He said:

  "Sacrifice and offering You did not
      desire,
    But a body You have prepared
      for Me.
6 In burnt offerings and *sacrifices* for
      sin
    You had no pleasure.
7 Then I said, 'Behold, I have come—
    In the volume of the book it is written
      of Me—
    To do Your will, O God.' "

8 Previously saying, "Sacrifice and offering, burnt offerings, and *offerings* for sin You did not desire, nor had pleasure *in them*" (which are offered according to the law), 9 then He said, "Behold, I have come to do Your will, O God." He takes away the first that He may establish the second. 10 By that will we have been sanctified through the offering of the body of Jesus Christ once *for all*.

11 And every priest stands ministering daily and offering repeatedly the same sacrifices, which can never take away sins. 12 But this Man, after He had offered one sacrifice for sins forever, sat down at the right hand of God, 13 from that time waiting till His enemies are made His footstool. 14 For by one offering He has

Jesus Christ did not come to found religion.   (SERMON MT.)

perfected forever those who are being sanctified.

15 But the Holy Spirit also witnesses to us; for after He had said before,

16 "This *is* the covenant that I will make with them after those days, says the LORD:

I will put My laws into their hearts, and in their minds I will write them," 17 *then He adds,* "Their sins and their lawless deeds I will remember no more." 18 Now where there is remission of these, *there is* no longer an offering for sin.

◆◆◆◆

Reading 319—The Ecstasy of His Doings
Psalm 126:3, 4

Whenever God brings His deliverances they are so supernatural that we are staggered with amazement. It is one of the most helpful spiritual exercises to reckon what God has done for us already. When God wanted to make His ancient people realize what manner of God He was, He said, "Remember the crossing of the Red Sea," and in the New Testament Paul says, "Remember, it is the God who raised Jesus from the dead." These two things are the unit of measurement of God's power. If I want to know what God can do, He is the God who made a way through the sea; if it is a question of power for my life, the measurement of that is the resurrection of Jesus.

"Bring back our captivity, O LORD, . . ." I call upon my soul to remember what God has done and it makes me bold to entreat Him to do it again. It is a crime to give way to self-pity, to be weak in God's strength when all this God is ours. . . . Robert Louis Stevenson asked God to forgive him if he had "shown no morning face"; and Dante places in the lowest circles of hell those who have been gloomy in the summer air.   (*GOOD*)

EZEKIEL 21:1—22:31

AND the word of the LORD came to me, saying, 2 "Son of man, set your face toward Jerusalem, preach against the holy places, and prophesy against the land of Israel; 3 and say to the land of Israel, 'Thus says the LORD: "Behold, I *am* against you, and I will draw My sword out of its sheath and cut off both righteous and wicked from you. 4 Because I will cut off both righteous and wicked from you, therefore My sword shall go out of its sheath against all flesh from south *to* north, 5 that all flesh may know that I, the LORD, have drawn My sword out of its sheath; it shall not return anymore." ' 6 Sigh therefore, son of man, with a breaking heart, and sigh with bitterness before their eyes. 7 And it shall be when they say to you, 'Why are you sighing?' that you shall answer, 'Because of the news; when it comes, every heart will melt, all hands will be feeble, every spirit will faint, and all knees will be weak *as* water. Behold,

it is coming and shall be brought to pass,' says the Lord GOD."

8 Again the word of the LORD came to me, saying, 9 "Son of man, prophesy and say, 'Thus says the LORD!' Say:

'A sword, a sword is sharpened
   And also polished!
10 Sharpened to make a dreadful
       slaughter,
   Polished to flash like lightning!
   Should we then make mirth?
   It despises the scepter of My son,
   As it does all wood.
11 And He has given it to be polished,
   That it may be handled;
   This sword is sharpened, and it is
       polished
   To be given into the hand of the
       slayer.'

12 "Cry and wail, son of man;
   For it will be against My people,
   Against all the princes of Israel.

Terrors including the sword will be
    against My people;
Therefore strike *your* thigh.

13 "Because *it is* a testing,
    And what if *the sword* despises even
        the scepter?
    The scepter shall be no *more*,"

says the Lord God.

14 "You therefore, son of man, prophesy,
    And strike *your* hands together.
    The third time let the sword do
        double *damage*.
    It *is* the sword *that* slays,
    The sword that slays the great *men*,
    That enters their private chambers.
15 I have set the point of the sword
        against all their gates,
    That the heart may melt and many
        may stumble.
    Ah! *It is* made bright;
    It is grasped for slaughter:

16 "Swords at the ready!
    Thrust right!
    Set your blade!
    Thrust left—
    Wherever your edge is ordered!

17 "I also will beat My fists together,
    And I will cause My fury to rest;
    I, the Lord, have spoken."

18 The word of the Lord came to me
again, saying: 19 "And son of man, appoint
for yourself two ways for the sword of the
king of Babylon to go; both of them shall
go from the same land. Make a sign; put
it at the head of the road to the city.
20 Appoint a road for the sword to go to
Rabbah of the Ammonites, and to Judah,
into fortified Jerusalem. 21 For the king of
Babylon stands at the parting of the road,
at the fork of the two roads, to use divination: he shakes the arrows, he consults the
images, he looks at the liver. 22 In his right
hand is the divination for Jerusalem: to set
up battering rams, to call for a slaughter,
to lift the voice with shouting, to set battering rams against the gates, to heap up a
siege mound, and to build a wall. 23 And
it will be to them like a false divination in
the eyes of those who have sworn oaths
with them; but he will bring their iniquity
to remembrance, that they may be taken.
24 "Therefore thus says the Lord God:
'Because you have made your iniquity to
be remembered, in that your transgressions
are uncovered, so that in all your doings

your sins appear—because you have come
to remembrance, you shall be taken in
hand.
25 'Now to you, O profane, wicked prince
of Israel, whose day has come, whose iniquity *shall* end, 26 thus says the Lord God:

"Remove the turban, and take off the
    crown;
Nothing *shall remain* the same.
Exalt the humble, and humble the
    exalted.

---

*B*eware of anything that puts you
in the place of the superior
person.   (Sermon Mt.)

---

27 Overthrown, overthrown,
    I will make it overthrown!
    It shall be no *longer*,
    Until He comes whose right it is,
    And I will give it *to Him*." '

28 "And you, son of man, prophesy and
say, 'Thus says the Lord God concerning
the Ammonites and concerning their reproach,' and say:

'A sword, a sword *is* drawn,
    Polished for slaughter,
    For consuming, for flashing—
29 While they see false visions for you,
    While they divine a lie to you,
    To bring you on the necks of the
        wicked, the slain
    Whose day has come,
    Whose iniquity *shall* end.

30 'Return *it* to its sheath.
    I will judge you
    In the place where you were created,
    In the land of your nativity.
31 I will pour out My indignation on
        you;
    I will blow against you with the fire
        of My wrath,
    And deliver you into the hands of
        brutal men *who are* skillful to
        destroy.
32 You shall be fuel for the fire;
    Your blood shall be in the midst of
        the land.
    You shall not be remembered,
    For I the Lord have spoken.' "

22 MOREOVER the word of the
Lord came to me, saying, 2 "Now,
son of man, will you judge, will you judge
the bloody city? Yes, show her all her abomi-

nations! 3 Then say, 'Thus says the Lord GOD: "The city sheds blood in her own midst, that her time may come; and she makes idols within herself to defile herself. 4 You have become guilty by the blood which you have shed, and have defiled yourself with the idols which you have made. You have caused your days to draw near, and have come to *the end of* your years; therefore I have made you a reproach to the nations, and a mockery to all countries. 5 *Those* near and *those* far from you will mock you as infamous *and* full of tumult.

6 "Look, the princes of Israel: each one has used his power to shed blood in you. 7 In you they have made light of father and mother; in your midst they have oppressed the stranger; in you they have mistreated the fatherless and the widow. 8 You have despised My holy things and profaned My Sabbaths. 9 In you are men who slander to cause bloodshed; in you are those who eat on the mountains; in your midst they commit lewdness. 10 In you men uncover their fathers' nakedness; in you they violate women who are set apart during their impurity. 11 One commits abomination with his neighbor's wife; another lewdly defiles his daughter-in-law; and another in you violates his sister, his father's daughter. 12 In you they take bribes to shed blood; you take usury and increase; you have made profit from your neighbors by extortion, and have forgotten Me," says the Lord GOD.

13 "Behold, therefore, I beat My fists at the dishonest profit which you have made, and at the bloodshed which has been in your midst. 14 Can your heart endure, or can your hands remain strong, in the days when I shall deal with you? I, the LORD, have spoken, and will do *it*. 15 I will scatter you among the nations, disperse you throughout the countries, and remove your filthiness completely from you. 16 You shall defile yourself in the sight of the nations; then you shall know that I *am* the LORD." ' "

17 The word of the LORD came to me, saying, 18 "Son of man, the house of Israel has become dross to Me; they *are* all bronze, tin, iron, and lead, in the midst of a furnace; they have become dross from silver. 19 Therefore thus says the Lord GOD: 'Because you have all become dross, therefore behold, I will gather you into the midst of Jerusalem. 20 *As men* gather silver, bronze, iron, lead, and tin into the midst of a furnace, to blow fire on it, to melt *it;* so I will gather *you* in My anger and in My fury, and I will leave *you there* and melt you. 21 Yes, I will gather you and blow on you with the fire of My wrath, and you shall be melted in its midst. 22 As silver is melted in the midst of a furnace, so shall you be melted in its midst; then you shall know that I, the LORD, have poured out My fury on you.' "

23 And the word of the LORD came to me, saying, 24 "Son of man, say to her: 'You *are* a land that is not cleansed or rained on in the day of indignation.' 25 The conspiracy of her prophets in her midst is like a roaring lion tearing the prey; they have devoured people; they have taken treasure and precious things; they have made many widows in her midst. 26 Her priests have violated My law and profaned My holy things; they have not distinguished between the holy and unholy, nor have they made known *the difference* between the unclean and the clean; and they have hidden their eyes from My Sabbaths, so that I am profaned among them. 27 Her princes in her midst *are* like wolves tearing the prey, to shed blood, to destroy people, and to get dishonest gain. 28 Her prophets plastered them with untempered *mortar,* seeing false visions, and divining lies for them, saying, 'Thus says the Lord GOD,' when the LORD had not spoken. 29 The people of the land have used oppressions, committed robbery, and mistreated the poor and needy; and they wrongfully oppress the stranger. 30 So I sought for a man among them who would make a wall, and stand in the gap before Me on behalf of the land, that I should not destroy it; but I found no one. 31 Therefore I have poured out My indignation on them; I have consumed them with the fire of My wrath; and I have recompensed their deeds on their own heads," says the Lord GOD.

PSALM 126:1–6

1   WHEN the LORD brought back the
     captivity of Zion,
     We were like those who dream.
2   Then our mouth was filled with
     laughter,
     And our tongue with singing.
     Then they said among the nations,
     "The LORD has done great things for
     them."
3   The LORD has done great things
     for us,
     And we are glad.

4   Bring back our captivity, O LORD,
     As the streams in the South.

5   Those who sow in tears
     Shall reap in joy.

> *Joy is not happiness; there is no mention in the Bible of happiness for a Christian.* (GLORIFY)

6 He who continually goes forth weeping,
   Bearing seed for sowing,
   Shall doubtless come again with rejoicing,
   Bringing his sheaves *with him*.

PROVERBS 28:23

23 HE who rebukes a man will find more favor afterward
   Than he who flatters with the tongue.

HEBREWS 10:19–39

THEREFORE, brethren, having boldness to enter the Holiest by the blood of Jesus, 20 by a new and living way which He consecrated for us, through the veil, that is, His flesh, 21 and *having* a High Priest over the house of God, 22 let us draw near with a true heart in full assurance of faith, having our hearts sprinkled from an evil conscience and our bodies washed with pure water. 23 Let us hold fast the confession of *our* hope without wavering, for He who promised *is* faithful. 24 And let us consider one another in order to stir up love and good works, 25 not forsaking the assembling of ourselves together, as *is* the manner of some, but exhorting *one another,* and so much the more as you see the Day approaching.

26 For if we sin willfully after we have received the knowledge of the truth, there no longer remains a sacrifice for sins, 27 but a certain fearful expectation of judgment, and fiery indignation which will devour the adversaries. 28 Anyone who has rejected Moses' law dies without mercy on the testimony of two or three witnesses. 29 Of how much worse punishment, do you suppose, will he be thought worthy who has trampled the Son of God underfoot, counted the blood of the covenant by which he was sanctified a common thing, and insulted the Spirit of grace? 30 For we know Him who said, "Vengeance is Mine, I will repay," says the Lord. And again, "The LORD will judge His people." 31 It is a fearful thing to fall into the hands of the living God.

32 But recall the former days in which, after you were illuminated, you endured a great struggle with sufferings: 33 partly while you were made a spectacle both by reproaches and tribulations, and partly while you became companions of those who were so treated; 34 for you had compassion on me in my chains, and joyfully accepted the plundering of your goods, knowing that you have a better and an enduring possession for yourselves in heaven. 35 Therefore do not cast away your confidence, which has great reward. 36 For you have need of endurance, so that after you have done the will of God, you may receive the promise:

37 "For yet a little while,
   And He who is coming will come
      and will not tarry.
38 Now the just shall live by faith;
   But if *anyone* draws back,
   My soul has no pleasure in him."

39 But we are not of those who draw back to perdition, but of those who believe to the saving of the soul.

◆◆◆◆

*Reading 320—*God's Own City
Hebrews 11:10

What a curious anomaly—a city of God! We could have understood if it had been the *country* of God, but a holy *city* is inconceivable to us. The city of Jerusalem, like the temple, was ordained of God, that is why the children of Israel were so certain the prophets were wrong in saying that God would ever leave Jerusalem; but God did leave it, He left it desolate on account of the sins of the people.

There is a time coming when we shall live in God's own city: Abraham looked for it; John saw it, coming down out of heaven. Our present-day communities are man's attempt at building up the city of God; man is confident that if only God will give him time enough he will build not only a holy city, but a holy community and establish peace on earth, and God is allowing him ample opportunity to try, until he is satisfied that God's way is the only way.   (GOOD)

EZEKIEL 23:1—24:27

THE word of the LORD came again to me, saying:

2   "Son of man, there were two women,
    The daughters of one mother.
3   They committed harlotry in Egypt,
    They committed harlotry in their
        youth;
    Their breasts were there embraced,
    Their virgin bosom was there
        pressed.
4   Their names: Oholah the elder and
        Oholibah her sister;
    They were Mine,
    And they bore sons and daughters.
    As for their names,
    Samaria *is* Oholah, and Jerusalem *is*
        Oholibah.

5   "Oholah played the harlot even
        though she was Mine;
    And she lusted for her lovers, the
        neighboring Assyrians,
6   *Who were* clothed in purple,
    Captains and rulers,
    All of them desirable young men,
    Horsemen riding on horses.
7   Thus she committed her harlotry
        with them,
    All of them choice men of Assyria;
    And with all for whom she lusted,
    With all their idols, she defiled
        herself.
8   She has never given up her harlotry
        brought from Egypt,
    For in her youth they had lain with
        her,
    Pressed her virgin bosom,
    And poured out their immorality
        upon her.

9   "Therefore I have delivered her
    Into the hand of her lovers,
    Into the hand of the Assyrians,
    For whom she lusted.
10 They uncovered her nakedness,
    Took away her sons and daughters,
    And slew her with the sword;

    She became a byword among
        women,
    For they had executed judgment on
        her.

11 "Now although her sister Oholibah
saw *this,* she became more corrupt in her
lust than she, and in her harlotry more corrupt than her sister's harlotry.

12 "She lusted for the neighboring
        Assyrians,
    Captains and rulers,
    Clothed most gorgeously,
    Horsemen riding on horses,
    All of them desirable young men.
13 Then I saw that she was defiled;
    Both *took* the same way.
14 But she increased her harlotry;
    She looked at men portrayed on the
        wall,
    Images of Chaldeans portrayed in
        vermilion,
15 Girded with belts around their waists,
    Flowing turbans on their heads,
    All of them looking like captains,
    In the manner of the Babylonians of
        Chaldea,
    The land of their nativity.
16 As soon as her eyes saw them,
    She lusted for them
    And sent messengers to them in
        Chaldea.

17 "Then the Babylonians came to her,
        into the bed of love,
    And they defiled her with their
        immorality;
    So she was defiled by them, and
        alienated herself from them.
18 She revealed her harlotry and
        uncovered her nakedness.
    Then I alienated Myself from her,
    As I had alienated Myself from her
        sister.

19 "Yet she multiplied her harlotry
    In calling to remembrance the days
        of her youth,
    When she had played the harlot in
        the land of Egypt.

20 For she lusted for her paramours,
    Whose flesh *is like* the flesh of
      donkeys,
    And whose issue *is like* the issue of
      horses.
21 Thus you called to remembrance the
      lewdness of your youth,
    When the Egyptians pressed your
      bosom
    Because of your youthful breasts.

22 "Therefore, Oholibah, thus says the
Lord GOD:

    'Behold, I will stir up your lovers
      against you,
    From whom you have alienated
      yourself,
    And I will bring them against you
      from every side:
23   The Babylonians,
    All the Chaldeans,
    Pekod, Shoa, Koa,
    All the Assyrians with them,
    All of them desirable young men,
    Governors and rulers,
    Captains and men of renown,
    All of them riding on horses.
24 And they shall come against you
    With chariots, wagons, and war-
      horses,
    With a horde of people.
    They shall array against you
    Buckler, shield, and helmet all
      around.

    'I will delegate judgment to them,
    And they shall judge you according
      to their judgments.
25 I will set My jealousy against you,
    And they shall deal furiously with
      you;
    They shall remove your nose and
      your ears,
    And your remnant shall fall by the
      sword;
    They shall take your sons and your
      daughters,
    And your remnant shall be devoured
      by fire.
26 They shall also strip you of your
      clothes
    And take away your beautiful
      jewelry.

27 'Thus I will make you cease your
      lewdness and your harlotry
    Brought from the land of Egypt,
    So that you will not lift your eyes
      to them,
    Nor remember Egypt anymore.'

28 "For thus says the Lord GOD: 'Surely I will deliver you into the hand of those you hate, into the hand *of those* from whom you alienated yourself. 29 They will deal hatefully with you, take away all you have worked for, and leave you naked and bare. The nakedness of your harlotry shall be uncovered, both your lewdness and your harlotry. 30 I will do these *things* to you because you have gone as a harlot after the Gentiles, because you have become defiled by their idols. 31 You have walked in the way of your sister; therefore I will put her cup in your hand.'

32 "Thus says the Lord GOD:

    'You shall drink of your sister's cup,
      The deep and wide one;
    You shall be laughed to scorn
      And held in derision;
    It contains much.
33 You will be filled with drunkenness
      and sorrow,
    The cup of horror and desolation,
    The cup of your sister Samaria.
34 You shall drink and drain it,
    You shall break its shards,
    And tear at your own breasts;
    For I have spoken,'
    Says the Lord GOD.

35 "Therefore thus says the Lord GOD:

    'Because you have forgotten Me and
      cast Me behind your back,
    Therefore you shall bear the *penalty*
    Of your lewdness and your
      harlotry.' "

36 The LORD also said to me: "Son of man, will you judge Oholah and Oholibah? Then declare to them their abominations. 37 For they have committed adultery, and blood *is* on their hands. They have committed adultery with their idols, and even sacrificed their sons whom they bore to Me, passing them through *the fire*, to devour *them*. 38 Moreover they have done this to Me: They have defiled My sanctuary on the same day and profaned My Sabbaths. 39 For after they had slain their children for their idols, on the same day they came into My sanctuary to profane it; and indeed thus they have done in the midst of My house. 40 "Furthermore you sent for men to come from afar, to whom a messenger *was* sent; and there they came. And you washed yourself for them, painted your eyes, and adorned yourself with ornaments. 41 You sat on a stately couch, with a table prepared

before it, on which you had set My incense and My oil. 42 The sound of a carefree multitude *was* with her, and Sabeans *were* brought from the wilderness with men of the common sort, who put bracelets on their wrists and beautiful crowns on their heads. 43 Then I said concerning *her who had grown old in adulteries*, 'Will they commit harlotry with her now, and she *with them?*' 44 Yet they went in to her, as men go in to a woman who plays the harlot; thus they went in to Oholah and Oholibah, the lewd women. 45 But righteous men will judge them after the manner of adulteresses, and after the manner of women who shed blood, because they *are* adulteresses, and blood *is* on their hands.

46 "For thus says the Lord God: 'Bring up an assembly against them, give them up to trouble and plunder. 47 The assembly shall stone them with stones and execute them with their swords; they shall slay their sons and their daughters, and burn their houses with fire. 48 Thus I will cause lewdness to cease from the land, that all women may be taught not to practice your lewdness. 49 They shall repay you for your lewdness, and you shall pay for your idolatrous sins. Then you shall know that I *am* the Lord God.'"

24 AGAIN, in the ninth year, in the tenth month, on the tenth *day* of the month, the word of the Lord came to me, saying, 2 "Son of man, write down the name of the day, this very day—the king of Babylon started his siege against Jerusalem this very day. 3 And utter a parable to the rebellious house, and say to them, 'Thus says the Lord God:

"Put on a pot, set *it* on,
        And also pour water into it.
4   Gather pieces *of meat* in it,
        Every good piece,
        The thigh and the shoulder.
        Fill *it* with choice cuts;
5   Take the choice of the flock.
        Also pile *fuel* bones under it,
        Make it boil well,
        And let the cuts simmer in it."

6 'Therefore thus says the Lord God:

"Woe to the bloody city,
        To the pot whose scum *is* in it,
        And whose scum is not gone
          from it!
        Bring it out piece by piece,
        On which no lot has fallen.
7   For her blood is in her midst;

        She set it on top of a rock;
        She did not pour it on the ground,
        To cover it with dust.
8   That it may raise up fury and take
          vengeance,
        I have set her blood on top of a
          rock,
        That it may not be covered."

9 'Therefore thus says the Lord God:

"Woe to the bloody city!
        I too will make the pyre great.
10   Heap on the wood,
        Kindle the fire;
        Cook the meat well,
        Mix in the spices,
        And let the cuts be burned up.

11   "Then set the pot empty on the coals,
        That it may become hot and its
          bronze may burn,
        That its filthiness may be melted
          in it,
        That its scum may be consumed.
12   She has grown weary with lies,
        And her great scum has not gone
          from her.
        Let her scum *be* in the fire!
13   In your filthiness *is* lewdness.
        Because I have cleansed you, and you
          were not cleansed,
        You will not be cleansed of your
          filthiness anymore,
        Till I have caused My fury to rest
          upon you.
14   I, the Lord, have spoken *it*;
        It shall come to pass, and I will
          do *it*;
        I will not hold back,
        Nor will I spare,
        Nor will I relent;
        According to your ways
        And according to your deeds
        They will judge you,"
        Says the Lord God.'"

15 Also the word of the Lord came to me, saying, 16 "Son of man, behold, I take away from you the desire of your eyes with one stroke; yet you shall neither mourn nor weep, nor shall your tears run down. 17 Sigh in silence, make no mourning for the dead; bind your turban on your head, and put your sandals on your feet; do not cover *your* lips, and do not eat man's bread *of sorrow.*"

18 So I spoke to the people in the morning, and at evening my wife died; and the next morning I did as I was commanded. 19 And the people said to me, "Will you

not tell us what these *things signify* to us, that you behave so?"

20 Then I answered them, "The word of the Lord came to me, saying, 21 'Speak to the house of Israel, "Thus says the Lord God: 'Behold, I will profane My sanctuary, your arrogant boast, the desire of your eyes, the delight of your soul; and your sons and daughters whom you left behind shall fall by the sword. 22 And you shall do as I have done; you shall not cover *your* lips nor eat man's bread *of sorrow*. 23 Your turbans shall be on your heads and your sandals on your feet; you shall neither mourn nor weep, but you shall pine away in your iniquities and mourn with one another. 24 Thus Ezekiel is a sign to you; according to all that he has done you shall do; and when this comes, you shall know that I *am* the Lord God.' "

25 'And you, son of man—*will it* not *be* in the day when I take from them their stronghold, their joy and their glory, the desire of their eyes, and that on which they set their minds, their sons and their daughters: 26 on that day one who escapes will come to you to let *you* hear *it* with *your* ears; 27 on that day your mouth will be opened to him who has escaped; you shall speak and no longer be mute. Thus you will be a sign to them, and they shall know that I *am* the Lord.' "

PSALM 127:1–5

1   UNLESS the Lord builds the house,
      They labor in vain who build it;
      Unless the Lord guards the city,
      The watchman stays awake in vain.
2   *It is* vain for you to rise up early,
      To sit up late,
      To eat the bread of sorrows;
      For so He gives His beloved sleep.

3   Behold, children *are* a heritage from
        the Lord,
      The fruit of the womb *is* a reward.
4   Like arrows in the hand of a warrior,
      So *are* the children of one's youth.
5   Happy *is* the man who has his quiver
      full of them;
      They shall not be ashamed,
      But shall speak with their enemies in
      the gate.

PROVERBS 28:24

24   WHOEVER robs his father or his
      mother,

And says, "*It is* no transgression,"
The same *is* companion to a destroyer.

HEBREWS 11:1–16

NOW faith is the substance of things hoped for, the evidence of things not seen. 2 For by it the elders obtained a *good* testimony.

3 By faith we understand that the worlds were framed by the word of God, so that the things which are seen were not made of things which are visible.

4 By faith Abel offered to God a more excellent sacrifice than Cain, through which he obtained witness that he was righteous, God testifying of his gifts; and through it he being dead still speaks.

5 By faith Enoch was taken away so that he did not see death, "and was not found, because God had taken him"; for before he was taken he had this testimony, that he pleased God. 6 But without faith *it is* impossible to please *Him*, for he who comes to God must believe that He is, and *that* He is a rewarder of those who diligently seek Him.

7 By faith Noah, being divinely warned of things not yet seen, moved with godly fear, prepared an ark for the saving of his household, by which he condemned the world and became heir of the righteousness which is according to faith.

8 By faith Abraham obeyed when he was called to go out to the place which he would receive as an inheritance. And he went out, not knowing where he was going. 9 By faith

---

*F*aith *never knows where it is being led, it knows and loves the One who is leading.* (NOT KNOWING)

---

he dwelt in the land of promise as *in* a foreign country, dwelling in tents with Isaac and Jacob, the heirs with him of the same promise; 10 for he waited for the city which has foundations, whose builder and maker *is* God.

11 By faith Sarah herself also received strength to conceive seed, and she bore a child when she was past the age, because she judged Him faithful who had promised. 12 Therefore from one man, and him as good as dead, were born *as many* as the stars of the sky in multitude—innumerable as the sand which is by the seashore.

13 These all died in faith, not having

received the promises, but having seen them afar off were assured of them, embraced *them* and confessed that they were strangers and pilgrims on the earth. 14 For those who say such things declare plainly that they seek a homeland. 15 And truly if they had called to mind that *country* from which they had come out, they would have had opportunity to return. 16 But now they desire a better, that is, a heavenly *country*. Therefore God is not ashamed to be called their God, for He has prepared a city for them.

◆◆◆

Reading 321—Strenuous Satisfaction
Psalm 128:2

This verse reveals the connection between the natural creation and the regenerated creation. . . . When we are born from above we are apt to despise the clay of which we are made. The natural creation and the creation of grace work together, and what we are apt to call the sordid things, laboring with our hands, and eating and drinking, have to be turned into spiritual exercises by obedience, then we shall "eat and drink, and do all to the glory of God." There must be a uniting in personal experience of the two creations. It cannot be done all at once, there are whole tracts of life which have to be disciplined. "Your body is the temple of the Holy Spirit," it is the handiwork of God, and it is in these bodies we are to find satisfaction, and that means strenuousness. Every power of mind and heart should go into the strenuousness of turning the natural into the spiritual by obeying the word of God regarding it. If we do not make the natural spiritual, it will become sordid; but when we become spiritual the natural is shot through with the glory of God.   (*Good*)

EZEKIEL 25:1—26:21

THE word of the LORD came to me, saying, 2 "Son of man, set your face against the Ammonites, and prophesy against them. 3 Say to the Ammonites, 'Hear the word of the Lord GOD! Thus says the Lord GOD: "Because you said, 'Aha!' against My sanctuary when it was profaned, and against the land of Israel when it was desolate, and against the house of Judah when they went into captivity, 4 indeed, therefore, I will deliver you as a possession to the men of the East, and they shall set their encampments among you and make their dwellings among you; they shall eat your fruit, and they shall drink your milk. 5 And I will make Rabbah a stable for camels and Ammon a resting place for flocks. Then you shall know that I *am* the LORD."

6 'For thus says the Lord GOD: "Because you clapped *your* hands, stamped your feet, and rejoiced in heart with all your disdain for the land of Israel, 7 indeed, therefore, I will stretch out My hand against you, and give you as plunder to the nations; I will cut you off from the peoples, and I will cause you to perish from the countries; I will destroy you, and you shall know that I *am* the LORD."

8 'Thus says the Lord GOD: "Because Moab and Seir say, 'Look! The house of Judah *is* like all the nations,' 9 therefore, behold, I will clear the territory of Moab of cities, of the cities on its frontier, the glory of the country, Beth Jeshimoth, Baal Meon, and Kirjathaim. 10 To the men of the East I will give it as a possession, together with the Ammonites, that the Ammonites may not be remembered among the nations. 11 And I will execute judgments upon Moab, and they shall know that I *am* the LORD."

12 'Thus says the Lord GOD: "Because of what Edom did against the house of Judah by taking vengeance, and has greatly offended by avenging itself on them," 13 therefore thus says the Lord GOD: "I will also stretch out My hand against Edom, cut off man and beast from it, and make it desolate from Teman; Dedan shall fall by the sword. 14 I will lay My vengeance

on Edom by the hand of My people Israel, that they may do in Edom according to My anger and according to My fury; and they shall know My vengeance," says the Lord God.

15 'Thus says the Lord God: "Because the Philistines dealt vengefully and took vengeance with a spiteful heart, to destroy because of the old hatred," 16 therefore thus says the Lord God: "I will stretch out My hand against the Philistines, and I will cut off the Cherethites and destroy the remnant of the seacoast. 17 I will execute great vengeance on them with furious rebukes; and they shall know that I *am* the Lord, when I lay My vengeance upon them." ' "

26 AND it came to pass in the eleventh year, on the first *day* of the month, *that* the word of the Lord came to me, saying, 2 "Son of man, because Tyre has said against Jerusalem, 'Aha! She is broken who *was* the gateway of the peoples; now she is turned over to me; I shall be filled; she is laid waste.'

3 "Therefore thus says the Lord God: 'Behold, I *am* against you, O Tyre, and will cause many nations to come up against you, as the sea causes its waves to come up. 4 And they shall destroy the walls of Tyre and break down her towers; I will also scrape her dust from her, and make her like the top of a rock. 5 It shall be *a place for* spreading nets in the midst of the sea, for I have spoken,' says the Lord God; 'it shall become plunder for the nations. 6 Also her daughter *villages* which *are* in the fields shall be slain by the sword. Then they shall know that I am the Lord.'

7 "For thus says the Lord God: 'Behold, I will bring against Tyre from the north Nebuchadnezzar king of Babylon, king of kings, with horses, with chariots, and with horsemen, and an army with many people. 8 He will slay with the sword your daughter *villages* in the fields; he will heap up a siege mound against you, build a wall against you, and raise a defense against you. 9 He will direct his battering rams against your walls, and with his axes he will break down your towers. 10 Because of the abundance of his horses, their dust will cover you; your walls will shake at the noise of the horsemen, the wagons, and the chariots, when he enters your gates, as men enter a city that has been breached. 11 With the hooves of his horses he will trample all your streets; he will slay your people by the sword, and your strong pillars will fall to the ground. 12 They will plunder your riches and pillage your merchandise; they will

break down your walls and destroy your pleasant houses; they will lay your stones, your timber, and your soil in the midst of the water. 13 I will put an end to the sound of your songs, and the sound of your harps shall be heard no more. 14 I will make you like the top of a rock; you shall be *a place for* spreading nets, and you shall never be rebuilt, for I the Lord have spoken,' says the Lord God.

15 "Thus says the Lord God to Tyre: 'Will the coastlands not shake at the sound of your fall, when the wounded cry, when slaughter is made in the midst of you? 16 Then all the princes of the sea will come down from their thrones, lay aside their robes, and take off their embroidered garments; they will clothe themselves with trembling; they will sit on the ground, tremble *every* moment, and be astonished at you. 17 And they will take up a lamentation for you, and say to you:

"How you have perished,
    O one inhabited by seafaring men,
    O renowned city,
    Who was strong at sea,
    She and her inhabitants,
    Who caused their terror *to be* on all
        her inhabitants!
18 Now the coastlands tremble on the
        day of your fall;
    Yes, the coastlands by the sea are
        troubled at your departure." '

19 "For thus says the Lord God: 'When I make you a desolate city, like cities that are not inhabited, when I bring the deep upon you, and great waters cover you, 20 then I will bring you down with those who descend into the Pit, to the people of old, and I will make you dwell in the lowest part of the earth, in places desolate from antiquity, with those who go down to the Pit, so that you may never be inhabited; and I shall establish glory in the land of the living. 21 I will make you a terror, and you *shall be* no *more;* though you are sought for, you will never be found again,' says the Lord God."

PSALM 128:1–6

1   BLESSED *is* every one who fears the
        Lord,
    Who walks in His ways.

2   When you eat the labor of your hands,
    You *shall be* happy, and *it shall be* well
        with you.

3 Your wife *shall be* like a fruitful vine
In the very heart of your house,
Your children like olive plants
All around your table.
4 Behold, thus shall the man be blessed
Who fears the LORD.

5 The LORD bless you out of Zion,
And may you see the good of
Jerusalem
All the days of your life.
6 Yes, may you see your children's
children.

Peace *be* upon Israel!

PROVERBS 28:25

25 HE who is of a proud heart stirs up
strife,
But he who trusts in the LORD will
be prospered.

HEBREWS 11:17–40

BY faith Abraham, when he was tested,
offered up Isaac, and he who had received
the promises offered up his only begotten
son, 18 of whom it was said, "In Isaac your
seed shall be called," 19 concluding that God
was able to raise *him* up, even from the
dead, from which he also received him in
a figurative sense.
20 By faith Isaac blessed Jacob and Esau
concerning things to come.
21 By faith Jacob, when he was dying,
blessed each of the sons of Joseph, and worshiped, *leaning* on the top of his staff.
22 By faith Joseph, when he was dying,
made mention of the departure of the children of Israel, and gave instructions concerning his bones.
23 By faith Moses, when he was born,
was hidden three months by his parents,
because they saw *he was* a beautiful child;

*If you have faith, prove it
by your life.*   (CONFORMED)

and they were not afraid of the king's
command.
24 By faith Moses, when he became of
age, refused to be called the son of Pharaoh's
daughter, 25 choosing rather to suffer affliction with the people of God than to enjoy
the passing pleasures of sin, 26 esteem-
ing the reproach of Christ greater riches
than the treasures in Egypt; for he looked
to the reward.
27 By faith he forsook Egypt, not fearing
the wrath of the king; for he endured as
seeing Him who is invisible. 28 By faith he
kept the Passover and the sprinkling of
blood, lest he who destroyed the firstborn
should touch them.
29 By faith they passed through the Red
Sea as by dry *land, whereas* the Egyptians,
attempting *to do* so, were drowned.
30 By faith the walls of Jericho fell down
after they were encircled for seven days.
31 By faith the harlot Rahab did not perish
with those who did not believe, when she
had received the spies with peace.
32 And what more shall I say? For the
time would fail me to tell of Gideon and
Barak and Samson and Jephthah, also *of*
David and Samuel and the prophets:
33 who through faith subdued kingdoms,
worked righteousness, obtained promises,
stopped the mouths of lions, 34 quenched
the violence of fire, escaped the edge of
the sword, out of weakness were made
strong, became valiant in battle, turned to
flight the armies of the aliens. 35 Women
received their dead raised to life again.
Others were tortured, not accepting deliverance, that they might obtain a better
resurrection. 36 Still others had trial of
mockings and scourgings, yes, and of chains
and imprisonment. 37 They were stoned,
they were sawn in two, were tempted, were
slain with the sword. They wandered about
in sheepskins and goatskins, being destitute,
afflicted, tormented— 38 of whom the
world was not worthy. They wandered in
deserts and mountains, *in* dens and caves
of the earth.
39 And all these, having obtained a good
testimony through faith, did not receive the
promise, 40 God having provided something better for us, that they should not
be made perfect apart from us.

Reading 322—Battle of the Margins
Hebrews 12:14–17

There is no effort about Esau, he is content with being once born; Jacob could not be satisfied with anything less than God. Jacob tried in a hundred and one ways, cunningly to satisfy himself, but it was of no use. Esau was a man who had no battles at all, or if he had any, he fought them all on the wrong side of the margins. A man is not brought up to the margins in an ordinary way, but only through an agony. We do not come near the margins until we are hit by a form of supreme suffering, and then we see we have been shutting our lives away from a great domain. If Jesus Christ is going to regenerate us, what is the problem He is up against? We have a heredity we had no say in, we are not holy, nor likely to be; Jesus Christ had the disposition of deity, and He says we have to be fathomlessly pure in heart. If all He can do is to tell me that I must be holy, be what I never can be, present me with an ideal I cannot come anywhere near, His teaching plants despair; He is nothing more than a tantalizer and I wish He had never come. But if He is a Regenerator, One who first of all can put into me His own heredity, then I see what He is driving at in the Sermon on the Mount—that the disposition He puts in is like His own. (SHAD. AGONY)

EZEKIEL 27:1—28:26

THE word of the LORD came again to me, saying, 2 "Now, son of man, take up a lamentation for Tyre, 3 and say to Tyre, 'You who are situated at the entrance of the sea, merchant of the peoples on many coastlands, thus says the Lord GOD:

"O Tyre, you have said,
'I *am* perfect in beauty.'
4 Your borders *are* in the midst of the
    seas.
    Your builders have perfected your
    beauty.
5 They made all *your* planks of fir trees
    from Senir;
    They took a cedar from Lebanon to
    make you a mast.
6 *Of* oaks from Bashan they made your
    oars;
    The company of Ashurites have inlaid
    your planks
    With ivory from the coasts of Cyprus.
7 Fine embroidered linen from Egypt
    was what you spread for your sail;
    Blue and purple from the coasts of
    Elishah was what covered you.

8 "Inhabitants of Sidon and Arvad were
    your oarsmen;
    Your wise men, O Tyre, were in you;
    They became your pilots.
9 Elders of Gebal and its wise men

Were in you to caulk your seams;
    All the ships of the sea
    And their oarsmen were in you
    To market your merchandise.

10 "Those from Persia, Lydia, and Libya
    Were in your army as men of war;
    They hung shield and helmet in you;
    They gave splendor to you.
11 Men of Arvad with your army *were*
        on your walls *all* around,
    And the men of Gammad were in
        your towers;
    They hung their shields on your walls
        all around;
    They made your beauty perfect.

12 "Tarshish *was* your merchant because of your many luxury goods. They gave you silver, iron, tin, and lead for your goods. 13 Javan, Tubal, and Meshech *were* your traders. They bartered human lives and vessels of bronze for your merchandise. 14 Those from the house of Togarmah traded for your wares with horses, steeds, and mules. 15 The men of Dedan *were* your traders; many isles *were* the market of your hand. They brought you ivory tusks and ebony as payment. 16 Syria *was* your merchant because of the abundance of goods you made. They gave you for your wares emeralds, purple, embroidery, fine linen, corals, and rubies. 17 Judah and the land of Israel *were* your traders. They traded for

your merchandise wheat of Minnith, millet, honey, oil, and balm. 18 Damascus *was* your merchant because of the abundance of goods you made, because of your many luxury items, with the wine of Helbon and with white wool. 19 Dan and Javan paid for your wares, traversing back and forth. Wrought iron, cassia, and cane were among your merchandise. 20 Dedan *was* your merchant in saddlecloths for riding. 21 Arabia and all the princes of Kedar *were* your regular merchants. They traded with you in lambs, rams, and goats. 22 The merchants of Sheba and Raamah *were* your merchants. They traded for your wares the choicest spices, all kinds of precious stones, and gold. 23 Haran, Canneh, Eden, the merchants of Sheba, Assyria, *and* Chilmad *were* your merchants. 24 These *were* your merchants in choice items—in purple clothes, in embroidered garments, in chests of multicolored apparel, in sturdy woven cords, which were in your marketplace.

25 "The ships of Tarshish were carriers of your merchandise.
You were filled and very glorious in the midst of the seas.
26 Your oarsmen brought you into many waters,
But the east wind broke you in the midst of the seas.

27 "Your riches, wares, and merchandise,
Your mariners and pilots,
Your caulkers and merchandisers,
All your men of war who *are* in you,
And the entire company which *is* in your midst,
Will fall into the midst of the seas on the day of your ruin.
28 The common-land will shake at the sound of the cry of your pilots.

29 "All who handle the oar,
The mariners,
All the pilots of the sea
Will come down from their ships *and* stand on the shore.
30 They will make their voice heard because of you;
They will cry bitterly and cast dust on their heads;
They will roll about in ashes;
31 They will shave themselves completely bald because of you,
Gird themselves with sackcloth,
And weep for you
With bitterness of heart *and* bitter wailing.
32 In their wailing for you

They will take up a lamentation,
And lament for you:
'What *city is* like Tyre,
Destroyed in the midst of the sea?

33 'When your wares went out by sea,
You satisfied many people;
You enriched the kings of the earth
With your many luxury goods and your merchandise.
34 But you are broken by the seas in the depths of the waters;
Your merchandise and the entire company will fall in your midst.
35 All the inhabitants of the isles will be astonished at you;
Their kings will be greatly afraid,
And *their* countenance will be troubled.
36 The merchants among the peoples will hiss at you;
You will become a horror, and *be* no more forever.' " ' "

28 THE word of the LORD came to me again, saying, 2 "Son of man, say to the prince of Tyre, 'Thus says the Lord GOD:

"Because your heart *is* lifted up,
And you say, 'I *am* a god,
I sit *in* the seat of gods,
In the midst of the seas,'
Yet you *are* a man, and not a god,
Though you set your heart as the heart of a god
3 (Behold, you *are* wiser than Daniel!
There is no secret that can be hidden from you!
4 With your wisdom and your understanding
You have gained riches for yourself,
And gathered gold and silver into your treasuries;
5 By your great wisdom in trade you have increased your riches,
And your heart is lifted up because of your riches),"

6 'Therefore thus says the Lord GOD:

"Because you have set your heart as the heart of a god,
7 Behold, therefore, I will bring strangers against you,
The most terrible of the nations;
And they shall draw their swords against the beauty of your wisdom,
And defile your splendor.
8 They shall throw you down into the Pit,

And you shall die the death of the
slain
In the midst of the seas.

9 "Will you still say before him who
slays you,
'I *am* a god'?
But you *shall be* a man, and not a
god,
In the hand of him who slays you.
10 You shall die the death of the
uncircumcised
By the hand of aliens;
For I have spoken," says the Lord
GOD.' "

11 Moreover the word of the LORD came
to me, saying, 12 "Son of man, take up a
lamentation for the king of Tyre, and say
to him, 'Thus says the Lord GOD:

"You *were* the seal of perfection,
Full of wisdom and perfect in beauty.
13 You were in Eden, the garden of
God;
Every precious stone *was* your
covering:
The sardius, topaz, and diamond,
Beryl, onyx, and jasper,
Sapphire, turquoise, and emerald
with gold.
The workmanship of your timbrels
and pipes
Was prepared for you on the day you
were created.

14 "You *were* the anointed cherub who
covers;
I established you;
You were on the holy mountain of
God;
You walked back and forth in the
midst of fiery stones.
15 You *were* perfect in your ways from
the day you were created,
Till iniquity was found in you.

16 "By the abundance of your trading
You became filled with violence
within,
And you sinned;
Therefore I cast you as a profane
thing
Out of the mountain of God;
And I destroyed you, O covering
cherub,
From the midst of the fiery stones.

17 "Your heart was lifted up because of
your beauty;
You corrupted your wisdom for the
sake of your splendor;

I cast you to the ground,
I laid you before kings,
That they might gaze at you.

18 "You defiled your sanctuaries
By the multitude of your iniquities,
By the iniquity of your trading;
Therefore I brought fire from your
midst;
It devoured you,
And I turned you to ashes upon the
earth
In the sight of all who saw you.
19 All who knew you among the peoples
are astonished at you;
You have become a horror,
And *shall be* no more forever." ' "

20 Then the word of the LORD came to
me, saying, 21 "Son of man, set your face
toward Sidon, and prophesy against her,
22 and say, 'Thus says the Lord GOD:

"Behold, I *am* against you, O Sidon;
I will be glorified in your midst;
And they shall know that I *am* the
LORD,
When I execute judgments in her and
am hallowed in her.
23 For I will send pestilence upon her,
And blood in her streets;
The wounded shall be judged in her
midst
By the sword against her on every
side;
Then they shall know that I *am* the
LORD.

24 "And there shall no longer be a prick-
ing brier or a painful thorn for the house
of Israel from among all *who are* around
them, who despise them. Then they shall
know that I *am* the Lord GOD."
25 Thus says the Lord GOD: "When I
have gathered the house of Israel from the
peoples among whom they are scattered,
and am hallowed in them in the sight of
the Gentiles, then they will dwell in their
own land which I gave to My servant Jacob.
26 And they will dwell safely there, build
houses, and plant vineyards; yes, they will
dwell securely, when I execute judgments
on all those around them who despise them.
Then they shall know that I *am* the LORD
their God." ' "

PSALM 129:1–4

1 "MANY a time they have afflicted me
from my youth,"

Let Israel now say—
2 "Many a time they have afflicted me from
   my youth;
   Yet they have not prevailed against me.
3 The plowers plowed on my back;
   They made their furrows long."
4 The LORD *is* righteous;
   He has cut in pieces the cords of the
   wicked.

PROVERBS 28:26

26 HE who trusts in his own heart is a
   fool,
   But whoever walks wisely will be
   delivered.

HEBREWS 12:1–29

THEREFORE we also, since we are surrounded by so great a cloud of witnesses,
let us lay aside every weight, and the sin
which so easily ensnares *us*, and let us run
with endurance the race that is set before
us, 2 looking unto Jesus, the author and
finisher of *our* faith, who for the joy that
was set before Him endured the cross, despising the shame, and has sat down at the
right hand of the throne of God.

---

*T*he domain in which Jesus Christ
lives is the domain of Bible
facts.   (PSY. REDEMP.)

---

3 For consider Him who endured such
hostility from sinners against Himself, lest
you become weary and discouraged in your
souls. 4 You have not yet resisted to
bloodshed, striving against sin. 5 And you
have forgotten the exhortation which speaks
to you as to sons:

"My son, do not despise the
   chastening of the LORD,
Nor be discouraged when you are
   rebuked by Him;
6 For whom the LORD loves He
   chastens,
And scourges every son whom He
   receives."

7 If you endure chastening, God deals
with you as with sons; for what son is there
whom a father does not chasten? 8 But if
you are without chastening, of which all
have become partakers, then you are illegitimate and not sons. 9 Furthermore, we have
had human fathers who corrected *us*, and
we paid *them* respect. Shall we not much
more readily be in subjection to the Father
of spirits and live? 10 For they indeed for
a few days chastened *us* as seemed *best* to
them, but He for *our* profit, that *we* may
be partakers of His holiness. 11 Now no
chastening seems to be joyful for the present, but painful; nevertheless, afterward it
yields the peaceable fruit of righteousness
to those who have been trained by it.

12 Therefore strengthen the hands which
hang down, and the feeble knees, 13 and
make straight paths for your feet, so that
what is lame may not be *dislocated*, but
rather be healed.

14 Pursue peace with all *people*, and holiness, without which no one will see the
Lord: 15 looking carefully lest anyone fall
short of the grace of God; lest any root
of bitterness springing up cause trouble,
and by this many become defiled; 16 lest
there *be* any fornicator or profane person
like Esau, who for one morsel of food sold
his birthright. 17 For you know that afterward, when he wanted to inherit the blessing, he was rejected, for he found no place
for repentance, though he sought it diligently with tears.

18 For you have not come to the mountain that may be touched and that burned
with fire, and to blackness and darkness
and tempest, 19 and the sound of a trumpet
and the voice of words, so that those who
heard *it* begged that the word should not
be spoken to them anymore. 20 (For they
could not endure what was commanded:
"And if so much as a beast touches the
mountain, it shall be stoned or shot with
an arrow." 21 And so terrifying was the sight
that Moses said, "I am exceedingly afraid
and trembling.")

22 But you have come to Mount Zion
and to the city of the living God, the heavenly Jerusalem, to an innumerable company
of angels, 23 to the general assembly and
church of the firstborn *who are* registered
in heaven, to God the Judge of all, to the
spirits of just men made perfect, 24 to Jesus
the Mediator of the new covenant, and to
the blood of sprinkling that speaks better
things than *that of* Abel.

25 See that you do not refuse Him who
speaks. For if they did not escape who refused Him who spoke on earth, much more
shall we not escape if we turn away from
Him who *speaks* from heaven, 26 whose
voice then shook the earth; but now He
has promised, saying, "Yet once more I
shake not only the earth, but also heaven."

27 Now this, "Yet once more," indicates the removal of those things that are being shaken, as of things that are made, that the things which cannot be shaken may remain.

28 Therefore, since we are receiving a kingdom which cannot be shaken, let us have grace, by which we may serve God acceptably with reverence and godly fear. 29 For our God *is* a consuming fire.

————————— ◆◆◆ —————————

Reading 323—The Highest Christian Love
Hebrews 13:12–14

The highest Christian love is not devotion to a work or to a cause, but to Jesus Christ. In the early days of our Lord's life the grief and astonishment of Mary and Joseph was caused by this very thing, "And He said to them, 'Why did you seek Me? Did you not know that I must be about My Father's business [in My Father's house]?' But they did not understand the statement which He spoke to them" (Luke 2:49, 50). Causes are good, and work is good, but love in these fails. The laying down of the life for Jesus Christ's sake exhibits the Christian love that never fails. Our Lord was viewed as wild and erratic because He did not identify Himself with the cause of the Pharisees or with the Zealots, yet He laid down His life as the servant of Yahweh. "Therefore Jesus also, that He might sanctify the people with His own blood, suffered outside the gate," and the writer immediately follows it up with the injunction, "Therefore let us go forth to Him, outside the camp, bearing His reproach. For here we have no continuing city, but we seek the one to come." (*Place Help*)

EZEKIEL 29:1—30:26

IN the tenth year, in the tenth *month,* on the twelfth *day* of the month, the word of the LORD came to me, saying, 2 "Son of man, set your face against Pharaoh king of Egypt, and prophesy against him, and against all Egypt. 3 Speak, and say, 'Thus says the Lord GOD:

"Behold, I *am* against you,
O Pharaoh king of Egypt,
O great monster who lies in the midst of his rivers,
Who has said, 'My River *is* my own; I have made *it* for myself.'
4   But I will put hooks in your jaws,
And cause the fish of your rivers to stick to your scales;
I will bring you up out of the midst of your rivers,
And all the fish in your rivers will stick to your scales.
5   I will leave you in the wilderness,
You and all the fish of your rivers;
You shall fall on the open field;

You shall not be picked up or gathered.
I have given you as food
To the beasts of the field
And to the birds of the heavens.

6   "Then all the inhabitants of Egypt
Shall know that I *am* the LORD,
Because they have been a staff of reed to the house of Israel.
7   When they took hold of you with the hand,
You broke and tore all their shoulders;
When they leaned on you,
You broke and made all their backs quiver."

8 'Therefore thus says the Lord GOD: "Surely I will bring a sword upon you and cut off from you man and beast. 9 And the land of Egypt shall become desolate and waste; then they will know that I *am* the LORD, because he said, 'The River *is* mine, and I have made *it.*' 10 Indeed, therefore, I *am* against you and against your rivers,

and I will make the land of Egypt utterly waste and desolate, from Migdol *to* Syene, as far as the border of Ethiopia. 11 Neither foot of man shall pass through it nor foot of beast pass through it, and it shall be uninhabited forty years. 12 I will make the land of Egypt desolate in the midst of the countries *that are* desolate; and among the cities *that are* laid waste, her cities shall be desolate forty years; and I will scatter the Egyptians among the nations and disperse them throughout the countries."

13 'Yet, thus says the Lord GOD: "At the end of forty years I will gather the Egyptians from the peoples among whom they were scattered. 14 I will bring back the captives of Egypt and cause them to return to the land of Pathros, to the land of their origin, and there they shall be a lowly kingdom. 15 It shall be the lowliest of kingdoms; it shall never again exalt itself above the nations, for I will diminish them so that they will not rule over the nations anymore. 16 No longer shall it be the confidence of the house of Israel, but will remind them of *their* iniquity when they turned to follow them. Then they shall know that I *am* the Lord GOD." ' "

17 And it came to pass in the twenty-seventh year, in the first *month,* on the first *day* of the month, *that* the word of the LORD came to me, saying, 18 "Son of man, Nebuchadnezzar king of Babylon caused his army to labor strenuously against Tyre; every head *was* made bald, and every shoulder rubbed raw; yet neither he nor his army received wages from Tyre, for the labor which they expended on it. 19 Therefore thus says the Lord GOD: 'Surely I will give the land of Egypt to Nebuchadnezzar king of Babylon; he shall take away her wealth, carry off her spoil, and remove her pillage; and that will be the wages for his army. 20 I have given him the land of Egypt *for* his labor, because they worked for Me,' says the Lord GOD.

21 'In that day I will cause the horn of the house of Israel to spring forth, and I will open your mouth to speak in their midst. Then they shall know that I *am* the LORD.' "

30 THE word of the LORD came to me again, saying, 2 "Son of man, prophesy and say, 'Thus says the Lord GOD:
   "Wail, 'Woe to the day!'

3   For the day *is* near,
     Even the day of the LORD *is* near;
     It will be a day of clouds, the time
        of the Gentiles.

4   The sword shall come upon Egypt,
     And great anguish shall be in
        Ethiopia,
     When the slain fall in Egypt,
     And they take away her wealth,
     And her foundations are broken
        down.

5 "Ethiopia, Libya, Lydia, all the mingled people, Chub, and the men of the lands who are allied, shall fall with them by the sword."

6 'Thus says the LORD:

   "Those who uphold Egypt shall fall,
     And the pride of her power shall
        come down.
     From Migdol *to* Syene
     Those within her shall fall by the
        sword,"
     Says the Lord GOD.

7   "They shall be desolate in the midst
        of the desolate countries,
     And her cities shall be in the midst
        of the cities *that are* laid waste.
8   Then they will know that I *am* the
        LORD,
     When I have set a fire in Egypt
     And all her helpers are destroyed.
9   On that day messengers shall go forth
        from Me in ships
     To make the careless Ethiopians
        afraid,
     And great anguish shall come upon
        them,
     As on the day of Egypt;
     For indeed it is coming!"

10 'Thus says the Lord GOD:

   "I will also make a multitude of Egypt
        to cease
     By the hand of Nebuchadnezzar
        king of Babylon.
11   He and his people with him, the most
        terrible of the nations,
     Shall be brought to destroy the
        land;
     They shall draw their swords against
        Egypt,
     And fill the land with the slain.
12   I will make the rivers dry,
     And sell the land into the hand of
        the wicked;
     I will make the land waste, and all
        that is in it,
     By the hand of aliens.
     I, the LORD, have spoken."

13 'Thus says the Lord GOD:

"I will also destroy the idols,
And cause the images to cease from Noph;
There shall no longer be princes from the land of Egypt;
I will put fear in the land of Egypt.
14 I will make Pathros desolate,
Set fire to Zoan,
And execute judgments in No.
15 I will pour My fury on Sin, the strength of Egypt;
I will cut off the multitude of No,
16 And set a fire in Egypt;
Sin shall have great pain,
No shall be split open,
And Noph *shall be in* distress daily.
17 The young men of Aven and Pi Beseth shall fall by the sword,
And these *cities* shall go into captivity.
18 At Tehaphnehes the day shall also be darkened,
When I break the yokes of Egypt there.
And her arrogant strength shall cease in her;
As for her, a cloud shall cover her,
And her daughters shall go into captivity.
19 Thus I will execute judgments on Egypt,
Then they shall know that I *am* the LORD." ' "

20 And it came to pass in the eleventh year, in the first *month,* on the seventh *day* of the month, *that* the word of the LORD came to me, saying, 21 "Son of man, I have broken the arm of Pharaoh king of Egypt; and see, it has not been bandaged for healing, nor a splint put on to bind it, to make it strong enough to hold a sword. 22 Therefore thus says the Lord GOD: 'Surely I *am* against Pharaoh king of Egypt, and will break his arms, both the strong one and the one that was broken; and I will make the sword fall out of his hand. 23 I will scatter the Egyptians among the nations, and disperse them throughout the countries. 24 I will strengthen the arms of the king of Babylon and put My sword in his hand; but I will break Pharaoh's arms, and he will groan before him with the groanings of a mortally wounded *man.* 25 Thus I will strengthen the arms of the king of Babylon, but the arms of Pharaoh shall fall down; they shall know that I *am* the LORD, when I put My sword into the hand of the king of Babylon and he stretches it out against the land of Egypt. 26 I will scatter the Egyptians among the nations and disperse them throughout the coun-

tries. Then they shall know that I *am* the LORD.' "

PSALM 129:5–8

5 LET all those who hate Zion
Be put to shame and turned back.
6 Let them be as the grass *on* the housetops,
Which withers before it grows up,
7 With which the reaper does not fill his hand,
Nor he who binds sheaves, his arms.
8 Neither let those who pass by them say,
"The blessing of the LORD *be* upon you;
We bless you in the name of the LORD!"

PROVERBS 28:27

27 HE who gives to the poor will not lack,
But he who hides his eyes will have many curses.

HEBREWS 13:1–25

LET brotherly love continue. 2 Do not forget to entertain strangers, for by so *doing* some have unwittingly entertained angels. 3 Remember the prisoners as if chained with them—those who are mistreated—since you yourselves are in the body also.

4 Marriage *is* honorable among all, and the bed undefiled; but fornicators and adulterers God will judge.

---

*Y*ou cannot have holiness without a chaste physical life.   (WORKMEN)

---

5 *Let your* conduct *be* without covetousness; *be* content with such things as you have. For He Himself has said, "I will never leave you nor forsake you." 6 So we may boldly say:

"The LORD *is* my helper;
I will not fear.
What can man do to me?"

7 Remember those who rule over you, who have spoken the word of God to you, whose faith follow, considering the outcome of *their* conduct. 8 Jesus Christ *is* the same yesterday, today, and forever. 9 Do not be carried about with various and strange doctrines. For *it is* good that the heart be established by grace, not with foods

which have not profited those who have been occupied with them.

10 We have an altar from which those who serve the tabernacle have no right to eat. 11 For the bodies of those animals, whose blood is brought into the sanctuary by the high priest for sin, are burned outside the camp. 12 Therefore Jesus also, that He might sanctify the people with His own blood, suffered outside the gate. 13 Therefore let us go forth to Him, outside the camp, bearing His reproach. 14 For here we have no continuing city, but we seek the one to come. 15 Therefore by Him let us continually offer the sacrifice of praise to God, that is, the fruit of *our* lips, giving thanks to His name. 16 But do not forget to do good and to share, for with such sacrifices God is well pleased.

17 Obey those who rule over you, and be submissive, for they watch out for your souls, as those who must give account. Let them do so with joy and not with grief,

for that would be unprofitable for you.

18 Pray for us; for we are confident that we have a good conscience, in all things desiring to live honorably. 19 But I especially urge *you* to do this, that I may be restored to you the sooner.

20 Now may the God of peace who brought up our Lord Jesus from the dead, that great Shepherd of the sheep, through the blood of the everlasting covenant, 21 make you complete in every good work to do His will, working in you what is well pleasing in His sight, through Jesus Christ, to whom *be* glory forever and ever. Amen.

22 And I appeal to you, brethren, bear with the word of exhortation, for I have written to you in few words. 23 Know that *our* brother Timothy has been set free, with whom I shall see you if he comes shortly.

24 Greet all those who rule over you, and all the saints. Those from Italy greet you.

25 Grace *be* with you all. Amen.

◆◆◆◆

Reading 324—Sin Seen in Unselfishness
James 1:15

How do we think about sin habitually, as Christians? If we have light views about sin we are not students in the school of Christ. The fact of sin is the secret of Jesus Christ's Cross; its removal is the secret of His risen and ascended life. Do we think along these lines? It is quite possible to be living in union with God through the Atonement and yet be traitors mentally. . . .

If you read carefully the modern statements regarding sin you will be amazed to find how often we are much more in sympathy with them than with the Bible statements. We have to face the problem that our hearts may be right with God while our heads have a startling affinity with a great deal that is antagonistic to the Bible teaching. What we need, and what we get if we go on with God, is an intellectual rebirth as well as a heart rebirth.

The trouble with the modern statements regarding sin is that they make sin far too slight. Sin according to the modern view simply means selfishness, and preachers and teachers are as dead against selfishness as the New Testament is. Immediately we come to the Bible we find that sin is much deeper than that. According to the Bible, sin in its final analysis is not a defect but a defiance, a defiance that means death to the life of God in us. Sin is seen not only in selfishness, but in what men call unselfishness. It is possible to have such sympathy with our fellowmen as to be guilty of red-handed rebellion against God. Enthusiasm for humanity as it is, is quite a different thing from the enthusiasm for the saints which the Bible reveals, namely, enthusiasm for readjusted humanity.   (*Bib. Ethics*)

EZEKIEL 31:1—32:32

NOW it came to pass in the eleventh year, in the third *month*, on the first *day* of the month, *that* the word of the LORD came to me, saying, 2 "Son of man, say to Pharaoh king of Egypt and to his multitude:

'Whom are you like in your greatness?
3 Indeed Assyria *was* a cedar in Lebanon,
With fine branches that shaded the forest,
And of high stature;
And its top was among the thick boughs.
4 The waters made it grow;
Underground waters gave it height,
With their rivers running around the place where it was planted,
And sent out rivulets to all the trees of the field.

5 'Therefore its height was exalted above all the trees of the field;
Its boughs were multiplied,
And its branches became long because of the abundance of water,
As it sent them out.
6 All the birds of the heavens made their nests in its boughs;
Under its branches all the beasts of the field brought forth their young;
And in its shadow all great nations made their home.

7 'Thus it was beautiful in greatness and in the length of its branches,
Because its roots reached to abundant waters.
8 The cedars in the garden of God could not hide it;
The fir trees were not like its boughs,
And the chestnut trees were not like its branches;
No tree in the garden of God was like it in beauty.
9 I made it beautiful with a multitude of branches,
So that all the trees of Eden envied it,
That *were* in the garden of God.'

10 "Therefore thus says the Lord GOD: 'Because you have increased in height, and it set its top among the thick boughs, and its heart was lifted up in its height, 11 therefore I will deliver it into the hand of the mighty one of the nations, and he shall surely deal with it; I have driven it out for its wickedness. 12 And aliens, the most terrible of the nations, have cut it down and left it; its branches have fallen on the mountains and in all the valleys; its boughs lie broken by all the rivers of the land; and all the peoples of the earth have gone from under its shadow and left it.

13 'On its ruin will remain all the birds of the heavens,
And all the beasts of the field will come to its branches—

14 'So that no trees by the waters may ever again exalt themselves for their height, nor set their tops among the thick boughs, that no tree which drinks water may ever be high enough to reach up to them.

'For they have all been delivered to death,
To the depths of the earth,
Among the children of men who go down to the Pit.'

15 "Thus says the Lord GOD: 'In the day when it went down to hell, I caused mourning. I covered the deep because of it. I restrained its rivers, and the great waters were held back. I caused Lebanon to mourn for it, and all the trees of the field wilted because of it. 16 I made the nations shake at the sound of its fall, when I cast it down to hell together with those who descend into the Pit; and all the trees of Eden, the choice and best of Lebanon, all that drink water, were comforted in the depths of the earth. 17 They also went down to hell with it, with those *slain* by the sword; and *those who were* its *strong* arm dwelt in its shadows among the nations.

18 'To which of the trees in Eden will you then be likened in glory and greatness? Yet you shall be brought down with the trees of Eden to the depths of the earth; you shall lie in the midst of the uncircumcised, with *those* slain by the sword. This *is* Pharaoh and all his multitude,' says the Lord GOD."

32 AND it came to pass in the twelfth year, in the twelfth *month,* on the first *day* of the month, *that* the word of the LORD came to me, saying, 2 "Son of man, take up a lamentation for Pharaoh king of Egypt, and say to him:

'You are like a young lion among the nations,
And you *are* like a monster in the seas,

Bursting forth in your rivers,
Troubling the waters with your feet,
And fouling their rivers.'

3 "Thus says the Lord GOD:

'I will therefore spread My net over
you with a company of many
people,
And they will draw you up in My
net.
4   Then I will leave you on the land;
I will cast you out on the open fields,
And cause to settle on you all the
birds of the heavens.
And with you I will fill the beasts
of the whole earth.
5   I will lay your flesh on the mountains,
And fill the valleys with your carcass.

6   'I will also water the land with the
flow of your blood,
Even to the mountains;
And the riverbeds will be full of you.
7   When *I* put out your light,
I will cover the heavens, and make
its stars dark;
I will cover the sun with a cloud,
And the moon shall not give her light.
8   All the bright lights of the heavens
I will make dark over you,
And bring darkness upon your land,'
Says the Lord GOD.

9 'I will also trouble the hearts of many
peoples, when I bring your destruction
among the nations, into the countries which
you have not known. 10 Yes, I will make
many peoples astonished at you, and their
kings shall be horribly afraid of you when
I brandish My sword before them; and they
shall tremble *every* moment, every man for
his own life, in the day of your fall.'
11 "For thus says the Lord GOD: 'The
sword of the king of Babylon shall come
upon you. 12 By the swords of the mighty
warriors, all of them the most terrible of
the nations, I will cause your multitude to
fall.

'They shall plunder the pomp of
Egypt,
And all its multitude shall be
destroyed.
13   Also I will destroy all its animals
From beside its great waters;
The foot of man shall muddy them
no more,
Nor shall the hooves of animals
muddy them.
14   Then I will make their waters clear,

And make their rivers run like oil,'
Says the Lord GOD.

15 'When I make the land of Egypt
desolate,
And the country is destitute of all
that once filled it,
When I strike all who dwell in it,
Then they shall know that I *am* the
LORD.

16   'This *is* the lamentation
With which they shall lament her;
The daughters of the nations shall
lament her;
They shall lament for her, for Egypt,
And for all her multitude,'
Says the Lord GOD."

17 It came to pass also in the twelfth year,
on the fifteenth *day* of the month, *that* the
word of the LORD came to me, saying:

18 "Son of man, wail over the multitude
of Egypt,
And cast them down to the depths
of the earth,
Her and the daughters of the famous
nations,
With those who go down to the Pit:
19 'Whom do you surpass in beauty?
Go down, be placed with the
uncircumcised.'

20 "They shall fall in the midst of *those*
slain by the sword;
She is delivered to the sword,
Drawing her and all her multitudes.
21   The strong among the mighty
Shall speak to him out of the midst
of hell
With those who help him:
'They have gone down,
They lie with the uncircumcised, slain
by the sword.'

22 "Assyria *is* there, and all her company,
With their graves all around her,
All of them slain, fallen by the sword.
23   Her graves are set in the recesses of
the Pit,
And her company is all around her
grave,
All of them slain, fallen by the sword,
Who caused terror in the land of the
living.

24 "There *is* Elam and all her multitude,
All around her grave,
All of them slain, fallen by the sword,
Who have gone down uncircumcised
to the lower parts of the earth,

Who caused their terror in the land
of the living;
Now they bear their shame with
those who go down to the Pit.
25 They have set her bed in the midst
of the slain,
With all her multitude,
With her graves all around it,
All of them uncircumcised, slain by
the sword;
Though their terror was caused
In the land of the living,
Yet they bear their shame
With those who go down to the Pit;
It was put in the midst of the slain.

26 "There *are* Meshech and Tubal and
all their multitudes,
With all their graves around it,
All of them uncircumcised, slain by
the sword,
Though they caused their terror in
the land of the living.
27 They do not lie with the mighty
Who are fallen of the uncircumcised,
Who have gone down to hell with
their weapons of war;
They have laid their swords under
their heads,
But their iniquities will be on their
bones,
Because of the terror of the mighty
in the land of the living.
28 Yes, you shall be broken in the midst
of the uncircumcised,
And lie with *those* slain by the
sword.

29 "There *is* Edom,
Her kings and all her princes,
Who despite their might
Are laid beside *those* slain by the
sword;
They shall lie with the uncircumcised,
And with those who go down to the
Pit.
30 There *are* the princes of the north,
All of them, and all the Sidonians,
Who have gone down with the slain
In shame at the terror which they
caused by their might;
They lie uncircumcised with *those*
slain by the sword,
And bear their shame with those who
go down to the Pit.

31 "Pharaoh will see them
And be comforted over all his
multitude,
Pharaoh and all his army,

Slain by the sword,"
Says the Lord GOD.

32 "For I have caused My terror in the
land of the living;
And he shall be placed in the midst
of the uncircumcised
With *those* slain by the sword,
Pharaoh and all his multitude,"
Says the Lord GOD.

PSALM 130:1–4

1 OUT of the depths I have cried
to You, O LORD;
2 Lord, hear my voice!
Let Your ears be attentive
To the voice of my supplications.

3 If You, LORD, should mark iniquities,
O Lord, who could stand?
4 But *there is* forgiveness with You,
That You may be feared.

PROVERBS 28:28

28 WHEN the wicked arise, men hide
themselves;
But when they perish, the righteous
increase.

JAMES 1:1–27

JAMES, a bondservant of God and of the
Lord Jesus Christ,

To the twelve tribes which are scattered
abroad:

Greetings.
2 My brethren, count it all joy when you
fall into various trials, 3 knowing that the

---

*If Jesus Christ can keep me
walking on the top of the waves,
He can keep me underneath
them.* (GOD'S WORKMANSHIP)

---

testing of your faith produces patience.
4 But let patience have *its* perfect work, that
you may be perfect and complete, lacking
nothing. 5 If any of you lacks wisdom, let
him ask of God, who gives to all liberally
and without reproach, and it will be given
to him. 6 But let him ask in faith, with no

doubting, for he who doubts is like a wave of the sea driven and tossed by the wind. 7 For let not that man suppose that he will receive anything from the Lord; 8 *he is* a double-minded man, unstable in all his ways.

9 Let the lowly brother glory in his exaltation, 10 but the rich in his humiliation, because as a flower of the field he will pass away. 11 For no sooner has the sun risen with a burning heat than it withers the grass; its flower falls, and its beautiful appearance perishes. So the rich man also will fade away in his pursuits.

12 Blessed *is* the man who endures temptation; for when he has been approved, he will receive the crown of life which the Lord has promised to those who love Him. 13 Let no one say when he is tempted, "I am tempted by God"; for God cannot be tempted by evil, nor does He Himself tempt anyone. 14 But each one is tempted when he is drawn away by his own desires and enticed. 15 Then, when desire has conceived, it gives birth to sin; and sin, when it is full-grown, brings forth death. 16 Do not be deceived, my beloved brethren. 17 Every good gift and every perfect gift is from above, and comes down from the Father of lights, with whom there is no variation or shadow of turning. 18 Of His own will He brought us forth by the word of truth, that we might be a kind of firstfruits of His creatures.

19 So then, my beloved brethren, let every man be swift to hear, slow to speak, slow to wrath; 20 for the wrath of man does not produce the righteousness of God.

21 Therefore lay aside all filthiness and overflow of wickedness, and receive with meekness the implanted word, which is able to save your souls.

22 But be doers of the word, and not hearers only, deceiving yourselves. 23 For if anyone is a hearer of the word and not a doer, he is like a man observing his natural face in a mirror; 24 for he observes himself, goes away, and immediately forgets what kind of man he was. 25 But he who looks into the perfect law of liberty and continues *in it*, and is not a forgetful hearer but a doer of the work, this one will be blessed in what he does.

26 If anyone among you thinks he is religious, and does not bridle his tongue but deceives his own heart, this one's religion *is* useless. 27 Pure and undefiled religion before God and the Father is this: to visit orphans and widows in their trouble, *and* to keep oneself unspotted from the world.

———————— ◆◆◆ ————————

Reading 325—Inability into Ability
James 2:10

Every man has an imperative something within him which makes him say "I ought" even in the most degraded specimens of humanity the "ought" is there, and the Bible tells us where it comes from—it comes from God. The modern tendency is to leave God out and make our standard what is most useful to man. The utilitarian says that these distinct laws of conduct have been evolved by man for the benefit of man—the greatest use to the greatest number. That is not the reason a thing is right; the reason a thing is right is that God is behind it. God's "ought's" never alter; we never grow out of them. Our difficulty is that we find in ourselves this attitude—"I ought to do this, but I won't;" "I ought to do that, but I don't want to." That puts out of court the idea that if you teach men what is right they will do it—they won't; what is needed is a power which will enable a man to do what he knows is right. We may say "Oh I won't count this time," but every bit of moral wrong is counted by God. The moral law exerts no coercion, neither does it allow any compromise. "For whoever shall keep the whole law, and yet stumble in one *point*, he is guilty of all." Once we realize this we see why it was necessary for Jesus Christ to come. The Redemption is the Reality which alters inability into ability.   (*Bib. Ethics*)

EZEKIEL 33:1—34:31

AGAIN the word of the LORD came to me, saying, 2 "Son of man, speak to the children of your people, and say to them: 'When I bring the sword upon a land, and the people of the land take a man from their territory and make him their watchman, 3 when he sees the sword coming upon the land, if he blows the trumpet and warns the people, 4 then whoever hears the sound of the trumpet and does not take warning, if the sword comes and takes him away, his blood shall be on his *own* head. 5 He heard the sound of the trumpet, but did not take warning; his blood shall be upon himself. But he who takes warning will save his life. 6 But if the watchman sees the sword coming and does not blow the trumpet, and the people are not warned, and the sword comes and takes *any* person from among them, he is taken away in his iniquity; but his blood I will require at the watchman's hand.'

7 "So you, son of man: I have made you a watchman for the house of Israel; therefore you shall hear a word from My mouth and warn them for Me. 8 When I say to the wicked, 'O wicked *man,* you shall surely die!' and you do not speak to warn the wicked from his way, that wicked *man* shall die in his iniquity; but his blood I will require at your hand. 9 Nevertheless if you warn the wicked to turn from his way, and he does not turn from his way, he shall die in his iniquity; but you have delivered your soul.

10 "Therefore you, O son of man, say to the house of Israel: 'Thus you say, "If our transgressions and our sins *lie* upon us, and we pine away in them, how can we then live?" ' 11 Say to them: '*As* I live,' says the Lord GOD, 'I have no pleasure in the death of the wicked, but that the wicked turn from his way and live. Turn, turn from your evil ways! For why should you die, O house of Israel?'

12 "Therefore you, O son of man, say to the children of your people: 'The righteousness of the righteous man shall not deliver him in the day of his transgression; as for the wickedness of the wicked, he shall not fall because of it in the day that he turns from his wickedness; nor shall the righteous be able to live because of *his righteousness* in the day that he sins.' 13 When I say to the righteous *that* he shall surely live, but he trusts in his own righteousness and commits iniquity, none of his righteous works shall be remembered; but because of the iniquity that he has committed, he

shall die. 14 Again, when I say to the wicked, 'You shall surely die,' if he turns from his sin and does what is lawful and right, 15 *if* the wicked restores the pledge, gives back what he has stolen, and walks in the statutes of life without committing iniquity, he shall surely live; he shall not die. 16 None of his sins which he has committed shall be remembered against him; he has done what is lawful and right; he shall surely live.

17 "Yet the children of your people say, 'The way of the LORD is not fair.' But it is their way which is not fair! 18 When the righteous turns from his righteousness and commits iniquity, he shall die because of it. 19 But when the wicked turns from his wickedness and does what is lawful and right, he shall live because of it. 20 Yet you say, 'The way of the LORD is not fair.' O house of Israel, I will judge every one of you according to his own ways."

21 And it came to pass in the twelfth year of our captivity, in the tenth *month*, on the fifth *day* of the month, *that* one who had escaped from Jerusalem came to me and said, "The city has been captured!"

22 Now the hand of the LORD had been upon me the evening before the man came who had escaped. And He had opened my mouth; so when he came to me in the morning, my mouth was opened, and I was no longer mute.

23 Then the word of the LORD came to me, saying: 24 "Son of man, they who inhabit those ruins in the land of Israel are saying, 'Abraham was only one, and he inherited the land. But we *are* many; the land has been given to us as a possession.'

25 "Therefore say to them, 'Thus says the Lord GOD: "You eat *meat* with blood, you lift up your eyes toward your idols, and shed blood. Should you then possess the land? 26 You rely on your sword, you commit abominations, and you defile one another's wives. Should you then possess the land?" '

27 "Say thus to them, 'Thus says the Lord GOD: "*As* I live, surely those who *are* in the ruins shall fall by the sword, and the one who *is* in the open field I will give to the beasts to be devoured, and those who *are* in the strongholds and caves shall die of the pestilence. 28 For I will make the land most desolate, her arrogant strength shall cease, and the mountains of Israel shall be so desolate that no one will pass through. 29 Then they shall know that I *am* the LORD, when I have made the land most desolate because of all their abominations which they have committed." '

30 "As for you, son of man, the children of your people are talking about you beside the walls and in the doors of the houses; and they speak to one another, everyone saying to his brother, 'Please come and hear what the word is that comes from the LORD.' 31 So they come to you as people do, they sit before you *as* My people, and they hear your words, but they do not do them; for with their mouth they show much love, *but* their hearts pursue their *own* gain. 32 Indeed you *are* to them as a very lovely song of one who has a pleasant voice and can play well on an instrument; for they hear your words, but they do not do them. 33 And when this comes to pass—surely it will come—then they will know that a prophet has been among them."

34 AND the word of the LORD came to me, saying, 2 "Son of man, prophesy against the shepherds of Israel, prophesy and say to them, 'Thus says the Lord GOD to the shepherds: "Woe to the shepherds of Israel who feed themselves! Should not the shepherds feed the flocks? 3 You eat the fat and clothe yourselves with the wool; you slaughter the fatlings, *but* you do not feed the flock. 4 The weak you have not strengthened, nor have you healed those who were sick, nor bound up the broken, nor brought back what was driven away, nor sought what was lost; but with force and cruelty you have ruled them. 5 So they were scattered because *there was* no shepherd; and they became food for all the beasts of the field when they were scattered. 6 My sheep wandered through all the mountains, and on every high hill; yes, My flock was scattered over the whole face of the earth, and no one was seeking or searching *for them*."

7 'Therefore, you shepherds, hear the word of the LORD: 8 "*As* I live," says the Lord GOD, "surely because My flock became a prey, and My flock became food for every beast of the field, because *there was* no shepherd, nor did My shepherds search for My flock, but the shepherds fed themselves and did not feed My flock"— 9 therefore, O shepherds, hear the word of the LORD! 10 Thus says the Lord GOD: "Behold, I *am* against the shepherds, and I will require My flock at their hand; I will cause them to cease feeding the sheep, and the shepherds shall feed themselves no more; for I will deliver My flock from their mouths, that they may no longer be food for them."

11 'For thus says the Lord GOD: "Indeed I Myself will search for My sheep and seek them out. 12 As a shepherd seeks out his flock on the day he is among his scattered sheep, so will I seek out My sheep and deliver them from all the places where they were scattered on a cloudy and dark day. 13 And I will bring them out from the peoples and gather them from the countries, and will bring them to their own land; I will feed them on the mountains of Israel, in the valleys and in all the inhabited places of the country. 14 I will feed them in good pasture, and their fold shall be on the high mountains of Israel. There they shall lie down in a good fold and feed in rich pasture on the mountains of Israel. 15 I will feed My flock, and I will make them lie down," says the Lord GOD. 16 "I will seek what was lost and bring back what was driven away, bind up the broken and strengthen what was sick; but I will destroy the fat and the strong, and feed them in judgment."

17 'And *as for* you, O My flock, thus says the Lord GOD: "Behold, I shall judge between sheep and sheep, between rams and goats. 18 *Is it* too little for you to have eaten up the good pasture, that you must tread down with your feet the residue of your pasture—and to have drunk of the clear waters, that you must foul the residue with your feet? 19 And *as for* My flock, they eat what you have trampled with your feet, and they drink what you have fouled with your feet."

20 'Therefore thus says the Lord GOD to them: "Behold, I Myself will judge between the fat and the lean sheep. 21 Because you have pushed with side and shoulder, butted all the weak ones with your horns, and scattered them abroad, 22 therefore I will save My flock, and they shall no longer be a prey; and I will judge between sheep and sheep. 23 I will establish one shepherd over them, and he shall feed them—My servant David. He shall feed them and be their shepherd. 24 And I, the LORD, will be their God, and My servant David a prince among them; I, the LORD, have spoken.

25 "I will make a covenant of peace with them, and cause wild beasts to cease from the land; and they will dwell safely in the wilderness and sleep in the woods. 26 I will make them and the places all around My hill a blessing; and I will cause showers to come down in their season; there shall be showers of blessing. 27 Then the trees of the field shall yield their fruit, and the earth shall yield her increase. They shall be safe in their land; and they shall know that I *am* the LORD, when I have broken the bands of their yoke and delivered them from the hand of those who enslaved them. 28 And they shall no longer be a prey for

the nations, nor shall beasts of the land devour them; but they shall dwell safely, and no one shall make *them* afraid. 29 I will raise up for them a garden of renown, and they shall no longer be consumed with hunger in the land, nor bear the shame of the Gentiles anymore. 30 Thus they shall know that I, the LORD their God, *am* with them, and they, the house of Israel, *are* My people," says the Lord GOD.' "

31 "You are My flock, the flock of My pasture; you *are* men, *and* I *am* your God," says the Lord GOD.

PSALM 130:5–8

5 I wait for the LORD, my soul waits,
And in His word I do hope.
6 My soul *waits* for the Lord
More than those who watch for the morning—
Yes, more than those who watch for the morning.

7 O Israel, hope in the LORD;
For with the LORD *there is* mercy,
And with Him *is* abundant redemption.
8 And He shall redeem Israel
From all his iniquities.

PROVERBS 29:1

1 HE who is often rebuked, *and* hardens *his* neck,
Will suddenly be destroyed, and that without remedy.

JAMES 2:1–26

MY brethren, do not hold the faith of our Lord Jesus Christ, *the Lord* of glory, with partiality. 2 For if there should come into

---

The glory of our Lord was the glory of a holy life. (ASK)

---

your assembly a man with gold rings, in fine apparel, and there should also come in a poor man in filthy clothes, 3 and you pay attention to the one wearing the fine clothes and say to him, "You sit here in a good place," and say to the poor man, "You stand there," or, "Sit here at my footstool,"

4 have you not shown partiality among yourselves, and become judges with evil thoughts?

5 Listen, my beloved brethren: Has God not chosen the poor of this world *to be* rich in faith and heirs of the kingdom which He promised to those who love Him? 6 But you have dishonored the poor man. Do not the rich oppress you and drag you into the courts? 7 Do they not blaspheme that noble name by which you are called?

8 If you really fulfill *the* royal law according to the Scripture, "You shall love your neighbor as yourself," you do well; 9 but if you show partiality, you commit sin, and are convicted by the law as transgressors. 10 For whoever shall keep the whole law, and yet stumble in one *point,* he is guilty of all. 11 For He who said, "Do not commit adultery," also said, "Do not murder." Now if you do not commit adultery, but you do murder, you have become a transgressor of the law. 12 So speak and so do as those who will be judged by the law of liberty. 13 For judgment is without mercy to the one who has shown no mercy. Mercy triumphs over judgment.

14 What *does it* profit, my brethren, if someone says he has faith but does not have works? Can faith save him? 15 If a brother or sister is naked and destitute of daily food, 16 and one of you says to them, "Depart in peace, be warmed and filled," but you do not give them the things which are needed for the body, what *does it* profit? 17 Thus also faith by itself, if it does not have works, is dead.

18 But someone will say, "You have faith, and I have works." Show me your faith without your works, and I will show you my faith by my works. 19 You believe that there is one God. You do well. Even the demons believe—and tremble! 20 But do you want to know, O foolish man, that faith without works is dead? 21 Was not Abraham our father justified by works when he offered Isaac his son on the altar? 22 Do you see that faith was working together with his works, and by works faith was made perfect? 23 And the Scripture was fulfilled which says, "Abraham believed God, and it was accounted to him for righteousness." And he was called the friend of God. 24 You see then that a man is justified by works, and not by faith only.

25 Likewise, was not Rahab the harlot also justified by works when she received the messengers and sent *them* out another way?

26 For as the body without the spirit is dead, so faith without works is dead also.

Reading 326—The Place for the Tongue

James 3:5, 6

Men never suffer because they live a godly life; they suffer for their speech. Humanly speaking, if our Lord had held His tongue, He would not have been put to death. "If I had not come and spoken to them, they would have no sin, but now they have no excuse for their sin." (*SEND I YOU*)

The tongue in our Lord Jesus Christ got to its right place because He never spoke from the spirit of His right to Himself; and our tongue and our brain will only be in the right place when we learn to obey the Spirit of God in thinking. (*BIB. PSYCH.*)

He who was the Wisdom of God Incarnate, said, "the words that I speak to you I do not speak on My own *authority*," that is, from the disposition of My right to Myself, but from My relationship to My Father. We are either too hasty or too slow; either we won't speak at all, or we speak too much, or we speak in the wrong mood. The thing that makes us speak is the lust to vindicate ourselves. (*SHADE*)

EZEKIEL 35:1—36:38

MOREOVER the word of the LORD came to me, saying, 2 "Son of man, set your face against Mount Seir and prophesy against it, 3 and say to it, 'Thus says the Lord GOD:

> "Behold, O Mount Seir, I *am* against you;
> I will stretch out My hand against you,
> And make you most desolate;
> 4 I shall lay your cities waste,
> And you shall be desolate.
> Then you shall know that I *am* the LORD.

5 "Because you have had an ancient hatred, and have shed *the blood of* the children of Israel by the power of the sword at the time of their calamity, *when* their iniquity *came to an* end, 6 therefore, *as* I live," says the Lord GOD, "I will prepare you for blood, and blood shall pursue you; since you have not hated blood, therefore blood shall pursue you. 7 Thus I will make Mount Seir most desolate, and cut off from it the one who leaves and the one who returns. 8 And I will fill its mountains with the slain; on your hills and in your valleys and in all your ravines those who are slain by the sword shall fall. 9 I will make you perpetually desolate, and your cities shall be uninhabited; then you shall know that I *am* the LORD.

10 "Because you have said, 'These two nations and these two countries shall be mine, and we will possess them,' although the LORD was there, 11 therefore, *as* I live," says the Lord GOD, "I will do according to your anger and according to the envy which you showed in your hatred against them; and I will make Myself known among them when I judge you. 12 Then you shall know that I *am* the LORD. I have heard all your blasphemies which you have spoken against the mountains of Israel, saying, 'They are desolate; they are given to us to consume.' 13 Thus with your mouth you have boasted against Me and multiplied your words against Me; I have heard *them*."

14 'Thus says the Lord GOD: "The whole earth will rejoice when I make you desolate. 15 As you rejoiced because the inheritance of the house of Israel was desolate, so I will do to you; you shall be desolate, O Mount Seir, as well as all of Edom—all of it! Then they shall know that I *am* the LORD." '

36 "AND you, son of man, prophesy to the mountains of Israel, and say, 'O mountains of Israel, hear the word of the LORD! 2 Thus says the Lord GOD: "Because the enemy has said of you, 'Aha! The ancient heights have become our possession,' " ' 3 therefore prophesy, and say, 'Thus says the Lord GOD: "Because they made *you* desolate and swallowed you up on every side, so that you became the possession of the rest of the nations, and you are taken up by the lips of talkers and slandered by the people"— 4 therefore, O mountains of Israel, hear the word of the

Lord GOD! Thus says the Lord GOD to the mountains, the hills, the rivers, the valleys, the desolate wastes, and the cities that have been forsaken, which became plunder and mockery to the rest of the nations all around— 5 therefore thus says the Lord GOD: "Surely I have spoken in My burning jealousy against the rest of the nations and against all Edom, who gave My land to themselves as a possession, with wholehearted joy *and* spiteful minds, in order to plunder its open country." '

6 "Therefore prophesy concerning the land of Israel, and say to the mountains, the hills, the rivers, and the valleys, 'Thus says the Lord GOD: "Behold, I have spoken in My jealousy and My fury, because you have borne the shame of the nations." 7 Therefore thus says the Lord GOD: "I have raised My hand in an oath that surely the nations that *are* around you shall bear their own shame. 8 But you, O mountains of Israel, you shall shoot forth your branches and yield your fruit to My people Israel, for they are about to come. 9 For indeed I *am* for you, and I will turn to you, and you shall be tilled and sown. 10 I will multiply men upon you, all the house of Israel, all of it; and the cities shall be inhabited and the ruins rebuilt. 11 I will multiply upon you man and beast; and they shall increase and bear young; I will make you inhabited as in former times, and do better *for you* than at your beginnings. Then you shall know that I *am* the LORD. 12 Yes, I will cause men to walk on you, My people Israel; they shall take possession of you, and you shall be their inheritance; no more shall you bereave them *of children.*"

13 'Thus says the Lord GOD: "Because they say to you, 'You devour men and bereave your nation *of children*,' 14 therefore you shall devour men no more, nor bereave your nation anymore," says the Lord GOD. 15 Nor will I let you hear the taunts of the nations anymore, nor bear the reproach of the peoples anymore, nor shall you cause your nation to stumble anymore," says the Lord GOD.' "

16 Moreover the word of the LORD came to me, saying: 17 "Son of man, when the house of Israel dwelt in their own land, they defiled it by their own ways and deeds; to Me their way was like the uncleanness of a woman in her customary impurity. 18 Therefore I poured out My fury on them for the blood they had shed on the land, and for their idols *with which* they had defiled it. 19 So I scattered them among the nations, and they were dispersed throughout the countries; I judged them according

to their ways and their deeds. 20 When they came to the nations, wherever they went, they profaned My holy name—when they said of them, 'These *are* the people of the LORD, *and* yet they have gone out of His land.' 21 But I had concern for My holy name, which the house of Israel had profaned among the nations wherever they went.

22 "Therefore say to the house of Israel, 'Thus says the Lord GOD: "I do not do *this* for your sake, O house of Israel, but for My holy name's sake, which you have profaned among the nations wherever you went. 23 And I will sanctify My great name, which has been profaned among the nations, which you have profaned in their midst; and the nations shall know that I *am* the LORD," says the Lord GOD, "when I am hallowed in you before their eyes. 24 For I will take you from among the nations, gather you out of all countries, and bring you into your own land. 25 Then I will sprinkle clean water on you, and you shall be clean; I will cleanse you from all your filthiness and from all your idols. 26 I will give you a new heart and put a new spirit within you; I will take the heart of stone out of your flesh and give you a heart of flesh. 27 I will put My Spirit within

---

The heart is the first thing to live in physical birth and in spiritual birth.　　(BIB. PSYCH.)

---

you and cause you to walk in My statutes, and you will keep My judgments and do *them.* 28 Then you shall dwell in the land that I gave to your fathers; you shall be My people, and I will be your God. 29 I will deliver you from all your uncleannesses. I will call for the grain and multiply it, and bring no famine upon you. 30 And I will multiply the fruit of your trees and the increase of your fields, so that you need never again bear the reproach of famine among the nations. 31 Then you will remember your evil ways and your deeds that *were* not good; and you will loathe yourselves in your own sight, for your iniquities and your abominations. 32 Not for your sake do I do *this*," says the Lord GOD, "let it be known to you. Be ashamed and confounded for your own ways, O house of Israel!"

33 'Thus says the Lord GOD: "On the day that I cleanse you from all your iniquities, I will also enable *you* to dwell in the

cities, and the ruins shall be rebuilt.
34 The desolate land shall be tilled instead
of lying desolate in the sight of all who
pass by. 35 So they will say, 'This land that
was desolate has become like the garden
of Eden; and the wasted, desolate, and
ruined cities *are now* fortified *and* inhabited.'
36 Then the nations which are left all around
you shall know that I, the LORD, have rebuilt the ruined places *and* planted what
was desolate. I, the LORD, have spoken *it,*
and I will do *it.*"

37 'Thus says the Lord GOD: "I will also
let the house of Israel inquire of Me to
do this for them: I will increase their men
like a flock. 38 Like a flock *offered as* holy
sacrifices, like the flock at Jerusalem on its
feast days, so shall the ruined cities be filled
with flocks of men. Then they shall know
that I *am* the LORD."'"

PSALM 131:1–3

1   LORD, my heart is not haughty,
    Nor my eyes lofty.
    Neither do I concern myself with great
        matters,
    Nor with things too profound for me.

2   Surely I have calmed and quieted my
        soul,
    Like a weaned child with his mother;
    Like a weaned child *is* my soul within
        me.

3   O Israel, hope in the LORD
    From this time forth and forever.

PROVERBS 29:2, 3

2   WHEN the righteous are in authority,
        the people rejoice;
    But when a wicked *man* rules, the
        people groan.

3   Whoever loves wisdom makes his
        father rejoice,
    But a companion of harlots wastes *his*
        wealth.

JAMES 3:1–18

MY brethren, let not many of you become
teachers, knowing that we shall receive a

stricter judgment. 2 For we all stumble in
many things. If anyone does not stumble
in word, he *is* a perfect man, able also
to bridle the whole body. 3 Indeed, we
put bits in horses' mouths that they may
obey us, and we turn their whole body.
4 Look also at ships: although they are
so large and are driven by fierce winds,
they are turned by a very small rudder
wherever the pilot desires. 5 Even so the
tongue is a little member and boasts great
things.

See how great a forest a little fire kindles!
6 And the tongue *is* a fire, a world of iniquity. The tongue is so set among our members that it defiles the whole body, and sets
on fire the course of nature; and it is set
on fire by hell. 7 For every kind of beast
and bird, of reptile and creature of the sea,
is tamed and has been tamed by mankind.
8 But no man can tame the tongue. *It is*
an unruly evil, full of deadly poison.
9 With it we bless our God and Father,
and with it we curse men, who have been
made in the similitude of God. 10 Out of
the same mouth proceed blessing and
cursing. My brethren, these things ought
not to be so. 11 Does a spring send forth
fresh *water* and bitter from the same
opening? 12 Can a fig tree, my brethren,
bear olives, or a grapevine bear figs?
Thus no spring yields both salt water and
fresh.

13 Who *is* wise and understanding
among you? Let him show by good conduct
that his works *are done* in the meekness of
wisdom. 14 But if you have bitter envy and
self-seeking in your hearts, do not boast
and lie against the truth. 15 This wisdom
does not descend from above, but *is* earthly,
sensual, demonic. 16 For where envy and
self-seeking *exist,* confusion and every evil
thing *are* there. 17 But the wisdom that is

---

*Spiritual muddle is only made plain
    by obedience.*   (UTMOST)

---

from above is first pure, then peaceable,
gentle, willing to yield, full of mercy and
good fruits, without partiality and without
hypocrisy. 18 Now the fruit of righteousness
is sown in peace by those who make
peace.

Reading 327—The Staggering Question
Ezekiel 37:3

Can that sinner be turned into a saint? Can that twisted life be put right? There is only one answer: "O Lord, You know, I don't." Never trample in with religious common sense and say—"Oh, yes, with a little more Bible reading and devotion and prayer, I see how it can be done."

It is much easier to *do* something than to trust in God; we mistake panic for inspiration. . . . We would far rather work for God than believe in Him. Am I quite sure that God will do what I cannot do? I despair of men in the degree in which I have never realized that God has done anything for me. Is my experience such a wonderful realization of God's power and might that I can never despair of anyone I see? Have I had any spiritual work done in me at all? The degree of panic is the degree of the lack of personal spiritual experience.

"Behold, O My people, I will open your graves." . . . If the Spirit of God has given you a vision of what you are apart from the grace of God (and He only does it when His Spirit is at work), you know there is no criminal who is half so bad in actuality as you know yourself to be in possibility. My "grave" has been opened by God and "I know that in me (that is, in my flesh) nothing good dwells." God's Spirit continually reveals what human nature is like apart from His grace. (*UTMOST*)

EZEKIEL 37:1—38:23

THE hand of the LORD came upon me and brought me out in the Spirit of the LORD, and set me down in the midst of the valley; and it *was* full of bones. 2 Then He caused me to pass by them all around, and behold, *there were* very many in the open valley; and indeed *they were* very dry. 3 And He said to me, "Son of man, can these bones live?"
So I answered, "O Lord GOD, You know."
4 Again He said to me, "Prophesy to these bones, and say to them, 'O dry bones, hear the word of the LORD! 5 Thus says the Lord GOD to these bones: "Surely I will cause breath to enter into you, and you shall live. 6 I will put sinews on you and bring flesh upon you, cover you with skin and put breath in you; and you shall live. Then you shall know that I *am* the LORD." ' "
7 So I prophesied as I was commanded; and as I prophesied, there was a noise, and suddenly a rattling; and the bones came together, bone to bone. 8 Indeed, as I looked, the sinews and the flesh came upon them, and the skin covered them over; but *there was* no breath in them.
9 Also He said to me, "Prophesy to the breath, prophesy, son of man, and say to the breath, 'Thus says the Lord GOD:

"Come from the four winds, O breath, and breathe on these slain, that they may live." ' " 10 So I prophesied as He commanded me, and breath came into them, and they lived, and stood upon their feet, an exceedingly great army.
11 Then He said to me, "Son of man, these bones are the whole house of Israel. They indeed say, 'Our bones are dry, our hope is lost, and we ourselves are cut off!' 12 Therefore prophesy and say to them, 'Thus says the Lord GOD: "Behold, O My people, I will open your graves and cause you to come up from your graves, and bring you into the land of Israel. 13 Then you shall know that I *am* the LORD, when I have opened your graves, O My people, and brought you up from your graves. 14 I will put My Spirit in you, and you shall live, and I will place you in your own land. Then you shall know that I, the LORD, have spoken *it* and performed *it*," says the LORD.' "
15 Again the word of the LORD came to me, saying, 16 "As for you, son of man, take a stick for yourself and write on it: 'For Judah and for the children of Israel, his companions.' Then take another stick and write on it, 'For Joseph, the stick of Ephraim, and *for* all the house of Israel, his companions.' 17 Then join them one to another for yourself into one stick, and they will become one in your hand.

18 "And when the children of your people speak to you, saying, 'Will you not show us what you *mean* by these?'— 19 say to them, 'Thus says the Lord GOD: "Surely I will take the stick of Joseph, which *is* in the hand of Ephraim, and the tribes of Israel, his companions; and I will join them with it, with the stick of Judah, and make them one stick, and they will be one in My hand." ' 20 And the sticks on which you write will be in your hand before their eyes.

21 "Then say to them, 'Thus says the Lord GOD: "Surely I will take the children of Israel from among the nations, wherever they have gone, and will gather them from every side and bring them into their own land; 22 and I will make them one nation in the land, on the mountains of Israel; and one king shall be king over them all; they shall no longer be two nations, nor shall they ever be divided into two kingdoms again. 23 They shall not defile themselves anymore with their idols, nor with their detestable things, nor with any of their transgressions; but I will deliver them from all their dwelling places in which they have sinned, and will cleanse them. Then they shall be My people, and I will be their God.

24 "David My servant *shall be* king over them, and they shall all have one shepherd; they shall also walk in My judgments and observe My statutes, and do them. 25 Then they shall dwell in the land that I have given to Jacob My servant, where your fathers dwelt; and they shall dwell there, they, their children, and their children's children, forever; and My servant David *shall be* their prince forever. 26 Moreover I will make a covenant of peace with them, and it shall be an everlasting covenant with them; I will establish them and multiply them, and I will set My sanctuary in their midst forevermore. 27 My tabernacle also shall

---

Whenever you obey God, His seal is always that of peace. (UTMOST)

---

be with them; indeed I will be their God, and they shall be My people. 28 The nations also will know that I, the LORD, sanctify Israel, when My sanctuary is in their midst forevermore." ' "

38 NOW the word of the LORD came to me, saying, 2 "Son of man, set your face against Gog, of the land of Magog, the prince of Rosh, Meshech, and Tubal, and prophesy against him, 3 and say, 'Thus

says the Lord GOD: "Behold, I *am* against you, O Gog, the prince of Rosh, Meshech, and Tubal. 4 I will turn you around, put hooks into your jaws, and lead you out, with all your army, horses, and horsemen, all splendidly clothed, a great company *with* bucklers and shields, all of them handling swords. 5 Persia, Ethiopia, and Libya are with them, all of them *with* shield and helmet; 6 Gomer and all its troops; the house of Togarmah *from* the far north and all its troops—many people *are* with you.

7 "Prepare yourself and be ready, you and all your companies that are gathered about you; and be a guard for them. 8 After many days you will be visited. In the latter years you will come into the land of those brought back from the sword *and* gathered from many people on the mountains of Israel, which had long been desolate; they were brought out of the nations, and now all of them dwell safely. 9 You will ascend, coming like a storm, covering the land like a cloud, you and all your troops and many peoples with you."

10 'Thus says the Lord GOD: "On that day it shall come to pass *that* thoughts will arise in your mind, and you will make an evil plan: 11 You will say, 'I will go up against a land of unwalled villages; I will go to a peaceful people, who dwell safely, all of them dwelling without walls, and having neither bars nor gates'— 12 to take plunder and to take booty, to stretch out your hand against the waste places *that are again* inhabited, and against a people gathered from the nations, who have acquired livestock and goods, who dwell in the midst of the land. 13 Sheba, Dedan, the merchants of Tarshish, and all their young lions will say to you, 'Have you come to take plunder? Have you gathered your army to take booty, to carry away silver and gold, to take away livestock and goods, to take great plunder?' " '

14 "Therefore, son of man, prophesy and say to Gog, 'Thus says the Lord GOD: "On that day when My people Israel dwell safely, will you not know *it?* 15 Then you will come from your place out of the far north, you and many peoples with you, all of them riding on horses, a great company and a mighty army. 16 You will come up against My people Israel like a cloud, to cover the land. It will be in the latter days that I will bring you against My land, so that the nations may know Me, when I am hallowed in you, O Gog, before their eyes." 17 Thus says the Lord GOD: "Are *you* he of whom I have spoken in former days by My servants the prophets of Israel, who prophesied for

years in those days that I would bring you against them?

18 "And it will come to pass at the same time, when Gog comes against the land of Israel," says the Lord GOD, "*that* My fury will show in My face. 19 For in My jealousy *and* in the fire of My wrath I have spoken: 'Surely in that day there shall be a great earthquake in the land of Israel, 20 so that the fish of the sea, the birds of the heavens, the beasts of the field, all creeping things that creep on the earth, and all men who *are* on the face of the earth shall shake at My presence. The mountains shall be thrown down, the steep places shall fall, and every wall shall fall to the ground.' 21 I will call for a sword against Gog throughout all My mountains," says the Lord GOD. "Every man's sword will be against his brother. 22 And I will bring him to judgment with pestilence and bloodshed; I will rain down on him, on his troops, and on the many peoples who *are* with him, flooding rain, great hailstones, fire, and brimstone. 23 Thus I will magnify Myself and sanctify Myself, and I will be known in the eyes of many nations. Then they shall know that I *am* the LORD." '

PSALM 132:1–9

1 LORD, remember David
    And all his afflictions;
2 How he swore to the LORD,
    And vowed to the Mighty One of
    Jacob:
3 "Surely I will not go into the chamber
    of my house,
    Or go up to the comfort of my bed;
4 I will not give sleep to my eyes
    Or slumber to my eyelids,
5 Until I find a place for the LORD,
    A dwelling place for the Mighty One
    of Jacob."

6 Behold, we heard of it in Ephrathah;
    We found it in the fields of the woods.
7 Let us go into His tabernacle;
    Let us worship at His footstool.
8 Arise, O LORD, to Your resting place,
    You and the ark of Your strength.
9 Let Your priests be clothed with
    righteousness,
    And let Your saints shout for joy.

PROVERBS 29:4

4 THE king establishes the land by
    justice,

But he who receives bribes
    overthrows it.

JAMES 4:1–17

WHERE do wars and fights *come* from among you? Do *they* not *come* from your *desires for* pleasure that war in your members? 2 You lust and do not have. You murder and covet and cannot obtain. You fight and war. Yet you do not have because you do not ask. 3 You ask and do not receive, because you ask amiss, that you may spend *it* on your pleasures. 4 Adulterers and adulteresses! Do you not know that friendship with the world is enmity with God? Whoever therefore wants to be a friend of the world makes himself an enemy of God. 5 Or do you think that the Scripture says in vain, "The Spirit who dwells in us yearns jealously"?

6 But He gives more grace. Therefore He says:

"God resists the proud,
    But gives grace to the humble."

7 Therefore submit to God. Resist the devil and he will flee from you. 8 Draw near to God and He will draw near to you. Cleanse *your* hands, *you* sinners; and purify *your* hearts, *you* double-minded. 9 Lament and mourn and weep! Let your laughter be turned to mourning and *your* joy to gloom. 10 Humble yourselves in the sight of the Lord, and He will lift you up.

11 Do not speak evil of one another, brethren. He who speaks evil of a brother and judges his brother, speaks evil of the law and judges the law. But if you judge the law, you are not a doer of the law but a judge. 12 There is one Lawgiver, who is able to save and to destroy. Who are you to judge another?

13 Come now, you who say, "Today or tomorrow we will go to such and such a city, spend a year there, buy and sell, and make a profit"; 14 whereas you do not know what *will happen* tomorrow. For what *is* your life? It is even a vapor that appears for a little time and then vanishes away.

Gracious uncertainty is the mark of the spiritual life. (UTMOST)

---

15 Instead you *ought* to say, "If the Lord wills, we shall live and do this or that."

16 But now you boast in your arrogance. All such boasting is evil.

17 Therefore, to him who knows to do good and does not do *it,* to him it is sin.

◆◆◆

Reading 328—The Patience of the Saints
James 5:7

Jesus says we are to keep the word of His patience. There are so many things in this life that it seems much better to be impatient about. The best illustration is that of an archer, he pulls the string further and further away from his bow with the arrow fixed, then, when it is adjusted, with his eye on the mark he lets fly. The Christian's life is like that. God is the archer; He takes the saint like a bow which He stretches, and we get to a certain point and say, "I can't stand any more, I can't stand this test of patience any longer"; but God goes on stretching. He is not aiming at our mark, but at His own, and the patience of the saints is that we hold on until He lets the arrow fly straight to His goal.   (*Place Help*)

The patience of the saints, like the patience of our Lord, puts the sovereignty of God over all the saint's career, and because the love of God is shed abroad in our hearts by the Holy Ghost, we choose by our free will what God predestinates, for the mind of God, the mind of the Holy Spirit, and the mind of the saint are all held together by a oneness of personal passionate devotion.   (*Chris. Dis. 2*)

EZEKIEL 39:1—40:49

"AND you, son of man, prophesy against Gog, and say, 'Thus says the Lord God: "Behold, I *am* against you, O Gog, the prince of Rosh, Meshech, and Tubal; 2 and I will turn you around and lead you on, bringing you up from the far north, and bring you against the mountains of Israel. 3 Then I will knock the bow out of your left hand, and cause the arrows to fall out of your right hand. 4 You shall fall upon the mountains of Israel, you and all your troops and the peoples who *are* with you; I will give you to birds of prey of every sort and *to* the beasts of the field to be devoured. 5 You shall fall on the open field; for I have spoken," says the Lord God. 6 "And I will send fire on Magog and on those who live in security in the coastlands. Then they shall know that I *am* the Lord. 7 So I will make My holy name known in the midst of My people Israel, and I will not *let them* profane My holy name anymore. Then the nations shall know that *I am* the Lord, the Holy One in Israel. 8 Surely it is coming, and it shall be done,"

says the Lord God. "This *is* the day of which I have spoken.

9 "Then those who dwell in the cities of Israel will go out and set on fire and burn the weapons, both the shields and bucklers, the bows and arrows, the javelins and spears; and they will make fires with them for seven years. 10 They will not take wood from the field nor cut down *any* from the forests, because they will make fires with the weapons; and they will plunder those who plundered them, and pillage those who pillaged them," says the Lord God.

11 "It will come to pass in that day *that* I will give Gog a burial place there in Israel, the valley of those who pass by east of the sea; and it will obstruct travelers, because there they will bury Gog and all his multitude. Therefore they will call *it* the Valley of Hamon Gog. 12 For seven months the house of Israel will be burying them, in order to cleanse the land. 13 Indeed all the people of the land will be burying, and they will gain renown for it on the day that I am glorified," says the Lord God. 14 "They will set apart men regularly employed, with the help of a search party, to pass through

the land and bury those bodies remaining on the ground, in order to cleanse it. At the end of seven months they will make a search. 15 The search party will pass through the land; and *when anyone* sees a man's bone, he shall set up a marker by it, till the buriers have buried it in the Valley of Hamon Gog. 16 *The* name of *the* city *will* also *be* Hamonah. Thus they shall cleanse the land." '

17 "And as for you, son of man, thus says the Lord GOD, 'Speak to every sort of bird and to every beast of the field:

"Assemble yourselves and come;
Gather together from all sides to My sacrificial meal
Which I am sacrificing for you,
A great sacrificial meal on the mountains of Israel,
That you may eat flesh and drink blood.
18 You shall eat the flesh of the mighty,
Drink the blood of the princes of the earth,
Of rams and lambs,
Of goats and bulls,
All of them fatlings of Bashan.
19 You shall eat fat till you are full,
And drink blood till you are drunk,
At My sacrificial meal
Which I am sacrificing for you.
20 You shall be filled at My table
With horses and riders,
With mighty men
And with all the men of war," says the Lord GOD.

21 "I will set My glory among the nations; all the nations shall see My judgment which I have executed, and My hand which I have laid on them. 22 So the house of Israel shall know that I *am* the LORD their God from that day forward. 23 The Gentiles shall know that the house of Israel went into captivity for their iniquity; because they were unfaithful to Me, therefore I hid My face from them. I gave them into the hand of their enemies, and they all fell by the sword. 24 According to their uncleanness and according to their transgressions I have dealt with them, and hidden My face from them." '

25 "Therefore thus says the Lord GOD: 'Now I will bring back the captives of Jacob, and have mercy on the whole house of Israel; and I will be jealous for My holy name— 26 after they have borne their shame, and all their unfaithfulness in which they were unfaithful to Me, when they dwelt safely in their *own* land and no one made *them* afraid. 27 When I have brought them

back from the peoples and gathered them out of their enemies' lands, and I am hallowed in them in the sight of many nations, 28 then they shall know that I *am* the LORD their God, who sent them into captivity among the nations, but also brought them back to their land, and left none of them captive any longer. 29 And I will not hide My face from them anymore; for I shall have poured out My Spirit on the house of Israel,' says the Lord GOD."

40 IN the twenty-fifth year of our captivity, at the beginning of the year, on the tenth *day* of the month, in the fourteenth year after the city was captured, on the very same day the hand of the LORD was upon me; and He took me there. 2 In the visions of God He took me into the land of Israel and set me on a very high mountain; on it toward the south *was* something like the structure of a city. 3 He took me there, and behold, *there was* a man whose appearance *was* like the appearance of bronze. He had a line of flax and a measuring rod in his hand, and he stood in the gateway.

4 And the man said to me, "Son of man, look with your eyes and hear with your ears, and fix your mind on everything I show you; for you *were* brought here so that I might show *them* to you. Declare to the house of Israel everything you see." 5 Now there was a wall all around the outside of the temple. In the man's hand was a measuring rod six cubits *long, each being a* cubit and a handbreadth; and he measured the width of the wall structure, one rod; and the height, one rod.

6 Then he went to the gateway which faced east; and he went up its stairs and measured the threshold of the gateway, *which was* one rod wide, and the other threshold *was* one rod wide. 7 Each gate chamber *was* one rod long and one rod wide; between the gate chambers *was a space of* five cubits; and the threshold of the gateway by the vestibule of the inside gate *was* one rod. 8 He also measured the vestibule of the inside gate, one rod. 9 Then he measured the vestibule of the gateway, eight cubits; and the gateposts, two cubits. The vestibule of the gate *was* on the inside. 10 In the eastern gateway *were* three gate chambers on one side and three on the other; the three *were* all the same size; also the gateposts were of the same size on this side and that side.

11 He measured the width of the entrance to the gateway, ten cubits; *and* the length of the gate, thirteen cubits. 12 *There was* a

space in front of the gate chambers, one cubit *on this side* and one cubit on that side; the gate chambers *were* six cubits on this side and six cubits on that side. 13 Then he measured the gateway from the roof of *one* gate chamber to the roof of the other; the width *was* twenty-five cubits, as door faces door. 14 He measured the gateposts, sixty cubits high, and the court all around the gateway *extended* to the gatepost. 15 *From* the front of the entrance gate to the front of the vestibule of the inner gate *was* fifty cubits. 16 *There were* beveled window *frames* in the gate chambers and in their intervening archways on the inside of the gateway all around, and likewise in the vestibules. *There were* windows all around on the inside. And on each gatepost *were* palm trees.

17 Then he brought me into the outer court; and *there were* chambers and a pavement made all around the court; thirty chambers faced the pavement. 18 The pavement was by the side of the gateways, corresponding to the length of the gateways; *this was* the lower pavement. 19 Then he measured the width from the front of the lower gateway to the front of the inner court exterior, one hundred cubits toward the east and the north.

20 On the outer court was also a gateway facing north, and he measured its length and its width. 21 Its gate chambers, three on this side and three on that side, its gateposts and its archways, had the same measurements as the first gate; its length *was* fifty cubits and its width twenty-five cubits. 22 Its windows and those of its archways, and also its palm trees, *had* the same measurements as the gateway facing east; it was ascended by seven steps, and its archway *was* in front of it. 23 A gate of the inner court was opposite the northern gateway, just as the eastern *gateway;* and he measured from gateway to gateway, one hundred cubits.

24 After that he brought me toward the south, and there a gateway was facing south; and he measured its gateposts and archways according to these same measurements. 25 *There were* windows in it and in its archways all around like those windows; its length *was* fifty cubits and its width twenty-five cubits. 26 Seven steps led up to it, and its archway *was* in front of them; and it had palm trees on its gateposts, one on this side and one on that side. 27 *There was* also a gateway on the inner court, facing south; and he measured from gateway to gateway toward the south, one hundred cubits.

28 Then he brought me to the inner court through the southern gateway; he measured the southern gateway according to these same measurements. 29 Also its gate chambers, its gateposts, and its archways *were* according to these same measurements; *there were* windows in it and in its archways all around; *it was* fifty cubits long and twenty-five cubits wide. 30 *There were* archways all around, twenty-five cubits long and five cubits wide. 31 Its archways faced the outer court, palm trees *were* on its gateposts, and going up to it *were* eight steps.

32 And he brought me into the inner court facing east; he measured the gateway according to these same measurements. 33 Also its gate chambers, its gateposts, and its archways *were* according to these same measurements; and *there were* windows in it and in its archways all around; *it was* fifty cubits long and twenty-five cubits wide. 34 Its archways faced the outer court, and palm trees *were* on its gateposts on this side and on that side; and going up to it *were* eight steps.

35 Then he brought me to the north gateway and measured *it* according to these same measurements— 36 also its gate chambers, its gateposts, and its archways. It had windows all around; its length *was* fifty cubits and its width twenty-five cubits. 37 Its gateposts faced the outer court, palm trees *were* on its gateposts on this side and on that side, and going up to it *were* eight steps.

38 *There was* a chamber and its entrance by the gateposts of the gateway, where they washed the burnt offering. 39 In the vestibule of the gateway *were* two tables on this side and two tables on that side, on which to slay the burnt offering, the sin offering, and the trespass offering. 40 At the outer side of the vestibule, as one goes up to the entrance of the northern gateway, *were* two tables; and on the other side of the vestibule of the gateway *were* two tables. 41 Four tables *were* on this side and four tables on that side, by the side of the gateway, eight tables on which they slaughtered *the sacrifices.* 42 *There were* also four tables of hewn stone for the burnt offering, one cubit and a half long, one cubit and a half wide, and one cubit high; on these they laid the instruments with which they slaughtered the burnt offering and the sacrifice. 43 Inside *were* hooks, a handbreadth wide, fastened all around; and the flesh of the sacrifices *was* on the tables.

44 Outside the inner gate *were* the chambers for the singers in the inner court, one facing south at the side of the northern

gateway, and the other facing north at the side of the southern gateway. 45 Then he said to me, "This chamber which faces south *is* for the priests who have charge of the temple. 46 The chamber which faces north *is* for the priests who have charge of the altar; these *are* the sons of Zadok, from the sons of Levi, who come near the LORD to minister to Him."

47 And he measured the court, one hundred cubits long and one hundred cubits wide, foursquare. The altar *was* in front of the temple. 48 Then he brought me to the vestibule of the temple and measured the doorposts of the vestibule, five cubits on this side and five cubits on that side; and the width of the gateway was three cubits on this side and three cubits on that side. 49 The length of the vestibule *was* twenty cubits, and the width eleven cubits; and by the steps which led up to it *there were* pillars by the doorposts, one on this side and another on that side.

PSALM 132:10–18

10 FOR Your servant David's sake,
 Do not turn away the face of Your
  Anointed.

11 The LORD has sworn *in* truth to
  David;
 He will not turn from it:
 "I will set upon your throne the fruit
  of your body.
12 If your sons will keep My covenant
 And My testimony which I shall teach
  them,
 Their sons also shall sit upon your
  throne forevermore."

13 For the LORD has chosen Zion;
 He has desired *it* for His dwelling
  place:
14 "This *is* My resting place forever;
 Here I will dwell, for I have
  desired it.
15 I will abundantly bless her provision;
 I will satisfy her poor with bread.
16 I will also clothe her priests with
  salvation,
 And her saints shall shout aloud for
  joy.
17 There I will make the horn of David
  grow;
 I will prepare a lamp for My Anointed.
18 His enemies I will clothe with shame,
 But upon Himself His crown shall
  flourish."

PROVERBS 29:5

5 A man who flatters his neighbor
 Spreads a net for his feet.

JAMES 5:1–20

COME now, *you* rich, weep and howl for your miseries that are coming upon *you!* 2 Your riches are corrupted, and your garments are moth-eaten. 3 Your gold and silver are corroded, and their corrosion will be a witness against you and will eat your flesh like fire. You have heaped up treasure in the last days. 4 Indeed the wages of the laborers who mowed your fields, which you kept back by fraud, cry out; and the cries of the reapers have reached the ears of the Lord of Sabaoth. 5 You have lived on the earth in pleasure and luxury; you have fattened your hearts as in a day of slaughter. 6 You have condemned, you have murdered the just; he does not resist you.

7 Therefore be patient, brethren, until the coming of the Lord. See *how* the farmer waits for the precious fruit of the earth, waiting patiently for it until it receives the early and latter rain. 8 You also be patient. Establish your hearts, for the coming of the Lord is at hand.

9 Do not grumble against one another, brethren, lest you be condemned. Behold, the Judge is standing at the door! 10 My brethren, take the prophets, who spoke in the name of the Lord, as an example of suffering and patience. 11 Indeed we count

---

*I*t is surely the patience of love,
 the patience of joyfulness,
 which knows that God
 reigns.   (CHRIS. DIS. 2)

---

them blessed who endure. You have heard of the perseverance of Job and seen the end *intended by* the Lord—that the Lord is very compassionate and merciful.

12 But above all, my brethren, do not swear, either by heaven or by earth or with any other oath. But let your "Yes" be "Yes," and *your* "No," "No," lest you fall into judgment.

13 Is anyone among you suffering? Let him pray. Is anyone cheerful? Let him sing psalms. 14 Is anyone among you sick? Let him call for the elders of the church, and let them pray over him, anointing him with oil in the name of the Lord. 15 And the

prayer of faith will save the sick, and the Lord will raise him up. And if he has committed sins, he will be forgiven. 16 Confess *your* trespasses to one another, and pray for one another, that you may be healed. The effective, fervent prayer of a righteous man avails much. 17 Elijah was a man with a nature like ours, and he prayed earnestly that it would not rain; and it did not rain

on the land for three years and six months. 18 And he prayed again, and the heaven gave rain, and the earth produced its fruit.

19 Brethren, if anyone among you wanders from the truth, and someone turns him back, 20 let him know that he who turns a sinner from the error of his way will save a soul from death and cover a multitude of sins.

◆◆◆◆

Reading 329—The Undefiled Inheritance
1 Peter 1:4

"Reserved in heaven for you"—This is a great conception of the New Testament, but it is a conception lost in modern evangelism. We are so much taken up with what God wants us to be here that we have forgotten heaven. There are one or two conceptions about heaven that have to be traced back to their home to find out whether they have their root in our faith or whether they are foreign flowers [having no root in Christianity]. . . . One of these is that heaven is a state and not a place; that is only a partial truth, for there cannot be a state without a place. The great New Testament conception of heaven is "hereafter" without the sin, "new heavens and a new earth in which righteousness dwells"—a conception beyond us. Peter is reminding every Christian that there is an undefiled inheritance awaiting us which has never yet been realized and that it has in it all we have ever hoped or dreamed or imagined, and a good deal more. It is always "better to come" in the Christian life until the "best of all" comes.   (*PLACE HELP*)

EZEKIEL 41:1—42:20

THEN he brought me into the sanctuary and measured the doorposts, six cubits wide on one side and six cubits wide on the other side—the width of the tabernacle. 2 The width of the entryway *was* ten cubits, and the side walls of the entrance *were* five cubits on this side and five cubits on the other side; and he measured its length, forty cubits, and its width, twenty cubits.

3 Also he went inside and measured the doorposts, two cubits; and the entrance, six cubits *high;* and the width of the entrance, seven cubits. 4 He measured the length, twenty cubits; and the width, twenty cubits, beyond the sanctuary; and he said to me, "This *is* the Most Holy Place."

5 Next, he measured the wall of the temple, six cubits. The width of each side chamber all around the temple *was* four cubits

on every side. 6 The side chambers *were* in three stories, one above the other, thirty chambers in each story; they rested on ledges which *were* for the side chambers all around, that they might be supported, but not fastened to the wall of the temple. 7 As one went up from story to story, the side chambers became wider all around, because their supporting ledges in the wall of the temple ascended like steps; therefore the width of the structure increased as one went up *from* the lowest *story* to the highest by way of the middle one. 8 I also saw an elevation all around the temple; it was the foundation of the side chambers, a full rod, *that is,* six cubits *high.* 9 The thickness of the outer wall of the side chambers *was* five cubits, and so also the remaining terrace by the place of the side chambers of the temple. 10 And between *it and* the *wall* chambers was a width of twenty cubits all around the temple on every side. 11 The doors of the side chambers opened on the terrace, one door toward the north and another toward the south; and the width of the terrace *was* five cubits all around.

12 The building that faced the separating courtyard at its western end *was* seventy cubits wide; the wall of the building *was* five cubits thick all around, and its length ninety cubits.

13 So he measured the temple, one hundred cubits long; and the separating courtyard with the building and its walls *was* one hundred cubits long; 14 also the width of the eastern face of the temple, including the separating courtyard, *was* one hundred cubits. 15 He measured the length of the building behind it, facing the separating courtyard, with its galleries on the one side and on the other side, one hundred cubits, as well as the inner temple and the porches of the court, 16 their doorposts and the beveled window frames. And the galleries all around their three stories opposite the threshold were paneled with wood from the ground to the windows—the windows were covered— 17 from the space above the door, even to the inner room, as well as outside, and on every wall all around, inside and outside, by measure.

18 And *it was* made with cherubim and palm trees, a palm tree between cherub and cherub. *Each* cherub had two faces, 19 so that the face of a man *was* toward a palm tree on one side, and the face of a young lion toward a palm tree on the other side; thus *it was* made throughout the temple all around. 20 From the floor to the space above the door, and on the wall of the sanctuary, cherubim and palm trees *were* carved.

21 The doorposts of the temple *were* square, *as was* the front of the sanctuary; their appearance was similar. 22 The altar *was* of wood, three cubits high, and its length two cubits. Its corners, its length, and its sides *were* of wood; and he said to me, "This *is* the table that *is* before the LORD."

23 The temple and the sanctuary had two doors. 24 The doors had two panels *apiece*, two folding panels: two *panels* for one door and two panels for the other *door*. 25 Cherubim and palm trees *were* carved on the doors of the temple just as they *were* carved on the walls. A wooden canopy *was* on the front of the vestibule outside. 26 *There were* beveled window *frames* and palm trees on one side and on the other, on the sides of the vestibule—also on the side chambers of the temple and on the canopies.

42 THEN he brought me out into the outer court, by the way toward the north; and he brought me into the chamber which *was* opposite the separating courtyard, and which *was* opposite the building toward the north. 2 Facing the length, *which was* one hundred cubits (the width was fifty cubits), was the north door. 3 Opposite the inner court of twenty *cubits,* and opposite the pavement of the outer court, *was* gallery against gallery in three *stories.* 4 In front of the chambers, toward the inside, *was* a walk ten cubits wide, at a distance of one cubit; and their doors faced north. 5 Now the upper chambers *were* shorter, because the galleries took away *space* from them more than from the lower and middle stories of the building. 6 For they *were* in three *stories* and did not have pillars like the pillars of the courts; therefore *the upper level* was shortened more than the lower and middle levels from the ground up. 7 And a wall which *was* outside ran parallel to the chambers, at the front of the chambers, toward the outer court; its length *was* fifty cubits. 8 The length of the chambers toward the outer court *was* fifty cubits, whereas that facing the temple *was* one hundred cubits. 9 At the lower chambers *was* the entrance on the east side, as one goes into them from the outer court.

10 Also *there were* chambers in the thickness of the wall of the court toward the east, opposite the separating courtyard and opposite the building. 11 *There was* a walk in front of them also, and their appearance *was* like the chambers which *were* toward the north; they *were* as long and as wide as the others, and all their exits and entrances *were* according to plan. 12 And corresponding to the doors of the chambers that *were* facing south, as one enters them, *there was* a door in front of the walk, the way directly in front of the wall toward the east.

13 Then he said to me, "The north chambers *and* the south chambers, which *are* opposite the separating courtyard, *are* the holy chambers where the priests who approach the LORD shall eat the most holy offerings. There they shall lay the most holy offerings—the grain offering, the sin offering, and the trespass offering—for the place *is* holy. 14 When the priests enter them, they shall not go out of the holy *chamber* into the outer court; but there they shall leave their garments in which they minister, for they *are* holy. They shall put on other garments; then they may approach *that* which *is* for the people."

15 Now when he had finished measuring

the inner temple, he brought me out through the gateway that faces toward the east, and measured it all around. 16 He measured the east side with the measuring rod, five hundred rods by the measuring rod all around. 17 He measured the north side, five hundred rods by the measuring rod all around. 18 He measured the south side, five hundred rods by the measuring rod. 19 He came around to the west side *and* measured five hundred rods by the measuring rod. 20 He measured it on the four sides; it had a wall all around, five hundred *cubits* long and five hundred wide, to separate the holy areas from the common.

PSALM 133:1–3

1   BEHOLD, how good and how
         pleasant *it is*
      For brethren to dwell together in unity!

2   *It is* like the precious oil upon the head,
         Running down on the beard,
      The beard of Aaron,
         Running down on the edge of his
           garments.
3   *It is* like the dew of Hermon,
         Descending upon the mountains of
           Zion;
      For there the LORD commanded the
           blessing—
      Life forevermore.

PROVERBS 29:6

6   BY transgression an evil man is snared,
      But the righteous sings and rejoices.

1 PETER 1:1–25

PETER, an apostle of Jesus Christ,

   To the pilgrims of the Dispersion in Pontus, Galatia, Cappadocia, Asia, and Bithynia, 2 elect according to the foreknowledge of God the Father, in sanctification of the Spirit, for obedience and sprinkling of the blood of Jesus Christ:

   Grace to you and peace be multiplied.

   3 Blessed *be* the God and Father of our Lord Jesus Christ, who according to His abundant mercy has begotten us again to a living hope through the resurrection of Jesus Christ from the dead, 4 to an inheritance incorruptible and undefiled and that

does not fade away, reserved in heaven for you, 5 who are kept by the power of God through faith for salvation ready to be revealed in the last time.

   6 In this you greatly rejoice, though now for a little while, if need be, you have been grieved by various trials, 7 that the genuineness of your faith, *being* much more precious than gold that perishes, though it is tested by fire, may be found to praise, honor, and glory at the revelation of Jesus Christ, 8 whom having not seen you love. Though now you do not see *Him,* yet believing, you rejoice with joy inexpressible and full of glory, 9 receiving the end of your faith— the salvation of *your* souls.

   10 Of this salvation the prophets have inquired and searched carefully, who prophesied of the grace *that would come* to you, 11 searching what, or what manner of time, the Spirit of Christ who was in them was indicating when He testified beforehand the sufferings of Christ and the glories that would follow. 12 To them it was revealed that, not to themselves, but to us they were ministering the things which now have been reported to you through those who have preached the gospel to you by the Holy Spirit sent from heaven—things which angels desire to look into.

   13 Therefore gird up the loins of your mind, be sober, and rest *your* hope fully upon the grace that is to be brought to you at the revelation of Jesus Christ; 14 as obedient children, not conforming yourselves to the former lusts, *as* in your ignorance; 15 but as He who called you *is* holy, you also be holy in all *your* conduct, 16 because it is written, "Be holy, for I am holy."

   17 And if you call on the Father, who without partiality judges according to each one's work, conduct yourselves throughout the time of your stay *here* in fear; 18 knowing that you were not redeemed with corruptible things, *like* silver or gold, from your aimless conduct *received* by tradition from your fathers, 19 but with the precious blood of Christ, as of a lamb without blemish and without spot. 20 He indeed was fore-

---

The death of Jesus Christ is the performance in history of the very mind of God.   (UTMOST)

---

ordained before the foundation of the world, but was manifest in these last times for you 21 who through Him believe in

God, who raised Him from the dead and gave Him glory, so that your faith and hope are in God. 22 Since you have purified your souls in obeying the truth through the Spirit in sincere love of the brethren, love one another fervently with a pure heart, 23 having been born again, not of corruptible seed but incorruptible, through the word of God which lives and abides forever, 24 because

"All flesh *is* as grass,
  And all the glory of man as the flower
    of the grass.
  The grass withers,
  And its flower falls away,
25 But the word of the Lord endures
    forever."

Now this is the word which by the gospel was preached to you.

◆◆◆

Reading 330—Follow His Steps
1 Peter 2:21–23

Peter makes it perfectly clear and unambiguous how we are to "follow His steps"—that is, in the way we suffer as Christians: "Who committed no sin, nor was deceit found in His mouth . . . when He suffered, He did not threaten.". . .

The following is distinctly limited to that one point: "Learn from Me; for I am gentle and lowly in heart." We are never told to be like the unique Being, the Lord Jesus Christ, who came into the world as God incarnate to put away sin. But when sin has been put away through the Atonement, we are to be conformed to His image. To follow His steps does not mean we have the belittling idea that we are to be Jesus Christ over again. It is not a question of "What would Jesus do?" but "What would Jesus have me do?" We have to exhibit over again the life He exhibited—in this particular instance, in the circumstance of suffering wrongfully. Suffering is the touchstone of saintliness, just as temptation is, and suffering wrongfully will always reveal the ruling disposition, because it takes us unawares.   (*GLORY*)

EZEKIEL 43:1—44:31

AFTERWARD he brought me to the gate, the gate that faces toward the east. 2 And behold, the glory of the God of Israel came from the way of the east. His voice *was* like the sound of many waters; and the earth shone with His glory. 3 *It was* like the appearance of the vision which I saw—like the vision which I saw when I came to destroy the city. The visions *were* like the vision which I saw by the River Chebar; and I fell on my face. 4 And the glory of the Lord came into the temple by way of the gate which faces toward the east. 5 The Spirit lifted me up and brought me into the inner court; and behold, the glory of the Lord filled the temple.

6 Then I heard *Him* speaking to me from the temple, while a man stood beside me.

7 And He said to me, "Son of man, *this is* the place of My throne and the place of the soles of My feet, where I will dwell in the midst of the children of Israel forever. No more shall the house of Israel defile My holy name, they nor their kings, by their harlotry or with the carcasses of their kings on their high places. 8 When they set their threshold by My threshold, and their doorpost by My doorpost, with a wall between them and Me, they defiled My holy name by the abominations which they committed; therefore I have consumed them in My anger. 9 Now let them put their harlotry and the carcasses of their kings far away from Me, and I will dwell in their midst forever.

10 "Son of man, describe the temple to the house of Israel, that they may be ashamed of their iniquities; and let them

measure the pattern. 11 And if they are ashamed of all that they have done, make known to them the design of the temple and its arrangement, its exits and its entrances, its entire design and all its ordinances, all its forms and all its laws. Write *it* down in their sight, so that they may keep its whole design and all its ordinances, and perform them. 12 This *is* the law of the temple: The whole area surrounding the mountaintop *is* most holy. Behold, this *is* the law of the temple.

13 "These are the measurements of the altar in cubits (the *cubit is* one cubit and a handbreadth): the base one cubit high and one cubit wide, with a rim all around its edge of one span. This *is* the height of the altar: 14 from the base on the ground to the lower ledge, two cubits; the width of the ledge, one cubit; from the smaller ledge to the larger ledge, four cubits; and the width of the ledge, *one* cubit. 15 The altar hearth *is* four cubits high, with four horns extending upward from the hearth. 16 The altar hearth *is* twelve cubits long, twelve wide, square at its four corners; 17 the ledge, fourteen *cubits* long and fourteen wide on its four sides, with a rim of half a cubit around it; its base, one cubit all around; and its steps face toward the east.

18 And He said to me, "Son of man, thus says the Lord GOD: 'These *are* the ordinances for the altar on the day when it is made, for sacrificing burnt offerings on it, and for sprinkling blood on it. 19 You shall give a young bull for a sin offering to the priests, the Levites, who are of the seed of Zadok, who approach Me to minister to Me,' says the Lord GOD. 20 You shall take some of its blood and put *it* on the four horns of the altar, on the four corners of the ledge, and on the rim around it; thus you shall cleanse it and make atonement for it. 21 Then you shall also take the bull of the sin offering, and burn it in the appointed place of the temple, outside the sanctuary. 22 On the second day you shall offer a kid of the goats without blemish for a sin offering; and they shall cleanse the altar, as they cleansed *it* with the bull. 23 When you have finished cleansing *it*, you shall offer a young bull without blemish, and a ram from the flock without blemish. 24 When you offer them before the LORD, the priests shall throw salt on them, and they will offer them up *as* a burnt offering to the LORD. 25 Every day for seven days you shall prepare a goat *for* a sin offering; they shall also prepare a young bull and a ram from the flock, both without blemish.

26 Seven days they shall make atonement for the altar and purify it, and so consecrate it. 27 When these days are over it shall be, on the eighth day and thereafter, that the priests shall offer your burnt offerings and your peace offerings on the altar; and I will accept you,' says the Lord GOD."

44 THEN He brought me back to the outer gate of the sanctuary which faces toward the east, but it *was* shut. 2 And the LORD said to me, "This gate shall be shut; it shall not be opened, and no man shall enter by it, because the LORD God of Israel has entered by it; therefore it shall be shut. 3 *As for* the prince, *because* he *is* the prince, he may sit in it to eat bread before the LORD; he shall enter by way of the vestibule of the gateway, and go out the same way."

4 Also He brought me by way of the north gate to the front of the temple; so I looked, and behold, the glory of the LORD filled the house of the LORD; and I fell on my face. 5 And the LORD said to me, "Son of man, mark well, see with your eyes and hear with your ears, all that I say to you concerning all the ordinances of the house of the LORD and all its laws. Mark well who may enter the house and all who go out from the sanctuary.

6 "Now say to the rebellious, to the house of Israel, 'Thus says the Lord GOD: "O house of Israel, let Us have no more of all your abominations. 7 When you brought in foreigners, uncircumcised in heart and uncircumcised in flesh, to be in My sanctuary to defile it—My house—and when you offered My food, the fat and the blood, then they broke My covenant because of all your abominations. 8 And you have not kept charge of My holy things, but you have set *others* to keep charge of My sanctuary for you." 9 Thus says the Lord GOD: "No foreigner, uncircumcised in heart or uncircumcised in flesh, shall enter My sanctuary, including any foreigner who *is* among the children of Israel.

10 "And the Levites who went far from Me, when Israel went astray, who strayed away from Me after their idols, they shall bear their iniquity. 11 Yet they shall be ministers in My sanctuary, *as* gatekeepers of the house and ministers of the house; they shall slay the burnt offering and the sacrifice for the people, and they shall stand before them to minister to them. 12 Because they ministered to them before their idols and caused the house of Israel to fall into iniquity, therefore I have raised My hand in an oath against them," says the Lord GOD,

"that they shall bear their iniquity. 13 And they shall not come near Me to minister to Me as priest, nor come near any of My holy things, nor into the Most Holy *Place;* but they shall bear their shame and their abominations which they have committed. 14 Nevertheless I will make them keep charge of the temple, for all its work, and for all that has to be done in it.

15 "But the priests, the Levites, the sons of Zadok, who kept charge of My sanctuary when the children of Israel went astray from Me, they shall come near Me to minister to Me; and they shall stand before Me to offer to Me the fat and the blood," says the Lord GOD. 16 "They shall enter My sanctuary, and they shall come near My table to minister to Me, and they shall keep My charge. 17 And it shall be, whenever they enter the gates of the inner court, that they shall put on linen garments; no wool shall come upon them while they minister within the gates of the inner court or within the house. 18 They shall have linen turbans on their heads and linen trousers on their bodies; they shall not clothe themselves with *anything that causes* sweat. 19 When they go out to the outer court, to the *outer* court to the people, they shall take off their garments in which they have ministered, leave them in the holy chambers, and put on other garments; and in their holy garments they shall not sanctify the people.

20 "They shall neither shave their heads, nor let their hair grow long, but they shall keep their hair well trimmed. 21 No priest shall drink wine when he enters the inner court. 22 They shall not take as wife a widow or a divorced woman, but take virgins of the descendants of the house of Israel, or widows of priests.

23 "And they shall teach My people *the difference* between the holy and the unholy, and cause them to discern between the unclean and the clean. 24 In controversy they shall stand as judges, *and* judge it according to My judgments. They shall keep My laws and My statutes in all My appointed meetings, and they shall hallow My Sabbaths.

25 "They shall not defile *themselves* by coming near a dead person. Only for father or mother, for son or daughter, for brother or unmarried sister may they defile themselves. 26 After he is cleansed, they shall count seven days for him. 27 And on the day that he goes to the sanctuary to minister in the sanctuary, he must offer his sin offering in the inner court," says the Lord GOD. 28 "It shall be, in regard to their inheritance, *that* I *am* their inheritance. You shall give them no possession in Israel, for I *am*

their possession. 29 They shall eat the grain offering, the sin offering, and the trespass offering; every dedicated thing in Israel shall be theirs. 30 The best of all firstfruits of any kind, and every sacrifice of any kind from all your sacrifices, shall be the priest's; also you shall give to the priest the first of your ground meal, to cause a blessing to rest on your house. 31 The priests shall not eat anything, bird or beast, that died naturally or was torn *by wild beasts.*

PSALM 134:1–3

1 BEHOLD, bless the LORD,
All *you* servants of the LORD,
Who by night stand in the house of
the LORD!

2 Lift up your hands *in* the sanctuary,
And bless the LORD.

3 The LORD who made heaven and earth
Bless you from Zion!

PROVERBS 29:7

7 THE righteous considers the cause of
the poor,
But the wicked does not understand
such knowledge.

1 PETER 2:1–25

THEREFORE, laying aside all malice, all deceit, hypocrisy, envy, and all evil speaking, 2 as newborn babes, desire the pure milk of the word, that you may grow thereby, 3 if indeed you have tasted that the Lord *is* gracious.

4 Coming to Him *as to* a living stone, rejected indeed by men, but chosen by God *and* precious, 5 you also, as living stones, are being built up a spiritual house, a holy priesthood, to offer up spiritual sacrifices acceptable to God through Jesus Christ. 6 Therefore it is also contained in the Scripture,

"Behold, I lay in Zion
A chief cornerstone, elect, precious,
And he who believes on Him will
by no means be put to shame."

7 Therefore, to you who believe, *He is* precious; but to those who are disobedient,

"The stone which the builders
rejected

Has become the chief
   cornerstone,"

8 and

   "A stone of stumbling
   And a rock of offense."

---

*T*he Jews were offended at Jesus
because they looked for a warrior
king in their coming
Messiah.   (GOD'S WORKMANSHIP)

They stumble, being disobedient to the
word, to which they also were appointed.

9 But you *are* a chosen generation, a royal
priesthood, a holy nation, His own special
people, that you may proclaim the praises
of Him who called you out of darkness
into His marvelous light; 10 who once *were*
not a people but *are* now the people of
God, who had not obtained mercy but now
have obtained mercy.

11 Beloved, I beg *you* as sojourners and
pilgrims, abstain from fleshly lusts which
war against the soul, 12 having your conduct
honorable among the Gentiles, that when
they speak against you as evildoers, they
may, by *your* good works which they observe, glorify God in the day of visitation.

13 Therefore submit yourselves to every
ordinance of man for the Lord's sake,
whether to the king as supreme, 14 or to
governors, as to those who are sent by him
for the punishment of evildoers and *for the*
praise of those who do good. 15 For this
is the will of God, that by doing good you
may put to silence the ignorance of foolish
men— 16 as free, yet not using liberty as a
cloak for vice, but as bondservants of God.
17 Honor all *people*. Love the brotherhood.
Fear God. Honor the king.

18 Servants, *be* submissive to *your* masters
with all fear, not only to the good and gentle, but also to the harsh. 19 For this *is* commendable, if because of conscience toward
God one endures grief, suffering wrongfully. 20 For what credit *is it* if, when you
are beaten for your faults, you take it patiently? But when you do good and suffer,
if you take it patiently, this *is* commendable
before God. 21 For to this you were called,
because Christ also suffered for us, leaving
us an example, that you should follow His
steps:

22 "Who committed no sin,
   Nor was deceit found in His
      mouth";

23 who, when He was reviled, did not revile
in return; when He suffered, He did not
threaten, but committed *Himself* to Him
who judges righteously; 24 who Himself
bore our sins in His own body on the tree,
that we, having died to sins, might live for
righteousness—by whose stripes you were
healed. 25 For you were like sheep going
astray, but have now returned to the Shepherd and Overseer of your souls.

◆◆◆◆

Reading 331—The Hope That Is in You
1 Peter 3:15

To give "a reason for the hope that is in you" is not at all the same thing
as convincing by reasonable argument why that hope is in us. The work
of the Spirit of God in us transcends reason, but never contradicts it, and
when a Christian says "the reason I am so-and-so is because I have received
the Holy Spirit," or, "I have received from God something which has made
this possible," it does not contradict reason, it transcends it, and is an answer
concerning the hope that is in you. The line we are continually apt to be
caught by is that of argumentative reasoning out why we are what we are; we
can never do that, but we can always say why the hope is in us.

Reason is the faculty of mind by which man draws conclusions. Every man
is always striving after a true expression of what he is. When a man is born
again his personality becomes alive to God as the Source of inspiration. Paul's

words "It is no longer I who live, but Christ lives in me" are the expression of the only worthy rationalism. . . .

As long as we use the image of our own salvation, our experience, the image of our feelings, or answers to prayer, we shall never begin to understand what Paul meant when he said "Christ lives in me." The exercise of man's essential reason is drawing on God as the Source of life.   (*GOD'S WORKMANSHIP*)

EZEKIEL 45:1—46:24

"MOREOVER, when you divide the land by lot into inheritance, you shall set apart a district for the LORD, a holy section of the land; its length *shall be* twenty-five thousand *cubits,* and the width ten thousand. It *shall be* holy throughout its territory all around. 2 Of this there shall be a square plot for the sanctuary, five hundred by five hundred *rods,* with fifty cubits around it for an open space. 3 So this is the district you shall measure: twenty-five thousand *cubits* long and ten thousand wide; in it shall be the sanctuary, the Most Holy *Place.* 4 It shall be a holy *section* of the land, belonging to the priests, the ministers of the sanctuary, who come near to minister to the LORD; it shall be a place for their houses and a holy place for the sanctuary. 5 *An area* twenty-five thousand *cubits* long and ten thousand wide shall belong to the Levites, the ministers of the temple; they shall have twenty chambers as a possession.

6 "You shall appoint as the property of the city *an area* five thousand *cubits* wide and twenty-five thousand long, adjacent to the district of the holy *section;* it shall belong to the whole house of Israel.

7 "The prince shall have *a section* on one side and the other of the holy district and the city's property; and bordering on the holy district and the city's property, extending westward on the west side and eastward on the east side, the length *shall be* side by side with one of the *tribal* portions, from the west border to the east border. 8 The land shall be his possession in Israel; and My princes shall no more oppress My people, but they shall give *the rest of* the land to the house of Israel, according to their tribes."

9 'Thus says the Lord GOD: "Enough, O princes of Israel! Remove violence and plundering, execute justice and righteousness, and stop dispossessing My people," says the Lord GOD. 10 "You shall have honest scales, an honest ephah, and an honest bath. 11 The ephah and the bath shall be of the same measure, so that the bath con-

tains one-tenth of a homer, and the ephah one-tenth of a homer; their measure shall be according to the homer. 12 The shekel *shall be* twenty gerahs; twenty shekels, twenty-five shekels, *and* fifteen shekels shall be your mina.

13 "This *is* the offering which you shall offer: you shall give one-sixth of an ephah from a homer of wheat, and one-sixth of an ephah from a homer of barley. 14 The ordinance concerning oil, the bath of oil, *is* one-tenth of a bath from a kor. A kor *is* a homer or ten baths, for ten baths *are* a homer. 15 And one lamb shall be given from a flock of two hundred, from the rich pastures of Israel. These shall be for grain offerings, burnt offerings, and peace offerings, to make atonement for them," says the Lord GOD. 16 "All the people of the land shall give this offering for the prince in Israel. 17 Then it shall be the prince's part *to give* burnt offerings, grain offerings, and drink offerings, at the feasts, the New Moons, the Sabbaths, and at all the appointed seasons of the house of Israel. He shall prepare the sin offering, the grain offering, the burnt offering, and the peace offerings to make atonement for the house of Israel."

18 'Thus says the Lord GOD: "In the first *month,* on the first *day* of the month, you shall take a young bull without blemish and cleanse the sanctuary. 19 The priest shall take some of the blood of the sin offering and put *it* on the doorposts of the temple, on the four corners of the ledge of the altar, and on the gateposts of the gate of the inner court. 20 And so you shall do on the seventh *day* of the month for everyone who has sinned unintentionally or in ignorance. Thus you shall make atonement for the temple.

21 "In the first *month,* on the fourteenth day of the month, you shall observe the Passover, a feast of seven days; unleavened bread shall be eaten. 22 And on that day the prince shall prepare for himself and for all the people of the land a bull *for* a sin offering. 23 On the seven days of the feast he shall prepare a burnt offering to the LORD, seven bulls and seven rams without

blemish, daily for seven days, and a kid of the goats daily *for* a sin offering. 24 And he shall prepare a grain offering of one ephah for each bull and one ephah for each ram, together with a hin of oil for each ephah.

25 "In the seventh *month*, on the fifteenth day of the month, at the feast, he shall do likewise for seven days, according to the sin offering, the burnt offering, the grain offering, and the oil."

46 'THUS says the Lord GOD: "The gateway of the inner court that faces toward the east shall be shut the six working days; but on the Sabbath it shall be opened, and on the day of the New Moon it shall be opened. 2 The prince shall enter by way of the vestibule of the gateway from the outside, and stand by the gatepost. The priests shall prepare his burnt offering and his peace offerings. He shall worship at the threshold of the gate. Then he shall go out, but the gate shall not be shut until evening. 3 Likewise the people of the land shall worship at the entrance to this gateway before the LORD on the Sabbaths and the New Moons. 4 The burnt offering that the prince offers to the LORD on the Sabbath day *shall be* six lambs without blemish, and a ram without blemish; 5 and the grain offering *shall be one* ephah for a ram, and the grain offering for the lambs, as much as he wants to give, as well as a hin of oil with every ephah. 6 On the day of the New Moon *it shall be* a young bull without blemish, six lambs, and a ram; they shall be without blemish. 7 He shall prepare a grain offering of an ephah for a bull, an ephah for a ram, as much as he wants to give for the lambs, and a hin of oil with every ephah. 8 When the prince enters, he shall go in by way of the vestibule of the gateway, and go out the same way.

9 "But when the people of the land come before the LORD on the appointed feast days, whoever enters by way of the north gate to worship shall go out by way of the south gate; and whoever enters by way of the south gate shall go out by way of the north gate. He shall not return by way of the gate through which he came, but shall go out through the opposite gate. 10 The prince shall then be in their midst. When they go in, he shall go in; and when they go out, he shall go out. 11 At the festivals and the appointed feast days the grain offering shall be an ephah for a bull, an ephah for a ram, as much as he wants to give for the lambs, and a hin of oil with every ephah.

12 "Now when the prince makes a voluntary burnt offering or voluntary peace offering to the LORD, the gate that faces toward the east shall then be opened for him; and he shall prepare his burnt offering and his peace offerings as he did on the Sabbath day. Then he shall go out, and after he goes out the gate shall be shut.

13 "You shall daily make a burnt offering to the LORD *of* a lamb of the first year without blemish; you shall prepare it every morning. 14 And you shall prepare a grain offering with it every morning, a sixth of an ephah, and a third of a hin of oil to moisten the fine flour. This grain offering is a perpetual ordinance, to be made regularly to the LORD. 15 Thus they shall prepare the lamb, the grain offering, and the oil, *as* a regular burnt offering every morning."

16 'Thus says the Lord GOD: "If the prince gives a gift *of some* of his inheritance to any of his sons, it shall belong to his sons; it is their possession by inheritance. 17 But if he gives a gift of some of his inheritance to one of his servants, it shall be his until the year of liberty, after which it shall return to the prince. But his inheritance shall belong to his sons; it shall become theirs. 18 Moreover the prince shall not take any of the people's inheritance by evicting them from their property; he shall provide an inheritance for his sons from his own property, so that none of My people may be scattered from his property.""'

19 Now he brought me through the entrance, which *was* at the side of the gate, into the holy chambers of the priests which face toward the north; and there a place *was* situated at their extreme western end. 20 And he said to me, "This *is* the place where the priests shall boil the trespass offering and the sin offering, *and* where they shall bake the grain offering, so that they do not bring *them* out into the outer court to sanctify the people."

21 Then he brought me out into the outer court and caused me to pass by the four corners of the court; and in fact, in every corner of the court *there was another* court. 22 In the four corners of the court *were* enclosed courts, forty *cubits* long and thirty wide; all four corners *were* the same size. 23 *There was* a row *of building stones* all around in them, all around the four of them; and cooking hearths were made under the rows of stones all around. 24 And he said to me, "These *are* the kitchens where the ministers of the temple shall boil the sacrifices of the people."

PSALM 135:1–7

1 PRAISE the LORD!

Praise the name of the LORD;
Praise *Him*, O you servants of the
  LORD!
2 You who stand in the house of the
  LORD,
In the courts of the house of our God,
3 Praise the LORD, for the LORD *is* good;
Sing praises to His name, for *it is*
  pleasant.
4 For the LORD has chosen Jacob for
  Himself,
Israel for His special treasure.

---

*The logic of mathematics does not
amount to anything in the spiritual
realm.* (SHADE)

---

5 For I know that the LORD *is* great,
And our Lord *is* above all gods.
6 Whatever the LORD pleases He does,
In heaven and in earth,
In the seas and in all deep places.
7 He causes the vapors to ascend from
  the ends of the earth;
He makes lightning for the rain;
He brings the wind out of His
  treasuries.

PROVERBS 29:8

8 SCOFFERS set a city aflame,
But wise *men* turn away wrath.

1 PETER 3:1–22

WIVES, likewise, *be* submissive to your
own husbands, that even if some do not
obey the word, they, without a word, may
be won by the conduct of their wives,
2 when they observe your chaste conduct
accompanied by fear. 3 Do not let your
adornment be *merely* outward—arranging
the hair, wearing gold, or putting on *fine*
apparel— 4 rather *let it be* the hidden person
of the heart, with the incorruptible *beauty*
of a gentle and quiet spirit, which is very
precious in the sight of God. 5 For in this
manner, in former times, the holy women
who trusted in God also adorned themselves, being submissive to their own husbands, 6 as Sarah obeyed Abraham, calling
him lord, whose daughters you are if you

do good and are not afraid with any terror.
7 Husbands, likewise, dwell with *them*
with understanding, giving honor to the
wife, as to the weaker vessel, and as *being*
heirs together of the grace of life, that your
prayers may not be hindered.
8 Finally, all *of you be* of one mind, having compassion for one another; love as
brothers, *be* tenderhearted, *be* courteous;
9 not returning evil for evil or reviling for
reviling, but on the contrary blessing,
knowing that you were called to this, that
you may inherit a blessing. 10 For

"He who would love life
  And see good days,
  Let him refrain his tongue from evil,
  And his lips from speaking deceit.
11 Let him turn away from evil and do
    good;
  Let him seek peace and pursue it.
12 For the eyes of the LORD *are* on the
    righteous,
  And His ears *are open* to their prayers;
  But the face of the LORD *is* against
    those who do evil."

13 And who *is* he who will harm you if
you become followers of what is good?
14 But even if you should suffer for righteousness' sake, *you are* blessed. "And do
not be afraid of their threats, nor be
troubled." 15 But sanctify the Lord God in
your hearts, and always *be* ready to *give* a
defense to everyone who asks you a reason
for the hope that is in you, with meekness
and fear; 16 having a good conscience, that
when they defame you as evildoers, those
who revile your good conduct in Christ
may be ashamed. 17 For *it is* better, if it is
the will of God, to suffer for doing good
than for doing evil.
18 For Christ also suffered once for sins,
the just for the unjust, that He might bring
us to God, being put to death in the flesh
but made alive by the Spirit, 19 by whom
also He went and preached to the spirits
in prison, 20 who formerly were disobedient, when once the Divine longsuffering
waited in the days of Noah, while *the* ark
was being prepared, in which a few, that
is, eight souls, were saved through water.

---

*God is amazingly
patient.* (GLORIFY)

---

21 There is also an antitype which now saves
us—baptism (not the removal of the filth

of the flesh, but the answer of a good conscience toward God), through the resurrection of Jesus Christ, 22 who has gone into heaven and is at the right hand of God, angels and authorities and powers having been made subject to Him.

◆◆◆◆

Reading 332—Suffering of the Sanctified
1 Peter 4:1

The sufferings of the sanctified are caused by growing into the idea of the will of God. God did not spare His own Son, and He does not spare His sanctified ones from the requirements of saintship. A child is a perfect specimen of the genus *homo*, so is a man. The child as it develops, suffers; it is a false mercy that spares a child any requirements of its nature to complete the full stature of manhood, and it is a false mercy that spares the sanctified child of God any of the requirements of its nature to complete "the measure of the stature of the fullness of Christ." We do not evolve into holiness, it is a gift—we evolve *in* it, attainment after attainment, becoming sons and daughters of God, brothers and sisters of the Lord Jesus. That is Paul's meaning in Philippians 3:12, 13, "reaching forward to those things which are ahead, I press toward the goal. . . ."

A child in the natural world is not fit for life unless it is perfectly healthy; sanctification is spiritual health, "perfect soundness." May the God of peace sanctify us wholly so that we are no longer sickly souls retarding His purposes, but made "perfect through suffering." Oh, that from every heart may rise the yearning longing, as from the apostle Paul.   (*GOD'S WORKMANSHIP*)

EZEKIEL 47:1—48:35

THEN he brought me back to the door of the temple; and there was water, flowing from under the threshold of the temple toward the east, for the front of the temple faced east; the water was flowing from under the right side of the temple, south of the altar. 2 He brought me out by way of the north gate, and led me around on the outside to the outer gateway that faces east; and there was water, running out on the right side.

3 And when the man went out to the east with the line in his hand, he measured one thousand cubits, and he brought me through the waters; the water *came up to my* ankles. 4 Again he measured one thousand and brought me through the waters; the water *came up to my* knees. Again he measured one thousand and brought me through; the water *came up to my* waist. 5 Again he measured one thousand, *and it was* a river that I could not cross; for the water was too deep, water in which one must swim, a river that could not be crossed. 6 He said to me, "Son of man, have you seen *this?*" Then he brought me and returned me to the bank of the river.

7 When I returned, there, along the bank of the river, *were* very many trees on one side and the other. 8 Then he said to me: "This water flows toward the eastern region, goes down into the valley, and enters the sea. *When it* reaches the sea, *its* waters are healed. 9 And it shall be *that* every living thing that moves, wherever the rivers go, will live. There will be a very great multitude of fish, because these waters go there; for they will be healed, and everything will live wherever the river goes. 10 It shall be *that* fishermen will stand by it from En Gedi to En Eglaim; they will be *places* for spreading their nets. Their fish will be of the same kinds as the fish of the Great Sea, exceedingly many. 11 But its swamps and marshes will not be healed; they will be given over to salt. 12 Along the bank of the river, on this side and that, will grow all *kinds of* trees used for food; their leaves will not

wither, and their fruit will not fail. They will bear fruit every month, because their water flows from the sanctuary. Their fruit will be for food, and their leaves for medicine."

13 Thus says the Lord GOD: "These *are* the borders by which you shall divide the land as an inheritance among the twelve tribes of Israel. Joseph *shall have two* portions. 14 You shall inherit it equally with one another; for I raised My hand in an oath to give it to your fathers, and this land shall fall to you as your inheritance.

15 "This *shall be* the border of the land on the north: from the Great Sea, *by* the road to Hethlon, as one goes to Zedad, 16 Hamath, Berothah, Sibraim (which *is* between the border of Damascus and the border of Hamath), to Hazar Hatticon (which *is* on the border of Hauran). 17 Thus the boundary shall be from the Sea to Hazar Enan, the border of Damascus; and as for the north, northward, it is the border of Hamath. *This is* the north side.

18 "On the east side you shall mark out the border from between Hauran and Damascus, and between Gilead and the land of Israel, along the Jordan, and along the eastern side of the sea. *This is* the east side.

19 "The south side, toward the South, *shall be* from Tamar to the waters of Meribah by Kadesh, along the brook to the Great Sea. *This is* the south side, toward the South.

20 "The west side *shall be* the Great Sea, from the *southern* boundary until one comes to a point opposite Hamath. This *is* the west side.

21 "Thus you shall divide this land among yourselves according to the tribes of Israel. 22 It shall be that you will divide it by lot as an inheritance for yourselves, and for the strangers who dwell among you and who bear children among you. They shall be to you as native-born among the children of Israel; they shall have an inheritance with you among the tribes of Israel. 23 And it shall be *that* in whatever tribe the stranger dwells, there you shall give *him* his inheritance," says the Lord GOD.

48 "NOW these *are* the names of the tribes: From the northern border along the road to Hethlon at the entrance of Hamath, to Hazar Enan, the border of Damascus northward, in the direction of Hamath, *there shall be* one *section for* Dan from its east to its west side; 2 by the border of Dan, from the east side to the west, one *section for* Asher; 3 by the border of Asher, from the east side to the west, one *section for* Naphtali; 4 by the border of Naphtali,

from the east side to the west, one *section for* Manasseh; 5 by the border of Manasseh, from the east side to the west, one *section for* Ephraim; 6 by the border of Ephraim, from the east side to the west, one *section for* Reuben; 7 by the border of Reuben, from the east side to the west, one *section for* Judah; 8 by the border of Judah, from the east side to the west, shall be the district which you shall set apart, twenty-five thousand *cubits* in width, and *in* length the same as one of the *other* portions, from the east side to the west, with the sanctuary in the center.

9 "The district that you shall set apart for the LORD *shall be* twenty-five thousand *cubits* in length and ten thousand in width. 10 To these—to the priests—the holy district shall belong: on the north twenty-five thousand *cubits in length,* on the west ten thousand in width, on the east ten thousand in width, and on the south twenty-five thousand in length. The sanctuary of the LORD shall be in the center. 11 *It shall be* for the priests of the sons of Zadok, who are sanctified, who have kept My charge, who did not go astray when the children of Israel went astray, as the Levites went astray. 12 And *this* district of land that is set apart shall be to them a thing most holy by the border of the Levites.

13 "Opposite the border of the priests, the Levites *shall have an area* twenty-five thousand *cubits* in length and ten thousand in width; its entire length *shall be* twenty-five thousand and its width ten thousand. 14 And they shall not sell or exchange any of it; they may not alienate this best *part* of the land, for *it is* holy to the LORD.

15 "The five thousand *cubits* in width that remain, along the edge of the twenty-five thousand, shall be for general use by the city, for dwellings and common-land; and the city shall be in the center. 16 These *shall be* its measurements: the north side four thousand five hundred *cubits,* the south side four thousand five hundred, the east side four thousand five hundred, and the west side four thousand five hundred. 17 The common-land of the city shall be: to the north two hundred and fifty *cubits,* to the south two hundred and fifty, to the east two hundred and fifty, and to the west two hundred and fifty. 18 The rest of the length, alongside the district of the holy *section, shall be* ten thousand *cubits* to the east and ten thousand to the west. It shall be adjacent to the district of the holy *section,* and its produce shall be food for the workers of the city. 19 The workers of the city, from

all the tribes of Israel, shall cultivate it. 20 The entire district *shall be* twenty-five thousand *cubits* by twenty-five thousand *cubits,* foursquare. You shall set apart the holy district with the property of the city.

21 "The rest *shall belong* to the prince, on one side and on the other of the holy district and of the city's property, next to the twenty-five thousand *cubits* of the *holy* district as far as the eastern border, and westward next to the twenty-five thousand as far as the western border, adjacent to the *tribal* portions; *it shall belong* to the prince. It shall be the holy district, and the sanctuary of the temple *shall be* in the center. 22 Moreover, apart from the possession of the Levites and the possession of the city *which are* in the midst of what *belongs* to the prince, *the area* between the border of Judah and the border of Benjamin shall belong to the prince.

23 "As for the rest of the tribes, from the east side to the west, Benjamin *shall have* one *section;* 24 by the border of Benjamin, from the east side to the west, Simeon *shall have* one *section;* 25 by the border of Simeon, from the east side to the west, Issachar *shall have* one *section;* 26 by the border of Issachar, from the east side to the west, Zebulun *shall have* one *section;* 27 by the border of Zebulun, from the east side to the west, Gad *shall have* one *section;* 28 by the border of Gad, on the south side, toward the South, the border shall be from Tamar *to* the waters of Meribah *by* Kadesh, along the brook to the Great Sea. 29 This *is* the land which you shall divide by lot as an inheritance among the tribes of Israel, and these *are* their portions," says the Lord GOD.

30 "These *are* the exits of the city. On the north side, measuring four thousand five hundred *cubits* 31 (the gates of the city *shall be* named after the tribes of Israel), the three gates northward: one gate for Reuben, one gate for Judah, and one gate for Levi; 32 on the east side, four thousand five hundred *cubits,* three gates: one gate for Joseph, one gate for Benjamin, and one gate for Dan; 33 on the south side, measuring four thousand five hundred *cubits,* three gates: one gate for Simeon, one gate for Issachar, and one gate for Zebulun; 34 on the west side, four thousand five hundred *cubits* with their three gates: one gate for Gad, one gate for Asher, and one gate for Naphtali. 35 All the way around *shall be* eighteen thousand *cubits;* and the name of the city from *that* day *shall be:* THE LORD *IS* THERE."

PSALM 135:8–14

8 HE destroyed the firstborn of Egypt,
   Both of man and beast.
9 He sent signs and wonders into the
      midst of you, O Egypt,
   Upon Pharaoh and all his servants.
10 He defeated many nations
   And slew mighty kings—
11 Sihon king of the Amorites,
   Og king of Bashan,
   And all the kingdoms of Canaan—
12 And gave their land *as* a heritage,
   A heritage to Israel His people.

13 Your name, O LORD, *endures* forever,
   Your fame, O LORD, throughout all
      generations.
14 For the LORD will judge His people,
   And He will have compassion on His
      servants.

PROVERBS 29:9

9 IF a wise man contends with a foolish
      man,
   Whether *the fool* rages or laughs, *there
      is* no peace.

1 PETER 4:1–19

THEREFORE, since Christ suffered for us in the flesh, arm yourselves also with the same mind, for he who has suffered in the flesh has ceased from sin, 2 that he no longer should live the rest of *his* time in the flesh for the lusts of men, but for the will of God. 3 For we *have spent* enough of our past lifetime in doing the will of the Gentiles—when we walked in lewdness, lusts, drunkenness, revelries, drinking parties, and abominable idolatries. 4 In regard to these, they think it strange that you do not run with *them* in the same flood of dissipation, speaking evil of *you.* 5 They will give an account to Him who is ready to judge the living and the dead. 6 For this reason the gospel was preached also to those who are dead, that they might be judged according to men in the flesh, but live according to God in the spirit.

7 But the end of all things is at hand; therefore be serious and watchful in your prayers. 8 And above all things have fervent love for one another, for "love will cover a multitude of sins." 9 *Be* hospitable to one another without grumbling. 10 As each one has received a gift, minister it to one an-

other, as good stewards of the manifold grace of God. 11 If anyone speaks, *let him speak* as the oracles of God. If anyone ministers, *let him do it* as with the ability which God supplies, that in all things God may be glorified through Jesus Christ, to whom belong the glory and the dominion forever and ever. Amen.

12 Beloved, do not think it strange concerning the fiery trial which is to try you, as though some strange thing happened to you; 13 but rejoice to the extent that you partake of Christ's sufferings, that when His glory is revealed, you may also be glad with exceeding joy. 14 If you are reproached for the name of Christ, blessed *are you*, for the Spirit of glory and of God rests upon you. On their part He is blasphemed, but on your part He is glorified. 15 But let none of you suffer as a murderer, a thief, an evildoer, or as a busybody in other people's matters. 16 Yet if *anyone suffers* as a Chris-

tian, let him not be ashamed, but let him glorify God in this matter.

17 For the time *has come* for judgment to begin at the house of God; and if *it begins* with us first, what will *be* the end of those who do not obey the gospel of God? 18 Now

> "If the righteous one is scarcely saved,
> Where will the ungodly and the
> sinner appear?"

That Christ died for me, therefore I go scot-free, is never taught in the New Testament. (UTMOST)

---

19 Therefore let those who suffer according to the will of God commit their souls *to Him* in doing good, as to a faithful Creator.

◆◆◆◆

Reading 333—Delivered from the Evil One
1 Peter 5:8, 9

The Bible holds man responsible for the introduction of Satan. Satan is the representative of the Devil, and the Devil is the adversary of God in the rule of man. When our Lord came face-to-face with Satan He dealt with him as representing the attitude man takes up in organizing his life apart from any consideration of God. (*SERVANT AS LORD*)

God does not deal with Satan direct, man must deal with Satan because man is responsible for his introduction. That is why God became Incarnate. Put it in any other way—why God could banish Satan in two seconds; but it is man who, through the Redemption, is to overcome Satan, and much more than overcome him, he is to do that which will exhibit the perfect fulfillment of this prophecy. Jesus Christ, the last Adam, took on Him our human form, and it is through His seed in that human form that Satan is to be overcome. (*GENESIS*)

Satan is not removed now from the presence of the saints, but the saint is still kept in the world where the Evil One rules; consequently, the saint is continually being badgered by the Evil One. Jesus prayed, not that we should be taken out of the world, but that we should be "delivered from the Evil One." (*SERVANT AS LORD*)

DANIEL 1:1—2:49

IN the third year of the reign of Jehoiakim king of Judah, Nebuchadnezzar king of Babylon came to Jerusalem and besieged it. 2 And the Lord gave Jehoiakim king of Judah into his hand, with some of the articles of the house of God, which he carried into the land of Shinar to the house of his god; and he brought the articles into the treasure house of his god.

3 Then the king instructed Ashpenaz, the

master of his eunuchs, to bring some of the children of Israel and some of the king's descendants and some of the nobles, 4 young men in whom *there was* no blemish, but good-looking, gifted in all wisdom, possessing knowledge and quick to understand, who *had* ability to serve in the king's palace, and whom they might teach the language and literature of the Chaldeans. 5 And the king appointed for them a daily provision of the king's delicacies and of the wine which he drank, and three years of training for them, so that at the end of *that time* they might serve before the king. 6 Now from among those of the sons of Judah were Daniel, Hananiah, Mishael, and Azariah. 7 To them the chief of the eunuchs gave names: he gave Daniel *the name* Belteshazzar; to Hananiah, Shadrach; to Mishael, Meshach; and to Azariah, Abed-Nego.

8 But Daniel purposed in his heart that he would not defile himself with the portion of the king's delicacies, nor with the wine which he drank; therefore he requested of the chief of the eunuchs that he might not defile himself. 9 Now God had brought Daniel into the favor and goodwill of the chief of the eunuchs. 10 And the chief of the eunuchs said to Daniel, "I fear my lord the king, who has appointed your food and drink. For why should he see your faces looking worse than the young men who *are* your age? Then you would endanger my head before the king."

11 So Daniel said to the steward whom the chief of the eunuchs had set over Daniel, Hananiah, Mishael, and Azariah, 12 "Please test your servants for ten days, and let them give us vegetables to eat and water to drink. 13 Then let our appearance be examined before you, and the appearance of the young men who eat the portion of the king's delicacies; and as you see fit, *so* deal with your servants." 14 So he consented with them in this matter, and tested them ten days.

15 And at the end of ten days their features appeared better and fatter in flesh than all the young men who ate the portion of the king's delicacies. 16 Thus the steward took away their portion of delicacies and the wine that they were to drink, and gave them vegetables.

17 As for these four young men, God gave them knowledge and skill in all literature and wisdom; and Daniel had understanding in all visions and dreams.

18 Now at the end of the days, when the king had said that they should be brought in, the chief of the eunuchs brought them in before Nebuchadnezzar. 19 Then the king

interviewed them, and among them all none was found like Daniel, Hananiah, Mishael, and Azariah; therefore they served before the king. 20 And in all matters of wisdom *and* understanding about which the king examined them, he found them ten times better than all the magicians *and* astrologers who *were* in all his realm. 21 Thus Daniel continued until the first year of King Cyrus.

2 NOW in the second year of Nebuchadnezzar's reign, Nebuchadnezzar had dreams; and his spirit was *so* troubled that his sleep left him. 2 Then the king gave the command to call the magicians, the astrologers, the sorcerers, and the Chaldeans to tell the king his dreams. So they came and stood before the king. 3 And the king said to them, "I have had a dream, and my spirit is anxious to know the dream."

4 Then the Chaldeans spoke to the king in Aramaic, "O king, live forever! Tell your servants the dream, and we will give the interpretation."

5 The king answered and said to the Chaldeans, "My decision is firm: if you do not make known the dream to me, and its interpretation, you shall be cut in pieces, and your houses shall be made an ash heap. 6 However, if you tell the dream and its interpretation, you shall receive from me gifts, rewards, and great honor. Therefore tell me the dream and its interpretation."

7 They answered again and said, "Let the king tell his servants the dream, and we will give its interpretation."

8 The king answered and said, "I know for certain that you would gain time, because you see that my decision is firm: 9 if you do not make known the dream to me, *there is only* one decree for you! For you have agreed to speak lying and corrupt words before me till the time has changed. Therefore tell me the dream, and I shall know that you can give me its interpretation."

10 The Chaldeans answered the king, and said, "There is not a man on earth who can tell the king's matter; therefore no king, lord, or ruler has *ever* asked such things of any magician, astrologer, or Chaldean. 11 *It is* a difficult thing that the king requests, and there is no other who can tell it to the king except the gods, whose dwelling is not with flesh."

12 For this reason the king was angry and very furious, and gave the command to destroy all the wise *men* of Babylon. 13 So the decree went out, and they began killing the wise *men;* and they sought Daniel and his companions, to kill *them.*

14 Then with counsel and wisdom Daniel answered Arioch, the captain of the king's guard, who had gone out to kill the wise *men* of Babylon; 15 he answered and said to Arioch the king's captain, "Why is the decree from the king so urgent?" Then Arioch made the decision known to Daniel.

16 So Daniel went in and asked the king to give him time, that he might tell the king the interpretation. 17 Then Daniel went to his house, and made the decision known to Hananiah, Mishael, and Azariah, his companions, 18 that they might seek mercies from the God of heaven concerning this secret, so that Daniel and his companions might not perish with the rest of the wise *men* of Babylon. 19 Then the secret was revealed to Daniel in a night vision. So Daniel blessed the God of heaven.

20 Daniel answered and said:

"Blessed be the name of God forever and ever,
For wisdom and might are His.
21 And He changes the times and the seasons;
He removes kings and raises up kings;
He gives wisdom to the wise
And knowledge to those who have understanding.
22 He reveals deep and secret things;
He knows what *is* in the darkness,
And light dwells with Him.

23 "I thank You and praise You,
O God of my fathers;
You have given me wisdom and might,
And have now made known to me what we asked of You,
For You have made known to us the king's demand."

24 Therefore Daniel went to Arioch, whom the king had appointed to destroy the wise *men* of Babylon. He went and said thus to him: "Do not destroy the wise *men* of Babylon; take me before the king, and I will tell the king the interpretation."

25 Then Arioch quickly brought Daniel before the king, and said thus to him, "I have found a man of the captives of Judah, who will make known to the king the interpretation."

26 The king answered and said to Daniel, whose name *was* Belteshazzar, "Are you able to make known to me the dream which I have seen, and its interpretation?"

27 Daniel answered in the presence of the king, and said, "The secret which the king has demanded, the wise *men*, the astrologers, the magicians, and the soothsayers cannot declare to the king. 28 But there is a God in heaven who reveals secrets, and He has made known to King Nebuchadnezzar what will be in the latter days. Your dream, and the visions of your head upon your bed, were these: 29 As for you, O king, thoughts came *to* your *mind while* on your bed, *about* what would come to pass after this; and He who reveals secrets has made known to you what will be. 30 But as for me, this secret has not been revealed to me because I have more wisdom than anyone living, but for *our* sakes who make known the interpretation to the king, and that you may know the thoughts of your heart.

31 "You, O king, were watching; and behold, a great image! This great image, whose splendor *was* excellent, stood before you; and its form *was* awesome. 32 This image's head *was* of fine gold, its chest and arms of silver, its belly and thighs of bronze, 33 its legs of iron, its feet partly of iron and partly of clay. 34 You watched while a stone was cut out without hands, which struck the image on its feet of iron and clay, and broke them in pieces. 35 Then the iron, the clay, the bronze, the silver, and the gold were crushed together, and became like chaff from the summer threshing floors; the wind carried them away so that no trace of them was found. And the stone that struck the image became a great mountain and filled the whole earth.

36 "This *is* the dream. Now we will tell the interpretation of it before the king. 37 You, O king, *are* a king of kings. For the God of heaven has given you a kingdom, power, strength, and glory; 38 and wherever the children of men dwell, or the beasts of the field and the birds of the heaven, He has given *them* into your hand, and has made you ruler over them all—you *are* this head of gold. 39 But after you shall arise another kingdom inferior to yours; then another, a third kingdom of bronze, which shall rule over all the earth. 40 And the fourth kingdom shall be as strong as iron, inasmuch as iron breaks in pieces and shatters everything; and like iron that crushes, *that kingdom* will break in pieces and crush all the others. 41 Whereas you saw the feet and toes, partly of potter's clay and partly of iron, the kingdom shall be divided; yet the strength of the iron shall be in it, just as you saw the iron mixed with ceramic clay. 42 And *as* the toes of the feet *were* partly of iron and partly of clay, *so* the kingdom shall be partly strong

and partly fragile. 43 As you saw iron mixed with ceramic clay, they will mingle with the seed of men; but they will not adhere to one another, just as iron does not mix with clay. 44 And in the days of these kings the God of heaven will set up a kingdom which shall never be destroyed; and the kingdom shall not be left to other people; it shall break in pieces and consume all these kingdoms, and it shall stand forever. 45 Inasmuch as you saw that the stone was cut out of the mountain without hands, and that it broke in pieces the iron, the bronze, the clay, the silver, and the gold—the great God has made known to the king what will come to pass after this. The dream is certain, and its interpretation is sure."

46 Then King Nebuchadnezzar fell on his face, prostrate before Daniel, and commanded that they should present an offering and incense to him. 47 The king answered Daniel, and said, "Truly your God *is* the God of gods, the Lord of kings, and a revealer of secrets, since you could reveal this secret." 48 Then the king promoted Daniel and gave him many great gifts; and he made him ruler over the whole province of Babylon, and chief administrator over all the wise *men* of Babylon. 49 Also Daniel petitioned the king, and he set Shadrach, Meshach, and Abed-Nego over the affairs of the province of Babylon; but Daniel *sat* in the gate of the king.

PSALM 135:15–21

15 THE idols of the nations *are* silver and gold,
   The work of men's hands.
16 They have mouths, but they do not speak;
   Eyes they have, but they do not see;
17 They have ears, but they do not hear;
   Nor is there *any* breath in their mouths.
18 Those who make them are like them;
   So is everyone who trusts in them.

19 Bless the LORD, O house of Israel!
   Bless the LORD, O house of Aaron!
20 Bless the LORD, O house of Levi!
   You who fear the LORD, bless the LORD!
21 Blessed be the LORD out of Zion,
   Who dwells in Jerusalem!

   Praise the LORD!

PROVERBS 29:10

10 THE bloodthirsty hate the blameless,
   But the upright seek his well-being.

1 PETER 5:1–14

THE elders who are among you I exhort, I who am a fellow elder and a witness of the sufferings of Christ, and also a partaker of the glory that will be revealed: 2 Shepherd the flock of God which is among you, serving as overseers, not by compulsion but willingly, not for dishonest gain but eagerly; 3 nor as being lords over those entrusted to you, but being examples to the flock; 4 and when the Chief Shepherd appears, you will receive the crown of glory that does not fade away.

5 Likewise you younger people, submit yourselves to *your* elders. Yes, all of *you* be submissive to one another, and be clothed with humility, for

   "God resists the proud,
      But gives grace to the humble."

6 Therefore humble yourselves under the mighty hand of God, that He may exalt you in due time, 7 casting all your care upon Him, for He cares for you.

8 Be sober, be vigilant; because your adversary the devil walks about like a roaring lion, seeking whom he may devour.

God grant the Devil may be kept off the brains of the saints. (BIB. ETHICS)

9 Resist him, steadfast in the faith, knowing that the same sufferings are experienced by your brotherhood in the world. 10 But may the God of all grace, who called us to His eternal glory by Christ Jesus, after you have suffered a while, perfect, establish, strengthen, and settle *you.* 11 To Him *be* the glory and the dominion forever and ever. Amen.

12 By Silvanus, our faithful brother as I consider him, I have written to you briefly, exhorting and testifying that this is the true grace of God in which you stand. 13 She who is in Babylon, elect together with *you,* greets you; and *so does* Mark my son. 14 Greet one another with a kiss of love.

   Peace to you all who are in Christ Jesus. Amen.

Reading 334—Tested by the Disagreeable
2 Peter 1:9

When Christ is formed in us we have to see that our human nature acts in perfect obedience to all that the Son of God reveals. God does not supply us with character, He gives us the life of His Son and we can either ignore Him and refuse to obey Him, or we can so obey Him, so bring every thought and imagination into captivity, that the life of Jesus is manifested in our mortal flesh. It is not a question of being saved from hell, but of being saved in order to manifest the Son of God in our mortal flesh. Our responsibility is to keep ourselves fit to manifest Him. . . .

The only way to keep yourself fit is by the discipline of the disagreeable. It is the disagreeable things which make us exhibit whether we are manifesting the life of the Son of God, or living a life which is antagonistic to Him. When disagreeable things happen, do we manifest the essential sweetness of the Son of God or the essential irritation of ourselves apart from Him? Whenever self comes into the ascendant, the life of the Son of God in us is perverted and twisted; there is irritation, and His life suffers. Growth in grace stops the moment we get huffed.   (*GROW*)

DANIEL 3:1—4:37

NEBUCHADNEZZAR the king made an image of gold, whose height *was* sixty cubits *and* its width six cubits. He set it up in the plain of Dura, in the province of Babylon. 2 And King Nebuchadnezzar sent *word* to gather together the satraps, the administrators, the governors, the counselors, the treasurers, the judges, the magistrates, and all the officials of the provinces, to come to the dedication of the image which King Nebuchadnezzar had set up. 3 So the satraps, the administrators, the governors, the counselors, the treasurers, the judges, the magistrates, and all the officials of the provinces gathered together for the dedication of the image that King Nebuchadnezzar had set up; and they stood before the image that Nebuchadnezzar had set up. 4 Then a herald cried aloud: "To you it is commanded, O peoples, nations, and languages, 5 *that* at the time you hear the sound of the horn, flute, harp, lyre, *and* psaltery, in symphony with all kinds of music, you shall fall down and worship the gold image that King Nebuchadnezzar has set up; 6 and whoever does not fall down and worship shall be cast immediately into the midst of a burning fiery furnace."

7 So at that time, when all the people heard the sound of the horn, flute, harp, *and* lyre, in symphony with all kinds of music, all the people, nations, and languages fell down *and* worshiped the gold image which King Nebuchadnezzar had set up.

8 Therefore at that time certain Chaldeans came forward and accused the Jews. 9 They spoke and said to King Nebuchadnezzar, "O king, live forever! 10 You, O king, have made a decree that everyone who hears the sound of the horn, flute, harp, lyre, *and* psaltery, in symphony with all kinds of music, shall fall down and worship the gold image; 11 and whoever does not fall down and worship shall be cast into the midst of a burning fiery furnace. 12 There are certain Jews whom you have set over the affairs of the province of Babylon: Shadrach, Meshach, and Abed-Nego; these men, O king, have not paid due regard to you. They do not serve your gods or worship the gold image which you have set up."

13 Then Nebuchadnezzar, in rage and fury, gave the command to bring Shadrach, Meshach, and Abed-Nego. So they brought these men before the king. 14 Nebuchadnezzar spoke, saying to them, "*Is it* true, Shadrach, Meshach, and Abed-Nego, *that* you do not serve my gods or worship the gold image which I have set up? 15 Now if you are ready at the time you hear the sound of the horn, flute, harp, lyre, *and* psaltery, in symphony with all kinds of music, and you fall down and worship the image which I have made, *good!* But if you do not worship, you shall be cast immediately into the midst of a burning fiery furnace. And who *is* the god who will deliver you from my hands?"

16 Shadrach, Meshach, and Abed-Nego answered and said to the king, "O Nebuchadnezzar, we have no need to answer you in this matter. 17 If that *is the case,* our God whom we serve is able to deliver us from the burning fiery furnace, and He will deliver *us* from your hand, O king. 18 But if not, let it be known to you, O king, that we do not serve your gods, nor will we worship the gold image which you have set up."

19 Then Nebuchadnezzar was full of fury, and the expression on his face changed toward Shadrach, Meshach, and Abed-Nego. He spoke and commanded that they heat the furnace seven times more than it was usually heated. 20 And he commanded certain mighty men of valor who *were* in his army to bind Shadrach, Meshach, and Abed-Nego, *and* cast *them* into the burning fiery furnace. 21 Then these men were bound in their coats, their trousers, their turbans, and their *other* garments, and were cast into the midst of the burning fiery furnace. 22 Therefore, because the king's command was urgent, and the furnace exceedingly hot, the flame of the fire killed those men who took up Shadrach, Meshach, and Abed-Nego. 23 And these three men, Shadrach, Meshach, and Abed-Nego, fell down bound into the midst of the burning fiery furnace.

24 Then King Nebuchadnezzar was astonished; and he rose in haste *and* spoke, saying to his counselors, "Did we not cast three men bound into the midst of the fire?"

They answered and said to the king, "True, O king."

25 "Look!" he answered, "I see four men loose, walking in the midst of the fire; and they are not hurt, and the form of the fourth is like the Son of God."

26 Then Nebuchadnezzar went near the mouth of the burning fiery furnace *and* spoke, saying, "Shadrach, Meshach, and Abed-Nego, servants of the Most High God, come out, and come *here.*" Then Shadrach, Meshach, and Abed-Nego came from the midst of the fire. 27 And the satraps, administrators, governors, and the king's counselors gathered together, and they saw these men on whose bodies the fire had no power; the hair of their head was not singed nor were their garments affected, and the smell of fire was not on them.

28 Nebuchadnezzar spoke, saying, "Blessed be the God of Shadrach, Meshach, and Abed-Nego, who sent His Angel and delivered His servants who trusted in Him, and they have frustrated the king's word,

and yielded their bodies, that they should not serve nor worship any god except their own God! 29 Therefore I make a decree that any people, nation, or language which speaks anything amiss against the God of Shadrach, Meshach, and Abed-Nego shall be cut in pieces, and their houses shall be made an ash heap; because there is no other God who can deliver like this."

30 Then the king promoted Shadrach, Meshach, and Abed-Nego in the province of Babylon.

4 NEBUCHADNEZZAR the king,

To all peoples, nations, and languages that dwell in all the earth:

Peace be multiplied to you.

2 I thought it good to declare the signs and wonders that the Most High God has worked for me.

Keep recounting the wonders God has done for you.   (PLACE HELP)

---

3 How great *are* His signs,
   And how mighty His wonders!
   His kingdom *is* an everlasting kingdom,
   And His dominion *is* from generation to generation.

4 I, Nebuchadnezzar, was at rest in my house, and flourishing in my palace. 5 I saw a dream which made me afraid, and the thoughts on my bed and the visions of my head troubled me. 6 Therefore I issued a decree to bring in all the wise *men* of Babylon before me, that they might make known to me the interpretation of the dream. 7 Then the magicians, the astrologers, the Chaldeans, and the soothsayers came in, and I told them the dream; but they did not make known to me its interpretation. 8 But at last Daniel came before me (his name *is* Belteshazzar, according to the name of my god; in him *is* the Spirit of the Holy God), and I told the dream before him, *saying:* 9 "Belteshazzar, chief of the magicians, because I know that the Spirit of the Holy God *is* in you, and no secret troubles you, explain to me the visions of my dream that I have seen, and its interpretation.

10 "These *were* the visions of my head
while on my bed:

I was looking, and behold,
A tree in the midst of the earth,
And its height was great.
11 The tree grew and became strong;
Its height reached to the heavens,
And it could be seen to the ends of
all the earth.
12 Its leaves *were* lovely,
Its fruit abundant,
And in it *was* food for all.
The beasts of the field found shade
under it,
The birds of the heavens dwelt in
its branches,
And all flesh was fed from it.

13 "I saw in the visions of my head
while on my bed, and there was a
watcher, a holy one, coming down
from heaven. 14 He cried aloud and
said thus:

'Chop down the tree and cut off its
branches,
Strip off its leaves and scatter its
fruit.
Let the beasts get out from
under it,
And the birds from its branches.
15 Nevertheless leave the stump and
roots in the earth,
Bound with a band of iron and
bronze,
In the tender grass of the field.
Let it be wet with the dew of heaven,
And *let* him graze with the beasts
On the grass of the earth.
16 Let his heart be changed from *that
of* a man,
Let him be given the heart of a beast,
And let seven times pass over him.

17 'This decision *is* by the decree of the
watchers,
And the sentence by the word of the
holy ones,
In order that the living may know
That the Most High rules in the
kingdom of men,
Gives it to whomever He will,
And sets over it the lowest of men.'

18 "This dream I, King
Nebuchadnezzar, have seen. Now
you, Belteshazzar, declare its
interpretation, since all the wise *men*
of my kingdom are not able to make
known to me the interpretation; but

you *are* able, for the Spirit of the
Holy God *is* in you."

19 Then Daniel, whose name was
Belteshazzar, was astonished for a
time, and his thoughts troubled him.
So the king spoke, and said,
"Belteshazzar, do not let the dream
or its interpretation trouble you."
Belteshazzar answered and said,
"My lord, *may* the dream concern
those who hate you, and its
interpretation concern your enemies!

20 "The tree that you saw, which grew
and became strong, whose height
reached to the heavens and which
could be seen by all the earth, 21 whose
leaves *were* lovely and its fruit
abundant, in which *was* food for all,
under which the beasts of the field
dwelt, and in whose branches the
birds of the heaven had their home—
22 it *is* you, O king, who have grown
and become strong; for your
greatness has grown and reaches to
the heavens, and your dominion to
the end of the earth.

23 "And inasmuch as the king saw a
watcher, a holy one, coming down
from heaven and saying, 'Chop down
the tree and destroy it, but leave its
stump and roots in the earth, *bound*
with a band of iron and bronze in
the tender grass of the field; let it
be wet with the dew of heaven, and
let him graze with the beasts of the
field, till seven times pass over him';
24 this is the interpretation, O king,
and this is the decree of the Most
High, which has come upon my lord
the king: 25 They shall drive you from
men, your dwelling shall be with the
beasts of the field, and they shall make
you eat grass like oxen. They shall
wet you with the dew of heaven, and
seven times shall pass over you, till
you know that the Most High rules
in the kingdom of men, and gives
it to whomever He chooses.

26 "And inasmuch as they gave the
command to leave the stump *and*
roots of the tree, your kingdom shall
be assured to you, after you come
to know that Heaven rules.
27 Therefore, O king, let my advice
be acceptable to you; break off your
sins by *being* righteous, and your
iniquities by showing mercy to *the*

poor. Perhaps there may be a lengthening of your prosperity."

28 All *this* came upon King Nebuchadnezzar. 29 At the end of the twelve months he was walking about the royal palace of Babylon. 30 The king spoke, saying, "Is not this great Babylon, that I have built for a royal dwelling by my mighty power and for the honor of my majesty?"

31 While the word *was still* in the king's mouth, a voice fell from heaven: "King Nebuchadnezzar, to you it is spoken: the kingdom has departed from you! 32 And they shall drive you from men, and your dwelling *shall be* with the beasts of the field. They shall make you eat grass like oxen; and seven times shall pass over you, until you know that the Most High rules in the kingdom of men, and gives it to whomever He chooses."

33 That very hour the word was fulfilled concerning Nebuchadnezzar; he was driven from men and ate grass like oxen; his body was wet with the dew of heaven till his hair had grown like eagles' *feathers* and his nails like birds' *claws.*

34 And at the end of the time I, Nebuchadnezzar, lifted my eyes to heaven, and my understanding returned to me; and I blessed the Most High and praised and honored Him who lives forever:

For His dominion *is* an everlasting dominion,
And His kingdom *is* from generation to generation.
35 All the inhabitants of the earth *are* reputed as nothing;
He does according to His will in the army of heaven
And *among* the inhabitants of the earth.
No one can restrain His hand
Or say to Him, "What have You done?"

36 At the same time my reason returned to me, and for the glory of my kingdom, my honor and splendor returned to me. My counselors and nobles resorted to me, I was restored to my kingdom, and excellent majesty was added to me. 37 Now I,

Nebuchadnezzar, praise and extol and honor the King of heaven, all of whose works *are* truth, and His ways justice. And those who walk in pride He is able to put down.

PSALM 136:1–9

1 OH, give thanks to the LORD, for *He is* good!
For His mercy *endures* forever.
2 Oh, give thanks to the God of gods!
For His mercy *endures* forever.
3 Oh, give thanks to the Lord of lords!
For His mercy *endures* forever:

4 To Him who alone does great wonders,
For His mercy *endures* forever;
5 To Him who by wisdom made the heavens,
For His mercy *endures* forever;
6 To Him who laid out the earth above the waters,
For His mercy *endures* forever;
7 To Him who made great lights,
For His mercy *endures* forever—
8 The sun to rule by day,
For His mercy *endures* forever;
9 The moon and stars to rule by night,
For His mercy *endures* forever.

PROVERBS 29:11

11 A fool vents all his feelings,
But a wise *man* holds them back.

2 PETER 1:1–21

SIMON Peter, a bondservant and apostle of Jesus Christ,

To those who have obtained like precious faith with us by the righteousness of our God and Savior Jesus Christ:

2 Grace and peace be multiplied to you in the knowledge of God and of Jesus our Lord, 3 as His divine power has given to us all things that *pertain* to life and godliness, through the knowledge of Him who called us by glory and virtue, 4 by which have been given to us exceedingly great and precious promises, that through these you may be partakers of the divine nature, having escaped the corruption *that is* in the world through lust.

5 But also for this very reason, giving all diligence, add to your faith virtue, to

virtue knowledge, 6 to knowledge self-control, to self-control perseverance, to perseverance godliness, 7 to godliness brotherly kindness, and to brotherly kindness love. 8 For if these things are yours and abound, *you will be* neither barren nor unfruitful in the knowledge of our Lord Jesus Christ. 9 For he who lacks these things is shortsighted, even to blindness, and has forgotten that he was cleansed from his old sins.

10 Therefore, brethren, be even more diligent to make your call and election sure, for if you do these things you will never stumble; 11 for so an entrance will be supplied to you abundantly into the everlasting kingdom of our Lord and Savior Jesus Christ.

12 For this reason I will not be negligent to remind you always of these things, though you know and are established in the present truth. 13 Yes, I think it is right, as long as I am in this tent, to stir you up by reminding *you,* 14 knowing that shortly I *must* put off my tent, just as our Lord Jesus Christ showed me. 15 Moreover I will be careful to ensure that you always have a reminder of these things after my decease.

16 For we did not follow cunningly devised fables when we made known to you the power and coming of our Lord Jesus Christ, but were eyewitnesses of His majesty. 17 For He received from God the Father honor and glory when such a voice came to Him from the Excellent Glory: "This is My beloved Son, in whom I am well pleased." 18 And we heard this voice which came from heaven when we were with Him on the holy mountain.

19 And so we have the prophetic word confirmed, which you do well to heed as a light that shines in a dark place, until the day dawns and the morning star rises in your hearts; 20 knowing this first, that no prophecy of Scripture is of any private interpretation, 21 for prophecy never came by the will of man, but holy men of God spoke *as they were* moved by the Holy Spirit.

◄◄◄◄

*Reading 335—*Obedience and Moral Crisis
Daniel 6:10

Moral problems are only solved by obedience. We cannot see what we see until we see it. Intellectually things can be worked out, but morally the solution is only reached by obedience. One step in obedience is worth years of study, and will take us into the center of God's will for us.

(*Shad. Agony*)

No one can tell us where the shadow of the Almighty is, we have to find it out for ourselves. When by obedience we have discovered where it is, we must abide there—"no evil shall befall you, nor shall any plague come near your dwelling." That is the life that is more than conqueror because the joy of the Lord has become its strength, and that soul is on the way to entering ultimately into the joy of the Lord. (*Glory*)

If for one whole day, quietly and determinedly, we were to give ourselves up to the ownership of Jesus and to obeying His orders, we should be amazed at its close to realize all He had packed into that one day. (*Send I You*)

DANIEL 5:1—6:28

BELSHAZZAR the king made a great feast for a thousand of his lords, and drank wine in the presence of the thousand. 2 While he tasted the wine, Belshazzar gave the command to bring the gold and silver vessels which his father Nebuchadnezzar had taken from the temple which *had been* in Jerusa-lem, that the king and his lords, his wives, and his concubines might drink from them. 3 Then they brought the gold vessels that had been taken from the temple of the house of God which *had been* in Jerusalem; and the king and his lords, his wives, and his concubines drank from them. 4 They drank wine, and praised the gods of gold and silver, bronze and iron, wood and stone.

5 In the same hour the fingers of a man's hand appeared and wrote opposite the lampstand on the plaster of the wall of the king's palace; and the king saw the part of the hand that wrote. 6 Then the king's countenance changed, and his thoughts troubled him, so that the joints of his hips were loosened and his knees knocked against each other. 7 The king cried aloud to bring in the astrologers, the Chaldeans, and the soothsayers. The king spoke, saying to the wise *men* of Babylon, "Whoever reads this writing, and tells me its interpretation, shall be clothed with purple and *have* a chain of gold around his neck; and he shall be the third ruler in the kingdom." 8 Now all the king's wise *men* came, but they could not read the writing, or make known to the king its interpretation. 9 Then King Belshazzar was greatly troubled, his countenance was changed, and his lords were astonished.

10 The queen, because of the words of the king and his lords, came to the banquet hall. The queen spoke, saying, "O king, live forever! Do not let your thoughts trouble you, nor let your countenance change. 11 There is a man in your kingdom in whom *is* the Spirit of the Holy God. And in the days of your father, light and understanding and wisdom, like the wisdom of the gods, were found in him; and King Nebuchadnezzar your father—your father the king—made him chief of the magicians, astrologers, Chaldeans, *and* soothsayers. 12 Inasmuch as an excellent spirit, knowledge, understanding, interpreting dreams, solving riddles, and explaining enigmas were found in this Daniel, whom the king named Belteshazzar, now let Daniel be called, and he will give the interpretation."

13 Then Daniel was brought in before the king. The king spoke, and said to Daniel, "*Are* you that Daniel who is one of the captives from Judah, whom my father the king brought from Judah? 14 I have heard of you, that the Spirit of God *is* in you, and *that* light and understanding and excellent wisdom are found in you. 15 Now the wise *men*, the astrologers, have been brought in before me, that they should read this writing and make known to me its interpretation, but they could not give the interpretation of the thing. 16 And I have heard of you, that you can give interpretations and explain enigmas. Now if you can read the writing and make known to me its interpretation, you shall be clothed with purple and *have* a chain of gold around your neck, and shall be the third ruler in the kingdom."

17 Then Daniel answered, and said before the king, "Let your gifts be for yourself, and give your rewards to another; yet I will read the writing to the king, and make known to him the interpretation. 18 O king, the Most High God gave Nebuchadnezzar your father a kingdom and majesty, glory and honor. 19 And because of the majesty that He gave him, all peoples, nations, and languages trembled and feared before him. Whomever he wished, he executed; whomever he wished, he kept alive; whomever he wished, he set up; and whomever he wished, he put down. 20 But when his heart was lifted up, and his spirit was hardened in pride, he was deposed from his kingly throne, and they took his glory from him. 21 Then he was driven from the sons of men, his heart was made like the beasts, and his dwelling *was* with the wild donkeys. They fed him with grass like oxen, and his body was wet with the dew of heaven, till he knew that the Most High God rules in the kingdom of men, and appoints over it whomever He chooses.

22 "But you his son, Belshazzar, have not humbled your heart, although you knew all this. 23 And you have lifted yourself up against the Lord of heaven. They have brought the vessels of His house before you, and you and your lords, your wives and your concubines, have drunk wine from them. And you have praised the gods of silver and gold, bronze and iron, wood and stone, which do not see or hear or know; and the God who *holds* your breath in His hand and owns all your ways, you have not glorified. 24 Then the fingers of the hand were sent from Him, and this writing was written.

25 "And this is the inscription that was written:

MENE, MENE, TEKEL, UPHARSIN.

26 This *is* the interpretation of *each* word. MENE: God has numbered your kingdom, and finished it; 27 TEKEL: You have been weighed in the balances, and found wanting; 28 PERES: Your kingdom has been divided, and given to the Medes and Persians." 29 Then Belshazzar gave the command, and they clothed Daniel with purple and *put* a chain of gold around his neck, and made a proclamation concerning him that he should be the third ruler in the kingdom.

30 That very night Belshazzar, king of the Chaldeans, was slain. 31 And Darius the Mede received the kingdom, *being* about sixty-two years old.

6 IT pleased Darius to set over the kingdom one hundred and twenty satraps, to be over the whole kingdom; 2 and over these, three governors, of whom Daniel *was* one, that the satraps might give account to them, so that the king would suffer no loss. 3 Then this Daniel distinguished himself above the governors and satraps, because an excellent spirit *was* in him; and the king gave thought to setting him over the whole realm. 4 So the governors and satraps sought to find *some* charge against Daniel concerning the kingdom; but they could find no charge or fault, because he *was* faithful; nor was there any error or fault found in him. 5 Then these men said, "We shall not find any charge against this Daniel unless we find *it* against him concerning the law of his God."

6 So these governors and satraps thronged before the king, and said thus to him: "King Darius, live forever! 7 All the governors of the kingdom, the administrators and satraps, the counselors and advisors, have consulted together to establish a royal statute and to make a firm decree, that whoever petitions any god or man for thirty days, except you, O king, shall be cast into the den of lions. 8 Now, O king, establish the decree and sign the writing, so that it cannot be changed, according to the law of the Medes and Persians, which does not alter." 9 Therefore King Darius signed the written decree.

10 Now when Daniel knew that the writing was signed, he went home. And in his upper room, with his windows open toward Jerusalem, he knelt down on his knees three times that day, and prayed and gave thanks before his God, as was his custom since early days.

Whichever way God engineers circumstances, the duty is to pray. (UTMOST)

---

11 Then these men assembled and found Daniel praying and making supplication before his God. 12 And they went before the king, and spoke concerning the king's decree: "Have you not signed a decree that every man who petitions any god or man within thirty days, except you, O king, shall be cast into the den of lions?"

The king answered and said, "The thing *is* true, according to the law of the Medes and Persians, which does not alter."

13 So they answered and said before the king, "That Daniel, who is one of the captives from Judah, does not show due regard for you, O king, or for the decree that you have signed, but makes his petition three times a day."

14 And the king, when he heard *these* words, was greatly displeased with himself, and set *his* heart on Daniel to deliver him; and he labored till the going down of the sun to deliver him. 15 Then these men approached the king, and said to the king, "Know, O king, that *it is* the law of the Medes and Persians that no decree or statute which the king establishes may be changed."

16 So the king gave the command, and they brought Daniel and cast *him* into the den of lions. *But* the king spoke, saying to Daniel, "Your God, whom you serve continually, He will deliver you." 17 Then a stone was brought and laid on the mouth of the den, and the king sealed it with his own signet ring and with the signets of his lords, that the purpose concerning Daniel might not be changed.

18 Now the king went to his palace and spent the night fasting; and no musicians were brought before him. Also his sleep went from him. 19 Then the king arose very early in the morning and went in haste to the den of lions. 20 And when he came to the den, he cried out with a lamenting voice to Daniel. The king spoke, saying to Daniel, "Daniel, servant of the living God, has your God, whom you serve continually, been able to deliver you from the lions?"

21 Then Daniel said to the king, "O king, live forever! 22 My God sent His angel and shut the lions' mouths, so that they have not hurt me, because I was found innocent before Him; and also, O king, I have done no wrong before you."

23 Now the king was exceedingly glad for him, and commanded that they should take Daniel up out of the den. So Daniel was taken up out of the den, and no injury whatever was found on him, because he believed in his God.

24 And the king gave the command, and they brought those men who had accused Daniel, and they cast *them* into the den of lions—them, their children, and their wives; and the lions overpowered them, and broke all their bones in pieces before they ever came to the bottom of the den.

25 Then King Darius wrote:

To all peoples, nations, and languages that dwell in all the earth:

Peace be multiplied to you.

26 I make a decree that in every dominion of my kingdom *men must*

tremble and fear before the God of Daniel.

For He *is* the living God,
And steadfast forever;
His kingdom *is the one* which shall not be destroyed,
And His dominion *shall endure* to the end.
27 He delivers and rescues,
And He works signs and wonders
In heaven and on earth,
Who has delivered Daniel from the power of the lions.

28 So this Daniel prospered in the reign of Darius and in the reign of Cyrus the Persian.

PSALM 136:10–26

10 TO Him who struck Egypt in their firstborn,
For His mercy *endures* forever;
11 And brought out Israel from among them,
For His mercy *endures* forever;
12 With a strong hand, and with an outstretched arm,
For His mercy *endures* forever;
13 To Him who divided the Red Sea in two,
For His mercy *endures* forever;
14 And made Israel pass through the midst of it,
For His mercy *endures* forever;
15 But overthrew Pharaoh and his army in the Red Sea,
For His mercy *endures* forever;
16 To Him who led His people through the wilderness,
For His mercy *endures* forever;
17 To Him who struck down great kings,
For His mercy *endures* forever;
18 And slew famous kings,
For His mercy *endures* forever—
19 Sihon king of the Amorites,
For His mercy *endures* forever;
20 And Og king of Bashan,
For His mercy *endures* forever—
21 And gave their land as a heritage,
For His mercy *endures* forever;
22 A heritage to Israel His servant,
For His mercy *endures* forever.

23 Who remembered us in our lowly state,
For His mercy *endures* forever;
24 And rescued us from our enemies,
For His mercy *endures* forever;
25 Who gives food to all flesh,
For His mercy *endures* forever.

26 Oh, give thanks to the God of heaven!
For His mercy *endures* forever.

PROVERBS 29:12, 13

12 IF a ruler pays attention to lies,
All his servants *become* wicked.

13 The poor *man* and the oppressor have this in common:
The LORD gives light to the eyes of both.

2 PETER 2:1–22

BUT there were also false prophets among the people, even as there will be false teachers among you, who will secretly bring in destructive heresies, even denying the Lord who bought them, *and* bring on themselves swift destruction. 2 And many will follow their destructive ways, because of whom the way of truth will be blasphemed. 3 By covetousness they will exploit you with deceptive words; for a long time their judgment has not been idle, and their destruction does not slumber.

4 For if God did not spare the angels who sinned, but cast *them* down to hell and delivered *them* into chains of darkness, to be reserved for judgment; 5 and did not spare the ancient world, but saved Noah, *one of* eight *people,* a preacher of righteousness, bringing in the flood on the world of the ungodly; 6 and turning the cities of Sodom and Gomorrah into ashes, condemned *them* to destruction, making *them* an example to those who afterward would live ungodly; 7 and delivered righteous Lot, *who was* oppressed by the filthy conduct of the wicked 8 (for that righteous man, dwelling among them, tormented *his* righteous soul from day to day by seeing and hearing *their* lawless deeds)—9 *then* the Lord knows how to deliver the godly out of temptations and to reserve the unjust under punishment for the day of judgment, 10 and especially those who walk according to the flesh in the lust of uncleanness and despise authority. *They are* presumptuous, self-willed. They are not afraid to speak evil of dignitaries, 11 whereas angels, who are greater in power and might, do not bring a reviling accusation against them before the Lord.

12 But these, like natural brute beasts made to be caught and destroyed, speak evil of the things they do not understand, and will utterly perish in their own corrup-

tion, 13 *and* will receive the wages of un-righteousness, *as* those who count it pleasure to carouse in the daytime. *They are* spots and blemishes, carousing in their own deceptions while they feast with you, 14 having eyes full of adultery and that cannot cease from sin, enticing unstable souls. *They have* a heart trained in covetous practices, *and are* accursed children. 15 They have forsaken the right way and gone astray, following the way of Balaam the *son* of Beor, who loved the wages of unrighteousness; 16 but he was rebuked for his iniquity: a dumb donkey speaking with a man's voice restrained the madness of the prophet.

17 These are wells without water, clouds carried by a tempest, for whom is reserved the blackness of darkness forever.

18 For when they speak great swelling *words* of emptiness, they allure through the lusts of the flesh, through lewdness, the ones who have actually escaped from those who live in error. 19 While they promise

them liberty, they themselves are slaves of corruption; for by whom a person is overcome, by him also he is brought into bondage. 20 For if, after they have escaped the pollutions of the world through the knowledge of the Lord and Savior Jesus Christ, they are again entangled in them and overcome, the latter end is worse for them than the beginning. 21 For it would have been

---

*J*esus Christ is Savior *and* Lord *in experience, and* Lord *and* Savior *in discernment.*   (BRILL. HERITAGE)

---

better for them not to have known the way of righteousness, than having known *it,* to turn from the holy commandment delivered to them. 22 But it has happened to them according to the true proverb: "A dog returns to his own vomit," and, "a sow, having washed, to her wallowing in the mire."

Reading 336—God Can Cleanse Us
2 Peter 3:14

I s it possible to be blameless in our spiritual relationship to Almighty God, to Jesus Christ and to the Holy Spirit? It is not only possible, but God's word tells us that that is what God does: "If we walk in the light, as He is in the light, . . . the blood of Jesus Christ His Son cleanses us from all sin" (1 John 1:7). That is cleansing not from conscious sin only but from infinitely more; it is cleansing to the depths of crystalline purity so that God Himself can see nothing impure. That is the work of the Lord Jesus Christ; to make His work anything less would be blasphemous. If God almighty cannot do that in your life and mine, we have followed "cunningly devised fables." Unless Jesus Christ can remake Himself in us, what is the meaning of those thirty years in Nazareth, those three years of His public life? What is the meaning of the cross of Jesus Christ, of His resurrection and ascension, if He cannot cleanse us from all sin? But, bless God, He can! The point is, have we let Him do it? Beware of praising Jesus Christ while all the time you cunningly refuse to let the Spirit of God work His salvation efficaciously in your life.

(*LOVE OF GOD*)

DANIEL 7:1—8:27

IN the first year of Belshazzar king of Babylon, Daniel had a dream and visions of his head *while* on his bed. Then he wrote down the dream, telling the main facts.

2 Daniel spoke, saying, "I saw in my vi-

sion by night, and behold, the four winds of heaven were stirring up the Great Sea. 3 And four great beasts came up from the sea, each different from the other. 4 The first *was* like a lion, and had eagle's wings. I watched till its wings were plucked off; and it was lifted up from the earth and made to stand on two feet like a man, and a man's heart was given to it.

5 "And suddenly another beast, a second, like a bear. It was raised up on one side, and *had* three ribs in its mouth between its teeth. And they said thus to it: 'Arise, devour much flesh!'

6 "After this I looked, and there was another, like a leopard, which had on its back four wings of a bird. The beast also had four heads, and dominion was given to it.

7 "After this I saw in the night visions, and behold, a fourth beast, dreadful and terrible, exceedingly strong. It had huge iron teeth; it was devouring, breaking in pieces, and trampling the residue with its feet. It *was* different from all the beasts that *were* before it, and it had ten horns. 8 I was considering the horns, and there was another horn, a little one, coming up among them, before whom three of the first horns were plucked out by the roots. And there, in this horn, *were* eyes like the eyes of a man, and a mouth speaking pompous words.

9   "I watched till thrones were put in
        place,
      And the Ancient of Days was seated;
      His garment *was* white as snow,
      And the hair of His head *was* like
        pure wool.
      His throne *was* a fiery flame,
      Its wheels a burning fire;
10   A fiery stream issued
      And came forth from before Him.
      A thousand thousands ministered to
        Him;
      Ten thousand times ten thousand
        stood before Him.
      The court was seated,
      And the books were opened.

11 "I watched then because of the sound of the pompous words which the horn was speaking; I watched till the beast was slain, and its body destroyed and given to the burning flame. 12 As for the rest of the beasts, they had their dominion taken away, yet their lives were prolonged for a season and a time.

13   "I was watching in the night visions,
      And behold, *One* like the Son of Man,
      Coming with the clouds of heaven!
      He came to the Ancient of Days,
      And they brought Him near before
        Him.
14   Then to Him was given dominion
        and glory and a kingdom,

      That all peoples, nations, and
        languages should serve Him.
      His dominion *is* an everlasting
        dominion,
      Which shall not pass away,
      And His kingdom *the one*
      Which shall not be destroyed.

15 "I, Daniel, was grieved in my spirit within *my* body, and the visions of my head troubled me. 16 I came near to one of those who stood by, and asked him the truth of all this. So he told me and made known to me the interpretation of these things: 17 'Those great beasts, which are four, *are* four kings *which* arise out of the earth. 18 But the saints of the Most High shall receive the kingdom, and possess the kingdom forever, even forever and ever.'

19 "Then I wished to know the truth about the fourth beast, which was different from all the others, exceedingly dreadful, *with* its teeth of iron and its nails of bronze, *which* devoured, broke in pieces, and trampled the residue with its feet; 20 and the ten horns that *were* on its head, and the other *horn* which came up, before which three fell, namely, that horn which had eyes and a mouth which spoke pompous words, whose appearance *was* greater than his fellows.

21 "I was watching; and the same horn was making war against the saints, and prevailing against them, 22 until the Ancient of Days came, and a judgment was made *in favor* of the saints of the Most High, and the time came for the saints to possess the kingdom.

23 "Thus he said:

      'The fourth beast shall be
      A fourth kingdom on earth,
      Which shall be different from all *other*
        kingdoms,
      And shall devour the whole earth,
      Trample it and break it in pieces.
24   The ten horns *are* ten kings
      Who shall arise from this kingdom.
      And another shall rise after them;
      He shall be different from the first
        ones,
      And shall subdue three kings.
25   He shall speak *pompous* words
        against the Most High,
      Shall persecute the saints of the
        Most High,
      And shall intend to change times
        and law.
      Then *the saints* shall be given into
        his hand
      For a time and times and half a time.

Holiness will bring persecution from those who are not holy. (PHIL. SIN)

26 'But the court shall be seated,
    And they shall take away his
        dominion,
    To consume and destroy *it* forever.
27 Then the kingdom and dominion,
    And the greatness of the kingdoms
        under the whole heaven,
    Shall be given to the people, the saints
        of the Most High.
    His kingdom *is* an everlasting
        kingdom,
    And all dominions shall serve and
        obey Him.'

28 "This *is* the end of the account. As for me, Daniel, my thoughts greatly troubled me, and my countenance changed; but I kept the matter in my heart."

8 IN the third year of the reign of King Belshazzar a vision appeared *to* me—to me, Daniel—after the one that appeared to me the first time. 2 I saw in the vision, and it so happened while I was looking, that I *was* in Shushan, the citadel, which *is* in the province of Elam; and I saw in the vision that I was by the River Ulai. 3 Then I lifted my eyes and saw, and there, standing beside the river, was a ram which had two horns, and the two horns *were* high; but one *was* higher than the other, and the higher *one* came up last. 4 I saw the ram pushing westward, northward, and southward, so that no animal could withstand him; nor *was there any* that could deliver from his hand, but he did according to his will and became great.

5 And as I was considering, suddenly a male goat came from the west, across the surface of the whole earth, without touching the ground; and the goat *had* a notable horn between his eyes. 6 Then he came to the ram that had two horns, which I had seen standing beside the river, and ran at him with furious power. 7 And I saw him confronting the ram; he was moved with rage against him, attacked the ram, and broke his two horns. There was no power in the ram to withstand him, but he cast him down to the ground and trampled him; and there was no one that could deliver the ram from his hand.

8 Therefore the male goat grew very great; but when he became strong, the large horn was broken, and in place of it four notable ones came up toward the four winds

of heaven. 9 And out of one of them came a little horn which grew exceedingly great toward the south, toward the east, and toward the Glorious *Land.* 10 And it grew up to the host of heaven; and it cast down *some* of the host and *some* of the stars to the ground, and trampled them. 11 He even exalted *himself* as high as the Prince of the host; and by him the daily *sacrifices* were taken away, and the place of His sanctuary was cast down. 12 Because of transgression, an army was given over *to the horn* to oppose the daily *sacrifices;* and he cast truth down to the ground. He did *all this* and prospered.

13 Then I heard a holy one speaking; and *another* holy one said to that certain *one* who was speaking, "How long *will* the vision *be, concerning* the daily *sacrifices* and the transgression of desolation, the giving of both the sanctuary and the host to be trampled underfoot?"

14 And he said to me, "For two thousand three hundred days; then the sanctuary shall be cleansed."

15 Then it happened, when I, Daniel, had seen the vision and was seeking the meaning, that suddenly there stood before me one having the appearance of a man. 16 And I heard a man's voice between *the banks of* the Ulai, who called, and said, "Gabriel, make this *man* understand the vision." 17 So he came near where I stood, and when he came I was afraid and fell on my face; but he said to me, "Understand, son of man, that the vision *refers* to the time of the end."

18 Now, as he was speaking with me, I was in a deep sleep with my face to the ground; but he touched me, and stood me upright. 19 And he said, "Look, I am making known to you what shall happen in the latter time of the indignation; for at the appointed time the end *shall be*. 20 The ram which you saw, having the two horns—*they are* the kings of Media and Persia. 21 And the male goat *is* the kingdom of Greece. The large horn that *is* between its eyes *is* the first king. 22 As for the broken *horn* and the four that stood up in its place, four kingdoms shall arise out of that nation, but not with its power.

23 "And in the latter time of their
        kingdom,
    When the transgressors have reached
        their fullness,
    A king shall arise,
    Having fierce features,
    Who understands sinister schemes.
24 His power shall be mighty, but not
    by his own power;

He shall destroy fearfully,
And shall prosper and thrive;
He shall destroy the mighty, and *also*
    the holy people.

25 "Through his cunning
    He shall cause deceit to prosper under
        his rule;
    And he shall exalt *himself* in his heart.
    He shall destroy many in *their*
        prosperity.
    He shall even rise against the Prince
        of princes;
    But he shall be broken without
        human means.

26 "And the vision of the evenings and
        mornings
    Which was told is true;
    Therefore seal up the vision,
    For *it refers* to many days *in the
    future*."

27 And I, Daniel, fainted and was sick
for days; afterward I arose and went about
the king's business. I was astonished by the
vision, but no one understood it.

PSALM 137:1–6

1   BY the rivers of Babylon,
    There we sat down, yea, we wept
    When we remembered Zion.
2   We hung our harps
    Upon the willows in the midst of it.
3   For there those who carried us away
        captive asked of us a song,
    And those who plundered us *requested*
        mirth,
    Saying, "Sing us *one* of the songs of
    Zion!"

4   How shall we sing the LORD's song
    In a foreign land?
5   If I forget you, O Jerusalem,
    Let my right hand forget *its skill!*
6   If I do not remember you,
    Let my tongue cling to the roof of my
        mouth—
    If I do not exalt Jerusalem
    Above my chief joy.

PROVERBS 29:14

14 THE king who judges the poor with
        truth,
    His throne will be established forever.

2 PETER 3:1–18

BELOVED, I now write to you this second
epistle (in *both of* which I stir up your pure
minds by way of reminder), 2 that you may
be mindful of the words which were spoken
before by the holy prophets, and of the
commandment of us, the apostles of the
Lord and Savior, 3 knowing this first: that
scoffers will come in the last days, walking
according to their own lusts, 4 and saying,
"Where is the promise of His coming? For
since the fathers fell asleep, all things continue as *they were* from the beginning of
creation." 5 For this they willfully forget:
that by the word of God the heavens were
of old, and the earth standing out of water
and in the water, 6 by which the world *that*
then existed perished, being flooded with
water. 7 But the heavens and the earth *which*
are now preserved by the same word, are
reserved for fire until the day of judgment
and perdition of ungodly men.

8 But, beloved, do not forget this one
thing, that with the Lord one day *is* as a
thousand years, and a thousand years as
one day. 9 The Lord is not slack concerning
His promise, as some count slackness, but
is longsuffering toward us, not willing that
any should perish but that all should come
to repentance.

10 But the day of the Lord will come as
a thief in the night, in which the heavens
will pass away with a great noise, and the
elements will melt with fervent heat; both
the earth and the works that are in it will
be burned up. 11 Therefore, since all these
things will be dissolved, what manner *of
persons* ought you to be in holy conduct
and godliness, 12 looking for and hastening
the coming of the day of God, because of
which the heavens will be dissolved, being
on fire, and the elements will melt with
fervent heat? 13 Nevertheless we, according
to His promise, look for new heavens and
a new earth in which righteousness dwells.

14 Therefore, beloved, looking forward
to these things, be diligent to be found
by Him in peace, without spot and blameless; 15 and consider *that* the longsuffering

*H*e came to put us right with
God that His own peace might
reign.   (SERVANT AS LORD)

of our Lord *is* salvation—as also our beloved
brother Paul, according to the wisdom

given to him, has written to you, 16 as also in all his epistles, speaking in them of these things, in which are some things hard to understand, which untaught and unstable *people* twist to their own destruction, as *they do* also the rest of the Scriptures.

17 You therefore, beloved, since you know *this* beforehand, beware lest you also fall from your own steadfastness, being led away with the error of the wicked; 18 but grow in the grace and knowledge of our Lord and Savior Jesus Christ.

To Him *be* the glory both now and forever. Amen.

◆◆◆◆

Reading 337—The Blood of Christ
1 John 1:7

When we speak of the blood of Jesus Christ cleansing us from all sin, we do not mean the physical blood shed on Calvary, but the whole life of the Son of God which was poured out to redeem the world. All the perfections of the essential nature of God were in that blood, and all the holiest attainments of mankind as well. It was the life of the perfection of deity that was poured out on Calvary, "the church of God which He purchased with His own blood" (Acts 20:28). We are apt to look upon the blood of Jesus Christ as a magic-working power instead of its being the very life of the Son of God poured forth for men. The whole meaning of our being identified with the death of Jesus is that His blood may flow through our mortal bodies. Identification with the death of Jesus Christ means identification with Him to the death of everything that never was in Him, and it is the blood of Christ, in the sense of the whole personal life of the Son of God, that comes into us and "cleanses us from all sin." (*PLACE HELP*)

DANIEL 9:1—10:21

IN the first year of Darius the son of Ahasuerus, of the lineage of the Medes, who was made king over the realm of the Chaldeans— 2 in the first year of his reign I, Daniel, understood by the books the number of the years *specified* by the word of the LORD through Jeremiah the prophet, that He would accomplish seventy years in the desolations of Jerusalem.

3 Then I set my face toward the Lord God to make request by prayer and supplications, with fasting, sackcloth, and ashes. 4 And I prayed to the LORD my God, and made confession, and said, "O Lord, great and awesome God, who keeps His covenant and mercy with those who love Him, and with those who keep His commandments,

In the Old Testament the prophet bases his prayer on the character of God. (ASK)

5 we have sinned and committed iniquity, we have done wickedly and rebelled, even by departing from Your precepts and Your judgments. 6 Neither have we heeded Your servants the prophets, who spoke in Your name to our kings and our princes, to our fathers and all the people of the land. 7 O Lord, righteousness *belongs* to You, but to us shame of face, as *it is* this day—to the men of Judah, to the inhabitants of Jerusalem and all Israel, those near and those far off in all the countries to which You have driven them, because of the unfaithfulness which they have committed against You.

8 "O Lord, to us *belongs* shame of face, to our kings, our princes, and our fathers, because we have sinned against You. 9 To the Lord our God *belong* mercy and forgiveness, though we have rebelled against Him. 10 We have not obeyed the voice of the LORD our God, to walk in His laws, which He set before us by His servants the prophets. 11 Yes, all Israel has transgressed Your law, and has departed so as not to obey Your voice; therefore

the curse and the oath written in the Law of Moses the servant of God have been poured out on us, because we have sinned against Him. 12 And He has confirmed His words, which He spoke against us and against our judges who judged us, by bringing upon us a great disaster; for under the whole heaven such has never been done as what has been done to Jerusalem.

13 "As *it is* written in the Law of Moses, all this disaster has come upon us; yet we have not made our prayer before the LORD our God, that we might turn from our iniquities and understand Your truth. 14 Therefore the LORD has kept the disaster in mind, and brought it upon us; for the LORD our God *is* righteous in all the works which He does, though we have not obeyed His voice. 15 And now, O Lord our God, who brought Your people out of the land of Egypt with a mighty hand, and made Yourself a name, as *it is* this day—we have sinned, we have done wickedly!

16 "O Lord, according to all Your righteousness, I pray, let Your anger and Your fury be turned away from Your city Jerusalem, Your holy mountain; because for our sins, and for the iniquities of our fathers, Jerusalem and Your people *are* a reproach to all *those* around us. 17 Now therefore, our God, hear the prayer of Your servant, and his supplications, and for the Lord's sake cause Your face to shine on Your sanctuary, which is desolate. 18 O my God, incline Your ear and hear; open Your eyes and see our desolations, and the city which is called by Your name; for we do not present our supplications before You because of our righteous deeds, but because of Your great mercies. 19 O Lord, hear! O Lord, forgive! O Lord, listen and act! Do not delay for Your own sake, my God, for Your city and Your people are called by Your name."

20 Now while I *was* speaking, praying, and confessing my sin and the sin of my people Israel, and presenting my supplication before the LORD my God for the holy mountain of my God, 21 yes, while I *was* speaking in prayer, the man Gabriel, whom I had seen in the vision at the beginning, being caused to fly swiftly, reached me about the time of the evening offering. 22 And he informed *me,* and talked with me, and said, "O Daniel, I have now come forth to give you skill to understand. 23 At the beginning of your supplications the command went out, and I have come to tell *you,* for you *are* greatly beloved; therefore consider the matter, and understand the vision:

24 "Seventy weeks are determined
   For your people and for your holy
      city,
   To finish the transgression,
   To make an end of sins,
   To make reconciliation for iniquity,
   To bring in everlasting righteousness,
   To seal up vision and prophecy,
   And to anoint the Most Holy.

25 "Know therefore and understand,
   That from the going forth of the
      command
   To restore and build Jerusalem
   Until Messiah the Prince,
   There shall be seven weeks and
      sixty-two weeks;
   The street shall be built again, and
      the wall,
   Even in troublesome times.

26 "And after the sixty-two weeks
   Messiah shall be cut off, but not for
      Himself;
   And the people of the prince who
      is to come
   Shall destroy the city and the
      sanctuary.
   The end of it *shall be* with a flood,
   And till the end of the war desolations
      are determined.
27 Then he shall confirm a covenant with
      many for one week;
   But in the middle of the week
   He shall bring an end to sacrifice and
      offering.
   And on the wing of abominations
      shall be one who makes desolate,
   Even until the consummation, which
      is determined,
   Is poured out on the desolate."

10 IN the third year of Cyrus king of Persia a message was revealed to Daniel, whose name was called Belteshazzar. The message *was* true, but the appointed time *was* long; and he understood the message, and had understanding of the vision. 2 In those days I, Daniel, was mourning three full weeks. 3 I ate no pleasant food, no meat or wine came into my mouth, nor did I anoint myself at all, till three whole weeks were fulfilled.

4 Now on the twenty-fourth day of the first month, as I was by the side of the great river, that *is,* the Tigris, 5 I lifted my eyes and looked, and behold, a certain man clothed in linen, whose waist *was* girded with gold of Uphaz! 6 His body *was* like beryl, his face like the appearance of lightning, his eyes like torches of fire, his arms

and feet like burnished bronze in color, and the sound of his words like the voice of a multitude.

7 And I, Daniel, alone saw the vision, for the men who were with me did not see the vision; but a great terror fell upon them, so that they fled to hide themselves. 8 Therefore I was left alone when I saw this great vision, and no strength remained in me; for my vigor was turned to frailty in me, and I retained no strength. 9 Yet I heard the sound of his words; and while I heard the sound of his words I was in a deep sleep on my face, with my face to the ground.

10 Suddenly, a hand touched me, which made me tremble on my knees and *on* the palms of my hands. 11 And he said to me, "O Daniel, man greatly beloved, understand the words that I speak to you, and stand upright, for I have now been sent to you." While he was speaking this word to me, I stood trembling.

12 Then he said to me, "Do not fear, Daniel, for from the first day that you set your heart to understand, and to humble yourself before your God, your words were heard; and I have come because of your words. 13 But the prince of the kingdom of Persia withstood me twenty-one days; and behold, Michael, one of the chief princes, came to help me, for I had been left alone there with the kings of Persia. 14 Now I have come to make you understand what will happen to your people in the latter days, for the vision *refers* to *many* days yet *to come.*"

15 When he had spoken such words to me, I turned my face toward the ground and became speechless. 16 And suddenly, *one* having the likeness of the sons of men touched my lips; then I opened my mouth and spoke, saying to him who stood before me, "My lord, because of the vision my sorrows have overwhelmed me, and I have retained no strength. 17 For how can this servant of my lord talk with you, my lord? As for me, no strength remains in me now, nor is any breath left in me."

18 Then again, *the one* having the likeness of a man touched me and strengthened me. 19 And he said, "O man greatly beloved, fear not! Peace *be* to you; be strong, yes, be strong!"

So when he spoke to me I was strengthened, and said, "Let my lord speak, for you have strengthened me."

20 Then he said, "Do you know why I have come to you? And now I must return to fight with the prince of Persia; and when I have gone forth, indeed the prince of Greece will come. 21 But I will tell you what is noted in the Scripture of Truth. (No one upholds me against these, except Michael your prince.

PSALM 137:7–9

7 REMEMBER, O LORD, against the
    sons of Edom
    The day of Jerusalem,
    Who said, "Raze *it,* raze *it,*
    To its very foundation!"

8 O daughter of Babylon, who are to be
    destroyed,
    Happy the one who repays you as you
    have served us!

9 Happy the one who takes and dashes
    Your little ones against the rock!

PROVERBS 29:15

15 THE rod and rebuke give wisdom,
    But a child left *to himself* brings shame
    to his mother.

1 JOHN 1:1–10

THAT which was from the beginning, which we have heard, which we have seen with our eyes, which we have looked upon, and our hands have handled, concerning the Word of life— 2 the life was manifested, and we have seen, and bear witness, and declare to you that eternal life which was with the Father and was manifested to us— 3 that which we have seen and heard we declare to you, that you also may have fellowship with us; and truly our fellowship *is* with the Father and with His Son Jesus Christ. 4 And these things we write to you that your joy may be full.

5 This is the message which we have heard from Him and declare to you, that God is light and in Him is no darkness at all. 6 If we say that we have fellowship with Him, and walk in darkness, we lie and do not practice the truth. 7 But if we walk in the light as He is in the light, we have fellowship with one another, and the blood of Jesus Christ His Son cleanses us from all sin.

---

*G*od judges us through the marvelous Atonement of Jesus Christ.   (SERMON MT.)

8 If we say that we have no sin, we deceive ourselves, and the truth is not in us. 9 If we confess our sins, He is faithful and just to forgive us *our* sins and to cleanse us from all unrighteousness. 10 If we say that we have not sinned, we make Him a liar, and His word is not in us.

◆◆◆◆

Reading 338—The Missionary Message
1 John 2:2

The key to the missionary message is the propitiation of Christ Jesus. Take any phase of Christ's work—the healing phase, the saving and sanctifying phase; there is nothing limitless about those. "The Lamb of God who takes away the sin of the world!"—that is limitless. The missionary message is the limitless significance of Jesus Christ as the propitiation for our sins, and a missionary is one who is soaked in that revelation.

The key to the missionary message is the remissionary aspect of Christ's life, not His kindness and His goodness, and His revealing of the Fatherhood of God; the great limitless significance is that He is the propitiation for our sins. . . .

A missionary is one who is wedded to the charter of his Lord and Master, he has not to proclaim his own point of view, but to proclaim the Lamb of God. It is easier to belong to a coterie which tells what Jesus Christ has done for me, easier to become a devotee to divine healing, or to a special type of sanctification, or to the baptism of the Holy Ghost. Paul did not say, "Woe is me if I do not preach what Christ has done for me," but "Woe is me if I do not preach the gospel!" This is the gospel—"The Lamb of God who takes away the sin of the world!"   (*Utmost*)

DANIEL 11:1—12:13

"ALSO in the first year of Darius the Mede, I, *even* I, stood up to confirm and strengthen him.) 2 And now I will tell you the truth: Behold, three more kings will arise in Persia, and the fourth shall be far richer than *them* all; by his strength, through his riches, he shall stir up all against the realm of Greece. 3 Then a mighty king shall arise, who shall rule with great dominion, and do according to his will. 4 And when he has arisen, his kingdom shall be broken up and divided toward the four winds of heaven, but not among his posterity nor according to his dominion with which he ruled; for his kingdom shall be uprooted, even for others besides these.

5 "Also the king of the South shall become strong, as well as *one* of his princes; and he shall gain power over him and have dominion. His dominion *shall be* a great dominion. 6 And at the end of *some* years they shall join forces, for the daughter of the king of the South shall go to the king of the North to make an agreement; but she shall not retain the power of her authority, and neither he nor his authority shall stand; but she shall be given up, with those who brought her, and with him who begot her, and with him who strengthened her in *those* times. 7 But from a branch of her roots *one* shall arise in his place, who shall come with an army, enter the fortress of the king of the North, and deal with them and prevail. 8 And he shall also carry their gods captive to Egypt, with their princes *and* their precious articles of silver and gold; and he shall continue *more* years than the king of the North.

9 "Also *the king of the North* shall come to the kingdom of the king of the South, but shall return to his own land. 10 However his sons shall stir up strife, and assemble a multitude of great forces; and *one* shall certainly come and overwhelm and pass

through; then he shall return to his fortress and stir up strife.

11 "And the king of the South shall be moved with rage, and go out and fight with him, with the king of the North, who shall muster a great multitude; but the multitude shall be given into the hand of his *enemy*. 12 When he has taken away the multitude, his heart will be lifted up; and he will cast down tens of thousands, but he will not prevail. 13 For the king of the North will return and muster a multitude greater than the former, and shall certainly come at the end of some years with a great army and much equipment.

14 "Now in those times many shall rise up against the king of the South. Also, violent men of your people shall exalt themselves in fulfillment of the vision, but they shall fall. 15 So the king of the North shall come and build a siege mound, and take a fortified city; and the forces of the South shall not withstand *him*. Even his choice troops *shall have* no strength to resist. 16 But he who comes against him shall do according to his own will, and no one shall stand against him. He shall stand in the Glorious Land with destruction in his power.

17 "He shall also set his face to enter with the strength of his whole kingdom, and upright ones with him; thus shall he do. And he shall give him the daughter of women to destroy it; but she shall not stand *with him*, or be for him. 18 After this he shall turn his face to the coastlands, and shall take many. But a ruler shall bring the reproach against them to an end; and with the reproach removed, he shall turn back on him. 19 Then he shall turn his face toward the fortress of his own land; but he shall stumble and fall, and not be found.

20 "There shall arise in his place one who imposes taxes *on* the glorious kingdom; but within a few days he shall be destroyed, but not in anger or in battle. 21 And in his place shall arise a vile person, to whom they will not give the honor of royalty; but he shall come in peaceably, and seize the kingdom by intrigue. 22 With the force of a flood they shall be swept away from before him and be broken, and also the prince of the covenant. 23 And after the league *is made* with him he shall act deceitfully, for he shall come up and become strong with a small *number of* people. 24 He shall enter peaceably, even into the richest places of the province; and he shall do *what* his fathers have not done, nor his forefathers: he shall disperse among them the plunder, spoil, and riches; and he shall devise his plans against the strongholds, but *only* for a time.

25 "He shall stir up his power and his courage against the king of the South with a great army. And the king of the South shall be stirred up to battle with a very great and mighty army; but he shall not stand, for they shall devise plans against him. 26 Yes, those who eat of the portion of his delicacies shall destroy him; his army shall be swept away, and many shall fall down slain. 27 Both these kings' hearts *shall be* bent on evil, and they shall speak lies at the same table; but it shall not prosper, for the end *will* still *be* at the appointed time. 28 While returning to his land with great riches, his heart shall be *moved* against the holy covenant; so he shall do *damage* and return to his own land.

29 "At the appointed time he shall return and go toward the south; but it shall not be like the former or the latter. 30 For ships from Cyprus shall come against him; therefore he shall be grieved, and return in rage against the holy covenant, and do *damage*.

"So he shall return and show regard for those who forsake the holy covenant. 31 And forces shall be mustered by him, and they shall defile the sanctuary fortress; then they shall take away the daily *sacrifices*, and place *there* the abomination of desolation. 32 Those who do wickedly against the covenant he shall corrupt with flattery; but the people who know their God shall be strong, and carry out *great exploits*. 33 And those of the people who understand shall instruct many; yet *for many* days they shall fall by sword and flame, by captivity and plundering. 34 Now when they fall, they shall be aided with a little help; but many shall join with them by intrigue. 35 And *some* of those of understanding shall fall, to refine them, purify *them*, and make *them* white, *until* the time of the end; because *it is* still for the appointed time.

36 "Then the king shall do according to his own will: he shall exalt and magnify himself above every god, shall speak blasphemies against the God of gods, and shall prosper till the wrath has been accomplished; for what has been determined shall be done. 37 He shall regard neither the God of his fathers nor the desire of women, nor regard any god; for he shall exalt himself above *them* all. 38 But in their place he shall honor a god of fortresses; and a god which his fathers did not know he shall honor with gold and silver, with precious stones and pleasant things. 39 Thus he shall act against the strongest fortresses with a foreign god, which he shall acknowledge, *and*

advance *its* glory; and he shall cause them to rule over many, and divide the land for gain. 40 "At the time of the end the king of the South shall attack him; and the king of the North shall come against him like a whirlwind, with chariots, horsemen, and with many ships; and he shall enter the countries, overwhelm *them,* and pass through. 41 He shall also enter the Glorious Land, and many *countries* shall be overthrown; but these shall escape from his hand: Edom, Moab, and the prominent people of Ammon. 42 He shall stretch out his hand against the countries, and the land of Egypt shall not escape. 43 He shall have power over the treasures of gold and silver, and over all the precious things of Egypt; also the Libyans and Ethiopians *shall follow* at his heels. 44 But news from the east and the north shall trouble him; therefore he shall go out with great fury to destroy and annihilate many. 45 And he shall plant the tents of his palace between the seas and the glorious holy mountain; yet he shall come to his end, and no one will help him.

12 "AT that time Michael shall stand up,
The great prince who stands *watch* over the sons of your people;
And there shall be a time of trouble, Such as never was since there was a nation,
Even to that time.
And at that time your people shall be delivered,
Every one who is found written in the book.
2 And many of those who sleep in the dust of the earth shall awake,
Some to everlasting life,
Some to shame *and* everlasting contempt.
3 Those who are wise shall shine
Like the brightness of the firmament,
And those who turn many to righteousness
Like the stars forever and ever.

4 "But you, Daniel, shut up the words, and seal the book until the time of the end; many shall run to and fro, and knowledge shall increase."

5 Then I, Daniel, looked; and there stood two others, one on this riverbank and the other on that riverbank. 6 And *one* said to the man clothed in linen, who *was* above the waters of the river, "How long shall the fulfillment of these wonders *be?*"

7 Then I heard the man clothed in linen, who *was* above the waters of the river, when

he held up his right hand and his left hand to heaven, and swore by Him who lives forever, that *it shall be* for a time, times, and half *a time;* and when the power of the holy people has been completely shattered, all these *things* shall be finished.

8 Although I heard, I did not understand. Then I said, "My lord, what *shall be* the end of these *things?*"

9 And he said, "Go *your way,* Daniel, for the words *are* closed up and sealed till the time of the end. 10 Many shall be purified, made white, and refined, but the wicked shall do wickedly; and none of the wicked shall understand, but the wise shall understand.

11 "And from the time *that* the daily *sacrifice* is taken away, and the abomination of desolation is set up, *there shall be* one thousand two hundred and ninety days. 12 Blessed *is* he who waits, and comes to the one thousand three hundred and thirty-five days.

13 "But you, go *your way* till the end; for you shall rest, and will arise to your inheritance at the end of the days."

PSALM 138:1–3

1 I will praise You with my whole heart;
Before the gods I will sing praises to You.
2 I will worship toward Your holy temple,
And praise Your name
For Your lovingkindness and Your truth;
For You have magnified Your word above all Your name.
3 In the day when I cried out, You answered me,
And made me bold *with* strength in my soul.

PROVERBS 29:16

16 WHEN the wicked are multiplied, transgression increases;
But the righteous will see their fall.

1 JOHN 2:1–29

MY little children, these things I write to you, so that you may not sin. And if anyone sins, we have an Advocate with the Father, Jesus Christ the righteous. 2 And He Himself is the propitiation for our sins, and not for ours only but also for the whole world.

3 Now by this we know that we know Him, if we keep His commandments. 4 He who says, "I know Him," and does not keep His commandments, is a liar, and the truth is not in him. 5 But whoever keeps His word, truly the love of God is perfected in him. By this we know that we are in Him. 6 He who says he abides in Him ought himself also to walk just as He walked.

7 Brethren, I write no new commandment to you, but an old commandment which you have had from the beginning. The old commandment is the word which you heard from the beginning. 8 Again, a new commandment I write to you, which thing is true in Him and in you, because the darkness is passing away, and the true light is already shining.

9 He who says he is in the light, and hates his brother, is in darkness until now. 10 He who loves his brother abides in the light, and there is no cause for stumbling in him. 11 But he who hates his brother is in darkness and walks in darkness, and does not know where he is going, because the darkness has blinded his eyes.

12 I write to you, little children,
    Because your sins are forgiven you
        for His name's sake.
13 I write to you, fathers,
    Because you have known Him *who
        is* from the beginning.
I write to you, young men,
    Because you have overcome the
        wicked one.
I write to you, little children,
    Because you have known the
        Father.
14 I have written to you, fathers,
    Because you have known Him *who
        is* from the beginning.
I have written to you, young men,
    Because you are strong, and the
        word of God abides in you,
    And you have overcome the
        wicked one.

15 Do not love the world or the things in the world. If anyone loves the world, the love of the Father is not in him. 16 For all that *is* in the world—the lust of the flesh, the lust of the eyes, and the pride of life—is not of the Father but is of the world. 17 And the world is passing away, and the lust of it; but he who does the will of God abides forever.

18 Little children, it is the last hour; and as you have heard that the Antichrist is coming, even now many antichrists have come, by which we know that it is the last hour. 19 They went out from us, but they were not of us; for if they had been of us, they would have continued with us; but *they went out* that they might be made manifest, that none of them were of us.

20 But you have an anointing from the Holy One, and you know all things. 21 I have not written to you because you do not know the truth, but because you know it, and that no lie is of the truth. 22 Who is a liar but he who denies that Jesus is the Christ? He is antichrist who denies the Father and the Son. 23 Whoever denies the Son does not have the Father either; he who acknowledges the Son has the Father also.

24 Therefore let that abide in you which you heard from the beginning. If what you heard from the beginning abides in you, you also will abide in the Son and in the Father. 25 And this is the promise that He has promised us—eternal life.

26 These things I have written to you concerning those who *try to* deceive you. 27 But the anointing which you have received from Him abides in you, and you do not need that anyone teach you; but as the same anointing teaches you concerning all things, and is true, and is not a lie, and just as it has taught you, you will abide in Him.

28 And now, little children, abide in Him, that when He appears, we may have confidence and not be ashamed before Him at His coming. 29 If you know that He is righ-

---

*T*here is no condition of life in which we cannot abide in Jesus. (BRILL. HERITAGE)

---

teous, you know that everyone who practices righteousness is born of Him.

Reading 339—Made into Bread for Others

1 John 3:16

A mother lays down her life for her child and for her home, but there is nothing advertised in her doing it. If the mother were to tell her child what she was doing, it would be an abortion of motherhood. The child will never recognize what the mother has done until in years to come the child is in the same place. Only then will the unadvertised substitution of the mother's life and love be recognized. This is what Jesus Christ has done in His redemptive work. "By this we know love, because He laid down His life for us. And we also ought to lay down *our* lives for the brethren." Jesus Christ was made broken bread and poured out wine for us, and He expects us to be made broken bread and poured out wine in His hands for others. If we are not thoroughly baked, we will produce indigestion because we are dough instead of bread. We have to be made into good nutritious stuff for other people. The reason we are going through the things we are is that God wants to know whether He can make us good bread with which to feed others. The stuff of our lives, not simply of our talk, is to be the nutriment of those who know us.   (*LOVE OF GOD*)

HOSEA 1:1—2:23

THE word of the LORD that came to Hosea the son of Beeri, in the days of Uzziah, Jotham, Ahaz, *and* Hezekiah, kings of Judah, and in the days of Jeroboam the son of Joash, king of Israel. 2 When the LORD began to speak by Hosea, the LORD said to Hosea:

"Go, take yourself a wife of harlotry
And children of harlotry,
For the land has committed great
    harlotry
By departing from the LORD."

3 So he went and took Gomer the daughter of Diblaim, and she conceived and bore him a son. 4 Then the LORD said to him:

"Call his name Jezreel,
For in a little *while*
I will avenge the bloodshed of Jezreel
    on the house of Jehu,
And bring an end to the kingdom
    of the house of Israel.
5   It shall come to pass in that day
That I will break the bow of Israel
    in the Valley of Jezreel."

6 And she conceived again and bore a daughter. Then *God* said to him:

"Call her name Lo-Ruhamah,
For I will no longer have mercy on
    the house of Israel,

But I will utterly take them away.
7   Yet I will have mercy on the house
        of Judah,
Will save them by the LORD their
        God,
And will not save them by bow,
Nor by sword or battle,
By horses or horsemen."

8 Now when she had weaned Lo-Ruhamah, she conceived and bore a son. 9 Then *God* said:

"Call his name Lo-Ammi,
For you *are* not My people,
And I will not be your *God*.

10 "Yet the number of the children of
        Israel
Shall be as the sand of the sea,
Which cannot be measured or
        numbered.
And it shall come to pass
In the place where it was said to them,
'You *are* not My people,'
There it shall be said to them,
'*You are* sons of the living God.'
11   Then the children of Judah and the
        children of Israel
Shall be gathered together,
And appoint for themselves one
        head;
And they shall come up out of the
        land,
For great *will be* the day of Jezreel!

2 SAY to your brethren, 'My people,'
And to your sisters, 'Mercy *is shown*.'

2 "Bring charges against your mother,
    bring charges;
For she *is* not My wife, nor *am* I
    her Husband!
Let her put away her harlotries from
    her sight,
And her adulteries from between her
    breasts;
3 Lest I strip her naked
And expose her, as in the day she
    was born,
And make her like a wilderness,
And set her like a dry land,
And slay her with thirst.

4 "I will not have mercy on her children,
For they *are* the children of harlotry.
5 For their mother has played the
    harlot;
She who conceived them has behaved
    shamefully.
For she said, 'I will go after my lovers,
Who give *me* my bread and my water,
My wool and my linen,
My oil and my drink.'

6 "Therefore, behold,
I will hedge up your way with thorns,
And wall her in,
So that she cannot find her paths.
7 She will chase her lovers,
But not overtake them;
Yes, she will seek them, but not find
    them.
Then she will say,
'I will go and return to my first
    husband,
For then *it was* better for me than
    now.'
8 For she did not know
That I gave her grain, new wine, and
    oil,
And multiplied her silver and gold—
Which they prepared for Baal.

9 "Therefore I will return and take away
My grain in its time
And My new wine in its season,
And will take back My wool and My
    linen,
Given to cover her nakedness.
10 Now I will uncover her lewdness in
    the sight of her lovers,
And no one shall deliver her from
    My hand.
11 I will also cause all her mirth to cease,
Her feast days,
Her New Moons,

Her Sabbaths—
All her appointed feasts.

12 "And I will destroy her vines and her
    fig trees,
Of which she has said,
'These *are* my wages that my lovers
    have given me.'
So I will make them a forest,
And the beasts of the field shall eat
    them.
13 I will punish her
For the days of the Baals to which
    she burned incense.
She decked herself with her earrings
    and jewelry,
And went after her lovers;
But Me she forgot," says the LORD.

14 "Therefore, behold, I will allure her,
Will bring her into the wilderness,
And speak comfort to her.
15 I will give her her vineyards from
    there,
And the Valley of Achor as a door
    of hope;
She shall sing there,
As in the days of her youth,
As in the day when she came up from
    the land of Egypt.

16 "And it shall be, in that day,"
    Says the LORD,
"*That* you will call Me 'My Husband,'
And no longer call Me 'My Master,'
17 For I will take from her mouth the
    names of the Baals,
And they shall be remembered by
    their name no more.
18 In that day I will make a covenant
    for them
With the beasts of the field,
With the birds of the air,
And *with* the creeping things of the
    ground.
Bow and sword of battle I will shatter
    from the earth,
To make them lie down safely.

19 "I will betroth you to Me forever;
Yes, I will betroth you to Me
In righteousness and justice,
In lovingkindness and mercy;
20 I will betroth you to Me in
    faithfulness,
And you shall know the LORD.

21 "It shall come to pass in that day
That I will answer," says the LORD;
"I will answer the heavens,
And they shall answer the earth.

22 The earth shall answer
     With grain,
     With new wine,
     And with oil;
     They shall answer Jezreel.

---

*Jesus never mentioned
unanswered prayer, He had the
boundless certainty that prayer is
always answered*.   (UTMOST)

---

23 Then I will sow her for Myself in
     the earth,
     And I will have mercy on *her who
     had* not obtained mercy;
     Then I will say to *those who were* not
     My people,
     'You *are* My people!'
     And they shall say, '*You are* my
     God!'"

PSALM 138:4–6

4 ALL the kings of the earth shall praise
    You, O LORD,
    When they hear the words of Your
    mouth.
5 Yes, they shall sing of the ways of the
    LORD,
    For great *is* the glory of the LORD.
6 Though the LORD *is* on high,
    Yet He regards the lowly;
    But the proud He knows from afar.

PROVERBS 29:17

17 CORRECT your son, and he will give
     you rest;
     Yes, he will give delight to your soul.

1 JOHN 3:1–24

BEHOLD what manner of love the Father
has bestowed on us, that we should be called
children of God! Therefore the world does
not know us, because it did not know Him.
2 Beloved, now we are children of God;
and it has not yet been revealed what we
shall be, but we know that when He is
revealed, we shall be like Him, for we shall
see Him as He is. 3 And everyone who has
this hope in Him purifies himself, just as
He is pure.
4 Whoever commits sin also commits lawlessness, and sin is lawlessness. 5 And you

know that He was manifested to take away
our sins, and in Him there is no sin.
6 Whoever abides in Him does not sin.
Whoever sins has neither seen Him nor
known Him.
7 Little children, let no one deceive you.
He who practices righteousness is righteous, just as He is righteous. 8 He who
sins is of the devil, for the devil has sinned
from the beginning. For this purpose the
Son of God was manifested, that He might
destroy the works of the devil. 9 Whoever
has been born of God does not sin, for
His seed remains in him; and he cannot
sin, because he has been born of God.
10 In this the children of God and the
children of the devil are manifest: Whoever
does not practice righteousness is not of
God, nor *is* he who does not love his
brother. 11 For this is the message that you
heard from the beginning, that we should
love one another, 12 not as Cain *who* was
of the wicked one and murdered his
brother. And why did he murder him? Because his works were evil and his brother's
righteous.

---

*The spirit of Cain is jealousy,
spite and envy.*   (GLORIFY)

---

13 Do not marvel, my brethren, if the
world hates you. 14 We know that we have
passed from death to life, because we love
the brethren. He who does not love *his*
brother abides in death. 15 Whoever hates
his brother is a murderer, and you know
that no murderer has eternal life abiding
in him.
16 By this we know love, because He laid
down His life for us. And we also ought
to lay down *our* lives for the brethren.
17 But whoever has this world's goods, and
sees his brother in need, and shuts up his
heart from him, how does the love of God
abide in him?
18 My little children, let us not love in
word or in tongue, but in deed and in truth.
19 And by this we know that we are of the
truth, and shall assure our hearts before
Him. 20 For if our heart condemns us, God
is greater than our heart, and knows all
things. 21 Beloved, if our heart does not
condemn us, we have confidence toward
God. 22 And whatever we ask we receive
from Him, because we keep His commandments and do those things that are pleasing
in His sight. 23 And this is His commandment: that we should believe on the name

of His Son Jesus Christ and love one another, as He gave us commandment.

24 Now he who keeps His command-

ments abides in Him, and He in him. And
by this we know that He abides in us, by
the Spirit whom He has given us.

◆◆◆

Reading 340—Antichrist
1 John 4:3

Every spirit that dissolves Jesus by analysis is antichrist. What is the spirit that dissolves Him? My claim to my right to myself does it. Is Jesus Christ "boss" or am I? God's order is that He is to be absolute sovereign over me, and I am to be absolute sovereign over everything that is not God, and sin is the switch off, for the time being, that makes me my own "boss" and consequently "boss" of nothing else. I only gain the absolute control God intended me to have when I am brought back into perfect union with God. If I want to know what the human race will be like on the basis of redemption, I shall find it mirrored in Jesus Christ, a perfect oneness between God and man, with no gap. In the meantime there is a gap. Sin, suffering, and the Book of God all bring a man to this realization, that there is something wrong at the basis of life, and that it cannot be put right by reason. If we make rationalism the basis of things, we shall find some great big tragedy will spit up and knock our theories to the winds. . . . Before we seal up our mind on any of these matters, Jesus Christ says, "Believe also in Me." (SHAD. AGONY)

HOSEA 3:1—4:19

THEN the LORD said to me, "Go again, love a woman *who is* loved by a lover and is committing adultery, just like the love of the LORD for the children of Israel, who look to other gods and love *the* raisin cakes *of the pagans.*"

2 So I bought her for myself for fifteen *shekels* of silver, and one and one-half homers of barley. 3 And I said to her, "You shall stay with me many days; you shall not play the harlot, nor shall you have a man—so, too, *will I be* toward you."

4 For the children of Israel shall abide many days without king or prince, without sacrifice or sacred pillar, without ephod or teraphim. 5 Afterward the children of Israel shall return and seek the LORD their God and David their king. They shall fear the LORD and His goodness in the latter days.

4 HEAR the word of the LORD,
You children of Israel,
For the LORD *brings* a charge against
the inhabitants of the land:

"There is no truth or mercy
Or knowledge of God in the land.
2   *By* swearing and lying,
Killing and stealing and committing
adultery,
They break all restraint,
With bloodshed upon bloodshed.
3   Therefore the land will mourn;
And everyone who dwells there will
waste away
With the beasts of the field
And the birds of the air;
Even the fish of the sea will be taken
away.

4   "Now let no man contend, or rebuke
another;
For your people *are* like those who
contend with the priest.
5   Therefore you shall stumble in the
day;
The prophet also shall stumble with
you in the night;
And I will destroy your mother.
6   My people are destroyed for lack of
knowledge.

Because you have rejected
  knowledge,
I also will reject you from being priest
  for Me;
Because you have forgotten the law
  of your God,
I also will forget your children.

7 "The more they increased,
  The more they sinned against Me;
  I will change their glory into shame.
8 They eat up the sin of My people;
  They set their heart on their iniquity.
9 And it shall be: like people, like priest.
  So I will punish them for their ways,
  And reward them for their deeds.
10 For they shall eat, but not have
  enough;
  They shall commit harlotry, but not
  increase;
  Because they have ceased obeying the
  LORD.

11 "Harlotry, wine, and new wine enslave
  the heart.
12 My people ask counsel from their
  wooden *idols,*
  And their staff informs them.
  For the spirit of harlotry has caused
  them to stray,
  And they have played the harlot
  against their God.
13 They offer sacrifices on the
  mountaintops,
  And burn incense on the hills,
  Under oaks, poplars, and terebinths,
  Because their shade *is* good.
  Therefore your daughters commit
  harlotry,
  And your brides commit adultery.

14 "I will not punish your daughters
  when they commit harlotry,
  Nor your brides when they commit
  adultery;
  For *the men* themselves go apart with
  harlots,
  And offer sacrifices with a ritual
  harlot.
  Therefore people *who* do not
  understand will be trampled.

15 "Though you, Israel, play the harlot,
  Let not Judah offend.
  Do not come up to Gilgal,
  Nor go up to Beth Aven,
  Nor swear an oath, *saying,* 'As the
  LORD lives'—

16 "For Israel is stubborn
  Like a stubborn calf;

Now the LORD will let them forage
  Like a lamb in open country.

17 "Ephraim *is* joined to idols,
  Let him alone.
18 Their drink is rebellion,
  They commit harlotry continually.
  Her rulers dearly love dishonor.
19 The wind has wrapped her up in its
  wings,
  And they shall be ashamed because
  of their sacrifices.

PSALM 138:7, 8

7 THOUGH I walk in the midst of
  trouble, You will revive me;
  You will stretch out Your hand
  Against the wrath of my enemies,
  And Your right hand will save me.
8 The LORD will perfect *that which*
  concerns me;
  Your mercy, O LORD, *endures* forever;
  Do not forsake the works of Your
  hands.

---

*G*od always ignores the present
perfection for the ultimate
perfection.   (UTMOST)

PROVERBS 29:18

18 WHERE *there is* no revelation, the
  people cast off restraint;
  But happy *is* he who keeps the law.

1 JOHN 4:1–21

BELOVED, do not believe every spirit, but
test the spirits, whether they are of God;
because many false prophets have gone out
into the world. 2 By this you know the Spirit
of God: Every spirit that confesses that Jesus
Christ has come in the flesh is of God,
3 and every spirit that does not confess that
Jesus Christ has come in the flesh is not
of God. And this is the *spirit* of the Antichrist, which you have heard was coming,
and is now already in the world.

    4 You are of God, little children, and have
overcome them, because He who is in you
is greater than he who is in the world.
5 They are of the world. Therefore they
speak *as* of the world, and the world hears
them. 6 We are of God. He who knows
God hears us; he who is not of God does

not hear us. By this we know the spirit of truth and the spirit of error.

7 Beloved, let us love one another, for love is of God; and everyone who loves is born of God and knows God. 8 He who does not love does not know God, for God is love. 9 In this the love of God was manifested toward us, that God has sent His only begotten Son into the world, that we might live through Him. 10 In this is love,

---

The Cross is the expression of the very heart of God. (BIB. ETHICS)

---

not that we loved God, but that He loved us and sent His Son *to be* the propitiation for our sins. 11 Beloved, if God so loved us, we also ought to love one another.

12 No one has seen God at any time. If we love one another, God abides in us, and His love has been perfected in us. 13 By this we know that we abide in Him,

and He in us, because He has given us of His Spirit. 14 And we have seen and testify that the Father has sent the Son *as* Savior of the world. 15 Whoever confesses that Jesus is the Son of God, God abides in him, and he in God. 16 And we have known and believed the love that God has for us. God is love, and he who abides in love abides in God, and God in him.

17 Love has been perfected among us in this: that we may have boldness in the day of judgment; because as He is, so are we in this world. 18 There is no fear in love; but perfect love casts out fear, because fear involves torment. But he who fears has not been made perfect in love. 19 We love Him because He first loved us.

20 If someone says, "I love God," and hates his brother, he is a liar; for he who does not love his brother whom he has seen, how can he love God whom he has not seen? 21 And this commandment we have from Him: that he who loves God *must* love his brother also.

Reading 341—Readjustment into Life
1 John 5:11

Sin interrupted the normal development of man, and it required another Man to take up the story where it was broken off and to complete it, without the sin. "You have no life in you," said Jesus (John 6:53). What life? The life He had, the life that is at the true Source. Eternal life means the life Jesus lived. "And this is the testimony: that God has given us eternal life, and this life is in His Son" (1 John 5:11). Eternal life is the life Jesus lived, the life of God in a mortal being, transformed by God's regenerating power into harmony with Himself.

"In Him was life, and the life was the light of men" (John 1:4). Why did Jesus live thirty-three years if all He came to do was to die for sin? He lived thirty-three years because He had to show what a normal man after God's pattern was like. He died that through His death we might have the source of life that was in Him (Rom. 5:17). That is why it is so absurd to say, "I accept Jesus as a teacher only." Try to apply the teachings of Jesus to your life without an understanding of His death, and you will find it cannot be done. It would either make you commit suicide or take you to the cross and give you an understanding of why it was necessary for Him to die. (*GLORY*)

HOSEA 5:1—6:11

1 "HEAR this, O priests!
Take heed, O house of Israel!
Give ear, O house of the king!
For yours *is* the judgment,
Because you have been a snare to
   Mizpah
And a net spread on Tabor.
2 The revolters are deeply involved in
   slaughter,
Though I rebuke them all.
3 I know Ephraim,
And Israel is not hidden from Me;
For now, O Ephraim, you commit
   harlotry;
Israel is defiled.

4 "They do not direct their deeds
Toward turning to their God,
For the spirit of harlotry is in their
   midst,
And they do not know the LORD.
5 The pride of Israel testifies to his face;
Therefore Israel and Ephraim
   stumble in their iniquity;
Judah also stumbles with them.

6 "With their flocks and herds
They shall go to seek the LORD,
But they will not find *Him;*
He has withdrawn Himself from
   them.
7 They have dealt treacherously with
   the LORD,
For they have begotten pagan
   children.
Now a New Moon shall devour them
   and their heritage.

8 "Blow the ram's horn in Gibeah,
The trumpet in Ramah!
Cry aloud *at* Beth Aven,
'*Look* behind you, O Benjamin!'
9 Ephraim shall be desolate in the day
   of rebuke;
Among the tribes of Israel I make
   known what is sure.

10 "The princes of Judah are like those
   who remove a landmark;
I will pour out my wrath on them
   like water.
11 Ephraim is oppressed *and* broken in
   judgment,
Because he willingly walked by
   human precept.
12 Therefore I *will be* to Ephraim like
   a moth,
And to the house of Judah like
   rottenness.

13 "When Ephraim saw his sickness,
And Judah *saw* his wound,
Then Ephraim went to Assyria
And sent to King Jareb;
Yet he cannot cure you,
Nor heal you of your wound.
14 For I *will be* like a lion to Ephraim,
And like a young lion to the house
   of Judah.
I, *even* I, will tear *them* and go away;
I will take *them* away, and no one
   shall rescue.
15 I will return again to My place
Till they acknowledge their offense.
Then they will seek My face;
In their affliction they will earnestly
   seek Me."

6 COME, and let us return to
   the LORD;
For He has torn, but He will heal
   us;
He has stricken, but He will bind
   us up.
2 After two days He will revive us;
On the third day He will raise
   us up,
That we may live in His sight.
3 Let us know,
Let us pursue the knowledge of the
   LORD.
His going forth is established as the
   morning;
He will come to us like the rain,
Like the latter *and* former rain to the
   earth.

4 "O Ephraim, what shall I do to you?
O Judah, what shall I do to you?
For your faithfulness is like a
   morning cloud,
And like the early dew it goes away.

---

*Character is made by things done
steadily and persistently, not by the exceptional or spasmodic.* (SERMON MT.)

---

5 Therefore I have hewn *them* by the
   prophets,
I have slain them by the words of
   My mouth;
And your judgments *are like* light
   that goes forth.
6 For I desire mercy and not sacrifice,
And the knowledge of God more
   than burnt offerings.

7 "But like men they transgressed the
   covenant;

There they dealt treacherously
with Me.

8 Gilead *is* a city of evildoers
And defiled with blood.

9 As bands of robbers lie in wait for
a man,
So the company of priests murder on
the way to Shechem;
Surely they commit lewdness.

10 I have seen a horrible thing in the
house of Israel:
There *is* the harlotry of Ephraim;
Israel is defiled.

11 Also, O Judah, a harvest is appointed
for you,
When I return the captives of My
people.

PSALM 139:1–6

1 O LORD, You have searched me and
known *me*.

2 You know my sitting down and my
rising up;
You understand my thought afar off.

3 You comprehend my path and my
lying down,
And are acquainted with all my ways.

4 For *there is* not a word on my tongue,
But behold, O LORD, You know it
altogether.

5 You have hedged me behind and before,
And laid Your hand upon me.

6 *Such* knowledge *is* too wonderful for
me;
It is high, I cannot *attain* it.

PROVERBS 29:19

19 A servant will not be corrected by
mere words;
For though he understands, he will
not respond.

1 JOHN 5:1–21

WHOEVER believes that Jesus is the
Christ is born of God, and everyone who
loves Him who begot also loves him who
is begotten of Him. 2 By this we know that
we love the children of God, when we love
God and keep His commandments.
3 For this is the love of God, that we keep
His commandments. And His commandments are not burdensome. 4 For whatever
is born of God overcomes the world. And
this is the victory that has overcome the
world—our faith. 5 Who is he who over-

comes the world, but he who believes that
Jesus is the Son of God?

6 This is He who came by water and
blood—Jesus Christ; not only by water, but
by water and blood. And it is the Spirit
who bears witness, because the Spirit is
truth. 7 For there are three that bear witness
in heaven: the Father, the Word, and the
Holy Spirit; and these three are one.
8 And there are three that bear witness on
earth: the Spirit, the water, and the blood;
and these three agree as one.

9 If we receive the witness of men, the
witness of God is greater; for this is the
witness of God which He has testified of
His Son. 10 He who believes in the Son
of God has the witness in himself; he who
does not believe God has made Him a liar,
because he has not believed the testimony
that God has given of His Son. 11 And this
is the testimony: that God has given us
eternal life, and this life is in His Son.
12 He who has the Son has life; he who
does not have the Son of God does not
have life. 13 These things I have written to

---

*Whenever Jesus speaks about life He
is referring to the life which is in
Himself.* (GLORY)

---

you who believe in the name of the Son
of God, that you may know that you have
eternal life, and that you may *continue to*
believe in the name of the Son of God.

14 Now this is the confidence that we
have in Him, that if we ask anything according to His will, He hears us. 15 And if we
know that He hears us, whatever we ask,
we know that we have the petitions that
we have asked of Him.

16 If anyone sees his brother sinning a
sin *which does* not *lead* to death, he will
ask, and He will give him life for those
who commit sin not *leading* to death. There
is sin *leading* to death. I do not say that
he should pray about that. 17 All unrighteousness is sin, and there is sin not *leading*
to death.

18 We know that whoever is born of God
does not sin; but he who has been born
of God keeps himself, and the wicked one
does not touch him.

19 We know that we are of God, and
the whole world lies *under the sway of* the
wicked one.

20 And we know that the Son of God
has come and has given us an understanding, that we may know Him who is true;
and we are in Him who is true, in His

Son Jesus Christ. This is the true God and eternal life.

21 Little children, keep yourselves from idols. Amen.

◆◆◆◆

Reading 342—The Security of Abandonment
Psalm 139:7

The psalmist states that the presence of God is the secure accompaniment of His knowledge; not only does God know everything about him, but He is with him in the knowledge. Where is the place that God is not?—hell? No, hell is God; if there were no God, there would be no hell. "If I make my bed in hell, behold, You *are there*." The first thing "the fool" does is to get rid of God ("The fool has said in his heart, *there* is no God," Ps. 14:1); then he gets rid of heaven and hell; then he gets rid of all moral consequences—no such thing as right and wrong. The psalmist is stating that wherever he may go in accordance with the indecipherable Providence of God, there the surprising presence of God will meet him. Immediately you begin to forecast and plan for yourself God will break up your program. He delights to do it, until we learn to live like children based on the knowledge that God is ruling and reigning and rejoicing, and His joy is our strength. When we say "even there Your hand shall lead me, and Your right hand shall hold me," there is no foreboding anxiety, because "His love in times past" enables us to rest confidently in Him. The only rest there is is in this abandon to the love of God. There is security from yesterday—"You have hedged me behind"; security for tomorrow—"and before"; and security for today, "and laid Your hand upon me." It was this knowledge that gave our Lord the imperturbable peace He always had.

(*Bib. Ethics*)

HOSEA 7:1—8:14

1 "WHEN I would have healed Israel,
Then the iniquity of Ephraim was
uncovered,
And the wickedness of Samaria.
For they have committed fraud;
A thief comes in;
A band of robbers takes spoil outside.
2 They do not consider in their hearts
That I remember all their wickedness;
Now their own deeds have
surrounded them;
They are before My face.
3 They make a king glad with their
wickedness,
And princes with their lies.

4 "They *are* all adulterers.
Like an oven heated by a baker—
He ceases stirring *the fire* after
kneading the dough,
Until it is leavened.
5 In the day of our king

Princes have made *him* sick, inflamed
with wine;
He stretched out his hand with
scoffers.
6 They prepare their heart like an oven,
While they lie in wait;
Their baker sleeps all night;
In the morning it burns like a flaming
fire.
7 They are all hot, like an oven,
And have devoured their judges;
All their kings have fallen.
None among them calls upon Me.

8 "Ephraim has mixed himself among
the peoples;
Ephraim is a cake unturned.
9 Aliens have devoured his strength,
But he does not know *it;*
Yes, gray hairs are here and there on
him,
Yet he does not know *it.*
10 And the pride of Israel testifies to
his face,

But they do not return to the LORD
their God,
Nor seek Him for all this.

11 "Ephraim also is like a silly dove,
without sense—
They call to Egypt,
They go to Assyria.
12 Wherever they go, I will spread My
net on them;
I will bring them down like birds
of the air;
I will chastise them
According to what their
congregation has heard.

13 "Woe to them, for they have fled
from Me!
Destruction to them,
Because they have transgressed
against Me!
Though I redeemed them,
Yet they have spoken lies against Me.
14 They did not cry out to Me with
their heart
When they wailed upon their beds.

"They assemble together for grain and
new wine,
They rebel against Me;
15 Though I disciplined *and*
strengthened their arms,
Yet they devise evil against Me;
16 They return, *but* not to the Most
High;
They are like a treacherous bow.
Their princes shall fall by the sword
For the cursings of their tongue.
This *shall be* their derision in the land
of Egypt.

8 "*SET* the trumpet to your mouth!
He shall come like an eagle against
the house of the LORD,
Because they have transgressed My
covenant
And rebelled against My law.
2 Israel will cry to Me,
'My God, we know You!'
3 Israel has rejected the good;
The enemy will pursue him.

4 "They set up kings, but not by Me;
They made princes, but I did not
acknowledge *them*.
From their silver and gold
They made idols for themselves—
That they might be cut off.
5 Your calf is rejected, O Samaria!
My anger is aroused against them—

How long until they attain to
innocence?
6 For from Israel *is* even this:
A workman made it, and it *is* not
God;
But the calf of Samaria shall be
broken to pieces.

7 "They sow the wind,
And reap the whirlwind.
The stalk has no bud;
It shall never produce meal.
If it should produce,
Aliens would swallow it up.
8 Israel is swallowed up;
Now they are among the Gentiles
Like a vessel in which *is* no pleasure.
9 For they have gone up to Assyria,
Like a wild donkey alone by itself;
Ephraim has hired lovers.
10 Yes, though they have hired among
the nations,
Now I will gather them;
And they shall sorrow a little,
Because of the burden of the king
of princes.

11 "Because Ephraim has made many
altars for sin,
They have become for him altars for
sinning.
12 I have written for him the great things
of My law,
But they were considered a strange
thing.
13 *For* the sacrifices of My offerings they
sacrifice flesh and eat *it,*
But the LORD does not accept them.
Now He will remember their iniquity
and punish their sins.
They shall return to Egypt.

14 "For Israel has forgotten his Maker,
And has built temples;
Judah also has multiplied fortified
cities;
But I will send fire upon his cities,
And it shall devour his palaces."

PSALM 139:7–12

7 WHERE can I go from Your Spirit?
Or where can I flee from Your
presence?
8 If I ascend into heaven, You *are* there;
If I make my bed in hell, behold, You
are there.
9 *If* I take the wings of the morning,
And dwell in the uttermost parts of the
sea,

*A*nywhere the man who is devoted to
Jesus Christ goes, Jesus Christ is there
with him.   (RUN)

10 Even there Your hand shall lead me,
    And Your right hand shall hold me.
11 If I say, "Surely the darkness shall fall
    on me,"
    Even the night shall be light about
    me;
12 Indeed, the darkness shall not hide from
    You,
    But the night shines as the day;
    The darkness and the light *are* both
    alike *to You.*

PROVERBS 29:20

20 DO you see a man hasty in his words?
    There is more hope for a fool than for
    him.

2 JOHN 1–13

THE Elder,

To the elect lady and her children, whom
I love in truth, and not only I, but also
all those who have known the truth,
2 because of the truth which abides in us
and will be with us forever:

3 Grace, mercy, *and* peace will be with
you from God the Father and from the
Lord Jesus Christ, the Son of the Father,
in truth and love.

4 I rejoiced greatly that I have found *some*
of your children walking in truth, as we
received commandment from the Father.

*A*ll God's commands are
enablings.   (PHIL. SIN)

5 And now I plead with you, lady, not as
though I wrote a new commandment to
you, but that which we have had from the
beginning: that we love one another.
6 This is love, that we walk according to
His commandments. This is the commandment, that as you have heard from the beginning, you should walk in it.

7 For many deceivers have gone out into
the world who do not confess Jesus Christ
as coming in the flesh. This is a deceiver
and an antichrist. 8 Look to yourselves, that
we do not lose those things we worked
for, but *that* we may receive a full reward.

9 Whoever transgresses and does not
abide in the doctrine of Christ does not
have God. He who abides in the doctrine
of Christ has both the Father and the Son.
10 If anyone comes to you and does not
bring this doctrine, do not receive him into
your house nor greet him; 11 for he who
greets him shares in his evil deeds.

12 Having many things to write to you,
I did not wish *to do so* with paper and ink;
but I hope to come to you and speak face
to face, that our joy may be full.

13 The children of your elect sister greet
you. Amen.

◆◆◆

Reading 343—Missionary Devotion
3 John 7

*O*ur Lord has told us how love to Him is to manifest itself. "Do you
love Me?" "Feed My sheep"—identify yourself with My interests in
other people, not, identify *Me* with *your* interests in other people. . . . The
test of my love for Jesus is the practical one, all the rest is sentimental jargon.

Loyalty to Jesus Christ is the supernatural work of redemption wrought in
me by the Holy Ghost who sheds abroad the love of God in my heart, and
that love works efficaciously through me in contact with everyone I meet. I
remain loyal to His name although every commonsense fact gives the lie to
Him, and declares that He has no more power than a morning mist.

The key to missionary devotion means being attached to nothing and no one saving our Lord Himself, not being detached from things externally. Our Lord was amazingly in and out among ordinary things; His detachment was on the inside toward God. External detachment is often an indication of a secret vital attachment to the things we keep away from externally. . . .

The men and women our Lord sends out on His enterprises are the ordinary human stuff, plus dominating devotion to Himself wrought by the Holy Ghost. (UTMOST)

HOSEA 9:1—10:15

1 DO not rejoice, O Israel, with joy like *other* peoples,
For you have played the harlot against your God.
You have made love *for* hire on every threshing floor.

2 The threshing floor and the winepress
Shall not feed them,
And the new wine shall fail in her.

3 They shall not dwell in the LORD's land,
But Ephraim shall return to Egypt,
And shall eat unclean *things* in Assyria.

4 They shall not offer wine *offerings* to the LORD,
Nor shall their sacrifices be pleasing to Him.
It shall be like bread of mourners to them;
All who eat it shall be defiled.
For their bread *shall be* for their *own* life;
It shall not come into the house of the LORD.

5 What will you do in the appointed day,
And in the day of the feast of the LORD?

6 For indeed they are gone because of destruction.
Egypt shall gather them up;
Memphis shall bury them.
Nettles shall possess their valuables of silver;
Thorns *shall be* in their tents.

7 The days of punishment have come;
The days of recompense have come.
Israel knows!
The prophet *is* a fool,
The spiritual man *is* insane,
Because of the greatness of your iniquity and great enmity.

8 The watchman of Ephraim *is* with my God;
But the prophet *is* a fowler's snare in all his ways—
Enmity in the house of his God.

9 They are deeply corrupted,
As in the days of Gibeah.
He will remember their iniquity;
He will punish their sins.

10 "I found Israel
Like grapes in the wilderness;
I saw your fathers
As the firstfruits on the fig tree in its first season.
But they went to Baal Peor,
And separated themselves *to that* shame;
They became an abomination like the thing they loved.

11 *As for* Ephraim, their glory shall fly away like a bird—
No birth, no pregnancy, and no conception!

12 Though they bring up their children,
Yet I will bereave them to the last man.
Yes, woe to them when I depart from them!

13 Just as I saw Ephraim like Tyre, planted in a pleasant place,
So Ephraim will bring out his children to the murderer."

14 Give them, O LORD—
What will You give?
Give them a miscarrying womb
And dry breasts!

15 "All their wickedness *is* in Gilgal,
For there I hated them.
Because of the evil of their deeds
I will drive them from My house;
I will love them no more.
All their princes *are* rebellious.

16 Ephraim is stricken,
Their root is dried up;
They shall bear no fruit.
Yes, were they to bear children,

I would kill the darlings of their
   womb."

17 My God will cast them away,
   Because they did not obey Him;
   And they shall be wanderers among
     the nations.

10

ISRAEL empties *his* vine;
   He brings forth fruit for himself.
According to the multitude of his
   fruit
He has increased the altars;
According to the bounty of his land
They have embellished *his* sacred
   pillars.

2 Their heart is divided;
   Now they are held guilty.
   He will break down their altars;
   He will ruin their sacred pillars.

3 For now they say,
   "We have no king,
   Because we did not fear the LORD.
   And as for a king, what would he
     do for us?"

4 They have spoken words,
   Swearing falsely in making a
     covenant.
   Thus judgment springs up like
     hemlock in the furrows of the
     field.

5 The inhabitants of Samaria fear
   Because of the calf of Beth Aven.
   For its people mourn for it,
   And its priests shriek for it—
   Because its glory has departed
     from it.

6 *The idol* also shall be carried to Assyria
   As a present for King Jareb.
   Ephraim shall receive shame,
   And Israel shall be ashamed of his
     own counsel.

7 *As for* Samaria, her king is cut off
   Like a twig on the water.

8 Also the high places of Aven, the sin
     of Israel,
   Shall be destroyed.
   The thorn and thistle shall grow on
     their altars;
   They shall say to the mountains,
     "Cover us!"
   And to the hills, "Fall on us!"

9 "O Israel, you have sinned from the
     days of Gibeah;
   There they stood.
   The battle in Gibeah against the
     children of iniquity

Did not overtake them.

10 When *it is* My desire, I will chasten
    them.
   Peoples shall be gathered against
    them
   When I bind them for their two
    transgressions.

11 Ephraim *is* a trained heifer
   That loves to thresh *grain;*
   But I harnessed her fair neck,
   I will make Ephraim pull *a plow.*
   Judah shall plow;
   Jacob shall break his clods."

12 Sow for yourselves righteousness;
   Reap in mercy;
   Break up your fallow ground,
   For *it is* time to seek the LORD,
   Till He comes and rains
    righteousness on you.

---

*When we lie like fallow ground, God
puts in new seeds.*   (RUN)

---

13 You have plowed wickedness;
   You have reaped iniquity.
   You have eaten the fruit of lies,
   Because you trusted in your own way,
   In the multitude of your mighty men.

14 Therefore tumult shall arise among
    your people,
   And all your fortresses shall be
    plundered
   As Shalman plundered Beth Arbel in
    the day of battle—
   A mother dashed in pieces upon *her*
    children.

15 Thus it shall be done to you,
   O Bethel,
   Because of your great wickedness.
   At dawn the king of Israel
   Shall be cut off utterly.

PSALM 139:13–16

13 FOR You formed my inward parts;
   You covered me in my mother's womb.

14 I will praise You, for I am fearfully *and*
    wonderfully made;
   Marvelous are Your works,
   And *that* my soul knows very well.

15 My frame was not hidden from You,
   When I was made in secret,
   And skillfully wrought in the lowest
    parts of the earth.

16 Your eyes saw my substance, being yet
    unformed.
   And in Your book they all were written,

The days fashioned for me,
When *as yet there were* none of them.

PROVERBS 29:21

21 HE who pampers his servant from
    childhood
    Will have him as a son in the end.

3 JOHN 1–14

THE Elder,

To the beloved Gaius, whom I love in
truth:

2 Beloved, I pray that you may prosper
in all things and be in health, just as your
soul prospers. 3 For I rejoiced greatly when

---

*H*ealth is simply the balance of our
bodily life with external
circumstances.   (PSY. REDEMP.)

---

brethren came and testified of the truth *that
is* in you, just as you walk in the truth.
4 I have no greater joy than to hear that
my children walk in truth.

5 Beloved, you do faithfully whatever you
do for the brethren and for strangers,
6 who have borne witness of your love before the church. *If* you send them forward
on their journey in a manner worthy of
God, you will do well, 7 because they went
forth for His name's sake, taking nothing
from the Gentiles. 8 We therefore ought
to receive such, that we may become fellow workers for the truth.

9 I wrote to the church, but Diotrephes,
who loves to have the preeminence among
them, does not receive us. 10 Therefore, if
I come, I will call to mind his deeds which
he does, prating against us with malicious
words. And not content with that, he himself does not receive the brethren, and for-
bids those who wish to, putting *them* out
of the church.

11 Beloved, do not imitate what is evil,
but what is good. He who does good is
of God, but he who does evil has not seen
God.

12 Demetrius has a *good* testimony from
all, and from the truth itself. And we also
bear witness, and you know that our testimony is true.

13 I had many things to write, but I do
not wish to write to you with pen and ink;
14 but I hope to see you shortly, and we
shall speak face to face.
Peace to you. Our friends greet you.
Greet the friends by name.

◆◆◆◆

Reading 344—Prayer Pervaded by Pentecost
Jude 20

W e have to pray relying upon what has been revealed by the sent-down
Holy Spirit, and the first revelation is that we do not know how to
pray. (See Rom. 8:26.) We have to learn to draw on our relationship to Jesus
Christ. As we do, we realize that the Holy Spirit keeps us in simple relationship
to our Lord while we pray. When we pray in the Holy Spirit we are released
from our petitions. "Your Father knows the things you have need of before
you ask Him" (Matt. 6:8).

Then why ask? The whole meaning of prayer is that we may know God.
The "asking and receiving" prayer is elementary; it is the part of prayer we
can understand. But it is not necessarily praying in the Holy Spirit. Those
who are not born again must ask and receive; but when we have received and
have become rightly related to God, we must maintain this simplicity of belief
in Him while we pray. Our minds must be saturated by the revelation of
prayer until we learn in every detail to pray in the Holy Spirit. Prayer is not
an exercise, it is life.   (*ASK*)

HOSEA 11:1—12:14

1 "WHEN Israel *was* a child, I loved
        him,
    And out of Egypt I called My son.
2 *As* they called them,
    So they went from them;
    They sacrificed to the Baals,
    And burned incense to carved
        images.

3 "I taught Ephraim to walk,
    Taking them by their arms;
    But they did not know that I healed
        them.
4 I drew them with gentle cords,
    With bands of love,
    And I was to them as those who take
        the yoke from their neck.
    I stooped *and* fed them.

5 "He shall not return to the land of
        Egypt;
    But the Assyrian shall be his king,
    Because they refused to repent.
6 And the sword shall slash in his cities,
    Devour his districts,
    And consume *them,*
    Because of their own counsels.
7 My people are bent on backsliding
        from Me.
    Though they call to the Most High,
    None at all exalt *Him.*

8 "How can I give you up, Ephraim?
    How can I hand you over, Israel?
    How can I make you like Admah?
    How can I set you like Zeboiim?
    My heart churns within Me;
    My sympathy is stirred.
9 I will not execute the fierceness of
        My anger;
    I will not again destroy Ephraim.
    For I *am* God, and not man,
    The Holy One in your midst;
    And I will not come with terror.

10 "They shall walk after the LORD.
    He will roar like a lion.
    When He roars,
    Then *His* sons shall come trembling
        from the west;
11 They shall come trembling like a bird
        from Egypt,
    Like a dove from the land of Assyria.
    And I will let them dwell in their
        houses,"
    Says the LORD.

12 "Ephraim has encircled Me with lies,
    And the house of Israel with deceit;

But Judah still walks with God,
    Even with the Holy One *who is*
        faithful.

12 "EPHRAIM feeds on the wind,
        And pursues the east wind;
    He daily increases lies and desolation.
    Also they make a covenant with the
        Assyrians,
    And oil is carried to Egypt.

2 "The LORD also *brings* a charge against
        Judah,
    And will punish Jacob according to
        his ways;
    According to his deeds He will
        recompense him.
3 He took his brother by the heel in
        the womb,
    And in his strength he struggled with
        God.
4 Yes, he struggled with the Angel and
        prevailed;
    He wept, and sought favor from
        Him.
    He found Him *in* Bethel,
    And there He spoke to us—
5 That is, the LORD God of hosts.
    The LORD *is* His memorable name.
6 So you, by *the help of* your God,
        return;
    Observe mercy and justice,
    And wait on your God continually.

7 "A cunning Canaanite!
    Deceitful scales *are* in his hand;
    He loves to oppress.
8 And Ephraim said,
    'Surely I have become rich,
    I have found wealth for myself;
    In all my labors
    They shall find in me no iniquity that
        is sin.'

9 "But I *am* the LORD your God,
    Ever since the land of Egypt;
    I will again make you dwell in tents,
    As in the days of the appointed feast.
10 I have also spoken by the prophets,
    And have multiplied visions;
    I have given symbols through the
        witness of the prophets."

11 Though Gilead *has* idols—
    Surely they are vanity—
    Though they sacrifice bulls in Gilgal,
    Indeed their altars *shall be* heaps in
        the furrows of the field.

12 Jacob fled to the country of Syria;
    Israel served for a spouse,
    And for a wife he tended *sheep.*

13 By a prophet the LORD brought Israel
   out of Egypt,
   And by a prophet he was preserved.
14 Ephraim provoked *Him* to anger
   most bitterly;
   Therefore his Lord will leave the guilt
   of his bloodshed upon him,
   And return his reproach upon him.

PSALM 139:17–24

17 HOW precious also are Your thoughts
   to me, O God!
   How great is the sum of them!
18 *If* I should count them, they would be
   more in number than the sand;
   When I awake, I am still with You.

19 Oh, that You would slay the wicked,
   O God!
   Depart from me, therefore, you
   bloodthirsty men.
20 For they speak against You wickedly;
   Your enemies take *Your name* in vain.
21 Do I not hate them, O LORD, who hate
   You?
   And do I not loathe those who rise
   up against You?
22 I hate them with perfect hatred;
   I count them my enemies.

23 Search me, O God, and know my heart;
   Try me, and know my anxieties;
24 And see if *there is any* wicked way
   in me,
   And lead me in the way everlasting.

PROVERBS 29:22

22 AN angry man stirs up strife,
   And a furious man abounds in
   transgression.

JUDE 1–25

JUDE, a bondservant of Jesus Christ, and
brother of James,

To those who are called, sanctified by
God the Father, and preserved in Jesus
Christ:

2 Mercy, peace, and love be multiplied
to you.
3 Beloved, while I was very diligent to
write to you concerning our common salvation, I found it necessary to write to you
exhorting you to contend earnestly for the
faith which was once for all delivered to
the saints. 4 For certain men have crept in
unnoticed, who long ago were marked out
for this condemnation, ungodly men, who
turn the grace of our God into lewdness
and deny the only Lord God and our Lord
Jesus Christ.

5 But I want to remind you, though you
once knew this, that the Lord, having saved
the people out of the land of Egypt, afterward destroyed those who did not believe.
6 And the angels who did not keep their
proper domain, but left their own abode,
He has reserved in everlasting chains under
darkness for the judgment of the great day;
7 as Sodom and Gomorrah, and the cities
around them in a similar manner to these,
having given themselves over to sexual immorality and gone after strange flesh, are
set forth as an example, suffering the vengeance of eternal fire.

8 Likewise also these dreamers defile the
flesh, reject authority, and speak evil of dignitaries. 9 Yet Michael the archangel, in con-
tending with the devil, when he disputed
about the body of Moses, dared not bring
against him a reviling accusation, but said,
"The Lord rebuke you!" 10 But these speak
evil of whatever they do not know; and
whatever they know naturally, like brute
beasts, in these things they corrupt themselves. 11 Woe to them! For they have gone
in the way of Cain, have run greedily in
the error of Balaam for profit, and perished
in the rebellion of Korah.

---

*C*ain's sin shattered him into
absolute solitariness.   (BIB. ETHICS)

---

12 These are spots in your love feasts,
while they feast with you without fear, serving *only* themselves. *They are* clouds without
water, carried about by the winds; late au-
tumn trees without fruit, twice dead, pulled
up by the roots; 13 raging waves of the sea,
foaming up their own shame; wandering
stars for whom is reserved the blackness
of darkness forever.
14 Now Enoch, the seventh from Adam,
prophesied about these men also, saying,
"Behold, the Lord comes with ten thousands of His saints, 15 to execute judgment
on all, to convict all who are ungodly among
them of all their ungodly deeds which they
have committed in an ungodly way, and
of all the harsh things which ungodly sinners have spoken against Him."
16 These are grumblers, complainers,
walking according to their own lusts; and

they mouth great swelling *words,* flattering people to gain advantage. 17 But you, beloved, remember the words which were spoken before by the apostles of our Lord Jesus Christ: 18 how they told you that there would be mockers in the last time who would walk according to their own ungodly lusts. 19 These are sensual persons, who cause divisions, not having the Spirit.

20 But you, beloved, building yourselves up on your most holy faith, praying in the Holy Spirit, 21 keep yourselves in the love of God, looking for the mercy of our Lord Jesus Christ unto eternal life.

22 And on some have compassion, making a distinction; 23 but others save with fear, pulling *them* out of the fire, hating even the garment defiled by the flesh.

24 Now to Him who is able to keep
you from stumbling,
And to present *you* faultless
Before the presence of His glory with
exceeding joy,
25 To God our Savior,
Who alone is wise,
Be glory and majesty,
Dominion and power,
Both now and forever.
Amen.

A Christian is one who trusts the wits and wisdom of God. (UTMOST)

Reading 345—Dawning Fear of His Deity
Revelation 1:17

These words were uttered by the disciple who knew Jesus most intimately, the one who laid his head on Jesus' bosom, the disciple "whom Jesus loved"—when he saw Him in His unveiled deity, he fell at His feet as one dead, paralyzed with amazement; then there came the voice he had learned to know in the days of His flesh, saying, "Do not be afraid; I am the First and the Last."

Has our discipleship to Jesus a sense of awe about it, or do we patronize Him? At the beginning we were sure that we knew all about Jesus, but now we are not quite so sure; He is taken up with a point of view we know nothing about, and we can no longer be familiar with Him. Instead of walking to triumph as the disciples expected Jesus to do, He goes to disaster; instead of bringing peace, He brings a sword. In every way Jesus enters into "somewhere" that fills us with awe. . . .

There are times when God cannot reveal Himself in any other way than in His majesty. And out of the midst of the terror there comes the voice we know, saying to us personally, "Do not be afraid." When once His touch comes like that, nothing can at all cast us into fear again. (*PLACE HELP*)

HOSEA 13:1—14:9

1 WHEN Ephraim spoke, trembling,
He exalted *himself* in Israel;
But when he offended through Baal
worship, he died.
2 Now they sin more and more,
And have made for themselves
molded images,
Idols of their silver, according to their
skill;

All of it *is* the work of craftsmen.
They say of them,
"Let the men who sacrifice kiss the
calves!"
3 Therefore they shall be like the
morning cloud
And like the early dew that passes
away,
Like chaff blown off from a
threshing floor
And like smoke from a chimney.

4 "Yet I *am* the LORD your God
Ever since the land of Egypt,
And you shall know no God but Me;
For *there is* no savior besides Me.
5 I knew you in the wilderness,
In the land of great drought.
6 When they had pasture, they were
filled;
They were filled and their heart was
exalted;
Therefore they forgot Me.

7 "So I will be to them like a lion;
Like a leopard by the road I will lurk;
8 I will meet them like a bear deprived
of *her cubs;*
I will tear open their rib cage,
And there I will devour them like a
lion.
The wild beast shall tear them.

9 "O Israel, you are destroyed,
But your help *is* from Me.
10 I will be your King;
Where *is any other,*
That he may save you in all your
cities?
And your judges to whom you said,
'Give me a king and princes'?
11 I gave you a king in My anger,
And took *him* away in My wrath.

12 "The iniquity of Ephraim *is* bound up;
His sin *is* stored up.
13 The sorrows of a woman in childbirth
shall come upon him.
He *is* an unwise son,
For he should not stay long where
children are born.

14 "I will ransom them from the power
of the grave;
I will redeem them from death.
O Death, I will be your plagues!
O Grave, I will be your destruction!
Pity is hidden from My eyes."

15 Though he is fruitful among *his*
brethren,
An east wind shall come;
The wind of the LORD shall come
up from the wilderness.
Then his spring shall become dry,
And his fountain shall be dried up.
He shall plunder the treasury of every
desirable prize.
16 Samaria is held guilty,
For she has rebelled against her God.
They shall fall by the sword,
Their infants shall be dashed in
pieces,

And their women with child ripped
open.

14 O Israel, return to the LORD your
God,
For you have stumbled because of
your iniquity;
2 Take words with you,
And return to the LORD.
Say to Him,
"Take away all iniquity;
Receive *us* graciously,
For we will offer the sacrifices of our
lips.
3 Assyria shall not save us,
We will not ride on horses,
Nor will we say anymore to the work
of our hands, '*You are* our gods.'
For in You the fatherless finds
mercy."

4 "I will heal their backsliding,
I will love them freely,
For My anger has turned away from
him.
5 I will be like the dew to Israel;
He shall grow like the lily,
And lengthen his roots like Lebanon.
6 His branches shall spread;
His beauty shall be like an olive tree,
And his fragrance like Lebanon.
7 Those who dwell under his shadow
shall return;
They shall be revived *like* grain,
And grow like a vine.
Their scent *shall be* like the wine of
Lebanon.

8 "Ephraim *shall say,* 'What have I to
do anymore with idols?'
I have heard and observed him.
I *am* like a green cypress tree;
Your fruit is found in Me."

9 Who *is* wise?
Let him understand these things.
Who is prudent?
Let him know them.
For the ways of the LORD *are* right;
The righteous walk in them,
But transgressors stumble in them.

PSALM 140:1–5

1 DELIVER me, O LORD, from evil
men;
Preserve me from violent men,
2 Who plan evil things in *their* hearts;
They continually gather together *for*
war.

3 They sharpen their tongues like a
    serpent;
  The poison of asps *is* under their lips.
                                    Selah

4 Keep me, O LORD, from the hands of
    the wicked;
  Preserve me from violent men,
  Who have purposed to make my steps
    stumble.
5 The proud have hidden a snare for me,
    and cords;
  They have spread a net by the wayside;
  They have set traps for me.   Selah

PROVERBS 29:23

23 A man's pride will bring him low,
  But the humble in spirit will retain
    honor.

REVELATION 1:1–20

THE Revelation of Jesus Christ, which God
gave Him to show His servants—things
which must shortly take place. And He sent
and signified *it* by His angel to His servant
John, 2 who bore witness to the word of
God, and to the testimony of Jesus Christ,
to all things that he saw. 3 Blessed *is* he
who reads and those who hear the words
of this prophecy, and keep those things
which are written in it; for the time *is* near.

4 John, to the seven churches which are
in Asia:

Grace to you and peace from Him who
is and who was and who is to come, and
from the seven Spirits who are before His
throne, 5 and from Jesus Christ, the faithful
witness, the firstborn from the dead, and
the ruler over the kings of the earth.

To Him who loved us and washed us
from our sins in His own blood, 6 and has
made us kings and priests to His God and
Father, to Him *be* glory and dominion forever and ever. Amen.

7 Behold, He is coming with clouds, and
every eye will see Him, even they who
pierced Him. And all the tribes of the earth
will mourn because of Him. Even so,
Amen.

8 "I am the Alpha and the Omega, *the*
Beginning and *the* End," says the Lord,
"who is and who was and who is to come,
the Almighty."

9 I, John, both your brother and companion in the tribulation and kingdom and patience of Jesus Christ, was on the island
that is called Patmos for the word of God
and for the testimony of Jesus Christ.
10 I was in the Spirit on the Lord's Day,
and I heard behind me a loud voice, as of
a trumpet, 11 saying, "I am the Alpha and
the Omega, the First and the Last," and,
"What you see, write in a book and send
it to the seven churches which are in Asia:
to Ephesus, to Smyrna, to Pergamos, to
Thyatira, to Sardis, to Philadelphia, and to
Laodicea."

12 Then I turned to see the voice that
spoke with me. And having turned I saw
seven golden lampstands, 13 and in the
midst of the seven lampstands *One* like the
Son of Man, clothed with a garment down
to the feet and girded about the chest with
a golden band. 14 His head and hair *were*
white like wool, as white as snow, and His
eyes like a flame of fire; 15 His feet *were*
like fine brass, as if refined in a furnace,
and His voice as the sound of many waters;
16 He had in His right hand seven stars,
out of His mouth went a sharp two-edged
sword, and His countenance *was* like the
sun shining in its strength. 17 And when I

---

*R*emain *true to God, although it
means the sword going through the
natural.*   (NOT KNOWING)

---

saw Him, I fell at His feet as dead. But
He laid His right hand on me, saying to
me, "Do not be afraid; I am the First and
the Last. 18 I *am* He who lives, and was
dead, and behold, I am alive forevermore.
Amen. And I have the keys of Hades and
of Death. 19 Write the things which you
have seen, and the things which are, and
the things which will take place after this.
20 The mystery of the seven stars which you
saw in My right hand, and the seven golden
lampstands: The seven stars are the angels
of the seven churches, and the seven lampstands which you saw are the seven
churches.

Reading 346—Healing the Past
Joel 2:25

We may have become born again, but what about those we have wronged? It is of no use to sit down and say, "It is irreparable now, I cannot alter it." Thank God, He can alter it! . . . If we are conscientious, the Holy Spirit will make us think about the past, and it is just here that the tyranny of nerves and the bondage of Satan comes in. The shores of life are strewn with ruined friendships, irreparable severances through our own blame or others, and when the Holy Spirit begins to reveal the tremendous twist, then comes the strange distress, "How can we repair it?" Many a sensitive soul has been driven into insanity through anguish of mind because he has never realized what Jesus Christ came to do, and all the asylums in the world will never touch them in the way of healing; the only thing that will is the realization of what the death of Jesus means, namely, that the damage we have done may be repaired through the efficacy of His cross. Jesus Christ has atoned for all, and He can make it good in us, not only as a gift but by a participation on our part. The miracle of the grace of God is that He can make the past as though it had never been; He can "restore to you the years that the swarming locust has eaten, the crawling locust, the consuming locust, and the chewing locust" (Joel 2:25). (PHIL. SIN)

JOEL 1:1—3:21

THE word of the LORD that came to Joel the son of Pethuel.

2 Hear this, you elders,
And give ear, all you inhabitants of the land!
Has *anything like* this happened in your days,
Or even in the days of your fathers?
3 Tell your children about it,
Let your children *tell* their children,
And their children another generation.

4 What the chewing locust left, the swarming locust has eaten;
What the swarming locust left, the crawling locust has eaten;
And what the crawling locust left, the consuming locust has eaten.

5 Awake, you drunkards, and weep;
And wail, all you drinkers of wine,
Because of the new wine,
For it has been cut off from your mouth.
6 For a nation has come up against My land,
Strong, and without number;
His teeth *are* the teeth of a lion,
And he has the fangs of a fierce lion.

7 He has laid waste My vine,
And ruined My fig tree;
He has stripped it bare and thrown *it* away;
Its branches are made white.

8 Lament like a virgin girded with sackcloth
For the husband of her youth.
9 The grain offering and the drink offering
Have been cut off from the house of the LORD;
The priests mourn, who minister to the LORD.
10 The field is wasted,
The land mourns;
For the grain is ruined,
The new wine is dried up,
The oil fails.

11 Be ashamed, you farmers,
Wail, you vinedressers,
For the wheat and the barley;
Because the harvest of the field has perished.
12 The vine has dried up,
And the fig tree has withered;
The pomegranate tree,
The palm tree also,
And the apple tree—
All the trees of the field are withered;

Surely joy has withered away from
the sons of men.

13 Gird yourselves and lament, you
priests;
Wail, you who minister before the
altar;
Come, lie all night in sackcloth,
You who minister to my God;
For the grain offering and the drink
offering
Are withheld from the house of your
God.

14 Consecrate a fast,
Call a sacred assembly;
Gather the elders
And all the inhabitants of the land
Into the house of the LORD your God,
And cry out to the LORD.

15 Alas for the day!
For the day of the LORD *is* at hand;
It shall come as destruction from the
Almighty.

16 Is not the food cut off before our
eyes,
Joy and gladness from the house of
our God?

17 The seed shrivels under the clods,
Storehouses are in shambles;
Barns are broken down,
For the grain has withered.

18 How the animals groan!
The herds of cattle are restless,
Because they have no pasture;
Even the flocks of sheep suffer
punishment.

19 O LORD, to You I cry out;
For fire has devoured the open
pastures,
And a flame has burned all the trees
of the field.

20 The beasts of the field also cry out
to You,
For the water brooks are dried up,
And fire has devoured the open
pastures.

2 BLOW the trumpet in Zion,
And sound an alarm in My holy
mountain!
Let all the inhabitants of the land
tremble;
For the day of the LORD is coming,
For it is at hand:

2 A day of darkness and gloominess,
A day of clouds and thick darkness,
Like the morning *clouds* spread over
the mountains.
A people *come,* great and strong,

The like of whom has never been;
Nor will there ever be any *such* after
them,
Even for many successive
generations.

3 A fire devours before them,
And behind them a flame burns;
The land *is* like the Garden of Eden
before them,
And behind them a desolate
wilderness;
Surely nothing shall escape them.

4 Their appearance is like the
appearance of horses;
And like swift steeds, so they run.

5 With a noise like chariots
Over mountaintops they leap,
Like the noise of a flaming fire that
devours the stubble,
Like a strong people set in battle
array.

6 Before them the people writhe in
pain;
All faces are drained of color.

7 They run like mighty men,
They climb the wall like men of war;
Every one marches in formation,
And they do not break ranks.

8 They do not push one another;
Every one marches in his own
column.
Though they lunge between the
weapons,
They are not cut down.

9 They run to and fro in the city,
They run on the wall;
They climb into the houses,
They enter at the windows like a thief.

10 The earth quakes before them,
The heavens tremble;
The sun and moon grow dark,
And the stars diminish their
brightness.

11 The LORD gives voice before His
army,
For His camp is very great;
For strong *is the One* who executes
His word.
For the day of the LORD *is* great and
very terrible;
Who can endure it?

12 "Now, therefore," says the LORD,
"Turn to Me with all your heart,
With fasting, with weeping, and with
mourning."

13 So rend your heart, and not your
garments;

Return to the LORD your God,
For He *is* gracious and merciful,
Slow to anger, and of great kindness;
And He relents from doing harm.
14 Who knows *if* He will turn and relent,
And leave a blessing behind Him—
A grain offering and a drink offering
For the LORD your God?

15 Blow the trumpet in Zion,
Consecrate a fast,
Call a sacred assembly;
16 Gather the people,
Sanctify the congregation,
Assemble the elders,
Gather the children and nursing
babes;
Let the bridegroom go out from his
chamber,
And the bride from her dressing
room.
17 Let the priests, who minister to the
LORD,
Weep between the porch and the
altar;
Let them say, "Spare Your people,
O LORD,
And do not give Your heritage to
reproach,
That the nations should rule over
them.
Why should they say among the
peoples,
'Where *is* their God?' "

18 Then the LORD will be zealous for
His land,
And pity His people.
19 The LORD will answer and say to His
people,
"Behold, I will send you grain and
new wine and oil,
And you will be satisfied by them;
I will no longer make you a reproach
among the nations.

20 "But I will remove far from you the
northern *army*,
And will drive him away into a barren
and desolate land,
With his face toward the eastern sea
And his back toward the western sea;
His stench will come up,
And his foul odor will rise,
Because he has done monstrous
things."

21 Fear not, O land;
Be glad and rejoice,
For the LORD has done marvelous
things!

22 Do not be afraid, you beasts of the
field;
For the open pastures are
springing up,
And the tree bears its fruit;
The fig tree and the vine yield their
strength.
23 Be glad then, you children of Zion,
And rejoice in the LORD your God;
For He has given you the former rain
faithfully,
And He will cause the rain to come
down for you—
The former rain,
And the latter rain in the first *month*.
24 The threshing floors shall be full of
wheat,
And the vats shall overflow with new
wine and oil.

25 "So I will restore to you the years that
the swarming locust has eaten,
The crawling locust,
The consuming locust,
And the chewing locust,
My great army which I sent among
you.
26 You shall eat in plenty and be
satisfied,
And praise the name of the LORD
your God,
Who has dealt wondrously with you;
And My people shall never be put
to shame.
27 Then you shall know that I *am* in
the midst of Israel:
I *am* the LORD your God
And there is no other.
My people shall never be put to
shame.

28 "And it shall come to pass afterward
That I will pour out My Spirit on
all flesh;
Your sons and your daughters shall
prophesy,
Your old men shall dream dreams,
Your young men shall see visions.
29 And also on *My* menservants and on
My maidservants
I will pour out My Spirit in those
days.

30 "And I will show wonders in the
heavens and in the earth:
Blood and fire and pillars of smoke.
31 The sun shall be turned into
darkness,
And the moon into blood,
Before the coming of the great and
awesome day of the LORD.

32 And it shall come to pass
    That whoever calls on the name of
       the LORD
    Shall be saved.
    For in Mount Zion and in Jerusalem
       there shall be deliverance,
    As the LORD has said,
    Among the remnant whom the LORD
       calls.

3 "FOR behold, in those days and at
       that time,
    When I bring back the captives of
       Judah and Jerusalem,
2   I will also gather all nations,
    And bring them down to the Valley
       of Jehoshaphat;
    And I will enter into judgment with
       them there
    On account of My people, My
       heritage Israel,
    Whom they have scattered among the
       nations;
    They have also divided up My land.
3   They have cast lots for My people,
    Have given a boy *as payment* for a
       harlot,
    And sold a girl for wine, that they
       may drink.

4   "Indeed, what have you to do
       with Me,
    O Tyre and Sidon, and all the coasts
       of Philistia?
    Will you retaliate against Me?
    But if you retaliate against Me,
    Swiftly and speedily I will return your
       retaliation upon your own head;
5   Because you have taken My silver and
       My gold,
    And have carried into your temples
       My prized possessions.
6   Also the people of Judah and the
       people of Jerusalem
    You have sold to the Greeks,
    That you may remove them far from
       their borders.

7   "Behold, I will raise them
    Out of the place to which you have
       sold them,
    And will return your retaliation upon
       your own head.
8   I will sell your sons and your
       daughters
    Into the hand of the people of
       Judah,
    And they will sell them to the
       Sabeans,
    To a people far off;
    For the LORD has spoken."

9   Proclaim this among the nations:
    "Prepare for war!
    Wake up the mighty men,
    Let all the men of war draw near,
    Let them come up.
10 Beat your plowshares into swords
    And your pruning hooks into spears;
    Let the weak say, 'I *am* strong.' "
11 Assemble and come, all you nations,
    And gather together all around.
    Cause Your mighty ones to go down
       there, O LORD.

12 "Let the nations be wakened, and
       come up to the Valley of
       Jehoshaphat;
    For there I will sit to judge all the
       surrounding nations.
13 Put in the sickle, for the harvest is
       ripe.
    Come, go down;
    For the winepress is full,
    The vats overflow—
    For their wickedness *is* great."

14 Multitudes, multitudes in the valley
       of decision!
    For the day of the LORD *is* near in
       the valley of decision.
15 The sun and moon will grow dark,
    And the stars will diminish their
       brightness.
16 The LORD also will roar from Zion,
    And utter His voice from Jerusalem;
    The heavens and earth will shake;
    But the LORD will be a shelter for
       His people,
    And the strength of the children of
       Israel.

17 "So you shall know that I *am* the LORD
       your God,
    Dwelling in Zion My holy mountain.
    Then Jerusalem shall be holy,
    And no aliens shall ever pass through
       her again."

18 And it will come to pass in that day
    That the mountains shall drip with
       new wine,
    The hills shall flow with milk,
    And all the brooks of Judah shall be
       flooded with water;
    A fountain shall flow from the house
       of the LORD
    And water the Valley of Acacias.

19 "Egypt shall be a desolation,
    And Edom a desolate wilderness,
    Because of violence *against* the
       people of Judah,

For they have shed innocent blood
in their land.
20 But Judah shall abide forever,
And Jerusalem from generation to
generation.
21 For I will acquit them of the guilt
of bloodshed, whom I had not
acquitted;
For the LORD dwells in Zion."

PSALM 140:6–13

6 I said to the LORD: "You *are* my God;
Hear the voice of my supplications,
O LORD.
7 O GOD the Lord, the strength of my
salvation,
You have covered my head in the day
of battle.
8 Do not grant, O LORD, the desires of
the wicked;
Do not further his *wicked* scheme,
Lest they be exalted.   Selah

9 *"As for* the head of those who
surround me,
Let the evil of their lips cover them;
10 Let burning coals fall upon them;
Let them be cast into the fire,
Into deep pits, that they rise not up
again.
11 Let not a slanderer be established in
the earth;
Let evil hunt the violent man to
overthrow *him*."

12 I know that the LORD will maintain
The cause of the afflicted,
And justice for the poor.
13 Surely the righteous shall give thanks
to Your name;
The upright shall dwell in Your
presence.

PROVERBS 29:24

24 WHOEVER is a partner with a thief
hates his own life;
He swears to tell the truth, but reveals
nothing.

REVELATION 2:1–29

"TO the angel of the church of Ephesus
write,
'These things says He who holds the
seven stars in His right hand, who walks
in the midst of the seven golden lampstands: 2 "I know your works, your labor,
your patience, and that you cannot bear
those who are evil. And you have tested
those who say they are apostles and are
not, and have found them liars; 3 and you
have persevered and have patience, and
have labored for My name's sake and have
not become weary. 4 Nevertheless I have
this against you, that you have left your

---

*People do not want to be devoted to
Jesus, but only to the cause He
started.* (UTMOST)

---

first love. 5 Remember therefore from
where you have fallen; repent and do the
first works, or else I will come to you quickly
and remove your lampstand from its place—
unless you repent. 6 But this you have, that
you hate the deeds of the Nicolaitans, which
I also hate.
7 "He who has an ear, let him hear what
the Spirit says to the churches. To him who
overcomes I will give to eat from the tree
of life, which is in the midst of the Paradise
of God." '
8 "And to the angel of the church in
Smyrna write,
'These things says the First and the Last,
who was dead, and came to life: 9 "I know
your works, tribulation, and poverty (but
you are rich); and *I know* the blasphemy
of those who say they are Jews and are
not, but *are* a synagogue of Satan. 10 Do
not fear any of those things which you are
about to suffer. Indeed, the devil is about
to throw *some* of you into prison, that you
may be tested, and you will have tribulation
ten days. Be faithful until death, and I will
give you the crown of life.
11 "He who has an ear, let him hear what
the Spirit says to the churches. He who
overcomes shall not be hurt by the second
death." '
12 "And to the angel of the church in
Pergamos write,
'These things says He who has the sharp
two-edged sword: 13 "I know your works,
and where you dwell, where Satan's throne
is. And you hold fast to My name, and
did not deny My faith even in the days in
which Antipas *was* My faithful martyr, who
was killed among you, where Satan dwells.
14 But I have a few things against you, because you have there those who hold the
doctrine of Balaam, who taught Balak to
put a stumbling block before the children
of Israel, to eat things sacrificed to idols,

and to commit sexual immorality. 15 Thus you also have those who hold the doctrine of the Nicolaitans, which thing I hate. 16 Repent, or else I will come to you quickly and will fight against them with the sword of My mouth.

17 "He who has an ear, let him hear what the Spirit says to the churches. To him who overcomes I will give some of the hidden manna to eat. And I will give him a white stone, and on the stone a new name written which no one knows except him who receives *it*." '

18 "And to the angel of the church in Thyatira write,

'These things says the Son of God, who has eyes like a flame of fire, and His feet like fine brass: 19 I know your works, love, service, faith, and your patience; and *as* for your works, the last *are* more than the first. 20 Nevertheless I have a few things against you, because you allow that woman Jezebel, who calls herself a prophetess, to teach and seduce My servants to commit sexual immorality and eat things sacrificed to idols. 21 And I gave her time to repent of her sexual immorality, and she did not repent.

22 Indeed I will cast her into a sickbed, and those who commit adultery with her into great tribulation, unless they repent of their deeds. 23 I will kill her children with death, and all the churches shall know that I am He who searches the minds and hearts. And I will give to each one of you according to your works.

24 "Now to you I say, and to the rest in Thyatira, as many as do not have this doctrine, who have not known the depths of Satan, as they say, I will put on you no other burden. 25 But hold fast what you have till I come. 26 And he who overcomes, and keeps My works until the end, to him I will give power over the nations—

27 'He shall rule them with a rod
        of iron;
    They shall be dashed to pieces like
        the potter's vessels'—

as I also have received from My Father; 28 and I will give him the morning star.

29 "He who has an ear, let him hear what the Spirit says to the churches." '

◆◆◆

Reading 347—Intelligent Witnessing
Revelation 3:2, 3

I do not think we have enough of the wondering spirit that the Holy Spirit gives. It is the child-spirit. A child is always wide awake with wonder. But as we get older we forget that a child's wonder is nearer the truth than our older knowledge. When through Jesus Christ we are rightly related to God, we learn to watch and wait, and wait wonderingly. "I wonder how God will answer this prayer." "I wonder how God will answer the prayer the Holy Spirit is praying in me." "I wonder what glory God will bring to Himself out of the strange perplexities I am in." "I wonder what new turn His providence will take in manifesting Himself in my ways."

The childlike wondering mind of the Holy Spirit, if I may say so reverently, was exhibited in the Lord Jesus Christ as everlasting wonder and expectancy at His Father's working. "I do not speak on My own *authority*," and "the Father who dwells in Me does the works" (John 14:10). Our Lord said that when the Holy Spirit is come, "He will not speak on His own *authority*, but whatever He hears He will speak." The Lord Jesus spoke and worked from the great big child-heart of God. God Almighty became incarnate as a little child, and Jesus Christ's message in us must become as that of little children.   (ASK)

AMOS 1:1—3:15

THE words of Amos, who was among the sheepbreeders of Tekoa, which he saw concerning Israel in the days of Uzziah king of Judah, and in the days of Jeroboam the son of Joash, king of Israel, two years before the earthquake.

2 And he said:

"The LORD roars from Zion,
And utters His voice from Jerusalem;
The pastures of the shepherds mourn,
And the top of Carmel withers."

3 Thus says the LORD:

"For three transgressions of
Damascus, and for four,
I will not turn away its *punishment*,
Because they have threshed Gilead
with implements of iron.
4 But I will send a fire into the house
of Hazael,
Which shall devour the palaces of
Ben-Hadad.
5 I will also break the *gate* bar of
Damascus,
And cut off the inhabitant from the
Valley of Aven,
And the one who holds the scepter
from Beth Eden.
The people of Syria shall go captive
to Kir,"
Says the LORD.

6 Thus says the LORD:

"For three transgressions of Gaza,
and for four,
I will not turn away its *punishment*,
Because they took captive the whole
captivity
To deliver *them* up to Edom.
7 But I will send a fire upon the wall
of Gaza,
Which shall devour its palaces.
8 I will cut off the inhabitant from
Ashdod,
And the one who holds the scepter
from Ashkelon;
I will turn My hand against Ekron,
And the remnant of the Philistines
shall perish,"
Says the Lord GOD.

9 Thus says the LORD:

"For three transgressions of Tyre,
and for four,
I will not turn away its *punishment*,

Because they delivered up the whole
captivity to Edom,
And did not remember the covenant
of brotherhood.
10 But I will send a fire upon the wall
of Tyre,
Which shall devour its palaces."

11 Thus says the LORD:

"For three transgressions of Edom,
and for four,
I will not turn away its *punishment*,
Because he pursued his brother with
the sword,
And cast off all pity;
His anger tore perpetually,
And he kept his wrath forever.
12 But I will send a fire upon Teman,
Which shall devour the palaces of
Bozrah."

13 Thus says the LORD:

"For three transgressions of the people
of Ammon, and for four,
I will not turn away its *punishment*,
Because they ripped open the women
with child in Gilead,
That they might enlarge their
territory.
14 But I will kindle a fire in the wall
of Rabbah,
And it shall devour its palaces,
Amid shouting in the day of battle,
And a tempest in the day of the
whirlwind.
15 Their king shall go into captivity,
He and his princes together,"
Says the LORD.

2 THUS says the LORD:

"For three transgressions of Moab,
and for four,
I will not turn away its *punishment*,
Because he burned the bones of the
king of Edom to lime.
2 But I will send a fire upon Moab,
And it shall devour the palaces of
Kerioth;
Moab shall die with tumult,
With shouting *and* trumpet sound.
3 And I will cut off the judge from
its midst,
And slay all its princes with him,"
Says the LORD.

4 Thus says the LORD:

"For three transgressions of Judah,
and for four,

I will not turn away its *punishment,*
Because they have despised the law
of the Lord,
And have not kept His
commandments.
Their lies lead them astray,
Lies which their fathers followed.
5   But I will send a fire upon Judah,
And it shall devour the palaces of
Jerusalem."

6 Thus says the Lord:

"For three transgressions of Israel, and
for four,
I will not turn away its *punishment,*
Because they sell the righteous for
silver,
And the poor for a pair of sandals.
7   They pant after the dust of the earth
which is on the head of the poor,
And pervert the way of the humble.
A man and his father go in to the
same girl,
To defile My holy name.
8   They lie down by every altar on
clothes taken in pledge,
And drink the wine of the
condemned *in* the house of their
god.

9   "Yet *it was* I *who* destroyed the Amorite
before them,
Whose height *was* like the height of
the cedars,
And he *was as* strong as the oaks;
Yet I destroyed his fruit above
And his roots beneath.
10 Also *it was* I *who* brought you up
from the land of Egypt,
And led you forty years through the
wilderness,
To possess the land of the Amorite.
11 I raised up some of your sons as
prophets,
And some of your young men as
Nazirites.
Is it not so, O you children of Israel?"
Says the Lord.
12 "But you gave the Nazirites wine to
drink,
And commanded the prophets
saying,
'Do not prophesy!'

13 "Behold, I am weighed down by you,
As a cart full of sheaves is weighed
down.
14 Therefore flight shall perish from the
swift,

The strong shall not strengthen his
power,
Nor shall the mighty deliver himself;
15 He shall not stand who handles the
bow,
The swift of foot shall not escape,
Nor shall he who rides a horse deliver
himself.
16 The most courageous men of might
Shall flee naked in that day,"
Says the Lord.

3 HEAR this word that the Lord has
spoken against you, O children of Israel, against the whole family which I
brought up from the land of Egypt, saying:

2   "You only have I known of all the
families of the earth;
Therefore I will punish you for all
your iniquities."

3   Can two walk together, unless they
are agreed?
4   Will a lion roar in the forest, when
he has no prey?
Will a young lion cry out of his den,
if he has caught nothing?
5   Will a bird fall into a snare on the
earth, where there is no trap
for it?
Will a snare spring up from the earth,
if it has caught nothing at all?
6   If a trumpet is blown in a city, will
not the people be afraid?
If there is calamity in a city, will not
the Lord have done *it?*

7   Surely the Lord God does nothing,
Unless He reveals His secret to His
servants the prophets.
8   A lion has roared!
Who will not fear?
The Lord God has spoken!
Who can but prophesy?

9   "Proclaim in the palaces at Ashdod,
And in the palaces in the land of
Egypt, and say:
'Assemble on the mountains of
Samaria;
See great tumults in her midst,
And the oppressed within her.
10 For they do not know to do right,'
Says the Lord,
'Who store up violence and robbery
in their palaces.'"

11 Therefore thus says the Lord God:

"An adversary *shall be* all around the
land;

He shall sap your strength from you,
And your palaces shall be plundered."

12 Thus says the LORD:

"As a shepherd takes from the mouth
  of a lion
Two legs or a piece of an ear,
So shall the children of Israel be taken
  out
Who dwell in Samaria—
In the corner of a bed and on the
  edge of a couch!
13 Hear and testify against the house
  of Jacob,"
Says the Lord GOD, the God of hosts,
14 "That in the day I punish Israel for
  their transgressions,
I will also visit *destruction* on the
  altars of Bethel;
And the horns of the altar shall be
  cut off
And fall to the ground.
15 I will destroy the winter house along
  with the summer house;
The houses of ivory shall perish,
And the great houses shall have an
  end,"
Says the LORD.

PSALM 141:1–4

1 LORD, I cry out to You;
  Make haste to me!
  Give ear to my voice when I cry out
    to You.
2 Let my prayer be set before You *as*
    incense,
  The lifting up of my hands *as* the
    evening sacrifice.

Silent prayer is, in reality, concentration on God.   (PLACE HELP)

---

3 Set a guard, O LORD, over my mouth;
  Keep watch over the door of my lips.
4 Do not incline my heart to any evil
    thing,
  To practice wicked works
  With men who work iniquity;
  And do not let me eat of their
    delicacies.

PROVERBS 29:25

25 THE fear of man brings a snare,
  But whoever trusts in the LORD shall
    be safe.

REVELATION 3:1–22

"AND to the angel of the church in Sardis
write,

'These things says He who has the seven
Spirits of God and the seven stars: "I know
your works, that you have a name that you
are alive, but you are dead. 2 Be watchful,
and strengthen the things which remain,
that are ready to die, for I have not found
your works perfect before God. 3 Remember therefore how you have received
and heard; hold fast and repent. Therefore
if you will not watch, I will come upon
you as a thief, and you will not know what
hour I will come upon you. 4 You have a
few names even in Sardis who have not
defiled their garments; and they shall walk
with Me in white, for they are worthy.
5 He who overcomes shall be clothed in
white garments, and I will not blot out
his name from the Book of Life; but I will
confess his name before My Father and before His angels.

6 "He who has an ear, let him hear what
the Spirit says to the churches." '

7 "And to the angel of the church in
Philadelphia write,

'These things says He who is holy, He
who is true, "He who has the key of David,
He who opens and no one shuts, and shuts
and no one opens": 8 I know your works.
See, I have set before you an open door,
and no one can shut it; for you have a
little strength, have kept My word, and have
not denied My name. 9 Indeed I will make
those of the synagogue of Satan, who say
they are Jews and are not, but lie—indeed
I will make them come and worship before
your feet, and to know that I have loved
you. 10 Because you have kept My command to persevere, I also will keep you
from the hour of trial which shall come
upon the whole world, to test those who
dwell on the earth. 11 Behold, I am coming
quickly! Hold fast what you have, that no
one may take your crown. 12 He who overcomes, I will make him a pillar in the temple
of My God, and he shall go out no more.
I will write on him the name of My God
and the name of the city of My God, the
New Jerusalem, which comes down out of
heaven from My God. And *I will write on
him* My new name.

---

*A disciple is one who has nothing
but a new name written all over
him.*   (BRILL. HERITAGE)

---

13 "He who has an ear, let him hear what the Spirit says to the churches." '

14 "And to the angel of the church of the Laodiceans write,

'These things says the Amen, the Faithful and True Witness, the Beginning of the creation of God: 15 "I know your works, that you are neither cold nor hot. I could wish you were cold or hot. 16 So then, because you are lukewarm, and neither cold nor hot, I will vomit you out of My mouth. 17 Because you say, 'I am rich, have become wealthy, and have need of nothing'—and do not know that you are wretched, miserable, poor, blind, and naked— 18 I counsel you to buy from Me gold refined in the fire, that you may be rich; and white garments, that you may be clothed, *that* the shame of your nakedness may not be revealed; and anoint your eyes with eye salve, that you may see. 19 As many as I love, I rebuke and chasten. Therefore be zealous and repent. 20 Behold, I stand at the door and knock. If anyone hears My voice and opens the door, I will come in to him and dine with him, and he with Me. 21 To him who overcomes I will grant to sit with Me on My throne, as I also overcame and sat down with My Father on His throne.

22 "He who has an ear, let him hear what the Spirit says to the churches." ' "

◆◆◆◆

Reading 348—Vision by Personal Character
Revelation 4:1

An elevated mood can only come out of an elevated habit of personal character. If in the externals of your life you live up to the highest you know, God will continually say—"Friend, go up higher. . . ." When the Devil puts you into an elevated place, he makes you screw your idea of holiness beyond what flesh and blood could ever bear, it is a spiritual acrobatic performance, you are just poised and dare not move; but when God elevates you by His grace into the heavenly places, instead of finding a pinnacle to cling to, you find a great tableland where it is easy to move.

Compare this week in your spiritual history with the same week last year and see how God has called you up higher. We have all been brought to see from a higher standpoint. Never let God give you one point of truth which you do not instantly live up to. Always work it out, keep in the light of it.

Growth in grace is measured not by the fact that you have not gone back, but that you have an insight into where you are spiritually; you have heard God say, "Come up higher," not to you personally, but to the insight of your character.

"Shall I hide from Abraham what I am doing?" God has to hide from us what He does until by personal character we get to the place where He can reveal it. (*UTMOST*)

AMOS 4:1—5:27

1 HEAR this word, you cows of
  Bashan, who *are* on the mountain
    of Samaria,
  Who oppress the poor,
  Who crush the needy,
  Who say to your husbands, "Bring
    wine, let us drink!"
2 The Lord GOD has sworn by His
    holiness:

"Behold, the days shall come upon you
  When He will take you away with
    fishhooks,
  And your posterity with fishhooks.
3 You will go out *through* broken *walls*,
  Each one straight ahead of her,
  And you will be cast into Harmon,"
  Says the LORD.

4 "Come to Bethel and transgress,
  At Gilgal multiply transgression;

Bring your sacrifices every morning,
Your tithes every three days.

5 Offer a sacrifice of thanksgiving with
leaven,
Proclaim *and* announce the freewill
offerings;
For this you love,
You children of Israel!"
Says the Lord God.

6 "Also I gave you cleanness of teeth
in all your cities.
And lack of bread in all your places;
Yet you have not returned to Me,"
Says the Lord.

7 "I also withheld rain from you,
When *there were* still three months
to the harvest.
I made it rain on one city,
I withheld rain from another city.
One part was rained upon,
And where it did not rain the part
withered.

8 So two *or* three cities wandered to
another city to drink water,
But they were not satisfied;
Yet you have not returned to Me,"
Says the Lord.

9 "I blasted you with blight and mildew.
When your gardens increased,
Your vineyards,
Your fig trees,
And your olive trees,
The locust devoured *them*;
Yet you have not returned to Me,"
Says the Lord.

10 "I sent among you a plague after the
manner of Egypt;
Your young men I killed with a
sword,
Along with your captive horses;
I made the stench of your camps
come up into your nostrils;
Yet you have not returned to Me,"
Says the Lord.

11 "I overthrew *some* of you,
As God overthrew Sodom and
Gomorrah,
And you were like a firebrand plucked
from the burning;
Yet you have not returned to Me,"
Says the Lord.

12 "Therefore thus will I do to you,
O Israel;
Because I will do this to you,
Prepare to meet your God, O Israel!"

13 For behold,
He who forms mountains,
And creates the wind,
Who declares to man what his
thought *is,*
And makes the morning darkness,
Who treads the high places of the
earth—
The Lord God of hosts *is* His name.

5 HEAR this word which I take up
against you, a lamentation, O house
of Israel:

2 The virgin of Israel has fallen;
She will rise no more.
She lies forsaken on her land;
There is no one to raise her up.

3 For thus says the Lord God:

"The city that goes out by a thousand
Shall have a hundred left,
And that which goes out by a
hundred
Shall have ten left to the house of
Israel."

4 For thus says the Lord to the house
of Israel:

"Seek Me and live;
5 But do not seek Bethel,
Nor enter Gilgal,
Nor pass over to Beersheba;
For Gilgal shall surely go into
captivity,
And Bethel shall come to nothing.
6 Seek the Lord and live,
Lest He break out like fire *in* the
house of Joseph,
And devour *it,*
With no one to quench *it* in Bethel—
7 You who turn justice to wormwood,
And lay righteousness to rest in the
earth!"

8 He made the Pleiades and Orion;
He turns the shadow of death into
morning
And makes the day dark as night;
He calls for the waters of the sea
And pours them out on the face of
the earth;
The Lord *is* His name.
9 He rains ruin upon the strong,
So that fury comes upon the fortress.

10 They hate the one who rebukes in
the gate,

And they abhor the one who speaks
    uprightly.
11 Therefore, because you tread down
    the poor
    And take grain taxes from him,
    Though you have built houses of
    hewn stone,
    Yet you shall not dwell in them;
    You have planted pleasant vineyards,
    But you shall not drink wine from
    them.
12 For I know your manifold
    transgressions
    And your mighty sins:
    Afflicting the just *and* taking bribes;
    Diverting the poor *from justice* at the
    gate.
13 Therefore the prudent keep silent at
    that time,
    For it *is* an evil time.

14 Seek good and not evil,
    That you may live;
    So the Lord God of hosts will be
    with you,
    As you have spoken.
15 Hate evil, love good;
    Establish justice in the gate.
    It may be that the Lord God of hosts
    Will be gracious to the remnant of
    Joseph.

16 Therefore the Lord God of hosts, the
Lord, says this:

   "*There shall be* wailing in all streets,
    And they shall say in all the highways,
   'Alas! Alas!'
    They shall call the farmer to
    mourning,
    And skillful lamenters to wailing.
17 In all vineyards *there shall be* wailing,
    For I will pass through you,"
    Says the Lord.

18 Woe to you who desire the day of
    the Lord!
    For what good *is* the day of the Lord
    to you?
    It *will be* darkness, and not light.
19 It *will be* as though a man fled from
    a lion,
    And a bear met him!
    Or *as though* he went into the house,
    Leaned his hand on the wall,
    And a serpent bit him!
20 *Is* not the day of the Lord darkness,
    and not light?
    Is it not very dark, with no brightness
    in it?

21 "I hate, I despise your feast days,
    And I do not savor your sacred
    assemblies.
22 Though you offer Me burnt offerings
    and your grain offerings,
    I will not accept *them,*
    Nor will I regard your fattened peace
    offerings.
23 Take away from Me the noise of your
    songs,
    For I will not hear the melody of
    your stringed instruments.
24 But let justice run down like water,
    And righteousness like a mighty
    stream.

25 "Did you offer Me sacrifices and
    offerings
    In the wilderness forty years,
      O house of Israel?
26 You also carried Sikkuth your king
    And Chiun, your idols,
    The star of your gods,
    Which you made for yourselves.
27 Therefore I will send you into
    captivity beyond Damascus,"
    Says the Lord, whose name *is* the
    God of hosts.

PSALM 141:5–10

5 LET the righteous strike me;
    It shall be a kindness.
    And let him rebuke me;
    It shall be as excellent oil;
    Let my head not refuse it.

    For still my prayer *is* against the deeds
    of the wicked.

---

*The very powers of darkness are
paralyzed by prayer.* (Run)

---

6 Their judges are overthrown by the
    sides of the cliff,
    And they hear my words, for they are
    sweet.
7 Our bones are scattered at the mouth
    of the grave,
    As when one plows and breaks up the
    earth.

8 But my eyes *are* upon You, O God
    the Lord;
    In You I take refuge;
    Do not leave my soul destitute.
9 Keep me from the snares they have laid
    for me,

And from the traps of the workers of
iniquity.
10 Let the wicked fall into their own nets,
While I escape safely.

PROVERBS 29:26

26 MANY seek the ruler's favor,
But justice for man *comes* from the
LORD.

---

*T*he man who looks for justice from
others is a fool.   (SHADE)

REVELATION 4:1–11

AFTER these things I looked, and behold,
a door *standing* open in heaven. And the
first voice which I heard *was* like a trumpet
speaking with me, saying, "Come up here,
and I will show you things which must
take place after this."
2 Immediately I was in the Spirit; and
behold, a throne set in heaven, and *One*
sat on the throne. 3 And He who sat there
was like a jasper and a sardius stone in appearance; and *there was* a rainbow around
the throne, in appearance like an emerald.
4 Around the throne *were* twenty-four
thrones, and on the thrones I saw twenty-
four elders sitting, clothed in white robes;
and they had crowns of gold on their heads.
5 And from the throne proceeded lightnings, thunderings, and voices. Seven lamps
of fire *were* burning before the throne,
which are the seven Spirits of God.
6 Before the throne *there was* a sea of glass,
like crystal. And in the midst of the throne,
and around the throne, *were* four living creatures full of eyes in front and in back.
7 The first living creature *was* like a lion,
the second living creature like a calf, the
third living creature had a face like a man,
and the fourth living creature *was* like a
flying eagle. 8 *The* four living creatures, each
having six wings, were full of eyes around
and within. And they do not rest day or
night, saying:

"Holy, holy, holy,
Lord God Almighty,
Who was and is and is to come!"

9 Whenever the living creatures give glory
and honor and thanks to Him who sits on
the throne, who lives forever and ever,
10 the twenty-four elders fall down before
Him who sits on the throne and worship
Him who lives forever and ever, and cast
their crowns before the throne, saying:

11 "You are worthy, O Lord,
To receive glory and honor and
power;
For You created all things,
And by Your will they exist and were
created."

◆◆◆◆

Reading 349—The Divine Paradox
Revelation 5:6

In the days of His flesh Jesus Christ exhibited this divine paradox of the
Lion and the Lamb. He was the Lion in majesty, rebuking the winds and
demons: He was the Lamb in meekness, "who, when He was reviled, did not
revile in return." He was the Lion in power, raising the dead: He was the
Lamb in patience—who was "led as a lamb to the slaughter, and as a sheep
before its shearers is silent, so He opened not His mouth." He was the Lion
in authority, "You have heard that it was said . . . But I say to you, ...":
He was the Lamb in gentleness, "Let the little children come to Me . . . and
He took them up in his arms, laid His hands on them, and blessed them."

   In our personal lives Jesus Christ proves Himself to be all this—He is the
Lamb to expiate our sins, to lift us out of condemnation and plant within us
His own heredity of holiness: He is the Lion to rule over us, so that we
gladly say, "the government of this life shall be upon His shoulders." And

what is true in individual life is to be true also in the universe at large. The time is coming when the Lion of the Tribe of Judah shall reign, and when "the kingdoms of this world have become *the kingdoms* of our Lord, and of His Christ."

One remaining paradox—In Revelation 6:16 "the wrath of the Lamb" is mentioned. We know what the wrath of a lion is like—but *the wrath of the Lamb!*—it is beyond our conception. All one can say about it is that the wrath of God is the terrible obverse side of the love of God.   (*CONFORMED*)

AMOS 6:1—7:17

1   WOE to you *who are* at ease in Zion,
And trust in Mount Samaria,
Notable persons in the chief nation,
To whom the house of Israel comes!

2   Go over to Calneh and see;
And from there go to Hamath the great;
Then go down to Gath of the Philistines.
Are you better than these kingdoms?
Or is their territory greater than your territory?

3   *Woe to* you who put far off the day of doom,
Who cause the seat of violence to come near;

4   Who lie on beds of ivory,
Stretch out on your couches,
Eat lambs from the flock
And calves from the midst of the stall;

5   Who sing idly to the sound of stringed instruments,
And invent for yourselves musical instruments like David;

6   Who drink wine from bowls,
And anoint yourselves with the best ointments,
But are not grieved for the affliction of Joseph.

7   Therefore they shall now go captive as the first of the captives,
And those who recline at banquets shall be removed.

8   The Lord GOD has sworn by Himself,
The LORD God of hosts says:
"I abhor the pride of Jacob,
And hate his palaces;
Therefore I will deliver up *the* city
And all that is in it."

9 Then it shall come to pass, that if ten men remain in one house, they shall die. 10 And when a relative *of the dead*, with one who will burn *the bodies*, picks up the bodies to take them out of the house, he will say to one inside the house, "*Are there any more with you?*"

Then someone will say, "None."

And he will say, "Hold your tongue! For we dare not mention the name of the LORD."

11   For behold, the LORD gives a command:
He will break the great house into bits,
And the little house into pieces.

12   Do horses run on rocks?
Does *one* plow *there* with oxen?
Yet you have turned justice into gall,
And the fruit of righteousness into wormwood,

13   You who rejoice over Lo Debar,
Who say, "Have we not taken Karnaim for ourselves
By our own strength?"

14 "But, behold, I will raise up a nation against you,
O house of Israel,"
Says the LORD God of hosts;
"And they will afflict you from the entrance of Hamath
To the Valley of the Arabah."

7 THUS the Lord GOD showed me: Behold, He formed locust swarms at the beginning of the late crop; indeed *it was* the late crop after the king's mowings. 2 And so it was, when they had finished eating the grass of the land, that I said:

"O Lord GOD, forgive, I pray!
Oh, that Jacob may stand,
For he *is* small!"

3   *So* the LORD relented concerning this.
"It shall not be," said the LORD.

4 Thus the Lord GOD showed me: Behold, the Lord GOD called for conflict by fire, and it consumed the great deep and devoured the territory. 5 Then I said:

"O Lord God, cease, I pray!
Oh, that Jacob may stand,
For he *is* small!"
6   *So* the Lord relented concerning this.
"This also shall not be," said the
Lord God.

7 Thus He showed me: Behold, the Lord
stood on a wall *made* with a plumb line,
with a plumb line in His hand. 8 And the
Lord said to me, "Amos, what do you see?"
And I said, "A plumb line."
Then the Lord said:

"Behold, I am setting a plumb line
In the midst of My people Israel;
I will not pass by them anymore.
9   The high places of Isaac shall be
desolate,
And the sanctuaries of Israel shall be
laid waste.
I will rise with the sword against the
house of Jeroboam."

10 Then Amaziah the priest of Bethel sent
to Jeroboam king of Israel, saying, "Amos
has conspired against you in the midst of
the house of Israel. The land is not able
to bear all his words. 11 For thus Amos
has said:

'Jeroboam shall die by the sword,
And Israel shall surely be led away
captive
From their own land.' "

12 Then Amaziah said to Amos:

"Go, you seer!
Flee to the land of Judah.
There eat bread,
And there prophesy.
13   But never again prophesy at Bethel,
For it *is* the king's sanctuary,
And it *is* the royal residence."

14 Then Amos answered, and said to
Amaziah:

"I *was* no prophet,
Nor *was* I a son of a prophet,
But I *was* a sheepbreeder
And a tender of sycamore fruit.
15   Then the Lord took me as I followed
the flock,
And the Lord said to me,
'Go, prophesy to My people Israel.'
16   Now therefore, hear the word of the
Lord:
You say, 'Do not prophesy against
Israel,

And do not spout against the house
of Isaac.'

17 "Therefore thus says the Lord:

'Your wife shall be a harlot in the
city;
Your sons and daughters shall fall by
the sword;
Your land shall be divided by *survey*
line;
You shall die in a defiled land;
And Israel shall surely be led away
captive
From his own land.' "

PSALM 142:1–7

1   I cry out to the Lord with my voice;
With my voice to the Lord I make
my supplication.
2   I pour out my complaint before Him;
I declare before Him my trouble.

3   When my spirit was overwhelmed
within me,
Then You knew my path.
In the way in which I walk
They have secretly set a snare for me.
4   Look on *my* right hand and see,
For *there is* no one who
acknowledges me;
Refuge has failed me;
No one cares for my soul.

5   I cried out to You, O Lord:
I said, "You *are* my refuge,
My portion in the land of the living.
6   Attend to my cry,
For I am brought very low;
Deliver me from my persecutors,
For they are stronger than I.
7   Bring my soul out of prison,
That I may praise Your name;
The righteous shall surround me,
For You shall deal bountifully
with me."

PROVERBS 29:27

27   AN unjust man *is* an abomination to
the righteous,
And *he who is* upright in the way *is* an
abomination to the wicked.

REVELATION 5:1–14

AND I saw in the right *hand* of Him who
sat on the throne a scroll written inside

and on the back, sealed with seven seals. 2 Then I saw a strong angel proclaiming with a loud voice, "Who is worthy to open the scroll and to loose its seals?" 3 And no one in heaven or on the earth or under the earth was able to open the scroll, or to look at it.

4 So I wept much, because no one was found worthy to open and read the scroll, or to look at it. 5 But one of the elders said to me, "Do not weep. Behold, the Lion of the tribe of Judah, the Root of David, has prevailed to open the scroll and to loose its seven seals."

There are no infallible principles, only an infallible Person. (DISCIPLES)

6 And I looked, and behold, in the midst of the throne and of the four living creatures, and in the midst of the elders, stood a Lamb as though it had been slain, having seven horns and seven eyes, which are the seven Spirits of God sent out into all the earth. 7 Then He came and took the scroll out of the right hand of Him who sat on the throne.

8 Now when He had taken the scroll, the four living creatures and the twenty-four elders fell down before the Lamb, each having a harp, and golden bowls full of incense, which are the prayers of the saints. 9 And they sang a new song, saying:

"You are worthy to take the scroll,
And to open its seals;

For You were slain,
And have redeemed us to God by
  Your blood
Out of every tribe and tongue and
  people and nation,
10 And have made us kings and priests
  to our God;
And we shall reign on the earth."

11 Then I looked, and I heard the voice of many angels around the throne, the living creatures, and the elders; and the number of them was ten thousand times ten thousand, and thousands of thousands, 12 saying with a loud voice:

"Worthy is the Lamb who was
  slain
To receive power and riches and
  wisdom,
And strength and honor and glory
  and blessing!"

13 And every creature which is in heaven and on the earth and under the earth and such as are in the sea, and all that are in them, I heard saying:

"Blessing and honor and glory and
  power
Be to Him who sits on the throne,
And to the Lamb, forever and
  ever!"

14 Then the four living creatures said, "Amen!" And the twenty-four elders fell down and worshiped Him who lives forever and ever.

◆◆◆◆

Reading 350—The Scriptural Trinity
Proverbs 30:4

The essential nature of God the Father, of God the Son and of God the Spirit is the same. The characteristics that marked God the Father in the old dispensation, and that marked God the Son when He lived on this earth, mark God the Holy Ghost in this present dispensation. (BIB. ETHICS)

The word "Trinity" is not a Bible word. Over and over again in the Bible the Triune God is revealed, so that the idea conveyed by the Trinity is thoroughly Scriptural. The following distinctions have existed from all eternity:

The Essence of Godhead (*esse*) usually known as God the Father;
The Existence of Godhead (*existere*) usually known as God the Son;
The Proceeding of Godhead (*procedere*) usually known as God the Holy Ghost. (BIB. PSYCH.)

Just as God the Father was rejected and spurned in the Old Testament dispensation, and Jesus Christ the Son was despised and spurned in His dispensation, so God the Holy Ghost is despised (as well as flattered) in this dispensation.   (BIB. PSYCH.)

AMOS 8:1—9:15

THUS the Lord GOD showed me: Behold, a basket of summer fruit. 2 And He said, "Amos, what do you see?"

So I said, "A basket of summer fruit."

Then the LORD said to me:

"The end has come upon My people Israel;
I will not pass by them anymore.
3   And the songs of the temple
Shall be wailing in that day,"
Says the Lord GOD—
"Many dead bodies everywhere,
They shall be thrown out in silence."

4   Hear this, you who swallow up the needy,
And make the poor of the land fail,

5 Saying:

"When will the New Moon be past,
That we may sell grain?
And the Sabbath,
That we may trade wheat?
Making the ephah small and the shekel large,
Falsifying the scales by deceit,
6   That we may buy the poor for silver,
And the needy for a pair of sandals—
Even sell the bad wheat?"

7   The LORD has sworn by the pride of Jacob:
"Surely I will never forget any of their works.
8   Shall the land not tremble for this,
And everyone mourn who dwells in it?
All of it shall swell like the River,
Heave and subside
Like the River of Egypt.

9   "And it shall come to pass in that day,"
says the Lord GOD,
"That I will make the sun go down at noon,
And I will darken the earth in broad daylight;
10   I will turn your feasts into mourning,
And all your songs into lamentation;
I will bring sackcloth on every waist,

And baldness on every head;
I will make it like mourning for an only *son*,
And its end like a bitter day.

11   "Behold, the days are coming," says the Lord GOD,
"That I will send a famine on the land,
Not a famine of bread,
Nor a thirst for water,
But of hearing the words of the LORD.
12   They shall wander from sea to sea,
And from north to east;
They shall run to and fro, seeking the word of the LORD,
But shall not find *it*.

13   "In that day the fair virgins
And strong young men
Shall faint from thirst.
14   Those who swear by the sin of Samaria,
Who say,
'As your god lives, O Dan!'
And, 'As the way of Beersheba lives!'
They shall fall and never rise again."

9 I saw the Lord standing by the altar, and He said:

"Strike the doorposts, that the thresholds may shake,
And break them on the heads of them all.
I will slay the last of them with the sword.
He who flees from them shall not get away,
And he who escapes from them shall not be delivered.

2   "Though they dig into hell,
From there My hand shall take them;
Though they climb up to heaven,
From there I will bring them down;
3   And though they hide themselves on top of Carmel,
From there I will search and take them;
Though they hide from My sight at the bottom of the sea,
From there I will command the serpent, and it shall bite them;

4   Though they go into captivity before
        their enemies,
    From there I will command the
        sword,
    And it shall slay them.
    I will set My eyes on them for harm
        and not for good."

5   The Lord GOD of hosts,
    He who touches the earth and it
        melts,
    And all who dwell there mourn;
    All of it shall swell like the River,
    And subside like the River of Egypt.
6   He who builds His layers in the sky,
    And has founded His strata in the
        earth;
    Who calls for the waters of the sea,
    And pours them out on the face of
        the earth—
    The LORD *is* His name.

7   "*Are* you not like the people of
        Ethiopia to Me,
    O children of Israel?" says the LORD.
    "Did I not bring up Israel from the
        land of Egypt,
    The Philistines from Caphtor,
    And the Syrians from Kir?

8   "Behold, the eyes of the Lord GOD
        are on the sinful kingdom,
    And I will destroy it from the face
        of the earth;
    Yet I will not utterly destroy the
        house of Jacob,"
    Says the LORD.

9   "For surely I will command,
    And will sift the house of Israel
        among all nations,
    As *grain* is sifted in a sieve;
    Yet not the smallest grain shall fall
        to the ground.
10 All the sinners of My people shall
        die by the sword,
    Who say, 'The calamity shall not
        overtake nor confront us.'

11 "On that day I will raise up
    The tabernacle of David, which has
        fallen down,
    And repair its damages;
    I will raise up its ruins,
    And rebuild it as in the days of old;
12 That they may possess the remnant
        of Edom,
    And all the Gentiles who are called
        by My name,"
    Says the LORD who does this thing.

13 "Behold, the days are coming," says
        the LORD,
    "When the plowman shall overtake the
        reaper,
    And the treader of grapes him who
        sows seed;
    The mountains shall drip with sweet
        wine,
    And all the hills shall flow *with it.*
14 I will bring back the captives of My
        people Israel;
    They shall build the waste cities and
        inhabit *them;*
    They shall plant vineyards and drink
        wine from them;
    They shall also make gardens and eat
        fruit from them.
15 I will plant them in their land,
    And no longer shall they be
        pulled up
    From the land I have given them,"
    Says the LORD your God.

PSALM 143:1–6

1   HEAR my prayer, O LORD,
    Give ear to my supplications!
    In Your faithfulness answer me,
    And in Your righteousness.
2   Do not enter into judgment with Your
        servant,
    For in Your sight no one living is
        righteous.

3   For the enemy has persecuted my soul;
    He has crushed my life to the ground;
    He has made me dwell in darkness,
    Like those who have long been dead.
4   Therefore my spirit is overwhelmed
        within me;
    My heart within me is distressed.

5   I remember the days of old;
    I meditate on all Your works;
    I muse on the work of Your hands.
6   I spread out my hands to You;
    My soul *longs* for You like a thirsty
        land.   Selah

PROVERBS 30:1–4

THE words of Agur the son of Jakeh, *his*
utterance. This man declared to Ithiel—to
Ithiel and Ucal:

2   Surely I *am* more stupid than *any*
        man,
    And do not have the understanding
        of a man.

3   I neither learned wisdom
    Nor have knowledge of the Holy One.

4   Who has ascended into heaven, or
        descended?
    Who has gathered the wind in His
        fists?
    Who has bound the waters in a
        garment?
    Who has established all the ends of
        the earth?
    What *is* His name, and what *is* His
        Son's name,
    If you know?

REVELATION 6:1–17

NOW I saw when the Lamb opened one of the seals; and I heard one of the four living creatures saying with a voice like thunder, "Come and see." 2 And I looked, and behold, a white horse. He who sat on it had a bow; and a crown was given to him, and he went out conquering and to conquer.

3 When He opened the second seal, I heard the second living creature saying, "Come and see." 4 Another horse, fiery red, went out. And it was granted to the one who sat on it to take peace from the earth, and that *people* should kill one another; and there was given to him a great sword.

5 When He opened the third seal, I heard the third living creature say, "Come and see." So I looked, and behold, a black horse, and he who sat on it had a pair of scales in his hand. 6 And I heard a voice in the midst of the four living creatures saying, "A quart of wheat for a denarius, and three quarts of barley for a denarius; and do not harm the oil and the wine."

7 When He opened the fourth seal, I heard the voice of the fourth living creature saying, "Come and see." 8 So I looked, and

behold, a pale horse. And the name of him who sat on it was Death, and Hades followed with him. And power was given to them over a fourth of the earth, to kill with sword, with hunger, with death, and by the beasts of the earth.

9 When He opened the fifth seal, I saw under the altar the souls of those who had been slain for the word of God and for the testimony which they held. 10 And they cried with a loud voice, saying, "How long, O Lord, holy and true, until You judge and avenge our blood on those who dwell on the earth?" 11 Then a white robe was given to each of them; and it was said to them that they should rest a little while longer, until both *the number of* their fellow servants and their brethren, who would be killed as they *were,* was completed.

12 I looked when He opened the sixth seal, and behold, there was a great earthquake; and the sun became black as sackcloth of hair, and the moon became like blood. 13 And the stars of heaven fell to the earth, as a fig tree drops its late figs when it is shaken by a mighty wind. 14 Then the sky receded as a scroll when it is rolled up, and every mountain and island was moved out of its place. 15 And the kings of the earth, the great men, the rich men, the commanders, the mighty men, every slave and every free man, hid themselves in the caves and in the rocks of the mountains, 16 and said to the mountains and rocks, "Fall on us and hide us from the face of Him who sits on the throne and from the wrath of the Lamb!

The wrath of the Lamb—*it is beyond our conception.*   (CONFORMED)

17 For the great day of His wrath has come, and who is able to stand?"

◆◆◆◆

Reading 351—The Bible As Our Native Air
Proverbs 30:5

A man's attitude to our Lord determines his attitude to the Bible. The "sayings" of God to a man not born from above are of no moment; to him the Bible is simply a remarkable compilation of literature—"that it is, and nothing more." All the confusion arises from not recognizing this. But to the soul born from above, the Bible is the universe of God's revealed will.

The Word of God to me is ever according to my spiritual character; it makes clear my responsibility to God as well as my individuality apart from Him. (CHRIS. DIS. 1)

When a soul is born from above and lifted to the atmosphere of the domain where our Lord lives, the Bible becomes its native air, its words become the storehouse of omnipotence, its commands and prophecies become alive, its limitless horizons brace the heart and mind to a new consciousness, its comforts in Psalms and prayers and exhortations delight the whole man. And better than all, the Lord Jesus Christ becomes the altogether Lovely One, it is in His light that we see light, it is in Him that we become new creatures. He who is the Word of God unfolds to us the revelation of God until we say in sacred rapture, "I hold in my hands the Thought of God."

(GOD'S WORKMANSHIP)

OBADIAH 1–21

THE vision of Obadiah.

Thus says the Lord GOD concerning Edom
(We have heard a report from the LORD,
And a messenger has been sent among the nations, *saying,*
"Arise, and let us rise up against her for battle"):

2 "Behold, I will make you small among the nations;
You shall be greatly despised.
3 The pride of your heart has deceived you,
You who dwell in the clefts of the rock,
Whose habitation is high;
You who say in your heart, 'Who will bring me down to the ground?'
4 Though you ascend *as* high as the eagle,
And though you set your nest among the stars,
From there I will bring you down," says the LORD.

5 "If thieves had come to you,
If robbers by night—
Oh, how you will be cut off!—
Would they not have stolen till they had enough?
If grape gatherers had come to you,
Would they not have left *some* gleanings?
6 "Oh, how Esau shall be searched out!
How his hidden treasures shall be sought after!
7 All the men in your confederacy
Shall force you to the border;
The men at peace with you

Shall deceive you *and* prevail against you.
Those who eat your bread shall lay a trap for you.
No one is aware of it.

8 "Will I not in that day," says the LORD,
"Even destroy the wise *men* from Edom,
And understanding from the mountains of Esau?
9 Then your mighty men, O Teman, shall be dismayed,
To the end that everyone from the mountains of Esau
May be cut off by slaughter.

10 "For violence against your brother Jacob,
Shame shall cover you,
And you shall be cut off forever.
11 In the day that you stood on the other side—
In the day that strangers carried captive his forces,
When foreigners entered his gates
And cast lots for Jerusalem—
Even you *were* as one of them.

12 "But you should not have gazed on the day of your brother
In the day of his captivity;
Nor should you have rejoiced over the children of Judah
In the day of their destruction;
Nor should you have spoken proudly
In the day of distress.
13 You should not have entered the gate of My people
In the day of their calamity.
Indeed, you should not have gazed on their affliction
In the day of their calamity,
Nor laid *hands* on their substance
In the day of their calamity.

14 You should not have stood at the crossroads
To cut off those among them who escaped;
Nor should you have delivered up those among them who remained
In the day of distress.

15 "For the day of the Lord upon all the nations *is* near;
As you have done, it shall be done to you;
Your reprisal shall return upon your own head.

16 For as you drank on My holy mountain,
So shall all the nations drink continually;
Yes, they shall drink, and swallow,
And they shall be as though they had never been.

17 "But on Mount Zion there shall be deliverance,
And there shall be holiness;
The house of Jacob shall possess their possessions.

---

*O*ur one desire is a hunger and thirst after nothing less than holiness.   (Brill. Heritage)

---

18 The house of Jacob shall be a fire,
And the house of Joseph a flame;
But the house of Esau *shall be* stubble;
They shall kindle them and devour them,
And no survivor shall *remain* of the house of Esau,"
For the Lord has spoken.

19 The South shall possess the mountains of Esau,
And the Lowland shall possess Philistia.
They shall possess the fields of Ephraim
And the fields of Samaria.
Benjamin *shall possess* Gilead.

20 And the captives of this host of the children of Israel
Shall possess the land of the Canaanites
As far as Zarephath.
The captives of Jerusalem who are in Sepharad
Shall possess the cities of the South.

21 Then saviors shall come to Mount Zion

To judge the mountains of Esau,
And the kingdom shall be the Lord's.

PSALM 143:7–12

7 ANSWER me speedily, O Lord;
My spirit fails!
Do not hide Your face from me,
Lest I be like those who go down into the pit.

8 Cause me to hear Your lovingkindness in the morning,
For in You do I trust;
Cause me to know the way in which I should walk,
For I lift up my soul to You.

9 Deliver me, O Lord, from my enemies;
In You I take shelter.

10 Teach me to do Your will,
For You *are* my God;
Your Spirit *is* good.
Lead me in the land of uprightness.

11 Revive me, O Lord, for Your name's sake!
For Your righteousness' sake bring my soul out of trouble.

12 In Your mercy cut off my enemies,
And destroy all those who afflict my soul;
For I *am* Your servant.

PROVERBS 30:5

5 EVERY word of God *is* pure;
He *is* a shield to those who put their trust in Him.

---

*N*ever drag down the word of God to anybody's understanding.   (Workmen)

REVELATION 7:1–17

AFTER these things I saw four angels standing at the four corners of the earth, holding the four winds of the earth, that the wind should not blow on the earth, on the sea, or on any tree. 2 Then I saw another angel ascending from the east, having the seal of the living God. And he cried with a loud voice to the four angels to whom it was granted to harm the earth and the sea, 3 saying, "Do not harm the earth, the sea, or the trees till we have sealed the servants of our God on their foreheads." 4 And I heard the number of those who were sealed. One hundred *and* forty-four thousand of all the tribes of the children of Israel *were* sealed:

5   of the tribe of Judah twelve thousand
     were sealed;
     of the tribe of Reuben twelve
     thousand *were* sealed;
     of the tribe of Gad twelve thousand
     were sealed;
6   of the tribe of Asher twelve thousand
     were sealed;
     of the tribe of Naphtali twelve
     thousand *were* sealed;
     of the tribe of Manasseh twelve
     thousand *were* sealed;
7   of the tribe of Simeon twelve
     thousand *were* sealed;
     of the tribe of Levi twelve thousand
     were sealed;
     of the tribe of Issachar twelve
     thousand *were* sealed;
8   of the tribe of Zebulun twelve
     thousand *were* sealed;
     of the tribe of Joseph twelve
     thousand *were* sealed;
     of the tribe of Benjamin twelve
     thousand *were* sealed.

9 After these things I looked, and behold, a great multitude which no one could number, of all nations, tribes, peoples, and tongues, standing before the throne and before the Lamb, clothed with white robes, with palm branches in their hands, 10 and crying out with a loud voice, saying, "Salvation *belongs* to our God who sits on

> *Thank God for the countless numbers of individuals who realize that the only Reality is Redemption.* (SEND I YOU)

the throne, and to the Lamb!" 11 All the angels stood around the throne and the elders and the four living creatures, and fell on their faces before the throne and worshiped God, 12 saying:

> "Amen! Blessing and glory and
>   wisdom,
> Thanksgiving and honor and power
>   and might,
> *Be* to our God forever and ever.
> Amen."

13 Then one of the elders answered, saying to me, "Who are these arrayed in white robes, and where did they come from?"
14 And I said to him, "Sir, you know."
So he said to me, "These are the ones who come out of the great tribulation, and washed their robes and made them white in the blood of the Lamb. 15 Therefore they are before the throne of God, and serve Him day and night in His temple. And He who sits on the throne will dwell among them. 16 They shall neither hunger anymore nor thirst anymore; the sun shall not strike them, nor any heat; 17 for the Lamb who is in the midst of the throne will shepherd them and lead them to living fountains of waters. And God will wipe away every tear from their eyes."

Reading 352—Faithful to God's Call
Jonah 1:1–3

The discernment of God's call does not come in every moment of life, but only in rare moments; the moments our Lord spoke of as "the light." We have to remain true to what we see in those moments; if we do not, we will put back God's purpose in our life. The undercurrent of regret arises when we confer with those who have not heard the call of God, and if we listen to them we get into darkness. (*NOT KNOWING*)

Arguers against obeying the call of God will arise in the shape of country and kindred, and if you listen to them you will soon dull your ears to God's call and become the dullest, most commonplace Christian imaginable, because you have no courage in your faith; you have seen and heard, but have not gone on. If you accept sympathy from those who have not heard the call of God, it will so blunt your own sense of His call that you become useless to Him.   (*NOT KNOWING*)

You hear the call of God and realize what He wants, then you begin to find reasons why you should not obey Him. Well, obey Him, because away in some other part of the world there are other circumstances being worked by God, and if you say—"I shan't, I wasn't made for this" you get out of touch with God. Your "goings" are not according to your mind, but according to God's mind. Remain true at all costs to what God is doing with you and don't ask why He is doing it.   (*NOT KNOWING*)

JONAH 1:1—4:11

NOW the word of the LORD came to Jonah the son of Amittai, saying, 2 "Arise, go to Nineveh, that great city, and cry out against it; for their wickedness has come up before Me." 3 But Jonah arose to flee to Tarshish from the presence of the LORD. He went down to Joppa, and found a ship going to Tarshish; so he paid the fare, and went down into it, to go with them to Tarshish from the presence of the LORD.

4 But the LORD sent out a great wind on the sea, and there was a mighty tempest on the sea, so that the ship was about to be broken up.

5 Then the mariners were afraid; and every man cried out to his god, and threw the cargo that *was* in the ship into the sea, to lighten the load. But Jonah had gone down into the lowest parts of the ship, had lain down, and was fast asleep.

6 So the captain came to him, and said to him, "What do you mean, sleeper? Arise, call on your God; perhaps your God will consider us, so that we may not perish."

The Holy Ghost is seeking to awaken men out of lethargy.   (BIB. ETHICS)

---

7 And they said to one another, "Come, let us cast lots, that we may know for whose cause this trouble *has come* upon us." So they cast lots, and the lot fell on Jonah. 8 Then they said to him, "Please tell us! For whose cause *is* this trouble upon us? What is your occupation? And where do you come from? What is your country? And of what people are you?"

9 So he said to them, "I *am* a Hebrew; and I fear the LORD, the God of heaven, who made the sea and the dry *land*."

10 Then the men were exceedingly afraid, and said to him, "Why have you done this?"

For the men knew that he fled from the presence of the LORD, because he had told them. 11 Then they said to him, "What shall we do to you that the sea may be calm for us?"—for the sea was growing more tempestuous.

12 And he said to them, "Pick me up and throw me into the sea; then the sea will become calm for you. For I know that this great tempest *is* because of me."

13 Nevertheless the men rowed hard to return to land, but they could not, for the sea continued to grow more tempestuous against them. 14 Therefore they cried out to the LORD and said, "We pray, O LORD, please do not let us perish for this man's life, and do not charge us with innocent blood; for You, O LORD, have done as it pleased You." 15 So they picked up Jonah and threw him into the sea, and the sea ceased from its raging. 16 Then the men feared the LORD exceedingly, and offered a sacrifice to the LORD and took vows.

17 Now the LORD had prepared a great fish to swallow Jonah. And Jonah was in the belly of the fish three days and three nights.

2 THEN Jonah prayed to the LORD his God from the fish's belly. 2 And he said:

"I cried out to the LORD because of
   my affliction,
And He answered me.

"Out of the belly of Sheol I cried,
   And You heard my voice.
3   For You cast me into the deep,
   Into the heart of the seas,
   And the floods surrounded me;
   All Your billows and Your waves
     passed over me.
4   Then I said, 'I have been cast out
    of Your sight;
   Yet I will look again toward Your
    holy temple.'

5 The waters surrounded me, *even* to
    my soul;
    The deep closed around me;
    Weeds were wrapped around my
    head.
6 I went down to the moorings of the
    mountains;
    The earth with its bars *closed* behind
    me forever;
    Yet You have brought up my life
    from the pit,
    O LORD, my God.

7 "When my soul fainted within me,
    I remembered the LORD;
    And my prayer went *up* to You,
    Into Your holy temple.

8 "Those who regard worthless idols
    Forsake their own Mercy.
9 But I will sacrifice to You
    With the voice of thanksgiving;
    I will pay what I have vowed.
    Salvation *is* of the LORD."

10 So the LORD spoke to the fish, and it
vomited Jonah onto dry *land*.

3 NOW the word of the LORD came to
Jonah the second time, saying,
2 "Arise, go to Nineveh, that great city, and
preach to it the message that I tell you."
3 So Jonah arose and went to Nineveh, according to the word of the LORD. Now
Nineveh was an exceedingly great city, a
three-day journey *in extent*. 4 And Jonah
began to enter the city on the first day's
walk. Then he cried out and said, "Yet forty
days, and Nineveh shall be overthrown!"
5 So the people of Nineveh believed God,
proclaimed a fast, and put on sackcloth,
from the greatest to the least of them.
6 Then word came to the king of Nineveh;
and he arose from his throne and laid aside
his robe, covered *himself* with sackcloth and
sat in ashes. 7 And he caused *it* to be proclaimed and published throughout Nineveh
by the decree of the king and his nobles,
saying,

Let neither man nor beast, herd nor
flock, taste anything; do not let them
eat, or drink water. 8 But let man
and beast be covered with sackcloth,
and cry mightily to God; yes, let every
one turn from his evil way and from
the violence that is in his hands.
9 Who can tell *if* God will turn and
relent, and turn away from His fierce
anger, so that we may not perish?

10 Then God saw their works, that they
turned from their evil way; and God relented from the disaster that He had said
He would bring upon them, and He did
not do it.

4 BUT it displeased Jonah exceedingly,
and he became angry. 2 So he prayed
to the LORD, and said, "Ah, LORD, was
not this what I said when I was still in
my country? Therefore I fled previously to
Tarshish; for I know that You *are* a gracious
and merciful God, slow to anger and abundant in lovingkindness, One who relents
from doing harm. 3 Therefore now, O
LORD, please take my life from me, for *it*
is better for me to die than to live!"
4 Then the LORD said, "*Is it* right for
you to be angry?"
5 So Jonah went out of the city and sat
on the east side of the city. There he made
himself a shelter and sat under it in the
shade, till he might see what would become
of the city. 6 And the LORD God prepared
a plant and made it come up over Jonah,
that it might be shade for his head to deliver
him from his misery. So Jonah was very
grateful for the plant. 7 But as morning
dawned the next day God prepared a worm,
and it *so* damaged the plant that it withered.
8 And it happened, when the sun arose,
that God prepared a vehement east wind;
and the sun beat on Jonah's head, so that
he grew faint. Then he wished death for
himself, and said, "*It is* better for me to
die than to live."
9 Then God said to Jonah, "*Is it* right
for you to be angry about the plant?"
And he said, "*It is* right for me to be
angry, even to death!"
10 But the LORD said, "You have had pity
on the plant for which you have not labored,
nor made it grow, which came up in a night
and perished in a night. 11 And should I
not pity Nineveh, that great city, in which
are more than one hundred and twenty
thousand persons who cannot discern between their right hand and their left—and
much livestock?"

PSALM 144:1–8

1 BLESSED *be* the LORD my Rock,
    Who trains my hands for war,
    And my fingers for battle—
2 My lovingkindness and my fortress,
    My high tower and my deliverer,
    My shield and *the One* in whom I take
    refuge,
    Who subdues my people under me.

3   LORD, what *is* man, that You take
       knowledge of him?
       Or the son of man, that You are mindful
       of him?
4   Man is like a breath;
       His days *are* like a passing shadow.

5   Bow down Your heavens, O LORD, and
       come down;
       Touch the mountains, and they shall
       smoke.
6   Flash forth lightning and scatter them;
       Shoot out Your arrows and destroy
       them.
7   Stretch out Your hand from above;
       Rescue me and deliver me out of great
       waters,
       From the hand of foreigners,
8   Whose mouth speaks lying words,
       And whose right hand *is* a right hand
       of falsehood.

PROVERBS 30:6–9

6   DO not add to His words,
       Lest He rebuke you, and you be found
       a liar.

7   Two *things* I request of You
       (Deprive me not before I die):
8   Remove falsehood and lies far from me;
       Give me neither poverty nor riches—
       Feed me with the food allotted to me;
9   Lest I be full and deny *You,*
       And say, "Who *is* the LORD?"
       Or lest I be poor and steal,
       And profane the name of my God.

REVELATION 8:1–13

WHEN He opened the seventh seal, there
was silence in heaven for about half an hour.
2 And I saw the seven angels who stand
before God, and to them were given seven
trumpets. 3 Then another angel, having a
golden censer, came and stood at the altar.
He was given much incense, that he should
offer *it* with the prayers of all the saints
upon the golden altar which was before
the throne. 4 And the smoke of the incense,

---

*A saint is never consciously a saint;
a saint is consciously dependent on
God.*   (UTMOST)

---

with the prayers of the saints, ascended before God from the angel's hand. 5 Then
the angel took the censer, filled it with fire
from the altar, and threw *it* to the earth.
And there were noises, thunderings, lightnings, and an earthquake.

6 So the seven angels who had the seven
trumpets prepared themselves to sound.

7 The first angel sounded: And hail and
fire followed, mingled with blood, and they
were thrown to the earth. And a third of
the trees were burned up, and all green
grass was burned up.

8 Then the second angel sounded: And
something like a great mountain burning
with fire was thrown into the sea, and a
third of the sea became blood. 9 And a third
of the living creatures in the sea died, and
a third of the ships were destroyed.

10 Then the third angel sounded: And a
great star fell from heaven, burning like a
torch, and it fell on a third of the rivers
and on the springs of water. 11 The name
of the star is Wormwood. A third of the
waters became wormwood, and many men
died from the water, because it was made
bitter.

12 Then the fourth angel sounded: And
a third of the sun was struck, a third of
the moon, and a third of the stars, so that
a third of them were darkened. A third of
the day did not shine, and likewise the
night.

13 And I looked, and I heard an angel
flying through the midst of heaven, saying
with a loud voice, "Woe, woe, woe to the
inhabitants of the earth, because of the remaining blasts of the trumpet of the three
angels who are about to sound!"

Reading 353—Happiness in God
Psalm 144:15

Happiness is not a sign that we are right with God; happiness is a sign of satisfaction, that is all, and the majority of us can be satisfied on too low a level. Jesus Christ disturbs every kind of satisfaction that is less than delight in God.   (*PERFECT*)

When a man is happy, he cannot pull a long face, he may try to, but it is the face of a clown; when he is happy inside he shows it on the outside. If you hear a Christian with a sad face saying, "Oh, I am so full of the joy of the Lord," well, you know it is not true. If I am full of the joy of the Lord, it will pour out of every cell of my body.   (*BIB. PSYCH.*)

Solomon rattles the bottom board out of every piece of deception. The only true joy in life, he says, is based on a personal relationship to God. You cannot find joy in being like animals, or in art, or aestheticism, in ruling or being ruled—the whole thing is passed in survey in a most ruthless examination by a man whose wisdom is profounder than the profoundest and has never been excelled, and in summing it all up he says that joy is only found in any of these things when a man is rightly related to God.   (*SHADE*)

MICAH 1:1—3:12

THE word of the LORD that came to Micah of Moresheth in the days of Jotham, Ahaz, *and* Hezekiah, kings of Judah, which he saw concerning Samaria and Jerusalem.

2   Hear, all you peoples!
Listen, O earth, and all that is in it!
Let the Lord GOD be a witness against you,
The Lord from His holy temple.

3   For behold, the LORD is coming out of His place;
He will come down
And tread on the high places of the earth.
4   The mountains will melt under Him,
And the valleys will split
Like wax before the fire,
Like waters poured down a steep place.
5   All this is for the transgression of Jacob
And for the sins of the house of Israel.
What *is* the transgression of Jacob?
Is it not Samaria?
And what *are* the high places of Judah?
Are they not Jerusalem?

6   "Therefore I will make Samaria a heap of ruins in the field,
Places for planting a vineyard;
I will pour down her stones into the valley,
And I will uncover her foundations.
7   All her carved images shall be beaten to pieces,
And all her pay as a harlot shall be burned with the fire;
All her idols I will lay desolate,
For she gathered *it* from the pay of a harlot,
And they shall return to the pay of a harlot."

8   Therefore I will wail and howl,
I will go stripped and naked;
I will make a wailing like the jackals
And a mourning like the ostriches,
9   For her wounds *are* incurable.
For it has come to Judah;
It has come to the gate of My people—
To Jerusalem.

10   Tell *it* not in Gath,
Weep not at all;
In Beth Aphrah
Roll yourself in the dust.
11   Pass by in naked shame, you inhabitant of Shaphir;
The inhabitant of Zaanan does not go out.
Beth Ezel mourns;
Its place to stand is taken away from you.

12 For the inhabitant of Maroth pined
for good,
But disaster came down from the
LORD
To the gate of Jerusalem.
13 O inhabitant of Lachish,
Harness the chariot to the swift steeds
(She *was* the beginning of sin to the
daughter of Zion),
For the transgressions of Israel were
found in you.

14 Therefore you shall give presents to
Moresheth Gath;
The houses of Achzib *shall be* a lie
to the kings of Israel.
15 I will yet bring an heir to you,
O inhabitant of Mareshah;
The glory of Israel shall come to
Adullam.
16 Make yourself bald and cut off your
hair,
Because of your precious children;
Enlarge your baldness like an eagle,
For they shall go from you into
captivity.

2 WOE to those who devise iniquity,
And work out evil on their beds!
At morning light they practice it,
Because it is in the power of their
hand.

---

*H*abit is the result of practice, by
continually doing a thing it becomes
second nature.   (SERMON MT.)

---

2 They covet fields and take *them* by
violence,
Also houses, and seize *them*.
So they oppress a man and his house,
A man and his inheritance.

3 Therefore thus says the LORD:

"Behold, against this family I am
devising disaster,
From which you cannot remove your
necks;
Nor shall you walk haughtily,
For this *is* an evil time.
4 In that day *one* shall take up a proverb
against you,
And lament with a bitter lamentation,
saying:
'We are utterly destroyed!
He has changed the heritage of my
people;
How He has removed *it* from me!

To a turncoat He has divided our
fields.' "

5 Therefore you will have no one to
determine boundaries by lot
In the assembly of the LORD.

6 "Do not prattle," *you say to those* who
prophesy.
So they shall not prophesy to you;
They shall not return insult for insult.
7 *You who are* named the house of
Jacob:
"Is the Spirit of the LORD restricted?
Are these His doings?
Do not My words do good
To him who walks uprightly?

8 "Lately My people have risen up as
an enemy—
You pull off the robe with the
garment
From those who trust *you*, as they
pass by,
Like men returned from war.
9 The women of My people you cast
out
From their pleasant houses;
From their children
You have taken away My glory
forever.

10 "Arise and depart,
For this *is* not *your* rest;
Because it is defiled, it shall destroy,
Yes, with utter destruction.
11 If a man should walk in a false spirit
And speak a lie, *saying,*
'I will prophesy to you of wine and
drink,'
Even he would be the prattler of this
people.

12 "I will surely assemble all of you,
O Jacob,
I will surely gather the remnant of
Israel;
I will put them together like sheep
of the fold,
Like a flock in the midst of their
pasture;
They shall make a loud noise because
of *so many* people.
13 The one who breaks open will come
up before them;
They will break out,
Pass through the gate,
And go out by it;
Their king will pass before them,
With the LORD at their head."

3 AND I said:

"Hear now, O heads of Jacob,
    And you rulers of the house of Israel:
    Is it not for you to know justice?
2   You who hate good and love evil;
    Who strip the skin from My people,
    And the flesh from their bones;
3   Who also eat the flesh of My people,
    Flay their skin from them,
    Break their bones,
    And chop *them* in pieces
    Like *meat* for the pot,
    Like flesh in the caldron."

4   Then they will cry to the LORD,
    But He will not hear them;
    He will even hide His face from them
        at that time,
    Because they have been evil in their
        deeds.

5   Thus says the LORD concerning the
        prophets
    Who make my people stray;
    Who chant "Peace"
    While they chew with their teeth,
    But who prepare war against him
    Who puts nothing into their mouths:
6   "Therefore you shall have night
        without vision,
    And you shall have darkness without
        divination;
    The sun shall go down on the
        prophets,
    And the day shall be dark for them.
7   So the seers shall be ashamed,
    And the diviners abashed;
    Indeed they shall all cover their lips;
    For *there is* no answer from God."

8   But truly I am full of power by the
        Spirit of the LORD,
    And of justice and might,
    To declare to Jacob his transgression
    And to Israel his sin.
9   Now hear this,

---

*M*ost of us talk piously, we have
    the practice but not the
    power.   (SERMON MT.)

    You heads of the house of Jacob
    And rulers of the house of Israel,
    Who abhor justice
    And pervert all equity,
10   Who build up Zion with bloodshed
    And Jerusalem with iniquity:
11   Her heads judge for a bribe,

Her priests teach for pay,
    And her prophets divine for money.
    Yet they lean on the LORD, and say,
    "Is not the LORD among us?
    No harm can come upon us."
12   Therefore because of you
    Zion shall be plowed *like* a field,
    Jerusalem shall become heaps of
        ruins,
    And the mountain of the temple
    Like the bare hills of the forest.

PSALM 144:9–15

9   I will sing a new song to You, O God;
    On a harp of ten strings I will sing
        praises to You,
10   *The One* who gives salvation to kings,
    Who delivers David His servant
    From the deadly sword.

11   Rescue me and deliver me from the
        hand of foreigners,
    Whose mouth speaks lying words,
    And whose right hand *is* a right hand
        of falsehood—
12   That our sons *may be* as plants grown
        up in their youth;
    That our daughters *may be* as pillars,
    Sculptured in palace style;
13   *That* our barns *may be* full,
    Supplying all kinds of produce;
    That our sheep may bring forth
        thousands
    And ten thousands in our fields;
14   *That* our oxen *may be* well laden;
    That there be no breaking in or going
        out;
    That there be no outcry in our streets.
15   Happy *are* the people who are in such
        a state;
    Happy *are* the people whose God *is*
    the LORD!

PROVERBS 30:10

10   DO not malign a servant to his master,
    Lest he curse you, and you be found
        guilty.

REVELATION 9:1–21

THEN the fifth angel sounded: And I saw
a star fallen from heaven to the earth. To
him was given the key to the bottomless
pit. 2 And he opened the bottomless pit,
and smoke arose out of the pit like the

smoke of a great furnace. So the sun and the air were darkened because of the smoke of the pit. 3 Then out of the smoke locusts came upon the earth. And to them was given power, as the scorpions of the earth have power. 4 They were commanded not to harm the grass of the earth, or any green thing, or any tree, but only those men who do not have the seal of God on their foreheads. 5 And they were not given *authority* to kill them, but to torment them *for* five months. Their torment *was* like the torment of a scorpion when it strikes a man. 6 In those days men will seek death and will not find it; they will desire to die, and death will flee from them.

7 The shape of the locusts was like horses prepared for battle. On their heads were crowns of something like gold, and their faces *were* like the faces of men. 8 They had hair like women's hair, and their teeth were like lions' *teeth*. 9 And they had breastplates like breastplates of iron, and the sound of their wings *was* like the sound of chariots with many horses running into battle. 10 They had tails like scorpions, and there were stings in their tails. Their power *was* to hurt men five months. 11 And they had as king over them the angel of the bottomless pit, whose name in Hebrew *is* Abaddon, but in Greek he has the name Apollyon.

12 One woe is past. Behold, still two more woes are coming after these things.

13 Then the sixth angel sounded: And I heard a voice from the four horns of the golden altar which is before God, 14 saying to the sixth angel who had the trumpet, "Release the four angels who are bound at the great river Euphrates." 15 So the four angels, who had been prepared for the hour and day and month and year, were released to kill a third of mankind. 16 Now the number of the army of the horsemen *was* two hundred million; I heard the number of them. 17 And thus I saw the horses in the vision: those who sat on them had breastplates of fiery red, hyacinth blue, and sulfur yellow; and the heads of the horses *were* like the heads of lions; and out of their mouths came fire, smoke, and brimstone. 18 By these three *plagues* a third of mankind was killed—by the fire and the smoke and the brimstone which came out of their mouths. 19 For their power is in their mouth and in their tails; for their tails *are* like serpents, having heads; and with them they do harm.

20 But the rest of mankind, who were not killed by these plagues, did not repent of the works of their hands, that they should not worship demons, and idols of gold, silver, brass, stone, and wood, which can neither see nor hear nor walk. 21 And they did not repent of their murders or their sorceries or their sexual immorality or their thefts.

◆◆◆◆

Reading 354—The Purpose of Mystery
Revelation 10:7

Mystery there must be, but the remarkable thing about the mysteries which the Bible reveals is that they never contradict human reason, they transcend it. The mysteries of other religions contradict human reason. The miracles which our Lord performed (a miracle simply means the public power of God) transcend human reason, but not one of them contradicts human reason.   (*Bib. Psych.*)

"O the depth of the riches both of the wisdom and the knowledge of God! how unsearchable are His judgments, and His ways past tracing out!" The purpose of mystery is not to tantalize us and make us feel that we cannot comprehend; it is a generous purpose, and meant to assure us that slowly and surely as we can bear it, the full revelation of God will be made clear.

(*Place Help*)

There are three big mysteries. The Mystery of the Triune God—Father, Son and Holy Ghost; the Mystery of our Lord Jesus Christ, who is both human and divine, and . . . the mystery that I, a sinner, can be made into the image of Jesus Christ by the great work of His atonement in my life.

(*Brill. Heritage*)

MICAH 4:1—5:15

1   NOW it shall come to pass in the
       latter days
       That the mountain of the LORD's
       house
       Shall be established on the top of
       the mountains,
       And shall be exalted above the hills;
       And peoples shall flow to it.
2   Many nations shall come and say,
       "Come, and let us go up to the
       mountain of the LORD,
       To the house of the God of Jacob;
       He will teach us His ways,
       And we shall walk in His paths."
       For out of Zion the law shall go forth,
       And the word of the LORD from
       Jerusalem.
3   He shall judge between many
       peoples,
       And rebuke strong nations afar off;
       They shall beat their swords into
       plowshares,
       And their spears into pruning hooks;
       Nation shall not lift up sword against
       nation,
       Neither shall they learn war anymore.

4   But everyone shall sit under his vine
       and under his fig tree,
       And no one shall make *them* afraid;
       For the mouth of the LORD of hosts
       has spoken.
5   For all people walk each in the name
       of his god,
       But we will walk in the name of the
       LORD our God
       Forever and ever.

6   "In that day," says the LORD,
       "I will assemble the lame,
       I will gather the outcast
       And those whom I have afflicted;
7   I will make the lame a remnant,
       And the outcast a strong nation;
       So the LORD will reign over them
       in Mount Zion
       From now on, even forever.
8   And you, O tower of the flock,
       The stronghold of the daughter of
       Zion,
       To you shall it come,
       Even the former dominion shall
       come,
       The kingdom of the daughter of
       Jerusalem."

9   Now why do you cry aloud?
       Is there no king in your midst?
       Has your counselor perished?

       For pangs have seized you like a
       woman in labor.
10 Be in pain, and labor to bring forth,
       O daughter of Zion,
       Like a woman in birth pangs.
       For now you shall go forth from the
       city,
       You shall dwell in the field,
       And to Babylon you shall go.
       There you shall be delivered;
       There the LORD will redeem you
       From the hand of your enemies.

11 Now also many nations have
       gathered against you,
       Who say, "Let her be defiled,
       And let our eye look upon Zion."
12 But they do not know the thoughts
       of the LORD,
       Nor do they understand His counsel;
       For He will gather them like sheaves
       to the threshing floor.

13 "Arise and thresh, O daughter of
       Zion;
       For I will make your horn iron,
       And I will make your hooves bronze;
       You shall beat in pieces many
       peoples;
       I will consecrate their gain to the
       LORD,
       And their substance to the Lord of
       the whole earth."

5   NOW gather yourself in troops,
       O daughter of troops;
       He has laid siege against us;
       They will strike the judge of Israel
       with a rod on the cheek.
2   "But you, Bethlehem Ephrathah,
       Though you are little among the
       thousands of Judah,
       Yet out of you shall come forth
       to Me
       The One to be Ruler in Israel,
       Whose goings forth *are* from of old,
       From everlasting."

---

*The new birth is illustrated by
the supernatural advent of our
Lord.*   (PSY. REDEMP.)

---

3   Therefore He shall give them up,
       Until the time *that* she who is in labor
       has given birth;
       Then the remnant of His brethren
       Shall return to the children of Israel.
4   And He shall stand and feed *His flock*
       In the strength of the LORD,

In the majesty of the name of the
LORD His God;
And they shall abide,
For now He shall be great
To the ends of the earth;
5 And this *One* shall be peace.

When the Assyrian comes into our
land,
And when he treads in our palaces,
Then we will raise against him
Seven shepherds and eight princely
men.
6 They shall waste with the sword the
land of Assyria,
And the land of Nimrod at its
entrances;
Thus He shall deliver *us* from the
Assyrian,
When he comes into our land
And when he treads within our
borders.

7 Then the remnant of Jacob
Shall be in the midst of many peoples,
Like dew from the LORD,
Like showers on the grass,
That tarry for no man
Nor wait for the sons of men.
8 And the remnant of Jacob
Shall be among the Gentiles,
In the midst of many peoples,
Like a lion among the beasts of the
forest,
Like a young lion among flocks of
sheep,
Who, if he passes through,
Both treads down and tears in pieces,
And none can deliver.
9 Your hand shall be lifted against your
adversaries,
And all your enemies shall be cut off.

10 "And it shall be in that day," says the
LORD,
"That I will cut off your horses from
your midst
And destroy your chariots.
11 I will cut off the cities of your land
And throw down all your
strongholds.
12 I will cut off sorceries from your
hand,
And you shall have no soothsayers.
13 Your carved images I will also cut
off,
And your sacred pillars from your
midst;
You shall no more worship the work
of your hands;
14 I will pluck your wooden images
from your midst;

Thus I will destroy your cities.
15 And I will execute vengeance in anger
and fury
On the nations that have not heard."

PSALM 145:1–9

1 I will extol You, my God, O King;
And I will bless Your name forever and
ever.
2 Every day I will bless You,
And I will praise Your name forever
and ever.
3 Great *is* the LORD, and greatly to be
praised;
And His greatness *is* unsearchable.

4 One generation shall praise Your works
to another,
And shall declare Your mighty acts.
5 I will meditate on the glorious splendor
of Your majesty,
And on Your wondrous works.
6 *Men* shall speak of the might of Your
awesome acts,
And I will declare Your greatness.
7 They shall utter the memory of Your
great goodness,
And shall sing of Your righteousness.

8 The LORD *is* gracious and full of
compassion,
Slow to anger and great in mercy.
9 The LORD *is* good to all,
And His tender mercies *are* over all His
works.

PROVERBS 30:11–14

11 *THERE is* a generation *that* curses its
father,
And does not bless its mother.
12 *There is* a generation *that is* pure in its
own eyes,
Yet is not washed from its filthiness.
13 *There is* a generation— oh, how lofty
are their eyes!
And their eyelids are lifted up.
14 *There is* a generation whose teeth *are*
like swords,
And whose fangs *are like* knives,
To devour the poor from off the earth,
And the needy from *among* men.

REVELATION 10:1–11

I saw still another mighty angel coming
down from heaven, clothed with a cloud.

And a rainbow *was* on his head, his face *was* like the sun, and his feet like pillars of fire. 2 He had a little book open in his hand. And he set his right foot on the sea and *his* left *foot* on the land, 3 and cried with a loud voice, as *when* a lion roars. When he cried out, seven thunders uttered their voices. 4 Now when the seven thunders uttered their voices, I was about to write; but I heard a voice from heaven saying to me, "Seal up the things which the seven thunders uttered, and do not write them."

5 The angel whom I saw standing on the sea and on the land raised up his hand to heaven 6 and swore by Him who lives forever and ever, who created heaven and the things that are in it, the earth and the things that are in it, and the sea and the things that are in it, that there should be delay no longer, 7 but in the days of the sounding of the seventh angel, when he is about to sound, the mystery of God would be finished, as He declared to His servants the prophets.

*B*y the word *"mystery"* we mean something known only to the initiated.   (BRILL. HERITAGE)

8 Then the voice which I heard from heaven spoke to me again and said, "Go, take the little book which is open in the hand of the angel who stands on the sea and on the earth."

9 So I went to the angel and said to him, "Give me the little book."

And he said to me, "Take and eat it; and it will make your stomach bitter, but it will be as sweet as honey in your mouth."

10 Then I took the little book out of the angel's hand and ate it, and it was as sweet as honey in my mouth. But when I had eaten it, my stomach became bitter. 11 And he said to me, "You must prophesy again about many peoples, nations, tongues, and kings."

◆◆◆◆

Reading 355—The Obliteration of Nations
Revelation 11:15

In these last days there is an idea that we are going to dominate everything by a perfect brotherhood. Any mind that expresses its view of the future says we are heading up into a federation of religions and nations when distinctions will be obliterated and there will be a great and universal brotherhood. The quarrels of nations make men look forward to the time when nations will be federated out of independent existence. That is a revolt which is a mental safety valve only. Peter says God is "longsuffering toward us" (2 Pet. 3:9). At present He is giving men opportunity to try every line they like in individual life as well as in the life of the nations at large. Some things have not been tried yet, and if God were to cut us off short we would say, "If You had left us a bit longer we could have realized our ideal of society and national life." God is allowing us to prove to the hilt that it cannot be done in any other way than Jesus Christ said; that is, by a personal relationship to God through Jesus Christ who is God and Man—One. When sooner or later we come to the end of our tether, we hear Jesus Christ say: "Blessed *are* the poor in spirit" (Matt. 5:3).   (*LOVE OF GOD*)

MICAH 6:1—7:20

HEAR now what the LORD says:

> "Arise, plead your case before the
> mountains,
> And let the hills hear your voice.
> 2 Hear, O you mountains, the LORD's
> complaint,
> And you strong foundations of the
> earth;
> For the LORD has a complaint
> against His people,
> And He will contend with Israel.
>
> 3 "O My people, what have I done to
> you?
> And how have I wearied you?
> Testify against Me.
> 4 For I brought you up from the land
> of Egypt,
> I redeemed you from the house of
> bondage;
> And I sent before you Moses, Aaron,
> and Miriam.
> 5 O My people, remember now
> What Balak king of Moab counseled,
> And what Balaam the son of Beor
> answered him,
> From Acacia Grove to Gilgal,
> That you may know the
> righteousness of the LORD."
>
> 6 With what shall I come before the
> LORD,
> *And* bow myself before the High
> God?
> Shall I come before Him with burnt
> offerings,
> With calves a year old?
> 7 Will the LORD be pleased with
> thousands of rams,
> Ten thousand rivers of oil?
> Shall I give my firstborn *for* my
> transgression,
> The fruit of my body *for* the sin of
> my soul?
>
> 8 He has shown you, O man, what *is*
> good;
> And what does the LORD require of
> you
> But to do justly,
> To love mercy,
> And to walk humbly with your
> God?
>
> 9 The LORD's voice cries to the city—
> Wisdom shall see Your name:
>
> "Hear the rod!
> Who has appointed it?

> 10 Are there yet the treasures of
> wickedness
> In the house of the wicked,
> And the short measure *that is* an
> abomination?
> 11 Shall I count pure *those* with the
> wicked scales,
> And with the bag of deceitful
> weights?
> 12 For her rich men are full of violence,
> Her inhabitants have spoken lies,
> And their tongue is deceitful in their
> mouth.
>
> 13 "Therefore I will also make *you* sick
> by striking you,
> By making *you* desolate because of
> your sins.
> 14 You shall eat, but not be satisfied;
> Hunger *shall be* in your midst.
> You may carry *some* away, but shall
> not save *them*;
> And what you do rescue I will give
> over to the sword.
>
> 15 "You shall sow, but not reap;
> You shall tread the olives, but not
> anoint yourselves with oil;
> And *make* sweet wine, but not drink
> wine.
> 16 For the statutes of Omri are kept;
> All the works of Ahab's house *are
> done*;
> And you walk in their counsels,
> That I may make you a desolation,
> And your inhabitants a hissing.
> Therefore you shall bear the reproach
> of My people."

7 WOE is me!
> For I am like those who gather
> summer fruits,
> Like those who glean vintage grapes;
> *There is no* cluster to eat
> Of the first-ripe fruit *which* my soul
> desires.
> 2 The faithful *man* has perished from
> the earth,
> And *there is* no one upright among
> men.
> They all lie in wait for blood;
> Every man hunts his brother with a
> net.
>
> 3 That they may successfully do evil
> with both hands—
> The prince asks *for gifts*,
> The judge *seeks* a bribe,
> And the great *man* utters his evil
> desire;
> So they scheme together.

4 The best of them *is* like a brier;
   The most upright *is sharper* than a
     thorn hedge;
   The day of your watchman and your
     punishment comes;
   Now shall be their perplexity.

5 Do not trust in a friend;
   Do not put your confidence in a
     companion;
   Guard the doors of your mouth
   From her who lies in your bosom.
6 For son dishonors father,
   Daughter rises against her mother,
   Daughter-in-law against her
     mother-in-law;
   A man's enemies *are* the men of his
     own household.
7 Therefore I will look to the LORD;
   I will wait for the God of my
     salvation;
   My God will hear me.

8 Do not rejoice over me, my enemy;
   When I fall, I will arise;
   When I sit in darkness,
   The LORD *will be* a light to me.
9 I will bear the indignation of the
     LORD,
   Because I have sinned against Him,
   Until He pleads my case
   And executes justice for me.
   He will bring me forth to the light;
   I will see His righteousness.
10 Then *she who is* my enemy will see,
   And shame will cover her who said
     to me,
   "Where is the LORD your God?"
   My eyes will see her;
   Now she will be trampled down
   Like mud in the streets.

11 *In* the day when your walls are to
     be built,
   In that day the decree shall go far
     and wide.
12 *In* that day they shall come to you
   From Assyria and the fortified cities,
   From the fortress to the River,
   From sea to sea,
   And mountain *to* mountain.
13 Yet the land shall be desolate
   Because of those who dwell in it,
   And for the fruit of their deeds.

14 Shepherd Your people with Your
     staff,
   The flock of Your heritage,
   Who dwell solitarily *in* a woodland,
   In the midst of Carmel;
   Let them feed *in* Bashan and Gilead,
   As in days of old.

15 "As in the days when you came out
     of the land of Egypt,
   I will show them wonders."

16 The nations shall see and be ashamed
     of all their might;
   They shall put *their* hand over *their*
     mouth;
   Their ears shall be deaf.
17 They shall lick the dust like a serpent;
   They shall crawl from their holes like
     snakes of the earth.
   They shall be afraid of the LORD our
     God,
   And shall fear because of You.
18 Who *is* a God like You,
   Pardoning iniquity
   And passing over the transgression
     of the remnant of His heritage?

   He does not retain His anger forever,
   Because He delights *in* mercy.
19 He will again have compassion
     on us,
   And will subdue our iniquities.

   You will cast all our sins
   Into the depths of the sea.
20 You will give truth to Jacob
   And mercy to Abraham,
   Which You have sworn to our fathers
   From days of old.

PSALM 145:10–16

10 ALL Your works shall praise You,
     O LORD,
   And Your saints shall bless You.
11 They shall speak of the glory of Your
     kingdom,
   And talk of Your power,
12 To make known to the sons of men
     His mighty acts,
   And the glorious majesty of His
     kingdom.
13 Your kingdom *is* an everlasting
     kingdom,
   And Your dominion *endures*
     throughout all generations.
14 The LORD upholds all who fall,
   And raises up all *who are* bowed down.
15 The eyes of all look expectantly to You,
   And You give them their food in due
     season.
16 You open Your hand
   And satisfy the desire of every living
     thing.

PROVERBS 30:15

15 THE leech has two daughters—
Give *and* Give!

There are three *things that* are never
satisfied,
Four never say, "Enough!":

REVELATION 11:1–19

THEN I was given a reed like a measuring
rod. And the angel stood, saying, "Rise and
measure the temple of God, the altar, and
those who worship there. 2 But leave out
the court which is outside the temple, and
do not measure it, for it has been given
to the Gentiles. And they will tread the
holy city underfoot *for* forty-two months.
3 And I will give *power* to my two witnesses, and they will prophesy one thousand
two hundred and sixty days, clothed in
sackcloth."

4 These are the two olive trees and the
two lampstands standing before the God
of the earth. 5 And if anyone wants to harm
them, fire proceeds from their mouth and
devours their enemies. And if anyone wants
to harm them, he must be killed in this
manner. 6 These have power to shut heaven,
so that no rain falls in the days of their
prophecy; and they have power over waters
to turn them to blood, and to strike the
earth with all plagues, as often as they
desire.

7 When they finish their testimony, the
beast that ascends out of the bottomless
pit will make war against them, overcome
them, and kill them. 8 And their dead bodies *will lie* in the street of the great city
which spiritually is called Sodom and
Egypt, where also our Lord was crucified.
9 Then *those* from the peoples, tribes,
tongues, and nations will see their dead bodies three-and-a-half days, and not allow their
dead bodies to be put into graves. 10 And
those who dwell on the earth will rejoice
over them, make merry, and send gifts to
one another, because these two prophets
tormented those who dwell on the earth.
11 Now after the three-and-a-half days the

breath of life from God entered them, and
they stood on their feet, and great fear fell
on those who saw them. 12 And they heard
a loud voice from heaven saying to them,
"Come up here." And they ascended to
heaven in a cloud, and their enemies saw
them. 13 In the same hour there was a great
earthquake, and a tenth of the city fell. In
the earthquake seven thousand people were
killed, and the rest were afraid and gave
glory to the God of heaven.

14 The second woe is past. Behold, the
third woe is coming quickly.

15 Then the seventh angel sounded: And
there were loud voices in heaven, saying,
"The kingdoms of this world have become
the kingdoms of our Lord and of His Christ,
and He shall reign forever and ever!"
16 And the twenty-four elders who sat before God on their thrones fell on their faces
and worshiped God, 17 saying:

"We give You thanks, O Lord God
Almighty,
The One who is and who was and
who is to come,
Because You have taken Your great
power and reigned.
18 The nations were angry, and Your
wrath has come,
And the time of the dead, that they
should be judged,
And that You should reward Your
servants the prophets and the
saints,
And those who fear Your name, small
and great,
And should destroy those who
destroy the earth."

---

*A saint is one in whom the life
of Jesus Christ is
formed.* (SERVANT AS LORD)

---

19 Then the temple of God was opened
in heaven, and the ark of His covenant was
seen in His temple. And there were lightnings, noises, thunderings, an earthquake,
and great hail.

Reading 356—Kingdom and Redemption
Revelation 12:10, 11

If we could only find some means of curing everybody of disease, of feeding them and putting them on a good social basis, what a marvelous thing it would be. That is the way we are being told that the kingdom of God is to be established on this earth. "We do not need any more of this talk about the Atonement, and the shedding of blood; what is needed today is to spend ourselves for others." That is the lure of the wrong road to the kingdom, and we cannot keep out of it if we forget to watch and pray. "Watch with Me," said Jesus; "Mine is the only road to the kingdom." (ASK)

In this dispensation the emphasis is on the kingdom within, but in another dispensation there is to be an external manifestation of the kingdom. To say that the kingdom is going to be brought in by the earth being swept clean through wars and cataclysms is not true; you cannot introduce the kingdom in that way, it is impossible. Nothing can bring in the kingdom saving the Redemption, which works in personal lives through the Cross and in no other way. (GOD'S WORKMANSHIP)

NAHUM 1:1—3:19

THE burden against Nineveh. The book of the vision of Nahum the Elkoshite.

2 God *is* jealous, and the LORD avenges;
The LORD avenges and *is* furious.
The LORD will take vengeance on His adversaries,
And He reserves *wrath* for His enemies;

3 The LORD *is* slow to anger and great in power,
And will not at all acquit *the wicked*.

The LORD has His way
In the whirlwind and in the storm,
And the clouds *are* the dust of His feet.

4 He rebukes the sea and makes it dry,
And dries up all the rivers.
Bashan and Carmel wither,
And the flower of Lebanon wilts.

5 The mountains quake before Him,
The hills melt,
And the earth heaves at His presence,
Yes, the world and all who dwell in it.

6 Who can stand before His indignation?
And who can endure the fierceness of His anger?
His fury is poured out like fire,

And the rocks are thrown down by Him.

7 The LORD *is* good,
A stronghold in the day of trouble;
And He knows those who trust in Him.

8 But with an overflowing flood
He will make an utter end of its place,
And darkness will pursue His enemies.

9 What do you conspire against the LORD?
He will make an utter end *of it*.
Affliction will not rise up a second time.

10 For while tangled *like* thorns,
And while drunken *like* drunkards,
They shall be devoured like stubble fully dried.

11 From you comes forth *one*
Who plots evil against the LORD,
A wicked counselor.

12 Thus says the LORD:

"Though *they are* safe, and likewise many,
Yet in this manner they will be cut down
When he passes through.
Though I have afflicted you,
I will afflict you no more;

13 For now I will break off his yoke
from you,
And burst your bonds apart."

14 The Lord has given a command
concerning you:
"Your name shall be perpetuated no
longer.
Out of the house of your gods
I will cut off the carved image and
the molded image.
I will dig your grave,
For you are vile."

15 Behold, on the mountains
The feet of him who brings good
tidings,
Who proclaims peace!
O Judah, keep your appointed feasts,
Perform your vows.
For the wicked one shall no more
pass through you;
He is utterly cut off.

2 HE who scatters has come up before
your face.
Man the fort!
Watch the road!
Strengthen *your* flanks!
Fortify *your* power mightily.

2 For the Lord will restore the
excellence of Jacob
Like the excellence of Israel,
For the emptiers have emptied them
out
And ruined their vine branches.

3 The shields of his mighty men *are*
made red,
The valiant men *are* in scarlet.
The chariots *come* with flaming
torches
In the day of his preparation,
And the spears are brandished.

4 The chariots rage in the streets,
They jostle one another in the broad
roads;
They seem like torches,
They run like lightning.

5 He remembers his nobles;
They stumble in their walk;
They make haste to her walls,
And the defense is prepared.

6 The gates of the rivers are opened,
And the palace is dissolved.

7 It is decreed:
She shall be led away captive,
She shall be brought up;

And her maidservants shall lead *her*
as with the voice of doves,
Beating their breasts.

8 Though Nineveh of old *was* like a
pool of water,
Now they flee away.
"Halt! Halt!" *they cry;*
But no one turns back.

9 Take spoil of silver!
Take spoil of gold!
There is no end of treasure,
Or wealth of every desirable prize.

10 She is empty, desolate, and waste!
The heart melts, and the knees shake;
Much pain *is* in every side,
And all their faces are drained of
color.

11 Where *is* the dwelling of the lions,
And the feeding place of the young
lions,
Where the lion walked, the lioness
and lion's cub,
And no one made *them* afraid?

12 The lion tore in pieces enough for
his cubs,
Killed for his lionesses,
Filled his caves with prey,
And his dens with flesh.

13 "Behold, I *am* against you," says the
Lord of hosts, "I will burn your chariots
in smoke, and the sword shall devour your
young lions; I will cut off your prey from
the earth, and the voice of your messengers
shall be heard no more."

3 WOE to the bloody city!
It *is* all full of lies *and* robbery.
Its victim never departs.

2 The noise of a whip
And the noise of rattling wheels,
Of galloping horses,
Of clattering chariots!

3 Horsemen charge with bright sword
and glittering spear.
There is a multitude of slain,
A great number of bodies,
Countless corpses—
They stumble over the corpses—

4 Because of the multitude of harlotries
of the seductive harlot,
The mistress of sorceries,
Who sells nations through her
harlotries,
And families through her sorceries.

5 "Behold, I *am* against you," says the
Lord of hosts;
"I will lift your skirts over your face,

I will show the nations your
    nakedness,
And the kingdoms your shame.
6   I will cast abominable filth upon you,
    Make you vile,
    And make you a spectacle.
7   It shall come to pass *that* all who
        look upon you
    Will flee from you, and say,
    'Nineveh is laid waste!
    Who will bemoan her?'
    Where shall I seek comforters for
        you?"

8   Are you better than No Amon
    That was situated by the River,
    That had the waters around her,
    Whose rampart *was* the sea,
    Whose wall *was* the sea?
9   Ethiopia and Egypt *were* her strength,
    And *it was* boundless;
    Put and Lubim were your helpers.
10 Yet she *was* carried away,
    She went into captivity;
    Her young children also were dashed
        to pieces
    At the head of every street;
    They cast lots for her honorable men,
    And all her great men were bound
        in chains.
11 You also will be drunk;
    You will be hidden;
    You also will seek refuge from the
        enemy.

12 All your strongholds *are* fig trees
        with ripened figs:
    If they are shaken,
    They fall into the mouth of the eater.
13 Surely, your people in your midst
        are women!
    The gates of your land are wide open
        for your enemies;
    Fire shall devour the bars of your
        gates.

14 Draw your water for the siege!
    Fortify your strongholds!
    Go into the clay and tread the mortar!
    Make strong the brick kiln!
15 There the fire will devour you,
    The sword will cut you off;
    It will eat you up like a locust.

    Make yourself many—like the locust!
    Make yourself many— like the
        swarming locusts!
16 You have multiplied your merchants
        more than the stars of heaven.
    The locust plunders and flies away.

17 Your commanders *are* like *swarming*
        locusts,
    And your generals like great
        grasshoppers,
    Which camp in the hedges on a cold
        day;
    When the sun rises they flee away,
    And the place where they *are* is not
        known.

18 Your shepherds slumber, O king of
        Assyria;
    Your nobles rest *in the dust*.
    Your people are scattered on the
        mountains,
    And no one gathers them.
19 Your injury *has* no healing,
    Your wound is severe.
    All who hear news of you
    Will clap *their* hands over you,
    For upon whom has not your
        wickedness passed continually?

PSALM 145:17–21

17 THE LORD *is* righteous in all His
        ways,
    Gracious in all His works.
18 The LORD *is* near to all who call upon
        Him,
    To all who call upon Him in truth.
19 He will fulfill the desire of those who
        fear Him;
    He also will hear their cry and save
        them.
20 The LORD preserves all who love Him,
    But all the wicked He will destroy.
21 My mouth shall speak the praise of the
        LORD,
    And all flesh shall bless His holy name
    Forever and ever.

PROVERBS 30:16

16 THE grave,
    The barren womb,
    The earth *that* is not satisfied with
        water—
    And the fire never says, "Enough!"

REVELATION 12:1–17

NOW a great sign appeared in heaven: a
woman clothed with the sun, with the moon
under her feet, and on her head a garland
of twelve stars. 2 Then being with child,
she cried out in labor and in pain to give
birth.

3 And another sign appeared in heaven: behold, a great, fiery red dragon having seven heads and ten horns, and seven diadems on his heads. 4 His tail drew a third of the stars of heaven and threw them to the earth. And the dragon stood before the woman who was ready to give birth, to devour her Child as soon as it was born. 5 She bore a male Child who was to rule all nations with a rod of iron. And her Child was caught up to God and His throne. 6 Then the woman fled into the wilderness, where she has a place prepared by God, that they should feed her there one thousand two hundred and sixty days.

7 And war broke out in heaven: Michael and his angels fought with the dragon; and the dragon and his angels fought, 8 but they did not prevail, nor was a place found for them in heaven any longer. 9 So the great dragon was cast out, that serpent of old, called the Devil and Satan, who deceives the whole world; he was cast to the earth, and his angels were cast out with him.

10 Then I heard a loud voice saying in heaven, "Now salvation, and strength, and the kingdom of our God, and the power of His Christ have come, for the accuser of our brethren, who accused them before our God day and night, has been cast down. 11 And they overcame him by the blood of the Lamb and by the word of their testimony, and they did not love their lives to the death. 12 Therefore rejoice, O heavens,

The Devil, sin, disease, spiritualism are all accurate facts, but they are not truthful facts. (MORAL FOUND.)

and you who dwell in them! Woe to the inhabitants of the earth and the sea! For the devil has come down to you, having great wrath, because he knows that he has a short time."

13 Now when the dragon saw that he had been cast to the earth, he persecuted the woman who gave birth to the male *Child.* 14 But the woman was given two wings of a great eagle, that she might fly into the wilderness to her place, where she is nourished for a time and times and half a time, from the presence of the serpent. 15 So the serpent spewed water out of his mouth like a flood after the woman, that he might cause her to be carried away by the flood. 16 But the earth helped the woman, and the earth opened its mouth and swallowed up the flood which the dragon had spewed out of his mouth. 17 And the dragon was enraged with the woman, and he went to make war with the rest of her offspring, who keep the commandments of God and have the testimony of Jesus Christ.

◆◆◆

Reading 357—Inviolable Walking
Habakkuk 2:1, 2

No longer watching and waiting, but actively set toward the divine goal to which God is calling.

Have you ever noticed the "wondering-ness" (if I may coin a word) of the people who go on with God? They never seem to be overanxious or overconcerned, and they always seem to be getting younger. What is the characteristic of the people of this world who have not got the child-heart? They are always sighing; they have mental and spiritual rheumatism and neuralgia, moral twists and perversities, and nothing can rouse them. Why? They need the child-spirit, the Spirit that was given to the disciples after the resurrection and in its fullness at Pentecost; then nothing will turn them aside. . . .

Thank God for every life that is running in the strength of the tremendous vision. Keep your eyes on your file leader, Jesus only, Jesus ever, "and make straight paths for your feet" (Heb. 12:13). Watch for His goings. When He stands and hides Himself in a cloud—stand, watch, and wait. When the meaning is clear, then you will run. A vision puts enthusiasm into you, a thrilling understanding of God's Word, and you soar above in tremendous ecstasy; then you come down and run without being weary, and then you come to the grandest days and walk without fainting.   (ASK)

HABAKKUK 1:1—3:19

THE burden which the prophet Habakkuk saw.

2   O LORD, how long shall I cry,
     And You will not hear?
     Even cry out to You, "Violence!"
     And You will not save.
3   Why do You show me iniquity,
     And cause *me* to see trouble?
     For plundering and violence *are*
         before me;
     There is strife, and contention arises.
4   Therefore the law is powerless,
     And justice never goes forth.
     For the wicked surround the
         righteous;
     Therefore perverse judgment
         proceeds.

5   "Look among the nations and watch—
     Be utterly astounded!
     For *I will* work a work in your days
     Which you would not believe, though
         it were told *you*.
6   For indeed I am raising up the
         Chaldeans,
     A bitter and hasty nation
     Which marches through the breadth
         of the earth,
     To possess dwelling places *that are*
         not theirs.
7   They are terrible and dreadful;
     Their judgment and their dignity
         proceed from themselves.
8   Their horses also are swifter than
         leopards,
     And more fierce than evening wolves.
     Their chargers charge ahead;
     Their cavalry comes from afar;
     They fly as the eagle *that* hastens to
         eat.
9   "They all come for violence;
     Their faces are set *like* the east wind.
     They gather captives like sand.
10 They scoff at kings,
     And princes are scorned by them.
     They deride every stronghold,
     For they heap up earthen *mounds* and
         seize it.
11 Then *his* mind changes, and he
         transgresses;

He commits offense,
Ascribing this power to his god."

12 Are You not from everlasting,
     O LORD my God, my Holy One?
     We shall not die.
     O LORD, You have appointed them
         for judgment;
     O Rock, You have marked them for
         correction.
13 *You are* of purer eyes than to behold
         evil,
     And cannot look on wickedness.
     Why do You look on those who deal
         treacherously,
     And hold Your tongue when the
         wicked devours
     A *person* more righteous than he?
14 *Why* do You make men like fish of
         the sea,
     Like creeping things *that have* no
         ruler over them?

15 They take up all of them with a hook,
     They catch them in their net,
     And gather them in their dragnet.
     Therefore they rejoice and are glad.
16 Therefore they sacrifice to their net,
     And burn incense to their dragnet;
     Because by them their share *is*
         sumptuous
     And their food plentiful.
17 Shall they therefore empty their net,
     And continue to slay nations without
         pity?

2   I will stand my watch
     And set myself on the rampart,
     And watch to see what He will say
         to me,
     And what I will answer when I am
         corrected.

2 Then the LORD answered me and said:

     "Write the vision
     And make *it* plain on tablets,
     That he may run who reads it.
3   For the vision *is* yet for an appointed
         time;
     But at the end it will speak, and it
         will not lie.
     Though it tarries, wait for it;

Because it will surely come,
It will not tarry.

4 "Behold the proud,
His soul is not upright in him;
But the just shall live by his faith.

We must keep in unbroken touch with God by faith. (MORAL FOUND.)

---

5 "Indeed, because he transgresses by wine,
He is a proud man,
And he does not stay at home.
Because he enlarges his desire as hell,
And he *is* like death, and cannot be satisfied,
He gathers to himself all nations
And heaps up for himself all peoples.

6 "Will not all these take up a proverb against him,
And a taunting riddle against him, and say,
'Woe to him who increases
What is not his—how long?
And to him who loads himself with many pledges'?

7 Will not your creditors rise up suddenly?
Will they not awaken who oppress you?
And you will become their booty.

8 Because you have plundered many nations,
All the remnant of the people shall plunder you,
Because of men's blood
And the violence of the land *and* the city,
And of all who dwell in it.

9 "Woe to him who covets evil gain for his house,
That he may set his nest on high,
That he may be delivered from the power of disaster!

10 You give shameful counsel to your house,
Cutting off many peoples,
And sin *against* your soul.

11 For the stone will cry out from the wall,
And the beam from the timbers will answer it.

12 "Woe to him who builds a town with bloodshed,
Who establishes a city by iniquity!

13 Behold, *is it* not of the LORD of hosts
That the peoples labor to feed the fire,
And nations weary themselves in vain?

14 For the earth will be filled
With the knowledge of the glory of the LORD,
As the waters cover the sea.

15 "Woe to him who gives drink to his neighbor,
Pressing *him to* your bottle,
Even to make *him* drunk,
That you may look on his nakedness!

16 You are filled with shame instead of glory.
You also—drink!
And be exposed as uncircumcised!
The cup of the LORD's right hand *will be* turned against you,
And utter shame will be on your glory.

17 For the violence *done to* Lebanon will cover you,
And the plunder of beasts *which* made them afraid,
Because of men's blood
And the violence of the land *and* the city,
And of all who dwell in it.

18 "What profit is the image, that its maker should carve it,
The molded image, a teacher of lies,
That the maker of its mold should trust in it,
To make mute idols?

19 Woe to him who says to wood, 'Awake!'
To silent stone, 'Arise! It shall teach!'
Behold, it is overlaid with gold and silver,
Yet in it there is no breath at all.

20 "But the LORD is in His holy temple.
Let all the earth keep silence before Him."

3 A prayer of Habakkuk the prophet, on Shigionoth.

Prayer does not fit us for the greater works; prayer is the greater work. (UTMOST)

---

2 O LORD, I have heard Your speech *and* was afraid;
O LORD, revive Your work in the midst of the years!

In the midst of the years make *it*
   known;
In wrath remember mercy.

3   God came from Teman,
   The Holy One from Mount Paran.
                Selah

His glory covered the heavens,
And the earth was full of His praise.
4   *His* brightness was like the light;
   He had rays *flashing* from His hand,
   And there His power *was* hidden.
5   Before Him went pestilence,
   And fever followed at His feet.

6   He stood and measured the earth;
   He looked and startled the nations.
   And the everlasting mountains were
      scattered,
   The perpetual hills bowed.
   His ways *are* everlasting.
7   I saw the tents of Cushan in affliction;
   The curtains of the land of Midian
      trembled.

8   O Lord, were *You* displeased with
      the rivers,
   Was Your anger against the rivers,
   Was Your wrath against the sea,
   That You rode on Your horses,
   Your chariots of salvation?
9   Your bow was made quite ready;
   Oaths were sworn over *Your* arrows.
                Selah

You divided the earth with rivers.
10   The mountains saw You *and*
      trembled;
   The overflowing of the water
      passed by.
   The deep uttered its voice,
   And lifted its hands on high.
11   The sun and moon stood still in their
      habitation;
   At the light of Your arrows they
      went,
   At the shining of Your glittering
      spear.

12   You marched through the land in
      indignation;
   You trampled the nations in anger.
13   You went forth for the salvation of
      Your people,
   For salvation with Your Anointed.
   You struck the head from the house
      of the wicked,
   By laying bare from foundation to
      neck.   .   Selah

14   You thrust through with his own
      arrows

The head of his villages.
They came out like a whirlwind to
   scatter me;
Their rejoicing was like feasting on
   the poor in secret.
15   You walked through the sea with
      Your horses,
   Through the heap of great waters.

16   When I heard, my body trembled;
   My lips quivered at *the* voice;
   Rottenness entered my bones;
   And I trembled in myself,
   That I might rest in the day of
      trouble.
   When he comes up to the people,
   He will invade them with his troops.

17   Though the fig tree may not blossom,
   Nor fruit be on the vines;
   Though the labor of the olive may
      fail,
   And the fields yield no food;
   Though the flock may be cut off from
      the fold,
   And there be no herd in the stalls—
18   Yet I will rejoice in the Lord,
   I will joy in the God of my salvation.

19   The Lord God is my strength;
   He will make my feet like deer's *feet,*
   And He will make me walk on my
      high hills.

To the Chief Musician. With my stringed
instruments.

PSALM 146:1–10

1   PRAISE the Lord!

Praise the Lord, O my soul!
2   While I live I will praise the Lord;
   I will sing praises to my God while I
      have my being.

3   Do not put your trust in princes,
   Nor in a son of man, in whom *there is*
      no help.
4   His spirit departs, he returns to his
      earth;
   In that very day his plans perish.

5   Happy *is he* who *has* the God of Jacob
      for his help,
   Whose hope *is* in the Lord his God,
6   Who made heaven and earth,
   The sea, and all that *is* in them;
   Who keeps truth forever,
7   Who executes justice for the oppressed,

Who gives food to the hungry.
The LORD gives freedom to the
    prisoners.

8   The LORD opens *the eyes of* the blind;
    The LORD raises those who are bowed
        down;
    The LORD loves the righteous.
9   The LORD watches over the strangers;
    He relieves the fatherless and widow;
    But the way of the wicked He turns
        upside down.

10 The LORD shall reign forever—
    Your God, O Zion, to all generations.

    Praise the LORD!

PROVERBS 30:17

17 THE eye *that* mocks *his* father,
    And scorns obedience to *his* mother,
    The ravens of the valley will pick it out,
    And the young eagles will eat it.

REVELATION 13:1-18

THEN I stood on the sand of the sea. And
I saw a beast rising up out of the sea, having
seven heads and ten horns, and on his horns
ten crowns, and on his heads a blasphemous
name. 2 Now the beast which I saw was
like a leopard, his feet were like *the feet of*
a bear, and his mouth like the mouth of a
lion. The dragon gave him his power, his
throne, and great authority. 3 And *I saw*
one of his heads as if it had been mortally
wounded, and his deadly wound was
healed. And all the world marveled and followed the beast. 4 So they worshiped the
dragon who gave authority to the beast;
and they worshiped the beast, saying, "Who
is like the beast? Who is able to make war
with him?"
5 And he was given a mouth speaking

great things and blasphemies, and he was
given authority to continue for forty-two
months. 6 Then he opened his mouth in
blasphemy against God, to blaspheme His
name, His tabernacle, and those who dwell
in heaven. 7 It was granted to him to make
war with the saints and to overcome them.
And authority was given him over every
tribe, tongue, and nation. 8 All who dwell
on the earth will worship him, whose names
have not been written in the Book of Life
of the Lamb slain from the foundation of
the world.
9 If anyone has an ear, let him hear.
10 He who leads into captivity shall go into
captivity; he who kills with the sword must
be killed with the sword. Here is the patience and the faith of the saints.
11 Then I saw another beast coming up
out of the earth, and he had two horns
like a lamb and spoke like a dragon.
12 And he exercises all the authority of the
first beast in his presence, and causes the
earth and those who dwell in it to worship
the first beast, whose deadly wound was
healed. 13 He performs great signs, so that
he even makes fire come down from heaven
on the earth in the sight of men. 14 And
he deceives those who dwell on the earth
by those signs which he was granted to
do in the sight of the beast, telling those
who dwell on the earth to make an image
to the beast who was wounded by the sword
and lived. 15 He was granted *power* to give
breath to the image of the beast, that the
image of the beast should both speak and
cause as many as would not worship the
image of the beast to be killed. 16 He causes
all, both small and great, rich and poor,
free and slave, to receive a mark on their
right hand or on their foreheads, 17 and
that no one may buy or sell except one
who has the mark or the name of the beast,
or the number of his name.
18 Here is wisdom. Let him who has understanding calculate the number of the
beast, for it is the number of a man: His
number *is* 666.

Reading 358—Actual Purity
Revelation 14:4

Actually pure in their natural walk, they followed the Lamb in their actual lives, and were consciously redeemed by the blood of Christ. There is a difference between innocence and purity. Innocence is the characteristic of a child, purity is the characteristic of a man or woman who knows what the tendencies and temptations to go wrong are, and who has overcome them. Virtue is not in the man who has not been tempted, neither is purity. When a man is tempted and remains steadfastly unspotted, then he is virtuous.

Jesus Christ says in effect, "If you will serve Me, you will keep your chastity," that means there has to be a fight; you realize that all the power of God is behind you as you make the fight. You may be pure and unsullied for months, when all of a sudden there will be the insinuation of an idea; grip it on the threshold of your mind in a vice instantly, and do not allow it any more. If I am to serve Jesus Christ, I have to remember that my body is the temple of the Holy Spirit. Talk about it being a "soft" thing to be a follower of Jesus Christ! It is about the sternest and most heroic thing a man ever "struck" in his life to keep himself absolutely undefiled, one who by chastity maintains his integrity. It is a discipline, and thank God for the discipline. (*PLACE HELP*)

ZEPHANIAH 1:1—3:20

THE word of the LORD which came to Zephaniah the son of Cushi, the son of Gedaliah, the son of Amariah, the son of Hezekiah, in the days of Josiah the son of Amon, king of Judah.

2 "I will utterly consume everything
From the face of the land,"
Says the LORD;
3 "I will consume man and beast;
I will consume the birds of the heavens,
The fish of the sea,
And the stumbling blocks along with the wicked.
I will cut off man from the face of the land,"
Says the LORD.

4 "I will stretch out My hand against Judah,
And against all the inhabitants of Jerusalem.
I will cut off every trace of Baal from this place,
The names of the idolatrous priests with the *pagan* priests—
5 Those who worship the host of heaven on the housetops;
Those who worship and swear *oaths* by the LORD,

But who *also* swear by Milcom;
6 Those who have turned back from *following* the LORD,
And have not sought the LORD, nor inquired of Him."

7 Be silent in the presence of the Lord GOD;
For the day of the LORD *is* at hand,
For the LORD has prepared a sacrifice;
He has invited His guests.

8 "And it shall be,
In the day of the LORD's sacrifice,
That I will punish the princes and the king's children,
And all such as are clothed with foreign apparel.
9 In the same day I will punish
All those who leap over the threshold,
Who fill their masters' houses with violence and deceit.

10 "And there shall be on that day," says the LORD,
"The sound of a mournful cry from the Fish Gate,
A wailing from the Second Quarter,
And a loud crashing from the hills.
11 Wail, you inhabitants of Maktesh!
For all the merchant people are cut down;
All those who handle money are cut off.

12 "And it shall come to pass at that time
      That I will search Jerusalem with
        lamps,
      And punish the men
      Who are settled in complacency,
      Who say in their heart,
      'The LORD will not do good,
      Nor will He do evil.'
13   Therefore their goods shall become
        booty,
      And their houses a desolation;
      They shall build houses, but not
        inhabit *them;*
      They shall plant vineyards, but not
        drink their wine."

14   The great day of the LORD *is* near;
      It is near and hastens quickly.
      The noise of the day of the LORD is
        bitter;
      There the mighty men shall cry out.
15   That day *is* a day of wrath,
      A day of trouble and distress,
      A day of devastation and desolation,
      A day of darkness and gloominess,
      A day of clouds and thick darkness,
16   A day of trumpet and alarm
      Against the fortified cities
      And against the high towers.

17 "I will bring distress upon men,
      And they shall walk like blind men,
      Because they have sinned against the
        LORD;
      Their blood shall be poured out like
        dust,
      And their flesh like refuse."

18   Neither their silver nor their gold
      Shall be able to deliver them
      In the day of the LORD's wrath;
      But the whole land shall be devoured
      By the fire of His jealousy,
      For He will make speedy riddance
      Of all those who dwell in the land.

2   GATHER yourselves together, yes,
        gather together,
      O undesirable nation,
2   Before the decree is issued,
      Or the day passes like chaff,
      Before the LORD's fierce anger comes
        upon you,
      Before the day of the LORD's anger
        comes upon you!
3   Seek the LORD, all you meek of the
        earth,
      Who have upheld His justice.
      Seek righteousness, seek humility.
      It may be that you will be hidden
      In the day of the LORD's anger.

4   For Gaza shall be forsaken,
      And Ashkelon desolate;
      They shall drive out Ashdod at
        noonday,
      And Ekron shall be uprooted.
5   Woe to the inhabitants of the
        seacoast,
      The nation of the Cherethites!
      The word of the LORD *is* against you,
      O Canaan, land of the Philistines:
      "I will destroy you;
      So there shall be no inhabitant."

6   The seacoast shall be pastures,
      With shelters for shepherds and folds
        for flocks.
7   The coast shall be for the remnant
        of the house of Judah;
      They shall feed *their* flocks there;
      In the houses of Ashkelon they shall
        lie down at evening.
      For the LORD their God will
        intervene for them,
      And return their captives.

8 "I have heard the reproach of Moab,
      And the insults of the people of
        Ammon,
      With which they have reproached My
        people,
      And made arrogant threats against
        their borders.
9   Therefore, as I live,"
      Says the LORD of hosts, the God of
        Israel,
      "Surely Moab shall be like Sodom,
      And the people of Ammon like
        Gomorrah—
      Overrun with weeds and saltpits,
      And a perpetual desolation.
      The residue of My people shall
        plunder them,
      And the remnant of My people shall
        possess them."

10   This they shall have for their pride,
      Because they have reproached and
        made arrogant threats
      Against the people of the LORD of
        hosts.
11   The LORD *will be* awesome to them,
      For He will reduce to nothing all
        the gods of the earth;
      People shall worship Him,
      Each one from his place,
      Indeed all the shores of the nations.

12 "You Ethiopians also,
      You shall be slain by My sword."

13   And He will stretch out His hand
        against the north,

Destroy Assyria,
And make Nineveh a desolation,
As dry as the wilderness.

14 The herds shall lie down in her midst,
Every beast of the nation.
Both the pelican and the bittern
Shall lodge on the capitals *of* her
  pillars;
Their voice shall sing in the windows;
Desolation *shall be* at the threshold;
For He will lay bare the cedar work.

15 This is the rejoicing city
That dwelt securely,
That said in her heart,
"I *am it,* and *there is* none besides me."
How has she become a desolation,
A place for beasts to lie down!
Everyone who passes by her
Shall hiss and shake his fist.

3 WOE to her who is rebellious and
    polluted,
To the oppressing city!

2 She has not obeyed *His* voice,
She has not received correction;
She has not trusted in the LORD,
She has not drawn near to her God.

3 Her princes in her midst *are* roaring
    lions;
Her judges *are* evening wolves
That leave not a bone till morning.

4 Her prophets are insolent,
    treacherous people;
Her priests have polluted the
    sanctuary,
They have done violence to the law.

5 The LORD *is* righteous in her midst,
He will do no unrighteousness.
Every morning He brings His justice
    to light;
He never fails,
But the unjust knows no shame.

6 "I have cut off nations,
Their fortresses are devastated;
I have made their streets desolate,
With none passing by.
Their cities are destroyed;
There is no one, no inhabitant.

7 I said, 'Surely you will fear Me,
You will receive instruction'—
So that her dwelling would not be
    cut off,
Despite everything for which I
    punished her.
But they rose early and corrupted all
    their deeds.

8 "Therefore wait for Me," says the
    LORD,

"Until the day I rise up for plunder;
My determination *is* to gather the
    nations
To My assembly of kingdoms,
To pour on them My indignation,
All My fierce anger;
All the earth shall be devoured
With the fire of My jealousy.

9 "For then I will restore to the peoples
    a pure language,
That they all may call on the name
    of the LORD,
To serve Him with one accord.

10 From beyond the rivers of Ethiopia
My worshipers,
The daughter of My dispersed ones,
Shall bring My offering.

11 In that day you shall not be shamed
    for any of your deeds
In which you transgress against Me;
For then I will take away from your
    midst
Those who rejoice in your pride,
And you shall no longer be haughty
In My holy mountain.

12 I will leave in your midst
A meek and humble people,
And they shall trust in the name of
    the LORD.

13 The remnant of Israel shall do no
    unrighteousness
And speak no lies,
Nor shall a deceitful tongue be found
    in their mouth;
For they shall feed *their* flocks and
    lie down,
And no one shall make *them* afraid."

14 Sing, O daughter of Zion!
Shout, O Israel!
Be glad and rejoice with all *your* heart,
O daughter of Jerusalem!

15 The LORD has taken away your
    judgments,
He has cast out your enemy.
The King of Israel, the LORD, *is* in
    your midst;
You shall see disaster no more.

16 In that day it shall be said to
    Jerusalem:
"Do not fear;
Zion, let not your hands be weak.

17 The LORD your God in your midst,
The Mighty One, will save;
He will rejoice over you with
    gladness,
He will quiet *you* with His love,
He will rejoice over you with
    singing."

18 "I will gather those who sorrow over
   the appointed assembly,
   Who are among you,
   To whom its reproach *is* a burden.
19 Behold, at that time
   I will deal with all who afflict you;
   I will save the lame,
   And gather those who were driven
      out;
   I will appoint them for praise and
      fame
   In every land where they were put
      to shame.
20 At that time I will bring you back,
   Even at the time I gather you;
   For I will give you fame and praise
   Among all the peoples of the earth,
   When I return your captives before
      your eyes,"
   Says the LORD.

PSALM 147:1–6

1 PRAISE the LORD!
   For *it is* good to sing praises to our
      God;
   For *it is* pleasant, *and* praise is beautiful.

2 The LORD builds up Jerusalem;
   He gathers together the outcasts of
      Israel.
3 He heals the brokenhearted
   And binds up their wounds.
4 He counts the number of the stars;
   He calls them all by name.
5 Great *is* our Lord, and mighty in power;
   His understanding *is* infinite.
6 The LORD lifts up the humble;
   He casts the wicked down to the
      ground.

PROVERBS 30:18, 19

18 THERE are three *things which* are too
   wonderful for me,
   Yes, four *which* I do not understand:
19 The way of an eagle in the air,
   The way of a serpent on a rock,
   The way of a ship in the midst of the
      sea,
   And the way of a man with a virgin.

REVELATION 14:1–20

THEN I looked, and behold, a Lamb standing on Mount Zion, and with Him one
hundred *and* forty-four thousand, having
His Father's name written on their foreheads. 2 And I heard a voice from heaven,
like the voice of many waters, and like the
voice of loud thunder. And I heard the
sound of harpists playing their harps.
3 They sang as it were a new song before
the throne, before the four living creatures,
and the elders; and no one could learn that
song except the hundred *and* forty-four
thousand who were redeemed from the
earth. 4 These are the ones who were not
defiled with women, for they are virgins.
These are the ones who follow the Lamb
wherever He goes. These were redeemed
from *among* men, *being* firstfruits to God
and to the Lamb. 5 And in their mouth
was found no deceit, for they are without
fault before the throne of God.

6 Then I saw another angel flying in the
midst of heaven, having the everlasting
gospel to preach to those who dwell on
the earth—to every nation, tribe, tongue,
and people— 7 saying with a loud voice,
"Fear God and give glory to Him, for the
hour of His judgment has come; and worship Him who made heaven and earth, the
sea and springs of water."

8 And another angel followed, saying,
"Babylon is fallen, is fallen, that great city,
because she has made all nations drink of
the wine of the wrath of her fornication."

9 Then a third angel followed them, saying with a loud voice, "If anyone worships
the beast and his image, and receives *his*
mark on his forehead or on his hand,
10 he himself shall also drink of the wine
of the wrath of God, which is poured out
full strength into the cup of His indignation. He shall be tormented with fire and
brimstone in the presence of the holy
angels and in the presence of the Lamb.
11 And the smoke of their torment ascends
forever and ever; and they have no rest day
or night, who worship the beast and his
image, and whoever receives the mark of
his name."

12 Here is the patience of the saints; here
are those who keep the commandments of
God and the faith of Jesus.

13 Then I heard a voice from heaven saying to me, "Write: 'Blessed *are* the dead
who die in the Lord from now on.' "

"Yes," says the Spirit, "that they may rest
from their labors, and their works follow
them."

14 Then I looked, and behold, a white
cloud, and on the cloud sat *One* like the
Son of Man, having on His head a golden
crown, and in His hand a sharp sickle.
15 And another angel came out of the temple, crying with a loud voice to Him who
sat on the cloud, "Thrust in Your sickle

At the throne of God, Jesus Christ has all power as Son of Man.   (PSY. REDEMP.)

---

and reap, for the time has come for You to reap, for the harvest of the earth is ripe."
16 So He who sat on the cloud thrust in His sickle on the earth, and the earth was reaped.
17 Then another angel came out of the temple which is in heaven, he also having a sharp sickle.

18 And another angel came out from the altar, who had power over fire, and he cried with a loud cry to him who had the sharp sickle, saying, "Thrust in your sharp sickle and gather the clusters of the vine of the earth, for her grapes are fully ripe."
19 So the angel thrust his sickle into the earth and gathered the vine of the earth, and threw *it* into the great winepress of the wrath of God. 20 And the winepress was trampled outside the city, and blood came out of the winepress, up to the horses' bridles, for one thousand six hundred furlongs.

◆◆◆◆

Reading 359—The Creed of Greatness
Haggai 2:23

A ll God's men are ordinary men made extraordinary by the matter He has given them. Unless we have the right matter in our minds intellectually and in our hearts affectionately, we will be hustled out of usefulness to God. We are not workers for God by choice. Many people deliberately choose to be workers, but they have no matter in them of God's almighty grace, no matter of His mighty word. Paul's whole heart and mind and soul were taken up with the great matter of what Jesus Christ came to do, he never lost sight of that one thing. We have to face ourselves with the one central fact—Jesus Christ and Him crucified.

"I have chosen you." Keep that note of greatness in your creed. It is not that you have got God but that He has got you. Here, in this college, God is at work, bending, breaking, molding, doing just as He chooses. Why He is doing it, we do not know; He is doing it for one purpose only—that He may be able to say, "This is My man, My woman." We have to be in God's hand so that He can plant men on the Rock as He has planted us.   (*UTMOST*)

HAGGAI 1:1—2:23

IN the second year of King Darius, in the sixth month, on the first day of the month, the word of the LORD came by Haggai the prophet to Zerubbabel the son of Sheal-tiel, governor of Judah, and to Joshua the son of Jehozadak, the high priest, saying, 2 "Thus speaks the LORD of hosts, saying:

In the Old Testament the prophet's calling is placed above that of king and of priest.   (SEND I YOU)

'This people says, "The time has not come, the time that the LORD's house should be built." ' "
3 Then the word of the LORD came by Haggai the prophet, saying, 4 "*Is it* time for you yourselves to dwell in your paneled houses, and this temple *to lie* in ruins?"
5 Now therefore, thus says the LORD of hosts: "Consider your ways!

6 "You have sown much, and bring in little;
    You eat, but do not have enough;
    You drink, but you are not filled with drink;

You clothe yourselves, but no one
  is warm;
And he who earns wages,
  Earns wages *to put* into a bag with
  holes."

7 Thus says the LORD of hosts: "Consider
your ways! 8 Go up to the mountains and
bring wood and build the temple, that I
may take pleasure in it and be glorified,"
says the LORD. 9 "*You* looked for much,
but indeed *it came to* little; and when you
brought it home, I blew it away. Why?"
says the LORD of hosts. "Because of My
house that *is in* ruins, while every one of
you runs to his own house. 10 Therefore
the heavens above you withhold the dew,
and the earth withholds its fruit. 11 For I
called for a drought on the land and the
mountains, on the grain and the new wine
and the oil, on whatever the ground brings
forth, on men and livestock, and on all the
labor of *your* hands."

12 Then Zerubbabel the son of Shealtiel,
and Joshua the son of Jehozadak, the high
priest, with all the remnant of the people,
obeyed the voice of the LORD their God,
and the words of Haggai the prophet, as
the LORD their God had sent him; and the
people feared the presence of the LORD.
13 Then Haggai, the LORD's messenger,
spoke the LORD's message to the people,
saying, "I *am* with you, says the LORD."
14 So the LORD stirred up the spirit of Zerubbabel the son of Shealtiel, governor of
Judah, and the spirit of Joshua the son of
Jehozadak, the high priest, and the spirit
of all the remnant of the people; and they
came and worked on the house of the LORD
of hosts, their God, 15 on the twenty-fourth
day of the sixth month, in the second year
of King Darius.

2 IN the seventh *month,* on the twenty-
first of the month, the word of the
LORD came by Haggai the prophet, saying:
2 "Speak now to Zerubbabel the son of
Shealtiel, governor of Judah, and to Joshua
the son of Jehozadak, the high priest, and
to the remnant of the people, saying:
3 'Who is left among you who saw this temple in its former glory? And how do you
see it now? In comparison with it, *is this*
not in your eyes as nothing? 4 Yet now be
strong, Zerubbabel,' says the LORD; 'and
be strong, Joshua, son of Jehozadak, the
high priest; and be strong, all you people
of the land,' says the LORD, 'and work; for
I *am* with you,' says the LORD of hosts.
5 '*According to* the word that I covenanted
with you when you came out of Egypt,

so My Spirit remains among you; do not
fear!'
6 "For thus says the LORD of hosts: 'Once
more (it *is* a little while) I will shake heaven
and earth, the sea and dry land; 7 and I
will shake all nations, and they shall come
to the Desire of All Nations, and I will
fill this temple with glory,' says the LORD
of hosts. 8 'The silver *is* Mine, and the gold
is Mine,' says the LORD of hosts. 9 'The
glory of this latter temple shall be greater
than the former,' says the LORD of hosts.
'And in this place I will give peace,' says
the LORD of hosts."

10 On the twenty-fourth *day* of the ninth
month, in the second year of Darius, the
word of the LORD came by Haggai the
prophet, saying, 11 "Thus says the LORD
of hosts: 'Now, ask the priests *concerning
the* law, saying, 12 "If one carries holy meat
in the fold of his garment, and with the
edge he touches bread or stew, wine or
oil, or any food, will it become holy?" ' "
Then the priests answered and said,
"No."
13 And Haggai said, "If *one who is* unclean
because of a dead body touches any of
these, will it be unclean?"
So the priests answered and said, "It shall
be unclean."
14 Then Haggai answered and said, " 'So
is this people, and so is this nation before
Me,' says the LORD, 'and so is every work
of their hands; and what they offer there
is unclean.
15 'And now, carefully consider from this
day forward: from before stone was laid
upon stone in the temple of the LORD—
16 since those *days,* when *one* came to a heap
of twenty ephahs, there were *but* ten; when
one came to the wine vat to draw out fifty
baths from the press, there were *but*
twenty. 17 I struck you with blight and mildew and hail in all the labors of your hands;
yet you did not *turn* to Me,' says the LORD.
18 'Consider now from this day forward,
from the twenty-fourth day of the ninth
month, from the day that the foundation
of the LORD's temple was laid—consider
it: 19 Is the seed still in the barn? As yet
the vine, the fig tree, the pomegranate, and
the olive tree have not yielded *fruit.* But
from this day I will bless *you.*' "

20 And again the word of the LORD came
to Haggai on the twenty-fourth day of the
month, saying, 21 "Speak to Zerubbabel,
governor of Judah, saying:

'I will shake heaven and earth.
22   I will overthrow the throne of
       kingdoms;

I will destroy the strength of the Gentile kingdoms.
I will overthrow the chariots
And those who ride in them;
The horses and their riders shall come down,
Every one by the sword of his brother.

23 'In that day,' says the LORD of hosts, 'I will take you, Zerubbabel My servant, the son of Shealtiel,' says the LORD, 'and will make you like a signet *ring;* for I have chosen you,' says the LORD of hosts."

PSALM 147:7–11

7   SING to the LORD with thanksgiving;
    Sing praises on the harp to our God,
8   Who covers the heavens with clouds,
    Who prepares rain for the earth,
    Who makes grass to grow on the mountains.
9   He gives to the beast its food,
    And to the young ravens that cry.
10 He does not delight in the strength of the horse;
    He takes no pleasure in the legs of a man.
11 The LORD takes pleasure in those who fear Him,
    In those who hope in His mercy.

PROVERBS 30:20

20 THIS *is* the way of an adulterous woman:
    She eats and wipes her mouth,
    And says, "I have done no wickedness."

REVELATION 15:1–8

THEN I saw another sign in heaven, great and marvelous: seven angels having the seven last plagues, for in them the wrath of God is complete.

2 And I saw *something* like a sea of glass mingled with fire, and those who have the victory over the beast, over his image and over his mark *and* over the number of his name, standing on the sea of glass, having harps of God. 3 They sing the song of Moses, the servant of God, and the song of the Lamb, saying:

"Great and marvelous *are* Your works,
  Lord God Almighty!
Just and true *are* Your ways,
  O King of the saints!

Saints have to become absolutely loyal to the disposition of Jesus Christ in their lives. (LOVE OF GOD)

4   Who shall not fear You, O Lord, and glorify Your name?
For *You* alone *are* holy.
For all nations shall come and worship before You,
For Your judgments have been manifested."

5 After these things I looked, and behold, the temple of the tabernacle of the testimony in heaven was opened. 6 And out of the temple came the seven angels having the seven plagues, clothed in pure bright linen, and having their chests girded with golden bands. 7 Then one of the four living creatures gave to the seven angels seven golden bowls full of the wrath of God who lives forever and ever. 8 The temple was filled with smoke from the glory of God and from His power, and no one was able to enter the temple till the seven plagues of the seven angels were completed.

*Reading 360—*Awaiting the Second Coming
Revelation 16:15

When our Lord does come, He will come quickly, and we will find He has been there all the time. One of the greatest strains in life is the strain of waiting for God. (GOD'S WORKMANSHIP)

The only way to wait for the Second Coming is to watch that you do what you should do so that *when* He comes is a matter of indifference. It is the attitude of a child, certain that God knows what He is about. When the Lord does come it will be as natural as breathing. God never does anything hysterical, and He never produces hysterics.   (GENESIS)

Ages will fade into foolish fancies beside the wonder of that blessed Age, that blessed period of Christ's reign among men. We have to remain steadfastly certain in Him, not go out of Him to see when He is coming; it is to be prophetic *living* as well as prophetic study. To the saint everything is instinct with the purpose of God. History is fulfilling prophecy all the time.

(GOD'S WORKMANSHIP)

ZECHARIAH 1:1—3:10

IN the eighth month of the second year of Darius, the word of the LORD came to Zechariah the son of Berechiah, the son of Iddo the prophet, saying, 2 "The LORD has been very angry with your fathers. 3 Therefore say to them, 'Thus says the LORD of hosts: "Return to Me," says the LORD of hosts, "and I will return to you," says the LORD of hosts. 4 "Do not be like your fathers, to whom the former prophets preached, saying, 'Thus says the LORD of hosts: "Turn now from your evil ways and your evil deeds." ' But they did not hear nor heed Me," says the LORD.

5 "Your fathers, where *are* they?
    And the prophets, do they live
        forever?
6   Yet surely My words and My
        statutes,
    Which I commanded My servants
        the prophets,
    Did they not overtake your fathers?

"So they returned and said:

'Just as the LORD of hosts
    determined to do to us,
According to our ways and
    according to our deeds,
So He has dealt with us.' " " "

7 On the twenty-fourth day of the eleventh month, which is the month Shebat, in the second year of Darius, the word of the LORD came to Zechariah the son of Berechiah, the son of Iddo the prophet: 8 I saw by night, and behold, a man riding on a red horse, and it stood among the myrtle trees in the hollow; and behind him *were* horses: red, sorrel, and white. 9 Then I said, "My lord, what *are* these?" So the angel who talked with me said to me, "I will show you what they *are*."

10 And the man who stood among the myrtle trees answered and said, "These *are* the ones whom the LORD has sent to walk to and fro throughout the earth."
11 So they answered the Angel of the LORD, who stood among the myrtle trees, and said, "We have walked to and fro throughout the earth, and behold, all the earth is resting quietly."
12 Then the Angel of the LORD answered and said, "O LORD of hosts, how long will You not have mercy on Jerusalem and on the cities of Judah, against which You were angry these seventy years?"
13 And the LORD answered the angel who talked to me, *with* good *and* comforting words. 14 So the angel who spoke with me said to me, "Proclaim, saying, 'Thus says the LORD of hosts:

"I am zealous for Jerusalem
    And for Zion with great zeal.
15 I am exceedingly angry with the
        nations at ease;
    For I was a little angry,
    And they helped—*but* with evil
        intent."

16 'Therefore thus says the LORD:

"I am returning to Jerusalem with
    mercy;
My house shall be built in it," says
    the LORD of hosts,
"And a *surveyor's* line shall be stretched
    out over Jerusalem." '

17 "Again proclaim, saying, 'Thus says the LORD of hosts:

"My cities shall again spread out
    through prosperity;
The LORD will again comfort Zion,
And will again choose Jerusalem." ' "

18 Then I raised my eyes and looked, and there *were* four horns. 19 And I said to the

angel who talked with me, "What *are* these?"

So he answered me, "These *are* the horns that have scattered Judah, Israel, and Jerusalem."

20 Then the LORD showed me four craftsmen. 21 And I said, "What are these coming to do?"

So he said, "These *are* the horns that scattered Judah, so that no one could lift up his head; but the craftsmen are coming to terrify them, to cast out the horns of the nations that lifted up *their* horn against the land of Judah to scatter it."

2 THEN I raised my eyes and looked, and behold, a man with a measuring line in his hand. 2 So I said, "Where are you going?"

And he said to me, "To measure Jerusalem, to see what *is* its width and what *is* its length."

3 And there *was* the angel who talked with me, going out; and another angel was coming out to meet him, 4 who said to him, "Run, speak to this young man, saying: 'Jerusalem shall be inhabited *as* towns without walls, because of the multitude of men and livestock in it. 5 For I,' says the LORD, 'will be a wall of fire all around her, and I will be the glory in her midst.'"

Wherever God's saints are in the world they are protected by a wall of fire.   (BIB. PSYCH.)

---

6 "Up, up! Flee from the land of the north," says the LORD; "for I have spread you abroad like the four winds of heaven," says the LORD. 7 Up, Zion! Escape, you who dwell with the daughter of Babylon."

8 For thus says the LORD of hosts: "He sent Me after glory, to the nations which plunder you; for he who touches you touches the apple of His eye. 9 For surely I will shake My hand against them, and they shall become spoil for their servants. Then you will know that the LORD of hosts has sent Me.

10 "Sing and rejoice, O daughter of Zion! For behold, I am coming and I will dwell in your midst," says the LORD. 11 "Many nations shall be joined to the LORD in that day, and they shall become My people. And I will dwell in your midst. Then you will know that the LORD of hosts has sent Me to you. 12 And the LORD will take possession of Judah as His inheritance in the Holy Land, and will again choose Jerusalem.

13 Be silent, all flesh, before the LORD, for He is aroused from His holy habitation!"

3 THEN he showed me Joshua the high priest standing before the Angel of the LORD, and Satan standing at his right hand to oppose him. 2 And the LORD said to Satan, "The LORD rebuke you, Satan! The LORD who has chosen Jerusalem rebuke you! *Is* this not a brand plucked from the fire?"

3 Now Joshua was clothed with filthy garments, and was standing before the Angel.

4 Then He answered and spoke to those who stood before Him, saying, "Take away the filthy garments from him." And to him He said, "See, I have removed your iniquity from you, and I will clothe you with rich robes."

5 And I said, "Let them put a clean turban on his head."

So they put a clean turban on his head, and they put the clothes on him. And the Angel of the LORD stood by.

6 Then the Angel of the LORD admonished Joshua, saying, 7 "Thus says the LORD of hosts:

'If you will walk in My ways,
  And if you will keep My command,
  Then you shall also judge My house,
  And likewise have charge of My
    courts;
  I will give you places to walk
  Among these who stand here.

8 'Hear, O Joshua, the high priest,
  You and your companions who sit
    before you,
  For they are a wondrous sign;
  For behold, I am bringing forth My
    Servant the BRANCH.
9 For behold, the stone
  That I have laid before Joshua:
  Upon the stone *are* seven eyes.
  Behold, I will engrave its inscription,'
  Says the LORD of hosts,
  'And I will remove the iniquity of
    that land in one day.
10 In that day,' says the LORD of hosts,
  'Everyone will invite his neighbor
  Under his vine and under his fig
    tree.'"

PSALM 147:12–20

12 PRAISE the LORD, O Jerusalem!
  Praise your God, O Zion!
13 For He has strengthened the bars of
  your gates;

He has blessed your children within
you.
14 He makes peace *in* your borders,
And fills you with the finest wheat.

15 He sends out His command *to the* earth;
His word runs very swiftly.
16 He gives snow like wool;
He scatters the frost like ashes;
17 He casts out His hail like morsels;
Who can stand before His cold?
18 He sends out His word and melts them;
He causes His wind to blow, *and* the
waters flow.

19 He declares His word to Jacob,
His statutes and His judgments to
Israel.
20 He has not dealt thus with any nation;
And *as for His* judgments, they have
not known them.

Praise the LORD!

PROVERBS 30:21–23

21 FOR three *things* the earth is perturbed,
Yes, for four it cannot bear up:
22 For a servant when he reigns,
A fool when he is filled with food,
23 A hateful *woman* when she is married,
And a maidservant who succeeds her
mistress.

REVELATION 16:1–21

THEN I heard a loud voice from the temple
saying to the seven angels, "Go and pour
out the bowls of the wrath of God on the
earth."
2 So the first went and poured out his
bowl upon the earth, and a foul and loathsome sore came upon the men who had
the mark of the beast and those who worshiped his image.
3 Then the second angel poured out his
bowl on the sea, and it became blood as
of a dead *man;* and every living creature
in the sea died.
4 Then the third angel poured out his
bowl on the rivers and springs of water,
and they became blood. 5 And I heard the
angel of the waters saying:

"You are righteous, O Lord,
The One who is and who was and
who is to be,
Because You have judged these
things.

6 For they have shed the blood of saints
and prophets,
And You have given them blood to
drink.
For it is their just due."

7 And I heard another from the altar saying, "Even so, Lord God Almighty, true
and righteous *are* Your judgments."
8 Then the fourth angel poured out his
bowl on the sun, and power was given to
him to scorch men with fire. 9 And men
were scorched with great heat, and they
blasphemed the name of God who has
power over these plagues; and they did not
repent and give Him glory.
10 Then the fifth angel poured out his
bowl on the throne of the beast, and his
kingdom became full of darkness; and they
gnawed their tongues because of the pain.
11 They blasphemed the God of heaven because of their pains and their sores, and
did not repent of their deeds.

*T*he entrance into the kingdom is
through the panging pains of
repentance.   (UTMOST)

12 Then the sixth angel poured out his
bowl on the great river Euphrates, and its
water was dried up, so that the way of the
kings from the east might be prepared.
13 And I saw three unclean spirits like frogs
coming out of the mouth of the dragon,
out of the mouth of the beast, and out of
the mouth of the false prophet. 14 For they
are spirits of demons, performing signs,
which go out to the kings of the earth and
of the whole world, to gather them to the
battle of that great day of God Almighty.
15 "Behold, I am coming as a thief.
Blessed *is* he who watches, and keeps his
garments, lest he walk naked and they see
his shame."
16 And they gathered them together to
the place called in Hebrew, Armageddon.
17 Then the seventh angel poured out his
bowl into the air, and a loud voice came
out of the temple of heaven, from the
throne, saying, "It is done!" 18 And there
were noises and thunderings and lightnings;
and there was a great earthquake, such a
mighty and great earthquake as had not
occurred since men were on the earth.
19 Now the great city was divided into three
parts, and the cities of the nations fell. And
great Babylon was remembered before God,
to give her the cup of the wine of the fierceness of His wrath. 20 Then every island fled

away, and the mountains were not found. 21 And great hail from heaven fell upon men, *each hailstone* about the weight of a

talent. Men blasphemed God because of the plague of the hail, since that plague was exceedingly great.

◆◆◆◆

Reading 361—Only God Knows Creation
Psalm 148:5

The Bible says that God created the world "by the breath of His mouth." Meditate for a moment on the word "creation," and see what a supernatural word it is. No philosopher ever thought of it, no expounder of natural history ever imagined such a word. We can understand "evolution" and "emanation," but we simply do not know what "creation" means. There is only one Being who knows, and that is God Himself, and the Bible says that God *created* the heavens and the earth.   (*Bib. Psych.*)

What God created is a satisfaction to God, but to no one less than God; consequently, until we come to know Him there is a great deal in His creation we shrug our shoulders over; but when we come to understand God we are as delighted with His creation as He is Himself.   (*God's Workmanship*)

ZECHARIAH 4:1—6:15

NOW the angel who talked with me came back and wakened me, as a man who is wakened out of his sleep. 2 And he said to me, "What do you see?"

So I said, "I am looking, and there *is* a lampstand of solid gold with a bowl on top of it, and on the *stand* seven lamps with seven pipes to the seven lamps. 3 Two olive trees *are* by it, one at the right of the bowl and the other at its left." 4 So I answered and spoke to the angel who talked with me, saying, "What *are* these, my lord?"

5 Then the angel who talked with me answered and said to me, "Do you not know what these *are*?"

And I said, "No, my lord."

6 So he answered and said to me:

"This *is* the word of the LORD to Zerubbabel:
'Not by might nor by power, but by My Spirit,'
Says the LORD of hosts.

7 'Who *are* you, O great mountain?
Before Zerubbabel *you shall become* a plain!
And he shall bring forth the capstone With shouts of "Grace, grace to it!" ' ".

8 Moreover the word of the LORD came to me, saying:

9 "The hands of Zerubbabel
Have laid the foundation of this temple;
His hands shall also finish *it*.
Then you will know
That the LORD of hosts has sent Me to you.

10 For who has despised the day of small things?
For these seven rejoice to see
The plumb line in the hand of Zerubbabel.
They are the eyes of the LORD,
Which scan to and fro throughout the whole earth."

11 Then I answered and said to him, "What *are* these two olive trees—at the right of the lampstand and at its left?" 12 And I further answered and said to him, "What *are these* two olive branches that *drip* into the receptacles of the two gold pipes from which the golden *oil* drains?"

13 Then he answered me and said, "Do you not know what these *are*?"

And I said, "No, my lord."

14 So he said, "These *are* the two anointed ones, who stand beside the Lord of the whole earth."

5 THEN I turned and raised my eyes, and saw there a flying scroll.

2 And he said to me, "What do you see?"

So I answered, "I see a flying scroll. Its length *is* twenty cubits and its width ten cubits."

3 Then he said to me, "This *is* the curse that goes out over the face of the whole earth: 'Every thief shall be expelled,' according *to* this side of *the scroll;* and, 'Every perjurer shall be expelled,' according *to* that side of it."

4   "I will send out *the curse,*" says the LORD of hosts;
"It shall enter the house of the thief
And the house of the one who swears falsely by My name.
It shall remain in the midst of his house
And consume it, with its timber and stones."

5 Then the angel who talked with me came out and said to me, "Lift your eyes now, and see what this *is* that goes forth."

6 So I asked, "What *is* it?" And he said, "It *is* a basket that is going forth."

He also said, "This *is* their resemblance throughout the earth: 7 Here *is* a lead disc lifted up, and this *is* a woman sitting inside the basket"; 8 then he said, "This *is* Wickedness!" And he thrust her down into the basket, and threw the lead cover over its mouth. 9 Then I raised my eyes and looked, and there *were* two women, coming with the wind in their wings; for they had wings like the wings of a stork, and they lifted up the basket between earth and heaven.

10 So I said to the angel who talked with me, "Where are they carrying the basket?"

11 And he said to me, "To build a house for it in the land of Shinar; when it is ready, *the basket* will be set there on its base."

6 THEN I turned and raised my eyes and looked, and behold, four chariots *were* coming from between two mountains, and the mountains *were* mountains of bronze. 2 With the first chariot *were* red horses, with the second chariot black horses, 3 with the third chariot white horses, and with the fourth chariot dappled horses—strong *steeds.* 4 Then I answered and said to the angel who talked with me, "What *are* these, my lord?"

5 And the angel answered and said to me, "These *are* four spirits of heaven, who go out from *their* station before the Lord of all the earth. 6 The one with the black horses is going to the north country, the white are going after them, and the dappled are going toward the south country."

7 Then the strong *steeds* went out, eager to go, that they might walk to and fro throughout the earth. And He said, "Go, walk to and fro throughout the earth." So they walked to and fro throughout the earth. 8 And He called to me, and spoke to me, saying, "See, those who go toward the north country have given rest to My Spirit in the north country."

9 Then the word of the LORD came to me, saying: 10 "Receive *the gift* from the captives—from Heldai, Tobijah, and Jedaiah, who have come from Babylon—and go the same day and enter the house of Josiah the son of Zephaniah. 11 Take the silver and gold, make an elaborate crown, and set *it* on the head of Joshua the son of Jehozadak, the high priest. 12 Then speak to him, saying, 'Thus says the LORD of hosts, saying:

"Behold, the Man whose name *is* the BRANCH!
From His place He shall branch out,
And He shall build the temple of the LORD;
13   Yes, He shall build the temple of the LORD.
He shall bear the glory,
And shall sit and rule on His throne;
So He shall be a priest on His throne,
And the counsel of peace shall be between them both." '

14 "Now the elaborate crown shall be for a memorial in the temple of the LORD for Helem, Tobijah, Jedaiah, and Hen the son of Zephaniah. 15 Even those from afar shall come and build the temple of the LORD. Then you shall know that the LORD of hosts has sent Me to you. And *this* shall come to pass if you diligently obey the voice of the LORD your God."

---

*A*s we obey God we find we have a wealth of power on the inside.   (PSY. REDEMP.)

PSALM 148:1–6

1   PRAISE the LORD!

Praise the LORD from the heavens;
Praise Him in the heights!
2   Praise Him, all His angels;

Praise Him, all His hosts!
3   Praise Him, sun and moon;
    Praise Him, all you stars of light!

---

*H*ad we but ears to hear the stars
singing.   (LOVE OF GOD)

---

4   Praise Him, you heavens of heavens,
    And you waters above the heavens!

5   Let them praise the name of the LORD,
    For He commanded and they were
    created.
6   He also established them forever and
    ever;
    He made a decree which shall not pass
    away.

PROVERBS 30:24–28

24 THERE are four *things which* are little
    on the earth,
    But they *are* exceedingly wise:
25 The ants *are* a people not strong,
    Yet they prepare their food in the
    summer;
26 The rock badgers are a feeble folk,
    Yet they make their homes in the crags;
27 The locusts have no king,
    Yet they all advance in ranks;
28 The spider skillfully grasps with its
    hands,
    And it is in kings' palaces.

REVELATION 17:1–18

THEN one of the seven angels who had
the seven bowls came and talked with me,
saying to me, "Come, I will show you the
judgment of the great harlot who sits on
many waters, 2 with whom the kings of the
earth committed fornication, and the inhabitants of the earth were made drunk with
the wine of her fornication."

3 So he carried me away in the Spirit
into the wilderness. And I saw a woman
sitting on a scarlet beast *which was* full of
names of blasphemy, having seven heads
and ten horns. 4 The woman was arrayed
in purple and scarlet, and adorned with gold
and precious stones and pearls, having in
her hand a golden cup full of abominations

and the filthiness of her fornication.
5 And on her forehead a name *was* written:

MYSTERY, BABYLON THE GREAT,
THE MOTHER OF HARLOTS AND
OF THE ABOMINATIONS OF THE
EARTH.

6 I saw the woman, drunk with the blood
of the saints and with the blood of the
martyrs of Jesus. And when I saw her, I
marveled with great amazement.

7 But the angel said to me, "Why did
you marvel? I will tell you the mystery of
the woman and of the beast that carries
her, which has the seven heads and the ten
horns. 8 The beast that you saw was, and
is not, and will ascend out of the bottomless
pit and go to perdition. And those who
dwell on the earth will marvel, whose names
are not written in the Book of Life from
the foundation of the world, when they
see the beast that was, and is not, and yet
is.

9 "Here *is* the mind which has wisdom:
The seven heads are seven mountains on
which the woman sits. 10 There are also
seven kings. Five have fallen, one is, *and*
the other has not yet come. And when he
comes, he must continue a short time.
11 The beast that was, and is not, is himself
also the eighth, and is of the seven, and is
going to perdition.

12 "The ten horns which you saw are ten
kings who have received no kingdom as
yet, but they receive authority for one hour
as kings with the beast. 13 These are of one
mind, and they will give their power and
authority to the beast. 14 These will make
war with the Lamb, and the Lamb will overcome them, for He is Lord of lords and
King of kings; and those *who are* with Him
are called, chosen, and faithful."

15 Then he said to me, "The waters which
you saw, where the harlot sits, are peoples,
multitudes, nations, and tongues. 16 And
the ten horns which you saw on the beast,
these will hate the harlot, make her desolate
and naked, eat her flesh and burn her with
fire. 17 For God has put it into their hearts
to fulfill His purpose, to be of one mind,
and to give their kingdom to the beast,
until the words of God are fulfilled.
18 And the woman whom you saw is that
great city which reigns over the kings of
the earth."

Reading 362—The Starved Imagination
Psalm 148:7–13

The people of God in Isaiah's day had starved their imagination by looking on the face of idols, and Isaiah made them look up at the heavens, that is, he made them begin to use their imagination aright. Nature to a saint is sacramental. If we are children of God, we have a tremendous treasure in nature. In every wind that blows, in every night and day of the year, in every sign of the sky, in every blossoming and in every withering of the earth, there is a real coming of God to us if we will simply use our starved imagination to realize it.

The test of spiritual concentration is bringing the imagination into captivity. Is your imagination looking on the face of an idol? Is the idol yourself? Your work? Your conception of what a worker should be? Your experience of salvation and sanctification? Then your imagination of God is starved, and when you are up against difficulties you have no power, you can only endure in darkness. If your imagination is starved, do not look back to your own experience; it is God whom you need. Go right out of yourself, away from the face of your idols, away from everything that has been starving your imagination. Rouse yourself, take the gibe that Isaiah gave the people, and deliberately turn your imagination to God.   (UTMOST)

ZECHARIAH 7:1—9:17

NOW in the fourth year of King Darius it came to pass *that* the word of the LORD came to Zechariah, on the fourth day of the ninth month, Chislev, 2 when *the people* sent Sherezer, with Regem-Melech and his men, *to* the house of God, to pray before the LORD, 3 *and* to ask the priests who *were* in the house of the LORD of hosts, and the prophets, saying, "Should I weep in the fifth month and fast as I have done for so many years?"

4 Then the word of the LORD of hosts came to me, saying, 5 "Say to all the people of the land, and to the priests: 'When you fasted and mourned in the fifth and seventh *months* during those seventy years, did you really fast for Me—for Me? 6 When you eat and when you drink, do you not eat and drink *for yourselves*? 7 *Should you* not *have obeyed* the words which the LORD proclaimed through the former prophets when Jerusalem and the cities around it were inhabited and prosperous, and the South and the Lowland were inhabited?' "

8 Then the word of the LORD came to Zechariah, saying, 9 "Thus says the LORD of hosts:

'Execute true justice,
    Show mercy and compassion
Everyone to his brother.

10 Do not oppress the widow or the fatherless,
    The alien or the poor.
    Let none of you plan evil in his heart
    Against his brother.'

11 But they refused to heed, shrugged their shoulders, and stopped their ears so that they could not hear. 12 Yes, they made their hearts like flint, refusing to hear the law and the words which the LORD of hosts had sent by His Spirit through the former prophets. Thus great wrath came from the LORD of hosts. 13 Therefore it happened, *that* just as He proclaimed and they would not hear, so they called out and I would not listen," says the LORD of hosts. 14 "But I scattered them with a whirlwind among all the nations which they had not known. Thus the land became desolate after them, so that no one passed through or returned; for they made the pleasant land desolate."

8 AGAIN the word of the LORD of hosts came, saying, 2 "Thus says the LORD of hosts:

'I am zealous for Zion with great zeal;
    With great fervor I am zealous for her.'

3 "Thus says the LORD:

'I will return to Zion,
And dwell in the midst of Jerusalem.
Jerusalem shall be called the City of
   Truth,
The Mountain of the LORD of hosts,
The Holy Mountain.'

4 "Thus says the LORD of hosts:

'Old men and old women shall again
   sit
In the streets of Jerusalem,
Each one with his staff in his hand
Because of great age.
5   The streets of the city
Shall be full of boys and girls
Playing in its streets.'

6 "Thus says the LORD of hosts:

'If it is marvelous in the eyes of the
   remnant of this people in these
   days,
Will it also be marvelous in My eyes?'
Says the LORD of hosts.

7 "Thus says the LORD of hosts:

'Behold, I will save My people from
   the land of the east
And from the land of the west;
8   I will bring them *back,*
And they shall dwell in the midst of
   Jerusalem.
They shall be My people
And I will be their God,
In truth and righteousness.'

9 "Thus says the LORD of hosts:

'Let your hands be strong,
You who have been hearing in these
   days
These words by the mouth of the
   prophets,
Who *spoke* in the day the foundation
   was laid
For the house of the LORD of hosts,
That the temple might be built.
10   For before these days
There were no wages for man nor any
   hire for beast;
There was no peace from the enemy
   for whoever went out or came in;
For I set all men, everyone, against
   his neighbor.

11 But now I *will* not *treat* the remnant of
this people as in the former days,' says the
LORD of hosts.

12 'For the seed *shall be* prosperous,
The vine shall give its fruit,

The ground shall give her increase,
And the heavens shall give their
   dew—
I will cause the remnant of this people
To possess all these.
13   And it shall come to pass
That just as you were a curse among
   the nations,
O house of Judah and house of Israel,
So I will save you, and you shall be
   a blessing.
Do not fear,
Let your hands be strong.'

14 "For thus says the LORD of hosts:

'Just as I determined to punish you
When your fathers provoked Me to
   wrath,'
Says the LORD of hosts,
'And I would not relent,
15   So again in these days
I am determined to do good
To Jerusalem and to the house of
   Judah.
Do not fear.
16   These *are* the things you shall do:
Speak each man the truth to his
   neighbor;
Give judgment in your gates for
   truth, justice, and peace;
17   Let none of you think evil in your
   heart against your neighbor;
And do not love a false oath.
For all these *are things* that I hate,'
Says the LORD."

18 Then the word of the LORD of hosts
came to me, saying, 19 "Thus says the LORD
of hosts:

'The fast of the fourth *month,*
The fast of the fifth,
The fast of the seventh,
And the fast of the tenth,
Shall be joy and gladness and cheerful
   feasts
For the house of Judah.
Therefore love truth and peace.'

20 "Thus says the LORD of hosts:

'Peoples shall yet come,
Inhabitants of many cities;
21   The inhabitants of one *city* shall go
   to another, saying,
"Let us continue to go and pray before
   the LORD,
And seek the LORD of hosts.
I myself will go also."
22   Yes, many peoples and strong nations

Shall come to seek the LORD of hosts
  in Jerusalem,
And to pray before the LORD.'

23 "Thus says the LORD of hosts: 'In those
days ten men from every language of the
nations shall grasp the sleeve of a Jewish
man, saying, "Let us go with you, for we
have heard *that* God *is* with you." ' "

9 THE burden of the word of the LORD
  Against the land of Hadrach,
  And Damascus its resting place
  (For the eyes of men
  And all the tribes of Israel
  Are on the LORD);
2   Also *against* Hamath, *which* borders
      on it,
    And *against* Tyre and Sidon, though
      they are very wise.

3   For Tyre built herself a tower,
    Heaped up silver like the dust,
    And gold like the mire of the streets.
4   Behold, the LORD will cast her out;
    He will destroy her power in the sea,
    And she will be devoured by fire.

5   Ashkelon shall see *it* and fear;
    Gaza also shall be very sorrowful;
    And Ekron, for He dried up her
      expectation.
    The king shall perish from Gaza,
    And Ashkelon shall not be inhabited.

6   "A mixed race shall settle in Ashdod,
    And I will cut off the pride of the
      Philistines.
7   I will take away the blood from his
      mouth,
    And the abominations from between
      his teeth.
    But he who remains, even he *shall
      be* for our God,
    And shall be like a leader in Judah,
    And Ekron like a Jebusite.
8   I will camp around My house
    Because of the army,
    Because of him who passes by and
      him who returns.
    No more shall an oppressor pass
      through them,
    For now I have seen with My eyes.

9   "Rejoice greatly, O daughter of Zion!
    Shout, O daughter of Jerusalem!
    Behold, your King is coming to you;
    He *is* just and having salvation,
    Lowly and riding on a donkey,
    A colt, the foal of a donkey.
10 I will cut off the chariot from
      Ephraim

And the horse from Jerusalem;
  The battle bow shall be cut off.
  He shall speak peace to the nations;
  His dominion *shall be* 'from sea to
    sea,
  And from the River to the ends of
    the earth.'

11 "As for you also,
    Because of the blood of your
      covenant,
    I will set your prisoners free from
      the waterless pit.
12 Return to the stronghold,
    You prisoners of hope.
    Even today I declare
    That I will restore double to you.
13 For I have bent Judah, My *bow,*
    Fitted the bow with Ephraim,
    And raised up your sons, O Zion,
    Against your sons, O Greece,
    And made you like the sword of a
      mighty man."

14 Then the LORD will be seen over
      them,
    And His arrow will go forth like
      lightning.
    The Lord GOD will blow the
      trumpet,
    And go with whirlwinds from the
      south.
15 The LORD of hosts will defend them;
    They shall devour and subdue with
      slingstones.
    They shall drink *and* roar as if with
      wine;
    They shall be filled *with blood* like
      basins,
    Like the corners of the altar.
16 The LORD their God will save them
      in that day,
    As the flock of His people.
    For they *shall be like* the jewels of a
      crown,
    Lifted like a banner over His land—
17 For how great is its goodness
    And how great its beauty!
    Grain shall make the young men
      thrive,
    And new wine the young women.

PSALM 148:7–14

7   PRAISE the LORD from the earth,
    You great sea creatures and all the
      depths;
8   Fire and hail, snow and clouds;
    Stormy wind, fulfilling His word;
9   Mountains and all hills;

Fruitful trees and all cedars;
10 Beasts and all cattle;
Creeping things and flying fowl;
11 Kings of the earth and all peoples;
Princes and all judges of the earth;
12 Both young men and maidens;
Old men and children.

13 Let them praise the name of the LORD,
For His name alone is exalted;
His glory *is* above the earth and heaven.

---

*E*verything that God has created
is like an orchestra praising
Him.   (APPROVED)

---

14 And He has exalted the horn of His
people,
The praise of all His saints—
Of the children of Israel,
A people near to Him.

Praise the LORD!

PROVERBS 30:29–31

29 THERE are three *things which* are
majestic in pace,
Yes, four *which* are stately in walk:
30 A lion, *which is* mighty among beasts
And does not turn away from any;
31 A greyhound,
A male goat also,
And a king *whose* troops *are* with him.

REVELATION 18:1–24

AFTER these things I saw another angel
coming down from heaven, having great
authority, and the earth was illuminated
with his glory. 2 And he cried mightily with
a loud voice, saying, "Babylon the great is
fallen, is fallen, and has become a dwelling
place of demons, a prison for every foul
spirit, and a cage for every unclean and hated
bird! 3 For all the nations have drunk of
the wine of the wrath of her fornication,
the kings of the earth have committed fornication with her, and the merchants of the
earth have become rich through the abundance of her luxury."

4 And I heard another voice from heaven
saying, "Come out of her, my people, lest
you share in her sins, and lest you receive
of her plagues. 5 For her sins have reached
to heaven, and God has remembered her

iniquities. 6 Render to her just as she rendered to you, and repay her double according to her works; in the cup which she
has mixed, mix double for her. 7 In the measure that she glorified herself and lived luxuriously, in the same measure give her torment and sorrow; for she says in her heart,
'I sit *as* queen, and am no widow, and will
not see sorrow.' 8 Therefore her plagues will
come in one day—death and mourning and
famine. And she will be utterly burned with
fire, for strong *is* the Lord God who judges
her.

9 "The kings of the earth who committed
fornication and lived luxuriously with her
will weep and lament for her, when they
see the smoke of her burning, 10 standing
at a distance for fear of her torment, saying,
'Alas, alas, that great city Babylon, that
mighty city! For in one hour your judgment
has come.'

11 "And the merchants of the earth will
weep and mourn over her, for no one buys
their merchandise anymore: 12 merchandise
of gold and silver, precious stones and
pearls, fine linen and purple, silk and scarlet,
every kind of citron wood, every kind of
object of ivory, every kind of object of most
precious wood, bronze, iron, and marble;
13 and cinnamon and incense, fragrant oil
and frankincense, wine and oil, fine flour
and wheat, cattle and sheep, horses and
chariots, and bodies and souls of men.
14 The fruit that your soul longed for has
gone from you, and all the things which
are rich and splendid have gone from you,
and you shall find them no more at all.
15 The merchants of these things, who became rich by her, will stand at a distance
for fear of her torment, weeping and wailing, 16 and saying, 'Alas, alas, that great
city that was clothed in fine linen, purple,
and scarlet, and adorned with gold and precious stones and pearls! 17 For in one hour
such great riches came to nothing.' Every
shipmaster, all who travel by ship, sailors,
and as many as trade on the sea, stood at
a distance 18 and cried out when they saw
the smoke of her burning, saying, 'What
is like this great city?'

19 "They threw dust on their heads and
cried out, weeping and wailing, and saying,
'Alas, alas, that great city, in which all who
had ships on the sea became rich by her
wealth! For in one hour she is made
desolate.'

20 "Rejoice over her, O heaven, and *you*
holy apostles and prophets, for God has
avenged you on her!"

21 Then a mighty angel took up a stone
like a great millstone and threw *it* into the

sea, saying, "Thus with violence the great city Babylon shall be thrown down, and shall not be found anymore. 22 The sound of harpists, musicians, flutists, and trumpeters shall not be heard in you anymore. No craftsman of any craft shall be found in you anymore, and the sound of a millstone shall not be heard in you anymore. 23 The light of a lamp shall not shine in you anymore, and the voice of bridegroom and bride shall not be heard in you anymore. For your merchants were the great men

of the earth, for by your sorcery all the nations were deceived. 24 And in her was found the blood of prophets and saints, and of all who were slain on the earth."

We are familiar with external martyrdom, but inner martyrdom is infinitely more vital. (PSY. REDEMP.)

◆◆◆◆

Reading 363—The Context of the Bible
Revelation 19:13

The revelation of God's will has been brought down to us in words. The Bible is not a book containing communications from God, it is God's revelation of Himself, in the interests of grace; God's giving of Himself in the limitation of words. The Bible is not a faery romance to beguile us for a while from the sordid realities of life, it is the divine complement of the laws of nature, of conscience and of humanity, it introduces us to a new universe of revelation facts not known to unregenerate common sense.

The context of the Bible is our Lord Jesus Christ, and personal relationship to Him. The *words* of God and the *Word* of God stand together; to separate them is to render both powerless. Any expounder of the words of God is liable to go off at a tangent if he or she does not remember this stern undeviating standard of exposition, namely, that no individual experience is of the remotest value unless it is up to the standard of the Word of God. . . .

The test of Truth is the revelation of the Son of God in me, not as a divine anticipation, but as a delightful activity *now*. It is perilously possible to praise our Lord as Savior and Sanctifier, and yet cunningly blind our own hearts to the necessity of His manifesting in our mortal flesh His peculiar salvation and sanctification.   (*GOD'S WORKMANSHIP*)

ZECHARIAH 10:1—12:14

1 ASK the LORD for rain
In the time of the latter rain.
The LORD will make flashing clouds;
He will give them showers of rain,
Grass in the field for everyone.

2 For the idols speak delusion;
The diviners envision lies,
And tell false dreams;
They comfort in vain.
Therefore *the people* wend their way
like sheep;
They are in trouble because *there is*
no shepherd.

3 "My anger is kindled against the
shepherds,
And I will punish the goatherds.
For the LORD of hosts will visit His
flock,
The house of Judah,
And will make them as His royal
horse in the battle.

4 From him comes the cornerstone,
From him the tent peg,
From him the battle bow,
From him every ruler together.

5 They shall be like mighty men,
Who tread down *their enemies*
In the mire of the streets in the battle.
They shall fight because the LORD
is with them,

And the riders on horses shall be put
to shame.

6 "I will strengthen the house of Judah,
And I will save the house of Joseph.
I will bring them back,
Because I have mercy on them.
They shall be as though I had not
cast them aside;
For I *am* the LORD their God,
And I will hear them.
7 *Those of* Ephraim shall be like a
mighty man,
And their heart shall rejoice as if with
wine.
Yes, their children shall see *it* and
be glad;
Their heart shall rejoice in the LORD.
8 I will whistle for them and gather
them,
For I will redeem them;
And they shall increase as they once
increased.

9 "I will sow them among the peoples,
And they shall remember Me in far
countries;
They shall live, together with their
children,
And they shall return.
10 I will also bring them back from the
land of Egypt,
And gather them from Assyria.
I will bring them into the land of
Gilead and Lebanon,
Until no *more room* is found for them.
11 He shall pass through the sea with
affliction,
And strike the waves of the sea:
All the depths of the River shall
dry up.
Then the pride of Assyria shall be
brought down,
And the scepter of Egypt shall depart.

12 "So I will strengthen them in the
LORD,
And they shall walk up and down
in His name,"
Says the LORD.

11 OPEN your doors, O Lebanon,
That fire may devour your cedars.

2 Wail, O cypress, for the cedar has
fallen,
Because the mighty *trees* are ruined.
Wail, O oaks of Bashan,
For the thick forest has come down.
3 *There is* the sound of wailing
shepherds!
For their glory is in ruins.

There is the sound of roaring lions!
For the pride of the Jordan is in ruins.

4 Thus says the LORD my God, "Feed
the flock for slaughter, 5 whose owners
slaughter them and feel no guilt; those who
sell them say, 'Blessed be the LORD, for I
am rich'; and their shepherds do not pity
them. 6 For I will no longer pity the inhabitants of the land," says the LORD. "But indeed I will give everyone into his neighbor's hand and into the hand of his king.
They shall attack the land, and I will not
deliver *them* from their hand."

7 So I fed the flock for slaughter, in particular the poor of the flock. I took for myself
two staffs: the one I called Beauty, and the
other I called Bonds; and I fed the flock.
8 I dismissed the three shepherds in one
month. My soul loathed them, and their
soul also abhorred me. 9 Then I said, "I
will not feed you. Let what is dying die,
and what is perishing perish. Let those that
are left eat each other's flesh." 10 And I took
my staff, Beauty, and cut it in two, that I
might break the covenant which I had made
with all the peoples. 11 So it was broken
on that day. Thus the poor of the flock,
who were watching me, knew that it *was*
the word of the LORD. 12 Then I said to
them, "If it is agreeable to you, give *me*
my wages; and if not, refrain." So they
weighed out for my wages thirty *pieces* of
silver.

13 And the LORD said to me, "Throw it
to the potter"—that princely price they set
on me. So I took the thirty *pieces* of silver
and threw them into the house of the LORD
for the potter. 14 Then I cut in two my
other staff, Bonds, that I might break the
brotherhood between Judah and Israel.

15 And the LORD said to me, "Next, take
for yourself the implements of a foolish
shepherd. 16 For indeed I will raise up a
shepherd in the land *who* will not care for
those who are cut off, nor seek the young,
nor heal those that are broken, nor feed
those that still stand. But he will eat the
flesh of the fat and tear their hooves in
pieces.

17 "Woe to the worthless shepherd,
Who leaves the flock!
A sword *shall be* against his arm
And against his right eye;
His arm shall completely wither,
And his right eye shall be totally
blinded."

12 THE burden of the word of the
LORD against Israel. Thus says the
LORD, who stretches out the heavens, lays

the foundation of the earth, and forms the spirit of man within him: 2 "Behold, I will make Jerusalem a cup of drunkenness to all the surrounding peoples, when they lay siege against Judah and Jerusalem. 3 And it shall happen in that day that I will make Jerusalem a very heavy stone for all peoples; all who would heave it away will surely be cut in pieces, though all nations of the earth are gathered against it. 4 In that day," says the LORD, "I will strike every horse with confusion, and its rider with madness; I will open My eyes on the house of Judah, and will strike every horse of the peoples with blindness. 5 And the governors of Judah shall say in their heart, 'The inhabitants of Jerusalem *are* my strength in the LORD of hosts, their God.' 6 In that day I will make the governors of Judah like a firepan in the woodpile, and like a fiery torch in the sheaves; they shall devour all the surrounding peoples on the right hand and on the left, but Jerusalem shall be inhabited again in her own place—Jerusalem.

7 "The LORD will save the tents of Judah first, so that the glory of the house of David and the glory of the inhabitants of Jerusalem shall not become greater than that of Judah. 8 In that day the LORD will defend the inhabitants of Jerusalem; the one who is feeble among them in that day shall be like David, and the house of David *shall be* like God, like the Angel of the LORD before them. 9 It shall be in that day *that* I will seek to destroy all the nations that come against Jerusalem.

10 "And I will pour on the house of David and on the inhabitants of Jerusalem the Spirit of grace and supplication; then they will look on Me whom they pierced. Yes, they will mourn for Him as one mourns for *his* only *son,* and grieve for Him as one grieves for a firstborn. 11 In that day there shall be a great mourning in Jerusalem, like the mourning at Hadad Rimmon in the plain of Megiddo. 12 And the land shall mourn, every family by itself: the family of the house of David by itself, and their wives by themselves; the family of the house of Nathan by itself, and their wives by themselves; 13 the family of the house of Levi by itself, and their wives by themselves; the family of Shimei by itself, and their wives by themselves; 14 all the families that remain, every family by itself, and their wives by themselves.

PSALM 149:1–4

1   PRAISE the LORD!

Sing to the LORD a new song,
And His praise in the assembly of saints.

2   Let Israel rejoice in their Maker;
Let the children of Zion be joyful in their King.
3   Let them praise His name with the dance;
Let them sing praises to Him with the timbrel and harp.
4   For the LORD takes pleasure in His people;
He will beautify the humble with salvation.

PROVERBS 30:32, 33

32   IF you have been foolish in exalting yourself,
Or if you have devised evil, *put your* hand on *your* mouth.
33   For *as* the churning of milk produces butter,
And wringing the nose produces blood,
So the forcing of wrath produces strife.

REVELATION 19:1–21

AFTER these things I heard a loud voice of a great multitude in heaven, saying, "Alleluia! Salvation and glory and honor and power *belong* to the Lord our God! 2 For true and righteous *are* His judgments, because He has judged the great harlot who corrupted the earth with her fornication; and He has avenged on her the blood of His servants *shed* by her." 3 Again they said, "Alleluia! Her smoke rises up forever and ever!" 4 And the twenty-four elders and the four living creatures fell down and worshiped God who sat on the throne, saying, "Amen! Alleluia!" 5 Then a voice came from the throne, saying, "Praise our God, all you His servants and those who fear Him, both small and great!"

6 And I heard, as it were, the voice of a great multitude, as the sound of many waters and as the sound of mighty thunderings, saying, "Alleluia! For the Lord God Omnipotent reigns! 7 Let us be glad and rejoice and give Him glory, for the marriage of the Lamb has come, and His wife has made herself ready." 8 And to her it was granted to be arrayed in fine linen, clean and bright, for the fine linen is the righteous acts of the saints.

9 Then he said to me, "Write: 'Blessed *are* those who are called to the marriage supper of the Lamb!'" And he said to me,

"These are the true sayings of God." 10 And I fell at his feet to worship him. But he said to me, "See *that you do* not *do that!* I am your fellow servant, and of your brethren who have the testimony of Jesus. Worship God! For the testimony of Jesus is the spirit of prophecy."

11 Now I saw heaven opened, and behold, a white horse. And He who sat on him *was* called Faithful and True, and in righteousness He judges and makes war. 12 His eyes *were* like a flame of fire, and on His head *were* many crowns. He had a name written that no one knew except Himself. 13 He *was* clothed with a robe dipped in blood, and His name is called The Word of God. 14 And the armies in heaven, clothed in fine linen, white and clean, followed Him on white horses. 15 Now out of His mouth goes a sharp sword, that with it He should strike the nations. And He Himself will rule them with a rod of iron. He Himself treads the winepress of the fierceness and wrath of Almighty God. 16 And He has on *His* robe and on His thigh a name written:

KING OF KINGS
AND LORD OF LORDS.

17 Then I saw an angel standing in the sun; and he cried with a loud voice, saying to all the birds that fly in the midst of heaven, "Come and gather together for the supper of the great God, 18 that you may eat the flesh of kings, the flesh of captains, the flesh of mighty men, the flesh of horses and of those who sit on them, and the flesh of all *people,* free and slave, both small and great."

19 And I saw the beast, the kings of the earth, and their armies, gathered together to make war against Him who sat on the horse and against His army. 20 Then the beast was captured, and with him the false prophet who worked signs in his presence, by which he deceived those who received the mark of the beast and those who worshiped his image. These two were cast alive into the lake of fire burning with

---

All we know about eternal life, about hell and damnation, the Bible alone tells us. (BIB. PSYCH.)

---

brimstone. 21 And the rest were killed with the sword which proceeded from the mouth of Him who sat on the horse. And all the birds were filled with their flesh.

◆◆◆

Reading 364—The Element of Judgment
Revelation 20:11–15

The Christian worker must never forget that salvation is God's thought, not man's; therefore it is an unfathomable abyss. Salvation is the great thought of God, not an experience. Experience is only a gateway by which salvation comes into our conscious life. Never preach the experience; preach the great thought of God behind. When we preach we are not proclaiming how man can be saved from hell and be made moral and pure; we are conveying good news about God.

In the teachings of Jesus Christ the element of judgment is always brought out, it is the sign of God's love. Never sympathize with a soul who finds it difficult to get to God, God is not to blame. It is not for us to find out the reason why it is difficult, but so to present the truth of God that the Spirit of God will show what is wrong. The great sterling test in preaching is that it brings everyone to judgment. The Spirit of God locates each one to himself.

If Jesus ever gave us a command He could not enable us to fulfill, He would be a liar; and if we make our inability a barrier to obedience, it means we are telling God there is something He has not taken into account. Every element of self-reliance must be slain by the power of God. Complete weakness and dependence will always be the occasion for the Spirit of God to manifest His power.   (*UTMOST*)

ZECHARIAH 13:1—14:21

"IN that day a fountain shall be opened for the house of David and for the inhabitants of Jerusalem, for sin and for uncleanness.

2 "It shall be in that day," says the LORD of hosts, "*that* I will cut off the names of the idols from the land, and they shall no longer be remembered. I will also cause the prophets and the unclean spirit to depart from the land. 3 It shall come to pass *that* if anyone still prophesies, then his father and mother who begot him will say to him, 'You shall not live, because you have spoken lies in the name of the LORD.' And his father and mother who begot him shall thrust him through when he prophesies.

4 "And it shall be in that day *that* every prophet will be ashamed of his vision when he prophesies; they will not wear a robe of coarse hair to deceive. 5 But he will say, 'I *am* no prophet, I *am* a farmer; for a man taught me to keep cattle from my youth.' 6 And *one* will say to him, 'What are these wounds between your arms?' Then he will answer, '*Those* with which I was wounded in the house of my friends.'

7 "Awake, O sword, against My
        Shepherd,
    Against the Man who is My
        Companion,"
    Says the LORD of hosts.
    "Strike the Shepherd,
        And the sheep will be scattered;
    Then I will turn My hand against
        the little ones.
8   And it shall come to pass in all the
        land,"
        Says the LORD,
    "*That* two-thirds in it shall be cut off
        and die,
    But *one*-third shall be left in it:
9   I will bring the *one*-third through the
        fire,
    Will refine them as silver is refined,
    And test them as gold is tested.
    They will call on My name,
    And I will answer them.
    I will say, 'This *is* My people';
    And each one will say, 'The LORD
        is my God.'"

14 BEHOLD, the day of the LORD is
            coming,

    And your spoil will be divided in your
        midst.
2   For I will gather all the nations to
        battle against Jerusalem;
    The city shall be taken,
    The houses rifled,
    And the women ravished.
    Half of the city shall go into captivity,
    But the remnant of the people shall
        not be cut off from the city.

3   Then the LORD will go forth
    And fight against those nations,
    As He fights in the day of battle.
4   And in that day His feet will stand
        on the Mount of Olives,
    Which faces Jerusalem on the east.
    And the Mount of Olives shall be
        split in two,
    From east to west,
    Making a very large valley;
    Half of the mountain shall move
        toward the north
    And half of it toward the south.

5   Then you shall flee *through* My
        mountain valley,
    For the mountain valley shall reach
        to Azal.
    Yes, you shall flee
    As you fled from the earthquake
    In the days of Uzziah king of Judah.

    Thus the LORD my God will come,
    And all the saints with You.

6   It shall come to pass in that day
    That there will be no light;
    The lights will diminish.
7   It shall be one day
    Which is known to the LORD—
    Neither day nor night.
    But at evening time it shall happen
    That it will be light.

8   And in that day it shall be
    That living waters shall flow from
        Jerusalem,
    Half of them toward the eastern sea
    And half of them toward the western
        sea;
    In both summer and winter it shall
        occur.
9   And the LORD shall be King over
        all the earth.
    In that day it shall be—

"The LORD *is* one,"
And His name one.

10 All the land shall be turned into a plain from Geba to Rimmon south of Jerusalem. *Jerusalem* shall be raised up and inhabited in her place from Benjamin's Gate to the place of the First Gate and the Corner Gate, and *from* the Tower of Hananel to the king's winepresses.

11   *The people* shall dwell in it;
And no longer shall there be utter destruction,
But Jerusalem shall be safely inhabited.

12 And this shall be the plague with which the LORD will strike all the people who fought against Jerusalem:

Their flesh shall dissolve while they stand on their feet,
Their eyes shall dissolve in their sockets,
And their tongues shall dissolve in their mouths.

13   It shall come to pass in that day
That a great panic from the LORD will be among them.
Everyone will seize the hand of his neighbor,
And raise his hand against his neighbor's hand;
14   Judah also will fight at Jerusalem.
And the wealth of all the surrounding nations
Shall be gathered together:
Gold, silver, and apparel in great abundance.

15   Such also shall be the plague
On the horse *and* the mule,
On the camel and the donkey,
And on all the cattle that will be in those camps.
So *shall* this plague *be.*

16 And it shall come to pass *that* everyone who is left of all the nations which came against Jerusalem shall go up from year to year to worship the King, the LORD of hosts, and to keep the Feast of Tabernacles. 17 And it shall be *that* whichever of the families of the earth do not come up to Jerusalem to worship the King, the LORD of hosts, on them there will be no rain. 18 If the family of Egypt will not come up and enter in, they *shall* have no *rain;* they shall receive the plague with which the LORD strikes the nations who do not come up to keep the Feast of Tabernacles. 19 This shall be the punishment of Egypt and the punishment of all the nations that do not come up to keep the Feast of Tabernacles.

20 In that day "HOLINESS TO THE LORD" shall be *engraved* on the bells of the horses. The pots in the LORD's house shall be like the bowls before the altar. 21 Yes, every pot in Jerusalem and Judah shall be holiness to the LORD of hosts. Everyone who sacrifices shall come and take them and cook in them. In that day there shall no longer be a Canaanite in the house of the LORD of hosts.

PSALM 149:5–9

5   LET the saints be joyful in glory;
Let them sing aloud on their beds.

If I am full of the joy of the Lord, it will pour out of every cell of my body.   (BIB. PSYCH.)

---

6   *Let* the high praises of God *be* in their mouth,
And a two-edged sword in their hand,
7   To execute vengeance on the nations,
And punishments on the peoples;
8   To bind their kings with chains,
And their nobles with fetters of iron;
9   To execute on them the written judgment—
This honor have all His saints.

Praise the LORD!

PROVERBS 31:1–9

THE words of King Lemuel, the utterance which his mother taught him:

2   What, my son?
And what, son of my womb?
And what, son of my vows?
3   Do not give your strength to women,
Nor your ways to that which destroys kings.

4   *It is* not for kings, O Lemuel,
It is not for kings to drink wine,
Nor for princes intoxicating drink;
5   Lest they drink and forget the law,
And pervert the justice of all the afflicted.

6 Give strong drink to him who is
      perishing,
   And wine to those who are bitter of
      heart.
7 Let him drink and forget his poverty,
   And remember his misery no more.

8 Open your mouth for the speechless,
   In the cause of all *who are* appointed
      to die.
9 Open your mouth, judge righteously,
   And plead the cause of the poor and
      needy.

REVELATION 20:1–15

THEN I saw an angel coming down from
heaven, having the key to the bottomless
pit and a great chain in his hand. 2 He laid
hold of the dragon, that serpent of old,
who is *the* Devil and Satan, and bound him
for a thousand years; 3 and he cast him into
the bottomless pit, and shut him up, and
set a seal on him, so that he should deceive
the nations no more till the thousand years
were finished. But after these things he must
be released for a little while.

4 And I saw thrones, and they sat on
them, and judgment was committed to
them. Then *I saw* the souls of those who
had been beheaded for their witness to Jesus
and for the word of God, who had not
worshiped the beast or his image, and had
not received *his* mark on their foreheads
or on their hands. And they lived and
reigned with Christ for a thousand years.
5 But the rest of the dead did not live again
until the thousand years were finished. This
is the first resurrection. 6 Blessed and holy
is he who has part in the first resurrection.
Over such the second death has no power,
but they shall be priests of God and of

Christ, and shall reign with Him a thousand
years.
7 Now when the thousand years have expired, Satan will be released from his prison
8 and will go out to deceive the nations
which are in the four corners of the earth,
Gog and Magog, to gather them together
to battle, whose number *is* as the sand of
the sea. 9 They went up on the breadth of
the earth and surrounded the camp of the
saints and the beloved city. And fire came
down from God out of heaven and devoured them. 10 The devil, who deceived
them, was cast into the lake of fire and brimstone where the beast and the false prophet
are. And they will be tormented day and
night forever and ever.

*T*he Devil is a bully, but he
cannot stand for a second before
God. (Ask)

11 Then I saw a great white throne and
Him who sat on it, from whose face the
earth and the heaven fled away. And there
was found no place for them. 12 And I saw
the dead, small and great, standing before
God, and books were opened. And another
book was opened, which is *the Book* of Life.
And the dead were judged according to
their works, by the things which were written in the books. 13 The sea gave up the
dead who were in it, and Death and Hades
delivered up the dead who were in them.
And they were judged, each one according
to his works. 14 Then Death and Hades
were cast into the lake of fire. This is the
second death. 15 And anyone not found
written in the Book of Life was cast into
the lake of fire.

◆◆◆◆

*Reading 365—*Unaging Youth
Revelation 22:13

Spiritually we never grow old; through the passing of the years we grow
so many years young. The characteristic of the spiritual life is its unaging
youth, exactly the opposite of the natural life. "I am . . . the First and the
Last." The Ancient of Days represents the Eternal Childhood. God Almighty
became the weakest thing in His own creation, a Baby. When He comes into
us in new birth we can easily kill His life in us, or else we can see to it that

His life is nourished according to the dictates of the Spirit of God so that we grow "to the measure of the stature of the fullness of Christ." The mature saint is just like a little child, absolutely simple and joyful and gay. Go on living the life that God would have you live and you will grow younger instead of older. There is a marvelous rejuvenescence when once you let God have His way. If you are feeling very old, then get born again and do more at it.   (*Psy. Redemp.*)

MALACHI 1:1—4:6

THE burden of the word of the LORD to Israel by Malachi.

2   "I have loved you," says the LORD.
    "Yet you say, 'In what way have You loved us?'
    Was not Esau Jacob's brother?"
    Says the LORD.
    "Yet Jacob I have loved;
3   But Esau I have hated,
    And laid waste his mountains and his heritage
    For the jackals of the wilderness."

4   Even though Edom has said,
    "We have been impoverished,
    But we will return and build the desolate places,"

Thus says the LORD of hosts:

    "They may build, but I will throw down;
    They shall be called the Territory of Wickedness,
    And the people against whom the LORD will have indignation forever.
5   Your eyes shall see,
    And you shall say,
    'The LORD is magnified beyond the border of Israel.'

6   "A son honors *his* father,
    And a servant *his* master.
    If then I am the Father,
    Where *is* My honor?
    And if I *am* a Master,
    Where *is* My reverence?
    Says the LORD of hosts
    To you priests who despise My name.

Nothing is so much resented as the idea that I am not to be my own master.   (CONFORMED)

    Yet you say, 'In what way have we despised Your name?'
7   "You offer defiled food on My altar,
    But say,
    'In what way have we defiled You?'
    By saying,
    'The table of the LORD is contemptible.'
8   And when you offer the blind as a sacrifice,
    Is it not evil?
    And when you offer the lame and sick,
    Is it not evil?
    Offer it then to your governor!
    Would he be pleased with you?
    Would he accept you favorably?"
    Says the LORD of hosts.

9   "But now entreat God's favor,
    That He may be gracious to us.
    While this is being *done* by your hands,
    Will He accept you favorably?"
    Says the LORD of hosts.
10 "Who *is there* even among you who would shut the doors,
    So that you would not kindle fire *on* My altar in vain?
    I have no pleasure in you,"
    Says the LORD of hosts,
    "Nor will I accept an offering from your hands.
11 For from the rising of the sun, even to its going down,
    My name *shall be* great among the Gentiles;
    In every place incense *shall be* offered to My name,
    And a pure offering;
    For My name shall be great among the nations,"
    Says the LORD of hosts.
12 "But you profane it,
    In that you say,
    'The table of the LORD is defiled;
    And its fruit, its food, *is* contemptible.'
13 You also say,
    'Oh, what a weariness!'

And you sneer at it,"
Says the LORD of hosts.
"And you bring the stolen, the lame,
    and the sick;
Thus you bring an offering!
Should I accept this from your
    hand?"
Says the LORD.

14 "But cursed *be* the deceiver
Who has in his flock a male,
And takes a vow,
But sacrifices to the Lord what is
    blemished—
For I *am* a great King,"
Says the LORD of hosts,
"And My name *is to be* feared among
    the nations.

2 "AND now, O priests, this
    commandment is for you.

2 If you will not hear,
And if you will not take *it* to heart,
To give glory to My name,"
Says the LORD of hosts,
"I will send a curse upon you,
And I will curse your blessings.
Yes, I have cursed them already,
Because you do not take *it* to heart.

3 "Behold, I will rebuke your
    descendants
And spread refuse on your faces,
The refuse of your solemn feasts;
And *one* will take you away with it.

4 Then you shall know that I have sent
    this commandment to you,
That My covenant with Levi may
    continue."
Says the LORD of hosts.

5 "My covenant was with him, *one* of
    life and peace,
And I gave them to him *that he might*
    fear *Me;*
So he feared Me
And was reverent before My name.

6 The law of truth was in his mouth,
And injustice was not found on his
    lips.
He walked with Me in peace and
    equity,
And turned many away from
    iniquity.

7 "For the lips of a priest should keep
    knowledge,
And *people* should seek the law from
    his mouth;
For he is the messenger of the LORD
    of hosts.

8 But you have departed from the way;

You have caused many to stumble
    at the law.
You have corrupted the covenant of
    Levi,"
Says the LORD of hosts.

9 "Therefore I also have made you
    contemptible and base
Before all the people,
Because you have not kept My ways
But have shown partiality in the law."

10 Have we not all one Father?
Has not one God created us?
Why do we deal treacherously with
    one another
By profaning the covenant of the
    fathers?

11 Judah has dealt treacherously,
And an abomination has been
    committed in Israel and in
    Jerusalem,
For Judah has profaned
The LORD's holy *institution* which He
    loves:
He has married the daughter of a
    foreign god.

12 May the LORD cut off from the tents
    of Jacob
The man who does this, being awake
    and aware,
Yet who brings an offering to the
    LORD of hosts!

13 And this is the second thing you do:
You cover the altar of the LORD with
    tears,
With weeping and crying;
So He does not regard the offering
    anymore,
Nor receive *it* with goodwill from
    your hands.

14 Yet you say, "For what reason?"
Because the LORD has been witness
Between you and the wife of your
    youth,
With whom you have dealt
    treacherously;
Yet she is your companion
And your wife by covenant.

15 But did He not make *them* one,
Having a remnant of the Spirit?
And why one?
He seeks godly offspring.
Therefore take heed to your spirit,
And let none deal treacherously with
    the wife of his youth.

16 "For the LORD God of Israel says
That He hates divorce,
For it covers one's garment with
    violence,"

Says the LORD of hosts.
"Therefore take heed to your spirit,
That you do not deal treacherously."

17 You have wearied the LORD with
your words;
Yet you say,
"In what way have we wearied *Him?*"
In that you say,
"Everyone who does evil
Is good in the sight of the LORD,
And He delights in them,"
Or, "Where *is* the God of justice?"

3 "BEHOLD, I send My messenger,
And he will prepare the way before
Me.
And the Lord, whom you seek,
Will suddenly come to His temple,
Even the Messenger of the covenant,
In whom you delight.
Behold, He is coming,"
Says the LORD of hosts.

2 "But who can endure the day of His
coming?
And who can stand when He
appears?
For He *is* like a refiner's fire
And like launderers' soap.
3 He will sit as a refiner and a purifier
of silver;
He will purify the sons of Levi,
And purge them as gold and silver,
That they may offer to the LORD
An offering in righteousness.

4 "Then the offering of Judah and
Jerusalem
Will be pleasant to the LORD,
As in the days of old,
As in former years.
5 And I will come near you for
judgment;
I will be a swift witness
Against sorcerers,
Against adulterers,
Against perjurers,
Against those who exploit wage
earners and widows and orphans,
And against those who turn away an
alien—
Because they do not fear Me,"
Says the LORD of hosts.

6 "For I *am* the LORD, I do not change;
Therefore you are not consumed,
O sons of Jacob.
7 Yet from the days of your fathers
You have gone away from My
ordinances

And have not kept *them*.
Return to Me, and I will return to
you,"
Says the LORD of hosts.
"But you said,
'In what way shall we return?'

8 "Will a man rob God?
Yet you have robbed Me!
But you say,
'In what way have we robbed You?'
In tithes and offerings.
9 You are cursed with a curse,
For you have robbed Me,
Even this whole nation.
10 Bring all the tithes into the
storehouse,
That there may be food in My house,
And try Me now in this,"
Says the LORD of hosts,
"If I will not open for you the
windows of heaven
And pour out for you *such* blessing
That *there will* not *be room* enough
to receive it.

11 "And I will rebuke the devourer for
your sakes,
So that he will not destroy the fruit
of your ground,
Nor shall the vine fail to bear fruit
for you in the field,"
Says the LORD of hosts;
12 And all nations will call you blessed,
For you will be a delightful land,"
Says the LORD of hosts.
13 "Your words have been harsh
against Me,"
Says the LORD,
"Yet you say,
'What have we spoken against You?'
14 You have said,
'It is useless to serve God;
What profit *is it* that we have kept
His ordinance,
And that we have walked as mourners
Before the LORD of hosts?
15 So now we call the proud blessed,
For those who do wickedness are
raised up;
They even tempt God and go free.' "

16 Then those who feared the LORD
spoke to one another,
And the LORD listened and heard
them;
So a book of remembrance was
written before Him
For those who fear the LORD
And who meditate on His name.

17 "They shall be Mine," says the LORD
of hosts,
"On the day that I make them My
jewels.
And I will spare them
As a man spares his own son who
serves him."

18 Then you shall again discern
Between the righteous and the
wicked,
Between one who serves God
And one who does not serve Him.

4 "FOR behold, the day is coming,
Burning like an oven,
And all the proud, yes, all who do
wickedly will be stubble.
And the day which is coming shall
burn them up,"
Says the LORD of hosts,
"That will leave them neither root nor
branch.

2 But to you who fear My name
The Sun of Righteousness shall arise
With healing in His wings;
And you shall go out
And grow fat like stall-fed calves.

3 You shall trample the wicked,
For they shall be ashes under the soles
of your feet
On the day that I do *this*,"
Says the LORD of hosts.

4 "Remember the Law of Moses, My
servant,
Which I commanded him in Horeb
for all Israel,
With the statutes and judgments.

5 Behold, I will send you Elijah the
prophet
Before the coming of the great and
dreadful day of the LORD.

6 And he will turn
The hearts of the fathers to the
children,
And the hearts of the children to their
fathers,
Lest I come and strike the earth with
a curse."

PSALM 150:1–6

1 PRAISE the LORD!

Praise God in His sanctuary;
Praise Him in His mighty firmament!

2 Praise Him for His mighty acts;
Praise Him according to His excellent
greatness!

3 Praise Him with the sound of the
trumpet;
Praise Him with the lute and harp!

4 Praise Him with the timbrel and dance;
Praise Him with stringed instruments
and flutes!

5 Praise Him with loud cymbals;
Praise Him with clashing cymbals!

6 Let everything that has breath praise
the LORD.

Praise the LORD!

PROVERBS 31:10–31

10 WHO can find a virtuous wife?
For her worth *is* far above rubies.

11 The heart of her husband safely trusts
her;
So he will have no lack of gain.

12 She does him good and not evil
All the days of her life.

13 She seeks wool and flax,
And willingly works with her hands.

14 She is like the merchant ships,
She brings her food from afar.

15 She also rises while it is yet night,
And provides food for her household,
And a portion for her maidservants.

16 She considers a field and buys it;
From her profits she plants a vineyard.

17 She girds herself with strength,
And strengthens her arms.

18 She perceives that her merchandise *is*
good,
And her lamp does not go out by night.

19 She stretches out her hands to the
distaff,
And her hand holds the spindle.

20 She extends her hand to the poor,
Yes, she reaches out her hands to the
needy.

21 She is not afraid of snow for her
household,
For all her household *is* clothed with
scarlet.

22 She makes tapestry for herself;
Her clothing *is* fine linen and purple.

23 Her husband is known in the gates,
When he sits among the elders of the
land.

24 She makes linen garments and sells
them,
And supplies sashes for the merchants.

25 Strength and honor *are* her clothing;
She shall rejoice in time to come.

26 She opens her mouth with wisdom,
And on her tongue *is* the law of
kindness.

27 She watches over the ways of her
household,
And does not eat the bread of idleness.
28 Her children rise up and call her blessed;
Her husband *also,* and he praises her:
29 "Many daughters have done well,
But you excel them all."
30 Charm *is* deceitful and beauty *is* passing,
But a woman *who* fears the LORD, she
shall be praised.
31 Give her of the fruit of her hands,
And let her own works praise her in
the gates.

REVELATION 21:1—22:21

NOW I saw a new heaven and a new earth,
for the first heaven and the first earth had
passed away. Also there was no more sea.
2 Then I, John, saw the holy city, New Jerusalem, coming down out of heaven from
God, prepared as a bride adorned for her
husband. 3 And I heard a loud voice from
heaven saying, "Behold, the tabernacle of
God *is* with men, and He will dwell with
them, and they shall be His people. God
Himself will be with them *and be* their God.
4 And God will wipe away every tear from
their eyes; there shall be no more death,
nor sorrow, nor crying. There shall be no
more pain, for the former things have passed
away."
5 Then He who sat on the throne said,
"Behold, I make all things new." And He
said to me, "Write, for these words are true
and faithful."
6 And He said to me, "It is done! I am
the Alpha and the Omega, the Beginning
and the End. I will give of the fountain
of the water of life freely to him who thirsts.
7 He who overcomes shall inherit all things,
and I will be his God and he shall be My
son. 8 But the cowardly, unbelieving, abominable, murderers, sexually immoral, sorcerers, idolaters, and all liars shall have their
part in the lake which burns with fire and
brimstone, which is the second death."
9 Then one of the seven angels who had
the seven bowls filled with the seven last
plagues came to me and talked with me,
saying, "Come, I will show you the bride,
the Lamb's wife." 10 And he carried me
away in the Spirit to a great and high mountain, and showed me the great city, the holy
Jerusalem, descending out of heaven from
God, 11 having the glory of God. Her light
was like a most precious stone, like a jasper
stone, clear as crystal. 12 Also she had a
great and high wall with twelve gates, and
twelve angels at the gates, and names writ-

ten on them, which are *the names* of the
twelve tribes of the children of Israel:
13 three gates on the east, three gates on
the north, three gates on the south, and
three gates on the west.
14 Now the wall of the city had twelve
foundations, and on them were the names
of the twelve apostles of the Lamb.

---

*What sounds mystical and
unpractical to anyone not born
again is a glorious reality to the
saint.*   (GOD'S WORKMANSHIP)

---

15 And he who talked with me had a gold
reed to measure the city, its gates, and its
wall. 16 The city is laid out as a square; its
length is as great as its breadth. And he
measured the city with the reed: twelve
thousand furlongs. Its length, breadth, and
height are equal. 17 Then he measured its
wall: one hundred *and* forty-four cubits,
according to the measure of a man, that is,
of an angel. 18 The construction of its wall
was *of* jasper; and the city *was* pure gold,
like clear glass. 19 The foundations of the
wall of the city *were* adorned with all kinds
of precious stones: the first foundation *was*
jasper, the second sapphire, the third chal-
cedony, the fourth emerald, 20 the fifth
sardonyx, the sixth sardius, the seventh
chrysolite, the eighth beryl, the ninth topaz,
the tenth chrysoprase, the eleventh jacinth,
and the twelfth amethyst. 21 The twelve
gates *were* twelve pearls: each individual
gate was of one pearl. And the street of
the city *was* pure gold, like transparent glass.
22 But I saw no temple in it, for the Lord
God Almighty and the Lamb are its temple.
23 The city had no need of the sun or of
the moon to shine in it, for the glory of
God illuminated it. The Lamb *is* its light.
24 And the nations of those who are saved
shall walk in its light, and the kings of the
earth bring their glory and honor into it.
25 Its gates shall not be shut at all by day
(there shall be no night there). 26 And they
shall bring the glory and the honor of the
nations into it. 27 But there shall by no
means enter it anything that defiles, or
causes an abomination or a lie, but only
those who are written in the Lamb's Book
of Life.

22 AND he showed me a pure river
of water of life, clear as crystal, proceeding from the throne of God and of
the Lamb. 2 In the middle of its street, and

on either side of the river, *was* the tree of life, which bore twelve fruits, each *tree* yielding its fruit every month. The leaves of the tree *were* for the healing of the nations. 3 And there shall be no more curse, but the throne of God and of the Lamb shall be in it, and His servants shall serve Him. 4 They shall see His face, and His name *shall be* on their foreheads. 5 There shall be no night there: They need no lamp nor light of the sun, for the Lord God gives them light. And they shall reign forever and ever.

6 Then he said to me, "These words *are* faithful and true." And the Lord God of the holy prophets sent His angel to show His servants the things which must shortly take place.

7 "Behold, I am coming quickly! Blessed *is* he who keeps the words of the prophecy of this book."

8 Now I, John, saw and heard these things. And when I heard and saw, I fell down to worship before the feet of the angel who showed me these things. 9 Then he said to me, "See *that you do not do that*. For I am your fellow servant, and of your brethren the prophets, and of those who keep the words of this book. Worship God." 10 And he said to me, "Do not seal the words of the prophecy of this book, for the time is at hand. 11 He who is unjust, let him be unjust still; he who is filthy, let him be filthy still; he who is righteous, let him be righteous still; he who is holy, let him be holy still."

12 "And behold, I am coming quickly, and My reward *is* with Me, to give to every one according to his work. 13 I am the Alpha and the Omega, *the* Beginning and *the* End, the First and the Last."

14 Blessed *are* those who do His commandments, that they may have the right to the tree of life, and may enter through the gates into the city. 15 But outside *are* dogs and sorcerers and sexually immoral and murderers and idolaters, and whoever loves and practices a lie.

16 "I, Jesus, have sent My angel to testify to you these things in the churches. I am the Root and the Offspring of David, the Bright and Morning Star."

17 And the Spirit and the bride say, "Come!" And let him who hears say, "Come!" And let him who thirsts come. Whoever desires, let him take the water of life freely.

18 For I testify to everyone who hears the words of the prophecy of this book: If anyone adds to these things, God will add to him the plagues that are written in this book; 19 and if anyone takes away from the words of the book of this prophecy, God shall take away his part from the Book of Life, from the holy city, and *from* the things which are written in this book.

20 He who testifies to these things says, "Surely I am coming quickly."

Amen. Even so, come, Lord Jesus!

21 The grace of our Lord Jesus Christ *be* with you all. Amen.

Personal Prayer
Concerns

The whole meaning of prayer is that we may know God.   (ASK)

Personal Prayer Concerns

When we cling to God we learn to kneel for the first time. (GENESIS)

Personal Prayer
Concerns

Prayer imparts the power to walk and not faint.   (Ask)

Personal Prayer
Concerns

Our prayers are heard, not because we are in earnest, not because we suffer, but because Jesus suffered. (ASK)

Personal Prayer
Concerns

We have to pray with our eyes on God, not on the difficulties. (GOD'S WORKMANSHIP)

Personal Prayer Concerns

The prayer of the saints is never self-important, but always God-important.   (DISCIPLES)

Personal Prayer
Concerns

*Prayer is the vital breath of the Christian; not the thing that
makes him alive, but the evidence that he is alive.*   (DISCIPLES)

Personal Prayer
Concerns

*Prayer is not logical; it is a mysterious moral working
of the Holy Spirit.* (CHRIS. DIS. 2)